bare

adjective **1** uncovered or
knees (***bald, exposed, nu***

Each definition in an entry numbered and on a separate line

2 plain or simple: *the bar*
stark, unadorned)

verb **3** to expose or uncov
bare *its teeth.*

headword, showing you how it is used in context

Word building: **bareness** *n*
Word history: Old English *bær*

Words often confused are explained in shaded entries

bare / bear

Don't confuse **bare** with **bear**, which is a large furry mammal. It can also mean 'to carry or support something':

I can't bear your weight any longer.

be

Grammar notes in shaded entries

The most common verb in English is the verb **to be**. It appears in several different forms, and some of them look quite different from **be**:

Present	*Past*
(I) **am**	(I, he, she, it) **was**
(we, you, they) **are**	(we, you, they) **were**
(he, she, it) **is**	
being (*present participle*)	**been** (*past participle*)

The verb **to be** can act on its own, or together with other verbs. That is, it can be a main verb or an auxiliary verb:

She is a doctor. (main verb)

They were here last week. (main verb)

He was walking to the beach. (auxiliary verb)

You are coming on Friday. (auxiliary verb)

The present and past forms, except for **am**, often form contractions with the word **not**. For example:

is not	becomes	*isn't*
are not	becomes	*aren't*
was not	becomes	*wasn't*
were not	becomes	*weren't*

Usage notes in shaded entries

You shouldn't contract **am not** to **amn't**. Instead, **am** contracts with *I* to become *I'm not*. Note that you should avoid using **ain't** unless you're writing down ungrammatical speech or dialogue.

bilby

noun a small bandicoot with big rabbit-like ears

Noun forms giving you the plural of the word if it is not formed by simply adding **-s** or **-es**

Noun forms: The plural is **bilbies**.
Word history: from Yuwaalaraay, an Australian Aboriginal language from the Lightning Ridge region

Word history telling you where the word came from

billabong

Label telling you where the word is used

noun Australian a waterhole which used to be part of a river

Interesting word histories given extended notes

Word history: from Wiradjuri, an Australian Aboriginal language of the Murrumbidgee-Lachlan region. The word *billa* meant 'river' and the ending *-bong* meant 'happening only after rain'. In the Aboriginal language this was the name of what the settlers called the Bell River, but it came to be used more widely for waterholes, particularly those that seemed to be separated from a flowing river.

Poppy Medcalf
7A

MACQUARIE SCHOOL DICTIONARY

THIRD EDITION

General Editor
Alison Moore

AUSTRALIA'S NATIONAL DICTIONARY

Third edition published 2010 by
John Wiley & Sons Australia, Ltd
42 McDougall Street, Milton, Qld 4064

First edition published 1995
Second edition published 2001

Typeset in 7/7 pt News Plantin MT Regular

National Library of Australia
Cataloguing-in-publication data

Title:	Macquarie school dictionary / Susan Butler, executive editor; Alison Moore, general editor.
Edition:	3rd ed.
ISBN:	978 1 7424 6073 4 (hbk.) 978 1 7424 6263 9 (pbk.)
Subjects:	English language — Dictionaries. English language — Australia — Dictionaries.
Dewey number:	423

Editorial Staff

General editor	Alison Moore		
Editorial staff	Ann Atkinson	Kris Burnet	Laura Davies
	Maree Frakes	Leila Jabbour	Lyn Jones
	Margaret McPhee	Victoria Morgan	Susanne Read
Computer systems	Andrew Doyle		
Editor, Macquarie Dictionary	Susan Butler		

Cover adapted from a design by Natalie Bowra

Cover image: © Robyn Mackenzie (gum leaves), used under licence from Shutterstock

Macquarie Dictionary
at

Typeset in India by Aptara

Printed in China by
Shenzhen Donnelley Printing Co., Ltd.

10 9 8 7 6 5 4 3 2

John Wiley & Sons Australia, Ltd, places great value on the environment and is actively involved in efforts to preserve it. The paper used in the production of this dictionary was supplied by mills that source their raw materials from sustainably managed forests.

Contents

To the teacher

The endpapers of this dictionary provide a guide to using the *Macquarie School Dictionary*. A close study will show that they describe some features not present in any other dictionary. These features have been included to make the dictionary a complete and accessible language resource for students.

Clarity of entries

Meanings of the headword are listed using a numbering system and a separate line for each meaning. Phrases or sentences to illustrate meanings are also provided as an integral part of definitions.

Vocabulary extension

Students are introduced to a wider choice of vocabulary through the inclusion of up to five thesaurus entries after the definition. Unlike other dictionaries, the *Macquarie School Dictionary* can be used to find alternatives for over-used words such as **big**, **nice** and **beautiful**. Thesaurus entries are also included for more difficult words, such as **ambivalent**, **buoyant** and **scrutinise**.

Grammar notes and language conventions

The *Macquarie School Dictionary* is unique in offering extended grammar and usage notes incorporated in special screened entries within the body of the dictionary. This provides a ready alphabetical reference for grammar rules and language conventions, eliminating the need for a supplementary reference text.

In addition, words likely to be confused because of similar pronunciation or spelling are explained in separate screened entries under the appropriate headwords. Examples and usage tips are also included.

Word origins

Students can better appreciate and understand the origins and history of the English language through expanded etymologies provided in the Word history feature.

Pronunciation key

Sometimes when a word is hard to say, a pronunciation guide is given in brackets after the headword. The following key will help you to understand the pronunciation guides.

Vowels

a sounds
a as in 'pat'
ah as in 'part', 'hurrah'
ay as in 'bay'

i sounds
i as in 'pit'
uy as in 'buy'
ear as in 'hear'

u sounds
u as in 'but'
oo as in 'book'
ooh as in 'boot'

e sounds
e as in 'pet'
ee as in 'feet'
air as in 'pair'

o sounds
o as in 'pot'
oh as in 'boat', 'oh'
aw as in 'paw'
ow as in 'how'
oy as in 'boy'
õ as in French 'bon voyage'

er sounds
er as in 'pert'
uh as in 'apart', 'batter'

Consonants

th as in '**th**in'
dh as in '**th**en'
sh as in '**sh**ow'
zh as in 'mea**s**ure'
ch as in '**ch**ase'
j as in '**j**ug'
g as in '**g**ame'
ng as in 'si**ng**'

Emphasis

Stress the part of the word which is underlined.

a
indefinite article a single, but not particular, member of a group: *She is **a** woman.*

Look up **articles in grammar: indefinite articles.**

aardvark (ahd-vahk)
noun a large African mammal, active at night, which digs burrows, lives on termites, and has a long tongue and ears
Word history: Afrikaans

aback
adverb **1** of a sail or ship, with wind blowing against the front, preventing forward movement
phrase **2 taken aback,**
a in sailing, caught by the wind in this way
b surprised (***bewildered, confused, disconcerted, thrown, unsettled***)
Word history: Middle English

abacus (ab-uh-kuhs)
noun a frame with rods through it which hold beads used for counting
Noun forms: The plural is **abacuses** or **abaci** (ab-uh-see).
Word history: Latin, from Greek

abalone (ab-uh-loh-nee)
noun a type of shellfish which you can eat, and whose shell is used for ornaments
Noun forms: The plural is **abalone.**
Word history: Spanish

abandon[1]
verb **1** to leave something and not mean to come back: *The woman **abandoned** her wrecked car.* (***desert, evacuate, forsake, vacate***)
2 to give something up: *to **abandon** hope / to **abandon** the cricket match because of rain* (***relinquish, renounce, surrender***)
Word history: Middle English, from Old French

abandon[2]
noun freedom from worry or care: *When the war was over people danced with **abandon**.*
Word use: The opposite of this is **inhibition** or **restraint.**
Word history: French

abase
verb to lower, degrade or humiliate: *The politician was forced to **abase** himself publicly and admit that he had lied.*
Word history: blend of *base* morally low or mean and Middle English *abesse(n)* (from Late Latin *bassus* low)

abashed (uh-basht)
adjective ashamed or embarrassed
Word history: Middle English, from Old French word meaning 'astonish'

abate (uh-bayt)
verb to become less strong: *The storm has **abated**.* (***diminish, peter out, wane***)
Word building: **abatement** *noun*
Word history: Middle English

abattoir (ab-uh-twah)
noun a building or place where animals are killed for food: *The **abattoir** has closed down.*
Word use: The form **abattoirs** is also used. Note that this can be thought of as singular (*An abattoirs is being built*) or plural (*The abattoirs were closed down*).
Word history: French

abbess
noun a nun in charge of a convent
Word use: Compare this with **abbot.**
Word history: Middle English, from Late Latin

abbey
noun a building or group of buildings where monks or nuns live (***convent, monastery***)
Word history: Middle English *abbeye*, from Old French *abaie*, from Late Latin *abbātia*

abbot
noun a monk in charge of a monastery
Word use: Compare this with **abbess.**
Word history: Middle English, from Late Latin, from Greek, from Aramaic *abbā* father

abbreviate
verb to make shorter by leaving something out: *We **abbreviate** 'Mister' to 'Mr'.* (***abridge, condense, sum up, summarise***)
Word history: Latin

abbreviation
noun a shortened form of a word used to stand for the whole word, for example, *Mon* for *Monday*
Word history: Latin

There are two main types of **abbreviation,** with different punctuation rules:

1 abbreviations that consist of the first one or more letters of the full word or words. For example:

p.	page
vol.	volume
cont.	continued
p.a.	per annum

(continued)

abbreviation *(continued)*

NSW	New South Wales
Mon	Monday
Rev	Reverend
ACTU	Australian Council of Trade Unions

2 abbreviations that start with the first letter of the full word and end with its last letter. These are called **contractions.** For example:

hcp	handicap
rd	road
vb	verb
figs	figures
Dr	Doctor
Mr	Mister
Fr	Father
Assn	Association

When do you use a full stop?

Contractions (type **2** above) never have a full stop. This applies whether or not the contraction begins with a capital letter.

Abbreviations like type **1** above do have a full stop if they begin with a lower-case letter. Those that begin with a capital letter also used to have full stops, but nowadays you can leave the stops out. So we write *cont.* with a full stop for *continued* but *Mon* or *Mon.* for *Monday.*

Acronyms, such as *ANZAC*, do not have stops either. Look up **acronym.**

Note that *a.m.* and *p.m.* can also be written without stops (*am* and *pm*), although they are not contractions. Look up **a.m.** and **p.m.**

There is one group of lower-case abbreviations which never have stops. They are the symbols for units of measurement. For example:

km	kilometre or kilometres
kg	kilogram or kilograms
ha	hectare or hectares

ABC
noun **1** the alphabet
2 the main or basic facts of any subject

abdicate
verb to give up a position, especially that of being king or queen: *King Edward VIII **abdicated** in 1936. | He **abdicated** the throne.*

Word building: **abdication** *noun*
Word history: Latin *abdicātus*, past participle

abdomen (ab-duh-muhn)
noun **1** the main part of the body that contains the stomach and other organs (***belly**, **tummy***)
2 the last section of the body of an insect or spider

Word building: **abdominal** (uhb-dom-uh-nuhl) *adjective*
Word history: Latin

abduct
verb to kidnap someone or carry them away by force (***capture**, **poach**, **rustle**, **shanghai**, **steal***)

Word building: **abduction** *noun* **abductor** *noun*
Word history: Latin

aberration (ab-uh-ray-shuhn)
noun a departure or lapse from what is normal, right or true: *I destroyed my latest painting in a moment of **aberration.***

Word building: **aberrant** (ab-uh-ruhnt, uh-be-ruhnt) *adjective*
Word history: Latin

abet
verb to help or encourage in committing something, usually something bad or undesirable: *She was **abetted** by her brother in her scheme to steal the money.*

Verb forms: I **abetted**, I have **abetted**, I am **abetting**
Word history: Middle English, from Old French

abeyance (uh-bay-uhns)
noun the state of being inactive or disused for a limited time

Word history: Anglo-French word meaning 'expectation', from Old French word meaning 'gape after'

abhor (uhb-haw)
verb to think of something with disgust and hate: *I **abhor** cruelty to animals.* (***abominate**, **despise**, **detest**, **loathe***)

Word use: The opposite of this is **love**.
Verb forms: I **abhorred**, I have **abhorred**, I am **abhorring**
Word history: late Middle English, from Latin

abhorrent (uhb-hor-uhnt)
adjective hateful or disgusting: *I find the idea of killing animals **abhorrent.***

Word use: The opposite of this is **admirable** or **desirable**.
Word building: **abhorrence** *noun*

abide
verb **1** to put up with: *I can't **abide** being laughed at.*
2 *Old-fashioned* to stay: ***Abide** with me.*
phrase **3 abide by,**
a to accept or act according to something: *to **abide by** the rules*
b to stand by: *to **abide by** a friend*

Verb forms: I **abode** or I **abided**, I have **abided**, I am **abiding**
Word history: Old English *ābīdan*

ability
noun **1** the power to do something or act in a certain way: *The baby has the **ability** to crawl now.*
2 skill: *She has great **ability** in music.* (***capability**, **expertise**, **flair**, **proficiency**, **talent***)

Noun forms: The plural is **abilities**.
Word history: Middle English, from French, from Latin

abiotic (ay-buy-ot-ik)
adjective having to do with the non-living parts of an ecosystem: *Temperature is an **abiotic** feature of an ecosystem.*

Word use: Compare this with **biotic**.

abject (ab-jekt)
adjective **1** wretched or miserable: ***abject** poverty*
2 humble: *an **abject** apology*
3 worthy of contempt or scorn: *an **abject** liar*

Word history: Middle English, from Latin

ablation (uh-blay-shuhn)
noun Geology the removal of surface structures of the earth by wind or water, especially the removal of snow or ice

Word history: from Latin word meaning 'a carrying away'

ablaze
adjective **1** on fire: *Look! Our hotel is* ***ablaze****.*
2 shining brightly: *The house is* ***ablaze*** *with lights.*

able
adjective **1** having enough power, skill, knowledge or opportunity: *Are you* ***able*** *to come to my party?*
2 having or showing special skills or knowledge: *He is an* ***able*** *pianist.* (***capable, experienced, expert, proficient***)
Word building: **ably** *adjective*
Word history: Middle English, from Latin *habilis* easy to handle, fit

able-bodied
adjective physically strong and healthy: *an* ***able-bodied*** *worker*

abled
adjective **1** having the usual range of human physical and mental abilities: *a sport for* ***abled*** *and disabled people*
phrase **2 differently abled**, having a variation from the usual range of abilities
Word use: Note that **differently abled** is the term that some people prefer to use instead of **disabled**, because it is more positive, stressing the possession of different abilities, rather than none at all.

ablution (uh-blooh-shuhn)
noun **1** a ceremonial washing of hands, body, or holy objects
2 ablutions, the act of washing yourself: *to perform your* ***ablutions***
Word history: Middle English, from Latin

abnegate (ab-nuh-gayt)
verb to refuse or give up: *to* ***abnegate*** *a right* (***abdicate, forgo, relinquish, renounce***)
Word building: **abnegation** *noun*
Word history: Latin

abnormal
adjective unusual: *Such severe heat is* ***abnormal*** *for this time of year.* (***bizarre, odd, peculiar, unconventional, weird***)
Word use: The opposite of this is **normal**.
Word building: **abnormality** *noun* (*plural* **abnormalities**)
Word history: Latin *abnormis* irregular + *-al*

aboard (uh-bawd)
adverb **1** on or in a ship, train, bus, etc.: *All* ***aboard!***
preposition **2** on: *We went* ***aboard*** *the boat.*

abode
noun **1** *Old-fashioned* your house or the place where you live
verb **2** past tense of **abide**
Word history: Old English, past tense of *ābīdan* abide

abolish
verb to put an end to something: *to* ***abolish*** *slavery* (***annul, break off, dissolve, finish, repeal***)
Word use: The opposite of this is **retain**.
Word building: **abolition** *noun*
Word history: French, from Latin word meaning 'perish'

abominable (uh-bom-uh-nuh-buhl, uh-bom-nuh-buhl)
adjective hateful or disgusting: *Slavery was an* ***abominable*** *practice.* (***abysmal, atrocious, monstrous, nasty, rotten***)
Word building: **abominably** *adverb*
Word history: Middle English, from Latin

abomination (uh-bom-uh-nay-shuhn)
noun **1** a person, thing or action causing great hate or disgust
2 extreme dislike (***abhorrence, aversion, detestation, loathing***)

aboriginal
adjective **1** having to do with the earliest inhabitants of a country: ***aboriginal*** *artefacts*
2 Aboriginal, having to do with Australian Aborigines
noun **3 Aboriginal**, an Australian Aborigine

aborigine (ab-uh-rij-uh-nee)
noun **1** one of the earliest inhabitants of a country
2 Aborigine, a member of a tribal people, the earliest known inhabitants of Australia
Word history: from Latin word meaning 'from the beginning'

Aborigine / Aboriginal

When the word **Aborigine** is used to refer to one of the earliest inhabitants of Australia, you write it with a capital letter. The plural is **Aborigines**.

When you write it with a lower-case a (**aborigine**), it means 'an original inhabitant of any country'. The plural is **aborigines**.

Aboriginal is the adjective from **Aborigine**:

an Aboriginal cave painting

Aboriginal is also sometimes used instead of **Aborigine** as a noun:

There were seven Aboriginals at the camp site.

The name **Aborigine** was given to these people by the British. Most Aboriginal people prefer to use a word from one of their own languages, such as *Koori*, *Murri* or *Yolngu*.

The adjective **Indigenous** is the preferred term when you want to talk about both **Aboriginal** people and Torres Strait Islander people.

abort (uh-bawt)
verb **1** of a foetus, to fail to develop completely, or to cause to be born before it is developed enough to live
2 to fail, or cause to fail, especially a military operation, test of a machine, etc.
Word history: Latin

abortion (uh-baw-shuhn)
noun **1** the birth or removal of a foetus from its mother's womb before it has grown enough to live on its own
2 anything which is a failure and which doesn't develop successfully
Word history: from Latin word meaning 'miscarriage'

abortive
adjective unsuccessful: *The injured bird made an* ***abortive*** *attempt to fly.*
Word history: Latin

abound
verb **1** to exist in great numbers: *Fish **abound** in this river.*
phrase **2 abound with,** to be filled with: *This river **abounds with** fish.*
Word history: Middle English, from Latin

about
preposition **1** of or concerning: *She wrote an essay **about** our polluted beaches.*
2 somewhere near or in: *He is **about** the house.*
adverb **3** approximately: ***about** 100 kilometres*
4 almost: ***about** ready*
5 around: *look **about** | move things **about***
phrase **6 about to,** on the point of: ***about to** leave*
7 up and about, active again after a sleep or illness
Word history: Old English *on būtan* on the outside (of)

above
adverb **1** in a higher place: *the blue sky **above***
2 earlier, especially in a book, document, etc.: *from what has been said **above***
preposition **3** over or higher than something or someone, in place, rank or power: *The spaceship flew **above** the earth. | A general is **above** a captain.*
4 more than, in number or quantity: *The petrol gauge was showing just **above** empty.*
5 not capable of, or too good for: *He is **above** telling lies. | She is **above** suspicion.*
6 too difficult for: *That question is **above** me.*
adjective **7** said or written earlier
phrase **8 above all,** most important of all
9 the above, something that was said or written earlier
Word history: Old English from *a-* + *bufan* above

abrade (uh-brayd)
verb to scrape off or wear down by rubbing
Word building: **abradant** *noun* **abradant** *adjective*
Word history: from Latin word meaning 'scrape off'

abrasion
noun a wound or sore that is caused by a scrape: *an **abrasion** on the knee*
Word history: Latin

abrasive
adjective **1** causing abrasion, as by rubbing or scraping: *an **abrasive** powder for kitchen cleaning*
2 annoying or irritating: *Her **abrasive** personality has cost her the job.*
noun **3** any material or substance used for rubbing, grinding or polishing, such as sand or emery
Word building: **abrasiveness** *noun*

abreast
adverb side by side: *They walked three **abreast**.*

abridge
verb to shorten by leaving some parts out: *to **abridge** the book for publication in a magazine* (***abbreviate, condense, sum up, summarise***)
Word history: Middle English, from Old French, from Latin word meaning 'shorten'

abroad
adverb **1** out of your own country: *to go **abroad***
2 out of doors: *The flying foxes are **abroad** at night.*
3 at large or in circulation: *There are bad rumours **abroad** in the school.*
Word history: Middle English *a-* + *broad* widely spread

abrogate (ab-ruh-gayt)
verb to abolish or bring officially to an end: *to **abrogate** a law* (***annul, cancel, quash, repeal***)
Word building: **abrogation** *noun*
Word history: Latin

abrupt
adjective **1** sudden or without warning: *an **abrupt** end to the story* (***impromptu, impulsive, snap, surprising***)
2 brief and impolite: *What an **abrupt** remark you made.* (***blunt, brusque, curt, rude, terse***)
Word use: The opposite of definition 1 is **gradual**. | The opposite of definition 2 is **polite**.
Word building: **abruptly** *adverb* **abruptness** *noun*
Word history: from Latin word meaning 'broken off'

abscess (ab-ses, ab-suhs)
noun a collection of pus in part of the body, which is usually caused by bacteria and which is often accompanied by swelling and inflammation: *an **abscess** under his tooth*
Word history: from Latin word meaning 'a going away'

abscissa (ab-sis-uh)
noun the distance of a point on a graph from the vertical axis (the *y*-axis)
Noun forms: The plural is **abscissae** (ab-sis-ee) or **abscissas**.
Word history: Latin, short for *linea abscissa* line cut off

abscond (ab-skond, uhb-skond)
verb to run away secretly, usually to avoid being caught by the police: *The treasurer **absconded** with the funds.* (***elope, escape, leave, nick off***)
Word history: from Latin word meaning 'put away'

abseil (ab-sayl)
verb to lower yourself down a cliff or wall, using a rope attached to a harness and a device to control downward movement
Word history: German

absence
noun **1** a state or period of being away: *I'll do your work during your **absence**.*
2 a lack of something: *The **absence** of evidence made the case hard to prove.*
Word history: Middle English, from Latin

absent (ab-suhnt)
adjective **1** away or not present: *to be **absent** from school*
2 missing or not found: *His usual smile was **absent** from his face.*
verb (uhb-sent) **3** to take or keep yourself away: *to **absent** yourself from the party*
Word history: Middle English, from Latin

absentee
noun a person who is away or not present: *The teacher noted the name of each **absentee** on the class roll.*

absenteeism
noun the practice of staying away from work or school

absentee vote
noun a vote lodged by a voter who is outside their electorate on election day, but still within their state or territory

Word use: You can also use **absent vote**.

absent-minded
adjective being forgetful or vague and not paying attention (***bemused***, ***half-asleep***, ***inattentive***, ***preoccupied***)

Word building: **absent-mindedly** *adverb*

absolute
adjective **1** complete or perfect: *He told the **absolute** truth.*
2 not limited in any way: *an **absolute** monarch | **absolute** command*

Word building: **absolutely** *adverb*
Word history: Middle English, from Latin word meaning 'loosened from'

absolute majority
noun the difference in number between the votes for the leading candidate in an election and the (lower) total of all other votes cast

absolute zero
noun the lowest possible theoretical temperature at which matter can exist; the temperature at which particles, whose movement is heat, would be at rest, defined as zero kelvin or -273.15 degrees Celsius

absolve
verb to free someone from blame, guilt, punishment, a duty, etc.: *We **absolve** you from responsibility in this instance.*

Word use: The opposite of this is **condemn**.
Word history: Latin word meaning 'loosen from'

absorb
verb to soak something up or drink in: *This sponge will **absorb** the spilt milk. | The student tried to **absorb** all the facts.* (***assimilate***, ***digest***, ***memorise***, ***take in***)

Word building: **absorbent** *adjective* **absorption** *noun*
Word history: Latin

absorbing
adjective very interesting: *an **absorbing** book*

Word use: The opposite of this is **boring**.

abstain
verb to keep yourself from doing something: *to **abstain** from smoking | to **abstain** from voting*

Word history: Middle English, from Latin

abstemious (uhb-stee-mee-uhs)
adjective careful or restrained in the use of food, drink, etc.

Word history: Latin

abstention
noun the act of abstaining, especially from voting

Word history: from Latin word meaning 'abstained'

abstinence
noun the habit or practice of abstaining, especially from drinking alcohol

Word history: Middle English, from Latin

abstract (ab-strakt)
adjective **1** having to do with ideas rather than things: *My essay was about desert landforms, but my friend wrote an **abstract** one about love.*
2 hard to understand: *an **abstract** argument*
noun (ab-strakt) **3** a summary or shortened form of a speech, experiment or essay
verb (uhb-strakt) **4** to remove something or take it away

Word use: The opposite of definition 1 is **concrete**.
Word history: from Latin word meaning 'drawn away'

abstract art
noun an art style which places great importance on design and colour, and avoids realistic representation of objects and figures

abstracted
adjective lost in thought: *She had an **abstracted** look on her face.* (***faraway***, ***preoccupied***, ***remote***)

abstraction (uhb-strak-shuhn)
noun **1** an abstract or general idea or expression
2 a state of being lost in thought

Word history: Latin

abstract noun
noun a word which refers to something that our five senses (touch, sight, hearing, smell and taste) can't pick up: *'Fear', 'love', 'size' and 'beauty' are all **abstract nouns**.*

Word use: The opposite of this is **concrete noun**.

For more information about **abstract nouns** and **concrete nouns**, look up **nouns**.

abstruse (uhb-stroohs)
adjective hard to understand: *an **abstruse** question*

Word history: from Latin word meaning 'concealed'

absurd
adjective **1** foolish or without common sense: *an **absurd** question* (***ludicrous***, ***nonsensical***, ***preposterous***, ***ridiculous***, ***silly***)
2 very funny: *an **absurd** clown* (***amusing***, ***comical***)

Word building: **absurdity** *noun*
Word history: Latin

abundant
adjective plentiful or more than enough: *The canteen has an **abundant** supply of sausage rolls.* (***ample***, ***bountiful***, ***copious***, ***prolific***)

Word use: The opposite of this is **scarce**, **deficient** or **insufficient**.
Word building: **abundance** *noun*
Word history: Middle English, from Latin

abuse (uh-byoohz)
verb **1** to speak to someone in a nasty way (***curse***, ***insult***, ***swear at***)
2 to use something wrongly: *to **abuse** a pencil by chewing it* (***damage***, ***exploit***, ***harm***, ***ill-treat***)
noun (uh-byoohs) **3** insults or hurtful language
4 wrong use: ***abuse** of textbooks by scribbling in them*
5 consumption of something in an excessive way: *drug **abuse** | alcohol **abuse***

Word building: **abusive** *adjective*
Word history: French, from Latin word meaning 'misuse'

abut (uh-but)
verb to touch at one end: *This piece of land* ***abuts*** *on a street. | My house* ***abuts*** *the park.* (***adjoin***, ***border***, ***verge***)

Verb forms: it **abutted**, it has **abutted**, it is **abutting**
Word history: Middle English, from Old French word meaning 'join end to end'

abysmal (uh-biz-muhl)
adjective so bad that it could not be worse: *an* ***abysmal*** *piece of work* (***abominable***, ***atrocious***, ***monstrous***, ***nasty***, ***rotten***)

abyss (uh-bis)
noun a hole or space that is too deep to measure

Word history: Latin *abyssus*, from Greek *ábyssos* without bottom

acacia (uh-kay-shuh, uh-kay-see-uh)
noun a small tree that grows in warm areas of the world, and has small ball-shaped yellow flowers

Word use: This is usually called **wattle** in Australia.
Word history: Latin, from Greek word meaning 'a thorny Egyptian tree'

academic
adjective **1** having to do with a college or university: ***academic*** *studies*
2 full of theory instead of practical common sense: *an* ***academic*** *argument*
3 having a strong ability for learning or study: *She's not very* ***academic***, *but she's a brilliant athlete.*
noun **4** someone who teaches or does research in a college or university

Word use: The opposite of definition 2 is **practical**.

academy
noun a school or society for learning

Noun forms: The plural is **academies**.
Word history: Latin, from Greek word meaning 'place sacred to *Akádēmos*' (a Greek hero)

accede (uhk-seed)
verb **1** to agree or consent: *I* ***accede*** *to your wishes.*
2 to come to an important position: *to* ***accede*** *to the throne*

Word history: from Latin word meaning 'go to'

accede / exceed
Don't confuse **accede** with **exceed**, which means 'to go beyond':
Don't exceed the speed limit.

accelerate (uhk-sel-uh-rayt)
verb **1** to make something move faster or speed up: *to* ***accelerate*** *a car | This drug will* ***accelerate*** *growth.*
2 *Physics* to change the amount and/or direction of the velocity of something

Word use: The opposite of this is **decelerate**.
Word building: **acceleration** *noun*
Word history: Latin

accelerator (uhk-sel-uh-ray-tuh)
noun a pedal in a car, which the driver presses to make the car go faster

accent (ak-sent)
noun **1** your own way of speaking: *I have an Australian* ***accent***.
2 a stress or stronger tone given to part of a word or a musical note, to make it different from the rest
3 a mark showing stress, or that a letter should be pronounced in a certain way
verb (ak-sent) **4** to stress or emphasise something: *to* ***accent*** *a note in a piece of music*

Word history: from Latin word meaning 'tone'

Some foreign languages use **accents** (definition 3 above) in their writing to show that certain letters have to be pronounced in a special way.
Look up **acute accent**, **cedilla**, **circumflex**, **dieresis**, **grave accent** and **umlaut**.

accentuate (uhk-sen-chooh-ayt)
verb to give importance to something: *The brown eye shadow* ***accentuates*** *your eyes.* (***emphasise***, ***highlight***, ***magnify***, ***stress***)

Word building: **accentuation** *noun*
Word history: Medieval Latin

accept (uhk-sept)
verb to take or receive something willingly: *to* ***accept*** *an invitation* (***adopt***, ***agree to***, ***consent to***)

Word use: The opposite of this is **decline** or **reject**.
Word history: Middle English, from Latin

accept / except
Don't confuse **accept** with **except**, which means 'excluding or leaving out':
Everyone understood the joke except me.

acceptable
adjective satisfactory, pleasing or worth accepting (***agreeable***, ***enjoyable***, ***good***, ***pleasant***, ***welcome***)

Word use: The opposite of this is **unacceptable**.

acceptance
noun **1** the act of taking, receiving or agreeing to something: *He sent his* ***acceptance*** *to the party invitation.*
2 approval or favourable reception: ***Acceptance*** *by the rest of the group was important to her.*
3 an agreement to pay an order or bill

accepted (uhk-sep-tuhd)
adjective according to custom: *It is* ***accepted*** *that Dad cooks dinner.* (***agreed***, ***approved***, ***confirmed***, ***established***, ***recognised***)

access (ak-ses)
noun **1** the right of coming to someone or something: *We have* ***access*** *to our principal at all times. | They have* ***access*** *to information about my finances.*
2 a way of getting to a place: *This street gives easy* ***access*** *to the highway.*
3 a parent's right to see a child, especially when a divorce has taken place
verb **4** to obtain information from: *to* ***access*** *a database*
5 to gain admittance to: *The building can be* ***accessed*** *from both sides. | to* ***access*** *a website*

accessible
adjective able to be reached or used
Word building: **accessibility** *noun*

accession
noun **1** the act of taking up an important position: *a king or queen's **accession** to the throne*
2 something added, that increases what was there before: *an **accession** of land | an **accession** of books to the library*
Word history: from Latin word meaning 'a joining', 'an increase'

accessory (uhk-ses-uh-ree)
noun **1** something added but not necessary: *My red handbag is an **accessory** that matches my red dress.*
2 someone who helps carry out a crime: *The person who hid the thief was charged with being an **accessory**.*
Noun forms: The plural is **accessories**.
Word history: Late Latin

accident (ak-suh-duhnt)
noun **1** an unwanted or unlucky happening: *a car **accident*** (***blow**, **disaster**, **mishap***)
2 something that happens by chance: *We met the boys by **accident**.*
Word history: Middle English, from Latin word meaning 'happening'

accidental (ak-suh-den-tl)
adjective **1** happening by accident or by chance: *an **accidental** meeting* (***chance**, **coincidental**, **fluky**, **haphazard**, **random***)
noun **2** *Music* any sign placed before a note showing a sharp, flat or natural not in the key signature

acclaim
verb **1** to praise with sounds of approval: *to **acclaim** the singer with shouts and clapping* (***applaud**, **cheer**, **clap**, **honour**, **toast***)
noun **2** praise or applause: *The singer was met with **acclaim**.*
Word building: **acclamation** *noun*
Word history: Latin

acclimatise
verb to get used to new conditions: *to **acclimatise** to living in the bush*
Word use: You can also use **acclimatize**.
Word building: **acclimatisation** *noun*
Word history: French

accolade (ak-uh-layd)
noun **1** the ceremonial touch of a sword on the shoulder of someone who is being made a knight
2 any way of showing praise or honour

accommodate
verb **1** to have space for someone or something: *This motel **accommodates** 200 people.*
2 to change or adapt: *to **accommodate** themselves to a new plan*
Word history: from Latin word meaning 'suited'

accommodation
noun a room for a visitor to stay, usually in a hotel or motel

accompaniment
noun **1** something less important or added for ornament: *The earring was the perfect **accompaniment** to the hairdo.*
2 *Music* a part written to play with a tune

accompany
verb **1** to go or be with someone: *to **accompany** a friend* (***associate with**, **chaperone**, **escort**, **hang around with**, **partner***)
2 to play or sing with someone: *My mother **accompanies** me on the piano while I play the violin.*
Verb forms: I **accompanied**, I have **accompanied**, I am **accompanying**
Word history: Middle English, from French

accomplice (uh-kum-pluhs, uh-kom-pluhs)
noun someone who shares in a crime: *The robber's **accomplice** drove the getaway car.*
Word history: earlier *complice*, from French, from Medieval Latin word meaning 'companion'; the phrase *a complice* became *accomplice* by people not recognising that it was two words

accomplish (uh-kum-plish, uh-kom-plish)
verb to carry out successfully: *to **accomplish** a task* (***achieve**, **attain**, **bring off**, **finish**, **perform***)
Word history: Middle English, from Late Latin

accomplished
adjective highly skilled: *an **accomplished** violinist*

accomplishment (uh-kum-plish-muhnt, uh-kom-plish-muhnt)
noun **1** completion or fulfilment: *the **accomplishment** of our desires*
2 an achievement or anything successfully done: *the **accomplishments** of scientists* (***attainment**, **exploit**, **feat**, **success***)
3 accomplishments, social arts, graces or skills

accord
noun **1** agreement or harmony: *The brothers are in **accord** with each other.*
2 a formal agreement or contract between two or more groups of people: *The Prices and Incomes **Accord** between the Australian Labor Party and the Australian Council of Trade Unions was reached in February 1983.*
phrase **3 of your own accord**, without being asked: *She put out the rubbish **of her own accord**.*
4 with one accord, with complete agreement: *They all stood up to cheer **with one accord**.*
Word building: **accord** *verb*
Word history: Late Latin

accordance
phrase **in accordance with**, in line with: ***in accordance with** your wishes*

according
phrase **according to 1** as set out in or conforming to: *to work **according to** the rules*
2 in relation or proportion to: *to be paid **according to** the age you are and the amount of experience you've had*
3 as told by: ***According to** him, the shark was as big as whale.*

accordion
noun a musical instrument which you squeeze to produce sound, and which you play using buttons or keys
Word history: *accord* agreement, harmony + *-ion*

accost
verb to come up and speak to, usually in an unpleasant way: *The bully* ***accosted*** *me in the playground today.*
Word history: French, from Late Latin word meaning 'put side by side'

account
noun **1** a sum of money in a bank or building society which you can add to or take away from
2 a record of money paid out and received by a person or business
3 *Computers* the right to access particular computing resources
4 a list of particular happenings: *I'll give you an* ***account*** *of my day at school.*
5 importance or value: *things of no* ***account***
6 judgement or consideration: *I will take that into* ***account.***
phrase **7 bring** (or **call**) **to account**, to ask someone to explain their actions
8 by all accounts, according to all reports
9 give a good account of (**yourself**), to do well
10 on account of, because of: *I can't go to the party* ***on account of*** *having a migraine.*
11 on (or **to**) **account**, as part payment: *I will pay $40* ***on account.***
12 account for, to explain: *That* ***accounts for*** *his disappearance.*
Word history: Middle English, from Late Latin

accountability
noun Commerce the responsibility, especially of a manufacturer or trader, to provide the information about, and guarantee the standard of quality or performance of something to match its value

accountable
adjective obliged to explain what you have done or how you have done something

accountant
noun someone whose job is to examine and record all the money that is earned and spent in a business
Word building: **accountancy** *noun*

accounting
noun the theory and system of setting up and looking after the books of a business, so that its financial position can be examined and the owners can find out how well it is doing

accounts payable
noun Commerce amounts owing to a creditor or creditors for goods they have delivered or services they have completed; part of the liabilities of a business

accounts receivable
noun Commerce amounts owed by a debtor or debtors for goods that have been delivered or services that have been completed; part of the assets of a business

accredit
verb **1** to attribute or consider as belonging: *They* ***accredit*** *this discovery to Edison.*
2 to give credentials to: *to* ***accredit*** *a representative*
phrase **3 accredit with**, to give credit to: *We* ***accredit*** *her* ***with*** *the plan.*
Word building: **accreditation** *noun*
Word history: French

accretion (uh-kree-shuhn)
noun **1** an increase in size by natural growth or by gradual addition
2 the growing together of separate parts into a single whole
Word history: Latin

accrual
noun Commerce the principle that income and expenses are entered into the accounts for the financial period in which they occur, rather than when the money is actually received or paid out

accrue
verb **1** to happen or result as a natural growth
2 to come as a regular addition: *Interest* ***accrues*** *on money in the bank.*
Word history: from *accrue*, obsolete noun, from French word meaning 'increase', from Latin

accumulate
verb to collect, or pile up: *He* ***accumulated*** *a large collection of stamps. | Don't let papers* ***accumulate*** *on your desk.* (***accrue, amass, gather, store***)
Word use: The opposite of this is **disperse**.
Word building: **accumulation** *noun*
Word history: from Latin word meaning 'heaped up'

accurate
adjective correct or exact: *an* ***accurate*** *copy | an* ***accurate*** *account of the accident* (***precise, right, true, valid***)
Word building: **accuracy** *noun* **accurately** *adverb*
Word history: from Latin word meaning 'cared for'

accursed (uh-ker-suhd, uh-kerst)
adjective **1** ruined or under a curse: *an* ***accursed*** *race of people*
2 detestable or worthy of curses: *I wish this* ***accursed*** *rain would stop.*

accusation (ak-yooh-zay-shuhn)
noun **1** a charge of doing wrong
2 the wrong with which someone is charged: *The* ***accusation*** *is murder.*
Word history: Latin

accuse
verb to blame openly for doing something wrong: *He* ***accused*** *his friend of cheating.* (***allege, charge, denounce, frame***)
Word history: Latin

accused (uh-kyoohzd)
noun someone charged with a crime: *The judge let the* ***accused*** *go free.*

accustom (uh-kus-tuhm)
phrase **accustom to**, to make used to: *He will* ***accustom*** *himself* ***to*** *the heat.*
Word history: Old French *a* to + *costume* custom

accustomed
adjective **1** usual: *The library opened at the* ***accustomed*** *time.*
phrase **2 accustomed to**, in the habit of: *She is* ***accustomed to*** *working hard.*

ace
noun **1** a playing card with a single spot: *the* ***ace*** *of spades*
2 a serve in tennis which the other player cannot touch with their racquet

3 an expert: *an* ***ace*** *at dancing | a flying* ***ace*** *from World War I* (***champion, genius, master, star***)

Word history: Middle English *as*, from Latin, supposedly from dialect. Greek, variant of Greek *heis* one

acerbity (uh-ser-buh-tee)
noun **1** sourness, with roughness or sharpness of taste
2 harshness or severity, of your temper, words, etc.

Word building: **acerbic** *adjective*
Word history: French, from Latin

acetate (as-uh-tayt)
noun Chemistry a salt formed from acetic acid

Word building: **acetated** *adjective*

acetic (uh-see-tik, uh-set-ik)
adjective having to do with, derived from, or producing vinegar or acetic acid

acetic / ascetic

Don't confuse **acetic** with **ascetic**, a word which describes the lifestyle of monks, nuns, hermits and others like them. They are strict about the way they live and deny themselves pleasures. We pronounce it *uh-set-ik*.

acetic acid (uh-see-tik as-uhd, uh-set-ik as-uhd)
noun a sour colourless acid, with a sharp smell, being the main compound in vinegar, used to make acetate fibre, etc.

Word use: Another name is **ethanoic acid**.
Word building: **acetous** *adjective*

acetone (as-uh-tohn)
noun a colourless, volatile, flammable liquid, known as a ketone, used as a solvent and in varnishes, etc.

acetylene (uh-set-uh-leen, uh-set-uh-luhn)
noun a gas which, when combined with oxygen, burns with a very hot flame and is used in welding

Word use: Acetylene is used in an **oxyacetylene torch**.

ache (ayk)
noun **1** a dull continuous pain: *a stomach* ***ache*** (***hurt, pang, soreness, throbbing***)
verb **2** to suffer continuous pain: *My leg is* ***aching***.

Word history: Old English *acan*, verb, *æce*, noun

achieve
verb to gain or bring about by effort: *to* ***achieve*** *an ambition* (***accomplish, attain, bring off, carry through, fulfil***)

Word building: **achievement** *noun*
Word history: Middle English, from Old French phrase *(venir) a chef* = Late Latin *ad caput venīre* come to a head

Achilles heel (uh-kil-eez heel)
noun a single major weakness or point open to attack

Word history: from the Greek legend of *Achilles*, hero of Homer's *Iliad*, whose only point of weakness was his heel

Achilles tendon (uh-kil-eez ten-duhn)
noun the tissue joining the calf muscles to the heel bone

Word history: Look up **Achilles heel**.

achromatic (ay-kruh-mat-ik)
adjective **1** without colour, as neutral greys
2 *Biology* containing or consisting of achromatin which is that part of the nucleus of a cell which stains less easily than the rest

Word history: from Greek word meaning 'colourless'

acid
noun **1** a chemical substance which can eat away metals. When you dissolve an acid in water, hydrogen ions with a positive charge are produced.
adjective **2** sour: *Lemons have an* ***acid*** *taste. | an* ***acid*** *remark* (***bitter, tart***)

Word building: **acidic** *adjective* **acidity** *noun*
Word history: from Latin word meaning 'sour'

acid test
noun **1** a test for gold using nitric acid
2 the final analysis or deciding test

acknowledge
verb **1** to admit to be real or true: *He* ***acknowledged*** *that he was to blame.* (***concede, confess, grant, reveal***)
2 to show that you have received: *to* ***acknowledge*** *a signal | to* ***acknowledge*** *an invitation*

Word building: **acknowledgement** *noun*
Word history: blend of obsolete *acknow* (Old English *oncnāwan* confess) and *knowledge*, verb, admit

acme (ak-mee)
noun the culmination or highest point: *the* ***acme*** *of success* (***apex, crest, peak, pinnacle, summit***)

Word history: Greek

acne (ak-nee)
noun a condition that is common in teenagers, caused by inflammation of those glands that secrete oil and resulting in pimples, especially on the face

acolyte (ak-uh-luyt)
noun **1** a minor helper in a church ceremony
2 a helper or attendant

Word history: Middle English, from Medieval Latin, from Greek word meaning 'follower'

acorn
noun a nut in a hardened scaly cup, which grows on an oak tree

Word history: Old English *æcern*

acoustic (uh-kooh-stik)
adjective **1** having to do with hearing or with the science of sound: *We need to lay* ***acoustic*** *insulation under the carpet to stop the noise problem from downstairs.*
2 having to do with musical instruments which are not electronically amplified: *I play an* ***acoustic*** *guitar but my brother plays electric guitar in a rock band.*

Word history: French, from Greek

acoustics (uh-kooh-stiks)
noun **1** the science or study of sound
2 the properties of a building which affect the quality of the sounds produced in it: *The concert hall has good* ***acoustics***.

acquaint
verb to tell, inform or make familiar: *You should* ***acquaint*** *the police with anything you know about a crime.*

Word building: **acquainted** *adjective*
Word history: Middle English, from Late Latin word meaning 'make known'

acquaintance
noun **1** knowledge: ***acquaintance*** *with the facts*
2 a person you know: *He is an* ***acquaintance****, but I wouldn't call him a friend.* (***associate****,* ***colleague****,* ***contact***)

acquiesce (ak-wee-es)
verb to agree or consent, especially in a quiet way: *to* ***acquiesce*** *in an opinion*

Word building: **acquiescence** *noun* **acquiescent** *adjective*
Word history: Latin

acquire
verb to get or obtain: *She has* ***acquired*** *a new bike.* (***gain****,* ***grab****,* ***procure****,* ***receive****,* ***win***)

Word use: The opposite of this is **lose**.
Word history: Latin

acquired immune deficiency syndrome
noun → **AIDS**

acquisition (ak-wuh-zish-uhn)
noun **1** something you have acquired: *This vase is my most precious* ***acquisition****.*
verb **2** to acquire something, such as books for a library, etc.

Word history: Latin

acquisitive
adjective eager to collect things

acquit
verb **1** to declare innocent: *They were* ***acquitted*** *by the jury.*
phrase **2 acquit yourself**, to perform: *He* ***acquitted himself*** *well in the exam.*

Verb forms: I **acquitted**, I have **acquitted**, I am **acquitting**
Word use: The opposite of definition 1 is **convict**.
Word building: **acquittal** *noun*

acre (ay-kuh)
noun a large area of land in the imperial system, that is equal to almost half a hectare

Word use: Look up **imperial system**.
Word building: **acreage** (ay-kuh-rij) *noun*
Word history: Old English *æcer*

acrid
adjective having a bitter or unpleasant taste or smell (***astringent****,* ***biting****,* ***pungent****,* ***sharp***)

Word history: Latin *ācer* sharp

acrimony (ak-ruh-muh-nee)
noun sharpness, harshness or bitterness of your temper or speech

Word building: **acrimonious** *adjective*
Word history: Latin

acrobat
noun someone who performs daring gymnastic tricks: *The* ***acrobat*** *at the circus walked the tightrope.*

Word building: **acrobatic** *adjective* **acrobatics** *noun*
Word history: French, from Greek word meaning 'walking on tiptoe'

acronym (ak-ruh-nim)
noun a word made from the first letters of other words: *'ANZAC' is an* ***acronym*** *from 'Australian and New Zealand Army Corps'.*

Word use: Compare this with **initialism**.
Word history: *acr(o)-* + Greek *ónyma* name

across
preposition **1** from side to side of: *a plank* ***across*** *a creek*
2 on the other side of: *I live* ***across*** *the lake.*
adverb **3** from one side to another: *I rowed* ***across*** *in a boat.*
4 on the other side: *We'll soon be* ***across****.*

acrostic (uh-kros-tik)
noun a set of words or lines, as a poem, in which the first, last or other particular letters form a word, phrase, the alphabet, etc.

Word history: Latin, from Greek

acrylic (uh-kril-ik)
noun **1** a synthetic material used for clothing
adjective **2** made of a material like this: *an* ***acrylic*** *jumper*
3 acrylics, synthetic colour used as a painting medium

Word history: *acr(olein)* + *-yl* + *-ic*

act
noun **1** something done or performed: *an* ***act*** *of bravery* (***achievement****,* ***action****,* ***deed****,* ***exploit****,* ***feat***)
2 a law or order: *an* ***act*** *of Parliament*
3 one of the main divisions of a stage play: *A ghost appeared in the third* ***act*** *of the play.*
4 a single performance in a concert: *a singing* ***act***
verb **5** to do something: *He* ***acted*** *quickly when danger was near.*
6 to do someone's duties when they are unable to: *to* ***act*** *as principal while she is away*
7 to play the part of: *to* ***act*** *Peter Pan in the school play*
8 to behave as: *to* ***act*** *the fool*
phrase **9 act on** (or **upon**),
a to follow: *Why don't you* ***act on*** *my suggestion?*
b to affect: *Alcohol* ***acts on*** *the brain.*
10 act out, to express an idea, a feeling, etc., by acting
11 act up, *Colloquial* to cause trouble (***make mischief****,* ***mess around****,* ***muck up***)

Word history: Middle English, from Latin *actum* a thing done

action
noun **1** an act or deed: *a brave* ***action*** (***achievement****,* ***exploit****,* ***feat***)
2 the state of being active: *The nurses went into* ***action*** *when the ambulance arrived.*
3 a way of moving: *the* ***action*** *of a horse*

Word history: Latin

action verb
noun → **dynamic verb**

activate
verb to make active or set in motion: *He* ***activated*** *the machine by pulling a lever.*

Word use: The opposite of this is **deactivate**.

active
adjective **1** taking part or doing things: *an **active** participant*
2 continuously busy: *He leads an **active** life.* (***energetic***, ***flat out***, ***hard-working***, ***hectic***, ***industrious***)
3 able to move quickly: *an **active** puppy*
4 highly involved in some area or activity: ***active** in the community* | *an **active** environmentalist*

Word use: The opposite of definition 1 is **passive**.
Word history: Latin

active verb
noun a type of verb form which indicates that the subject of the verb is doing the action

Look up **verbs: active verbs**.

activist
noun someone who works very hard for something they believe in: *Alex is an **activist** for peace.*

activity
noun a thing you do, often energetically: *The main **activity** for the day was swimming.*

Noun forms: The plural is **activities**.

actor
noun someone who acts the part of a character in a play or film, or on television: *The **actor** who played the killer was frightening.*

Word building: **actress** *feminine noun*
Word history: Latin

The word **actor** is used for both males and females. The term **actress**, to describe a female actor, is not used as much nowadays as it has been in the past. For more information, look up **non-sexist language**.

actual
adjective real or existing (***concrete***, ***material***, ***physical***, ***tangible***)

Word building: **actually** *adverb*
Word history: from Late Latin word meaning 'active', 'practical'

actuality (ak-chooh-al-uh-tee)
noun reality or actual existence

actuary (ak-chooh-uh-ree)
noun in economics, insurance, etc., someone who calculates risks, rates of payment, etc., based on statistics or recorded facts

Noun forms: The plural is **actuaries**.
Word building: **actuarial** *adjective*
Word history: Latin

actuate (ak-chooh-ayt)
verb to move to action: *He was **actuated** by selfish feelings.*

Word building: **actuation** *noun*
Word history: Medieval Latin

acuity (uh-kyooh-uh-tee)
noun sharpness or acuteness: ***acuity** of sight* | ***acuity** of thought*

Word history: Medieval Latin

acumen (ak-yuh-muhn)
noun good judgement: *His business **acumen** helped him to make money.*

Word history: Latin

acupuncture (ak-yuh-pungk-chuh, ak-uh-pungk-chuh)
noun a Chinese type of medicine which treats illness or pain by sticking needles into certain parts of the body

Word building: **acupuncturist** *noun*
Word history: Latin *acu(s)* needle + *puncture*

acute
adjective **1** very sudden and severe: *an **acute** attack of asthma*
2 clever and to the point: *an **acute** remark*
3 having less than 90°: *an **acute** angle*

Word history: from Latin word meaning 'sharpened'

acute / chronic
Look up **chronic / acute**.

acute accent
noun a mark (´) used in some languages to show that certain vowels have to be pronounced in a certain way

Acute accents are used in writing French, Spanish, Greek and other languages.

In French, an acute accent over an e means that it should be pronounced *ay*, to rhyme with *day*. For example, the French word *début*, meaning 'first public appearance', is pronounced *day-booh*, which explains why the English spelling, *debut*, is pronounced this way too.

In other languages, such as Spanish and Greek, acute accents are used to show that a vowel is stressed.

acute angle
noun Geometry an angle of less than 90°

AD
abbreviation short for *anno domini*, Latin words meaning *'in the year of our Lord'*: *A person first walked on the moon in **AD** 1969.*

Word history: Latin

Our calendar dates events from the year of Jesus Christ's birth. Years after this are labelled **AD**, and the years before are labelled **BC**.

You can write **AD** before or after the numbers showing the date, although some people do regard putting it after as a mistake. This is because AD stands for *anno domini*, Latin for 'in the year of our Lord', and if you expand the abbreviation it sounds odd to have it after the year. But, nowadays, more and more people find it sensible to have AD matching BC, which always comes after the numbers.

The abbreviation **CE** (as in *1427 CE*) is sometimes used if the speaker or writer wants to avoid the reference to Christ. It stands for *(of the) Common Era*.

adage (ad-ij)
noun a wise saying: *'More haste less speed' is a common **adage**.* (***epigram***, ***maxim***, ***motto***, ***proverb***)

Word history: French, from Latin *adagium*

adagio (uh-dah-zhee-oh, uh-dah-jee-oh)
adverb played or sung slowly and calmly

Word history: Italian

adamant (ad-uh-muhnt)
adjective staying firm in what you decide: *She was **adamant** that she would not go.* (***determined***, ***inflexible***, ***obstinate***, ***persistent***, ***uncompromising***)

Word history: Latin, from Greek

Adam's apple
noun a projection of the thyroid cartilage at the front of a man's throat

adapt
verb **1** to change or adjust: *We **adapted** the design of our model aeroplane so that it flew better.* (***alter***, ***convert***, ***transform***, ***vary***)
phrase **2 adapt to**, to become used to: *She found it hard to **adapt to** a new school.*

Word building: **adaptable** *adjective*
Word history: Latin

adaptation
noun **1** an adjustment of some kind: *an **adaptation** of a piece of music for three guitars instead of one*
2 *Literature* a work rewritten to be presented in a different way: *an **adaptation** of a book for the stage*
3 *Biology* the alteration of the structure or work of an organism so that it can live and work if the conditions in which it lives changes

adaptor
noun an extra part which changes a machine or tool to a different use

add
verb **1** to join so as to increase: *to **add** another bead to the necklace* (***append***, ***attach***, ***insert***, ***supplement***, ***tack on***)
2 to find the sum of: *to **add** up all the numbers* (***calculate***, ***number***, ***tally***, ***total***)
phrase **3 add to**, to increase or make bigger: *to **add to** his surprise*
4 add up,
a to amount to: *The detective thinks it **adds up** to murder.*
b *Colloquial* to make sense: *These facts don't **add up**.*

Word history: Middle English, from Latin

added value
noun something added to a product or process which increases its value

addendum (uh-den-duhm)
noun something added, especially an appendix to a book

Noun forms: The plural is **addenda**.
Word history: Latin

adder
noun a small venomous snake

Word history: variant of Middle English *nadder* (*a nadder* being taken as *an adder*), Old English *nǣdre*

addict (ad-ikt)
noun someone who can't do without something, especially drugs: *a coffee **addict***

Word building: **addiction** *noun* **addicted** *adjective*
Word history: from Latin word meaning 'devoted'

addictive
adjective habit-forming or causing dependence, especially in the case of drugs

addition
noun **1** something added which increases the size or number of things: *A new bathroom is the latest **addition** to our house.*
2 *Mathematics*, the act of adding numbers together (denoted by the symbol +)
phrase **3 in addition to**, besides or as well as: *I have other friends **in addition to** you.*

Word use: The opposite of definition 2 is **subtraction**.
Word building: **additional** *adjective*
Word history: Latin *additio*

additive
noun something which is added, especially a chemical added to food to keep it fresh

Word history: Latin

address (uh-dres, ad-res)
noun **1** the details of the place where you live
2 a formal speech: *to give an **address** at a meeting*
3 *Computers*, a number or symbol which indicates the location of a piece of information in a computer's memory
verb (uh-dres) **4** to write the receiver's name, street and town on: *I **addressed** the letter wrongly.*
5 to speak to: *The politician **addressed** the meeting.*
6 to deal with: *These are the issues you should **address** in your essay.*

Word history: Middle English, from Latin *ad* to + *directus* straight

adduce (uh-dyoohs)
verb to bring forward in argument or give as proof: *to **adduce** reasons*

Word building: **adducible** *adjective*
Word history: from Latin word meaning 'lead to'

adenoids (ad-uh-noydz)
plural noun the mass of soft growths at the back of the nose which sometimes block it and have to be removed: *My **adenoids** were removed when I was ten.*

Word history: from Greek word meaning 'glandular'

adept
adjective skilful: *She was **adept** at ball games.*

Word history: from Latin word meaning 'having attained'

adequate (ad-uh-kwuht)
adjective suitable or enough: *That light jacket isn't **adequate** for this cold weather.* (***satisfactory***, ***sufficient***)

Word building: **adequacy** *noun*
Word history: from Latin word meaning 'equalised'

adhere
verb to stick firmly: *The grass seeds **adhered** to our socks. | They **adhered** strictly to the rules.*

Word building: **adherence** *noun*

adherent (uhd-hear-ruhnt, uhd-he-ruhnt)
noun **1** someone who follows or supports a person or idea
adjective **2** sticking or clinging

Word history: Latin

adhesive
noun **1** a substance which sticks things together (***cement***, ***gum***, ***mortar***, ***paste***)
adjective **2** sticky: *an **adhesive** bandage*

Word building: **adhesion** *noun*

ad hoc (ad hok)
adjective **1** for this, usually a special purpose: *An **ad hoc** committee is one set up to deal with one subject only.*
2 made or done without preparation: *An **ad hoc** decision is one made with regard to urgent needs of the moment.*

Word history: Latin

ad infinitum (ad in-fuh-nuy-tuhm)
adverb endlessly or forever

Word history: Latin

adjacent (uh-jay-suhnt)
adjective lying near or close: *Our block of land was **adjacent** to the railway line.* (***beside***, ***bordering***, ***joining***, ***neighbouring***, ***next***)

Word history: Latin

adjective
noun Grammar a word which describes a noun, such as 'tall' in *a tall building*

Word building: **adjectival** *adjective*
Word history: Latin

adjectives

You use **adjectives** to describe a noun in more detail:

the wall

the long wall

The only wall that is over 2000 km long.

Adjectives are one of the major word classes.

An adjective doesn't have to come immediately before the noun it is describing:

a long snake

The wall is long.

George is a good surfer.

George's surfing is good.

In fact, a few adjectives can only come straight after the noun they're describing:

bargains galore or *president elect*

And some others can only come after a verb:

The snake is awake.

The zookeeper is asleep.

Using adjectives in writing
You can use adjectives to make very precise descriptions of things, but they are also useful for showing how you feel about something or how you judge it:

The wave was large, curling and crystal clear.

George said it was unreal.

But Kim thought it was an uncatchable wave.

The first example is an impersonal, precise description of a wave. The second sentence shows how George felt about the wave, and the third shows how Kim judged or assessed it.

Comparing with adjectives
Adjectives can change their form to show how two or more things compare. You can use an -er ending with some adjectives to compare two things:

Which of the two snakes is longer?

You can add -est to some adjectives to compare three or more things:

the longest snake in the world

With adjectives of more than two syllables you can't add -er or -est. Instead, you use more or most before the adjective to show the comparison:

Which of the two snakes is more beautiful?

Which is the most beautiful snake in the world?

The ending -er and the word more are used to form what is called the comparative degree of an adjective. Most and -est form the superlative degree.

Adjectives that never make comparisons
Some adjectives do not have a comparative or superlative. For example, you can't be *more first* in a race than someone else, you can't be the *deadest* corpse in the morgue, and one pot can't be *more iron* than another. When an adjective (like *first*, *dead* or *iron*) describes something that is complete, perfect or absolute, it can have no degrees of comparison.

adjoin (uh-joyn)
verb to be in contact with or next to: *His land **adjoins** the lake. | The houses **adjoin**.*

Word building: **adjoining** *adjective*
Word history: Middle English, from Latin word meaning 'join to'

adjourn (uh-jern)
verb **1** to put off: *We will **adjourn** the meeting until tomorrow.* (***delay***, ***postpone***, ***shelve***, ***suspend***)
2 to move: *Shall we **adjourn** to the living room?*

Word building: **adjournment** *noun*
Word history: Middle English, from Old French phrase *a jorn nome* until an appointed day

adjudicate (uh-jooh-duh-kayt)
verb to act as judge: *The principal **adjudicated** in our debate.* (***decide***, ***determine***, ***evaluate***, ***referee***, ***umpire***)

Word building: **adjudication** *noun* **adjudicator** *noun*
Word history: Latin

adjunct (aj-ungkt)
noun **1** something added to another thing
2 an assistant in some duty or work

Word history: Latin

adjure (uh-jooh-uh)
verb to urge or command, seriously and solemnly, often under oath

Word history: Middle English, from Latin

adjust
verb to cause to fit or work properly: *I **adjusted** my belt. | I **adjusted** the tuning on the TV.*

Word building: **adjustable** *adjective* **adjustment** *noun*
Word history: French (obsolete) *adjuster*, from Late Latin *adjuxtāre*

adjutant (aj-uh-tuhnt)
noun Military a staff officer who assists the commanding officer

Word building: **adjutancy** *noun*
Word history: from Latin word meaning 'aiding'

ad lib
adverb **1** freely or impromptu
adjective **2** spoken or done without preparation

Word history: Latin *ad libitum*

administer
verb **1** to run or have charge of: *An accountant* ***administered*** *the business.*
2 to give: *The vet* ***administered*** *a big dose of medicine to the sick horse.*

Word history: Latin

administration
noun the people that run a business or government: *If you don't like the rules, complain to the* ***administration****.*

Word building: **administrative** *adjective*
administrator *noun*

admirable (<u>ad</u>-muh-ruh-buhl)
adjective worthy of admiration: *an* ***admirable*** *effort*

Word building: **admirably** *adverb* **admirer** *noun*

admiral
noun the highest ranking officer in the Navy

Word history: variant of Middle English *amiral*, from Old French, from Arabic *amīr al* (chief of); variant *admiral* arose by association with Latin *admīrābilis* admirable

admire
verb to think very highly of (***appreciate***, ***esteem***, ***respect***)

Word building: **admiration** *noun* **admirer** *noun*
Word history: from Latin word meaning 'wonder at'

admissible (uhd-<u>mis</u>-uh-buhl)
adjective allowable or acceptable as evidence in a court of law

admission (uhd-<u>mish</u>-uhn)
noun **1** the process of entering, dependent on permission or help given, or on the removal of problems: *My* ***admission*** *into hospital took three hours.*
2 the price paid for entrance, such as to the theatre, etc.
3 confession of a charge, error or crime: *His* ***admission*** *of the mistake solved the mystery.*

Word history: Latin

admit
verb **1** to let in: *Only* ***admit*** *one car at a time.*
2 to agree to the truth of: *He* ***admitted*** *his guilt.* (***acknowledge***, ***concede***, ***confess***, ***reveal***)

Verb forms: I **admitted**, I have **admitted**, I am **admitting**
Word building: **admittance** *noun*
Word history: Latin

admonish (uhd-<u>mon</u>-ish)
verb **1** to warn or caution: *We* ***admonished*** *the boys not to be noisy.*
2 to reprimand or scold, especially mildly: *He* ***admonished*** *the children for their lateness.* (***rebuke***, ***reprove***, ***rouse on***, ***tell off***)

Word building: **admonition** (ad-muh-<u>ni</u>-shuhn) *noun*
Word history: Latin

ad nauseam (ad <u>naw</u>-zee-uhm, ad <u>naw</u>-zay-uhm)
adverb to the point of disgust or boredom: *She rambled on and on* ***ad nauseam****.*

Word history: Latin

ado
noun **1** bustle or fuss
phrase **2 much ado about nothing**, a great fuss about very little

Word history: Middle English *at do* to do

adolescence (ad-uh-<u>les</u>-uhns)
noun the time between reaching puberty and being an adult

Word building: **adolescent** *adjective*, *noun*

adopt
verb **1** to take (a baby or a child) as legally your own: *They* ***adopted*** *the baby when he was eight weeks old.*
2 to choose and take for yourself: *She* ***adopted*** *a new name.* | *The school council decided to* ***adopt*** *a new uniform.* (***accept***, ***assume***, ***select***, ***take on***)

Word use: Compare definition 1 with **foster**.
Word building: **adoption** *noun*
Word history: Latin

adoptive
adjective related by adoption: ***adoptive*** *parents*

adoration
noun **1** worship or homage
2 strong and faithful love

adore
verb to feel very strong love for: *The children* ***adored*** *their puppy.* (***cherish***, ***dote on***, ***worship***)

Word history: from Latin word meaning 'address', 'worship'

adorn
verb to decorate or make more attractive: *New furniture* ***adorned*** *the room.* (***beautify***, ***embellish***, ***ornament***)

Word history: Latin

adrenaline (uh-<u>dren</u>-uh-luhn, uh-<u>dren</u>-uh-leen)
noun **1** a hormone produced by the adrenal glands, which is sent into the blood when the body is undergoing stress or activity. It increases your heart rate, blood pressure and blood sugar levels.
2 this substance purified from animals and used as a drug to achieve the effects listed above

Word use: You can also use **adrenalin**.

adrift
adjective **1** not fastened by any kind of moorings and so at the mercy of winds and currents
2 influenced by any chance impulse
3 *Colloquial* confused or wide of the mark

adroit (uh-<u>droyt</u>)
adjective clever or skilful in using your hands or mind

Word building: **adroitly** *adverb* **adroitness** *noun*
Word history: Anglo-French *à droit* rightly

adulate (<u>aj</u>-uh-layt)
verb to show pretended devotion or praise too much

Word building: **adulation** *noun* **adulator** *noun* **adulatory** *adjective*
Word history: Latin

adult
adjective **1** grown-up or mature: *This film is only suitable for an* ***adult*** *audience.*
noun **2** someone who is fully grown
3 *Law* a person who has reached 18 years of age

Word building: **adulthood** *noun*
Word history: Latin

adulterate
verb to spoil by adding something inferior: *to* ***adulterate*** *food*

Word building: **adulteration** *noun*
Word history: from Latin word meaning 'defiled'

adultery
noun a sexual relationship in which at least one of the two people is married to someone else

Word building: **adulterer** *noun* **adulterous** *adjective*
Word history: Latin

advance
verb **1** to move or bring forwards: *He* ***advanced*** *his chess piece across the board. | She* ***advanced*** *to the front of the room.* (***proceed***, ***progress***)
2 to improve or develop: *The new students are* ***advancing*** *rapidly in Maths.* (***forge ahead***, ***make headway***, ***proceed***, ***progress***, ***push on***)
noun **3** progress or movement forwards
4 a loan: *an* ***advance*** *of $10*
phrase **5 in advance**,
a in front or before: ***in advance*** *of other pupils*
b ahead of time: *They paid the rent* ***in advance***.

Word building: **advancement** *noun*
Word history: Middle English, from Late Latin *abante* from before

advanced
adjective above average in progress: *an* ***advanced*** *class in Italian*

advantage
noun **1** something that puts you ahead of others: *Her strong arms gave her an* ***advantage*** *in swimming.* (***asset***, ***benefit***, ***boon***, ***help***, ***plus***)
2 benefit or profit: *It is to his* ***advantage*** *to be tall if he wants to play basketball.*
3 *Tennis* the first point following the score of deuce (when both players have 40 points)
phrase **4 take advantage of**,
a to make use of: *You should* ***take advantage of*** *this chance to go overseas.*
b to impose or make too many demands on someone: *to* ***take advantage of*** *his kindness*

Word building: **advantageous** (ad-van-<u>tay</u>-juhs) *adjective*
Word history: Middle English *avantage*, from Old French *avant* before, forward, from Late Latin

advent (<u>ad</u>-vent)
noun an arrival: *the* ***advent*** *of scientific methods of treatment*

Word history: Middle English from Latin word meaning 'arrival'

adventitious (ad-ven-<u>tish</u>-uhs)
adjective accidentally obtained or added from outside

Word history: Latin word meaning 'coming from abroad'

adventure
noun an exciting experience (***escapade***, ***exploit***)

Word history: Middle English, from Latin *(rēs) adventūra*, future perfect, (a thing) about to happen

adventurer
noun **1** a person who looks out for adventure
2 a person who takes risks in business

adventurous
adjective **1** wanting to take part in adventures: *an* ***adventurous*** *child* (***adventuresome***, ***audacious***, ***bold***, ***daring***)
2 needing courage to perform: *an* ***adventurous*** *act*

adverb
noun Grammar a word which tells you something extra about a verb, an adjective or another adverb, such as 'beautifully' in *singing beautifully*

Word building: **adverbial** *adjective*
Word history: Latin

adverbs

You use **adverbs** to say something extra about a verb, an adjective or another adverb. Many of them end in <u>-ly</u>, though some common ones don't. Adverbs often answer questions like 'How?', 'Where?' or 'When?' for verbs:

How?
Sherlock Holmes strode <u>rapidly</u> across the room.

How?
He could see the traces of tobacco <u>well</u> through his magnifying glass.

Where?
He could tell that the tobacco was grown <u>locally</u>.

Where?
Holmes looked for Watson, but he had gone off <u>somewhere</u>.

When?
He <u>immediately</u> rang the police.

When?
They <u>soon</u> came.

Each of the underlined words in these examples is an adverb, including the common words *well* and *soon* which don't end in <u>-ly</u>.

You can see that adverbs may come before or after the word they describe, and that they may appear next to that word or quite a distance away. Adverbs may also strengthen or weaken an adjective or adverb:

The murderer kept <u>very</u> quiet in the bushes outside the window.

He was <u>really</u> scared.

He was <u>fairly</u> certain that Holmes was on to him.

Some adverbs look just like adjectives:

The murderer knew he had to move <u>fast</u>. (adverb)

There was a <u>fast</u> train to London in five minutes. (adjective)

But when the adverb is not the same as the adjective, it cannot be used instead of the adjective. For example, *well* is the adverb that relates to the adjective *good*, so *good* is not generally used as an adverb:

He made a <u>good</u> getaway and was soon sitting in the train beside a tall quiet man. (adjective)

(continued)

adverbs *(continued)*

But the man was Holmes, who smiled and said: 'These handcuffs will fit you well.' (adverb)
NOT *'These handcuffs will fit you good.'*

adversary (ad-vuh-suh-ree)
noun someone you compete against or fight with (***antagonist, enemy, foe, opponent, rival***)

Word use: The opposite of this is **friend, supporter** or **comrade.**
Noun forms: The plural is **adversaries.**
Word history: Middle English, from Latin

adverse (ad-vers, uhd-vers)
adjective **1** threatening or hostile: ***adverse** criticism*
2 opposing your interests or wishes: ***adverse** influences*

Word history: Middle English, from Latin word meaning 'turned against'

adversity (uhd-ver-suh-tee)
noun hardship or misfortune: *a time of great **adversity***

advert (uhd-vert)
phrase **advert to,** to call attention or refer to: *He briefly **adverted to** the events of the day.*

Word history: from Latin word meaning 'turn to'

advertise (ad-vuh-tuyz)
verb to praise or draw attention to, especially in order to sell: *We **advertised** our car in the newspapers.* (***broadcast, promote, publicise***)

Word history: Middle English, from Latin

advertisement (uhd-ver-tuhs-muhnt)
noun a notice telling you about an event that is coming, or about something lost or for sale

Word history: Middle English, from Middle French

advertorial (ad-vuh-taw-ree-uhl)
noun an item in a newspaper or magazine which looks like a news or feature article but which is written and paid for by an advertiser

advice (uhd-vuys)
noun an opinion someone gives you to help you decide what to do: *George gave me **advice** about the best way to fix my bike.* (***counsel, guidance***)

Word history: late Middle English, from Latin *ad-* + *vīsum*, past participle neuter, what seems best

advisable
adjective sensible: *It's **advisable** not to take the steep, dangerous track.*

advise (uhd-vuyz)
verb to tell what you think should be done: *We **advised** them not to go to the desert in summer.* (***guide, recommend, suggest, warn***)

Word building: **adviser, advisor** *noun*
Word history: Late Latin

advisory
adjective **1** giving advice: *an **advisory** council / an **advisory** talk*
noun **2** a statement that offers advice: *A travel **advisory** from the government warned against making unnecessary journeys to the cyclone devastated country.*

Noun forms: The plural is **advisories.**

advocate (ad-vuh-kuht)
noun **1** someone who speaks in favour of a person or cause: *the criminal's **advocate** / an **advocate** of peace* (***backer, campaigner, champion, spokesperson, supporter***)
verb (ad-vuh-kayt) **2** to speak in favour of: *We **advocate** peace rather than war.* (***champion, endorse, hold with, promote, support***)

Word use: The opposite of definition 1 is **opponent.** | The opposite of definition 2 is **oppose.**
Word building: **advocacy** *noun*
Word history: from Latin word meaning 'one summoned to help another (in legal case)'

aegis (eej-uhs)
noun protection or sponsorship: *under the **aegis** of the Australian government*

Word history: Latin, from Greek word meaning '(a goatskin) the shield of Zeus' (a Greek god)

aeon (ee-on, ee-uhn)
noun a long period of time: ***aeons** ago when dinosaurs lived*

Word use: You can also use **eon.**
Word history: Latin, from Greek word meaning 'lifetime', 'age'

aerate (air-rayt)
verb **1** to charge or treat with air or gas, especially with carbon dioxide
2 to expose to the free action of air, especially to freshen, or remove unpleasant smells

Word building: **aeration** *noun*

aerial
noun **1** a wire or rod that you put up to receive radio or television signals
adjective **2** living in or reaching into the air: *The plant has **aerial** roots.*

Word history: Latin word meaning 'airy' (from Greek) + *-al*

aerobics
plural noun exercises done to improve your physical fitness and strengthen your heart and lungs

Word building: **aerobic** *adjective*

aerodrome
noun a landing field for aeroplanes which is smaller than an airport but which has hangars and other buildings

aerodynamics (air-roh-duy-nam-iks)
noun the study of air in motion and of forces acting on solids in motion relative to the air through which they move

Word building: **aerodynamic** *adjective*

aeronautics
noun the science of flight

Word building: **aeronautical** *adjective*
Word history: plural of *aeronautic*, from Neo-Latin word meaning 'relating to sailing in the air'

aeroplane
noun a winged machine which is driven through the air by its propellers or jet engines

aerosol (air-ruh-sol)
noun **1** a smoke or fog
2 a container from which liquids kept under pressure, such as household cleaner, paint, etc., can be sprayed

Word use: You can also use **spray can** for definition 2.
Word history: *aero-* a word part indicating 'air', 'atmosphere', 'gas' + *sol* a fluid suspension of solid in a liquid

aerospace
noun the earth's atmosphere and the space beyond it

aesthete (uhs-theet, ees-theet, es-theet)
noun someone who is very aware of the beauties of art or nature
Word use: You can also use **esthete**.
Word history: from Greek word meaning 'one who perceives'

aesthetic (uhs-thet-ik)
adjective **1** having to do with the idea of what is beautiful, or with the study of beauty
2 being aware of what is beautiful, or having a love of beauty
Word use: You can also use **esthetic**.
Word history: from Greek word meaning 'perceptive'

aesthetics (uhs-thet-iks)
noun the study of beauty, especially in art
Word use: You can also use **esthetics**.

aetiology (ee-tee-ol-uh-jee)
noun the study of the causes of anything, especially of diseases
Word building: **aetiologist** *noun*
Word history: Latin, from Greek *aitía* cause + *-logy*

afar
adverb **1** far away: *He came from* ***afar***.
2 at or to a distance
Word history: Middle English *a fer*

affable
adjective friendly and approachable: *The* ***affable*** *old man told the children stories of his travels.*
Word building: **affability** *noun* **affably** *adverb*
Word history: French, from Latin word meaning 'able to be spoken to'

affair
noun **1** an event or matter: *Tell us about the whole* ***affair***.
2 a sexual relationship between two people
Word history: French *à faire* to do

affect[1]
verb to cause a change in: *His sad story* ***affected*** *our mood. | The heat* ***affected*** *the milk and turned it bad.*
Word history: from Latin word meaning 'influenced'

affect / effect

Don't confuse **affect** with **effect**. They are rather alike in meaning but **affect** is usually a verb and **effect** is usually a noun.

Warm weather affects me and makes me sleepy.

The effect of the warm weather is to make me sleepy.

Note that **effect** can be a verb meaning 'to make happen'.

affect[2]
verb to pretend or make a show of: *He* ***affected*** *not to know what we were talking about, though we knew he really did.* (***feign***)
Word history: French, from Latin

affectation
noun an exaggerated sort of behaviour: *Her friends thought her way of talking was an* ***affectation***.
Word history: from Latin word meaning 'a pursuit after'

affected[1]
adjective **1** influenced: *I can't help being* ***affected*** *by what my parents think.*
2 moved or touched: *She was* ***affected*** *by the music.*
Word history: past participle of *affect*[1]

affected[2]
adjective artificial: *The actress's voice was very* ***affected***. (***la-di-da***, ***pretentious***, ***proud***, ***snooty***, ***uppity***)
Word use: The opposite of this is **natural**.
Word history: past participle of *affect*[2]

affection
noun warm feelings of love or liking
Word building: **affectionate** *adjective*
Word history: Latin

affidavit (af-uh-day-vuht)
noun Law a written statement sworn or affirmed which may be used as a substitute for oral evidence in court
Word history: from Latin word meaning 'he has made oath'

affiliate
verb to connect as a branch or part, or to associate with: *The union was* ***affiliated*** *with the international organisation.*
Word building: **affiliate** *noun* **affiliation** *noun*
Word history: from Late Latin word meaning 'adopted as a son'

affinity
noun a natural liking or sense of closeness: *She felt an* ***affinity*** *for the girl her own age.*
Noun forms: The plural is **affinities**.
Word history: Middle English, from Latin

affirm
verb to declare definitely: *The minister* ***affirmed*** *his support for the poor.*
Word building: **affirmation** *noun*
Word history: Latin

affirmative
adjective agreeing: *an* ***affirmative*** *reply*
Word use: The opposite is **negative**.
Word history: Late Latin

affix (uh-fiks)
verb **1** to fix, fasten or join: *to* ***affix*** *stamps to a letter*
2 to stamp or press on: *to* ***affix*** *an official seal or stamp*
noun (af-iks) **3** *Grammar* a meaningful part (prefix or suffix) added to the stem or base of a word
Word building: **affixture** *noun*
Word history: from Latin word meaning 'fasten to'

affixes in grammar

Many long words, and some short ones, have a root or core element, and some smaller 'extras' added to it which we call **affixes**. They may be either in front of the root, as in *undress*, or after it, as in *dressing*. Those in front are called **prefixes**, and those which come after are called **suffixes**. English has many more suffixes than prefixes. A word may have several suffixes attached to it, but usually only one or two prefixes.

For more about this, look up **prefix** and **suffix**.

afflict
verb to trouble greatly or cause pain: *He was **afflicted** with sickness.*
Word building: **affliction** *noun*
Word history: from Latin word meaning 'thrown down'

affluent (af-looh-uhnt)
adjective wealthy or rich: *an **affluent** country* (***loaded***, ***prosperous***, ***well-off***)
Word use: The opposite of this is **poor**.
Word building: **affluence** *noun*
Word history: Middle English, from Latin word meaning 'flowing to'

afford
verb to have enough money to pay for: *They couldn't **afford** a new car.*
Word history: Old English *geforthian* further, accomplish

afforestation
noun the conversion of bare or uncultivated land into forest, originally to provide hunting grounds but nowadays to prevent soil erosion
Word building: **afforest** *verb*
Word history: Middle Latin

affront
noun something that hurts your pride or your feelings: *His rudeness was an **affront** to the visitors.*
Word building: **affront** *verb*
Word history: Middle English, from Late Latin

affronted
adjective offended: *I was **affronted** when he ignored me.*

Afghan hound
noun a breed of greyhound with very long silky hair

afield
adverb away: *You should search further **afield**.*

afloat
adjective **1** floating on the water: *The ship is **afloat**.*
2 flooded: *The main deck was **afloat**.*

afraid
adjective **1** frightened or feeling fear (***fearful***, ***nervous***, ***panicky***, ***petrified***, ***scared***)
2 feeling sorry or regretful: *I'm **afraid** I can't come.*
Word history: Middle English

afresh
adverb again: *After each interruption she started the book **afresh**.*

aft (ahft)
adverb at or towards the back of a ship: *He went **aft** to his cabin.*
Word use: The opposite is **fore**.
Word history: Old English *æftan* from behind

after
preposition **1** behind, or at the end of: *She always tags **after** me.* | *You can play your piece **after** me.*
2 about: *I want to ask **after** his health.*
3 in the style of: *She paints Ned Kelly **after** Sir Sidney Nolan.*
4 with the name of: *He was called Robert **after** his uncle.*
adverb **5** behind or in the rear: *We all followed **after**.*
6 afterwards: *happy ever **after***
adjective **7** rear: *the **after** deck of a boat*
conjunction **8** following the time that: *She was very tired **after** the baby was born.*
Word history: Old English *æfter* (from *æf-* away from + *-ter*, comparative suffix)

afterbirth
noun the placenta and foetal membranes expelled from the uterus after the birth of offspring

aftermath
noun conditions which follow a disaster: *the **aftermath** of the fire*
Word history: *after* + *math* a mowing (Old English *mæth*)

afternoon
noun the time from midday till evening

afterwards
adverb subsequently or at a later time
Word use: You can also use **afterward**.
Word history: Old English

again
adverb **1** once more or another time: *He has to do it all over **again**.*
2 on the other hand: *I might be his girlfriend but then **again** I might not.*
Word history: Old English *ongegn*, adverb and preposition, opposite (to), towards, again, from *on* in + *gegn* straight

against
preposition **1** towards or upon: *The rain beat **against** the window.*
2 pressing on: *Prop it up **against** the wall.*
3 opposed or hostile to: *twenty votes **against** ten*
4 in preparation for: *He saved money **against** losing his job.*
Word history: *again* + *-(e)s*, adverb genitive suffix + *-t* added later

agape (uh-gayp)
adverb **1** showing wonder or eagerness, with your mouth wide open
adjective **2** wide open

agate (ag-uht)
noun a type of hard stone which is often marked with stripes or swirls of colour
Word history: French, from Latin, from Greek

age
noun **1** the length of time that someone or something has existed: *Joe is fourteen years of **age**.*
2 a period of historical time: *the Middle **Ages*** | *the Elizabethan **age***

3 a stage of human life: *old* ***age***
verb **4** to grow old or look older: *Our grandmother has* ***aged*** *since her illness.*
phrase **5 act** (or **be**) **your age,** *Colloquial* to behave in the way that people expect for someone your age
6 of age, *Law* at an age (usually 18) at which you get certain legal rights, such as the right to vote
7 under age, not old enough to do something, such as drink alcohol or drive a car, legally

Verb forms: I **aged,** I have **aged,** I am **ageing** or I am **aging**

aged (ayjd, ay-juhd)
adjective very old: *an* ***aged*** *woman* (***elderly, geriatric, mature***)

Word history: Middle English, from Old French, from Latin

ageism (ay-jiz-uhm)
noun an attitude which assumes what a person is like, especially an elderly person, according to age, or which discriminates against people on the basis of age, especially old age

Word building: **ageist** *adjective, noun*

agency
noun an organisation which helps or acts for people: *You can go to an employment* ***agency*** *if you need help finding a job.*

Noun forms: The plural is **agencies.**

agenda
noun **1** the list or plan of what has to be done or talked about, especially at a meeting: *There were three items for discussion on the* ***agenda.***
2 a set of strong reasons for doing something: *There's a political* ***agenda*** *behind the decision to build that new road. | Her comments made me think she has a hidden* ***agenda.***

Word history: Latin

Agenda is a singular word in English, and the verb and pronoun we use when referring to it should also be singular:

The agenda for the meeting was very long. It took us the whole day to work through it.

For more information, look up **agreement in grammar.**

agent
noun **1** someone who acts or organises things for you: *a travel* ***agent***
2 something used for a special purpose: *a cleaning* ***agent***
3 a secret agent; spy

Word history: from Latin word meaning 'driving', 'doing'

agent orange
noun a highly dangerous chemical, in military use for stripping leaves from trees

age spot
noun → **liver spot**

agglomerate (uh-glom-uh-rayt)
verb **1** to collect or gather into a mass
adjective (uh-glom-uh-ruht) **2** gathered together into a lump or mass
noun (uh-glom-uh-ruht) **3** a mass of things clustered together
4 *Geology* a type of rock made of large angular volcanic pieces

Word building: **agglomeration** *noun* **agglomerative** *adjective*
Word history: from Latin word meaning 'wound into a ball'

agglutinate (uh-glooh-tuh-nayt)
verb **1** to cause to stick on or together, as if with glue
adjective (uh-glooh-tuh-nuht) **2** joined by or as if by glue

Word history: from Latin word meaning 'pasted to'

aggrandise (uh-gran-duyz)
verb **1** to make larger or wider
2 to make greater or appear greater in power, wealth or honour

Word use: You can also use **aggrandize.**
Word building: **aggrandisement** *noun* **aggrandiser** *noun*
Word history: French, from Latin *ad-* + *grandīre* make great

aggravate (ag-ruh-vayt)
verb **1** to make worse: *Tiredness* ***aggravated*** *his bad temper.* (***exaggerate, heighten, inflame, intensify, magnify***)
2 to annoy: *Don't* ***aggravate*** *the teacher by shuffling your feet.* (***exasperate, get on someone's nerves, irritate, rub up the wrong way***)

Word use: The opposite of definition 1 is **soothe** or **alleviate.** | Note that some people feel that definition 2 is not a correct use.
Word building: **aggravation** *noun*
Word history: from Latin word meaning 'added to the weight of'

aggregate
noun the total or sum of single things: *the* ***aggregate*** *of all your marks in the exam*

Word history: from Latin word meaning 'added to'

aggression
noun **1** any hostile action, such as the action of a country that invades another and takes it over by force
2 hostile behaviour or the making of attacks

Word history: Latin

aggressive
adjective **1** likely to attack: *an* ***aggressive*** *guard dog* (***belligerent, combative, hostile, pugnacious, warlike***)
2 (to do with medical conditions) vigorous and intensive, as of a fast-growing cancer or an in-depth course of medical treatment
3 of a high-risk investment plan which may bring a high profit

Word building: **aggressively** *adverb* **aggressiveness** *noun*

aggressor
noun a person or country that attacks or invades first

Word history: Latin

aggrieved
adjective feeling hurt or wronged: *She was* ***aggrieved*** *that no-one asked her to join the party.*

aghast (uh-gahst)
adjective shocked and frightened: *They were* ***aghast*** *at the unexpected result of their plan.*

Word history: from Middle English word meaning 'terrify'

agile (aj-uyl)
adjective lively and active: *an* ***agile*** *gymnast* (***athletic***, ***light***, ***nimble***, ***sprightly***, ***spry***)
Word building: **agility** *noun*
Word history: Latin

agistment (uh-jist-muhnt)
noun in farming, the action of taking in and feeding or pasturing someone else's sheep, cattle, etc., for payment: *His cattle are out on* ***agistment*** *because of the drought.*
Word building: **agist** *verb* **agistor** *noun*
Word history: Middle English, from Old French *à* to + *giste* resting-place

agitate
verb **1** to disturb or shake about: *to* ***agitate*** *the water*
2 to try to get public support: *to* ***agitate*** *for a change of government*
Word use: The opposite of definition 1 is **calm**.
Word building: **agitation** *noun*
Word history: from Latin word meaning 'aroused', 'excited'

agitator
noun **1** someone who stirs people up and makes them excited in order to influence them: *a political* ***agitator***
2 a machine for mixing or shaking things about

agnostic (ag-nos-tik)
noun someone who believes that you can't know anything about God
Word use: Compare this with **atheist**.
Word building: **agnostic** *adjective* **agnosticism** *noun*
Word history: *a-* + Greek *gnōstikós* knowing. Coined in 1869 by English biologist, anthropologist and philosopher, TH Huxley

ago
adverb past: *some time* ***ago*** | *long* ***ago***
Word history: Old English *āgān* go by, pass

agog (uh-gog)
adjective excited and eager: *Santa's sleigh arrived and the little children were all* ***agog***.
Word history: French *en gogues* in a merry mood

agonise
verb **1** to suffer great pain
2 to struggle or make a very great effort: *to* ***agonise*** *over your project*
Word use: You can also use **agonize**.
Word history: Medieval Latin, from Greek word meaning 'contend'

agonist (ag-uh-nuhst)
noun an actively contracting muscle considered in relation to its opposing muscle (the **antagonist**)

agony
noun great pain or suffering (***anguish***, ***distress***, ***torment***)
Noun forms: The plural is **agonies**.
Word history: Middle English, from Greek word meaning 'contest', 'anguish'

agrarian (uh-grair-ree-uhn)
adjective having to do with the land or farming: *an* ***agrarian*** *way of life* (***outback***, ***pastoral***, ***rural***, ***rustic***)
Word history: from Latin word meaning 'pertaining to land'

agree
verb **1** to say yes: *I* ***agreed*** *to share my lollies.* (***acquiesce***, ***assent***, ***comply***, ***consent***)
2 to have the same opinion (***be of the same mind***, ***concur***, ***see eye to eye***)
3 to arrange: *We* ***agreed*** *to meet after lunch.*
phrase **4 agree with,**
a to suit: *The food doesn't* ***agree with*** *me.*
b to think like
Word history: Middle English, from Old French phrase *a gré* at pleasure

agreeable
adjective **1** pleasant or likeable: ***agreeable*** *weather* (***amiable***, ***charming***, ***friendly***, ***good-natured***, ***nice***)
2 willing to agree: *We will go now if you are* ***agreeable***. (***acquiescent***, ***amenable***, ***consenting***, ***in accord***)
Word building: **agreeableness** *noun*

agreement
noun **1** the same way of thinking: *John and I are in* ***agreement*** *about that film.* (***accord***, ***concord***, ***concurrence***, ***harmony***)
2 arrangement: *They came to an* ***agreement*** *about sharing the bike.* (***compact***, ***contract***, ***deal***, ***pact***, ***settlement***)
Word use: The opposite of definition 1 is **disagreement**.

agreement in grammar

In a piece of writing or in speech some words are linked in special ways. Subjects and their verbs are linked. So are nouns or pronouns, and the pronouns that refer to them. They show this connection by **agreement**.

1 *My favourite surfboard is electric orange.*

2 *My friend Peta's boards are striped with green.*

In these sentences the subjects and verbs agree in number. Example 1 has a singular subject, *surfboard*, so the verb, *is*, must be singular. Example 2 has a plural subject, *boards*, so the verb, *are*, must be plural.

3 *We want to paint them with our own designs.*

4 *But the paint is expensive, so we can't afford it!*

In example 3 the speaker is referring to all the boards so she uses the plural pronoun *them*. The second speaker is talking about one item, paint, so he uses the singular pronoun *it*.

Agreement with collective nouns

Collective nouns, such as *herd*, *class*, *flock* and *family*, can be thought of as either singular or plural. Your choice depends on whether you are thinking of them as a single unit or whether you are thinking of the individuals who make up the group.

5 *My whole family has decided to help me pay for the paint.*

6 *We are going to pay them back when we can.*

In example 5 the *family* is thought of as one thing, so it takes the singular verb *has decided*. However, in example 6 the speaker wants to think of them as many individuals so he uses the pronoun *them*, even though that pronoun still refers to the *family*.

Agreement when the subject consists of several words

When you have a number of subjects joined by the word *and*, as in example 7, you use the plural of the verb.

7 *Peta and I are sharing the money.*

But when you use most other joining words or phrases (like *with* in example 8), things are different. The nouns that follow such words are not part of the subject, and so they don't affect the agreement of the verbs.

8 *The paint with all the painting equipment is going to cost $100.*

Other phrases that act in this way are *together with*, *as well as* and *in addition to*.

Beware!

Sometimes the subject is so far away from the verb that we forget how the agreement should be.

9 *The colour we chose for my board and Peta's board are really wild.*

Example 9 is wrong because the subject (*the colour*) is singular, and so the verb should be the singular *is*, not the plural *are*.

Agreement with *everyone*

Even though pronouns like *everyone* are singular, you can often use the plural pronoun *they* with them.

10 *Everyone we know thinks they should have the first surf on our 'new' boards.*

This used to be frowned on, but it's common in speech, and is used more and more in writing. It avoids having to choose between the singular pronouns *he* and *she* when you either don't know or don't wish to specify the sex of the person you're referring to. Other pronouns like this are *everybody*, *anybody*, *anyone*, *somebody*, *someone*, *no-one* and *nobody*.

Look up **non-sexist language**.

Some nouns, like *data* and *media*, raise special questions of agreement. For more about these, look up **data** and **media**.

agribusiness
noun any business activity that has to do with agriculture

agriculture
noun farming: *Much of Australia's wealth comes from **agriculture**.*

Word use: Another name is **agronomy**.
Word building: **agricultural** *adjective* **agriculturalist** *noun*
Word history: Latin *agrī*, gen. of *ager* land + *cultūra* cultivation

agronomy (uh-gron-uh-mee)
noun **1** soil science and plant science as applied to farming, especially crops
2 → **agriculture**

Word building: **agronomist** *noun*

ahead
adverb **1** in front or forward
phrase **2 be ahead**, to be better off or be winning: *I **am** well **ahead** in the deal.*
3 get ahead of, to pass or beat someone at something

aid
noun **1** help or support (***assistance***, ***backing***, ***charity***, ***relief***)
2 a helper
phrase **3 in aid of**, for or intended to achieve: *What are all these presents **in aid of?***

Word history: Middle English, from Latin

aide-de-camp (ayd-duh-komp)
noun a personal assistant, especially a military officer, to a general, governor, etc.

Noun forms: The plural is **aides-de-camp**.
Word use: You can also use **aide**.
Word history: from French word meaning 'camp assistant'

AIDS (aydz)
noun a disease caused by a virus (HIV) which breaks down the body's natural defences, resulting in severe infections, skin tumours and death

Word history: *a*(*cquired*) *i*(*mmune*) *d*(*eficiency*) *s*(*yndrome*)

ailing
adjective unwell or sickly: *an **ailing** child* (***crook***, ***ill***, ***indisposed***, ***off-colour***)

Word history: Old English *eglan*

ailment
noun an illness: *She has a serious **ailment**.*

aim
verb **1** to direct or point: *to **aim** that remark at him* | *to **aim** a gun carefully before firing* (***level***)
2 to try very hard: *We **aim** to succeed.* (***intend***, ***mean***, ***plan***, ***seek***)
noun **3** a purpose or target: *Our **aim** was to win the race.*
phrase **4 take aim**, to point a weapon

Word history: Middle English, from Latin word meaning 'estimate'

aimless
adjective without purpose: *an **aimless** conversation*

Word building: **aimlessly** *adverb*

ain't
informal contraction of **am not**, **are not** or **is not**

Look up **be**. Also look up **contractions in grammar**.

air
noun **1** the mixture of gases which surrounds the earth and which we breathe
2 appearance: *She has an **air** of success.* (***aspect***, ***aura***, ***manner***, ***style***)
3 a tune or melody
4 *Colloquial* air conditioning in a motor vehicle: *Has your new car got **air**?*
verb **5** to let air into: *Open the window to **air** the room.*
6 to make known to people: *The meeting was a chance for her to **air** her views.*
phrase **7 clear the air**, to sort out a disagreement
8 give yourself airs or **put on airs**, to pretend to be important or behave in a conceited way
9 into thin air, without a trace or completely out of sight
10 on the air, broadcasting or being broadcast on the radio
11 (**up**) **in the air**, not decided or uncertain: *Our travel plans are still **up in the air**.*
12 walk on air, to feel very happy or delighted

Word history: Middle English, from Latin, from Greek word meaning 'air', 'mist'

air / heir

Don't confuse **air** with **heir**, which is a person who inherits something.

airbag
noun in a motor vehicle, a bag which inflates in front of the driver or a passenger immediately after the vehicle has a crash, to give them protection from injury

air conditioning
noun a system of treating air in buildings or vehicles to assure temperature, humidity, etc., remain the same

Word use: You can also use **air-conditioning**.
Word building: **air-conditioned** *adjective* **air conditioner** *noun*

aircraft
noun any machine that can fly, such as an aeroplane or helicopter

airfare
noun the price of a flight in a commercial aircraft

air force
noun the part of a country's armed forces which uses planes for attack and defence

air guitar
noun an imaginary guitar which someone pretends to hold and play, usually to rock music

air kiss
noun Colloquial an exaggerated kiss of greeting or farewell in which your lips do not touch the face of the other person

airline
noun a company which provides a regular plane service for passengers and goods

airlock
noun **1** an airtight compartment at the entrance of a chamber that has air under pressure, as in a spacecraft, where the airlock prevents that air escaping into space
2 *Engineering* an air bubble in a pipe which stops the flow of liquid

airplay
noun the amount of time given to broadcasting a recording

airport
noun a large area where planes land and take off, usually with buildings for staff, passengers and planes

airtight
adjective tightly closed so that air can't get in or out: *an **airtight** jar*

airtime
noun **1** the amount of television or radio broadcasting time given to a particular subject, person, etc.: *Each major political party was allotted equal **airtime**.*
2 the amount of time a mobile phone is able to be used, especially that permitted under a mobile phone contract: *unlimited **airtime***

airy
adjective **1** having air moving through it: *an **airy** room*
2 careless or light-hearted: *He went off with an **airy** wave of his hand.*

Adjective forms: **airier**, **airiest**
Word building: **airiness** *noun*

aisle (uyl)
noun a clear path between seats in a church, hall, aeroplane, etc.

Word history: variant of *isle*, translation of late Medieval Latin *insula* aisle (in Latin island)

aisle / isle

Don't confuse **aisle** with **isle**, which is a small island. This is an old-fashioned word, but you will still find it in some placenames, as in the *Isle of Wight*.

ajar
adverb partly open: *Leave the door **ajar**.*

Word history: Middle English *on char* on the turn

akimbo
adverb with your hands on your hips and your elbows pointing out: *to stand with arms **akimbo***

Word history: Middle English

akin
adjective related or alike: *Emus are **akin** to ostriches.* (***comparable***, ***corresponding***, ***similar***)

Word history: *a-* a reduced form of Old English *of* + *kin* all your relatives taken as a group

alabaster (al-uh-<u>bas</u>-tuh, <u>al</u>-uh-bas-tuh)
noun **1** a fine variety of gypsum, often white and translucent, used for ornamental objects such as lamp bases, small statues, etc.
adjective **2** made of alabaster
3 smooth and white like alabaster: *her **alabaster** throat*

Word history: Middle English, from Latin, from Greek word meaning 'an alabaster box'

alacrity (uh-<u>lak</u>-ruh-tee)
noun cheerful willingness: *Jane went to do the messages with **alacrity**.*

Word history: Latin

alarm
noun **1** a warning sound or signal (***alert***, ***siren***)
2 sudden fear caused by discovering that you're in danger: *The smell of smoke filled me with **alarm**.* (***apprehension***, ***fright***, ***nervousness***, ***trepidation***)
verb **3** to frighten: *The sudden shout **alarmed** him.* (***petrify***, ***scare***, ***shock***, ***terrify***)

Word building: **alarming** *adjective*
Word history: Middle English, from Old French, from Italian word meaning 'tumult', 'fright', from *al l'arme* to arms

alas (uh-<u>las</u>, uh-<u>lahs</u>)
interjection an exclamation of sorrow, pity, concern, or recognition of evil

Word history: Middle English, from Old French *a, ha* ah + *las* miserable, from Latin *lassus* weary

albatross
noun a very large seabird that can fly long distances

Noun forms: The plural is **albatrosses**.
Word history: variant of *algatross*, from Portuguese *alcatraz* seafowl, cormorant; perhaps change of *-g-* to *-b-* by association with Latin *alba* white (the bird's colour)

albeit (awl-bee-it)
conjunction although: *a necessary **albeit** cowardly course*

Word history: Middle English *al be it* although it be

albino (al-bee-noh)
noun a human or an animal with pale skin, white hair and pink eyes because of an absence of pigmentation or colouring matter

Noun forms: The plural is **albinos**.
Word history: Portuguese, from Latin word meaning 'white'

album
noun **1** a book with blank pages used for keeping things like photographs and stamps
2 a long-playing recording on which there is a collection of songs or pieces

Word history: Latin

albumen (al-byuh-muhn)
noun **1** the white of an egg
2 *Botany* the substance about the embryo in a seed which is its food
3 → **albumin**

Word history: Latin, from *albus* white

albumin (al-byuh-muhn)
noun Biochemistry any of a class of water-soluble proteins found in milk, egg, blood and in animal and vegetable tissue

Word use: You can also use **albumen**.
Word history: Latin

alchemy (al-kuh-mee)
noun the medieval form of chemistry which tried to find ways of changing all metals into gold

Word building: **alchemist** *noun*
Word history: Middle English, from Old French, from Medieval Latin, from Arabic

alcohol
noun **1** a colourless liquid which is found in some drinks and which makes you drunk if you have too much
2 any drink containing alcohol

Word history: Medieval Latin word originally meaning 'fine powder'; hence, essence, from Arabic word meaning 'the powdered antimony', 'kohl'

alcoholic
noun **1** someone who continually drinks too much alcohol
adjective **2** having to do with, or containing alcohol: *an **alcoholic** drink* / ***alcoholic** poisoning*
3 suffering from alcoholism

alcoholism
noun a disease caused by drinking too much alcohol for a long time

alcopop (al-koh-pop)
noun a commercially-sold alcoholic drink based on a soft drink, such as lemonade, etc., to which alcohol has been added

alcove
noun a small space or recess set off the main part, especially in a room

Word history: French, from Spanish, from Arabic

alderman
noun a man or woman elected to a local council: *He complained to the **alderman** about the holes in the footpaths.*

Noun forms: The plural is **aldermen**.
Word history: Old English, from *ealdor* chief, elder + *mann* man

On the whole, the word **alderman** has been replaced with **councillor**, a more neutral term for both women and men, as it does not include the element **-man**.

ale
noun a type of beer

Word history: Old English

alert
adjective **1** watchful and quick to react: *The guards are **alert** to any danger.* (***attentive***, ***awake***, ***inquisitive***, ***observant***)
phrase **2 on the alert**, watchful or ready for danger

Word building: **alertness** *noun*
Word history: French, from Italian word meaning 'on the lookout'

Alexandrine (al-uhg-zan-dreen, al-uhg-zan-druyn)
noun **1** in poetry, a verse or line of poetry of six iambic feet
2 in French poetry, a verse of alternate couplets of twelve and thirteen syllables

Word history: French *alexandrin*, from poems in this metre about *Alexander the Great*, 356–323 BC, king of Macedonia, conqueror of Greek city-states and Persian Empire from Asia Minor and Egypt to India

alga (al-guh)
noun the singular form of **algae**

algae (al-jee, al-gee)
plural noun one or many-celled chlorophyll-containing plants, such as seaweed or pondweed

Noun forms: The singular is **alga**.
Word building: **algal** *adjective*
Word history: from Latin word meaning 'seaweed'

algebra
noun the branch of mathematics which uses letters to stand for numbers

Word building: **algebraic** *adjective*
Word history: Medieval Latin, from Arabic word meaning 'bone-setting', 'reunification' (referring to the solving of algebraic equations)

ALGOL (al-gol)
noun a language in which computer programs are written, in algebraic notation

Word use: You can also use **Algol**.
Word history: *algo(rithmic) l(anguage)*

algorism (al-guh-riz-uhm)
noun a sum in arithmetic

Word history: Middle English, from the name of a ninth century Arab mathematician, author of a famous treatise on algebra translated into Medieval Latin

algorithm (al-guh-ridh-uhm)
noun a step-by-step method for doing a sum

Word history: variant of *algorism* by association with *arithmetic*

alias (<u>ay</u>-lee-uhs)
noun **1** a false name: *The criminal is said to be living under an **alias** in South America.* (***nickname, pen-name, pseudonym, title***)
adverb **2** also called: *Superman, **alias** Clark Kent*
Word history: from Latin word meaning 'at another time or place'

alibi (<u>al</u>-uh-buy)
noun a defence by someone that they were somewhere else when a crime was committed
Word history: from Latin word meaning 'elsewhere'

alien (<u>ay</u>-lee-uhn)
noun **1** someone who is not a citizen of the country in which they are living
2 (in science fiction) a being from outer space
adjective **3** strange or foreign: ***alien** speech* (***ethnic, exotic, imported, migrant***)
phrase **4 alien to**, opposed or repugnant: *ideas **alien to** our way of thinking*
Word history: Middle English, from Latin word meaning 'belonging to another'

alienate
verb to make unfriendly: *The Prime Minister **alienated** his supporters.*
Word building: **alienation** *noun*
Word history: from Latin word meaning 'estranged'

alight[1] (uh-<u>luyt</u>)
verb **1** to get down from a horse or out of a vehicle (***disembark, dismount, touch down***)
2 to settle or stay after descending: *a bird **alights** on a tree*
phrase **3 alight on** (or **upon**), to come accidentally, or without design: *Walking through the park you will **alight upon** places of great beauty.*
Word use: The opposite of definition 1 is **board**.
Verb forms: I **alighted** or I **alit** (uh-<u>lit</u>), I have **alighted** or I have **alit**, I am **alighting**
Word history: Old English

alight[2] (uh-<u>luyt</u>)
adjective burning: *The fire is **alight**.*
Word history: Middle English

align (uh-<u>luyn</u>)
verb to bring into line: *to **align** the pictures on the wall*
Word building: **alignment** *noun*
Word history: French

alike
adverb **1** in the same manner: *She treats all pupils **alike**.*
adjective **2** similar: *Their clothes are **alike**.* (***akin, comparable, corresponding, related***)
Word use: The opposite of definition 1 is **differently**. | The opposite of definition 2 is **different**.
Word history: Middle English, from Scandinavian

alimentary canal
noun the digestive passage in any animal, which extends from the mouth to the anus

alimony (<u>al</u>-uh-muh-nee)
noun a US word for **maintenance** (definition 3)
Word history: from Latin word meaning 'sustenance'

alive
adjective **1** living
2 in force or operation: *keep a memory **alive***
3 lively: ***alive** with laughter*
4 swarming or teeming: *The place was **alive** with ants.*
phrase **5 alive to**, aware of: ***alive to** the possibility of defeat*
Word use: The opposite of definition 1 is **dead**.
Word history: Old English *on līfe* in life

alkali (<u>al</u>-kuh-luy)
noun a chemical that reduces the effect of acid
Word building: **alkaline** *adjective*
Word history: Middle English, from Arabic word meaning 'ashes of certain beach plants'

all
adjective **1** the whole of: ***all** Australians | **all** year round | **all** my books*
2 many: ***all** kinds of people*
3 any: *beyond **all** doubt*
pronoun **4** whole amount or number: *to eat **all** your banana | **all** of us*
5 everything: *Is that **all**?*
noun **6** a whole or everything: *I gave him my **all**.*
phrase **7 above all**, before everything else
8 after all,
a after everything has been thought of
b in spite of everything: *He lost his true love **after all**.*
9 all in all, everything taken together, as a whole
10 at all, in any way: *not bad **at all** | no offence **at all***
11 for good and all, finally or forever
12 in all, all included: *I'm inviting twenty people **in all**.*
13 once and for all, for the final time: *Be quiet, **once and for all**.*
Word history: Old English *all, eall*

allay (uh-<u>lay</u>)
verb to make less or relieve: *to **allay** suspicion | to **allay** the pain*
Word history: Old English word meaning 'put down', 'suppress', from *ā-*, *'a-'* + *lecgan* lay

allege (uh-<u>lej</u>)
verb to declare without proof: *Kim **alleged** that Mandy broke the window.* (***assert, charge, claim, maintain***)
Word building: **allegation** (<u>al</u>-uh-gay-shuhn) *noun*
Word history: Middle English, from Latin

allegiance (uh-<u>lee</u>-juhns)
noun loyalty or faithfulness: *They swore **allegiance** to the queen.*
Word history: Middle English, from Old French

allegory (<u>al</u>-uh-guh-ree, <u>al</u>-uh-gree)
noun a story which seems simple but has an extra underlying or symbolic meaning
Noun forms: The plural is **allegories**.
Word building: **allegorical** *adjective*
Word history: Middle English, from Latin, from Greek

allegro
adverb played or sung at a fast speed

Word history: Italian, from Latin word meaning 'brisk'

allergen (al-uh-juhn)
noun something which causes an allergic reaction

Word history: *aller(gy)* + *-gen* something that produces

allergy (al-uh-jee)
noun an unusual sensitivity to things that are normally harmless, like pollen, dust and certain foods: *I sneezed in the pet shop because of my **allergy** to cats.*

Noun forms: The plural is **allergies**.
Word building: **allergic** (uh-ler-jik) *adjective*
Word history: Neo-Latin, from Greek

alleviate (uh-lee-vee-ayt)
verb to make easier to bear: *The aspirin has **alleviated** the pain.* (***ease***, ***lighten***, ***relieve***, ***soothe***)

Word use: The opposite of this is **aggravate**.
Word building: **alleviation** *noun*
Word history: Late Latin

alley
noun **1** a narrow lane between buildings
2 a long narrow enclosure with a smooth wooden floor for games like tenpin bowling
phrase **3 up your alley**, perfectly suited to what you like or to what you are good at: *Babysitting is **up my alley** because I love children.*

Noun forms: The plural is **alleys**.
Word history: Middle English, from Old French word meaning 'a going', 'passage', from *aler* go

alliance (uh-luy-uhns)
noun an agreement to work together: *Australia has a military **alliance** with the United States of America. | The local people are in **alliance** to prevent the building of a freeway.*

Word history: Middle English, from Old French

alligator
noun an animal like a crocodile, but with a broader snout, found mainly in America

Word history: Spanish *el lagarto* the 'lizard', from Latin word meaning 'lizard'

alliteration
noun the repeated use of the same letter or sound to start two or more words in a group, as in 'Around the rugged rocks the ragged rascal ran'

Word use: Compare this with **assonance**.
Word building: **alliterative** *adjective*
Word history: *al-* + Latin *lītera* letter + *-ation*

allocate
verb to set apart for a special purpose: *to **allocate** some of your pocket money for sweets* (***allot***, ***assign***, ***earmark***, ***share out***)

Word building: **allocation** *noun*
Word history: Medieval Latin, from Latin *al-* + *locāre* place

allot
verb **1** to hand out or distribute: *to **allot** equal shares* (***allocate***, ***assign***, ***earmark***, ***share out***)
2 to set apart: *to **allot** money for the new park*

Verb forms: I **allotted**, I have **allotted**, I am **allotting**
Word history: Middle French *a* to + *loter* divide by lot

allotment
noun **1** a section, share, or thing allotted (***allocation***, ***cut***, ***helping***, ***part***, ***quota***)
2 a block of land: *vacant **allotment***

allotrope (al-uh-trohp)
noun one of two or more forms of a chemical element: *Charcoal, graphite and diamonds are **allotropes** of carbon.*

Word building: **allotropic** (al-uh-trop-ik) *adjective*

allow
verb **1** to give permission to or for: *Will your parents **allow** you to come?* (***authorise***, ***license***, ***permit***, ***suffer***, ***tolerate***)
2 to set aside: *to **allow** space for a margin*
phrase **3 allow for**, to provide for: *I took enough money to **allow for** lunch.*

Word use: The opposite of definition 1 is **forbid** or **ban**.
Word history: Middle English, from Old French word meaning 'assign'

allowance
noun **1** money given for a special purpose: *a travelling **allowance***
phrase **2 make allowance for**, to take into account: *Please **make allowance for** my broken arm.*

allowed
adjective permitted: *Are you **allowed** to stay the night?*

alloy
noun a metal made by mixing different metals together: *Bronze is an **alloy** of copper and tin.*

Word history: Old French, from Latin word meaning 'combine'

all right
adjective **1** all correct: *Your answers were **all right**.*
2 satisfactory: *Are you feeling **all right** now? | The meal was **all right**, but not fantastic.*

Word use: You can also use **alright** for definition 2.

allude
verb to refer casually: *She **alluded** to his late arrival.* (***hint***, ***imply***, ***insinuate***, ***mention***, ***suggest***)

Word building: **allusive** *adjective*
Word history: from Latin word meaning 'play with'

> **allude / elude**
> Don't confuse **allude** with **elude**, which means 'to escape or avoid' as in *to elude the guard.*

allure
noun **1** temptation or attraction: *the **allure** of the glamorous clothing*
verb **2** to tempt by offering something attractive

Word building: **alluring** *adjective*
Word history: Middle English, from Old French *a* to + *lurer* lure

allusion
noun a passing mention of something

Word history: from Latin word meaning 'playing with'

allusion / illusion
Don't confuse **allusion** with **illusion**, which is something that seems to be true but isn't:
I thought the puppet was really speaking but it was an illusion.

alluvial
adjective made of sand or mud which has been washed down by a river: ***alluvial** soil*

Word history: Latin *alluvium*

alluvium (uh-looh-vee-uhm)
noun **1** a deposit of sand, mud, etc., formed by flowing water
2 sedimentary matter deposited in this way within recent times, especially in valleys of large river

Noun forms: The plural is **alluvia** or **alluviums**.
Word history: Latin, neuter of *alluvius* washed towards

all-wheel drive
noun **1** a system which gives a constant connection of all four wheels of a motor vehicle to the source of power
2 a motor vehicle which has such a system

Word use: The abbreviation is **AWD**.

ally (<u>al</u>-uy)
noun **1** a country which has signed an agreement to help another country: *an **ally** in times of war*
2 a friend or supporter (***helper***, ***partner***)
verb (uh-<u>luy</u>) **3** to join together to help one another (***combine***, ***unite***)

Noun forms: The plural is **allies**.
Verb forms: it **allied,** it has **allied,** it is **allying**
Word history: French, from Latin word meaning 'bind to'

almanac (<u>awl</u>-muh-nak, <u>al</u>-muh-nak)
noun a calendar which gives information about the sun, moon, tides, weather or other special information

Word history: Middle English, from Medieval Latin, from Spanish, perhaps from Arabic

almighty
adjective **1** very powerful: *an **almighty** king*
2 very great: *to be in **almighty** trouble*

Word history: Old English *ælmihtig*, *ealmihtig* all mighty

almond (<u>ah</u>-muhnd)
noun an oval-shaped nut with a cream-coloured kernel and a sweet taste

Word history: Middle English, from Latin, from Greek

almost (<u>awl</u>-mohst)
adverb very nearly: *She's **almost** an adult now.*

Word history: Old English, *æl mæst* nearly

alms (ahmz)
plural noun Old-fashioned money and other gifts given to poor people (***charity***, ***contribution***, ***donation***, ***legacy***, ***present***)

Word history: Old English, from Late Latin, from Greek word meaning 'compassion', 'alms'

aloft
adverb **1** high up in the air or above ground
2 in sailing ships, in the upper rigging towards the top of the mast

Word history: Middle English, from Scandinavian

alone
adjective **1** by yourself: *to live **alone** (**apart**, **isolated**, **solitary**, **unaccompanied**)*
2 only: *She **alone** knows the real story.*
adverb **3** apart from others
phrase **4 leave alone,**
a to let a person be by themselves
b to not interfere with
5 stand alone, to be special or outstanding because of your ability or something like this

Word history: Middle English *al one* all (wholly) one

along
preposition **1** from one end to the other of: *to walk **along** the driveway*
adverb **2** in company or together with: *Can we come **along**?*
phrase **3 all along,** all the time: *I've been here **all along**.*
4 along with, as well as: *Please take those books, along with this bag, to the table.*
5 get along, *Colloquial*
a to leave or go
b to be friendly: *I **get along** with all of them.*
c to cope or manage well
6 go along with, to agree with

Word history: Old English *andlang*

aloof (uh-<u>loohf</u>)
adjective **1** withdrawn and proud: *She seems **aloof** and unfriendly, but she's really only shy.* (***antisocial***, ***cold***, ***inhospitable***, ***stand-offish***)
adverb **2** at a distance apart: *to stand **aloof** from the crowd*

Word use: The opposite of definition 1 is **approachable** or **friendly**.

aloud
adverb **1** in a normal speaking voice: *to read **aloud***
2 loudly: *to cry **aloud** with pain*

alp
noun **1** a high mountain
2 alps, a high mountain range, usually covered with snow, such as 'the Australian Alps' or 'the Swiss Alps'

alphabet
noun all the letters of a language arranged in their usual order

Word history: Latin, from Greek *álpha* A + *bêta* B

alphabetical
adjective in the order of the alphabet

alpha male
noun **1** *Zoology* the dominant male in a group of animals that live together
2 *Colloquial* a forceful, dominant man

Word history: *Alpha* is the first letter in the Greek alphabet (equivalent to English *A*), and is often used in science to refer to the first or highest item in a series or group. The term **alpha male** was first used in zoology to describe dominant male animals (as in definition 1), and was later extended to describe human males who behave in a similar way.

alphanumeric
adjective **1** (of a set of characters) conveying information by using both letters and numerals: *The data was sent in **alphanumeric** code.*

noun **2** a character which is either a letter or a number

Word history: blend of *alpha(bet)* + *numerical*

alpine
adjective having to do with a cold mountainous place: ***alpine** flowers*

Word history: Latin *Alpīnus*, from the Alps

already
adverb **1** by or before this or that time: *Her bicycle had **already** been fixed.*
2 sooner than expected: *You're not leaving **already**?*

Word history: Middle English *al redy* all ready

already / all ready

Don't confuse **already** with **all ready**.

If a group of people are **all ready** to do something, each one is prepared or ready:

The musicians were all ready to start playing.

alright
adjective satisfactory: *The book was **alright**, but I didn't like the film.*

Word use: You can also use **all right**.

alright / all right

Both **alright** and **all right** mean 'satisfactory or okay'. Some people feel that writing it as a single word is incorrect, but there is really no good reason for this, as **alright** follows the pattern of the accepted words *already* and *altogether*.

Alsatian (al-<u>say</u>-shuhn)
noun a large, strong, wolf-like dog, often trained as a guard dog and used by the police

Word use: Another name is **German shepherd**.

also
adverb too or in addition

Word history: Old English *alswā*, *ealswā* all (wholly or quite) so

altar
noun a table which is used for religious ceremonies in a church or temple

Word history: Old English *altar(e)*, from Late Latin

alter
verb to change: *Your appearance **alters** as you grow up.* | *She has **altered** her hairstyle again.* (***adapt***, ***convert***, ***transform***, ***vary***)

Word history: French, from Latin word meaning 'other'

alteration
noun **1** the act of changing something or making it different: *The kitchen needs some **alteration** to make room for the new fridge.*
2 a change: *The first **alteration** will be to knock down that wall.*

altercation
noun an angry disagreement or dispute (***conflict***, ***controversy***, ***difference***, ***quarrel***)

alternate (<u>awl</u>-tuh-nayt, <u>ol</u>-tuh-nayt)
verb **1** to follow one another in turn: *Day and night **alternate** with each other.*
adjective (awl-<u>ter</u>-nuht, ol-<u>ter</u>-nuht) **2** every second one of a series: *They visit their grandmother on **alternate** weekends.*

Word history: Latin

alternate / alternative

The adjective definitions of these two words are closely related, but they have different meanings.

Alternate refers to every second (or every other) thing in a series, whereas **alternative** describes a choice between options.

Note that **alternative** used to be limited to a choice between just two options. Nowadays it can apply to two or more.

alternating current
noun a current that reverses direction in regular cycles

Word use: The abbreviation is **AC** or **a.c.**

alternative (awl-<u>ter</u>-nuh-tiv, ol-<u>ter</u>-nuh-tiv)
noun **1** one of two or more choices: *to provide orange juice as an **alternative** to milk* | *a list of **alternatives*** (***elective***, ***option***, ***preference***, ***selection***)
adjective **2** giving a choice between one thing and another, or between several things: *the **alternative** route to Brisbane* (***other***, ***second***, ***substitute***)

Word history: Medieval Latin

alternative energy
noun energy, such as wind energy or solar energy, which is not derived from fossil fuels

alternative medicine
noun any of a number of practices and treatments, often based on traditional remedies, which fall outside the scope of mainstream medicine

alternator (<u>awl</u>-tuh-nay-tuh, <u>ol</u>-tuh-nay-tuh)
noun a generator of alternating current

although
conjunction even though

Word history: Middle English, from *al* even + *though*

altimeter (<u>al</u>-tuh-meet-uh)
noun the instrument which measures altitude or height

altitude
noun height above sea level: *to fly at a high **altitude***

Word history: Middle English, from Latin word meaning 'height'

alto (<u>al</u>-toh)
noun **1** the range of musical notes which can be sung by a female singer with a low voice: *She sings **alto** in the choir.*
2 a woman with a low singing voice
adjective **3** in or having to do with this range: *He plays **alto** saxophone.*

Word use: A similar word is **contralto.** | **Alto** range is higher than **bass, baritone** and **tenor** but lower than **soprano**.
Word history: Italian, from Latin word meaning 'high'

altogether
adverb **1** completely or totally: *to be* ***altogether*** *correct*
2 in total: *That costs $10* ***altogether****.*
3 on the whole: ***Altogether****, I'm glad its over.*

Word history: Middle English *al* all, adjective + *togeder* together

> **altogether / all together**
> Don't confuse **altogether** with **all together** which is used when a lot of things are grouped close to each other:
> *The sporting goods were all together in one section of the shop.*

altruism (<u>al</u>-trooh-iz-uhm)
noun the principle or practice of seeking the welfare of others

Word building: **altruist** *noun* **altruistic** *adjective*
Word history: French, from Italian word meaning 'of or to others'

aluminium
noun a light-weight silver-grey metal which is used to make drink cans and cooking utensils and can be rolled into thin sheets of silver foil

Word history: Neo-Latin, from Latin *alūmen* alum

always
adverb **1** all the time or without interruption
2 every time: *She* ***always*** *sings in the shower.*

Word history: Middle English

Alzheimer's disease (<u>alts</u>-huy-muhz duh-zeez)
noun a progressive, organic disease involving degeneration of the brain, resulting in confusion and disorientation

Word history: named after Alois *Alzheimer*, 1864–1915, German physician

a.m.
abbreviation short for *ante meridiem*, Latin words meaning *'before noon'*: *I get up at 6* ***a.m.***

Word use: You can also use **am**.
Word history: Latin

amalgam (uh-<u>mal</u>-guhm)
noun **1** a mixture or combination
2 an alloy of mercury mixed with another metal or metals
3 a rare mineral, an alloy of silver and mercury, occurring as silver-white crystals or grains

Word history: Middle English, from Latin word meaning 'poultice', from Greek

amalgamate (uh-<u>mal</u>-guh-mayt)
verb to mix together or combine: *to* ***amalgamate*** *two classes | The classes* ***amalgamated*** *when the teacher was away.* (***assemble***, ***blend***, ***fuse***, ***join***, ***merge***)

Word use: The opposite of this is **divide** or **separate**.
Word building: **amalgamation** *noun*

amanuensis (uh-man-yooh-<u>en</u>-suhs)
noun a person employed as a secretary to take down what another dictates, etc.

Noun forms: The plural is **amanuenses**.
Word history: Latin word meaning 'secretary', originally adjective from *(servus) ā manū* secretary + *-ensis* belonging to

amass
verb **1** to gather for yourself: *to* ***amass*** *a fortune*
2 to collect or bring together into a mass or pile (***accumulate***, ***pile up***, ***rake in***, ***store***)

Word history: French, from Latin word meaning 'lump (of dough, etc.)'

amateur (<u>am</u>-uh-tuh, <u>am</u>-uh-chuh)
noun **1** someone who does something for enjoyment and not to earn money from it
2 an athlete who does not earn money from playing sport: *The tournament was open to* ***amateurs*** *only.*
3 someone who does a job unskilfully: *This fence must have been built by an* ***amateur****.*

Word use: Compare this with **professional**.
Word building: **amateur** *adjective* **amateurish** *adjective*
Word history: French, from Latin word meaning 'lover'

amatory (<u>am</u>-uh-tree)
adjective having to do with lovers or lovemaking: ***amatory*** *poems | an* ***amatory*** *look*

Word history: Latin *amātōrius*

amaze
verb to surprise and astonish: *Peter's friends were* ***amazed*** *when he won the race.* (***astound***, ***dumbfound***, ***shock***, ***stun***)

Word building: **amazement** *noun* **amazing** *adjective*
Word history: Old English *āmasian*

amazon (<u>am</u>-uh-zuhn)
noun a tall powerful woman

Word history: Middle English, from Latin, from the Greek name for one of a race of female warriors in Greek legend

ambassador
noun **1** the chief official who is sent by a government to represent it in a foreign country
2 someone, such as a famous singer or sports star, who brings credit to their own country while visiting another

Word building: **ambassadorial** *adjective*
Word history: Middle English, from French, from Italian *ambasciatore*; probably of Celtic origin

amber
noun **1** a hard yellow-brown substance which can be polished as a gem stone
2 the yellowish colour used as the warning light of a traffic signal

Word building: **amber** *adjective*
Word history: Middle English, from Medieval Latin, from Arabic

ambergris (<u>am</u>-buh-grees, <u>am</u>-buh-gris)
noun a waxy substance taken from the intestines of the sperm whale, used in making perfume

Word history: late Middle English, from French *ambre gris* grey amber

ambidextrous
adjective able to use both hands equally well

Word building: **ambidexterity** *noun*

ambience (<u>am</u>-bee-uhns)
noun **1** the environment or atmosphere that surrounds you

2 the mood, character, quality, atmosphere, etc., as of a place or setting

Word history: French

ambient (<u>am</u>-bee-uhnt)
adjective **1** completely surrounding: ***ambient** air*
2 having to do with a style of music designed to calm and soothe the listener

Word history: Latin *ambiens*, past participle, going around

ambiguous (am-<u>big</u>-yooh-uhs)
adjective with more than one meaning: *to give an **ambiguous** reply* (***bewildering***, ***indefinite***, ***perplexing***, ***puzzling***, ***unclear***)

Word building: **ambiguity** *noun* (*plural* **ambiguities**)
Word history: from Latin word meaning 'doubtful'

ambit
noun **1** boundary or limits
2 scope or extent

Word history: Middle English, from Latin word meaning 'scope'

ambition
noun **1** strong desire for something in the future, especially money or fame: *to be poor but filled with **ambition***
2 the object that is desired: *His **ambition** is to win the race.*

Word building: **ambitious** *adjective*
Word history: Middle English, from Latin word meaning 'striving for honours'. Ultimately it came from the Latin *ambire* meaning 'to go around and about' with reference to the kind of asking for votes that people did, going from one person to another, on their way to winning office.

ambivalence (am-<u>biv</u>-uh-luhns)
noun **1** the presence in a person of opposite and conflicting feelings towards someone or something
2 an uncertainty, especially due to an inability to make up your mind

ambivalent (am-<u>biv</u>-uh-luhnt)
adjective having opposite and conflicting feelings towards someone or something: *Although I enjoy parties I am **ambivalent** about going to one without my friend.* (***doubtful***, ***equivocal***, ***in two minds***, ***uncertain***, ***undecided***)

amble
verb to walk at a relaxed or comfortable pace (***saunter***, ***stroll***)

Word history: Middle English, from Latin word meaning 'walk'

ambulance
noun a vehicle which is specially equipped to carry sick or injured people and which is driven by experts in first aid

Word history: French (*hôpital*) *ambulant* walking (hospital)

ambush
verb **1** to attack after lying in wait in a hidden place (***snare***, ***take by surprise***, ***trap***, ***waylay***)
noun **2** a sudden attack from a hidden place

Word history: Middle English, from Old French, from *bûche* bush, of Germanic origin

ameliorate (uh-<u>mee</u>-lee-uh-rayt, uh-<u>meel</u>-yuh-rayt)
verb to make or become better

Word building: **amelioration** *noun*
Word history: French

amen (ah-<u>men</u>, ay-<u>men</u>)
interjection at the end of a prayer, hymn, etc., it is so or so be it

Word history: Old English, from Late Latin, from Greek, from Hebrew word meaning 'certainty', 'truth'

amenable (uh-<u>men</u>-uh-buhl, uh-<u>meen</u>-uh-buhl)
adjective agreeable and cooperative: ***amenable** to the idea of a picnic*

Word history: French *à* to + *mener* bring, from Latin *minãre* drive + *-able*

amend
verb **1** to alter: *to **amend** a law*
2 to improve or correct: *to **amend** bad behaviour* (***rectify***, ***reform***, ***remedy***, ***repair***, ***revise***)

Word history: Middle English, from Latin word meaning 'correct'

amendment
noun **1** correction or improvement: *The bill will need **amendment** before all the members of parliament will accept it.*
2 a change made by correcting something or by adding extra material to it: *The **amendments** suggested are acceptable to all the parties.*

amends
phrase **make amends**, to make up for some wrong or injury that has been done: *to **make amends** for hurting someone*

Word history: Middle English, from Old French word meaning 'reparation'

amenity (uh-<u>men</u>-uh-tee, uh-<u>meen</u>-uh-tee)
noun anything which makes a place more comfortable and pleasant: *a motel with such **amenities** as hot showers, laundry, swimming pool and restaurant*

Noun forms: The plural is **amenities**.
Word use: The plural is used more often than the singular.
Word history: late Middle English, from Latin

amethyst (<u>am</u>-uh-thuhst)
noun a purple-coloured precious stone

Word history: Latin, from Greek word literally meaning 'without drunkenness' (from the belief that the stone prevented intoxication)

amiable (<u>aym</u>-ee-uh-buhl)
adjective friendly and good-natured: *an **amiable** conversation* (***agreeable***, ***charming***, ***good-humoured***, ***likeable***, ***nice***)

Word building: **amiability** *noun*
Word history: Middle English, from Latin word meaning 'friendly'

amicable (<u>am</u>-ik-uh-buhl)
adjective friendly: *an **amicable** settlement*

Word building: **amicability** *noun*
Word history: Latin

amid
preposition among or surrounded by: *a block of flats **amid** all the houses*

Word use: You can also use the old-fashioned **amidst.**
Word history: Old English *on middan* in the middle

> **amid / among**
> These words both mean 'surrounded by', but you use them with different kinds of nouns.
> **Amid** nowadays seems rather poetic and even old-fashioned. But it can go with any kind of noun, whether it is
> a <u>count</u> noun (a noun which refers to things that can be counted): *amid the trees*
> or
> a <u>mass</u> noun (a noun which refers to things that can't be counted): *amid the scrub*
> **Among** only goes with count nouns. We can say *among the trees*, but not *among the scrub.* Instead we have to say something like 'in the middle of the scrub'.
> **Amongst** is another form of **among**, used more in literary styles of writing than elsewhere.

amino acid (uh-<u>mee</u>-noh <u>as</u>-uhd, <u>am</u>-uh-noh <u>as</u>-uhd)
noun an organic compound forming the building blocks for proteins

amiss
adjective **1** wrong or out of order: *There is something **amiss** with it.*
phrase **2 not come** (or **go**) **amiss,** to be welcome: *Some new clothes would**n't come amiss** with me.*
3 take amiss, to be offended at: *Don't **take** my comments **amiss.***

Word history: Middle English *a-* + *mis* wrong

> **Amiss** (definition 1) always comes <u>after</u> the noun, not before it.

amity (<u>am</u>-uh-tee)
noun friendship or good relations, especially between nations

Word history: Middle English, from Latin word meaning 'friend'

ammeter (<u>am</u>-ee-tuh)
noun an instrument for measuring the strength of electric currents in amperes

Word history: *am(pere)* + *-meter*

ammonia
noun a strong-smelling gas, a compound of nitrogen and hydrogen, often dissolved in water to make a liquid which may be used for cleaning

Word history: Neo-Latin, obtained from *ammoniac*, a substance found near shrine of the Egyptian divinity *Ammon*, in Libya

ammunition
noun powder or bullets used in firing guns or other weapons

Word history: French (obsolete)

amnesia
noun loss of memory: *He suffered from **amnesia** after he hit his head in the accident.*

Word history: Neo-Latin, from Greek word meaning 'forgetfulness'

amnesty
noun a pardon, usually granted for offences against a government (***acquittal, release, reprieve***)

Noun forms: The plural is **amnesties.**
Word history: Latin, from Greek word meaning 'forgetfulness'

amoeba (uh-<u>mee</u>-buh)
noun a one-celled animal which can only be seen with a microscope and which changes shape as it moves and absorbs food

Word use: You can also use **ameba.**
Noun forms: The plural is **amoebas** or **amoebae** (uh-<u>mee</u>-bee).
Word building: **amoebic** *adjective*
Word history: Neo-Latin, from Greek word meaning 'change'

amok (uh-<u>muk</u>)
phrase **run amok,** to rush about wildly

Word use: You can also use **amuck.**
Word history: Malay

among
preposition **1** surrounded by: *She was **among** friends.*
2 one included in a group of: *That's **among** the songs we'll sing.*
3 between more than two people: *Distribute these pencils **among** you.* | *They should settle the dispute **among** themselves.*

Word use: You can also use **amongst.**
Word history: Old English *on (ge)mang* in the crowd, in the midst of

> **among / between**
> These words are similar in meaning but they are sometimes used in different ways.
> If there are only two things or people, you should use **between. Among** is never used for only two:
> *There was a fight between Luke and Elisabeth over the last cake.*
> NOT
> *There was a fight among Luke and Elisabeth over the last cake.*
> When you are talking about more than two people or things, you can use **among** or **between**:
> *Share the lollies among all the kids.*
> *A war broke out between the four countries.*

amoral (ay-<u>mor</u>-uhl)
adjective neither moral nor immoral

Word history: *a-* + *moral*

> **amoral / immoral**
> Don't confuse **amoral** with **immoral**. These words both have <u>moral</u> as their base word, and have very similar meanings.
> **Amoral** is used to describe someone who doesn't know or doesn't care about the difference between good and bad or right and wrong.
> **Immoral** describes someone who knows the difference but who chooses to act in a way which is bad or wrong.

amorous (am-uh-ruhs)
adjective feeling or showing love, especially of a sexual kind: *an **amorous** boy | an **amorous** smile*

Word history: Middle English, from Old French, from Latin word meaning 'love'

amorphous (uh-maw-fuhs)
adjective without a fixed shape or form

Word history: Greek

amortise (uh-maw-tuyz, am-uh-tuyz)
verb Commerce to end a debt, or something similar, by making regular payments of part of the amount into a sinking fund

Word use: You can also use **amortize**.
Word building: **amortisation** *noun*
Word history: Middle English, from Old English word meaning 'deaden', 'buy out', from *mort* death

amount
noun **1** quantity or extent: *Is there a large or small **amount** of food left?*
2 total of two or more things: *What is the **amount** of the bill?*
phrase **3 amount to,** to add up to or be equal to: *The cost of her shopping trip **amounted to** $20. | Her advice didn't **amount to** much in the end.*

Word history: Middle English, from Old French phrase *a mont* to the mountain

ampere (am-pair)
noun the base SI unit of electric current

Word use: The symbol is **A**, without a full stop.
Word history: named after AM *Ampère*, 1775–1836, French physicist

ampersand (am-puh-sand)
noun the sign '&' which is used to mean 'and' as in *Cobb & Co*

The **ampersand** is usually found only in titles and company names. For more information, look up **and.**

amphetamine (am-fet-uh-meen)
noun a drug used to relieve nasal congestion or to stimulate the central nervous system

amphibian
noun an animal that begins life in the water and lives on land as an adult, such as a frog or a newt

Word history: Neo-Latin, from Greek word meaning 'living a double life'

amphibious
adjective able to live, move or operate both on land and in water: *an **amphibious** creature | an **amphibious** vehicle*

Word history: from Greek word meaning 'living a dual life'

amphitheatre
noun a round building with an open area in the centre and rows of seats rising around it: *The ancient Romans watched plays in **amphitheatres**.*

Word history: Latin, from Greek

ample
adjective **1** more than enough in size or amount: *There was **ample** space for us all to fit in.* (***abundant**, **bountiful**, **copious**, **plentiful**, **prolific***)
2 large or well filled out: *She has an **ample** figure.* (***bulky**, **generous**, **huge**, **substantial***)

Word history: Middle English, from Latin

amplifier
noun **1** *Electronics* an instrument that makes the electric waves that are fed into it stronger
2 an instrument used to make the sound of a radio, CD player, or a musical instrument, like the electric guitar, louder

amplify (am-pluh-fuy)
verb **1** to make louder: *The microphone will **amplify** my speech.*
2 to enlarge or expand by adding details: *Please **amplify** your story so that I can understand what happened.* (***add to**, **augment**, **boost**, **elaborate**, **increase***)

Verb forms: I **amplified**, I have **amplified**, I am **amplifying**
Word building: **amplification** *noun*
Word history: Middle English, from Latin word meaning 'enlarge'

amplitude (amp-luh-choohd)
noun **1** breadth or extent
2 *Electronics* the maximum strength of an alternating current during its cycle (different from the mean or effective strength)
3 *Physics* the distance or range from the maximum or minimum point of a wave pattern to the middle point

Word history: Latin

amplitude modulation
noun a system of radio transmission in which the amplitude of the carrier wave is varied in accordance with the frequency of the signal

Word use: Compare this with **frequency modulation.** | The abbreviation is **AM.**

amputate
verb to cut off in a medical operation: *The doctor **amputated** the patient's injured leg.*

Word building: **amputation** *noun*
Word history: Latin

amputee
noun someone who has had a limb amputated

amuck
adverb → **amok**

amuse
verb **1** to entertain so that the time passes pleasantly: *She **amused** herself reading.* (***interest**, **occupy***)
2 to make laugh or smile: *His jokes **amused** them.*

Word history: late Middle English, from Middle French *amuser* occupy with trifles, divert

amusement
noun **1** the feeling of being amused
2 something which amuses, such as a concert or a merry-go-round

Word history: French

an
indefinite article the form of **a** before a vowel sound

Look up **articles in grammar: indefinite articles.**

anachronism (uh-nak-ruh-niz-uhm)
noun **1** the mistake of placing something in the wrong (usually earlier) period of time, as in *Captain Cook filmed the east coast of Australia.*
2 something that is out of its proper time or out of date

Word building: **anachronistic** *adjective*
Word history: Greek

anaconda (an-uh-kon-duh)
noun a large South American snake of the boa family

anaemia (uh-nee-mee-uh)
noun a lack of red blood cells or their haemoglobin content, causing paleness and weakness

Word use: You can also use **anemia**.
Word building: **anaemic** *adjective*
Word history: Neo-Latin, from Greek word meaning 'want of blood'

anaesthesia (an-uhs-thee-zhuh, an-uhs-thee-zee-uh)
noun **1** *Medicine* a general or local inability to feel pain, etc., brought about by certain drugs
2 a general loss of ability to feel pain, heat, cold, touch, etc.

Word use: You can also use **anesthesia**.
Word history: Neo-Latin, from Greek word meaning 'insensibility'

anaesthetic (an-uhs-thet-ik)
noun a drug that makes you unable to feel pain: *He was given an **anaesthetic** before the operation.*

Word use: You can also use **anesthetic**.
Word building: **anaesthetise** (uh-nees-thuh-tuyz) *verb* **anaesthetist** (uh-nees-thuh-tuhst) *noun*

anagram
noun a word made by changing the order of the letters in another word: *'Caned' is an **anagram** of 'dance'.*

Word history: Neo-Latin, from Greek word meaning 'transposition of letters'

anal (ay-nuhl)
adjective having to do with or near the anus

analgesic (an-uhl-jee-zik)
noun **1** a medicine that removes or lessens pain
adjective **2** causing the removal of pain: *an **analgesic** drug*

Word building: **analgesia** *noun*

analog
adjective **1** showing measurement by the use of a continuously moving needle or pointer, such as the hands on a clock face
2 *Electronics* measuring or representing by use of a quantity that keeps changing, such as a voltage

Word use: Compare this with **digital**.

analogous (uh-nal-uh-guhs, uh-nal-uh-juhs)
adjective similar or comparable in some way: *The processor of a computer is **analogous** with the human brain.*

Word history: Latin, from Greek word meaning 'proportionate'

analogue (an-uh-log)
noun **1** something similar or comparable to something else
2 *Biology* an organ or part that is similar to another

Word history: French, from Greek *análogon*

analogy (uh-nal-uh-jee)
noun a likeness between two or more things which makes you compare them: *Teachers sometimes draw an **analogy** between the heart and a pump.*

Noun forms: The plural is **analogies**.
Word history: Latin, from Greek word meaning 'origin', 'equality of ratios', 'proportion'

analyse
verb **1** to examine in detail in order to find out the meaning: *to **analyse** behaviour* | *to **analyse** a story* (***assess***, ***inspect***, ***investigate***, ***review***, ***study***)
2 to separate into parts: *The scientist **analysed** the strange liquid.*

analysis (uh-nal-uh-suhs)
noun **1** the act of analysing (***examination***, ***investigation***, ***study***, ***test***)
2 separation into parts

Noun forms: The plural is **analyses** (uh-nal-uh-seez).
Word use: Compare definition 2 with **synthesis**.
Word building: **analytical** (an-uh-lit-ik-uhl) *adjective*
Word history: Medieval Latin, from Greek word meaning 'a breaking up'

analyst (an-uh-luhst)
noun someone who is skilled in analysis

Anangu (uh-nang-gooh)
noun an Aboriginal person from Central Australia

Word use: Compare this with **Koori**, **Murri**, **Nunga**, **Nyungar**, **Yamatji** and **Yolngu**.

anaphylactic shock (an-uh-fuh-lak-tik shok)
noun a sudden and potentially life-threatening allergic reaction to a food, insect bite, medicine, etc., that causes rapid swelling of body tissues and breathing difficulties

anarchist (an-uh-kuhst)
noun a person who wants to destroy the order in a society provided by a government but not replace what has been destroyed with any other system

anarchy (an-uh-kee)
noun **1** a society where there is no government or law
2 any situation where there is no control or rules: *There was **anarchy** in the classroom when the teacher was not there.*

Word use: The opposite of definition 2 is **order**.
Word history: from Greek word meaning 'lack of a ruler'

anathema (uh-nath-uh-muh)
noun **1** a formal curse of Christian churches, excommunicating someone or declaring something evil
2 someone or something hated or loathed: *She is **anathema** to me.*

Noun forms: The plural is **anathemas**.
Word use: Note that definition 2 is usually used without the article *an*.
Word history: Late Latin, from Greek word meaning 'something devoted (to evil)'

anatomy
noun **1** the structure of an animal or plant: *Bones are an important part of the human **anatomy**.*
2 the study or science of the structure of animals and plants

Word building: **anatomical** *adjective*
Word history: Late Latin, from Greek word meaning 'dissection'

ancestor
noun someone related to you who lived long ago: *What country did your **ancestors** come from?* (***antecedent***, ***forebear***, ***forefather***, ***predecessor***)

Word use: The opposite of this is **descendant**. | The study of who your ancestors were is called **genealogy**.
Word building: **ancestral** *adjective*
Word history: Middle English, from Latin word meaning 'predecessor'

ancestry
noun **1** descent from your ancestors, especially when they are noble
2 a line of ancestors: *Many people are eager to trace their **ancestry**.*

Noun forms: The plural is **ancestries**.

anchor (ang-kuh)
noun **1** a heavy object chained to a boat and dropped into the water to stop the boat from floating away
2 *TV*, *Radio* the person who links different parts of a program (***compere***, ***presenter***)
3 *Sport* a person who is most heavily relied upon in a team, such as the last runner in a relay race, etc.
verb **4** to hold tightly by an anchor
5 to fix or fasten firmly
6 *TV*, *Radio* to act as the anchor of a program
phrase **7 cast anchor**, to let down the anchor
8 weigh anchor, to take up the anchor

Word history: Old English *ancor*, from Latin, from Greek

anchorage (ang-kuh-rij)
noun **1** a place where you can anchor
2 a fee charged for anchoring

anchorite (ang-kuh-ruyt)
noun someone who lives alone in an isolated place for religious reasons (***hermit***, ***recluse***)

Word history: Middle English, from Medieval Latin

anchovy (an-chuh-vee, an-choh-vee)
noun a small fish with a very salty taste, often made into a paste for eating

Noun forms: The plural is **anchovies**.
Word history: Spanish and Portuguese, probably from Italian (Genoese), from Late Latin, from Greek

ancient (ayn-shuhnt, ayn-chuhnt)
adjective **1** happening or living long ago: ***ancient** history | the **ancient** Romans*
2 very old: *an **ancient** tree* (***aged***, ***antique***, ***old-fashioned***, ***prehistoric***)

Word history: Middle English, from Late Latin word meaning 'former', 'old', from Latin *ante* before

ancillary (an-sil-uh-ree)
noun **1** someone who or something that acts as a help or support: *He is an **ancillary** to our unit.*
adjective **2** acting as helpers or supports: ***ancillary** staff at a school*

Noun forms: The plural is **ancillaries**.
Word history: from Latin word meaning 'a handmaid'

and
conjunction **1** with: *pens **and** pencils*
2 as a result: *Practise harder **and** your piano playing will improve.*
3 afterwards: *Go to the movie **and** come straight home.*
4 as well as: *nice **and** warm*
5 to: *try **and** do it*

Word use: Definition 5 is used between verbs.
Word history: Old English; related to German *und*

Is it wrong to begin sentences with **and**?

Not really, though it's better not to begin a lot of sentences with **and**. If you use **and** (or any other word) again and again at the start of your sentences, it gets very monotonous.

But now and then you may want to link a point from one sentence with the beginning of the next sentence, and **and** is very handy for this. For example:

She was extremely good at sport. And she was intelligent…

It is something we often do when speaking, to add a separate but closely related point to whatever went before. There's nothing wrong with using it occasionally in writing.

As with *but*, some people argue that because **and** is a conjunction, it must link items inside the sentence. Yet its power to link things certainly reaches across from one sentence to the next. Look up **link word**.

The 'and' signs **&** (called the **ampersand**) and *&* are usually found only in titles and company names. People often use + for 'and' when they're making rough notes, but it shouldn't appear in the final version.

andante (an-dan-tay, an-dan-tee)
adverb played or sung fairly slowly and evenly

Word history: Italian word literally meaning 'walking'

anecdote (an-uhk-doht)
noun a short account of a funny or interesting person or event: *I can tell you a lot of **anecdotes** about our holiday.*

Word building: **anecdotal** *adjective*
Word history: Middle Latin, from Greek word meaning 'things unpublished'

anemone (uh-nem-uh-nee)
noun **1** an animal that lives in the sea and catches food with its tentacles
2 a small flower, usually red, blue or white

Word use: You can also use **sea anemone** for definition 1.
Word history: Latin, from Greek word literally meaning 'windflower'

aneroid barometer (an-uh-royd buh-rom-uh-tuh)
noun an instrument for measuring atmospheric pressure by recording the action of air pressure on the elastic top of a box emptied of air

aneurysm (an-yuh-riz-uhm)
noun an abnormal widening of the wall of a blood vessel weakened by disease

Word use: You can also use **aneurism**.
Word history: from Greek word meaning 'dilatation'

anew
adverb **1** again: *The sequel tells* ***anew*** *the circumstances of their meeting, for those who missed the first book.*
2 in a new way or form: *After the flaw was found, the design of the building was drawn* ***anew.***
Word history: Old English *ofniowe*

angel
noun **1** in Judaism, Christianity and Islam, one of God's messengers or attendants, usually pictured to look like a human with wings
2 someone who is very kind, good or beautiful
Word building: **angelic** *adjective*
Word history: Middle English, from Latin, from Greek *ángelos*, messenger

angel / angle
Don't confuse **angel** with **angle**, which is the point where two lines or surfaces meet.

anger
noun **1** a strong feeling of annoyance caused by thinking that something wrong has been done to you (***fury, ire, rage, temper, wrath***)
verb **2** to make or feel angry: *Jack's rudeness* ***angered*** *them.* (***annoy, enrage, incense, infuriate, irritate***)
Word history: Middle English, from Scandinavian

angle[1]
noun **1** the pointed shape made when two straight lines or surfaces meet each other: *The streets met at a sharp* ***angle.***
2 point of view: *a new* ***angle*** *on the problem*
verb **3** to bend, move or place at an angle: *He* ***angled*** *the ball away from the fielder.*
4 to put a bias or slant on: *He* ***angled*** *the question to suit himself.*
phrase **5 at an angle,** sloping or not at a right angle to: *Straighten the picture because it's* ***at an angle.***
Word history: Middle English, from French, from Latin

angle[2]
verb **1** to fish with a hook and line
phrase **2 angle for,** to try to get something in a dishonest or sly way: *to* ***angle for*** *the lead role in a play*
Word history: Old English *angul* fishhook

angler
noun someone who enjoys fishing
Word history: *angle*[2] + *-er*

Angora (ang-gaw-ruh)
noun **1** a type of goat or rabbit with long silky hair
2 → **mohair**
Word history: from *Angora*, variant of *Ankara*, capital of Turkey

angry
adjective **1** feeling or showing anger: *an* ***angry*** *woman | an* ***angry*** *look* (***annoyed, furious, indignant, irate, livid***)
2 inflamed: *The sore on your knee is looking very* ***angry.***
Adjective forms: **angrier, angriest**
Word history: Middle English

You are **angry** *with* or *at* a person, but you are **angry** *about* or *at* something that has happened:
I'm angry with you about what you did yesterday.

anguish (ang-gwish)
noun very great pain, sorrow or worry: *She suffered* ***anguish*** *over her daughter's disappearance.* (***agony, grief, heartbreak, misery, torment***)
Word building: **anguish** *verb*
Word history: from Middle English word meaning 'straits', 'distress'

angular
adjective having a pointed or sharp shape like an angle: *His face had* ***angular*** *features.*
Word building: **angularity** *noun*
Word history: Latin

animal
noun **1** a living thing that is not a plant and can feel and move about
2 any animal except a human being: *Many people keep* ***animals*** *as pets.*
3 someone who is rough and badly-behaved
Word history: from Latin word meaning 'living being'

animate (an-uh-mayt)
verb **1** to make lively and energetic: *The thought of going to the beach* ***animated*** *her.*
2 to make move as if alive: *to* ***animate*** *drawings to produce cartoons*
adjective (an-uh-muht) **3** alive: ***animate*** *creatures*
Word use: The opposite of definition 3 is **dead.**
Word history: Latin

animated
adjective **1** lively or full of life: *an* ***animated*** *face*
2 having to do with a film, or part of a film, which consists of a series of drawings, each slightly different from the ones before and after it, so that, when run through a projector, they produce a moving image

animation
noun **1** the act of creating an animated film
2 an animated film

anime (an-uh-may)
noun → **manga movie**
Word history: Japanese, but originally from the French word *animer*, meaning 'to animate'.

animosity
noun a strong feeling of dislike or unfriendliness: *She looked at her enemy with* ***animosity.*** (***antipathy, aversion, hatred, hostility***)
Word history: late Middle English, from Latin word meaning 'courage'

anion (an-uy-uhn)
noun Chemistry a negatively charged ion which is attracted to the anode in electrolysis
Word history: from Greek word meaning 'going up'

aniseed
noun a strong-smelling seed which is used in cooking and medicines

ankle
noun the part of the body which joins the foot to the leg
Word history: Middle English, from Scandinavian

anklet
noun an ornament worn around the ankle

annals (<u>an</u>-uhlz)
plural noun historical records that are kept year by year
Word building: **annalist** *noun*
Word history: Latin *annālēs* (*librī*) (books) yearly records

anneal (uh-<u>neel</u>)
verb to heat to free from or prevent internal stress: *to* ***anneal*** *glass, pottery or metals*
Word history: Old English *an* on + *ǣlan* burn

annex
verb to obtain and join to what is already owned: *The farmer* ***annexed*** *the neighbouring land.* (***appropriate***, ***occupy***, ***take over***)
Word building: **annexation** *noun*
Word history: Middle English, from Latin word meaning 'joined'

annexe
noun a building added on to a larger building
Word history: French

annihilate (uh-<u>nuy</u>-uh-layt)
verb to destroy or defeat completely: *They* ***annihilated*** *the enemy's army.* (***demolish***, ***eradicate***, ***exterminate***, ***wipe out***)
Word building: **annihilation** *noun*
Word history: Late Latin

anniversary
noun a yearly celebration of something which took place in an earlier year: *our fifth wedding* ***anniversary***
Noun forms: The plural is **anniversaries**.
Word history: Latin

annotate (<u>an</u>-uh-tayt)
verb to supply with notes or make remarks upon: *to* ***annotate*** *works of Bacon*
Word building: **annotation** *noun*
Word history: Latin

announce
verb to tell or make known in public: *Kata* ***announced*** *that she was leaving school.* (***advise***, ***notify***, ***proclaim***, ***publish***, ***reveal***)
Word building: **announcement** *noun*
Word history: Middle English, from Old French, from Latin

announcer
noun someone on radio or television who talks about or introduces a program

annoy
verb to irritate or make cranky: *Very loud music* ***annoys*** *me.* (***aggravate***, ***bother***, ***exasperate***, ***get on someone's nerves***, ***madden***)
Word history: Middle English, from Old French word meaning 'displease', from Late Latin *in odiō* in hatefulness

annoyance
noun **1** a nuisance or something that annoys
2 the feeling you have when you are annoyed

annual
adjective **1** happening once a year: *Our school sports day is an* ***annual*** *event.*
noun **2** a plant that lives for one season or year
3 a book or magazine published once a year
Word building: **annually** *adverb*

annuity (uh-<u>nyooh</u>-uh-tee)
noun **1** a sum of money paid regularly (especially once each year) to a person, often for life
2 the right to receive such income
Noun forms: The plural is **annuities**.
Word history: Middle English, from Latin word meaning 'yearly'

annul (uh-<u>nul</u>)
verb to abolish or put an end to, used especially of laws, etc.: *to* ***annul*** *a marriage* (***break off***, ***dissolve***, ***finish***, ***repeal***)
Verb forms: it **annulled**, it has **annulled**, it is **annulling**
Word building: **annulment** *noun*
Word history: Middle English, from Late Latin

annunciate (uh-<u>nun</u>-see-ayt)
verb to announce
Word building: **annunciation** *noun*
Word history: Middle English word meaning 'announced', from Medieval Latin

anode
noun **1** a positively charged electrode which attracts electrons, as in a radio valve
2 a positive electrode of a cell
Word use: The opposite of definition 2 is **cathode**.
Word history: from Greek word meaning 'way up'

anoint
verb to put ointment or oil on: *The priest* ***anointed*** *the dying man.*
Word history: Middle English, from Old French, from Latin

anomaly (uh-<u>nom</u>-uh-lee)
noun a variation from what is normal
Noun forms: The plural is **anomalies**.
Word building: **anomalous** (uh-<u>nom</u>-uh-luhs) *adjective*
Word history: Latin, from Greek

anonymous (uh-<u>non</u>-uh-muhs)
adjective having no name given: *The book was written by an* ***anonymous*** *author.*
Word use: The abbreviation is **anon.**
Word building: **anonymity** (an-uh-<u>nim</u>-uh-tee) *noun*
Word history: Greek

anorexia (an-uh-<u>reks</u>-ee-uh)
noun an eating disorder marked by weight loss, usually because of failure to eat for fear of growing fat
Word use: Another name is **anorexia nervosa**.
Word building: **anorexic** *adjective*, *noun*
Word history: Greek

another
adjective **1** second or additional: ***another*** *piece of fruit*
2 different: ***another*** *day* | ***another*** *woman*
pronoun **3** one more: *Please take* ***another***.
4 something different: *The butterfly flitted from one flower to* ***another***.
Word history: Middle English; originally *an other*

answer
noun **1** a reply or response (***acknowledgement***, ***feedback***)
2 a solution to a problem
verb **3** to respond or reply: *She* ***answered*** *with a nod.*
4 to reply to: *Hurry up and* ***answer*** *the question.*
phrase **5 answer back**, to make a rude or cheeky reply
Word history: Old English *and-* against + *swaru*, related to *swerian* swear

answerable
adjective **1** responsible: *I am* ***answerable*** *for my child's safety.*
2 able to be solved or answered

ant
noun a small insect that usually lives in a large family group or community called a colony
Word history: Old English *æmete*

antagonise (an-tag-uh-nuyz)
verb to make angry or make an enemy of: *The bully* ***antagonised*** *the children by spoiling their game.*
Word use: The opposite of this is **pacify** or **appease**. | You can also use **antagonize**.

antagonism
noun active opposition to someone or something: *She expressed her* ***antagonism*** *towards me by kicking my chair.*
Word history: Greek

antagonist
noun **1** an enemy or opponent (***adversary***, ***foe***, ***rival***)
2 a muscle which acts in opposition to another muscle (the **agonist**)
Word building: **antagonistic** *adjective*
Word history: Greek

antarctic (ant-ahk-tik)
adjective having to do with the area near the South Pole
Word use: You can also use **Antarctic**.
Word history: Latin, from Greek word meaning 'opposite the north'

anteater
noun an animal with a long sticky tongue that feeds on ants or termites
Word use: Different varieties are called **echidnas** or **numbats**.

antecedent (ant-uh-see-duhnt)
noun anything that goes before another
Word history: Latin

antedate
verb **1** to be of older date than: *The Peruvian Empire* ***antedates*** *that of Mexico.* (***forego***, ***precede***)
2 to fix an earlier date to

antelope
noun a slight swift animal which has horns, chews its cud and is related to cattle, sheep and goats
Word history: Middle English, from Medieval Latin, from Late Greek

antenna
noun **1** a sense organ or feeler found on the head of insects or crabs
2 a radio or television aerial
Noun forms: The plural for definition 1 is **antennae** (an-ten-ee); the plural for definition 2 is **antennas.**
Word history: from Latin word meaning 'a sailyard'

anterior (an-tear-ree-uh)
adjective **1** placed before or found more towards the front: *the* ***anterior*** *hump of a whale*
2 earlier or going before in time: *an* ***anterior*** *age* (***antecedent***, ***preceding***, ***previous***)
Word use: The opposite of definition 1 is **posterior.**
Word building: **anteriority** *noun* **anteriorly** *adverb*
Word history: Latin word meaning comparative adjective from *ante* before

anthem
noun a ceremonial song for an organisation or country: *'Advance Australia Fair' is Australia's national* ***anthem***.
Word history: Old English *antemn(e)*, *antefn(e)*, from Vulgar Latin, from Late Latin, from Greek

anthology
noun a collection of poems, plays or short stories by various authors or from various books
Noun forms: The plural is **anthologies**.
Word history: Greek word literally meaning 'a flower-gathering'

anthropogenic (an-thruh-puh-jen-ik)
adjective caused by human beings: ***anthropogenic*** *climate change*

anthropoid (an-thruh-poyd)
adjective **1** like a human being
noun **2** an ape that resembles a human, such as a gorilla, chimpanzee, etc.
Word history: Greek

anthropology
noun the scientific study of the beginnings and development of humans
Word building: **anthropologist** *noun*

antibiotic
noun a drug capable of killing bacteria and other germs
Word building: **antibiotic** *adjective*

antibody
noun Medicine a protein produced in the human body in response to the presence of an antigen (a protein not usually found in the body), or introduced when someone is immunised against a disease
Noun forms: The plural is **antibodies.**

anticipate
verb **1** to know or realise in advance what is going to happen or what to expect: *to* ***anticipate*** *the*

*disaster | to **anticipate** the excitement of Christmas* (***count on, foresee, look forward to***)
2 to think of or mention before the proper time: *To **anticipate** your objection, I think you're being too cautious.*

Word building: **anticipation** *noun*
Word history: Latin

anticlimax (an-tee-kluy-maks)
noun something you find disappointing, especially when you compare it with what has gone before: *The ending of the play was a real **anticlimax**.* (***blow, fizzer, letdown, setback***)

Word building: **anticlimactic** *adjective*

anticlockwise
adjective going round in the opposite direction to the hands on a clock face

Word use: The opposite of this is **clockwise**.

antics
plural noun odd or silly behaviour

Word history: Italian *antico* old (but used as if Italian *grottesco* grotesque), from Latin

antidote
noun something to stop the bad effects caused by a disease or a poison: *The doctor gave Ji Soo the **antidote** for the spider bite.*

Word history: Latin, from Greek word meaning 'given against'

antigen
noun any substance which when injected into an animal causes an antibody to form

Word history: *anti(body) + -gen*

antimony (an-tuh-muh-nee)
noun a brittle white metallic element used chiefly in alloys and (in compounds) in medicine

Word history: late Middle English, from Medieval Latin

antioxidant
noun **1** any substance inhibiting oxidation
2 such a substance in the body, which neutralises free radicals formed when body cells burn oxygen for energy, keeping the immune system healthy and reducing the risk of cancer and other diseases

Word use: You can also use **anti-oxidant**.

antipathy (an-tip-uh-thee)
noun a feeling of strong dislike: *The dog had a strong **antipathy** to strangers.* (***animosity, aversion, hatred, hostility***)

Word use: The opposite of this is **liking**.

antipodes (an-tip-uh-deez)
plural noun a place or places directly opposite another on the earth: *Australia is the **antipodes** of Britain.*

Word building: **antipodean** (an-tip-uh-dee-uhn) *adjective*
Word history: Latin, from Greek word meaning 'with feet opposite'

antiquary (an-tuh-kwuh-ree)
noun an expert on ancient things; a student or collector of extremely old things

Noun forms: The plural is **antiquaries**.
Word building: **antiquarian** *adjective*
Word history: from Latin word meaning 'of antiquity'

antiquated (an-tuh-kway-tuhd)
adjective old-fashioned or out of date: *an **antiquated** textbook* (***archaic, dated, obsolete, old, outmoded***)

antique (an-teek)
noun **1** an object of art or piece of furniture which was made long ago: *I collect **antiques** from Japan.*
adjective **2** dating from earlier times: *an **antique** vase made over two centuries ago* (***ancient, old-fashioned, prehistoric, vintage***)

Word history: from Latin word meaning 'old'

antiquity (an-tik-wuh-tee)
noun ancient times or the early stages of history

antiseptic
noun **1** a chemical used to kill germs that produce disease
adjective **2** having to do with such chemicals: *an **antiseptic** cream*

antisocial (an-tee-soh-shuhl)
adjective **1** unwilling or unable to mix normally with people (***aloof, cold, inhospitable, stand-offish***)
2 opposed or damaging to social order, or to the principles on which society is built

Word building: **antisocially** *adverb*

antithesis (an-tith-uh-suhs)
noun **1** the direct opposite: *Sinead was the **antithesis** of a good student.*
2 a contrast between two opposites: *the **antithesis** between light and dark*

Noun forms: The plural is **antitheses**.
Word history: Late Latin, from Greek word meaning 'opposition'

antitoxin (an-tee-tok-suhn)
noun a substance formed in the body, which fights a particular poison, often used in treating or immunising (protecting) against certain infectious diseases

antivenene (an-tee-vuh-neen)
noun an injection to fight the venom from a spider or snake bite

antler
noun a long, hard, branch-like horn on the head of a male deer and other similar animals

Word history: Middle English, from Latin word meaning 'before eye'

antonym (an-tuh-nim)
noun a word which has an opposite meaning to another word: *'Fast' is the **antonym** of 'slow'.*

Word history: *ant(i)-* + Greek *ónyma* name; modelled on *synonym*

Some examples of **antonyms** are: *quick* and *slow*, *hot* and *cold*, *dead* and *alive*, *buy* and *sell*. Although they mean the opposite, antonyms always have a common denominator between them, such as:

speed (for *quick* and *slow*)
temperature (for *hot* and *cold*)
life (for *dead* and *alive*)
exchange of goods (for *buy* and *sell*).

Antonyms contrast with **synonyms**.

anus (<u>ay</u>-nuhs)
noun the opening at the lower end of the alimentary canal, where waste material from the bowel comes out

Word history: Latin

anvil
noun a heavy iron block with a smooth surface on which hot metals are hammered and shaped before they go cold and hard

Word history: Old English *anfilt(e)*

anxiety (ang-<u>zuy</u>-uh-tee)
noun worry or uneasy feelings: *A mother feels* ***anxiety*** *if her child becomes lost.*

Word history: Latin

anxious (<u>ang</u>-shuhs)
adjective **1** full of anxiety or worry: *She was very* ***anxious*** *about her sick dog.* (***apprehensive***, ***concerned***, ***nervous***, ***tense***, ***uneasy***)
2 eager: *He was* ***anxious*** *to please his father.* (***avid***, ***keen***, ***willing***)

Word history: from Latin word meaning 'troubled'

any
adjective **1** one or some: *Ask* ***any*** *of my friends.*
2 every: ***Any*** *Australian knows that.*
3 great or unlimited in amount: ***any*** *number of things*
pronoun **4** any person or thing: *He is more responsible than* ***any*** *before him.*
adverb **5** at all: *Do you feel* ***any*** *better?*

Word history: Old English *ǣnig*, from *ān* one

Any can be used with both plural and singular verbs, pronouns and nouns. This is because it can refer to a whole group or an individual member of it:

If any of the boys <u>are</u> available, <u>they</u> can come.

If any of the boys <u>is</u> available, <u>he</u> can come.

anybody
pronoun any person

anybody / anyone
For information on how to use verbs and pronouns with these words, look up **agreement in grammar**.

anyhow
adverb **1** in any case
2 in a careless way: *He threw down his clothes* ***anyhow.***

anyone
pronoun any person

anything
pronoun any thing whatever

anyway
adverb in any case

anywhere
adverb in, at, or to any place

Anzac (<u>an</u>-zak)
noun a soldier from Australia or New Zealand

Word history: an acronym, made up of the initials of *A(ustralian and) N(ew) Z(ealand) A(rmy) C(orps)*. It was originally used to refer to those Australian and New Zealand soldiers who served as members of this Corps during World War I, but is now often used more widely to refer to any Australian or New Zealand soldier.

Anzac biscuit
noun a biscuit made from wheat flour, rolled oats, desiccated coconut, and golden syrup

Word use: You can also use **anzac biscuit.**

A1 (ay-<u>wun</u>)
adjective Colloquial **1** first class or excellent
2 in good health

Word use: You can also use **A-1** or **A-one.**

aorta (ay-<u>aw</u>-tuh)
noun the main artery carrying blood from the left side of the heart to nearly all parts of the body

Word history: New Latin, from Greek

apart
adverb **1** to pieces: *He took the calculator* ***apart*** *to see how it worked.*
2 separated or not together: *You must keep these animals* ***apart.***
adjective **3** separate or independent: *a class* ***apart***
phrase **4 apart from**, aside from or leaving out: ***Apart from*** *my boyfriend, I love you the best.*

Word history: Middle English, from Latin *ad partem* to the side

apartheid (uh-<u>pah</u>-tuyd, uh-<u>pah</u>-tayt)
noun a policy of keeping races separate. In a country with such a policy, people of different races do not catch the same transport, go to the same schools, etc.

Word history: Afrikaans

apartment
noun a set of rooms for living in, usually among others in a building

Word history: French, from Italian

apathy (<u>ap</u>-uh-thee)
noun no feeling for, or interest in things other people find interesting or exciting: *He was sunk in* ***apathy*** *after his father's death.*

Word use: The opposite of this is **interest.**
Word building: **apathetic** (ap-uh-<u>thet</u>-ik) *adjective*
Word history: Latin, from Greek word meaning 'insensibility'

apatosaurus (uh-<u>pat</u>-uh-saw-ruhs)
noun a very large, amphibious, plant-eating dinosaur, with a long neck and tail and a relatively small head

Word use: This is popularly known as a **brontosaurus.**

ape
noun **1** a large monkey without a tail
verb **2** to imitate or copy: *The child* ***aped*** *the strange way the clown was walking.* (***caricature***, ***impersonate***, ***send up***)
phrase **3 go ape over**, *Colloquial* to react with too much pleasure, excitement, etc.: *He* ***went ape over*** *the CD I bought him.*

Word building: **apelike** *adjective* **apish** *adjective*
Word history: Old English *apa*

aperture (ap-uh-chuh)
noun a hole, crack or other opening, especially the opening in a camera that limits the amount of light it lets in (***break***, ***chink***, ***gap***, ***perforation***, ***slit***)

Word history: Latin

apex
noun the peak, summit or highest point: *Every mountain has an* ***apex***. (***crest***, ***pinnacle***, ***top***)

Noun forms: The plural is **apexes** or **apices** (ay-puh-seez).
Word history: from Latin word meaning 'point', 'summit'

aphid (ay-fuhd)
noun a small insect which sucks the sap from plants

Word use: You can also use **aphis**.
Word history: Neo-Latin

aphorism (af-uh-riz-uhm)
noun a short saying containing a general truth

Word building: **aphoristic** *adjective* **aphorist** *noun*
Word history: Medieval Latin, from Greek word meaning 'definition'

aphrodisiac (af-ruh-diz-ee-ak)
noun a drug or food that wakes or increases sexual desire

Word history: Greek

apiary (ay-pee-uh-ree)
noun a place where beehives are kept

Noun forms: The plural is **apiaries**.
Word building: **apiarist** *noun*
Word history: Latin

apiece
adverb each: *an orange* ***apiece*** | *costing a dollar* ***apiece***

Word history: originally two words, *a* to or for each + *piece*

aplomb (uh-plom)
noun the ability to handle difficult or unusual situations: *The boy introduced the guest speaker with* ***aplomb***.

Word history: French

apocalypse (uh-pok-uh-lips)
noun the discovery or revealing of some great event, such as the end of the world

Word building: **apocalyptic** *adjective*
Word history: from Greek word meaning 'revelation'

apocryphal (uh-pok-ruh-fuhl)
adjective **1** of doubtful authorship
2 false (***fictitious***, ***legendary***, ***mythical***)

apologetic
adjective full of regret, or showing that you are sorry: *an* ***apologetic*** *glance*

Word history: Late Latin, from Greek

apologise
verb to say you are sorry: *She* ***apologised*** *for being late.*

Word use: You can also use **apologize**.

apology
noun **1** an expression of regret or sadness that you offer when you have done something wrong: *Please accept my* ***apology***.
2 a poor example of something: *an* ***apology*** *for a hat*

Noun forms: The plural is **apologies**.
Word history: Latin, from Greek word meaning 'speech in defence'

apoplexy (ap-uh-plek-see)
noun **1** a noticeable loss of someone's body function due to damage of the blood-supply to their brain (***fit***, ***stroke***)
2 *Colloquial* a fit of extreme anger: *Just thinking about her behaviour gives him* ***apoplexy***.

Word building: **apoplectic** *adjective*
Word history: Middle English, from Latin, from Greek word meaning 'disable by a stroke'

apostasy (uh-pos-tuh-see)
noun a total desertion of your religion, principles, party, cause, etc.

Noun forms: The plural is **apostasies**.
Word building: **apostate** *noun*
Word history: Middle English, from Latin, from Greek word meaning 'revolt'

apostle (uh-pos-uhl)
noun **1** someone who strongly supports a new idea: *an* ***apostle*** *of change in education*
2 any important Christian teacher or missionary

Word history: Old English *apostol*, from Latin, from Greek word meaning 'one sent away'

apostrophe (uh-pos-truh-fee)
noun a sign (') used to show that a letter has been left out, or that something is owned

Word history: Latin, from Greek word meaning 'a turning away'

There are two reasons why we use **apostrophes**:

1 to show that something has been left out of a word: *they've gone*

2 to show ownership: *Gavin's hang-glider*

1 We use an apostrophe to show that we have left a letter (or sometimes more than one letter) out of a word or phrase:

it's	it is
she'll	she will
John'll	John will (*or* shall)
I've	I have
might've	might have

These are called contractions. They are quite common in speech, but usually avoided in formal writing.

2 We use an apostrophe when we want to show that something belongs to a person or thing.

(**a**) When a word is singular, whether it already ends in an s or not, we add an apostrophe and then an s at the end of the word:

The bike's wheel came loose.

Here is Chris's dog.

(**b**) When a word is plural, if it already ends in an s, we simply add an apostrophe at the end of the word, not an s as well:

All the girls' fathers came to the meeting.

(continued)

apostrophes *(continued)*

(**c**) When a word is plural but does not end in an s, we add an apostrophe and then an s as well:

The children's playground was unsafe.

Note that apostrophes are often not used in the titles of institutions, organisations, etc.:

Boys High School

Secondary Teachers College

These days apostrophes are often left out of plural words in expressions of time:

five weeks time

two months holiday

However the apostrophe should be there if the time word is singular:

a week's time

one month's holiday

Its and it's

A tricky point to remember is that *it's* is short for *it is*, whereas *its* (without an apostrophe) shows ownership.

The dog wagged its tail.

It's raining cats and dogs.

One way of remembering this is to remind yourself that *its* is a pronoun like *her* and *his*, and they don't have apostrophes for ownership.

Beware!

Never use an apostrophe with ordinary plural words. For example, you wouldn't write *Banana's for sale.* But when letters are used as words, we use apostrophes to avoid confusion and to make the text easier to read:

Dot the i's and cross the t's.

apothecary (uh-poth-uh-kree)
noun Old-fashioned a chemist, a mixer of drugs

Noun forms: The plural is **apothecaries**.
Word history: Middle English, from Late Latin word meaning 'shopkeeper'

appal
verb to horrify: *The thought of atomic war* ***appals*** *me.* | *The violence in that film appals many people.*

Verb forms: it **appalled**, it has **appalled**, it is **appalling**
Word history: Middle English, from Old French word meaning 'become or make pale'

apparatus (ap-uh-rah-tuhs, ap-uh-ray-tuhs)
noun a collection of tools or machines used for a particular purpose: *the* ***apparatus*** *used by firefighters* (***equipment***, ***gear***)

Word history: from Latin word meaning 'preparation'

apparel
noun your outer clothing (***attire***, ***dress***, ***garb***, ***wardrobe***)

Word use: An old-fashioned word for this is **raiment**.
Word history: Middle English, from Latin word meaning 'make ready'

apparent
adjective **1** able to be seen or understood: *My spelling error was* ***apparent*** *when I checked in the dictionary.* (***clear***, ***distinct***, ***evident***, ***plain***, ***visible***)
2 seeming, not necessarily real: *the* ***apparent*** *motion of the sun*

Word building: **apparently** *adverb*
Word history: from Latin word meaning 'appearing'

apparition (ap-uh-rish-uhn)
noun something that appears in an unusual way: *A ghostly* ***apparition*** *in the empty house frightened me.* (***phantom***, ***spectre***, ***spook***, ***wraith***)

Word history: Latin

appeal
noun **1** a call or request for something needed: *The school made an* ***appeal*** *for money for a new library.* (***entreaty***, ***plea***)
2 the ability to attract or interest: *Sport has an* ***appeal*** *for most people.* (***allure***, ***attraction***, ***charm***, ***draw***, ***fascination***, ***pull***)
verb **3** to make an appeal: *The refugees* ***appealed*** *for help.* (***ask***, ***plead***)

Word history: Middle English, from Latin word meaning 'approach', 'summon'

appear
verb **1** to come into view: *The sun* ***appeared*** *over the horizon.* (***emerge***, ***loom***, ***materialise***, ***show up***)
2 to seem or have a certain look: *The boy* ***appears*** *to be sick.*
3 to come or be placed before the public: *His biography* ***appeared*** *last year.*

Word history: Middle English, from Latin *appārēre* come forth

appearance
noun **1** the act of appearing
2 the look of something or what you see on the outside: *a woman of noble* ***appearance*** (***air***, ***aspect***, ***complexion***, ***manner***, ***presence***)
3 outward show: *We don't want to give the* ***appearance*** *of being poor.*
phrase **4 keep up appearances**, to continue to act in an acceptable way while keeping some unpleasant things hidden
5 to all appearances, so far as can be seen or noticed

appease
verb **1** to make peaceful, quiet or happy: *He* ***appeased*** *the angry customer.* (***calm***, ***comfort***, ***mollify***, ***placate***, ***quieten***)
2 to satisfy: *to* ***appease*** *hunger*

Word use: The opposite of definition 1 is **antagonise**. | The opposite of definition 2 is **intensify**.
Word building: **appeasement** *noun*
Word history: Middle English, from Old French *a* to + *pais* (from Latin *pax*) peace

appellation (ap-uh-lay-shuhn)
noun **1** a name or title
2 the giving of such a name

Word history: from Latin word meaning 'name'

append (uh-pend)
verb to add, as an extra part (***attach***, ***supplement***, ***tack on***)

Word building: **appendage** *noun* **appendant** *adjective*
Word history: from Latin word meaning 'hang (something) on'

appendicitis (uh-pen-duh-suy-tuhs)
noun a painful inflammation of the appendix

Word history: Latin *appendix* + *-ītis*

appendix
noun **1** a section added to the main part of a book to give extra information
2 a short, narrow tube without openings, protruding from the large intestine in the lower right-hand part of the abdomen in humans, and having no known useful function

Word use: The full name of definition 2 is **vermiform appendix**.
Word history: from Latin word meaning 'something that hangs on'

The plural may be spelt either **appendixes** or **appendices** when you're referring to the sections of writing at the back of a book.

When you are using the word in a medical or anatomical way, the plural is spelt **appendixes**.

appetising
adjective looking or smelling good to eat: *the **appetising** smell of roast lamb* (***luscious***, ***more-ish***, ***mouth-watering***, ***scrumptious***)

Word use: You can also use **appetizing**.

appetite
noun the wish for food or drink: *Exercise gives you a good **appetite**.*

Word history: Middle English, from Latin word meaning 'onset', 'desire for'

applaud (uh-plawd)
verb to praise or express approval, especially by clapping your hands or calling out: *The audience **applauded** the actors in the play.* (***acclaim***, ***cheer***, ***clap***, ***honour***, ***toast***)

Word building: **applause** *noun*
Word history: Latin

apple
noun a crisp round fruit with thin red or green skin

Word history: Old English *æppel*

applet
noun *Internet* a small Java program that can be transferred over the internet, running on the client machine rather than the server

Word history: from *appl(ication)* (definition 3) + diminutive ending *-et*

appliance
noun a tool which has a motor worked by electricity: *We have some useful kitchen **appliances**.*

applicable (uh-plik-uh-buhl)
adjective suitable or able to be used: *a rule only **applicable** to children.*

applicant
noun someone who asks or requests: *an **applicant** for a job* (***candidate***, ***claimant***)

Word history: Latin

application
noun **1** a request: *to make an **application** for a job*
2 something put or laid on: *an **application** of paint*
3 *Computers* a program which is written to perform a specific task

Word history: from Latin word meaning 'a joining to'

apply (uh-pluy)
verb **1** to ask: *to **apply** for a job*
2 to put on: *to **apply** make-up*
3 to put to use: *to **apply** rules*
4 to give full attention to: *I **apply** my mind to my lessons.*

Verb forms: I **applied**, I have **applied**, I am **applying**
Word history: Middle English, from Latin word meaning 'attach'

appoint
verb to choose for special duties: *The principal **appointed** the school captain.* (***commission***, ***elect***, ***install***, ***select***)

Word history: Middle English, from Old French *a-* + *pointer* point

appointment
noun **1** the arrangement of a special time: *an **appointment** to see the dentist*
2 the placing of someone in a special position: *the **appointment** of a new school captain*
3 the job or special position to which someone is appointed

apportion (uh-paw-shuhn)
verb to share out in fair divisions: *to **apportion** costs*

Word building: **apportionment** *noun*
Word history: French *à* to + *portionner* portion, verb

apposite (ap-uh-zuht)
adjective suitable or well-adapted: *an **apposite** answer* (***applicable***, ***appropriate***, ***apt***, ***pertinent***, ***relevant***)

Word history: from Latin word meaning 'put to'

apposition (ap-uh-zish-uhn)
noun the act of placing together (***juxtaposition***)

Word building: **appositional** *adjective* **appose** *verb*

appraise
verb to judge the value of: *The judges **appraised** the paintings in the competition.*

Word building: **appraisal** *noun*
Word history: blend of *apprize* (from Middle English *aprise(n)*, from Old French *apriser*, from phrase *à pris* for sale) and *praise*

appraise / apprise

Don't confuse **appraise** with **apprise**, which is to inform or advise about something:

I will apprise you of the situation as soon as I have some news.

appreciable (uh-preesh-uh-buhl)
adjective **1** able to be seen or noticed: *There has been an **appreciable** increase in the number of people who do not smoke.* (***detectable***, ***discernible***, ***noticeable***, ***pronounced***)
2 fairly large: *We have travelled an **appreciable** distance.*

Word building: **appreciably** *adverb*

appreciate
verb **1** to think highly of: *I **appreciate** your help.* (***be grateful for, enjoy, esteem, value, welcome***) **2** to increase in value: *This antique vase continues to **appreciate** the longer I keep it.*

Word use: The opposite of definition 2 is **depreciate**.
Word building: **appreciation** *noun* **appreciative** *adjective*
Word history: from Latin word meaning 'appraised'

apprehend
verb to take into keeping: *The police **apprehended** the thieves.* (***abduct, arrest, grab, pick up, trap***)

Word use: The opposite of this is **release**.
Word history: from Latin word meaning 'seize'

apprehension
noun fear that something might happen: *I went to the doctor in **apprehension**.*

apprehensive
adjective afraid or uneasy about something that may happen: ***apprehensive** of being attacked in the dark streets* (***anxious, edgy, frightened, tense, uneasy***)

apprentice
noun someone who is working for a tradesperson and in return is being taught that trade

Word building: **apprenticeship** *noun*
Word history: Middle English, from Old French *a(p)rendre* teach, learn, *apprehend*

apprise (uh-pruyz)
verb to inform or advise: *I will **apprise** him of the situation.*

Word history: French *a(p)pris*, past participle of *a(p)prendre* learn, teach

apprise / appraise
Don't confuse **apprise** with **appraise**, which is to assess or judge the value of something.

approach
verb **1** to come near to: *to **approach** your house* **2** to come to with a request or an idea: *I **approached** the boss for permission to leave.*

Word history: Middle English *aproche(n)*, from Old French *aprochier*, from Late Latin *appropiāre*

approachable
adjective friendly and easy to talk to: *My teacher is very **approachable**.*

approbation (ap-ruh-bay-shuhn)
noun approval or praise: *Her project earned the teacher's **approbation**.*

appropriate (uh-proh-pree-uht)
adjective **1** suitable for a particular use: ***appropriate** clothes for wet weather*
verb (uh-proh-pree-ayt) **2** to take for your own use: *She **appropriated** Mario's desk.* (***annex, borrow, confiscate, grab, steal***)

Word use: The opposite of definition 1 is **inappropriate**.
Word history: from Latin word meaning 'made one's own'

approval
noun **1** agreement or permission: *The teacher needed the principal's **approval** before sending the class home.* (***clearance, consent, dispensation, leave***)
phrase **2 on approval**, of goods for sale, taken by the customer for examination, with the choice of returning them to the shop or of buying them

Word use: The opposite of definition 1 is **disapproval**.

approve
verb **1** to agree to: *My father **approved** my plan.* (***authorise, endorse, give the go-ahead to, sanction***)
phrase **2 approve of**, to consider good or satisfactory: *I **approve of** your attitude.* (***admire, advocate, hold with, respect, support***)

Word use: The opposite of definition 1 is **reject** or **veto**. | The opposite of definition 2 is **disapprove of**.
Word history: Middle English, from Latin

approximate
adjective nearly right: *Tell me the **approximate** number of children in the class.* (***estimated, loose, rough***)

Word use: The opposite of this is **exact**.
Word building: **approximately** *adverb*
Word history: Latin

apricot
noun a small, round, yellow fruit with soft juicy flesh and one large seed inside

Word history: Latin *praecoqua* apricots

April
noun the fourth month of the year, containing thirty days

Word history: Latin

apron
noun **1** a piece of clothing worn in front to protect the clothes underneath it
phrase **2 tied to someone's apron strings**, dependent on someone for your emotional needs, such as your mother, your wife, etc.

Word history: Middle English *napron* (*napron* being later taken as *an apron*), from Old French, from Latin word meaning 'napkin', 'cloth'

apse (aps)
noun Architecture a semicircular or many-sided recess in a building with an arched roof, especially at the east end of a church

Word history: Latin *apsis*, from Greek word meaning 'circle', 'arch', 'apse'

apt
adjective **1** likely or inclined: *Our baby is **apt** to cry when we leave the room.* (***disposed, liable, prone***) **2** suitable or appropriate: *an **apt** remark* (***applicable, fitting, relevant, to the point***) **3** quick to learn: *an **apt** pupil* (***astute, bright, intelligent, sharp, smart***)

Word history: Middle English, from Latin word meaning 'joined', 'fitted'

aptitude
noun the ability to learn quickly: *an **aptitude** for music* (***flair, gift, talent***)

Word history: Medieval Latin, from Latin

aqualung
noun a cylinder of air strapped to the back of a diver, with a tube that takes air to the mouth or nose

aquamarine
noun **1** a greenish-blue stone used in jewellery
2 a light blue-green or greenish-blue colour

Word building: **aquamarine** *adjective*
Word history: Latin *aqua marīna* sea water

aquarium (uh-kwair-ree-uhm)
noun a glass tank in which fish and water plants are kept

Noun forms: The plural is **aquariums** or **aquaria**.
Word history: Latin

aquatic (uh-kwot-ik)
adjective **1** living or growing in water
2 done in or on water: ***aquatic** sports*

Word history: from Latin word meaning 'watery'

aqueduct (ak-wuh-dukt)
noun a bridge built for carrying a water pipe or channel across a valley

Word history: Latin *aquae ductus* conveyance of water

aqueous (ak-wee-uhs, ay-kwee-uhs)
adjective **1** of, like or containing water
2 formed of matter deposited in or by water: ***aqueous** rocks*

aquiline (ak-wuh-luyn)
adjective curved or hooked like an eagle's beak: *an **aquiline** nose*

Word history: Latin

Arabic numerals (a-ruh-bik nyooh-muh-ruhlz)
plural noun the characters 0, 1, 2, 3, 4, 5, 6, 7, 8, 9

Word use: You can also use **Arabic figures**.

arable (a-ruh-buhl)
adjective suitable for growing crops: ***arable** land*

Word history: Latin *arābilis* that can be ploughed

arachnid (uh-rak-nid)
noun a class of arthropods with eight legs, that includes spiders, scorpions, mites, etc.

Word history: Neo-Latin *Arachnida*, from Greek word meaning 'spider', 'spider's web'

arbiter (ah-buh-tuh)
noun **1** a person in a position to decide points of disagreement (***adjudicator, judge, referee, umpire***)
2 someone who has complete control of something

Word history: from Latin word meaning 'witness', 'judge'

arbitrary (ah-buh-truh-ree, ah-buh-tree)
adjective based on your own feelings and ideas rather than on rules or reasons: *an **arbitrary** decision* (***illogical, inconsistent, personal, random, subjective***)

Word history: from Latin word meaning 'uncertain'

arbitrate
verb to decide or settle a matter for others, often a disagreement or a dispute (***determine, judge, mediate, referee, umpire***)

Word history: Latin

arbitration
noun the settling of a disagreement by someone chosen to do so

arbitrator
noun a person appointed to examine all the facts in a dispute and decide what the outcome should be

Word use: You can also use **arbiter**.

arboreal (ah-baw-ree-uhl)
adjective having to do with, or living in trees: *Monkeys are **arboreal** animals.*

arbour
noun a shady place formed by trees and shrubs

Word use: You can also use **arbor**.
Word history: Middle English, from Latin *herba* plant

arc
noun a curved line

Word history: Middle English, from Latin *arcus* bow

arc / ark

Don't confuse **arc** with **ark**, which is a vessel like the one that Noah and the animals lived in during the Flood, as the story is told in the Bible.

arcade
noun **1** a covered passage with shops on either side
2 *Architecture*
a a series of arches supported on columns
b a part of a building with an arched roof

Word history: French, from Italian word meaning 'bow', 'arch', from Latin

arcane (ah-kayn)
adjective mysterious or understood only by a few

Word history: from Latin word meaning 'shut up', 'keep'

arch
noun **1** a curved structure which helps support a bridge or building or forms the top of a doorway
verb **2** to curve or make into a curved shape: *A horse **arches** its neck.*

Verb forms: it **arches**, it **arched**, it has **arched**, it is **arching**
Word history: Middle English, from Latin *arcus* bow

archaeology (ah-kee-ol-uh-jee)
noun the study of the people and customs of ancient times, made by digging up and describing the remains of buried cities

Word use: You can also use **archeology**.
Word building: **archaeologist** *noun* **archaeological** *adjective*
Word history: from Greek word meaning 'knowledge of ancient things'

archaic (ah-kay-ik)
adjective so old-fashioned that it is not used any more: *an **archaic** word* (***antiquated, obsolete, old, out-of-date, outmoded***)

Word building: **archaism** *noun*
Word history: from Greek word meaning 'antique'

archangel (ahk-ayn-juhl)
noun one of the chief angels

Word history: Middle English, from Latin, from Greek word meaning 'chief angel'

archbishop
noun a head bishop

Word history: Old English *arcebiscop* (representing *hēahbiscop* high bishop)

archenemy
noun a chief enemy: *They are* ***archenemies,*** *and never speak to each other. | Drought is the* ***archenemy*** *of the farmer.*

Noun forms: The plural is **archenemies**.

archer
noun someone who shoots with a bow and arrows

Word history: Middle English, from Latin *arcus* bow

archery
noun the sport, art or skill of an archer

archetype (ah-kuh-tuyp)
noun a typical example or original model: *He was the* ***archetype*** *of all great rulers.* (***paradigm, prototype, standard***)

Word building: **archetypal** *adjective*
Word history: Latin, from Greek word meaning 'first-moulded', 'original'

Archimedes' Principle (ah-kuh-mee-deez)
noun the principle that the weight of the liquid displaced by a floating object is equal to the weight of the object

Word history: discovered by *Archimedes*, 287?–212 BC, Greek mathematician, physicist and inventor

archipelago (ah-kuh-pel-uh-goh)
noun **1** a large body of water with many islands
2 a group of islands in a sea

Noun forms: The plural is **archipelagos** or **archipelagoes**.
Word history: Italian *arcipelago*, literally, chief sea

architect (ah-kuh-tekt)
noun someone whose job is to plan and design new buildings and make sure they are built correctly

Word history: Latin, from Greek word meaning 'chief builder'

architecture
noun the art or science of drawing up plans for buildings

Word building: **architectural** *adjective*
Word history: Latin

architrave (ah-kuh-trayv)
noun the frame around a doorway or window

Word history: Italian *archi-* + *trave* (from Latin word meaning 'beam')

archives (ah-kuyvz)
plural noun a collection of historical documents about a family, business or country: *The* ***archives*** *are kept in the library.*

Word building: **archivist** (ah-kuh-vuhst) *noun*
Word history: French, from Latin, from Greek

arch rival
noun the chief rival: *For the second year running, the* ***arch rivals*** *will meet in the grand final.*

arctic (ahk-tik)
adjective **1** having to do with the area near the North Pole
2 very cold

Word use: You can also use **Arctic** for definition 1.
Word history: Latin, from Greek word meaning 'of the Bear (constellation)', 'northern'

ardent
adjective enthusiastic, or full of feeling: *an* ***ardent*** *campaigner for saving the koalas |* ***ardent*** *promises of love*

Word history: from Latin word meaning 'burning'

ardour (ah-duh)
noun **1** a very strong feeling: *the* ***ardour*** *of love for your country*
2 eagerness or enthusiasm: *Rain does not dampen his* ***ardour*** *for bushwalking.*

Word use: You can also use **ardor**.
Word history: Middle English, from Old French, from Latin

arduous (ahd-zhooh-uhs)
adjective needing a lot of hard work: *Climbing mountains is an* ***arduous*** *sport.* (***demanding, strenuous, tough***)

Word history: Latin

are
verb present plural of **be**

area
noun **1** a particular part of land, of a town, etc.: *a suburban* ***area*** (***precinct, quarter, section, zone***)
2 a particular part of anything: *a sensitive* ***area*** *of the body*
3 the size of a flat or curved surface: *The* ***area*** *of this hall is 100 square metres.*

Word history: from Latin word meaning 'piece of level ground', 'open space'

arena
noun **1** an enclosed space for sports events
2 any activity that involves competition: *Is it wise to enter the* ***arena*** *of politics?*

Word history: from Latin word meaning 'sand', 'sandy place'

aren't
contraction of **are not**

Look up **contractions in grammar**.

argon
noun a colourless, odourless, chemically inactive, gaseous element

Word history: Neo-Latin, from Greek word meaning 'idle'

argot (ah-goh)
noun the peculiar language or slang of any class or group, formerly that of thieves

Word history: French

arguable
adjective **1** able to be proved by argument: *He put forward an* ***arguable*** *case for having classroom monitors.*
2 doubtful

Word building: **arguably** *adverb*

argue
verb to quarrel or disagree: *James* ***argued*** *with Lisa about which film to see.* (***clash***, ***conflict***, ***dispute***, ***row***, ***squabble***)

Verb forms: I **argued**, I have **argued**, I am **arguing**
Word history: Middle English, from Latin *argūtāre*, from *arguere* show

argument
noun **1** a quarrel or disagreement (***altercation***, ***conflict***, ***controversy***, ***difference***, ***dispute***)
2 a reason: *a good* ***argument*** *for doing exercises*
3 a discussion in which reasons for and against something are stated

Word history: Middle English, from Latin word meaning 'proof'

argumentative
adjective liking to argue or quarrelsome: *an* ***argumentative*** *person* (***aggressive***, ***cantankerous***, ***contrary***, ***defiant***, ***stroppy***)

aria (ah-ree-uh)
noun a song sung by one person in an opera

Word history: Italian, from Latin word meaning 'air'

arid
adjective dry and hot: *an* ***arid*** *desert* (***dehydrated***, ***desiccated***, ***parched***)

Word use: The opposite of this is **lush**.
Word building: **aridity** *noun*
Word history: from Latin word meaning 'dry'

arise
verb **1** to appear or come into being: *The question of new school colours may* ***arise***. (***come about***, ***happen***, ***occur***, ***transpire***)
2 to rise or move upwards: *He told them to* ***arise*** *and follow him.*

Verb forms: I **arose**, I have **arisen**, I am **arising**
Word history: Old English *ā-* up + *rīsan* rise

aristocracy (a-ruh-stok-ruh-see)
noun the people of highest rank (***elite***, ***nobility***, ***peerage***, ***upper class***)

Word history: Latin, from Greek word meaning 'rule of the best'

aristocrat (a-ruh-stuh-krat)
noun someone who belongs to the nobility of a country, such as a duke or an earl

Word building: **aristocratic** *adjective*

arithmetic (uh-rith-muh-tik)
noun **1** calculation with numbers
adjective (a-rith-met-ik) **2** having to do with arithmetic

Word use: You can also use **arithmetical** for definition 2.
Word building: **arithmetician** *noun*
Word history: Latin, from Greek word meaning 'of or for reckoning'

ark
noun in the Bible, the large covered boat built by Noah to escape from the Flood

Word history: Old English *arc*, *earc*, from Latin *arca* a chest, coffer

ark / arc
Don't confuse **ark** with **arc** which is a curved line.

arm[1]
noun **1** the part of your body from shoulder to hand
2 the part of a chair on which your arm rests
3 a branch of an organisation

Word history: Old English *arm, earm*

arm[2]
noun **1** Look up **arms**.
verb **2** to supply weapons to
3 to prepare (a thing) for any specific purpose: *Please* ***arm*** *the cabin doors for take-off.*

Word use: The opposite of definitions 2 and 3 is **disarm**.
Word history: Middle English, from Latin

armada (ah-mah-duh)
noun a large fleet of warships

Word history: Spanish, from Latin word meaning 'armed forces'

armadillo (ah-muh-dil-oh)
noun a South American burrowing animal with a covering of bony plates

Word history: Spanish, diminutive of *armado* armed, from Latin

armament
noun the weapons on an aeroplane or warship

Word history: from Latin word meaning 'equipment', 'ship's tackle'

armature (ah-muh-chuh)
noun **1** *Biology* the protective covering of an animal or plant
2 *Electronics*
a the iron or steel placed across the poles of a permanent magnet to close it, or to the poles of an electromagnet to carry mechanical force
b the part of an electrical machine which includes the coils carrying the current
c a part of an electrical machine that vibrates when activated by a magnetic field

Word history: from Latin word meaning 'armour'

armchair
noun **1** a chair with supports at the side for your forearms or elbows
adjective **2** basing ideas on theory or reading, rather than practical experience: *an* ***armchair*** *critic* | *an* ***armchair*** *traveller*

armed
adjective **1** having weapons: *the* ***armed*** *forces*
2 prepared and ready

armed services
plural noun the principal military forces of a country or countries including army, navy, air force, etc.

Word use: You can also use **armed forces**.

armistice (ahm-uh-stuhs)
noun an agreement between countries at war to stop fighting and talk about peace (***ceasefire***, ***truce***)

Word history: Neo-Latin, from Latin word meaning '*armi-*' (combining form of *arma* arms) + *-stitium* (from *sistere* stop)

armour
noun **1** metal or leather covering that knights used to wear when fighting
2 the protective plates on warships and planes
3 any protective covering, such as the scales of a fish

Word use: You can also use **armor**.
Word history: Middle English, from Latin

armoured
adjective having a protective covering: *an **armoured** car*

Word use: You can also use **armored**.

armoury
noun a place for storing weapons

Word use: You can also use **armory**.
Noun forms: The plural is **armouries**.
Word history: Middle English *armurie*

armpit
noun the hollow part under your arm at the shoulder

arms
plural noun **1** weapons: *The soldiers were given **arms** to fight with.*
phrase **2 bear arms**, to serve as a soldier
3 take (**up**) **arms**, to prepare to fight
4 up in arms, angry or indignant: *We're **up in arms** at the way the Premier refuses to talk to us.*

Word history: Middle English, from Latin

army
noun **1** the part of a country's armed forces which is trained to fight on land
2 a large number: *An **army** of workers cleaned up after the fire.*

Noun forms: The plural is **armies**.
Word history: Middle English, from Latin word meaning 'armed forces'

army reserve
noun the part of a country's fighting force not in active service, but used as a further means of defence in case of necessity

aroma (uh-roh-muh)
noun a pleasant smell: *the **aroma** of coffee* (***bouquet***, ***fragrance***, ***scent***)

Word history: Latin, from Greek word meaning 'spice', 'sweet herb'

aromatic (a-ruh-mat-ik)
adjective **1** having a pleasant smell: *an **aromatic** oil*
noun **2** a plant, herb, or medicine with an aroma

arose
verb past tense of **arise**

around
adverb **1** in a circle on every side: *to gather **around***
2 about or here and there: *to travel **around***
3 with a circular movement: *the wheels go **around***
preposition **4** surrounding: *a scarf **around** her head*
5 on the other side of: *a house **around** the corner*
6 *Colloquial* approximately: *to meet **around** ten o'clock*

Word history: *a-* + *round*

arouse
verb **1** to bring into being: *to **arouse** doubts*
2 to wake from sleep

Word building: **arousal** *noun*
Word history: *rouse*, modelled on *arise*

arpeggio (ah-pej-ee-oh)
noun a musical chord played by sounding its notes one after the other

Noun forms: The plural is **arpeggios**.
Word history: Italian word meaning 'play on the harp'

arrange
verb **1** to put in order: *to **arrange** books on a shelf* (***classify***, ***file***, ***group***, ***organise***, ***sort***)
2 to plan: *to **arrange** a party* (***devise***, ***organise***, ***prepare***)

Word building: **arrangement** *noun*
Word history: Middle English, from Old French *a-* + *rangier* range, verb

arrant (a-ruhnt)
adjective complete or utter: *an **arrant** fool* | ***arrant** nonsense*

Word history: variant of *errant*

array
verb **1** to put into position: *The soldiers were **arrayed** for battle.*
noun **2** a group of things on show: *an excellent **array** of children's art*

Word history: Middle English, from Old French *a* to + *rei* order, of Germanic origin

arrear (uh-rear)
noun **1** something that is owed or overdue
phrase **2 in arrear** or **in arrears**, behind in payments, etc.

Word use: The plural form of this word is usually used.
Word history: Middle English, from Latin *ad-* + *retrō* backwards

arrest
verb **1** to take prisoner: *The police officer **arrested** the thief.* (***apprehend***, ***grab***, ***hijack***, ***pick up***, ***trap***)
2 to stop: *The sandbags **arrested** the flood waters.*
noun **3** capture by police: *under **arrest***

Word history: Middle English, from Latin *ad-* + *restāre* stop

arrival
noun **1** the act of arriving: *time of **arrival***
2 a person or thing that arrives: *a new **arrival** at school*

Word use: The opposite of definition 1 is **departure**.

arrive
verb **1** to reach the end of a journey (***berth***, ***land***, ***reach***, ***surface***, ***turn up***)
2 to come: *The moment has **arrived**.* (***appear***, ***happen***, ***occur***)

Word history: Middle English, from Late Latin word meaning 'come to shore'

arrogant (a-ruh-guhnt)
adjective showing that you think you are very important (***conceited***, ***haughty***, ***pompous***, ***snobbish***, ***supercilious***)

Word building: **arrogance** *noun*
Word history: Middle English, from Latin word meaning 'assuming'

arrow
noun **1** a thin pointed piece of wood shot from a bow
2 a sign used to point the way to go

Word history: Middle English and Old English *arwe*

arrowroot
noun a white floury substance used in cooking

arsenal
noun a place for making or storing weapons and ammunition

Word history: from Italian word meaning 'dock'

arsenic (ah-suh-nik)
noun a poisonous chemical substance

Word history: Middle English, from Latin, from Greek *arsenikon* from Arabic *az-zarnik* in which the root word is the Persian *zar* which means 'gold'. Originally it referred to arsenic sulphide which was a yellow dye and colouring agent.

arson
noun the deliberate burning of a building or other valuable property

Word building: **arsonist** *noun*
Word history: Anglo-French, from Late Latin word meaning 'a burning'

art
noun **1** the production and expression of what is beautiful, especially by painting, drawing or sculpture
2 the beautiful things people make: *Our city has a building where works of* ***art*** *are kept.*
3 a skill: *There is an* ***art*** *in making good furniture.*

Word history: Middle English, from Old French, from Latin word meaning 'skill', 'art'

Art Deco (aht dek-oh, aht day-koh)
noun a style of ornament, architecture, furniture and the like, originating in the 1920s and 1930s, marked by geometrical forms and the use of such materials as plastic, glass, etc.

Word use: You can also use **art deco**.
Word history: French *Art Déco*, short form of *Exposition Internationale des Arts Décoratifs*, Paris, 1925

artefact (ah-tuh-fakt)
noun a useful thing made by someone, such as a tool or a work of art

Word use: You can also use **artifact**.
Word history: Latin

arterial
adjective having to do with or like an artery: ***arterial*** *blood* | *an* ***arterial*** *road*

arteriosclerosis (ah-tear-ree-oh-skluh-roh-suhs)
noun Medicine a disease marked by loss of elasticity and thickening of the artery walls

Word history: Neo-Latin, from Greek *artērio-* artery + *sklērōsis* hardening

artery
noun a blood vessel which takes blood from the heart to other parts of the body

Noun forms: The plural is **arteries**.
Word history: Middle English, from Latin, from Greek

artesian basin (ah-tee-zhuhn bay-suhn)
noun Geology a series of rocks formed in such a way that water is held by them under pressure

artesian bore
noun a well sunk through a layer of water-bearing rock in which pressure rather than pumping keeps water rising above the ground

Word use: You can also use **artesian well**.
Word history: French *artésien* pertaining to *Artois*, former province of France where such wells were bored

arthritis (ah-thruy-tuhs)
noun a disease that causes swelling and pain in the joints of the body

Word building: **arthritic** *adjective*
Word history: Latin, from Greek word meaning 'joint disease'

arthropod (ahth-ruh-pod)
noun one of the group of invertebrates, having jointed legs and a segmented body, as the insects, arachnids, crustaceans, etc.

arthroscope (ah-thruh-skohp)
noun Medicine a thin, tubular instrument which is inserted into the cavity between bones to examine a joint and perform surgical procedures

artichoke
noun a thick round flower which grows on a thistle-like plant and is used as a vegetable

Word history: Italian, from Provençal, from Arabic

article
noun **1** a particular thing: *an* ***article*** *of clothing* (***item***, ***object***, ***piece***)
2 a piece of writing about a particular subject in a newspaper or magazine
3 *Grammar* a word, such as 'a', 'an' and 'the', which comes before a noun to show if it relates to one particular person or thing

Word history: Middle English, from French, from Latin *articulus*, diminutive of *artus* joint

articles in grammar

1 definite articles

The **definite article** comes before a noun, and you use it when the noun has already been referred to, or when the noun is about to be identified. For example:

Johnny Rocker released a new single last week.
The song is already number one in the charts.
The rumour that you were leaving school ...

2 indefinite articles

The **indefinite articles** in English are *a* or *an* for singular count nouns, and *some* for plural nouns or mass nouns:

I want a banana and an apple for lunch. (singular count)
There are some apples in the bowl. (plural)
There is some butter in the dish. (mass)
Some is optional — it can be left out before plural nouns or mass nouns:
There are apples in the bowl. (plural)
There is butter in the dish. (mass)

(continued)

articles in grammar *(continued)*

You use an **indefinite article** in front of a noun that has not been referred to before in your writing. The **definite article** (*the*), on the other hand, comes before nouns that have already been referred to or which are clearly identified:

Where are the apples you promised?

articulate (ah-tik-yuh-layt)
verb **1** to speak clearly: *He* ***articulated*** *every word so that everyone could hear.* (***enunciate, sound, utter, voice***)
adjective (ah-tik-yuh-luht) **2** able to put your ideas clearly into words (***coherent, eloquent, fluent, lucid, well-spoken***)

Word use: The opposite of definition 2 is **incoherent** or **unclear**.
Word building: **articulation** *noun*
Word history: Latin

articulated
adjective having joints or divisions: *A semitrailer is an* ***articulated*** *truck.*

artifice (ah-tuh-fuhs)
noun **1** a clever trick or device
2 trickery or deception

Word history: French, from Latin

artificial
adjective **1** made by human beings: ***artificial*** *flowers* (***manufactured, synthetic***)
2 not genuine: ***artificial*** *sorrow* (***affected, counterfeit, fake, sham***)

Word building: **artificiality** *noun*
Word history: Middle English, from Latin

artillery
noun **1** large guns on wheels
2 the part of an army that uses these guns

Word history: Middle English, from Old French word meaning 'implements of war'

artisan
noun a skilled worker who makes things

Word history: French, from Italian *arte* guild

artist
noun **1** someone who creates beautiful things, such as a painter or sculptor
2 a performer or entertainer
3 someone who uses the skills of art in their work: *a commercial* ***artist*** | *an* ***artist*** *with words*

Word history: French, from Italian, from Late Latin

artistic
adjective able to create beautiful things

Word building: **artistically** *adverb*

artistry
noun the skill you need to create beautiful things or to perform in a memorable way

Art Nouveau (aht nooh-voh)
noun a style of art, architecture and ornament of the 1890s, marked by patterns of twisting flower and vegetable forms, based on ideas of naturalistic representation

Word use: You can also use **art nouveau**.
Word history: from French word meaning 'new art'

art union
noun Australian, NZ a lottery, usually with non-cash prizes

arvo
noun Australian, NZ Colloquial afternoon

Word history: modified short form of *afternoon* + *-o*

as
adverb **1** to the same amount or degree (followed by the conjunction *as*): ***as*** *good as gold*
conjunction **2** like or in the way that: *Speak* ***as*** *he does* | ***as*** *I hear it*
3 though: *Bad* ***as*** *it is, you can't blame him.*
4 when or while: ***As*** *he came towards me, the clock began to chime.*
5 since or because: ***As*** *I am here, I might as well stay for dinner.*
6 for instance: *forms of transport,* ***as*** *ferry, train, bus, etc.*
phrase **7 as for** or **as to**, with regard to: ***As for*** *him, you'd best forget he exists.*
8 as if or **as though**, as it would be if: *It was* ***as if*** *I had wings.*
9 as it were, in a way, or so to speak
10 as yet, up to now: ***As yet*** *I haven't told anybody.*

Word history: Old English *alswā*, *ealswā* all so, quite so

As has more than one meaning, and you often need to make clear which one you intend.

We came home as the wind was rising.

In this sentence, it isn't clear whether the wind was the reason why people returned, or just something that happened when they returned. **As** is a conjunction which can express either cause or time (or comparison). In our example the meaning could be made clear by using either

because (if you are thinking about the reason)

or

when (if you are thinking about the timing of events).

In a novel this ambiguity might be useful. But if you were writing up a scientific experiment, it would be important to sort the matter out. **As** is best avoided in factual and argumentative writing.

Look up **like / as**.

asbestos (uhs-bes-tuhs, as-bes-tuhs)
noun a grey substance of fine fibres, which is used for making heat-resistant and fireproof materials

Word history: Latin, from Greek word meaning 'unquenchable'

ascend
verb to climb or go upwards: *I* ***ascended*** *the ladder.* | *Smoke* ***ascended*** *from the chimney.* (***clamber, mount, scale, shin***)

Word use: The opposite of this is **descend**
Word history: Middle English, from Latin word meaning 'climb up'

ascendant (uh-sen-duhnt)
noun **1** a position of power or control: *to be in the* ***ascendant***
adjective **2** predominant or more powerful
3 rising

Word use: You can also use **ascendent**.
Word building: **ascendancy** *noun*

ascension
noun an upward movement
Word history: Middle English, from Latin

ascent
noun **1** an upward movement
2 an upward slope
Word use: The opposite of this is **descent**.
Word history: from *ascend*, modelled on *descent*

ascent / assent
Don't confuse **ascent** with **assent**, which has to do with permission:
I assent to your proposal.
The proposal got my assent.

ascertain (as-uh-tayn)
verb to find out or determine: *to **ascertain** the truth* (***discover***, ***establish***, ***glean***, ***learn***, ***understand***)
Word building: **ascertainable** *adjective* **ascertainment** *noun*
Word history: Middle English, from Old French word meaning 'make certain'

ascetic (uh-set-ik)
noun someone who, for religious reasons, lives simply without many of the usual comforts of life
Word building: **asceticism** *noun*
Word history: from Greek word meaning 'monk', 'hermit' (originally 'athlete')

ascetic / acetic
Don't confuse **ascetic** with **acetic**, which has to do with vinegar or acid.

ASCII (as-kee)
noun Computers a standard code for representing alphanumeric characters
Word history: *A(merican) S(tandard) C(ode for) I(nformation) I(nterchange)*

ascorbic acid (uhs-kaw-bik as-uhd)
noun a water-soluble vitamin, vitamin C, which has a major role in the formation of bones, blood vessels and connective tissues; occurring naturally in citrus fruits, tomatoes, capsicum, and green vegetables, but also produced synthetically

ascribe (uh-skruyb)
verb **1** to consider as connected to a cause, origin, or something like this: *The alphabet is usually **ascribed** to the Phoenicians.*
2 to consider to belong: *to **ascribe** wisdom to old age*
Word building: **ascription** *noun*
Word history: from Latin word meaning 'add to a writing'

aseptic (ay-sep-tik)
adjective free from the living germs of disease, fermentation or rotting
Word building: **aseptically** *adverb* **asepsis** *noun*

asexual
adjective **1** not sexual: *an **asexual** relationship*
2 having no sex or organs for sex: *These cells duplicate themselves by **asexual** reproduction.*

ash[1]
noun **1** the powder left after something has been burnt: *cigarette **ash** | The **ashes** are in the fireplace.*
2 ashes, what is left after a human body has been cremated
Word history: Old English *asce*, *æsce*

ash[2]
noun a tree from which we get a valuable hard timber
Word history: Old English *æsc*

ashamed
adjective **1** feeling shame or sorrow: *After I hit her I felt **ashamed**.*
2 unwilling because you're afraid of being laughed at: ***ashamed** to answer the question*

ashen
adjective **1** grey or ash-coloured
2 consisting of ashes

ashore
adverb on to the land: *We went **ashore** at sunset. | The wreckage of the ship was washed **ashore**.*

aside
adverb **1** on or to one side: *to turn **aside***
noun **2** words spoken quietly so that only some people present can hear: *'Curses! Foiled again,' said the villain in an **aside** to the audience.*

asinine (as-uh-nuyn)
adjective stupid or obstinate
Word building: **asininity** *noun*
Word history: from Latin word meaning 'ass'

ask
verb **1** to enquire: *I will **ask** the way.*
2 to put a question to: *I will **ask** him.* (***interrogate***, ***query***)
3 to attempt by words to obtain: *She **asked** a favour. | He **asked** for advice.* (***beg***, ***beseech***, ***entreat***, ***implore***, ***request***)
4 to invite: *I will **ask** her to the party.*
phrase **5 ask for trouble** (or **it**), *Colloquial* to behave in a way that seems to invite trouble to come
6 a big ask, *Australian*, *NZ*, *Colloquial* an extremely difficult task: *Winning the match tomorrow is **a big ask**.*
Word history: Old English *āscian*

askance (uhs-kans)
adverb showing distrust: *He looked **askance** at my offer.*

askew (uhs-kyooh)
adverb out of position: *He knocked my hat **askew**.* (***aslant***, ***awry***, ***cockeyed***, ***crooked***)

asleep
adverb **1** in or into a state of sleep: *I fell **asleep**.*
adjective **2** sleeping: *He is **asleep**.*
3 numb: *My foot is **asleep**.*
Word use: The opposite of definition 2 is **awake**.

asp
noun a small venomous snake, especially the Egyptian cobra
Word history: Latin, from Greek

asparagus
noun a plant with long green shoots, used as a vegetable
Word history: Latin, from Greek

aspect
noun **1** the way a thing appears: *the burnt* ***aspect*** *of the land after the bushfire | to think about every* ***aspect*** *of a problem* (***appearance, condition, look, view***)
2 the direction a building faces: *a northern* ***aspect***
3 *Grammar* a verb form which shows that the action is either continuous or complete
Word history: Middle English, from Latin word meaning 'look at'

For more information about **aspect** (definition 3), look up **verbs: aspect.**

Asperger's syndrome (as-per-guhz sin-drohm, as-per-juhz, as-per-guhz, as-per-juhz)
noun a form of autism characterised by a tendency to social isolation and inappropriate behaviour
Word history: named after Hans *Asperger*, an Austrian paediatrician who first described it in 1944 after observing these patterns of behaviour in some children he was studying. He later opened a school for children with this condition.

asperity (as-pe-ruh-tee, uhs-pe-ruh-tee)
noun roughness or harshness of manner: *He looked at me with some* ***asperity***.
Word history: from Latin word meaning 'roughness'

aspersion
noun a harmful remark or criticism: *He cast* ***aspersions*** *on my character.*

asphalt (ash-felt, as-felt)
noun a black sticky substance like tar, mixed with crushed rock and used for making roads
Word history: Late Latin, from Greek

asphyxia (uhs-fik-see-uh)
noun the extreme medical condition caused by lack of oxygen and too much carbon dioxide in the blood, caused by interruption to breathing, such as in choking
Word building: **asphyxiant** *noun* **asphyxiate** *verb*
Word history: from Greek word meaning 'stopping of the pulse'

aspic
noun a jelly used for setting fish, meat or vegetables in a mould
Word history: French

aspirate (as-puh-rayt)
verb **1** *Phonetics* to begin a word or syllable with an *h* sound, as in *howl*, opposed to *owl*
2 *Medicine* to remove fluids from body cavities by suction

aspiration
noun an ambition to strive towards

aspire
verb to aim eagerly: *to* ***aspire*** *to be school captain*
Word building: **aspirant** *noun*
Word history: Middle English, from Latin word meaning 'breathe on'

aspirin
noun a drug used for stopping pain
Word history: German (originally trademark)

ass
noun a long-eared animal in the same family as the horse (***donkey***)
Word history: Old English, from Old Welsh *asyn* ass, from Latin

assail (uh-sayl)
verb **1** to attack violently
2 to attack with arguments, requests, insults, etc.
Word building: **assailant** *noun*
Word history: Middle English, from Vulgar Latin, from Latin *ad-* + *salīre* leap

assassin (uh-sas-uhn)
noun someone who sets out to murder a well-known person, especially for political or religious reasons, or for a reward
Word history: named after one of an order of Muslim fanatics, active in Persia and Syria from about 1090 to 1272, whose chief object was to assassinate Crusaders; French, from Medieval Latin, from Arabic word meaning 'hashish eaters'

assassinate
verb **1** to kill suddenly or secretly after careful planning, especially for political or religious reasons: *to* ***assassinate*** *the Prime Minister* (***execute, murder, put down, slay***)
2 to ruin or destroy in a disloyal way: *to* ***assassinate*** *someone's character*
Word building: **assassination** *noun*
Word history: Medieval Latin

assault
noun **1** an attack: *to make an* ***assault*** *on the fort* (***ambush, blitz, foray, onslaught***)
2 *Law* an unlawful attack or threatened attack on someone, with or without a weapon
verb **3** to attack or try to attack, often in a sexual way (***beat up, get stuck into, invade, violate***)
Word building: **assaulter** *noun*
Word history: Middle English, from Old French word meaning 'assail'

assay (uh-say)
verb **1** to examine by trial, evaluate or put to test: *to* ***assay*** *his ability | to* ***assay*** *a drug for its strength* (***check, investigate, sample, screen, try***)
2 to attempt or endeavour
noun (uh-say, as-ay) **3** the determination of the strength, purity, etc., of a drug or something similar
4 an examination, trial or attempt
Word building: **assayer** *noun* **assayable** *adjective*
Word history: Middle English, from Old French, from Late Latin word meaning 'weighing'

assemblage (uh-sem-blij)
noun **1** a group
2 *Art* a method of forming a three-dimensional work of art by combining different elements on a hanging surface or in a free position
Word history: French

assemble
verb **1** to bring or put together: *to* ***assemble*** *a machine* (***construct, fabricate, fit together, piece together***)

2 to come together: *We **assembled** in the playground.* (***congregate***, ***collect***, ***gather***, ***rally***)

Word history: Middle English, from Old French, from Late Latin word meaning 'compare', 'imitate'

assembly

noun **1** a number of people gathered together for a special purpose (***conference***, ***congregation***, ***crowd***, ***gathering***, ***meeting***)
2 the putting together of something that is in parts: *a factory for the **assembly** of cars*

Noun forms: The plural is **assemblies**.
Word history: Middle English, from Old French

assembly line

noun an arrangement of machines, tools and workers in which each worker performs a special operation on an incomplete unit

assent

verb to agree: *to **assent** to her suggestion* (***acquiesce***, ***comply***, ***concur***, ***consent***, ***go along with***)

Word building: **assent** *noun*
Word history: Middle English, from Latin

assent / ascent

Don't confuse **assent** with **ascent**, which is a journey up, usually up a mountain:

Sir Edmund Hillary and Tenzing Norgay made the first ascent of Mount Everest.

assert

verb to state or declare strongly: *to **assert** your innocence*

Word use: The opposite of this is **deny**.
Word history: from Latin word meaning 'joined to'

assertion

noun a strong positive statement

assertiveness

noun the quality of expressing yourself strongly: *It was the **assertiveness** of our third speaker that helped us win the debate.*

Word use: The opposite of this is **submissiveness**.
Word building: **assertive** *adjective*

assess

verb to work out the value of: *to **assess** your work* (***analyse***, ***investigate***, ***review***, ***study***, ***test***)

Word building: **assessment** *noun* **assessor** *noun*
Word history: Middle English, from Late Latin word meaning 'fix a tax'

asset

noun **1** something you own: *A house is a valuable **asset**.*
2 anything of value: *Good health is an **asset**.*

assets

noun Commerce property or possessions owned by a person or a business, such as machinery, buildings, cash, etc. (***belongings***, ***goods***, ***reserves***, ***resources***, ***valuables***)

Word use: Compare this with **liabilities**.
Word history: Middle English, from Old French word meaning 'enough', from Latin *ad-* + *satis* enough

assiduous (uh-sid-jooh-uhs)

adjective **1** continual or without stopping: ***assiduous** reading*
2 attentive or devoted

Word history: from Latin word meaning 'sitting down to'

assign

verb **1** to distribute or allot: *to **assign** rooms at the hotel*
2 to appoint or choose: *to **assign** you to do the cleaning | to **assign** a day for the picnic*
3 *Law* to transfer property

Word building: **assignable** *adjective* **assigner** *noun*
Word history: Middle English, from Old French, from Latin

assignation (as-ig-nay-shuhn)

noun **1** an appointment for a meeting, nowadays especially a forbidden love-meeting (***date***, ***rendezvous***, ***tryst***)
2 the act of assigning

assignment

noun a particular task: *Our **assignment** was to write a composition.*

assimilate

verb to take in and make part of yourself: *I **assimilated** the information.* (***absorb***, ***incorporate***)

Word history: from Latin word meaning 'likened'

assimilation (uh-sim-uh-lay-shuhn)

noun **1** the act or process of assimilating
2 the state or condition of being assimilated
3 *Biology* the absorption and transformation of food, etc., into tissue
4 the process in which individuals or groups of differing origins take on the basic attitudes, habits and life-styles of another culture

Word building: **assimilative** *adjective* **assimilatory** *adjective*

assist

verb to help: *She **assisted** me with my homework.* (***aid***, ***lend a hand***, ***support***)

Word building: **assistance** *noun*
Word history: French, from Latin word meaning 'stand by'

assistant

noun a helper, usually of some higher-ranking person: *an **assistant** to the manager* (***aide***, ***attendant***, ***deputy***, ***offsider***)

associate (uh-soh-see-ayt)

verb **1** to connect in your mind: *I **associate** the beach with holidays.* (***identify***, ***link***, ***relate***)
2 to spend time with or to work with: *I **associate** with people who enjoy the same hobbies.* (***accompany***, ***hang around with***, ***mix with***)
noun (uh-soh-see-uht) **3** a partner or someone who shares your interests: *She is my **associate** in business.* (***collaborator***, ***colleague***, ***comrade***, ***friend***, ***helper***)

Word history: Middle English, from Latin word meaning 'joined to'

association

noun **1** a group of people interested in the same thing: *an **association** of stamp collectors* (***alliance***, ***assembly***, ***club***, ***league***, ***society***)
2 the connection of ideas in your mind: *the **association** of sleep with bed*

assonance (<u>as</u>-uh-nuhns)
noun the repetition of the same vowel sound in words close together, as in 'fly high'

Word use: Compare this with **alliteration.**
Word building: **assonant** *adjective*
Word history: French, from Latin word meaning 'sounding to'

assorted
adjective **1** arranged in sorts or varieties: ***assorted*** *biscuits*
2 including various different kinds: ***assorted*** *flower seeds* (***diverse, miscellaneous, mixed, motley***)
3 matched or suited: *What a strangely* ***assorted*** *pair.*

assortment
noun a collection of things of various kinds: *an* ***assortment*** *of lollies* (***hotchpotch, jumble, medley, miscellany***)

assuage (uh-<u>swayj</u>)
verb **1** to ease or make less severe: *to* ***assuage*** *grief*
2 to satisfy or fill the needs of: *to* ***assuage*** *appetite and thirst*
3 to pacify or calm

Word history: Middle English, from Old French, from Latin *ad-* + *suāvis* sweet

assume
verb **1** to believe without proof: *Don't* ***assume*** *that he'll come — ask him!* (***accept, take for granted, think, trust***)
2 to agree to carry out: *to* ***assume*** *the duties of school captain*

Word history: late Middle English, from Latin word meaning 'take up'

assumption
noun **1** the act of assuming
2 something you take for granted: *the* ***assumption*** *that your parents love you*

assurance
noun **1** a promise or guarantee: *to give an* ***assurance*** *of continuing support*
2 confidence or faith in your own ability: *to do something with* ***assurance***

assure
verb **1** to tell with certainty: *He* ***assured*** *us he would come.*
2 to make sure or certain: *His good marks* ***assured*** *him of a place in the top class.*

Word history: Middle English, from Late Latin

> **assure / ensure / insure**
> Look up **ensure / insure / assure.**

asterisk (<u>as</u>-tuh-risk)
noun a star shape (*) used in printing or writing to show that something has been written as a footnote at the bottom of the page, or been left out, etc.

Word history: Late Latin, from Greek word meaning 'star'

astern
adverb behind or at the back of

Word use: This word is only used of ships or boats.

asteroid
noun any one of the hundreds of tiny planets lying between Mars and Jupiter

Word history: from Greek word meaning 'starlike'

asthma (<u>as</u>-muh)
noun a breathing disorder which causes wheezing, coughing and a feeling of tightness in the chest

Word history: from Greek word meaning 'panting'

asthmatic (as-<u>mat</u>-ik)
adjective **1** having to do with or suffering from asthma: *an* ***asthmatic*** *condition* | *an* ***asthmatic*** *child*
noun **2** someone who suffers from asthma

astonish
verb to amaze or surprise greatly (***astound, dumbfound, stagger, stun***)

Word building: **astonishment** *noun* **astonishing** *adjective*
Word history: Old English *stunian* resound

astound
verb to overcome with amazement (***astonish, dumbfound, stagger, stun***)

Word building: **astounding** *adjective*
Word history: past participle of obsolete *astone, astun*

astral
adjective having to do with or coming from the stars (***stellar***)

Word history: Latin word meaning 'star', from Greek

astray
adverb away from the proper path: *to go* ***astray***

astride
adverb with the legs on either side of: *He stood* ***astride*** *the low fence.*

astringent (uh-<u>strin</u>-juhnt)
noun **1** a liquid put on the skin to tighten it and cause it to tingle
adjective **2** tightening and refreshing the skin: *an* ***astringent*** *after-shave lotion*
3 harsh or bitter: ***astringent*** *remarks about their behaviour*

Word building: **astringency** *noun*
Word history: Latin

astrology
noun the study of the possible effects of the stars and planets on our lives

Word use: An astrological forecast or chart is called a **horoscope.**
Word building: **astrologer** *noun* **astrological** *adjective*
Word history: Middle English, from Latin *astrologia*, from Greek

> **astrology / astronomy**
> Don't confuse **astrology** with **astronomy.** These subjects both have to do with the stars but there is a difference.
>
> **Astrology** is a study which assumes that heavenly bodies have an influence on human beings, and tries to explain what that effect is.
>
> **Astronomy** is the science of the stars and planets, in which they are identified and described as closely as possible. Remember that <u>-nomy</u> is a word part meaning 'naming'.

astronaut
noun someone specially trained to travel in a spaceship

Word use: Astronauts from Russia are called **cosmonauts**.
Word history: *astro-* star + Greek *naútēs* sailor

astronautics (as-truh-naw-tiks)
noun the science of flight in space

astronomical
adjective **1** having to do with astronomy
2 very large: *The patient got an **astronomical** bill from the hospital.*

astronomy
noun the scientific study of the sun, moon, stars and planets

Word building: **astronomer** *noun*
Word history: Middle English, from Latin, from Greek

astronomy / astrology
Look up **astrology / astronomy.**

astute
adjective having clear and quick understanding: *an **astute** manager* (***canny***, ***clever***, ***knowing***, ***shrewd***, ***sharp***)

Word building: **astuteness** *noun*
Word history: from Latin word meaning 'adroitness', 'cunning'

asunder
adverb Old-fashioned in or into pieces: *to tear **asunder***

Word history: Old English *on sundran* apart

asylum (uh-suy-luhm)
noun **1** protection or safety: *seeking **asylum***
2 a shelter that offers safety or care (***haven***, ***retreat***, ***sanctuary***)

Word history: Latin, from Greek word meaning 'inviolable'

asystole (ay-sis-tuh-lee)
noun Medicine the absence of the normal rhythmical contraction of the heart, so that there is no blood flow, leading to death

at
preposition **1** used to state a place, time, order, experience, etc.: ***at** home* | ***at** noon* | ***at** zero* | ***at** work*
phrase **2 at it again**, acting in a way you expect
3 at that, as things are at the moment: *Let it go **at that**.*

Word history: Old English *æt*

atavism (at-uh-viz-uhm)
noun **1** *Biology* the reappearance after many generations of characteristics of some far-removed ancestor
2 a return to an earlier type

Word building: **atavist** *noun* **atavistic** *adjective*
Word history: Latin *atavus* ancestor + *-ism*

ate
verb past tense of **eat**: *I eat meat today but I **ate** bread last week.*

The British pronunciation of **ate** is *et* but in Australian English it is more commonly pronounced to sound like *eight*.

atheist (ay-thee-uhst)
noun someone who believes that there is no God

Word use: Compare this with **agnostic**.
Word building: **atheism** *noun* **atheistic** *adjective*
Word history: Greek *átheos* without a god + *-ist*

athlete (ath-leet)
noun someone who trains in sports such as running and jumping

Word history: Latin, from Greek word meaning 'contestant in games'

athletic (ath-let-ik)
adjective **1** having an active and strong body: *an **athletic** teenager* (***able-bodied***, ***fit***, ***robust***, ***strong***, ***vigorous***)
2 of an athlete or athletics: ***athletic** excellence* | ***athletic** events*

athletics
noun events that take place on a track, such as running and hurdling, javelin throwing and the high jump: *The **athletics** at the Olympic Games are exciting to watch.*

atlas
noun a book of maps

ATM
noun an automatic teller machine; a computer-operated machine from which you can withdraw money from your bank account and do other basic banking transactions

Word history: abbreviation

atmosphere
noun **1** the air that surrounds the earth
2 a feeling or mood: *an unpleasant **atmosphere** in the room after a quarrel*

Word building: **atmospheric** *adjective*
Word history: Neo-Latin, from Greek *atmó(s)* vapour + *sphaîra* sphere

atoll
noun a coral island with a salt-water lake in the middle

Word history: Maldive *atol*

atom
noun the smallest part that an element can be divided into and still keep its special qualities or take part in a chemical reaction. An atom is made up of protons, neutrons and electrons.

Word history: Latin, from Greek word meaning 'indivisible'

atomic
adjective **1** having to do with atoms
2 driven by atomic energy: *an **atomic** submarine*
3 using atomic weapons: ***atomic** warfare*

atomic bomb
noun a bomb which explodes with great force because of the energy released from the splitting of atoms

atomic energy
noun → **nuclear energy**

atomiser (at-uh-muy-zuh)
noun an apparatus for reducing liquids to a fine spray

Word use: You can also use **atomizer**.

atonal (ay-<u>tohn</u>-uhl)
adjective not in any musical key: *The composer wrote a piece of* ***atonal*** *music for the school orchestra.* (***cacophonous, dissonant, flat, sharp***)

Word building: **atonality** *noun* **atonally** *adverb*

atone
verb to make up or show you are sorry: *I* ***atoned*** *for my laziness by helping with the housework.*

Word building: **atonement** *noun*
Word history: backformation from *atonement*

atrocious (uh-<u>troh</u>-shuhs)
adjective **1** terribly wicked or cruel: *an* ***atrocious*** *crime* (***barbaric, brutal, savage, vicious, violent***)
2 very bad or lacking in taste: ***atrocious*** *taste in clothes* (***abominable, abysmal, monstrous, nasty, rotten***)

Word building: **atrociousness** *noun*
Word history: *atroci(ty)* + *-ous*

atrocity (uh-<u>tros</u>-uh-tee)
noun a terribly wicked or cruel act

Noun forms: The plural is **atrocities**.
Word history: Latin

atrophy (<u>at</u>-ruh-fee)
verb to lose strength or size: *Muscles* ***atrophy*** *if they aren't used.* (***contract, decrease, dwindle, shrivel, wither***)

Verb forms: it **atrophied**, it has **atrophied**, it is **atrophying**
Word history: Latin, from Greek word meaning 'lack of nourishment'

attach
verb **1** to fasten or join: ***Attach*** *the label to the suitcase.* (***append, tack on***)
2 *Computers* to join a file to another document such as an email: *He* ***attached*** *the minutes of the meeting to the email to committee members.*
phrase **3 be attached to,** to like or love: *She* ***is*** *very* ***attached to*** *to her elder brother.*

Word building: **attachment** *noun*
Word history: Middle English, from Old French

attaché (uh-<u>tash</u>-ay)
noun a person appointed to an official staff, as a government representative, especially an ambassador in a foreign country

Word history: French *attacher* attach

attaché case (uh-<u>tash</u>-ay kays)
noun a briefcase

attack
verb **1** to begin to use force or weapons: *The army* ***attacked*** *at dawn.* (***charge, strike***)
2 to use force or weapons against: *to* ***attack*** *the enemy* (***assail, assault, lay into, raid, set upon***)
3 to go to work on strongly: *to* ***attack*** *a difficult task* (***tackle, try, undertake***)
noun **4** a military operation which aims to overcome an enemy and destroy its forces (***ambush, assault, blitz, foray, onslaught***)
5 the first movement in a contest
6 *Music* vigour or flair in the way you present a piece of music

Word building: **attacker** *noun*
Word history: French, from Italian

attain
verb to reach or achieve by trying hard: *He* ***attained*** *a high grade in English.* (***accomplish, bring off, carry through, gain, secure***)

Word building: **attainable** *adjective*
Word history: Middle English, from Latin word meaning 'touch upon'

attainment
noun **1** the act of achieving something
2 something that someone achieves

attempt
verb **1** to try: *to* ***attempt*** *to swim* (***endeavour, seek, strive***)
2 to try to do: *to* ***attempt*** *a course of study* (***attack, have a go at, tackle, undertake, work towards***)
noun **3** an effort or try: *I said I would make an* ***attempt*** *to climb the mountain.* (***bid, crack, endeavour, stab***)

Word history: from Latin word meaning 'try'

attend
verb **1** to be present at
2 to look after: *The nurse* ***attended*** *the patient.*
3 to pay attention or take notice: *to* ***attend*** *to your teacher* (***consider, focus on, heed, mind, note***)

Word history: Middle English, from Latin word meaning 'stretch towards'

attendance
noun **1** the act of being present at something
2 the number of people present: *The* ***attendance*** *at the play is good tonight.*
3 the number of times that someone is present: *Your* ***attendance*** *at school hasn't been good lately.*

attendant
noun someone who helps or looks after someone else: *a cloakroom* ***attendant*** (***aide, assistant, guide, helper, servant***)

attention
noun **1** the act of concentrating or fixing your mind on something: *This job needs all your* ***attention.***
2 a position in which you stand straight and still: *The soldiers stood at* ***attention.***

Word history: Middle English, from Latin

attentive
adjective observant or paying attention (***awake, concentrating, inquisitive, mindful, watchful***)

attenuate (uh-<u>ten</u>-yooh-ayt)
verb **1** to make or become thin or fine
2 to weaken or reduce in force, quantity or value

Word building: **attenuation** *noun*
Word history: from Latin word meaning 'made thin'

attest (uh-<u>test</u>)
verb **1** to declare to be correct, true or genuine: *to* ***attest*** *the truth of a statement*
2 to give proof of: *His works* ***attest*** *his industry.*

Word building: **attestation** *noun* **attester** *noun* **attestor** *noun*
Word history: from Latin word meaning 'bear witness'

attic
noun a room or a space directly under the roof of a building: *We store junk in the* ***attic.*** (***garret, loft***)

Word history: French, from Latin; originally applied to a square column in building

attire
verb **1** to dress, particularly for a special occasion: *to* ***attire*** *yourself in your best*
noun **2** clothes, especially rich or splendid ones (***apparel***, ***dress***, ***garb***, ***wardrobe***)

Word history: Middle English, from Old French word meaning 'put in order'

attitude
noun **1** a way of holding your body: *He stood in a threatening* ***attitude***. (***bearing***, ***carriage***, ***pose***, ***posture***, ***stance***)
2 the way you think or behave: *Ben has a helpful* ***attitude*** *to small children.* (***conviction***, ***outlook***, ***stand***, ***viewpoint***)

Word history: French, from Italian, from Medieval Latin word meaning 'aptitude'

attorney (uh-ter-nee)
noun **1** a person, usually a solicitor, appointed by someone to do business for them (***advocate***, ***counsel***)
phrase **2 power of attorney**, legal permission to make decisions or sign documents for another person

Noun forms: The plural is **attorneys**.
Word history: Middle English, from Old French word meaning 'assign'

attract
verb to pull or draw: *A magnet* ***attracts*** *steel pins. | His smile* ***attracts*** *people.* (***charm***, ***entice***, ***lure***, ***magnetise***)

Word history: from Latin word meaning 'drawn to'

attraction
noun **1** the act or power of attracting
2 something that attracts: *the main* ***attraction*** *at the fair*
3 *Physics* a force which pulls two or more objects together or which makes them revolve around a central point

Word use: The opposite of definitions 1 and 3 is **repulsion**.

attractive
adjective **1** pleasing: *an* ***attractive*** *idea* (***agreeable***, ***appealing***, ***charming***, ***pleasant***, ***tempting***)
2 pleasing to look at: *an* ***attractive*** *man* (***beautiful***, ***fair***, ***good-looking***, ***handsome***)

attribute (uh-trib-yooht)
verb **1** to think of as belonging or due: *The crop failure may be* ***attributed*** *to the drought.*
noun (at-ruh-byooht) **2** something thought of as belonging: *Wisdom is one of her* ***attributes***.

Word building: **attribution** *noun* **attributive** *adjective*
Word history: Middle English, from Latin word meaning 'assigned'

attrition (uh-trish-uhn)
noun **1** a rubbing against (***chafing***, ***friction***, ***grating***, ***scraping***)
2 a wearing down or away by friction (***abrasion***, ***erosion***)
3 a reduction of effectiveness of force caused by loss of people and material: *a war of* ***attrition***

Word history: Latin

atypical (ay-tip-ik-uhl)
adjective not typical, or different from usual: *Anna's grumpiness is* ***atypical*** *of her usual pleasant nature.*

aubergine (oh-buh-zheen)
noun → **eggplant**

Word history: French

auburn
adjective of a reddish-brown colour: ***auburn*** *hair*

Word building: **auburn** *noun*
Word history: Middle English, from Latin *alburnus* whitish, from *albus* white

auction (ok-shuhn)
noun **1** a public sale at which things are sold to the person who offers the most money
verb **2** to sell by auction: *They decided to* ***auction*** *the cottage.*

Word history: from Latin word meaning 'an increasing'

auctioneer
noun someone whose job is to sell things by auction

audacious (aw-day-shuhs)
adjective bold or daring: *an* ***audacious*** *reply to the teacher | an* ***audacious*** *attempt on Mount Everest*

Word building: **audacity** *noun*
Word history: *audaci(ty)* + *-ous*

audible
adjective able to be heard: *His voice was barely* ***audible*** *over the noise of the stereo.*

Word use: The opposite of this is **inaudible**.
Word building: **audibility** *noun*
Word history: Medieval Latin, from Latin word meaning 'hear'

audience
noun **1** a group of people listening or watching
2 an interview with someone important: *an* ***audience*** *with the Queen*

Word history: Middle English, from Latin word meaning 'attention', 'hearing'

audio
adjective having to do with hearing and sound, especially with the machines that use the sound waves that can be heard by the human ear, such as tape-recorders or CD players

audiology (aw-dee-ol-uh-jee)
noun the study of the process of hearing, especially diagnosis and measurement

Word building: **audiological** *adjective* **audiologist** *noun*

audio system
noun a combination of a tape deck, amplifier, loudspeakers, CD player, etc., for listening to music

audiovisual
adjective having to do with use of your ears and eyes at the same time: *an* ***audiovisual*** *aid for teaching science*

audit
noun an inspection and checking of business accounts, usually once a year

Word building: **audit** *verb* **auditor** *noun*
Word history: Middle English, from Latin word meaning 'a hearing'

audition
noun **1** a test given to see how suitable an actor or performer is for a particular job: *Elsa is having an* ***audition*** *for a part in the new play.*
verb **2** to test by giving an audition to: *The bandleader* ***auditioned*** *two new trumpet players.*
3 to give a trial performance: *They* ***auditioned*** *for the choir.*
Word use: An audition for a part in a film is called a **film test**.
Word history: from Latin word meaning 'a hearing'

auditorium
noun a hall or other large space for meetings or concerts
Word history: Latin

auditory (aw-duh-tree, aw-duh-tuh-ree)
adjective having to do with hearing or the ears: *an* ***auditory*** *signal*
Word history: Latin

auger (aw-guh)
noun a carpenter's tool, larger than a gimlet, with a spiral groove for drilling holes in wood or in the ground
Word history: Middle English, variant of *nauger* (*a nauger* being taken as *an auger*), Old English *nafogār*

augment
verb to make larger: *He works at night to* ***augment*** *his income.* (***amplify***, ***boost***, ***enlarge***, ***expand***, ***increase***)
Word building: **augmentation** *noun*
Word history: Middle English, from Latin word meaning 'increase'

augmented
adjective of an interval in music, greater by one semitone than the perfect or major interval of the same name: *an* ***augmented*** *third*

augur (aw-guh)
noun **1** in ancient Rome, one of a body of officials charged with observing and explaining omens for guidance in public affairs
verb **2** to be a sign, or bode well or ill
Word building: **augural** *adjective* **augurship** *noun*
Word history: Latin

august (aw-gust)
adjective causing you to feel awe and respect: *the* ***august*** *atmosphere of Canberra's War Memorial*
Word history: Latin *augustus*

August
noun the eighth month of the year, containing 31 days
Word history: named after Augustus Caesar

aunt
noun **1** the sister of your father or mother
2 your uncle's wife
Word use: You can also use **aunty** or **auntie**.

auntie
noun **1** *Aboriginal English*
a a female relative of an older generation
b a closely-connected non-Aboriginal woman
2 → **aunty**
Word use: You can also use **aunty**.

aunty
noun **1** another form of **aunt**
2 *Aboriginal English* → **auntie**
Noun forms: The plural is **aunties.**

aura
noun a special character or atmosphere: *The garden has an* ***aura*** *of peace.*
Word history: Latin, from Greek word meaning 'breath of air'

aural (aw-ruhl)
adjective having to do with hearing or listening: *The first part of the music exam was an* ***aural*** *test.*

> **aural / oral**
> Don't confuse **aural** with **oral**, which has to do with the mouth.
> An **oral** exam is one in which you speak your answers. **Oral** rhymes with *moral.*

auriferous (aw-rif-uh-ruhs)
adjective yielding or containing gold
Word history: Latin *aurifer* gold-bearing + *-ous*

aurora (uh-raw-ruh)
noun a natural display of moving lights in the sky

auspices (aws-puhs-uhz)
phrase **under the auspices of**, with the support or help of: ***under the auspices of*** *the Australian Red Cross Society*
Word history: Latin *auspicium*

auspicious
adjective favourable or showing signs of success: *an* ***auspicious*** *occasion* (***fortunate***, ***happy***, ***promising***)

austere (os-tear)
adjective **1** severely simple: *The nuns live in* ***austere*** *surroundings.*
2 stern or grim: *The doctor had an* ***austere*** *manner.* (***firm***, ***harsh***, ***rigid***, ***straitlaced***)
Word history: Middle English, from Latin, from Greek

austerity
noun a lack of wealth or finery or a severe way of living: *the* ***austerity*** *of her clothing* | ***austerities*** *imposed during the war*
Noun forms: The plural is **austerities**.

Australian Business Number
noun an 11-digit number allocated by the government to a business, which must be shown on invoices, receipts, letterheads, etc.
Word use: You can also use **ABN**.

Australian crawl
noun → **freestyle** (definition 1)

Australian Rules
plural noun a type of football requiring two teams of 18 players, which originated in Australia
Word use: You can also use **Australian National Football**, **Australian Football** or **Aussie Rules**.

Australian silky terrier
noun a small, lightly built dog of medium length with erect ears and a long, silky, blue or grey-blue coat with tan markings
Word use: Another name is **Sydney silky**.

autarchy (aw-tah-kee)
noun self-government

Noun forms: The plural is **autarchies.**
Word building: **autarchic** *adjective*
Word history: from Greek word meaning 'self-rule'

authentic
adjective genuine or real: *an **authentic** diamond* (***actual***, ***factual***, ***legitimate***, ***proven***, ***true***)

Word use: The opposite of this is **fake**.
Word history: Late Latin, from Greek word meaning 'warranted'

authenticate
verb to prove to be genuine: *to **authenticate** a will*

authenticity
noun genuineness or reliability: *the **authenticity** of the car dealer*

author
noun **1** someone who writes a book, article or poem
2 the creator of anything: *Wellington was the **author** of Napoleon's downfall.*

Word building: **authorship** *noun*
Word history: Middle English, from Latin *auctor* originator

authorise
verb **1** to give legal power to: *He **authorised** the deputy to decide the question.* (***license***, ***permit***)
2 to approve officially: *The grant for the new library has been **authorised**.* (***ratify***, ***sanction***)

Word use: You can also use **authorize**.
Word building: **authorisation** *noun*

authoritarian (aw-tho-ruh-tair-ree-uhn, uh-tho-ruh-tair-ree-uhn)
adjective acting without considering people's freedom: *an **authoritarian** government* (***autocratic***, ***dictatorial***, ***imperious***, ***overbearing***, ***tyrannical***)

Word building: **authoritarianism** *noun*

authoritative (aw-tho-ruh-tuh-tiv, uh-tho-ruh-tuh-tiv)
adjective having or giving authority

authority
noun **1** the right to decide or judge: *The courts have **authority** over people who come before them.*
2 a right that gives power: *The police have **authority** to control traffic.*
3 a reliable source of information: *She is an **authority** on gardening.* (***expert***, ***specialist***)

Noun forms: The plural is **authorities**.
Word history: Middle English, from Latin

autistic (aw-tis-tik)
adjective suffering from a mental illness in which you have severe difficulty communicating with other people and acting socially

Word building: **autism** *noun*

autobiography
noun your own life story written by yourself

Noun forms: The plural is **autobiographies**.
Word use: Compare this with **biography**.
Word building: **autobiographical** *adjective*

autocracy (aw-tok-ruh-see)
noun **1** unlimited rule by one person over others (***despotism***, ***tyranny***)
2 a country ruled by someone with unlimited power (***autarchy***, ***dictatorship***)

Noun forms: The plural is **autocracies**.
Word history: Greek

autocrat (aw-tuh-krat)
noun someone who rules alone, without taking advice from other people

Word building: **autocratic** *adjective*
Word history: from Greek word meaning 'ruling by oneself'

autograph
noun **1** someone's own handwriting, especially their signature
verb **2** to write your name on or in: *to **autograph** a book*

Word history: Latin, from Greek

autoimmune system
noun the system within the body which produces antibodies

Word use: You can also use **auto-immune system**.

automatic
adjective **1** working or going by itself: *an **automatic** washing machine*
2 like a machine: *Their reaction to the bell was **automatic**.*
noun **3** a car with a gear change that works automatically when you are driving

Word building: **automatically** *adverb*
Word history: Greek *autómatos* self-acting + *-ic*

automation (aw-tuh-may-shuhn)
noun the use of machines instead of people to do jobs in factories

Word history: blend of *autom(atic)* + *(oper)ation*

automaton (aw-tom-uh-tuhn)
noun a robot or someone who acts like a robot

Noun forms: The plural is **automatons** or **automata** (aw-tom-uh-tuh).

automobile
noun a car

Word history: French

automotive (aw-tuh-moh-tiv)
adjective **1** driven by a self-contained power plant
2 having to do with motor vehicles

autonomous (aw-ton-uh-muhs)
adjective self-governing: *Papua New Guinea is now an **autonomous** nation.* (***independent***, ***self-ruling***, ***sovereign***)

Word history: Greek

autopsy
noun the examination of a dead body to discover the cause of death (***dissection***, ***post-mortem***)

Noun forms: The plural is **autopsies**.
Word history: from Greek word meaning 'seeing with one's own eyes'

autotrophic (aw-tuh-tro-fik)
adjective (of plants) able to make their own food: *an **autotrophic** organism*

Word use: Compare this with **heterotrophic**.

autumn (aw-tuhm)
noun the season of the year following summer, when the leaves change colour and fall from some trees

Word building: **autumnal** (aw-tum-nuhl) *adjective*
Word history: Latin

auxiliary (og-zil-yuh-ree, awg-zil-yuh-ree)
adjective **1** aiding or helping: *an **auxiliary** verb*
2 kept in case it is needed or in reserve: *an **auxiliary** engine*
noun **3** a helper

Noun forms: The plural is **auxiliaries**.
Word building: **auxiliary** *noun*
Word history: from Latin word meaning 'aid'

auxiliary verb
noun Grammar a verb usually found before certain forms of other verbs, used to express time, aspect, etc., as *am, have*, etc., in *I am going* and *we have spoken*

Look up **verbs: auxiliary verbs**.

avail (uh-vayl)
verb **1** to serve or be of use
2 to be of value or profit
phrase **3 avail yourself of**, to make use of: *to **avail yourself of** all the facilities offered*

Word history: Middle English, from Latin word meaning 'be strong', 'have effect'

available
adjective ready, or able to be used: *There are three tennis courts **available**. | Peter is **available** to help.*

Word building: **availability** *noun*

avalanche
noun a large mass of snow sliding or falling suddenly down a mountain slope

Word history: French: blend of dialect *avaler* go down (from Latin *ad-* + *vallis* valley) and French (Swiss) *lavenche* of pre-Latin origin

avarice (av-uh-ruhs)
noun greediness for money

Word building: **avaricious** *adjective*
Word history: Middle English, from Old French, from Latin word meaning 'greed'

avatar (av-uh-tah)
noun Internet the representation of a person in virtual reality: *Tim chose a white swan for his chat room **avatar**.*

Word history: Hindi for the form in which a Hindu god appeared on earth, either as a human being or an animal

avenge
verb to get revenge for: *'I will **avenge** my father's murder!' cried the knight as he drew his sword.*

Word building: **avenger** *noun*
Word history: Middle English, from Latin word meaning 'punish'

avenge / revenge
Don't confuse **avenge** with **revenge**. These words have the same basic meanings but are usually different parts of speech.
Avenge is always used as a verb.
Revenge is most often used as a noun.

avenue
noun a street or road, especially one lined with trees

Word history: French, from Latin word meaning 'come to'

aver (uh-ver)
verb to affirm or declare in a positive manner

Verb forms: I **averred**, I have **averred**, I am **averring**
Word history: Middle English, from Latin *ad-* + *vērus* true

average
noun **1** the result of dividing the sum of two or more quantities by the number of quantities: *The **average** of 1, 6 and 8 is 5.*
2 an ordinary amount, kind, quality or rate: *Her ability is well above the **average**.*
verb **3** to do or have an average: *to **average** twelve kilometres a week on your bike | to **average** four meals a day*
phrase **4 average out**, *Colloquial* to divide or sort out, more or less evenly

Word history: from French, from Arabic word meaning 'damages'

averse
adjective opposed or not willing: ***averse** to work* (***disinclined**, **hesitant**, **loath**, **reluctant***)

Word history: from Latin word meaning 'turned away'

aversion
noun **1** a strong dislike: *I have an **aversion** to spinach.* (***animosity**, **antipathy**, **hatred**, **hostility**, **loathing***)
2 a person or thing disliked: *Smoking is my pet **aversion**.*

Word use: The opposite of definition 1 is **liking**.

avert
verb **1** to turn away: *She **averted** her eyes.*
2 to prevent: *to **avert** danger*

Word history: Middle English, from Latin word meaning 'turn away'

avian flu
noun → **avian influenza**

avian influenza
noun any of a wide range of influenza viruses affecting birds, some forms of which can be transmitted from birds to humans

Word use: You can also use **avian flu** or **bird flu**.

aviary (ay-vuh-ree, ayv-yuh-ree)
noun a large cage or enclosure where birds are kept

Noun forms: The plural is **aviaries**.
Word history: Latin *avis* bird

aviation
noun the science or act of flying in a plane: *Amy Johnson was a pioneer of **aviation**.*

Word history: French

aviator
noun a pilot

avid
adjective keen or eager: *an **avid** swimmer* (***ardent**, **enthusiastic**, **fervent***)

Word building: **avidity** *noun* **avidly** *adverb*
Word history: from Latin word meaning 'eager'

avocado
noun a green, pear-shaped fruit used in salads

Noun forms: The plural is **avocados**.
Word history: Spanish, from Nahuatl word literally meaning 'testicle'

Avogadro's hypothesis (av-uh-gad-rohz huy-poth-uh-suhs)
noun the hypothesis which states that equal volumes of gases under the same conditions of temperature and pressure contain equal numbers of molecules

Word history: named after Count Amedeo *Avogadro*, 1776–1856, Italian physicist and chemist

Avogadro's number
noun the number of atoms or molecules in a mole of substance; $6.022\ 52 \times 10^{23}$ per mole

Word use: You can also use **Avogadro's constant**.
Word history: named after Count Amedeo *Avogadro*, 1776–1856, Italian physicist and chemist

avoid
verb to keep away from: *to **avoid** danger | to **avoid** a boring film* (***elude, evade, miss, shirk, steer clear of***)

Word building: **avoidable** *adjective* **avoidance** *noun*
Word history: Middle English, from Old French word meaning 'empty out'

avow (uh-vow)
verb **1** to admit or acknowledge frankly or openly (***confess, own***)
2 to state or declare (***affirm, assert, aver, profess, swear***)

Word building: **avowal** *noun* **avowed** *adjective*
Word history: Middle English, from Latin word meaning 'summon'

avuncular (uh-vungk-yuh-luh)
adjective like an uncle: ***avuncular** regard*

Word history: from Latin word meaning 'uncle'

await
verb **1** to wait for: *I **await** your commands.*
2 to be ready for: *Supper **awaits** you.*

Word history: Middle English, from Old Northern French *a-* + *waitier* watch

awake
verb **1** to wake up: *When I **awoke** the sun was shining.*
2 to excite or stir up: *to **awake** his interest*
adjective **3** not sleeping: *The baby is **awake**.*

Word use: The opposite of definition 3 is **asleep**.
Verb forms: I **awoke**, I have **awoken**, I am **awaking**
Word history: Old English *awacen*

awaken
verb to wake up or alert: *A kookaburra **awakened** the campers. | Frank **awakened** them to their danger.*

Word history: Old English

awakening
noun **1** a waking up from sleep
2 a renewing of interest: *an **awakening** among the people in the cause of peace*

award
verb **1** to give for merit or achievement: *to **award** prizes* (***confer, donate, grant, present***)
noun **2** something won by merit or achievement: *an **award** for bravery* (***medal, pennant, prize, trophy***)
3 a ruling about wages and conditions of work given by an industrial tribunal: *the metal industry **award***

Word history: Middle English, from Anglo-French word meaning 'observe', 'decide', from Latin

aware
adjective having a feeling or knowledge: *He was **aware** of a stealthy step behind him.*

Word building: **awareness** *noun*
Word history: Old English *gewær* watchful

away
adverb **1** off: *to go **away***
2 at a distance: *to stand **away** from the wall*
3 from your possession: *to give money **away***
4 at once: *right **away***
adjective **5** absent: ***away** from home*
6 distant: *six kilometres **away***
phrase **7 do away with**, to kill
8 make away with, to steal

Word history: Old English *aweg*, earlier *on weg* on way

awe
noun a feeling of great respect mixed with fear: *The convicts were in **awe** of the overseer's whip.*

Word building: **awe** *verb*
Word history: Middle English, from Scandinavian

awe / oar / or / ore

Don't confuse **awe** with the other three words that sound the same.

You use an **oar** for rowing a boat.

You use **or** to connect alternative words, phrases or clauses:

I don't know which colour to choose — red, yellow or green.

Ore is a rock or mineral which is mined for the metal it contains.

awesome
adjective filling you with feelings of respect and fear: *an **awesome** height above the valley*

awful
adjective very bad or unpleasant: *an **awful** mess* (***horrible, repulsive, revolting, vile, yucky***)

Word history: Middle English

This word used to mean the same as **awesome**, but it was overused and lost much of its force.

awfully
adverb **1** very badly: *He treats his dogs **awfully**.*
2 a word used to add emphasis to an adjective or adverb: ***awfully** good | an **awfully** long way*

awkward
adjective **1** clumsy: *an **awkward** girl who is always bumping into things* (***accident-prone, all thumbs, gangling, heavy-handed, incompetent***)
2 inconvenient: *an **awkward** room to furnish | an **awkward** time*

Word building: **awkwardness** *noun*
Word history: *auk* backhanded (from Scandinavian) + *-ward*

awl
noun a small pointed instrument for making holes in leather, wood, etc.
Word history: Old English *æl*

awning
noun a roof-like shelter over a window or door, etc., to give protection from the weather: *a shop* ***awning***

awoke
verb past tense of **awake**

awry (uh-ruy)
adverb **1** turned to one side: *to wear your hat* ***awry*** */ to look* ***awry*** (***askew***, ***aslant***, ***cockeyed***, ***crooked***)
2 wrong or amiss: *Our plans went* ***awry***.
Word history: Middle English *on wry*

axe
noun **1** a tool with a blade for chopping
verb **2** *Colloquial* to dismiss from a position, usually a job
phrase **3 have an axe to grind**, to have private or selfish reasons for doing things
4 the axe, *Colloquial*
a a cutting down or reduction of spending
b the sack or dismissal from a job
Word history: Old English *æx*

axes (ak-seez)
noun plural of **axis**

axial (ak-see-uhl)
adjective **1** having to do with or forming an axis
2 found on an axis

axiom
noun something that is obviously true
Word building: **axiomatic** *adjective*
Word history: Latin, from Greek word meaning 'a requisite'

axis
noun **1** an imaginary line which something revolves around: *The earth rotates on its* ***axis*** *once every 24 hours.*
2 a central line that divides something exactly in half: *an* ***axis*** *of symmetry*
Noun forms: The plural is **axes** (ak-seez).
Word history: from Latin word meaning 'axle', 'axis', 'board'

axle
noun the rod in the middle of a wheel on which the wheel turns
Word history: Old English *eaxl(e)* shoulder

axolotl (aks-uh-lot-l)
noun an amphibian with a long tail and short legs, found in Mexican lakes: *We kept our* ***axolotl*** *in the tank with our goldfish.*

ayatollah (uy-uh-tol-uh)
noun the name given to a Muslim religious leader in Iran

azalea (uh-zayl-yuh)
noun a shrub with attractive flowers that bloom in spring
Word history: Neo-Latin, from Greek word meaning (feminine adjective) 'dry'; so named as growing in dry soil

azure (ay-zhuh, a-zyoo-uh)
adjective of a pale blue or sky-blue colour
Word building: **azure** *noun*
Word history: Middle English, from Arabic, from Persian word meaning 'lapis lazuli'

baba ganoush (bub-uh guh-noosh)
noun a food made from cooked eggplant, herbs and garlic, made into a paste
Word use: You can also use **baba ghanoush.**
Word history: Arabic

babble
verb **1** to speak quickly and unclearly: *The shy boy* ***babbled*** *his answer.* (***jabber, talk rubbish, waffle, yak***)
2 to to make a soft, continuous, murmuring sound the way a brook or stream does
Word building: **babble** *noun*
Word history: Middle English; imitative

baboon
noun a large monkey with a mouth like a dog and a short tail, found in Africa and Arabia
Word history: Middle English, from Old French word meaning 'stupid person'

baby
noun **1** a very young child or animal
adjective **2** like or suitable for a baby: *a* ***baby*** *face* | ***baby*** *clothes*
verb **3** to treat someone like a baby: *Stop* ***babying*** *me — I'm sixteen years old!*
Noun forms: The plural is **babies**.
Verb forms: I **babied**, I have **babied**, I am **babying**
Word history: Middle English

babysit
verb to look after (a child) while the parents are out
Verb forms: I **babysat**, I have **babysat**, I am **babysitting**
Word building: **babysitter** *noun* **babysitting** *noun*

baccarat (bak-uh-rah, bak-uh-rah)
noun a card game played for money
Word history: French; origin unknown

bach
verb Australian, NZ Colloquial to keep house alone or with a companion when neither is accustomed to housekeeping: *She was* ***baching*** *with a friend near the university.*
Word use: You can also use **batch**.
Word history: abbreviation of *bachelor*

bachelor
noun **1** a man who isn't married
2 Bachelor, the first or lowest degree awarded to a person at university: *He's got a* ***Bachelor*** *of Arts.*
Word history: Middle English, from Old French, from Medieval Latin word meaning 'small dairy farmer'

bacillus (buh-sil-uhs)
noun any of the group of rod-shaped bacteria
Word history: from Late Latin word meaning 'small rod'

back[1]
noun **1** the part of something that is farthest from the front: *the* ***back*** *of the room*
2 the rear part of your body, from your neck to the bottom of your spine
3 a defending player in football and other games
verb **4** to reverse: *Dad* ***backed*** *the car into the garage.*
5 to support: *They* ***backed*** *their local team.* (***advocate, assist, champion, side with, sponsor***)
6 to bet on: ***Back*** *a horse in the next race.*
adjective **7** found or situated at the rear: *the* ***back*** *door* | *my* ***back*** *pocket*
8 having to do with the past: ***back*** *issues of the magazine*
phrase **9 back down**, to give up your point of view in an argument, etc.
10 back out of, to avoid fulfilling or carrying out something: *to* ***back out of*** *an agreement*
11 back up,
a to support or encourage someone: *My mother will* ***back*** *me* ***up*** *in this argument.*
b to make a copy of the data you key into a computer on a tape or disk, so that it doesn't get lost
12 behind someone's back, in secret or without anyone knowing
13 be (or **get**) **on someone's back**, *Colloquial* to nag at someone in order to make them do something
14 break the back of, to finish the hardest part of something
15 get your back up, to become annoyed
16 put your back into, to do something with all your strength
17 see the back of, to be rid of a person, a job, etc.
18 turn your back on, to ignore or have nothing further to do with a person or thing
Word history: Old English *bæc*

back[2]
adverb **1** at or to the rear: *to step* ***back***
2 in reply or in return: *to write* ***back*** | *to pay* ***back***
3 in or towards an earlier time or place: *to go* ***back*** *to your old home*
phrase **4 back and forth**, first in one direction and then the other
Word history: variant of *aback*

backbench
noun the parliamentary members of a particular political party who are not ministers or shadow ministers
Word building: **backbencher** *noun*

backbone
noun **1** the spine of your body or the similar set of bones in other animals
2 courage to stand up for what you believe
3 *Computers* a high-speed connection or series of connections forming a major pathway in a network

backburner
noun **1** the rear burner of a stove, often used to keep food warm
phrase **2 put on the backburner**, to postpone doing something for the time being: *Ella's dream of playing in a band has been **put on the backburner** until she finishes high school.*

backdate
verb to date earlier or to make effective from an earlier date: *We shall **backdate** the pay rise.*

backfire
verb to have a very different effect from what you intended: *Our plan **backfired** and we became hopelessly lost.*

backgammon
noun a board game in which two people play on a special double board which has 12 spaces each side; each player has fifteen pieces which they take turns to move after throwing dice

Word history: *back*[1], adjective + Old English *gamen* game; game so called because the pieces often go back and re-enter

background
noun **1** the back part of a view or scene: *in the **background** of the picture*
2 the events and conditions that lead up to and explain something: *the **background** of today's disaster*
3 your social position, experience and education
phrase **4 in the background**, out of sight, or not noticed

Word use: The opposite of definition 1 is **foreground**.

backhand
noun **1** a stroke, in a game such as tennis, by a right-handed player from the left of the body (or the reverse for a left-handed player), with the back of the hand turned forwards
2 writing which slopes backwards or to the left

backing
noun **1** support of any kind, such as a piece of material placed behind another to strengthen it, or money made available to help a project (***aid***, ***assistance***, ***endorsement***, ***sponsorship***)
2 musical background for a singer

backlash
noun **1** any sudden, violent or unexpected backward movement, such as that of a wave, the wheels of a machine, etc.
2 a strong political or social movement, sometimes sudden and violent, against a previous development

backload
noun **1** a load which can be transported by a truck back to its base once its main load has been dropped off, thus making the truck's journey more profitable
2 the passengers transported by an airline on a return trip from a major destination

Word building: **backload** *verb*

backlog
noun a piling up of things that need to be done or looked at: *There is a **backlog** of letters to be answered.* (***accumulation***, ***oversupply***, ***stock***)

backpack
noun a light, strong bag designed to be carried on the back, especially by travellers, walkers, etc. (***haversack***, ***knapsack***, ***rucksack***)

backpacker
noun someone who travels with their clothes, etc., in a backpack, usually staying in low-priced accommodation

backroom
adjective doing important work without public notice or in secret: ***backroom** workers in the lab*

backslash
noun a short diagonal line (\), either printed or on a computer screen

backslide
verb to return to former bad behaviour

Verb forms: it **backslid**, it has **backslid**, it is **backsliding**
Word building: **backslider** *noun*

backstage
adverb out of view of the audience in a theatre, such as behind the scenes or in the dressing rooms

Word building: **backstage** *adjective*

backstop
noun **1** *Sport* a person or fence placed to prevent the ball going too far
2 someone who or something that is relied on for help when all else fails: *I have $500 as a **backstop**.*

backstroke
noun a stroke in swimming in which you lie on your back and move your arms backwards in turn

back-to-back
adjective **1** consecutive: *She had four **back-to-back** wins.*
adverb **2** consecutively: *They played two games **back-to-back**.*

backtrack
verb **1** to return over the same course
2 to change your mind about an agreement, plan, opinion, etc.

Word building: **backtracker** *noun*

backup
noun **1** support or help: *His plan received a lot of **backup**.*
2 something kept for use when needed
3 a build-up, especially of a liquid: *the **backup** of floodwater*
4 the process of copying data so that a version is available if the original data is lost or damaged: *We do a **backup** at the end of each day.*

backward
adjective **1** turned or moving towards the back: *a **backward** look* | *a **backward** step*
2 behind the others in growth, or ability to learn: *a **backward** reader* (***illiterate***, ***innumerate***, ***retarded***, ***slow***, ***uneducated***)
adverb **3** → **backwards**

Word use: The opposite of this is **forward**.
Word history: Middle English

backwards
adverb **1** towards the back
2 with the back first
3 opposite to the usual or right way: *to spell **backwards***
4 towards the past
5 towards a less advanced condition: *My work is going **backwards**.*
phrase **6 backwards and forwards**, first in one direction and then the other
7 bend (or **lean**) **over backwards**, *Colloquial* to try hard to please, help, etc.

Word use: The opposite of definitions 1 to 5 is **forwards**. | You can also use **backward** for definitions 1 to 5.
Word history: Middle English

backwater
noun **1** a pool of still, stale water that is joined to a river but not reached by its current
2 a place where nothing seems to happen

backwoods
plural noun **1** country areas with small populations
2 any little known area: *the **backwoods** of English literature*

backyard
noun **1** the enclosed area behind a house
2 *Colloquial* your own neighbourhood, community, or society

bacon
noun the salted meat from the back and sides of a pig

Word history: Middle English, from Old French, from Germanic

bacteria
plural noun microscopic living bodies with one cell, which multiply by dividing themselves in two and which can cause disease and decay

Noun forms: The singular is **bacterium**.
Word building: **bacterial** *adjective*
Word history: Neo-Latin, from Greek word meaning 'little stick'

You will sometimes see **bacteria** used with a singular verb. Some people feel that this is not acceptable as **bacteria** is the plural form of **bacterium**.

Look up **germ / bacterium / virus**.

bad
adjective **1** not good: ***bad** behaviour* (***abominable***, ***abysmal***, ***atrocious***, ***nasty***, ***rotten***)
2 of poor quality: *a **bad** film | a **bad** shot in golf* (***defective***, ***faulty***, ***inferior***, ***unsatisfactory***)
3 serious or severe: *a **bad** accident | a **bad** mistake*
4 sick or unhealthy: *I feel **bad** today.*
5 rotten or decayed: ***bad** meat*
6 upset or sorry: *I feel **bad** about your accident.*
7 *Colloquial* excellent or good
phrase **8 go bad**, decay: *My apple has **gone bad**.*
9 not bad, *Colloquial* quite good or fair in quality

Adjective forms: **worse**, **worst**
Word building: **badness** *noun* **badly** *adverb*
Word history: Middle English *badde*; perhaps a backformation from Old English *bæddel* effeminate person

bad cholesterol
noun the cholesterol which has a tendency to clog blood vessels, and is associated with an increased risk of coronary artery disease

Word use: Compare this with **good cholesterol**.

bad debt
noun a debt that you know will never be paid and which you have written off

bade (bad)
verb Old-fashioned past tense of **bid**

badge
noun **1** a disc or label that you wear on your clothes to show people what you're a member or supporter of, or what rank you hold
verb **2** to mark with an insignia or brand: *to **badge** a website*

Word history: Middle English *bage, bagge*

badger
noun **1** a burrowing mammal found in Europe and America, which has a white mark on its head
verb **2** to pester or annoy someone: *He **badgered** his parents with questions.*

Word history: perhaps from *badge* (with allusion to white mark on head) + *-ard*

badinage (bad-uh-nahzh, bad-uh-nahj)
noun light, playful talk or banter

Word history: French word meaning 'fool', from Provençal word meaning 'gape', from Late Latin

badminton
noun a game in which two players hit a feathered shuttlecock over a high net

Word history: named after *Badminton*, village in Gloucestershire, England

baffle
verb **1** to confuse or puzzle someone: *The unusual question **baffled** me.* (***bewilder***, ***confound***, ***mystify***, ***perplex***)
noun **2** a screen or something similar used to control the flow of gases, sounds, liquids, etc.

Word building: **bafflement** *noun* **baffling** *adjective*

bag
noun **1** a container for holding or carrying things: *a **bag** of cement | a shopping **bag***
2 bags, *Colloquial* plenty or a lot of: *She's got **bags** of money.*

Word building: **bag** *verb* (**bagged**, **bagging**)
Word history: Middle English *bagge*, probably from Scandinavian

bagel (bay-guhl)
noun a small hard bread roll, in the shape of a ring

Word history: Yiddish

baggage
noun **1** the suitcases and boxes which belong to a traveller: *I left my **baggage** with a porter.* (***belongings***, ***bags***, ***luggage***, ***suitcases***)
2 negative feelings carried over from previous experiences that influence a person's attitudes and the way they behave: *guilt and other emotional **baggage***

bagpipes
plural noun a musical instrument you play by blowing into a bag with pipes attached

bail[1]
noun **1** money which must be paid so that someone who is charged with a crime can go free until they are tried in court
phrase **2 bail out**,
a to help someone get their freedom by giving bail
b to help someone out of trouble: *He lent me some money to* ***bail*** *me* ***out*** *until I get paid.*
3 jump bail, to fail to appear in court at the appointed time and lose your bail as a result

Word history: Middle English, from Latin word meaning 'carry'

bail[2]
verb **1** to empty a boat with a bucket or can: *They* ***bailed*** *furiously after each wave hit them.*
phrase **2 bail out**, to jump from a plane with a parachute: *When the engine failed he* ***bailed out.***

Word use: You can also use **bale**.
Word history: Middle English, from Old French word meaning 'bucket', from Vulgar Latin word meaning 'vessel'

bail[3]
noun **1** one of the two small pieces of wood that rest on top of cricket stumps
2 a framework for holding a cow's head during milking
phrase **3 bail up**, *Australian*, *NZ*
a to hold up and rob: *Bushrangers would often* ***bail up*** *early settlers travelling through the bush.*
b to delay someone by talking to them: *She* ***bailed*** *me* ***up*** *just as I was leaving.*

bail / bale

Don't confuse **bail** with **bale**, which refers to a large bundle of goods, such as *a bale of wool.*

The word may be spelt **bale** or **bail** when it is used with *out* to mean either 'to remove water from a boat with a bucket', or 'to jump from a plane with a parachute'.

bailiff (bay-luhf)
noun a law officer employed to deliver court orders, collect payments of debts, etc.

Word history: Middle English, from Old French word meaning 'govern'

bails
plural noun Look up **bail**[3] (definition 1).

bait
noun **1** food used on a hook, or in a trap, to catch fish or animals
2 food with poison in it, used to kill or drug animals
verb **3** to use bait: *to* ***bait*** *a trap*
4 to tease someone in order to upset or annoy them

Word history: Middle English, from Scandinavian

bake
verb **1** to cook in an oven
2 to make hard by heating: *to* ***bake*** *pots in a kiln*

Word history: Old English *bacan*

baker
noun someone whose job is to bake bread and cakes

baker's dozen
noun thirteen

bakery
noun the place where bread and cakes are baked

baking powder
noun any of various powders used in baking to make dough rise, made of sodium bicarbonate and an acid substance (such as cream of tartar), which together react with water to give out carbon dioxide

baking soda
noun → **sodium bicarbonate**

baklava (buh-klah-vuh, bak-luh-vuh)
noun a cake made from thin pastry, nuts and honey

Word history: Turkish

balaclava (bal-uh-klah-vuh)
noun a knitted cap that pulls down over your head and under your chin: *Your grey* ***balaclava*** *looks like a helmet.*

Word history: named after *Balaclava*, a port on the Black Sea, scene of the charge of the Light Brigade in the Crimean War, 1854

balalaika (bal-uh-luy-kuh)
noun a Russian musical instrument like a triangular guitar

Word history: Russian

balance
verb **1** to make or keep steady: *I can't* ***balance*** *on my new skates. | He* ***balanced*** *a stick on his nose.*
2 to be equal to something else, especially in weight: *Do these scales* ***balance****?*
3 *Bookkeeping*
a to find or make equal the difference between the debit and the credit sides of an account
b to arrange accounts so that the total of the debit and the credit side is equal
noun **4** steadiness: ***balance*** *of judgement | I can't keep my* ***balance****.* (***equilibrium***, ***poise***, ***stability***)
5 the difference between the total of the money paid into, and the money taken out of, a bank account
6 an instrument for weighing, often a swaying bar with containers hanging at the ends (***scales***, ***weighing machine***)
7 in a work of art, an arrangement of the shapes, colour, etc., that is pleasing to the viewer

Word history: Middle English, from Late Latin word meaning 'having two scales'

balanced
adjective **1** having weight evenly distributed: *a* ***balanced*** *load*
2 of a discussion, opinion, etc., taking everything into account in a fair, well-judged way: *a* ***balanced*** *report on climate change*
3 of a diet, having different kinds of food in the correct proportion to maintain health

balance of nature
noun a balanced food web where there is no danger to the existence of any species

Word use: Look up **food web**.

balance of payments
noun the difference between a nation's total payments (debits) to and total receipts (credits) from foreign countries

balance of trade
noun the difference between the value of goods going out of a country (exports) and those coming in (imports)

balance sheet
noun a statement summarising the financial position of a business or other organisation at a given date by showing the assets balancing against the liabilities and capital

balcony
noun **1** an upstairs verandah that often has a roof and railings
2 the highest floor of seats in a theatre
Noun forms: The plural is **balconies**.
Word history: Italian word meaning 'scaffold', from Old High German

bald
adjective **1** without hair: *a **bald** head | a **bald** man*
2 plain and to the point: *a **bald** statement* (***blunt***, ***direct***, ***downright***, ***unadorned***)
Word building: **balding** *adjective* **baldness** *noun*
Word history: Middle English from obsolete *ball* white spot

bale[1]
noun a large amount of goods to be stored or transported, such as wool, hay or straw, tied up tightly with cords or wire
Word history: Middle English, from Flemish, from Old French, from Germanic

bale[2]
verb → **bail**[2]

bale / bail
Don't confuse **bale** with **bail**.
The word **bail** in its legal sense is the money left with a court to ensure that an accused person comes back for trial. To **bail** someone out means 'to help someone get out of trouble'. **Bail** in its cricketing sense is part of a wicket.
The word may be spelt **bale** or **bail** when it is used (often with 'out') to mean 'to remove water from a boat with a bucket', or (always with 'out') 'to jump from a plane with a parachute'.

baleful
adjective full of hate: *The bull watched him with a **baleful** expression before charging.*
Word history: Old English

ball[1]
noun **1** a round or egg-shaped object which you can bounce, or which you can kick, catch, or hit in games
2 something which is shaped like a ball: *a **ball** of string | a **ball** of wool* (***globe***, ***globule***, ***orb***, ***sphere***)
3 a rounded part of your body: *the **ball** of your thumb*
phrase **4 ball of muscle** (or **strength**), *Colloquial* a person who is very healthy and strong
5 have the ball in your court, *Colloquial* to have the chance or the responsibility of making the next move
6 on the ball, *Colloquial* quick to learn, understand or take action
7 start (or **keep**) **the ball rolling**, *Colloquial* to start or keep something going
Word history: Middle English, from Scandinavian

ball[2]
noun a very grand or formal dance: *My parents wore their best evening clothes to the **ball**.*
Word history: French, from Late Latin

ball / bawl
Don't confuse **ball** with **bawl**. When people **bawl** they cry noisily.

ballad
noun a simple poem with short verses, which tells a story and is often turned into a song
Word history: Middle English, from Provençal word meaning 'dance', from Late Latin

ballast
noun heavy material carried by a ship to keep it steady, or by a balloon to control its height (***counterbalance***, ***counterweight***, ***stabiliser***, ***weight***)
Word history: Middle Low German *bal* bad + *last* load

ball bearing
noun a bearing in which moving parts turn or run on rolling steel balls

ballerina (bal-uh-ree-nuh)
noun a girl or woman ballet dancer
Word history: Italian

ballet (bal-ay)
noun a formal sort of dancing, performed by a group, who act out a story, using graceful and controlled movements
Word history: French, from Italian word meaning 'little ball'

ballistic
adjective **1** having to do with ballistics
phrase **2 go ballistic**, *Colloquial* to become extremely angry: *Dad will **go ballistic** when he sees this mess.*

ballistics
noun the study of the movement of missiles, bullets, or other objects fired from guns

balloon
noun **1** a small rubber bag which is filled with air or gas and used as a toy
2 a large bag filled with hot air or other light gas, which may have a basket for passengers and can rise and float in the air
verb **3** to swell out: *The sail **ballooned** in the wind.*
Word history: Italian *balla* ball

balloonist
noun someone who travels by balloon

ballot
noun **1** a ticket or paper you must fill in to record your vote: *They counted our **ballots** to see who had won the election.*
2 a secret way of voting
verb **3** to vote by ballot
4 to draw lots: *to **ballot** for duties in the classroom*
Verb forms: I **balloted**, I have **balloted**, I am **balloting**
Word use: You can also use **ballot paper** for definition 1. | You can also use **secret ballot** for definition 2.
Word history: Italian *balla* ball

ballpoint pen
noun a pen whose point is a small ball which rolls around

Word use: Another name is **biro**.

balm (bahm)
noun **1** a sweet-smelling ointment or oil which heals or makes something less painful
2 something soothing: *The good news was **balm** to the anxious parents.*

Word history: Middle English, from Latin word meaning 'balsam'

Balmain bug
noun an edible flattened crustacean first discovered in Port Jackson (Sydney Harbour); similar to the Moreton Bay bug

Word history: named after *Balmain*, a suburb of Sydney, New South Wales

balmy (bah-mee)
adjective fine or pleasant: *In the **balmy** spring weather they often ate outdoors.* (***fair***, ***mild***, ***sunny***, ***temperate***)

Adjective forms: **balmier**, **balmiest**

balsa (bawl-suh)
noun very light wood, often used in crafts

Word history: Spanish

balsam (bawl-suhm, bol-suhm)
noun **1** a sweet-smelling gum that comes from some trees (***balm***, ***oil***, ***resin***)
2 a kind of garden plant with red, pink or white flowers

Word history: Old English, from Latin, from Greek

balustrade (bal-uh-strayd)
noun a rail with a row of short pillars holding it up, usually part of a balcony or staircase

bamboo
noun a woody, tree-like plant whose hollow stem is used for building and making light furniture

Word history: Dutch, from Malay *mambu*

bamboozle
verb to confuse or deceive: *He **bamboozled** them with conjuring tricks.* (***baffle***, ***befuddle***, ***distract***, ***muddle***, ***puzzle***)

Word history: perhaps from thieves' jargon

ban
verb to bar or forbid: *Our teacher **banned** chewing gum from the classroom.* (***censor***, ***disqualify***, ***exclude***, ***outlaw***, ***prevent***)

Word use: The opposite of this is **allow**.
Verb forms: I **banned**, I have **banned**, I am **banning**
Word history: Middle English, from Scandinavian

banal (buh-nahl, bay-nuhl)
adjective ordinary and unoriginal: *The TV film was so **banal** that we turned it off.* (***clichéd***, ***commonplace***, ***hackneyed***, ***trite***, ***unimaginative***)

Word building: **banality** *noun*
Word history: French, from Germanic word meaning 'proclamation'

banana
noun a long curved fruit with a yellow skin

Word history: Portuguese, Spanish, from native name in Guinea

banana republic
noun any small tropical country considered backward, politically unstable, etc., and dependent on the trade of rich foreign nations

band[1]
noun **1** a group of people acting together: *a **band** of outlaws* (***bunch***, ***crowd***, ***gang***, ***huddle***, ***troop***)
2 a group of musicians: *a rock **band** | a **brass** band*
verb **3** to join in a group: *to **band** together to protect the environment*

Word history: French, from Germanic

band[2]
noun **1** a strip of material for tying, binding or decorating: *a hat **band** | a rubber **band***
2 a narrow strip that contrasts with its surroundings: *a **band** of red paint* (***line***, ***stripe***)
3 *Mining* a layer of stone containing ore or a similar valuable material, such as opal (***deposit***, ***seam***, ***stratum***, ***vein***)
4 *Radio* a defined or specified range of frequencies: *The radio station I listen to is part of the FM **band**.*

Word history: Middle English, from French

bandage
noun a strip of cotton or elastic material used to bind up a wound

Word building: **bandage** *verb*
Word history: French

bandaid
noun a small adhesive cover put over an abrasion or sore to protect it

bandana (ban-dan-uh)
noun a bright scarf: *The cowboy wore a red **bandana** around his neck.*

Word use: You can also use **bandanna**.
Word history: apparently from Hindustani *bandhnu*, mode of dyeing in which the cloth is tied so as to prevent parts from receiving the dye

banded
adjective striped: *Another name for a numbat is a **banded** anteater.*

bandicoot
noun a rat-like Australian marsupial which feeds at night on insects, worms and plant roots

Word history: Telugu *pandikokku* pig-rat of India and Sri Lanka

bandit
noun an armed robber (***brigand***, ***buccaneer***, ***bushranger***, ***criminal***, ***thief***)

Word history: Italian *bandito*, from *bandire* proscribe

bandwidth
noun the volume of information that can be transmitted by a communications channel, usually measured in bits per second

bandy[1]
verb to exchange: *The rivals **bandied** insults, then punches.*

Verb forms: I **bandied**, I have **bandied**, I am **bandying**
Word history: origin obscure

bandy²
adjective (of legs) bending outwards at the knees: *The old jockey has **bandy** legs from so much riding.*
Word history: origin obscure

bandy-legged
adjective having crooked legs

bane
noun someone or something that ruins or destroys: *The school bully is the **bane** of my life.*
Word building: **baneful** *adjective*
Word history: Old English *bana* slayer

bang
noun **1** a sudden loud noise
verb **2** to hit or shut noisily: *They **banged** the cymbals together. | The door **banged**.* (***hammer***, ***punch***, ***smack***, ***thrash***, ***thump***)
Word history: probably from Scandinavian

bangle
noun a band worn as an ornament round your wrist or ankle
Word history: Hindustani

banish
verb to send away as a punishment: *The evil magician was **banished** from his country forever.* (***deport***, ***evict***, ***exile***, ***isolate***, ***throw out***)
Word building: **banishment** *noun*
Word history: Middle English, from Late Latin word meaning 'ban', of Germanic origin

banister
noun the rail that runs along a stairway: *She slid down the **banister**.*
Word use: You can also use **bannister**.
Word history: variant of *baluster*, support for railing

banjo
noun a musical instrument with a round body which you play by plucking or strumming its strings
Noun forms: The plural is **banjos**.
Word building: **banjoist** *noun*
Word history: variant of *bandore*, from Late Latin, from Greek word meaning 'musical instrument with three strings'

bank¹
noun **1** a pile or mass: *a **bank** of earth | a huge cloud **bank***
2 the land beside a river or stream
verb **3** to make into a pile or mass: *to **bank** up the snow* (***gather***, ***hoard***, ***save***, ***stockpile***, ***stow***)
4 to tip or slope sideways: *The aeroplane **banked** steeply, then straightened out.*
Word history: Middle English, probably from Scandinavian

bank²
noun **1** a place where you can keep your money and take it out again when you wish
verb **2** to place in a bank
phrase **3 bank on**, to rely on: *I'm **banking on** you to help.*
4 bank up, to gather or accumulate: *The cars **banked up** in a line behind us.*
Word history: Middle English, from French, from Italian *banca*, originally bench, table; of Germanic origin

bankbook
noun a book given by a bank to customers as a record of how much money they have (***passbook***)

banker¹
noun **1** a person or company which receives customers' money and pays it out again on loan
2 a person employed by a bank, especially as an executive or senior official

banker²
noun **1** a bank-high flood
phrase **2 run a banker**, (of a river) to be flowing up to the top of the banks

banknote
noun paper money issued by a bank

bankrupt
adjective **1** unable to pay money you owe to other people: *He became **bankrupt** when his business failed.* (***destitute***, ***impecunious***, ***insolvent***, ***poor***, ***ruined***)
noun **2** someone who is unable to pay their debts
verb **3** to make someone bankrupt
Word building: **bankruptcy** *noun*
Word history: French, from Italian *banca* bank + *rotta*, broken, from Latin

banksia
noun an Australian shrub or tree with leathery, notched leaves and tiny, yellow flowers massed together in spikes
Word history: Neo-Latin, named after Sir Joseph *Banks*, 1743–1820, English explorer and botanist in Australia

banner
noun **1** a flag which sometimes has a message or slogan on it: *The marchers carried a big **banner** which said 'Peace'.*
2 *Internet* a large advertisement placed on a web page, intended to direct users to the internet website of the advertiser
Word history: Middle English, from Late Latin word meaning 'standard', of Germanic origin

banns
plural noun in a church, the public announcement of an intended marriage, formerly required by English law

banquet
noun a large formal dinner for many guests: *At the jubilee **banquet** there was good food but too many speeches.* (***feast***, ***repast***, ***spread***)
Word building: **banquet** *verb* (**banqueted**, **banqueting**)
Word history: French, from Italian word meaning 'table', 'sumptuous meal', diminutive of *banco* bench

bantam
noun a breed of small domestic fowl
Word history: from *Bantam*, a village in western Java where the fowls are said to have originated

banter
noun playful teasing: *Their **banter** never led to a fight.*
Word building: **banter** *verb*

baobab (bay-oh-bab)
noun → **boab**
Word history: Neo-Latin probably from a central African language

baptism
noun **1** a Christian ceremony in which someone is sprinkled with, or put under, water to show that they are accepted as a member of the church (***christening***)
phrase **2 baptism of fire,**
a a soldier's first battle
b any severe test or vital ordeal: *He had to go through a **baptism of fire** before he was allowed to join the special squadron.*
Word building: **baptise** *verb* **baptismal** *adjective*

bar[1]
noun **1** a long plank or piece of metal or other hard material, often used as a barrier: *the top **bar** of the fence*
2 the counter in a hotel where drinks are served
3 a band or stripe: *a **bar** of light | a **bar** of colour*
4 *Music*
a one of the upright lines drawn across the stave in written music, to separate the groups of beats
b the part between two of these lines
5 in law,
a a division in a courtroom separating the public from the members of the legal profession
b barristers thought of as a group
verb **6** to stop or prevent: *Guards **barred** them from entering.* (***ban, hinder, obstruct, prevent***)
phrase **7 not to have a bar of,** *Australian, NZ* not to put up with: *I **will not have a bar of** your rudeness.*
Verb forms: I **barred**, I have **barred**, I am **barring**
Word use: You can also use **bar-line** for definition 4a.
Word history: Middle English, from Late Latin *barra*, of disputed origin

bar[2]
noun a unit for measuring pressure in the metric system, equal to 10 units per square metre
Word use: Look up **metric system.**
Word history: from Greek word meaning 'weight'

barb
noun **1** the sharp point that sticks out backwards on a fish-hook, arrowhead or fence wire
2 a hurtful remark
Word history: Middle English, from Latin word meaning 'beard'

barbarian (bah-bair-ree-uhn)
noun **1** in ancient Greek and Roman times, a person belonging to a backward culture that had no form of writing
2 someone with bad manners and not much education: *Those **barbarians** burnt all the books that they didn't agree with.*
adjective **3** of or like a barbarian: *The invading **barbarian** tribes destroyed the town's statues.*
Word history: French, from Latin word meaning 'barbarous country'

barbaric (bah-ba-rik)
adjective wild, savage or cruel: ***barbaric** acts of torture* (***brutal, callous, ruthless, vicious, violent***)
Word building: **barbarically** *adverb*
Word history: Middle English, from Latin, from Greek word meaning 'foreign', 'barbaric'

barbarity (bah-ba-ruh-tee)
noun **1** the sort of savage cruelty that an ancient barbarian might have committed: *Such an act of **barbarity** will never be allowed to happen again.*
2 a barbarian act or product: *I won't have such **barbarity** between members of my team.*
Word use: You can also use **barbarism.**

barbarous (bah-buh-rus)
adjective crude or rough in manners or style: ***barbarous** behaviour*
Word history: Middle English, from Latin, from Greek word meaning 'foreign', 'barbaric'

barbecue
noun **1** a fireplace or metal frame for cooking meat over an open fire
2 an outdoor meal or party where the food is cooked on a barbecue
Word use: You can also use **barbeque.**
Word building: **barbecue** *verb*
Word history: Spanish, from Haitian *barboka*

barbed
adjective **1** having sharp points sticking out
2 sharp or pointed like a barb: *a **barbed** remark*

barbed wire
noun steel wire with barbs at short intervals, used for fences

barber
noun someone whose job is to cut men's hair and to shave or trim their beards
Word history: Middle English, from Latin *barba* beard

barbie (bah-bee)
noun Australian, NZ Colloquial a barbecue
Word use: You can also use **barby.**

barbiturate (bah-bit-chuh-ruht)
noun a drug used to ease pain or to calm and soothe someone, which you can get addicted to

barcode
noun a printed code which consists of a series of vertical bars that identify each item being sold, and which a computerised cash register can scan
Word building: **barcoding** *noun*

bard
noun Old-fashioned a poet or singer
Word building: **bardic** *adjective*
Word history: Middle English, from Celtic

bare
adjective **1** uncovered or naked: ***bare** walls | **bare** knees* (***bald, exposed, nude, unclad***)
2 plain or simple: *the **bare** truth* (***basic, essential, stark, unadorned***)
verb **3** to expose or uncover: *The fierce dog began to **bare** its teeth.*
Word building: **bareness** *noun*
Word history: Old English *bær*

bare / bear
Don't confuse **bare** with **bear**, which is a large furry mammal. It can also mean 'to carry or support something':
I can't bear your weight any longer.

barely
adverb just, or no more than: *She is **barely** 14.*

bargain
noun **1** something bought cheaply: *The shoes were a* ***bargain*** *at half price.*
2 an agreement or arrangement to buy or sell something
verb **3** to argue for a better price: *to* ***bargain*** *with the stallholders*
phrase **4 bargain for**, to expect or be prepared for: *to get more than you* ***bargain for*** (***anticipate, count on, foresee, look forward to***)
5 bargain on, to rely or count on
6 into the bargain, more than what is stated or agreed
7 strike a bargain, to agree on a deal
Word building: **bargainer** *noun*
Word history: Middle English, from Old French

barge
noun **1** a flat-bottomed boat that carries cargo
verb **2** to make way by pushing or shoving: *He* ***barged*** *through the crowd.*
phrase **3 barge in**, to push in or interrupt
4 barge into, to bump into: *to* ***barge into*** *the sofa*
Word history: Middle English, from Latin, from Greek word meaning '(Egyptian) boat or barge'

bar graph
noun a graph made up of bars whose lengths correspond to the quantity they represent in a set of data

barista (buh-<u>ris</u>-tuh)
noun a person skilled in making espresso coffee in a cafe or restaurant
Noun forms: The plural is **baristas** or **baristi**.
Word history: Italian for a bartender, or someone who owned or worked in a bar. It later came to mean someone skilled in making espresso coffee, and is now also used in English with that more recent meaning.

baritone
noun **1** the range of musical notes which can be sung by a male singer with a fairly deep voice: *He sings* ***baritone*** *in the choir.*
2 a man with a fairly deep singing voice
Word use: **Baritone** range is higher than a **bass** but lower than **soprano**, **alto** and **tenor**.
Word building: **baritone** *adjective*
Word history: from Greek word meaning 'deep sounding'

barium (<u>bair</u>-ree-uhm)
noun **1** a whitish metallic element
phrase **2 barium enema**, an injection of barium sulfate into the rectum before an X-ray to show up any abnormality in the large intestine or rectum
3 barium meal, a preparation of barium sulfate which is swallowed before an X-ray to show up any abnormality of the stomach
Word history: Neo-Latin; from *bar(ytes)* + *-ium*

bark[1]
verb **1** to make the noise of a dog
2 to speak abruptly and harshly: *to* ***bark*** *an order*
noun **3** the harsh cry of a dog or other similar animal
Word history: Old English *beorcan*

bark[2]
noun **1** the outer covering of a tree
verb **2** to scrape or graze: *She* ***barked*** *her elbow on the edge of the table.*
Word history: Middle English, from Scandinavian

barley
noun a grain used as food, and in making beer and whisky
Word history: Old English *bærlīc*

bar mitzvah (bah <u>mits</u>-vuh)
noun **1** in the Jewish religion, a boy aged 13, when he acquires religious duties
2 the ceremony and feast marking this
Word history: from Hebrew word meaning 'son of the commandment'

barn
noun a shed to store hay or shelter animals
Word history: Old English *bere* barley + *ærn* place, house

barnacle
noun a shellfish which clings to the bottoms of ships and other underwater objects
Word history: late Middle English *bernacle*

barometer
noun an instrument that measures air pressure, used to help work out what height you're at and what changes in the weather can be expected: *The* ***barometer*** *is falling which means the weather is getting bad.*
Word use: When you use a barometer to see what height you're at, it is called an **altimeter**.
Word building: **barometric** *adjective*

baron
noun **1** a nobleman or peer of the lowest titled rank in the United Kingdom
2 in feudal times, a lord who held his lands under the direct authority of the monarch: *The* ***baron*** *left his castle to fight for the king.*
3 a rich and powerful man: *a newspaper* ***baron***
Word building: **baronial** *adjective*
Word history: Middle English, from Medieval Latin word meaning 'man', 'free man'

baroness
noun **1** the female counterpart of a baron
2 the wife of a baron

baronet (<u>ba</u>-ruh-net)
noun a member of the British hereditary rank of commoners

baroque (buh-<u>rok</u>, buh-<u>rohk</u>)
adjective **1** *Art, Architecture* very ornate and richly decorated, as in the style developed in Italy during the 16th century
2 *Music* highly ornamented and involved as in the style developed in Europe during the 17th and early 18th centuries
Word use: You can also use **Baroque**.
Word history: French, from Portuguese word meaning 'irregular'

barrack
verb to shout encouragement: *We* ***barracked*** *for our favourite team.*
Word building: **barracker** *noun*
Word history: perhaps Northern Ireland dialect *barrack* to brag, boast of fighting powers

barracks
plural noun the buildings where soldiers live
Word history: French, from Italian

barracouta (ba-ruh-kooh-tuh)
noun a long, cold-water, southern fish, caught for sport and food

Word use: You can also use the colloquial word **couta**.
Word history: from *barracuda*

barracuda (ba-ruh-kooh-duh)
noun any of various fierce, warm-water fishes, some of which are caught for food

Word use: Another name is **sea-pike**.
Word history: Spanish, from West Indian

barrage (ba-rahzh, ba-rahj)
noun an overwhelming attack, especially of gunfire: *a **barrage** of questions | a **barrage** of bullets*

Word building: **barrage** *verb*
Word history: French *barrer*, verb, bar

barramundi (ba-ruh-mun-dee)
noun a large, silvery grey fish, valued as a food, found in coastal rivers of tropical northern Australia and the Indo-Pacific

Word use: Another name is **giant perch**.
Word history: from an Australian Aboriginal language

barrel
noun **1** a large container made of vertical strips of wood held together with hoops
2 a unit of volume equal to 35 gallons (about 160 litres)
3 the metal tube of a gun

Word history: Middle English, from Old French

barren
adjective **1** *Old-fashioned* unable to produce children: *a **barren** woman*
2 unable to produce crops: ***barren** land*

Word use: The opposite of this is **fertile**.
Word history: Middle English, from Old French, of pre-Latin origin

barricade
noun **1** a barrier or wall, especially one built in a hurry: *a **barricade** to stop traffic | The street fighters hid behind a **barricade** of rubble.*
verb **2** to block or defend with a barricade (***bar***, ***blockade***, ***close***, ***fortify***, ***obstruct***)

Word history: French, probably from Provençal *barricada* a barricade, originally made of casks filled with earth, from *barrica* cask

barrier
noun anything which bars or blocks the way: *a road **barrier** | a trade **barrier*** (***obstruction***)

Word history: Middle English, from Anglo-French word meaning 'bar'

barrier reef
noun a long, narrow, offshore ridge of coral close to or above the surface of the sea

barrister
noun a lawyer whose main work is to present cases in court

Word use: Compare this with **solicitor**.
Word history: *barri-* (combining form of *bar*[1]) + *-ster*

barrow[1]
noun **1** a street seller's cart
2 a wheelbarrow

Word history: Old English *bearwe*

barrow[2]
noun an ancient or prehistoric burial mound

Word history: Old English *beorg* hill, mound

barter
verb to trade by swapping food and other goods instead of using money

Word building: **barter** *noun*
Word history: Middle English, from Old French word meaning 'exchange', 'cheat'

basalt
noun a dark, dense, volcanic rock, often with columnar structure

Word building: **basaltic** *adjective*
Word history: Latin *basaltes* a dark, hard marble of Ethiopia

base[1]
noun **1** the bottom part of anything, which gives support: *the **base** of a statue* (***bed***, ***floor***, ***foot***, ***foundation***)
2 the centre of operations: *Report back to **base** when you finish your mission.*
3 *Mathematics*
a the starting point for a counting system, such as ten in the decimal system
b a number which when raised to a certain power has a logarithm (based on that number) equal to that power: *The logarithm to **base** 10 of 10 000 is 4.*
c the side or face which forms the bottom of a geometric figure
4 *Chemistry* a compound which reacts with an acid to form a salt
5 one of the four fixed positions in baseball which the players run to
verb **6** to rest or fix: *to **base** an argument on facts*

Word history: Middle English, from Latin, from Greek word meaning 'a stepping', 'a step', 'pedestal', 'base'

base[2]
adjective *Old-fashioned* morally low, mean or selfish: *a **base** trick*

Word history: Middle English, from Late Latin *bassus* low

base / bass
Don't confuse **base** with **bass**, which is the lowest voice, singer or instrument in a group. Note that **bass** with this meaning rhymes with *case*. When **bass** rhymes with *lass*, it means a type of fish.

baseball
noun **1** a game played by two teams with a bat and a ball, on a field with four bases which the batter must pass to score a run
2 the ball used in this game

basement
noun a room or area of a building below the ground floor

bash
verb **1** to hit hard or wildly: *The boys **bashed** each other. | He **bashed** the ball.*
noun **2** *Colloquial* a try or attempt: *Give it a **bash**.*

bashful
adjective very modest or shy: *She felt **bashful** about making a speech.* (***coy***, ***demure***, ***diffident***, ***reticent***)

Word use: The opposite of this is **bold**.
Word building: **bashfully** *adverb* **bashfulness** *noun*

basic
adjective main or most important: *The **basic** ingredient for toffee is sugar.* (***essential**, **fundamental**, **key**, **primary**, **vital***)
Word building: **basically** *adverb*

BASIC (bay-sik)
noun a fairly simple computer programming language
Word use: You can also use **Basic**.
Word history: an acronym for *B(eginner's) A(ll-purpose) S(ymbolic) I(nstruction) C(ode)*

basil
noun a herb used in cooking and salads
Word history: Middle English, from Latin, from Greek word meaning 'royal'

basilica (buh-sil-ik-uh, buh-zil-ik-uh)
noun an oblong building, especially a church with the nave higher than the aisles
Word history: Latin, from Greek word meaning 'royal'; in ancient Rome, a large oblong building near the Forum, used as a hall of justice and public meeting place

basin
noun **1** a sink or container that holds water for washing
2 a bowl for mixing or cooking
3 an area of water surrounded by land: *a river **basin*** (***bay**, **dam**, **lagoon**, **reservoir**, **swamp***)
4 land drained by a river
Word history: Middle English, from Late Latin word meaning 'water vessel'

basis
noun **1** a foundation or support that forms the base of something: *The **basis** of the story was an incident that really took place.*
2 the main part or ingredient
Noun forms: The plural is **bases** (bay-seez).
Word history: Latin, from Greek

bask (bahsk)
verb **1** to lie in or enjoy warmth: *to **bask** in the sun*
2 to enjoy something pleasant: *to **bask** in the warmth of his praise*
Word history: Middle English, from Scandinavian

basket
noun a woven container for storing or carrying: *a clothes **basket** | a shopping **basket***
Word history: Middle English

basketball
noun **1** a game played by two teams who try to score points by shooting a ball through a hoop or basket at the top of the other team's goal post
2 the ball used in this game

basmati rice (baz-mah-tee ruys)
noun a kind of rice which has long grains which separate easily when cooked
Word history: from Hindi word meaning 'fragrant'

basque (bahsk)
noun a tightly knitted band on the lower edge and cuffs of a jumper
Word history: French

bas-relief (bah-ruh-leef)
noun a carving on a flat surface, in which the figures are raised only slightly from the background; sculpture in low relief
Word history: French, from Italian *basso-rilievo* low relief

bass (bays)
noun **1** the range of musical notes which can be sung by a male singer with a deep voice: *He sings **bass** in the choir.*
2 a man with a deep singing voice
Word use: **Bass** range is lower than a **soprano**, **alto**, **tenor** and **baritone**.
Word building: **bass** *adjective*
Word history: Middle English *bas* low

bass / base
Don't confuse **bass** with **base**, which is the bottom of anything, or a centre of operations where things are organised.

basset
noun a long-bodied dog with short legs and long ears, used for hunting foxes and badgers
Word use: You can also use **basset hound**.
Word history: French, originally diminutive of *bas* low

bassinette
noun the basket in which a very young baby sleeps
Word use: You can also use **bassinet**.
Word history: French

bassoon (buh-soohn)
noun a bass woodwind instrument

bastard
noun **1** *Old-fashioned* someone whose parents were not married when he or she was born
2 someone or something who is very unpleasant
Word use: The use of this word might offend people.
Word history: Middle English, from Old French word, probably from *bast* saddle used for carrying goods + *-ard*

baste[1] (bayst)
verb in sewing, to tack
Word history: Middle English, from Old German

baste[2] (bayst)
verb to moisten while cooking, with hot fat, etc.: *to **baste** meat*
Word history: perhaps French

bastion (bas-tee-uhn)
noun **1** a fortified place
2 a strong supporter: *He is a **bastion** of the environmental movement.*
Word history: French, from Italian word meaning 'build'

bat[1]
noun **1** the stick used to hit the ball in games like cricket and baseball
verb **2** to hit with or as if with a bat: *to **bat** the ball in cricket* (***beat**, **clip**, **knock**, **strike**, **tap***)
phrase **3 off your own bat**, on your own, without help or advice

Verb forms: I **batted**, I have **batted**, I am **batting**
Word building: **batter** *noun* **batsman** *masculine noun*
Word history: Old English *batt* cudgel

bat[2]
noun **1** a mouse-like winged mammal which is active at night
phrase **2 have bats in the belfry**, *Colloquial* to be crazy or to have mad ideas
3 like a bat out of hell, *Colloquial* very fast
Word history: variant of Middle English *bakke*, from Scandinavian

batch
noun a number of things made at the same time or grouped together: *a **batch** of biscuits | this year's **batch** of students*
Word history: Old English *bacan* bake

bath
noun **1** a container for washing yourself in, which is large enough for you to sit or lie in
2 the water used in the bath
verb **3** to put or wash in a bath: *to **bath** the baby*
Word history: Old English *bæth*

bathe
verb **1** to wash clean: ***Bathe** your sore eye in salty water.*
2 *Old-fashioned* to swim: *We **bathed** in the creek.*
Word history: Old English *bæth* bath

bather
noun Old-fashioned a swimmer

bathers
plural noun Australian a swimming costume

bathos (bay-thos)
noun **1** an abrupt change in style from a lofty to a common way of writing or speaking, usually with a comical effect
2 ordinariness or unimportance
3 insincere emotion
Word building: **bathetic** *adjective*
Word history: from Greek word meaning 'depth'

bathroom
noun **1** a room fitted with a bath or a shower (or both), and sometimes with a toilet and basin for washing the face and hands
2 a room fitted with a toilet

batik (bah-teek, ba-tik)
noun **1** a way of dyeing cloth in which the parts not to be coloured are covered with wax
2 cloth dyed in this way
Word history: Malay (Javanese)

batman
noun an army officer's servant
Noun forms: The plural is **batmen**.

bat mitzvah (bat mits-vuh)
noun **1** in the Jewish religion, a girl aged 13, when she acquires religious duties
2 the ceremony and feast marking this
Word use: You can also use **bas mitzvah**.
Word history: from Hebrew word meaning 'daughter of the commandment'

baton
noun **1** a thin stick used by the conductor of an orchestra to beat time
2 a short stick, especially one handed by one runner to the next in a relay race
Word history: French, from Late Latin *bastum*

batt
noun a rectangular sheet of matted fibreglass, cottonwool, etc., used for insulation
Word use: You can also use **bat**.

battalion
noun an army unit of three or more smaller groups of soldiers known as companies
Word history: French, from Italian

batten
noun **1** a light strip of wood, used to strengthen or support something, such as a sail
verb **2** in sailing, to fasten with battens or tarpaulins: *to **batten** down the hatches*
Word history: Scandinavian

batter[1]
verb to beat or hit hard or often: *to **batter** on the door*
Word building: **battering** *noun*
Word history: Middle English from *bat*

batter[2]
noun a mixture of flour, eggs and milk or water beaten together for use in cooking
Word history: late Middle English use of *batter*[1]

batter[3]
noun in cricket, baseball and some other ball games, the person who hits the ball with the bat

battery
noun **1** a group of electric cells connected together to make or store electricity: *a torch **battery** | a car **battery***
2 a group of guns or machines to be used together
3 a large number of cages in which chickens and other animals are kept
4 the act of beating or battering someone
Noun forms: The plural is **batteries**.
Word history: from French word meaning 'beat'

battle
noun a large-scale or serious fight: *a **battle** between armies | a **battle** to save the old building* (***brawl**, **combat**, **conflict**, **fray**, **skirmish***)
Word building: **battle** *verb*
Word history: French, from Latin *battuere* meaning 'to strike, to beat'

battleaxe (bat-uhl-aks)
noun **1** an axe used as weapon of war
2 *Colloquial* a tough or aggressive woman

battlement
noun a wall with openings for shooting through: *The archers shot their arrows from the **battlement**.*
Word use: This word is often used as a plural noun, as in *The soldiers stormed the battlements.*
Word history: Middle English, perhaps from Old French word meaning 'fortify'

battler
noun Australian, NZ Colloquial an honest, hardworking person who tries hard to make a good living and who is brave in the face of bad times

battleship
noun a heavily armed warship

bauble (baw-buhl)
noun a cheap bright ornament: *to hang **baubles** on the Christmas tree*

Word history: Middle English, from Old French word meaning 'toy', probably from Latin *bellus* pretty

baulk (bawk)
verb to stop and refuse to do something: *The horse **baulked** at the jump. | to **baulk** at making a speech*

Word history: Old English *balca* ridge

bauxite (bawk-suyt)
noun a rock which is the main ore of aluminium

Word history: Les *Baux*, in southern France + *-ite*

bawdy
adjective containing rough talk and jokes about sex: *a **bawdy** story*

Adjective forms: **bawdier**, **bawdiest**
Word building: **bawdily** *adverb* **bawdiness** *noun*

bawl
verb **1** to cry noisily: *He **bawled** when the ball hit him.* (***blubber***, ***sob***, ***wail***, ***weep***)
2 to shout out loudly: *to **bawl** from across the playground* (***bellow***, ***belt out***, ***roar***, ***shriek***, ***yell***)
phrase **3 bawl out**, to scold harshly: *to **bawl** someone **out** for lying* (***admonish***, ***rebuke***, ***reprimand***, ***rouse on***, ***tick off***)

Word building: **bawl** *noun*
Word history: Middle English, probably from Medieval Latin *baulāre* bark as a dog

bawl / ball

Don't confuse **bawl** with **ball**, which is a round object or a formal dance.

bay[1]
noun a sheltered part of a sea or lake, formed by a curve in its shore (***bight***, ***cove***, ***estuary***, ***gulf***, ***inlet***)

Word history: Middle English, from Late Latin

bay[2]
verb **1** to howl like a dog: *to **bay** at the moon*
noun **2** the deep long bark of a hunting dog
phrase **3 at bay**,
a forced to stand and face an enemy: *The kangaroo stood **at bay**.*
b away or at a distance: *I kept my sad thoughts **at bay** by working hard.*

Word history: Middle English, from Late Latin word meaning 'gape'

bay[3]
noun a space, section or area: *a bomb **bay** | a parking **bay***

Word history: Middle English, from Old French

bay[4]
noun the European laurel, a small evergreen tree whose leaves are used as a herb in cooking

Word history: Middle English, from Latin word meaning 'berry'

bay[5]
adjective of a reddish-brown colour: *a **bay** horse*

Word building: **bay** *noun*
Word history: Middle English, from Latin

bayonet (bay-nuht, bay-uh-nuht)
noun a blade for stabbing which can be joined to the end of a rifle

Word history: French, from *Bayonne*, in France, where such weapons were first manufactured

bazaar (buh-zah)
noun **1** a market with stalls selling many different kinds of goods
2 a sale to raise money for charity

Word history: French, from Arabic, from Persian

bazaar / bizarre

Don't confuse **bazaar** with **bizarre** which means 'very strange':

She looks bizarre wearing that red and green wig.

BC
abbreviation before Christ: *Julius Caesar invaded Britain in 55 **BC**.*

Our calendar dates events from the year of Jesus Christ's birth. Years before this are called **BC** and years after this are **AD**. When you are writing **BC**, you should put it after the number showing the date.

be
verb **1** to exist or have reality: *He **is** no more.*
2 to take place or happen: *The wedding **was** last week.*
3 to be found or located: *Do you know where the children **are**?*
4 a word connecting a subject either with a predicate or with adjectives, in statements, questions, and commands: *You **are** late. | Tomorrow **is** Thursday. | **Is** he here? | **Be** good at school today.*
5 a word serving to form certain phrases, as in
a infinitive phrases: *(I wanted) to **be** a dancer.*
b participial phrases: *(the art of) **being** agreeable*
6 a word used as an auxiliary verb with a present participle of another verb, to form the continuous aspect: *I **am** waiting. | She **was** running.*
7 a word used as an auxiliary verb with a past participle, in passive forms of transitive verbs: *The date **was** fixed.*

Word history: Middle English *been*, Old English *beon*, from Indo-European *bheu-* become

The most common verb in English is the verb **to be**. It appears in several different forms, and some of them look quite different from **be**:

Present	*Past*
(I) **am**	(I, he, she, it) **was**
(we, you, they) **are**	(we, you, they) **were**
(he, she, it) **is**	
being (*present participle*)	**been** (*past participle*)

The verb **to be** can act on its own, or together with other verbs. That is, it can be a main verb or an auxiliary verb:

She is a doctor. (main verb)
They were here last week. (main verb)
He was walking to the beach. (auxiliary verb)
You are coming on Friday. (auxiliary verb)

(continued)

be *(continued)*

The present and past forms, except for **am**, often form contractions with the word **not**. For example:

is not	becomes	*isn't*
are not	becomes	*aren't*
was not	becomes	*wasn't*
were not	becomes	*weren't*

You shouldn't contract **am not** to **amn't**. Instead, **am** contracts with *I* to become *I'm not*. Note that you should avoid using **ain't** unless you're writing down ungrammatical speech or dialogue.

beach

noun **1** the sandy or pebbly land at the edge of a sea, lake or river
verb **2** to drive or pull onto the beach from the water: *We* ***beached*** *the boat when we reached the shore.*

Word history: perhaps from Old English *bece* brook

beach / beech

Don't confuse **beach** with **beech**, which is a kind of tree.

beachcomber (beech-koh-muh)

noun **1** someone who lives on or near a beach, gathering things washed up by the sea
2 a long rolling wave

beacon

noun **1** a signal which shows the way or warns of danger: *We lit a fire on the hill to serve as a* ***beacon*** *for the fishermen.*
2 a lighthouse

Word history: Old English *bēac(e)n*

bead

noun **1** a small ball with a hole through the middle, that can be threaded on a string
2 a drop of liquid: ***beads*** *of sweat*
3 beads, a necklace

Word history: Middle English *bede* prayer, rosary bead, variant of *ibed*, Old English *gebed* prayer

beady

adjective small, round and shiny like a bead: ***beady*** *little eyes*

Adjective forms: **beadier**, **beadiest**

beagle

noun a small hunting dog with short legs and long ears

Word history: Middle English *begle*; origin uncertain

beak

noun the hard horny part of a bird's mouth (***bill***, ***nib***)

Word building: **beaked** *adjective*
Word history: Middle English, from Latin *beccus*, of Celtic origin

beaker

noun **1** a large cup or mug
2 a glass container with a pouring lip shaped like a beak, used in laboratories

Word history: variant (influenced by *beak*) of dialect English *bicker*, Middle English *biker*, from Scandinavian

beam

noun **1** a long strong piece of wood, concrete or metal, often used as a support: ***beams*** *supporting the floor | a balancing* ***beam*** *for gymnastics*
2 the widest part of a ship: *ten metres across the* ***beam***
3 a ray of light: *the* ***beam*** *of a search light | a sun****beam***
4 a radio or other similar signal, used to guide pilots through the darkness or in bad weather
verb **5** to send out rays of light (***blaze***, ***burn***, ***flare***, ***glow***, ***sparkle***)
6 to smile happily: *She* ***beamed*** *when she heard the good news.*
phrase **7 off beam**, *Colloquial* wrong: *The answer was completely* ***off beam***.
8 on beam, *Colloquial* correct or just right

Word history: Old English *bēam* tree, piece of wood, ray of light

bean

noun **1** a plant with smooth seeds growing in a long pod
2 the seed or pod of a bean plant which can be eaten fresh or cooked
phrase **3 full of beans**, *Colloquial* full of energy: *The children are* ***full of beans*** *now the holidays have started.*
4 spill the beans, *Colloquial* to let out a secret

Word history: Old English *bēan*

bean / been

Don't confuse **bean** with **been**, which is the past participle of the verb **be**:

I have been sick.
Have you been waiting long?

beanbag

noun **1** a large cushion that you can sit on, filled with pellets
2 a small cloth bag filled with beans and thrown in catching games

beanie

noun a kind of close-fitting knitted cap, sometimes with a pompom or other decoration on top

Word history: This word comes from the colloquial use of the word *bean* meaning 'head', because a **beanie** is made to fit snugly on your head to keep it warm.

bear[1]

verb **1** to hold up or carry: *a branch strong enough to* ***bear*** *your weight | The swimmer was* ***borne*** *along on the tide.*
2 to put up with or tolerate: *I can't* ***bear*** *pain. | I can't* ***bear*** *people who tell tales.*
3 to produce or give birth to: *This tree* ***bears*** *oranges. | She* ***bore*** *three children.* (***breed***, ***grow***, ***yield***)
4 to have or show: *The sisters* ***bear*** *no resemblance to each other. | to* ***bear*** *signs of damage*
phrase **5 bear out**, to prove right: *The facts* ***bear*** *me* ***out***. (***confirm***, ***corroborate***, ***substantiate***, ***verify***)
6 bear up, to stay strong and firm during a time of difficulty

7 bear witness, to be or give evidence or proof of something: *His tears* ***bear witness*** *to his grief.*
8 bring to bear, to apply or cause to have an effect: *He had to give in after pressure was* ***brought to bear*** *on him.*

Verb forms: I **bore**, I have **borne** or I have **born**, I am **bearing**
Word history: Old English *beran*

bear[2]
noun a large heavy mammal with short rough fur and a very short tail

Word history: Old English *bera*

bear / bare
Don't confuse **bear** with **bare**. Someone is **bare** when they are naked.

beard
noun **1** the hair that grows on a man's chin and face
2 a beardlike tuft, such as that on a goat's jaw, below a bird's beak and growing on wheat

Word building: **bearded** *adjective*
Word history: Old English *beard*

bearer
noun someone who brings or carries something: *the* ***bearer*** *of good news | the* ***bearer*** *of gifts*

bearing
noun **1** the way you stand or behave: *a king of noble* ***bearing*** (***appearance***, ***attitude***, ***carriage***, ***posture***, ***stance***)
2 a supporting part of a machine
3 bearings, direction or position: *We lost our* ***bearings*** *in the dark.*
phrase **4 bearing on**, connection or relevance to: *This information has no* ***bearing on*** *the problem.*

beast
noun **1** a four-footed animal
2 a rough cruel person, especially someone you dislike

Word history: Middle English, from Late Latin

beastly
adjective **1** like a beast
2 *Colloquial* horrible or nasty

Word building: **beastliness** *noun*

beat
verb **1** to hit again and again: *to* ***beat*** *a drum | to* ***beat*** *someone severely | The rain* ***beat*** *on the window.* (***bang***, ***hammer***, ***punch***, ***smack***, ***thrash***, ***thump***)
2 to make any movement over and over again: *My heart* ***beat*** *loudly. | A bird was* ***beating*** *its wings.*
3 to stir thoroughly: *to* ***beat*** *cream*
4 to defeat: *She* ***beat*** *him in the race.* (***conquer***, ***lick***, ***thrash***, ***vanquish***)
noun **5** a sound made over and over again: *the* ***beat*** *of a drum*
6 regular rhythm in music: *The conductor kept the* ***beat*** *while the orchestra played.* (***swing***, ***tempo***, ***time***)
7 a path or route which someone usually takes: *A police officer walks a* ***beat***.
phrase **8 beat about the bush**, *Colloquial* to avoid coming to the point: *Stop* ***beating about the bush*** *and tell me what really happened.*
9 beat a retreat, to withdraw or run away
10 beat down, *Colloquial* to get a lower price from someone
11 beat it, to leave: *We'd better* ***beat it*** *before someone comes.*
12 beat up, to attack and hurt: *The school bully* ***beat*** *him* ***up***. (***assault***, ***charge***, ***get stuck into***, ***mug***)

Verb forms: I **beat**, I have **beaten**, I am **beating**
Word building: **beating** *noun*
Word history: Old English *bēatan*

beat / beet
Don't confuse **beat** with **beet**, which is a kind of vegetable.

beatific (bee-uh-<u>tif</u>-ik)
adjective **1** joyful or blissful: *a* ***beatific*** *smile*
2 giving blessedness

Word history: Late Latin

beatify (bee-<u>at</u>-uh-fuy)
verb **1** to make very happy
2 in the Roman Catholic Church, to declare (a dead person) among the blessed in heaven, therefore worthy of special religious honour

Verb forms: it **beatified**, it has **beatified**, it is **beatifying**
Word history: French, from Latin word meaning 'make happy'

Beaufort scale (<u>boh</u>-fuht skayl)
noun a scale of numbers for showing the force or speed of wind, from 0 for calm to 12 for hurricane, or speeds over 120 km/h

Word history: named after Sir Francis *Beaufort*, 1774–1857, British admiral who devised it

beaut
adjective Australian, NZ Colloquial very good and enjoyable: *a* ***beaut*** *party*

beautician
noun someone who works in a beauty salon

beautiful
adjective pleasing and enjoyable to look at, touch, smell, taste or hear: ***beautiful*** *music | a* ***beautiful*** *face* (***exquisite***, ***gorgeous***, ***lovely***, ***pretty***, ***stunning***)

beautify
verb to decorate something or make it more beautiful: *to help* ***beautify*** *a city by planting trees*

Verb forms: I **beautified**, I have **beautified**, I am **beautifying**

beauty
noun **1** the quality of being beautiful: *a garden famous for its* ***beauty***
2 a beautiful person or thing: *My new bike is a* ***beauty***.
3 advantage: *The* ***beauty*** *of this machine is that it runs on batteries.*

Word use: The opposite of definition 1 is **ugliness**.
Noun forms: The plural is **beauties**.
Word building: **beauteous** *adjective*
Word history: Middle English, from Old French *beau*

beaver
noun a brown furry animal of North America, with sharp teeth, webbed back feet and a wide flat tail, which builds dams in streams

Word history: Old English *beofor*

became
verb past tense of **become**

because
conjunction **1** for the reason that: *The game was abandoned **because** it rained.*
phrase **2 because of**, by reason or on account: *The game was abandoned **because of** rain.*

Word history: Middle English *bi cause* by cause

beckon
verb to signal by waving your hand, or nodding your head: *He **beckoned** them to follow.*

Word history: Old English *bēacen* sign

become
verb **1** to come to be: *to **become** hungry*
2 *Old-fashioned* to suit or look good on: *That dress **becomes** you.*
phrase **3 become of**, happen to: *What will **become of** me?*

Verb forms: I **became,** I have **become,** I am **becoming**
Word history: Old English *becuman* come about, happen

becoming
adjective Old-fashioned **1** proper or suitable: *behaviour which is **becoming** to a ten year old*
2 flattering or making you look attractive: *a **becoming** dress*

Word use: The opposite of this is **unbecoming**.

bed
noun **1** a place to sleep, especially a piece of furniture with a mattress, pillow and covers
2 a plot of earth in a garden: *a flower **bed***
3 the ground under a sea or river: *a river **bed***
4 a base or foundation (***floor***, ***foot***, ***support***)
5 a layer of rock
verb **6** to fix or place in a base or foundation: *to **bed** the pebbles in cement*
7 to fix or plant in a plot of earth: *to **bed** the roses*
phrase **8 bed down,** to go to bed: *The hikers **bedded down** in an old cabin.*

Verb forms: I **bedded,** I have **bedded,** I am **bedding**
Word history: Old English *bedd*

bedding
noun the things you make your bed with, especially sheets and blankets

bedlam
noun a scene of great noise and confusion: *There was **bedlam** in the room when the teacher was away.*

Word history: Middle English *bedlem*, alteration of *Bethlehem*, from the former Royal Bethlehem Hospital, a lunatic asylum in South East London

Bedouin (bed-ooh-uhn)
noun a member of any of the nomadic tribes of Arabs in the deserts of North Africa or the Middle East

Word use: You can also use **bedouin**.
Word history: French, from Arabic word meaning 'desert dweller'

bedraggled (buh-drag-uhld)
adjective wet, dirty and hanging limply: *long **bedraggled** hair* (***dishevelled***, ***sloppy***, ***unkempt***, ***untidy***)

bedridden (bed-rid-uhn)
adjective forced to stay in bed: *I was **bedridden** with the flu.*

Word history: Old English, literally, bed-rider

bedrock
noun **1** the solid, unbroken rock under the top layers of soil
2 the bottom level of anything: *The team's spirits hit **bedrock** when they lost another match.*

bedroom
noun a room with a bed or beds for sleeping in

bee[1]
noun **1** a stinging insect with four wings, which collects nectar and pollen from flowers to make into honey
phrase **2 bee in your bonnet**, an idea, sometimes a slightly silly one, that is firmly fixed in your brain

Word use: The place where bees live is called a **beehive** or **hive,** and a group of bees together is called a **swarm.**
Word history: Old English *bēo*

bee[2]
noun **1** a small group of people gathered together for some type of work: *a sewing **bee***
2 a contest: *a spelling **bee***

Word history: Middle English *bene* a favour

beech
noun a tree with smooth grey bark and triangular nuts, whose hard wood is useful for making furniture

Word history: Old English *bēce*

beech / beach
Don't confuse **beech** with **beach,** which is the sandy or pebbly shore of a river, sea or lake.

beef
noun the meat from a cow or bull: *roast **beef** for dinner*

Word history: Middle English, from Old French *boef*, from Latin word meaning 'ox'

beefy
adjective solid and with plenty of muscles (***burly***, ***heavy***, ***squat***, ***stumpy***, ***thickset***)

Adjective forms: **beefier, beefiest**
Word building: **beefiness** *noun*

beeline
noun a direct line, like the course bees take when returning to the hive: *The children made a **beeline** for the food.*

been
verb past participle of **be**

been / bean
Don't confuse **been** with **bean,** which is a vegetable.

beer
noun an alcoholic drink made from malt and flavoured with hops
Word history: Old English *bēor*

beet
noun a plant with a root that is good to eat and from which sugar can be made
Word history: Old English, from Latin

beet / beat
Don't confuse **beet** with **beat**, which is a regular rhythm, such as a heartbeat or the beat of music. It is also a verb with many meanings:
Beat the eggs.
This yacht can beat them in the race.
The cruel man beat his horse.

beetle
noun **1** a large insect with two pairs of wings, one of which is hard and protects the delicate flying wings underneath
verb **2** *Colloquial* to move swiftly: *The car* ***beetled*** *along the highway.*
Word history: Old English *bitula* literally, biter

beetroot
noun the red root of a beet plant, which is eaten as a vegetable

befall
verb to happen to: *Whatever* ***befalls*** *us, we will be together.*
Verb forms: it **befell**, it has **befallen**, it is **befalling**
Word history: Old English

befit
verb to be suitable or appropriate for: *The old jeans he wore did not* ***befit*** *the formal occasion.*
Verb forms: I **befitted**, I have **befitted**, I am **befitting**
Word building: **befitting** *adjective*

before
adverb **1** earlier, or at an earlier time: *Have you been here* ***before****? | Begin writing when I tell you, not* ***before****.*
2 ahead or in front: *She went* ***before*** *to prepare the way.*
preposition **3** earlier than: ***before*** *the earthquake*
4 *Old-fashioned* in front of: *They knelt* ***before*** *the altar.*
5 ahead of: *Parents put their children's needs* ***before*** *their own.*
6 in the presence or sight of: ***before*** *an audience*
7 under consideration of: *The case is* ***before*** *the judge.*
conjunction **8** rather than: *I'll scrap the whole project* ***before*** *I give in to your demands.*
Word history: Old English *be* by + *foran* before

beforehand
adverb in advance: *Let me know* ***beforehand****.*

befriend
verb to aid or be friendly towards: *to* ***befriend*** *a stray kitten* (***champion***, ***defend***, ***help***, ***side with***, ***stand by***)
Word use: The opposite of this is **shun**.

befuddle
verb **1** to make stupidly drunk
2 to confuse, as with smooth-sounding argument (***bamboozle***, ***distract***, ***fluster***, ***muddle***, ***puzzle***)

befuddled
adjective confused or muddled: *We felt* ***befuddled*** *by so many people talking at once.*

beg
verb **1** to ask humbly: *I* ***beg*** *you to forgive me. | to* ***beg*** *for money to buy food* (***beseech***, ***demand***, ***entreat***, ***implore***, ***request***)
phrase **2 beg off**, to excuse yourself from doing something
3 beg the question,
a to assume something which supports a point of view, even though this assumption may not be proven: *Saying that criminal parents produce criminal children begs the question of the influence of heredity on the development of a child.*
b to prompt or raise the question: *Saying that people should be paid to stay at home and do housework begs the question of who is to fund it.*
4 beg your pardon or **beg yours**, a polite apology or a request for the repetition of something not clearly heard
5 go begging, to not be wanted or claimed by anyone: *Have the last chocolate biscuit — it's* ***going begging****.*
Verb forms: I **begged**, I have **begged**, I am **begging**
Word history: Old English *bedecian*

began
verb past tense of **begin**

beget
verb **1** to produce: *to* ***beget*** *a child*
2 to cause: *Jealousy* ***begets*** *unhappiness.*
Verb forms: I **begot**, I have **begotten** or I have **begot**, I am **begetting**
Word use: Definition 1 is used mainly of a male parent.
Word history: Middle English

beggar
noun **1** someone who lives by begging
2 *Colloquial* someone you feel sorry for: *You poor* ***beggar****.*
verb **3** to reduce to poverty
4 to make seem powerless or inadequate: *Her good looks* ***beggar*** *description.*
Word history: Middle English

beggarly
adjective **1** very poor
2 mean or miserly: *a* ***beggarly*** *amount of food*

begin
verb to start or commence: *Please* ***begin*** *work now. | How did the trouble* ***begin****?* (***embark on***, ***initiate***, ***institute***, ***open***, ***set about***)
Verb forms: I **began**, I have **begun**, I am **beginning**
Word history: Old English

beginner
noun someone who is just learning something
Word use: The opposite of this is **expert** or **veteran**.

beginning
noun the time or place when something begins (***commencement***, ***onset***, ***origin***, ***outset***, ***start***)

begrudge
verb **1** to envy: *They* ***begrudged*** *him his luck.*
2 to be unwilling to give: *The boss* ***begrudged*** *her the money she earned.*

beguile (buh-guyl)
verb **1** to charm or enchant: *The children were* ***beguiled*** *by the witch's magic.* (***attract***, ***bewitch***, ***entice***, ***fascinate***, ***mesmerise***)
2 to deceive or mislead

beguiling
adjective charming: *a* ***beguiling*** *smile*

behalf
phrase **on behalf of**, on the side of or for: *to speak* ***on behalf of*** *my friend*

Word history: Middle English *behalve* beside, in Old English a phrase, *be healfe (him)* by (his) side

behave
verb **1** to act: *to* ***behave*** *like a child* (***acquit yourself***, ***carry yourself***, ***conduct yourself***, ***perform***)
phrase **2 behave yourself**, to act properly or in an acceptable way: *to* ***behave yourself*** *in school*

Word history: late Middle English, apparently from *be-* + *have* hold yourself a certain way

behaviour
noun the way you behave

Word use: You can also use **behavior**.
Word building: **behavioural** *adjective*

behead
verb to cut off the head of: *They* ***beheaded*** *many people during the French Revolution.* (***decapitate***, ***guillotine***)

behest (buh-hest)
noun command: *It was done at the* ***behest*** *of the commander-in-chief.*

Word history: Old English *behǣs* promise

behind
preposition **1** at the back of: ***behind*** *the garden shed*
2 after or later than: *I'm* ***behind*** *schedule with my homework.*
3 less advanced than: ***behind*** *his class in woodwork*
adverb **4** at or towards the back: *She lagged* ***behind.***
5 late: *She's* ***behind*** *with her essay.*
noun **6** your buttocks
7 *Australian Rules*, a score of one point, made when you put the ball between a goal post and an outer post

Word history: Old English

behold
verb Old-fashioned to look at or see: *You will* ***behold*** *a child.*

Verb forms: I **beheld**, I have **beheld**, I am **beholding**
Word building: **beholder** *noun*
Word history: Old English *behaldan* keep

behove (buh-hohv)
verb to be necessary or proper for: *It* ***behoves*** *me to see him.*

Word history: Old English *behōfian* need

beige (bayzh)
adjective of a very light brown colour

Word building: **beige** *noun*
Word history: French

being
noun **1** something which lives: ***beings*** *from outer space | a human* ***being***
2 existence or life: *to come into* ***being***

belated
adjective happening or arriving too late: *I forgot her birthday so I sent a* ***belated*** *birthday card.*

belch
verb **1** to pass wind noisily from your stomach through your mouth: *Fizzy drink makes me* ***belch.*** (***bring up wind***, ***burp***)
2 to throw out violently: *The volcano* ***belched*** *out lava.*
noun **3** the rumbling noise you make when belching

Word history: Middle English

belfry (bel-free)
noun a tower with a bell hanging in it: *the* ***belfry*** *of the local church*

Noun forms: The plural is **belfries**.
Word history: Middle English, from Old French, from Germanic

belie (buh-luy)
verb **1** to give a false account of: *His face* ***belied*** *his thoughts.*
2 to show to be false: *Her trembling* ***belied*** *her calm words.*
3 to fail to justify: *His exam results* ***belie*** *his earlier promise.*

Verb forms: it **belied**, it has **belied**, it is **belying**
Word history: Old English *be-* + *lēogan* lie

belief
noun **1** something that you believe and accept as true: *It is my* ***belief*** *that children should enjoy school. | a religious* ***belief*** (***doctrine***, ***dogma***, ***faith***, ***tenet***)
2 trust or faith: *children's* ***belief*** *in their parents*

Word history: Middle English

believe
verb **1** to trust or have confidence in: *I can't* ***believe*** *that story.* (***accept***, ***credit***)
2 to think: *I* ***believe*** *they will be late.* (***assume***, ***conjecture***, ***presume***, ***reckon***, ***suppose***)
phrase **3 believe in**, to accept as real or true: *Do you* ***believe in*** *ghosts?*
4 make believe, to pretend: *The little kids like to* ***make believe*** *they're creatures from outer space.*

Word building: **believable** *adjective*
believer *noun*
Word history: Middle English, from Old English *lēfan*

belittle
verb to make seem unimportant: *She hurt their feelings when she* ***belittled*** *their work.* (***decry***, ***deride***, ***disparage***, ***slight***)

bell
noun **1** a hollow metal cup with a clapper hanging inside which can hit the side of the cup and make a ringing sound
2 the ringing sound of a bell
3 something which makes the sound of a bell
phrase **4 ring a bell**, *Colloquial* to sound familiar: *Her name* ***rings a bell.***

Word history: Old English *belle*

belladonna (bel-uh-don-uh)
noun **1** deadly nightshade
2 a drug obtained from this plant

Word history: Italian word literally meaning 'fair lady'

bellbird
noun a small bird that has a clear ringing call like the sound of a bell and lives in bushy areas along the east coast of Australia

bellicose (bel-uh-kohs)
adjective warlike or keen to fight (***aggressive***, ***bloodthirsty***, ***hawkish***, ***militant***, ***pugnacious***)

Word building: **bellicosity** *noun*
Word history: from Latin word meaning 'war'

belligerent (buh-lij-uh-ruhnt)
adjective **1** angry and aggressive: *We were surprised by her* ***belligerent*** *behaviour.* (***argumentative***, ***combative***, ***hostile***, ***pugnacious***, ***warlike***)
2 involved in a war: *a* ***belligerent*** *country*

Word building: **belligerence** *noun*
Word history: Latin

bellow
verb to cry or roar loudly: *to* ***bellow*** *an answer | The bull* ***bellowed*** *with anger.* (***bawl***, ***belt out***, ***shout***, ***shriek***, ***yell***)

Word history: Middle English, apparently blend of Old English *bellan* bell and *bylgan* bellow

bellows
noun an instrument for pumping air: *We pumped the* ***bellows*** *to make the fire burn brightly.*

Word history: Old English

bellwether (bel-wedh-uh)
noun **1** a wether or other male sheep that leads the flock, often wearing a bell so that the whereabouts of the flock is known
2 a person whom others follow blindly

belly
noun **1** the front part of the body containing the stomach and the intestines: *to hit someone in the* ***belly*** (***abdomen***, ***tummy***)
2 the inside of anything: *the* ***belly*** *of a ship* (***centre***, ***contents***, ***guts***, ***interior***)

Word history: from Old English word meaning 'bag', 'skin'

belong
verb **1** to have a rightful place: *It just doesn't* ***belong*** *here.*
phrase **2 belong to,**
a to be the property of: *The book* ***belongs to*** *him.*
b to be part of: *That cover* ***belongs to*** *this jar.*

Word history: Middle English *be-* + *longen* belong, from Old English *gelang* belonging to

belongings
plural noun things you own: *Our* ***belongings*** *are stored in a warehouse.* (***assets***, ***gear***, ***paraphernalia***, ***possessions***)

beloved (buh-luv-uhd, buh-luvd)
adjective **1** much loved: *a* ***beloved*** *friend*
noun Old-fashioned **2** someone you love very much: *to kiss your* ***beloved***

below
adverb **1** beneath: *The rain fell onto the parched earth* ***below.***
2 downstairs: *the floor* ***below***
3 at a later point on a page or in your writing: *See* ***below*** *for further examples.*
4 in a lower rank or grade: *the form* ***below***
preposition **5** lower than: ***below*** *the knee |* ***below*** *the usual price*

Word history: Middle English *biloghe* by low

belt
noun **1** a strip of strong material, often worn around your waist or hips
2 a large strip of land where a particular thing is grown: *the wheat* ***belt*** *| a* ***belt*** *of trees*
verb **3** to fasten with a belt
4 to beat or hit very hard: *to* ***belt*** *someone as a punishment*
phrase **5 below the belt**, unfair or against the rules: *That comment was* ***below the belt!***
6 belt out, *Colloquial* to sing very loudly
7 belt up, *Colloquial*
a to be quiet: *Why don't you* ***belt up?***
b to fasten a safety belt

Word history: Old English, perhaps from Latin

belting
noun a beating

bemused (buh-myoohzd)
adjective **1** muddled or confused
2 lost in thought: *a* ***bemused*** *look on her face* (***absent-minded***, ***half-asleep***, ***inattentive***, ***preoccupied***)

bench
noun **1** a seat long enough for several people: *a park* ***bench***
2 a strong work-table: *a carpenter's* ***bench***
3 a seat for members of parliament or judges in court
phrase **4 the bench**,
a the position or office of a judge: *He has been appointed to* ***the bench.***
b the group of people sitting as judges: *The prisoner stood before* ***the bench.***

Word history: Old English *benc*

benchmark
noun **1** a point of known height, usually a mark cut into some lasting material, to serve as a reference point in running a line of levels for the determination of other heights
2 a standard from which quality or excellence is measured

bend
verb **1** to turn or curve in a particular direction: *to* ***bend*** *a piece of wire | The road* ***bends*** *to the left.* (***curl***, ***deflect***, ***flex***, ***loop***)
2 to stoop: *to* ***bend*** *over to pick up something*
noun **3** a curve or change in direction: *a* ***bend*** *in the road*
phrase **4 bend over backwards**, to try as hard as you can: *I* ***bent over backwards*** *to get you a ticket to the concert.*
5 round the bend, *Colloquial* mad
6 the bends, a dangerous disorder where nitrogen bubbles form in your blood because of a sudden drop in the surrounding pressure, especially common in divers who have come to the surface too quickly

Verb forms: I **bent,** I have **bent,** I am **bending**
Word history: Old English *bendan* bind, bend (a bow)

beneath
adverb **1** below, or underneath: *Snow fell onto the freezing ground* ***beneath****. | the heaven above and the earth* ***beneath***
preposition **2** under, or underneath: ***beneath*** *the same roof | He sat on the branch* ***beneath*** *me.*
3 not worthy of: *That comment is* ***beneath*** *my notice.*

Word history: Old English *be* by + *neothan* below

benediction (ben-uh-dik-shuhn)
noun the blessing at the end of a church service

Word history: Middle English, from Latin

benefactor
noun someone who gives help or money to those who need it

Word history: Latin

beneficent (buh-nef-uh-sunt)
adjective doing good, especially by acting kindly towards other people and giving help if it is needed

Word building: **beneficence** *noun*

beneficial
adjective helpful: ***beneficial*** *advice | the* ***beneficial*** *effect of a good night's sleep* (***advantageous, handy, profitable, useful, valuable***)

beneficiary (ben-uh-fish-uh-ree)
noun someone who receives assistance, especially money left in a will

Noun forms: The plural is **beneficiaries.**

benefit
noun **1** anything that is good for you: *the* ***benefits*** *of education* (***advantage, asset, boon***)
2 a concert to raise money for charity
verb **3** to be good for: *A holiday will* ***benefit*** *you greatly.* (***advance, advantage, assist, help, further***)

Verb forms: I **benefited,** I have **benefited,** I am **benefiting**
Word history: Latin *bene* + *factum* thing done

benevolent (buh-nev-uh-luhnt)
adjective **1** wanting to help other people
2 intended for doing good rather than making a profit: *The Red Cross is a* ***benevolent*** *organisation.*

Word use: The opposite of definition 1 is **malevolent.**
Word building: **benevolence** *noun*
Word history: from Latin word meaning 'well-wishing'

benighted (buh-nuy-tuhd)
adjective backward in learning or in morals

Word history: past participle of *benight*, verb

benign (buh-nuyn)
adjective **1** kind and gentle: *a* ***benign*** *smile*
2 not harmful to the body: *The lump taken out of her neck by the doctor was* ***benign****.*

Word use: The opposite of definition 2 is **malignant.**
Word history: Middle English, from Latin word meaning 'kind'

bent
adjective **1** crooked or curved: *a* ***bent*** *hairpin* (***buckled, distorted, twisted, warped***)
noun **2** a liking or preference: *a* ***bent*** *for painting*
phrase **3 bent on,** determined or set on: ***bent on*** *playing football*

Word history: past participle of *bend*

bequeath (buh-kweedh, buh-kweeth)
verb to hand down or pass on to someone who comes after you: *to* ***bequeath*** *money in a will*

Word history: Old English *be-* + *cwethan* say

bequest
noun money or other personal property left by someone in a will

Word history: Old English

berate (buh-rayt)
verb to scold

bereaved
adjective **1** sad because of someone's death: *The* ***bereaved*** *husband wept at his wife's funeral.*
phrase **2 the bereaved,** the person or people who are suffering because someone they loved is dead

Word history: Old English *be-* + *rēafian* rob

bereavement
noun the loss of someone dear to you

bereft
adjective **1** suffering loss: ***bereft*** *of family |* ***bereft*** *of hope*
2 lacking: ***bereft*** *of meaning*

beret (be-ray)
noun a soft round cap

Word history: French, from Béarn dialect, from Late Latin word meaning 'cloak'

berry
noun a small fruit, often brightly coloured

Noun forms: The plural is **berries.**
Word history: Old English *berie*

> **berry / bury**
> Don't confuse **berry** with **bury,** which means 'to put something in the ground and cover it with earth'.

berserk (buh-zerk)
adjective uncontrollably crazy and wild: *The dogs went* ***berserk*** *when they were untied.*

berth
noun **1** a place to sleep on a boat or train: *Our cabin has four* ***berths****.*
2 a place where a ship can tie up
verb **3** to tie up at a dock: *The ship* ***berthed*** *at 7 o'clock.*
phrase **4 give a wide berth to,** to avoid or keep away from

Word history: probably from *bear*

> **berth / birth**
> Don't confuse **berth** with **birth,** which is the beginning of a life.

beryl (be-ruhl)
noun **1** the mineral group which includes the emerald
2 a pale bluish-green colour

Word building: **beryl** *adjective*
Word history: Middle English, from Latin, from Greek

beseech
verb to ask anxiously: *Help me, I **beseech** you!* (***beg***, ***demand***, ***entreat***, ***implore***, ***request***)

Verb forms: I **besought** or I **beseeched**, I have **besought** or I have **beseeched**, I am **beseeching**
Word history: Old English *sēcan* seek

beset
verb **1** to attack on all sides: *to **beset** the enemy.* (***assail***, ***besiege***, ***harass***)
adjective **2** surrounded: ***beset** by difficulties.*

Verb forms: it **beset**, it has **beset**, it is **besetting**
Word history: Old English, from *be-* + *settan* set

beside
preposition **1** near or at the side of: *Sit down **beside** me.*
2 compared with: ***Beside** her, he is tall.*
3 nothing to do with: ***beside** the point*
phrase **4 beside yourself**, too upset to think clearly or act rationally: *He's **beside himself** with grief.*

Word history: Old English *be sīdan* by side

besides
preposition **1** in addition to: *Did anyone turn up **besides** you? | It was a badly made film **besides** being violent.*
2 other than: *I have no other friend **besides** you.*
adverb **3** moreover or beyond what has been said: ***Besides,** you are too sick to go.*

besiege
verb **1** to crowd round and surround: *The enemy troops **besieged** the town for three weeks.*
2 to set upon or attack: *The speaker was **besieged** with questions.*

besotted (buh-sot-uhd)
adjective **1** filled with foolish love: *He was **besotted** with her.*
2 made stupid, or drunk

best
adjective **1** of the finest or highest quality (***chief***, ***first-class***, ***leading***, ***supreme***, ***top***)
2 favourite: *my **best** friend*
adverb **3** most successfully: *She swims **best**.*
4 most: *I like him **best**.*
noun **5** your nicest clothes: *to put on your **best** for the party*
phrase **6 all the best**, something you say when you want to wish someone well
7 at best, in the most favourable or promising conditions: ***At best** he'll make you do it again but he'll probably punish you.*
8 for the best,
a having an unexpectedly good result
b with good intentions or motives
9 had best, would be wiser or safer to: *You **had best** come in out of the rain.*
10 make the best of, to manage as well as you can in difficult conditions

Word use: **Best** is one of the forms of the adjective **good** and the adverb **well**. It is the *superlative* form. The other form (the *comparative*) of both **good** and **well** is **better**.
Word history: Old English *betst*

bestial (bes-tee-uhl)
adjective **1** savage like a beast can be
2 inhuman or brutal

Word building: **bestially** *adverb* **bestialise** *verb*
Word history: Middle English, from Latin

best man
noun the chief attendant or helper of the bridegroom at a wedding

bestow
verb to give as a gift or reward: *The queen **bestowed** a medal on the soldier for bravery.*

Word building: **bestowal** *noun*

bet
noun **1** a promise that you will give money or something similar to someone whose opinion differs from yours, if that person is right and you are wrong: *Ann made a **bet** that she was taller than Kate.*
2 the money or thing that you promised: *She lost her **bet**.*
verb **3** to risk as part of a bet: *I **bet** you fifty cents I can jump this fence.*
4 to make a bet

Verb forms: I **bet** or I **betted**, I have **bet** or I have **betted**, I am **betting**

betide
verb Old-fashioned to befall or happen to: *Woe **betide** the villain!*

Word history: Old English *tīdan* betide

betray
verb **1** to be unfaithful or disloyal to: *The spy **betrayed** his country by selling important secrets to the enemy.* (***blab***, ***dob on***, ***doublecross***, ***give up***, ***sell out***)
2 to show or reveal: *His face **betrayed** his anger. | to **betray** a secret* (***disclose***, ***expose***, ***make public***, ***publish***)

Word building: **betrayal** *noun* **betrayer** *noun*
Word history: Middle English, from Old French, from Latin *trādere* give over

betrothal (buh-trohdh-uhl)
verb Old-fashioned a promise to marry (***engagement***)

Word building: **betroth** *verb* **betrothed** *noun* **betrothed** *adjective*
Word history: Old English *trēowth* pledge

better
adjective **1** of higher quality, or of more value: *This furniture is made of **better** wood than that.*
2 larger, or greater: *It took him the **better** part of his life to build his house.*
3 improved in health: *I hope you are feeling **better** today.*
adverb **4** in an improved or more suitable manner: *She behaved **better** today.*
verb **5** to improve: *He **bettered** his score in the first round by ten points.* (***amend***, ***enhance***, ***forward***, ***raise***, ***reform***)
phrase **6 better off**, in better conditions: *I'm **better off** living near the station.*
7 better yourself, to improve your education or your position in society: *She went back to night school to try and **better herself**.*
8 had better, would be wiser or safer to: *You **had better** stay at home in such bad weather.*
9 think better of, to reconsider and decide more wisely: *to **think better of** going barefoot on the hot sand*

Word use: **Better** is one of the forms of the adjective **good** and the adverb **well**. It is the *comparative* form. The other form (the *superlative*) of both **good** and **well** is **best**. Note that, because **better** is already the comparative, you should not say *more better*.
Word history: Old English *betera*

bettong (<u>bet</u>-ong)
noun a very small kangaroo that looks like a small wallaby with a short nose

Word history: from Dharug, an Australian Aboriginal language spoken by the people living near Sydney Cove in the early days of European settlement

between
preposition **1** within the space, time or amount separating two or more things: *a path **between** the houses | a break **between** exams | a difference **between** prices*
2 connecting: *a link **between** parts*
3 concerning or involving: *a war **between** nations*
4 by joint action or possession of: *to carry it **between** them | to own land **between** them*
phrase **5 between you and me** or **between ourselves**, in secret

Word history: Old English *be* by + *-twēonan*, *-twēonum*, from *twā* two

between / among
These words are similar in meaning but they are sometimes used in different ways.
If there are only two things or people, you should use **between. Among** is never used for only two:
There was a fight between Luke and Elisabeth over the last cake.
NOT
There was a fight among Luke and Elisabeth over the last cake.
When you are talking about more than two people or things, you can use **among** or **between**:
Share the lollies among all the kids.
A war broke out between the four countries.

betwixt
preposition, adverb **1** *Old-fashioned* between
phrase **2 betwixt and between**, neither one thing nor the other

Word history: Old English *betweox*

bevel (<u>bev</u>-uhl)
noun **1** the slope that one line or surface makes with another when not at right angles
2 a woodworking tool used to make such a slope
verb **3** to cut or slope at an angle

Verb forms: I **bevelled**, I have **bevelled**, I am **bevelling**
Word building: **beveller** *noun*

beverage
noun a drink of any kind

Word history: Middle English, from Latin word meaning 'drink'

bevy (<u>bev</u>-ee)
noun **1** a flock of birds, especially of quail
2 a group, especially of girls or women

Noun forms: The plural is **bevies.**
Word history: Middle English *bevey*

beware
verb be careful of: *If you go in, **beware** of the dog.*

bewilder
verb to confuse or puzzle: *The maze completely **bewildered** him.* (***baffle, confound, mystify, perplex***)

Word building: **bewilderment** *noun*
Word history: *be-* + *wilder* to cause to lose one's way

bewitch
verb **1** to put under a magic spell
2 to charm: *The little girl **bewitched** the audience with her delightful appearance.* (***attract, beguile, entice, fascinate, mesmerise***)

beyond
preposition **1** farther on or more distant than: ***beyond** the horizon | **beyond** the house*
2 past: ***beyond** human understanding*
3 more than or in excess of: *They spend **beyond** their income.*

Word history: Old English *be* by + *geondan* beyond

biannual (buy-<u>an</u>-yooh-uhl)
adjective taking place twice a year

biannual / biennial
Don't confuse **biannual** with **biennial.**
Something is **biennial** if it happens every two years.

bias (<u>buy</u>-uhs)
noun **1** a strong opinion which often stops you from seeing the other side of an argument: *The teacher's **bias** towards football was obvious.* (***bigotry, intolerance, one-sidedness, partiality, prejudice***)
2 a slanting line or direction
verb **3** to prejudice or influence, usually unfairly (***brainwash, condition, manipulate, persuade***)

Word use: The opposite of definition 1 is **impartiality.**
Verb forms: it **biased**, it has **biased**, it is **biasing**
Word history: French word meaning 'slant', probably from Latin *biaxius* having two axes

biased
adjective inclined or prejudiced: ***biased** towards maths | **biased** against racists* (***bigoted, intolerant, one-sided, partial, predisposed***)

Word use: The opposite of this is **unbiased** or **impartial.**

bib
noun **1** a small cloth tied under a baby's chin to protect its clothes at mealtime
2 the part of an apron or pair of overalls above the waist

Word history: Middle English; origin uncertain, perhaps from Latin *bibere* drink

bible
noun **1 Bible,** the sacred book of the Christian religion, consisting of the Old and New Testaments
2 a book accepted as authoritative or as favourite reading: *His **bible** was his book of orchids.*

Word building: **biblical** *adjective*
Word history: Middle English, from Medieval Latin, from Greek word meaning 'book'

bibliography (bib-lee-<u>og</u>-ruh-fee)
noun **1** a list of all the books read or used by a writer when writing a book or essay
2 a list of everything written by a particular writer, or about a particular subject: *a **bibliography** of Australian wildlife*

Noun forms: The plural is **bibliographies**.
Word building: **bibliographer** *noun* **bibliographic** *adjective* **bibliographical** *adjective*

bicameral
adjective having two chambers or houses: *The Federal Parliament of Australia is **bicameral** — its lower house is the House of Representatives and its upper house is the Senate.*

bicarbonate (buy-kah-buh-nuht, buy-kah-buh-nayt)
noun a salt of carbonic acid, containing the HCO_3^- ion

bicentenary (buy-suhn-teen-uh-ree, buy-suhn-ten-uh-ree)
noun a 200th anniversary: *Australia had its **bicentenary** of white settlement in 1988.*

Noun forms: The plural is **bicentenaries**.
Word building: **bicentennial** *adjective*

biceps (buy-seps)
noun a large muscle at the top of your arm or the back of your thigh that helps you to bend your elbow or knee

Word history: from Latin word meaning 'two-headed'

bicker
verb to squabble or argue about little things (***differ***, ***dispute***, ***dissent***, ***wrangle***)

Word history: Middle English

bicycle
noun a two-wheeled machine for riding on, which you steer by handlebars and drive by pushing pedals

Word use: You can also use the colloquial word **bike**.
Word building: **bicyclist** *noun*
Word history: French, from *bi-* + Greek *kýklos* circle, wheel

bid
verb **1** *Old-fashioned* to order or command: *The king **bids** his people to do as he wishes.*
2 *Old-fashioned* to say or tell: *I **bid** you farewell.*
3 to offer or make an offer to buy at an auction: *She **bid** $200 for the table. | He **bid** for the chair.*
noun **4** the amount offered for something, especially at an auction (***proposal***, ***proposition***, ***suggestion***, ***tender***)
5 an attempt to achieve a goal or purpose

Verb forms: I **bade** or, for definition 3, I **bid**, I have **bidden** or, for definition 3, I have **bid**, I am **bidding**
Word building: **bidder** *noun* **bidding** *noun*
Word history: Old English *(ge)bidden* beg, ask, pray

biddy
noun *Colloquial* a woman, especially one who is old

Noun forms: The plural is **biddies**.

bide
phrase **bide your time**, to wait for a favourable chance

Word history: Old English *bīdan*

bidet (bee-day)
noun a small low basin, with running water, for washing the genital area

Word history: French

biennale (bee-uh-nah-lee)
noun a major exhibition or festival held every two years

Word use: We pronounce the final 'e' in this word because it has come into English from Italian.
Word history: Italian

biennial (buy-en-ee-uhl)
adjective **1** happening every two years
2 living for two years: *Onions and parsnips are **biennial** plants.*

Word building: **biennial** *noun*
Word history: Latin *biennium* two-year period + *-al*

> **biennial / biannual**
> Don't confuse **biennial** with **biannual**.
> Something is **biannual** if it happens twice a year.

bier (beer)
noun a stand on which a dead body, or the coffin holding it, rests before it is buried

Word history: Old English *bēr, bær*

bifocals
plural noun a pair of glasses with lenses which have two parts, one for seeing things far away and one for seeing things close to you

Word building: **bifocal** *adjective*

big
adjective **1** large in size or amount: *a **big** overdraft at the bank* (***ample***, ***bulky***, ***generous***, ***huge***, ***substantial***)
2 elder: *her **big** brother*
3 important: ***big** business*
adverb **4** *Colloquial* boastfully: *to talk **big***
phrase **5 big on**, knowing a lot and eager about: *She's **big on** computers.*

Adjective forms: **bigger**, **biggest**
Word history: Middle English

bigamy (big-uh-mee)
noun the crime of marrying someone while you are still married to someone else

Word use: Compare this with **monogamy** and **polygamy**.
Word building: **bigamist** *noun* **bigamous** *adjective*
Word history: Middle English, from Old French

Big Brother
noun a ruler, especially one who tries to control people's private lives and thoughts

Word history: from a character in the novel *1984*, by George Orwell

bight (buyt)
noun **1** a bend or curve in the shore of the sea
2 a body of water bounded by such a bend or curve (***cove***, ***estuary***, ***gulf***, ***inlet***)

Word history: Old English *byht* a bend

> **bight / bite / byte**
> Don't confuse **bight** with **bite** or **byte**.
> A **bite** is a mouthful of something or a wound made using teeth or something similar.
> A **byte** is a unit of information stored in a computer.

bigot (big-uht)
noun a person unreasonably convinced of the rightness of a particular opinion, practice, etc.

Word building: **bigotry** *noun*
Word history: French

bigoted
adjective intolerant of people with different opinions, lifestyles, etc. (***biased***, ***dogmatic***, ***narrow-minded***, ***prejudiced***)

big-time
adjective Colloquial **1** at the top level in any business or activity: *the **big-time** operators*
adverb Colloquial **2** greatly: *She loves you **big-time**.*

bike
noun Colloquial a bicycle or motorcycle

bikini (buh-kee-nee)
noun a two-piece swimming costume for women

Word history: named in 1946 by French designer Louis Reard after *Bikini Atoll* in the Marshall Islands in the northern Pacific, prominent as a site for US nuclear bomb tests, 1946–58, from a comparison of the effect the swimming costume would have with the devastating effects of the nuclear explosion

bilateral
adjective of or affecting two sides: *The two countries came to a **bilateral** agreement about trade.*

bilby
noun a small bandicoot with big rabbit-like ears

Noun forms: The plural is **bilbies**.
Word history: from Yuwaalaraay, an Australian Aboriginal language from the Lightning Ridge region

bile
noun a bitter yellowish liquid which is produced by the liver and which helps you digest food

Word use: Another name is **gall**.
Word history: French, from Latin

bilge
noun **1 a** either of the rounded parts at either side of a ship's hull
b the lowest part of a ship's hold
c water that collects in a ship's bilge
2 *Colloquial* nonsense (***bunkum***, ***piffle***, ***rot***, ***rubbish***)

Word use: You can also use **bilge water** for definition 1c.

bilingual (buy-ling-gwuhl)
adjective able to speak two languages fluently

Word building: **bilingualism** *noun*
Word history: from Latin word meaning 'speaking two languages'

bilious (bil-yuhs)
adjective **1** having, or caused by, too much bile: *a **bilious** attack*
2 feeling sick in the stomach

Word building: **biliousness** *noun*
Word history: from Latin word meaning 'full of bile'

bill[1]
noun **1** a written statement telling you how much money you owe for something
2 a poster or advertisement on display
3 a plan for a new law to be presented to Parliament
verb **4** to advertise by poster or advertisement: *The new actor was **billed** for next week.*
5 to send someone an account for the goods they have bought

Word history: Middle English, from Anglo-Latin *billa*, variant of Medieval Latin *bulla* seal

bill[2]
noun a bird's beak

Word history: Old English *bile* beak

billabong
noun Australian a waterhole which used to be part of a river

Word history: from Wiradjuri, an Australian Aboriginal language of the Murrumbidgee-Lachlan region. The word *billa* meant 'river' and the ending *-bong* meant 'happening only after rain'. In the Aboriginal language this was the name of what the settlers called the Bell River, but it came to be used more widely for waterholes, particularly those that seemed to be separated from a flowing river.

billet (bil-uht)
noun **1** a place for someone to live for a while, usually in someone else's home: *The soldier was given a **billet** in the captain's own home.*
verb **2** to provide accommodation for: *We **billeted** a student from Japan in our home.*

Verb forms: I **billeted**, I have **billeted**, I am **billeting**
Word history: Middle English, from Old French

billiards (bil-yuhdz)
noun a game played by two or more people on a rectangular table, with hard balls hit by a long stick called a cue

Word history: French *bille* log

billion (bil-yuhn)
noun **1 a** a thousand times a million, or 10^9
b a million times a million, or 10^{12}
2 *Colloquial* a large amount
adjective **3** amounting to a billion in number

Word use: Definition 1b is becoming rare, with people everywhere tending to use **billion** in the sense of 'a thousand millions'.
Word building: **billionth** *adjective* **billionth** *noun*
Word history: French, from *bi-* + *(mi)llion*, that is the second power of one million

billionaire
noun someone who has a billion dollars or more

bill of rights
noun a formal statement of the basic rights of the people of a nation

billow
noun **1** a large wave: *the **billows** of the ocean*
verb **2** to swirl or rise like billows: *Smoke **billowed** from the chimney.*

Word building: **billowy** *adjective*
Word history: Scandinavian

billy
noun Australian, NZ a tin container with a lid, used for boiling water

Noun forms: The plural is **billies**.
Word history: probably from Scottish dialect *bally* a milk-pail

billycart
noun Australian, NZ a four-wheeled cart which has a box for a seat and which you steer by ropes attached to its front axle

billy goat
noun a male goat

bin
noun a box or container used to store things: *Put the empty packet in the garbage* ***bin.***

Word history: Old English *binn(e)* crib

binary (buy-nuh-ree)
adjective **1** made up of two parts or things
2 using the numbers 0 and 1: ***binary*** *code*

Word history: from Latin word meaning 'consisting of two things'

bind (buynd)
verb **1** to tie up or fasten: *The girls* ***bind*** *their hair with ribbons.*
2 to cover or bandage: *to* ***bind*** *up her arm*
3 to cause to harden or stick together: *to* ***bind*** *the flour and sugar with eggs*
4 to fasten with a cover: *to* ***bind*** *a book*
noun **5** *Colloquial* a nuisance or a bore: *Doing the dishes is a* ***bind.***

Verb forms: I **bound**, I have **bound**, I am **binding**
Word history: Old English *bindan*

binder
noun **1** something or someone that binds, such as the cement used for joining bricks
2 a cover for keeping loose papers in

bindi-eye
noun a small spiky weed

Word use: You can also use **bindi**.
Word history: from Kamilaroi and Yuwaalaraay, Australian Aboriginal languages of NSW

binding
noun **1** anything that binds, such as the covering around the pages of a book, or the band sewn along the edge of cloth to keep it from fraying
adjective **2** having the power to bind someone to do something: *a* ***binding*** *agreement*

binge
noun Colloquial a period of too much eating, drinking or spending money

Word history: Dialect from Lincolnshire in England, meaning 'to soak'. Its meaning was later extended to cover a period of metaphorically 'soaking' yourself in something, such as too much food, drink, spending, etc.

binge drinking
noun a pattern of alcohol consumption in which a person punctuates periods of total abstinence with sessions in which a large amount of alcohol is consumed in a short period of time and with the primary intention of becoming intoxicated: *His ill health was due to* ***binge drinking.***

Word building: **binge drinker** *noun*

bingo
noun a gambling game in which you cross numbers, called in any order, off a card (***housie-housie***, ***lotto***)

binoculars (buh-nok-yuhl-uhz)
plural noun double magnifying glasses for both eyes, used for making distant objects seem nearer (***field-glasses***)

binomial (buy-noh-mee-uhl)
noun Mathematics a combination of two numbers or symbols with no equals sign, which are added together or subtracted, such as $3x + 2y$ or $x^2 - 4x$

biochar
noun charcoal that is produced by an oxygen-free burning process and which can be used to store carbon dioxide and to fertilise the soil

biochemistry (buy-oh-kem-uhs-tree)
noun that branch of chemistry concerned with living matter

Word building: **biochemical** *adjective*
biochemist *noun*

bioclimatology
noun the study of the effect of climate on the life and health of animals, especially humans

biodegradable
adjective able to be broken down by the action of very small living things like bacteria: *Most detergents are* ***biodegradable.***

biodiesel
noun a biodegradable, nonflammable fuel, made from vegetable oils, especially from recycled cooking oil

biodiverse
adjective exhibiting biodiversity: *a* ***biodiverse*** *region*

biodiversity
noun the variety of types of organisms living within an area: *threats to coastal* ***biodiversity***

biodynamic
adjective having to do with methods of improving the soil and vegetation without the use of chemical fertilisers in a way that is environmentally sound and sustainable: ***biodynamic*** *farming practices*

biofuel
noun a fuel, such as methane and biodiesel, that is derived from renewable sources such as biological matter

biogenesis (buy-oh-jen-uh-suhs)
noun **1** the theory that living organisms come from other living organisms only
2 the development of living organisms from earlier living organisms

Word building: **biogenetic** *adjective*

biography
noun the story of a person's life, written by someone else

Noun forms: The plural is **biographies**.
Word use: Compare this with **autobiography**.
Word building: **biographer** *noun* **biographical** *adjective*
Word history: Greek

biohazard
noun any biological material likely to cause human or animal disease or environmental contamination

Word use: You can also use **bio-hazard**.
Word building: **biohazardous** *adjective*

biological
adjective **1** having to do with biology
2 having to do with a family member who is related to you by birth rather than by adoption, fostering, etc.: *She met her* ***biological*** *mother when she was eighteen.*

biological clock
noun a system built into living organisms, which controls the timing of the cycle of biological processes (biorhythms) and which is not dependent on outside time

biological warfare
noun warfare which uses living organisms, such as bacteria, or poisons produced from them to harm people, domestic animals, or food crops

Word use: Another name is **germ warfare**.

biology
noun the science or study of all living things

Word building: **biologist** *noun*

biomass
noun organic matter used as a source of energy, such as the residue of farming activity, landfill, compressed household waste, etc.

bionic ear
noun → **cochlear implant**

biopsy
noun the removal of a small piece of tissue from someone's body to test for signs of disease

Noun forms: The plural is **biopsies**.
Word history: from French

biorhythm (buy-oh-ridh-uhm)
noun **1** the theory that human energy is based on three separate, in-built cycles, those of the body, the emotions, and the mind
2 the pattern of one such cycle

biosecurity
noun **1** security measures taken to prevent the transmission of disease to the plants or animals of a particular region
2 security measures taken against bioterrorism

biotech (buy-oh-tek)
noun biotechnology

biotechnology
noun the use of microorganisms to produce desirable products, such as drugs, and services, such as waste recycling

Word building: **biotechnological** *adjective*
biotechnologist *noun*

bioterrorism
noun terrorism that involves the use of biological agents, such as bacteria and viruses, which have a harmful effect on humans, domestic animals or food crops

Word building: **bioterrorist** *noun*

biotic
adjective having to do with the animal and plant life of an ecosystem: *The rainforest was dense with **biotic** matter.*

Word use: You can also use **biotical**. | Compare this with **abiotic**.
Word history: Greek *biōtikos* of or relating to life

bioweapon
noun a weapon which uses a living organism to cause the death of humans or the destruction of crops

bipartite (buy-pah-tuyt)
adjective **1** being in two parts
2 concerning two parties (***bilateral***)

Word history: from Latin word meaning 'divided into two parts'

bipolar disorder (buy-poh-luh dis-aw-duh)
noun a mental disorder marked by alternating periods of mood elevation and depression

Word use: Another name is **manic depression**.

birch
noun a tree of cold countries with slender branches and smooth white bark

Word history: Old English *bierce*

bird
noun **1** a two-legged creature which lays eggs and has wings and feathers
2 *Colloquial* a person: *He's a funny old **bird**.*
3 *Colloquial* a girl

Word history: Old English *brid(d)* young bird, chick

bird flu
noun → **avian influenza**

bird of paradise
noun **1** a type of song bird found in Australia and the island of New Guinea, noted for the fine, brightly coloured feathers of the male
2 a tropical plant with purple stems opening out into orange flowers similar in shape to birds' heads

bird's-eye view
noun a view from above, as of terrain, landscape, etc.: *a **bird's-eye view** of the city*

biro (buy-roh)
noun → **ballpoint pen**

Word history: Trademark

birth
noun **1** the act of being born
2 any beginning: *the **birth** of a nation.*

Word history: Middle English, from Scandinavian

> **birth / berth**
> Don't confuse **birth** with **berth**, which is the bunk or room where a traveller sleeps on a ship or train. It can also be the space for a ship to tie up at a dock.

birth control
noun the control by methods of contraception of the number of children a woman has

birthday
noun **1** the day on which someone is born
2 the annual celebration of the day of someone's birth: *It is my fourteenth **birthday** today.*

birthrate
noun a number of births for every 100 or 1000 people in a given area during a given time

birthright
noun any right or property to which a person is entitled by birth

biscuit (bis-kuht)
noun a small thin cake which has been baked until it is crisp

Word history: Middle English, from Latin *bis* twice + *coquere* cook

bisect
verb to cut or divide into two parts or two equal parts
Word building: **bisection** *noun*

bisexual
noun **1** an animal, human or plant which has both male and female sex organs
2 someone who is sexually attracted to both males and females

bishop
noun **1** a church minister of high rank, in charge of a whole district
2 a chess piece which can only move diagonally
Word use: **Episcopal** is the adjective meaning 'having to do with a bishop' (definition 1).
Word history: Old English, from Vulgar Latin, from Greek word meaning 'overseer'

bishopric (bish-uhp-rik)
noun the district the bishop is in charge of
Word use: Compare this with **see**[2].
Word history: Old English *bisceop* bishop + *rīce* dominion

bison (buy-suhn)
noun a large American buffalo with high shoulders and shaggy hair
Noun forms: The plural is **bison.**
Word history: Latin, from Germanic

bistro (bis-troh)
noun a small restaurant or wine bar (***cafe***, ***cafeteria***, ***canteen***, ***diner***)
Noun forms: The plural is **bistros**.

bit[1]
noun **1** a metal bar placed in a horse's mouth and attached to the reins, used to help control it
2 the part of some tools which is used for cutting and making holes
Word history: Old English *bite* action of biting

bit[2]
noun a small piece or amount of something
Word history: Old English *bita* bit, morsel

bit[3]
noun a single basic unit of information, used in connection with computers
Word history: abbreviation for '*b(inary dig)it*'

bit[4]
verb past tense of **bite**

bitch
noun **1** a female dog, fox or wolf
2 *Colloquial* an unpleasant or bad-tempered woman
verb **3** *Colloquial* to complain: *He was **bitching** about his teacher.*
Word use: The use of this word as in definition 2 may offend people.
Word building: **bitchiness** *noun* **bitchy** *adjective*
Word history: Old English *bicce*

bite
verb **1** to grab or cut or take a piece out with your teeth: *He **bit** the apple.*
2 to hurt or sting: *The mosquitoes are **biting** tonight.*
3 to take the bait: *The fish were **biting** well yesterday.*
noun **4** a wound made by biting
5 a snack or small amount of food: *I'll just have a **bite** to eat at the restaurant.*
6 the act of biting: *The baby had one or two **bites** of the biscuit.*
phrase **7 bite back**, to hold back: *to **bite back** angry words*
8 bite the dust, *Colloquial*
a to fall down dead
b to fail: *Another good plan **bites the dust.***
Verb forms: I **bit**, I have **bitten**, I am **biting**
Word history: Old English *bītan*

bite / bight / byte
Don't confuse **bite** with **bight** or **byte**.
A **bight** is a bay, as in the *Great Australian Bight.*
A **byte** is a unit of information stored by a computer.

bitmap
noun Computers a graphical image consisting of rows and columns of dots stored as bits
Word building: **bitmapped** *adjective* **bitmapping** *noun*

bitonality
noun in musical composition, the use of two keys at the same time

bitter
adjective **1** having a sharp unpleasant taste (***acid***, ***sharp***, ***sour***, ***tart***)
2 hard to accept or bear: *He felt a **bitter** sorrow when his mother died.* (***cruel***, ***galling***, ***harsh***, ***intense***, ***severe***)
3 very cold: *a **bitter** wind.* (***freezing***, ***frosty***, ***icy***, ***nippy***, ***wintry***)
4 filled with sour feelings: *She felt **bitter** when her friend betrayed her.* (***angry***, ***hostile***, ***resentful***, ***sore***, ***sullen***)
Word building: **bitterness** *noun*
Word history: Old English *biter*; related to *bite*

bittersweet
adjective **1** both bitter and sweet to the taste
2 both pleasant and painful

bitumen (bit-chuh-muhn)
noun **1** a sticky black mixture, like tar or asphalt, used to make roads
2 a tarred road: *You must ride your bike on the **bitumen**, not on the footpath.*
Word history: Latin

bitzer (bit-suh)
noun Australian, NZ Colloquial a mongrel
Word use: You can also use **bitser**.
Word history: from the informal pronunciation of the phrase *bits of*, a shortened form of *bits of this and bits of that*, used to describe a dog or other animal that is a mix of different breeds or kinds.

bivalve
noun Zoology a shellfish with two shells jointed together, such as the oyster
Word building: **bivalve** *adjective*

bivouac (biv-ooh-ak)
noun **1** a camp set up for a short time: *The soldiers had their **bivouac** in the bush.*
verb **2** to camp out: *The cadets **bivouacked** by the stream.*

Verb forms: they **bivouacked**, they have **bivouacked**, they are **bivouacking**
Word history: French, probably from dialect German

bizarre (buh-zah)
adjective very strange or unusual (***abnormal***, ***odd***, ***peculiar***, ***unconventional***, ***weird***)
Word history: French word meaning 'odd', from Spanish word meaning 'brave', probably from Basque *bizar* beard

bizarre / bazaar
Don't confuse **bizarre** with **bazaar**, which is a market where you can buy a variety of goods.

blab
verb **1** to talk too much: *My friend* ***blabbed*** *for hours.* (***chatter***, ***gossip***, ***jabber***, ***prattle***)
2 to tell or reveal without thinking (***betray***, ***give away***, ***let out***, ***let slip***, ***spill***)
Verb forms: I **blabbed**, I have **blabbed**, I am **blabbing**

black
adjective **1** completely dark, or without colour and brightness: *a* ***black*** *night* | *a* ***black*** *dress* (***dark***, ***ebony***, ***inky***, ***jet-black***, ***pitch-black***)
2 having dark-coloured skin
3 sad or gloomy: *It was a* ***black*** *day for the children when their dog died.*
4 angry: *He gave me a* ***black*** *look.*
5 evil or wicked: *Murder is a* ***black*** *deed.*
6 without milk or cream: *I have my coffee* ***black***.
noun **7** a black colour
8 someone who has dark-coloured skin
verb **9** to make black or put black on: *to* ***black*** *your shoes*
phrase **10 be in someone's black books**, to be out of favour with someone
11 black out,
a to hide news or something similar from the public
b to lose consciousness
12 in the black, in credit or not owing money to anyone
Word history: Old English *blæc*

blackball
verb **1** to keep out of a group, club, etc.
2 to vote against
noun **3** a negative vote

black ban
noun Australian a refusal by a group, as of producers, trade unions, buyers, etc., to supply or buy goods or services

blackberry
noun a prickly plant which grows in tangled bushes or its small, sweet, black or purple fruit
Noun forms: The plural is **blackberries**.

blackbird
noun a European songbird of the thrush family, now introduced into Australia

blackboard
noun a smooth dark board, used for writing or drawing on with chalk

black box
noun a unit, not always coloured black, for storing and protecting electronic equipment, especially equipment which automatically records information about the journey of a plane or train and which may be looked at after a crash

blackbutt
noun a type of Australian gum tree with dark bark at the base of the trunk

blackcurrant
noun a small black fruit which grows on a shrub

blacken
verb **1** to darken or make black: *to* ***blacken*** *his face*
2 to say bad or unpleasant things about: *to* ***blacken*** *a person's reputation*

black eye
noun bruising round the eye, resulting from a blow, etc.

blackguard (blag-ahd)
noun Old-fashioned a dishonourable man

blackhead
noun a small, black-tipped pimple, usually on your face

black hole
noun a region thought to arise from the collapse of a star under its own gravity and from which no radiation or matter can escape

black ice
noun a thin, barely visible coating of newly formed ice, as on a road

blackjack
noun **1** in the past, a large cup or jug for beer, etc., originally made of leather covered with tar
2 the black flag of a pirate ship
3 → **pontoon**^{2}

blackleg
noun **1** → **scab** (definition 2)
2 a cheat, especially in racing or gambling
3 *Veterinary Science* an infectious, usually fatal disease of cattle and sheep with painful swellings in the leg
Word building: **blackleg** *verb* (**blacklegged**, **blacklegging**)

blacklist
noun **1** a list of people, groups, etc., considered fit for punishment, disapproval, or exclusion
verb **2** to put on a blacklist
Word building: **blacklisted** *adjective*

black magic
noun magic used for evil purposes

blackmail
noun the act of demanding money from someone by threatening to reveal secrets about them (***bribe***, ***coerce***, ***extort***, ***hold to ransom***)
Word building: **blackmail** *verb* **blackmailer** *noun*
Word history: *black* + *mail* coin, rent (Middle English, from Old French)

black market
noun an illegal market which does not keep to price controls, rationing, etc.
Word building: **black marketeer** *noun*

blackout
noun **1** an electrical power failure
2 a loss of memory, consciousness or sight which lasts for a short time

black prince
noun Colloquial a large Australian cicada coloured black with some green markings on its back

black sheep
noun someone thought to be a disappointment or failure, compared to the other members of their family or other group

blacksmith
noun someone who makes or repairs things made of iron

Word history: *black* (in reference to iron or black metal) + *smith*

black spot
noun any of various fungal infections of plants, particularly of roses, that cause black spots on the leaves

bladder
noun **1** the part of your body which stores urine until it is passed out
2 any bag that gets bigger if you fill it with air or liquid, like the rubber bag inside a football

Word history: Old English *blædre* bladder, blister

blade
noun **1** the flat cutting part of a knife, sword or dagger
2 the leaf of a plant: *a* ***blade*** *of grass*
3 the thin flat part of something, like an oar or a bone
4 blades, *Colloquial* rollerblades
verb **5** *Colloquial* to rollerblade

Word history: Old English

blame
noun **1** the responsibility for a mistake: *He shares the* ***blame*** *for the accident.*
verb **2** to place blame on

Word building: **blameless** *adjective* **blameworthy** *adjective*
Word history: Middle English, from Old French from Late Latin word meaning 'blaspheme'

blanch (blanch, blahnch)
verb **1** to make white by removing colour
2 to put in boiling water for a very short time, in order to preserve colour, remove skins, etc.: *to* ***blanch*** *vegetables, meat and nuts*
3 to become pale, from sickness, fear or something like this
4 *Horticulture* to make white or prevent from becoming green by keeping out light

Word history: Middle English, from Old French *blanc* white

blancmange (bluh-monzh, bluh-monj)
noun a sweet, jelly-like dessert made with thickened and flavoured milk

Word history: Middle English, from Old French word literally meaning 'white food'

bland
adjective **1** pleasant or polite but often without real feeling: *a* ***bland*** *smile*
2 smooth and mild: ***bland*** *food* (***flat***, ***insipid***, ***plain***, ***tasteless***)

Word history: Latin

blandish
verb to flatter or please with admiring words or actions

Word building: **blandishment** *noun*
Word history: Middle English, from Latin word meaning 'flatter'

blank
adjective **1** not written or printed on: *a* ***blank*** *piece of paper* (***clear***, ***unmarked***, ***vacant***, ***void***)
2 showing no understanding or interest: *He had a* ***blank*** *look on his face.*
noun **3** an empty space left for someone to fill in: *Just fill in the* ***blanks*** *on this form please.*
4 a gun cartridge which has powder inside it but no bullet: *The army uses* ***blanks*** *for its practice shooting.*
phrase **5 draw a blank**, to be unsuccessful, especially when looking for someone or something, or trying to find out about something: *I've* ***drawn a blank*** *on finding out her name for you.*

Word history: Middle English, from Old French *blanc* white, from Germanic

blanket
noun **1** a large piece of soft woollen or cotton material, used as a bed covering
2 any layer or covering that hides something: *There was a* ***blanket*** *of snow covering the ground.*

Word building: **blanket** *verb* (**blanketed**, **blanketing**)
Word history: Middle English, from Old French *blanc* white, with reference to the undyed woollen cloth used for clothes and bed coverings

blare (blair)
verb **1** to make a loud harsh sound: *The car horns* ***blared.***
noun **2** any loud noise: *the* ***blare*** *of traffic*

Word history: Middle English, from Middle Dutch

blasé (blah-zay, blah-zay)
adjective not caring about and bored by the enjoyments and pleasures of life (***apathetic***, ***indifferent***, ***uninterested***, ***world-weary***)

Word use: The opposite of this is **excited** or **enthusiastic**.
Word history: from French word meaning 'exhausted', 'satiated'

blaspheme (blas-feem)
verb to speak without respect about God or sacred things

Word building: **blasphemous** (blas-fuh-muhs) *adjective* **blasphemy** (blas-fuh-mee) *noun*
Word history: Late Latin, from Greek word meaning 'speak ill'

blast
noun **1** a sudden strong gust of wind or air
2 the shrill sound of a whistle or horn
3 an explosion
4 *Colloquial* a severe criticism: *The teacher gave him a* ***blast*** *for being late.*
verb **5** to set off explosives
6 *Colloquial* to criticise: *Her mother* ***blasted*** *her for being rude.*

Word history: Old English *blæst*

blast furnace
noun a furnace which uses a forced blast of air to produce molten iron which may be made into other forms of iron or steel

blatant (blay-tuhnt)
adjective very obvious: *a **blatant** lie*

Word history: coined by English poet Edmund Spenser (c. 1552–99)

blaze[1]
noun **1** a bright flame or fire
2 a gleam or glow of brightness: *a sudden **blaze** of sunlight*
3 a bright or sparkling display: *The garden was a **blaze** of colour.*
4 sudden fury: *a **blaze** of temper*
verb **5** to burn brightly: *The fire **blazed** in the fireplace.*
6 to shine or glow like a flame: *The oval **blazed** with lights during the match.* (***beam**, **burn**, **flare**, **sparkle***)

Word history: Old English *blase* torch, flame

blaze[2]
noun **1** a white patch on the face of a horse or cow
2 a mark made on a tree to point out a path
verb **3** to mark a path with blazes: *The scouts **blazed** a trail through the bush.*

Word history: Low German *bläse* a white mark on the head of a horse or steer

blazer
noun a jacket, sometimes with a crest sewn on the pocket

bleach
verb **1** to make white, pale or colourless: *My mother **bleached** the stains out of my dress.*
noun **2** a chemical used for bleaching

Word history: Old English *blæcean*

bleak
adjective **1** cold and harsh: *A **bleak** winter wind was blowing.* (***chill**, **chilly**, **glacial**, **raw***)
2 empty and dreary: *A prisoner in jail has a **bleak** life.* (***cheerless**, **cloudy**, **depressing**, **dismal**, **grey***)

Word history: Middle English *bleke* pale, from Old English

bleary
adjective dimmed from tears or tiredness: ***bleary** eyes*

Adjective forms: **blearier, bleariest**
Word building: **blearily** *adverb*
Word history: Middle English; origin uncertain

bleat
verb **1** to make the cry of a sheep or goat
2 to complain

Word building: **bleat** *noun*
Word history: Old English *blætan*

bleed
verb **1** to lose blood
2 to draw or drain blood, liquid or air from: *to **bleed** the brakes of a car*
3 to get money from someone by using force, threats or some other illegal means: *to **bleed** someone dry*

Verb forms: I **bled**, I have **bled**, I am **bleeding**
Word building: **bleeding** *noun*
Word history: Old English *blōd* blood

blemish
verb **1** to spoil or tarnish the perfection of: *to **blemish** her good reputation* (***blot**, **mar**, **stain**, **taint***)
noun **2** a spot, stain or other defect: *a **blemish** on your skin | a **blemish** on the skin of the peach*

Word history: Middle English, from Old French word meaning 'make livid'

blend
verb to mix or combine: *He **blended** the flour and water. | The flour and water **blended** well.* (***amalgamate**, **assemble**, **fuse**, **join**, **merge***)

Word building: **blend** *noun*
Word history: Old English

blender
noun an electric appliance which chops and mixes food

bless
verb **1** to make sacred: *The bishop **blessed** the church.* (***consecrate**, **sanctify***)
2 to give good things to: *to **bless** our country with peace*
3 in the Christian church, to make the sign of the cross over

Verb forms: I **blessed** or I **blest**, I have **blessed** or I have **blest**, I am **blessing**
Word history: Old English word meaning 'consecrate' (originally with blood), from *blōd* blood

blessed (bles-uhd, blest)
adjective **1** holy or sacred: *a **blessed** sacrament* (***hallowed**, **religious**, **saintly***)
2 happy or fortunate: *He led a happy life **blessed** with four lovely children.*

Word use: We usually say 'bles-uhd' when this word comes before the noun and 'blest' when it comes after the noun.
Word building: **blessedness** *noun*

blessings
plural noun good things given by God: ***blessings** from heaven*

blew (blooh)
verb past tense of **blow**

> **blew / blue**
> Don't confuse **blew** with **blue**, which is a colour.

blight
noun **1** a plant disease: *tomato **blight***
2 something that damages or destroys
verb **3** to destroy, ruin or frustrate: *The rain came this morning to **blight** our picnic.*

blind
adjective **1** not able to see
2 unwilling to understand or be fair: *He was **blind** with anger.*
verb **3** to make unable to see
noun **4** a window cover which keeps out light
5 a cover for hiding the truth

Word building: **blindly** *adverb* **blindness** *noun*
Word history: Old English

blindfold
verb **1** to cover the eyes of, to prevent from seeing: *His captors **blindfolded** him.*
noun **2** a cover for the eyes: *We wear a **blindfold** for this game.*

Word history: *blind* + *fold* wrap up

blindside
verb **1** *Football* to manoeuvre a player into a position where their view of an approaching opponent is obstructed
2 to catch unawares with an unforeseen decision or strategy: *Drivers* ***blindsided*** *by the council's sudden change to parking regulations complained bitterly about their fines.*

Verb forms: I **blindsided**, I am **blindsiding**

bling
noun showy jewellery, especially when worn in large quantity

Word use: You can also use **bling-bling.**
Word history: US English. It first became popular through its use in rap music, including in the 1999 song *Bling Bling* by US rap singer BG.

blink
verb **1** to shut and open the eyes quickly and often: *I* ***blinked*** *in the bright sunlight.*
2 to shine or twinkle: *The lights of the city are* ***blinking*** *in the distance.*
noun **3** a blinking of the eye
4 a gleam or glimmer
phrase **5 on the blink,** *Colloquial* not working properly

Word history: from Middle English word meaning 'blench' (to flinch)

blinker
noun **1** one of a set of flashing lights on a vehicle used to indicate a change of direction, such as turning a corner or changing lanes (***indicator***)
2 blinkers, a pair of flaps on a bridle to prevent a horse from seeing sideways

bliss
noun great happiness

Word building: **blissful** *adjective* **blissfully** *adverb*
Word history: Old English *blīthe* blithe

blister
noun **1** a small watery swelling on your skin
verb **2** to cause blisters on: *The hot sun* ***blistered*** *my bare shoulders.*
3 to get blisters: *My shoulders* ***blistered*** *at the beach.*

Word building: **blistery** *adjective*
Word history: Middle English, probably from Old French word meaning 'clod', 'lump'

blithe
adjective *Old-fashioned* happy or cheerful (***glad, gleeful, jolly, joyful, merry***)

Word history: Old English *blīthe* kind, joyous

blitz
noun a sudden attack: *a* ***blitz*** *on a city in wartime | a* ***blitz*** *on drivers who drink* (***ambush, assault, foray, onslaught***)

Word history: from German word meaning 'lightning'

blizzard
noun a snowstorm with strong winds

Word history: variant of dialect *blizzer* blaze, flash, blinding flash of lightning

bloated
adjective swollen: *a* ***bloated*** *stomach | the* ***bloated*** *bodies of dead animals | to feel* ***bloated*** *after eating too much*

Word building: **bloat** *verb*
Word history: Middle English *blout* puffy, from Scandinavian

bloc
noun a group of countries sharing the same political ideas: *a trading* ***bloc***

Word history: French

block
noun **1** a solid piece of hard material: *a child's building* ***block***
2 *Australian* a piece of land on which a house is built
3 a group of buildings or houses surrounded by streets
4 an amount or part thought of or dealt with at one time: *a* ***block*** *of tickets*
verb **5** to be in the way of: *The accident* ***blocked*** *the traffic.* (***bar, barricade, blockade, hinder, obstruct***)
phrase **6 lose** (or **do**) **your block,** *Colloquial* to become very angry

Word building: **blockage** *noun*
Word history: Middle English, apparently from Old French *bloc* block, mass, from Germanic

blockade
noun **1** the shutting off of a place, especially a port or harbour, by enemy ships or soldiers to stop supplies going in or out (***barricade, siege***)
2 a similar barricading of a place carried out by any group, usually as a form of protest

Word building: **blockade** *verb*

blockbuster
noun **1** an aerial bomb containing high explosives used in World War II to destroy large areas
2 *Colloquial* anything large and exciting, such as a lavish theatrical production, successful political campaign, etc.

blockout
noun → **sunscreen** (definition 1)

Word history: Trademark

blog
noun **1** a record of items of interest found on the internet, presented as a website with comments and links
2 a personal diary published on the internet
3 an online forum

Word building: **blogger** *noun*
Word history: a shortened form of the term *web log*, made up of *web*, meaning the World Wide Web or the internet, and *log*, meaning the daily record of a voyage or flight kept by the captain of a ship or plane

bloke
noun *Colloquial* a man

blond
adjective **1** having light-coloured hair and skin
noun **2** a blond person

Word building: **blonde** *noun*
Word history: French, from Medieval Latin *blondus* yellow

The spelling **blonde** (usually a noun) refers to females with fair hair and was originally taken from the French who add an 'e' to some words when they refer to women:

I saw a blonde drive away from the accident.

(continued)

blonde *(continued)*

Nowadays there is a trend towards using the spelling **blond** (as a noun) to refer to men and women but you will still see the 'e' spelling used for women.

blood
noun **1** the fluid that flows through the arteries and veins of your body
2 responsibility for a person's death: *He has **blood** on his hands.*
3 your temper or state of mind: *person of hot **blood***
4 descent from the same ancestors: *related by **blood***
phrase **5 in cold blood**, calmly and without feeling

Word history: Old English *blōd*

blood bank
noun a place where blood is stored, for use in blood transfusions in operations or at the scene of an accident, etc.

bloodbath
noun the cruel killing of a large number of people (***carnage, extermination, massacre, slaughter***)

blood count
noun a count of the number of red or white blood cells in a certain volume of blood

bloodcurdling
adjective very frightening and horrible: *a **bloodcurdling** tale of evil and murder*

blood group
noun one of several sections into which blood may be grouped according to its clotting reactions

Word use: You can also use **blood type**.

bloodhound
noun a large dog with a good sense of smell, used for hunting animals or finding lost people

blood pressure
noun the pressure of blood against the inner walls of blood vessels

bloodshed
noun slaughter or the taking of life

bloodshot
adjective showing streaks of blood: ***bloodshot** eyes*

bloodstream
noun the blood flowing through the circulatory system

blood sugar
noun glucose in the blood

Word use: You can also use **blood glucose**.

bloodthirsty
adjective wanting to kill: *The **bloodthirsty** pirates took no prisoners.* (***brutal, cruel, murderous, savage***)

blood type
noun → **blood group**

blood vessel
noun any of the vessels in the body (arteries, veins, capillaries) through which blood circulates

bloody
adjective **1** with blood on it: *a **bloody** nose*
2 causing loss of life: *a **bloody** battle*
3 *Colloquial* very great: *a **bloody** pest* | *a **bloody** miracle*

Adjective forms: **bloodier, bloodiest**
Word use: The use of this word as in definition 3 might offend people.
Word history: Old English *blōdig*

bloom
verb **1** to produce flowers: *The rose bush **blooms** in summer.* (***blossom, bud, flower***)
noun **2** a flower

Word history: Middle English, from Scandinavian

bloomers
plural noun Old-fashioned **1** loose underpants, worn by women
2 women's sports briefs worn over underwear and under a skirt

Word history: named after a Mrs Amelia *Bloomer* of New York, about 1850

blossom
noun **1** the flower of a fruit tree
verb **2** to produce flowers
3 to develop: *He **blossomed** into a fine athlete.* (***bloom, flower, flourish, mature, progress***)

blot
noun **1** a spot of ink on paper
2 a blemish on someone's character or reputation
verb **3** to dry or soak up: *to **blot** the ink*
phrase **4 blot out**, to take away: *to **blot out** a bad memory*

Verb forms: I **blotted**, I have **blotted**, I am **blotting**
Word history: Old English *blōs(t)m(a)* flower

blotch
noun a large, unevenly shaped mark

Word building: **blotchy** *adjective* (**blotchier, blotchiest**)
Word history: blend of *blot* and *botch*

blouse (blowz)
noun a loosely fitting shirt usually gathered, or tucked in, at the waist

Word history: French, probably from Provençal *(lano) blouso* short (wool)

blow[1]
noun **1** a hard stroke with the hand or something held in it
2 a sudden shock or disappointment: *a **blow** to your pride* | *Her resignation was a **blow** to her employers.* (***affliction, calamity, reverse, setback, upset***)
phrase **3 come to blows**, to start a fight

Word history: northern Middle English *blaw*

blow[2]
verb **1** to be in motion: *The winds **blow**.*
2 to be moved by the wind: *Dust **blew** down the street.*
3 to produce a current of air, with bellows or your mouth: ***Blow** on the fire.* (***heave, pant, puff, wheeze***)
4 to make a noise by blowing into: ***Blow** the whistle.*
5 to burn out or burst: *The light bulb has **blown**.* | *The tyre **blew**.*

6 to put out with a puff of air: ***Blow** out the candle.*
noun **7** a storm with strong wind
phrase **8 blow in**, *Colloquial* to drop in or make an unexpected visit to: *His friend **blew in** to see him.* (***call**, **drop in**, **look in**, **stop by***)
9 blow out, *Economics* to go beyond the limits of your budget
10 blow over,
a to cease: *The storm has **blown over** now.*
b to be forgotten: *I'll tell him when the row has **blown over**.*
11 blow up,
a to force air into: *to **blow up** a balloon*
b to destroy with explosives: *to **blow up** a bridge*
c to come into being: *The storm **blew up** suddenly.*

Verb forms: I **blew**, I have **blown**, I am **blowing**
Word history: Old English *blāwan*

blowfly
noun a fly which lays its eggs on meat and rubbish

Noun forms: The plural is **blowflies**.

blowhole
noun **1** an opening for letting out air or gas
2 either of two nostrils in the head of whales through which they breathe
3 a hole in the ice to which whales or seals come to breathe
4 a hole in the coastal rock formation up through which sea water is forced violently by tide or wave

blowlamp
noun a small portable apparatus which gives a hot flame by forcing kerosene under pressure through a small nozzle and burning it in air

blowout
noun **1** the bursting of a car tyre
2 the burning out of an electrical fuse
3 a sudden or violent escape of air, steam, oil or gas from a well, or the like
4 an excess on the limits of a budget

Word use: You can also use **blow-out**.

blow-up
noun **1** an explosion or other violent happening
2 an outburst of temper
3 *Photography* an enlargement

blubber
noun **1** the fat of a whale or similar sea animal
verb **2** to cry noisily (***bawl**, **sob**, **wail**, **weep***)

Word history: Middle English; apparently imitative

bludge
verb Australian, NZ Colloquial **1** to avoid doing what you should: *While others worked, he **bludged**.* (***idle**, **loaf**, **loll**, **not pull your weight**, **rest***)
phrase **2 bludge on**, to take unfair advantage of others

Word building: **bludger** *noun*
Word history: British underworld slang of the late 1800s *bludger*, which was originally a shortened form of *bludgeoner*, used to refer to a thug who used a bludgeon to bully other people and steal their money

bludgeon (bluj-uhn)
noun **1** a short heavy piece of wood used as a weapon
verb **2** to hit with a bludgeon

blue
adjective **1** having the colour of a clear sky (***aqua**, **azure**, **navy**, **sapphire***)
2 *Colloquial* sad and depressed: *I'm feeling **blue**.* (***depressed**, **despondent**, **forlorn**, **glum**, **heart-broken***)
3 obscene: *a **blue** movie*
noun **4** a blue colour
5 *Australian, NZ Colloquial* a mistake (***blunder**, **boo-boo**, **error**, **slip***)
6 *Australian, NZ Colloquial* a nickname for a red-headed person
phrase **7 out of the blue**, unexpectedly: *It arrived one afternoon **out of the blue**.*
8 true blue, loyal

Adjective forms: **bluer**, **bluest**
Word history: Middle English, from Germanic

blue / blew
Don't confuse **blue** with **blew**, which is the past tense of **blow**:
The wind blew the blue banners down.

bluebottle
noun **1** a small, blue sea animal with long tentacles which can sting you
2 a large blue and green fly

Word use: Another name for definition 1, especially in the US and Britain, is **Portuguese man-of-war**.

blue-collar
adjective belonging or having to do with industrial workers or manual labourers

Word use: Compare this with **white-collar**.
Word history: from the blue shirt traditionally worn as part of a uniform by people in such positions

blue heeler
noun a type of purebred Australian cattle dog

blueprint
noun **1** a copy of a building plan printed in white on blue paper
2 any detailed plan which can be copied at a later time

blue-ribbon
adjective **1** *Politics* having to do with an electorate that is safe, or sure to be held by a particular party
2 having to do with a prize-winner

blue-ringed octopus
noun a small octopus of eastern Australia with blue to purple bands on the tentacles and a highly poisonous bite

blues
plural noun **1** feelings of sadness: *to have the **blues***
2 a style of music, first performed by African Americans, usually sad in character and slow in tempo

Word history: short for *blue devils*

blue-tongue
noun a large Australian lizard with a broad blue tongue

bluetooth wireless technology
noun a short-range radio technology used for connecting and transferring information between devices such as mobile phones, mobile computers, or portable handheld devices, and the internet

Word use: You can also use **bluetooth**.
Word history: **Bluetooth** is a trademark. The inventor of this technology named it after *Harald Bluetooth*, a Viking king who peacefully united two Scandinavian kingdoms into a single kingdom, referring to the fact that this technology joins mobile phones, computers and other devices into a single communication network.

blue whale
noun a whale of northern and southern oceans, with yellowish underparts; the largest known mammal

bluff¹
noun a wide steep cliff

Word history: probably from Low German *blaf* flat

bluff²
verb **1** to trick by showing you aren't afraid: *She **bluffed** her way past the guard, whistling as she went.* (***deceive***, ***fool***, ***hoax***, ***kid***)
2 to pretend you aren't afraid hoping you will get your own way: *Don't take any notice of him, he's only **bluffing**.*
noun **3** a pretence of having no fear: *It was a big **bluff**.*
phrase **4 call someone's bluff**, to encourage someone to go ahead and do something they've been threatening to do when you know that they probably won't do it

blunder
noun **1** a silly mistake (***blue***, ***boo-boo***, ***error***, ***slip***)
verb **2** to make a silly mistake
3 to move or act clumsily: *I **blundered** into the cupboard.*

Word history: Middle English, from Scandinavian

blunt
adjective **1** not sharp: *a **blunt** knife*
2 plain or direct: *a **blunt** refusal* (***brusque***, ***curt***, ***frank***, ***straightforward***, ***terse***)

Word building: **bluntly** *adverb* **bluntness** *noun*
Word history: Middle English

blur
verb **1** to make unclear or confused: *Tears **blurred** my sight.*
noun **2** something that is unclear or confused: *We drove so fast the countryside was a **blur**.*

Verb forms: it **blurred**, it has **blurred**, it is **blurring**
Word building: **blurry** *adjective* (**blurrier**, **blurriest**)
Word history: probably related to *blear*

blurb
noun information about a book, CD, etc., often printed on its cover

Word history: coined by Gelett Burgess, 1866–1951, US humorist and illustrator

blurt (blert)
phrase **blurt out**, to tell suddenly or thoughtlessly: *to **blurt out** an answer* (***blab***, ***disclose***, ***reveal***, ***spill***)

Word history: probably imitative

blush
verb to become red in the face when you're embarrassed or ashamed

Word building: **blush** *noun*
Word history: Old English *blyscan* redden

bluster
verb **1** to speak or act in a noisy or violent way: *He **blustered** when he was criticised.*
2 to force by blustering: *He **blustered** his way through.*

Word building: **bluster** *noun*
Word history: Middle English, probably from Low German

blustery
adjective loud and violent: *a **blustery** wind* | *a **blustery** manner*

BMX
noun a strongly-built bicycle, good for riding in rough areas

Word use: **BMX** probably comes from *B(icycle) M(oto)cross*, with *cross* changed to *X* and pronounced as the letter 'x'.

BO
noun Colloquial body odour

boa (boh-uh)
noun **1** a type of non-venomous snake which winds round its victim to crush and kill it
2 a long, snake-shaped garment of feathers, etc., worn about the neck by women

Noun forms: The plural is **boas**.
Word history: Latin

boab (boh-ab)
noun a large tree with a very thick trunk, native to northern Australia and tropical Africa

Word use: You can also use **baobab**.

boa constrictor
noun a boa of Central and South America, up to four metres long

boar
noun a male pig

Word history: Old English *bār*

> **boar / bore / boor**
> Don't confuse these three words which sound the same but mean different things.
> A **boar** is a male pig.
> A **bore** is either a tedious and uninteresting person, or a hole made by drilling. **Bore** is also the past tense of the verb **bear**.
> A **boor** is a person who lacks manners and refinement.

board
noun **1** a flat piece of wood, cut into long thin pieces: *a floor **board***
2 a thin flat piece of wood or other material made for a special purpose: *a chess **board*** | *an ironing-**board*** | *a notice**board***
3 a group of people who are in charge of a business or organisation: *the **board** of the club* (***committee***, ***council***, ***directorate***, ***panel***)
verb **4** to get on: *to **board** a ship or bus*
5 to pay for the use of a room, or for a room and meals: *I **board** at the hotel.* (***lodge***, ***quarter***, ***room***)

phrase **6 across the board**, affecting everything or everybody concerned: *The new regulations apply* ***across the board***.
7 on board, on or in a ship, aeroplane or vehicle

Word history: Old English *bord* board, table, shield

board / bored

Don't confuse **board** with **bored**.

To be **bored** is to feel no interest in something.

Wood has been **bored** when a hole has been made through it with a drill.

boarder

noun **1** a pupil who lives at a school
2 someone who pays for meals and a room to sleep in: *Mrs Smith takes in* ***boarders***.

boarder / border

Don't confuse **boarder** with **border**, which is the edge of something, like a boundary line separating one country from another.

boarding school

noun a school where pupils live and are provided with meals

board shorts

plural noun shorts with extra-long legs, often made of quick-drying fabric, which were originally designed to protect surfers from their waxed surfboards

boast

verb **1** to speak with too much pride: *She* ***boasted*** *about her ability.* (***blow your own trumpet***, ***brag***, ***crow***, ***skite***, ***talk big***)
noun **2** something which is spoken of with pride

Word building: **boaster** *noun* **boastful** *adjective*
Word history: Middle English

boat

noun **1** a small vessel for carrying people or things over water
2 a dish shaped like a boat: *a gravy* ***boat***
phrase **3 in the same boat**, in the same situation, usually a bad one: *We're both* ***in the same boat*** *now that we've both broken our legs.*

Word history: Old English *bāt*

boater

noun a straw hat with a hard flat brim

boating

noun travelling in boats, especially for sport or pleasure: ***Boating*** *is my favourite sport.*

boat people

plural noun people who decide to leave South-East Asian countries, setting out for Australia or other countries in boats

boatswain (<u>boh</u>-suhn)

noun an officer on a ship in charge of a deck crew and equipment

Word use: You can also use **bo's'n** or **bosun**.
Word history: Old English *bātswegen* boatman

bob[1]

noun **1** a short quick movement: *a* ***bob*** *of the head*
verb **2** to make a short quick movement up and down: *The float* ***bobbed*** *in the water.*
phrase **3 bob up**, to come into sight suddenly: *He* ***bobbed up*** *from behind the tree.*

Verb forms: it **bobbed**, it has **bobbed**, it is **bobbing**
Word history: Middle English

bob[2]

noun **1** a short haircut for women and children
verb **2** to cut short: *He* ***bobbed*** *the horse's tail.*

Verb forms: I **bobbed**, I have **bobbed**, I am **bobbing**
Word history: from Middle English word meaning 'bunch', 'cluster', 'knob'

bobbin

noun a small reel on which thread is wound for use in a sewing machine or in spinning

Word history: from French word meaning 'wind up'

bobby pin

noun a metal hairpin which closes tightly on itself to hold the hair

bocconcini (bok-uhn-<u>chee</u>-nee)

noun a small, round, fresh cheese with soft, white curd

bodice (<u>bod</u>-uhs)

noun the part of a woman's dress above the waist

Word history: variant of *bodies*, plural of *body*

bodkin (<u>bod</u>-kuhn)

noun **1** a small, pointed instrument for making holes in cloth, etc.
2 a blunt needle for drawing cord, etc., through a hem, etc.
3 a long hairpin

Word history: from Middle English word meaning 'dagger'

body

noun **1** the whole physical structure of a person or animal
2 the physical part of a person or animal without the head, arms or legs (***torso***, ***trunk***)
3 a dead person or animal (***cadaver***, ***carcass***, ***corpse***, ***remains***)
4 the main part: *the* ***body*** *of a car | the* ***body*** *of the speech*
5 a group of people or things: *a* ***body*** *of friends*

Noun forms: The plural is **bodies**.
Word history: Old English *bodig*

body art

noun the artistic modification of the body by piercing, tattooing, scarring or painting

bodyguard

noun a person or a group of people acting as a personal guard for a high official, etc.

body image

noun the picture that a person has in their mind of their own body, particularly in relation to whether they see themselves as fat or thin, good-looking or not

body language

noun communication with others through movements of your body and through your facial expressions rather than with words

body mass index
noun a measure of body mass that is calculated by weight in kilograms divided by height in metres squared. It is used to estimate the total amount of body fat in relation to health risk.

Word use: The abbreviation is **BMI**.

body politic
noun the people of a nation considered as forming a single political body under an organised government

bodysurfing
noun the sport of swimming in the surf, and especially of riding waves, by holding the body stiff, usually with the arms outstretched, and allowing yourself to be carried along by the force of the water

Word building: **bodysurf** *verb* **bodysurfer** *noun*

bog
noun **1** an area of muddy ground (***lake***, ***marsh***, ***mire***, ***quagmire***)
verb **2** to make or become stuck: *The mud* ***bogged*** *the car. | The car was* ***bogged*** *in the mud.*

Verb forms: it **bogged**, it has **bogged**, it is **bogging**
Word building: **boggy** *adjective* (**boggier**, **boggiest**)
Word history: from Irish or Gaelic word meaning 'soft'

bogey[1] (<u>boh</u>-gee)
noun Golf a score of one over par

Noun forms: The plural is **bogeys**.
Word history: from *The Bogey Man*, a popular song of about 1908, thought of as a feared and invincible opponent

bogey[2] (<u>boh</u>-gee)
noun Australian **1** a swim
2 a swimming hole

Word use: You can also use **bogie**.
Word history: from Dharug, an Australian Aboriginal language spoken by the people living near Sydney Cove in the early days of European settlement

boggle
verb to show fear or surprise

Verb forms: I **boggled**, I have **boggled**, I am **boggling**
Word history: variant of *bug* bugbear

bogie (<u>boh</u>-gee)
noun **1** a small trolley used by workers on a railway line
2 a set of wheels supporting a railway engine or carriage

Word history: perhaps variant of *bogy*

bogong moth (<u>boh</u>-gong moth)
noun a large, dull-coloured, Australian moth

Word history: from Ngarigo, an Australian Aboriginal language of the Snowy Mountains region, in which *bugong* means 'high plains'

bogus (<u>boh</u>-guhs)
adjective not real or true: *The* ***bogus*** *doctor was arrested by the police.* (***counterfeit***, ***false***, ***phoney***, ***sham***)

Word use: The opposite of this is **genuine**.

bogy (<u>boh</u>-gee)
noun anything that frightens or worries you

Noun forms: The plural is **bogies**.
Word history: from obsolete *bog*

bohemian (boh-<u>hee</u>-mee-uhn)
noun **1** a person, especially an artist or a writer, who lives and acts without regard for convention
adjective **2** having to do with or typical of bohemians (***alternative***, ***nonconformist***, ***radical***, ***unconventional***)

Word building: **bohemianism** *noun*

boil[1]
verb **1** to cause to become so hot that bubbles form and steam comes off: *I* ***boiled*** *water for tea.*
2 to become as hot as that: *The water* ***boiled***.
3 to hold, or be in, a boiling liquid: *The kettle is* ***boiling***. | *The peas are* ***boiling***.
4 to cook by boiling: *I* ***boiled*** *the potatoes.* (***braise***, ***coddle***, ***poach***, ***simmer***, ***stew***)
phrase **5 boil down**,
a to reduce or make less by boiling: *to* ***boil down*** *a liquid*
b to shorten an account or an explanation and only leave the most important parts
6 boil down to, to have as the most important part: *The situation* ***boils down to*** *the fact that I don't really like her.*
7 boil over,
a to overflow while boiling
b to be unable to control strong feelings of anger, excitement, etc.

Word history: Middle English, from Latin

boil[2]
noun an infected, swollen sore under your skin

Word history: Old English *bȳl*

boiler
noun **1** a container with a lid used for boiling things
2 a closed container in which steam is produced to drive engines

boiler suit
noun overalls with sleeves, used when doing hard dirty work

boiling point
noun **1** the temperature at which a liquid boils at a given pressure
2 a high state of excitement or emotion

boisterous
adjective rough and noisy: *a* ***boisterous*** *welcome* | *a* ***boisterous*** *crowd of friends*

Word history: Middle English

bok choy
noun a vegetable with long green leaves and thick, pale stems

bold
adjective **1** without fear (***brave***, ***courageous***, ***fearless***, ***heroic***, ***valiant***)
2 having no shame or modesty (***brazen***, ***forward***, ***fresh***, ***pert***, ***unashamed***)
3 rude
4 easy to see: ***bold*** *handwriting*

Word building: **boldly** *adverb* **boldness** *noun* **embolden** *verb*
Word history: Old English *b(e)ald*

bolder
adjective comparative of **bold**

bolder / boulder
Don't confuse **bolder** with **boulder**, which is a large smooth rock.

bolster (<u>bohl</u>-stuh)
noun **1** a long round pillow
2 a support: *a* ***bolster*** *to your courage*
verb **3** to help make strong: *Success* ***bolstered*** *his shattered pride.*

Word history: Old English *bolster*

bolt
noun **1** a sliding bar which fastens a door or gate
2 a thick metal pin which holds pieces of wood or metal together
verb **3** to fasten with a bolt
4 to run away because you are afraid: *They* ***bolted*** *when they saw the police.*
phrase **5 a bolt of lightning**, a flash in the sky, with thunder
6 bolt out of (or **from**) **the blue**, something that happens suddenly and when you least expect it
7 bolt upright, stiffly and completely upright or erect

Word use: You can also use **thunderbolt** for definition 5.
Word history: Old English

bomb
noun **1** a container filled with an explosive and used as a weapon
2 *Australian, NZ Colloquial* an old car
verb **3** to attack with bombs
phrase **4 go like a bomb**, *Colloquial* to go very fast or with a lot of success: *The vine I planted is* ***going like a bomb.***

Word history: French, from Italian, from Latin word meaning 'booming sound', from Greek

bombard
verb **1** to attack with heavy guns or bombs: *to* ***bombard*** *the city*
2 *Physics* to point a stream of high-speed particles towards
3 to keep on attacking: *to* ***bombard*** *a politician with questions*

Word building: **bombardment** *noun*
Word history: Middle English, from Old French word meaning 'cannon', from Latin word meaning 'loud noise'

bombast
noun words or remarks that sound important but are often not sincere: *His speech was full of* ***bombast.***

Word building: **bombastic** *adjective*
Word history: French, from Latin *bombyx* silkworm, silk, from Greek

bomber
noun **1** someone who throws or sets bombs
2 an aeroplane which carries and drops bombs

bombora (bom-<u>baw</u>-ruh)
noun a submerged reef of rocks

Word history: from an Australian Aboriginal language, perhaps from Dharug, a language spoken by the people living near Sydney Cove in the early days of European settlement

bombshell
noun **1** a bomb
2 something which causes surprise and shock: *Her marriage came as a* ***bombshell*** *to us.*

bona fide (boh-nuh <u>fuy</u>-dee)
adjective genuine or without falseness: *a* ***bona fide*** *reason for being late*

Word use: You can also use **bona-fide**.
Word history: Latin

bona fides (boh-nuh <u>fuy</u>-deez)
plural noun something that proves your genuine intention or position: *Her* ***bona fides*** *were quite acceptable to the employment agency.*

Word history: Latin

bond
noun **1** something that joins or holds together: *a* ***bond*** *of friendship*
2 a promise or agreement: *to sign a* ***bond*** *to work for the government*
3 a certificate of government debt to an individual, usually at a fixed rate of interest
4 *Chemistry* any connection between the atoms making up any molecule, or between the atoms and molecules in any substance
verb **5** to join or hold together: *to* ***bond*** *with glue*

Word history: Middle English

bondage
noun the state of being controlled by someone or something (***captivity***, ***slavery***, ***subjection***, ***subjugation***)

bond money
noun money additional to rent which a person pays when first renting a property and which is held as security against damage or failure to pay rent

bone
noun **1** one of the separate pieces of hard tissue that form a skeleton: *a hip* ***bone***
verb **2** to take out the bones of: *to* ***bone*** *a fish*
phrase **3 bare bones**, the most important parts or facts presented in their simplest form: *the* ***bare bones*** *of an argument*
4 bone of contention, something which causes people to disagree: *My allowance is a* ***bone of contention*** *between my parents and myself.*
5 bone up on, *Colloquial* to study hard or get information about
6 feel in your bones, to have a strong feeling about something without knowing why
7 have a bone to pick, to have something to argue about
8 make no bones about, to be open or honest about: *to* ***make no bones about*** *an illness*
9 point the bone at,
a in tribal Aboriginal culture, to cause a guilty person to lose the will to live by pointing a bone at them
b *Australian Colloquial* to wish bad luck upon

Word building: **bony** *adjective* (**bonier**, **boniest**)
Word history: Old English *bān*

bonfire
noun a large outdoor fire

Word history: earlier *bonefire*; heaps of wood and bones were burnt at certain old festivals

bongo
noun one of a pair of small drums, which you play by beating with your fingers
Noun forms: The plural is **bongos** or **bongoes**.
Word history: American Spanish

bonnet
noun **1** a close-fitting hat, tied under the chin: *a baby's **bonnet***
2 any other hood or protective covering, such as the metal cover over the engine of a car
Word history: Middle English, from Old French word meaning 'cap'

bonsai (bon-suy)
noun **1** the art of keeping trees and shrubs very small by cutting their roots and branches
2 a tree or shrub grown this way
Word history: Japanese *bon* bowl, pot + *sai* to plant

bonus
noun extra money paid to a worker as a reward for good work (***bounty***, ***commission***, ***dividend***, ***reward***)
Word history: from Latin word meaning 'good'

bonzer
adjective Australian, NZ Colloquial excellent or pleasing: *a **bonzer** picnic*
Word use: You can also use **bonza**.

boob (boohb)
noun Colloquial **1** a foolish person
2 a foolish mistake
verb Colloquial **3** to make a mistake (***err***, ***go wrong***, ***make a slip***, ***miscalculate***, ***trip up***)
Word use: You can also use **boo-boo**.

boobook
noun a small brownish owl with a white-spotted back and wings, found in Australia and New Zealand

booby prize
noun a prize given in fun to the worst performer in a game or competition

booby trap
noun **1** an object so placed as to fall on or trip up a person who is off guard (***lure***, ***net***, ***snare***)
2 a hidden bomb or mine placed so that it will be set off by anyone who walks on, or drives over it

boogie board (booh-gee bawd, boo-gee bawd)
noun a small flexible lightweight surfboard, usually ridden lying down
Word history: Trademark

book
noun **1** a number of pages bound together inside a cover, for writing in or for reading (***publication***, ***text***, ***tome***, ***volume***)
verb **2** to reserve or buy early: *They **booked** seats on the train. | to **book** theatre tickets*
3 to record or take the name of: *A police officer **booked** Joe for speeding.*
phrase **4 bring to book**, to demand an explanation from
5 by the book, in the correct and proper way: *We must run this meeting **by the book**.*
6 take a leaf out of someone's book, to do what someone else has already done: ***Take a leaf out of my book** and get another job.*
7 throw the book at, *Colloquial*
a to charge an offender with every offence you can think of
b to punish someone severely
Word history: Old English *bōc*

bookend
noun **1** a support placed at the end of a row of books to hold them upright
verb **2** to act as a marker at the beginning and end of a period, process, activity, etc.: *The year was **bookended** by bushfires.*

booking
noun **1** an order for rooms, tickets, etc., which you make in advance
2 an engagement to perform somewhere

bookish
adjective eager to read or study: *The athletic girls teased Jane for being **bookish**.*

bookkeeping
noun the job of keeping records of all the money earned and spent in a business
Word building: **bookkeeper** *noun*

bookmaker
noun someone who takes the bets of other people, especially at a racecourse
Word building: **bookmaking** *noun*

bookmark
noun **1** a strip of cardboard, ribbon, etc., placed between the pages of a book to mark a place
2 *Internet* a website address stored in a file by a browser for ease of future access: *I have **bookmarks** for all the chess sites I visit frequently.*
verb **3** *Internet* to store the address of (a frequently used website) in a file for ease of future access: *I'll **bookmark** that site — it seems to be quite useful.*

bookworm
noun someone who loves reading

Boolean (booh-lee-uhn)
adjective **1** having to do with Boolean algebra: ***Boolean** logic*
2 expressed or executed by means of Boolean algebra: *a **Boolean** equation*
Word history: from the name of George *Boole*, the English mathematician and logician who invented the system of logic now known as *Boolean algebra*

Boolean algebra
noun a mathematical system of representing statements in logic using operators such as 'and', 'or' and 'not', in which each element or variable has one of only two possible values, as 'true' or 'false'. Boolean algebra is used in computer science for programming and information retrieval.

Boolean operator
noun an operator (definition 3), as 'and', 'or', or 'not', used in computer programming and to phrase queries in database searches

Boolean search
noun a search of a computer database in which Boolean operators may be used

boom[1]
verb **1** to make a deep echoing noise: *His voice **boomed** in the cave.*

2 to suddenly do very well: *During the gold rush business was* ***booming****.* (**bloom**, **blossom**, ***flourish***, ***prosper***)
noun **3** a loud deep sound, like that made by waves or distant guns
4 a rapid increase in the amount of business done or in anything like this

Word history: imitative

boom[2]
noun **1** a long pole, used to keep the bottom of a sail straight
2 a movable arm that holds a microphone or floodlight above the actors in a television or film studio

Word history: from Dutch word meaning 'tree', 'beam'

boomer
noun Australian a large male kangaroo

boomerang
noun one of a number of kinds of curved sticks used as weapons, some of which return to your hand if you throw them properly

Word history: from Dharug, an Australian Aboriginal language spoken by the people living near Sydney Cove in the early days of European settlement

boon
noun a help or advantage: *The car is a* ***boon*** *now that I live so far from the city.*

Word history: Middle English, from Scandinavian

boor
noun someone who is rude or inconsiderate

Word building: **boorish** *adjective*
Word history: Dutch *boer* peasant

boor / bore / boar

Don't confuse **boor** with **bore** or **boar**.

A **bore** is either a tedious and uninteresting person, or a hole made by drilling.

Bore is also the past tense of the verb **bear**.

A **boar** is a male pig.

boost
verb **1** to lift: *He* ***boosted*** *the child onto his shoulders.* (***elevate***, ***hoist***, ***raise***)
2 to increase or improve: *The teacher's praise* ***boosted*** *the nervous boy's confidence.* (***add to***, ***augment***, ***expand***, ***heighten***, ***promote***)
noun **3** an upward push

Word history: blend of *boom* and *hoist*

booster
noun something which gives an increase, such as an electronic device that increases the voltage in a circuit, or an extra injection of a substance that increases your immunity to a particular infection

boot[1]
noun **1** a shoe which covers part of the leg
2 a separate space for baggage at the back of a car

Word history: Middle English, from Old French; of Germanic origin

boot[2]
verb to put the system that operates a computer into its memory so that the computer can be used

Word use: You can also use **boot up**.
Word history: Old English *bōt* advantage

bootee
noun a knitted shoe for a baby

bootee / booty

Don't confuse **bootee** with **booty**, which is anything taken or won.

booth
noun a small closed-in place usually made just big enough for one person: *a telephone* ***booth*** | *a ticket* ***booth*** | *a voting* ***booth***

Word history: Middle English, from Scandinavian

bootleg
adjective made illegally: *The old man went to jail for making* ***bootleg*** *whisky.*

Word history: arose from the practice of concealing illegal spirits in the leg of the boot

bootscoot
verb to dance in a linedance

Word building: **bootscooting** *noun*

booty
noun anything taken or won, especially in times of war: *The pirates shared their* ***booty*** *of gold.* (***loot***, ***pickings***, ***plunder***, ***spoils***)

Word history: late Middle English

booty / bootee

Don't confuse **booty** with **bootee**, which is a knitted shoe for a baby.

booze
noun Colloquial alcoholic drink: *They bought some* ***booze*** *for the party.*

Word history: Middle English, from Middle Dutch

border
noun **1** the edge or side of anything: *to sew a pattern around the* ***border*** (***brim***, ***brink***, ***margin***, ***outskirts***, ***rim***)
2 a boundary line that separates one country or state from another

Word building: **border** *verb*
Word history: Middle English, from Old French word meaning 'side', 'edge'; of Germanic origin

border / boarder

Don't confuse **border** with **boarder**, which is commonly a student at a boarding school.

borderline
adjective close to a limit or edge: *a* ***borderline*** *pass in the exam*

bore[1]
verb **1** to make a round hole: *to* ***bore*** *through wood*
noun **2** a deep hole drilled to reach an underground water supply

Word history: Old English *borian*

bore[2]
verb **1** to tire or weary: *She* ***bores*** *me with her complaints.*
noun **2** a dull person
Word building: **boredom** *noun* **bored** *adjective* **boring** *adjective*

bore[3]
verb past tense of **bear**[1]

bore / boar / boor
Don't confuse these three words which sound the same but mean different things.
A **bore** is either a tedious and uninteresting person, or a hole made by drilling. **Bore** is also the past tense of the verb **bear**.
A **boar** is a male pig.
A **boor** is a person who lacks manners and refinement.

bored / board
Don't confuse **bored** with **board**, which is commonly a long piece of wood.
To **board** a bus is to get on it.
Board has many other meanings.

borer
noun an insect that bores into wood

born
adjective **1** brought into being by birth: *I was* ***born*** *in Tasmania.*
verb **2** *Old-fashioned* past participle of **bear**[1]

borne (bawn)
verb past participle of **bear**[1]

boronia (buh-roh-nee-uh)
noun an Australian shrub with small pink or brown flowers
Word history: after Italian botanist Francesco *Borone*, 1769–94

borough (bu-ruh)
noun **1** in Britain, an urban community incorporated by royal charter
2 in Victoria, an area of land similar to a municipality in the other states of Australia
Word history: Old English *burg* stronghold

borrow
verb to take or get on the understanding that you have to return it: *Could I please* ***borrow*** *your pen for a moment? I've lost mine.*
Word use: Compare this with **lend** (definition 1).
Word building: **borrower** *noun*
Word history: Old English *borg* a pledge

bosom (booz-uhm)
noun someone's chest or breast, especially a woman's
Word history: Old English *bōsm*

boss
noun **1** someone who employs and directs people, or controls a business (***chief***, ***manager***, ***overseer***, ***supervisor***)
verb **2** to order around
Word history: Dutch *baas* master

bossy
adjective acting like a boss (***authoritarian***, ***autocratic***, ***dictatorial***, ***imperious***, ***overbearing***)
Adjective forms: **bossier**, **bossiest**

botanist
noun someone who studies plants

botany
noun the study of plants
Word building: **botanical** *adjective*
Word history: Medieval Latin *botanicus*, from Greek

botch
verb to spoil or bungle: *He* ***botched*** *the cake by taking it out of the oven too soon.* (***fluff***, ***fumble***, ***muck up***, ***muff***)
Word building: **botch** *noun*
Word history: Middle English *bocchen*; origin uncertain

both
adjective **1** two together: *Give* ***both*** *dates.*
pronoun **2** the one and the other: ***Both*** *had been there.*
adverb **3** equally: *He is* ***both*** *ready and willing.*
Word history: Middle English, from Scandinavian

bother
verb **1** to annoy or pester: *The flies* ***bothered*** *them so much they couldn't concentrate.* (***aggravate***, ***exasperate***, ***get on someone's nerves***, ***hassle***, ***irritate***)
2 to worry or confuse: *The maths problem* ***bothered*** *him.* (***alarm***, ***concern***, ***distress***, ***upset***)
Word building: **bothersome** *adjective*
Word history: Irish *bodhaire* meaning 'deafness', from *bodhraim* meaning 'to deafen, annoy'. Originally the nuisance was constant noise from people chattering but gradually the meaning extended to cover anything which was annoying.

bottle
noun **1** a container used for holding liquids, usually made of glass or plastic: *milk* ***bottles*** | *a* ***bottle*** *of soft drink*
verb **2** to put in a bottle: *to* ***bottle*** *fruit to make preserves*
phrase **3 bottle up**, to shut in or keep in check: *to* ***bottle up*** *your feelings*
Word history: Middle English, from Late Latin word meaning 'butt' (cask or barrel)

bottlebrush
noun an Australian shrub with brush-like flowers

bottleneck
noun a place where progress becomes slow, especially the narrow part of a road where traffic cannot flow freely

bottom
noun **1** the lowest or deepest part of anything, opposite to the top: *the* ***bottom*** *of a hill* | *the* ***bottom*** *of the sea* (***base***, ***bed***, ***floor***, ***foot***, ***foundation***)
2 the place of least honour or achievement: *the* ***bottom*** *of the class*
3 the lowest or first gear of a motor
4 the underside: *the* ***bottom*** *of an iron*
5 *Colloquial* the buttocks
6 the basic part: *the* ***bottom*** *of my heart*
adjective **7** lowest: *the* ***bottom*** *stair*
phrase **8 at bottom**, in reality
Word history: Old English *botm*

bougainvillea (boh-guhn-vil-ee-uh)
noun a tropical climbing plant with brilliantly coloured bracts, widely grown in parts of Australia

Word history: named after Louis Antoine de *Bougainville*, 1729–1811, French scientist and explorer of the Pacific

bough (bow)
noun one of the larger main branches of a tree

Word history: from Old English word meaning 'shoulder', 'bough'

> **bough / bow**
> Don't confuse **bough** with **bow**, which is the bending movement you make to indicate respect. Note that **bow** with this meaning is pronounced to rhyme with *cow*. When **bow** rhymes with *so*, it's a different word, as in *bow and arrow* or *a bow in your hair*.

bought (bawt)
verb past tense and past participle of **buy**

> **bought / brought**
> Don't confuse **bought** with **brought**, which is the past form of the verb **bring**:
> *I brought the lollies home before I ate them.*
> Remember the two r's go together, **brought** and **bring**.

boulder
noun a large smooth rock

Word history: short for *boulder stone*, Middle English *bulder-* from Scandinavian

> **boulder / bolder**
> Don't confuse **boulder** with **bolder**, which is the comparative of **bold**:
> *Frank is a bold boy in class, but Jack is bolder.*

boulevard (booh-luh-vahd)
noun a wide avenue or city street lined with trees

Word use: You can also use **boulevarde**.
Word history: French, from Middle Low German

bounce
verb **1** to strike against and return: *The ball* ***bounced*** *on the pavement.*
2 to throw against and cause to return: *He* ***bounced*** *the ball along the footpath.*
3 *Colloquial* to be returned unpaid: *His cheque* ***bounced****.*

Word building: **bounce** *noun*
Word history: Middle English word meaning 'thump', from Low German, *bums!* thump!

bouncing
adjective big, strong and healthy: *a* ***bouncing*** *baby*

bound[1]
adjective **1** tied up: *The prisoner held out his* ***bound*** *hands.*
2 fastened within a cover: *a nicely* ***bound*** *book*
3 sure: *If you don't put the bike away, it's* ***bound*** *to be stolen.*
4 having a duty, or under an obligation: *Once you've promised, you're really* ***bound*** *to help.*

Word history: past participle of *bind*

bound[2]
verb **1** to move with big steps or leaps: *to* ***bound*** *over a fence | to* ***bound*** *after a ball* (***frisk***, ***leap***, ***lollop***, ***spring***, ***vault***)
noun **2** a leap

Word history: from French word meaning 'leap', originally 'resound'

boundary
noun **1** a dividing line or limit: *the* ***boundary*** *between states | He rode around the farm's* ***boundary****.* (***border***, ***edge***, ***frontier***, ***outskirts***, ***perimeter***)
2 a hit in cricket which sends the ball beyond the boundary of the field

Noun forms: The plural is **boundaries**.

bounds
plural noun **1** boundaries or limits: *the* ***bounds*** *of space and time*
phrase **2 out of bounds**, forbidden or not to be entered

Word history: Middle English, from Late Latin

bounteous (bown-tee-uhs)
adjective plentiful or generous: *We experienced nature's* ***bounteous*** *rewards as we regarded the view spread before us.*

Word use: This word means the same as **bountiful** but is more literary or poetic.
Word building: **bounteousness** *noun*
Word history: *bounte* (earlier variant of *bounty*) + *-ous*

bountiful
adjective plentiful or generous: *The rains produced a* ***bountiful*** *harvest.* (***abundant***, ***ample***, ***bounteous***, ***copious***, ***prolific***)

Word building: **bountifully** *adverb*

bounty
noun **1** generosity
2 a reward given for a special purpose: *There was a* ***bounty*** *for the killing of wild pigs which were causing damage.*

Noun forms: The plural is **bounties**.
Word history: Middle English, from Latin word meaning 'goodness'

bouquet (booh-kay, boh-kay)
noun **1** a bunch of flowers
2 an aroma or smell which is typical of wine, brandy, etc. (***fragrance***, ***scent***)

Word use: The 't' is silent because **bouquet** came from French.
Word history: French word meaning 'bunch', 'clump of trees', from Old French word meaning 'wood'

bourbon (ber-buhn)
noun a type of whisky distilled from corn

Word history: originally the whisky produced in *Bourbon* County, Kentucky

bourgeois (boouh-zhwah, booh-zhwah)
noun **1** a member of the middle class, the social class between the wealthy and the working class
adjective **2** belonging to or consisting of the middle class

Noun forms: The plural is **bourgeois**.
Word history: French

bourgeoisie (boohuh-zhwah-zee)
noun the middle class or the social group between the rich (upper class) and the poor (working class)
Word history: French

bout
noun **1** a contest: *a wrestling* ***bout*** (***championship, competition, game, match***)
2 a period or spell: *a* ***bout*** *of hard work | a* ***bout*** *of flu*
Word history: variant of obsolete *bought* bend, turn, from *bow*

boutique (booh-teek)
noun a small shop, especially one that sells expensive or fashionable clothes
Word history: French

bovine (boh-vuyn)
adjective having to do with the family of cud-chewing animals that includes cattle and oxen
Word history: Latin *bōs* ox

bow[1] (bow)
verb **1** to bend or stoop down: *The men* ***bowed*** *and the women curtsied to the queen.*
phrase **2 bow and scrape**, to behave like a servant
3 bow out, to retire or leave the scene: *She* ***bowed out*** *after ten years as manager.*
Word building: **bow** *noun*
Word history: Old English *būgan*

> **bow / bough**
> Don't confuse **bow** with **bough**, which is a branch of a tree.

bow[2] (boh)
noun **1** a piece of wood bent by a string stretched between its ends, which is used to shoot arrows
2 a knot, made up of two loops and two ends
3 the special stick used to play stringed instruments like the violin
Word history: Old English *boga*

bow[3] (bow)
noun the front end of a boat
Word history: Low German or Dutch

bowel
noun the long tube in your body which carries food from the stomach out of the body (***gut, intestine***)
Word use: Note that people often use the plural and speak of this tube as your **bowels**.
Word history: Middle English, from Latin *botulus* sausage

bower
noun a leafy shelter
Word history: Old English *būan* dwell

bowerbird
noun an Australian bird which makes a bower-like shelter where it keeps special objects and courts its mate

bowl[1]
noun **1** a deep round dish used for holding food or liquid
2 something shaped like a bowl: *the* ***bowl*** *of a pipe*
Word history: Middle English *bolle*, from Old English, from Icelandic *bolli*

bowl[2]
verb **1** to throw or roll: *to* ***bowl*** *a hoop along the ground*
2 to throw a cricket ball, keeping your arm straight, towards the person batting
3 to get out by bowling: *He* ***bowled*** *the opening batsman with his first ball.*
noun **4** a heavy, weighted or biased ball used in the game of bowls
Word history: Middle English *boule*, from Old French word meaning 'ball', from Latin *bulla* bubble

bowler[1]
noun a hard, felt hat with a rounded top and a narrow brim
Word history: *bowl*[1] + *-er*

bowler[2]
noun **1** someone who bowls
2 someone who plays bowls

bowls
noun **1** a game in which heavy balls are rolled across a lawn
2 a similar game, but one which is played indoors
Word use: You can also use **lawn bowls** for definition 1. | You can also use **carpet bowls** for definition 2.

bowser
noun Australian, NZ a pump at a service station for putting fuel into motor vehicles
Word history: a trademark from the name of Sylvanus *Bowser*, the US engineer who invented the self-measuring fuel pump. His company, SF Bowser & Company, then exported these pumps around the world.

box[1]
noun **1** a wooden or cardboard container with a lid
2 a small room or raised stand: *a* ***box*** *at the theatre | a witness* ***box***
verb **3** to put into a box
phrase **4 box in,**
a to build a box around
b to surround or imprison: *to be* ***boxed in*** *by the traffic* (***confine, coop up, encircle, enclose, surround***)
5 the box, *Colloquial* a television set

box[2]
verb **1** to hit with your hand or fist, especially on the ear
2 to spar or fight with your fists
Word building: **boxing** *noun*
Word history: Middle English

boxer
noun someone who fights with the fists as a sport

box jellyfish
noun a type of jellyfish found in tropical seas, the common Australian species being highly poisonous
Word use: Another name is **sea wasp**.

box office
noun the place in a theatre where tickets are sold

boy
noun a male child
Word building: **boyish** *adjective*
Word history: Middle English;

boy / buoy
Don't confuse **boy** with **buoy**, which is a marker which floats on water.

boycott
verb **1** to refuse to go to: *to* ***boycott*** *a meeting*
2 to stop buying or using: *to* ***boycott*** *the new soap powder*

Word history: from Captain Charles C *Boycott*, 1832–97, land agent for the Earl of Erne, County Mayo, Ireland, ostracised by the tenants

boyfriend
noun a male who you have a steady romantic relationship with

boysenberry (boy-zuhn-be-ree, boy-zuhn-bree)
noun a blackberry-like fruit with a flavour similar to raspberries

Noun forms: The plural is **boysenberries**.
Word history: named after R *Boysen*, US botanist

bra
noun underwear which supports the breasts

Word history: abbreviation of brassiere

brace
noun **1** something which holds parts together or in place
2 braces,
a wires placed on your teeth to help straighten them
b straps worn over your shoulders for holding up your trousers
verb **3** to steady: *He* ***braced*** *himself against the wall so that he wouldn't fall over.* (***balance***, ***fix***, ***secure***, ***stabilise***, ***support***)

Word history: Middle English *brase(n)* from Old French *bracier* embrace

bracelet (brays-luht)
noun an ornamental chain or band for wearing around your wrist

Word history: Middle English, from Latin word meaning 'arm'

brachiosaurus (brak-ee-uh-saw-ruhs)
noun a dinosaur with a very large, sloping body

bracken
noun a fern which is often found in the wetter parts of Australia

Word history: Middle English, from Scandinavian

bracket
noun **1** a support of wood, metal, etc., often in the shape of a right angle, placed under a shelf or the like
2 *Architecture* an ornamental support for a statue, etc.
3 either of two sets of signs **()** or **[]** used to group words or figures together, as in *John (the butcher's son) brought meat to our barbecue.*
4 a grouping of persons, musical items, etc.: *low income* ***bracket*** | *a* ***bracket*** *of songs*
verb **5** to furnish with or support by a bracket or brackets
6 to enclose or place within brackets
7 to classify or group together

Word history: French, from Provençal, or Spanish, from Latin word meaning 'breeches', of Celtic origin

Brackets are used in writing to include a thought or expression which may not be necessary, but which explains the topic further or adds interest to it. For example:

Perth (the capital of Western Australia) is one of Australia's cleanest cities.

My uncle (who just turned 93) used to be a top-ranking tennis player.

Commas or dashes may be used instead of brackets. In the two examples above, you could change the brackets to commas or dashes without changing the meaning. But brackets seem to separate information more than commas or dashes. Look up **comma** and **dash**.

Brackets with other punctuation
If the sentence should have a punctuation mark where the brackets are, then include it after the brackets. Otherwise, there is no need for other punctuation marks with the brackets. The example below would need a comma after *skateboard* if the brackets weren't used, so you should still include it, but put it after the closing bracket. That way you're not separating related bits from one another:

Daniel grabbed his skateboard (which he had recently painted), jammed his money into his pocket and took off with his friend.

If the words inside the brackets need punctuation of their own, just follow the normal punctuation rules:

Although my schoolbag was so brightly coloured (green with purple stripes, would you believe?), I couldn't find it in the giant pile of bags near the door.

Other types of brackets
Round brackets (or **parentheses**) are also used to enclose a number or letter which is introducing items in a list.

The apparatus needed for this experiment includes:
(a) a bunsen burner
(b) a pipette
(c) litmus paper.

Square brackets [ ] are used in writing to include something which is not meant to be read as part of the text:

'Felicity, you'll have to hurry if you're going to the party,' called Anne as she [Anne] closed the door.

If you want to use one set of brackets inside another, square brackets can be used inside round brackets to avoid confusion:

Patrick and Ben were meant to be going to the party too, but they had to mind Louis (their cousin down from Dubbo [a town in north-western NSW] for a few days) because he was too young to be left alone.

Square brackets can also be used to include additional information like:

[turn to back of book for solution]
[continued on p. 7]

Three other special types of brackets are:

braces { }
angle brackets < >
slash brackets / /.

brackish
adjective slightly salty: *The cattle wouldn't drink the* ***brackish*** *water.*

Word history: Dutch *brak* + *-ish*

bract
noun a specialised leaf or leaf-like part, usually found at the base of a flower

brag
verb to boast (***blow your own trumpet***, ***crow***, ***skite***, ***talk big***)

Verb forms: I **bragged**, I have **bragged**, I am **bragging**
Word history: Scandinavian

braggart
noun someone who is always boasting

braid
verb **1** to weave or plait
noun **2** a plait: *She wore her hair in one long* ***braid.***
3 a woven trimming: *The officer's uniform was edged with* ***braid.***

Word history: Old English *bregdan* move to and fro, weave

braille (brayl)
noun a system of printing using raised dots which people who are vision-impaired can read by touch

Word history: named after Louis *Braille*, 1809–52, its inventor

brain
noun **1** the soft, greyish mass of nerve cells inside your skull, which controls feeling, thinking and movement
2 understanding or intelligence: *He has a good* ***brain.***
3 a very clever or well-informed person: *She's a real* ***brain.***
phrase **4 pick someone's brains**, to use another person's work or ideas to do yourself good

Word use: Definition 2 is often plural as in *He has brains.* | **Cerebral** is a word meaning 'having to do with the brain'.
Word history: Old English *bregen*

brainiac (<u>bray</u>-nee-ak)
noun Colloquial a very intelligent person

Word history: **Brainiac** was the name of a fictional villain in the *Superman* comics who first appeared as a character in the 1950s.

brainstorm
noun a sudden brilliant idea

brainwash
verb to indoctrinate so intensely that beliefs, especially political, are changed (***bias***, ***condition***, ***manipulate***, ***persuade***, ***prejudice***)

Word building: **brainwashing** *noun*

brainy
adjective clever (***bright***, ***brilliant***, ***intelligent***, ***shrewd***, ***smart***)

Adjective forms: **brainier**, **brainiest**

braise
verb to fry quickly in a pan, then stew gently in a covered pot

Word history: from French word meaning 'hot charcoal'; of Germanic origin

brake
noun **1** something which slows or stops a machine
verb **2** to slow or stop

Word history: Middle English, from Middle Low German and/or Middle Dutch; similar to *break*

brake / break
Don't confuse **brake** with **break**. Look up **break**.

bramble
noun any thorny bush growing wild

Word building: **brambly** *adjective*
Word history: Old English *brōm* broom

bran
noun the outer shell of wheat or rye, sometimes used in breakfast cereal

Word history: Middle English, from Old French

branch
noun **1** the limb of a tree or shrub
2 a part or section which divides from the main part: *the* ***branch*** *of a river*
3 part of a large organisation: *the local* ***branch*** *of my bank*
verb **4** to divide or separate
phrase **5 branch out**, to develop in a new direction

Word history: Middle English, from Late Latin *branca* paw, claw

brand
noun **1** the mark or label on something which shows where it comes from or who makes it (***sticker***, ***tab***, ***tag***, ***ticket***)
2 the particular kind or make of something: *my favourite* ***brand*** *of jam*
verb **3** to mark with a brand: *to* ***brand*** *the cattle*

Word history: Old English; similar to *burn*

brandish
verb to shake or wave: *The soldiers* ***brandished*** *their swords.*

Word history: Middle English, from Old French *brand* sword; of Germanic origin

brandy
noun a strong alcoholic drink made from wine

Noun forms: The plural is **brandies.**
Word history: short for *brandywine*, from Dutch *brandewijn* burnt (that is distilled) wine

brash
adjective bold or over-confident: *The* ***brash*** *youth offended everyone with his bragging.*

Word use: The opposite of this is **self-effacing.**
Word building: **brashly** *adverb*

brass
noun **1** a yellowish metal mixed from copper and zinc
2 the group name for the trumpet and horn family of musical instruments: *The conductor brought in the strings, the woodwinds and then the* ***brass.***
adjective **3** made of brass: ***brass*** *instruments*

Word building: **braze** *verb*
Word history: Old English *bræs*

brassiere (<u>braz</u>-ee-uh, <u>bras</u>-ee-uh)
noun underwear which supports the breasts

Word use: The short form is **bra**.
Word history: French

brassy
adjective **1** made of or like brass, especially in colour: ***brassy*** *hair*
2 harsh and loud: *a* ***brassy*** *voice*
3 too bright and showy to be in good taste: *a* ***brassy*** *appearance* | ***brassy*** *behaviour*
Adjective forms: **brassier, brassiest**

brat
noun a child: *She told the woman to quieten her* ***brats****.*
Word use: This word is usually used in an unfriendly way.
Word history: compare dialect *brat* rag, trash, Old English *bratt* cloak

bravado (bruh-vah-doh)
noun bravery and confidence which is often pretended: *He was full of* ***bravado*** *until the time came for him to perform.*
Word history: Spanish. Look up **brave**.

brave
adjective **1** full of courage (***bold, courageous, fearless, heroic, valiant***)
verb **2** to meet or face with courage: *to* ***brave*** *misfortunes*
3 to dare or defy: *to* ***brave*** *the storm*
phrase **4 brave it out,** to ignore or stand up to all opposition
Word building: **bravely** *adverb* **braveness** *noun* **bravery** *noun*
Word history: French, from Italian *bravo* brave, from Spanish word meaning 'vicious' (first applied to bulls)

brawl
noun a noisy quarrel or fight (***battle, combat, conflict, fray, skirmish***)
Word building: **brawl** *verb*
Word history: Old English *brēothan* go to ruin

brawn
noun **1** well-developed muscles or muscular strength: *to be all* ***brawn*** *and no brains*
2 cooked meat, pressed in a mould and set in its own jelly, used with salads and in sandwiches
Word history: Middle English, from Old French, from Germanic

brawny
adjective strong and muscly: *a* ***brawny*** *sailor* (***hardy, husky, robust, wiry***)
Adjective forms: **brawnier, brawniest**

bray
noun the loud harsh noise a donkey makes
Word building: **bray** *verb*
Word history: Middle English, from Old French

brazen
adjective **1** made of brass
2 cheeky or rude: ***brazen*** *behaviour* (***forward, insolent, pert, saucy, unashamed***)
Word history: Old English *bræs* brass

brazier
noun a metal container for holding burning fuel and used for heating or cooking
Word history: French *braise* live coals

breach
noun **1** a failure to keep or observe: *a* ***breach*** *of promise* | *a* ***breach*** *of the law*
2 a gap or opening: *a* ***breach*** *in the line of defence*
Word building: **breach** *verb*
Word history: Middle English, from Old French, from Germanic

bread (bred)
noun **1** a food made by baking flour and water, usually with yeast to make it rise: *a loaf of* ***bread***
2 a general word for food: *to earn our daily* ***bread***
3 *Colloquial* money
Word history: Old English *brēad*

breadcrumb trail
noun Internet the information which visitors to a website leave about who they are and their patterns of behaviour, in particular their buying patterns

breadline
noun **1** a line of poor people waiting to receive free food
phrase **2 on the breadline,** living at the barest level, usually supported by public help

breadth
noun the distance from one side to the other (***span, spread, width***)
Word history: Old English *brǣdu* + *-th*

breadwinner
noun someone who earns the money to keep a family

break
verb **1** to divide into pieces violently
2 to fail to keep: *to* ***break*** *a promise*
3 to crack a bone of: *to* ***break*** *a leg*
4 to do better than: *to* ***break*** *a record in running*
5 to interrupt: *to* ***break*** *the silence*
6 to make known: *to* ***break*** *the news*
7 to change in tone: *His voice* ***broke****.*
8 to begin racing before the starting signal has been given: *Two swimmers* ***broke****.*
noun **9** a gap: *a* ***break*** *in the fence* (***crack, crevice, fissure, hole, split***)
10 an attempt to escape: *a* ***break*** *for freedom*
11 a short rest or spell: *They took a* ***break*** *from work.*
phrase **12 break away,**
a *Football* to run faster than the defending players and run towards the opposing goal
b to move and keep away from another person
13 break down,
a to collapse
b to overcome
c to stop working properly
14 break in,
a to interrupt
b to get a horse used to being handled by people
c to enter a house using force
15 break into,
a to interrupt
b to enter using force
16 break new ground, to try out a new idea or activity
17 break off,
a to separate by breaking: *to* ***break off*** *some bread* (***detach, disconnect, divide, free***)
b to put a stop to: *to* ***break off*** *an engagement* (***abolish, annul, dissolve, finish, repeal***)
c to stop suddenly: *to* ***break off*** *a conversation*

18 to break out,
a in certain diseases, to erupt on the surface of the skin: *to* ***break out*** *in a rash*
b to escape: *Two prisoners* ***broke out*** *of prison last night.*
19 break up,
a to separate or finish: *to* ***break up*** *a marriage*
b to finish a school term for the holidays
c *Colloquial* to explode into laughter (***fall about***, ***guffaw***)

Verb forms: I **broke**, I have **broken**, I am **breaking**
Word building: **breakable** *adjective*
Word history: Old English *brecan*

break / brake

Don't confuse **break** with **brake**, which is a device for stopping a wheel going round.

breakage
noun **1** the breaking of something
2 an allowance for the loss or damage of any articles that get broken

breakaway
noun **1** the act of breaking away, as of a political or similar group
2 *Rugby Union* either of two players who pack down on either side of the back row in a scrum
3 a panic rush of a mob of cattle, horses, etc.
adjective **4** having to do with something which has broken away: *a* ***breakaway*** *political party*

breakdown
noun **1** a collapse or failure: *a nervous* ***breakdown***
2 separation into simple parts: *the* ***breakdown*** *of soil*
3 an analysis: *a* ***breakdown*** *of all our accounts*

breakfast
noun **1** the first meal of the day
verb **2** to have breakfast

Word history: Middle English *brek* break + *fast* a limiting of your food

breakneck
adjective dangerous: *to drive at a* ***breakneck*** *speed*

breakthrough
noun any important new development which allows for further progress to take place: *a* ***breakthrough*** *in finding a cure for cancer*

breakwater
noun a structure built to break the force of waves, as before a harbour

bream (brim)
noun an Australian saltwater fish which is good for eating

Noun forms: The plural is **bream**.
Word history: Middle English, from Old French, of Germanic origin

breast
noun **1** a milk gland, especially of a woman, or of female animals
2 *Old-fashioned* your chest
phrase **3 make a clean breast of**, to confess something completely

Word history: Old English *brēost*

breaststroke
noun a way of swimming in which your arms move outwards and back from your chest and your legs kick in a frog-like manner

breath
noun **1** the air taken into your lungs and let out again: *short of* ***breath***
2 an act of breathing once: *Take a deep* ***breath***.
3 a light current: *A* ***breath*** *of air cooled the stuffy room.*
phrase **4 below** (or **under**) **your breath**, in a whisper
5 out of breath, finding it difficult to breathe, the way you do after strenuous exercise
6 take your breath away, to surprise or astound

Word building: **breathy** *adjective* **breathless** *adjective*
Word history: Old English *brǣth* smell, exhalation

breathalyser
noun a machine used to measure the amount of alcohol in someone's breath, used by police as a first test for drivers and administered by the side of the road

breathe
verb **1** to draw in and give out air: *We* ***breathe*** *without thinking.*
2 to speak softly: *He* ***breathed*** *a word of warning.*
3 to live or exist: *Everything that* ***breathed*** *was destroyed in the flood.*
phrase **4 breathe freely**, to relax or be freed from worry or fear

breathtaking
adjective causing excitement or pleasure: *a* ***breathtaking*** *adventure* | ***breathtaking*** *beauty* (***exhilarating***, ***rousing***, ***stimulating***, ***thrilling***)

breath test
noun a test to determine the level of alcohol in a driver's blood, which is given at a police station to someone with a positive reading on a breathalyser

Word building: **breath-test** *verb*

bred
verb past tense and past participle of **breed**

breech
noun the barrel of a gun

Word history: Old English *brēc*, plural

breeches (brich-uhz)
plural noun trousers covering the hips and thighs: *riding* ***breeches***

breed
verb **1** to produce young: *Rats were* ***breeding*** *in the garbage.* (***multiply***, ***procreate***, ***reproduce***)
2 to produce, by keeping the parents for the purpose: *He* ***breeds*** *prize bulls.*
3 to cause: *Dirt* ***breeds*** *disease.* (***create***, ***generate***, ***give rise to***, ***produce***)
noun **4** a type or kind: *a* ***breed*** *of sheep*

Verb forms: I **bred**, I have **bred**, I am **breeding**
Word history: Old English *brōd* brood

breeder
noun someone who breeds animals

breeding
noun **1** the mating and rearing of animals
2 good manners which are the result of training

breeze
noun **1** a light wind or movement of air
2 *Colloquial* an easy task: *It's a* ***breeze****.*
phrase **3 breeze along** (or **in**), to move in a relaxed way
4 breeze through, *Colloquial* to do something easily: *to* ***breeze through*** *the exams*

Word history: Spanish (and Portuguese) *briza*

breezy
adjective **1** windy
2 cheerful or sprightly: *a* ***breezy*** *greeting*

Adjective forms: **breezier, breeziest**
Word building: **breezily** *adverb* **breeziness** *noun*

brethren (<u>bredh</u>-ruhn)
plural noun *Old-fashioned* brothers

brevity (<u>brev</u>-uh-tee)
noun shortness or briefness: *the* ***brevity*** *of life* | *The* ***brevity*** *of his speech surprised us.*

Word history: Latin *brevis* short

brew
verb **1** to make or prepare by soaking, boiling, or fermenting: *Let's* ***brew*** *a pot of tea.* | *to* ***brew*** *a stronger beer*
2 to cause or bring about: *to* ***brew*** *trouble*
3 to be forming or gathering: *Trouble is* ***brewing****.*

Word building: **brew** *noun* **brewer** *noun*
Word history: Old English *brēowan*

brewery
noun a place where beer is made

Noun forms: The plural is **breweries.**

briar (<u>bruy</u>-uh)
noun a prickly bush

Word history: French word meaning 'heath', from Late Latin derivative of Gallic *brūcus* heather

bribe
noun **1** money or a gift given to someone if they promise to do something they shouldn't for you
verb **2** to give or promise a bribe to: *He tried to* ***bribe*** *the police to let him go.*

Word building: **bribery** *noun*
Word history: Middle English

bric-a-brac (<u>brik</u>-uh-brak)
noun various articles of old-fashioned, ornamental, or other interest

Word use: You can also use **bric-à-brac.**
Word history: French

brick
noun **1** a small hard block of baked clay, used for building
2 something shaped like a brick: *a* ***brick*** *of ice-cream*

Word history: Middle English, from Middle Dutch

bricklayer
noun someone whose job is to build with bricks

bride
noun a woman who is going to be married or who has just been married

Word building: **bridal** *adjective*
Word history: Old English *brȳd*

bridegroom
noun a man who is going to be married or who has just been married

Word use: The short form is **groom.**
Word history: Old English *brȳd* bride + *guma* man

bridesmaid
noun a woman who helps a bride on her wedding day

bridge[1]
noun **1** a structure built over a river, road or railway line, to provide a way of getting from one side to the other
2 a raised platform above the deck of a ship for the captain or other senior officers
3 the upper part of your nose
verb **4** to make a bridge over: *When the government* ***bridged*** *the river, ferries were no longer needed.* (***ford, span, traverse***)

Word history: Old English *brych*

bridge[2]
noun a card game for two pairs of players

bridle
noun **1** the leather straps, bit and reins fitted around the head of a horse and used to control it
verb **2** to put a bridle on
3 to react with anger or resentment: *She* ***bridled*** *at the suggestion that she was not a good driver.*

Word history: Old English *brīdel*

bridle / bridal
Don't confuse **bridle** with **bridal,** which relates to a bride or a wedding:
a bridal veil | *a bridal feast*

brief
adjective **1** short: *a* ***brief*** *visit* | *a* ***brief*** *speech* | *a* ***brief*** *skirt* (***abridged, concise, condensed***)
noun **2** an outline of information or instructions on a subject, especially for use by a barrister conducting a legal case (***argument, data, precis, summary, synopsis***)
verb **3** to instruct or show using a brief: *The solicitor's job is to* ***brief*** *the barrister.*
phrase **4 in brief,** in as few words as possible, or in a shortened form: ***In brief,*** *here is an outline of the problem.* | *the news* ***in brief***

Word building: **brevity** *noun* **briefness** *noun* **briefly** *adverb*
Word history: French, from Latin

briefcase
noun a flat rectangular case for carrying books and papers

briefing
noun a short exact summary of all the details of a plan or a mission, such as the one given to a military unit or the crew of an aircraft, before it carries out the mission

briefs
plural noun close-fitting underpants without legs

brig
noun a two-masted ship with square sails on both masts

Word history: short form of *brigantine*

brigade
noun **1** a large group of soldiers
2 a group of people trained for a special purpose: *a fire* ***brigade***

Word history: French, from Italian word meaning 'troop', from *brigare* strive, contend

brigadier
noun an army officer in charge of a brigade
Word history: French, from *brigade* a group of soldiers

brigalow
noun a type of acacia that grows in Queensland and northern New South Wales, and which has strong heavy wood used by the Aboriginal people for carving
Word history: from an Australian Aboriginal language, perhaps Kamilaroi of northern NSW

brigand (brig-uhnd)
noun one of a gang of robbers who live in mountain or forest areas (***bushranger, criminal, highwayman, thief***)
Word history: Middle English, from Old French, from Italian

bright
adjective **1** shining or giving a strong light: *a **bright** silver coin | a **bright** lamp* (***brilliant, dazzling, glaring, illuminated***)
2 clever: *a **bright** pupil* (***brainy, brilliant, intelligent, shrewd, smart***)
3 cheerful and happy: *Sad people need **bright** company.* (***blithe, glad, jolly, joyful, merry***)
Word building: **brightly** *adverb* **brightness** *noun*
Word history: Old English *brhyt, beorht*

brighten
verb to become or make bright or brighter

brilliant (bril-yuhnt)
adjective **1** shining brightly (***bright, dazzling, glaring, illuminated***)
2 extraordinarily clever: *a **brilliant** plan | a **brilliant** pianist* (***exceptional, glorious, magnificent, outstanding, superb***)
Word building: **brilliance** *noun* **brilliantly** *adverb*
Word history: French, perhaps from Latin *bēryllus* beryl

brim
noun **1** the top edge or rim of something hollow: *He filled the glass to the **brim**.* (***border, brink, margin, outskirts***)
2 the outer edge of a hat
Word history: Old English *brim* sea

brindle
adjective grey or brownish-yellow with darker streaks or spots

brine
noun strongly salted water, often used in preserving some foods
Word history: Old English *brȳne*

bring
verb **1** to carry: *I will **bring** the book.*
2 to cause to come: *The drought **brought** suffering to everyone.*
phrase **3 bring about,**
a to cause: *to **bring about** change*
b in sailing, to bring a ship onto the opposite tack or into a different position in relation to the wind
4 bring back, to remind you of: *to **bring back** memories*
5 bring down,
a to cause something to fall: *The hard tackle **brought down** the footballer. | The plane was **brought down** by the enemy fire.*
b to reduce a price
6 bring in, to introduce: *to **bring in** new ideas*
7 bring on, to cause: *Too much sun will **bring on** sunstroke.*
8 bring out,
a to encourage a timid person: *Perhaps acting will **bring** her **out**.*
b to publish: *to **bring out** a book*
9 bring round,
a to persuade someone to have the same opinion as you about something
b to bring back to consciousness
10 bring to, to bring back to consciousness
11 bring up,
a to care for during childhood
b to mention or introduce in a conversation or at a meeting
c to vomit
Verb forms: I **brought**, I have **brought**, I am **bringing**
Word history: Old English *bringan*

brink
noun the edge of a steep or dangerous place or time: *the **brink** of a cliff | on the **brink** of war* (***threshold, verge***)
Word history: Middle English, from Scandinavian

brinkmanship
noun Colloquial the practice of risking disaster, especially war, to achieve a goal

briny
adjective salty: *the **briny** sea*
Adjective forms: **brinier, briniest**

brisk
adjective fast and lively: *a **brisk** walk | a **brisk** breeze*
Word use: The opposite of this is **slow**.
Word building: **briskly** *adverb* **briskness** *noun*
Word history: perhaps similar to *brusque*

brisket
noun **1** the breast of an animal
2 the meat from this
Word history: Middle English, from Old French, from Germanic

bristle
noun **1** a short stiff hair or hairlike material: *pigs' **bristles** | the **bristles** of a brush*
verb **2** to raise the bristles: *The dog **bristled** when it saw the burglar.*
3 to show anger: *He **bristled** at the idea.*
Word building: **bristly** *adjective*
Word history: Middle English

brittle
adjective likely to break easily: ***brittle** shells* (***breakable, delicate, fragile, frail***)
Word building: **brittleness** *noun*
Word history: Old English *brēotan* break

broach
verb to ask about for the first time: *I **broached** the subject of buying a dictionary.*
Word history: Middle English, from Latin *brocc(h)us* projecting

broach / brooch

Don't confuse **broach** with **brooch**, which is an ornament made to be fastened to your clothes with a pin.

broad
adjective **1** very wide: *a* ***broad*** *river* | ***broad*** *knowledge* (***deep***, ***extensive***, ***outspread***, ***widespread***)
2 widely spread or complete: ***broad*** *daylight*
3 not detailed: *the* ***broad*** *outline of the story*
4 having a strong accent: *He speaks* ***broad*** *Australian.*
Word building: **broaden** *verb* **broadly** *adverb*
Word history: Old English *brād*

broadband
noun high-speed internet access having a bandwidth sufficient to carry multiple voice, video, and data channels simultaneously
Word history: This word, which is made up of *broad*, meaning 'wide', and *band*, meaning 'a range of radio frequencies', refers to the fact that this form of internet access uses a wide range of frequencies to transmit a large volume of information at the same time, making it very fast when downloading or sending data.

broadbased
adjective taking into account a wide range of factors: *a* ***broadbased*** *approach*

broad bean
noun an annual plant grown for its large seeds, which are used as a vegetable

broadbrush
adjective widely ranging and general in treatment: *a* ***broadbrush*** *policy outline*

broadcast
verb **1** to send by radio or television: *to* ***broadcast*** *a program*
2 to send radio or television programs: *They are* ***broadcasting*** *now.*
noun **3 a** the sending out of sound and images on radio or television
b a radio or television program
Verb forms: it **broadcast**, it has **broadcast**, it is **broadcasting**
Word building: **broadcaster** *noun*

broadleaf
noun any of various trees or shrubs having broad leaves
Word building: **broadleaf** *adjective*

broad-minded
adjective able to accept or understand other people's ideas and ways (***liberal***, ***permissive***, ***tolerant***, ***unconventional***)

broadsheet
noun **1** a sheet of paper, usually large, printed on one side only, for handing out or posting
2 a ballad, song, etc., printed, or originally printed, on a broadsheet
3 a newspaper printed on the standard sheet size of paper

broadside
noun **1** the firing of all the guns on one side of a ship
2 an abusive verbal attack on someone

brocade (bruh-kayd)
noun cloth woven with a raised pattern on it
Word building: **brocaded** *adjective*
Word history: Spanish word meaning 'interweave with gold or silver', from Latin

broccoli (brok-uh-lee, brok-uh-luy)
noun a green vegetable similar to a cauliflower
Word history: Italian, plural of *broccolo* sprout, from Latin word meaning projecting

brochure (broh-shuh, bruh-shoouh)
noun a small book with a paper cover, containing information or advertisements (***booklet***, ***circular***, ***flyer***, ***handbill***, ***pamphlet***)
Word history: from French word meaning 'stitching', with reference to little booklets that were roughly stitched together rather than properly bound

brogue[1] (brohg)
noun a broad accent, especially an Irish one
Word history: special use of *brogue*[2]

brogue[2] (brohg)
noun a strongly made, comfortable shoe
Word history: Irish, Gaelic *brōg* shoe

broil (broyl)
verb to grill or cook by direct heat
Word use: This is mostly used in the US.
Word history: Middle English, probably from Old French word meaning 'burn', from Late Latin

broke
adjective Colloquial having no money (***bankrupt***, ***destitute***, ***impecunious***, ***insolvent***, ***poor***)
Word use: This word comes from the verb **break**.

broken
verb **1** past participle of **break**
adjective **2** separated into pieces: *a* ***broken*** *plate* (***fragmented***, ***shattered***, ***smashed***)
3 not working because of the breaking of one of the parts: *a* ***broken*** *watch* | *a* ***broken*** *arm* (***damaged***)
4 not kept or obeyed: *a* ***broken*** *promise* | ***broken*** *rules*
5 imperfectly spoken: *He spoke* ***broken*** *English.*
Word use: This word comes from the verb **break**.

broker
noun **1** someone who buys or sells things for someone else: *a share* ***broker*** (***dealer***, ***merchant***, ***retailer***, ***vendor***)
verb **2** to negotiate: *to broker a deal*

brokerage
noun **1** the business of a broker
2 the sum or commission paid to a broker for any services provided

brolga
noun a large silvery-grey bird with long legs, which dances, perhaps as part of its courtship display
Word use: This name for the bird is mostly used now, instead of the old name, **native companion**.
Word history: from Kamilaroi, an Australian Aboriginal language of northern NSW

brolly
noun Colloquial umbrella

bronchitis (brong-kuy-tuhs)
noun an inflammation of the membrane lining of the bronchial tubes which are the air passages in your chest

Word history: Neo-Latin; from *bronch(us)-* + *-itis*

brontosaurus (bron-tuh-saw-ruhs)
noun → **apatosaurus**

Word history: *bronto-*, combining form from Greek *brontē* thunder + *-saurus*

bronze
noun **1** a brown-coloured metal mixed from copper and tin
2 a dark reddish-brown colour

Word building: **bronze** *adjective*
Word history: French, from Italian

brooch (brohch)
noun an ornament made to be fastened to your clothes with a pin

Word history: variant of *broach*, noun

brooch / broach
Don't confuse **brooch** with **broach**, which means 'to introduce or mention something for the first time':
It's time to broach the small matter of the washing up.

brood
noun **1** a number of young animals, especially birds, hatched at the same time
verb **2** to sit on eggs to hatch them
phrase **3 brood on**, to worry about: *She* ***brooded on*** *her failure.* (***agonise over***, ***dwell on***, ***fret about***, ***mull over***)

Word history: Old English *brōd*

broody
adjective **1** likely or tending to sit on eggs: *a* ***broody*** *hen*
2 moody

Adjective forms: **broodier, broodiest**

brook
noun a British word for **creek**

Word history: Old English *brōc* stream

broom
noun a brush with a long handle, used for sweeping

Word history: Old English *brōm*

broth
noun a thin soup of fish, meat or vegetables

Word history: Old English

brothel
noun a house where prostitutes work

brother
noun **1** a male relative who has the same parents as you
2 a fellow worker or colleague: *They are* ***brothers*** *in the fight against crime.*
3 a male member of certain church organisations

Word building: **brotherhood** *noun* **brotherly** *adjective*
Word history: Old English *brōthor*

brother-in-law
noun **1** the brother of your husband or your wife
2 the husband of your sister
3 the husband of the sister of your wife or husband

Noun forms: The plural is **brothers-in-law**.

brought (brawt)
verb past tense and past participle of **bring**

brought / bought
Don't confuse **brought** with **bought**, which is the past form of the verb **buy**:
I bought some lollies at the shop.

brow
noun **1** the bony ridge over your eye (***forehead***, ***temples***)
2 the edge or top of a steep place: *the* ***brow*** *of a hill*

Word history: Old English *brū*

browbeat
verb to bully

Verb forms: I **browbeat**, I have **browbeaten**, I am **browbeating**

brown
noun **1** the colour of earth, a mixture of red, yellow and black
adjective **2** of a brown colour: *a* ***brown*** *horse* (***beige***, ***fawn***, ***sepia***, ***tan***)
3 having skin of that colour: *The Polynesians are a* ***brown*** *people.*
4 sunburned or tanned
verb **5** to make or become brown

Word history: Old English *brūn*

brownfield
adjective having to do with an urban site which has been previously developed or used: *a* ***brownfield*** *redevelopment*

Word use: Compare this with **greenfield**.

brownfields site
noun a site which needs to be cleared of existing industrial and commercial facilities with the accompanying risk of contamination

brownie
noun a thick brown biscuit

brownout
noun a partial blackout, resulting in a dimming of lights, sometimes imposed deliberately to conserve electricity or, as in World War II, to reduce the glare in the sky of big industrial cities

browse
verb **1** to glance casually through a book or at the goods in a shop (***flip through***, ***leaf through***, ***skim***, ***peruse***)
2 to feed or graze: *The cattle* ***browsed*** *in the clover.*

Word building: **browse** *noun*
Word history: Middle French word meaning 'young sprout', from Germanic

browser
noun computer software which enables you to use the World Wide Web

Word use: You can also use **web browser**.

bruise
verb **1** to cause a discoloured mark on the body: *The punch **bruised** my arm.*
2 to develop such a bruised mark: *I **bruise** easily.*
noun **3** the discoloured mark or injury caused

Word history: Old English *brȳsan* crush

bruiser
noun **1** a boxer
2 *Colloquial* a bully who is strong and tough

brumby
noun Australian, NZ a wild horse living freely in the bush

Noun forms: The plural is **brumbies**.
Word history: ? from Irish *bromach* colt;? from Lieutenant *Brumby* a horse-breeder of the early 1800s

brunch
noun a meal in midmorning instead of breakfast and lunch

Word history: blend of *br(eakfast* and *l)unch*

brunette
noun a woman or girl with dark hair

brunt
noun the main shock or force: *to bear the **brunt** of an attack*

Word history: Middle English

bruschetta (broos-ket-uh, broo-shet-uh)
noun grilled slices of bread brushed with olive oil and fresh garlic, often served with various toppings

Word history: from Italian word meaning 'to roast over coals'

brush[1]
noun **1** an instrument made of hair or bristles set in a handle: *a paint **brush** | a hair **brush***
2 an act of brushing: *Give my coat a **brush**.*
3 an argument: *I had a **brush** with him over using my pens.*
verb **4** to use a brush on: ***Brush** your hair every day.*
5 to touch lightly: *She **brushed** me as she passed.*
phrase **6 brush aside**, to ignore: *He **brushed** my arguments **aside**.*
7 brush up,
a to smarten or polish up
b to improve your skill in: *to **brush up** your French*

Word history: Middle English, from Old French, from Germanic

brush[2]
noun a thick growth of bushes

Word history: Middle English, from Old French *broce*

brush turkey
noun a large mound-building bird of the wooded regions of eastern Australia

Word use: You can also use **scrub turkey**.

brusque (brusk, broosk)
adjective quick to say something and not very polite: *His **brusque** manner upsets people.* (***abrupt**, **blunt**, **curt**, **short**, **terse***)

Word history: French, from Italian word meaning 'rude', 'sharp' from Latin word meaning 'broom'

brussels sprout
noun a green vegetable like a tiny cabbage

Word use: You can also use **sprout**.

brutal
adjective savagely cruel: *a **brutal** blow* (***barbaric**, **callous**, **ruthless**, **vicious**, **violent***)

Word use: The opposite of this is **humane**.
Word building: **brutality** (broo-tal-uh-tee) *noun* **brutally** *adverb*

brute
noun **1** an animal or beast
2 a cruel person

Word history: French, from Latin word meaning 'dull'

bubble
noun **1** a small ball of air or gas rising through liquid
2 a small ball of air in a fine coating of liquid: *to blow **bubbles***
verb **3** to send up bubbles

Word history: Middle English

bubble-and-squeak
noun left-over vegetables, or meat and vegetables, fried together

bubblegum
noun chewing gum which can be blown into bubbles

bubbler
noun Australian a small fountain which sends up a short stream of drinking water

bubble wrap
noun a plastic wrapping material consisting of numerous small, sealed air-pockets, used for protecting delicate items during transport or storage

bubbly
adjective **1** containing, or like bubbles: *a **bubbly** drink | a **bubbly** personality*
noun **2** *Colloquial* champagne

bubonic plague (byooh-bon-ik playg)
noun a contagious epidemic disease with chills, fevers and inflamed swellings, which is carried by fleas from rats

buccaneer
noun Old-fashioned a pirate

Word history: French *boucanier* a hunter of wild oxen

buck[1]
noun a male deer, rabbit or hare

Word use: The female animal is called a **doe**.
Word history: Middle English

buck[2]
verb **1** to jump with arched back and stiff legs: *The young horse **bucked** the first time he was saddled.*
2 to throw by bucking: *The horse **bucked** his rider off.*

Word history: special use of *buck*[1]

buck[3]
phrase **pass the buck**, *Colloquial* to shift the responsibility or blame to another person

Word history: from *buck (horn knife)*, formerly an object commonly placed in the kitty during a game of poker to remind the winner of some privilege or duty when it is his or her turn to deal next

buck[4]
noun Colloquial **1** a dollar
phrase **2 a fast buck,** money earned with little effort, often by dishonest means

Word use: This word was first used in this way in the US but is becoming quite common in Australia.
Word history: short form of *buckskin*, an accepted form of exchange in the US frontier

bucket
noun a round open container with a flat bottom and a handle

Word building: **bucketful** *noun*
Word history: Middle English, from Old French *bucket* pail, tub

buckle
noun **1** a clasp for fastening a belt or strap
2 a bend or bulge in a sheet of hard material
verb **3** to fasten with a buckle
4 to cause to bend or bulge: *The heat* ***buckled*** *the road.*
5 to bend or bulge: *The heat caused the road to* ***buckle.***
phrase **6 buckle under,** to yield or give way

Word history: Middle English, from French word meaning 'buckle', 'boss of a shield', from Latin *bucca* cheek, mouth

Buckley's
noun Colloquial **1** *Australian, NZ* a very slim chance or hope: *You've got* ***Buckley's*** *of winning the race, mate!*
phrase **2 Buckley's and none,** *Australian* (said in a joking way) two chances amounting to next to no chance

Word use: You can also use **Buckley's chance** or **Buckley's hope** for definition 1.
Word history: This expression probably began as a reference to William *Buckley*, a British-born convict who escaped from prison and went to live with the Aboriginal people; despite having little chance of survival in the bush, he managed to live and was later employed as a liaison officer between the Aboriginal people and the British settlers. Definition 2 might also have been influenced by a pun on *Buckley and Nunn*, the name of a Melbourne department store, referring to the fact that to have **Buckley's** chance of something is just slightly better than having none.

bucktooth
noun a tooth in your upper jaw that sticks out

Noun forms: The plural is **buckteeth.**
Word building: **bucktoothed** *adjective*

bucolic (byooh-kol-ik)
adjective having to do with farming or the country: *living in* ***bucolic*** *isolation* (***pastoral, rural, rustic***)

Word history: Latin, from Greek word meaning 'rustic'

bud
noun **1** a flower or leaf before it has fully opened
2 a small shoot on the stem of a plant which will grow into a leaf or flower
verb **3** to produce buds

Verb forms: it **budded,** it has **budded,** it is **budding**
Word history: Middle English *budde*

Buddhism (bood-iz-uhm)
noun a world religion, founded by the teacher Buddha who lived in India about the sixth century BC, which teaches that life is full of suffering and that supreme happiness and peace (Nirvana) is gained by destroying greed, hatred, and delusion

Word building: **Buddhist** *noun, adjective*
Word history: named after *Buddha*, a Sanskrit name meaning 'wise' or 'enlightened'

buddy
noun **1** *Colloquial* a friend or mate: *my best* ***buddy***
2 someone who acts as a partner to another, as to provide support with a particular task

Noun forms: The plural is **buddies.**

budge
verb to move: *I won't* ***budge*** *until you return.* | *I can't* ***budge*** *that heavy table.* (***shift, stir***)

Word use: This is usually used with the word **not.**
Word history: French, from Latin word meaning 'to boil'

budgerigar (buj-uh-ree-gah)
noun a small yellow and green parakeet found in inland parts of Australia, but also kept in cages and bred to produce other colours

Word use: The short form is **budgie.**
Word history: from Kamilaroi, an Australian Aboriginal language of northern NSW

budget
noun **1** a plan showing what money you will earn and how you will spend it
verb **2** to make such a plan
adjective **3** not costing much: ***budget*** *clothes*

Verb forms: I **budgeted,** I have **budgeted,** I am **budgeting**

buff
adjective **1** of a light yellow colour: ***buff*** *envelopes*
noun **2** a buff colour
3 an expert: *a film* ***buff***
verb **4** to polish by rubbing hard (***burnish, shine, smooth, wax***)

Word history: late Middle English, from French *bouge* bag, from Latin

buffalo
noun a kind of ox sometimes used for pulling heavy loads

Noun forms: The plural is **buffaloes** or **buffalos.**
Word history: Italian *bufalo*, from dialect Latin

buffer
noun something that softens a blow, especially one of the two springs at each end of a railway carriage to take the shock of a collision

Word history: from *buff*, to blow or slap + *-er*

buffet[1] (buf-uht)
verb **1** to strike, shake or knock about: *The big waves* ***buffeted*** *the boat.*
noun **2** a blow or a slap

Verb forms: it **buffeted,** it has **buffeted,** it is **buffeting**
Word history: Middle English, from Old French *buffe* a blow

buffet[2] (<u>buf</u>-ay, <u>boof</u>-ay)
noun **1** a table or counter holding food
2 a low cupboard for holding cups and plates
adjective **3** set out on a table from which you serve yourself: *a* ***buffet*** *dinner*

Word history: from French word meaning 'chair', 'table'

buffoon (buh-<u>foohn</u>)
noun someone who acts the fool

Word building: **buffoonery** *noun* **buffoonish** *adjective*
Word history: French, from Italian *buffone* jester, from *buffa* a jest

bug
noun **1** any tiny insect
2 *Colloquial* an illness caused by an infection
3 *Colloquial* something that is going wrong: *There's a* ***bug*** *in my system.*
4 a hidden microphone
5 an error in a computer program
6 *Australian* a type of seafood you can eat, sometimes called a Moreton Bay bug or a Balmain bug
verb **7** to hide a microphone in: *The spy* ***bugged*** *the room.*
8 *Colloquial* to annoy: *Your silliness* ***bugs*** *me.* (***goad***, ***irritate***, ***pique***, ***provoke***, ***vex***)

Verb forms: I **bugged**, I have **bugged**, I am **bugging**
Word history: Middle English *bugge*

bugbear
noun something that worries or annoys you: *Exams are my* ***bugbear***.

Word history: *bug* a bogy + *bear*[2]

buggy
noun a light carriage with two wheels, pulled by one horse

Noun forms: The plural is **buggies**.

bugle (<u>byooh</u>-guhl)
noun a wind instrument, used in the army to sound signals

Word building: **bugler** *noun*
Word history: Middle English, from Old French, from Latin word meaning 'ox'

build (bild)
verb **1** to make by joining parts together: *to* ***build*** *a house* | *to* ***build*** *a model aeroplane* (***construct***, ***erect***, ***fashion***, ***put up***, ***shape***)
noun **2** the shape of someone's body: *a heavy* ***build*** (***figure***, ***form***, ***physique***, ***structure***)
phrase **3 build up**, to increase or make stronger
4 build up to, to prepare or get ready for: *The music is* ***building up to*** *a climax.*

Verb forms: I **built**, I have **built**, I am **building**
Word building: **builder** *noun*
Word history: Old English *bold* dwelling, house

building
noun something built for people to live or work in, such as a house or an office block

building society
noun an organisation that uses money, deposited as savings by its members, as a fund for lending money to members to buy or build a house

build-up
noun **1** any gradual increase
2 a gathering of large numbers of troops, etc., for a military attack
3 an advertising campaign for a person or a product

built (bilt)
verb past tense and past participle of **build**

built-up area
noun an area of high population density where low speed-limits apply to traffic

bulb
noun **1** the rounded root-like stem of certain plants, such as the onion
2 anything with a shape like that: *an electric light* ***bulb***

Word history: Latin, from Greek

bulbous
adjective bulging or shaped like a bulb: *a* ***bulbous*** *nose*

bulge
noun a round part that swells out (***bump***, ***lump***, ***protuberance***, ***swelling***)

Word building: **bulge** *verb*
Word history: Middle English, from Latin word meaning 'bag', of Celtic origin

bulimia (buh-<u>lee</u>-mee-uh)
noun an eating disorder marked by periods of overeating followed by forced vomiting

Word building: **bulimic** *adjective*, *noun*
Word history: Neo-Latin, from Greek word meaning 'great hunger'

bulk
noun **1** the size of something including its length, width and depth: *a ship's* ***bulk***
2 the main part: *The* ***bulk*** *of the work has been done.*

Word building: **bulky** *adjective* (**bulkier**, **bulkiest**)
Word history: Middle English *bolke* heap, from Scandinavian

bull[1]
noun **1** a male of the ox family
2 a male elephant, whale or seal

Word history: Old English *bula*

bull[2]
noun in the Roman Catholic Church, a formal written order or letter from the Pope, with his seal on it

Word history: Middle English, from Medieval Latin word meaning 'seal', 'document', from Latin word meaning 'bubble', 'knob'

bull[3]
noun Colloquial **1** nonsense
2 something someone says that is dishonest or boastful

Bullamakanka (bool-uh-muh-<u>kang</u>-kuh)
noun an imaginary and remote town

bull ant
noun a large ant which can give a painful bite

bulldog
noun a type of dog with a large head and a small strong body

bulldozer
noun a powerful tractor with a blade in front, used to move trees and rocks, and to level land

Word building: **bulldoze** *verb*

bullet
noun a small piece of metal shot from a small gun
Word history: from French word meaning 'little ball'

bulletin
noun a short written or spoken news report: *the latest* ***bulletin*** *on the floods* (***announcement***, ***communication***, ***message***, ***news flash***, ***statement***)
Word history: French, from Italian

bulletin board
noun **1** a board attached to a wall, used for the display of notices, etc.
2 *Internet* an electronic message system which allows users to leave messages and to read and reply to messages left by other users

bullfight
noun an entertainment in which a person fights with, and usually kills, a bull
Word building: **bullfighter** *noun*

bull-headed
adjective blindly determined or obstinate

bullion (<u>bool</u>-yuhn)
noun bars of gold or silver
Word history: Middle English, from Anglo-French word meaning 'mint', from *bouillir* 'boil', from Latin

bullock
noun a bull that has had its sex organs removed (***ox***, ***steer***)
Word history: Old English *bulluc*

bullocky
noun Australian, *NZ* the driver of a bullock team

bullroarer
noun a thin piece of wood on a string, which is whirled in the air to make a roaring noise and which is traditionally used for religious services by Australian Aboriginal people (***churinga***, ***thunder stick***)

bullseye
noun **1** the central spot on a target
2 a round hard sweet

bull-terrier
noun a strongly built, short-haired breed of dog produced by crossing the bulldog and the terrier

bully
noun **1** someone who hurts, frightens or orders about smaller or weaker people
verb **2** to behave as a bully towards (***bulldoze***, ***coerce***, ***intimidate***, ***threaten***, ***tyrannise***)
Noun forms: The plural is **bullies**.
Verb forms: they **bullied**, they have **bullied**, they are **bullying**
Word history: Dutch *boele* lover

bulrush
noun **1** in the Bible, papyrus
2 a type of tall rushlike plant from which mats, seats of chairs, etc., are made
Word history: *bull* large + *rush* a grass-like plant

bulwark (<u>bool</u>-wuhk)
noun **1** a wall of earth or other material situated round a place as a defence (***embankment***, ***rampart***)
2 anything serving as a protection or defence (***bastion***, ***buffer***, ***buttress***, ***fortification***, ***safeguard***)
3 bulwarks, in ships, a solid part of a ship's side reaching up above the level of the deck
Word history: Middle English

bum
Colloquial
noun **1** the buttocks
2 a lazy and irresponsible person
verb **3** to obtain something from someone else with no intention of repayment: *to* ***bum*** *some money*
adjective **4** of poor quality
phrase **5 bum around**, to live as a bum
Verb forms: I **bummed**, I have **bummed**, I am **bumming**
Word history: related to *bump*

bumble
verb Colloquial **1** to move, perform or speak clumsily: *She* ***bumbled*** *through her speech.*
2 to manage badly

bumblebee
noun a large hairy kind of bee
Word history: *bumble* buzz + *bee*

bump
verb **1** to knock against: *I* ***bumped*** *the table.*
2 to hit: *I* ***bumped*** *my head on the tree.*
noun **3** a light hit or knock
4 a small raised area: *a* ***bump*** *on the head* | *a* ***bump*** *on the road*
phrase **5 bump into**, to meet by chance (***come across***, ***encounter***, ***join up with***, ***run into***)
6 bump off, *Colloquial* to kill (***assassinate***, ***execute***, ***murder***, ***put down***, ***slay***)
7 bump up, *Colloquial* to increase: *to* ***bump up*** *prices*
Word building: **bumpy** *adjective* (**bumpier**, **bumpiest**)
Word history: imitative

bumper bar
noun the bar across the front or back of a car which protects it in a collision

bumpkin
noun someone who is awkward and clumsy
Word history: from Middle Dutch word meaning 'little barrel'

bumptious (<u>bump</u>-shuhs)
adjective showing your importance in a way that offends people: *a* ***bumptious*** *young man*
Word building: **bumptiously** *adverb* **bumptiousness** *noun*
Word history: *bump* + *-tious*, modelled on *fractious*, etc.

bun
noun **1** a kind of round bread roll which can be plain or sweetened
2 hair arranged at the back of your head in the shape of a bun
Word history: Middle English

bunch
noun **1** a group of things joined or gathered together: *a* ***bunch*** *of grapes* | *a* ***bunch*** *of roses* (***assortment***, ***batch***, ***clump***, ***cluster***, ***stack***)
verb **2** to gather together
Word history: Middle English

bundle
noun **1** a group of things loosely held together: *a* ***bundle*** *of sticks*
verb **2** to put together loosely: *I* ***bundled*** *the books into my bag.*
3 to send away quickly: *I* ***bundled*** *them out of the room.*

phrase **4 drop your bundle,** *Australian, NZ* to lose hope or control of your mind, etc.

Word history: Middle English, from Middle Dutch; related to Old English *byndele* binding together

bundy (<u>bun</u>-dee)
noun a clock which marks the arrival and departure times of employees on a card pushed into it

Word history: Trademark

bung[1]
noun **1** a stopper for the hole in a wine cask
verb **2** to close with a bung, or to block with any obstruction: *The drain is* ***bunged*** *up.*
3 *Colloquial* to throw or toss: ***Bung*** *it over here, Bruce!*

Word history: Middle English, from Middle Dutch

bung[2]
adjective Australian, NZ Colloquial broken, or in poor working order: *My watch is* ***bung*** *— could you please tell me the time?*

Word history: from Yagara, an Australian Aboriginal language of the Brisbane region

bungalow
noun a house with only one storey

Word history: from Hindustani word meaning 'of Bengal'

bungee jumping (<u>bun</u>-jee jumping)
noun a sport in which you throw yourself from a high place such as a bridge to which you are attached by an elasticised cord (a **bungee**)

Word use: You can also use **bungy jumping**.
Word building: **bungee jumper** *noun*

bungle
verb **1** to do badly: *He* ***bungled*** *the job.* (***botch, fluff, fumble, muck up, muff***)
noun **2** something badly done

Word history: probably imitative

bunion (<u>bun</u>-yuhn)
noun a swelling of a joint on the foot, especially on the big toe

bunk
noun **1** a bed built like a shelf, in a ship's cabin
2 one of a pair of beds built one above the other

bunker
noun **1** a fortified shelter, often underground
2 a sandy hollow on a golf course
3 a chest or box; a large bin or receptacle

Word history: origin uncertain; ? Scottish *bunkart*

bunkum (<u>bung</u>-kuhm)
noun insincere or foolish talk (***nonsense, piffle, rot, rubbish***)

Word history: alteration of *Buncombe*, a county in the US, in North Carolina, from its Congressional representative's phrase, 'talking for Buncombe'

bunny
noun Colloquial **1** a rabbit
2 a foolish or unlucky person, especially someone left with the responsibility for a situation

Noun forms: The plural is **bunnies**.

Bunsen burner
noun a type of gas burner with a very hot, blue flame, used widely in laboratories

Word history: named after RW *Bunsen*, 1811–99, German chemist

bunting
noun brightly coloured cloth used to make flags for decoration

Word history: compare German *bunt*, of various colours

bunyip
noun an imaginary creature of Aboriginal legend, said to live in swamps and billabongs

Word history: from Wembawemba, an Australian Aboriginal language of western Victoria

buoy (boy)
noun **1** a float anchored in the water, which marks channels and hidden rocks
2 a ring used to help people stay afloat
verb **3** to keep afloat
4 to encourage or lift the spirits of: *The thought of a hot dinner* ***buoyed*** *them up.*

Word use: You can also use **lifebuoy** for definition 2.
Word history: Middle English, from Middle Dutch word meaning 'buoy', from Latin word meaning 'fetter'

buoy / boy
Don't confuse **buoy** with **boy**, which is a male child.

buoyant (<u>boy</u>-uhnt)
adjective **1** able to float: *This rubber ring will keep you* ***buoyant****.*
2 light-hearted and cheerful (***confident, happy-go-lucky, hopeful, optimistic, positive***)

Word building: **buoyancy** *noun*

burble
verb **1** to make a bubbling sound
2 to speak quickly and unclearly
noun **3** a bubbling gentle sound
4 a flow of excited unclear speech

Word history: probably imitative

burden
noun **1** a load: *to carry a heavy* ***burden*** (***encumbrance, weight***)
2 a difficult job that you don't really want to do: *The children found looking after the animals a* ***burden****.* (***onus, responsibility, strain, trial, trouble***)
verb **3** to load: *I won't* ***burden*** *you with my problems.*

Word building: **burdensome** *adjective*
Word history: Old English *byrthen*

bureau (<u>byooh</u>-roh, byooh-<u>roh</u>)
noun **1** a writing-desk with drawers
2 a government office where people can get information: *a tourist* ***bureau***

Noun forms: The plural is **bureaus** or **bureaux**.
Word history: French word meaning 'desk', 'office', Old French word meaning 'cloth-covered table', 'kind of woollen cloth', from Latin word meaning 'long-haired woollen cloth'

bureaucracy (byooh-<u>rok</u>-ruh-see)
noun **1** unnecessary rules about the way things have to be done in government offices
phrase **2 the bureaucracy**, the people who make these rules

Noun forms: The plural is **bureaucracies**.
Word history: French

bureaucrat (byooh-ruh-krat)
noun a member of the bureaucracy, especially one who follows the rules without thinking about what they mean

Word building: **bureaucratic** *adjective*

burgeon (ber-juhn)
verb **1** to begin to grow by putting out buds, shoots, as a plant does: *The seedlings **burgeoned** forth after the rain.*
2 to grow rapidly: *The population of the town **burgeoned.***

Word use: You can also use **bourgeon.**
Word history: Middle English, from Old French, perhaps from Germanic

burglary (ber-gluh-ree)
noun the crime of breaking into a building to steal things

Noun forms: The plural is **burglaries.**
Word building: **burglar** *noun* **burgle** *verb*

burgundy
noun **1** a type of red wine
2 a rich, dark red colour

Word building: **burgundy** *adjective*

burial (be-ree-uhl)
noun the act of putting a dead person into a grave: *We all went to the cemetery for grandfather's **burial.***

Word history: *bury* + *-al*

burka (ber-kuh)
noun → **burqa**

burl
noun Australian, NZ Colloquial **1** a try (***attempt, crack, effort, endeavour, stab***)
phrase **2 burl along,** to move quickly

Word history: northern British dialect *birl* to spin

burlesque (ber-lesk)
noun a play or a book which makes people laugh by making fun of serious matters

Word history: French, from Italian *burlesco*, from *burla* jest, mockery

burly
adjective big and solidly built: *a **burly** footballer* (***beefy, fat, heavy, stocky, thickset***)

Adjective forms: **burlier, burliest**
Word history: Middle English; origin uncertain

burn
verb **1** to set or be on fire: *to **burn** the wood | The wood is **burning.***
2 to give out heat and light: *This sand **burns.** | The lights **burn** all night.* (***beam, blaze, flare, glow, shine***)
3 to turn black or red by heat or fire: *Put on a sunhat in case your face **burns.** | to **burn** the toast*
4 to hurt by heat or fire: *to **burn** your fingers in the fire*
5 to feel strongly: *to **burn** with anger*
6 to copy (data) onto a compact disc: *I'll **burn** those files for archiving | Can you **burn** a disc of the family photos?*
noun **7** a sore made by something hot: *She had a bad **burn** from the iron.*
phrase **8 burn off,** to clear land by setting fire to the trees
9 burn your fingers, to suffer because you have interfered or tried to help

Verb forms: it **burnt** or it **burned,** it has **burnt** or it has **burned,** it is **burning**
Word history: Old English

burner
noun the part of a stove or lamp where the flame comes out

burning
adjective very interesting and important: *a **burning** question*

burnish
verb to make bright and shiny by polishing: *to **burnish** the copper kettle* (***buff, shine, smooth, wax***)

Word history: Middle English, from Old French word meaning 'make brown', 'polish', from *brun* brown, from Germanic

burnished
adjective bright, smooth and glossy: *Her hair shone like **burnished** gold.*

burnt
verb past tense and past participle of **burn**

burp
verb **1** to noisily pass wind from your stomach through your mouth: *Drinking lemonade makes me **burp.***
2 to help to burp, especially by patting on the back: *to **burp** the baby after its feed*

Word building: **burp** *noun*
Word history: imitative

burqa (ber-kuh)
noun a traditional Muslim garment for women, thought to have originated in the Arabian peninsula, covering the entire body, including the face, and with a narrow opening for the eyes

Word use: Another name is **chador.** Also look up **hijab.**

burr
noun the prickly case around some seeds, such as a chestnut seed

Word history: Middle English, from Scandinavian

burrito (buh-ree-toh)
noun a Mexican food made of a tortilla folded around a filling of meat, cheese or beans

burrow
noun **1** a hole in the ground dug by an animal, to live and shelter in: *The wombat was hiding in its **burrow.***
verb **2** to dig a burrow
3 to search with a digging movement: *She **burrowed** in her bag.*

Word history: Middle English

bursar (ber-suh)
noun someone in charge of money and accounts, especially in a college or university

Word history: from Medieval Latin word meaning 'purse'

bursary
noun money given to a student to help pay for school fees, textbooks, uniforms and other expenses

Noun forms: The plural is **bursaries.**
Word history: Medieval Latin

burst
verb **1** to split or break open: *The sausages* ***burst*** *when we cooked them. | to* ***burst*** *a balloon*
2 to rush suddenly: *The children* ***burst*** *into the room.*
3 to be full or overflowing: *The shopping basket was* ***bursting*** *with goodies.*
4 to express your feelings suddenly: *to* ***burst*** *out laughing*
noun **5** a sudden effort or action: *a* ***burst*** *of speed | a* ***burst*** *of clapping*

Verb forms: it **burst**, it has **burst**, it is **bursting**
Word history: Old English *berstan*

burst / bust

These words look similar and they can mean the same thing.

To **burst** is to split or break open:

The sausages have started to burst and splatter all over the oven.

My balloon has burst.

Note that this word stays the same for its past forms and doesn't add -ed to make *bursted*. So don't get it confused with **busted**.

Bust is an informal word meaning 'break':

Did you bust my pink balloon?

He busted my new headphones.

Although the word is often used this way in speech, you should avoid it in your essays.

bury (be-ree)
verb **1** to put in the ground and cover with earth: *Dogs* ***bury*** *their bones.*
2 to cover over completely: *Her books were* ***buried*** *under a pile of clothing.*
phrase **3 bury yourself**, to occupy yourself completely so that you don't notice anything else: *to* ***bury yourself*** *in a book*

Verb forms: I **buried**, I have **buried**, I am **burying**
Word history: Old English *byrgan*

bury / berry

Don't confuse **bury** with **berry**, which is a small juicy fruit.

bus
noun **1** a long vehicle with many seats, for carrying passengers: *to catch the* ***bus*** *to school*
2 a circuit in a computer to which any device (the central processing unit, disk drive, etc.) may be connected to transfer information
verb **3** to travel by bus
4 to transport people by bus

Noun forms: The plural is **buses** or **busses**.
Verb forms: they **bussed** or they **bused**, they have **bussed** or they have **bused**, they are **bussing** or they are **busing**
Word history: short for *omnibus*

bush
noun **1** a plant like a small tree with many branches coming out from the trunk near the ground: *a rose* ***bush***
2 a tree-covered area of land
phrase **3 beat about the bush**, to take a long time coming to the point in a conversation
4 go bush,
a to live close to nature
b to disappear suddenly from the places you usually go
5 take to the bush, to disappear suddenly from the places you usually go
6 the bush, *Australian* the country as opposed to the city: *Our cousins live in* ***the bush.***

Word history: Middle English; unexplained variant of *busk*, from Scandinavian

bush band
noun a group of musicians who perform Australian folk music, using instruments such as the accordion and guitar

bushcare
noun the care of fragments of native bush or the replanting of land with native trees, often done by landowners and community groups: *She volunteered to help once a month with* ***bushcare.***

Word history: *bush + (land)care*
Word building: **bushcarer** *noun*

bushcraft
noun Australian, NZ knowledge of how to live in and travel through rough bush country

bush dance
noun Australian a dance held in traditional Australian bush style with country music and dancing

bushed
adjective **1** very tired: *We are* ***bushed*** *after a hard day's work.* (***exhausted, fatigued, lethargic, weary, worn***)
2 lost or confused: *I was completely* ***bushed*** *when I couldn't find her house.*

bushel
noun Old-fashioned an imperial measure of large quantities of goods such as grain or fruit, equal to 8 gallons ($36.368\,72 \times 10^{-3}\,m^3$)

Word history: Middle English, from Old French, from Gallic word meaning hollow of the hand

bushfire
noun Australian, NZ a fire in the bush or forest

bushie
noun Australian, NZ Colloquial someone who lives in the bush or in a rural area

bushman
noun Australian, NZ someone who lives in the bush and knows how to survive there

Word building: **bushmanship** *noun*

bushranger
noun Australian, NZ in the past, someone who hid in the bush and lived by robbing travellers: *Ned Kelly was a famous Australian* ***bushranger.*** (***brigand, criminal, highwayman, thief***)

Word building: **bushranging** *noun*

bush regeneration
noun the regeneration of areas of bush in which native plants have been destroyed, either by encouraging native bush to regrow or by planting with species that are thought to be part of the original ecology

bush tucker
noun Australian **1** simple food, as eaten by one living in the bush

2 food from native Australian plants and trees
3 traditional Aboriginal food, especially food caught or collected using traditional Aboriginal methods

bush turkey
noun → **brush turkey**

bushwalking
noun Australian walking through the bush for exercise or pleasure

Word building: **bushwalk** *noun* **bushwalker** *noun*

bushwhacker
noun Australian, NZ Colloquial someone who lives in the bush

bushy
adjective thick or dense like a bush: *a fox's **bushy** tail*

Adjective forms: **bushier, bushiest**

business (biz-nuhs)
noun **1** the work someone does to earn a living (***career, job, occupation, profession, vocation***)
2 buying and selling goods to make a profit: *to be in **business***
3 a matter which someone has a right to know about: *My exam mark is none of your **business.***
phrase **4 mean business,** to be serious: *Those guard dogs look as if they **mean business.***

Noun forms: The plural is **businesses.**
Word history: Old English (North) *bisignes*

business / busyness
Don't confuse **business** with **busyness**, which refers to the state of being busy:

There was a great deal of busyness as the children prepared for the fete.

business activity statement
noun a statement which a business is required to submit to the government agency on a regular basis, containing an account of transactions and allowing the calculation of tax payable, especially GST

Word use: You can also use **BAS.**

businesslike
adjective practical and well-organised

business model
noun an outline of the structure and operations of a business, which sets out precisely the means by which it aims to generate revenue

businessperson
noun someone who works in commercial business or trade

Noun forms: The plural is **businesspeople.**
Word building: **businessman** *masculine noun* **businesswoman** *feminine noun*

business plan
noun a plan set out for a commercial organisation which details its projected financial development over a number of years

busker
noun a musician who performs in the street hoping to get donations of money from people passing by

Word building: **busk** *verb*

bust[1]
noun **1** a woman's breasts or chest
2 a sculpture of someone's head and shoulders

Word history: French, from Italian *busto*

bust[2]
verb Colloquial **1** to break or burst: *to **bust** a balloon*
2 to arrest: *He was **busted** for selling drugs.*
phrase **3 bust in,** to rush in suddenly
4 bust up, to quarrel and separate: *I have **busted up** with my boyfriend.*
5 go bust, to lose all your money: *His business has **gone bust.***

Word history: dialect or colloquial variant of *burst*

bustard (bust-uhd)
noun a large heavy bird which can run fast and lives in the grassy plains of Australia and New Guinea

Word history: Middle English, from Old French, from Latin *avis tarda* slow bird

busted
adjective Colloquial broken or ruined

bustle[1]
verb to move or act busily: *She **bustled** about tidying the house.*

Word history: probably variant of obsolete *buskle*

bustle[2]
noun a pad or wire frame worn in the olden days to puff out the back of a woman's skirt

Word history: probably from *bustle*[1]

busy
adjective **1** fully occupied: *I can't come now as I am **busy** doing my homework.* (***active, engaged, flat out, hard-working, industrious***)
2 full of activity: *Saturday morning is a **busy** time at the shops.* (***hectic, hustling, lively***)
3 already in use: *The telephone was **busy.*** (***engaged, occupied***)
verb **4** to make or keep busy: *I shall **busy** myself tidying up my room.*

Adjective forms: **busier, busiest**
Verb forms: I **busied**, I have **busied**, I am **busying**
Word building: **busily** *adverb* **busyness** *noun*
Word history: Old English *bysig* busy

busybody
noun somebody who interferes in other people's business

Noun forms: The plural is **busybodies.**

but
conjunction **1** on the contrary: *All my friends went, **but** I didn't.*
2 except: *Nothing would please her **but** that I should stay the night.*
preposition **3** except or save: *No one answered **but** me.*
adverb **4** only: *I have **but** one true friend.*
5 however: ***But** this isn't the end of the story.*
phrase **6 all but,** almost: *The war has **all but** finished.*
7 but for, were it not for: *She would have died **but for** you.*

Word history: Old English *b(e)ūta(n)* on the outside, without

but / butt

Don't confuse **but** with **butt**, which is the end of something such as a rifle or a cigarette.

butane (byooh-tayn)
noun an inflammable gas made from petroleum and used as a fuel when in liquid form

Word history: *but(yl)* + *-ane*

butch
adjective Colloquial **1** of a woman or homosexual man, having masculine characteristics
2 showing such characteristics: *a **butch** haircut*

Word history: probably from *butcher*

butcher
noun **1** someone who prepares and cuts up meat to sell
2 a cruel and violent murderer
verb **3** to kill violently: *The murderer **butchered** his victims.*
4 to make a terrible mess of: *That new hairdresser **butchered** my hair.*

Word building: **butchery** *noun*
Word history: Middle English, from Old French *boc* he-goat, from Germanic

butcherbird
noun a black or grey Australian bird which hangs its dead prey on branches

butler
noun the head male servant in a large house

Word history: Middle English, from Anglo-French *bouteille* bottle

butt[1]
noun **1** the thick blunt end of a weapon or tool: *the **butt** of a rifle*
2 an end which is not used up: *a cigarette **butt***
3 *Colloquial* the buttocks

Word history: Middle English; apparently short for *buttock*

butt[2]
noun **1** someone who is a target: *He is always the **butt** of their jokes.*
2 a wall of earth which stops bullets or arrows fired at targets in front of it

Word history: Middle English, from Old French word meaning 'end', 'extremity', of Germanic origin

butt[3]
verb to push with the head or horns: *The goat **butted** me.*

Word building: **butt** *noun*
Word history: Middle English, from Old French, strike, thrust, abut, touch, from *bout* end, of Germanic origin

butter
noun **1** soft yellow spread made from cream
verb **2** to spread butter on

Word building: **buttery** *adjective*
Word history: Old English *butere*, from Latin, from Greek

butterfly
noun **1** an insect with large wings which are often brightly coloured
2 a stroke in swimming in which both your arms are lifted together from the water and thrown forward

Noun forms: The plural is **butterflies**.
Word use: You can also use **butterfly stroke** for definition 2.
Word history: Old English *buttorflēoge*, probably originally used of a butter-coloured (yellow) species

buttermilk
noun a sour liquid left after butter has been made from cream

butterscotch
noun a kind of toffee or flavouring

buttock
noun either of the two rounded parts of the body at the base of your back

Word history: Old English *buttuc*

button
noun **1** a small, usually round, object sewn onto clothing to join two parts together
2 anything shaped like a button, such as a small knob you press to ring a bell, or a small outlined area on a computer screen you can click on
verb **3** to fasten with a button: *I **buttoned** my cardigan.*

Verb forms: I **buttoned**, I have **buttoned**, I am **buttoning**
Word history: Middle English, from Old French word meaning 'thrust'

buttonhole
noun **1** a slit in a garment through which buttons are passed to fasten a garment
2 a flower worn in a buttonhole on the lapel of a coat

buttress
noun a support for a wall or building

Word building: **buttress** *verb*
Word history: Old French *bouterez*, plural, from *bouter* thrust, abut

buxom (buks-uhm)
adjective plump and attractive: *She's a **buxom** woman.*

Word history: Old English *būgan* bend, bow

buy
verb **1** to get by paying money for (***acquire***, ***procure***, ***purchase***)
2 to accept: *I don't **buy** that idea.*
noun **3** something bought: *a good **buy***
phrase **4 buy into**,
a to buy shares in a company or something similar
b *Colloquial* to decide to become involved: *to **buy into** an argument*
5 buy off, to bribe: *The developer tried to **buy off** anyone who stood in his way.*
6 buy out, to buy all the shares belonging to a partner in, or the owner of, a company
7 buy up, to buy as much as you can of: *to **buy up** all the oil in the world*

Verb forms: I **bought**, I have **bought**, I am **buying**
Word history: Old English *bycgan*

buy / by / bye

Don't confuse **buy** with **by** or **bye**.

By means 'near or close to something':

The table is by the door.

By has many other meanings which you should look up.

A **bye** in sport is when your team doesn't have to play in a particular round of a contest.

Bye can also mean 'goodbye'.

buyer
noun **1** someone who buys: *We have a* ***buyer*** *for our old car.* (***consumer***, ***customer***, ***patron***, ***purchaser***, ***shopper***)
2 someone whose job it is to buy stock for a store: *He is chief* ***buyer*** *for a supermarket.*

Word use: The opposite of definition 1 is **seller** or **vendor**.

buzz
noun **1** a low, humming sound: *the* ***buzz*** *of bees | a* ***buzz*** *of conversation*
verb **2** to make a buzzing noise (***drum***, ***palpitate***, ***pulsate***, ***throb***, ***whirr***)
phrase **3 buzz off**, *Colloquial* to go or leave

Word history: imitative

buzzard
noun any of various birds of prey related to but smaller than eagles

buzzer
noun an electrical device that makes a buzzing noise as a signal

buzzword
noun Colloquial a jargon word used to impress a listener, especially by showing that the speaker is up-to-date

Word use: You can also use **buzz word**.

by
preposition **1** near to: *I live* ***by*** *the school.*
2 via or using as a way: *to come in* ***by*** *the main gate | to travel* ***by*** *train*
3 past (something nearby): *to go* ***by*** *the swimming pool*
4 during: ***by*** *night |* ***by*** *day*
5 not later than: *Be home* ***by*** *midnight.*
adverb **6** near: *I live close* ***by***.
7 past something nearby: *The car sped* ***by***.
phrase **8 by and by**, *Old-fashioned* presently or before long: *I'll be with you* ***by and by***.
9 by and large, in general: *She dresses very well* ***by and large***.

Word history: Old English *bī*

bye[1] (buy)
noun **1** *Sport* a state of having no opponent in a contest where competitors are in pairs, bringing the right to compete in the next round
2 *Cricket* a run made from a ball not struck by the person batting
phrase **3 by the bye**, by the way, or, incidentally

Word use: You can also use **by the by** for definition 3.
Word history: variant spelling of *by*, preposition, in noun use

bye[2]
interjection goodbye

by-election
noun an extra election held to fill the seat of a member of parliament who has died or retired

bygone (<u>buy</u>-gon)
adjective **1** past or gone by: ***bygone*** *days* (***former***, ***late***, ***previous***, ***sometime***)
noun **2** something which is past

by-law
noun a rule of a local government authority with legal effect only within the area covered by that authority

Word history: Middle English *by* town from Scandinavian

BYO
adjective **1** of a party, dinner, etc., to which you bring your own alcoholic drinks
noun Australian, *NZ* **2** a restaurant which allows people to bring their own alcoholic drinks

Word use: You can also use **BYOG**.
Word history: abbreviation of *b(ring) y(our) o(wn) g(rog)*

bypass
noun **1** a road built to go around a town or a busy traffic area
verb **2** to use or make a bypass

by-product
noun something produced in addition to the main product: *Asphalt is a* ***by-product*** *of making petrol.*

byre (<u>buy</u>-uh)
noun a cowhouse or shed

Word history: Old English *būr* hut

bystander
noun someone who happens to be present at, but takes no part in, what is occurring

byte (buyt)
noun a unit of information stored by a computer

byte / bite / bight

Don't confuse **byte** with **bite** or **bight**.

A **bite** is a mouthful of something, or a wound made using teeth or something similar.

A **bight** is a bay, as in the *Great Australian Bight*.

byway
noun a road not used very often

byword
noun **1** the name of a person or thing which is thought of as representing some quality or idea: *His name is a* ***byword*** *for courage.*
2 a common saying (***adage***, ***dictum***, ***maxim***, ***proverb***)

Word history: Old English *bīword*

Byzantine (<u>biz</u>-uhn-teen, <u>biz</u>-uhn-tuyn, buh-<u>zan</u>-tuyn, buh-<u>zan</u>-tuhn)
adjective having to do with the style of art or architecture of the Byzantine Empire, especially of the fifth and sixth centuries, featuring the rich use of mosaics, domes, decoration, etc.

Word history: Latin

Cc

C
noun Computers a programming language which combines the flexibility of a high-level language with the direct machine programming ability of a low-level language

C++ (see-plus-plus)
noun Computers a programming language with features that enable object-oriented software development

cab
noun **1** a taxi
2 the covered part of a truck where the driver sits
Word history: short for *cabriolet*, a type of horse-drawn carriage, from French word meaning 'caper' (with reference to its movement)

cabaret (kab-uh-ray)
noun a musical or comedy show performed at a restaurant or club
Word history: from French word meaning 'cellar'

cabbage
noun a kind of vegetable with large green leaves wrapped tightly around a short stem
Word history: Middle English, from French, probably from Provençal *cap* head, from Latin

cabbage tree
noun a tall palm with large leaves and with edible buds, found along the coast of eastern Australia
Word use: Another name is **cabbage tree palm**.

cabernet sauvignon (kab-uh-nay soh-vin-yõ)
noun **1** a claret-style wine
2 the grape widely used to make this wine

cabin
noun **1** a small house or hut
2 a room in a ship where passengers sleep
3 the space inside a plane where the crew and passengers sit
Word history: Middle English, from French, from Provençal, from Late Latin

cabinet
noun **1** a piece of furniture with shelves and drawers
2 in parliament, the group of ministers from the ruling political party who advise the leader and are responsible for the government of a state or nation
Word use: You can also use **Cabinet** for definition 2.
Word history: French, from Italian

cable
noun **1** thick strong rope, chain or several wires twisted together
2 a bundle of insulated wires that carry electricity
Word history: Middle English

cable television
noun a system of broadcasting television programs by sending them through electrical cables
Word use: The short form is **cable TV**.

cabriolet (kab-ree-oh-lay)
noun **1** a type of car resembling a coupé, with a folding top; a convertible coupé
2 a light, hooded one-horse carriage with two seats

cacao (kuh-kay-oh, kuh-kah-oh)
noun **1** a small, evergreen, tropical American tree grown for its seeds, from which cocoa and chocolate are made
2 the seeds of this tree
Noun forms: The plural is **cacaos**.
Word use: Compare this with **cocoa**.
Word history: Spanish, from Nahuatl

cache (kash)
noun **1** a hiding place for storing things
2 the things that are hidden in a cache
Word history: from French word meaning 'hide'

> **cache / cash**
> Don't confuse **cache** with **cash**, which is money, particularly in the form of notes or coins.

cache memory (kaysh mem-ree)
noun Computers memory which is used to temporarily store data so that it can be accessed very quickly

cackle
verb to laugh or talk with the kind of noisy sound that a hen makes after laying an egg (***chortle***, ***chuckle***)
Word building: **cackle** *noun*
Word history: Middle English *cackelen*; imitative

cacophony (kuh-kof-uh-nee)
noun a loud unmusical sound: *The dogs started a **cacophony** of barking.*
Word history: Neo-Latin, from Greek

cactus (kak-tuhs)
noun a spiky plant which stores water in its thick skin and grows in hot dry places
Noun forms: The plural is **cacti** (kak-tuy) or **cactuses**.
Word history: Latin, from Greek word meaning 'kind of prickly plant'

cad
noun Old-fashioned a man who does not behave like a gentleman
Word building: **caddish** *adjective*

cadaver (kuh-dav-uh, kuh-dah-vuh)
noun a dead body, particularly of a human being (***corpse***, ***remains***)

Word history: Latin

caddie
noun someone who is paid to carry a golfer's playing clubs and find the ball

Word use: You can also use **caddy**.
Word history: French *cadet* cadet

caddy[1]
noun a small box or tin in which tea is kept

Noun forms: The plural is **caddies**.
Word history: Malay

caddy[2]
noun → **caddie**

Noun forms: The plural is **caddies**.
Word history: French *cadet* cadet

cadence (kay-duhns)
noun **1** the rising and falling of sounds, especially in the sound of your voice when reading poetry
2 a group of musical notes or chords which show the end of a section or piece of music

Word history: Middle English, from French, from Italian *cadenza*, from Latin word meaning 'falling'

cadet (kuh-det)
noun someone who is being trained in a job or an organisation, like the army or a school military group

Word history: French word meaning 'chief', from Latin word meaning 'head'

cadetship
noun a training position in an organisation often accompanied by a scholarship to attend a course of study

cadge (kaj)
verb to borrow or get, especially from a friend, usually with no intent to repay: *May I **cadge** a cigarette?*

cadmium (kad-mee-uhm)
noun Chemistry a white metallic element which looks like tin, used in electroplating and in making some alloys. It is also used in control rods of nuclear reactors.

Word history: Neo-Latin, from Latin, from Greek

cadre (kah-duh)
noun a key group of people needed to establish and train a new military, political or other unit

Word history: French word meaning 'frame', from Italian, from Latin word meaning 'a square'

caesarean section (suh-zair-ree-uhn sek-shuhn)
noun an operation for delivering a baby, in which the womb and the walls of a woman's abdomen are cut through (said to have been performed at the birth of Julius Caesar)

Word use: You can also use **caesarian**.

caesar salad (see-zuh sal-uhd)
noun a salad containing lettuce, bread croutons, parmesan cheese and sometimes anchovies, seasoned and dressed with egg, oil and vinegar

caesium (see-zee-uhm)
noun Chemistry a rare, extremely active, soft, metallic element. The radioactive isotope, **caesium-137**, is used in radiotherapy.

Word use: You can also use **cesium**.
Word history: from Latin word meaning 'bluish grey'

cafe (kaf-ay)
noun a restaurant where coffee and small meals are served (***bistro***, ***cafeteria***, ***canteen***, ***diner***)

Word history: French

The 'e' at the end of **cafe** is pronounced because the word comes from the French *café*, which means 'coffee'.

cafe latte (kaf-ay lah-tay)
noun an Italian style of coffee in which espresso coffee is combined with hot milk in a large glass: *For morning tea she had a nice big **cafe latte**.*

Word use: You can also use **caffe latte** or **latte**.

cafeteria
noun a cheap self-service restaurant (***bistro***, ***cafe***, ***canteen***, ***diner***)

Word history: from American Spanish word meaning 'coffee shop'

caffeine (kaf-een)
noun a stimulating drug found in coffee and tea which stops you falling asleep

Word history: French *café* coffee

caftan (kaf-tan)
noun **1** a man's long garment, with long sleeves and tied at the waist, worn under a coat in the Middle East
2 a similar garment, worn by women (and men) in western countries

Word history: Turkish, Persian *qaftān*

cage
noun **1** an enclosure made of wires or bars, in which animals or birds can be kept
2 anything that is like a prison
verb **3** to put someone or something in, or as if in, a cage: *The prisoner was **caged** in his cell.*

Word history: Middle English, from Latin word meaning 'enclosure'

cagey
adjective careful not to tell very much: *He became very **cagey** when the police questioned him.* (***guarded***, ***secretive***, ***wary***)

Word use: You can also use **cagy**.
Adjective forms: **cagier**, **cagiest**
Word building: **cagily** *adverb* **caginess** *noun*

caiman (kay-muhn)
noun a tropical American reptile resembling and related to the alligators, but with overlapping abdominal plates

Word use: You can also use **cayman**.

cajole (kuh-johl)
verb to persuade by praising or making promises (***coax***, ***inveigle***, ***wheedle***)

Word history: French *cajoler*, perhaps blend of *caresser* caress and *enjôler* capture

cake
noun **1** a sweet food, usually made with butter or margarine, flour, sugar, eggs, and a flavouring, which is baked in an oven
2 a small mass of something with a definite shape: *a fish **cake** | a **cake** of soap*
verb **3** to cover with a thick crust of something: *She **caked** her face with make-up.*
phrase **4 have your cake and eat it**, *Colloquial* to have all the advantages of something without any of its disadvantages
5 piece of cake, *Colloquial* something which is done or obtained easily: *The maths exam was a **piece of cake**.*
6 take the cake, *Colloquial* to win the prize or be the best: *This rudeness **takes the cake**.*

Word history: Middle English, from Scandinavian

calamari (kal-uh-mah-ree)
noun squid used as food

Word history: Italian

calamine (kal-uh-muyn)
noun a liquid soothing to the skin, prepared from mixture of zinc oxide with ferric oxide

Word history: French, from Medieval Latin

calamity
noun a terrible happening or disaster (***catastrophe***, ***debacle***, ***misfortune***, ***tragedy***)

Noun forms: The plural is **calamities**.
Word building: **calamitous** *adjective*
Word history: late Middle English, from Latin

calcify (kal-suh-fuy)
verb to make or become hardened by the deposit of calcium salts or lime, such as happens in the tissues of your body or in rocks

Verb forms: it **calcified**, it has **calcified**, it is **calcifying**
Word building: **calcification** *noun*
Word history: Latin *calx* lime + -(*i*)*fy*

calcium (kal-see-uhm)
noun a soft, silver-white metal, which is found in limestone and chalk, and in teeth and bones

Word history: Neo-Latin, from Latin *calx* lime + *-ium*

calculate
verb **1** to work out using mathematics: *He got out his ruler and **calculated** the area of the square.* (***compute***, ***count***, ***figure***, ***measure***, ***reckon***)
2 to work out by thinking about: *She **calculated** that it was worth taking the risk.*

Word building: **calculation** *noun*
Word history: from Latin word meaning 'counted'

calculated
adjective done deliberately or with careful planning: *a **calculated** insult*

calculating
adjective very careful and shrewd: *a **calculating** look*

calculator
noun a small electronic machine that can be used to do mathematical operations

Word history: Latin

calculus (kal-kyuh-luhs)
noun the branch of mathematics concerned with the measurement of quantities which are continually changing, by treating continuous change as if it were made up of many small parts

Word history: from Latin word meaning 'stone used in counting', diminutive of *calx* small stone, lime

calendar
noun a chart that shows the days and weeks of each month of the year

Word history: from Latin word meaning 'account book'

calf[1] (kahf)
noun a young cow, whale, elephant or seal

Noun forms: The plural is **calves**.
Word history: Old English

calf[2] (kahf)
noun the back part of your leg, below the knee

Noun forms: The plural is **calves**.
Word history: Middle English, from Scandinavian

calibrate (kal-uh-brayt)
verb **1** to work out, check, or adjust the scale of any measuring instrument
2 to measure the calibre of something

Word building: **calibration** *noun*

calibre (kal-uh-buh)
noun **1** the diameter of something round, like a bullet or the barrel of a gun
2 the ability or character of a person: *You can't rely on a person of that **calibre**.*

Word use: The US spelling is **caliber**.
Word history: French, from Italian, from Arabic word meaning 'mould'

calico (kal-ik-oh)
noun a rough cotton cloth, usually whitish in colour

Word history: named after *Calicut*, a city on the coast of Malabar, India

caliper
noun a metal splint used as a support for an injured leg or arm

Word use: You can also use **calliper**.
Word history: variant of *calibre*

call
verb **1** to cry out in a loud voice (***bawl***, ***roar***, ***shout***, ***yell***)
2 to order to happen: *The principal **called** a staff meeting.* (***announce***, ***proclaim***, ***require***, ***stipulate***)
3 to read out aloud: *The teacher **called** the roll.*
4 to shout out to someone
5 to ask or order to come: *We'd better **call** a doctor.*
6 to telephone: *Please **call** me tonight.*
7 to give a name to someone or something: *His parents **called** him Jacques.* (***christen***, ***dub***, ***tag***, ***title***)
8 to describe as something particular: *She **called** me a cheat.*
9 to make a short visit: *Maria **called** at the shop on her way home.* (***blow in***, ***drop in***, ***look in***, ***stop by***)
noun **10** a shout or cry
11 a short visit
12 a telephone conversation: *a long-distance **call***
phrase **13 call for**,
a to need or be suitable for: *His success **calls for** a party.*
b to go and collect something: *I have to **call for** my new shoes on the way home.*

14 call off, to cancel or postpone: *They* ***called off*** *the sports carnival because of rain.*
15 call on, to make a short visit: *Why don't we* ***call on*** *Sergio?*
16 call up,
a to demand payment of something: ***call up*** *all your debts*
b to send for someone for military service
c to bring to your mind: *He* ***called up*** *all the great holidays they'd shared.*
17 on call, *Commerce*
a something which can be returned or is payable without advance notice being needed
b available for duty at short notice

Word building: **caller** *noun*
Word history: Middle English *calle(n)*

call centre
noun a location at which operators receive and make phone calls for client organisations, as for marketing, information services, etc.

callgirl
noun a prostitute who makes appointments by telephone

calligraphy (kuh-lig-ruh-fee)
noun the art of doing beautiful handwriting

Word building: **calligrapher** *noun*
Word history: Greek

calling
noun someone's job, profession or trade

callisthenics (kal-uhs-then-iks)
noun **1** the practice or art of exercising muscles to make yourself healthy, strong, and graceful: ***Callisthenics*** *is very good for your body.*
2 the exercises used: *These* ***callisthenics*** *are very hard at first.*

Word use: You can also use **calisthenics.** | Note that definition 1 is usually treated as singular and definition 2 is usually treated as plural.
Word building: **callisthenic** *adjective*
Word history: Greek *kállos* beautiful + *sthénos* strength + *-ics*

callous
adjective showing no concern for another person's feelings: *She gave a* ***callous*** *answer to his call for help.* (***cold-blooded, cruel, hard-hearted, insensitive, unfeeling***)

Word building: **callousness** *noun*
Word history: from Latin word meaning 'hard-skinned'

callous / callus
Don't confuse **callous** with **callus**, which is a piece of your skin which has grown thick and hard.

callow
adjective young and inexperienced: *a* ***callow*** *youth* (***amateur, incompetent, naive, raw, untrained***)

Word building: **callowness** *noun*
Word history: Old English *calu, calw-*

callus
noun a hard thick part of your skin caused by something rubbing against it: *I've got a* ***callus*** *on my thumb from the handle of my tennis racquet.*

Word history: from Latin word meaning 'hardened skin'

calm
adjective **1** still, with no rough movements: *a* ***calm*** *sea*
2 not windy: *a* ***calm*** *day*
3 not getting excited or upset: *He always stays* ***calm*** *when there is trouble.*
verb **4** to make or become calm: *to* ***calm*** *someone's fears* | *to* ***calm*** *down after a fight* (***appease, comfort, mollify, pacify, quieten***)

Word use: The opposite of definition 4 is **agitate.**
Word building: **calm** *noun* **calmness** *noun* **calmly** *adverb*
Word history: Middle English *calme*, from Old French, from Italian *calma* (as if originally, heat of the day, hence, time for resting, quiet)

calorie (kal-uh-ree)
noun a measurement of heat or the energy value of food: *That cake is full of* ***calories.***

Word use: Nowadays **kilojoule** is used instead of **calorie.** It is the metric unit.
Word history: French, from Latin word meaning 'heat'

calumny (kal-uhm-nee)
noun a false statement designed to hurt someone or give him or her a bad name (***aspersion, defamation, libel, slander, smear***)

Noun forms: The plural is **calumnies.**
Word history: Latin

calve (kahv)
verb to give birth to young: *The cow in the top paddock is about to* ***calve.***

Word history: Middle English

calve / carve
Don't confuse **calve** with **carve**, which means 'to cut meat up into slices'.

calyx (kay-liks, kal-liks)
noun Botany the outermost group of the parts of a flower, usually green in colour

Noun forms: The plural is **calyces** (kal-uh-seez, kay-luh-seez) or **calyxes.**
Word use: The calyx is made up of **sepals.**
Word history: Latin, from Greek word meaning 'covering', 'husk', 'calyx'

camaraderie (kam-uh-rah-duh-ree)
noun close friendship or mateship

Word history: French, from comrade

came
verb past tense of **come**

camel
noun an animal with a humped back, used to carry people and loads across the desert

Word history: Middle English and Old English, from Latin, from Greek *kámēlos*; of Semitic origin

cameo (kam-ee-oh)
noun **1** a piece of jewellery made from a stone or shell which has been carved so that the design stands out from its background
2 a small part in a film or play acted by a celebrity

Word history: Italian

camera
noun a machine with which you take photographs

Word history: Medieval Latin word meaning 'chamber', from Latin word meaning 'arch', 'vault'

camisole (kam-uh-sohl)
noun **1** a woman's decorative undergarment, originally designed to cover the corset
2 a woman's simple top with narrow shoulder straps

Word history: French, from Spanish word meaning 'little shirt'

camouflage (kam-uh-flahzh, kam-uh-flahj)
noun a kind of disguise, either natural or manufactured, that makes something hard to see against its surroundings: *The colour of that insect gives it a good* ***camouflage****.*

Word building: **camouflage** *verb*
Word history: from French word meaning 'disguise'

camp[1]
noun **1** a group of tents, caravans or shelters for outdoor living
2 a place for these kinds of shelters
verb **3** to live for a while in a tent: *We* ***camped*** *in the bush during our holidays.*

Word building: **camper** *noun*
Word history: French, from Italian *campo* field, from Latin

camp[2]
adjective **1** in an exaggerated or amusing style: *The new play is very* ***camp****. | a* ***camp*** *hairstyle*
2 homosexual

Word history: from French *se camper* behave in an exaggerated manner

campaign (kam-payn)
noun **1** a series of planned attacks by an army, in a particular area or for a particular purpose: *How many soldiers fought in that* ***campaign****?*
2 any planned series of actions with a particular purpose: *They started a* ***campaign*** *to change the school uniform.*

Word building: **campaign** *verb* **campaigner** *noun*
Word history: French, from Latin *campus* plain

camphor (kam-fuh)
noun a whitish translucent substance with a strong smell, used in medicine, the production of celluloid, etc.

Word history: Medieval Latin, from Arabic, from Malay *kāpūr*

campus
noun the grounds of a university or technical college

Word history: from Latin word meaning 'field'

can[1]
verb **1** to be able to: *You* ***can*** *lift that box.*
2 to have permission to: ***Can*** *I speak to you a moment?*

Verb forms: I **can**, I **could**
Word use: This is a auxiliary verb, always used with another one.
Word history: Old English *cann, can*

can / may

Can and **may** have slightly different meanings, though they often overlap.

Can means 'is able':

It can fly faster than the speed of sound.

May means

1 'it's allowed':

You may turn the TV on if you've finished your homework.

2 'it's possible':

It may rain tomorrow.

In conversation, this difference is often ignored:

You can go to the beach.

This sentence could mean either that you are able to go to the beach, or that you're allowed to.

In questions, **can** can also take on the first meaning of may. For example:

Can I go to the beach?

In this question, you are probably asking whether you are allowed to go to the beach. But note that some people feel it is more polite to ask:

May I go to the beach?

can[2]
noun **1** a tin container for food and drink: *a* ***can*** *of oil | a* ***can*** *of apples*
verb **2** to put in a can
phrase **3 carry the can**, *Colloquial* to take the blame

Verb forms: I **canned**, I have **canned**, I am **canning**
Word building: **canned** *adjective*
Word history: Old English *canne*

canal (kuh-nal)
noun a constructed waterway for ships or barges

Word history: late Middle English, from Latin word meaning 'pipe', 'groove'

canary
noun a small yellow bird that sings sweetly and is often kept as a pet

Noun forms: The plural is **canaries**.
Word history: named after the *Canary Islands*. In Latin the name for these islands was *canaria insula*, literally 'island of dogs', from the Latin word *canis* meaning 'dog' and *insula* meaning 'island'. In Roman times one of the islands had a large number of dogs on it.

canasta
noun a card game played by two to six people

Word history: Spanish

cancel
verb **1** to call off: *to* ***cancel*** *a picnic (****abolish****,* ***annul****,* ***dissolve****,* ***quash****,* ***repeal****)*
2 to cross out by drawing lines through: *He* ***cancelled*** *my name on the list of competitors.*

Verb forms: I **cancelled**, I have **cancelled**, I am **cancelling**
Word building: **cancellation** *noun*
Word history: late Middle English, from Latin word meaning 'to make like a lattice', 'to strike out a writing'

cancer
noun the harmful growth of a group of cells in someone's body, which destroys the nearby cells and can spread throughout the whole body, often causing death

Word building: **cancerous** *adjective*
Word history: from Latin word meaning 'crab', 'tumour'

candelabrum (kan-duh-lah-bruhm)
noun an ornamental holder for a number of candles

Noun forms: The plural is **candelabra**.
Word history: from Latin word meaning 'candle'

candid
adjective **1** honest and sincere: *He gave a **candid** answer to the judge's question.* (***direct***, ***forthright***, ***frank***, ***genuine***, ***straightforward***)
2 taken without people knowing: ***candid** photos*

Word history: Latin *candidus* white, sincere

candidate
noun **1** someone sitting for an examination
2 someone who is applying for a job, an award or a place in parliament

Word building: **candidacy** *noun* **candidature** *noun*
Word history: Latin *candidātus* clad in white, as a Roman candidate for office

candied
adjective cooked in sugar: ***candied** fruit* (***glacé***, ***sugary***, ***sweet***)

candle
noun **1** a piece of wax containing a wick which is burnt to give light
phrase **2 burn the candle at both ends**, to try to do too much and wear yourself out
3 can't hold a candle to, *Colloquial* to be inferior to

Word history: Old English *candel*, from Latin

candour (kan-duh)
noun honesty and sincerity: *He answered with complete **candour**.*

Word use: The opposite of this is **reserve**. | You can also use **candor**.
Word history: from Latin word meaning 'radiance', 'purity', 'candour'

candy
noun **1** a sweet made of boiled sugar
verb **2** to cook in sugar syrup so as to preserve

Noun forms: The plural is **candies**.
Verb forms: I **candied**, I have **candied**, I am **candying**
Word history: French *sucre candi* candied sugar *candi* from Arabic *qand* sugar, from Persian

cane
noun **1** the thin, woody stem of bamboo, sugar cane and other similar plants
verb **2** to beat with a cane (***flog***, ***lash***, ***scourge***, ***thrash***, ***whip***)
3 *Colloquial* to defeat soundly in a competition: *We **caned** the other team!*

Word history: Middle English, from Old French, from Provençal or Italian, from Latin, from Greek word meaning 'reed'

cane toad
noun a toad brought into Queensland to get rid of cane beetles and which is now a pest

canine (kay-nuyn)
adjective **1** having to do with dogs
noun **2** any animal belonging to the dog family: *Foxes and wolves are **canines**.*
3 the pointed tooth on each side of your upper and lower jaws

Word history: from Latin word meaning 'of a dog'

canister
noun a small container, often made of metal: *a tea **canister***

Word history: Latin, from Greek word meaning 'wicker basket'

cannabis (kan-uh-buhs)
noun the dried flowers and leaves of Indian hemp (***marijuana***)

Word history: from Latin word meaning 'hemp'

cannibal
noun someone who eats human flesh

Word building: **cannibalise** *verb* **cannibalism** *noun*
Word history: Spanish

cannon
noun a large gun on wheels

Word history: French, from Italian word meaning 'large tube', from Latin

cannot
a form of **can not**

cannula (kan-yuh-luh)
noun a metal tube which is put into the body, for things like keeping a passage open, or to draw off fluid, or to pass medication through

canny (kan-ee)
adjective **1** not taking risks (***careful***, ***cautious***, ***sensible***)
2 wise (***astute***, ***clever***, ***knowing***, ***shrewd***, ***sharp***)

Adjective forms: **cannier**, **canniest**
Word building: **canniness** *noun*
Word history: apparently from *can*[1]

canoe (kuh-nooh)
noun a light narrow boat that you move by using paddles

Word building: **canoe** *verb* (**canoed**, **canoeing**) **canoeist** *noun*
Word history: Spanish, from Carib

canon[1]
noun **1** a law or rule
2 a set of church laws
3 a piece of music in which the same tune is played or sung by two or more parts overlapping each other

Word history: Middle English and Old English, from Latin word meaning 'rule', 'canon', from Greek word meaning 'straight rod', 'rule', 'standard'

canon[2]
noun a member of the clergy connected with a cathedral

Word history: Middle English, from Medieval Latin

canopy (kan-uh-pee)
noun an ornamental or protective covering: *a bed* ***canopy*** | *a* ***canopy*** *of trees*

Noun forms: The plural is **canopies**.
Word building: **canopied** *adjective*
Word history: Middle English, from Latin word meaning 'net curtains', from Greek word meaning 'mosquito net'

cant[1] (kant)
noun **1** insincere expressions of goodness or high morals
2 words, phrases, etc., used by a particular group of people: *thieves'* ***cant*** | *sociological* ***cant*** (***argot***, ***jargon***, ***lingo***)

Word history: from Latin word meaning 'song'

cant[2] (kant)
noun a slope, or slant

Word history: Middle Dutch, or Middle Low German *kant*, both probably from Old Northern French, from Latin word meaning 'corner', 'side'

can't
contraction of **cannot**

Look up **contractions in grammar**.

cantaloupe (kan-tuh-loohp)
noun → **rockmelon**

Word use: You can also use **cantaloup**.
Word history: French, from Italian *Cantalupo*, a former estate of the Pope near Rome, where it was first grown in Europe

cantankerous (kan-tang-kuh-ruhs)
adjective bad-tempered and quarrelsome: *a* ***cantankerous*** *neighbour* (***aggressive***, ***argumentative***, ***contrary***, ***defiant***, ***stroppy***)

Word history: perhaps from Middle English *contek* contention

canteen
noun **1** a cafeteria or a counter where food is sold in a factory, office, or school (***bistro***, ***cafe***, ***diner***)
2 a box holding cutlery
3 a small container for carrying drinking water

Word history: French, from Italian *cantina* cellar, wine cellar, from Latin

canter
noun the movement of a horse which is a little slower than a gallop

Word building: **canter** *verb*
Word history: short for *Canterbury gallop* (as of pilgrims to Canterbury, England)

canton (kan-ton, kan-ton)
noun a division of a country, especially Switzerland

Word history: French word meaning 'corner', from Latin

canvas
noun **1** heavy cotton cloth used for sails, tents and other similar articles
2 a piece of this used for painting on: *an artist's* ***canvas***

Word history: Middle English, from Latin *cannabis* hemp

canvass
verb to ask for votes or support from: *The candidate* ***canvassed*** *the voters in her electorate.*

Word building: **canvasser** *noun*
Word history: variant of *canvas*, noun; originally meaning to toss (someone) in a canvas sheet

canyon
noun a deep valley with steep sides

Word history: Spanish word meaning 'tube', from Latin word meaning 'reed'

canyoning
noun the sport of following a river down a canyon, usually on a raft, and involving rockclimbing, abseiling, etc.

Word building: **canyoner** *noun*

cap
noun **1** a soft, close-fitting hat with a peak to shade the face
2 membership of a particular sports team: *He got his* ***cap*** *in the rowing team.*
3 a lid or top
4 a small explosive used in toy guns to make a loud bang
5 an upper limit on a price, salary, etc.
verb **6** to put a cap or top on
7 to improve upon: *He* ***capped*** *his previous record in the high jump.*
phrase **8 cap in hand**, humbly

Verb forms: I **capped**, I have **capped**, I am **capping**
Word history: Old English *cæpe*, from Late Latin word meaning 'cap', 'hooded cloak', 'cape', apparently from *caput* head

capable
adjective **1** having ability or skill: *He is a* ***capable*** *cook.* (***competent***, ***experienced***, ***expert***, ***good***, ***proficient***)
phrase **2 capable of**,
a able to: *He is* ***capable of*** *running a kilometre.*
b likely to do: *He is* ***capable of*** *murder.*

Word use: The opposite of definition 1 is **incapable**. | The opposite of definition 2 is **incapable of**.
Word building: **capability** *noun*
Word history: Late Latin

capacious (kuh-pay-shuhs)
adjective able to hold a lot: *a* ***capacious*** *bag*

Word building: **capaciousness** *noun*
Word history: *capaci(ty)* + *-ous*

capacity
noun **1** the quantity or amount which can be held or contained: *This jug's* ***capacity*** *is one litre.*
2 mental ability: *a pupil's* ***capacity*** *to learn a language*
3 the position or standing of someone: *I am arresting you in my* ***capacity*** *as a police officer.*

Noun forms: The plural is **capacities**.
Word history: Middle English, from Latin

cap-and-trade
adjective having to do with an emissions trading scheme in which a cap is set for allowable emissions in a particular area, and individual emitters are given their allocation of emission permits which they can use or sell provided the overall cap is not breached

cape[1]
noun a loose cloak which is fastened at your neck and hangs over your shoulders

Word history: French, from Spanish, from Late Latin

cape[2]
noun a piece of land jutting out into the sea

Word history: Middle English, from French, from Provençal, from Latin *caput* head

caper
verb **1** to jump or dance about (***frisk***, ***gambol***, ***leap***, ***prance***, ***skip***)
noun **2** a prank or a foolish action

Word history: figurative use of Latin *caper* he-goat

capillary (kuh-pil-uh-ree)
noun one of the smallest blood vessels in your body

Noun forms: The plural is **capillaries**.
Word history: from Latin word meaning 'relating to the hair'

capital
noun **1** the city which is the official seat of government of a state or country: *Canberra is the* ***capital*** *of Australia.*
2 a large letter: *People's names start with a* ***capital***.
3 the amount of money owned by a business or person
4 any form of wealth used to produce more wealth (***assets***, ***funds***, ***investments***, ***principal***, ***stock***)
adjective **5** chief or main: *a* ***capital*** *city*

Word history: Middle English, from Latin *capitālis* relating to the head or to life, chief

capitalise
verb **1** to print in capital letters, or to begin with a capital
2 to take advantage of: *to* ***capitalise*** *on your opportunities*

Word use: You can also use **capitalize**.
Word building: **capitalisation** *noun*

capitalism
noun the economic system under which industries are owned privately and not by the government

Word use: Compare this with **communism** and **socialism**.
Word building: **capitalist** *noun*

capital letters

Capital letters are the large-sized letters used at the beginning of a sentence or as the first letter of a proper name. Capital letters are also called upper case letters. Some are just larger versions of the lower case letter, like *O*, *o*. Others are different in their shape as well as being larger in size. For example *Q*, *q* and *R*, *r*.

Capitals are used in the titles of books, films, plays, etc. The following are the types of words which are spelt most commonly with a capital letter:

1 the names and titles of specific people, organisations and institutions:

Sir Neville Bonner	Lady Fairfax
Mr Joe Williams	Ms Gina Curtis
Reserve Bank	Con Savalas

Australian Broadcasting Corporation
University of Sydney
Standards Association of Australia
College of Tourism and Hospitality
Look up **abbreviation** also.

2 the names of places, whether they are countries, states or suburbs:

Italy	United States of America
Fremantle	Brisbane
Kew	Tasmania
Liverpool	Beijing

3 national and ethnic names, and the names of religious and language groups:

Buddhist	Chinese
Fijian	English
African American	Christian
Aboriginal	Swahili

4 the names of historical periods or events, as well as the names of holidays or ceremonies:

the Second World War	Australia Day
the French Revolution	Queen's Birthday
the Eureka Stockade	Christmas Day
the Renaissance	Ramadan

Note that geographical and other names often lose their capital letters when they are shortened:

The Building Workers' Industrial Union was formed in 1942.

After the war, the union grew rapidly.

Building Workers' Industrial Union becomes just *union* if that word is used on its own.

The Murray River rises in the Great Dividing Range. The river is approximately 2600 kilometres in length.

Murray River becomes just *river*; however, if you shortened it to *the Murray*, the capital letter would be retained.

The general rule is that the capital letters are abandoned when you shorten the name to just the common noun in it.

Look up **common noun**.

capital punishment
noun death as punishment for a crime (***death penalty***, ***execution***)

capitulate (kuh-pich-uh-layt)
verb to give in or surrender: *The enemy* ***capitulated***. (***submit***, ***succumb***, ***yield***)

Word building: **capitulation** *noun*
Word history: Medieval Latin word meaning 'arrange in chapters', from Latin word meaning 'head'

cappuccino (kap-uh-cheen-oh)
noun coffee with frothy milk added, made in a special machine

Word history: from Italian word meaning 'hood'

caprice (kuh-prees)
noun a sudden change of mind without an apparent reason (***fancy***, ***impulse***, ***whim***)

Word building: **capricious** *adjective* **capriciousness** *noun*
Word history: French, from Italian *capriccio* a lively dance

capsicum (kap-suh-kuhm)
noun a type of pepper plant and its green or red fruit, which is used in salads or to flavour food

Word history: Latin *capsa* box

capsicum spray
noun an aerosol spray derived from capsicum, which irritates the face, especially the eyes: *The police used **capsicum spray** to subdue the offender.*

Word use: You can also use **pepper spray**.

capsize
verb to turn over: *The boat **capsized**. | The large waves **capsized** the boat.* (***keel over***, ***overturn***, ***tip over***, ***turn turtle***)

capsule
noun **1** a small case or covering, like the one that holds a dose of powdered medicine
2 the part of a spaceship which holds the crew or instruments

Word history: from Latin word meaning 'little box'

captain
noun **1** a leader: ***captain** of the basketball team*
2 someone who commands a group of soldiers
3 someone who is in charge of a ship or aeroplane

Word building: **captaincy** *noun*
Word history: Middle English, from Old French word meaning 'chief', from Latin word meaning 'head'

caption
noun a heading for a newspaper article or a title for a picture or cartoon

Word building: **caption** *verb*
Word history: Latin

captivate
verb to charm and delight: *She **captivated** the audience with her singing.*

Word building: **captivation** *noun*
Word history: from Late Latin word meaning 'taken captive'

captive
noun **1** someone who has been taken prisoner
adjective **2** made or held prisoner, or kept confined: ***captive** animals*

Word use: The opposite of definition 2 is **free**.
Word building: **captive** *adjective* **captivity** *noun*
Word history: Latin

captive breeding
noun the breeding of wild animals in an enclosure, sometimes to prevent extinction of a species

captor
noun someone who captures

capture
verb to take by force (***abduct***, ***apprehend***, ***arrest***, ***catch***, ***seize***)

Word building: **capture** *noun*
Word history: French, from Latin

car
noun **1** a passenger vehicle driven by its own power, usually by an internal-combustion or diesel engine, and used for road travel
2 a carriage running on rails or cable
3 the part of a lift, in which passengers or freight are carried

Word history: Middle English, from Latin, of Celtic origin

carafe (kuh-rahf, kuh-raf)
noun a glass bottle used for serving water, wine or fruit juice at a meal table

Word history: French, from Italian, from Arabic word meaning 'drinking vessel'

caramel
noun **1** a type of sweet, or a colouring or flavouring made from burnt sugar
2 a light brown colour

Word building: **caramel** *adjective*
Word history: French, from Spanish

carat
noun **1** a unit of weight for measuring gems, equal to 200 milligrams
2 a measure of the purity of gold: *Pure gold is 24 **carats**.*

Word history: French, from Italian word meaning 'light weight', from Greek word meaning 'carob bean', 'carat', diminutive of *kéras* horn

carat / caret / carrot

Don't confuse **carat** with **caret** or **carrot**.

A **caret** is the omission mark you use in writing (^) to show where something has to be added.

A **carrot** is a kind of vegetable.

caravan
noun **1** a covered van that can be pulled by a car, and in which you can live, especially when you are on holidays
2 a group of people travelling together, especially across a desert

Word history: French, from Persian

caraway
noun a herb, whose small seeds are used in cooking

Word history: late Middle English, from Medieval Latin, from Arabic

carbine
noun a rifle with a short barrel

Word history: French

carbohydrate
noun a chemical compound containing oxygen, hydrogen and carbon, such as sugar or starch, which is present in all living things

carbon
noun **1** a common element found in all living things as well as in such substances as diamonds, graphite and coal
2 carbon dioxide: ***carbon** sequestration*

Word history: French, from Latin word meaning 'coal', 'charcoal'

carbon cap
noun an upper limit of carbon dioxide production that is permitted by a government or international body which has set the limit in an attempt to reduce the risk of climate change

carbon capture
noun the process of removing carbon dioxide from places like power plants, where it is released, so that it can then be prevented from entering the atmosphere See **carbon sequestration**.

carbon capture and storage
noun the technology of storing carbon dioxide captured from a process that involves its production as a by-product in something like a rock formation so as to prevent its release into the atmosphere

Word use: The abbreviation is **CCS**.

carbon credit
noun a credit earned in schemes set up to decrease the levels of carbon dioxide in the atmosphere, such as in actions like planting forests, etc.

carbon dioxide
noun a colourless gas which has no smell and does not burn, formed when we breathe, when things are burnt, and when organic matter decomposes; used in industry as dry ice and in fizzy drinks; a greenhouse gas

carbon emissions
plural noun the amounts of carbon dioxide released into the atmosphere by coal-fired power generators, transport, forest burning, etc.: *A council was set up to monitor the city's* ***carbon emissions****.*

carbon footprint
noun the carbon dioxide emissions for which an individual or organisation can be held responsible, in things like travel, fuel consumption, diet, energy requirements, etc.: *She aimed to reduce her* ***carbon footprint*** *by half.*

carbon monoxide
noun a colourless poisonous gas which has no smell

carbon-neutral
adjective having achieved carbon neutrality

carbon neutrality
noun a state in which an organisation or country balances its carbon emissions against its carbon reductions to achieve zero net emissions of carbon dioxide

carbon offset
noun a way to make up for greenhouse gases produced in some part of the economy, such as by planting enough trees to compensate for gases produced by airline travel

Word building: **carbon offsetting** *noun*

carbon paper
noun paper that is coated with carbon, used between sheets of writing or typing paper to make copies

carbon reduction
noun a reduction in greenhouse gas emissions, usually as part of a plan to achieve carbon neutrality

carbon sequestration
noun the process by which carbon dioxide is removed from the atmosphere, either naturally by plants in their growth, or artificially by various means whereby it is prevented from returning to the atmosphere by the creation of products containing it which have long-term use, as timber from forests, or by storing it in sealed reservoirs, as by injecting it into underground geological formations

carbon sink
noun a large area of vegetation which absorbs carbon dioxide from the atmosphere, thus reducing the level of greenhouse gases

carbon tax
noun a tax on the consumption of fossil fuels, designed to recoup the costs of managing and repairing the environmental damage caused by such fuels

carbon trading
noun trading in carbon credits on a carbon market

carbuncle (kah-bung-kuhl)
noun a painful pus-filled swelling, like a large boil

Word history: Middle English, from Old Northern French, from Latin *carbunculus*, diminutive of *carbo* (live) coal

carburettor (kah-byuh-ret-uh)
noun the part of an engine in which fuel and air are mixed together to form an explosive gas

carcass (kah-kuhs)
noun the dead body of an animal

Word use: You can also use **carcase**.
Word history: French, from Italian

carcinogen (kah-sin-uh-juhn)
noun any substance which tends to produce a cancer in a body

Word building: **carcinogenic** *adjective*

card[1]
noun **1** a piece of stiff paper or cardboard, usually small and rectangular in shape: *a birthday* ***card*** *| a business* ***card***
2 one of a set of cards used for playing games such as rummy or bridge
3 *Computers* a circuit board: *a sound* ***card*** *| a video* ***card***
4 *Colloquial* an amusing person: *She's a real* ***card****, always making us laugh.*
phrase **5 on the cards**, likely to happen
6 put (or **lay**) **your cards on the table**, to speak openly

Word history: Middle English, from Latin *c(h)arta* paper, from Greek word meaning 'leaf of paper'

card[2]
noun a type of comb, used to get the knots out of wool or cotton before it is spun

Word building: **card** *verb*
Word history: late Middle English, from Latin word meaning 'thistle'

cardboard
noun a thick, stiff sort of paper

cardiac
adjective having to do with the heart: *a* ***cardiac*** *disease*

Word history: Latin *cardiacus* of the heart, from Greek *kardiakós*

cardigan
noun a knitted jacket with buttons down the front

Word history: named after the 7th Earl of *Cardigan*, 1797–1868

cardinal
adjective **1** chief or of first importance: *a **cardinal** point to remember* (***basic, fundamental, essential, key, primary***)
noun **2** a high-ranking priest in the Roman Catholic Church

Word history: Middle English, from Latin word meaning 'chief'

cardinal number
noun a term used in mathematics for a number such as '1', '2', '3', etc., which tells you how many things are in a given set but not the order in which they appear

Word use: Compare this with **ordinal number**. | For information on how to write and punctuate numbers, look up **number**.

cardiogram
noun → **electrocardiogram**

cardiograph (<u>kah</u>-dee-uh-graf)
noun → **electrocardiograph**

cardiology (kah-dee-<u>ol</u>-uh-jee)
noun the study of the heart and the work it does

Word building: **cardiologist** *noun*

cardiopulmonary resuscitation
(kah-dee-oh-pul-muhn-ree ruh-sus-uh-<u>tay</u>-shuhn)
noun an emergency life-support procedure using a combination of mouth-to-mouth resuscitation and external cardiac massage: *We learned about **cardiopulmonary resuscitation** in our life saving classes.*

Word use: The abbreviation is **CPR**.

cardiovascular (kah-dee-oh-<u>vas</u>-kyuh-luh)
adjective having to do with the heart and blood vessels

care
noun **1** worry or anxiety: *She was worn out by **care**.*
2 thoughtful attention: *Do your work with **care**.*
3 protection or charge: *under the **care** of a doctor*
verb **4** to worry: *I **care** about the future.*
phrase **5 care for**,
a to like or love (***be fond of, enjoy, prize***)
b to look after: *We must help **care for** the sick.*
6 care of, at the address of: *You can write to him **care of** his mother.*

Word building: **carefree** *adjective*
Word history: Old English *c(e)aru*

careen (kuh-<u>reen</u>)
verb to go forward while swaying from side to side: *The train **careened** down the mountain.*

Word history: French, from Latin word meaning 'keel'

career
noun **1** the job or profession in which you earn your living: *a business **career** | a **career** in law* (***occupation, vocation, work***)
verb **2** to move rapidly and wildly: *The car's brakes failed and it **careered** down the hill.*

Word history: French, from Italian, from Latin

careful
adjective **1** taking care to avoid risks: *a **careful** driver* (***cautious, wary, watchful***)
2 putting time and effort into your work (***attentive, conscientious, diligent, fussy***)

Word use: The opposite of this is **careless**.
Word building: **carefully** *adverb* **carefulness** *noun*

careless
adjective **1** done without paying enough attention: ***careless** work* (***casual, hasty, heedless, lax, negligent, sloppy***)
2 done or said without thinking: *A **careless** remark can be hurtful.* (***inconsiderate, thoughtless, unmindful, unthinking***)

Word use: The opposite of definition 1 is **careful**. | The opposite of definition 2 is **thoughtful**.
Word building: **carelessly** *adverb* **carelessness** *noun*

caress (kuh-<u>res</u>)
noun **1** an action which shows affection, such as a gentle touch, a hug or a kiss
verb **2** to touch with affection

Word history: French, from Italian, from Latin word meaning 'dear'

caret
noun a mark (^) you make in writing or printing to show where something has to be added

Word history: from Latin word meaning 'there is lacking'

caret / carrot / carat

Don't confuse **caret** with **carrot** or **carat**.

A **carrot** is a kind of vegetable.

Carat is a measurement used to express the fineness of gold and the weight of gemstones:

My watch is ten carat gold.

caretaker
noun someone who looks after a thing or a place, especially a building

cargo
noun the goods carried on a ship, aircraft, truck, etc.

Noun forms: The plural is **cargoes**.
Word history: from Spanish word meaning 'load'

caribou (<u>ka</u>-ruh-booh)
noun any of several kinds of reindeer from North America

Noun forms: The plural is **caribou**.
Word history: Canadian French, from Algonquian *xalibu* pawer, scratcher

caricature (<u>ka</u>-rik-uh-choouh)
noun a picture or description of someone or something which makes fun of their unusual or characteristic features (***cartoon, lampoon, parody, send-up, take-off***)

Word building: **caricature** *verb*
Word history: French, from Italian word meaning '(over)load', 'exaggerate'

caricaturist
noun someone who draws caricatures

caries (<u>kair</u>-reez)
noun decay, especially of bone or teeth

Word building: **carious** *adjective*
Word history: Latin

carillon (kuh-ril-yuhn)
noun a set of bells hung in a tower and used to play tunes

Word history: French word meaning 'chime of (originally four) bells', from Latin *quattuor* four

carillonist
noun someone who plays carillon bells

caring
adjective thoughtful and sympathetic: *People liked him for his **caring** nature.*

carjack
verb to steal (a car) by forcing the driver to get out, or by forcing the driver to drive to a chosen destination

Word use: You can also use **car-jack**.
Word building: **carjacker** *noun* **carjacking** *noun*

car kit
noun a hands-free mobile phone system installed in a vehicle

carmine
noun **1** a crimson or purplish red colour
2 a crimson colouring obtained from cochineal

Word building: **carmine** *adjective*
Word history: Medieval Latin, from Spanish word meaning 'crimson'

carnage
noun the killing of many people: *the **carnage** of war* (***butchery***, ***massacre***, ***slaughter***)

Word history: French, from Italian word meaning 'meat', from Latin word meaning 'flesh'

carnal
adjective having to do with the body

Word history: Middle English, from Latin word meaning 'flesh'

carnation
noun a garden plant with red, pink, or white flowers

Word history: from Latin word meaning 'fleshiness'

carnival
noun **1** a period of time during which sporting events are held: *an athletics **carnival** | a surfing **carnival***
2 a time of processions and public merry-making, usually for a special occasion: *The city is holding a New Year **Carnival** in the main street.* (***festival***, ***fiesta***, ***mardi gras***)

Word history: from Italian word meaning 'stop (eating) meat'

carnivore (kah-nuh-vaw)
noun an animal that eats meat: *Cats and dogs are **carnivores**.*

Word use: Compare this with **herbivore**, **insectivore** and **omnivore**.
Word building: **carnivorous** *adjective*

carob (ka-ruhb)
noun a tree which bears a long pod with seeds in a sweet pulp

Word history: French, from Arabic

carol
noun a joyful song, especially a Christmas song or hymn

Word building: **carol** *verb* (**carolled**, **carolling**) **caroller** *noun*
Word history: Middle English, from Old French

carotid (kuh-rot-uhd)
adjective having to do with either of the two large arteries, one on each side of the neck, which carry blood to the head

Word history: from Greek word meaning 'stupor' (thought to be caused by compression of these arteries)

carouse (kuh-rowz)
noun **1** a noisy or drunken feast
verb **2** to drink deeply and behave noisily and drunkenly

Word history: German *gar aus* (drink a cup) wholly out

carousel (ka-ruh-sel)
noun **1** a merry-go-round
2 the continuously moving belt from which travellers get their bags at the end of a journey by ship, aeroplane or bus

Word history: French, from Italian, from Latin word meaning 'cart'

carp
noun a large, freshwater fish that is good to eat

Noun forms: The plural is **carp**.
Word history: Middle English, from Provençal, from Late Latin *carpa*; of Germanic origin

car park
noun an area of land or a specially designed building where you are permitted to park your car

carpenter
noun someone who makes things out of wood and puts up wooden parts of a building

Word history: Middle English, from Late Latin word meaning 'wagon-maker', from Latin *carpentum* wagon

carpentry
noun → **woodwork**

carpet
noun **1** a thick, woven floor covering
verb **2** to cover with a carpet
phrase **3 on the carpet**, being or about to be blamed

Verb forms: I **carpeted**, I have **carpeted**, I am **carpeting**
Word history: Middle English, from Latin word meaning 'card' (wool)

carpet snake
noun a large, non-venomous Australian snake that kills by crushing, often used in barns to control rats, mice, etc.

car pool
noun an arrangement whereby a group of people travel together in one car on a regular basis, taking turns to transport the rest of the group each in their own car

Word use: You can also use **carpool**.

carpool
verb to take part in a car pool: *The parents decided to **carpool** to reduce traffic around the school.*

carriage
noun **1** one of the passenger-carrying cars on a train
2 a vehicle on wheels for carrying people, pulled by a horse or horses
3 the way you hold your head and body when you walk or stand (***attitude***, ***bearing***, ***deportment***, ***posture***, ***stance***)
Word history: Middle English, from Old Northern French

carrier
noun **1** someone or something that carries
2 an organisation which provides telecommunication services

carrion
noun the rotting flesh of dead animals
Word history: Middle English, Old French, from Latin *caro* flesh

carrot
noun an orange-coloured root vegetable
Word history: French, from Latin, from Greek

carrot / carat / caret
Don't confuse **carrot** with **carat** or **caret**.
Carat is a measurement used to express the fineness of gold and the weight of gemstones:
My watch is ten carat gold.
A **caret** is the omission mark you use in writing (^) to show where something has to be added.

carry
verb **1** to take from one place to another: *to **carry** something in your pocket* | *to **carry** cargo by ship* (***convey***, ***deliver***, ***transfer***, ***transport***)
2 to take or bring: *sounds **carried** by the wind* | *electricity **carried** by cables* (***bear***, ***conduct***, ***relay***, ***transmit***)
3 to bear the weight or burden of: *The bag was almost too heavy for him to **carry**.* (***hold up***, ***shoulder***, ***support***, ***sustain***)
4 to walk, stand or behave: *She **carries** herself well.*
phrase **5 carry away**, to excite: *She was **carried away** by the beautiful music.*
6 carry off,
a to win: *to **carry off** the prize*
b to handle boldly and successfully: *to **carry off** a situation*
c to cause the death of: ***carried off** by cancer*
7 carry on,
a to conduct: *to **carry on** a business*
b to continue: ***Carry on** with what you were doing.*
8 carry out, to complete: *to **carry out** a plan*
9 carry over, to put off until later
10 carry through,
a to complete (***accomplish***, ***achieve***, ***attain***, ***bring off***, ***finish***)
b to support: *She'll **carry** them **through** their hard times.*
Verb forms: I **carried**, I have **carried**, I am **carrying**
Word history: Middle English, from Late Latin word meaning 'convey by wagon', from Latin

cart
noun **1** a small vehicle, sometimes pulled by a horse, used for carrying a load
verb **2** to carry in or as if in a cart: *She **carted** the baby around all day.*
Word building: **carter** *noun*
Word history: Old English *cræt*

cartel (kah-<u>tel</u>)
noun a group formed of various firms to fix prices, etc., in some field of business
Word history: French, from Italian, from Latin *charta* paper

Cartesian coordinates
plural noun Mathematics numbers given to a point to identify its position, being the perpendicular distances of the point from two (or three) axes
Word history: from *Cartesius* a Latinised version of the name René *Descartes*, a mathematician and philosopher

cartilage
noun a firm, elastic substance forming part of your bone structure
Word history: French, from Latin *cartilāgo* gristle

cartography (kah-<u>tog</u>-ruh-fee)
noun the making of maps or charts
Word building: **cartographic** *adverb*
Word history: Medieval Latin *carta* chart, map + *-graphy*

carton
noun a cardboard box often used for packaging food: *a milk **carton*** | *a **carton** of tinned fish*
Word history: French

cartoon
noun **1** a funny drawing
2 a comic strip
3 a film made of many slightly different drawings which give the effect of movement when put through a projector
Word building: **cartoonist** *noun*
Word history: French, from Italian word meaning 'pasteboard', 'cartoon', from Latin word meaning 'paper'

cartridge
noun **1** a case which holds the explosive powder and often also the bullet, for a rifle or other gun
2 a container, as for ink for some types of fountain pens, or as toner for computer printers, or for recording tape for tape recorders, etc.

cartwheel
noun **1** the wheel of a cart, usually large and wooden, with spokes and metal tyres
2 a sideways somersault with legs and arms outstretched

carve
verb **1** to shape by cutting: *He **carved** a doll from a piece of wood.*
2 to cut up or cut into slices: *to **carve** a turkey* | *to **carve** a leg of lamb*
Word building: **carved** *adjective* **carver** *noun*
Word history: Old English *ceorfan* cut

carve / calve
Don't confuse **carve** with **calve**, which means 'to produce a calf'.

carving
noun **1** the act of making something by carving
2 a carved design or work

casanova (kas-uh-noh-vuh, kaz-uh-noh-vuh)
noun a man notable for his amorous adventures

Word history: from Giovanni Jacopo *Casanova*, 1725–98, Italian amorous adventurer and writer

cascade
noun **1** a waterfall over steep rocks
verb **2** to fall like a cascade: *The ferns* ***cascaded*** *down the cliff face.*

Word history: French, from Italian, from Latin word meaning 'fall'

case[1]
noun **1** an example of the existence or occurrence of something: *a* ***case*** *of forgetfulness | a* ***case*** *of measles*
2 a list of facts or reasons: *This is our* ***case*** *for a new library.*
3 an action against someone in a court of law
4 *Grammar* the form of a noun or pronoun which shows its relation to other words in a sentence
phrase **5 in any case**, anyhow or under any circumstances

Word use: For definition 4 the three cases are **subjective**, **objective** and **possessive**.
Word history: Middle English, from Latin word meaning 'a falling', 'occurrence'

case[2]
noun **1** a container: *a pencil* ***case*** *| a* ***case*** *of apples*
2 a suitcase: *My* ***case*** *is packed with my holiday clothes.*

Word history: Middle English, from Latin word meaning 'box', 'receptacle'

casement
noun a hinged window which opens like a door

Word history: *case[2]* + *-ment*

cash
noun **1** money in notes or coins, rather than cheques: *Have you any* ***cash*** *in your pocket?*
2 money available straight away: *Will you pay* ***cash*** *or charge it?*
verb **3** to give or get cash for: *to* ***cash*** *a cheque*

Word use: Compare definition 2 with **credit**.
Word history: French, from Provençal, from Latin word meaning 'box'

cash / cache

Don't confuse **cash** with **cache**, which is a hidden store of provisions or weapons:

The bushranger had a cache of supplies and guns in the bush.

cashew
noun a small, curved nut that you can eat

Word history: French, from Brazilian Portuguese, from Tupi

cash flow
noun the amount of cash coming in and out of a company or other enterprise in a given period

cashier
noun someone who is in charge of the money in a shop or bank

Word history: from French word meaning 'cash box'

cashmere (kash-mear)
noun fine wool obtained from the Kashmir goats of India, often used to make clothes

casino (kuh-see-noh)
noun a building or large room where gambling games are played

Noun forms: The plural is **casinos**.
Word history: Italian word meaning 'little house', from Latin word meaning 'cottage'

cask
noun a barrel for holding wine or other liquids

Word history: French, from Spanish word meaning 'skull', 'helmet', 'cask' (for wine, etc.), from Late Latin word meaning 'break', 'shake'

casket
noun a small chest or box

cassava (kuh-sah-vuh)
noun a family of tropical plants whose roots are used for food

Word history: Spanish, from Haitian

casserole
noun **1** a covered baking dish
2 the food, usually a mixture of meat and vegetables, cooked in it

Word history: French *casse* pan, ladle, from Late Latin, from Greek word meaning 'little cup'

cassette
noun **1** the plastic container holding the recording tape used in videos and tape-recorders
adjective **2** designed for playing cassettes: *a* ***cassette*** *recorder*

cassock
noun a long garment worn by members of the clergy

Word history: French, from Italian

cassowary (kas-uh-wuh-ree)
noun a large, three-toed bird found in Australia, New Guinea and nearby islands, which is almost as large as an ostrich and cannot fly

Noun forms: The plural is **cassowaries**.
Word history: Malay

cast
verb **1** to throw out or fling: *to* ***cast*** *a fishing line | to* ***cast*** *a stone*
2 to cause to fall: *The sun* ***cast*** *a shadow over the field.*
3 to throw off or shed: *A snake* ***casts*** *its old skin.*
4 to select for a play: *They* ***cast*** *him as the dragon.*
5 to form in a mould: *The decorative iron railings were* ***cast*** *in 1900.*
noun **6** all the actors in a play
7 a mould of plaster around a broken limb
8 a permanent squint: *He has a* ***cast*** *in his eye.*
phrase **9 cast about**,
a to search with your mind: *to* ***cast about*** *for a reason*
b to scheme
10 cast back, to refer to something past: *to* ***cast back*** *to happier times*
11 cast off,
a to reject or get rid of
b in knitting, to make the final row of stitches
12 cast on, in knitting, to make the first row of stitches

Verb forms: I **cast**, I have **cast**, I am **casting**
Word history: Middle English, from Scandinavian

castanets
plural noun a pair of shell-shaped pieces of ivory or wood which you hold in the palm of your hand and strike together in time to music and dancing

Word history: Spanish, from Latin word meaning 'chestnut'

castaway
noun someone who has been shipwrecked, especially someone who has escaped from the ship to an island or other remote, lonely place

caste
noun **1** one of the social groups or divisions into which Hindus are born
2 any strictly followed system of social divisions

Word history: Spanish, Portuguese *casta* breed, race, from Latin word meaning 'pure', 'chaste'

castigate
verb to criticise or punish severely

Word building: **castigation** *noun* **castigator** *noun*
Word history: Latin

cast iron
noun an alloy of iron, carbon and other elements made by casting in a mould

castle
noun **1** a large strongly-built fort, used as a home by royalty and the nobility, especially long ago
2 a piece in chess, shaped like a castle (***rook***)

Word history: Middle English, from Latin word meaning 'fortress'

castor
noun **1** a small wheel attached to the bottom of a bed or under the legs of some tables and chairs to make them easier to move
2 a bottle with holes in the top, for holding sugar

Word history: Latin, from Greek word meaning 'beaver'

castor oil
noun a sticky oil pressed from the seeds of a plant and used as a medicine

castrate
verb to remove the testicles from: *to **castrate** the bull*

Word building: **castration** *noun*
Word history: Latin

casual
adjective **1** happening by chance: *a **casual** meeting*
2 without thinking: *a **casual** remark* (***nonchalant***, ***offhand***, ***thoughtless***)
3 informal: *I wear **casual** clothes on holidays.* (***easygoing***, ***relaxed***, ***unofficial***)
4 employed only irregularly: *a **casual** worker* (***fill-in***, ***interim***, ***makeshift***, ***provisional***, ***temporary***)
noun **5** a worker employed only irregularly

Word building: **casually** *adverb*
Word history: Late Latin *cāsuālis* by chance

casualty
noun **1** someone hurt or killed in an accident or war
2 the section of a hospital where accident or emergency cases are taken for immediate treatment

Noun forms: The plural is **casualties.**

casuarina (kazh-yuh-ree-nuh)
noun an Australian tree or shrub with jointed stems and no real leaves

Word use: Another name is **she-oak**.

cat
noun **1** a small, furry animal often kept as a pet
2 a member of the cat family, which includes lions, tigers and other similar animals (***feline***)
3 a spiteful girl or woman
phrase **4 let the cat out of the bag**, to give out information, often without meaning to
5 rain cats and dogs, to rain heavily

Word history: Old English *catt, catte*

cataclysm (kat-uh-kliz-uhm)
noun **1** any violent upheaval, especially one of social or political nature
2 *Geology* a sudden and violent physical action producing changes in the earth's surface

Word building: **cataclysmic** *adjective*
cataclysmal *adjective*
Word history: Latin, from Greek word meaning 'deluge'

catacomb (kat-uh-kohm, kat-uh-koohm)
noun a series of underground tunnels and caves or rooms, once used as burial places

Word history: Old English *catacumbe*, from Late Latin

catalogue (kat-uh-log)
noun a list, usually in alphabetical order, of names, books or articles on sale or display and some information about them: *a **catalogue** of artists | a library **catalogue** | a sales **catalogue***

Word building: **catalogue** *verb* **cataloguer** *noun*
Word history: French, from Late Latin, from Greek word meaning 'a list'

catalyst (kat-uh-luhst)
noun **1** *Chemistry* a substance which is added to accelerate a chemical change but which is not permanently affected by the reaction it causes
2 someone or something that causes a change or a reaction

Word building: **catalyse** *verb* **catalysis** *noun*
catalytic *adjective*

catamaran (kat-uh-muh-ran)
noun a boat with two hulls

Word history: from Tamil word meaning 'tied tree or wood'

catapult
noun **1** a Y-shaped stick with a length of elastic joined to the prongs, used for shooting stones at things (***shanghai***, ***sling***, ***slingshot***)
2 a device for launching planes from the deck of a ship
verb **3** to throw or be thrown, as if from a catapult

Word history: Latin, from Greek

cataract
noun **1** a large waterfall
2 a disease of the eye in which the lens becomes clouded, causing loss of sight

Word history: Middle English, from Latin word meaning 'waterfall', from Greek word meaning 'down rushing'

catarrh (kuh-tah)
noun an inflammation of the mucous membrane, resulting in over-secretion of mucus, especially in the respiratory tract

Word building: **catarrhal** *adjective*
Word history: Latin, from Greek word meaning 'running down'

catastrophe (kuh-tas-truh-fee)
noun a sudden disaster (***calamity***, ***debacle***, ***misfortune***, ***tragedy***)

Word building: **catastrophic** *adjective*
Word history: from Greek word meaning 'overturning'

catch
verb **1** to capture, especially after a chase (***ambush***, ***apprehend***, ***snare***, ***trap***, ***waylay***)
2 to take in the hands: *to **catch** a ball*
3 to be in time for: *to **catch** a bus*
4 to get or contract: *to **catch** a cold*
5 to surprise or come upon suddenly: *I **caught** him stealing.*
noun **6** anything worth getting: *It was a great **catch**.*
7 something that's been caught, such as a quantity of fish
8 a fragment: *a **catch** of song*
9 *Cricket* the catching and holding of the ball after it has been batted and before it touches the ground
10 a difficulty, usually one that you don't see: *What's the **catch**?*
phrase **11 catch it**, *Colloquial* to get into trouble
12 catch on,
a to become popular
b to understand
13 catch out,
a to trap into revealing a secret, showing ignorance, etc.: *to **catch** someone **out***
b to surprise
14 catch up, to reach or become level: *He **caught up** with the rest of the class. | I ran and **caught up** to the leaders.*

Verb forms: I **caught**, I have **caught**, I am **catching**
Word building: **catcher** *noun*
Word history: Middle English, from Old Northern French, from Latin word meaning 'take'

catchment area
noun **1** *Geography* the drainage area, especially of a reservoir or river
2 the area from which people may come to a school, hospital, etc.

Word use: You can also use **catchment basin** for definition 1.

catchphrase
noun a phrase adopted and repeated, often meaninglessly, while it is in fashion

catchword
noun **1** a word or phrase repeated for effect, especially by a political party
2 a word printed at the top of a page in a dictionary or other reference book to point to the first or last article on that page

catchy
adjective easy to remember: *a **catchy** tune*

Adjective forms: **catchier**, **catchiest**

catechism (kat-uh-kiz-uhm)
noun a book of questions and answers meant to help you learn about your religion

Word building: **catechise** *verb* **catechist** *noun*
Word history: Late Latin

categorical
adjective clear and plain, with no doubt: *Her response is **categorical**.*

category
noun a group or division of people or things

Noun forms: The plural is **categories**.
Word building: **categorise** *verb*
Word history: Latin, from Greek word meaning 'assertion'

cater
verb to supply food and drink: *My mother is **catering** for my party.*

Word history: Middle English *catour*, 'buyer of provisions', from Old French word meaning 'buyer'

caterer
noun a supplier, especially of food

caterpillar
noun the worm-like grub or larva of a moth or butterfly

Word history: Middle English

caterwaul (kat-uh-wawl)
verb to cry or howl like quarrelling cats

Word history: Middle English, *cater* (compare German *Kater* tomcat) + *wrawen* howl

catharsis (kuh-thah-suhs)
noun **1** a getting rid of feelings that trouble you, especially when brought about by art, drugs or psychiatric therapy
2 *Medicine* a purging, especially of your bowels

Word building: **cathartic** *adjective*
Word history: Neo-Latin, from Greek word meaning 'a cleansing'

cathedral
noun the main church in a district which acts as a bishop's headquarters

catheter (kath-uh-tuh)
noun *Medicine* a hollow tube used to drain fluids from body cavities, especially urine from the bladder

Word history: Late Latin, from Greek word meaning 'let down'

cathode
noun **1** an electrode with a negative charge, which sends out electrons, such as a radio valve
2 the negative electrode of a cell

Word use: The opposite of definition 2 is **anode**.
Word history: from Greek word meaning 'way down'

cathode ray
noun a stream of electrons generated at the cathode during an electric discharge in a vacuum tube

catholic (kath-lik, kath-uh-lik)
adjective **1** universal, or of interest to all
2 broad-minded, or liberal: *to be **catholic** in your tastes and interests*

Word history: Latin, from Greek

cation (<u>kat</u>-uy-uhn)
noun **1** an ion with a positive charge, which is attracted to the cathode in electrolysis
2 any ion, radical or molecule with a positive charge

Word history: Greek *katión*, going down

CAT scanner (<u>kat</u> skan-uh)
noun a machine which produces a series of X-rays, and is often used for medical investigation

Word history: the word CAT is an acronym for *c(omputerised) a(xial) t(omography)*

cattle
noun farm animals such as cows, bulls and oxen: *The **cattle** are grazing in the far paddock.*

Word history: Middle English, from Latin word meaning 'wealth', 'stock'

cattle dog
noun a dog trained to guard and round up cattle

catty
adjective spiteful: *a **catty** remark*

Adjective forms: **cattier, cattiest**

catwalk
noun a long narrow platform on which models walk to display clothes (***runway***)

caucus (<u>kaw</u>-kuhs)
noun a meeting of the members of parliament belonging to a particular political party

Word history: Native American *caucauasa* adviser

caught (kawt)
verb past tense and past participle of **catch**

caught / court
Don't confuse **caught** with **court**, as in tennis court and law court.

cauldron (<u>kawl</u>-druhn)
noun a large rounded kettle or boiler with a lid and handles

Word history: Middle English, from Latin word meaning 'hot'

cauliflower
noun a vegetable with a large round head of white flowers

Word history: half adoption, half translation of Neo-Latin *caulifl̄ōra*, literally, cabbage-flower

caulk (kawk)
verb **1** to make watertight or airtight by filling seams or cracks with tar, etc.: *to **caulk** a sailing vessel* | *to **caulk** a window*
2 to fill or close so as to make watertight, airtight, etc.: *to **caulk** seams* | *to **caulk** cracks*

Word history: Middle English, from Latin word meaning 'tread', 'press'

causality (kaw-<u>zal</u>-uh-tee)
noun **1** the relation of cause and effect
2 the quality of being a cause

Noun forms: The plural is **causalities**.

causation (kaw-<u>zay</u>-shuhn)
noun **1** the action of causing or producing
2 the relation of cause to effect
3 anything that produces an effect

cause
noun **1** someone or something which brings about an effect or result: *His joke was the **cause** of all the laughter.*
2 something that you believe in: *Peace is a **cause** worth working for.*
verb **3** to bring about: *to **cause** trouble*

Word building: **causal** *adjective*
Word history: Middle English, from Latin *causa*

causeway
noun a raised road or path across low or wet ground

Word history: variant of *causey* way, from Middle English, from Late Latin *calciāta* paved road

caustic (<u>kos</u>-tik)
adjective **1** capable of burning or eating away living cells: ***caustic** soda*
2 critical or sarcastic: *a **caustic** remark*

Word history: Latin, from Greek word meaning 'capable of burning'

cauterise (<u>kaw</u>-tuh-ruyz)
verb to burn with a hot instrument, especially to kill germs: *to **cauterise** a wound*

Word use: You can also use **cauterize**.
Word building: **cauterisation** *noun*

caution
noun **1** great care when there is danger: *Use **caution** in crossing city streets.*
2 a warning
verb **3** to warn (***admonish, advise, alert, forewarn, tip off***)

Word building: **cautionary** *adjective* **cautious** *adjective*
Word history: Latin

cavalcade
noun a procession, especially of people on horseback or in horse-drawn carriages

Word history: French, from Italian, from Late Latin word meaning 'ride on horseback'

cavalier (kav-uh-<u>lear</u>)
noun Old-fashioned **1** a soldier or knight on horseback
2 a gallant or a courtly gentleman
adjective **3** not caring about important things: *He had a **cavalier** attitude to his work.*

Word history: French, from Italian, from Latin

cavalry
noun the group of soldiers within an army which used to be mounted on horseback, and now are often equipped with armoured vehicles

Word history: French, from Italian word meaning 'knighthood'

cave
noun **1** a hollow place in a hillside
verb **2** to explore caves
phrase **3 cave in**, to fall or sink: *The ground **caved in** under their feet.*

Word history: Middle English, from Latin *cava* hollow (places)

cavern (<u>kav</u>-uhn)
noun a large cave

Word building: **cavernous** *adjective*
Word history: Middle English, from Latin *caverna* cave

caviar (kav-ee-ah, kav-ee-ah)
noun the salted eggs of sturgeon or other large fish

Word history: French, from Italian, from Turkish

cavil (kav-uhl)
verb to raise stupid and trivial objections, or find fault without a reason

Verb forms: I **cavilled**, I have **cavilled**, I am **cavilling**
Word building: **caviller** *noun*
Word history: French, from Latin word meaning 'a jeering'

cavity
noun an empty space or hollow: *a **cavity** in a wall* | *a **cavity** in a tooth*

Noun forms: The plural is **cavities**.
Word history: French, from Late Latin word meaning 'hollowness'

cavort (kuh-vawt)
verb to dance or jump about

CB radio
noun radio communication with transmitters and receivers suitable for individual use, as by truck drivers, etc.

Word use: You can also use **CB**.
Word history: *c(itizen) b(and) radio*

C clef
noun in written music, the sign showing where middle C is on the stave

CD
noun a disc about 12 cm in diameter, for storing digitally encoded information which can be read by a laser beam and then transmitted to a hi-fi system, a computer monitor or a television set

Word use: The full form is **compact disc**.

CD-ROM (see dee rom)
noun Computers a compact disc which is used to store and retrieve large amounts of data, sound and images, and which may be written to only once

Word history: the word ROM is an acronym for *R(ead) O(nly) M(emory)*

cease
verb to stop: *The noise **ceased**.* | *We will **cease** work now.* (***end***, ***expire***, ***finish***, ***terminate***)

Word history: Middle English, from Latin word meaning 'go', 'yield'

ceasefire
noun **1** an order to stop firing (***armistice***, ***truce***)
2 a ceasing of active warfare

cedar (see-duh)
noun a type of tree, often used for making furniture

Word history: Old English, from Latin, from Greek

cede (seed)
verb to yield or give up by means of a treaty or formal agreement: *to **cede** land*

Word history: from Latin word meaning 'go', 'withdraw', 'yield', 'grant'

cedilla (suh-dil-uh)
noun a mark placed under the letter 'c' in languages such as French and Portuguese

A **cedilla** shows that the 'c' should be pronounced like an s, not a *k*. For example, the French word *garçon* (boy) is pronounced with an *s* sound in the middle.

ceiling
noun **1** the inside lining that covers the top of a room
2 the top limit that something can reach: *We should put a **ceiling** on the price of bread.*

Word history: Middle English *ceil*

ceiling / sealing
Don't confuse **ceiling** with **sealing**, which comes from the verb seal, to close or fasten tightly:
I am sealing the jam jars with wax.

celebrant
noun **1** a priest or minister who leads a religious ceremony
2 an official who isn't a priest or minister but who has the authority to conduct a marriage ceremony, funeral, etc.

Word building: **celebrancy** *noun*

celebrate
verb **1** to honour with ceremonies and festivities: *Christians **celebrate** the birth of Jesus at Christmas.*
2 to perform solemnly: *to **celebrate** mass*
3 to have a party: *When exams are over, we're going to **celebrate**.* (***party on***, ***rejoice***, ***revel***, ***whoop it up***)

Word building: **celebration** *noun*
Word history: Latin

celebrated
adjective famous: *a **celebrated** writer* (***important***, ***notable***, ***noted***, ***renowned***)

celebrity (suh-leb-ruh-tee)
noun a famous or well-known person (***VIP***, ***hero***, ***household name***, ***personality***, ***star***)

Noun forms: The plural is **celebrities**.

celerity (suh-le-ruh-tee)
noun great speed or swiftness

Word history: Middle English, from Latin

celery
noun a vegetable, of the parsley family, with long green stalks that are good to eat

Word history: French, from dialect Italian, from Late Latin, from Greek word meaning 'parsley'

celestial
adjective having to do with heaven

Word history: Middle English, from Latin *caelestis* heavenly

celibacy (sel-uh-buh-see)
noun the condition of being unmarried and refraining from sexual intercourse: *Some priests live under vows of **celibacy**.*

Word building: **celibate** *adjective* **celibate** *noun*

cell
noun **1** a small room in a prison or a convent (***compartment***, ***cubicle***, ***den***)
2 the tiny basic parts of all living matter, enclosed by a membrane in animals and a cell wall in plants: *plant **cells*** | *blood **cells*** | *nerve **cells***

3 part of an electric battery
4 an area covered by one radio transmitter in a cellular telephone network

Word history: Old English *cell*, from Latin word meaning 'room'

cell / sell

Don't confuse **cell** with **sell**. To **sell** something is to hand it over to someone in exchange for money.

cellar
noun **1** an underground room or store
2 a supply of wines

Word history: from Latin word meaning 'pantry'

cellar / seller

Don't confuse **cellar** with **seller**, which is someone who sells things.

cello (<u>chel</u>-oh)
noun an instrument shaped like a large violin, which has four strings and is held upright on the floor between the knees of the player

Word use: The **cello** sounds lower than the **violin** and **viola** and higher than the **double bass**.
Word building: **cellist** (<u>chel</u>-uhst) *noun*
Word history: short form of *violoncello*

cell phone
noun → **cellular telephone**

cellular (<u>sel</u>-yuh-luh)
adjective having many small holes or cells

Word history: from Latin word meaning 'little room'

cellular telephone
noun a type of telephone, usually portable or for use in a car, which sends or receives signals controlled by a radio transmitter. Each transmitter covers a specific area (**cell**) and is linked to other transmitters by a computer network, thus allowing a service over a large area.

Word use: You can also use **cell phone**.

cellulite (<u>sel</u>-yuh-luyt)
noun fatty deposits, giving a dimply appearance to the skin, which apparently cannot be removed by dieting or exercise

celluloid (<u>sel</u>-yuh-loyd)
noun **1** *Chemistry* a plastic consisting mainly of a cellulose salt and camphor, used for toys, toilet articles, photographic film, etc.
2 films, or cinema
adjective **3** having to do with films: *a **celluloid** hero*
4 unreal, or synthetic

Word history: Trademark; *cellul(ose)* + *-oid*

cellulose (<u>sel</u>-yuh-lohs)
noun important material that forms the cell walls of plants and is found in wood, cotton, hemp and paper

Word history: Latin *cellula* little cell + *-ose*

Celsius
adjective having to do with a scale of temperature in which 0° is the melting point of ice and 100° is the boiling point of water

Word use: The symbol is **C**, without a full stop.
Word history: named after A *Celsius*, 1701–44, Swedish astronomer

cement
noun **1** a mixture of clay and limestone, used for making concrete
2 a type of glue (***adhesive***, ***gum***, ***mortar***, ***paste***)
verb **3** to unite or join together

Word history: from Latin word meaning 'rough stone'

cemetery (<u>sem</u>-uh-tree)
noun a burial ground or graveyard

Noun forms: The plural is **cemeteries**.
Word history: Middle English, from Late Latin, from Greek *koimetirion* meaning 'dormitory', from *koiman* meaning 'to put to sleep'

cenotaph (<u>sen</u>-uh-tahf)
noun a public memorial to those killed in war

Word history: Latin, from Greek word meaning 'an empty tomb'

censor
noun **1** someone who is specially chosen to decide what books, films or news reports are to be made available to the public
verb **2** to remove as not being suitable for the public: *to **censor** paragraphs from a book* (***ban***, ***bar***, ***exclude***, ***outlaw***, ***prevent***)

Word building: **censorial** *adjective*
Word history: Latin

censor / sensor

Don't confuse **censor** with **sensor**, which is something that detects changes in heat, light and moisture.

censorious (sen-<u>saw</u>-ree-uhs)
adjective critical and fault-finding

censorship
noun the act or practice of censoring

censure (<u>sen</u>-shuh)
verb to find fault with, or condemn: *The manager **censured** the clerk for being late so often.*

Word building: **censure** *noun*
Word history: Middle English, from Latin word meaning 'censorship', 'judgement'

census
noun an official counting of all the people who live in a place or country

Word history: Latin

cent
noun a coin worth 100th of a dollar

Word history: Latin, short for *centēsimus* hundredth

cent / sent / scent

Don't confuse **cent** with **sent** or **scent**.

Sent is the past form of the verb send:

He sent me this postcard.

A **scent** is the smell that flowers and perfume have.

centaur (<u>sen</u>-taw)
noun a creature of Greek legend, said to be half man and half horse

Word history: Middle English, from Latin, from Greek

centenarian
noun someone who is 100 years old

Word history: Latin

centenary (sen-<u>teen</u>-uh-ree, sen-<u>ten</u>-uh-ree)
noun a 100th anniversary

Noun forms: The plural is **centenaries.**
Word history: Latin *centēnārius* of or containing 100

centennial (sen-<u>ten</u>-ee-uhl)
adjective **1** marking the end of 100 years
2 lasting 100 years
3 taking place every 100 years

Word history: Latin *centennium* 100 years + *-al*; modelled on *biennial*

Centigrade
adjective an old-fashioned word for **Celsius**

Word history: French

centimetre
noun a unit of length in the metric system, equal to 0.01 metre

Word use: The symbol is **cm**, without a full stop. | Look up **metric system**. | The US spelling is **centimeter**.

centipede
noun a small insect-like creature with a long thin body and many pairs of legs

Word history: from Latin word meaning 'hundred-footed insect'

central
adjective **1** of or forming a centre
2 in, at or near the centre
3 most important: *the **central** character in a novel | a **central** idea*

Word use: The opposite of this is **central.**
Word history: Latin

centralisation
noun **1** the concentration of administrative power in a central government
2 the drawing or moving of people, businesses, etc., towards a centre

Word use: You can also use **centralization.**

centralise
verb **1** to bring under one control, especially in government
2 to come together at a centre

Word use: You can also use **centralize.**

central nervous system
noun → **nervous system** (definition 2a)

centre
noun **1** the middle point of an area: *the **centre** of a circle* (***core***, ***focus***, ***heart***, ***hub***, ***nucleus***)
2 a place for a particular activity: *a shopping **centre***
verb **3** to bring or come to a centre: *She **centred** her mind on the job. | All the attention **centred** on the winner.*

Word use: The US spelling is **center.**
Word history: Middle English, from Latin, from Greek word meaning 'sharp point', 'centre'

centrefold
noun the double page in the middle of a magazine, usually having a large photograph for pinning up on a wall

centre of gravity
noun the point through which forces of gravity act on an object, keeping it evenly balanced in any position

centrifugal (sen-<u>trif</u>-uh-guhl, sen-truh-<u>fyooh</u>-guhl)
adjective moving outwards from the centre: ***centrifugal** force*

Word history: Neo-Latin *centrifugus* centre-fleeing + *-al*

centrifugal force
noun an apparent force exerted on an object moving in a curved path, which seems to be pulling the object outwards

centripetal force
noun a force acting on a body, which causes it to move in a circle or curve by pulling it towards the centre

centurion
noun in the ancient Roman army, the leader of 100 soldiers

Word history: Middle English, from Latin

century
noun **1** a period of 100 years
2 any group of 100: *He scored a **century** in the cricket match.*

Word history: Latin *centuria* a division of a hundred things

cephalic (suh-<u>fal</u>-ik)
adjective having to do with the head

Word history: Latin, from Greek word meaning 'of the head'

ceramic (suh-<u>ram</u>-ik)
adjective **1** made of clay: *a **ceramic** pot*
noun **2 ceramics**, the craft of making things out of clay: ***Ceramics** is taught at the art school.*
3 the things made: *We sell **ceramics** in our craft shop.*

Word history: from Greek word meaning 'pottery'

cereal (<u>sear</u>-ree-uhl)
noun **1** a grain plant, such as wheat, corn or rice
2 a food made from grain, especially a breakfast food

Word history: Latin *Cereālis* pertaining to Ceres, ancient Italian goddess of agriculture and corn

cereal / serial
Don't confuse **cereal** with **serial,** which is a story you get one part at a time at regular intervals.

cerebral (<u>se</u>-ruh-bruhl, suh-<u>ree</u>-bruhl)
adjective having to do with the brain

Word history: Neo-Latin

cerebral palsy
noun a form of paralysis caused by brain damage

Word use: People who suffer from this paralysis are sometimes called **spastics**. However, because some people use **spastic** to refer informally to someone they think is foolish, the term has taken on negative and offensive overtones. For that reason, it is avoided by many people when referring to sufferers of cerebral palsy.

ceremonial
adjective belonging to or used for a ceremony (***formal***, ***ritual***, ***stately***)

ceremonious
adjective elaborately polite: *a **ceremonious** welcome*

ceremony
noun **1** the solemn actions performed on an important occasion: *a wedding **ceremony** | the opening **ceremony** for the new school*
phrase **2 stand on ceremony**, to be too formal or polite

Noun forms: The plural is **ceremonies**.
Word history: from Latin word meaning 'sacred rite'

cerise (suh-<u>rees</u>, suh-<u>reez</u>)
adjective red like the colour of a cherry

Word building: **cerise** *noun*
Word history: French

certain
adjective **1** confident or having no doubt: *She was **certain** that she had seen him.* (***clear***, ***convinced***, ***definite***, ***positive***, ***sure***)
2 sure: *It is **certain** to happen.* (***bound***, ***fated***, ***inevitable***)
3 definite or particular, but not named: *a **certain** person*

Word use: The opposite of this is **uncertain**.
Word building: **certainly** *adverb* **certainty** *noun*
Word history: Middle English, from Latin word meaning 'fixed', 'certain'

certificate
noun a written paper stating certain facts: *a **certificate** of health | a birth **certificate***

Word history: Middle English, from Medieval Latin

certify
verb to state in writing or declare as fact

Verb forms: I **certified**, I have **certified**, I am **certifying**
Word building: **certification** *noun*
Word history: Middle English, from French, from Medieval Latin

certitude (<u>ser</u>-tuh-tyoohd)
noun total belief, or certainty

cervix (<u>ser</u>-viks)
noun the entrance to the womb

Noun forms: The plural is **cervices** (suh-<u>vuy</u>-seez) or **cervixes**.
Word building: **cervical** *adjective*
Word history: Latin

cessation
noun a pause or stopping

Word history: Latin

cession (<u>sesh</u>-uhn)
noun a giving up of rights, territory, etc., to another by treaty or agreement

Word history: Latin

cesspool
noun **1** a pit or cistern for holding the drainage or sewerage from a house
2 any filthy place for keeping things: *a **cesspool** of iniquity | His mind is a **cesspool**.*

cetacean (suh-<u>tay</u>-shuhn)
adjective **1** belonging to the class of marine mammals that includes the whales, dolphins, porpoises, etc.
noun **2** a cetacean mammal

Word building: **cetaceous** *adjective*
Word history: Neo-Latin *Cetācea*

CGI
noun Computers a standard for communication between a server and a host

Word history: *C(ommon) G(ateway) I(nterface)*

chador (<u>chah</u>-duh)
noun → **burqa**

chafe
verb **1** to wear down or make sore by rubbing: *This saddle **chafes** my horse.* (***abrade***, ***coarsen***, ***rasp***, ***roughen***)
2 to become impatient: *She **chafed** at the delay.*

Word history: Middle English, from Late Latin contraction of Latin *calefacere* make hot

chaff (chahf)
noun **1** the husks or dry outer coverings of grain: *to separate the wheat from the **chaff***
2 straw cut up small and used for animal feed

Word history: Old English *ceaf*

chagrin (shuh-<u>grin</u>, <u>shag</u>-ruhn)
noun a feeling of anger and disappointment: *She found to her **chagrin** that they had already left.*

Word history: French

chain
noun **1** a series of metal rings joined together
2 a series of connected things: *a mountain **chain** | a **chain** of events* (***course***, ***cycle***, ***sequence***, ***succession***)
3 a number of shops, hotels or theatres that belong to one owner
verb **4** to fasten with a chain
phrase **5 drag the chain**, *Australian, NZ Colloquial* to avoid or fall behind in your share of work or responsibility

Word history: Middle English, from Latin

chain-reaction
noun **1** *Physics* a nuclear reaction which produces enough neutrons to continue the reaction
2 *Chemistry* a reaction which results in a product necessary for the continuing of the reaction
3 *Colloquial* a series of reactions brought about by one event: *A pay-increase for railway workers would cause a **chain-reaction** of wage claims.*

chainsaw
noun a saw which has teeth on a revolving chain driven by a motor

chair
noun **1** a seat with a back and often with arms
verb **2** to act as a chairperson: *to **chair** a meeting*
phrase **3 take the chair**, to act as chairperson at a meeting

Word history: Middle English, from Latin word meaning 'seat', from Greek *kathédra*

chairlift
noun a line of chairs hung from a motor-driven, revolving cable, for carrying people up or down mountains

chairperson
noun someone who controls a meeting

Word building: **chairman** *noun* **chairwoman** *noun*

> **chairperson / chairman / chairwoman**
> The non-sexist word **chairperson** is often used to refer to the person who controls a meeting or a committee. The ending -person applies equally to both men and women.
> **Chairman** is the traditional name for this person, but because it ends in -man it seems to favour men.
> **Chairwoman** is the feminine alternative to **chairman**, but it has never been used very much. It does not solve the problem of finding a word that refers to both men and women.
> An alternative solution is to find a completely different word for the position — *moderator*, *convener* and *the chair* have all been offered as suggestions.
> Look up **non-sexist language**.

chalet (shal-ay)
noun a mountain cottage, sometimes used as a holiday house

Word history: French (Swiss)

chalice (chal-uhs)
noun a cup for wine in Christian religious services

Word history: Middle English, from Latin *calix* cup

chalk
noun **1** soft, white limestone
2 a stick of this for drawing or writing on blackboards
verb **3** to write with chalk
phrase **4 by a long chalk**, by far
5 chalk up,
a to score: *to* ***chalk up*** *360 runs in cricket*
b to credit: *We can* ***chalk*** *it* ***up*** *to experience.*

Word history: Old English *cealc*, from Latin word meaning 'lime'

challenge
verb **1** to invite to take part or compete in a test of skill or strength: *to* ***challenge*** *someone to fight*
2 to make demands on: *This job will* ***challenge*** *your abilities.*

Word building: **challenge** *noun* **challenger** *noun*
Word history: Middle English, from Latin *calumnia* calumny, slander

chamber
noun **1** *Old-fashioned* a room, often a private room or bedroom: *in my lady's* ***chamber***
2 chambers, rooms of barristers and judges

Word history: Middle English, from Latin

chamberlain (chaym-buh-luhn)
noun the official in charge of the household of a sovereign or member of the nobility

Word history: Middle English, from Old French, from Old German

chamber magistrate
noun a solicitor employed in a Court of Petty Sessions, who gives free legal advice

chamber music
noun music for a small group of players, suitable for playing in a room rather than in a large concert hall

chamber of commerce
noun an association, mainly of business people, to protect and improve business in an area

chamber-pot
noun a portable bowl used in the past in bedrooms as a toilet

chameleon (kuh-mee-lee-uhn, shuh-mee-lee-uhn)
noun a lizard that can change its skin colour to blend into its surroundings

Word history: Middle English, from Latin, from Greek word meaning 'ground lion'

chamois
noun **1** (sham-wah) a goatlike antelope, of the high mountains of Europe and south-western Russia
2 (sham-ee) soft leather made from various skins or synthetics (originally chamois skin) treated with oil

Word use: You can also use **chammy** or **shammy** for definition 2.
Word history: French, from Late Latin *camox*

chamomile (kam-uh-muyl)
noun a herb with strongly scented leaves and flowers which are used in teas and medicines

Word use: You can also use **camomile**.
Word history: Late Latin, from Greek word meaning 'earth apple'

champ[1]
verb **1** to bite upon, especially impatiently: *Horses* ***champ*** *the bit.*
2 to munch, or chew noisily
phrase **3 champ at the bit**, to be anxious to begin

Word history: perhaps nasalised variant of *chop* bite at, from *chap, chop* jaw

champ[2]
noun *Colloquial* champion

champagne (sham-payn)
noun a bubbly white wine, originally produced in Champagne, France

champignon (sham-pin-yon)
noun a mushroom, picked when very small, while the cap still meets the stem

Word history: French, from Latin *campus* field

champion
noun **1** someone or something that holds first place in a sport or contest (***conqueror, hero, title holder, victor, winner***)
2 someone who fights for a cause: *She is a* ***champion*** *of women's rights.* (***advocate, backer, defender, patron, supporter***)

Word building: **champion** *adjective* **champion** *verb*
Word history: Middle English, from Latin *campus* field (of battle)

championship
noun **1** the position or honour of being a champion
2 a contest held to decide who the champion will be (***bout***, ***competition***, ***game***, ***match***, ***race***)
3 defence of someone or something

chance
noun **1** the absence of any known reason for something happening: *They met by* ***chance****.* (***accident***, ***destiny***, ***fortune***, ***luck***, ***providence***)
2 risk: *to take a* ***chance***
3 opportunity: *Now is your* ***chance*** *to tell him.*

Word history: Middle English, from Late Latin *cadentia* a falling out

chancellor (chan-suh-luh, chahn-suh-luh)
noun **1** mainly in Britain, the title of various legal and other high officials
2 the chief minister of state in German-speaking countries
3 the honorary head of a university

Word building: **chancellorship** *noun*
Word history: Middle English, from Late Latin *cancellārius*, originally officer stationed at a tribunal

chandelier (shan-duh-lear)
noun a branched holder for a number of lights, hanging from the ceiling

Word history: French

change
verb **1** to alter or make different: *You must* ***change*** *your habits.* (***adapt***, ***convert***, ***transform***, ***vary***)
2 to become different: *She has* ***changed*** *since her illness.*
3 to exchange, especially for something else
4 to give or get smaller money for: *to* ***change*** *a $10 note*
5 to change your clothes: *It is time you* ***changed*** *for the party.*
noun **6** something different from before: *a* ***change*** *in the weather*
7 the money you get back when what you've bought costs less than the amount you handed over
8 coins of small value: *I need* ***change*** *for the bus.*
phrase **9 change hands**, to pass from one owner to another

Word building: **changeable** *adjective* **changeless** *adjective*
Word history: Middle English, from Late Latin

changeling (chaynj-ling)
noun a child supposedly exchanged secretly for another, especially by fairies (***elfchild***)

channel
noun **1** a waterway: *a stormwater* ***channel*** (***ditch***, ***furrow***, ***groove***, ***rut***, ***trench***)
2 a passage which ships use to travel between two seas
3 a frequency band for radio, television and the internet
4 a television station
5 a way of communicating: *He approached the Minister through the usual* ***channels****.*
verb **6** to make pass through a channel
7 to direct towards an end: *to* ***channel*** *your interests*

Verb forms: I **channelled**, I have **channelled**, I am **channelling**
Word history: Middle English, from Latin *canālis* canal

chant
noun **1** a simple tune, often repeating one note, for church singing
2 words repeated in a sing-song way

Word building: **chant** *verb*
Word history: Middle English, from Latin word meaning 'sing'

chaos (kay-os)
noun total disorder

Word use: The opposite of this is **order**.
Word building: **chaotic** *adjective*
Word history: Latin, from Greek

chap
noun Colloquial a man or boy

Word history: short for *chapman* pedlar

chapel
noun a small church or part of a large one

Word history: Middle English, from Late Latin *cappella* sanctuary for relics (such as the cape of St Martin), diminutive of *capa, cappa* cape

chaperone (shap-uh-rohn)
verb to accompany in order to ensure respectable behaviour: *The teacher will* ***chaperone*** *the children at the school dance.* (***attend***, ***escort***, ***shepherd***, ***watch over***)

Word use: You can also use **chaperon**.
Word building: **chaperone** *noun*
Word history: from French word meaning 'hood'

chaplain
noun a member of the clergy who works in a school, hospital or the armed forces (***minister***, ***parson***, ***priest***, ***vicar***)

Word history: Middle English, from Late Latin *capella* chapel

chapped
adjective cracked and made rough: *She has* ***chapped*** *hands from the wind.*

chapter
noun one of the main divisions of a book, usually with a number and a title

Word history: Middle English, from Latin word meaning 'small head', 'capital of column', 'chapter'

char
verb **1** to burn to charcoal
2 to scorch or burn slightly

Verb forms: it **charred**, it has **charred**, it is **charring**
Word history: perhaps short for *charcoal*

character
noun **1** someone in a story or play
2 the special things about you that make you different from someone else
3 an odd or interesting person: *He's quite a* ***character****.*
4 honesty, or high moral standards: *a person of* ***character***
5 a mark, letter or other symbol, used in writing and printing

Word history: Latin, from Greek word meaning 'instrument for marking', 'mark'

characterise
verb to be typical of or describe the character of

Word use: You can also use **characterize**.
Word building: **characterisation** *noun*

characteristic
adjective **1** typical or showing the special qualities: *That boasting is **characteristic** of him.*
noun **2** a special feature: *Large loops are a **characteristic** of her handwriting.*

Word building: **characteristically** *adverb*

charade (shuh-rahd)
noun **1** any silly pretence which obviously isn't working: *The government should stop this **charade**, and get on with running the country.*
2 charades, a game in which half the players have to guess a word acted out by the others in a series of short scenes

Word history: French, from Provençal word meaning 'entertainment'

charcoal
noun partly burnt wood used as a fuel or in sticks for drawing

Word history: Middle English

chardonnay (shah-duh-nay)
noun a dry white wine

Word history: French

charge
verb **1** to blame or accuse: *The police **charged** her with speeding.* (***allege***, ***book***, ***denounce***, ***frame***)
2 to write down as a debt: ***Charge** it to my account.*
3 to ask as the price: *They **charge** a dollar each for mangoes.*
4 to supply with electrical energy: *to **charge** a battery*
5 to attack by rushing violently (***assail***, ***assault***, ***storm***)
noun **6** an accusation or blame
7 cost or price (***expense***, ***outlay***, ***rate***)
8 an amount of explosive to be let off all at once
phrase **9 in charge**, in control: *Ky-Long is **in charge** of the tickets.*

Word history: Middle English, from Late Latin *carricāre* load

charge account
noun an arrangement with a department store, etc., by which the cost of goods purchased is recorded for payment at a later date

chargé d'affaires (shah-zhay duh-fair)
noun an official placed in charge during the temporary absence of an ambassador

Noun forms: The plural is **chargés d'affaires**.
Word use: You can also use **chargé**.
Word history: French word literally meaning 'entrusted with affairs'

charger
noun a war-horse

chariot
noun a two-wheeled carriage used in ancient times

Word history: Middle English, from Old French

charisma (kuh-riz-muh)
noun the power to attract and influence people: *A successful leader should have **charisma**.* (***appeal***, ***charm***, ***magnetism***)

Word building: **charismatic** *adjective*
Word history: from Greek word meaning 'gift'

charity
noun **1** the giving of help or money to people who need it (***aid***, ***assistance***, ***backing***, ***benefaction***, ***relief***)
2 an organisation for providing help: *Several **charities** have put up shelters for the homeless.*

Noun forms: The plural is **charities**.
Word building: **charitable** *adjective*
Word history: Middle English, from Latin *cāritas* affection

charlatan (shah-luh-tuhn)
noun someone who claims to have knowledge or skill that they don't really have: *He was treated by a **charlatan** and now his rash is worse than ever.* (***con man***, ***impostor***, ***quack***)

Word history: French, from Italian word meaning 'chatter'

charm
noun **1** the power of pleasing and attracting: *The new assistant has a great deal of **charm**.*
2 a magic spell
3 an ornament or trinket supposed to bring good luck
verb **4** to enchant, or attract powerfully by beauty, etc. (***beguile***, ***bewitch***, ***entice***, ***fascinate***, ***mesmerise***)
phrase **5 like a charm**, perfectly or successfully

Word building: **charming** *adjective*
Word history: Middle English, from Latin *carmen* song, incantation

chart
noun **1** a printed sheet giving information, often as a table or with pictures
2 a map, especially of the sea and waterways
3 charts, an up-to-date list of the best-selling popular music
verb **4** to make a chart of: *to **chart** unknown seas*
5 to plan a course of action

Word history: French, from Latin *c(h)arta* paper, from Greek word meaning 'leaf of paper'

charter
noun **1** a document giving certain legal rights: *The settlers were given a land **charter**.*
verb **2** to hire: *They **chartered** a boat for their holiday.*

Word history: Middle English, from Latin

chary (chair-ree)
adjective **1** careful, or wary
2 shy
phrase **3 chary of**, not giving freely: ***chary of** his praise*

Adjective forms: **charier**, **chariest**
Word building: **charily** *adverb*
Word history: Old English *cearig* sorrowful

chase
verb **1** to follow quickly in order to catch or overtake (***pursue***, ***seek***, ***shadow***, ***tag***, ***track***)
noun **2** a hunt or pursuit
3 a large area of land set aside for plants and animals

Word history: Middle English, from Old French, from Latin word meaning 'seize'

chasm (kaz-uhm)
noun a deep gap or opening in the ground

Word history: Latin, from Greek

chassis (shaz-ee)
noun the frame, wheels and sometimes the machinery of a car or truck, designed to support its body

Noun forms: The plural is **chassis**.
Word history: from French word meaning 'frame'

chaste
adjective **1** pure and without sexual experience
2 decent and clean: ***chaste** language*

Word history: Middle English, from Latin word meaning 'pure'

chasten (chay-suhn)
verb Old-fashioned to punish so as to bring about improvement: *to **chasten** a puppy for biting* (***chastise**, **discipline**, **upbraid***)

Word history: Old French *chastier*, from Latin

chastened (chay-suhnd)
adjective subdued or restrained: *to be **chastened** by the experience*

chastise
verb to punish or scold: *His father **chastised** him for breaking the window.* (***chasten**, **correct**, **discipline**, **penalise**, **upbraid***)

Word building: **chastisement** *noun*
Word history: Middle English

chastity
noun purity in your sexual life, having no sexual relations at all, or only with your husband or wife: *The knights of old took vows of **chastity**.*

chat
verb **1** to talk in a friendly way: *The sisters **chatted** about their recent holidays.* (***confer**, **converse**, **gossip**, **yak**, **yarn***)
2 *Computers* to communicate with someone over a network on a real-time basis
noun **3** informal conversation
4 *Computers* a session of real-time communication with someone over a network
5 a small Australian bird which catches insects on the ground and which has a harsh cry

Verb forms: I **chatted**, I have **chatted**, I am **chatting**
Word building: **chatty** *adjective* (**chattier**, **chattiest**)
Word history: short for *chatter*

chat room
noun Internet a channel where a group of users can chat (definition 2) to each other

Word history: an extension of the notion of actually talking in an actual place together

chattel (chat-uhl)
noun **1** something you own, which can be moved
2 *Old-fashioned* a slave

Word history: Middle English, from Old French

chatter
verb **1** to talk quickly, often without making sense (***babble**, **gab**, **jabber**, **natter**, **prattle***)
2 to make a rapid clicking noise: *Her teeth were **chattering** with the cold.*

Word building: **chatter** *noun*
Word history: Middle English; imitative

chatterbox
noun someone who talks a lot

chauffeur (shoh-fuh, shoh-fer)
noun someone whose job is to drive you in a car: *The **chauffeur** drives the judge to the court every day.*

Word history: French word meaning 'stoker', from *chauffer* heat

chauvinism (shoh-vuh-niz-uhm)
noun unthinking support of any cause or group: *male **chauvinism***

Word building: **chauvinist** *noun* **chauvinistic** *adjective*
Word history: French; from Nicolas *Chauvin*, an old soldier and overenthusiastic admirer of Napoleon I

cheap
adjective **1** of a low price: *You can buy **cheap** fruit at the market.* (***dirt-cheap**, **discount**, **inexpensive**, **no-frills**, **reduced***)
2 of poor quality: *Those shirts are made of **cheap** material.*

Word use: The opposite of definition 1 is **costly** or **expensive**.
Word building: **cheapness** *noun*
Word history: Old English *cēap* bargain

cheapen
verb **1** to make cheap or cheaper
2 to act in a way that lessens your dignity or reputation: *I would not **cheapen** myself by behaving like that.*

cheat
verb **1** to be dishonest or deceive: *to **cheat** in an exam | to **cheat** at cards*
2 to take from by tricking: *to **cheat** someone out of $10* (***defraud**, **fleece**, **rip off**, **swindle**, **trick***)
noun **3** someone who cheats

Word history: Middle English, variant of *escheat*, from Old French word meaning 'fall to one's share'

check
verb **1** to stop or prevent: *The fallen tree across the road **checked** their progress.* (***arrest**, **end**, **halt**, **hinder**, **obstruct***)
2 to find out the correctness of: *Please **check** the names on this list.* (***examine**, **investigate**, **sample**, **screen**, **try***)
noun **3** something that stops or holds back: *The accident was a **check** to her career.* (***bar**, **control**, **curb**, **impediment**, **obstruction***)
4 a test for correctness (***audition**, **check-up**, **exam**, **trial***)
5 a pattern of squares
6 *Chess* the position of the king when it is threatened with a direct attack
7 the US spelling of **cheque**
phrase **8 check in**, to record your arrival at a hotel or something like this
9 check out,
a to leave a hotel or something similar
b *Colloquial* to have a look at

Word building: **checked** *adjective*
Word history: Middle English, from Old French *eschec*

check / cheque

Don't confuse **check** with **cheque**.

A **cheque** is a money order that you write to your bank on a special form, instructing them to pay a specific amount to someone.

Check is the way this word is spelt in the US.

checkmate
noun Chess the act of trapping your opponent's king, so ending the game
Word building: **checkmate** *verb*
Word history: Middle English *chek mat*, from Arabic *shāh māt* the king is dead

check-up
noun a test to make sure that all is in order, especially your health: *She went to the doctor for her yearly **check-up**.*

cheddar
noun a fairly hard, yellow cheese
Word history: *Cheddar*, a town in Somerset, England

cheek
noun **1** either side of your face, below your eyes
2 boldness or lack of respect: *He had the **cheek** to tell me to mind my own business.*
phrase **3 cheek by jowl**, close together
4 tongue in cheek, in a mocking or insincere way
Word history: Old English *cēace*

cheeky
adjective impudent or lacking respect: *Her **cheeky** behaviour annoyed the teacher.* (***bold***, ***impolite***, ***insolent***, ***insulting***, ***rude***)
Adjective forms: **cheekier**, **cheekiest**
Word building: **cheekily** *adverb* **cheekiness** *noun*

cheep
verb **1** to make weak high sounds, the way a chicken does (***peep***)
noun **2** a small weak sound
Word history: imitative of the sound itself

cheer
noun **1** a shout of encouragement or approval
verb **2** to greet with shouts of approval: *They **cheered** the winner.* (***acclaim***, ***applaud***, ***hail***, ***praise***, ***toast***)
phrase **3 cheer up**, to make or become happier: *The news of his arrival **cheered** us **up**. / We **cheered up** when we heard the news.*
Word building: **cheerful** *adjective* **cheery** *adjective* (**cheerier**, **cheeriest**)
Word history: Middle English, from Old French word meaning 'face', from Late Latin

cheese
noun a food made from milk curds
Word building: **cheesy** *adjective* (**cheesier**, **cheesiest**)
Word history: Old English *cēse*

cheetah
noun a leopard-like animal that belongs to the cat family and is the fastest animal on earth
Word history: Hindustani

chef (shef)
noun a cook, especially the head cook in a restaurant
Word history: French

chemical
adjective **1** having to do with chemistry
noun **2** a substance obtained by or used in chemistry

chemical reaction
noun a process involving two or more substances in which the make-up of their molecules is altered

chemical warfare
noun warfare with poisonous gases, defoliants, etc.

chemist
noun **1** a scientist who studies and does research in chemistry
2 someone who has studied drugs and medicines and keeps a shop selling them (***pharmacist***)
Word history: variant of *alchemist*

chemistry
noun the science of what substances are made of and the ways they react with each other

chemotherapy (kem-oh-ther-uh-pee, kee-moh-ther-uh-pee)
noun the treatment of disease using chemicals, especially in treating cancer
Word building: **chemotherapist** *noun*

chenille (shuh-neel)
noun a fabric with short tufts of cotton which form a pattern, used for bedspreads, etc.
Word history: from French word meaning 'hairy caterpillar'

cheongsam (chong-sam)
noun a straight dress, often made of silk and sometimes with a slit skirt, originally worn by Chinese women

cheque (chek)
noun a written order asking a bank to pay a certain amount of money to a particular person
Word history: altered spelling of *check*

cheque account
noun a bank account from which money may be withdrawn by cheque at any time by the customer

cheque-book
noun a book of printed forms for cheques

chequer
noun a pattern of squares
Word history: Middle English, from Anglo-French word meaning 'chessboard'

chequered
adjective **1** marked with squares
2 marked by changes in good or bad luck: *a **chequered** career*

cherish
verb to look after tenderly: *He **cherishes** his pet rabbit.* (***adore***, ***care for***, ***dote on***, ***like***, ***worship***)
Word history: Middle English, from French *cher* dear, from Latin *cārus*

cheroot (shuh-rooht)
noun a cigar with cut ends

Word history: French, from Tamil word meaning 'a roll'

cherry
noun **1** a small, juicy fruit with a stone in the middle, varying in colour from pink to black
2 a bright red colour

Noun forms: The plural is **cherries**.
Word building: **cherry** *adjective*
Word history: Middle English, backformation from Old English *ciris* (the *-s* being taken for plural sign), from Vulgar Latin from Latin word meaning 'cherry tree', from Greek *kerasós*

cherub
noun **1** an angel, pictured as a child with wings
2 a child with a chubby face

Noun forms: The plural for definition 1 is **cherubim**; the plural for definition 2 is **cherubs**.
Word history: Old English *cherubin*, plural, ultimately from Hebrew word meaning 'sing'

cherubic
adjective round and innocent-looking: *a **cherubic** face*

chess
noun a game played by two people, each with sixteen pieces, on a chequered board

Word history: Middle English, from Old French

chessman
noun one of the pieces used in the game of chess

Noun forms: The plural is **chessmen**.

chest
noun **1** the front part of your body from your neck to your waist
2 a box, usually large and strong with a hinged lid
phrase **3 get (something) off your chest**, to talk about something that is worrying you

Word history: Old English *cest*, *cist*, from Latin, from Greek word meaning 'box'

chestnut
noun **1** a European tree or its hard brown nuts
2 a reddish-brown colour

Word building: **chestnut** *adjective*
Word history: obsolete *chesten* chestnut (Old English *cisten-*, from West Germanic, from Latin, from Greek *kastanéa*) + *nut*

chew
verb to bite and crush with your teeth (***chomp***, ***eat***, ***masticate***, ***munch***, ***nibble***)

Word building: **chewy** *adjective* (**chewier**, **chewiest**)
Word history: Old English *cēowan*

chewing gum
noun a sweetened gum for chewing

Word use: You can also use the colloquial word **chewie**.

chic (sheek)
adjective attractive and stylish: *Your new dress is very **chic**.* (***dapper***, ***elegant***, ***fashionable***, ***nifty***, ***smart***)

Word history: French

chicanery (shuh-kay-nuh-ree)
noun the use of legal tricks or misleading arguments, usually to take advantage of someone

Noun forms: The plural is **chicaneries**.

chick
noun a young chicken or other bird

chicken
noun **1** a hen or rooster, or its meat: *roast **chicken** for dinner*
2 *Colloquial* a coward: *He's too much of a **chicken** to climb that tree.* (***cry-baby***, ***scaredy-cat***, ***sissy***, ***sook***)
adjective **3** *Colloquial* cowardly
phrase **4 chicken out**, to back out because you are scared (***cower***, ***flinch***, ***quail***, ***waver***)
5 play chicken, to do something because of a dare

Word history: Old English *cicen*, *ciken*

chickenpox
noun a viral disease, common in children, causing fever and itchy blisters

chick flick
noun *Colloquial* a film seen as appealing more to female than to male viewers, especially a romance

chick lit
noun *Colloquial* a genre of popular fiction appealing usually to young women, often set in a stylish urban business environment and featuring romance: *After the exam all she wanted was to curl up with a chocolate bar and a bit of **chick lit**.*

chickpea
noun a small, round, yellow vegetable, like a pea

chide
verb to scold or find fault with: *She **chided** me for not tidying my room.*

Word history: Old English *cīdan*

chief
noun **1** the head person or boss in a group (***manager***, ***master***, ***overseer***, ***supervisor***)
adjective **2** most important or main: *My **chief** problem is my spelling.* (***fundamental***, ***key***, ***major***, ***primary***, ***significant***)

Word building: **chiefly** *adverb*
Word history: Middle English, from Latin word meaning 'head'

chieftain (cheef-tuhn)
noun the leader of a tribe

Word history: Middle English, from Late Latin

chiffon (shuh-fon, shif-on)
noun light, see-through material made of silk or nylon

Word history: French *chiffe* rag

chihuahua (chuh-wow-wuh, chuh-wah-wuh)
noun a Mexican breed of very small dog

chilblain
noun a red swelling on your fingers or toes caused by the cold

Word history: *chil(l)* + *blain* swelling, from Old English

child
noun **1** a boy or girl
2 a son or daughter
phrase **3 with child**, *Old-fashioned* pregnant

Noun forms: The plural is **children**.
Word history: Middle English *child*, plural *childre(n)*, Old English *cild*, plural *cild(ru)*

childbirth
noun the act of giving birth to a baby: *Women don't die in* ***childbirth*** *nearly as frequently as they used to.*

childcare centre
noun a place where children, especially young children, are looked after while their parents work

childcare worker
noun a person who is professionally employed to look after children

childhood
noun the time spent as a child

childish
adjective **1** silly or stupid: ***childish*** *behaviour*
2 of, or like a child: ***childish*** *laughter* (***immature, infantile, juvenile, youthful***)
Word history: Old English *cildisc*

childproof
adjective made so that children can't use or damage it

chill
noun **1** coldness: *There's a* ***chill*** *in the air.*
2 a cold, shivery feeling, often the first stage of a cold: *Take off your wet clothes before you catch a* ***chill.***
verb **3** to make or become cold (***cool, freeze, refrigerate***)
adjective **4** cold: *a* ***chill*** *wind* (***bleak, chilly, glacial, raw, wintry***)
Word building: **chilly** *adjective* (**chillier, chilliest**)
Word history: Old English *ciele, cile* coolness

chilly / chilli

These words sound the same but have different meanings.

A **chilly** breeze makes you feel cold. If someone gives you a **chilly** look, you know they feel unfriendly towards you.

A **chilli** is a type of small, hot capsicum.

chilli
noun a type of small capsicum which tastes hot
Word use: The US spelling is **chili**.
Word history: American Spanish, from Nahuatl

chime
noun **1** a ringing, musical sound: *the* ***chime*** *of the church bells*
2 chimes, a set of metal tubes or bells which make musical sounds when rung
verb **3** to sound in harmony like a set of bells (***knell, peal, ring, toll***)
phrase **4 chime in,** to break suddenly into a conversation, usually to say that you agree
Word history: Old English, from Latin *cymbalum* cymbal

chimney
noun a long tube running from a fireplace to the roof of a building, which draws smoke away from the fire
Noun forms: The plural is **chimneys.**
Word history: Middle English, from Latin word meaning 'furnace', from Greek

chimpanzee
noun a small African ape which is very intelligent and can easily be trained to perform tricks
Word history: a Bantu language in Angola, West Africa

chin
noun **1** the part of your face below your mouth
2 the point of the lower jaw
Word history: Old English *cin*

china (chuy-nuh)
noun **1** plates, cups and bowls made from porcelain clay: *We use the best* ***china*** *when guests come for dinner.* (***crockery***)
adjective **2** made of porcelain
Word history: named after *China* where such porcelain came from originally

chink[1]
noun **1** a crack: *a* ***chink*** *in the wall* (***aperture, fissure, gap, perforation, slit***)
2 a narrow opening: *a* ***chink*** *in the curtains*
Word history: Old English *cinu, cine* crack, fissure + *-k*, suffix

chink[2]
verb **1** to make, or cause to make, a short, sharp, ringing sound: *to* ***chink*** *coins or glasses by striking them together*
noun **2** a chinking sound
Word history: imitative of the sound itself

chintz (chints)
noun shiny, brightly-patterned, cotton material, used to make curtains and furniture coverings
Word history: Hindustani *chīnt*

chintzy
adjective shiny and cheap-looking
Adjective forms: **chintzier, chintziest**

chip
noun **1** a small piece chopped or split off something larger: *a* ***chip*** *of wood* | *chocolate* ***chips***
2 a gap where a small piece has broken off: *This plate has a* ***chip*** *in it.*
3 a thin slice of fried potato eaten cold
4 a tiny square which contains electronic circuits, used in a computer, watch or electronic game: *a silicon* ***chip***
verb **5** to cut or break off in small pieces
phrase **6 a chip off the old block,** *Colloquial* a person who is like one or both their parents
7 a chip on the shoulder, *Colloquial* a long-standing grievance
8 chip in, *Colloquial*
a to contribute money or help: *We all* ***chipped in*** *to buy her birthday present.*
b to interrupt: *It's rude to* ***chip in*** *while others are talking.* (***butt in, interject***)
Verb forms: I **chipped**, I have **chipped**, I am **chipping**
Word use: You can also use **crisp** for definition 3.
Word history: Old English *cippian*

chipboard
noun **1** a board made from waste wood, sawdust, resin, etc., used in sheets for light structural work
2 a board, usually made of wastepaper, used in box-making, etc.
Word use: Another name for definition 1 is **particle board.**

chipmunk
noun a type of small, striped squirrel that lives in the forests of North America and Asia

Word history: from Native American word meaning 'squirrel'

chiropody (kuh-rop-uh-dee, shuh-rop-uh-dee)
noun the treatment of minor foot problems, such as corns, bunions, etc.

Word building: **chiropodist** *noun*
Word history: *chiro-* + Greek *-podia*, from *poús* foot

chiropractic (kuy-ruh-prak-tik)
noun the method used by chiropractors of treating disease based on the idea that disease is caused by something being wrong with the nerves in the spine

Word history: *chiro-* + Greek *praktikós* practical

chiropractor (kuy-ruh-prak-tuh)
noun someone trained to treat back pain and other types of illness by massaging and adjusting the spine

chirp (cherp)
verb to make a short high sound like a bird or insect

Word use: You can also use **chirrup**.
Word building: **chirp** *noun*

chirpy
adjective lively and cheerful

Adjective forms: **chirpier**, **chirpiest**
Word building: **chirpily** *adverb*

chirrup
verb → **chirp**

Verb forms: it **chirruped**, it has **chirruped**, it is **chirruping**
Word building: **chirrup** *noun*
Word history: variant of *chirp*

chisel
noun **1** a cutting tool with a sharp end, used to shape wood and stone
verb **2** to cut with or use a chisel
3 *Colloquial* to cheat or trick: *He **chiselled** me out of my savings.*

Verb forms: I **chiselled**, I have **chiselled**, I am **chiselling**
Word history: Middle English, from Latin word meaning 'cut'

chiseller
noun Colloquial a cheat or swindler

chit[1]
noun **1** a voucher showing money owed for food, drink, etc.
2 a voucher allowing admittance to a restricted area, such as a military base
3 a note, or short memorandum

Word history: Hindustani *chitthī*

chit[2]
noun a young person, especially an impudent girl: *She's a **chit** of a girl.*

Word history: perhaps like *kitten*

chivalry (shiv-uhl-ree)
noun **1** polite respectful behaviour, especially of a man towards a woman
2 the qualities of courtesy and bravery which were valued amongst medieval knights

Word building: **chivalrous** *adjective*
Word history: Middle English, from Old French *chevalier* knight, cavalier

chives
plural noun a small, grass-like herb which tastes like onion and is used in cooking

Word history: Middle English, from Latin word meaning 'onion'

chloride (klaw-ruyd)
noun a compound of two elements only, one of which is chlorine

chlorinate (klo-ruhn-ayt)
verb to disinfect with chlorine: *to **chlorinate** a swimming pool*

Word building: **chlorination** *noun*

chlorine (klaw-reen)
noun a poisonous, greenish-yellow gas with a strong irritating smell, which is dissolved in water and used to bleach clothes or to disinfect swimming pools

chlorofluorocarbon
(klaw-roh-floo-uh-roh-kah-buhn)
noun a chemical containing chlorine, fluorine, and carbon, the use of which as a coolant in refrigerators and a propellant in spray cans is being phased out because of the damage it does to the ozone layer

Word use: The abbreviation is **CFC**.

chloroform (klo-ruh-fawm)
noun **1** a colourless liquid, which used to be used as an anaesthetic and which is now used as a solvent
verb **2** to anaesthetise with chloroform

chlorophyll (klo-ruh-fil)
noun the green colouring in leaves and plants, which traps the energy of sunlight and is sometimes used as a dye

chock
noun a block of wood wedged under something to stop it moving: *Put a **chock** under the door to stop it closing.*

Word history: Old Northern French *choque* log or block of wood

chocolate
noun **1** a sweet food or drink made from the seeds of a small, tropical American tree
2 a dark brown colour
adjective **3** made with or from chocolate
4 of a chocolate colour

Word history: Spanish, from Nahuatl *chocolatl* bitter water

choice
noun **1** the act of choosing or selecting (***discrimination***, ***selection***)
2 the thing chosen: *The blue one is my **choice**.* (***alternative***, ***elective***, ***option***, ***pick***, ***preference***)
3 a number of things from which you can choose: *a wide **choice** of colours*
adjective **4** excellent or worthy of being chosen: *a **choice** apple*

Word history: Middle English, from Old French *choisir* choose, of Germanic origin

choir (<u>kwuy</u>-uh)
noun an organised group of people who sing together, especially in a church (***chorus***)
Word history: Middle English, from Latin *chorus*

choke
verb **1** to suffocate or stop breathing: *This tight collar is **choking** me.* | *He **choked** on a fishbone.* (***asphyxiate***, ***smother***, ***stifle***, ***strangle***)
2 to clog up or congest: *Mud and leaves are **choking** the drain.*
noun **3** a device used when starting an engine, which controls the amount of air that is mixed with the petrol
Word history: Old English *acēocian*

choker
noun a tight necklace or band around the neck

choko (<u>choh</u>-koh)
noun a green, pear-shaped vegetable with a prickly skin, which grows on a vine
Noun forms: The plural is **chokos** or **chokoes**.

cholera (<u>kol</u>-uh-ruh)
noun an infectious tropical disease of the digestive tract, marked by diarrhoea, vomiting, cramp, etc., and which can kill you
Word history: Latin, from Greek

cholesterol (kuh-<u>les</u>-tuh-rol)
noun an organic compound found in the liver, blood and brain, the yolk of eggs, and elsewhere. A high level of cholesterol in the bloodstream has been linked to a greater risk of heart and artery disease.
Word history: *chol(e)*- gall or bile + Greek *ster(eós)* solid

chook
noun Australian, NZ Colloquial a domestic chicken
Word history: British English, originally an imitation of the clucking sound made by chickens. Other bird names have arisen in a similar way, including *boobook* (from the Aboriginal language Dharug), *cuckoo* (from Middle English) and *kookaburra* (from the Aboriginal language Wiradjuri).

choose
verb **1** to pick out or select: ***Choose** a number between one and ten.* | *Don't rush me while I'm **choosing**.* (***elect***, ***opt for***, ***settle on***)
2 to decide or prefer: *She **chose** not to go to the party.* (***determine***, ***resolve***)
Verb forms: I **chose**, I have **chosen**, I am **choosing**
Word history: Old English *ceōsan*

choosy
adjective Colloquial hard to please
Word use: You can also use **choosey**.

chop
verb **1** to cut by hitting with quick heavy blows: *to **chop** wood with an axe*
noun **2** a quick cutting stroke
3 a slice of meat with bone in it: *lamb **chops***
phrase **4 get the chop**, *Colloquial*
a to be killed
b to be dismissed from work
Verb forms: I **chopped**, I have **chopped**, I am **chopping**
Word history: variant of *chap* a crack in the skin

chopper
noun Colloquial **1** a helicopter
2 a motorcycle with the front wheel moved forward, a long, curved seat and high handlebars

choppy
adjective forming short broken waves: *a **choppy** sea*
Adjective forms: **choppier**, **choppiest**

chopsticks
plural noun a pair of thin smooth sticks, used in Asia instead of a knife and fork to pick up food
Word history: ? transferred sense of earlier *chopstick* a stick attached to a deep-sea fishing line

choral (<u>ko</u>-ruhl)
adjective sung by a choir or a chorus
Word building: **chorally** *adverb*
Word history: Medieval Latin, from Latin *chorus*

choral / coral
Don't confuse **choral** with **coral**, which is the hard skeleton of small sea animals.

chord (kawd)
noun three or more musical notes played together: *to play **chords** on a guitar*
Word history: Latin word meaning 'cord', 'string', from Greek word meaning 'gut', 'string of a musical instrument'

chord / cord / cored
Don't confuse **chord** with **cord** or **cored**.
A **cord** is a kind of light rope.
Cored is the past form of **core**, to remove the centre from a piece of fruit.

chore (chaw)
noun a boring or unpleasant job (***assignment***, ***duty***, ***errand***, ***mission***, ***task***)
Word history: Old English *cyrr*

choreography (ko-ree-<u>og</u>-ruh-fee)
noun the art of designing ballets and dances
Word building: **choreograph** *verb* **choreographer** *noun*
Word history: *choreo*- (combining form representing Greek *choreía* dance) + *-graphy*

chorister (<u>ko</u>-ris-tuh)
noun someone who sings in a choir
Word history: Medieval Latin *chorista* chorister + *-er*

chortle (<u>chaw</u>-tuhl)
verb to laugh softly and with glee (***cackle***, ***chuckle***)
Word history: blend of *chuckle* and *snort*; coined by Lewis *Carroll* in *Through the Looking-Glass* (1871)

chorus (<u>kaw</u>-ruhs)
noun **1** the part of a song that is repeated after each verse (***refrain***)
2 a piece of music for several people to sing together
3 a group of people or a choir singing together
verb **4** to sing or say all together

Word history: Latin, from Greek *chorós* dance, band of dancers, chorus

chose
verb past tense and obsolete past participle of **choose**

chowder
noun a kind of soup or stew made of shellfish, fish or vegetables, with potatoes, onions and seasoning

Word history: probably from French word meaning 'cauldron', from Late Latin *caldus, calidus* hot

christen (kris-uhn)
verb **1** to give a name to, especially at baptism: *We **christened** the baby Peter William. | We **christened** the new boat Mary-Belle.* (**call**, **dub**, **tag**, **title**)
2 *Colloquial* to use for the first time: *Have you **christened** your new bike yet?*

Word history: Old English *cristnian* make Christian (by baptism)

christening
noun the ceremony of baptism

Christianity
noun a world religion which is based on belief in Jesus Christ as the Son of God who lived on earth as a man, died and came back to life on earth before going to heaven. It is also based on Jesus's teachings as written in the New Testament of the Bible, which emphasised kind, good and unselfish behaviour as a response to God's love for the world.

Word building: **Christian** *noun*, *adjective*
Word history: named after Jesus *Christ*, from a Hebrew name meaning 'anointed'

Christian name
noun your first or given name: *His **Christian names** are Robert James and his surname is Bell.*

People who are not Christians prefer to use **first name** or **given name**.

Christmas beetle
noun a beetle with rainbow colours on its wings, usually seen in Australia in mid-summer

Christmas bush
noun an Australian shrub or small tree with white flowers and red sepals, flowering at Christmas and used for decoration

Christmas tree
noun **1** a tree, usually pine or fir, hung with decorations at Christmas
2 a tree of the mistletoe family, native to western Australia

chromatic
adjective **1** having to do with a musical scale that moves by small steps, using all of the twelve semitones
2 having to do with colour

Word history: Latin, from Greek word meaning 'relating to colour' (chiefly in musical sense)

chrome
noun a hard, shiny, silver-coloured metal used to cover other metals to protect them and to stop rust

Word use: This is short for **chromium**.
Word history: from Greek word meaning 'colour'

chrome-plated
adjective covered in chrome

chromium (kroh-mee-uhm)
noun a shiny, hard, brittle metallic element found in compounds used for making pigments and also in corrosion-resisting chromium plating

Word history: Greek *chrôm(a)* colour + *-ium*

chromosome (kroh-muh-sohm)
noun a tiny threadlike body found in the nucleus of all living cells, which carries the genetic codes for the characteristics of the organism: *A human cell has 23 pairs of **chromosomes**.*

Word use: Look up **X chromosome** or **Y chromosome**.

chronic
adjective **1** constant or continuing for a long time: *She has **chronic** asthma. | **chronic** depression*
2 *Colloquial* very bad: *a **chronic** sense of humour*

Word building: **chronically** *adverb*
Word history: Latin, from Greek

chronic / acute

These two words do not mean the same thing. In fact they are opposites when they refer to disease.

A **chronic** illness is one that continues for a long time.

An **acute** illness is brief and severe:

I had an acute attack of appendicitis and was rushed to hospital.

chronic fatigue syndrome
noun a condition of extreme fatigue and depression lasting months or years following an apparently mild viral infection

Word use: Another name is **ME** which is short for **myalgic encephalomyelitis**.

chronicle
noun **1** a record or history of events in the order they happened: *the **chronicles** of Ancient Rome*
verb **2** to record events

Word history: Middle English, from Old French *cronique*, from Medieval Latin, from Greek word meaning 'annals'

chronicler
noun someone who records the events of their times

chronological
adjective arranged in order according to when it happened: *I wrote down the most important events in my life in **chronological** order.*

chronology
noun a record of past events in order of time

Noun forms: The plural is **chronologies**.

chronometer (kruh-nom-uh-tuh)
noun a very accurate clock for measuring time, used especially at sea

chrysalis (kris-uh-luhs)
noun the form that a butterfly or moth takes when changing from a grub to an adult insect, inside a hard-shelled cocoon (***pupa***)

Noun forms: The plural is **chrysalids** or **chrysalises**.
Word history: Latin, from Greek word meaning 'gold-coloured sheath of butterflies'

chrysanthemum (kruh-santh-uh-muhm, kruh-zanth-uh-muhm)
noun a tall plant with big white or brightly coloured flowers, often given as a present on Mother's Day

Word history: Latin, from Greek word meaning 'golden flower'

chubby
adjective plump and round: *a **chubby** baby*

Adjective forms: **chubbier, chubbiest**
Word building: **chubbiness** *noun*

chuck
verb Colloquial **1** to throw or fling: *to **chuck** the ball over the fence* (***hurl, pitch, toss***)
2 to vomit
noun Colloquial **3** a toss or throw
phrase **4 chuck it in**, to give up without finishing: *I'm bored with playing football so I'll **chuck it in**.*

Word history: imitative

chuckle
verb to laugh softly (***cackle, chortle***)

Word building: **chuckle** *noun*

chum
noun **1** a close friend or companion: *boyhood **chums*** (***comrade, mate, pal***)
phrase **2 chum up with**, to meet and become friendly with

Verb forms: I **chummed**, I have **chummed**, I am **chumming**

chump
noun **1** *Colloquial* a stupid person
2 the section of lamb, between the leg and the loin, which is cut into chops

chunder
verb Australian, NZ Colloquial to vomit

chunk
noun a thick piece or lump: *a **chunk** of fresh bread*

Word history: nasalised variant of *chuck* noun, a cut of beef

chunky
adjective thick or bulky (***dense, heavy, solid***)

Adjective forms: **chunkier, chunkiest**
Word building: **chunkiness** *noun*

church
noun **1** a building where Christians gather to worship
2 the worship of God in a church
3 Church, an organisation of Christians who share the same religious beliefs: *the Catholic **Church** | the Anglican **Church***

Word history: Old English *cir(i)ce, cyrice* from Greek *kȳriakón* (*dôma*) Lord's (house)

churinga (chuh-ring-guh)
noun a sacred representation of an Aboriginal totemic object, usually made of wood or stone (***bullroarer, thunderstick***)

Word use: You can also use **churunga** or **tjuringa**.
Word history: from Arrernte, an Australian Aboriginal language of central Australia

churlish (cherl-ish)
adjective rude and surly

Word history: Old English *ceorl* freeman of the lowest rank + *-ish*

churn
noun **1** a large metal container for milk
2 a machine for making butter from cream or milk
verb **3** to shake or stir in order to make into butter: *to **churn** cream*
4 to move about violently: *Her stomach **churned** with excitement.*

Word history: Old English *cyrin*

chute (shooht)
noun a sloping channel or passage for sending or carrying things to a lower level: *a laundry **chute***

Word history: blend of French *chute* a fall (from Latin *cadere*) and English *shoot*

chute / shoot
Don't confuse **chute** with **shoot**, which is a new part that grows from a plant. You **shoot** at something when you fire a gun at it.

chutney
noun a spicy jam-like food made from fruit, sugar, spices and vinegar

Word history: Hindustani

cicada (suh-kah-duh, suh-kay-duh)
noun a large flying insect which is found in trees in the summer and which makes a very loud shrill sound in hot weather

Word history: Latin

cicatrice (sik-uh-truhs)
noun the scar left by a wound

Word use: You can also use **cicatrix.**
Noun forms: The plural is **cicatrices** (sik-uh-truy-seez) or **cicatrixes.**
Word building: **cicatricial** *adjective* **cicatricose** *adjective*

cider (suy-duh)
noun a drink, sometimes containing alcohol, made from apples

Word history: Middle English, from Late Latin, from Greek, from Hebrew word meaning 'strong drink'

cigar (suh-gah)
noun tobacco leaves rolled tightly together

Word history: Spanish perhaps from *cigarra* grasshopper, from Latin

cigarette
noun a roll of shredded tobacco, for smoking, inside a cylinder of very thin paper

Word history: from French word meaning 'little cigar'

cinch (sinch)
noun **1** a strong girth for a saddle or pack
2 *Colloquial* something certain or easy: *This exam's a **cinch**.*

Word building: **cinchy** *adjective* (**cinchier, cinchiest**)
Word history: Spanish, from Latin word meaning 'girdle'

cinder
noun a burnt and blackened piece of wood or coal

Word history: Old English *sinder* cinder, slag

cinema
noun **1** a theatre where films are shown
2 films in general or the art of making films: *the history of Australian* ***cinema***

Word history: short for *cinematograph*. This was a word made up by the French brothers Auguste and Louis Jean Lumière to describe the apparatus that showed moving pictures. The first part of it is from the Greek word *kinein* meaning 'to move'.

cinematic (sin-uh-mat-ik)
adjective **1** having to do with the cinema
2 suited to a film treatment or presentation: *the* ***cinematic*** *quality of the landscape*

Word building: **cinematically** *adverb*

cinnamon (sin-uh-muhn)
noun a yellowish or reddish-brown spice made from the inner bark of certain trees and used in cooking

Word history: Late Latin, from Greek

cipher (suy-fuh)
noun **1** secret writing or a code: *The message was sent in* ***cipher*** *so the enemy could not understand it.*
verb **2** to write in code

Word use: You can also use **cypher**.
Word history: Middle English, from Medieval Latin, from Arabic word meaning 'empty'

circadian rhythm (ser-kay-dee-uhn ridh-uhm)
noun the roughly 24-hour cycle in which physiological processes like eating and sleeping occur

circle
noun **1** a perfectly round shape
2 anything that has the shape of a circle or part of a circle: *Sit in a* ***circle*** *to listen to the story.*
3 a group of people who do things together: *a sewing* ***circle***
4 the upper section of seats in a theatre or cinema: *the dress* ***circle***
verb **5** to move around in a circle: *The plane* ***circled*** *the airport. | The plane* ***circled*** *three times before landing.*

Word building: **encircle** *verb*
Word history: from Latin word meaning 'little circle', 'ring'

circle graph
noun → **pie graph**

circuit (ser-kuht)
noun **1** a circular path or roundabout journey: *The visitors made a* ***circuit*** *of the school.*
2 a circular racing track
3 an arrangement of wires joined so as to carry an electric current: *a closed* ***circuit***
4 a number of venues or events at which an entertainer, etc., performs in turn: *the RSL* ***circuit*** *| the talk show* ***circuit***
5 a course regularly travelled: *The airline now flies the Perth-Singapore-London* ***circuit*** *twice weekly.*

Word history: Middle English, from Latin

circuit board
noun Electronics an insulated board on which circuits are mounted or printed, which can be inserted into a piece of electronic equipment such as a computer

Word use: You can also use **printed circuit board**.

circuitous (ser-kyooh-uh-tuhs)
adjective roundabout, not direct: *a* ***circuitous*** *route home*

Word use: The opposite of this is **direct**.

circular
adjective **1** round or shaped like a circle
noun **2** a letter or notice sent to a number of people

Word building: **circularity** *noun* **circularly** *adverb*
Word history: from Latin word meaning 'circle'

circulate
verb **1** to move in a circle or circuit: *Blood* ***circulates*** *through your body.*
2 to pass from place to place or person to person: *The news* ***circulated*** *quickly. | We* ***circulated*** *a petition.*

Word history: from Latin word meaning 'gathered into a circle'

circulation
noun **1** continuous circular movement: *the* ***circulation*** *of blood through the body*
2 the number of copies of a newspaper or magazine sent out: *The local paper has a* ***circulation*** *of 20 000.*

circumcise
verb to cut away the skin around the end of the penis of: *to* ***circumcise*** *a baby boy*

Word building: **circumcision** *noun*
Word history: Middle English, from Latin word meaning 'cut around'

circumference
noun the distance around something, especially around a circle or circular object: *You can measure the* ***circumference*** *of a tree trunk with a tape measure.* (***border, perimeter, periphery, rim***)

Word history: Latin

circumflex
noun a mark (ˆ) placed over a vowel in some languages

> The **circumflex** can tell you something about how the vowel is pronounced, and also about the word's history.
>
> In French, the circumflex usually shows that the vowel sound is slightly longer. Often it also means that a letter has dropped out from the spelling. Commonly, the letter left out was s. So French words like *hôtel* and *fête* are words which used to be spelt with an s (*hostel* and *feste*).

circumlocution (ser-kuhm-luh-kyooh-shuhn)
noun **1** a roundabout way of speaking, or the use of too many words
2 a roundabout expression: *He used a* ***circumlocution*** *to hide his embarrassment.*

Word history: Latin

circumnavigate
verb to sail round: *to* ***circumnavigate*** *the earth*

Word building: **circumnavigation** *noun*

circumscribe
verb **1** to surround, or encircle
2 to limit, or confine, especially in a narrow way: *Their knowledge is strictly **circumscribed**.*
3 *Geometry* to draw round another figure so as to touch as many points as possible: *to **circumscribe** a square*

Word building: **circumscription** *noun*
Word history: from Latin word meaning 'draw a line round', 'limit'

circumspect
adjective cautious and watchful

Word building: **circumspection** *noun*
Word history: late Middle English, from Latin word meaning 'considerate', 'wary'

circumstance
noun **1** a condition which influences a person or an event
2 circumstances, financial position: *They used to be rich, but now their **circumstances** have changed.*

Word history: Middle English, from Latin word meaning 'surrounding conditions'

circumvent (ser-kuhm-vent)
verb **1** to get around or avoid: ***circumvent** a problem*
2 to outwit, or get the better of by cleverness: ***circumvent** the law*

Word history: Latin *circumventus*, past participle, surrounded

circus
noun **1** a travelling show with performing animals, clowns, jugglers and acrobats
2 an open area with seats on all sides, used for chariot races and other sports in ancient Rome

Word history: Latin, from Greek *kírkos* ring

cirrhosis (si-roh-suhs, suh-roh-suhs)
noun a serious disease which alters the make-up of the liver

Word history: Neo-Latin, from Greek *kirrhós* tawny + *-osis*

cirrus (si-ruhs)
noun high feathery cloud

Word history: from Latin word meaning 'curl', 'tuft', 'fringe'

cistern (sis-tuhn)
noun a tank for holding water, such as the one above a toilet

Word history: Middle English, from Latin word meaning 'box'

citadel
noun a fort or strongly defended place, built to protect or control a city

Word history: French, from Italian word meaning 'city'

citation
noun **1** the act of quoting
2 the quoting of a passage, book, author, etc.
3 a quotation or a passage cited

cite
verb to mention or refer to: *The soldier was **cited** for bravery in the official dispatch. | The teacher **cited** three examples to explain the meaning of the word.*

Word history: Middle English, from Latin word meaning 'move', 'excite', 'call'

cite / sight / site
Don't confuse **cite** with **sight** or **site**.
Your **sight** is your ability to see things. It can also be something worth seeing: *a great sight.*
A **site** is the land where something is built or will soon be built.

citizen
noun **1** a member of a nation who has certain rights and duties: *All Australian **citizens** over the age of eighteen must vote in the election.*
2 someone who lives in a particular place: *a **citizen** of Adelaide*

Word building: **citizenship** *noun*
Word history: Middle English, from Old French *citeain*, from *cite* city

citric acid
noun an organic acid occurring in small amounts in almost all living cells as part of the citric acid cycle, and in greater amounts in many fruits, especially in limes and lemons

citrus
noun **1** a small evergreen tree such as the lemon, orange, lime, grapefruit or mandarin
adjective **2** having to do with trees like this: ***citrus** fruit*

Word history: Latin

city
noun **1** a large or important town (***metropolis**, **municipality***)
2 the people who live in a city: *The whole **city** turned out to watch the parade.*

Noun forms: The plural is **cities**.
Word history: Middle English, from Old French, from Latin *cīvitas* citizenship, the state, a city

city council
noun the local administrative body which serves a capital city or large country town

Word use: Compare this with **municipal council** and **shire council**.

civet (siv-uht)
noun **1** a yellow, oily substance with a strong musk-like smell, obtained from civets (definition 2) and used in making perfume
2 a cat-like, meat-eating mammal of southern Asia and Africa, that has glands in the genital area that secrete civet

Word history: French, from Italian, from Arabic

civic
adjective having to do with a city or citizens: *The council buildings are in the **civic** centre. | It is your **civic** duty to put litter in the bins provided.* (***communal**, **public***)

Word history: Latin *cīvis* citizen

civil
adjective **1** having to do with the state or state authorities: *It was a matter for the **civil** authorities, not the religious ones.*
2 having to do with citizens or the people: ***civil** liberties*
3 polite or courteous: *His way of asking was so **civil** that we did what he wanted.*

Word building: **civilly** *adverb*
Word history: Middle English, from Latin

civilian
adjective **1** having to do with ordinary life: *The soldier left the army and entered* ***civilian*** *life as a bus driver.*
noun **2** a person in ordinary life, as opposed to a soldier, etc.

civilisation
noun the highly developed life of a particular people, including their science, art and writing: *The ancient Greeks brought* ***civilisation*** *to the tribes they ruled. | Chinese* ***civilisation***

Word use: You can also use **civilization**.

civilise
verb to refine, or bring out of a savage state

Word use: You can also use **civilize**.
Word history: Medieval Latin

civilised
adjective **1** highly developed: *The Chinese have been a* ***civilised*** *race for thousands of years.*
2 polite and controlled: *They expected him to be angry but he wrote a very* ***civilised*** *letter.*

Word use: The opposite is **uncivilised**. | You can also use **civilized**.

civility
noun **1** politeness or courtesy
2 civilities, polite conversation: *The two executives exchanged* ***civilities*** *before they got down to business.*

Noun forms: The plural is **civilities**.

civil liberty
noun freedom of opinion, movement, etc., limited only by the public good

civil rights
plural noun the personal rights of the citizen in society

civil war
noun a war between people living in the same country

civvies (siv-eez)
plural noun Colloquial civilian clothes

clack
verb to make a quick, sharp sound

Word history: Middle English imitative

clad
adjective **1** dressed or clothed in: *He arrived at the meeting* ***clad*** *in a black suit.*
2 covered with: *a tree* ***clad*** *with creepers*

Word use: This word is often used with other words to form compound adjectives: *leather-clad young men | ivy-clad walls.*

claim
verb **1** to ask for, as if it's your right: *He* ***claims*** *his share of the money.* (***call for***, ***demand***, ***require***)
2 to say definitely: *She* ***claims*** *that her story is true.* (***assert***, ***declare***, ***hold***, ***insist***, ***profess***)
noun **3** a demand: *The children make too many* ***claims*** *on her.*
4 the right to something: *After all your hard work you have a* ***claim*** *to some holidays.*
5 something claimed, such as a piece of land for mining

Word history: Middle English, from Latin word meaning 'call'

clairvoyant (klair-voy-uhnt)
adjective claiming to be able to see into the future

Word building: **clairvoyance** *noun*
clairvoyant *noun*
Word history: French *clair* clear + *voyant*, seeing

clam
noun a large shellfish whose two shells are hinged and can be tightly closed

Word history: from Old English word meaning 'band', 'bond'

clamber
verb to climb up with difficulty: *He* ***clambered*** *onto the roof.* (***ascend***, ***mount***, ***scale***, ***shin***)

Word history: Middle English *clambren*

clammy
adjective cold, damp and sticky

Adjective forms: **clammier**, **clammiest**
Word building: **clamminess** *noun*
Word history: perhaps Flemish *klammig* sticky

clamour (klam-uh)
noun **1** the loud noise of many voices: *an angry* ***clamour***
verb **2** to make a loud noise or ask noisily

Word use: You can also use **clamor**.
Word building: **clamorous** *adjective*
Word history: Middle English, from Latin word meaning 'a cry', 'shout'

clamp
noun **1** a tool which holds things tightly together (***brace***, ***cramp***, ***grip***, ***vice***)
verb **2** to hold tightly: *He* ***clamped*** *his teeth together in anger.*
3 to press down: *The lid was* ***clamped*** *onto the box then locked.*
phrase **4 clamp down**, *Colloquial* to become more strict

Word history: Middle Dutch

clan
noun a group of related families who share a common ancestor

Word history: Gaelic *clann* family, stock

clandestine (klan-des-tuhn)
adjective secret and unlawful: *The freedom fighters held* ***clandestine*** *meetings away from the town.*

Word history: Latin

clang
verb to ring loudly

Word history: imitates the sound

clangour (klang-uh, klang-guh)
noun a loud metallic sound

Word use: You can also use **clangor**.
Word building: **clangorous** *adjective*
Word history: Latin

clannish
adjective very close, like the members of a clan

clap
verb **1** to hit your hands together noisily, especially in applause
2 to show approval or enjoyment of, by clapping: *We* ***clapped*** *our favourite actor.* (***acclaim***, ***applaud***, ***cheer***, ***honour***)

3 to shut away immediately: *The recaptured prisoner was **clapped** into jail.*
noun **4** a loud sudden noise: *There was a **clap** of thunder.*
5 a sign of approval, by clapping: *They've done well — let's give them a **clap**.*

Verb forms: I **clapped**, I have **clapped**, I am **clapping**
Word history: Old English *clæppan*

clapper
noun something that claps, especially the tongue of a bell

claret (kla-ruht)
noun **1** the red (originally light red or yellowish) table wine of Bordeaux, France
2 a similar wine made elsewhere
3 a deep purplish red colour

Word building: **claret** *adjective*
Word history: Middle English, from Old French word meaning 'somewhat clear', 'light-coloured', from Latin

clarify
verb to make clear: *to **clarify** butter | to **clarify** the answer to the problem* (***elucidate***, ***explain***, ***illustrate***, ***interpret***, ***spell out***)

Word use: The opposite of this is **confuse**.
Verb forms: I **clarified**, I have **clarified**, I am **clarifying**
Word building: **clarification** *noun*
Word history: Middle English, from Old French, from Late Latin

clarinet
noun a musical instrument belonging to the woodwind family which makes a deeper sound than the flute

Word history: from French word meaning 'little clarion'

clarinettist
noun a clarinet player

clarion (kla-ree-uhn)
noun an old type of trumpet used for high-sounding passages

Word history: Middle English, from Medieval Latin, from Latin *clārus* clear

clarity
noun clearness: *You could see the riverbed because of the **clarity** of the water. | The **clarity** of her arguments convinced us she was right.*

Word history: Latin

clash
verb **1** to make a loud harsh noise
2 to disagree, differ or conflict: *Their opinions **clashed**.*
3 to happen at the same time: *Their favourite television shows **clashed**.*

Word building: **clash** *noun*
Word history: ? imitative

clasp
noun **1** something which fastens things together
2 a firm hold
verb **3** to hold tightly (***cling to***, ***clutch***, ***grasp***, ***grip***, ***hug***)

Word history: Middle English *claspe(n)*

class
noun **1** a group of people or things which are alike in some way (***kind***, ***set***, ***sort***, ***species***, ***type***)
2 a group of pupils who are taught together (***form***, ***grade***, ***year***)
3 someone's place in society, judged by their possessions or their family: *the middle **class*** (***level***, ***rank***, ***station***)
4 the level of comfort in travel: *First **class** is more expensive than business **class**.*
verb **5** to put in a group

Word history: French, from Latin *classis* class (of people, etc.), army, fleet

classic
adjective **1** of high quality: *That vintage car is a **classic** model in perfect condition.*
2 typical: *The actor had a **classic** case of nerves.*
noun **3** someone or something known to be excellent: *'Gone With The Wind' is now considered a film **classic**.*
4 classics, the writings and language of ancient Greece and Rome

Word history: from Latin word meaning 'of the first or highest class'

classical
adjective **1** classic
2 traditional: *a **classical** outfit*
3 *Music*
a belonging to a period in which several traditional forms, such as the sonata, the symphony, etc., developed
b following strict rules of style and form, especially referring to music composed before 1800
4 Classical, in keeping with the classics, especially ancient Greek and Roman models in literature and art, or with later systems of principles modelled on them

Word use: Compare definition 3a with **romantic**.

classicism (klas-uh-siz-uhm)
noun **1** the principles of classical literature or art
2 the classical style in literature or art, which pays special attention to form, with the general effect of regularity, simplicity, balance, proportion and controlled emotion

Word building: **classicist** *noun*

classification
noun **1** the act or result of classifying
2 the placing of plants and animals into groups according to structure, origin, etc.
3 one of several degrees (such as restricted, top secret, etc.) of security protection for government papers and other similar documents
4 in libraries, a system for arranging books and other reading material, according to their subject matter

classified advertisement
noun a short advertisement in a newspaper, usually advertising a job or something for sale

Word use: You can also use **classified ad**.

classify
verb to group according to quality or likeness: *When we had **classified** the documents, the new ones were filed and the old ones thrown out.* (***arrange***, ***file***, ***list***, ***order***, ***sort***)

Verb forms: I **classified**, I have **classified**, I am **classifying**
Word building: **classifiable** *adjective* **classified** *adjective*

classroom
noun a room in a school or college where lessons take place

clatter
verb **1** to rattle loudly
noun **2** disturbance

Word history: Old English *clatrian*, of imitative origin

clause (klawz)
noun Grammar a group of words which contains a subject and a verb, which may be a part of a sentence or a whole sentence, such as *after the boy arrived* and *She heard the news.*

Word history: Middle English, from Medieval Latin

A **clause** is the most important unit in the structure of a sentence. Whatever else is there, the sentence must have a clause. And the clause always contains a verb with a subject. This is how it differs from a **phrase**. For example:

on the corner	phrase
standing on the corner	phrase
I was standing on the corner	clause

Only the third example has a complete verb (*was standing*), with its subject (*I*), and therefore it is the only one that is a clause.

There are two major types of clause: **main clauses** (also called **principal clauses**) and **dependent clauses** (also called **subordinate clauses**).

Main clauses

These always have a main verb in them. They can stand alone as a sentence, as in:

I'm going home.

When the main clause stands alone, as in the sentence above, it is known as a simple sentence. A main clause can also join with a dependent clause to form a longer sentence, as in:

After we've had lunch, I'm going home.

Another name for main clauses is **principal clauses.**

Dependent clauses

A dependent clause does not make a complete message by itself. That is, it cannot stand as a sentence on its own:

While I was standing on the corner…

There are three major types of dependent clause: adjectival clauses, adverbial clauses and noun clauses. You can tell from their names that they are clauses that do the work of adjectives, adverbs and nouns.

In the following examples you can see how the clauses replace the word in each part of speech. Notice that the clauses give you the chance to add in extra information:

the winning horse	adjective
the horse that won this race	adjectival clause
they came late	adverb
they came after it had started	adverbial clause
he said his farewell	noun
he said that he was going now	noun clause

Adjectival clauses normally begin with pronouns like *who*, *whom*, *whose*, *which* and *that*. These are all relative pronouns:

The car which hurtled past was green.

The banana that was thrown out struck me.

The driver who threw the banana was my uncle.

Adverbial clauses answer the questions 'when?' 'where?' 'how?' or 'why?':

After he threw the banana he laughed. When? (adverbial clause of time)

He drove round the corner where I couldn't see him. Where? (adverbial clause of place)

As an eagle swoops on its prey I hurtled after him. How? (adverbial clause of manner)

I slipped over because a banana peel lay on the gutter. Why? (adverbial clause of reason)

noun clauses usually explain what people are thinking, feeling or saying:

I suspect that I have a broken leg.

I hope that my uncle enjoyed his supper.

He says that bananas are good for you.

I know what you're going to say.

For more about the way clauses work, look up **adjectives**, **adverbs** and **nouns**.

claustrophobia (klos-truh-foh-bee-uh)
noun the fear of being shut in a small place

Word building: **claustrophobic** *adjective*
Word history: Neo-Latin, from Latin *claustrum* enclosure + *-phobia*

claves (klayvz, klah-vayz)
plural noun a simple musical instrument which consists of two wooden sticks which are hit together

clavichord (klav-uh-kawd)
noun an early type of piano, whose strings are softly struck with metal blades

Word history: Medieval Latin, from Latin *clāvi(s)* key + *chord(a)* string

clavicle (klav-uh-kuhl)
noun either of two slender bones each connecting the breastbone with a shoulderblade and forming the front part of the shoulder

Word use: A more common term for this is **collarbone.**
Word building: **clavicular** *adjective*
Word history: from Latin word meaning 'little key'

claw
noun **1** the sharp curved nail on the foot of an animal or bird
2 the sharp pincers of crabs and lobsters
verb **3** to scratch or seize with nails or claws

Word history: Old English *clawian*

clay
noun a dense earth which holds water and is used in making pottery and bricks

Word building: **clayey** *adjective*
Word history: Old English *clǣg*

claymation (klay-may-shuhn)
noun an animation technique using clay figures as the basis for the film rather than drawn figures

clean
adjective **1** without dirt or stains (***hygienic***, ***immaculate***, ***pure***, ***spick-and-span***, ***spotless***)
2 fair: *It was a **clean** fight.*
3 without a mark: *She started a **clean** page.*
4 not using illegal drugs: *Although once an addict, he has been **clean** for years.*
5 with a smooth edge: *It was a **clean** cut that would heal easily.*
verb **6** to remove dirt from: *She **cleaned** herself in the shower.* (***cleanse***, ***mop up***, ***scrub***, ***sterilise***, ***wash***)
phrase **7 clean up,**
a to tidy up or put in order
b to finish up or reach the end of
c *Colloquial* to make money
d in sport, to defeat crushingly
8 come clean, to make a full confession

Word use: The opposite of definitions 1 and 2 is **dirty**.
Word building: **cleaner** *noun* **cleanliness** *noun* **cleanly** *adverb*
Word history: Middle English *clene*, Old English *clǣne* pure, clear, related to Dutch and German *klein* small

clean coal
noun coal which has been processed to make it less damaging to the environment

clean-cut
adjective **1** clearly outlined
2 well-shaped: *a **clean-cut** haircut*
3 definite: *a **clean-cut** answer*
4 neatly dressed and well-presented: *a **clean-cut** worker*

clean fuel
noun a fuel which produces minimal greenhouse gas emissions

cleanse (klenz)
verb to make clean or pure: *to **cleanse** the skin* (***mop up***, ***purify***, ***scrub***, ***sterilise***, ***wash***)

Word history: Old English, from *clǣne* clean

clean-shaven
adjective without a beard or moustache: *a **clean-shaven** young man*

clear
adjective **1** light or bright: *It was a **clear** sunny day.*
2 transparent: ***clear** glass* (***limpid***, ***sheer***, ***translucent***)
3 easily understood: *The children need **clear** examples.* (***evident***, ***explicit***, ***obvious***, ***plain***, ***straightforward***)
4 without doubt: *a **clear** win* (***certain***, ***confident***, ***definite***, ***positive***)
5 open or free from obstacles: *a **clear** road*
verb **6** to become light or bright: *After a cloudy morning the sky **cleared**.*
7 to free from blockage: *He **cleared** the gutters on the roof.*
8 to free from blame: *The jury's verdict **cleared** her of guilt.* (***excuse***, ***let off***, ***pardon***, ***spare***)
adverb **9** entirely: *to get **clear** away*
phrase **10 clear up,** to make easier to understand: *Can you **clear up** this point for me?*

Word building: **clearly** *adverb*
Word history: Middle English, from Latin

clearance
noun **1** the space between two things: *The truck had a **clearance** of ten centimetres under the bridge.*
2 permission to go ahead with something: *They needed a **clearance** from the council to build their home of mud bricks.* (***approval***, ***consent***, ***dispensation***, ***leave***)

clearing
noun a piece of cleared land in the middle of bush or forest

clearway
noun a busy street or highway on which cars may stop only in case of emergency

cleat
noun **1** a wedge-shaped piece of wood or metal which a climber drives into a steep mountain side to make a foothold
2 a projecting piece of metal fastened under a shoe to increase grip or to preserve the sole

Word history: Middle English *clete* wedge

cleavage
noun a division or split

cleave[1]
phrase **cleave to,** *Old-fashioned* **1** to stick, cling or hold fast
2 to be attached or faithful: *to **cleave to** your friends through thick and thin*

Word history: Old English *cleofian*

cleave[2]
verb **1** to divide or part by a cutting blow, especially along the grain or any other natural line of division
2 to make by or as by cutting: *to **cleave** a path through the wilderness*
3 to separate or sever by, or as if by, splitting

Verb forms: it **cleft** or it **cleaved** or it **clove**, it has **cleft** or it has **cleaved** or it has **cloven**, it is **cleaving**
Word history: Old English *clēofan*

cleaver
noun a chopper with a long blade, used by butchers for cutting meat

clef
noun a symbol placed on a line of music that shows the height or pitch of the notes: *treble **clef***

Word history: French, from Latin word meaning 'key'

cleft
noun a narrow opening or split

Word history: Middle English *clift*, Old English *geclyft* split, crack, fissure

clench
verb to close or press tightly: *to **clench** your teeth in pain | to **clench** your fist in anger*

Word history: Old English *beclencan* hold fast

clergy
noun the priests and ministers of Christian churches

Word history: Middle English, from Late Latin *clēricus* cleric

clergyman
noun someone who belongs to the clergy (***chaplain***, ***minister***, ***parson***, ***priest***, ***vicar***)

If you don't know the sex of the person you're referring to, it is best to use the term **member of the clergy**.

cleric
noun a member of the clergy

Word history: Late Latin, from Greek word meaning 'clergy', 'origin', 'lot', 'allotment'

clerical
adjective **1** having to do with office workers and clerks: *a* ***clerical*** *error*
2 having to do with the clergy: *a* ***clerical*** *collar*

Word history: Late Latin

clerk (klahk)
noun someone who works in an office, keeping records and accounts and sorting letters and papers

Word history: Old English *clerc, cleric*, from Late Latin word meaning 'cleric'

clever
adjective **1** good at thinking quickly (***brainy***, ***bright***, ***intelligent***, ***shrewd***, ***smart***)
2 able or skilful: *He's* ***clever*** *with his hands.*

Word building: **cleverly** *adverb*
cleverness *noun*
Word history: Middle English *cliver*

cliché (<u>klee</u>-shay)
noun a saying which has become stale or dull because it has been used too often, such as *as old as the hills*

Word building: **clichéd** *adjective*
Word history: French, past participle of *clicher* to stereotype

click
noun **1** a slight sharp sound
verb **2** to make a click or series of clicks
3 *Colloquial* to fall into place, or be understood: *His story suddenly* ***clicked.***
4 *Colloquial* to understand: *I finally* ***clicked*** *and realised that he was lying.*
5 *Computers* to operate the mouse button to select (something on screen): ***Click*** *the red button to start the game.*

Word history: imitating the sound

client
noun **1** someone who uses the services of a business or a person such as a lawyer or accountant
2 *Internet* a computer which accesses the resources of another computer, the server, via a network

Word history: Middle English, from Latin *cliens* retainer

clientele (klee-uhn-<u>tel</u>)
noun all the customers, clients, etc., of a business or a person such as a lawyer or accountant

Word history: Latin

cliff
noun a steep rocky slope

Word history: Old English *clif*

climactic
adjective having to do with a climax, the highest point or most important part of anything: *the* ***climactic*** *scene of the play | the* ***climactic*** *battle of the war*

Word building: **climactically** *adverb*

climactic / climatic
Don't confuse **climactic** and **climatic**. **Climatic** is to do with climate, the weather of a particular place, whereas **climactic** is to do with a **climax**, the highest point or most important part of anything:

The climactic scene of the film is when the hero rescues his friend from the jaws of a giant ant.

climate
noun the usual weather of a particular place

Word history: Middle English, from Late Latin, from Greek word meaning 'clime', 'zone', literally 'slope' (of the earth from equator to pole)

climate change
noun a significant change in the usual climatic conditions, especially such a change thought to be caused by global warming

climate refugee
noun someone who escapes for safety, especially to a foreign country, due to catastrophic climate change in their own country

climatic
adjective having to do with weather: ***climatic*** *conditions in the south of the state*

Word building: **climatically** *adverb*

climax
noun the highest or most important and exciting point of anything: *The* ***climax*** *of the show was a fireworks display at night.*

Word history: Latin, from Greek *klîmax* ladder, staircase, climax

climb
verb **1** to move up something, especially by using your hands and feet: *She* ***climbed*** *the ladder.* (***ascend***, ***clamber***, ***mount***, ***scale***, ***shin***)
2 to move upwards: *The aeroplane* ***climbs*** *slowly into the sky.* (***ascend***, ***mount***, ***rise***, ***soar***)
3 to slope upwards: *The mountain* ***climbs*** *to a sharp peak.*

Word building: **climb** *noun* **climber** *noun*
Word history: Old English *climban*

clinch
verb **1** to settle once and for all: *They* ***clinched*** *the sale by signing the papers.*
noun **2** a close hold in boxing, which slows your opponent's punches

Word building: **clincher** *noun*
Word history: later variant of *clench*

cling
verb to hold tightly: *The child was* ***clinging*** *to his mother.* (***clasp***, ***clutch***, ***grasp***, ***grip***, ***hug***)

Verb forms: I **clung**, I have **clung**, I am **clinging**
Word building: **clingy** *adjective* (**clingier, clingiest**)
Word history: Old English *clingan* stick or draw together, shrivel

clinic
noun **1** a medical centre where you can go to see a doctor or have special tests or treatment, such as an X-ray
2 an organised session of instruction in a particular activity or subject: *a **basketball** clinic*

Word history: Late Latin word meaning 'of a bed', from Greek

clinical
adjective **1** having to do with a clinic, sick room or hospital
2 concerned with the observation and personal treatment of disease in a patient: *a **clinical** diagnosis*
3 scientific, detached or unemotional in your approach to life: *He has a **clinical** attitude to death.*

Word building: **clinically** *adverb*

clink[1]
verb **1** to make a light, sharp, ringing sound, such as glasses make when they are hit together
noun **2** the rather piercing cry of some birds

Word history: Middle English

clink[2]
noun *Colloquial* a prison (***compound***, ***jail***, ***lockup***, ***penitentiary***)

Word history: apparently from *Clink* prison in Clink St, Southwark, London

clip[1]
verb **1** to cut off or shorten with scissors or shears: *The shearer **clipped** the sheep's wool. | Dad **clipped** the ends of his moustache.* (***shear***, ***snip***, ***tear***, ***trim***)
2 to punch a hole in: *The bus conductor **clipped** our tickets.*
3 to give a sharp hit: *He **clipped** the man on the jaw.* (***bat***, ***beat***, ***knock***, ***strike***, ***tap***)
noun **4** a trimming: *Please give my hair a **clip**.*
5 → **wool clip**
6 a short section of a film: *The actors saw **clips** of the film as it was being made.*
7 *Colloquial* → **video clip**

Verb forms: I **clipped**, I have **clipped**, I am **clipping**
Word building: **clipped** *adjective* **clipping** *noun*
Word history: Middle English, from Scandinavian

clip[2]
noun **1** something which holds things in place: *My bag is open because the **clip** keeps coming undone.*
verb **2** to fasten

Word history: Old English *clyppan* embrace

clipper
noun **1** a cutting tool, especially for your hair or nails
2 a fast sailing ship

Word use: You can also use **clippers** for definition 1.

clique (kleek)
noun a small close group of people who keep themselves apart from others

Word building: **cliquey** *adjective* (**cliquier**, **cliquiest**)
Word history: French, *claque*, hired applauders in a theatre

clitoris (klit-uh-ruhs)
noun the small organ of a woman's vulva, corresponding anatomically to a man's penis

Word history: Neo-Latin, from Greek word meaning 'shut'

cloak
noun **1** a sleeveless coat or cape which does up at your neck
verb **2** to hide or keep hidden: *to **cloak** your feelings*

Word history: Middle English, from Medieval Latin word meaning 'cloak', originally 'bell'; perhaps of Celtic origin

clock
noun **1** something which measures and tells you the time
verb **2** to time

Word history: Middle English, from Middle Dutch word meaning 'instrument for measuring time'

clockwise
adjective going around in the same direction as the hands on a clock face

Word use: The opposite is **anticlockwise**.

clockwork
noun **1** the workings of a clock or a wind-up toy
phrase **2 like clockwork**, smoothly and without interruption: *Our travel plans went **like clockwork**.*

clod
noun **1** a lump, especially of earth
2 *Old-fashioned* a dull or stupid person

Word history: Old English *clodd*

cloddish
adjective dull or stupid

clodhopper
noun **1** a clumsy stupid person (***bumpkin***, ***oaf***, ***rustic***)
2 clodhoppers, strong heavy shoes

clog
verb **1** to block or become blocked: *Leaves **clogged** the gutter.*
noun **2** a heavy wooden shoe

Verb forms: it **clogged**, it has **clogged**, it is **clogging**
Word history: Middle English *clog, clogge*

cloister (kloy-stuh)
noun **1** a covered path by the side of a building such as a church
2 a place where nuns or priests live quietly, away from the rest of the world

Word building: **cloister** *verb*
Word history: Middle English, from Old French, blend of *cloison* partition and Latin *claustrum* enclosed place

clone
noun the offspring of a plant or animal which is exactly the same as its parent and has been formed, not by the joining of male and female cells, but from one of its parent's own cells

Word building: **clone** *verb*
Word history: Greek word meaning 'slip', 'twig', 'cutting from a plant'

close (klohz)
verb **1** to block off: *Heavy snow **closed** the road.* (***bar***, ***barricade***, ***blockade***, ***obstruct***)
2 to shut: *The door **closed** in the wind. | She **closed** the window.*
3 to refuse entry to: *Police **closed** the sports ground.*

4 to end: *After two hours the meeting finally* ***closed.*** | *He* ***closed*** *his show with a song.* (***conclude, finish, terminate***)
noun (klohz) **5** conclusion
adjective (klohs) **6** narrow or tight: *The shoes are a* ***close*** *fit.* (***confined, cramped***)
7 hard to breathe: *The air in the hot room was too* ***close*** *and someone fainted.*
8 near or nearby: *The school is* ***close*** *to the park.* | *The children are* ***close*** *in age.* (***adjacent, neighbouring, next***)
9 having by a strong shared feeling: *a* ***close*** *friendship* | *They felt* ***close*** *after all they had been through together.* (***affectionate, intimate, loving***)
10 thorough: *This book needs* ***close*** *study.* (***comprehensive, detailed, exhaustive, in-depth, intensive***)
phrase **11 close in,** to surround and come towards gradually, the way you do when you are trying to capture a place

Word use: The opposite of definitions 1 to 4 is **open.** | The opposite of definition 8 is **far.**
Word building: **close** *adverb* **closed** *adjective* **closely** *adverb* **closeness** *noun*
Word history: Middle English, from French, from Latin *clausum* enclosed place

closet (kloz-uht)
noun **1** a cupboard or small room where things are stored
2 a toilet

Word history: Middle English, from Old French word meaning 'little enclosed place', from Latin

closure (kloh-zhuh)
noun **1** the act of closing or shutting
2 the state of being closed
3 a conclusion
4 the method of closing debate in parliament and causing an immediate vote to be taken on a question under discussion

Word use: You can also use **closure motion** for definition 4.
Word history: Middle English, from Latin word meaning 'shut'

clot
noun **1** a solid lump: *a blood* ***clot***
2 *Colloquial* a fool
verb **3** to thicken or form into clots: *The blood from his cut began to* ***clot*** *and dry up.* (***coagulate, congeal, curdle***)

Verb forms: it **clotted,** it has **clotted,** it is **clotting**
Word history: Old English *clott* lump

cloth
noun **1** a piece of material: *Her skirt was made of woollen* ***cloth.*** | *He wiped the milk up with a* ***cloth.*** (***fabric, stuff, textile***)
phrase **2 the cloth,** the clergy

Word history: Old English *clath*

cloth / clothe

Don't confuse **cloth** with **clothe.** To **clothe** someone is to give them clothes to wear.

clothe (klohdh)
verb to provide with clothes: *to* ***clothe*** *the needy children*

Word building: **clothing** *noun*
Word history: Old English *clāthian*

clothes (klohdhz)
plural noun the things you wear

Word history: originally, plural of *cloth*

cloud
noun **1** a white or grey mass of water vapour, ice, smoke or dust that floats in the air
2 anything which looks or acts like a cloud: *a* ***cloud*** *of steam* | *a* ***cloud*** *of sandflies*
verb **3** to darken or become darker: *Anger* ***clouded*** *her face.* | *The mirror* ***clouded*** *with steam.*

Word building: **cloudiness** *noun* **cloudy** *adjective* (**cloudier, cloudiest**)
Word history: Old English *clūd* rock, hill

clout
noun **1** *Colloquial* a hit with the hand: *He gave the boy a* ***clout*** *on the shoulder.*
2 power or influence: *You need some* ***clout*** *to get a good job like that.* (***authority, pull, standing, sway, weight***)
verb **3** *Colloquial* to hit

Word history: Old English *clūt* piece of cloth or metal

clove
noun the dried flower bud of a tropical tree, used as a spice

Word history: Middle English, from Old French *clou de girofle* nail of clove, so called from the shape

cloven
verb **1** past participle of **cleave**[2]
adjective **2** cleft, split or divided: ***cloven*** *feet* | ***cloven*** *hoofs*

clover
noun a plant with leaves divided into three parts and a small flower, often used as food for cattle

Word history: Old English *clāfre*

clown
noun **1** someone in a circus, often dressed up with a white face, a red nose and silly clothes, who makes people laugh (***buffoon, harlequin, jester***)
verb **2** to act the fool

Word building: **clowning** *noun* **clownish** *adjective*

cloy (kloy)
verb to weary by too much food, sweetness, pleasure, etc. (***glut, sate, satiate***)

Word building: **cloying** *adjective*
Word history: from obsolete *acloy* to stop up, drive in a nail, perhaps from Middle French, from Latin *clāvus* nail

club
noun **1** a heavy stick, used as a weapon
2 a stick used to hit the ball in games like golf
3 a group of people who have joined together because they share a particular interest or hobby: *We started a chess* ***club*** *at school.* (***association, guild, society, union***)
4 a place run by a group, which offers entertainment and cheap food and drink to those who belong
5 the clover-shaped black sign on some playing cards
verb **6** to beat with a club
phrase **7 club in,** to join together: *Everyone in the office* ***clubbed in*** *to buy her a card.*

Verb forms: I **clubbed,** I have **clubbed,** I am **clubbing**
Word history: Middle English, from Scandinavian

cluck
verb to make the sound a hen makes when calling her chicks

Word history: variant of *clock* (now Scottish and dialect), from Old English *cloccian*

clucky
adjective Australian, NZ Colloquial feeling a strong desire to have children

clue
noun something which helps to explain a puzzle or mystery: *a **clue** in a detective story* (***guide***, ***marker***, ***pointer***, ***sign***)

clump
noun a group of things growing together, such as trees or grasses

Word building: **clump** *verb*
Word history: Old English *clympre*

clumsy
adjective **1** awkward in the way you move about (***accident-prone***, ***bumbling***, ***gangling***, ***uncoordinated***)
2 without skill: *a **clumsy** worker* (***incompetent***, ***inept***, ***inexpert***)

Adjective forms: **clumsier**, **clumsiest**
Word building: **clumsily** *adverb* **clumsiness** *noun*
Word history: from obsolete verb *clumse* be benumbed with cold, from Scandinavian

clung
verb past tense and past participle of **cling**

cluster
noun **1** a number of things growing or placed close together: *a **cluster** of grapes | a **cluster** of stars*
verb **2** to gather in close groups

Word history: Old English *clyster* bunch

clutch
verb **1** to seize or hold tightly: *The baby **clutched** the kitten.* (***clasp***, ***cling to***, ***grasp***, ***grip***, ***hug***)
noun **2** a tight hold
3 part of a machine which is used in changing gears
4 **clutches**, power: *Now the witch had Ivan in her **clutches**.*
phrase **5** **clutch at**, to try to seize: *He **clutched at** the rope.*

Word history: Old English *clyccan* crook or bend, close (the hand), clench

clutter
verb to make untidy: *Papers **clutter** the dining room table.*

Word building: **clutter** *noun*
Word history: variant of *clotter*, from *clot*

coach
noun **1** a closed carriage pulled by horses
2 a tourist bus
3 a railway carriage
4 someone who trains athletes
verb **5** to train (***drill***, ***educate***, ***instruct***, ***tutor***)

Word history: French, from Hungarian

coagulate (koh-<u>ag</u>-yuh-layt)
verb to change from a liquid into a thick lump, such as a clot (***condense***, ***congeal***, ***curdle***)

Word building: **coagulation** *noun*
Word history: from Latin word meaning 'curdled'

coal
noun **1** a black or dark brown rock, formed from the remains of ancient trees, used as fuel
phrase **2** **haul** (**someone**) **over the coals**, to scold severely

Word history: Old English *col* live coal

coalesce (koh-uh-<u>les</u>)
verb to grow or join together: *The many small groups **coalesced** into one strong party.*

Word building: **coalescence** *noun* **coalescent** *adjective*
Word history: Latin

coalition (koh-uh-<u>lish</u>-uhn)
noun the joining together of two or more groups, at least for a while: *a **coalition** of political parties*

Word building: **coalitionist** *noun*
Word history: Medieval Latin, from Latin word meaning 'coalesce'

coarse (kaws)
adjective **1** thick or rough: ***coarse** material | **coarse** sand* (***bristly***, ***bumpy***, ***shaggy***, ***unfinished***, ***unrefined***)
2 rude or offensive: ***coarse** jokes | **coarse** manners* (***common***, ***crude***, ***tasteless***, ***uncouth***, ***vulgar***)

Word use: The opposite of definition 1 is **fine**. | The opposite of definition 2 is **refined**.
Word building: **coarsely** *adverb* **coarseness** *noun*
Word history: adjectival variant of *course*, noun, with the sense of ordinary

> **coarse / course**
> Don't confuse **coarse** with **course**, which is usually a noun and has several meanings.
> For example, a **course** is one part of a meal, as *in the main course.*
> A **course** is also the ground or stretch of water where a race is held.

coast
noun **1** the seashore or the land beside the sea
verb **2** to go downhill in a car or on a bike, without using power (***drift***, ***glide***)
phrase **3** **the coast is clear**, the danger has gone

Word building: **coastal** *adjective*
Word history: Middle English, from Latin *costa* rib, side

coastguard
noun someone whose job is to patrol the coast of a country, helping ships in danger and looking out for smugglers or illegal fishing boats

coat
noun **1** a piece of clothing with sleeves, which you wear over other clothes
2 the fur or wool of an animal
3 a layer: *The house needs a **coat** of paint.*
verb **4** to cover: *to **coat** with paint* (***daub***, ***plaster***, ***smear***, ***spread***)

Word history: Middle English, from Old French, from Germanic

coathanger
noun a curved or triangular piece of wood, plastic, etc., with a hook attached at the top, for hanging clothes on

coating
noun a covering: *a **coating** of batter* | *a **coating** of flour* (***crust***, ***film***, ***glaze***, ***skin***, ***veneer***)

coat of arms
noun the special design, often with a motto, belonging to a noble family or nation: *The knight had his **coat of arms** painted on his tunic and his shield.*

Word history: translation of French *cotte d'armes*

coax (kohks)
verb to persuade gently and patiently: *She **coaxed** the sick child to eat.* (***cajole***, ***encourage***, ***induce***, ***talk into***)

Word building: **coaxer** *noun*
Word history: from obsolete *cokes*, noun, fool

cob
noun **1** a stocky horse with short legs
2 a male swan
3 the head on which corn seeds grow: *a **cob** of corn*

Word history: Middle English

cobalt (koh-bawlt, koh-bolt)
noun a silver-white metal which gives a blue colouring to pottery

Word history: from German word meaning 'goblin'

cobber
noun Australian, *NZ Colloquial* a friend or mate

Word history: British dialect *cob*, meaning 'to form a friendship with'.

cobble
noun **1** a rounded paving stone
2 a badly completed job of sewing, mending, etc.
verb **3** to mend or patch roughly
4 to pave with cobblestones

Word use: You can also use **cobblestone** for definition 1.
Word history: perhaps *cob*, lump, heap

cobbler
noun Old-fashioned someone who mends shoes

COBOL (koh-bol)
noun a language for writing computer programs for commercial use

Word use: You can also use **Cobol**.
Word history: an acronym for *Co(mmon) B(usiness) O(riented) L(anguage)*

cobra (kob-ruh, koh-bruh)
noun a venomous snake which can spread out the skin of its neck like a hood

Word history: short for Portuguese *cobra* (from Latin *colubra* serpent) *de capello* hood snake

cobweb
noun **1** the fine thread spun by a spider to catch insects
2 something very light or fine

Word building: **cobwebby** *adjective*
Word history: Middle English *coppe* spider + *web*

cocaine (koh-kayn)
noun a bitter drug which is made from the leaves of a South American shrub

coccyx (kok-siks, kok-iks)
noun a small, triangular bone forming the lower end of the spinal column in humans

Noun forms: The plural is **coccyges** (kok-suy-jeez).
Word building: **coccygeal** *adjective*
Word history: Latin, from Greek word meaning 'coccyx', originally 'cuckoo'

cochineal (koch-uh-neel, koch-uh-neel)
noun **1** an insect which lives on cacti of Mexico and other warm regions of Central America
2 a dye, crimson in colour, produced from the dried bodies of this insect

Word history: French, from Spanish word meaning 'slater', from *cochino* pig

cochlear implant (kok-lee-uhr im-plant)
noun an artificial hearing device which takes digitally encoded sound from the outer ear to the inner ear and stimulates inner-ear nerves, thus restoring some hearing to people with severe damage to nerves in their inner ear

Word use: Another name is **bionic ear**.

cock[1]
noun **1** a rooster or male bird
2 the hammer of a gun

Word history: Old English *cocc*

cock[2]
verb to set or turn upwards or to one side, often in a jaunty or significant manner: *He wore his hat **cocked** to one side.* | *The dog **cocked** his ears attentively.*

Word history: perhaps a special use of *cock*[1]

cockatiel (kok-uh-tee-uhl)
noun a small, crested, long-tailed cockatoo, common in inland areas of Australia

Word history: Dutch

cockatoo
noun a crested parrot

Word history: Dutch, from Malay *kakatuwa* which might be a word made up to copy the sound that the bird makes, or it may be related to the Malay word meaning 'pincers' with reference to the birds way of holding things with its beak

cockerel (kok-uh-ruhl, kok-ruhl)
noun a young domestic cock

Word history: diminutive of *cock*, rooster

cocker spaniel
noun a type of small spaniel trained for use in hunting or kept as pets

cockeyed (kok-uyd)
adjective **1** crooked: *Your tie is **cockeyed**.*
2 foolish or absurd: *a **cockeyed** plan*
3 having a squinting eye

cockfight
noun a fight between gamecocks, usually with metal spurs attached to their legs, on the outcome of which spectators place bets

Word building: **cockfighting** *noun*

cockle
noun **1** a shellfish found in Europe, which is good to eat
2 cockles, the inmost or deepest parts: *Their kindness warms the **cockles** of your heart.*

Word history: Middle English, from French, from Greek word meaning 'little mussel or cockle'

cockpit
noun **1** the front end of a plane where the pilots sit
2 the driver's seat in a racing car

cockroach
noun an insect, usually active at night, with a flattened body and long feelers, which is a common household pest

cockscomb (kok-skohm)
noun the fleshy part on the head of a cock

Word use: You can also use **coxcomb**.

cocksure (kok-shaw)
adjective too certain, often in an arrogant way

cocktail (kok-tayl)
noun **1** a short, mixed, alcoholic drink, usually chilled and often sweetened
2 any mix of ingredients, especially one that is dangerous: *a **cocktail** of drugs | a dangerous **cocktail** of enthusiasm and ignorance*
adjective **3** small enough to be eaten with your fingers: ***cocktail** sausage*

cocky[1]
adjective Colloquial too confident or smart: *The new workers on the job are **cocky**, until they find out how hard it is.* (***cocksure**, **overconfident***)

Adjective forms: **cockier**, **cockiest**
Word building: **cockily** *adverb* **cockiness** *noun*

cocky[2]
noun **1** *Australian* a cockatoo
2 *Australian, NZ* a farmer, especially of a small farm

Noun forms: The plural is **cockies**.
Word history: abbreviation of *cockatoo*

cocoa (koh-koh)
noun **1** the crushed and powdered seeds of the cacao tree
2 a drink made from the brown powder which is also used to make chocolate

Word history: variant of *cacao*

coconut
noun the large hard nut of the coconut palm, which is lined with white flesh and contains a clear milk

cocoon (kuh-koohn)
noun **1** the covering which grubs such as the silkworm spin around themselves for their chrysalis stage before their next stage of growth
verb **2** to cover or protect

Word history: French *coque* shell

cod
noun any of a number of freshwater and saltwater fishes valued as a food

Word history: Middle English

coda (koh-duh)
noun the part which finishes a piece of music

Word history: Italian, from Latin *cauda* tail

coddle
verb **1** to pamper, or look after very well: *His parents **coddled** him after he was sick.*
2 to cook in water very slowly: *to **coddle** eggs* (***braise**, **poach**, **simmer***)

Word history: from *caudle* kind of gruel, from Old Northern French, from Latin *calidus* hot

code
noun **1** a set of rules or laws: *a legal **code** | a **code** of honour*
2 a secret language, or a system such as the dots and dashes used in morse code
verb **3** to put in a code

Word building: **decode** *verb* **encode** *verb*
Word history: Middle English, from French, from Latin *cōdex*

codger (koj-uh)
noun a man, especially elderly and slightly odd: *a lovable old **codger***

Word history: perhaps variant of *cadger*

codicil (kod-uh-sil)
noun a supplement to a will, containing an addition, change, explanation, etc.

Word building: **codicillary** *adjective*
Word history: Latin

codify (koh-duh-fuy, kod-uh-fuy)
verb to arrange in a code: *to **codify** laws*

Verb forms: I **codified**, I have **codified**, I am **codifying**
Word building: **codifier** *noun* **codification** *noun*

coeducation (koh-ed-juh-kay-shuhn)
noun joint education, especially of both sexes in the same institution and classes

Word building: **coeducational** *adjective*

coefficient (koh-uh-fish-uhnt)
noun **1** something that acts together with another thing to produce a result
2 *Mathematics* a number in an algebraic expression by which a quantity is multiplied: *3 is the **coefficient** of x in 3x.*
3 *Physics* a quantity, constant for a given substance, body or process under particular conditions, used as the measure of one of its properties: *the **coefficient** of friction*

coelenterate (suh-len-tuh-rayt, suh-len-tuh-ruht)
noun one of a group of invertebrate animals that includes the hydras, jellyfishes, sea anemones, corals, etc., marked by a single internal cavity which is used for digestion, excretion, and other functions

coeliac (see-lee-ak)
adjective **1** having to do with the cavity of the abdomen
2 having to do with coeliac disease
noun **3** a person suffering from coeliac disease: *When she found out she was a **coeliac** she had to change her diet.*

Word use: You can also use **celiac**.

coeliac disease
noun a disorder which causes diarrhoea in people whose bowels are not able to process gluten

Word use: You can also use **celiac disease**.

coerce (koh-<u>ers</u>)
verb to force: *The shopkeeper was **coerced** at gun point to open the cash register.* (***bully***, ***compel***, ***make***)

Word building: **coercion** *noun* **coercive** *adjective*
Word history: from Latin word meaning 'hold together'

coffee
noun **1** a drink made from the roasted and ground beans of a tropical shrub
2 the brown powder you use to make this drink

Word history: Turkish, from Arabic

coffer
noun **1** a box or chest, especially one for valuables
2 coffers, a treasury, or funds

Word history: Middle English, from Old French word meaning 'chest', from Latin word meaning 'basket'

coffin
noun the box in which a dead body is buried or cremated

Word history: Middle English, from Old French word meaning 'small basket', 'coffin', from Latin, from Greek word meaning 'basket'

cog
noun **1** one of the toothlike parts sticking out of a gearwheel which connects it with another wheel
2 one of many unimportant people in an organisation

Word history: Middle English

cogent (<u>koh</u>-juhnt)
adjective so convincing that you are forced to agree: *a **cogent** argument*

Word building: **cogency** *noun*
Word history: from Latin word meaning 'forcing'

cogitate (<u>koj</u>-uh-tayt)
verb to think hard

Word building: **cogitation** *noun* **cogitative** *adjective*
Word history: Latin

cognac (<u>kon</u>-yak)
noun a high quality brandy

Word history: from *Cognac*, town in France where it was first made

cognate (kog-<u>nayt</u>)
adjective **1** having the same parents, descent, origins, etc.: ***cognate** languages* / ***cognate** species*
noun **2** someone or something cognate with another

Word history: Latin

cognisance (<u>kog</u>-nuh-zuhns)
noun knowledge, or notice: *to take **cognisance** of a fact*

Word building: **cognisant** *adjective*
Word history: Middle English, from Latin word meaning 'come to know'

cognition (kog-<u>nish</u>-uhn)
noun **1** the act or process of knowing (***perception***, ***thought***)
2 something known

Word building: **cognitive** *adjective*
Word history: Middle English, from Latin

cohabit (koh-<u>hab</u>-uht)
verb to live together in a sexual relationship

Word building: **cohabitation** *noun*
Word history: from Late Latin word meaning 'dwell with'

coherent (koh-<u>hear</u>-ruhnt)
adjective **1** agreeing or well thought out: *a **coherent** argument*
2 sticking together firmly: ***coherent** surfaces*

Word use: The opposite of definition 1 is **incoherent**.
Word building: **cohere** *verb* **coherence** *noun* **coherently** *adverb*
Word history: from Latin word meaning 'stick together'

cohesion (koh-<u>hee</u>-zhuhn)
noun **1** the state of sticking together or being connected
2 in English, the linking of sentences in speech or writing to make a connected whole

Word building: **cohesive** *adjective*

cohort (<u>koh</u>-hawt)
noun **1** one of the ten divisions of a legion in an ancient Roman army
2 a group or company, especially of soldiers or fighters
3 a supporter or helper (***accomplice***, ***ally***, ***follower***)
4 a group of people at the same level, as in education, skill development, etc.

Word history: from Latin word meaning 'enclosure'

coiffure (kwu-<u>fyoo</u>-uh)
noun **1** a style of arranging the hair
2 a head covering, or headdress

Word history: from French word meaning 'furnish with a coif'

coil
verb **1** to wind into loops: *to **coil** ropes*
2 to form into loops: *The snake **coiled** itself and struck.*
noun **3** a loop (***curl***, ***spiral***, ***twist***)

Word history: French word meaning 'gather', from Latin

coin
noun **1** a metal piece of money
verb **2** to make coins
3 to invent: *to **coin** a word* (***create***, ***devise***, ***make up***, ***originate***)

Word building: **coinage** *noun*
Word history: Latin *cuneus* wedge

coincide (koh-uhn-<u>suyd</u>)
verb **1** to happen together by chance
2 to agree: *Our opinions **coincide** on this point.*

Word history: Latin *co-* + *incidere* fall on

coincidence (koh-<u>in</u>-suh-duhns)
noun the surprising fact of things happening together by chance: *It was just a **coincidence** that we were on the same ship to Italy.*

Word building: **coincidental** *adjective*

coke
noun a solid fuel made from heating coal

Word history: Middle English *colk* core

cola (<u>koh</u>-luh)
noun a soft drink containing an extract prepared from the cola nut

Word history: Latinisation of *Kola, Kolla, Goora*, in Negro languages of West Africa

colander (<u>kul</u>-uhn-duh, <u>kol</u>-uhn-duh)
noun a bowl with many small holes, which is used in the kitchen for draining off liquid

Word use: You can also use **cullender**.
Word history: Latin *cōlāre* strain

cold
adjective **1** having or feeling a lack of warmth: *It's a **cold** day. | My hands are **cold**.* (***freezing***, ***frigid***, ***frosty***, ***icy***, ***wintry***)
2 unfriendly: *Our neighbours were **cold** towards us at first.* (***aloof***, ***antisocial***, ***inhospitable***)
noun **3** the absence of heat
4 a viral illness which usually comes with a blocked or runny nose, sore throat, coughing, etc.
phrase **5 cold comfort**, almost no comfort at all
6 cold feet, the loss of the courage you had for carrying something out
7 in cold blood, on purpose and without any pity: *They carried out the murder **in cold blood**.*
8 in the cold, ignored or left out
9 leave (**someone**) **cold**, to fail to make someone feel good about or positive towards something: *That painting **leaves me cold**.*
10 throw cold water on, to discourage

Word building: **coldly** *adverb* **coldness** *noun*
Word history: Old English *cald*

cold-blooded
adjective **1** without feelings of pity: *a **cold-blooded** murder* (***cruel***, ***hard-hearted***, ***insensitive***, ***stony***, ***unfeeling***)
2 having a blood temperature which changes as the temperature of the surrounding air or water changes: *Reptiles and fish are **cold-blooded** animals.*

Word use: The opposite of definition 2 is **warm-blooded**.

cold-call
verb to attempt to sell a product or service by making a telephone call to a person who has not asked for contact to be made and may or may not not be interested: *She was employed to **cold-call** people between 7 and 9 o'clock each evening.*

Word building: **cold-calling** *noun*

cold case
noun a crime that has remained unsolved for a long period of time

cold-shoulder
verb to ignore, or act coldly towards (***avoid***, ***exclude***, ***expel***, ***ostracise***, ***shun***)

Word history: from the phrase *give (someone) the cold shoulder*

cold sore
noun a blister-like sore on the face, often appearing during a cold

Word use: The medical name is **herpes simplex**.

cold turkey
noun Colloquial **1** a blunt or matter-of-fact statement of procedure
2 the sudden and complete withdrawal of a drug as a treatment for drug addiction

Word building: **cold-turkey** *verb*

cold war
noun a serious economic and political conflict between nations, etc., stopping just short of military action

coleslaw
noun a salad made with sliced raw cabbage

Word history: Dutch *koolsla*, from *kool* cabbage + *sla*, from *salade* salad

colic
noun a sharp pain in your stomach

Word building: **colicky** *adjective*
Word history: Middle English, from Latin, from Greek word meaning 'relating to the colon'

coliform (<u>kol</u>-uh-fawm)
noun **1** a group of bacteria that live in the intestine and which, if they are found in water, for instance, indicate there is faecal contamination
adjective **2** having to do with these bacteria: *The water was tested for levels of **coliform** bacteria.*

collaborate
verb **1** to work together: *They **collaborated** on the project.* (***combine***, ***cooperate***, ***team up***, ***unite***)
2 to work together with an enemy inside your own country: *He **collaborated** with the invaders.*

Word building: **collaboration** *noun* **collaborative** *adjective* **collaborator** *noun*
Word history: Late Latin

collage (kuh-<u>lahzh</u>)
noun a picture made from various materials, such as pieces of paper, cloth or other materials, pasted onto paper or board

collapse
verb **1** to fall down or fall apart suddenly: *The old man **collapsed** in the street. | The whole building **collapsed** when the wall gave way.* (***cave in***, ***crumple***, ***give way***, ***subside***)
2 to be made so that parts can be folded flat together: *This chair **collapses**.*

Word building: **collapse** *noun* **collapsible** *adjective*
Word history: from Latin word meaning 'fallen together'

collar
noun **1** the part of a piece of clothing that is worn around your neck
2 a leather band put around an animal's neck
verb **3** *Colloquial* to seize by the collar or neck: *The police officer **collared** the escaping criminal.*

Word history: Latin word meaning 'neckband', 'collar', from *collum* neck

collarbone
noun → **clavicle**

collate (kuh-<u>layt</u>)
verb to gather together in proper order: *I must **collate** the pages of my story.*

Word building: **collation** *noun*
Word history: from Latin word meaning 'brought together'

collateral (kuh-<u>lat</u>-uh-ruhl)
adjective **1** positioned at the side
2 parallel, or running side by side: ***collateral** agreements*
3 accompanying or supporting the main thing: ***collateral** security*

4 descended from the same ancestor, but through a different line and so not directly related
noun **5** an asset, pledged as security for the payment of a loan

Word history: Middle English, from Middle Latin

collateral damage
noun unintended destruction or injury, especially unintended civilian casualties in a military operation: *The **collateral damage** to the local villagers was appalling.*

colleague (kol-eeg)
noun someone you work with, usually in the same profession or office (***associate***, ***collaborator***, ***comrade***, ***partner***)

Word history: French, from Latin word meaning 'one chosen with another'

collect
verb **1** to gather together: *Please **collect** all the rubbish from the floor.* (***accumulate***, ***amass***, ***pile up***)
2 to assemble: *A crowd **collected** around the smashed car.* (***cluster***, ***congregate***, ***converge***)
3 to gather and keep examples of: *She **collects** stamps as a hobby.*
4 to gather money: *We are **collecting** for the poor.*
5 to call for and take away: *Please **collect** the parcel at the post office.*

Word building: **collection** *noun* **collector** *noun*
Word history: from Latin word meaning 'gathered together'

collected
adjective self-controlled: *She walked into the exam room looking very cool, calm and **collected**.*

collective
adjective **1** having to do with a group of people taken as a whole: *It will be done more quickly if we make a **collective** effort.* (***common***, ***communal***, ***general***)
noun **2** a group of people who share what they own and who work together for the good of them all

collective noun
noun *Grammar* a noun that is singular in its form but that expresses a grouping of individual objects or people: *Words like 'family', 'jury' and 'clergy' are all **collective nouns**.*

collectivism (kuh-lekt-uh-viz-uhm)
noun the principle of control by the people as a whole, or by the state, of all production or economic activities

Word building: **collectivist** *noun* **collectivist** *adjective*

college
noun **1** a place for learning, rather like a university, that you can go to after you finish high school
2 a place within a university where students live
3 a large private school

Word history: Middle English, from Latin *collēgium* association, a society

collide
verb to crash together: *The cars **collided**.*

Word building: **collision** *noun*
Word history: Latin

collie
noun a kind of dog with long thick hair and a bushy tail, often used in other countries to guard sheep

colliery (kol-yuh-ree)
noun a coalmine with all its buildings and equipment

Noun forms: The plural is **collieries**.

collocation (kol-uh-kay-shuhn)
noun **1** the act or result of placing things together or in proper order
2 *Linguistics* the joining together of particular words, such as *green as grass*

Word building: **collocate** *verb*

colloid
noun *Chemistry* a substance in solution which is of large particle size, that is, between a true solution and a coarse suspension

Word building: **colloidal** *adjective*
Word history: Greek *kólla* glue + *-oid*

colloquial (kuh-loh-kwee-uhl)
adjective suitable for casual, informal, or everyday language: *'Arvo' is a **colloquial** way of saying 'afternoon'.*

Word use: The opposite of this is **formal**.

colloquialism
noun an expression that you use when talking and chatting, or when you're not taking your written language too seriously

Examples of **colloquialisms** are:

He was a whizz at making pancakes.

They wanted to shoot through as soon as the meal finished.

Such expressions have an informal character, and if you use them in writing, they give an informal flavour to it. You would probably use them when writing dialogue, but not in formal essays.

collusion (kuh-looh-zhuhn)
noun a secret agreement made to deceive someone or to do something wrong (***conspiracy***, ***intrigue***)

Word building: **collusive** *adjective*
Word history: Middle English, from Latin word meaning 'a playing together'

cologne (kuh-lohn)
noun a kind of perfume

Word use: You can also use **eau de Cologne**.
Word history: short for *Cologne water* (made at *Cologne*, Germany, since 1709)

colon[1] (koh-luhn)
noun a punctuation mark (:) which is used to separate the main part of a sentence from a list of examples or an explanation

Word history: Latin, from Greek word meaning 'limb', 'clause'

We use the **colon** to show that we are going to explain, or give examples of, whatever we have just written. For instance:

The kennels cared for a number of breeds of dog: terriers, spaniels, corgis, labradors and German shepherds.

(continued)

colon *(continued)*

In informal writing, a dash could have been used in the above example instead of a colon. Look up **dash**.

Colons can be used before quoting someone's speech:

The teacher said: 'Sit down in that chair!'

Instead of a colon, you can use a comma here, or you can leave out the punctuation altogether. Look up **quotation mark**.

colon² (koh-luhn)
noun the part of bowel which is made up of most of the large intestine

Noun forms: The plural is **colons** or **cola**.
Word building: **colonic** *adjective*
Word history: Middle English, from Latin, from Greek word meaning 'food', 'colon'

colonel (ker-nuhl)
noun a senior officer in the army

Word history: French, from Italian word meaning 'little column'

colonel / kernel

Don't confuse **colonel** with **kernel**, which sounds the same but is the name for the hard centre of a nut or fruit.

colonial
noun someone who lives in a colony

Word building: **colonial** *adjective*

colonise
verb to start a colony in: *England **colonised** Australia.* (***occupy***, ***populate***, ***settle***)

Word use: You can also use **colonize**.
Word building: **colonisation** *noun* **colonist** *noun*

colonnade (kol-uhn-ayd, kol-uh-nayd)
noun **1** a series of columns set at a regular distance apart, and usually supporting a roof, series of arches, etc.
2 a long row of trees

Word history: French, from Italian, from Latin *columna* column

colony (kol-uh-nee)
noun **1** a group of people who have left their home and formed a settlement in a new land ruled by the parent country
2 the land settled in this way: *The early European settlements in Australia were **colonies** of Britain.*
3 a group of animals or plants of the same kind that live close together

Noun forms: The plural is **colonies**.
Word building: **colonial** *adjective*
Word history: Middle English, from Latin

colossal
adjective **1** very great in size (***enormous***, ***gigantic***, ***huge***, ***massive***, ***vast***)
2 *Colloquial* splendid or marvellous: *That film was **colossal**.*

colossus (kuh-los-uhs)
noun **1** a huge statue
2 a thing or person of great size or importance

Noun forms: The plural is **colossi** (kuh-los-uy) or **colossuses**.
Word history: Middle English, from Latin, from Greek

colostomy (kuh-los-tuh-mee)
noun a surgical operation to form an artificial anus or opening from the bowel through the stomach wall

Noun forms: The plural is **colostomies**.

colour
noun **1** the look that something has which is caused by the way light is reflected by it: *The main **colours** are red, orange, yellow, green, blue, indigo and violet.*
2 the colour of someone's skin
3 something used to give colour, such as paint or dye
4 details that make something interesting: *That story has a lot of **colour**.*
verb **5** to put colour on to (***dye***, ***paint***, ***stain***, ***tint***)
6 to go red in the face
7 to influence or change: *His jealousy **coloured** the way he told the story.*
phrase **8 show your true colours**, to show what sort of person you really are
9 with flying colours, very successfully

Word use: You can also use **color**.
Word building: **colourful** *adjective* **colouring** *noun* **colourless** *adjective*
Word history: Middle English, from Old French, from Latin

colour-bar
noun economic, political or social restrictions separating peoples of different colour, especially non-whites from whites

Word use: You can also use **color-bar**.

colour blindness
noun a fault in someone's eyesight that stops them from being able to tell the difference between some colours, such as red and green

Word use: You can also use **color blindness**.
Word building: **colour blind** *adjective*

colt
noun a male horse that is younger than four years old

Word history: Old English

column (kol-uhm)
noun **1** a long upright support or pillar
2 anything with a similar shape to a column: *a **column** of smoke | The children formed two **columns**.*
3 an upright row of numbers or of print going down a page
4 a piece of writing on a particular subject that appears regularly in a newspaper or magazine: *I like reading the fashion **column**.*

Word history: Middle English, from Old French, from Latin word meaning 'pillar', 'post'

columnist (kol-uhm-uhst, kol-uhm-nuhst)
noun a writer or organiser of a special column in a newspaper, etc.

coma
noun a very long, deep unconsciousness, which may be caused by disease, injury, poison, etc.

Word building: **comatose** *adjective*
Word history: from Greek word meaning 'deep sleep'

comb
noun **1** a piece of plastic or metal with a set of thin pointed teeth, which is used to tidy or hold back hair
2 a comb-shaped part on the head of a hen, rooster or turkey
verb **3** to tidy with a comb
4 to search carefully: *They **combed** the room for the missing purse.*

Word history: Old English

combat
verb **1** to fight against: *He must **combat** his liking for sweets. | The army was trained to **combat** an air attack.*
noun **2** a fight or struggle (***battle**, **brawl**, **conflict**, **fray**, **skirmish***)

Word building: **combatant** *noun* **combatant** *adjective*
Word history: French, from Latin *com-* + *batt(u) ere* beat

combine
verb to mix or join together: *You **combine** flour and water to make paste. | The two schools decided to **combine**.* (***amalgamate**, **assemble**, **blend**, **fuse**, **merge***)

Word use: The opposite of this is **separate**.
Word building: **combination** *noun*
Word history: Middle English, from Late Latin word meaning 'join together'

combo
noun Colloquial any small band of musicians

combustible
adjective able to burn

Word history: from Latin word meaning 'burnt up'

combustion
noun the process of catching alight or burning

come
verb **1** to move towards a person or place: *Please **come** here.*
2 to arrive or happen: *Christmas **comes** in December. | I hope my turn will **come** soon.*
3 to appear: *The light **comes** and goes.* (***emerge**, **loom**, **materialise**, **show up***)
4 to reach or extend: *I want the dress to **come** below my knees.*
phrase **5 come about**, to occur or happen in due course (***arise**, **fall**, **transpire***)
6 come across, to meet or find: *I **came across** her at the shops.* (***bump into**, **encounter**, **join up with**, **run into***)
7 come along, to hurry (***get a move on**, **hasten**, **shake a leg***)
8 come (a)round,
a to regain consciousness
b to change, especially your opinion or direction
9 come at,
a to rush at and attack
b *Colloquial* to agree to do
10 come by,
a to get or obtain
b to stop for a visit
11 come down with, to become ill with: *to **come down with** a disease*
12 come from, to live in or be born into: *I **come from** Australia. | I **come from** an Italian family.*
13 come good, *Colloquial* to improve after a bad beginning
14 come into, to inherit
15 come off,
a to happen or occur
b to reach the end
c to become unfastened
16 come out with, to tell or make known
17 come over, to happen to or have an effect on: *What has **come over** her to make her so quiet?*
18 come to, to add up to or equal: *What does the bill **come to**?*
19 come up, to arise or present itself: *to **come up** for discussion*
20 come upon, to meet by chance (***bump into**, **come across**, **encounter**, **join up with**, **run into***)
21 come up with, to suggest or produce: *Nicole **came up with** a very good idea.*

Verb forms: I **came**, I have **come**, I am **coming**
Word history: Old English *cuman*

comedian (kuh-mee-dee-uhn)
noun someone who performs or writes comedy shows (***comic**, **humorist**, **jester***)

> **comedian / comedienne**
> These used to be the masculine and feminine forms of the word. A **comedian** was a man, and a **comedienne** was a woman. Nowadays **comedian** is used for both men and women. You might come across **comedienne** in your reading, but try to avoid it in your own writing. Look up **non-sexist language**.

comedown
noun an unexpected or humiliating descent from dignity, importance, or prosperity: *What a **comedown** after all his bragging!*

comedy
noun **1** a play, film, story or other entertainment that is funny or makes you feel happy
2 any funny event or series of events

Noun forms: The plural is **comedies**.
Word history: Middle English, from Latin, from Greek *kômos* mirth + *ōidós* singer

comely (kum-lee)
adjective Old-fashioned pleasant in appearance (***attractive**, **beautiful**, **good-looking***)

Adjective forms: **comelier**, **comeliest**
Word building: **comeliness** *noun*
Word history: Old English *cȳmlic*

comet
noun an object in space that moves around the sun and has a bright central part surrounded by a misty part that finishes in the shape of a tail

Word history: Middle English, from Latin, from Greek word meaning 'long-haired'

comfort (kum-fuht)
verb **1** to cheer or make feel less sad or worried: *He **comforted** the baby by cuddling her.* (***console**, **pacify**, **reassure**, **relieve**, **soothe***)
noun **2** a feeling of being less sad or worried (***consolation**, **relief**, **solace***)
3 someone or something that comforts: *My mother is a **comfort** to me.*

4 pleasant enjoyment with no troubles or unfulfilled needs: *They live a life of* ***comfort.*** (***ease***, ***luxury***, ***wellbeing***)

Word building: **comforter** *noun* **comforting** *adjective*
Word history: Middle English, from Old French, from Latin word meaning 'strengthen'

comfortable
adjective **1** giving comfort: *a* ***comfortable*** *armchair | a* ***comfortable*** *way of life*
2 feeling comfort in your body or mind: *I am quite* ***comfortable*** *sitting here. | I am* ***comfortable*** *about those problems now.* (***complacent***, ***content***, ***relaxed***, ***satisfied***)
3 having adequate income or wealth: *they aren't rich but they are* ***comfortable.***
4 easily achieved, as a victory: *a* ***comfortable*** *win.*

comfort zone
noun a set of conditions which make you feel confident in your ability to handle a situation, giving you a sense of being in control: *I was right outside my* ***comfort zone*** *up on the stage and could feel my hands getting more and more clammy.*

comic
adjective **1** having to do with comedy: *He is a* ***comic*** *actor.*
2 funny or amusing: *She had a* ***comic*** *look on her face.*
noun **3** a magazine containing a series of drawings that tell a funny story or an adventure story
4 a comic actor or person

Word history: Latin, from Greek

comical
adjective funny or amusing: *She put on a* ***comical*** *voice to make us laugh.* (***amusing***, ***droll***, ***hilarious***, ***humorous***)

Word use: The opposite of this is **serious**.

comic strip
noun a series of cartoon drawings, telling a funny story, adventure story, etc.

comma
noun a punctuation mark (,) that is used to show small breaks in a sentence

Word history: Latin, from Greek word meaning 'short clause'

You use a **comma** to separate one item from another within a list:

Bob ran through the final checklist for the party: drinks, food, CDs and the birthday cake.

You use a comma when you want to separate one section of a sentence from another to make it easier to read:

Many of his guests were going first to the beach, then on to the party. You may also want to separate one section of a sentence from another to ensure the reader doesn't misread words from one phrase to the next:

All along, the beach was covered in bluebottles.

Without the comma, this sentence would not work for the reader. It would seem to lack a subject.

Commas sometimes mark off a part of a sentence which adds more information. This may be a phrase, for example:

The lifesavers scraped all the bluebottles, large and small, into a hole and covered them with sand.

Or it may be a clause:

This meant that all of Bob's guests, who were already in their swimming costumes, could race in for a quick swim before the party.

Note that without the commas in the above example, the meaning of the sentence would be different. It would then mean that only those of Bob's guests who were already in their swimming costumes could have a swim.

For information about the use of commas in numbers, look up **number**.

command
verb **1** to order or direct, usually with the right to be obeyed: *The teacher* ***commanded*** *silence. | He* ***commanded*** *them to come immediately.* (***bid***, ***demand***, ***require***)
2 to be in charge of: *He* ***commanded*** *the army during the battle.* (***control***, ***govern***, ***head***, ***preside over***, ***rule***)
3 to deserve and get: *Her position* ***commands*** *respect.*
noun **4** an order: *He gave the* ***command*** *to stop.* (***decree***, ***direction***, ***edict***, ***instruction***)
5 power to give orders or be in charge: *Who is in* ***command*** *of these people?*

Word history: Middle English from Old French, from Latin *com-* + *mandāre* enjoin

commandant
noun in the army, a commanding officer of a place or group

Word history: from French word meaning 'commanding'

commandeer
verb to take or seize officially

Word history: Afrikaans, from French word meaning 'command'

commander
noun **1** a chief officer, or someone who has power to direct (***captain***, ***leader***, ***ruler***)
2 the chief commissioned officer (regardless of rank) of a military unit
3 a rank in certain modern orders of knighthood

Word building: **commandership** *noun*

commandment
noun Old-fashioned a command or order

commando
noun someone who belongs to a small fighting force that is specially trained to make quick attacks inside enemy areas

Noun forms: The plural is **commandos** or **commandoes**.
Word history: Afrikaans, from Portuguese

commemorate
verb to keep alive or honour the memory of: *This stone* ***commemorates*** *the opening of the school. | Anzac Day* ***commemorates*** *those who have fought for our country.*

Word building: **commemoration** *noun* **commemorative** *adjective*
Word history: from Latin word meaning 'brought to remembrance'

commence
verb to begin or start: ***Commence*** *work now.* (***embark on***, ***initiate***, ***set about***)

Word use: The opposite of this is **finish**.
Word building: **commencement** *noun*
Word history: Middle English, from Old French, from Late Latin *com-* + *initiāre* begin

commend
verb **1** to suggest as being suitable for trust, a reward, or a job: *She* ***commended*** *her friend as a babysitter. | He was* ***commended*** *for a medal after the war.* (***recommend***, ***speak well of***)
2 to praise: *I* ***commend*** *you for your good work.* (***acclaim***, ***applaud***, ***approve***, ***compliment***)

Word history: Middle English, from Latin word meaning 'commit'

commendable
adjective deserving praise: *a* ***commendable*** *action*

commendation
noun praise for something you have done well

Word building: **commendatory** *adjective*

commensurate (kuh-<u>men</u>-shuh-ruht)
adjective having the same measure, size or value

Word building: **commensuration** *noun*
Word history: Latin *com-* + *mensūrātus*, measured

comment
noun a short note or remark that gives an opinion or explanation

Word building: **comment** *verb*
Word history: Middle English, from Late Latin *commentum* exposition, Latin word meaning 'contrivance', 'invention'

> **comment / commentate**
> Don't confuse **comment** with **commentate**, which means 'to make running commentaries, or write them, as a way of earning a living'.
> The people who do this sort of work are called **commentators**.

commentary (<u>kom</u>-uhn-tuh-ree, <u>kom</u>-uhn-tree)
noun a series of written or spoken comments: *He is listening to the sports* ***commentary*** *on the radio.*

Noun forms: The plural is **commentaries**.

commentate
verb to act as a commentator

Word history: backformation from *commentator*

commentator
noun a writer or broadcaster who makes remarks that explain or comment on news and events, or who describes sporting events, etc.

commerce
noun the buying and selling of goods, especially as carried on between different countries or between different parts of the same country (***trade***)

Word history: French, from Latin word meaning 'trade'

commercial (kuh-<u>mer</u>-shuhl)
adjective **1** having to do with commerce: *Australia established a* ***commercial*** *relationship with China.*
2 likely to be sold in great numbers: *We need products that are* ***commercial****.*
3 aimed at making money rather than keeping to standards of high quality: *That is a very* ***commercial*** *film.*
4 relying on money from advertising: *a* ***commercial*** *TV station*
noun **5** an advertisement on radio or television

Word building: **commercialism** *noun* **commercialise** *verb*

commercial artist
noun someone whose job it is to produce illustrations for commercial use, particularly advertising

commiserate
verb to share someone's sorrow or disappointment: *He* ***commiserated*** *with her when she failed the exam.* (***feel for***, ***sympathise***)

Word building: **commiseration** *noun*
Word history: Latin

commissar (<u>kom</u>-uh-sah)
noun formerly, the head of a government department in the Soviet Union

Word history: Russian, from French

commission
noun **1** an order, direction or particular duty, given by someone who is in charge
2 a written paper giving someone a particular duty or rank in the army or navy
3 a group of people who have been given particular official duties: *A* ***commission*** *was set up to investigate traffic accidents.*
4 use or service: *Is your car out of* ***commission*** *today?*
5 a sum of money given to an employee, such as a salesperson for each successful effort: *He received 10 per cent* ***commission*** *on each car he sold.* (***cut***, ***fee***, ***percentage***)
verb **6** to give a duty or task to: *The teacher* ***commissioned*** *her to hand out the books each day.*

Word history: Middle English, from Latin

commissionaire (kom-ish-uh-<u>nair</u>)
noun a uniformed messenger or doorkeeper at a hotel, office, theatre, etc.

commissioner
noun **1** someone who is a member of an official commission
2 someone who is in charge of a government department (***administrator***, ***director***, ***superintendent***)

commit
verb **1** to give into someone's charge or trust: *I am* ***committing*** *these important papers to you.*
2 to put into a particular form in order to keep: *She* ***committed*** *the poem to memory.*
3 to hand over for punishment: *The judge* ***committed*** *him to prison.*
4 to do or perform: *He* ***committed*** *a crime.*
phrase **5 commit yourself**, to bind yourself by making a promise: *Don't* ***commit yourself*** *before you are sure you like the job.*

Verb forms: I **committed**, I have **committed**, I am **committing**
Word building: **commitment** *noun* **committed** *adjective* **committal** *noun*
Word history: Middle English, from Latin word meaning 'bring together', 'join', 'entrust'

committee
noun a group of people selected from a larger group to discuss or make decisions about a particular subject: *A* ***committee*** *was chosen to run the school magazine.*

Word history: from Anglo-French word meaning 'committed'

commode (kuh-mohd)
noun a chair containing a chamber-pot

Word history: French, from Latin *commodus* fit, convenient, useful

commodious (kuh-moh-dee-uhs)
adjective convenient and roomy: *a* ***commodious*** *house* (***expansive, open, roomy, spacious, wide***)

Word history: Middle English, from Middle Latin

commodity (kuh-mod-uh-tee)
noun something useful, especially something that is bought and sold: *This shop has a wide range of stoves, refrigerators and other household* ***commodities.***

Noun forms: The plural is **commodities.**

commodore
noun **1** a senior captain in the navy
2 the president of a boat club

Word history: possibly from Dutch, from French word meaning 'command'

common
adjective **1** shared by two or more people: ***common*** *property* | ***common*** *action*
2 general or shared by all: ***common*** *knowledge* (***collective, communal, popular, public***)
3 found or happening often: *a* ***common*** *flower* | *a* ***common*** *event* (***prevalent, widespread***)
4 *Old-fashioned* impolite or vulgar (***coarse, crude, rude, tasteless, uncouth***)
5 ordinary or not having any special rank: *the* ***common*** *people* (***average, plain, regular, simple, standard***)

Word use: The opposite of definition 3 is **rare** or **uncommon.**
Word building: **commonly** *adverb*
Word history: Middle English, from Old French, from Latin word meaning 'common', 'general'

commoner
noun an ordinary person, who is not one of the ruling class in a society

common fraction
noun Mathematics a fraction with the numerator above and the denominator below a straight line

Word use: Compare this with **decimal fraction.**

common law
noun **1** the system of law originating in England as distinct from the civil or Roman law and the canon or ecclesiastical law
2 the unwritten law, especially of England, based on custom or court decision, as distinct from statute law
3 the law administered through the system of writs, as distinct from equity, etc.

common-law
adjective **1** based on or having to do with the common law
2 a having to do with a marriage that in law is recognised to exist because the partners have lived together for a certain period of time even though they have not taken part in a formal marriage
b having to do with one of the partners in this type of marriage: *a* ***common-law*** *wife*

common market
noun a group of countries agreeing to trade with one another without the taxing of goods

common noun
noun Grammar a noun which can be used of any one of a class of things and which does not have a capital letter: *'Robert' is not a* ***common noun,*** *but 'boy' is.*

Word use: Compare this with **proper noun.**

For more information, look up **nouns: common nouns.**

commonplace
adjective **1** ordinary, or not special: *a* ***commonplace*** *person*
2 used or said too often: *a* ***commonplace*** *remark*
noun **3** a well-known, customary, or obvious remark
4 anything common, ordinary, or uninteresting

Word history: translation of Latin *locus commūnis,* Greek (*koinós*) *topós* a stereotyped topic, argument, or passage in literature

common room
noun in schools, universities, etc., a sitting room for the use of the teaching staff and sometimes the students

common sense
noun the ability to behave sensibly and make sensible decisions

Word use: You can also use **commonsense.**
Word building: **commonsensical** *adjective*

commonwealth
noun **1** all the people of a country or state
2 Commonwealth, a country that is made up of several states, in which there is one government for the whole country as well as a government for each of the states: *the* ***Commonwealth*** *of Australia*
3 a group of people or countries united by a common interest

commotion
noun a wild or noisy disturbance: *There was a great* ***commotion*** *in the classroom when the teacher went out.* (***fuss, hullaballoo, riot, tumult, turmoil***)

communal
adjective shared by several people: *The flats have their own bathrooms but a* ***communal*** *laundry.* (***collective, common, general, popular, public***)

commune[1] (kuh-myoohn)
verb to talk together so that each person understands the other's thoughts or feelings

Word history: Middle English, from Old French word meaning 'share', from *comun* common

commune[2] (kom-yoohn)
noun a group of people who live together, sharing their property and work, and following their own rules and standards (***collective***)

Word history: French, feminine of *commun* common

communicate
verb **1** to pass on or make known to someone: *We will **communicate** the news to her.*
2 to share thoughts or feelings: *They **communicate** well with each other.*

Word building: **communicator** *noun*
Word history: from Latin word meaning 'shared'

communication
noun **1** the passing on or sharing of thoughts, ideas or information
2 something that is communicated, such as a piece of news
3 communications, ways of passing on information, such as by telephone, radio or television

communicative
adjective talkative, or willing to communicate (***chatty***, ***expansive***, ***forthcoming***, ***loquacious***, ***voluble***)

communion
noun **1** the sharing of thoughts, feelings or interests: *I enjoy the **communion** of my friends.*
2 Communion, a Christian ceremony in which bread and wine are blessed and eaten as the body and blood of Christ or as symbols of them

Word use: You can also use **Holy Communion** for definition 2.
Word history: Middle English, from Latin word meaning 'fellowship'

communiqué (kuh-myoohn-uh-kay)
noun an official news report (***bulletin***, ***dispatch***)

Word history: French

communism
noun **1** a way of living in which all property is owned equally by all the people in a society
2 a way of organising a country, in which there is only one political party and all trade and business is run by the government

Word use: Compare this with **capitalism** and **socialism**.
Word building: **communist** *adjective* **communist** *noun*
Word history: French

community
noun a group of people who live in one area, have the same government, and often share a common history or culture

Noun forms: The plural is **communities**.
Word history: Latin

commute
verb **1** to travel regularly between home and work: *I **commute** by bus.*
2 to change and make less punishing: *The judge **commuted** his death sentence to life imprisonment.*

Word building: **commuter** *noun*
Word history: from Latin word meaning 'change wholly'

compact (kom-pakt, kom-pakt)
adjective **1** fitted or packed closely together
verb (kom-pakt) **2** to join or pack closely together
noun (kom-pakt) **3** a small case containing a mirror and face powder

Word history: from Latin word meaning 'joined together'

compact disc
noun → **CD**

companion
noun **1** someone who goes out with or travels with another: *Are you taking a **companion** to the party?* (***associate***, ***colleague***, ***consort***, ***friend***, ***partner***)
2 someone or something that matches or goes with another: *I wish I could find the **companion** to this sock.* (***fellow***, ***pair***, ***twin***)

Word building: **companionship** *noun*
Word history: Late Latin, from Latin *com-* with + *pānis* bread

companionable
adjective friendly

company (kum-puh-nee)
noun **1** a group of people brought together for a purpose, such as to run a business organisation: *a **company** that makes fridges | a theatrical **company*** (***corporation***, ***firm***, ***organisation***, ***outfit***, ***syndicate***)
2 guests: *We've got **company** tonight.*
3 a group of soldiers forming part of an army
phrase **4 keep company**, to go or associate with
5 part company,
a to stop being friends with
b to leave or separate from

Noun forms: The plural is **companies**.
Word history: Middle English, from Old French

comparable
adjective **1** able to be compared: ***comparable** systems of education* (***akin***, ***alike***, ***corresponding***, ***related***, ***similar***)
2 worthy of comparison: *a **comparable** essay*

comparative
adjective **1** having to do with comparison
2 relative or judged by comparison: *They live in **comparative** poverty.* (***relative***)
3 *Grammar* having to do with the form of an adjective or adverb which expresses a greater degree: *'Smoother' is the **comparative** form of 'smooth' and 'more easily' is the **comparative** form of 'easily'.*

Word use: Compare definition 3 with **superlative**.

comparatively
adverb relative to or compared with others: *They are **comparatively** poor.*

compare (kuhm-pair)
verb **1** to show to be similar: *You can **compare** the heart to a pump.*
2 to look for the similarities and differences of: *He **compared** his new bike with John's.*
3 to be as good as: *Australian beaches **compare** with any in the world.*

Word history: Middle English, from French, from Latin word meaning 'bring together'

compare / compere

Don't confuse **compare** with **compere.** A compere is someone who introduces the acts in a show. We pronounce this word with a stress on the first syllable, whereas **compare** has its stress on the second syllable.

compare / contrast

Don't confuse **compare** with **contrast.** To **contrast** two things is to show what they do not have in common.

comparison
noun **1** the result of comparing
2 an estimate or statement of what is similar and what is different between certain things
Word history: Middle English, from Old French, from Latin

compartment
noun a separate space, room or section: *a **compartment** in a railway carriage* (***cell, chamber, cubicle, den***)
Word history: French, from Italian, from Late Latin word meaning 'divide'

compass (kum-puhs)
noun **1** an instrument with a magnetic needle pointing to north which is used to find direction
2 extent or range: *a wide **compass** of knowledge | the **compass** of a singer's voice*
3 an instrument with two legs, used for measuring and drawing circles
Word use: You can also use **pair of compasses** for definition 3.
Word history: Middle English, from Old French word meaning 'divide exactly', from Latin word meaning 'equal step'

compassion
noun a feeling of sorrow or pity for someone (***kindness, mercy, sympathy, tenderness***)
Word building: **compassionate** *adjective*
Word history: Middle English, from Late Latin word meaning 'sympathy'

compatible
adjective **1** able to agree or exist side by side: *a **compatible** married couple | **compatible** ideas*
2 able to be used together: *The two computers are **compatible** with each other.*
Word use: The opposite of this is **incompatible.**
Word building: **compatibility** *noun*
Word history: Medieval Latin, from Late Latin word meaning 'suffer with'

compatriot
noun someone from your own country: *I met a lot of my **compatriots** while I was in Greece.*
Word history: Latin

compel
verb **1** to force to do something: *They can **compel** you to attend school.* (***bully, coerce, drive, make***)
2 to bring about as if by force: *His angry look **compelled** an immediate answer.*
Verb forms: I **compelled**, I have **compelled**, I am **compelling**
Word history: Middle English, from Latin

compelling
adjective **1** holding your attention forcefully
2 convincing: *a **compelling** argument*

compensate
verb **1** to make up to: *We will **compensate** you for your expenses.* (***pay back, recompense, refund, reimburse, reward***)
phrase **2 compensate for,** to make up for: *Nothing can **compensate for** his loss.*
Word history: from Latin word meaning 'counterbalanced'

compensation
noun **1** the act of compensating
2 something you receive to make up for debt, loss or suffering you have experienced

compere (kom-pair)
noun someone who introduces the acts in a show
Word building: **compere** *verb*
Word history: French

compere / compare

Don't confuse **compere** with **compare.** When we **compare** things we look for the similarities and differences between them, or we show how they are similar:

Don't bother to compare your new hairstyle with hers.
You can compare your eye to a camera.

compete
verb to set yourself against one or more people to gain or win something: *The shops lowered their prices to **compete** for customers.* (***contend, contest, vie***)
Word history: from Latin word meaning 'contend for'

competent
adjective able or skilful: *He is a **competent** rider.* (***capable, experienced, expert, good, proficient***)
Word use: The opposite of this is **incompetent.**
Word building: **competence** *noun* **competency** *noun*
Word history: from Latin word meaning 'being fit'

competition
noun **1** a test or situation in which people compete against each other (***championship, contest, game, match, tournament***)
2 a feeling or act of competing: *There is a lot of **competition** between the top runners.* (***contention, rivalry, struggle***)
3 the people against whom someone competes: *What's the **competition** like?*
Word history: Latin

competitive
adjective **1** having to do with or decided by competition: *a **competitive** exam*
2 liking competition: *a **competitive** person*

competitor
noun someone who competes

compile
verb **1** to collect and put together into one list, account or book
2 *Computers* to create (a set of computer instructions) from a high-level language, using a compiler

Word building: **compilation** *noun*
Word history: Middle English, from Old French, from Latin word meaning 'snatch together and carry off'

compiler
noun Computers a program which translates programming languages into the basic commands acted upon by the computer

complacent
adjective pleased or satisfied with yourself (***comfortable***, ***content***, ***satisfied***, ***unconcerned***)

Word building: **complacency** *noun*

complain
verb **1** to find fault
2 to tell about your illnesses, troubles or pains: *She is always* ***complaining***. (***gripe***, ***grumble***, ***nag***, ***whine***, ***whinge***)

Word history: Middle English, from Old French, from Late Latin word meaning 'lament'

complaint
noun **1** an expression of dissatisfaction, blame or pain: *He made a* ***complaint*** *about the poor service in the shop.*
2 a sickness or illness

Word history: Middle English, from Old French

complement (kom-pluh-muhnt)
noun **1** something which completes or makes perfect: *The flute was a perfect* ***complement*** *to the sound of the guitar.*
2 the number that is required: *The hockey team now has its full* ***complement*** *of players.*
3 *Geometry* the angle needed to bring a given angle to a right angle
4 *Mathematics* all the members of any set, class or space of elements, that is not a given subset
verb (kom-pluh-ment) **5** to complete

Word building: **complementary** *adjective*
Word history: Middle English, from Latin word meaning 'that which fills up'

complement / compliment

These words sound the same but are different in meaning. Don't confuse **complement** with **compliment**, which is a flattering remark:

Her performance drew compliments from all her listeners.

To **compliment** someone is to say something nice about them.

Complimentary is the adjective from **compliment**.

complementary angle
noun the angle which, together with the given angle, adds up to 90°

complementary medicine
noun the range of treatments and procedures of an alternative nature which are considered to assist mainstream medical treatments and procedures

complete
adjective **1** having all its parts: *a* ***complete*** *set of coloured pencils* (***full***, ***intact***, ***perfect***, ***whole***)
2 finished: *My piano practice is* ***complete***.
3 total or absolute: *Your bedroom is a* ***complete*** *mess.*
verb **4** to finish: *She* ***completed*** *her homework.*
5 to make whole or entire: *to* ***complete*** *a set of tools*

Word building: **completion** *noun*
Word history: Middle English, from Latin word meaning 'filled up', 'completed'

complex
adjective **1** made up of parts connected with each other
2 difficult to understand or explain: *Maths is too* ***complex*** *for me.* (***complicated***, ***involved***)
noun **3** a group of buildings or shops: *a shopping* ***complex***
4 a fixed idea, often of concern: *He has a* ***complex*** *about his height.* (***fetish***, ***hang-up***, ***phobia***)

Word use: The opposite of definitions 1 and 2 is **simple**.
Word building: **complexity** *noun*
Word history: from Latin word meaning 'having embraced'

complexion
noun **1** the colour and appearance of your skin, especially of your face
2 aspect or character: *The new evidence puts a different* ***complexion*** *on the murder case.*

Word history: Middle English, from Late Latin word meaning 'constitution', Latin combination

complex sentence
noun a sentence which consists of at least two clauses, one of which is a dependent clause

Look up **sentences: complex sentence.**

compliance (kuhm-pluy-uhns)
noun **1** the act of agreeing
2 the state of being too willing to agree
phrase **3 in compliance with**, in keeping with: ***in compliance with*** *the rules*

compliant (kuhm-pluy-uhnt)
adjective agreeable or willing to do what is asked or required (***docile***, ***dutiful***, ***obedient***, ***submissive***, ***tractable***)

complicate
verb to make harder to understand or deal with: *Too many directions can* ***complicate*** *a map.*

Word building: **complicated** *adjective*
complication *noun*
Word history: from Latin word meaning 'folded together'

complicit (kuhm-plis-uht)
adjective involved with a degree of guilt: *a company* ***complicit*** *in safety abuses*

complicity
noun the state of being a partner or taking part: ***complicity*** *in crime*

Noun forms: The plural is **complicities**.

compliment (kom-pluh-muhnt)
noun **1** words or actions expressing praise and admiration: *She paid him a* ***compliment*** *about his new jumper.*

verb (kom-pluh-ment) **2** to pay a compliment to (***commend, congratulate, praise, speak well of***)

Word history: French, from Italian, from Spanish word meaning 'fulfil', from Latin

compliment / complement
Look up **complement / compliment.**

complimentary
adjective **1** praising, or expressing a compliment **2** free or without cost: *He gave them* ***complimentary*** *tickets to the show.*

comply
verb to act in agreement with a request, wish, command or rule (***acquiesce, consent, heed, obey, submit***)

Verb forms: I **complied**, I have **complied**, I am **complying**
Word history: Italian word meaning 'fulfil', 'complete', from Spanish, from Latin word meaning 'complete'

compo
noun Australian, NZ Colloquial → **workers compensation**

component
noun a part of a whole: *The silicon chip is an important* ***component*** *of a computer.*

Word building: **component** *adjective*
Word history: from Latin word meaning 'composing'

compose
verb **1** to make by putting parts together (***assemble, build, fashion, form, frame***)
2 to make up or form: *Smog is* ***composed*** *of smoke and fog.*
3 to write music or poetry
phrase **4 compose yourself,** to make your mind and body quiet and calm

Word history: Middle English, from Old French

composed
adjective calm and in control of your feelings: *They were* ***composed*** *and dignified throughout the funeral.* (***cool, placid, serene, tranquil***)

composer
noun a person who writes music

composite (kom-puh-zuht)
noun **1** something made up of different parts
adjective **2** made up of various parts: *a* ***composite*** *picture*

Word history: Latin *compōnere* put together, compound, compose

composite number
noun Mathematics a whole number greater than one which is able to be divided with no remainder by a whole number other than itself and one

composition
noun **1** the putting together of parts to make a whole
2 the way in which parts are combined: *What is the* ***composition*** *of smog?* (***constitution, make-up, structure***)
3 something that has been composed, such as a piece of music
4 a short essay, written as a school exercise
5 the arrangement of the parts of a work of art so that they fit well together in relation to each other and to the whole

compositor (kuhm-poz-uh-tuh)
noun in printing, a person who puts together the type for a printed page

compost
noun a mixture of rotting materials, like old vegetable peelings, leaves and manure, used as a fertiliser for the garden

Word history: Middle English, from Old French, from Latin word meaning 'compounded'

composure (kuhm-poh-zhuh)
noun calmness of mind, or self-control

compound[1] (kom-pownd)
adjective **1** made up of two or more parts: *'Bedroom' is a* ***compound*** *word.*
noun (kom-pownd) **2** a mixture
3 a chemical substance made by joining two or more chemicals: *When hydrogen and oxygen are joined together, they form a* ***compound*** *called water*
verb (kuhm-pownd) **4** to mix or combine
5 to add to, or increase

Word history: Middle English, from Old French, from Latin word meaning 'put together'

compound[2] (kom-pownd)
noun a closed-off area with buildings where people can stay or be kept: *a prison* ***compound*** (***enclosure, jail, lockup, penitentiary***)

Word history: Malay *kampong* enclosure

compound interest
noun interest earned on a sum of money made up of the original amount of capital (the principal) and the interest that has been earned on it and added to it in the meantime

Word use: Compare this with **simple interest**.

compound sentence
noun a sentence which consists of at least two main clauses

Look up **sentences: compound sentence.**

compound tense
noun a tense, the aspect of which is shown by the use of auxiliary verbs with the main verb

Look up **verbs: compound tense.**

comprehend
verb **1** to understand the meaning of: *I can't* ***comprehend*** *the story.* (***fathom, grasp, make out, perceive, realise***)
2 to take in or include: *The new National Park* ***comprehends*** *all the old reserves.*

Word history: Middle English, from Latin *comprehendere* seize

comprehension
noun **1** the ability to understand or the act of understanding: *Computers are beyond my* ***comprehension.***
2 a school exercise in reading and understanding, usually tested by a set of short questions

Word history: Latin

comprehensive
adjective including a great deal (***detailed, exhaustive, in-depth, intensive, whole***)

compress (kuhm-pres)
verb **1** to press together, or force into less space: *Wool is **compressed** into bales ready for transportation.* (***condense***, ***cram***, ***jam***, ***squash***, ***squeeze***)
2 *Computers* to encode (data) into a format which uses less storage
noun (kom-pres) **3** a soft pad of cloth applied to an injury and held in place with a bandage

Word use: Another term for definition 2 is **zip**.
Word building: **compression** *noun*
Word history: Middle English, from Latin

comprise
verb to include or be composed of: *This school **comprises** an infants section and a primary section.* (***contain***, ***cover***, ***embrace***, ***incorporate***, ***involve***)

Word history: Middle English, from French, from Latin word meaning 'seize'

compromise (kom-pruh-muyz)
noun **1** the settlement of an argument by both sides agreeing to give way a bit: *Our **compromise** is to take turns on the bike.*
2 something midway between two other things: *Jogging is a **compromise** between walking and running.*
verb **3** to lay open to suspicion or bad comments from others: *You will **compromise** yourself as class captain if you talk like that.*

Word history: Middle English, from French, from Latin word meaning 'a mutual promise to abide by a decision'

compulsion
noun the use of force or pressure

Word history: Middle English, from Late Latin

compulsive
adjective **1** unable to break a given habit: *She is a **compulsive** eater.*
2 forcing you to continue, especially of pleasurable activities: ***compulsive** reading*

compulsory
adjective forced or required: *Attendance at school is **compulsory** for all children.*

Word use: The opposite of this is **optional** or **voluntary**.

compunction (kuhm-pungk-shuhn)
noun uneasiness of your conscience or feelings: *Shame on you. Have you no **compunction**?* (***contrition***, ***regret***, ***remorse***)

Word history: Middle English, from Late Latin word meaning 'remorse'

compute
verb to calculate or to work out using mathematics: *to **compute** the distance of the moon from the earth* (***count***, ***derive***, ***figure***, ***measure***, ***reckon***)

Word building: **computation** *noun*
Word history: from Latin word meaning 'reckon'

computer
noun an electronic machine which does mathematical calculations very quickly, and which stores and gives out information, according to a set of stored instructions called a program

Word building: **computerise** *verb*

computer geek
noun → **geek** (definition 2)

computer language
noun any artificial language coded in text or graphics that can be interpreted by a machine, particularly a computer

Word use: Another name is **programming language**.

computer programming
noun the process of writing, testing, debugging, and maintaining the source code of computer programs to achieve a specified outcome using a computer

Word building: **computer programmer** *noun*

computer terminal
noun a machine linked up to a computer and used for receiving or giving information

Word use: You can also use **terminal**.

computing
noun **1** the science or study of the principles and uses of computers
2 the field of computer technology: *to have a job in **computing***
adjective **3** having to do with computers: ***computing** skills*

comrade (kom-rayd, kom-ruhd)
noun a close friend or mate (***collaborator***, ***colleague***, ***helper***, ***partner***)

Word use: The opposite of this is **enemy**.
Word history: French, from Spanish *camarada*, literally, a group living in one room, from Latin *camera* chamber

con
Colloquial
noun **1** a trick or swindle (***hoax***, ***plot***, ***prank***, ***ruse***)
adjective **2** having to do with the gaining of someone's confidence in order to swindle them: *a **con** man / a **con** game*

Word building: **con** *verb* (**conned**, **conning**)
Word history: short for *confidence trick* or *confidence man*

concave
adjective hollow and curved like the inside of a circle: *A saucer is slightly **concave**.*

Word use: The opposite of this is **convex**.
Word history: Latin

conceal
verb **1** to hide or keep from sight: *He **concealed** the knife in his coat pocket.* (***camouflage***, ***cover***, ***disguise***, ***mask***)
2 to keep secret: *She **concealed** her real reason for coming.*

Word use: The opposite of this is **reveal**.
Word building: **concealment** *noun*
Word history: Middle English, from Old French, from Latin word meaning 'hide'

concede
verb **1** to admit as true or certain: *Everyone **concedes** that the earth is round.*
2 to allow someone to have or do something: *He **conceded** us the right to choose our own team.*

Word building: **concession** *noun*
Word history: Latin

conceit
noun pride in yourself and your own importance or ability

Word building: **conceited** *adjective*
Word history: Middle English

conceive
verb **1** to think of: *to **conceive** a plan* (***concoct, contrive, create, devise, formulate***)
2 to become pregnant

Word building: **conceivable** *adjective*
Word history: Middle English, from Old French, from Latin word meaning 'take in'

concentrate
verb **1** to focus or direct towards one point: *She **concentrated** the light on his face.*
2 to direct your attention to one subject: *to **concentrate** on watching the ball* (***attend to, consider, focus on, put your mind to***)
3 to make stronger or purer: *Some detergents have been **concentrated** by removing some of the water from them.*
noun **4** a substance that has been concentrated

Word history: *con-* + Latin *centrum* centre + *-ate*

concentration
noun **1** the act of concentrating
2 total attention to one object
3 *Chemistry* the amount of a particular substance in a given space or a stated unit of a mixture, solution or ore; expressed as a per cent by weight or by volume

concentration camp
noun a prison camp for prisoners of war or enemies of a country

concentric
adjective having the same centre: *When you drop a stone into water, the ripples form **concentric** circles.*

concept
noun a general idea or understanding of something: *My **concept** of computer programming is very vague.* (***image, notion, theory***)

Word building: **conceptual** *adjective* **conceptualise** *verb*
Word history: from Latin word meaning 'a conceiving'

conception
noun **1** an idea or thought: *Her **conception** of how the house should look was different to his.*
2 the beginning of pregnancy, or the act of conceiving a child

concern
verb **1** to be of interest or importance: *This problem **concerns** us all.*
2 to be anxious or troubled: *I am **concerned** about your cough.*
noun **3** a matter of interest or importance: *It's no **concern** of mine.*
4 worry or anxiety: *The father's **concern** for his child's safety was obvious.*

Word history: Latin *con-* + *cernere* separate, have respect to

concert
noun **1** a public musical performance by one or more musicians or other performers (***eisteddfod, jam session, prom concert, soiree***)
2 agreement in a plan or action: *The children acted in **concert** to recover the stolen money.*

Word history: French, from Italian word meaning 'be in accord', from Latin word meaning 'contend'

concertina
noun **1** a small musical instrument like an accordion
verb **2** to fold up or collapse like a concertina

Verb forms: it **concertinaed**, it has **concertinaed**, it is **concertinaing**
Word history: *concert* + *-ina*, diminutive suffix

concerto (kuhn-sher-toh, kuhn-cher-toh)
noun a piece of music for one or more solo instruments, such as a piano or violin, and an orchestra

Noun forms: The plural is **concertos** or **concerti** (kuhn-sher-tee, kuhn-cher-tee).
Word history: Italian

concession
noun something that you agree to do or to give, especially to end some conflict, or as a special right: *Tax **concessions** were granted to industry.*

Word history: Latin

conch (konch, kongk)
noun **1** the spiral shell of a sea snail, which makes a sound when you blow it
2 any of several sea gastropods

Noun forms: The plural is **conchs** (kongks) or **conches** (kon-chuhz).
Word history: Latin, from Greek word meaning 'mussel or cockle', 'shell-like part or thing', 'external ear'

conciliate
verb to make friendly or calm (***propitiate, reconcile***)

Word building: **conciliator** *noun* **conciliatory** *adjective*
Word history: from Latin word meaning 'brought together'

conciliation
noun the working out of a dispute with the help of a person (the conciliator) who is not involved in it, especially between trade unions and employers

concise
adjective expressing a lot in a few words: ***a concise** account of what happened* (***abridged, condensed, brief, short, to the point***)

Word use: The opposite of this is **verbose** or **wordy**.
Word building: **conciseness** *noun*
Word history: from Latin word meaning 'cut up or off'

conclave (kon-klayv, kong-klayv)
noun **1** any private meeting
2 a private meeting of the cardinals of the Roman Catholic Church for the election of a pope

Word history: Middle English, from Latin word meaning 'lockable place'

conclude
verb **1** to finish: *After a short speech, she **concluded**.* (***cease, stop***)
2 to bring to an end: *The teacher **concluded** the lesson with two examples.* (***close, complete, finalise, terminate***)
3 to arrange or settle: *The two leaders **concluded** an agreement.*

4 to decide by working out: *After reading the whole book she* ***concluded*** *that jealousy was the real reason for the murder.* (***deduce, gather, infer, solve***)

Word history: Middle English, from Latin word meaning 'shut up'

conclusion

noun **1** the end or the last part: *The* ***conclusion*** *of the novel is where all the points made by the author are summed up.* (***close, finale, finish, termination***)
2 a result or outcome: *a foregone* ***conclusion*** (***consequence, effect***)
3 a final decision, or a deduction reached after considering all the facts available
phrase **4 in conclusion**, finally

Word history: Middle English, from Latin

conclusive

adjective convincing, or decisive

Word use: The opposite of this is **inconclusive** or **unconvincing**.

concoct

verb **1** to make up or invent: *He* ***concocted*** *a story to cover up for his absence.* (***contrive, cook up, devise, think up***)
2 to make up by combining parts, or to prepare: *She* ***concocted*** *a quick, easy meal.*

Word building: **concoction** *noun*
Word history: from Latin word meaning 'cooked together', 'digested'

concomitant (kuhn-<u>kom</u>-uh-tuhnt, kuhng-<u>kom</u>-uh-tuhnt)

adjective **1** concurrent, or happening together
noun **2** a concomitant quality, condition, person, or thing

Word building: **concomitance** *noun*
Word history: from Late Latin word meaning 'accompanying'

concord

noun **1** agreement between people
2 peace
3 *Music* harmony of sounds (***consonance***)

Word history: Middle English, from French, from Latin word meaning 'agreement'

concourse (<u>kon</u>-kaws, <u>kohng</u>-kaws)

noun **1** a coming together or assembly of people
2 an open space or main hall in a public building, especially in a railway station or airport
3 grounds for racing, athletic sports, etc.
4 a running or coming together, usually of water, etc.

Word history: Middle English, from Old French, from Latin word meaning 'running together'

concrete

noun **1** a mixture of cement, sand, water and gravel, that hardens as it dries and is used in building
adjective **2** made of this mixture: *a* ***concrete*** *floor.*
3 real or existing as an actual thing, not just an idea: *A wedding ring is a* ***concrete*** *object, but the feeling of love is not.* (***material, physical, tangible***)

Word use: The opposite of definition 3 is **abstract**.
Word building: **concrete** *verb*
Word history: from Latin word meaning 'grown together', 'hardened'

concrete noun

noun Grammar a word which refers to something that our five senses (touch, sight, hearing, smell and taste) can pick up: *'Boat', 'sun' and 'dog' are all* ***concrete nouns.***

Word use: The opposite of this is **abstract noun**.

For more information, look up **nouns: common nouns**.

concubine (<u>kong</u>-kyooh-buyn)

noun a man's second or other wife, in a country where a man can be married to more than one woman at a time

Word history: Middle English, from Latin

concur

verb to agree: *I* ***concur*** *with that decision.* (***assent, see eye to eye***)

Verb forms: I **concurred**, I have **concurred**, I am **concurring**
Word history: Middle English, from Latin word meaning 'run together'

concurrent

adjective **1** occurring together: ***concurrent*** *events*
2 *Geometry* passing through the same points: *four* ***concurrent*** *lines*

concussion

noun **1** a shock, or violent shaking caused by a blow or collision
2 an injury or jarring of the brain or spine caused by a blow or fall

Word building: **concuss** *verb*
Word history: from Latin word meaning 'shock'

condemn (kuhn-<u>dem</u>)

verb **1** to express strong disapproval of: *He* ***condemned*** *the child's bad behaviour.* (***censure, criticise***)
2 to judge someone to be guilty or sentence them to punishment: *The murderer was* ***condemned*** *to death.* (***convict, damn, doom***)
3 to decide something is no longer fit for use: *The old building was* ***condemned*** *by council.*

Word use: The opposite of definition 1 is **praise**. | The opposite of definition 2 is **absolve**.
Word building: **condemnation** *noun*
Word history: Middle English, from Old French, from Latin

condensation

noun **1** the changing of a gas to a liquid or solid: *When steam hits something cold,* ***condensation*** *occurs.*
2 something that has been condensed: *This book is a* ***condensation*** *of a much larger novel.*

condense

verb **1** to make thicker or reduce the volume of: *to* ***condense*** *milk* (***concentrate, thicken***)
2 to change from a gas to a liquid or solid: *to* ***condense*** *steam to get water*
3 to say or write something in fewer words: *He* ***condensed*** *his story into just a few pages.* (***abbreviate, abridge, shorten, sum up, summarise***)

Word building: **condenser** *noun*
Word history: Middle English, from Latin word meaning 'make thick'

condescend
verb **1** to agree, even though it's below your social level: *The queen* ***condescended*** *to have a meal with her servants.*
2 to act as if you are in a higher social position than others

Word building: **condescending** *adjective*
Word history: Middle English, from French, from Late Latin word meaning 'stoop'

condiment (kon-duh-muhnt)
noun something used to give an extra taste to food, such as a sauce or seasoning

Word history: from Latin word meaning 'spice'

condition
noun **1** the state of someone or something: *The runner was in top* ***condition*** *before the race. | The car was rusty and in very poor* ***condition.***
2 anything that is required before another thing can be done: *Having a licence is a* ***condition*** *for driving a car.*
verb **3** to put in a fit state: *Long-distance runners* ***condition*** *themselves for their races by training.*
4 to influence or affect: *What we are taught by our parents and teachers* ***conditions*** *the way we live.*
phrase **5 on condition that,** if, or provided that

Word history: Middle English, from Latin *condicio* (erroneously *conditio*) agreement, stipulation, circumstances

conditional
adjective depending on something else: *They made a* ***conditional*** *agreement to go to the beach only if the weather was good.*

conditional aspect
noun a grammatical aspect which expresses what may happen if certain conditions are true

Look up **verbs: aspect.**

conditional clause
noun Grammar a clause which expresses the condition which must be met for the action of the main verb to take place, as in *If you visit, we will meet.*

Word use: You can also use **if-clause.**

condolences (kuhn-dohl-uhn-suhs)
plural noun expressions of sympathy with a person in sorrow: *He offered the widow his* ***condolences.***

condom (kon-dom)
noun a thin sheath, usually of rubber, worn over the penis during intercourse, used as a contraceptive and to prevent passing on disease

Word history: perhaps named after *Condom*, 18th century English physician said to have devised it

condominium (kon-duh-min-ee-uhm)
noun **1** joint rule over a territory by several foreign states: *Vanuatu was once an Anglo-French* ***condominium*** *before it became a republic.*
2 *Chiefly US*
a a block of high-rise apartments or units
b an apartment or unit in such a block

Word use: You can also use the colloquial word **condo** for definition 2.
Word history: Neo-Latin, from Latin *con-* with, jointly + Latin *dominium* lordship

condone
verb to pardon, excuse or overlook: *His parents* ***condoned*** *his boldness because they thought he might be sick.*

Word history: from Latin word meaning 'give up'

conducive (kuhn-dyooh-siv)
adjective leading to or helping to bring about (a result): *Lots of exercise is* ***conducive*** *to good health.*

conduct (kon-dukt)
noun **1** someone's behaviour or way of acting: *Her* ***conduct*** *was very rude all evening.*
verb (kuhn-dukt) **2** to behave: *He* ***conducted*** *himself well today.* (***acquit yourself, carry yourself, perform***)
3 to manage or carry on: *The politician* ***conducted*** *a well-planned campaign.*
4 to direct or lead an orchestra or choir
5 to lead: *The mayor* ***conducted*** *us on a tour of the city.*
6 to be a channel for electricity, heat or sound: *The air* ***conducts*** *sound waves to our ears.*

Word history: from Latin word meaning 'bring together'

conduction
noun Physics the conducting or channelling of heat, electricity, sound, etc., through something

conductivity (kon-duk-tiv-uh-tee)
noun the ability of a substance to conduct heat, electricity or sound: *Copper has a high* ***conductivity.***

Noun forms: The plural is **conductivities.**

conductor
noun **1** a guide or a leader
2 someone who collects fares on a tram, train or bus
3 a person who directs the playing of an orchestra or chorus, especially with a baton
4 something that easily conducts heat, electricity or sound: *Copper is a good* ***conductor*** *of heat.*

conductor / conductress
People used to distinguish between the men and the women who sold or collected tickets on a bus, tram or train, by calling the man a **conductor** and the woman a **conductress.** Nowadays we consider that it is the job that counts, not the sex of the person doing it, and so we refer to both men and women as **conductors.** You may come across conductress in your reading but don't use it yourself.
Look up **non-sexist language.**

conduit (kon-jooh-uht)
noun **1** a pipe, tube, etc., for carrying water, gas, etc.
2 a pipe that encloses electrical wires to protect them from damage

Word history: Middle English, from Old French, from Late Latin word meaning 'brought together'

Condy's crystals (kon-deez kris-tuhlz)
plural noun Chemistry potassium permanganate, a powerful oxidant, formerly used as a disinfectant, etc.

Word history: named after Henry Bollman *Condy*, 19th century English physician

cone
noun **1** a solid shape with a flat round bottom, whose sides meet at the top in a point
2 anything shaped like this: *an ice-cream **cone***
3 the cone-like fruit of pine and fir trees

Word history: Latin, from Greek

confectionery
noun lollies, candies or sweets

Noun forms: The plural is **confectionaries**.

confederacy
noun a group of people or countries joined together for a common purpose or reason

Noun forms: The plural is **confederacies**.
Word building: **confederation** *noun*

confederate
noun an ally or supporter

Word building: **confederate** *adjective*
Word history: Middle English, from Late Latin word meaning 'united in a league'

confer
verb **1** to give as a gift, favour or honour: *The queen **conferred** a medal for bravery on the boy.* (***award***, ***donate***, ***grant***, ***present***)
2 to talk together: *We **conferred** for some time about the situation.* (***consult***, ***converse***, ***deliberate***, ***discuss***)

Verb forms: I **conferred**, I have **conferred**, I am **conferring**
Word history: from Latin word meaning 'bring together'

conference
noun a meeting arranged to discuss something special (***assembly***, ***congress***, ***convention***, ***council***)

Word building: **conference** *verb*

confess
verb **1** to admit or own up: *I **confess** that I broke the cup.* | *The prisoner **confessed**.* (***acknowledge***, ***concede***)
2 to tell your mistakes or sins, especially to a priest

Word building: **confession** *noun*
Word history: Middle English from Latin

confessor
noun **1** someone who confesses
2 someone to whom someone confesses

Word use: You can also use **confesser**.

confetti
noun small bits of coloured paper, thrown at weddings or carnivals

Word history: Italian, plural of *confetto* meaning 'sweets', from the practice of throwing little sweets on such festival occasions. Later this was plaster balls which shattered into a cloud of white dust, and then little bits of coloured paper.

confidante (kon-fuh-<u>dant</u>, <u>kon</u>-fuh-duhnt)
noun someone you confide in

Word history: French, from Italian, from Latin word meaning 'trusting'

confide
verb to trust or tell, as a secret: *She **confided** in her best friend.* | *He **confided** all his secrets to his brother.*

Word history: Middle English, from Latin word meaning 'trust altogether'

confidence
noun **1** trust or faith in someone
2 a belief in yourself and what you can do: *She played the tournament with plenty of **confidence**.*
3 a secret: *He told me his **confidences** after school.*
phrase **4 in confidence**, as a secret or private matter: *I told him that **in confidence**.*

confidence trick
noun a swindle in which the victim's trust is gained and used to persuade them to part with their money

confident
adjective having a strong belief or feeling certain: *I am **confident** that he will arrive soon.* (***clear***, ***convinced***, ***definite***, ***positive***, ***sure***)

confidential
adjective **1** secret or not public: *The police officer wrote out a **confidential** report.* (***classified***, ***hush-hush***, ***private***)
2 trusted with secrets or private matters: *The director of the company had a **confidential** secretary.*

configuration (kuhn-fig-uh-<u>ray</u>-shuhn, kuhn-fig-yuh-<u>ray</u>-shuhn)
noun **1** the arrangement of the parts of something
2 the shape or outline that results from this
3 *Astronomy* the relative position or arrangement of the stars, planets, etc.
4 *Chemistry* the relative position in space of the atoms in a molecule

Word building: **configurational** *adjective* **configurative** *adjective*
Word history: from Latin word meaning 'shape after some pattern'

confine (kuhn-<u>fuyn</u>)
verb **1** to restrict or keep within limits: *I **confine** myself to one chocolate a day.* (***hold back***, ***limit***, ***restrain***)
2 to shut or keep in: *He was **confined** to prison for three months.* (***box in***, ***coop up***, ***enclose***, ***imprison***, ***incarcerate***)

Word building: **confinement** *noun*
Word history: French, from Italian word meaning 'bordering', from Latin

confirm
verb **1** to make certain or sure: *He **confirmed** our table booking at the restaurant.*
2 to strengthen or make firm: *What you have told me **confirms** what I already thought.* (***bear out***, ***corroborate***, ***prove***, ***substantiate***, ***verify***)
3 to admit as a member of a church in a special ceremony

Word use: The opposite of definition 2 is **contradict**.
Word building: **confirmation** *noun*
Word history: from Latin word meaning 'make firm'

confirmed
adjective firmly settled in a habit or condition

confiscate
verb to take and keep: *The teacher **confiscated** my comic.* (***appropriate***, ***commandeer***, ***seize***)

Word building: **confiscation** *noun*
Word history: from Latin word meaning 'put away in a chest'

conflict (kuhn-flikt)
verb **1** to disagree or clash: *Our ideas **conflict** because we are too different.*
noun (kon-flikt) **2** a fight or disagreement: *a **conflict** between nations* (***argument, battle, feud, quarrel, war***)

Word use: The opposite of definition 2 is **peace**.
Word history: from Latin word meaning 'struck together'

conflicted
verb **1** past participle of **conflict**
adjective **2** feeling uneasy due to conflicting wants: *She was **conflicted** when she had to choose between the gorgeous puppy or the older dog whose tail was wagging so frantically.* (***torn***)

conflicting
verb **1** present participle of **conflict**
adjective **2** in disagreement: ***Conflicting** opinions were tearing our group apart.*
3 generating conflict: *The proposal to change the uniform was **conflicting** for the school body.*

conform
verb **1** to act according to rules or laws
2 to be like or similar to: *Her hairstyle **conforms** to the latest fashion trend.*

Word use: The opposite of definition 1 is **rebel**.
Word building: **conformist** *noun* **conformity** *noun*
Word history: Middle English, from French, from Latin word meaning 'fashion', 'shape after'

confound
verb to surprise or puzzle: *He **confounded** the experts by solving the problem.* (***baffle, bewilder, confuse, mystify, perplex***)

Word history: Middle English, from Old French, from Latin word meaning 'pour together', 'mix', 'confuse'

confront
verb **1** to meet face to face: *He turned the corner and was **confronted** by his mother.*
2 to face boldly or bravely: *She **confronted** her problem without hesitation.*

Word building: **confrontation** *noun*
Word history: French, from Latin *con-* with + *frons* forehead

confronting
adjective intimidating or challenging: *a **confronting** documentary*

confuse
verb **1** to mix up or puzzle: *The teacher's instructions have **confused** me.* (***baffle, bamboozle, befuddle, muddle, perplex***)
2 to be unable to tell the difference between: *I always **confuse** one type of car with another.*

Word building: **confusion** *noun*
Word history: Middle English, from Latin word meaning 'confounded'

congeal (kuhn-jeel)
verb to thicken or become solid: *Cooking fat or dripping **congeals** as it cools.* (***clot, coagulate, condense, curdle***)

Word history: Middle English, from Latin word meaning 'cause to freeze together'

congenial (kuhn-jee-nee-uhl)
adjective pleasant or agreeable: *a more **congenial** job | **congenial** friends*

Word history: *con-* with + Latin *genius* spirit

congenital (kuhn-jen-uh-tl)
adjective existing at or from birth: ***congenital** heart disease*

Word history: from Latin word meaning 'born together with'

congest
verb to fill too much or to become overcrowded: *Cars are **congesting** the road.*

Word building: **congestion** *noun*
Word history: from Latin word meaning 'brought together'

conglomerate (kuhn-glom-uh-ruht, kuhng-glom-uh-ruht)
noun **1** anything made of various materials or elements
2 *Geology* a rock consisting of small round stones held together by clay, etc.
3 a company which controls production of a wide range of different products, often created by the merging of different businesses
adjective (kuhn-glom-uh-ruht, kuhng-glom-uh-ruht) **4** gathered into, or made up of a rounded mass
5 *Geology* like a conglomerate: ***conglomerate** material*
verb (kuhn-glom-uh-rayt, kuhng-glom-uh-rayt) **6** to make into or cause to become a ball or rounded mass

Word history: from Latin word meaning 'rolled together'

congratulate
verb to praise and show pleasure to: *They **congratulated** her on her victory.*

Word building: **congratulation** *noun*
Word history: Latin

congregate
verb to gather together: *The people **congregated** on the river bank.* (***assemble, convene, meet, rally, turn out***)

Word history: Middle English, from Latin word meaning 'collected into a flock'

congregation
noun a group of people gathered together, especially in a church (***assembly, crowd, flock***)

congress
noun a meeting of people to discuss ideas of interest to them all: *A **congress** of health workers was held here last week.* (***assembly, conference, convention, council***)

Word history: from Latin word meaning 'a meeting'

congruent
adjective **1** agreeing: ***congruent** opinions*
2 *Geometry* being exactly the same shape and size: ***congruent** triangles*

Word building: **congruence** *noun*

conifer
noun an evergreen tree which grows cones, like the pine or fir

Word building: **coniferous** *adjective*
Word history: from Latin word meaning 'cone-bearing'

conjecture (kuhn-jek-chuh)
noun **1** the forming or expressing of an opinion without enough information
2 a guess
verb **3** to conclude or suppose without enough information to be reliable

Word building: **conjectural** *adjective*
Word history: Middle English, from Latin word meaning 'a throwing together', 'inference'

conjoined twins
plural noun twins who are born joined together in any manner: *The **conjoined twins** were joined at the head.*

Word use: Another name is **Siamese twins**, although this is not used much nowadays.

conjugal (kon-juh-guhl, kon-jooh-guhl)
adjective concerning a husband and wife (***connubial***, ***marital***)

Word building: **conjugality** *noun*
Word history: Latin *conjunx* husband or wife

conjugate (kon-juh-gayt)
verb **1** *Grammar* to give various forms of a verb, depending on person, tense, number, etc.
2 *Biology* in the sexual reproduction of single-celled animals and plants, to unite temporarily to exchange nuclear material at the point of joining
adjective (kon-juh-guht, kon-juh-gayt) **3** joined together, especially in a pair or pairs (***coupled***, ***matched***, ***paired***)
4 having a common origin: ***conjugate** words*

Word building: **conjugative** *adjective*
conjugation *noun*
Word history: from Latin word meaning 'joined together', 'yoked'

conjunction
noun **1** a combination or joining together: *the **conjunction** of two rivers*
2 *Grammar* a word, such as 'and' or 'because', used for joining items together

conjunctions

You use **conjunctions** in your writing to join together words, phrases, clauses and sentences. *And, but, or, since*, if and when are examples of conjunctions.

There are two types of conjunctions, **coordinating** and **subordinating**.

Coordinating conjunctions join items of the same grammatical type:

table and chair (noun + noun)

up the street or down the road (phrase + phrase)

He was tired but she was lively. (main clause + main clause)

She said she could dance all night. And she was right. (sentence + sentence)

Subordinating conjunctions connect items of different types, such as a main clause and a dependent clause:

I went to the door (main clause) *when I heard someone knocking* (dependent clause).

Subordinating conjunctions tend to express a closer logical tie between the items:

The weather's terrible and I won't go.
coordinating conjunction

The weather's terrible so I won't go.
subordinating conjunction

In the second sentence, *so* indicates that there is a link of cause and effect between the clauses, while in the first sentence that link is not actually stated.

For more about the function of conjunctions, look up **link word**.

conjunctive
adjective **1** connective
2 joint, or joined together

conjunctivitis (kuhn-jungk-tuh-vuy-tuhs)
noun Medicine a painful disease of the very fine membrane that covers and protects the inside of the eyelid and the surface of the eye, causing redness and swelling

Word history: New Latin

conjure (kun-juh)
verb **1** to do magic tricks
phrase **2 conjure up,**
a to call or bring into existence by magic
b to recall or bring to mind

Word building: **conjurer** *noun*
Word history: Middle English, from Latin word meaning 'swear together'

conk
Colloquial
noun **1** a nose
2 a blow, or violent stroke
verb **3** to hit or strike, especially on the head
phrase **4 conk out,**
a to stop, or break down: *The engine **conked out** in the middle of the freeway.*
b to collapse, or become tired suddenly: *I **conked out** when I came home from shopping.*

Word history: probably alteration of *conch*

connect
verb **1** to join or unite: ***Connect** this wire to the end of that rod. | These wires should **connect** somewhere.* (***combine***, ***couple***, ***knit***, ***link***)
phrase **2 be connected with,** to have to do or be associated with: ***Are you connected with** the church?*

Word building: **connective** *adjective*
Word history: from Latin word meaning 'join', 'tie'

connection (kuh-nek-shuhn)
noun **1** the act of joining
2 the state of being joined
3 anything that joins: *telephone **connection***
4 an association, or relationship
5 a meeting of one means of transport with another, such as a bus system with a railway
6 connections, influential friends, relatives, etc.

Word use: You can also use **connexion**.
Word history: Latin

connive (kuh-nuyv)
phrase **1 connive at,** to avoid noticing or reporting something you should oppose: *The policeman **connived at** the prisoner's escape.*

2 connive with, to work together secretly (***collude, conspire, intrigue, plan, scheme***)

Word building: **connivance** *noun*
Word history: from Latin word meaning 'shut the eyes'

connoisseur (kon-uh-ser)
noun someone who has a special interest or knowledge of a particular subject: *a* ***connoisseur*** *of stained glass | a* ***connoisseur*** *of wine*

Word history: French, from Latin word meaning 'come to know'

connote (kuh-noht)
verb to suggest a meaning in addition to the main meaning

Word building: **connotation** *noun*
Word history: Latin *con-* + *notāre* mark

connote / denote

Don't confuse **connote** with **denote.** If one thing denotes another then it is a sign or indication of it:

Your furrowed brow denotes your great anxiety.

When you talk about a word denoting something, you mean that the word is a sign or symbol for something that exists in reality. The word 'dog' **denotes** a furry creature that eats bones and goes 'woof'. This 'woofing' creature is the **denotation** of the word 'dog'.

If a word **connotes** something then it calls to mind a certain feeling, mood or set of associations. **Connotations** of words are often very personal, because the emotional quality or colour that you attach to words comes from your own experiences:

For me, the colour purple connotes mystery and sadness.

Racist words have bad connotations.

conquer
verb to overcome by force: *The Allies* ***conquered*** *Germany in World War II.* (***beat, defeat, lick, thrash, vanquish***)

Word building: **conqueror** *noun* **conquest** *noun*
Word history: Middle English, from Latin word meaning 'seek for'

conscience (kon-shuhns)
noun the ability to see the difference between right and wrong in what you do

Word history: Middle English, from Old French, from Latin *conscientia* joint knowledge

conscientious (kon-shee-en-shuhs)
adjective **1** careful and particular: *a* ***conscientious*** *worker* (***attentive, diligent, fussy, painstaking, reliable***)
2 doing or controlled by what you believe to be right: *a* ***conscientious*** *objector to war*

Word building: **conscientiousness** *noun*

conscious (kon-shuhs)
adjective **1** aware or having knowledge: *I was not* ***conscious*** *of the bell.*
2 aware of what is happening around you: *The injured driver was still* ***conscious.***

Word building: **consciousness** *noun*
Word history: from Latin word meaning 'knowing'

conscript (kuhn-skript)
verb **1** to force to join the army, navy or air force
noun (kon-skript) **2** someone who has been conscripted

Word building: **conscription** *noun*
Word history: from Latin word meaning 'enrolled'

consecrate
verb **1** to declare holy: *The bishop* ***consecrated*** *the new church.*
2 to devote: *They* ***consecrated*** *themselves to God.*

Word building: **consecration** *noun*
Word history: Middle English, from Latin word meaning 'dedicated'

consecutive
adjective following one after another: *The instructions were given in* ***consecutive*** *order.*

Word history: French, from Latin word meaning 'having followed after'

consensus
noun a general agreement

Word history: from Latin word meaning 'agreement'

consent
verb **1** to agree: *They* ***consented*** *to go with him.*
noun **2** agreement: *By common* ***consent*** *they all came to the meeting.*

Word use: The opposite of definition 1 is **refuse.** | The opposite of definition 2 is **refusal.**
Word history: Middle English, from Old French, from Latin word meaning 'feel together'

consequence (kon-suh-kwuhns)
noun **1** an outcome or result: *This mess is the* ***consequence*** *of your foolishness.* (***conclusion, effect, sequel***)
2 importance or value: *a matter of no* ***consequence***

consequent (kon-suh-kwuhnt)
adjective **1** following as an effect or result
2 logically consistent

Word history: Latin

consequential (kon-suh-kwen-shuhl)
adjective following as an effect or result, or as a logical conclusion

conservation
noun the protection, management or restoration of things, especially natural resources and historic objects

Word building: **conservationist** *noun*
Word history: Latin

conservation / conversation

Don't confuse **conservation** with **conversation,** which is a talk or discussion.

conservatism
noun **1** opposition to change or to new ideas
2 the ideals and actions of the members of right-wing political parties who are conservative in their outlook

conservative
adjective **1** careful or moderate: *a* ***conservative*** *opinion |* ***conservative*** *dress*
2 opposed to new ideas and sudden change of any kind: *a* ***conservative*** *political party*

Word use: The opposite of definition 1 is **bold**. | The opposite of definition 2 is **progressive**
Word building: **conservative** *noun*

conservatorium
noun a school where you can study music

conservatory
noun a room or building made of glass, where plants are displayed

Noun forms: The plural is **conservatories**.

conserve (kuhn-serv)
verb **1** to keep from being lost or wasted: *to **conserve** petrol*
noun (kon-serv) **2** fruit preserved in a jam

Word use: The opposite of definition 1 is **waste**.
Word history: Middle English, from Latin word meaning 'preserve'

consider
verb **1** to think about: *I will **consider** the problem.* (***attend to**, **contemplate**, **focus on**, **ponder**, **take notice of***)
2 to think or believe: *I **consider** him to be the fastest swimmer.*

Word history: Middle English, from Latin word meaning 'examine closely'

considerable
adjective large or important enough to think about

considerate
adjective thoughtful of other people's needs and feelings (***kind**, **nice**, **unselfish**, **well-meaning***)

consideration
noun **1** careful thought: *I will give the problem my **consideration**.*
2 something taken, or that should be taken, into account
3 thoughtfulness for others

consign (kuhn-suyn)
verb **1** to hand over: *I am **consigning** the running of the school to my deputy.*
2 to send, often by public carrier: *to **consign** a message*
3 to hand over or deliver formally: *to **consign** him to prison*

Word history: French, from Latin word meaning 'furnish or mark with a seal'

consignment (kon-suyn-muhnt)
noun **1** the act of consigning
2 something consigned: *a **consignment** of art materials*
phrase **3 on consignment**, sent to an agent for sale: *goods **on consignment***

consist
verb to be made up: *The book **consists** of two parts.*

Word history: from Latin word meaning 'place oneself'

consistency
noun **1** agreement or harmony: *There is a **consistency** about his story which is convincing.*
2 the density, or degree of thickness: *Mix the ingredients until they are the **consistency** of cream.*

Noun forms: The plural is **consistencies**.

consistent
adjective **1** agreeing: *The message is **consistent** with what we heard before.*
2 acting or thinking in the same way throughout: *He is always **consistent** in applying the rules.*

console[1] (kuhn-sohl)
verb to comfort or cheer up: *He tried to **console** her for the loss of the kitten.*

Word building: **consolation** *noun*
Word history: from Latin word meaning 'comfort'

console[2] (kon-sohl)
noun **1** a desk-like structure containing the keyboards, pedals, etc., of an organ, from which it is played
2 a control panel for an electric or electronic system such as a computer

Word history: French

consolidate (kuhn-sol-uh-dayt)
verb **1** to make solid or firm: *to **consolidate** gains*
2 to unite, or bring together: *to **consolidate** two companies of troops*

Word building: **consolidator** *noun* **consolidation** *noun*
Word history: from Latin word meaning 'made solid'

consommé (kon-suh-may, kuhn-so-may)
noun a clear soup made from meat or vegetable stock

Word use: You can also use **consomme**.
Word history: French, from Latin *consummāre* finish

consonance
noun **1** agreement
2 harmony of sounds
3 *Music* a chord which seems harmonically at rest

Word use: The opposite of definition 3 is **dissonance**.

consonant
noun **1** a speech sound made by blocking the flow of your breath by the tongue or lips
2 any letter of the alphabet, except *a*, *e*, *i*, *o* or *u*

Word use: Compare this with **vowel**.
Word history: Middle English, from Latin word meaning 'sounding together'

consort (kon-sawt)
noun **1** the husband of a ruling queen or the wife of a king
verb (kuhn-sawt) **2** to associate or keep company: *The police warned him about **consorting** with criminals while he was still on parole.*

Word history: Middle English, from French word meaning 'mate', from Latin *consors* partner, sharer

consortium (kuhn-saw-tee-uhm, kuhn-saw-shee-uhm)
noun **1** an association of business institutions, etc., for carrying into effect some special operation needing large amounts of capital
2 an association or union

Noun forms: The plural is **consortia** or **consortiums**.
Word history: from Latin word meaning 'partnership'

conspicuous
adjective noticeable or standing out: *She was **conspicuous** in her red jumper and purple shoes.* (***exposed**, **obvious**, **prominent**, **visible***)

Word history: from Latin word meaning 'visible', 'striking'

conspire
verb to plan secretly together, especially to do something wrong or illegal: *The group* ***conspired*** *to hijack a plane.* (***collude***, ***connive***, ***intrigue***, ***plot***, ***scheme***)

Word building: **conspiracy** *noun* (*plural* **conspiracies**)
conspirator *noun* **conspiratorial** *adjective*
Word history: Middle English, from Latin word meaning 'breathe together'

constable (kun-stuh-buhl)
noun a police officer of the lowest rank

Word history: Middle English, from Old French, from Late Latin *comes stabulī* count of the stable, master of the horse

constant
adjective **1** going on without stopping: *Her success has been a* ***constant*** *source of pleasure.* (***endless***, ***interminable***, ***permanent***, ***persistent***, ***steady***)
2 faithful: *He has been* ***constant*** *in looking after his mother.* (***devoted***, ***loyal***, ***reliable***, ***steadfast***, ***trustworthy***)

Word use: The opposite of definition 1 is **intermittent** or **occasional**.
Word building: **constancy** *noun*
Word history: Middle English, from Latin word meaning 'standing firm'

constellation
noun a group of stars

Word history: Middle English, from Late Latin *constellātio* group of stars

consternation
noun a sudden amazement that causes you to feel shock or fear: *We were thrown into* ***consternation*** *at the news of his disappearance.*

Word history: Latin

constipation
noun the unpleasant condition of not being able to empty your bowels regularly or easily

constituency
noun the people represented by an elected member of parliament

Noun forms: The plural is **constituencies**.

constituent (kon-stit-shooh-uhnt)
adjective **1** one of the components that make up a thing: ***constituent*** *parts*
2 having the power to put together or alter a political constitution: *a* ***constituent*** *assembly*
noun **3** *Grammar* an element that forms part of a sentence, clause, phrase, etc.
4 a person who lives in a constituency or electorate who is entitled to vote in an election

Word history: Latin

constitute
verb to make up or form: *His absences, lateness, and general lack of interest* ***constitute*** *quite a problem.*

Word history: from Latin word meaning 'set up', 'established'

constitution
noun **1** the health or condition of your body: *Jim has a strong* ***constitution.***
2 a set of basic rules for governing a state, society or other organisation: *the Australian* ***constitution*** | *the* ***constitution*** *of the rowing club*

Word building: **constitutional** *adjective*
Word history: Middle English, from Latin

constitutional monarchy
noun a form of monarchy in which the power of the sovereign is limited by a constitution, whether written (as in Australia) or unwritten (as in Britain)

Word use: You can also use **limited monarchy**.

constrain (kuhn-strayn)
verb **1** to compel, or persuade with force: *to* ***constrain*** *to agree*
2 to repress or restrain

Word history: Middle English, from Old French, from Latin word meaning 'draw together'

constraint
noun **1** something that limits or controls the way you behave or what you can do at certain times: *There are legal* ***constraints*** *on doctors not to advertise for patients.*
2 control or the keeping back of your natural feelings and impulses: *We are trying to save money so we are acting with* ***constraint*** *and not going out much.*

constrict
verb to make tighter or narrower: *a drug to* ***constrict*** *the blood vessels*

Word use: The opposite of this is **dilate**.
Word building: **constriction** *noun*
Word history: from Latin word meaning 'drawn together'

construct
verb to build: *to* ***construct*** *a house* | *to* ***construct*** *a theory* (***erect***, ***fashion***, ***make***, ***put up***, ***shape***)

Word history: from Latin word meaning 'constructed', 'piled or put together'

construction (kuhn-struk-shuhn)
noun **1** the act or art of constructing
2 the way in which something is put together: *objects of similar* ***construction*** (***composition***, ***form***, ***structure***)
3 *Geometry*
a the process of drawing a figure so as to satisfy certain conditions
b extra parts added to show a proof
4 *Grammar* the arrangement of two or more forms in a grammatical unit
5 the explanation of a law or text, etc. (***interpretation***, ***reading***)

Word building: **constructional** *adjective*

constructive
adjective helpful or useful: *to make* ***constructive*** *suggestions*

construe (kuhn-strooh)
verb **1** to explain, or put a particular interpretation on
2 to deduce by construction or interpretation (***infer***, ***read***)

Word history: Middle English, from Latin word meaning 'build up', 'pile together'

consul
noun an official sent by a government to represent it in a foreign country

Word building: **consular** *adjective* **consulship** *noun*

consulate
noun the offices officially used by a consul
Word history: Latin

consult
verb to seek advice from: *to **consult** a doctor* | *to **consult** a dictionary*
Word history: from Latin word meaning 'deliberate', 'take counsel'

consultant (kuhn-sul-tuhnt)
noun **1** a person who consults
2 a person who gives professional or expert advice
3 a medical or surgical specialist

consultation (kon-suhl-tay-shuhn)
noun **1** the act of consulting
2 a meeting to discuss or plan something
3 an application for professional advice, especially to a doctor
Word building: **consultative** *adjective*

consumable
adjective **1** able to be consumed
2 (of an item of equipment or supply) normally consumed in use: *Pens, folders and printer cartridges were on the list of **consumable** office supplies that had to be restocked.*
noun **3** a consumable product or supply: ***Consumables** are products that people buy over and over because they use them up.*

consume
verb **1** to eat: *to **consume** a meat pie* (***absorb**, **devour**, **digest**, **swallow***)
2 to use up or destroy: *They **consumed** the stock of paper.* | *The building was **consumed** by fire.*
Word history: Middle English, from Latin word meaning 'take up completely'

consumer
noun someone who buys and uses goods and services: *Advertising is designed to make **consumers** buy more.* (***buyer**, **customer**, **patron**, **purchaser**, **shopper***)

consumerism (kuhn-syooh-muh-riz-uhm)
noun **1** a movement which aims at making consumers aware of their rights and also protecting their interests from dishonest trading practices
2 a theory that the economy of a capitalist society needs people to consume more and more goods

consumer price index
noun a measure of inflation, which compares the cost of a standard basket of retail goods over certain periods of time
Word use: The abbreviation is **CPI**.

consummate (kon-syooh-mayt)
verb **1** to bring to completion or perfection
2 to fulfil through sexual intercourse: *to **consummate** a marriage*
adjective (kon-syooh-muht, kuhn-sum-uht)
3 complete or perfect: *a **consummate** performance of music*
Word building: **consummation** *noun*
Word history: late Middle English, from Latin word meaning 'brought to the highest degree'

consumption
noun **1** eating or using up
2 an old-fashioned word for **tuberculosis**
Word history: Middle English, from Latin word meaning 'a wasting'

contact
noun **1** a meeting or touching: *to make **contact** with someone*
2 the moving part of a switch that completes and breaks an electrical circuit
3 a useful person to meet: *a business **contact***
Word history: from Latin word meaning 'a touching'

contact lenses
plural noun small, usually plastic lenses to improve your sight, which fit closely over the iris or coloured part of your eye and are held in place by fluid from the eye

contagious (kuhn-tay-juhs)
adjective catching or easily spread from one person to another: *Chickenpox is a **contagious** disease.* | *Happiness is **contagious**.*
Word history: Middle English, from Late Latin

contagious / infectious

Both these words mean something similar, but there is a difference when you use them to describe a disease.

An **infectious** illness is one that can spread from one person to another:

Influenza is an infectious disease but appendicitis isn't.

A **contagious** disease is an **infectious** disease which is spread by contact, either by direct contact with the sick person or by indirect contact with their clothes or bedding.

contain
verb to have inside itself: *This jug **contains** milk.* | *This book **contains** instructions.*
Word history: Middle English, from Old French, from Latin word meaning 'hold together', 'hold back'

container
noun **1** anything that contains or can contain
2 a very large crate for carrying goods on ships or trucks

contaminate
verb to make dirty or impure: *This meat has been **contaminated** by flies.* (***corrupt**, **damage**, **foul**, **pollute**, **taint***)
Word building: **contamination** *noun*
contaminant *noun*
Word history: Latin

contemplate
verb to look at or consider thoughtfully: *He **contemplated** the letter for several minutes.* | *She is **contemplating** going to Melbourne.* (***meditate on**, **mull over**, **ponder**, **reflect on***)
Word building: **contemplation** *noun*
Word history: from Latin word meaning 'having surveyed'

contemplative (kon-tuhm-play-tiv, kon-temp-luh-tiv)
adjective **1** used to, or known for considering things in a thoughtful way (***meditative**, **pensive**, **reflective***)
noun **2** a person devoted to religious contemplation

contemporaneous
(kuhn-tem-puh-ray-nee-uhs)
adjective taking place at the same time, or in the present
Word history: Latin

contemporary
adjective **1** existing at the same time: *Francis Greenway was* ***contemporary*** *with Governor Macquarie.*
2 modern or existing now: *The room was decorated in* ***contemporary*** *style.* (***current, late, new, recent, up-to-date***)
Word use: The opposite of definition 2 is **old-fashioned**.
Word building: **contemporary** *noun* (*plural* **contemporaries**)
Word history: *con-* + *temporary*

contempt
noun the feeling that someone or something is mean and disgraceful: *They felt* ***contempt*** *for the person who had robbed the vision-impaired woman.* (***derision, disdain, disrespect, scorn***)
Word history: Middle English, from Latin word meaning 'scorn'

contemptible
adjective deserving contempt: *Tripping up the other runner was a* ***contemptible*** *action.* (***despicable, mean, nasty, shabby, unkind***)

contemptible / contemptuous
Don't confuse **contemptible** with **contemptuous**, which means 'treating someone or something with contempt'.
The person who is doing the despising is **contemptuous**:
The bullies were contemptuous of his attempts at football.

contemptuous
adjective showing contempt: *She was* ***contemptuous*** *of Lisa's clumsy attempts to dance.* (***disdainful, scornful, supercilious***)
Word history: Latin *contemptu(s)* scorn + *-ous*

contend
verb **1** to fight or struggle: *She had to* ***contend*** *with illness.*
2 to say firmly: *He* ***contends*** *that he is only having a look.*
Word building: **contender** *noun* **contention** *noun*
Word history: from Latin word meaning 'stretch out'

content[1] (kon-tent)
noun **1** whatever is inside or contained in: *the* ***contents*** *of a bottle* | *The* ***contents*** *of a book are often listed in an index.* | *the* ***content*** *of a web page*
2 the volume, capacity, or amount contained
Word history: Medieval Latin *contentum* that which is contained

content[2] (kuhn-tent)
adjective **1** pleased or satisfied: *He is* ***content*** *with what he has.* (***comfortable, complacent, fulfilled, satiated***)
verb **2** to please or satisfy: *She* ***contented*** *herself with a quick snack.*
Word building: **contentment** *noun*
Word history: Middle English, from Latin word meaning 'satisfied'

contention (kuhn-ten-shuhn)
noun **1** strife, or rivalry
2 a competition, or contest
Word building: **contentious** *adjective*
Word history: Middle English, from Latin word meaning 'strife'

contest (kon-test)
noun **1** a competition
verb (kuhn-test) **2** to struggle for and try to win: *He* ***contested*** *the leadership.*
3 to argue against or object to: *They* ***contested*** *my idea.* | *She is going to* ***contest*** *the will.*
Word history: French, from Latin word meaning 'call to witness', 'bring a legal action'

contestant (kuhn-test-uhnt)
noun a person who takes part in a contest or a competition
Word history: French

context
noun the surrounding circumstances or words: *It was unfair to take his remarks about his brother out of* ***context***.
Word building: **contextual** *adjective*
Word history: Middle English, from Latin word meaning 'connection'

contiguous (kuhn-tig-yooh-uhs)
adjective **1** in contact, or touching
2 near, or very close without actually touching
Word building: **contiguousness** *noun* **contiguity** *noun*
Word history: Latin touching

continence (kon-tuh-nuhns)
noun **1** moderation or self-restraint, especially in regard to sexual activity
2 the ability to control your natural functions, especially urination and defecation
Word use: The opposite of definition 2 is **incontinence**.
Word history: Middle English, from Latin

continent
noun one of the main land masses of the world: *Australia is one of the seven* ***continents***.
Word building: **continental** *adjective*
Word history: Middle English, from Latin word meaning 'holding together'

continental climate
noun a type of climate associated with continental interiors and characterised by extremely hot, sunny summers, bitterly cold winters, and little rainfall occurring mainly in early summer

continental crust
noun Geology that portion of the lithosphere which comprises the earth's continents and the shallow seabeds surrounding the continents
Word use: Look up **oceanic crust**.

continental drift
noun the movement of continents away from the original single landmass to their present position

continental quilt
noun → **doona**

continental shelf
noun that portion of a continent found under a shallow sea, in contrast with the deep ocean basins from which it is separated by a steep slope of earth

contingency (kuhn-tin-juhn-see)
noun **1** a chance event, conditional on something uncertain
2 uncertainty

Noun forms: The plural is **contingencies.**

contingent (kuhn-tin-juhnt)
adjective **1** dependent for existence, occurrence, character, etc., on something that is not yet certain: *The new sports program is* ***contingent*** *on the approval of the principal.*
2 happening by chance or without known cause
noun **3** a group of people with a single purpose, as troops sent on a particular mission

Word history: Middle English, from Latin word meaning 'touching', 'bordering on', 'reaching', 'befalling'

continual
adjective happening often: *He got into trouble for his* ***continual*** *lateness.*

Word use: The opposite of this is **intermittent.**
Word history: Medieval Latin

continual / continuous

Don't confuse **continual** with **continuous.** These words are very similar in meaning, but there can be a difference.

Something is **continual** if it is more or less constant over a period of time, that is, if it happens again and again:

Your continual moaning is driving me mad.

The implication here is not that you moan from the moment you get up in the morning till the moment you go to bed. You do spend time on other things like eating and going to school. But you do moan so much that it is a fairly constant factor.

Something is **continuous** if it goes on without a break. If your moaning had been **continuous** you would not have paused to eat or go to school — you would have just moaned all the time.

Continuous lines go on and on without a break, and **continuous** surfaces have no gaps or holes in them.

continue
verb **1** to keep on: *They* ***continued*** *to walk in the rain.* (***carry on, persist in, stick at***)
2 to go on after being interrupted: *We will* ***continue*** *tomorrow.*
3 to go on with: *to* ***continue*** *a story | to* ***continue*** *a journey tomorrow* (***pick up, recommence, resume, return to, take up***)

Word building: **continuation** *noun*
Word history: Middle English, from Latin word meaning 'make continuous'

continuity (kon-tuh-nyooh-uh-tee)
noun **1** the condition or quality of being continuous
2 a continuous or connected whole

Noun forms: The plural is **continuities.**

continuous
adjective going on without stopping: *the* ***continuous*** *sound of his breathing* (***constant, endless, permanent, persistent, steady***)

Word use: The opposite of this is **intermittent.**
Word history: from Latin word meaning 'hanging together'

continuous / continual

Look up **continual / continuous.**

continuous aspect
noun the grammatical aspect which shows that something is continuing, such as 'am running' in *I am running*

For more information, look up **verbs: aspect.**

continuum (kuhn-tin-yooh-uhm)
noun **1** a continuous extent, series, or whole
phrase **2 four-dimensional continuum,** in the theory of relativity in physics, the three dimensions of space and the dimension of time considered together

Noun forms: The plural is **continua** or **continuums.**

contort
verb to twist out of shape

Word building: **contortion** *noun* **contortionist** *noun*
Word history: from Latin word meaning ' twisted'

contour (kon-toouh, kon-taw)
noun **1** the shape or outline: *the* ***contour*** *of the land*
2 a line on a map joining points of equal height

Word history: French, from Italian, from Latin *con-* with + *tornāre* turn

contraband
noun goods imported or exported illegally

Word history: Spanish

contrabass
noun **1** in any family of musical instruments, the member below the bass
2 in the violin family, the double bass

Word building: **contrabassist** *noun*

contraception
noun the prevention of pregnancy (***birth control***)

Word building: **contraceptive** *adjective* **contraceptive** *noun*
Word history: *contra-* against + *(con)ception*

contract (kon-trakt)
noun **1** an agreement, especially a legal one: *They signed the* ***contract*** *for building the house.*
verb (kuhn-trakt) **2** to become smaller: *Metal* ***contracts*** *when it is cooled.* (***decrease, dwindle, reduce, shrink***)
3 to make an agreement
4 to acquire, whether you want it or not: *to* ***contract*** *a disease | to* ***contract*** *debts*

Word building: **contractor** *noun*
Word history: Middle English, from Late Latin word meaning 'agreement'

contraction
noun **1** the act of contracting or the state of being contracted
2 a shortened form of a word, such as *can't* for *cannot*
3 one of the movements of a woman's uterus during labour

contractions in grammar

When you drop letters from the middle of a word or phrase to make it shorter, you're using a **contraction**. There are two types of **contraction**.

1 One type of **contraction** is an abbreviation. If a shortened form of a word begins with the first letter of the word and ends with its last letter, it is a contraction. Some examples are:

Dr	Doctor	Mr	Mister
rd	road	rm	room
hcp	handicap	cmdr	commander

Note that contractions do not have full stops. For more about this, look up **abbreviation**.

2 The other type of **contraction** is where letters are dropped from a two-word phrase, joining the words together. The position of the missing letters is marked by an apostrophe. Examples of contractions are underlined in the following sentences:

It's raining today. (it is)
We can't ride our horses. (cannot)
The horses don't like getting wet. (do not)
We should've gone yesterday. (should have)
Rain's a pain sometimes. (rain is)
Maybe it'll stop tonight. (it will)

Note that can't is a contraction of this type even though *cannot* is only one word.

Contractions give an informal tone to your writing. This can be useful for some kinds of writing, but doesn't suit more formal styles such as essay writing.

contractual
adjective having to do with a contract

contra deal
noun an agreement involving an exchange of goods or services, rather than money

contradict
verb **1** to deny or say the opposite of: *Whatever he says, you* ***contradict*** *it.* (***challenge, counter, oppose***)
2 to be the direct opposite of: *This experiment* ***contradicts*** *the results we got before.* (***negate, rebut, refute***)

Word use: The opposite of this is **confirm**.
Word building: **contradiction** *noun* **contradictory** *adjective*
Word history: from Latin word meaning 'said against'

contralto
noun **1** the lowest range of musical notes which can be sung by a female singer
2 a woman who sings contralto

Word use: You can also use **alto**. | A **contralto** is higher than a **tenor, baritone** or **bass** but lower than a **soprano**.
Word history: Italian

contraption
noun a complicated gadget or piece of machinery: *Sam has invented a* ***contraption*** *for exercising his pet mice.* (***apparatus, device, mechanism***)

contrary
adjective **1** (kon-truh-ree) opposed or different: *My opinion is* ***contrary*** *to yours.* (***antithetical, conflicting, contradictory, converse***)
2 (kuhn-trair-ree) perverse or self-willed: *a* ***contrary*** *child* (***argumentative, cantankerous, defiant, quarrelsome, stroppy***)
noun (kon-truh-ree) **3** the opposite: *You say he is right, but I can prove the* ***contrary.***
phrase **4 on the contrary**, in opposition to what has been said: ***On the contrary,*** *you are wrong.*

Word history: Middle English, from Anglo-French, from Latin word meaning 'opposite', 'hostile'

contrast (kuhn-trahst)
verb **1** to examine in order to show differences: ***Contrast*** *last year's result with this year's.*
2 to show a difference in comparison: *The red flowers of the grevillea* ***contrast*** *with its green leaves.*
noun (kon-trahst) **3** a marked difference: *a colour* ***contrast*** | *a* ***contrast*** *in attitude*

Word history: French, from Italian, from Late Latin word meaning 'withstand', 'oppose'

contrast / compare

Don't confuse **contrast** with **compare**. To **compare** two things is to look at them to see how they are alike.

contravene (kon-truh-veen)
verb **1** to oppose, or come or be in conflict with
2 to break, or infringe: *to* ***contravene*** *the law*

Word building: **contravention** *noun*
Word history: from Latin word meaning 'oppose'

contribute (kuhn-trib-yooht)
verb **1** to donate or pay a share: *to* ***contribute*** *to a fund*
2 to give to, or write for, a magazine or newspaper: *I have* ***contributed*** *a story to the school magazine.*

Word building: **contribution** *noun* **contributor** *noun*
Word history: from Latin word meaning 'brought together'

contrite
adjective feeling a strong sense of regret or guilt: *He knew he had done wrong and was very* ***contrite.*** (***sorry***)

contrition (kuhn-trish-uhn)
noun real sorrow for any bad things you have done

Word history: Middle English, from Latin

contrive
verb to invent or plan cleverly: *He* ***contrived*** *to be absent at the time.* (***arrange, manage, manoeuvre, plot, scheme***)

Word building: **contrivance** *noun* **contrived** *adjective*
Word history: Middle English, from Old French *con-* + *trover* find

control
verb **1** to be in charge of or direct: *Peter and Maria* ***control*** *the library.* (***govern, manage, rule, run, supervise***)
2 to adjust as necessary: *This tap* ***controls*** *the flow of water.*
3 to keep in check: *to* ***control*** *your temper* (***curb, inhibit, restrain, restrict, stifle***)
noun **4** command or check: *Keep your dog under* ***control.***

Verb forms: I **controlled**, I have **controlled**, I am **controlling**
Word building: **controllable** *adjective* **controller** *noun*
Word history: French, from Old French *contre-* counter- + *rolle* roll

control order
noun an order issued by a court which restricts a person's movements and associations, and may also require home detention, the wearing of a tracking device, reporting to police stations at specified times, etc.

control panel
noun **1** a panel in which the controls of a device, vehicle, etc., are fitted
2 *Computers* an interface (definition 2) for setting system parameters on a computer, made to resemble a control panel (definition 1) on the screen

controversy (kon-truh-ver-see, kuhn-trov-uh-see)
noun an argument or difference of opinion: *The position of the new airport is a matter of* ***controversy.*** (***altercation, conflict, debate, dispute, quarrel***)

Noun forms: The plural is **controversies**.
Word building: **controversial** *adjective*
Word history: Latin *contrōversia* debate, contention

contuse (kuhn-tyoohz)
verb to bruise, often with a blunt instrument, or something like this

Word building: **contusion** *noun*
Word history: from Latin word meaning 'beaten together'

conundrum (kuh-nun-druhm)
noun a riddle or puzzle

convalesce (kon-vuh-les)
verb to grow stronger after an illness: *He is* ***convalescing*** *at home after a long stay in hospital.* (***pick up, rally, recover, recuperate***)

Word building: **convalescence** *noun* **convalescent** *adjective* **convalescent** *noun*
Word history: from Latin word meaning 'grow strong'

convection
noun the spreading of heat by the movement of heated air or water

Word building: **convector** *noun*
Word history: Late Latin, from Latin word meaning 'carry together'

convene
verb to call or gather together: *to* ***convene*** *a meeting | to* ***convene*** *for a quick talk about tactics*

Word building: **convener, convenor** *noun*
Word history: Middle English, from Latin word meaning 'come together'

convenient
adjective **1** suited to your needs: *a* ***convenient*** *time* (***appropriate, fitting, suitable***)
2 easy to use, access, etc.: *a* ***convenient*** *house*

Word building: **convenience** *noun*
Word history: Middle English, from Latin word meaning 'agreeing', 'suiting'

convent
noun **1** a group of buildings where nuns live
2 a school run by nuns

Word history: from Latin word meaning 'meeting', 'assembly', 'company'

convention
noun **1** a large meeting: *A science* ***convention*** *was held at the university.* (***assembly, conference, council***)
2 a rule, often unwritten, which everyone accepts: *There are certain* ***conventions*** *about the use of the tennis courts.* (***formula, law, precept, regulation, tradition***)

Word building: **conventional** *adjective*
Word history: from Latin word meaning 'a meeting'

converge
verb **1** to move towards each other, or to meet at a common point: *A number of ambulances* ***converged*** *on the scene of the accident. | The beams from the search lights* ***converged*** *on the enemy plane.*
2 to tend towards a common result, conclusion, etc.

Word building: **convergence** *noun* **convergent** *adjective*
Word history: from Late Latin word meaning 'incline together'

conversant (kuhn-vers-uhnt, kon-vuhs-uhnt)
phrase **conversant with**, familiar by use or study: *I'm not* ***conversant with*** *law terms.*

Word history: Middle English, from Latin word meaning 'associating with'

conversation
noun talk among people: *We had an interesting* ***conversation*** *about a new film.* (***chat, dialogue, discussion, exchange***)

Word building: **conversational** *adjective* **conversationalist** *noun*
Word history: Middle English, from Old French, from Latin word meaning 'frequent use', 'intercourse'

conversation / conservation
Don't confuse **conversation** with **conservation**, which is the protection of nature or historic buildings.
Someone who cares a lot about nature and wants it protected is called a conservationist.

converse[1] (kuhn-vers)
verb to have a talk: *We* ***conversed*** *about music.* (***chat, confer, exchange views***)

Word history: Middle English, from Old French, from Latin word meaning 'associate with'

converse[2] (kon-vers)
adjective **1** turned about or opposite: *to go in a* ***converse*** *direction* (***antithetical, conflicting, contradictory, contrary***)
noun **2** the opposite: *He says it is possible but the* ***converse*** *is true.*

Word history: from Latin word meaning 'turned about'

convert (kuhn-vert)
verb **1** to change completely: *Cinderella's fairy godmother* ***converted*** *her rags into a ball gown.* (***alter, transform***)
2 to change the belief of: *His friends* ***converted*** *him from rugby to soccer.*
noun (kon-vert) **3** someone who has changed their religion or other beliefs

Word history: Middle English, from Latin word meaning 'turn about', 'change'

convertible
adjective **1** able to be changed
2 having a top that you can remove: *a* ***convertible*** *car*
noun **3** *Colloquial* a convertible car

Word building: **conversion** *noun*

convex
adjective curved or bulging outwards like the outer surface of a circle

Word use: The opposite is **concave**.
Word building: **convexity** *noun*
Word history: from Latin word meaning 'vaulted', 'arched'

convey (kuhn-vay)
verb to carry: *The bus* ***conveyed*** *us to town. | His words* ***conveyed*** *a message of sympathy.* (***bear, deliver, send, transfer, transport***)

Word building: **conveyable** *adjective*
Word history: Middle English, from Old French (from Latin *via* way, journey)

conveyance
noun Old-fashioned a car or other vehicle

conveyancing
noun that branch of the law concerned with examining titles, giving opinions as to their validity, and preparing deeds, etc., for transfer of real property from one person to another

Word building: **conveyancer** *noun*

conveyor belt
noun a flexible band passing around two or more wheels, etc., used to move objects from one place to another

convict (kuhn-vikt)
verb **1** to find guilty of a crime, especially after a legal trial: *to* ***convict*** *a criminal*
noun (kon-vikt), *Old-fashioned* **2** someone who has been found guilty of a crime: *English* ***convicts*** *used to be sent to Australia to serve their sentences.* (***captive, criminal, internee, prisoner***)

Word use: The opposite of definition 1 is **acquit**.
Word history: Middle English, from Latin word meaning 'overcome', 'convicted'

conviction
noun **1** the occasion of being found guilty: *As it was his first* ***conviction*** *he was let off with a warning.*
2 strong belief: *He spoke with a voice filled with* ***conviction.*** (***assurance, certainty, confidence, faith***)

convince
verb to make feel sure, or persuade: *We finally* ***convinced*** *him that he was wrong.*

Word building: **convincing** *adjective* **convincingly** *adverb*
Word history: from Latin word meaning 'overcome by argument or proof', 'convict of error or crime', 'prove'

convivial (kuhn-viv-ee-uhl)
adjective **1** fond of feasting, drinking, and merry company (***genial, jovial, sociable***)
2 festive or having to do with a feast
3 agreeable, or merry

Word building: **conviviality** *noun*
Word history: from Latin word meaning 'of a feast'

convolution (kon-vuh-looh-shuhn)
noun **1** a rolled up or coiled state
2 a rolling or coiling together
3 a whorl, or turn of anything coiled: *the* ***convolutions*** *of the brain | the* ***convolutions*** *of a shell*

convoy
noun **1** a number of ships or vehicles travelling together, sometimes for protection: *The ocean liner set sail with a* ***convoy*** *of small boats.*
verb **2** to travel with as an escort

Word history: Middle English, from French word meaning 'convey'

convulse
verb **1** to agitate, or shake violently
2 to cause to suffer violent spasms of your muscles: *to* ***convulse*** *with laughter*

Word building: **convulsion** *noun*
Word history: from Latin word meaning 'shattered'

coo
verb **1** to make the soft, murmuring sound of pigeons or doves
2 to murmur or talk fondly: *to bill and* ***coo***

Word building: **coo** *noun*
Word history: imitating the sound

cooee
noun Australian, NZ **1** a long clear call rising at the end, used especially in the bush as a signal
verb Australian, NZ **2** to make the call 'cooee'
phrase **3 not within cooee**, far from achieving a given goal
4 within cooee, within calling distance

Verb forms: I **cooeed**, I have **cooeed**, I am **cooeeing**
Word history: from Dharug, an Australian Aboriginal language spoken by the people living near Sydney Cove in the early days of European settlement

cook
verb **1** to prepare food by boiling, baking, roasting, etc.
2 to heat until ready for eating
noun **3** someone who cooks or prepares food

Word history: Old English *cōc*, from Late Latin

cookery
noun the art of cooking

cookie
noun **1** *Computers* a small file sent by a server to a browser, which the server can use when being accessed in the future
2 the US word for **biscuit**

cooktop
noun a group of electric hotplates or gas burners for cooking, fitted into a benchtop

Cooktown orchid
noun an attractive, purple orchid found on rocks and trees in far northern Queensland; the floral emblem of Queensland

cool
adjective **1** not too cold: *a **cool** morning*
2 a calm or unexcited: *She remained **cool**.* (***composed***, ***peaceful***, ***placid***, ***poised***, ***relaxed***)
b unfriendly: *to be **cool** towards someone you distrust*
3 *Colloquial* attractive or fashionable: *It's not **cool** to wear trousers like that.*
verb **4** to become or make cool (***chill***, ***freeze***, ***refrigerate***)
noun **5** a cool time, place, etc.: *in the **cool** of the evening*
6 *Colloquial* calmness in the way you conduct yourself: *to keep your **cool** in times of great stress*

Word building: **coolly** *adverb*
Word history: Old English *cōl*

coolamon (kooh-luh-mon)
noun a wooden dish traditionally made and used by some Aboriginal peoples

Word history: from Kamilaroi, an Australian Aboriginal language of northern NSW

coolant (koohl-uhnt)
noun **1** a substance, usually a liquid or gas, used to reduce heat in an engine, etc.
2 a lubricant used to reduce heat caused by friction

Word history: *cool* + *-ant*

Coolgardie safe
noun a cabinet for keeping food, which cools by allowing a breeze to blow through wet material, such as hessian

Word use: You can also use **cool safe** or **Coolgardie cooler**.
Word history: from *Coolgardie*, town in Western Australia

coolibah (kooh-luh-bah)
noun a gum tree found in inland Australia which has short twisted branches

Word use: You can also use **coolabah**.
Word history: from Yuwaalaraay, an Australian Aboriginal language from the Lightning Ridge region

cool temperate rainforest
noun a mainly broad-leaved forest which exists under a mean annual temperature of about 12°C; carrying such species as Antarctic beech, southern sassafras, and leatherwood (in Tasmania)

Word use: You can also use **cool temperate forest**. | Look up **warm temperate rainforest**.

coop
noun **1** a small cage for hens
phrase **2 coop up**, to keep in a small place: *We were all **cooped up** in one room.* (***box in***, ***cage***, ***confine***, ***shut in***)

cooperate (koh-op-uh-rayt)
verb **1** to work together: *The two city councils **cooperated** to build a new pool.* (***collaborate***, ***combine***, ***team up***, ***unite***)
2 to be helpful: *When we complained about the noise, they **cooperated** by turning down the volume.*

Word building: **cooperation** *noun*
Word history: from Late Latin word meaning 'having worked together'

cooperative (koh-op-uh-ruh-tiv, koh-op-ruh-tiv)
adjective **1** helpful: ***cooperative** children* (***accommodating***, ***obliging***, ***responsive***, ***supportive***)
2 having to do with economic cooperation: *a **cooperative** farm*
noun **3** a business which is owned and controlled by a group of members and which is formed to provide them with work or with goods at reasonable prices
4 a farm run on a communal basis, or which shares with others the use of marketing facilities, machinery, labour, etc.

Word use: The opposite of definition 1 is **uncooperative**. | You can also use **cooperative society** for definition 3. | You can also use **cooperative farm** for definition 4.

coordinate (koh-aw-duhn-ayt)
verb **1** to combine or put together: *It's hard to **coordinate** the different things I want to do.*
2 to match or go well together: *The colours of your coat and blouse do not **coordinate**.*
3 to move together smoothly: *When he dances he can't **coordinate** his feet.*
noun (koh-aw-duhn-uht) **4** *Mathematics* any of the numbers which define the position of a point, line, etc., by reference to a fixed figure, system of lines, etc.

Word building: **coordination** *noun* **coordinator** *noun*

cop
Colloquial
noun **1** a member of the police force
verb **2** to get: *He **copped** a punch on the nose.*
phrase **3 cop it**, to get into trouble
4 cop out,
a to choose not to do or opt out of: *to **cop out** of the cleaning*
b to fail completely
5 cop this!, look at this!
6 not much cop, not worthwhile

Verb forms: I **copped**, I have **copped**, I am **copping**
Word history: Old English *coppian* lop, steal

cope
verb to manage or get on: *How are you **coping** in your new job?*

Word history: Middle English, from French word meaning 'strike'

copious (koh-pee-uhs)
adjective **1** abundant or plentiful: *a **copious** supply of milk* (***ample***, ***bountiful***, ***lavish***, ***prolific***)
2 having or giving an abundant supply: *a **copious** vegetable garden*
3 showing an ability to produce a large amount, of thoughts or words, etc.: *a **copious** writer*

Word history: Middle English, from Latin word meaning 'plentiful'

cop-out
noun Colloquial an easy but irresponsible way out of a difficult situation

copper
noun **1** a fairly soft, reddish-brown metal
2 a reddish-brown colour

Word building: **copper** *adjective*
Word history: Old English *coper*, *copor* from Latin *aes Cyprium* Cyprian metal

copperplate
noun **1** a plate of polished copper on which writing, a picture or a design is made by engraving or etching
2 a print or impression from such a plate
3 an engraving or printing of this kind
4 a formal, rounded, heavily sloping style of handwriting, formerly much used in engravings
adjective **5** sloping, rounded and formal: ***copperplate** handwriting*

copra
noun the dried flesh of the coconut, from which coconut oil is pressed

Word history: Portuguese, from Malayalam, an Indian language

copulate
verb to have sexual intercourse

Word building: **copulation** *noun*
Word history: from Latin word meaning 'coupled'

copy
noun **1** something which is made the same as something else: *The secretary took my letter and made two **copies**.* (***duplicate***, ***facsimile***, ***imitation***, ***replica***, ***reproduction***)
2 a single example of the same book or magazine
verb **3** to do or make the same as: ***Copy** me until you've learned the steps.* | *to **copy** a set of numbers* (***duplicate***, ***match***, ***reproduce***, ***simulate***, ***trace***)

Noun forms: The plural is **copies**.
Verb forms: I **copied**, I have **copied**, I am **copying**
Word history: Middle English, from Latin word meaning 'plenty', Medieval Latin word meaning 'transcript'

copybook
noun **1** a book in which examples of handwriting are printed for learners to imitate
adjective **2** excellent, or according to the rules: *The plane made a **copybook** landing.* | ***copybook** tennis*
phrase **3 blot your copybook**, to spoil or hurt your reputation or record

copyright
noun **1** the exclusive right, given by law for a fixed period of time, to make and sell copies of, and to control in other ways, a book, play or film, or a musical or other artistic work
adjective **2** protected by copyright
verb **3** to have a copyright put on something

copyright law
noun the law which says who may use or copy someone's books, music, films or computer programs

coral
noun the hard, colourful shapes formed from the skeletons of small sea animals

Word history: Middle English, from Old French, from Latin, from Greek word meaning 'red coral'

> **coral / choral**
> Don't confuse **coral** with **choral**. Music is **choral** if it is sung by a choir or a chorus.

cord
noun **1** a strong string, not as thick as rope
2 wire, which is protected by cloth or plastic, used to connect electrical goods to a power point (***flex***)
3 a ribbed material, especially corduroy: *He was wearing a jacket of **cord**.*

Word history: Middle English, from Latin, from Greek word meaning 'gut'

> **cord / chord / cored**
> Don't confuse **cord** with **chord** or **cored**.
> A **chord** is a set of musical notes sounded together.
> **Cored** is the past form of **core**, to remove the centre from a piece of fruit.

cordial
adjective **1** warmly friendly: *a **cordial** welcome*
noun **2** a fruit-flavoured syrup that you mix with water to make a drink

Word building: **cordiality** *noun* **cordially** *adverb*
Word history: Middle English, from Latin *cor* heart

corduroy
noun a cotton material with a pattern of ridges

Word history: obsolete *duroy*, a kind of coarse woollen fabric

core
noun **1** the inner or middle part, especially of fruit
2 the primary memory of a computer
verb **3** to remove the core

> **core / corps**
> Don't confuse **core** with **corps**, a word which sounds the same but means a unit of soldiers.

core dump
noun Computers the copying of the contents of a computer's memory to the hard disk, a tape, etc., such as when a system error occurs

Word use: You can also use **memory dump**.

corella (kuh-<u>rel</u>-uh)
noun an Australian cockatoo with a predominantly white plumage tinged with pink or red

corgi (<u>kaw</u>-gee)
noun a dog with short legs and a thick body

Noun forms: The plural is **corgis**.

coriander
noun a herb with strong-smelling, seedlike fruit and leaves, used in cooking and medicine

cork[1]
noun **1** the outer bark of a tree (the **cork oak**), used for making stoppers of bottles, floats, etc.

2 a piece of cork, or other material (such as rubber), used as a stopper for a bottle, etc.
3 a small float to buoy up a fishing line or to show when a fish bites
phrase **4 cork up**, to stop with, or as if with, a cork

Word history: Spanish *alcorque* shoe with cork, from Arabic, from Latin word meaning 'oak'

cork[2]
verb to receive a damaging blow to: *to **cork** your thigh*

corkage
noun a charge made by a restaurant, etc., for serving liquor brought in by the customer

corkscrew
noun a sharp metal spiral with a handle, for pulling corks out of bottles

cormorant (kaw-muh-ruhnt)
noun a fish-eating bird with a small head, long thin neck and long pointed bill, widespread in Australia and in other places

Word use: Another name is **shag**.
Word history: Middle English, from Old French *corp* raven + *marenc* marine, from Latin *corvus marinus*

corn[1]
noun **1** a grain plant that you can eat as a vegetable or grind to make flour
verb **2** to preserve by salting: *to **corn** beef*

Word use: Definition 1 is often called **maize** in the US.
Word history: Old English

corn[2]
noun a hard, painful lump on your toes or other parts of your feet

Word history: Old French word meaning 'horn', from Latin *cornū*

cornea (kaw-nee-uh, kaw-nee-uh)
noun the transparent outer covering of your eye, covering the iris and the pupil

Noun forms: The plural is **corneas** (kaw-nee-uhz) or **corneae** (kaw-nee-ee).
Word building: **corneal** *adjective*
Word history: from Latin word meaning 'horny'

corner
noun **1** a place where two lines or surfaces meet and form an angle: *a street **corner** | the **corner** of a room | the **corners** of a table*
2 a place or region: *The travellers come from all the **corners** of the earth.*
3 *Soccer, Hockey, etc.* a free kick or hit from the corner of the field: *She took the penalty shot from the left corner.*
verb **4** to trap: *The dog **cornered** the cat in a narrow lane.*
5 to turn a corner, especially at speed: *This car **corners** well.*
adjective **6** placed at the junction of two roads: *a **corner** shop*
phrase **7 corner the market**, to have control of an area of activity so that no-one else can have success in that area
8 cut corners,
a to do something with as little time, effort or money as possible
b to bypass an official procedure, or something like this
9 round the corner, so close that you can walk there
10 turn the corner, to begin to get well

Word history: Middle English, from Latin word meaning 'horn', 'corner'

cornerstone
noun **1** a stone built into a corner of the foundation of an important building as the official start of building, usually laid with formal ceremonies
2 someone or something of basic importance

cornet
noun **1** a wind instrument like the trumpet, but smaller
2 a small cone, such as for ice-cream

Word history: Middle English, from Old French, from Latin word meaning 'horn'

cornflour
noun the fine flour made from rice or corn which is used in cooking, especially to thicken sauces

cornice (kawn-uhs)
noun *Architecture* a long piece of wood or plaster which covers the join between the walls and ceiling of a room

Word history: French, from Italian, from Medieval Greek word meaning 'summit', Greek word meaning 'anything curved or bent'

corny (kaw-nee)
adjective **1** too well known and silly: *a **corny** joke*
2 sentimental

Adjective forms: **cornier**, **corniest**

corollary (kuh-rol-uh-ree)
noun **1** a proposition that follows, without needing further proof, from one that has already been proved
2 something that follows naturally from something else

Noun forms: The plural is **corollaries**.
Word history: Middle English, from Late Latin word meaning 'corollary', Latin word meaning 'gift', originally 'garland'

corona (kuh-roh-nuh)
noun **1** a coloured circle of light seen round the sun or moon, caused by the bending of light by water drops in the earth's atmosphere (***halo***)
2 the outer part of the sun's atmosphere, seen as a shining circle around the sun during an eclipse
3 *Botany* a crown-like part, especially on the inner side of a flower's petals, such as the daffodil

Noun forms: The plural is **coronas** or **coronae** (kuh-roh-nee).
Word history: from Latin word meaning 'garland'

coronary (ko-ruhn-ree)
adjective **1** of or like a crown
2 *Anatomy*
a encircling like a crown, such as certain blood vessels
b having to do with the arteries which supply the heart tissues and which originate in the root of the aorta
noun **3** a heart attack

Word history: Latin

coronation
noun the crowning of a king or queen

coronavirus
noun a virus affecting mammals, the cause in humans of the common cold, but, in other animals, of respiratory and intestinal disorders which can be fatal

coroner
noun the official who is in charge of a court inquiry into the cause of sudden or unexplained deaths

Word building: **coronial** *adjective*
Word history: Middle English, from Anglo-French word meaning 'officer of the crown'

coronet
noun a small crown

Word history: from Old French word meaning 'little crown'

corporal[1]
noun physical or having to do with the body

Word history: Middle English, from Latin word meaning 'body'

corporal[2]
noun a junior officer in the army or air force

Word history: French, from Italian *caporale*, from Latin word meaning 'head'

corporal punishment
noun any punishment that causes pain or injury to the body, such as caning or smacking

corporate (kaw-puh-ruht, kaw-pruht)
adjective **1** having to do with a corporation: *a **corporate** body*
2 united in one body
3 shared by all persons in a group: ***corporate** ownership*

Word history: from Latin word meaning 'formed into a body'

corporation
noun a business or other united group of people: *The children's parents formed a **corporation** to run their own school.* (***company***, ***firm***, ***organisation***, ***outfit***, ***syndicate***)

corporeal (kaw-paw-ree-uhl)
adjective **1** bodily, or having the nature of the physical body: ***corporeal** existence*
2 having the nature of matter: ***corporeal** goods* (***material***, ***physical***, ***tangible***)

Word building: **corporeality** *noun* **corporealness** *noun*
Word history: Latin *corporeus* of the nature of body + *-al*

corps (kaw)
noun **1** a unit of soldiers
2 a group of people in the same job: *the press **corps***

Word history: French

corps / core
Don't confuse **corps** with **core**. A **core** is at the centre of something, like the **core** of an apple.

corpse
noun a dead body, especially of a human being (***cadaver***, ***remains***)

Word history: Middle English, from Old French, from Latin *corpus* body

corpse / corps
Don't confuse **corpse** with **corps**, which is pronounced to rhyme with *door* and refers to a unit of soldiers.

corpulence (kaw-pyuh-luhns)
noun bulkiness or largeness of body

Word building: **corpulent** *adjective*
Word history: Middle English, from French, from Latin

corpus (kaw-puhs)
noun **1** a large or complete collection or body of writings, laws, etc.
2 the bulk, or main part

Noun forms: The plural is **corpora** (kaw-puh-ruh) or **corpuses**.
Word history: Latin

corpuscle (kaw-puh-suhl)
noun **1** one of the very small bodies in the blood (**blood corpuscles**, both red and white), the lymph (**lymph corpuscles**, white only), etc.
2 a very small particle

Word use: You can also use **corpuscule** (*say* kaw-pus-kyoohl).
Word building: **corpuscular** *adjective*
Word history: from Latin word meaning 'a little body'

correct
verb **1** to remove or point out the mistakes of
adjective **2** free from mistakes (***accurate***, ***certain***, ***right***, ***true***, ***valid***)
3 acceptable or proper: ***correct** behaviour*

Word building: **correction** *noun* **corrective** *adjective*
Word history: Middle English, from Latin word meaning 'made straight', 'directed'

correlate (ko--ruh-layt)
verb **1** to match, usually one thing against another, or establish in orderly connection: *to **correlate** one set of figures with another*
2 to have a mutual relation: *These figures do not **correlate** easily with those.*
noun **3** either of two related things, especially when one implies the other: *Lung cancer is thought to be a **correlate** of smoking.*

Word history: *cor-* + *relate*

correlation (ko-ruh-lay-shuhn)
noun **1** the mutual relation of two or more things, parts, etc.
2 *Statistics* the degree of relationship of two attributes or measurements on the same group of elements

correspond
verb **1** to match or be similar: *Those figures almost **correspond**.*
2 to write letters: *We used to **correspond** every week.*

Word building: **corresponding** *adjective*
Word history: Latin *cor-* + *rēspondēre* answer

correspondence
noun **1** letters
2 similarity: *Is there any* ***correspondence*** *between the two accounts of what happened?*

correspondent (ko-ruh-spon-duhnt)
noun **1** someone who writes letters
2 a reporter paid to send in articles and news reports from a distant place

corridor
noun **1** a connecting passage in a building
2 a passage into which several rooms, apartments, or railway compartments open

Word history: French word meaning 'long passageway', from Italian *corridore* covered way, from Spanish, from Latin word meaning 'run'

corroborate (kuh-rob-uh-rayt)
verb to confirm, or make more certain: *The witness's story* ***corroborates*** *what the police officer said.* (***bear out***, ***prove***, ***substantiate***, ***verify***)

Word building: **corroborative** *adjective* **corroboratory** *adjective* **corroborator** *noun*
Word history: from Latin word meaning 'strengthened'

corroboree (kuh-rob-uh-ree)
noun an Aboriginal ceremony with dancing and singing

Word history: from Dharug, an Australian Aboriginal language spoken by the people living near Sydney Cove in the early days of European settlement

corrode (kuh-rohd)
verb to gradually eat away: *Rust had* ***corroded*** *the old car.*

Word building: **corrosion** *noun* **corrosive** *adjective*
Word history: from Latin word meaning 'gnaw away'

corrugate
verb to wrinkle: *to* ***corrugate*** *cardboard*

Word building: **corrugation** *noun*
Word history: from Latin word meaning 'wrinkled'

corrugated
adjective ridged or bumpy: *The roof was made of* ***corrugated*** *iron.*

corrupt
adjective **1** dishonest or able to be bribed (***crooked***, ***degenerate***, ***depraved***, ***immoral***, ***perverted***)
verb **2** to make dishonest, especially by bribery
3 to change from good to bad: *to* ***corrupt*** *the language* (***contaminate***, ***damage***, ***foul***, ***pollute***, ***taint***)

Word building: **corruptible** *adjective* **corruption** *noun*
Word history: Middle English, from Latin word meaning 'broken in pieces', 'destroyed'

corsage (kaw-sahzh)
noun a small bunch of flowers, especially worn pinned to a dress

Word history: from French word meaning 'body'

corset
noun underwear which gives shape or firm support to the body

Word history: Middle English, from French

cortege (kaw-tairzh, kaw-tayzh)
noun **1** a procession
2 a retinue, group of attendants

Word use: You can also use **cortège**.
Word history: French, from Italian word meaning 'court'

cortex (kaw-teks)
noun **1** *Botany* the inner bark
2 *Anatomy*, *Zoology* the outer layer of some organs, especially that of the grey matter of the brain

Noun forms: The plural is **cortices** (kaw-tuh-seez).
Word building: **cortical** *adjective*
Word history: from Latin word meaning 'bark', 'rind', 'shell'

cosh
noun **1** a blunt weapon
verb **2** to hit with a cosh

cosine (koh-suyn)
noun *Mathematics* the sine of the complement of a given angle

Word use: The short form is **cos**.

cosmetic
adjective **1** meant to improve the look of your skin and hair: *the* ***cosmetic*** *effect of lipstick*
noun **2** a beauty aid

Word building: **cosmetically** *adverb*
Word history: from Greek word meaning 'relating to adornment'

cosmic
adjective having to do with the universe: ***cosmic*** *laws*

Word building: **cosmically** *adverb*
Word history: from Greek word meaning 'of the world'

cosmonaut
noun → **astronaut**

Word history: *cosmo-* universe + Greek *naútēs* sailor

cosmopolitan (koz-muh-pol-uh-tuhn)
adjective **1** having people or customs from many parts of the world: *a* ***cosmopolitan*** *city*
2 feeling at home in many parts of the world: *a* ***cosmopolitan*** *outlook*

cosmos (koz-mos)
noun the universe

Word history: Neo-Latin, from Greek *kósmos* order, form, the world or universe as an ordered whole, ornament

cosset (kos-uht)
verb to pamper, or treat as a pet

Word history: compare Old English *cossetung* kissing

cossie (koz-ee)
noun a swimming costume

Word use: You can also use **cozzie**.

cost
noun **1** the price to be paid for something (***charge***, ***expense***, ***outlay***, ***rate***)
2 a loss or expense: *The battle was won at the* ***cost*** *of many lives.*
verb **3** to end in a particular loss: *It* ***cost*** *him his life.*
4 to estimate the price of

Word history: Middle English, from Old French, from Latin word meaning 'stand together'

cost / costed

These words are both possible past forms of the verb **cost**. But they do not mean the same thing.

We use the verb **cost** to give the price paid for something:

My book cost me $40.

His laziness has cost him the top job.

If you want the word to mean 'to estimate the price of something', then you use **costed**:

She has costed the job and decided that it is too expensive.

costly
adjective expensive or costing a great deal (***dear***, ***exorbitant***, ***pricey***)

Word use: The opposite of this is **cheap** or **inexpensive**.
Adjective forms: **costlier**, **costliest**
Word building: **costliness** *noun*

cost of living
noun the average retail prices of food, clothing, and other needs, paid by a person, family, etc., in order to live at their usual standard

cost price
noun **1** the price at which goods are bought for resale
2 the cost of production

costume
noun a set of clothes, especially for dressing up or for a particular purpose: *The actors had very simple* ***costumes****.* | *a swimming* ***costume***

Word history: French, from Italian word meaning 'habit', 'fashion', from Latin word meaning 'custom'

cosy
adjective **1** close and friendly: *There was a* ***cosy*** *atmosphere in the room.* (***comfortable***, ***inviting***, ***pleasant***, ***snug***, ***warm***)
noun **2** a knitted cover for keeping a teapot warm

Adjective forms: **cosier**, **cosiest**
Word building: **cosily** *adverb* **cosiness** *noun*
Word history: originally Scottish; probably from Scandinavian

cot
noun a child's bed with enclosed sides

Word history: Anglo-Indian, from Hindustani

cot death
noun → **sudden infant death syndrome**

coterie (koh-tuh-ree)
noun a close group of friends or people with common interests (***circle***, ***clique***, ***gang***)

Word history: from French word meaning 'set', 'association of people'

cottage
noun a small one-storey house

cottage cheese
noun a cheese made from curdled, skimmed milk

cottage industry
noun an industry done in the home of the worker, such as knitting, pottery or weaving

cotton
noun **1** a light material made from the soft white hairs covering the seeds of the cotton plant
2 a thread used for sewing

Word history: Middle English, from Old French, from Italian, from Arabic

cottonwool
noun cotton in a soft and fluffy state used especially for cleaning your skin and dressing wounds

couch
noun **1** a seat like a wide armchair for two or more people (***sofa***, ***lounge***, ***settee***)
2 a padded bed without sides, often used in a doctor's surgery
verb **3** to put into words: *The message is* ***couched*** *in very difficult language.*

Word history: Middle English, from Latin word meaning 'lay in its place'

cougar (kooh-guh)
noun → **puma**

Word history: French, from Neo-Latin, from South American Indian

cough (kof)
noun the noisy blast of air from your lungs which you get in some illnesses, or when something is stuck in, or irritates your throat

Word building: **cough** *verb*
Word history: Old English *cohhetan* cough

could (kood)
verb past tense of **can[1]**

Word history: Old English

could / might

Could can mean 'was able':

I could climb a coconut palm when I was younger.

Could is also used in polite questions and requests:

Could you help me please?

Could and **might** both mean that something is possible:

If the weather is fine, they could go to the beach.

If the weather is fine, they might go to the beach.

When the possibility is in the past, you could use **could have**, **might have** or even **may have**:

I might have been near Central Station when it happened.

I could have been near Central Station when it happened.

I may have been near Central Station when it happened.

couldn't
contraction of **could not**

Look up **contractions in grammar**.

could've
contraction of **could have**

When you say 'could've' it may sound like the words 'could of'. In fact it is short for 'could have', so **could've** is the correct way to write it, not **could of**. For more information, look up **of / have** and **contractions in grammar**.

coulomb (kooh-lom)
noun the derived SI unit of electric charge, defined as the quantity of electricity transferred by 1 ampere of electric current in 1 second

Word use: The symbol is **C**, without a full stop.
Word history: named after CA de *Coulomb*, 1736–1806, French physicist

council
noun **1** a group of people that meets regularly to discuss or decide certain things (***board***, ***caucus***, ***conference***, ***congress***, ***senate***)
2 the government of a small area such as a city or its suburbs: *She was elected to the shire* ***council***.

Word history: Middle English, from Old French, from Latin word meaning 'assembly'

councillor
noun a member of a council

counsel
noun **1** advice
2 a lawyer who is paid to give advice to someone in a court case (***advocate***, ***attorney***, ***barrister***, ***solicitor***)
verb **3** to advise: *to* ***counsel*** *against the trip*

Verb forms: I **counselled**, I have **counselled**, I am **counselling**
Word history: Middle English, from Old French, from Latin word meaning 'consultation', 'plan'

counsellor
noun an adviser, especially a psychologist (***guide***, ***guru***, ***mentor***, ***teacher***)

count[1]
verb **1** to add up: *He* ***counted*** *the trucks as they passed.* (***calculate***, ***number***, ***sum up***, ***tally***, ***total***)
2 to name the numbers: *She had to* ***count*** *up to ten slowly.*
3 to include: *That makes five of us,* ***counting*** *Alex.*
4 to matter: *What you want doesn't* ***count*** *in prison.*
phrase **5 count on,** to depend on: *The boss is* ***counting on*** *us being on time.* (***anticipate***, ***bargain for***, ***expect***, ***rely on***, ***trust in***)
6 count out, to disregard or leave out: *You can* ***count*** *me* ***out***.

Word building: **count** *noun*
Word history: Middle English, from Old French, from Latin word meaning 'calculate', 'reckon'

count[2]
noun a European noble

Word building: **countess** *feminine noun*
Word history: Anglo-French, from Latin word meaning 'companion'

countenance
noun your face or its expression: *a happy* ***countenance***

Word history: Middle English, from Old French word meaning 'bearing', from Medieval Latin word meaning 'demeanour', Latin word meaning 'restraint'

counter[1]
noun **1** a long shelf or bar where goods are sold or food is eaten
2 something used for keeping count, especially in a game
phrase **3 over the counter,** (in relation to medicines) without a prescription: *You can buy these tablets* ***over the counter***.
4 under the counter,
a not on show and available only when asked for
b secretly

Word history: Middle English, from Anglo-French word meaning 'counting house', 'counting table', from Old French word meaning 'count'

counter[2]
adverb **1** in the opposite direction
verb **2** to move against: *He* ***countered*** *their plan with strong arguments.* (***defy***, ***obstruct***, ***oppose***, ***resist***, ***withstand***)
adjective **3** opposite or opposed: *a* ***counter*** *attack*

counteract (kown-tuhr-akt)
verb to act against, or prevent the effect of by opposite action

Word building: **counteraction** *noun*
counteractive *adjective*

counterbalance
noun **1** a weight balancing another weight
verb **2** to weigh or act against with equal force

counterfeit (kown-tuh-fuht, kown-tuh-feet)
adjective **1** made to imitate or look like, especially to deceive: ***counterfeit*** *money* (***bogus***, ***fake***, ***false***, ***phoney***, ***sham***)
noun **2** an imitation: *That painting is a* ***counterfeit***.

Word building: **counterfeit** *verb*
Word history: Middle English from Old French word meaning 'imitated', from *contre* against + *faire* do (from Latin)

counterintuitive
adjective contrary to what one would normally think or expect: *It seems* ***counterintuitive*** *but many experienced sailors head for the open sea when the weather turns bad.*

Word building: **counterintuitively** *adverb*
counterintuitiveness *noun*

countermand
verb **1** to cancel or change (an order, etc.), especially by issuing a new command: *to* ***countermand*** *the instructions given yesterday*
noun **2** a command or order cancelling an earlier one

Word history: Middle English, from Old French *contre* + *mander* command, (from Latin word meaning 'enjoin')

counterpart
noun one of two people or things which matches or looks like the other

counterpoint
noun Music **1** the art of combining different tunes in harmony
2 a melody composed to be combined with another melody

Word history: French *contrepoint*, from Medieval Latin (*cantus*) *contrā punctus* (song) pointed against

countersign
noun **1** *Military* a password or signal given in order to pass a guard
verb **2** to sign in addition to another signature, especially in confirmation: *to **countersign** a document*

Word building: **countersignature** *noun*
Word history: Old French, from Italian

counterterrorism
noun measures taken by a government to prevent or control terrorism, etc., involving activities like intelligence gathering, police operations, maintenance of security provisions, etc.

Word building: **counterterrorist** *noun* **counterterrorist** *adjective*

countless
adjective too many to count (***endless***, ***infinite***, ***myriad***, ***umpteen***, ***untold***)

count noun
noun a noun that refers to things that can be counted: *Dog, table and letter are **count nouns**.*

For more information, look up **nouns: count nouns.**

country
noun **1** an area of land separated from other areas, usually with its own government: *Europe is divided into different **countries**.* (***nation***, ***state***, ***territory***)
2 the land where someone is born
3 the land beyond the towns and cities
4 (as used by Indigenous Australians) traditional land with its embedded cultural values relating to the Dreaming: *the importance of **country***

Noun forms: The plural is **countries.**
Word history: Middle English, from Old French, from Late Latin word meaning 'what lies opposite', from Latin

country and western
noun a type of music that first came from the southern and western areas of the US and which consists of songs about country life, accompanied by a stringed instrument such as a guitar or fiddle

Word use: You can also use **country music**.

countryside
noun a country area (***farmland***, ***hinterland***, ***outback***, ***the bush***, ***the sticks***)

county
noun a large area within a state, bigger than a shire

Noun forms: The plural is **counties.**
Word history: Middle English, from Old French

coup (kooh)
noun a plan carried out suddenly and successfully: *The generals have been in power since the army **coup**.* (***rebellion***, ***revolt***, ***revolution***, ***strike***, ***uprising***)

Word history: French, from Late Latin word meaning 'blow', from Greek

coup d'état (kooh day-tah)
noun a sudden takeover of government, especially illegally or by force

Word history: from French word meaning 'stroke of state'

coupe[1] (koo-pay)
noun a fruit dessert served in a shallow glass or bowl

Word history: French, from Old French, from Late Latin *cuppa* cup

coupe[2] (koohp)
noun a single defined area of forest, usually less than 50 hectares, from which trees are, or will be, harvested for wooden boards or woodchips

coupé (kooh-pay)
noun **1** a two-door car often with front seats only
2 a short, four-wheeled, closed, horse-drawn carriage

Word history: from French word meaning 'cut'

couple (kup-uhl)
noun **1** two people, especially if married: *the **couple** next door*
2 any two things: *a **couple** of apples*
verb **3** to join or link together: *The carriages had to be **coupled** before the train could leave.* (***combine***, ***connect***, ***hitch***, ***knit***, ***unite***)

Word building: **coupling** *noun*
Word history: Middle English, from Latin word meaning 'band', 'bond'

couplet (kup-luht)
noun a pair of lines of poetry which rhyme

Word history: from French word meaning 'little couple'

coupon (kooh-pon)
noun **1** a ticket or card which you can exchange for goods or money
2 a form which must be filled in to order goods, or enter a competition

Word history: French

courage (ku-rij)
noun the strength to do or face something you find frightening: *She hasn't the **courage** to learn to drive.* (***bravery***, ***daring***, ***nerve***, ***valour***)

Word history: Middle English, from Old French word meaning 'heart', from Latin *cor*

courageous
adjective brave: *a **courageous** warrior* (***bold***, ***fearless***, ***heroic***, ***valiant***)

courgette (kaw-zhet)
noun → **zucchini**

Word history: French

courier (koo-ree-uh)
noun **1** someone who carries messages or parcels for others (***envoy***, ***herald***, ***mail deliverer***, ***messenger***)
2 someone who looks after a group of tourists and their travel arrangements

Word history: French, from Italian word meaning 'runner', from Latin word meaning 'run'

course (kaws)
noun **1** one stage of a meal: *We had meat and potatoes for the main **course**.*
2 a series, especially of lessons: *I'm doing a **course** of exercises.* (***curriculum***, ***program***)
3 the ground or water on which a race takes place
4 movement or progress: *the ship's **course** | in the **course** of the year* (***passage***, ***path***, ***route***, ***track***)
verb **5** to race
phrase **6 in due course**, at the right time
7 of course, certainly: ***Of course** you will come.*

Word history: French

course / coarse

Don't confuse **course** with **coarse**, which is an adjective.

We call someone **coarse** if their behaviour is rude and offensive.

We call a substance **coarse** if it has large rather than fine grains, as in *coarse sand.*

court (kawt)
noun **1** the hard ground where games such as tennis and basketball are played
2 the palace of a king or queen and the people who live or work there
3 the place where legal cases and trials are heard
4 a courtyard or space enclosed by walls
verb **5** *Old-fashioned* to try to win love or favour: *My grandfather **courted** my grandmother for a year before they became engaged.* (***pay suit to***, ***woo***)

Word history: Middle English, from Old French, from Latin word meaning 'enclosure'

court / caught

Don't confuse **court** with **caught**, which is the past form of the verb **catch**:

He threw the ball and I caught it.

courteous (<u>ker</u>-tee-uhs)
adjective well-mannered or polite: *a **courteous** boy | a **courteous** reply* (***chivalrous***, ***gallant***, ***gracious***)

Word use: The opposite of this is **rude**.
Word building: **courteously** *adverb*
Word history: Middle English, from Old French word meaning 'court'

courtesan (<u>kaw</u>-tuh-zan)
noun **1** a mistress of a king, nobleman, etc.
2 a prostitute

Word history: French, from Italian word meaning 'woman of the court'

courtesy (<u>ker</u>-tuh-see)
noun **1** politeness and good manners
2 permission: *The poems are printed by **courtesy** of the author.*

Word use: The opposite of definition 1 is **rudeness.**
Word history: Middle English, from Old French word meaning 'courteous'

courtier
noun someone who serves the king or queen at court

courtly
adjective polite: ***courtly** manners*

Adjective forms: **courtlier**, **courtliest**
Word building: **courtliness** *noun*

court martial
noun a court of officers which tries anyone in the armed forces who breaks the military law

Noun forms: The plural is **courts martial** or **court martials.**
Word building: **court-martial** *verb* (**court-martialled, court-martialling**)

courtroom
noun a room in a court in which a legal trial is held

courtship (<u>kawt</u>-ship)
noun the act or period of courting

courtyard
noun an area enclosed by walls or buildings

couscous (<u>koos</u>-koos)
noun small grains comprising largely semolina but with some flour and salt added

cousin (<u>kuz</u>-uhn)
noun a son or daughter of your uncle or aunt

Word history: French, from Latin word meaning 'mother's sister's child'

couturier (kooh-<u>tooh</u>-ree-uh)
noun a person who designs, makes and sells high-fashion clothes

Word building: **couturière** *feminine noun*
Word history: from French word meaning 'sewing'

cove
noun a small bay or inlet (***bight***, ***estuary***, ***gulf***)

Word history: Old English *cofa* chamber

coven (<u>kuv</u>-uhn)
noun a gathering of witches

Word history: variant of *convent*

covenant
noun a solemn promise: *The **covenant** between the nations' leaders led to a peace treaty.*

Word history: Middle English, from Old French, from Latin word meaning 'agree'

cover
verb **1** to hide: *She **covered** her face with her hands.* (***conceal***, ***screen***)
2 to lie over or be spread over: *A quilt **covered** the bed.* (***blanket***, ***envelop***, ***overlay***, ***shroud***)
3 to protect: *to be **covered** by insurance*
4 to include: *This list **covers** everything we need.* (***comprise***, ***embrace***, ***incorporate***, ***involve***)
5 to be enough to pay for: *Ten dollars should **cover** expenses.*
6 to get news of: *Three reporters were **covering** the fire.*
7 to travel over: *We **covered** a long distance today.*
noun **8** something which covers: *a book **cover***
9 shelter: *The rabbit ran for **cover** into its burrow.*
phrase **10 break cover**, to come out, especially suddenly, from hiding
11 take cover, to hide or shelter yourself
12 under cover, secret or secretly: *to go on a mission **under cover***

Word building: **covering** *noun*
Word history: Middle English, from Old French, from Latin word meaning 'cover over'

coverage
noun **1** the reporting of an event or a series of events by journalists for the media: *the cricket **coverage** on television*
2 the total amount of risk, in the event of fire or an accident, covered by an insurance policy

cover charge
noun an extra amount added to a charge for food and drink by a restaurant, nightclub, etc.

cover note
noun a document providing temporary insurance until a policy is prepared

covert (kuv-uht, koh-vert)
adjective **1** covered, or sheltered
2 hidden, or secret
noun **3** a shelter, or hiding place
Word history: Middle English, from Old French word meaning 'covered'

covet (kuv-uht)
verb to want very much to have: *John* ***covets*** *that car of yours.* (***crave***, ***desire***, ***fancy***, ***long for***, ***yearn for***)
Word history: Middle English, from Latin word meaning 'desire'

covetous
adjective having a strong desire to possess something, especially something that doesn't belong to you (***acquisitive***, ***envious***, ***greedy***, ***jealous***, ***possessive***)

cow
noun the female of cattle and of some other large animals, such as the whale
Word history: Old English *cu*

coward
noun someone who acts badly or weakly out of fear (***chicken***, ***sissy***, ***sook***)
Word building: **cowardice** *noun* **cowardly** *adverb*
Word history: Middle English, from Old French word meaning 'tail', from Latin, through comparison with an animal with its 'tail' between its legs

cowboy
noun a man who looks after cattle in the American west

cower
verb to draw away in fear: *The puppy was* ***cowering*** *under a table.* (***cringe***, ***flinch***, ***quail***, ***shrink***, ***tremble***)
Word history: Middle English, from Scandinavian

cowry
noun the shell of various sea snails, used as money or ornament
Noun forms: The plural is **cowries**.
Word use: You can also use **cowrie**.
Word history: Hindustani *kaurī*

coxcomb (koks-kohm)
noun **1** → **cockscomb**
2 a conceited dandy

coxswain (kok-suhn)
noun the person who steers a boat, especially in rowing
Word use: The short form is **cox**.
Word history: Middle English *cock* ship's boat + *swain* servant

coy
adjective shy, or pretending to be shy (***bashful***, ***demure***, ***diffident***, ***modest***, ***reticent***)
Word building: **coyly** *adverb* **coyness** *noun*
Word history: Middle English, from French, from Latin word meaning 'at rest'

coyote (koy-oh-tee)
noun a North American wild dog which howls at night
Word history: Mexican Spanish, from South American Indian

crab
noun a hard-shelled sea animal with five pairs of legs, the last two with pincers, around a flattish body
Word history: Old English *crabba*

crack
verb **1** to split, often with a sharp noise: *The glass jug* ***cracked****.*
2 to flick with a loud noise: *The drover* ***cracked*** *the whip.*
3 to give up: *At first he would not confess but finally he* ***cracked****.*
4 to break into: *The robbers* ***cracked*** *the safe.*
5 to find the answer to: *to* ***crack*** *a code*
6 to tell: *to* ***crack*** *a joke*
noun **7** a sudden sharp noise
8 the line of a split: ***Cracks*** *appeared but the bowl didn't break.* (***chink***, ***crevice***, ***fissure***, ***fracture***, ***rift***)
9 a hard blow: *He gave himself a* ***crack*** *with the hammer.*
adjective **10** first-rate: *a* ***crack*** *shot at darts*
phrase **11 crack down on**, *Colloquial* to become strict with: *to* ***crack down on*** *people who break school rules*
12 crack up, *Colloquial*
a to break down, especially mentally: *She* ***cracked up*** *when she failed her exams.*
b to laugh uncontrollably: *We* ***cracked up*** *when we heard the joke.*
13 get cracking, *Colloquial* to start or get going: *Let's* ***get cracking*** *or we'll never finish.*
14 not what (or **as good as**) **it's cracked up to be**, *Colloquial* not as good as it has been described or praised as being: *I know she is an international star but her singing is* ***not what it's cracked up to be****.*
Word building: **cracked** *adjective*
Word history: Old English *cracian* resound

cracker
noun **1** a thin, crisp, unsweetened biscuit
2 a firework
3 a twisted roll of paper with a surprise inside, which explodes when you pull it (***bonbon***)

crackle
verb to make a crunching sound: *The dry leaves* ***crackled*** *underfoot.*
Word building: **crackle** *noun*
Word history: from *crack*

crackling
noun crisp, cooked pork skin

cradle
noun **1** a baby's small bed, usually on rockers
2 a frame which supports or protects: *The window cleaners were in a* ***cradle*** *halfway up a building.*
3 a box on rockers used to separate gold dust from sand and dirt
verb **4** to hold or rock, as if in a cradle (***cuddle***, ***embrace***, ***hug***, ***nurse***)
Word history: Old English *cradol*

craft
noun **1** skilfulness (***art***, ***artistry***, ***technique***)
2 cunning
3 a job or trade needing special skill with your hands
4 a boat or an aircraft
verb **5** to make individually
Noun forms: The plural for definition 4 is **craft**.
Word history: Old English *cræft*

crafty
adjective clever in a tricky or cunning way (***artful***, ***devious***, ***dishonest***, ***sly***, ***wily***)
Adjective forms: **craftier**, **craftiest**
Word building: **craftily** *adverb* **craftiness** *noun*

crag
noun a steep rock sticking up from a cliff or mountain
Word building: **craggy** *adjective* (**craggier**, **craggiest**)
Word history: Middle English, from Celtic

cram
verb **1** to stuff tightly: *Sue **crammed** the papers under her bed.*
2 to fill very full, especially with food
Verb forms: I **crammed**, I have **crammed**, I am **cramming**
Word history: Old English *crammian*, from *crimman* insert

cramp[1]
noun a sudden painful tightening of a muscle in your body: *a stomach **cramp*** (***spasm***, ***stitch***, ***twinge***)
Word history: Middle English, from Middle Dutch

cramp[2]
noun **1** a metal bar with bent ends, for holding together wood, stone, etc.
verb **2** to confine or restrict
phrase **3 cramp someone's style**, *Colloquial* to prevent someone from showing their ability, etc.
Word history: from Middle Dutch word meaning 'hook', 'clamp'

crane
noun **1** a large bird with long legs, neck and bill, which feeds in shallow water
2 a machine with a long moving arm, which can lift and move heavy weights around
verb **3** to stretch in order to see: *to **crane** your neck*
Word history: Old English *cran*

cranium (kray-nee-uhm)
noun **1** the skull of a vertebrate
2 the part of the skull which encloses the brain
Noun forms: The plural is **crania** (kray-nee-uh).
Word building: **cranial** *adjective*
Word history: Medieval Latin, from Greek

crank
noun **1** a bar for winding or levering: *He used the **crank** to jack up his car.*
2 an odd person
Word history: Old English *cranc*, in *crancstæf* weaving implement, crank

crankshaft
noun a shaft driving or driven by a crank, especially the main shaft of an engine carrying cranks to which the connecting rods are joined

cranky
adjective bad-tempered or irritable (***angry***, ***annoyed***, ***dissatisfied***, ***grumpy***, ***vexed***)
Adjective forms: **crankier**, **crankiest**
Word building: **crankily** *adverb* **crankiness** *noun*

cranny
noun a narrow opening, especially in rock
Noun forms: The plural is **crannies**.
Word history: Middle English, from French word meaning 'fissure' (from *crener* cut away, from Latin)

crash
verb **1** to run into or hit noisily: *The car **crashed** into the tree.*
2 to fall and smash: *The aeroplane **crashed**.*
noun **3** the noise of breaking or hitting
4 an accident or collision
Word history: Middle English

crass (kras)
adjective **1** stupid, or gross: ***crass** ignorance*
2 coarse, or rude
Word history: from Latin word meaning 'solid', 'thick', 'dense', 'fat'

crate
noun a large wooden box
Word history: from Latin word meaning 'wicker-work'

crater
noun **1** the cup-shaped opening at the top of a volcano
2 a round hole in the ground, like one made by a meteorite or a bomb
Word history: Latin, from Greek word originally meaning 'a bowl for mixing wine and water'

cravat (kruh-vat)
noun a man's scarf, loosely tied at the throat
Word history: French *cravate*; so called because adopted from the Croats (French *Cravates*)

crave
verb to want desperately: *The thirsty man **craved** a drink. | I **crave** one favour.* (***covet***, ***desire***, ***long for***, ***yearn for***)
Word building: **craving** *noun*
Word history: Old English *crafian*

craven (kray-vuhn)
adjective Old-fashioned cowardly: *a **craven** fool*
Word history: Middle English, from Old French, blend of *crav(anté)* overthrown and *(recre)ant* recreant

crawl
verb **1** to go slowly, especially on hands and knees
2 to flatter or be nice to someone to gain an advantage: *He is **crawling** to the teacher so that he'll be chosen for the team.*
noun **3** a crawling movement
4 → **freestyle** (definition 1)
Word building: **crawler** *noun*
Word history: Middle English, from Scandinavian

crayfish
noun a hard-shelled, freshwater animal which looks like a small lobster: *The yabby is a small Australian **crayfish**.*

Noun forms: The plural is **crayfishes** or **crayfish**.
Word history: Middle English *crevice*, from Old French, from Old High German word meaning 'crab'

crayon
noun a stick of coloured wax, chalk, etc., used for drawing and colouring

Word history: French, from Latin word meaning 'chalk'

craze
verb **1** to madden: *The wind **crazed** the horses.*
noun **2** a short-lived fashion: *a **craze** for yoyos* (***fad***, ***rage***, ***trend***, ***vogue***)

Word history: Middle English *crase(n)* break, from Scandinavian

crazy
adjective **1** mad or insane (***loony***, ***maniacal***, ***nutty***, ***silly***)
2 odd or irregular: ***crazy** paving*

Adjective forms: **crazier**, **craziest**
Word building: **crazily** *adverb* **craziness** *noun*

creak
verb to make a squeaking noise: *The floor boards **creaked**.*

Word building: **creaky** *adjective* (**creakier**, **creakiest**)
Word history: Middle English *creken*, compare Old English crācettan *croak*

creak / creek
Don't confuse **creak** with **creek**, which is a small stream.

cream
noun **1** the fatty part of milk, which rises to the surface
2 anything which is thick and smooth: *face **cream***
3 the top or best part: *Only the **cream** of athletes go to the Olympic Games.*
4 a yellowish white colour
adjective **5** having a cream colour
verb **6** to make smooth like cream: *to **cream** the butter and sugar*

Word building: **creamy** *adjective* (**creamier**, **creamiest**)
Word history: Middle English, from French, from Late Latin word meaning 'chrism'

cream of tartar
noun an acid powder used in baking

crease
noun **1** a sharp line or fold especially in material or paper
verb **2** to fold or wrinkle: *to **crease** paper* | *to **crease** your brows*

Word building: **creased** *adjective*

create (kree-<u>ayt</u>)
verb **1** to make or invent (***compose***, ***concoct***, ***design***, ***develop***, ***improvise***)
2 to make into: *He was **created** a knight.*

Word building: **creativity** *noun* **creator** *noun*
Word history: from Latin word meaning 'brought into being'

creation (kree-<u>ay</u>-shuhn)
noun **1** something which has been made or invented
2 the act of creating

creative
adjective good at making or inventing things

creature (<u>kree</u>-chuh)
noun any living thing: *Noah took two of every **creature** onto his ark.*

Word history: Middle English, from Old French, from Late Latin word meaning 'a thing created'

creche (kraysh, kresh)
noun a nursery for babies and young children

Word history: French, from Old High German word meaning 'crib'

cred
noun Colloquial respect or credibility: *street **cred*** | *He has a lot of **cred** with the students.*

Word history: short form of *credibility*

credence (<u>kree</u>-dns)
noun belief: *to give **credence** to a statement*

Word history: Middle English, from Medieval Latin word meaning 'belief', from Latin word meaning 'believing'

credential (kruh-<u>den</u>-shuhl)
noun **1** something which gives the right to belief or trust
2 credentials, a letter or certificate showing the holder's right to a position of trust or authority

Word history: Medieval Latin *crēdentia* belief + *-al*

credible (<u>kred</u>-uh-buhl)
adjective **1** believable (***conceivable***, ***likely***, ***plausible***, ***possible***, ***probable***)
2 worthy of belief or trust

Word building: **credibility** *noun* **credibleness** *noun*
Word history: Middle English, from Latin

credit
noun **1** praise or approval: *Give her **credit** for trying.*
2 trust or belief: *I don't put much **credit** in his promise to pay.*
3 (in some educational institutions) a result in an examination which shows performance higher than that necessary to pass
4 the amount someone is allowed to spend or borrow: *How much **credit** do I have?*
5 the amount of money in your favour in an account
6 *Bookkeeping*
a an entry of payments or value received, in an account
b the right-hand side of an account, where credit entries are made
verb **7** to believe or accept: *Hal was so surprised he couldn't **credit** what he heard.*
phrase **8 on credit**, with agreement to pay later

Verb forms: I **credited**, I have **credited**, I am **crediting**
Word use: Compare definition 5 with **debit**. | Compare definition 8 with **cash**.
Word history: French, from Italian, from Latin word meaning 'believed'

creditable
adjective something which brings praise: *a **creditable** performance in gymnastics*

credit card
noun a card enabling the holder to obtain goods and services on credit

credit note
noun a document issued to a customer, stating that some previous charge has been wholly or partly cancelled, as for example when goods are returned, and the customer receives credit, but not cash, to the same value as the cost of those goods

creditor
noun someone you owe money to

Word use: Compare this with **debtor**.

credit union
noun a financial organisation for receiving and lending money, usually formed by the workers in some industry or at a place where many people are employed

credulous (kred-zhuh-luhs)
adjective ready to believe things, especially without good reasons

Word building: **credulity** *noun* **credulousness** *noun*
Word history: from Latin word meaning 'apt to believe'

creed
noun a statement of belief

Word history: Old English *crēda*, from Latin *crēdo* I believe

creek
noun a small stream

Word history: Middle English, from Scandinavian

creek / creak

Don't confuse **creek** with **creak**, which is a sharp, rough or squeaking sound. To **creak** is to make this sound.

creep
verb **1** to go very slowly and quietly: *She **crept** out of the house so as not to wake anyone.*
2 to crawl along the ground
noun **3** *Colloquial* an unpleasant person: *He's a real **creep**.*
phrase **4 the creeps**, a feeling of fear or disgust

Verb forms: I **crept**, I have **crept**, I am **creeping**
Word history: Old English *crēopan*

creeper
noun a plant which climbs walls or grows along the ground

creepy
adjective frightening or unpleasant (***forbidding***, ***grim***, ***horrible***, ***scary***, ***weird***)

Adjective forms: **creepier**, **creepiest**
Word building: **creepiness** *noun*

cremate
verb to burn to ashes: *The dead man had asked for his body to be **cremated**.*

Word building: **cremation** *noun*
Word history: from Latin word meaning 'consumed by fire'

crematorium (krem-uh-taw-ree-uhm)
noun the place where bodies are cremated

crenellated (kren-uh-lay-tuhd)
adjective having square indentations or battlements, such as some castles have

Word building: **crenellation** *noun*
Word history: from French word meaning 'little notch'

creole (kree-ohl)
noun **1** a pidgin which has become the first language of a group of people
adjective **2** a style of cooking associated with New Orleans, often using tomatoes, onions, capsicum and rice

Word history: French, from Spanish word meaning 'native to the locality', from Portuguese word meaning 'bring up', from Latin word meaning 'create'

crepe (krayp)
noun **1** a light crinkled material made of cotton or silk
2 a finely wrinkled paper
3 a thin pancake

Word history: French, from Latin word meaning 'curled'

crept
verb past tense and past participle of **creep**

crescendo (kruh-shen-doh)
adverb increasingly loud or forceful

Word use: This is an instruction in music.
Word history: Italian word meaning 'increasing', from Latin

crescent (kres-uhnt, krez-uhnt)
noun **1** the shape of the moon in its first or last quarter
2 anything of a similar shape, especially a street

Word history: from Latin word meaning 'increasing'

cress
noun a fast-growing herb whose leaves are used in salads

Word history: Old English *cresse*

crest
noun **1** the feathers or growth on the top of the heads of some birds
2 the very top of anything: *on the **crest** of success* (***apex***, ***peak***, ***pinnacle***, ***summit***)
3 part of a coat of arms which is used as a badge: *Their blazer pockets were embroidered with the school **crest**.*
verb **4** to reach the top of: *to **crest** a wave*

Word use: The opposite of definition 2 is **base**.
Word building: **crested** *adjective*
Word history: Middle English, from Old French, from Latin word meaning 'tuft'

crestfallen
adjective disappointed or sad: *He looks quite **crestfallen** at missing the train.*

cretin (kret-uhn)
noun Colloquial a very stupid person

Word building: **cretinous** *adjective*
Word history: from *cretin* a person suffering from a disease causing dwarfism and idiocy; French, from dialectal *crestin*, from Latin *Christiānus* Christian

crevasse (kruh-vas)
noun a deep crack in a glacier or river of ice

Word history: French

crevice (krev-uhs)
noun a crack forming an opening: *a **crevice** in a rock* (***chink***, ***cleft***, ***fissure***, ***rift***, ***split***)

Word history: Middle English, from Old French word meaning 'burst', from Latin word meaning 'crack'

crew
noun **1** the group of people who work on a ship or aeroplane
verb **2** to provide with a crew: *to **crew** a boat*

Word history: Middle English, from Old Northern French word meaning 'increase', from Latin word meaning 'grow'

crew cut
noun a very short haircut

crib
noun **1** a baby's cot
2 a box or rack used to hold food for cattle and horses
3 *Australian*, *NZ* a meal, packed in a container and taken to work by a miner, construction worker, etc.

Word history: Old English *crib(b)*

crick
noun **1** a muscle cramp, especially in your neck or back
verb **2** to cause a crick in: *I've **cricked** my neck.*

cricket[1]
noun a leaping insect, similar to a grasshopper, which makes a loud noise by rubbing its wings on its abdomen

Word history: Middle English, from Old French *criquet*; imitative

cricket[2]
noun a team game played with ball, bat and wickets

Word history: Old French *criquet* stick

crime
noun **1** an act which breaks the law
2 the breaking of laws: ***Crime** is a serious problem in most cities.*

Word history: Middle English, from Latin word meaning 'offence'

criminal
adjective **1** having to do with crime: ***criminal** activities* (***dishonest***, ***felonious***, ***fraudulent***, ***illegal***, ***illicit***)
noun **2** someone who is guilty of a crime (***bandit***, ***crook***, ***felon***, ***offender***, ***outlaw***)

Word history: Latin

criminalise
verb to make into a criminal offence: *to **criminalise** racism*

Word use: You can also use **criminalize**.
Word building: **criminalisation** *noun*

criminology (krim-uh-nol-uh-jee)
noun the science dealing with the causes of crime and the treatment of criminals

Word building: **criminologist** *noun*
Word history: Latin *crīmen* crime + *-o-* + *-logy*

crimp
verb to make curly: *to **crimp** hair*

Word history: Old English *gecrympan* curl (from *crump* crooked)

crimson
adjective of a deep, purplish-red colour

Word building: **crimson** *noun*
Word history: Middle English, from Italian or from Spanish, both from Arabic *qirmiz* the name of the insect whose dried body was ground up to make the deep red dye

cringe
verb to bend or bow down in fear (***cower***, ***flinch***, ***quail***, ***shrink***)

Word history: Old English *cringan* yield, fall (in battle)

crinkle
verb to wrinkle or crease: *His face **crinkled** with laughter.*

Word building: **crinkle** *noun*
Word history: Old English *crincan* bend, yield

crinoline (krin-uh-luhn)
noun **1** a petticoat of stiff material, worn by women under a full skirt, especially in the 19th century
2 a hoop skirt

Word history: French, from Italian

cripple
noun **1** someone who has lost the use of one or more limbs
verb **2** to damage or make lame (***disable***, ***incapacitate***, ***paralyse***, ***weaken***)

Word history: Old English *crypel*; akin to *creep*

crisis (kruy-suhs)
noun **1** a time of danger or trouble
2 a turning point, especially in the course of an illness

Noun forms: The plural is **crises** (kruy-*seez*).
Word history: Latin, from Greek word meaning 'decision'

crisp
adjective **1** hard, dry and easily broken: ***crisp** biscuits* (***brittle***, ***crunchy***)
2 cool, dry and fresh: ***crisp** air* (***chilly***, ***nippy***)
3 clean and neat: *a **crisp** uniform*
noun **4** → **chip** (definition 3)

Word building: **crispy** *adjective* (**crispier**, **crispiest**)
crispness *noun*
Word history: Old English, from Latin word meaning 'curled'

criteria (kru-tear-ree-uh)
noun the plural of **criterion**

criterion (kruy-tear-ree-uhn)
noun a standard or rule for testing something

Noun forms: The plural is **criteria**.
Word history: Greek *kritērion* test, standard

critic
noun **1** someone who is a judge of quality or excellence: *The newspaper's literary* ***critic*** *praised the author's latest novel.*
2 someone who finds fault

Word history: Latin, from Greek word meaning 'skilled in judging'

critical
adjective **1** likely to find fault
2 having to do with a crisis: *He kept calm at the* ***critical*** *moment.* (***crucial***, ***deciding***, ***key***, ***momentous***, ***significant***)

critically
adverb dangerously: ***critically*** *ill*

critically endangered species
noun a threatened species that is facing an extremely high risk of extinction in the wild in the immediate future

Word use: Compare this with **endangered species** and **vulnerable species**.

criticise (krit-uh-suyz)
verb to find fault with: *to* ***criticise*** *someone's manners*

Word use: You can also use **criticize**.
Word building: **criticism** *noun*

critique (kruh-teek, kri-teek)
noun **1** an article or essay criticising something
2 the art or practice of criticism

Word history: French, from Greek word meaning 'the critical art'

croak
verb to make a low hoarse sound: *The frogs* ***croaked*** *in the pond.*

Word building: **croaky** *adjective* (**croakier**, **croakiest**)
Word history: Old English *crācettan*

crochet (kroh-shuh, kroh-shay)
verb to make a lace-like material using a special hook and yarn

Verb forms: I **crocheted**, I have **crocheted**, I am **crocheting**
Word building: **crochet** *noun*
Word history: French word meaning 'hooked implement', from Old French word meaning 'little hook'

crock[1]
noun an earthenware pot or jar

Word history: Old English *croc(c)*, *crocca* pot

crock[2]
noun **1** an old worn-out horse or ewe
2 *Colloquial* a broken-down old person

Word history: related to *crack* verb

crockery
noun cups, plates, dishes and similar articles made of china or pottery (***china***)

crocodile
noun a large, lizard-like reptile found living in the waters of tropical countries

Word history: Latin, from Greek word meaning 'lizard'

croissant (krwus-õ)
noun a roll of yeast dough or puff pastry, shaped into a crescent and baked

crone (krohn)
noun an old woman

Word history: Middle Dutch *croonje*, from Old North French *carogne* carcass

crony (kroh-nee)
noun a close friend

Noun forms: The plural is **cronies**.
Word history: perhaps from Greek word meaning 'longlasting', from *chrónos* time

cronyism (kroh-nee-iz-uhm)
noun unfair preference shown by someone for their friends, especially in making political appointments

crook
noun **1** a bent or curved part: *the* ***crook*** *of your elbow*
2 a stick with a bend or curve at one end: *a shepherd's* ***crook***
3 *Colloquial* a dishonest person (***cheat***, ***criminal***, ***fraud***, ***knave***, ***rogue***)
adjective Australian, NZ **4** *Colloquial* sick: *I feel* ***crook***. (***ailing***, ***ill***, ***indisposed***, ***off-colour***, ***unwell***)
5 unpleasant: *Scrubbing floors is a* ***crook*** *job.*
verb **6** to bend or curve: *to* ***crook*** *your finger*

Word history: Middle English, from Scandinavian; definition 5 from English dialect

crooked (krook-uhd)
adjective **1** bent: *a* ***crooked*** *stick* (***buckled***, ***distorted***, ***twisted***, ***warped***)
2 *Colloquial* dishonest: ***crooked*** *dealings* (***corrupt***, ***deceitful***, ***illegal***, ***shady***, ***shifty***)

Word history: Old English *gecrōcod*

croon
verb to sing or hum in a soft or sentimental way

Word building: **crooner** *noun*
Word history: Middle English, from Middle Dutch word meaning 'murmur'

crop
noun **1** products grown in the ground: *a good wheat* ***crop*** | *a* ***crop*** *of apples*
2 a short whip used by horse riders
verb **3** to cut short: *to* ***crop*** *a horse's tail*
phrase **4 crop up**, to come as a surprise: *A problem* ***cropped up***.

Verb forms: I **cropped**, I have **cropped**, I am **cropping**
Word history: Old English

cropper (krop-uh)
noun **1** someone or something that crops
2 a plant which yields a crop: *This variety is a good* ***cropper***.
phrase **3 come a cropper**, *Colloquial*
a to fall heavily
b to fail, or to meet with an accident

crop rotation
noun the system of growing different crops one after the other in the same piece of ground, in order to keep the soil fertile

croquet (kroh-kay, kroh-kee)
noun a game played by hitting wooden balls with mallets through metal arches set in a lawn

Word history: from French dialect word meaning 'hockey stick'

cross
noun **1** anything in the shape made by two lines going through each other such as '+' or '×'
2 the result of mixing breeds of animals or plants: *My dog is a* ***cross*** *between a terrier and a beagle.*
verb **3** to draw a line across: *to* ***cross*** *a cheque*
4 to form a cross with: ***cross*** *your fingers* (***crisscross, intersect***)
5 to pass in the way of: *He* ***crossed*** *my path.*
6 to go from one side of to another: *The bridge* ***crosses*** *the river.* (***bridge, ford, span, traverse***)
adjective **7** lying or passing across: *a* ***cross*** *wind*
8 annoyed: *My aunt was* ***cross*** *with me.* (***angry, cranky, dissatisfied, grumpy, vexed***)
phrase **9 cross out**, to draw a line through
10 cross the floor, in parliament, to vote with the opposing political party
11 cross your mind, to come as an idea, or occur to you

Word history: Old English *cros*, from Old Irish, from Latin *crux*

cross-country
noun a running race which is run across fields, parks etc., and not on a prepared track

cross-examine
verb to question in order to check the truth of something already stated

cross-eyed (kros-uyd)
adjective having both eyes turned towards your nose

cross-fire
noun **1** *Military* a line of fire from two or more positions, crossing one another
2 a lively exchange of words or opinions

crosshatch
verb Art to shade with two or more groups of parallel lines that cross over each other

Word building: **crosshatching** *noun*

crossing
noun **1** a moving across: *The first* ***crossing*** *of the Blue Mountains by Europeans took place in 1813.*
2 a place where a road, river or railway line can be crossed

cross-purpose
noun **1** an opposing or contrary purpose
phrase **2 be at cross-purposes**, to misunderstand each other

cross-section
noun **1** a cutting across anything, especially at right angles to its length
2 a piece cut off in this way
3 a drawing of the surface that would be shown by this cutting: *a* ***cross-section*** *of the leg showing skin, nerves, muscles and bone*
4 a typical selection, or a sample showing all characteristic parts: *a* ***cross-section*** *of Australian opinion*

Word building: **cross-section** *verb* **cross-sectional** *adjective*

crossword
noun a puzzle in which words are to be worked out from clues and fitted, running across or down, into an arrangement of numbered squares

Word use: You can also use **crossword puzzle**.

crotch
noun a forked piece, or part, such as of the human body or a pair of trousers where the two legs join

Word building: **crotched** *adjective*
Word history: variant of *crutch*

crotchet (krot-chuht)
noun a musical note equal to the time of one beat

Word history: Middle English, from Old French

crotchety
adjective bad-tempered or irritable (***angry, cantankerous, cross, snappy, touchy***)

crouch
verb to bend your knees and lean forward: *I* ***crouched*** *behind the shrub to hide myself.*

Word building: **crouch** *noun*
Word history: Middle English, from Old French word meaning 'become bent', from *croche* hook

croupier (krooh-pee-uh)
noun someone who takes and pays out the money at a gambling table

Word history: French; originally, someone who rides behind on the croup of another's horse

crow[1]
noun a bird with shiny black plumage and a harsh-sounding call

Word history: Old English *crawe*

crow[2]
verb **1** to make the sound of a rooster
2 to boast (***blow your own trumpet, brag, skite, talk big***)

Verb forms: it **crowed** or it **crew**, it has **crowed**, it is **crowing**
Word history: Old English *crāwen*; imitative

crowbar
noun an iron bar used as a lever or to break hard ground

crowd
noun **1** a large number of people or things gathered closely together (***flock, herd, mob, pack, throng***)
verb **2** to gather in large numbers: *Children* ***crowded*** *around the clown.*
3 to squeeze or push: *They* ***crowded*** *into the room.*

Word building: **crowded** *adjective*
Word history: Old English *crūdan*

crowd-surfing
noun an activity at a rock concert or party in which someone is held up by the main group and moved about over their heads

Word building: **crowd-surf** *verb* **crowd-surfer** *noun*

crown
noun **1** an ornament made of gold and jewels worn on the head of a king or queen
2 the sovereign as the head of state
3 the top or highest part: *the* ***crown*** *of your head*
verb **4** to put a crown on: *The Archbishop* ***crowned*** *the new king.*
5 to honour or reward: *Success* ***crowned*** *his efforts.*

Word use: You can also use **Crown** for definition 2.
Word history: Middle English, from Anglo-French, from Latin word meaning 'garland', 'crown'

crown-of-thorns starfish
noun a starfish with sharp, stinging spines, found widely in tropical waters, especially on the Great Barrier Reef, where it destroys coral

crucial (krooh-shuhl)
adjective of greatest importance: *a **crucial** decision* (***critical, pivotal***)

Word history: Latin, from *crux* cross

cruciate ligament (kroohsh-ee-uht lig-uh-muhnt)
noun one of two major ligaments of the knee which connect the femur to the tibia and give stability to the knee

crucible (krooh-suh-buhl)
noun **1** a container used for heating substances to high temperatures
2 a severe test

Word history: from Medieval Latin word meaning 'night lamp', 'melting pot'

crucifix (krooh-suh-fiks)
noun a cross with the figure of Jesus on it

Word history: Middle English, from Late Latin word meaning 'fixed to a cross'

crucify (krooh-suh-fuy)
verb to put to death by nailing to a cross

Word building: **crucifixion** *noun*
Word history: Middle English, from Old French, from Late Latin word meaning 'fix to a cross'

crude
adjective **1** in a natural state: ***crude** oil*
2 rude and not in good taste: *a **crude** joke* (***coarse, common, tasteless, uncouth, vulgar***)
3 not carefully done: *a **crude** drawing*

Word use: The opposite of definition 1 is **refined**. | The opposite of definition 2 is **polite**.
Word building: **crudely** *adverb* **crudeness** *noun* **crudity** *noun*
Word history: Middle English, from Latin word meaning 'raw', 'crude', 'rough'

crude oil
noun oil as it is found in nature, usually brown or black, and often in association with natural gas which forms a cap above it and saline water which collects underneath it

cruel
adjective liking or likely to cause pain: *a **cruel** person* | *a **cruel** remark* (***brutal, callous, harsh, savage, vicious***)

Word use: The opposite of this is **kind**.
Word building: **cruelly** *adverb*
Word history: Middle English, from Old French, from Latin word meaning 'hard', 'cruel', related to *crudus* crude

cruelty
noun behaviour that causes pain or hardship to others

Word use: The opposite of this is **kindness**.
Noun forms: The plural is **cruelties**.

cruet (krooh-uht)
noun a set of small containers for salt, pepper and mustard

Word history: Middle English, from Old French word meaning 'little pitcher', 'pot', from Germanic

cruise
verb **1** to sail from place to place: *The battleship **cruised** in enemy waters.* (***coast, float, glide, skim***)
2 to travel at a moderate speed
3 *Colloquial* to move around an urban area, in search of excitement
noun **4** a voyage in which you sail from place to place: *a holiday **cruise***

Word building: **cruiser** *noun*
Word history: from Dutch word meaning 'cross', 'cruise'

cruise missile
noun a self-propelled, guided missile which uses external air in its combustion and which carries a conventional or a nuclear warhead

cruisy
adjective *Colloquial* easy; not taxing: *a **cruisy** job*

Word use: You can also use **cruisey**.

crumb
noun **1** a small piece of bread, cake or other dry food
verb **2** to break into crumbs
3 to coat with crumbs: *to **crumb** steak*

Word history: Old English *cruma*

crumble
verb to break into small pieces: *I **crumbled** the cake.* | *The wall was **crumbling** with age.* (***crush, grind, mill, pound, pulverise***)

Word building: **crumbly** *adjective* (**crumblier, crumbliest**)
Word history: Old English *gecrymman* crumble (from *cruma* crumb)

crummy
adjective *Colloquial* of poor quality or in poor condition (***defective, dud, inferior, shoddy, worthless***)

Adjective forms: **crummier, crummiest**
Word use: You can also use **crumby**.

crumpet
noun a kind of flat cake, eaten toasted and buttered

Word history: short for *crumpet cake* curled cake, Middle English *crompid*, crimped

crumple
verb **1** to crush into wrinkles: *I **crumpled** the paper in my hands.*
2 to break down or collapse: *Her face **crumpled** into tears.* | *The building **crumpled** after the blast.*

Word history: Middle English *crimplen* wrinkle

crunch
verb to crush or grind noisily

Word history: blend of *craunch* and *crush*

crusade
noun a strong movement of support: *a **crusade** to save the park*

Word building: **crusade** *verb* **crusader** *noun*
Word history: blend of Old French and Spanish word meaning 'bear the cross', from Latin *crux* cross

crush
verb **1** to press or squeeze together between hard surfaces
2 to break into small pieces: *to **crush** rocks* (***grind***, ***mill***, ***pound***, ***pulverise***)
3 to defeat totally: *to **crush** a rebellion*
noun **4** a strong liking which often doesn't last long: *to have a **crush** on a film star*

Word history: Middle English, from Old French word meaning 'break', 'crush'

crust
noun **1** the outside surface of bread, or a piece of it
2 any hard outer surface

Word history: Middle English, from Latin word meaning 'rind'

crustacean (krus-<u>tay</u>-shuhn)
noun a type of animal with a hard shell instead of a skeleton, such as a crab or crayfish, usually living in water

crustal plate
noun → **tectonic plate**

crusty
adjective **1** like or having a crust
2 rough or sour-tempered; gruff or surly: *a **crusty** old man | a **crusty** remark*

Adjective forms: **crustier**, **crustiest**
Word building: **crustiness** *noun*

crutch
noun a stick which fits under the arm to help an injured person walk

Word history: Old English *crycc*

crux (kruks)
noun a vital, basic, or decisive point

Word history: from Latin word meaning 'cross', 'torment', 'trouble'

cry
verb **1** to shed tears (***bawl***, ***blubber***, ***sob***, ***wail***, ***weep***)
2 to shout: *We **cried** for help.*
noun **3** a fit of weeping
4 a shout: *A great **cry** went up.*
phrase **5 a far cry**,
a a long distance
b very different: *That colour paint is **a far cry** from the one I chose.*
6 cry down,
a to speak poorly of: *to **cry down** the new maths program*
b to stop from speaking, especially by talking loudly: *to **cry down a** speaker at the rally*
7 cry off, to break: *to **cry off** a promise or agreement*

Verb forms: I **cried**, I have **cried**, I am **crying**
Noun forms: The plural is **cries**.
Word history: Middle English, from Latin word meaning 'wail'

cryogen (<u>kruy</u>-uh-juhn)
noun a freezing mixture, or a substance for producing low temperatures

Word building: **cryogenic** *adjective*

crypt (kript)
noun an underground room under a church, often used as a burial place

Word history: Latin, from Greek word meaning 'hidden'

cryptic (<u>krip</u>-tik)
adjective mysterious, or difficult to understand: *a **cryptic** message*

crystal
noun **1** a clear mineral which looks like ice
2 a single grain or piece of this
3 a substance with a geometric form due to the regular arrangement of atoms, ions or molecules it has
4 clear sparkling glass
adjective **5** made of or like crystal: *a **crystal** bowl*

Word building: **crystalline** *adjective*
Word history: Middle English, from Old French

crystallise
verb **1** to form into crystals
2 to coat with sugar

Word use: You can also use **crystallize**.
Word building: **crystallisation** *noun*

cub
noun the young of certain animals such as the lion and bear

Word history: variant of *cob*

cubbyhouse
noun Australian a child's playhouse

cube
noun **1** a solid shape with six equal square sides
2 the result of multiplying a number by itself twice: *The **cube** of 3 is 3 × 3 × 3, or 27.*

Word history: Latin, from Greek word meaning 'die', 'cube'

cube root
noun the number which, when multiplied by itself twice, gives the cube: *The **cube root** of 27 is 3.*

cubic
adjective **1** solid or having three dimensions (height, breadth and depth): *A **cubic** metre is the volume of a cube with edges each one metre long.*
2 *Mathematics* having to do with the third power or degree

cubicle
noun a partly enclosed small space: *a toilet **cubicle*** (***cell***, ***chamber***, ***compartment***, ***den***)

Word history: from Latin word meaning 'bedchamber'

cuckold (<u>kuk</u>-uhld)
noun Old-fashioned **1** a man whose wife has had sexual intercourse with another man
verb Old-fashioned **2** to make a cuckold of: *to **cuckold** a husband*

Word building: **cuckoldry** *noun*
Word history: Middle English *cokewold*

cuckoo (<u>koo</u>-kooh)
noun a bird which is known for its habit of laying its eggs in the nests of other birds

Word history: Middle English *cucu* (imitative of its call)

cucumber
noun a fruit which is usually long and thin with green skin and white flesh, used as a vegetable in salads, and for pickling

Word history: French, from Latin

cud
noun food which cattle and some other animals return from their first stomach to chew a second time

Word history: Old English *cudu*

cuddle
verb to hug gently (***cradle***, ***embrace***, ***fondle***, ***pet***)

Word building: **cuddle** *noun* **cuddly** *adjective* (**cuddlier, cuddliest**)
Word history: obsolete *couth*, friendly + *-le*

cudgel
noun a short thick stick used as a weapon

Word history: Old English *cycgel*

cue[1]
noun anything said or done as a signal for what follows, especially in a play: *The ringing of a bell was the maid's **cue** to enter.*

Word building: **cue** *verb* (**cued, cueing**)
Word history: perhaps spelling of abbreviation *q.* or *qu.* for Latin *quando* when

cue[2]
noun a long stick used to hit the ball in billiards and other similar games

Word building: **cue** *verb* (**cued, cueing**)
Word history: variant of *queue*, from French

cue / queue
Don't confuse **cue** with **queue**, which is a line of people or cars waiting in turn.

cuff[1]
noun **1** a band or fold at the wrist of a sleeve
2 a part turned up at the end of a trouser leg
phrase **3 off the cuff**, on the spur of the moment or without preparation: *to speak **off the cuff***

Word history: Middle English *cuffe* glove

cuff[2]
verb to hit with your open hand

Word history: compare Swedish *kuffa* thrust, push

cul-de-sac (<u>kul</u>-duh-sak)
noun a short street which is closed at one end

Word history: from French word meaning 'bottom of sack'

culinary (<u>kul</u>-uhn-ree, <u>kul</u>-uhn-uh-ree)
adjective having to do with the kitchen or cookery

Word history: from Latin word meaning 'kitchen'

cull (kul)
verb **1** to pick out the best from: *to **cull** the main points from the long report*
2 to gather
3 to kill (animals, such as deer, kangaroos, etc.), with a view to controlling numbers
noun **4** the killing of animals in order to reduce their numbers: *the annual seal **cull***

Word history: Middle English, from Old French, from Latin word meaning 'collect'

culminate
verb to reach the highest point: *His efforts **culminated** in success.*

Word history: from Late Latin word meaning 'crowned'

culottes
plural noun trousers which are cut wide to look like a skirt

Word history: French

culpable (<u>kul</u>-puh-buhl)
adjective deserving blame: *a **culpable** act of negligence*

Word building: **culpability** *noun* **culpableness** *noun*
Word history: from Latin word meaning 'blameworthy'

culprit
noun someone who has done something wrong: *After breaking the shop window the **culprit** ran away.*

Word history: origin uncertain; traditionally explained as from Latin *cul(pābilis)*, guilty + Anglo-French *pri(s)t* ready, such as the prosecution is ready to prove guilt

cult
noun **1** a religion
2 a strong, almost religious devotion to a person or thing: *the **cult** of jogging*

Word history: from Latin word meaning 'care', 'worship'

cultivate
verb **1** to dig the soil for planting and growing: *He **cultivates** wheat on his farm.* (***till***)
2 to develop or improve: *to **cultivate** the mind*

Word building: **cultivation** *noun*
Word history: Medieval Latin word meaning 'tilled', from Latin word meaning 'till'

cultivated
adjective **1** produced or improved by cultivating: *a **cultivated** crop of plants*
2 educated or knowing about culture (***erudite***, ***knowledgeable***, ***learned***, ***refined***, ***well-informed***)

cultural
adjective having to do with culture: ***cultural** achievements*

Word building: **culturally** *adverb*

cultural context
noun the setting of something, such as a piece of prose, within the confines of a particular society, with all its ideas, customs and art being expressed through the words and actions of the characters

culture
noun **1** the state or stage of civilisation of a particular people at a certain time: *Greek **culture***
2 skills, arts, beliefs and customs passed on from one generation to another: *the **culture** of Japan*
3 the raising of plants or animals, especially to improve or develop them
4 *Biology* the growth of cells, such as bacteria or human tissue, for scientific studies, medical use, etc.

Word history: Middle English, from French, from Latin word meaning 'tending', 'cultivation'

cumbersome
adjective awkward to handle: *a **cumbersome** parcel*

cumquat (<u>kum</u>-kwot)
noun a fruit like a small mandarin, but not as sweet, used chiefly in jams

Word use: You can also use **kumquat**.
Word history: from Chinese word meaning 'gold orange'

cumulative (<u>kyoohm</u>-yuh-luh-tiv)
adjective **1** increasing, growing, or formed by adding something on a regular basis
2 to be served one after another: ***cumulative** prison sentences*

cumulus (<u>kyooh</u>-myuh-luhs)
noun a cloud, usually white, which is flat at the bottom and has round heaps at the top

cuneiform (<u>kyooh</u>-nuh-fawm)
adjective **1** wedge-shaped
noun **2** characters used in writing in ancient Persia and some nearby countries

Word history: Latin *cuneus* wedge + *-i-* + *-form*

cunning
noun skill used in a clever plan, or in tricking other people (***artfulness**, **deceit**, **guile**, **shrewdness**, **trickery***)

Word building: **cunning** *adjective*
Word history: Old English *cunnung*, from *cunnan* know (how)

cup
noun **1** a small, round, open container, often with a handle on the side, used mainly to drink from
2 an ornamental bowl, usually of silver or gold, given as a prize
3 a unit of volume, measuring 250 millilitres
verb **4** to form into the shape of a cup: *to **cup** your hands*

Verb forms: I **cupped**, I have **cupped**, I am **cupping**
Word history: Old English *cuppe*, from Late Latin word meaning 'cup', from Latin word meaning 'tub', 'cask'

cupboard (<u>kub</u>-uhd)
noun a piece of furniture or a built-in space with doors, used for storing things

Word history: Middle English, from *cup* + *board*

cur (ker)
noun **1** a fierce or worthless dog
2 *Old-fashioned* a low, hateful person

Word history: Middle English *curre*; imitative

curacy
noun the position or work of a curate

Noun forms: The plural is **curacies**.

curate[1] (<u>kyooh</u>-ruht)
noun a member of the clergy who helps a rector or vicar

Word history: Middle English, from Medieval Latin

curate[2] (kyooh-<u>rayt</u>)
verb **1** to supervise and maintain (an art collection, museum, etc.)
2 to collect and prepare works of art for (an exhibition): *She has **curated** some important exhibitions.*

curator (kyooh-<u>ray</u>-tuh)
noun someone who looks after a museum, art gallery or similar kind of collection

Word history: from Latin word meaning 'overseer', 'guardian'

curb
verb **1** to control or hold back: ***Curb** your temper.* (***check**, **inhibit**, **limit**, **restrict**, **stifle***)
noun **2** anything that holds back or controls

Word history: Middle English, from French word meaning 'curved', from Latin word meaning 'bent', 'crooked'

> **curb / kerb**
> Don't confuse **curb** with **kerb**, which is a line of concrete or stones at the edge of a road.

curd
noun a jelly-like substance formed in milk which has been treated with an acid, eaten fresh or used for making cheese

Word history: Middle English

curdle
verb to form into curd: *I **curdled** the custard by accidentally letting it boil. | The milk **curdled** on the hot day.* (***clot**, **coagulate**, **congeal**, **thicken***)

Word history: related to *curd*

cure
noun **1** a medicine or treatment which gets rid of an illness or disability
verb **2** to bring back to good health
3 to treat so as to preserve or finish properly: *to **cure** meat | to **cure** concrete*

Word building: **curable** *adjective* **curative** *adjective*
Word history: Middle English, from Old French, from Latin word meaning 'care', 'treatment', 'concern'

curfew
noun an order which says people are not allowed to be out on the streets after a certain time at night

Word history: Middle English, from Old French *cuevre-feu* cover-fire

curie (<u>kyooh</u>-ree)
noun the non-SI unit of measurement of radioactivity

Word history: named after Marie *Curie*, 1867–1934, Polish-born physicist and chemist

curious
adjective **1** wanting to learn: *to be **curious** about butterflies* (***enquiring**, **inquisitive**, **questioning***)
2 interesting because strange or new: *a **curious** custom*

Word building: **curiosity** *noun* (*plural* **curiosities**)
Word history: Middle English, from Old French, from Latin word meaning 'careful', 'inquiring', 'inquisitive'

curl
noun **1** a small ring of hair
2 a curved or twisted shape: *There were **curls** of chocolate on the cake.* (***coil**, **loop**, **spiral**, **twist***)
verb **3** to twist or curl: *The vine **curled** round the tree.* (***curve**, **deflect**, **flex**, **loop**, **turn***)
phrase **4 curl your lip**, to show contempt or scorn

Word building: **curly** *adjective* (**curlier**, **curliest**)
Word history: Middle English, from Middle Dutch or Middle Flemish

curlew (<u>ker</u>-lyooh)
noun a type of long-legged shorebird

Word history: Middle English, from Old French; imitative

currajong (<u>kur</u>-uh-jong)
noun → **kurrajong**

currant
noun a small, dried, seedless grape

Word history: Middle English, from Anglo-French (*raisins de*) *Corauntz* (raisins of) Corinth

> **currant / current**
> Don't confuse **currant** with **current**, which means 'belonging to the present' or 'a flow or movement'.

currawong
noun a large, black-and-white or greyish Australian bird with a large pointed bill and a loud ringing call

Word history: from an Australian Aboriginal language, perhaps from the Yagara language of the Brisbane region

currency
noun money in current use in a country

Noun forms: The plural is **currencies.**

current
adjective **1** belonging to the present: ***current*** *problems* | *the* ***current*** *month* (***contemporary***, ***late***, ***new***, ***recent***, ***up-to-date***)
noun **2** a flow or movement: *a strong* ***current*** *in the river* | *a* ***current*** *of air from a fan* | *a* ***current*** *of electricity*

Word history: from Latin word meaning 'running'

curriculum (kuh-<u>rik</u>-yuh-luhm)
noun a set of courses of study: *the school* ***curriculum***

Noun forms: The plural is **curricula** or **curriculums.**
Word building: **curricular** *adjective*
Word history: from Latin word meaning 'running', 'course'

curry[1]
noun **1** a spicy sauce or dish of meat and vegetables which tastes hot
verb **2** to prepare with this sauce: *to* ***curry*** *meat*

Noun forms: The plural is **curries.**
Verb forms: I **curried,** I have **curried,** I am **currying**
Word history: Tamil *kari* sauce

curry[2]
verb **1** to rub with a brush or comb to clean: *to* ***curry*** *a horse*
phrase **2 curry favour,** to try to gain favour by kindness, flattery, politeness, etc.

Verb forms: I **curried,** I have **curried,** I am **currying**
Word history: Middle English, from Old French word meaning 'put in order', from *con-* + *-reder* make ready (from Germanic)

curse
noun **1** a wish that evil will happen to someone: *to put a* ***curse*** *on someone*
2 a swear word or blasphemy: *to utter a* ***curse***

Word building: **curse** *verb*
Word history: Old English *curs,* from *cūrsian,* verb, curse, reprove, from Old Irish *cūrsagim* I blame

cursive
noun **1** writing or print with the letters joined together
adjective **2** in a flowing style with the letters joined in this way

Word history: Medieval Latin, from Latin word meaning 'a running'

cursor
noun **1** the sliding part of a measuring tool
2 a moving dot or line on a computer video screen showing where the next letter or other character will appear

cursory (<u>ker</u>-suh-ree)
adjective short and rapid, without noticing details: *a* ***cursory*** *inspection* (***casual***, ***desultory***, ***offhand***, ***superficial***)

Word building: **cursoriness** *noun*
Word history: from Latin word meaning 'of a runner or a race'

curt
adjective rudely brief in speech or manner: *He gave me a* ***curt*** *nod.* (***abrupt***, ***blunt***, ***brusque***, ***short***, ***terse***)

Word history: from Latin word meaning 'cut short', 'clipped'

curtail
verb to cut short: *We had to* ***curtail*** *our holiday.* (***abbreviate***, ***abridge***, ***reduce***, ***shorten***, ***trim***)

Word history: obsolete *curtal,* verb, 'dock', from French word meaning 'short', from Latin

curtain
noun a piece of material hanging from a rod over a window or across the front of a stage

Word building: **curtain** *verb*
Word history: Middle English, from Old French, from Late Latin word meaning 'curtain'

curtsy
noun a respectful bow made by a woman bending her knees, often with one foot in front of the other

Noun forms: The plural is **curtsies.**
Word use: You can also use **curtsey,** and the plural of this is **curtseys.**
Word building: **curtsy** *verb* (**curtsied, curtsying**)
Word history: variant of *courtesy*

curvature (<u>ker</u>-vuh-chuh)
noun **1** the act of curving
2 a curved condition, often abnormal: ***curvature*** *of the spine*

curve
noun a bending line or shape with no angles: *a* ***curve*** *in a road* | *the* ***curves*** *of the letter 's'*

Word building: **curve** *verb* **curvy** *adjective* (**curvier, curviest**)
Word history: Latin *curvus* bent, curved

cuscus (<u>kus</u>-kus)
noun a small furry animal like a possum, which has a long tail and lives in New Guinea and northern Queensland

cushion
noun **1** a soft pad used to sit on, or lean against, especially on a chair
verb **2** to place on a cushion
3 to lessen the force or effect of: *Thick bushes* ***cushioned*** *his fall.*

Word history: Middle English, from Old French, perhaps from Latin *culcita* cushion

cusp
noun **1** a pointed end
2 a point sticking out or up, such as on the crown of a tooth
3 the point of a crescent, especially of the moon
4 *Astrology* the period of change from one sign to the next: *to be born on the* ***cusp***
Word building: **cusped** *adjective*
Word history: Latin *cuspis* point

custard
noun a food made of milk, eggs and sugar, and eaten as a dessert
Word history: earlier *crustarde* a kind of patty, from Old English *croste* crust

custard apple
noun the soft-fleshed fruit of any of several tropical trees

custodian
noun a keeper, or guardian: *a* ***custodian*** *at the museum*

custody
noun **1** keeping or care: *The family jewels are in safe* ***custody*** *at the bank.*
2 imprisonment: *The police officer took the suspect into* ***custody****.*
Word building: **custodial** *adjective*
Word history: Latin

custom
noun **1** habit or usual practice
2 customs,
a a tax paid on goods brought into the country
b the government department that collects these taxes
Word history: Middle English, from Old French, from Latin word meaning 'custom'

customary
adjective usual or according to custom (***conventional***, ***normal***, ***orthodox***, ***regular***, ***traditional***)
Word history: Medieval Latin, from Old French word meaning 'custom'

custom-built
adjective made in the way you ordered

customer
noun someone who buys goods from other people (***buyer***, ***consumer***, ***patron***, ***purchaser***, ***shopper***)

custom-made
adjective made to individual order: ***custom-made*** *shoes*

cut
verb **1** to make an opening in with something sharp: *to* ***cut*** *your finger* (***gash***, ***nick***, ***pierce***, ***slash***, ***slit***)
2 to separate or make shorter with something sharp: *to* ***cut*** *a string* (***chop***, ***clip***, ***hack***, ***lop***, ***trim***)
3 to cross: *One line* ***cut*** *another at right angles. | The river rose and* ***cut*** *the road.*
4 to lower: *to* ***cut*** *prices* (***decrease***, ***moderate***, ***reduce***)
5 to be able to cut: *This knife* ***cuts*** *well.*
noun **6** the result of cutting: *a* ***cut*** *on your leg* (***gash***, ***incision***, ***notch***, ***opening***, ***slit***)
7 a piece cut off: *a* ***cut*** *of meat*
8 a reduction or lowering: *a* ***cut*** *in the price*
phrase **9 a cut above,** *Colloquial* better than another in some way
10 cut and dried,
a already fixed or settled
b without interest or freshness
11 cut back,
a to reduce or shorten (***decrease***, ***lessen***, ***lower***, ***minimise***)
b in a novel or film, to return suddenly to events that happened earlier
12 cut in,
a to interrupt (***break in***, ***butt in***, ***intrude***)
b to pull in between other cars too soon after overtaking
13 cut off, to stop: *He* ***cut*** *me* ***off*** *before I finished speaking.*
14 cut out,
a to omit or leave out
b to remove and take the place of: *to* ***cut out*** *a rival*
c to cease or stop (***halt***, ***hesitate***, ***pause***, ***quit***, ***stall***)
d to form or make by cutting: *to* ***cut out*** *a dress*
e to switch off when overloaded: *The heater suddenly* ***cut out.***
15 cut out for (or **to be**), well fitted for an occupation, role, etc.: *I don't think I was* ***cut out to be*** *a dancer.*
Verb forms: I **cut**, I have **cut**, I am **cutting**
Word history: Middle English *cutten, kytten, kitten*

cutaneous (kyooh-tay-nee-uhs)
adjective having to do with affecting the skin: *The rash was a symptom of a* ***cutaneous*** *disease.*

cute (kyooht)
adjective **1** *Colloquial* pleasingly pretty
2 clever, or shrewd
Word building: **cuteness** *noun*
Word history: variant of *acute*

cuticle
noun the skin around the edges of a fingernail or toenail
Word history: from Latin word meaning 'skin'

cutlass
noun a short, heavy, slightly curved sword
Word history: French, from Latin word meaning 'small knife'

cutlery
noun the knives, forks and spoons used for eating
Word history: French

cutlet
noun a small cut of meat, usually lamb or veal, that contains a rib
Word history: French word meaning 'little rib', from Latin

cuttlefish
noun a mollusc with two gills, ten sucker-bearing arms and the power of sending out a black, ink-like liquid when attacked
Noun forms: The plural is **cuttlefish** or **cuttlefishes.**
Word history: Old English *cudele*

cyanide
noun a very poisonous salt

cyber attack
noun an attack on a computer or telecommunications network

cybernetics (suy-buh-net-iks)
noun the scientific study of those methods of control and communication which are shared by living organisms and machines, especially having to do with the operations of computers

Word building: **cybernetic** *adjective*
Word history: Greek *kybernētēs* helmsman + *-ics*

cybersecurity
noun protection provided for an information system, such as computer and telecommunications networks, against cyberthreats

cyberspace
noun the sites that you reach on the internet, thought of as existing in a separate world

Word history: coined by US science-fiction writer William Gibson in 1982

cyberterrorism
noun a type of terrorism in which computer networks, data, etc., are damaged or altered to harm a targeted group or country

Word building: **cyberterrorist** *noun*

cyberthreat
noun an attack on a computer network, as a worm (definition 3), a virus (definition 3), hacker intrusion, etc.

cyclamate (suy-kluh-muht)
noun an artificial sweetener

cyclamen (suy-kluh-muhn)
noun a plant with nodding white, purple, pink, or red flowers, the petals of which fold backwards

Word history: Neo-Latin, from Greek

cycle
noun **1** a series of events happening in a regular repeating order: *the **cycle** of the seasons* (***chain**, **course**, **sequence**, **succession***)
2 a bicycle
verb **3** to ride a bicycle

Word building: **cyclist** *noun*
Word history: Latin, from Greek word meaning 'ring', 'circle'

cyclic
adjective occurring again and again in cycles: *a **cyclic** process*

Word building: **cyclical** *adjective*
Word history: Latin, from Greek word meaning 'circular'

cyclone
noun a tropical storm with strong winds

Word history: from Greek word meaning 'moving in a circle'

cygnet (sig-nuht)
noun a young swan

Word history: Middle English, from Latin *cygnus* swan (from Greek) + *-et*

cylinder
noun **1** a tube-shaped object, either hollow or solid, with perfectly circular ends
2 the part of an engine in which the piston moves

Word history: Latin, from Greek word meaning 'cylinder'

cylindrical
adjective shaped like a cylinder: *a **cylindrical** object*

cymbal
noun one of a pair of curved brass plates which are struck together to make a sharp, musical, ringing sound

Word building: **cymbalist** *noun*
Word history: Old English, from Latin, from Greek word meaning 'cup', 'bowl'

cymbal / symbol
Don't confuse **cymbal** with **symbol**, which is a token or character used to represent something:
The dove is a symbol of peace.
The symbol for a heart is ♥.

cynic
noun someone who does not believe in the goodness of people or events and is often scornful of them

Word building: **cynical** *adjective* **cynicism** *noun*
Word history: from 'Cynic' (a school of Greek philosophers founded around 400 BC), Latin, from Greek word meaning 'dog-like', 'churlish'

cypher (suy-fuh)
noun, verb → **cipher**

cypress
noun an evergreen cone-bearing tree with dark overlapping leaves

Word history: from Greek

cyst (sist)
noun Medicine **1** a closed sac formed in animal tissues, often containing liquid
2 a bladder, or sac

Word building: **cystic** *adjective*
Word history: Neo-Latin, from Greek word meaning 'bladder', 'bag', 'pouch'

cystitis (sis-tuy-tuhs)
noun inflammation of the urinary bladder

czar (zah)
noun the emperor of Russia in former times

Word use: You can also use **tsar**.
Word history: Russian, from Latin *Caesar*

Dd

dab
verb **1** to put on gently: *She **dabbed** a little perfume behind her ears.*
noun **2** a small amount: *a **dab** of lipstick*

Verb forms: I **dabbed**, I have **dabbed**, I am **dabbing**
Word history: Middle English

dabble
verb **1** to splash in water: *to **dabble** your toes*
phrase **2 dabble in**, to do as a hobby: *to **dabble in** painting*

Word history: Flemish

dachshund (daks-uhnd, dash-huhnd)
noun a small dog with a long body and very short legs

Word history: German *Dachs* badger + *Hund* dog

dad
noun Colloquial **1** a father: *Is your **dad** feeling better?*
2 Dad, a word used when you address your father: *Hurry up **Dad**, or we'll be late!*

Word use: Children often use **daddy** or **Daddy**.

daddy-long-legs
noun Australian, NZ a spider with a small body and long, very thin legs

Word use: The plural form is the same as the singular.

daemon (dee-muhn)
noun Computers a process that runs in the background and can be called upon to perform specified operations by the operating system

daffodil (daf-uh-dil)
noun a plant which has yellow bell-shaped flowers in spring

Word history: unexplained variant of Middle English *affodille*, from Greek *asphódelos*

daft (dahft)
adjective foolish or slightly mad

Word history: Old English *gedæfte* mild, meek

dag[1]
noun Australian, NZ wool, usually dirty, from a sheep's hindquarters

dag[2]
noun Australian, NZ Colloquial **1** an odd or amusing person
2 a person lacking in style

Word building: **daggy** *adjective* (**daggier**, **daggiest**)

dagger
noun a weapon with a short pointed blade for stabbing

Word history: Middle English

daily
adjective done or happening every day: *our **daily** chores*

Word building: **daily** *adverb*

dainty
adjective small and delicate: *to take **dainty** steps* (***elfin***, ***petite***)

Adjective forms: **daintier**, **daintiest**
Word building: **daintily** *adverb* **daintiness** *noun*
Word history: Middle English, from Old French, from Latin word meaning 'worthiness'

dairy
noun **1** the place on a farm where cows are milked
2 a cool place where milk and cream are stored and made into butter and cheese
adjective **3** having to do with or made in a dairy: ***dairy** cows* | ***dairy** products*

Noun forms: The plural is **dairies**.
Word history: Middle English *dei* female servant + *-erie* -ery

> **dairy / diary**
> Don't confuse **dairy** with **diary**, which is a book in which you write what happens each day.

dais (day-uhs)
noun a raised platform at the end of a hall for a speaker's desk and microphone, and for seats of the guests of honour, etc.

Word history: Middle English, from Old French, from Late Latin word meaning 'table'

daisy
noun a common plant which has brightly coloured flowers with many petals surrounding a yellow centre

Noun forms: The plural is **daisies**.
Word history: Old English *daegesēage* day's eye

daks
plural noun Australian Colloquial trousers: *He was wearing a collared shirt with navy **daks**.*

Word history: Trademark, coined by Alexander Simpson, of Simpsons clothing store in Piccadilly, London, in 1934, by blending 'dad' and 'slacks'

dale
noun a small open valley
Word history: Old English *dæl*

dally
verb **1** to waste time (***delay, linger, loiter, tarry***)
2 to make love playfully
phrase **3 dally with**, to consider something, but not in a serious way, without trying to make up your mind: *I am **dallying with** the idea of taking a few days off work next week.*

Verb forms: I **dallied**, I have **dallied**, I am **dallying**
Word building: **dalliance** *noun*
Word history: Middle English, from Old French word meaning 'talk'

Dalmatian (dal-may-shuhn)
noun a breed of dog having a white colour with many dark-coloured spots

dam[1]
noun **1** a lot of water held back by a strong wall built across a river (***reservoir, weir***)
2 the wall itself
3 *Australian, NZ* a waterhole dug out of the ground on a farm
verb **4** to hold back: *They **dammed** the river to provide water for the town.*

Verb forms: I **dammed**, I have **dammed**, I am **damming**
Word history: Middle English

dam[2]
noun the mother of a four-legged animal, such as a horse

Word history: Middle English variant of *dame*

dam / damn

Don't confuse **dam** with **damn**. To **damn** is to ruin with fierce criticism, as in *a damning report.* It also means 'to curse':

He damned the weather and everything.

damage (dam-ij)
verb **1** to harm or injure (***mar, spoil, vandalise, wreck***)
noun **2** harm or injury
3 damages, money that a court says you should get to make up for an injury or loss: *The court awarded her **damages** of a million dollars.*

Word history: Middle English, from Old French

damage control
noun **1** measures to limit damage, as during or after a disaster: ***Damage control** involved calling in as many firefighters as could be found.*
2 attempts to mitigate the unpleasant consequence of an event, action, etc.: *We went into **damage control** when we heard that the story had been leaked.*

Word use: You can also use **damage limitation**.

damask (dam-uhsk)
noun a fabric of linen, silk, cotton, or wool, woven with wavy patterns, often used as table linen

Word history: Middle English, from Latin, from Greek word meaning 'Damascus'

dame
noun **1 Dame**, the title used to address a woman awarded a high rank: ***Dame** of the Order of Australia*
2 *Colloquial* a woman: *There were no **dames** at the party.*

Word use: Definition 2 is mostly used in the US by men and may offend some women.
Word history: Middle English, from Latin word meaning 'mistress', 'lady'

damn (dam)
verb **1** to wish extreme suffering and misery upon: *to **damn** him for his evil deeds*
2 to declare something or someone to be the target of your anger: ***Damn** you for your stupidity!* (***censure, condemn***)
interjection **3** an expression of anger or annoyance, as in 'Damn! I've missed the last train.'

Word history: Middle English, from Latin word meaning 'condemn', 'doom'

damnation
noun everlasting punishment in hell

damned (damd)
adjective **1** condemned to punishment in hell: *a **damned** soul*
2 *Colloquial* very great: *She's a **damned** nuisance.*
adverb **3** *Colloquial* very or extremely: *She's **damned** late.*

Word use: Definitions 2 and 3 are used by some people to express strong feeling.

damp
adjective **1** slightly wet or moist (***dank, clammy***)
noun **2** moisture in the air or in clothes, or other objects like this
verb **3** to moisten or dampen: *to **damp** the clothes for ironing*
4 *Music* to dull or deaden the sound of, often by stopping or slowing down the vibrations of an instrument's strings, such as those inside a piano

Word building: **dampness** *noun*
Word history: Middle English, from Middle Flemish word meaning 'vapour'

dampen
verb **1** to moisten or make damp
2 to deaden or make dull: *to **dampen** sound | to **dampen** enthusiasm*

damper
noun bread made from flour and water mixed to make a dough and baked in the coals of an open fire

Word history: British dialect

dance
noun **1** a series of rhythmical steps, usually performed in time to music
2 a party for dancing: *A new band played at the **dance** on Saturday.*
3 dancing as an art or profession: *She is studying dance.*
verb **4** to move your feet and body in a rhythmic way, usually with music (***caper, gambol, prance***)
5 to perform or take part in a dance: *to **dance** a waltz*

Word building: **dancer** *noun*
Word history: Middle English, from Old French; probably of Germanic origin

dance music
noun any of various genres of pop music with a strong beat, designed for dancing at nightclubs, dance parties, etc.

D and C
noun dilation and curettage, a surgical method for the removal of tissue from the uterus by scraping

Word history: abbreviation

dandelion (dan-dee-luy-uhn, dan-duh-luy-uhn)
noun a wild plant with bright yellow flowers which form light downy balls when they go to seed

Word history: French *dent de lion* lion's tooth (with allusion to the toothed leaves)

dandruff
noun small white flakes of dead skin from your scalp

dandy
noun **1** a man who is too concerned about clothes and appearance (***fop, show pony, lair***)
adjective **2** *Colloquial* very good or fine

Noun forms: The plural is **dandies.**
Adjective forms: **dandier, dandiest**

danger
noun **1** a possible cause of harm or injury: *A careless driver is a* ***danger*** *on the road.*
2 a situation in which harm or injury may happen: *When the volcano erupted the people were in great* ***danger.***

Word history: Middle English, from Late Latin word meaning 'lordship'

dangerous
adjective full of or causing danger: *a* ***dangerous*** *mission | a* ***dangerous*** *weapon* (***hazardous, perilous, risky***)

Word use: The opposite of this is **safe.**

dangle
verb to hang so as to swing to and fro

Word history: Scandinavian

dank
adjective unpleasantly damp or moist: *a* ***dank*** *cave*

Word building: **dankness** *noun*
Word history: Middle English

dapper
adjective neat and smart (***elegant, fashionable, nifty***)

Word history: from Middle English word meaning 'pretty', 'elegant'

dapple
verb to mark with spots or patches: *Sunlight* ***dappled*** *the leaves.*

Word building: **dappled** *adjective*
Word history: origin uncertain

dare (dair)
verb **1** to be bold or courageous enough: *The teacher was so angry that nobody* ***dared*** *to speak.*
2 to challenge: *I* ***dare*** *you to jump off the roof.*
noun **3** a challenge to do something risky
phrase **4 dare say,** to think something is likely: *I* ***dare say*** *you'll go to a college when you finish school.*

Verb forms: I **dared,** I have **dared,** I am **daring**
Word history: Old English *durran*

daredevil
noun someone who is very daring or reckless

daren't (dairnt, dair-ruhnt)
contraction of **dare not**

Look up **contractions in grammar.**

daring
adjective bold and adventurous: *a* ***daring*** *explorer*

Word use: The opposite of this is **cautious.**

dark
adjective **1** with very little or no light: *the* ***dark*** *cave* (***inky, jet-black, pitch-black***)
2 more like black than white: *a* ***dark*** *colour*
3 angry-looking or gloomy: *He gave us a* ***dark*** *look.*
noun **4** absence of light: *My little brother is afraid of the* ***dark.***
5 night: *Please come home before* ***dark.***
phrase **6 in the dark,** ignorant or knowing nothing

Word building: **darkness** *noun*
Word history: Old English *deorc*

darken
verb **1** to make dark (***dim, obscure, shade***)
2 to become dark: *The sky* ***darkened.***

dark horse
noun **1** an unexpected winner in a race, competition, etc.
2 a person whose abilities may be greater than they are known to be

dark matter
noun theoretically postulated matter of unknown nature that comprises 90 per cent or more of the mass of the universe

darkroom
noun a room which is sealed so that no light can get in, used for developing and printing film

darling
noun someone who is loved very much: *Our new baby is a* ***darling.***

Word building: **darling** *adjective*
Word history: Old English *dēore* dear + *-ling*

darn
verb **1** to mend with crossing rows of stitches: *to* ***darn*** *a hole in my socks* (***stitch, tack, work***)
noun **2** a darned patch in clothing

Word history: Old English *dernan* hide

dart
noun **1** a small metal arrow which is thrown by hand, usually as part of a game or sport
verb **2** to move suddenly or quickly (***hurry, scamper, scoot, scurry***)

Word history: Middle English, from Old French, from Germanic

Darwinism
noun the theory of Charles Darwin which holds that all species developed from parent forms, with only those which have best adapted to their environment surviving to continue to breed

Word building: **Darwinist** *noun* **Darwinist** *adjective*
Word history: from Charles *Darwin*, 1809–82, English naturalist

dash
verb **1** to rush or move quickly: *to* ***dash*** *across the road* (***dart, hasten, speed***)
2 to throw or smash violently: *to* ***dash*** *a cup to the floor*
3 to spoil or ruin: *to* ***dash*** *someone's hopes*
noun **4** a sudden or speedy rush
5 a small amount: *a* ***dash*** *of milk* (***drop, hint, skerrick***)

6 a horizontal line (—) used as punctuation to show a break in a sentence
phrase **7 dash off,** to write quickly: *to **dash off** a letter* (***draft***, ***pen***, ***scribble***)

Word history: Middle English

Dashes (definition 6) are punctuation marks which are used:

1. to mark off a part of a sentence which may not be necessary, but which explains the topic further or adds interest to it. In this case, dashes work the same way as commas or brackets:

   The fashion parade lasted so long — about three hours — that Prince Charles fell asleep.

2. to show an abrupt break or pause in the structure of a sentence:

   And suddenly, at the end of the film she — but I won't spoil it for you by telling you the ending.

3. instead of colons at the beginning of an informal list:

   He emptied out the contents of his pencil case — a rubber, two pencils, a pencil sharpener and a stapler.

Look up **comma** and **bracket.**

dashboard
noun the panel in a car or plane which is in front of the driver's seat and has instruments for measuring things like speed, the distance you have travelled and the temperature of the engine

Word use: The short form is **dash**.

dashing
adjective smartly dressed and high-spirited: *a **dashing** young man*

data (day-tuh, dah-tuh)
plural noun **1** facts or information: *to gather **data** for a report on schools in Australia*
2 *Computers* digital information

Noun forms: The singular is **datum**.

Data can mean one block of information, or many individual items. So you may use it as a singular or plural noun.

Whichever you choose, remember that the verb and pronoun you use should be in agreement:

The data was analysed carefully and results were calculated on the basis of it. (**data** as a singular noun)

or

As the data were collected they were quickly classified. (**data** as a plural noun)

Look up **agreement in grammar**. Note that one piece of information is sometimes called a **datum** in technical language.

database
noun a collection of information stored in a computer and organised in categories so that it can be retrieved easily

datacast
verb to broadcast digital information: *The technician had to **datacast** the pictures for the evening news.*

Verb forms: I **datacast**, I have **datacasted**, I am **datacasting**
Word building: **datacaster** *noun* **datacasting** *noun*

date[1]
noun **1** the day or year of something happening, or a statement of it in numbers: *What's the **date** of Easter next year? | Today's **date** is the 29th.*
2 the period of time to which something belongs: *This old coin is valuable because of its early **date**.*
3 an appointment made for a particular time: *a **date** with the dentist* (***assignation***, ***rendezvous***, ***tryst***)
4 someone with whom you have an arrangement to go out, especially someone you are romantically interested in: *Do you have a date for the dance on Saturday?*
verb **5** to mark with a date: *to **date** a letter*
6 to belong to a particular time: *This vase **dates** from 50 BC*
7 to go out with someone in whom you have romantic interest: *Are you dating anyone at present?*
phrase **8 out of date,** old-fashioned: *The dress I bought last year is already **out of date**.*
9 to date, to the present time

Word history: Middle English, from French, from Latin word meaning 'things given'

date[2]
noun the small brown fruit that grows on the date palm tree, which tastes very sweet and is often dried for eating

Word history: Middle English, from Old French, from Latin, from Greek word meaning 'date', originally 'finger'

dated
adjective old-fashioned: ***dated** clothes*

date line
noun **1** a line in a letter, newspaper article, etc., giving the date (and often the place) of origin
2 an imaginary line running approximately along the meridian 180° from Greenwich, England, the areas on either side of which are counted as differing by one calendar day

Word use: You can also use **International Date Line** for definition 2.

datum (day-tuhm, dah-tuhm)
noun **1** any given statement which forms a basis for further reasoning
2 any fact taken to be a matter of direct observation

Noun forms: The plural is **data**.
Word use: You will find this in technical writing — look up **data**, which is used much more commonly.
Word history: from Latin word meaning 'something given'

daub (dawb)
verb **1** to cover or coat, especially with something soft or sticky like paint or mud: *to **daub** a canvas with paint* (***plaster***, ***smear***)
noun **2** sticky clay or mud: *a hut made of wattle and **daub***

Word history: Middle English, from Old French, from Latin word meaning 'whiten', 'plaster'

daughter (daw-tuh)
noun someone's female child: *My parents have two* ***daughters.***

Word history: Old English *dohtor*

daughter-in-law
noun the wife of your son

Noun forms: The plural is **daughters-in-law**.

daunt (dawnt)
verb to discourage or make frightened: *We're not* ***daunted*** *by the rain.*

Word building: **daunting** *adjective*
Word history: Middle English, from Old French, from Latin word meaning 'tame', 'subdue'

dauntless
adjective fearless or bold

dauphin (daw-fuhn, doh-fan)
noun the title of the eldest son of the king of France, from 1349 to 1830

Word history: French, apparently originally a proper name used as a surname; often identified with Latin *delphīnus* dolphin

dawdle
verb to waste time by being slow: *to* ***dawdle*** *on your way home* (***dally, delay, linger, loiter, tarry***)

Word building: **dawdler** *noun*
Word history: perhaps a variant of *daddle* toddle

dawn
noun **1** the time of day when it begins to get light (***sunrise***)
2 the beginning of anything: *the* ***dawn*** *of civilisation* (***outset, start***)
verb **3** to begin: *A new day has* ***dawned.***
phrase **4 dawn on**, to begin to be understood by: *It finally* ***dawned on*** *him that he needs to practise.*

Word history: Middle English *dawening* dawn, apparently from Scandinavian

day
noun **1** the time between sunrise and sunset when the sky is light
2 the 24 hour period between midnight of one day and the following midnight: *There are seven* ***days*** *in a week.*
3 the time when you are actively doing things: *Have you had a good* ***day****?*
4 a particular time or period: *There were no mobile phones in my grandmother's* ***day.***
phrase **5 call it a day**, to finish doing something for the time being
6 day by day, daily, or each day
7 day in, day out, all day, every day for a period of time

Word use: Definition 4 can also be used in the plural form as in *the olden days* or *in those days*.
Word history: Old English

daybreak
noun dawn or the first appearance of light in the morning

daydream
verb to dreamily imagine pleasant things: *I often* ***daydream*** *about horses.* (***be lost in thought, let your thoughts wander, muse, switch off***)

Word building: **daydream** *noun* **daydreamer** *noun*

daylight saving
noun a system of putting the clock forward by one or more hours during the summer months so as to add more hours of daylight to the time that most people are awake: *6 o'clock in standard time becomes 7 o'clock in* ***daylight saving*** *or summertime.*

daze
verb **1** to stun, confuse, or bewilder: *He was* ***dazed*** *by a knock on the head. | Success* ***dazed*** *him.*
noun **2** a confused state or condition: *to be in a* ***daze***

Word history: Middle English, from Scandinavian

dazzle
verb **1** to lessen (someone's) vision by a sudden intense brightness
2 to amaze or surprise: *The children* ***dazzled*** *the audience with their display of gymnastics.*

Word building: **dazzling** *adjective*
Word history: from *daze*

D-day
noun the day set for the beginning of a previously planned attack, especially the day (6 June 1944) of the Allied entry into Normandy in World War II

DDT
noun a very powerful insecticide

Word history: abbreviation of *d(ichloro-) d(iphenyl-)t(richloroethane)*

deacon (dee-kuhn)
noun someone who assists a priest and has certain duties in the Christian churches

Word building: **deaconess** *feminine noun*
Word history: Old English *dēacon, diacon*, from Late Latin, from Greek word meaning 'servant', 'minister', 'deacon'

dead
adjective **1** no longer alive or useful: ***dead*** *leaves | a* ***dead*** *match* (***deceased, lifeless***)
2 numb or unable to feel anything: *to be* ***dead*** *to pain after an anaesthetic*
3 very tired or exhausted: *She felt* ***dead*** *after chopping wood all day.*
4 complete or absolute: ***dead*** *silence*
adverb **5** completely or absolutely: *You're* ***dead*** *right. | He stopped* ***dead.***
phrase **6 dead to the world**, *Colloquial* very deeply asleep

Word use: The opposite of definition 1 is **alive**.
Word history: Old English *dēad*

dead centre
noun in a piston-driven engine or pump, either of two positions of the crank in which the connecting rod has no power to turn it, occurring when the piston is at the top or bottom of its stroke

deaden
verb to weaken or dull: *Carpet* ***deadens*** *the sound of footsteps.*

dead end
noun a street that is closed at one end so that traffic cannot go through

dead heat
noun a race in which two or more competitors finish together

dead letter
noun **1** a law or something similar, which has lost its force, but is not formally done away with
2 a letter which lies unclaimed at a post office, usually because of incorrect address, etc.

Word building: **dead-letter** *adjective*

deadline
noun the latest time for finishing something: *The **deadline** for your project is next Friday.*

deadlock[1]
noun the point which people reach in an argument when neither side will give way (***stalemate***, ***standstill***, ***impasse***)

deadlock[2]
noun a lock with a bolt which can be fixed in place after the door is shut. It is more secure than a spring-loaded bolt.

deadly
adjective **1** likely to cause death: *a **deadly** poison* (***lethal***, ***malignant***, ***terminal***)
2 *Colloquial* wonderful; excellent

Adjective forms: **deadlier**, **deadliest**

deadpan
adjective Colloquial **1** lacking expression, especially when telling jokes
adverb **2** without expression or in a deadpan way

deaf (def)
adjective **1** not able to hear, partially or wholly
phrase **2 turn a deaf ear**, to refuse to listen

Word building: **deafness** *noun*
Word history: Old English *dēaf*

deafen
verb to make deaf: *That **drilling** is starting to deafen me.*

Word building: **deafening** *adjective*

deal
verb **1** to give out or hand out: *to **deal** the cards* (***dispense***, ***distribute***)
2 to do business or trade: *to **deal** with a biscuit company | to **deal** in rare books*
noun **3** quantity or amount: *a great **deal** of noise*
4 an arrangement or agreement: *We made a **deal** not to fight any more.*
phrase **5 deal with**,
a to be about: *This book **deals with** Australian explorers.*
b to take action against: *The teacher will **deal with** the children who broke the window.*
c to treat or behave towards: *Our teacher always **deals** fairly **with** us.*

Verb forms: I **dealt**, I have **dealt**, I am **dealing**
Word history: Old English *dǣlan* divide, share

dealer
noun **1** someone who buys and sells things: *a car **dealer*** (***broker***, ***merchant***, ***retailer***, ***vendor***)
2 the player who gives out the cards in a card game

dealings
plural noun business or connections between people

dean
noun **1** the head priest in charge of a cathedral
2 the head of a university faculty

Word history: Middle English, from Old French, from Late Latin word meaning 'chief of ten'

dear
adjective **1** greatly loved: *a **dear** friend*
2 costing too much (***costly***, ***exorbitant***, ***expensive***)
3 Dear, (at the beginning of a letter) a word put before the name of the person you are writing to, as the conventional polite way of starting a letter: *Dear Mr Matthews*
noun **4** someone you love: *my **dear***

Word building: **dearly** *adverb* **dearness** *noun*
Word history: Old English *dēore*

dear / deer
Don't confuse **dear** with **deer**, which is a large grass-eating animal.

dearth (derth)
noun **1** a very small supply or lack (***deficiency***, ***deficit***, ***insufficiency***, ***shortage***)
2 a famine or a small supply of food

Word history: Old English *dēor*, hard, rigorous

death
noun **1** the end of life: *A car accident caused his **death**.*
2 the end or destruction of anything: *the **death** of our hopes of winning a gold medal*
phrase **3 do to death**,
a to kill
b to repeat until all meaning seems to be lost
4 put to death, to kill or execute
5 sick to death of, bored and annoyed with

Word history: Old English *dēath*

death adder
noun a venomous snake of Australia and Papua New Guinea with a thick body and broad head

Word use: This snake is commonly known as **deaf adder**.

death duty
noun a tax paid on property received through a will

Word use: This word is usually used in its plural form **death duties**.

deathly
adverb like or as in death: ***deathly** pale*

Word history: Old English *dēathlīc*

debacle (day-<u>bah</u>-kuhl, duh-<u>bah</u>-kuhl)
noun a sudden break-up, overthrow, collapse, or crushing disaster (***calamity***, ***catastrophe***, ***misfortune***, ***tragedy***)

Word history: French *dé-* + *bâcler* bar, from Latin word meaning 'stick', 'rod'

debar
verb **1** to prevent from being present or involved: *to **debar** him from appearing in court*
2 to prevent or disallow: *to **debar** an action*

Verb forms: I **debarred**, I have **debarred**, I am **debarring**
Word history: Old French *des-* + *barrer* bar

debase
verb **1** to reduce in quality (***adulterate***, ***contaminate***)
2 to lower in rank

Word building: **debasement** *noun*

debatable
adjective open to question or discussion: *The Government's latest stand on that issue is* ***debatable.***

Word use: You can also use **debateable.**

debate
noun **1** an organised discussion: *a* ***debate*** *in parliament*
2 an organised contest in which two teams of speakers put forward opposite views on a chosen subject
verb **3** to argue or discuss: *to* ***debate*** *the issue*

Word building: **debater** *noun*
Word history: Middle English, from Old French

debauched (duh-bawcht)
adjective living a life of too much sex, drinking, drug-taking, etc.: *a* ***debauched*** *lifestyle*

Word building: **debauchery** *noun*
Word history: Old French word meaning 'seduce from duty'

debenture
noun **1** a note saying that you owe someone money
2 money that is lent to a business at a fixed rate of interest and that has a guarantee of repayment

Word history: from Latin word meaning 'there are owing'

debilitate (duh-bil-uh-tayt)
verb to make weak, weaken or enfeeble

Word building: **debilitation** *noun* **debility** *noun*
Word history: from Latin word meaning 'weakened'

debit (deb-uht)
noun **1** the recording of a debt in an account
2 *Bookkeeping*
a an entry recording a debt
b the left-hand side of an account, where debit entries are made
verb **3** to charge with a debt: *The shop will* ***debit*** *her for the purchase.*
4 to enter on the debit side of an account

Word use: Compare definition 2 with **credit.**
Word history: from Latin word meaning 'something owed'

debonair (deb-uh-nair)
adjective Old-fashioned cheerful and with pleasant manners

Word history: Middle English, from Old French phrase *de bon aire* of good disposition

debrief (dee-breef)
verb to question after a mission: *to* ***debrief*** *a soldier, astronaut or diplomat*

Word building: **debriefing** *noun*

debris (deb-ree, day-bree, duh-bree)
noun the rubbish left when something is broken or destroyed (***garbage***, ***junk***, ***refuse***, ***trash***)

Word use: The 's' is silent because this word comes from French.
Word history: Old French

debt (det)
noun **1** anything that you owe someone else
phrase **2 bad debt,** a debt that will not be paid: *The shopkeeper was owed $1000 in* ***bad debts.***

Word building: **indebted** *adjective*
Word history: Middle English, from Old French *dete*, from Latin word meaning 'thing owed'

debtor (det-uh)
noun someone who owes money: *He is my* ***debtor*** *because he owes me money.*

Word use: Compare this with **creditor.**

debug
verb Colloquial **1** to find and remove faults in: *to* ***debug*** *an electronic system*
2 to remove electronic listening devices from: *to* ***debug*** *a room*

Verb forms: I **debugged,** I have **debugged,** I am **debugging**

debunk
verb Colloquial to make fun or show up the falseness of

debut (day-booh, duh-booh)
noun **1** a first appearance in public, on stage, etc.
2 a formal introduction and entrance into society

Word history: from French word meaning 'make the first stroke in a game', 'make one's first appearance'

debutant (deb-yuh-tont)
noun Sport a young player making their first appearance at a particular level

debutante (deb-yuh-tont)
noun a girl making her debut into society

Word building: **debutant** *masculine noun*
Word history: French

decade (dek-ayd)
noun a period of time lasting ten years

Word history: French, from Latin, from Greek word meaning 'a group of ten'

decadence (dek-uh-duhns)
noun **1** decay, deterioration, or the act or process of falling into a lower state
2 luxurious self-indulgence: *the* ***decadence*** *of a luxury holiday.*

Word building: **decadent** *adjective* **decadent** *noun*
Word history: French, from Latin *dē* + *cadere* fall

decaffeinated (dee-kaf-uhn-ay-tuhd)
adjective with the drug caffeine taken out: ***decaffeinated*** *coffee*

decagon (dek-uh-gon, dek-uh-guhn)
noun a flat shape with ten straight sides

Word building: **decagonal** *adjective*
Word history: Medieval Latin *deca-* + *-gon*

decahedron (dek-uh-heed-ruhn)
noun a solid shape with ten flat faces

Noun forms: The plural is **decahedrons** or **decahedra.**

decant
verb to pour gently from one container into another

Word history: Medieval Latin

decanter (duh-kan-tuh)
noun a container, usually a specially made glass bottle with a stopper, for serving wine, water or juice at the table

decapitate
verb to cut off the head of

Word building: **decapitation** *noun*

Word history: Medieval Latin, from Latin *caput* head

decathlon (duh-kath-luhn, duh-kath-lon)
noun a contest in which athletes compete for the highest score in ten different events

Word building: **decathlete** *noun*
Word history: Greek *deca-* + *âthlon* contest

decay (duh-kay)
verb to rot or go bad (***decompose***, ***deteriorate***, ***fester***, ***perish***, ***putrefy***)

Word building: **decay** *noun*
Word history: Middle English, from Old French *de-* + *cair* (from Latin word meaning 'fall')

decease (duh-sees)
noun death: *After his wife's **decease** Bob stayed home to care for the children.*

Word history: Middle English, from Old French, from Latin word meaning 'departure', 'death'

deceased
adjective **1** dead: *a **deceased** person* (***departed***, ***late***)
phrase **2 the deceased**, the dead person or people: *The will of **the deceased** was read.*

deceased / diseased

Don't confuse **deceased** with **diseased**. If someone or something has a disease, they are **diseased**:

After years of smoking, my uncle's lungs are diseased.

deceit
noun **1** the ability to trick or mislead someone (***cunning***, ***guile***, ***trickery***, ***wiles***)
2 a trick or other act meant to deceive someone (***subterfuge***, ***ploy***, ***deception***)

Word building: **deceitful** *adjective* **deceitfulness** *noun*
Word history: Middle English, from Old French word meaning 'deceive'

deceive
verb to trick or mislead: *She **deceived** us by saying she'd found the money when she'd really stolen it.* (***cheat***, ***delude***, ***dupe***, ***hoodwink***)

Word building: **deception** *noun*
Word history: Middle English, from Old French, from Latin word meaning 'catch', 'deceive'

decelerate (dee-sel-uh-rayt)
verb to decrease in velocity or speed

Word use: The opposite is **accelerate**.
Word building: **deceleration** *noun*
Word history: *de-* + *(ac)celerate*

December
noun the twelfth month of the year, containing 31 days

Word history: Latin: the tenth month of the early Roman year

decency
noun **1** the condition or quality of being decent: *He showed his **decency** by looking after me when I was sick.*
2 decencies, standards of behaviour that people think are respectable: *All the **decencies** were observed at his funeral.*

Noun forms: The plural is **decencies**.

decent (dee-suhnt)
adjective **1** respectable or proper: ***decent** behaviour* (***ethical***, ***honest***, ***moral***, ***upright***)
2 reasonable or good enough: *to earn a **decent** wage* (***adequate***, ***satisfactory***)
3 kind and helpful: *It was **decent** of you to give me a lift home.*

Word use: The opposite of definition 1 is **indecent**. | The opposite of definition 2 is **inadequate** or **unreasonable**.
Word building: **decently** *adverb*
Word history: from Latin word meaning 'fitting'

decentralise
verb **1** to spread out from an area where a lot of people live to an area without many people: *Industry has been **decentralised** and many companies have now built new plants in country areas.*
2 to spread administration more evenly: *to **decentralise** an organisation | to **decentralise** government*

Word use: You can also use **decentralize**.
Word building: **decentralisation** *noun*

deception
noun a trick or something that deceives

Word building: **deceptive** *adjective* **deceptively** *adverb*
Word history: Middle English, from Late Latin word meaning 'deceive'

decibel (des-uh-bel)
noun a measure of loudness used to show how much louder one sound is than another

decide
verb **1** to make up your mind: *I couldn't work out whether to go or not, but I've **decided** now.* (***conclude***, ***resolve***, ***arrive at a decision***)
2 to judge or settle: *We will ask the teacher to **decide** the argument.* (***arbitrate***, ***determine***, ***adjudge***, ***make a ruling on***)

Word building: **decision** *noun*
Word history: Middle English, from Latin word meaning 'cut off', 'determine'

decided
adjective **1** definite and obvious: *a **decided** difference between my writing and yours*
2 having firmly made up your mind: *He felt quite **decided** about not going to the party.*

decidedly
adverb definitely: *Your work has **decidedly** improved.*

deciduous (duh-sid-jooh-uhs)
adjective of a plant, losing the leaves every year: *They have a nice mix of **deciduous** trees and evergreens in their garden.*

Word use: Compare this with **evergreen**.
Word history: from Latin word meaning 'falling down'

decimal
adjective **1** based on tenths or on the number ten: ***decimal** currency*
noun **2** a decimal fraction or number

Word history: Latin *decimus* tenth + *-al*

decimal fraction
noun a fraction in which the bottom number is 10, 100, 1000, 10 000, etc., usually written with just the top number and a dot in front of it, as $0.4 = \frac{4}{10}$, $0.04 = \frac{4}{100}$

Word use: Compare this with **common fraction**.

decimal number
noun a number consisting of a whole number and a decimal fraction, separated by a dot, such as *4.23*

decimal point
noun the dot in a decimal fraction

decimate
verb to destroy every tenth one or a great number: *The soldiers* ***decimated*** *the enemy in a fierce battle.*

Word history: Latin, from the Roman practice of punishing soldiers who mutinied by drawing them up in ranks and executing one in every ten

decipher (duh-suy-fuh)
verb to solve or find the meaning of: *to* ***decipher*** *a code*

decipherable
adjective able to be understood or read

Word use: The opposite is **indecipherable**.

decision
noun **1** the act of making up your mind: *a difficult* ***decision***
2 an opinion or judgement: *The judge's* ***decision*** *is final.*
3 firmness and certainty in all you think and do: *a woman of* ***decision***

Word history: from Latin word meaning 'a cutting down', 'decision'

decisive
adjective **1** ending all argument or with the power of deciding: *a* ***decisive*** *victory*
2 able to make decisions easily; determined

Word use: The opposite of definition 2 is **indecisive**.

deck
noun **1** the floor of a ship or bus
2 an open, raised platform or verandah, usually made of wood
verb **3** to decorate or dress: *to* ***deck*** *the Christmas tree with tinsel*
phrase **4 hit the deck**, *Colloquial* to fall on the ground or the floor
5 on deck, on duty or ready for action

Word history: from Middle Dutch word meaning 'cover'

declaim (duh-klaym)
verb **1** to make a formal speech
2 to speak violently: *to* ***declaim*** *against the new law*

Word building: **declamation** *noun* **declamatory** *adjective*
Word history: Middle English, from Latin word meaning 'cry aloud'

declaration
noun an announcement

declare (duh-klair)
verb **1** to announce or make known officially: *The government* ***declared*** *war.* (***advertise***, ***broadcast***, ***proclaim***, ***report***, ***reveal***)
2 to close a cricket innings before all ten wickets have fallen

Word history: Middle English, from Latin word meaning 'make clear'

declension (duh-klen-shuhn)
noun **1** *Grammar*
a the form (inflection) of a noun, pronoun or adjective that shows its case, number or gender, for example *who, whose, whom*
b a class of such words having similar sets of forms, as the second declension in Latin
2 a bending, sloping, or moving downward

Word history: from Latin word meaning 'a bending aside', 'inflection'

decline (duh-kluyn)
verb **1** to refuse politely: *She* ***declined*** *the opportunity to say anything more.* (***reject***, ***renounce***, ***pass up***)
2 to turn down an offer or invitation politely: *I asked him to the party but he* ***declined***. (***beg off***, ***refuse***)
3 to become worse or less: *His health has* ***declined***. | *School attendance* ***declines*** *in wet weather.* (***degenerate***, ***worsen***)
noun (duh-kluyn, dee-kluyn) **4** a slope going down
5 a deterioration or slow loss in health, strength, value, or something like this

Word use: The opposite of definition 2 is **accept**. | The opposite of definition 3 is **improve**.
Word history: Middle English, from Latin word meaning 'bend from', 'avoid', 'inflect'

decode
verb to translate from code into the original language or form: *to* ***decode*** *a message*

Word use: The opposite of this is **encode**.
Word building: **decoder** *noun*

decommission
verb **1** to remove (something or someone) from service: *After many years of navy service, the vessel was finally* ***decommissioned***.
2 to close down (a facility, like a power station, sewerage plant, etc.)

decompose
verb to rot or break up: *Leaves* ***decomposed*** *under the forest trees.* (***decay***, ***deteriorate***, ***perish***)

Word building: **decomposition** *noun*
Word history: French *dé-* + *composer* compose

decomposer
noun Ecology a bacterium or a fungus which breaks down the cells of dead plants and animals into simpler substances

decompress
verb **1** to reduce the pressure in
2 to return to the normal pressure of the atmosphere in a decompression chamber: *to* ***decompress*** *a diver*
3 *Computers* to decode (data) from a compressed storage format into its original format

Word use: Another term for definition 3 is **unzip**.
Word building: **decompression** *noun*

decompression chamber
noun a room in which pressure can be changed slowly so that people who have been under high pressure, such as divers, etc., can gradually be returned to atmospheric pressure

Word use: Another name is **hyperbaric chamber**.

decongestant (dee-kuhn-jest-uhnt)
noun **1** a drug that relieves congestion or stuffiness of your nose or chest caused by a virus or allergy
adjective **2** relieving stuffiness and congestion: *a **decongestant** cough mixture*

decontaminate
verb to remove dangerous chemicals or make them safe: *to **decontaminate** an object | to **decontaminate** an area*

decor (day-kaw, dek-aw)
noun the way a room is decorated or furnished

Word history: French, from Latin word meaning 'decorate'

decorate
verb **1** to make bright and pretty by adding something like paint, wallpaper, beautiful objects, or streamers: *to **decorate** a room | to **decorate** the Christmas tree* (***adorn**, **embellish***)
2 to honour with a medal or badge: *to be **decorated** for bravery*

Word building: **decorative** *adjective*
Word history: Latin

decoration
noun **1** the act of decorating
2 something that decorates: *party **decorations***
3 a badge, medal or something like this, given and worn as a sign of honour

decorator
noun a person whose job is to decorate, especially the inside of a house or building

decorous (dek-uh-ruhs)
adjective behaving properly

Word building: **decorously** *adverb* **decorousness** *noun*

decorum (duh-kaw-ruhm)
noun proper behaviour, speech or dress: *to act with **decorum** at school assembly*

Word history: from Latin word meaning 'something decorous'

decoy (dee-koy)
noun something or someone that tempts or lures, especially into danger or into a trap: *The police officer was used as a **decoy** to trap the bag thief.*

Word building: **decoy** *verb*
Word history: variant of *coy* (now a dialect word), both from Dutch *(de) kooi* (the) cage, from Latin *cavea* cage

decrease (duh-krees)
verb **1** to make less: *I have **decreased** the amount of sugar I take in my tea.* (***cut back**, **diminish**, **lower**, **reduce***)
2 to become less gradually: *Cinema audiences have **decreased**.* (***diminish**, **lessen**, **wane***)
noun (dee-krees, duh-krees) **3** a gradual lessening or reduction: *There has been a **decrease** in bus services.*

Word history: Middle English, from Old French, from Latin word meaning 'grow less'

decree
noun an official order or command: *a government **decree*** (***command**, **regulation***)

Word building: **decree** *verb* (**decreed**, **decreeing**)
Word history: Middle English, from Old French, from Latin word meaning 'decree'

decrepit
adjective made weak or broken down by old age: *a **decrepit** old man | a **decrepit** car* (***crumbling**, **infirm**, **moth-eaten**, **threadbare**, **timeworn***)

Word building: **decrepitude** *noun*
Word history: from Latin word meaning 'noiseless'

decry (duh-kruy)
verb to speak badly of

Verb forms: I **decried**, I have **decried**, I am **decrying**
Word building: **decrial** *noun*
Word history: French *dé-* + *crier* cry

dedicate
verb **1** to devote or give up completely: *land **dedicated** for public use | She **dedicated** her life to helping the poor.*
2 to put the name of someone on, as a sign of thanks or respect: *The author **dedicated** the book to his wife.*

Word building: **dedication** *noun*
Word history: from Latin word meaning 'proclaimed', 'devoted'

deduce
verb to work out by reasoning: *We **deduced** that he would be late.* (***gather**, **infer**, **reason***)

Word building: **deducible** *adjective* **deductive** *adjective*
Word history: from Latin word meaning 'lead down', 'derive'

deduct
verb to take away: *I'm going to **deduct** a dollar from your pocket money.* (***remove**, **subtract***)

Word use: The opposite of this is **add**.
Word building: **deductible** *adjective*
Word history: from Latin word meaning 'led down', 'withdrawn'

deduction
noun **1** an amount taken away: *a **deduction** from my wages*
2 a conclusion or answer worked out from the facts

deed
noun **1** something done: *a good **deed*** (***achievement**, **act**, **action**, **exploit**, **feat***)
2 a signed agreement, usually about ownership of land

Word history: Old English *dēd*

deed poll
noun **1** a formal declaration of a person's act and intention, especially to change his or her name
2 a deed or signed agreement showing this

deem
verb **1** to judge, think or have an opinion
2 to regard or hold as an opinion

Word history: Old English *dēman*

deep
adjective **1** going far down, in, or back: *a **deep** pool | a **deep** wound | a **deep** shelf* (***bottomless**, **gaping**, **cavernous**, **profound***)
2 being a certain distance down, in, or back: *a tank two metres **deep***
3 intense or great in amount: *a **deep** blue | a **deep** sleep | **deep** sorrow*
4 hard to understand: *This book is too **deep** for me.*
5 low in pitch: *a **deep** voice*
phrase **6 go off the deep end**, *Colloquial* to become very angry or excited
7 in deep water, *Colloquial* in trouble or great difficulty

Word building: **deepen** *verb* **depth** *noun*
Word history: Old English *dēop*

deep-fry
verb to cook food in a pan, using enough fat or oil to completely cover it while it is being cooked

Verb forms: I **deep-fried**, I have **deep-fried**, I am **deep-frying**
Word building: **deep-fried** *adjective*

deer
noun a large grass-eating animal with hooves, the male of which has branching horns or antlers

Noun forms: The plural is **deer**.
Word history: Old English *dēor*

deer / dear
Don't confuse **deer** with **dear**, which means 'greatly loved' or 'costing a lot'.

deface
verb to damage the appearance of: *Someone has **defaced** the building by spraying paint on it.*

Word building: **defacement** *noun*
Word history: Middle English, from French

de facto
adjective actually existing although not official or legal: *They decided to recognise the **de facto** government of the rebels.*

Word history: Latin: from the fact, used to describe something that exists as a fact even though it is not legally recognised. This is why it is often used to describe couples who are not legally married but who live together in the same way as couples who are legally married.

defame
verb to damage the good name of: *The local newspaper **defamed** the mayor.* (***libel**, **malign**, **slander**, **slur**, **smear***)

Word building: **defamation** *noun* **defamatory** *adjective*
Word history: Middle English, from Medieval Latin

default (duh-fawlt)
noun **1** neglect or failure to act
2 failure to pay debts
3 *Law* failure to perform an act legally required, especially failure to appear in a law court when required, or failure to pay a debt
4 failure to take part in or finish something, as a competition
5 want, lack, or absence: *owing to **default** of funds*
6 *Computers* a course which a program automatically follows when there are no other specific instructions
verb **7** to fail in fulfilling or satisfying an engagement, claim, or obligation
8 to fail to pay debts, or to account properly for money, etc., in your care
9 *Law* to fail to appear in court or to lose by failure to appear in court
10 a to fail to take part in or finish something, such as a match
b to lose a match by default

Word history: Middle English from Old French

defeat
verb **1** to overcome or beat in a battle or contest (***conquer**, **thrash**, **vanquish***)
noun **2** the state of being beaten: *Our **defeat** on Saturday was the first of the season.*

Word history: Middle English, from Old French word meaning 'undone'

defecate (def-uh-kayt)
verb to pass waste material from the bowel

Word building: **defecation** *noun*
Word history: Latin word meaning 'cleansed from dregs'

defect (dee-fekt)
noun **1** a fault or weakness: *a **defect** in the glass | a **defect** of character*
verb (duh-fekt) **2** to leave your country without permission, not intending to return

Word building: **defection** *noun* **defector** *noun*
Word history: from Latin word meaning 'want', 'defect'

defective
adjective not perfect of having faults: *a **defective** radio* (***faulty**, **shoddy**, **substandard**, **unsound***)

defence
noun **1** a protection against attack: *A moat was part of the castle's **defence**.* (***safeguard**, **security**, **shield***)
2 an argument in support of something or in answer to a charge in court: *her **defence** of Aboriginal land rights | His **defence** was that he was ill.*

Word use: The US spelling is **defense**.
Word building: **defensible** *adjective*
Word history: Middle English, from Old French, from Late Latin word meaning 'prohibition', from Latin word meaning 'ward off'

defend
verb **1** to protect or keep safe, especially from attack: *to **defend** a fort | to **defend** a title* (***guard**, **screen**, **secure**, **shield***)
2 to give support to: *He **defended** me against their unfair criticisms.* (***champion**, **side with**, **stand by**, **stick up for***)

Word history: Middle English, from Old French, from Latin word meaning 'ward off'

defendant
noun a person against whom a charge is brought in a court of law

defensive
adjective **1** designed to defend or protect: ***defensive** armour*
2 made or carried to resist an attack: ***defensive** weapons*
3 acting as if you are being attacked or are expecting to be attacked: *a **defensive** attitude*

defer[1]
verb to put off until another time: *to **defer** the exam* (***adjourn**, **delay**, **postpone**, **shelve**, **suspend***)

Verb forms: I **deferred**, I have **deferred**, I am **deferring**
Word history: Middle English, from Latin word meaning 'delay'

defer²
phrase **defer to**, to give way to in judgement, opinion, or will, especially with respect: *to **defer to** wiser heads than mine*

Verb forms: I **deferred**, I have **deferred**, I am **deferring**
Word history: French from Latin word meaning 'carry from', 'report', 'accuse'

defer / differ
Don't confuse **defer** with **differ**, which is to be different or to disagree.

deferred share
noun Commerce a share sold on the understanding that buyers must accept a delay in payment of dividends if this is necessary

defiance
noun a daring challenge to authority or any opposing force

Word building: **defiant** *adjective*

deficient
adjective lacking: ***deficient** in vitamins*

Word use: The opposite of this is **abundant** or **sufficient**.
Word building: **deficiency** *noun* (*plural* **deficiencies**)

deficit (def-uh-suht)
noun an amount of money lacking: *There is a **deficit** in the accounts.*

Word use: The opposite of this is **surplus**.
Word history: from Latin word meaning 'there is wanting'

defile
verb to make dirty: *Their minds were **defiled** by reading racist literature.*

Word history: Old English *befȳlan* make foul

define
verb **1** to explain the meaning or nature of: *The easiest words are the hardest to **define**.*
2 to fix the limits of: *to **define** a problem*

Word history: Middle English, from French, from Latin word meaning 'limit', 'determine', 'explain', 'terminate'

definite
adjective **1** clearly stated or exact
2 clear or certain: *It is a **definite** advantage to be able to run fast.* (***unmistakable**, **sure**, **positive***)

Word history: from Latin word meaning 'limited', 'determined'

definite article
noun the word *the* in English

Look up **articles in grammar: definite articles**.

definition
noun **1** the act of making something definite or clear
2 a statement of the meaning of a word or phrase: *a dictionary **definition***
3 the clearness of a shape, colour, or sound: *The **definition** in this photo is poor.*

definitive
adjective final, or most accurate and complete: *the **definitive** battle in the war | a **definitive** history of our times*

deflate
verb **1** to let the air out of: *Someone **deflated** his tyres.*
2 to lower or reduce: *to **deflate** prices*
3 to make feel less important: *The criticism **deflated** him.*

Word use: The opposite of this is **inflate**.

deflation
noun **1** the act of deflating
2 a lowering in the price of goods or services, especially when the cost of making these goods is not also lowered

Word use: The opposite of this is **inflation**.

deflect
verb to turn aside: *The armour **deflected** the bullet.* (***divert**, **head off***)

Word building: **deflection** *noun*
Word history: Latin

defoliant
noun a chemical used to cause the leaves to fall from a tree

defoliate
verb to strip of leaves: *The plague of caterpillars **defoliated** the trees.*

Word building: **defoliation** *noun*
Word history: Medieval Latin, from Latin *folium* leaf

deforestation (dee-for-uhst-ay-shuhn)
noun the permanent removal of forests or trees from a large area, usually for commercial purposes

deform (duh-fawm)
verb to disfigure, spoil, or put out of shape

Word building: **deformation** *noun*
Word history: Middle English, from Latin word meaning 'disfigure'

deformed
adjective out of shape: *a **deformed** leg*

deformity
noun **1** the state of being out of shape or spoiled in the way something looks
2 something that is out of shape or spoiled in some way

Noun forms: The plural is **deformities**.

defrag (dee-frag)
Colloquial
verb **1** to defragment a computer disk: ***Defragging** the disk made it easier to find the information they were looking for.*
noun (dee-frag) **2** the process of defragmenting a computer disk: *Try doing a **defrag**.*

Word use: Look up **defragment**.

defragment
verb to reorganise the data stored on (a computer disk) so that whole files are stored in the same place, to eliminate fragmentation (definition 2): *Information was easier to search through after the disks were **defragmented**.*

Word use: You can also use the colloquial word **defrag**.
Word building: **defragmentation** *noun*

defraud
verb to cheat, especially of money (***deceive***, ***fleece***, ***rip off***, ***swindle***, ***trick***)

Word history: Middle English, from Latin

defray (duh-fray)
verb to bear or pay: *to **defray** costs*

Word building: **defrayal** *noun* **defrayment** *noun*
Word history: French, Old French word meaning 'pay costs', from *des-* + *frai* cost

defrost
verb **1** to remove ice from: *to **defrost** a refrigerator*
2 to thaw out: ***Defrost** the chicken before cooking it.*

deft
adjective quick and neat: ***deft** movements*

Word history: Middle English; variant of *daft*

defunct (duh-fungkt)
adjective **1** dead or extinct
2 no longer in use or not operative

Word history: from Latin word meaning 'discharged', 'finished'

defuse
verb **1** to remove the fuse from: *The army expert **defused** the bomb.*
2 to calm: *to **defuse** a tense situation* (***quell***, ***quieten***)

defy
verb **1** to disregard or resist boldly: *A small group **defied** the conqueror.* (***obstruct***, ***oppose***, ***withstand***)
2 to dare: *She **defied** him to do his worst.*

Verb forms: I **defied**, I have **defied**, I am **defying**
Word history: Middle English, from Old French *de-* + *fier* (from Latin word meaning 'trust')

degenerate (duh-jen-uh-rayt)
verb **1** to become bad or worse than before (***decline***, ***rot***, ***waste away***, ***worsen***)
adjective (duh-jen-uh-ruht) **2** corrupt or weak: *a **degenerate** king* (***depraved***, ***perverted***)

Word building: **degeneracy** *noun*
Word history: Latin word meaning 'departed from its race'

degrade
verb to lower or make worse in character or nature

Word building: **degradation** *noun*
Word history: Middle English, from ecclesiastical Late Latin word meaning 'reduce in rank', from Latin *gradus* grade

degree
noun **1** a step or stage: *He recovered by **degrees**.*
2 a level: *She experienced some **degree** of satisfaction.*
3 *Geometry* a unit of measurement of angles, one degree equalling $\frac{1}{360}$ of the circumference of a circle
4 a unit of measurement for temperature
5 a unit of measurement for latitude or longitude
6 an award given by a university

Word use: The symbol for definitions 3, 4 and 5 is °.
Word history: Middle English, from Old French, from Latin *gradus* step, degree

dehydrate
verb to cause to lose water or other fluids: *to **dehydrate** vegetables to preserve them* | *to be **dehydrated** by the desert sun*

Word building: **dehydration** *noun*

deify (dee-uh-fuy, day-uh-fuy)
verb **1** to make a god of
2 to look upon or worship as a deity: *to **deify** money*

Verb forms: I **deified**, I have **deified**, I am **deifying**
Word building: **deification** *noun*
Word history: Middle English, from Old French, from Late Latin

deign (dayn)
verb to stoop or lower yourself: *The duchess **deigned** to answer her servant.*

Word history: Middle English, from Old French, from Latin word meaning 'deem worthy'

deity (dee-uh-tee, day-uh-tee)
noun a god or goddess

Noun forms: The plural is **deities**.
Word history: Middle English, from Old French, from Late Latin

dejected
adjective unhappy or depressed

Word building: **dejection** *noun*

delay
verb **1** to make or be late: *The breakdown **delayed** us.* | *Don't **delay**!* (***dally***, ***linger***, ***loiter***, ***tarry***)
2 to put off or postpone: *We don't want to **delay** our visit.* (***adjourn***, ***postpone***, ***shelve***, ***suspend***)
noun **3** a hold-up or stoppage: *The **delay** was due to a signal failure.*

Word history: Middle English, from Old French, from Latin word meaning 'loosen'

delectable
adjective delicious: ***delectable** food*

Word history: Middle English, from Latin

delegate (del-uh-gayt)
verb **1** to give or pass on to someone else: *The manager **delegated** her authority to the foreman.*
noun (del-uh-guht) **2** a representative or deputy: *There were 50 **delegates** at the conference.*

Word history: from Latin word meaning 'sent', 'deputed'

delegation (del-uh-gay-shuhn)
noun **1** an act of delegating
2 a group of people officially appointed to represent another, or others

delete
verb to strike or wipe out: ***Delete** their names from the list.* (***cross out***, ***drop***, ***leave out***, ***obliterate***)

Word use: The opposite of this is **insert**.
Word building: **deletion** *noun*
Word history: from Latin word meaning 'done away with', 'destroyed'

deleterious (del-uh-tear-ree-uhs)
adjective harmful to health

Word history: Neo-Latin, from Greek

deliberate (duh-lib-uh-ruht)
adjective **1** intentional or carefully considered (***planned***, ***premeditated***, ***purposeful***)

verb (duh-lib-uh-rayt) **2** to consider, or think carefully

Word building: **deliberation** *noun*
Word history: from Latin word meaning 'weighed well'

delicacy (del-uh-kuh-see)
noun **1** fineness: *the **delicacy** of the lace cloth*
2 a tasty or expensive food: *Caviar is a **delicacy**.*

Noun forms: The plural is **delicacies**.

delicate
adjective **1** finely-made or sensitive: ***delicate** lace / a **delicate** measuring instrument*
2 easily damaged or weakened: ***delicate** china / **delicate** health* (***breakable, brittle, frail***)
3 pale or soft: *a **delicate** face / a **delicate** shade of blue* (***feathery, fine, flimsy, gauzy***)

Word history: Middle English, from Latin word meaning 'delightful', 'luxurious', 'soft'

delicatessen (del-uh-kuh-tes-uhn)
noun a shop which sells a variety of foods, including cheeses, sausages, and other prepared goods

Word use: You can also use the colloquial word **deli**.
Word history: German word meaning 'delicacies', from French, from Italian word meaning 'delicate'

delicious (duh-lish-uhs)
adjective very pleasing to smell or taste: *a **delicious** meal* (***appetising, luscious, mouth-watering, scrumptious***)

Word history: Middle English, from Old French, from Latin word meaning 'delight'

delight
noun **1** great enjoyment or pleasure: *The children's faces lit up with **delight** when they saw their presents.*
verb **2** to give great pleasure: *Their singing **delighted** everyone.* (***appeal to, attract, charm, satisfy***)
phrase **3 delight in**, to take great pleasure in: *I **delighted in** helping them.*

Word building: **delighted** *adjective* **delightful** *adjective* **delightfully** *adverb*
Word history: from Latin word meaning 'allure'

delineate (duh-lin-ee-ayt)
verb **1** to draw the outline or shape of
2 to describe or show in words

Word building: **delineable** *adjective* **delineation** *noun*
Word history: from Latin word meaning 'sketched out'

delinquent (duh-ling-kwuhnt)
adjective **1** guilty of a lapse from good behaviour or from conformity to the law (***insubordinate, unruly***)
noun **2** someone, usually a young person, who is in trouble with the law

Word building: **delinquency** *noun*
Word history: Latin

delirious (duh-lear-ree-uhs)
adjective restless, excited, and seeing things that aren't there, as when you have a fever

Word building: **deliriously** *adverb*

delirium
noun **1** a disorder of the mind (which is usually only temporary) caused by a high fever or by being intoxicated with alcohol, etc., during which the sufferer is restless, excited, and sometimes sees things that aren't there
2 a state of wild excitement or emotion

Noun forms: The plural is **deliriums** or **deliria**.
Word history: from Latin word meaning 'be deranged', literally 'go out of the furrow'

deliver
verb **1** to carry and hand over (***convey, transfer, transport***)
2 to help at the birth of: *The doctor **delivered** her baby.*
3 to cause to move in a certain direction: *The bowler **delivered** a fast ball.*
4 to give or declare: *to **deliver** a verdict*
5 to save or set free: *The army **delivered** the besieged town.* (***emancipate, liberate, release, rescue***)

Word building: **deliverance** *noun*
Word history: Middle English, from French, from Late Latin word meaning 'set free'

delivery
noun **1** the delivering of letters, goods, etc.
2 a way of speaking: *a clear **delivery***
3 an act or way of delivering: *the **delivery** of a ball by the bowler in cricket*
4 the act of giving birth to a baby

Noun forms: The plural is **deliveries**.

delta
noun the flat rich land between outspreading river branches at the mouth of a river

Word history: from one form of the Greek letter delta which is triangular in shape. Originally it referred to a triangular area enclosed by the Nile between the two main branches at its mouth, but then it came to mean any such river mouth.

delude
verb to trick or mislead: *He has **deluded** them into thinking that he is an honest man.* (***dupe, hoodwink, mislead, take for a ride***)

Word history: from Latin word meaning 'play false'

deluge (del-yoohj)
noun **1** a great flood or downpour
2 anything that pours out like a flood: *a **deluge** of words*

Word building: **deluge** *verb*
Word history: Middle English, from Old French, from Latin

delusion (duh-looh-zhuhn, duh-lyooh-zhuhn)
noun false belief

delusion / illusion

These words are often confused, partly because they look and sound alike and partly because they both have to do with mistaken notions about reality.

An **illusion** is when our eyes deceive us about something. When a magician pulls a rabbit out of a hat, that is an **illusion**. It can also mean 'a false impression', as when you have an **illusion** of freedom.

(continued)

delusion *(continued)*

The word **delusion** suggests that your own beliefs and perceptions are distorted. If you think that you are Napoleon then you are suffering from a **delusion**. To have *delusions of grandeur* is to think that you are more important than you really are.

Illusions are usually fleeting things whereas **delusions** are often established over a long period of time.

deluxe (duh-luks)
adjective of expensive high quality: *a **deluxe** hotel with gold taps in the bathrooms* (***excellent, high-class, prize, quality***)

Word history: from French word meaning 'of luxury'

delve
phrase **delve into**, to search deeply: *He **delved into** the cupboard for clean socks.* (***explore, probe***)

Word history: Old English *delfan*

demagogue (dem-uh-gog)
noun a leader who gains popularity by stirring up the emotions and prejudices of the people

Word building: **demagogic** (dem-uh-gog-ik) *adjective*
Word history: Greek *dêmos* people + *agōgós* leader

demand
verb **1** to ask for, as if it's your right: *He **demands** an apology.* (***insist on, order, require, stipulate***)
2 to need: *This job **demands** a lot of patience.*
noun **3** a request or need: *a **demand** for information | a big **demand** for sandals* (***call, requirement***)
4 a question
phrase **5 on demand**,
a *Commerce* required to be payed when someone asks: *cash **on demand***
b as required

Word history: French, from Medieval Latin word meaning 'demand', from Latin word meaning 'give in charge', 'entrust'

demarcation (dee-mah-kay-shuhn)
noun **1** the marking off of the boundaries of something
2 a division between things, especially between types of work carried out by members of different trade unions
3 separation by clear boundaries

Word history: from Spanish word meaning 'mark out the bounds of'

demean
verb to lower in people's opinion: *Don't **demean** yourself by having tantrums at your age.*

Word history: *de-* + *mean*, modelled on *debase*

demeanour (duh-mee-nuh)
noun the way you behave, and the impression this gives people of what you are like: *Everyone was upset by his sad **demeanour**.*

Word use: You can also use **demeanor**.
Word history: Middle English, from Old French, from *de-* + *mener* lead

demented
adjective mad: *For a while she was **demented** with grief.*

Word building: **dementedly** *adverb*

dementia (duh-men-shuh)
noun madness or a loss of mental powers: *She suffers from a form of **dementia**.*

Word history: from Latin word meaning 'madness'

demerit (dee-mer-uht)
noun **1** a failing in behaviour
2 a mark against a person for bad behaviour

Word history: Medieval Latin word meaning 'fault', from Latin word meaning 'deserve'

demilitarised zone
noun an area in which the gathering of, or control by, military forces is not allowed

Word use: You can also use **demilitarized zone**.

demise (duh-muyz)
noun death

Word history: from Old French word meaning 'sent or put away'

demister (dee-mis-tuh)
noun an apparatus that blows air, usually heated, onto the windscreen of a car to clear it of mist

democracy (duh-mok-ruh-see)
noun **1** a way of governing a country, in which the people elect representatives to govern the country on their behalf
2 a country with such a government
3 the idea that everyone in a country has equal rights: ***Democracy** demands that everyone should have the right to vote.*

Word building: **democratic** *adjective*
Word history: French, from Greek *dēmokratía* popular government, from *dēmo-* + *-kratía* rule, authority

democrat
noun someone who supports democracy

demography (duh-mog-gruh-fee)
noun the science of population statistics, as of births, deaths, diseases, marriages, etc.

Word building: **demographer** *noun* **demographic** *adjective* **demographics** *noun*

demolish
verb to knock down or destroy: *to **demolish** an old building | to **demolish** an argument* (***annihilate, eradicate, exterminate, wipe out***)

Word building: **demolition** *noun*
Word history: French, from Latin word meaning 'throw down', 'destroy'

demon (dee-muhn)
noun **1** an evil spirit
2 someone who does something with great energy: *She's a **demon** for tidiness.*

Word building: **demonic** *adjective*
Word history: Middle English, from Late Latin word meaning 'evil spirit', from Latin word meaning 'spirit', from Greek word meaning 'divine power', 'fate', 'god'

demonstrate
verb to show clearly: *She **demonstrated** how she felt by bursting into tears.* (***display, exhibit, parade***)

Word history: from Latin word meaning 'showed', 'proved'

demonstration
noun **1** a march or other act to show support: *There was a big* ***demonstration*** *for land rights.*
2 a public showing in order to advertise: *There is a* ***demonstration*** *of power tools in the hardware store.*

demonstrative (duh-mon-struh-tiv)
adjective **1** characterised by or given to open showing of feelings, etc.
2 serving to demonstrate, explain or illustrate
3 *Grammar* of a word, pointing out the thing referred to
noun **4** *Grammar* a demonstrative word, such as *this*, *that* or *these*

For more information on definition 4, look up **pronouns: demonstrative pronouns / adjectives.**

demoralise
verb to destroy the confidence of: *Their jeering* ***demoralised*** *him.*
Word use: You can also use **demoralize.**
Word building: **demoralisation** *noun*
Word history: French

demote (duh-moht, dee-moht)
verb to reduce to a lower class or position
Word use: The opposite of this is **promote.**
Word building: **demotion** *noun*
Word history: *de-* + *mote*, modelled on *promote*

demur (duh-mer)
verb to object or take exception
Verb forms: I **demurred**, I have **demurred**, I am **demurring**
Word building: **demurral** *noun*
Word history: Middle English, from Old French, from Latin word meaning 'linger'

demure
adjective shyly well-behaved: *a* ***demure*** *child* (***bashful***, ***coy***, ***diffident***, ***modest***, ***reticent***)
Word building: **demurely** *adverb*
Word history: Middle English, from Old French word meaning 'grave', 'ripe', from Latin word meaning 'mature'

den
noun **1** an animal's burrow or shelter
2 a quiet room or place separate from other rooms: *He's reading in his* ***den***. (***cell***, ***chamber***, ***compartment***, ***cubicle***, ***study***)
Word history: Old English *denn*

denial (duh-nuy-uhl)
noun an act of denying

denigrate (den-uh-grayt)
verb to devalue the importance or worth of
Word building: **denigration** *noun* **denigrator** *noun*
Word history: from Latin word meaning 'blackened'

denim
noun a heavy cotton material used to make jeans and other clothes
Word history: French, short for *serge de Nîmes* serge of Nîmes

denizen (den-uh-zuhn)
noun a person, animal or plant that lives or grows in a particular place
Word history: Middle English, from Anglo-French, from Latin word meaning 'from within'

denomination
noun a religious group, especially in the Christian churches
Word building: **denominational** *adjective*

denominator
noun the number under the line in a fraction which shows how many equal parts it may be divided into: *In the fraction ¾, 4 is the* ***denominator***. (***divisor***)
Word use: Compare this with **numerator.**

denote
verb to mean or show: *A yellow flag on a ship* ***denotes*** *illness on board.*
Word building: **denotation** *noun*
Word history: French, from Latin word meaning 'mark out'

denote / connote
Look up **connote / denote.**

denouement (duh-nooh-mõ)
noun the end of the story, where everything is explained
Word history: French *de-* + *nouer*, from Latin word meaning 'knot', 'tie'

denounce
verb to speak out against: *He will* ***denounce*** *the traitors.* (***bring to book***, ***charge***)
Word building: **denunciation** *noun*
Word history: Middle English, from Latin word meaning 'threaten'

dense
adjective **1** closely packed or thick: *a* ***dense*** *crowd* | *a* ***dense*** *fog* (***chunky***, ***heavy***, ***solid***)
2 foolish or stupid (***dull***, ***dumb***, ***silly***, ***slow***, ***thick***)
Word history: from Latin word meaning 'thick', 'thickly set'

density
noun **1** the state or quality of being thick or closely packed
2 *Physics*
a the mass per unit of volume
b the amount per unit or area of any physical quantity: *energy* ***density*** | *current* ***density***
Noun forms: The plural is **densities.**

dent
noun a small hollow scarring a surface: *The stones made* ***dents*** *on the car.*
Word building: **dent** *verb*
Word history: Middle English

dental
adjective having to do with teeth or dentists
Word history: Latin *dens* tooth

dentist
noun someone who is trained to treat your teeth
Word history: French

dentistry
noun the work that a dentist does

dentition (den-tish-uhn)
noun **1** teething or the growing of teeth
2 the type, number, and arrangement of the teeth of any animal, including humans

Word history: from Latin word meaning 'teething'

denture
noun a plate with a false tooth or teeth attached, which fits into your mouth

Word history: French

denude (duh-nyoohd)
verb to strip or make naked or bare: *Trees were **denuded** of leaves.*

Word building: **denudation** *noun*
Word history: from Latin word meaning 'lay bare'

denunciation (duh-nun-see-ay-shuhn)
noun an open and harsh condemnation of someone or something you think is evil

deny (duh-nuy)
verb **1** to say to be untrue: *Henry **denies** that he stole the fruit.*
2 to refuse: *She **denied** us permission to go.*

Verb forms: I **denied,** I have **denied,** I am **denying**
Word building: **denial** *noun*
Word history: Middle English, from French, from Latin

deodorant (dee-oh-duh-ruhnt)
noun something which prevents or removes bad smells

deodorise (dee-oh-duh-ruyz)
verb to take away a nasty smell from: *to **deodorise** the carpet*

Word use: You can also use **deodorize.**

depart
verb to go away or leave (***retire***, ***retreat***, ***withdraw***)

Word history: Middle English, from Old French *de-* + *partir* leave, divide (from Latin)

department
noun a division in a large organisation such as a government, a school, a college, or a retail store: *The toy **department** was on the second floor.*

Word building: **departmental** *adjective*

department store
noun a large shop selling a range of different goods in separate sections of the shop

departure
noun **1** a going away or a setting out: *Our **departure** is scheduled for 4 o'clock.*
2 a change from what is usual: *A holiday in the country is quite a **departure** for our family.*

Word use: The opposite of definition 1 is **arrival.**

depend
verb **1** to rely: *They **depend** on us to help them.*
phrase **2 depend on,** to be determined by: *Whether we can afford it **depends on** how much money we have.*

Word building: **dependable** *adjective*
Word history: Middle English, from Old French, from Latin word meaning 'hang upon'

dependant
noun someone who relies on or needs the support of another (***hanger-on***, ***parasite***, ***protégé***, ***satellite***)

> **dependant / dependent**
> Don't confuse **dependant** with **dependent.** These words are related, but **dependant** is the noun and **dependent** is the adjective.

dependency (duh-pen-duhn-see)
noun **1** dependence or the state of being dependent
2 a small country ruled by another

Noun forms: The plural is **dependencies.**

dependent
adjective needing support: *a **dependent** child*

Word use: The opposite of this is **independent.**
Word building: **dependence** *noun*

depict
verb to describe or show in words or pictures: *The artist had **depicted** a country scene.* (***portray***, ***represent***)

Word building: **depiction** *noun*
Word history: from Latin word meaning 'portrayed'

depilatory (duh-pil-uh-tree)
noun **1** a substance for removing hair
adjective **2** for removing hair: *a **depilatory** cream*

Noun forms: The plural is **depilatories.**

deplete (duh-pleet)
verb to reduce or lessen: *to **deplete** our natural resources*

Word building: **depletion** *noun* **depletive** *adjective*
Word history: from Latin word meaning 'emptied out'

deplorable (duh-plaw-ruh-buhl)
adjective **1** causing grief or regret: *a **deplorable** action*
2 wretched or worthy of blame: *They live in **deplorable** conditions.*

deplore
verb to regret or be sorry for: *We **deplore** the bad condition of the house.*

Word history: from Latin word meaning 'bewail'

deploy (duh-ploy)
verb **1** to spread out to form a wide front: *to **deploy** troops or military units*
2 make careful or effective use of: *to **deploy** your resources*

Word building: **deployment** *noun* **deployable** *adjective*
Word history: French, from Latin word meaning 'fold'

deport
verb to send out of the country as a punishment: *The judge **deported** the thief who was born overseas.* (***banish***, ***evict***, ***exile***, ***isolate***, ***throw out***)

Word building: **deportation** *noun* **deportee** *noun*
Word history: French, from Latin word meaning 'carry away', 'transport', 'banish'

deportment
noun the way you stand (***bearing***, ***carriage***)

depose
verb to remove from a high position by force: *The general **deposed** the king.*

Word history: Middle English, from Old French word meaning 'put down'

deposit
verb **1** to put down: *She **deposited** her basket on a chair.* (***lodge***, ***park***, ***position***, ***rest***, ***set down***)
2 to put away for safekeeping: *She **deposited** her money in the bank.*
noun **3** an amount given as the first part of a payment, or as a promise to pay
4 money placed in a bank
5 a layer which collects on a surface: *There was a fine **deposit** of dust on the furniture.*
6 a layer of ore, oil, etc., found in the earth (***band***, ***seam***, ***stratum***, ***vein***)

Word history: from Latin word meaning 'put away or down', 'deposited', Medieval Latin 'testified'

deposition
noun **1** *Law* a statement someone makes under oath, which is written down and which may be used in court instead of calling the witness
2 the removal of someone from an important position: *the **deposition** of a prime minister*

depot (dep-oh)
noun **1** a place where goods are stored or unloaded
2 a place where buses or trams are kept

Word history: French, from Latin word meaning 'a putting down'

deprave
verb to make evil in character: *Films showing violence might **deprave** others.*

Word building: **depraved** *adjective* **depravity** *noun*

deprecate (dep-ruh-kayt)
verb to protest against or say that you disapprove of: *to **deprecate** a scheme*

Word building: **deprecatory** *adjective* **deprecation** *noun*
Word history: from Latin word meaning 'having prayed against'

depreciate (duh-pree-shee-ayt, duh-pree-see-ayt)
verb **1** to go down in value
2 to belittle or lessen the value of

Word use: The opposite of this is **appreciate**.
Word building: **depreciatingly** *adverb* **depreciator** *noun* **depreciatory** *noun*
Word history: from Late Latin word meaning 'undervalued'

depreciation
noun **1** a lowering in the value of goods, property, etc., due to wear and tear, decrease in price or something like this
2 a lowering in the amount that money can buy, and of what it is worth when you exchange it for foreign currency

depredation (dep-ruh-day-shuhn)
noun **1** a robbery
2 a destruction

depress
verb **1** to make miserable: *The bad news **depressed** him.*
2 to press down: *I **depressed** the lever.*
3 to cause to sink lower in level: *to **depress** the value of their houses*

Word building: **depressed** *adjective* **depressive** *adjective*
Word history: Middle English, from Old French, from Latin word meaning 'pressed down'

depressant
noun **1** a sedative that slows down the functions of the human body
adjective **2** having the ability to slow down the body's activities

depression
noun **1** the state of being miserable (***anguish***, ***gloom***, ***melancholy***, ***sorrow***)
2 a hollow or a sunken place: *a **depression** in the ground*
3 a time when the economy is slow and many people are without a job
4 in the weather, an area of low air pressure

Word history: Middle English, from Latin

depression / recession
When used in economics, these terms refer to similar circumstances, but there is a difference.
A **recession** is a downturn in the economy for a short period of time.
A **depression** is a downturn in the economy lasting for a long period of time. It is a major economic and social crisis.

deprive
verb to take away or keep from: *to **deprive** someone of their freedom*

Word building: **deprivation** *noun*
Word history: Middle English, from Old French, from Latin word meaning 'deprive'

deprived
adjective lacking affection, a good education, etc.: *a **deprived** child*

depth
noun **1** deepness or distance downward
2 strength, especially of colour or feeling: *No-one knew the **depth** of his hatred.*
3 depths, the deepest part, especially of the sea
phrase **4 in depth**, without missing anything: *to study a subject **in depth***
5 out of your depth,
a in water so deep that you can't stand up
b beyond what you can do or understand

Word history: Middle English, from *dep-* (Old English *dēop* deep) + *-th*

deputation
noun people chosen to speak on behalf of the group they belong to (***delegation***, ***mission***)

deputy (dep-yuh-tee)
noun someone who assists or acts for another person: *While the principal was sick, her **deputy** took assembly.* (***aide***, ***assistant***, ***associate***, ***offsider***)

Noun forms: The plural is **deputies**.
Word building: **deputise** *verb* **deputy** *adjective*
Word history: Middle English, from Old French word meaning 'deputed' (appointed or assigned)

der (der)
interjection Colloquial a word you say to point out that someone has stated something obvious: *'Your hair is red.' '**Der!**'*

derail
verb to run off the tracks or rails on which it is travelling or to cause to run off the tracks: *The train **derailed** in the bad weather. | The train was **derailed** by a rock thrown onto the tracks.*
Word building: **derailment** *noun*

deranged (duh-raynjd)
adjective thrown into confusion or made insane: *The **deranged** man forgot where he lived.*
Word use: The opposite of this is **sane**.
Word building: **derange** *verb* **derangement** *noun*
Word history: French, from Old French

derelict (de-ruh-likt)
adjective **1** empty and run-down: *They found **derelict** houses in the abandoned mining town.*
noun **2** a poor, homeless, and neglected person
Word history: from Latin word meaning 'forsaken utterly'

dereliction
noun extreme or serious neglect: ***dereliction** of duty*

deride
verb to mock or laugh at
Word history: from Latin word meaning 'laugh'

derision
noun the act of laughing at or making fun of someone (***mockery***, ***ridicule***)
Word building: **derisive** *adjective*
Word history: Latin

derivation
noun origin: *the **derivation** of a word*

derivative
adjective coming from something else: *That's not a new idea, it's **derivative**.*

derive
verb **1** to take or receive from somewhere: *She **derives** her income from two jobs.*
2 to get by working out: *I **derived** the answer by adding the figures together.* (***compute***, ***figure out***, ***make out***, ***reckon***)
Word history: French, from Latin word meaning 'lead off'

dermatitis (der-muh-tuy-tuhs)
noun an inflammation of the skin making it itchy or painful

derogatory (duh-rog-uh-tree, duh-rog-uh-tuh-ree)
adjective unfairly critical: *She was upset by **derogatory** remarks about her family.*

derrick
noun **1** a type of crane for lifting and moving heavy weights
2 a tower-like framework over an oil-well
Word history: named after *Derrick*, a hangman at Tyburn, London, about 1600

desalination (dee-sal-uh-nay-shuhn)
noun the removal of salt from sea water so that it becomes suitable for drinking or for irrigation

descant (des-kant)
noun a tune played or sung above the main tune
Word history: Middle English, from Old Northern French (from Latin *cantus* song)

descend
verb **1** to go or climb down: *She began to **descend** the tree.*
2 to pass from a higher to a lower place: *The path **descends** steeply here.* (***drop***, ***sink***)
3 to pass from the earlier to later times
phrase **4 descend on** (or **upon**),
a to approach with haste and often with anger: *The police **descended upon** the thieves.*
b to arrive at as a crowd: *My whole class **descended on** our house for the party.*
Word use: The opposite of definitions 1 and 2 is **ascend**.
Word building: **descendent** *adjective*
Word history: Middle English, from Old French, from Latin

descendant
noun offspring: *I'm a **descendant** of his.* (***issue***, ***progeny***, ***young***)
Word use: The opposite of this is **ancestor**.
Word history: from French word meaning 'descending'

descended
phrase **descended from**, having as your ancestors: *I'm **descended from** one of the first convicts to arrive in Australia from England.*

descent (duh-sent)
noun **1** the act of coming or going down: *The old lady's **descent** of the stairs was very shaky.*
2 the downward slope of a mountain or stairway
Word use: The opposite of this is **ascent**
Word history: Middle English, from Old French

describe
verb to give a picture of someone or something using written or spoken words: *He **described** what happened after we left.* (***depict***, ***portray***, ***represent***)
Word building: **descriptive** *adjective*
Word history: from Latin word meaning 'copy off', 'sketch off', 'describe'

description
noun **1** a representation by written or spoken words: *Can you give a **description** of the thief?*
2 sort or kind: *people of that **description***
3 *Geometry* the act of describing a shape
Word history: Middle English, from Latin

desecrate (des-uh-krayt)
verb to use in an unworthy way: *to **desecrate** a holy place*
Word building: **desecrater** *noun* **desecration** *noun*
Word history: *de-* + *-secrate*, modelled on *consecrate*

deselect
verb Computers to cancel the selection of (an item, a set of items, highlighted text, etc.) by clicking the mouse outside or inside what is selected (where to click depending on the program operating): *She **deselected** the text that she didn't want.*

desert[1] (dez-uht)
noun a sandy or stony place without enough rainfall to grow many plants
Word history: Middle English, from Old French, from Latin word meaning 'abandoned'

desert[2] (duh-zert)
verb **1** to run away from without intending to return (***quit***, ***evacuate***, ***vacate***)
2 to leave behind in trouble or danger (***abandon***, ***forsake***)
Word building: **deserter** *noun* **desertion** *noun*
Word history: French, from Latin word meaning 'abandon'

desert / dessert
Don't confuse **desert** with **dessert**. A **dessert**, pronounced with the stress on the second syllable, is a sweet dish served at the end of a meal.

desertification (duh-zer-tuh-fuh-kay-shuhn)
noun the creation of deserts in areas that were once fertile, either by natural or artificial changes to the environment

deserts (duh-zerts)
plural noun something which is deserved, either as a reward or a punishment
Word history: Middle English, from Old French word meaning 'deserved'

deserve
verb to be worthy of
Word building: **deserving** *adjective* **deserved** *adjective*
Word history: Middle English, from Old French, from Latin word meaning 'serve zealously'

desiccate (des-uh-kayt)
verb to dry thoroughly, often in order to preserve: *to* ***desiccate*** *food*
Word building: **desiccation** *noun*
Word history: from Latin word meaning 'completely dried'

desiccated (des-uh-kayt-uhd)
adjective **1** dehydrated or powdered: ***desiccated*** *coconut* | ***desiccated*** *milk.*
2 completely dried out: *The* ***desiccated*** *body of a rat was stuck in a crack in the rock.*

design (duh-zuyn)
verb **1** to draw plans for: *An architect* ***designed*** *the house.*
2 to invent: *He's* ***designed*** *a new type of motor.* (***concoct***, ***develop***, ***improvise***)
noun **3** a sketch or plan: *Here is my* ***design*** *for a long skirt.*
4 a pattern: *There is a* ***design*** *of roses on the plates.* (***figure***, ***form***, ***shape***, ***structure***)
5 *Art* the ability to combine the parts of a picture or other work of art into a pleasing visual whole: *a school of* ***design***
phrase **6 by design**, on purpose: *He met me here* ***by design.***
Word building: **designer** *noun*
Word history: French word meaning 'designate', from Latin word meaning 'mark out'

designate (dez-ig-nayt)
verb **1** to mark or point out: *You should* ***designate*** *an area for parking.*
2 to suggest appointment for duty, office, purpose, etc.: *to* ***designate*** *a successor in the job*
adjective (dez-ig-nuht, dez-ig-nayt) **3** appointed to office but not yet holding it: *the ambassador* ***designate***
Word building: **designative** *adjective* **designator** *noun* **designation** *noun*
Word history: from Latin word meaning 'marked out'

designated driver
noun a member of a group of people attending a place where alcohol will be drunk, who agrees not to drink alcohol and to be responsible for driving the other members home

desirable
adjective good or beautiful enough to be wanted: *It's a* ***desirable*** *property in the best part of town.*
Word building: **desirability** *noun* **desirably** *adverb*

desire
verb **1** to want very much (***covet***, ***crave***, ***fancy***, ***long for***)
2 to ask for: *The king* ***desired*** *their presence at the palace.*
noun **3** need or craving: *They had a strong* ***desire*** *to laugh.* | *She has a* ***desire*** *for chocolate.* (***inclination***, ***yen***, ***wish***)
4 request: *Tell us your* ***desires*** *and we shall try to grant them.*
Word building: **desirous** *adjective*
Word history: Middle English, from Old French, from Latin word meaning 'want'

desist (duh-zist)
verb to stop doing something: *They asked him not to kick his football against their wall and he* ***desisted.***
Word history: Old French, from Latin word meaning 'leave off'

desk
noun **1** a writing table, often with drawers or small spaces for papers
2 the place, usually at the front of an office or hotel, where information is given: *Ask at the* ***desk*** *if there is a room vacant.*

desktop
noun **1** the background image displayed on a computer screen by some computer programs, which includes icons representing programs, documents, etc.
adjective **2** of computers, office equipment, etc., designed to be used at a desk: *a* ***desktop*** *computer*

desktop publishing
noun the production of printed material using a personal computer, software and a laser printer, all of which can be operated in a normal office

desolate (des-uh-luht, dez-uh-luht)
adjective **1** deserted or without people: *The streets are* ***desolate*** *at 3 a.m.*
2 sad and hopeless: *They felt* ***desolate*** *after losing all their possessions.*
Word building: **desolate** *verb* **desolation** *noun*
Word history: Middle English, from Latin word meaning 'left alone', 'forsaken'

despair
noun **1** a feeling of hopelessness: *We were filled with* ***despair*** *when the train left without us.*
verb **2** to lose or give up hope: *Don't* ***despair,*** *I'll help you!*

Word history: Middle English, from Old French, from Latin word meaning 'be without hope'

desperate
adjective **1** ready to run any risk: *a* ***desperate*** *criminal*
2 tried as a last attempt: *a* ***desperate*** *plan*
3 very bad or dangerous: *a* ***desperate*** *illness*

Word building: **desperately** *adverb* **desperation** *noun*
Word history: late Middle English, from Latin word meaning 'given up', 'despaired of'

despicable
adjective deserving scorn: *a* ***despicable*** *action | a* ***despicable*** *person* (***contemptible, mean, nasty***)

Word history: Late Latin, from Latin word meaning 'despise'

despise
verb to look down on, especially with hate or scorn: *They* ***despised*** *him for not daring to face the enemy.* (***abhor, abominate, detest, loathe***)

Word history: Middle English, from Old French, from Latin word meaning 'look down upon', 'despise'

despite (duh-spuyt)
preposition in spite of or notwithstanding

Word building: **despite** *noun*
Word history: Middle English, from Old French, from Latin word meaning 'a looking down upon'

despondent
adjective depressed or down-hearted: *He looks so* ***despondent*** *after losing his game.* (***forlorn, glum, heart-broken, sad***)

Word building: **despondency** *noun*

despot
noun a cruel and unjust ruler

Word building: **despotic** *adjective* **despotically** *adverb*
Word history: Greek *despótēs* master

dessert (duh-zert)
noun the fruit or sweets eaten at the end of a meal

Word history: from French word meaning 'clear the table'

dessert / desert
Look up **desert / dessert.**

destination
noun the place you're travelling to, or to which something is sent

Word use: The opposite of this is **origin**.

destined
adjective meant by fate: *We were* ***destined*** *to meet.*

destiny (des-tuh-nee)
noun fate, or something that had to happen: *To die by dragon's breath was his* ***destiny.*** (***chance, fortune, luck***)

Noun forms: The plural is **destinies**.
Word building: **destine** *verb*
Word history: Middle English, from Old French

destitute
adjective without money or the means of getting any: *The father died leaving his family* ***destitute.*** (***impecunious, insolvent, poor, ruined***)

Word building: **destitution** *noun*
Word history: Middle English, from Latin word meaning 'put away', 'abandoned'

destroy
verb **1** to wreck completely: *Bombs* ***destroyed*** *the city.* (***annihilate, demolish, eradicate, exterminate, wipe out***)
2 to kill an animal for humane reasons: *The horse with the broken leg was* ***destroyed.*** (***put down, put to sleep***)

Word building: **destroyer** *noun*
Word history: Middle English, from Old French, from Latin word meaning 'pull down', 'destroy'

destruction
noun the act of destroying or being destroyed: *Nuclear* ***destruction*** *is a real possibility. | Logging in the wilderness areas is responsible for the* ***destruction*** *of our rainforests.*

Word building: **destructive** *adjective*
Word history: Middle English, from Latin

desultory (des-uhl-tree, dez-uhl-tree)
adjective **1** moving from one thing to another: ***desultory*** *conversation*
2 without plan: ***desultory*** *thought*

Word history: Latin word meaning 'relating to or like someone who leaps', 'superficial' (leaping from one thing to another)

detach
verb to separate or unfasten: *You* ***detach*** *the top copy and keep it.* (***break off, disconnect,*** 0***free***)

Word building: **detachable** *adjective*
Word history: French, from Old French word meaning 'nail'

detached
adjective **1** separate or standing apart: ***detached*** *houses*
2 unconcerned and aloof (***disinterested, noncommittal***)

detachment
noun **1** the ability to stand aside and not let your judgement be affected by your feelings
2 a force of soldiers or naval ships set aside for a special task

detail
noun **1** one of the single or small parts which go to make up a whole: *the* ***details*** *of a story*
2 fine delicate work: *There is a lot of* ***detail*** *in his drawings.*
verb **3** to report fully: *She was asked to* ***detail*** *her plans.*

Word history: from French word meaning 'cut in pieces'

detain
verb **1** to delay or hold up: *I won't* ***detain*** *you much longer.*
2 to keep under control or in prison

Word building: **detainee** *noun* **detention** *noun*
Word history: Middle English, from Old French, from Latin word meaning 'keep back'

detect
verb to discover or notice: *to **detect** someone stealing* (***locate***, ***trace***, ***unearth***)

Word building: **detection** *noun* **detector** *noun*
Word history: from Latin word meaning 'discovered', 'uncovered'

detectable
adjective noticeable: *a **detectable** rash*

detective
noun a person, usually a police officer, who is trained to discover who committed a crime

Word building: **detective** *adjective*

detention
noun **1** a keeping under guard
2 the keeping in of a pupil after school hours as a punishment

deter (duh-<u>ter</u>)
verb to prevent or stop from doing (***advise against***, ***dissuade***, ***talk out of***)

Verb forms: I **deterred**, I have **deterred**, I am **deterring**
Word history: Latin word meaning 'frighten from'

detergent
noun powder or liquid used for cleaning

Word building: **detergent** *adjective*

deteriorate (duh-<u>tear</u>-ree-uh-rayt)
verb to become worse: *His health **deteriorated** as he grew older.* (***decline***, ***degenerate***, ***worsen***)

Word building: **deterioration** *noun*
Word history: Late Latin

determination
noun firmness of purpose: *a **determination** to win*

determine
verb to settle on or decide: *I have **determined** my future course of study.*

Word history: Middle English, from Old French, from Latin word meaning 'limit'

determined
adjective firm in purpose: *a **determined** effort*

determiner
noun Grammar a word which comes before a noun to show which particular person, thing, etc., is being referred to

deterrent (duh-<u>te</u>-ruhnt, duh-<u>ter</u>-ruhnt)
noun something that has a discouraging effect: *They are making nuclear weapons as a **deterrent** to invaders.*

Word building: **deterrence** *noun*

detest
verb to hate or loathe (***abhor***, ***abominate***, ***despise***)

Word building: **detestable** *adjective* **detestation** *noun*
Word history: French, from Latin word meaning 'curse while calling a deity to witness'

detonate
verb to explode or cause to explode

Word building: **detonation** *noun* **detonator** *noun*
Word history: from Latin word meaning 'thundered forth'

detour (<u>dee</u>-toouh, <u>dee</u>-taw)
noun **1** a different way round, used when a road is closed
verb **2** to go by way of a detour

Word history: from French word meaning 'turn aside'

detract
phrase **detract from**, to take away some of, or reduce the value of: *Lying will **detract from** your good name.*

Word building: **detraction** *noun* **detractor** *noun*
Word history: from Latin word meaning 'drawn away or down'

detriment (<u>det</u>-ruh-muhnt)
noun **1** loss, damage, or physical hurt: *He spoke to the **detriment** of his friends.*
2 a cause of loss or damage

Word building: **detrimental** *adjective*
Word history: from Latin word meaning 'loss', 'damage'

detritus (duh-<u>truy</u>-tuhs)
noun **1** particles worn or broken away from rock by water or glacial ice
2 any broken up material or debris

Word history: from Latin word meaning 'a rubbing away'

deuce (dyoohs)
noun **1** a playing card, or the side of a dice, marked with two spots: *the **deuce** of hearts*
2 a stage in a game of tennis when both players have a score of 40

Word history: from Old French word meaning 'two'

devalue
verb to lower the worth or value of: *to **devalue** someone's efforts | to **devalue** the Australian dollar*

Word use: The opposite of this is **revalue.**
Word building: **devaluation** *noun*

devastate
verb to turn into a wasteland: *The fire **devastated** a large area of bush.*

Word building: **devastation** *noun*
Word history: Latin

develop
verb **1** to make or grow larger: *Exercise **develops** the muscles. | Muscles **develop** with exercise.*
2 to advance or expand: *Her mind **developed** with age.*
3 to work out or expand on: *In this piece the composer **develops** the theme.* (***amplify***, ***embellish***, ***embroider***, ***flesh out***)
4 to bring into being: *The gardener **developed** a new type of rose.*
5 *Photography* to treat with chemicals so as to bring out the picture: *to **develop** a photograph*

Word building: **developer** *noun*
Word history: French *dé-* + *voluper* wrap

developed
adjective **1** having undergone development: *The **developed** site featured new office blocks where there was nothing but scrub before.*
2 of a country, industrialised: *a **developed** nation*

developing
adjective **1** undergoing development: *a **developing** storm*
2 of a country, in the early stages of developing an industrial economy: *aid for a **developing** country*

development
noun **1** growth or expansion: *What we need is faster **development** of our manufacturing industries.*
2 a large building project, such as a housing estate, an office block, etc.

deviant (<u>dee</u>-vee-uhnt)
adjective **1** departing from what is accepted as normal
noun **2** someone who is deviant, usually in their sexual behaviour

Word building: **deviance** *noun*

deviate
verb to swerve or turn aside: *The rocket **deviated** from its planned course.* | *to **deviate** from normal behaviour*

Word building: **deviate** *noun*
Word history: Latin *de-* + *via* way

deviation
noun **1** the act of swerving or turning aside
2 *Statistics* the difference between one set of values and the mean or middle amount of that set

device
noun **1** an invention: *This **device** opens the garage door by remote control.* (***contraption***, ***gadget***, ***machine***)
phrase **2 leave someone to their own devices**, to allow someone to do whatever they want

Word history: Middle English, from Old French, from Latin word meaning 'divided'

device driver
noun a program in a computer that lets the operating system recognise devices, such as a modem, a printer, and a mouse, which are not part of the computer

Word use: The short form is **driver**.

devil
noun **1** a wicked person
phrase **2 between the devil and the deep blue sea**, faced with two things that are both unpleasant
3 give the devil his due, to be fair to a person you dislike
4 speak (or **talk**) **of the devil**, here comes the person you were just talking about

Word building: **devilish** *adjective* **devilment** *noun* **devilry** *noun*
Word history: Old English *deofol*, from Latin, from Greek word meaning 'Satan', originally 'slanderer'

devious
adjective tricky or deceitful: *His **devious** ways made a lot of enemies.* (***artful***, ***crafty***, ***dishonest***, ***sly***, ***wily***)

Word building: **deviousness** *noun*
Word history: from Latin word meaning 'out of the way'

devise
verb **1** to think out, invent or plan: *to **devise** a new system of collecting taxes* (***conceive***, ***concoct***, ***create***, ***originate***)
2 to form a plan

Word history: Middle English, from Old French, from Latin word meaning 'separate'

devoid
phrase **devoid of**, free from, or without: *The street was **devoid of** shade.*

Word history: from Old French word meaning 'empty out'

devolve
verb **1** to pass on, transfer or delegate to or upon another: *to **devolve** a duty or responsibility*
2 *Law* to pass by inheritance or legal succession

Word building: **devolvement** *noun*
Word history: from Latin word meaning 'roll down'

devon
noun *Australian* a large, smooth sausage, usually sliced and eaten cold

devote
verb to set apart for a particular purpose: *to **devote** an hour to a hobby*

Word history: from Latin word meaning 'vowed'

devoted
adjective loving and loyal: *a **devoted** parent* (***affectionate***, ***fond***, ***tender***)

devotion
noun a serious attachment: ***devotion** to duty* | ***devotion** to a friend* (***regard***, ***veneration***)

Word history: Middle English, from Latin

devour
verb to eat hungrily (***consume***, ***gobble***, ***gulp***)

Word history: Middle English, from Old French, from Latin word meaning 'swallow down'

devout
adjective sincerely religious (***god-fearing***, ***holy***, ***pious***, ***reverent***)

Word history: Middle English, from Old French, from Latin word meaning 'devoted'

dew
noun small drops of water that form during the night on any cool surfaces out of doors

Word building: **dewy** *adjective* (**dewier**, **dewiest**)
Word history: Old English *dēaw*

dew / due

Don't confuse **dew** with **due**. Your **due** is what is owed to you:

When the goodies are handed out you will get your due.

Due also means 'expected to arrive':

The maths assignment is due on Friday.

Dewey decimal classification (<u>dyooh</u>-ee)
noun in libraries, a system of classifying and arranging books into ten main subject classes

Word use: You can also use **decimal classification**.
Word history: named after Melvil *Dewey*, 1851–1931, US librarian

dexterity
noun skill or cleverness, especially in using your hands

Word building: **dexterous** *adjective*

dhal (dahl)
noun an Indian food made from cooked lentils, herbs and spices

diabetes (duy-uh-bee-teez)
noun a disease in which your body finds it difficult to use sugar and passes it out in your urine

Word building: **diabetic** *noun* **diabetic** *adjective*
Word history: Neo-Latin, from Greek word meaning 'a passer through'

diabolical
adjective **1** devilish or wicked (***fiendish***, ***satanic***) **2** very difficult or unpleasant

Word use: You can also use **diabolic**.
Word history: Late Latin, from Greek

diagnosis
noun the working out of what disease a patient has

Word building: **diagnose** *verb* **diagnostic** *adjective*
Word history: Neo-Latin, from Greek word meaning 'a distinguishing'

diagnosis / prognosis

These are both medical terms, although they have more general meanings.

A **diagnosis** is a doctor's analysis of what is wrong with a patient.

A **prognosis** is the next step that the doctor takes after making a **diagnosis**. It is an informed guess as to what course the illness will take:

The doctor's prognosis is that you will have a fever for two weeks.

diagonal
noun a sloping line joining opposite angles of a rectangle or square

Word building: **diagonal** *adjective* **diagonally** *adverb*
Word history: Latin, from Greek word meaning 'from angle to angle'

diagram
noun a drawing which explains how something works or is laid out: *a **diagram** of the engine | a **diagram** of a racecourse*

Word building: **diagrammatic** *adjective*
Word history: Latin, from Greek word meaning 'that which is marked out by lines'

dial
noun **1** the face of a clock, radio, or measuring instrument: *a speedometer **dial***
verb **2** to enter numbers into a telephone so as to make a call: *to **dial** a telephone number*

Verb forms: I **dialled**, I have **dialled**, I am **dialling**
Word history: Middle English, from Medieval Latin word meaning 'daily', from Latin word meaning 'day'

dialect
noun a variety of a language spoken in a particular area or by a particular group of people (***jargon***, ***pidgin***, ***slang***, ***tongue***)

Word history: Latin, from Greek word meaning 'discourse', 'language', 'dialect'

dialogue
noun a conversation between two or more people, especially in a play or story (***debate***, ***discussion***)

Word history: French, from Latin, from Greek

dial-up
adjective able to be accessed by telephone line: *a **dial-up** connection to the internet | a **dial-up** health service*

Word use: You can also use **dialup**.

dialysis (duy-al-uh-suhs)
noun **1** *Chemistry* the separation of smaller molecules from larger ones in a solution by selective diffusion through a semipermeable membrane
2 *Medicine* in cases where someone has a problem with their kidneys, the removal of waste products from the blood by causing them to diffuse through a semipermeable membrane

Noun forms: The plural is **dialyses** (duy-al-uh-seez).
Word building: **dialyse** *verb*
Word history: from Greek word meaning 'separation', 'dissolution'

diameter (duy-am-uh-tuh)
noun **1** the straight line which goes through the centre of a circle from one side to the other
2 the length of such a line

Word history: Middle English, from Latin, from Greek word meaning 'diagonal', 'diameter'

diametric (duy-uh-met-rik)
adjective **1** having to do with a diameter
2 direct or absolute, as of opposite sides, viewpoints, etc.: ***diametric** opposites*

Word use: You can also use **diametrical**.
Word building: **diametrically** *adverb*

diamond
noun **1** a very hard precious stone which is clear and sparkling like glass
2 the red four-sided shape on some playing cards

Word history: Middle English, from Latin *adamas* adamant,which was a legendary rock or mineral which was very hard. Later this rock was identified with the diamond because of its hardness. The form of the word 'adamant' was altered to 'diamond'.

diaphanous (duy-af-uh-nuhs)
adjective transparent or translucent: ***diaphanous** material*

Word history: Medieval Latin, from Greek

diaphragm (duy-uh-fram)
noun **1** the sheet of muscle inside your body between your chest and abdomen
2 a thin sheet or membrane, especially in a telephone or microphone

Word history: Late Latin, from Greek word meaning 'midriff', 'barrier'

diarrhoea (duy-uh-ree-uh)
noun the frequent and excessive emptying of watery fluid from your bowel

Word use: You can also use **diarrhea**.
Word history: from Greek word meaning 'a flowing through'

diary
noun a book in which you write down daily events or thoughts (***journal***, ***notebook***)

Noun forms: The plural is **diaries**.
Word history: from Latin word meaning 'daily allowance', 'journal'

> **diary / dairy**
> Don't confuse **diary** with **dairy**. A **dairy** farm is one where cows are milked.

diastole (duy-uhs-tohl)
noun the normal rhythmical relaxation of the heart

Word use: Compare this with **systole**.
Word building: **diastolic** *adjective*
Word history: Late Latin, from Greek word meaning 'lengthening'

diatonic
adjective Music involving the tones, intervals, or harmonies of the major or minor scale you are playing in, without using accidental notes outside the scale

Word history: Late Latin, from Greek

diatribe (duy-uh-truyb)
noun a bitter and violent attack or criticism

Word history: Latin, from Greek word meaning 'pastime', 'study', 'discourse'

dibbler
noun a small mouse with spots, found in Western Australia, now almost extinct

Word history: from Nyungar, an Australian Aboriginal language of the Perth-Albany region

dice
plural noun **1** small cubes marked on each side with a different number of spots, from one to six, used in games
2 any small cubes
verb **3** to cut into small cubes: *to **dice** carrots*

Noun forms: The singular is **die**.

dichotomy (duy-kot-uh-mee)
noun a division into two parts

Noun forms: The plural is **dichotomies**.
Word history: from Greek word meaning 'a cutting in two'

dictate
verb **1** to say or read aloud for somebody else to write down: *The manager **dictated** a letter to her secretary.*
2 to give orders
3 to influence or control something, such as a decision, action, etc.

Word building: **dictation** *noun*
Word history: from Latin word meaning 'pronounced', 'dictated'

dictator
noun someone who has total power, especially in governing a country

Word building: **dictatorial** *adjective*
Word history: Latin

dictatorship
noun a country or government in which one person has complete power

diction
noun **1** a style of spoken or written expression: *good **diction** | a Latin **diction***
2 clearness in speech

Word history: from Latin word meaning 'a saying'

dictionary
noun a book with an alphabetical list of words, their meanings, and sometimes other information such as their pronunciations and history

Noun forms: The plural is **dictionaries**.
Word history: Medieval Latin word meaning 'a word-book', from Late Latin word meaning 'word'

did
verb past tense of **do**

didactic (duy-dak-tik, duh-dak-tik)
adjective **1** meant to teach something, especially a moral or a lesson about life: ***didactic** poetry*
2 wanting to teach or lecture others too much: *a **didactic** old lady*

Word building: **didactically** *adverb* **didacticism** *noun*
Word history: from Greek word meaning 'apt at teaching'

diddle
verb Colloquial to cheat or swindle

Word building: **diddler** *noun*
Word history: origin uncertain

didjeridu (dij-uh-ree-dooh)
noun a long, pipe-shaped, Aboriginal wind instrument made of wood

Word use: You can also use **didgeridoo**.
Word history: from an imitation of the sound it makes

didn't
contraction of **did not**

> Look up **contractions in grammar**.

die[1]
verb **1** to stop living (***be no more***, ***breathe your last***, ***expire***, ***pass away***, ***perish***)
phrase **2 die down**, to pass or fade slowly away: *The wind **died down**.*
3 die off, to die one after the other until there are hardly any left
4 die out, to become extinct or no longer live on earth

Verb forms: he **died**, he has **died**, he is **dying**
Word history: Middle English *deghen*

die[2]
noun **1** a tool for cutting, stamping, or shaping coins or other metal objects
2 the singular form of **dice**

Noun forms: The plural for definition 1 is **dies**.
Word history: Middle English, from Old French, from Latin word meaning 'given' (apparently in sense of given by fortune)

> **die / dye**
> Don't confuse **die** with **dye**. To **dye** something is to colour it with a **dye** or colouring agent:
> *I'm sick of my brown hair — I'm going to dye it black.*

dieresis (duy-er-uh-suhs)
noun a mark (¨) used to show that two vowels side by side are pronounced separately

In English you might use a **dieresis** with names like *Chloë* and *Noël*. It is placed over the second of the two vowels.
Although it looks like an umlaut in German, its function is different. Look up **umlaut**.
The plural of **dieresis** is spelt **diereses**, with the last syllable rhyming with *seas*.

diesel
noun the oil left after petrol and kerosene have been taken from crude petroleum; used in diesel engines

diesel engine
noun an internal combustion engine which burns heavy oil, not petrol, with air inside one of its working cylinders
Word history: named after Rudolf *Diesel*, 1859–1913, German inventor

diet (duy-uht)
noun **1** the food you usually eat: *Your* ***diet*** *affects your health.*
2 a particular selection of foods: *a slimming* ***diet*** | *a low fat* ***diet***
verb **3** to choose what you eat in order to lose weight or improve your health
Verb forms: I **dieted**, I have **dieted**, I am **dieting**
Word building: **dietary** *adjective* **dieter** *noun*
Word history: Middle English, from Latin, from Greek word meaning 'way of living', 'diet'

dietitian
noun someone trained to give advice about the food you eat
Word use: You can also use **dietician**.

differ
verb **1** to be unlike or not the same
2 to disagree (***argue***, ***bicker***, ***dispute***, ***dissent***, ***wrangle***)
Word history: French, from Latin word meaning 'bear apart', 'put off', 'be different'

differ / defer
Don't confuse **differ** with **defer.** To **defer** is to put off to another time:
My exams have been deferred for another month.
If you **defer to** someone's wishes, you do what they want rather than what you want.

difference
noun **1** a way of being unlike: *The* ***difference*** *between my sister and me is in our height.*
2 a disagreement or quarrel (***altercation***, ***conflict***, ***controversy***, ***dispute***)
3 the amount by which two things differ: *The* ***difference*** *between 6 and 1 is 5.*
Word history: Old English, from Latin

different to / from / than
You will see the word **different** followed by **to, from** and **than.**
Different from has traditionally been the form that people prefer:
That kitten is different from the rest of the litter.
Different to is often used as a perfectly acceptable alternative:
Your uniform is different to mine.
While **different than** is commonly used in speech, it is still discouraged in written work.

different
adjective **1** dissimilar or having unlike qualities
2 separate or distinct
3 various or several: *It comes in* ***different*** *colours*
4 striking or not ordinary
Word use: The opposite of definition 1 is **alike**.
Word history: Middle English, from Latin

differential (dif-uh-ren-shuhl)
adjective **1** having to do with difference
2 distinguishing or distinctive: *a* ***differential*** *feature*
noun **3** a set of gears in a car which permit the driving wheels to revolve at different speeds when the car is turning
Word history: Medieval Latin, from Latin word meaning 'difference'

differentiate
verb to see the difference between: *I can* ***differentiate*** *him from his brother.*

difficult
adjective hard to do or understand (***arduous***, ***complex***, ***demanding***, ***tough***)
Word use: The opposite of this is **easy**.
Word building: **difficulty** *noun* (*plural* **difficulties**)

diffident
adjective not confident or sure of yourself: *He is* ***diffident*** *about speaking in public.* (***bashful***, ***coy***, ***demure***, ***modest***, ***reticent***)
Word building: **diffidence** *noun*
Word history: from Latin word meaning 'mistrusting'

diffraction (duh-frak-shuhn)
noun **1** the effect on light or other radiation when it passes by the edge of an opaque body, or is sent through small holes, resulting in the formation of a series of light and dark bands, colour, spectra, etc. It is caused by interference due to the wave nature of radiation.
2 a similar effect on soundwaves when passing by the edge of a building or other large body
Word building: **diffractive** *adjective*

diffuse (duh-fyoohz)
verb **1** to pour out or spread over: *A blush* ***diffused*** *her face.*
adjective (duh-fyoohs) **2** scattered or spread out thinly
3 using too many words: *a* ***diffuse*** *speech*
Word history: Middle English, from Latin word meaning 'poured out'

diffusion
noun Physics
1 the filling of any space by a fluid, or the mixing of fluids due to the way their particles or molecules move freely
2 the process of being scattered

dig
verb **1** to break up or turn over with a spade: *to **dig** the soil* (***excavate, gouge, mine***)
2 to make by digging: *to **dig** a tunnel | to **dig** a garden*
3 to push or poke: *She **dug** me in the ribs.*
phrase **4 dig in,**
a to dig trenches for defence against the enemy in battle
b to hold your position or opinion firmly
5 dig into, *Colloquial* to begin with enthusiasm: *to **dig into** your dinner*

Verb forms: I **dug**, I have **dug**, I am **digging**
Word history: Middle English, probably from French, of Germanic origin

digest
verb **1** to break down in your stomach and intestines for use by your body: *to **digest** food*
2 to think over and take in mentally: *to **digest** information* (***absorb, assimilate, comprehend***)

Word building: **digestive** *adjective*
Word history: Middle English, from Latin word meaning 'separated', 'arranged', 'dissolved'

digestion
noun **1** the act of or process by which you digest food
2 the ability to digest food

digger
noun **1** a miner: *a **digger** on the goldfields*
2 *Colloquial* an Australian soldier, especially one from World War I

Word history: This word was originally used to refer to miners who dug for gold; they worked hard together with a strong sense of mateship because mining was impossible to do alone. During World War I the meaning of **digger** shifted to refer to soldiers who dug trenches and fought together on the front line, the sense of hard work and mateship taking on even more significance because of the dangerous and serious circumstances involved.

diggings
plural noun a place where miners dig

digit
noun **1** any of the numerals from 0 to 9 (***figure, number***)
2 a finger or toe

Word history: from Latin word meaning 'finger', 'toe'

digital
adjective **1** having fingers or toes
2 using digits or numbers but no pointers to show time, amount, etc.: *a **digital** clock*
3 *Electronics* having to do with information represented by patterns made up from qualities existing in two states only, on and off: ***digital** signals*

Word use: Compare this with **analog**.
Word building: **digitally** *adverb*

digital camera
noun a camera which stores pictures as digital files

digital signature
noun a unique code, in the form of a series of characters, used to verify the identity of the sender of an electronic document, and to ensure that the document has not been altered before reaching the receiver

Word use: You can also use **e-signature**.

digitise
verb Computers to put (analog information) into digital form: *If you scan the photos, they will be **digitised** and you can email them to me.*

Word use: You can also use **digitize**.

dignified
adjective calm and controlled in a way that brings respect: *He managed to remain **dignified** in spite of being cold and hungry.*

dignitary
noun someone who is in a high position in government or a church

Noun forms: The plural is **dignitaries**.

dignity
noun **1** nobleness of mind or manner: *She acted with great **dignity** despite the rudeness of the others.*
2 a high rank or noble position

Word history: from Latin word meaning 'worthiness', 'rank'

digress
verb to wander away from the main subject when writing or speaking (***diverge, stray***)

Word building: **digression** *noun*
Word history: from Latin word meaning 'having departed'

dike
noun → **dyke**

dilapidated
adjective shabby and in need of repair: *a **dilapidated** house*

Word building: **dilapidation** *noun*

dilate
verb to make or become wider or larger: *The drops **dilated** the pupils of my eyes. | The pupils of her eyes **dilated**.*

Word use: The opposite is **constrict**.
Word building: **dilation** *noun* **dilator** *noun*
Word history: from Latin word meaning 'spread out'

dilatory (dil-uh-tree)
adjective slow or tending to delay: *a **dilatory** person*

Word history: from Latin word meaning 'delayer'

dilemma
noun a situation in which you have to choose between two alternatives: *Her **dilemma** was that going to the pictures meant missing Justine's party.*

Word history: Late Latin, from Greek word meaning 'double proposition'

diligent
adjective paying careful and unceasing attention: *a **diligent** scholar* (***attentive, conscientious***)

Word building: **diligence** *noun* **diligently** *adverb*
Word history: Middle English, from Latin word meaning 'choosing', 'liking'

dill[1]
noun a plant bearing a seedlike fruit used in medicine and cooking

Word history: Old English *dile-*

dill[2]
noun Colloquial a fool

dillybag
noun **1** *Australian* a small bag used for carrying food or your belongings
2 a bag of twisted grass or fibre, traditionally used by some Aboriginal peoples

Word history: *dilly* from Yagara, an Australian Aboriginal language of the Brisbane region + *bag*

dilute
verb to make thinner or weaker by adding water: *to* ***dilute*** *disinfectant*

Word history: from Latin word meaning 'washed to pieces', 'dissolved', 'diluted'

dilution
noun **1** the act of diluting
2 something that has been diluted

dim
adjective **1** not bright: *a* ***dim*** *light | a* ***dim*** *room* (***murky***, ***obscure***, ***shadowy***)
2 not clear to the mind: *a* ***dim*** *idea*
verb **3** to make less bright: *to* ***dim*** *the lights of a room* (***obscure***, ***shade***)

Verb forms: I **dimmed**, I have **dimmed**, I am **dimming**
Word history: Old English *dim(m)*

dimension
noun size measured in a particular direction

Word history: from Latin word meaning 'a measuring'

diminish
verb to become smaller (***abate***, ***moderate***, ***peter out***, ***wane***)

Word use: The opposite of this is **grow** or **increase**.

diminuendo (duh-min-yooh-en-doh)
adverb gradually reducing in force or loudness

Word use: This is an instruction in music.
Word history: Italian

diminutive
adjective **1** very small
noun **2** a word which tells you something is small: *'Booklet' is the* ***diminutive*** *of 'book'.*

Word history: Middle English, from Latin word meaning 'lessened'

dimmer
noun a device you use to vary the strength of lights

dimple
noun a small hollow in your cheek

Word building: **dimple** *verb*
Word history: Middle English, related to Middle High German word for 'pool'

dim sim
noun a Chinese food made of seasoned meat wrapped in thin dough and steamed or fried

Word use: You can also use **dim sum**.

din
noun loud noise that goes on and on (***commotion***, ***hubbub***, ***pandemonium***, ***racket***, ***uproar***)

Word history: Old English *dyne, dynn*

dine
verb to have dinner

Word building: **diner** *noun*

ding
verb **1** to strike or beat
2 to ring or sound the way a bell does, especially over and over again
3 to cause to ring, as by striking
4 *Australian, NZ Colloquial* to smash or damage
noun **5** a blow or stroke
6 the sound of bell, etc.
7 *Australian, NZ Colloquial* a minor accident with a car, bike, etc.

Word history: imitative

dinghy (ding-gee)
noun a small rowing boat, especially one that belongs to a launch or ship

Noun forms: The plural is **dinghies**.
Word history: Hindustani

dingo
noun an Australian wild dog which is brownish-yellow, has pointed ears and a bushy tail and makes a yelping noise

Noun forms: The plural is **dingoes** or **dingos**.
Word use: Another name is **warrigal**.
Word history: from Dharug, an Australian Aboriginal language spoken by the people living near Sydney Cove in the early days of European settlement. It was the word used for the domesticated dogs in the Dharug camps, the wild dogs being referred to as *warrigals*.

dingy (din-jee)
adjective having a dull dirty colour or looking shabby: *a* ***dingy*** *room* (***gloomy***, ***mousy***, ***sombre***)

Adjective forms: **dingier**, **dingiest**

dinkum (ding-kuhm)
adjective Australian, NZ Colloquial **1** honest and sincere: *a* ***dinkum*** *friend*
interjection Australian, NZ Colloquial **2** truly!

Word use: You can also use **dinky-di** for definition 1. | You can also use **fair dinkum** for definition 2.
Word history: British dialect

dinner
noun **1** the main meal of the day, usually eaten about noon or in the evening
2 a formal meal in honour of someone or something

Word history: Middle English, from French

dinner jacket
noun a man's jacket for formal evening wear, usually black and part of a dinner suit

dinner suit
noun a man's suit for formal evening wear, usually black and often worn with a bow tie

dinosaur (duy-nuh-saw)
noun any of a number of very large lizard-like animals which died out millions of years ago
Word history: from Neo-Latin word meaning 'terrible lizard'

dint
noun **1** force; power: *by **dint** of argument*
2 a dent
verb **3** to make a dint in
Word history: Old English *dynt*

diocese (duy-uh-suhs)
noun the district, and the people who live in it, under the care of a bishop
Word building: **diocesan** *adjective*
Word history: Middle English, from Old French, from Latin word meaning 'district', from Greek word meaning 'housekeeping', 'administration', 'province'

diorama (duy-uh-rah-muh)
noun a miniature scene reproduced in three dimensions, with coloured backgrounds, models and sometimes lights

dip
verb **1** to put into a liquid for a short time: *I **dipped** my hand in the river.* (***sink***, ***submerge***)
2 to slope down
noun **3** a soft tasty mixture that you dip biscuits into before you eat them
4 a downward slope or hollow: *a **dip** in the road*
5 a short swim
Verb forms: I **dipped**, I have **dipped**, I am **dipping**
Word building: **dipper** *noun*
Word history: Old English *dyppan*; related to *deep*

diphtheria (dif-thear-ree-uh)
noun a serious infectious disease affecting your throat which makes it hard to breathe and which causes a high fever
Word history: Neo-Latin, from Greek *diphthéra* skin, leather + *-ia*

diphthong (dif-thong)
noun a speech sound made by the tongue gliding from one vowel to another in the same syllable, such as *ei* in *vein*
Word history: Late Latin, from Greek word meaning 'having two sounds'

diploid (dip-loyd)
Biology
adjective **1** having two similar sets of chromosomes
noun **2** an organism or cell with chromosomes that have paired in preparation for cell-division
Word use: Compare this with **haploid**.

diploma (duh-ploh-muh)
noun an official paper proving that you are qualified in a particular field of study: *a **diploma** in librarianship*
Word history: Latin, from Greek word meaning 'paper folded double', 'letter of recommendation', 'licence', etc.

diplomacy (duh-ploh-muh-see)
noun skill in managing relations between nations or people and keeping them friendly
Word history: French

diplomat
noun **1** someone whose job is to represent their country overseas
2 someone who is tactful

diplomate
noun a holder of a diploma

diplomatic
adjective **1** skilled in achieving things in a tactful way, without causing offence: *She was very **diplomatic** and managed to avoid an argument.*
2 having to do with diplomacy between nations: *She had a **diplomatic** job at her country's embassy in China.*

diplomatic corps
noun a body of diplomats officially attached to a state or capital

diplomatic immunity
noun the freedom from local court action, taxation, etc., which is the right of official representatives of a foreign state

dipsomania (dip-suh-may-nee-uh)
noun an irresistible desire for alcoholic drink
Word building: **dipsomaniac** *noun*
Word history: Neo-Latin, from Greek *dípso(s)* thirst + *manía* mania

dip switch
noun a switch which lowers the beams of a vehicle's headlights
Word use: You can also use **dipper switch**.

DIP switch (dip swich)
noun in a computer, one of a number of small switches which may be set as a group to define a parameter, such as a printer default
Word history: the word DIP is an acronym for *D(ual) I(n-line) P(ackage)*

dire (duy-uh)
adjective **1** causing great fear or suffering
phrase **2 in dire straits**, in great difficulty or danger
Word history: Latin

direct
verb **1** to show or tell the way: *I **directed** the lost motorist to the police station.*
2 to give orders to (***command***, ***order***, ***tell***)
3 to have control over (***govern***, ***rule***, ***run***, ***supervise***)
adjective **4** going in a straight line or by the shortest way: *a **direct** route*
5 forthright and honest: *Her comments are refreshingly **direct**.* (***candid***, ***straightforward***)
6 quoting the exact words said: ***direct** speech*
Word use: The opposite of definition 4 is **circuitous** or **roundabout**.
Word building: **directness** *noun*
Word history: Middle English, from Latin

direct current
noun *Electronics* a relatively steady current in one direction in a circuit
Word use: The abbreviations for this are **DC** and **d.c.**

direction
noun **1** the line towards a certain point or area: *a northerly **direction** / We went in the **direction** of the sea.*

2 directions, guidance or instruction: *We got here quickly following your **directions**.*

Word building: **directional** *adjective*

directive

adjective **1** serving to direct
noun **2** an instruction or order

directly

adverb immediately

Word use: The opposite of this is **later**.

direct object

noun *Grammar* the person or thing which is acted on by the verb

For more information, look up **objects in grammar**.

director

noun **1** someone who directs (***administrator***, ***boss***, ***commissioner***, ***superintendent***)
2 *Commerce* one of the group of people chosen to control the affairs of a company or a corporation
3 a person in charge of the production of a play or film

Word building: **directorship** *noun*

directory

noun **1** a book containing an alphabetical list of names and addresses, maps, or other types of information: *a telephone **directory** | a street **directory***
2 *Computers* (in some operating systems) a defined area on a computer disk used to store files

Word use: Another word for definition 2 is **folder**.
Noun forms: The plural is **directories**.
Word history: from Latin word meaning 'that directs'

direct speech

noun a way of recording or writing down what someone said

When you want to record or write down what someone said, you can do it either directly or indirectly. With **direct speech** you would quote the words actually spoken, as in:

Whitlam said: 'Maintain your rage.'

The quotation marks show that these were exactly the words used. This is the most dramatic way to present speech, because it is written in the same direct way as it was uttered.

A less direct way of doing it is to write it as **indirect speech**:

Whitlam said that everyone should maintain their rage.

In this version there are no quotation marks because the man's remarks have been translated a little by the writer. Notice how the impact of the original command has been lost, and the *your* (second person) has become *their* (third person).

For more information, look up **indirect speech**.

dirge (derj)

noun a funeral song or tune, or one expressing grief

Word history: form of the Latin word used at the start of a ceremony for the dead

dirt

noun **1** loose earth or soil: *He fell in the **dirt**.* (***ground***, ***loam***)
2 anything that is not clean: *I can't get the **dirt** out of your jumper.*
adjective **3** made of dirt: *a **dirt** road*

Word history: Middle English *drit*, from Scandinavian

dirt bike

noun a motorcycle designed for off-road riding, with a high engine and exhaust system, often of especially light construction

Word use: Another name is **trail bike**.

dirty

adjective **1** covered with dirt (***filthy***, ***grimy***, ***grotty***, ***grubby***, ***polluted***)
2 unfair or mean: *a **dirty** fight*

Adjective forms: **dirtier**, **dirtiest**
Word use: The opposite of this is **clean**.
Word building: **dirtiness** *noun*

disability

noun a lack of strength or power in part of your body, or a physical or mental problem which makes it hard for you to do some things: *His short leg was a **disability** which he struggled to overcome.*

Noun forms: The plural is **disabilities**.

disable

verb to cripple or make unable (***incapacitate***, ***paralyse***)

Word building: **disablement** *noun*

disabled

adjective having been made unable or unfit: ***Disabled** soldiers receive a pension.* (***crippled***, ***incapacitated***)

disadvantage

noun something that makes what you do more difficult: *Lack of education is a **disadvantage**.*

Word use: The opposite of this is **advantage** or **benefit**.
Word building: **disadvantage** *verb* **disadvantageous** *adjective*

disagree

verb **1** to differ or fail to agree: *The two reports of the disaster **disagree** on the number of casualties.* (***contrast***, ***bear no resemblance***, ***vary***)
2 to quarrel (***argue***, ***bicker***, ***wrangle***)

Word building: **disagreement** *noun*

disagreeable

adjective **1** not to your liking: *a **disagreeable** task*
2 unpleasant or unfriendly in manner: *a **disagreeable** person*

Word use: The opposite of this is **agreeable**.
Word building: **disagreeableness** *noun*

disallow

verb to refuse to allow or admit: *The referee **disallowed** the goal because the players were offside.*

disappear

verb **1** to go out of sight: *He **disappeared** around the corner.* (***dematerialise***, ***dissolve***, ***fade***, ***melt***, ***vanish***)
2 to cease to exist: *His fear **disappeared** when he saw his father coming.*

Word building: **disappearance** *noun*

disappoint
verb to fail to satisfy the hopes of: *I **disappointed** my friends when I lost the race.*

Word history: Old French

disappointment
noun **1** the feeling of being disappointed: ***Disappointment** showed on his face when he heard the news.* (***discontent, dismay, dissatisfaction***)
2 someone or something that disappoints you: *That new movie is a real **disappointment** after all the advertising hype.* (***anticlimax, fizzer, letdown, setback***)

disapprove
phrase **disapprove of,** to find fault with: *My father **disapproves of** my plan to be an actor.* (***frown on, take a dim view of, take exception to***)

Word use: The opposite of this is **approve of.**
Word building: **disapproval** *noun* **disapproving** *adjective* **disapprovingly** *adverb*

disarm
verb **1** to take weapons from
2 to reduce the size of armed forces and weapon supplies
3 to take away anger from: *Her smile **disarmed** him.*
4 to take out of a state of readiness for any particular purpose: *Please disarm the cabin doors.*

Word use: The opposite of definitions 1 and 4 is **arm.**
Word building: **disarming** *adjective*
Word history: Old French

disarmament
noun a reduction in the size of a country's armed forces and of its supplies of weapons

disarray
verb **1** to put out of order: *The wind **disarrayed** her hair.*
noun **2** disorder or confusion: *Her clothes were in a state of **disarray**.*

disassociate (dis-uh-<u>soh</u>-shee-ayt, dis-uh-<u>soh</u>-see-ayt)
verb → **dissociate**

Word building: **disassociation** (dis-uh-soh-shee-<u>ay</u>-shuhn, dis-uh-soh-see-<u>ay</u>-shuhn) *noun*

disaster (duh-<u>zah</u>-stuh)
noun any sudden terrible happening which causes great suffering and damage (***calamity, catastrophe, debacle, misfortune, tragedy***)

Word building: **disastrous** *adjective*
Word history: from Italian word meaning 'not having a (lucky) star'

disavow
verb to refuse to admit knowledge of, connection with, or responsibility for

Word building: **disavowal** *noun*
Word history: Middle English, from Old French

disband
verb to break up: *to **disband** a military force*

Word building: **disbandment** *noun*
Word history: Middle French

disbar
verb to remove from a lawyer the right to practise law

Verb forms: I **disbarred**, I have **disbarred**, I am **disbarring**
Word building: **disbarment** *noun*

disbelieve
verb to refuse to believe (***distrust, query, question, take with a grain of salt***)

Word building: **disbelief** *noun*

disburse
verb to pay out or expend: *to **disburse** money*

Word building: **disbursement** *noun*
Word history: Old French *des-* + *bourse* purse (from Late Latin)

disc
noun **1** any thin, flat, circular object
2 *Computers* → **disk**
3 a plate of cartilage in your body, such as between joints or between vertebrae

Word history: Latin *discus* discus

> **disc / disk**
> Look up **disk / disc.**

discard
verb to throw away: *to **discard** old clothes | to **discard** an ace in a card game* (***ditch, dump, jettison, scrap, shed***)

Word building: **discard** *noun*

discern (duh-<u>sern</u>)
verb **1** to see, recognise, or understand clearly
2 to discriminate or to recognise as separate or different: *He can **discern** good from bad.*

Word building: **discernible** *adjective* **discernment** *noun*
Word history: Middle English, from French, from Latin word meaning 'separate', 'set apart'

discharge
verb **1** to unload: *The ship **discharged** its cargo.*
2 to fire: *He **discharged** the gun at the intruder. | The gun **discharged**.*
3 to give out or off: *The pipe **discharged** water and steam. | The chimney **discharged** smoke.*
4 to dismiss from a job
5 to fulfil or pay: *I **discharged** all my debts.*

Word building: **discharge** *noun*
Word history: Middle English, from Old French

disciple (duh-<u>suy</u>-puhl)
noun a follower of any set of ideas or of the person who puts them forward: *a **disciple** of the peace movement*

Word history: Middle English, from Old French, from Latin

disciplinarian
noun someone who believes in strict discipline

discipline (<u>dis</u>-uh-pluhn)
noun **1** training given to teach good conduct or behaviour: *Schools hope their **discipline** will make us good citizens.*
2 orderliness resulting from this training: *Our teacher keeps good **discipline** in the class room.*
3 punishment
verb **4** to train or control
5 to punish (***chastise, correct, penalise, scold***)

Word building: **disciplinary** *adjective*
Word history: Middle English, from Latin word meaning 'instruction'

disc jockey
noun → **DJ**

disclaim
verb **1** to claim no interest in or connection with: *She will **disclaim** all knowledge.*
2 *Law* to give up a claim or right to

Word history: Anglo-French *des-* + *clamer* claim

disclose
verb to allow to be seen or known: *I **disclosed** my secret.* (***expose***, ***make public***, ***publish***, ***reveal***)

Word building: **disclosure** *noun*
Word history: Middle English, from Old French from Latin word meaning 'close'

disco
noun a place or club in which people dance to recorded music

Noun forms: The plural is **discos.**
Word use: You can also use **discotheque.**
Word building: **disco** *adjective*
Word history: abbreviation of French *discothèque*

discolour
verb **1** to change the colour of: *The spilt coffee **discoloured** the cloth.*
2 to change colour or fade: *The carpet **discoloured** with age.*

Word use: You can also use **discolor.**
Word building: **discolouration** *noun*

discomfit
verb **1** to throw into confusion and unease or to disconcert
2 to upset the plans of
3 *Old-fashioned* to defeat completely

Word building: **discomfiture** *noun*
Word history: Middle English, from Old French *des-* + *confire* make, accomplish (from Latin)

discomfort
noun **1** lack of comfort or pleasure: *Much to my **discomfort**, I was asked to recite a poem.*
2 pain or uneasiness: *The accident caused me a lot of **discomfort**.*

Word history: Middle English, from Old French

disconcert (dis-kuhn-<u>sert</u>)
verb to cause feelings of embarrassment or distress: *Her accusation **disconcerted** me.*

Word building: **disconcerted** *adjective* **disconcerting** *adjective*

disconnect
verb to detach or to break the connection of or between (***cut off***, ***unplug***)

Word building: **disconnected** *adjective* **disconnection** *noun*

disconsolate (dis-<u>kon</u>-suh-luht)
adjective not being able to be comforted when you are in trouble

Word history: Medieval Latin

discontinue (dis-kuhn-<u>tin</u>-yooh)
verb to cause to finish or to come to an end: *The school principal **discontinued** the swimming carnival because of the rain. | The magazine was **discontinued** after only a week.*

Word building: **discontinuation** *noun* **discontinuity** *noun*

discord
noun **1** lack of agreement: ***discord** between the two friends*
2 a combination of musical notes which is unpleasant to listen to

Word building: **discordance** *noun* **discordant** *adjective*
Word history: Middle English, from Old French, from Latin word meaning 'be at variance'

discotheque (<u>dis</u>-kuh-tek)
noun → **disco**

discount
verb **1** (<u>dis</u>-kownt) to take an amount off the set price: *They **discounted** everything in the store by half.*
2 (dis-<u>kownt</u>) to disregard or take no notice of: *to **discount** someone's explanation*
noun **3** (<u>dis</u>-kownt) an amount taken off, usually in order to sell something quickly: *a **discount** of $10*

Word history: Old French *des-* + *conter* count

discourage
verb **1** to cause to lose spirit or courage: *Their defeat **discouraged** the team.* (***daunt***, ***demoralise***, ***dishearten***, ***dismay***)
2 to try to prevent: *He will **discourage** her attempts at hang-gliding.*

Word use: The opposite of this is **encourage.**
Word building: **discouragement** *noun* **discouraging** *adjective*
Word history: Old French

discourse (<u>dis</u>-kaws, dis-<u>kaws</u>)
noun **1** a conversation or a sharing of thought by words
2 a formal discussion of a subject in speech or writing
verb (dis-<u>kaws</u>) **3** to take part in talking or to converse
4 to discuss a subject formally in speech or writing

Word history: Middle English, from French, from Latin

discover
verb to find or find out, especially for the first time: *I **discovered** a shorter way home. | He **discovered** he could run very fast.* (***detect***, ***locate***, ***trace***, ***unearth***)

Word building: **discoverer** *noun* **discovery** *noun*
Word history: Middle English, from Old French *des-* + *covrir* cover

discredit
verb **1** to lower other people's opinion of: *His rudeness **discredited** him and his family.*
2 to show to be unworthy of belief: *The new discovery **discredited** the old ideas.*

Word history: *dis-* + *credit*

discreet
adjective **1** careful not to upset people: ***discreet** behaviour* (***judicious***, ***tactful***)
2 able to keep secrets: *You can confide in a **discreet** friend.*

Word use: The opposite of definition 1 is **tactless.**
Word history: Middle English, from Old French, from Latin word meaning 'separated'

discreet / discrete
Don't confuse **discreet** with **discrete**. If something is **discrete** it is separate from other things.

discrepancy (dis-krep-uhn-see)
noun a difference or an inconsistency: *There is a **discrepancy** between their two stories.*
Noun forms: The plural is **discrepancies**.
Word history: Old French, from Latin word meaning 'dissimilarity'

discrete (dis-kreet)
adjective **1** distinct or separate from others
2 made up of a number of individual and separate parts: ***discrete** data*
Word history: from Latin word meaning 'separated'

discretion (dis-kresh-uhn)
noun **1** the ability to be discreet: *I can rely on her **discretion**.*
2 the ability or right to do what should be done: *Use your own **discretion**.*
phrase **3 at your discretion**, as you wish or decide: *The choice will be made **at your discretion**.*
Word building: **discretionary** *adjective*

discriminate
verb **1** to be able to tell a difference: *A music lover can **discriminate** between good and bad playing.*
phrase **2 discriminate against**, to treat unfairly: *We should not **discriminate against** people because of the colour of their skin.*
Word history: from Latin word meaning 'divided', 'distinguished'

discriminating
adjective having good judgement, especially in regard to matters of taste: *a **discriminating** woman*

discrimination
noun **1** the act of judging well and noticing differences
2 prejudice in certain cases, usually in the form of unfair treatment against a person or thing: *Racial **discrimination** should not be tolerated in any society.*
3 the ability to make good judgements and notice differences

discriminatory
adjective showing an unfair prejudice for one person or group over another: ***discriminatory** laws* (***inequitable**, **partial**, **prejudiced**, **unjust***)

discursive (dis-ker-siv)
adjective passing rapidly or freely from one subject to another
Word building: **discursiveness** *noun* **discursion** *noun*

discus (dis-kuhs)
noun a circular plate for throwing in athletic contests
Noun forms: The plural is **discuses**.
Word history: Latin, from Greek word meaning 'discus', 'disc'

discuss
verb to talk over; to examine the arguments for and against (***canvass**, **debate***)
Word building: **discussion** *noun*
Word history: Middle English, from Latin word meaning 'struck asunder'

disdain
verb **1** to look down on with scorn
noun **2** a feeling of dislike for anything thought of as unworthy (***contempt**, **derision**, **disrespect***)
Word building: **disdainful** *adjective*
Word history: Middle English, from Old French *des-* + *deignier* deign

disease
noun a sickness which can affect a part or all of any living thing: *a skin **disease** | a bone **disease** | a plant **disease***
Word history: Middle English, from Old French *des-* + *aise* ease

diseased
adjective affected with a disease: *a **diseased** kidney*

diseased / deceased
Don't confuse **diseased** with **deceased**. If someone is **deceased** they have died.

disembark
verb to leave a ship or plane (***alight**, **dismount***)
Word use: The opposite of this is **embark**.
Word building: **disembarkation** *noun*

disembowel (dis-uhm-bow-uhl)
verb to remove the intestines from
Verb forms: I **disembowelled**, I have **disembowelled**, I am **disembowelling**
Word building: **disembowelment** *noun*

disenfranchise (dis-uhn-fran-chuyz)
verb to take certain rights away from, especially the right to vote
Word building: **disenfranchisement** *noun* **disenfranchised** *adjective*

disengage (dis-uhn-gayj)
verb to free or release: *to **disengage** a clutch*
Verb forms: I **disengaged**, I have **disengaged**, I am **disengaging**
Word building: **disengagement** *noun*

disentangle
verb to free from knots, tangles, etc.: *They had to **disentangle** the fishing lines before they could start.* (***sort out**, **unravel**, **untangle***)
Word building: **disentanglement** *noun*

disfigure
verb to spoil the appearance or beauty of: *Vandals **disfigured** the monument with paint. | Scars **disfigured** his face.*
Word building: **disfigurement** *noun*
Word history: Middle English, from Old French

disgorge (dis-gawj)
verb to throw out from or as if from your throat: *He **disgorged** his meal. | The train **disgorged** its passengers.*
Word history: Middle English, from Old French

disgrace
noun **1** shame or dishonour
2 a cause of shame: *Unsportsmanlike behaviour is a* ***disgrace*** *to the team.*
phrase **3 in disgrace**, looked at with disapproval: *He is* ***in disgrace*** *because of his lying.*

Word building: **disgrace** *verb* **disgraceful** *adjective*
Word history: French, from Italian *disgrazia*

disgruntled
adjective annoyed and sulky: *He was very* ***disgruntled*** *when he lost the election.* (***discontented***, ***displeased***, ***querulous***)

disguise
verb to change the appearance of: *He grew a beard and dyed his hair to* ***disguise*** *himself.* (***camouflage***, ***conceal***, ***cover***, ***mask***)

Word building: **disguise** *noun*
Word history: Middle English, from Old French *des-* + *guise* guise

disgust
verb **1** to cause complete dislike in: *Cruelty* ***disgusts*** *me.* (***horrify***, ***nauseate***, ***offend***, ***revolt***, ***sicken***)
noun **2** strong dislike

Word building: **disgusted** *adjective* **disgusting** *adjective*
Word history: Middle French

dish
noun **1** an open and rather shallow container for serving food
2 a particular kind of food prepared for eating: *a meat and vegetable* ***dish***

Word history: Old English *disc* dish, plate, bowl, from Latin *discus* dish, discus

dishevelled (di-shev-uhld)
adjective untidy or in disorder: *a* ***dishevelled*** *appearance | Her hair was* ***dishevelled****.* (***bedraggled***, ***sleazy***, ***sloppy***, ***unkempt***)

Word history: French *chevel* meaning 'hair', from Latin *capillus*, with the idea that one's hair is all messed up

dishonest
adjective **1** likely to lie, cheat or steal: *a* ***dishonest*** *man* (***crooked***, ***deceitful***, ***hypocritical***)
2 showing a lack of honesty: *a* ***dishonest*** *action*

Word use: The opposite of this is **honest**.
Word building: **dishonesty** *noun*

dishonour (dis-on-uh)
noun **1** a lack of respect: *His actions show* ***dishonour*** *to his school.*
2 shame or disgrace: *Her actions brought* ***dishonour*** *on her country.*
verb **3** to bring shame on or disgrace to: *to* ***dishonour*** *his team*
4 to not pay a cheque, or something like this, when you should

Word use: You can also use **dishonor**.
Word building: **dishonourable** *adjective*
Word history: Medieval Latin, from Old French, from Latin

dishwasher
noun a machine that washes dishes automatically

disillusion (dis-uh-looh-zhuhn)
verb to disenchant or to free from false ideas: *The audience was* ***disillusioned*** *when they discovered how the stunt had been done.*

Word building: **disillusion** *noun* **disillusionment** *noun*

disinfect
verb to get rid of germs or any other cause of infection: *to* ***disinfect*** *rooms | to* ***disinfect*** *clothes*

disinfectant
noun any chemical substance which kills germs

disinherit
verb to cut out from a will someone who was to receive property, etc.: *She* ***disinherited*** *her grandson.*

Word building: **disinheritance** *noun*

disintegrate
verb to break up into small parts: *The building* ***disintegrated*** *when the bomb exploded.*

Word building: **disintegration** *noun*

disinterested
adjective not directly involved: *It is wise to get a* ***disinterested*** *outsider to settle an argument.* (***detached***, ***impartial***, ***uncommitted***)

Word use: The opposite of this is **biased**.

disinterested / uninterested

Don't confuse **disinterested** with **uninterested**.

A **disinterested** person is one who is free from bias and self-interest:

A judge has to act as the disinterested controller of a court.

Uninterested means 'not interested' and is the opposite of **interested**:

She was so uninterested in the proceedings that she left the courtroom.

disjointed
adjective not fitting together: *a* ***disjointed*** *account of an adventure* (***disconnected***, ***incoherent***, ***rambling***)

Word history: Old French, from Latin word meaning 'disconnect'

disk
noun Computers a thin, flat, circular object used for storing data

Word use: You can also use **floppy disk** or **diskette**.

disk / disc

Disk is the spelling we usually use when we are referring to the circular object used in computers.

Disc is the spelling we use for other flat circular objects, such as compact discs, and for the discs in the spine, as in *slipped disc*.

disk drive
noun Computers a mechanism for rotating disks so that data can be accessed

dislike
verb **1** not to like
noun **2** distaste or the feeling of not liking: *I have taken a strong* ***dislike*** *to him.* (***animosity***, ***antipathy***, ***aversion***, ***hatred***, ***hostility***)

dislocate
verb **1** to put out of place: *I* ***dislocated*** *my shoulder when I fell.*
2 to throw into disorder: *The accident* ***dislocated*** *traffic.*
Word building: **dislocation** *noun*
Word history: Medieval Latin, from Latin

dislodge
verb to remove or go from a place of rest: *The mountaineer* ***dislodged*** *a number of small stones from the cliff face as he climbed.*
Word building: **dislodgement** *noun*

disloyal (dis-loy-uhl)
adjective treacherous or not loyal (***false***, ***fickle***, ***slippery***, ***traitorous***)
Word building: **disloyalty** *noun*
Word history: Old French *des-* + *loial* law-abiding (from Latin)

dismal (diz-muhl)
adjective feeling deep sadness: *He was quite* ***dismal*** *about his failure.* (***bleak***, ***depressed***, ***gloomy***)
Word history: Middle English *dismall*; origin uncertain

dismantle
verb to take apart: *We* ***dismantled*** *the engine.*
Word history: French (obsolete)

dismay
verb to fill with disappointment or fear
Word building: **dismay** *noun* **dismayed** *adjective*
Word history: Middle English, probably from Old French

dismember
verb **1** to divide limb from limb
2 to separate into parts
Word building: **dismemberment** *noun*
Word history: Middle English, from Old French

dismiss
verb **1** to order or allow to leave: *He* ***dismissed*** *his dishonest employee.* | *to* ***dismiss*** *the class*
2 to cause to be out in cricket: *The wicket-keeper* ***dismissed*** *the batsman.*
Word building: **dismissal** *noun*
Word history: from Medieval Latin word meaning 'sent away'

dismount
verb **1** to get off or down from something such as a horse, bicycle, etc. (***alight***, ***disembark***)
2 to remove something from its support or setting: *The statue was* ***dismounted*** *from its stand.*

disobedient
adjective refusing to obey: *a* ***disobedient*** *child* (***defiant***, ***delinquent***, ***insubordinate***, ***unruly***, ***wilful***)
Word building: **disobedience** *noun*

disobey
verb to refuse to obey: *to* ***disobey*** *an order* | *to* ***disobey*** *a teacher* (***defy***, ***flout***, ***transgress***, ***violate***)
Word history: Middle English, from Old French

disorder
noun **1** confusion or lack of order: *The* ***disorder*** *in my room took hours to clean up.*
2 violence and noise in public: *There was* ***disorder*** *in the streets.*
Word building: **disorder** *verb* **disordered** *adjective* **disorderly** *adjective*

disorganise
verb to throw into a state of confusion or disorder (***disrupt***, ***disturb***, ***mess up***)
Word use: You can also use **disorganize**.

disorganised
adjective in confusion or disorder: *He has such a* ***disorganised*** *mind it takes him ages to finish a job.* | *a* ***disorganised*** *procession* (***chaotic***, ***haywire***, ***higgledy-piggledy***)
Word use: You can also use **disorganized**.

disorientate (dis-or-ee-uhn-tayt)
verb to confuse, especially geographically
Word use: You can also use **disorient**.
Word building: **disorientation** *noun*

disown
verb to declare or imply that something or someone doesn't belong to you: *After she had caused so much trouble her family* ***disowned*** *her.*

disparage (duhs-par-ij)
verb to speak of or treat as of little value: *His painting was* ***disparaged*** *by many critics.*
Word building: **disparagingly** *adverb* **disparagement** *noun*
Word history: Middle English, from Old French *des-* + *parage* equality (from Latin)

disparate (dis-puh-ruht)
adjective unlike or different in kind
Word building: **disparity** *noun*
Word history: from Latin word meaning 'separated'

dispassionate
adjective impartial or free from strong feeling or bias: *a* ***dispassionate*** *witness*

dispatch
verb **1** to send off: *to* ***dispatch*** *a letter* | *to* ***dispatch*** *a messenger* (***forward***, ***pass on***, ***relay***, ***transmit***)
2 to put to death or kill (***assassinate***, ***execute***, ***murder***, ***slay***)
Word use: You can also use **despatch**.
Word building: **dispatch** *noun*
Word history: Italian or Spanish, from Old French word meaning 'set free', from Latin

dispel
verb to drive off or scatter: *He* ***dispelled*** *my fears.* (***dissipate***, ***rout***)
Verb forms: I **dispelled**, I have **dispelled**, I am **dispelling**
Word history: from Latin word meaning 'drive asunder'

dispensable
adjective able to be done without (***expendable***, ***peripheral***, ***unimportant***)

dispensary
noun the part of a chemist's shop or hospital where medicines are made up and given out
Noun forms: The plural is **dispensaries**.

dispensation
noun **1** the act of giving out or the distribution of something: *the* ***dispensation*** *of justice*
2 a ruling or permission: *a judge's* ***dispensation*** (***approval***, ***clearance***, ***consent***, ***leave***)

3 in the Roman Catholic Church, the relaxation or removal of a church law for a particular occasion

dispense
verb **1** to deal out: *The courts **dispense** justice.* (***allocate***, ***allot***, ***issue***)
2 to make up from a prescription and give out: *Any pharmacy will **dispense** that medicine for you.*
phrase **3 dispense with**,
a to do without
b to get rid of

Word building: **dispenser** *noun*
Word history: Middle English, from Old French, from Latin word meaning 'weigh out'

disperse
verb **1** to scatter around: *The wind **dispersed** the leaves on the ground.* (***dissipate***, ***distribute***, ***spread***, ***strew***)
2 to separate and move in different directions: *The crowd **dispersed**.*

Word use: The opposite of this is **gather** or **accumulate**.
Word building: **dispersal** *noun*
Word history: French, from Latin word meaning 'scattered'

dispersion
noun **1** the act of being dispersed: *the **dispersion** of seeds*
2 *Physics* the splitting or separation of light into the colours of the spectrum
3 *Statistics* the scattering of scores in a set or group around an average score
4 *Chemistry* a group of particles suspended in a fluid

Word use: You can also use **dispersal** for definition 1.

displace
verb **1** to put out of the usual place: *War often **displaces** families.*
2 to take the place of: *Weeds **displaced** the flowers in the old garden.*

displacement
noun **1** the act of displacing: *the **displacement** of families*
2 *Physics*
a the displacing or replacing of one thing with another, usually in a fluid: *the **displacement** of water in the bath when I get in*
b the weight of the fluid displaced by a floating object, equal to the weight of that object: *The ship has a **displacement** of 10 000 tonnes.*
3 *Geology* the distance of rocks from where they started off, caused by movement along a fault line or split under the surface of the earth

display
verb to show or exhibit: *His face **displayed** anger.* | *He **displayed** his prize roses.* (***demonstrate***, ***flaunt***, ***parade***)

Word building: **display** *noun*
Word history: Middle English, from Old French word meaning 'deploy'

displease
verb to annoy or cause to be unhappy or angry: *My bad behaviour **displeased** my parents.*

Word building: **displeasing** *adjective* **displeasure** *noun*

dispose
verb **1** *Old-fashioned* to influence or make willing: *The sunny weather **disposed** her to go to the beach.*
phrase **2 dispose of**, to get rid of: *I **disposed of** my old books.*

Word building: **disposable** *adjective* **disposal** *noun* **disposed** *adjective*
Word history: Middle English, from Old French

disposition
noun **1** your personality or particular character: *a happy **disposition***
2 arrangement in an order: *the **disposition** of troops*

Word history: Latin

dispossess
verb to deprive someone of possession, especially of land or property: *The natives were **dispossessed** of their ancient hunting grounds.*

Word building: **dispossession** *noun*

disproportion
noun a lack of proportion

Word building: **disproportionate** *adjective*

disprove
verb to prove a claim, argument, etc., to be false or wrong: *The theory that the world is flat was **disproved** centuries ago.* (***contradict***, ***invalidate***, ***rebut***, ***refute***)

Word history: Middle English, from Old French

disputable
adjective open to argument

disputation
noun discussion

dispute
verb **1** to argue loud and long (***debate***, ***wrangle***)
2 to argue about or against: *to **dispute** what to do* | *to **dispute** a claim*
noun **3** an argument (***altercation***, ***conflict***, ***controversy***, ***difference***, ***quarrel***)

Word history: Middle English, from Latin

disqualify
verb **1** to prevent or make unsuitable: *His income will **disqualify** him from getting a pension.* (***bar***, ***exclude***)
2 to declare unable to compete because a rule has been broken

Verb forms: I **disqualified**, I have **disqualified**, I am **disqualifying**
Word building: **disqualification** *noun*

disquiet
verb **1** to disturb or to make uneasy
noun **2** an uneasiness or anxiety

Word building: **disquieting** *adjective* **disquietude** *noun*

disregard
verb **1** to leave out or pay no attention to: *They selected only the blue balloons and **disregarded** all the rest.* (***leave out***, ***omit***, ***overlook***)
2 to treat without due regard or respect
noun **3** neglect or lack of attention
4 lack of due regard

disrepair
noun the state of being neglected or needing repair: *The shed fell into **disrepair**.*

disreputable (dis-rep-yuh-tuh-buhl)
adjective **1** having a bad name: *a* ***disreputable*** *company*
2 not respectable: ***disreputable*** *clothes*

disrepute (dis-ruh-pyoot)
noun discredit or the loss or lack of good opinion: *That idea is in* ***disrepute*** *now.*

disrespect
noun rudeness or lack of respect (***contempt***, ***derision***, ***disdain***)
Word building: **disrespectful** *adjective*

disrupt
verb to interrupt or throw into disorder: *The demonstrators* ***disrupted*** *the meeting.* (***break up***, ***disturb***, ***mess up***, ***upset***)
Word building: **disruption** *noun* **disruptive** *adjective*
Word history: Latin

dissatisfy
verb to make discontented
Verb forms: I **dissatisfied**, I have **dissatisfied**, I am **dissatisfying**
Word building: **dissatisfied** *adjective*

dissect
verb to cut apart for close examination: *We* ***dissect*** *plants in biology class.*
Word building: **dissector** *noun* **dissection** *noun*
Word history: from Latin word meaning 'cut asunder'

dissemble (duh-sem-buhl)
verb **1** to hide your true feelings: *He* ***dissembled*** *his nervousness by talking a lot.*
2 to put on the appearance of or pretend: *The worried parent* ***dissembled*** *calm.*
Word history: *dis-* + *semble*, modelled on *resemble*

disseminate
verb to spread abroad or to scatter, as seed in sowing: *to* ***disseminate*** *information*
Word building: **dissemination** *noun* **disseminator** *noun*
Word history: Latin

dissent
verb **1** to disagree or have a different opinion: *to* ***dissent*** *from the chairperson's ruling* (***differ***, ***demur***, ***object***)
2 to refuse to accept the power and authority of the established church
noun **3** a difference of opinion
4 a breaking away from the established church
Word building: **dissension** *noun* **dissenter** *noun* **dissenting** *adjective*
Word history: Middle English, from Latin word meaning 'differ in opinion'

dissertation (dis-uh-tay-shuhn)
noun **1** a written essay or thesis
2 a formal talk

disservice
noun harm, injury, or an ill turn: *He did her a* ***disservice****, though he meant to be kind.*
Word building: **disserviceable** *adjective*

dissident
noun someone who has a different opinion or belief, especially about a particular political system (***antagonistic***, ***rebellious***, ***recalcitrant***)
Word building: **dissident** *adjective*
Word history: from Latin word meaning 'differing', 'sitting apart'

dissimilar
adjective different or not similar
Word building: **dissimilarity** *noun*

dissimulate (duh-sim-yuh-layt)
verb **1** to disguise or hide (your feelings, etc.) under a false appearance
2 to feign or pretend: *Be yourself and don't* ***dissimulate****.* (***dissemble***, ***put on an act***)
Word building: **dissimulation** *noun*
Word history: Latin

dissipate
verb **1** to scatter or disappear in different directions: *The smoke* ***dissipated*** *in the wind.*
2 to scatter or use wastefully: *He* ***dissipated*** *his money by gambling.*
Word building: **dissipation** *noun*
Word history: from Latin word meaning 'scattered', 'demolished'

dissociate (di-soh-shee-ayt, di-soh-see-ayt)
verb to separate or to withdraw from the association of: *They* ***dissociated*** *themselves from such a noisy group.*
Word use: You can also use **disassociate**.
Word building: **dissociative** *adjective*
Word history: Latin

dissociative disorder
noun → **multiple personality disorder**

dissolute (dis-uh-looht)
adjective having a wasteful and immoral way of life
Word history: from Latin word meaning 'loosened'

dissolution
noun **1** the breaking down of a thing into its parts
2 the undoing or breaking up of a tie, bond, assembly, etc.
3 in government, an order issued by the head of state terminating a parliament and making a new election necessary
Word use: Compare definition 3 with **double dissolution**.

dissolve
verb **1** to mix or become mixed in a liquid: *I* ***dissolved*** *the sugar in the water.* | *Salt* ***dissolves*** *in water.*
2 to bring to an end: *The Queen* ***dissolved*** *Parliament.* | *The court* ***dissolved*** *the partnership.* (***abolish***, ***annul***, ***break off***, ***finish***, ***repeal***)
Word history: Middle English, from Latin word meaning 'loosen', 'disunite'

dissonance
noun **1** sound that is harsh and unpleasant
2 a combination of musical notes that doesn't sound pleasant
Word building: **dissonant** *adjective*

dissuade (di-swayd)
phrase **dissuade from**, to advise or persuade not to do something: *We* ***dissuaded*** *him* ***from*** *leaving home.* (***advise against***, ***deter from***, ***talk out of***)

Word building: **dissuasion** *noun* **dissuasive** *adjective*
Word history: from Latin word meaning 'advise against'

distance
noun **1** the length of a space: *the **distance** between Adelaide and Perth*
2 a part of the landscape which is far away: *The **distance** was hidden in mist.*
phrase **3 go the distance**, to finish or complete something
4 keep your distance, to be aloof or keep yourself apart from others

distant
adjective far off: *a **distant** town | the **distant** future* (***faraway***, ***isolated***, ***outlying***, ***remote***)
Word history: French, from Latin word meaning 'being distant', 'standing apart'

distaste
noun a dislike: *He has a **distaste** for showing his feelings in public.*
Word building: **distasteful** *adjective*

distemper[1]
noun Veterinary Science an infectious viral disease of young dogs
Word history: Middle English, from Medieval Latin

distemper[2]
noun **1** a water paint used on interior walls and ceilings, especially one containing glue or casein
verb **2** to paint with distemper
Word history: Old French, from Latin

distend
verb to swell or stretch: *Their stomachs **distended** from overeating.*
Word building: **distension** *noun* **distensible** *adjective*
Word history: Latin

distil
verb **1** to make pure and more concentrated by heating to a gas and then turning the gas back into a liquid: *to **distil** liquid*
2 to separate by doing this: *to **distil** kerosene from petroleum*
Word use: You can also use **distill**.
Verb forms: I **distilled**, I have **distilled**, I am **distilling**
Word history: Middle English, from Latin word meaning 'drip down'

distillate (dis-tuh-luht, dis-tuh-layt)
noun a product obtained by distillation

distillation
noun **1** the process of distilling
2 the end product or what you end up with when you finish distilling
3 something brought to its purest form, leaving only what is most important: *His last book contains the **distillation** of his thought.*
Word use: You can also use **distillate** for definition 2.

distilled
adjective made pure: ***distilled** water*

distillery
noun a place for distilling, especially alcoholic spirits
Noun forms: The plural is **distilleries**.

distinct
adjective **1** separate or different: *They were in **distinct** groups. | The new uniform is quite **distinct** from the old one.* (***disparate***, ***unrelated***)
2 clear and unmistakable: *a **distinct** difference* (***apparent***, ***evident***, ***plain***, ***visible***)
Word building: **distinctly** *adverb* **distinctness** *noun*

distinction
noun **1** difference, or a marking of something as different: *The **distinction** between sprinting and jogging is easy to see. | The **distinction** between the two sets of sports clothes is obvious because they are different colours.*
2 a mark of special favour: *the **distinction** of shaking hands with a film star*
3 greatness or superior quality: *a writer of **distinction***
4 the highest grade awarded at some universities and colleges

distinctive
adjective noticeable, and therefore distinguishing from others: *Each bird has the **distinctive** purple beak of the species.* (***characteristic***, ***identifying***)

distinguish
verb **1** to mark off as different: *A leopard's spots **distinguish** it from a tiger.*
2 to recognise a difference: *I can **distinguish** between the twins by their heights.*
3 to make well-known: *My sister **distinguished** herself as an athlete.*
Word history: from Latin word meaning 'separate', 'distinguish'

distinguished
adjective famous or of high standing: *a **distinguished** musician* (***aristocratic***, ***eminent***, ***superior***)

distort
verb **1** to twist out of shape: *Pain **distorted** her face.*
2 to change and make incorrect: *to **distort** the truth* (***exaggerate***, ***falsify***, ***slant***, ***twist***)
Word building: **distorted** *adjective*
Word history: Latin

distortion
noun **1** the act of distorting: *the **distortion** of an argument*
2 anything that has been distorted: *The **distortion** of the human body as portrayed by that artist is ugly to me.*

distract
verb **1** to draw away the attention of: *The noise outside the room **distracted** the class.*
2 to trouble or disturb: *Worry **distracted** her to the point of illness.* (***bamboozle***, ***befuddle***, ***fluster***, ***muddle***, ***puzzle***)
Word building: **distraction** *noun*
Word history: from Latin word meaning 'pulled asunder'

distracted
adjective nervous and troubled

distraught (duhs-<u>trawt</u>)
adjective distracted or greatly troubled in mind: *The child became more and more* ***distraught*** *as the daylight faded.*

Word history: variant of an obsolete meaning of *distract*, adjective

distress
noun **1** great pain, worry or sorrow (***anguish, misery***)
2 poverty: *The donations assist families in* ***distress.*** (***deprivation, destitution, need, want***)
3 danger or difficulty: *The lifesaver went to the surfer in* ***distress.***

Word building: **distress** *verb*
Word history: Middle English, from Old French, from Latin word meaning 'drawn tight'

distribute
verb **1** to give or share out: *Santa Claus* ***distributed*** *gifts to the children.* (***allocate, allot, dispense, issue, ration out***)
2 to scatter or spread: ***Distribute*** *the manure evenly over the garden.*

Word history: Latin

distribution
noun **1** the act of distributing: *The* ***distribution*** *of presents made everyone excited.*
2 the way in which something is distributed: *the* ***distribution*** *of rainforests along the east coast*
3 arrangement: ***distribution*** *into types of insect*

distributor
noun **1** someone or something that distributes things
2 *Commerce* someone whose work is to sell and circulate goods
3 the part of a petrol engine which sends electric current to the spark plugs in a certain order
4 *Australian* a main road designed to take traffic quickly from the centre of a city towards the outer suburbs

district
noun **1** a particular area, region or neighbourhood: *What* ***district*** *do you live in?*
2 an area marked out for some official purpose: *a postal* ***district***

Word history: from Medieval Latin word meaning 'territory under jurisdiction', special use of Latin word meaning 'constrained'

distrust
noun **1** doubt or lack of trust
verb **2** to regard with doubt or suspicion: *He* ***distrusted*** *computers until he learned more about them.* (***disbelieve, query, question, take with a grain of salt***)

Word building: **distrustful** *adjective*

disturb
verb **1** to interrupt the quiet, rest or peace of (***intrude on, distract***)
2 to move or unsettle: *The wind* ***disturbed*** *the smooth surface of the lake.* (***agitate, ruffle***)

Word history: from Latin word meaning 'throw into disorder', 'disturb'

disturbance
noun **1** the act of disturbing or the state of being disturbed: *The* ***disturbance*** *of the water brought mud to the surface. | Horror films always cause me* ***disturbance.***
2 a commotion or an outbreak of disorder: *a* ***disturbance*** *in the clouds | The rioters caused a* ***disturbance.***
3 something that disturbs: *Her mere presence was a* ***disturbance.***
4 *Geology* the bending or faulting of rock from its original position

disturbing
adjective worrying: ***disturbing*** *news*

disuse (dis-<u>yoohs</u>)
noun a stopping of use: *The stables fell into* ***disuse*** *when the horse was sold.*

Word building: **disuse** (dis-<u>yoohz</u>) *verb* **disused** *adjective*

ditch
noun **1** a long narrow hollow dug in the earth, used as a drain or channel for carrying water to dry land (***furrow, gutter, rut, trench***)
verb **2** *Colloquial* to get rid of: *to* ***ditch*** *your boyfriend* (***dump, jettison, scrap, shed***)

Word history: Old English *dīc*

dither
verb Colloquial to be nervous and confused: *They* ***dithered*** *over what to do next.*

Word building: **dither** *noun*
Word history: variant of *didder*, Middle English *diddir*; origin obscure

ditto
noun **1** the same, used in lists, etc., to avoid repeating something you've already mentioned
adverb **2** likewise or as already stated

Noun forms: The plural is **dittos.**
Word use: The abbreviation for definition 1 is **do**
Word building: **ditto** *verb* (**dittoed, dittoing**)
Word history: Italian word meaning 'said', 'already said' from Latin word meaning 'said'

ditto marks
noun in writing, marks (") which indicate that the word above them is to be repeated

> The **ditto marks** in the following example mean that Alex also ate four potatoes.
>
> *Sarah ate four potatoes.*
> *Alex " " "*
>
> Some people disapprove of ditto marks in general writing, though their use can sometimes make tables easier to read. As with all writing, your use of ditto marks should be to make things as clear and simple for the reader as possible.

ditty
noun **1** a poem intended to be sung
2 a short, simple song

Noun forms: The plural is **ditties.**
Word history: Middle English, from Old French, from Latin word meaning 'thing composed or recited'

ditzy (<u>dit</u>-see)
adjective Colloquial flighty; appearing to have no brains: *She's so* ***ditzy,*** *she believes anything anyone says.*

Word use: You can also use **ditsy.**

diurnal (duy-<u>er</u>-nuhl)
adjective **1** daily
2 active or out by day, as certain birds, insects, flowers, etc.

Word use: The opposite of definition 2 is **nocturnal**.
Word history: from Late Latin word meaning 'daily'

divan (duh-<u>van</u>)
noun a low bed or couch without a back or arms

Word history: Turkish, from Persian

dive
verb **1** to jump, especially headfirst, into water
2 to go down suddenly: *The aeroplane* ***dived****.*

Word building: **dive** *noun* **diver** *noun* **diving** *adjective*
Word history: Old English *dȳfan*, dip

diverge
verb to branch off: *The road* ***diverged*** *to the left.* (***digress***, ***turn***, ***wander***)

Word building: **divergence** *noun* **divergent** *adjective*
Word history: Neo-Latin, from Latin

diverse
adjective of many different kinds or forms (***assorted***, ***miscellaneous***, ***mixed***, ***motley***, ***various***)

Word building: **diverseness** *noun* **diversity** *noun*
Word history: from variant of *divers*, a word meaning 'several', 'sundry'

diversify (duy-<u>ver</u>-suh-fuy, duh-<u>ver</u>-suh-fuy)
verb **1** to vary or to make diverse
2 to extend your activities, especially in business, over more than one field

Verb forms: I **diversified**, I have **diversified**, I am **diversifying**
Word building: **diversification** *noun* **diversified** *adjective*
Word history: French, from Medieval Latin, from Latin *dīversi-* diverse + *-ficāre* make

diversion
noun **1** a turning aside from something you are doing
2 a detour you have to take on a road to avoid roadworks or something similar
3 an amusement or entertainment that takes your mind off more serious matters
4 a military action intended to draw the attention of the enemy away from where the main attack will take place

Word building: **diversionary** *adjective*

divert
verb **1** to turn aside from a path or course: *Police* ***diverted*** *the traffic.*
2 to draw off: *I'll* ***divert*** *their attention from you.*

Word history: Old French, from Latin word meaning 'turn aside', 'separate'

divest
verb **1** to take off the clothing, etc., of someone
2 to strip or deprive of anything: *The new laws* ***divested*** *the police of much of their power.*

Word history: Medieval Latin, from Old French

divide
verb **1** to split up or separate into parts (***carve up***, ***pull apart***, ***segment***, ***subdivide***)
2 to share out: *I* ***divided*** *the books among the children.* (***allocate***, ***parcel out***)
3 to separate into equal parts, using mathematics: *to* ***divide*** *69 by 3*

Word use: The opposite of definition 1 is **amalgamate**.
Word history: Middle English, from Latin word meaning 'force asunder'

dividend
noun **1** the number which is divided by another number: *In the sum 16 ÷ 4, 16 is the* ***dividend****.*
2 your share of some money which is being given out, especially from the profits of a business (***bonus***, ***pay***, ***proceeds***, ***return***, ***royalty***)

Word use: Compare definition 1 with **divisor** and **quotient**.
Word history: from Latin word meaning 'thing to be divided'

divine
adjective **1** having to do with God
2 religious or sacred: *the* ***divine*** *service on Sunday morning radio*
3 *Colloquial* wonderful or excellent: *Isn't the weather* ***divine****?* (***exceptional***, ***fantastic***, ***great***, ***sensational***, ***terrific***)
verb **4** to discover by instinct, magic or guessing: *The gypsy fortune-teller used a crystal ball to* ***divine*** *the future.* (***foresee***, ***foretell***, ***prophesy***)
5 to discover things, such as water or metal, with the help of a divining rod

Word history: Middle English, from Latin

diviner
noun someone who finds things by instinct, magic or by guessing: *A water* ***diviner*** *uses a rod to find underground water.*

divining rod
noun a forked stick which is said to tremble when a diviner holds it over a place where there is water or metal underground

divinity
noun **1** a god or divine being
2 the study of religion: *a student of* ***divinity*** (***theology***)

Noun forms: The plural is **divinities**.

divisible
adjective able to be divided: *20 is* ***divisible*** *by 10*

division
noun **1** the act of dividing one number by another number in mathematics (denoted by the symbol ÷)
2 a separation or distribution: ***division*** *of the class into four teams*
3 a section or group: *an army* ***division*** | *He plays football in the under-twelve* ***division****.*

Word use: The opposite of definition 1 is **multiplication**.
Word building: **divisional** *adjective*
Word history: Latin

divisive
adjective creating disagreement or discord: *a* ***divisive*** *policy*

divisor (duh-<u>vuy</u>-zuh)
noun a number by which you divide another number: *In the sum 16 ÷ 4, 4 is the* ***divisor****.*

Word use: Compare this with **dividend** and **quotient**.

divorce
noun the ending of a marriage by a court of law

Word building: **divorce** *verb*
Word history: Middle English, from French, from Latin word meaning 'separation', 'dissolution'

divorcee
noun someone who is divorced

divulge
verb to tell or reveal: *I'll tell you a secret if you promise not to* ***divulge*** *it.*

Word history: from Latin word meaning 'make common'

dizzy
adjective having or causing the feeling that you are spinning around: *Don't all talk at once — you make me* ***dizzy****. | She climbed to a* ***dizzy*** *height.* (***giddy***, ***unsteady***)

Adjective forms: **dizzier, dizziest**
Word building: **dizziness** *noun* **dizzily** *adverb*
Word history: Old English *dysig* foolish

DJ
noun **1** someone who presents programs of recorded music on radio
2 someone who presents recorded music at a live venue or function, usually providing spoken links

Word use: You can also use **deejay**.
Word history: *d(isc) j(ockey)*

DNA
noun Biochemistry one of a class of large molecules which are found in the nuclei of cells and viruses and are responsible for passing on genetic characteristics

Word history: abbreviation of *d(eoxyribo)n(ucleic) a(cid)*

DNS
noun → **domain name system**

do
verb **1** to perform or carry out
2 to be the cause of: *to* ***do*** *harm*
3 to deal with: *to* ***do*** *the dishes*
4 to travel: *We* ***did*** *30 kilometres today.*
5 to serve or be all right for: *This room will* ***do*** *us.*
noun **6** *Colloquial* a party: *We are having a* ***do*** *next week.*
phrase **7 can** (or **could**) **do with**, to need or get benefit from: ***I could do with*** *more sleep.*
8 do away with,
a abolish or to put an end to: ***do away with*** *school uniforms*
b to kill
9 do for,
a to defeat, ruin or cause the death of
b *Colloquial* to cook and keep house for
10 do in, *Colloquial*
a to kill or murder
b to exhaust or tire out
11 do or die, to make a last great effort
12 do over,
a to renovate or redecorate: *to* ***do over*** *her bedroom*
b *Colloquial* to beat up
13 do up, to renovate: *to* ***do up*** *the house*
14 make do, to manage with what you've got

Word history: Old English *dōn*

One of the most common verbs in English is the verb **to do**. It appears in several different forms:

Present	*Past*
(I, you, we, they) **do**	(I, you, he, she, it, we, they) **did**
(he, she, it) **does**	
doing (*present participle*)	**done** (*past participle*)

The past participle of **do** is **done**, and this shouldn't be used without **has, have** or **had** before it, unless you're writing down ungrammatical speech or dialogue:

Who done it? WRONG
Who has done it? RIGHT
Who did it? RIGHT

Do is also used as a modal verb (a type of auxiliary verb). We use it to form questions and negative statements:

They know *becomes* Do they know? (question). *and* They do not know (negative).

dob
phrase **1 dob in,**
a *Australian, NZ Colloquial* to betray; report (someone), as for a misdeed: *He* ***dobbed*** *them* ***in*** *for breaking the window.* (***blow the whistle on***, ***expose***, ***rat on***, ***shelf***)
b *Australian Colloquial* to name (someone absent) for an unpleasant task: *We* ***dobbed*** *Jiro* ***in*** *to do the late shift.*
2 dob on, *Australian Colloquial* to inform against; betray: *He* ***dobbed on*** *them for breaking the window.*

Verb forms: I **dobbed,** I have **dobbed,** I am **dobbing**
Word history: British English dialect *dob* to knock someone over or, figuratively, to put someone down

Doberman pinscher (doh-buh-muhn pin-chuh)
noun a breed of large, smooth-coated terriers, usually black and tan or brown, with long forelegs and wide hindquarters

Word use: You can also use **Doberman**.

docile (doh-suyl)
adjective quiet and easily handled: *a* ***docile*** *horse* (***compliant***, ***dutiful***, ***submissive***, ***tractable***, ***well-behaved***)

Word building: **docility** *noun* **docilely** *adverb*
Word history: Middle English, from Latin

dock[1]
noun **1** a wharf or pier where a ship ties up when it's in port
2 the part of a large building where trucks can enter to load or unload goods
verb **3** to come or bring into a dock for loading or repair: *The ship* ***docks*** *at 3 o'clock today.*
4 to join together while in orbit: *The spaceships* ***docked*** *successfully.*

Word history: origin uncertain

dock[2]
verb to cut off or take away a part of: *to* ***dock*** *a dog's tail | They* ***docked*** *his wages because he came to work late.* (***curtail***, ***reduce***)

Word history: Old English *-docca*, in *fingerdocca* finger muscle

dock[3]
noun the part of a courtroom where the person on trial is put
Word history: Flemish *dok* cage

docket
noun **1** a ticket or label on a package stating what is inside
2 a receipt, like one from a cash register, proving that you have paid for goods
Word history: Middle English *doket*; origin obscure

doctor
noun **1** someone who has learned about diseases and is allowed by law to look after sick people and give them medicine
2 someone who has received the highest degree given by a university: *After many years of research he was made a* ***Doctor*** *of Philosophy.*
Word history: from Latin word meaning 'teacher'

doctrine (dok-truhn)
noun something that is believed or taught: *a religious* ***doctrine***
Word building: **doctrinal** (dok-truy-nuhl) *adjective*
Word history: Middle English, from French, from Latin word meaning 'teaching', 'learning'

document (dok-yuh-muhnt)
noun **1** a paper giving information or evidence: *Keep an important* ***document*** *like your birth certificate in a safe place.* (***bulletin***, ***dossier***, ***statement***)
2 a file produced by a computer, especially one made by word-processing software
verb (dok-yooh-ment) **3** to support or back up with documents: *You must* ***document*** *your case well if you hope to convince the judge.*
Word history: Middle English, from Latin word meaning 'lesson', 'example'

documentary (dok-yooh-men-tree)
noun a film or radio program about a real event or someone's everyday life
Noun forms: The plural is **documentaries.**

documentation
noun the documents provided to support a case

dodge
verb **1** to duck or move aside quickly, so as to avoid something: *He* ***dodged*** *the ball just in time. | She* ***dodged*** *when she saw the ball coming towards her.*
noun **2** a dishonest trick

dodgy
adjective awkward or tricky

doe
noun the female of animals such as a deer, rabbit or kangaroo
Word use: The male animal is usually called a **buck.**
Word history: Middle English *do*, Old English *dā*

> **doe / dough**
> Don't confuse **doe** with **dough**. **Dough** is a mixture of flour and water or milk which is baked to make bread or pastry. It is also an informal word for money.

does (duz, duhz)
verb **1** third person singular present indicative of **do**
phrase **2 that does it!**, an exclamation showing exasperation, defeat, etc.

doesn't
contraction of **does not**

> Look up **contractions in grammar.**

doff
verb to remove or take off: *to* ***doff*** *your hat*
Word use: The opposite of this is **don.**
Word history: contraction of *do off*

dog
noun **1** a four-legged mammal which eats meat and may live in the wild, like a dingo or wolf, or may be kept as a pet, like a terrier or German Shepherd (***canine***)
2 the male of this type of animal
verb **3** to pursue or follow closely: *Bad luck* ***dogged*** *him all his life.*
phrase **4 dog in the manger**, a selfish person who refuses to hand over something that someone else wants to use, even though he or she has no particular use for it
5 go to the dogs, *Colloquial* to go to ruin
6 lead a dog's life, to have an unhappy existence
7 let sleeping dogs lie, to leave things alone that may cause trouble
Verb forms: I **dogged**, I have **dogged**, I am **dogging**
Word use: The female animal is a **bitch.**
Word history: Old English *docga*

dogged (dog-uhd)
adjective determined not to give in: ***dogged*** *perseverance* (***single-minded***, ***stubborn***, ***tenacious***, ***unflagging***)
Word building: **doggedly** *adverb*

doggerel (dog-uh-ruhl)
adjective **1** (of poetry) comic and usually poorly written
noun **2** badly written poetry
Word history: Middle English

dogma
noun a belief or principle which many people hold to be true: *religious* ***dogma***
Word history: Latin, from Greek

dogmatic
adjective saying what you think very forcefully and expecting others to accept it as true
Word building: **dogmatism** *noun* **dogmatist** *noun*

doily
noun a small fancy mat that can be put under a cake on a plate or under a vase of flowers
Noun forms: The plural is **doilies.**
Word history: named after a 17th century draper of London

Dolby system (dol-bee sis-tuhm)
noun a method of reducing noise in recording and playing of magnetic tapes
Word history: Trademark

doldrums (dol-druhmz)
plural noun **1** an area of calm near the equator
phrase **2 in the doldrums**, period of inactivity, depression, etc.

dole
phrase **1 the dole**, money paid by the government to help people who are out of work
2 dole out, to give out in small amounts: *to **dole out** the soup* (***allocate***, ***allot***, ***apportion***)
3 go (or **be**) **on the dole**, to receive this government money
Word history: Old English *dāl* part, portion

doleful
adjective very sad: *a puppy with **doleful** eyes* (***glum***, ***miserable***, ***unhappy***)
Word building: **dolefully** *adverb*

doll
noun **1** a child's toy which is made to look like a person
phrase **2 doll up**, to dress in your best clothes
Word use: Children often use **dolly** for definition 1.
Word history: from *Doll*, *Dolly*, for *Dorothy*, woman's name

dollar
noun a unit of money, either a coin or a banknote, which is equal to 100 cents and is used in Australia, the US and some other countries
Word use: The symbol for the dollar is '$'.
Word history: High German *Thaler*, for *Joachimsthaler* coin of Joachimsthal, town in Bohemia where they were coined

dolphin
noun an intelligent, playful sea mammal with a long sharp nose
Word use: You can also use **porpoise** for some types of dolphin.
Word history: Middle English, from Old French, from Latin, from Greek *delphís*

domain (duh-mayn)
noun **1** a territory or realm that is owned or controlled: *The land between the mountains and the sea is in the king's **domain**.*
2 an area of interest or knowledge: *Geology is not my **domain**.*
Word history: French, from Latin word meaning 'that belonging to a lord'

domain name
noun Internet the name of a server connected to the internet

domain name server
noun Internet a server which keeps a record of domain names and IP addresses

domain name system
noun Internet a system for naming servers on the internet and mapping them to IP addresses
Word use: You can also use **domain name service** or the abbreviation **DNS**.

dome
noun a roof shaped like the top half of a hollow sphere or ball: *The **dome** of the cathedral stands out from all the other buildings.*
Word building: **domed** *adjective*
Word history: Latin *domus* house

domestic (duh-mes-tik)
adjective **1** having to do with the home or family: *Cooking, cleaning and washing are **domestic** tasks.*
2 tame or living with people: *Dogs and cats are **domestic** animals.*
3 for or from your own country: *Some of the wheat is for **domestic** use and the rest will be sold overseas.*
noun Old-fashioned **4** a servant paid to do housework
Word use: The opposite of definition 2 is **wild**. | The opposite of definition 3 is **foreign**.
Word building: **domesticity** *noun*
Word history: from Latin word meaning 'belonging to the household'

domesticate (duh-mes-tuh-kayt)
verb **1** to tame or to train to live with people: *to **domesticate** an animal*
2 to cause someone to enjoy home life
Verb forms: I **domesticated**, I have **domesticated**, I am **domesticating**
Word building: **domestication** *noun* **domesticity** *noun*

domicile (dom-uh-suyl)
noun **1** someone's home or a place of residence
2 *Law* the country which is a person's legal permanent place of residence
Word history: French, from Latin word meaning 'habitation', 'dwelling'

dominant
adjective **1** most important or influential (***forceful***, ***potent***)
noun **2** *Music* the fifth note in a scale
Word building: **dominance** *noun*
Word history: French, from Latin

dominate
verb **1** to rule over or control
2 to tower above or overshadow: *The huge gum tree **dominates** the park.*
Word building: **domination** *noun*
Word history: Latin

domineer (dom-uh-near)
verb to tyrannise or to govern or command without considering the wishes of others
Word history: Dutch, from French, from Latin word meaning 'rule'

domineering
adjective bossy and overbearing (***despotic***, ***oppressive***, ***repressive***, ***totalitarian***)

dominion (duh-min-yuhn)
noun **1** power to rule or govern: *Australia has **dominion** over these islands.*
2 the land ruled by one person or government: *Britain and all her **dominions***
Word history: Middle English, from French (obsolete), from Latin word meaning 'lordship', 'ownership'

domino
noun a flat piece of wood or plastic marked with a number of dots and used for playing a game
Noun forms: The plural is **dominoes**.

domino theory
noun the theory that a particular political event in one country will lead to its repetition in others, as a communist takeover of one South-East Asian country leading to a similar takeover of countries near it

don
verb to put on: *to **don** clothing*
Verb forms: I **donned**, I have **donned**, I am **donning**
Word use: The opposite of this is **doff**.
Word history: contraction of *do on*

donate
verb to give as a gift: *to **donate** books to the school library* (***confer***, ***present***)

donation
noun a gift, usually of money (***alms***, ***contribution***, ***legacy***, ***present***)

done
verb **1** past participle of **do**
adjective **2** completed or finished
3 worn out or used up
4 socially acceptable: *Wearing thongs just isn't **done**.*
phrase **5 have** (or **be**) **done with**, to have finished with

doner kebab (<u>don</u>-uh kuh-bab)
noun → **kebab** (definition 2)
Word history: Turkish, from *dōner* a turning + *kebab*

donkey
noun **1** a long-eared mammal, related to a horse (***ass***)
2 someone who is stupid or stubborn
phrase **3 donkey's years**, a long time
Noun forms: The plural is **donkeys**.
Word history: perhaps a familiar variant of *Duncan*, man's name

donkey vote
noun a vote cast unthinkingly, giving the order of preferences from the top to bottom on the ballot paper

donor
noun someone who gives or donates something: *The Blood Bank is calling for blood **donors**.*
Word history: Middle English, from Anglo-French, Latin word meaning 'give'

don't
contraction of **do not**

Look up **contractions in grammar.**

doodle
verb to draw or scribble while you are thinking about something else (***scratch***, ***scrawl***)
Word building: **doodle** *noun* **doodler** *noun*

doom
noun **1** a dreadful outcome, fate or death: *The ship struck an iceberg and all the passengers went to their **doom**.*
verb **2** to force or condemn to unhappiness, ruin, or a difficult situation: *The accident **doomed** him to life in a wheelchair.*
Word building: **doomed** *adjective*
Word history: Old English *dōm* judgement, sentence, law

doona (<u>dooh</u>-nuh)
noun Australian a quilted bedcover often used instead of top sheets and blankets
Word use: Other names are **continental quilt** and **duvet**.
Word history: Trademark

door
noun **1** a large piece of wood, metal or other material, which can be moved to open or close the entrance to a house, room, cupboard, car, plane, etc.
2 the entrance to a room or house
3 a house or building: *He lives two **doors** down the street.*
phrase **4 lay at the door of**, to blame someone for
5 next door to,
a in the next house to
b very near
6 out of doors, outside
Word use: You can also use **doorway** for definition 2.
Word history: Old English *duru*

dope
noun Colloquial **1** a stupid person
2 an illegal drug
3 the actual facts or information: *Give me the **dope** on that new computer.*
Word building: **dope** *verb* **dopey** *adjective*
Word history: Dutch *doop* a dipping, sauce

Doppler effect (<u>dop</u>-luhr uh-fekt)
noun Physics a change in the frequency and wavelength of sound or light waves which seems to occur as the distance between the source and the observer changes
Word history: named after CJ *Doppler*, 1803–53, Austrian physicist

dork
noun Colloquial **1** an annoying or stupid person
2 a person lacking in style; a person who is not cool (definition 3)
Word history: US colloquial *dork* penis

dormant
adjective not active, as if asleep or resting: *Some animals are **dormant** during winter. | This volcano has been **dormant** for two hundred years.*
Word use: The opposite of this is **active**.
Word building: **dormancy** *noun*
Word history: Middle English, from Old French, from Latin word meaning 'sleep', 'be inactive'

dormitory
noun a big room with many beds, especially in a boarding school or hostel
Noun forms: The plural is **dormitories**.
Word history: Latin

Dorothy Dixer
noun a question asked in parliament specifically to allow a minister to reply with political propaganda
Word history: from *Dorothy Dix*, pen-name of an American journalist who wrote an advice column responding to letters from readers; it was thought that she wrote her more intriguing letters herself

dorsal
adjective Zoology having to do with the back of an organ or part of an animal or plant: ***dorsal** nerves | a **dorsal** fin*
Word history: Latin *dorsum* back

dose
noun **1** the amount of medicine taken at one time
2 an amount of something unpleasant: *a **dose** of the flu*

Word building: **dosage** *noun* **dose** *verb*
Word history: French, from Medieval Latin, from Greek word meaning 'giving', 'portion', 'dose'

doss
Colloquial
noun **1** a place to sleep, especially in a cheap lodging house
phrase **2 doss down**, to make a temporary sleeping place for yourself

Word history: French word meaning 'back', from Latin

dossier (dos-ee-uh)
noun a bundle of documents containing information about a person or subject: *The police kept a **dossier** on the bank robber.* (***file, catalogue***)

Word history: from French word meaning 'a bundle of papers with a label on the back'

dot
noun **1** a small spot or a speck: *The car soon became a **dot** on the horizon.*
2 *Music*
a a point placed after a note or rest showing that its length is to be increased one half
b a point placed under or over a note showing that it is to be shortened
verb **3** to mark or cover with a dot or dots
phrase **4 dot your i's and cross your t's,** *Colloquial* to give attention to all the details
5 in the year dot, *Colloquial* long ago
6 on the dot, *Colloquial* exactly on time

Verb forms: I **dotted,** I have **dotted**, I am **dotting**
Word history: Old English *dott* head of a boil

dot art
noun a style of Aboriginal art in which ochre or other pigment is applied as a series of dots to build up a composite picture

dotcom
noun **1** a company trading over the internet
2 a company involved in the information technology industry
adjective **3** having to do with a dotcom
4 (of a company) trading over the internet

Word use: You can also use **dot com, dot-com** or **dot.com.**
Word history: from the suffix *.com* which appears at the end of the domain names of commercial businesses on the internet

dote
phrase **dote on**, to love so much that you appear to be silly: *She **dotes on** horses and talks about them all the time.* (***adore, care for, cherish, worship***)

Word history: Middle English

doting
adjective being too fond or showing too much love: ***doting** parents*

Word building: **dotingly** *adverb*

dot painting
noun a picture in the style of dot art: *The American tourists invested in a number of **dot paintings.***

Word use: Look up **dot art.**
Word building: **dot painter** *noun*

dotty
adjective Colloquial mad or crazy

Adjective forms: **dottier, dottiest**

double
adjective **1** twice as big, heavy or strong: *a **double** helping of mashed potato | a **double** bed* (***dual, duplicate, twin, two-piece***)
2 with two parts: *a **double** ice-cream | a word with a **double** meaning*
noun **3** anything that is doubled: *Four is the **double** of two.*
4 someone who looks almost the same as someone else: *You look so much like my sister you could be her **double**.*
verb **5** to make or become twice as much: *You **double** four to get eight. | The bread dough **doubled** in size.*
6 to bend or fold in two: *She **doubled** up with laughter. | to **double** over the handkerchiefs neatly for ironing*
7 to serve or be used in two ways: *The swimming pool **doubles** as a skating rink in winter.*
8 *Australian, NZ* to carry on a bike or horse: *She **doubled** me home from school.*
phrase **9 double back**, to turn back the way you came
10 on the double, very quickly: *Get in here **on the double.***

Word history: Middle English, from Old French, from Latin *duplus*

double bass
noun the largest instrument of the violin family, which has a very deep sound

doublecross
verb to betray or deceive by pretending to act in agreement with someone but doing the opposite (***knife in the back, sell out***)

Word building: **doublecross** *noun*

double dissolution
noun Australian in government, an order given by a governor-general dissolving both houses of parliament and causing a new election for all senators and members to be called

Word use: Compare this with **dissolution.**

double negative
noun Grammar the use of two negatives when only one is needed

Look up **negatives: double negatives.**

double standard
noun any principle, moral code, etc., which permits greater freedom to one person or group than to another, especially that which imposes stricter sexual morals on women than men

double take
noun a surprised reconsideration of something, caused by the realisation that what you have just witnessed is unusual in some way: *He glanced quickly out the window, then did a **double take** as he realised that there was an elephant in the garden.*

doubt (dowt)
verb **1** to be uncertain or unsure: *I **doubt** that you will get there on time.* (***disbelieve, query, question***)
noun **2** a feeling of uncertainty or suspicion: *There is some **doubt** about his honesty.*

Word history: Middle English, from Latin word meaning 'hesitate', 'doubt'

doubtful
adjective uncertain (***debatable***, ***dubious***, ***questionable***)

Word building: **doubtfully** *adverb*

doubtless
adverb **1** certainly or unquestionably: *She told me her story, which was* ***doubtless*** *true, but had very little to do with my research.*
2 probably: *He does well in his exams,* ***doubtless*** *because he studies hard.*

douche (doohsh)
noun **1** a stream of water forced into or onto any part of the body to wash or medicate it
2 an instrument for forcing a stream like this
verb **3** to give a douche to

Word history: French, from Italian word meaning 'conduit', 'shower', from Latin word meaning 'lead'

dough (doh)
noun **1** a mixture of flour and water or milk which is baked to make bread or pastry
2 *Colloquial* money

Word history: Old English *dāh*

dough / doe
Don't confuse **dough** with **doe**, which is the female of animals such as deer, rabbits and kangaroos.

doughnut
noun a ring-shaped cake which is deep-fried and covered in sugar or icing

Word use: You can also use **donut**.
Word history: *dough* + *nut*, in allusion to the original shape

dour (dow-uh, doohuh)
adjective gloomy or stern: *He looks* ***dour*** *and unfriendly.* (***grave***, ***serious***, ***sober-minded***)

Word history: Scottish dialect, from Latin word meaning 'hard'

douse (dows)
verb to throw water on: *to* ***douse*** *a fire to put it out*

dove (duv)
noun a bird like a pigeon

Word history: Old English *dūfe*-, related to *dive*, verb

dowager (dow-uh-juh)
noun **1** a woman of rank who holds some title or property from her dead husband
2 *Colloquial* a dignified elderly woman

Word history: Middle French word meaning 'woman with a dower', from Latin word meaning 'dowry'

dowdy
adjective shabby and unfashionable: *She wore* ***dowdy*** *old clothes.*

Word building: **dowdiness** *noun*
Word history: Middle English *doude*; origin obscure

dowel (dow-uhl)
noun **1** a pin, usually round, fitting into corresponding holes in two pieces of wood, etc., to join them or to prevent slipping
2 long, thin, wooden rods suitable for this purpose

Word use: You can also use **dowel pin** for definition 1. | You can also use **dowelling** for definition 2.
Word history: compare German *Döbel* peg, plug, pin

down[1]
adverb **1** from higher to lower: *Climb* ***down*** *quickly!*
2 on or to the ground: *He fell* ***down***.
3 to a quiet or inactive point: *Her career is winding* ***down***.
4 from an earlier to a later time: *The song had come* ***down*** *from my grandmother's day.*
preposition **5** to or at a lower place on or in: ***down*** *the stairs* | ***down*** *the ladder*
6 along: *to sail* ***down*** *the river* | *walking* ***down*** *the street*
adjective **7** downwards: *From here the path is* ***down*** *for about 3 km.*
8 in bed because you're sick: *He's* ***down*** *with flu.*
9 (of a machine, computer system or factory) not operational: *My laptop is* ***down***. | *The server is* ***down***.
10 unhappy: *I'm* ***down*** *at the moment.*
noun **11** a time of bad luck or depression: *Life has many ups and* ***downs***.
12 a grudge or a feeling of dislike: *He has a* ***down*** *on me.*
phrase **13 down and out**, *Colloquial* without friends, money or any hope of things improving in the future
14 down at heel, poor and shabby
15 down in the mouth, feeling that life is too much for you
16 down on, too quick to find faults and punish them
17 down to earth, with a practical or realistic approach to life (***matter-of-fact***, ***pragmatic***, ***sensible***)
18 down with, let us get rid of: ***Down with*** *the tyrant!*

Word history: Old English *of dūne* from (the) hill

down[2]
noun fine soft hair or feathers: ***down*** *on his face* | *the* ***down*** *of a duck*

Word building: **downy** *adjective*
Word history: Middle English, from Old Norse

downfall
noun **1** disgrace or ruin: *Greediness was her* ***downfall***.
2 a heavy fall of rain or snow

download
Computers
verb **1** to transfer or copy (data) from one computer to another, or from a computer to a disk, etc.: *She* ***downloaded*** *the data to her USB stick so she could take it with her.*
noun **2** an act of downloading data
3 a set of data that has been downloaded

Word building: **downloadable** *adjective*

down-market
adjective inferior in status, quality or price

Word use: The opposite of this is **up-market**.

down payment
noun a deposit on a purchase made on an instalment plan or mortgage

downpour
noun a heavy fall of rain

downs
plural noun open hilly country, usually covered with grass

Word history: Old English *dūn* hill

downstairs
adverb **1** down the stairs
2 to or on a lower floor
adjective **3** having to do with or situated on a lower floor: *a **downstairs** toilet*
noun **4** the lower floor of a house: *There were noises coming from **downstairs**.*

Down syndrome
noun a genetic condition resulting from a third chromosome on the 21st chromosomal pairing, characterised by varying degrees of intellectual and physical impairment

Word use: You can also use **Down's syndrome**.
Word history: from John Langdon-*Down*, 1828–96, English physician

downtime
noun **1** time during which equipment is out of order or otherwise not able to be used productively
2 time in which a factory, plant, etc., is not operating because of machine failure or maintenance
3 time in which a computer or a computerised system is not operational: *experiencing server **downtime***

Word use: You can also use **down time**.

downward
adjective **1** moving or going towards a lower place or condition: *The plane made a sudden **downward** movement. | a **downward** trend in the share market*
adverb **2** → **downwards**

downwards
adverb from a higher to a lower place or condition: *The road started to wind **downwards**.*

Word use: You can also use **downward**.

dowry
noun money or property that a woman in some cultures brings to her husband when she marries

Noun forms: The plural is **dowries**.
Word history: Middle English, from Anglo-French

doyen (doy-uhn)
noun the senior member of a body, class, profession, etc.

Word building: **doyenne** *feminine noun*
Word history: French

doze
verb to fall into a light sleep, often without meaning to (***drowse***, ***nap***, ***slumber***, ***snooze***)

Word building: **doze** *noun*
Word history: Old English *dwǣsian* become stupid

dozen
noun a group of twelve

Noun forms: The plural is **dozen** or **dozens**.
Word history: Middle English, from Old French word meaning 'twelve', from Latin

drab
adjective dull or uninteresting: ***drab** life* (***dingy***, ***gloomy***, ***mousy***, ***sombre***)

Adjective forms: **drabber**, **drabbest**
Word history: French *drap* cloth

draft
noun **1** a rough sketch or piece of writing
verb **2** to write as a draft: *to **draft** a letter of reply*
3 to force to join the armed forces: *My grandfather was **drafted** into the army when he was 20.*
phrase **4 the draft**, the forcing of people to join the armed forces

Word history: Old English *dragan* draw

> **draft / draught**
>
> Don't confuse **draft** with **draught**, which is a current of air or wind. It is also a rather old-fashioned word for a drink.
>
> It is slightly confusing because American English uses the spelling **draft** for both words. Australian English is starting to follow this trend, so you will sometimes see the meanings listed under **draught** spelt **draft**.

draftsman
noun someone who makes drawings of the plans or designs of things such as bridges, roads, and buildings

Noun forms: The plural is **draftsmen**.
Word use: You can also use **draughtsman**.

> **draftsman / draughtsman**
>
> You might note that these words both end with the suffix -man. Nowadays this is thought to be a sexist ending because it favours men. The word **drafter** avoids this problem and is favoured by the professional drafting organisations.
>
> Look up **non-sexist language**.

drag
verb **1** to pull slowly and heavily along: *to **drag** a cupboard across the room | His feet are **dragging** after walking so far.* (***draw***, ***haul***, ***lug***, ***tow***)
2 to pass or move slowly: *The speech **dragged** on and on.*
3 to search with nets: *The police **dragged** the river for the body.*
noun **4** something that holds you back
5 *Colloquial* someone or something very boring: *The party was a **drag** so we left early.*
6 *Colloquial* women's clothes when worn by men: *to be dressed in **drag***
7 *Colloquial* a car race to see which car can accelerate fastest from a standstill
phrase **8 drag the chain**, *Australian, NZ Colloquial* to hold someone up by doing something slowly
9 drag your feet, to do things very slowly so as to annoy someone

Verb forms: I **dragged**, I have **dragged**, I am **dragging**
Word history: Middle English

dragnet
noun **1** a net to be drawn along the bottom of a river, pond, etc., or along the ground, to catch fish, find a dead body, etc.
2 anything that serves to catch someone or drag them in, such as a police system

dragon
noun **1** an imaginary fire-breathing monster which was supposed to look like a huge lizard with wings and fierce claws

2 *Colloquial* a very strict and bossy old woman
3 a type of lizard like the frill-necked lizard or bearded dragon

Word history: Middle English, from Old French, from Latin, from Greek word meaning 'serpent'

dragonfly
noun a large harmless insect with a long thin body and two pairs of long delicate wings of the same length

Noun forms: The plural is **dragonflies**.

drain
verb **1** to draw or flow away gradually: *to **drain** water from the swimming pool | The colour **drained** from her face.*
2 to make or become dry by water flowing away: *The dishes are **draining** on the sink.*
noun **3** a pipe or channel which carries liquid away
4 anything which uses up or exhausts: *Buying that new car was a **drain** on our bank account.*
phrase **5 go down the drain**, *Colloquial*
a to be wasted: *all the lives that **go down the drain** in war*
b to become worthless: *years of hard work **going down the drain***

Word history: from Old English word meaning 'drain', 'strain out'

drainage
noun **1** the act or process of draining
2 a system of drains, artificial or natural
3 something which is drained off

drainage basin
noun the whole area drained by a river and all the smaller streams flowing off it

Word use: You can also use **drainage area**.

drake
noun a male duck

Word use: The female is called a **duck**.
Word history: Middle English

dram
noun **1** a unit of measurement in the imperial system, equal to approximately 1.772 grams
2 a small drink of liquor
3 a small quantity of anything

Word history: Middle English, from Old French, from Latin word meaning 'drachma'

drama
noun **1** an exciting, sad or serious play acted on stage, radio or television
2 any exciting event: *the **drama** of a bank robbery*

Word history: Late Latin word meaning 'a play', from Greek word meaning 'deed', 'play'

dramatic
adjective **1** having to do with drama: ***dramatic** art*
2 using the same form or technique that is used in drama: *the **dramatic** structure of a novel*
3 full of excitement or conflict: ***dramatic** events*

dramatics
plural noun **1** a play or other dramatic production put on by amateur performers rather than by professional actors
2 exaggerated behaviour that reminds you of an actor's behaviour in a dramatic production: *She's having an attack of **dramatics** again.*

dramatise
verb **1** to take a story and make it into a play
2 to express or show in an exaggerated way: *He **dramatises** his sadness.*

Word use: You can also use **dramatize**.
Word building: **dramatisation** *noun* **dramatist** *noun*

drank
verb past tense and former past participle of **drink**

drape
verb **1** to hang in loose folds: *to **drape** a blanket around your shoulders | That material **drapes** nicely.*
2 to put casually: *Don't **drape** your legs over the arm of the sofa.*
noun **3 drapes**, curtains

Word history: French word meaning 'cloth', from Late Latin

draper
noun Old-fashioned a shopkeeper who sells material, such as cotton or linen

Word history: Middle English, from Anglo-French

drapery
noun **1** material or cloth
2 a shop selling material or cloth

Noun forms: The plural is **draperies**.

drastic
adjective violent, harsh or extreme: *In an emergency we may need to take **drastic** action.*

Word building: **drastically** *adverb*
Word history: Greek *drastikós* efficacious

draught (drahft)
noun **1** a current of air or wind
2 *Old-fashioned* a drink: *a long **draught** of water*
3 the depth of water which a ship needs so that it can float: *a **draught** of 30 m*
4 draughts, a game played by two people each with twelve pieces which they move diagonally across a chequered board (***checkers***)

Word history: Middle English *draht*

Look up **draft / draught.**

draught horse
noun a big strong horse used for pulling heavy loads

Word use: You can also use **draughthorse**.

draughtsman
noun → **draftsman**

draughty
adjective windy or breezy: *a **draughty** corridor*

Adjective forms: **draughtier, draughtiest**

draw
verb **1** to sketch or make a picture with a pen or pencil
2 to pull, move or take in a particular direction: *to **draw** your hand away | The ship **draws** near. | The crowd **drew** together. | to **draw** money from the bank* (***drag, haul, lug, tow***)
3 to attract: *The tennis match **drew** a big crowd.* (***charm, lure, magnetise, pull in***)
noun **4** the act of drawing or picking: *a lottery **draw***
5 something that is picked or drawn: *a lucky **draw***

6 a contest where neither side wins: *The match ended in a **draw**.*
phrase **7 draw a blank**, to be unsuccessful, especially when looking for someone or something, or trying to find out about something: *I thought my watch was in lost property but I **drew a blank**.*
8 draw out,
a to make longer: *to **draw out** a conversation*
b to encourage somebody to talk: *Try and **draw** that shy new girl **out**.*
9 draw up,
a to come to a stop: *The car **drew up** ouside my hotel.*
b to prepare or set out, such things as documents or plans: *to **draw up** an agreement for peace*
c to arrange, especially in the sort of formation used by the military

Verb forms: I **drew**, I have **drawn**, I am **drawing**
Word building: **drawer** *noun* **drawn** *adjective*
Word history: Old English *dragan*

drawback
noun a disadvantage or inconvenience: *The plan is excellent except for one **drawback**.* (***barrier***, ***handicap***, ***hindrance***, ***hitch***)

drawbridge
noun a bridge which can be raised or lowered: *After the knights rode into the castle, they pulled up the **drawbridge**.*

drawer
noun **1** a container shaped like a box that slides in and out of furniture such as cupboards or desks
2 drawers, *Old-fashioned* roomy underpants

drawing
noun **1** a sketch or picture
2 money or the trading stock of a business owned by one person taken and used by the owner for things not to do with business

drawing board
noun **1** a rectangular board which you can attach paper to for drawing
phrase **2 back to the drawing board**, back to the start
3 on the drawing board, being prepared: *The plans are still **on the drawing board**.*

drawing-pin
noun a short broad-headed tack designed to be pushed in by the thumb (***thumbtack***)

drawing room
noun a room where guests are entertained, especially after dinner

Word history: obsolete *drawing* withdrawing + *room*

drawl
verb to speak very slowly so that the sounds are long and drawn out

Word building: **drawl** *noun*
Word history: from *draw*

drawn
verb **1** the past participle of **draw**
adjective **2** looking tired and tense
3 closed or pulled together
4 in a game, equal in score
5 pulled out of its sheath or holster: *They attacked with weapons **drawn**.*

dray
noun a low horse-drawn cart without sides, used for carrying heavy loads

Word history: Middle English *draye* sledge without wheels

dread
verb **1** to be very much afraid of: *to **dread** the exams*
noun **2** great fear or deep awe

Word history: Old English *drǣdan*

dreadful
adjective **1** causing great dread or terror: *a **dreadful** giant* (***frightening***, ***horrendous***, ***terrible***)
2 extremely bad or unpleasant: *The film was **dreadful** so we left early.*

Word building: **dreadfully** *adverb*

dream
noun **1** the thoughts and pictures that pass through your mind when you are sleeping
2 a hope or ambition: *His **dream** is to become a famous actor.*
verb **3** to have a dream
4 to imagine (***make believe***, ***pretend***)
phrase **5 dream up**, *Colloquial* invent or plan in your imagination

Verb forms: I **dreamed** or I **dreamt**, I have **dreamed** or I have **dreamt**, I am **dreaming**
Word building: **dreamer** *noun*
Word history: Old English *drēam* mirth, noise

Dreaming
noun (also lower case) **the**, (in Aboriginal mythology) the time in which the earth received its present form and in which the patterns and cycles of life and nature were initiated

Word use: You can also use **the Dreamtime**.

dreamy
adjective vague or lost in dreams (***absent-minded***, ***bemused***, ***preoccupied***)

Adjective forms: **dreamier**, **dreamiest**

dreary
adjective dull or depressing: *a **dreary** afternoon | a **dreary** sight* (***bleak***, ***cheerless***, ***depressing***, ***dismal***, ***gloomy***)

Adjective forms: **drearier**, **dreariest**
Word building: **drearily** *adverb* **dreariness** *noun*
Word history: Old English *drēorig* gory, cruel, sad

dredge
noun **1** a machine for drawing up sand or mud from the bottom of a river or harbour
verb **2** to use a dredge to clear out the bottom of: *to **dredge** the harbour*
phrase **3 dredge up**, to find with difficulty: *She finally **dredged up** some ideas for her story.*

Word history: late Middle English *dreg*, related to Old English *dragan* draw

dregs
plural noun **1** the solid parts that settle at the bottom of a drink: *She drank the cup of tea down to the **dregs**.* (***lees***, ***sediment***)
2 a useless or worthless part of something: *the **dregs** of society*

Word history: Middle English, from Scandinavian

drench
verb to soak or make very wet: *The rain* ***drenched*** *my clothes.* (***flood***, ***inundate***, ***swamp***)

Word history: Old English *drencan*, make drink

dress
noun **1** a piece of clothing worn by a woman, which covers her body from her shoulders to her legs
2 clothing in general: *The pictures in that book show the* ***dress*** *of the Middle Ages.* (***apparel***, ***attire***, ***garb***)
verb **3** to put clothes on: *Please* ***dress*** *now.* | *Wait while I* ***dress*** *the baby.*
4 to treat by cleaning and bandaging: *The nurse* ***dressed*** *the wound.*
5 to arrange or decorate: *They* ***dressed*** *the shop window for Christmas.*
adjective **6** for a formal occasion: *a* ***dress*** *suit*
phrase **7 dress up,**
a to put on your best clothes
b to put on fancy dress or a costume that disguises you

Word history: Middle English, from Old French word meaning 'arrange', from Latin word meaning 'straight'

dressage (dres-ahzh)
noun the art of training a horse in obedience, deportment, and responses

dress circle
noun the curved section of seats upstairs in a theatre or cinema

dresser
noun a piece of furniture with shelves and drawers for dishes, knives, and forks

Word history: Middle English, from Old French

dressing
noun **1** an act of getting dressed: ***Dressing*** *takes her hours.*
2 a sauce for foods: *salad* ***dressing***
3 a bandage for a wound

dressing-gown
noun a coat that is worn over your nightclothes

dressing table
noun a piece of furniture for your bedroom, usually with drawers and a mirror

drew
verb past tense of **draw**

dribble
verb **1** to flow in small drops: *Sweat* ***dribbled*** *down his forehead.* (***ooze***, ***seep***, ***trickle***)
2 to let spit flow from your mouth: *Babies are always* ***dribbling***.
3 to move a ball along by a series of kicks or pushes, used in soccer, hockey, and other games

Word building: **dribble** *noun*
Word history: obsolete *drib* drip

dried
verb past tense and past participle of **dry**

drier
adjective **1** the comparative form of **dry**
noun **2** → **dryer**

drift
verb **1** to be carried along by the movement of water or air
2 to wander without any particular aim or direction: *She has spent the last three years just* ***drifting*** *about.*
noun **3** a general movement or trend: *The* ***drift*** *of public opinion is towards the government.*
4 the general meaning: *Did you get the* ***drift*** *of his argument?* (***essence***, ***gist***, ***sense***, ***significance***)

Word history: Middle English *drift* act of driving

driftwood
noun wood that is floating on water or has been washed ashore

drill
noun **1** a tool for making or boring holes
2 a strict way of training or exercise that is repeated regularly: *The soldiers were doing their marching* ***drill***. | *We must do fire* ***drill*** *once a month.* (***rehearsal***, ***run-through***, ***practice***)
verb **3** to pierce using a drill
4 to train by giving repeated exercises: *She* ***drilled*** *them in their lines for the play.* (***coach***, ***instruct***)

Word history: Dutch *drillen* bore, drill

drink
verb **1** to swallow liquid (***imbibe***, ***quaff***, ***sip***)
2 to drink alcohol
noun **3** any liquid that can be drunk
4 an alcoholic drink: *We had a* ***drink*** *to celebrate.*
phrase **5 drink in,** to take in by paying attention: *We* ***drank in*** *his words.* (***absorb***, ***digest***)

Verb forms: I **drank**, I have **drunk**, I am **drinking**
Word history: Old English *drincan*

drip
verb **1** to let drops fall: *That tap* ***drips*** *all the time.* (***dribble***, ***ooze***, ***seep***, ***trickle***)
2 to fall in drops: *Rain is* ***dripping*** *from the leaves.*
noun **3** a falling drop of liquid or the sound it makes
4 a slow injection of liquid into the veins of a sick person
5 *Colloquial* a dull or boring person

Verb forms: it **dripped**, it has **dripped**, it is **dripping**
Word history: Middle English, from Scandinavian

dripping
noun fat that has dripped from meat during cooking and that is kept to be used again

drive
verb **1** to force to go: *to* ***drive*** *the mice away* | *He* ***drives*** *himself hard.*
2 to control the movement of: *Can you* ***drive*** *a car?*
3 to take, go, or travel in a car or other vehicle: *I will* ***drive*** *you home.* | *We are* ***driving*** *from Melbourne to Sydney.*
noun **4** a trip in a car or other vehicle
5 a road up to a private house: *The car was parked in the* ***drive***.
6 energy: *She has a lot of* ***drive***.
7 an effort by many people to get something done: *The club is having a* ***drive*** *to get more members.*

Verb forms: I **drove**, I have **driven**, I am **driving**
Word history: Old English *drīfan*

drive-in
noun **1** an outdoor cinema where people watch films from their cars
adjective **2** serving customers in their cars: *a* ***drive-in*** *bank*

drivel
verb **1** to let saliva flow from the mouth
2 to talk childishly or stupidly
noun **3** childish or silly talk

Verb forms: I **drivelled**, I have **drivelled**, I am **drivelling**
Word history: Old English *dreflian*

driven
verb **1** past participle of **drive**
adjective **2** pursuing a goal with fanatical determination: *The girl was so* ***driven*** *that her mother worried about her getting ill.*

driver
noun **1** someone who drives a vehicle
2 a golf club for hitting the ball long distances
3 → **device driver**

drizzle
verb to rain lightly

Word building: **drizzle** *noun* **drizzly** *adjective*
Word history: Old English *drēosan* fall

droll
adjective amusingly odd or comical (***amusing***, ***hilarious***, ***humorous***)

Word building: **drollness** *noun* **drolly** *adverb* **drollery** *noun*
Word history: French, from Middle Dutch word meaning 'little man'

drone[1]
noun **1** a male bee which does not make honey and has no sting
2 someone who is lazy and won't work

Word history: Old English *dran*

drone[2]
verb **1** to make a dull continuous sound: *His voice* ***droned*** *on and on.*
noun **2** a humming sound

Word history: Look up **drone[1]**.

drool
verb **1** to let spit fall from your mouth: *He was* ***drooling*** *with hunger.*
phrase **2 drool over**, to have a greedy interest in: *She* ***drooled over*** *her friend's new car.*

droop
verb **1** to bend or hang down: *His head* ***drooped*** *with tiredness.* (***collapse***, ***loll***, ***slump***)
2 to lose courage: *Their spirits* ***drooped*** *when the boat's engine stopped.*

Word building: **droop** *noun* **drooping** *adjective* **droopy** *adjective*
Word history: Middle English, from Scandinavian

drop
noun **1** a small rounded amount of liquid which falls
2 a small amount of anything, especially liquid: *a* ***drop*** *of milk*
3 the distance or length by which anything falls: *That cliff has a big* ***drop****. | What is the* ***drop*** *of those curtains?*
4 a fall in amount or value: *There has been a* ***drop*** *in prices.*
verb **5** to fall or let fall: *He* ***dropped*** *onto the chair. | She* ***dropped*** *her pencil.*
6 to set down from a car or other vehicle: *I'll* ***drop*** *you at the corner.*
7 to make lower: *to* ***drop*** *your voice | to* ***drop*** *the hem of the dress*
phrase **8 drop in** or **drop by**, to visit for a short time (***blow in***, ***call***, ***look in***, ***stop by***)
9 drop off,
a to get smaller or less: *Sales have* ***dropped off****.*
b to fall asleep

Verb forms: I **dropped**, I have **dropped**, I am **dropping**
Word history: Old English *dropa*

drop-dead
adjective Colloquial extremely attractive: *a* ***drop-dead*** *hunk*

Word use: You can also use **drop-dead gorgeous**.

drop-down menu
noun → **pull-down menu**

dropout
noun **1** someone who decides to leave college or university, or to leave ordinary society and practise another life-style
2 *Computers* the loss of information stored on magnetic tape files

Word use: You can also use **drop-out**.

droppings
plural noun the dung of animals

dross
noun **1** a waste product taken off molten metal during smelting
2 waste matter

Word history: Old English *drōs*

drought (drowt)
noun a long period of dry weather

Word history: Old English *drūgath*, related to *drȳge* dry

droughtproof
verb **1** to ensure a supply of drinking water for: *to* ***droughtproof*** *the city*
adjective **2** designed so as to be unaffected by drought: *a* ***droughtproof*** *garden*

drove[1]
verb past tense of **drive**

drove[2]
verb to drive cattle or sheep over long distances: *He was* ***droving*** *in Queensland for many years.*

Word building: **drover** *noun*
Word history: Old English *drāf* act of driving, herd, company

drown
verb **1** to die from being under water for too long: *He* ***drowned*** *in the river.*
2 to kill by holding under water
3 to cover up by making a louder sound: *The noise of the traffic* ***drowned*** *her cries.*

Word history: Old English *druncnian*

drowsy
adjective sleepy: *She felt very* ***drowsy*** *after the large meal.*

Adjective forms: **drowsier**, **drowsiest**
Word building: **drowse** *verb* **drowsiness** *noun*
Word history: Old English *drūsian* droop, become sluggish

drudge
noun someone who does boring or hard work

Word building: **drudge** *verb* **drudgery** *noun*
Word history: origin unknown

drug
noun **1** a chemical substance given to someone to prevent or cure a disease
2 a substance that is habit-forming
verb **3** to mix a drug with: *His enemies had **drugged** his drink.*
4 to poison or make unconscious with a drug

Verb forms: I **drugged**, I have **drugged**, I am **drugging**
Word history: Middle English, from Old French, perhaps from Dutch *drog* dry thing

drug mule
noun → **mule** (definition 3)

drum
noun **1** a musical instrument with a round hollow body covered with a tightly stretched skin, which makes a deep sound when it is hit
2 a container for petrol or other liquid, in the shape of a drum
verb **3** to beat or play a drum
4 to beat on anything continuously: *She **drummed** on the desk with her fingers.*
phrase **5 the drum**, *Australian, NZ Colloquial* information or advice: *I'm new here so you'd better give me the **drum**.* (***dope***, ***gossip***, ***intelligence***, ***news***)

Verb forms: I **drummed**, I have **drummed**, I am **drumming**
Word building: **drummer** *noun*
Word history: 16thC English *drumslade* drummer, from Low German word meaning 'drumbeat'

drunk
adjective **1** having had too much alcoholic drink
noun **2** someone who is drunk

drunkard
noun someone who is often drunk

drunken
adjective **1** drunk or affected by alcohol
2 resulting from drinking too much alcohol: *a **drunken** sleep | **drunken** driving*

Word building: **drunkenly** *adverb* **drunkenness** *noun*

dry
adjective **1** not wet or damp (***arid***, ***dehydrated***, ***desiccated***, ***parched***)
2 having little or no rain: *It has been a very **dry** winter.*
3 thirsty or making thirsty: *This is **dry** work.*
4 not sweet: *a **dry** wine* (***acid***, ***bitter***, ***green***, ***tart***)
5 dull or boring: *Her speech was very **dry**.* (***flat***, ***humourless***, ***lacklustre***)
6 funny and able to be expressed in a few words: *She has a **dry** sense of humour.*
verb **7** to make or become dry

Adjective forms: **drier, driest**
Verb forms: I **dried**, I have **dried**, I am **drying**
Word building: **dryly, drily** *adverb* **dryness** *noun*
Word history: Old English *drȳge*

dry-clean
verb to clean with chemicals rather than water

Word building: **dry-cleaning** *noun* **dry-cleaner** *noun*

dry dock
noun a dock from which water can be emptied so that the undersides of ships can be repaired or cleaned

dryer
noun something which makes things dry: *a clothes **dryer** | a hair **dryer***

Word use: You can also use **drier**.

dry ice
noun solid frozen carbon dioxide which is used to keep things cold

dryland
adjective **1** having to do with land which is often dry, especially land having sandy soil: *The **dryland** soil was no good to grow roses in.*
noun **2** such a tract of land

Word use: You can also use **drylands** for definition 2.

dryland farming
noun a method of cultivation of land which receives little rainfall, such as leaving the stubble of some plants on the ground to provide nutrients and preserve water

dry run
noun a test exercise or practice

dry season
noun the period of an annual cycle in the tropics when there is little rainfall and the days are hot and sunny, usually as a result of the change in the prevailing winds

Word use: Compare this with **wet season**.

dual (dyooh-uhl)
adjective having to do with two or having two parts: *That plane has **dual** controls. | This book has a **dual** purpose — to teach you and to entertain you.* (***duplicate***, ***twin***, ***two-piece***)

Word building: **duality** (dyooh-al-uh-tee) *noun*
Word history: from Latin word meaning 'containing two'

dual / duel
Don't confuse **dual** with **duel**, which is a fight or contest between two people using swords or pistols.

dub[1]
verb **1** to tap with a sword when making a knight: *The queen **dubbed** him Sir James.*
2 to give a name to: *We **dubbed** him 'The Rat'.* (***call***, ***christen***, ***tag***, ***title***)

Verb forms: I **dubbed**, I have **dubbed**, I am **dubbing**
Word history: Old English *dubbian*

dub[2]
verb to give a new soundtrack in a different language to: *They **dubbed** the French film so that it could be understood in Australia.*

Verb forms: I **dubbed**, I have **dubbed**, I am **dubbing**
Word history: short for *double*

dubious (<u>dyooh</u>-bee-uhs)
adjective **1** uncertain or doubtful: *I feel* ***dubious*** *about my chances in the exam.* (***diffident, unsure***)
2 open to suspicion or question: *His intentions were* ***dubious****.* (***debatable, questionable***)

Word use: The opposite of definition 1 is **certain** or **sure**.
Word building: **dubiously** *adverb* **dubiousness** *noun*
Word history: from Latin word meaning 'doubtful'

duchess
noun **1** the wife or widow of a duke
2 a woman who holds the same position as a duke

Word history: Middle English, from French

duck[1]
noun **1** a waterbird with a flat bill, short legs and webbed feet
2 a female duck

Word use: The male of this bird is a **drake**.
Word history: Old English *dūce* diver

duck[2]
verb **1** to lower suddenly: *She* ***ducked*** *her head just in time to avoid being hit.*
2 to push under water for a moment: *You are not allowed to* ***duck*** *people in this pool.*
phrase **3 duck out** (or **off**), *Colloquial* to go away for a short time: *I am just* ***ducking out*** *to the shop.*

Word building: **duck** *noun*
Word history: Middle English *douke*

duck[3]
noun a batsman's score of zero in cricket

duckling
noun a young duck

duct
noun **1** any tube or channel by which liquids are carried
2 a tube in your body that carries liquid: *a tear* ***duct***

Word history: from Latin word meaning 'leading', 'conduct', 'conduit'

ductile (<u>duk</u>-tuyl)
adjective **1** able to be hammered out thin, as certain metals
2 able to be drawn out into wire or threads, as gold
3 easily influenced

Word building: **ductility** *noun*
Word history: Middle English, from Latin word meaning 'that may be led'

dud
noun Colloquial something which turns out to be a failure (***disaster, fiasco, flop, write-off***)

Word building: **dud** *adjective*

dude (doohd)
noun Colloquial a man or boy: *Some* ***dude*** *was looking for you this morning.*

dudgeon (<u>dud</u>-juhn)
phrase **in high dudgeon**, in a state of anger or indignation: *He stalked out of the meeting* ***in high dudgeon****.*

due
adjective **1** owing and waiting to be payed: *This bill will be* ***due*** *in a month's time.*
2 proper or suitable: *Please treat these glasses with* ***due*** *care.*
3 expected to be ready or arrive: *The train is* ***due*** *at 7 o'clock.*
noun **4** something that is owed or deserved, especially praise or credit: *We must give him his* ***due****.*
5 dues, payment or fees: *Members must pay their* ***dues*** *next meeting.*
adverb **6** directly or straight: *He sailed* ***due*** *east.*
phrase **7 due to**, caused by: *There was a traffic delay* ***due to*** *an accident.*

Word history: Middle English, from Old French, from Latin word meaning 'owe'

due / dew
Don't confuse **due** with **dew**. **Dew** appears as beads of water on the grass in the early morning.

duel (<u>dyooh</u>-uhl)
noun **1** an arranged fight with special rules, between two people with weapons such as pistols and swords
2 any fight or contest between two sides

Word building: **duel** *verb* (**duelled, duelling**) **duellist** *noun*
Word history: from Medieval Latin word meaning 'a combat between two'

duel / dual
Don't confuse **duel** with **dual**, which has to do with two, or having two parts:
This computer game has dual controls.

duet (dyooh-<u>et</u>)
noun a musical piece for two voices or two performers

Word history: from an Italian word meaning 'two'

duffer
noun Colloquial a stupid person

Word history: perhaps a Scottish *duffar* a stupid, inactive fellow

dug
verb past tense and past participle of **dig**

dugong (<u>dooh</u>-gong)
noun a tropical plant-eating water mammal, having flipper-like forelimbs

Word history: Malay

dugout
noun **1** a rough shelter dug into the ground or the face of a river bank
2 a boat made by hollowing out a log

duke
noun **1** a prince who rules a small country
2 a nobleman of the next highest rank to a prince

Word building: **dukedom** *noun* **duchess** *feminine noun*
Word history: Middle English *duc*, from Old French, from Latin *dux* leader

dulcet (<u>dul</u>-suht)
adjective especially of sounds, pleasing or soothing

Word history: Middle English, from Old French, from Latin word meaning 'sweet'

dulcimer (dul-suh-muh)
noun an old-fashioned musical instrument with metal strings that you strike with light hammers
Word history: Middle English, from Old French

dull
adjective **1** boring or uninteresting: *a **dull** talk | a **dull** trip* (***banal, flat, lacklustre, tedious, wearisome***)
2 stupid or unintelligent (***dense, dumb, silly, slow, thick***)
3 not bright or clear: *a **dull** light | a **dull** rainy afternoon* (***dreary, foggy, hazy, misty, overcast***)
4 not sharply felt: *a **dull** pain*
Word building: **dull** *verb* **dullness** *noun* **dully** *adverb*
Word history: Middle English *dul, dull*; related to Old English *dol* foolish, stupid

duly (dyooh-lee)
adverb **1** properly or as deserved: *He was **duly** awarded the prize.*
2 at the proper time: *The train **duly** arrived.*

dumb (dum)
adjective **1** not able to speak
2 silent: *She was **dumb** with surprise.*
3 *Colloquial* stupid or unintelligent: *That was a **dumb** answer.* (***dense, dull, silly, slow, thick***)
Word history: Old English

dumbfound
verb to make unable to speak, usually because of amazement
Word history: blend of *dumb* and *confound*

dummy
noun **1** a copy or model of something used for display or to show off clothes: *He was dressing the **dummy** in the shop window.*
2 a rubber teat given to a baby to suck
Noun forms: The plural is **dummies**.

dump
verb **1** to throw down or put down heavily
2 to hand over or get rid of: *He **dumps** all the worst jobs on me. | They decided to **dump** the captain when the team kept on losing.* (***ditch, jettison, scrap, shed***)
noun **3** a place where something is dumped or stored: *a rubbish **dump** | an ammunition **dump***
4 *Colloquial* a place or a house that is untidy and in bad condition
Word history: Middle English, from Scandinavian

dumper
noun a wave that dumps surfers to the bottom

dumpling
noun **1** a small ball of dough cooked with stewed meat or soup
2 a type of fruit pudding
Word history: perhaps originally *lumpling* little lump

dumps
phrase **down in the dumps**, *Colloquial* in an unhappy state of mind
Word history: British obsolete *dump* a slow dance, sad tune

dumpy
adjective short and fat: *She has a **dumpy** figure.*
Adjective forms: **dumpier, dumpiest**

dun
adjective of a dull or greyish brown colour
Word building: **dun** *noun*
Word history: Old English *dunn*

dunce
noun a stupid or unintelligent person
Word history: from John *Duns* Scotus, born about 1265, died about 1308, scholastic theologian; his system was attacked as foolish by the humanists

dune
noun a sandhill formed by wind, near the beach or in deserts
Word history: Old English *dūn*

dung
noun waste product from the bowels of animals (***droppings, manure***)
Word history: Old English *dung*

dungarees (dung-guh-reez)
plural noun work clothing, usually overalls, made from a rough cotton cloth
Word history: Hindustani

dungeon (dun-juhn)
noun a dark small prison or cell, usually underground: *The prisoners were thrown into the **dungeon** of the castle.*
Word history: Middle English, from Old French, from Late Latin word meaning 'dominion', 'tower', from Latin word meaning 'master', 'lord'

dunk
verb to dip into a liquid: *I like to **dunk** biscuits in my coffee.*
Word history: from German word meaning 'dip'

dunnart (dun-aht)
noun a type of mouse found only in Australia
Word history: from Nyungar, an Australian Aboriginal language of the Perth-Albany region

dunny
noun Australian, NZ Colloquial a toilet, especially an outside one
Noun forms: The plural is **dunnies**.
Word history: British English dialect; a shortened form of the word *dunnekin*, made up of *dunne*, meaning 'dung', and *ken*, meaning 'house' or 'place', so literally 'dung house' or 'dung place'

duo
noun a pair, especially of musicians: *a new singing **duo***
Word history: Italian, from Latin word meaning 'two'

dupe
verb **1** to trick or deceive: *They **duped** him into believing that they would share the money with him.* (***cheat, delude, hoodwink, mislead, take for a ride***)
noun **2** someone who has been tricked or deceived
Word history: Latin *upupa* stupid bird

duplex
noun Australian, US a building consisting of two separate dwellings, arranged either on each storey of a two-storey building, or as a pair of semidetached cottages

duplicate (dyooh-pluh-kuht)
adjective **1** exactly like another thing: *I would like a* ***duplicate*** *copy of this letter.* (***copy, match, twin***)
noun (dyooh-pluh-kuht) **2** something which is exactly the same as something else, usually a copy: *Get me a* ***duplicate*** *of this letter please.* (***likeness, model, replica***)
verb **3** to make an exact copy of: *The secretary* ***duplicated*** *each letter.* (***copy, match, replicate, reproduce***)

Word history: from Latin word meaning 'doubled'

duplicity (dyoo-plis-uh-tee)
noun **1** the quality or state of being double
2 double-dealing or deceitfulness in speech or action

Noun forms: The plural is **duplicities**.
Word history: Late Latin word meaning 'doubleness', from Latin word meaning 'twofold'

durable
adjective lasting for a long time: *School clothes should be made of* ***durable*** *material.* (***heavy-duty, rugged, strong, sturdy, tough***)

Word building: **durability** *noun*
Word history: Middle English, from Latin word meaning 'lasting'

duration
noun the length of time that anything continues for: *They went away for the* ***duration*** *of the holidays. | Hold the notes in your piece of music for their full* ***duration.***

Word history: Middle English, from Latin word meaning 'last'

duress (dyooh-res)
noun **1** the use of threats or force
2 imprisonment or the loss of freedom by force

Word history: Middle English, from Latin word meaning 'hardness'

during (dyooh-ring)
preposition **1** throughout the whole course of: *It is hot* ***during*** *the day.*
2 at some time in the course of: *He visited me* ***during*** *the day.*

Word history: Middle English, from French, from Latin word meaning 'endure'

dusk
noun the time of the evening when it is half light and half dark (***gloaming, twilight***)

Word history: variant of Old English *dux, dox* dark, related to Latin *fuscus* dark brown

dust
noun **1** a fine dry powder of earth or other matter
verb **2** to wipe dust away from
3 to cover lightly: *She* ***dusted*** *her arms with powder..*
phrase **4 bite the dust,** *Colloquial*
a to fall down dead
b to fail: *Another good plan* ***bites the dust.***

Word building: **duster** *noun* **dusty** *adjective* (**dustier, dustiest**)
Word history: Old English *dūst*

Dutch courage
noun courage that comes from drinking alcohol

Dutch oven
noun **1** a large, heavy pot with a close-fitting lid used for slow cooking
2 a metal container, open in front, for roasting meat, etc., before an open fire

Dutch treat
noun a meal or outing in which each person pays for their own costs

Word use: You can also use **Dutch shout**.

Dutch uncle
noun someone who corrects or scolds another severely and openly

duty
noun **1** what someone feels is the right thing to do: *She decided it was her* ***duty*** *to stay with her sick mother.* (***assignment, chore, errand, mission***)
2 what someone has to do because of their position: *These are your* ***duties*** *as leader of the group.*
3 a tax charged by the government: *customs* ***duty***
phrase **4 off duty,** not at work
5 on duty, at work

Noun forms: The plural is **duties**.
Word building: **dutiful** *adjective*
Word history: Middle English, from Anglo-French word meaning 'due'

duty-free
adjective of goods, bought without any tax charges, especially by travellers: *a* ***duty-free*** *camera*

duty of care
noun Law a legal obligation to avoid causing harm to another person by taking reasonable care to avoid causing injury to that person when that injury might be reasonably expected

duvet (dooh-vay, dyooh-vay)
noun NZ, British → **doona**

Word history: from French word meaning 'down'

dux
noun Australian, NZ the top student at a school

Word history: from a Latin word meaning 'leader', originally referring to a military leader. In Australia and some other countries it is now used to refer to the leading student in a school.

DVD
noun **1** a high-capacity optical disc, usually 12 cm in diameter, with enough capacity to store the video and audio data for a full-length movie
2 the technology related to this storage
adjective **3** having to do with this technology: *a* ***DVD*** *player | a* ***DVD*** *film*

Word history: an acronym for *D(igital) V(ideo) D(isc)*, but later said to stand for *D(igital) V(ersatile) D(isc)*, because of its ability to store audio and other data as well as video images

dwarf (dwawf)
noun **1** a person suffering from a genetic condition resulting in short stature
2 someone or something much smaller than normal
3 a small manlike creature in fairy stories: *Snow White and the Seven* ***Dwarfs***
verb **4** to make seem small: *The tower* ***dwarfed*** *the surrounding buildings.*

Noun forms: The plural is **dwarfs** or **dwarves.**
Word building: **dwarfish** *adjective*
Word history: Old English *dweorg*

dwell
verb **1** *Old-fashioned* to live: *They* ***dwell*** *in peace and harmony.*
phrase **2 dwell on**, to continue thinking, speaking, or writing about: *It does no good to* ***dwell on*** *your troubles.* (***brood over***, ***concentrate on***, ***focus on***, ***pore over***)
Verb forms: I **dwelt**, I have **dwelt**, I am **dwelling**
Word history: Old English *dwellan, dwelian* lead astray, hinder, delay

dwelling
noun a place where someone lives

dwindle
verb to become smaller or less: *Our hopes are* ***dwindling***. (***atrophy***, ***contract***, ***decrease***, ***shrivel***, ***wither***)
Word history: Old English *dwīnan* languish

dye
noun **1** a liquid that is used to colour cloth, hair, and other things
verb **2** to colour with a dye: *I think I will* ***dye*** *this dress red.* (***stain***, ***tint***)
Verb forms: I **dyed**, I have **dyed**, I am **dyeing**
Word history: Old English *dēagian*

dye / die
Don't confuse **dye** with **die.** To **die** is to exit from life.

dyeing / dying
Don't confuse **dyeing** with **dying.**
Dyeing is a form of the verb **dye.**
Dying is a form of the verb **die,** meaning 'to stop living'.

dyke
noun **1** a bank built to hold back the water of a sea or river
2 *Australian, NZ Colloquial* a toilet
Word use: You can also use **dike.**
Word history: Middle English, from Scandinavian

dynamic (duy-nam-ik)
adjective **1** having to do with dynamics (***kinetic***, ***mobile***)
2 energetic and forceful: *a* ***dynamic*** *person* (***busy***, ***full of beans***, ***lively***, ***spirited***, ***vigorous***)
Word history: from Greek word meaning 'powerful'

dynamics
plural noun **1** the science that studies the forces that make things move
2 the forces that are at work in any situation: *the* ***dynamics*** *of government*
3 *Music* changes in the loudness of sound

dynamic verb
noun Grammar a verb which indicates an action or process, as *The child jumps*, or *The light fades.*
Word use: You can also use **action verb.** | Compare this with **stative verb.**

dynamite
noun **1** a substance that makes a powerful explosion when set off: *We will blow up the building with* ***dynamite.***
2 *Colloquial* anyone or anything likely to be dangerous or cause trouble
verb **3** to destroy with dynamite

dynamo (duy-nuh-moh)
noun a machine which produces electrical energy
Noun forms: The plural is **dynamos.**

dynasty (din-uh-stee)
noun a series of rulers who are members of the same family
Noun forms: The plural is **dynasties.**
Word building: **dynastic** *adjective* **dynastical** *adjective*
Word history: Latin, from Greek word meaning 'lord', 'chief'

dyne (duyn)
noun a unit of force in the centimetre-gram-second system, equal to 10^{-5} newtons
Word history: French, from Greek word meaning 'force'

dysentery (dis-uhn-tree)
noun an infectious disease marked by an inflammation of the lower bowels, and diarrhoea with mucus and blood
Word history: Latin, from Greek

dyslexia (dis-lek-see-uh)
noun a disability that makes it difficult to learn to read
Word building: **dyslectic** *adjective* **dyslexic** *adjective*

dyspepsia (dis-pep-see-uh)
noun → **indigestion**
Word building: **dyspeptic** *adjective*
Word history: Latin, from Greek

Ee

each (eetch)
adjective **1** every, when you consider two or more things one by one: ***each** hair on my head*
adverb **2** apiece or for every piece or person: *The tickets cost five dollars **each**.*

Word history: Old English *ǣlc*, from *ā* ever + *(ge)līc* like

eager
adjective keenly wanting or longing: ***eager** to help* (***avid, enthusiastic, keen, willing***)

Word building: **eagerly** *adverb* **eagerness** *noun*
Word history: Middle English, from Old French, from Latin word meaning 'sharp'

eagle
noun a large, sharp-sighted, hunting bird with a strong curved beak and claws

Word history: Middle English, from Old French, from Latin

ear[1]
noun **1** the part of the body used for hearing
2 the ability to notice differences of sound: *Marina has a good **ear**.*
phrase **3 be all ears**, to listen very carefully
4 by ear, without looking at written music
5 have an ear to the ground, to know a lot about a topic
6 turn a deaf ear, to refuse to help: *to **turn a deaf ear** to her cries*

Word history: Old English *ēare*

ear[2]
noun the top part of a plant such as corn, on which the grain grows

Word history: Old English *ēar*

eardrum
noun a membrane separating the middle ear from the passage of the outer ear

earl (erl)
noun a British nobleman

Word history: Middle English *erl*, Old English *eorl* man, warrior

early
adverb **1** before the set time: *I arrived **early** for my dental appointment and had to wait for 20 minutes.*
2 at or near the beginning: ***Early** in her talk she showed slides.*
3 in or near the beginning part of the day: *We've got a long drive so let's start **early**.*
adjective **4** happening before the set time: *an **early arrival***
5 taking place in or near the beginning part of the day: *an **early** appointment*

Adverb forms: **earlier, earliest**
Adjective forms: **earlier, earliest**
Word building: **earliness** *noun*
Word history: Old English *ǣrlīce* (from *ǣr* soon + *-līce* -ly)

earn (ern)
verb **1** to receive in return for working: *They **earn** $15 a morning.*
2 to deserve to get: *She **earned** her reputation as a hard worker.*

Verb forms: I **earned** or I **earnt**, I have **earned** or I have **earnt**, I am **earning**
Word history: Old English *earnian*

> **earn / urn**
> Don't confuse **earn** with **urn**, which is a kind of vase. It is also a container with a tap, for heating water.

earnest (er-nuhst)
adjective serious or sincere: *I think he is **earnest** in his desire to help.*

Word use: The opposite of this is **insincere**.
Word building: **earnestly** *adverb* **earnestness** *noun*
Word history: Old English *eornost*

earnings (er-ningz)
plural noun money earned, either your wages or profits from investments

Word history: Old English *earnung*

earphone
noun a small listening device placed in or over the ear

earring
noun a ring or other ornament worn on or through the outer part of your ear

earshot
noun reach or range of hearing: *within **earshot***

earth
noun **1** the planet we live on
2 dry land: *Sea used to cover some parts of the **earth**.*
3 soil, rather than rocks or sand (***dirt, loam***)
4 a wire connecting an electrical appliance to the ground, for added safety
phrase **5 cost the earth**, *Colloquial* to cost a lot; be very expensive
6 down to earth, practical or blunt in your approach to things
7 on earth, *Colloquial* an expression used to add emphasis to questions: *What **on earth** are you doing? | Why **on earth** would they want to buy that house?*

Word history: Old English *eorthe*

earthenware
noun goods, such as pots, made of baked clay

earthquake
noun a shaking of the ground caused by movement of rock under the earth's surface

earthworm
noun a worm with a body divided into segments, which burrows in soil and feeds on soil and rotting plants and animals

earthy (erth-ee)
adjective **1** made up of or like earth or soil: *an* ***earthy*** *smell*
2 coarse: ***earthy*** *jokes*
3 direct or robust in your approach to life
4 sensual in a natural way
Adjective forms: **earthier**, **earthiest**
Word building: **earthiness** *noun*

ease
noun **1** freedom from any problem or discomfort: *He learned to ride with* ***ease****.*
2 a free and relaxed manner: *Her* ***ease*** *with people overcame their shyness.*
verb **3** to give relief or comfort (***alleviate***, ***lighten***, ***relieve***, ***soothe***)
4 to make less difficult
5 to move slowly and carefully: *The old man* ***eased*** *himself into a chair.* (***insert***, ***insinuate***, ***slip***)
phrase **6 at ease**,
a in the armed forces, a position in which soldiers may relax but may not talk or leave
b in a relaxed state of mind
Word use: The opposite of definition 1 is **difficulty**. | The opposite of definition 2 is **awkwardness**.
Word history: Middle English, from Old French, from Late Latin word meaning 'near'

easel
noun a stand for holding an artist's canvas or a blackboard
Word history: Dutch *ezel*, from German *Esel* easel, literally, ass; related to *ass*

easement (eez-muhnt)
noun **1** something that gives ease
2 *Law* a right held by one person to make use of part of the land of another

east
noun the direction from which the sun rises
Word use: The opposite direction is **west**.
Word building: **east** *adjective* **east** *adverb* **eastern** *adjective*
Word history: Old English *ēast*

easterly
adjective **1** towards the east: *We travelled in an* ***easterly*** *direction.*
2 of the wind, from the east: *an* ***easterly*** *wind*
noun **3** a wind blowing from the east: *An* ***easterly*** *sprang up in the late afternoon.*
Noun forms: The plural is **easterlies**.

easy
adjective **1** not difficult: *an* ***easy*** *book to read* (***cinchy***, ***foolproof***, ***simple***, ***uncomplicated***)
2 not formal or stiff: *an* ***easy*** *manner*
3 *Colloquial* having no strong feelings about something: *I'm* ***easy****.*
4 moderate: *an* ***easy*** *pace*
adverb **5** *Colloquial* in an easy manner: *Take it* ***easy****.*
phrase **6 go easy on** (or **with**), *Colloquial*
a to not be harsh or severe: ***Go easy on*** *the children.*
b to use only a small amount: ***Go easy with*** *the honey.*
Word use: The opposite of definition 1 is **difficult**.
Adjective forms: **easier**, **easiest**
Word building: **easily** *adverb* **easiness** *noun*
Word history: Middle English, from Old French

easygoing
adjective approaching life in a relaxed and unworried way (***casual***, ***informal***)

eat
verb **1** to chew and swallow (***consume***, ***devour***, ***gobble***, ***gulp***)
2 to have a meal: *We* ***eat*** *at twelve.*
3 to wear away
Verb forms: I **ate**, I have **eaten**, I am **eating**
Word history: Old English *etan*

eating disorder
noun a pattern of compulsive over-eating or abstinence carried to such an extent that it affects your physical and mental health: *diagnosed with an* ***eating disorder***

eaves
plural noun the overhanging lower edges of a roof: *Pigeons have built a nest under the* ***eaves****.*
Word history: Old English *efes*

eavesdrop
verb to listen secretly
Verb forms: I **eavesdropped**, I have **eavesdropped**, I am **eavesdropping**
Word building: **eavesdropper** *noun*
Word history: literally, be on the *eavesdrop* (of a house), earlier *eavesdrip* ground on which falls the drip from the eaves, Old English *yfesdrype*

ebb
verb **1** to flow back or away: *The tide turned and began to* ***ebb****.* (***go out***, ***recede***)
2 to fade away: *Her strength was quickly* ***ebbing****.*
Word building: **ebb** *noun*
Word history: Old English *ebba*

ebony (eb-uh-nee)
noun a hard, black, shiny wood which is sought after for ornamental carving
Word history: Middle English, from Latin, from Greek

e-book
noun a book in an electronic format

ebullient (uh-bool-yuhnt, uh-bul-yuhnt, uh-byoohl-yuhnt)
adjective **1** overflowing with eagerness, excitement, etc. (***ardent***, ***enthusiastic***, ***zestful***)
2 bubbling like a boiling liquid
Word building: **ebullience** *noun*
Word history: from Latin word meaning 'boiling up or out'

eccentric (uhk-<u>sen</u>-trik)
adjective **1** not usual or normal: ***eccentric*** *behaviour*
noun **2** an eccentric person: *He's a real* ***eccentric****.*

Word use: The opposite of definition 1 is **conventional**.
Word building: **eccentrically** *adverb*
eccentricity *noun*
Word history: Late Latin, from Greek word meaning 'off centre'

ecclesiastic (uh-klee-zee-<u>as</u>-tik)
noun **1** a member of the clergy
adjective **2** having to do with the church

Word use: You can also use **ecclesiastical** for definition 2.
Word history: Late Latin, from Greek word meaning 'of the assembly or church'

echelon (<u>esh</u>-uh-lon)
noun **1** a level of command: *in the higher* ***echelons***
2 a steplike formation of troops, ships, planes, etc.

echidna (uh-<u>kid</u>-nuh)
noun a spiny, ant-eating animal found only in Australia, which lays eggs and feeds its young with its own milk

Word use: Another name is **spiny anteater**.
Word history: Neo-Latin, from Greek word meaning 'viper'

echinacea (ek-uh-<u>nay</u>-shuh)
noun a North American plant often used in herbal medicine: ***Echinacea*** *is effective as a cold remedy.*

echo (<u>ek</u>-oh)
noun **1** a repeating sound, when the sound waves bounce off something hard
verb **2** to repeat or act as an echo: *Our voices* ***echoed*** *in the bare room.*
3 to imitate or repeat: *You are just* ***echoing*** *someone else's ideas.*

Noun forms: The plural is **echoes**.
Verb forms: I **echoed**, I have **echoed**, I am **echoing**
Word history: Latin, from Greek word meaning 'sound'

echocardiogram (ek-oh-<u>kah</u>-dee-uh-gram)
noun an ultrasound image of the heart

echocardiograph (ek-oh-<u>kah</u>-dee-uh-graf, ek-oh-<u>kah</u>-dee-uh-grahf)
noun an ultrasound device for the examination of the heart

Word building: **echocardiographic** *adjective*
echocardiography *noun*

eclectic (e-<u>klek</u>-tik)
adjective **1** choosing from various sources
2 made up of what is chosen from different sources
noun **3** someone who follows an eclectic method, such as in their philosophy

Word building: **eclectically** *adverb*
eclecticism *noun*
Word history: from Greek word meaning 'selective'

eclipse
noun **1** the darkness caused when the sun's light is blocked by the moon, or when the moon's light is blocked by the earth's shadow
verb **2** to do very much better than: *The brilliant pianist* ***eclipsed*** *everyone else's performance.*

Word history: Middle English, from Old French, from Latin, from Greek word meaning 'a failing'

eco (<u>ee</u>-koh)
adjective having to do with environmentally friendly practices, materials, technology, etc.: *an* ***eco*** *house*

ecological footprint
noun a measure of the demands put on the environment by humans, as in growing food, providing fuel, etc., in terms of the global hectares required to sustain one person, taking into account the emissions produced in the production of food and goods and services, as well as those produced in fuel consumption and household requirements such as heating, cooling, etc.

Word use: You can also use **footprint**.

ecology (uh-<u>kol</u>-uh-jee)
noun the study of the relationship between living things and their environment

Word building: **ecological** *adjective*
ecologist *noun*
Word history: Greek *oîko(s)* house + *-logy*

> **ecology / environment**
> Don't confuse **ecology** with **environment.**
> Your **environment** is everything that surrounds you:
> *They grew up in a rural environment.*
> It can also be the physical conditions of a place, such as weather, water, vegetation and buildings.

e-commerce
noun commerce transacted via the internet

Word use: You can also use **e-business**.

economical (ek-uh-<u>nom</u>-i-kuhl, eek-uh-<u>nom</u>-i-kuhl)
adjective not wasteful: *She is an* ***economical*** *housekeeper.* (***careful***, ***frugal***, ***provident***, ***thrifty***)

Word building: **economically** *adverb*

economics (ek-uh-<u>nom</u>-iks, eek-uh-<u>nom</u>-iks)
noun the science of how money is used

Word building: **economic** *adjective* **economist** *noun*

economise (uh-<u>kon</u>-uh-muyz)
verb **1** to manage economically or use sparingly
2 to avoid waste

Word use: You can also use **economize**.

economy (uh-<u>kon</u>-uh-mee)
noun **1** careful management of money or materials (***frugality***, ***thrift***)
adjective **2** at the cheaper end of a range of prices: ***economy*** *brands* | ***economy*** *fare.*

Word history: Latin, from Greek word meaning 'management of a household or of the state'

ecosphere (<u>eek</u>-oh-sfear, <u>ek</u>-oh-sfear)
noun **1** the global ecosystem of a planet
2 the part of the atmosphere of a planet or other heavenly body which can sustain life

ecosystem (eek-oh-sis-tuhm)
noun a community of organisms plus the environment in which they live and interact, such as a pond, forest, etc.

ecowarrior
noun an environmental activist, especially one who takes public action for their cause

ecstasy (eks-tuh-see)
noun a sudden feeling of great joy

Word building: **ecstatic** *adjective*
Word history: Middle English, from Old French, from Medieval Latin, from Greek word meaning 'distraction of mind'

ecumenical (eek-yuh-men-uh-kuhl, ek-yuh-men-uh-kuhl)
adjective **1** universal, especially including or involving all Christian churches
2 tending or intended to work towards unity among all Christian churches: *the **ecumenical** movement*

Word use: You can also use **ecumenic**.
Word building: **ecumenicalism** *noun*
Word history: Late Latin, from Greek word meaning 'general', 'universal'

eczema (ek-suh-muh)
noun an itchy or painful rash in which the skin becomes red and flaky

Word history: Neo-Latin, from Greek word meaning 'a cutaneous eruption'

eddy
noun a current moving in a circle, especially in a river

Noun forms: The plural is **eddies**.
Word building: **eddy** *verb* (**eddied**, **eddying**)
Word history: Old English *ed-* turning + *ēa* stream

edema (uh-dee-muh)
noun → **oedema**

edge
noun **1** a border or a line where two parts or surfaces meet: *the horizon's **edge** | the **edge** of a box* (***brink***, ***margin***, ***rim***)
2 the thin cutting part of something sharp, such as a knife
verb **3** to move slowly and gradually: *to **edge** your way through the crowd*
4 to put an edge on
phrase **5 have the edge**, *Colloquial* to have the advantage
6 on edge, unpleasantly excited and nervous: *He was **on edge** about starting school.* (***apprehensive***, ***edgy***, ***jittery***, ***jumpy***, ***nervous***)

Word history: Old English *ecg*

edgy
adjective anxious or nervous (***apprehensive***, ***jittery***, ***jumpy***, ***upset***)

Adjective forms: **edgier**, **edgiest**
Word building: **edginess** *noun*

edible
adjective able or fit to be eaten: *an **edible** mushroom*

Word history: from Latin word meaning 'eat'

edict (ee-dikt)
noun an order given by a ruler or other authority

Word history: from Latin word meaning 'declared', 'proclaimed'

edifice (ed-uh-fuhs)
noun a building, especially a large or impressive one

Word history: French, from Latin word meaning 'building'

edify (ed-uh-fuy)
verb to build up or increase the faith, morality, etc., of

Verb forms: it **edified**, it has **edified**, it is **edifying**
Word building: **edification** *noun* **edifying** *adjective*
Word history: Middle English, from Old French, from Latin word meaning 'build'

edit
verb **1** to be in charge of the publication of: *She **edits** a magazine.*
2 to read and correct the mistakes of: *She found a lot of spelling mistakes when she **edited** his story.*

Verb forms: I **edited**, I have **edited**, I am **editing**

editing
noun **1** the process of reading text and correcting any mistakes
2 the job of an editor

edition
noun **1** one printing of a book or newspaper: *The afternoon **edition** of the paper has not come out yet.*
2 the total number of copies of a book or a work of art that is printed from one set of type or one engraving plate

Word history: Latin

editor
noun **1** someone who gets written material, such as a book or an article, ready for publication
2 someone who is responsible for what goes into a newspaper, and who puts forward an opinion about world affairs, etc., in the name of the paper
3 someone who edits films, sound recordings, etc.

Word history: Latin

editorial
noun a newspaper article written by an editor, which expresses the editor's or the paper's views (***leader***)

Word building: **editorial** *adjective*

educate
verb **1** to instruct or give knowledge to: *He also **educates** the boys in skills such as fencing.* (***coach***, ***drill***, ***teach***, ***train***)
2 to train: *She has **educated** her taste away from sweet foods.*

Word building: **educated** *adjective* **education** *noun* **educational** *adjective* **educator** *noun*
Word history: from Latin word meaning 'brought up', 'trained', 'educated'

eel
noun an edible snakelike fish

Word history: Old English *ēl*

EEPROM (ee-prom)
noun a computer memory chip the contents of which can be erased electronically and reprogrammed for other purposes

Word history: an acronym for *E(lectrically) E(rasable) P(rogrammable) R(ead-)O(nly) M(emory)*

eerie (ear-ree)
adjective frighteningly strange: *The thick fog produced an* ***eerie*** *atmosphere in the mountains.*

Adjective forms: **eerier, eeriest**
Word building: **eerily** *adverb* **eeriness** *noun*
Word history: Old English *earg* cowardly

eerie / eyrie
Don't confuse **eerie** with **eyrie**, which is the lofty nest of a bird of prey. It can also be a house or castle built so high up that it is hard to reach.

efface (uh-fays)
verb **1** to destroy or wipe out: *It is hard to* ***efface*** *some memories.*
2 to make not noticeable: *There is no need to* ***efface*** *yourself.*

Word building: **effacement** *noun*
Word history: Middle English, from French, *ef-* (from Latin *ex-* ex- + *face* face

effect
noun **1** something which is produced by some cause: *Wrinkles are an* ***effect*** *of age.* (***consequence, outcome, result***)
2 the power to produce results: *Threats have no* ***effect*** *on us.*
verb **3** to make happen: *to* ***effect*** *a change*
phrase **4 for effect,** for the sake of an impression you wish to make: *I dress like this* ***for effect.***
5 in effect,
a in fact or reality: *What will happen* ***in effect*** *is that I will be acting principal.* (***actually, in reality***)
b working or in operation: *The new law will be* ***in effect*** *from tomorrow.*

Word history: Middle English, from Latin word meaning 'brought about'

effect / affect
Don't confuse **effect** with **affect**. They are rather alike in meaning but **effect** is usually a noun and **affect** is usually a verb.

The effect of the warm weather is to make me sleepy.
Warm weather affects me and makes me sleepy.

effective
adjective having the intended result: *an* ***effective*** *way of doing a job*

Word use: The opposite of this is **ineffective**.
Word building: **effectiveness** *noun*

effective rate
noun **1** the actual interest rate paid or received after all other charges or costs have been taken into account
2 the annual interest rate corresponding to a nominal interest over a shorter period, such as a month: *The monthly nominal rate of 1.5 per cent is equivalent to 19.72 per cent* ***effective rate*** *per annum.*

effectual (uh-fek-chooh-uhl)
adjective **1** adequate or producing an intended effect
2 binding or valid: *an* ***effectual*** *agreement*

Word history: Late Latin

effeminate (uh-fem-uh-nuht)
adjective having qualities thought to be more suited to a woman: *Joseph is* ***effeminate*** *in the way he dresses.*

Word history: from Latin word meaning 'made womanish'

effeminate / female / feminine / feminist
Don't confuse **effeminate** with **female, feminine** or **feminist.**

A man is described as **effeminate** when he is thought to have too many characteristics that are regarded as feminine. You would not describe a woman as **effeminate.**

You use the word **female** when you just wish to identify the sex of a person or an animal. A woman is female.

A person who is **feminine** has the attributes which are traditionally linked to the female sex, such as gentleness, kindness, or frailty. A man or a woman could be described as having feminine characteristics. **Feminine** is also used as the adjective from **female,** as in *feminine endings of words* and *the feminine sex.*

A **feminist** is someone who believes that women should have the same rights and opportunities as men. Note that **feminist** and **feminine** do not mean the same thing.

effervesce (ef-uh-ves)
verb **1** to give off bubbles of gas, as fermenting liquors
2 to show excitement, liveliness, etc.

Word history: from Latin word meaning 'boil up'

effervescent (ef-uh-ves-uhnt)
adjective fizzy

Word building: **effervescence** *noun*

effete (uh-feet)
adjective **1** exhausted or worn out
2 sterile or unable to produce

Word history: from Latin word meaning 'exhausted'

efficacy (ef-uh-kuh-see)
noun ability to produce effects

Noun forms: The plural is **efficacies.**
Word building: **efficacious** *adjective*
Word history: Latin

efficient (uh-fish-uhnt)
adjective **1** having and using the necessary knowledge, skill, and industry to do something quickly and well (***capable, competent, practised***)
2 producing an effect

Word use: The opposite of this is **inefficient.**
Word building: **efficiency** *noun*
Word history: from Latin word meaning 'accomplishing'

effigy (ef-uh-jee)
noun a picture or statue of a person (***likeness, model, replica***)

Noun forms: The plural is **effigies.**
Word history: French, from Latin

effluent (<u>ef</u>-looh-uhnt)
adjective **1** flowing out
noun **2** something that flows out, as liquid waste from industry, sewage works, etc.
3 a stream flowing out of another stream, lake, etc.

Word building: **effluence** *noun*
Word history: Latin

effort
noun **1** the use of physical strength: *It takes a great deal of **effort** to push a car.* (***exertion***, ***labour***, ***work***)
2 a serious attempt: *If you made an **effort** you could learn these words.* (***bid***, ***endeavour***)

Word building: **effortless** *adjective*
Word history: French, from Old French *es-* (from Latin *ex-* + *force* strength

effrontery (uh-<u>frun</u>-tuh-ree)
noun cheeky rudeness or impudence: *She had the **effrontery** to tell me I was an old prune!*

Word history: French, from Old French word meaning 'shameless'

effusive (uh-<u>fyooh</u>-siv, uh-<u>fyooh</u>-ziv)
adjective unduly expressive of feeling: ***effusive** emotion* | *an **effusive** person*

Word building: **effusiveness** *noun*

EFTPOS
noun electronic funds transfer at point of sale; a system of electronic funds transfer from a customer's account to a business's account: *She paid using **EFTPOS**.*

e.g.
abbreviation short for *exempli gratia*, Latin words meaning *'for example'*: *Australia has many wildflowers, **e.g.** the flannel flower.*

egalitarian (uh-gal-uh-<u>tair</u>-ree-uhn)
adjective **1** showing or believing in the equality of all people
noun **2** someone who expresses or believes in the equality of all people

Word building: **egalitarianism** *noun*
Word history: French *égal* equal

egg
noun **1** a roundish object produced by a female animal, bird or fish, which contains or grows into its young: *There was a mass of frogs' **eggs** in the pond.*
2 a bird's egg, especially a hen's: ***eggs** for breakfast*

Word history: Scandinavian

eggplant
noun a large, dark purple, more or less egg-shaped fruit used as a vegetable

Word use: Another name is **aubergine**.

ego (<u>ee</u>-goh)
noun **1** the 'I' or self of someone: *The **ego** plays a part in all our thoughts.*
2 conceit or self-importance: *Nothing you say can damage his **ego**.*

Noun forms: The plural is **egos**.
Word building: **egoism** *noun* **egoist** *noun* **egoistic** *adjective*
Word history: from Latin word meaning 'I'

egotism
noun the habit of thinking and talking about yourself all the time: *His **egotism** has lost him all his friends.*

Word building: **egotist** *noun* **egotistic** *adjective*

egress (<u>ee</u>-gres)
noun **1** the act of going out
2 an exit or a way out
3 the right to go out

Word history: from Latin word meaning 'go out'

egret (<u>ee</u>-gruht)
noun any of various herons found throughout the world and bearing long plumes in the breeding season

Word history: Middle English, from Old French

eh (ay)
interjection a questioning sound, sometimes expressing surprise or doubt: *Wasn't it lucky, **eh**?*

eiderdown
noun a quilt filled with feathers and down

Word building: **eiderdown** *adjective*
Word history: Icelandic

eight
noun **1** a cardinal number, seven plus one (7 + 1)
2 the symbol for this number, as 8 or VIII
3 a set of eight people or things, especially a rowing crew
adjective **4** amounting to eight in number

Word building: **eighth** *adjective* **eighth** *noun*
Word history: Old English *eahta*

eighteen
noun **1** a cardinal number, ten plus eight (10 + 8)
2 the symbol for this number, as 18 or XVIII
3 a set of eighteen people or things
4 *Australian Rules* a team of eighteen players
adjective **5** amounting to eighteen in number

Word building: **eighteenth** *adjective* **eighteenth** *noun*
Word history: Old English *eahtatēne*

eighty
noun **1** a cardinal number, ten times eight (10 × 8)
2 the symbol for this number, as 80 or LXXX
3 a set of eighty persons or things
4 eighties, the numbers from 80 to 89 of a series, especially someone's age, or the years of a century: *a man in his **eighties***
adjective **5** amounting to eighty in number

Noun forms: The plural is **eighties**.
Word building: **eightieth** *adjective* **eightieth** *noun*
Word history: Old English *eahtatig*

eisteddfod (uh-<u>sted</u>-fuhd)
noun Australian a competition of singing, playing music and reciting poetry

Noun forms: The plural is **eisteddfods** or **eisteddfodau** (uh-<u>sted</u>-fuh-duy).
Word use: The second plural is unusual because the word comes from Welsh.
Word history: Welsh: session, from Welsh *eistedd*, meaning 'to sit'. Originally an **eisteddfod** was a competitive festival of music and poetry in Wales, but the word is now used in Australia to refer to any such competition.

either
adjective **1** one or the other of two: *Sit at **either** table.*
2 both one and the other: *There were trees on **either** side.*
pronoun **3** one or the other but not both: *Take **either**.*
conjunction **4** used together with **or** to show one of two equal alternatives: ***Either** come **or** write.*

Word history: Old English *ā* always + *gehwæther* each of two

> **either ... or**
> The verb that follows the **either ... or** construction agrees with only one of the alternatives, usually the first:
> *Either this or that is the one you want.*
> *Either you or I are going to come first.*
> Look up **agreement in grammar.**

ejaculate (uh-jak-yuh-layt)
verb **1** to say or shout suddenly and shortly (***cry out, exclaim***)
2 *Old-fashioned* to throw or send out suddenly and quickly
3 to discharge semen

Word building: **ejaculation** *noun* **ejaculator** *noun* **ejaculatory** *adjective*
Word history: from Latin word meaning 'having cast out'

eject
verb to put or send out: *They **ejected** him from the meeting.*

Word building: **ejection** *noun*
Word history: from Latin word meaning 'thrown out'

eke (eek)
phrase **eke out 1** to make enough by adding to it or using it carefully: *to **eke out** the last of the butter*
2 to make with difficulty: *They **eked out** a living in the barren land.*

Word history: Old English *ēcan*

elaborate (uh-lab-uh-ruht)
adjective **1** worked out in great detail: *an **elaborate** scheme | an **elaborate** pattern* (***complicated, convoluted, fiddly, intricate, involved***)
phrase **2 elaborate on,** to add details to: *He **elaborated on** the story.*

Word building: **elaboration** *noun*
Word history: from Latin word meaning 'worked out'

elapse
verb of time, to pass: *Two weeks **elapsed** before I saw her again.*

Word history: Latin

elastic
adjective able to be stretched and go back into shape again: *an **elastic** band* (***bouncy, resilient, springy, stretchy***)

Word building: **elasticity** *noun*
Word history: Neo-Latin, from Greek word meaning 'propulsive'

elated (uh-lay-tuhd)
adjective in high spirits: *She was **elated** at the thought of the trip to Hong Kong.* (***blissful, ecstatic, joyful, jubilant, rapturous***)

Word building: **elation** *noun*
Word history: Middle English, from Latin word meaning 'brought out', 'raised', 'exalted'

elbow
noun the joint between the upper and lower arm

Word history: Old English *elneboga*

elder
adjective **1** older: *Michael is Con's **elder** brother.*
noun **2** an older or senior person: *Listen carefully to your **elders**.*
3 a senior person of status in an Aboriginal community, especially one who holds knowledge of traditional language and culture
4 an older person of high standing and influence in another traditional community, clan, tribe, etc., often a chief or ruler

Word history: Old English *eldra*, etc. (comparative of *ald, eald* old)

elderly
adjective old or aged: *It is often interesting to hear **elderly** people talk about their lives.* (***geriatric***)

eldest
adjective oldest or firstborn

Word building: **eldest** *noun*
Word history: Old English *eldest(a)*, superlative of *ald, eald* old

elect
verb to choose by vote: *to **elect** a member of parliament*

Word building: **election** *noun* **elector** *noun*
Word history: Middle English, from Latin word meaning 'chosen', 'picked out'

elective
adjective **1** filled by an election: *an **elective** position*
2 not required but optional: *an **elective** subject at school*
noun **3** something preferred or chosen: *I'm doing art as an **elective**.* (***choice, option, preference, selection***)

electoral (uh-lek-tuh-ruhl)
adjective having to do with electors or election

electorate (uh-lek-tuh-ruht)
noun the area, or the people in it, which a member of parliament represents: *The Prime Minister is very clever at appealing to the **electorate**.*

electric
adjective **1** having to do with or produced by electricity: *an **electric** current | an **electric** shock*
2 run by electricity: *an **electric** bell*
3 very exciting: *an **electric** performance*
4 of musical instruments, made louder by an electronic device built into them: *an **electric** guitar*

Word building: **electrical** *adjective*
Word history: Neo-Latin, from Latin, from Greek word meaning 'amber' (as a substance that develops electricity under friction)

> **electric / electronic**
> Don't confuse **electric** with **electronic.** Equipment which is **electronic** makes use of transistors or integrated circuits, as an *electronic calculator* does.

electrician
noun someone who works with electrical appliances and wiring

electricity
noun a form of energy from electrons, which can be used for heating, lighting, driving a motor, and other things

electrify
verb **1** to equip for use with electricity: *The railway line has been **electrified**.*
2 to thrill or excite: *Her news **electrified** us.*

Verb forms: it **electrified**, it has **electrified**, it is **electrifying**
Word building: **electrification** *noun*

electrocardiogram
(uh-lek-troh-kah-dee-uh-gram)
noun Medicine the graphic record produced by an electrocardiograph

Word use: The abbreviation is **ECG**. | The short form is **cardiogram**.

electrocardiograph
(uh-lek-troh-kah-dee-uh-graf)
noun a machine which picks up and records the electrical activity of the heart

Word use: The abbreviation is **ECG**. | The record produced is called an **electrocardiogram**.

electrocute
verb to kill by electricity: *A faulty electric toaster could **electrocute** you.*

Word building: **electrocution** *noun*

electrode
noun a conductor through which electric current enters or leaves a battery, circuit or valve

electroencephalograph
(uh-lek-troh-en-sef-uh-luh-graf)
noun a machine which picks up and records the electrical activity of the brain

Word use: The abbreviation is **EEG**. | The record produced is called an **electroencephalogram**.
Word building: **electroencephalographic** *adjective* **electroencephalography** *noun*

electrolysis (e-luhk-tro-luh-suhs, uh-lek-tro-luh-suhs)
noun Chemistry the breaking down of a chemical compound in solution into its basic parts, by passing an electric current through it

electromagnet
noun a magnet with a core made of iron and steel with wire coiled around it, through which an electric current is passed

electromagnetic
adjective having to do with the relationship between magnetic forces and electric currents: ***electromagnetic** radiation* / ***electromagnetic** waves*

electromagnetic radiation
noun heat, light, X-rays, radio waves and other forms of radiation made up of electromagnetic waves. These waves are produced by the acceleration of an electric charge and have an electric field and a magnetic field at right angles to each other.

electron
noun a very tiny particle which orbits the nucleus in all atoms and which has a type of negative energy that balances the energy of a proton

Word use: Compare this with **neutron** and **proton**.

electronic (el-uhk-tron-ik, uh-lek-tron-ik)
adjective worked or produced by small changes in voltage: *an **electronic** calculator*

Word use: This word does not mean the same as **electric**, which relates to electric current or energy.
Word building: **electronically** *adverb*

electronic funds transfer
noun a computerised banking system for the transfer of money from one account to another

electronics (el-uhk-tron-iks, uh-lek-tron-iks)
noun the study and application of the effects of the movement of electrons in valves and semiconductors

electronic tag
noun → **e-tag**

electronic whiteboard
noun a whiteboard with a digital capability: *The teacher printed out what was showing on the **electronic whiteboard**.*

elegant
adjective graceful or stylish: ***elegant** manners* / ***elegant** clothes* (***chic**, **dapper**, **fashionable**, **nifty**, **smart***)

Word building: **elegance** *noun*
Word history: from Latin word meaning 'fastidious', 'nice', 'fine', 'elegant'

elegy (el-uh-jee)
noun a poem expressing sorrow over someone's death

Noun forms: The plural is **elegies**.
Word building: **elegiac** (el-uh-juy-uhk) *adjective*
Word history: Latin, from Greek word meaning 'lament'

element
noun **1** a substance that can't be broken down into anything else: *The compound copper sulfate can be broken down into the **elements** copper and sulfur.* (***component**, **constituent***)
2 a wire that is the heating unit of an electric heater, jug or similar electric appliance
3 the natural or ideal surroundings of any person or thing: *He's in his **element**.*
4 elements, the weather or atmospheric forces: *protected from the **elements***

Word history: Middle English, from Latin word meaning 'a first principle', 'rudiment'

elementary
adjective simple or basic

elephant
noun a very large animal of Africa or India, with a thick skin, a long grasping trunk, and long curved tusks

Word history: Latin, from Greek word meaning 'elephant', 'ivory'

elevate
verb to lift or raise: *The idea of an outing **elevated** her spirits.*

Word history: Middle English, from Latin

elevation (el-uh-vay-shuhn)
noun **1** height above sea or ground level
2 a high or raised place
3 grandeur or dignity
4 *Architecture*
a a scale drawing of an object or structure, especially the face of a building, showing it without perspective, every point being drawn as if looked at horizontally
b the front, side, or back of a building
5 *Surveying* the angle between the line from an observer to an object above the observer and a horizontal line

elevator
noun **1** a building for storing grain
2 the US word for **lift** (definition 2)
Word history: Late Latin

eleven
noun **1** a cardinal number, ten plus one (10 + 1)
2 the symbol for this number, as 11 or XI
3 a set of eleven people or things
4 a team of eleven players, as in soccer, cricket, hockey, etc.
adjective **5** amounting to eleven in number
Word building: **eleventh** *adjective* **eleventh** *noun*
Word history: Middle English, Old English, literally, one left (after counting ten)

elf
noun a small being in fairy stories who often plays tricks on people
Noun forms: The plural is **elves.**
Word history: Old English *elfen* nymph (feminine elf)

elicit (uh-lis-uht)
verb to draw or bring out: *to* ***elicit*** *the truth*
Word building: **elicitation** *noun*
Word history: Latin

eligible (el-uh-juh-buhl)
adjective **1** ready or qualified: *You are* ***eligible*** *to vote when you are eighteen years old.*
2 suitable to be chosen, especially as a husband or wife: *an* ***eligible*** *bachelor*
Word use: The opposite of this is **ineligible**.
Word building: **eligibility** *noun*
Word history: French, from Latin word meaning 'pick out'

eliminate
verb to get rid of or remove: *The early rounds of the tournament will* ***eliminate*** *the weakest players.*
Word building: **elimination** *noun*
Word history: from Latin word meaning 'turned out of doors'

elite (uh-leet)
noun **1** the group of people with the most money, power, and other advantages: *Only the* ***elite*** *can afford to live in that neighbourhood.*
2 the group of people with the most talent or skill: *the sporting* ***elite***
adjective **3** belonging to the group of people with the most talent or skill: *elite athletes*
Word history: French word meaning 'choose', from Latin

elitism
noun the idea that a certain group of people should have special advantages

elixir (uh-liks-uh)
noun **1** a sweet liquid medicine: *a cough* ***elixir***
2 a liquid remedy formerly believed to cure all ills, or to have special, almost magical effects: ***elixir*** *of life* | ***elixir*** *of love*
Word history: Middle English, from Medieval Latin, from Arabic *el, al* the + *iksīr* philosopher's stone, probably from Late Greek word meaning 'a drying powder for wounds'

elk
noun a large deer found in Europe and Asia
Word history: Old English *ealh* elk

ellipse
noun an oval shape
Word building: **elliptical** *adjective*
Word history: Latin

ellipsis (uh-lip-suhs)
noun **1** *Grammar* the omission from a sentence of a word or words which would make it more complete or clear
2 in writing or printing, the marks (. . .) which show that something has been left out
Noun forms: The plural is **ellipses.**
Word history: Latin, from Greek word meaning 'omission'

> You use an **ellipsis** (...) in writing to show that letters or words have deliberately been left out as the text was being copied from the original.
>
> You can use an ellipsis
>
> **1** within a sentence:
>
> *She needed time . . . before she could reply to his letter.*
>
> **2** at the beginning of a piece of text:
>
> *. . . words which she knew would hurt him.*
>
> Note that in this case you may have to put a capital letter on the first word after the ellipsis. This is because it may become the first word in a new sentence, whatever it was in the original:
>
> *. . . She knew it was the beginning of the end.*
>
> **3** at the end of a sentence:
>
> *She never heard from him again . . .*
>
> Note that when the ellipsis comes at the end of a sentence, you don't add a full stop.

ellipsoid (uh-lip-soyd)
noun a solid oval, the shape of a football

elm
noun any of a group of large trees of northern Europe or tropical Asia which lose their leaves in winter; used for timber
Word history: Old English

El Niño (el nin-yoh)
noun a climatic event involving a rapid warming of the surface of the southern Pacific Ocean causing a change in normal wind and current movements, and having often disastrous effects on the world's weather, marked in Australia by drought on the eastern coast
Word use: Compare this with **La Niña**
Word history: Spanish: the (Christ) child; alluding to the appearance of the current off South America near Christmas

elocution
noun the study of good clear speaking

Word history: from Latin word meaning 'a speaking out'

elongated
adjective drawn out to a greater length than usual: *an **elongated** shape | an **elongated** period of illness*

Word history: Late Latin

elope
verb to run away with a lover, usually so that you can get married without the permission of your parents

Word history: Middle English *a-* + *lopen* lope

eloquent (el-uh-kwuhnt)
adjective able to speak in a flowing, expressive manner (***articulate***, ***fluent***, ***silver-tongued***, ***slick***, ***smooth***)

Word building: **eloquence** *noun*
Word history: Middle English, from Latin word meaning 'speaking out'

else
adverb **1 a** instead or other than the person or the thing mentioned: *somebody **else** | who **else**?*
b in addition: *What **else** shall I do? | Who **else** is going?*
2 other than yours: *somebody **else's** child | nobody **else's** business*
3 otherwise: *Run, or **else** you will be late.*

Word history: Old English *elles*

elsewhere
adverb somewhere else

elucidate (uh-looh-suh-dayt)
verb to explain, or make understandable or clear (***clarify***, ***spell out***)

Word building: **elucidation** *noun* **elucidatory** *adjective*
Word history: from Late Latin word meaning 'made light'

elude (uh-loohd)
verb **1** to avoid or escape, especially by skill or trickery: *to **elude** the guard | to **elude** the law* (***evade***, ***miss***, ***steer clear of***)
2 to momentarily escape your memory: *The name of that plant **eludes** me at the moment.*

Word building: **eluder** *noun* **elusion** *noun*
Word history: from Latin word meaning 'finish play', 'deceive'

elude / allude
Don't confuse **elude** with **allude**. When you **allude** to a person or thing, you mention them casually.

elusive
adjective hard to find or get hold of: *an **elusive** person | an **elusive** memory*

Word building: **elusiveness** *noun*

emaciated (uh-may-see-ayt-uhd)
adjective very thin, because of or as if because of disease: *The pictures of **emaciated** children made us realise how severe the famine in Africa had been.*

Word history: Latin

email (ee-mayl)
noun **1** messages sent on a telecommunications system linking computers or terminals
verb **2** to send (a message) by email: *to **email** a response*
3 to send such messages to (someone): *He **emailed** me last night.*

Word use: You can also use **e-mail**, and for definition 1 you can also use **electronic mail**.

emanate (em-uh-nayt)
verb to flow or come out (***originate***, ***start from***)

Word building: **emanation** *noun*
Word history: Latin

emancipate (uh-man-suh-payt)
verb to set free: *to **emancipate** a slave* (***deliver***, ***liberate***, ***release***)

Word building: **emancipation** *noun*
Word history: Latin

emancipist
noun Australian History a convict pardoned by the governor in early colonial times

emasculate (uh-mas-kyuh-layt)
verb **1** to castrate
2 to weaken: *Bankruptcy seemed to **emasculate** the previously powerful man.*

Word building: **emasculation** *noun*
Word history: Latin

embalm (em-bahm)
verb to treat a corpse with chemicals in order to preserve it

Word history: Middle English, from French *em-* + *baume* balm

embankment
noun a mound of earth and stones to keep back water or to carry a road or railway

embargo
noun a ban, usually placed by a government on trade of some kind: *an **embargo** on the export of parrots*

Noun forms: The plural is **embargoes**.
Word history: Spanish word meaning 'restrain', from Romance word meaning 'bar'

embark
verb **1** to go on board a ship for a voyage: *We **embarked** in Brisbane.*
phrase **2 embark on**, to start: *They **embarked on** a new project.* (***commence***, ***initiate***, ***set about***, ***start***)

Word use: The opposite of definition 1 is **disembark**.
Word building: **embarkation** *noun*
Word history: French

embarrass
verb to cause to feel uncomfortable: *My mother's old-fashioned ideas **embarrassed** me in front of my friends.*

Word building: **embarrassment** *noun*
Word history: from French word meaning 'block', 'obstruct'

embassy
noun the office and house of an ambassador

Noun forms: The plural is **embassies**.
Word history: Middle French, from Late Latin word meaning 'office'

embattled
adjective caught in a battle or an argument

embellish
verb to make beautiful by decorating: *Carved figures* ***embellished*** *the box.* (***decorate, embroider***)

Word building: **embellishment** *noun*
Word history: Middle English, from Old French

ember (em-buh)
noun **1** a small live piece of coal, wood, etc., such as in a dying fire
2 embers, the remains of a fire

Word history: Old English *ǣmerge*

embezzle
verb to steal, usually by making false entries in accounts: *The clerk* ***embezzled*** *$1000.*

Word building: **embezzlement** *noun*
Word history: Middle English, from Anglo-French *en-* em- + *beseler* destroy, dissipate

emblem
noun a badge or something that serves as a sign or symbol: *A horseshoe is an* ***emblem*** *of good luck.* (***token, totem***)

Word building: **emblematic** *adjective*
Word history: Latin word meaning 'inlaid work', 'ornamentation', from Greek word meaning 'an insertion'

emboss
verb to decorate with a design which stands out from its background

Word history: Middle English, from Old French word meaning 'swell in protuberances'

embrace
verb to hug or cuddle

Word building: **embrace** *noun*
Word history: Middle English, from Old French *em-* + *bras* arm (from Latin)

embroider
verb **1** to sew decorative patterns on: *to* ***embroider*** *a cushion-cover* (***sew, stitch, work***)
2 to make more interesting with untruthful additions: *to* ***embroider*** *a story* (***amplify, develop, embellish, expand on***)

Word building: **embroidery** *noun*

embroil
verb **1** to involve: *to* ***embroil*** *in an argument*
2 to complicate or throw into confusion

Word building: **embroilment** *noun*
Word history: French *em-* + *brouiller* disorder

embryo (em-bree-oh)
noun a young animal or human in the very early stages of growing in the womb

Noun forms: The plural is **embryos**.
Word use: Compare this with **foetus**.
Word building: **embryonic** *adjective*
Word history: Medieval Latin, from Greek

emend (uh-mend)
verb **1** to correct or free from faults or errors
2 to correct or change by removing errors: *to* ***emend*** *the text of his novel*

Word building: **emendable** *adjective* **emendation** *noun*
Word history: from Latin word meaning 'correct'

emerald
noun **1** a green precious stone
2 a clear bright green colour

Word building: **emerald** *adjective*
Word history: Middle English, from Old French, from Latin word meaning 'a green precious stone', from Greek

emerge
verb to come out into view: *She* ***emerged*** *from behind the trees.* (***appear, loom, materialise, show up***)

Word use: The opposite of this is **disappear**.
Word building: **emergence** *noun*
Word history: from Latin word meaning 'rise out'

emergency
noun an unexpected serious happening that needs action at once

Noun forms: The plural is **emergencies**.
Word history: from Medieval Latin word meaning 'a coming up'

emergent (uh-mer-juhnt)
adjective **1** emerging
2 recently independent and generally in an early stage of development: *an* ***emergent*** *nation*

emery (em-uh-ree)
noun a granular mineral substance, consisting typically of corundum mixed with magnetite or hematite, used for grinding and polishing

Word history: French *émeri*, from Greek *smêris*

emetic (uh-met-ik)
noun a medicine or substance causing vomiting

Word building: **emetic** *adjective*
Word history: Latin, from Greek

emigrate
verb to leave your own country to go to live in another

Word use: The opposite of this is **immigrate**.
Word building: **emigrant** *noun* **emigration** *noun*
Word history: Latin

emigrate / immigrate / migrate

Don't confuse **emigrate** with **immigrate**.

To **immigrate** is to come to live in a new country.

An **emigrant** goes away from a place (**emigration**) and an **immigrant** comes into a place (**immigration**).

To **migrate** can be to **emigrate** or to **immigrate**. In Australia it is common to call immigrants **migrants**.

When birds **migrate** they change their place of living at regular times each year. The journey of these **migratory** creatures is **migration**.

eminence
noun **1** a high rank or standing: *She was in a position of* ***eminence*** *in her profession.*
2 a high place: *The house stood on an* ***eminence***.

eminent
adjective important or high in rank (***famous, great, pre-eminent, prestigious, prominent***)

Word history: from Latin word meaning 'standing out'

eminent / imminent
Don't confuse **eminent** with **imminent**.
If something is **imminent**, it is likely to happen at any moment:
The flashes of lightning show that a thunderstorm is imminent.

emir (e-<u>mear</u>, <u>e</u>-mear)
noun **1** a Muslim or Arabic chieftain or prince
2 a title of honour of the descendants of Mohammed
Word use: You can also use **emeer**.
Word history: Arabic *amīr* commander

emirate (<u>em</u>-uh-ruht)
noun a territory under the control of an emir

emissary (<u>em</u>-uhs-uh-ree, <u>em</u>-uhs-ree)
noun someone sent on mission (***envoy, representative***)
Noun forms: The plural is **emissaries**.
Word history: from Latin word meaning 'scout'

emission (uh-<u>mish</u>-uhn, ee-<u>mish</u>-uhn)
noun **1** the act of emitting
2 something that is emitted; a discharge; an emanation
3 such a discharge, especially of pollutants such as greenhouse gases, into the environment

emission credit
noun a credit purchased within an emissions trading scheme, as from a scheme achieving a reduction in carbon dioxide in the atmosphere, to offset the carbon emission of the buyer

emissions trading
noun trading in emission permits under a system by which countries or organisations not using their quotas are able to sell their excess permits to others exceeding their quota
Word use: Look up **carbon cap**.

emit
verb **1** to discharge or send forth: *to **emit** liquid, light, heat, sound, etc.*
2 to issue: *to **emit** an order or decree*
3 to utter: *to **emit** an opinion*
Verb forms: it **emitted**, it has **emitted**, it is **emitting**
Word building: **emitter** *noun*
Word history: from Latin word meaning 'send out'

emo (<u>ee</u>-moh)
adjective **1** having to do with a music style derived from hardcore punk but with lyrics expressing personal emotional experiences
2 having to do with a style of dress associated with fans of emo music: *dressed **emo** style all in black*
noun **3** emo music
4 a fan of emo music
5 *Colloquial* a person who is overly pessimistic and emotional

emollient (uh-<u>moh</u>-lee-uhnt)
noun a medicine or substance with the power to soften or soothe living tissues, especially your skin
Word history: Latin

emotion
noun a feeling, such as love, hate, happiness, misery or anger
Word history: French word meaning 'excite', from Latin

emotional
adjective **1** having to do with or affected by your emotions
2 appealing to the emotions: *It was an **emotional** request to the judge.*
3 caused or determined by emotion rather than reason: *an **emotional** decision*
4 showing too much emotion (***agitated, overwrought***)
Word use: The opposite of definition 2 is **unemotional**. | The opposite of definition 4 is **impassive**.
Word building: **emotionally** *adverb* **emotionalism** *noun*

emotive
adjective **1** showing or having to do with emotion
2 sparking off emotion

empathy
noun emotional or mental understanding of the feelings or spirit of someone: *She has an **empathy** with children.*
Word building: **empathic** *adjective* **empathically** *adverb* **empathise** *verb*
Word history: Greek

emperor
noun a man who rules over a group of countries or peoples: *Augustus was the first Roman **emperor**.*
Word history: Middle English, from Old French, from Latin word meaning 'ruler'

emphasis (<u>em</u>-fuh-suhs)
noun stress or importance: *The manager placed great **emphasis** on punctuality.*
Noun forms: The plural is **emphases** (<u>em</u>-fuh-seez).
Word building: **emphasise** *verb* **emphatic** *adjective*
Word history: Latin, from Greek

empire
noun **1** a group of countries or peoples ruled by an emperor or empress
2 a large and powerful business group controlled by a single person or group of people
Word building: **imperial** *adjective*
Word history: Middle English, from French, from Latin *imperium* a command, authority, realm

empirical (em-<u>pir</u>-ik-uhl)
adjective **1** taken from or guided by experience or experiment
2 depending upon experience or observation rather than using science or theory
Word building: **empirically** *adverb*

employ
verb **1** to provide work for: *The factory **employs** 100 people.*
2 to use: *to **employ** a spade for digging | to **employ** your spare time in reading*
Word building: **employment** *noun*
Word history: French, from Latin word meaning 'enfold'

employee
noun someone who is paid to work by an employer

employer
noun someone who hires and provides paid work for others

empress
noun **1** the woman ruler of an empire
2 the wife of an emperor
Word history: Middle English, from Old French, from Latin

empty
adjective containing nothing (***blank***, ***deserted***, ***vacant***, ***void***)
Adjective forms: **emptier**, **emptiest**
Word building: **empty** *verb* (**emptied**, **emptying**) **emptiness** *noun*
Word history: Old English *ǣmtig*, from *ǣmetta* leisure + *-ig* -y

emu (<u>eem</u>-yooh)
noun a large Australian bird which can't fly and is related to the cassowary
Word history: Portuguese *ema* ostrich, cassowary

emulate (<u>em</u>-yooh-layt, <u>em</u>-yuh-layt)
verb to try to imitate or be like: *She wanted to* ***emulate*** *the great inventors of the past.*
Word building: **emulation** *noun*
Word history: from Latin word meaning 'having rivalled'

emulsion (uh-<u>mul</u>-shuhn)
noun **1** a milk-like mixture formed when one liquid is suspended rather than dissolved in another, such as of oil in water
2 *Photography* a light-sensitive layer on a photographic film, plate, or paper
Word building: **emulsify** *verb* (**emulsified**, **emulsifying**)
Word history: Neo-Latin *ēmulsio*, from Latin *ēmulsus*, past participle, milked out

enable
verb to make able: *The bridge* ***enables*** *you to cross the harbour.*

enact
verb **1** to make into an act or statute
2 to order or decree
3 to act the part of: *to* ***enact*** *Hamlet*
Word building: **enactment** *noun*

enamel
noun **1** a very hard coating applied to metal
2 a glossy paint
Word history: Middle English, from Anglo-French

encapsulate
verb **1** to enclose in or as if in a capsule
2 to put in shortened form (***abridge***, ***condense***)
Word building: **encapsulation** *noun*

enchant
verb **1** to cast a magic spell on
2 to delight or charm: *Her singing* ***enchanted*** *us.*
Word building: **enchantment** *noun*
Word history: Middle English, from Old French, from Latin word meaning 'chant a magic formula against'

encircle
verb to surround or enclose in a circle

enclave
noun a country, or an outlying portion of it, completely surrounded by foreign land
Word history: French word meaning 'shut in', from Latin

enclose
verb **1** to shut or close in on all sides: *A wall* ***enclosed*** *the orchard.* (***box in***, ***confine***, ***coop up***, ***surround***)
2 to put in: *I* ***enclose*** *a photograph with this letter.* (***add***, ***insert***, ***slip in***)
Word building: **enclosure** *noun*
Word history: Old French

encode
verb to put in a code: *to* ***encode*** *a message*
Word use: The opposite of this is **decode**.

encompass
verb **1** to surround or form a circle about
2 to enclose or contain

encore (<u>on</u>-kaw, <u>ong</u>-kaw)
interjection **1** once more!
noun **2** an extra piece of music performed in answer to continued clapping by the audience
Word history: French word meaning 'still', 'yet', 'besides', from Latin word meaning 'within this hour'

encounter
verb to meet: *to* ***encounter*** *an old enemy* | *to* ***encounter*** *an unexpected problem* (***bump into***, ***come across***, ***run into***)
Word building: **encounter** *noun*
Word history: Middle English, from Old French, from Latin *in-* + *contrā* against

encourage
verb to cheer up or cheer on: *We* ***encouraged*** *him after his defeat.* | *We* ***encouraged*** *the team with shouts and flag-waving.* (***inspire***, ***motivate***, ***urge***)
Word building: **encouragement** *noun*
Word history: Middle English, from Old French *en-* + *corage* courage

encroach
verb to go beyond your own area and onto someone else's: *The neighbour's garage* ***encroaches*** *on our land.*
Word building: **encroachment** *noun*
Word history: Middle English, from Old French *en-* + *croc* hook

encumber
verb **1** to impede or hold back
2 to block up or fill with what is obstructive or unnecessary
3 to burden or weigh down: *to* ***encumber*** *with debts* | *to* ***encumber*** *with parcels*
Word building: **encumbrance** *noun*
Word history: Middle English, from Old French *en-* + *combre* barrier (from Late Latin, from Gallic *comberos* a bringing together)

encyclopedia
noun a book, usually in several volumes, of information arranged alphabetically

Word use: You can also use **encyclopaedia**.
Word building: **encyclopedic** *adjective*
Word history: Late Latin, from pseudo-Greek *enkyklopaideía*, for *enkýklios paideía* general education, complete round or course of learning

end
noun **1** the finishing point (***close***, ***conclusion***, ***finale***, ***finish***)
2 aim or purpose: *To what* ***end*** *are you doing this?*
verb **3** to stop or finish (***cease***, ***finish***, ***terminate***)
phrase **4 at a loose end**, not busy enough or having nothing to do
5 make both ends meet, to spend no more than you earn
6 on end,
a upright: *Her hair stood* ***on end***.
b without stopping: *It has rained for days* ***on end***.

Word history: Old English *ende*

endanger
verb to put in danger or at risk: *They will* ***endanger*** *their lives if they go to sea in that leaky boat.* (***compromise***, ***expose***, ***jeopardise***, ***put at risk***)

Word building: **endangered** *adjective*

endangered species
noun a threatened species that is facing a very high risk of extinction in the near future

Word use: Compare this with **critically endangered species**, **vulnerable species**.

endear
verb to make dear or beloved: *He* ***endeared*** *himself to his friends.*

Word building: **endearing** *adjective* **endearment** *noun*

endeavour
verb to try or attempt: *We* ***endeavour*** *to do our best.*

Word use: You can also use **endeavor**.
Word building: **endeavour** *noun*
Word history: Middle English *putten en deveren* to make one's duty

endemic (en-<u>dem</u>-ik)
adjective **1** limited to a particular group or place, as a disease may be
noun **2** an endemic disease or plant

Word building: **endemically** *adverb*
Word history: Greek *éndēmos* belonging to a people + *-ic*

endive
noun a herb, probably of Indian origin with its leaves now widely used in salads and as a cooked vegetable

Word history: Middle English, from Latin

endocrine gland (<u>en</u>-duh-kruhn gland)
noun a gland, such as the thyroid gland, which produces certain important secretions (hormones) which are carried by the blood to other parts of the body, where they regulate organ functions

endorse
verb **1** to sign your name on: *to* ***endorse*** *a petition*
2 to approve of or support: *to* ***endorse*** *an action* | *to* ***endorse*** *a candidate* (***advocate***, ***bless***, ***sanction***)

Word building: **endorsement** *noun*
Word history: Middle English, from Old French *en-* on + *dos* (from Latin *dorsum* back)

endow (en-<u>dow</u>)
verb **1** to give money, especially to a school, hospital, etc.
2 to give or equip: *Nature has* ***endowed*** *him with great ability.*

Word building: **endowment** *noun*
Word history: Middle English, from Old French *en-* + *douer*, (from Latin word meaning 'endow')

endure
verb **1** to put up with, especially for a long time (***stick***, ***suffer***, ***tolerate***)
2 to last well: *This car is so strong it should* ***endure*** *for years.* (***continue***, ***hold out***, ***persist***, ***survive***)

Word use: The opposite of definition 1 is is **succomb**.
Word building: **endurance** *noun*
Word history: Middle English, from Latin word meaning 'harden'

enema (<u>en</u>-uh-muh)
noun Medicine a fluid injected into someone's rectum to cause their bowels to empty

Word history: from Greek word meaning 'injection'

enemy
noun **1** someone who hates someone else, or wishes to harm them (***adversary***, ***antagonist***, ***foe***, ***opponent***)
2 an unfriendly armed force which is prepared to fight: *The country was invaded by the* ***enemy***.

Noun forms: The plural is **enemies**.
Word building: **enmity** *noun* **inimical** *adjective*
Word history: Middle English, from Old French, from Latin word meaning 'unfriendly', 'hostile'

energetic (en-uh-<u>jet</u>-ik)
adjective strong and active: *Puppies are very* ***energetic***. (***busy***, ***dynamic***, ***full of beans***, ***lively***, ***vigorous***)

Word use: The opposite of this is **inactive**.
Word building: **energetically** *adverb*
Word history: from Greek word meaning 'active'

energy (<u>en</u>-uh-jee)
noun **1** ability to be vigorous and active: *I haven't the* ***energy*** *for another game.* (***drive***, ***verve***, ***vitality***)
2 electrical or other power: *It's wasting* ***energy*** *to leave the lights on.*
3 *Physics* the capacity for doing work, existing in various forms: *kinetic* ***energy*** | *nuclear* ***energy***

Word use: The unit used for measuring energy (definition 3) is the **joule**.
Word history: Late Latin, from Greek word meaning 'agency', 'force'

enervate (<u>en</u>-uh-vayt)
verb to take away the energy, force, or strength of: *This hot weather completely* ***enervates*** *me.* (***sap one's strength***, ***weaken***)

Word building: **enervation** *noun* **enervator** *noun* **enervative** *adjective*
Word history: Latin

enforce
verb **1** to make sure of obedience to: *to* ***enforce*** *laws | to* ***enforce*** *rules*
2 to obtain by force: *to* ***enforce*** *payment of a debt*
3 to force upon a person: *to* ***enforce*** *a way of life on his children*
4 to impress, state or urge in a forceful way: *to* ***enforce*** *a point of view*

Word building: **enforceable** *adjective* **enforcedly** *adverb* **enforcer** *noun* **enforcement** *noun*
Word history: Middle English, from Old French, from Latin *in-* + *fortis* strong

enfranchise (en-fran-chuyz, uhn-fran-chuyz)
verb **1** to grant the rights of citizenship, especially the right of voting
2 to give the right of being represented in Parliament
3 to set free, as from slavery

Word building: **enfranchisement** *noun*
Word history: Middle French

engage
verb **1** to employ: *The old lady* ***engaged*** *a gardener.*
2 to attract or hold the attention of: *She* ***engaged*** *everyone with her witty conversation.*
3 to connect or interlock: *Have you* ***engaged*** *the gears?*
verb **4** to fight: *The two armies* ***engaged*** *in battle.*

Word history: French *en-* + *gage* pledge

engaged
adjective **1** busy or occupied: *Her telephone is giving the* ***engaged*** *signal.*
2 having decided to be married: *an* ***engaged*** *couple*

engagement
noun **1** the act of engaging
2 a pledge or agreement, especially to marry someone
3 a time or position of employment
4 an appointment or arrangement, often to do with business

engaging
adjective attractive or pleasing: *an* ***engaging*** *smile*

Word building: **engagingly** *adverb*

engender
verb **1** to produce, cause, or give rise to: *Hatred* ***engenders*** *violence.*
2 to come into existence

Word building: **engenderer** *noun* **engenderment** *noun*
Word history: Middle English, from Latin word meaning 'beget'

engine
noun **1** a machine which changes energy from sources like petrol or steam into movement: *The factory replaced its old steam* ***engines*** *with electric motors.*
2 a railway locomotive

Word history: Middle English, from Latin word meaning 'invention'

engineer (en-juhn-ear)
noun someone who is trained to design and build things and to use machinery: *His father was an* ***engineer*** *who built roads and bridges. | an electrical* ***engineer*** *| a chemical* ***engineer***

English muffin
noun → **muffin** (definition 1)

English spinach
noun → **spinach**

engrave
verb **1** to cut with a sharp tool: *The jeweller* ***engraved*** *my name on my watch.*
2 to fix firmly: *The words of the song are* ***engraved*** *in our memory.*

Word building: **engraver** *noun*

engraving
noun **1** the act or art of printing from a flat surface that has had a design cut into it
2 the design that has been cut
3 a print made from the design cut onto the flat plate or block

engross (en-grohs)
verb to occupy the mind or attention of completely: *That book* ***engrossed*** *her for days.* (***absorb***, ***fascinate***)

Word building: **engrossing** *adjective*
Word history: Middle English, from Anglo-French word meaning 'write large'

engulf
verb to swallow up: *The tidal wave* ***engulfed*** *the coastal village. | Darkness* ***engulfed*** *the houses.* (***inundate***, ***overwhelm***, ***smother***, ***swamp***)

enhance
verb to increase or improve: *A coat of paint should* ***enhance*** *the value of the house.* (***better***, ***enrich***, ***perfect***, ***upgrade***)

Word history: Middle English, from Old French *en-* + *haucier* raise

enigma (uh-nig-muh)
noun someone or something difficult or impossible to understand

Word history: Latin, from Greek word meaning 'riddle'

enigmatic (en-ig-mat-ik)
adjective puzzling

enjoy
verb **1** to get happiness from: ***Enjoy*** *your holiday.* (***appreciate***, ***relish***)
2 to have as a good quality or state of being: *to* ***enjoy*** *a good reputation | to* ***enjoy*** *good health*
phrase **3 enjoy yourself**, to have a good time

Word building: **enjoyable** *adjective* **enjoyment** *noun*
Word history: Middle English, from Old French *en-* + *joir* joy, verb

enlarge
verb **1** to increase in size: *She wants to* ***enlarge*** *the photos.* (***amplify***, ***augment***, ***boost***, ***expand***)
2 to give more details: *Could you please* ***enlarge*** *on your first point?*

Word use: The opposite of definition 1 is **reduce** or **shrink**.
Word building: **enlargement** *noun*
Word history: Middle English, from Old French *en-* + *large* large

enlighten
verb to make something clear to: *Would you care to* ***enlighten*** *me?*

enlightened
adjective having knowledge or information

enlightenment
noun **1** the act of being enlightened
phrase **2 the Enlightenment**, an 18th-century philosophical movement marked by a belief in human reason

enlist
verb to join the army, navy, or air force

Word building: **enlistment** *noun*

enmity
noun strong dislike or hatred

Noun forms: The plural is **enmities**.
Word history: Middle English, from Latin word meaning 'enemy'

enormity
noun **1** something outrageous or atrocious
2 hugeness

enormous
adjective of an unusually large size: *an **enormous** house with many rooms* (***colossal***, ***gigantic***, ***huge***, ***massive***, ***vast***)

Word history: from Latin word meaning 'huge'

enough
adjective **1** as much as is wanted or needed: *I've had **enough** food. | Are there **enough** people to make a team?* (***adequate***, ***decent***, ***satisfactory***, ***sufficient***)
noun **2** the amount or quantity wanted or needed
adverb **3** in a quantity or degree that fulfils a need or desire
4 fully or quite: *ready **enough***
5 fairly or tolerably: *He sings well **enough**.*

Word history: Old English *genōh*

enquire
verb to try to gain by asking: *'What should we do next?' I **enquired**. | I need to **enquire** about information for our holiday.*

Word use: You can also use **inquire**.
Word building: **enquirer** *noun*

enquiry
noun a question

Noun forms: The plural is **enquiries**.

> **enquiry / inquiry**
> You can use either of these spellings for this word. But note that **enquiry** is often used as a formal word for 'a question' and **inquiry** for 'an investigation', as in *a government inquiry*.

enrage
verb to make very angry: *Her cheeky questions **enraged** the teacher.* (***drive someone up the wall***, ***incense***, ***infuriate***)

Word history: Middle French

enrich
verb **1** to supply with more money
2 to improve the quality of: *Farmers **enrich** the soil with fertiliser.* (***better***, ***enhance***, ***improve***, ***perfect***, ***upgrade***)

Word building: **enrichment** *noun*
Word history: Middle English, from Old French *en-* + *riche* rich

enrol
verb **1** to put your name down: *He **enrolled** to study Italian.*
2 to record the name of: *The teachers **enrol** everyone on the first day.*

Verb forms: I **enrolled**, I have **enrolled**, I am **enrolling**
Word building: **enrolment** *noun*
Word history: Middle English, from Old French *en-* + *rolle* roll, noun

enrolled nurse
noun a nurse with a qualification from a nursing college, TAFE college, etc.

Word use: The abbreviation is **EN**. | Compare this with **registered nurse**.

ensconce (en-skons)
verb to settle comfortably or firmly: *I **ensconced** myself in an armchair.*

Word history: *en-* + *sconce* shelter

ensemble (on-som-buhl)
noun **1** all the parts of something taken together as a whole
2 a whole set of clothing
3 *Music*
a a complete performance with all the musicians, singers, etc., involved
b the group that performs this way: *a string **ensemble***

Word history: Middle English, from French, from Late Latin word meaning 'at the same time'

ensign (en-suyn)
noun a flag or banner

Word history: Middle English, from Old French, from Latin word meaning 'insignia'

ensue
verb **1** to follow in order or come immediately afterwards
2 to follow as a result

Word history: Middle English, from Old French, from Latin word meaning 'follow close upon'

ensuite (on-sweet)
noun Australian, NZ a small bathroom joined to a bedroom

Word history: French

ensure (en-shaw)
verb to make certain

Word history: Middle English, from Anglo-French *en-* + Old French *seur* sure

> **ensure / insure / assure**
> Don't confuse **ensure** with **insure** or **assure**.
> To **ensure** is to make certain of something:
> *I'm reminding you now to ensure that you return the book tomorrow.*
> To **insure** is to arrange a guarantee that your property will be replaced if it is lost, stolen or damaged.
> The most common meaning of **assure** is to tell someone something with certainty:
> *They assure us that the roof is on.*

entail
verb **1** to bring on by necessity or as a result: *That idea will **entail** a lot of work.*
2 *Law* in former times, to cause to be inherited by a fixed line of heirs: *to **entail** property*
3 to involve as a logical deduction: *Being a bachelor **entails** being unmarried.*

Word building: **entail** *noun*
Word history: from Old French word meaning 'tax'

entangle
verb to twist or catch: *The horse **entangled** his legs in wire.*

Word building: **entanglement** *noun*

entente (on-tont)
noun an understanding, such as one between nations

Word history: French

enter
verb **1** to come or go in: *We **entered** the house. | They **entered** after us.*
2 to start in: *She **entered** the race.*
3 to insert or write, as on a list (***log***, ***note***, ***record***, ***register***)
4 to type (data, text, etc.) into a computer file
phrase **5 enter into,**
a to take an interest or part in: *to **enter into** the party spirit*
b to begin to think about: *to **enter into** a subject*
c to sympathise with: *to **enter into** a person's feelings*
d to form part of: *This suggestion should **enter into** your plans.*

enterprise (en-tuh-pruyz)
noun **1** something to be done, especially something which involves effort or courage: *Running the school fete was quite an **enterprise**.* (***job***, ***project***, ***undertaking***, ***venture***)
2 the energy and skill you need to do something like that: *She is full of **enterprise**.*

Word history: Middle English, from Old French, from Latin word meaning 'go into'

enterprise information portal
noun → **information portal**

enterprising
adjective resourceful or able to carry out new, important or difficult projects

entertain
verb **1** to interest and amuse
2 to have as a guest: *They are **entertaining** us on Friday night.*

Word building: **entertainer** *noun* **entertaining** *adjective* **entertainment** *noun*
Word history: Middle English, from French from *entre-* inter- + *tenir* (from Latin word meaning 'hold')

enthral (en-thrawl)
verb to enchant or hold the whole attention of: *Her beauty **enthrals** him. | The story **enthralled** us.*

Verb forms: it **enthralled**, it has **enthralled**, it is **enthralling**

enthusiasm (en-thooh-zee-az-uhm)
noun lively interest: *She is full of **enthusiasm** for her new job.* (***get-up-and-go***, ***zeal***)

Word use: The opposite of this is **apathy**.
Word building: **enthuse** *verb* **enthusiast** *noun* **enthusiastic** *adjective*
Word history: Late Latin *enthūsiasmus*, from Greek *enthousiasmós*

entice
verb to tempt or persuade with promises of money or other advantages (***attract***, ***beguile***)

Word building: **enticement** *noun* **enticing** *adjective*
Word history: Middle English, from Old French word meaning 'incite', from Latin word meaning 'firebrand'

entire
adjective whole or unbroken: *She bought the **entire** set.* (***complete***, ***full***, ***total***)

Word building: **entirety** *noun*
Word history: Middle English from Latin word meaning 'untouched', 'whole'

entirely
adverb quite: *That allegation is **entirely** without truth.*

entitle
verb **1** to give a title, right, or claim to something: *This driver's licence **entitles** me to drive.*
2 to call by a particular title or name

Word history: Middle English, from Old French, from Latin *in-* + *titulus* title

entity
noun **1** something that has a real existence
2 being or existence
3 *Commerce* a person or company about whom or which financial statements are prepared

Noun forms: The plural is **entities**.
Word history: Late Latin

entomology (en-tuh-mol-uh-jee)
noun a branch of zoology that deals with insects

Word building: **entomological** *adjective* **entomologist** *noun*

entomology / etymology
Don't confuse **entomology** with **etymology**.
Etymology is the study of the history and derivation of words.
One way to remember this is that the ent- in **entomology** sounds a bit like *ant*, which is an insect.

entourage (on-tuh-razh)
noun a group of people attending and helping someone, especially an important person

Word history: from French word meaning 'surround'

entrails
plural noun the intestines

Word history: Middle English, from French, from Late Latin word meaning 'intestines', from Latin word meaning 'within'

entrance[1] (en-truhns)
noun **1** the act of entering: *to make an **entrance** at a party*
2 the way in: *The **entrance** was bolted.*

Word use: The opposite of definition 1 is **departure.** | The opposite of definition 2 is **exit.**
Word history: Old French

entrance[2] (en-trans, en-trahns)
verb to fill with delight: *The dancers **entranced** the crowds with their grace.*

entrant
noun someone who takes part in a competition: *an **entrant** in the race*

Word history: French

entreat
verb to beg: *I **entreat** you to come.* (***beseech, implore***)

Word history: Middle English, from Old French *en-* + *traitier* treat

entreaty
noun a serious request: *The doctor came as a result of their **entreaty**.*

Noun forms: The plural is **entreaties.**

entree (on-tray)
noun a small serving of food eaten before the main course of a meal

Word history: French

entrenched
adjective firmly established: ***entrenched** beliefs*

entrepot (on-truh-poh)
noun **1** a warehouse
2 a commercial centre, such as a port, for the collection or distribution of goods, or for the transferring of these from one ship to another

Word use: You can also use **entrepôt.**

entrepreneur (on-truh-pruh-ner)
noun someone who organises a business enterprise, especially a risky one

Word building: **entrepreneurial** *adjective*
Word history: from French word meaning 'undertake'

entrust
verb **1** to give a trust or responsibility to: *I **entrusted** him with her care.*
2 to give with trust for care, use, etc.: *She **entrusted** her fortune to him. | He **entrusted** his life to a thin rope.*

entry
noun **1** the act of coming or going in: *The space shuttle made a safe **entry** into the earth's atmosphere.*
2 the way in: *The **entry** was blocked by a car.*
3 a written record: *In her diary there were few **entries** for that month.*
4 someone or something entered in a competition: *How many **entries** are there in the essay competition?*

Noun forms: The plural is **entries.**
Word history: Middle English, from French

enumerate (uh-nyooh-muh-rayt)
verb **1** to name one by one (***itemise, list***)
2 to count or find the number of

Word building: **enumeration** *noun*
Word history: from Latin word meaning 'counted out'

enunciate (uh-nun-see-ayt)
verb **1** to speak or pronounce, especially in a particular manner: *He **enunciates** his words clearly.* (***articulate, utter, voice***)
2 to state definitely, as a theory
3 to declare or announce

Word building: **enunciation** *noun*
Word history: Latin

envelop (en-vel-uhp)
verb to wrap or cover: *He **enveloped** the baby in a large blanket.* (***blanket, cover, enclose, shroud, wreathe***)

Word building: **enveloping** *adjective* **envelopment** *noun*
Word history: Middle English, from Old French *en-* + *voluper* wrap

envelope (en-vuh-lohp, on-vuh-lohp)
noun a folded paper cover for a letter

Word history: French

enviable
adjective worth wanting

envious
adjective full of envy (***covetous, desirous, jealous***)

Word history: Middle English, from Old French word meaning 'envy'

environment
noun **1** the whole surroundings of your life: *He grew up in a country town **environment**.* (***environs, habitat, scene, setting***)
2 all the geographical features of an area, such as trees, land, water, etc., and the system connecting these

Word building: **environmental** *adjective*

environment / ecology
Don't confuse **environment** with **ecology.**
Ecology is the study of the relationship between living things and their environment.

environmentalist (en-vuy-ruhn-ment-uhl-uhst)
noun someone who is concerned about protecting the natural environment

environs (en-vuy-ruhnz)
plural noun the surrounding districts: *the **environs** of Brisbane* (***locale, surroundings***)

Word history: French

envisage (en-viz-ij)
verb to form a mental image of, especially a future event

Word history: French *en-* + *visage* face, appearance

envoy
noun someone sent as a representative: ***Envoys** from each country met to discuss trade.*

Word history: from French word meaning 'one sent'

envy
noun the desire for someone else's possessions or success: *Instead of enjoying what he has, he is full of **envy** of others.*

Word building: **envy** *verb* (**envied, envying**) **enviable** *adjective* **envious** *adjective*
Word history: Middle English, from Old French, from Latin

enzyme (en-zuym)
noun an animal protein which produces a chemical change: ***Enzymes** help to digest the food we eat.*

Word history: from Medieval Greek word meaning 'leavened'

eon
noun → **aeon**

epaulet (ep-uh-let)
noun a fancy shoulder piece worn on uniforms

Word history: French word meaning 'shoulder', from Latin

ephemeral (uh-fem-uh-ruhl)
adjective not lasting long: ***ephemeral** styles in fashion* (***fleeting***, ***momentary***, ***passing***, ***transitory***)

Word use: The opposite of this is **lasting**.

epic
noun **1** a long poem about heroic deeds
adjective **2** grand or heroic: *an **epic** journey across the desert*

Word history: Latin, from Greek word meaning 'word', 'tale', 'song'

epicentre
noun the point from which earthquake waves seem to go out, directly above the true centre of the disturbance

Word use: You can also use **epicentrum**.
Word history: Neo-Latin, from Greek word meaning 'on the centre'

epicure (ep-uh-kyooh-uh)
noun **1** someone who has refined tastes, as in food, drink, art, music, etc.
2 someone who enjoys luxury and sensuous pleasures

Word building: **epicurean** *adjective* **epicurean** *noun*
Word history: originally anglicised form of *Epicurus*, born about 342 BC, died 270 BC, Greek philosopher who held that the highest good in life is pleasure

epidemic
noun a lot of cases of an illness in a short period of time: *There is an **epidemic** of measles at the school.*

Word building: **epidemic** *adjective*
Word history: Late Latin, from Greek word meaning 'prevalence of an epidemic'

epidermis (ep-uh-derm-uhs)
noun **1** the outer non-sensitive layer of your skin
2 the outermost living layer of an animal, usually formed of one or more layers of cells
3 the outer cell layer of plants with sap

Word building: **epidermal** *adjective*
Word history: Late Latin, from Greek word meaning 'outer skin'

epidural anaesthetic (ep-ee-dyooh-ruhl an-uhs-thet-ik)
noun an injection of an agent into the outer covering of the spinal cord to deaden feeling in the lower part of the body, especially in childbirth

Word use: You can also use **epidural** or **epidural anesthetic**.

epigram
noun a short and witty saying (***adage***, ***maxim***, ***motto***, ***proverb***)

Word building: **epigrammatic** *adjective*
Word history: Latin, from Greek word meaning 'an inscription'

epilepsy
noun an illness which produces fits of unconsciousness and uncontrollable movements of the body

Word building: **epileptic** *adjective* **epileptic** *noun*
Word history: Late Latin, from Greek word meaning 'a seizure'

epilogue (ep-uh-log)
noun a short section at the end of a play or written work which acts as a conclusion: *The author has added his more recent views as an **epilogue** to his book.*

Word history: French, from Latin, from Greek word meaning 'a conclusion'

episcopal (uh-pis-kuh-puhl)
adjective having to do with a bishop: ***episcopal** robes*

Word building: **episcopacy** *noun*

episode
noun **1** an event in your life: *an **episode** from my past*
2 one in a series of scenes or chapters: *They watched the last **episode** of the serial on TV last night.*

Word building: **episodic** *adjective*
Word history: from Greek word meaning 'coming in besides'

epistle (uh-pis-uhl)
noun a letter (***communiqué***, ***dispatch***)

Word use: This is old-fashioned and mostly used jokingly.
Word history: Old English *epistol*, from Latin, from Greek word meaning 'message', 'letter'

epitaph (ep-uh-tahf)
noun the words, sometimes in verse, written on a gravestone in memory of the dead person

Word history: Middle English, from Latin, from Greek word meaning 'funeral oration'

epithet (ep-uh-thet)
noun **1** an adjective or phrase used to describe a person or thing, as in Alexander *the Great*
2 an insulting word or phrase: *She hurled choice **epithets** at his departing figure.*

Word building: **epithetic** *adjective* **epithetical** *adjective*
Word history: Latin, from Greek word meaning 'added'

epitome (uh-pit-uh-mee)
noun the most typical example of: *With his fair hair and his suntan he is the **epitome** of a surfer.*

Word use: The opposite of this is **antithesis**.
Word building: **epitomise** *verb*
Word history: Latin, from Greek word meaning 'cut into', 'abridge'

epoch (ee-pok, ep-ok)
noun a period of time in history or geology: *in the **epoch** of the Napoleonic wars*

Word history: Medieval Latin, from Greek word meaning 'check', 'pause', 'position', 'epoch'

Epsom salts
plural noun hydrated magnesium sulfate, used as a very strong laxative, etc.

Word history: so called because first prepared from the water of the mineral springs at *Epsom*, England

equable (ek-wuh-buhl)
adjective **1** of motion, temperature, etc., uniform or free from change
2 uniform in operation, etc.: ***equable*** *laws*
3 calm, tranquil or not easily disturbed: *an* ***equable*** *mind*

Word history: from Latin word meaning 'that can be made equal'

equal
adjective **1** of the same number, value, or other quality: *Everyone's share is* ***equal****.* (***equivalent****,* ***level****,* ***similar****,* ***uniform***)
2 evenly matched: *It's an* ***equal*** *fight.*
verb **3** to add up to the same number as: *I know that 5 plus 3* ***equals*** *8.*
4 to match: *The hurdler couldn't* ***equal*** *the record.*

Verb forms: I **equalled**, I have **equalled**, I am **equalling**
Word building: **equal** *noun* **equalise** *verb* **equality** *noun*

equanimity (eek-wuh-nim-uh-tee, ek-wuh-nim-uh-tee)
noun evenness of mind or temper (***calmness****,* ***composure***)

Word history: from Latin word meaning 'of an even mind'

equate
verb **1** to state the equality of, or between, as in an equation
2 to regard, treat, or represent as equal: *He* ***equates*** *money with happiness.*

Word history: from Latin word meaning 'made equal'

equation
noun **1** the act of making something equal
2 an equally balanced state
3 a mathematical expression in which two quantities are said to be equal, such as $12 \div 4 = 3$

equator (uh-kway-tuh)
noun the imaginary circle around the earth, halfway between the poles, where the climate is mostly hot and wet

Word building: **equatorial** *adjective*
Word history: Middle English, from Late Latin word meaning 'equaliser' (of day and night, as when the sun is on the equator)

equestrian (uh-kwes-tree-uhn)
adjective having to do with horses or horse-riding

Word history: from Latin word meaning 'horseman'

equidistant
adjective equally distant: *The two stations are* ***equidistant*** *from my house.*

Word building: **equidistance** *noun* **equidistantly** *adverb*

equilateral (eek-wuh-lat-uh-ruhl)
adjective equal-sided: *an* ***equilateral*** *triangle*

Word history: Late Latin

equilibrium (eek-wuh-lib-ree-uhm, ek-wuh-lib-ree-uhm)
noun **1** equal balance: *The children kept the see-saw in* ***equilibrium****.*
2 steadiness of feelings: *At first she was upset but soon recovered her* ***equilibrium****.*

Word use: The opposite of definition 1 is **imbalance**. | The opposite of definition 2 is **disequilibrium**.

equine (ek-wuyn)
adjective of or like a horse

Word history: Latin *equus* horse

equine influenza
noun a viral respiratory disease which causes flu-like symptoms in horses

Word use: The abbreviation is **EI**. | Another name is **horse flu**.

equinox (ee-kwuh-noks)
noun the time when the sun is directly over the earth's equator, making night and day all over the earth of equal length, occurring about 21 March and 22 September

Word history: from Latin word meaning 'equality between day and night'

equip
verb to provide with whatever is needed to do something: *to* ***equip*** *with camping gear*

Verb forms: I **equipped**, I have **equipped**, I am **equipping**
Word history: Old French, probably from Scandinavian

equipment
noun anything used to equip for a job, etc., especially a collection of tools, machines, resources, skills, etc.

equity
noun **1** fairness
2 anything that is fair and just
3 *Law*
a a group of laws which make up for the weaknesses in the common law
b a claim or right that is fair and just
4 equities, the shares issued by a company that denote ownership of the company

Noun forms: The plural is **equities**.
Word building: **equitable** *adjective*
Word history: from Latin word meaning 'equality', 'justice'

equivalent (uh-kwiv-uh-luhnt)
adjective equal or matching: *An admiral in the navy is* ***equivalent*** *to a general in the army.*

Word building: **equivalence** *noun*
Word history: Middle English, from Late Latin word meaning 'having equal power'

equivocal (uh-kwiv-uh-kuhl)
adjective **1** uncertain: *an* ***equivocal*** *attitude*
2 of doubtful character
3 having two or more meanings (***ambiguous****,* ***to be taken both ways***)

Word history: Middle English, from Late Latin word meaning 'ambiguous'

equivocate (uh-kwiv-uh-kayt)
verb to use words having more than one meaning, especially in order to mislead (***fence***, ***hedge***, ***prevaricate***, ***quibble***)

Word building: **equivocation** *noun*

era (ear-ruh)
noun any long period of time with a special characteristic: *the **era** of the steam train*

Word history: from Late Latin word meaning 'number or epoch by which reckoning is made'

eradicate
verb to root out or destroy: *to **eradicate** crime* (***annihilate***, ***demolish***, ***exterminate***, ***wipe out***)

Word building: **eradication** *noun*
Word history: from Latin word meaning 'rooted out'

erase
verb to rub out: *Use a rubber to **erase** your mistakes.* (***obliterate***, ***wipe out***)

Word building: **eraser** *noun* **erasure** *noun*
Word history: from Latin word meaning 'scratched out'

e-reader
noun an electronic device for reading publications in electronic form: *a handheld **e-reader***

Word use: You can also use **e-book reader**.

erect
adjective **1** upright: *to sit with an **erect** back*
verb **2** to build: *They have **erected** a house on the spare block.* (***construct***, ***put up***)

Word building: **erection** *noun*
Word history: Middle English, from Latin word meaning 'set upright', 'built'

ermine (er-muhn)
noun the white winter fur of the stoat

Word history: Middle English, from Old French, from Germanic

erode
verb **1** to form by eating or wearing away: *to **erode** a channel*
2 to destroy slowly: *Misfortune **eroded** his confidence.*

Word use: Definition 1 is used especially in geology, when referring to the wearing away of soil, etc., by wind and water.
Word building: **erosive** *adjective*
Word history: from Latin word meaning 'gnaw off'

erogenous (uh-roj-uh-nuhs)
adjective **1** tending to arouse sexual desire
2 sensitive to sexual stimulation: ***erogenous** zones*

erosion
noun the cracking and wearing away of the soil by weather

Word history: Latin

erotic
adjective having to do with sexual love

Word history: Greek

err
verb **1** to make a mistake: *I must have **erred** about the street number.* (***go wrong***, ***make a slip***, ***miscalculate***)
2 to do wrong: *He admitted that he had **erred** by telling a lie.*

Word building: **erring** *adjective*
Word history: Middle English, from Latin word meaning 'wander'

errand
noun a small task you are sent to do: *I went to town on an **errand** for my father.* (***assignment***, ***chore***, ***duty***, ***mission***)

Word history: Old English *ærende*

errant (e-ruhnt)
adjective **1** travelling, in search of adventure, etc.: *a knight **errant***
2 deviating from the regular course

Word history: Middle English, from Old French word meaning 'travel' (from Vulgar Latin word meaning 'journey')

erratic (uh-rat-ik)
adjective unsteady and irregular in your behaviour or movements (***changeable***, ***eccentric***, ***unstable***)

Word use: The opposite of this is **consistent** or **regular**.
Word building: **erratically** *adverb*
Word history: Middle English, from Latin word meaning 'wander', 'err'

erroneous (uh-roh-nee-uhs)
adjective incorrect or containing a mistake: ***erroneous** information* (***false***, ***inaccurate***, ***off beam***, ***untrue***)

Word history: Middle English, from Latin word meaning 'straying'

error
noun **1** a mistake (***blunder***, ***boo-boo***, ***miscalculation***, ***slip***)
2 wrongdoing: *She has seen the **error** of her ways.*

Word history: Latin

erudite (e-ruh-duyt)
adjective learned or scholarly: *an **erudite** professor* (***clever***, ***cultivated***, ***educated***, ***knowledgeable***, ***well-informed***)

Word building: **eruditely** *adverb*
Word history: from Latin word meaning 'instructed'

erudition (e-ruh-dish-uhn)
noun learning or scholarship, especially in literature, history, etc.

erupt
verb to explode or burst out: *The volcano has **erupted**.*

Word building: **eruption** *noun*
Word history: from Latin word meaning 'burst forth'

escalate (es-kuh-layt)
verb to make or become larger or more intense: *to **escalate** a war | Prices will **escalate**.*

Word building: **escalation** *noun*

escalator (es-kuh-lay-tuh)
noun a continuously moving stairway

Word history: from Latin word meaning 'ladder'

escapade (es-kuh-payd, es-kuh-payd)
noun a reckless adventure

Word history: French, from Spanish, or from Italian

escape
verb **1** to get away: *He **escaped** from prison.* (***abscond***, ***flee***, ***nick off***, ***take to your heels***)
2 to avoid: *She **escaped** injury.*

Word building: **escape** *noun* **escapee** *noun*
Word history: Middle English, from Old Northern French, from Latin word meaning 'cloak'

escapee
noun someone who has escaped, especially from prison (***absconder***, ***fugitive***, ***runaway***, ***truant***)

escarpment (uhs-kahp-muhnt)
noun **1** a long cliff-like ridge of rock usually formed by faulting or fracturing of the earth's crust
2 ground that has been cut into a steep slope around a fortification, castle, etc.

eschew (uhs-chooh)
verb to avoid or shun: *to **eschew** evil*

Word building: **eschewal** *noun*
Word history: Middle English, from Old French, from Germanic

escort
noun **1** someone who goes along with someone else as a guard or to show respect: *a police **escort***
2 someone who goes with you to a dance or party: *Her **escort** for the dinner was late.*

Word building: **escort** *verb*
Word history: French, from Italian word meaning 'guide', from Latin

esky
noun Australian a container for keeping things cold: *There are some drinks in the **esky**.*

Word history: Trademark

esophagus (uh-sof-uh-guhs)
noun → **oesophagus**

esoteric (es-uh-te-rik, ees-uh-te-rik)
adjective understood by, meant for, or belonging to a select few or to a special field of study

Word building: **esoterically** *adverb*
Word history: from Greek word meaning 'inner'

ESP
noun perception or communication outside the normal activity of your five senses, such as in telepathy and clairvoyance

Word use: You can also use **e.s.p.** or **extrasensory perception**.
Word history: abbreviation of *E(xtra) S(ensory) P(erception)*

especially
adverb particularly or more than usually: *He did well, **especially** in maths.*

espionage (es-pee-uh-nahzh)
noun the practice of spying

Word history: French word meaning 'spy upon', from *espion* spy, from Italian, from Germanic

esplanade (es-pluh-nayd, es-pluh-nahd)
noun any open level space for public walks, etc., especially one by the sea

Word history: French, from Spanish, from Latin word meaning 'level'

espresso
noun coffee made in a machine which forces steam through crushed coffee beans

Word history: Italian word meaning 'expressed (coffee)'

esquire
noun Old-fashioned the polite title after a man's name, usually shortened to 'Esq', which is sometimes used instead of 'Mr' or 'Dr': *Robert Jones, **Esq***

Word history: Middle English *esquier*, from Old French, from Late Latin *scūtārius* shield-bearer, from Latin *scūtum* shield

essay
noun a short piece of writing on a particular subject: *The teacher hasn't marked our **essays** on the causes of World War I.*

Word history: Middle French, from Late Latin word meaning 'a weighing'

essence
noun **1** the basic nature: *The artist has caught the **essence** of the Prime Minister in that portrait.* (***drift***, ***gist***, ***meaning***, ***sense***, ***significance***)
2 the concentrated liquid from a substance: *vanilla **essence***

Word history: Middle English, from Latin

essential (uh-sen-shuhl)
adjective **1** absolutely necessary: *Flour is an **essential** ingredient in bread.* (***crucial***, ***imperative***, ***obligatory***, ***vital***)
2 *Biology* obtained from the diet: *an **essential** fatty acid*

Word building: **essentially** *adverb*
Word history: Middle English, from Late Latin *essentiālis*.

establish
verb **1** to set up: *They have **established** a new school.* (***begin***, ***found***, ***institute***)
2 to settle: *We have **established** ourselves in the new neighbourhood.*
3 to prove: *We can't **establish** the truth of what he says.*

Word history: Middle English, from Old French, from Latin word meaning 'make stable'

establishment
noun **1** the act of establishing
2 something established, such as an organisation
phrase **3 the Establishment**, the group of people whose opinions are said to have a lot of influence in society and government

estate
noun **1** an area of land in the country, especially a large and valuable one: *On her **estate** she breeds racehorses.*
2 the possessions and property of a person who has died

Word history: Middle English, from Old French, from Latin

estate agent
noun someone who sells or manages properties, especially houses, as an agent for the owners

esteem
verb **1** to respect or think highly of: *The judge always **esteemed** your father.*
noun **2** high opinion (***devotion***, ***honour***, ***regard***, ***respect***, ***veneration***)

Word history: Middle English, from Middle French, from Latin

ester (<u>es</u>-tuh)
noun an organic compound formed by the reaction between an organic acid and an alcohol, with water also being produced

Word building: **esterify** *verb* **esterification** *noun*
Word history: coined by L Gmelin, 1788–1853, German chemist

estimable (<u>es</u>-tuh-muh-buhl)
adjective **1** deserving respect
2 able to be estimated

estimate (<u>es</u>-tuh-mayt)
verb **1** to roughly work out the value, size, or other qualities: *We **estimated** the cost to be $20.* (***calculate***, ***gauge***, ***judge***, ***measure***)
noun (<u>es</u>-tuh-muht) **2** a rough valuation

Word building: **estimation** *noun*
Word history: from Latin word meaning 'valued', 'rated'

estranged (uh-<u>straynjd</u>)
adjective not living with the person you are married to any more: *She had a meeting with her **estranged** husband today to discuss the children.*

Word building: **estrangement** *noun*
Word history: Middle English, from Middle French, from Latin word meaning 'foreign'

estrogen (<u>ees</u>-truh-juhn, <u>es</u>-truh-juhn)
noun → **oestrogen**

estrous cycle (<u>ees</u>-truhs suy-kuhl)
noun → **oestrous cycle**

estuary (<u>es</u>-chooh-uh-ree, <u>es</u>-chuh-ree)
noun the mouth or lower part of a river which is affected by high tides

Noun forms: The plural is **estuaries**.
Word history: from Latin word meaning 'a heaving motion', 'surge', 'tide'

e-tag
noun an electronic device in a vehicle which causes a toll to be debited from the customer's account: *The **e-tag** beeped when the car went through the toll gate.*

Word use: You can also use **etag** or **electronic tag**.

etc. (et-<u>set</u>-ruh)
abbreviation et cetera, Latin words meaning 'and other things': *I need pens, papers, ink, **etc**.*

etch
verb **1** to cut or eat into metal, as acid does
2 to print from a design which has been etched
3 to produce a clear and therefore lasting effect: *Fear has **etched** those events on my memory.*

Word building: **etching** *noun*
Word history: Dutch, from German word meaning 'feed', 'corrode', 'etch'

eternal
adjective lasting forever: ***eternal** life* (***everlasting***, ***immortal***, ***perennial***, ***permanent***, ***perpetual***)

Word building: **eternally** *adverb*
Word history: Middle English, from Latin

eternity
noun **1** time without end: *A lifetime seems short when you try to imagine **eternity**.*
2 a very long time: *We had to wait an **eternity**.*

Noun forms: The plural is **eternities**.
Word use: Definition 2 is used jokingly.
Word history: Middle English, from Old French, from Latin

ethanol (<u>eeth</u>-uh-nol, <u>eth</u>-uh nol)
noun an alcohol produced from crops and used as a biofuel

ether (<u>ee</u>-thuh)
noun a chemical which used to be used to put a patient to sleep during an operation, but is now used to dissolve other substances

Word history: Latin, from Greek word meaning 'upper air', 'sky'

ethereal (uh-<u>thear</u>-ree-uhl)
adjective **1** light or airy (***ghostly***, ***intangible***, ***nebulous***, ***shadowy***)
2 extremely delicate or refined: ***ethereal** beauty*
3 heavenly

ethical (<u>eth</u>-uh-kuhl)
adjective morally right (***decent***, ***honest***, ***moral***)

Word building: **ethically** *adverb*

ethics
plural noun the system of beliefs and rules, used to judge human action: *He is a very honourable person who always acts according to his **ethics**.*

ethnic
adjective having to do with the history, language and customs of a particular group: ***ethnic** dancing*

Word history: Middle English, from Late Latin, from Greek word meaning 'national', 'gentile', 'heathen'

ethos (<u>ee</u>-thos)
noun **1** character
2 *Sociology* the basic spiritual character of a culture

Word history: Neo-Latin, from Greek word meaning 'character'

etiquette (<u>et</u>-ee-kuht)
noun behaviour which is thought of as polite and correct: *business **etiquette***

Word history: French

etymology (et-uh-<u>mol</u>-uh-jee)
noun **1** the study of the changes in words over a long period of time
2 an explanation of the history of a word, showing all the changes it has gone through

Noun forms: The plural is **etymologies**.
Word building: **etymological** *adjective*
Word history: Latin, from Greek

etymology / entomology
Don't confuse **etymology** with **entomology**, which is the study of insects.

eucalyptus (yooh-kuh-<u>lip</u>-tuhs)
noun a type of tree with many different varieties, found mostly in Australia, used for its timber and its strong oil

Word use: Other names are **eucalypt**, **eucalyptus tree**, **gum** or **gum tree**.
Noun forms: The plural is **eucalyptuses** or **eucalypti**.
Word building: **eucalyptus** *adjective*
Word history: Neo-Latin, from *eu-* + Greek *kalyptós* covered (with allusion to the cap covering the buds)

eulogy (<u>yooh</u>-luh-jee)
noun **1** a speech or writing in praise of a person or thing, especially one to honour a dead person
2 high praise

Noun forms: The plural is **eulogies**.
Word building: **eulogise** *verb*
Word history: Medieval Latin, from Greek word meaning 'praise'

eunuch (<u>yooh</u>-nuhk)
noun a castrated man

Word history: Middle English, from Latin, from Greek word meaning 'chamber attendant'

euphemism (<u>yooh</u>-fuh-miz-uhm)
noun a mild word or phrase chosen to replace one that is more direct but less pleasant: *'To pass away' is a* ***euphemism*** *for 'to die'.*

Word building: **euphemistic** *adjective*
Word history: from Greek word meaning 'use fair words'

euphoria (yooh-<u>faw</u>-ree-uh)
noun a feeling or state of wellbeing, especially one of unnatural joy

Word building: **euphoric** *adjective*
Word history: Neo-Latin, from Greek word meaning 'bearing well'

euro[1] (<u>yooh</u>-roh)
noun a stocky type of kangaroo

Noun forms: The plural is **euros**.
Word history: from Adnyamathanha, an Australian Aboriginal language of the Flinders Ranges area in South Australia

euro[2] (<u>yooh</u>-roh)
noun the monetary unit of the European Union, introduced as legal tender in most of the member nations in 2002

Noun forms: The plural is **euros**.

Eustachian tube (yooh-<u>stay</u>-shuhn tyoohb)
noun a canal leading from the middle ear to the pharynx (at the back of the mouth)

Word use: Another name is **auditory canal**.
Word history: from Bartolommeo *Eustachio*, died 1574, Italian anatomist

euthanase
verb to subject to euthanasia: *The vet thought it would be kindest to* ***euthanase*** *the badly injured possum.*

Verb forms: I **euthanased**, I have **euthanased**, I am **euthanasing**
Word use: You can also use **euthanise**.

euthanasia (yooh-thuh-<u>nay</u>-zhuh)
noun the act of helping or letting someone die when they want to, because their pain or suffering has become too great

Word history: Neo-Latin, from Greek word meaning 'an easy death'

evacuate (uh-<u>vak</u>-yooh-ayt)
verb **1** to move out of for a time in order to escape danger: *They* ***evacuate*** *their house during earthquakes.* (***abandon***, ***desert***, ***quit***, ***vacate***)
2 to send to safety, especially by emptying a building or area which is dangerous: *They* ***evacuated*** *the people from the flooded suburbs.*
3 to empty out, especially waste from the bowel (***excrete***, ***void***)

Word building: **evacuation** *noun*
Word history: Latin *evacuatus* emptied out

evacuee (uh-vak-yooh-<u>ee</u>)
noun someone who is taken away from a dangerous place

evade
verb **1** to get round or escape from by trickery: *He* ***evaded*** *pursuit.* (***avoid***, ***elude***, ***steer clear of***)
2 to avoid doing: *She* ***evades*** *work.*

Word history: from Latin word meaning 'pass over', 'go out'

evaluate
verb to test and find the value or quality of: *to* ***evaluate*** *your answer* (***adjudicate***, ***appraise***, ***judge***, ***measure***, ***size up***)

Word building: **evaluation** *noun*
Word history: French, from Old French word meaning 'be worth', from Latin

evangelist (uh-<u>van</u>-juh-luhst)
noun someone who travels from place to place teaching from the Gospels

Word building: **evangelistic** *adjective*
Word history: from Greek word meaning 'good messenger'

evaporate
verb **1** to turn or change to vapour
2 to give off moisture, or take moisture from
3 to dry up: *The water has* ***evaporated***. | *The sun* ***evaporates*** *the puddles.*

Word building: **evaporation** *noun* **evaporator** *noun*
Word history: from Late Latin word meaning 'dispersed in vapour'

evasion (uh-<u>vay</u>-zhuhn)
noun **1** the act or means of escaping something by trickery or cleverness: ***evasion*** *of your duty*
2 the avoiding of an argument, question, etc.
3 a way of evading (***deception***, ***subterfuge***)

Word building: **evasive** *adjective* **evasively** *adverb*
Word history: Middle English, from Late Latin

eve
noun **1** the day before: *Today is Christmas* ***eve***.
2 the time just before an event takes place: *They left the country on the* ***eve*** *of war.*

Word history: variant of *even* an old-fashioned word for evening

even
adjective **1** able to be divided by two: *Four, six, eight and ten are* ***even*** *numbers.*
2 equal in size: *She cut the cake in* ***even*** *slices.*
3 fairly matched: *It is an* ***even*** *contest.*
4 calm and steady: *He has an* ***even*** *temper.*
5 smooth or level: *The cricket pitch is not* ***even***. (***flat***, ***horizontal***)
adverb **6** still or yet: *School is* ***even*** *better now.*
7 however unlikely it may seem: ***Even*** *my little brother was quiet when the beautiful music began.*
verb **8** to make even, level or smooth
phrase **9 break even**, to have your gains and losses equal
10 get even, to get your revenge: *to* ***get even*** *with someone*

Verb forms: I **evened**, I have **evened**, I am **evening**
Word history: Old English *efen*

evening
noun **1** the late afternoon and early night
adjective **2** having to do with the evening: ***evening*** *dress*

Word history: Old English *ǣfnung*, from *ǣfnian* draw towards evening

event
noun **1** something which happens, especially something important: *The fete is a big* ***event.*** | *the day's* ***events***
2 one of the items in a sports competition: *The last* ***event*** *was an egg-and-spoon race.*
phrase **3 at all events** or **in any event**, in any case or whatever happens

Word building: **eventful** *adjective*
Word history: from Latin word meaning 'occurrence', 'issue'

eventual
adjective final or last: *The* ***eventual*** *result was a draw.*

Word building: **eventually** *adverb*

eventuality (uh-ven-chooh-al-uh-tee)
noun a possible event or circumstance

Noun forms: The plural is **eventualities**.

eventuate (uh-ven-chooh-ayt)
verb **1** to result: *The delay* ***eventuated*** *in our missing the plane.*
2 to happen or come about: *Did your promotion* ***eventuate?***

ever
adverb **1** at all times: *He is* ***ever*** *ready to help.*
2 continuously or without ceasing: ***ever*** *since then*
3 at any time: *Did you* ***ever*** *see anything like this?*
4 at all: *How did he* ***ever*** *manage it?*

Word history: Old English *ǣfre*, probably related to *ā* ever

evergreen
adjective of a plant, having leaves all year long: *an* ***evergreen*** *tree*

Word use: Compare this with **deciduous**.
Word building: **evergreen** *noun*

every
adjective **1** each: *We go swimming* ***every*** *day.*
2 all possible: *He has* ***every*** *chance of success.*
phrase **3 every bit**, *Colloquial* in all respects: ***every bit*** *as good*
4 every now and then or **every now and again** or **every once in a while**, from time to time
5 every other, every second, or alternate: *I catch the bus home* ***every other*** *day.*

Word history: Old English *ǣfre ǣlc* ever, each

everybody
pronoun every person

everyday
adjective having to do with ordinary or casual situations, rather than formal ones: ***everyday*** *language*

everyone
pronoun every person or everybody

everyone / everybody / everything

All of these words have to be followed by a singular verb:

everyone is ...
everybody is ...
everything is ...

A following pronoun, though, sometimes causes problems:

Everyone has to do his or her best.

The *his or her* construction is awkward, and for speech and most styles of writing it's acceptable to use a plural pronoun instead:

Everyone has to do their best.

everything
pronoun **1** every thing or detail of a group or total
2 something very important: *This news means* ***everything*** *to us.*

everywhere
adverb in every place or part; in all places: *I have looked* ***everywhere*** *for my keys.*

evict
verb to turn out or remove: *The landlord* ***evicted*** *the tenants for not paying the rent.* (***expel, throw out***)

Word building: **eviction** *noun*
Word history: from Latin word meaning 'overcome completely', '(property) recovered by judicial decision'

evidence
noun **1** something seen or heard that shows something else to be true
2 a clear sign of something: *The daffodils are the first* ***evidence*** *of spring.*
3 *Law* the information or objects recognised by witnesses, and presented to the court or jury to help prove the facts being argued
verb **4** to support using evidence: *A historian needs to* ***evidence*** *any historical claims with documents to prove these to be true.*
phrase **5 in evidence**, able to be easily seen

evident
adjective clear, or easily seen or understood: *It's* ***evident*** *you don't know what you are talking about.* (***explicit, obvious, plain, straightforward***)

Word use: The opposite of this is **unclear**.
Word building: **evidently** *adverb*
Word history: Latin

evil
adjective **1** wicked and harmful (***heinous, sinful, villainous***)
noun **2** anything evil

Word history: Old English *yfel*

evince
verb to show the possession of (a quality, trait, etc.): *She* ***evinces*** *pleasure in her new horse.*

Word history: from Latin word meaning 'overcome completely', 'prove', 'demonstrate'

evoke (uh-vohk)
verb **1** to call up, or produce: *The music* ***evoked*** *calmness.*
2 to draw or bring out: *That discussion* ***evoked*** *a response.* (***elicit, induce, inspire, produce, provoke***)

Word building: **evocation** *noun* **evocative** *adjective*
Word history: from Latin word meaning 'call forth'

evolution (ev-uh-looh-shuhn, eev-uh-looh-shuhn)
noun **1** any process in which something grows or develops over time: *the* ***evolution*** *of humans*
2 a product which has evolved
3 *Biology* the gradual continuous genetic change of plants and animals to adapt to the environment

Word building: **evolutionary** *adjective* **evolutionist** *noun*

evolve (uh-volv)
verb **1** to develop gradually: *to* ***evolve*** *a theory*
2 *Biology* to develop gradually to a more complex or advanced condition

Word building: **evolvement** *noun* **evolution** *noun*
Word history: from Latin word meaning 'roll out', 'unroll', 'unfold'

ewe (yooh)
noun a female sheep

Word history: Middle English and Old English

> **ewe / you / yew**
> Don't confuse **ewe** with **you** or **yew**.
> **You** is the person being spoken to.
> A **yew** is an evergreen tree.

ewer (yooh-uh)
noun a jug with a wide spout

Word history: Middle English, from Anglo-French, from Latin word meaning 'vessel for water'

exacerbate (ek-sas-uh-bayt)
verb to increase or aggravate the strength or violence of: *Stress will only* ***exacerbate*** *his medical condition.*

Word building: **exacerbation** *noun*
Word history: from Latin word meaning 'irritated'

exact
adjective **1** absolutely right in every detail: *She wants an* ***exact*** *fit.* (***accurate***, ***precise***, ***spot-on***)
verb **2** to demand, sometimes by force: *The government* ***exacts*** *tax from everyone.*

Word use: The opposite of definition 1 is **approximate**.
Word building: **exactness** *noun*
Word history: from Latin word meaning 'forced out', 'required', 'measured by a standard'

exacting
adjective demanding: *an* ***exacting*** *job*

exaggerate (uhg-zaj-uh-rayt)
verb **1** to speak of something as greater than it is: *She* ***exaggerates*** *her wealth.* (***magnify***, ***overstate***)
2 to increase even more: *Tiredness* ***exaggerates*** *his limp.*

Word building: **exaggerated** *adjective* **exaggeration** *noun*
Word history: from Latin word meaning 'heaped up'

exalt (uhg-zawlt)
verb **1** to raise in rank, honour, power, character, etc.: *They* ***exalted*** *him to the position of president.*
2 to praise: *to* ***exalt*** *someone to the skies*

Word building: **exaltation** *noun*
Word history: from Latin word meaning 'lift up'

exam
noun an examination (definition 2)

examination
noun **1** an act of careful looking and testing: *The dentist's* ***examination*** *of her teeth revealed a broken filling.* (***analysis***, ***investigation***)
2 a test of knowledge or skill which often has to be passed before the next stage of learning begins

Word history: Latin

examine
verb **1** to inspect or look at carefully (***analyse***, ***assess***, ***investigate***, ***review***, ***study***)
2 to test the knowledge, reactions, or abilities of, especially with questions or tasks: *to* ***examine*** *a student*
3 *Law* to question about actions or knowledge of facts: *to* ***examine*** *a witness* (***cross-examine***, ***interrogate***)

Word building: **examiner** *noun*
Word history: Middle English, from French, from Latin word meaning 'weigh accurately', 'test'

example
noun **1** a sample which makes something clear: *He gave an* ***example*** *of what he wanted us to do.* (***guide***, ***model***, ***pattern***, ***specimen***)
2 a model to be followed: *You aren't setting a very good* ***example*** *to the younger children.*

Word history: Middle English, from Old French, from Latin

exasperate
verb to annoy very much (***aggravate***, ***get on someone's nerves***, ***irritate***, ***upset***)

Word building: **exasperation** *noun*
Word history: from Latin word meaning 'roughened'

excavate (eks-kuh-vayt)
verb **1** to make a hole or cavity in (***dig***, ***gouge***, ***hollow out***, ***mine***, ***scoop***)
2 to make by removing material: *to* ***excavate*** *a tunnel*
3 to dig or scoop out: *to* ***excavate*** *earth*
4 to lay bare or uncover by digging: *to* ***excavate*** *an ancient city*

Word use: The opposite of this is **bury**.
Word building: **excavation** *noun* **excavator** *noun*
Word history: Latin *excavātus* meaning 'hollowed out'

exceed
verb to go beyond: *You shouldn't* ***exceed*** *the speed limit.*

Word history: Middle English, from French, from Latin word meaning 'go out'

> **exceed / accede**
> Don't confuse **exceed** with **accede** which means 'to agree or consent to something':
> *The company had to accede to the workers' demands for air conditioning.*

exceedingly
adverb extremely: *It's an* ***exceedingly*** *hot day.*

excel (uhk-sel)
verb to be very good: *He* ***excels*** *at swimming.*

Verb forms: I **excelled**, I have **excelled**, I am **excelling**
Word history: Latin

excellence (ek-suh-luhns)
noun **1** the fact or state of excelling (***pre-eminence, superiority***)
2 an excellent quality or feature
3 Excellence → **Excellency**

Excellency (ek-suh-luhn-see)
noun a title of honour given to certain high officials, as governors and ambassadors

Word use: You can also use **Excellence**.

excellent (ek-suh-luhnt)
adjective very good or of a very high quality: *He is an* ***excellent*** *cook.* (***exceptional, fantastic, outstanding, sensational, terrific***)

Word building: **excellently** *adverb*
Word history: Middle English, from Latin

except
preposition **1** leaving or taking out: *They all went* ***except*** *me.*
conjunction **2** with the exclusion: *All the songs sounded the same,* ***except*** *that the last track on the album was much slower than the rest.*
3 otherwise than: *The room was all red* ***except*** *in the corner near the fireplace.*

except / accept
Don't confuse **except** with **accept**, which means 'to take or receive something willingly'.

excepted
adjective excluded or left out: *All my friends are* ***excepted*** *from this rule.*

Word history: from Latin word meaning 'taken out'

exception (uhk-sep-shuhn)
noun someone or something which doesn't follow the general rule or pattern: *They behaved themselves, with only a few* ***exceptions****.*

Word history: Latin

exceptional
adjective unusually good (***outstanding, superior***)

Word building: **exceptionally** *adverb*

excerpt (ek-serpt)
noun a piece quoted from a book or shown from a film

Word history: from Latin word meaning 'picked out'

excess (uhk-ses, ek-ses)
noun **1** an extreme amount (***glut, oversupply, surplus***)
2 in insurance, the first portion of a loss which the insured agrees to pay in connection with any claim against a policy
adjective (ek-ses) **3** more than necessary or usual: ***excess*** *baggage*

Word history: Middle English, from Latin word meaning 'a departure'

excessive
adjective more than the usual or proper limit: ***excessive*** *good spirits* (***extra, redundant, superfluous, surplus***)

exchange
verb **1** to give one thing in return for another: *We'll* ***exchange*** *with you.* (***substitute, swap, transpose***)
2 to give to each other: *They* ***exchanged*** *insults.*
noun **3** the act of exchanging
4 a central office where letters and calls are received and sorted: *a telephone* ***exchange***

Word history: Middle English, from Anglo-French, from Late Latin

exchange rate
noun the rate at which one currency can be exchanged for another on the international money market

exchequer (uhks-chek-uh)
noun a treasury, especially of a state or nation

Word history: Middle English, from Old French word meaning 'chess board' (so called with reference to the table-cover marked with squares on which accounts were reckoned with counters). Look up **chequer.**

excise[1] (ek-suyz)
noun **1** a tax or duty on certain locally made goods, etc.: *an* ***excise*** *on tobacco*
2 a tax payable for a licence to carry on certain forms of work, to play certain sports, etc.
verb (ek-suyz) **3** to place an excise on

Word history: Middle Dutch, from Old French word meaning 'a tax', from Late Latin word meaning 'tax'

excise[2] (ek-suyz)
verb to cut out or off: *The doctor* ***excised*** *the lump.* (***remove***)

Word building: **excision** *noun*
Word history: Latin *excisus* cut out

excite (uhk-suyt)
verb to cause eager feelings in: *Your visit has* ***excited*** *them.*

Word building: **excited** *adjective* **excitement** *noun* **exciting** *adjective*
Word history: Middle English, from Latin word meaning 'call forth', 'rouse'

exclaim
verb to cry out suddenly in fright or pleasure

Word history: Latin *exclamare* call out

exclamation
noun something said or cried out suddenly in fright or pleasure (***interjection, outburst***)

exclamation mark
noun a punctuation mark (!) used after an exclamation

We use an **exclamation mark** when we write down an utterance to show that it has been said
1 as a command:
Look out!
Come here!

2 as an expression of pleasure, surprise, fright, or some other strong feeling:

Oh no!

What a pity!

How lovely!

Note that if you are using an exclamation mark, you don't use a full stop as well.

If you have an exclamation which is also a question, the exclamation mark comes after the question mark:

You mean you're going to the party?!

exclude
verb to shut or keep out: *Blinds **exclude** light from rooms. | All children under ten are **excluded** from our club.* (***ban***, ***delete***, ***leave out***)

Word building: **exclusion** *noun*
Word history: Middle English, from Latin

exclusive
adjective **1** fashionable: *an **exclusive** club | an **exclusive** suburb*
2 not shared with others: *an **exclusive** interview* (***single***, ***sole***, ***unique***)

Word history: from Medieval Latin word meaning 'excluded'

excommunicate
verb to cut off from receiving Communion or being a member of a church

Word building: **excommunication** *noun*
Word history: from Late Latin word meaning 'put out of the community'

excrement (eks-kruh-muhnt)
noun waste matter from your body

Word history: from Latin word meaning 'what is evacuated'

excrescence (eks-kres-uhns)
noun **1** an abnormal outgrowth, usually harmless, on an animal or vegetable body
2 a normal outgrowth such as hair

Word building: **excrescent** *adjective*

excrete
verb to pass out from the body: *The caterpillar **excreted** a green slime after I trod on it.*

Word building: **excretion** *noun*
Word history: from Latin word meaning 'sifted out', 'discharged'

excruciating (uhks-krooh-shee-ay-ting)
adjective very painful or causing great suffering

excursion
noun a short journey or trip usually taken for a special reason: *Our class went on an **excursion** to the zoo.* (***expedition***, ***jaunt***, ***tour***)

Word history: from Latin word meaning 'a running out'

excuse (uhk-skyoohz)
verb **1** to pardon or forgive (***let off***, ***spare***)
2 to free from duty or let off: *He **excused** her from the washing up.*
noun (uhk-skyoohs) **3** a reason, sometimes a pretended one, for being excused

Word history: Middle English, from Latin word meaning 'allege in excuse'

executable (ek-suh-kyooh-tuh-buhl)
adjective **1** that can be executed or carried out: *an **executable** command*
2 *Computers* having to do with a version of an application that can be directly read by a computer: *an **executable** program*
noun **3** (*plural*) *Computers* the executable version of a program

executable code
noun Computers the low-level programming language version of an application, able to be directly read by a computer

Word use: Compare this with **source code**.

executable file
noun a version of computer application that can be read by the computer

Word use: You can also use the colloquial term **exe file.**

execute
verb **1** to do or carry out: *to **execute** a plan*
2 to put to death (***assassinate***, ***kill***, ***murder***, ***slay***)

Word building: **execution** *noun*
Word history: Middle English, from Latin word meaning 'having followed out'

executive (uhg-zek-yuh-tiv)
noun **1** someone responsible for carrying out plans, especially in a business
adjective **2** having to do with managing things

executor (uhg-zek-yuh-tuh)
noun Law the person named in a will to carry out its requests

Word building: **executorship** *noun*
Word history: Middle English, from Latin word meaning 'one who follows out'

exemplary (uhg-zemp-luh-ree)
adjective **1** worthy of being copied: ***exemplary** conduct*
2 used as a warning: *an **exemplary** penalty*
3 used as a model or pattern
4 typical or used as an example

Word building: **exemplariness** *noun*

exemplify (uhg-zemp-luh-fuy)
verb **1** to show or make clearer by example: *He **exemplified** his point with a diagram.*
2 to serve as an example of: *This mistake **exemplifies** the whole problem.*

Verb forms: it **exemplified**, it has **exemplified**, it is **exemplifying**
Word building: **exemplification** *noun*
Word history: Middle English, from Latin *exempli-* example + *ficāre* make

exempt
verb to make free from a duty or rule: *She was **exempted** from sport because she was sick.*

Word building: **exempt** *adjective* **exemption** *noun*
Word history: Middle English, from Latin

exercise
noun **1** an activity of the body or mind to train or improve it
2 a putting into practice: *It will be an **exercise** of your willpower to stop eating cake.*

Word building: **exercise** *verb*
Word history: Middle English, from Old French, from Latin

exercise / exorcise
Don't confuse **exercise** with **exorcise**, which means 'to drive away evil spirits by prayers or a religious ceremony'.

exert (uhg-zert)
verb to use or put into action: *She **exerted** all her strength to lift the bricks.*
Word history: Latin

exertion
noun effort: *The **exertion** of her long swim was too much for her.* (***industry, labour, work***)

exhale
verb to breathe out
Word building: **exhalation** *noun*
Word history: Middle English, from French, from Latin word meaning 'breathe out'

exhaust (uhg-zawst)
verb **1** to tire or wear out: *I have **exhausted** myself working.* (***fatigue, strain, weaken, weary***)
2 to empty or use up completely: *I have **exhausted** all my patience.*
noun **3** the used gases given off by an engine
Word use: The opposite of definition 1 is **energise**.
Word building: **exhaustion** *noun*
Word history: from Latin word meaning 'drained out'

exhaustive
adjective thorough: *an **exhaustive** search* (***comprehensive, detailed, in-depth, intensive***)

exhaustive / exhausting
Don't confuse **exhaustive**, meaning 'thorough', with **exhausting**.
Something is **exhausting** if it is tiring or if it wears you out, as in *an exhausting day at school*.

exhibit (uhg-zib-uht)
verb **1** to show or display (***demonstrate, flaunt, parade***)
noun **2** something shown or displayed to the public (***display, exhibition***)
Word history: Latin

exhibition
noun **1** a public show or display: *an **exhibition** of paintings* (***demonstration, parade***)
2 a display to demonstrate skill as in sport, games, or something similar

exhilarate (uhg-zil-uh-rayt)
verb to fill with energy or excitement: *His swim in the cold surf **exhilarated** him.*
Word building: **exhilaration** *noun*
Word history: Latin

exhort (uhg-zawt)
verb to urge, advise, or ask urgently: *to **exhort** someone to take care*
Word building: **exhortation** *noun*
Word history: Middle English, from Latin word meaning 'urge', 'encourage'

exhume (eks-hyoohm)
verb to dig the earth, usually to find something buried: *to **exhume** a dead body* (***disentomb, disinter***)
Word building: **exhumation** *noun*
Word history: Latin *ex-* + *humus* earth, ground

exigency (uhg-zij-uhn-see)
noun **1** a state of urgency
2 exigencies, the urgent needs or demands of a particular occasion: *the **exigencies** of war*
3 a situation which demands immediate action (***crisis, emergency***)
Noun forms: The plural is **exigencies**.
Word building: **exigent** *adjective*

exile
verb **1** to force to leave your home or country: *The king **exiled** her for treason.* (***banish, evict, expel, throw out***)
noun **2** a long separation from your country or home
3 someone who has been forced to leave their country or home
Word history: Middle English, from Old French, from Latin word meaning 'banishment'

exist
verb **1** to be: *The earth has **existed** for millions of years.* (***live, remain, survive***)
2 to have life or be real: *Do ghosts **exist**?*
3 to continue to live: *We cannot **exist** without water.*
Word building: **existence** *noun*
Word history: from Latin word meaning 'stand forth', 'arise', 'be'

exit
noun **1** a way out: *The building had a number of **exits**.*
2 a going away or a departure: *Anne said 'goodbye' and made a quick **exit**.*
verb **3** to go away or out
Word history: special use of stage direction *exit* he goes out, influenced by association with Latin *exitus* a going out

exit strategy
noun a plan for the termination of a project: *a sound **exit strategy***

exodus
noun a going out or a departure, usually of a large number of people
Word history: Middle English, from Latin, from Greek *éxodos* a going out

exonerate (uhg-zon-uh-rayt)
verb **1** to free from blame
2 to free from a responsibility, duty, etc.
Word building: **exoneration** *noun*
Word history: from Latin word meaning 'disburdened'

exorbitant (uhg-zaw-buh-tuhnt)
adjective going beyond what is normal, right, or reasonable: *an **exorbitant** price | an **exorbitant** demand* (***costly, dear, expensive***)
Word building: **exorbitance** *noun*
Word history: from Late Latin word meaning 'going out of the track'

exorcise (ek-saw-suyz)
verb to free from evil spirits by prayers or a religious ceremony: *to **exorcise** a haunted house*

Word building: **exorcism** *noun* **exorcist** *noun*
Word history: Late Latin, from Greek

exorcise / exercise
Look up **exercise / exorcise.**

exotic
adjective **1** foreign or not belonging to your own country: *an **exotic** plant* (***alien, foreign, imported***)
2 strange, or unusually colourful or beautiful: *When we were overseas we saw many **exotic** places and ate **exotic** food.*

Word building: **exotic** *noun*
Word history: Latin, from Greek word meaning 'foreign', 'alien'

expand
verb **1** to increase in size or to swell: *Daniel **expanded** the sentence into a whole paragraph. | The balloon **expanded** with air.* (***amplify, develop, embellish, embroider, pad out***)
2 to spread, stretch out or unfold: *A bird **expands** its wings to fly.*

Word building: **expansion** *noun*
Word history: from Latin word meaning 'spread out'

expanse
noun a large open space or widespread area: *Australia has vast **expanses** of desert.*

expatiate (uhks-pay-shee-ayt)
phrase **expatiate on**, to enlarge in speech or writing: *to **expatiate on** an idea*

Word building: **expatiation** *noun*
Word history: from Latin word meaning 'extended', 'spread out'

expatriate (eks-pat-ree-uht)
noun someone who has left their own country to live in another

Word history: Late Latin

expect
verb **1** to look forward to (***anticipate, count on, foresee***)
2 to look for with good reason: *I **expect** you to do your duty.*
3 to be pregnant: *My mother is **expecting**.*

Word building: **expectancy** *noun*
Word history: from Latin word meaning 'look for'

expectant
adjective **1** full of anticipation or looking forward to: *an **expectant** audience*
2 waiting for the birth of a baby: *an **expectant** mother*

expectation
noun **1** the great hope that something will happen: *the **expectation** that he will come*
2 a strong wish for someone to live or behave in a certain way: *I can't live up to their **expectations**.*

expectorate (uhk-spek-tuh-rayt)
verb **1** to cough or spit out from the throat or lungs: *to **expectorate** phlegm*
2 to spit

Word building: **expectoration** *noun*
Word history: Latin word meaning 'banished from the breast'

expedient
adjective useful or suitable for a particular purpose: *It would be **expedient** for you to go to the meeting.*

Word building: **expediency** *noun*
Word history: Middle English, from Latin word meaning 'dispatching'

expedite (eks-puh-duyt)
verb to hurry up or to do quickly: *We must **expedite** this matter so it will be ready on time.*

Word building: **expeditious** *adjective*
Word history: from Latin word meaning 'extricated', 'helped forwards', 'sent off or dispatched'

expedition
noun **1** a journey made for a special purpose, such as a war or exploration (***excursion, jaunt, trip***)
2 the group of people and the transport used to go on such a journey

expel
verb **1** to drive out or away with force: *When you blow up a balloon you **expel** air from your lungs.* (***banish, evict, exile, throw out***)
2 to dismiss or send away from a club or a school

Verb forms: I **expelled**, I have **expelled**, I am **expelling**
Word building: **expulsion** *noun*
Word history: Middle English, from Latin word meaning 'drive out'

expend
verb **1** to use up: *I **expended** all my energy climbing the hill.* (***employ, utilise***)
2 to pay out or spend (***fork out, outlay***)

Word use: The opposite of this is **conserve**.
Word history: from Latin word meaning 'weigh out', 'pay out'

expendable
adjective not so important that it can't be sacrificed for a good reason: *They considered those soldiers to be **expendable**.* (***dispensable, peripheral, unimportant***)

expenditure
noun everything that is spent or used up: *We need to work out our monthly **expenditure** today.*

expense
noun **1** cost or charge: *the **expense** of our holiday | We had our meal at his **expense**.*
2 expenses,
a the costs you have to pay out for your work
b the money you pay to cover these costs: *She receives a good salary plus **expenses**.*
phrase **3 at the expense of**, involving the loss or injury of: *They chose quantity **at the expense of** quality.*

Word use: The opposite of this is **savings**.
Word history: Middle English, from Anglo-French, from Late Latin word meaning 'paid or weighed out'

expensive
adjective costing a great deal: *an **expensive** meal* (***costly, dear, exorbitant***)

Word use: The opposite of this is **cheap** or **inexpensive**.

experience (uhks-pear-ree-uhns)
noun **1** something that happens to you: *I had many strange **experiences** on my trip.*
2 the knowledge or practice you get from doing or seeing things
verb **3** to meet with, or have happen to you: *She **experienced** a lot of friendliness on her trip.* (***feel, perceive, sense***)

Word history: Middle English, from Old French, from Latin word meaning 'trial', 'proof', 'knowledge'

experiment
verb **1** to try or test to find something out: *Doctors are **experimenting** with drugs to find a cure.*
noun **2** a test or a trial carried out to discover something

Word building: **experimental** *adjective* **experimentation** *noun*
Word history: Middle English, from Latin word meaning 'a trial', 'test'

expert
noun **1** someone who has a lot of skill or knowledge about a special thing (***authority, consultant, specialist***)
adjective **2** having a lot of special skill or knowledge (***experienced, proficient***)

Word use: The opposite of definition 1 is **beginner** or **novice**.
Word history: Middle English, from Latin word meaning 'having tried'

expertise (eks-per-teez)
noun expert skill or knowledge

expiate (eks-pee-ayt)
verb to make up for by repayment, accepting punishment, etc.: *to **expiate** a sin or wrongdoing*

Word building: **expiation** *noun* **expiatory** *adjective*
Word history: Latin

expire
verb **1** to come to an end: *The contract has almost **expired**.* (***cease, finish, terminate***)
2 *Old-fashioned* to die (***become extinct, breathe your last, kick the bucket, pass away, perish***)
3 (of food products) to be beyond the use-by date: *This milk has **expired**.*

Word building: **expiration** *noun* **expiry** *noun*
Word history: Middle English, from French, from Latin word meaning 'breathe out'

expiry / expiration

Don't confuse **expiry** with **expiration**.

The **expiry** of something is its ending after a fixed period of time. We usually use it in relation to legal documents or agreements that are no longer valid at the end of that time:

The date of expiry for my passport has gone by.

We use **expiration** in formal writing to mean 'the close of a period':

The expiration of his academic career caused him great sorrow.

Expiration can also be the action of breathing air out through your lungs.

explain
verb **1** to make clear or easy to understand (***clarify, elucidate, interpret, spell out***)
2 to give the reason for or cause of: *Please **explain** your absence.* (***justify, vindicate***)
phrase **3 explain away**, to give excuses or reasons for: *Don't try to **explain away** your absence.*

Word history: from Latin word meaning 'make plain', 'flatten out'

explanation
noun **1** something which explains or gives the meaning of: *This book contains an **explanation** of the causes of World War I.*
2 a written or spoken text type or form which describes how something operates or why something happens

Word building: **explanatory** *adjective*
Word history: Latin

expletive (uhk-splee-tiv)
noun a violent exclamation or swearword

Word history: from Late Latin word meaning 'serving to fill out'

explicate (eks-pluh-kayt)
verb to make plain or clear (***explain, interpret***)

Word building: **explication** *noun* **explicative** *adjective* **explicatory** *adjective*
Word history: from Latin word meaning 'unfolded'

explicit (uhk-splis-uht)
adjective clearly stated and fully set out: *The recipe was so **explicit** that even I could follow it.* (***clear, evident, obvious, plain, straightforward***)

Word use: The opposite of this is **ambiguous** or **vague**.
Word history: from Latin word meaning 'unfolded'

explicit / implicit

These words are opposites.

Something is **implicit** if it is suggested or implied but not actually stated:

We had an implicit agreement even though nothing was signed.

It is the prefixes ex- and im- that make these words opposites.

explode
verb **1** to blow up or burst into pieces with a loud noise: *The bomb **exploded**.*
2 to burst out with a sudden expression of feeling: *She **exploded** with laughter when she saw it.*

Word history: from Latin word meaning 'drive out by clapping'

exploit[1] (eks-ployt)
noun a notable or daring deed (***achievement, act, action***)

Word history: Middle English, from Old French, from Latin word meaning 'unfolded'

exploit[2] (uhk-sployt)
verb **1** to use unfairly or selfishly: *She **exploits** her little brother.*
2 to put to good use: *The earth is **exploited** for its oil and minerals.*

Word building: **exploitation** *noun*
Word history: Middle English, from Old French, from Latin word meaning 'unfold'

explore
verb **1** to travel over an area to discover things or places: *They* ***explored*** *the bush to see if it had any caves.*
2 to examine or go over carefully: *The doctor* ***explored*** *every symptom in order to make a diagnosis.* (***delve into***, ***investigate***, ***probe***, ***research***, ***scrutinise***)

Word building: **exploration** *noun* **exploratory** *adjective* **explorer** *noun*
Word history: Latin

explosion
noun **1** a blowing up or exploding: *The* ***explosion*** *scattered rubbish everywhere.*
2 a sudden burst of noise: *There was an* ***explosion*** *of laughter around the dinner table.*

Word building: **explosive** *adjective* **explosive** *noun*
Word history: from Latin word meaning 'a driving off by clapping'

exponent (uhk-spoh-nuhnt)
noun **1** someone or something that explains, or interprets
2 someone or something that supports and promotes: *an* ***exponent*** *of free trade*
3 *Mathematics* a symbol placed above and at the right of another symbol (the base), to show the power it is to be raised to, as in x^3

Word history: from Latin word meaning 'putting forth'

exponential (eks-puh-nen-shuhl)
adjective increasing at a very fast rate, especially when the rate of increase is itself growing all the time: ***exponential*** *financial growth* | ***exponential*** *growth in population*

Word building: **exponentially** *adverb*

export (uhk-spawt, ek-spawt)
verb **1** to send to other countries for sale: *Australia* ***exports*** *a lot of wool every year.*
noun (ek-spawt) **2** something exported: *Sugar is one of Australia's* ***exports***.

Word use: The opposite of this is **import**.
Word building: **exportation** *noun*
Word history: from Latin word meaning 'carry away'

export / import
Don't confuse **export** with **import**.
To **export** goods is to send them out of a country.
To **import** goods is to bring them into a country.

expose (uhk-spohz)
verb **1** to uncover (***disclose***, ***make public***, ***reveal***, ***unfold***)
2 to let light onto, when taking a photograph: *He* ***exposed*** *several films which he developed himself.*

Word use: The opposite of this is **cover**.
Word history: Old French *ex-* + *poser* put

exposé (eks-poh-zay)
noun **1** a formal explanation or exposition: *He gave an* ***exposé*** *on the folly of going to war.*
2 a public exposure of some wrongdoing

Word history: French

exposition (eks-puh-zish-uhn)
noun **1** a large public show of products of art, manufacture, etc.
2 a written or spoken text type which gives a detailed statement or explanation
3 the act of presenting to view
4 *Music* a part of a fugue or a sonata form, in which the subject or main themes are first stated

expostulate (uhk-spos-chooh-layt)
verb to reason seriously with a person against something that person intends to do or has done: *They* ***expostulated*** *with him on the foolishness of his actions.*

Word building: **expostulation** *noun*
Word history: Latin

exposure
noun **1** the revealing of something private, secret or criminal: *public* ***exposure*** *of his dishonesty*
2 publicity given to a person or an event: *media* ***exposure***
3 the state of being able to be affected very strongly by something or someone, often in a harmful way: ***exposure*** *to radiation* | ***exposure*** *to new ideas*
4 the harmful effect of cold weather on someone's body: *He died from* ***exposure*** *on the mountain.*
5 *Photography* the length of time that film, or any other photographic medium, is exposed to the light

expound (uhk-spownd)
verb **1** to set forth or state in detail: *He* ***expounded*** *his new theory.*
2 to interpret or explain

Word history: Middle English, from Old French, from Latin word meaning 'put out', 'expose', 'set forth', 'explain'

express
verb **1** to put into words: *I* ***expressed*** *my opinion.* (***depict***, ***describe***, ***state***)
2 to show or make known: *Her face* ***expressed*** *her joy.*
3 to make known your feelings or thoughts: *He* ***expresses*** *himself well in English.*
adjective **4** sent or travelling direct, and fast, without stopping: *an* ***express*** *parcel*
5 clearly stated or definite: *an* ***express*** *purpose*
noun **6** an express train or bus

Word history: Middle English, from Latin word meaning 'pressed out', 'described'

expression
noun **1** the act of putting into words: *an* ***expression*** *of opinion*
2 the look on someone's face: *Your* ***expression*** *is grim.*
3 feeling or emotion: *Put some* ***expression*** *into the music.*
4 *Mathematics* a combination of numbers and symbols with no equals sign, which represents a number or something like this

expressive
adjective full of emotion or meaning: *an* ***expressive*** *smile* | *an* ***expressive*** *piece of music*

Word building: **expressiveness** *noun*

expressway
noun a road on which traffic can travel fast (***freeway***, ***motorway***)

expropriate (eks-<u>proh</u>-pree-ayt)
verb to take from a private owner, especially for public use: *to* ***expropriate*** *property*

Word building: **expropriation** *noun*
Word history: from Late Latin word meaning 'deprived of property'

expulsion (uhk-<u>spul</u>-shuhn)
noun **1** the act of driving out or expelling
2 the state of being expelled

Word building: **expulsive** *adjective*
Word history: Latin

expunge (uhk-<u>spunj</u>)
verb to rub out: ***expunge*** *guilt* (***erase***, ***obliterate***)

Word building: **expunction** *noun*
Word history: from Latin word meaning 'prick out', 'strike out'

expurgate (<u>eks</u>-puh-gayt)
verb to remove parts thought to be offensive from: *to* ***expurgate*** *a book*

Word building: **expurgation** *noun*
Word history: from Latin word meaning 'purged'

exquisite
adjective delicately beautiful: *an* ***exquisite*** *vase* (***gorgeous***, ***lovely***, ***stunning***)

extant (ek-<u>stant</u>, <u>ek</u>-stuhnt)
adjective still in existence, not destroyed or lost

Word history: from Latin word meaning 'standing out'

extempore (uhk-<u>stem</u>-puh-ree)
adverb **1** without preparation: *to speak* ***extempore***
adjective **2** impromptu: *an* ***extempore*** *performance*

Word history: from Latin word meaning 'out of the time'

extend
verb **1** to stretch out: *We will* ***extend*** *the coil of rope to its full length. | This road* ***extends*** *for twenty kilometres.* (***run***, ***spread***)
2 to make longer or larger: *to* ***extend*** *shopping hours | to* ***extend*** *a house*

Word history: Middle English, from Latin

extension
noun **1** a stretching out or lengthening
2 something added on: *an* ***extension*** *to our house*
3 an extra telephone connected to the one you already have
adjective **4** able to be extended: *an* ***extension*** *ladder*

Word history: Latin

extensive
adjective **1** large in amount or size: ***extensive*** *knowledge | an* ***extensive*** *wheat farm* (***broad***, ***outspread***, ***wide***)
2 carried out as far as possible: *an* ***extensive*** *search*

extent
noun length, area or volume: *to its full* ***extent***

Word history: Middle English, from Anglo-French, from Latin word meaning 'extend'

extenuating (uhk-<u>sten</u>-yooh-ay-ting)
adjective serving to explain away or reduce the seriousness of: ***extenuating*** *circumstances*

Word building: **extenuate** *verb* **extenuation** *noun*
Word history: from Latin word meaning 'made thin'

exterior (uhk-<u>stear</u>-ree-uh)
adjective **1** being on the outside of: *the* ***exterior*** *walls of the house*
noun **2** the outside: *the* ***exterior*** *of the building* (***facade***, ***face***, ***surface***)

Word use: The opposite of this is **interior**.
Word history: Latin, comparative of *exter*, *exterus* outer, outward

exterminate
verb to get rid of, especially by destroying: *to* ***exterminate*** *white ants* (***annihilate***, ***demolish***, ***destroy***, ***eradicate***, ***wipe out***)

Word building: **extermination** *noun* **exterminator** *noun*
Word history: from Latin word meaning 'driven beyond the boundaries'

external
adjective **1** on the outside: *Her* ***external*** *injuries included a black eye.*
2 coming from outside: *The* ***external*** *support for the school's project came mainly from local businesses.*

Word use: The opposite of this is **internal**.
Word history: Latin *extern(us)* outward + *-al*

extinct
adjective **1** no longer existing: *Dinosaurs are an* ***extinct*** *type of reptile.*
2 no longer active: *an* ***extinct*** *volcano*

Word building: **extinction** *noun*
Word history: Middle English, from Latin word meaning 'destroyed', 'put out'

extinguish
verb to put out: *Always* ***extinguish*** *your camp fire before leaving.* (***douse***, ***quench***, ***smother***)

Word building: **extinguisher** *noun*
Word history: Latin *ex(s)tinguere* put out, quench, destroy + *-ish*

extirpate (<u>ek</u>-stuh-payt)
verb **1** to remove completely or do away with
2 to pull up by the roots (***exterminate***, ***eradicate***)

Word building: **extirpation** *noun*
Word history: from Latin word meaning 'rooted out'

extol (uhk-<u>stohl</u>)
verb to praise highly (***eulogise***, ***laud***)

Verb forms: I **extolled**, I have **extolled**, I am **extolling**
Word use: You can also use **extoll**.
Word building: **extoller** *noun*
Word history: from Latin word meaning 'lift out or up'

extort (uhk-<u>stawt</u>)
verb **1** to take from a person by violence, threats, etc.
2 to take illegally under cover of your job or position: *to* ***extort*** *money form the bank where you work*

Word building: **extortion** *noun* **extortionist** *noun* **extortionary** *adjective*
Word history: from Latin word meaning 'twisted or wrested out'

extra
adjective **1** more than is usual or necessary (***redundant***, ***superfluous***, ***surplus***, ***unnecessary***)
noun **2** something added

3 someone playing a minor part in a film, usually as part of a crowd

Word history: probably originally short for *extraordinary*

extract (uhk-strakt)
verb **1** to pull or take out: *to **extract** a tooth* (***dislodge, remove, withdraw***)
noun (eks-trakt) **2** something taken out or separated: *I read an **extract** from her latest book. | a drink made from beef **extract***

Word history: from Latin word meaning 'drawn out'

extraction
noun **1** a separation or taking out: *the **extraction** of a tooth*
2 your descent or lineage: *She's of Japanese **extraction**.*

extradition (ek-struh-dish-uhn)
noun the giving up of a prisoner by one state or authority to another

Word building: **extradite** *verb* **extraditable** *adjective*
Word history: French, from Latin *ex-* + *trāditio* a giving over

extraneous (uhk-stray-nee-uhs)
adjective not belonging or proper to a thing (***external, foreign***)

Word building: **extraneously** *adverb* **extraneousness** *noun*
Word history: from Latin word meaning 'that is without', 'foreign'

extraordinary (uhk-straw-duhn-ree)
adjective **1** more than ordinary: *He is a man of **extraordinary** strength.* (***astonishing, fabulous, incredible, marvellous, phenomenal***)
2 unusual or remarkable: *We have been having **extraordinary** weather.* (***rare, singular, uncommon***)
3 *Commerce* having to do with gains and losses arising from activities outside the normal operations of a business

Word building: **extraordinarily** *adverb*
Word history: from Latin word meaning 'out of the common order'

extrapolate (ek-strap-uh-layt)
verb **1** *Statistics* to calculate a quantity which depends on one or more variables by extending the variables beyond their established ranges
2 to make a guess about something you don't know using the things you do know as a basis (***conjecture, infer***)

Word building: **extrapolation** *noun*
Word history: *extra-* + *-polate* of *interpolate*

extrasensory (eks-truh-sen-suh-ree)
adjective outside the normal senses

Word use: Look up **ESP**.

extrasensory perception
noun → **ESP**

extravagant (uhk-strav-uh-guhnt)
adjective **1** spending money excessively or wastefully: *an **extravagant** person*
2 too high or exorbitant: ***extravagant** expenses | **extravagant** prices* (***excessive***)
3 showing lack of restraint: ***extravagant** praise | **extravagant** gifts* (***lavish***)
4 going beyond the bounds of reason: ***extravagant** demands or actions* (***excessive***)
5 very elaborate or flamboyant: *an **extravagant** dress*

Word building: **extravagance** *noun*
Word history: Middle English, from Medieval Latin word meaning 'wander beyond', from Latin

extravaganza (uhk-strav-uh-gan-zuh)
noun an artistic production, as a comic opera or musical comedy, marked by wild and irregular form and feeling with detailed staging and costume

Word history: blend of *extravagance* and Italian *stravaganza* odd behaviour

extreme
adjective **1** very great: *She was in **extreme** pain.*
2 outermost: *We saw him at the **extreme** edge of the cricket field.*

Word building: **extremely** *adverb*
Word history: Middle English, from Latin *extrēmus*, superlative of *exter* outer, outward

extreme sport
noun a sport which involves a high degree of physical risk: *Canyoning is categorised as an **extreme sport**.*

extremism (uhk-stree-miz-uhm)
noun a tendency to go to extremes, especially in politics

Word building: **extremist** *noun*

extremity
noun **1** the extreme point or part of something
2 one of the limbs of the body
3 extremities, the end part of the limbs, such as your hands or feet

Noun forms: The plural is **extremities**.

extricate (ek-struh-kayt)
verb to free or disentangle: *He will **extricate** the butterfly from the web. | Can you **extricate** them from this unhappy situation?*

Word building: **extrication** *noun*
Word history: from Latin word meaning 'disentangled'

extrovert
noun someone who is lively and outgoing

Word use: The opposite is **introvert**.
Word building: **extroverted** *adjective*
Word history: Latin

extrude (ek-stroohd)
verb **1** to force or press out
2 in making metals, plastics, etc., to form into a desired shape by forcing through a shaped opening: *to **extrude** tubing*
3 to jut out

Word building: **extrusion** *noun*
Word history: from Latin word meaning 'thrust out'

exuberant (uhg-zyoohb-uh-ruhnt)
adjective **1** with great warmth of feeling: *an **exuberant** welcome* (***effusive, emotional, heartfelt***)
2 full of high spirits: *The soldiers were **exuberant** after their victory.*

Word building: **exuberance** *noun*
Word history: from Latin word meaning 'being fruitful'

exude (uhg-zyoohd)
verb to come or send out gradually in drops like sweat through pores or small openings
Word history: Latin

exult
verb **1** to rejoice greatly: *He **exulted** to find that he had won.*
phrase **2 exult in,** to take great pleasure in: *to **exult in** one's strength.*
Word building: **exultant** *adjective* **exultation** *noun*
Word history: from Latin word meaning 'leap out or up'

eye
noun **1** the organ or part of the body with which we see
2 the iris or coloured part of this organ: *She has blue **eyes**.*
3 a close or careful watch: *Keep an **eye** on my books for me.*
4 an ability to use your eyes effectively: *You have a good **eye** for ball games.*
phrase **5 an eye for an eye,** the paying back of an injury in the same form that you received it
6 catch someone's eye, to attract someone's attention
7 have an eye for, to be a good judge of
8 keep an eye on, to watch carefully
9 keep an eye out for, to be looking out for
10 see eye to eye, to agree
11 shut (or **close**) **your eyes to,** to disregard or refuse to see
12 turn a blind eye to, to ignore or pretend not to see
Word history: Old English *ēge*

eyeball
noun **1** the ball or globe of the eye
phrase **2 eyeball to eyeball,** face to face in an angry way

eyebrow
noun the arch of hair on the bony ridge over your eye

eyelash
noun one of the short curved hairs growing on the edge of an eyelid
Word use: The short form is **lash**.

eyelid
noun the lid of skin which moves up and down over your eye when you blink
Word use: The short form is **lid**.

eyesight
noun the power of seeing

eyesore
noun something unpleasant to look at: *The shabby picnic shed was an **eyesore** in the park.*

eyewitness
noun **1** someone who actually sees a particular action or happening
adjective **2** given by an eyewitness: *an **eyewitness** account*

eyrie (ear-ree, air-ree)
noun **1** the high nest of a bird of prey, as an eagle, or of any large bird
2 a building, such as a house or castle, built up high
Word history: *aerie*, from Latin word meaning 'level ground'

eyrie / eerie
Don't confuse **eyrie** with **eerie**, which means 'strange and frightening':
I crept into the twilight of that eerie cave.

ezine (ee-zeen)
noun a magazine in HTML format on the World Wide Web
Word use: You can also use **e-zine**.

fable
noun a short story, often about animals, that teaches a lesson about how to behave: *the **fable** of the tortoise and the hare*

Word history: Middle English, from Latin word meaning 'narrative'

fabric
noun cloth made by weaving, knitting or pressing fibres together: *wool **fabric** | felt **fabric*** (***material, stuff, textile***)

Word history: Middle English, from Latin word meaning 'workshop', 'art', 'fabric'

fabricate (fab-ruh-kayt)
verb **1** to construct by art and labour
2 to make by fitting together standard parts or sections
3 to invent: *to **fabricate** a legend or a lie*

Word building: **fabricator** *noun* **fabrication** *noun*
Word history: from Latin word meaning 'having made'

fabulous (fab-yooh-luhs)
adjective **1** *Colloquial* very good or wonderful: *We had a **fabulous** time.* (***astonishing, extraordinary, incredible, marvellous, phenomenal***)
2 told about in fables or myths: *a **fabulous** creature*

Word history: Latin *fabula* meaning 'a story'

facade (fuh-sahd)
noun **1** the front of a building (***exterior, face, outside, surface***)
2 an appearance, especially a misleading one: *Behind his **facade** of generosity, he hides a cruel nature.*

Word history: French

face
noun **1** the front of your head from the forehead to the chin
2 a look or expression: *a sad **face***
3 a surface of something: *the **face** of a cube | the **face** of a watch* (***exterior, facade, outside***)
verb **4** to look towards
5 to come into contact with or meet: *to **face** difficulties*
phrase **6 face to face,** meeting with or standing in the way of: ***face to face** with death*
7 face up to, to meet or acknowledge: *to **face up to** the facts*
8 in the face of, in spite of: *to do well **in the face of** sickness*
9 lose face, to have your dignity or standing amongst your friends damaged
10 on the face of it, judging by outward appearances
11 save face, to have your dignity or standing amongst your friends restored

Word history: Middle English, from French, from Vulgar Latin word meaning 'form', 'face'

face lift
noun **1** plastic surgery on the face for removing age lines, etc.
2 any improvement in appearance: *a **face lift** for an old building*

Word use: You can also use **facelift.**

facet (fas-uht)
noun **1** a side or part of something complicated like a personality, an argument or a structure: *The conservation argument has many **facets.***
2 one of the small, flat, polished surfaces of a gemstone

Word history: from French word meaning 'little face'

facetious (fuh-see-shuhs)
adjective meant to be or trying to be amusing, at the wrong time or in an unsuitable way: *a **facetious** remark | a **facetious** person*

Word building: **facetiously** *adverb* **facetiousness** *noun*
Word history: from Latin word meaning 'witticisms'

face value
noun **1** the value stated on the face of a financial or legal document
2 apparent value: *to accept promises at **face value***

face washer
noun a small piece of soft cloth used for washing the face or body

Word use: You can also use **washer.** | Another name is **flannel.**

facial
adjective **1** of or for your face: *a **facial** expression | a **facial** cream*
noun **2** a beauty treatment for your face

facile (fas-uyl)
adjective **1** moving, acting, working, etc., with ease: *a **facile** hand | a **facile** tongue*
2 easily done, performed, used, etc.: *a **facile** victory | a **facile** method*
3 smooth but shallow: *a **facile** expression* (***glib, slick***)

Word history: from Latin word meaning 'easy to do', 'easy'

facilitate (fuh-sil-uh-tayt)
verb to make easier: *He took my hand to **facilitate** my progress up the steep rock.* (***advance, ease, further, help, promote***)

Word use: The opposite of this is **hinder.**

facility (fuh-<u>sil</u>-uh-tee)
noun **1** a quality or ability possessed by something to enable a function to be performed: *The taxation office has a translation **facility**.*
2 skill or cleverness: *Her **facility** with words impressed us.*
3 facilities,
a equipment, aids, etc., attached to a building or place that make it easier to do something: *sporting **facilities** | banking **facilities***
b bathroom and toilet: *a hotel room with **facilities***
Noun forms: The plural is **facilities**.
Word history: Latin

facility / faculty
Don't confuse **facility** with **faculty**.
A **faculty** is any one of the five senses.
To have all your **faculties** is to be in full possession of all your mental powers.

facsimile (fak-<u>sim</u>-uh-lee)
noun **1** an exact copy: *a **facsimile** of an old document*
2 → fax
Word history: Latin *fac*, imperative, make + *simile* (neuter) like

fact
noun **1** something that is true or real
phrase **2 in fact**, really: ***In fact**, what happened was he pushed me.*
Word building: **factual** *adjective*
Word history: from Latin word meaning 'thing done'

faction
noun a small group of people within a larger group, who hold a different opinion to the larger group
Word building: **factional** *adjective* **factionalism** *noun*
Word history: from Latin word meaning 'a doing or making', 'action', 'party'

faction / fraction
Don't confuse **faction** with **fraction**, which is a part of a whole number, or a small piece or amount of something:
$\frac{1}{4}$ is a fraction.
Open the window a fraction.

factor
noun **1** one of the things that brings about a result: *Hard work was a **factor** in her success.*
2 one of two or more numbers which, when multiplied together, give the product: ***Factors** of 18 are 3 and 6.*
Word history: from Latin word meaning 'doer', 'maker'

factorial (fak-<u>taw</u>-ree-uhl)
Mathematics
noun **1** the product of an integer multiplied by all integers lower than itself: *The **factorial** of 4 (written 4!) is $4 \times 3 \times 2 \times 1 = 24$*
adjective **2** having to do with factors or factorials

factory
noun a building or group of buildings where goods are made
Noun forms: The plural is **factories**.
Word history: Medieval Latin, from Latin *factor*

faculty
noun **1** one of the powers that you are born with: *the **faculty** of hearing | He's turned 100, but he's still got all his **faculties**.*
2 the ability to do something in particular: *a **faculty** for getting into trouble*
Noun forms: The plural is **faculties**.
Word history: Middle English, from Latin word meaning 'ability', 'means'

fad
noun something that is popular for a short time: *Yoyos are a **fad** that comes and goes.* (***craze**, **fashion**, **rage**, **trend**, **vogue***)
Word building: **faddish** *adjective*
Word history: noun use of dialect *fad*, verb, be busy about trifles

fade
verb **1** to lose colour or strength: *The carpet **faded**.*
2 to disappear slowly: *The smile **faded** from her face.* (***dematerialise**, **dissolve**, **melt**, **vanish***)
3 to cause to fade: *Sunshine **faded** the carpet.*
Word history: Middle English, from Old French word meaning 'pale', 'weak', from blend of Latin *vapidus* flat and *fatuus* insipid

faeces (<u>fee</u>-seez)
plural noun waste matter discharged from the intestines (***excrement***)
Word use: You can also use **feces**.
Word building: **faecal** *adjective*
Word history: from Latin word meaning 'dregs'

fag
noun **1** tiresome work
2 in the British school system, a younger boy at a public school required to perform certain services for an older pupil
3 *Colloquial* a cigarette

fagged
adjective Colloquial exhausted: *She was completely **fagged** after a day of hard work.*
Word use: You can also use **fagged out**.

faggot
noun a bundle of sticks, etc., bound together and used for fuel, etc.
Word history: Middle English, from Old French; origin uncertain

Fahrenheit (<u>fa</u>-ruhn-huyt)
adjective having to do with a scale of temperature in which the melting point of ice is 32° above zero and the boiling point is 212° above zero
Word use: The symbol is **F**, without a full stop.
Word history: named after Gabriel *Fahrenheit*, 1686–1736, German physicist, who devised this scale and introduced the use of mercury in thermometers

fail
verb **1** to be unsuccessful: *He **failed** in maths.* (***bomb out**, **do no good**, **not make the grade***)
2 to be less than expected: *The wheat crop **failed** this year.*
Word history: Middle English, from Old French, from Latin word meaning 'deceive', 'disappoint'

failing
noun a weakness: *His **failing** in mathematics is not knowing his tables.*

failure
noun lack of success: *All his efforts ended in **failure**.* (***disaster***, ***dud***, ***fiasco***, ***flop***, ***write-off***)

Word history: Old French *faillir* fail

faint
adjective **1** lacking strength: *a **faint** light | a **faint** sound* (***indistinct***, ***low***, ***muffled***, ***quiet***, ***soft***)
2 weak and dizzy: *I feel **faint**.*
verb **3** to lose consciousness for a short time (***black out***, ***pass out***, ***swoon***)
noun **4** a brief loss of consciousness

Word history: Middle English, from Old French word meaning 'feigned', 'hypocritical', 'sluggish', 'spiritless'

fair[1]
adjective **1** not showing favouritism: *a **fair** judge*
2 done according to the rules: *a **fair** fight*
3 not cloudy: ***fair** weather* (***balmy***, ***fine***, ***mild***, ***sunny***, ***temperate***)
4 of light colour: ***fair** hair*
adverb **5** in a way that keeps to the rules: *to play **fair***
phrase **6 fair and square**,
a directly: *to hit someone **fair and square** on the chin*
b honestly or in a just way

Word history: Old English *fæger*

fair[2]
noun **1** a group of sideshows and similar entertainments set up for a short time in one place
2 a regular gathering of buyers and sellers of a particular type of goods: *a book **fair** | a cattle **fair***

Word history: Middle English, from Old French, from Late Latin word meaning 'holiday'

fair / fare
Don't confuse **fair** with **fare**, which is the money you pay for a ticket on a bus, train, or the like.

fair dinkum
adjective Australian, NZ Colloquial true or genuine: *a **fair dinkum** Australian*

fairway
noun **1** that part of a golf course between a tee and the green, where the grass is kept short
2 a channel in a harbour or river, which vessels can pass through

fairy
noun **1** a tiny imaginary creature with magical powers
phrase **2 away** (or **off**) **with the fairies**, out of touch with reality

Noun forms: The plural is **fairies**.
Word history: Middle English, from Old French *faerie*, from *fae* fay, fairy. Ultimately this word goes back to the Roman Fata, the Fates. These were the three goddesses who controlled the life of human beings.

fairytale
noun **1** a story about fairies
2 a story that's untrue or hard to believe: *Her excuse was a bit of a **fairytale**.*

Word building: **fairytale** *adjective*

faith
noun **1** trust in someone or something
2 the collection of beliefs of a religion: *the Christian **faith** | the Jewish **faith*** (***belief***, ***denomination***, ***religion***)

Word history: Middle English, from Old French, from Latin *fides*

faithful
adjective loyal or trustworthy: *a **faithful** friend | a **faithful** worker* (***constant***, ***devoted***, ***steadfast***, ***trusty***)

Word building: **faithfully** *adverb*

fake
verb **1** to make in such a way as to trick other people: *to **fake** money*
2 to pretend: *to **fake** illness*
adjective **3** designed to deceive or cheat: *He sold fake watches.*

Word use: The opposite of definition 3 is **authentic**.
Word building: **fake** *noun* **fake** *adjective*

falafel (fuh-luf-uhl, -laf-)
noun fried balls of ground chickpeas and spices, often eaten with a sauce, bread and salad

Word use: You can also use **felafel**.

falcon (fal-kuhn, fawl-kuhn, faw-kuhn)
noun a kind of hunting bird which captures its prey in flight

Word history: Latin *falx* sickle

falconry
noun the training and use of falcons

fall
verb **1** to drop from a higher to a lower place (***overbalance***, ***pitch forward***, ***topple***)
2 to become less or lower: *Prices **fall** when there is a glut. | The temperature **fell** today.* (***abate***, ***decrease***, ***diminish***)
3 to come to be: *to **fall** asleep | to **fall** in love*
noun **4** an act of falling or dropping
phrase **5 fall back on**, to use when something else hasn't worked: *If these scones don't come out right, I'll have to **fall back on** an old recipe of Mum's.*
6 fall behind, to slow down or not keep up with: *to **fall behind** the leader*
7 fall down, *Colloquial* to fail: *to **fall down** on the job*
8 fall for, *Colloquial*
a to be deceived or taken in by: *to **fall for** his tricks*
b to come to be in love with: *to **fall for** the new boy in my class*
9 fall in with, to agree to: *to **fall in with** his plans*
10 fall on (or **upon**), to attack: *The thugs **fell upon** the boys.* (***assault***, ***beat up***, ***get stuck into***, ***mug***)
11 fall out, to quarrel (***fight***, ***squabble***, ***wrangle***)
12 fall short, to fail to achieve something that was important to you: *to **fall short** of a world record in swimming*
13 fall through, to be unsuccessful: *Our plans **fell through**.* (***collapse***, ***fail***, ***miscarry***)

Verb forms: I **fell**, I have **fallen**, I am **falling**
Word history: Old English *feallan*

fallacy (fal-uh-see)
noun **1** a deceptive, misleading, or false idea, belief, etc.: *a popular **fallacy***
2 a misleading or unsound argument

Noun forms: The plural is **fallacies.**
Word building: **fallacious** *adjective*
Word history: Middle English *falacye*, from Latin *fallācia* deceit; replacing Middle English *fallace*, from Old French

fallible (fal-uh-buhl)
adjective likely to make a mistake

Word history: Medieval Latin, from Latin word meaning 'deceive'

fallopian tubes (fuh-loh-pee-uhn tyoohbz)
plural noun the uterine tubes, a pair of slender oviducts leading from the ovaries to the uterus, for the transport and fertilisation of ova

Word history: named after Gabriello *Fallopio*, 1523–62, Italian anatomist

fallout
noun dangerous radioactive dust falling from the air, after a nuclear explosion

fallow
adjective ploughed but left unseeded to improve its quality: *If we leave this land **fallow**, we should get a good crop next season.*

Word history: Old English *fealga*, plural, fallow land

fallow cropping
noun the growing and ploughing back of a green crop, on an area of land temporarily set aside from cropping production, to fertilise the soil

false
adjective **1** not true or correct: *a **false** statement* (***erroneous**, **inaccurate**, **incorrect**, **off beam**, **untrue***)
2 not faithful: *a **false** friend* (***disloyal**, **fickle**, **traitorous**, **treacherous**, **unfaithful***)
3 not real: ***false** teeth* (***bogus**, **counterfeit**, **fake**, **phoney**, **sham***)

Word building: **falseness** *noun* **falsity** *noun*
Word history: Old English *fals*, from Latin word meaning 'feigned', 'deceptive', 'false'

false alarm
noun a warning given when in fact the supposed emergency, accident, etc., has not happened: *We were told the building was on fire but it was a **false alarm**.*

falsehood
noun a statement that is not true

false pretences
plural noun the use of false records, untruthful information, or similar illegal devices to get what you want

falsetto (fawl-set-oh)
noun **1** a very high-pitched voice, especially in a man
adjective **2** high-pitched: *a **falsetto** voice* (***soprano**, **treble***)

Noun forms: The plural is **falsettos.**
Word history: Italian, diminutive of *falso* false

falsify
verb to make false or incorrect, especially to deceive someone: *to **falsify** the evidence* (***distort**, **misrepresent**, **slant**, **twist***)

Verb forms: I **falsified**, I have **falsified**, I am **falsifying**
Word history: Middle English, from Latin word meaning 'that acts falsely'

falter
verb to move or speak weakly or unsteadily

Word building: **falteringly** *adverb*
Word history: Middle English, perhaps from Scandinavian

fame
noun the state of being widely known: *His **fame** spread after he won an Olympic medal.*

Word history: Middle English, from obsolete French, from Latin word meaning 'report', 'fame'

familiar
adjective **1** well-known: *a **familiar** story*
phrase **2 familiar with**, having knowledge of: *I am **familiar with** the success he has achieved.*

Word building: **familiarise** *verb* **familiarity** *noun*

family
noun **1** parents and their children (***flesh and blood**, **kin**, **relations**, **relatives***)
2 a wider group of related people including grandparents, uncles, aunts and cousins
3 a group of related things: *the human **family** | a tree of the acacia **family***
adjective **4** having to do with the family
5 suitable for a family

Noun forms: The plural is **families.**
Word history: Middle English, from Latin *familia* the servants of a household, household, family

family name
noun the name that you share with the rest of your family: *His **family name** is Ivanov and his given name is Peter.*

Word use: You can also use **surname.**

family tree
noun a genealogical chart showing ancestry, descent, and relationship of the members of a family, as of people, animals, languages, etc.

famine (fam-uhn)
noun a serious shortage of food, usually caused by drought

Word history: Middle English, from French, from Latin

famished
adjective very hungry

Word use: The opposite of this is **replete** or **sated.**

famous
adjective well-known (***acclaimed**, **celebrated**, **distinguished**, **illustrious**, **legendary**, **notable**, **noted**, **prominent**, **renowned***)

fan[1]
noun **1** something designed to move the air and make you feel cooler
verb **2** to cool by moving the air: *We **fanned** her with a folded paper.*

Verb forms: I **fanned**, I have **fanned**, I am **fanning**
Word history: Old English *fann*, from Latin *vannus* fan for winnowing grain

fan[2]
noun someone who is an eager supporter: *a football* ***fan***

Word history: short for *fanatic*, although the original meaning has now changed

fanatic (fuh-nat-ik)
noun someone who is too enthusiastic, often in an unthinking way, about something they believe in: *a* ***fanatic*** *about health foods*

Word building: **fanatical** *adjective* **fanaticism** *noun*
Word history: Latin *fānāticus* relating to a temple, inspired by a divinity, frantic

fanbelt
noun the belt which drives the cooling fan of a motor

fancy
noun **1** a liking: *She took a* ***fancy*** *to me.*
2 something imagined: *It was only a* ***fancy*** *though it seemed real at the time.*
verb **3** to imagine: *I* ***fancied*** *I saw myself in a beautiful palace.* (***dream, make believe, pretend***)
4 to like or want: *I* ***fancy*** *fish for tea.* (***covet, crave, desire, long for***)
5 to believe without being certain: *I* ***fancied*** *she said she would come.*
adjective **6** ornamental: ***fancy*** *gold braid*

Noun forms: The plural is **fancies.**
Verb forms: I **fancied**, I have **fancied**, I am **fancying**
Adjective forms: **fancier, fanciest**
Word history: contraction of *fantasy*

fanfare
noun a short, loud piece of music usually played on trumpets, used to mark the beginning of an event or the arrival of someone important

Word history: French

fang
noun **1** one of the long, sharp, hollow teeth of a snake, by which it injects venom
2 a canine tooth

Word history: Old English

fanlight
noun a fan-shaped window above a door or other opening

fantastic
adjective **1** strange or unusual: ***fantastic*** *ornaments*
2 imaginary: ***fantastic*** *fears* (***fanciful, fictitious, made-up***)
3 *Colloquial* very good or wonderful: *a* ***fantastic*** *party* (***exceptional, outstanding, sensational, terrific***)

Word history: Middle English, from Medieval Latin word meaning 'imaginary', from Greek

fantasy
noun **1** imagination: *the world of* ***fantasy***
2 the making of pleasant mental pictures: *a* ***fantasy*** *in which I'm a famous pilot* (***daydream, pipedream, vision***)

Noun forms: The plural is **fantasies.**
Word building: **fantasise** *verb*
Word history: Middle English, from Old French, from Latin word meaning 'idea', 'fancy', from Greek word meaning 'impression', 'image'

fantasy fiction
noun a fiction genre based on fantasy worlds

FAQ[1]
adjective of reasonable or average quality, especially applied to products as wheat, meat, etc.

Word use: You can also use **faq.**
Word history: abbreviation of *F(air) A(verage) Q(uality)*

FAQ[2]
noun especially in computers, a frequently asked question

Word history: abbreviation

far
adverb **1** at or to a great distance or point: *He went* ***far*** *away.*
adjective **2** distant: *a* ***far*** *city*
3 the more distant of two: *the* ***far*** *side of the river*
phrase **4 as far as,** to the distance or degree that: ***as far as*** *I am concerned*
5 by far, very much: ***By far*** *the best thing you can do is to go home.*
6 far and away, very much
7 far gone, in an advanced or extreme state, usually of something bad, such as an illness or an addiction
8 so far, up to now

Word use: The opposite of definition 2 is **close** or **near.**
Adjective forms: **farther** or **further, farthest** or **furthest**
Adverb forms: **farther** or **further, farthest** or **furthest**
Word history: Old English *feor*

faraway
adjective **1** distant or remote: *a* ***faraway*** *country* (***isolated, outlying***)
2 dreamy: *a* ***faraway*** *look*

farce
noun **1** a comedy in which the humour depends on a ridiculous and unlikely situation
2 foolish show or mockery: *Her unkindness made a* ***farce*** *of her friendship for me.*

Word history: Middle English, from French, from Latin word meaning 'stuff'

farcical (fah-suh-kuhl)
adjective ridiculous or unlikely: *a* ***farcical*** *situation* (***absurd, ludicrous, nonsensical, preposterous, silly***)

fare
noun **1** the price of travelling on a public vehicle: *a bus* ***fare*** | *a train* ***fare***
2 *Old-fashioned* food: *The* ***fare*** *at the hotel was good.*
verb **3** to get on or manage: *We* ***fared*** *well.*

Word history: Old English *faran*

fare / fair
Don't confuse **fare** with **fair.** A **fair** is a carnival. For other meanings look up **fair.**

farewell
noun **1** a saying of goodbye: *a sad **farewell***
verb **2** to say goodbye to

Word history: originally two words, *fare well.* Look up **fare** (definition 3).

far-fetched
adjective exaggerated or removed from everyday life: *a **far-fetched** story* (***implausible***, ***improbable***, ***incredible***, ***unbelievable***, ***unlikely***)

farm
noun **1** an area of land used for growing crops or raising animals
verb **2** to cultivate the soil, or run a farm

Word building: **farmer** *noun* **farming** *noun*
Word history: Middle English, from French word meaning 'fix', from Latin

fart
Colloquial
noun **1** an amount of wind coming out from the anus, usually smelly and often producing a noise
verb **2** to produce a fart

farther
adverb **1** at or to a greater distance, degree, point
2 additionally or further
adjective **3** more distant or remote
4 additional or further

Word use: This word is the comparative form in the set **far, farther, farthest.**
Word history: Middle English *ferther*

> **farther / further**
>
> People have tried to make distinctions between these two words but in fact they are just different ways of spelling the same word. In Australia the more popular spelling seems to be **further**:
>
> *I can go no further down the track.*
>
> *I will give you no further advice.*
>
> The superlative is either **furthest** or **farthest.**

farthing
noun **1** a former British coin of bronze, worth one quarter of a penny, which ceased to be legal tender from 1 January 1961
2 something of very small value

Word history: Old English *fēorthung*

fascia (fay-shuh, fay-shee-uh) for definitions 1, 2 and 4; (fash-ee-uh) for definition 3
noun (*plural* **fascias** or, for definition 3, **fasciae** (fash-ee-ee))
1 a band or fillet
2 *Architecture*
a a long, flat member or band
b a long flat board covering the ends of rafters
3 *Anatomy*, *Zoology* a band or sheath of connective tissue investing, supporting, or binding together internal organs or parts of the body
4 the plastic covering for the face of a mobile phone, often coloured, decorated or branded

Word use: You can also use **facia.**

fascinate (fas-uh-nayt)
verb to attract and hold the interest of completely: *She **fascinated** us with her stories.*

Word building: **fascinating** *adjective* **fascination** *noun*
Word history: from Latin word meaning 'enchanted'

fascism (fash-iz-uhm)
noun **1** a government system with strong centralised power, permitting no opposition, controlling all the industrial, commercial and other affairs of the nation, together with an aggressive nationalism; first established in Italy by Mussolini in 1922
2 *Colloquial* any extreme right-wing ideology, especially one involving racism

Word use: You can also use **Fascism** for definition 1. | Definition 2 is usually used in a disapproving way.
Word building: **fascist** *noun*
Word history: Italian *Fascismo*, from *fascio* group, bundle, from Latin *fascis* a bundle of rods containing an axe, a Roman emblem of official power, later adopted by the Italian Fascist party

fashion
noun **1** the custom or style of dress, behaviour, etc., of a particular time: *Those sunglasses are the latest **fashion**.* (***craze***, ***fad***, ***trend***, ***vogue***)
2 manner or way: *He spoke to me in a rude **fashion**.*
verb **3** to shape or form: *He **fashioned** a crib for the baby.* (***build***, ***construct***, ***erect***, ***make***, ***put up***)

Word building: **fashionable** *adjective*
Word history: Middle English, from Old French, from Latin word meaning 'a doing or making'

fast[1]
adjective **1** able to move quickly: *a **fast** runner* (***speedy***, ***swift***)
2 finished in a short time: *a **fast** race*
3 ahead of the correct time: *My clock is **fast**.*
4 fixed firmly in place: *He made the boat **fast** to the wharf.*
adverb **5** tightly: *Hold **fast** to that rope.*
6 soundly: *I was **fast** asleep.*
7 quickly or swiftly: *He ran **fast**.*

Word use: The opposite of definitions 1 to 3 is **slow.** | The opposite of definition 7 is **slowly.**
Word building: **fastener** *noun*
Word history: Old English *fæst*

fast[2]
noun a period of time when no food is eaten, usually for religious or health reasons

Word building: **fast** *verb*
Word history: Old English *fæstan*

fasten
verb to fix firmly in place

Word history: Old English *fæstnian*

fast food
noun food for sale, as chicken, chips, hamburgers, etc., which can be provided without delay

fastidious (fas-tid-ee-uhs)
adjective fussy or hard to please: *He is **fastidious** about cleanliness.*

Word history: Latin *fastīdiōsus*, from *fastīdium* loathing, disgust

fat
noun **1** the white or yellowish greasy substance found in or around the flesh of animals and in some plants: *Cut the **fat** from the chops.*
adjective **2** plump or obese (***heavy***, ***portly***, ***stocky***, ***stout***, ***tubby***)
3 having much edible flesh: *a **fat** lamb*

Adjective forms: **fatter**, **fattest**
Word building: **fatten** *verb* **fatty** *adjective*
Word history: Old English *fætt*

FAT
noun Computers an area on a disk when you are using DOS, which is copied onto the disk when you format it. The FAT creates an empty directory called the root directory. On each of your disks, the directories store the files and the FAT keeps track of where they are. The FAT also allocates the free space on your disks so that you have enough room to create new files.

Word history: abbreviation of *F(ile) A(llocation) T(able)*

fatal
adjective **1** causing death: *a **fatal** injury* (***deadly**, **lethal**, **malignant**, **terminal***)
2 likely to have very important results: *a **fatal** decision*

Word history: Middle English, from Latin word meaning 'belonging to fate'

fatalism (fay-tuhl-iz-uhm)
noun the belief that all events are influenced by fate and are therefore inevitable

Word building: **fatalist** *noun* **fatalistic** *adjective*

fatality
noun **1** a disaster that ends in death
2 someone who is killed in an accident, or something like this
3 deadliness or the quality of causing death or disaster: *the **fatality** of illnesses such as AIDS*

Noun forms: The plural is **fatalities**.

fate
noun **1** the cause beyond your control that seems to control the things that happen to you: *It was **fate** that we should meet.* (***chance**, **destiny**, **fortune**, **luck**, **providence***)
2 the end, outcome or final result: *the **fate** of our plans*

Word history: Middle English, from Latin word meaning 'a prophetic declaration', 'fate'

fate / fete
Don't confuse **fate** with **fete**. A **fete** is a kind of fair to raise money for a school or church or the like. Note that this can also be written **fête**.

fateful
adjective important because of deadly or disastrous consequences: *the **fateful** day of the earthquake* (***critical**, **memorable**, **momentous**, **significant***)

father
noun **1** a male parent
2 someone who shows the interest of a father: *a **father** to the neighbourhood children*
3 someone who invents or begins something: *King Alfred was the **father** of the English navy.*
verb **4** to be the father of
5 to act as a father towards

Word building: **fatherhood** *noun* **fatherly** *adjective*
Word history: Old English *fæder*

father-in-law
noun the father of your husband or wife

Noun forms: The plural is **fathers-in-law**.

fathom (fadh-uhm)
noun **1** a measure of the depth of water in the imperial system, equal to 6 feet, or nearly 2 metres in the metric system
verb **2** to understand completely: *I couldn't **fathom** maths until my brother helped me.* (***comprehend**, **get the hang of**, **grasp**, **make out***)

Word use: Look up **imperial system**.
Word history: Old English *fæthm*

fatigue (fuh-teeg)
noun **1** severe mental or physical tiredness
2 weakening of material, especially metal, as a result of strain put on it by long use

Word use: The opposite of definition 1 is **energy**.
Word building: **fatigue** *verb* (**fatigued**, **fatiguing**)
Word history: French, from Latin word meaning 'tire'

fatuous (fa-chooh-uhs)
adjective foolish without knowing it (***idiotic**, **inane**, **silly**, **stupid***)

Word building: **fatuousness** *noun*
Word history: Latin

fault
noun **1** responsibility or cause for blame: *It was my **fault** we were late.*
2 a mistake or blemish: *I returned the shirt to the shop because there was a **fault** in the collar.*
3 a failure to serve a ball according to the rules in tennis and similar games
4 *Geology* a break or fracture in rock, along which movement has occurred
verb **5** to find something wrong with: *They couldn't **fault** his wonderful singing.* (***censure**, **condemn**, **criticise**, **disapprove of**, **pick to pieces***)
phrase **6 at fault**, open to blame: *If the battery's flat we'll all know who's **at fault**.*
7 find fault, to find something wrong: *He's already **found fault** with the new car.*
8 to a fault, to a great extent: *He was generous **to a fault**.*

Word history: Middle English, from Old French, from Latin word meaning 'deceive'

fault line
noun **1** *Geology* the line along which the movement in an earthquake is liable to occur
2 *Sociology* a difference which may become socially divisive, such as class, gender, race, etc.

Word use: You can also use **faultline**.

faulty
adjective having faults or something wrong: *We realised the new heater was **faulty** as soon as we tried to turn it on.* (***defective**, **broken**, **unsound**, **substandard**, **shoddy***)

fauna (faw-nuh)
noun the animals of a particular area or period of time: *Australian **fauna** includes koalas, kookaburras and blue-tongue lizards.*

Word use: Compare this with **flora**.
Word history: Neo-Latin, special use of *Fauna*, name of sister of *Faunus*, in Roman mythology a woodland deity identified with Pan

faux fur (foh fer)
noun imitation fur: *the resurgence of the popularity of leather and **faux fur***
Word history: from French word meaning 'false' + *fur*

faux pas (foh pah, foh pah)
noun a slip in your manners or a blunder you make in public
Noun forms: The plural is **faux pas** (foh pahz, foh pah).
Word history: from French words meaning 'false step'

favour
noun **1** a kind act: *Will you do me a **favour**?*
2 a state of being thought well of: *in **favour** with the teacher*
verb **3** to think of with approval: *to **favour** an idea*
4 to prefer unfairly: *He **favours** his youngest child.* (***like best, single out***)
5 to show favour to: *Will you **favour** us by coming to our meeting?*
phrase **6 in favour of,**
a on the side of: *He is **in favour of** our idea.*
b payable to: *a cheque **in favour of** the Red Cross*
Word use: You can also use **favor.**
Word building: **favoured** *adjective*
Word history: Middle English, from Old French, from Latin

favourable
adjective **1** giving help: *a **favourable** wind for the boats*
2 saying what you want to hear: *a **favourable** answer*
Word use: You can also use **favorable.**

favourite
noun **1** someone or something most highly thought of: *This picture is my **favourite**.*
2 a competitor who is expected to win
3 someone who is treated as being better than others without really deserving it: *the teacher's **favourite***
Word use: You can also use **favorite.**
Word building: **favourite** *adjective*
Word history: French, from Italian *favorito*, from Latin

favouritism
noun **1** the favouring of one person in a group of people who should be treated equally
2 the state of being treated better than others
Word use: You can also use **favoritism.**

fawn[1]
noun **1** a young deer, under a year old
2 a pale yellowish-brown colour
adjective **3** having a fawn colour (***beige, light brown, sepia, tan***)
Word history: Middle English, from Old French, from Latin word meaning 'offspring', 'young'

fawn[2]
verb **1** to try to get special treatment from someone by flattery
2 to show affection by wagging the tail, licking and jumping around as a dog does
Word history: Old English *fægnian* rejoice, fawn

fax
noun **1** a way of sending documents or pictures along a telephone line
2 a document or picture sent this way
verb **3** to send by fax: *to **fax** a document*
Word use: You can also use **facsimile** for definitions 1 and 2.
Word history: a respelling of the first part of *facs(imile)*

faze
verb Colloquial to upset or disturb: *That doesn't **faze** me at all.*
Word history: variant of obsolete *feeze* disturb, worry

fear
noun **1** a feeling that danger or something unpleasant is near
verb **2** to be afraid of (***be frightened of, be scared of***)
3 to feel anxious: *I **fear** for his safety.*
phrase **4 for fear of,** in order to avoid or stop
Word building: **fearful** *adjective* **fearless** *adjective* **fearlessness** *noun*
Word history: Old English *fǣr* sudden attack, sudden danger

fearsome
adjective causing fear: *a **fearsome** storm*

feasible (feez-uh-buhl)
adjective likely to work: *a **feasible** plan* (***possible, practicable, viable, workable***)
Word use: The opposite of this is **impossible.**
Word building: **feasibility** *noun* **feasibly** *adverb*
Word history: Middle English, from Old French, from Latin word meaning 'do', 'make'

feast
noun **1** a large meal set out for many guests (***banquet, repast, spread***)
2 a large quantity of anything eaten or giving pleasure: *a **feast** of ice-cream | a **feast** of music*
3 something very pleasant: *a **feast** for the eyes*
Word building: **feast** *verb*
Word history: Middle English, from Old French, from Latin word meaning 'festal' (befitting a feast)

feasting
noun the eating of a large meal in the company of many people: *It was a night of **feasting**.*

feat
noun a deed of great skill, courage or strength (***accomplishment, achievement***)
Word history: Middle English, from Old French, from Latin word meaning 'thing done'

feat / feet
Look up **feet / feat.**

feather
noun **1** one of the growths that make up the covering of a bird's body
phrase **2 a feather in your cap,** an honour or mark of merit you have earned
3 feather your nest, to provide for yourself or make yourself rich
4 make the feathers fly, to cause confusion

Word building: **feathered** *adjective* **feathery** *adjective*
Word history: Middle English and Old English *fether*

feature
noun **1** any part of your face: *His nose is his best **feature**.*
2 an outstanding part or quality: *The lovely scenery was a **feature** of our trip.*
verb **3** to give special importance to: *to **feature** a tenor on a concert program*
4 to be an outstanding or distinguishing part: *Gum trees **feature** in his paintings.*

Word building: **featured** *adjective*
Word history: Middle English, from Old French, from Latin word meaning 'making', 'formation'

February (<u>feb</u>-rooh-uh-ree, <u>feb</u>-yuh-ree)
noun the second month of the year, containing 28 days, but 29 in leap years

Word history: Latin *Februārius*, from *februa*, plural, the Roman festival of purification, celebrated 15 February

feckless (<u>fek</u>-luhs)
adjective lacking any purpose in life, money or possessions (***careless***, ***irresponsible***)

Word history: Scottish

fed
verb **1** past tense and past participle of **feed**
phrase **2 fed up**, annoyed or frustrated: *I'm **fed up** with this nonsense.* (***angry***, ***infuriated***, ***vexed***)

federal
adjective having to do with a central government rather than state governments: ***federal** politics*

Word history: from Latin word meaning 'compact', 'league'

federate
verb to join in a league or federation

federation
noun the forming of a nation by a number of states who give some of their powers and responsibilities to a central government

fee
noun the money you owe, such as to a doctor, lawyer or private school for their services

Word history: Middle English, from Anglo-French; of Germanic origin

feeble
adjective **1** weak in body or mind (***frail***, ***helpless***, ***invalid***, ***weedy***)
2 lacking strength or brightness: *a **feeble** voice | **feeble** light* (***faltering***, ***powerless***, ***sickly***, ***washed-out***, ***weak***)

Word building: **feebleness** *noun* **feebly** *adverb*
Word history: Middle English, from Old French, from Latin word meaning 'lamentable'

feed
verb **1** to give food to
2 to supply with the means of growth: *to **feed** a fire | Two creeks **feed** the river.*
3 to be food for: *This leg of lamb will **feed** six people.*
4 to supply to: *to **feed** corn to chickens*
noun **5** food, especially for animals: *horses' **feed***
6 *Colloquial* a meal (***bite to eat***, ***repast***, ***snack***, ***spread***)

Verb forms: I **fed**, I have **fed**, I am **feeding**
Word history: Old English *fēdan*

feedback
noun **1** information passed back about something that has been done or said: *I've had a lot of **feedback** about my new book.* (***acknowledgement***, ***reaction***, ***response***)
2 the return of part of the sound put out by a loudspeaker into the microphone so that a high-pitched noise is made

feel
verb **1** to know or examine by touching: ***Feel** the wool. | We **felt** our way in the dark.* (***finger***, ***handle***, ***touch***)
2 to sense or experience: *She **feels** the cold. | She **felt** sadness at the news.*
3 to know that you are: *She **feels** happy. | I **felt** ill.*
4 to believe: *I **feel** that you are wrong.*
noun **5** the way something is sensed when you touch it: *a silky **feel***
phrase **6 feel for**, to have sympathy for: *I **feel for** her in her distress.*
7 feel like, to want or wish for: *to **feel like** a walk* (***desire***, ***fancy***, ***favour***)
8 feel up to, *Colloquial* to be able to cope with: *to **feel up to** a walk*

Verb forms: I **felt**, I have **felt**, I am **feeling**
Word history: Old English *fēlan*

feeler
noun **1** a thin, armlike growth on some animals, especially those without a backbone, which is used for touching or grasping
2 a remark made to find out what someone else is thinking

feeling
noun **1** a particular sensation or emotion: *a **feeling** of warmth | a **feeling** of fear* (***awareness***, ***impression***, ***perception***, ***sense***)
2 a belief or idea: *I have a **feeling** it will turn out well.*

feet
noun plural of **foot**

> **feet / feat**
> Don't confuse **feet** with **feat**.
> You stand on your two **feet**.
> A **feat** is an achievement or an accomplishment, usually of something difficult to do:
> *It was quite a feat to scale the face of that cliff.*

feign (fayn)
verb **1** to pretend to have: *to **feign** illness*
2 to make up or invent: *to **feign** an excuse*

Word history: Middle English, from Old French, from Latin word meaning 'form', 'conceive', 'devise'

feint (faynt)
noun **1** a movement made with the object of deceiving an opponent
2 feigned appearance
verb **3** to make a feint

Word history: from French word meaning 'feign'

feisty (<u>fuy</u>-stee)
adjective **1** easy to excite or cause to argue: *She had a **feisty** personality.*
2 lively: *a **feisty** little dog*

felicitous (fuh-lis-uh-tuhs)
adjective well-chosen or apt: *a* ***felicitous*** *word in a poem* | *He is a most* ***felicitous*** *choice for the job.*

felicity (fuh-lis-uh-tee)
noun **1** the state of happiness or bliss
2 aptness or skilfulness of expression

Word history: Middle English, from Latin word meaning 'happiness'

feline (fee-luyn)
adjective having to do with cats or the cat family

Word building: **feline** *noun*
Word history: from Latin word meaning 'of a cat'

fell[1]
verb past tense of **fall**

fell[2]
verb to cut down or cause to fall: *to* ***fell*** *a tree* | *The boxer* ***felled*** *his opponent.*

fell[3]
adjective Old-fashioned **1** fierce or cruel: *a* ***fell*** *blow*
2 destructive or deadly: *a* ***fell*** *poison* | *a* ***fell*** *disease* | *one* ***fell*** *swoop*

Word history: Middle English, from Old French word meaning 'base'

fellow
noun **1** a man or a boy
2 Fellow, a member of a professional society: *a* ***Fellow*** *of the Royal College of Surgeons*
adjective **3** having the same position or occupation: *my* ***fellow*** *workers*

Word building: **fellowship** *noun*
Word history: late Old English *fēolaga*, from Scandinavian

felony (fel-uh-nee)
noun a serious crime, such as murder or burglary

Noun forms: The plural is **felonies**.
Word building: **felon** *noun* **felonious** *adjective*

felt
noun cloth made of wool, fur or hair which is not woven but pressed firmly together: *soft toys made of* ***felt***

Word building: **felt** *adjective*

felt pen
noun a pen with a thick nib made of felt, usually in a bright colour, used for colouring in, etc.

Word use: You can also use **felt-tip pen.** | Another name is **texta.**

female
adjective **1** of the sex which is able to give birth to young
noun **2** a female person or animal

Word use: The opposite is **male.**
Word history: Middle English, from Old French, from Latin word *femella* meaning little woman, from *femina* woman.

female / feminine / feminist / effeminate

These words are all related in meaning but there are important differences.

You use the word **female** when you just wish to identify the sex of a person or an animal. A woman is female.

A person who is **feminine** has the attributes which are traditionally linked to the female sex, such as gentleness, kindness, or frailty. A man or a woman could be described as having feminine characteristics. **Feminine** is also used as the adjective from **female,** as in *feminine endings of words* and *the feminine sex.*

A **feminist** is someone who believes that women should have the same rights and opportunities as men. Note that **feminist** and **feminine** do not mean the same thing.

A man is described as **effeminate** when he is thought to have too many characteristics that are regarded as feminine. You would not describe a woman as **effeminate.**

feminine (fem-uh-nuhn)
adjective **1** female
2 having qualities such as softness and gentleness, thought to be typical of women

Word use: The opposite is **masculine.**
Word building: **femininity** *noun*
Word history: Middle English, from Latin word meaning 'woman'

feminism
noun the principle that women deserve the same rights and opportunities as men

feminist
noun someone who holds the belief that women deserve the same rights and opportunities as men

femur (fee-muh)
noun Anatomy the bone of the thigh, the longest bone in the body

Noun forms: The plural is **femurs** or **femora** (fem-uh-ruh).
Word history: from Latin word meaning 'thigh'

fence
noun **1** a wall or barrier put up around something to separate it from its surroundings
2 *Colloquial* someone who earns a living by buying and selling stolen goods
verb **3** to enclose or separate by a fence: *to* ***fence*** *a garden*
4 to fight with a sword: *to* ***fence*** *in a sports tournament*
phrase **5 over the fence**, *Australian* not reasonable in your behaviour
6 sit on the fence, to avoid taking sides in an argument

Word building: **fencer** *noun*
Word history: a variant of *defence* in which the *de-* (an unstressed syllable) has gradually disappeared

fencing
noun **1** the sport of sword fighting
2 material, such as wood or wire, used to build fences

fend
phrase **1 fend for**, to look after or protect
2 fend off, to fight off or resist: *He **fended off** the savage dog.*

Word history: variant of *defend*

fender
noun **1** something which wards something off
2 a guard or screen before an open fireplace, to keep back falling coals or to prevent children falling in
3 a US word for **mudguard**

Word history: variant of *defender*

feng shui (fuhng shwee)
noun a practice in Chinese culture of placing yourself in a good relationship with the physical world around you so as to increase good luck, especially by following rules in relation to the design and location of buildings, the position of objects and furniture in a room, etc.

Word history: Mandarin word literally meaning 'wind and water'

fennel (fen-uhl)
noun **1** a plant with yellow flowers, which bears strongly-smelling seeds used in cookery and medicine and which you can eat as a vegetable
2 the seeds of this plant

Word history: Old English *fenol*, from Latin word meaning 'fennel'

feral (fe-ruhl)
adjective **1** wild or untamed: ***Feral** dogs roamed the countryside.*
noun **2** *Australian Colloquial* someone who supports the environmental movement and who chooses to live close to nature in simple conditions without taking any notice of normal social customs with regard to clothing, cleanliness, etc.

Word history: from Latin word meaning 'wild beast'

ferment (fuh-ment)
verb **1** to change in taste and appearance, because yeast or bacteria has turned sugar into alcohol and gas: *Yeast **ferments** grape juice and turns it into wine. | The apple juice was standing there so long it **fermented**.*
noun (fer-ment) **2** a state of excitement and activity

Word history: from Latin word meaning 'agitation'

fermentation (fer-men-tay-shuhn)
noun **1** the act or process of fermenting
2 the breakdown of complex molecules brought about by a state of activity, such as when grape sugar is changed into ethyl alcohol by yeast enzymes
3 excitement or agitation

fern
noun a green leafy plant that does not have flowers and grows in damp shady places

Word history: Old English *fearn*

ferocious (fuh-roh-shuhs)
adjective fierce, savage and cruel: ***ferocious** animals | a **ferocious** attack (**forceful**, **furious**, **violent**, **wild**)*

Word building: **ferocity** *noun*

ferret
noun **1** an animal with a long thin body used in hunting rabbits
phrase **2 ferret out**, to search out: *We **ferreted out** the truth.*

Word history: Middle English, from Old French, from Latin word meaning 'thief'

ferrous (fe-ruhs)
adjective having to do with or containing iron

ferry
noun **1** a boat that carries people or cars across a river or harbour
verb **2** to transport from one place to another

Noun forms: The plural is **ferries**.
Verb forms: it **ferried**, it has **ferried**, it is **ferrying**
Word history: Old English *ferian*

fertile
adjective **1** richly productive and abundant: ***Fertile** land grows healthy crops. | Her stories are most interesting because of her **fertile** imagination.*
2 able to have babies

Word use: The opposite is **sterile** or **barren**.
Word building: **fertility** *noun*
Word history: Middle English, from Latin word meaning 'fruitful'

fertilise
verb **1** to make fertile or enrich: *to **fertilise** the vegetable garden with cow manure*
2 to combine with in order to create new life: *The male sperm **fertilises** the female egg to start the development of a baby.*

Word use: You can also use **fertilize**.
Word building: **fertilisation** *noun*

fertiliser
noun a material used to enrich the soil, especially a commercial or chemical manure

Word use: You can also use **fertilizer**.

fertility (fer-til-uh-tee)
noun **1** the state or quality of being fertile
2 *Biology* the ability to produce offspring; power of reproduction
3 (of soil) the quality of supplying nutrients in proper amounts for plant growth when other factors are favourable

fervour (fer-vuh)
noun great enthusiasm or passion: *She spoke with **fervour** against nuclear bombs.*

Word use: You can also use **fervor**.
Word building: **fervent** *adjective* **fervently** *adverb*
Word history: Middle English, from Old French, from Latin word meaning 'heat', 'passion'

fester
verb **1** to form pus: *The wound began to **fester**.* (***decay***, ***putrefy***, ***rot***, ***suppurate***)
2 to rankle or cause irritation: *Resentment towards the bosses began to **fester** in the hearts of the employees.*

Word building: **fester** *noun*
Word history: Middle English, from Old French, from Latin word meaning 'ulcer'

festival
noun **1** a joyful celebration with processions, exhibitions and performances of music, dance and drama (***carnival***, ***fair***, ***fete***, ***gala***)
2 a time of religious celebration: *the **festival** of Christmas*

Word history: Middle English, from Latin word meaning 'festive'

festive
adjective merry and joyful: *to be in a **festive** mood*

Word history: from Latin word meaning 'merry', 'lively'

festivity
noun **1** a festival
2 festivities, festive activities: *Come and join in the **festivities**.*

Noun forms: The plural is **festivities**.

festoon
noun **1** a streamer, or ribbon hung as a decoration
verb **2** to drape or adorn: *to **festoon** the Christmas tree with lights*

Word history: French, from Italian word meaning 'festival', 'feast'

fetch
verb **1** to go and bring back: ***Fetch** the ball Fido!*
2 to sell for or bring in: *That gold watch should **fetch** a high price.*
phrase **3 fetch and carry**, to do small unimportant jobs

Word history: Old English *feccan*

fetching
adjective *Old-fashioned* charming and attractive: *a **fetching** smile*

fete (fayt)
noun **1** a small fair held to raise money for a school or charity
verb **2** to treat as special and important: *They **feted** the overseas visitors with champagne.*

Word use: You can also use **fête**.
Word history: French

fete / fate
Look up **fate / fete**.

fetid (fet-uhd, feet-uhd)
adjective stinking, especially something rotting or decaying (***high***, ***putrid***, ***rank***)

Word use: You can also use **foetid**.
Word building: **fetidness** *noun* **fetidity** *noun*
Word history: Latin

fetish (fet-ish)
noun **1** an object believed to have magical powers or to be the place where a powerful spirit lives
2 an obsession or fixation, usually expressed in behaviour that is religious or very structured in nature

Word history: French, from Portuguese, from Latin word meaning 'made by art'

fetlock
noun the part of a horse's leg with a tuft of hair just above the hoof

Word history: Middle English

fetta (fet-uh)
noun a soft, white, Greek-style cheese which has been preserved by being soaked in salted water

Word use: You can also use **feta**.
Word history: from Latin word meaning 'mouthful' or 'bite'

fetter
noun **1** a chain or shackle tied around the ankles
2 anything that restricts or stops you from doing what you want
verb **3** to confine or restrict

Word use: Definition 2 is often used in the plural form, as in *to shake off your fetters.*
Word history: Old English *feter*; related to *foot*

fettle (fet-uhl)
noun state or condition: *in fine **fettle***

Word history: Middle English, from Old English *fetel* belt

fettuccine (fet-uh-chee-nee)
noun a kind of pasta that has been cut into wide flat strips

feud (fyoohd)
noun a bitter, long-lasting quarrel, especially between two families: *He had never met his cousins because of the family **feud**.* (***conflict***, ***row***, ***vendetta***)

Word building: **feud** *verb*
Word history: Middle English, from Old French, from Old High German

feudal (fyooh-duhl)
adjective having to do with a way of life in which ordinary people lived on and used the land of a nobleman, giving him military and other service in return

Word use: We talk about the **feudal system** which was in force in medieval Europe.
Word building: **feudalism** *noun*

fever
noun **1** an unusually high body temperature caused by illness
2 great excitement: *The crowd waiting for the rock group worked itself up into a **fever**.*
phrase **3 fever pitch**, the height of excitement: *It didn't take the crowd long to reach **fever pitch**.*

Word history: Old English, from Latin

feverish
adjective hot or restless

Word building: **feverishness** *noun*

few
adjective **1** not many: ***Few** people go swimming in winter.*
phrase **2 a good few** or **quite a few**, a fairly large number
3 the few, a small number or minority: *In the old days, education was only for **the few**.*

Adjective forms: **fewer, fewest**
Word history: Old English *fēawe*

fewer / less

Both of these words have to do with 'a smaller quantity'.

Many people use *less* on every occasion, and never use *fewer* at all.

In careful writing though, **fewer** should be used with nouns that refer to things you can count (count nouns), and **less** with nouns that refer to things that aren't countable (mass nouns):

fewer chairs *less water*
fewer people *less butter*

fey (fay)
adjective **1** having or showing magical or supernatural qualities, such as second sight, etc.
2 light-headed or slightly crazy (***away with the fairies, eccentric***)
Word history: Old English *fǣge* doomed to die, timid

fiancé (fee-on-say)
noun the man to whom a woman is engaged
Word history: French word meaning 'betroth', from Latin

fiancée (fee-on-say)
noun the woman to whom a man is engaged to be married: *She is Tony's **fiancée**.*
Word history: French word meaning 'betroth', from Latin

fiasco (fee-as-koh)
noun an embarrassing or ridiculous failure (***disaster, failure, flop, write-off***)
Word history: from a 19th-century Italian theatrical phrase *far fiasco* literally meaning 'to make a bottle', which was idiomatic for 'to be a disaster'

fib
noun a lie about something that's not very important
Word building: **fib** *verb* (**fibbed, fibbing**) **fibber** *noun*
Word history: short for *fibble-fable*, reduplication of *fable*

fibre (fuy-buh)
noun **1** a fine thread of wool, cotton or other material
2 the part of food that can't be digested: *Celery has a lot of **fibre**.*
Word use: The US spelling is **fiber**.
Word history: Middle English, from Latin word meaning 'fibre', 'filament'

fibreglass
noun material made of fine glass fibres which is used to insulate buildings against heat and cold or mixed with plastic and used to make surfboards and boats
Word history: Trademark

fibro
noun Australian, NZ strong building material made of asbestos and cement
Word history: Trademark

fibrous
adjective stringy or indigestible

fibula (fib-yuh-luh)
noun **1** *Anatomy* the outer and thinner of the two bones of the lower leg
2 *Zoology* a similar bone of the leg or hind limb of other animals
Noun forms: The plural is **fibulae** (fib-yuh-lee) or **fibulas**.
Word history: from Latin word meaning 'clasp', 'buckle', 'pin'

fickle
adjective changeable or likely to have changes of mind: *a **fickle** wind | a **fickle** friend* (***capricious, flighty, mercurial, temperamental, unfaithful***)
Word building: **fickleness** *noun*
Word history: from Old English word meaning 'deceitful', 'treacherous'

fiction
noun a story which isn't true but is made up from the imagination
Word use: The opposite is **nonfiction**.
Word building: **fictional** *adjective*
Word history: Middle English, from Latin word meaning 'a making', 'fashioning'

fictitious
adjective not real or genuine: *a **fictitious** character* (***fanciful, imaginary, made-up, mythical***)
Word history: from Latin word meaning 'artificial'

fiddle
verb **1** to move your hands around restlessly
2 to play a violin
noun **3** a violin
phrase **4 fiddle with**, to play around with or attempt to make (something) work
5 fit as a fiddle, in very good health
6 play second fiddle, to take an unimportant or minor part
Word building: **fiddler** *noun*
Word history: Middle English

fiddly
adjective needing to be done with care and practice (***complicated, convoluted, elaborate, intricate, involved***)

fidelity (fuh-del-uh-tee)
noun **1** the strict carrying out of promises, duties, etc.
2 loyalty
3 faithfulness in marriage
4 strict holding to truth or fact: *The **fidelity** of people concerns their honesty and truthfulness. | The **fidelity** of descriptions has to do with their likeness to the original.*
5 *Electronics* the ability of an amplifier, transmitter, radio, etc., to reproduce a high quality sound
Noun forms: The plural is **fidelities**.
Word use: The opposite of definition 2 is **disloyalty**.
Word history: from Latin word meaning 'faithfulness'

fidget (fij-uht)
verb **1** to move about restlessly (***squirm, toss and turn, wriggle, writhe***)
noun **2** someone who fidgets
phrase **3 the fidgets**, restlessness because you're bored or nervous
Word building: **fidgety** *adjective*
Word history: obsolete *fidge*, variant of dialect *fitch*

field
noun **1** a piece of open ground or space: *a **field** of wheat | a football **field***
2 an area of interest or activity: *to study in the **field** of chemistry*
3 *Physics* an area or space influenced by some force or thing: *an electric **field** | a magnetic **field** | a gravitational **field***
4 *Computers* an area on a record that has been specified in some way
verb **5** to stop or catch the ball in cricket and other similar sports
adjective **6** happening on a sports field rather than on a running track: *Long jump is a **field** event.*

Word building: **fielder** *noun*
Word history: Middle English and Old English

field day
noun **1** a day spent in outdoor activities or sports
2 a day when scientific explorations, investigations, etc., are carried on in the field
3 an occasion of total enjoyment, amusement, etc.

field glasses
plural noun → **binoculars**

fiend (feend)
noun **1** an evil spirit
2 a nuisance or troublemaker
3 someone who spends a lot of time or energy in playing a game or sport: *a chess **fiend***

Word history: Old English *fēond*

fiendish
adjective evil or cruel

fierce
adjective **1** wild or violent: ***fierce** animals | **fierce** winds* (***ferocious, forceful, furious, intense, violent***)
2 very strong or intense: ***fierce** competition for the prize*

Word building: **fiercely** *adverb* **fierceness** *noun*
Word history: Middle English, from Old French, from Latin word meaning 'wild', 'fierce', 'cruel'

fiery (fuy-uh-ree)
adjective **1** having the bright colour or intense heat of fire: ***fiery** red* (***blazing, scorching***)
2 showing strong feelings: *a **fiery** speech*

Adjective forms: **fierier**, **fieriest**

fiesta (fee-es-tuh)
noun a holiday or festival, especially on a religious occasion

Word history: Spanish, from Latin word meaning 'festive'

fife
noun a high-pitched flute often played in military bands

Word history: from German word meaning 'pipe'

fifteen
noun **1** a cardinal number, ten plus five (10 + 5)
2 a symbol for this number, as 15 or XV
3 a set of fifteen people or things, as a Rugby Union team
adjective **4** amounting to fifteen in number

Word building: **fifteenth** *adjective* **fifteenth** *noun*
Word history: Old English *fīf* five + *-tēne* -teen

fifth
adjective **1** next after the fourth
2 being one of five equal parts
noun **3** a fifth part, especially of one ($\frac{1}{5}$)
4 the fifth member of a series
5 *Music* a note on the fifth degree from a given note (counted as the first)

Word history: Old English *fifta*

fifty
noun **1** a cardinal number, ten times five (10 × 5)
2 a symbol for this number, as 50 or L
3 a set of fifty persons or things
4 fifties, the numbers from 50 to 59 of a series, especially the years of someone's age or the years of a century
adjective **5** amounting to fifty in number

Noun forms: The plural is **fifties.**
Word building: **fiftieth** *adjective* **fiftieth** *noun*
Word history: Old English *fīf* five + *-tig* -ty

fig
noun a small, soft, pear-shaped fruit containing many tiny seeds which is eaten fresh or dried

Word history: Middle English, from Old French, from Latin

fight
noun **1** a quarrel, especially one in which people attack each other physically: *a **fight** in the playground* (***brawl, conflict, fray, skirmish***)
2 an intense effort to overcome something: *the **fight** against poverty* (***battle, struggle***)
verb **3** to try to defeat: *to **fight** feelings of hunger*
4 to take part in a physical conflict: *We **fought** to the end.* (***come to blows, grapple, scuffle, struggle, tussle***)
phrase **5 fight it out**, to struggle till a clear result is reached

Verb forms: I **fought**, I have **fought**, I am **fighting**
Word building: **fighter** *noun*
Word history: Old English *fe(o)htan*

figment
noun something that's only imaginary: *a **figment** of your imagination*

Word history: Latin *figmentum* image, fiction, anything made

figurative (fig-yuh-ruh-tiv, fig-uh-ruh-tiv)
adjective **1** involving a figure of speech, especially a metaphor: ***figurative** expression* (***metaphorical***)
2 representing by means of a figure or likeness, as you do in drawing or sculpture
3 representing by a figure or emblem

figuratively / literally

These words have opposite meanings.

If someone is speaking **figuratively**, then they are giving words an abstract or imaginative meaning rather than the ordinary one. So, for example, if someone says 'you're being led up the garden path' then they mean that you're being deceived.

If you take something **literally** then you take it at face value. So, for example, if someone offered 'to lead you up the garden path', you would follow them.

figure
noun **1** a symbol that stands for a number: *the **figure** 3*
2 an amount or sum of money: *They paid a large **figure** for the new car.*
3 a shape, form, or pattern: *The dancer has a graceful **figure**. | The **figures** on my socks are squares and triangles.* (***design***, ***outline***)
4 a person or character: *The Prime Minister is an important **figure**.*
5 figures, calculations or sums: *I'm not good at **figures**.*
verb **6** to work out or calculate: *to **figure** the cost to be $150* (***compute***, ***count***, ***make***, ***reckon***)
phrase **7 figure out**, to understand or decide: *I can't **figure out** where I made the mistake in this sum.* (***puzzle out***, ***work out***)
Word history: Middle English, from French, from Latin word meaning 'form', 'shape'

figurehead
noun **1** someone who has an important position in an organisation but has no real power
2 a carved figure, often a woman, which decorates the bow of a sailing ship

figure of speech
noun an expression in which words are used out of their usual meaning for special effect, like a metaphor or simile: *Calling it a one-horse town was just a **figure** of speech.*

figurine (fig-yooh-reen)
noun a small statue or model
Word history: French, from Italian word meaning 'little figure'

filament
noun a very thin thread: *a **filament** of cotton | The wire **filament** in a light bulb glows when electricity passes through it.*
Word building: **filamentous** *adjective*
Word history: Late Latin, from Latin word meaning 'thread'

filch
verb Colloquial to steal, especially something of small value (***lift***, ***pilfer***)
Word building: **filcher** *noun*

file[1]
noun **1** an orderly collection of papers or the folder they are kept in
2 an ordered collection of data stored on tape or disk for a computer
3 a line of people or things one behind the other: *to stand in single **file*** (***queue***, ***rank***, ***row***, ***string***)
verb **4** to put or arrange in a file: *to **file** letters in order according to the date they were received* (***classify***, ***grade***, ***group***, ***sort***)
5 to walk or march one after the other
phrase **6 on file**, neatly arranged for easy use
Word history: French word meaning 'thread', 'string' from Latin

file[2]
noun a steel tool whose surface is covered with ridges for smoothing or cutting metal and other materials
Word building: **file** *verb*
Word history: dialect Old English *fil*

filename
noun Computers a sequence of characters that identifies a file on a computer

file transfer protocol
noun → **ftp**

filial (fil-ee-uhl)
adjective **1** having to do with a son or daughter: ***filial** duty*
2 being a child to a parent
Word history: Late Latin, from Latin *filius* son, *filia* daughter

filibuster (fil-uh-bus-tuh)
verb to delay the business in a parliament by making long speeches
Word history: Spanish, from Dutch word meaning 'freebooter' (a pirate or buccaneer)

filigree (fil-uh-gree)
noun a delicate lacelike design made out of metal thread, used in jewellery
Word building: **filigree** *adjective* **filigreed** *adjective*
Word history: French, from Italian

fill
verb **1** to supply or have as much of something as can be held: *to **fill** the bath to the top*
2 to take up all the space or time: *Smoke **filled** the room. | The movie was **filled** with excitement.*
3 to take or occupy: *to apply to **fill** the position of caretaker*
noun **4** earth and rocks used to fill a hole in the ground
phrase **5 fill in**,
a to complete by writing in the blank spaces: *to **fill in** an entry form for the competition*
b to stand in for, or replace: *The principal **filled in** for our teacher when he was away sick.*
6 fill out,
a to stretch: *The wind **filled out** the sails.*
b to become larger or grow fat: *Her figure has **filled out** lately.*
c to finish the details of: *to **fill out** a design*
7 fill the bill, to be just what is needed (***qualify***, ***serve***, ***suffice***, ***suit***)
Word history: Old English *fyllan*

fillet
noun a slice of fish or meat without the bone
Word building: **fillet** *verb*
Word history: Middle English, from French word meaning 'little thread', from Latin

filling
noun something put in to fill something: *The pie has a lemon **filling**. | I have a **filling** in one of my teeth.*

filly
noun a female horse less than four years old
Noun forms: The plural is **fillies**.
Word history: Scandinavian

film
noun **1** a thin sheet or layer of material: *to wrap sandwiches in plastic **film** | a **film** of oil on water* (***coating***, ***glaze***, ***skin***, ***veneer***)
2 material which is sensitive to light and is used in a camera for taking photographs
3 a moving picture which is shown on a screen: *to see a **film** about life in China* (***flick***, ***picture***, ***movie***)
Word building: **film** *verb*
Word history: Old English *filmen*

filmography
noun a listing of films selected on the basis of containing the work of a particular actor, director, etc., or of dealing with a particular subject

Word building: **filmographic**, **filmographical** *adjective* **filmographer** *noun*

filmy
adjective light and transparent: *The dancers' costumes were made of **filmy** material.*

Adjective forms: **filmier**, **filmiest**
Word building: **filminess** *noun*

filo pastry (fee-loh pay-stree, fuy-loh)
noun a very thin pastry made from flour and water, often used in Greek cookery

filter
noun **1** a device for straining liquids or air to remove unwanted material: *A **filter** in a swimming pool keeps the water clean.*
verb **2** to remove by the action of a filter: *to **filter** debris from the water*
3 to pass through a filter: *to **filter** liquid*

Word history: Middle English, from Old French, from Medieval Latin word meaning 'felt' (used as a filter), from Germanic

filth
noun something that is disgustingly dirty, repulsive or obscene

Word history: from Old English word meaning 'foul'

filthy
adjective **1** very dirty: ***filthy** clothes* (***grimy***, ***grotty***, ***grubby***, ***polluted***)
phrase **2 filthy rich**, very or extremely rich

Adjective forms: **filthier**, **filthiest**
Word building: **filthiness** *noun*

filtrate
noun the liquid which has been strained through a filter

filtration
noun the process of filtering

fin
noun **1** one of the flap-like structures on the body of a fish which is used for moving through the water
2 a small triangular or fin-shaped part on a surfboard, plane or boat to help with steering or balancing

Word history: Old English *finn*

final
adjective **1** last or coming at the end: *the **final** match of the season | I say 'no', and my word is **final**.*
noun **2** the one at the end of a series, especially of races or competitions: *to play in the grand **final***

Word building: **finality** *noun* **finally** *adverb*
Word history: Middle English, from Latin word meaning 'end'

finale (fuh-nah-lee)
noun the last part of a concert, opera or ballet (***close***, ***conclusion***, ***finish***)

Word history: Italian

finalise
verb to end or conclude

Word use: You can also use **finalize**.

finalist
noun a competitor who takes part in the last round of a contest

finance
noun **1** the management of money: *an expert in banking and **finance***
2 finances, money supplies or revenue: *I'm sorry I can't lend you any money as my **finances** are rather low.*
verb **3** to fund or pay for: *to **finance** a new business venture*

Word building: **financial** *adjective*
Word history: Middle English, from Old French word meaning 'ending', 'payment', 'revenue'

financial year (fuh-nan-shuhl year)
noun any 12-monthly period at the end of which a government, company, etc., balances its accounts and determines its financial condition (***fiscal year***)

financier (fuh-nan-see-uh)
noun someone whose business is lending money

Word history: from French word meaning 'finance'

finch
noun a type of small bird with a large beak for eating seeds

Word history: Old English *finc*

find
verb **1** to come upon by chance or after a search: *to **find** shells at the beach | to **find** a lost umbrella* (***detect***, ***discover***, ***locate***, ***trace***, ***unearth***)
2 to discover or learn: *to **find** the answer to a question*
noun **3** a valuable discovery
phrase **4 find out**, to discover by asking, searching or experiencing
5 find your feet, to be able to act without help from other people
6 find yourself, to learn what you are capable of

Verb forms: I **found**, I have **found**, I am **finding**
Word building: **finder** *noun*
Word history: Old English *findan*

findings
plural noun data or information

fine[1]
adjective **1** excellent or of high quality: *a **fine** musician* (***distinguished***, ***great***, ***outstanding***)
2 sunny, or without rain: ***fine** weather* (***balmy***, ***fair***, ***mild***, ***sunny***, ***temperate***)
3 very thin or slender: *a **fine** thread*
4 made up of tiny particles: *Sugar is **fine** but salt is **finer**.*
5 sharp: *a **fine** point on a pencil*
6 well or healthy (***fit***, ***robust***, ***sound***)

Word use: The opposite of definitions 3 and 4 is **coarse**.
Word history: Middle English, from Old French, from Latin word meaning 'finish'

fine[2]
noun a sum of money paid as a penalty for doing something wrong

Word building: **fine** *verb*
Word history: Middle English, from Old French, from Latin word meaning 'boundary', 'end', Medieval Latin word meaning 'settlement', 'fine'

fine arts
plural noun those arts, such as architecture, sculpture, painting, music, etc., which aim to express qualities of beauty

fine motor skills
plural noun those physical skills required for coordinated small muscle movements, such as picking up small items between the thumb and a finger
Word use: Compare this with **gross motor skills**.

finery
noun fine or showy clothes, ornaments, etc.

finesse (fuh-nes)
noun fine skill or clever management: *to conduct business dealings with* ***finesse***
Word history: French

finger
noun **1** any one of the five, long, end parts of your hand, especially one that's not your thumb
2 something shaped like a finger: *the* ***finger*** *of a glove | a* ***finger*** *of toast*
verb **3** to touch lightly: *Don't* ***finger*** *your food.* (***feel***, ***handle***, ***stroke***)
phrase **4 burn your fingers**, to get hurt or suffer from something you have done
5 not lift a finger, to do nothing
Word history: Old English

fingerprint
noun the pattern made by the curved lines on the tips of your fingers

finicky
adjective **1** very fussy or choosy
2 fiddly or full of small, unimportant detail: *This embroidery is very* ***finicky***.

finish
verb **1** to come to an end (***close***, ***conclude***)
2 to bring to an end (***complete***, ***terminate***)
noun **3** the end or conclusion (***close***, ***finale***, ***termination***)
4 the surface layer of wood or metal or the substance put on it: *to polish the car to give it a brilliant* ***finish***
phrase **5 finish off**,
a to totally use up or complete: *to* ***finish off*** *your dinner*
b to kill or destroy (***assassinate***, ***execute***, ***kill***, ***murder***, ***put down***, ***slay***)
Word history: Middle English, from French, from Latin word meaning 'bound', 'end'

finite (fuy-nuyt)
adjective having limits which can be measured or counted: *Is the number of stars in the universe* ***finite****?*
Word use: The opposite is **infinite**.
Word building: **finitely** *adverb* **finiteness** *noun*
Word history: from Latin word meaning 'bounded'

fink
noun Chiefly US Colloquial a contemptible person, especially someone who goes back on a promise
Word history: ? German slang *Fink* a student not belonging to the student's association

fiord (fee-awd)
noun → **fjord**

fir
noun a tree, like a traditional Christmas tree, which has needle-like leaves and produces cones
Word history: Old English *fyrh*

> **fir / fur**
> Don't confuse **fir** with **fur**, which is hair on an animal.

fire
noun **1** the heat, light and flames produced by burning: *You could see the* ***fire*** *from far away.*
2 a mass of burning material, such as in a fireplace: *to light a* ***fire*** *to keep warm*
3 enthusiasm or passion: *a speech full of* ***fire***
4 the shooting of guns: *to open* ***fire*** *on the enemy soldiers*
verb **5** to set on fire or make very hot: *to* ***fire*** *the furnace | to* ***fire*** *pottery in a kiln*
6 to shoot: *to* ***fire*** *a gun*
7 *Colloquial* to dismiss or sack from a job: *The boss* ***fired*** *him for not doing his work properly.*
8 to inspire or excite: *The speaker's words* ***fired*** *the audience with enthusiasm.*
phrase **9 catch fire**, to start burning
10 play with fire, to play with something dangerous in a careless way
11 under fire,
a exposed to or in the line of enemy fire
b under attack or suffering criticism from someone
Word building: **fiery** *adjective* (**fierier**, **fieriest**)
Word history: Old English *fȳr*

firearm
noun any type of gun

firebreak
noun a strip of land which has been cleared of grass and trees to stop a fire from spreading

fire brigade
noun an organisation set up to fight fires

fire-engine
noun a motor vehicle equipped with water and hoses for fighting fires

fire-escape
noun a fireproof staircase often on the outside of a building by means of which people can escape if there is a fire

fire extinguisher
noun a device for putting out fires, that you can carry around

firefighter
noun a person employed to put out or prevent fires
Word use: You can also use **fireman** or **fire officer**.

> **firefighter / fireman**
> **Firefighter** is now the preferred word for a person who fights fires. It is replacing **fireman** since it allows for the possibility that both men and women can do this job.

firefly
noun a soft-bodied, nocturnal beetle with light-producing organs. A luminous larva or wingless female is called a **glow-worm**.

Noun forms: The plural is **fireflies**.

fireman
noun **1** → **firefighter**
2 a person employed to tend fires, such as the fire on a steam-engine (***stoker***)

Noun forms: The plural is **firemen**.

fireplace
noun an open place, built of brick or stone, for lighting fires in

fireproof
adjective not able to burn or be set on fire easily: ***fireproof*** *walls* | ***fireproof*** *clothing*

firestick farming
noun the burning of areas of bush using a lighted stick, traditionally used by Aboriginal peoples, to make way for new grass to grow as a food source for kangaroos, wallabies, etc.

firestorm
noun **1** an atmospheric phenomenon caused by a large fire, as after the mass bombing of a city, in which a rising column of air above the fire draws in strong winds creating an inferno
2 a huge and uncontrollable bushfire

firewall
noun Computers software designed to prevent unauthorised connection to a computer on a network

fireworks
plural noun **1** containers filled with a powder that burns or explodes giving out brilliantly coloured sparks
2 an outburst of anger or bad temper

firey (fuy-uh-ree, fuy-ree)
noun Colloquial a firefighter

Word use: You can also use **firie**.

firing line
noun **1** a position in a battle in which you are close enough to fire upon the enemy, etc.
2 the troops that fight in such a position
3 the forefront or most vulnerable part of any activity

firing squad
noun a group of soldiers, etc., with the duty of putting a condemned person to death by shooting them

firm[1]
adjective **1** solid, hard, or stiff (***rigid***, ***tough***)
2 not wavering in your beliefs or opinions (***reliable***, ***staunch***, ***steadfast***, ***stout-hearted***, ***sturdy***)
3 strong, definite, and unchanging: *to speak in a* ***firm*** *voice* | *a* ***firm*** *belief* (***fixed***, ***secure***, ***stable***, ***steady***)

Word building: **firm** *verb* **firm** *adverb* **firmly** *adverb*
Word history: Latin *firmus*

firm[2]
noun a business company (***corporation***, ***organisation***, ***outfit***, ***syndicate***)

Word history: Italian, Spanish word meaning 'signature', from Latin word meaning 'confirm'

firmament (ferm-uh-muhnt)
noun in poetry, the sky or the heavens

Word history: Middle English, from Late Latin word meaning 'firmament', Latin word meaning 'a support', 'prop'

first
adjective **1** being number one or coming before all others in time, order or importance: *She was the* ***first*** *one to arrive.*
adverb **2** before anyone or anything else in time, order or importance: *He arrived* ***first***.
3 for the first time: *They* ***first*** *met at a party.*
phrase **4 first up**, before all others: *You're performing* ***first up***.

Word building: **first** *noun* **firstly** *adverb*
Word history: Old English *fyrst*

first aid
noun emergency treatment given to someone who is hurt or taken ill

first-class
adjective **1** of the best quality, best-equipped or most expensive: *a* ***first-class*** *restaurant*
adverb **2** in the best part of a vehicle: *to travel* ***first-class***

firsthand
adverb directly from the source: *We got the information* ***firsthand***.

Word building: **firsthand** *adjective*

first name
noun the name that comes before the family name or surname: *My* ***first name*** *is Mario and my family name is Rossi.*

Word use: You can also use **given name**, which is more appropriate when the family name comes first, as with some Asian names.

first person
noun the class of a pronoun or verb in which the person speaking is the subject

> A story such as this, which is told from the narrator's point of view, using such pronouns as *I*, *we* and *me*, is said to be in the **first person**.
>
> *Scenes of violent death leave me unmoved.*
>
> *But we were quite unprepared for the sight that greeted us as I opened the door to my office.*
>
> For more information, look up **person in grammar**.

fiscal (fis-kuhl)
adjective **1** having to do with the public treasury or revenues
2 having to do with financial matters in general

Word history: from Latin word meaning 'belonging to the state treasury'

fish
noun **1** a cold-blooded animal which lives in water, breathes through gills, swims by means of fins and has scales on its body
verb **2** to catch or try to catch fish
3 to feel around for and find: *to* ***fish*** *some money out of your pocket*
phrase **4 fish for**, to try to get indirectly: *to* ***fish for*** *information*

Noun forms: The plural is **fishes** or **fish**.
Word history: Old English *fisc*

fisherman
noun someone who fishes, either as a job or for pleasure

Noun forms: The plural is **fishermen**.
Word use: A similar word for someone who fishes for pleasure is **angler**.

Because **fisherman** seems to exclude women, some people use the term **fisher**.

fishy
adjective **1** having a fishlike smell or taste
2 *Colloquial* strange or causing suspicion: *There was something **fishy** about his disappearance, so I wondered what he was up to.*

Adjective forms: **fishier**, **fishiest**

fission
noun **1** *Biology* the division of an organism into new organisms, such as in the process of reproduction
2 *Physics* the splitting of the nucleus of a heavy atom, such as uranium, to form the nuclei of lighter atoms

Word history: from Latin word meaning 'a cleaving'

fissure (<u>fish</u>-uh)
noun a crack or split: *The rock had a deep **fissure** in it.* (***break***, ***crevice***, ***rift***)

Word building: **fissure** *verb*
Word history: French, from Latin word meaning 'a cleft'

fist
noun your hand when the fingers are closed tightly into the palm

Word history: Old English *fȳst*

fisticuffs (<u>fis</u>-tee-kufs)
plural noun fighting with the fists

fistula (<u>fis</u>-chuh-luh)
noun Medicine **1** an abnormal passage or duct, present from birth or caused by disease or injury, leading from an organ to another organ, to a body cavity, or to the exterior of the body
2 such a passage surgically created for a medical procedure

Noun forms: The plural is **fistulas** or **fistulae** (<u>fis</u>-chuh-lee).

fit[1]
adjective **1** suitable or good enough: *Those clothes are not **fit** to be worn.*
2 right or proper: *Picking up papers is a **fit** punishment for littering.*
3 healthy (***robust***, ***sound***, ***well***)
verb **4** to be suitable or the right size or shape for (***fill the bill***, ***qualify***, ***serve***, ***suffice***, ***suit***)
5 to make or have space for: *We can **fit** five people in the car.*
6 to put into place: *I am **fitting** a new handle on to this door.*
noun **7** the way in which something fits: *This shirt is a perfect **fit**.*
phrase **8 fit in**, to be or become suited: *Do you think this chair **fits in** with the rest of the furniture?*
9 fit out, to provide with clothing or equipment

Adjective forms: **fitter**, **fittest**
Verb forms: I **fitted**, I have **fitted**, I am **fitting**
Word building: **fitter** *noun* **fitness** *noun*
Word history: Middle English *fyt*

fit[2]
noun **1** a sudden outburst: *She hit him in a **fit** of rage.* | *He had a **fit** of coughing.*
2 a sudden sickness in which your body twists uncontrollably and you sometimes become unconscious

Word history: Old English *fitt* fight, struggle

fitful
adjective stopping and starting: *a **fitful** sleep* (***erratic***, ***intermittent***, ***irregular***, ***sporadic***)

Word building: **fitfully** *adverb*

fitting
adjective **1** suitable or proper
noun **2** a trying on of clothes for a proper fit
3 the size of clothes or shoes: *What is your **fitting**?*
4 fittings, furnishings or equipment: *Their house has beautiful **fittings**.*

five
noun **1** a cardinal number, four plus one (4 + 1)
2 the symbol for this number, as 5 or V
3 a set of five persons or things
adjective **4** amounting to five in number

Word building: **fifth** *adjective* **fifth** *noun*
Word history: Old English *fīf*

fix
verb **1** to make firm or put securely in place: *We've got to **fix** the poles into the ground before we put up the tent.* (***secure***, ***stabilise***, ***steady***)
2 to settle or decide: *Let's **fix** a price for this car.*
3 to mend or repair (***correct***, ***improve***, ***patch up***, ***restore***)
noun **4** *Colloquial* a difficult situation: *I'm in such a **fix** that I don't know what to do.*
phrase **5 fix on**, to decide on (***choose***, ***pick***, ***prefer***, ***select***)
6 fix up,
a to arrange properly: *Please **fix up** the books on your desk.*
b *Australian, NZ* to put right; solve or repair: *Can you **fix up** the mess I've made of this job?*

Word building: **fixed** *adjective* **fixedly** *adverb* **fixer** *noun*
Word history: Middle English, from Latin word meaning 'fix'

fixation (fik-<u>say</u>-shuhn)
noun **1** the act or result of fixing
2 *Psychology* a stopping of the emotional development of someone's personality at an early stage

Word history: Middle English, from Latin word meaning 'fix'

fixed asset
noun Commerce a business asset, such as land or machinery, which is bought for continued use in manufacture

Word use: You can also use **capital asset**.

fixed interest
noun an interest rate which is payable on a loan and which does not change for the entire period of the loan

fixture
noun **1** something fixed in place, especially in a house or other building
2 a sporting event that is to be held on a particular date

fizz
verb to bubble and make a hissing sound: *I like it when lemonade **fizzes** up your nose.*
Word building: **fizz** *noun* **fizzy** *adjective* (**fizzier**, **fizziest**)

fizzle
verb **1** to make a hissing or spluttering sound
phrase **2 fizzle out**, *Colloquial* to fail after a good start: *Our plans have **fizzled out**.* (***collapse***, ***fail***, ***fall through***, ***miscarry***)
Word building: **fizzle** *noun*
Word history: obsolete *fise* from Scandinavian

fjord (fee-awd)
noun a deep, narrow inlet of the sea with steep cliffs on each side: *Norway is famous for its **fjords**.*
Word use: You can also use **fiord**.
Word history: Norwegian

flab
noun *Colloquial* extra fat on your body
Word building: **flabbiness** *noun*

flabbergast (flab-uh-gast, flab-uh-gahst)
verb to astound or overcome with surprise
Word building: **flabbergasted** *adjective*
Word history: perhaps *flabb(y)* + *aghast*

flabby
adjective having soft fatty flesh: ***flabby** arms* | *a **flabby** man*
Adjective forms: **flabbier**, **flabbiest**
Word building: **flabbiness** *noun*
Word history: compare earlier *flappy* (from *flap* + *-y* in same sense

flaccid (flas-uhd)
adjective soft and loose: ***flaccid** muscles* (***flabby***, ***limp***, ***slack***)
Word history: Latin

flag[1]
noun **1** a piece of cloth with a particular design used as a symbol of a country or an organisation, or as a signal: *The Australian **flag** has the Southern Cross on it.* | *A red **flag** is used to signal danger.*
verb **2** to signal, mark or warn with a flag
Verb forms: I **flagged**, I have **flagged**, I am **flagging**
Word history: apparently blend of *flap*, noun, and obsolete *fag*, noun, flap, flag

flag[2]
verb to grow weak or tired: *The walkers began to **flag** at the end of the day.*
Verb forms: I **flagged**, I have **flagged**, I am **flagging**
Word history: late Middle English *flagge* turf, probably from Scandinavian

flag[3]
noun **1** a flagstone
verb **2** to pave with flagstones
Verb forms: I **flagged**, I have **flagged**, I am **flagging**

flagellate (flaj-uh-layt)
verb **1** to whip, flog, or lash
adjective **2** *Biology* having long whip-like tails, called flagella, to swim with
Word use: You can also use **flagellated** for definition 2.
Word building: **flagellation** *noun*
Word history: from Latin word meaning 'whipped'

flagellum (fluh-jel-uhm)
noun a long tail which looks like a whip, that bacteria, sperm, protozoans, etc., use to swim with
Noun forms: The plural is **flagella** or **flagellums**.
Word history: from Latin word meaning 'whip', 'scourge'

flagon
noun a large bottle
Word history: Middle English, from Old French

flagrant (flay-gruhnt)
adjective obvious in a shameless way: *a **flagrant** lie* | ***flagrant** disobedience*
Word history: from Latin word meaning 'blazing', 'burning'

flagship
noun a ship which carries the commander of a fleet, squadron, etc., and flies this officer's flag

flail (flayl)
noun **1** a tool for threshing grain, consisting of a handle with a free-swinging stick
verb **2** to thresh with a flail
3 to hit or whip
4 to flap about: *She ran blindly with her arms **flailing**.*
Word history: Old English *flygel*

flair
noun **1** natural talent: *She has a **flair** for maths.*
2 smart style: *He dresses with **flair**.*
Word history: French word meaning 'smell', from Latin

> **flair / flare**
> Don't confuse **flair** with **flare**, which is a kind of light, usually short-lived and very bright.

flak
noun **1** anti-aircraft fire
2 strong criticism or abuse
Word history: from German, abbreviation of *Fl(ieger)a(bwehr)k(anone)* anti-aircraft gun

flake[1]
noun **1** a small, flat, thin piece of anything: *a **flake** of skin* | *a **flake** of snow*
verb **2** to peel off in flakes: *This paint is **flaking**.*
3 *Colloquial* to lie down or fall asleep from tiredness: *I **flaked** after the race.*
Word building: **flaky** *adjective* (**flakier**, **flakiest**)
Word history: Old English *flac-*, which occurs in *flacor* flying (said of arrows)

flake[2]
noun shark meat sold as food

flamboyant
adjective dazzlingly bright and showy (***eye-catching***, ***gaudy***, ***opulent***, ***ostentatious***, ***spectacular***)

Word use: The opposite of this is **understated**.
Word history: French, from Old French word meaning 'small flame'

flame
noun **1** a tongue of fire: ***Flames*** *licked around the base of the tree. | The candle burnt with a low* ***flame****.*
2 *Internet* an email expressing anger or hatred

Word building: **flame** *verb*
Word history: Middle English, from Old French, from Latin

flamenco (fluh-meng-koh)
noun a type of Spanish music or dance, especially of gypsy style

Noun forms: The plural is **flamencos**.

flameproof
adjective **1** not easily burnt: ***flameproof*** *clothing*
2 safe for use over flames: *a* ***flameproof*** *dish*

flame tree
noun an ornamental Australian tree with scarlet, bell-shaped flowers

Word use: You can also use **Illawarra flame tree**.

flamingo (fluh-ming-goh)
noun a water bird with a very long neck, long legs and dark pink feathers

Noun forms: The plural is **flamingos** or **flamingoes**.
Word history: Portuguese, from Spanish, from Provençal

flammable
adjective easily set on fire: *Be careful not to wear a* ***flammable*** *dressing gown.*

Word building: **flammability** *noun*

flammable / inflammable

There used to be just one word, **inflammable**, which referred to something which was likely to burst into flames. The in- of this word meant 'into'. But people confused it with in- meaning 'not', as in *insoluble* (not soluble). And so there was confusion about the label **inflammable**. Did it mean 'bursting into flames' or 'not bursting into flames'?

Because this confusion was dangerous it was decided to drop the label **inflammable** and invent a new word, **flammable**, about which there could be no mistake. So while you may still find the old word **inflammable** in its original meaning, it is now replaced by **flammable**. Something which doesn't burn is therefore not **flammable**.

flan
noun a large tart with a sweet or savoury filling

Word history: French

flange (flanj)
noun an edge, rim, or ridge on an object for keeping it in place, strengthening it, etc.

Word history: from Old French word meaning 'bend'

flank
noun **1** the side of an animal between the ribs and hip
2 the side of anything
verb **3** to be at the side of: *The president was* ***flanked*** *by two guards.*

Word history: Old English *flanc*, from Old French, from Germanic

flannel
noun **1** a warm soft cloth, usually made of wool: *a* ***flannel*** *suit*
2 a face washer

flannelette
noun a cotton cloth treated on one side to look and feel like flannel

flannel flower
noun an Australian plant with light-cream flowers and leaves that feel like flannel

flap
verb **1** to swing about loosely, especially with a noise: *The curtain is* ***flapping*** *in the wind.*
2 to move up and down: *The bird* ***flapped*** *its wings.* (***flutter***, ***wave***)
noun **3** something flat and thin that is joined to something else on one side only and hangs loose
4 *Colloquial* a feeling of nervousness or excitement: *Don't get yourself into a* ***flap****.*

Verb forms: I **flapped**, I have **flapped**, I am **flapping**
Word history: Middle English *flappe(n)*, probably of imitative origin

flare
verb **1** to burn brightly and suddenly: *The fire* ***flared*** *up.* (***blaze***, ***glow***, ***shine***, ***sparkle***)
2 to burst with a sudden strong feeling
3 to curve outwards like the end of a trumpet: *Her skirt* ***flared*** *at the bottom.*
noun **4** bright light used as a signal: *The stranded bushwalkers sent up a* ***flare****.*

Word history: originally meaning spread out, display; blend of *fly* and *bare*

flare / flair

Look up **flair / flare**.

flash
noun **1** a sudden short burst of flame or light: *a* ***flash*** *of lightning*
2 a short moment: *He was gone in a* ***flash****.*
3 a short, important piece of news on radio or television
adjective **4** quick or sudden: *a* ***flash*** *flood*

Word building: **flash** *verb*
Word history: Middle English *flasche(n)* rush (said of tidal waters); blend of *flow* (or *flood*) and *wash*

flashback
noun a part of a film or story that shows an event that happened at an earlier time

flash flood
noun a sudden, destructive short-lived flood, usually due to heavy rain

flashforward
noun a representation of an event or scene from some future time: *The film used a* ***flashforward*** *to show the future.*

flashlight
noun a bulb that gives a flash of very bright light, used when taking photographs inside or at night

flash memory
noun Computers a type of EEPROM which is erased and reprogrammed in large blocks, making it faster in the handling of large amounts of data

flash memory stick
noun → **memory stick**

flashpacker
noun Colloquial a backpacker who travels in relative luxury

Word building: **flashpacking** *noun*

flashy
adjective bright and showy: ***flashy*** *jewellery | a* ***flashy*** *car*

flask (flahsk)
noun a small flat bottle

Word history: Old English *flasce, flaxe*

flat[1]
adjective **1** even or smooth: *It is easier to run on* ***flat*** *ground.* (***horizontal***, ***level***)
2 lying spread out: *I found her* ***flat*** *on the bed.*
3 not high: *a shoe with* ***flat*** *heels*
4 emptied of air: *a* ***flat*** *tyre* (***deflated***)
5 clear and absolute: *He answered with a* ***flat*** *refusal.* (***definite***, ***firm***, ***outright***)
6 boring or dull (***humdrum***, ***monotonous***, ***stale***, ***tedious***)
7 no longer bubbly or fizzy
8 not shiny: ***flat*** *paint* (***dull***, ***lacklustre***, ***matt***)
9 lowered in pitch by a semitone: *The musical note B* ***flat*** *is a semitone lower than the note B.*
adverb **10** in a flat position: *Please lay the paper out* ***flat***.
noun **11** a flat side or part of anything: *She hit him with the* ***flat*** *of her hand.*
12 flat ground: *Be careful to stay on the* ***flat***.
13 a a note that is one semitone below a given note
b the music sign '♭' which lowers a note by a semitone when it is placed before it
phrase **14 fall flat**, to fail: *The party* ***fell flat***.
15 flat out,
a as fast or hard as possible
b very busy

Word use: The opposite of definitions 9 and 13 is **sharp**.
Word building: **flatly** *adverb* **flatness** *noun*
Word history: Middle English, from Scandinavian

flat[2]
noun **1** a group of rooms for living in, usually part of a larger building and often rented (***apartment***, ***home unit***, ***unit***)
verb Australian, NZ **2** to live in a flat: *I* ***flat*** *with two friends.*

Verb forms: I **flatted**, I have **flatted**, I am **flatting**
Word history: Old English *flet* floor, house, hall

flathead
noun any of various long fishes living on the sea bottom which have flattened, ridged heads

flatline
verb Colloquial to die: *In the movie the patient* ***flatlined*** *before they reached the hospital.*

Verb forms: he **flatlined**, he has **flatlined**, he is **flatlining**
Word history: This word is descriptive of the line that appears on a hospital monitor that is registering a person's heart or brain function. The line normally moves up and down, reflecting the person's heart or brain activity. If the person dies, the line becomes flat.

flat pack
noun a product which is sold in its unassembled pieces

flat rate
noun a rate of payment which is fixed at a single price and which is the same in all circumstances: *There is a* ***flat rate*** *of $80 per day for the hire of a car — nothing extra is charged for the number of kilometres you drive.*

flatter
verb **1** to try to please by compliments or praise even if you do not mean them (***butter up***, ***make up to***, ***soft-soap***, ***suck up to***, ***sweet-talk***)
2 to show or describe as being more attractive than is really so: *This photo* ***flatters*** *her.*

Word building: **flatterer** *noun* **flattery** *noun*
Word history: perhaps Old French *flat(t)er* caress with the hand, smooth, flatter, of Frankish origin

flatulence (flach-uh-luhns)
noun **1** bubbles of gas in your stomach, intestines, etc., causing burping or wind
2 talk that has little meaning, does not sound sincere or uses too many words

Word building: **flatulent** *adjective*
Word history: French, from Latin word meaning 'a blowing'

flaunt (flawnt)
verb to show off boldly: *She was always* ***flaunting*** *her parents' wealth.* (***demonstrate***, ***display***, ***exhibit***, ***parade***)

Word history: Scandinavian

flaunt / flout
Don't confuse **flaunt** with **flout.** To **flout** a rule is to deliberately ignore it. It rhymes with *stout*:
You have flouted the school rule that you must wear a tie.

flautist (flaw-tuhst)
noun someone who plays the flute

Word history: from Italian word meaning 'flute'

flavour
noun **1** taste, especially the special taste that something has: *Do you like the* ***flavour*** *of lemon?*
2 the nature or quality of something: *The outdoor tables gave the restaurant a French* ***flavour***. (***air***, ***aspect***, ***character***, ***feel***, ***feeling***, ***quality***, ***spirit***)
verb **3** to add flavour to: *She* ***flavoured*** *the stew with salt and pepper.* (***season***)

Word use: You can also use **flavor**.
Word building: **flavouring** *noun*
Word history: Middle English, from Old French, from Latin word meaning 'emit an odour'

flaw
noun **1** a fault: *Laziness is the biggest* ***flaw*** *in my character.*
2 a crack or scratch: *There is a* ***flaw*** *in this plate.*

Word building: **flaw** *verb*
Word history: Middle English, from Scandinavian

flaw / floor
Don't confuse **flaw** with **floor**. The **floor** of a room is what you walk on.

flax
noun a plant with narrow leaves and blue flowers, grown for its fibre which is made into linen and for its seeds which contain oil
Word history: Old English *fleax*

flaxen
adjective having a pale yellow colour: ***flaxen** hair*

flay
verb **1** to strip off the skin or outer covering of
2 to criticise or scold unmercifully
Word history: Old English *flēan*

flea
noun a small wingless insect which moves by jumping and which sucks blood from mammals and birds
Word history: Old English *flēah, flēa*

flea market
noun a market where usually second-hand or cheap articles are sold

fleck
noun a spot or small patch of something
Word building: **fleck** *verb*
Word history: Scandinavian

fled
verb past tense and past participle of **flee**

fledgling
noun **1** a young bird that has just become able to fly
2 someone who is young or new to something
Word use: You can also use **fledgeling**.

flee
verb to run away or escape (***abscond**, **elope**, **nick off**, **take to your heels***)
Verb forms: I **fled**, I have **fled**, I am **fleeing**
Word history: Old English *flēon*

fleece
noun **1** the coat of wool that covers a sheep or other animal
verb **2** to take money or belongings from by cheating: *They **fleeced** him of all his earnings.* (***cheat**, **deceive**, **defraud**, **rip off**, **swindle**, **trick***)
Word building: **fleecy** *adjective* (**fleecier**, **fleeciest**) **fleeciness** *noun*
Word history: Old English *flēos*

fleet[1]
noun **1** a large group of naval ships, usually under the command of one officer
2 a group of other boats, aeroplanes, or vehicles: *a **fleet** of company cars*
Word use: Compare this with **flotilla**.
Word history: Old English *flēot* ship, craft, from *flēotan* float

fleet[2]
adjective very fast or swift
Word building: **fleetness** *noun*
Word history: Old English *flēotan* float

fleeting
adjective passing quickly: *He only gave my homework a **fleeting** glance.* (***brief**, **momentary**, **transient**, **transitory***)

flesh
noun **1** the soft part of an animal body, which is made up of fat and muscle
2 the human body when you think of it as separate from the mind or the spirit: *Meat feeds the **flesh** and books feed the mind.*
3 the soft part of a fruit or vegetable
phrase **4 in the flesh,**
a alive
b in person: *I saw my favourite TV star **in the flesh**.*
5 pound of flesh, what a person is owed, taken without mercy or regard to the feelings of others
Word history: Old English *flǣsc*

flew (flooh)
verb past tense of **fly**[1]

flew / flu / flue
Don't confuse **flew** with **flu** or **flue**.
Flu is the short form of **influenza**.
A **flue** is a passage made for air or gases.

flex
verb **1** to bend: *to **flex** a piece of wire* (***curl**, **loop**, **turn***)
noun **2** a cord containing an electric wire
Word use: The opposite of definition 1 is **straighten**.
Word history: Latin

flexible
adjective **1** easily bent or stretched: ***flexible** wire* (***pliable**, **supple***)
2 able to be changed easily: *My plans are **flexible**.* (***alterable**, **malleable***)
Word use: The opposite of this is **rigid**.
Word building: **flexibility** *noun* **flexibly** *adverb*
Word history: Latin *flexibilis*

flexitime
noun an arrangement in which workers can choose their starting and finishing times, as long as they work the right number of hours altogether

flick
noun a sudden light blow: *He gave the table a **flick** with the duster.*
Word building: **flick** *verb*
Word history: Middle English *flykke*; apparently imitative

flicker
verb **1** to burn unsteadily: *The candle **flickered**.* (***glimmer**, **twinkle***)
2 to move quickly to and fro
Word building: **flicker** *noun*
Word history: Old English *flicorian* flutter

flight[1]
noun **1** an act of flying or the way in which something flies: *The **flight** of my paper plane wasn't what I expected.*
2 a number of things flying together: *A **flight** of gulls landed on the water.*
3 a journey by aeroplane
4 a series of steps or stairs

Word history: Old English *flyht*

flight[2]
noun **1** a running away or fleeing
phrase **2 put to flight**, to force to run away: *to **put** an invading army **to flight***
3 take flight, to run away

Word history: Middle English

flight attendant
noun a person employed to look after passengers on an aircraft

flighty
adjective often changing your mind or feelings: *I wish you'd stop being so **flighty**.* (***capricious***, ***fickle***, ***frivolous***, ***mercurial***, ***temperamental***)

Adjective forms: **flightier**, **flightiest**

flimsy
adjective **1** not strongly made: *a **flimsy** fence* (***delicate***, ***fragile***)
2 weak or not carefully thought out: *a **flimsy** excuse* (***feeble***, ***insubstantial***, ***slight***, ***tenuous***)

Adjective forms: **flimsier**, **flimsiest**
Word use: The opposite of definition 1 is **sturdy**. | The opposite of definition 2 is **convincing** or **strong**.
Word building: **flimsiness** *noun*
Word history: *film* (by metathesis) + *-sy*, adjective suffix

flinch
verb to draw back from something dangerous, difficult, or unpleasant: *They did not **flinch** when they saw the enemy.* (***chicken out***, ***cower***, ***quail***, ***waver***)

Word history: perhaps nasalised variant of dialect *flitch* flit, shift (your) position

fling
verb **1** to throw, usually forcefully or impatiently: *He **flung** the blunt pencil to the floor.* (***chuck***, ***hurl***, ***pitch***, ***toss***)
2 to move quickly or violently: *She would **fling** out of the room when she was annoyed.*
noun **3** a time of pleasure or fun: *Let's have a last **fling** before the exams.*
4 an attempt or try: *I will have one more **fling** at jumping that height.*

Verb forms: I **flung**, I have **flung**, I am **flinging**
Word history: Middle English

flint
noun a hard kind of stone, which can start a fire when struck with steel

Word building: **flinty** *adjective*
Word history: Old English

flip
verb **1** to move or throw with a snap of a finger and thumb: *She **flipped** the coin to see who would go first.*
2 to move with a jerk: *He **flipped** over the pages of the book.*
noun **3** a flipping movement: *a **flip** of the wrist*
4 a somersault: *a backwards **flip***
phrase **5 flip your lid**, *Colloquial* to become angry

Verb forms: I **flipped**, I have **flipped**, I am **flipping**
Word history: probably imitative

flippant (flip-uhnt)
adjective not suitably serious: *This is not the time to make **flippant** remarks.*

Word building: **flippancy** *noun*

flipper
noun **1** the broad flat limb of an animal such as a seal or whale that is used for swimming
2 a piece of rubber shaped like a flipper and worn on your foot to help in swimming

flirt
verb to amuse yourself by pretending to be romantically interested in someone

Word building: **flirt** *noun* **flirtation** *noun* **flirtatious** *adjective*
Word history: imitative

flit
verb to move lightly and quickly: *The birds **flitted** from tree to tree.* (***dart***, ***flutter***)

Verb forms: I **flitted**, I have **flitted**, I am **flitting**
Word history: Middle English, from Scandinavian

float
verb **1** to rest or move gently on the top of a liquid: *He swam and then **floated** on his back.*
2 to move freely and easily: *The idea **floated** through her mind.* (***skim***, ***waft***)
noun **3** something that floats, such as an air-filled rubber mattress that you lie on in the water, or the cork on a fishing line
4 a platform on wheels that carries a display in a procession
5 a van or trailer for carrying horses

Word history: Old English *flotian*

flock
noun **1** a number of animals of the same kind that live and feed together, especially sheep and birds
verb **2** to gather together or go in a flock: *Everyone **flocked** around him to hear the story.*

Word history: Old English *floc*

floe
noun a large piece of ice floating on the sea

Word history: perhaps Norwegian *flo*

flog
verb **1** to beat hard with a whip or stick: *The soldier **flogged** the convict.* (***cane***, ***lash***, ***scourge***, ***thrash***)
2 *Colloquial* to sell or try to sell: *He **flogs** used cars.* (***hawk***, ***peddle***)
3 *Colloquial* to steal: *I bet she **flogged** that money.* (***nick***, ***pilfer***, ***pinch***, ***take***, ***thieve***)
phrase **4 flog a dead horse**, to make useless efforts to do something

Verb forms: I **flogged**, I have **flogged**, I am **flogging**
Word history: perhaps blend of *flay* and *jog*, variant of *jag*, verb meaning 'prick', 'slash'

flood (flud)
noun **1** a great overflow of water, especially over land which is usually dry: *Many houses were washed away in the **flood**.*

2 any great outpouring: *a **flood** of words* | *a **flood** of tears*
verb **3** to cover with water, as in a flood (***engulf***, ***inundate***, ***swamp***)
4 to rise or flow in a flood
5 to supply in great numbers: *They **flooded** us with gifts.*

Word history: Old English *flōd*

floodlight
noun **1** a light that gives a strong beam, used especially outside
verb **2** to light up with a floodlight: *to **floodlight** a sportsground at night*

Verb forms: I **floodlit**, I have **floodlit**, I am **floodlighting**

flood plain
noun a flat plain along the course of a stream that floods when the water level rises

floor
noun **1** the lowest flat part of a room or other place: *Don't drop crumbs on the **floor**.* | *The ship sank to the **floor** of the sea.* (***base***, ***bed***, ***bottom***)
2 one of the different levels of a building: *That office block has thirty **floors**.* (***level***, ***storey***)
verb **3** to knock down or defeat: *The boxer **floored** his opponent.*
4 *Colloquial* to confuse or puzzle completely: *This question will **floor** you.*

Word history: Old English *flōr*

floor / flaw

Don't confuse **floor** with **flaw**, which is a fault or defect.

flooring
noun material used to make floors

flop
verb **1** to fall or drop suddenly, especially with a noise: *He **flopped** into a chair.*
2 *Colloquial* to prove to be a failure (***bomb out***, ***fail***, ***fall through***)
noun **3** the movement or sound of flopping: *She sat down with a **flop**.*
4 *Colloquial* something that is a failure: *That film was a complete **flop**.* (***disaster***, ***dud***, ***failure***, ***fiasco***, ***write-off***)

Verb forms: I **flopped**, I have **flopped**, I am **flopping**
Word building: **floppily** *adverb* **floppiness** *noun* **floppy** *adjective*
Word history: variant of *flap*

floppy disk
noun a flexible plastic disk used for storing information in a computer. Floppy disks are usually encased in square, plastic cases to protect them.

flora (flaw-ruh)
noun the plants of a particular area or period of time: *Australian **flora** includes waratahs and banksias.*

Word use: Compare this with **fauna**.
Word history: Neo-Latin, from Latin *Flora* goddess of flowers

floral (flo-ruhl, flaw-ruhl)
adjective having to do with or made of flowers

Word history: from Latin word meaning 'flower'

florid
adjective **1** red-coloured: ***florid** cheeks* (***bloodshot***, ***flushed***, ***inflamed***, ***ruddy***)
2 too showy or flowery: ***florid** music* | ***florid** writing* (***decorated***, ***ornate***)

Word history: from Latin word meaning 'flowery'

florin
noun in former times, a silver coin worth two shillings

Word history: Middle English, from French, from Italian *fiorino* a Florentine coin stamped with a lily, from Latin word meaning 'flower'

florist
noun someone who arranges and sells flowers

floristry
noun the art of arranging flowers: *She studied **floristry** at TAFE.*

floss
noun **1** a cottony fibre yielded by silk-cotton trees
2 a soft waxed thread used for cleaning between the teeth

Word use: You can also use **floss silk** for definition 1. | You can also use **dental floss** for definition 2.
Word history: Scandinavian

flotation (floh-tay-shuhn)
noun **1** the act or state of floating
2 the floating of a business, loan, etc., especially by selling shares

Word use: You can also use **floatation**.
Word history: variant of *floatation*

flotilla
noun a group of small naval ships, or a small group of any boats

Word use: Compare this with **fleet**.
Word history: Spanish word meaning 'little fleet', from French, from Old English *flota*

flotsam and jetsam (flot-suhm uhn jet-suhm)
noun **1** the wreckage of a ship and its cargo found either floating upon the sea or washed ashore
2 odds and ends

Word history: The word *flotsam* is from the French *floter* meaning 'to float'. The word *jetsam* is from the Old French *getaison* meaning 'goods thrown overboard to lighten a ship in distress', and is ultimately from the Latin *jactare* to throw.

flounce[1]
verb to move with an impatient or angry jerk of your body: *She **flounced** out of the room in a rage.*

Word building: **flounce** *noun*
Word history: Scandinavian

flounce[2]
noun a strip of material gathered together and used to decorate the bottom of a skirt or other clothing

Word building: **flouncing** *noun* **flouncy** *adjective*
Word history: Old French word meaning 'a wrinkle', 'fold', from Germanic

flounder[1]
verb **1** to struggle along with stumbling movements: *They **floundered** through the mud.*
2 to struggle helplessly because of embarrassment or confusion

Word history: perhaps blend of *flounce* to fling your body about angrily and *founder* to sink or fail

> **flounder / founder**
> Don't confuse **flounder** with **founder**. A boat **founders** if it fills with water and sinks.

flounder[2]
noun a kind of fish, eaten as food

Noun forms: The plural is **flounder**.
Word history: Middle English, from Anglo-French, from Scandinavian

flour
noun a fine powder made by grinding wheat or other grain and used in cooking

Word building: **floury** *adjective* (**flourier, flouriest**)
Word history: Middle English; special use of *flower*

> **flour / flower**
> Don't confuse **flour** with **flower**, which is the blossom of a plant.
> When Dr Johnson wrote his dictionary in 1755, he gave **flower** with both these meanings. The flower of grain was the edible part of it. But at some point in the 1700s the two meanings became established with different spellings.

flourish (flu-rish)
verb **1** to grow strongly (***bloom, blossom, flower, thrive***)
2 to wave about in a showy way: *She **flourished** her prize.* (***brandish, shake***)
noun **3** a waving movement: *He gave a **flourish** of his sword.*
4 anything used for show such as a curve used to decorate handwriting

Word building: **flourishing** *adjective*
Word history: Middle English, from Old French, from Latin word meaning 'bloom'

flout (flowt)
verb to show no respect for: *He always **flouts** the rules.* (***defy, disobey, infringe, transgress, violate***)

Word building: **flouter** *noun* **floutingly** *adverb*
Word history: Middle English *floute(n)*, variant of *flute*, verb

> **flout / flaunt**
> Don't confuse **flout** with **flaunt**, which means 'to show off boldly'. It rhymes with *haunt*.
> *She flaunted her new bike before her friends at school.*

flow
verb **1** to move along in a stream: *The river **flows** out to the sea.* (***gush, spurt, stream, surge***)
2 to go along continuously and smoothly like a stream: *Her thoughts **flowed** smoothly onto the page.*
3 to fall or hang loosely: *Her hair **flowed** in the breeze.*

Word building: **flow** *noun*
Word history: Old English *flōwan*

flow chart
noun a diagram showing how something works or develops, stage by stage

flower
noun the blossom or part of a plant that produces the seed

Word building: **flower** *verb*
Word history: Middle English, from Old French, from Latin

> **flower / flour**
> Look up **flour / flower.**

flowerbed
noun a small plot of ground in a garden where flowers are grown

flowery
adjective **1** covered with flowers
2 using a lot of fancy words: *a **flowery** speech*

Adjective forms: **flowerier, floweriest**

flown
verb past participle of **fly**[1]

flu
noun → **influenza**

Word history: abbreviation

> **flu / flue / flew**
> Look up **flew / flu / flue.**

fluctuate (fluk-chooh-ayt)
verb to change all the time: *The temperature keeps **fluctuating**.* (***chop and change, vacillate***)

Word building: **fluctuation** *noun*
Word history: from Latin word meaning 'undulated'

flue (flooh)
noun a tube or pipe or any space for air or smoke to pass through

Word history: Old English *flēwsa* a flowing

fluent (flooh-uhnt)
adjective **1** flowing smoothly and easily: *to speak **fluent** French*
2 able to speak easily: *to be **fluent** in French* (***articulate, eloquent, silver-tongued, slick, smooth***)

Word building: **fluency**
Word history: from Latin word meaning 'flowing'

fluff
noun **1** light, soft, tiny pieces from materials like cotton or wool: *Woollen jumpers often have **fluff** on them.*
2 *Colloquial* an error or mistake (***boo-boo, gaff, fumble***)

Word building: **fluff** *verb*
Word history: perhaps blend of *flue* fluff and puff

fluid
noun **1** a substance that can flow, either a liquid or a gas
adjective **2** changing easily or not fixed: *Our plans are **fluid** at this early stage.*

Word building: **fluidity** *noun*
Word history: from Latin word meaning 'flow'

fluke[1]
noun Colloquial any accidental advantage or stroke of good luck, especially in sport

Word building: **fluke** *verb* **fluky** *adjective* (**flukier**, **flukiest**)

fluke[2]
noun **1** one of the flat triangular pieces on an anchor which catch in the ground
2 one of the triangular halves of a whale's tail

flung
verb past tense and past participle of **fling**

flunk
Colloquial
verb **1** to fail: *I hope he doesn't* ***flunk*** *this time. | I'm sure I'll* ***flunk*** *the exam.*
phrase **2 flunk out**, to give up or back out

Word history: perhaps related to *flinch, funk*

flunkey
noun **1** a male servant in uniform
2 someone who tries to win favour with another in a crawling, servile way (***crawler***, ***toady***)

Noun forms: The plural is **flunkeys**.
Word history: perhaps alteration of *flanker*, meaning 'someone or something on the outer edge of something'

fluorescence (floouh-res-uhns, fluh-res-uhns)
noun **1** the ability that certain substances have to give out light when exposed to radiation or a stream of high energy particles, such as electrons
2 the light or luminosity produced this way

fluorescent
adjective giving off light when hit by a stream of particles, such as electrons: *a* ***fluorescent*** *tube*

fluoridation
noun the addition of fluoride to toothpaste, to the water supply, etc., to help prevent tooth decay

Word history: *fluorid(e)* + *-ation*

fluoride
noun a chemical compound which protects your teeth from decay

Word building: **fluoridate** *verb* **fluoride** *adjective*

fluorine (floouh-reen, flooh-reen)
noun a pale yellow corrosive gas which can be found occurring in nature combined with other elements, especially in fluorspar, cryolite, phosphate rock, and other minerals

fluoro (flu-ro)
adjective of a very bright colour: *I thought her* ***fluoro*** *pants were a bit too bright.*

Word use: This is a short way of saying **fluorescent**.

flurry
noun **1** sudden excitement or confusion: *In all the* ***flurry*** *I forgot my bag.*
2 a sudden gust of wind

Word building: **flurry** *verb* (**flurried**, **flurrying**)
Word history: blend of *flutter* and *hurry*

flush[1]
verb **1** to blush or become red in the face
2 to flood with water, especially for cleaning: *to* ***flush*** *the toilet*

Word building: **flush** *noun*

flush[2]
adjective **1** even or level: *That brick should be* ***flush*** *with this one.*
2 having plenty of something, especially money: *Let's eat out tonight, I'm* ***flush*** *at the moment.*

Word building: **flush** *adverb*
Word history: special use of *flush[1]*

fluster
verb to make nervous or confused (***bamboozle***, ***befuddle***, ***confuse***)

Word building: **fluster** *noun*
Word history: compare Icelandic *flaustr* hurry, bustle

flute
noun **1** a musical wind instrument played by blowing across a hole near its end
verb **2** to make long grooves in: *The potter* ***fluted*** *the edges of his new pot.*

Word building: **fluted** *adjective*
Word history: Middle English, from Old French, from Provençal, from Latin word meaning 'blown'

flutter
verb **1** to flap or wave: *The flags* ***fluttered*** *in the breeze.*
2 to move with quick uneven movements: *Her heart* ***fluttered*** *with excitement.*
noun **3** a flapping movement
4 a wave of nervous excitement or confusion: *A* ***flutter*** *of excitement went through the class when the visitor arrived.*

Word history: Old English *floterian* float

flux
noun **1** a flowing or flow
2 the flowing in of the tide
3 a continuous movement or change: *to be in a state of* ***flux***
4 *Physics* the rate of flow of a liquid, heat, etc.

Word history: Middle English, from Latin word meaning 'a flowing'

fly[1]
verb **1** to move through the air with the help of wings, wind or some other force (***flit***, ***hover***, ***soar***)
2 to move very quickly: *The runner was* ***flying*** *down the track.* (***dart***, ***hurtle***, ***pelt***, ***speed***, ***streak***)
3 to make fly: *The children were* ***flying*** *a kite.*
4 to operate, or travel in, an aircraft or spacecraft
noun **5** a flap of material hiding a zipper in clothing, especially in trousers
6 a piece of material that forms the door or outer roof of a tent
phrase **7 fly at**, to attack (***assault***, ***charge***, ***get stuck into***)
8 fly in the face of, to refuse to obey or take notice of: *to* ***fly in the face of*** *our mother's warning*
9 let fly,
a to throw (***chuck***, ***fling***, ***hurl***, ***pitch***, ***toss***)
b to allow to flow out, especially an attack of words: *She* ***let fly*** *when I dropped the plate.*

Verb forms: I **flew**, I have **flown**, I am **flying**
Noun forms: The plural is **flies**.
Word history: Old English *flēogan*

fly[2]
noun **1** an insect with two wings
2 a fish hook made to look like an insect
phrase **3 fly in the ointment**, a slight fault that reduces the value of or your pleasure in something

Noun forms: The plural is **flies.**
Word history: Old English *flēoge, flȳge*

flyer
noun **1** someone or something that flies
2 a single sheet of printed material distributed as an advertisement or to announce something

flying fox
noun **1** a large bat which has a foxlike head and feeds on fruit
2 *Australian, NZ* a machine which is worked by an overhead cable and is used to carry you over water or rough land

flying saucer
noun a disc-shaped flying object said to be a spaceship from outer space

Word use: Another name is **UFO**.

flyleaf
noun a blank page at the beginning or end of a book

Noun forms: The plural is **flyleaves**.

foal
noun a young horse or donkey, either male or female

Word history: Old English *fola*

foam
noun **1** a collection of very small bubbles
2 a spongy material made by putting gas bubbles into plastic or rubber

Word building: **foam** *verb*
Word history: Old English *fām*

fob[1]
noun **1** a small pocket just below the waistline in men's trousers or waistcoat to hold a watch, etc.
2 a short chain or ribbon tied to a watch and worn hanging from a pocket like this

Word use: You can also use **fob pocket** for definition 1.

fob[2]
phrase **fob off 1** to get rid of by tricking someone: *to* ***fob off*** *a stolen watch on a person*
2 to put off with tricks, lies, etc.: *Don't try to* ***fob*** *me* ***off*** *with promises.*

Verb forms: I **fobbed**, I have **fobbed**, I am **fobbing**

focaccia (fuh-kah-chee-uh)
noun flat Italian bread which can be eaten with various fillings or toppings

Word history: Italian

focal length
noun the distance from the optical centre of a mirror or lens to the focal point

focal point
noun **1** the focus for a beam of light rays
2 *Colloquial* the main point of interest, attraction, activity, etc.

focus (foh-kuhs)
noun **1** a point at which rays of light meet after they have been reflected or bent
2 the adjustment of something like a camera lens to get a clear, sharp picture
3 the main point of interest or attraction: *The new girl was the* ***focus*** *of attention.* (***centre, core, heart, hub, nucleus***)
verb **4** to adjust a lens so that the image is made clear: *He* ***focused*** *his camera.*
5 to bring rays of light together to a point: *He used his magnifying glass to* ***focus*** *the sun's rays onto the paper to burn it.*
phrase **6 focus on**, to concentrate on (***attend to, centre on, consider, ponder***)

Noun forms: The plural is **focuses** or **foci** (foh-suy, foh-kuy).
Verb forms: I **focused** or I **focussed**, I have **focused** or I have **focussed**, I am **focusing** or I am **focussing**
Word building: **focal** *adjective*
Word history: from Latin word meaning 'hearth', 'fireplace'

fodder
noun food like hay or straw for cattle and horses

Word history: Old English *fodder, fōdor*

foe
noun *Old-fashioned* an enemy (***adversary, antagonist, opponent, rival***)

Word use: The opposite of this is **friend** or **ally**.
Word history: Old English *(ge)fā(h)* enemy

foetus (fee-tuhs)
noun a young human or animal during its development in an egg or in its mother's womb, especially in the later stages

Word use: You can also use **fetus**. | Compare this with **embryo**.
Word building: **foetal** *adjective*
Word history: from Latin word meaning 'a bringing forth', 'offspring', 'young'

fog
noun a cloudlike layer that forms close to the earth's surface and is made up of drops of water (***mist, smog***)

Word building: **fog** *verb* (**fogged, fogging**) **foggy** *adjective* (**foggier, foggiest**)
Word history: from obsolete *foggy* marshy, thick, murky

fogey (foh-gee)
noun an old-fashioned person

Noun forms: The plural is **fogies** or **fogeys**.
Word use: You can also use **fogy** and the plural of this is **fogies**.

foghorn
noun a loud horn or siren used for warning ships in foggy weather

fogy (foh-gee)
noun → **fogey**

Noun forms: The plural is **fogies**.

foible
noun a slight weakness in someone's character: *He has several* ***foibles*** *but no major faults.*

Word history: from French word meaning 'feeble'

foil[1]
verb to stop from being successful: *She **foiled** him in his plans to run away.*
Word history: Middle English *foile(n)*, from Old French word meaning 'trample'

foil[2]
noun **1** metal which has been beaten, hammered or rolled out into very thin sheets: *aluminium **foil***
2 anything that shows up the good qualities of something else by contrast with it
Word history: Middle English *foile*, from Old French, from Latin word meaning 'leaf'

foil[3]
noun a light thin sword with a button on the point which prevents injury in fencing
Word history: origin uncertain

foist (foyst)
verb **1** to sell or pass off by trickery, usually something of low quality: *He **foisted** damaged goods onto the customer.*
2 to bring or put secretly or dishonestly: *She **foisted** stolen goods into the room.*
Word history: probably from Dutch word meaning 'to take in hand'

fold[1]
verb **1** to bend one part of something over another part: *They **folded** their blankets neatly on the bed.*
2 to wrap up: *He **folded** the present in paper.*
3 to cross: *to **fold** your arms*
noun **4** a part that is folded or a layer of something folded
5 a crease made by folding
6 *Geology* a part of a rock bed which is folded or bent, or which connects two horizontal rock beds of different levels
Word history: Old English *faldan*

fold[2]
noun Old-fashioned a closed-off pen for keeping animals like sheep
Word history: Old English *fald, falod*

folder
noun **1** a holder or cover for papers usually made of a folded sheet of cardboard
2 (in some operating systems) a defined area on a computer disk used to store related files

fold mountains
plural noun mountains formed by massive bending and lifting up of the earth's crust, caused by compression

foliage (<u>foh</u>-lee-ij)
noun the leaves of a plant
Word history: French, from Latin word meaning 'leaf'

folio (<u>foh</u>-lee-oh)
noun **1** a sheet of paper folded once to make two leaves (four pages) of a book
2 a volume having pages of the largest size
3 a leaf of a book, etc., numbered only on the front side
Noun forms: The plural is **folios.**
Word history: from Latin word meaning 'leaf'

folk (fohk)
noun **1** people in general
2 the people of a particular group: *City **folk** and country **folk** should be friends.*
3 folks, *Colloquial* someone's own family
adjective **4** belonging to ordinary people: ***folk** craft*
Word history: Old English *folc*

folklore (<u>fohk</u>-law)
noun the beliefs, stories and customs of a people or a tribe passed down from each generation

folk music
noun **1** music, often of simple nature, coming from and handed down amongst the common people
2 music coming from urban America of the 1940s and 1950s, which concentrates on words that have a strong social comment

folk song
noun a song, often of simple nature, coming from and handed down amongst the common people
Word building: **folk singer** *noun*

follicle (<u>fol</u>-ik-uhl)
noun **1** a dry one-celled seed vessel that splits along only one side to let out its seed, such as the fruit of the columbine
2 a small cavity, sac, or gland in your body: *a hair **follicle***
Word building: **follicular** (fuh-<u>lik</u>-yuh-luh) *adjective*
Word history: from Latin word meaning 'little bellows', 'bag'

follow
verb **1** to come or go after: *You go ahead and I'll **follow**.*
2 to pursue, especially in secret: *The detective **followed** the suspect.* (***shadow**, **tag**, **track***)
3 to accept as a guide: *I'll **follow** your instructions.* (***comply with**, **heed**, **obey**, **observe***)
4 to move forward or go along: ***Follow** this path through the woods.*
5 to come after as a result: *It **follows** from this that he must be innocent. | If you do that, disaster will **follow**.*
6 to understand: *Do you **follow** this lesson?* (***comprehend**, **fathom**, **grasp***)
7 to watch the movements of something or the way something is developing: *She **follows** the news carefully.*
phrase **8 follow out**, to carry out to the end
9 follow through, to carry through completely an action, a stroke in tennis, etc.
10 follow up,
a to investigate or examine closely: *to **follow up** a lead in a murder case*
b to do something more at a later stage, especially to increase the effect of what has already been done: *The social worker will **follow up** with more counselling after the family goes home.*

folly
noun **1** foolishness
2 a foolish or silly act
Noun forms: The plural is **follies.**
Word history: Middle English *folie*, from Old French word meaning 'mad'

foment (fuh-<u>ment</u>)
verb **1** to cause or help the growth or development of: *to **foment** discord or rebellion*
2 to put warm or medicated liquid, cloths dipped in this liquid, etc., on to to lessen pain: *to **foment** a boil on your leg*
Word history: Late Latin, from Latin word meaning 'warm application'

fond
adjective **1** loving or affectionate: *a **fond** look* (***caring***, ***devoted***, ***tender***)
phrase **2 fond of**, liking: ***fond of** children*

Word history: Middle English *fonned* be foolish

fondle
verb to stroke or caress lovingly: *to **fondle** a puppy*

fondue (fon-dyooh, fon-dooh)
noun a meal cooked at the table in which pieces of food are speared on the end of long forks and cooked in melted cheese or hot oil

Word history: from French word meaning 'melt'

font[1]
noun a large stone bowl in a church which holds the water used in baptism

Word history: Old English, from Latin word meaning 'baptismal font', 'spring', 'fountain'

font[2]
noun a style of printing type: *Let's use a different **font** for the quotation.*

food
noun **1** anything that can be eaten to keep your body alive and help it grow (***chow***, ***grub***, ***provisions***, ***tucker***, ***victuals***)
phrase **2 food for thought**, something that might inspire new ideas

Word history: Old English *fōda*

food chain
noun a series of organisms in which the smallest is eaten by a larger one, which in turn is eaten by a still larger one, etc.

food mile
noun a unit of measurement used to work out how far a food product has to travel before it is consumed

food web
noun a series of food chains that are interrelated by the habits of the predators (the organisms that do the eating) and their prey (the organisms that are eaten)

fool
noun **1** someone who is silly or without common sense
verb **2** to trick or deceive: *She **fooled** him into believing she was older than she really was.* (***con***, ***hoax***, ***swindle***)
3 to play around or waste time: *Stop **fooling** around and come and finish your homework.*

Word history: Middle English *fol*, from Old French, from Late Latin word meaning 'empty-headed fellow', from Latin word meaning 'bellows'

foolhardy
adjective reckless and foolishly adventurous (***harebrained***, ***hasty***, ***impetuous***, ***rash***)

Adjective forms: **foolhardier**, **foolhardiest**
Word building: **foolhardiness** *noun*

foolish
adjective silly or unwise: *a **foolish** person | a **foolish** action* (***idiotic***, ***irrational***, ***mad***, ***ridiculous***, ***senseless***, ***stupid***)

Word use: The opposite of this is **wise** or **sensible**.
Word building: **foolishness** *noun*

foolproof
adjective designed not to fail or break, even when wrongly used (***cinchy***, ***easy***, ***simple***, ***uncomplicated***)

foolscap (foohlz-kap)
noun a paper size

Word history: so called from its former watermark, the outline of a fool's cap

foot
noun **1** the part of your body at the end of your leg, which is used for standing and walking
2 the end or bottom part, rather than the top or head part: *the **foot** of a mountain*
3 a unit of length in the imperial system, equal to about 30 centimetres
verb **4** to pay: *to **foot** the bill*
phrase **5 fall on your feet**, to be lucky
6 put your foot down, to be strict or firm
7 put your foot in your mouth (or **in it**), *Colloquial* to say or do something embarrassing

Noun forms: The plural is **feet**.
Word use: For definition 3 look up **imperial system**.
Word history: Old English *fōt*

footage (foot-ij)
noun **1** a length of film; the film used for a scene or scenes: *The **footage** was destroyed in the fire.*
2 the sequence of scenes shown on a length of film: *We watched the **footage** and couldn't see what all the fuss was about.*

football
noun **1** a game in which a ball is kicked or thrown, such as soccer, Australian Rules, Rugby Union and Rugby League
2 the ball used in these games

Word building: **footballer** *noun*

footing
noun **1** a firm position or foothold, especially for your feet
2 a foundation on which anything is established
3 the condition of a relationship: *He is on a friendly **footing** with her.*

footlights
plural noun the row of lights at the front of the stage in a theatre

footloose
adjective free to go or travel about without any responsibilities, etc.

footman
noun a male servant who attends the door, carriage, table, etc.

Noun forms: The plural is **footmen**.

footnote
noun a note at the bottom of a page, usually in small printing, which tells you more about something in the main text

footpath
noun a strip, usually laid with concrete, for walking on next to a road or street

footprint
noun **1** a track or mark made by a foot
2 the surface area covered by a structure or device, as a building on an area of land, or a computer on a desk
3 → **ecological footprint**

footstep
noun **1** the sound made by a step of the foot
phrase **2 follow in someone's footsteps**, to copy or follow someone in their work or way of life

fop
noun a man who is too concerned about his manners and appearance

for
preposition **1** with the purpose of: *to go **for** a walk*
2 intended to be used by or in connection with: *a book **for** children | a box **for** gloves*
3 in order to obtain: *a law suit **for** damages*
4 with a tendency towards: *to long **for** a thing | to have an eye **for** beauty*
5 in return for: *Thank you **for** your efforts.*
6 suitable for: *a subject **for** argument*
7 during: ***for** a long time*
8 in support of: *to stand **for** honest government*
9 in place of: *a substitute **for** butter*
10 with the purpose of reaching: *to start **for** Perth*
11 such as results in: *his reason **for** going*
12 to the extent or amount of: *to walk **for** a kilometre*
conjunction **13** because or since: *She laughed, **for** she suddenly felt happy.*
Word history: Old English

for / four / fore
These words sound the same but have different meanings.
For is a preposition with a wide range of meanings. Here is one example:
This apple is for the teacher.
Four is the number that comes after three.
Fore is in the phrase **come to the fore** meaning 'to come to the front of everything else'. It is also what golfers shout when they are warning someone that a ball is coming and they are in danger of being hit by it.

forage (fo-rij)
verb **1** to search around for food or other supplies: *to **forage** in the refrigerator*
noun **2** food or fodder for animals
Word history: Middle English, from Old French word meaning 'fodder', from Germanic

foray
noun **1** a raid or attack in order to steal: *to make a **foray** into the enemy camp* (***assault, excursion, onslaught, sally, sortie***)
2 a first attempt: *to make a **foray** into a different kind of work*
Word building: **foray** *verb*
Word history: Middle English

forbear (faw-bair)
verb **1** to keep yourself back from or refrain from: *I will **forbear** punishing you.*
2 to refrain or hold back
3 to be patient
Verb forms: I **forbore**, I have **forborne**, I am **forbearing**
Word building: **forbearance** *noun*
Word history: Old English *forberan*

forbid
verb to not allow: *I **forbid** you to go.* (***ban, prohibit***)
Word use: The opposite of this is **allow**.
Verb forms: I **forbade** or I **forbad**, I have **forbidden**, I am **forbidding**
Word history: Old English *forbēodan*

forbidding
adjective unpleasant, dangerous, or frightening (***creepy, grim, horrible, scary***)

force
noun **1** strength or power: *the **force** of the wind | to use **force** to get your own way* (***might, muscle***)
2 an organised group of people working together: *the police **force***
3 a something which produces or tends to produce a motion or a change of motion
b the strength of this thing
verb **4** to make or compel, often by using threats or violence: *The thief **forced** them to hand over the money.* (***bully, coerce, compel, drive***)
5 to use, move or do with force or effort: *to **force** the lid off a box*
phrase **6 in force**,
a operating or effective: *The new rules are **in force** from today.*
b all together: *Her friends came to see her **in force**.*
Word history: Middle English, from French, from Vulgar Latin, from Latin word meaning 'strong'

forceful
adjective strong and powerful (***dominant, mighty, potent***)
Word use: The opposite of this is **weak**.
Word building: **forcefully** *adverb*

forceps (faw-suhps)
noun a pair of tongs or tweezers used for grasping and holding objects, especially in operations
Noun forms: The plural is **forceps**.
Word history: Latin

forcible
adjective **1** using force: ***forcible** entry into the premises*
2 convincing: *a **forcible** argument*

ford
noun **1** a shallow part of a river where you can walk or ride across
verb **2** to cross or traverse by a ford: *to **ford** a stream*
Word history: Old English

fore
noun **1** the front part
adverb **2** at or towards the bow of a ship
phrase **3 to the fore**, to or at the front or best position: *He always pushes himself **to the fore**.*
Word use: The opposite of definition 2 is **aft**.

fore / for / four
Look up **for / four / fore.**

forearm
noun the part of your arm between the elbow and the wrist

forebear (faw-bair)
noun → **ancestor**
Word history: Middle English (Scottish)

forebode (faw-bohd)
verb **1** to be an omen or sign of: *clouds that **forebode** a storm*
2 to have a feeling that warns of: *to **forebode** evil*
Word building: **foreboding** *noun* **foreboding** *adjective*

forecast
verb **1** to predict or warn about for the future: *The Weather Bureau **forecasts** rain for the weekend.*
noun **2** a prediction, especially about the weather
Verb forms: I **forecast**, I have **forecast**, I am **forecasting**
Word building: **forecaster** *noun*

foreclose
verb Law to take away from someone the right to recover the mortgage on a property, a pledge, etc.: *The bank has **foreclosed** on me because I couldn't keep up my repayments.*
Word building: **foreclosure** *noun*
Word history: Middle English, from Old French, from Latin

forefinger
noun the finger next to your thumb (***index finger***)

forego
verb to go before
Verb forms: I **forewent**, I have **foregone**, I am **foregoing**
Word building: **foregoing** *adjective* **foregone** *adjective*
Word history: Old English *foregān* go before

foreground
noun the part of a view or picture nearest the front or the viewer: *We could see the river in the **foreground** with the mountains in the distance.*
Word use: The opposite is **background**.

forehand
Tennis, etc.
adjective **1** of a stroke, made to or from the right side of your body, if you are right-handed
noun **2** a stroke made from the right side of your body, if you are right-handed, with the palm of your hand facing the front

forehead (fo-ruhd)
noun the part of your face above your eyes and below where your hair starts growing (***brow***, ***temples***)
Word history: Old English *forhēafod*

foreign (fo-ruhn)
adjective **1** from a country other than your own: *a **foreign** language* (***alien***, ***ethnic***, ***exotic***, ***imported***, ***migrant***)
2 not belonging in the place where it is found: *a **foreign** substance in your eye*
Word history: Middle English, from Old French, from Latin word meaning 'out of doors', 'outside'

foreigner
noun someone from another country

forelock
noun the lock of hair that grows from the front of the head

foreman
noun **1** a man who is placed in charge of other workers in a factory (***overseer***)
2 the member of a jury who chairs the jury's discussions and acts as its representative
Noun forms: The plural is **foremen**.
Word use: If you are not referring specifically to a man it is best to use a term like **supervisor** for definition 1. You can also use **foreperson** for both definitions, but **foreman** remains the word generally used in courts for the jury leader, applying to both men and women.

foremost
adjective first or top: *The world's **foremost** athletes compete in the Olympic Games.*
Word building: **foremost** *adverb*

forensic (fuh-ren-sik, fuh-ren-zik)
adjective having to do with or used in courts of law or public argument: ***forensic** evidence used in a murder case*
Word building: **forensically** *adverb*
Word history: from Latin word meaning 'of the forum'

foreperson
noun → **foreman**
Noun forms: The plural is **forepersons**.

foresee
verb to expect or see in advance: *to **foresee** trouble* (***anticipate***, ***bargain for***, ***count on***, ***look ahead to***)
Verb forms: I **foresaw**, I have **foreseen**, I am **foreseeing**
Word history: Old English *foresēon*

foreshore
noun **1** the part of the shore between the ordinary high-water mark and low-water mark
2 the ground between the water's edge and the land used for crops or building

foresight
noun care or thought for the future

forest
noun land thickly covered with trees
Word history: Middle English, from Old French, from Latin word meaning 'outside'

forestall (faw-stawl)
verb **1** to prevent by taking some action first: *to **forestall** someone before they had a chance to complain*
2 to deal with, meet, or recognise in advance of the natural or proper time
Word history: Old English *foresteall* intervention (to defeat justice), waylaying

forestry (fo-ruhs-tree)
noun the science of planting and taking care of forests

forever
adverb **1** without ever ending (***eternally***, ***everlastingly***)
2 continually: *He's **forever** complaining.* (***incessantly***, ***interminably***, ***perpetually***)

foreword (faw-werd)
noun a short introduction at the front of a book (***preface***)

foreword / forward
Don't confuse **foreword** with **forward**, meaning 'ahead or towards the front'.

forfeit (faw-fuht)
noun **1** something paid or lost because of carelessness, disobedience, or crime: *According to the rules of the game, you pay a **forfeit** if you give the wrong answer.*
verb **2** to lose or be likely to lose because of a fault, crime, etc.: *You'll have to **forfeit** your turn because you cheated.*
Word building: **forfeit** *adjective* **forfeiter** *noun*
Word history: Middle English, from Old French

forgave (fuh-gayv)
verb past tense of **forgive**

forge[1]
verb **1** to copy in order to trick or deceive: *to **forge** a signature*
2 to form or make by heating and hammering: *A blacksmith **forges** horseshoes.*
3 to form or make in any way: *I didn't like her much at first, but over the years we've **forged** a firm friendship.*
noun **4** a furnace for softening metal before shaping it to make tools and other things
Word building: **forger** *noun*
Word history: Middle English, from Old French, from Latin word meaning 'workshop'

forge[2]
phrase **forge ahead**, to move forward with great effort: *to **forge ahead** through thick bush* (***advance***, ***make headway***, ***proceed***, ***progress***, ***push on***)

forgery
noun the crime of making an imitation and passing it off as genuine
Noun forms: The plural is **forgeries**.

forget
verb **1** to not remember: *I **forgot** my homework.* | *I **forgot** to clean my teeth.* (***disregard***, ***neglect***, ***omit***, ***overlook***)
2 to not remember something: *However often you tell him, he always **forgets**.*
phrase **3 forget yourself**,
a to say or do something rude or thoughtless
b to become absent-minded
c to stop thinking of your own feelings
Verb forms: I **forgot**, I have **forgotten**, I am **forgetting**
Word building: **forgetful** *adjective* **forgetfulness** *noun*
Word history: Old English *forg(i)etan*

forget-me-not (fuh-get-mee-not)
noun a small plant with a light blue flower, regarded as a symbol of continuing love

forgive
verb to excuse without holding any bad feelings: *He will **forgive** you if you say you are sorry.* (***let off***, ***pardon***, ***spare***)
Verb forms: I **forgave**, I have **forgiven**, I am **forgiving**
Word building: **forgiveness** *noun* **forgiving** *adjective*
Word history: Old English *forgiefan*

forgo
verb to do without or give up: *I'll **forgo** dinner to come and collect you.* (***shun***, ***renounce***)
Verb forms: I **forwent**, I have **forgone**, I am **forgoing**
Word history: Old English

forgot
verb past tense and past participle of **forget**

fork
noun **1** an instrument with prongs for lifting food, digging the garden, and other things
2 a place in a tree, road, or river where it divides into several parts: *Turn left at the **fork** in the road.*
3 a divided part like the prongs of a fork
Word building: **fork** *verb*
Word history: Old English *forca*, from Latin

forked
adjective **1** divided into parts or branches: *the **forked** tongue of a snake* | *a **forked** path*
2 zigzag: ***forked** lightning*

forklift
noun a small truck with two horizontal arms or prongs for lifting and carrying heavy loads

forlorn (fuh-lawn)
adjective left all alone and miserable: *a **forlorn** puppy* (***blue***, ***depressed***, ***despondent***, ***glum***, ***heart-broken***, ***sad***)
Word history: Old English *forlēosan* lose, destroy

form
noun **1** shape or appearance: *a birthday cake in the **form** of a '6'* (***design***, ***figure***, ***structure***)
2 condition or fitness: *How's his **form**?* | *They were in good **form** for the big match.*
3 a printed paper with blank spaces to fill in: *an entry **form** for the competition*
4 behaviour or conduct: *It is not good **form** to talk with your mouth full.*
5 the set of classes in high school for students of about the same age
6 a long seat or bench
7 *Art* the organisation and relationship of lines, colours, shapes, etc., in order to create a well-balanced image
verb **8** to make, build or produce: *to **form** an idea* | *to freeze water to **form** ice*
9 to develop or be made: *Buds are **forming** on the trees.*
phrase **10 a matter of form**, an everyday activity
Word history: Middle English, from Old French, from Latin word meaning 'form', 'figure', 'model', 'mould', 'sort'

formal
adjective **1** not relaxed or casual: *He greeted us in a **formal** manner.* | ***formal** clothes* (***ceremonial***, ***official***, ***ritual***)
2 following the official or proper procedure: *to make a **formal** complaint in writing*
noun **3** a dance or ball at which evening dress is to be worn
Word building: **formally** *adverb*

formally / formerly

These words sound the same but mean different things.

Formally is the adverb from **formal**:

We have to dress formally for the dinner tonight.

Formerly is the adverb from **former** and means 'previously' or 'in the past':

Now we can wear ordinary clothes to school. Formerly we had to wear school uniforms.

formaldehyde (faw-mal-duh-huyd)
noun a gas used in solution, as a disinfectant and preservative, and in the manufacture of resins and plastics

Word use: You can also use **formaldehyd.**
Word history: *form(ic acid) + aldehyde*

formality
noun **1** a way of thinking and behaving that is formal and not relaxed
2 something done only because it fits in with formal or polite behaviour: *Everybody knew she'd win, so the announcement was just a* ***formality.***

Noun forms: The plural is **formalities.**

formal language
noun speech or writing that does not include colloquialisms, contractions, and the like

format (faw-mat)
noun **1** shape, plan or style: *The book is now available in a new* ***format*** *with a soft cover and bigger print.*
2 *Computers* a neat arrangement of data elements to form a larger body of information such as a file
verb **3** to organise into a particular format: *to* ***format*** *data*

Verb forms: it **formatted,** it has **formatted,** it is **formatting**
Word history: French, from Latin word meaning 'formed' (in a certain way)

formation
noun **1** the process of making or producing: *the* ***formation*** *of ice from water*
2 something which has formed: *a rock* ***formation***
3 a planned arrangement or pattern: *planes flying in* ***formation***

formative
adjective shaping or moulding

former
adjective **1** earlier or past: *a* ***former*** *marriage* (***bygone, sometime***)
2 being the first one of two: *They served both tea and coffee but I chose the* ***former.***

Word use: The opposite of definition 2 is **latter.**
Word history: Old English *forma* first + *-er*

formerly
adverb in the past

formidable (faw-muh-duh-buhl, faw-mid-uh-buhl)
adjective **1** very difficult and needing much hard work: *To clean up such a messy bedroom is a* ***formidable*** *task.*
2 frightening: *a* ***formidable*** *enemy*

Word building: **formidably** *adverb*
Word history: French, from Latin word meaning 'causing fear'

formula (faw-myuh-luh)
noun **1** a rule or recipe to be followed: *The* ***formula*** *for mixing the baby's milk is one part milk powder to five parts water.*
2 *Chemistry* the representation of the atoms in a molecule by symbols: *The* ***formula*** *for water is* H_2O.

Noun forms: The plural is **formulas** or **formulae** (faw-myuh-lee).
Word history: Latin

formulate
verb to state clearly or exactly

Word building: **formulation** *noun*

fornication (faw-nuh-kay-shuhn)
noun sexual intercourse between people who are not married

forsake
verb to give up or abandon (***desert, leave behind***)

Verb forms: I **forsook,** I have **forsaken,** I am **forsaking**
Word building: **forsaken** *adjective*
Word history: Old English *forsacan* deny, give up

fort
noun **1** a place like a castle, which is strongly built and armed against enemy attack
phrase **2 hold the fort,** to look after things for someone while they are away

Word use: You can also use **fortress** for definition 1.
Word history: French, from Latin word meaning 'strong'

fort / fought

Don't confuse **fort** with **fought,** which is the past tense of the verb **fight:**

They fought well in the last war.

forte[1] (faw-tay)
noun something that you do particularly well: *Music is her* ***forte.***

Word history: French

forte[2] (faw-tay)
adverb loudly: *This passage of music is played* ***forte.***

Word use: This is an instruction in music written as 'f'. | The opposite is **piano.**
Word history: Italian, from Latin word meaning 'strong'

forth
adverb **1** forwards: *to set* ***forth*** *into battle*
2 onwards: *from that day* ***forth***
phrase **3 and so forth,** and so on

Word history: Middle English and Old English

forth / fourth

Don't confuse **forth** with **fourth,** which is the next number after third.

forthcoming
adjective **1** happening or coming soon: *our* ***forthcoming*** *visit to the zoo*
2 ready when needed: *We wanted to buy a boat but the money was not* ***forthcoming.***

forthright
adjective speaking your mind openly and honestly (***candid***, ***direct***, ***frank***, ***honest***, ***straightforward***)

Word building: **forthrightly** *adverb*

forthwith
adverb immediately or at once

fortify (<u>faw</u>-tuh-fuy)
verb to make strong so as to resist attack, damage and other harmful things: *to build strong walls to **fortify** the castle | to drink hot soup to **fortify** yourself against the cold* (***prop up***, ***reinforce***, ***shore up***, ***steady***, ***strengthen***)

Verb forms: I **fortified**, I have **fortified**, I am **fortifying**
Word use: The opposite of this is **weaken**.
Word building: **fortification** *noun*
Word history: Middle English, from French, from Late Latin word meaning 'make'

fortissimo
adverb very loudly: *This passage of music is played **fortissimo**.*

Word use: This is an instruction in music written as 'ff'. | The opposite is **pianissimo**.
Word history: Italian, superlative of *forte*. Look up **forte**[2].

fortitude (<u>faw</u>-tuh-tyoohd)
noun patient courage in times of sickness, hardship, etc.

Word history: Latin

fortnight
noun two weeks, or fourteen days and nights

Word building: **fortnightly** *adjective* **fortnightly** *adverb*
Word history: Old English *fēowertēne niht* fourteen nights

fortress
noun → **fort** (definition 1)

Word history: Middle English, from Old French word meaning 'strong'

fortuitous (faw-<u>tyooh</u>-uh-tuhs)
adjective accidental or happening by chance or by good luck

Word history: from Latin word meaning 'casual'

fortunate
adjective lucky or having good fortune: *You were **fortunate** to find the money you lost.*

Word building: **fortunately** *adverb*
Word history: Middle English, from Latin word meaning 'made prosperous or happy'

fortune
noun **1** a great amount of money or property: *to make a **fortune** buying and selling land* (***riches***, ***treasure***, ***wealth***)
2 luck: *We had the good **fortune** to have fine weather for the sports carnival.*
3 fate or destiny: *to tell someone's **fortune***

Word history: Middle English, from French, from Latin word meaning 'chance', 'luck', 'fortune'

forty
noun **1** a cardinal number, ten times four (10 × 4)
2 a symbol for this number, as 40 or XL or XXXX
3 a set of forty persons or things
4 forties, the numbers from 40 to 49 of a series, especially years of a person's age, or the years of a century
adjective **5** amounting to forty in number

Noun forms: The plural is **forties**.
Word building: **fortieth** *adjective* **fortieth** *noun*
Word history: Old English *fēowertig*

forum
noun **1** a public meeting to discuss matters of general interest
2 the main square or marketplace of an ancient Roman town

Word history: Latin

forward
adjective **1** ahead or towards the front: *a **forward** step | the **forward** part of a boat*
2 behaving boldly usually in order to be noticed by others: *She is quite **forward** but her sister is very shy.* (***bold***, ***brazen***, ***fresh***, ***saucy***)
adverb **3** → **forwards**
verb **4** to send on: *to **forward** a letter to the new address* (***dispatch***, ***pass on***, ***relay***, ***transmit***)
noun **5** someone who plays in an attacking position in sports such as football and hockey

Word use: The opposite of definitions 1 and 3 is **backward**. | The opposite of definition 2 is **reticent**.
Word history: Middle English and Old English *for(e)ward*

forward / foreword
Don't confuse **forward** with **foreword**, which is an introduction in a book. It is the <u>word</u> you say be<u>fore</u> the book begins.

forwards
adverb **1** towards or at a place, point, or time in advance; onwards; ahead: *to move **forwards***
2 towards the front: *Please allow the children at the back to move **forwards** so that they can see.*
3 into view or consideration: *The pushed their views **forwards**.*

Word use: The opposite of definitions 1 and 2 is **backwards**. | You can also use **forward**.

forward slash
noun a punctuation mark (/)

Word use: The technical term for this is **solidus**.

fossick
verb Australian, *NZ* **1** to try to find gold or precious stones in ground that has already been worked over by others
2 to search or hunt: *to **fossick** through a drawer for a pencil*

Word building: **fossicker** *noun*
Word history: This word comes from a dialect of Cornish, where it originally meant 'a troublesome person' or 'to bustle or fuss about'.

fossil
noun **1** the remains of an animal or plant from long ago, preserved as rock
2 *Colloquial* someone who has old-fashioned ideas

Word building: **fossilise** *verb* **fossilised** *adjective*
Word history: from Latin word meaning 'dug up'

fossil fuel
noun coal and oil which have formed underground from the remains of plants and animals millions of years old

foster
verb **1** to take into a family and care for: *to **foster** an orphan child*
2 to help or encourage to grow: *to **foster** friendship between nations*
adjective **3** having to do with fostering: *a **foster** child | a **foster** home*
Word use: Compare definition 1 with **adopt**.
Word history: Middle English; Old English *fōster* nourishment

fought (fawt)
verb past tense and past participle of **fight**

> **fought / fort**
> Look up **fort / fought.**

foul
adjective **1** very nasty, dirty or unpleasant: *a **foul** smell | **foul** weather | **foul** language* (***grotesque***, ***hideous***, ***monstrous***, ***repulsive***, ***ugly***)
verb **2** to make dirty or unpleasant (***contaminate***, ***corrupt***, ***pollute***, ***spoil***, ***taint***)
3 to make or become jammed or caught: *Our propeller **fouled** on a fishing line.*
4 to play unfairly or break the rules in sport
noun **5** an unfair action in sport
phrase **6 fall foul of,** to have or be in trouble with
7 foul up, *Colloquial* to spoil or mess up
Word building: **foulness** *noun*
Word history: Old English *fūl*

> **foul / fowl**
> Don't confuse **foul** with **fowl**, which is a bird kept for eating or for its eggs, like a chicken or a turkey.

found
verb to set up or start: *to **found** a new settlement* (***establish***, ***institute***, ***launch***, ***pioneer***)
Word building: **founder** *noun* **founding** *adjective*
Word history: Old English *funde*

foundation
noun **1** the founding or setting up of something
2 a base on which something rests or stands: *the stone **foundations** of a building | the **foundations** of society* (***framework***, ***skeleton***, ***support***)
adjective **3** having an association from the beginning: *a **foundation** member of the club*

founder[1]
noun someone who begins or establishes something

founder[2]
verb **1** of a ship, to fill with water and sink
2 of buildings, etc., to fall or sink down
3 to fail completely
4 to trip, break down, or go lame
Word history: Middle English, from Old French, from Latin word meaning 'bottom'

> **founder / flounder**
> Don't confuse **founder** with **flounder**, which means 'to do something clumsily and with great difficulty'.

foundling
noun a baby found abandoned, without a parent or guardian
Word history: Middle English

foundry
noun a place producing castings, in which molten metal is poured into moulds
Noun forms: The plural is **foundries**.
Word history: French

fount
noun **1** in poetry, a spring of water or a fountain
2 origin or source: *a **fount** of all wisdom*
Word history: short for *fountain*

fountain
noun **1** a place where water spurts upward or streams downward from a water pipe
2 the origin or source: *the **fountain** of wisdom*
Word history: late Middle English, from Old French, of or from a spring

fountain pen
noun a pen which has a small container inside for supplying ink to the nib

four
noun **1** a cardinal number, three plus one (3 + 1)
2 a symbol of this number, as 4 or IV or IIII
3 a set of four persons or things
4 *Rowing* a crew of four rowers
5 *Chemistry* a hit scoring four runs, when the ball is hit to the boundary, but first touches the ground
adjective **6** amounting to four in number
phrase **7 on all fours**, on your hands and feet (or knees)
Word building: **fourth** *adjective* **fourth** *noun*
Word history: Old English *fēower*

> **four / for / fore**
> These words sound the same but have different meanings.
> **Four** is the number that comes after three.
> **For** is a preposition with a wide range of meanings. Here is one example:
> *This apple is for the teacher.*
> **Fore** is in the phrase **come to the fore** meaning 'to come to the front of everything else'. It is also what golfers shout when they are warning someone that a ball is coming and they are in danger of being hit by it.

fourteen
noun **1** a cardinal number, ten plus four (10 + 4)
2 a symbol for this number, as 14 or XIV or XIIII
3 a set of fourteen people or things
adjective **4** amounting to fourteen in number
Word building: **fourteenth** *adjective* **fourteenth** *noun*
Word history: Old English *fēowertēne*

fourth
adjective next after the third: *He missed out on a medal but was presented with an encouragement award for coming* ***fourth****.*

fourth / forth
Don't confuse **fourth** with **forth**.
Forth is rather old-fashioned and means 'forwards':
Go forth and conquer the world.

four-wheel drive
noun a car or truck which can travel over rough country or soft ground because all four wheels are driven by the engine
Word use: The abbreviation is **4WD**.

fowl
noun a bird kept for eating or for its eggs, such as a hen, duck, or turkey
Noun forms: The plural is **fowl** or **fowls**.
Word history: Middle English *foule*, Old English *fugel*

fowl / foul
Look up **foul / fowl**.

fox
noun **1** a small wild dog with red-brown fur, a long bushy tail and pointed ears
2 someone who is sly or cunning
Word history: Old English

foxy
adjective sly and cunning
Adjective forms: **foxier**, **foxiest**

foyer (foy-uh, foy-yuh)
noun the large entrance hall of a theatre or hotel
Word history: French word meaning 'hearth', 'fireside' (originally a room to which theatre audiences went for warmth between the acts), from Latin word meaning 'hearth'

fracas (fra-kah)
noun a noisy disturbance or fight (***commotion***, ***dust-up***, ***free-for-all***, ***hubbub***, ***uproar***)
Word history: French, from Italian word meaning 'smash', from Latin

fraction
noun **1** a part of a whole number: $\frac{3}{4}$ *is a* ***fraction***
2 a small piece or amount: *to open the door a* ***fraction***
Word use: Compare definition 1 with **integer**.
Word building: **fractional** *adjective* **fractionally** *adverb*
Word history: Middle English, from Latin word meaning 'break'

fraction / faction
Don't confuse **fraction** with **faction**, which is a small group of people within a larger group, who hold a different opinion to that of the larger group.

fractious (frak-shuhs)
adjective bad-tempered and uncooperative: *a* ***fractious*** *child*
Word history: *fracti(on)* (in obsolete sense of discord) + *-ous*

fracture
verb to crack or break: *to fall over and* ***fracture*** *your arm | The rock* ***fractured*** *when we hit it.*
Word building: **fracture** *noun*
Word history: French, from Latin word meaning 'breach'

fragile
adjective delicate and easily damaged or broken: *a* ***fragile*** *china cup* (***breakable***, ***brittle***, ***frail***)
Word building: **fragility** *noun*
Word history: Latin

fragment (frag-muhnt)
noun **1** a part that has been broken off or left unfinished: *a* ***fragment*** *of glass | a* ***fragment*** *of a poem* (***particle***, ***piece***, ***scrap***, ***sliver***, ***trace***)
verb (frag-ment) **2** to break into small pieces
Word building: **fragmentary** *adjective*
Word history: Latin

fragmentation
noun **1** the act or process of fragmenting
2 *Computers* the process where data is broken into parts
3 fragments from an exploded bomb or grenade

fragrant
adjective sweet-smelling: *a* ***fragrant*** *perfume*
Word building: **fragrance** *noun*
Word history: from Latin word meaning 'smelling sweet'

frail
adjective weak or delicate: *to be* ***frail*** *after a long illness* (***feeble***, ***helpless***, ***invalid***)
Word building: **frailness** *noun*
Word history: Middle English, from Old French, from Latin word meaning 'fragile'

frailty
noun weakness
Noun forms: The plural is **frailties**.

frame
noun **1** the structure which fits around or supports something and gives it shape: *a picture* ***frame*** *| a house with a wooden* ***frame*** *| the human* ***frame***
2 one of the small pictures that make up a strip of film
verb **3** to form or put together: *to* ***frame*** *a plan*
4 to put into a frame or surround like a frame: *to* ***frame*** *a picture | Curly hair* ***framed*** *her face.*
5 *Colloquial* to make seem guilty: *The gangster* ***framed*** *his innocent friend.*
phrase **6 frame of mind**, mood: *to be in a good* ***frame of mind***
Word history: from Old English word meaning 'avail', 'profit'

framework
noun a supporting frame (***base***, ***foundation***, ***skeleton***, ***support***)

franchise (fran-chuyz)
noun **1** a citizen's right to vote
2 permission given by a manufacturer to a shopkeeper to sell the manufacturer's products

Word history: Middle English, from Old French word meaning 'free'

frangipani (fran-juh-pan-ee)
noun **1** a shrub or tree with thick fleshy branches, grown for its strongly scented yellow, white or pink flowers
2 a perfume prepared from, or imitating this scent

Noun forms: The plural is **frangipanis**.
Word use: You can also use **frangipanni**.
Word history: French, after the Marquis *Frangipani* of Rome, who invented a perfume for scenting gloves in the 16th century

frank
adjective **1** open or not pretending in what you say: *to give a **frank** answer* (***candid***, ***forthright***, ***honest***, ***sincere***, ***straightforward***)
noun **2** a mark put on a letter in place of a postage stamp to show that postage has already been paid
verb **3** to put such a mark on: *to **frank** a letter*

Word building: **frankness** *noun*
Word history: Middle English, from Old French, from Late Latin word meaning 'free'

frankfurt
noun a spicy red-coloured sausage, usually eaten with a bread roll (***frankfurter***, ***hot dog***, ***saveloy***)

Word history: from *Frankfurt*, a city in central Germany

frankly
adverb openly: *I'll tell you quite **frankly** what you want to know.*

frantic
adjective wild with excitement, fear, worry or pain

Word use: The opposite of this is **calm**.
Word building: **frantically** *adverb*
Word history: Middle English, from Old French, from Latin word meaning 'delirious', from Greek

fraternal
adjective of or like a brother

Word history: from Latin word meaning 'brotherly' + *-al*

fraternise
verb to be friendly: *to **fraternise** with your teachers*

Word use: You can also use **fraternize**.

fraternity
noun a group of people, often men, with the same interests or goals: *the legal **fraternity***

Noun forms: The plural is **fraternities**.
Word history: Middle English, from Old French, from Latin word meaning 'brotherhood'

fraud (frawd)
noun **1** deliberate trickery or cheating (***deceit***, ***guile***)
2 someone or something that is not what they pretend to be (***cheat***, ***con man***, ***knave***, ***rogue***, ***shark***)

Word building: **fraudulent** *adjective* **fraudulently** *adverb*
Word history: Middle English, from Old French, from Latin word meaning 'cheating', 'deceit'

fraught (frawt)
adjective **1** involving or full of: *an undertaking **fraught** with danger | a heart **fraught** with grief*
2 *Colloquial* upset, anxious or tense

Word history: Middle English, from Middle Dutch or Middle Low German word meaning 'freight money'

fray[1]
noun a noisy fight or quarrel: *When the older children joined the **fray** the whole playground was in an uproar.* (***battle***, ***brawl***, ***combat***, ***conflict***, ***skirmish***)

Word history: variant of *affray*

fray[2]
verb to wear out: *My shirt collar is **fraying**. | A hard day's work **frayed** her temper.*

Word history: French, from Latin word meaning 'rub'

frazzle
verb **1** to fray or wear to threads or shreds
2 to tire out or weary
noun **3** the condition of being completely worn out or burnt: *worn to a **frazzle** | burnt to a **frazzle***

Word history: blend of *fray*[2] and *fazzle*, Middle English *faselin* unravel

freak
noun **1** someone or something that is extremely strange or unusual
adjective **2** unusual: *a **freak** storm* (***extraordinary***, ***rare***, ***remarkable***, ***strange***, ***uncommon***)

Word history: perhaps related to Old English *frīcian* dance

freakish
adjective weird: ***freakish** behaviour*

freckle
noun a small brown spot on your skin caused by the sun: *People with red hair usually have **freckles**.*

Word building: **freckle** *verb* **freckled** *adjective*
Word history: blend of obsolete *frecken* freckle (from Scandinavian) and *speckle*, noun

free
adjective **1** costing nothing: ***free** tickets to the pictures*
2 not confined or restricted: *The bird flew out of the cage and is **free**. | a **free** choice*
3 not being used: *The room is **free** now.*
4 not restrained or inhibited: *He is **free** in manner.* (***open***, ***spontaneous***, ***uninhibited***)
adverb **5** loose or not captive: *to set the bird **free***
phrase **6 free and easy**, casual or not formal (***easygoing***, ***informal***, ***relaxed***)
7 make free with, to treat or use in a way that is too familiar: *He **makes free with** my possessions without asking me.*

Word building: **free** *verb* (**freed**, **freeing**) **freely** *adverb*
Word history: Old English *frēo*, originally, dear, favoured

free / for free

If something is **free**, you can have it or use it without paying for it:

The biscuits were free.

In this sentence **free** is an adjective.

You do something **for free** if you do it without being paid:

She said she'd babysit for free.

You get something **for free** if you get it without having to pay:

I got the pen for free.

In these sentences **for free** is a phrase used as an adverb. People used to frown on the use of **for free** and say that it was wrong. Nowadays so many people use it that it is becoming more acceptable.

freedom
noun **1** the right to act or speak out as you wish (***autonomy***, ***independence***, ***liberty***)
2 the state of being free rather than being in captivity or in prison or another kind of confinement

Word history: Old English *frēodōm*

free enterprise
noun the belief in or practice of a minimum amount of government control of private business and industry

freehand
adjective drawn by hand, and not traced, or drawn with a ruler, compass, or other instruments: *a **freehand** drawing*

Word building: **freehand** *adverb*

freehold
noun **1** ownership or holding of property for an unlimited time and without any conditions
2 an estate held in this way

Word building: **freehold** *adjective*

freelance
noun someone, especially a writer, who doesn't work for a wage but who sells work to more than one employer

Word building: **freelance** *verb* **freelance** *adjective*

free market
noun an economic system that allows unrestricted supply and demand: *The prices were determined by the **free market**.*

Word building: **free marketeer** *noun*

free radical
noun a molecule or ion with one or more unpaired electrons

free-range
adjective able to walk around and feed freely, rather than being kept in a cage: ***free-range** chickens*

free selection
noun Australian in the past, land chosen, especially for farming use, and taken up by lease or licence under various land acts, or after crown auction, as opposed to land granted by the Crown or taken by squatting

freesia (free-zhuh)
noun a plant native to southern Africa, cultivated for its fragrant white, yellow, or sometimes other coloured, tubular flowers

Word history: Neo-Latin; named after EM *Fries*, 1794–1878, Swedish botanist

free speech
noun the right to express your opinions in public

freestyle
noun **1** a fast style of swimming in which your head and the front of your body are kept flat to the water, with legs kicking and your arms used in turn
2 a swimming race in which you can use any style you like, usually the freestyle because it is the fastest

Word use: Other names for definition 1 are **Australian crawl** and **crawl**.
Word building: **freestyle** *adjective*

free trade
noun trade between different countries, free from the restrictions or duties imposed by governments

free verse
noun poetry without regular rhythms or rhymes

free vote
noun in a house of parliament, a vote on a motion in which members are free to vote according to their own judgement without being bound by any party policy or decision

Word use: You can also use **conscience vote**.

freeway
noun a road on which traffic can travel fast (***expressway***, ***motorway***)

free will
noun **1** free choice or your own decision
2 the doctrine that says that the way human beings behave is decided by them and is not imposed on them by physical or divine forces

freeze
verb **1** to turn to ice: *The puddles **froze**. | We **froze** our drinks.*
2 to be or feel very cold
3 to keep fresh by putting in a freezer: *She **froze** the meat.*
4 to keep very still, as with fear: *Thinking she heard footsteps, she **froze**.*
5 of a computer system, to stop outputting or accepting input
noun **6** a period of very cold weather
7 a period in which no change is allowed in something, such as prices or wages

Verb forms: I **froze**, I have **frozen**, I am **freezing**
Word history: Old English *frēosan*

freeze / frieze

Don't confuse **freeze** with **frieze**, which is a band around the top of a wall, often decorated with a painted or sculpted pattern.

freezer
noun a refrigerated cabinet for keeping food below freezing temperature

freight (frayt)
noun **1** goods sent by air, sea or land
2 the charge for sending goods

Word building: **freight** *verb*

freighter
noun a ship or plane that carries goods

Word history: Middle English, from Middle Dutch or Middle Low German word meaning 'freight money'

French cricket
noun a game played with a ball and a cricket bat, in which the bat is held in front of the legs and the person batting can only be dismissed if the ball hits their legs or they are caught

French fries
plural noun thin strips of potato, fried

Word use: You can also use **french fries.**

French horn
noun a brass wind instrument with a mellow tone

frenetic (fruh-net-ik)
adjective insane or frantic: ***frenetic** activity*

Word use: You can also use **phrenetic.**
Word building: **frenetically** *adverb*
Word history: variant of *phrenetic*

frenzy
noun a wildly or furiously excited state: *The dog was in a **frenzy** barking at all the cars.*

Word building: **frenzied** *adjective*
Word history: Middle English, from Old French, from Late Latin, from Greek

frequency (free-kwuhn-see)
noun **1** the fact of happening often: *He was annoyed by the **frequency** of her visits.*
2 the rate at which something happens: *the **frequency** of a pulse*
3 the rate of cycles or vibrations of a wave movement: *His radio only picks up stations on a high **frequency**.*

Noun forms: The plural is **frequencies.**
Word history: Latin

frequency modulation
noun a broadcasting system, relatively free from static, in which the frequency of the transmitted wave is modulated or varied in accordance with the amplitude and pitch of the signal

Word use: Compare this with **amplitude modulation.** | The abbreviation is **FM.**

frequent (free-kwuhnt)
adjective **1** happening often: *They make **frequent** visits to the beach.* (***periodic, recurrent, regular, repeated***)
verb (fruh-kwent) **2** to visit often: *She **frequents** the cinema.*

Word building: **frequently** *adverb*
Word history: from Latin word meaning 'crowded'

fresco
noun a painting done on a freshly plastered wall or ceiling before it has dried, so that the colours sink in

Noun forms: The plural is **frescoes** or **frescos.**
Word history: Italian word meaning 'cool', from Germanic

fresh
adjective **1** in a natural state: *Sometimes we have **fresh** fruit and sometimes stewed fruit.*
2 new: ***fresh** milk* | ***fresh** footprints*
3 original: *a **fresh** style of writing* (***innovative, new, novel***)
4 cool: *It's a **fresh** morning.* (***nippy, sharp***)
5 not salt: ***fresh** water*
6 strong and not tired or faded: ***fresh** colour* | *She looks **fresh** after her holiday.*
7 just arrived: ***fresh** from home*
8 *Old-fashioned* cheeky: *Don't get **fresh** with me!* (***bold, forward, pert, saucy***)

Word building: **fresh** *noun* **freshly** *adverb*
Word history: Old English *fersc*

freshen
phrase **freshen up**, to make yourself fresh, by washing, etc.: *to **freshen up** before dinner*

Word building: **freshener** *noun*

freshwater
adjective of or living in water that is fresh, or not salt: *a **freshwater** crocodile*

fret[1]
verb to be worried or annoyed: *He **frets** about things not being done properly.* (***bother, fuss***)

Verb forms: I **fretted,** I have **fretted,** I am **fretting**
Word history: Old English *fretan*

fret[2]
noun one of the bars across the neck of a stringed instrument, such as a guitar, which marks off the notes

fretwork
noun **1** ornamental work consisting of interlacing perforated parts
2 any pattern of dark and light, as sunlight and shadow

Word history: Middle English *frette*

Freudian slip
noun a mistake people make when they speak, which is taken to reveal their true or subconscious thoughts

Word history: from Sigmund *Freud*, 1856–1939, Austrian physician and founder of modern psychoanalysis

friable (fruy-uh-buhl)
adjective easily crumbled: ***friable** rock*

Word building: **friability** *noun*
Word history: Latin

friar
noun a member of a Christian religious order, such as the Dominicans or the Franciscans, who lives a simple life of prayer

Word history: Middle English, from Old French, from Latin word meaning 'brother'

friction
noun **1** the rubbing of one thing against another: *There is some **friction** where the wheel touches the mudguard.*
2 *Physics* the resistance to the relative motion or sliding and rolling of the surfaces of bodies that are touching each other
3 a clash or struggle: *There was **friction** between the sisters.*

Word history: from Latin word meaning 'a rubbing'

Friday
noun the sixth day of the week, following Thursday

Word history: Middle English, Old English *Frīgedæg* Freo's day (Old English goddess identified with Venus)

fridge
noun → **refrigerator**

Word history: abbreviation

fridge magnet
noun a magnet, usually decorative, used for attaching notes, etc., to a refrigerator door

friend (frend)
noun someone you like and who likes you (***companion***, ***mate***, ***pal***, ***playmate***)

Word use: The opposite of this is **adversary**, **enemy** or **foe**.
Word building: **friendly** *adjective* **friendship** *noun*
Word history: Old English *frēond*, *frēogan* love

frieze (freez)
noun a band around the top of a wall which is often decorated with a painted or sculpted pattern

Word history: French, from Medieval Latin word meaning 'embroidery'

> **frieze / freeze**
> Don't confuse **frieze** with **freeze**, which means 'to turn to ice', or 'to feel very cold'.

frigate (<u>frig</u>-uht)
noun a warship, often used as an escort vessel

Word history: French, from Italian

fright
noun **1** a sudden feeling of fear or shock: *She crept up to give him a* ***fright****.*
2 someone or something of a shocking or silly appearance: *to look a* ***fright***

Word history: Old English *fryhto*

frighten
verb **1** to scare or terrify (***alarm***, ***petrify***, ***shock***, ***terrorise***)
phrase **2 frighten off** (or **away**), to drive off or away by scaring: *The cat* ***frightened off*** *the bird by stalking it.*

Word building: **frightened** *adjective*

frightful
adjective **1** alarming or unpleasant: *They had a* ***frightful*** *time trying to cross the flooded river.* (***dreadful***, ***frightening***, ***horrible***, ***terrible***)
2 very bad: *We saw a* ***frightful*** *film.*

frightfully
adverb very: *That music is* ***frightfully*** *loud.*

frigid (<u>frij</u>-uhd)
adjective **1** very cold: *a* ***frigid*** *climate* (***freezing***, ***frosty***, ***icy***, ***wintry***)
2 stiff or unfriendly: *His* ***frigid*** *manner puts people off.*

Word history: Latin

frigidity
noun coldness

frigidly
adverb stiffly: *She smiled* ***frigidly*** *at me when I said I was sorry.*

frill
noun a ruffled edge, used to decorate something like the hem or neck of a dress

Word building: **frill** *verb*
Word history: perhaps from Flemish word meaning 'frill' (of a collar)

fringe
noun **1** a border of loose or bunched threads on something like a scarf or rug
2 hair which has been cut across the forehead
3 the edge or outer part: *We live on the* ***fringe*** *of the town.*

Word building: **fringe** *verb*
Word history: Middle English, from Old French, from Late Latin word meaning 'border', 'fringe'

fringe benefit
noun a reward received in addition to wages, as a car, travel allowance, etc.

frisbee
noun a flat plastic disc with a rim, designed to stay in the air for some time when thrown with horizontal spin, usually as part of a game

Word history: Trademark

frisk
verb **1** to leap around playfully, as a lamb or kitten does (***caper***, ***dance***, ***gambol***, ***prance***, ***skip***)
2 *Colloquial* to search for hidden weapons: *After the bomb scare, guards* ***frisked*** *the visitors.*

frisky
adjective lively (***energetic***, ***frolicsome***, ***playful***)

Adjective forms: **friskier**, **friskiest**
Word history: Old French, from Germanic

frittata (fri-<u>tah</u>-tuh)
noun a thick omelette containing vegetables, cheese, seasonings, etc.

Word history: Italian word meaning 'fried'

fritter[1]
verb to waste gradually: *She* ***fritters*** *her money away on useless things.*

Word history: earlier *fitter*, from *fit* part

fritter[2]
noun a small piece of food, often fruit, fried in batter: *banana* ***fritter***

Word history: Middle English, from Old French word meaning 'fry'

frivolous (<u>friv</u>-uh-luhs)
adjective not serious: *He is in trouble for giving* ***frivolous*** *answers to the questions.*

Word building: **frivolity** (fruh-<u>vol</u>-uh-tee) *noun* **frivolously** *adverb*
Word history: from Latin word meaning 'silly', 'trifling', 'paltry'

frizz
verb **1** to form into small, tight curls or little tufts
noun **2** the condition of being frizzed
3 frizzed hair

Verb forms: it **frizzed**, it has **frizzed**, it is **frizzing**
Noun forms: The plural is **frizzes**.
Word history: backformation from *frizzle*

fro
phrase **to and fro 1** back and forwards
2 here and there

Word history: Middle English, from Scandinavian

frock
noun a dress

Word history: Middle English, from Old French, of Germanic origin

frog
noun a tailless creature with webbed feet and long back legs for jumping, which lives in water or on land

Word history: Old English *frogga*

frolic
noun happy play: *After school they had a good* ***frolic*** *outside.*

Word building: **frolic** *verb* (**frolicked, frolicking**)
frolicsome *adjective*
Word history: from Dutch word meaning 'joyful'

from
preposition a word that marks a starting point, used to express **1** distance in regard to space, time, order, etc.: *The train runs west* ***from*** *Sydney.* | ***from*** *that moment on* | *to stop yourself* ***from*** *laughing*
2 difference or distinction: *What is 5* ***from*** *10?* | *to tell black* ***from*** *white*
3 source or origin: *to get an idea* ***from*** *my friend* | *to draw sketches* ***from*** *real life*
4 cause or reason: *to die* ***from*** *starvation*

Word history: Old English *fram*, preposition, from, as adverb, forwards, forth

from / off
These words are both often used as prepositions in the following way:
I'll buy that book from you.
I'll buy that book off you.
Note that some people consider this use of **off** to be incorrect so it's better to avoid it in formal essays.

frond
noun the divided leaf of plants such as ferns and palms

Word history: from Latin word meaning 'leafy branch'

front (frunt)
noun **1** the part or surface facing forward or most often seen: *The door is at the* ***front.***
2 the battle line: *Many soldiers died at the* ***front.***
3 land facing a road or shore: *No-one owns the lake* ***front.***
4 in weather, a surface where two air-masses with different temperatures, etc., meet
verb Australian, NZ Colloquial **5** to arrive or turn up: *We waited an hour but they didn't bother to* ***front.***

Word building: **front** *adjective*
Word use: You can also use **front up** for definition 5.
Word history: Middle English, from Latin word meaning 'forehead', 'front'

front bench
noun the members of parliament who are government ministers or opposition spokespersons

Word building: **frontbencher** *noun*

frontier (frun-tear)
noun **1** the border of a country or state
2 the end of known territory: *The early settlers explored the* ***frontier.*** (***boundary, edge, limit***)

Word history: Middle English *frountere*, from Old French

frost
noun **1** extreme cold
2 the covering of ice formed when dew freezes
verb **3** to ice: *The baker* ***frosted*** *the cake.*

Word building: **frosted** *adjective* **frosty** *adjective* (**frostier, frostiest**)
Word history: Old English *frost*

frostbite
noun damage done by the freezing of exposed parts of your body in very cold conditions

Word building: **frostbitten** *adjective*

frosting
noun **1** a fluffy cake icing
2 a frostlike coating on glass, metal or other surfaces

froth
noun the mass of tiny bubbles that rise to the top of some liquids (***bubbles, foam***)

Word building: **froth** *verb* **frothy** *adjective* (**frothier, frothiest**)
Word history: Middle English *frothe*

frown
verb **1** to wrinkle your forehead in a look of worry or displeasure (***glare, glower, scowl***)
phrase **2 frown on,** to disapprove of (***find fault with, take a dim view of, take exception to***)

Word building: **frown** *noun*
Word history: Middle English *froune(n)*, from Old French word meaning 'surly expression'; of Celtic origin

froze
verb past tense of **freeze**

frozen
verb **1** past participle of **freeze**
adjective **2** made solid by cold: ***frozen*** *yoghurt*
3 covered with ice: *a* ***frozen*** *landscape*

Word use: This word comes from the verb **freeze**.

frugal (frooh-guhl)
adjective **1** very careful not to waste anything (***economical, provident, thrifty***)
2 poor or cheap: *They had a* ***frugal*** *meal of bread and tomatoes.*

Word use: The opposite of definition 1 is **wasteful.**
Word building: **frugality** *noun* **frugally** *adverb*
Word history: from Latin word meaning 'economical'

fruit
noun **1** the edible part which grows from the flowers of trees and plants, such as apples, oranges, pineapples, and many others
2 the result: *Her book is the* ***fruit*** *of years of work.*
verb **3** to bear fruit: *When will the apple tree* ***fruit?***

Word history: Middle English, from Old French, from Latin word meaning 'enjoyment', 'proceeds', 'fruit'

fruit-fly
noun a small two-winged fly which lays its eggs in developing fruit and which is a serious pest

fruitful
adjective producing pleasing, useful results: *a **fruitful** partnership* | *a **fruitful** discussion* (***productive***)

fruition (frooh-ish-uhn)
noun **1** the reaching of a goal or production of results: *the **fruition** of his labours*
2 the bearing of fruit

Word history: Middle English, from Late Latin word meaning 'enjoyment'

fruitless
adjective useless; not achieving anything: *a **fruitless** search* | *a **fruitless** attempt*

fruity
adjective **1** like fruit in taste or smell
2 rich or mellow in tone: *a **fruity** voice*

Adjective forms: **fruitier**, **fruitiest**

frump
noun an untidy, unfashionably dressed woman

Word building: **frumpish** *adjective* **frumpy** *adjective* (**frumpier**, **frumpiest**)

frustrate
verb to prevent or put difficulties in the way of: *She **frustrates** his attempts to help by doing everything herself.* (***block***, ***hamper***, ***hinder***, ***impede***, ***inhibit***)

Word building: **frustrated** *adjective* **frustration** *noun*
Word history: from Latin word meaning 'having disappointed or deceived'

fry
verb to cook in a pan, using fat or oil

Verb forms: I **fried**, I have **fried**, I am **frying**
Word building: **fried** *adjective*
Word history: Middle English *frye(n)*, from French, from Latin

ftp
noun **1** a computer program which enables the transfer of data from one computer to another via a communications network
verb **2** to transfer (data) this way: *to **ftp** the files to India*

Word history: abbreviation of *f(ile) t(ransfer) p(rotocol)*

fuchsia (fyooh-shuh)
noun a small shrub grown for its showy hanging flowers, usually pink, red, or purple

Word history: Neo-Latin, named after Leonhard *Fuchs*, 1501–66, German botanist

fudge
noun a soft sweet made from sugar, butter and milk

fuel
noun **1** anything, such as wood, petrol or kerosene, which is burnt to give heat or to make an engine work
verb **2** to get or supply with fuel

Verb forms: I **fuelled**, I have **fuelled**, I am **fuelling**
Word history: Middle English, from Old French, from Latin word meaning 'hearth', 'fireplace'

fuel cell
noun a continuously fed battery in which a chemical reaction is used directly to produce electricity, the fuel being on the anode side and the oxidant on the cathode side

fugitive (fyooh-juh-tiv)
noun someone who is running away (***absconder***, ***escapee***, ***runaway***, ***truant***)

Word building: **fugitive** *adjective*
Word history: from Latin word meaning 'fleeing'

fugue (fyoohg)
noun a piece of music in which a short melody is played or sung and then copied by other instruments or voices

Word history: French, from Italian, from Latin word meaning 'flight'

fulcrum (foolk-ruhm)
noun the point on which something balances or turns: *A bent pipe made a **fulcrum** for the seesaw.*

Noun forms: The plural is **fulcrums** or **fulcra**.
Word history: from Latin word meaning 'bedpost'

fulfil
verb **1** to carry out: *He **fulfilled** his promise to pay.* (***carry through***, ***live up to***)
2 to satisfy: *Each weekend she **fulfils** her need to paint.*

Verb forms: I **fulfilled**, I have **fulfilled**, I am **fulfilling**
Word use: The opposite of definition 1 is **neglect**.
Word building: **fulfilled** *adjective* **fulfilling** *adjective* **fulfilment** *noun*
Word history: Old English *fullfyllan*

full
adjective **1** filled up (***bursting***, ***crammed***, ***packed***)
2 whole or complete: *Jason has collected the **full** series of cards.* (***entire***, ***total***)
3 wide or loose: *She is wearing a **full** skirt.*
adverb **4** completely
phrase **5 full of**, very interested in or involved with: *She's **full of** her new job.* (***enthusiastic about***, ***keen on***)
6 full of yourself, very vain or self-centred
7 full up, having eaten enough
8 in full,
a to or for the full amount: *You must pay **in full**.*
b not shortened or reduced: *to read a book **in full***
9 on the full, of a ball, as it is flying through the air before bouncing: *Catch it **on the full**.*
10 to the full, to the utmost extent: *She enjoys life **to the full**.*

Word building: **fully** *adverb*
Word history: Old English *full*, *ful*

Full Bench
noun a sitting of a court or commission for an important matter, with all the judges of the court, etc., or several of them representing all

full-on
Colloquial
adjective **1** full of life, enthusiasm, energy, etc.; with nothing held back: *She's a **full-on** sort of person.* | ***full-on** rock'n'roll*
adverb **2** with complete effort, strength, etc.: *The car ran **full-on** into the fence.*

full preferential voting
noun a form of preferential voting in which voters must indicate their order of preference for all the candidates

Word use: Compare this with **partial preferential voting** and **optional preferential voting**.

full stop
noun a punctuation mark (.) which is used at the end of a sentence or, sometimes, to show that a word has been shortened

Word use: Other names are **full point** and **period**.

You use a **full stop** at the end of a sentence except where a question mark or an exclamation mark is needed:

The dog bit the man.

Sometimes, if you are reporting a conversation, you may use a short phrase which, although it is not a sentence, can make sense on its own and can have a full stop:

'Which hat do you like?'

'This one.'

'Did you see him?'

'No.'

Full stops are used in some abbreviations. Look up **abbreviation** for a full explanation.

full-time
adjective working most of the week at any job: *a **full-time** mother | a **full-time** actor*

fulminate (<u>fool</u>-muh-nayt)
verb **1** to explode with a loud noise
phrase **2 fulminate against**, to shout out disapprovingly or angrily at

Word building: **fulmination** *noun*
Word history: from Latin word meaning 'struck by lightning'

fulsome
adjective **1** overdone or insincere: ***fulsome** praise*
2 lavish; unlimited: *We showered her with **fulsome** praise for her amazing effort.*

Word use: Note that some people feel that definition 2 is not a correct use.
Word history: Middle English *fulsum*

fumble
verb to handle clumsily: *He **fumbled** the catch and dropped the ball.* (**botch**, **bungle**, ***fluff***)

Word building: **fumbler** *noun* **fumbling** *adjective*
Word history: Low German

fume
verb **1** to give out fumes
2 to be very angry: *I **fume** whenever I think of the government's waste of money.*
noun **3 fumes**, smoke or gas which can be easily seen or smelt

Word building: **fuming** *adjective*
Word history: Middle English, from Old French, from Latin word meaning 'smoke', 'steam', 'fume'

fumigate (<u>fyooh</u>-muh-gayt)
verb to treat with chemical fumes to get rid of insect pests

Word building: **fumigation** *noun* **fumigator** *noun*
Word history: from Latin word meaning 'smoked'

fun
noun **1** enjoyment: *We had **fun** at the pool this morning.*
adjective **2** *Colloquial* providing enjoyment or entertainment; lively: *a **fun** place to be | a **fun** person.*
phrase **3 like fun**, *Colloquial* an expression used to mean that that there is absolutely no chance of something happening: ***Like fun** I'll give you breakfast in bed!*
4 make fun of, to make jokes about or make people laugh at someone or something: *They all **made fun of** my new hairdo. | He **made fun of** her because of her accent.*

Word history: perhaps dialect variant of obsolete *fon*, verb, befool

function
noun **1** what someone or something is meant to do: *one of the **functions** of a treasurer | the **function** of a vehicle*
2 a social or official occasion, such as a dinner to raise money
3 *Mathematics* a quantity whose value depends upon values of other quantities, called variables of the function
verb **4** to work or go: *The heater isn't **functioning**.*

Word history: from Latin word meaning 'performance'

functional
adjective **1** designed to perform some function rather than for decoration: *These shoes aren't very attractive, but they're **functional**.*
2 useful or efficient: *a **functional** design*
3 operating (correctly): *How many **functional** keyboards do we have in the office?*

functional grammar
noun a grammar in which the analysis begins with the functions of language and words rather than their forms

functionality
noun **1** the purpose designed to be fulfilled by a device, tool, machine, etc.
2 *Computers* the range of functions which an application has

function key
noun one of a set of keys (usually ten or twelve) on a computer keyboard, which can be programmed to perform certain functions, often to save you having to press several other keys to perform the same function

fund
noun **1** a supply of money: *They have a **fund** which pays for their holidays.*
2 a supply: *His **fund** of experience is helpful.*
verb **3** to pay for: *to **fund** a new project*

Word history: from Latin word meaning 'bottom'

fundamental
adjective **1** most important or basic: *You have to learn the **fundamental** rules of the road before you can get a licence.* (***cardinal***, ***chief***, ***key***, ***main***, ***primary***)
noun **2** the basic rule or principle underlying any system: *He is learning the **fundamentals** of computer programming.*

Word history: Neo-Latin, from Latin word meaning 'foundation'

fundamentally
adverb basically

fund manager
noun **1** a commercial organisation that manages investors' money for a fee
2 someone who manages an investment portfolio

funeral
noun a ceremony held to honour someone who has died and to take their body to the place where it will be buried or cremated

Word history: Middle English, from Medieval Latin, from Latin word meaning 'funeral', 'death'

funereal (fyooh-near-ree-uhl)
adjective gloomy as a funeral

Word history: from Latin word meaning 'of a funeral' + *-al*

fungi (fung-gee)
noun plural of **fungus**

fungus
noun a simple plant, such as the mushroom, mould or yeast, which grows in dark or damp places

Noun forms: The plural is **fungi** or **funguses**.
Word history: from Latin word meaning 'mushroom', 'fungus'

funicular railway (fuh-nik-yuh-luh rayl-way)
noun a short railway system operating up steep slopes, in which cars or trains on cables move up and down at the same time, balancing each other's weight

Word history: Latin *fūniculus* little rope + *-ar*

funk[1]
noun Old-fashioned, Colloquial fear or a condition of terror: *He was in a **funk** about his exams.*

Word building: **funk** *verb*
Word history: perhaps Flemish

funk[2]
noun an up-tempo style of soul music, influenced by jazz, with a lot of syncopation

funnel
noun **1** an open-ended cone used for pouring liquid or dry goods into a container with a narrow opening
2 the wide tube which forms the chimney of a ship or steam-engine
verb **3** to pour through a funnel

Verb forms: I **funnelled**, I have **funnelled**, I am **funnelling**
Word history: Middle English *fonel*, from Old French, from Latin

funnel-web
noun a large black venomous spider of eastern Australia, which builds a funnel-shaped web

funny
adjective **1** amusing or comical (***droll***, ***hilarious***, ***humorous***)
2 strange: *There's something **funny** about this recipe.*

Adjective forms: **funnier**, **funniest**
Word building: **funnily** *adverb*

funny bone
noun the point of your elbow which tingles when it is hit

fur
noun **1** the hairy coat of some animals, such as dogs, cats and possums
2 the skin of some animals, such as rabbits, minks and foxes, which is treated and made into a garment: *The ladies wore **furs**.*

Word building: **furry** *adjective* (**furrier**, **furriest**)
Word history: Middle English *furre*, from Old French word meaning 'line with fur', from Germanic

fur / fir
Don't confuse **fur** with **fir**, which is a kind of tree.

furious
adjective **1** extremely angry (***annoyed***, ***indignant***, ***irate***, ***livid***)
2 strong or violent: *A **furious** wind knocked the trees over.* (***ferocious***, ***fierce***, ***forceful***, ***intense***, ***wild***)

Word building: **furiously** *adverb* **fury** *noun* **infuriate** *verb*
Word history: Middle English, from Latin word meaning 'raging'

furl
verb to roll up: *The sailors lowered and **furled** the flag.*

Word history: Old French word meaning 'to bind firm', from Latin

furlong
noun a unit of distance in the imperial system, just over 200 metres long

Word use: Look up **imperial system**.
Word history: Old English *furlang*, from *furh* furrow + *lang* long

furlough (fer-loh)
noun leave of absence from duty, especially for soldiers

Word history: variant of *furloff*, from Dutch word meaning 'leave'

furnace
noun a structure for producing heat, as in the steel industry or for heating buildings

Word history: Middle English *furneise*, from Old French, from Latin word meaning 'oven'

furnish
verb **1** to decorate with furniture and other fittings: *They have **furnished** the sitting room with cane chairs.*
2 to provide: *The attendant will **furnish** you with pens and paper.*

Word building: **furnisher** *noun*
Word history: Middle English *furnisshe(n)*, from Old French word meaning 'accomplish', 'furnish', from Germanic

furniture
noun the chairs, beds, tables and other fittings of a room or house

Word history: from French word meaning 'furnish'

furore (fyooh-raw)
noun an outburst of noisy disorder

Word use: You can also use **furor**.
Word history: from Latin word meaning 'a raging'

furphy (fer-fee)
noun Australian a piece of gossip

Noun forms: The plural is **furphies**.
Word history: from John *Furphy*, manufacturer in Victoria of water and sanitation carts, which during World War I were centres of gossip

furrow
noun **1** a groove, especially one made by a plough (***channel, ditch, rut, trench***)
verb **2** to wrinkle: *A frown* ***furrowed*** *her brow.*

Word history: Old English *furh*

further
adverb **1** at or to a greater distance: *I ran* ***further*** *than you.*
2 in addition
adjective **3** more distant: *The* ***further*** *house is ours.*
4 more: *Do you want* ***further*** *advice?*
verb **5** to help to advance: *He will try to* ***further*** *my career.* (***facilitate, further, promote***)

Word use: This word is the comparative form in the set **far, further, furthest**.
Word history: Old English *furthor*

further / farther

People have tried to make distinctions between these two words but in fact they are just different ways of spelling the same word. In Australia the more popular spelling seems to be **further**:

I can go no further down the track.

I will give you no further advice.

The superlative is either **furthest** or **farthest**.

Note, however, that you can't use **farther** for the verb **to further** (see definition 5).

further education
noun any form of education beyond the school system, such as at colleges, universities, etc.

furtive
adjective stealthy or sly: *She took a* ***furtive*** *look to see if anyone was watching.* (***cagey, secretive, surreptitious, underhand***)

Word building: **furtively** *adverb*
Word history: from Latin word meaning 'stolen'

fury
noun extreme or violent anger: *He smashed the door in his* ***fury***. (***ill temper, ire, rage, vexation, wrath***)

Noun forms: The plural is **furies**.
Word history: Middle English, from Latin word meaning 'rage', 'madness'

fuse[1]
noun **1** the wick which sets off an explosive when it is lit
2 the safety wire in an electrical circuit which cuts off the power if there is a fault
verb **3** to blow a fuse: *The lights* ***fused*** *and everything went dark.*

Word history: Italian, from Latin word meaning 'spindle'

fuse[2]
verb **1** to melt into one: *He* ***fused*** *the two metals by heating them.* | *The burnt wires* ***fused***.
2 to join inseparably: *The two powers* ***fused*** *their forces to fight the common enemy.* (***blend, combine, merge***)

Word history: Latin *fūsus*, past participle, poured, melted, cast

fuselage (fyooh-zuh-lahzh, fyooh-zuh-lij)
noun the body of an aircraft

Word history: French word meaning 'spindle-shaped', from Latin

fusion
noun the coming together of two light atomic nuclei, for example deuterium, to form a single nucleus together with a release of energy

Word use: You can also use **nuclear fusion**.
Word history: from Latin word meaning 'a pouring out'

fuss
noun **1** unnecessary bother: *She does everything without* ***fuss***.
2 a noise or disturbance: *When they couldn't get the seats they wanted, they made a great* ***fuss***. (***commotion, hullaballoo, riot, tumult, turmoil***)

fussy
adjective busy or worrying about unimportant things (***attentive, careful, conscientious, diligent***)

Adjective forms: **fussier, fussiest**
Word use: The opposite of this is **easygoing**.

futile
adjective useless and ineffective: *The dog made* ***futile*** *jumps at the cat up in the tree.* (***impossible, ineffectual, useless, vain***)

Word history: from Latin word meaning 'untrustworthy', 'vain', literally 'that easily pours out'

futility
noun uselessness

future
noun the time which has not yet come: *You shouldn't worry about the* ***future***.

Word building: **future** *adjective*
Word history: Middle English, from Latin word meaning the future sense of the word 'to be'

future tense
noun the form of a verb which shows that something is going to happen

For information about **future tense**, look up **verbs: future tense**.

futuristic (fyooh-chuh-ris-tik)
adjective **1** having to do with an artistic and literary movement (**futurism**), started in Italy in 1909, which expressed the movement and speed of the machine age
2 of a work of art, in a modern style or not traditional: *a* ***futuristic*** *painting*
3 of design in clothes, furniture, etc., looking towards the space age

fuzz
noun **1** a fluffy mass or coating
2 *Colloquial* the police

fuzzy
adjective blurred: *a* ***fuzzy*** *photograph*

Adjective forms: **fuzzier, fuzziest**

FX
plural noun in films, radio, etc., special effects, for example, bombs exploding, snow falling, etc.

Gg

gabble
verb **1** to talk or speak so rapidly that no-one can understand you: *to* ***gabble*** *an answer | I can't understand when you* ***gabble*** *like that.*
2 of geese, etc., to cackle or make noisy high sounds
noun **3** rapid talk which cannot be understood

Word building: **gabbler** *noun*
Word history: from *gab*

gaberdine (gab-uh-<u>deen</u>, <u>gab</u>-uh-deen)
noun closely woven cloth made of wool, cotton or spun rayon

Word use: You can also use **gabardine**.
Word history: Spanish, from Middle High German word meaning 'pilgrimage'

gable
noun the triangular part of a wall between the two slopes of a roof

Word history: Middle English, probably from Scandinavian

gad
phrase **gad about**, to move with no particular purpose from place to place, often hoping to find pleasure

Verb forms: I **gadded**, I have **gadded**, I am **gadding**

gadget
noun a small invention or useful piece of machinery which performs a particular job: *a* ***gadget*** *for slicing carrots*

gaffe (gaf)
noun a mistake you make in public

Word history: French

gaffer tape
noun a strong adhesive cloth tape

Word history: from *gaffer*, a film or television lighting technician. Gaffers traditionally use this tape to attach things together temporarily, to stick cables to the floor so people don't trip over them, etc.

gag[1]
verb **1** to cover someone's mouth to stop them from speaking or making a sound
2 to be unable to swallow, and make sounds as though you are vomiting
noun **3** something pushed into or tied round your mouth to prevent you from speaking

Verb forms: I **gagged**, I have **gagged**, I am **gagging**
Word history: probably imitative of the sound of choking

gag[2]
noun a joke or trick (***crack***, ***jest***, ***laugh***, ***wisecrack***)

Word building: **gagger** *noun*

gaggle
noun a flock of geese

Word history: imitative

gaiety (<u>gay</u>-uh-tee)
noun cheerfulness or high spirits (***glee***, ***happiness***, ***merriment***, ***mirth***)

Word history: French

gaily
adverb merrily and happily

gain
verb **1** to get or win: *to* ***gain*** *top marks in an exam | to* ***gain*** *a prize* (***acquire***, ***procure***)
2 to catch up: *He* ***gained*** *rapidly on the fat man.*
noun **3** a profit: *a* ***gain*** *of $2 on the sale*
4 an increase or advance: *His marks showed a substantial* ***gain*** *over the last term.*
phrase **5 gain ground**, to advance or get an advantage: *Our troops began to* ***gain ground*** *in enemy territory.*

Word building: **gainful** *adjective*
Word history: Old French word meaning 'to get possession of', from Germanic word meaning 'to plunder'

gait
noun way of walking or moving: *an old man's* ***gait*** *| a horse's* ***gait***

> **gait / gate**
> Don't confuse **gait** with **gate.** You close a **gate** to block the way.

gaiter (<u>gay</u>-tuh)
noun a cloth or leather covering for the ankle and instep, and sometimes also the lower leg

Word history: French

gala (<u>gah</u>-luh)
noun a celebration or special occasion: *a swimming* ***gala***

Word history: French, from Italian word meaning 'festal pomp', 'finery', from Old French word meaning 'joy', 'pleasure', from Middle Dutch word meaning 'riches'

galah (guh-<u>lah</u>)
noun **1** an Australian cockatoo with pink and grey feathers
2 *Australian Colloquial* a foolish person

Word history: from Yuwaalaraay, an Australian Aboriginal language of the Lightning Ridge region

galaxy
noun **1** a large group of stars held together by gravitation and separated from any other system by large areas of space
2 a gathering of famous people

Noun forms: The plural is **galaxies**.
Word building: **galactic** *adjective*
Word history: Middle English, from Medieval Latin, from Greek word meaning 'milk'

gale
noun a very strong wind

gall (gawl)
noun **1** → **bile**
2 something very bitter or severe: *Losing the race was* ***gall*** *to his pride.*
3 boldness: *You have a lot of* ***gall*** *to say that.*

Word history: Old English *galla*

gallant (gal-uhnt, guh-lant)
adjective **1** brave and noble
2 very polite and courteous (***chivalrous***, ***gracious***)

Word history: Old French word meaning 'splendid', 'magnificent', from *galer* to rejoice

gallantry
noun **1** noble courage
2 polite attention to women

Noun forms: The plural is **gallantries**.

gall bladder
noun a part of your body attached to your liver, which stores bile

galleon (gal-i-uhn, gal-yuhn)
noun a kind of large Spanish sailing ship

Word history: from Spanish word meaning 'large galley'

> **galleon / gallon**
> Don't confuse **galleon** with **gallon**, which is an old-fashioned measure of liquid, equal to about 4.5 litres.

gallery
noun **1** an upper floor or balcony where you can sit, especially in a theatre
2 a room or building where you can see paintings and sculptures
3 a place where you can practise shooting
phrase **4 play to the gallery**, to seek approval by doing popular things rather than things that have been carefully thought out

Noun forms: The plural is **galleries**.
Word history: Italian, from Medieval Latin word meaning 'vestibule'

> **gallery / galley**
> Don't confuse **gallery** with **galley**, which is a long low ship propelled by oars. It is also the kitchen in a ship or an aeroplane.

galley
noun **1** a long low ship propelled by oars
2 the kitchen in a ship or aeroplane

Noun forms: The plural is **galleys**.
Word history: Middle English, from Medieval Latin, from Late Greek

gallivant (gal-uh-vant)
verb to go from place to place in a carefree way, seeking amusement

Word use: You can also use **galavant**.
Word history: perhaps a humorous alteration of *gallant*

gallon
noun a measure of liquid in the imperial system, equal to about 4.5 litres

Word use: Look up **imperial system**.

gallop
noun **1** the fastest movement of a horse
verb **2** to ride a horse at full speed: *The drovers* ***galloped*** *after the cattle.*

Word history: French, from Old Low German word meaning 'run well'

gallows
noun a wooden frame for hanging criminals

Word history: Old English *galgan*, plural of *g(e)alga* gallows

gallstone
noun a stone formed in the bile ducts or gall bladder

gallup poll
noun the questioning of a representative cross-section of the population in order to work out public opinion

Word history: after George Horace *Gallup*, 1901–84, US statistician

galore
adjective in great numbers: *There were cakes* ***galore*** *at the party.*

Word use: This word is only used after nouns.
Word history: Irish *go leōir* to sufficiency

galoshes (guh-losh-uhz)
plural noun a pair of overshoes made of a waterproof substance

Word history: Middle English, from Latin word meaning 'Gallic sandal'

galvanise (gal-vuh-nuyz)
verb **1** to coat with zinc to prevent rust: *to* ***galvanise*** *iron*
2 to cause to move by, or as if by, an electric current: *to* ***galvanise*** *into action*

Word use: You can also use **galvanize**.

galvanometer (gal-vuh-nom-uh-tuh)
noun an instrument for finding an electric current and measuring its strength and direction

gambit (gam-buht)
noun **1** an opening in chess, in which the player seeks by giving up a pawn or other piece to obtain some advantage
2 any act or course of action designed to obtain some advantage

Word history: French, from Italian word meaning 'a tripping-up'

gamble
verb **1** to play a game in which you risk losing something, especially money
2 to take a chance: *I* ***gambled*** *on his being away that day.*

Word building: **gambler** *noun* **gambling** *noun*
Word history: perhaps Old English *gamenian* to sport, play

gambol (gam-buhl)
verb to jump about in a playful manner: *The children **gambolled** in the shallow water.* (***caper***, ***dance***, ***frisk***, ***prance***, ***skip***)

Verb forms: I **gambolled**, I have **gambolled**, I am **gambolling**
Word history: French word meaning 'leap', from Italian word meaning 'a kick'

game
noun **1** something you can play, usually with set rules: *a **game** of football | a **game** of cards*
2 wild animals, including birds and fish, hunted for food or as a sport: *a book of recipes for cooking **game***
adjective **3** brave and courageous: *as **game** as Ned Kelly* (***bold***, ***fearless***, ***heroic***, ***valiant***)
4 *Colloquial* willing to do something difficult or dangerous: *I'm **game** if you are.*
phrase **5 give the game away**,
a to give up
b to reveal a secret
6 have the game sewn up, to be in charge of the situation
7 off your game, not giving your best performance
8 play the game, to act fairly, or according to the rules

Word history: Old English *gamen*

gamelan (gum-uh-lun, gam-uh-lan)
noun **1** a South-East Asian tuned percussion instrument
2 an orchestra comprising a number of gamelans, with some woodwind and strings

Word history: Malay

gamete (gam-eet, guh-meet)
noun either of the two germ cells which unite to form a new organism

Word building: **gametic** *adjective*
Word history: Neo-Latin, from Greek *gametē* wife or *gametēs* husband

gamma rays
plural noun rays similar to X-rays, but of higher frequency and shorter wavelength, forming part of the radiation of radioactive substances

gammon
noun **1** ham which is smoked or cured
2 meat from the lower end of a side of bacon

Word history: Middle English, from Old Northern French word meaning 'ham', from *gambe* hoof, leg, from Late Latin

gamut (gam-uht)
noun the whole scale or range: *A good actor can express the whole **gamut** of emotion.*

Word history: Medieval Latin, contraction of *gamma ut*, from *gamma*, used to represent the first or lowest tone (G) in the medieval scale + *ut* (later *do*)

gander
noun a male goose

Word use: The female is called a **goose**.
Word history: Old English *gan(d)ra*

gang
noun **1** a band or group: *a **gang** of children* (***bunch***, ***mob***)
2 a group of people working together: *a **gang** of labourers*
phrase **3 gang up on**, to combine against: *We all decided to **gang up on** the bully.*

Word history: Old English *gongan, gangan*

gangling (gang-gling)
adjective awkwardly tall and thin: *a **gangling** youth who had grown out of his clothes*

Word history: related to obsolete *gangrel* gangling person, from *gang*

gangly
adjective tall, thin, and awkward in movement: *a **gangly** teenager*

Word use: You can also use **gangling**.
Word building: **gangliness** *noun*

gangplank
noun a movable board used as a bridge for going on and off a ship

Word use: You can also use **gangway**.

gangrene (gang-green)
noun the rotting of flesh caused by the blood supply being cut off

Word building: **gangrenous** *adjective*
Word history: Latin, from Greek word meaning 'an eating sore'

gangster
noun a member of a gang of criminals (***bandit***, ***criminal***, ***crook***, ***hood***, ***outlaw***)

gangway
noun **1** a passageway, especially on a ship
2 → **gangplank**

Word history: Old English *gangweg*

gannet
noun any of several large coastal birds which dive from great heights to catch fish

Word history: Middle English and Old English *ganet*

gantry (gan-tree)
noun **1** a bridge-like framework, such as the ones holding railway signals above the tracks, etc.
2 a wheeled frame supporting something, such as a rocket or a travelling crane

Noun forms: The plural is **gantries**.
Word history: dialect *gawn* (contraction of gallon) + *-tree* supporting frame

gaol (jayl)
noun → **jail**

Word history: Middle English *gay(h)ole, gaile*, from Old Northern French, from Latin word meaning 'cavity', 'enclosure', 'cage'

gaol / goal

Don't confuse **gaol** (an alternative spelling for **jail**) with **goal**.

A **goal** is what you aim the ball at, in games such as football and basketball.

Whatever you aim towards can be your **goal**:

His goal is to play for Australia.

gap
noun **1** a break or opening: *a **gap** in the fence* (***aperture**, **chink**, **hole**, **slit***)
2 a blank or unfilled space: *a **gap** in my memory | a **gap** between words*
Word history: Middle English, from Scandinavian

gape
verb **1** to stare with your mouth wide open: *They all **gaped** at her green hair.* (***gawk**, **gaze**, **goggle***)
2 to split or become open: *Your jeans are **gaping** at the seams.*
Word history: Middle English *gapen*, from Scandinavian

garage
noun **1** a building for keeping a car, bus or truck
2 a place where cars are repaired and petrol is sold (***petrol station**, **service station***)
Word history: French word meaning 'put in shelter', from Provençal word meaning 'keep', 'heed', from Germanic

garb
noun **1** clothes, especially of a special style or kind (***apparel**, **attire**, **clothing**, **dress***)
2 covering or form
verb **3** to dress or clothe
Word history: French, from Italian word meaning 'grace', from Germanic

garbage
noun rubbish or waste material (***debris**, **junk**, **refuse**, **trash***)

garble
verb to mix up and so make hard to understand: *to **garble** a message*
Word history: Italian, from Arabic word meaning 'sift', perhaps from Late Latin word meaning 'little sieve'

garden
noun **1** an area, usually with trees and plants, used for pleasure and as a place to relax: *the front **garden** | a botanical **garden***
2 a flower bed: *a herb **garden***
Word building: **gardener** *noun*
Word history: Middle English, from Old Northern French, of Germanic origin

gardenia (gah-deen-yuh, gah-dee-nee-uh)
noun an evergreen tree or shrub native to China, South Africa, etc., including species grown for their sweet-smelling, waxlike, white flowers
Word history: Neo-Latin; named after Dr Alexander *Garden*, 1730–91, US physician

garfish
noun a fish found in Australian seas and estuaries, with a slender body and the lower jaw forming a needle-like point
Noun forms: The plural is **garfishes** or **garfish**.
Word history: Middle English *garfysshe*, from *gar* (Old English *gār* spear) + *fysshe* fish

gargle
verb to move a liquid around inside your throat without swallowing
Word history: from French word meaning 'throat'

gargoyle
noun a spout, often carved in the shape of an ugly head with an open mouth, which carries rainwater off a roof
Word history: Middle English, from Old French word meaning 'throat'

garish (gair-rish, gah-rish)
adjective bright and attracting attention: ***garish** colours* (***colourful**, **gaudy**, **rich**, **vivid***)
Word history: from Middle English word meaning 'stare'

garland
noun a string of flowers or leaves you wear as an ornament
Word history: Middle English, from Old French

garlic
noun a plant whose strong-smelling bulb is used in cooking and sometimes as a medicine
Word history: Old English *gār* spear +*lēac* leek

garment
noun a piece of clothing, such as a dress or shirt
Word history: Middle English, from Old French word meaning 'equip'

garnet (gah-nuht)
noun **1** any of a group of hard, silicate minerals of which a deep red variety is used as a gem
2 a deep red colour
Word building: **garnet** *adjective*
Word history: Middle English, from Medieval Latin word meaning 'garnet', 'pomegranate', literally 'having grains or seeds'

garnish
verb to make more pleasing to taste or look at: ***Garnish** the fish with parsley and lemon.*
Word use: This word is used mostly in cookery.
Word building: **garnish** *noun*
Word history: Middle English, from Old French word meaning 'prepare'

garret
noun a room just under the roof of a house (***attic***)
Word history: Middle English, from Old French word meaning 'watchtower'

garrison
noun **1** a group of soldiers who are ready to defend a fort or town
2 a place that has been strengthened against attack
Word building: **garrison** *verb*
Word history: Middle English, from Old French word meaning 'defence'

garrotte (guh-rot)
noun **1** a method of killing, originally with an instrument causing strangulation, later by one breaking the neck
2 the instrument used
verb **3** to kill by the garrotte
4 to strangle, especially for the purpose of robbery
Verb forms: I **garrotted**, I have **garrotted**, I am **garrotting**
Word use: You can also use **garotte** or **garrote**.
Word history: Spanish word originally meaning 'a stick' (formerly used in drawing a cord tight), from Provençal word meaning 'cudgel', 'stick for twisting a cord tight', from Celtic *garra* leg

garrulous (ga-ruh-luhs)
adjective very talkative (***chatty***, ***loquacious***, ***voluble***)

Word history: from Latin word meaning 'talkative'

garter
noun a band made of elastic worn around your leg to hold up your long socks

Word history: Middle English, from Old Northern French word meaning 'the bend of the knee', from Celtic word meaning 'leg'

gas[1]
noun **1** any air-like substance that will take up the whole of the space that contains it
2 coal gas or natural gas used as a fuel: *We use **gas** for cooking.*
verb **3** to make sick or kill with a poisonous gas

Noun forms: The plural is **gases**.
Verb forms: I **gassed**, I have **gassed**, I am **gassing**
Word building: **gaseous** *adjective* **gassy** *adjective*
Word history: coined by JB van Helmont, 1577–1644, Flemish chemist; suggested by Greek *cháos* chaos

gas[2]
noun a US word for **petrol**

Word history: short for *gasoline*

gash
noun a long deep cut: *a **gash** in her leg* (***incision***, ***opening***, ***slit***)

Word building: **gash** *verb*
Word history: Old Northern French *garser* scarify

gasket
noun a metal or rubber fitting used to seal a joint, especially one in a car engine

gasp
noun **1** a sudden short intake of breath: *He gave a **gasp** of horror.*
verb **2** to catch your breath or struggle for breath with your mouth open (***blow***, ***heave***, ***pant***, ***puff***, ***wheeze***)

Word history: Middle English, from Scandinavian; related to Old English *gipian* yawn, *gipung* open mouth

gastric
adjective having to do with your stomach: ***gastric** juices* | ***gastric** pains*

gastric bypass
noun a surgical procedure for the treatment of obesity in which the stomach is stapled to make it smaller

gastroenteritis (gas-troh-en-tuh-ruy-tuhs)
noun inflammation of the stomach and intestines

gastronomy (gas-tron-uh-mee)
noun the art or science of good eating

Word building: **gastronomic, gastronomical** *adjective*
Word history: French, from Greek

gastropod (gas-truh-pod)
noun any of a class of molluscs including the snails, slugs and whelks, having a flattened muscular foot on which they move about

Word history: *gastro-* stomach + *-pod* foot

gate
noun **1** a movable frame for closing an entrance or blocking a passageway
2 an opening through which you can enter an enclosed area
3 the number of people who pay for admission to a sporting event

Word history: Old English *gatu* gates, plural of *geat* opening in a wall

> **gate / gait**
> Don't confuse **gate** with **gait**. Your **gait** is the way you walk.

gatecrash
verb to enter or be present at without paying or being invited: *to **gatecrash** the tennis tournament* | *to **gatecrash** a party*

gateway
noun Computers **1** a piece of software or hardware which translates between two protocols
2 → **router**

gather
verb **1** to collect or pick: *to **gather** fruit* (***accumulate***, ***amass***, ***pile up***, ***rake in***, ***store***)
2 to understand: *I **gather** that he is an expert.* (***conclude***, ***deduce***, ***infer***, ***reason***)
3 to draw into small folds on a thread: *to **gather** a skirt at the waist*
4 to come together: *A crowd **gathered** to see the fire.* (***assemble***, ***congregate***, ***meet***, ***rally***)

Word use: The opposite of definitions 1 and 4 is **disperse**.
Word history: Old English *gaderian*, from *geador* together

gauche (gohsh)
adjective clumsy and awkward: ***gauche** manners*

Word building: **gaucherie** *noun*
Word history: French

gaudy
adjective bright and attracting attention: *a **gaudy** beach towel* (***flashy***, ***loud***, ***showy***, ***spectacular***)

Adjective forms: **gaudier, gaudiest**
Word building: **gaudiness** *noun*
Word history: originally attributive use of *gaudy* large bead of rosary, feast

gauge (gayj)
verb **1** to judge or make a guess at: *to **gauge** the public reaction*
2 to measure: *to **gauge** the height of the building* (***calculate***, ***estimate***, ***judge***)
noun **3** thickness, especially of thin objects: *wire of a fine **gauge***
4 an instrument for measuring: *a pressure **gauge***
5 the distance between the two lines of a railway track

Word history: Middle English, from Old Northern French word meaning 'measuring rod'; of Celtic origin

gaunt
adjective very thin and tired-looking in appearance

Word history: Middle English, from French word meaning 'yellowish'

gauntlet[1] (<u>gawnt</u>-luht)
noun **1** a metal glove worn in medieval times to protect the hand
2 a glove with a long cuff for the wrist
phrase **3 take up the gauntlet**, to accept challenge, originally to a duel
4 throw down the gauntlet, to give out a challenge, originally to a duel

Word history: Middle English, from Old French word meaning 'little glove', from Germanic

gauntlet[2] (<u>gawnt</u>-luht)
phrase **run the gauntlet 1** to be forced to run between two rows of men who strike with weapons as someone passes. This was a former common military punishment.
2 to expose yourself to danger, criticism, etc.

Word history: Swedish *gatlopp*, literally, lane run

gauze
noun **1** thin transparent cloth
2 similar material with an open weave, such as wire

Word building: **gauzy** *adjective* (**gauzier, gauziest**)
Word history: French *gaze*, named after *Gaza*, an eastern Mediterranean seaport

gave
verb past tense of **give**

gavel (<u>gav</u>-uhl)
noun a small hammer used by the person in charge of a meeting to signal for quiet

gawk (gawk)
noun **1** an awkward foolish person
verb **2** *Colloquial* to stare stupidly (***gape, gawp, gaze, goggle***)

Word history: Old English *gagol* foolish + *-oc* -ock

gawky (<u>gaw</u>-kee)
adjective awkward: *a **gawky** teenager* (***clumsy, ungainly***)

Adjective forms: **gawkier, gawkiest**

gay
adjective **1** homosexual: ***gay** men*
2 having to do with homosexuals: ***gay** literature*
3 cheerful or bright: ***gay** music* | ***gay** colours* (***colourful, rich, vivid***)
noun **4** a homosexual, especially a male

Word history: Middle English, from Old French

> As long ago as 1935 the adjective **gay** was being used to mean 'homosexual'.
>
> Nowadays this is accepted by most people as standard. This usage also extends to the noun, although this is mainly reserved for male homosexuals:
>
> *Gays and lesbians attended the march.*
>
> Homosexuals adopted the word as an acceptable or positive alternative to words of abuse like 'poofter', 'queer' and 'pansy'.
>
> While this is understandable, it has made people reluctant to use the word gay in its original meaning of 'cheerful' or 'bright'. They feel that they may be misinterpreted. This can certainly happen with literature written before World War II. Remember that if an author writing then refers to *a gay young man*, it most probably means that the man is full of youthful good cheer.

gaze
verb to look long and steadily (***regard, stare***)

Word building: **gaze** *noun*
Word history: Middle English, from Scandinavian

gazebo (guh-<u>zee</u>-boh)
noun a structure having a wide view, especially a turret, pavilion, or summerhouse

Noun forms: The plural is **gazebos** or **gazeboes**.
Word history: perhaps pseudo-Latin coinage on *gaze*, verb, after Latin *vidēbō* I shall see

gazelle
noun a small antelope with large eyes

Word history: French, from Arabic

gazette
noun **1** an official government magazine containing lists of people the government has appointed, etc.
verb **2** to announce or list in a gazette

Word history: French, from Italian, originally a Venetian coin (the price of the gazette)

gazump (guh-<u>zump</u>)
verb **1** in real estate, to bypass by selling at a higher price to another buyer: *to **gazump** a buyer with whom a price has been agreed*
2 to force a buyer to accept a price higher than that previously agreed upon

Word history: originally, to pound; imitative of an explosion or heavy blow

gear
noun **1** a group of toothed wheels, or one of the wheels, that connect with each other to pass on or change the movement of a machine, such as those that carry power from the engine to the wheels of a car
2 equipment: *climbing **gear*** | *cricket **gear*** (***belongings, paraphernalia, possessions, property***)
3 *Colloquial* clothes (***apparel, attire, clothing, dress, garb***)

Word history: Middle English, from Scandinavian

gearbox
noun a case in which gears of a motor are enclosed

gearstick
noun a lever for connecting and disconnecting gears in a car

Word use: You can also use **gearlever** or **gearshift**.

gecko
noun a small lizard which is mostly active at night

Noun forms: The plural is **geckos** or **geckoes**.
Word history: Malay *gēkoq*; imitative

gee[1] (jee)
interjection a mild exclamation of surprise or delight: *Gee! I wasn't expecting that.*

gee[2] (jee)
phrase **gee up**, a command to horses or other animals directing them to go faster: *The jockey tried to **gee up** his horse but he still came last.*

geek
noun Colloquial **1** a person who has an awkward personality and dresses in a conservative way; a person who is not cool (definition 3)
2 a person whose lifestyle revolves around computers

Word history: originally US slang (1900s); from British dialect, variant of *geck* (16thC) a fool, simpleton

geese
noun plural of **goose**

Geiger counter (guy-guh kown-tuh)
noun an instrument for measuring radioactivity, especially after the explosion of an atom bomb

Word history: named after Hans *Geiger*, 1882–1947, German physicist

geisha (gay-shuh)
noun a Japanese girl, trained to amuse men with singing, dancing and conversation

Word history: Japanese

gel (jel)
noun a type of jelly that you can use to help shape your hairstyle

Word history: short for *gelatine*

gelatine
noun a colourless tasteless substance, used to make jellies and glues

Word building: **gelatinous** *adjective*
Word history: French, from Italian word meaning 'jelly', from Latin word meaning 'frozen', 'congealed'

gelato (juh-lah-toh)
noun an iced sweet made from cream, milk or water, with fruit or other flavouring, and whipped at a very low temperature

Word history: Italian

geld (geld)
verb to castrate, especially animals: *to **geld** a colt*

Verb forms: I **gelded** or I **gelt**, I have **gelded** or I have **gelt**, I am **gelding**
Word history: Middle English, from Scandinavian

gelding (gel-ding)
noun a male horse that has had its sex organs removed

Word history: Middle English, from Scandinavian

gelignite (jel-uhg-nuyt)
noun an explosive substance used in mining

gem
noun a stone used in jewellery, after it has been cut and polished

Word history: Middle English, from French, from Latin word meaning 'bud', 'jewel'

gen (jen)
Colloquial
noun **1** all the necessary information about a subject
phrase **2 gen up on**, to get information about: *to **gen up on** a subject*

Verb forms: I **genned**, I have **genned**, I am **genning**
Word history: short form of *general information*

gender
noun **1** *Grammar*
a a set of classes, such as masculine, feminine, and neuter, which together include all nouns
b one class of such a set
2 the condition of being male or female: *The job is open to anyone, regardless of **gender**.*

Word history: Middle English, from Latin word meaning 'race', 'kind', 'sort', 'gender'

gene
noun one of the units in your body which is responsible for passing on characteristics, like blue eyes, from parents to their children

Word building: **genetic** *adjective*
Word history: from Greek word meaning 'breed', 'kind'

> **genes / jeans**
> Don't confuse **genes** (the plural of **gene**) with **jeans**, which are trousers made of denim or other strong material.

genealogy (jee-nee-al-uh-jee)
noun a study or record of the ancestors and relations in your family

Noun forms: The plural is **genealogies**.
Word building: **genealogist** *noun* **genealogical** (jee-nee-uh-loj-i-kuhl) *adjective*
Word history: Middle English, from Late Latin, from Greek word meaning 'tracing of descent'

gene mapping
noun the identification of the place on one of the twenty-three pairs of human chromosomes where a particular gene lies

gene pool
noun the total amount of genetic information, and thus of possibilities for future evolutionary development, held by all the individuals in a specified population

genera (jen-uh-ruh)
noun plural of **genus**

general
adjective **1** concerning all or most people: *a **general** election* (***collective***, ***common***, ***communal***, ***popular***, ***public***)
2 common or widespread: *a **general** feeling of unhappiness*
3 not limited to particular details or information: ***general** instructions*
noun **4** an officer of the highest rank in the Australian army
5 a military commander: *Julius Caesar was a great **general**.*
phrase **6 in general**,
a having to do with the whole group referred to
b usually or commonly

Word building: **generally** *adverb*
Word history: Middle English, from Latin word meaning 'of or belonging to a (whole) race', 'kind'

general anaesthetic
noun a drug which makes your whole body unable to feel pain and makes you lose consciousness

Word use: You can also use **general anesthetic**.

general election
noun a parliamentary election, in which all seats in the house are thrown open, as a federal or state election for the Lower House

generalise
verb to make up a general rule from a limited number of examples

Word use: You can also use **generalize**.

generality
noun **1** a general or vague statement: *to speak in **generalities***
2 a general principle, rule or law
3 the greater part or majority: *the **generality** of people*

Noun forms: The plural is **generalities**.

general practitioner
noun a doctor who does not specialise in any particular branch of medicine but is responsible for the general health of a number of people in a district

Word use: The abbreviation is **GP**.

generate
verb to produce or bring into existence: *The sun **generates** heat.*

Word history: from Latin word meaning 'begotten'

generation
noun **1** all of the people born about the same time: *the younger **generation***
2 the period of years, usually about 25 to 30, thought of as the difference between one generation of a family and another

Word history: Middle English, from Latin

generation text
noun the generation that has grown up using mobile phones: *Kids in **generation text** are so quick at sending SMS messages.*

generation X
noun the generation born in the late 1960s and 1970s: *People think those from **generation X** are more cynical than previous generations.*

Word use: You can also use **X generation** or **gen X**.
Word building: **generation Xer** *noun*

generation Y
noun the generation born in the 1980s and 1990s: *People from **generation Y** have a reputation for being focused on themselves.*

Word use: You can also use **Y generation** or **gen Y**.

generation Z
noun the generation born in the early 2000s: ***Generation Z** is characterised as being at ease with computer technology and the newest communication systems among other things.*

generator
noun a machine for producing electricity

Word history: Latin

generic (juh-<u>ne</u>-rik)
adjective **1** having to do with a genus
2 referring to all the members of a genus or class
3 (of a product) sold under the brand name of a retailing chain, usually for a cheaper price than if it appeared under the brand name of the producer

Word history: Latin *genus* kind + *-ic*

generous
adjective unselfish or ready to give freely: *a **generous** person* (***charitable***, ***kind***, ***lavish***, ***liberal***, ***magnanimous***)

Word building: **generosity** *noun*
Word history: from Latin word meaning 'of noble birth'

gene shears
plural noun molecules developed to target and destroy specific RNA within plant and animal cells and so to prevent an undesirable gene from carrying out its work

genesis (<u>jen</u>-uh-suhs)
noun a coming into being: *the **genesis** of the Australian nation*

Word history: Middle English, from Latin, from Greek word meaning 'origin', 'creation'

genetic
adjective **1** having to do with genetics
2 determined by genes as opposed to environment
3 having to do with origin

Word history: from Greek word meaning 'generative'

genetically-modified
adjective (of an animal or plant) having had its genetic material altered by technological means, usually to change certain characteristics and thereby improve the organism for some purpose: ***genetically-modified** food*

Word use: You can also use **GM**.

genetic code
noun the code, based on the arrangement of the molecular elements of the chromosomes, by which hereditary characteristics are passed on

genetics
noun the science which studies the passing on of special characteristics from parents to their offspring

Word use: This word is singular, like **mathematics**.
Word building: **geneticist** *noun*

genial
adjective having a warm and friendly manner (***agreeable***, ***kindly***, ***outgoing***, ***sociable***)

Word building: **geniality** *noun*
Word history: from Latin word meaning 'festive', 'jovial', 'pleasant'; literally 'relating to generation or to marriage'

genie (<u>jee</u>-nee)
noun a spirit in Arabian stories

Word history: French, from Latin *genius*. Look up **genius**.

genitals
plural noun the parts of your body which are used for sexual intercourse

genius
noun a very talented or clever person (***mastermind***, ***sage***, ***scholar***, ***whiz kid***)

Noun forms: The plural is **geniuses**.
Word history: from Latin word meaning 'guardian spirit', 'any spiritual being', 'disposition', originally a male generative or creative principle

genius / genus
Don't confuse **genius** with **genus**.
A **genus** in biology is one of the main subdivisions of a family of animals or plants.

genocide (<u>jen</u>-uh-suyd)
noun the planned killing of all the people belonging to one race or nation

Word building: **genocidal** *adjective*
Word history: Greek *géno(s)* race + *-cide*; coined by Dr Raphael Lemkin, 1944

genome (<u>jee</u>-nohm)
noun the complete genetic material for any cell

genre (<u>zhon</u>-ruh)
noun **1** a kind or sort
2 *Literature* the different forms or types of writing that we recognise, such as poetry, drama and prose

Word history: from French word meaning 'kind'

A language **genre** is a particular way in which people within a culture exchange spoken or written information. Each genre has a characteristic **structure** to enable a specific **purpose** to be achieve.

Genres can be divided into **literary** (story, biography, play, poem) and **non-literary** (apology, invitation, news report, advertisement) and can be either written or spoken. **Literary** genres can be further divided in **narrative** and **non-narrative** with a general purpose of **creating** or **entertaining. Non-literary** genres can be further divided into **transactional, procedural, report, expository** and **persuasive** genres with a general purpose to **communicate** or **inform.**

genteel (jen-<u>teel</u>)
adjective very polite and careful in your manners, speech and behaviour (***refined, superior***)

Word building: **gentility** *noun*
Word history: French

gentile (<u>jen</u>-tuyl)
noun someone who is not Jewish, especially a Christian

Word history: Middle English, from Latin word meaning 'belonging to a people', 'national', Late Latin word meaning 'foreign'

gentle
adjective **1** kind and patient (***compassionate, humane, lenient, merciful, mild***)
2 not rough or violent: *a **gentle** wind | a **gentle** tap* (***peaceful, serene, tranquil***)
3 gradual: *a **gentle** slope*
4 soft or low: *a **gentle** sound*

Word history: Middle English, from Old French word meaning 'of good family', 'noble', 'excellent', from Latin

gentleman
noun **1** any man: *Good morning, ladies and **gentlemen**.*
2 a man with polite manners: *I want you to behave like a **gentleman**.*

Noun forms: The plural is **gentlemen**.
Word use: Definition 1 is used as a polite form of speech. | This word used to mean 'a man born into a family with a high social standing' and a woman of the same kind was called a **gentlewoman**.

gentry (<u>jen</u>-tree)
noun **1** *Old-fashioned* people of high birth or social position
2 in Britain, the land-owning class below the nobility

Word history: Middle English, from *gent* noble + *-ry*

genuflect (<u>jen</u>-yuh-flekt)
verb to bend your knee or knees, especially as a mark of respect or worship

Word history: Latin *genū* knee + *flectere* bend

genuine (<u>jen</u>-yooh-uhn)
adjective **1** true or real: ***genuine** sorrow | a **genuine** diamond* (***authentic, legitimate, proven***)
2 having real, not pretended, feelings: *a **genuine** person* (***candid, direct, honest, sincere, straightforward***)

Word use: The opposite of this is **bogus** or **fake**.
Word history: from Latin word meaning 'native', 'natural', 'authentic', 'genuine'

genus (<u>jeen</u>-uhs)
noun **1** a kind, sort or class
2 *Biology* the main subdivision of a family or subfamily of animals or plants, usually consisting of more than one species, basically very similar to one another and regarded as very closely related

Noun forms: The plural is **genera**.
Word history: from Latin word meaning 'race', 'stock', 'kind', 'sort', 'gender'

genus / genius
Don't confuse **genus** with **genius.**
A **genius** is a very talented or clever person.

geochemistry (jee-oh-<u>kem</u>-uhs-tree)
noun the science dealing with chemical structure of and changes in the earth, especially the crust

Word building: **geochemist** *noun*

geoengineering
noun the use of large-scale projects to produce specific effects on climate, usually to act against the effects of global warming, such as encouraging the growth of phytoplankton that will absorb carbon dioxide from the atmosphere

geography (jee-<u>og</u>-ruh-fee)
noun the study of the earth, including its land forms, peoples, climates, soils and plants

Word building: **geographer** *noun* **geographical** *adjective*
Word history: Latin, from Greek

geology (jee-<u>ol</u>-uh-jee)
noun the study of the rocks which form the earth

Word building: **geological** *adjective* **geologist** *noun* **geological** *adjective*
Word history: Neo-Latin

geometry (jee-<u>om</u>-uh-tree)
noun the part of mathematics that studies shapes such as squares and triangles

Word building: **geometric** *adjective* **geometrical** *adjective*
Word history: Middle English, from Latin, from Greek

geophysics (jee-oh-fiz-iks)
noun the physics of the earth, especially the study by instruments of the parts of the earth which cannot be reached by people

Word building: **geophysicist** *noun*

geranium (juh-ray-nee-uhm)
noun a common garden plant with red, pink or purple flowers

Word history: Latin, from Greek word meaning 'crane's-bill'

geriatric (je-ree-at-rik)
adjective **1** having to do with old people or their care: *a **geriatric** hospital*
noun **2** someone who is old, especially if they are sick

Word building: **geriatrician** *noun*
Word history: Greek *gêras* old age + *iātrikós* of medicine

geriatrics
noun the medical care of old people

germ
noun **1** a tiny living thing which can only be seen with a microscope and which causes disease
2 the beginning of anything: *The **germ** of an idea came into his mind.*

Word history: French

germ / bacterium / virus

These words all refer to the cause of a disease.

A **germ** is an everyday term that nonscientists might use to describe a bacterium or virus which causes an infectious illness.

A **bacterium** is a single-celled microorganism. Some bacteria cause infectious diseases and others take part in the process of fermentation or rotting.

A **virus** is a strand of genetic material (DNA or RNA). It reproduces by infecting living cells and undermining their cellular structure so as to make more virus. As viruses do not use up energy it is debatable whether they are living things or merely complicated biochemical molecules.

germane (jer-mayn)
adjective closely related: *a remark **germane** to the question* (***pertinent***, ***relevant***)

Word use: This word is usually used after nouns.
Word history: variant of *german* having the same father and mother

German measles
noun a disease which gives you a temperature and a rash and is usually not serious except for a woman who is having a baby

Word use: You can also use **rubella**.

German shepherd
noun → **Alsatian**

germinate
verb to begin to grow or develop: *Water is needed to **germinate** plant seeds. | The idea **germinated** in her mind.* (***bloom***, ***blossom***, ***flourish***, ***flower***, ***sprout***)

Word building: **germination** *noun*
Word history: Latin

gerrymander
Politics
noun **1** an arrangement of the political divisions of an electorate, etc., made so as to give one party an unfair advantage in elections
verb **2** to arrange in such a way

Word history: *Gerry* (governor of Massachusetts, US, whose party in 1812 redistributed the electoral boundaries of Massachusetts) + (*sala*) *mander* (from a fancied resemblance to this animal of the gerrymandered map of Massachusetts)

gerund (je-ruhnd)
noun *Grammar* the present participle of a verb used as a noun

Word history: Latin *gerere* bear, conduct

The -ing form of verbs, the present participle, is often used as a noun. When this happens, the participle can be called a **gerund**:

I love jogging.
Does my whistling annoy you?

Compare these two sentences:

He gets really annoyed at my whistling.
He gets really annoyed at me whistling.

Some people argue that the second example isn't correct because if *whistling* is a noun it has to have the possessive pronoun, *my*, rather than *me* in front of it. Except in the most formal writing, though, both are acceptable.

gestate (jes-tayt)
verb to carry in the uterus from conception to birth

Word history: from Latin word meaning 'carried'

gesticulate (jes-tik-yuh-layt)
verb to make movements with part of your body, especially your hands, in order to express a feeling or idea

Word building: **gesticulation** *noun*
Word history: from Latin word meaning 'having made mimic gestures'

gesture (jes-chuh)
noun **1** a movement of part of your body to express a feeling or idea: *He tossed his head in a **gesture** of impatience.*
2 something done to express a feeling or idea: *a **gesture** of friendship*

Word history: Middle English, from Latin word meaning 'bear', 'conduct'

get
verb **1** to obtain or receive: *to **get** a new dress | to **get** a present* (***acquire***, ***gain***, ***procure***)
2 to bring or fetch: *I'll go and **get** it.*
3 to hear or understand: *I didn't **get** what you said.* (***comprehend***, ***fathom***, ***grasp***, ***make out***)
4 to reach: *I've phoned his house but I can't **get** him.*
5 to cause to be or do: *I must **get** my hair cut. | I can't **get** the car to start.*
6 to prepare or make ready: *She's **getting** the dinner.*
7 to arrive: *When did you **get** here?* (***come***, ***reach***, ***turn up***)
8 to become or grow: *I am **getting** tired.*
phrase **9 get about,**
a to move about
b of news, etc., to become known

10 get across, to make understood
11 get ahead, to make progress or be successful (***advance***, ***forge ahead***, ***make headway***, ***proceed***, ***push on***)
12 get at,
a to reach
b *Colloquial* to imply or suggest (***hint***, ***insinuate***)
c *Colloquial* to cause to be dishonest by using bribery, etc.
13 get away,
a to escape: *The fish* ***got away***. (***abscond***, ***flee***, ***nick off***, ***take to your heels***)
b to go away, usually on a holiday
14 get away with, to escape punishment for: *They* ***got away with*** *the crime.*
15 get by, to manage: *I don't know how I'll* ***get by*** *without a car.*
16 get down to, to concentrate on
17 get off, to escape punishment
18 get on,
a to become old
b to make progress (***advance***, ***forge ahead***, ***make headway***)
c to be friendly: *Anna* ***gets on*** *well with the rest of the class.*
19 get over,
a to defeat or find a way around (***beat***, ***conquer***, ***lick***)
b to recover from
20 get round,
a to get into favour with: *to* ***get round*** *your teacher*
b to overcome: *to* ***get round*** *difficulties*
21 get round to, to come at last to: *to* ***get round to*** *washing the car*
22 get through to,
a to connect on the telephone with
b *Colloquial* to make understand: *I can't* ***get through to*** *her at all.*
23 get up,
a to sit up or stand
b to rise from bed
24 get up to, to take part in: *to* ***get up to*** *something bad*

Verb forms: I **got**, I have **got**, I am **getting**
Word history: Middle English *geten*, from Scandinavian

Get is among the commonest verbs in English, though more so for speakers than writers. When talking, we use it almost as often as the auxiliary verbs *be*, *have* and *do*. We often use **get** instead of the verb *be* in expressions such as:

My brother is getting married on Saturday.

My brother is being married on Saturday.

The second sentence sounds rather formal. It has what we call the passive form of the verb. (Look up **verbs: passive verbs**.)

In conversation, we also use **get** instead of the more formal *become*:

My parents get angry when I mention money.

My parents become angry when I mention money.

Among its other uses, **get** often replaces other more specific verbs, such as: *buy*, *borrow*, *fetch*, *obtain* and *prepare*, again when a speaker isn't trying to be too formal. In these cases **get** is working as a main verb, not an auxiliary.

People sometimes worry about **get** appearing too often in writing. It may indeed be a pity if it is overused as a main verb in writing which is supposed to be precise and formal. (If you are looking for alternatives to **get**, a thesaurus would help you to find some.) But if you're aiming at an informal style, **get** is quite natural.

geyser (gee-zuh, guy-zuh)
noun a hot spring that sometimes sends up jets of water and steam into the air

Word history: Icelandic *Geysir* gusher, name of a hot spring in Iceland, from *geysa* rush furiously, gush

ghastly (gahst-lee)
adjective very bad or unpleasant: *a* ***ghastly*** *mess | a* ***ghastly*** *smell* (***awful***, ***horrible***)

Adjective forms: **ghastlier**, **ghastliest**
Word history: Old English *gāstlic* spectral

gherkin (ger-kuhn)
noun a small, pickled cucumber

Word history: variant of *gurchen* (from German)

ghetto (get-oh)
noun the part of a city where a group of people, such as poor people or people from another country, live together

Noun forms: The plural is **ghettos** or **ghettoes**.
Word history: Italian (Venetian), blend of Hebrew *ghēt* separation and Italian *ge(t)to* foundry, the name of Jewish quarter in Venice in the 16th Century

ghost
noun **1** the spirit of someone who has died, imagined as visiting living people (***apparition***, ***phantom***, ***spectre***, ***spook***, ***wraith***)
2 a very small amount or trace: *She hasn't a* ***ghost*** *of a chance.*
3 an annoying double image on a television picture

Word building: **ghostly** *adjective* **ghostliness** *noun*
Word history: Old English *gāst*

ghost town
noun a deserted or nearly deserted town, such as a formerly wealthy goldmining town

ghostwriter
noun someone who writes speeches, stories, etc., for another who takes the credit

ghoul (goohl)
noun **1** an evil spirit imagined to feed on human bodies
2 someone who enjoys what others find revolting

Word building: **ghoulish** *adjective*
Word history: Arabic *ghūl*

GI
noun Colloquial a soldier, usually not an officer, in any of the US armed forces

Word history: abbreviation originally of *galvanised iron*, used in US Army book-keeping entries of articles made of it; then, by association with *government issue*, of the full range of articles issued and, finally, of the soldiers themselves

giant
noun **1** an imaginary creature that looks like a human but is much bigger and stronger
2 someone or something of great size, importance or ability: *a sporting* ***giant***
adjective **3** huge or gigantic: *a* ***giant*** *plant*

Word building: **giantess** *feminine noun*
Word history: Middle English, from Old French, from Latin, from Greek

giant perch
noun → **barramundi**

giardia (jee-ah-dee-uh, gee-ah-dee-uh)
noun an organism which is a parasite of the intestines: *She was diagnosed with* ***giardia.***

gibber[1] (jib-uh)
verb to speak quickly and without making much sense

Word building: **gibberish** *noun*
Word history: perhaps from the obsolete word *gib*, verb, caterwaul, behave like a cat

gibber[2] (gib-uh)
noun Australian a stone or rock

Word history: from Dharug, an Australian Aboriginal language spoken by the people living near Sydney Cove in the early days of European settlement

gibbon
noun a kind of small ape with long arms

Word history: French, apparently from a dialect of India

gibe (juyb)
verb **1** to use mocking words (***taunt, scoff at***)
noun **2** a taunting or sarcastic remark (***quip, wisecrack, witticism***)

Word use: You can also use **jibe**.
Word history: perhaps from Old French word meaning 'handle roughly', 'shake'

giblets (jib-luhts)
plural noun the inside parts of a fowl, such as the gizzard, heart and neck, usually cooked separately

Word history: Middle English, from Old French word meaning 'dish of game'

giddy
adjective having a feeling of whirling or spinning (***faint, dizzy, swimming***)

Adjective forms: **giddier, giddiest**
Word building: **giddily** *adverb* **giddiness** *noun*
Word history: Old English *gydig* mad, from *god*; original sense presumably god-possessed, in a state of divine frenzy

GIF
noun Computers **1** a data format for image files
2 a file in this format

Word history: *G(raphic) I(nterface) F(ormat)*

gift
noun **1** something that is given as a present (***bequest, favour, offering***)
2 a special ability: *She has a* ***gift*** *for singing.* (***flair, talent***)

Word history: Middle English, from Scandinavian

gifted
adjective having special natural abilities: *a* ***gifted*** *artist*

gig[1]
noun a light, two-wheeled carriage pulled by one horse

gig[2]
noun Colloquial a job for a musician, usually a booking for one show

gigabyte
noun a measure of computer memory equal to approximately one billion bytes

Word use: You can also use the colloquial word **gig.** | The abbreviation is **G** or **GB** with full stops.

gigantic (juy-gan-tik)
adjective very large or huge: *a* ***gigantic*** *man* | *a* ***gigantic*** *rock* (***colossal, enormous, massive, vast***)

Word use: The opposite of this is **tiny**.
Word history: from Latin word meaning 'giant' + *-ic*

giggle
verb to laugh in a silly way (***cackle, chortle, chuckle, guffaw***)

Word building: **giggle** *noun* **giggler** *noun* **giggly** *adjective*

gigolo (jig-uh-loh)
noun **1** a man supported by a woman, especially a young man supported by an older woman, in return for companionship
2 a male professional dancing partner

Noun forms: The plural is **gigolos**.
Word history: French

gild
verb to cover with a layer of gold or something gold-coloured

Verb forms: I **gilded** or I **gilt**, I have **gilded** or I have **gilt**, I am **gilding**
Word building: **gilding** *noun*
Word history: Old English *gyldan*, from *gold*

gill
noun the part of the body that fish and other sea creatures use for breathing

Word history: Middle English, from Scandinavian

gilt
adjective **1** golden-coloured or covered with gold: *a* ***gilt*** *vase*
noun **2** the gold or other material used in gilding

gilt / guilt
Don't confuse **gilt** with **guilt**, which is the feeling you have when you know you've done something wrong.

gimlet (gim-luht)
noun **1** a small tool for making holes, with a pointed screw at one end and a handle at the other
2 a tree found in western Australia, with a twisted furrowed trunk
adjective **3** deeply penetrating, or thought to be deeply penetrating: ***gimlet*** *eyes*

Word history: Middle English, from Old French word meaning 'little wimble'

gimmick
noun an unusual action or trick, usually used to get attention

Word building: **gimmicky** *adjective*
Word history: perhaps a blend of *gimmer* trick finger-ring and magic

gin (jin)
noun a strong alcoholic drink

Word history: Dutch *genever*, from Old French, from Latin word meaning 'juniper'

ginger
noun **1** a plant root which is used in cooking as a spice and in medicine
2 a reddish-brown colour

Word building: **ginger** *adjective*
Word history: Old English, from Latin, from Greek word meaning 'ginger', apparently from Prakrit (an old Indian language)

ginger ale
noun a soft drink flavoured with ginger, often used to mix with brandy, etc.

ginger beer
noun a soft drink made of water, sugar, yeast, etc., flavoured with ginger

gingerbread
noun **1** a type of cake flavoured with ginger and treacle or golden syrup
2 something showy but cheap and without taste

Word history: alteration of Middle English word meaning 'preserved ginger', from Medieval Latin

gingerly
adverb with great care: *He walked **gingerly** over the slippery rocks.*

gingery
adjective spicy, like ginger: *a **gingery** taste*

gingham (ging-uhm)
noun a cotton cloth with a striped or checked pattern

Word history: French, from Malay word meaning 'striped'

ginkgo (ging-koh)
noun **1** a large tree with fan-shaped leaves, originally of China
2 an extract from these leaves often used in herbal medicine

Noun forms: The plural is **gingkoes**.
Word use: You can also use **gingko**, or, for definition 1, **gingko biloba**.

gipsy
noun → **gypsy**

giraffe
noun an African animal with spots, a very long neck and long legs

Word history: French, from Arabic, probably of African origin

gird (gerd)
verb Old-fashioned **1** to fasten a belt or girdle around the waist
2 to prepare for action: *to **gird** yourself up for the fight*

Verb forms: I **girt** or I **girded**, I have **girt** or I have **girded**, I am **girding**
Word use: You can also use **gird up** for definition 2.
Word history: Old English *gyrdan*

girder
noun a thick beam used as a support in building

Word history: *gird* + *-er*

girdle
noun Old-fashioned **1** a belt or cord worn around your waist
2 a piece of elastic underwear that supports your stomach and hips

Word history: Old English *gyrdel*

girl
noun a female child or a young woman

Word history: Middle English *gurle, girle* child, young person, Old English *gyrl-* in *gyrlgyden* virgin goddess

girlfriend
noun **1** a female who you have a steady romantic or sexual relationship with
2 a female friend of a woman or girl: *She's going to the pictures with her **girlfriends**.*

girl guide
noun → **guide** (definition 5)

girth
noun **1** the measurement around anything: *They measured the **girth** of the tree trunk.*
2 a band placed under the stomach of a horse to hold a saddle or pack onto its back

Word history: Middle English, from Scandinavian

gist (jist)
noun the most important part: *I understand the **gist** of your argument.* (***drift***, ***essence***, ***meaning***, ***sense***, ***significance***)

Word history: Old French word meaning 'lie', 'rest', from Latin

give
verb **1** to hand over freely: *to **give** someone a present* (***confer***, ***donate***, ***grant***)
2 to pay: *I'll **give** you $1 for those stamps.*
3 to allow or grant: ***Give** him one more chance.*
4 to present or organise: *to **give** a concert | to **give** a party*
5 to provide with: *to **give** help | to **give** a baby a name*
6 to make, especially a movement: *She **gave** a jump.*
phrase **7 give away**,
a to give as a present
b to betray or allow to become known (***blab***, ***let out***, ***let slip***, ***reveal***, ***spill***)
8 give in, to admit defeat (***capitulate***, ***submit***, ***succumb***, ***surrender***, ***yield***)
9 give off, to send out or emit: *to **give off** fumes*
10 give out,
a to become worn out or used up
b to hand out or distribute
11 give over,
a to transfer
b to keep free for a special purpose: *to **give over** an evening for study*
12 give up,
a to lose all hope
b to stop: *You should **give up** smoking.* (***cease***, ***quit***)
c to surrender

Verb forms: I **gave**, I have **given**, I am **giving**
Word building: **giver** *noun*
Word history: Middle English, from Scandinavian

given name
noun the name you are given when you are born, which is different from the names of other members of your family: *Her* ***given name*** *is Irena and her family name is Popov.*

gizzard (giz-uhd)
noun the second, grinding or muscular, stomach of birds

Word history: Middle English, from Old French, from Latin word meaning 'cooked entrails of poultry'

glacial
adjective **1** having large masses of ice
2 icy or cold as ice (***chill, chilly, icy, freezing, raw***)

Word history: from Latin word meaning 'icy'

glacier
noun a large area of ice which moves slowly down a valley or mountain

Word history: French word meaning 'ice', from Latin

glacier / glazier
Don't confuse **glacier** with **glazier**, which is someone who fits glass into windows.

glad
adjective **1** delighted or pleased (***happy, joyful, thrilled, tickled pink***)
phrase **2 glad of**, grateful for: *I would be* ***glad of*** *a little help*

Adjective forms: **gladder, gladdest**
Word building: **gladden** *verb* **gladly** *adverb* **gladness** *noun*
Word history: Old English

glade
noun an open space in a forest

Word history: related to *glad* in its obsolete sense 'bright'

gladiator
noun a man in ancient Rome who fought as a public entertainment

Word building: **gladiatorial** *adjective*
Word history: Latin

gladiolus (glad-ee-oh-luhs)
noun a plant native mainly to South Africa, with upright leaves and spikes of coloured flowers

Noun forms: The plural is **gladiolus** or **gladioli** or **gladioluses**.
Word use: Another name is **sword lily**.
Word history: from Latin word meaning 'little sword'

glamour
noun an exciting charm or beauty: *That job has a lot of* ***glamour****. | Her clothes always have* ***glamour****.*

Word use: You can also use **glamor**.
Word building: **glamorous** *adjective*
Word history: from *grammar* in obsolete sense of 'occult learning', 'magic'

glance
verb **1** to look quickly
2 to hit and go off at an angle: *The ball* ***glanced*** *off the cricket bat.*

Word building: **glance** *noun*
Word history: Middle English word meaning 'strike a glancing blow', from Old French word meaning 'slip'

gland
noun a part of your body that makes a substance that is used by another part of your body or eliminated from your body altogether: *Sweat is made by* ***glands****.*

Word building: **glandular** *adjective*
Word history: Old French, from Latin word meaning 'acorn'

glare
noun **1** a strong bright light: *the* ***glare*** *of car headlights*
2 an angry look

Word building: **glare** *verb*
Word history: Middle English

glaring
adjective very obvious: *a* ***glaring*** *mistake* (***apparent, clear, distinct, evident, plain***)

glass
noun **1** a hard transparent substance used for such things as windows, bottles and drinking containers
2 something made of glass, such as a drinking container or a mirror

Word history: Old English

glasses
plural noun two lenses in a frame which are worn over your eyes to help you see more clearly (***goggles, spectacles***)

glassy
adjective **1** like glass
2 of eyes, having a fixed or unintelligent stare

Adjective forms: **glassier, glassiest**

glaze
verb **1** to fit or cover with glass: *to* ***glaze*** *windows*
2 to cover with a thin coat of a clear shiny substance: *to* ***glaze*** *pottery*
noun **3** a smooth, shiny coating or surface
phrase **4 glaze over**, to become glassy: *His eyes* ***glazed over*** *as he sat daydreaming.*

Word history: Middle English *glasen*

glazier
noun someone who fits glass into windows

Word history: Middle English *glasier*, from *glas* glass + *-ier*

glazier / glacier
Don't confuse **glazier** with **glacier**. A glacier is a large area of ice which moves slowly down a valley or mountain.

gleam
noun **1** a flash of light (***flicker, glimmer***)
2 a dim light: *the* ***gleam*** *of polished wood*
3 a short burst: *A* ***gleam*** *of interest came into his eyes.*

Word building: **gleam** *verb*
Word history: Old English

glean
verb to gather, usually slowly and bit by bit: *to **glean** grain after it has been reaped | to **glean** information* (***ascertain**, **discover**, **learn**, **tumble to**, **understand***)

Word building: **gleaner** *noun*
Word history: Middle English, from Old French, from Late Latin, of Celtic origin

glee
noun a feeling of joy (***gaiety**, **happiness**, **high spirits**, **merriment**, **mirth***)

Word building: **gleeful** *adjective* **gleefully** *adverb*
Word history: Old English

glen
noun a small narrow valley

Word history: Middle English, from Gaelic

glib
adjective speaking or spoken easily though often insincerely: *a **glib** speaker | a **glib** tongue | **glib** words*

Adjective forms: **glibber**, **glibbest**
Word history: Dutch

glide
verb to move or make to move along smoothly (***coast**, **cruise**, **float**, **sail**, **skim***)

Word building: **glide** *noun*
Word history: Old English

glider
noun **1** an aeroplane without an engine that flies by using air-currents
2 a small tree-dwelling marsupial with a flap of skin joining the feet on each side which it uses to help it jump from branch to branch

glimmer
noun **1** a faint or flickering light (***flicker**, **glitter**, **shimmer**, **twinkle***)
2 a faint hint or suggestion: *a **glimmer** of hope* (***gleam**, **ray***)

Word building: **glimmer** *verb* **glimmering** *noun*
Word history: from Middle English word meaning 'gleam'

glimpse
noun a quick sighting: *I caught a **glimpse** of him as he ran past.*

Word building: **glimpse** *verb*
Word history: Middle English *glymsen*

glint
noun **1** a flash or glow of light: *the **glint** of metal*
2 a look showing amusement or a secret idea: *a **glint** in his eyes*

Word building: **glint** *verb*
Word history: Middle English, variant of obsolete Scandinavian

glisten (glis-uhn)
verb to shine with a sparkling light: *Her gold ring **glistened** in the sunlight.* (***glitter**, **sparkle**, **twinkle***)

Word history: from Old English word meaning 'glitter'

glitch
noun Colloquial an extra electric current or signal, especially one that interferes in some way with the working of a system

glitter
verb to shine with a bright sparkling light: *Her eyes **glittered** with excitement.* (***sparkle**, **twinkle***)

Word building: **glitter** *noun* **glittery** *adjective*
Word history: Middle English, from Scandinavian

gloat
verb to look at or think about something or someone in a very satisfied way: *He **gloated** over his enemy's defeat.*

Word building: **gloating** *adjective*
Word history: perhaps from Scandinavian word meaning 'grin', 'smile scornfully'

global
adjective **1** round; spherical
2 world-wide: ***global** war*
3 all-inclusive; comprehensive
4 *Computers* an action operating over an entire database, set of records, or an entire document etc.

global hectare
noun a unit of measurement of the rate at which resources are used, arrived at by adding up all the hectares of land in which resources are produced and waste is absorbed in a sustainable way and dividing it by the number of hectares on the earth

Word use: The abbreviation is **gha**.

globalisation
noun the process of becoming international: *the **globalisation** of the English language*

Word use: You can also use **globalization**.
Word building: **globalise** *verb*

globalism
noun **1** the pursuit of globalisation
2 the worldwide integration of economies which pose threats to national cultural and political independence

Word building: **globalist** *noun*, *adjective*

global positioning system
noun → **GPS**

global warming
noun the significant rise in temperature of the whole of the earth's atmosphere

globe
noun **1** a round ball-shaped map of the earth
2 anything shaped like a round ball (***orb**, **sphere***)
3 *Australian*, *NZ* an electric light bulb
phrase **4 the globe**, the earth: *They travelled all over **the globe**.*

Word building: **global** *adjective*
Word history: French, from Latin word meaning 'round body or mass', 'ball', 'globe'

globule (glob-yoohl)
noun a small ball-shaped object, especially a drop of liquid

Word building: **globular** *adjective*
Word history: French, from Latin word meaning 'little globe'

glockenspiel (glo-kuhn-speel, glo-kuhn-shpeel)
noun a musical instrument with steel bars set in a frame, which you hit with hammers

Word history: from German word meaning 'bell' + 'play'

gloom[1]
noun darkness or dimness

Word history: from Old English word meaning 'twilight'

gloom[2]
noun a feeling of unhappiness or depression (***anguish***, ***melancholy***, ***misery***, ***sorrow***)

Word building: **gloomy** *adjective* (**gloomier**, **gloomiest**)
Word history: from Middle English word meaning 'frown'

glorify
verb to praise or honour: *to* ***glorify*** *God*

Verb forms: I **glorified**, I have **glorified**, I am **glorifying**
Word building: **glorification** *noun*
Word history: Middle English, from Old French, from Late Latin

glorious
adjective **1** beautiful, wonderful or delightful: *It is a* ***glorious*** *day. | We had a* ***glorious*** *time.*
2 giving or having glory: *a* ***glorious*** *victory*

Word building: **gloriously** *adverb* **gloriousness** *noun*
Word history: Middle English, from Anglo-French, from Latin word meaning 'full of glory'

glory
noun **1** praise and honour (***acclamation***, ***distinction***, ***fame***, ***kudos***, ***prestige***, ***renown***)
2 something that is a cause of pride or honour: *Beautiful beaches are one of the* ***glories*** *of Australia.* (***splendour***, ***wonder***)
3 splendid or divine beauty: *the* ***glory*** *of God*

Noun forms: The plural is **glories**.
Word history: Middle English, from Old French, from Latin word meaning 'glory', 'fame', 'boasting'

gloss
noun **1** the shine on the outside of something: *the* ***gloss*** *of satin*
verb **2** to put a gloss on
phrase **3 gloss over**, to cover up or try to make seem unimportant: *He* ***glossed over*** *his mistakes.*

Word building: **glossy** *adjective* (**glossier**, **glossiest**) **glossiness** *noun*
Word history: Scandinavian

glossary
noun a list of special or difficult words about a particular subject, with their definitions: *This textbook has a* ***glossary*** *at the back.*

Noun forms: The plural is **glossaries**.
Word history: Latin

glove
noun a covering for your hand, usually with a separate part for each finger and for the thumb

Word history: Old English

glove box
noun a small space in a car, set into the dashboard, for storing small objects, as gloves, maps, etc.

glow
noun **1** the light given out by something extremely hot (***radiance***)
2 brightness of colour
3 a pleasant warm feeling: *a* ***glow*** *of happiness*

Word building: **glow** *verb*
Word history: Old English

glower
verb **1** to stare with sullen dislike (***glare***, ***scowl***)
noun **2** a frown or a glowering look

Word history: obsolete *glow* stare

glow-worm
noun a kind of insect whose body glows in the dark

glucosamine (glooh-<u>koh</u>-suh-meen)
noun a compound used in the treatment of osteoarthritis

glucose
noun a natural sugar which is the major energy source for most living cells

Word history: French, from Greek word meaning 'sweet' + *-ose*

glue
noun **1** a paste used to stick things together (***adhesive***, ***cement***, ***gum***, ***mortar***)
verb **2** to stick with glue

Word building: **gluey** *adjective*
Word history: Middle English, from Old French, from Late Latin

glum
adjective unhappy or depressed (***dejected***, ***gloomy***, ***miserable***, ***morose***, ***sad***)

Adjective forms: **glummer**, **glummest**
Word history: from Middle English word meaning 'to look glum or solemn'

glut
noun an oversupply: *a* ***glut*** *of tomatoes* (***excess***, ***surplus***)

Word use: The opposite of this is **scarcity** or **shortage**.
Word building: **glut** *verb* (**glutted**, **glutting**)
Word history: Middle English word meaning 'glutton', from Old French word meaning 'greedy'

gluten (<u>glooh</u>-tuhn)
noun **1** a tough, sticky substance left when the flour of wheat or other grain is washed to remove the starch
2 glue, or some gluey substance

Word building: **glutenous** *adjective*
Word history: from Latin word meaning 'glue'

glutinous (<u>glooh</u>-tuh-nuhs)
adjective sticky, like glue

Word history: from Latin word meaning 'gluey', 'viscous'

glutton
noun someone who eats too much

Word building: **gluttonous** *adjective* **gluttony** *noun*
Word history: Middle English, from Old French, from Latin

glycerol (<u>glis</u>-uh-rol)
noun a colourless, odourless, sweet, liquid alcohol obtained from natural fats and oils, and used as a solvent, plasticiser, or sweetener

glycogen (gluy-kuh-juhn)
noun a form of sugar found in liver and muscle which provides the body with energy
Word building: **glycogenic** (gluy-kuh-jen-ik) *adjective*

GM
abbreviation genetically-modified

gnarled (nahld)
adjective **1** twisted and having many woody lumps: *a* ***gnarled*** *old tree*
2 rough and worn by the weather: ***gnarled*** *hands* (***coarse***, ***weathered***)
Word history: variant of *knurled*, ridged

gnash (nash)
verb to grind together: *He* ***gnashed*** *his teeth in anger.*
Word history: Scandinavian

gnat (nat)
noun a kind of small insect with only one pair of wings
Word use: Compare this with **midge**.
Word history: Old English

gnaw (naw)
verb to chew or bite: *The lion* ***gnawed*** *at its food.*
Word building: **gnawing** *adjective* **gnawing** *noun*
Word history: Old English

gnome (nohm)
noun a small being in fairy stories, usually imagined as a little old man
Word history: French, from Neo-Latin

gnomic (noh-mik, nom-)
adjective **1** like or containing short, wise, pithy expressions of a general truth
2 having to do with someone noted for use of gnomic expressions
Word history: Greek

gnu (nooh)
noun a kind of antelope with curved horns and a long tail
Noun forms: The plural is **gnus** or **gnu**.

go
verb **1** to move or pass along: *Where are you* ***going****?*
2 to move away or depart: *I want you to* ***go*** *now.*
3 to work properly: *The engine won't* ***go****.*
4 to become: *She* ***goes*** *red with anger.*
5 to reach or lead: *That road* ***goes*** *to Brisbane.*
6 *Internet* to access a site on the internet: *The results were available when I went to the university site this morning.*
7 to pass or happen: *Time* ***goes*** *quickly. | The party* ***went*** *well.*
8 to belong or have a place: *Where do the knives and forks* ***go****?*
9 to fit or be contained: *Two litres of milk will* ***go*** *into this jug.*
10 to be used up or finished: *The food* ***went*** *quickly.*
11 to make a particular sound or movement: *The gun* ***went*** *bang.*
noun **12** energy: *He has plenty of* ***go****.*
13 a turn or try: *It's Jane's* ***go*** *on the swing.*
phrase **14 all the go**, *Colloquial* in the current fashion
15 from the word go, *Colloquial* from the very beginning
16 go along with, to accept or agree
17 go back on, *Colloquial* to fail to keep: *to* ***go back on*** *a promise*
18 go for,
a to attack: *That dog will* ***go for*** *children.*
b to be attracted to: *to* ***go for*** *heavy metal music*
c to aim for: *to* ***go for*** *the top job*
d to apply to: *That rule* ***goes for*** *all of us.*
19 go in for, to be interested in: *He* ***goes in for*** *surfing.*
20 go off,
a to explode: *The gun* ***went off****.*
b to become bad: *The meat has* ***gone off****.*
c to stop liking
21 on the go, active and energetic
Verb forms: I **went**, I have **gone**, I am **going**
Noun forms: The plural is **goes**.
Word history: Old English

One of the most common functions of the verb **to go** is to help to indicate future time in English:

I'm going to be sick.

They are going to look pretty silly.

Going to can sometimes be written as **gonna** or **gunna** if you are trying to represent colloquial dialogue, but these contractions shouldn't be used in your normal writing.

Note that you don't use **went** straight after *have*, *has*, *had* or *having*:

He should have went yesterday.	WRONG
He should have gone yesterday.	RIGHT
He went yesterday.	RIGHT

goad
noun **1** a stick with a pointed end used to prod cattle and other animals into moving
verb **2** to drive with a goad
3 to tease or anger (***annoy***, ***bug***, ***irritate***, ***provoke***, ***vex***)
Word history: Old English

go-ahead
noun **1** permission to do something: *We are still waiting to get the* ***go-ahead*** *before we can start.*
adjective **2** using new methods enthusiastically in order to succeed or develop: *They want their children to go to that* ***go-ahead*** *school in the next suburb.*

goal
noun **1** an area, basket or something similar at which you aim the ball, in sports such as football, basketball and others
2 the score made by doing this: *We got three* ***goals****.*
3 something you aim towards: *My* ***goal*** *is to be a doctor.* (***aim***, ***ambition***, ***mission***, ***objective***, ***target***)
Word history: from Middle English word meaning 'boundary', 'limit'

goal / gaol
Don't confuse **goal** with **gaol**, which is another spelling for **jail**, the place where criminals are imprisoned.

goanna (goh-an-uh)
noun any of a number of large Australian lizards
Word history: from *iguana*

goat
noun a small cud-chewing animal with horns, which is able to live in rocky mountainous areas and is domesticated throughout the world
Word history: Old English

goatee (goh-tee)
noun a man's beard cut to a point on the chin

gob[1]
noun **1** a mass or lump
verb **2** to spit
Word history: Middle English word meaning 'lump', 'mass', from Old French

gob[2]
noun Colloquial the mouth: *Shut your **gob**.*
Word history: Gaelic or Irish

gobble
verb to swallow or eat quickly in large pieces: *to **gobble** food* (***devour***, ***gulp***)
Word history: from *gob*[1]

gobbledegook (gob-uhl-dee-gook, gob-uhl-dee-goohk)
noun Colloquial language marked by the use of too many words, roundabout expression, and jargon: *the **gobbledegook** of government reports*

go-between
noun someone who acts as an agent between people or parties

goblet
noun a cup or glass with a stem and a base
Word history: Middle English, from Old French word meaning 'little cup'; of Celtic origin

goblin
noun an ugly elf in fairy stories who usually makes trouble for people
Word history: Middle English, from French, from Middle High German word meaning 'goblin'

go-cart
noun **1** a small cart with wheels, which children use to ride in
2 → **go-kart**

god
noun **1** a supernatural being who is believed to have power to control human affairs and the world of nature and is worshipped according to particular religious beliefs: *Thor is the Old Norse **god** of thunder.*
2 an idol or statue of a god
3 someone or something which is given too much attention: *Money is his **god**.*
4 God, the supreme maker and ruler of the universe worshipped by people who believe in one god
Word history: Old English god, German

godchild
noun someone for whom a person (godparent) takes responsibility at baptism
Noun forms: The plural is **godchildren**.

goddess
noun **1** a female god or deity
2 a very beautiful or adored woman

godly
adjective following God's laws: *a **godly** man*

goggle
verb to stare with your eyes wide open (***gape***, ***gawk***)
Word history: from Middle English word meaning 'look aside'

goggles
plural noun glasses with rims and side pieces used to protect your eyes from wind, dust, glare or water

going concern
noun Commerce the assumption that a business will stay in operation indefinitely, and especially that it will still be in business for the next accounting period

goitre (goy-tuh)
noun an enlargement of the thyroid gland, on the front and sides of the neck
Word history: French, from Latin word meaning 'throat'

go-kart
noun a small, light, low-powered car for racing
Word use: You can also use **go-cart**.

gold
noun **1** a precious yellow metal
2 money or wealth
3 something highly valued: *a heart of **gold***
4 a yellow colour, like gold
adjective **5** made of gold, or like gold
6 of a gold colour
Word building: **golden** *adjective*
Word history: Middle English and Old English

golden retriever
noun one of a breed of retriever dogs with a thick, wavy, golden coat

golden syrup
noun a sweet gold-coloured syrup used in cooking and as a sauce for desserts, etc.

goldfish
noun small fish often kept in aquariums or pools
Noun forms: The plural is **goldfishes** or **goldfish**.

goldmine
noun **1** a place where gold is mined
2 a plentiful source of something very useful: *She is a **goldmine** of information.*
Word building: **goldminer** *noun* **goldmining** *noun*

golf
noun an outdoor game in which a small ball is hit with special clubs around a set course
Word history: Middle English (Scottish)

gonad (goh-nad)
noun the sex gland, male or female, in which the reproductive cells are produced
Word history: Neo-Latin, from Greek word meaning 'offspring', 'seed'

gondola (gon-duh-luh)
noun **1** a long narrow boat with high pointed ends, used on the canals of Venice in Italy
2 the basket beneath a balloon, for carrying passengers
Word history: Italian (Venetian), from Roman root *dond-* to rock

gondolier (gon-duh-lear)
noun the person who rows a gondola

gone
verb **1** past participle of **go**
adjective **2** lost or without hope
3 *Colloquial* in a state of excitement, from the influence of drugs, music, etc.
phrase **4 far gone**, *Colloquial* deeply involved
5 gone on, *Colloquial* having strong feelings for: *He is **gone on** rock music.*

gong
noun a bronze disc which is struck with a soft-headed stick to give a loud ringing sound
Word history: Malay

gonorrhoea (gon-uh-ree-uh)
noun a contagious disease of the sex organs
Word history: Greek *gono-* + *rhoia* a flow

good
adjective **1** excellent or right (***fine***, ***great***, ***grouse***, ***neat***, ***satisfactory***)
2 of fine quality
3 well-behaved
4 helpful or useful: *a knife **good** for cutting* (***advantageous***, ***beneficial***, ***handy***)
5 enjoyable or pleasant: *a **good** holiday*
6 sufficient or ample: *a **good** supply*
7 clever or skilful: *a **good** farmer*
noun **8** advantage or benefit: *It's for your own **good**.*
9 excellent qualities or proper actions: *Look for **good** in others.*
10 goods,
a possessions
b products or articles that you can buy: ***goods** from a factory*
phrase **11 as good as**, almost: *I'm **as good as** finished.*
12 good for,
a legal or valid: *This ticket is **good for** a month.*
b giving someone a right to: *That coupon is **good for** a free meal.*
13 for good, for ever
14 make good,
a to fulfil or carry out: *to **make good** a promise*
b to be successful
Adjective forms: **better**, **best**
Word history: Old English *gōd*; perhaps originally meaning fitting, suitable, and related to *gather*

good / well
These two words are different parts of speech — **good** is an adjective, and **well** is the adverb that relates to it. So, generally, **good** belongs with nouns and **well** with verbs, as in the following sentences:

You did a good job. — *good* + noun
You did it well. — verb + *well*

We do not say
You did a well job. or *You did it good.*
There are, however, common expressions using **good** as an adverb that are generally accepted:
That sounds good.
And there's a distinction in meaning between
You're looking well. (a comment on health)
and
You're looking good. (a comment on looks)
Note that even though **goodly** looks like the adverb from **good** (because of its -ly ending), it is actually an old-fashioned adjective meaning 'good'.

goodbye
interjection a word you use when you leave someone
Word history: short form of *God be with you (ye)*

good cholesterol
noun the cholesterol that has a tendency to unclog blood vessels, and which is associated with a reduced risk of coronary artery disease
Word use: Compare this with **bad cholesterol**.

good-looking
adjective having a pleasing appearance: *a **good-looking** woman | He's very **good-looking**.* (***attractive***, ***beautiful***, ***handsome***)

good-natured
adjective having a pleasant personality; friendly and helpful to other people: *His **good-natured** disposition made it easy for everyone to get along with him.*

goodwill
noun **1** friendly feelings
2 *Commerce* the value to a business of its reputation for good service and of the skill of its staff, as distinct from the value of its products and all the property it owns
Word history: Middle English, from Old English

google
verb **1** to search for information on the internet
2 to search the internet for information about: *to **google** the homework topic*
noun **3** an instance of such a search: *to have a quick **google***
Verb forms: I **googled**, I have **googled**, I am **googling**

goose
noun **1** a large bird with webbed feet and a long neck, sometimes kept on farms
2 the female of this bird, as distinct from the male
3 a silly person: *Don't be a **goose**.*
Noun forms: The plural is **geese**.
Word use: The male is called a **gander**. | A young goose is called a **gosling**.
Word history: Old English *gōs* (plural *gēs*)

gooseberry (gooz-buh-ree, gooz-bree)
noun a small, sour-tasting, round berry
Noun forms: The plural is **gooseberries**.

goose pimples
plural noun small lumps on your skin that appear when you are cold or frightened
Word use: You can also use **goose bumps** or **goose flesh**.

goosestep
noun an unusual marching step in which your legs are swung high while your knees are kept straight and stiff

gore[1]
noun blood from a wound, especially when it has clotted

Word building: **gory** *adjective* (**gorier, goriest**)
Word history: Old English *gor* dung, dirt

gore[2]
verb to pierce with horns or tusks: *The bull* ***gored*** *him.*

Word history: Middle English *goren*

gorge
noun **1** a narrow valley with steep rocky walls, often with a river running through it
verb **2** to stuff by over-eating: *He* ***gorged*** *himself.*

Word history: Middle English, from Old French word meaning 'throat', from Late Latin blend of Latin *gurges* stream, abyss and *gula* throat

gorgeous
adjective beautiful or attractive: *a* ***gorgeous*** *sunset | a* ***gorgeous*** *little boy | The bride looked* ***gorgeous***. (***exquisite, lovely, stunning***)

Word history: Middle English, from Old French word meaning 'fashionable', 'gay'

gorilla
noun the largest kind of ape

Word history: Neo-Latin, from Greek; said to be of African origin

> **gorilla / guerilla / griller**
> Don't confuse **gorilla** with **guerilla** or **griller**.
> A **guerilla** is a member of a small band of soldiers that makes surprise raids and attacks on the enemy.
> A **griller** is the part of a stove or kitchen appliance which cooks meat by direct heat.

gormless
adjective Colloquial dull or stupid: *a* ***gormless*** *person*

Word building: **gormlessness** *noun*
Word history: dialect *gaum* attention, heed

gosling
noun a young goose

Word history: Middle English, from Scandinavian

go-slow
noun Colloquial the intentional action of workers in an industrial struggle of slowing down the rate of work

gospel
noun anything that is considered to be completely true

Word history: Old English *gōd* good + *spell* tidings

gossamer (gos-uh-muh)
noun **1** a fine cobweb lying on grass or bushes or floating in the air
2 any very fine material

Word history: Middle English *gos(e)-somer* ('goose summer'); possibly first used as a name for late mild autumn (Indian summer), a time when goose was a favourite dish, then transferred to the filmy cobwebs also commonly found in that season

gossip
noun **1** silly, and sometimes unkind, chatter about other people's business (***hearsay, rumour, talk, the drum, the whisper***)
2 someone who talks gossip

Word building: **gossip** *verb* **gossiper** *noun* **gossipy** *adjective*
Word history: Old English *godsipp*, godparent

got
verb past tense and past participle of **get**

> **got / gotten**
> These are both past forms of the verb **get**, though they are used in slightly different ways.
> **Got** is the past tense, as in:
> *She got hungry and he got a pizza on the way home.*
> It is used this way by English speakers everywhere in the world.
> In Australia, **got** is also used as the past participle, as in:
> *She had got hungry and he had got a pizza …*
> In the US, the past participle is normally **gotten**:
> *She had gotten hungry and he had gotten a pizza …*
> This usage is becoming more common in Australia.

> **got to**
> This is a common way of saying that someone must do something:
> *I've got to make some lamingtons.*
> *The school's got to raise money for computers.*
> The two words are often run together as they are said, and so they're sometimes written as **gotta**. But this spelling is only used in writing that is meant to look colloquial. More formal ways of saying **I've got to** are:
> *I have to   I ought to   I must   I should*

Gothic
adjective **1** having to do with a style of building found in western Europe from the 12th to 16th century, having pointed arches, a rib-like (vaulted) roof, etc.
2 having horrible and frightening images, especially in literature: *a* ***Gothic*** *novel*
3 of a typeface in printing, having elaborate pointed letters

Word building: **Gothically** *adverb*
Word history: Late Latin *Gothicus*

gotten
verb a past participle of **get**: *He planned to give his sister a key after he'd* ***gotten*** *a copy made.*

gouge (gowj)
noun **1** a sharp curved tool used for making grooves in wood
2 a hole made by this tool

Word building: **gouge** *verb*
Word history: French, from Late Latin

goulash (gooh-lash)
noun a meat stew containing onions and paprika

Word history: Hungarian

gourd (goouhd, gawd)
noun **1** the fruit of a climbing plant
2 the shell of this plant, dried and used as a bottle, bowl or container

Word history: Middle English, from French, from Latin

gourmet (goouh-may, gaw-may)
noun someone who knows a lot about good food

Word history: French, from Old French word meaning 'wine merchant's man'

gout (gowt)
noun a disease of the joints, especially of the hands and feet, causing pain and swelling

Word history: Middle English, from Old French, from Latin word meaning 'a drop', 'Medieval Latin' word meaning 'gout'

govern
verb to rule by authority, such as laws (***control***, ***direct***, ***manage***, ***run***, ***supervise***)

Word history: Middle English, from Latin, from Greek word meaning 'steer', 'guide', 'govern'

governess
noun a woman who teaches children in their own homes, usually because they live too far from a school

government
noun **1** the group of people who rule or govern a country or state: *the Labor* ***government*** *| the* ***government*** *of Tasmania*
2 rule or control: *A country prospers under good* ***government***.

governor
noun the representative of the king or queen in a state of the Commonwealth of Australia

Word history: Middle English, from Latin word meaning 'steersman', 'director'

governor-general
noun the main representative of the king or queen in Australia and some other British Commonwealth countries

Noun forms: The plural is **governor-generals** or **governors-general**.

gown
noun **1** a dress worn by women on important occasions
2 a loose, flowing garment worn by judges, lawyers, members of the clergy, and others

Word history: Middle English, from Late Latin

GPS (jee pee es)
noun **1** a navigational system which relies on information from satellites to provide an object's latitude and longitude
2 a device which determines location

Word use: You can also use **global positioning system**.

grab
verb **1** to take suddenly (***nab***, ***nail***, ***seize***, ***snap up***, ***snatch***)
2 *Colloquial* affect or impress: *How does that* ***grab*** *you?*

Verb forms: I **grabbed**, I have **grabbed**, I am **grabbing**
Word history: Medieval Dutch and Middle Low German *grabben*

grace
noun **1** beauty of appearance or movement
2 favour or goodwill
3 a short prayer of thanks to God said before or after a meal

Word use: The opposite of definition 1 is **awkwardness**.
Word building: **graceful** *adjective*
Word history: Middle English, from Latin word meaning 'favour', 'gratitude', 'agreeableness'

gracious
adjective showing kindness and courtesy: *a* ***gracious*** *hostess | a* ***gracious*** *act* (***courteous***, ***gallant***, ***polite***)

Word use: The opposite of this is **rude**.
Word history: Middle English, from Latin word meaning 'enjoying or showing favour'

gracious / graceful
Don't confuse **gracious** with **graceful**. A movement or shape is **graceful** if it is elegant or attractive to look at.

gradation
noun any change taking place through a series of stages, by degrees, or gradually

Word building: **gradate** *verb*

grade
noun **1** a stage or step on a scale of positions, quality or value: *There are several* ***grades*** *of clerks in the Public Service. | Eggs are sold according to* ***grade***. (***class***, ***level***, ***rank***)
2 a class in a school arranged according to age and ability
verb **3** to arrange or sort according to grade (***classify***, ***file***, ***group***, ***list***)
4 to make level and smooth: *to* ***grade*** *a road*
phrase **5 make the grade**, to reach a desired standard

Word history: French, from Latin *gradus* step, stage, degree

grader
noun **1** someone or something that sorts or groups: *a fruit* ***grader***
2 a vehicle with a blade in front used for levelling roads

gradient
noun **1** the amount of slope or steepness in a road, railway or path (***camber***, ***pitch***, ***tilt***)
2 a sloping surface (***incline***, ***slope***)

Word history: from Latin word meaning 'walking', 'going'

gradual
adjective taking place little by little

Word use: The opposite of this is **abrupt** or **sudden**.
Word history: from Latin *gradus* step, grade

graduate (<u>graj</u>-ooh-uht)
noun **1** someone who has passed a course of study at a university or college
verb (<u>graj</u>-ooh-ayt) **2** to receive a degree after passing a course of study at a university or college
3 to divide into regular divisions: *to **graduate** a thermometer*

Word building: **graduate** *adjective* **graduation** *noun*
Word history: Medieval Latin word meaning 'admit to an academic degree', from Latin *gradus* step, grade

graffiti (gruh-<u>fee</u>-tee)
plural noun drawings or words written without permission on walls in public places

Noun forms: The singular is **graffito**.
Word history: Italian word meaning 'a scratch', from Greek word meaning 'mark', 'draw', 'write'

graft[1] (grahft)
noun **1** part of a plant placed in a slit in another plant so that the first is fed by the second plant and becomes part of it
2 a piece of living tissue cut by a doctor from one part of your body and placed somewhere else in your body: *a skin **graft** | a bone **graft***

Word building: **graft** *verb*
Word history: Middle English, from Old French word meaning 'stylus', 'pencil', from Late Latin, from Greek word meaning 'stylus'

graft[2] (grahft)
noun **1** work, especially hard work
2 the gaining of money unfairly, by the dishonest use of your position: ***graft** and corruption*
verb **3** to work hard

Word history: British dialect

Grail (grayl)
noun → **Holy Grail**

Word history: Middle English, from Old French, from Medieval Latin word meaning 'plate', 'bowl'

grain
noun **1** a small hard seed of one of the cereal plants: *wheat **grain***
2 any small hard particle: *a **grain** of gold | a **grain** of sand*
3 a very small amount of something: *a **grain** of truth in his story*
4 the direction of the fibres in wood or cloth

Word building: **grainy** *adjective* (**grainier**, **grainiest**) **granular** *adjective* **granulate** *verb*
Word history: Middle English, from Old French, from Latin word meaning 'grain', 'seed'

gram
noun a measure of weight in the metric system

Word use: The symbol is **g**, without a full stop. | Look up **metric system**.
Word history: French, from Late Latin, from Greek word meaning 'a small weight', originally 'something drawn'

gramma (<u>gram</u>-uh)
noun a type of pumpkin, the fruit of which has an orange flesh and skin

grammar
noun **1** the parts of a language, such as sounds and words, and the way they are combined into phrases and sentences
2 the description of this or a book containing such a description

Word building: **grammarian** *noun* **grammatical** *adjective*
Word history: Middle English, from Old French, from Latin, from Greek word meaning 'relating to letters or literature'

grampus
noun **1** a mammal of the dolphin family, found in northern seas
2 any of various related marine mammals as the killer whale

Word history: Old French, from Medieval Latin word meaning 'fat fish'

granary (<u>gran</u>-uh-ree)
noun a storehouse for grain

Noun forms: The plural is **granaries**.
Word history: Latin

grand
adjective **1** important-looking (***dignified***, ***distinguished***, ***lordly***, ***majestic***, ***stately***)
2 noble or fine: *a **grand** old man*
3 complete: *the **grand** total*
4 highest in importance

Word history: Middle English, from Latin word meaning 'large', 'full-grown', 'great', 'grand'

grandchild
noun the child of someone's daughter or son

Noun forms: The plural is **grandchildren**.

granddaughter
noun a daughter of your son or daughter

Word use: You can also use **grand-daughter**.

grandeur (<u>gran</u>-juh)
noun imposing greatness or grandness: *The **grandeur** of the occasion was overwhelming.*

grandfather
noun the father of your father or mother

grandiloquent (gran-<u>dil</u>-uh-kwuhnt)
adjective speaking in a grand or over-important style (***bombastic***, ***inflated***, ***overblown***, ***pompous***)

grandiose (<u>gran</u>-dee-ohs)
adjective too grand or splendid: ***grandiose** schemes*

Word use: The opposite of this is **humble** or **unimposing**.
Word history: French, from Italian

grandmother
noun the mother of your father or mother

grandparent
noun a parent of one of your parents

grandson
noun a son of your son or daughter

grandstand
noun a building with seats rising in tiers, at a sports field or similar outdoor entertainment

granite (<u>gran</u>-uht)
noun a hard rock used for carving monuments and for buildings

Word history: Italian word meaning 'grained', from Latin word meaning 'grain'

Granny Smith
noun a type of apple with green skin, suitable for eating raw or cooking

Word history: from Maria Ann *Smith*, died 1870, who first produced them at Eastwood, Sydney

grant
verb **1** to give or allow: *I* ***granted*** *him permission to leave.* | *to* ***grant*** *land* (***award***, ***bestow***, ***confer***, ***donate***, ***present***)
2 to agree to: *to* ***grant*** *a request*
noun **3** something which is given, such as land or money: *a* ***grant*** *for research into kidney disease*
phrase **4 take for granted**, to accept without questioning or appreciating: *to* ***take*** *freedom of speech* ***for granted***

Word history: Middle English, from Anglo-French word meaning 'promise', 'authorise', 'confirm', 'approve', from Latin word meaning 'trust', 'believe'

granular (gran-yuh-luh)
adjective **1** made of or like granules or grains
2 having a grainy structure or surface

Word building: **granularity** (gran-yuh-lar-uh-tee) *noun*

granulate (gran-yuh-layt)
verb to form into or become grains or particles

Word building: **granulation** *noun*
Word history: *granul(e)* + *-ate*

granule (gran-yoohl)
noun a little grain or particle

Word history: from Latin word meaning 'little grain'

grape
noun a small, round, green or purple fruit which grows in bunches on a vine and is used for eating or making wine

Word history: Middle English, from Old French word meaning 'cluster of fruit or flowers'; of Germanic origin

grapefruit
noun a large, round, yellow-skinned citrus fruit with sour juicy flesh

grapevine
noun **1** a vine that bears grapes
2 *Colloquial* an informal way in which information is carried, especially rumour: *I heard it on the* ***grapevine***.

graph
noun a diagram which shows the relationship between two or more things by dots, lines or bars

Word building: **graph** *verb*
Word history: short for *graphic formula*

graphic
adjective **1** vivid or true to life: *a* ***graphic*** *description*
2 having to do with the use of diagrams or graphs
noun **3** a graphic image or icon: *computer* ***graphics***

Word building: **graphically** *adverb*
Word history: Latin, from Greek word meaning 'drawing', 'writing'

graphical user interface
noun *Computers* an interface which uses graphic displays, such as icons and pull-down menus

Word use: You can also use **graphic interface** or the abbreviation **GUI**.

graphic arts
plural noun forms of art, for example design, drawing, painting, engraving, used to express ideas artistically

Word building: **graphic artist** *noun*

graphic designer
noun a designer who uses print styles, other typographical symbols, images, etc., as design elements: *We hired a* ***graphic designer*** *to design the book cover.*

Word building: **graphic design** *noun*

graphics
noun **1** the art of drawing, especially in mathematics, engineering, etc.
2 the use of diagrams for calculation
3 the production of patterns and diagrams by computer
4 design combining diagrams or pictures with printing or writing

Word history: *graph* + *-ics*

graphite (graf-uyt)
noun a soft blackish form of carbon used in lead pencils

Word history: German, from Greek word meaning 'mark', 'draw', 'write' + *-ite*

grapnel (grap-nuhl)
noun **1** a tool consisting of one or more claws for hooking and holding something
2 a small anchor with three or more hooks

Word use: You can also use **grapple** for definition 1. | A nautical name for definition 2 is **grappling iron**.
Word history: Middle English, from Old French word meaning 'little hook'

grapple
verb **1** to wrestle or struggle: *He* ***grappled*** *with the thief.* | *to* ***grapple*** *with a problem* (***struggle***, ***tussle***)
noun **2** a tool with one or more claws used for hooking or holding something

Word history: from Old English word meaning 'seize'

grasp
verb **1** to seize and hold with your hands (***clasp***, ***clutch***, ***grab***, ***grip***)
2 to understand or take into your mind: *I* ***grasped*** *his meaning.* (***comprehend***, ***fathom***, ***make out***)

Word building: **grasp** *noun*
Word history: Middle English

grasping
adjective greedy (***avaricious***, ***insatiable***, ***rapacious***, ***voracious***)

grass
noun **1** a plant which you can grow to make a lawn
2 any of a number of plants with long narrow leaves, including wheat, oats and bamboo
3 *Colloquial* marijuana

Word building: **grassy** *adjective* (**grassier**, **grassiest**)
Word history: Old English

grasshopper
noun a type of plant-eating insect with large back legs for jumping

grassroots (grahs-roohts, grahs-roohts)
plural noun Colloquial **1** the basics
adjective Colloquial **2** coming from ordinary people

grate[1]
noun **1** a frame of metal bars for holding wood or coal when burning in a fireplace
2 a frame of parallel or crossing bars used as a cover or guard: *a **grate** over a drain*

Word use: You can also use **grating** for definition 2.
Word history: Middle English, from Italian, from Latin word meaning 'wickerwork', 'hurdle'

grate[2]
verb **1** to rub together making a rough sound: *Chalk **grates** on the blackboard.*
2 to rub into small pieces against a surface with many sharp-edged openings: *to **grate** cheese*
phrase **3 grate on**, to irritate or annoy

Word history: Middle English, from Old French, of Germanic origin

> **grate / great**
> Don't confuse **grate** with **great**, meaning 'large', as in *a great crowd of people*, or 'very good' as in *a really great film.*

grateful
adjective feeling thankful or showing thanks (***appreciative***, ***indebted***, ***obliged***)

Word building: **gratitude** (grat-uh-tyoohd) *noun*
Word history: obsolete *grate* pleasing, thankful, from Latin

gratify (grat-uh-fuy)
verb **1** to give pleasure or satisfaction to: *to **gratify** people*
2 to satisfy or indulge: *to **gratify** desire*

Verb forms: I **gratified**, I have **gratified**, I am **gratifying**
Word building: **gratification** *noun* **gratifying** *adjective*
Word history: French, from Latin word meaning 'do a favour to', 'oblige', 'gratify'

gratuitous (gruh-tyooh-uh-tuhs)
adjective **1** freely given or obtained
2 without reason, cause, or excuse: *a **gratuitous** insult*

Word building: **gratuitousness** *noun*
Word history: from Latin word meaning 'free', 'spontaneous'

gratuity (gruh-tyooh-uh-tee)
noun **1** a gift, usually of money, for service given (***handout***, ***tip***)
2 something given without being owed or demanded

Noun forms: The plural is **gratuities**.

grave[1]
noun a hole dug in the earth for burying a dead body

Word history: Old English

grave[2]
adjective **1** solemn or without humour: *a **grave** expression* (***dour***, ***serious***, ***sober***, ***stern***)
2 serious or dangerous: *a **grave** situation*
3 important: *a **grave** decision*

Word history: French, from Latin word meaning 'heavy'

grave accent (grahv ak-sent)
noun an accent (`) used in languages such as French and Italian to show that a vowel is altered in some way

> In Italian a **grave accent** shows that the vowel is stressed. In French it is used mostly with e to show that it sounds like the vowel of *met* (rather than *mate*).
>
> It is also used sometimes in English in the editing of poetry, to show that the last part of verbs ending in -ed should be pronounced as a separate syllable. For example *crossèd* would be pronounced as two syllables rather than just one, as you would normally say it. Putting the accent over the e shows how the poet originally intended the word to be pronounced, and is important for the rhythm and rhyme of the poem.

gravel
noun small stones mixed with sand

Word building: **gravelly** *adjective*
Word history: Middle English, from Old French word meaning 'little sandy shore'; of Celtic origin

gravitate (grav-uh-tayt)
verb **1** to move or tend to move under the influence of gravity
phrase **2 gravitate to** (or **towards**), to tend to move or be attracted

Word history: from Latin word meaning 'heavy'

gravitation (grav-uh-tay-shuhn)
noun **1** *Physics*
a a force of attraction between all particles or bodies, or the acceleration of one towards the other. One example is the falling of objects to the earth.
b a falling or moving caused by gravitation
2 an attraction or tendency to move towards

Word building: **gravitational** *adjective*

gravity
noun **1** the force that attracts or causes everything to fall towards the centre of the earth
2 seriousness or solemnity: *the **gravity** of the occasion*

Word history: from Latin word meaning 'heaviness'

gravy
noun a sauce made from the juices that drip from meat during cooking, mixed with flour and water

Word history: Middle English, from Old French word meaning 'kind of dressing'

graze[1]
verb to feed on growing grass

Word history: from Old English word meaning 'grass'

graze[2]
verb **1** to touch lightly in passing
2 to scratch the skin of: *I fell and **grazed** my knee.* (***cut***, ***nick***, ***scrape***, ***scratch***)

Word building: **graze** *noun*

grazier
noun Australian, NZ a farmer who usually has a large area of land on which cattle or sheep are grazed

grease (grees)
noun **1** melted animal fat
2 any fatty or oily substance
3 a substance used to keep machinery running smoothly
verb (greez, grees) **4** to put grease on
Word building: **greasy** *adjective* (**greasier**, **greasiest**)
Word history: Middle English, from Old French, from Latin word meaning 'fat'

great
adjective **1** large: *a **great** wave of water* | *a **great** crowd of people* (***huge***, ***enormous***, ***massive***)
2 unusual or extreme: ***great** joy*
3 notable or important: *a **great** composer* (***eminent***, ***famous***, ***pre-eminent***, ***prominent***)
4 *Colloquial* very good or fine: *We had a **great** time.* (***exceptional***, ***fantastic***, ***sensational***, ***terrific***)
Word history: Old English

great / grate
Look up **grate / great.**

great circle
noun a circle on a sphere formed by the plane passing through the centre of the sphere. The shortest distance between any two points on the sphere is along the great circle passing through them.

Great Dane
noun one of a breed of large, powerful, short-haired dogs

greed
noun great or unreasonable desire for food or money
Word building: **greediness** *noun* **greedy** *adjective* (**greedier**, **greediest**)
Word history: Old English

green
adjective **1** of the colour of growing leaves (***emerald***, ***hazel***, ***lime***, ***olive***, ***turquoise***)
2 not ripe: *a **green** plum* (***acid***, ***bitter***, ***dry***, ***sour***, ***tart***)
3 *Colloquial* jealous (***covetous***, ***envious***)
4 characterised by, or having to do with, a concern for environmental issues: *a **green** political party*
noun **5** a green colour
6 the part of a golf course surrounding a hole
7 the smooth level lawn on which bowls is played
8 **greens**, green vegetables
Word history: Old English

green ban
noun Australian, NZ the refusal by building workers to do work which would result in the destruction of anything of natural or historical importance

green belt
noun an area of parkland or native bush near a town or city, on which building is strictly controlled or not allowed

green energy
noun energy derived from environmentally friendly sources, such as wind power, solar power, etc.

greenfield
adjective having to do with a location for a business where there has not previously been any building: *a **greenfield** site*
Word use: Compare this with **brownfield.**

greenfields
plural noun parkland or agricultural land on the outskirts of a city

green footprint
noun an ecological footprint which is environmentally friendly

greengrocer
noun someone who sells fresh vegetables and fruit

greenhouse
noun a building used for growing plants, which is made mainly of glass so that it will store the sun's heat

greenhouse effect
noun the increase in the temperature of the earth caused by its atmosphere acting as the glass of a greenhouse does; the increase may become greater as pollution adds more and more carbon dioxide to the atmosphere

greenhouse gas
noun a gas, such as carbon dioxide or methane, which contributes to the greenhouse effect

greenie
noun Colloquial someone who believes that the natural environment should be conserved, that our food should be produced without chemicals, and that we should live more simply

green room
noun a room set aside for use of artists in a theatre, television studio, etc., in which they can relax and entertain when not performing

greenstick
noun a type of make-up with a slight green hue to it which covers up redness on the skin

greenstick fracture
noun a partial fracture of a bone of a young person or animal, in which only one side of the bone is broken

greet
verb to welcome or receive, usually with friendly words
Word history: Old English

greeting
noun **1** the act or words of someone who greets
2 **greetings**, a friendly message: *to send **greetings***

gregarious (gruh-gair-ree-uhs)
adjective fond of the company of other people (***sociable***, ***outgoing***)
Word use: The opposite of this is **shy** or **unfriendly**.
Word history: Latin

gremlin
noun something that causes mischief or trouble: *a **gremlin** in the engine*

grenade
noun a small bomb thrown by hand or fired from a rifle

Word history: French, from Spanish *granada* pomegranate, from *granado* having grains, from Latin

grevillea (gruh-vil-ee-uh)
noun any of a number of types of Australian shrubs or trees, many of which have spiky bright-coloured flowers

Word history: Neo-Latin, from Charles French *Greville*, died 1809, Scottish botanist

grew
verb past tense of **grow**

grey
adjective **1** of a colour between black and white (***charcoal***, ***slate***, ***steel***)
2 dark and overcast: *a **grey** day*

Word building: **grey** *noun*
Word history: Old English *græg*

grey area
noun an issue or subject which is vague or not made absolutely clear

greyhound
noun a type of tall slender dog used for racing

Word history: Middle English *gre(i)hound*, apparently from Scandinavian

greywater
noun untreated domestic or industrial wastewater that can be used for watering lawns and gardens, or for other purposes: *We wash our clothes in **greywater**.*

grid
noun **1** a grating of crossed bars
2 a network of cables and pipes supplying electricity, gas or water
3 a network of crossed lines on a map, designed to give fixed points of reference for finding a place easily
4 *Mathematics* a pattern of evenly-spaced squares used in calculations

griddle
noun a flat heavy pan for cooking on top of the stove

Word history: Middle English, from Old French word meaning 'gridiron' (a cooking utensil)

grief (greef)
noun **1** deep suffering in your mind because of sorrow or loss (***grieving***, ***lamentation***, ***mourning***)
phrase **2 come to grief**, to turn out badly in the end

Word history: Middle English, from Old French word meaning 'grieve'

grievance
noun a feeling of anger or annoyance caused by something unfair that has happened

grieve (greev)
verb to feel grief: *I **grieved** when my aunt died.* (***brood***, ***lament***, ***mope***, ***mourn***, ***pine away***)

Word history: Middle English, from Old French, from Latin word meaning 'weigh down'

grievous (gree-vuhs)
adjective **1** causing grief or sorrow: ***grievous** news*
2 very bad or atrocious: *a **grievous** fault* | ***grievous** bodily harm*

Word history: Middle English, from Old French

griffin
noun in mythology, a monster, usually having the head and wings of an eagle and the body of a lion

Word history: Middle English, from Latin, from Greek

grill
noun **1** a meal, mainly of meat, which has been grilled
2 a griller
verb **3** to cook under or in a griller
4 *Colloquial* to question harshly and closely (***interrogate***, ***interview***, ***pump***, ***question***, ***quiz***)

Word history: French *gril* gridiron (a cooking utensil), from Latin word meaning 'wickerwork', 'hurdle'

grille (gril)
noun a screen of metal bars, sometimes ornamental, for a window, gate or the front of a car

Word history: from French word meaning 'grating'

griller
noun the part of a stove or kitchen appliance for cooking meat by direct heat

griller / gorilla / guerilla
Don't confuse **griller** with **gorilla** or **guerilla**.
A **gorilla** is the largest kind of ape.
A **guerilla** is a member of a small band of soldiers that makes surprise raids and attacks on the enemy.

grim
adjective **1** having a fierce or forbidding appearance (***frightening***, ***horrible***)
2 causing fear or disgust: *the **grim** facts of war*

Adjective forms: **grimmer, grimmest**
Word history: Middle English and Old English

grimace (grim-uhs, gruh-mays)
noun an unnatural or twisted look on your face showing fear, hatred and other such emotions

Word building: **grimace** *verb*
Word history: French, from Spanish word meaning 'panic', 'fear', from Gothic

grime
noun dirt or filth, especially on a surface: *the **grime** on the walls*

Word building: **grimy** *adjective* (**grimier, grimiest**)
Word history: apparently special use of Old English *grīma* mask, to denote layer of dust, etc., that forms on the face and elsewhere

grin
verb **1** to smile broadly
phrase **2 grin and bear it**, *Colloquial* to suffer without complaining

Verb forms: I **grinned,** I have **grinned,** I am **grinning**
Word building: **grin** *noun*
Word history: Old English *grennian*

grind
verb **1** to crush into fine particles: *to **grind** wheat* (***crumble***, ***crush***, ***mill***, ***pound***, ***pulverise***)
2 to produce by grinding: *to **grind** flour*
3 to grate together: *to **grind** your teeth*
4 to smooth, shape or sharpen by rubbing with a tool: *to **grind** a lens* | *to **grind** an axe* (***plane***, ***polish***, ***rub down***, ***sand***)
noun **5** *Colloquial* hard or boring work

Verb forms: I **ground**, I have **ground**, I am **grinding**
Word building: **grinder** *noun*
Word history: Old English *grindan*

grip
noun **1** a firm hold
2 control: *She is in the **grip** of her emotions.*
verb **3** to grasp or seize firmly (***clasp***, ***cling to***, ***clutch***, ***grab***, ***hold***)
4 to hold the interest of: *His story **gripped** us.*
phrase **5 come** (or **get**) **to grips with**, to deal with or tackle: *to **come to grips with** a problem* | *to **get to grips with** an enemy*

Verb forms: I **gripped**, I have **gripped**, I am **gripping**
Word history: Old English *gripe* grasp

gripe
verb *Colloquial* to complain or grumble (***nag***, ***whine***, ***whinge***)

Word building: **gripe** *noun*
Word history: Old English *grīpan*

grisly (griz-lee)
adjective horrible or frightening: *a **grisly** murder*

Word history: Old English *grislic* horrible

grist
noun **1** corn to be ground
phrase **2 it's all grist to the mill**, everything available can be used

Word history: Old English *grīst*, from *grindan grind*

gristle
noun a firm elastic tissue in animals or humans (***cartilage***)

Word history: Middle English and Old English

grit
noun **1** fine, hard, stony particles
2 strength of character or courage: *He showed a lot of **grit** in overcoming his injury.* (***endurance***, ***perseverance***, ***persistence***, ***stamina***, ***tenacity***)
verb **3** to clamp tightly: *to **grit** your teeth*

Verb forms: I **gritted**, I have **gritted**, I am **gritting**
Word building: **gritty** *adjective* (**grittier**, **grittiest**)
Word history: Old English *grēot*

grizzle
verb to whimper or whine

grizzly
adjective greyish in colour: *a **grizzly** head of hair*

Word history: Middle English, from Old French word meaning 'grey'

groan
noun **1** a low sad sound, usually expressing pain or sorrow (***moan***)
verb **2** to utter a groan (***moan***)

Word history: Old English *grānian*

groan / grown
Don't confuse **groan** with **grown**, which is a past form of **grow**, to increase in size.

grocer
noun a shopkeeper with a small store who sells flour, tea, canned and other foods, as well as other household goods

Word history: Middle English, from Old French, from Late Latin *grossus* gross

grocery
noun **1** a grocer's store or business
2 groceries, food and other household goods bought at a shop or supermarket

Noun forms: The plural is **groceries**.

grog
noun *Australian*, *NZ Colloquial* alcoholic drink: *Just bring a bottle of **grog**.*

Word history: originally a shortened form of the word *grogram*, which was the material used to make the cloak of the British naval officer Admiral Vernon, who was known as 'Old Grog'. In 1740, he ordered that water must be mixed with the pure spirits given to sailors to drink. Historically, the word **grog** was used to refer to a mixture of rum and water. It later came to mean any alcoholic drink, especially of a cheap or poor quality kind.

groggy
adjective staggering from tiredness, injury or too much alcoholic drink

Adjective forms: **groggier**, **groggiest**

groin
noun the hollow where your thigh joins your abdomen

Word history: Middle English *grynde*

grommet[1]
noun a small, plastic tube inserted through the eardrum into the middle ear to assist in preventing infection

Word history: French, from Late Latin word meaning 'throat'

grommet[2]
noun *Colloquial* **1** a young surfer
2 a young snowboarder

Word history: Old French *gromet* or *groumet*, which originally meant 'servant' or 'shop-boy', reflecting the fact that young surfers don't yet have the same level of respect as older, more experienced surfers

groom
noun **1** someone who looks after horses
2 → **bridegroom**
verb **3** to brush, comb and generally keep clean and neat in appearance: *to **groom** a horse* | *to **groom** yourself*

Word history: Middle English *grom(e)* boy, groom

groomsman
noun a man who accompanies a bridegroom at his wedding

Noun forms: The plural is **groomsmen**.

groove
noun **1** a long narrow cut made by a tool: ***a groove** in wood* (***channel, furrow***)
2 the track in a record (definition 4) in which the needle moves
verb **3** to furrow or cut a groove in

Word history: Middle English *grofe, groof* mining shaft, Old English *grōf* ditch, sewer

groovy
adjective Colloquial exciting or satisfying

Adjective forms: **groovier, grooviest**

grope
verb **1** to feel about with your hands
2 to search uncertainly: *I **groped** for an answer*

Word history: Old English *grāpian*, from *grāp*, noun, grasp

groper (groh-puh)
noun any of several species of large Australian or New Zealand fish with an enormously wide mouth opening

Noun forms: The plural is **gropers** or **groper**.
Word history: Portuguese *garupa*

gross (grohs)
adjective **1** whole or total, without anything having been taken out: ***gross** income*
2 very bad or shocking: ***gross** injustice*
noun **3** twelve dozen or 144
verb **4** to earn a total of: *The company **grossed** ten million dollars last year.*

Noun forms: The plural is **gross**.
Word history: Middle English, from Old French word meaning 'large', from Late Latin word meaning 'thick'

gross motor skills
plural noun the physical skills considered basic to human activity, such as locomotion, balance, spatial placement, etc.

Word use: Compare this with **fine motor skills**.

gross profit
noun Commerce the total amount from sales revenue, minus payments of wages, salaries, rent, raw materials, bills, etc. This represents the difference between the money received and the money outlayed in carrying on the operation of a firm.

grotesque (groh-tesk)
adjective odd or unnatural in shape, form or appearance: *the **grotesque** figures in a nightmare* (***foul, hideous, monstrous, repulsive***)

Word history: French, from Italian word meaning 'grotesque decoration', such apparently as was found in ancient excavated dwellings, from *grotta* grotto.

grotto
noun Old-fashioned a cave

Noun forms: The plural is **grottoes** or **grottos**.
Word history: Italian *grotta*, from Vulgar Latin word meaning 'crypt', from Greek word meaning 'vault'

grotty
adjective Colloquial **1** dirty (***filthy, grimy, grubby, polluted***)
2 useless

Adjective forms: **grottier, grottiest**
Word history: alteration of *grotesque*

grouch
noun Colloquial a bad-tempered person

Word building: **grouchy** *adjective*
Word history: variant of obsolete *grutch*, from Old French *groucher* grumble

ground
noun **1** firm or dry land: *high **ground***
2 earth or soil: *stony **ground*** (***dirt, loam***)
3 the land surrounding a building or group of buildings: *school **ground** | hospital **grounds***
4 basis or reason: *He has no **ground** for complaint.*
verb **5** to run on to the shore: *The boat **grounded** in the storm.*
6 to stop from flying: *to **ground** a pilot*
phrase **7 common ground**, matters of agreement
8 gain ground, to make progress (***advance, forge ahead, make headway, proceed, push on***)
9 lose ground, to lose what has been gained
10 run to ground, to hunt or track down
11 stand your ground, to keep to your opinion

Word history: Old English *grund*

groundwater
noun the water beneath the surface of the ground, which eventually drains into rivers, lakes or wetlands: *The heavy rains made the **groundwater** rise.*

group
noun **1** a number of people or things gathered together and thought of as being connected in some way (***band, bunch, crowd, gang***)
2 a number of musicians who play together: *a pop **group***

Word building: **group** *verb* **grouping** *noun*
Word history: French, from Italian, of Germanic origin

group certificate
noun a certificate given by an employer to an employee at the end of the financial year or at the end of a period of employment, setting out gross income, tax paid, contributions to superannuation, etc.

group therapy
noun the treatment of a group of psychiatric patients in sessions where problems are shared and discussed

grouse[1]
noun a fowl-like bird of the Northern Hemisphere, with a plump body and protective (often brown) colouring; hunted for game

grouse[2]
verb Colloquial to grumble or complain (***complain, gripe, nag, whine, whinge***)

Word building: **grouse** *noun*

grouse[3]
adjective Australian, NZ Colloquial very good (***excellent, fine, great, satisfactory***)

grout (growt)
noun a thin coarse cement poured into the joint between tiles and brickwork

Word building: **grout** *verb*
Word history: Old English *grūt*

grove
noun a small group of trees
Word history: Old English *grāf*

grovel (grov-uhl)
verb **1** to humble yourself in an undignified way
2 to lie or crawl face down, especially in fear
Verb forms: I **grovelled**, I have **grovelled**, I am **grovelling**
Word history: obsolete *grufe* face down (from Scandinavian)

grow
verb **1** to increase in size (***accumulate***, ***expand***, ***increase***, ***mount***, ***multiply***)
2 to develop: *Plants **grow** from seeds.*
3 to become gradually: *to **grow** older | to **grow** richer*
4 to cause to grow: *I **grow** roses.*
phrase **5 grow on**,
a to gain an increasing influence, effect, etc.
b to win the admiration of bit by bit
6 grow out of,
a to become too big for
b to develop from
7 grow up, to become mature
Verb forms: I **grew**, I have **grown**, I am **growing**
Word history: Old English *grōwan*

grown / groan
Don't confuse **grown** with **groan**.
Grown is a past form of **grow**.
To **groan** is to make a low, sad sound, often because you are in pain.

growl
verb **1** to make a deep angry sound
2 to complain or grumble angrily
Word building: **growl** *noun*
Word history: Middle English *groule* rumble (said of the bowels)

grown-up
noun someone who is fully grown or mature (***adult***)

growth
noun **1** gradual increase or development
2 something that grows or has grown
3 *Medicine* a diseased mass of tissue, such as a tumour
Word use: The opposite of definition 1 is **decline**.

grub
noun **1** the young or larva of some insects
2 *Colloquial* food (***chow***, ***food***, ***provisions***, ***tucker***, ***victuals***)
verb **3** to dig
Word history: Middle English *grubbe(n)* dig

grubby
adjective dirty or untidy: *a **grubby** house* (***filthy***, ***grimy***, ***grotty***)
Adjective forms: **grubbier**, **grubbiest**
Word history: *grub*, noun + *-y*

grudge
noun a feeling of anger caused by someone hurting or insulting you: *to bear a **grudge***
Word history: from Old French word meaning 'murmur', 'grumble'

gruel (grooh-uhl)
noun Old-fashioned a thin mixture like porridge, cooked in water or milk
Word history: Middle English, from Old French word meaning 'meal', from Germanic

gruelling (grooh-uh-ling)
adjective very tiring: *a **gruelling** race*

gruesome
adjective causing feelings of horror: *a **gruesome** story*
Word history: *grue*, verb, shudder + *-some*

gruff
adjective **1** hoarse or low and harsh
2 rough or unfriendly: *He had a **gruff** cranky manner.*
Word history: Dutch, from *ge-* prefix + *rof*, related to Old English *hrēof* rough

grumble
verb to complain crankily (***gripe***, ***nag***, ***whine***, ***whinge***)
Word history: Old English *grymman* wail, mourn

grumpy
adjective bad-tempered (***cross***, ***crotchety***, ***irritable***, ***snappy***, ***touchy***)
Adjective forms: **grumpier**, **grumpiest**
Word building: **grump** *noun*
Word history: British dialect *grump* grumble

grunge
noun **1** *Colloquial* any dirty substance
2 a type of modern rock music
3 a fashion in which clothes are worn which are normally considered shabby or unfashionable, such as those bought at second-hand shops
Word building: **grungy** *adjective*

grunt
verb **1** to make a deep sound like a pig
noun **2** the sound of grunting
3 *Colloquial* the power of an engine or mechanism: *a car with **grunt***
Word history: Old English *grunian* grunt

G-string
noun an item of clothing consisting of a narrow piece of material passing between the legs and supported by a strap around the waist, giving minimal cover for the genitals

guacamole (gwok-uh-moh-lee, gwahk-uh-moh-lee)
noun a dip consisting of mashed avocado, seasonings, and lemon or lime juice

guano (gwah-noh)
noun **1** a manure mainly made up of the excrement of seabirds
2 the droppings of bats, used as a fertiliser

guarantee (ga-ruhn-tee)
noun **1** a promise to replace or repair something if it is faulty: *My new television set has a* ***guarantee*** *for the next four years.*
2 a pledge, or promise accepting responsibility for someone else's debts, liabilities, obligations, etc.
3 anything which is taken or presented as security: *I'll leave my watch as a* ***guarantee*** *that I'll return.*
4 a promise: *Wealth is no* ***guarantee*** *of happiness.*
verb **5** to give a promise or guarantee

Verb forms: I **guaranteed**, I have **guaranteed**, I am **guaranteeing**
Word history: from Anglo-French word meaning 'warrant'

guarantee / warranty
When these words have to do with a person's legal rights as a buyer of goods, they are similar in meaning.
A **guarantee** is an assurance, especially in writing, given by a manufacturer that the goods you have purchased will last for a certain time and perform at a certain standard.
A **warranty**, more commonly issued with second-hand goods, emphasises the limits of the seller's liability. It may define what sort of faults will be repaired, what time period is covered, etc.

guarantor (ga-ruhn-taw)
noun someone who makes or gives a guarantee

guard (gahd)
verb **1** to protect or keep safe from harm (***defend***, ***screen***, ***secure***, ***shield***)
2 to keep from escaping
3 to keep in control: *to* ***guard*** *your tongue*
4 to make safe: *The pool fence* ***guards*** *the pool.*
noun **5** someone who protects or keeps watch
6 a careful watch: *That prisoner should be kept under close* ***guard****.*
7 something that guards from harm or injury: *Each footballer should wear a mouth* ***guard****.*

Word history: Middle English *garde*, from French, of Germanic origin

guardian
noun **1** someone who guards, protects or takes care of someone or something
2 someone who is appointed by law to take care of another person and their property
adjective **3** guarding or protecting: *a* ***guardian*** *angel*

Word building: **guardianship** *noun*
Word history: Middle English, from Anglo-French

guava (gwah-vuh)
noun an American tree or shrub with a fruit used for making jam and jelly

Word history: Spanish, from South American name

guerilla (guh-ril-uh)
noun **1** a member of a small band of soldiers which worries the enemy by surprise raids and attacks
adjective **2** having to do with soldiers like these or to their way of fighting: ***guerilla*** *warfare*

Word use: You can also use **guerrilla**.
Word history: Spanish, diminutive of *guerra*, war

guerilla / gorilla / griller
Don't confuse **guerilla** with **gorilla** or **griller**.
A **gorilla** is the largest kind of ape.
A **griller** is the part of a stove or kitchen appliance which cooks meat by direct heat.

guernsey (gern-zee)
noun **1** a close-fitting knitted jumper, often worn by sailors, footballers, etc.
phrase **2 get a guernsey**, *Australian*
a to be selected for a football team
b *Colloquial* to succeed, win approval

Word history: This word comes from the name of the island of *Guernsey*, in the English Channel, where these sailors' knitted jumpers originated. The word is now also used to refer to footballers' jumpers and similar garments. The phrase **get a guernsey** was originally used literally, meaning to be selected for a football team and so be given a team guernsey. It is now also used in a more general sense, meaning to win success or approval of any kind.

guess (ges)
verb **1** to give an answer when you don't really know
2 to think or believe: *I* ***guess*** *I can get there in time* (***conclude***, ***imagine***, ***reckon***, ***suppose***)
noun **3** a judgement or opinion formed without really knowing

Word history: Middle English, probably from Scandinavian

guest (gest)
noun **1** a visitor or someone who is entertained at your house
2 someone well-known who visits and performs at a club or show
3 someone who stays at a hotel or motel
adjective **4** of a performer, invited to make an appearance in one of a series of broadcasts, concerts, etc.: *a* ***guest*** *artist*

Word history: Middle English, from Scandinavian

guffaw (gu-faw, guh-faw)
noun **1** a noisy laugh
verb **2** to laugh loudly and noisily (***cackle***, ***chortle***, ***chuckle***)

GUI
noun *Computers* an interface which uses graphic displays, such as icons and pull-down menus, to guide the user and initiate commands

Word history: *G(raphical) U(ser) I(nterface)*

guidance
noun advice, guiding or leadership

guide (guyd)
verb **1** to show the way
2 to tell what to do (***advise***, ***counsel***)
noun **3** someone who shows the way, often for money
4 someone who offers advice and useful information (***adviser***, ***counsellor***, ***guru***, ***mentor***, ***teacher***)
5 a member of an organisation of girls which aims at developing health, character, and practical skills
6 a book with information for travellers or tourists

Word use: You can also use **Guide** or **girl guide** for definition 5.
Word history: Middle English, from Old French, from Germanic

guide dog
noun a dog specially trained to lead or guide a person who is vision-impaired

guild (gild)
noun Old-fashioned an organisation or society of people who have similar jobs or interests

Word history: Middle English, from Scandinavian

guile (guyl)
noun cleverness or cunning in the way you deceive somebody (***deceit***, ***trickery***)

Word building: **guileless** *adjective*
Word history: Middle English, from Old French; of Germanic origin

guillotine (gil-uh-teen)
noun **1** a machine with a heavy blade that falls between two grooved posts and is used for cutting off someone's head
2 a machine with a long blade used for trimming paper

Word building: **guillotine** *verb*
Word history: French; named after JI *Guillotin*, 1738–1814, French physician, who urged its use

guilt (gilt)
noun **1** the position of having committed a crime or being wrong: *His **guilt** was proved by the court.*
2 a feeling that something is your fault: *We should all share the **guilt** of our school's disgrace.*

Word use: The opposite of this is **innocence**.
Word history: Old English *gylt* offence

guilt / gilt
Don't confuse **guilt** with **gilt**, which is the gold or other material used to decorate precious objects like vases.

guilty
adjective **1** marked by or showing a sense of guilt: ***guilty** intent* | *a **guilty** conscience*
phrase **2 guilty of**, justly charged with: ***guilty of** murder*

Adjective forms: **guiltier**, **guiltiest**

guinea pig (gin-ee pig)
noun **1** a short-eared short-tailed animal kept as a pet and also used for scientific experiments
2 someone used in experiments: *The children were used as **guinea pigs** to test the new soft drink.*

Word history: *Guinea* + *pig*; the reason for associating the animal with Guinea is unknown

guise (guyz)
noun the outside appearance, usually only pretended, of someone or something: *The robber walked into the bank in the **guise** of a priest.*

Word history: Middle English, from Old French, from Germanic

guitar (guh-tah)
noun a violin-shaped musical instrument with a long neck and strings which you pluck

Word history: Spanish, from Greek word meaning 'cithara' (an ancient Greek musical instrument)

gulf
noun **1** a part of an ocean which is partly bounded by land
2 a deep hollow or split in the earth
3 any wide separation: *The **gulf** between the two boys widened after the fight.*

Word history: Middle English, from Old French, from Italian, from Greek word meaning 'bosom', 'gulf'

gull
noun → **seagull**

Word history: Middle English

gullet
noun the tube-like part of your body, by which the food and drink you swallow pass to your stomach

Word history: Middle English, from Old French, from Latin word meaning 'throat'

gullible
adjective easily deceived or cheated (***believing***, ***naive***, ***simple***, ***trusting***)

Word use: The opposite of this is **discerning**.

gully
noun **1** a small valley cut out of the earth by running water
2 a ditch or a gutter

Noun forms: The plural is **gullies**.
Word history: variant of *gullet*

gulp
verb **1** to swallow quickly: *to **gulp** water* | *to **gulp** with fear* (***consume***, ***devour***, ***gobble***)
noun **2** an amount swallowed at one time

Word history: Middle English *gulpe(n)*

gum[1]
noun **1** a sticky liquid which oozes from plants or trees
2 → **gum tree**
3 a sticky flavoured sweet for chewing
4 a glue (***adhesive***, ***cement***, ***mortar***, ***paste***)
verb **5** to cover or stick together with gum

Verb forms: I **gummed**, I have **gummed**, I am **gumming**
Word use: You can also use **chewing gum** for definition 3.
Word history: Middle English, from Latin, from Greek

gum[2]
noun the firm flesh around the bottom of your teeth

Word use: Often used as a plural **gums**.
Word history: Old English *gōma* palate, inside of the mouth

gumboot
noun a rubber boot sometimes reaching to your knee or thigh

gumption (gump-shuhn)
noun Colloquial **1** courage or resourcefulness
2 practical common sense

Word history: originally Scottish

gum tree
noun a tree or shrub used for its timber and strong oil, and which grows mostly in Australia

Word use: The short form is **gum**. | Other names are **eucalyptus** or **eucalypt**.

gun
noun **1** a weapon with a long metal tube for firing bullets or other ammunition
2 anything which is similar to a gun in its shape or in the way it is used: *a spray* ***gun*** *for paint*
verb **3** to shoot: *The thief* ***gunned*** *down the policeman.*
phrase **4 jump the gun**, to begin very early
5 stick to your guns, to keep your position in an argument, when faced with opposition, etc.

Verb forms: I **gunned**, I have **gunned**, I am **gunning**
Word history: Middle English *gunne, gonne*, apparently short for *Gunilda* (Latin), *gonnyld* (Middle English), name for engine of war, from Scandinavian

gunnery
noun the art and science of making and managing (large) guns

gunpowder
noun a mixture of chemical powders that explodes when set off by a gun or by fire

gunwale (gun-uhl)
noun the upper edge of the side of a ship or boat

Word use: You can also use **gunnel**.
Word history: *gun* + *wale* plank; so called because guns were set upon it

gunyah (gun-yuh)
noun a hut traditionally made by Aboriginal people from tree branches and bark (***humpy***, ***mia mia***)

Word use: You can also use **gunya**.
Word history: from Dharug, an Australian Aboriginal language spoken by the people living near Sydney Cove in the early days of European settlement.

guppy
noun a small brightly coloured fish which is often kept in home aquariums

Noun forms: The plural is **guppies**.

gurgle
verb **1** to flow with a noisy bubbling sound
2 to make or imitate this sound

Word building: **gurgle** *noun*
Word history: perhaps imitative

guru (goo-rooh, gooh-rooh)
noun a wise and powerful teacher (***adviser***, ***coach***, ***trainer***, ***tutor***)

Word history: from Hindi, a language of India

gush
verb **1** to flow suddenly in large amounts: *The sea* ***gushed*** *through the hole the torpedo had made.* (***spurt***, ***stream***, ***surge***, ***wash***)
2 to have a large sudden flow of something: *The wound* ***gushed*** *blood.* | *Her eyes* ***gushed*** *tears.*
3 *Colloquial* to express yourself in a rush of emotional talk (***chatter***, ***gasbag***, ***harp on***, ***rant***, ***rave***, ***yak***)

Word history: Middle English *gusche*

gusset (gus-uht)
noun an angular piece of material inserted in a garment to strengthen, enlarge or give freedom of movement to some part of it

Word history: Middle English, from Old French word meaning 'pod', 'husk'

gust
noun a sudden strong blast or rush: *a* ***gust*** *of wind*

Word history: Scandinavian

gusto
noun hearty enjoyment

Word history: Italian, from Latin word meaning 'taste', 'relish'

gut
noun **1** → **intestine**
2 the tough string made from the gut of an animal and used for things like violin strings or tennis racquet strings
3 guts, *Colloquial*
a your stomach
b courage
c most important part or contents: *the* ***guts*** *of the motor*
verb **4** to take out the stomach, intestines, etc., of something
5 to destroy the inside of something: *Fire* ***gutted*** *the inside of the building.*

Verb forms: it **gutted**, it has **gutted**, it is **gutting**
Word building: **gut** *adjective*
Word history: Old English *guttas*, plural, related to *gēotan* pour

gutter
noun **1** a channel, usually along the side of a street, for carrying away water
2 a channel along the eaves or roof of a building for carrying off rainwater

Word use: You can also use **guttering** for definition 2.
Word history: Middle English, from Old French, from Latin word meaning 'a drop'

guttural (gut-uh-ruhl)
adjective **1** having to do with your throat
2 harsh and throaty

Word history: Neo-Latin, from Latin word meaning 'throat'

guy[1]
noun Colloquial **1** a man or a boy
2 any person

Word history: from *Guy* Fawkes, the leader of the *Gunpowder Plot*

guy[2]
noun a rope or wire attached to something to guide, steady or secure it

Word history: Middle English, from Old French word meaning 'a guide'

guzzle
verb to eat or drink noisily and greedily

gym (jim)
noun **1** a centre providing fitness equipment and classes
2 → **gymnasium**
3 → **gymnastics**

Word history: abbreviation

gymkhana (jim-kah-nuh)
noun horse-riding events with games and contests

Word history: from Hindustani word meaning 'ball house', 'racquet-court'

gymnasium (jim-nay-zee-uhm)
noun a building or room specially equipped for gymnastics and sport

Word use: The short form is **gym**.
Word history: Latin, from Greek

gymnast (jim-nuhst)
noun someone especially trained and skilled in gymnastics

gymnastic (jim-nas-tik)
adjective having to do with physical exercises which develop your muscle strength and tone up your body

gymnastics (jim-nas-tiks)
noun the performance of gymnastic exercises

Word use: The short form is **gym**.

gynaecology (guy-nuh-kol-uh-jee)
noun the area of medicine which deals with the functions and diseases of women, especially those affecting the reproductive organs

Word use: You can also use **gynecology**.
Word building: **gynaecologist** *noun*

gyp (jip)
verb Colloquial **1** to cheat or swindle (***deceive***, ***fool***, ***hoax***, ***kid***, ***trick***)
noun Colloquial **2** a swindle (***con***, ***hoax***, ***ruse***, ***trick***)

Verb forms: I **gypped**, I have **gypped**, I am **gypping**
Word use: You can also use **gip**.

gypsum (jip-suhm)
noun a very common mineral, hydrated calcium sulfate, used especially to make plaster of Paris

Word history: Latin, from Greek word meaning 'chalk', 'gypsum'

gypsy
noun (*often upper case*) **1** → **Romani**
2 someone who has an unconventional or nomadic lifestyle

Noun forms: The plural is **gypsies**.
Word use: You can also use **gipsy**.
Word history: from *gipcyan*, variant of *Egyptian*

gyrate (juy-rayt)
verb to whirl or move in a circle (***spin***, ***swirl***, ***turn***, ***twirl***, ***whirr***)

Word building: **gyration** *noun*
Word history: from Latin word meaning 'wheeled round', 'turned'

gyre (juy-uh)
noun **1** a ring or circle
2 a circular course or motion

gyroscope (juy-ruh-skohp)
noun a rotating wheel inside a frame which lets the wheel's axis keep its original direction even though the frame is moved around, used to help make such instruments as stabilisers in ships

Word history: French

habeas corpus (hay-bee-uhs kaw-puhs)
noun a written order that a person being kept in prison must be brought before a court which will then decide whether the imprisonment is legal

Word history: from Latin word meaning 'you may have the body' (the first words of the order)

haberdasher
noun someone who sells buttons, needles, ribbons, etc.

Word building: **haberdashery** *noun*
Word history: from Anglo-French word meaning 'kind of fabric'

habit
noun **1** a certain usual way of behaving: *It is a **habit** of mine to read in bed.*
2 the dress of someone in a religious order, like a nun or a monk

Word building: **habitual** *adjective*
Word history: from Latin word meaning 'condition', 'appearance', 'dress'

habitable
adjective able to be lived in

habitat
noun the place where a plant or animal naturally lives or grows (***environment***, ***environs***, ***setting***, ***surroundings***)

Word history: from Latin word meaning 'it inhabits'

habitation
noun a home or a place of living

habituate (huh-bich-ooh-ayt)
verb to make used to: *Police horses are **habituated** to traffic.* (***accustom***, ***condition***, ***familiarise***, ***inure***)

Word history: Late Latin word meaning 'bring into a condition', from Latin word meaning 'habit'

háček (hach-ek)
noun a mark (ˇ) over a letter used especially in the spelling of Slavic languages to represent particular phonetic qualities

Word history: Czech

hack[1]
verb **1** to cut or chop with rough heavy blows
noun **2** a rough cut or gash

Word history: from Old English word meaning 'hack to pieces'

hack[2]
noun **1** an old or worn-out horse
2 a riding horse kept for hire or ordinary riding
3 someone who does poor quality writing for a living
verb **4** *Colloquial* to put up with

Word building: **hack** *adjective*
Word history: short for *hackney* a horse for ordinary riding

hacker
noun Colloquial a person who gains access to a computer system and without permission uses or changes information

hackle
noun **1** the long neck feather or feathers of a rooster
2 hackles, the hair on the back of a dog's neck
phrase **3 with your hackles up**, very angry and ready to fight

Word history: Middle English *hakell*

hackneyed (hak-need)
adjective made commonplace or stale by overuse: *a **hackneyed** expression* (***cliched***, ***trite***)

hacksaw
noun a saw for cutting metal, consisting of a narrow, fine-toothed blade fixed in a frame

hackwork
noun the routine side of creative or artistic work, thought of as mundane, especially in the literary field

had
verb **1** past tense and past participle of **have**
phrase **2 be had**, to be cheated or deceived: *I **was had**.*
3 have had, to be extremely annoyed with: *I **have had** this government.*

haddock (had-uhk)
noun a fish, valued as a food, found in the northern Atlantic and related to, but smaller than the cod

Noun forms: The plural is **haddocks** or **haddock**.
Word history: Middle English *haddoc*

hades (hay-deez)
noun hell

Word history: from *Hades*, (in Greek mythology) the gloomy underground place of the dead, ruled over by Pluto

hadn't
contraction of **had not**

Look up **contractions in grammar**.

had've
contraction of **had have**

Word use: This is considered to be ungrammatical.

Occasionally you'll hear people say phrases like these:

If I had have gone ...

If I had've gone ...

These are irregular versions of:

If I had gone...

The *have* serves no useful purpose in such a phrase, so it's better not to use it in your writing.

Some people even write (or say) *had of*, which makes even less sense than the original mistake. *Could of* and *should of* are similar mistakes. Avoid all three.

Look up **contractions in grammar**.

haemoglobin (hee-muh-gloh-buhn)
noun a protein in blood which carries oxygen to the tissues. When combined with oxygen, it gives the bright red colour to blood which flows through the arteries. When it is without oxygen the result is the blue-red colour of the blood which flows in the veins.

Word use: You can also use **hemoglobin**.

haemophilia (hee-muh-fil-ee-uh)
noun a hereditary disease, carried by females but showing itself in males, which makes you bleed for a long time if you cut yourself because the blood does not clot as it should

Word use: You can also use **hemophilia**.
Word building: **haemophiliac** *noun*
Word history: Neo-Latin, from Greek

haemorrhage (hem-uh-rij)
noun a sudden flow of blood like one from a burst blood vessel

Word use: You can also use **hemorrhage**.
Word building: **haemorrhage** *verb*
Word history: Latin, from Greek word meaning 'a violent bleeding'

haemorrhoids (hem-uh-roydz)
plural noun painful swellings of a vein or veins around the anus (***piles***)

Word use: You can also use **hemorrhoids**.
Word history: Latin word meaning 'piles', from Greek

haft
noun the handle, especially of a knife, sword, dagger, etc.

Word history: Middle English, from Old English *hæft*

hag
noun an ugly old woman

Word history: from Old English word meaning 'fury', 'witch'

haggard (hag-uhd)
adjective looking worn out from hunger, sickness or worry

Word history: origin uncertain, perhaps French

haggis (hag-uhs)
noun a food, originally Scottish, made of the heart, liver, etc., of a sheep or calf, minced with suet and oatmeal, seasoned, and boiled in a bag made from the stomach of the animal

Word history: perhaps from Old English word meaning 'meat'

haggle
verb to bargain or argue about the price of something

Word history: from *hag* cut, hew, hack, from Scandinavian

haiku (huy-kooh)
noun a Japanese form of poem which has 17 syllables and three lines

hail[1]
verb **1** to greet or welcome
2 to attract attention by calling out: *to **hail** a taxi*
noun **3** a shout or call to attract attention
phrase **4 hail from**, to come from or belong to: *He **hails from** Tasmania.*

Word history: Middle English word meaning 'health', from Scandinavian

hail[2]
noun **1** a shower of small balls of ice from the clouds, like frozen rain
2 a shower of anything hard: *a **hail** of bullets*
verb **3** to pour down hail or to fall like hail

Word history: Old English *hægl*

hair
noun **1** a fine threadlike growth from the skin of people and animals: *There's a **hair** in my soup. | She pulled a **hair** out of my head.*
2 the mass of these which cover the human head or the body of an animal: *Please get your **hair** cut.*
phrase **3 let your hair down**, to behave in a relaxed or free manner
4 split hairs, to make unnecessary or petty distinctions
5 tear your hair out, to show great emotion, such as anger or anxiety
6 without turning a hair, remaining calm and showing no emotion

Word history: Middle English *ha(i)re*, from Scandinavian

hair / hare

Don't confuse **hair** with **hare**, which is a rabbit-like animal.

hairdo (hair-dooh)
noun the style in which someone's hair is arranged, cut, tinted, etc.

Noun forms: The plural is **hairdos**.

hairdresser
noun someone who arranges or cuts hair, especially women's hair

Word use: Compare this with **barber**.

hairline fracture
noun a break or fault in a bone, metal casting, etc., which shows itself as a very thin line on the surface

hairpiece
noun a full or partial wig

hair's-breadth
noun **1** a very small space or distance
adjective **2** very narrow or close: *a **hair's-breadth** escape*

Word use: You can also use **hairsbreadth** or **hairbreadth**.

hairstyle
noun the style in which someone's hair is arranged

hairy
adjective **1** covered with hair
2 *Colloquial* difficult: *a **hairy** problem*
3 *Colloquial* frightening: *a **hairy** manoeuvre* (***dangerous***, ***scary***)

Adjective forms: **hairier, hairiest**

haji (hah-jee)
noun a Muslim who has made their pilgrimage to Mecca

Noun forms: The plural is **hajis**.
Word use: You can also use **hadji** or **hajji**.

hake (hayk)
noun any of several saltwater fishes, valued as food, related to the cod

hakea (hay-kee-uh)
noun a type of Australian shrub or tree that has hard woody fruit with winged seeds

halal (hal-al)
adjective having to do with meat from animals that have been killed according to the special food rules of Islamic religious practice: ***halal** meat* | *a **halal** butcher*

Word history: from Arabic word meaning 'lawful'

halcyon (hal-see-uhn)
noun **1** in mythology, a bird, usually said to be the kingfisher, supposed to have the power of calming winds and waves
adjective **2** calm, peaceful or tranquil
3 carefree or joyous

Word history: Latin, from Greek word meaning 'kingfisher'

hale[1]
adjective healthy and robust

Word history: Old English *hāl*

hale[2]
verb to drag or bring by force: *to **hale** a man into court*

Word history: Middle English, from Old French word meaning 'hale', 'haul', from Germanic

half (hahf)
noun **1** one of two equal parts into which anything can be divided
adjective **2** being about half the full amount: ***half** speed*
adverb **3** in part or partly: *The house was only **half** built.*
phrase **4 by half**, by a great deal or by too much: *too clever **by half***
5 the half of it, the more important part: *You don't know **the half of it**!*

Noun forms: The plural is **halves**.
Word history: Old English

half of

There is often disagreement over whether *half of* is followed by a singular or a plural verb. Should we say

Half of X is ...

or

Half of X are ...?

The answer is simple: it depends on the number of *X*. If *X* is singular, so is the verb that follows:

Half of my apple is gone.

If *X* is plural, so is the verb:

Half of my apples are gone.

half-back
noun **1** *Rugby* the player who puts the ball in the scrum, and tries to catch it as it comes out
2 *Australian Rules* any of the three players on the line between the centre-line and the full-back line
3 *Soccer* one of the three players in the next line behind the forward line

half-baked
adjective **1** not cooked enough
2 *Colloquial*
a not completed: *a **half-baked** plan*
b lacking wisdom or experience

half-brother
noun a brother who is related to you through one parent only

half-hearted
adjective having not much interest or willingness: *He made a **half-hearted** attempt to join in.* (***apathetic***, ***indifferent***, ***lukewarm***, ***passive***)

half-life
noun the time taken for half of a sample of radioactive substance to decay

half-sister
noun a sister who is related to you through one parent only

halfway
adverb **1** with half the distance covered: *to go **halfway** to a place*
2 to or at half the distance: *The rope reaches only **halfway**.*
adjective **3** midway, as between two places or points: ***halfway** mark*
4 incomplete: ***halfway** measures*
phrase **5 meet halfway**, to compromise

halfway house
noun a place for people who have left an institution, such as a prison or hospital, to live in while undergoing rehabilitation and adjusting to independent living

halfwit
noun someone who is considered stupid

halibut (hal-uh-buht)
noun **1** a dark brown fish, valued as a food, found in tropical waters of Australia and elsewhere
2 either of two kinds of large flatfishes, valued as a food, found in the North Atlantic and the North Pacific

Noun forms: The plural is **halibuts** or **halibut**.
Word history: from Old English word meaning *hälig* holy + *butte* kind of fish; so called because eaten on holy days

halitosis (hal-uh-toh-suhs)
noun bad breath

Word history: Neo-Latin, from Latin word meaning 'breath'

hall
noun **1** a corridor or passage inside the front door of a house, from which you can get to the other rooms
2 a large building or room used for such things as public meetings or dances

Word history: Old English

hall / haul
Don't confuse **hall** with **haul**. To **haul** something is to drag it along. A **haul** is something you grab or drag in:
We went fishing and got a good haul of whiting.

hallelujah (hal-uh-looh-yuh)
interjection a cry which expresses praise to God

Word history: from Hebrew word meaning 'praise ye Jehovah'

hallmark
noun **1** an official mark or stamp indicating a standard of purity, used in marking gold and silver articles
2 any mark or special sign of genuineness, good quality, etc.
3 any outstanding feature or characteristic

Word history: from Goldsmiths' *Hall*, London, the seat of the Goldsmiths' Company which tested and marked gold and silver articles

hallowed
adjective greatly honoured because it is part of a tradition, etc.: *the **hallowed** halls of the ancient university*

Word history: Old English *hālgian*, from *hālig* holy

hallucination (huh-looh-suh-nay-shuhn)
noun something which someone imagines they have seen or heard: *Some drugs can make you have **hallucinations**.* (***fantasy***, ***illusion***)

Word building: **hallucinate** *verb*

halo (hay-loh)
noun **1** a ring of light surrounding the head of a holy person in paintings of saints or angels
2 a circle of light seen around the sun or moon

Noun forms: The plural is **haloes** or **halos**.
Word use: You can also use **nimbus** for definition 1.
Word history: Latin word meaning from Greek word meaning 'disc', 'halo', 'threshing floor' (on which the oxen trod out a circular path)

haloumi (huh-looh-mee)
noun a soft, firm, Greek-style cheese, which has been preserved by being soaked in salted water

Word use: You can also use **halloumi**.

halt
verb to stop (***pull up***, ***stall***)

Word building: **halt** *noun*
Word history: from German word meaning 'stoppage'

halter
noun a rope or a strap for leading or tying horses or cattle

Word history: Old English *hælftre*

halve (hahv)
verb **1** to divide in halves: *She **halved** the apple for the two boys.*
2 to cut down or reduce to half

Word use: The opposite of this is **double**.
Word history: Middle English *halven*, from *half*

halves (hahvz)
noun **1** plural of **half**
phrase **2 by halves**,
a incompletely
b half-heartedly
3 go halves, divide equally, share

halyard (hal-yuhd)
noun the rope or tackle used to raise or lower a sail, yard, flag, etc.

Word use: You can also use **halliard**.
Word history: from Middle English word meaning 'that which hales or hauls'

ham
noun **1** salted or smoked meat from the upper part of a pig's leg
2 *Colloquial* an actor who overacts
3 someone whose hobby is sending and receiving radio messages around the world
verb **4** *Colloquial* to overact or act in an exaggerated way

Word history: Old English *hamm*

hamburger
noun a bread roll containing a fried, flattened lump of minced beef

Word history: from *Hamburg*, a city in Germany

hamlet
noun a very small village

Word history: Middle English *hamlet*, from Old French, from Germanic word meaning 'land'

hammer
noun **1** a tool with a heavy metal head and a handle, used for banging nails into wood and for beating things
2 anything shaped or used like a hammer
verb **3** to hit or work with a hammer
4 to hit with force, or to pound: *She **hammered** the table with her fist.* (***bang***, ***beat***, ***punch***, ***smack***, ***thump***)

Word history: Old English *hamor*

hammerhead
noun **1** the head of a hammer
2 a shark with a head shaped like a double-headed hammer

hammock
noun a hanging bed made of canvas or netlike material

Word history: Spanish *hamaca*; of West Indian origin

hamper[1]
verb to hold back or hinder: *Heavy rain **hampered** the search for the lost child.* (***impede***, ***inhibit***, ***prevent***)

Word history: Middle English *hampren*

hamper[2]
noun **1** a large box or basket, sometimes with a cover
2 such a basket filled with food, and given as a gift, prize, etc.

Word history: Middle English *hampere*

hamster
noun a small short-tailed animal belonging to the rat family, which looks like a very small guinea pig

Word history: German

hamstring
noun **1** in humans, any of the tendons at the back of the knee: *He injured his* ***hamstring*** *playing football.*
2 in quadrupeds, the large sinew at the back of the hock
verb **3 a** to cripple by cutting the hamstring or hamstrings
b to make useless or thwart: *Lack of money will* ***hamstring*** *the project.*

Verb forms: I **hamstrung**, I have **hamstrung**, I am **hamstringing**

hand
noun **1** the end part of your arm below your wrist, used for touching and holding things
2 something like a hand: *the* ***hands*** *of a clock*
3 a worker or labourer: *a factory* ***hand***
4 help or cooperation: *Give me a* ***hand.***
5 a side or a point in an argument: *on the other* ***hand***
6 a unit of measurement, about 10 centimetres, for giving the height of horses: *This horse is sixteen* ***hands.***
7 a burst of clapping or applause for a performer: *Give him a big* ***hand.***
8 hands, power or control: *Your fate is in my* ***hands.***
verb **9** to deliver or pass with your hand: ***Hand*** *me the jam please.*
phrase **10 at hand**, near or ready
11 change hands, to pass from one owner to another
12 free hand, freedom to act as desired
13 hand out, to distribute
14 hand over, to give control and responsibility to someone else
15 hands down, totally, completely or very easily: *to win* ***hands down***
16 in hand, under control
17 keep your hand in, to keep in practice
18 old hand, an experienced person: *The* ***old hands*** *made quick work of the shearing.*
19 throw in your hand, to stop doing something or give up

Word history: Old English

handbag
noun a small bag used for holding money and small articles

handball
noun **1** a game in which two teams of seven players move a ball around a court with their hands, trying to hit the ball into their opponents' goal
2 a game in which a small ball is batted against a wall with the hand
3 a game, often played in school playgrounds, in which a tennis ball is batted with the hand to an opponent across a line, the ball bouncing before crossing the line
4 (in soccer) the offence of a player other than the goalkeeper in the penalty area touching the ball with the hand
verb **5** *Australian Rules* to hold the ball in one hand and hit it away with the fist of the other: *to* ***handball*** *to the opposition*

handbook
noun a small book that gives advice or instructions: *a* ***handbook*** *of car maintenance* (***guidebook***, ***manual***)

handcuff
noun one of a pair of connected steel rings or bracelets put around someone's wrists to stop them using their hands

Word building: **handcuff** *verb*

handicap
noun **1** a physical disability
2 any disadvantage that makes success harder (***barrier***, ***drawback***, ***hindrance***, ***hitch***, ***obstacle***)
3 a race or contest in which the better competitors are given a disadvantage, such as a greater distance to run
4 the disadvantage given to these competitors, such as the extra distance: *Last year's winner was given a* ***handicap*** *of three metres.*

Word building: **handicap** *verb* (**handicapped**, **handicapping**) **handicapped** *adjective*
Word history: originally *hand i' cap* (with *i'* for *in* before a consonant), referring to the deposit of stakes or forfeits in a cap or hat

handicraft
noun an occupation or art in which you use your hands: *Pottery and weaving are* ***handicrafts.***

Word history: Old English *handcræft*, modelled on *handiwork*

handiwork
noun **1** work done with the hands
2 the work or art of making things with the hands (***craft***, ***manual labour***)

Word use: You can also use **handwork**.
Word history: Old English *handgeweorc*

handkerchief (<u>hang</u>-kuh-cheef)
noun a small, usually square piece of cloth used for wiping your nose

handle
noun **1** a part of something, used to hold it by or open it with: *the* ***handle*** *of a knife* | *a door* ***handle***
verb **2** to touch or feel with your hand (***finger***, ***pat***, ***stroke***)
3 to use: *He* ***handles*** *a paintbrush with skill.*
4 to manage or control: *The captain cannot* ***handle*** *his soldiers.*

Word history: Old English *handlian* from *hand*

handlebars
plural noun the curved bar at the front of a bike that you steer it with

handout
noun **1** a prepared written statement such as given to the press for publication
2 a free sample
3 food, money or the like given to those in need: *There was a queue for* ***handouts*** *after the earthquake.*

handsome
adjective **1** good-looking (***attractive***, ***beautiful***)
2 large or generous: *a* ***handsome*** *gift* (***lavish***, ***liberal***, ***magnanimous***)

Word use: Definition 1 is used mostly of men.
Word history: Middle English, easy to handle

handwriting
noun writing done with your hand, especially your own style of writing: *very neat **handwriting***

Word building: **handwritten** *adjective*

handy
adjective **1** close at hand: *Is the glue **handy**?* (***adjacent***, ***near***)
2 skilful with your hands
3 useful or convenient: *a **handy** tool* (***advantageous***, ***beneficial***, ***helpful***, ***valuable***)

Adjective forms: **handier**, **handiest**
Word history: Middle English

hang
verb **1** to fix or be fixed at the top but not at the bottom: ***Hang** the picture on that hook.* | *The vine is **hanging** from the top of the fence.*
2 to put to death by dropping with a rope around the neck
3 to bend downwards: *I **hung** my head in shame.*
phrase **4 hang around with**, to spend time with (***accompany***, ***associate with***)
5 hang back, to hesitate or be reluctant to go on (***pause***, ***stall***)
6 hang on, to wait
7 hang together, to be consistent: *His statements do not **hang together**.*
8 hang up, to break off a phone conversation

Verb forms: I **hung** or, for definition 2, I **hanged**, I have **hung** or, for definition 2, I have **hanged**, I am **hanging**
Word history: Old English *hangian*

When talking about death by hanging, the usual past form used to be **hanged**, rather than **hung**. However, nowadays, except in legal use, the past form often used for this meaning is **hung**.

She hung herself from the chandelier.

Hung is also the past form for all other senses of **hang**.

He hung out the washing.

hangar
noun a large shed that planes are kept in

Word history: French, perhaps from Germanic

hangar / hanger

Don't confuse **hangar** with **hanger**, which is something on which you hang your clothes, as in *coathanger*.

hanger
noun a curved piece of wood, plastic or metal with a hook attached, used for hanging clothes

Word use: You can also use **coathanger**.

hang-glider
noun a large type of kite which you hang on to and guide as you glide through the air

hangover
noun **1** the feeling of sickness and headache that you get after drinking too much alcohol
2 something remaining or left over

hang-up
noun Colloquial something which worries you and which you can't get off your mind (***obsession***, ***phobia***)

hank
noun **1** a coil, as of thread or yarn
2 a definite length of thread or yarn

Word history: Middle English, from Scandinavian

hanker
phrase **hanker after**, to have an unsatisfied longing

Word building: **hankering** *noun*
Word history: perhaps from Dutch

hanky-panky
noun Colloquial **1** trickery
2 sexual play

haphazard (hap-haz-uhd)
adjective happening by chance, or not planned: *a **haphazard** remark* (***accidental***, ***chance***, ***fluky***, ***random***)

Word use: The opposite of this is **ordered** or **systematic**.
Word history: archaic *hap* chance + *hazard*

hapless (hap-luhs)
adjective unfortunate or unlucky (***cursed***, ***star-crossed***, ***wretched***)

haploid (hap-loyd)
Biology
adjective **1** having a single set of chromosomes
noun **2** an organism or cell having only one complete set of chromosomes

Word use: Compare this with **diploid**.

happen
verb **1** to take place or occur, sometimes by chance (***arise***, ***come about***, ***transpire***)
2 to have the luck or the occasion: *I **happened** to see him just in time.*

Word history: Middle English, from Old Norse *happ* chance

happy
adjective **1** delighted, pleased or glad about something (***blithe***, ***cheerful***, ***gleeful***, ***joyful***, ***merry***)
2 fortunate or lucky: *a **happy** coincidence* (***auspicious***, ***promising***)

Adjective forms: **happier**, **happiest**
Word history: Middle English; from *hap*, chance

harangue (huh-rang)
noun a long, noisy and scolding speech

Word building: **harangue** *verb*
Word history: French, from Germanic

harass (ha-ruhs, huh-ras)
verb **1** to trouble by attacking or raiding again and again
2 to continually annoy or worry

Word building: **harassed** *adjective*
harassment *noun*
Word history: Old French *harer* set a dog on

harbinger (hah-bin-juh)
noun a person or thing that comes before or announces a future event (***herald***, ***omen***)

Word history: Middle English, from Old French word meaning 'provide lodging for'

harbour (<u>hah</u>-buh)
noun **1** a sheltered part of the sea along the shore, deep enough for ships to be protected from wind and waves
2 a place of shelter
verb **3** to give shelter to

Word use: You can also use **harbor**.
Word history: Old English *herebeorg* lodgings, quarters, from *here* army + *(ge)beorg* refuge

hard
adjective **1** solid and firm to the touch: *Rocks and wood are **hard**.* (***rigid***, ***stiff***, ***tough***)
2 difficult to do or explain: *a **hard** problem* (***arduous***, ***complex***, ***demanding***, ***tough***)
3 needing much effort or energy: ***hard** work*
4 (of water) containing salts from minerals which make it difficult for soap to lather
adverb **5** with a lot of effort or energy: *to work **hard***
phrase **6 hard up**, *Colloquial* urgently in need of something, especially money (***broke***, ***disadvantaged***, ***impoverished***, ***needy***, ***poor***)

Word history: Old English *heard*

hardball
phrase **play hardball**, *Colloquial* to use tough, ruthless tactics

hard disk
noun Computers a rigid magnetic storage disk, built into the computer, with a higher recording density than a floppy disk and providing fast access to more data

hard drive
noun a disk drive for a hard disk

harden
verb **1** to make or become hard or harder: *The cold **hardened** the plastic. | The glue slowly **hardened**.* (***freeze***, ***petrify***, ***set***, ***solidify***, ***stiffen***)
2 to make or become unfeeling or unkind: *He **hardened** his heart against the poor animal. | Her feelings **hardened** when she saw the evidence.*

hard-hit
adjective severely affected: ***hard-hit** by the floods*

hardline
adjective not turning from a set idea or policy: *a **hardline** attitude to drugs*

hardly
adverb **1** almost not at all: *The fog was so thick, we could **hardly** see.*
2 probably not: *He'd **hardly** come now, would he?*

Hardly is a special negative adverb commonly used with *any*:

There are hardly any flowers in the garden.

Because **hardly** functions as a negative, it does not need another negative as well. The following is wrong:

There aren't hardly any flowers in the garden.

Note that *hardly* is one of the few adverbs that require you to change around the word order when a verb follows it:

Hardly <u>had I</u> gone when … RIGHT
Hardly <u>I had</u> gone when … WRONG

hard sell
noun a method of advertising or selling which is direct, forceful, and demanding

Word use: Compare this with **soft sell**.

hardship
noun unpleasantness or suffering in the way you live: *Being poor involves much **hardship**.* (***adversity***, ***misfortune***, ***troubles***)

hardware
noun **1** building materials or tools
2 the mechanical parts of a computer
3 the equipment needed for carrying out an activity: *military **hardware***

Word use: Compare definition 2 with **software**.

hardwired
adjective **1** *Computers* (of a circuit) permanently wired into a computer
2 (of people) inherently equipped to act in a certain way: *Humans are **hardwired** for language.*
3 not modifiable

Word use: You can also use **hard-wired**.

hardy
adjective able to stand up to hard or severe treatment or conditions (***durable***, ***heavy-duty***, ***rugged***, ***sturdy***, ***tough***)

Adjective forms: **hardier**, **hardiest**
Word history: Middle English, from Old French word meaning 'hardened', from Germanic

hare
noun a rabbit-like animal with long ears and long back legs

Word history: Old English *hara*

hare / hair
Don't confuse **hare** with **hair. Hair** is what grows on your head.

harebrained
adjective reckless or without sense (***foolhardy***, ***hasty***, ***impetuous***, ***rash***)

harelip
noun a lip, usually the upper one, which at birth has a vertical gap in it, similar to the divided lip of a hare

harem (<u>hair</u>-ruhm, hah-<u>reem</u>)
noun **1** formerly, in some Muslim societies, the wives, mistresses, female servants, etc., of a household
2 the part of the household where these women lived

Word history: from Arabic word meaning 'forbidden'

harem pants
plural noun long loose trousers gathered at the ankle, worn by women

hark
verb **1** *Old-fashioned* to listen
phrase **2 hark back**, to return to a previous point or subject

Word use: Definition 1 is mainly found as a command.
Word history: Middle English *herk(i)en*

harlequin (<u>hah</u>-luh-kwuhn)
adjective having bright, fanciful or varied colours
Word history: from *Harlequin* a traditional character in early Italian comedy and pantomime, usually masked, dressed in muliticoloured spangled tights, and carrying a wooden sword or magic wand

harlot (<u>hah</u>-luht)
noun Old-fashioned a promiscuous woman
Word history: Middle English, from Old French word meaning 'rogue', 'knave'

harm
noun damage or hurt (***injure***, ***maim***, ***mutilate***, ***wound***)
Word building: **harm** *verb*
Word history: Old English *hearm*

harmonic
adjective having to do with harmony, as opposed to melody and rhythm
Word history: Latin, from Greek word meaning 'skilled in music'

harmonica (hah-<u>mon</u>-ik-uh)
noun a small wind instrument with metal reeds, which you play by blowing (***mouth organ***)

harmonics
plural noun **1** the science or study of musical sounds
2 those notes produced by a vibrating string or column of air, depending on whether it is vibrating as a single unit through its whole length, or whether certain fractions of the string are vibrating ($\frac{1}{2}$, $\frac{1}{3}$, $\frac{1}{4}$, etc.). If the whole length is vibrating, we call this the fundamental tone or the first harmonic, while the other parts are the second, third, fourth harmonic, etc. (***overtones***)

harmonise
verb Music to sing or play notes that are different to the main tune to produce an overall sound which is pleasing to the ear
Word use: You can also use **harmonize**.

harmony
noun **1** agreement in feelings, actions or ideas
2 a pleasing combination of musical notes sounding together
Noun forms: The plural is **harmonies**.
Word use: The opposite of this is **discord**.
Word building: **harmonious** *adjective*
Word history: Middle English, from Latin, from Greek word meaning 'a joining', 'concord', 'music'

harness
noun **1** the leather straps, bands, etc., used to control a horse, or to attach a cart or load to it
2 a similar arrangement worn by people for safety: *a parachute **harness***
verb **3** to put a harness on
4 to put to work: *We have **harnessed** water to produce electricity.*
phrase **5 in harness**,
a side by side or together
b at your job or working
Word history: Middle English, from Old French, perhaps from Old High German

harp
noun a musical instrument with a triangular frame and strings which are plucked with the fingers
Word history: Old English *hearpe*

harpoon
noun a spear-like weapon attached to a rope, used to catch large fish
Word building: **harpoon** *verb*
Word history: Dutch, from French word meaning 'grapple', of Germanic origin

harpsichord (<u>hahp</u>-suh-kawd)
noun an old-fashioned musical instrument which looks like a piano
Word history: French, *harpe* harp + *chorde* string

harpy (<u>hah</u>-pee)
noun **1** a greedy, snatching person
2 an unattractive, bad-tempered, old woman
Word history: from *Harpy*, in Greek mythology, an unpleasant, greedy, and filthy monster with a woman's head and a bird's body; Late Greek word meaning 'snatcher'

harridan (<u>ha</u>-ruh-duhn)
noun a bad-tempered violent woman

harrow (<u>ha</u>-roh)
noun **1** a heavy frame set with teeth, spikes, etc., drawn over ploughed land to break up the dirt and level it
verb **2** to break up or level land with a harrow
3 to torment or distress
Word history: Middle English *haru, harwe*

harrowing
adjective causing emotional pain or suffering: *a **harrowing** film | a **harrowing** sight*

harry (<u>ha</u>-ree)
verb to worry or torment
Verb forms: I **harried**, I have **harried**, I am **harrying**
Word history: Old English *her(g)ian* ravage (from *here* army)

harsh
adjective **1** rough and unpleasant: *a **harsh** voice*
2 cruel or severe: *a **harsh** winter* (***austere***, ***firm***, ***rigid***, ***straitlaced***, ***strict***)
Word use: The opposite of definition 1 is **smooth**.
Word history: Middle English *harsk*

hart
noun a male deer

hart / heart
Don't confuse **hart** with **heart**, which is an organ in your body.

harvest
noun the gathering or picking of crops
Word building: **harvest** *verb*
Word history: Old English *hærfest*

has
verb third person singular present of **have**

hash[1]
noun **1** a mixture of chopped, cooked meat, reheated in a sauce
phrase **2 make a hash of**, to spoil or make a mess of

Word history: French *hache* axe

hash[2]
noun → **hashish**

Word history: short form of *hashish*

hashish (ha-<u>sheesh</u>, <u>ha</u>-shish)
noun a drug made from the purified resin of the flowers, seeds and leaves of Indian hemp

Word use: The short form is **hash**.
Word history: Arabic

hasn't
contraction of **has not**

Look up **contractions in grammar**.

hasp (hasp, hahsp)
noun a fastening for a door, lid, etc., especially one passing over a hook and fastened by a pin or a padlock

Word history: Old English *hæsp, hæpse*

hassle
verb Colloquial to worry or annoy: *Don't **hassle** me about money.* (***nag***, ***pester***, ***pursue***)

hassock
noun **1** a thick, firm cushion used for kneeling
2 a thick clump of grass

Word history: Old English *hassuc* coarse grass

haste
noun **1** action in a hurry
phrase **2 in haste**, with speed, quickly
3 make haste, to force yourself to do something quickly

Word building: **hasty** *adjective* (**hastier**, **hastiest**)
Word history: Middle English, from Old French, from Germanic

hasten (<u>hay</u>-suhn)
verb to hurry: *He **hastened** to her side.* (***rush***, ***speed***)

hat
noun **1** a shaped covering for the head, usually worn outdoors
phrase **2 at the drop of a hat**, without thinking or pausing
3 eat your hat, *Colloquial* to be very surprised if a certain event happens
4 old hat, *Colloquial* of ideas, etc., old-fashioned
5 talk through your hat, *Colloquial* to speak without knowledge of the true facts
6 under your hat, *Colloquial* secret: *Keep this information **under your hat**.*

hatch[1]
verb **1** to break out of an egg: *Two new chicks **hatched** this morning.*
2 to make up or arrange: *They have **hatched** a plan.* (***concoct***, ***contrive***, ***cook up***, ***create***, ***invent***)

Word history: Middle English *hacche*

hatch[2]
noun **1** an opening in a floor, a roof or a ship's deck
2 a cover for this opening

Word history: Old English *hæcc* grating, hatch

hatch[3]
verb to mark with lines, especially closely set parallel lines

Word building: **hatching** *noun*
Word history: French *hacher* chop, hash, hatch

hatchback
noun a car fitted with a top-hinged door at the back which includes the rear-vision window

hatchet
noun **1** a small short-handled axe (***tomahawk***)
phrase **2 bury the hatchet**, to make peace

Word history: Middle English, from French word meaning 'little axe', from Germanic

hate
verb **1** to regard with a strong dislike (***abhor***, ***abominate***, ***despise***, ***detest***, ***loathe***)
2 to dislike or be unwilling: *I **hate** to do it.*
noun **3** strong dislike
4 the object of hatred
adjective **5** given over to expressing dislike: *a **hate** session*

Word history: Old English *hatian*

hateful
adjective so nasty or unpleasant as to deserve or cause a feeling of hate: *a **hateful** action* | *a **hateful** job*

hat-trick
noun **1** *Cricket* the taking of three wickets with three successive balls
2 three goals, tries, etc., achieved by a player in a single game
3 a feat involving a set of three successes

haughty (<u>haw</u>-tee)
adjective too proud of yourself and scornful of others (***arrogant***, ***conceited***, ***pompous***, ***snobbish***, ***supercilious***)

Adjective forms: **haughtier**, **haughtiest**
Word history: from French word meaning 'high'

haul
verb **1** to pull hard: *to **haul** a load of rubbish* | *to **haul** on the rope* (***drag***, ***draw***, ***lug***, ***tow***)
noun **2** a strong pull
3 the amount won, taken or caught at one time: *a **haul** of fish*

Word history: Middle English *hale(n)*, from Germanic

haul / hall
Don't confuse **haul** with **hall**, which is a large assembly room.

haunch
noun **1** the part of your body around your hip
2 the back part of an animal

Word history: Middle English *hanche*, from Germanic

haunt
verb **1** to keep visiting as a ghost or spirit
2 to continually return to: *His memories* ***haunted*** *him.*
noun **3** a place visited often: *The cave had been one of his favourite* ***haunts*** *in his childhood.*

Word history: Middle English *haunten*, from Germanic

have
verb **1** to own: *I* ***have*** *a diamond ring.*
2 to possess: *I* ***have*** *an uncle in Darwin.*
3 to possess as a characteristic: *to* ***have*** *red hair*
4 to get, receive or take: *Can I* ***have*** *your attention?*
5 to experience: *to* ***have*** *a good time*
6 to eat or drink: *to* ***have*** *a glass of water*
7 to invite or expect visitors: *We* ***have*** *friends coming for lunch.*
8 to give birth to: *to* ***have*** *twins*
phrase **9 have had it**, *Colloquial*
a to be extremely annoyed
b to be extremely tired
10 have it out, to have an argument or discussion
11 have on,
a to be wearing
b to have arranged: *What do you* ***have on*** *tomorrow?*
12 have someone on, *Colloquial* to tease or deceive: *Are you* ***having me on****?*
13 have to do with,
a to have dealings with: *She will* ***have*** *nothing* ***to do with*** *me.*
b to concern: *This* ***has*** *nothing* ***to do with*** *you.*

One of the most common verbs in English is the verb **to have**. It appears in several different forms:

Present	*Past*
(I, you, we, they) **have**	(I, you, he, she, it, we, they) **had**
(he, she, it) **has**	
having	**had**
(*present participle*)	(*past participle*)

The verb **to have** can work both on its own (as a *main verb*), or it can combine with other verbs (as an *auxiliary verb*):

I have an apple. (main verb)
I have returned. (auxiliary)

Have often forms contractions with *not*. For example:

has not *becomes* hasn't
have not haven't
had not hadn't

Have also combines with *to*, as a substitute for *must*, to express a need or a duty:

I have to go now.

A common error is to write *of* instead of **have**. Look up **had've**.

haven (<u>hay</u>-vuhn)
noun a place of shelter or safety (***asylum***, ***refuge***, ***retreat***, ***sanctuary***)

Word history: Old English *hæfen*

haven't
contraction of **have not**

Look up **contractions in grammar**.

haversack (<u>ha</u>-vuh-sak)
noun Old-fashioned a backpack

Word history: French *havresac*, from Low German word meaning 'oat sack'

havoc
noun **1** great damage or devastation
phrase **2 play havoc with**, to destroy or totally confuse

Word history: Middle English, from Anglo-French, variant of Old French *havot*, used especially in phrase *crier havot* cry havoc, give the call for pillaging; probably from Germanic

hawk[1]
noun a hunting bird with a hooked beak and large claws

Word history: Old English *hafoc*

hawk[2]
verb to offer things for sale in the street or by calling at people's homes (***flog***, ***peddle***)

Word building: **hawker** *noun*
Word history: Middle Low German *hoker*

hawthorn
noun a small thorny tree grown in hedges, with white or pink blossoms and bright fruit

Word history: Old English *haguthorn*

hay
noun grass which has been cut and dried to use as animal feed

Word history: Middle English; Old English *hēg*, *hīeg*

hay fever
noun an allergy affecting the mucous membranes of the eyes, nose and throat, caused by pollen, usually in spring and summer

haywire
adjective out of control or crazy (***chaotic***, ***disorganised***, ***higgledy-piggledy***)

hazard (<u>haz</u>-uhd)
noun **1** a risk or danger: *Smoking is a health* ***hazard****.*
verb **2** to risk or take a chance on: *to* ***hazard*** *a guess*

Word building: **hazardous** *adjective*
Word history: Middle English, from Old French, from Arabic *az-zahr* the die

haze
noun bits of dust, smoke, etc., which combine and look like a thin mist

Word building: **hazy** *adjective* (**hazier**, **haziest**)

hazel
noun **1** a small tree which has light brown nuts that people eat
2 a greenish-brown colour

Word building: **hazel** *adjective*
Word history: Old English *hæs(e)l*

HB
adjective **1** of pencils, hard and black
noun **2** a hard black pencil

he
pronoun the personal pronoun used to refer to a particular male: ***He*** *married my sister yesterday.*

He is a third person singular pronoun in the subjective case.
For more information, look up **pronouns: personal pronouns**.

head
noun **1** the top part of your body with your brain, eyes, ears, nose and mouth; it is joined to the rest of your body by your neck
2 a similar part of an animal's body
3 the brain or mind: *a good* ***head*** *for figures*
4 the top or front part of anything: *the* ***head*** *of a page | the* ***head*** *of a procession*
5 a leader or a chief
6 a person or animal as one of a number: *ten* ***head*** *of cattle | She charged $10 a* ***head*** *for dinner.*
7 heads, the side of a coin with a picture of a head on it: ***Heads*** *or tails?*
verb **8** to go or be at the head of or in front of: *She* ***heads*** *the list of winners.*
9 to turn towards a certain direction: ***Head*** *your horse down the other track. | Let's* ***head*** *for home.*
10 to give a heading or title to
adjective **11** being in a position of leadership or authority: *the* ***head*** *cook* (***leading, top***)
phrase **12 come to a head,** to reach an important point or crisis
13 go to your head,
a to make you confused
b to make you too proud or pleased with yourself
14 head off, to intercept and make change direction: *The stockman was able to* ***head off*** *the mob of cattle before they reached the hills.*
15 lose your head, to panic, especially in an emergency
16 make head or tail of, to understand
17 over your head, beyond your understanding
18 turn someone's head, to make someone vain

Word history: Old English *hēafod*

headache
noun **1** a pain in your head
2 *Colloquial* a troublesome or worrying problem

heading
noun the words written as a title at the top of a page or at the beginning of a piece of writing

headland
noun a high piece of land which juts out into a sea or lake (***promontory***)

head lice
plural noun very small insects that can live in your hair and make your head itchy, laying eggs called nits

Word use: The short form is **lice**.

headlight
noun one of the powerful lights on the front of a car or truck

headline
noun **1** a line in big print at the top of a newspaper article, saying what it is about
2 headlines, important news: *Drought is in the* ***headlines*** *again.*

headlong
adverb at great speed and without thought or consideration: *He raced* ***headlong*** *into the surf.*

headmaster
noun the male teacher in charge of a school

headmistress
noun the female teacher in charge of a school

> **headmaster / headmistress**
> Many schools now prefer to call the head teacher the **principal**. This has the advantage of giving the position a title which does not specify the sex of the person holding it. It does not make it seem that your gender is a part of your job, as **head<u>master</u>** and **head<u>mistress</u>** do.
> Look up **non-sexist language**.

headphones
plural noun a listening device for a radio made of earphones held on by a band over your head

Word use: You can also use **headset**.

headquarters (<u>hed</u>-kwaw-tuhz, hed-<u>kwaw</u>-tuhz)
noun the place where the people in charge of a large organisation work: *police* ***headquarters***

headscarf
noun **1** a scarf worn around the head
2 → hijab

Noun forms: The plural is **headscarfs** or **headscarves**.

head start
noun an advantage at the start of a race or competition

headstone
noun a stone set at the head of a grave

headstrong
adjective hard to control or determined to have your own way (***delinquent, insubordinate, unruly, wilful***)

heads-up
noun Colloquial a quick issuing of information ahead of time: *The school committee was given a* ***heads-up*** *by the principal on the minister's proposed visit.*

headway
noun forward motion: *The car made little* ***headway*** *in the heavy fog.*

headwind
noun a wind that blows in the opposite direction to the course of a ship

heady
adjective **1** thoughtlessly hasty
2 exciting or intoxicating

Adjective forms: **headier, headiest**

heal
verb to make or become whole or well again

Word history: Old English *hǣlan*, from *hāl* hale, whole

> **heal / heel**
> Don't confuse **heal** with **heel**, which is the rounded back of your foot.

health
noun **1** freedom from disease or sickness
2 the general state of your body: *in poor* ***health***

Word building: **healthy** *adjective* (**healthier, healthiest**)
Word history: Old English *hǣlth*, from *hāl* hale, whole

health care
noun medical and other services provided for the maintenance of health, prevention of disease, etc.
Word use: You can also use **health-care** or **healthcare**.

heap
noun **1** a group of things lying one on top of the other: *a **heap** of stones* (***mass, mound, pile, stack***)
2 *Colloquial* a great quantity or number: *He has made a **heap** of money.* (***abundance, lot, mass***)
3 *Colloquial* something very old and broken down: *His car was a real **heap**.*
phrase **4 give someone heaps**, *Australian, NZ Colloquial* to give someone a lot of insults or trouble
Word building: **heap** *verb*
Word history: Old English *hēap* heap, multitude, troop

hear
verb **1** to be able to sense sounds through your ear
2 to be informed of or to receive information: *Have you **heard** the news yet?*
phrase **3 hear someone out**, to listen to until the end: *Don't say anything until you **hear me out**.*
4 hear things, to imagine noises
Verb forms: I **heard** (herd), I have **heard**, I am **hearing**
Word history: Old English *hēran*

hear / here
Don't confuse **hear** with **here**. If you are **here** in this place, you are not there in that place.

heard / herd
Don't confuse **heard**, the past form of **hear**, with **herd**, which is a mob of cattle.

hearing
noun **1** the process by which sounds are sensed by your ear
2 the opportunity to speak or be heard: *Give our next speaker a decent **hearing**.*
3 the distance or range within which a sound can be heard: *I must tell you this while he is out of **hearing**.*

hearing-impaired
adjective deficient in the ability to hear, ranging from complete to partial hearing loss

hearsay
noun gossip or rumour (***talk, the drum, the whisper***)

hearse (hers)
noun a special car used in a funeral for carrying a coffin
Word history: Middle English, from Old French word meaning 'harrow', 'frame'

heart
noun **1** the organ in your body that pumps the blood and keeps it circulating through your body
2 emotions, affections or feelings: *She won his **heart**.*
3 courage or enthusiasm: *He showed plenty of **heart** when he went on to win.*
4 the middle part of something: *the **heart** of a lettuce* (***centre, core, hub, nucleus***)
5 the most important part: *the **heart** of the matter*
6 a figure said to be shaped like a heart, as on playing cards
phrase **7 after your own heart**, having the same tastes, opinions, likes and dislikes: *She enjoys bushwalking — a girl **after my own heart**!*
8 by heart, from memory: *to learn a poem off **by heart***
9 close to your heart, deeply affecting your interests and affections: *Saving the native forests is an issue **close to his heart**.*
10 have a heart, to be reasonable
11 have your heart in your mouth, to be very frightened
12 take heart, to find new courage or strength
13 take to heart, to be deeply affected by: *Don't **take** their comments **to heart**.*
Word use: **Cardiac** is a medical word meaning 'having to do with the heart'.
Word history: Old English *heorte*

heart / hart
Don't confuse **heart** with **hart**, which is a male deer.

heart attack
noun a sudden stopping of the blood supply to the heart muscles, caused by a blockage in an artery (***coronary occlusion, coronary thrombosis, myocardial infarct***)

heartburn
noun a burning sensation in the abdomen or chest, caused by too much acid in the stomach

hearten
verb to cheer up or give courage to

hearth (hahth)
noun the floor of a fireplace, which usually extends a little way onto the floor of the room
Word history: Old English *he(o)rth*

heart-rending
adjective causing great sorrow

hearty
adjective **1** warm-hearted, enthusiastic and sincere: *a **hearty** welcome | **hearty** approval*
2 large and satisfying: *a **hearty** meal*
Adjective forms: **heartier**, **heartiest**
Word building: **heartily** *adverb*

heat
noun **1** warmth or the quality of being hot
2 excitement or anger: *the **heat** of an argument*
3 a race or competition run to decide who will be in the final: *If you come in the first three in your **heat** you have to run in the final.*
Word building: **heat** *verb* **heated** *adjective*
Word history: Old English *hǣtu*

heath (heeth)
noun **1** an area of open land with a lot of low shrubs growing on it
2 a small, low shrub which grows on such land
Word history: Old English *hæth*

heathen (<u>hee</u>-dhuhn)
noun **1** someone who does not believe in the Christian, Jewish or Muslim God (***infidel***, ***pagan***)
2 *Old-fashioned* someone who is not religious or who shows disrespect and dislike for religion

Noun forms: The plural is **heathens** or **heathen.**
Word building: **heathen** *adjective*
Word history: Old English *hǣthen*; commonly explained as originally meaning heath-dweller

heather (<u>he</u>-dhuh)
noun any of the shrubs called heaths, usually with small light-purple flowers

Word history: blend of *heath* and obsolete *hadder* heather

heave
verb **1** to raise or lift using effort or force
2 to drag, haul or pull: *The sailors **heaved** the anchor on board. | They **heaved** on the ropes.*
3 to rise and fall: *His chest **heaved** with the effort of breathing after the race.*

Word building: **heave** *noun*
Word history: Old English *hebban*

heaven
noun **1** a place where God and the angels live, and where good people are said to go when they die
2 a place or condition of great happiness or pleasure

Word use: **Celestial** is a word meaning 'having to do with heaven'.
Word building: **heavenly** *adjective*
Word history: Old English *hefen, heofon*

heavens
interjection an exclamation expressing surprise

heavy
adjective **1** of great weight and, as a result, hard to lift or carry (***hefty***, ***ponderous***, ***solid***, ***weighty***)
2 larger or greater than usual: ***heavy** rain* (***dense***, ***solid***, ***thick***)
3 serious: *a **heavy** responsibility*
4 filled or weighed down: *air **heavy** with moisture | Her heart was **heavy** with sorrow.*
noun **5** *Colloquial* someone important in a particular area: *He is one of the **heavies** of the television world.*

Adjective forms: **heavier**, **heaviest**
Word building: **heavily** *adverb*
Word history: Old English *hefig*, from *hefe* weight

heavy metal
noun a style of fast, hard rock music with a strong beat and noisy electric guitars

heckle
verb to torment and bother a speaker with annoying questions and comments (***rib***, ***taunt***, ***tease***)

Word history: Middle English *hechele*

hectare (<u>hek</u>-tair)
noun a unit of measurement of land in the metric system, equal to 10 000 square metres, or about 2½ acres

Word use: The symbol is **ha**, without a full stop. | Look up **metric system.**
Word history: French *hecto-* from Greek word meaning 'hundred' + French *are* from Latin word meaning 'a measure of area equal to one hundred square metres'

hectic
adjective full of excitement, activity and confusion: *a **hectic** day* (***active***, ***busy***, ***chaotic***, ***intense***)

Word history: Late Latin, from Greek word meaning 'habitual', 'hectic'

hector (<u>hek</u>-tuh)
verb to bully or bother aggressively

he'd
contraction of **he had** or **he would**

Look up **contractions in grammar.**

hedge
noun **1** a row of bushes or small trees planted close together to form a fence
verb **2** to enclose or separate by a hedge or barrier
3 to avoid making a direct answer: *Stop **hedging** and say what you want.*

Word history: Old English

hedgehog
noun a spiny, insect-eating animal found mostly in Europe, which is active at night

Word history: late Middle English

hedonism (<u>he</u>-duhn-iz-uhm, <u>hee</u>-duhn-iz-uhm)
noun the belief that pleasure or happiness is the most important thing in life

Word building: **hedonist** *noun* **hedonist** *adjective* **hedonistic** *adjective*

heed
verb **1** to pay attention to, or to notice (***comply with***, ***follow***, ***obey***, ***observe***)
noun **2** careful attention

Word history: Old English *hēdan*

heel[1]
noun **1** the rounded back part of your foot below your ankle
2 the part of a sock or shoe that fits over your heel
verb **3** to follow by walking close to your heels: *to train a dog to **heel***
phrase **4 dig your heels in,** to stubbornly refuse to change your position
5 down at heel, shabby and poor-looking
6 on the heels of, closely following
7 take to your heels, to run away quickly

Word history: Old English *hēl(a)*, apparently from *hōh* hock

heel[2]
verb of a ship, to lean to one side (***tilt***, ***yaw***)

Word history: Old English *h(i)eldan* bend, incline

heel / heal
Don't confuse **heel** with **heal**, which is to become whole or well again.

heeler
noun a dog trained to round up sheep or cattle by chasing them and biting at their heels

hefty
adjective Colloquial big, strong and heavy: *a **hefty** bloke* (***solid***, ***stocky***)

Adjective forms: **heftier**, **heftiest**

hegemony (heg-uh-muh-nee, hej-uh-muh-nee)
noun the leadership or dominance of one state or country over others

Noun forms: The plural is **hegemonies**.
Word building: **hegemonic** *adjective*
Word history: Greek

heifer (hef-uh)
noun a young cow that has not had a calf

Word history: Old English

height (huyt)
noun **1** the distance from bottom to top
2 a cliff or mountain peak or other very high place
3 the greatest part or amount: *the **height** of her career | the **height** of stupidity*

Word use: **Height** is the noun from the adjective **high**.
Word history: Old English

heighten
verb to increase or make higher

Heimlich manoeuvre (huym-lik muh-nooh-vuh)
noun a method of assisting someone who is choking: *The **Heimlich manoeuvre** dislodged the food that was caught in her throat.*

heinous (hay-nuhs, hee-nuhs)
adjective hateful for its wickedness: *a **heinous** offence* (***atrocious***, ***gross***, ***iniquitous***, ***unpardonable***, ***villainous***)

Word history: Middle English, from Old French word meaning 'hatred'; of Germanic origin

heir (air)
noun someone who inherits a dead person's money, property or title

Word building: **heiress** *feminine noun*
Word history: Middle English, from Old French, from Latin

heir / air
Don't confuse **heir** with **air**, which is what we breathe.

heirloom (air-loohm)
noun something valuable that is handed down from generation to generation in a family

Word history: *heir* + *loom*, originally a tool or implement

heist (huyst)
noun a robbery (***burglary***, ***theft***)

Word use: This word is more common in the US.

held
verb past tense and past participle of **hold**[1]

helicopter
noun an aircraft without wings which flies by means of a large propeller mounted on the top

Word history: French, *helix* + Greek *pterón* wing

helicopter parenting
noun a style of child rearing where the parents are excessively involved in the lives of their children

Word building: **helicopter parent** *noun*
Word history: This expression comes from the idea that parents who practise this kind of child rearing are always hovering over their children like a helicopter.

heliport
noun a place for helicopters to take off and land

helium (hee-lee-uhm)
noun a gas which is lighter than air and is often used to fill balloons

Word history: Greek *hēlios* sun

helix (heel-iks, hel-iks)
noun a spiral or curve

Noun forms: The plural is **helices** (hel-uh-seez, heel-uh-seez) or **helixes**.
Word history: Latin, from Greek word meaning 'anything of spiral shape'

hell
noun **1** a dreadful place where evil people are said to go for punishment after death
phrase **2 for the hell of it**, for no particular reason, for fun
3 hell for leather, at top speed
4 hell to pay, serious trouble
5 raise hell, to cause very great trouble

Word building: **hellish** *adjective*
Word history: Old English *hel(l)*

he'll
contraction of **he will** or **he shall**

Look up **contractions in grammar**.

hello
interjection a word you use when you greet someone or when you answer the telephone

Word use: You can also use **hallo**.
Word history: from French *holà* ho there!

helm
noun **1** the wheel or handle which is used to steer a boat
phrase **2 at the helm**, in charge: *The company has a new manager **at the helm**.*

Word building: **helmsman** *noun*
Word history: Old English *helma*

helmet
noun a hard hat worn to protect your head

Word history: Middle English, from Old French, from Germanic

help
verb **1** to aid or give assistance (***assist***, ***oblige***, ***support***)
2 avoid or keep from: *We couldn't **help** laughing.*
noun **3** someone or something that aids or assists: *He was no **help** at all.* (***aid***, ***assistance***, ***backing***, ***relief***)
phrase **4 help out**, to aid or assist in a time of difficulty: *He is **helping out** while his mother is away.*
5 help yourself to, to take for yourself

Word history: Old English *helpan*

help desk
noun a service providing assistance or guidance within an organisation: *He called the **help desk** after his computer crashed.*

Word use: You can also use **helpdesk**.

helper
noun someone who helps (***aide***, ***assistant***, ***associate***, ***attendant***, ***offsider***)

helpful
adjective willing to help (***accommodating***, ***cooperative***, ***obliging***, ***supportive***)

helping
noun a serving of food (***plateful***, ***portion***, ***share***)

helpless
adjective **1** weak or unable to do anything (***feeble***, ***frail***)
2 without help or assistance: ***helpless*** *victims of the earthquake*

Word building: **helplessly** *adverb* **helplessness** *noun*

helter-skelter
adverb with great haste and confusion: *The crowds ran **helter-skelter** from the surf when the shark alarm sounded.*

Word history: imitative

hem
verb **1** to fold back and sew the edge of: *to **hem** a dress*
noun **2** a folded and sewn edge of material
phrase **3 hem in,** to surround or enclose: *Enemy soldiers **hemmed** the prisoners **in**.*

Verb forms: I **hemmed**, I have **hemmed**, I am **hemming**
Word history: Old English *hem*

hemisphere (hem-uhs-fear)
noun half of a round or spherical shape such as the earth: *When it is spring in the southern **hemisphere** it is autumn in the northern **hemisphere**.*

Word building: **hemispherical** *adjective*
Word history: Latin, from Greek

hemlock
noun **1** a poisonous herb with spotted stems, finely divided leaves, and small white flowers, used in medicine as a powerful sedative drug
2 a poisonous drink made from this herb

Word history: Old English *hemlic*, from *hymele* hop plant + *-k* suffix. Both hemlock and hops have a sedative effect.

hemp
noun a plant which is grown for its strong fibres which are used to make rope and sacks, and also for the leaves which are used as a drug

Word history: Old English *henep, hænep*

hen
noun a female bird, especially a domestic chicken

Word use: The male is called a **cock** or, for domestic chickens, a **rooster**.
Word history: Old English *hen(n)* (from Old English *hana* cock)

hence
adverb **1** for this reason
2 from this time: *a month **hence***

henchman (hench-muhn)
noun a faithful supporter or follower, especially one who obeys a leader without regard for principle or honesty

Noun forms: The plural is **henchmen**.
Word history: Middle English *henchemanne, henxtman*, probably originally meaning groom, and apparently from Old English *hengest* stallion + *mann* man

hendra virus
noun a virus affecting horses and human beings, the natural host being the fruit bat

henna
noun a reddish-orange dye which is used to colour hair

Word history: Arabic

hepatitis (hep-uh-tuy-tuhs)
noun a serious disease characterised by inflammation or enlargement of the liver, appearing in various forms caused by different viruses, each form being identified by a letter of the alphabet

Word history: Neo-Latin, from Greek

hepatitis A
noun a form of hepatitis caused by the hepatitis A virus, occurring mainly in young children and spread by contaminated food or eating utensils

hepatitis B
noun a form of hepatitis caused by the hepatitis B virus, which enters the blood of the recipient from infected blood (or blood products) or other body fluids, and which can be transmitted through sexual contact and contaminated needles and instruments

hepatitis C
noun a form of hepatitis caused by the hepatitis C virus, which is transmitted by infected body fluids and occurs mainly in intravenous drug users

heptagon (hep-tuh-gon, hep-tuh-guhn)
noun a flat shape with seven sides

Word building: **heptagonal** (hep-tag-uh-nuhl) *adjective*
Word history: from Greek word meaning 'seven-cornered'

her
pronoun **1** the personal pronoun used, usually after a verb or preposition, to refer to a particular female: *I saw **her** yesterday. | Give it to **her**.*
2 the possessive form of **she**, used before a noun: *That is **her** book.*

Her is a third person singular pronoun. Definition 1 is in the objective case. Definition 2 is sometimes called a *determiner* or a *possessive adjective*.

For more information, look up **pronouns: personal pronouns** and **pronouns: possessive pronouns**.

herald
noun **1** somebody or something that carries messages or announces coming events (***courier***, ***envoy***, ***messenger***)
verb **2** to announce: *Dawn **heralds** the new day.*

Word history: Medieval Latin *heraldus* (of Germanic origin)

heraldry (he-ruhl-dree)
noun the investigation and recording of coats of arms and the histories of the families to which they belong

Word building: **heraldic** (huh-ral-dik) *adjective*

herb
noun a flowering plant used in cooking or medicines

Word history: Middle English, from French, from Latin word meaning 'grass', 'herb'

herbal
adjective having to do with or made of herbs: *a **herbal** remedy | **herbal** tea*

Word building: **herbalist** *noun*

herbicide
noun a chemical that kills plants

herbivore (her-buh-vaw)
noun an animal that eats plants

Word use: Compare this with **carnivore**, **insectivore** and **omnivore**.
Word building: **herbivorous** *adjective*

herd
noun **1** a large group of animals: *a **herd** of cattle being driven to new pasture* (***bunch***, ***mob***)
verb **2** to drive or move together as a group

Word history: Old English *heord*

herd / heard
Don't confuse **herd** with **heard**, which is the past form of the verb **hear**:
Don't shout. I heard you the first time.

here
adverb **1** in this place: *Put it **here**.*
2 to or towards this place: *Come **here**!*
3 at this point: ***Here** the speaker paused.*
phrase **4 here and now**, immediately
5 here and there, in or to various places: *The fish darted **here and there** amongst the coral.*
6 neither here nor there, not important: *The colour is **neither here nor there** so long as it is warm and waterproof.*

here/ hear
Don't confuse **here** with **hear**. You **hear** sounds with your ears.

hereditary (huh-red-uh-tree)
adjective inherited or passing down from parent to offspring: *a **hereditary** disease | **hereditary** ownership of land*

Word history: from Latin word meaning 'of an inheritance'

heredity (huh-red-uh-tee)
noun the passing on of characteristics from parents to offspring: ***Heredity** is to blame for my big nose.*

Noun forms: The plural is **heredities**.
Word history: from Latin word meaning 'heirship', 'inheritance'

heresy (he-ruh-see)
noun a belief, especially about religion, which goes against the teaching of the church or religious system

Noun forms: The plural is **heresies**.
Word building: **heretic** *noun* **heretical** *adjective*
Word history: Middle English, from Latin, from Greek word meaning 'a taking', 'choice'

heritage
noun something which is passed on to you because you have been born of a particular family or country (***birthright***, ***inheritance***)

Word history: Middle English, from Old French word meaning 'inherit', from Late Latin

hermaphrodite (her-maf-ruh-duyt)
noun a person, animal or flower with both male and female reproductive organs

Word building: **hermaphroditic** *adjective*
Word history: Middle English, from Latin, from Greek *hermaphrόdītos*. In Greek mythology, *Hermaphrodites* was the son of the gods Hermes and Aphrodite. He became united in body with the nymph Salmacis while bathing in her fountain.

hermit
noun someone who lives alone and keeps away from other people (***introvert***, ***loner***, ***recluse***, ***solitary***)

Word history: Middle English, from Late Latin, from Greek word meaning 'of the desert'

hermit crab
noun any of a group of crustaceans which protect their soft bodies by living in the empty shells of certain molluscs

hernia
noun the pushing out of an organ in your body, through a tear or opening in the tissue that surrounds it (***rupture***)

Word history: Middle English, from Latin

hero
noun **1** a person who has done a very brave or difficult thing (***angel***, ***champion***, ***a jewel***, ***the tops***)
2 the person, usually a man or boy, who has the main part in a book, film or play (***leading man***, ***star***)

Noun forms: The plural is **heroes**.
Word building: **heroic** *adjective*
Word history: Middle English *heroës*, plural, from Latin, from Greek

hero / heroine
Hero used to be used only for men and boys, and **heroine** was reserved for females.
Nowadays it is the thing achieved that is most important and not the sex of the person who does it. This is why it is common to find both women and men referred to as **heroes**. **Heroine**, on the other hand, is still used only for women.

heroin (her-uh-wuhn)
noun a dangerously addictive, illegal drug made from morphine

Word history: Trademark (effect of drug is to make someone feel like a 'hero'); German, from Greek

heroine (her-uh-wuhn)
noun **1** a woman or girl who has done a very brave thing
2 the woman or girl who has the main part in a book, film or play (***leading lady, star***)

Word history: Latin, from Greek word meaning 'hero'

heroism
noun the qualities of a hero or heroine

heron
noun a water bird with long legs, a long neck and a long bill

Word history: Middle English, from Old French, from Germanic

herpes (her-peez)
noun an infection which causes small blisters to break out on your skin

Word history: Latin, from Greek word meaning 'a creeping'

herring (he-ring)
noun a small fish which is caught in the seas of the northern hemisphere and eaten either fresh, cooked or pickled

Noun forms: The plural is **herrings** or **herring.**
Word history: Old English *hǣring*

herringbone
noun **1** a pattern of joining rows of parallel lines so arranged that any two rows have the form of a V or an upside down V; used in needlework, bricklaying, etc.
2 a sewing stitch similar to cross-stitch

hers
pronoun **1** the possessive form of **she**, without a noun following: *That book is **hers**.*
2 the person(s) or thing(s) belonging to her: ***Hers** is the best work I've seen.*

Hers is a third person singular pronoun in the possessive case.
For more information, look up **pronouns: personal pronouns** and **pronouns: possessive pronouns.**

herself
pronoun **1** the reflexive form of **she**: *She made **herself** some dinner.*
2 a form of **her** or **she** used for emphasis: *She did it **herself**.*
3 her normal state of mind: *She didn't feel **herself** for a few days after the operation.*

For more information, look up **pronouns: reflexive pronouns.**

he's
contraction of **he is** or **he has**

Look up **contractions in grammar**.

hesitate
verb to wait or pause before doing something, as if you are not sure if you should go on: *to **hesitate** before you speak* (***dither, halt, stall***)

Word building: **hesitancy** *noun* **hesitant** *adjective* **hesitantly** *adverb* **hesitation** *noun*
Word history: from Latin word meaning 'stuck fast'

hessian (hesh-uhn)
noun strong rough cloth often used to make sacks

heterodox (het-uh-ruh-doks, het-ruh-doks)
adjective not agreeing with established teachings or opinions, especially in religion (***nonconformist, unorthodox***)

Word building: **heterodoxy** *noun*
Word history: from Greek word meaning 'of another opinion'

heterogeneous (het-uh-roh-jee-nee-uhs)
adjective **1** different in kind
2 made of parts of different kinds

Word building: **heterogeneity** *noun*
Word history: Medieval Latin, from Greek word meaning 'of different kinds'

heterosexual (het-uh-roh-sek-shooh-uhl)
noun **1** someone who has sexual feelings for people of the opposite sex
adjective **2** having to do with a heterosexual

Word use: Compare this with **homosexual**.

heterotrophic (het-uh-roh-tro-fik)
adjective (of an organism) needing an outside supply of organic material as food: *The **heterotrophic** plant withered without sustenance.*

Word use: Compare this with **autotrophic**.

heuristic (hyooh-ris-tik)
adjective helping to find out, or encouraging investigation

Word history: Greek *heurís(kein)* find out

hew (hyooh)
verb to chop or cut: *The statue had been **hewn** out of local rock.*

Verb forms: I **hewed**, I have **hewn**, I am **hewing**
Word history: Old English *hēawan*

hew / hue
Don't confuse **hew** with **hue**, which is another word for 'colour':
This fabric is of such a pretty hue.

hex (heks)
noun **1** an evil spell or charm
2 a powerful evil influence over someone or something
verb **3** to wish or bring misfortune on, as if by an evil spell

Word history: German *Hexe* witch

hexagon
noun a flat shape with six straight sides

Word building: **hexagonal** *adjective*

hey (hay)
interjection an exclamation used to call attention, give encouragement, etc.

heyday
noun the stage or period of highest success or fullest strength

Word history: alteration of *high day*

hiatus (huy-ay-tuhs)
noun an interruption or a break, with a part missing: *a **hiatus** in a text | a **hiatus** in a discussion*

Noun forms: The plural is **hiatuses** or **hiatus.**
Word history: from Latin word meaning 'gap'

hibernate (huy-buh-nayt)
verb to hide away and sleep through the winter: *Many animals in cold climates* ***hibernate*** *when food is scarce during the winter.*

Word building: **hibernation** *noun*
Word history: from Latin word meaning 'wintered'

hibiscus (huy-bis-kuhs)
noun a shrub or small tree with large brightly coloured flowers

Word history: Latin, from Greek word meaning 'mallow'

hiccup
noun a sudden movement in your chest which causes a quick intake of breath and a short sharp sound

Word use: You can also use **hiccough**.

hickory
noun any of a group of deciduous North American trees, some of which bear sweet nuts such as the pecan, and others which yield valuable hard wood such as the shagbark

Noun forms: The plural is **hickories**.
Word history: Native American

hid
verb past tense and past participle of **hide**[1]

hide[1]
verb to keep from being seen (***camouflage***, ***conceal***, ***cover***, ***disguise***, ***mask***)

Verb forms: I **hid**, I have **hidden**, I am **hiding**
Word use: The opposite of this is **reveal**.
Word history: Old English *hȳdan*

hide[2]
noun **1** the skin of an animal: *Cow* ***hide*** *is used to make leather shoes.* (***pelt***)
phrase **2 neither hide nor hair**, not even the smallest trace: *We could see* ***neither hide nor hair*** *of them.*

Word history: Old English *hȳd*

hideous (hid-ee-uhs)
adjective **1** very ugly: *a* ***hideous*** *monster* (***foul***, ***grotesque***, ***monstrous***, ***repulsive***)
2 shockingly dreadful: *a* ***hideous*** *crime*

Word building: **hideousness** *noun*
Word history: Middle English, from Anglo-French word meaning 'horror', 'fear'

hiding
noun **1** a severe beating as a punishment
2 a thorough defeat or loss in a game: *They gave their opponents a* ***hiding*** *in the final.*

hierarchy (huy-uh-rah-kee)
noun a system which arranges people or things in grades from the highest to the lowest

Noun forms: The plural is **hierarchies**.
Word building: **hierarchical** *adjective*

hieroglyphic (huy-uh-ruh-glif-ik)
noun **1** a picture or symbol used in a writing system, particularly that of the ancient Egyptians, to represent a word or sound
2 hieroglyphics,
a writing using such pictures
b writing that is difficult to read
adjective **3** having to do with or written in hieroglyphics

Word history: Late Latin, from Greek

hi-fi
noun a stereo sound system for the home

Word use: This is short for **high-fidelity**.
Word building: **hi-fi** *adjective*

high
adjective **1** reaching far above the ground (***elevated***, ***lofty***, ***towering***)
2 from bottom to top: *a wall two metres* ***high***
3 being above the normal level or amount: *The river is* ***high*** *after the rain.* | ***high*** *prices*
4 sharp or shrill in sound: *to sing in a* ***high*** *voice* (***falsetto***, ***high-pitched***, ***soprano***, ***treble***)
5 excited or happy: *The children are in* ***high*** *spirits.*
6 bad-smelling: *This fish is* ***high***. (***fetid***, ***putrid***, ***rank***, ***smelly***, ***stinking***)
phrase **7 high and dry**, *Colloquial* left without help
8 high and low, everywhere
9 high and mighty, proud or haughty
10 on a high, in an excitedly happy state

Word building: **height** *noun* **high** *adverb*
Word history: Old English *hēah*

highbrow
Colloquial
noun **1** a person who has or thinks he or she has good taste in artistic or intellectual matters
adjective **2** approved of by highbrows: *a* ***highbrow*** *play*

high five
noun a form of greeting in which two people slap the palms of their hands together, often to express shared delight in a victory

high-five
verb to give or perform a high five: *They* ***high-fived*** *each other after they won the game.*

Verb forms: I **high-fived**, I have **high-fived**, I am **high-fiving**

high frequency
noun a radio frequency between 3 and 30 megacycles per second

Word use: The abbreviation is **h.f.**

high-frequency
adjective of a sound which is high in pitch

Word building: **high-frequency** *adjective*

high-handed
adjective overbearing and using power without consideration: *a* ***high-handed*** *manner*

Word building: **high-handedness** *noun*

highland
noun **1** an area of high ground
2 highlands, the high, mountainous part of a country: *the New Guinea* ***Highlands*** (***plateau***, ***upland***)

Word building: **highlander** *noun*

high-level language
noun Computers a language used for writing programs which is closer to human language than to machine language

Word use: Compare this with **low-level language**.

highlight
verb **1** to emphasise or make stand out (***accentuate***, ***magnify***, ***stress***)
2 to use a highlighter to emphasise (written or printed text)
noun **3** the best, brightest or most outstanding part: *The **highlight** of the trip was seeing some dolphins swim near our boat.*

highlighter
noun a pen which puts a translucent colour over parts of a page to draw attention to these parts

highly strung
adjective tense and nervous

Word use: You can also use **high-strung**.

highness
noun **1** the state of being high
2 Highness, a title of honour given to members of a royal family with 'His', 'Her', 'Your', etc.

high-rise
adjective having to do with a building that has many storeys: *a **high-rise** apartment*

high school
noun → **secondary school**

high treason
noun treason against king, queen or state

highway
noun a main road built to carry a lot of traffic

highwayman
noun a bandit, usually on horseback, who used to hold up travellers on the road (***bandit***, ***brigand***, ***buccaneer***, ***bushranger***)

Noun forms: The plural is **highwaymen**.

hijab (huh-jahb)
noun the traditional Islamic headscarf worn by women, which covers the hair, neck and shoulders

Word use: You can also use **hejab**.

hijack
verb to seize by using threats or violence: *to **hijack** a plane* (***abduct***, ***apprehend***, ***capture***, ***grab***)

Word building: **hijacker** *noun*
Word history: perhaps from *high(wayman)* + *jack* hunt by night with the aid of a jacklight

hike
noun **1** a very long walk, usually for pleasure: *We went on a **hike** through the mountains.*
2 a sudden increase: *a **hike** in the price of petrol*

Word building: **hike** *verb* **hiker** *noun*
Word history: perhaps related to *hitch*

hilarious (huh-lair-ree-uhs)
adjective **1** noisily cheerful
2 extremely funny: *a **hilarious** story* (***amusing***, ***comical***, ***droll***, ***humorous***)

Word building: **hilarity** *noun*

hill
noun **1** a naturally raised part of the earth's surface, smaller than a mountain
2 a heap or pile made by humans or animals
phrase **3 as old as the hills**, *Colloquial* very old
4 over the hill, *Colloquial* past the peak of physical or other condition
5 take to the hills, *Colloquial* to run away and hide

Word history: Old English *hyll*

hillbilly
noun an unsophisticated person living in the country, especially in the mountains away from other people

Word use: This word was first used in North America. | An Australian word with a similar meaning is **bushie**.
Word history: *hill* + *Billy*, pet variant of *William*, man's name

hilt
noun **1** the handle of a sword or dagger
phrase **2 to the hilt**, completely

Word history: Old English *hilt, hilte*

him
pronoun the personal pronoun used, usually after a verb or preposition, to refer to a particular male: *I saw **him** yesterday. | Give it to **him**.*

> **Him** is a third person singular pronoun in the objective case.
> For more information, look up **pronouns: personal pronouns**.

> **him / hymn**
> Don't confuse **him** with **hymn**, which is a religious song.

himself
pronoun **1** the reflexive form of **he**: *He made **himself** a cup of tea.*
2 a form of **him** or **he** used for emphasis: *He did it **himself**.*
3 his normal state of mind: *He is now **himself** again.*

> For more information, look up **pronouns: reflexive pronouns**.

hind[1]
adjective placed behind or at the back: *Kangaroos have very strong **hind** legs.*

Word history: perhaps short for *behind*, but compare Old English *hindan*, adverb, from behind

hind[2]
noun a female deer

Word history: Old English

hinder (hin-duh)
verb to slow down or make difficult: *Fog **hindered** our progress.* (***block***, ***frustrate***, ***hamper***, ***impede***, ***retard***)

Word use: The opposite of this is **facilitate** or **help**.
Word building: **hindrance** *noun*
Word history: Old English *hindrian* behind, back

hindsight (huynd-suyt)
noun the ability to understand what you should have done in an event, after it has happened

Hinduism (hin-dooh-iz-uhm)
noun the main religion of India, in which followers worship many gods and goddesses and in which there is a complex body of religious, social, cultural, and philosophical beliefs, and a strict system of castes (social ranks)

Word building: **Hindu** *noun*, *adjective*

hinge
noun **1** a movable joint like the one which attaches a door to a door post, allowing the door to swing backwards and forwards
verb **2** to join by a hinge
3 to depend: *Everything **hinges** on your decision.*

Word history: Old English *hencg*

hint
noun **1** a roundabout or indirect suggestion: *to drop a **hint** that you would like an invitation to the party*
2 a piece of helpful advice

Word building: **hint** *verb*
Word history: from an obsolete British word *hent*, verb, seize

hinterland
noun the land lying just inland from the coast: *Very few people settled in the **hinterland**.*

Word history: from German word meaning 'hinder land', 'land behind'

hip
noun the projecting part at each side of your body, just below the waist, formed by the top of the pelvic bone

Word history: Old English *hype*

hippie
noun a person who is part of a general movement that promotes peace and living with nature and rejects narrow social conventions, especially such a person living in the 1960s

Word use: You can also use **hippy**.

Hippocratic oath (hip-uh-kra-tik <u>ohth</u>)
noun the oath stating the duties and obligations of doctors, sometimes taken by medical graduates

Word history: named after *Hippocrates*, about 460–357 BC, Greek physician, known as the father of medicine

hippopotamus
noun a large mammal with short legs and a heavy hairless body, that lives around lakes and rivers in Africa

Noun forms: The plural is **hippopotamuses** or **hippopotami**.
Word use: The short form is **hippo**.
Word history: Latin, from Late Greek word meaning 'the horse of the river'

hire
verb to pay money to use, or employ: *to **hire** a car | to **hire** a butler*

Word building: **hire** *noun*
Word history: Old English *hȳr*

hire / rent / lease / let

These words have similar meanings but there are some differences.

To **hire** something is to have temporary use of it in return for payment:

We are hiring a hall for the wedding.

To **hire** something is also to give others the temporary use of it in return for payment. Often this is **hire out**:

I will hire out this hall to you for the wedding.

To **hire** someone is to employ them:

We are hiring a band for the occasion.

To **rent** or **lease** property is to have the use of it in return for payments made to the owner:

I am renting a flat in town from a millionaire.

I am leasing a television rather than buying it.

To **rent** or **lease** property is also to give temporary possession of it to someone else. Sometimes this is **rent out**:

I will rent (out) my flat in town to you.

The verb **rent** has developed from the noun **rent**, the payment made to the owner. The document you sign when **renting** a property is a **lease**.

To **let** property is to put it up for rent:

I have made the decision to let my flat in town. If you want it I will rent it to you.

Property which is available for rental in this way is said to be **to let**:

My flat in town is to let.

hirsute (her-<u>syooht</u>)
adjective **1** hairy
2 covered with long, stiff hairs

Word history: from Latin word meaning 'rough', 'hairy'

his
pronoun **1** the possessive form of **he**, used before a noun: *That is **his** book.*
2 the possessive form of **he**, without a noun following: *That book is **his**.*
3 the person(s) or thing(s) belonging to him: ***His** are the green ones on the left.*

His is a third person singular pronoun. Definition 2 is in the possessive case, and definition 1 is sometimes called a *determiner* or a *possessive adjective*.

For more information, look up **pronouns: personal pronouns** and **pronouns: possessive pronouns**.

hiss
verb to make the sound 'ssss', like a snake, especially as a way of showing you don't like something: *The play was so boring that the audience **hissed** and booed the actors.*

Word building: **hiss** *noun*
Word history: Old English *hyscan* jeer at, rail

hissy fit
noun Colloquial an outburst of bad temper: *She threw a **hissy fit** when she didn't get her way.*

histamine (<u>his</u>-tuh-meen)
noun a crystalline substance released by animal and plant tissues in allergic reactions

Word history: *hist(idine)* + *amine*

histogram
noun Statistics a graph of a frequency distribution in which a vertical column shows the frequency or number of units for each equal division marked on the horizontal axis

historian
noun someone who studies history and writes about it

historic
adjective memorable; likely to go down in history: *the **historic** opening of the Sydney Harbour Bridge*

historic / historical

Although both these words are linked to **history**, they do mean different things.

Historic means 'memorable'. A **historic** occasion is one felt to be so important that it will go down in history.

A **historical** event is one that really happened and is part of history.

historical
adjective having to do with history or past events

history
noun **1** the events which have happened in the past, or the study of them
2 a description of important things which have happened in the past

Noun forms: The plural is **histories**.
Word history: Middle English, from Latin, from Greek word meaning 'a learning or knowing by inquiry'

histrionics (his-tree-on-iks)
plural noun artificial or melodramatic behaviour

hit
verb **1** to strike or give a blow to (***beat***, ***clip***, ***knock***, ***tap***)
2 *Colloquial* to reach or arrive at: *The school building fund **hit** $1000.*
noun **3** a blow or stroke
4 a great success: *That new song is sure to be a **hit**.*
5 *Internet* a connection made to a website
adjective **6** successful: *a **hit** song*
phrase **7 hit home**, to have the desired effect on someone
8 hit it off, *Colloquial* to get on well together: *I can't seem to **hit it off** with the new neighbours.*
9 hit on, to find by chance: *to **hit on** a good idea*
10 hit the nail on the head, to state or sum up exactly
11 hit the road (or **trail**), to depart: *time to **hit the road***
12 hit the roof, *Colloquial* to show extreme anger

Verb forms: I **hit**, I have **hit**, I am **hitting**
Word history: Old English, from Scandinavian

hitch
verb **1** to tie or fasten: *to **hitch** a horse to a cart*
noun **2** a kind of knot that can be undone easily
3 something that obstructs or makes things difficult: *a **hitch** in our plans* (***barrier***, ***drawback***, ***handicap***, ***hindrance***, ***obstacle***)
phrase **4 hitch up**, to pull or tug up: *to **hitch up** your trousers*

Word history: Middle English *hytche(n)*

hitchhike
verb to travel free of charge by getting lifts in passing cars or trucks

Word use: You can also use the colloquial word **hitch**.
Word building: **hitchhiker** *noun*

hither
adverb **1** to or towards this place: *to come **hither***
adjective **2** on or towards this side: *the **hither** side of the hill*
phrase **3 hither and thither**, this way and that

Word history: Old English *hider*

hitherto (hi-dhuh-tooh)
adverb until now or up to this time: *a fact **hitherto** unknown*

HIV
noun the virus that causes AIDS

Word history: h(uman) i(mmunodeficiency) v(irus)

hive
noun **1** a place that bees live in
2 a place full of busy people

Word history: Old English *hȳf*

hives
noun a rash, usually due to eating or touching something to which you are allergic: *Oranges give me **hives**.*

Word history: originally Scottish

hoard
verb **1** to save up and hide away in a secret place: *Squirrels **hoard** nuts for the winter.* (***gather***, ***stockpile***, ***store***, ***stow away***)
noun **2** a secret store

Word building: **hoarder** *noun*
Word history: Old English

hoard / horde

Don't confuse **hoard** with **horde**, which is a large group of people or animals.

hoarding
noun **1** a large board for putting up advertisements or notices
2 a temporary fence made of boards around a building site

Word history: obsolete *hoard*, noun, apparently from Middle English word meaning 'hurdle'

hoarse (haws)
adjective rough or croaky: *to shout until your voice becomes **hoarse***

Word building: **hoarseness** *noun*
Word history: Middle English *hoors*, apparently from Scandinavian

hoarse / horse

Don't confuse **hoarse** with **horse**, which is a four-legged animal that you can ride on and can be trained to pull loads.

hoary (haw-ree)
adjective **1** grey or white, especially with age
2 very old or venerable

Adjective forms: **hoarier**, **hoariest**
Word building: **hoariness** *noun*

hoax
noun a trick or practical joke (***con***, ***prank***, ***ruse***, ***swindle***)

Word building: **hoax** *verb* **hoaxer** *noun*
Word history: contraction of *hocus(-pocus)*

hobble
verb to walk with difficulty: *to **hobble** around with a sprained ankle* (***limp***, ***shuffle***, ***stagger***, ***totter***)

Word history: from Middle English word meaning 'protuberance', 'uneven ground'

hobby
noun something that you enjoy doing in your spare time: *My **hobby** is collecting stamps.* (***interest***, ***pastime***)

Noun forms: The plural is **hobbies**.
Word history: Middle English *hoby, hobyn*, probably for *Robin*, or *Robert*, common name for horse

hobgoblin (<u>hob</u>-gob-luhn)
noun **1** a mischievous goblin
2 a bogy or anything causing superstitious fear

hobnob
verb to associate with on very friendly terms: *He **hobnobbed** with the boss to try to get a promotion.*

Verb forms: I **hobnobbed**, I have **hobnobbed**, I am **hobnobbing**
Word history: earlier *hab or nab* alternately, literally, have or have not

hobo (<u>hoh</u>-boh)
noun **1** a tramp or vagrant
2 a travelling worker

Noun forms: The plural is **hobos** or **hoboes**.
Word history: rhyming formation, perhaps based on *beau* fop, used as a (sarcastic) word of greeting, for example, in *hey, bo!*

hock
noun the joint in the hind leg of a horse or similar animal, corresponding to the ankle in a human, but raised from the ground and protruding backwards when bent

Word history: Old English *hōh* hock, heel

hockey
noun a game played on a field or on ice in which two teams compete to hit a ball into a goal using a stick with a curved end

Word history: *hock* stick with hook at one end, variant of *hook*

hod
noun a long, narrow container for carrying bricks, etc., fixed on a pole and carried on the shoulder

Word history: Middle Dutch *hodde* basket

hoe
noun **1** a garden tool with a long handle and flat thin blade, which you use to break up the soil
phrase **2 hoe in**, *Australian, NZ Colloquial* to begin doing something energetically
3 hoe into, *Australian, NZ*
a to eat heartily
b to attack strongly, usually with words: *If your parents find out you have been wagging, they will **hoe into** you.*
c to take up with energy

Word history: Middle English, from Old French, from Germanic

hog
noun **1** a pig
2 *Colloquial* someone who is greedy or dirty
verb **3** *Colloquial* to take more than your share of: *to **hog** the biscuits*
phrase **4 go the whole hog**, *Colloquial* to do something completely: *He **went the whole hog** and spent all his pocket money on sweets.*

Verb forms: I **hogged**, I have **hogged**, I am **hogging**
Word history: Old English *hogg*

hogget
noun **1** a young sheep, from ten months to the cutting of its first two adult teeth
2 the meat from such a sheep

hoist
verb **1** to lift up or raise: *to **hoist** a flag* (***elevate***, ***jack up***, ***lever up***, ***raise aloft***)
noun **2** a lift or other machine that raises things off the ground

Word history: later form of dialect *hoise*

hold[1]
verb **1** to have or keep in your arms or hands (***cling to***, ***clutch***, ***grab***, ***grasp***, ***grip***)
2 to own: *to **hold** land in the country* (***have all to yourself***, ***occupy***, ***own***, ***possess***)
3 to contain: *The petrol tank **holds** 50 litres.*
4 to fasten or stay fastened: *A paper clip **holds** pages together. | The anchor will not **hold** in rough seas.*
5 to have or conduct: *to **hold** a meeting*
noun **6** a grip: *The wrestler locked his opponent in a firm **hold**.*
7 control or influence: *to have a **hold** on your audience*
phrase **8 hold down**, to continue to hold even though there are difficulties: *to **hold down** a job*
9 hold forth, to speak long and loudly about something
10 hold in, to check or restrain (***constrain***, ***control***, ***curb***, ***rein in***, ***repress***)
11 hold off,
a to keep apart or at a distance
b to keep from doing something
12 hold on,
a to keep a firm hold on something
b to continue (***endure***, ***hold out***, ***last***, ***persist***, ***survive***)
c *Colloquial* to stop or wait
13 hold out,
a to offer or present
b to stretch forth
c to last: *I hope the bread **holds out** till Monday.*
d to refuse to yield or submit
14 hold up,
a to display
b to delay
c to rob
d to cope in distressing circumstances

Verb forms: I **held**, I have **held**, I am **holding**
Word building: **holder** *noun*
Word history: Old English *h(e)aldan*

hold[2]
noun the part of a ship, below the deck, where cargo is carried

Word history: variant of *hole*

holding
noun property owned, especially stocks and shares or land

Word use: This word is often used as a plural.

hold-up
noun **1** a robbery
2 a delay

hole
noun **1** an opening through something (***aperture***, ***break***, ***chink***, ***gap***, ***perforation***)
2 a hollow space
3 *Colloquial* a dirty or unpleasant place: *This restaurant is a **hole**.*
phrase **4 hole up**, to hide, often from the police
Word history: Old English *hol* hole, cave, den

hole / whole
Don't confuse **hole** with **whole**. Something is **whole** if it is complete or entire:
I have a whole packet of biscuits to myself.

holey
adjective full of holes: ***holey** socks*

holey / holy / wholly
Don't confuse **holey** with **holy** or **wholly**. **Wholly** means 'entirely':
I am wholly committed to this new project.
Something is **holy** if it is sacred or religious.
Something is **holey** if it is full of **holes**:
Your socks are so holey it's a wonder they don't fall apart.
Note that the **holey dollar** was indeed a dollar with a hole in it. It was issued by Governor King in colonial times and was a Spanish silver dollar with the middle cut out of it. The circular piece from the centre was called a *dump*.

holiday
noun **1** a day's break from work or school, usually to celebrate or remember an important event: *a public **holiday** on Anzac Day*
2 holidays, a much longer break from your daily work (***vacation***)
verb **3** to take a holiday: *She will **holiday** on the Gold Coast.*
Word history: Old English *hāligdæg* holy day

hollow
adjective **1** having empty space inside: *a **hollow** log*
2 empty of meaning: ***hollow** promises*
noun **3** a hole or a dip, especially in the ground
Word building: **hollow** *verb* **hollowness** *noun*
Word history: Old English *holh* hollow (place)

holly
noun a small tree with shiny prickly leaves and bright red berries in winter
Noun forms: The plural is **hollies**.
Word history: Old English *holegn*

holocaust (hol-uh-kost, hol-uh-kawst)
noun great loss of life, especially when caused by a bad fire
Word history: Greek *holókauston* a burnt offering

holster
noun a leather case for a gun, worn on a belt
Word history: Swedish

holy
adjective **1** sacred or dedicated to God: *Easter is a **holy** festival.* (***blessed***, ***hallowed***, ***religious***, ***saintly***)
2 religious or pious: *a **holy** priest*
Adjective forms: **holier**, **holiest**
Word building: **holiness** *noun*
Word history: Old English *hālig*, *hāleg*

holy / wholly / holey
Look up **holey / holy / wholly**.

Holy Grail
noun **1** in medieval legend, the cup used by Jesus at the Last Supper
2 your ultimate objective: *Winning gold at the Olympics was his **Holy Grail**.*
Word use: You can also use **Grail**.

homage (hom-ij)
noun respect or honour: *to pay **homage** to a leader*
Word history: Middle English, from Old French, from Late Latin *homo* vassal, Latin man

home
noun **1** the place where you live or were born: *Australia is my **home**.*
2 a house or other dwelling
3 a place where people can be cared for: *an old people's **home***
adverb **4** to or at home: *to come straight **home** after school*
adjective **5** something to do with your home, town, or country: *the **home** team*
phrase **6 at home**,
a in a familiar or comfortable situation
b prepared to receive visitors
c familiar with or accustomed to
d *Sport* in your own town or grounds
7 bring home to, to make aware of: *His mother's sadness **brought** his misdeeds **home to** him.*
8 home in on, to find as if by radar
Word history: Old English *hām* home, dwelling

home / hone
These two entirely unrelated words tend to be confused in the phrase **home in on** something, meaning 'to focus on or target something'.
To **hone** is to sharpen something, such as a knife. There is no such phrase as *hone in on*.

homeboy
noun Colloquial a member of a youth gang
Word history: originally used in Black American English to mean a boy from your home district or town

homegrown terrorism
noun terrorist activities carried out within a country by people who have lived there all or most of their lives
Word building: **homegrown terrorist** *noun*

homeless
adjective having nowhere to live: *a shelter for **homeless** men*
Word building: **homelessness** *noun*

homely
adjective **1** plain and simple: ***homely** food*
2 not pretty or good-looking: *a **homely** face*
Adjective forms: **homelier**, **homeliest**
Word building: **homeliness** *noun*
Word history: Middle English

homely / homey

Don't confuse **homely** with **homey**. If you describe a place as **homey** then you mean that it is comfortable and makes you feel **at home**. You will also find this word spelt **homy**.

homemade
adjective made at home, as opposed to made commercially: *a **homemade** cake*

homeopath (<u>hoh</u>-mee-uh-path)
noun a practitioner of homeopathy

Word use: You can also use **homoeopath**.

homeopathy (hoh-mee-<u>op</u>-uh-thee)
noun a method of treating disease by drugs, given in minute doses, which produce in a healthy person symptoms similar to those of the disease

Word use: You can also use **homoeopathy**.
Word building: **homeopathic** (hoh-mee-uh-<u>path</u>-ik) *adjective*

home page
noun the main screen of a website from which you can get to all the information available on the site

home rule
noun self-government in internal affairs by those living in a dependent country

homesick
adjective unhappy and wanting to be at home (***pining***)

Word building: **homesickness** *noun*

homestead
noun the main house on a sheep or cattle station or a large farm

home truth
noun a disagreeable statement of fact that hurts the feelings

home unit
noun Australian, NZ → **unit** (definition 4)

homeward
adverb towards home

homework
noun **1** work set for a student to do at home, not in class
phrase **2 do your homework**, *Colloquial* to prepare for a meeting, interview, discussion, etc., by finding out what you need to know: *She obviously had **done her homework** — she was able to answer all the questions they asked at the meeting.*

homey
adjective of a place, comfortable: *She made the new place feel **homey**.*

Word use: You can also use **homy**.

homicidal (hom-uh-<u>suy</u>-duhl)
adjective having a tendency towards homicide: *a **homicidal** maniac*

homicide (<u>hom</u>-uh-suyd)
noun the crime of killing someone on purpose

Word history: Middle English, from Old French, from Latin

homily (<u>hom</u>-uh-lee)
noun **1** a religious talk addressed to people
2 words aimed to advise or give direction

Noun forms: The plural is **homilies**.
Word building: **homiletic** *adjective*
Word history: Medieval Latin, from Greek word meaning 'discourse'

homing
adjective returning home: *a **homing** device* | ***homing** pigeons*

hommos (<u>hoom</u>-uhs, <u>hom</u>-uhs)
noun → **hummus**

homogeneous (hoh-muh-<u>jee</u>-nee-uhs, hom-uh-<u>jee</u>-nee-uhs)
adjective made up of parts which are all of the same kind: *You shouldn't treat the class as a **homogeneous** group – the children have many different personalities and interests.*

Word use: You can also use **homogenous**. | The opposite of this is **different** or **diverse**.
Word history: from Greek word meaning 'of the same kind'

homogeneous / homogenous

There is often confusion about which of these words should be used.

The original meaning of **homogeneous** (of which **homogenous** is a variant) was 'having the same origin', and this has been extended to 'having like parts throughout'.

There is a tendency to always use **homogenous** for mass nouns, like *milk* and *butter*. Otherwise either word can be used, although **homogeneous** is generally more common in Australian English.

homogenise (huh-<u>moj</u>-uh-nuyz)
verb to mix evenly so that all parts are alike

Word use: You can also use **homogenize**.

homogenous (huh-<u>moj</u>-uh-nuhs)
adjective **1** similar in structure because from the same origin
2 → **homogeneous**

homologous (huh-<u>mol</u>-uh-guhs)
adjective **1** similar in shape or position
2 *Biology* corresponding in type of structure and in origin, but not necessarily in use: *The wing of a bird and the foreleg of a horse are **homologous**.*
3 *Chemistry* of the same chemical type or series, but differing by a fixed increase in certain constituents: *The alkanes are a **homologous** series.*

Word history: from Greek word meaning 'agreeing', 'of one mind'

homonym (<u>hom</u>-uh-nim)
noun a word which has the same sound or the same spelling as another but has a different meaning

Word use: If two homonyms are spelt the same, like *bear* (the animal) and *bear* (to carry), they're called **homographs**; if two homonyms sound the same, like *heir* and *air*, they're called **homophones**.
Word history: Latin word meaning 'having the same name', from Greek

Homo sapiens (hoh-moh sap-ee-uhnz)
noun the single, surviving species of the genus *Homo* or modern human beings

Word history: Neo-Latin, from Latin *homo* man + *sapiens* intelligent, wise

homosexual (hoh-muh-sek-shooh-uhl, hom-uh-sek-shooh-uhl)
noun **1** someone who has sexual feelings for people of the same sex as themselves
adjective **2** having to do with a homosexual

Word use: Compare this with **heterosexual**.
Word building: **homosexuality** *noun*

hone (hohn)
noun **1** a fine, dense stone, especially one for sharpening razors
verb **2** to sharpen on or as if on a hone
3 to trim or cut back

Word history: Old English *hān* stone, rock

hone / home
Look up **home / hone.**

honest (on-uhst)
adjective truthful and fair (***frank***, ***scrupulous***, ***sincere***, ***upright***)

Word building: **honestly** *adverb* **honesty** *noun*
Word history: Middle English, from Latin *honestus* honourable, worthy, virtuous

honey (hun-ee)
noun a sweet, sticky liquid made by bees from the nectar of flowers

Word history: Old English *hunig*

honeycomb
noun a wax structure made up of many rows of tiny compartments, made by bees for holding eggs, honey and pollen in the hive

Word history: Old English *hunigcamb*

honeydew melon
noun a sweet-flavoured, green-fleshed melon with a smooth, white skin

honeyeater
noun any of many, mainly Australasian birds with a beak and tongue able to get nectar from flowers

honeymoon
noun a holiday spent by a bride and groom straight after their wedding

Word building: **honeymoon** *verb*
Word history: traditionally referred to an equation between the changes of love and the phases of the moon

honeysuckle (hun-ee-suk-uhl)
noun a type of climbing shrub grown for its sweet-smelling white, yellow, or red tube-shaped flowers

Word history: Old English

honk
noun **1** the cry of the wild goose
2 any similar sound, as a car horn
verb **3** to make a honk

Word history: imitative

honorarium (on-uh-rair-ree-uhm)
noun a payment given in recognition of professional services on which no price is set

Noun forms: The plural is **honorariums** or **honoraria**.
Word history: from Latin word meaning 'honorary'

honorary (on-uh-ruh-ree)
adjective not paid for what you do: *the **honorary** secretary of the club*

Word history: from Latin word meaning 'relating to honour'

honorific (on-uh-rif-ik)
adjective **1** doing or giving honour
noun **2** in certain languages, as Chinese and Japanese, a form of words used to show respect, especially in conversation
3 a title of respect, as *Professor, Right Honourable*, etc.

Word history: Latin

honour
noun **1** fame or glory: *to bring **honour** to the school*
2 respect or esteem: *to be treated with **honour*** (***regard***, ***veneration***)
3 honesty and high morals: *a person of **honour***
verb **4** to revere or hold in high respect (***idolise***, ***venerate***, ***worship***)
5 to keep or fulfil: *to **honour** a promise*
phrase **6 do honour to,**
a to show respect to
b to be a credit to
7 do the honours, to act as host
8 on your honour, accepting personal responsibility for your actions or the truthfulness of your words

Word use: You can also use **honor.**
Word building: **honourable** *adjective*

honourable / honorary
These words are both linked to **honour,** but they have different meanings.
An **honourable** person is one who has a sense of **honour** and who acts accordingly. An **honourable** action is one which is in accordance with that sense of **honour**.
An **honorary** position is an unpaid one you take purely for the **honour** it confers on you.

hood[1]
noun **1** a loose kind of hat, usually attached to a coat, which covers your head and neck
2 a folding roof for a car or baby's pram

Word building: **hooded** *adjective*
Word history: Old English *hōd*

hood[2]
noun *Colloquial* a hoodlum

hoodie
noun *Colloquial* a jacket with a hood

hoodlum (hoohd-luhm)
noun a rough destructive young person

hoodwink (hood-wingk)
verb to trick or deceive (***cheat***, ***delude***, ***dupe***, ***mislead***, ***take for a ride***)

hoof
noun the hard covering which protects the feet of some animals such as horses, cows and pigs

Noun forms: The plural is **hoofs** or **hooves.**
Word history: Old English *hōf*

hook
noun **1** a piece of metal or some other material bent or curved so as to hold or catch something
2 a punch in boxing, made with the arm bent
verb **3** to hold or be fastened by a hook
4 to hit a ball so that it curves to the left if you are right-handed
phrase **5 by hook or by crook**, by any way possible
6 off the hook,
a out of trouble
b with the receiver lifted: *The telephone is **off the hook**.*

Word use: The opposite of definition 4 is **slice**.
Word history: Old English *hōc*

hookah (hook-uh)
noun a pipe with a long tube by which the smoke of tobacco, etc., is drawn through a container of water and cooled

Word use: You can also use **hooka**.
Word history: from Arabic word meaning 'box', 'vase', 'pipe for smoking'

hooked
adjective **1** hook-shaped or bent like a hook
2 made with or having a hook
3 caught with a hook: *The **hooked** fish struggled to get off the line.*
4 *Colloquial* married
phrase **5 hooked on**, *Colloquial* addicted to or obsessed with

hook-up
noun a link-up or connection, as between radio or television stations or telephones

hooligan
noun a rough and noisy young person who causes trouble

Word history: variant of *Houlihan*, Irish surname which came to be associated with rowdies

hoop
noun **1** a ring or circular band made of wire, wood or plastic
phrase **2 jump through hoops**, to obey without question
3 put through the hoops, to force into a series of often unreasonable tests

Word history: late Old English *hōp*

hooray
interjection **1** an expression or cry of joy or approval: ***Hooray**! I've won the lottery.*
verb **2** to shout 'hooray'

Word use: You can also use **hoorah** or **hurray**.

hoot
verb **1** to cry out or shout, especially in disapproval
2 to utter the cry of an owl
3 to make a similar sound especially in disapproval or derision
4 to blow a horn or factory hooter
5 to laugh
noun **6** the cry of an owl or a similar sound
7 a cry or shout, especially of disapproval

Word history: Middle English *huten*

hooves (hoohvz)
noun plural of **hoof**

hop[1]
verb **1** to jump, especially on one foot
phrase **2 hop into**, *Colloquial*
a to set about energetically: *He **hopped into** the job at once.*
b to put on quickly: *He **hopped into** his coat.*
3 hop it, *Colloquial* to move quickly: ***Hop it** or you will be late!*
4 hop to, to come or act quickly: ***Hop to** it!*
5 on the hop,
a unprepared: *caught **on the hop***
b busy or moving

Verb forms: I **hopped**, I have **hopped**, I am **hopping**
Word building: **hop** *noun*
Word history: Old English *hoppian*

hop[2]
noun a climbing plant whose flowers are used to flavour beer

Word history: Middle English *hoppe*, from Middle Dutch

hope
verb **1** to look forward to or expect, especially something good
noun **2** a wish or desire that something good will happen: *We all expressed a **hope** for their safety.*
3 an expectation or likelihood: *no **hope** of finding the lost money*

Word building: **hopeless** *adjective*
hopelessness *noun*
Word history: Old English *hope*

hopeful
adjective **1** expressing hope: ***hopeful** words*
2 promising advantage or success: *a **hopeful** outlook*
noun **3** a promising young person

Word use: The opposite of definition 1 is **despairing** or **pessimistic**.
Word building: **hopefully** *adverb* **hopefulness** *noun*

Hopefully is often used to mean 'I hope that'. For example:

Hopefully the flood waters will subside by tomorrow.

This could have been phrased as follows:

I hope that the flood waters will subside by tomorrow.

Some people consider that the first example really means that the flood waters were 'full of hope', and that therefore the sentence is illogical. But logic does not always apply to idiomatic expressions. Most people use **hopefully** in speech to mean 'I hope that', and an increasing number are using it this way in their writing. There seems no point in avoiding such a useful idiom which has gained wide acceptance, but be aware that some people will still object quite strongly to it.

hopscotch
noun a children's game in which a player throws a stone or other small flat object into a pattern of numbered squares drawn on the ground and then hops from one square to another without touching a line

horde
noun a great crowd: *a **horde** of flies buzzing around the barbecue*
Word use: This word often appears in the plural form **hordes** as in: *I had hordes of visitors while I was in hospital.*
Word history: Polish, from Turkic word meaning 'camp'

horde / hoard
Don't confuse **horde** with **hoard**, which is a secret supply collected over some period of time:
I have a private hoard of biscuits in my room.

horizon (huh-<u>ruy</u>-zuhn)
noun **1** the line where the earth or sea appears to meet the sky
2 the limit or boundary to knowledge: *Reading broadens your **horizons**.*
Word history: Latin, from Greek word meaning 'bounding circle', 'horizon'

horizontal (ho-ruh-<u>zon</u>-tuhl)
adjective **1** parallel, or in line, with the horizon
2 lying down flat (***even***, ***level***, ***smooth***)
Word use: Compare this with **vertical**.
Word building: **horizontally** *adverb*

hormone
noun a chemical substance made by a gland in the body, which travels through the blood and affects other parts of the body
Word building: **hormonal** *adjective*
Word history: from Greek word meaning 'setting in motion'

horn
noun **1** a hard pointed growth on the forehead of animals like cows, sheep and deer
2 the bonelike material making up horns or hoofs
3 a musical wind instrument: *a French **horn***
4 a device for sounding a warning signal: *to blow the car's **horn***
verb **5** to wound or stab with the horns

hornet
noun a large wasp with a very painful sting
Word history: Old English *hyrnet(u)*

horny
adjective tough or hardened, as if made by horn
Adjective forms: **hornier**, **horniest**

horoscope (<u>ho</u>-ruh-skohp)
noun **1** a diagram showing the position of the planets in the sky at a particular time and thought by some people to be an aid in forecasting the future
2 a forecast of the future based on such a diagram
Word history: Old English, from Latin, from Greek word meaning 'sign in the ascendant at time of birth'

horrendous
adjective horrible and dreadful (***frightening***, ***frightful***, ***terrible***)
Word history: from Latin word meaning 'bristle', 'shudder'

horrible
adjective terrible, dreadful or very unpleasant (***frightening***, ***frightful***, ***nasty***)
Word building: **horribly** *adverb*
Word history: Middle English, from Old French, from Latin word meaning 'terrible', 'fearful'

horrid
adjective nasty or horrible
Word history: from Latin word meaning 'bristling', 'rough'

horrific (ho-<u>rif</u>-ik, huh-<u>rif</u>-ik)
adjective causing horror
Word history: Latin

horrify
verb to shock or fill with horror: *The violent film **horrified** me.* (***disgust***, ***nauseate***, ***offend***, ***revolt***, ***sicken***)
Verb forms: it **horrified**, it has **horrified**, it is **horrifying**
Word building: **horrifying** *adjective*
Word history: from Latin word meaning 'cause horror'

horror
noun **1** a strong feeling of fear or disgust: *a **horror** of spiders*
2 *Colloquial* someone or something thought to be bad or ugly: *Her brother is a little **horror**.*
Word history: Latin

hors d'oeuvre (aw <u>derv</u>)
noun a small piece of food such as an olive, a nut or a savoury, served before a main meal as an appetiser
Word history: French word meaning 'aside from (the main body of the) work'

horse
noun **1** a large, four-legged animal with hoofs, which is easily trained for riding, racing or pulling loads
phrase **2 a dark horse**, a person of unknown ability
3 eat like a horse, to have a big appetite
4 hold your horses, to wait and not rush ahead
5 horse about (or **around**), to act or play roughly
Word history: Old English *hors*

horse / hoarse
Don't confuse **horse** with **hoarse**. If your voice is **hoarse**, then it sounds rough and distorted.

horse flu
noun → **equine influenza**

horseplay
noun rough noisy play

horsepower
noun a unit for measuring power in the imperial system: *a 50 **horsepower** engine*
Word use: Look up **imperial system**.

horseradish
noun a plant whose strongly flavoured root is used in cooking

horseshoe
noun **1** a U-shaped iron plate nailed to a horse's hoof to protect it
2 something shaped like a horseshoe
3 a sign of good luck
adjective **4** in the shape of a horseshoe

horticulture (haw-tuh-kul-chuh)
noun the growing of garden plants for their fruit, vegetables and flowers
Word building: **horticultural** *adjective* **horticulturalist** *noun* **horticulturist** *noun*
Word history: *horti-* (combining form of Latin *hortus* garden) + *culture*

hose
noun **1** a flexible tube for carrying water
2 → **hosiery**
verb **3** to water or wet with a hose
Word history: Old English

hosiery (hoh-zhuh-ree, hoh-zuh-ree)
noun clothing for your legs and feet, such as socks or stockings
Word use: You can also use **hose**.

hospice
noun a hospital for patients who are dying, often run by a church
Word history: French, from Latin word meaning 'hospitality'

hospital
noun a place where sick and injured people are given medical treatment
Word history: Middle English, from Old French, from Late Latin word meaning 'inn', from Latin word meaning 'pertaining to guests', 'hospitable'

hospitalise
verb to put into hospital
Word use: You can also use **hospitalize**.

hospitality (hos-puh-tal-uh-tee)
noun kindness and generosity shown to guests
Word building: **hospitable** *adjective*

host[1] (hohst)
noun **1** someone who entertains guests: *The* ***host*** *of a party.*
2 an animal or plant on which a parasite lives: *A dog is* ***host*** *to many fleas.*
3 a computer connected to the internet with its own IP address
Word use: You can also use **host computer** for definition 3.
Word building: **host** *verb*
Word history: Middle English, from Old French, from Latin word meaning 'host', 'guest', 'stranger'

host[2] (hohst)
noun a great number or crowd: *a* ***host*** *of household chores | a* ***host*** *of angels*
Word history: Middle English, from Old French, from Medieval Latin word meaning 'army', from Latin word meaning 'stranger', 'enemy'

hostage (hos-tij)
noun someone held prisoner by an enemy or terrorist until certain conditions are met or ransom money is paid
Word history: Middle English, from Old French word meaning 'guest', from Latin

hostel (hos-tuhl, hos-tel)
noun a place where people can get meals and a room to sleep for the night at a low cost
Word history: Middle English, from Old French word meaning 'guest'

hostess (hohs-tes)
noun a woman who receives guests

hostile
adjective unfriendly or acting like an enemy (***aggressive***, ***belligerent***, ***combative***, ***pugnacious***)
Word use: The opposite of this is **friendly**.
Word building: **hostility** *noun*
Word history: late Middle English, from Latin word meaning 'enemy'

hot
adjective **1** having a high temperature and giving out heat (***blazing***, ***fiery***)
2 strong or burning to taste: *a* ***hot*** *curry*
3 angry, violent or passionate: *a* ***hot*** *temper*
phrase **4 hot under the collar**, angry (***annoyed***, ***furious***, ***indignant***, ***irate***, ***livid***)
5 not so hot, *Colloquial*
a not very good: *He's* ***not so hot*** *at maths.*
b not very well: *I'm* ***not*** *feeling* ***so hot***.
Word history: Old English *hāt*

hot air
noun Colloquial empty, exaggerated talk or writing

hotchpotch (hoch-poch)
noun **1** a jumble or unordered mixture (***assortment***, ***medley***, ***miscellany***)
2 a thick soup made from meat and vegetables
Word use: You can also use **hodgepodge**.
Word history: rhyming variant of *hotchpot*, from Old French; stew

hot dog
noun a long, red sausage served hot in a bread roll

hotel
noun a place which provides rooms and meals for paying guests, and which has special rooms where people can go to drink beer and other alcoholic drinks
Word history: from French word meaning 'hostel'

hotelier (hoh-tel-ee-uh)
noun someone who manages a hotel or hotels

hotline
noun a telephone line which connects people directly to special services that can give advice or organise help, as in times of emergency

hotplate
noun a metal plate on an electric stove or barbecue which can be heated and used to cook food

hot seat
noun Colloquial **1** the electric chair
2 a position in which there are difficulties or dangers

hound
noun **1** a dog, especially a hunting dog
verb **2** to hunt or pursue continually: *The dogs **hounded** the fox into the trap.*
3 to keep on making demands to: *Her parents always have to **hound** her to do her homework.* (***berate, chase up, nag, pursue***)

Word history: Old English *hund*

hound's-tooth (howndz-toohth)
adjective **1** printed, decorated, or woven with a pattern of broken checks
noun **2** a pattern of contrasting jagged checks

hour
noun **1** a unit of measurement of time equal to 60 minutes
2 a particular time: *The **hour** has come.*
3 hours, the usual times for work or business: *School **hours** are 9 a.m. to 3.30 p.m. | office **hours***
phrase **4 the eleventh hour**, the very last possible moment: *They were rescued at **the eleventh hour**.*
5 the small hours, the hours just after midnight

Word history: Middle English, from Old French, from Latin word meaning 'time', 'season', 'hour', from Greek

hourglass (ow-uh-glahs)
noun **1** an instrument for measuring time, consisting of two bulbs of glass joined by a narrow passage through which a quantity of sand (or mercury) runs in just an hour
adjective **2** having a narrow waist

hourly
adjective **1** happening or done each hour: *an **hourly** broadcast*
adverb **2** every hour: *The radio station broadcasted the news **hourly**.*

house (hows)
noun **1** a building where people live
2 a building for any purpose: *Parliament **House** | a **house** of worship*
3 a section of a school, made up of children from all classes, formed for sport and other competitions
4 the group of people forming a parliament or one of its divisions: *the upper **house** | the lower **house***
5 a family seen as consisting of ancestors and descendants: *the royal **house** of Windsor*
6 an audience in a theatre: *The performers played to a full **house**.*
verb (howz) **7** to provide space or accommodation for: *to **house** refugees*
phrase **8 keep house**, to look after a home
9 on the house, free, as a gift from the management

Word history: Old English *hūs*

houseboat
noun a boat which is fitted up for people to live on

household
noun **1** all the people who live together in a house
adjective **2** belonging to, or having to do with, a house or family: ***household** furniture | **household** chores*

Word building: **householder** *noun*

housekeeper
noun someone in charge of the cleaning, cooking, etc., for a household, especially when paid as an employee

housewife
noun the woman in charge of a household, especially a wife who does no other job

Noun forms: The plural is **housewives**.
Word building: **housewifely** *adjective*
Word history: Middle English

housework
noun the work of cleaning, cooking, etc.

housie-housie
noun → **bingo**

housing
noun **1** houses or dwellings in general: *a shortage of **housing***
2 a protective covering or support for a machine

hovel
noun a small dirty house or hut

Word history: Middle English *hovel, hovyl*

hover (hov-uh)
verb **1** to stay in one spot in the air as if hanging: *The bees were **hovering** over the flowers.*
2 to linger or stay close to: *The children **hovered** around a bowl of chocolates.*

Word history: Middle English *hoveren*

hovercraft
noun a vehicle which can travel over land or water, supported on a cushion of air

how
adverb **1** in what way or manner: ***How** did it happen?*
2 to what extent or amount: ***How** late will you be?*
3 in what state or condition: ***How** are you?*
phrase **4 and how**, *Colloquial* very much indeed: *I liked that film **and how**.*

Word building: **how** *conjunction*
Word history: Old English

however
conjunction **1** nevertheless
adverb **2** no matter how far, much, etc.: ***However** hard he tries, he'll never win.*
3 in no matter what condition, state, or manner: *Go there **however** you like.*

Word history: Middle English

howl
verb to make a long, loud, wailing noise like a dog or wolf

Word building: **howl** *noun*
Word history: Middle English; imitative

HTML
noun a computer mark-up language, similar to SGML, used primarily to create documents for the World Wide Web

http
noun Internet the protocol used for moving files on the World Wide Web

Word history: *h(yper)t(ext) t(ransfer) p(rotocol)*

hub
noun **1** the centre part of a wheel
2 any busy or important centre: *The city is a **hub** of activity.* (***centre, focus, nucleus***)

Word use: The opposite of this is **periphery**.

huddle
verb **1** to crowd closely together: *to **huddle** by the fire to keep warm*
noun **2** a few people crowded together to discuss something in private (***bunch***, ***group***)

hue (hyooh)
noun a colour or shade of colour: *the **hues** of the rainbow*

Word history: Old English *hīw* form, appearance, colour

hue / hew
Don't confuse **hue** with **hew**. To **hew** wood is to chop it up into pieces.

huff
noun **1** a sudden surge of anger or fit of resentment: *to leave in a **huff***
verb **2** to puff or blow

Word building: **huffish** *adjective* **huffy** *adjective*
Word history: imitative

hug
verb **1** to clasp tightly in the arms, especially with fondness (***cuddle***, ***embrace***, ***hold***, ***nurse***)
2 to keep close to, as in sailing, horseracing or going along: *The boat **hugged** the shore.*
noun **3** a tight clasp with the arms

Verb forms: I **hugged**, I have **hugged**, I am **hugging**
Word history: perhaps from Old Norse word meaning 'console'

huge
adjective very, very large: *a **huge** mountain* (***colossal***, ***enormous***, ***gigantic***, ***massive***, ***vast***)

Word building: **hugeness** *noun*
Word history: Middle English

hulk
noun someone or something that is bulky, heavy or clumsy

Word building: **hulking** *adjective*
Word history: Old English *hulc*, probably from Medieval Latin, from Greek word meaning 'trading vessel'

hull[1]
noun the shell, husk, or outer covering of a seed or fruit

Word history: Middle English from Old English *hulu* husk, pod

hull[2]
noun the body of a ship or boat: *to paint the **hull***

hullabaloo (hul-uh-buh-<u>looh</u>)
noun an uproar or loud noisy disturbance (***commotion***, ***fuss***, ***riot***, ***tumult***, ***turmoil***)

hum
verb **1** to make a buzzing or droning sound
2 to sing with your lips closed
3 to be busy and active: *The factory **hummed** all day and night.*

Verb forms: I **hummed**, I have **hummed**, I am **humming**
Word building: **hum** *noun*
Word history: Middle English; imitative

human
noun **1** a man, woman or child
adjective **2** characteristic of humans: ***human** nature* | *the **human** form*
3 having the weaknesses of ordinary people: ***human** error*

Word history: from Latin word meaning 'of a man'

humane (hyooh-<u>mayn</u>)
adjective showing feelings of pity and tenderness: *It would be **humane** to help him.* (***compassionate***, ***humanitarian***)

Word use: The opposite of this is **inhumane** or **cruel**.
Word history: variant of *human*

humanism
noun any system of thought or values based on human effort or achievements rather than religion

humanist
noun **1** a student of human nature or affairs
2 someone who favours the thought and practice of humanism

Word use: You can also use **Humanist** for definition 2.
Word building: **humanistic** *adjective*

humanitarian
adjective concerned with the interests and wellbeing of all humanity

Word building: **humanitarian** *noun* **humanitarianism** *noun*

humanity
noun **1** all humans
2 sympathy and kindness towards other people and animals

Word history: Middle English, from French, from Latin

humankind
noun all human beings

humble
adjective **1** modest and meek: *She was too **humble** to expect the famous writer to speak to her.* (***lowly***, ***self-effacing***)
2 poor and lowly: *He came from a **humble** home.*

Word building: **humility** *noun*
Word history: Middle English, from Old French, from Latin word meaning 'low', 'humble'

humbug
noun **1** the quality of being false or deceitful
2 someone who tricks others by cheating
3 a type of hard, peppermint sweet

humdrum
adjective dull and ordinary: *a **humdrum** existence* (***boring***, ***monotonous***, ***stale***, ***tedious***)

Word history: variation of *hum* repeated

humerus (<u>hyooh</u>-muh-ruhs)
noun **1** in humans, the single, long bone in the arm which goes from the shoulder to the elbow
2 a similar bone in the forelimbs of other animals or in the wings of birds

Noun forms: The plural is **humeri** (<u>hyooh</u>-muh-ruy).
Word history: from Latin word meaning 'shoulder'

humid (<u>hyooh</u>-muhd)
adjective moist and damp, especially when it's also warm: *a **humid** day* (***close***, ***muggy***, ***oppressive***, ***sultry***)

Word history: from Latin word meaning 'moist'

humidifier
noun a device for regulating air moisture content and temperature in an air-conditioned room or building

humidity
noun **1** a state of being damp and moist
2 in relation to weather, a condition of the atmosphere concerned with the amount of water-vapour present

humiliate (hyooh-<u>mil</u>-ee-ayt)
verb to cause to feel ashamed or foolish: *His rude remarks **humiliated** her.* (***belittle***, ***insult***, ***slight***, ***snub***)

Word building: **humiliation** *noun*
Word history: from Late Latin word meaning 'humbled'

humility
noun the quality of being modest about yourself and your own importance

Word history: Middle English, from French, from Latin

hummingbird
noun a very small American bird with a slender bill, colourful feathers, and narrow wings whose rapid movement produces a hum

hummock
noun a small hill rising above the general level of a marshy area

Word building: **hummocky** *adjective*

hummus (<u>hoom</u>-uhs, <u>hom</u>-uhs)
noun a Middle Eastern dish made with chickpeas, lemon juice and garlic

Word use: You can also use **hommos** or **hommus.**
Word history: from Arabic word meaning 'chickpea'; also used to refer to this dish because it is a traditional way of eating chickpeas

humorous
adjective **1** amusing or funny: *the **humorous** side of things* (***comical***, ***droll***, ***facetious***)
2 having or showing humour: *a **humorous** person*

humour
noun the quality of being funny or amusing: *a sense of **humour** | Standing there dripping wet, he couldn't see the **humour** in the situation.*

Word use: You can also use **humor**. | The opposite of this is **seriousness**.
Word history: Middle English, from Anglo-French, from Latin word meaning 'moisture', 'liquid'

hump
noun **1** a bulge on the back: *a camel's **hump***
2 a rounded rise in the ground or on a road: *a speed **hump***
verb **3** to carry: *to **hump** a swag*

Word history: from *humpbacked*

humpy
noun an Aboriginal bush shelter

Word history: from Yagara, an Australian Aboriginal language of the Brisbane region

humungous (hyooh-<u>mung</u>-guhs)
adjective *Colloquial* very large: *The little kid had a **humungous** glass of soft drink.*

Word history: perhaps blend of *huge* and *monstrous*

humus (<u>hyooh</u>-muhs)
noun dark nourishing material in soil, formed by the rotting of animal and vegetable matter

Word history: from Latin word meaning 'earth', 'ground'

hunch
verb **1** to push out or up: *to **hunch** your shoulders*
noun **2** *Colloquial* a belief, usually without the knowledge of the facts: *I had a **hunch** that something would happen.*

Word history: apparently from *hunchbacked*

hundred
noun **1** a cardinal number, 10 times 10
2 a symbol for this number, as 100 or C
3 a set of a hundred persons or things
adjective **4** amounting to one hundred in number

Word use: The plural is **hundreds** or, after a numeral, **hundred.**
Word building: **hundredth** *adjective* **hundredth** *noun*
Word history: Old English *hundred*

hung
verb past tense and past participle of **hang**

hunger
noun an uncomfortable feeling of the need for food

Word building: **hungry** *adjective* (**hungrier**, **hungriest**)
Word history: Middle English, Old English *hungor*

hunk
noun **1** a large rough piece: *They ate **hunks** of bread with the cheese.*
2 *Colloquial* a very handsome man with a good physique

hunt
verb **1** to chase for food or sport
2 to search: *I **hunted** everywhere for my pencil.* (***quest***, ***seek***)

Word building: **hunt** *noun* **hunter** *noun* **huntress** *feminine noun*
Word history: Old English *huntian*

huntsman spider
noun any of numerous species of medium to large spiders with flattened, brown or grey, hairy bodies (***tarantula***)

Huon pine (hyooh-on <u>puyn</u>)
noun a large coniferous (cone-bearing) timber tree found in Tasmania

Word history: named after the river *Huon* in Tasmania

hurdle
noun a movable fence over which horses or people have to jump in a race

Word history: Old English *hyrdel*

hurl
verb to throw (***chuck***, ***fling***, ***pitch***, ***toss***)

Word history: Middle English

hurricane
noun a violent, tropical storm with a very strong wind

Word history: Spanish, from Caribbean

hurricane lamp
noun a kerosene lamp, the flame of which is protected by a glass chimney or other similar device

hurry
verb to act quickly to save time: ***Hurry** or you will be late!* (***get a move on, hasten, shake a leg***)

Verb forms: I **hurried**, I have **hurried**, I am **hurrying**
Word building: **hurried** *adjective* **hurriedly** *adverb* **hurry** *noun*
Word history: perhaps imitative

hurt
verb **1** to cause pain or damage to: *I **hurt** my leg. | My thoughtlessness **hurt** Jan.* (***harm, injure, maim, mutilate, wound***)
2 to be painful: *My leg **hurts**.*

Word building: **hurt** *noun* **hurtful** *adjective*
Word history: Middle English, probably from Old French word meaning 'strike against'

hurtle
verb to rush noisily: *We **hurtled** along in the train.* (***dart, pelt, race, speed, streak***)

Word history: Middle English; from *hurt*

husband
noun the man to whom a woman is married (***partner, spouse***)

Word history: Old English *hūsbōnda*, from *hūs* house + *bōnda* householder

husbandry
noun **1** the business of agriculture or farming
2 careful management, without waste (***frugality, thrift***)

hush
verb **1** to make quiet or silent: ***Hush** your voice. | **Hush** the baby.*
2 to become quiet: *The crowd **hushed**.*

Word building: **hush** *noun*

hush money
noun a payment of money used to keep someone silent about something

husk
noun the dry outside covering of grain

Word history: Middle English *huske*, from Old English

husky[1]
adjective **1** low and hoarse: *a **husky** voice*
2 big and strong: *a **husky** lifesaver* (***brawny, hardy, muscly, robust***)

Adjective forms: **huskier, huskiest**
Word building: **huskiness** *noun*
Word history: from *husk* + *-y*

husky[2]
noun a dog used by people in Arctic regions for pulling sleds

Word history: perhaps a shortened variant of *Eskimo*

hussy (hu-see, hu-zee)
noun **1** an ill-behaved girl
2 a rude woman

Noun forms: The plural is **hussies**.
Word history: colloquial variant of *housewife*

hustings
plural noun speeches and other proceedings connected with political elections: *The candidate spent the day on the **hustings**.*

Word history: Middle English, from Scandinavian

hustle (hus-uhl)
verb **1** to push along roughly or hurriedly: *They **hustled** him out of the room.*
2 to hurry

hut
noun a small house-like shelter: *a beach **hut***

Word history: French, from German

hutch
noun a coop or house for small animals: *a rabbit **hutch***

Word history: Middle English, from Old French, from Medieval Latin word meaning 'chest'

hyacinth (huy-uh-suhnth)
noun a type of plant, growing from a bulb, widely cultivated for its spikes of fragrant, white or coloured, bell-shaped flowers

Word history: Latin, from Greek word meaning 'kind of flower', also 'a gem'

hybrid (huy-brid, huy-bruhd)
noun **1** an animal or plant that is the result of breeding between different types
2 (anything) produced from many sources, or made of different elements: *a **hybrid** computer | a **hybrid** car*

Word building: **hybridise** *verb*
Word history: from Latin word meaning 'offspring of a tame sow and wild boar', 'a mongrel'

hybrid car
noun a car which has both an electric and a petrol engine, the latter being required at higher speeds

hydrangea (huy-drayn-juh)
noun a shrub which has large, colourful clusters of flowers and loses its leaves in winter

Word history: Neo-Latin

hydrant
noun a point where a hose can be connected to a water main

hydraulic (huy-drol-ik)
adjective worked by the pressure of water, oil or other liquid: ***hydraulic** brakes*

Word history: Latin, from Greek word meaning 'pertaining to the water organ', 'an ancient musical instrument'

hydraulics
noun the science dealing with the laws governing water and other liquids in motion and the application of these laws in engineering

Word history: plural of *hydraulic*

hydrocarbon
noun any of a class of organic compounds containing only hydrogen and carbon, such as methane, ethylene, acetylene, (aliphatic hydrocarbons), and benzene, (an aromatic hydrocarbon)

hydrochloric acid
noun a colourless, poisonous, fuming liquid formed by the solution of hydrogen chloride in water, used extensively in chemical and industrial processes

Word use: The name of the commercial form is **muriatic acid**.

hydrochlorofluorocarbon
(huy-droh-klaw-roh-floo-uh-roh-kah-buhn)
noun a chemical containing hydrogen, chlorine, fluorine, and carbon; used instead of the earlier chlorofluorocarbon as a coolant in refrigerators and a propellant in spray cans because it does not damage the ozone layer as much

Word use: The abbreviation is **HCFC**.

hydro-electric
adjective relating to the making of electricity by water power

Word building: **hydro-electricity** *noun*

hydrofluorocarbon
(huy-droh-floo-uh-roh-kah-buhn)
noun a chemical containing hydrogen, fluorine, and carbon; used instead of the earlier chlorofluorocarbon as a coolant in refrigerators and a propellant in spray cans because it does not deplete the ozone layer but it is, nevertheless, a greenhouse gas with a high global warming potential

Word use: The abbreviation is **HFC**.

hydrofoil
noun **1** a ski-like attachment which raises the hull of a boat above the surface of the water when a certain speed has been reached
2 a boat with hydrofoils

hydrogen
noun a gas which combines with oxygen to make water

Word history: French

hydrogen fuel cell
noun a non-polluting fuel cell which produces electricity, the only waste product being water

Word use: The abbreviation is **HFC**.

hydrolysis (huy-drol-uh-suhs)
noun chemical decomposition by which a compound is changed into other compounds by taking up the elements of water, as salts of weak acids, etc.

Noun forms: The plural is **hydrolyses** (huy-drol-uh-seez).

hydroplane (huy-druh-playn)
noun a light, high-powered boat designed to skim along the surface of the water at high speed

hydroponics (huy-druh-pon-iks)
noun the growing of plants in water rather than soil

Word building: **hydroponic** *adjective*

hyena
noun a doglike animal that eats the flesh of dead animals

Word history: Latin, from Greek word meaning 'hog'

hygiene (huy-jeen)
noun **1** the science of preserving health
2 the cleanliness necessary for preserving health

hygienic (huy-jeen-ik, huy-jen-ik)
adjective **1** clean and sanitary
2 having to do with the science of hygiene

hygrometry (huy-grom-uh-tree)
noun the branch of physics that studies humidity

hymen (huy-muhn)
noun the membrane that usually partly covers the opening of the vagina until it is broken, often at first sexual intercourse

Word history: from Greek word meaning 'thin skin', 'membrane'

hymn (him)
noun a song praising God (***anthem***)

Word history: Late Latin, from Greek

hymn / him
Don't confuse **hymn** with **him**, which is a form of the pronoun **he**:
I saw him going down the street.

hype[1]
noun exaggeration, especially as used in advertising or the media

Word history: origin unknown, first used in the US

hype[2]
phrase **hype up**, *Colloquial* **1** to increase the power, speed, etc., of a car engine, etc.: *He **hyped up** his Holden.*
2 to persuade or exhort to greater achievement or success: *The coach **hyped up** his team before the match.*

Word history: short form of *hypodermic* needle

hyperactive
adjective unable to rest calmly or quietly because your body makes you maintain a very high level of activity: *a **hyperactive** child*

hyperbola (huy-per-buh-luh)
noun a plane curve formed by the intersection of a cone by a plane which makes a greater angle to the base than the side does

Noun forms: The plural is **hyperbolas**.
Word building: **hyperbolic** *adjective*
Word history: Neo-Latin, from Greek word meaning 'a throwing beyond'

hyperbole (huy-per-buh-lee)
noun an obvious over-statement made for effect and not intended to be taken literally, such as *I've told you a million times not to do that!*

Word building: **hyperbolic** *adjective*
Word history: Latin, from Greek word meaning 'a throwing beyond', 'excess', 'hyperbole'

hyperlink
noun Computers a connection created in hypertext

Word use: You can also use **link**.

hypertension (huy-puh-ten-shuhn)
noun high blood pressure, the chief sign of disease of the arteries

Word building: **hypertensive** *adjective*

hypertext
noun Computers text created in HTML which has highlighted links to other documents or other areas within the same document

hypertext transfer protocol
noun the protocol used for transferring files on the World Wide Web

Word use: The abbreviation is **HTTP** or **http**.

hyperthermia
noun an abnormally high body temperature: ***Hyperthermia*** *can lead to coma and death if not treated.*

hyperventilation (huy-puh-ven-tuh-lay-shuhn)
noun abnormally fast breathing which exposes the lungs to too much oxygen resulting in a rapid loss of carbon dioxide from the blood

Word building: **hyperventilate** *verb*

hyphen
noun a short line (-) used to link words which should be read together, or to link the parts of a word when it has to be split at the end of a line

Word history: Late Latin, from Greek word meaning 'together'

Hyphens often link the two parts of a compound, as in *baby-sitter*, *icy-cold* and *(to) cold-shoulder*.

With adjective and verb compounds (like *cold-shoulder* and *icy-cold*) the hyphen has an important role to play in making sure that both parts are read in the right grammatical 'slot' in the sentence. Compare the following sentences:

With icy cold turkey soup, it was a queer meal.

With icy-cold turkey soup, it was a queer meal.

If the hyphen is missing, you're not sure at first which word 'cold' goes with. It's the same in these examples:

They will cold shoulder anyone from outside.

They will cold-shoulder anyone from outside.

The hyphen helps to show that 'cold' is part of a compound verb.

With noun compounds the hyphen is usually less important:

The baby sitter did the washing up.

The baby-sitter did the washing up.

The compound won't suffer from misreading whether there is a hyphen there or not.

Hyphens can also help to keep apart the two parts of a compound or complex word, which would otherwise be misread. You may be puzzled or misled by the following:

sealegs shakeout reice coop

But with hyphens, their meaning is plain:

sea-legs shake-out re-ice co-op

Hyphens and wordbreaks. Hyphens are also used when we divide a word at the end of a line, because the whole word won't fit in. The hyphen shows that the rest of the word is on the next line. Look up **wordbreak**.

Note that hyphens are the punctuation mark we use within words. The similar but longer mark we use in punctuating sentences is the **dash**. Look up **dash**.

hypnosis
noun a sleep-like state brought about by cooperating with someone who is then able to control your mind and actions

Word building: **hypnotic** *adjective*
Word history: Neo-Latin, from Greek word meaning 'put to sleep'

hypnotise
verb to put under hypnosis: *The doctor* ***hypnotised*** *the patient.*

Word use: You can also use **hypnotize**.
Word building: **hypnotism** *noun*

hypochondria (huy-puh-kon-dree-uh)
noun the state of being very anxious about your health or imagining yourself ill

Word building: **hypochondriac** *adjective* **hypochondriac** *noun*
Word history: from Late Latin word meaning (plural), 'the abdomen', thought to be the seat of melancholy

hypocrisy (hip-ok-ruh-see)
noun the act of pretending to have a character or beliefs, principles, etc., that you do not possess

Noun forms: The plural is **hypocrisies**.
Word use: The opposite of this is **sincerity**.
Word history: Middle English, from Old French, from Late Latin, from Greek word meaning 'acting of a part', 'pretence'

hypocrite (hip-uh-krit)
noun someone who pretends to be better than they are

Word building: **hypocritical** *adjective*
Word history: Middle English, from Old French, from Late Latin, from Greek word meaning 'actor', 'pretender', 'hypocrite'

hypodermic (huy-puh-der-mik)
adjective injecting under the skin: *a* ***hypodermic*** *needle*

hypotenuse (huy-pot-uh-nyoohz)
noun the side opposite the right angle in a right-angled triangle

Word history: Late Latin, from Greek word meaning 'extending under'

hypothermia (huy-puh-ther-mee-uh)
noun **1** an abnormally low body temperature
2 the artificial reduction of body temperature, usually to make heart surgery possible

hypothesis (huy-poth-uh-suhs)
noun a proposition or theory which is taken as a useful starting point for a discussion or scientific investigation

Noun forms: The plural is **hypotheses** (huy-poth-uh-seez).
Word building: **hypothesise** *verb* **hypothetical** *adjective*
Word history: Neo-Latin, from Greek word meaning 'supposition', 'basis'

hysterectomy (his-tuh-rek-tuh-mee)
noun the surgical removal of the uterus

Noun forms: The plural is **hysterectomies**.

hysteria (his-tear-ree-uh)
noun **1** senseless, emotional frenzy
2 a mental disorder characterised by violent emotional outbreaks, affecting sensory and motor functions

hysteric (his-te-rik)
noun **1** a person suffering from hysteria
2 hysterics, a fit of hysteria

Word history: Latin, from Greek

hysterical
adjective **1** suffering from hysteria
2 extremely and wildly emotional
3 laughing uncontrollably
4 *Colloquial* very funny or amusing: *The show was* ***hysterical****.*

Word history: Latin

Ii

I
pronoun the personal pronoun used by a speaker to refer to himself or herself: ***I** heard that.*

> **I** is a first person singular pronoun in the subjective case.
> For more information, look up **pronouns: personal pronouns.**

iamb (uy-amb, uy-am)
noun a metrical foot of two syllables, a short one followed by a long one, or an unaccented by an accented. In *Come live with me and be my love*, there are four iambs.
Word building: **iambic** *adjective*
Word history: from Latin word meaning 'an iambic verse or poem'

ibidem (ib-uh-dem, i-buy-duhm)
adverb (in citations, bibliographies, etc.) in the same book, chapter or page
Word history: Latin

ibis (uy-buhs)
noun a wading bird with a long, thin, down-curved beak
Noun forms: The plural is **ibises**.
Word history: Latin, from Greek; of Egyptian origin

ice
noun **1** frozen water
verb **2** to become frozen: *The pond has **iced** over.*
3 to cover with icing: *to **ice** a cake*
phrase **4 on ice**, waiting or in readiness: *He kept the plan **on ice** for some time.*
5 on thin ice, in a risky situation
Word history: Old English *īs*

iceberg
noun a large mass of ice broken off from a glacier and floating in the sea
Word history: half Anglicisation, half adoption of Dutch word meaning 'ice mountain'

ice cap
noun a mass of ice which typically feeds a number of glaciers at its edge
Word use: You can also use **icecap**.

icecap
noun a cap of ice over an area, sometimes a very large area, sloping in all directions from the centre

ice-cream
noun a sweet, frozen food made with cream or milk

ice sheet
noun **1** a broad, thick sheet of ice covering an extensive area of land, sometimes running down to the sea floor, for a long period of time
2 a glacier covering a large part of a continent
Word use: You can also use **icesheet**.

ice shelf
noun a thick floating platform of ice which forms where a glacier flows to a coastline and onto the ocean surface
Word use: You can also use **iceshelf**.

ice skate
noun a special boot with a blade running from the front of the sole to the back of the sole to allow the wearer to glide over ice
Word building: **ice-skate** *verb* **ice-skater** *noun*

ichthyology (ik-thee-ol-uh-jee)
noun the branch of zoology that deals with fishes
Word building: **ichthyologic** *adjective* **ichthyological** *adjective* **ichthyologist** *noun*

icicle (uy-si-kuhl)
noun a hanging tapering piece of ice formed by the freezing of dripping water
Word history: Old English *īsgicel*

icing
noun a mixture of sugar and water or other ingredients for covering cakes

icon (uy-kon)
noun Computers a small picture or symbol on the screen that represents a process, a group of files, and such things: *Select the calculator **icon** if you want to use the computer as a calculator.*

iconoclast (uy-kon-uh-klast)
noun **1** a person who destroys sacred or religious images
2 a person who attacks established beliefs
Word building: **iconoclastic** *adjective* **iconoclasm** *noun*
Word history: Late Latin, from Late Greek

I'd
contraction of **I had** or **I would**

> Look up **contractions in grammar.**

idea (uy-dear)
noun a thought or picture in the mind (***concept, notion, theory***)
Word history: Latin, from Greek word meaning 'see'

ideal
noun **1** an idea of something at its most perfect: *She is my **ideal** of a doctor.*
2 a high ambition or standard: *He works hard towards his **ideals**.*

adjective **3** perfect and seen as a standard: ***ideal*** *beauty* | ***ideal*** *behaviour* (***faultless***, ***immaculate***, ***impeccable***)

Word history: Late Latin, from Latin word meaning 'idea'

idealise
verb to represent in an ideal form: *She* ***idealises*** *her dead father.*

Word use: You can also use **idealize**.

idealism
noun the representing of things as you think they ought to be rather than as they are

Word use: Compare this with **realism**.

idealist
noun someone who believes they can achieve their ideals or who believes the world can be made a better place, even when these beliefs are not realistic: *She was an* ***idealist*** *when she was young but now she has become more realistic.*

Word use: Compare this with **realist**.
Word building: **idealistic** *adjective*

idem (id-em, uy-dem)
pronoun the same

Word building: **idem** *adjective*
Word history: Latin

identical
adjective exactly alike: ***identical*** *twins*

identify
verb to recognise or prove as being a particular thing or person: *Can you* ***identify*** *your keys?* (***discern***, ***pick out***, ***spot***)

Verb forms: I **identified**, I have **identified**, I am **identifying**
Word building: **identifiable** *adjective* **identification** *noun*

identikit (uy-dent-ee-kit)
noun **1** pictures of parts of faces, such as eyes, nose, chin, etc., which can be put together to make a likeness of someone being sought by police
2 a picture so made up

Word history: Trademark

identity
noun **1** the condition of being a certain person or thing: *The group kept its* ***identity*** *under different leaders.*
2 a well-known personality: *an* ***identity*** *in the cricket club*

Noun forms: The plural is **identities**.
Word history: Late Latin, apparently from Latin word meaning 'repeatedly the same'

identity theft
noun the theft of identification, as in banking or government documents, passports or credit card details, so it can be used to commit fraud or theft: *She was charged with* ***identity theft***.

ideology (uy-dee-ol-uh-jee)
noun a set of beliefs or way of thinking of a social or political movement or group: *Marxist* ***ideology***

Word building: **ideological** *adjective* **ideologist** *noun*

ides (uydz)
plural noun in the ancient Roman calendar, the 15th day of March, May, July or October, and the 13th day of the other months

Word history: French, from Latin

idiom (id-ee-uhm)
noun a form of expression peculiar to a language, especially one having a meaning other than its literal one, such as *It's raining cats and dogs.*

Word history: Late Latin, from Greek word meaning 'a peculiarity'

idiomatic (id-ee-uh-mat-ik)
adjective **1** peculiar to or typical of a language: ***idiomatic*** *expressions*
2 showing the typical ways of expression of a speaker, group, or dialect: ***idiomatic*** *English*

idiosyncrasy (id-ee-oh-sing-kruh-see)
noun a peculiarity of someone's character or behaviour: *He has an* ***idiosyncrasy*** *of writing with purple ink.*

Noun forms: The plural is **idiosyncrasies**.
Word building: **idiosyncratic** *adjective*
Word history: Greek

idiot
noun **1** a very stupid person (***dunce***, ***fool***, ***imbecile***, ***moron***, ***simpleton***)
2 a person who is extremely subnormal intellectually

Word use: The opposite of this is **genius**.
Word building: **idiocy** *noun* **idiotic** *adjective*
Word history: Middle English, from Latin, from Greek word meaning 'a private, non-professional, or ignorant person'

idle
adjective **1** not doing or wanting to do anything: ***idle*** *workers* (***indolent***, ***lazy***, ***lethargic***, ***slack***, ***slothful***)
2 not being used: ***idle*** *machinery* | ***idle*** *time*

Word building: **idler** *noun*
Word history: Middle English and Old English *īdel*

idol
noun **1** a statue worshipped as a god
2 any person or thing which is blindly or excessively adored: *a sporting* ***idol*** (***celebrity***, ***hero***, ***household name***, ***star***, ***VIP***)

Word building: **idolatry** *noun*
Word history: Middle English, from Old French, from Latin, from Greek word meaning 'image', 'phantom', 'idol'

idolise
verb to worship or adore: *He* ***idolises*** *his daughter.* (***be besotted with***, ***be infatuated with***, ***dote on***)

Word use: You can also use **idolize**.

idyll (uy-duhl, id-uhl)
noun a poem, piece of prose or piece of descriptive music concerned with pleasant country scenes

Word building: **idyllic** *adjective*
Word history: Latin, from Greek diminutive word meaning 'form'

i.e.
abbreviation short for *id est*, Latin words meaning 'that is': *Please bring to the exam all your stationery needs,* ***i.e.*** *pencils, paper and ruler.*

if
conjunction **1** on condition that: *I'll come **if** you want me to.*
2 even though: ***If** you did say it, I didn't hear you.*
3 whether: *I don't know **if** I can do it.*
noun **4** a condition: ***ifs** and buts*
5 *Colloquial* something doubtful: *At this stage the plan is a big **if**.*
phrase **6 if only**, used to introduce a phrase expressing a wish, especially one that probably cannot be fulfilled: ***If only** I had known!*

Word history: Middle English; Old English *gif*

iffy
adjective Colloquial uncertain; seeming like there is something wrong: *I don't know – it seems a bit **iffy** to me.*

igloo
noun a dome-shaped hut built of blocks of hard snow

Word history: from Inuit word meaning 'house'

igneous (ig-nee-uhs)
adjective having to do with fire

Word history: from Latin word meaning 'of fire'

igneous rock
noun rock formed from magma which has cooled and solidified

Word use: Compare this with **metamorphic rock** and **sedimentary rock**.

ignite
verb to set on fire

Word use: The opposite of this is **extinguish**.
Word history: Latin

ignition (ig-nish-uhn)
noun **1** the act of setting on fire
2 a system for setting on fire, especially that of the electrical sparks which ignite the fuel in the cylinders in a car engine

ignoble (ig-noh-buhl)
adjective of low character and behaviour

Word use: This is the opposite of **noble**.
Word history: from Latin word meaning 'unknown', 'of low birth'

ignominy (ig-nuh-muh-nee)
noun disgrace or dishonour

Word building: **ignominious** *adjective*
Word history: from Latin word meaning 'disgrace', 'dishonour'

ignoramus (ig-nuh-ray-muhs)
noun someone who knows little or nothing

Noun forms: The plural is **ignoramuses**.
Word history: from Latin word meaning 'we do not know', 'we disregard'

ignorant
adjective **1** uneducated (***backward**, **illiterate**, **innumerate**, **stupid***)
2 having no knowledge: ***ignorant** of Russian*

Word building: **ignorance** *noun*
Word history: Middle English, from Latin word meaning 'not knowing'

ignore
verb to take no notice of

Word history: from Latin word meaning 'not to know', 'disregard'

iguana (i-gwah-nuh)
noun a large lizard of tropical America

Word history: Spanish, from Native American

ilk
adjective **1** same
noun **2** family, class, or kind: *he and all his **ilk***

Word history: Old English *elc, ylc, each*

ill
adjective **1** sick (***ailing**, **crook**, **indisposed**, **off-colour***)
2 bad: ***ill** feeling*
adverb **3** badly: *to treat someone **ill***
noun **4** an evil: *the **ills** of our society*

Word building: **illness** *noun*
Word history: Middle English, from Scandinavian

I'll
contraction of **I will** or **I shall**

Look up **contractions in grammar**.

Illawarra flame tree
noun → **flame tree**

illegal
adjective not allowed by the law (***criminal**, **felonious**, **illicit***)

Word use: The opposite of this is **legal**.
Word history: Medieval Latin, from Latin

illegible
adjective not able to be read: ***illegible** writing*

Word use: The opposite is **legible**.
Word building: **illegibility** *noun*

illegitimate (il-uh-jit-uh-muht)
adjective **1** born to parents who are not legally married
2 against the law or not allowed

Word use: The opposite of this is **legal** or **legitimate**.
Word building: **illegitimacy** *noun*

ill-gotten
adjective gained in unlawful ways: ***ill-gotten** gains*

illicit (i-lis-uht)
adjective not lawful: ***illicit** drugs* (***black-market**, **contraband**, **illegal***)

Word history: from Latin word meaning 'forbidden'

illiterate
adjective unable to read and write

Word use: The opposite is **literate**.
Word building: **illiteracy** *noun*
Word history: from Latin word meaning 'unlettered'

illuminate (i-looh-muh-nayt)
verb **1** to light up
2 to give knowledge to or inform: *Would you care to **illuminate** me on this point?*

Word use: The opposite of definition 1 is **darken**.
Word building: **illumination** *noun*
Word history: Latin

illusion (i-looh-zhuhn)
noun a false idea or daydream: ***illusions** of becoming a rock singer*

Word use: The opposite of this is **reality**.
Word history: Middle English, from Latin word meaning 'mocking', 'illusion'

illusion / allusion
Don't confuse **illusion** with **allusion**, which is a passing mention of something, often made while speaking about something else.

illusion / delusion
Look up **delusion / illusion**.

illustrate (il-uhs-trayt)
verb **1** to provide with pictures: *The author **illustrated** her book with photographs.*
2 to make clear by giving examples: *He **illustrated** his theory about leadership with accounts of the lives of some famous explorers.* (***clarify***, ***elucidate***, ***explain***, ***spell out***)
Word building: **illustrative** *adjective* **illustrator** *noun*
Word history: from Latin word meaning 'illuminated'

illustration
noun **1** the act of explaining or making clear
2 a photograph or drawing in a book, magazine or newspaper

illustrious
adjective famous or distinguished: *an **illustrious** family in the nation's history*
Word history: from Latin word meaning 'lit up', 'bright'

I'm
contraction of **I am**

Look up **contractions in grammar**.

image
noun **1** a picture in the mind: *I have an **image** of the perfect house.*
2 reflection: *your **image** in the mirror*
3 an exact likeness: *She is the **image** of her mother.*
Word history: Middle English, from French, from Latin word meaning 'copy', 'image'

imagery
noun **1** the technique through which a writer creates pictures in the reader's mind to make the words more vivid. The two main types of imagery are metaphors and similes.
2 the forming of images, figures, or likenesses of things, often in your imagination, in dreams, etc.
Noun forms: The plural is **imageries**.

imaginary
adjective not real, existing only in the imagination: *an **imaginary** illness* (***fanciful***, ***fictitious***, ***made-up***, ***mythical***)
Word use: The opposite of this is **real**.

imagination (i-maj-uh-nay-shuhn)
noun the ability to form pictures in your mind or to make up interesting stories
Word history: Middle English, from Latin

imaginative
adjective having to do with using the imagination in a creative or unusual way: *an **imaginative** approach to the problem*

imagine
verb **1** to form a picture of in the mind: *to **imagine** a scene at the beach* (***conjure up***, ***dream up***, ***fantasise about***, ***have visions of***, ***picture***)
2 to think or believe: *I **imagine** she'll be happy when she hears the good news.* (***conclude***, ***reckon***, ***suppose***)
Word history: Middle English, from French, from Latin word meaning 'picture to oneself', 'fancy'

imaging
noun the process of making an image or picture of a scan of the body taken by such a device as an ultrasound or a CAT scanner

imam (im-ahm)
noun an Islamic religious leader

imbalance
noun lack of balance (***lopsidedness***, ***unevenness***)

imbecile (im-buh-seel, im-buh-suyl)
noun someone who is mentally deficient
Word building: **imbecile** *adjective*
Word history: French, from Latin word meaning 'weak', 'feeble'

imbibe (im-buyb)
verb to drink, absorb, or take in: *Don't drive if you **imbibe** too much alcohol! | to **imbibe** ideas*
Word history: Middle English, from Latin word meaning 'drink in'

imbue (im-byooh)
verb **1** to soak or fill, as with feelings, opinions, etc.
2 to soak with moisture, fill with colour, etc.
Verb forms: I **imbue**, I have **imbued**, I am **imbuing**
Word history: Latin

imitate
verb to copy or use as a model (***ape***, ***impersonate***, ***mimic***)
Word building: **imitative** *adjective*
Word history: from Latin word meaning 'having copied'

imitation
noun **1** an act of imitating: ***imitation** of his behaviour*
2 a copy or reproduction
adjective **3** made to look like something real or superior: ***imitation** pearls* (***counterfeit***, ***fake***)

immaculate (i-mak-yuh-luht)
adjective spotlessly clean (***pure***, ***spotless***)
Word history: late Middle English, from Latin word meaning 'unspotted'

immaterial (im-uh-tear-ree-uhl)
adjective **1** unimportant: *It's **immaterial** to me whether you come or not.* (***inconsequential***, ***irrelevant***)
2 not having a physical or material form (***insubstantial***, ***spiritual***)
Word history: Medieval Latin, from Late Latin, from French

immature
adjective not mature, ripe, developed, or perfected

Word building: **immaturity** *noun*
Word history: from Latin word meaning 'unripe'

immediate
adjective happening straight away: *an* ***immediate*** *reply*

Word use: The opposite of this is **delayed.**
Word building: **immediacy** *noun* **immediately** *adverb*
Word history: from Medieval Latin word meaning 'not mediate'

immemorial
adjective reaching back beyond memory, record, or knowledge: *from time* ***immemorial***

Word history: Medieval Latin, from Latin

immense
adjective extremely large

Word history: from Latin word meaning 'boundless', 'unmeasured'

immerse
verb to put below the surface of a liquid: *He* ***immersed*** *his hand in the warm water.*

Word building: **immersion** *noun*
Word history: from Latin word meaning 'dipped'

immigrate
verb to come to live in a new country

Word use: The opposite of this is **emigrate.**
Word building: **immigrant** *noun* **immigration** *noun*
Word history: Latin

immigrate / emigrate / migrate
Look up **emigrate / immigrate / migrate.**

imminent (i-muh-nuhnt)
adjective likely to happen at any moment (***impending***, ***looming***)

Word history: from Latin word meaning 'projecting over'

imminent / eminent
Don't confuse **imminent** with **eminent.**
We call someone **eminent** if they are important or have a high rank.

immobile (i-moh-buyl)
adjective **1** not able to be moved
2 not moving; motionless (***stationary***, ***steady***, ***still***)

Word building: **immobilise** *verb* **immobility** *noun*
Word history: Latin

immolate (im-uh-layt)
verb to kill as a sacrifice

Word building: **immolation** *noun*
Word history: from Latin word meaning 'sacrificed' (originally 'sprinkled with sacrificial meal')

immoral
adjective wrong or wicked (***corrupt***, ***degenerate***, ***depraved***, ***indecent***, ***perverted***)

Word use: The opposite of this is **moral.**
Word building: **immorality** *noun*

immoral / amoral
Don't confuse **immoral** with **amoral.** These words both have moral as their base word, and have very similar meanings.
Immoral describes someone who knows the difference between good and bad but who chooses to act in a way which is bad or wrong.
Amoral is used to describe someone who doesn't know or doesn't care about the difference between good and bad or right and wrong.

immorality / immortality
Don't confuse **immorality** with **immortality**, which is the power to live forever.

immortal
adjective living or lasting forever: *the* ***immortal*** *works of Banjo Paterson* (***ageless***, ***deathless***, ***evergreen***, ***everlasting***, ***undying***)

Word use: The opposite of this is **mortal** or **passing.**
Word building: **immortalise** *verb* **immortality** *noun*
Word history: Middle English, from Latin word meaning 'undying'

immovable
adjective **1** not able to be moved: *an* ***immovable*** *rock* (***fixed***, ***rigid***, ***permanent***)
2 not moving; motionless: *A kangaroo stood* ***immovable*** *on a rock.*
3 not able to be changed: *an* ***immovable*** *regulation*
4 unyielding: *He's* ***immovable*** *in his decision.* (***confirmed***, ***inflexible***, ***steadfast***)

immune
adjective **1** protected from a disease: *She is* ***immune*** *to mumps now.*
2 protected from distress or misfortune: ***immune*** *from harm* (***safe***, ***secure***, ***sheltered***, ***shielded***)

Word use: The opposite of this is **susceptible.**
Word building: **immunise** *verb* **immunisation** *noun* **immunity** *noun*
Word history: Middle English, from Latin word meaning 'exempt'

immunodeficiency
(im-yuh-noh-duh-fish-uhn-see)
noun an impairment in the autoimmune system resulting in poor immunity to infection

Word building: **immunodeficient** *adjective*

immunology (im-yooh-nol-uh-jee)
noun the science that deals with protection from diseases

Word building: **immunologist** *noun*

immure (i-myooh-uh)
verb **1** to enclose within walls
2 to confine or shut in (***imprison***, ***incarcerate***, ***wall in***)

Word history: Medieval Latin, from Latin

immutable (i-myooht-uh-buhl)
adjective changeless (***fixed***, ***unalterable***)

Word building: **immutability** *noun*

imp
noun **1** a little devil
2 a child who misbehaves a bit
Word building: **impish** *adjective*
Word history: Middle English and Old English *impe* a shoot, a graft

impact
noun the hitting of one thing against another: *I heard the* ***impact*** *of the cars at the corner.*
Word history: from Latin word meaning 'to strike against'

impacted
adjective **1** wedged in, or tightly packed
2 of a tooth, firmly embedded in the jawbone and not able to grow out: *an* ***impacted*** *wisdom tooth*

impair
verb to spoil, make worse, or lessen in value
Word use: The opposite of this is **improve**.
Word building: **impairment** *noun*
Word history: Middle English, from Old French, from Latin

impale
verb to fix upon or pierce through with a sharp, pointed object
Word building: **impalement** *noun*
Word history: Medieval Latin, from Latin

impart
verb **1** to tell or make known: *to* ***impart*** *a secret* (***communicate***, ***convey***, ***relay***)
2 to give or bestow: *to* ***impart*** *satisfaction | to* ***impart*** *wisdom*
3 to give out a part or share of
Word building: **imparter** *noun*
Word history: Middle English, from Latin word meaning 'share'

impartial
adjective not taking one side or the other: *an* ***impartial*** *judge* (***disinterested***, ***neutral***, ***objective***)
Word use: The opposite of this is **biased**.
Word building: **impartiality** *noun*

impasse (im-pahs)
noun **1** a position from which there is no escape
2 a road or way that has no outlet
Word history: French

impassioned
adjective filled with passion: *The student made an* ***impassioned*** *speech against war.* (***ardent***, ***passionate***)

impassive
adjective not showing any emotion: *His face remained* ***impassive*** *as she told her story.*
Word use: The opposite of this is **emotional**.
Word building: **impassivity** *noun*

impatient
adjective **1** unwilling to wait (***eager***, ***enthusiastic***, ***keen***)
2 short-tempered: *I am often* ***impatient*** *with noisy children.* (***cranky***, ***cross***, ***crotchety***, ***grumpy***, ***irritable***)
Word building: **impatience** *noun*
Word history: Middle English, from Latin word meaning 'not bearing or enduring'

impeach
verb **1** to question the credibility of: *to* ***impeach*** *a witness*
2 to accuse a government official of a serious crime in connection with their job
Word building: **impeachable** *adjective* **impeachment** *noun*
Word history: Middle English, from Old French word meaning 'hinder', from Late Latin word meaning 'catch', 'entangle', from Latin word meaning 'fetter'

impeccable
adjective without any faults: *His work was* ***impeccable***. (***faultless***, ***ideal***, ***immaculate***, ***perfect***)
Word history: Late Latin

impecunious (im-puh-kyooh-nee-uhs)
adjective having no money (***broke***, ***destitute***, ***insolvent***, ***penniless***, ***poor***)
Word building: **impecuniousness**, **impecuniosity** *noun*

impede
verb to slow down or block the way of: *The demonstration* ***impeded*** *the traffic.* (***hamper***, ***hinder***, ***inhibit***)
Word history: from Latin word meaning 'entangle', 'hamper' (originally, 'as to the feet')

impediment
noun **1** an obstruction or obstacle (***difficulty***, ***hindrance***)
2 a physical defect, especially a speech disorder

impel
verb **1** to drive or urge forward
2 to drive, or cause to move, onwards (***propel***, ***shove***, ***thrust***)
Verb forms: I **impelled**, I have **impelled**, I am **impelling**
Word history: Latin

impending
adjective about to happen: *Bushfire smoke on the horizon alerted us to the* ***impending*** *disaster.* (***imminent***, ***looming***, ***threatening***)
Word history: from Latin word meaning 'hang over'

imperative (im-pe-ruh-tiv)
adjective **1** essential or compulsory: *an* ***imperative*** *duty* (***crucial***, ***necessary***, ***obligatory***, ***vital***)
2 commanding: *an* ***imperative*** *tone of voice*
3 *Grammar* having to do with the verb mood used in commands
Word building: **imperative** *noun*
Word history: Latin

> For more information about the **imperative** mood (definition 3), look up **verbs: mood**.

imperfect
adjective faulty or not perfect
Word history: from Latin word meaning 'unfinished'

imperfect aspect
noun another name for the **continuous aspect** of verbs

> For more information, look up **verbs: aspect**.

imperial (im-pear-ree-uhl)
adjective belonging to an empire: *the **imperial** throne*
Word history: Middle English, from Latin word meaning 'of the empire or emperor'

imperialism
noun a system in which one country dominates another, either directly by holding it as a colony or indirectly by military or economic influence
Word building: **imperialist** *adjective*

imperial system
noun a system of weights and measures set up in Britain and used in Australia before the metric system was introduced in 1970

imperious
adjective arrogant or bossy: *The director had an **imperious** manner.* (***authoritarian***, ***autocratic***, ***dictatorial***, ***overbearing***, ***tyrannical***)
Word history: from Latin word meaning 'commanding'

impermeable (im-per-mee-uh-buhl)
adjective not allowing fluids to pass through: *an **impermeable** membrane*
Word building: **impermeability** *noun* **impermeableness** *noun*

impersonal
adjective **1** not influenced by or showing any personal feelings: *Her remarks were cool and **impersonal**.*
2 not having a personality or existing as a person: *an **impersonal** god*

impersonate
verb to pretend to be: *The thief **impersonated** a detective to persuade the old lady to let him in.* (***ape***, ***imitate***, ***mimic***)
Word building: **impersonation** *noun* **impersonator** *noun*

impertinent
adjective cheeky or rude
Word building: **impertinence** *noun*

impervious (im-per-vee-uhs)
adjective **1** not allowing fluids to pass through: ***impervious** to water* (***impermeable***)
phrase **2 impervious to**, not moved or affected by: ***impervious to** reason*

impetigo (im-puh-tuy-goh)
noun a contagious skin disease, especially of children
Word history: from Latin word meaning 'attack'

impetuous
adjective acting hastily and thoughtlessly (***foolhardy***, ***harebrained***, ***hasty***, ***rash***, ***reckless***)
Word building: **impetuosity** *noun*
Word history: Middle English, from Latin word meaning 'an attack'

impetus (im-puh-tuhs)
noun **1** a moving force or stimulus: *a fresh **impetus***
2 a force that starts a body moving or tends to keep it moving and resisting changes in its motion
Noun forms: The plural is **impetuses**.
Word history: from Latin word meaning 'onset'

impinge (im-pinj)
verb to go beyond the proper limits (***infringe***, ***trespass***)
Word history: from Latin word meaning 'drive in or at', 'strike against'

implacable (im-plak-uh-buhl)
adjective not able to be appeased or calmed: *an **implacable** enemy*
Word building: **implacability** *noun* **implacableness** *noun*

implant (im-plant, im-plahnt)
verb **1** to teach or instil so as to fix it firmly in the mind: ***implant** sound principles*
noun (im-plant, im-plahnt) **2** *Medicine* any substance, such as grafted tissue, an electronic device, a drug, etc., put into the body
Word building: **implantation** *noun*

implausible (im-plawz-uh-buhl)
adjective seeming not to be true or believable (***far-fetched***, ***improbable***, ***incredible***, ***unbelievable***, ***unlikely***)
Word building: **implausibility** *noun*

implement (im-pluh-muhnt)
noun **1** a tool: *a kitchen **implement***
verb (im-pluh-ment) **2** to put into effect: *to **implement** a plan*
Word building: **implementation** *noun*
Word history: Middle English, from Late Latin word meaning 'a filling up'

implicate (im-pluh-kayt)
verb to involve in or with something: *to be **implicated** in a crime*
Word history: from Latin word meaning 'entangled', 'involved'

implication (im-pluh-kay-shuhn)
noun something suggested as naturally to be understood without actually being stated: *The **implication** was that he had not told the truth.*

implicit (im-plis-uht)
adjective **1** suggested or implied but not actually stated: *an **implicit** understanding*
2 absolute or unquestioning: ***implicit** reliance on his friend*
Word use: The opposite of definition 1 is **explicit**. | The opposite of definition 2 is **limited** or **qualified**.
Word history: from Latin word meaning 'entangled', 'involved'

implicit / explicit
Look up **explicit / implicit**.

implore
verb to beg or plead (***ask***, ***beseech***, ***entreat***, ***request***)
Word history: from Latin word meaning 'invoke with tears'

imply (im-pluy)
verb **1** to mean: *What do these words **imply**?*
2 to suggest without actually stating: *He did not say it was urgent but his manner **implied** it.* (***hint***, ***insinuate***)

Word history: Middle English, from Old French, from Latin word meaning 'enfold', 'entangle', 'involve'

imply / infer

To **imply** something is to suggest it without actually stating it. For example, the two statements *Brisbane is in Australia* and *Toowong is a suburb of Brisbane* imply a third — *Toowong is in Australia.*

To **infer** something is to work it out from the information provided or from what has been said by other people.

When the great detective states confidently that the woman before him is a plumber he has drawn an **inference** from the facts that the woman has mud on her shoes and that she arrived in a truck which advertised Wilson's Plumbing.

You can make an **inference** which is not correct. For example, the woman might have dirty shoes because she is a gardener and she just borrowed the truck from her friend, Mr Wilson, the plumber. Appearances can be deceiving.

Sometimes we make statements which are not clear and which allow for misinterpretation. There is not much room for error or confusion in the statements about Toowong and Brisbane, but we are not always so precise. So it is possible for others to **infer** things from what we say which we did not mean to **imply**. The **implication** may or may not have been there.

impolite
adjective having bad manners (***abrupt***, ***impudent***, ***insolent***, ***insulting***, ***rude***, ***vulgar***)

import (im-pawt)
verb **1** to bring in from another country: *Australia* ***imports*** *clothing from Hong Kong.*
noun (im-pawt) **2** something that is brought in from another country
3 meaning: *to get the full* ***import*** *of a statement*
4 importance or consequence: *The shock announcement was of* ***import*** *to us all.*

Word use: The opposite of definitions 1 and 2 is **export**.
Word building: **importation** *noun*
Word history: Middle English, from Latin word meaning 'bring in', 'bring about'

import / export

Don't confuse **import** with **export**.

To **export** goods is to send them out of a country.

To **import** goods is to bring them into a country.

important
adjective **1** having great meaning or effect: *an* ***important*** *message | an* ***important*** *event*
2 leading or powerful: *an* ***important*** *visitor* (***distinguished***, ***eminent***, ***famous***, ***prestigious***, ***prominent***)

Word building: **importance** *noun*
Word history: French, from Medieval Latin word meaning 'be of consequence', Latin word meaning 'bring in', 'cause'

importune (im-paw-choohn, im-paw-tyoohn)
verb to trouble or annoy with persistent, urgent demands

Word building: **importunity** *noun*
Word history: Middle English, from Middle French, from Latin word meaning 'unfit', 'inconvenient', 'troublesome'

impose
verb **1** to set officially as something to be obeyed or paid: *to* ***impose*** *a tax | to* ***impose*** *a new law*
2 to push or force yourself on others: *We don't want to* ***impose*** *on you by staying the night.*

Word history: French

imposing
adjective making an impression on your mind: *an* ***imposing*** *building | an* ***imposing*** *woman*

Word use: The opposite of this is **unimposing**.

imposition (im-puh-zish-uhn)
noun **1** the laying or placing on of something
2 something placed on someone, as a burden, task or punishment
3 a deceiving or taking advantage of

impossible (im-pos-uh-buhl)
adjective **1** not able to be, exist, or happen (***impracticable***, ***unattainable***, ***unthinkable***)
2 not able to be done or effected: *It is* ***impossible*** *for my son to carry me.*
3 not able to be true
4 not to be done, put up with, etc.: *an* ***impossible*** *situation*
5 hopelessly unsuitable: *an* ***impossible*** *person*

Word building: **impossibility** *noun*
Word history: Middle English, from Latin

impostor (im-pos-tuh)
noun someone who deceives other people by pretending to be someone else

Word history: from Latin word meaning 'impose'

impotent (im-puh-tuhnt)
adjective not having the power to do things (***feeble***, ***gutless***, ***incapacitated***, ***powerless***, ***useless***)

Word building: **impotence** *noun*

impound
verb **1** to shut up in a pound: *to* ***impound*** *a stray dog*
2 to confine within an enclosure or within limits: *The soldiers* ***impounded*** *the prisoners.*
3 to confiscate legally, such as taking a document for evidence

impoverish (im-pov-uh-rish, im-pov-rish)
verb **1** to cause to become poor: *The country was* ***impoverished*** *by war.*
2 to make poor in quality, strength, or richness: *to* ***impoverish*** *the soil*

Word history: Middle English, from Old French

impregnable (im-preg-nuh-buhl)
adjective **1** strong enough to resist attack: *an* ***impregnable*** *fort*
2 not to be overcome or overthrown: *an* ***impregnable*** *argument*

Word building: **impregnability** *noun*
Word history: Middle English, from French

impregnate (<u>im</u>-preg-nayt)
verb **1** to make pregnant
2 to fertilise
3 to saturate: *The cottonwool was* ***impregnated*** *with disinfectant.*

Word building: **impregnation** *noun*
Word history: from Late Latin word meaning 'made pregnant'

impress
verb **1** to fill with admiration: *His musical talent* ***impressed*** *all who heard him.*
2 to fix firmly in the mind: *She* ***impressed*** *her news on us.*

Word history: Middle English, from Latin word meaning 'pressed upon'

impression
noun **1** a mark made by pressure: *the* ***impression*** *of a rubber stamp.*
2 a strong effect made on the mind or feelings: *His story made an* ***impression*** *on the audience.*
3 a vague feeling or indication: *I had the* ***impression*** *she was unhappy. | The picture gave an* ***impression*** *of sunlight and leaves.* (***awareness, perception, sensation, sense***)

Word building: **impressionistic** *adjective*
Word history: Middle English, from Latin

impressionable
adjective easily influenced

impressionism
noun a style of music, painting or literature that aims to convey the mood or feeling of a subject

impressive
adjective having the ability to impresses you; causing admiration or wonder: *an* ***impressive*** *building | Her first speech in parliament was very* ***impressive.***

Word building: **impressively** *adverb* **impressiveness** *noun*

imprint
verb to fix firmly: *The warning* ***imprinted*** *itself on his mind.*

Word history: Middle English, from Old French, from Latin word meaning 'impress', 'imprint'

imprison
verb to put into prison (***confine, intern, jail, lock up, restrain***)

Word use: The opposite of this is **release** or **free**.
Word building: **imprisonment** *noun*

improbable (im-<u>prob</u>-uh-buhl)
adjective unlikely to be true or to happen (***far-fetched, implausible, incredible, unbelievable***)

impromptu (im-<u>prompt</u>-yooh)
adjective made up or done on the spur of the moment: *an* ***impromptu*** *speech | an* ***impromptu*** *party* (***impulsive, sudden***)

Word use: The opposite of this is **planned** or **prepared.**
Word history: French, from Latin word meaning 'in readiness'

improper
adjective **1** not really right or belonging: *an* ***improper*** *use for a thing*
2 not in accordance with correct behaviour, manners, etc.: ***improper*** *language*
3 unsuitable: ***improper*** *tools*

improve
verb **1** to make better (***correct, enhance, enrich, repair, upgrade***)
2 to become better: *the patient's condition has* ***improved***

Word history: Anglo-French, from Old French

improvement
noun any change or addition that improves or adds beauty or value

improvisation
noun **1** the act of inventing or composing on the spot
2 anything that is improvised

improvise (<u>im</u>-pruh-vuyz)
verb **1** to make do with what is available: *He* ***improvised*** *a meal from the leftovers in the fridge.*
2 to invent or compose on the spot: *to* ***improvise*** *a little tune* (***concoct, create, extemporise, make up***)

Word history: French, from Italian, from Latin word meaning 'unforeseen', 'unexpected'

impudent (<u>im</u>-pyuh-duhnt)
adjective cheeky or insolent (***abrupt, bold, impolite, insulting, rude***)

Word building: **impudence** *noun*
Word history: from Latin word meaning 'shameless'

impugn (im-<u>pyoohn</u>)
verb to call into doubt or challenge as false

Word building: **impugnable** *adjective*
Word history: Middle English, from Old French, from Latin word meaning 'attack'

impulse
noun a sudden desire: *He felt an* ***impulse*** *to run.*

Word history: from Latin word meaning 'a push against'

impulsive
adjective acting on sudden thoughts or desires (***capricious, hasty, rash***)

Word building: **impulsiveness** *noun*

impunity (im-<u>pyooh</u>-nuh-tee)
noun freedom from any punishment or harm that might result from your actions: *I can speak with* ***impunity.***

Word history: from Latin word meaning 'omission of punishment'

impute (im-<u>pyooht</u>)
verb **1** to blame with or for: *I* ***impute*** *to him the disaster which followed.*
2 to consider as coming from a cause or source: *We* ***impute*** *her happiness to her new job.*

Word building: **imputation** *noun*
Word history: Middle English, from Latin word meaning 'bring into the reckoning'

in
preposition a word that expresses the following:
1 containment within a place: ***in*** *the city |* ***in*** *politics*
2 containment within a certain period of time: ***in*** *ancient days |* ***in*** *ten minutes*
3 condition or situation: ***in*** *darkness |* ***in*** *love*
adjective **4** in fashion: *Short hair is* ***in*** *this year.*
5 in season: *Oranges are* ***in*** *now.*
phrase **6 be in it**, to be part of an action

7 in for, about to experience: *We are **in for** another hot day.*
8 in for it, about to be punished
9 in on, having a share or a part of, especially something secret: *She's **in on** the plot.* | ***in on** the secret*
10 in that, for the reason that
11 nothing in it, in a competition, very close in performance
12 well in with, on good terms with

inability
noun the fact of not being able to do something: *an **inability** to make friends* | *an **inability** to lie*

inaccuracy (in-ak-yooh-ruh-see)
noun **1** the quality of being incorrect
2 something which is incorrect

Word building: **inaccurate** *adjective*

inadequate
adjective not enough to fill a need: ***inadequate** food* (***deficient**, **incomplete**, **insufficient***)

Word building: **inadequacy** *noun*

inadvertent (in-uhd-ver-tuhnt)
adjective **1** not paying attention
2 unintentional: *an **inadvertent** insult* (***accidental**, **unintended***)

inane
adjective silly or senseless: *an **inane** remark* (***fatuous**, **foolish**, **idiotic**, **irrational**, **ridiculous***)

Word building: **inanity** *noun* (*plural* **inanities**)
Word history: from Latin word meaning 'empty', 'vain'

inanimate
adjective not living: ***inanimate** objects*

Word use: The opposite of this is **animate**.

inaugurate (in-awg-yuh-rayt)
verb to bring into public use with an opening ceremony

Word building: **inauguration** *noun*
Word history: from Latin word meaning 'consecrated or installed with augural ceremonies'

inborn
adjective natural or possessed from birth: *an **inborn** clumsiness* (***innate**, **natural***)

inbred
adjective **1** inborn
2 having to do with or resulting from breeding with close relatives

inbreeding
noun production of offspring resulting from the mating of closely related individuals such as cousins, brother-sister, or self-fertilising plants

Word building: **inbreed** *verb*

incalculable (in-kal-kyuh-luh-buhl)
adjective **1** not able to be calculated (***countless**, **endless**, **infinite**, **myriad***)
2 not able to be forecast

in camera (in kam-uh-ruh)
adjective **1** of a legal case, heard in a judge's private room or in court with the public kept out
2 in secret: *The meeting was held **in camera**.*

Word history: from Latin word meaning 'in the chamber'

incandescence (in-kan-des-uhns)
noun the state of a body caused by near white heat, when it may be used as a source of artificial light

Word use: Compare this with **luminescence**.

incandescent (in-kan-des-uhnt)
adjective glowing with white heat (***bright**, **flaming**, **luminous**, **shining***)

Word history: from Latin word meaning 'growing hot'

incantation (in-kan-tay-shuhn)
noun **1** the chanting of words thought to have magical power
2 a spell (***charm**, **hocus-pocus**, **magic words***)

Word history: Middle English, from Late Latin word meaning 'enchantment'

incapable (in-kayp-uh-buhl)
adjective **1** not able
phrase **2 incapable of**, not having the ability or power for a certain act: *He is just **incapable of** keeping his desk tidy!*

Word history: Late Latin

incapacitate (in-kuh-pas-uh-tayt)
verb to make unable or unfit: *Illness **incapacitated** him.* (***cripple**, **disable**, **paralyse***)

Word building: **incapacitation** *noun*

incarcerate (in-kahs-uh-rayt)
verb to imprison (***confine**, **jail***)

Word building: **incarceration** *noun*
Word history: Medieval Latin, from Latin

incarnate (in-kah-nuht, in-kah-nayt)
adjective with a human body: *the devil **incarnate***

Word building: **incarnation** *noun*
Word history: Middle English, from Late Latin word meaning 'made flesh'

incendiary (in-senj-uh-ree)
adjective **1** used or made for setting property on fire: ***incendiary** bombs*
2 having to do with the criminal setting on fire of property
3 likely to cause trouble, discontent, etc.: ***incendiary** speeches* (***inflammatory**, **rabble-rousing***)
noun **4** in the army, etc., a shell or bomb that contains phosphorus or a similar material and which is capable of starting fires
5 someone who stirs up trouble, discontent, etc. (***agitator***)

Word history: from Latin word meaning 'causing fire'

incense[1] (in-sens)
noun a substance which gives off a sweet smell when burnt

Word history: from Late Latin word meaning 'incense'

incense[2] (in-sens)
verb to make angry (***anger**, **drive someone up the wall**, **enrage**, **infuriate***)

Word history: Middle English, from Latin word meaning 'set on fire', 'kindled'

incentive
noun something that encourages and gives a motive: *The scholarship was an **incentive** for her to work hard.*

Word use: The opposite of this is **disincentive** or **deterrent**.

inception (in-sep-shuhn)
noun a beginning or start

incessant (in-ses-uhnt)
adjective continuing without stopping: *an **incessant** noise*

Word history: from Late Latin word meaning 'unceasing'

incest
noun sexual intercourse between closely related people

Word building: **incestuous** *adjective*
Word history: Middle English, from Latin word meaning 'unchaste'

inch
noun **1** a unit of length in the imperial system, equal to 25.4 millimetres
verb **2** to move by a short distance at a time: *to **inch** along the cliff*
phrase **3 within an inch of**, almost or very near to: *She came **within an inch of** being killed.*

Word use: For definition 1 look up **imperial system**.
Word history: Middle English; Old English *ynce*, from Latin word meaning 'twelfth part', 'inch', 'ounce'

inchoate (in-koh-ayt)
adjective just begun and not fully formed: ***inchoate** political ideas*

Word history: from Latin word meaning 'begun'

incidence
noun **1** the extent of a thing or the range within which it happens: *the **incidence** of disease*
2 the falling, or direction or manner of falling, of a ray of light, etc., on a surface

incident
noun an event or happening

Word history: Middle English, from Latin word meaning 'befalling'

incidental (in-suh-den-tuhl)
adjective happening at the same time as something more important: ***incidental** results*

incinerate (in-sin-uh-rayt)
verb to burn to ashes: *We **incinerated** the rubbish. / The house was **incinerated** in the bushfire.*

Word history: Medieval Latin, from Latin

incinerator
noun a container for burning things in (***furnace***)

incipient (in-si-pee-uhnt)
adjective just beginning to exist or appear

Word building: **incipience** *noun*
Word history: Latin

incise (in-suyz)
verb to cut marks, etc., upon

Word building: **incised** *adjective*
Word history: French, from Latin word meaning 'cut into'

incision (in-sizh-uhn)
noun **1** a cut, gash, or notch (***opening***, ***score***, ***slit***)
2 a cutting into, especially for medical purposes
3 sharpness, especially of wit, etc.

Word history: Middle English, from Latin

incisive (in-suy-siv)
adjective **1** sharp and penetrating: *an **incisive** tone of voice* (***biting***, ***keen***)
2 clear and acute: ***incisive** thoughts*
3 used for cutting: *the **incisive** teeth*

Word building: **incisiveness** *noun*

incisor (in-suy-zuh)
noun a tooth in the front part of the jaw, used for cutting or biting

Word history: Neo-Latin

incite (in-suyt)
verb to urge on or stir up: *He **incited** the crowd to riot.*

Word history: late Middle English, from Latin word meaning 'set in motion'

incite / insight
Don't confuse **incite** with **insight**, which is an intuition or sudden understanding that you have. It is pronounced with the stress on the first syllable in-:

Her books reveal an insight into the problems of growing up.

incitement
noun **1** the act of inciting
2 something that incites: *The film was criticised for being an **incitement** to violence.*

inclination (in-kluh-nay-shuhn)
noun a tendency or preference of the mind or will: *They showed little **inclination** to do as they were told.* (***desire***, ***willingness***, ***wish***)

incline (in-kluyn)
verb **1** to slant or lean (***list***, ***slope***, ***tilt***, ***tip***)
2 to lean or tend towards in your mind
noun (in-kluyn) **3** a slope (***gradient***, ***pitch***)

Word history: Latin

include
verb to consist of or contain as a part: *Education **includes** what we learn both at home and at school.* (***comprise***, ***cover***, ***embrace***, ***incorporate***, ***involve***)

Word building: **inclusion** *noun*
Word history: Middle English, from Latin word meaning 'shut in'

inclusive
adjective **1** being included for consideration: *everyone from ages six to ten **inclusive***
2 including a great deal: *an **inclusive** coverage of the story* (***comprehensive***, ***wide-ranging***)

inclusive language
noun language which does not discriminate against a person for any reason, for example, race, sex, age, religion

Look up **non-sexist language** and **racist language**.

incognito (in-kog-nee-toh)
adverb with your name or appearance changed so you won't be recognised: *He's travelling **incognito**.*

Word history: Italian, from Latin word meaning 'unknown'

incoherent (in-koh-hear-ruhnt)
adjective **1** not arranged or connected properly: *an **incoherent** sentence* (***disjointed***, ***rambling***)
2 showing unordered thought or language: ***incoherent** with rage*

income
noun the money someone earns from their work or investments (***commission***, ***earnings***, ***profit***, ***salary***, ***wage***)

income tax
noun a tax which the government sets each year, based on how much money you earn

incommunicado (in-kuh-myooh-nuh-kah-doh)
adjective especially of a prisoner, not allowed any communication with others

Word history: from Spanish word meaning 'deprived of communication'

incomparable (in-kom-puh-ruh-buhl, in-kom-pruh-buhl)
adjective not able to be equalled: ***incomparable** beauty*

incompatible (in-kuhm-pat-uh-buhl)
adjective **1** not able to exist together in peace
2 of two or more propositions, not logically able to be true at the same time (***inconsistent***, ***irreconcilable***)

Word use: The opposite of this is **compatible**.

incompetent (in-kom-puh-tuhnt)
adjective **1** lacking the necessary skill or ability: *an **incompetent** worker* (***amateurish***, ***clumsy***, ***fumbling***, ***inept***, ***unskilful***)
noun **2** an incompetent person

Word use: The opposite of definition 1 is **competent** or **skilled**.
Word building: **incompetence** *noun*
Word history: from Late Latin word meaning 'insufficient'

inconclusive (in-kuhn-klooh-siv)
adjective **1** not sufficient as to settle a question: ***inconclusive** evidence*
2 without final results: ***inconclusive** experiments*

Word use: The opposite of this is **conclusive**.

incongruous (in-cong-grooh-uhs)
adjective out of place or unsuitable: *The man in the business suit looked **incongruous** at the barbecue.*

Word building: **incongruity** *noun*
Word history: Latin

inconsequential
adjective **1** of little or no importance (***insignificant***, ***trivial***)
2 not logical or relevant (***incoherent***, ***irrational***)

inconsiderate (in-kuhn-sid-uh-ruht, in-kuhn-sid-ruht)
adjective **1** without proper regard for the rights or feelings of others: *It was **inconsiderate** of him to forget.* (***self-centred***, ***selfish***, ***thoughtless***)
2 thoughtless

inconsistent
adjective **1** lacking agreement between the different parts or elements: *an **inconsistent** argument.* (***illogical***, ***self-contradictory***)
2 lacking agreement or not making sense when taken together: *His story was **inconsistent** with the evidence.* | *The dry ground was **inconsistent** with the rainy weather.* (***contradictory***, ***discordant***, ***incompatible***, ***incongruous***)

Word building: **inconsistency** *noun*

inconvenient
adjective awkward or causing trouble: *an **inconvenient** time* | *an **inconvenient** way to travel*

Word building: **inconvenience** *noun*
Word history: Middle English, from Latin word meaning 'not agreeing'

incorporate (in-kaw-puh-rayt)
verb to include and make part of: *We **incorporated** several ideas into the design of the house.* (***embrace***, ***involve***, ***subsume***, ***take in***)

Word history: Middle English, from Late Latin word meaning 'embodied'

incorrect
adjective wrong or false: *Her answer was **incorrect**.* | *an **incorrect** statement*

incorrigible (in-ko-ruhj-uh-buhl)
adjective too bad to ever improve: *an **incorrigible** liar* (***brazen***, ***obdurate***, ***obstinate***, ***shameless***)

increase
verb **1** to make greater: *to **increase** your knowledge* (***amplify***, ***augment***, ***boost***, ***enlarge***, ***expand***)
2 to become greater or more in number: *Australia's population **increases** every year.* (***grow***, ***mount***, ***multiply***, ***redouble***)

Word building: **increase** *noun*
Word history: Middle English, from Anglo-French, from Latin

incredible
adjective hard to believe: ***incredible** bravery* | *an **incredible** story* (***far-fetched***, ***implausible***, ***improbable***, ***unbelievable***, ***unlikely***)

Word building: **incredibility** *noun*

incredulous
adjective **1** not willing to believe
2 showing lack of belief: *an **incredulous** smile* (***disbelieving***, ***sceptical***)

Word building: **incredulity** *noun*

increment (in-kruh-muhnt, ing-kruh-muhnt)
noun **1** something added or gained
2 profit
3 an increase in salary as payment for increases in skill or experience
4 *Mathematics*
a the difference between two values of a variable
b the increase of a function due to this

Word building: **incremental** *adjective*
Word history: Middle English, from Latin word meaning 'an increase'

incriminate (in-krim-uh-nayt)
verb **1** to charge with a crime or fault
2 to involve in crime or wrongdoing, or appear to do so: *Her evidence at the trial **incriminated** him.*

Word use: The opposite of this is **exonerate**.
Word building: **incriminatory** *adjective*
Word history: from Medieval Latin word meaning 'accused of a crime'

incubate (<u>in</u>-kyooh-bayt, <u>ing</u>-kyooh-bayt)
verb to hatch by keeping warm naturally or artificially: *The hen **incubated** the eggs by sitting on them for three weeks. | We are **incubating** these eggs under a warm lamp.*

Word building: **incubation** *noun*
Word history: from Latin word meaning 'hatched', 'sat on'

incubator
noun **1** an apparatus for hatching eggs artificially, usually a case heated by a lamp
2 a boxlike apparatus in which prematurely born babies are kept at the right temperature for them

inculcate (<u>in</u>-kul-kayt)
verb to place in the mind by repeated statement: *At each assembly the rules were **inculcated** into the students.* (***impress, instil***)

Word history: from Latin word meaning 'stamped in', 'impressed upon'

incumbent (in-<u>kum</u>-buhnt)
adjective **1** resting on you as an obligation: *Visiting my aunt is a duty **incumbent** upon me. | It is **incumbent** on you to warn of the danger.*
noun **2** the holder of an office: *She's done a better job than the last **incumbent**.*

Word history: Middle English, from Latin word meaning 'leaning upon'

incur
verb to bring upon yourself: *to **incur** someone's anger | to **incur** debts*

Verb forms: I **incurred**, I have **incurred**, I am **incurring**
Word history: Middle English, from Latin word meaning 'run into', 'or against'

incursion
noun a sudden, uninvited, attacking entrance: *an **incursion** into enemy territory | an **incursion** on my privacy* (***attack, invasion, sortie***)

Word history: Middle English, from Latin word meaning 'onset'

indebted (in-<u>det</u>-uhd)
adjective **1** owing money
2 feeling that you owe a debt of gratitude for help, a favour, or the like: *I am **indebted** to you for helping me with my studies.* (***appreciative, beholden, grateful, obliged, thankful***)

Word building: **indebtedness** *noun*

indecent
adjective **1** not proper or in good taste: *His swearing was **indecent**.*
2 obscene: *He was had up for **indecent** behaviour.* (***corrupt, degenerate, depraved, immoral, perverted***)

Word building: **indecency** *noun*

indeed
adverb truly or in fact: ***Indeed** he did it.*

indefatigable (in-duh-<u>fat</u>-ig-uh-buhl)
adjective not able to be tired out: *an **indefatigable** worker*

Word history: Latin

indefensible
adjective **1** not able to be excused or justified: *an **indefensible** remark*
2 not able to be defended by military force: *an **indefensible** coastline*

indefinite (in-<u>def</u>-uh-nuht)
adjective **1** without fixed limit: *an **indefinite** number*
2 not clear or vague: *an **indefinite** feeling | an **indefinite** figure* (***approximate, faint, hazy, uncertain, woolly***)
3 *Grammar* not limiting or making particular, as the indefinite pronoun *some*

indefinite article
noun an article (*a, an* or *some*) which implies that the noun is not yet identified

Look up **articles in grammar: indefinite articles.**

indelible (in-<u>del</u>-uh-buhl)
adjective **1** not able to be removed: *He made an **indelible** impression on us.*
2 making marks which can't be removed or rubbed out: *an **indelible** pencil*

Word history: from Latin word meaning 'that cannot be destroyed'

indelicate
adjective offensive to a sense of what is proper or modest: *an **indelicate** suggestion* (***coarse, unrefined***)

Word building: **indelicacy** *noun*

indemnify (in-<u>dem</u>-nuh-fuy)
verb **1** to pay back for damage, loss, costs, etc.
2 to promise to pay for possible loss, damage, etc. (***cover, insure***)

Verb forms: I **indemnified**, I have **indemnified**, I am **indemnifying**

indemnity (in-<u>dem</u>-nuh-tee)
noun **1** protection or security, for example through insurance, against damage or loss
2 payment for damage or loss
3 legal exemption from normal penalties, often given to public officers, etc.

Noun forms: The plural is **indemnities**.
Word history: late Middle English, from Latin word meaning 'unharmed'

indent
verb to set in or back from the margin: *to **indent** the first line of a paragraph*

Word building: **indentation** *noun*
Word history: Middle English, from Old French word meaning 'tooth'

indenture
noun **1** a formal, written agreement
2 an agreement by which a person, such as an apprentice, is bound to work for another
verb **3** to bind by indenture, especially an apprentice

Word history: Middle English, from Old French word meaning 'indentation'

independent
adjective **1** able to make up your own mind
2 not needing or relying on the help of others (***autonomous, self-sufficient***)
3 having to do with popular music which is not mainstream but produced by an independent label
4 having to do with a film which is produced independently rather than by an established studio

Word use: The opposite of definitions 1 and 2 is **dependent**.
Word building: **independence** *noun*

indeterminate (in-duh-ter-muh-nuht)
adjective **1** not fixed, definite or certain: *an **indeterminate** date in the future*
2 *Mathematics* of a quantity, having no fixed value

index
noun **1** an alphabetical list of names, places or subjects in a book, showing their page numbers
2 in maths, the small number which shows how many times another number has to be multiplied by itself. For example, in 10^4 (10 to the power of 4, which means 10 × 10 × 10 × 10) the index is ^{4}.
verb **3** to provide with an index: *to **index** a book*

Noun forms: The plural is **indexes** or, especially for definition 2, **indices** (in-duh-seez).
Word history: Middle English, from Latin word meaning 'index', 'forefinger', 'sign'

indexation
noun the adjustment of one variable in the light of changes in another variable

Word use: Look up **wage indexation**.

index finger
noun → **forefinger**

Indian summer
noun **1** a period of summer weather coming after the end of the summer season
2 a happy and peaceful time experienced in old age

indicate
verb **1** to point out or point to: *I **indicated** the right way to go.*
2 to be a sign of, or show: *His tiredness **indicates** he is not well.*

Word building: **indication** *noun*
Word history: Latin

indicative (in-dik-uh-tiv)
adjective **1** *Grammar* having to do with the verb mood used in statements of actuality, questions, etc., as opposed to statements of possibility, wish, etc. In the sentence *John plays football*, the verb *plays* is in the indicative mood.
phrase **2 indicative of**, showing: *Shiny hair is **indicative of** good health.*

Word history: late Middle English, from Latin

For more information about the **indicative** mood (definition 1), look up **verbs: mood**.

indicator
noun **1** something that points to or shows something: *This rain is an **indicator** that the drought is over.* (***clue***, ***guide***, ***marker***, ***pointer***, ***sign***)
2 *Chemistry* a substance which shows (for example, by changing its colour) the point at which a certain reaction is completed

indices (in-duh-seez)
noun a plural of **index**

indict (in-duyt)
verb to charge with an offence or crime (***bring to book***, ***accuse***)

Word building: **indictment** *noun*
Word history: Middle English, from Anglo-French word meaning 'accuse', 'indict'

indifferent
adjective **1** showing no interest or concern: *When I spoke of my grief she was **indifferent**.* (***callous***, ***hard-hearted***, ***impervious***, ***unfeeling***)
2 not very good: *She is an **indifferent** actress. / He is in **indifferent** health.* (***inferior***, ***mediocre***, ***ordinary***, ***second-rate***)

Word building: **indifference** *noun*
Word history: Middle English, from Latin

indigenous (in-dij-uh-nuhs)
adjective **1** native to a particular area or country: *Kangaroos are **indigenous** to Australia but rabbits are not.*
2 Indigenous, having to do with Aboriginal and Torres Strait Islander people: *Indigenous issues*

Word building: **indigene** *noun*
Word history: from Latin word meaning 'native'

indigent (in-duh-juhnt)
adjective needy (***destitute***, ***poor***)

Word building: **indigence** *noun*
Word history: Middle English, from Latin

indigestible (in-duh-jes-tuh-buhl)
adjective not able to be digested: *Unripe fruit is **indigestible**.*

indigestion (in-duh-jes-chuhn, in-duy-jes-chuhn)
noun pain in your stomach caused by difficulty in digesting food

Word use: Another name is **dyspepsia**.

indignation
noun anger at something you think is unjust or wicked

Word building: **indignant** *adjective*

indignity (in-dig-nuh-tee)
noun treatment which makes you feel embarrassed and foolish: *the **indignity** of being sent from the room*

Noun forms: The plural is **indignities**.
Word history: from Latin word meaning 'unworthiness'

indigo (in-dig-oh)
noun **1** a blue dye
2 a deep violet blue colour

Word building: **indigo** *adjective*
Word history: Spanish or Portuguese, from Latin word meaning 'indigo'

indirect object
noun *Grammar* the person or thing that receives something through the action of the verb

Compare these sentences:
Buy your friend the book.
Give me the book.
The phrases *your friend* and *me* are **indirect objects**, and *the book* is the **direct object**.
Indirect objects can always be replaced by a phrase beginning with *to* or *for*:
Buy the book for your friend.
Give the book to me.
In a sense, this object is only 'indirectly' acted upon by the verb. For more information on this, look up **objects in grammar**.

indirect question
noun a question which is reported rather than quoted directly

Indirect questions are those which are reported rather than quoted directly.

'Why are you doing that?' he asked. (direct question)

He asked me why I was doing that. (indirect question)

Notice that in the indirect question, there is a shift of tense. The reported question is moved into the past tense to match the main verb in the sentence (*asked*). Note also that there is no question mark in the indirect question.

For more information, look up **indirect speech**.

indirect speech
noun speech which is reported from the viewpoint of the witness, rather that in the actual words used by the speaker

When a masked man says to his accomplice:

'You get the keys of the safe.' (direct speech)

it might be reported as:

The masked man told his assistant to get the keys of the safe. (indirect speech)

You can see the small but quite important differences. The indirect speech of the report puts it all into the past tense, making it narrative rather than drama. ('Says' becomes 'told'.) The word 'told' also shows the reader that what the man said was a kind of command. Indirect speech gives you the gist of what was said, but does not claim to tell you the actual words. That's why there are no quotation marks in indirect speech.

For more discussion of this, look up **direct speech**.

Note that another name for indirect speech is **reported speech**.

indiscreet
adjective not discreet: ***indiscreet** behaviour*

Word building: **indiscreetly** *adverb*

indiscretion
noun **1** lack of discretion
2 an indiscreet act or step

indiscriminate (in-duhs-krim-uh-nuht)
adjective making no choices or distinction: ***indiscriminate** in his friendships* | ***indiscriminate** killing* (***arbitrary**, **haphazard**, **hit-and-miss**, **random***)

indispensable
adjective absolutely necessary

Word building: **indispensability** *noun*

indisposed
adjective slightly sick or unwell: ***indisposed** with a cold* (***ailing**, **crook**, **ill**, **off-colour**, **out of sorts***)

Word building: **indisposition** *noun*

individual
adjective **1** single or separate: *the **individual** members of the class*
2 meant for one person or thing only: ***individual** servings* | ***individual** attention*
noun **3** a single person or thing
4 *Colloquial* a person: *a strange **individual***

Word use: The opposite of definitions 1 and 2 is **collective**.
Word building: **individually** *adverb*
Word history: Middle English, from Latin word meaning 'indivisible'

individuality (in-duh-vij-ooh-al-uh-tee)
noun the quality that makes you different from other people

indoctrinate (in-dok-truh-nayt)
verb to instruct so thoroughly that the ideas are accepted without question

Word building: **indoctrination** *noun*
Word history: from Latin word meaning 'teaching'

indolent (in-duh-luhnt)
adjective tending to avoid work (***idle**, **lazy**, **slack**, **slothful***)

Word building: **indolence** *noun*
Word history: from Late Latin word meaning 'not suffering'

indomitable (in-dom-uh-tuh-buhl)
adjective not able to be defeated or overcome: *an **indomitable** person* | ***indomitable** courage*

Word history: from Latin word meaning 'tame'

indoor
adjective happening, used, living, etc., inside a house or building: ***indoor** games* | ***indoor** plant*

indoors
adverb inside a house or building: *Let's go **indoors** to have dinner.*

indubitable (in-dyooh-buh-tuh-buhl)
adjective not able to be doubted (***certain**, **incontrovertible**, **undeniable***)

induce
verb **1** to persuade or cause to decide: *I will **induce** him to go.* (***coax**, **convince**, **influence**, **talk into***)
2 to cause or bring on: *Bad news **induces** anxiety.* (***incur**, **occasion**, **produce**, **provoke***)

Word building: **inducement** *noun*
Word history: Middle English, from Latin word meaning 'lead in', 'bring in', 'persuade'

induct
verb to install, especially formally, in a place, office, etc.

Word history: Middle English, from Latin

induction (in-duk-shuhn)
noun Physics the process by which a body with electrical or magnetic properties produces such properties in a nearby body without touching it directly

Word history: Middle English, from Latin

indulge
verb **1** to give in to: *I **indulged** his wish for a lazy afternoon.*
phrase **2 indulge in**, to satisfy your own desire for: *to **indulge in** chocolates*

Word history: from Latin word meaning 'be kind', 'yield', 'grant'

indulgence
noun **1** the act or process of indulging or satisfying a desire: *Too much **indulgence** in eating is not good for you.*
2 the act of indulging the wishes or behaviour of others: *She showed **indulgence** towards her children.*

Word building: **indulgent** *adjective*

industrial
adjective **1** having to do with industry or industries: ***industrial** waste* | ***industrial** training* | ***industrial** worker*
2 having many manufacturing industries: *an **industrial** nation*

industrial action
noun organised action such as a strike or go-slow, taken by a group of workers, to gain better pay, conditions, etc., or an objective thought to be in the general public good

industrialise
noun to introduce industry into an area or country on a large scale

Word use: You can also use **industrialize.**
Word building: **industrialisation** *noun*

industrialist
noun someone who owns or manages an industrial business

industrial revolution
noun **1** the social, economic and physical changes that happen in a country when mechanised industry is introduced on a wide scale
2 the period in history when such a development took place in England in the late 18th and early 19th centuries

Word use: You can also use **Industrial Revolution** for definition 2.

industrious
adjective hard-working: *He is an **industrious** student.* (***busy***, ***diligent***, ***energetic***, ***flat out***)

Word history: from Latin word meaning 'diligent'

industry (<u>in</u>-duhs-tree)
noun **1** all businesses that produce or manufacture things: *the growth of **industry** in Australia*
2 a particular type of manufacturing business: *the steel **industry***
3 any large-scale business activity: *the tourist **industry** | the pastoral **industry***
4 hard, careful and conscientious work (***efforts***, ***exertions***, ***labour***)

Noun forms: The plural is **industries.**
Word history: Middle English, from Latin word meaning 'diligence'

inebriated (in-<u>ee</u>-bree-ayt-uhd)
adjective drunk (***befuddled***, ***intoxicated***)

Word history: Latin

ineffable (in-<u>ef</u>-uh-buhl)
adjective **1** not able to be spoken or expressed, because of extreme emotion, etc.: ***ineffable** joy*
2 too holy to be spoken

Word history: Middle English, from Latin

ineffectual (in-uh-<u>fek</u>-chooh-uhl)
adjective **1** without satisfactory effect: *an **ineffectual** remedy | an **ineffectual** effort* (***futile***, ***impractical***, ***ineffective***, ***useless***, ***vain***)
2 powerless: *an **ineffectual** person* (***feeble***, ***gutless***, ***impotent***, ***powerless***, ***useless***)

inept
adjective awkward or unskilful: *an **inept** attempt to chop wood* (***amateurish***, ***clumsy***, ***inexperienced***, ***fumbling***, ***incompetent***)

Word use: The opposite of this is **competent**.
Word building: **ineptitude** *noun*
Word history: Latin

inequality
noun **1** the condition of being unequal or uneven
2 *Mathematics* an expression of two unequal quantities connected by the sign > or <, for example, $a > b$, 'a is greater than b'; $a < b$, 'a is less than b'

Word history: late Middle English, from Medieval Latin word meaning 'unevenness'

inert (in-<u>ert</u>)
adjective **1** having no power of action, movement, or resistance: ***inert** matter*
2 without active properties: *an **inert** drug*

Word building: **inertness** *noun*
Word history: from Latin word meaning 'unskilled', 'idle'

inertia (in-<u>er</u>-shuh)
noun **1** sluggishness or lack of energy: ***Inertia** overcame us in the midday heat.*
2 *Physics*
a the tendency of matter to continue in a state of rest or to move uniformly in a straight line
b a similar property of a force: *electric **inertia***

Word use: The opposite of definition 1 is **energy**.
Word history: from Latin word meaning 'lack of skill', 'inactivity'

inestimable (in-<u>est</u>-uh-muh-buhl)
adjective too great to be measured or estimated

Word history: Middle English, from French, from Latin

inevitable
adjective not able to be avoided: *an **inevitable** result*

Word building: **inevitability** *noun* **inevitably** *adverb*
Word history: Middle English, from Latin

inexcusable
adjective so bad that it cannot be forgiven: *It was an **inexcusable** invasion of their privacy.*

inexorable (in-<u>eks</u>-uh-ruh-buhl, in-<u>egz</u>-uh-ruh-buhl)
adjective **1** not able to be changed: ***inexorable** facts*
2 not to be persuaded, or influenced by prayers or begging (***firm***, ***unyielding***)

Word building: **inexorability** *noun*
Word history: Latin

inexpensive
adjective not costing much: *an **inexpensive** toy* (***cheap***, ***dirt-cheap***, ***discount***, ***no-frills***)

infallible (in-<u>fal</u>-uh-buhl)
adjective **1** never being wrong or making a mistake: *an **infallible** judge of character*
2 able to be relied on completely: *an **infallible** law of nature | an **infallible** cure for hiccups*

Word building: **infallibility** *noun* **infallibly** *adverb*
Word history: late Middle English, from Medieval Latin

infamous (<u>in</u>-fuh-muhs)
adjective deserving or causing a very bad name or reputation: *an **infamous** act*

Word building: **infamy** *noun*
Word history: Middle English, from Latin

infancy
noun the time of being an infant

infant
noun a baby or very young child

Word history: from Latin word meaning 'young child', properly adjective, 'not speaking'

infantile (<u>in</u>-fuhn-tuyl)
adjective **1** having to do with infants: ***infantile** diseases*
2 childish or like an infant: ***infantile** behaviour*

Word use: The opposite of this is **mature**.
Word history: Late Latin

infantry
noun soldiers who fight on foot with hand weapons

Word history: French, from Italian word meaning 'youth', 'foot soldier'

infatuated (in-<u>fat</u>-chooh-ayt-uhd)
adjective blindly or foolishly in love

Word building: **infatuate** *verb* **infatuation** *noun*

infect
verb **1** to give germs or a disease to: *to **infect** a wound | She had measles and **infected** the whole family.*
2 to affect by spreading from one to another: *His discontent **infected** the class.*

Word history: Middle English, from Latin word meaning 'put in', 'dyed', 'imbued', 'infected'

infection
noun **1** an infecting with germs of disease
2 something, such as a germ, that infects
3 the state of being infected

infectious
adjective **1** passed on by infection: *an **infectious** disease*
2 tending to spread from one to another: *Laughter is **infectious**.*

Word building: **infectiousness** *noun*

infectious / contagious

Both these words mean something similar, but there is a difference when you use them to describe a disease.

An **infectious** illness is one that can spread from one person to another:

> *Influenza is an infectious disease but appendicitis isn't.*

A **contagious** disease is an **infectious** disease which is spread by contact, either by direct contact with the sick person or by indirect contact with their clothes or bedding.

infer (in-<u>fer</u>)
verb to form an opinion after considering all the facts and information: *He **inferred** from the spy's report that the enemy would attack.* (**conclude**, **deduce**, **gather**, **reason**)

Verb forms: I **inferred**, I have **inferred**, I am **inferring**
Word history: from Latin word meaning 'bring in or on', 'infer'

infer / imply

Look up **imply / infer**.

inference
noun Mathematics the process of reaching a conclusion by logical reasoning from a set of premises

inferior (in-<u>fear</u>-ree-uh)
adjective **1** lower in rank or position: *an **inferior** officer*
2 lower in value or quality: ***inferior** work* (***crummy***, ***defective***, ***mediocre***, ***poor***, ***shoddy***)

Word building: **inferiority** *noun*
Word history: Middle English, from Latin

inferno
noun a place that seems like hell because of heat or fire

Noun forms: The plural is **infernos**.
Word history: Italian word meaning 'hell', from Latin word meaning 'underground'

infest
verb to spread or swarm over in great numbers: *Snakes **infest** this part of the bush.*

Word building: **infestation** *noun*
Word history: late Middle English, from Latin word meaning 'assail', 'molest'

infidel (<u>in</u>-fuh-del)
noun Old-fashioned someone who doesn't accept a particular religious faith (***heathen***, ***pagan***)

Word use: This is a word that Christians and Muslims used of each other in the past.
Word building: **infidel** *adjective*
Word history: late Middle English, from Latin word meaning 'unfaithful', Late Latin word meaning 'unbelieving'

infidelity (in-fuh-<u>del</u>-uh-tee)
noun **1** unfaithfulness, especially within a sexual relationship
2 an act of unfaithfulness
3 lack of religious faith

Noun forms: The plural is **infidelities**.

infiltrate
verb to secretly join or enter, usually to work against: *She **infiltrated** the enemy camp.*

Word building: **infiltration** *noun* **infiltrator** *noun*

infinite (<u>in</u>-fuh-nuht)
adjective endless or having no limits: *The desert seemed **infinite** to the weary travellers.* (***boundless***, ***limitless***, ***never-ending***)

Word use: The opposite is **finite**.
Word building: **infinity** *noun*
Word history: Middle English, from Latin

infinitesimal (in-fin-uh-<u>tez</u>-muhl, in-fin-uh-<u>tes</u>-uh-muhl)
adjective immeasurably small

infinitive (in-<u>fin</u>-uh-tiv)
noun **1** the grammatical form of a verb that you use after certain other verbs or after 'to', such as 'come' in *I didn't come* and *I wanted to come*
2 having to do with the infinitive: *an **infinitive** verb*

Word history: late Middle English, from Late Latin word meaning 'unlimited', 'indefinite'

infirm
adjective weak in body or health (***ailing***, ***debilitated***, ***failing***, ***infirm***, ***peaky***)

Word building: **infirmity** *noun*
Word history: Middle English, from Latin

infirmary
noun a kind of hospital: *the school's **infirmary***

Noun forms: The plural is **infirmaries**.
Word history: from Latin word meaning 'infirm'

inflame
verb to make angry or passionate: *The Prime Minister **inflamed** the crowd with her fiery speech.*

Word building: **inflammatory** *adjective*
Word history: Middle English, from Old French, from Latin word meaning 'set on fire'

inflammable
adjective flammable

Word building: **inflammability** *noun*

inflammable / flammable
Look up **flammable / inflammable**.

inflammation
noun a red, painful, and often swollen area on the body, caused by an infection

Word building: **inflamed** *adjective*

inflate
verb **1** to swell with gas or air: *to **inflate** a balloon | The rubber boat **inflated**.*
2 to cause a large rise in: *to **inflate** prices*

Word use: The opposite of this is **deflate**.
Word building: **inflatable** *adjective* **inflationary** *adjective*
Word history: from Latin word meaning 'puffed up'

inflation
noun an economic condition in which there is a large rise in prices and cost of living

Word use: The opposite is **deflation**.
Word building: **inflationary** *adjective*

inflection (in-<u>flek</u>-shuhn)
noun **1** change in pitch or tone of voice (***modulation***, ***transition***)
2 *Grammar*
a the putting of an ending on to the basic part of a word to make the word do a different job in a sentence
b the set of forms of a single word changed in this way
3 a curve or angle

Word use: You can also use **inflexion**.
Word building: **inflectional** *adjective*

inflict
verb to cause to be experienced or suffered: *to **inflict** a wound*

Word building: **infliction** *noun*
Word history: from Latin word meaning 'struck against'

influence
noun some force or power that affects or produces a change in someone or something else: *He is a good **influence** on his brother.*

Word building: **influence** *verb* **influential** *adjective*
Word history: Middle English, from Medieval Latin word meaning 'a flowing in', from Latin

influenza
noun a sickness caused by a virus which affects the nose and throat and causes high temperatures and tiredness

Word use: The short form is **flu**.
Word history: Italian word meaning 'influx of disease', 'epidemic', 'influenza'

influx
noun a flowing in: ***influx** of water | There was an **influx** of migrants to Australia when gold was discovered.*

Word history: from Latin word meaning 'flow in'

inform
verb to give news or knowledge to: *I **informed** him of your success.* (***advise***, ***instruct***, ***notify***, ***put in the picture***, ***tell***)

Word building: **informative** *adjective*
Word history: Latin

informal
adjective **1** casual or without ceremony or formality: *an **informal** visit* (***easygoing***, ***relaxed***, ***unofficial***)
2 *Australian*, *NZ* (of a vote) invalid: *an **informal** vote*
phrase **3 vote informal**, *Australian* to mark a ballot paper incorrectly so that the vote will not be counted

Word building: **informality** *noun*

informal language
noun language which is suited to informal conversation, including colloquialisms, contractions, and the like

informant
noun someone who informs or gives information

information
noun knowledge or news: *tourist **information*** (***gossip***, ***intelligence***, ***the dope***, ***the drum***)

Word history: Latin

information portal
noun a website which provides information about an organisation: *I found her contact number on the company's **information portal**.*

Word use: You can also use **enterprise information portal**.

information report
noun a written or spoken text type which presents facts about an entire class of people, animals or objects

information technology
noun → **IT**

informer
noun someone who tells on someone else, especially to the police

infra-red
noun the invisible part of the spectrum of light which has a wavelength longer than that of visible red light

Word building: **infra-red** *adjective*

infrastructure (<u>in</u>-fruh-struk-chuh)
noun the basic framework or underlying foundation: *the **infrastructure** of an organisation or a system*

infringe
verb to disobey: *to* ***infringe*** *a law* | *They* ***infringed*** *the rules of the club.* (***defy***, ***flout***, ***transgress***, ***violate***)

Word building: **infringement** *noun*
Word history: from Latin word meaning 'break off'

infuriate (in-fyooh-ree-ayt)
verb to make very angry (***anger***, ***drive someone up the wall***, ***enrage***, ***incense***)

Word building: **infuriating** *adjective* **infuriation** *noun*
Word history: from Medieval Latin word meaning 'enraged'

infuse
verb to soak in hot water to draw out the flavour: *to* ***infuse*** *tea*

Word building: **infuser** *noun* **infusion** *noun*
Word history: Middle English, from Latin word meaning 'poured in or on'

ingenious (in-jeen-ee-uhs)
adjective **1** cleverly made or invented: *an* ***ingenious*** *machine*
2 clever at working out ways of doing and making things: *an* ***ingenious*** *inventor*

Word building: **ingenuity** *noun*
Word history: Middle English, from Latin word meaning 'of good natural talents'

ingenuous (in-jen-yooh-uhs)
adjective open, straightforward, sometimes easily deceived (***artless***, ***innocent***)

Word history: from Latin word meaning 'native', 'innate', 'freeborn', 'noble', 'frank'

ingest (in-jest)
verb to put or take into the body: *to* ***ingest*** *food*

Word building: **ingestion** *noun*
Word history: from Latin word meaning 'carried', or 'poured in'

ingot (ing-guht)
noun a block of metal which has been melted and poured into a mould

Word history: from Middle English word meaning 'mould for metal'

ingrained
adjective fixed firmly and deep: ***ingrained*** *habits* | ***ingrained*** *dirt*

ingrate
noun an ungrateful person

Word history: Middle English, from Latin word meaning 'unpleasing', 'not grateful'

ingratiate (in-gray-shee-ayt)
verb to act in a way that will make others pleased with you: *He* ***ingratiated*** *himself with his boss.*

Word building: **ingratiatingly** *adverb* **ingratiation** *noun*
Word history: Latin

ingratitude
noun failure to be grateful

ingredient
noun one of the parts of a mixture or a whole: *an* ***ingredient*** *in a cake* | *An* ***ingredient*** *of his success was his hard work.*

Word history: late Middle English, from Latin word meaning 'entering'

inhabit
verb to live or dwell in: *Aboriginal people* ***inhabited*** *Australia long before Europeans came.* (***occupy***, ***populate***)

Word building: **inhabitable** *adjective* **inhabited** *adjective* **inhabitant** *noun*
Word history: Latin

inhale
verb to breathe in: *to* ***inhale*** *the fresh country air* | ***Inhale*** *deeply for good health.*

Word use: The opposite of this is **exhale**.
Word building: **inhalant** *noun* **inhalation** *noun*
Word history: Latin

inhaler
noun → **puffer**

inherent (in-he-ruhnt, in-hear-ruhnt)
adjective existing in something as a permanent and inseparable part or quality

Word history: from Latin word meaning 'sticking in or to'

inherit
verb **1** to receive as a gift from someone who has died: *Susan* ***inherited*** *some money and a stamp collection from her aunt.*
2 to get, as a family characteristic, through your parents: *He has* ***inherited*** *his mother's blue eyes.*

Word building: **inheritance** *noun*
Word history: Middle English, from Old French, from Latin word meaning 'inherit'

inhibit
verb to hold back or hinder: *Black plastic spread around your plants should* ***inhibit*** *the growth of weeds.* (***block***, ***frustrate***, ***hamper***, ***impede***, ***retard***)

Word building: **inhibition** *noun*
Word history: late Middle English, from Latin word meaning 'held back', 'restrained'

inhibited
adjective shy: *an* ***inhibited*** *young boy*

inhuman (in-hyooh-muhn)
adjective **1** lacking natural human feeling or sympathy for others (***brutal***, ***callous***)
2 not human

Word history: late Middle English, from Latin

inhumane (in-hyooh-mayn)
adjective lacking humanity or kindness

Word use: The opposite of this is **humane**.

inimical
adjective acting as an enemy or in an unfavourable way: *an* ***inimical*** *attitude* | *a climate* ***inimical*** *to health* (***hostile***, ***unfriendly***)

Word history: late Latin, from Latin word meaning 'unfriendly', 'an enemy'

inimitable (i-nim-it-uh-buhl)
adjective not able to be imitated, unique

Word building: **inimitability** *noun* **inimitableness** *noun*

iniquity (in-ik-wuh-tee)
noun wickedness: *He will be punished for his* ***iniquity***.

Noun forms: The plural is **iniquities**.
Word building: **iniquitous** *adjective*
Word history: Middle English, from Latin word meaning 'injustice'

initial
adjective **1** having to do with the beginning: *The **initial** plan was later changed.*
noun **2** the first letter of a word or name
verb **3** to mark or sign with the initials of your name

Verb forms: I **initialled**, I have **initialled**, I am **initialling**
Word history: from Latin word meaning 'of the beginning'

initialism
noun an abbreviation formed from the initial letters of a sequence of words, with each letter pronounced separately: *LPG is an **initialism** of 'liquefied petroleum gas'.*

Word use: Compare this with **acronym**.

initiate (i-nish-ee-ayt)
verb **1** to begin or set going: *I want to **initiate** an annual fun run at our school.* (***establish***, ***found***, ***institute***, ***launch***, ***pioneer***)
2 to admit into a society or club with a formal ceremony

Word building: **initiate** (i-nish-ee-uht, i-nish-ee-ayt) *noun* **initiation** *noun* **initiator** *noun*
Word history: from Latin word meaning 'begun', 'initiated'

initiative (i-nish-ee-uh-tiv)
noun **1** a first act or step: *to take the **initiative***
2 readiness or ability to set something going (***enterprise***, ***get-up-and-go***)

inject
verb to use a syringe and needle to force a fluid into: *The doctor **injected** him with a pain-killing drug.*

Word building: **injection** *noun*
Word history: from Latin word meaning 'thrown or put in'

injunction (in-jungk-shuhn)
noun **1** *Law* an order by a judge or court telling someone to do a particular thing
2 a command, order or direction

Word history: from Late Latin word meaning 'command'

injure
verb to hurt or cause harm to: *The sharp rock **injured** him when he fell. | Gossip often **injures** innocent people.* (***damage***, ***hurt***, ***maim***)

Word building: **injury** *noun* (*plural* **injuries**) **injured** *adjective* **injurious** *adjective*

injustice
noun **1** something that is unfair or unjust
2 unfairness or lack of justice

Word use: The opposite of this is **justice**.
Word history: Middle English, from French, from Latin

ink
noun a dark fluid used for writing or printing

Word building: **ink** *verb*
Word history: Middle English, from Old French, from Late Latin, from Greek word meaning 'kind of ink'

inkling
noun a vague or uncertain idea: *I had an **inkling** of what might happen.*

Word history: from Middle English word meaning 'to hint at'

inlaid
adjective set in the surface of something: *an **inlaid** pattern in wood*

inland
adjective **1** having to do with, or situated in parts of a country away from the coast or border: ***inland** towns*
adverb **2** in or towards the inner part of a country: *We went **inland**.*
noun **3** the inner part of a country, away from the coast or border: *We went to the **inland** for our trip.*

Word history: Middle English and Old English

in-law
noun a relative by marriage

inlay
verb **1** to decorate with thin layers of fine materials: *The wooden tray was **inlaid** with silver.*
noun **2** work or decoration made by inlaying
3 a layer of fine material set in something else

Verb forms: I **inlaid**, I have **inlaid**, I am **inlaying**

inlet
noun a small narrow bay or cove

inline skate
noun → **rollerblade**

Word building: **inline skating** *noun*

inmate
noun someone who has to stay in a hospital, prison or other institution

inn
noun a small hotel especially one for travellers

Word history: Old English *inn* house

innards (in-uhdz)
plural noun the inward parts of the body (***entrails***, ***guts***, ***viscera***)

innate (in-ayt)
adjective **1** existing or as if existing in someone from birth: ***innate** shyness* (***inborn***, ***inherited***, ***natural***)
2 basic to the character of something
3 arising naturally from the mind, rather than learned from experience: ***innate** ideas*

Word building: **innateness** *noun*
Word history: late Middle English, from Latin word meaning 'inborn'

inner
adjective **1** further in: *an **inner** door*
2 private or personal: ***inner** thoughts*

Word history: Old English *inne* within

innermost
adjective furthest inwards

Word use: You can also use **inmost**.
Word history: Middle English

innings
noun **1** the turn of a member of a cricket team to bat
2 the whole team's turn at batting: *The first **innings** was interrupted by rain.*

> Although this word ends in -s, it can be singular as well as plural:
>
> *One innings is all you play in a one-day match.* (singular)
>
> *Three innings have been played so far.* (plural)

innocent
adjective **1** free from guilt or from having done anything wrong
2 harmless: ***innocent*** *fun* (***blameless***, ***simple***)

Word building: **innocence** *noun* **innocently** *adverb*
Word history: Middle English, from Latin word meaning 'harmless'

innocuous (in-ok-yooh-uhs)
adjective not harmful (***harmless***, ***safe***)

Word history: Latin

innovate (in-uh-vayt)
verb to bring in something new

Word building: **innovative** *adjective* **innovator** *noun*
Word history: from Latin word meaning 'renewed', 'altered'

innovation (in-uh-vay-shuhn)
noun a new method, practice or custom

innovative (in-uh-vuh-tiv)
adjective new and original: *an* ***innovative*** *idea*

Word use: You can also use **innovatory.**
Word building: **innovativeness** *noun* **innovatively** *adverb*

innuendo (in-yooh-en-doh)
noun a remark that suggests something unpleasant about someone without actually saying it

Noun forms: The plural is **innuendos** or **innuendoes.**
Word history: from Latin word meaning 'intimation'

innumerable (i-nyooh-muh-ruh-buhl, i-nyoohm-ruh-buhl)
adjective too many to be counted (***countless***, ***infinite***, ***myriad***, ***numerous***, ***umpteen***)

inoculate (i-nok-yooh-layt)
noun to protect from a disease, by introducing germs which give you a very mild form of the disease (***vaccinate***)

Word building: **inoculation** *noun*
Word history: late Middle English, from Latin word meaning 'grafted', 'implanted'

inopportune (in-op-uh-tyoohn)
adjective of a time, event, etc., not suitable: *an* ***inopportune*** *visit* (***inappropriate***, ***inconvenient***)

inordinate (in-awd-uh-nuht)
adjective not within proper limits: ***inordinate*** *demands* (***excessive***, ***extreme***)

Word history: Middle English, from Latin word meaning 'disordered'

inorganic
adjective **1** not having the basic form which living bodies all have
2 *Chemistry* having to do with compounds not containing carbon, excepting cyanides and carbonates

Word use: Compare definition 2 with **organic** (definition 2).
Word building: **inorganically** *adverb*

inpatient
noun a patient who lives at a hospital while being treated

input
noun anything that is put in to be used, especially by a machine

Word use: The opposite of this is **output**.

input/output
noun Computers the section of the system which controls the passage of information into and out of a computer

Word use: The abbreviation is **I/O**.

inquest
noun an official inquiry to find out how someone died

Word history: Middle English, from Old French, from Latin word meaning '(a thing) inquired into'

inquire
verb **1** to ask
phrase **2 inquire into**, to search or examine the particulars of: *to* ***inquire into*** *the cause of the explosion*

Word use: You can also use **enquire**.
Word building: **inquirer** *noun*
Word history: Latin

inquiry
noun an investigation (***analysis***, ***examination***, ***probe***, ***review***, ***survey***)

Noun forms: The plural is **inquiries**.
Word building: **inquiring** *adjective*

> **inquiry / enquiry**
> You can use either of these spellings for this word. But note that **inquiry** is often used to mean 'an investigation', and **enquiry** is often used as a formal word for 'a question'.

inquisition (in-kwuh-zish-uhn)
noun a thorough investigation and questioning

Word building: **inquisitor** *noun*
Word history: Middle English, from Latin word meaning 'a searching into'

inquisitive (in-kwiz-uh-tiv)
adjective wanting to find out all about something: ***inquisitive*** *onlookers* (***curious***, ***enquiring***, ***nosy***, ***questioning***, ***snoopy***)

inroads
plural noun forcible entry which reduces the area, amount, etc., of something: ***inroads*** *on our savings*

insane
adjective mentally ill or mad: *He's* ***insane***. | *an* ***insane*** *act* (***crazy***, ***loony***, ***maniacal***, ***nutty***)

Word use: The opposite of this is **sane**.
Word building: **insanity** *noun*

insatiable (in-say-shuh-buhl)
adjective never having enough: *an* ***insatiable*** *appetite* (***greedy***, ***rapacious***, ***voracious***)

inscribe
verb to write or cut: *I* ***inscribed*** *his name on the metal plaque.*

Word building: **inscription** *noun*
Word history: from Latin word meaning 'write in or upon'

inscrutable (in-<u>skrooh</u>-tuh-buhl)
adjective mysterious or not easily understood: *an **inscrutable** expression on his face*

Word history: late Middle English, from Late Latin

insect
noun a small creature with its body clearly divided into three parts with three pairs of legs and usually two pairs of wings

Word use: Bees, ants and flies are insects; spiders and ticks are not, even though some people call them insects.
Word history: from Latin word meaning 'cut in or up' (because of their segmented form)

insecticide (in-<u>sek</u>-tuh-suyd)
noun a chemical substance used to kill insects

Word history: Latin

insectivore (in-<u>sek</u>-tuh-vaw)
noun a bird or animal that eats insects

Word use: Compare this with **herbivore**, **carnivore** and **omnivore**.
Word history: Neo-Latin, from Latin

insectivorous
adjective having to do with an animal that eats insects: *Lizards are **insectivorous**.*

insecure
adjective **1** not firm or safe: *He had an **insecure** hold on the rope.*
2 afraid or unsure: *She feels **insecure** if she can't see her mother.* (***exposed***, ***susceptible***, ***vulnerable***)

Word building: **insecurity** *noun*

inseminate (in-<u>sem</u>-uhn-ayt)
verb **1** to place or introduce seed into
2 to fertilise or make pregnant (***impregnate***)

Word building: **insemination** *noun*
Word history: from Latin word meaning 'sown', 'planted in'

insensible
adjective **1** incapable of feeling or sensing
2 unconscious, unaware, or unappreciative: *We are not **insensible** of your kindness.*
3 not able to be noticed by the senses: ***insensible** changes*
4 unresponsive or lacking in feeling

Word building: **insensibly** *adverb* **insensibility** *noun*

insensitive
adjective lacking in feeling (***callous***, ***cold-blooded***, ***hard-hearted***, ***stony***, ***unfeeling***)

insert (in-<u>sert</u>)
verb to put or set inside: ***Insert** the key in the lock.* | *to **insert** an advertisement in a newspaper*

Word use: The opposite of this is **remove** or **withdraw**.
Word building: **insert** (<u>in</u>-sert) *noun* **insertion** *noun*
Word history: from Latin word meaning 'put in'

in-service
adjective having to do with training provided by employers, in connection with a person's current work

inset (<u>in</u>-set)
noun **1** something put or set into or inside something else
verb (in-<u>set</u>) **2** to set in (***infix***, ***insert***)

Verb forms: I **inset**, I have **inset**, I am **insetting**

inside
preposition **1** on the inner side of: ***inside** the box*
noun **2** the inner part or side: *She put the label on the **inside**.*
3 insides, *Colloquial* your stomach and intestines and other inner parts of your body
adjective **4** being on or in the inside: ***inside** walls*
5 coming from within a place: ***inside** information*
adverb **6** indoors, or in or into the inner part: *She's working **inside**.*
phrase **7 inside out**,
a with the inner side turned to face outward
b thoroughly or completely: *She knows her job **inside out**.*

insidious (in-<u>sid</u>-ee-uhs)
adjective **1** intended to trap or deceive: *an **insidious** plot*
2 operating unnoticed but with serious effect: *an **insidious** disease*

Word history: from Latin word meaning 'cunning', 'artful'

insight (<u>in</u>-suyt)
noun an understanding of the inner nature of someone or something: *I gained an **insight** into the working of her mind.*

> **insight / incite**
> Don't confuse **insight** with **incite**. To **incite** someone to do something is to stir them up so that they will take action. The word is pronounced with the stress of the second syllable <u>-cite</u>.

insignia (in-<u>sig</u>-nee-uh)
noun badges or special marks of a position someone holds

Word history: from Latin word meaning 'mark', 'badge'

> This noun can take a singular or plural verb:
> *The mayor's insignia are so heavy and elaborate that she rattles when she walks.* (plural)
> *The insignia of that airline is an eagle flying through a cloud.* (singular)

insinuate
verb **1** to suggest something unpleasant without saying so outright: *By asking where my sales docket was, he **insinuated** that I had stolen the shoes.* (***hint***, ***imply***)
phrase **2 insinuate yourself into**, to get into gradually and slyly: *Wahid **insinuated himself into** the boss's favour.* (***ease yourself into***, ***slip into***)

Word building: **insinuation** *noun*
Word history: from Latin word meaning 'brought in by windings or turnings'

insipid (in-<u>si</u>-puhd)
adjective without noticeable, interesting, or attractive qualities (***bland***, ***flat***, ***mild***, ***plain***, ***tasteless***)

Word history: from Late Latin word meaning 'tasteless'

insist
verb to demand firmly: *I **insist** that you come.* (***require, stipulate***)

Word building: **insistence** *noun* **insistent** *adjective*
Word history: from Latin word meaning 'insist', 'stand or press upon'

insolent (<u>in</u>-suh-luhnt)
adjective insulting and rude (***bold, cheeky, impolite, impudent***)

Word building: **insolence** *noun*
Word history: Middle English, from Latin word meaning 'unaccustomed', 'unusual', 'excessive', 'arrogant'

insoluble (in-<u>sol</u>-yooh-buhl)
adjective **1** not able to be dissolved: ***insoluble** salts*
2 that cannot be worked out: *an **insoluble** problem*

Word use: The opposite of this is **soluble**.
Word building: **insolubility** *noun*
Word history: Middle English, from Latin

insolvent (in-<u>sol</u>-vuhnt)
adjective **1** not able to pay your debts (***bankrupt, broke, destitute, impecunious***)
noun **2** someone who is unable to pay their debts

Word building: **insolvency** *noun*

insomnia (in-<u>som</u>-nee-uh)
noun sleeplessness

Word building: **insomniac** *noun* **insomniac** *adjective*
Word history: Latin

inspect
verb **1** to look carefully at or over (***examine, scan, survey***)
2 to look at formally or officially: *The general **inspected** the soldiers.*

Word building: **inspection** *noun*
Word history: Latin

inspector
noun **1** a person who inspects, such as an inspector of taxes
2 a police officer who ranks above sergeant and below chief inspector

Word history: Latin

inspiration
noun **1** an action, influence, person or thing that has an encouraging and uplifting effect: *Her determination was an **inspiration** to us all.*
2 an action, influence, person or thing that arouses ideas, feelings or impulses that lead to creative activity

Word building: **inspirational** *adjective*

inspire
verb **1** to have an encouraging and uplifting effect on: *His courage **inspired** his followers.* (***encourage, motivate, set an example to, urge on***)
2 to produce or give rise to: *She **inspires** love in all her friends.* (***cause, evoke, induce, provoke***)

Word building: **inspirer** *noun* **inspiring** *adjective*
Word history: Middle English, from Latin word meaning 'breathe into'

inspired
adjective influenced by inspiration: *an **inspired** idea*

install
verb **1** to put into place for use: *to **install** a new stove* (***establish, locate, position, site, station***)
2 to place in an official position with a ceremony: *to **install** the new club president*
3 *Computers* to load (a software program) onto a hard disk

Word use: The opposite of definition 1 is **remove.** | The opposite of definition 2 is **decommission** or **oust.** | The opposite of definition 3 is **uninstall.**
Word history: Medieval Latin

installation
noun **1** the act of installing
2 something installed, such as a group of machines placed in position for use
3 a permanent military base with buildings, soldiers and equipment

instalment
noun **1** a single payment in a series which is meant to pay off a debt
2 a single part of a story being published in several parts in a magazine or newspaper

instance
noun an example or case: *Looking after his friend's dog was another **instance** of his kindness.*

Word history: Middle English, from Anglo-French, from Latin word meaning 'presence', 'urgency'

instant
noun **1** a very short space of time (***minute, moment, second***)
2 a particular point of time: *At that **instant** the door slammed.* (***juncture, moment***)
adjective **3** happening immediately: ***instant** relief*
4 in a form that makes preparation quick and easy: ***instant** coffee*

Word history: late Middle English, from Latin word meaning 'standing upon', 'insisting', 'being at hand'

instantaneous (in-stuhn-<u>tayn</u>-ee-uhs)
adjective occurring, done, or completed in an instant

instant messaging
noun text-based instant communication between people using the internet

instead
adverb in place of someone or something else: *She sent me **instead**.*

Word history: originally two words, *in stead* in place

instep
noun the upper part of your foot between your toes and ankle

instigate (<u>in</u>-stuh-gayt)
verb **1** to encourage some action: *to **instigate** a riot*
2 to bring about by urging: *Your presence is sure to **instigate** a quarrel.* (***cause, provoke, set off***)

Word building: **instigator** *noun* **instigation** *noun*
Word history: Latin

instil
verb to inject slowly or by degrees into the mind or feeling: *Manners must be **instilled** in childhood.*

Verb forms: I **instilled**, I have **instilled**, I am **instilling**
Word building: **instiller** *noun* **instillation** *noun*
Word history: from Latin word meaning 'pour in by drops'

instinct
noun **1** a natural urge or tendency that is there when you are born: *a bird's* ***instinct*** *to migrate in winter*
2 a natural knowledge or skill: *He has an* ***instinct*** *for making friends.*
Word building: **instinctive** *adjective*
Word history: late Middle English, from Latin word meaning 'instigation', 'impulse'

institute
verb **1** to set up or establish: *to* ***institute*** *a new government department* | *to* ***institute*** *rules of conduct* (***initiate***, ***launch***, ***pioneer***)
noun **2** an organisation or society set up to carry on a particular activity: *a literary* ***institute***
Word history: Middle English word meaning 'set up', 'established', from Latin

institution
noun **1** an organisation set up for a worthwhile cause: *an* ***institution*** *for the care of the aged*
2 a building used by an organisation like this
3 a setting up or establishing: *the* ***institution*** *of democratic government*
Word building: **institutional** *adjective* **institutionalise** *verb*

instruct
verb **1** to teach or train (***coach***, ***drill***)
2 to order or command (***advise***, ***tell***)
Word building: **instructor** *noun*
Word history: late Middle English, from Latin word meaning 'built', 'prepared', 'furnished', 'instructed'

instruction
noun **1** the act of instructing or teaching
2 knowledge or information that is passed on by teaching
3 instructions, orders or directions: *Read the* ***instructions*** *before you start.*

instructive
adjective serving to instruct or inform: *an* ***instructive*** *booklet*

instrument (<u>in</u>-struh-muhnt)
noun **1** a mechanical device or tool: *a doctor's* ***instrument***
2 something made to produce musical sounds: *Horns and clarinets are wind* ***instruments***.
3 an electrical device which gives information about the state of some part of an aeroplane, car or other vehicle: *The pilot checked the* ***instruments*** *on the panel in front of him.*
Word history: Middle English, from Latin

instrumental (in-struh-<u>men</u>-tuhl)
adjective **1** serving as a means: *Money was* ***instrumental*** *in her decision to take the job.*
2 performed on or written for a musical instrument

instrumentalist (in-struh-<u>men</u>-tuhl-uhst)
noun a person who performs on a musical instrument

insubordinate (in-suh-<u>baw</u>-duh-nuht)
adjective not obeying those in authority (***defiant***, ***delinquent***, ***disobedient***)
Word building: **insubordination** *noun*

insubstantial (in-suhb-<u>stan</u>-shuhl)
adjective **1** not great in amount (***inconsequential***, ***slight***, ***trivial***)
2 without reality: *the* ***insubstantial*** *stuff of dreams*

insufferable
adjective unbearable or not able to be tolerated: *He is an* ***insufferable*** *gossip.*

insufficient
adjective not enough; not as much or as many as wanted or needed: ***insufficient*** *cash* | ***insufficient*** *students* (***inadequate***, ***scant***, ***meagre***, ***paltry***, ***skimpy***)
Word building: **insufficiency** *noun*

insular (<u>in</u>-syooh-luh, <u>in</u>-shooh-luh)
adjective **1** having to do with an island or islands
2 narrow-minded
Word building: **insularity** *noun*
Word history: from Late Latin word meaning 'of an island'

insulate (<u>in</u>-shuh-layt)
verb **1** to cover with something to stop the escape of electric current: *to* ***insulate*** *the electric toaster cord*
2 to put a special material in the roof to keep in warmth in winter and keep out heat in summer: *We* ***insulated*** *our house.*
Word building: **insulation** *noun*
Word history: from Latin word meaning 'made into an island'

insulator
noun anything that insulates, especially against electricity

insulin (<u>in</u>-shuh-luhn, <u>in</u>-syuh-luhn, <u>in</u>-suh-luhn)
noun a substance your body produces to help it use the sugar in the food you eat
Word use: **Diabetes** results if your body does not make enough insulin.
Word history: from Latin word meaning 'island' (with reference to the islands of the pancreas)

insult (in-<u>sult</u>)
verb **1** to act or speak rudely or offensively to (***affront***, ***offend***, ***slight***, ***snub***)
noun (<u>in</u>-sult) **2** a rude or offensive action or remark
Word building: **insulting** *adjective*
Word history: from Latin word meaning 'leap on or at', 'insult'

insuperable (in-<u>sooh</u>-puh-ruh-buhl)
adjective not able to be passed over, overcome, or beaten: *an* ***insuperable*** *barrier*

insurance
noun a system of paying money to a company that says it will pay you a sum of money if you suffer a loss from fire, burglary, accident or the like

insure (in-<u>shaw</u>, in-<u>shoouh</u>)
verb to guarantee against the risk of loss or damage
Word building: **insured** *noun* **insurer** *noun*
Word history: variant of *ensure*

insure / ensure / assure
Don't confuse **insure** with **ensure** or **assure**.
To **insure** is to arrange a guarantee that your property will be replaced if it is lost, stolen or damaged.
To **ensure** is to make certain of something:
I'm reminding you now to ensure that you return the book tomorrow.
The most common meaning of **assure** is to tell someone something with certainty:
They assure us that the roof is on.

insurgent (in-ser-juhnt)
noun **1** someone who revolts against or fights against lawful authority, such as a government
adjective **2** rebellious
Word building: **insurgence** *noun* **insurgency** *noun*
Word history: from Latin word meaning 'rising on or up'

insurrection
noun the act of fighting or showing open resistance against established authority, such as a government
Word history: late Middle English, from Latin word meaning 'rise up'

intact
adjective unharmed, unchanged or whole: *The parcel arrived **intact**.*
Word history: late Middle English, from Latin

intaglio (in-tah-lee-oh)
noun decorative art done by carving into the surface of a gem, piece of jewellery, etc.
Word history: Italian, from *intagliare* cut in, engrave

intake
noun **1** the act of taking in: *There is a new **intake** of students at the beginning of each year.*
2 the amount or quantity that is taken in

intangible (in-tan-juh-buhl)
adjective **1** non-material or not able to be sensed by touching
2 not definite or clear to the mind: ***intangible** arguments | **intangible** fears* (***ethereal, nebulous, shadowy***)
noun **3** something intangible
4 *Commerce* an asset with no easily identifiable material form, such as goodwill, research and development, or a franchise

integer (in-tuh-juh)
noun any whole number (***digit, figure, number, numeral***)
Word use: Compare this with **fraction**.
Word history: from Latin word meaning 'untouched', 'whole', 'entire'

integral (in-tuh-gruhl)
adjective **1** necessary to the completeness of: *Saliva is an **integral** part of the digestive system.*
2 *Mathematics* having to do with a whole number
Word history: Late Latin

integrate
verb to bring together to make a united whole: *I've tried to **integrate** all these facts into one powerful argument. | The government is working to **integrate** the two races to bring harmony.*
Word building: **integration** *noun*
Word history: from Latin word meaning 'made whole'

integrated circuit
noun an arrangement of interconnected circuit elements integrated with or deposited on a single semiconductor base
Word use: The abbreviation is **IC**.

integrity (in-teg-ruh-tee)
noun honesty and trustworthiness
Word history: late Middle English, from Latin

intellect (in-tuh-lekt)
noun the power of your mind to think, reason and understand: *to have a fine **intellect*** (***brain, intelligence, mind***)
Word history: Middle English, from Latin word meaning 'a discerning', 'perceiving'

intellectual (in-tuh-lek-chooh-uhl)
adjective **1** of interest to the mind or intellect: *He prefers **intellectual** hobbies such as chess.*
2 making much use of the mind: *an **intellectual** writer*
noun **3** an intellectual person (***philosopher, sage, scholar***)
Word building: **intellectuality** *noun* **intellectually** *adverb*
Word history: Middle English, from Latin

intelligence (in-tel-uh-juhns)
noun **1** the ability to learn, understand and reason: *Your **intelligence** enables you to solve problems.*
2 good mental ability: *a woman of **intelligence***
Word use: The opposite of this is **stupidity**.
Word building: **intelligent** *adjective*

intelligent / intellectual
Although you need to be **intelligent** to be an **intellectual**, these words have different meanings.
An **intelligent** person is someone who has the power to reason and learn and think things out.
An **intellectual** person spends a lot of time studying and thinking.

intelligentsia (in-tel-uh-jent-see-uh)
plural noun intellectual people viewed as a social class
Word history: Russian, from Latin *intelligentia* intelligence

intelligible (in-tel-uh-juh-buhl)
adjective able to be understood (***clear, comprehensible***)
Word history: Middle English, from Latin

intemperate (in-tem-puh-ruht, in-tem-pruht)
adjective **1** having the habit of drinking too much
2 not in control of your own passions, appetites, etc.
Word building: **intemperance** *noun*

intend
verb to have in mind or to mean: *I **intended** to do it.* | *I **intend** no harm.* (***choose***, ***have in mind***, ***mean***, ***plan***, ***vow***)

Word history: Middle English, from Latin word meaning 'extend', 'intend'

intended
adjective **1** designed or meant: *a tool **intended** for cutting*
noun **2** *Colloquial* the person whom someone is planning to marry: *He is Jane's **intended**.*

intense
adjective **1** very great or strong: ***intense** pain* | ***intense** joy* (***passionate***, ***profound***, ***severe***, ***violent***, ***vivid***)
2 showing strong feeling: *an **intense** expression*

Word use: The opposite of definition 1 is **moderate**. | The opposite of definition 2 is **mild**.
Word building: **intensify** *verb* (**intensified**, **intensifying**) **intenseness** *noun*
Word history: Middle English, from Latin word meaning 'stretched tight', 'intense'

intensity
noun **1** great strength, especially of feeling: *the **intensity** of the wind* | *the **intensity** of his emotions*
2 high degree: *the **intensity** of the cold*

intensive
adjective with a lot of attention or work: ***intensive** care of a seriously ill person* (***comprehensive***, ***detailed***, ***exhaustive***, ***in-depth***, ***thorough***)

Word history: Medieval Latin

intent[1]
noun purpose, or what you intend: *He acted with criminal **intent**.*

Word history: Middle English, from Old French, from Latin

intent[2]
adjective having your mind firmly fixed: *He was **intent** on his book.*

Word history: from Latin word meaning 'stretched', 'intent'

intention
noun a firm plan or purpose

Word building: **intentional** *adjective*
Word history: Latin

inter (in-ter)
verb to place (a dead body, etc.) in a grave or tomb

Verb forms: I **interred**, I have **interred**, I am **interring**
Word history: Middle English, from Old French

interact
verb to act on or have an effect on each other: *Some chemicals **interact** to form gases.*

Word building: **interaction** *noun* **interactive** *adjective*

intercede (in-tuh-seed)
verb to act on behalf of someone in trouble: *to **intercede** with the governor for a thief* (***arbitrate***, ***intervene***, ***mediate***, ***negotiate***)

Word history: from Latin word meaning 'intervene'

intercept (in-tuh-sept)
verb **1** to take or seize on the way from one place to another: *to **intercept** a letter*
noun (in-tuh-sept) **2** an act of intercepting, such as gaining possession of the ball in a football game

Word building: **interception** *noun*
interceptor *noun*
Word history: Latin

interchange (in-tuh-chaynj)
verb **1** to cause to change places: *I **interchanged** the two names on the list.*
noun (in-tuh-chaynj) **2** an act of interchanging or sharing: *an **interchange** of ideas*
3 a major road junction
4 a point where it is possible to change from one form of public transport to another

Word building: **interchangeable** *adjective*
Word history: *inter-* (prefix meaning 'between', 'among') + *change*

intercom
noun a system for sending spoken messages throughout a place such as a school or office

Word use: This is short for **intercommunication system.**

intercourse
noun **1** exchange of ideas, thoughts and feelings between people
2 → **sexual intercourse**

interdict (in-tuh-dikt, in-tuh-duyt)
noun **1** in civil law, any ruling of a court or an official which forbids an act
verb (in-tuh-dikt, in-tuh-duyt) **2** to forbid (***prohibit***, ***outlaw***)

Word history: Latin

interest
noun **1** the feeling you have when your attention is held by something: *to have an **interest** in stamp collecting*
2 importance: *The results of the election were of great **interest** to us all.*
3 money paid to you by a bank or building society for the use of the money you have put into your account
verb **4** to hold the attention of

Word use: The opposite of definition 4 is **bore.**
Word building: **interested** *adjective* **interesting** *adjective*
Word history: late Middle English, from Latin

interface (in-tuh-fays)
noun **1** a surface which is the common boundary between two bodies or spaces
2 *Computers* a system which enables you to instruct a computer to perform different functions, such as creating and storing documents, accessing the internet, etc.
3 any point of communication or contact: *The conference provided a useful **interface** between the various community groups.*
verb (in-tuh-fays) **4** to cause to act on each other

interfere (in-tuh-fear)
verb **1** to take a part in someone else's affairs without being asked: *Our neighbours **interfere** all the time.* (***butt in***, ***chip in***, ***interject***, ***intrude***, ***meddle***)
2 to clash or get in the way: *His plans **interfere** with mine.*

Word history: from Old French word meaning 'strike each other'

interference
noun **1** the act of interfering
2 *Physics* the action of light waves, sound waves, etc., of strengthening or cancelling each other when they meet
3 *Radio* the jumbling of radio signals with similar frequencies coming from more than one source

intergalactic (in-tuh-guh-lak-tik)
adjective existing or happening between different galaxies in space: ***intergalactic** warfare*

interim (in-tuh-ruhm)
noun **1** a time coming between: *Rattan's between jobs at the moment — he's gone surfing in the **interim**.*
adjective **2** temporary: *an **interim** solution* (***casual***, ***fill-in***, ***makeshift***, ***provisional***)
3 *Commerce* calculated for a period that is not the final period, usually the first six months of the financial year: ***interim** accounts* | ***interim** dividends*

Word history: from Latin word meaning 'in the meantime'

interior (in-tear-ree-uh)
adjective **1** being within: *the **interior** rooms*
noun **2** an inner or inside area: *the **interior** of a house* | *the **interior** of the country*

Word use: The opposite of this is **exterior**.
Word history: from Latin word meaning 'inner'

interject (in-tuh-jekt)
verb **1** to throw in quickly between other things: *to **interject** a careless remark*
2 to interrupt a conversation or speech (***butt in***, ***heckle***)

Word building: **interjector** *noun*
Word history: Latin

interjection
noun a remark made to interrupt a conversation or speech, such as *Oh!*, *yuk!* and *struth!* (***exclamation***, ***outburst***)

interlace (in-tuh-lays)
verb **1** to cross one another as if woven together: ***interlacing** branches*
2 to place so as to go across one another: *to **interlace** threads* (***intertwine***, ***plait***)

interlock (in-tuh-lok)
verb **1** to connect with each other: *The pieces of a jigsaw **interlock**.*
2 to fit into each other, as parts of machinery
noun (in-tuh-lok) **3** a smooth knitted fabric, especially one made of cotton thread

interlope (in-tuh-lohp)
verb to force yourself into the affairs of others

Word building: **interloper** *noun*
Word history: *inter-* (prefix meaning 'between', 'among') + *lope*

interlude
noun **1** a short period of time, especially of restfulness: *Our picnic by the river was a pleasant **interlude**.*
2 a short performance, especially of music between two acts of a play

Word history: Middle English, from Medieval Latin

intermediate
adjective being or happening between two times, places, or stages: *an **intermediate** class* | *an **intermediate** product*

Word history: Medieval Latin, from Latin word meaning 'between'

interminable (in-term-uhn-uh-buhl)
adjective without end: ***interminable** talks* (***constant***, ***continuous***, ***endless***, ***persistent***)

Word history: Middle English, from Late Latin

intermission
noun an interval, especially during a film

Word history: Latin

intermittent
adjective stopping and starting: *There was **intermittent** rain all day.* (***erratic***, ***fitful***, ***irregular***, ***sporadic***, ***unsteady***)

Word use: The opposite of this is **constant**, **continual** or **continuous**.

intern[1] (in-tern)
verb to keep in an enclosed and guarded area, especially prisoners of war (***confine***, ***imprison***, ***jail***, ***lock up***)

Word building: **internment** *noun*
Word history: from French *interner*, from Latin word meaning 'internal'

intern[2] (in-tern)
noun a doctor who has recently finished university and is working full-time in a hospital

Word history: from French *interne*, from Latin word meaning 'internal'

internal
adjective **1** having to do with the inside: *the **internal** organs of our bodies*
2 happening within: *the **internal** affairs of a country*

Word use: The opposite of this is **external**.
Word history: Medieval Latin, from Latin word meaning 'inward'

international
adjective between or among nations: ***international** sporting events*

international law
noun the body of rules that nations adhere to in their conduct towards one another: *binding **international law***

International System of Units
noun an internationally recognised system of metric units, now used as the basis of Australia's metric system, in which the seven base units are the metre, kilogram, second, ampere, kelvin, mole and candela

Word use: The abbreviation is **SI**, which is based on the French name **Système International d'Unitès**. | Also look up **metric system**.

international waters
plural noun areas of ocean which are outside any national jurisdiction

internecine (in-tuh-nee-suyn)
adjective having to do with much killing and destruction

Word history: from Latin word meaning 'slaughter'

internet
noun **the**, the communications system created by the interconnecting networks of computers around the world

Word use: You can also use **the Net** or **the net**.

internet cafe
noun a business which offers connection to the internet for a fee, sometimes also providing the usual services of a cafe

internet portal
noun → **web portal**

internet relay chat
noun Internet an online discussion forum available through the internet, in which multiple users can conduct real-time communication by means of typing text

Word use: The abbreviation is **IRC**.

internet service provider
noun a company which provides access to the internet, usually for a fee

Word use: The short form is **service provider**, **provider** or **ISP**.

interplay (in-tuh-play)
noun **1** the effect of actions on each other
verb (in-tuh-play) **2** to have an effect on each other

interpolate (in-ter-puh-layt)
verb to put in or introduce as an addition to other things or parts: *He **interpolated** quotations into his speech.* (***interject***, ***interpose***)

Word building: **interpolation** *noun* **interpolator** *noun*
Word history: from Latin word meaning 'altered', 'falsified'

interpose (in-tuh-pohz)
verb **1** to place between: *to **interpose** yourself between two fighters*
2 to interrupt a conversation or speech with: *to **interpose** a comment*
3 to step in between people opposing each other: *She **interposed** in their argument.* (***intervene***, ***mediate***)

Word building: **interposition** *noun*
Word history: French from *inter-* (prefix meaning 'between', 'among') + *pose*

interpret (in-ter-pruht)
verb **1** to explain the meaning of: *to **interpret** dreams* (***clarify***, ***elucidate***, ***spell out***)
2 to translate what is said in a foreign language

Verb forms: I **interpreted**, I have **interpreted**, I am **interpreting**
Word history: Middle English, from Latin word meaning 'explain'

interpretation
noun **1** the act of interpreting or explaining
2 a particular explanation: *to put a wrong **interpretation** on a message*
3 the performing of a piece of music, a part in a play, etc., so as to give a particular idea of it

interpreter
noun **1** someone who explains or interprets, such as someone whose work is translating from one language to another
2 *Computers* a program which causes a computer to obey instructions in some code different from the basic code of the computer

interregnum (in-tuh-reg-nuhm)
noun **1** a period of time between the close of a king or queen's rule and the beginning of the next rule
2 any period during which a state has no ruler or only a short-term governing body
3 any pause or interruption in continuity

Noun forms: The plural is **interregnums** or **interregna**.
Word building: **interregnal** *adjective*
Word history: Latin

interrogate (in-te-ruh-gayt)
verb to question closely to find out something: *The police **interrogated** the suspect.* (***grill***, ***interview***, ***pump***, ***question***, ***quiz***)

Word building: **interrogation** *noun*
Word history: late Middle English, from Latin

interrogative (in-tuh-rog-uh-tiv)
adjective **1** having to do with a question or suggesting a question: *an **interrogative** look*
2 *Grammar* forming a question: *an **interrogative** pronoun* | *an **interrogative** sentence*

For more information on definition 2, look up **pronouns: interrogative pronouns**.

interrupt (in-tuh-rupt)
verb to stop or break into in the middle of: *She **interrupted** my speech.* | *to **interrupt** someone's work* (***disturb***, ***intervene in***)

Word building: **interruption** *noun* **interruptive** *adjective*
Word history: Middle English, from Latin word meaning 'broken apart'

intersect (in-tuh-sekt)
verb **1** to cut or divide by passing through or across: *This line **intersects** the circle.*
2 to cross: *There is a signpost where the streets **intersect**.*

Word history: from Latin word meaning 'cut off'

intersection
noun a place where streets cross

intersperse (in-tuh-spers)
verb to scatter here and there among other things

Word history: from Latin word meaning 'strewn'

interstate (in-tuh-stayt)
adjective **1** between states: *an **interstate** competition*
adverb (in-tuh-stayt) **2** *Australian* to or from another state: *She wants to send a letter **interstate**.*

interstice (in-ter-stuhs)
noun a small or narrow space between things or parts (***chink***, ***crack***, ***crevice***, ***slit***)

Noun forms: The plural is **interstices** (in-ter-stuh-seez).
Word history: from Latin word meaning 'space between'

interval (in-tuh-vuhl)
noun **1** the length of time between events: *an **interval** of 50 years*
2 a pause or break, especially halfway through a program of films or music
3 the space between things
4 the difference in pitch between two notes

Word history: Middle English, from Latin

intervene (in-tuh-veen)
verb to step in, in order to change or solve: *The government **intervened** in the industrial dispute.* (***intercede***, ***mediate***, ***negotiate***)

Word building: **intervention** *noun*
Word history: from Latin word meaning 'come between'

interview (in-tuh-vyooh)
noun a meeting in which someone is asked questions about something: *The Prime Minister gave an **interview** about the election. | a job **interview***

Word building: **interview** *verb* **interviewer** *noun*
Word history: from Old French *entrevue* see (each other)

intestate (in-tes-tayt, in-tes-tuht)
adjective **1** without having made a valid will: *He died **intestate**.*
noun **2** someone who has died intestate

Word history: Middle English, from Latin word meaning 'having made no will'

intestine (in-tes-tuhn)
noun the long tube that carries food from your stomach to your anus. The **large intestine** is the broader and shorter part containing the colon and rectum, and the **small intestine** is the narrower and longer part containing the duodenum.

Word use: This word usually occurs in the plural form **intestines**. | Another name is **gut**.
Word building: **intestinal** *adjective*
Word history: from Latin word meaning 'entrails'

intimate[1] (in-tuh-muht)
adjective **1** very close: ***intimate** friends*
2 secret or deep: ***intimate** thoughts*
3 very thorough: *an **intimate** knowledge*
noun **4** a close friend

Word building: **intimacy** *noun*
Word history: from Late Latin word meaning 'put or pressed into'

intimate[2] (in-tuh-mayt)
verb **1** to make known indirectly, by hinting or suggesting
2 to make known, especially by a formal announcement

Word building: **intimation** *noun*
Word history: from Late Latin word meaning 'put or pressed into', 'announced'

intimidate
verb **1** to make frightened or nervous
2 to frighten in order to force someone into doing something (***blackmail***, ***bludgeon***, ***cow***, ***menace***, ***threaten***)

Word building: **intimidation** *noun*
Word history: from Medieval Latin word meaning 'made afraid'. Look up **timid**.

into
preposition **1** a word expressing:
a movement or direction towards the inner part: *to run **into** the room*
b involvement or placement within: *to be well **into** a book*
c change to new conditions, etc.: *to turn **into** a frog*
2 *Mathematics* being the divisor of: *2 **into** 10 equals 5*

into / in to

There's a slight difference in meaning between sentences like these:

I drove into the carpark.

I drove in to work.

The first sentence with **into** is simply about bringing the car into a carpark. The second, which sets **in** apart from **to**, draws special attention to **in**. It carries the extra hint that the driver was coming from out of town, and that he or she had a special purpose in heading for work.

Whenever **in** is set apart from **to**, it highlights the act of moving in towards the centre or towards a particular focus. You'll notice it being used this way sometimes after a number of common verbs, such as *come*, *go*, *run* and *walk*.

intolerance
noun **1** unwillingness to tolerate different opinions or beliefs: ***intolerance** of other religions*
2 inability to bear or endure: ***intolerance** of heat*
3 an abnormal sensitivity or allergy to something: *a lactose **intolerance***

intonation
noun the pattern of changes of pitch in speech or music

intone
verb to speak or recite at one pitch level, as when chanting in a religious ceremony

Word history: late Middle English, from Medieval Latin

intoxicant
noun something which causes drunkenness, such as liquor or some drugs

intoxicate
verb to make drunk

Word building: **intoxicated** *adjective*
intoxication *noun*
Word history: Middle English, from Medieval Latin word meaning 'poisoned'

intractable
adjective hard to deal with or manage (***obstinate***, ***recalcitrant***, ***stubborn***)

Word building: **intractability** *noun*
intractableness *noun* **intractably** *adverb*

intranet
noun Computers a website or group of websites belonging to an organisation, accessible only to organisation members, employees, etc., or people authorised by them

intransigent (in-tran-suh-juhnt)
adjective **1** keeping firmly to your own ideas or position (***uncompromising***, ***unmoved***)
noun **2** someone who is firm or immovable in this way

Word building: **intransigence** *noun*
intransigency *noun*
Word history: French, from Spanish

intransitive verb
noun a verb like 'come' that needs no object for it to make sense

Word use: The opposite is a **transitive verb**.

intrastate (<u>in</u>-truh-stayt)
adjective within a state: ***intrastate** trade*

intravenous (in-truh-<u>vee</u>-nuhs)
adjective into a vein: *The sick baby had **intravenous** feeds through a tube in her arm.*

Word building: **intravenously** *adverb*

intrepid (in-<u>trep</u>-uhd)
adjective very brave: *an **intrepid** explorer*

Word building: **intrepidly** *adverb*
Word history: from Latin word meaning 'not alarmed'

intricate (<u>in</u>-truh-kuht)
adjective finely detailed: ***intricate** lace* (***complicated**, **convoluted**, **elaborate**, **fiddly**, **involved***)

Word building: **intricacy** *noun* **intricateness** *noun*
Word history: late Middle English, from Latin word meaning 'entangled'

intrigue (in-<u>treeg</u>)
verb **1** to interest or make curious because of puzzling or unusual qualities: *The strange sounds **intrigued** her.*
2 to plan secretly (***connive**, **conspire**, **plot**, **scheme***)

Word building: **intrigue** (<u>in</u>-treeg) *noun* **intriguing** *adjective*
Word history: French, from Italian from Latin word meaning 'entangle', 'perplex'

intrinsic (in-<u>trin</u>-zik, in-<u>trin</u>-sik)
adjective belonging to a thing by its very nature: ***intrinsic** merit*

Word history: from Medieval Latin word meaning 'inward'

introduce
verb **1** to bring into notice, knowledge, use, etc.: *to **introduce** a fashion*
2 to bring forward for consideration, as a bill in parliament, etc.
3 to present or bring forward with material that explains or prepares for the main part: *to **introduce** a book with a long preface*
4 to lead, bring or put into a place, surroundings, etc.: *to **introduce** a figure into a design | to **introduce** a subject of conversation*
5 to present to another person: *He **introduced** his sister to us.*
phrase **6 introduce to**, to bring to the knowledge or experience of something: *to **introduce** a person **to** chess*

Word history: late Middle English, from Latin word meaning 'lead in'

introduced species
noun a species of plant or animal which has been brought to a particular area, by accident or design, often resulting in the loss of a native species

Word use: You can also use **naturalised species** or **exotic species**. | Compare this with **native species**

introduction
noun **1** the act of making known for the first time: *We had our **introduction** to sailing during the holidays.*
2 the first part of a book or essay which leads up to the main subject

Word use: The opposite of definition 2 is **conclusion**.
Word building: **introductory** *adjective*
Word history: Middle English, from Latin

introspection
noun examination of your own mental states or feelings

introvert (<u>in</u>-truh-vert)
noun someone concerned mainly with their own thoughts or mental states, often shy and withdrawn

Word use: The opposite is **extrovert**.
Word building: **introverted** *adjective*
Word history: Latin

intrude
verb to enter or force yourself in when you are not wanted or invited (***butt in**, **chip in**, **interfere**, **meddle***)

Word building: **intrusion** *noun*
Word history: from Latin word meaning 'thrust in'

intruder
noun someone who intrudes onto someone else's property: *The **intruder** stole our TV.*

intrusive
adjective **1** intruding
2 *Geology* having to do with rocks that have been forced, while molten, into cracks or between layers of other rocks

intuition (in-chooh-<u>ish</u>-uhn)
noun a strong feeling about something without any real reason that you know of: *My **intuition** tells me that she's not well.*

Word building: **intuitive** *adjective*
Word history: Medieval Latin, from Latin word meaning 'look at', 'consider'

inundate (<u>in</u>-un-dayt)
verb to overwhelm with a flood or with something like a flood: *to **inundate** surrounding country | to be **inundated** with work* (***deluge**, **engulf**, **flood**, **swamp***)

Word building: **inundation** *noun*
Word history: from Latin word meaning 'overflowed'

inure
phrase **inure to**, to make used to by toughening or hardening: *to **inure** someone **to** danger | to **inure** someone **to** hard work* (***accustom**, **habituate***)

Word building: **inurement** *noun*
Word history: late Middle English

invade
verb **1** to attack and enter: *Caesar **invaded** Britain.*
2 to force yourself in on: *to **invade** someone's privacy*

Word building: **invader** *noun*
Word history: late Middle English, from Latin word meaning 'go into', 'attack'

invalid[1] (<u>in</u>-vuh-lid)
noun **1** someone who is sick or weak
adjective **2** weak or sick: *an **invalid** son* (***feeble**, **frail**, **sickly**, **weedy***)

Word history: from Latin word meaning 'infirm', 'not strong'

invalid[2] (in-val-uhd)
adjective not correct, especially legally: ***invalid** arguments* | *an **invalid** will*

Word use: The opposite of this is **valid**.
Word history: *in-* + *valid*

invaluable
adjective with a value too great to be measured: *an **invaluable** painting* | ***invaluable** help* (***precious**, **priceless**, **treasured***)

invaluable / valuable / valueless

Don't confuse **invaluable** with **valuable** or **valueless.**

Something **valuable** is of great worth or value.

Something **valueless** is worthless and has no value at all.

invariable
adjective **1** always the same (***constant**, **fixed**, **unchanging***)
noun **2** an invariable quantity

invasion
noun **1** the act of invading or entering by attack: ***invasion** of enemy territory*
2 the coming of anything troublesome or harmful, such as disease or pests
3 the act of intruding or interfering: ***invasion** of privacy*

Word building: **invasive** *adjective*
Word history: from Late Latin word meaning 'an attack'

invective
noun a strong verbal attack putting blame on someone (***abuse**, **denunciation**, **recriminations***)

Word history: Middle English, from Late Latin word meaning 'abusive'

inveigh (in-vay)
verb to attack strongly in words: *to **inveigh** against democracy* (***denounce**, **fulminate against**, **rail against***)

Word history: Middle English, from Latin word meaning 'carry or bear into', 'assail'

inveigle (in-vay-guhl)
verb to persuade by flattery, etc.: *to **inveigle** a person into playing bridge* | *to **inveigle** someone from attending* (***beguile**, **cajole***)

Word history: late Middle English, from French word meaning 'blind', 'delude'

invent
verb to make or think up: *She **invented** a machine for cleaning windows.* | *He **invented** an excuse.* (***coin**, **conceive**, **concoct**, **create**, **devise***)

Word building: **inventive** *adjective* **inventor** *noun*
Word history: late Middle English, from Latin word meaning 'discovered', 'found out'

invention
noun **1** the act of inventing or creating
2 something invented
3 the power of inventing, creating, or being imaginative

inventory (in-vuhn-tree, in-ven-tuh-ree)
noun **1** a detailed list of articles, goods, etc., held in a shop, a furnished flat, etc.
2 *Commerce* a business's stock of finished goods, raw materials and work in progress

Noun forms: The plural is **inventories**.

inverse
adjective **1** turned in the opposite position or direction
noun **2** the opposite

Word history: from Latin word meaning 'turned about'

invert
verb **1** to turn upside down, inside out, or inwards (***overturn**, **tip over**, **upset***)
2 to turn in the opposite position, direction, or order

Word building: **inversion** *noun*
Word history: from Latin word meaning 'turn about', 'upset'

invertebrate (in-ver-tuh-bruht, in-ver-tuh-brayt)
adjective without a backbone: *A worm is an **invertebrate** animal.*

Word building: **invertebrate** *noun*

inverted comma
noun → **quotation mark**

inverted commas
plural noun quotation marks

For more on how to use **inverted commas**, look up **quotation mark**.

invest
verb **1** to spend money on something in the hope of making more money: *She **invested** in real estate and made a big profit.*
2 to use or spend: *to **invest** time and effort*

Word building: **investor** *noun*
Word history: late Middle English, from Latin word meaning 'clothe'

investigate
verb to look into or examine closely: *She heard a noise and went to **investigate**.* | *The police **investigated** the crime.* (***delve into**, **explore**, **probe**, **research**, **scrutinise***)

Word building: **investigation** *noun* **investigative** *adjective* **investigator** *noun*
Word history: from Latin word meaning 'tracked', 'traced out'

investiture (in-ves-ti-chuh)
noun **1** the formal act of giving certain rights or powers, or installing into office
2 an official government ceremony in which someone is given public honours and awards

Word history: Middle English, from Medieval Latin

investment
noun the investing of money in order to make a profit

inveterate (in-vet-uh-ruht)
adjective **1** being firmly established in a habit, practice, feeling, etc.: *an **inveterate** gambler*
2 firmly established over a long time

Word building: **inveterately** *adverb* **inveterateness** *noun*
Word history: Middle English, from Latin word meaning 'rendered old'

invidious (in-vid-ee-uhs)
adjective **1** attracting hatred or envy: *an **invidious** honour*
2 meant to excite ill will or resentment or give offence: ***invidious** remarks* | ***invidious** comparisons*
Word building: **invidiousness** *noun*
Word history: from Latin word meaning 'envious'

invigorate
verb to fill with energy and strength: *The exercises should **invigorate** you.*
Word building: **invigorating** *adjective*

invincible (in-vin-suh-buhl)
adjective unable to be defeated or beaten
Word building: **invincibly** *adverb*
Word history: Middle English, from Latin

inviolable (in-vuy-uh-luh-buhl)
adjective **1** sacred or not to be broken or violated: *an **inviolable** sanctuary* | ***inviolable** rights*
2 indestructible or unable to be injured
Word building: **inviolability** *noun* **inviolableness** *noun* **inviolably** *adverb*

inviolate (in-vuy-uh-luht, in-vuy-uh-layt)
adjective free from attack, injury, disturbance, etc.: ***inviolate** peace* | ***inviolate** laws*
Word building: **inviolacy** *noun* **inviolateness** *noun*

invisible
adjective unable to be seen (***imperceptible***, ***unseen***)
Word building: **invisibility** *noun* **invisibly** *adverb*

invite
verb **1** to ask to visit or take part: *We **invited** Linh for dinner.* | *They **invited** us to help in the garden.*
2 to act so as to produce a certain result: *to **invite** danger*
Word building: **invitation** *noun*
Word history: Latin

inviting
adjective especially attractive or tempting

in vitro (in vit-roh)
adjective in artificial surroundings, like a test tube: ***in vitro** fertilisation*
Word history: Neo-Latin word literally meaning 'in glass'

invoice
noun a bill for things you've bought, listing all their prices separately
Word building: **invoice** *verb*
Word history: from French word meaning 'sending', 'thing sent'

invoke (in-vohk)
verb **1** to call for with earnest desire: *to **invoke** God's mercy*
2 to appeal to, for confirmation or justification: *to **invoke** the constitution*
3 to put into effect: *to **invoke** the power of a law*
Word building: **invoker** *noun*
Word history: late Middle English, from Latin

involve
verb to include as a necessary part of something: *The job of an art gallery guide **involves** a knowledge of art history.*
Word history: Middle English, from Latin word meaning 'roll in or on', 'enwrap', 'involve'

involved
adjective **1** complicated, or very difficult to sort out: *an **involved** plan* (***convoluted***, ***elaborate***, ***fiddly***, ***intricate***)
2 deeply interested: ***involved** in music*
3 closely connected or associated, especially romantically
Word building: **involvement** *noun*

inward
adjective **1** going towards the inside or interior: *an **inward** gaze*
2 situated inside: *an **inward** room*
3 mental or spiritual: ***inward** peace*
adverb **4** → **inwards**
Word history: Old English

inwards
adverb **1** towards the inside or interior: *The cell faced **inwards** over the courtyard.*
2 into the mind or spirit: *to direct your thoughts **inwards***
Word use: You can also use **inward**.

in-your-face
adjective Colloquial forcing you to think about things you might find unpleasant: ***in-your-face** humour*

iodine (uy-uh-deen, uy-uh-duyn)
noun a chemical element which produces a purple antiseptic when heated
Word history: French, from Greek word properly meaning 'rust-coloured', but taken to mean 'violet-like'

ion (uy-uhn)
noun a tiny particle, such as an atom, which has an electric charge
Word history: from Greek word meaning 'go'

ion / iron
Look up **iron / ion.**

ionosphere (uy-on-uhs-fear)
noun the outer regions of the earth's atmosphere, beyond the stratosphere, made up of a succession of ion-containing layers

iota (uy-oh-tuh)
noun a very small quantity
Word history: from *iota, the ninth and smallest letter of the Greek alphabet*

IOU
noun a written acknowledgement of a debt
Word history: from the pronunciation of 'I owe you'

IP (uy pee)
noun Computers a protocol for communication between networks
Word history: *i(nternet) p(rotocol)*

IP address
noun Internet a unique set of numbers which identifies a computer on the internet
Word use: You can also use **IP number**.

IQ
noun the relation of a person's mental age to actual age. A child with a mental age of 12 years and an actual age of 10 years has an intelligence rating of 1.2; this is usually expressed as 120.
Word history: abbreviation of *i(ntelligence) q(uotient)*

irascible (i-ras-uh-buhl)
adjective **1** easily made angry: *an **irascible** old man*
2 marked by, excited by or coming from anger: *an **irascible** nature*
Word building: **irascibility** *noun* **irascibleness** *noun* **irascibly** *adverb*
Word history: Latin

irate
adjective angry (***annoyed***, ***furious***)
Word history: Latin

IRC
noun → **internet relay chat**

ire
noun anger or rage (***fury***, ***wrath***)
Word building: **ireful** *adjective*
Word history: Middle English, from Old French, from Latin

iridescent (ir-uh-des-uhnt)
adjective showing lustrous, changing rainbow colours
Word building: **iridescence** *noun*
Word history: from Latin word meaning 'rainbow'

iris
noun **1** the coloured part of the eye around the pupil
2 a large, brightly coloured flower
Noun forms: The plural is **irises.**
Word history: Middle English, from Latin, from Greek

irk
verb to annoy or trouble: *It **irked** him to wait.*
Word building: **irksome** *adjective*
Word history: Middle English, from Scandinavian

iron (uy-uhn)
noun **1** a metallic element used in the making of tools and machinery, and which is also found in some foods and is used by the body in the making of blood
2 a tool with a handle which can be heated and used to remove the creases from clothes
3 a golf club with an iron head
adjective **4** made of iron
5 strong and unyielding: *an **iron** will*
verb **6** to remove creases with an iron
phrase **7 iron out,**
a to remove with an iron: *to **iron out** creases from a skirt*
b to smooth over and remove in other ways: *They have managed to **iron out** their problems.*
8 strike while the iron is hot, to act quickly while the opportunity is still there
Word history: Old English *iren, īsen, īsern*

> **iron / ion**
> Don't confuse **iron** with **ion**, which is a small particle of matter with an electric charge.

ironbark
noun a gum tree with hard dark grey bark

ironic (uy-ron-ik)
adjective **1** showing irony: *an **ironic** remark*
2 using irony or in the habit of using irony: *an **ironic** speaker*
Word use: You can also use **ironical.**
Word building: **ironically** *adverb*

iron lung
noun a chamber in which high and low pressure can be used alternately to force normal lung movements, used especially to treat someone with poliomyelitis

ironman
noun **1** a contestant in a sporting event in which male competitors swim, ride bikes and run
adjective **2** having to do with such an event: ***ironman** competition*
Word use: You can also use **iron man.**
Word building: **ironwoman** *feminine noun*

irony (uy-ruh-nee)
noun a humorous way of speaking in which the real meaning is the opposite of what is said: *'How nice!' he said with **irony** in response to her bitter comment.*
Word history: Latin, from Greek word meaning 'dissimulation', 'understatement'

irradiate (i-ray-dee-ayt)
verb **1** to throw light on (***illuminate***, ***spotlight***)
2 to shine with light
3 to heat with radiant energy
4 to cure or treat by exposure to radiation, such as that of ultraviolet light
5 to expose to radiation
Word building: **irradiation** *noun* **irradiator** *noun*
Word history: from Latin word meaning 'illumined'

irrational
adjective absurd or unreasonable: *Jan has an **irrational** fear of water.* (***arbitrary***, ***groundless***, ***illogical***, ***unreasonable***)
Word use: The opposite of this is **rational.**
Word building: **irrationally** *adverb*
Word history: late Middle English, from Latin

irregular
adjective **1** not having an even pace or rhythm: *The patient's pulse was **irregular**.* (***broken***, ***erratic***, ***fluctuating***, ***intermittent***, ***spasmodic***)
2 not following an even line: ***irregular** walls* (***lopsided***, ***unbalanced***, ***unequal***)
3 not usual or normal (***extraordinary***, ***singular***, ***strange***, ***uncommon***)
Word use: This is the opposite of **regular.**
Word building: **irregularity** *noun* **irregularly** *adverb*
Word history: Medieval Latin

irregular verb
noun a verb whose different forms do not follow the usual pattern

> Look up **verbs: irregular verbs.**

irrelevant
adjective **1** not connected with the current topic or issue: *an **irrelevant** remark*

2 not important because not connected with a situation, person, etc.: *Age is **irrelevant** to how well you can do this job – it is skill which is important.*

Word building: **irrelevance** *noun*

irresistible
adjective so tempting that you cannot fight against it: *an **irresistible** impulse | I find sweet food **irresistible**.*

irrespective
phrase **irrespective of**, without regard to or independent of: ***irrespective of** all rights*

irresponsible
adjective not reliable, or not able to be trusted; not responsible: *He is too **irresponsible** to be left in charge of the children.*

Word building: **irresponsibility** *noun*

irrevocable (uh-rev-uh-kuh-buhl, i-ruh-voh-kuh-buhl)
adjective not able to be cancelled or revoked: *an **irrevocable** order*

Word building: **irrevocably** *adverb*

irrigate
verb to supply with water using a system of canals and pipes in order to increase productivity: *to **irrigate** land*

Word building: **irrigation** *noun*
Word history: Latin

irritable
adjective easily annoyed: *I am tired and **irritable**.* (***cross***, ***crotchety***, ***grumpy***, ***snappy***, ***touchy***)

Word building: **irritability** *noun*
Word history: Latin

irritant
noun something which irritates: *The loud music was a continual **irritant** to her.*

irritate
verb **1** to annoy or make angry: *The audience's chatter **irritated** the musicians.* (***bug***, ***goad***, ***pique***, ***provoke***, ***vex***)
2 to make sore: *She **irritates** the mosquito bites by scratching them.*

Word building: **irritating** *adjective* **irritation** *noun*
Word history: Latin

is
part of the verb **to be**

For more information, look up **be**.

Islam
noun a world religion based on the teachings of the prophet Mohammed and set down in the holy book of Islam, the Koran, which teaches that its followers should live their lives according to the wishes of Allah (God)

Word building: **Islamic** *adjective*
Word history: from Arabic word meaning 'submission (to the will of God)'

island (uy-luhnd)
noun a piece of land completely surrounded by water

Word history: Old English *īland, īgland*

islander
noun someone who lives on an island

isle (uyl)
noun a small island

Word history: Middle English, from Old French, from Latin

isle / aisle
Don't confuse **isle** with **aisle**, which is a clear path between seats in a church, hall, aeroplane, etc.

isn't
contraction of **is not**

Look up **contractions in grammar**.

isobar (uy-suh-bah)
noun **1** *Meteorology* a line drawn on a weather map, etc., connecting all points having the same barometric pressure
2 *Physics, Chemistry* one of two or more elements of different atomic number, but the same atomic weight

Word history: from Greek word meaning 'of equal weight'

isolate
verb **1** to keep quite separate or apart: *Distance **isolates** the farmers.*
2 to track down: *They **isolated** the fault.*

Word building: **isolated** *adjective* **isolation** *noun*

isolationism
noun the policy of keeping a nation separate from others by not taking part in international affairs

Word building: **isolationist** *noun*

isometric
adjective having to do with or having equal measurements

Word use: You can also use **isometrical**.
Word history: from Greek word meaning 'of equal measure'

isometrics
plural noun a system of exercises in which muscles are tensed against each other or against a fixed object

Word use: **Isometrics** is used with a singular verb.

isosceles (uy-sos-uh-leez)
adjective with two sides equal: *an **isosceles** triangle*

Word history: Late Latin, from Greek word meaning 'with equal legs'

isotope
noun any of two or more forms of a chemical element which have the same number of protons in the nucleus and therefore the same atomic number, but which have different numbers of neutrons in the nucleus and therefore different atomic weights. Isotopes of an element have almost identical properties.

Word building: **isotopic** *noun*
Word history: *iso-* (prefix meaning 'equal') + Greek *tópos* place

ISP
noun → **internet service provider**

issue
noun **1** a lively or important topic of discussion
2 something published or sent out at a certain time: *the November **issue** of our school magazine*
3 a complaint; objection: *Do you have an issue with this decision?*
4 *Old-fashioned* your children or descendants (***offspring***, ***progeny***, ***young***)
verb **5** to give or send out: *The teachers **issued** pens and paper.* (***allocate***, ***dispense***, ***distribute***)
6 to publish
phrase **7 at issue**, in disagreement: *The point **at issue** is how much we'll be paid.*
8 take issue, to disagree: *They **took issue** over wages.*

Word history: Middle English, from Old French, from Latin word meaning 'go out'

isthmus (is-muhs)
noun a narrow strip of land, with water on both sides, joining two larger pieces of land

Noun forms: The plural is **isthmuses**.
Word history: Latin, from Greek word meaning 'narrow passage', 'neck', 'isthmus'

it
pronoun **1** the personal pronoun used to refer to a thing, or to a person or animal whose sex you don't know: *The desk is ready. You can pick **it** up today.* | *The baby is awake. I can hear **it** crying.*
2 the personal pronoun used as the impersonal subject of a sentence whose logical subject is a phrase or clause which usually follows: ***It** was agreed that she would go.* | ***It's** amazing how often he rings her.*
3 the personal pronoun used as the impersonal subject in sentences which refer to such things as the weather, the time and distances: ***It** is raining.* | ***It** is six o'clock.* | ***It** is nearly 20 kilometres to his house.*

It is a third person singular pronoun. It can be in the subjective case (*It is crying*) or the objective case (*Pick it up*).

Note that **its** is the possessive form of **it**, without any apostrophe. (Look up **its / it's**.)

Because **it** never refers to people, it is sometimes called the impersonal pronoun. In fact, it can be used to avoid mentioning people at all. Compare these two sentences:

The staff all agreed to abolish the cane.

It was agreed that the cane should be abolished.

In the second version there is no sign as to who did the agreeing. It is as if the decision to abolish the cane took place without human intervention! **It** doesn't stand as a pronoun for anything at all there. It is just a 'dummy' subject for the sentence. It helps to keep people out of the subject role, and to create an impersonal style.

For more information, look up **pronouns: personal pronouns.**

IT (uy tee)
noun the technology concerned with storing and presenting information using computers

Word use: The full form is **information technology.**

italics (it-al-iks)
plural noun printing which slopes to the right (as *italics*), often used for emphasis

Word building: **italic** *adjective*
Word history: Latin

itch (ich)
verb **1** to have a feeling on the skin which makes you want to scratch: *My leg **itches**.*
2 to want very much: *He is **itching** to play.*

Word building: **itch** *noun*
Word history: Old English *gicc(e)an*

itchy
adjective **1** having an itching sensation: *Her arm was **itchy** where the mosquito had bitten her.*
phrase **2 have an itchy palm,**
a to be willing to take bribes
b to be expecting to receive a sum of money
3 have itchy feet, to have the desire to travel

Adjective forms: **itchier, itchiest**
Word building: **itchiness** *noun*

it'd
contraction of **it had** or **it would**

Look up **contractions in grammar.**

item (uy-tuhm)
noun **1** one thing, especially among a number: *I have five **items** on my list.*
2 a piece of news: *Here is an interesting **item** on page one.*

Word history: Middle English, from Latin word meaning (adverb) 'just so', 'likewise'

itemise
verb to list one by one: *He **itemised** his complaints.* (***enumerate***, ***list***, ***record***, ***tabulate***)

Word use: You can also use **itemize.**

itinerant (uy-tin-uh-ruhnt)
adjective travelling from place to place, especially to find work: *an **itinerant** fruit picker*

Word history: Late Latin

itinerary (uy-tin-uh-ree)
noun the program or plan of a trip, listing places to be visited, times of journeys, etc.

Noun forms: The plural is **itineraries.**

it'll
contraction of **it will** or **it shall**

Look up **contractions in grammar.**

its
pronoun possessive form of **it**: ***its** collar*

its / it's

Its is the special possessive form of **it**, and never has an apostrophe: *The dog chewed its bone.*

Just remember that for this pair of words you only use an apostrophe when you leave something out — the i of *is* in **it is.**

For more information, look up **pronouns: personal pronouns** and **pronouns: possessive pronouns.**

it's
contraction of **it is**: ***It's** wet.*

Look up **contractions in grammar.**

itself

pronoun **1** the reflexive form of **it**: *The dog hurt **itself** on the barbed-wire fence.*
2 a form of **it** used for emphasis: *The play **itself** was not worth watching.*

For more information, look up **pronouns: reflexive pronouns**.

IUD

noun a contraceptive device, usually made of metal or plastic, inserted into the uterus

Word history: abbreviation of *i(ntra)-u(terine) d(evice)*

I've

contraction of **I have**

Look up **contractions in grammar**.

IVF

noun the fertilisation of an egg, especially a human ovum by a sperm in a test tube, after which the embryo is implanted in a uterus

Word use: The full form is **in-vitro fertilisation**.
Word history: abbreviation of *i(n)-v(itro) f(ertilisation)*

ivory

noun **1** the valuable creamy white tusk of elephants, from which ornaments are carved
2 a creamy white colour
adjective **3** made of ivory
4 of an ivory colour (***cream***, ***off-white***, ***pale***)

Word history: Middle English, from Old French, from Latin word meaning 'made of ivory'

ivy

noun a climbing plant with smooth, shiny, evergreen leaves

Word history: Middle English; Old English *īfig*

Jj

jab
verb to push or poke with something sharp: *He **jabbed** the boy in the ribs with his elbow.*
Verb forms: I **jabbed**, I have **jabbed**, I am **jabbing**
Word building: **jab** *noun*
Word history: Scottish variant of Middle English *jobbe(n)*; ? imitative

jabber
verb **1** to speak quickly, unclearly, or foolishly (***babble***, ***chatter***, ***gabble***, ***rave***, ***yabber***)
noun **2** rapid or foolish talk (***gibberish***, ***gobbledeygook***)
Word history: apparently imitative

jabiru (jab-uh-<u>rooh</u>)
noun a type of white stork found in Australia that has a green-black head, neck and tail
Word history: This bird was originally called the *New Holland jabiru*, because it reminded people of the South American stork which is similarly large and black and white, but which has a red collar. The name of that bird was borrowed from a South American Indian language.

jacaranda (jak-uh-<u>ran</u>-duh)
noun a tall tree with pale purple flowers
Word history: South American Indian

jack
noun **1** a tool used for lifting up heavy weights, such as a car
2 a playing card that has a picture of the knave or prince on it
phrase **3 every man jack**, everyone without exception
4 jack of, *Australian Colloquial* tired of
5 jack up,
a to lift with a jack (***elevate***, ***hoist***, ***lever up***, ***raise***)
b *Australian Colloquial* to refuse to do something: *We asked him to help but he **jacked up**.*
Word history: originally proper name *Jack*, earlier *Jacken*

jackal (<u>jak</u>-uhl)
noun a wild dog of Asia and Africa which hunts in packs at night
Word history: Turkish, from Persian

jackaroo
noun someone who is learning to work on a cattle or sheep station
Word use: You can also use **jackeroo**.
Word building: **jackaroo** *verb*
Word history: origin unknown; perhaps a blend of *Jack* Christian name + *(kanga)roo*

jackass
noun **1** a male donkey
2 a very stupid or foolish person
Word history: *jack* male (from the given name *Jack*) + *ass*

jacket
noun **1** a short coat
2 a book's paper cover which can be taken off
3 the skin of a potato
Word history: Middle English, from Old French

jackhammer
noun a handheld machine used for drilling rocks, road surfaces, etc., driven by compressed air

jack-in-the-box
noun a toy figure on a spring which pops out of its box when the lid is opened

jackknife
noun **1** a large knife whose blade folds into its handle
2 a dive in which you bend your body so that your hands touch your toes
verb **3** to bend or fold up, like a jackknife
4 of a semitrailer, to go out of control in such a way that the trailer swings around at a sharp angle
Noun forms: The plural is **jackknives**.

jackpot
noun the biggest prize that you can win in a lottery or other competition

jade
noun **1** a precious, usually green, stone used for carving and jewellery
2 a bluish-green to yellowish-green colour
Word building: **jade** *adjective*
Word history: French, from Spanish, from Latin

jaded
adjective worn out with tiredness

jaffle
noun Australian a sandwich cooked by being pressed between two hot metal plates

jagged (<u>jag</u>-uhd)
adjective rough and sharp-edged: *He tore his hands on the **jagged** rocks.* (***pointed***, ***rough***, ***serrated***, ***uneven***)

jaguar (<u>jag</u>-yooh-uh)
noun a large, fierce, spotted cat found in tropical America

jail
noun **1** the place where prisoners are kept while they serve their sentences (***clink***, ***compound***, ***lockup***, ***penitentiary***, ***prison***)
verb **2** to put into prison (***confine***, ***imprison***, ***intern***, ***lock up***, ***restrain***)

Word use: You can also use **gaol**.
Word history: Middle English, from Old French word meaning 'prison', 'cage', from Latin word meaning 'cavity', 'enclosure', 'cage'

jalopy (juh-lop-ee)
noun Colloquial an old car
Noun forms: The plural is **jalopies**.

jam[1]
verb **1** to become stuck: *The door **jammed** in the wet weather.*
2 to push or force into a space tightly (***compress***, ***press***, ***squash***, ***squeeze***)
noun **3** people or things crowded together: *a traffic **jam***
4 *Colloquial* a difficult situation: *He got into a bit of a **jam**.*
Verb forms: I **jammed**, I have **jammed**, I am **jamming**

jam[2]
noun a food made of fruit and sugar which you spread on bread or scones

jamb (jam)
noun the side piece of a doorway or window
Word history: Middle English, from French word meaning 'leg', 'jamb', from Late Latin word meaning 'hoof'

jamboree
noun a large gathering of Scouts or Guides

jangle (jang-guhl)
verb **1** to make a hard, metallic sound: *The keys **jangled**. | He **jangled** the keys.*
2 to cause to become upset or tense: *The argument **jangled** my nerves.*
noun **3** a hard metallic sound
Word history: Middle English, from Old French word meaning 'chatter', 'tattle'

janitor
noun a North American word for **caretaker**
Word history: from Latin word meaning 'doorkeeper', with reference to the Roman god *Janus*

January
noun (*plural* **-ries**)
the first month of the year, containing 31 days
Word history: Latin: the month of *Janus*, a Roman god presiding over doors and gates, beginnings and endings, commonly represented with 2 faces looking in opposite directions

jar[1]
noun a glass or earthenware container, usually cylindrical and with a wide opening
Word history: French, from Provençal or Spanish, from Arabic word meaning 'earthen vessel'

jar[2]
verb **1** to make a harsh, unpleasant, grating sound
2 to jolt or shake about roughly or painfully
3 to upset or shock
Verb forms: it **jarred**, it has **jarred**, it is **jarring**

jargon (jah-guhn)
noun the words and phrases used only by people in a particular job or group: *computer **jargon*** (***dialect***, ***language***, ***pidgin***, ***slang***, ***tongue***)
Word history: Middle English from Old French

jarrah (ja-ruh)
noun a large tree found in western Australia with a hard, dark, red wood
Word history: from Nyungar, an Australian Aboriginal language of the Perth-Albany region

jasmine (jaz-muhn)
noun a shrub or climbing plant with sweet-smelling flowers
Word history: French, from Arabic, from Persian

jasper
noun an opaque, often highly coloured, variety of quartz, commonly used in ornamental carvings
Word history: Middle English, from Old French, from Latin, from Greek

jaundice (jawn-duhs)
noun **1** a diseased condition of the body due to increased bile in the blood, characterised by yellowness of the skin and the whites of the eyes, and by tiredness
2 a state of feeling in which your ideas or judgement are influenced by bitterness, jealousy, etc.
Word history: Middle English, from Old French, from Latin word meaning 'greenish yellow'

jaunt (jawnt)
noun a short trip, usually for fun: *They had a **jaunt** on the harbour.* (***excursion***, ***expedition***, ***journey***, ***tour***)
Word building: **jaunt** *verb*
Word history: perhaps a nasalised variant of *jot* jog, jolt

jaunty
adjective **1** lively and confident: *a **jaunty** step* (***energetic***, ***frisky***, ***frolicsome***, ***playful***, ***vivacious***)
2 smart: *She is wearing a **jaunty** outfit.*
Adjective forms: **jauntier**, **jauntiest**
Word building: **jauntily** *adverb* **jauntiness** *noun*
Word history: earlier *janty*, from French *gentil*

Java (jah-vuh)
noun Computers a high-level object-oriented programming language which can run on most computers and is particularly suited to the World Wide Web

javelin (jav-uh-luhn)
noun a spear which is thrown in sporting contests
Word history: French *javeline*; probably from Celtic

jaw
noun one of the two bones between your chin and nose which contain your teeth
Word history: Middle English, from Old French word meaning 'cheek', 'jaw'

jay
noun **1** any of a number of Australian birds such as certain currawongs and cuckoo-shrikes
2 any of several birds of Europe and America, all of them gaily coloured and noisy
3 *Colloquial* a simple-minded or foolish person
Word history: Middle English, from Old French

jaywalk
verb to cross a street carelessly, taking no notice of traffic lights, etc.
Word history: US slang *jay* a fool + *walk*

jazz
noun **1** a type of music with strong rhythms, first played by black Americans
phrase **2 jazz up**, *Colloquial* to make brighter or more lively: *She has* ***jazzed up*** *her room with new curtains.*

Word building: **jazz** *adjective*
Word history: origin obscure; said to have been long used by Negroes of the southern US, especially those of Louisiana

jealous (jel-uhs)
adjective wanting what other people have, or not wanting to lose what you've already got: *Sam is* ***jealous*** *of his brother's popularity.* | *a* ***jealous*** *husband* (***covetous***, ***envious***, ***green***, ***possessive***)

Word building: **jealously** *adverb* **jealousy** *noun*
Word history: Middle English, from Old French, from Latin, from Greek word meaning 'zeal'

jeans
plural noun trousers made of denim or other strong material

Word history: probably from French *Gênes* Genoa, a city in Italy

jeans / genes

Don't confuse **jeans** with **genes**. **Genes** are the units in your body which are responsible for passing on physical characteristics, like blue eyes, from parents to their children.

jeep
noun a small strong car for driving in rough conditions

Word history: perhaps a special use of *jeep*, name of fabulous animal in comic strip 'Popeye', or an alteration of *GP* (for General Purpose Vehicle)

jeer
verb to mock or insult

Word building: **jeer** *noun*
Word history: perhaps from Old English *cēir* clamour

Jekyll-and-Hyde (jek-uhl-uhn-huyd)
adjective of a person, having both very good and very bad qualities

Word history: from *Dr Jekyll and Mr Hyde* (1886), a novel by RL Stevenson

jelly
noun a soft food, set with gelatine so that it wobbles when it is moved

Noun forms: The plural is **jellies**.
Word building: **jelly** *verb* (**jellied**, **jellying**)
Word history: Middle English, from Old French, from Latin word meaning 'frozen'

jellyfish
noun a soft-bodied sea animal, especially one with an umbrella-shaped body and long tentacles

Noun forms: The plural is **jellyfishes** or **jellyfish**.

jemmy
noun **1** a short crowbar
verb **2** to force open with a jemmy: *The burglars* ***jemmied*** *the window to get in the house.*

Noun forms: The plural is **jemmies**.
Verb forms: I **jemmied**, I have **jemmied**, I am **jemmying**
Word history: apparently a form of *James*

jeopardise (jep-uh-duyz)
verb to risk (***compromise***, ***endanger***, ***expose***, ***put at risk***, ***threaten***)

Word use: You can also use **jeopardize**.

jeopardy (jep-uh-dee)
noun danger: *The illness put his life in* ***jeopardy***.

Word history: Middle English, from Old French *jeu parti*, divided game, even game or chance

jerk
noun **1** a sudden rough movement
2 *Colloquial* a stupid or annoying person
verb **3** to move with a jerk

Word building: **jerkily** *adverb* **jerkiness** *noun* **jerky** *adjective*

jerry-build
verb to build cheaply and poorly

Verb forms: I **jerry-built**, I have **jerry-built**, I am **jerry-building**
Word building: **jerry-built** *adjective*

jerry can
noun an oblong can for carrying liquids, especially petrol

jersey
noun **1** a long-sleeved knitted pullover
2 Jersey, a breed of cattle which produces rich milk

Word history: from the island of *Jersey*, in the English Channel

jest
noun **1** a joke (***crack***, ***gag***, ***laugh***, ***wisecrack***)
verb **2** to speak jokingly

Word history: variant of *gest*, from Latin word meaning 'perform'

jester
noun a clown who entertained royalty in medieval times

jet[1]
noun **1** a fast-flowing spurt or stream of liquid or gas: *The fountain sent a* ***jet*** *of water into the air.*
2 the opening for a stream of liquid or gas: *She lit the gas* ***jets***.
3 a plane which is powered by engines that work by having hot gas forced at high speed through an opening at the back
verb **4** to rush out in a stream or to spout
5 to travel by jet

Word use: You can also use **jet plane** for definition 3.
Word building: **jet** *verb* (**jetted**, **jetting**)
Word history: French

jet[2]
noun a hard black coal which is polished and used to make buttons, jewellery and the like

Word history: Middle English, from Old French, from Latin, from Greek, from *Gágai*, town in Lycia, Asia Minor

jet lag
noun bodily discomfort caused by the change in normal patterns of eating and sleeping during a long plane journey

jettison (jet-uh-suhn)
verb **1** to throw overboard, especially to lighten a ship or aircraft: *to* ***jettison*** *cargo* (***discard***, ***ditch***, ***dump***, ***scrap***, ***shed***)

noun **2** the act of throwing cargo, etc., overboard to lighten a ship or aircraft

Word history: from Anglo-French variant of an Old French word meaning 'throw'

jetty
noun a long structure, jutting out into a river or the sea, that boats or ships can be tied to (***pier***, ***wharf***)

Noun forms: The plural is **jetties**.
Word history: Middle English, from Old French word meaning 'throw'

Jew
noun **1** a person descended from the Hebrews
2 a person whose religion is Judaism

Word building: **Jewish** *adjective*

jewel (jooh-uhl)
noun **1** a precious stone, such as a diamond, a ruby or an emerald, which has been cut and polished
2 an ornament, such as a brooch or ring, made of precious stones, pearls, gold or other valuable materials

Word history: Middle English, from Anglo-French, from Latin word meaning 'jest', 'sport'

jewellery (jooh-uhl-ree)
noun articles made of gold, silver, precious stones, etc., for personal ornament

Word use: You can also use **jewels**. | The US spelling is **jewelry**.
Word building: **jeweller** *noun*

jewfish
noun any of several types of large, marine, Australian fishes valued as food and for sport, such as the mulloway

Noun forms: The plural is **jewfishes** or **jewfish**.

jib
verb **1** to stop suddenly, like a horse when it is frightened (***baulk***, ***shy***)
phrase **2 jib at**, to be unwilling to do: *He will wash up but he* ***jibs at*** *cooking.*

Verb forms: I **jibbed**, I have **jibbed**, I am **jibbing**
Word history: perhaps related to *gibbet*

jiffy
noun Colloquial a very short time: *I'll have it done in a* ***jiffy***.

Noun forms: The plural is **jiffies**.

jig
noun **1** a very lively dance, usually in triple time
verb **2** to move with a jerky action
3 to dance, play, or sing a jig

Verb forms: I **jigged**, I have **jigged**, I am **jigging**
Word history: variant of *gauge*

jigger
noun **1** any of various mechanical devices, many of which have a jerky movement
2 in billiards, etc., a long-handled support for a cue
3 a measure for alcohol

jiggle (jig-uhl)
verb **1** to move up and down with short, quick jerks
noun **2** a jiggling movement

jigsaw
noun a narrow saw for cutting curves

jigsaw puzzle
noun a puzzle made up of many differently shaped pieces which fit together to form a picture

jihad (jee-had, jee-hahd)
noun **1** in Islam
a the spiritual struggle to be righteous and follow God's path: *his personal* ***jihad***
b a struggle or holy war in support of Islam against unbelievers
2 any vigorous campaign on behalf of a principle, etc.: *a* ***jihad*** *against smokers*

Word history: Arabic: effort or struggle. It can refer to either a spiritual or moral effort or struggle within yourself, or an effort or struggle against someone or something else.

jillaroo
noun a female worker on a sheep or cattle station

Word use: You can also use **jilleroo** or **jill**.
Word history: modelled on *jackaroo*

jilt
verb to reject or cast aside after a close friendship or engagement

jingle
verb **1** to clink or tinkle: *Her keys* ***jingle*** *when she runs. | He* ***jingled*** *his coins impatiently.*
noun **2** a tinkling sound (***clink***, ***rattle***, ***tinkle***)
3 a bright simple song of the sort used in radio or television commercials

Word history: Middle English; apparently imitative

jingoism (jing-goh-iz-uhm)
noun strong, extreme love for your country

Word building: **jingoist** *noun* **jingoistic** *adjective*
Word history: *jingo*, used in a song urging a warlike British policy against Russia in 1878 + *ism*

jinx
noun someone or something which is supposed to bring bad luck

Word building: **jinx** *verb*
Word history: variant of *jynx*, from Latin, from Greek word meaning 'bird' (woodpecker) used in witchcraft, hence 'a spell'

jitter
verb **1** to behave nervously
phrase **2 the jitters**, *Colloquial* nervousness

Word history: variant of *chitter* shiver

jive
noun **1** a lively dance performed to music with a strong beat
verb **2** to dance to rhythmic music

job[1]
noun **1** a piece of work or a task (***engagement***, ***enterprise***, ***project***, ***undertaking***, ***venture***)
2 paid employment (***occupation***, ***position***, ***work***)
phrase **3 a good job**, *Colloquial* a lucky state of affairs: *It was* ***a good job*** *I didn't lose my way in the dark.*
4 just the job, *Colloquial* exactly what is needed: *That spanner is* ***just the job***.
5 the devil's own job, a very difficult experience: *It was* ***the devil's own job*** *undoing the knot.*

job[2]
verb Australian Colloquial to hit: *Shut up or I'll **job** you.* (***hit***, ***punch***)

Verb forms: I **jobbed**, I have **jobbed**, I am **jobbing**
Word history: Middle English; perhaps imitative

jockey
noun someone who rides horses in races

Word history: diminutive of *Jock*, Scottish variant of *Jack*

jockstrap
noun Colloquial a support for the male genitals. Jockstraps are usually made of elastic cotton webbing, and are worn by athletes, dancers, etc.

Word history: from obsolete British colloquial *jock* penis

jocose (juh-kohs)
adjective characterised by joking (***humorous***, ***jesting***)

Word building: **jocosity** *noun*
Word history: Latin

jocular
adjective joking or playful: *a **jocular** mood*

Word building: **jocularity** *noun*
Word history: Latin

jocund (jok-uhnd)
adjective cheerful (***merry***, ***mirthful***)

Word building: **jocundity** *noun*
Word history: Middle English, from Late Latin word meaning 'pleasant'

jodhpurs (jod-puhz)
plural noun riding trousers which are close fitting below the knee

Word history: named after *Jodhpur* a city in India

joey
noun Australian a young animal, especially a young kangaroo which is carried in its mother's pouch

jog
verb **1** to run or go along at a slow regular pace
2 to push or nudge: *to **jog** someone's elbow*

Verb forms: I **jogged**, I have **jogged**, I am **jogging**
Word building: **jog** *noun* **jogger** *noun*
Word history: a blend of *jot* jolt and *shog* shake (both now British dialect)

jogger
noun **1** a person who jogs for sport or exercise
2 a type of shoe suitable for jogging

Word use: You can also use **jogging shoe** for definition 2.

John Dory
noun a thin, deep-bodied, high quality food fish of Australian waters

join
verb **1** to put together: *She **joins** the pieces with glue.* (***combine***, ***connect***, ***couple***, ***knit***, ***link***, ***unite***)
2 to come together: *This is where the parts **join**.*
3 to meet up with: *I'll **join** you for lunch.* (***bump into***, ***come across***, ***encounter***, ***join up with***, ***meet***, ***run into***)
4 to become a member of
phrase **5 join up**, to enlist in one of the armed forces

Word building: **join** *noun*
Word history: Middle English, from Old French, from Latin word meaning 'join', 'yoke'

joiner
noun someone who makes wooden furniture and house fittings such as window frames

joint
noun **1** the place where two things or parts are joined: *She hurt her elbow **joint**.*
2 a cut of meat: *She put a **joint** of lamb in the oven.*
adjective **3** shared: *a **joint** account*
phrase **4 out of joint**,
a out of position: *I had an accident and put my knee **out of joint**.*
b in a state of confusion or disorder: *Our plans are all completely **out of joint**.*

Word history: Middle English, from Old French, from Latin

joist
noun a length of wood or metal used to support floors, ceilings or other structures

Word history: Middle English, from Old French, from Latin word meaning 'lie'

joke
noun something which is said or done to make people laugh (***crack***, ***gag***, ***jest***, ***wisecrack***)

Word building: **joke** *verb*
Word history: from Latin word meaning 'jest', 'sport'

joker
noun **1** someone who jokes
2 an extra playing card in a pack, used in some games, often counting as the highest card

jolly
adjective **1** good-humoured and full of fun: *He is a **jolly** old man.* (***blithe***, ***cheerful***, ***gleeful***, ***happy***, ***merry***)
adverb **2** *Colloquial* very: *You've done **jolly** well.*

Word history: Middle English, from Old French

jolt
verb to bump or shake roughly

Word building: **jolt** *noun*
Word history: blend of British dialect *jot* jolt and obsolete *joll* knock about

jonquil (jong-kwuhl)
noun a flowering plant of the narcissus group with long, narrow leaves and sweet-smelling yellow or white flowers

Word history: French, from Spanish, from Latin word meaning 'a rush'

jostle (jos-uhl)
verb to push roughly or rudely: *People were **jostling** to see the parade.*

Word history: Middle English

jot
verb **1** to write briefly or scribble down: *I'll **jot** down a few thoughts.*
noun **2** a little bit: *He doesn't care a **jot**.*

Verb forms: I **jotted**, I have **jotted**, I am **jotting**
Word building: **jotter** *noun* **jotting** *noun*
Word history: from Latin word meaning 'iota'

joule (joohl)
noun a measure of work or energy in the metric system

Word use: The symbol is **J**, without a full stop. | Look up **metric system**.
Word history: named after JP *Joule*, 1818–89, British physicist

journal (jer-nuhl)
noun **1** a newspaper or magazine
2 a daily record of events
3 a book in which the financial transactions of the day are recorded (***daybook***)

Word history: Middle English, from Old French, from Late Latin word meaning 'diurnal'

journalese (jer-nuh-leez)
noun a hackneyed style of newspaper writing

journalism (jer-nuh-liz-uhm)
noun the work of writing and running newspapers and magazines

journalist (jer-nuh-luhst)
noun someone who works for a newspaper or magazine

journey (jer-nee)
noun a trip, especially by land: *We made a car **journey** to the mountains.* (***excursion***, ***expedition***, ***jaunt***, ***tour***)

Word building: **journey** *verb*
Word history: Middle English, from Old French, from Latin word meaning 'of the day', 'daily'

joust (jowst)
noun a contest between two knights on horseback to see which can unseat the other with his spear

Word history: Middle English, from Old French, from Latin word meaning 'near'

jovial (joh-vee-uhl)
adjective cheerful and friendly

Word building: **joviality** *noun*
Word history: from Latin word meaning 'of Jupiter', because in astrology the planet is regarded as exerting a happy influence

jowl
noun a fold of flesh which hangs below the cheek or jaw

Word history: Middle English, from Old English *ceole* throat

joy
noun **1** great happiness or delight (***bliss***, ***ecstasy***, ***joyfulness***)
phrase **2 not to have any joy**, to be unsuccessful

Word building: **joyful** *adjective* **joyfully** *adverb* **joyous** *adjective* **joyously** *adverb*
Word history: Middle English, from Old French, from Latin plural word meaning 'joy', 'gladness'

joy-ride
noun Colloquial a pleasure ride, as in a car, especially when the car is driven wildly or stolen

Word building: **joy-rider** *noun* **joy-riding** *noun adjective*

joystick
noun **1** the control stick of a plane
2 *Computers* a lever used to control the movement of the cursor and other images in computer games, or the arrangement of graphics on a screen

JPEG (jay-peg)
noun Computers a standard format used to store images as data, especially useful for photographs

Word history: *J(oint) P(hotographic) E(xperts) G(roup)*

jube
noun a chewy fruit-flavoured lolly made with gelatine

jubilant (jooh-buh-luhnt)
adjective extremely happy or joyful: *He was **jubilant** at winning the race.* (***blissful***, ***ecstatic***, ***elated***, ***rapturous***)

Word building: **jubilation** *noun*
Word history: Latin

jubilee
noun a celebration, especially of the anniversary of something which happened a long time ago

Word history: Middle English, from French, from Late Latin, from Greek, from Hebrew word meaning 'ram', 'ram's horn' (used as a trumpet)

Judaism (jooh-day-iz-uhm)
noun the religion of the Jewish people, based on the writings of the Old Testament and the teaching of the rabbis, which say that there is only one God

Word building: **Judaic** *adjective*

judas (jooh-duhs)
noun someone disloyal enough to act against a friend (***snake in the grass***, ***traitor***)

Word history: from *Judas Iscariot*, the disciple who, in the Bible, betrayed Jesus

judge (juj)
noun **1** someone whose job is to hear and decide cases in a court of law
2 someone who gives an opinion or a decision on the winner of a contest or competition
verb **3** to hear and decide a case in a court of law
4 to act as a judge: *to **judge** a contest*
5 to form a judgement or opinion on or upon: *I **judge** that it will take the rest of the day.* (***adjudicate***, ***appraise***, ***evaluate***, ***size up***)

Word history: Middle English, from Old French, from Latin

judgement
noun **1** an opinion or conclusion: *Your **judgement** of her is too harsh.*
2 the ability to make right decisions: *That driver has good **judgement**.*
3 the decision in a court case: *The **judgement** was 'guilty'.*

Word use: You can also use **judgment**.

judicial (jooh-dish-uhl)
adjective having to do with judges or law courts: *There is to be a **judicial** enquiry.*

Word history: Middle English, from Latin word meaning 'of a court of justice'

judiciary (jooh-dish-uh-ree)
noun the system of courts and judges

judicious (jooh-dish-uhs)
adjective showing good or wise judgement

Word building: **judiciously** *adverb*
Word history: French, from Latin word meaning 'judgement'

judo
noun a type of self-defence based on jujitsu

Word history: from Japanese word meaning 'soft way'

jug
noun a container with a handle and pouring lip

Word history: perhaps a special use of *Jug*, variant of *Joan* or *Joanna*

juggernaut (jug-uh-nawt)
noun **1** anything in which you have blind faith, but which may cause you harm
2 any large, destructive force, especially a vehicle

Word history: from an Indian idol *Jagannath* lord of the world, annually drawn on an enormous vehicle under whose wheels devotees are said to have thrown themselves to be crushed; Hindustani, from Sanskrit

juggle
verb to throw several things into the air and keep them moving, without dropping any

Word building: **juggler** *noun*
Word history: Middle English, from Old French, from Latin word *jocus* meaning 'jest'

jugular (jug-yooh-luh)
adjective having to do with or situated in the throat or neck: ***jugular** vein*

Word history: Neo-Latin, from Latin word meaning 'collarbone', 'throat'

juice
noun **1** the liquid part of a plant, especially fruit: *orange **juice***
2 *Colloquial* petrol: *We're out of **juice**.*

Word building: **juicy** *adjective* (**juicier**, **juiciest**)
Word history: Middle English, from Old French, from Latin word meaning 'broth'

jujitsu (jooh-jit-sooh)
noun a Japanese way of self-defence without weapons

Word history: from Japanese word meaning 'soft art'

jukebox
noun a coin-operated machine which plays selected musical items

July (juh-luy)
noun (*plural* **-lies**)
the seventh month of the year, containing 31 days

Word history: Middle English, Old English *Julius*, from Latin; named after Julius Caesar, who was born in this month

jumble
verb **1** to muddle or confuse
noun **2** a confused mixture (***medley***, ***miscellany***)
3 a state of confusion or disorder (***clutter***, ***litter***, ***mess***, ***muddle***, ***shambles***)

Word history: perhaps a blend of *join* and *tumble*

jumbo
noun Colloquial **1** an elephant
2 a very large jet, or anything bigger than usual
adjective Colloquial **3** very large

Word history: from *Jumbo*, an elephant at the London Zoo, subsequently sold to Phineas T Barnum

jumbuck
noun Australian, *NZ Colloquial* a sheep

Word use: This is a word that we know mainly from the song 'Waltzing Matilda'.

jump
verb **1** to leap or spring from the ground (***bound***, ***frisk***, ***lollop***, ***vault***)
2 to make a sudden movement due to fear or surprise: *She **jumped** at the noise.*
3 to move irregularly: *Her argument **jumps** from one point to another.*
noun **4** a leap
5 something to be leapt over
6 a sudden move from one state or thing to another: *a **jump** in price*
7 a sudden nervous movement
phrase **8 jump at**, accept eagerly: *She **jumped at** the chance of a new job.*
9 jump on (or **upon**), to scold (***go crook at***, ***reprimand***, ***upbraid***)
10 jump the gun, *Colloquial* to get an unfair advantage
11 jump the queue, to get something out of your proper turn
12 jump to it, *Colloquial* to hurry

Word history: apparently imitative

jumper[1]
noun a piece of clothing, usually made of wool, and worn on the top half of the body, often over other clothes (***jersey***, ***pullover***, ***sweater***)

jumper[2]
noun Computers a short length of conductor used to make a connection, usually temporary, between electrical terminals

jumpsuit
noun trousers and top which are joined at the waist

jumpy
adjective nervous or frightened in mood or behaviour: *The storm makes the animals **jumpy**.* (***anxious***, ***apprehensive***, ***edgy***, ***jittery***, ***upset***)

Adjective forms: **jumpier**, **jumpiest**
Word building: **jumpily** *adverb* **jumpiness** *noun*

junction (jungk-shuhn)
noun the place where two or more things, especially roads or railway tracks, meet or cross

Word history: from Latin word meaning 'a joining'

juncture (jungk-chuh)
noun **1** a particular point in time: *At this **juncture** let us finish.*
2 the junction or joining point of two things

Word history: Middle English, from Latin word meaning 'joining', 'joint'

June
noun the sixth month of the year, containing thirty days

Word history: Middle English; Old English *Iuni*, from Latin

jungle
noun the thick trees and vegetation which grow in warm, damp, tropical conditions

Word history: Hindustani, from Sanskrit word meaning 'dry', 'desert'

junior
adjective **1** younger or smaller: *the **junior** members*
noun **2** a person who is younger than another
3 a person of the lowest rank
4 *Law* any barrister who is not a Senior Counsel or Queen's Counsel

Word history: from Latin word meaning 'young'

juniper (<u>jooh</u>-nuh-puh)
noun an evergreen shrub or tree with purple berries which are used in making gin and in medicine

Word history: Middle English, from Latin

junk[1]
noun old or unwanted things (***debris***, ***garbage***, ***refuse***, ***rubbish***, ***trash***)

junk[2]
noun a Chinese flat-bottomed boat

Word history: Portuguese *junco*, from Malay *jong*, *ajong*, apparently from Javanese *jong*

junket
noun a milk pudding made by setting sweetened warm milk

Word history: Middle English, from Latin

junk food
noun food which has little value to the health of your body: *A lot of fast food is also **junk food**.*

junkie
noun **1** *Colloquial* a drug addict
2 a person who is enthusiastic about something specified: *a sci-fi **junkie***

junta (<u>jun</u>-tuh)
noun a small group of people ruling a country, especially as the result of a revolution

Word history: Spanish, from Latin word meaning 'joined'

jurisdiction (jooh-ruhs-<u>dik</u>-shuhn)
noun the legal power to settle matters: *The soldiers come under military **jurisdiction**.*

Word history: Middle English, from Latin word meaning 'administration of the law', 'authority'

jurisprudence (jooh-ruhs-<u>prooh</u>-duhns)
noun **1** the science or philosophy of law
2 a body or system of laws

Word history: from Latin word meaning 'the science of the law'

jurist (<u>jooh</u>-ruhst, <u>joouh</u>-ruhst)
noun an expert in the law

Word building: **juristic** *adjective*
Word history: Medieval Latin, from Latin word meaning 'right', 'law'

juror
noun a member of a jury

jury
noun **1** the group of people chosen to hear and try to decide the outcome of a court case
2 a group chosen to judge a competition and award prizes

Word history: Middle English, from Anglo-French, from Latin word meaning 'swear'

just
adjective **1** fair or rightly judged: *a **just** decision* (***impartial***, ***neutral***, ***objective***, ***right***)
adverb **2** by a very little: *You have **just** missed him.*
3 exactly: *That's **just** what I think.*
4 only: *He is still **just** a boy.*

Word history: Middle English, from Latin word meaning 'righteous'

justice
noun **1** what is right and fair: *They trust his sense of **justice**.*
2 judgement by a court of law
phrase **3 do justice to,**
a to show in favourable terms: *The colour of that dress does not **do justice to** your eyes.*
b to deal with properly: *We didn't have the time to **do justice to** the exhibition*

Word use: The opposite of this is **injustice**.
Word history: Middle English, from Old French, from Latin

justify
verb to try to defend or show to be right: *She can **justify** her argument.* (***excuse***, ***explain***, ***vindicate***, ***warrant***)

Verb forms: I **justified**, I have **justified**, I am **justifying**
Word building: **justifiable** *adjective* **justifiably** *adverb* **justification** *noun*
Word history: Middle English, from Old French, from Late Latin word meaning 'act justly towards'

jut
phrase **jut out,** to stick out: *The rock **juts out** sharply here.* (***bulge***, ***project***, ***protrude***)

Verb forms: it **jutted**, it has **jutted**, it is **jutting**
Word history: variant of *jet*[1], verb

jute
noun a strong fibre which is used for making rope or sacks

Word history: Bengali, from Sanskrit word meaning 'braid of hair'

juvenile (<u>jooh</u>-vuh-nuyl)
adjective **1** young or for the young
2 childish
noun **3** a young person

Word history: from Latin word meaning 'of youth'

juxtapose
verb to place close together

Word building: **juxtaposition** *noun*

K
abbreviation Computers 2^{10} words, bytes or bits

kadaitja man (kuh-duy-chuh man)
noun in some traditional Aboriginal cultures, a man who has the power to take revenge for a wrong felt by a member of his community

Word use: You can also use **kadaicha man** or **kurdaitcha man**.
Word history: from Arrernte, an Australian Aboriginal language of central Australia

kadaitja shoes
plural noun in certain central Australian Aboriginal groups, shoes made of human hair, string and emu feathers, matted with human blood, worn by the kadaitja man so that his footsteps may not be traced

Word use: You can also use **kadaicha shoes** or **kurdaitcha shoes**.

kaftan
noun → **caftan**

kaleidoscope (kuh-luy-duh-skohp)
noun a tube with mirrors and pieces of coloured glass in one end, which shows different patterns when it is turned around

Word building: **kaleidoscopic** *adjective*
Word history: Greek

kamikaze (kam-uh-kah-zee)
noun Colloquial dangerous or suicidal: *his **kamikaze** driving*

Word history: *Kamikaze* was the name of members of a Japanese air force corps in World War II whose mission was to crash their aircraft, loaded with explosives, into an enemy target, killing themselves. The word itself means 'divine wind' in Japanese.

Kanaka (kuh-nak-uh)
noun in the past, a Pacific islander kidnapped and brought to Australia as a labourer

Word use: The use of this word to refer to Pacific islanders nowadays will offend people.
Word history: Hawaiian word literally meaning 'man'

kangaroo
noun an Australian animal with a small head, short front limbs, and a large tail and back legs for leaping

Word use: The short form is **roo**. | The kangaroo belongs to a class of animals called **marsupials**.
Word history: from *gangurru*, from the Australian Aboriginal language Guugu Yimidhirr, from the Cooktown region in Queensland

kangaroo court
noun Colloquial a court set up without proper authority and held in mock or informal manner, by prisoners in a gaol, or by trade unionists in judging workers who do not follow union decisions

Word history: originally a British and US colloquialism

kapok (kay-pok)
noun a cotton-like substance from the seeds of trees in south-east Asia, Africa and tropical America, used for stuffing pillows, etc.

Word history: Malay

kaput (ka-poot, kuh-poot)
adjective Colloquial ruined or not working

Word history: German

karaoke (ka-ree-oh-kee)
noun **1** the entertainment of singing to a karaoke machine: *That restaurant offers **karaoke**.*
adjective **2** of bars, restaurants, etc., equipped with a karaoke machine

Word history: Japanese word meaning 'no orchestra', from *kara* absent + *oke* orchestra

karaoke machine
noun a music system which simultaneously plays a video clip of a song with subtitled lyrics and the backing tape of the song, and which is equipped with microphones for the use of a singer

Word use: You can also use **karaoke unit**.

karate (kuh-rah-tee)
noun a Japanese form of self-defence which uses only hands, elbows, feet and knees as weapons

Word history: Japanese word literally meaning 'empty hand'

karma
noun **1** in Hinduism, Buddhism, etc., the justice by which a person has a status in life according to his or her actions in the last life
2 fate or destiny

Word history: from Sanskrit word meaning 'deed', 'action'

karri (ka-ree)
noun a western Australian gum tree with hard lasting wood

Word history: from Nyungar, an Australian Aboriginal language of the Perth-Albany region

kauri (kow-ree)
noun a tall New Zealand cone-bearing tree, which is valued for its wood and its resin

Word history: Maori

kayak (kuy-ak)
noun **1** a light canoe, like the watertight skin-covered hunting canoe made by Inuit people
verb **2** to travel in a kayak

Word history: Inuit

kebab (kuh-bab)
noun **1** small pieces of meat cooked on a skewer, sometimes with vegetables
2 a dish of cooked meat and salad rolled up in a piece of flat bread

Word use: You can also use **shish kebab** for definition 1 and **doner kebab** for definition 2.

keel
noun **1** a long piece of timber or metal which stretches along the bottom of a ship, holding it together
phrase **2 keel over,** to turn over or upside down: *The yacht **keeled over** in the strong breeze.* (***capsize***, ***overbalance***)

Word history: Middle English, from Scandinavian

keen[1]
adjective **1** strong or clear in feelings or senses: *a **keen** disappointment | a **keen** eye*
2 full of enthusiasm: *He's **keen** to start the job.* (***anxious***, ***avid***, ***eager***, ***enthusiastic***, ***willing***)
3 sharp: *a **keen** blade*
phrase **4 keen on,** fond of: *She's **keen on** cakes.*

Word building: **keenly** *adverb* **keenness** *noun*
Word history: Old English *cēne*

keen[2]
noun **1** a wailing lament for the dead
verb **2** to wail in lamentation for the dead

Word history: from Irish word meaning 'lament'

keep
verb **1** to continue or make continue in the same way or state: *to **keep** calm | to **keep** the house clean* (***maintain***, ***preserve***, ***retain***, ***sustain***)
2 to retain or hang on to: *I'll **keep** one dress and send the others back.*
3 to have and look after: *to **keep** hens*
4 to obey, follow or carry out: *to **keep** a promise | to **keep** the law*
noun **5** the basic needs of living, like food and shelter: *to earn your **keep***
6 the central tower of a medieval castle
phrase **7 for keeps,** *Colloquial* permanently or forever: *We've broken up **for keeps**.*
8 keep at, to continue or persist in: *Try to **keep at** your homework.*
9 keep down,
a to prevent from rising or appearing: *She managed to **keep down** her emotions.*
b to continue to hold: *to **keep down** a job*
10 keep on, to continue or persist: *She **kept on** running in spite of the heat.*
11 keep time,
a to record time as a watch or clock does
b to beat out or follow the rhythmic accents of music
12 keep to, to follow or stick to: *to **keep to** an agreement | to **keep to** the truth*
14 keep up, to have an equal rate of speed or progress with another: *We are going to work quickly so you will have to concentrate if you want to **keep up**.*

Verb forms: I **kept**, I have **kept**, I am **keeping**
Word history: Old English *cēpan*, observe, heed, regard, await, take

keeper
noun **1** someone who keeps, guards, or watches
2 the person in charge of something valuable, for example an attendant in a zoo, museum, etc.

keeping
noun **1** care or possession: *He gave his watch into my **keeping**.*
phrase **2 in keeping with,** suitable for: *clothes **in keeping with** the situation*

keepsake
noun something kept to remember a person or event by: *She took the program as a **keepsake** of the concert.* (***memento***, ***souvenir***, ***token***, ***trophy***)

keg
noun a barrel, especially for beer

Word history: late Middle English, from Scandinavian

kelp
noun a greenish-brown seaweed which grows in thick strands

Word history: Middle English; ultimate origin unknown

kelpie
noun a breed of Australian sheepdog

Word history: probably from the name of an early specimen of the breed

kelvin
noun the base SI unit of thermodynamic temperature, equal to the fraction $\frac{1}{273.16}$ of the temperature of the triple point of water. As a unit of temperature interval, one kelvin is equivalent to one degree Celsius.

Word use: The symbol is **K**, without a full stop. | Also look up **Celsius** and **absolute zero**.
Word history: named after Lord *Kelvin*, 1824–1907, British physicist and mathematician

Kelvin scale
noun a scale of temperature based on thermodynamic principles, in which zero is equivalent to –273.16°C or –459.69°F

kennel
noun a house or shelter built for a dog

Word history: Middle English, from Anglo-French, from Vulgar Latin, from Latin word meaning 'dog'

kept
verb past tense and past participle of **keep**

kerb
noun the line of stones or concrete at the edge of a street

Word history: variant spelling of *curb* something that controls or borders, Middle English, from French word meaning 'curved', from Latin word meaning 'bent', 'crooked'

kerb / curb

Don't confuse **kerb** with **curb**. When you **curb** something, you control it or hold it back. It is worth noting that the line of concrete at the edge of a road is usually spelt **curb** in the US, and you will sometimes see it spelt this way in Australia.

kernel
noun **1** the inner part of a nut which you can eat
2 a grain, as of wheat or corn
3 *Computers* the essential parts of an operating system

Word history: Old English *cyrnel*, diminutive of *corn* seed, grain

kernel / colonel

Don't confuse **kernel** with **colonel**. A **colonel** is an officer in the army.

kero
noun Australian, NZ Colloquial → **kerosene**

kerosene
noun a liquid used as a fuel for lamps, engines and heaters

Word use: You can also use **kerosine.** | You can also use the colloquial word **kero.**
Word history: from Greek word meaning 'wax'

ketchup
noun a sauce: *tomato **ketchup***

Word use: This word is used more in the US.
Word history: apparently from Chinese (Amoy dialect) word meaning 'brine of pickled fish'

kettle
noun a pot with a spout, a lid and a handle, used for boiling water

Word history: Middle English, from Scandinavian, from Latin diminutive word meaning 'bowl', 'pot'

kettledrum
noun a drum with a skin stretched over a brass or copper bowl

key
noun **1** a small, specially-shaped piece of metal that can open a lock
2 something which helps you to read or understand such things as a map, a code, or a puzzle
3 one of the notes on a piano
4 the set of notes, starting and ending on one particular note, used to make up a piece of music: *This piece is in the **key** of C major.*
5 one of a set of parts pressed in working a typewriter or computer terminal
adjective **6** main or important: *a **key** piece of information* (***chief***, ***fundamental***, ***major***, ***significant***)

Word building: **keyer** *noun*
Word history: Old English *cǣg*

key / quay

Don't confuse **key** with **quay**, which is a wharf where ships load or unload passengers and cargo.

keyboard
noun a row or set of keys such as on a piano, typewriter or computer

keynote
noun **1** the note on which a musical key or scale is based (***base note***, ***tonic***)
2 the main element or principle: *The **keynote** of her speech was the fight against poverty.*

Word building: **keynote** *adjective*

key signature
noun the sharps or flats placed after the clef to show what key a piece of music is in

Word use: Compare this with **time signature.**

keystone
noun the wedge-shaped stone at the top of an arch which is thought to hold the other stones in place

khaki (kah-kee, kah-kee)
noun **1** a dull greenish-brown colour, used especially for soldiers' uniforms
2 a heavy cotton cloth of this colour, worn especially by soldiers

Word building: **khaki** *adjective*
Word history: from Hindustani word meaning 'dusty'

kibble
verb **1** to grind into small particles
adjective **2** having to do with wheat, grain, etc., which has been kibbled

kibbutz (ki-boots)
noun an Israeli farming settlement whose management, work and products are shared

Noun forms: The plural is **kibbutzim.**
Word history: from Modern Hebrew word meaning 'gathering'

kick
verb **1** to hit, move or drive with the foot: *That horse **kicks.** | to **kick** a ball*
2 to spring back: *The rifle **kicked** into her shoulder.*
noun **3** a hit or thrust with the foot
4 a sudden, strong movement backwards, especially of a gun
5 *Colloquial* a feeling of pleasure or satisfaction: *She gets a **kick** out of dancing.*
phrase **6 kick on,** *Australian* to continue: *She felt tired but decided to **kick on** with the work. | We were having such a good time that we **kicked on** until dawn.*
7 kick upstairs, to promote to a position with a high-sounding title but no real power

Word history: Middle English

kid[1]
noun **1** a young goat
2 *Colloquial* a child

Word history: Middle English, apparently from Old Norse

kid[2]
verb Colloquial to tease or trick: *He's only **kidding.*** (***bluff***, ***cheat***, ***deceive***, ***fool***, ***hoax***)

Verb forms: I **kidded,** I have **kidded,** I am **kidding**
Word history: perhaps special use of *kid*, meaning 'child'

kidnap
verb to take someone away by force and hold them prisoner until money is paid, or some other condition is met (***abduct***, ***capture***, ***shanghai***)

Verb forms: I **kidnapped,** I have **kidnapped,** I am **kidnapping**
Word building: **kidnapper** *noun*
Word history: *kid*[1] + obsolete *nap* seize

kidney
noun one of the two bean-shaped organs in your body which get rid of waste from the blood

Noun forms: The plural is **kidneys.**
Word history: Middle English

kidney bean
noun a small dark-red bean with a curved shape

kikuyu (kuy-kooh-yooh)
noun a tough grass which is used for lawns and pasture

kill
verb **1** to cause the death of (***assassinate, execute, murder, slay***)
2 to stop or destroy: *He will **kill** any suggestion you make.*
3 to eliminate an opponent, etc., in a computer game

Word building: **kill** *noun* **killer** *noun*
Word history: Middle English, apparently from Old English *-colla* (in *morgen-colla* morning slaughter)

killjoy
noun a person or thing that spoils the joy or enjoyment of others

kiln
noun a big oven or furnace for baking bricks or pottery

Word history: Old English *cyl(e)n*, from Latin word meaning 'kitchen'

kilo (kee-loh)
noun → **kilogram**

Noun forms: The plural is **kilos**.

kilobit
noun a unit of measurement of computer storage equal to 1024 bits

Word use: The abbreviation is **Kb**.

kilobyte
noun a unit of measurement of computer storage equal to 1024 bytes

Word use: The abbreviation is **KB** or **kbyte**.

kilogram
noun a unit of weight in the metric system, equal to 1000 grams

Word use: The symbol is **kg**, without a full stop. | You can also use the colloquial word **kilo**. | Look up **metric system**.
Word history: *kilo-* (a prefix meaning 1000) + *gram*

kilojoule
noun a measure of work or energy in the metric system, equal to 1000 joules or the amount of food needed to produce it

Word use: The symbol is **kJ**, without a full stop. | Look up **metric system**.
Word history: *kilo-* (a prefix meaning 1000) + *joule*

kilometre (kil-uh-mee-tuh, kuh-lom-uh-tuh)
noun a unit of length in the metric system, equal to 1000 metres

Word use: The symbol is **km**, without a full stop. | Look up **metric system**. | The US spelling is **kilometer**.
Word history: *kilo-* (a prefix meaning 1000) + *metre*

kilowatt
noun 1000 watts

Word use: The symbol is **kW**, without a full stop.
Word history: *kilo-* (a prefix meaning 1000) + *watt*

kilt
noun a pleated skirt of tartan cloth, sometimes worn by men in the Scottish Highlands

Word history: Middle English, probably from Scandinavian

kilter
phrase **out of kilter**, not in good condition or out of order: *The engine was **out of kilter**.*

kimono (ki-muh-noh, kuh-moh-noh)
noun a wide-sleeved Japanese robe which is tied at the waist

Noun forms: The plural is **kimonos**.
Word history: Japanese

kin
noun your relatives: *Her mother's **kin** were Irish.* (***family, flesh and blood, relations***)

Word building: **kin** *adjective*
Word history: Middle English; Old English *cynn* from Germanic root equivalent to Latin *gen-*, Greek *gen-*, Sanskrit *jan-* beget, produce

kind[1]
adjective warm-hearted, friendly and well-wishing (***considerate, thoughtful, unselfish, well-meaning***)

Word use: The opposite of this is **cruel**.
Word building: **kindly** *adverb* **kindness** *noun*
Word history: Old English *gecynd* nature from where *kind*[2] also comes

kind[2]
noun **1** a group of things or people of the same nature or type (***category, class, genre, sort, variety***)
2 something not quite exact: *They used the shed as a **kind** of house.*

Word history: Old English *gecynd*

kind of / kinds of

When you are using **kind** as a noun to mean 'sort', remember that it is a singular noun. This is especially important when you use it with a collective noun such as *people*, *team*, and *crowd*, which stands for a group of things taken as a whole.

So while it is correct to write *this kind of fruit*, it is wrong to write *these kind of fruit*.

If you want to talk about more than one type of fruit, you should use **kinds of**, as in *these kinds of fruit*.

kindergarten
noun a school or class for very young children which prepares them for primary school

Word history: German word literally meaning 'children's garden'

kindle
verb **1** to set alight or ablaze: *She **kindled** the fire with dry leaves.*
2 to light up: *The sticks began to **kindle**.* | *His eyes **kindled**.*

Word use: The opposite of this is **extinguish**.
Word history: Middle English, probably from Scandinavian

kindling
noun the twigs and other material used to start a fire

kindred
noun **1** your relatives
adjective **2** like or related: *They talked about war and **kindred** matters.*
Word history: Middle English from *kin* + *-red* (a suffix indicating condition)

kinetic (kuh-net-ik, kuy-net-ik)
adjective having to do with movement (***dynamic***, ***mobile***, ***moving***)
Word history: Greek

kinetic energy
noun Science energy which a body has because it is moving, or energy which a system has because its parts are moving
Word use: Compare this with **potential energy**.

king
noun **1** a man, from a royal family, who rules over a country or empire
2 someone who is powerful or outstanding: *a cattle **king** | He is a **king** among men.*
3 a playing card with a picture of a king on it
4 the chess piece whose capture ends the game
adjective **5** large: ***king** size*
Word building: **kingly** *adjective*
Word history: Middle English from Old English *cyng, cyning*

kingdom
noun **1** a country or government ruled over by a king or queen (***dominion***, ***realm***)
2 a section of nature, especially one of the three great divisions of natural objects: *the animal, vegetable and mineral **kingdoms***
Word history: Middle English from Old English *cyningdōm*

kingfisher
noun a brilliantly coloured bird which eats fish or insects in water

king parrot
noun a large parrot of eastern Australia

kink
noun **1** a wrinkle or fault
2 an unusual taste or whim
Word building: **kinky** *adjective* (**kinkier**, **kinkiest**)
Word history: from Dutch word meaning 'twirl'

kinship
noun relationship by family or other ties: *He claims **kinship** with my cousin. | The girls found a **kinship** in stamp collecting.*

kiosk (kee-osk)
noun a small shop or stall which sells such things as newspapers, souvenirs and light refreshments
Word history: from Turkish word meaning 'pavilion'

kip
noun Colloquial sleep

kipper
noun a dried fish, usually herring or salmon, which has been salted and smoked
Word history: perhaps from Old English *cypera* spawning salmon

kirk
noun a church
Word use: This is used in Scotland.
Word history: Middle English, from Scandinavian

kismet (kiz-muht, kis-muht)
noun fate or destiny
Word history: Turkish, from Persian, from Arabic word meaning 'divide'

kiss
verb **1** to touch or press with the lips, in a sign of greeting, affection, etc.
2 to touch gently or lightly
noun **3** the act of kissing
4 a slight touch
Word history: Old English *cyssan* from *coss* a kiss

kiss of life
noun **1** mouth-to-mouth resuscitation
2 anything which offers new hopes of success to a failing enterprise

kit
noun **1** a set of tools, supplies or parts for a special purpose: *climbing **kit** | first-aid **kit***
2 a set of parts to be put together: *We bought the furniture as a **kit**.*
Word history: Middle English, apparently from Middle Dutch word meaning 'kind of tub'

kitchen
noun the room or place where food is cooked and prepared
Word history: Old English *cycene*, from Latin

kite
noun **1** a light frame covered by a thin material, which is flown in the wind at the end of a long string
2 a medium-sized hawk with long wings and tail
Word history: Old English *cȳta*

kiteboard
noun **1** a small surfboard used in kitesurfing
verb **2** to take part in kitesurfing: *They **kiteboarded** until the wind dropped.*
Word building: **kiteboarder** *noun*

kitesurfing
noun the sport of riding a kiteboard while being propelled by a large controllable kite
Word use: You can also use **kiteboarding**.

kitsch (kich)
adjective in art, literature, etc., showy, self-important, and worthless (***flashy***, ***gaudy***, ***loud***, ***tawdry***)
Word history: German

kitten
noun a young cat
Word history: Middle English, from a dialect of Old French

kitty
noun **1** a collection, usually of small amounts of money, used for a special purpose by a group of people
2 *Cards* a pool of money into which each player places a stake
Noun forms: The plural is **kitties**.
Word history: from *kitcot*, variant of *kidcot* prison, from *kid* (in the sense of a slave or criminal) + *cot* (in the old sense of a hut or shelter)

kiwi (kee-wee)
noun **1** a New Zealand bird with thick legs and a long, thin bill, and which cannot fly
2 *Colloquial* someone from New Zealand
Word history: Maori

kiwifruit
noun a small, oval, hairy fruit with light green flesh
Word use: Another name is **Chinese gooseberry**.

klaxon (klak-suhn)
noun a loud horn once used in motor cars
Word history: Trademark

kleptomania (klep-tuh-mayn-ee-uh)
noun an uncontrollable urge to steal things
Word building: **kleptomaniac** *noun*
Word history: Neo-Latin, from Greek

knack (nak)
noun the skill for doing a particular thing
Word history: Middle English

knacker (nak-uh)
noun someone who buys old or useless horses to kill for pet meat
Word building: **knackery** *noun*
Word history: Scandinavian

knapsack (nap-sak)
noun Old-fashioned a backpack
Word history: Low German

knave (nayv)
noun Old-fashioned a dishonest man or boy (***cheat***, ***crook***, ***fraud***, ***rascal***, ***rogue***)
Word building: **knavish** *adjective*
Word history: Middle English; Old English *cnafa*

knead (need)
verb to press and push with your hands: *The baker **kneaded** the dough.*
Word history: Old English *cnedan*

knead / need
Don't confuse **knead** with **need**. To **need** something is to want it urgently:
I need help. Quick!

knee (nee)
noun the joint between the upper and lower leg
Word history: Old English *cnēo(w)*

kneecap
noun the flat movable bone which covers the knee joint

kneejerk
phrase **kneejerk reaction**, an instinctive response

kneel (neel)
verb to go down on your knees
Verb forms: I **knelt** or I **kneeled**, I have **knelt** or I have **kneeled**, I am **kneeling**
Word history: Old English *cnēow* knee

knell (nel)
noun a slow bell ringing for a death or funeral
Word history: Old English *cnyllan* strike, ring (a bell)

knew (nyooh)
verb past tense of **know**

knew / new
Don't confuse **knew** with **new**. People or things are **new** if they have arrived recently or have just come into being.

knickerbockers (nik-uh-bok-uhz)
plural noun loose, short trousers which are gathered in at the knees
Word history: from *Knickerbocker*, a descendant of the Dutch settlers of New York

knickers (nik-uhz)
plural noun underpants, usually for girls or women
Word history: short form of *knickerbockers*

knick-knack (nik-nak)
noun a small ornament

knife (nuyf)
noun **1** a tool with a sharp blade for cutting
verb **2** to wound with a knife
Noun forms: The plural is **knives**.
Word history: Old English *cnīf*

knight (nuyt)
noun **1** a nobleman who pledged to serve and fight for a king in medieval times
2 an honour, with the title 'Sir', given to a man by a king or queen for service to his country
3 a chess piece shaped like a horse's head
Word building: **knight** *verb* **knighthood** *noun* **knightly** *adjective*
Word history: Old English *cniht* boy, manservant

knight / night / nite
Don't confuse **knight** with **night** or **nite**.
Night is the time between sunset and sunrise, when it is dark.
Nite is another spelling for **night** that is used in informal writing and advertising.

knit (nit)
verb **1** to make out of long strands of wool, using a pair of long pointed needles: *to **knit** a jumper*
2 to join together: *He has to wait for the bones to **knit** after his fracture.* (***combine***, ***connect***, ***couple***, ***link***, ***unite***)
3 to wrinkle up: *She **knits** her brow when she is thinking.*
Verb forms: I **knitted**, I have **knitted**, I am **knitting**
Word building: **knitter** *noun*
Word history: Old English *cynttan* tie

knit / nit
Don't confuse **knit** with **nit**, which is the egg or young of an insect, such as a louse, living in human hair.

knob (nob)
noun **1** a round handle, as on a drawer or door
2 a rounded lump: *a **knob** of butter*
Word building: **knobby** *adjective* **knobbly** *adjective*
Word history: Middle English

knock (nok)
verb **1** to tap or beat: ***Knock*** *on the door.* (***hit***, ***strike***)
2 to bump or strike: *She* ***knocked*** *the leg of the table.* | *He* ***knocked*** *the nail in.*
3 *Colloquial* to criticise or find something wrong with: *She is always* ***knocking*** *their efforts.*
phrase **4 knock back**, *Colloquial*
a to eat or drink up quickly: *He* ***knocked back*** *two pies.*
b *Australian*, *NZ* to refuse: *They have* ***knocked back*** *my job application.* (***decline***, ***rebuff***, ***reject***)
5 knock down,
a to strike to the ground with a blow
b to reduce the price of: *These items will be* ***knocked down*** *during the sale.*
6 knock off, *Colloquial*
a to stop an activity, especially work
b to steal (***nick***, ***pilfer***, ***pinch***, ***take***, ***thieve***)
c to kill (***assassinate***, ***execute***, ***murder***)
7 knock out, to strike someone so hard that he or she loses consciousness
8 knock together, to put together quickly or roughly: *to* ***knock together*** *a cubby* | *to* ***knock together*** *a plan*
9 knock up,
a to arouse or wake up
b to put together quickly or roughly
c to score: *to* ***knock up*** *points*
d to wear out or exhaust

Word building: **knock** *noun*
Word history: Old English *cnocian*

knocker
noun **1** a hinged knob, bar, etc., on a door, for use in knocking
phrase **2 on the knocker**, *Australian*, *NZ Colloquial* at the right time, punctual: *He was there at 4 o'clock* ***on the knocker***.

knockout
noun **1** the act of knocking someone unconscious
2 a blow that knocks someone unconscious
3 *Colloquial* something or someone who is extremely attractive or successful

Word use: The abbreviation of definition 2 is **KO**.

knoll (nol)
noun a small, rounded hill (***hillock***, ***mound***)

Word history: Old English *cnol(l)*

knot (not)
noun **1** a piece of thread, rope or the like, tied or tangled
2 a fault or join in the grain of wood
3 a measure of speed, used especially for ships, about equal to 1.85 kilometres per hour

Word building: **knot** *verb* (**knotted**, **knotting**) **knotty** *adjective*
Word history: Old English *cnotta*

> **knot / not**
> Don't confuse **knot** with **not**. We use **not** to express something negative, or to deny or refuse something:
>
> *I am not a fool.*

know (noh)
verb **1** to feel certain that something is a fact or the truth
2 to have learned and understood
3 to have met before: *I* ***know*** *that face.*
phrase **4 in the know**, having inside knowledge

Verb forms: I **knew**, I have **known**, I am **knowing**
Word history: Old English *(ge)cnāwan*

> **know / no**
> Don't confuse **know** with **no**, which is the opposite of *yes*.
>
> We use it to deny, disagree with or refuse something.

knowable
adjective able to be known: *The future is not* ***knowable***.

know-all
noun someone who says they know everything, or everything about a particular subject (***boaster***, ***exhibitionist***, ***show-off***, ***skite***, ***smart alec***)

knowing
adjective sharp or shrewd: *He gave her a* ***knowing*** *look.* (***astute***, ***canny***)

knowledge (nol-ij)
noun what is or can be known: *Do you have any* ***knowledge*** *of what took place?* | *She passed on her* ***knowledge*** *to her daughters.*

Word building: **knowledgeable** *adjective*
Word history: Middle English

known (nohn, noh-uhn)
verb past participle of **know**

knuckle (nuk-uhl)
noun a finger joint, especially the bottom joint where the finger meets the rest of the hand

Word history: Middle English

KO
noun → **knockout** (definition 2)

Word use: You can also use **k.o.**
Word history: abbreviation

koala (koh-ah-luh)
noun a furry, grey, Australian animal without a tail, which lives and feeds in certain types of gum tree

Word use: The koala belongs to a class of animals called **marsupials**.
Word history: from Dharug, an Australian Aboriginal language spoken by the people living near Sydney Cove in the early days of European settlement

kohl (kohl)
noun a powder, used to darken the eyelids, emphasise eyebrows, etc.: *brown* ***kohl***

komodo dragon
noun a large lizard found in Komodo, an island in Indonesia

kookaburra
noun an Australian kingfisher whose call sounds like human laughter

Word use: Other names are **laughing kookaburra** and **laughing jackass**.
Word history: from Wiradjuri, an Australian Aboriginal language of the Murrumbidgee-Lachlan region

Koori (koor-ee)
noun an Aboriginal person from southern NSW or Victoria

Word use: Compare this with **Anangu**, **Murri**, **Nunga**, **Nyungar**, **Yamatji** and **Yolngu**.

Koran (kaw-rahn, kuh-rahn)
noun the holy book of Islam, which Muslims believe came directly from Allah through the prophet Mohammed

Word history: from Arabic word meaning 'reading' or 'recitation'

kosher (koh-shuh, kosh-uh)
adjective **1** lawful, prepared or cleaned according to the Jewish law
2 selling or using kosher food
3 *Colloquial* proper or correct

Word use: Definition 1 is used mainly about meat, etc. | Definition 2 is used mainly about shops, houses, etc.
Word history: from Hebrew word meaning 'fit', 'proper', 'lawful'

kowari (kuh-wah-ree)
noun a small, yellow-brown animal with a black bushy tail, found in the Australian desert

Word history: from Diyari, an Australian Aboriginal language of a region east of Lake Eyre

kowtow (kow-tow)
verb **1** to kneel touching the forehead to the ground in respect or worship
2 to try very hard to please, especially in an overeager way

Word history: from Chinese (Mandarin) word meaning 'knock-head', literally 'knock the head'

kris (krees)
noun a short sword or heavy knife, used in Malaysia

Word history: Malay

krypton (krip-ton)
noun an inert, gaseous element

Word history: Neo-Latin, from Greek word meaning 'hidden'

kudos (kyooh-dos)
noun glory or fame: *She only does something if it will bring her **kudos**.*

Word history: Greek

kumquat (kum-kwot)
noun → **cumquat**

kung-fu (koong-fooh, kung-fooh)
noun a Chinese form of karate

kurrajong (ku-ruh-jong)
noun a flowering tree of eastern Australia

Word use: You can also use **currajong**.
Word history: from Dharug, an Australian Aboriginal language spoken by the people living near Sydney Cove in the early days of European settlement

kylie
noun a boomerang with one side flat and the other curved

Word history: from Nyungar, an Australian Aboriginal language of the Perth-Albany region

label
noun **1** a piece of paper put on something to show what it is, who owns it, or where it is going: *a* ***label*** *for a suitcase | a* ***label*** *for a jar* (***sticker***, ***tab***, ***tag***, ***ticket***)
verb **2** to mark or describe with a label: *The bottle was* ***labelled*** *'poison'.* (***brand***, ***identify***, ***tag***)

Verb forms: I **labelled**, I have **labelled**, I am **labelling**
Word history: Middle English, from Old French, perhaps from Germanic

laboratory (luh-bo-ruh-tree)
noun a building or room for doing scientific tests or for making chemicals or medicines

Noun forms: The plural is **laboratories.**
Word history: from Medieval Latin word meaning 'workshop'

laborious (luh-baw-ree-uhs)
adjective needing a lot of effort: ***laborious*** *work*

Word history: Middle English, from Latin

labour
noun **1** hard or tiring work: *the* ***labour*** *of building a house* (***effort***, ***exertion***, ***industry***)
2 people who are employed to do such work, especially when organised into trade unions: *Organised* ***labour*** *will push for reform.*
3 the pain and effort of giving birth to a baby
verb **4** to work or toil (***slave***, ***slog***, ***strain***)

Word use: You can also use **labor.**
Word building: **labourer** *noun*
Word history: Middle English from Old French, from Latin word meaning 'toil', 'distress'

labrador
noun a kind of large dog with short black or golden hair

Word history: named after *Labrador*, a peninsula in north-eastern North America, where the breed originated

labyrinth (lab-uh-rinth)
noun a twisting set of passages in which it is hard to find your way (***maze***)

Word history: Latin *labyrinthus*, from Greek *labýrinthos*

lace
noun **1** a material with a fine netlike design of threads: *a wedding dress made of* ***lace***
2 a cord for pulling and holding something together: *shoe* ***laces***
verb **3** to tie together with a lace: *to* ***lace*** *your shoe*

Word building: **lacy** *adjective* (**lacier**, **laciest**)
Word history: Middle English, from Old French word meaning 'noose', 'string', from Latin word meaning 'noose', 'snare'

lacerate (las-uh-rayt)
verb to tear roughly or cut: *The broken glass* ***lacerated*** *his hands.* (***gash***, ***rip***, ***scratch***, ***slash***)

Word building: **laceration** *noun*
Word history: Latin

lack
noun **1** a shortage or absence of something you need or want: *a* ***lack*** *of food | a* ***lack*** *of interest* (***dearth***, ***deficiency***, ***deficit***, ***insufficiency***)
verb **2** to be without: *to* ***lack*** *strength*

Word history: Middle English, from Middle Low German or Middle Dutch word meaning 'deficiency'

laconic (luh-kon-ik)
adjective using few words: *She gave a* ***laconic*** *reply.* (***quiet***, ***reserved***, ***reticent***, ***taciturn***)

Word history: Latin, from Greek word meaning 'Laconian' (of Sparta, whose inhabitants were noted for brief, pithy speech)

lacquer (lak-uh)
noun a clear coating put on something to protect it or to make it shiny

Word building: **lacquer** *verb* **lacquered** *adjective*
Word history: French, from Arabic, from Persian

lactate
verb to produce milk

Word building: **lactation** *noun*

lad
noun *Old-fashioned* **1** a boy or youth
2 *Colloquial* a young man typically wearing clothing with brand names and presenting an image of an aggressive troublemaker

Word history: Old English *Ladda* (nickname), of obscure origin

ladder
noun **1** a structure made of wood, metal or rope, with rungs or steps you use to climb up or down
2 a line in a stocking or pair of tights where the stitches have come undone

Word history: Old English

laden
adjective loaded: ***laden*** *with fruit |* ***laden*** *with responsibilities* (***crushed***, ***packed***, ***weighed down***)

Word history: Old English

ladle
noun a cup-shaped spoon with a long handle, for serving liquids: *a soup* ***ladle***

Word building: **ladle** *verb*
Word history: from Old English word meaning *lade* load

lady
noun **1** a polite name for a **woman**
2 a woman of good family or social position, or of good breeding, refinement, etc.: *She always behaves like a* ***lady****.*

Noun forms: The plural is **ladies**.
Word history: Old English word perhaps originally meaning 'loaf-kneader'

lady / woman

People used to save the title **lady** for women of the upper classes. In a class-conscious society it was important to know who was from the 'best' families and who was part of the common herd. Nowadays the distinction is not so important and the term **lady** refers either to a woman who has good manners and is very polite, or simply to any woman.

This genteel term has, however, turned up in efforts to deal with a new problem. Many occupations have names which do not indicate the gender of the person doing the job. And so where, for example, a doctor or a plumber is a woman, some people are tempted to indicate gender by such clumsy expressions as *a lady doctor* and *a lady plumber*. In most cases like this the fact that the person is female is irrelevant. It is their occupation that is important. For more information, look up **non-sexist language**.

ladybird
noun a small beetle whose orange or red back is spotted with black

Word history: *lady* (Virgin Mary) + *bird*; (our) Lady's bird

lady-in-waiting
noun a woman in attendance upon a queen or princess

Noun forms: The plural is **ladies-in-waiting**.

lag
verb **1** to become less or decrease: *My interest in work is beginning to* ***lag****.* (***abate***, ***decrease***, ***diminish***, ***peter out***, ***wane***)
phrase **2 lag behind**, to fall behind or drop back: *He's always* ***lagging behind*** *when we go for a walk.*

Verb forms: I **lagged**, I have **lagged**, I am **lagging**
Word use: The opposite of this is **lead**.
Word history: Scandinavian

lager (lah-guh)
noun a kind of light beer

Word history: German

lagerphone (lah-guh-fohn)
noun a homemade percussion instrument made of beer bottle tops loosely nailed to a broom handle

lagoon
noun a pond of shallow water, often separated from the sea by low banks of sand

Word history: Italian, Spanish, from Latin word meaning 'pool', 'pond'

laid
verb past tense and past participle of **lay**[1]

laid-back
adjective at ease (***casual***, ***easygoing***, ***informal***, ***nonchalant***, ***relaxed***)

Word use: You can also use **laidback**.

lain
verb past participle of **lie**[2]

lain / lane

Look up **lane / lain**.

lair[1]
noun the den or shelter of a wild animal

Word history: Old English

lair[2]
noun Australian, NZ Colloquial **1** a flashily dressed young man of bold and sometimes rude behaviour
phrase **2 lair it up**, to behave in a bold and rude manner

Word building: **lairy** *adjective*

laissez faire (lay-say fair)
noun **1** the idea that government should not interfere in the economic affairs of a country
2 the idea of leaving people to conduct their own affairs

Word use: You can also use **laisser faire**.
Word building: **laissez-faire** *adjective*
Word history: from French word meaning 'allow to act'

laity (lay-uh-tee)
noun **1** ordinary people who are not members of the clergy
2 people outside any profession as different from those within it

lake
noun a large area of water surrounded by land

Word history: from Old English word meaning 'stream', 'pool', 'pond'

laksa (luk-suh)
noun a spicy Malaysian dish of thin rice noodles, vegetables, meat or seafood, tofu, etc., served in a soup

lama (lah-muh)
noun a Buddhist priest or monk

Word history: Tibetan

lama / llama

Don't confuse **lama** with **llama**, a native animal of South America related to the camel and used for carrying loads.

lamb
noun a young sheep or its meat

Word history: Old English

lame
adjective **1** having something wrong with your foot or leg that causes you to limp (***crippled***, ***disabled***, ***handicapped***)
2 weak or poor: *a* ***lame*** *excuse*

Word building: **lame** *verb* **lamely** *adverb* **lameness** *noun*
Word history: Old English

lamé (lah-may)
noun an ornamental fabric in which metallic threads are woven with silk, wool, etc.

Word history: French word meaning 'laminated', from Old French word meaning 'gold or silver thread or wire'

lament (luh-ment)
verb **1** to feel or show sorrow for: *She* ***lamented*** *her husband's death.* (***brood over***, ***grieve for***, ***mourn***)
noun **2** a poem or song expressing sorrow

Word use: The opposite of definition 1 is **celebrate**.
Word building: **lamentable** *adjective* **lamentation** *noun*
Word history: from Latin word meaning 'wail', 'weep'

laminate
verb **1** to separate into thin sheets or layers
2 to cover with thin layers

Word building: **laminate** *adjective* **laminated** *adjective* **lamination** *noun*
Word history: *lamin(a)* + *-ate*

lamington
noun a square of sponge cake covered with chocolate icing and grated coconut

Word history: probably named after Baron *Lamington*, 1860–1940, governor of Queensland, 1895–1901

lamp
noun a kind of light, often one which you can move or carry around: *a kerosene* ***lamp***

Word history: Middle English, from Old French, from Latin, from Greek word meaning 'torch', 'light', 'lamp'

lampoon (lam-poohn)
noun **1** the use of sarcasm to attack a person, government, etc., in either prose or verse
verb **2** to attack with sarcasm

Word building: **lampooner** *noun* **lampoonist** *noun*
Word history: French

lamprey (lam-pree)
noun a type of eel-like fish, some species of which attach themselves to fish and suck their blood

Noun forms: The plural is **lampreys**.
Word history: Middle English, from Old French, from Late Latin

lance
noun **1** a long spear
verb **2** to cut open with a sharp instrument: *The doctor* ***lanced*** *my boil.* (***nick***, ***score***)

Word history: Middle English, from French, from Latin

land
noun **1** the part of the earth's surface not covered by water
2 a particular area of ground: *We own the house and the* ***land*** *around it.*
3 a country or nation: *Our* ***land*** *is called Australia.*
verb **4** to come or bring to land or shore (***alight***, ***disembark***, ***dismount***, ***touch down***)
5 to come to rest in any place or position: *Where did the ball* ***land****?*
6 *Colloquial* to gain or obtain: *He* ***landed*** *a good job.*
phrase **7 land on your feet**, to be successful in a situation which might have gone badly

Word history: Old English

landcare
noun the sustainable management of the environment and natural resources in agriculture

landfall
noun **1** an approach to, or sighting of land
2 land sighted or reached

landfill
noun material such as garbage, building refuse, etc., deposited under layers of earth to raise the level of a site

landform
noun any of the many features which make up the surface of the earth, such as plains, mountains, valleys, etc.

landing
noun **1** the act of landing
2 the area at the top or bottom of a flight of stairs

landlady
noun a woman who owns and rents out land, houses, flats or rooms

landline
noun **1** a telecommunications line running under or over the ground
2 a telephone using a landline

Word use: You can also use **fixed line**, or, for definition 2, **landline telephone**.

landlocked
adjective shut in more or less completely by land

landlord
noun a man who owns and rents out land, houses, flats or rooms

landlubber
noun someone who is not used to boats or sailing

landmark
noun **1** something on land that is easily seen and is used as a guide to travellers
2 an event that stands out as important: *The Eureka Stockade was a* ***landmark*** *in Australia's history.*

landmass
noun a sizeable body of land surrounded by water: *a tree-shaped* ***landmass***

Word use: You can also use **land mass**.

landmine
noun an explosive device buried in the ground

land rights
plural noun the rights of those first living in a country to possess land, especially sacred tribal grounds

landscape
noun **1** a view of country scenery (***outlook***, ***prospect***, ***scene***, ***vista***)
2 a painting of country scenery
verb **3** to arrange to make look like a landscape: *to* ***landscape*** *a garden*

Word history: earlier *landskap*, from Dutch

landslide
noun **1** the sliding down of a mass of rocks and soil from a steep slope

2 an easy win in an election: *The government won in a **landslide**.*

lane
noun **1** a narrow passage or road between fences, walls or houses (***alley***)
2 a strip of road marked out for a single line of vehicles
3 a strip marked out on a running track or swimming pool for one runner or swimmer in a race

Word history: Old English

lane / lain
Don't confuse **lane** with **lain**, which is a past form of the verb **lie**:
She felt refreshed after she had lain down for half an hour.

language
noun **1** the arrangement of words we use when we speak and write (***dialect***, ***jargon***, ***tongue***)
2 any set of signs or symbols used to pass on information: *sign **language** | computer **language***
3 the language of a particular country or group of people: *French is the **language** of France.*

Word history: Middle English, from Old French word meaning 'tongue', from Latin

languid (lang-gwuhd)
adjective weak, tired, or slow-moving (***apathetic***, ***inert***, ***lethargic***, ***listless***, ***sluggish***)

Word use: The opposite of this is **energetic** or **vigorous.**
Word building: **languidly** *adverb*
Word history: Latin

languish (lang-gwish)
verb to become weak or without interest

Word use: The opposite of this is **thrive.**
Word history: Middle English, from French, from Latin

La Niña (lah neen-yuh)
noun the reverse of an El Niño, marked in Australia by heavy rain on the eastern coast

Word use: Compare this with **El Niño.**
Word history: Spanish: feminine gender of **El Niño** to indicate the contrast of heavy rain to drought

lank
adjective **1** too long and thin: *Your plants will grow very **lank** without sunlight.*
2 straight and dull: ***lank** hair*

Word building: **lanky** *adjective* (**lankier**, **lankiest**) **lankiness** *noun* **lankness** *noun*
Word history: Old English

lanolin (lan-uh-luhn)
noun a fatty substance from wool used in ointments

Word use: You can also use **lanoline** (lan-uh-leen).
Word history: from Latin word meaning 'wool'

lantana (lan-tahn-uh)
noun any of several tropical plants, including one with yellow or orange flowers which has become a troublesome weed in temperate and tropical areas

Word history: Neo-Latin

lantern
noun a glass case that holds a light and protects it from wind and rain

Word history: Middle English, from French, from Latin, from Greek word meaning 'a light torch'

lap[1]
noun the front of your body from your waist to your knees, when you are sitting down: *She sat the child on her **lap**.*

Word history: Old English *læppa*

lap[2]
noun **1** a single round of a racing track or a single length of a swimming pool (***circuit***, ***course***)
verb **2** to fold over or about: *She **lapped** the bandage around her sprained ankle.*
3 in sport, to get a lap or more ahead of another competitor

Verb forms: I **lapped**, I have **lapped**, I am **lapping**

lap[3]
verb **1** to hit with a gentle splashing: *The water **lapped** against the side of the boat.*
2 to drink using the tongue: *The cat **lapped** the milk.*

Verb forms: it **lapped**, it has **lapped**, it is **lapping**
Word history: Old English *lapian*

lapel (luh-pel)
noun the part of a coat collar that is folded back over your chest

Word history: little *lap[1]*

lapidary (lap-uh-duh-ree)
noun **1** a person who cuts and polishes precious stones
2 an expert on precious stones
adjective **3** having to do with the cutting of precious stones

Noun forms: The plural is **lapidaries.**
Word history: Middle English, from Latin word meaning 'of stones or stone'

lapse
noun **1** a mistake or failure: *a **lapse** of memory*
2 the passing of time: *I saw him again after a **lapse** of two years.*
verb **3** to pass slowly or gradually: *She **lapsed** into unconsciousness.*
4 to fall or sink into: *He **lapsed** into bad habits.* (***descend***, ***slip***)

Word history: late Middle English, from Latin word meaning 'a fall', 'slip'

laptop
noun a portable computer, small enough to be operated while held on your knees

larceny (lah-suh-nee)
noun the stealing of someone else's goods

Noun forms: The plural is **larcenies.**
Word building: **larcenous** *adjective*
Word history: Middle English, from Latin word meaning 'robbery'

lard
noun pig fat prepared for use in cooking

Word history: Middle English, from Old French, from Latin word meaning 'fat of pork'

larder
noun a room or cupboard where food is kept (***pantry***, ***store***)
Word history: Middle English, from Old French word meaning 'lard'

large
adjective **1** of more than usual size, amount or extent: *a **large** dog* | *a **large** family* (***ample***, ***bulky***, ***generous***, ***substantial***)
phrase **2 at large**,
a free: *The murderer is **at large**.*
b as a whole: *This is important for the school **at large**.*
Word building: **largeness** *noun*
Word history: Middle English, from Old French, from Latin word meaning 'abundant', 'liberal'

largely
adverb to a great extent

largesse (lah-jes)
noun **1** gifts or a gift generously given
2 *Old-fashioned* generosity
Word use: You can also use **largess**.
Word history: Middle English, from Old French word meaning 'large'

lark[1]
noun a kind of bird that lives in northern areas of the world and often sings while flying
Word use: Another name is **skylark**.
Word history: Old English

lark[2]
noun something done for fun or as a joke: *We hid under the bed for a **lark**.*

larrikin
noun Australian, NZ Colloquial someone, usually young, who behaves in a noisy, wild way
Word building: **larrikinism** *noun*
Word history: perhaps from British (Warwickshire and Worcestershire) dialect word meaning 'mischievous youth'

larva
noun the young of any insect which changes the form of its body before becoming an adult: *A caterpillar is the **larva** of a butterfly.*
Noun forms: The plural is **larvae** (lah-vee).
Word building: **larval** *adjective*
Word history: from Neo-Latin, special use of Latin word meaning 'ghost', 'skeleton', 'mask'

> **larva / lava**
> Don't confuse **larva** with **lava**. **Lava** is molten rock from a volcano.

laryngitis (la-ruhn-juy-tuhs)
noun a soreness and swelling in your larynx that often makes you lose your voice for a while
Word history: Neo-Latin

larynx (la-ringks)
noun the box-like space at the top of your windpipe that contains the vocal cords which you use when speaking
Noun forms: The plural is **larynges** or **larynxes**.
Word use: You can also use the colloquial term **voice box**.
Word history: Neo-Latin, from Greek

lasagne (luh-sahn-yuh)
noun **1** a type of pasta cut into rectangular sheets
2 a dish made with this, often with mince meat, tomato and cheese between layers of the pasta

lascivious (luh-siv-ee-uhs)
adjective **1** full of strong and often uncontrolled sexual appetite
2 tending to cause lustful feelings
Word building: **lasciviousness** *noun*
Word history: Late Latin, from Latin word meaning 'wantonness'

laser (lay-zuh)
noun a device which produces a very narrow beam of intense light
Word history: *l(ight) a(mplification by) s(timulated) e(mission of) r(adiation)*

lash
noun **1** the cord part of a whip
2 a blow with a whip or something similar: *He got six **lashes**.*
3 → **eyelash**
verb **4** to strike with a whip or something similar (***beat***, ***cane***, ***flog***, ***scourge***, ***thrash***)
5 to tie with a rope or cord
6 to beat violently against: *Waves **lashed** the side of the ship.*
Word history: Middle English

lashing[1]
noun **1** a whipping
2 a severe scolding
phrase **3 lashings of**, *Colloquial* large quantities of

lashing[2]
noun **1** a binding or fastening with a rope or the like
2 the rope, cord, twine, etc., used

lass
noun Old-fashioned a girl or young woman
Word history: Middle English

lassitude (las-uh-tyoohd)
noun weariness of body or mind (***languor***, ***lethargy***)
Word history: from Latin word meaning 'weariness'

lasso (la-sooh)
noun a long rope with a loop at one end which tightens when pulled, used to catch horses and other animals
Noun forms: The plural is **lassos** or **lassoes**.
Word building: **lasso** *verb* (**lassoed**, **lassoing**)
Word history: Spanish, from Latin word meaning 'noose', 'snare'

last[1]
adjective **1** coming after everything else in time, order or place
2 latest or most recent: ***last** night*
adverb **3** after all the others: *I came **last** in the race.*
noun **4** something that is at the end: *This is the **last** of the questions.*
phrase **5 at last**, eventually, or after a long time: *We waited patiently and **at last** the bus arrived.*
Word building: **lastly** *adverb*
Word history: Old English superlative form of *læt* late

last[2]
verb **1** to go on or continue: *This lesson will **last** half an hour.*
phrase **2 last out**, to keep on in the face of difficulty: *I'm afraid we can't **last out** much longer.* (***endure***, ***hold out***, ***persist***, ***survive***)

Word building: **lasting** *adjective*
Word history: from Old English word meaning 'follow', 'perform', 'continue'

last-ditch
adjective final, or most extreme, made when everything else has failed: *a **last-ditch** attempt to revive him*

latch
noun **1** a bar which slides or falls into a slot, used to keep a door or gate closed
verb **2** to close or fasten with a latch
phrase **3 latch on to**, *Colloquial* to understand: *He **latched on to** what she meant.*

Word history: from Old English word meaning 'take hold of', 'catch', 'take'

late
adjective **1** coming or continuing after the usual or proper time: *a **late** arrival | a **late** dinner*
2 far advanced in time: *a **late** hour | the **late** afternoon*
3 having died: *the **late** king* (***bygone***, ***deceased***, ***departed***, ***former***, ***sometime***)
adverb **4** after the usual or proper time: *They came **late**.*
phrase **5 of late**, recently: *She has been working hard **of late**.*

Word building: **lateness** *noun*
Word history: Old English *læt* slow, late

lately
adverb recently

latent
adjective present but not active or able to be seen: *a **latent** disease | a **latent** talent* (***dormant***, ***hidden***)

Word building: **latency** *noun*
Word history: from Latin word meaning 'lying hid'

later
adjective, *adverb* comparative form of **late**

> **later / latter**
> These words look similar but have different meanings.
> **Later** is one of the forms of **late**:
> *Dinner will be later than usual.*
> *I'll go to a later session of the film.*
> **Latter** refers to the second thing mentioned out of two (as opposed to *former*):
> *I prefer the latter of the recipes you read out.*

lateral
adjective having to do with the side: *a **lateral** view | a **lateral** root of a plant*

Word history: from Latin word meaning 'side'

lateral thinking
noun a way of thinking by making associations with other apparently unrelated areas, rather than by following one logical train of thought

latest
adjective newest: *the **latest** fashion*

latex (lay-teks)
noun a milky liquid present in certain plants, such as those from which indiarubber is produced

Word history: from Latin word meaning 'liquid'

lathe (laydh)
noun a machine which holds and turns a piece of wood or metal while it is being cut or shaped

Word history: Middle English, from Scandinavian

lather (la-dhuh)
noun **1** foam made from soap and water
2 froth caused by heavy sweating
verb **3** to become covered with a lather

Word history: Old English

latitude
noun **1** the distance by which a point on the earth is north or south of the equator, measured in degrees
2 freedom, or room to move: *Give your horse a bit of **latitude** and he'll find his own way home.*

Word building: **latitudinal** *adjective*
Word history: Middle English, from Latin word meaning 'breadth'

latrine (luh-treen)
noun a toilet, especially in an army camp

Word history: French, from Latin

latte (lah-tay)
noun → **cafe latte**

latter
adjective **1** the second out of two things mentioned: *I prefer the **latter** idea.*
2 recent, or in a period of time, towards the end: *Things have been going well in **latter** days. | the **latter** years of his life*

Word use: The opposite of definition 1 is **former**.
Word building: **latterly** *adverb*
Word history: Old English

lattice (lat-uhs)
noun a frame made of crossed wooden or metal strips with diamond-shaped spaces in between, used as a screen or as a support for plants

Word history: Middle English, from Old French, from Germanic

laugh (lahf)
verb **1** to make the sounds that show amusement, happiness, or scorn (***chortle***, ***chuckle***, ***guffaw***)
phrase **2 laugh off**, to treat lightly or with scorn: *He **laughed off** her accusations.* (***make light of***, ***minimise***, ***play down***, ***trivialise***)

Word building: **laugh** *noun* **laughter** *noun*
Word history: Old English

laughable
adjective funny or foolish

launch[1] (lawnch)
noun a strong open boat, usually with a motor

Word history: Spanish, Portuguese

launch[2]
verb **1** to send into the water: *to **launch** a ship*
2 to send up into the air: *to **launch** a rocket*
3 to set going or start: *to **launch** an attack | to **launch** out on a new career* (***begin***, ***establish***, ***found***, ***initiate***, ***institute***)
4 to introduce a new project, product, etc., with publicity: *to launch a book*

Word building: **launch** *noun*
Word history: Middle English, from Old Northern French word meaning 'lance'

launder
verb to wash and iron: *to **launder** shirts*

laundromat
noun a public laundry with washing machines and spin-driers which you operate by putting coins in the slot of each machine

Word history: Trademark

laundry
noun **1** a room in a house for washing clothes
2 clothes that are ready to be washed or have been washed
3 a business where laundry is done commercially

laurel (lo-ruhl)
noun **1** a small evergreen tree with leaves that are used as a herb in cooking
2 the leaves of this tree made into a wreath, used as a sign of victory
phrase **3 rest on your laurels**, to be happy with what you have already done and not want to try for any more achievements

Word history: Middle English, from French, from Old French, from Latin word meaning 'laurel'

lava (lah-vuh)
noun **1** the hot liquid rock which comes out of a volcano
2 the hard rock formed when this becomes cool and solid

Word history: Italian (Neapolitan) word meaning 'stream'

lava / larva
Look up **larva / lava**.

lavatory (lav-uh-tree)
noun a toilet, or a room with a toilet in it

Noun forms: The plural is **lavatories**.
Word history: Middle English, from Late Latin

lavender
noun **1** a small shrub with pale purple flowers that have a strong but pleasing smell
2 a pale bluish-purple colour

Word building: **lavender** *adjective*
Word history: Middle English, from Anglo-French, from Medieval Latin

lavish (lav-ish)
adjective **1** plentiful or abundant: *__lavish__ gifts*
2 generous in giving or using: *He is **lavish** with his money.* (***liberal***, ***magnanimous***)

Word building: **lavish** *verb* **lavishly** *adverb* **lavishness** *noun*
Word history: Middle English word meaning 'profusion', from Old French word meaning 'deluge'

law
noun **1** a rule or set of rules, especially those made by a government or ruler (***convention***, ***formula***, ***precept***, ***regulation***)
2 the area of knowledge or the occupation that has to do with these rules: *to study **law** | to practise **law** in a law court*
3 a statement describing what always happens under certain conditions: *the **law** of gravity*

Word history: Old English, from Scandinavian

law / lore
Don't confuse **law** with **lore**. **Lore** is learning or knowledge about a particular subject, as in *the lore of herbs.*

lawful
adjective allowed by law: *a **lawful** marriage* (***authorised***, ***legal***, ***legitimate***, ***permitted***, ***proper***)

Word use: The opposite of this is **unlawful**.

lawless
adjective not controlled by or not obeying the law

lawn
noun an area of mown, grass-covered land, usually part of a garden

Word history: from Old French word meaning 'wooded ground'; of Celtic origin

lawn bowls
noun a game in which the players roll weighted balls along a very smooth lawn in an effort to make them stop as near as possible to a target ball called the jack

lawsuit
noun the prosecution of a claim in a law court

lawyer
noun someone whose work is to give advice about the law and to argue on behalf of people in law courts (***advocate***, ***attorney***, ***barrister***, ***counsel***)

Word use: A lawyer can be a **barrister**, who presents cases in court, or a **solicitor**, who advises clients and prepares cases for barristers to present.

lax (laks)
adjective **1** careless or not strict: *__lax__ behaviour | **lax** rules* (***casual***, ***irresponsible***, ***negligent***, ***thoughtless***)
2 loose or slack: *__lax__ muscles*

Word use: The opposite of definition 1 is **strict**. | The opposite of definition 2 is **rigid** or **tense**.
Word history: Middle English, from Latin word meaning 'loose', 'slack'

laxative (laks-uh-tiv)
noun a medicine for helping you pass waste matter from your bowels easily and without pain

Word building: **laxative** *adjective*
Word history: from Latin word meaning 'loosening'

lay[1]
verb **1** to put down or place: *to **lay** the book on the table | He **laid** his hand on her arm.*
2 to produce an egg
3 to prepare: *to **lay** the table | to **lay** plans*
noun **4** the way in which something lies or is laid: *the **lay** of the land*

phrase **5 lay it on** (**with a trowel**) or (**a bit thick**), *Colloquial* to exaggerate
6 lay off,
a to dismiss from a job: *The boss* ***laid off*** *five workers.*
b *Colloquial* to stop: *Let's* ***lay off*** *work now.*
7 lay out,
a to arrange in order, or prepare
b to spend: *to* ***lay out*** *a fortune*
c *Colloquial* to knock unconscious
8 lay up,
a to store for future use
b to cause to stay in bed or indoors

Verb forms: I **laid**, I have **laid**, I am **laying**
Word history: Old English

lay / lie

The past forms of these verbs are often confused.

Lay, meaning 'to put down', always needs an object — you lay something somewhere. It's an irregular verb, with *laid* as its past form:

I now lay my heart before you. (present)
I laid the table last night. (past)
I had laid the old map open on the desk. (past participle)

Lie is another irregular verb, meaning 'to be or rest in a flat position'. It never has an object — you just lie somewhere. Its past tense is **lay**, and its past participle **lain**:

Every day I lie in the sun for a while. (present)
I lay down for a sleep this morning. (past)
I had lain in the sun for an hour. (past participle)

Lie is also a verb meaning 'to tell an untruth'. Its past forms are regular: **I lied, I have lied.**

lay[2]

verb past tense of **lie[2]**

lay[3]

adjective **1** having to do with ordinary people or laity, as distinguished from the clergy: *a* ***lay*** *preacher*
2 not belonging to a particular profession, especially to the law or medicine: *a* ***lay*** *opinion*

Word history: Middle English, from Old French, from Late Latin

lay-by

noun Australian, NZ **1** a system of buying something by paying out part of the cost and then making further payments until it has been fully paid for and may be collected: *I'll put this dress on* ***lay-by.***
2 something bought in this way

Word building: **lay-by** *verb*

layer

noun a single thickness or coating: *a cake with three* ***layers*** | *a* ***layer*** *of paint* (***band***, ***deposit***, ***seam***, ***stratum***, ***vein***)

Word building: **layer** *verb*
Word history: Middle English, from *lay[1]* + *-er*

layette (lay-et)

noun a complete outfit of clothes for a newborn baby

Word history: from French word meaning 'box', 'drawer'

layman

noun **1** a man who is not a member of the clergy
2 a man who is not a member of a particular profession
phrase **3 in layman's terms** (or **language**), in ordinary plain English without using any jargon: *Could you please repeat that for me* ***in layman's terms?***

layout

noun the way something is arranged: *the* ***layout*** *of a newspaper page* | *the* ***layout*** *of a kitchen*

layperson

noun **1** someone who is not a member of the clergy
2 someone who is not a member of a particular profession: *It is difficult for the* ***layperson*** *to understand computer jargon.*

Noun forms: The plural is **laypeople.**

laze

verb **1** to idle or lounge lazily: *to* ***laze*** *in the sun* (***bludge***, ***loaf***, ***loll***, ***rest***)
noun **2** the act of lazing
phrase **3 laze away**, to pass lazily: *to* ***laze away*** *the hours*

lazy

adjective **1** not liking work or effort: *a* ***lazy*** *student* (***idle***, ***indolent***, ***slack***, ***slothful***)
2 slow-moving: *a* ***lazy*** *stream* (***leisurely***, ***slow***, ***unhurried***)
3 not spent in work or effort: *a* ***lazy*** *afternoon*

Adjective forms: **lazier**, **laziest**
Word building: **lazily** *adverb* **laziness** *noun*

leach (leech)

verb to remove soluble matter from ashes, soil, etc., by filtering: *Heavy rain* ***leaches*** *the soil.*

Word history: variant of Old English *leccan* moisten, wet

leach / leech

Don't confuse **leach** with **leech**. A **leech** is a small worm that sucks the blood of humans or animals.

lead[1] (leed)

verb **1** to guide, often in a particular direction or to a particular place
2 to go or be at the front of
3 to command or be in charge of: *to* ***lead*** *an army* | *to* ***lead*** *a discussion*
noun **4** the front position: *Margaret is in the* ***lead.***
5 amount or distance ahead: *a* ***lead*** *of five metres*
6 a strap for holding an animal: *Put the dog on its* ***lead.***
7 a clue: *The police haven't got any* ***leads*** *about the murder.*
phrase **8 lead someone on,** to make someone continue in a foolish belief or action
9 lead to, to be a way of getting to: *The next track* ***leads to*** *the river.*
10 lead up to, to prepare gradually for

Verb forms: I **led**, I have **led**, I am **leading**
Word use: The opposite of definitions 1 and 2 is **follow.**
Word history: Old English

lead[2] (led)
noun **1** a heavy bluish-grey metal used to make pipes, petrol, paint and bullets
2 a thin stick of carbon used in pencils

Word building: **lead** *adjective*
Word history: Old English

leaded petrol
noun petrol that contains small amounts of the metal lead and therefore is environmentally damaging

leaden (led-uhn)
adjective heavy and grey like lead: ***leaden** storm clouds*

leader (leed-uh)
noun **1** someone or something that leads
2 an article in a newspaper that gives the opinion of the newspaper or its editor on events happening at the moment (***editorial***)
3 the main violinist in an orchestra, who helps the conductor

Word use: The opposite of definition 1 is **follower.**

leadership
noun **1** the position of a leader
2 the ability to lead

leading question
noun a question worded so as to suggest the desired answer

leaf
noun **1** the flat, usually green, part of a plant that grows out from its stem
2 a page of a book
3 a thin sheet of metal: *gold **leaf***
phrase **4 leaf through,** to turn the pages of (***browse through, skim***)
5 take a leaf out of someone's book, to follow someone's example
6 turn over a new leaf, to begin new and better behaviour

Noun forms: The plural is **leaves.**
Verb forms: I **leafed,** he/she **leafs,** I have **leafed,** I am **leafing**
Word building: **leafy** *adjective* (**leafier, leafiest**)
Word history: Old English

leaflet
noun a small sheet of printed information: *They handed out **leaflets** advertising the school fete.* (***handout, pamphlet, tract***)

league (leeg)
noun **1** a group of people, countries or organisations who have made an agreement between themselves (***alliance, association, bloc, coalition, confederation, federation, union***)
2 League, a kind of football game
phrase **3 in league,** having an agreement: *They are **in league** with each other.*

Word use: You can also use **Rugby League** for definition 2.
Word history: Middle English, from Old French, from Italian, from Latin word meaning 'bind'

league table
noun **1** in sports, the table of scores for teams in a competition
2 the rankings given to individual people, organisations, etc., within a group: *the **league table** of sales managers*

leak
noun **1** a hole or crack that lets liquid or gas in or out accidentally: *This bucket has a **leak.***
2 the amount of liquid or gas that escapes through a leak: *There has been a huge **leak** from this bucket.*
3 the giving out of secret information: *a government **leak***
verb **4** to let a substance in or out through a leak: *The roof **leaks.***
5 to pass in or out through a leak: *Gas is **leaking.***

Word building: **leaky** *adjective* (**leakier, leakiest**) **leakiness** *noun*
Word history: Middle English, from Scandinavian

leak / leek
Don't confuse **leak** with **leek.** A **leek** is a vegetable that is related to the onion.

leakage
noun **1** the act or process of leaking
2 the amount which leaks in or out

lean[1]
verb **1** to be or to put in a sloping position: *The door was **leaning** off its hinge. | She **leaned** her head out the window.* (***list, slant, slope, tilt, tip***)
2 to rest against or on something for support
phrase **3 lean on,** to put pressure on: *I'll **lean on** him for a quick decision.*

Verb forms: I **leaned** or I **leant** (lent), I have **leaned** or I have **leant** (lent), I am **leaning**
Word history: Old English *hleonian*

leant / lent
Don't confuse **leant** (a past form of the verb **lean**) with **lent.** The word **lent** is the past form of the verb **lend,** to let someone use something of yours for a short time.
Note that **Lent** (with a capital L) is the period of forty days before Easter.

lean[2]
adjective **1** thin: *a **lean** athlete* (***skinny, slender, slight, slim, spindly***)
2 with little or no fat: ***lean** meat*

Word building: **lean** *noun* **leanness** *noun*
Word history: Old English *hlǣne*

leap
verb **1** to jump or move quickly: *to **leap** over a puddle | to **leap** away from burning fat* (***bound, spring, vault***)
2 to jump over: *He **leapt** the fence.*
noun **3** a jump
4 a sudden rise: *a **leap** in prices*
phrase **5 leap at,** to accept eagerly: *He **leapt at** the chance to go horse riding.*

Verb forms: I **leapt** (lept) or I **leaped,** I have **leapt** (lept) or I have **leaped,** I am **leaping**
Word history: from Old English word meaning 'leap', 'run'

leap year
noun a year of 366 days every fourth year, with the extra day on 29 February

learn

verb **1** to come to have knowledge of or skill in: *to* ***learn*** *Italian | to* ***learn*** *piano* (***absorb***, ***assimilate***, ***digest***, ***memorise***, ***take in***)
2 to get knowledge or skill: *She* ***learns*** *quickly.*

Verb forms: I **learned** or I **learnt**, I have **learned** or I have **learnt**, I am **learning**
Word building: **learner** *noun*
Word history: Old English *leornian*

learn / teach
Don't confuse **learn** with **teach**.
To **teach** is to instruct or help others in particular skills or areas of knowledge. So you *teach someone Italian*, or *teach someone to play the saxophone*.
This is why we don't say *She learned me Italian* — because someone else has helped to give you that knowledge. The correct thing to say would be *She taught me Italian.*

learned (<u>lern</u>-uhd)

adjective having a lot of knowledge from study: *a* ***learned*** *woman* (***clever***, ***cultivated***, ***erudite***, ***knowledgeable***, ***well-informed***)

learning

noun the gaining of knowledge by study or the knowledge gained this way

lease (lees)

noun **1** a written agreement which gives someone the right to use land or live in a building in return for rent
verb **2** to give or have the use of by a lease

Word history: Middle English, from Anglo-French, from Old French, from Latin word meaning 'loosen'

lease / let / hire / rent
Look up **hire / rent / lease / let.**

leash

noun a strap for holding a dog

Word building: **leash** *verb*
Word history: Middle English, from Old French, from Latin word meaning 'loose', 'lax'

least

adjective **1** smallest: *Our geography teacher gives us the* ***least*** *amount of homework.* (***lowest***, ***minimum***, ***slightest***)
noun **2** the smallest in amount, extent or importance: *That is the* ***least*** *of my problems.*
phrase **3 at least,**
a at the lowest calculation or judgement: *He must be* ***at least*** *fifty years old.*
b at any rate: *I feel awful but* ***at least*** *I don't have to go to school.*

Word use: For other forms of the adjective look up **little**.
Word history: from Old English *lǣst*, superlative form of *lǣs(sa)* less

leather (<u>ledh</u>-uh)

noun the skin of animals prepared by tanning and used to make such things as shoes and bags

Word building: **leathery** *adjective*
Word history: Old English *lether* (in compounds)

leave[1]

verb **1** to go away from: *She* ***left*** *the room.* (***depart***, ***leave***, ***quit***, ***retire from***, ***withdraw from***)
2 to depart or go away: *When do we* ***leave****?*
3 to allow to stay or remain in a particular place or condition: *to* ***leave*** *the books on the table | to* ***leave*** *the door unlocked*
4 to give for use after you have died: *He* ***left*** *her all his money.* (***bequeath***, ***hand down***)
phrase **5 leave alone,** to stop interfering with: ***Leave*** *me* ***alone.***

Verb forms: I **left**, I have **left**, I am **leaving**
Word history: Old English *lǣfan*

leave[2]

noun **1** permission: *May I have* ***leave*** *to go home?* (***approval***, ***clearance***, ***consent***, ***dispensation***)
2 the time during which someone has permission to be absent: *My teacher is away on six weeks'* ***leave.***
phrase **3 take leave of,** to say goodbye to

Word history: Old English *lēaf*

leaven (<u>lev</u>-uhn)

noun **1** a mass of fermenting dough kept for producing fermentation in a new batch of dough
2 something which works in another thing to produce change
verb **3** to produce bubbles of gas in (a dough or batter)

Word building: **leavening** *noun*
Word history: Middle English, from Old French, from Latin word meaning 'that which raises'

lecher (<u>lech</u>-uh)

noun a man who continually looks for sexual experiences

Word building: **lecherous** *adjective* **lechery** *noun*
Word history: Middle English, from Old French word meaning 'gourmand', 'sensualist'

lectern (<u>lek</u>-tuhn)

noun a reading desk, especially in a church

Word history: Middle English *lettrun*, from Old French, from Medieval Latin, from Latin word meaning 'read'

lecture

noun **1** a speech that you prepare and give before an audience or a class in order to teach or inform: *a* ***lecture*** *on Australian history* (***address***, ***talk***)
2 a long talk that's a warning or a scolding: *She gave me a* ***lecture*** *about my lateness.*

Word building: **lecture** *verb*
Word history: Middle English, from Late Latin, from Latin word meaning 'read'

lecturer

noun a person who gives lectures, especially at a university or college

led

verb past tense and past participle of **lead**[1]

ledge

noun a narrow, flat shelf sticking out from something upright: *a window* ***ledge***

Word history: Old English *lecg* (exact meaning not clear), from *lecgan* lay[1]

ledger

noun an account book used to record money that is paid out and paid in

Word history: Middle English

lee
noun a side or part that is sheltered or turned away from the wind: *the **lee** of a hill*
Word building: **lee** *adjective* **leeward** *adjective* **leeward** *adverb*
Word history: Old English *hlēo* shelter

leech
noun a small worm that sucks the blood of humans or animals and was once used by doctors to take blood from sick people
Word history: Old English *lǣce*

leech / leach
Don't confuse **leech** with **leach**. When soil is **leached**, chemicals are washed out of it by the passage of water.

leek
noun a vegetable that tastes like an onion and has a white bulb and wide, green leaves
Word history: Old English *lēac*

leek / leak
Don't confuse **leek** with **leak**. A **leak** is a hole or crack that lets liquid or gas in or out accidentally.

leer
noun an unpleasant kind of smile that suggests thoughts of sex, cruelty or cunning
Word building: **leer** *verb*
Word history: special use of obsolete *leer* cheek, Old English *hlēor*

leeway
noun **1** the distance by which a ship or plane is blown off course by the wind
2 extra space, time or money that allows freedom of action and choice

left[1]
adjective **1** having to do with the side of a person or thing which is turned toward the west when they are facing north: *Raise your **left** hand.*
noun **2** the left side: *Turn to the **left**.*
phrase **3 the Left**, a political party or group that believes in the equal distribution of wealth and supports workers rather than companies
Word use: The opposite is **right**. | You can also use **the left** or **left wing** for definition 3.
Word history: Middle English; special use of Old English dialect *left* (Old English *lyft*) meaning 'weak', 'infirm'

left[2]
verb **1** past tense and past participle of **leave**[1]
adjective **2** remaining

left-handed
adjective naturally inclined to use the left hand to do things: *One-sixth of the class was **left-handed**.*

leftist
noun **1** a member of a socialist or radical party or a person in agreement with their ideas
adjective **2** having socialist or radical political ideas

left wing
noun → **left**[1] (definition 3)
Word building: **left-wing** *adjective* **left-winger** *noun*

leg
noun **1** one of the parts of a body which is used for support and for walking
2 one of the supports of a piece of furniture: *the **leg** of a table*
3 one of the sections of a journey, race or competition: *The first **leg** of the flight was to Singapore.*
4 → **leg side**
phrase **5 not have a leg to stand on**, to have no good reason or excuse
6 pull someone's leg, to tease or make fun of someone
Word history: Middle English, from Scandinavian

legacy
noun **1** a gift of money or property made after someone's death through their will: *He left her a **legacy** of $500.* (***bequest***, ***inheritance***)
2 anything that is handed down from the past or happens as a result of something in the past: *The refugee problem is a **legacy** of war.*
Noun forms: The plural is **legacies**.
Word history: Middle English, from Old French, from Latin word meaning 'legate'

legal (lee-guhl)
adjective **1** allowed or decided by law: *a **legal** action* (***authorised***, ***lawful***, ***legitimate***, ***permitted***, ***proper***)
2 having to do with law: *a **legal** secretary*
Word use: The opposite of definition 1 is **illegal**.
Word building: **legality** *noun* **legally** *adverb*
Word history: from Latin word meaning 'relating to law'

legalise
verb to make legal
Word use: You can also use **legalize**.

legate (leg-uht)
noun **1** an official representative of the pope in a foreign country
2 in ancient Rome, an assistant to a general in the army or to the governor of a province
Word history: Middle English, from Latin word meaning 'deputy'

legatee (leg-uh-tee)
noun someone to whom a legacy is given

legation (luh-gay-shuhn)
noun the house and offices of a diplomatic minister and staff when the minister is not of the rank of an ambassador
Word history: late Middle English, from Latin word meaning 'embassy'

legend (lej-uhnd)
noun a story that comes from long ago in the past and which is thought by many people to be at least partly true: *the **legend** of King Arthur and the Knights of the Round Table*
Word building: **legendary** *adjective*
Word history: Middle English, from Old French, from Medieval Latin word meaning 'things to be read'

leggings
plural noun an outer covering for the legs, usually tight-fitting

legible (<u>lej</u>-uh-buhl)
adjective able to be read easily: ***legible** handwriting*

Word use: The opposite is **illegible.**
Word building: **legibility** *noun* **legibly** *adverb*
Word history: Middle English, from Latin word meaning 'read'

legion (<u>lee</u>-juhn)
noun **1** a unit of soldiers in the ancient Roman army
2 any large group of soldiers
3 any great number: *She has a **legion** of friends.*

Word building: **legionary** *noun* **legionary** *adjective*
Word history: Middle English, from Old French, from Latin

legislation (lej-uhs-<u>lay</u>-shuhn)
noun **1** the making of laws: *Parliament is responsible for **legislation**.*
2 a law or all the laws made: *Parliament passed new **legislation** to increase parking fines.*

Word building: **legislate** *verb* **legislator** *noun*
Word history: from Latin word meaning 'the proposing of a law'

legislature (<u>lej</u>-uhs-lay-chuh, <u>lej</u>-uhs-luh-chuh)
noun an organisation, such as a parliament, that makes laws

Word building: **legislative** *adjective*

legitimate (luh-<u>jit</u>-uh-muht)
adjective **1** in accordance with law: *a **legitimate** document* (***authorised***, ***formal***, ***lawful***, ***legal***, ***proper***)
2 born to parents who are legally married: *a **legitimate** child*

Word building: **legitimacy** *noun*
Word history: late Middle English, from Latin word meaning 'lawful'

leg side
noun Cricket that half of the field that is behind the person who is batting

Word use: You can also use **leg**. | Compare this with **off side.**

legume (<u>leg</u>-yoohm)
noun **1** any of a family of flowering plants which have pods as fruits, especially those used for feed, food, or a soil-improving crop
2 a member of this family, such as peas, beans, etc., used as a vegetable

Word building: **leguminous** *adjective*
Word history: French, from Latin word meaning 'something gathered (or picked)'

leisure (<u>lezh</u>-uh)
noun **1** time that is free from work
phrase **2 at leisure**, without hurry

Word use: The opposite of definition 1 is **work**.
Word history: Middle English, from Old French, from Latin word meaning 'be permitted'

leisurely
adjective unhurried (***lazy***, ***plodding***, ***slow***)

lemming
noun a small, mouse-like animal of far northern areas, such as Norway, Sweden, and elsewhere, noted for its mass migrations in times of population increases

Word history: Norwegian

lemon
noun **1** a yellow fruit with a sour taste
2 a clear light-yellow colour

Word building: **lemon** *adjective*
Word history: Middle English, from Old French, from Arabic, Persian

lemonade
noun a fizzy soft drink made with lemons, sugar and water

Word history: from French word meaning 'lemon'

lemur (<u>lee</u>-muh)
noun any of various small mammals, related to the monkeys, that live in trees, are mainly active at night, usually have a foxlike face and woolly fur, and are found chiefly in Madagascar

Word history: Neo-Latin, from Latin word meaning 'ghosts', 'spectres'; so called because of nocturnal habits

lend
verb **1** to give the use of, for a short time: *Could you please lend me your pen for a moment? I've lost mine.* (***loan***)
phrase **2 lend itself to,** to be well suited for: *This room **lends itself to** study.*

Verb forms: I **lent**, I have **lent**, I am **lending**
Word use: Compare definition 1 with **borrow**.
Word building: **lender** *noun* **loan** *noun*
Word history: Old English *lǣnan*, from *lǣn* meaning 'loan'

lend / loan
It is usual to use **lend** as a verb, and **loan** as either a noun or a verb:

My father won't lend me his new sports jacket.

I asked him so nicely for a loan of it.

I'd loan him mine if I owned one.

In casual talk you will often hear people use **lend** as a noun:

He said he'd give me a lend of his red sports car instead.

length
noun **1** the measure from end to end: *This room is four metres in **length**.* (***extent***)
2 a piece of something long: *a **length** of rope*
phrase **3 at length,**
a in full detail: *She told the story **at length**.*
b at last or finally: ***At length** the train arrived.*

Word building: **lengthen** *verb* **lengthiness** *noun* **lengthy** *adjective*
Word history: Middle English and Old English, from *lang*, long[1]

lenient (<u>lee</u>-nee-uhnt)
adjective gentle or not hard in treatment: *a **lenient** punishment* (***compassionate***, ***humane***, ***merciful***, ***mild***)

Word use: The opposite of this is **harsh**.
Word building: **lenience** *noun* **leniency** *noun*
Word history: from Latin word meaning 'softening'

lens
noun a piece of glass or other material with two opposite surfaces, either or both curved, used for bringing together or spreading light rays, so as to make objects look larger or for use in glasses to correct bad eyesight

Noun forms: The plural is **lenses.**
Word history: from Latin word meaning 'a lentil' (which is shaped like a biconvex lens)

lent
verb past tense and past participle of **lend**

lent / leant
Don't confuse **lent** with **leant. Leant** is a past form of the verb **lean**, to rest on or against something for support:
He leant his head on my shoulder.

lentil
noun a kind of plant with a seed that is used as food, similar to peas and beans

Word history: Middle English, from French, from Latin word meaning 'a lentil'

leonine (<u>lee</u>-uh-nuyn)
adjective having to do with, or like a lion

Word history: Middle English, from Latin

leopard (<u>lep</u>-uhd)
noun a large, fierce, spotted animal of the cat family

Word building: **leopardess** *feminine noun*
Word history: Middle English, from Old French, from Late Latin, from Late Greek

leotard (<u>lee</u>-uh-tahd)
noun a close-fitting piece of clothing worn for dancing or doing exercises

Word history: named after Jules *Léotard*, 19th century French acrobat

leper (<u>lep</u>-uh)
noun someone who has leprosy

Word history: Middle English, from Old French, from Latin, from Greek word meaning 'scaly'

leprechaun (<u>lep</u>-ruh-kawn)
noun a fairy in Irish folk stories, in the shape of a little man

Word history: from Irish *lupracān* a little sprite

leprosy (<u>lep</u>-ruh-see)
noun an infectious disease which can cause sores on your skin, the loss of your fingers and toes, and the loss of feeling in parts of your body

Word history: Late Latin

lesbian (<u>lez</u>-bee-uhn)
noun **1** a female homosexual
adjective **2** having to do with a lesbian

Word building: **lesbianism** *noun*
Word history: from *Lesbos* (Lesvos), a Greek island which was the birthplace of Sappho, a homosexual poetess of the sixth century BC

lesion (<u>lee</u>-zhuhn)
noun a wound (***cut***, ***injury***)

Word history: late Middle English, from Latin word meaning 'an injury'

less
adjective **1** smaller in size, amount or extent: *I want **less** talking.*
adverb **2** to a smaller extent or in a smaller amount: *Choose a **less** expensive present.*

Word use: For other forms look up **little.**
Word history: Old English *lǣs(sa)*

less / fewer
Both of these words have to do with 'a smaller quantity'.
Many people use **less** on every occasion, and never use **fewer** at all.
In careful writing, though, **fewer** should be used with nouns that refer to things you can count (count nouns), and **less** with nouns that refer to things that aren't countable (mass nouns):
fewer chairs *less water*
fewer people *less butter*

lessee (le-<u>see</u>)
noun someone to whom the lease of a property is given

lessen
verb to make less: *This medicine will **lessen** the pain.* (***cut back***, ***decrease***, ***lower***, ***minimise***, ***reduce***)

Word use: The opposite of this is **increase.**

lesser
adjective being smaller in size, amount, importance, etc., than another: *a **lesser** evil*

Word history: late Middle English, from *less* + *-er*

lesson
noun **1** the time during which a pupil or a class is taught one subject
2 anything that you learn, or from which you learn: *a **lesson** in crossing roads | The accident taught me a **lesson**.*

Word history: Middle English, from Old French, from Latin word meaning 'a reading'

lessor (le-<u>saw</u>, <u>le</u>-saw)
noun someone who gives a lease of a property

lest
conjunction for fear that: *He did not move **lest** he fall*

Word history: Old English

let
verb **1** to allow or permit (***authorise***, ***license***, ***suffer***, ***tolerate***)
2 to rent or hire out: *We have a room to **let**.*
phrase **3 let alone** or **let be**, to stop bothering, arguing with, etc.
4 let down, to disappoint: *You will **let** us **down** if you don't come.*
5 let go, *Colloquial*
a to freely express anger or other emotion
b to stop holding onto someone or something
6 let know, to inform or tell: *I'll **let** you **know** the news.*
7 let off,
a to excuse (***forgive***, ***pardon***, ***spare***)
b to make explode: *We have a whole bag of fireworks to **let off**.*

8 let off steam, to express your anger or other strong emotion in a free and harmless manner
9 let out,
a to tell: *He **let out** our secret.* (***blab***, ***give away***, ***let slip***, ***reveal***, ***spill***)
b to make larger: *to **let out** the waist of a skirt*
c to give out: *He **let out** a laugh.*
d to free: *to **let** a bird **out** of a cage*

Verb forms: I **let**, I have **let**, I am **letting**
Word history: Old English *lǣtan*

let / lease / hire / rent
Look up **hire / rent / lease / let.**

lethal (leeth-uhl)
adjective causing death: *a **lethal** poison* (***deadly***, ***fatal***, ***malignant***, ***terminal***)

Word history: Latin

lethargy (leth-uh-jee)
noun a state of sleepy laziness: *The hot weather has filled me with **lethargy**.*

Word use: The opposite of this is **energy**.
Word building: **lethargic** *adjective*
Word history: Late Latin, from Greek word meaning 'drowsiness'

let's
contraction of **let us**

Look up **contractions in grammar.**

letter
noun **1** a message in writing or printing addressed to a person or group (***dispatch***, ***note***)
2 one of the signs used in writing and printing to stand for a speech sound: *'A' is the first **letter** of the alphabet.*

Word history: Middle English, from Old French, from Latin *littera* alphabetic character, plural *litterae* epistle, writings

lettuce
noun a plant with large green leaves which are used in salads

Word history: Middle English, from Old French, from Latin

leukaemia (looh-kee-mee-uh)
noun a disease in which your body produces too many white blood cells and which often causes death

Word use: You can also use **leukemia**.
Word history: Neo-Latin, from Greek word meaning 'white'

levee (lev-ee)
noun **1** a raised bank of earth and sand built up by a river during floods
2 a bank built to keep a river from overflowing

Word history: from French word meaning 'raise'

level
adjective **1** even, or having no part higher than another: *a **level** surface* (***flat***, ***horizontal***, ***smooth***)
2 horizontal, not sloping: ***level** ground*
3 equal: *They are **level** in intelligence.* (***equal***, ***equivalent***, ***similar***)
noun **4** a horizontal or level position or surface
5 a ranking whether high or low: *He was given a job at the top **level** in the Company.* (***class***, ***grade***, ***rank***, ***stage***)
6 an instrument for finding out whether something is exactly flat or horizontal
verb **7** to make or become level or equal
8 to aim or point: *He **levelled** the gun at her chest.*
phrase **9 find your level**, to find the most suitable place for yourself, especially in regard to the people around
10 on the level, *Colloquial* honest: *Are you sure he is **on the level**?*
11 your level best, *Colloquial* your very best

Verb forms: I **levelled**, I have **levelled**, I am **levelling**
Word building: **leveller** *noun*
Word history: Middle English, from Old French, from Latin word meaning 'a balance', 'level'

lever (lee-vuh)
noun **1** a bar supported at one point along its length, which lifts a weight at one end when you press or pull down the other
verb **2** to move with a lever: *to **lever** a rock out of the ground* (***force***, ***prise***)

Word history: Middle English, from Old French word meaning 'raise', from Latin word meaning 'lighten', 'lift', 'raise'

leverage (leev-uh-rij)
noun **1** the action of a lever
2 the mechanical power gained by using a lever
3 means of influence: *His position gives him a lot of **leverage**.*

levitate (lev-uh-tayt)
verb to rise or float in the air as if by magic

Word building: **levitation** *noun*
Word history: *levit(y)* + *-ate*; modelled on *gravitate*

levity
noun a lack of seriousness in the way you think and behave

Word use: The opposite of this is **gravity**.
Word history: Latin

levy (lev-ee)
verb **1** to place or impose by law: *to **levy** a tax on cigarettes and beer*
noun **2** a fee or a tax which has to be paid: *The club imposed a **levy** on members to pay for the Christmas party.*

Verb forms: I **levied**, I have **levied**, I am **levying**
Noun forms: The plural is **levies**.
Word history: Middle English, from French word meaning 'raise'

lewd (loohd, lyoohd)
adjective marked by, or exciting, obscene sexual desire: *a **lewd** look | a **lewd** song*

Word building: **lewdness** *noun*
Word history: Middle English word meaning 'ignorant', from Old English word meaning 'of the people'

lexicography (leks-uh-kog-ruh-fee)
noun the writing or compiling of dictionaries

Word building: **lexicographic** *adjective* **lexicographical** *adjective* **lexicographer** *noun*

lexicon (<u>leks</u>-uh-kuhn)
noun **1** a dictionary, especially of Greek, Latin, or Hebrew
2 a list of words belonging to a particular subject, language, etc.

Word history: Medieval Latin (much used in Latin titles of dictionaries), from Greek word meaning 'of or for words'

liability
noun **1** something or someone that causes difficulty rather than being helpful: *New shoes are a **liability** on a long walk because they can make your feet sore.*
2 legal responsibility: *He accepted **liability** for the accident.*
3 liabilities, debts

Noun forms: The plural is **liabilities.**
Word use: The opposite of definition 1 is **advantage.** | Compare definition 3 with **assets.**

liable (<u>luy</u>-uh-buhl)
adjective **1** likely: *Problems are **liable** to come up.* (***apt***, ***expected***, ***odds-on***)
2 having a legal responsibility: *He was **liable** for the accident and had to pay the repair costs.*

Word history: late Middle English, from French word meaning 'bind'

liaise (lee-<u>ayz</u>)
phrase **liaise with**, to communicate and act together

liaison (lee-<u>ay</u>-zuhn)
noun a connection or communication between people or groups: *The school captain acted as a **liaison** between teachers and pupils.*

Word history: French, from Latin word meaning 'a binding'

liar
noun someone who tells lies (***fibber***, ***storyteller***)

liar / lyre
Don't confuse **liar** with **lyre**, which is a stringed musical instrument like a harp, used in ancient Greece.

libel (<u>luy</u>-buhl)
noun a written or printed statement which damages someone's reputation: *The politician sued the newspaper for **libel**.* (***defamation***, ***slander***, ***slur***, ***smear***)

Word building: **libel** *verb* (**libelled, libelling**) **libeller** *noun* **libellous** *adjective*
Word history: Middle English, from Latin word meaning 'book'

libel / slander
Don't confuse **libel** with **slander. Slander** is a <u>spoken</u> statement which damages someone's reputation or good name.

liberal
adjective **1** happy to see change and development, especially in social and religious matters
2 broad-minded or accepting a wide range of ideas: *a **liberal** thinker* (***permissive***, ***relaxed***, ***tolerant***, ***unconventional***)
3 generous: *a **liberal** gift | a **liberal** giver* (***lavish***, ***magnanimous***)

Word use: The opposite of definition 2 is **narrow-minded.** | The opposite of definition 3 is **stingy.**
Word building: **liberality** *noun*
Word history: Middle English, from Latin word meaning 'relating to a free man'

liberalism
noun any liberal principles and practices, especially in a political party or a religious movement

liberate
verb to set free: *The army **liberated** the country from enemy control.* (***deliver***, ***emancipate***, ***free***, ***release***)

Word building: **liberation** *noun* **liberator** *noun*
Word history: Latin

libertarian (lib-uh-<u>tair</u>-ree-uhn)
noun someone who believes in freedom of thought, behaviour, etc.

Word building: **libertarianism** *noun*

libertine (<u>lib</u>-uh-teen)
noun someone who does not exercise self-control, especially in moral or sexual matters

Word building: **libertinism** *noun*
Word history: Middle English, from Latin word meaning 'freed man'

liberty
noun **1** freedom from imprisonment, or from a cruel or foreign government
2 freedom to do, think, or speak as you choose
3 a rude or disrespectful freedom in behaviour or speech: *Don't think that you can take **liberties** with me.*
phrase **4 at liberty**, free, or having permission to do a particular thing

Noun forms: The plural is **liberties.**
Word history: Middle English, from Old French, from Latin

libido (luh-<u>bee</u>-doh)
noun **1** *Psychology* all of the instinctive energies and desires which come from the unconscious mind
2 the sexual urge

Word building: **libidinal** *adjective*
Word history: from Latin word meaning 'pleasure', 'longing'

librarian (luy-<u>brair</u>-ree-uhn)
noun a person in charge of a library

library
noun **1** a room or building where books and other reading or study materials are kept for people to use or borrow
2 a collection of books, or of films, recordings or music: *She has a good **library** at home.*

Noun forms: The plural is **libraries.**
Word history: Middle English, from Latin word meaning 'place to keep books'

lice (luys)
noun plural of **louse** See **head lice.**

licence
noun **1** official permission to do something or a certificate showing this permission: *a driving **licence***

2 uncontrolled freedom of behaviour: *That teacher allows the children too much* ***licence.***

Word history: Middle English, from Old French, from Latin

license

verb to give official permission to: *He is* ***licensed*** *to sell guns.* (***authorise, permit***)

Word building: **licensee** *noun*

licentious (luy-sen-shuhs)

adjective uncontrolled in sexual behaviour

Word history: Medieval Latin

lichen (luy-kuhn)

noun a moss-like plant that grows in patches, usually on rocks or tree trunks

Word history: Latin, from Greek

lick

verb **1** to pass your tongue over: *David* ***licked*** *the back of the stamp.*
2 to pass over or touch lightly: *Flames* ***licked*** *the logs of wood.*
3 *Colloquial* to defeat: *We* ***licked*** *the other team.* (***beat, conquer, thrash, vanquish***)

Word building: **lick** *noun*
Word history: Old English *liccian*

licorice (lik-uh-rish, lik-rish)

noun a sweet-tasting substance made from the root of a plant and used in making sweets and some medicines

Word use: You can also use **liquorice**.
Word history: Middle English, from Anglo-French, from Late Latin, from Greek

lid

noun **1** a movable top for covering a container
2 → **eyelid**

Word history: Old English *hlid*

lie[1]

noun a deliberate untruth (***falsehood, fib, half-truth, invention***)

Word building: **lie** *verb* (**lied, lying**)
Word history: Old English *lēogan*

lie[2]

verb **1** to be or to rest in a flat horizontal position: *I would like to* ***lie*** *in bed all day.* | *A book is* ***lying*** *on the table.*
2 to remain in a certain position or condition: *The money* ***lay*** *forgotten in the bank for many years.*
3 to be found or to be located: *The trouble with the bike* ***lies*** *with the gears.* | *Our land* ***lies*** *beside the river.*
phrase **4 lie low**, to be in hiding
5 take lying down, to submit without resistance or protest

Verb forms: I **lay**, I have **lain**, I am **lying**
Word history: Old English *licgan*

lie / lay
Look up **lay / lie.**

lieu (looh, lyooh)

phrase **in lieu of**, instead of

Word history: Middle English, from French, from Latin word meaning 'place'

lieutenant (lef-ten-uhnt), *US* (looh-ten-uhnt)

noun an officer in the army or navy, lower in rank than a captain

Word history: Middle English, from French *lieutenant:* holding a place, from Latin

life

noun **1** the condition that makes animals and plants different from dead things and from other objects like rocks, liquids, machines, etc.
2 the time you are alive, from your birth to your death
3 living things as a group: ***life*** *on earth*
4 lively activity or interest: *Her speech was full of* ***life.***

Noun forms: The plural is **lives**.
Word use: The opposite of definitions 1 and 2 is **death**.
Word history: Old English *līf*

lifeboat

noun a boat carried on a large ship and used if the ship sinks or catches fire

life cycle

noun the development of a living thing from the beginning of its life to the time it becomes an adult

life expectancy

noun the probable life span of a person, determined by statistics and affected by things such as sex, race, heredity, habitat, occupation, etc.

lifeguard

noun someone who is paid to patrol a place where people swim, such as a public pool, beach, etc., and to rescue people if necessary and give them first aid

lifeline

noun **1** a line or rope for saving life, such as one attached to a lifeboat
2 a route over which supplies can be sent to an area otherwise cut off
3 anything supplying emergency help, communication, counselling, etc.

lifesaver

noun Australian someone who makes sure that people swim at the safe part of a beach and who rescues swimmers in difficulty

lifesaving

noun rescue and resuscitation methods that deal with emergency situations in or near the water

lifestreaming

noun the online recording of one's daily life by means of webcam or personal blogs, microblogs, etc.

lifestyle

noun the way or manner of living: ***lifestyles*** *of the rich and famous* | *an* ***exciting*** *lifestyle*

lift

verb **1** to raise or bring upwards (***elevate, hoist, jack up, set aloft***)
noun **2** a moving platform or cage for bringing people from one level of a building to another
3 a free ride in a vehicle: *Can you give me a* ***lift*** *home?*

Word use: Another name for definition 2, which is more common in the US, is **elevator**.
Word history: Middle English, from Scandinavian

lift-off
noun the moment when a space shuttle or rocket leaves the ground

ligament (lig-uh-muhnt)
noun a band of tissue, usually white and fibrous, for connecting bones, holding organs in place, etc.

Word history: Middle English, from Latin word meaning 'a tie', 'band'

ligature (lig-uh-chuh)
noun **1** anything that you use for binding or tying up, such as a band, bandage, or cord
2 in surgery, a thread or wire for tying blood vessels, etc.

Word history: Middle English, from Latin word meaning 'bind'

light[1]
noun **1** a form of radiation produced by some objects such as the sun or fire, which bounces off other things and so lets us see them
2 one of those things which give off light, such as an electric light globe or the sun
3 one of the set of coloured lights that is used to control traffic at intersections
4 new knowledge or information: *Can you throw any* ***light*** *on this mystery?*
adjective **5** having light, rather than darkness: *a* ***light*** *room* (***bright***, ***illuminated***)
6 pale in colour: ***light*** *blue*
verb **7** to set burning or start to burn: *He* ***lit*** *a fire. | The match won't* ***light***.
8 to give light to: *They took a torch to* ***light*** *their way.*
phrase **9 bring to light**, to discover (***expose***, ***reveal***)
10 in the light of, taking into account or considering: ***in the light of*** *this experience*
11 light up,
a to make brighter: *A smile* ***lit up*** *her face.*
b to become bright with light or colour: *The city* ***lights up*** *at night.*
12 see the light,
a to come into existence
b to be made public, or to be published: *Will the committee's findings ever* ***see the light****?*
c to realise the truth of something

Verb forms: I **lit** or I **lighted**, I have **lit** or I have **lighted**, I am **lighting**
Word building: **lightness** *noun* **lighten** *verb*
Word history: Old English *lēoht*

light[2]
adjective **1** of little weight: *a* ***light*** *load*
2 small in amount, force or depth: *a* ***light*** *meal | * ***light*** *rain |* ***light*** *sleep*
3 not heavy or serious: ***light*** *reading*
4 cheerful: *a* ***light*** *heart*
phrase **5 make light of**, to treat as being of little importance: *He* ***made light of*** *his troubles.*

Word building: **lightly** *adverb* **lightness** *noun* **lighten** *verb*
Word history: Old English *lēoht*

lighthouse
noun a tower with a strong light that guides ships at sea and warns them of any dangerous rocks nearby

lighting
noun **1** in a theatre, in films, etc., the arrangement and effect of lights
2 the way light falls upon a face, object, etc., especially in a picture

lightning
noun a sudden flash of light in the sky caused by electricity in the air during a thunderstorm

lightning / lightening

Lightning should not be confused with **lightening**, a form of the verb **lighten**, to make less dark, or to make less in weight:

I've been lightening the paint but it's still too red.

light-year
noun the distance travelled by light in one year, used in measuring distances between stars

ligneous (lig-nee-uhs)
adjective woody

Word history: from Latin word meaning 'wooden'

like[1]
adjective **1** similar or able to be compared in some way
noun **2** something that is similar: *oranges, lemons and the* ***like***
3 a similar person or thing: *No-one has seen his* ***like*** *before.*

Word building: **likeness** *noun*
Word history: from Old English word meaning 'of the same body or form'

like / as

In traditional grammar **like** is a preposition, used to introduce a noun or something standing for a noun. So we would write:

She walks like a duck.

As is a conjunction and we use it to link a new clause with one already there:

She walks as ducks do.

These two sentences mean the same thing.

Nowadays people use **like** in many cases when it is formally wrong because it sounds better than **as**:

She acts like witches do.

Here **like** is acting as a conjunction which people used to think was wrong.

This is an example of a word taking on a new role in grammar.

like[2]
verb **1** to find pleasant or agreeable: *I* ***like*** *picnics. | I* ***like*** *her.* (***appreciate***, ***enjoy***, ***fancy***, ***welcome***)
2 to wish or want: *Do it whenever you* ***like***.

Word history: Old English

likely
adjective **1** probable: *a* ***likely*** *account of what happened* (***apt***, ***believable***, ***possible***, ***probable***)
adverb **2** probably: *He was very* ***likely*** *right.*

Word building: **likelihood** *noun*
Word history: Middle English, from Scandinavian

liken
verb to compare

likes
plural noun preferences: *to have* ***likes*** *and dislikes*

likewise
adverb **1** also
2 in the same or similar manner
Word history: abbreviation of *in like wise*

liking
noun preference: *I have a* ***liking*** *for skating.*
Word use: The opposite of this is **antipathy** or **aversion**.

lilac (luy-luhk)
noun **1** a purple or white flower with a pleasant smell, which grows in clusters on a shrub
2 a pale purple colour
Word building: **lilac** *adjective*
Word history: French, from Arabic, from Persian word meaning 'bluish'

Lilliputian (lil-uh-pyooh-shuhn)
adjective **1** tiny
noun **2** a tiny person
Word history: from *Lilliput*, an imaginary island inhabited by tiny people, in *Gulliver's Travels* (1726) by Jonathan Swift

lilt
verb to sing or play in a light rhythmic manner
Word building: **lilt** *noun* **lilting** *adjective*
Word history: Middle English

lily
noun a plant with a bulb and a funnel-shaped flower which can be found in many colours, although most people think of lilies as being white
Word history: Old English, from Latin

lima bean (luy-muh been)
noun a kind of bean with a broad, flat seed that you can eat

limb
noun **1** your arm or leg, or the similar part of an animal's body, such as a wing (***member***)
2 the large main branch of a tree (***bough***)
Word history: Old English *lim*

limber
phrase **limber up**, to exercise or warm up in order to make yourself flexible and relaxed: *Always remember to* ***limber up*** *before a race.*

limbo[1] (lim-boh)
noun a place where people or things are regarded as being put when cast aside, forgotten, past, or out of date
Noun forms: The plural is **limbos**.
Word history: Middle English, from Medieval Latin *in limbo* on the border (of hell), where some souls had to wait because they were not wicked and didn't deserve to go to Hell, but they were also not fit to enter Heaven because they had not been baptised or saved

limbo[2]
noun a type of dance where each dancer in turn bends backwards in order to pass underneath a horizontal bar which is gradually lowered
Word history: West Indian native name

lime[1]
noun **1** a white powder obtained by heating limestone, that is used in making cement
2 a calcium mixture used to improve crop-growing soil
Word history: Old English *līm*

lime[2]
noun **1** a small greenish-yellow citrus fruit
2 a greenish-yellow colour
Word building: **lime** *adjective*
Word history: French, from Spanish

limelight
noun **1** a strong light, made by heating a cylinder of lime in a flame of mixed gases, which used to be directed upon the stage to light up particular persons or objects
phrase **2 in the limelight**, to be at the centre of public interest: *He was really* ***in the limelight*** *after the trial.* (***famous***, ***in the spotlight***)
3 steal the limelight, to make yourself the centre of attention

limerick (lim-uh-rik)
noun a funny rhyming poem of five lines
Word history: named after *Limerick* a county in Ireland; originally from a song with refrain, 'Will you come up to Limerick?'

limestone
noun a soft, white, chalky rock

limit
noun **1** the end or furthest part: *to reach the* ***limit*** *of your patience*
2 a boundary or line that you should not pass: *You may only ride up to the* ***limit*** *I have set you.* (***edge***, ***frontier***, ***perimeter***)
verb **3** to keep within a certain amount or space: *to* ***limit*** *your pocket money | to* ***limit*** *the playing area* (***control***, ***curb***, ***restrict***)
Verb forms: I **limited**, I have **limited**, I am **limiting**
Word building: **limitation** *noun*
Word history: Middle English, from Old French, from Latin word meaning 'boundary'

limousine (lim-uh-zeen, lim-uh-zeen)
noun any large, comfortable car, especially one driven by a paid driver
Word history: French word meaning 'cloak', from *Limousin*, a former province in central France

limp[1]
verb to walk with difficulty because of an injured leg or foot (***hobble***, ***shuffle***, ***stagger***, ***totter***)
Word building: **limp** *noun*
Word history: Middle English

limp[2]
adjective not stiff or firm: ***limp*** *material*
Word use: The opposite of this is **firm** or **stiff**.

limpet
noun a cone-shaped shellfish that sticks very firmly to rocks
Word history: Old English, from Late Latin word meaning 'limpet', 'lamprey'

limpid
adjective clear or transparent: ***limpid*** *pools of water*
Word history: Latin

linchpin
noun **1** a pin or rod put through the end of an axle to stop the wheel from falling off
2 the main point of a plan, argument, etc.
3 the main or key person or event, in a play, etc.

Word use: You can also use **lynchpin**.
Word history: Old English

line[1]
noun **1** a thin mark or stroke made on paper, wood or some other surface
2 something arranged like a line: *a **line** of trees | a **line** of words on a page* (***file***, ***row***, ***string***)
3 a wrinkle on someone's face
4 a strip of railway track: *the railway **line***
5 a type of goods which a shop sells: *We don't stock that **line**.*
6 *Art* a mark from a crayon, pencil or brush in a work of graphic art, which shows direction and marks the edges of forms, used either singly or with other lines to make shading
7 a continuous stretch of length, straight or curved, without breadth or thickness
8 lines, the words of an actor's part in a play: *Have you learned your **lines**?*
verb **9** to form a line along: *Trees **lined** the street.*
phrase **10 bring into line**, to make conform
11 get your lines crossed, to misunderstand
12 in line,
a conforming
b with a good chance: ***in line** for a promotion*
13 out of line, not according to standard practice or agreement
14 line up,
a to take a position in a line or queue
b to bring into a line

Word history: Middle English, partly from Old French, from Vulgar Latin, from Latin word meaning 'thread', 'line'

line[2]
verb to cover the inside of: *to **line** a coat with silk*

Word history: Old English, from Latin

lineage (lin-ee-ij)
noun descent from a line of ancestors (***ancestry***)

lineal (lin-ee-uhl)
adjective of a descendant, ancestor, etc., being in the direct line of descent

Word history: Middle English, from Latin word meaning 'line[1]'

linear (lin-ee-uh)
adjective **1** having to do with lines or length: *a **linear** measure*
2 arranged in a line: *a **linear** series*
3 narrow, like a line: *a **linear** leaf*
4 having to do with a line that can be shown on a graph and described by an equation such as $x + y = 3$

linedance
noun a dance to country music in which dancers perform a repeated sequence of steps while facing the same direction in a line

Word building: **linedancing** *noun*

linen
noun **1** cloth made from flax
2 articles made from linen or cotton, such as sheets and table cloths

Word history: Old English *linnen*

line of credit
noun Finance a borrowing facility extended on an indefinite basis: *He could borrow whenever the need arose due to his **line of credit**.*

liner[1]
noun a large passenger ship

liner[2]
noun something used as a lining: *nappy **liner***

linesman
noun **1** → **linesperson**
2 someone who puts up or repairs telephone or electric power lines

Noun forms: The plural is **linesmen**.

linesperson
noun a sports official who helps a referee or umpire decide if the ball has landed inside or outside one of the lines on the field of play

Noun forms: The plural is **linespeople**.
Word use: You can also use **linesman**.

line-up
noun **1** the members of a particular order or grouping of people or things, for action, inspection, etc., as in a sporting team, a music band, etc.
2 a sequence of programs or events: *Tonight's TV **line-up** is a knockout.*

Word use: You can also use **lineup**.

linger
verb to stay on in a place because you don't want to leave (***dally***, ***dawdle***, ***delay***, ***loiter***, ***tarry***)

Word history: from Old English word meaning 'delay'

lingerie (lon-zhuh-ray)
noun women's underwear or nightwear

Word history: French, from Latin word meaning 'flax'

lingo (ling-goh)
noun Colloquial language

Noun forms: The plural is **lingoes**.
Word history: Lingua Franca, from Latin

linguist (ling-gwuhst)
noun a person who studies language

linguistic (ling-gwis-tik)
adjective having to do with language

linguistics (ling-gwis-tiks)
noun the study of language, including sounds, words and grammar: ***Linguistics** is a subject studied at university.*

liniment
noun an oily liquid for rubbing on bruises, sprains or sore muscles

Word history: Middle English, from Late Latin

lining
noun a covering for an inside surface: *The **lining** of the coat is grey silk.*

link
noun **1** one of the separate rings which make up a chain
2 anything which is a bond or connecting part: *Our love of football is a strong **link** between us.* (***connection***, ***tie***)
3 → **hyperlink**

Word building: **link** *verb*
Word history: Middle English, from Scandinavian

linkage
noun **1** the act of linking
2 a system of links

linkbait
verb **1** to create points of interest in a website so that other sites will link to it: *They wanted to **linkbait** the new website so more people would visit it.*
noun **2** such a feature of a site

Word building: **linkbaiting** *noun*

link word
noun a word which is used to connect ideas between sentences

Any good piece of writing will connect and develop ideas from one sentence to another. The connecting links in these chains of ideas are often **link words**. They may seem small and unimportant, but they can do a great deal to make your writing cohesive.

(Some of the link words in the paragraph you've just read are *these*, *they*, *if* and *but*.)

Link words include:

1 this that these those
(**demonstratives**)

2 he she it his him her hers its they them their
(third person **pronouns**)

3 although and as because but if nor or since so when while yet
(**conjunctions**)

4 also besides consequently furthermore hence however likewise nevertheless next otherwise neither similarly still then therefore thus
(connective **adverbs**)

All these words, and others like them, make links with something already mentioned. The demonstratives and pronouns link up with things and people named earlier. The conjunctions and connective adverbs link ideas and statements with each other, either within a sentence, or from one sentence to the next.

linoleum (luh-<u>noh</u>-lee-uhm, luy-<u>noh</u>-lee-uhm)
noun a floor covering made of a mixture of oil, cork and rosin pressed into a strong cloth backing

Word use: The short form is **lino**.
Word history: Latin

linseed
noun the seed of the flax plant from which an oil is made

Word history: Old English *līn* flax + *sǣd* seed

lint
noun **1** a soft material for dressing wounds, etc., made from specially treated linen cloth
2 bits of thread or fluff

Word history: perhaps from Old English *linwyrt*, from *līn* flax + *wyrt* wort

lintel
noun a horizontal piece of wood or stone to support the bricks, etc., above an opening such as a window or a door

Word history: Middle English, from Old French, from Vulgar Latin word meaning 'boundary'

lion (<u>luy</u>-uhn)
noun **1** a large, honey-coloured member of the cat family, living in Africa and southern Asia, the male of which usually has a mane
2 a man of great strength, courage, etc.
3 a well-known and important person many people want to meet: *a literary **lion***
phrase **4 the lion's share**, the largest share or portion of anything

Word history: Middle English, from Old French, from Latin, from Greek

lioness (<u>luy</u>-uh-nes)
noun a female lion

lip
noun **1** either of the two fleshy parts or folds forming the edges of the mouth and important for speech
2 lips, these parts as the organs of speech
3 a lip-like part or structure
4 any edge or rim
phrase **5 bite your lip**, to try hard, and succeed, in not showing your feelings, especially of anger or annoyance
6 give someone lip, to talk, especially to someone in a higher position, in a cheeky or insolent manner
7 keep a stiff upper lip, to face trouble or pain without showing your feelings

Word history: Old English

lip-read
verb to understand spoken words by watching the movement of a speaker's lips

lip-service
noun the saying of something without meaning it; insincere profession of devotion or goodwill

lipstick
noun a cosmetic for colouring your lips

liquefy (<u>lik</u>-wuh-fuy)
verb to make or become liquid

Word use: You can also use **liquify**. | The opposite of this is **solidify**.
Verb forms: it **liquefied**, it has **liquefied**, it is **liquefying**
Word history: late Middle English, from Latin word meaning 'make liquid'

liqueur (luh-<u>kyooh</u>-uh, luh-<u>ker</u>)
noun a type of alcoholic drink, usually strong, sweet and highly flavoured, and usually drunk in small quantities after a meal

Word history: French

liqueur / liquor

These words look similar but refer to different types of alcoholic drink.

Liqueur should not be confused with **liquor**, which is any strong alcoholic drink distilled from wine, such as brandy, or from grain, such as whisky.

liquid
adjective **1** flowing like water (***fluid***, ***molten***, ***runny***)
2 having to do with liquids: *a **liquid** measuring jug*
noun **3** any liquid substance

Word history: Middle English, from Latin

liquid assets
plural noun Economics **1** that part of a trading bank's assets which consist of its notes and coins, its cash with the Reserve Bank of Australia, and its Commonwealth Treasury bills
2 cash and assets that can be easily changed into cash

liquidate (lik-wuh-dayt)
verb **1** to settle or pay: *to **liquidate** a debt*
2 to pay off debts and finish doing business
3 to get rid of, especially by killing: *to **liquidate** political prisoners*

Word history: Medieval Latin, from Latin

liquidation (lik-wuh-day-shuhn)
noun the process of winding up the affairs of a business, etc., by changing liquid assets into cash and settling debts: *The company went into **liquidation**.*

liquidator (lik-wuh-day-tuh)
noun a person appointed to carry out the winding up of a company and the settling of the debts

liquidity (luh-kwid-uh-tee)
noun **1** a liquid state or quality
2 condition of having assets either in cash or readily convertible into cash

liquid oxygen
noun oxygen in its liquid state which is a pale blue liquid which boils at –182.9°C. It is used in rocket engines

liquor (lik-uh)
noun a strong alcoholic drink such as brandy or whisky

Word history: from Latin word meaning 'liquid (state)', 'liquid'

liquorice
noun → **licorice**

lisp
noun the inability to pronounce 's', making it sound like the 'th' in *thin*

Word building: **lisp** *verb*
Word history: Old English *wlisp* lisping

lissom (lis-uhm)
adjective lithe, especially of your body (***active***, ***agile***, ***limber***, ***supple***)

Word history: variant of *lithesome*

list[1]
noun **1** a set of the names of things written down one under the other, so that you'll remember them: *a shopping **list***
2 any set of names, words, etc., written down: *She had to keep a list of all the parcels that were sent out that day.* (***catalogue***, ***record***, ***register***)

Word building: **list** *verb* **listing** *noun*

list[2]
verb to lean to one side: *The ship **listed** to starboard.* (***bank***, ***incline***, ***slant***, ***slope***, ***sway***, ***tilt***, ***tip***)

Word building: **list** *noun*

listen (lis-uhn)
verb to pay attention so that you are able to hear something

Word building: **listener** *noun*
Word history: Old English *hlysnan*

listless
adjective having no energy or interest in anything (***apathetic***, ***languid***, ***lazy***, ***lethargic***, ***sluggish***, ***tired***)

Word building: **listlessly** *adverb* **listlessness** *noun*
Word history: late Middle English

listserv
noun Computers an automatic mailing list server. An email message is sent to a central computer which then sends the message to all the addresses on your mailing list.

lit
verb past tense and past participle of **light**[1]

litany (lit-uh-nee)
noun **1** a form of prayer consisting of a series of prayerful requests, etc., followed by responses
2 a long and boring account: *The opposition recited a **litany** of the government's mistakes.*

Noun forms: The plural is **litanies**.
Word history: Late Latin, from Greek word meaning 'litany', 'an entreating'

literacy (lit-uh-ruh-see)
noun the ability to read and write

literal
adjective **1** true to fact and not exaggerated: *a **literal** account of what happened*
2 following or referring to the exact or actual words that are written or spoken: *a **literal** translation*

Word building: **literally** *adverb*
Word history: Middle English, from Late Latin word meaning 'letter'

literally (lit-ruh-lee, lit-uh-ruh-lee)
adverb **1** word for word: *to translate **literally***
2 in the literal sense: *parachutists dropping in, **literally***

literally / figuratively
Look up **figuratively / literally**.

literary
adjective having to do with books and literature: *a **literary** critic*

literary / literally
These words look similar but they have different meanings.
A **literary** person has a knowledge or love of literature.
A common meaning of **literally** is 'actually or without exaggeration':

There were literally thousands of ants swarming in the kitchen.

literate (lit-uh-ruht)
adjective able to read and write

Word use: The opposite is **illiterate**.
Word history: Middle English, from Latin word meaning 'lettered'

literature
noun **1** books, poems, plays and other forms of writing of a high standard: *Australian **literature***
2 what is written about a particular subject: *the **literature** of home decorating*

Word history: Middle English, from French, from Latin word meaning 'learning'

lithe (luydh)
adjective supple or bending easily: *She has a **lithe** figure.*

Word history: Old English *līthe*

lithium (lith-ee-uhm)
noun a soft, silver-white metallic element. It is the lightest metal.

Word history: Neo-Latin, from Greek word meaning 'stone'; so named because found in minerals

lithography (li-thog-ruh-fee)
noun the art or process of printing a picture, writing, etc., from a flat surface of aluminium, zinc or stone, with some greasy or oily substance

Word building: **lithograph** *noun* **lithographer** *noun* **lithographic** *adjective*

lithosphere (lith-uhs-fear)
noun the crust or solid part of the earth, in contrast to the hydrosphere and the atmosphere, comprising the continental crust, oceanic crust and the brittle part of the upper mantle

Word use: Look up **continental crust** and **oceanic crust**.

litigant (lit-uh-guhnt)
noun a person concerned in a lawsuit

Word building: **litigant** *adjective*
Word history: Latin

litigate (lit-uh-gayt)
verb **1** to contest at law
2 to carry on a lawsuit

Word building: **litigable** *adjective* **litigation** *noun* **litigator** *noun*
Word history: Latin

litmus (lit-muhs)
noun a blue colouring matter obtained from certain lichens. In alkaline solutions litmus turns blue, in acid solutions it turns red. Strips of paper soaked in a solution of litmus are used for this test.

Word history: Middle English, from Scandinavian

litre (lee-tuh)
noun a measure of liquid in the metric system

Word use: The symbol is **L** or **l**, without a full stop. | Look up **metric system**. | The US spelling is **liter**.
Word history: French, from Late Latin, from Greek word meaning 'pound'

litter
noun **1** things, especially rubbish, scattered about (***clutter***, ***jumble***, ***mess***, ***muddle***, ***shambles***)
2 a number of baby animals born at the same time: *a **litter** of puppies*
verb **3** to make untidy by scattering rubbish: *The picnickers **littered** the beach with cans.*
4 to be scattered around: *Bottles **littered** the park.*

Word history: Middle English, from Anglo-French, from Latin

litterbug
noun someone who drops rubbish, especially in public places

little
adjective **1** small in size: *a **little** boy* (***miniature***, ***minute***, ***short***, ***tiny***)
2 not much or small in amount: ***little** hope*
3 short or brief: *a **little** time*
phrase **4 make little of**,
a to treat as unimportant
b to understand only partly: *I can **make little of** your writing.*

Adjective forms: for definition 1, **littler**, **littlest**; for definitions 2 and 3, **less**, **least**
Word history: Middle English and Old English *lytel*

liturgy (lit-uh-jee)
noun **1** a form of public worship: *Greek Orthodox **liturgy*** (***rites***, ***ritual***)
2 a particular arrangement of services: *the Easter **liturgy***

Noun forms: The plural is **liturgies**.
Word building: **liturgical** *adjective* **liturgist** *noun*
Word history: Medieval Latin, from Greek word meaning 'public duty', 'public'

live[1] (liv)
verb **1** to be alive or have life (***breathe***, ***exist***, ***remain***, ***survive***)
2 to keep life going: *to **live** on bread and water*
3 to have your home in a particular place: *to **live** in Australia* (***dwell***, ***lodge***, ***reside***)
phrase **4 live and learn**, to learn through experience
5 live down, to live so as to cause something bad or shameful to be forgotten: *to **live down** a mistake*

Word history: Old English *lifian, libban*

live[2] (luyv)
adjective **1** living or alive
2 broadcast or televised as it is being performed: *a **live** broadcast of the town hall concert*
3 charged with electricity: *a **live** wire*
4 unexploded: *a **live** bullet*
adverb **5** of a radio or television program, broadcast at the time of its happening: *This race is brought to you **live** from the Olympic swimming pool.*

Word history: variant of *alive*

livelihood (luyv-lee-hood)
noun a way of earning money to live: *He makes a **livelihood** from fishing.*

Word history: from Old English word meaning 'life-support'

lively (luyv-lee)
adjective full of energy or spirit: *a **lively** puppy* (***energetic***, ***frisky***, ***frolicsome***, ***jaunty***, ***vivacious***)

Word building: **liveliness** *noun*
Word history: Old English *līflīc*

liven
verb to make more lively or energetic

liver (liv-uh)
noun the part of your body that makes bile which helps digest your food

Word history: Old English *lifer*

liver spot
noun a brownish patch on the skin, usually of an elderly person

Word use: Another name is **age spot**.

livery (liv-uh-ree)
noun **1** the distinctive clothes worn by servants, or formerly by a lord's retainers
2 the feeding or stabling of horses for pay

Noun forms: The plural is **liveries.**
Word history: Middle English, from Anglo-French, from Latin word meaning 'liberate'

livestock
noun all the animals kept on a farm or station property

Word use: You can also use **stock**.

livid (liv-uhd)
adjective **1** very angry: *He was **livid** when we told him.* (***furious, irate***)
2 discoloured by bruises

Word history: Latin

living
adjective **1** alive (***animate, breathing, existent, live***)
2 in existence or use: *German is a **living** language.*
3 having to do with living beings: *The floods were the worst in **living** memory.*
noun **4** livelihood: *to earn a **living***
phrase **5 the living image**, the exact likeness or copy: *He's **the living image** of his father.*

living room
noun a room in a home with comfortable seats, for relaxing or entertaining guests

Word use: Another name is **lounge room**.

lizard
noun a reptile with a long, thin body, four legs and a long tail

Word history: Middle English, from Old French, from Latin

llama (lah-muh)
noun a South American animal related to the camel and used for carrying loads

Word history: Spanish, from South American Indian

llama / lama
Don't confuse **llama** with **lama,** a Buddhist priest or monk.

load
noun **1** something carried (***ballast, burden, encumbrance, weight***)
2 the quantity carried: *a **load** of soil*
verb **3** to put a load on or in
4 to take on as a load: *The ship is **loading** wheat now.*
5 to put bullets into, or a film into: *to **load** a gun / to **load** a camera*
phrase **6 get a load of,** *Colloquial*
a to look at
b to listen

Word history: Middle English

load / lode
Don't confuse **load** with **lode,** a geological word for a strip of minerals running along a joint in rocks.

loaded
adjective **1** carrying a load: *a **loaded** ship*
2 charged: *a **loaded** gun*
3 *Colloquial* very wealthy: *They must be **loaded** to be able to buy a yacht like that.*

loading
noun **1** a load, or the act of loading
2 an extra payment to employees in recognition of some aspect of their work, as shift work, special conditions, etc., or as a holiday bonus
3 an extra premium for something seen as a risk by an insurance company

loaf[1]
noun **1** an amount of bread or cake baked in a particular shape
2 any food made into a loaf shape: *a meat **loaf***

Noun forms: The plural is **loaves.**
Word history: from Old English word meaning 'loaf', 'bread'

loaf[2]
verb **1** to be lazy or do nothing: *I **loafed** all day.* (***bludge, idle, laze, loll, rest***)
noun **2** a restful, lazy time

Verb forms: I **loafed,** he/she **loafs,** I have **loafed,** I am **loafing**
Word history: perhaps from German word meaning 'tramp', 'vagabond'

loam
noun loose, very fertile soil (***dirt, earth, ground***)

Word building: **loamy** *adjective* (**loamier, loamiest**)
Word history: Old English *lām*

loan
noun **1** the giving of something to be used for a short time before being returned to the owner: *I made him a **loan** of my book.*
2 money given for a short time, usually to be repaid with interest: *a bank **loan*** (***advance, credit***)
verb **3** to lend

Word history: Old English, apparently from Scandinavian

loan / lend
It is usual to use **lend** as a verb, and **loan** as either a noun or a verb:

My father won't lend me his new sports jacket.
I asked him so nicely for a loan of it.
I'd loan him mine if I owned one.

In casual talk you will often hear people use **lend** as a noun:

He said he'd give me a lend of his red sports car instead.

loan / lone
Don't confuse **loan** with **lone,** which means 'not with anyone', as in *a lone traveller*. It can also mean 'standing apart', as in *a lone tree.*

loath (lohth)
adjective unwilling or not inclined: *I am **loath** to lend her anything.* (***averse, disinclined, hesitant, reluctant, unwilling***)

Word use: The opposite of this is **glad** or **willing**.
Word history: from Old English word meaning 'hostile', 'hateful'

loathe (lohdh)
verb to hate or detest very much

Word use: The opposite of this is **love**.
Word building: **loathsome** *adjective*
Word history: from Old English word meaning 'be hateful'

lob
verb **1** to hit or throw a ball high into the air, as in tennis
phrase **2 lob in**, *Colloquial* to arrive, often without warning

Verb forms: I **lobbed**, I have **lobbed**, I am **lobbing**
Word building: **lob** *noun*
Word history: from Middle English word meaning 'a fish'; later, 'country bumpkin'; as verb, 'move clumsily'

lobby
noun **1** an entrance hall
2 a group of people trying to get support for a particular cause: *a **lobby** for cancer research*
verb **3** to try to influence lawmakers: *to **lobby** for conservation of rainforests* (***campaign***, ***crusade***)

Noun forms: The plural is **lobbies**.
Word building: **lobbyist** *noun*
Word history: from Medieval Latin word meaning 'covered walk'; of Germanic origin

lobe
noun **1** a roundish part which stands out, as of an organ, leaf, etc.
2 the soft, hanging, lower part of your ear

Word history: French, from Late Latin, from Greek

lobotomy (luh-<u>bot</u>-uh-mee)
noun the cutting into or across a lobe of the brain to alter the way the brain works, especially in the treatment of mental disorders

Noun forms: The plural is **lobotomies**.

lobster
noun a large shellfish with ten legs and a long tail, which turns pink when cooked

Word history: Latin *locusta* influenced by Old English *loppestre*, from *loppe* spider (both creatures having many projecting parts)

local
adjective **1** having to do with a particular place: *a **local** custom*
2 having to do with the area you are living in rather than the whole town or state: ***local** government | the **local** school* (***community***, ***district***, ***municipal***, ***neighbourhood***, ***regional***)
3 acting on only part of the body: *a **local** anaesthetic*
noun **4** someone who lives in a particular place: *He's one of the **locals**.*

Word building: **localise** *verb* **locally** *adverb*
Word history: Middle English, from Late Latin, from Latin word meaning 'place'

locale (loh-<u>kahl</u>)
noun a place or locality, especially with direction of attention to events or conditions connected with it

Word history: French

local government
noun the management of the affairs of some particular area smaller than that of a state, such as a shire, municipality, town, etc., by officers elected by the residents and ratepayers of that area

locality (loh-<u>kal</u>-uh-tee)
noun a particular place or area: *We are now in the **locality** where Ned Kelly lived.*

Noun forms: The plural is **localities**.

locate
verb **1** to find the place of: *to **locate** the fault in the engine* (***detect***, ***discover***, ***trace***, ***track down***, ***unearth***)
2 to put in a place or area: *to **locate** the Post Office near the shops* (***establish***, ***install***, ***position***, ***site***, ***station***)

Word history: from Latin word meaning 'placed'

location
noun **1** a place or position: *a house in a fine **location*** (***site***, ***spot***, ***venue***)
2 in film-making, a place, outside the studio, which has suitable surroundings for photographing plays, events, etc.

locavore
noun a person who eats only food that is locally produced

loch (lok)
noun a Scottish word for **lake**

Word history: Gaelic

lock[1]
noun **1** a device for fastening a door, gate, lid or drawer, which needs a key to open it
2 a part of a canal with gates at each end allowing ships to be raised from one level to another
verb **3** to fasten or become fastened with a key
phrase **4 lock up**, to shut up or put into a place of safety or imprisonment (***confine***, ***imprison***, ***intern***, ***jail***, ***restrain***)

Word history: from Old English word meaning 'fastening'

lock[2]
noun a short length or curl of hair (***ringlet***, ***strand***)

Word history: from Old English word meaning 'lock of hair'

lockdown
noun **1** the confining of prisoners to the cells
2 a state of security alert where access is cut off and movement of people is halted
3 a state of restricted access to a communications system: *a temporary **lockdown** of the network*

locker
noun a cupboard that may be locked, especially one for your own use

locket
noun a small case for a small picture or lock of hair, usually worn on a chain hung around your neck

Word history: Middle English, from French word meaning 'latch', 'catch', from Old French word meaning 'little lock', from Germanic

lockjaw
noun an old-fashioned word for **tetanus**

locksmith
noun someone who makes or mends locks and keys

locomotion (loh-kuh-moh-shuhn)
noun the act or power of moving from place to place

Word history: from Latin word meaning 'place' + *motion*

locomotive (loh-kuh-moh-tiv)
noun the engine which pulls railway carriages or trucks

Word history: from Latin word meaning 'place' + *motive*

locum (loh-kuhm)
noun a temporary stand-in for a doctor, lawyer, etc.

Word use: You can also use **locum tenens** (loh-kuhm ten-uhnz).
Word history: from Medieval Latin word meaning 'one holding the office (of another)'

locus (lok-uhs, lohk-uhs)
noun **1** a place
2 *Mathematics* a curve or other figure considered as produced by a point which moves according to a fixed law

Noun forms: The plural is **loci** (lok-ee, lohk-ee, lohk-uy).
Word history: from Latin word meaning 'place'

locust (loh-kuhst)
noun a type of grasshopper which moves from one place to another in large numbers and destroys crops

Word history: Middle English, from Latin *locusta* which also referred to a lobster. The lobster and the locust were thought to resemble each other in that they had many protruding legs.

lode
noun **1** *Mining* a veinlike deposit, usually yielding metal
2 any body of ore set off from the rock formations next to it

Word history: from Old English word meaning 'way', 'course', 'carrying'

lode / load
Look up **load / lode**.

lodge
noun **1** a building used as a holiday house: *a ski **lodge***
2 a meeting place of a branch of a secret society
verb **3** to board or live for a while in someone else's home: *I **lodge** at Mrs Smith's house.*
4 to be put, caught or placed: *A speck of dirt **lodged** in my eye.*
5 to put for safe keeping: *to **lodge** valuables with a bank* (***deposit***, ***park***, ***place***)

Word building: **lodger** *noun* **lodgings** *noun* **lodgement** *noun*
Word history: Middle English, from Old French word meaning 'hut', originally 'leafy shelter', from Germanic

loft
noun **1** the space in a building between the roof and the ceiling
2 an upper level of a church or hall made for a special purpose: *a choir **loft***

Word history: Old English, from Scandinavian

lofty
adjective **1** reaching high into the air: ***lofty** mountains* (***elevated***, ***grand***, ***tall***, ***towering***)
2 noble or high in character: *He has **lofty** ideals.* (***ambitious***, ***far-reaching***, ***uplifting***)
3 proud or haughty: *a **lofty** manner* (***arrogant***, ***pompous***, ***supercilious***)

Adjective forms: **loftier**, **loftiest**

log
noun **1** a large branch or the trunk of a tree which has fallen or been cut down
2 the daily record of a voyage or flight kept by the captain of a ship or plane
verb **3** to cut down trees or cut them into logs
4 to enter information in the log of a ship or plane (***record***, ***register***)
phrase **5 log in** (or **on**), to begin a session on a computer by typing in a name and password
6 log off (or **out**), to end a session on a computer

Verb forms: I **logged**, I have **logged**, I am **logging**
Word building: **logger** *noun* **logging** *noun*
Word history: Middle English

loganberry
noun a large, dark-red berry you can eat, or the plant it grows on

Word history: named after JH *Logan*, 1841–1928, of California, US, by whom the berry was first grown

logarithm (log-uh-ridh-uhm)
noun the exponent of that power to which a fixed number, called the *base*, must be raised in order to produce a given number: *From $2^3 = 8$, it can be seen that 3 is the **logarithm** of 8 to the base 2.*

Word history: Neo-Latin, from Greek *lógos* proportion + *arithmós* number

logbook
noun a book in which the record of a journey made by a ship or plane is entered

logic (loj-ik)
noun correct reasoning: *His argument was based on **logic**.*

Word building: **logician** *noun*
Word history: Middle English, from Medieval Latin, from Greek word meaning 'pertaining to reason'

logical
adjective **1** based on correct reasoning: *a **logical** answer* (***coherent***, ***sound***, ***well-balanced***, ***well-reasoned***)
2 reasonably to be expected: *War was the **logical** consequence of such threats.*

Word use: The opposite of this is **illogical**.

login (log-in)
noun the act of beginning a computer session, usually gaining access by inputting a username and password

Word use: You can also use **logon**.

logistics (luh-jis-tiks)
noun the branch of military science concerned with the mathematics of transportation and supply, and the movement of troops
Word history: from French word meaning 'lodging'

logo (loh-goh)
noun a trademark or symbol designed to identify a company, organisation, etc.

logoff
noun → **logout**

logon (log-on)
noun → **login**

logout (log-owt)
noun the act of ending a computer session, usually by selecting a command
Word use: You can also use **logoff**.

loin (loyn)
noun **1** the part of your body between your lowest rib and the top of either thigh
2 the similar part of a four-legged animal: *a* ***loin*** *of lamb*
phrase **3 gird up your loins**, to get ready for action
Word history: Middle English, from Old French, from Latin

loiter
verb to move about aimlessly or stay in the one place: *I* ***loitered*** *on the street corner waiting for my friend.* (***dally***, ***dawdle***, ***delay***, ***linger***, ***tarry***)
Word building: **loiterer** *noun*
Word history: perhaps from Middle English word meaning 'lurk'

loll
verb **1** to lean in a lazy manner: *He* ***lolled*** *against the post.*
2 to hang loosely: *The dog's tongue* ***lolled*** *from its mouth as it panted.*
Word history: Middle English *lolle*

lollipop
noun a kind of boiled sweet, often fixed to the end of a stick

lollop (lol-uhp)
verb to move with jumping, awkward springs (***bound***, ***frisk***, ***spring***)
Word history: extension of *loll*, in this sense perhaps influenced by *gallop*

lolly
noun **1** *Australian*, *NZ* any sweet, especially a boiled one (***candy***)
2 *Colloquial* your head
3 *Colloquial* money
Noun forms: The plural is **lollies**.

lone
adjective **1** being alone or not with anyone: *a* ***lone*** *traveller*
2 standing apart from others: *a* ***lone*** *tree*
Word history: variant of *alone*

> **lone / loan**
> Don't confuse **lone** with **loan**, the giving of something to be used for a short time and then returned to the owner:
> *Can I have a loan of your ruler?*

lonely
adjective **1** alone or without friendly company: *A lighthouse keeper's job is a* ***lonely*** *one.* (***reclusive***, ***solitary***)
2 far away from where people are: ***lonely*** *beaches*
3 feeling sad because of being alone: *The old man was* ***lonely*** *when his wife died.*
Word building: **loneliness** *noun*

loner
noun someone who likes to be alone

lonesome (lohn-suhm)
adjective depressed by a sense of being alone: *to feel* ***lonesome***

long[1]
adjective **1** having a great distance from one end to the other (***extended***, ***extensive***, ***lengthy***)
2 lasting a great amount of time (***drawn-out***, ***interminable***, ***lengthy***, ***prolonged***, ***protracted***)
3 having a stated distance or time: *a road ten kilometres* ***long*** | *a speech an hour* ***long***
adverb **4** for a great amount of time: *Did he stay* ***long****?*
5 for or throughout a certain amount of time: *How* ***long*** *did he stay?*
phrase **6 before long**, soon
7 in the long run, in the final result
8 the long and short of, the main part of: ***The long and short of*** *it is that we decided to go.*
Word building: **length** *noun*
Word history: Old English

long[2]
phrase **long for**, to want or desire very much: *I* ***long for*** *a pet.* (***crave***, ***yearn for***)
Word building: **longing** *noun*
Word history: Old English *langian* seem long, arouse desire in

longevity (lon-jev-uh-tee)
noun **1** length or duration of life
2 long life

longhand
noun writing of the ordinary kind, in which the words are written out in full

longitude (long-guh-tyood)
noun the distance, measured in degrees, by which a point on the earth is east or west of Greenwich in England
Word building: **longitudinal** *adjective*
Word history: Middle English, from Latin word meaning 'length'

long-life
adjective having to do with any product which has been treated to last beyond the normal length of time: ***long-life*** *milk*

long paddock
noun a stock route or open road where people unable to afford their own grazing land or driven off it by drought can graze their horses, cattle, etc.

longwinded
adjective talking for too long or using more words than necessary: *He's always so* ***longwinded*** *in his explanations.* (***lengthy***, ***long-drawn-out***, ***rambling***, ***tedious***, ***wordy***)

loo
noun Colloquial a toilet: *The* ***loo*** *is down the hall.*

loofah (<u>looh</u>-fuh)
noun **1** a tropical, climbing herb
2 the fibrous network of its fruit, used as a bath sponge
Word history: Arabic

look
verb **1** to use your eyes in order to see
2 to examine by searching: *to **look** through papers*
3 to appear or seem: *He **looked** happy.*
4 to face towards: *The house **looks** east.*
noun **5** the act of looking: *a **look** of enquiry*
6 looks, general appearance: *good **looks***
phrase **7 look after**, to take care of
8 look down on, to despise or scorn (***disapprove of***, ***frown on***, ***spurn***, ***take a dim view of***)
9 look for, to search for
10 look forward to, to expect with pleasure (***anticipate***, ***bargain on***, ***count on***)
11 look out, to be on guard or be watchful: *to **look out** for danger*
12 look to,
a to give attention to: ***Look to** your children.*
b to direct your hopes to someone or something for a thing that you desire: *We **look to** you for the answer.*
13 look up to, to admire or respect
Word history: Old English *lōcian*

lookout
noun **1** a watch kept for something that may come or happen
2 someone who keeps such a watch or the place from which they watch
3 a place on a high point, especially a mountain, from which you can admire the view

loom[1]
noun a machine or apparatus for weaving cloth
Word history: from Old English word meaning 'tool', 'implement'

loom[2]
verb to appear, often in a large or frightening form: *The hedge suddenly **loomed** in front of the young horse rider.* (***appear***, ***emerge***, ***materialise***, ***show up***)
Word history: similar to dialect Swedish *loma* move slowly

loop
noun **1** a more or less oval shape twisted in a piece of string, ribbon or something similar (***coil***, ***curl***, ***spiral***, ***twist***)
2 anything shaped like this: *a **loop** in a railway track*
Word building: **loop** *verb*
Word history: Middle English *loupe*

loophole
noun **1** an opening, especially in a wall to allow light in or to fire weapons through
2 a way or means of escape

loose (loohs)
adjective **1** free from being fastened: *a **loose** end of string*
2 not bound together: *a **loose** bundle of papers*
3 not in a container: ***loose** peanuts*
4 not firm: *a **loose** rein*
5 not fitting tightly: *a **loose** sweater*
verb **6** to free from check or control
phrase **7 at a loose end**, having nothing to do
8 on the loose, free from check or control: *a lion **on the loose***
Word building: **loosely** *adverb*
Word history: Middle English, from Scandinavian

loose / loosen

As verbs, these words have slightly different meanings, though both are related to the adjective **loose**.

To **loose** is to set someone or something free. The opposite of this is *bind*:

I don't think you should loose such a dangerous animal.

This way of using **loose** is becoming less common than it once was. Nowadays it is more common in the form **let loose**, as in *to let the horses loose.*

To **loosen** something is to make it less tight. The opposite of this is *tighten*:

I've eaten so much that I'll have to loosen my belt.

The distinction between **loose** and **loosen** becomes less clear when we speak of loosing or loosening a knot. To loose a knot is to undo it, but to loosen a knot is to make it less tight. There isn't much difference between these two actions.

Note that **<u>un</u>loose** means the same as **loose.** It is <u>not</u> the opposite as you might expect from the <u>un-</u> at the beginning. This is an old-fashioned word and you will usually find it in sayings such as *unloose the dogs of war.*

<u>Un</u>loosen means the same as **loosen**, but it seems to be becoming more common than **loosen**:

Why don't you unloosen your belt?

loose / lose

These words look similar but mean different things. Something is **loose** if it is not fastened, but when you **lose** something, you can't find it. This word rhymes with *chews.*

loosen (<u>looh</u>-suhn)
verb to make or become looser

loot
noun anything that has been stolen, especially from an enemy in war (***booty***, ***pickings***, ***plunder***, ***spoils***)
Word building: **loot** *verb* **looter** *noun*
Word history: Hindustani

loot / lute

Don't confuse **loot** with **lute**, which is an old-fashioned musical instrument with strings like a guitar.

lop
verb **1** to cut off: *to **lop** branches from a tree*
2 to cut branches from: *to **lop** trees*
Verb forms: I **lopped**, I have **lopped**, I am **lopping**
Word building: **lopper** *noun*
Word history: from Middle English word meaning 'small branch', identical in its word history with obsolete *lop* spider, both objects being marked by many projecting parts

lope
verb to move with long easy steps
Word building: **lope** *noun*
Word history: Middle English, variant of obsolete *loup* leap, from Scandinavian

lopsided
adjective **1** leaning to one side (***irregular***, ***unbalanced***, ***unequal***, ***uneven***)
2 larger or heavier on one side than the other

loquacious (luh-kway-shuhs)
adjective talkative (***chatty***, ***communicative***, ***garrulous***, ***voluble***)
Word building: **loquaciousness** *noun*

loquat (loh-kwot, loh-kwuht)
noun a small, evergreen tree native to China and Japan, but grown elsewhere for ornament and for its yellow plumlike fruit
Word history: from Cantonese word meaning 'rush orange'

lord
noun **1** a British nobleman with a title in front of his name
2 someone who has power over others
phrase **3 lord it over someone**, to behave in an arrogant or domineering manner towards someone
Word building: **lordly** *adjective*
Word history: Old English *hlāf* loaf[1] + *weard* keeper

lore
noun learning or knowledge, especially on a particular subject: *family **lore** | the **lore** of herbs*
Word history: Old English *lār*

lore / law
Don't confuse **lore** with **law**, a set of rules made by a government or a ruler.

lorikeet (lo-ruh-keet)
noun a small brightly coloured parrot that has a brush-like tongue for feeding on nectar
Word history: *lory* (from Malay *luri*) a type of parrot + *(para)keet*

lorry
noun → **truck**
Noun forms: The plural is **lorries**.

lose (loohz)
verb **1** to come to be without for some reason, and not be able to find (***mislay***, ***misplace***)
2 to have taken away by death: *to **lose** an uncle*
3 to fail to get or win
phrase **4 lose face**, to lose worth or dignity by having a mistake or foolish action made public
Verb forms: I **lost**, I have **lost**, I am **losing**
Word building: **loser** *noun*
Word history: Old English *leōsan*

lose / loose
Don't confuse **lose** with **loose**, which means 'free from being fastened'.

loss
noun **1** the losing of something: *the **loss** of his wallet | the **loss** of her friends*
2 something that is lost
phrase **3 a dead loss**, a completely useless person or thing
4 at a loss, confused or uncertain: *He was **at a loss** as to what to do.*
Word use: The opposite of this is **gain**.
Word history: from Old English word meaning 'destruction'

lost
adjective **1** no longer in your possession
2 not knowing the way
3 wasted or not used: ***lost** time*
Word use: The opposite of this is **found**.

lot
noun **1** a large number
2 your fate in life: *Illness seems to be her **lot**.*
3 the drawing of an object from a hat or box to decide something by chance: *We decided by **lot** who would go first.*
phrase **4 a lot**, much: *That is **a lot** better.*
5 the lot, the whole amount
Word history: Old English *hlot*

lotion (loh-shuhn)
noun a liquid that you use to heal, clean, or feed your skin
Word history: Middle English, from Latin word meaning 'a washing'

lottery
noun a kind of raffle in which the prize is usually money
Noun forms: The plural is **lotteries**.
Word history: Italian word meaning 'lot', from French, from Germanic

lotto
noun → **bingo**
Word history: Italian

lotus (loh-tuhs)
noun a kind of water-lily which grows in Asia and Egypt
Word history: Latin, from Greek

loud
adjective **1** producing a lot of sound so that you can hear it easily: *a **loud** radio | **loud** knocking* (***blaring***, ***deafening***, ***raucous***, ***resonant***, ***shrill***)
2 very colourful, usually in an unpleasant way: *a **loud** tie* (***flashy***, ***gaudy***, ***showy***, ***tawdry***)
adverb **3** with a lot of sound
Word building: **loudly** *adverb*
Word history: Old English *hlūd*

loud / loudly
Loud can be used as an adjective and an adverb:
What a loud voice you have! (adjective)
There's no need to shout so loud. (adverb)
Loudly is only ever used as an adverb:
There's no need to shout so loudly.

loudspeaker
noun a device which makes speech, music, etc., more easily heard throughout a room, hall, etc.

lounge
verb **1** to lie back lazily: *to* ***lounge*** *in a chair*
noun **2** → **lounge room**
3 the most expensive seats in a theatre
4 a large room in a hotel, airport, etc., used by guests or passengers for relaxation purposes or while waiting for a flight, etc.
5 a sofa or couch

Word history: perhaps from obsolete *lungis* laggard, from Old French word meaning 'one who is long' (taken to mean slow)

lounge room
noun Australian a room in a house for relaxing, entertaining guests, etc.

Word use: You can also use **lounge** or **living room.**

louse
noun **1** a small wingless insect which lives in the hair or skin and sucks blood
2 *Colloquial* someone who is hateful or not to be trusted

Noun forms: The plural for definition 1 is **lice.**
Word history: Old English *lūs* (plural *lȳs*)

lousy (<u>low</u>-zee)
adjective **1** having many lice
2 *Colloquial* mean or hateful
phrase **3 feel lousy,** *Colloquial* to be sick or unwell

lout
noun a rough, rude, and sometimes violent young man

Word building: **loutish** *adjective*
Word history: perhaps from obsolete *lout* stoop, bow low

louvre (<u>looh</u>-vuh)
noun an arrangement of overlapping, sloping glass panels which form a window and can be adjusted to allow in air but which keep out rain

Word history: Middle English, from Old French

lovable
adjective inspiring love

love
noun **1** strong or warm feelings of affection: ***love*** *for a parent* | ***love*** *for a friend* (***adoration, devotion, fondness***)
2 sexual desire
3 strong liking: ***love*** *of reading*
4 no score in tennis and similar games: *The score is 30* ***love.***
phrase **5 in love with,** feeling deep passion for: *They are* ***in love with*** *each other.*
6 make love, to have sexual intercourse

Word building: **beloved** *adjective* **love** *verb*
Word history: Old English *lufu*

love affair
noun → **affair** (definition 2)

lovebird
noun Colloquial a budgerigar

lovelorn
adjective sorrowing from unhappiness in love

lovely
adjective **1** having a beautiful appearance or personality (***beautiful, exquisite, gorgeous, stunning***)
2 very pleasant or enjoyable: *a* ***lovely*** *day*

Adjective forms: **lovelier, loveliest**
Word history: from Old English word meaning 'amiable'

lover
noun **1** a person who is in love with another
2 a sexual partner, especially someone having a love affair
3 a person who has a strong liking for something: *a* ***lover*** *of music* | *a* ***lover*** *of nature*

loving
adjective affectionate (***devoted, fond, tender***)

low[1]
adjective **1** not far above the ground, floor, or base
2 lying below the average level: ***low*** *ground* | *The river is* ***low*** *because of the drought.*
3 small in amount: *a* ***low*** *number*
4 deep in pitch: *a* ***low*** *voice*
5 difficult to hear because of lack of volume or deepness of pitch: *a* ***low*** *buzz* (***faint, indistinct, muffled, quiet, soft***)
6 of lesser rank, quality or importance: ***low*** *birth*

Word building: **low** *adverb*
Word history: Middle English, from Scandinavian

low[2]
verb to make the sound that cattle make (***moo***)

Word building: **low** *noun* **lowing** *noun*
Word history: Old English *hlōwan*

lowboy
noun a piece of furniture for holding clothes, similar to but lower than a wardrobe

lowbrow
noun Colloquial a person uninterested in higher forms of music, art, etc.

low-down
adjective mean or dishonourable

lowdown
noun Colloquial the actual facts or truth on some subject

lower
verb **1** to make less: *to* ***lower*** *the price of bread* (***cut back, decrease, lessen, minimise, reduce***)
2 to make less loud: *to* ***lower*** *the voice*
3 to let down: *to* ***lower*** *a rope* (***drop, let fall***)

Word use: The opposite is **raise.**

lower case
noun the printing type that makes small, not capital, letters

Word use: Compare this with **upper case.**
Word building: **lower-case** *adjective*
Word history: from the arrangement of cases of type in a printery (small letters in lower case, capitals in upper case)

lower class
noun the group of people in a society who have the lowest income

Word use: Compare this with **upper class** and **middle class.**
Word building: **lower-class** *adjective*

lower house
noun one of the bodies in a parliament of two houses (upper and lower), usually larger and more directly representative of the people

Word use: You can also use **lower chamber.**

low frequency
noun a radio frequency in the range 30 to 300 kilohertz

Word building: **low-frequency** *adjective*

low-key (<u>loh</u>-kee)
adjective **1** done in a quiet way: *a **low-key** performance*
2 of a person, not given to displays of feeling (***restrained, reticent, unobtrusive***)

low-level language
noun Computers a language used for writing programs which is closer to machine language than human language

Word use: Compare this with **high-level language**.

lowly (<u>loh</u>-lee)
adjective **1** humble in station, condition, or nature: *a **lowly** mortal*
2 low in growth or position (***insignificant, junior, minor, subordinate, subsidiary***)
adverb **3** in a low position, manner, or degree
4 humbly

Adjective forms: **lowlier, lowliest**
Word building: **lowliness** *noun*

low profile
noun a deliberately understated position or style of behaviour

lowry (<u>low</u>-ree)
noun → **rosella**

Word history: variant of *lory* (from Malay *luri*) a type of parrot

loyal
adjective faithful and true: *a **loyal** friend* (***devoted, reliable, steadfast, trustworthy, trusty***)

Word building: **loyalty** *noun*
Word history: French, from Latin word meaning 'legal'

lozenge (<u>loz</u>-uhnj)
noun a small sweet, usually used to soothe a sore throat

Word history: Middle English, from Old French, apparently from Provençal word meaning 'stone slab'

LPG
noun a mixture of hydrocarbon gases, such as butane and propane, liquefied and stored under pressure for use as a gas fuel (***bottled gas, liquefied petroleum gas***)

Word history: abbreviation of *l(iquefied) p(etroleum) g(as)*

L-plate (<u>el</u>-playt)
noun the letter L, shown front and back on a car, motor cycle, etc., being driven by someone who is learning to drive

Word history: *l(earner) + plate*

LSD
noun lysergic acid diethylamide, a drug which produces heightened perception as well as temporary hallucinations and sometimes a schizophrenia-like state

Word history: abbreviation of *l(y)s(ergic acid) d(ethylamide)*

lubricate (<u>looh</u>-bruh-kayt)
verb to oil or grease the moving parts of, so that they will move more easily: *to **lubricate** an engine*

Word building: **lubricant** *noun, adjective* **lubrication** *noun*
Word history: from Latin word meaning 'made slippery'

lucerne (<u>looh</u>-suhn)
noun a plant used to feed cattle (***alfalfa***)

Word history: French, from Provençal, from Latin word meaning 'light'

lucid (<u>looh</u>-suhd)
adjective **1** clear or easy to understand: *a **lucid** explanation*
2 having clear understanding: *He was still **lucid** despite the severe blow to his head.*

Word use: The opposite of definition 1 is **unclear** or **vague**.
Verb forms: I **abhorred**, I have **abhorred**, I am **abhorring**
Word history: Latin

luck
noun **1** something which happens to a person by chance (***destiny, fate, fortune, providence***)
2 good fortune: *She wished me **luck**.*
phrase **3 down on your luck**, in poor or unfortunate circumstances
4 no such luck, unfortunately not
5 push your luck, to take another risk in the hope that you'll be lucky yet again

Word history: Middle English, from Low German or Dutch

lucky
adjective (**luckier, luckiest**)
1 having good luck; fortunate.
2 happening fortunately: *a **lucky** accident.*
3 bringing or predicting good luck, or supposed to do so: *a **lucky** penny.*

Word use: The opposite of this is **unlucky**.

lucrative (<u>looh</u>-kruh-tiv)
adjective producing good profits or paying well: *a **lucrative** business*

Word use: The opposite of this is **unprofitable**.
Word history: Middle English, from Latin

lucre (<u>looh</u>-kuh)
noun gain or money as the object of mean and selfish desire

Word history: Middle English, from Latin word meaning 'gain'

ludicrous (<u>looh</u>-duh-kruhs)
adjective so silly as to cause laughter: *a **ludicrous** remark* (***absurd, farcical, nonsensical, preposterous, ridiculous***)

Word history: Latin

lug
verb to pull along or carry with effort (***drag, draw, haul, tow***)

Verb forms: I **lugged**, I have **lugged**, I am **lugging**
Word history: Middle English, from Scandinavian

luggage
noun the suitcases and other containers you use when travelling (***baggage, gear***)

Word history: *lug + -age*

lugubrious (luh-gooh-bree-uhs)
adjective mournful (***gloomy***, ***dismal***)

Word history: from Latin word meaning 'mournful'

lukewarm
adjective **1** a bit warm
2 not very enthusiastic: *a **lukewarm** response* (***apathetic***, ***half-hearted***, ***indifferent***)

Word history: Middle English *lukewarme*, from *luke* tepid (from Old English) + *warme* warm

lull
verb **1** to put to sleep by singing or rocking
2 to calm or quiet: *to **lull** someone's fears*
noun **3** a period of calm: *the **lull** before the storm*

Word use: The opposite of definition 1 is **rouse**.
Word history: Middle English *lulle*

lullaby
noun a song sung to put a baby to sleep

Noun forms: The plural is **lullabies**.
Word history: Middle English interjection *lulla!* (from *lull*) + *-by* (from *bye-bye*)

lumbar (lum-buh)
adjective having to do with the lower part of the back

Word history: Neo-Latin, from Latin word meaning 'loin'

lumber[1]
noun timber sawn into boards

lumber[2]
verb to move clumsily or heavily: *The bear **lumbered** alongside the river.*

lumberjack
noun someone who cuts down trees

Word use: This word is mostly used in the US and Canada.

luminary (looh-muhn-uh-ree, looh-muhn-ree)
noun **1** a heavenly body, as the sun or moon
2 a body or thing that gives light
3 a person whose learning, etc., enlightens others
4 a famous person or celebrity

Noun forms: The plural is **luminaries**.
Word history: Middle English, from Medieval Latin word meaning 'a light', 'lamp', 'heavenly body'

luminescence (looh-muh-nes-uhns)
noun light given out from a substance, but not as a result of a process which involves the production of heat. It includes phosphorescence, fluorescence, etc.

Word use: Compare this with **incandescence**.
Word building: **luminescent** *adjective*

luminous (looh-muh-nuhs)
adjective giving off or reflecting light: *a **luminous** clock face* (***bright***, ***gleaming***, ***phosphorescent***, ***shining***, ***shiny***)

Word use: The opposite of this is **dull**.
Word building: **luminosity** *noun*
Word history: Middle English, from Latin

lump
noun **1** a mass of solid matter: *a **lump** of clay*
2 a swelling: *a **lump** on the head*
adjective **3** including a number of things taken together: *a **lump** sum of money*
4 in the form of a lump: ***lump** sugar*
phrase **5 have a lump in the throat**, to feel as if you're about to cry

Word history: Middle English *lumpe*

lunacy (looh-nuh-see)
noun **1** any form of insanity
2 foolishness: *Her decision to leave was total **lunacy**.*

Word use: The opposite of definition 1 is **sanity**.
Noun forms: The plural is **lunacies**.
Word history: *lun(atic)* + *-acy*

lunar (looh-nuh)
adjective having to do with the moon

Word history: from Latin word meaning 'of the moon', 'crescent'

lunatic (looh-nuh-tik)
noun **1** someone who is mad
adjective **2** mad: *a **lunatic** idea*

Word use: At one time it was thought that people were sent mad by the full moon, which is called *luna* in Latin.
Word history: Middle English, from Late Latin word meaning 'mad', from Latin word meaning 'moon'

lunch
noun a light midday meal

Word building: **lunch** *verb*
Word history: short for *luncheon*

luncheon (lun-chuhn)
noun a formal occasion at which lunch is served: *There was a **luncheon** to welcome the new principal.*

Word history: blend of *lump* and dialect *nuncheon*

lung
noun either of the two saclike organs in the chest of humans and other vertebrates, used for breathing

Word history: Old English *lungen*

lunge
verb to make a sudden forward movement or attack: *I **lunged** at him with a stick.*

Word building: **lunge** *noun*
Word history: French word meaning 'lengthen', 'extend', from Latin

lurch[1]
noun **1** a sudden or unsteady movement, especially to one side
verb **2** to stagger or make a lurch (***reel***, ***shake***, ***sway***, ***wobble***)

Word history: first in nautical use

lurch[2]
phrase **leave in the lurch**, to leave someone in a helpless situation: *You've really **left** me **in the lurch** with twenty hungry children to feed.*

Word history: from French word meaning 'discomfited'

lure
noun **1** something that attracts: *The shop offered free child-minding as a **lure** to customers.* (***attraction***, ***enticement***)
2 a device used to attract fish

Word building: **lure** *verb*
Word history: Middle English, from Old French, from Germanic

lurid (looh-ruhd)
adjective **1** shining with an unnatural glare: *the **lurid** city lights*
2 horrifying or frightening: ***lurid** tales* | ***lurid** crimes*

Word history: from Latin word meaning 'pale yellow', 'wan'

lurk
verb **1** to stay or move about secretly: *to **lurk** in the darkness*
noun Australian, NZ Colloquial **2** an easy and often sly way of doing a job or earning a living
phrase **3 lurks and perks**, advantages that come with having a particular job, position, etc., gained honestly or dishonestly: *Cheap travel is one of the **lurks and perks** of working for the airlines.* | *Many **lurks and perks** come with being a politician.*

Word history: Middle English

luscious (lush-uhs)
adjective tasting very pleasant: *a **luscious** pie* (***appetising***, ***delicious***, ***more-ish***, ***mouth-watering***, ***scrumptious***)

Word history: late Middle English; perhaps a variant of *delicious*

lush
adjective with strong-growing plants and trees: *the **lush** undergrowth of the forest*

Word use: The opposite of this is **arid**.
Word history: Middle English, from Old French word meaning 'loose', 'slack'

lust
noun **1** strong desire: *to have a **lust** for power*
2 uncontrolled sexual desire

Word building: **lust** *verb* **lustful** *adjective*
Word history: Old English

lustre (lus-tuh)
noun **1** shining brightness: *the **lustre** of a new silver coin*
2 brightness or glory: *His bravery added **lustre** to his name.*

Word use: The US spelling is **luster**.
Word building: **lustrous** *adjective*
Word history: French, from Italian word meaning 'to shine', from Latin word meaning 'illuminate'

lusty
adjective **1** full of or having healthy fitness
2 hearty or large and enjoyable: *a **lusty** meal*

Adjective forms: **lustier, lustiest**
Word building: **lustily** *adverb* **lustiness** *noun*
Word history: Middle English

lute (looht)
noun an old-fashioned musical instrument with strings like a guitar

Word building: **lutenist** *noun*
Word history: Middle English, from Old French, from Provençal, from Arabic

lute / loot
Don't confuse **lute** with **loot**, which means 'anything that has been stolen, especially from an enemy in wartime'.

luxuriant (lug-zhooh-ree-uhnt)
adjective strong in growth: ***luxuriant** vines*

Word history: from Latin word meaning 'growing rank'

luxuriant / luxurious
These related words have different meanings.
Luxuriant means 'plentiful or growing strongly'.
We say that something is **luxurious** if it is very comfortable, beautiful and expensive, as in *a luxurious hotel.*

luxuriate (lug-zhooh-ree-ayt)
verb to enjoy as a luxury

luxurious (lug-zhooh-ree-uhs)
adjective characterised by luxury: *a **luxurious** home*

luxury (luk-shuh-ree)
noun **1** anything that makes life extremely pleasant or comfortable
2 enjoyment of costly food, clothing, and living generally: *He lives a life of **luxury**.*

Noun forms: The plural is **luxuries**.
Word history: Middle English word meaning 'lust', from Latin

lychee (luy-chee)
noun a small Chinese fruit with a thin shell covering a sweet jelly-like pulp

Word history: Chinese

lymph (limf)
noun a clear, yellowish, slightly alkaline fluid coming from the tissues of the body by way of a system of capillaries and vessels, through the lymph glands, and then passing into the blood

Word history: from Latin word meaning 'water'

lymph gland
noun any of the glandlike bodies in the lymphatic system, such as the tonsils, where antibodies and white blood cells (*lymphocytes*) are produced, and where bacteria are destroyed

Word use: You can also use **lymph node** or **lymphatic gland**.

lynch (linch)
verb to put to death, usually by hanging, without a trial: *The mob **lynched** the murderer before the police arrived.*

Word building: **lynching** *noun*
Word history: named after Captain William *Lynch*, 1742–1820, of Virginia, US, who introduced the practice

lynx (lingks)
noun a type of wildcat with long limbs and a short tail

Noun forms: The plural is **lynxes** or **lynx**.
Word history: Middle English, from Latin, from Greek

lyre (luy-uh)
noun a stringed musical instrument of ancient Greece

Word history: Middle English, from Old French, from Latin, from Greek

lyre / liar
Don't confuse **lyre** with **liar**, someone who tells lies.

lyrebird (luy-uh-berd)
noun a type of Australian bird which can mimic other sounds and is known for the long beautiful tails which the males display when courting the females

Word history: Louis-Claude Desaules de Freycinet, a French naval explorer who made two journeys to Australia in 1802 and then later in 1817–18, named this bird in his account of his expeditions published in 1824. He called it *oiseau-lyre*, literally 'bird-lyre', or *lyre magnifique*, literally 'lyre magnificent', because, as he said, it put its tail feathers into an elegant lyre shape.

lyric (li-rik)
adjective **1** having the form and musical quality of a song: ***lyric** poetry*
noun **2** a lyric poem
3 the words of a song

Word use: You can also use **lyrical** for definition 1. | Definition 3 is often used in the plural.
Word history: Latin, from Greek word meaning 'of a lyre'

lyricist (li-ruh-suhst)
noun someone who writes lyrics

macabre (muh-kahb)
adjective horrible in a gruesome way: ***macabre*** *crimes* (***dreadful***, ***frightening***, ***frightful***, ***horrendous***, ***terrible***)
Word history: Middle English, from French, perhaps from Arabic word meaning 'graveyard'

macadamia (mak-uh-day-mee-uh)
noun **1** a hard-shelled, edible nut
2 a tree, originally from eastern Australia, which bears this nut

macaroni
noun thick short tubes of pasta which are boiled and served in a sauce
Word history: Italian, from Late Greek word meaning 'food of broth and pearl barley', originally 'happiness'

macaw (muh-kaw)
noun a colourful, tropical American parrot with a long tail and a harsh voice
Word history: Portuguese *macao*; of Brazilian origin

mace (mays)
noun **1** a club-like weapon of war often with a spiked metal head, used in former times
2 a staff carried before or by certain officials as a symbol of office
Word history: Middle English, from Old French

machete (muh-shet-ee)
noun a large knife with a broad blade used for slashing thick plants
Word history: Spanish, from Latin word meaning 'slaughter'

Machiavellian (mak-ee-uh-vel-ee-uhn)
adjective **1** supporting the use of or using trickery and deceit in politics
2 with secretive and dishonest cunning (***artful***, ***crafty***, ***devious***, ***sly***, ***wily***)
Word history: from Niccolò di Bernardo *Machiavelli*, 1469–1527, Italian statesman and writer; supported the use of trickery and deceit to achieve a political goal

machinate (mash-uh-nayt, mak-uh-nayt)
verb to plan or scheme, especially with evil purpose (***collude***, ***connive***, ***conspire***, ***intrigue***, ***plot***)
Word building: **machinator** *noun*
machination *noun*
Word history: Latin

machine (muh-sheen)
noun **1** a device which is made up of parts that work together and which is used to perform a task: *a washing* ***machine***
verb **2** to make or do by machine: *Could you* ***machine*** *this hem for me?*
Word history: French, from Latin, from Greek

machine gun
noun a gun which can fire a rapid stream of bullets

machine language
noun Computers a low-level, complex binary code which is a precise set of operating instructions for a computer

machinery (muh-sheen-uh-ree)
noun **1** machines in general: *Farm* ***machinery*** *such as ploughs have made work on the land easier.*
2 the parts of a machine: *the* ***machinery*** *of a clock*

macho (mach-oh, mahch-oh)
adjective strongly masculine
Word history: Mexican Spanish

mackerel
noun a shiny greenish fish which is used for food
Word history: Middle English, from Old French

macramé (muh-krah-mee)
noun the craft of making things by knotting thread or cord in patterns

macro[1]
noun a single-word computer command which sets in train a number of other commands

macro[2]
noun broad and comprehensive: *at the* ***macro*** *level*
Word use: Compare this with **micro**.

macroclimate
noun the climate affecting a large geographical region
Word use: Compare this with **microclimate**.

macrocosm (mak-ruh-koz-uhm)
noun the great world, or universe
Word use: Compare this with **microcosm**.
Word history: French, from Medieval Latin

macrofauna
noun small animal organisms found in the soil or at the bottom of bodies of water, measuring at least 1 mm in length
Word use: Look up **microfauna**.

mad
adjective **1** insane or mentally unbalanced: *She went* ***mad***. (***crazy***, ***loony***, ***maniacal***, ***nutty***, ***silly***)
2 *Colloquial* angry: *He gets* ***mad*** *if you tease him.* (***annoyed***, ***cranky***, ***grumpy***, ***infuriated***, ***vexed***)
3 wild or excited
phrase **4 be mad about**, *Colloquial* to like a lot: *I'm* ***mad about*** *chocolate.*
5 like mad, *Colloquial*
a with great haste etc.
b in great amounts: *to sweat* ***like mad***
Word building: **madly** *adverb* **madness** *noun*
Word history: Old English

madam
noun a polite term of address to a woman: *May I help you, **madam**?*
Word history: Middle English, from Old French, originally *ma dame* my lady

made
verb **1** past tense and past participle of **make**
adjective **2** produced by making, preparing, etc.: *a **made** dish*
3 certain of success or fortune: *a **made** man / You've got it **made**.*

made / maid
Don't confuse **made** with **maid**, a woman who tidies guests' rooms in a hotel.

maelstrom (mayl-struhm)
noun **1** a large whirlpool
2 a state of great confusion or agitation (***commotion***, ***hullaballoo***, ***tumult***, ***turbulence***, ***turmoil***)
Word history: from *Maelstrom*, famous whirlpool off the coast of Norway

maestro (muy-stroh)
noun **1** a master of any art, especially a great or famous musical composer, teacher, or conductor
2 Maestro, a title of respect for such a person
Noun forms: The plural is **maestros** or **maestri** (muy-stree).
Word history: Italian word meaning 'master'

magazine
noun **1** a paper or journal containing stories, articles and advertisements, usually issued once a week or once a month (***bulletin***, ***periodical***, ***review***)
2 a place where explosives are kept (***arsenal***)
Word history: French, from Italian word meaning 'storehouse', from Arabic

magenta (muh-jen-tuh)
adjective of a reddish purple colour
Word building: **magenta** *noun*

maggot
noun the small, white grub which turns into a fly or other similar insect
Word history: Middle English

magic (maj-ik)
noun **1** power which is supernatural or which can't be explained normally (***sorcery***, ***witchcraft***, ***wizardry***)
2 an act in which seemingly impossible tricks are done for entertainment
Word building: **magic** *adjective* **magical** *adjective* **magically** *adverb*
Word history: Middle English, from Late Latin, from Latin *magicus* meaning 'relating to magic', from Greek *magos* 'a wise man'

magic bullet
noun Colloquial **1** any drug or treatment which acts effectively against a disease and has no harmful or unpleasant side effects
2 any remedy which is remarkably effective

magician (muh-jish-uhn)
noun someone who practises magic or magic tricks
Word history: Middle English, from Old French, from Latin

magisterial (maj-uhs-tear-ree-uhl)
adjective **1** full of authority: *a **magisterial** pronouncement* (***authoritative***, ***imperious***, ***masterly***)
2 having to do with a magistrate or the position of magistrate
Word history: Medieval Latin, from Latin word meaning 'master'

magistrate (maj-uh-struht, maj-uh-strayt)
noun someone who acts as a judge in some less important court cases: *She had to appear before a **magistrate** for not paying her fines.*
Word history: Middle English, from Latin word meaning 'the office of a chief'

magma
noun Geology the very hot molten rock under the solid crust of the earth, and from which igneous rocks are formed
Word building: **magmatic** *adjective*
Word history: Latin, from Greek word meaning 'a salve'

magnanimous (mag-nan-uh-muhs)
adjective nobly unselfish and generous: *He is too **magnanimous** to hold a grudge.* (***big-hearted***, ***charitable***, ***kind***, ***lavish***, ***liberal***)
Word building: **magnanimity** (mag-nuh-nim-uh-tee) *noun* **magnanimously** *adverb*
Word history: from Latin word meaning 'great-souled'

magnate (mag-nayt, mag-nuht)
noun someone who is very powerful and successful, especially in business (***captain of industry***, ***tycoon***)
Word history: late Middle English, from Late Latin, from Latin word meaning 'great'

magnesium
noun a light silver-white metal
Word history: Neo-Latin

magnet
noun **1** a piece of iron or steel which draws iron objects to it
2 anything that attracts something else
Word building: **magnetically** *adverb* **magnetism** *noun*
Word history: late Middle English, from Latin word meaning 'lodestone', 'magnet', from Greek word meaning '(stone) of Magnesia' (in Thessaly)

magnetic (mag-net-ik)
adjective **1** having to do with a magnet or magnetism: *a **magnetic** field*
2 strongly attractive: *a **magnetic** personality* (***alluring***, ***charismatic***, ***irresistible***, ***seductive***)
Word building: **magnetically** *adverb*

magnetic field
noun the area of force around a magnet or a wire or coil carrying electric current which shows itself as a force on magnetic objects within that space

magnetic north
noun the direction in which the needle of a compass points, differing in most places from true north

magnetic pole
noun **1** a pole of a magnet
2 either of the two points on the earth's surface where the compass needle stands vertical, one in the Arctic, the other in the Antarctic

magnetic resonance imaging
noun a technique used for medical diagnosis in which an image of internal organs is produced by exposing the body to an extremely strong magnetic field. Different types of tissue absorb different amounts of magnetism, so a picture can be created of the composition of the tissues examined.
Word use: The abbreviation is **MRI**.

magnetic tape
noun tape which is used to record sound for a tape-recorder, pictures for a video cassette, or data for a computer

magneto (mag-nee-toh)
noun a small electric generator, the poles of which are permanent magnets, used especially for producing sparks in a car engine
Noun forms: The plural is **magnetos**.
Word history: short for *magneto-electric* (*machine*)

magnification (mag-nuh-fuh-kay-shuhn)
noun **1** the act or result of magnifying
2 the power to magnify

magnificent (mag-nif-uh-suhnt)
adjective **1** grand in appearance: ***magnificent*** *robes* (***imposing***, ***lavish***, ***majestic***, ***resplendent***, ***splendid***)
2 excellent: *a* ***magnificent*** *dinner* (***fabulous***, ***great***, ***marvellous***, ***superb***, ***wonderful***)
Word building: **magnificence** *noun*
magnificently *adverb*
Word history: Old French, from Latin

magnify (mag-nuh-fuy)
verb to make larger or greater: *This lens will* ***magnify*** *the insect so you'll be able to see its eyes. / He* ***magnifies*** *his troubles.* (***amplify***, ***augment***, ***boost***, ***enlarge***, ***exaggerate***)
Verb forms: I **magnified**, I have **magnified**, I am **magnifying**
Word history: Middle English, from Latin word meaning 'make much of'

magnitude
noun **1** size: *They measured the* ***magnitude*** *of the angles.*
2 greatness or importance: *She finally realised the* ***magnitude*** *of her loss.*
Word history: Middle English, from Latin word meaning 'greatness'

magnolia (mag-noh-lee-uh)
noun a large shrub or small tree with large, showy, perfumed flowers in white, purple, etc.
Word history: Neo-Latin; named from P *Magnol*, 1638–1715, French botanist

magnum (mag-nuhm)
noun a wine bottle holding about 2.25 litres
Word history: from Latin word meaning 'great'

magpie
noun a black-and-white bird with a large beak, which is found throughout Australia and New Guinea
Word history: from *Mag*, familiar variant of *Margaret*, woman's name + *pie* (look up **pied**)

magpie lark
noun a common Australian black-and-white bird which builds its mud nest high in a tree
Word use: Another name is **peewee**.

maharajah (mah-huh-rah-juh)
noun the title of certain great ruling princes in India
Word use: You can also use **maharaja**.
Word history: Sanskrit

maharani (mah-huh-rah-nee)
noun the wife of a maharajah
Word history: Hindustani: great queen

mahjong (mah-zhong)
noun a game of Chinese origin, usually for four persons, with 136 (or sometimes 144) domino-like pieces or tiles, counters and dice
Word history: from Chinese (Mandarin) word meaning 'sparrow', literally 'hemp-bird', pictured on the first tiles of one of the suits

mahogany (muh-hog-uh-nee)
noun a hard reddish-brown wood, used for making furniture
Word history: perhaps West Indian

maid
noun **1** *Old-fashioned* a girl or unmarried woman
2 a female servant
3 a woman who tidies guests' rooms in a hotel or the like
Word history: variant of *maiden*

maid / made
Don't confuse **maid** with **made**, which is the past tense and past participle of **make**.

maiden
noun **1** *Old-fashioned* a young unmarried woman
adjective **2** unmarried: *my* ***maiden*** *aunt*
3 done or used for the first time: *a* ***maiden*** *voyage*
Word history: Old English

maiden name
noun a woman's surname before she is married

mail[1]
noun **1** letters and packages sent by post
2 a train or boat which carries mail, often at night: *the North Coast* ***Mail***
Word building: **mail** *verb* **mail** *adjective*
Word history: Middle English word meaning 'bag', from Old French, from Germanic

mail[2]
noun armour made of linked metal rings, which was worn in medieval times
Word history: Middle English, from Old French, from Latin word meaning 'mesh of a net'

mail / male
Don't confuse **mail** with **male**, which is an animal of the masculine gender. A man is a **male**, and so is a boy.

mailing list
noun **1** a list consisting of the names and addresses of people to whom information, etc., is sent by post
2 *Computers* a list of email addresses assembled under one email address, allowing a user to send a message to all of those on the list simultaneously

maim
verb to damage or cripple (***harm***, ***hurt***, ***injure***, ***mutilate***, ***wound***)
Word building: **maimed** *adjective*
Word history: variant of *mayhem*

main
adjective **1** most important or biggest: *the* ***main*** *course* | *the* ***main*** *reason* (***chief***, ***fundamental***, ***key***, ***major***, ***primary***)
noun **2** the largest pipe in a gas or water system
Word use: You can also use **mains** for definition 2.
Word building: **mainly** *adverb*
Word history: from Old English word meaning 'strength', 'power'

main / main
Don't confuse **main** with **mane**, which is long hair growing on the neck of an animal like a horse or a lion.

main clause
noun a clause that includes a main verb

Look up **clause.**

mainframe
noun a large and powerful multi-user computer

mainland
noun a large land mass, as distinct from the islands around it: *Tasmanians sometimes go to the* ***mainland*** *for a holiday.*

mainstay
noun **1** a rope supporting the main mast of a ship from in front
2 chief support: *His interest is the* ***mainstay*** *of the group.* (***anchor***, ***backbone***, ***linchpin***, ***prop***)

mainstream
noun the chief trend or tendency in an area: *in the* ***mainstream*** *of rock music*

maintain
verb **1** to keep up or keep in good condition: *to* ***maintain*** *a correspondence* | *to* ***maintain*** *the roads* (***preserve***, ***prolong***, ***retain***, ***sustain***)
2 to hold onto: *to* ***maintain*** *a lead*
Word history: Middle English, from French, from Latin word meaning 'hold in the hand'

maintenance (mayn-tuh-nuhns)
noun **1** the act of maintaining or condition of being maintained
2 a means of support (***keep***, ***livelihood***, ***sustenance***)
3 *Law* money paid for the support of a spouse or children after divorce

main verb
noun a verb which tells what action or process is or was taking place in a sentence

Look up **verbs: main verbs.**

maize
noun a tall cereal plant with heads of yellow grain
Word use: This is usually called **corn** in Australia.
Word history: Spanish, from Taino, a West Indian language

maize / maze
Don't confuse **maize** with **maze**, which is a confusing network of connecting paths or passages.

majestic (muh-jes-tik)
adjective dignified or grand (***distinguished***, ***lofty***, ***lordly***, ***regal***, ***stately***)
Word building: **majestically** *adverb*

majesty (maj-uh-stee)
noun **1** greatness or dignity: *The* ***majesty*** *of the view left them speechless.*
2 Majesty, the title given to a king or queen: *Your* ***Majesty***
Noun forms: The plural is **majesties.**
Word history: Middle English, from French, from Latin word meaning 'greatness', 'grandeur'

major
noun **1** an officer in the army
adjective **2** greater in size or importance: *His* ***major*** *work is on language.* (***chief***, ***key***, ***leading***, ***primary***)
Word history: Middle English, from Latin word meaning 'greater', 'larger', 'superior'

majority (muh-jo-ruh-tee)
noun **1** the greater number or more than half: *The* ***majority*** *of people stayed at home.* (***most***, ***bulk***)
2 the age at which the law says you are an adult and can vote in elections
Noun forms: The plural is **majorities.**
Word use: The opposite is **minority.**
Word history: French, from Medieval Latin, from Latin word meaning 'major'

majority / minority
When you use **majority** and **minority** the verb will be either singular or plural depending on the sense you want to emphasise. This is the same as with words like *government*, *team* or *crowd* which refer either to a single unit or to a collection of individuals:

A large majority of teachers was present.

A tiny minority of protesters were present.

Major Mitchell
noun a handsome white and pink cockatoo found in dry regions of Australia

major scale
noun any musical scale which has semitones between the third and fourth notes and between the seventh and eighth notes
Word use: Such a scale is said to be in a *major key.* | Compare this with **minor scale.**

make
verb **1** to bring into being or create: *She* ***makes*** *her own clothes.* | *Who* ***makes*** *the laws?* (***build***, ***form***, ***manufacture***, ***produce***)

2 to produce an effect: *The rain **makes** the road slippery.*
3 to prepare for use: *to **make** a bed*
4 to win or get: *to **make** a friend* (***acquire***, ***gain***, ***procure***)
5 to be or become: *The box will **make** a useful container.*
6 to add up to: *I know that 3 and 3 **make** 6.*
7 to reach or attain: *They **made** the shore at last.* | *She will **make** the finals.*
noun **8** a type or brand: *What **make** of car does she drive?*
phrase **9 make a face**, to grimace
10 make believe, to pretend (***dream***, ***feign***, ***imagine***)
11 make do, to manage with the means available, however small or inadequate
12 make for, to try to reach: *Let's **make for** home.*
13 make good,
a to achieve a goal
b to become a success
14 make it,
a to achieve your object
b to arrive successfully: *I didn't think I'd **make it**.*
15 make off, to run away (***disappear***, ***escape***, ***flee***, ***leave***, ***nick off***)
16 make out,
a to write out a bill, cheque, form, etc.
b to see and understand: *I can't **make out** your handwriting.* (***decipher***, ***read***)
c to present as: *He **made** me **out** to be a liar.*
17 make up,
a to form or complete: *We need three more players to **make up** a team.*
b to invent: *He **makes up** stories.* (***coin***, ***conceive***, ***concoct***, ***create***, ***devise***)
c to become friendly again after a quarrel
d to apply cosmetics to: *She **made up** her face.*

Verb forms: I **made**, I have **made**, I am **making**
Word history: Old English *macian*

makeover
noun **1** a treatment to radically improve someone's appearance, usually involving a new hairstyle, make-up, etc.
2 the improvement of a house, yard, etc., by completely changing its appearance

makeshift
adjective used in place of something else: *He had to use a brick as a **makeshift** hammer.*

make-up
noun **1** cosmetics
2 physical or mental constitution: *his emotional **make-up***

making
noun **1** the act or process of being made
2 a means or cause of success: *to be the **making** of someone*
3 the possibility of being: *She has the **makings** of a fine singer.* (***capacity***, ***potential***)
phrase **4 in the making**, being made; not yet finished

Word use: Definition 3 is often used in the plural.

malady (<u>mal</u>-uh-dee)
noun an illness or disease

Word history: Middle English, from Old French word meaning 'sick', from Late Latin word meaning 'ill-conditioned'

malapropism (<u>mal</u>-uh-prop-iz-uhm)
noun a word used by mistake for a similar-sounding word, so that the effect is funny: *It is a **malapropism** to say 'Beethoven wrote nine sympathies' since the right word is 'symphonies'.*

Word history: from Mrs *Malaprop*, a character in a play *The Rivals* (1775) by Irish dramatist RB Sheridan, who uses words in this way

malaria (muh-<u>lair</u>-ree-uh)
noun an illness which gives you fever, chills and sweating, and which is spread by mosquitoes

Word history: Italian, contraction of *mala aria* bad air

male
adjective **1** belonging to the sex which fertilises the female egg
noun **2** a male person or animal

Word use: The opposite of this is **female**.
Word history: Middle English, from Old French, from Latin

male / mail
Don't confuse **male** with **mail**, which is all the letters, parcels, etc., that are sent by post.

malevolent (muh-<u>lev</u>-uh-luhnt)
adjective full of ill will: *a **malevolent** sneer*

Word use: The opposite of this is **benevolent**.
Word building: **malevolence** *noun* **malevolently** *adverb*
Word history: from Latin word meaning 'wishing ill'

malformation
noun faulty formation or structure, especially in a living body: *a **malformation** of the bones*

Word building: **malformed** *adjective*

malibu (<u>mal</u>-uh-booh)
noun a long surfboard, offering more stability than a shorter board

Word use: You can also use **malibu board**.

malice (<u>mal</u>-uhs)
noun the desire to harm or hurt someone: *She broke his pen out of **malice**.* (***animosity***, ***hatred***, ***hostility***, ***ill will***, ***spite***)

Word use: The opposite of this is **kindness**.
Word building: **malicious** (muh-<u>lish</u>-uhs) *adjective* **maliciously** *adverb*
Word history: Middle English, from Old French, from Latin word meaning 'badness', 'spite'

malign (muh-<u>luyn</u>)
verb to speak ill of (***defame***, ***insult***, ***libel***, ***slander***, ***smear***)

malignant (muh-<u>lig</u>-nuhnt)
adjective **1** dangerous or deadly: *a **malignant** cancer* (***fatal***, ***lethal***, ***terminal***)
2 wanting to harm or hurt someone: *a **malignant** look* (***hostile***, ***malevolent***, ***malicious***, ***spiteful***, ***vicious***)

Word use: The opposite is **benign**.
Word building: **malignancy** *noun*
Word history: from Late Latin word meaning 'injuring maliciously'

malinger (muh-ling-guh)
verb to pretend to be sick or injured, especially to avoid duty, work, etc.

Word history: from French word meaning 'sickly', 'ailing'

mall (mawl, mal)
noun an area without traffic where people can stroll and shop (***arcade, plaza***)

Word history: Middle English, from Old French, from Latin word meaning 'hammer'; by association, an alley where the game *pall-mall* was played (using a mallet)

mall / maul

Don't confuse **mall** with **maul**. To **maul** something or someone is to attack them savagely.

The lion mauls a carcass.

Maul is always pronounced to rhyme with *ball*.

malleable (mal-ee-uh-buhl)
adjective easily worked into a different shape: *Some metals are more **malleable** than others.* (***flexible, pliable, supple***)

Word use: The opposite of this is **rigid**.
Word building: **malleability** *noun*
Word history: Middle English, from Old French, from Latin word meaning 'beat with a hammer'

mallee
noun **1** a wiry Australian gum tree which has several thin stems which grow from a large underground root
phrase **2 the mallee**, *Australian*
a country where these trees grow
b any remote, isolated or unsettled area

Word history: from Wembawemba, an Australian Aboriginal language of western Victoria

mallet
noun **1** a hammer made of wood
2 the wooden stick used to hit the ball in croquet or polo

Word history: Middle English, from Old French

malnutrition (mal-nyooh-trish-uhn)
noun an illness caused by not having enough of the right food

malpractice
noun improper or criminal action by a professional person, such as a doctor, accountant, etc.

malt
noun grain which is used in making beer and whisky

Word history: Old English

maltreat
verb to treat roughly or cruelly (***abuse, exploit, mistreat, misuse, victimise***)

Word history: French

mamma (mam-uh)
noun the organ in female mammals which forms milk (***breast, udder***)

Noun forms: The plural is **mammae** (mam-ee).
Word building: **mammary** *adjective*
Word history: Old English, from Latin word meaning 'breast'

mammal
noun an animal whose young feeds on its mother's milk

Word building: **mammalian** (mam-ayl-ee-uhn) *adjective, noun*
Word history: from Late Latin word meaning 'of the breast'

mammoth
noun **1** a type of large hairy elephant with long curved tusks, which died out a long time ago
adjective **2** huge: *a **mammoth** sale* (***colossal, enormous, gigantic, massive, vast***)

Word history: Russian

man
noun **1** a grown-up male human being
2 human beings in general
3 a piece in a game such as chess or draughts
verb **4** to provide with workers: *to **man** a ship*

Noun forms: The plural is **men**.
Verb forms: I **manned**, I have **manned**, I am **manning**
Word history: Old English

This old English word is the first part of quite a lot of compounds and longer words. The following are a sample of them:

man-eating	*manful*	*manhood*
manhandle	*manhole*	*manhours*
manhunt	*mankind*	*manly*
man-made	*manpower*	*man-sized*
manslaughter		

Two meanings of **man** are:

1 an adult male
2 people in general

These two different meanings are not always recognised. In words like *manful*, *manhood* and *manly*, the first part clearly means 'adult male'. In others, such as *manhandle*, *manhunt* and *man-sized*, the word **man** seems to mean 'adult male', because the whole word refers to something which normally involves men.

But in quite a lot of similar words, **man** is intended to mean 'people in general'. This is so in *man-eating*, *manhole*, *manhours*, *mankind*, *man-made*, *manpower*, *manslaughter*, etc. Man-eating tigers certainly don't limit their diet to adult males! And women help to make up the *manpower* which turns out *man-made* products in a given number of *manhours*. These words, like *mankind* itself, are intended to refer to people in general, not a single sex.

Still, it is easy enough to avoid words in which **man** may seem to be exclusive. For example, you could use:

humankind or *the human race* (instead of *mankind*)

workforce (instead of *manpower*)

artificial (instead of *man-made*)

Note that in words such as the ones below, the letters man- are the Latin root for 'hand':

manicure	*manufacture*
manoeuvre	*manual*
manuscript	*manipulate*

They have nothing to do with either adult males or people at large.

For more about **man**, look up **-man** and **non-sexist language**.

-man

This old English word appears in the names of many job titles. For example:

alderman	*foreman*	*salesman*
fireman	*postman*	*stockman*
policeman	*sportsman*	*draughtsman*
spokesman	*chairman*	*newsman*
businessman	*linesman*	

Though **man** can mean either 'adult male' or 'human being', it tends to be understood as 'adult male' in such words. So they seem to exclude women from doing the job they refer to.

The difficulty can be avoided in one of two ways:

1 by using an alternative term to cover both men and women.

For example:

executive	for	*businessman/woman*
chairperson or *chair*		*chairman/woman*
firefighter		*fireman/woman*
supervisor		*foreman/woman*
journalist or *reporter*		*newsman/woman*
salesperson or *assistant*		*salesman/woman*
competitor or *athlete*		*sportsman/woman*

2 by using a parallel term with -woman (when you know that you are referring to a woman or women), for example:

businessman	*businesswoman*
chairman	*chairwoman*
policeman	*policewoman*
sportsman	*sportswoman*

For more about this, look up **non-sexist language**.

manacle (man-uh-kuhl)
noun **1 manacles**, a pair of iron rings linked by a chain, used on prisoners' wrists (***handcuffs***, ***irons***)
2 any restraint
Word history: Middle English, from Old French word meaning 'handcuff', from Latin word meaning 'hand'

manage (man-ij)
verb **1** to be able to: *Can he **manage** to feed himself?*
2 to take charge of or control: *The young stockman cannot **manage** the cattle.* (***direct***, ***govern***, ***rule***, ***run***, ***supervise***)
3 to bring about, or succeed in accomplishing: *He **managed** to see the governor.*
Word building: **manageable** *adjective*
Word history: Italian word meaning 'handle', 'train (horses)', from Latin word meaning 'hand'

management
noun **1** the running of something: *He leaves the **management** of the business to her.*
2 the person or people who run something, such as a business or hotel: *This shop is under new **management**.*
3 such people taken as a whole: *discussions between labour and **management***

manager
noun **1** someone who runs a business (***administrator***, ***boss***, ***director***, ***official***, ***superintendent***)
2 someone who looks after the business interests of an entertainer or a sporting team
Word building: **managerial** *adjective*

manchester (man-ches-tuh)
noun sheets, towels, etc., as sold in shops
Word history: from *Manchester*, a city in England known for its textile industry

mandarin
noun **1** a small, soft-skinned, orange-coloured citrus fruit
2 in former times, a public official in the Chinese Empire
Word use: You can also use **mandarine** for definition 1.
Word history: Chinese pidgin English, from Portuguese, from Sanskrit word meaning 'thought', 'counsel'

mandate
noun **1** a commission given to one nation to administer the government, affairs, etc., of a territory or colony
2 a command (***decree***, ***order***, ***summons***, ***warrant***, ***writ***)
3 an instruction or permission from the electorate for a certain policy: *The Government has no **mandate** for higher taxes.*
verb **4** to give a territory or colony to the charge of a particular nation under a mandate
Word building: **mandator** *noun*
Word history: from Latin word meaning 'commit', 'enjoin', 'command'

mandatory (man-duh-tree, man-duh-tuh-ree)
adjective **1** having to do with a mandate
2 obligatory (***compulsory***, ***essential***, ***imperative***, ***necessary***, ***required***)
3 *Law* allowing no choice
Word use: The opposite of definition 2 and 3 is **optional**.

mandible (man-duh-buhl)
noun **1** a bone of the lower jaw
2 in birds,
a the lower part of the beak
b mandibles, the upper and lower parts of the beak
3 in insects, etc., one of the pair of biting mouth parts
Word history: from Late Latin word meaning 'jaw'

mandolin (man-duh-lin)
noun a musical instrument with a pear-shaped wooden body and metal strings which you pluck
Word history: French, from Italian

mane
noun the long hair on a male lion's head or along the neck of a horse
Word history: Old English *manu*

mane / main

Don't confuse **mane** with **main**, which means 'the most important or biggest'.

manga
noun the Japanese form of comic book, which has a wide variety of subject areas, catering for both children and adults

Word history: Japanese *manga*, originally the title of a sketchbook drawn by the Japanese artist Katsushika Hokusai in 1812. It comes from the Japanese words *man*, meaning 'aimless', 'involuntary' or 'indiscriminate', and *ga*, meaning 'picture', referring to the free-flowing, non-traditional nature of this style of illustration.

manga movie
noun a Japanese animated film, made in the style of the Japanese comic books

Word use: Another name is **anime**.

manganese (mang-guh-neez)
noun a hard, brittle, greyish-white metallic element used in alloys with steel and other metals to give them toughness

Word history: French, from Italian, from Medieval Latin word meaning 'magnesia'

mange (maynj)
noun a skin disease, mainly of animals, in which the skin becomes rough and red and loses its hair

Word building: **mangy** *adjective* (**mangier**, **mangiest**)
Word history: Middle English, from Old French word meaning 'itch', ultimately from Latin word meaning 'chew'

manger (mayn-juh)
noun a box from which cattle or horses eat

Word history: Middle English, from Old French, from Latin word meaning 'chew'

mangle
verb to crush, cut, or ruin (***damage***, ***destroy***, ***spoil***, ***vandalise***, ***wreck***)

Word history: Middle English, from Anglo-French, perhaps from Old French word meaning 'maim'

mango
noun a sweet, yellow tropical fruit

Noun forms: The plural is **mangoes** or **mangos**.
Word history: Portuguese, from Malay, from Tamil

mangrove
noun a tree which grows thickly along the water's edge sending up roots through the mud or sand

Word history: Spanish

manhandle
verb **1** to handle roughly
2 to move by human effort, without machines

manhole
noun a covered hole, as in a footpath or ceiling, that you can climb through to get at pipes and wires

mania (may-nee-uh)
noun **1** great enthusiasm or excitement: *He has a **mania** for collecting matchboxes.*
2 a violent or excitable form of insanity

Word building: **manic** (man-ik) *adjective*
Word history: Middle English, from Latin, from Greek word meaning 'madness'

maniac (may-nee-ak)
noun someone who is mad, or who acts wildly or dangerously

Word building: **maniacal** (muh-nuy-uh-kuhl) *adjective*

manic depression (man-ik duh-presh-uhn)
noun → **bipolar disorder**

Word building: **manic depressive** *adjective*, *noun*

manicure
noun treatment of your hands and fingernails

Word building: **manicurist** *noun*
Word history: French, from Latin word meaning 'hand care'

manifest (man-uh-fest)
adjective **1** obvious: *a **manifest** error | Dislike was **manifest** on his face.* (***apparent***, ***clear***, ***distinct***, ***evident***, ***plain***)
verb **2** to show plainly: *His dislike **manifested** itself in rudeness.* (***display***, ***exhibit***, ***expose***, ***express***, ***reveal***)
noun **3** a list of cargo carried by land, sea or air

Word history: Middle English, from Latin word meaning 'palpable', 'evident'

manifesto (man-uh-fest-oh)
noun a public statement by a government or group, setting out its ideas or goals: *the Communist **manifesto***

Noun forms: The plural is **manifestos** or **manifestoes**.
Word history: Italian word meaning 'manifest' (noun)

manifold (man-uh-fohld)
adjective **1** of many and various kinds: ***manifold** duties* (***assorted***, ***diverse***, ***miscellaneous***, ***mixed***, ***motley***)
noun **2** a pipe or chamber with several inlets or outlets

Word history: Old English *manigfeald*

manipulate (muh-nip-yuh-layt)
verb **1** to use, especially with skill: *to **manipulate** the puppets with strings* (***handle***, ***operate***, ***ply***, ***wield***, ***work***)
2 to influence cleverly and unfairly: *She **manipulates** people.*
3 to use the hands to treat as a chiropractor does: *to **manipulate** the spine*

Word building: **manipulative** *adjective* **manipulator** *noun*
Word history: French, from Latin word meaning 'handful'

manipulation (muh-nip-yuh-lay-shuhn)
noun **1** the act of manipulating
2 skilful or artful influencing of situations or other people

mankind
noun all human beings

Look up **man**.

mannequin (man-uh-kuhn, man-uh-kwuhn)
noun **1** someone who wears new clothes to show them to customers
2 a human-sized figure used by dressmakers and window dressers to fit or model clothes

Word history: French, from Dutch word meaning 'little man'

manner
noun **1** a way of being or doing: *Hold the pencil in this* ***manner****.* (***method***, ***mode***, ***style***)
2 manners, behaviour or way of behaving, especially according to standards of politeness: *good* ***manners*** | *bad* ***manners***
3 a way of behaving towards others: *a pleasant* ***manner*** (***air***, ***bearing***, ***carriage***, ***comportment***, ***demeanour***)
Word history: Middle English, from Anglo-French word originally meaning 'way of handling', from Latin word meaning 'of or for the hand'

manner / manor
Don't confuse **manner** with **manor**, which is a mansion surrounded by a large estate.

mannerism
noun a habit of doing something a little strange: *He has a funny little* ***mannerism*** *— he pulls his ear every time he starts to speak.*

manoeuvre (muh-nooh-vuh)
noun **1** a clever move: *She won the game by an unbeatable* ***manoeuvre****.*
2 manoeuvres, military exercises: *The soldiers are out on* ***manoeuvres****.*
Word building: **manoeuvre** *verb* **manoeuvrability** *noun* **manoeuvrable** *adjective*
Word use: **Maneuver** is the usual spelling in the US.
Word history: French word meaning 'manipulation', from Late Latin word meaning 'work by hand'

manor
noun a large British country house with its land, originally the home of a lord
Word history: Middle English, from Old French word meaning 'dwell', from Latin word meaning 'remain'

mansion
noun a large or grand house
Word history: Middle English, from Old French, from Latin *mansio* meaning 'a place where someone stays', from *manere* to stay

manslaughter (man-slaw-tuh)
noun the accidental killing of someone

mantelpiece
noun the shelf above a fireplace

mantis
noun a long, stick-like, brown or green insect which holds its front legs doubled up as if in prayer
Word use: You can also use **praying mantis.**
Word history: Neo-Latin, from Greek word meaning 'prophet', 'kind of insect'

mantle
noun **1** a loose cloak or cover
2 *Geology* the layer of the earth between the crust and the core, consisting of solid rock
verb **3** to cover or be covered: *Snow* ***mantled*** *the peaks.*
Word history: Old English *mæntel*, from Latin word meaning 'cloak'

manual (man-yooh-uhl)
adjective **1** done by hand: ***manual*** *work*
noun **2** a book which tells you how to do or use something
3 a car which has gears that you change by hand
Word building: **manually** *adverb*
Word history: from Latin word meaning 'of the hand'

manufacture
verb **1** to make or produce by hand or machine, especially in large numbers (***build***, ***create***, ***form***, ***frame***)
noun **2** the making of goods by hand or by machinery, especially on a large scale
Word history: French, from Latin

manufacturing
noun production of goods in a factory: *Our economy is based on farming,* ***manufacturing****, and tourism.*
Word building: **manufacturing** *adjective*

manure (muh-nyooh-uh)
noun animal waste, especially when used as fertiliser
Word history: Middle English, from Anglo-French word meaning 'work by hand', from Old French

manuscript (man-yuh-skript)
noun a book, letter or piece of music, written by hand
Word history: from Medieval Latin word meaning 'handwritten'

many (men-ee)
adjective **1** forming a large number: ***many*** *people* (***countless***, ***innumerable***, ***manifold***, ***numerous***)
2 relatively numerous: *Six may be too* ***many****.*
pronoun **3** a great number: *Many attended the meeting.*
phrase **4 a good** (or **great**) **many,** a large number
Adjective forms: **more, most**
Word history: Old English *manig*

map
noun **1** a drawing or diagram of an area showing where certain things are, such as towns, roads, mountains and borders (***chart***)
verb **2** to represent in a map
3 to make a logical connection between two things
phrase **4 map out,** to plan something: *She has* ***mapped out*** *a new career path.*
5 off the map, out of existence: *Whole cities were wiped* ***off the map****.*
6 put on the map, to make famous or widely known: *The discovery of gold* ***put*** *the valley* ***on the map****.*
Verb forms: I **mapped,** I have **mapped,** I am **mapping**
Word history: Medieval Latin word meaning 'map', from Latin word meaning 'napkin'

maple
noun a tree that grows in cold countries, used for its wood and its sap which produces a sweet syrup
Word history: Old English

mar
verb to spoil: *His bad temper* ***mars*** *his good performance.* (***damage***, ***hurt***, ***ruin***, ***wreck***)
Word use: The opposite of this is **improve.**
Verb forms: I **marred,** I have **marred,** I am **marring**
Word history: Old English *merran* hinder, waste

marathon
noun **1** a long-distance foot race, officially of 42 195 metres
2 any activity or pursuit that continues for a long period of time: *a movie* ***marathon***

Word history: from *Marathon*, a plain in Attica, north-east of Athens, from which, following the defeat of the Persians there in 490 BC, a runner took the news to Athens, about forty kilometres away

marauding (muh-rawd-ing)
adjective searching for things to steal, destroy, etc. *The car windows had been smashed by a* ***marauding*** *gang of louts.*

Word building: **marauder** *noun* **maraud** *verb*
Word history: from French word meaning 'rogue', 'vagabond'

marble
noun **1** a hard mottled limestone of various colours, used in building and sculpture
2 a small glass ball used in a game

Word building: **marble** *adjective*
Word history: Middle English, from Old French, from Latin

marbled
adjective patterned with different coloured patches like marble (***dappled***, ***flecked***, ***mottled***, ***speckled***, ***stippled***)

march
verb **1** to walk like a soldier, with even steps and swinging arms (***parade***, ***stride***, ***strut***)
2 to make someone march: *She* ***marched*** *them out to the playground.*
noun **3** the act of marching: *He joined the* ***march.***
4 the distance covered by a march: *The town is three days'* ***march*** *away.*
5 a lively rhythmical piece of music suited to marching

Word building: **marcher** *noun*
Word history: French word meaning 'go', earlier 'trample', from Latin word meaning 'hammer'

March
noun the third month of the year, containing 31 days

Word history: Middle English, from Anglo-French, from Latin *Martius*, a word meaning the month 'of Mars'

Mardi gras (mah-dee grah)
noun a festive carnival

Word use: You can also use **mardi gras**.
Word history: from French word meaning 'meat-eating Tuesday', referring to 'Shrove Tuesday', the last day before Lent, which is celebrated with special carnival activities

mare (mair)
noun a fully grown female horse

Word history: Old English *mere, myre* feminine of *mearh* horse

> **mare / mayor**
> Don't confuse **mare** with **mayor**, which is the chief official of a local government.

margarine
noun a butter-like spread made from vegetable oil

Word history: French, from Greek word meaning 'white of pearl'

margin (mah-juhn)
noun **1** an edge or border, such as the blank space beside the writing on a page (***brim***, ***brink***, ***outskirts***, ***rim***)
phrase **2 margin of error**, an extra amount allowed in calculations, such as of time or money, to cover mistakes

Word building: **marginal** *adjective*
Word history: Middle English, from Latin word meaning 'border', 'edge'

marijuana (ma-ruh-wah-nuh)
noun the dried leaves and flowers of the Indian hemp plant which contain a drug

Word history: American Spanish

marinade (ma-ruh-nayd)
noun **1** a liquid in which food may be soaked before cooking or serving, to add flavour
verb (ma-ruh-nayd) **2** → **marinate**

Word history: from French word meaning 'pickle in brine'

marinate (ma-ruh-nayt)
verb to add flavour to a food by soaking it in a liquid before cooking or serving

Word use: You can also use **marinade**.
Word history: French

marine (muh-reen)
adjective **1** having to do with the sea: ***marine*** *creatures*
noun **2** a soldier who serves on ship and on land

Word history: Middle English, from Latin word meaning 'of the sea'

mariner (ma-ruh-nuh)
noun someone who has gained experience in sailing from a life at sea (***sailor***, ***seafarer***)

Word history: Middle English, from French

marital (ma-ruh-tuhl)
adjective having to do with marriage

Word history: Latin

maritime (ma-ruh-tuym)
adjective having to do with the sea or shipping: ***maritime*** *law* (***marine***, ***nautical***, ***oceanic***)

Word history: from Latin word meaning 'of the sea'

maritime climate
noun a type of climate characterised by little temperature change, high cloud cover, and precipitation, and associated with coastal areas

mark
noun **1** something like a spot, line, scratch or stain on anything
2 a sign or label which tells something about an object, such as who made it or who owns it (***sticker***, ***tab***, ***tag***, ***ticket***)
3 a symbol, such as a letter of the alphabet, used to judge behaviour or work: *a good* ***mark*** *for an essay*
4 a target: *His arrow hit the* ***mark.***
verb **5** to make marks on (***blemish***, ***blot***, ***scar***, ***scratch***, ***spot***, ***stain***)

6 to be a special feature of: *Violence **marked** the opening of the football season.*
7 to judge, by a number or other sign, the value of work: *He **marks** fairly.*
phrase **8 make your mark**, to become famous or successful
9 mark down, to reduce the price of
10 mark off, to separate, as by a line or limit
11 mark up,
a to mark with numbers or signs
b to increase the price of
12 overstep the mark, to go beyond the accepted bounds of behaviour; go too far: *You **overstepped the mark** when you criticised her sister.*
13 wide of the mark, incorrect: *You're a bit **wide of the mark** with that statement.* (***erroneous***, ***false***, ***inaccurate***, ***untrue***)

Word building: **marker** *noun*
Word history: Old English *mearc* boundary, landmark

market
noun **1** a place where things are bought and sold, often at many different stalls (***bazaar***, ***fair***)
2 the demand for goods: *There's no **market** for furs.*
3 a group of people trading in particular goods: *the fish **market***
4 current price or value: *a rising **market***
verb **5** to sell
phrase **6 in the market for**, ready to buy: *We're **in the market for** a new car.*
7 on the market, for sale or available

Word history: Middle English and late Old English, from Latin word meaning 'trading', 'traffic', 'market'

marketing
noun the organised selling of a product or service, including advertising

market research
noun the gathering of information on what is the likely market for a product before putting a product on the market, on how well a product is known, etc.

mark-up
noun the amount or percentage added to the cost of an article to fix the selling price: *a 50 per cent **mark-up** on cameras*

mark-up language
noun a computer language in which various elements of a document, database, etc., are marked with tags, providing a flexible means of arranging and retrieving data

Word use: Look up **HTML** and **SGML**.

marlin
noun a large, powerful fish with an upper jaw like a spear

marmalade
noun a jam made of citrus fruits, such as oranges and grapefruit

Word history: Middle English, from French, from the Portuguese word *marmelada* meaning 'quince jam', from Latin *malomellum* sweet apple, from Greek

maroon (muh-rohn, muh-roohn)
adjective of a dark brownish-red colour

Word building: **maroon** *noun*
Word history: French, from Italian word meaning 'chestnut'

marooned (muh-roohnd)
adjective left somewhere that you can't get away from: *They were **marooned** on an island for two months. | I was **marooned** at the shops with no money and no car.*

Word history: French

marquee (mah-kee)
noun a big tent used for outdoor parties, circuses, etc.

marriage (ma-rij)
noun **1** the legal union of a man with a woman for life (***matrimony***, ***wedlock***)
2 the legal or religious ceremony of marriage (***nuptials***, ***wedding***)
3 any close union: *a **marriage** of ideas*

Word building: **marriageable** *adjective*
Word history: Middle English, from Old French

marrow
noun **1** the soft tissue inside bones which is important in producing red blood cells
2 a large white, yellow or green vegetable

Word history: Old English *mearg*

marry
verb **1** to join together as husband and wife (***wed***)
2 to take as a husband or wife: *My sister is **marrying** my best friend's brother.*

Verb forms: I **married**, I have **married**, I am **marrying**
Word history: Middle English, from French, from Latin word meaning 'wed'

marsh
noun low-lying wet land (***bog***, ***lake***, ***mire***, ***quagmire***, ***swamp***)

Word building: **marshy** *adjective*
Word history: Old English *mere* pool + *-isc*

marshal
noun **1** someone who organises the activities at a show or other public occasion
verb **2** to organise in rows or ranks

Verb forms: I **marshalled**, I have **marshalled**, I am **marshalling**
Word history: Middle English, from Old French, from Vulgar Latin word meaning 'groom', from Germanic

marshal / martial

Don't confuse **marshal** with **martial**, which means 'to do with fighting or war', as in *martial arts.*

marshmallow
noun a soft sweet made from gelatine, sugar and flavouring

Word history: Old English *merscmealwe*

marsupial (mah-sooh-pee-uhl, mah-syooh-pee-uhl)
noun a mammal such as a kangaroo which keeps and feeds its young in a pouch for a few months after birth

Word history: Latin

marsupial mouse
noun any of various small Australian marsupials looking rather like mice or rats

martial (<u>mah</u>-shuhl)
adjective having to do with war or fighting: ***martial** arts* (***bellicose**, **military**, **warlike***)
Word history: Middle English, from Latin word meaning 'of Mars'

martial art
noun any of various methods of training for combat, mostly coming from Asia, which are now often also practised as forms of sport

martial law
noun law placed upon an area by military forces when the civil authority has broken down

martyr (<u>mah</u>-tuh)
noun **1** someone who is killed or suffers a great deal for the sake of their beliefs
2 someone who goes to great trouble for others, just so they can feel self-righteous and receive pity
Word building: **martyr** *verb* **martyrdom** *noun*
Word history: Old English *martyr*, from Latin, from Greek word meaning 'witness'

marvel
noun **1** something which causes delight and wonder
verb **2** to wonder at or be filled with wonder: *I **marvel** at her skill.*
Verb forms: I **marvelled**, I have **marvelled**, I am **marvelling**
Word history: Middle English, from French, from Latin word meaning 'wonderful things'

marvellous
adjective wonderful (***excellent**, **fabulous**, **great**, **incredible**, **phenomenal***)

marzipan
noun a sweet made of crushed almonds and sugar
Word history: German

mascara
noun a substance used to colour the eyelashes
Word history: from Spanish word meaning 'a mask'

mascot
noun something which is supposed to bring good luck
Word history: French, from Provençal word meaning 'witch'; of Germanic origin

masculine (<u>mas</u>-kyuh-luhn)
adjective having qualities thought to be typical of a male
Word use: The opposite is **feminine.**
Word building: **masculinity** (mas-kyuh-<u>lin</u>-uh-tee) *noun*
Word history: Middle English, from Latin *masculīnus* male

mash
verb to pound down or crush (***pulp**, **pulverise**, **squash***)
Word history: Old English *māsc-* (in compounds)

mask
noun **1** a covering for your face, worn as a disguise or for protection
verb **2** to hide or disguise (***camouflage**, **cloak**, **conceal**, **cover**, **veil***)
Word history: French, from Italian, from Late Latin

masochism (<u>mas</u>-uh-kiz-uhm)
noun a condition in which a person looks for and sometimes takes pleasure from suffering
Word building: **masochist** *noun* **masochistic** (mas-uh-<u>kis</u>-tik) *adjective*
Word history: named after Leopold von Sacher *Masoch*, 1836–95, Austrian novelist, who described the condition

mason
noun someone who builds or works with stone
Word building: **masonry** *noun*
Word history: Middle English, from Old French, from Late Latin word meaning 'beat'; of Germanic origin

masquerade (mas-kuh-<u>rayd</u>)
noun **1** a party at which the guests wear masks and fancy dress
2 a false outward show
Word building: **masquerade** *verb*
Word history: French, from Italian word meaning 'mask'

mass[1]
noun **1** a quantity of matter of no particular shape or size: *a **mass** of snow* | *a cloud **mass***
2 a large number or quantity: *a **mass** of papers* | *a **mass** of water*
3 the amount of matter in a body
phrase **4 the masses,** the common people
Word history: Middle English, from Latin *massa* mass, lump

mass[2]
noun a religious service in the Roman Catholic and some other Christian churches
Word history: Old English *mæsse*, from Latin

massacre (<u>mas</u>-uh-kuh)
noun the killing of a large number of people: *When the troops arrived they discovered there had been a **massacre**, and most of the villagers were dead.* (***butchery**, **carnage**, **extermination**, **slaughter***)
Word building: **massacre** *verb* (**massacred, massacring**)
Word history: French, from Old French word meaning 'to butcher'

massage (<u>mas</u>-ahzh, <u>mas</u>-ahj)
noun the act of rubbing and pressing the body, to relax it or ease pain
Word building: **massage** *verb*
Word history: from French word meaning 'knead'

masseur (ma-<u>ser</u>)
noun a man skilled in massage

masseuse (ma-<u>serz</u>, muh-<u>soohs</u>)
noun a woman skilled in massage

massive
adjective large and heavy: *a **massive** load* (***colossal**, **enormous**, **gigantic**, **huge**, **vast***)
Word history: Middle English, from French

mass media
plural noun radio, television, newspapers and magazines, by which information is passed on to large numbers of people

Look up **media.**

mass noun
noun a noun which refers to a thing which occurs as a mass and is not normally counted or used in the plural

For more information, look up **nouns: common nouns.**

mass-produce
verb to make in large quantities with machines in factories

Word building: **mass-production** *noun*

mast
noun **1** a tall pole rising from the deck of a ship, to which sails are attached
2 any upright pole: *a radio-transmitting* ***mast***

Word history: Old English *mæst*

mastectomy (mas-tek-tuh-mee)
noun the operation of removing a breast

Noun forms: The plural is **mastectomies.**

master
noun **1** someone who has control or special skill: *He is a* ***master*** *of several languages.* (***ace, champion, expert, wizard***)
2 the owner of a dog or other animal
3 a male teacher, especially one who is head of a department
verb **4** to get control of

Word history: Old English *magister*, from Latin

masterful
adjective **1** domineering
2 showing great skill

masterful / masterly
These words are both linked to **master** but mean different things.
A **masterful** person is one who takes command of things.
To do something in a **masterly** way is to do it like an expert.

masterly
adjective showing great skill

master of ceremonies
noun someone who directs the entertainment at a party, dinner, wedding reception, etc.

Word use: The abbreviation is **MC.**

masterpiece
noun the most excellent piece of work of an artist, musician or writer

mastery
noun **1** command or control: ***mastery*** *of a situation*
2 expert skill or knowledge

masticate (mas-tuh-kayt)
verb to chew (***chomp, munch***)

Word building: **mastication** *noun*
Word history: from Late Latin word meaning 'chewed'

masturbate (mas-tuh-bayt)
verb to rub the genitals to produce a pleasant sensation

Word building: **masturbation** *noun*

mat
noun **1** a piece of material of some kind used to cover the floor or part of it: *a bath* ***mat*** | *a rubber* ***mat*** (***carpet, rug***)
2 a small piece of cork or fabric for putting under a plate or ornament
verb **3** to make or become a thick and tangled mass

Verb forms: it **matted,** it has **matted,** it is **matting**
Word building: **matting** *noun*
Word history: Old English *meatt(e)*, from Late Latin

mat / matt
Don't confuse **mat** with **matt,** which means 'not shiny' or 'unpolished'.
The kitchen wall has a matt finish.

matador
noun the bullfighter who kills the bull

Word use: Compare this with **picador.**
Word history: Spanish, from Latin word meaning 'slayer'

match[1]
noun a short, thin piece of wood tipped with a chemical substance which produces fire when you scrape it on a rough surface

Word history: Middle English, from Old French

match[2]
noun **1** someone or something that equals or looks like another in some way (***companion, fellow, mate, pair***)
2 a contest or game: *a football* ***match*** (***bout, championship, competition***)
verb **3** to agree exactly: *These colours don't* ***match.***
4 to place in opposition: *They are* ***matched*** *in the semi-final.*

Word use: The opposite of definition 3 is **differ.**
Word history: Old English *gemæcca* mate, fellow

mate
noun **1** a friend: *Joe is a real* ***mate.*** (***comrade, pal***)
2 *Australian, NZ* a word you use to address a friend or when you want to sound friendly: *G'day,* ***mate.***
3 the male or the female of a pair of animals: *the fox and its* ***mate***

Word building: **mateship** *noun*
Word history: Middle English, from Middle Low German, variant of *gemate*

material (muh-tear-ree-uhl)
noun **1** the substance which is used to make something: *building* ***materials*** | *painting* ***materials***
2 cloth: *curtain* ***material*** (***fabric, stuff, textile***)
adjective **3** existing in a form you can touch (***actual, concrete, physical, real, tangible***)

Word history: Middle English, from Late Latin word meaning 'matter'

materialise (muh-tear-ree-uhl-uyz)
verb to appear in a physical shape: *Her figure* ***materialised*** *out of the mist.* (***emerge, loom, show up, turn up***)

Word use: The opposite of this is **disappear**. | You can also use **materialize**.

materialism (muh-tear-ree-uhl-iz-uhm)
noun concern for material rather than spiritual objects, needs, etc.

Word building: **materialist** *noun*

maternal
adjective belonging to or like a mother: ***maternal*** *feelings*

Word history: Middle English, from Latin word meaning 'of a mother'

maternity (muh-tern-uh-tee)
adjective **1** having to do with pregnancy or childbirth
noun **2** motherhood

mathematics
noun the science dealing with numbers and the size of things: ***Mathematics*** *is fun.*

Word building: **mathematical** *adjective* **mathematician** *noun*
Word use: The short form is **maths**.
Word history: plural of *mathematic*, from Latin, from Greek word meaning 'pertaining to science'

maths
noun → **mathematics**

matinee (mat-uh-nay)
noun an afternoon performance of a play or showing of a film

Word history: French

matriarch (may-tree-ahk, mat-ree-ahk)
noun a woman leader in a family, tribe or any field of activity

Word building: **matriarchal** *adjective*

matriarchy (may-tree-ah-kee, mat-ree-ah-kee)
noun a form of social organisation in which the mother is head of the family and in which descent is through the female line, the children belonging to the mother's clan

Noun forms: The plural is **matriarchies**.

matrices (may-truh-seez)
noun a plural of **matrix**

matriculate (muh-trik-yuh-layt)
verb **1** to be admitted to membership, especially of a university or the like
2 to pass matriculation

Word history: from Late Latin word meaning 'public register', 'roll'

matriculation (muh-trik-yuh-lay-shuhn)
noun an examination which must be passed before you can enrol at a university

matrimony (mat-ruh-muh-nee)
noun marriage

Word building: **matrimonial** *adjective*
Word history: Middle English, from Latin word meaning 'marriage'

matrix (may-triks)
noun **1** the rock in which a crystallised mineral is embedded
2 *Printing* a mould in which type is cast
3 *Mathematics, Computers* an ordered array of numbers

Noun forms: The plural is **matrices** (may-truh-seez) or **matrixes**.

matron
noun **1** a middle-aged married woman
2 *Old-fashioned* the most senior nurse in a hospital
3 a woman in charge of household arrangements in a school or other institution

Word use: Definition 2 is not used much nowadays. The term *Director of Nursing* is usually used instead.
Word building: **matronly** *adjective*
Word history: Middle English, from Old French, from Latin word meaning 'married woman'

matt
adjective having a dull surface: ***matt*** *paint*

Word history: French, *mat* dead

matt / mat
Don't confuse **matt** with **mat**, which is a small floor covering.

matter
noun **1** the substance of which things are made
2 a particular kind of substance: *colouring* ***matter***
3 an affair or subject: *a* ***matter*** *of life and death*
4 trouble or difficulty: *What is the* ***matter****?*
verb **5** to be of importance: *It doesn't* ***matter****.*
phrase **6 as a matter of fact**, actually: ***As a matter of fact****, I quite like that colour.*
7 for that matter, as far as that is concerned
8 matter of course, a logical and certain outcome of events: *You will be sent the results as a* ***matter of course****.*

Word history: Middle English, from Old French, from Latin word meaning 'stuff', 'material'

matter-of-fact
adjective ordinary, not excited or imaginative: *a* ***matter-of-fact*** *voice* (***down-to-earth, practical, pragmatic, realistic, sensible***)

mattock (mat-uhk)
noun a tool for loosening the soil, like a pick but with a blade instead of a point

Word history: Old English *mattuc*

mattress
noun a soft and springy covering for the base of a bed

Word history: Middle English, from Old French, from Italian, from Arabic word meaning 'mat', 'cushion'

mature (muh-tyoouh)
adjective **1** fully grown or developed: *a* ***mature*** *tree* | *a* ***mature*** *woman* (***adult***)
2 ripe: ***mature*** *fruit*
3 having the understanding and attitudes which an adult should have

Word use: The opposite of this is **immature**.
Word building: **mature** *verb* **maturity** (muh-tyoouh-ruh-tee) *noun*
Word history: Middle English, from Latin word meaning 'ripe', 'timely', 'early'

matzo (mat-soh)
noun a biscuit made of bread without yeast, eaten by Jewish people during the Feast of the Passover
Noun forms: The plural is **matzos**.

maudlin (mawd-luhn)
adjective tearfully or weakly emotional or sentimental
Word history: from *Maudlin*, variant of *Magdalen* (Mary Magdalene), often represented in art as weeping

maul (mawl)
verb to handle roughly
Word history: variant of *mall*

maul / mall
Don't confuse **maul** with **mall,** which is an area without traffic where people can stroll and shop.

mausoleum (maws-uh-lee-uhm, mawz-uh-lee-uhm)
noun **1** a stately and magnificent tomb
2 *Colloquial* a large unwelcoming building
Noun forms: The plural is **mausoleums** or **mausolea** (maws-uh-lee-uh, mawz-uh-lee-uh).
Word history: Latin, from Greek word meaning 'the tomb of Mausolus' (King of Caria) erected at Halicarnassus in Asia Minor in 350 BC and one of the Seven Wonders of the World

mauve (mohv)
adjective of a light purple colour
Word building: **mauve** *noun*
Word history: French, from Latin

mawkish (maw-kish)
adjective characterised by feelings expressed in a foolish, over-emotional way
Word history: *mawk* maggot (from Scandinavian)

max (maks)
phrase **to the max**, *Colloquial* to the greatest extent possible: *He's cool **to the max**.*

maxilla (mak-sil-uh)
noun the jaw or jawbone, especially the upper one
Noun forms: The plural is **maxillae** (mak-sil-ee).
Word building: **maxillary** *adjective*
Word history: from Latin word meaning 'jaw'

maxim
noun a saying containing a general truth or rule: *'Look before you leap' is a wise **maxim**.* (***adage**, **epigram**, **motto**, **proverb***)
Word history: Middle English, from Old French, from Latin *maxima (prōpositio)*, words meaning 'greatest (proposition)'

maximise
verb to increase to the greatest possible amount or degree
Word use: The opposite of this is **minimise**. | You can also use **maximize**.
Word building: **maximisation** *noun*

maximum
noun the greatest number or amount possible: *The hall holds a **maximum** of 500 people.* | *The bottle is filled to the **maximum**.*
Noun forms: The plural is **maximums** or **maxima**.
Word use: The opposite is **minimum**.
Word building: **maximum** *adjective*
Word history: from Latin word meaning 'the greatest'

may
verb **1** to be allowed to: *You **may** go now.*
2 could possibly: *They **may** arrive this afternoon.*
Word use: This verb is an auxiliary verb, always used with another one in the form **may** or **might**. Look up **might**[1].
Word history: Old English *mæg*

may / can
Look up **can / may**.

May
noun the fifth month of the year, containing 31 days
Word history: Middle English; Old English *Maius*, from Latin

maybe
adverb perhaps
Word history: short for *it may be*

mayday
noun an international radio signal for help, used by ships or aircraft
Word history: French; alteration of *m'aider* help me

mayhem
noun disorder or confusion
Word history: Middle English, from Old French word meaning 'injury'

mayonnaise (may-uh-nayz)
noun a thick, cold sauce made from eggs and oil and eaten with salad
Word history: French, from *Mahon*, a port of the Balearic Islands

mayor (mair)
noun the head of a city, town or suburban council
Word history: Middle English *maire*, from French, from Latin *mājor* greater

mayor / mare
Don't confuse **mayor** with **mare**, which is a female horse.

maze
noun a confusing and complicated arrangement of many crossing paths or lines that you have to find a way through
Word history: Middle English; variant of *amaze*

maze / maize
Don't confuse **maze** with **maize**, which is another name for corn.

MC (em see)
noun → **master of ceremonies**
Word history: abbreviation

me
pronoun the personal pronoun used, usually after a verb or preposition, by a speaker to refer to himself or herself: *She passed **me** in the street.* | *Give it to **me**.*

> **Me** is a first person singular pronoun in the objective case.
> For more information, look up **pronouns: personal pronouns**.

ME (em <u>ee</u>)
noun → **chronic fatigue syndrome**

Word history: *m(yalgic) e(ncephalomyelitis)*

meadow (<u>med</u>-oh)
noun a paddock

Word use: This word is used mostly in England.
Word history: Middle English *medwe*, Old English *mǣdw-*

meagre (<u>mee</u>-guh)
adjective small or of poor quality: *a **meagre** meal* (***insufficient**, **paltry**, **scant**, **skimpy**, **sparse***)

Word use: The US spelling is **meager**.
Word history: Middle English, from Old French, from Latin word meaning 'lean'

meal[1]
noun food served at more or less fixed times each day: *Breakfast is my favourite **meal**.* (***repast***)

Word history: Old English *mæl* measure, fixed time, occasion, meal

meal[2]
noun grain which has been ground or crushed

Word history: Old English *melu*

mealy-mouthed
adjective avoiding the use of plain terms, because of shyness or insincerity

mean[1]
verb **1** to intend or have the purpose: *I **mean** to talk to him.* (***have in mind**, **plan**, **propose***)
2 to signify or indicate: *'Vermicelli' literally **means** 'little worms'.* | *His arrival **means** trouble.*

Verb forms: I **meant**, I have **meant**, I am **meaning**
Word history: Old English *mǣnan*

mean[2]
adjective **1** stingy or not willing to give anything away (***miserly**, **penny-pinching**, **thrifty**, **tight***)
2 nasty: ***mean** motives* (***contemptible**, **despicable**, **shabby**, **unkind***)

Word history: Old English *gemǣne*

mean[3]
noun **1** something halfway between two end points
2 *Mathematics* the average

Word building: **mean** *adjective*
Word history: Middle English, from Old French, from Late Latin word meaning 'in the middle'

meander (mee-<u>an</u>-duh)
verb to wind or wander about: *The river **meandered** through the valley.* (***ramble**, **stray***)

Word history: Latin, from Greek word meaning 'a winding', originally the name of a winding river (now Menderes) in western Asia Minor (now Turkey)

meaning
noun something which is intended to be, or actually is, said or shown (***connotation**, **import**, **significance***)

Word building: **meaningful** *adjective*

means
noun **1** a method or way used to reach an end: *a **means** of transport* (***agency**, **instrument**, **mode**, **procedure**, **technique***)
2 a supply of money: *Our **means** are not enough for our needs.*
phrase **3 by all means**, certainly: *Go, **by all means**.*
4 by any means, in any way: *She's no beauty **by any means**.*
5 by means of, by the use of: *She achieved this result **by means of** hard work.*
6 by no means, not at all: ***By no means** can you go to the party.*

> When the word **means** is a noun with the sense 'a way of achieving something', it can be treated as either a singular or a plural:
> *A means of transport <u>is</u> vital.*
> *Our means of communication <u>were</u> quite varied.*
> When the word refers to money, it's always treated as a plural:
> *They lived comfortably, because their means <u>were</u> considerable.*

means test
noun an inquiry into the income and resources of a person, to determine their right to gain a pension, allowance, etc.

meantime
adverb **1** meanwhile
phrase **2 in the meantime**, in the period of time between two events: *He left yesterday and will be back next week. **In the meantime** we have to paint the house.*

meanwhile (<u>meen</u>-wuyl, meen-<u>wuyl</u>)
adverb at the same time

measles
noun a type of infectious disease with fever and a rash

Word history: Middle English, from German word meaning 'spot'

> Although this looks like a plural noun, it is actually singular: *Measles is a very dangerous disease.*

measure (<u>mezh</u>-uh)
noun **1** the size or quantity of something
2 an agreed unit or standard: *A metre is a **measure** of length.*
3 a means to an end: *to take **measures** to prevent illness*
verb **4** to decide the size or quantity of, usually by using a special instrument such as a ruler or scales (***calculate**, **estimate**, **gauge***)
phrase **5 for good measure**, as an extra precaution
6 measure up to, to be suitable for (***qualify**, **serve**, **suffice**, **suit***)

Word history: Middle English, from Old French, from Latin

measurement
noun **1** the act of measuring
2 the extent, size, etc., of something, as determined by measuring: *What are your **measurements**?*

meat
noun **1** the flesh of animals as used for food
2 the edible part of a fruit, nut, etc.
3 the main substance of something, as an argument
Word history: Middle English and Old English *mete*

meat / meet
Don't confuse **meat** with **meet**.
To **meet** someone is to come across them, either by accident or by arrangement.

Mecca (mek-uh)
noun a place regarded as a centre of interest or activity and visited by many people
Word use: You can also use **mecca**.
Word history: from *Mecca*, city in Saudi Arabia to which Muslim pilgrims journey

mechanic (muh-kan-ik)
noun a skilled worker with tools or machines
Word history: Middle English, from Latin, from Greek word meaning 'of machines'

mechanical (muh-kan-ik-uhl)
adjective **1** having to do with or worked by machinery or tools
2 like a machine: *to answer in a **mechanical** way*

mechanical advantage
noun the ratio of the force performing the work done, to the input force

mechanics
noun **1** the branch of knowledge concerned with machinery
2 the science dealing with the action of forces on bodies and with movement

mechanise (mek-uh-nuyz)
verb to change over to the use of machines in: *to **mechanise** the furniture industry*
Word use: You can also use **mechanize**.

mechanism (mek-uh-niz-uhm)
noun a piece of machinery
Word history: Neo-Latin, from Greek

mechatronics (mek-uh-tron-iks)
noun a branch of technology used especially in the design and manufacture of products and processes controlled by intelligent computers, such as robots performing certain tasks, air conditioners, etc.

medal
noun a metal disc or cross given as a reward for bravery or as a prize
Word history: French, from Italian, from Latin word meaning 'metal'

medal / meddle
Don't confuse **medal** with **meddle**, which is to interfere in things that do not concern you.

medallion (muh-dal-yuhn)
noun a large medal, or something shaped like one, used as part of a design such as on a building
Word history: French, from Italian word meaning 'large medal'

meddle
noun to interfere with something that doesn't concern you (***intrude***, ***pry***)
Word history: Middle English, from Old French, from Latin word meaning 'mix'

medevac (med-ee-vak)
noun **1** the evacuation of a seriously ill or wounded person, usually by aircraft
verb **2** to evacuate (such a person): *The helicopter was called to **medevac** the patient.*
Verb forms: I **medevaced**, I have **medevaced**, I am **medevacing**
Word use: You can also use **medivac**.

media
noun the means of communication, including radio, television, newspapers and magazines

Media is the Latin plural of the noun **medium**, and is used because the word originally came into English from Latin.
In this plural form, the word often refers to the various means of mass communication in our society, including radio, television and newspapers (the **mass media**). **Media** is now often thought of as a singular noun:
What is the media doing about this?
In the past, people regarded that as a mistake, because they knew it was a Latin plural. However, in English, it behaves like a collective noun and can take either a singular or plural verb.

mediaeval
adjective → **medieval**

medial (meed-ee-uhl)
adjective **1** in the middle or having to do with the middle
2 of an average
3 ordinary (***average***, ***fair***, ***mediocre***, ***nondescript***, ***standard***)
Word history: Late Latin, from Latin word meaning 'middle'

median (mee-dee-uhn)
adjective **1** coming in the middle
noun **2** *Mathematics* the middle number in a given series of numbers
3 a line through the vertex of a triangle dividing the opposite side into two equal parts
Word history: from Latin word meaning 'in the middle'

median strip
noun a dividing area, usually raised, which separates opposing lanes of traffic on a highway
Word use: Note that some people call this a *medium strip*, but this is not regarded as correct.

mediate (mee-dee-ayt)
verb to come between people or groups who are arguing to try to get them to agree: *to **mediate** in a dispute* (***arbitrate***, ***conciliate***)
Word building: **mediation** *noun* **mediator** *noun*
Word history: Middle English, from Late Latin word meaning 'divided', 'situated in the middle'

medical
adjective having to do with medicine or its practice: *a **medical** examination* | *a **medical** book*
Word history: Late Latin, from Latin word meaning 'of healing'

medicate (med-uh-kayt)
verb to treat with medicine
Word building: **medicative** *adjective*
Word history: from Latin word meaning 'cured'

medication
noun a substance used to treat an illness, such as a liquid medicine or tablets

medicine (med-uh-suhn, med-suhn)
noun **1** a substance used in treating disease: *cough **medicine***
2 the art or science of treating disease: *skilled in **medicine*** (***healing***)
Word building: **medicinal** (muh-dis-uh-nuhl) *adjective*
Word history: Middle English, from Latin

medicine man
noun (in some societies) a man who has power over a tribe because they think he can do magic

medieval (med-ee-ee-vuhl)
adjective belonging to or having to do with the Middle Ages, that is, from about the fifth to the fifteenth century: ***medieval** music*
Word use: You can also use **mediaeval**.
Word history: Neo-Latin *medi(um) aev(um)* middle age + *-al*

mediocre (mee-dee-oh-kuh, mee-dee-oh-kuh)
adjective neither good nor bad: ***mediocre** abilities* (***indifferent***, ***mundane***, ***ordinary***, ***second-rate***)
Word building: **mediocrity** (mee-dee-ok-ruh-tee) *noun*
Word history: French, from Latin word meaning 'in a middle state'

meditate (med-uh-tayt)
verb to think long and deeply: *to **meditate** on a problem* (***deliberate***, ***muse***, ***ponder***, ***reflect***)
Word building: **meditation** *noun* **meditative** (med-uh-tay-tiv, med-uh-tuh-tiv) *adjective*
Word history: Latin

medium
adjective **1** average in size, degree, quality, etc.: *a man of **medium** height*
noun **2** the way in which something is done or communicated: *an advertising **medium*** | *the **medium** of television*
3 the material or method used by an artist
4 someone who claims to be able to communicate with the spirits of dead people
Noun forms: The plural for definitions 2 and 3 is **media**; the plural for definition 4 is **mediums**.
Word history: from Latin word meaning 'middle', 'intermediate'

medley
noun a mixture: *He played a **medley** of songs on his guitar.* (***assortment***, ***hotchpotch***, ***jumble***, ***miscellany***)
Noun forms: The plural is **medleys**.
Word history: Middle English, from Old French word meaning 'a mixing'

meek
adjective patient and obeying readily: *She was too **meek** to object to the unfair arrangements.* (***humble***, ***modest***, ***self-effacing***, ***submissive***, ***unassuming***)
Word use: The opposite of this is **assertive**.
Word building: **meekly** *adverb* **meekness** *noun*
Word history: Middle English *make, meoc*, from Scandinavian

meet
verb **1** to come face to face with: *I **met** Laura in the street.* (***bump into***, ***come across***, ***encounter***, ***run into***)
2 to welcome on arrival: *to **meet** a friend at the airport*
3 to come together so as to touch or cross: *The paths **met** near the river.* (***connect***, ***converge***, ***join***)
4 to come together as a group for talks or other purposes: *The class representatives **meet** every Thursday.* (***assemble***, ***congregate***, ***gather***)
phrase **5 meet someone halfway**, to reach an agreed compromise
Verb forms: I **met**, I have **met**, I am **meeting**
Word history: Old English *mētan, gemētan*, from *mōt, gemōt* meeting

meet / meat
Don't confuse **meet** with **meat**.
Meat is the flesh of animals.

meeting
noun a coming together for a purpose: *a **meeting** of the chess club* | *a business **meeting*** (***assembly***, ***conference***, ***convention***, ***gathering***)

mega-
an informal word part meaning 'extreme' or 'extremely': *a **mega**hit* | ***mega**cool*

megabit
noun a unit of measurement of computer memory size equal to one million bits
Word use: The symbol for **megabit** is **Mb**, without a full stop.

megacity
noun a metropolitan area, often formed when two or more large cities grow together, with a population in excess of 10 million people

megafauna
noun **1** the group of large animals, over 500 kg, existing in a particular region or geological period
2 a group of such animals that are now extinct

megalith (meg-uh-lith)
noun a stone of great size, especially one in ancient constructions or prehistoric monumental remains
Word use: Compare this with **monolith**.
Word building: **megalithic** *adjective*

megalitre
noun a unit of capacity in the metric system, equal to 1×10^6 litres
Word use: The symbol for **megalitre** is **ML**, without a full stop. | The US spelling is **megaliter**.

megalomania (meg-uh-luh-may-nee-uh)
noun a mental illness in which the patients falsely believe they are great and powerful

Word history: from Greek word meaning 'great', 'bigness' + *mania*

megalomaniac
noun a person suffering from megalomania

megaphone
noun a funnel-shaped device for increasing or directing sound

megapixel
noun one million pixels, usually in reference to the resolution of a digital camera

megawatt
noun a unit of power, equal to one million watts

Word use: The symbol for **megawatt** is **MW**, without a full stop.

meh (me)
Colloquial
interjection **1** an expression of resigned acceptance, indifference, etc.
adjective **2** boring; mediocre

meiosis (muy-oh-suhs)
noun Biology a type of cell division in sex cells in which the pairs of chromosomes are divided, resulting in half the number of chromosomes for each new cell

Word use: Compare this with **mitosis**.

melaleuca (mel-uh-looh-kuh)
noun a type of tree or shrub mainly found in Australia, usually on river banks or in swamps (***paperbark***, ***tea-tree***)

Word history: Neo-Latin, from Greek *méla(s)* black + *leukós* white, with reference to the black trunk and white branches

melancholy (mel-uhn-kol-ee)
adjective feeling sad or depressed (***dejected***, ***gloomy***)

Word use: The opposite of this is **cheerful**.
Word building: **melancholy** *noun*
Word history: Middle English, from Late Latin, from Greek word meaning 'black bile'

melanin (mel-uh-nuhn)
noun the dark pigment in the body of humans and certain animals, found in the hair, skin, etc.

melatonin (mel-uh-toh-nuhn)
noun a hormone which causes lightening of the skin in some animals and the tendency to sleep

melee (me-lay, me-lee)
noun a confused and noisy fight (***brawl***, ***conflict***, ***fray***, ***skirmish***)

Word history: French

mellifluous (muh-lif-looh-uhs)
adjective sweetly or smoothly flowing: ***mellifluous*** *voices* (***honeyed***, ***mellifluent***, ***mellow***, ***sweet***)

Word history: Middle English, from Late Latin word meaning 'flowing with honey'

mellow
adjective **1** soft and rich: *a* ***mellow*** *voice* | *a* ***mellow*** *flavour*
2 softened by time: *a* ***mellow*** *attitude to life*

Word building: **mellow** *verb* **mellowness** *noun*
Word history: Old English *meru* tender, soft

melodic (muh-lod-ik)
adjective having to do with melody as distinguished from harmony and rhythm (***lyrical***, ***melodious***, ***tuneful***)

melodrama (mel-uh-drah-muh)
noun a play, novel, television series etc., that is too dramatic to be real

Word history: French, from Italian word meaning 'musical drama', from Greek word meaning 'music drama'

melodramatic
adjective excessively emotional and dramatic: *Don't be so* ***melodramatic*** *about it – it's just a slight problem.*

melody
noun a tune (***air***)

Word building: **melodious** (muh-loh-dee-uhs) *adjective*
Word history: Middle English, from Old French, from Late Latin, from Greek word meaning 'singing', 'choral song'

melon
noun a large, juicy fruit with a thick skin

Word history: Middle English, from Old French, from Late Latin, from Greek word meaning 'apple-like gourd'

melt
verb **1** to make or become liquid by heating: ***Melt*** *the fat in the pan.* | *The snow* ***melted*** *in the spring.*
2 to fade gradually: *The mountain ridge* ***melted*** *into the clouds.* (***dematerialise***, ***disappear***, ***dissolve***, ***vanish***)
3 to fill with tender feeling: *His heart* ***melted***.

Word history: Old English *meltan*

meltwater
noun water made from melted snow or ice

member
noun **1** each of the people forming a society, parliament, or other group
2 a part of a whole, such as a limb of your body (***piece***, ***portion***, ***section***, ***segment***)

Word history: Middle English, from Old French, from Latin word meaning 'limb', 'part'

membrane (mem-brayn)
noun a thin sheet or film: *The eardrum is a* ***membrane*** *between the outer and middle ear.*

Word building: **membranous** (mem-bruh-nuhs) *adjective*
Word history: from Latin word meaning 'the skin that covers the several members of the body', 'parchment'

memento (muh-men-toh)
noun something that acts as a reminder of what is past: *She gave them a book as a* ***memento*** *of her visit.* (***keepsake***, ***souvenir***, ***token***, ***trophy***)

Noun forms: The plural is **mementos** or **mementoes**.
Word history: from Latin word meaning 'remember'

This word is sometimes spelt *momento*, but this is not regarded as correct.

memo (mem-oh, mee-moh)
noun a message from someone in an organisation to another person: *She sent me a* ***memo*** *about tomorrow's meeting.*

Noun forms: The plural is **memos**.
Word use: This is short for **memorandum**.

memoirs (<u>mem</u>-wahz)
plural noun a record of the life and times of somebody, based on the personal experience of the writer (***autobiography***, ***diary***, ***journal***)

Word history: French

memorabilia (mem-uh-ruh-<u>bil</u>-ee-uh)
plural noun **1** matters or events worth being remembered
2 things collected for the sake of memory

Word history: Latin

memorable
adjective worth remembering (***famous***, ***historic***, ***important***, ***momentous***, ***notable***)

Word use: The opposite of this is **forgettable**.
Word history: Latin

memorandum
noun → **memo**

Noun forms: The plural is **memorandums** or **memoranda**.
Word history: Latin

memorial
noun something to remind people of a person or event: *a **memorial** to Burke and Wills* (***commemoration***, ***monument***)

Word history: Middle English, from Latin word meaning 'of memory'

memorise
verb to put into the memory or learn by heart: *I finally **memorised** the poem.*

Word use: You can also use **memorize**.

memory
noun **1** the ability to store things in your mind and recall them when needed
2 something remembered: *a **memory** of home* (***recollection***, ***remembrance***)
3 part of a computer in which information is stored until needed
phrase **4 in memory of**, in order to remind people of: *a monument **in memory of** Captain Cook*

Word history: Middle English, from Latin

memory dump
noun → **core dump**

memory stick
noun a small portable data storage device that plugs into the USB port of a computer: *I copied the file onto my **memory stick** so I could look at it at home.*

Word use: You can also use **flash memory stick** or **USB stick**.

men
noun plural of **man**

menace (<u>men</u>-uhs)
noun **1** something dangerous
2 a threatening attitude: *to speak with **menace***
3 *Colloquial* a nuisance
verb **4** to threaten (***bully***, ***intimidate***, ***terrorise***)

Word history: Middle English, from Old French, from Latin word meaning 'a threat'

menagerie (muh-<u>naj</u>-uh-ree)
noun *Old-fashioned* a collection of wild animals in cages for show

Word history: from French word meaning 'management of a household'

mend
verb **1** to make right or put into working order again (***correct***, ***fix***, ***renovate***, ***repair***, ***restore***)
2 to get better: *His broken arm is **mending**.*

Word history: variant of *amend*

Mendel's laws (<u>men</u>-duhlz lawz)
plural noun the basic principles of heredity, stating: **1** that the pairs of hereditary units carried by each cell separate completely during meiosis
2 that the separation of each pair happens independently of that of any other pair

Word building: **Mendelian** (men-<u>deel</u>-ee-uhn) *adjective* **Mendelism** *noun*
Word history: named after Gregor *Mendel*, 1822–84, Austrian biologist, founder of the study of genetics

menial (<u>mee</u>-nee-uhl)
adjective having to do with or fit for servants: ***menial** work*

Word building: **menial** *noun*
Word history: Middle English, from Anglo-French, from Latin word meaning 'household'

meninges (muh-<u>nin</u>-jeez)
plural noun the three membranes that surround the brain and spinal cord

Noun forms: The singular is **meninx** (<u>meen</u>-ingks).
Word history: New Latin, from Greek word meaning 'membrane', especially of the brain

meningitis (men-uhn-<u>juy</u>-tuhs)
noun an inflammation of the meninges

Word building: **meningitic** *adjective*
Word history: Neo-Latin, from Greek

meningococcal disease (muh-nin-juh-<u>kok</u>-uhl duh-zeez)
noun a form of meningitis marked by its rapid onset, with flu-like symptoms and a sometimes fatal outcome

meniscus (muh-<u>nis</u>-kuhs)
noun **1** something in the shape of a quarter moon (***crescent***)
2 the curved upper surface of a column of liquid

Noun forms: The plural is **menisci** (muh-<u>nis</u>-uy).
Word history: New Latin, from Greek word meaning 'crescent', 'little moon'

menopause (<u>men</u>-uh-pawz)
noun the time in a woman's life when her monthly periods stop altogether

Word building: **menopausal** *adjective*

men's business
noun **1** in Aboriginal societies, matters, especially cultural traditions, which are the exclusive domain of men
2 *Colloquial* (*humorous*) activities seen to be especially favoured or understood by men

Word use: You can also use **secret men's business**.

menstrual cycle
noun the approximately monthly cycle of ovulation and menstruation

menstruate (<u>men</u>-strooh-ayt)
verb to have a flow of blood and mucus from the womb, usually monthly

Word building: **menstrual** *adjective* **menstruation** *noun*

mental
adjective having to do with the mind (***cerebral***, ***intellectual***, ***psychological***)

Word history: Middle English, from Late Latin

mentality
noun **1** mental ability: *a person of average **mentality*** (***intellect***, ***intelligence***)
2 way of thinking: *to understand the Japanese **mentality***

mention
verb to briefly speak or write about

Word building: **mention** *noun*
Word history: from Latin word meaning 'a calling to mind', 'mention'

mentor (<u>men</u>-taw)
noun **1** a wise and trusted adviser: *Her mother has been her **mentor** for many years.* (***counsellor***, ***guide***, ***teacher***)
2 (in an organisation, school, etc.) an experienced senior employee or student who advises and assists a new employee or student

Word history: from *Mentor*, friend of Odysseus and guardian of his household when he went to Troy

mentoring
noun the pairing up of those with experience and knowledge with those who lack it: *He hoped that **mentoring** from the country's leader would help him in his career.*

menu
noun **1** a list of the dishes served at a meal or in a restaurant
2 *Computers* a list of options presented to an operator by a computer

Word history: French word meaning 'detailed list', originally an adjective, 'small', from Latin word meaning 'minute'

mercantilism (muh-<u>kan</u>-tuhl-iz-uhm, <u>mer</u>-kuhn-tuyl-iz-uhm)
noun a political and economic system of former times in which a state sought to gain political supremacy in its rivalry with other states by building up a supply of precious metals, boosting exports, limiting imports, and prohibiting the export of precious metals

mercenary (<u>mers</u>-uhn-ree, <u>mer</u>-suhn-uh-ree)
adjective **1** working or caring only for money: *She has a **mercenary** attitude to her art.*
noun **2** a soldier who is paid to fight in a foreign army

Noun forms: The plural is **mercenaries**.
Word history: from Latin word meaning 'hired for pay'

merchandise (<u>mer</u>-chuhn-duys)
noun **1** goods for sale
verb (<u>mer</u>-chuhn-duyz) **2** to buy and sell

Word history: Middle English, from Old French word meaning 'merchant'

merchant
noun someone who buys and sells goods (***broker***, ***dealer***, ***retailer***, ***seller***, ***vendor***)

Word building: **merchant** *adjective*
Word history: Middle English, from Old French, from Latin word meaning 'trade'

merchant bank
noun a bank which conducts banking for businesses and other large organisations, rather than individual customers

Word use: Compare this with **retail bank**.
Word building: **merchant banker** *noun* **merchant banking** *noun*

merchant navy
noun **1** the trading ships of a nation
2 the people working on these ships

Word use: You can also use **mercantile marine** or **merchant marine**.

mercurial (mer-<u>kyooh</u>-ree-uhl)
adjective rapidly changing in mood (***capricious***, ***erratic***, ***fickle***, ***flighty***, ***temperamental***)

mercury
noun a silvery, metallic element which is liquid instead of solid at ordinary temperatures

Word use: An old-fashioned word for this is **quicksilver**.
Word history: Middle English, from Latin *Mercurius*

mercy
noun kindness shown by not punishing or not being cruel (***clemency***, ***compassion***, ***forgiveness***, ***leniency***, ***pity***)

Noun forms: The plural is **mercies**.
Word building: **merciful** *adjective* **merciless** *adjective*
Word history: Middle English, from Old French word meaning 'favour', 'thanks', from Latin word meaning 'pay', Medieval Latin word meaning 'mercy'

mere
adjective being nothing more than: *You are a **mere** child.*

Word history: Middle English, from Latin word meaning 'pure', 'unmixed', 'mere'

merely
adverb only or just

merge (merj)
verb to unite or blend together: *The colours **merged**.* (***amalgamate***, ***combine***, ***fuse***, ***join***, ***mix***)

Word use: The opposite of this is **separate**.
Word history: from Latin word meaning 'dip', 'plunge', 'sink'

merger
noun a joining of two companies in business

meridian (muh-<u>rid</u>-ee-uhn)
noun a line of longitude

Word history: from Latin word meaning 'of midday', 'of the south'

meringue (muh-<u>rang</u>)
noun a mixture of sugar and beaten eggwhites used in cakes and sweets

Word history: French, perhaps from German word meaning 'cake of Mehringen'

merino (muh-<u>ree</u>-noh)
noun a type of sheep that has very fine wool

Noun forms: The plural is **merinos**.
Word history: Spanish, from Latin (*ariēs*) *mājōrīnus* (male sheep) of the larger sort

merit
noun **1** excellence: *a painting of* ***merit***
2 merits, the qualities or features of something or someone, whether good or bad: *Let's take each case on its* ***merits.***
verb **3** to deserve: *Her work* ***merits*** *praise.*

Verb forms: it **merited**, it has **merited**, it is **meriting**
Word history: Middle English, from French, from Latin word meaning 'deserved', 'earned'

meritorious (me-ruh-<u>taw</u>-ree-uhs)
adjective deserving of reward or praise

Word history: Middle English, from Medieval Latin word meaning 'meritorious', Latin word meaning 'serving to earn money'

mermaid
noun an imaginary sea creature, a woman from the waist up and a fish from the waist down

Word building: **merman** *masculine noun*
Word history: Middle English, from *mere* lake, from Latin + *maid*

merry
adjective cheerful or happy (***blithe***, ***glad***, ***gleeful***, ***jolly***, ***joyful***)

Word building: **merriment** *noun* **merrymaking** *noun*
Word history: Old English *myr(i)ge* pleasant, delightful

merry-go-round
noun a revolving circular platform with wooden horses or similar things on it, which people ride on for fun (***carousel***, ***roundabout***)

mesh
noun **1** a net or network: *nylon* ***mesh*** *for an insect screen | caught in the* ***meshes*** *of the law*
2 the space between the threads of a net, wire netting, etc.: *This net has a wide* ***mesh.***

Word building: **mesh** *verb* **enmesh** *verb*

mesmerise (<u>mez</u>-muh-ruyz)
verb to completely hold the attention of: *The beauty of the scenery* ***mesmerised*** *him.*

Word use: You can also use **mesmerize.** | This word once used to mean **hypnotise.**
Word building: **mesmerisation** *noun*

mess
noun **1** a dirty or untidy state (***clutter***, ***jumble***, ***litter***, ***muddle***, ***shambles***)
2 a difficult or confused state: *His life is in a* ***mess.***
3 a dining room, especially in the army
phrase **4 mess about** (or **around**), to waste time doing useless things

Word history: Middle English, from Old French word meaning 'put (on the table)', from Latin word meaning 'sent', 'put'

message
noun **1** information sent from one person to another (***communiqué***, ***dispatch***, ***note***, ***word***)
2 the meaning of something such as a book or what it tries to teach you
phrase **3 get the message**, to understand

Word history: Middle English, from Old French word meaning 'envoy', from Latin word meaning 'sent'

messenger
noun someone who carries a message (***courier***, ***envoy***, ***herald***, ***mail deliverer***)

Word history: Middle English, from Old French word meaning 'message'

Messiah (muh-<u>suy</u>-uh)
noun **1 a** (in Judaism) the expected deliverer of the Jewish people
b (in Christianity) Jesus, seen as this deliverer
2 any expected deliverer

Word building: **Messianic** (mes-ee-<u>an</u>-ik) *adjective*
Word history: variant of Latin *Messīas* (Vulgate), from Greek form of Hebrew word meaning 'anointed'

met
verb past tense and past participle of **meet**

metabolism (muh-<u>tab</u>-uh-liz-uhm)
noun all the processes and chemical changes happening in your body or any living thing

Word building: **metabolic** (met-uh-<u>bol</u>-ik) *adjective*
Word history: *meta-* + Greek *bolē* change + *-ism*

metadata (<u>met</u>-uh-day-tuh, <u>met</u>-uh-dah-tuh)
noun information about data, especially in relation to its structure and organisation

metal
noun an element such as iron, copper or gold which is shiny, able to be shaped or worked, and is a good conductor of electricity

Word building: **metallic** *adjective* **metalwork** *noun*
Word history: Middle English, from Old French, from Latin word meaning 'mine', 'mineral', 'metal', from Greek word meaning 'mine'

metal / mettle
Don't confuse **metal** with **mettle.** To be on your **mettle** is to be keyed up to do your very best. Something that tests your **mettle** is something that tests your courage or spirit.

metallurgy (<u>met</u>-uh-ler-jee, muh-<u>tal</u>-uh-jee)
noun the study of metals

metamorphic rock (met-uh-<u>maw</u>-fik rok)
noun a rock which shows changes in structure or composition caused by natural forces such as pressure and heat, as marble does

Word use: Compare this with **igneous rock** and **sedimentary rock.**

metamorphosis (met-uh-<u>maw</u>-fuh-suhs)
noun a change from one form to another: *the* ***metamorphosis*** *of a caterpillar into a butterfly*

Word building: **metamorphic** *adjective*
Word history: Latin, from Greek word meaning 'transformation'

metaphor (<u>met</u>-uh-faw, <u>met</u>-uh-fuh)
noun a figure of speech in which something is spoken of as if it were something else: *'Knowledge is a key that opens many doors' is a* ***metaphor.***

Word use: Compare this with **simile.**
Word building: **metaphorical** *adjective*
Word history: Latin word meaning from Greek word meaning 'a transfer'

metaphysical (met-uh-fiz-ik-uhl)
adjective having to do with subjects beyond the measurable physical world, such as the meaning of life, how the world began, what truth is, etc.

Word building: **metaphysics** *noun*
Word history: Medieval Latin, from Medieval Greek word meaning 'the (works) after the physics'; with reference to the arrangement of Aristotle's writings

metastasise (muh-tas-tuh-suyz)
verb (of a tumour) to invade other regions of the body by spreading cancerous cells: *The doctor didn't think that her tumour would* ***metastasise****.*

Verb forms: it **metastasised**, it has **metastasised**, it is **metastasising**
Word use: You can also use **metastasize**.

meteor (mee-tee-uh, mee-tee-aw)
noun a small, rocklike object from outer space which enters the earth's atmosphere making a fiery streak across the sky

Word history: late Middle English, from Neo-Latin, from Greek word meaning 'raised', 'high in air'

meteoric (mee-tee-o-rik)
adjective brilliant, fast, or passing quickly, like a meteor (***dazzling***, ***flashing***, ***fleeting***, ***rapid***, ***spectacular***)

meteorite
noun a mass of stone or metal that has reached the earth from outer space

meteoroid (meet-ee-uh-royd)
noun any of the small bodies, often remnants of comets, travelling through space, which, when meeting the earth's atmosphere, are heated to the point where they light up, thus becoming meteors

meteorology (mee-tee-uh-rol-uh-jee)
noun the study of weather and climate

Word building: **meteorological** *adjective* **meteorologist** *noun*
Word history: Greek

meter
noun an instrument that measures, especially one that measures the amount of gas, electricity or water passing through it (***dial***, ***gauge***)

Word history: Middle English

meter / metre
Don't confuse **meter** with **metre**, which is a unit of length, equal to 100 centimetres.

methadone (meth-uh-dohn)
noun a synthetic substitute for morphine, used in the treatment of morphine addiction

methamphetamine (meth-uhm-fet-uh-meen)
noun a synthetic drug which acts as a powerful central nervous system stimulant

methane (mee-thayn)
noun a colourless, odourless, flammable gas, the main constituent of marsh gas and firedamp of coal mines, the first member of the alkane series of hydrocarbons; a greenhouse gas

metho (meth-oh)
noun Colloquial → **methylated spirits**

Word history: modified shortened form of *methylated* + *-o*

method
noun a way of going about something, especially an orderly way: *a* ***method*** *for doing a sum* (***approach***, ***means***, ***mode***, ***procedure***, ***technique***)

Word history: Latin word meaning 'mode of procedure', 'method', from Greek word meaning 'a following after', 'method'

method acting
noun an acting technique where actors immerse themselves in the character they are portraying

Word building: **method actor** *noun*

methodical (muh-thod-ik-uhl)
adjective done or acting in a careful, ordered way: *That scientist achieved great results from* ***methodical*** *study.* (***disciplined***, ***organised***, ***planned***, ***structured***, ***systematic***)

Word use: The opposite of this is **haphazard**.

methylated spirits (meth-uh-lay-tuhd spi-ruhts)
noun a liquid used for cleaning and sometimes as a fuel

meticulous (muh-tik-yuh-luhs)
adjective careful about small details: *He was* ***meticulous*** *in his personal appearance.* (***exact***, ***fastidious***, ***fussy***, ***particular***, ***thorough***)

Word use: The opposite of this is **careless**.
Word history: from Latin word meaning 'fearful'

metre[1] (mee-tuh)
noun a unit of length in the metric system

Word use: The symbol for **metre** is **m**, without a full stop. **Metre** is the spelling recommended by the Standards Association of Australia, but you may sometimes find the spelling **meter** used for this word. This is the usual spelling in the US. | Look up **metric system**.
Word history: French, from Greek word meaning 'measure'

metre[2] (mee-tuh)
noun the arrangement of words in poetry into lines or verses with certain rhythmic patterns

Word building: **metrical** (met-rik-uhl) *adjective*
Word history: Middle English, from French, from Latin

metre / meter
Look up **meter / metre**.

metric (met-rik)
adjective belonging to the system of measurement based on the metre

Word building: **metricate** *verb*
Word history: French

metrication (met-ruh-kay-shuhn)
noun the process of conversion from British or imperial units to the metric system

metric system
noun the international standard system of weights and measures based on the number 10 which uses units such as the metre, kilometre, kilogram and litre. It was introduced into Australia in 1970 and replaced the imperial system.

Word use: Look up **imperial system**.

metronome (met-ruh-nohm)
noun an instrument that can be set to beat at a fixed rate and so give the right speed of performance for a piece of music

Word history: from Greek word meaning 'measure'

metropolis (muh-trop-uh-luhs)
noun a large city, not necessarily the capital, in a country, state, or region

Word history: Late Latin, from Greek word meaning 'a mother state or city'

metropolitan (met-ruh-pol-uh-tuhn)
adjective having to do with a large city (***urban***)

metrosexual
noun **1** a heterosexual male who devotes considerable attention to his appearance and presentation
adjective **2** having to do with such a male

Word building: **metrosexuality** *noun*

mettle
noun **1** the quality of someone's character, especially when spirited or brave: *We need a woman of **mettle** for this job.*
phrase **2 on your mettle**, eager to do your best

Word history: variant of metal

mettle / metal
Don't confuse **mettle** with **metal**, which is a hard substance like gold, silver, copper or iron.

Mexican wave
noun a wave-like motion among spectators at a sporting match, rock concert, etc., achieved by having sections of the crowd stand up with their arms above their heads and then sit down, in sequence

Word history: from the soccer World Cup finals in Mexico, June 1986, where it was first performed

mezzanine (mez-uh-neen, mez-uh-neen)
noun a balcony-like floor in a building, usually between the ground floor and the next

Word history: French, from Italian, from Latin word meaning 'median'

mica (muy-kuh)
noun any member of a group of minerals, complex silicates of aluminium with other bases, chiefly potassium, magnesium, iron and lithium, that separate easily by cleavage into thin, tough, often transparent sheets

Word building: **micaceous** *adjective*
Word history: from Neo-Latin, special use of Latin word meaning 'crumb', 'grain', 'little bit'

mice (muys)
noun a plural of **mouse**

micro
adjective individual or particular: *at the **micro** level*

Word use: Compare this with **macro**.

microbe
noun a tiny living creature which is so small that it can only be seen under a microscope, and which usually carries disease

Word history: French, from Greek word meaning 'small life'

microbiology (muy-kroh-buy-ol-uh-jee)
noun the science and study of microscopic organisms

Word building: **microbiological** *adjective* **microbiologist** *noun*
Word history: from Greek word meaning 'small' + *biology*

microblog
noun **1** an internet posting which is extremely short, usually up to 140 characters
verb **2** to issue such an internet posting: *She **microblogged** her latest news.*

Verb forms: I **microblogged**, I have **microblogged**, I am **microblogging**
Word building: **microblogging** *noun* **microblogger** *noun*

microbusiness
noun a small business operated by one person

microchip
noun a very small electronic chip

microclimate
noun the climate affecting a localised region, often created by terrain or conditions which are not prevalent throughout the wider area, ranging from something as small as a garden bed to something as large as a valley

Word use: Compare this with **macroclimate**.
Word building: **microclimatic** *adjective* **microclimatically** *adverb*

microcomputer
noun a small computer that will fit on your desk, and is meant for only one person to use at a time

microcosm (muy-kruh-koz-uhm)
noun **1** a little world
2 anything regarded as a world in miniature

Word use: Compare this with **macrocosm**.
Word building: **microcosmic** *adjective*
Word history: French, from Late Latin, from Late Greek word meaning 'little world'

microfauna
noun very small animals, usually too small to be seen with the naked eye

Word use: Look up **macrofauna**.

microfiche (muy-kroh-feesh)
noun a sheet of transparent plastic about the size of a filing card which may have many pages of print on it that can be read with a special projector

Word history: French

microfilm
noun a photographic film with very small images which can be enlarged when projected, and which is used for storing information

microlight aircraft
noun an ultralight aircraft with weight shift controls for stabilisation

Word use: You can also use **microlight**.

micrometer (muy-krom-uh-tuh)
noun a device for measuring very small distances, angles, etc., used with a telescope or microscope

Word building: **micrometry** *noun*

microorganism (muy-kroh-awg-uhn-iz-uhm)
noun a microscopic animal or vegetable organism

microphone
noun an instrument which changes sound waves into electrical waves, often used in equipment that makes sounds louder or records them

microprocessor
noun the most important electronic chip in a microcomputer

microscope
noun an instrument used for looking at extremely tiny things that you normally can't see

Word history: from *micro-* very small + Greek word meaning 'view'

microscopic (muy-kruh-skop-ik)
adjective extremely small

microwave
noun **1** an electromagnetic wave of very high frequency, with a wavelength range from 50 cm to 1 mm
2 a microwave oven

microwave oven
noun an oven which cooks food very quickly by passing high-speed microwaves through it

mid
adjective at or near the middle point: *in the **mid** nineties of the last century* (***central***)

Word history: Middle English; Old English *midd*

midair
noun **1** any raised position above the ground
2 a position or state where things are not decided or finished: *She was left in **midair**, not knowing what was going to happen.*

midday
noun twelve o'clock in the middle of the day (***noon***)

Word history: Middle English; Old English *middæg*

middle
noun a halfway point: *the **middle** of the road | the **middle** of the discussion* (***centre***, ***core***, ***heart***, ***hub***, ***nucleus***)

Word building: **middle** *adjective*
Word history: Middle English and Old English *middel*

middle-aged
adjective between youth and old age: *They were a **middle-aged** couple with children at university.*

middle class
noun a social grouping of people who are neither very rich, nor come from a long established and well-off family, nor very poor, but work at a job that pays them well enough to live comfortably, such as businesspeople, doctors, lawyers, teachers, public servants, etc.

Word use: Compare this with **lower class** and **upper class**.
Word building: **middle-class** *adjective*

middleman
noun **1** a person who makes a profit by buying from producers and selling to retailers or consumers
2 someone who acts as an intermediary between others

Noun forms: The plural is **middlemen**.
Word use: You can also use **middle man**.

middling (mid-ling)
adjective medium in size, quality, grade, rank, etc.: *of **middling** height*

middy (mid-ee)
noun *Australian* a medium size glass, mainly used for serving beer

Noun forms: The plural is **middies**.

midge (mij)
noun a type of two-winged insect, some kinds of which bite

Word use: Compare this with **gnat**.
Word history: Old English *mycg*

midget
noun a very small person or thing

midnight
noun twelve o'clock at night

midriff
noun the part of your body between the chest and the waist

Word history: Old English *midd* mid + *hrif* belly

midshipman (mid-ship-muhn)
noun a probationary rank held by naval cadets to see whether they can qualify as officers

Noun forms: The plural is **midshipmen**.

midst
noun **1** the position of anything surrounded by other things or parts, or coming in the middle of a period of time, course of action, etc.
2 the middle point, part, or stage
phrase **3 in our midst**, among us: *We have a genius **in our midst**!*

Word history: Middle English *middes* middle

midwife
noun a nurse specially trained to help a woman while she is giving birth to a baby

Noun forms: The plural is **midwives**.
Word building: **midwifery** (mid-wif-uh-ree) *noun*
Word history: Middle English, from *mid* with, + *wife*

might[1]
verb **1** past tense of **may**
2 could possibly: *He **might** be lost.*

Word use: This is an auxiliary verb, always used with another one.

might[2]
noun power or force (***strength***, ***vigour***)

Word history: Old English

> **might / could**
> Look up **could / might**.

> **might / mite**
> Don't confuse **might** with **mite**, which is a small insect.

might've
contraction of **might have**

> Look up **contractions in grammar**.

mighty
adjective **1** powerful: *a **mighty** king* (***dominant***, ***forceful***, ***potent***, ***strong***)
2 huge: *a **mighty** mountain* (***colossal***, ***enormous***, ***gigantic***, ***massive***, ***vast***)

migraine (muy-grayn)
noun a very bad headache which makes you feel ill
Word history: French

migrant (muy-gruhnt)
noun someone who leaves their own country to go and live in another (***emigrant***, ***immigrant***)
Word history: Latin

migrate (muy-grayt)
verb **1** to change the place of living at regular times each year, as some birds do
2 to go to live in another country: *Many people have **migrated** from South-East Asia to Australia.*
Word building: **migratory** *adjective*
Word history: Latin

> **migrate / emigrate / immigrate**
> Look up **emigrate / immigrate / migrate**.

migration (muy-gray-shuhn)
noun **1** the act of migrating
2 a number of persons or animals migrating together

mild
adjective **1** gentle: *a **mild** voice* (***calm***, ***kind***, ***quiet***, ***soft***)
2 not severe: ***mild** pain*
3 not sharp or strong: *a **mild** flavour*
Word building: **mildness** *noun*
Word history: Old English

mildew
noun a coating or growth which appears on damp cloth, paper, leather and other materials

mile
noun a unit of length in the imperial system, equal to about 1.6 kilometres
Word use: Look up **imperial system**.
Word history: Old English, from Latin word meaning 'a thousand'

mileage (muy-lij)
noun **1** the total length or distance stated in miles
2 advantageous use: *The opposition got a lot of **mileage** out of the scandal involving the Prime Minister.*

milestone
noun **1** (formerly) a stone set up to mark the distance to or from a town or city, especially along a highway
2 an event marking an important point in someone's life or career

milieu (mee-lyer)
noun the total surrounding area, state or atmosphere in which someone lives or operates: *the social **milieu** | the cultural **milieu*** (***environment***, ***environs***, ***habitat***, ***surroundings***)
Word history: French, from Latin

militant
adjective fighting or ready to fight, especially for a cause: *a **militant** supporter of Aboriginal land rights* (***aggressive***, ***combative***)
Word building: **militancy** *noun* **militant** *noun*
Word history: Middle English, from Latin word meaning 'serving as a soldier'

military
adjective having to do with soldiers: *a **military** hospital*
Word history: Latin

militate
verb to influence or affect: *Poor weather **militated** against the climbers' plans of reaching the summit. | an activist group **militating** in favour of a change in the law*

militia (muh-lish-uh)
noun **1** a group of part-time citizen soldiers
2 one such soldier
Word history: from Latin word meaning 'military service'

milk
noun the white liquid produced by female mammals to feed their young, especially cow's milk
Word building: **milky** *adjective*
Word history: Old English

milk bar
noun a shop where drinks, especially milkshakes, ice-cream, sandwiches, etc., are sold

milkshake
noun a frothy drink made of milk, flavouring and ice-cream, shaken together

milk tooth
noun one of the temporary or first teeth of a mammal which are replaced by the permanent teeth (***baby tooth***)

mill
noun **1** a building with machinery for grinding grain into flour
2 a small grinding machine: *a coffee **mill** | a pepper **mill***
3 a factory, especially one for spinning or weaving: *a woollen **mill***
verb **4** to grind, work or shape in or with a mill (***crumble***, ***crush***, ***pound***, ***pulverise***)
phrase **5 go through the mill**, to undergo a difficult experience: *She's really **gone through the mill** since the death of her husband.*
Word building: **miller** *noun*
Word history: Old English, from Latin word meaning 'millstone', 'mill'

millennium
noun a period of 1000 years
Word history: Neo-Latin, from Latin *mīlle* thousand + *-ennium*

> This word is often spelt *millenium*, but this is not regarded as correct.

millet
noun a cereal grain grown in Asia and southern Europe
Word history: Middle English, from French, from Latin

millibar
noun in the metric system, a unit of measurement for air pressure, especially in the atmosphere

Word use: Look up **metric system**.

milligram
noun in the metric system, a unit of weight equal to 0.001 gram

Word use: The symbol is **mg**, without a full stop. | Look up **metric system**.

millilitre
noun in the metric system, a unit of measurement of liquid equal to 0.001 litre

Word use: The symbol is **ml**, without a full stop. | Look up **metric system**. | The US spelling is **milliliter**.

millimetre
noun in the metric system, a unit of length equal to 0.001 metre

Word use: The symbol is **mm**, without a full stop. | Look up **metric system**. | The US spelling is **millimeter**.

milliner (mil-uh-nuh)
noun someone who makes or sells hats for women

Word history: variant of obsolete *Milaner*, an inhabitant of Milan, a dealer in articles from Milan

million
noun **1** a cardinal number, one thousand times one thousand, 1 000 000 or 10^6
2 a very great number
adjective **3** amounting to a million in number

Word building: **millionth** *adjective* **millionth** *noun*

millionaire
noun someone who has a million dollars or more

Word history: from French word meaning 'million'

millipede
noun a small creature like a caterpillar with a long body made up of many parts, most of which have two pairs of legs

Word history: from Latin word meaning 'wood louse'

millstone
noun **1** in the past, either of a pair of large, circular stones between which grain or other substance was ground, as in a mill
phrase **2 a millstone around your neck**, something which causes you continuing problems (***encumbrance***, ***load***, ***weight***)

mime
noun **1** a form of acting in which the actors tell the story by using movements of their body and face instead of words
2 a play in which the performers use this form of acting

Word building: **mime** *verb*
Word history: Latin, from Greek

MIME
noun Computers an encoding method for converting non-ASCII data into ASCII data and back to the original format so that the data can be emailed

Word history: *M(ultipurpose) I(nternet) M(ail) E(xtensions)*

mimic
verb **1** to copy or imitate (***ape***, ***caricature***, ***impersonate***, ***mock***, ***send up***)
noun **2** someone who is good at imitating the voice and movements of others

Verb forms: I **mimicked**, I have **mimicked**, I am **mimicking**
Word building: **mimicry** *noun*
Word history: Latin, from Greek word meaning 'belonging to mimes'

minaret (min-uh-ret, min-uh-ret)
noun a tall tower attached to a Muslim mosque, from which the muezzin (crier) calls the people to prayer

Word history: Spanish, from Arabic word meaning 'lighthouse'

mince
verb **1** to cut or chop into very small pieces
2 to speak, walk or move in a dainty way
noun **3** meat that has been minced
phrase **4 not mince (your) words**, to tell someone something unpleasant without trying to soften what you are saying to avoid upsetting them: *I'm sorry you're hurt, but you know that I don't **mince words**.*

Word history: Middle English, from Old French word meaning 'make small', from Latin word meaning 'small'

mincemeat
noun **1** a mixture composed of minced apples, suet, candied peel, raisins, currants, etc., for filling a pie
2 meat that has been minced
phrase **3 make mincemeat of**, *Colloquial* to successfully attack: *The opposition **made mincemeat of** the Prime Minister during the debate.*

mind
noun **1** the part of you that thinks and feels, using judgement, memory, etc.
2 intelligence, understanding or mental ability
3 memory: *Keep this in **mind**.*
4 your opinion or what you think or feel: *Feel free to speak your **mind**.*
verb **5** to look after: *Will you **mind** the baby?*
6 to dislike or feel bad about: *Do you **mind** the cold weather?*
phrase **7 make up your mind**, to come to a decision
8 out of your mind, severely disturbed or upset (***crazy***, ***insane***, ***loony***, ***maniacal***, ***nutty***, ***unbalanced***)
9 presence of mind, ability to act quickly and effectively when faced with danger or difficulty

Word history: from Old English word meaning 'memory', 'thought'

mindful
phrase **mindful of**, careful about: *She is usually **mindful of** other people's feelings.* (***alert to***, ***attentive to***, ***awake to***, ***aware of***)

mind game
noun **1** a contest in which psychological pressure is critical in deciding the outcome: *Golf is the ultimate **mind game**.*
phrase **2 play mind games**, to exert psychological pressure: *to **play mind games** with the opposition*

mindless
adjective done without thinking

mind map
noun a visual representation of the way in which concepts are related around a central key word or idea

mine[1]
noun **1** a large hole dug in the earth to remove precious stones, coal, etc.
2 a rich store of anything: *This book is a* ***mine*** *of information.*
3 a bomb placed underground or in the sea to blow up the enemy or their ships

Word history: Old English

mine[2]
pronoun **1** the possessive form of **I**, used without a noun following: *That black dog is* ***mine****.*
2 the person(s) or thing(s) belonging to me: ***Mine*** *is that black dog over there.*

> **Mine** is a first person singular pronoun in the possessive case.
> For more information, look up **pronouns: personal pronouns** and **pronouns: possessive pronouns.**

miner[1]
noun someone who works in a mine

miner[2]
noun a type of bird with a yellow beak and yellow or yellow-brown legs: *noisy* ***miner***

> **miner / minor**
> Don't confuse **miner** with **minor**, which means 'lesser in size, extent, or importance' as in *a minor share* or a *minor weakness.* A **minor** is also someone under the legal adult age.

mineral
noun a substance such as stone, ore or coal which is obtained by mining

Word building: **mineral** *adjective*
Word history: Middle English, from Medieval Latin word meaning 'of a mine', from Old French word meaning 'mine'

mineral water
noun water containing dissolved mineral salts and gases

minestrone (min-uh-stroh-nee)
noun a soup made with vegetables, herbs, pasta, etc.

Word history: Italian, from a Latin word meaning 'serve' or 'wait on'

mingle
verb **1** to become mixed: *Her tears* ***mingled*** *with the rain on her face.* (***blend***, ***combine***, ***intermix***, ***merge***)
2 to take part with others or to associate with: *She* ***mingled*** *with the rest of the guests.*

Word history: Old English *mengan*

> **mini-**
> is a fairly new prefix, meaning 'small in size'. You'll find it in *mini-budget*, *minibus*, *minigolf*, *mini-series*, *miniskirt*, *mini-van* and other words.

> Because mini- is still quite new, people often use a hyphen when writing words with it (for example, *mini-budget*, *mini-van*). But as the words and the prefix become more familiar, the hyphen tends to disappear.

miniature (min-uh-chuh)
noun **1** a very small copy or model of something: *Some model aeroplanes are exact* ***miniatures*** *of the real thing.*
2 a very small painting, especially a portrait
adjective **3** on a very small scale or much reduced in size (***baby***, ***diminutive***, ***dwarf***, ***pocket-sized***, ***scaled-down***)

Word history: Italian, from Latin

minibus
noun a motor vehicle designed to carry between five and ten passengers

Noun forms: The plural is **minibuses**.

minigolf
noun a form of golf played on a very small course with contrived obstacles and hazards

minim
noun a note in music equal to half a semibreve in length

Word history: Middle English, from Latin word meaning 'least', 'smallest'

minimise
verb to reduce to the smallest possible amount (***cut back***, ***decrease***, ***lessen***, ***lower***, ***shrink***)

Word use: The opposite of this is **maximise**. | You can also use **minimize**.
Word building: **minimisation** *noun*

minimum
noun **1** the smallest number or amount possible: *You have to get a* ***minimum*** *of four points to qualify.*
2 the lowest number

Noun forms: The plural is **minimums** or **minima**.
Word use: The opposite is **maximum**.
Word building: **minimal** *adjective* **minimum** *adjective*
Word history: Latin

miniskirt
noun a very short skirt

Word use: You can also use **mini**.

minister
noun **1** a member of the clergy who conducts services in a church (***chaplain***, ***clergyman***, ***parson***, ***priest***, ***vicar***)
2 a member of parliament who is in charge of a government department
phrase **3 minister to**, to give service or care to: *He* ***ministered*** *to the sick people.* (***aid***, ***assist***, ***help***, ***support***, ***tend***)

Word building: **ministerial** (min-uh-stear-ree-uhl) *adjective*
Word history: from Latin word meaning 'servant'

ministry
noun **1** the service, work or profession of a minister of religion
2 in parliament, the service, work, department, or headquarters of a minister of state

Noun forms: The plural is **ministries**.

mink
noun **1** a small, furry, meat-eating animal of Asia, Europe and North America
2 the valuable fur of this animal
Word history: Scandinavian

minor
adjective **1** lesser in size or importance: *a **minor** share | His plan had only a few **minor** faults.* (***insignificant***, ***secondary***, ***slight***, ***trifling***, ***trivial***)
noun **2** someone who is under the legal adult age
Word history: from Latin word meaning 'less', 'inferior', 'younger'

minor / miner
Look up **miner / minor**.

minority (muy-no-ruh-tee)
noun **1** the smaller part or number, or less than half
2 a group of people whose views are different to the views of most other people: *There will always be a **minority** which does not agree with the laws of this country.*
Noun forms: The plural is **minorities**.
Word use: The opposite of this is **majority**.

minority / majority
Look up **majority / minority**.

minor scale
noun any musical scale which has a semitone between the second and third notes
Word use: Such a scale is said to be in a *minor key*. | Compare this with **major scale**.

minstrel
noun a musician in the Middle Ages who sang or recited poetry while playing an instrument
Word history: Middle English, from Old French word meaning 'servant', from Late Latin

mint[1]
noun **1** a herb with leaves that are used in cooking
2 a peppermint
Word history: Old English, from Latin, from Greek

mint[2]
noun **1** a place where money is made by the government
verb **2** to make money in a mint
phrase **3 in mint condition**, new or looking like new: *The second-hand car was **in mint condition**.*
Word history: Old English word meaning 'coin', from Latin word meaning 'money'

minuet (min-yooh-et)
noun **1** a slow, stately dance of French origin
2 a piece of music for such a dance or in its rhythm
Word history: from French word meaning 'very small' (with reference to the small steps taken in the dance)

minus
preposition **1** *Mathematics* subtracting or taking away: *5 **minus** 2 is 3.*
2 of a temperature, below zero on the scale: *It's too cold to go out to play — it's **minus** 10° outside.*
3 without or missing: *We arrived **minus** our luggage.*
noun **4** a negative point or disadvantage: *Our new car doesn't have power steering — that's a big **minus**.*
Word history: Latin

minuscule (min-uhs-kyoohl)
adjective **1** having to do with letters, small, not capital
2 tiny (***diminutive***, ***microscopic***, ***miniature***, ***minute***)
Word history: from Latin word meaning 'rather small'

This is sometimes spelt *miniscule*, probably because some people associate the word with **mini-**; this is usually thought of as incorrect.

minute[1] (min-uht)
noun **1** a sixtieth part of an hour
2 any short space of time: *Wait a **minute**.* (***instant***, ***moment***)
3 minutes, the official record of what has been discussed in a meeting
phrase **4 up to the minute**, very up-to-date
Word history: Middle English, from Old French, from Medieval Latin word meaning 'small part or division', from Latin

minute[2] (muy-nyooht)
adjective extremely small: *She got a **minute** piece of dirt in her eye.* (***diminutive***, ***microscopic***, ***miniature***, ***minuscule***, ***tiny***)
Word history: Middle English, from Latin word meaning 'made smaller'

minutiae (muh-nyooh-shee-uy)
plural noun small or unimportant details
Word history: plural of Late Latin *minutia* smallness

miracle
noun **1** an event which can't be explained by natural or scientific evidence or arguments: *The Bible tells of many wonderful **miracles**.*
2 a wonderful or remarkable thing: *It was a **miracle** that the lost child was found.* (***marvel***, ***wonder***)
Word building: **miraculous** (muh-rak-yuh-luhs) *adjective*
Word history: Middle English, from Old French, from Latin

mirage (muh-rahzh)
noun an illusion or false vision in which someone sees distant things as much closer than they really are, or even sees things that are not there at all
Word history: French word meaning 'look at (oneself) in a mirror', 'see reflected', from Vulgar Latin

mire (muy-uh)
noun **1** wet, swampy ground (***bog***, ***marsh***, ***quagmire***, ***swamp***)
2 deep mud
Word building: **miry** *adjective*
Word history: Middle English, from Scandinavian

mirror
noun **1** glass that has been treated so that you can see yourself reflected in it
2 something that gives a true picture of something else: *This story is a **mirror** of my true feelings.*
3 *Internet* an exact copy of a website, often set up in a position remote from the original so that users can access the information from the site which is physically closer to them

Word building: **mirror** *verb*
Word history: Middle English, from Old French, from Medieval Latin word meaning 'wonder at', 'admire'

mirth (merth)
noun amusement and laughter: ***Mirth** rippled through the audience.* (***gaiety**, **glee**, **happiness**, **high spirits**, **merriment***)

Word history: Old English *myr(g)th*, *myrigth*, from *myrige* merry

misadventure
noun **1** bad luck or a piece of ill fortune
2 an accident or mishap

misanthropic (miz-uhn-<u>throp</u>-ik)
adjective hating people in general

Word building: **misanthropy** (miz-<u>an</u>-thruh-pee) *noun*
Word history: from Greek word meaning 'hating humankind'

misappropriate (mis-uh-<u>proh</u>-pree-ayt)
verb **1** to put to a wrong use
2 to use wrongfully or dishonestly: *to **misappropriate** money*

Word building: **misappropriation** *noun*

misbehave
verb to behave badly: *I was embarrassed when he **misbehaved** at the party.*

Word building: **misbehaviour** *noun*

miscarriage
noun **1** the failure to get the right result or decision: *a **miscarriage** of justice*
2 the birth of a dead baby, especially early in a pregnancy

Word building: **miscarry** *verb* (**miscarried**, **miscarrying**)

miscellaneous (mis-uh-<u>lay</u>-nee-uhs)
adjective made up of a mixture of different kinds: *He kept a **miscellaneous** collection of items like bottle tops, pens and clips in his desk.* (***assorted**, **diverse**, **mixed**, **motley**, **various***)

Word history: from Latin word meaning 'mixed'

miscellany (muh-<u>sel</u>-uh-nee)
noun **1** a miscellaneous collection of pieces by several writers, dealing with various topics
2 a miscellaneous collection of objects

Noun forms: The plural is **miscellanies**.

mischief (<u>mis</u>-chuhf)
noun **1** behaviour meant to tease or annoy
2 harm, injury or trouble

Word building: **mischievous** *adjective*
Word history: Middle English, from Old French word meaning 'succeed ill'

miscommunicate
verb **1** to fail in communicating (a message, idea, etc.), so that the recipient has no understanding or a wrong understanding of the message
2 to fail in communicating in this way

Verb forms: I **miscommunicated**, I have **miscommunicated**, I am **miscommunicating**
Word building: **miscommunication** *noun*

misdemeanour (mis-duh-<u>meen</u>-uh)
noun an instance of bad behaviour (***misdeed**, **offence**, **transgression***)

Word use: You can also use **misdemeanor**.

miser (<u>muy</u>-zuh)
noun **1** someone who lives very poorly so as to save and store up money
2 someone who is mean and greedy

Word use: The opposite of definition 1 is **spendthrift**. | The opposite of definition 2 is **generous**.
Word building: **miserly** *adjective*
Word history: from Latin word meaning 'wretched', 'unhappy', 'sick', 'bad'

miserable (<u>miz</u>-ruh-buhl, <u>miz</u>-uh-ruh-buhl)
adjective **1** very unhappy or uncomfortable (***depressed**, **despondent**, **forlorn**, **glum**, **sad***)
2 causing unhappiness or discomfort: ***miserable** weather* (***bleak**, **cheerless**, **depressing**, **dismal**, **dreary***)
3 mean and stingy (***miserly**, **penny-pinching**, **thrifty**, **tight***)

Word history: from Latin word meaning 'pitiable'

misery (<u>miz</u>-uh-ree)
noun great unhappiness (***anguish**, **depression**, **gloom**, **melancholy**, **sorrow***)

Noun forms: The plural is **miseries**.

misfire
verb **1** to fail to fire or explode properly
2 to go wrong or to fail: *His plan to take over **misfired**.* (***collapse**, **fall through**, **miscarry***)

misfit
noun someone who does not fit in or get along well in their job or with other people

misfortune
noun **1** bad luck
2 an instance of bad luck (***accident**, **blow**, **calamity**, **disaster**, **mishap***)

misgiving
noun a feeling of doubt or worry

mishap (<u>mis</u>-hap)
noun an unfortunate accident (***blow**, **disaster**, **mischance**, **misfortune***)

mishmash
noun a disordered mass of things thrown together (***clutter**, **jumble**, **mess**, **muddle**, **shambles***)

mislay
verb to put in a place which you forget afterwards: *I have **mislaid** my pen again.*

Verb forms: I **mislaid**, I have **mislaid**, I am **mislaying**

mislead
verb **1** to lead or guide wrongly (***deceive**, **delude**, **dupe**, **hoodwink**, **trick***)
2 to influence badly or to lead into error or wrongdoing: *His friends were **misleading** him into bad habits.*

Verb forms: I **misled**, I have **misled**, I am **misleading**
Word building: **misleading** *adjective*

misnomer (mis-noh-muh)
noun a name or designation used wrongly: *Calling him an expert is a bit of a **misnomer**.*

Word history: Middle English, from Old French

misogyny (muh-soj-uh-nee)
noun hatred of women

Word building: **misogynist** *noun* **misogynous** *adjective*
Word history: Greek

misprint (mis-print)
noun **1** a mistake in printing
verb (mis-print) **2** to print incorrectly

misrepresent
verb to describe or show someone or something in an incorrect or false way

Word building: **misrepresentation** *noun*

miss[1]
verb **1** to fail to hit, meet, catch, see, hear, etc.
2 to fail to attend
3 to notice or feel sad about the absence or loss of: *She **missed** her sister when she went away.*
4 to escape or avoid (***elude***, ***evade***, ***shirk***, ***steer clear of***)
phrase **5 miss out**, to fail to be present, as at a function, or to fail to receive, especially something you particularly want

Word building: **miss** *noun*
Word history: Old English

miss[2]
noun **1** a girl or young unmarried woman
2 Miss, a title sometimes put before an unmarried woman's name

Look up **Ms**.

misshapen (mis-shayp-uhn)
adjective badly shaped (***bent***, ***crooked***, ***deformed***, ***distorted***)

missile (mis-uyl)
noun an object or weapon that can be thrown or shot (***projectile***)

Word history: from Latin word meaning 'something which can be thrown'

missing
adjective absent or not found

mission (mish-uhn)
noun **1** a group of people sent out, usually to another country, to do government or religious work
2 a duty someone is sent to carry out (***assignment***, ***errand***, ***task***)

Word history: from Latin word meaning 'a sending'

missionary (mish-uhn-ree)
noun someone sent out, often to another country, on religious work

Noun forms: The plural is **missionaries**.

mission statement
noun a formal statement of the goals of an organisation

mist
noun a cloud-like collection of water vapour, like a very thin fog

Word history: Old English

mistake
noun **1** an error or misunderstanding (***blue***, ***blunder***, ***misconception***)
verb **2** to believe to be someone or something different: *He always **mistakes** me for my sister.*
3 to misunderstand: *She **mistook** my meaning.* (***misinterpret***, ***misread***)

Verb forms: I **mistook**, I have **mistaken**, I am **mistaking**
Word history: Middle English, from Scandinavian

mister
noun **1** *Colloquial* a form of address for a man: *Hello **mister**, what's your name?*
2 Mister, a title put before a man's name

Word use: **Mister** is usually written **Mr**, without a full stop.
Word history: variant of *master*

mistletoe (mis-uhl-toh)
noun **1** a plant with small, white berries which feeds and grows on the branches of other trees, and is often used for Christmas decorations
2 a parasitic plant which grows on Australian trees

Word history: Old English *mistel* meaning 'bird droppings' and *tan* twig, from the fact that little mistletoe shoots came out of bird droppings, the birds having eaten the seeds

mistreat
verb to treat cruelly or in an incorrect way

Word building: **mistreatment** *noun*

mistress
noun **1** a woman in charge of a household, servants, etc.
2 a female owner of an animal like a dog or a horse
3 *Australian* a female teacher in charge of a particular subject or department at school
4 a woman who has a sexual relationship with a man who is married to someone else

Word history: Middle English, from Old French, feminine of *maistre* master

mistrust
noun suspicion, or a lack of trust or confidence (***distrust***, ***doubt***, ***scepticism***, ***wariness***)

Word use: The opposite of this is **trust** or **believe**.
Word building: **mistrust** *verb* **mistrustful** *adjective*

misunderstanding
noun **1** a failure to understand correctly: *There seems to be some **misunderstanding** about the date of the birthday party.*
2 a disagreement or quarrel

Word building: **misunderstand** *verb* (**misunderstood**, **misunderstanding**)

misuse (mis-yoohs)
noun **1** wrong use: ***Misuse** of some medicines can be dangerous.*
verb (mis-yoohz) **2** to use in the wrong way
3 to treat badly

mite
noun a tiny, insect-like creature which lives in food like cheese or flour or feeds off plants and animals

Word history: Old English

mite / might

Don't confuse **mite** with **might**, which is power, as in the phrase *with all your might*.

Might is also the paste tense of **may**.

mitigate (mit-uh-gayt)
verb to make less intense or severe: *medication to* ***mitigate*** *pain* (***cut back***, ***decrease***, ***lessen***, ***lower***, ***reduce***)

Word building: **mitigator** *noun* **mitigation** *noun*
Word history: Middle English, from Medieval Latin

mitosis (muy-toh-suhs)
noun an asexual method of cell division in which the chromosomes in the cell nucleus double and then separate to form two identical cells

Word use: Compare this with **meiosis.**
Word building: **mitotic** *adjective*
Word history: New Latin, from Greek word meaning 'a thread' + *osis*

mitre (muy-tuh)
noun **1** the tall headdress worn by a bishop
2 the angle cut at the ends of two pieces of wood which are then joined together

Word history: Middle English, from Latin, from Greek word meaning 'belt', 'headband', 'headdress'

mitten
noun a kind of glove which covers the four fingers together and the thumb separately

Word history: Middle English, from Old French, from Gallo-Romance word meaning 'half (glove)', from Latin word meaning 'middle'

mix
verb **1** to combine or blend together: *You can* ***mix*** *flour and water to make paste.* | *He* ***mixes*** *business with pleasure.* (***amalgamate***, ***fuse***, ***join***, ***merge***, ***unite***)
2 to make by combining different things: *She* ***mixed*** *a cake.*
noun **3** a mixture, such as a prepared blend of ingredients to which it is necessary to add only water
phrase **4 mix up in**, to involve in: *How did you get* ***mixed up in*** *his plan?*
5 mix with, to be friends with or associate with: *She's* ***mixing with*** *some really nice people at university.*

Word building: **mix** *noun* **mixer** *noun*
Word history: French, from Latin word meaning 'mixed'

mixed farming
noun farming which involves more than one type of activity, often growing crops and raising livestock

mixed marriage
noun a marriage between persons of different religions or races

mixture
noun **1** something made up of mixed or combined things (***assortment***, ***hotchpotch***, ***jumble***, ***medley***, ***miscellany***)
2 *Chemistry*, *Physics* two or more substances not chemically united, and which are mixed in no fixed proportion to each other

Word history: Latin

mix-up
noun a muddle, or confused state of things

mnemonic (nuh-mon-ik)
noun a verse or the like intended to help the memory

Word history: from Greek word meaning 'of memory'

moan
noun **1** a long, low sound of sorrow or pain
2 any similar sound: *the* ***moan*** *of the wind*
3 *Colloquial* a complaint: *Thanks for listening — I needed to have a bit of a* ***moan*** *about school.* (***grumble***, ***whinge***)

Word building: **moan** *verb*
Word history: from Old English word meaning 'complain of', 'lament'

moan / mown

Don't confuse **moan** with **mown**, which is a past form of the verb **mow**, meaning 'to cut something off or down':

Have you mown the lawn yet?

moat
noun a deep, wide trench or ditch, usually filled with water, surrounding a town or castle to help protect it from invaders

Word history: Middle English word meaning 'moat', earlier 'mound', from Old French word meaning 'mound', 'eminence'; probably from Celtic or Germanic

mob
noun **1** a large crowd which is sometimes rowdy or violent (***flock***, ***herd***, ***pack***, ***throng***)
2 a group of friends
3 *Australian*, *NZ* a group of animals
4 *Aboriginal English* a group of people connected by family or tribal relationship
verb **5** to crowd around: *The fans* ***mobbed*** *the rock star at the concert.*
6 to surround and attack violently: *The people* ***mobbed*** *the bus and destroyed it.*

Verb forms: they **mobbed**, they have **mobbed**, they are **mobbing**
Word history: short for Latin *mōbile vulgus* the movable (meaning 'excitable') common people

mobile
adjective **1** able to be moved (***dynamic***, ***kinetic***, ***manoeuvrable***, ***moving***)
2 changing easily: *The clown had a* ***mobile*** *face which he could change from happy to sad.*
noun **3** a hanging decoration made up of delicately balanced movable parts
4 a mobile phone

Word building: **mobility** *noun*
Word history: from Latin word meaning 'movable'

mobile / movable

These words both have to do with movement but they are used in different ways.

We say that things are **mobile** if they can move freely or are designed to move easily:

These mobile army tanks can be driven over any terrain.

We say that people are **mobile** if they can move or travel about easily:

He's not mobile yet after breaking both his legs.

I'm more mobile now that I've bought this car.

We say that someone has a **mobile** face if their expression changes as their feelings change.

Movable objects normally stay in one place but can be moved from one place or position to another, as in *a movable screen* or *a movable wardrobe.*

mobile phone
noun a portable cellular telephone

mobilise
verb to get ready for duty or use: *The general **mobilised** his troops.*

Word use: You can also use **mobilize**.
Word building: **mobilisation** *noun*
Word history: French

moccasin (mok-uh-suhn)
noun a shoe made completely of soft leather

Word history: Native American

mock
verb **1** to make fun of (***heckle***, ***insult***, ***ridicule***, ***taunt***, ***tease***)
adjective **2** being a copy or imitation: ***mock** battle* (***counterfeit***, ***fake***, ***false***, ***phoney***, ***sham***)

Word history: Middle English, from Old French

mockery
noun an action or speech that unkindly laughs at something of a serious nature (***contempt***, ***derision***, ***disdain***, ***ridicule***, ***scorn***)

mockumentary (mok-yooh-men-tree)
noun a parody of the documentary genre

mock-up
noun a model, built to scale, used for testing or teaching (***example***, ***guide***, ***pattern***, ***sample***, ***specimen***)

modal verb
noun a type of auxiliary verb which indicates how probable something is (*I might come*, *The sun will rise*) or how necessary something is (*He should speak more loudly*, *The court must decide*)

Word use: Look up **auxiliary verb**.

mod cons
plural noun Colloquial modern conveniences, such as toasters, alarm clocks, hot and cold running water, etc.

mode[1]
noun **1** a method or way: *a **mode** of travel* (***approach***, ***means***, ***procedure***, ***technique***)
2 *Music* the arrangement of the diatonic tones of an octave
3 *Mathematics* the category with the highest frequency in a distribution

Word building: **modal** *adjective*
Word history: Middle English, from Latin word meaning 'due measure', 'manner'

mode[2]
noun **1** customary or normal usage in manners, dress, etc.
2 the style or fashion of the moment (***trend***, ***vogue***)

Word history: French, from Latin word meaning 'mode[1]'

model
noun **1** an example used for copying or comparing: *Her work was used as a **model** by the teachers.* (***guide***, ***pattern***, ***sample***, ***specimen***)
2 a small copy: *a **model** of an aeroplane*
3 someone who poses for a painter or photographer
4 someone employed to wear and show new clothes to customers
5 a particular style or form: *This bike is the latest **model**.*
adjective **6** excellent, or worthy to serve as a model: *She was a **model** student.* (***exemplary***, ***ideal***)
verb **7** to form, shape or make: *He **modelled** a vase out of clay.*
8 to be employed as a model

Verb forms: I **modelled**, I have **modelled**, I am **modelling**
Word history: French, from Italian, from Latin word meaning 'mode[1]'

modem (moh-dem, moh-duhm)
noun a device that converts data stored in one computer into a form which can be transmitted over a telecommunications system to another computer

Word history: from *mo(dulator) dem(odulator)*

moderate (mod-ruht, mod-uh-ruht)
adjective **1** reasonable or not extreme: *a **moderate** request* (***modest***, ***restrained***, ***temperate***)
2 fair, average or medium: *a **moderate** income* (***mediocre***, ***nondescript***, ***ordinary***, ***standard***)
noun **3** someone who is moderate in opinions or actions
verb (mod-uh-rayt) **4** to make or become less violent or severe (***abate***, ***decrease***, ***diminish***, ***peter out***, ***wane***)

Word building: **moderation** *noun* **moderately** *adverb*
Word history: Middle English, from Latin

moderator
noun **1** someone or something that moderates
2 a chairperson

modern
adjective belonging to or used in the present time (***contemporary***, ***current***, ***new***, ***recent***, ***up-to-date***)

Word building: **modernise** *verb*
Word history: Late Latin, from Latin word meaning 'just now'

modest
adjective **1** having a moderate opinion of yourself and your abilities (***humble***, ***meek***, ***self-effacing***, ***unassuming***)
2 moderate or reasonable: *a* ***modest*** *home* | *a* ***modest*** *request* (***restrained***, ***temperate***)
3 behaving in a proper or decent way

Word use: The opposite of definition 1 is **boastful.** | The opposite of definition 2 is **excessive.**
Word building: **modesty** *noun*
Word history: from Latin word meaning 'keeping due measure'

modicum (mod-uh-kuhm)
noun a small quantity

Word history: Middle English, from Latin

modify
verb **1** to change a little bit: *He* ***modified*** *his plan to fit in with the new rules.* (***adapt***, ***adjust***, ***alter***, ***vary***)
2 to reduce or make less severe or extreme: *She* ***modified*** *her strong language.* (***soften***, ***temper***, ***tone down***)
3 to limit or add more detail to the meaning of a word: *Adverbs* ***modify*** *verbs.*

Verb forms: I **modified**, I have **modified**, I am **modifying**
Word building: **modification** *noun*
Word history: Middle English, from Latin word meaning 'set limits to'

modular (mo-juh-luh)
adjective **1** having to do with a module
2 composed of standardised units for easy building or arrangement: ***modular*** *furniture*

modulate (mo-juh-layt)
verb **1** to tone down or adjust
2 to change the pitch or loudness of your voice when you speak

Word history: from Latin word meaning 'having measured'

modulation (mo-juh-lay-shuhn)
noun **1** the act of modulating
2 the state of being modulated
3 *Music* transition from one key to another

module (mo-joohl)
noun a part of something which can be separated from the rest and be used on its own

Word history: from Latin word meaning 'a small measure'

mogul (moh-guhl)
noun an important person: *a media* ***mogul*** (***baron***, ***magnate***, ***notable***, ***tycoon***, ***VIP***)

Word history: from the *Moguls*, a people who conquered India and ruled from 1526 to 1857

mohair
noun **1** the coat of an Angora goat
2 fabric made from this hair

Word history: obsolete *mo(cayare)* mohair (from Arabic) + *hair*

mohawk
noun a type of hairstyle, with a long strip of upright hair along the middle of the head, and the sides of the head shaved

Word history: the name of a Native American people

Mohs scale (mohz skayl)
noun a scale for measuring the hardness of a mineral by determining its ability to withstand scratching by other minerals of known hardness

Word history: after Friedrich *Mohs*, 1773–1839, German mineralogist

moiety (moy-uh-tee)
noun **1** a half
2 *Anthropology* one of two units into which a tribe is divided on the basis of descent through one parent only

Noun forms: The plural is **moieties**.
Word history: Middle English, from Old French, from Late Latin word meaning 'half', Latin word meaning 'the middle'

moist
adjective damp or slightly wet (***clammy***, ***dank***, ***humid***, ***soggy***)

Word building: **moisten** (moy-suhn) *verb*
Word history: Middle English, from Old French word meaning 'moist', 'mouldy'

moisture (moys-chuh)
noun water or other liquid making anything moist

molar
noun one of the large teeth at the back of your mouth used for grinding

Word building: **molar** *adjective*
Word history: from Latin word meaning 'grinder'

molasses
noun the syrup taken from raw sugar

Word history: Portuguese, from Late Latin word meaning 'honey'

mole[1]
noun a small spot, usually dark, on your skin

Word history: Old English

mole[2]
noun **1** a small, furry animal that feeds on insects and lives mainly underground
2 a person who has a job in the government of the enemy in order to act as a spy

Word history: Middle English

mole[3]
noun Chemistry the amount of a substance whose weight, in grams, is equal to the molecular weight of the substance, for example, one mole of carbon-12 weighs 12 grams

Word use: The symbol is **mol**, without a full stop. | You can also use **gram-molecule.**
Word history: German, from *Molekül* molecule

molecular weight
noun the average weight of a molecule of an element or compound measured in units based on one twelfth of the weight of an atom of carbon-12

molecule (mol-uh-kyoohl)
noun the smallest unit or particle into which something can be divided without changing its features: *A* ***molecule*** *of water has two hydrogen atoms and one oxygen atom.*

Word building: **molecular** (muh-lek-yuh-luh) *adjective*
Word history: from Latin word meaning 'mass'

molest (muh-<u>lest</u>)
verb to annoy or interfere with so as to hurt

Word building: **molestation** *noun*
Word history: Middle English, from Latin

mollify
verb to make calmer or less angry: *He managed to* ***mollify*** *her with apologies.* (***appease***, ***calm***, ***pacify***, ***placate***, ***quieten***)

Verb forms: I **mollified**, I have **mollified**, I am **mollifying**
Word use: The opposite of this is **upset**.
Word history: Middle English, from Latin word meaning 'soften'

mollusc (<u>mol</u>-uhsk)
noun an animal with a soft body, a hard shell, and no backbone, such as a snail or octopus

Word history: Neo-Latin, from Latin word meaning 'soft' (applied to a thin-shelled nut)

mollycoddle
verb to treat too carefully or tenderly: *Her mother* ***mollycoddled*** *her even when she was a teenager.*

Word history: *Molly* (variant of *Mary*) + *coddle*

molten
adjective made into liquid by heat: ***molten*** *steel*

moment
noun **1** a very short space of time: *I'll be there in a* ***moment***. (***flash***, ***instant***, ***minute***, ***second***)
2 the present or another particular time: *I can't come at the* ***moment***. | *I was going out the door at that* ***moment***.
3 importance: *This is a decision of great* ***moment***.

Word history: Middle English, from Latin word meaning 'movement', 'moment of time', etc.

momentary
adjective **1** lasting for only a moment: *a* ***momentary*** *flash of light* (***brief***, ***ephemeral***, ***fleeting***, ***passing***)
2 happening at every moment: *He lives in* ***momentary*** *fear of discovery.*

Word use: The opposite of defnition 1 is **perpetual**.
Word building: **momentarily** *adverb*

momentous
adjective of great importance: *The opening of the bridge was a* ***momentous*** *occasion.* | *a* ***momentous*** *decision* (***critical***, ***crucial***, ***historic***, ***memorable***, ***pivotal***)

momentous / monumental

These words both have to do with <u>importance</u> but they have different meanings.

Something is **momentous** if it is very important at the moment:

Will this momentous question ever be answered?

We use **momentous** to refer to abstract nouns.

A work of art is **monumental** if it is large in size and great enough to have lasting value. We use **monumental** to refer to concrete nouns.

momentum (muh-<u>ment</u>-uhm)
noun **1** a measure of the movement in a body which is equal to its mass multiplied by the speed at which it moves
2 force, as of a moving body

Word history: Latin

monarch (<u>mon</u>-uhk, <u>mon</u>-ahk)
noun a ruler of a country who inherits the position, such as a king or queen (***sovereign***)

Word history: Middle English, from Late Latin, from Greek word meaning 'ruling alone'

monarchy (<u>mon</u>-uh-kee)
noun **1** a country or government ruled by a monarch
2 the power of a monarch

Noun forms: The plural is **monarchies**.

monastery (<u>mon</u>-uhs-tree, <u>mon</u>-uhs-tuh-ree)
noun a place where a group of monks live and work

Noun forms: The plural is **monasteries**.
Word history: Middle English, from Late Latin, from Late Greek word meaning 'solitary dwelling'

monastic (muh-<u>nas</u>-tik)
adjective having to do with monasteries or monks

Monday
noun the second day of the week, following Sunday

Word history: from Middle English, Old English word meaning 'moon's day'

monetary (<u>mun</u>-uh-tree)
adjective having to do with money, or money matters

Word history: from Latin word meaning 'relating to the mint'

money
noun **1** metal coins or banknotes
2 property or wealth: *That is a family with lots of* ***money***. (***capital***, ***fortune***, ***riches***, ***treasure***)

Noun forms: The plural is **moneys** or **monies**.
Word history: Middle English, from Old French, from Latin word meaning 'mint', 'money'

Money usually stays singular even when you are writing about several pieces of money:

I've got lots of money in my pocket.

When it is used in this way **money** is a mass noun.

Money does sometimes need to be plural, though. Usually this is when you are comparing different types or units of currency:

The moneys of the world are many and varied.

money laundering
noun the illegal practice of making illegally obtained funds appear legitimate, usually by depositing them as cash in a bank account and then drawing on the account for legal transactions

Word building: **money launderer** *noun*

money market
noun a financial market in which large amounts of money are borrowed and lent for short periods of time

money order
noun an order for payment which can be exchanged for money at a post office

mongrel (<u>mung</u>-gruhl)
noun a plant or animal, especially a dog, that is a mix of different breeds or kinds

Word history: obsolete English *mong* mixture (Old English *gemang*) + *-rel*

monitor
noun **1** a pupil who has particular jobs to help the teacher
2 something that keeps a check or gives warning
3 a computer screen
4 a kind of television set used in TV studios to check the quality of the broadcast
5 a kind of large lizard which is supposed to warn that crocodiles are near
verb **6** to keep a careful check on: *We must **monitor** our spending.* (***audit, check***)

Word history: Latin

monk (mungk)
noun a male member of a religious group living a life of religious devotion away from the rest of the world

Word history: Old English, from Late Latin, from Late Greek word meaning 'solitary'

monkey
noun a kind of animal that has a long tail and lives in trees in tropical areas

Noun forms: The plural is **monkeys**.
Word history: apparently from Low German

monochromatic (mon-uh-kruh-mat-ik)
adjective producing or having to do with one colour or one wavelength

monochrome (mon-uh-krohm)
noun **1** a painting or drawing in different shades of a single colour
2 the art or method of making these
3 a black-and-white photograph

Word history: from Greek word meaning 'of one colour'

monocle
noun a glass lens for one eye only

Word history: French, from Late Latin word meaning 'one-eyed'

monogamy (muh-nog-uh-mee)
noun **1** marriage to one person at a time
2 the practice of remaining faithful to a single sexual partner

Word use: Compare this with **polygamy** and **bigamy**.
Word building: **monogamous** *adjective*

monogram
noun a design made up of two or more letters, usually your initials

Word history: Late Latin, from Late Greek word meaning 'single-lettered character'

monolith
noun a single huge rock or stone, such as Uluru

Word use: Compare this with **megalith**.
Word building: **monolithic** *adjective*
Word history: Late Latin, from Greek word meaning 'made of one stone'

monologue (mon-uh-log)
noun a long talk by one person

Word history: French, from Greek word meaning 'speaking alone'

monopolise (muh-nop-uh-luyz)
verb to get, have, or exercise complete control of: *to **monopolise** a market | to **monopolise** a conversation* (***dominate***)

Word use: You can also use **monopolize**.
Word building: **monopolisation** *noun*

monopoly (muh-nop-uh-lee)
noun the complete control of something, especially the supply of a product or service

Noun forms: The plural is **monopolies**.
Word history: Latin, from Greek word meaning 'a right of exclusive sale'

monorail (mon-uh-rayl)
noun a railway with carriages running on a single, usually overhead, rail

monosodium glutamate (mon-uh-soh-dee-uhm glooh-tuh-mayt)
noun a sodium salt used in cooking to make the natural flavour of a dish stronger

Word use: The abbreviation is **MSG**.

monosyllable (mon-uh-sil-uh-buhl)
noun a word of one syllable, as *yes*

Word building: **monosyllabic** *adjective*

monotone
noun a series of spoken or sung sounds in one unchanging tone: *She spoke in a dreary **monotone**.*

Word history: Neo-Latin, from Late Greek word meaning 'of one tone'

monotonous (muh-not-uh-nuhs)
adjective unvarying in any way: *a **monotonous** day* (***boring, dull, humdrum, stale, tedious***)

monotony (muh-not-uh-nee)
noun lack of change or variety, which produces boredom

Word history: Late Greek

monotreme (mon-uh-treem)
noun the egg-laying mammals, the platypus and the echidna, that are found only in Australia and its near regions

Word history: from *mono-* + Greek word meaning 'hole'

mono-unsaturated
adjective having to do with a fat or oil based on fatty acids having only one double bond per molecule: ***mono-unsaturated** olive oil*

monsoon
noun **1** any major wind system which reverses in direction at different times of the year, usually creating a difference between dry and rainy seasons
2 a rainy season associated with a monsoon, as the wet season of northern Australia from December to March

Word building: **monsoonal** *adjective*
Word history: Dutch, from Portuguese, from Arabic word meaning 'season', 'seasonal wind', 'monsoon'

monsoon forest
noun a semi-deciduous tropical forest occurring in areas which experience a monsoon climate, marked by dry periods followed by torrential rain

monster
noun **1** someone or something that is frighteningly horrible or cruel
2 someone or something of huge size

Word history: Middle English, from Old French, from Latin word meaning 'omen', 'prodigy'

monstrous
adjective **1** huge or great: *a **monstrous** amount of money* (***colossal**, **enormous**, **gigantic**, **massive**, **vast***)
2 frightful or shocking: *a **monstrous** face | a **monstrous** idea* (***abominable**, **abysmal**, **atrocious**, **grotesque**, **terrible***)

Word building: **monstrosity** *noun*
Word history: Middle English, from Late Latin word meaning 'strange'

montage (mon-tahzh)
noun **1** the art or method of arranging different pictures, or parts of pictures, in one composition
2 a technique of film editing in which several shots are partially superimposed to form a single image

Word history: from French word meaning 'mounting', 'putting together'

montane (mon-tayn)
adjective **1** mountainous: *a **montane** region.*
2 *Biology* (of a species) found in a mountainous habitat

month
noun **1** any of the twelve parts into which the year is divided
2 a period of about four weeks or 30 days

Word history: Old English

monthly
adjective **1** having to do with a month, or with each month: *a **monthly** magazine*
adverb **2** once a month: *They come **monthly**.*

monument
noun **1** something made in memory of a person or event, such as a statue
2 something from the past, such as an ancient building: *the **monuments** of ancient Greece*

Word history: Middle English, from Latin

monumental
adjective great in size or importance (***awe-inspiring**, **memorable**, **outstanding**, **tremendous**, **unforgettable***)

monumental / momentous
Look up **momentous / monumental.**

MOO
noun Computers a game on the internet, similar to a MUD, but in which the users are able to modify the conditions under which the game is being played

Word history: *M(UD) O(bject) O(riented)*

mooch
verb Colloquial to walk around in an aimless and unhappy way

Word history: Middle English

mood
noun **1** the way you feel at a particular time: *You never know if she will be in a good or bad **mood**.* (***disposition**, **frame of mind**, **humour**, **spirit***)
2 *Grammar* the type of expression as shown by a verb

Word history: from Old English word meaning 'mind', 'spirit', 'mood'

For more information about **mood** (definition 2), look up **verbs: mood.**

moody
adjective **1** angry or unhappy (***gloomy**, **glum**, **morose**, **sullen**, **surly***)
2 changeable in mood or feelings (***grumpy**, **prickly**, **sensitive**, **temperamental**, **touchy***)

Adjective forms: **moodier, moodiest**
Word building: **moodily** *adverb* **moodiness** *noun*

moon
noun **1** the round body that circles the earth every month and can be seen as a light in the sky at night
2 this body as it appears at different stages of the month: *the new **moon** | the full **moon***

Word use: **Lunar** is the adjective meaning 'having to do with the moon'.
Word history: Old English

moonlight
noun **1** the light of the moon
adjective **2** having to do with moonlight
3 lit by moonlight
4 happening by moonlight
verb **5** *Colloquial* to work at a second job, often at night

moor[1]
noun an open area of damp, wild land in Britain, usually covered with low, rough, plant growth

Word history: Old English

moor[2]
verb to make stay in the same position with ropes or an anchor: *to **moor** a ship*

Word building: **mooring** *noun* **moorings** *plural noun*
Word history: Old English

moor / more
Don't confuse **moor** with **more**, which is the opposite of **less**.

moose
noun a large animal of the deer family

Noun forms: The plural is **moose.**
Word history: Native American

moot
adjective **1** doubtful (***debatable**, **dubious**, **open to question**, **questionable**, **uncertain***)
verb **2** to bring forward (any point, subject, etc.) for discussion

Word history: from Old English word meaning 'meeting', 'assembly'

moot point
noun a matter which is uncertain and open to debate

mop
noun **1** a loose bundle of cloth or strings fixed to the end of a stick, and used for washing floors or dishes
2 a cleaning or wiping with a mop
3 a thick mass: *a **mop** of hair*
verb **4** to clean or wipe up with a mop or something similar (***blot**, **sponge**, **swab**, **towel**, **wipe***)

Verb forms: I **mopped,** I have **mopped,** I am **mopping**
Word history: Middle English

mope
verb to be in an unhappy mood (***brood***, ***fret***, ***grieve***, ***moon***, ***pine***)

Word history: variant of obsolete *mop* make a wry face

mopoke (moh-pohk)
noun a kind of owl found in Australia and New Zealand

Word history: imitative

moral
adjective **1** having to do with the knowledge of what is right and wrong: *This is a* ***moral*** *question.*
2 acting according to the rules of what is thought to be right, especially in sexual behaviour: *a* ***moral*** *person* (***decent***, ***ethical***, ***honest***, ***proper***, ***respectable***)
noun **3** the lesson taught by story or experience: *The* ***moral*** *is 'Slow and steady wins the race'.*
4 morals, beliefs or ways of behaviour that have to do with right and wrong

Word building: **moralistic** *adjective* **morally** *adverb*
Word history: Middle English, from Latin word meaning 'relating to manners', 'customs'

morale (muh-rahl)
noun the amount of optimism or confidence felt by a person or group: *We must keep the cricket team's* ***morale*** *high.*

Word history: French

moralise
verb to make moral judgements

Word use: You can also use **moralize**.

morality (muh-ral-uh-tee)
noun **1** a set of standards for behaviour based on what is considered right and wrong, honest and dishonest, etc.
2 moral quality or character (***integrity***)

moratorium (mo-ruh-taw-ree-uhm)
noun any official delay, such as in making a political decision

Noun forms: The plural is **moratoriums** or **moratoria**.
Word history: Neo-Latin, from Latin word meaning 'delay'

morbid
adjective **1** showing an unhealthy interest in gruesome things
2 caused by or having to do with disease

Word building: **morbidity** *noun* **morbidly** *adverb* **morbidness** *noun*
Word history: from Latin word meaning 'sickly'

more
adjective **1** in greater quantity, measure, degree, or number
2 in or to a greater degree: ***more*** *slowly*
pronoun **3** an extra quantity or amount: *Could I have more, please?*

Word use: This is a form of the adjective **much**.
Word history: Old English

> **more / moor**
> Don't confuse **more** with **moor**.
> A **moor** is an open area of wild land in Britain.
> To **moor** a boat is to fix it in position with ropes or an anchor.

> **more / most**
> Both these words can act as either a singular pronoun or a plural pronoun, depending on what they're referring to. So be careful to use the correct form of the verb with them:
> *You've put in a lot of effort, but more [more effort] is needed.* (singular)
> *You've collected a lot of stamps, but more [more stamps] are needed.* (plural)
> *Is most of the pavlova eaten now?* (singular)
> *Are most of the strawberries eaten now?* (plural)

moreover
adverb beyond what has been said: *He's coming to the meeting.* ***Moreover***, *he's going to make a speech.* (***besides***, ***further***)

mores (maw-rayz)
plural noun unquestioned customs and moral views of a group

Word history: from Latin word meaning 'customs'

Moreton Bay bug
noun an edible, flattened crustacean found in northern Australian waters; similar to the Balmain bug

morgue (mawg)
noun a place where the bodies of dead people are kept until their funerals (***funeral parlour***, ***mortuary***)

Word history: French; originally name of building in Paris so used

morning (maw-ning)
noun **1** the beginning of day (***dawn***, ***daybreak***, ***sunrise***)
2 the first part of the day, from dawn, or from midnight, to noon
adjective **3** having to do with morning: ***morning*** *sun*

Word history: Middle English

> **morning / mourning**
> Don't confuse **morning** with **mourning**. Someone is in **mourning** if they are grieving over the death of someone they love.

moron (maw-ron)
noun **1** someone with below normal intelligence
2 *Colloquial* someone who is stupid

Word building: **moronic** (muh-ron-ik) *adjective*
Word history: from Greek word meaning 'dull', 'foolish'

morose (muh-rohs)
adjective bad-tempered or unfriendly because of unhappiness (***gloomy***, ***glum***, ***moody***, ***sullen***, ***surly***)

Word building: **morosely** *adverb* **moroseness** *noun*
Word history: from Latin word meaning 'fretful'

morph
verb **1** of a computerised image, to change shape as a result of morphing
2 *Colloquial* to change appearance, personality, etc.: *Lately he's* ***morphed*** *from a selfish pig to a really nice guy.*

morphine (maw-feen)
noun a drug used to stop pain and to help you to sleep

Word history: from *Morpheus*, the Greek god of dreams

morphing
noun Computers the manipulation of digitised images to produce a sequence whereby one image changes into another

morphology (maw-fol-uh-jee)
noun **1** the study of form, structure, and the like
2 that branch of biology which deals with the form and structure of animals and plants
3 the study of the physical form of lands, areas, or towns

Word building: **morphological** *adjective*

morse code
noun a system of signalling in which different groups of short and long sounds or flashes of light, called dots and dashes, stand for each letter in a word

Word history: named after US inventor Samuel *Morse*, 1791–1872, who designed it

morsel
noun a very small piece or amount (***crumb***, ***fragment***, ***grain***, ***particle***, ***scrap***)

Word history: Middle English, from Old French word meaning 'a small bite', from Latin word meaning 'bite'

mortal
adjective **1** having to die eventually: *All humans are **mortal**.*
2 causing death: *a **mortal** wound* (***deadly***, ***fatal***, ***lethal***)
3 deadly or extreme: *a **mortal** enemy*
noun **4** a human being

Word history: Middle English, from Latin word meaning 'subject to death'

mortality (maw-tal-uh-tee)
noun **1** the condition of being mortal or human: *His death made me think about my own **mortality**.*
2 death, or rate of death: *Child **mortality** is high in some countries.*

mortar[1]
noun **1** a heavy bowl in which food or other substances are ground to a powder with a pestle
2 a short cannon designed to fire shells to a great height

Word history: Old English, from Latin word meaning 'vessel in which substances are pounded', or 'one in which *mortar*[2] is made'

mortar[2]
noun a mixture of lime or cement, sand and water, used for joining bricks together

Word history: Middle English, from French, from Latin

mortgage (maw-gij)
noun a promise that a property will be given over if a loan is not repaid to a bank or the like: *We have a **mortgage** on our house.*

Word building: **mortgage** *verb*
Word history: Middle English, from Old French *mort* dead + *gage* pledge

mortgagee (maw-guh-jee)
noun someone to whom property is mortgaged: *The **mortgagee** of my house is the bank.*

mortgagor (maw-guh-jaw)
noun someone who mortgages property

mortice (maw-tuhs)
noun a deep, rectangular hole in one piece of wood, etc., into which is fitted another piece of wood, so as to form a joint. The joint formed in this way is called a mortice and tenon joint.

Word history: Middle English, from Old French, perhaps from Arabic word meaning 'made fast'

mortify
verb to severely embarrass or hurt the feelings or pride of: *My mother **mortified** me by treating me like a baby in front of my friends.*

Verb forms: I **mortified**, I have **mortified**, I am **mortifying**
Word building: **mortification** *noun*
Word history: Middle English, from Old French, from Late Latin word meaning 'kill', 'destroy'

mortuary (maw-chuh-ree)
noun a place where the bodies of dead people are kept until their funerals (***funeral parlour***, ***morgue***)

Noun forms: The plural is **mortuaries**.
Word history: Middle English, from Latin word meaning 'belonging to the dead'

mosaic (moh-zay-ik, muh-zay-ik)
noun a picture or pattern made of small pieces of different coloured stone or glass

Word history: Middle English, from Medieval Latin word meaning 'of the Muses', 'artistic'

moselle (moh-zel)
noun a light white wine originally from the Rhine Valley in Germany

mosh
verb Colloquial to dance at a concert in a very tightly packed group in front of the stage

mosque (mosk)
noun a Muslim place of worship

Word history: French, from Italian, from Arabic word meaning 'prostrate oneself', 'worship'

mosquito
noun a small, flying insect, the female of which sucks the blood of animals and humans, and by this passes on some diseases, such as malaria

Noun forms: The plural is **mosquitoes** or **mosquitos**.
Word history: Spanish, from Latin word meaning 'a fly'

moss
noun a plant with very small leaves that grows in patches on damp ground, tree trunks or rocks

Word building: **mossy** *adjective*
Word history: from Old English word meaning 'bog'

most
adjective **1** in the greatest quantity, degree, amount or number: *the **most** votes*
pronoun **2** the greatest quantity, amount or degree
adverb **3** in or to the greatest range or degree: *It was the **most** horrible thing I had ever seen.*

Word use: This is a form of the adjective **much**.
Word history: Old English

most / more
Look up **more / most**.

mostly (mohst-lee)
adverb **1** for the most part: *Tomorrow the weather will be* ***mostly*** *fine.*
2 almost all: *The drink is* ***mostly*** *made of orange juice.*

motel
noun a roadside hotel which provides accommodation for travellers and parking for their cars

moth
noun a flying insect, similar to a butterfly, that is active at night
Word history: Old English

mothball
noun a small ball of a chemical substance which is stored with clothes to kill moths

mother
noun **1** a female parent
2 the head of a convent of nuns
verb **3** to treat too protectively or tenderly: *Stop* ***mothering*** *him — he's 25 years old!*
Word building: **motherhood** *noun* **motherliness** *noun* **motherly** *adjective*
Word history: Old English

motherboard
noun Computers a printed circuit board plugged into the back of a computer into which other boards can be slotted so that the computer can operate a range of peripherals

mother-in-law
noun the mother of your husband or wife
Noun forms: The plural is **mothers-in-law**.

mother-of-pearl
noun the hard, shiny lining of some shells, used for ornaments

mothership
noun **1** a large ship which services the group of smaller ships with which it sails
2 a spacecraft which is the main vehicle providing resources and services to a fleet of smaller craft
Word use: You can also use **mother ship**.

motif (moh-teef, moh-tuhf)
noun **1** an idea that is repeated in various ways throughout a piece of writing or music or in the work of an artist
2 a part of a design that is repeated, such as in wallpaper
Word history: French

motion
noun **1** movement or the power of movement
2 an idea put forward at a meeting to be voted on: *He moved a* ***motion*** *in Parliament.*
verb **3** to direct by a movement of the hand or head: *He* ***motioned*** *her to leave the room.*
Word history: Middle English, from Latin word meaning 'a moving'

motivate (moh-tuh-vayt)
verb to provide with a strong reason for doing something: *Ambition* ***motivates*** *her to work hard.* (***encourage***, ***drive***, ***impel***, ***inspire***, ***stimulate***)
Word building: **motivation** *noun*

motive
noun a strong reason for doing something: *Jealousy was the* ***motive*** *for the murder.*
Word building: **motivated** *adjective* **motivation** *noun*
Word history: Medieval Latin word meaning 'a moving cause', from Latin word meaning 'moved'

motley (mot-lee)
adjective made up of different parts or colours: *a* ***motley*** *collection of people* (***assorted***, ***diverse***, ***miscellaneous***, ***mixed***, ***various***)
Word history: Middle English

motocross
noun cross-country motorcycle racing

motor
noun **1** an internal combustion engine, especially that of a car or boat
2 a device which receives and modifies energy from some natural source in order to utilise it to drive machinery, etc.
Word history: from Latin word meaning 'one who moves'

motor car
noun a car

motorcycle
noun a large, heavy bicycle with an engine
Word use: You can also use **motorbike**.

motorist
noun someone who owns and drives a car

motorway
noun a road on which traffic can travel fast (***expressway***, ***freeway***)

mottled
adjective covered with different coloured spots or patches: *a* ***mottled*** *book jacket* | ***mottled*** *skin*

motto
noun a short saying, often taken as summing up the aims or beliefs of a particular organisation or group: *The* ***motto*** *of the Scouts is 'Be prepared'.* (***adage***, ***epigram***, ***maxim***, ***proverb***)
Noun forms: The plural is **mottos** or **mottoes**.
Word history: Italian

mould[1] (mohld)
noun **1** a hollow form which gives shape to melted or soft material which hardens inside it: *a pottery* ***mould*** | *a jelly* ***mould***
verb **2** to give a particular shape or character to
Word use: The US spelling is **mold**.
Word history: Middle English, from Old French, from Latin word meaning 'module'

mould[2] (mohld)
noun a furry growth on something that is too damp or is decaying: *This bread has* ***mould*** *on it.*
Word building: **mouldy** *adjective* (**mouldier**, **mouldiest**)
Word use: The US spelling is **mold**.
Word history: Middle English

moult (mohlt)
verb to lose or throw off old feathers, fur or skin: *Some birds* ***moult*** *in spring.*
Word use: You can also use **molt**.
Word history: Old English, from Latin word meaning 'change'

mound
noun **1** a heap: *a* ***mound*** *of earth*
2 a small hill
Word history: Old English

mount
verb **1** to go up something: *She* ***mounted*** *the stairs.* (***ascend***, ***clamber***, ***climb***, ***scale***, ***shin***)
2 to move upwards (***ascend***, ***rise***, ***soar***)
3 to get up on: *He* ***mounted*** *the horse.*
4 to fix on or in a position or setting: *to* ***mount*** *a painting on a wall | to* ***mount*** *a jewel*
5 to rise or increase: *Prices are* ***mounting***. (***accumulate***, ***expand***, ***grow***, ***multiply***, ***pile up***)
noun **6** a horse for riding
7 a backing or setting: *We should put this photograph on a white* ***mount***.
Word use: The opposite of definition 3 is **dismount**.
Word history: Middle English, from Old French, from Latin word meaning 'mountain'

mountain
noun **1** a large natural raised part of the earth, higher than a hill (***elevation***, ***peak***)
2 something like this in size, shape or amount: *a* ***mountain*** *of reading*
Word use: This is sometimes called a **mount**, especially in a name as in *Mount Kosciuszko*.
Word building: **mountainous** *adjective*
Word history: Middle English, from Old French word meaning 'mountain', from Latin

mountain devil
noun **1** a spiny, grotesque-looking lizard found in lowland and mountain regions of southern, central and western Australia
2 a woody shrub of sandstone areas of New South Wales

mountaineer
noun someone who climbs mountains

mourn (mawn)
verb to feel or show sorrow over, especially over someone's death or the loss of something: *He* ***mourned*** *the death of his wife. | She* ***mourned*** *the loss of her car.* (***grieve about***, ***lament***)
Word building: **mourner** *noun* **mournful** *adjective* **mournfully** *adverb*
Word history: Old English

mourning
noun **1** the act of someone who mourns (***lamentation***, ***sorrowing***)
phrase **2 in mourning**, having recently suffered the death of a loved one: *She was* ***in mourning*** *after the death of her husband.*

mourning / morning
Don't confuse **mourning** with **morning**, which is the first part of the day.

mouse
noun **1** a small animal with sharp teeth and a long tail
2 *Computers* a small object which you hold and move to position the cursor on the screen
Noun forms: The plural for definition 1 is **mice**; the plural for definition 2 is **mouses**.
Word history: Old English *mūs* (plural *mȳs*)

mouse potato
noun Colloquial someone who likes to spend a large proportion of their time on the internet

moussaka (mooh-sah-kuh)
noun a dish from Greece, Turkey and other countries near them, with layers of minced meat, tomatoes and eggplant, with a thick white sauce on top
Word history: Turkish, from Arabic

mousse (moohs)
noun **1** a food made of whipped cream, beaten eggs, gelatine and a sweet or savoury flavouring: *chocolate* ***mousse*** *| fish* ***mousse***
2 a foam-like substance used for cosmetic purposes, such as styling the hair or cleansing the skin: *shaving* ***mousse*** *| hair* ***mousse***
Word history: from French word meaning 'froth'

moustache (muh-stahsh)
noun the hair that grows on the upper lip of a man
Word history: French, from Italian, from Greek word meaning 'upper lip', 'moustache'

mousy
adjective shy and quiet (***bashful***, ***demure***, ***modest***, ***reticent***, ***unassuming***)
Word use: You can also use **mousey**.

mouth (mowth)
noun **1** the opening in the face used for eating, drinking and talking
2 an opening in anything
3 the place where a river flows into the sea
verb (mowdh) **4** to move the lips as if talking, but make no sound
phrase **5 down in the mouth**, unhappy or glum
Word history: Old English

mouthful
noun as much as you can fit into your mouth at one time

mouth organ
noun → **harmonica**

mouthpiece
noun the part of a wind instrument which you blow into or the part of a telephone which you speak into

movable / mobile
Look up **mobile / movable**.

move
verb **1** to change from one place or position to another: *Stand still and do not* ***move***! (***budge***, ***shift***, ***stir***)
2 to cause to change position: *to* ***move*** *the chair across the room* (***carry***, ***shift***, ***transfer***, ***transport***)
3 to cause strong feelings in: *His sad story* ***moved*** *me.*
4 to make a formal request at a meeting
noun **5** a movement or change of position
6 a player's turn in a game: *Throw the dice and make your* ***move***.
phrase **7 get a move on**, *Colloquial* hurry up
8 move in, to settle into a house
9 move out, to leave a house
10 on the move, moving
Word building: **movable** *adjective*
Word history: Middle English, from Anglo-French, from Latin

movement
noun **1** a moving or changing from one place or position to another
2 an organised group of people working towards a particular goal: *the **movement** against uranium mining*
3 one of the sections of a long piece of music: *This symphony has four **movements**.*

movie
noun **1** → **film** (definition 3)
phrase **2 go to the movies**, to go to a showing of a film in a cinema

mow
verb **1** to cut off or down: *to **mow** the lawn* (***clip***, ***shear***, ***snip***, ***trim***)
phrase **2 mow down**, to knock down: *The runaway car **mowed down** people on the footpath.*

Verb forms: I **mowed**, I have **mown** or I have **mowed**, I am **mowing**
Word history: Old English

> **mown / moan**
> Don't confuse **mown** with **moan**, which is a long, low sound of sorrow or pain.

mozzarella (mot-suh-rel-uh)
noun a soft, white cheese which melts easily and is often used on pizzas and in other Italian foods

Word history: Italian word meaning 'a slice'

MPEG
noun Computers
1 a standard for encoding electronic video data
2 a file stored in this format

Word history: *M(oving) P(ictures) E(xpert) G(roup)*

MP3 (em pee three)
noun **1** a digital audio file
adjective **2** having to do with such a file: *to download an **MP3** file*

Word use: You can also use **mp3**.

MP3 player
noun a device for downloading, storing, and playing MP3s

Mr (mis-tuh)
noun a title put before a man's name

Word history: abbreviation of *mister*

Mrs (mis-uhz)
noun a title often put before a married woman's name

Word history: variant of *mistress*

> Look up **Ms.**

Ms (miz, muhz)
noun a title put before a woman's name

> **Ms** is used to avoid mentioning whether a woman is married or not. It gives women a title equal to *Mr*, which refers to the man in question and not to his marital status. Because of this, **Ms** is also useful when you're writing to a woman whose marital status is unknown to you. But if you know that a woman prefers to be addressed as *Mrs* or *Miss*, it is polite to use the preferred title.
>
> Note that **Ms** is not an abbreviation of some other word as *Mr* is of *Mister*, and it doesn't have a full stop after it.
>
> For more information, look up **non-sexist language.**

MS
noun → **multiple sclerosis**

Word history: abbreviation

much
adjective **1** in great quantity, amount, measure or degree: ***much** work*
noun **2** a great quantity or amount: ***Much** of this is true.*
phrase **3 to make much of,**
a to treat as of great importance
b to treat with attention or fondness: ***to make much of** an old friend*

Adjective forms: **more**, **most**

muck
noun **1** dirt or filth
verb **2** to make dirty: *Be careful not to **muck** your new shirt.* (***smear***, ***smudge***, ***soil***, ***spoil***, ***spot***)
phrase **3 muck about** (or **around**), *Colloquial* to fool about
4 muck out, to remove muck from: *to **muck out** the stables*
5 muck up, *Colloquial*
a *Australian* to misbehave (***act up***, ***make mischief***, ***mess around***)
b make a mess of (***botch***, ***bungle***, ***fluff***, ***fumble***, ***muff***)

Word building: **mucky** *adjective* (**muckier**, **muckiest**)
Word history: Middle English, from Scandinavian

mucous (myooh-kuhs)
adjective **1** having to do with mucus
2 containing or producing mucus: *the **mucous** membrane*

Word building: **mucosity** *noun*
Word history: from Latin word meaning 'slimy'

mucus (myooh-kuhs)
noun thick, slimy liquid which builds up in your nose and throat when you have a cold

Word history: Latin

mud
noun wet, soft, sticky earth (***bog***, ***mire***, ***slush***)

Word building: **muddy** *adjective* (**muddier**, **muddiest**)
Word history: Middle English

MUD
noun Computers a game on the internet in which a user assumes an identity and interacts with other users

Word history: *M(ulti)U(ser) D(imension)*

muddle
verb **1** to mix up or confuse (***bamboozle***, ***befuddle***, ***bewilder***, ***fluster***, ***puzzle***)
noun **2** a confused mess (***clutter***, ***disarray***, ***jumble***, ***shambles***)

Word use: The opposite of definition 2 is **order**.
Word history: *mud* + *-le*

mudflat
noun an area of muddy ground covered by water at high tide

mudguard
noun a cover for the wheel of a car or bicycle to stop mud and water splashing up

muesli (myoohz-lee, moohz-lee)
noun breakfast cereal made from oats, chopped fruit and nuts

Word history: Swiss German

muesli bar
noun a snack made from a muesli mixture, usually sweetened and set in a bar shape

muff
noun **1** a rolled up piece of fur or woollen material into which you can put your hands to keep them warm
verb **2** *Colloquial* to bungle or miss: *to **muff** an easy catch* (***botch, fluff, fumble***)

Word history: Dutch, from French

muffin
noun **1** a flat cake which is toasted and eaten topped with butter
2 a type of small sweet cake

Word use: You can also use **English muffin** for definition 1.

muffin top
noun Colloquial the fold of fat on a woman's hips and stomach which spills out over the top of tight-fitting pants or skirts

muffle
verb **1** to wrap in scarves, shawls and other warm clothes
2 to deaden the sound of: *to **muffle** drums*

Word building: **muffled** *adjective*
Word history: Middle English, from Old French

muffler
noun **1** a device which fits onto the exhaust pipe of a car to deaden the noise of the engine
2 a thick, warm scarf

mufti (muf-tee)
noun everyday clothes as opposed to a uniform

mug
noun **1** a large drinking cup
2 *Colloquial* your face
3 *Colloquial* someone who is easily fooled
verb **4** *Colloquial* to attack and rob (***assault, beat up***)

Verb forms: they **mugged**, they have **mugged**, they are **mugging**
Word building: **mugger** *noun*
Word history: Middle English, from Scandinavian

muggy
adjective unpleasantly warm and humid: ***muggy** weather* (***close, oppressive, sultry***)

Adjective forms: **muggier, muggiest**
Word history: dialect *mug* mist, from Scandinavian

mulberry (mul-bree)
noun **1** a tree which has sweet, dark-purple fruit like blackberries, and leaves which are eaten by silkworms
2 the fruit of this tree

Noun forms: The plural is **mulberries.**
Word history: Old English, from Latin

mulch
noun straw, grass clippings, leaves or similar material spread on gardens to protect and feed the plants

Word building: **mulch** *verb*
Word history: from Middle English word meaning 'soft', Old English word meaning 'mellow'

mule
noun **1** the offspring of a female horse and a male donkey
2 *Colloquial* someone who is stupid or stubborn
3 *Colloquial* a courier of illegal drugs

Word use: You can also use **drug mule** for definition 3.
Word building: **mulish** *adjective*
Word history: Middle English, from Old French, from Latin

mulga
noun **1** a type of wattle tree found in dry inland areas of Australia
phrase **2 up (in) the mulga,** *Australian* away out in the bush or outback: *He's been living **up the mulga** for twenty years now.*

Word history: from a number of Australian Aboriginal languages of inland NSW and South Australia

mulgara (mul-gah-ra)
noun a small marsupial that looks like a mouse with a black hairy tail, found in desert areas of Australia

Word history: from Wangganguru, an Australian Aboriginal language of the region north of Lake Eyre

mull
phrase **mull over,** to think about: *She **mulled over** the problem.* (***contemplate, meditate on, ponder, pore over, reflect on***)

Word history: perhaps originally British dialect word meaning 'muddle', 'crumble', from Middle Dutch

mullet
noun **1** a type of fish commonly found in the rivers and sea around Australia
2 a type of hairstyle, long at the back and cut short on the top and sides

Noun forms: The plural is **mullets** or **mullet**.
Word history: Middle English, from Old French, from Latin word meaning 'red mullet'

multicultural (mul-tee-kulch-uh-ruhl)
adjective having to do with a society that has within it several large groups of people of different cultures and races

multifarious (mul-tuh-fair-ree-uhs)
adjective having many different parts or kinds

Word history: from Latin word meaning 'manifold'

multilateral (mul-tee-lat-uh-ruhl, mul-tee-lat-ruhl)
adjective **1** having many sides
2 in government, indicating an agreement or arrangement between three or more nations

Word use: You can also use **multipartite** for definition 2.

multimedia
adjective **1** having to do with or involving several different kinds of media, such as television, radio and newspapers: *a **multimedia** advertising campaign*
2 combining text, sound, video, etc.: *a **multimedia** encyclopedia on CD-ROM*

multinational
adjective involving many different countries: *a **multinational** business company*

multipartite (mul-tee-pah-tuyt)
adjective **1** divided into many parts
2 multilateral (definition 2)

Word history: from Latin word meaning 'much-divided'

multiple
adjective **1** having many parts
noun **2** a number formed by multiplying one number by another: *6, 9 and 12 are **multiples** of 3*

Word history: French, from Late Latin word meaning 'manifold'

multiple personality disorder
noun a rare psychotic disorder in which the patient develops several distinct, independent personalities which emerge at different times

Word use: Another name is **dissociative disorder**. | You will sometimes find **split personality** used but its use is not generally approved.

multiple sclerosis (mul-tuh-puhl skluh-roh-suhs)
noun a disease of the central nervous system which may affect many different bodily functions, especially walking, sight and coordination, as well as memory, mental functions and personality

Word use: The abbreviation is **MS**.

multiplex
noun a cinema complex with multiple screens and auditoriums

multiplication (mul-tuh-pluh-kay-shuhn)
noun **1** the act of multiplying or the state of being multiplied
2 *Arithmetic* the process (denoted by the symbol ×) of finding the number (called the product) resulting from the addition of a given number (the multiplicand) to itself as many times as there are units in another given number (the multiplier); 4 × 3 means 4 + 4 + 4

Word use: The opposite of this is **division**.

multiplicity (mul-tuh-plis-uh-tee)
noun a large number

multiplier
noun a number by which another number is multiplied

multiply
verb **1** to increase in amount or number: *to **multiply** your savings by putting them in the bank | Rabbits **multiply** quickly.* (***expand***, ***proliferate***)
2 to add a number to itself a number of times to get a total or product: ***Multiply** 4 by 3 to get 12.*

Verb forms: I **multiplied**, I have **multiplied**, I am **multiplying**
Word history: Middle English, from Old French, from Latin

multiracial
adjective having people of many different races or nationalities: *a **multiracial** society*

multi-tasking
noun **1** the execution by a computer of a number of different tasks at the same time, such as processing data, printing, etc.
2 the performance of a number of different jobs by one person

multitude
noun a great number or crowd: *a **multitude** of people* (***flock***, ***herd***, ***mob***, ***pack***, ***throng***)

Word building: **multitudinous** (mul-tuh-tyooh-duh-nuhs) *adjective*
Word history: Middle English, from Latin

multi-user
adjective of a computer system, allowing more than one user at the same time

mum[1]
noun Colloquial **1** a mother: *Will your **mum** pick us up?*
2 Mum, a word used when you address your mother

Word use: Children often use **mummy** or **Mummy**.

mum[2]
phrase **keep mum about**, *Old-fashioned* to say nothing about: *to **keep mum about** the plan*

Word history: Middle English; imitative

mumble
verb to speak softly and unclearly (***murmur***, ***mutter***)

Word history: from Middle English word meaning 'make inarticulate sounds'

mumbo jumbo
noun meaningless words, especially when thought to have a magical effect

Word history: from the name of a god formerly worshipped by certain West African tribes

mummify
verb **1** to make a dead body into a mummy
2 to dry or shrivel up

Verb forms: I **mummified**, I have **mummified**, I am **mummifying**

mummy[1]
noun a dead body that has been specially treated to stop it from decaying: ***Mummies** were found in the pyramids of Egypt.*

Word history: Middle English, from Medieval Latin, from Arabic, from Persian word meaning 'asphalt'

mummy[2]
noun → **mum**[1]

mumps
plural noun a disease caused by a virus which makes the glands around your mouth and neck very sore and swollen: ***Mumps** is a disease which can be serious if not properly treated.*

Word history: originally meaning 'grimace'

> Although **mumps** is a plural noun, it is followed by a singular verb: *Mumps was a common childhood illness.*

munch
verb to chew noisily: *Horses **munch** apples.* (***chomp***, ***crunch***)

Word history: from Middle English word meaning 'eat', 'chew'

mundane
adjective ordinary or boring: *to lead a very* ***mundane*** *life* (***banal***, ***commonplace***, ***everyday***, ***humdrum***)

Word history: from Latin word meaning 'of the world'

municipal
adjective having to do with a municipality: *the* ***municipal*** *library*

Word history: Latin

municipal council
noun a local administrative body which serves a municipality, predominantly in a rural town or city suburban area

Word use: Compare this with **city council** and **shire council**.

municipality (myooh-nuh-suh-pal-uh-tee)
noun a district which has its own local government: *The council collects the garbage from all houses in the* ***municipality***.

munitions
plural noun weapons and ammunition used in war

mural
noun a picture painted on a wall or ceiling

Word history: French, from Latin

murder
noun **1** the crime of deliberately killing someone (***assassination***, ***homicide***, ***slaughter***, ***slaying***)
2 *Colloquial* a very hard or unpleasant job: *It's* ***murder*** *trying to comb the knots out of your hair.*

Word building: **murder** *verb* **murderer** *noun* **murderous** *adjective*
Word history: Old English

murky
adjective dark and gloomy: *a* ***murky*** *cave* | ***murky*** *water* (***cloudy***, ***foggy***, ***shadowy***)

Adjective forms: **murkier**, **murkiest**
Word building: **murk** *noun* **murkiness** *noun*
Word history: Old English

murmur
noun a whispering sound or conversation: *the* ***murmur*** *of the wind in the trees* | *the* ***murmur*** *of the children in school assembly* (***rustle***, ***sigh***, ***undertone***)

Word building: **murmur** *verb* (**murmured**, **murmuring**) **murmuring** *adjective*
Word history: Middle English, from Latin

Murri (mur-ee)
noun an Aboriginal person from parts of Qld and NSW

Word use: Compare this with **Anangu**, **Koori**, **Nunga**, **Nyungar**, **Yamatji** and **Yolngu**.
Word history: from Kamilaroi, an Australian Aboriginal language of northern NSW

muscle (mus-uhl)
noun **1** the parts of the body which give it the strength and power to move
2 strength or force: (***might***, ***power***, ***vigour***)

Word building: **muscly** *adjective* **muscular** *adjective* **muscularity** *noun*
Word history: French, from Latin word meaning 'little mouse' (from the appearance of certain muscles)

muscle / mussel
Don't confuse **muscle** with **mussel**, which is a type of shellfish that you can eat.

muse[1]
verb to meditate or be lost in thought: *to* ***muse*** *on what might happen* (***daydream***, ***let your thoughts wander***, ***ponder***, ***switch off***)

Word history: Middle English, from Old French word meaning 'ponder', 'loiter'

muse[2]
noun a person who inspires a creative force in someone: *I actually wrote the poems but she was my* ***muse***.
Word history: from the nine *Muses* who, in Greek mythology, were the goddesses in charge of writing, painting and science

museum
noun a place where rare and interesting things are displayed (***gallery***)

Word history: Latin, from Greek word meaning 'seat of the Muses', 'place of study', 'library'

mush
noun **1** something thick and soft like porridge (***mash***, ***pulp***, ***slush***)
2 *Colloquial* something very sentimental, such as a film or book

Word building: **mushy** *adjective* (**mushier**, **mushiest**)
Word history: blend of (obsolete) *moose* thick vegetable porridge and *mash*

mushroom
noun **1** a type of fungus shaped like an umbrella which grows very quickly in damp soil and which you can eat
verb **2** to spread or grow quickly: *Interest in the new book* ***mushroomed*** *after the author appeared on television.*

Word use: Compare definition 1 with **toadstool**.
Word history: late Middle English, from French, from Late Latin

music
noun **1** sounds combined together using melody, rhythm and harmony to express ideas and feelings
2 written notes and signs which represent sounds which can be sung or played on a musical instrument
phrase **3 face the music**, to face the unpleasant results of your actions

Word history: Middle English, from Latin, from Greek *mousikē* (*technē*) originally, any art over which the Muses presided

musical
adjective **1** producing music or like music: ***musical*** *instruments* | *a* ***musical*** *voice* (***lyrical***, ***melodious***, ***tuneful***)
2 fond of music or able to play an instrument or sing well
noun **3** a play or film with a lot of singing and dancing

musician
noun someone who plays or composes music

music sticks
plural noun two wooden sticks which are hit together rhythmically to make music (***song sticks***)

musk
noun a strong perfume produced by a type of deer

Word building: **musky** *adjective* (**muskier, muskiest**)
Word history: Middle English, from Late Latin, from Late Greek, from Persian

musket
noun an old-fashioned type of gun from which the modern rifle has developed

Word history: French, from Italian

Muslim (mooz-luhm, muz-luhm)
noun **1** a person whose religion is Islam
adjective **2** having to do with the Islamic religion: ***Muslim** law*

Word use: You can also use **Moslem.**
Word history: from Arabic word meaning 'submission' or 'someone who accepts Islam'

muslin (muz-luhn)
noun a soft, fine, cotton material

Word history: French, from Italian word meaning 'muslin', from *Mussolo* Mosul, city in Iraq

mussel
noun a type of shellfish which has two black shells hinged together and which you can eat

Word history: Middle Low German

mussel / muscle

Don't confuse **mussel** with **muscle**. Your **muscles** are the parts of your body which give it the ability to move.

must
verb **1** to have to: *I **must** tidy my room.*
2 to be definitely: *She **must** be nearly 90.*
noun **3** something that is thought to be necessary: *This new book is a **must** for all children.* (***essential, necessity, requirement***)

Word use: The verb form is always used with another verb and is called an *auxiliary* (helping) verb.
Word history: Old English

must-
an informal word part used to indicate something which is considered a necessity: *a **must**-see film* / *a **must**-have dress*

mustard
noun **1** a yellow-brown powder or paste made from the seeds of a herb, which is used as a hot spice in cooking
phrase **2 keen as mustard**, very eager

Word history: Middle English, from Old French

muster
verb **1** to make gather into a group: *to **muster** sheep* (***assemble, marshal, round up***)
2 to gather together: *The soldiers **mustered** on the parade ground.* (***assemble, congregate, meet, rally, turn out***)
noun **3** a gathering up or rounding up into a group
phrase **4 pass muster**, to come up to a certain standard: *Those dirty fingernails certainly won't **pass muster**.*

Word building: **musterer** *noun*
Word history: Middle English, from Old French, from Latin word meaning 'show'

musty
adjective smelling stale: *Yuusuke opened the windows to air the **musty** room.*

Adjective forms: **mustier, mustiest**

mutant
noun a new type of organism produced by mutation

Word building: **mutant** *adjective*

mutate
verb to change or alter from one appearance, kind, or quality, to another (***adapt, evolve, metamorphose***)

mutation
noun **1** a plant or animal which becomes different in appearance or nature because of a change in genes
2 the process of changing

Word history: Middle English, from Latin

mute
noun **1** someone who can't speak
2 something which can be put in or on a musical instrument to soften the sound
adjective **3** silent: *a **mute** stare*
verb **4** to deaden the sound
5 to soften or reduce in volume

Word history: from Latin word meaning 'silent', 'dumb'

mutilate (myooh-tuh-layt)
verb to injure, damage or disfigure very badly (***maim, mangle, wound***)

Word building: **mutilation** *noun* **mutilator** *noun*
Word history: from Latin word meaning 'cut off', 'maimed'

mutiny (myooh-tuh-nee)
noun rebellion against authority, especially of sailors or soldiers against their officers

Noun forms: The plural is **mutinies.**
Word building: **mutiny** *verb* (**mutinied, mutinying**) **mutinous** *adjective*

mutt
noun Colloquial **1** a dog, especially a mongrel
2 a stupid person (***dolt, fool, idiot, imbecile, simpleton***)

Word history: origin uncertain; perhaps short from *muttonhead*

mutter
verb to speak or grumble in a low voice that is hard to understand (***mumble, murmur***)

Word building: **mutter** *noun*
Word history: from Middle English word meaning 'speak', 'murmur', Old English word meaning 'speak in public'

mutton
noun the meat from a sheep

Word history: Middle English, from Old French; of Celtic origin

mutton-bird
noun any of various species of petrel, the chicks of which are commercially harvested for their oil, feathers and flesh, especially the short-tailed shearwater of the Pacific Ocean, which in summer nests in Tasmania, South Australia, Victoria, and the islands of Bass Strait

Word use: You can also use **muttonbird.**

mutual (<u>myooh</u>-chooh-uhl)
adjective shared or common: *our **mutual** friend*

Word building: **mutuality** *noun*
Word history: Middle English, from Latin word meaning 'reciprocal'

muzak (<u>myooh</u>-zak)
noun recorded background music played continuously in places of work, hotels, lifts, etc., or over the telephone, and meant to make people feel happy and at ease

Word history: Trademark

muzzle
noun **1** the jaws, mouth and nose of an animal (***snout***)
2 a small wire cage which can be fastened over an animal's mouth to stop it biting
3 the open front end of a gun
verb **4** to put a muzzle on the mouth of an animal
5 to stop someone speaking or expressing an opinion (***gag***, ***silence***, ***suppress***)

Word history: Middle English, from Old French word meaning 'little muzzle'

my
pronoun the possessive form of **I**, used before a noun: ***my** dog*

My is a first person singular pronoun. It is sometimes called a *determiner* or a *possessive adjective.*

For more information, look up **pronouns: personal pronouns** and **pronouns: possessive pronouns.**

myall (<u>muy</u>-awl)
noun **1** any of several wattle trees
2 a hard fine-grained wood of such a tree used for carving

Word history: from Dharug, an Australian Aboriginal language spoken by the people living near Sydney Cove in the early days of European settlement

myna (<u>muy</u>-nuh)
noun a noisy, chocolate-brown bird with a black head, and yellow beak and legs, introduced from Asia and now common around large cities and cane-growing areas in eastern Australia

Word use: You can also use **Indian myna**.
Word history: from Hindustani word meaning 'a starling'

myocardial infarct (muy-oh-kah-dee-uhl <u>in</u>-fahkt)
noun → **heart attack**

myopia (muy-<u>oh</u>-pee-uh)
noun a condition of the eyes which stops you from clearly seeing things in the distance

Word building: **myopic** (muy-<u>op</u>-ik) *adjective*
Word history: Neo-Latin, from Greek word meaning 'short-sighted'

myriad (<u>mi</u>-ree-uhd)
noun a very great number: ***myriads** of tiny beetles | a **myriad** stars in the sky*

Word building: **myriad** *adjective*
Word history: from Greek word meaning 'ten thousand'

myself
pronoun **1** the reflexive form of **I**: *I cut **myself**.*
2 a form of **me** or **I** used for emphasis: *I did it **myself**.*
3 your normal or proper self: *I don't feel **myself** today.*

For more information, look up **pronouns: reflexive pronouns.**

mysterious (muh-<u>stear</u>-ree-uhs)
adjective puzzling or full of mystery: *a **mysterious** smile* (***ambiguous***, ***bewildering***, ***confusing***, ***perplexing***)

mystery (<u>mis</u>-tree, <u>mis</u>-tuh-ree)
noun something that is puzzling or secret or can't be explained: *the **mystery** of UFOs* (***enigma***, ***puzzle***)

Word history: Middle English, from Latin, from Greek

mystic (<u>mis</u>-tik)
noun someone who prays or meditates in order to know the mysteries of God and the universe

Word building: **mysticism** *noun*
Word history: Middle English, from Latin, from Greek word meaning 'mystic', 'secret'

mystical (<u>mis</u>-tik-uhl)
adjective **1** having to do with mystics or mysticism: *a **mystical** experience*
2 of occult character, power, or significance: *a **mystical** formula*
3 spiritually significant or symbolic
4 inspiring a sense of spiritual mystery or wonder: *the **mystical** power of nature*
5 of the nature of or having to do with mysteries known only to the initiated: ***mystical** rites*
6 of obscure or mysterious character or significance

Word building: **mystically** *adverb* **mysticalness** *noun*

mystify (<u>mis</u>-tuh-fuy)
verb to bewilder or puzzle (***baffle***, ***confound***, ***confuse***, ***perplex***)

Verb forms: I **mystified**, I have **mystified**, I am **mystifying**
Word history: French

mystique (mis-<u>teek</u>)
noun an air of mystery or mysterious power surrounding some person, object, belief, etc.

Word history: French

myth
noun an ancient story about gods, heroes and supernatural happenings, which may try to explain natural events like the weather, sunrise and sunset, etc. (***fable***, ***legend***)

Word building: **mythological** *adjective*
Word history: Neo-Latin, from Late Latin, from Greek word meaning 'word', 'speech', 'tale', 'legend', 'myth'

mythical
adjective **1** having to do with myths: *The bunyip is a **mythical** creature.*
2 having no foundation in fact: *His claim to be related to royalty is completely **mythical**.*

Word use: The opposite of definition 2 is **real**.

mythology
noun all the myths of a particular culture

myxomatosis (mik-suh-muh-<u>toh</u>-suhs)
noun a very infectious disease which kills rabbits

naan (nahn)
noun a slightly leavened Indian bread, usually round

Word use: You can also use **nan**.

nab
verb to catch or seize suddenly (***capture, grab, nail, snap up, snatch, take***)

Verb forms: I **nabbed**, I have **nabbed**, I am **nabbing**

nachos
plural noun a snack made from corn chips with tomato, chilli, and melted cheese on top

Word history: Mexican Spanish

nadir (nay-dear)
noun **1** the point of the celestial sphere directly beneath any place or observer and opposite to the zenith
2 the lowest point of anything, such as of misfortune

Word use: Compare this with **zenith**.
Word history: Middle English, from Arabic word meaning 'corresponding', 'opposite' (that is, to the zenith)

nag[1]
verb to keep on finding fault, complaining or making demands (***gripe, grumble, whine, whinge***)

Verb forms: I **nagged**, I have **nagged**, I am **nagging**
Word history: Scandinavian

nag[2]
noun Colloquial a horse, especially one that is old or worn out

Word history: Middle English *nagge*

nail
noun **1** a small, metal spike, usually with a flattened end, used to fasten pieces of wood together
2 the thin, horny end of your finger or toe
verb **3** to fasten with nails
phrase **4 hit the nail on the head**, to say or do exactly the right thing

Word history: Old English *nægl*

naive (nuy-eev)
adjective simple, innocent and ignorant: *a **naive** comment* (***gullible, unsophisticated, unworldly***)

Word building: **naivety** *noun*
Word history: French, from Latin word meaning 'native', 'natural'

naivety / nativity

These words look similar but have different meanings. **Nativity** means 'birth'.

The **Nativity** (always written with a capital N) is the birth of Christ.

naked (nay-kuhd)
adjective unclothed or bare: *a **naked** body | the **naked** truth* (***bald, exposed, nude***)

Word building: **nakedness** *noun*
Word history: Old English *nacod*

naltrexone (nal-trek-sohn)
noun a drug used to treat drug addiction

name
noun **1** what someone or something is called
2 reputation or fame: *She has made her **name** as a trumpet player.*
verb **3** to give a name to: *They **named** the baby Angelo.* (***call, christen, dub***)
4 to mention by name: *The report **named** three business people.*
phrase **5 in the name of,**
a with appeal to: ***In the name of** mercy, stop screaming!*
b by the authority of
6 to someone's name, belonging to someone: *not a cent **to my name***

Word history: Old English *nama*

namely
adverb that is to say: *two cities, **namely,** Sydney and Melbourne*

namesake
noun someone having, or given, the same name as another

Word history: alteration of *name's sake*

naming ceremony
noun **1** a ceremony at which someone or something is officially named
2 an occasion at which a child is named, guardians (or godparents) appointed, etc.

Noun forms: The plural is **naming ceremonies**.

nanna
noun Colloquial a grandmother

Word use: You can also use **nana** or **nan**.

nanny
noun a woman who lives in your house to look after your children

Noun forms: The plural is **nannies**.
Word history: alteration of female first name *Ann*

nanny goat
noun a female goat

nanomedicine
noun medical treatments which use nanotechnology, such as the use of controllable micro-sized robots to perform medical procedures

nanometre
noun one billionth (10^{-9}) of a metre

nanoparticle
noun a microscopic particle whose size is measured in nanometres

nanoscience
noun the science concerned with objects of the smallest dimensions

nanotechnology
noun technology generated from nanoscience

Word building: **nanotechnologist** *noun*

nap[1]
verb to have a short sleep (***doze***, ***drowse***, ***sleep***, ***slumber***, ***snooze***)

Verb forms: I **napped**, I have **napped**, I am **napping**
Word building: **nap** *noun*
Word history: Old English *hnappian*

nap[2]
noun **1** the short ends of fibres on the surface of cloth drawn up by brushing
2 any soft, hairy coating, as on plants

Word history: Old English *-hnoppe* (in *wullhnoppa* tuft of wool)

napalm (nay-pahm, na-pahm)
noun a substance which is mixed with petrol and used in flame throwers and fire bombs

Word history: *na(phtha)* a petrol product + *palm(itate)* salt from palm oil

nape
noun the back of the neck

Word history: Middle English

naphthalene (naf-thuh-leen)
noun a white crystalline solid, used in making dyes, as a moth repellent, etc.

Word use: You can also use **naphthaline** or **naphthalin.**
Word history: *naphth(a)* petrol product + *al(cohol)* + *-ene*

napkin
noun a serviette

Word history: Middle English word meaning 'little tablecloth', from French, from Latin word meaning 'cloth'

nappy
noun a piece of cloth or a pad of paper tissue fastened round a baby's waist and legs to soak up its urine and contain the waste matter from its bowels

Word history: alteration of *napkin*

narcissism (nar-suh-siz-uhm)
noun self love, especially love of your own appearance

Word building: **narcissistic** *adjective*
Word history: Greek

narcissus (nar-sis-uhs)
noun any of a group of bulbous plants bearing flowers with a cup-shaped corona, such as the wild daffodil

Noun forms: The plural is **narcissuses** or **narcissi** (nar-sis-uy).
Word history: Latin, from the Greek *Narcissos*, the name of the beautiful youth who fell in love with his own relfection in a pool of water and pined away with longing. A flower grew up on the spot where he died which was given his name.

narcosis (nah-koh-suhs)
noun a state of sleep, drowsiness, or unconsciousness, especially produced by a drug

Word history: Neo-Latin, from Greek word meaning 'a benumbing'

narcotic
noun any drug which can relieve pain and make you sleepy

Word building: **narcotic** *adjective*
Word history: from Greek word meaning 'making stiff or numb'

nark
noun Colloquial **1** an informer or spy, especially for the police
2 a person who continually complains and spoils the pleasure of others
verb Colloquial **3** to annoy or irritate
4 to act as an informer

Word history: from Romani word meaning 'nose'

narrate
verb to tell a particular story in speech or writing (***describe***, ***outline***, ***recount***, ***relate***)

Word building: **narration** *noun* **narrator** *noun*
Word history: Latin

narrative (na-ruh-tiv)
noun **1** a story of events, experiences, etc. (***tale***)
2 the act or art of narrating
adjective **3** using the form of a narrative: *a **narrative** poem*
4 having to do with narration: ***narrative** skill*

narrative genre
noun the type of writing which involves the telling of a story

narrow
adjective **1** not wide: ***narrow** stairs* (***confined***, ***cramped***, ***small***, ***tight***)
2 only just succeeding: *a **narrow** escape*
3 small-minded and lacking understanding of other people or the world: *a **narrow** person* (***biased***, ***bigoted***, ***intolerant***, ***narrow-minded***, ***prejudiced***)

Word history: Old English *nearu*

narrow-minded
adjective not liking or understanding people, customs, etc., that are different to yours: ***narrow-minded** views*

Word use: The opposite of this is **broad-minded**.

nasal
adjective **1** having to do with your nose: *a **nasal** spray*
2 sounded through your nose: *a **nasal** voice*

Word building: **nasality** *noun*
Word history: from Latin word meaning 'nose'

nascent (nay-suhnt, nas-uhnt)
adjective beginning to exist or develop: *the **nascent** republic*

Word building: **nascence** *noun* **nascency** *noun*
Word history: from Latin word meaning 'being born'

nasturtium (nuh-ster-shuhm)
noun a garden plant with red, yellow or orange flowers and round leaves

Word history: from Latin word meaning 'a type of cress'

nasty
adjective **1** unpleasant or disgusting: ***nasty** weather* | *a **nasty** smell* (***awful***, ***repulsive***, ***revolting***, ***yucky***)
2 unkind or cruel: *She was very **nasty** to her little brother.* (***mean***, ***shabby***)

Adjective forms: **nastier**, **nastiest**
Word building: **nastiness** *noun*
Word history: Middle English, origin uncertain

natal (nay-tuhl)
adjective having to do with someone's birth

Word history: Middle English, from Latin

nation
noun **1** a large group of people living in one country under one government (***kingdom***, ***power***, ***realm***, ***republic***)
2 a group of people who have the same customs, history, and language, though they may not have their own government: *an elder of the Gurindji **nation***

Word building: **national** *adjective*
Word history: Middle English, from Latin word meaning 'birth'

nationalise
verb to bring under public ownership or government control: *to **nationalise** the health system*

Word use: You can also use **nationalize.**
Word building: **nationalisation** *noun*

nationalise / naturalise

Don't confuse **nationalise** with **naturalise.** To **naturalise** someone is to make them a full citizen of a country.

nationalism
noun **1** patriotism or love of your own country: *His **nationalism** took the form of singing bush ballads.*
2 a strong wish for the growth, freedom and independence of your country or nation
3 extreme, unreasoning devotion to your own nation

Word building: **nationalist** *noun* **nationalistic** *adjective*

nationality
noun membership or connection that someone has with a country: *I have Australian **nationality**.* (***citizenship***)

Noun forms: The plural is **nationalities**.

national park
noun an area of land set aside by the government to preserve the flora and fauna of a region, and open to the public for enjoyment and education

native
adjective **1** of your birth: *your **native** land*
2 belonging to the place you were born: ***native** language*
3 belonging to the country it is in: *a **native** plant*
noun **4** someone born in a particular place: *a **native** of Adelaide*
5 one of the people who have lived in a country for hundreds of years: *a **native** of Italy*
6 a plant or animal in its own country

Word history: from Latin word meaning 'native', 'innate', 'natural'

native species
noun a species of plant or animal which is endemic to an area

native title
noun the legal right held by an Aboriginal or Torres Strait Islander person to land or water that they have maintained connection with

nativity
noun **1** birth
phrase **2 the Nativity**, the birth of Jesus Christ

Noun forms: The plural is **nativities.**
Word history: Middle English, from Late Latin

nativity / naivety

Don't confuse **nativity** with **naivety**.

We say that someone has an air of **naivety** if they are not sophisticated and have a childlike approach to life.

natural
adjective **1** found in or formed by nature: *a **natural** harbour*
2 inborn or given by nature: ***natural** talent*
3 real and without pretence: *a **natural** manner* (***plain***, ***simple***, ***unaffected***)
noun **4 a** a note that is not a sharp or flat
b the sign in music (♮) that is placed before a note to show it is a natural

Word use: The opposite of definition 3 is **affected.**
Word history: Middle English, from Latin word meaning 'by birth', 'in accordance with nature'

natural gas
noun a combustible gas formed naturally in the earth, usually consisting of methane and other gases, used as a fuel and in making organic compounds

naturalise
verb to make a full citizen of a country

Word use: You can also use **naturalize.**

naturalist
noun a person who studies nature

natural selection
noun a process of evolution in which those with characteristics best adapted to their surroundings survive in the struggle for existence, thus passing on their characteristics to the next generation

nature
noun **1** the world around us made up of earth, sky and sea, especially when untouched by human beings: *Lovers of **nature** enjoy bushwalking.*

2 the make-up and qualities of a person or thing: *She has a kind* ***nature.*** | *The* ***nature*** *of glue is to stick.*
3 kind or sort: *These books are of the same* ***nature.***

Word history: Middle English, from Latin word meaning 'birth', 'natural character'

naturopathy (nach-uh-rop-uh-thee)
noun a system of treating disease in ways considered natural, especially by use of herbs, natural foods, etc.

Word building: **naturopath** *noun*

naught (nawt)
noun Old-fashioned **1** nothing
2 destruction, ruin or complete failure: *to bring to* ***naught*** | *to come to* ***naught***
phrase **3 set at naught**, to regard or treat as of no importance

Word history: Old English *nā*, no[2] + *wiht* thing

naught / nought

Don't confuse **naught** with **nought**, the sign in maths (0) which stands for zero.

naughty (naw-tee)
adjective badly behaved (***incorrigible***, ***mischievous***, ***perverse***, ***uncooperative***)

Adjective forms: **naughtier, naughtiest**

nausea (naw-zee-uh, naw-see-uh)
noun a feeling of wanting to vomit

Word building: **nauseate** *verb* **nauseous** *adjective*
Word history: Latin, from Greek *naus* a ship, which gave rise to *nausia* seasickness

nautical
adjective having to do with ships, sailors or sailing (***maritime***, ***naval***, ***seafaring***, ***seagoing***)

Word history: Latin, from Greek word meaning 'relating to ships or sailors'

nautilus (naw-tuhl-uhs)
noun a kind of squid or octopus with a spiral shell divided into many sections

Word history: Latin, from Greek word meaning 'sailor'

naval
adjective having to do with a navy: *a* ***naval*** *battle* | ***naval*** *uniform*

naval / navel

Don't confuse **naval** with **navel**, the small, round hollow in the stomach.

nave
noun the middle part, lengthwise, of a church, usually having the aisles on either side and reaching from the entrance to the chancel

Word history: Medieval Latin

navel
noun **1** the small, round hollow in the middle of the stomach, which is where the umbilical cord is attached at birth
phrase **2 navel orange**, a kind of seedless orange that has a hollow at the top rather like a navel

Word history: Old English *nafela*

navigate
verb **1** to steer or direct on a course: *to* ***navigate*** *a ship*
2 *Internet* to find your way around (a website)

Word building: **navigable** *adjective* **navigation** *noun* **navigator** *noun*
Word history: Latin

navy (nay-vee)
noun **1** the part of a country's armed forces that is trained to fight at sea (***fleet***)
2 a very dark blue colour, as of a naval uniform
adjective **3** of a navy colour: ***navy*** *shorts*

Noun forms: The plural is **navies.**
Word use: You can also use **navy blue** for definitions 2 and 3.
Word history: Middle English, from Old French, from Latin word meaning 'ship'

nay
adverb **1** *Old-fashioned* no
2 *Old-fashioned* not only but also: *many good,* ***nay,*** *noble qualities*
noun **3** a refusal or denial
4 a negative vote or voter, as in Parliament

Word history: Middle English, from Scandinavian

nazi (naht-see)
noun (*plural* **Nazis**)
1 (*also upper case*) someone who believes in racist policies, or has racist beliefs, especially ones aimed at Jewish people
2 (*also upper case*) *Colloquial*
a someone who is extremely domineering and unwilling to compromise
b someone who displays a dictatorial attitude about how people should think or behave with regard to a particular topic or thing: *a kitchen* ***Nazi***

Word history: from the name given to members of the National Socialist German Workers' party, which established a dictatorship over Germany in 1933 under Adolf Hitler.

NB
abbreviation note well

NB is used when you want to draw your reader's attention to some particular point:

NB: There are several studies on this subject not yet published.

As it is an abbreviation, you should avoid using it in your essays where it is best not to use shorthand expressions.

You might sometimes see this abbreviation written **n.b.** Because the letters are lower-case here, full stops are needed. For more about this, look up **abbreviation**.

neap
noun one of the tides, midway between spring tides, which have the least height

Word use: You can also use **neap tide**.
Word history: Old English *nēpflōd* neap flood

near
adverb **1** at or to a short distance: *Stand* ***near.*** | *Come* ***near.***
adjective **2** being at a short distance in place or time: *The shops are* ***near.*** | *Christmas is* ***near.*** (***adjacent***, ***close***, ***neighbouring***, ***next***)
3 less distant: *the* ***near*** *side*

verb **4** to come close to or approach: *We* ***neared*** *the wharf. | The storm is* ***nearing.***

Word history: Old English *nēar*, comparative of *nēah* nigh

nearby
adjective **1** near: *a* ***nearby*** *building*
adverb **2** not far off: *The school is* ***nearby.***

nearly
adverb **1** almost: *We* ***nearly*** *reached the top.*
2 closely: ***nearly*** *related*

neat
adjective **1** tidy and ordered: *a* ***neat*** *room* (***methodical, orderly, shipshape, trim***)
2 well thought out and put together: *a* ***neat*** *plan*

Word building: **neatness** *noun*
Word history: French word meaning 'clean', from Latin word meaning 'bright', 'fine', 'neat'

nebula (neb-yuh-luh)
noun a cloudlike patch in the night sky, consisting of a galaxy of stars, or of materials from which such galaxies are being formed

Noun forms: The plural is **nebulas** or **nebulae** (neb-yuh-lee).
Word history: from Latin word meaning 'mist', 'vapour', 'cloud'

nebulise (neb-yuh-luyz)
verb **1** to reduce to fine spray: ***nebulised*** *liquid in the air*
2 to administer medication by means of a nebuliser: *The doctor advised that it was more effective to* ***nebulise*** *the medication.*

Verb forms: I **nebulised**, I have **nebulised**, I am **nebulising**
Word use: You can also use **nebulize**.

nebuliser
noun Medicine a device which reduces a liquid medication to a fine mist which is then inhaled into the lungs

Word use: You can also use **nebulizer**.

nebulous (neb-yuh-luhs)
adjective cloudy or vague: *a* ***nebulous*** *shape | a* ***nebulous*** *idea* (***ethereal, ghostly, intangible, shadowy***)

Word history: Middle English, from Latin

necessary (nes-uhs-uh-ree, nes-uhs-ree)
adjective **1** unable to be done without: *Water is* ***necessary*** *for life.* (***crucial, essential, imperative, obligatory, vital***)
2 that must happen: *a* ***necessary*** *result of his illness*
noun **3** something necessary

Noun forms: The plural is **necessaries**.
Word building: **necessarily** *adverb*
Word history: Middle English, from Latin word meaning 'unavoidable', 'indispensable'

necessitate (nuh-ses-uh-tayt)
verb to make necessary: *The breakdown of the motor* ***necessitated*** *a halt.*

necessity (nuh-ses-uh-tee)
noun **1** something that cannot be done without: *A car is a* ***necessity*** *in the country.*
2 the state of being poor: ***Necessity*** *caused him to steal.*

Noun forms: The plural is **necessities**.
Word history: Middle English, from Latin word meaning 'exigency'

neck
noun **1** the part of the body of an animal or human which joins the head to the rest
2 any narrow connecting part: *the* ***neck*** *of a bottle | the* ***neck*** *of a violin*
phrase **3 neck and neck**, completely even in a race
4 neck of the woods, a particular area or place: *We don't often see you in this* ***neck of the woods.***
5 stick your neck out, to act, speak, etc., so as to leave yourself open to criticism or risk

Word history: Old English *hnecca*

necklace
noun a string of beads or other ornament worn round your neck

necromancy (nek-ruh-man-see)
noun **1** magic in general
2 the foretelling of the future through supposed communication with the dead

Word building: **necromancer** *noun*
Word history: Latin, from Greek

nectar
noun **1** a sweet liquid produced by plants and made into honey by bees
2 the drink of the gods of classical mythology
3 any delicious drink

Word history: Latin, from Greek

nectarine
noun a kind of peach with a smooth skin

Word history: *nectar* + *-ine*

nee (nay)
adjective born

Word use: You can also use **née**. | This is placed after the name of a married woman to introduce her maiden name.
Word history: French

need
noun **1** something that you have to have: *The immediate* ***needs*** *of the flood victims are food and shelter.* (***necessity, requirement***)
2 an urgent want: *a* ***need*** *for food | a* ***need*** *for improvement*
3 a situation or time when you want something: *a friend in* ***need***
verb **4** to have a need for: *You* ***need*** *help.*
5 to have to do: *I* ***need*** *to cut my lawn*

Word building: **needful** *adjective* **needless** *adjective*
Word history: Old English *nēd*

need / knead
Don't confuse **need** with **knead**, which means 'to press and push something with your hands':

The pastry chef kneaded the dough.

needle
noun **1** a small, thin, pointed tool, usually made of steel and with a hole at one end for thread, used for sewing
2 a thin rod for knitting, or one hooked at the end for crocheting
3 a pointer on a dial: *a compass* ***needle***
4 a thin tube sharp enough to pierce your skin, used for giving injections

5 anything sharp and shaped like a needle: *a pine* ***needle***
6 → **stylus** (definition 2)

Word history: Old English dialect *nēdl*

needlework
noun the act or product of working with a needle in sewing or embroidery

needn't
contraction of **need not**

Look up **contractions in grammar**.

needy
adjective very poor: *a* ***needy*** *family* (***disadvantaged***, ***hard up***, ***impoverished***)

Adjective forms: **needier**, **neediest**

nefarious (nuh-fair-ree-uhs)
adjective very wicked or iniquitous: ***nefarious*** *practices*

Word history: from Latin word meaning 'impious'

negate (nuh-gayt)
verb **1** to remove the effect of: *to* ***negate*** *a ruling*
2 to prove untrue: *to* ***negate*** *a belief*

Word building: **negatory** *adjective*

negative
adjective **1** saying or meaning no: *a* ***negative*** *answer*
2 minus or smaller than nothing: *a* ***negative*** *number*
3 having an excess of electrons: *the* ***negative*** *poles of an electric cell*
noun **4** a photographic film which is used to make prints and has the light and dark of the picture reversed

Word use: The opposite of definition 1 is **affirmative**.
Word building: **negation** *noun*
Word history: Middle English, from Latin word meaning 'denying'

negatives

There are several words in English which are used to make **negative** sentences. They include *no*, *not* and *never*.

You have to be careful not to use more negatives than you really need, since two negatives may be said to equal a positive.

I've never done nothing like that.

is not the same as:

I've never done anything like that.

double negatives

There have been times in the history of our language when it was possible to stack up negative words in a sentence (like *no*, *not*, *never*) to emphasise your point. It is not possible to do that today in standard English — people will say that two negatives make a positive, as in maths:

I haven't got no money.

This sentence could be taken to mean that you have got some money! Even words like *hardly* and *scarcely* are regarded as negatives:

I can't hardly do it.

Sentences like this are not acceptable in standard writing or speech (although there may be occasions when you want to include them in informal dialogue to indicate emphasis).

Note also that the use of double negatives can be quite deliberate in formal writing. It can give a quality of understatement to your writing:

I was not unimpressed by the sight of Uluru at dawn.

negative space
noun Art the background areas in a composition or design which contrast with the main shapes or positive space

neglect
verb **1** to pay no attention to: *He* ***neglected*** *his piano practice.* (***disregard***, ***forget***, ***leave out***, ***omit***, ***overlook***)
2 to fail to look after: *to* ***neglect*** *a dog*

Word building: **neglect** *noun* **neglectful** *adjective*
Word history: from Latin word meaning 'unheeded'

negligee (neg-luh-zhay)
noun a woman's dressing-gown, especially one made of thin material

Word history: from French word meaning 'neglected'

negligence (neg-luh-juhns)
noun the failure to take proper care: *They showed* ***negligence*** *towards their family.*

negligent (neg-luh-juhnt)
adjective careless or neglectful (***casual***, ***irresponsible***, ***lax***, ***thoughtless***)

Word use: The opposite of this is **careful**.

negligible (neg-luh-juh-buhl)
adjective unimportant enough to be ignored: *The amount of wine spilt was* ***negligible***.

negotiable (nuh-goh-shuh-buhl)
adjective able to be negotiated: *The terms of the contract are* ***negotiable***.

negotiate (nuh-goh-shee-ayt)
verb to arrange by discussion: *The government has* ***negotiated*** *a treaty.* (***broker***, ***mediate***)

Word building: **negotiation** *noun*
Word history: Latin

neigh (nay)
noun the sound a horse makes

Word building: **neigh** *verb*
Word history: Old English *hnǣgan*

neighbour
noun (nay-buh) someone who lives near you

Word use: You can also use **neighbor**.
Word building: **neighbourly** *adjective*
Word history: Old English *nēah* nigh + *gebūr* dweller, countryman

neighbourhood
noun (nay-buh-hood) **1** the region near or round about some place or thing (***locality***, ***vicinity***)
2 a part of a town or city, often marked by some quality: *a fashionable* ***neighbourhood***
3 a number of persons living near one another or in a particular place: *The whole* ***neighbourhood*** *was there.*

Word use: You can also use **neighborhood**.

neither (nuy-dhuh, nee-dhuh)
adjective **1** not one or the other: ***Neither** statement is true.*
pronoun **2** not the one or the other: ***Neither** of the statements is true.*
conjunction **3** not either: ***Neither** you nor I know the answer.*

neither ... nor

Neither is said to be a singular word so in very formal writing you say **neither** (of them) is, not **neither** (of them) are. However, in speech and in informal styles of writing, **neither** is often treated as if it were plural:

Neither of the boys are getting paid.

The same applies to **neither...nor**:

Neither Tony nor Anna is going.

Neither Tony nor Anna are going.

This is also the best solution when **neither... nor** is used with two words which would take different verbs:

Neither he nor I...

We couldn't complete the sentence with *is going* or *am going*. Neither of these sounds quite right. The usual way out is to finish with *...are going.*

nemesis (nem-uh-suhs)
noun fate, especially one that punishes

Noun forms: The plural is **nemeses** (nem-uh-seez).
Word history: named after *Nemesis*, who, in classical mythology, was the goddess of retribution or vengeance; Latin, from Greek

neologism (nee-ol-uh-jiz-uhm)
noun **1** a new word or phrase
2 the introduction or use of new words, or new meanings of words

Word history: French

neon
noun a gas which glows when an electric current is put through it, and so is used in lights

Word history: Neo-Latin, from Greek word meaning 'new'

neophyte (nee-uh-fuyt)
noun **1** a person being trained in the first steps of religious worship
2 a beginner in anything

Word building: **neophytic** *adjective*
Word history: Late Latin, from Greek word meaning 'newly planted'

nephew (nef-yooh, nev-yooh)
noun the son of your brother or sister, or of your husband's or wife's brother or sister

Word history: Middle English, from Old French, from Latin word meaning 'grandson', 'nephew'

nephritis (nuh-fruy-tuhs)
noun inflammation of the kidneys

Word building: **nephritic** *adjective*

nepotism (nep-uh-tiz-uhm)
noun the favouring of a relation or friend by giving them a job or promotion

Word history: French, from Italian, from Latin word meaning 'descendant'

nerd
noun Colloquial a person who has an awkward personality and dresses in a conservative way; a person who is not cool (definition 3)

Word history: perhaps from the name of a character appearing in Dr Seuss's children's book *If I ran the Zoo* (1950)

nerve
noun **1** a fibre or bundle of fibres that carries messages from your brain to other parts of your body so that you can move and feel
2 courage, especially when you are facing a difficult situation: *You need **nerve** to walk a tightrope.*
3 nerves, nervousness or shakiness: *I had an attack of **nerves** before the school play.*

Word history: Middle English, from Latin

nervous
adjective **1** having to do with the nervous system
2 excited, uneasy or frightened (***anxious**, **apprehensive**, **edgy**, **jittery**, **jumpy**, **nervy***)

Word building: **nervousness** *noun*

nervous system
noun **1** the system of nerves and nerve centres in an animal
phrase **2** a particular part of this system:
a central nervous system or **cerebrospinal nervous system**, the brain and spinal cord
b peripheral nervous system, the system of nerves derived from the central system, comprising the cranial nerves, the spinal nerves, the various sense organs, etc.
c autonomic nervous system, the system of nerves which supply the walls of the vascular system and the various viscera and glands

nervy
adjective **1** → **nervous** (definition 2)
2 becoming easily excited or angry (***edgy**, **irritable***)

Adjective forms: **nervier, nerviest**

nest
noun a shelter built or a place used by a bird to lay its eggs and bring up its young

Word building: **nest** *verb* **nestling** *noun*
Word history: Middle English and Old English

nest egg
noun a sum of money saved for special times or emergencies

nestle (nes-uhl)
verb to lie close, like a bird in a nest

Word history: Old English *nestlian*

net[1]
noun **1** a material made of fine threads knotted or woven together with holes in between
2 a fabric like this, made of cord or rope
3 an object that uses this material to catch something or to keep something out: *a fishing **net** | a mosquito **net***
4 a piece of net used in some sports, such as tennis
verb **5** to catch in a net

Verb forms: I **netted**, I have **netted**, I am **netting**
Word history: Old English *net(t)*

net[2]
adjective **1** not counting packaging: *The **net** weight of these baked beans is 250 grams.*

2 after expenses have been paid: ***net** profit*
3 after all calculations have been made, or all additions and subtractions have had their effect

Word use: You can also use **nett**.
Word history: from French word meaning 'clean', 'clear'

netball
noun **1** a game played by two teams of seven players, in which players try to score points by throwing the ball through a hoop attached to a pole at the opponents' end of a rectangular court
2 the ball used in this game

nether (nedh-uh)
adjective **1** lying, or thought of as lying, beneath the earth's surface: *the **nether** world*
2 lower or under: *his **nether** lip*

Word history: Middle English; Old English *neothera*

netiquette (net-ee-ket)
noun the generally accepted code of behaviour on the internet

Word history: blend of *(Inter)net* and *etiquette*

netizen
noun someone who uses the internet frequently

Word history: blend of *(inter)net* and *(cit)izen*

Netspeak
noun the language style that has evolved in online communication

nett
adjective → **net**[2]

nettle
noun **1** a common weed with hairs on its leaves and stem which cause a rash if you touch them
verb **2** to irritate: *His criticisms **nettled** me.*

Word history: Middle English; Old English *netele*

network
noun **1** a netlike arrangement of connected lines, passages or channels: *a **network** of drainage ditches*
2 a group of radio or television stations, sometimes having the same owner, that can broadcast the same programs
3 *Computers* a system of connecting computer systems or peripheral devices, each one remote from the others
4 a group of people linked by a shared interest or occupation: *a **network** of friends*
verb **5** to establish social contact with particular people because it is thought that they may prove to be useful

Word building: **networking** *noun*

neural (nyooh-ruhl)
adjective having to do with a nerve or the nervous system

neuralgia (nyooh-ral-juh)
noun a sharp and paroxysmal pain along a nerve

Word building: **neuralgic** *adjective*
Word history: New Latin *neur(o)-* nerve + *-algia* pain

neurology (nyooh-rol-uh-jee)
noun the science of the nerves or the nervous system, especially its diseases

Word building: **neurological** *adjective* **neurologist** *noun*

neurosis (nyooh-roh-suhs)
noun an emotional disorder in which someone suffers feelings of anxiety, obsessional thoughts, compulsive acts, and physical complaints without any real evidence of disease

Noun forms: The plural is **neuroses** (nyooh-roh-seez).

neurotic (nyooh-rot-ik)
adjective on edge and behaving strangely, because of a disorder of the mind

neurotoxin (nyooh-roh-tok-suhn)
noun a chemical, often highly toxic, which stops or slows down the function of the nervous system

neuter (nyooh-tuh)
adjective being neither masculine nor feminine

Word history: from Latin word meaning 'neither'

neutral (nyooh-truhl)
adjective **1** not taking one side or the other: *Sweden was **neutral** in World War II.* (***detached**, **disinterested**, **even-handed**, **noncommittal***)
2 greyish or of no particular colour (***bleached**, **faded**, **pale***)
noun **3** a person or country that does not take sides in a war
4 the position of gears in a car where they are not ready to be driven by the engine

Word building: **neutrality** (nyooh-tral-uh-tee) *noun*
Word history: Middle English, from Latin

neutralise (nyooh-truh-luyz)
verb **1** to make neutral
2 to make ineffective or counteract
3 to declare a country neutral
4 *Chemistry* to make chemically neutral, as when you add an acid to an alkali

Word use: You can also use **neutralize**.
Word building: **neutralisation** *noun*

neutron (nyooh-tron)
noun a part of an atom with the same mass as a proton but no charge

Word use: Compare this with **electron** and **proton**.
Word history: *neutr(al)* neither positive nor negative + *-on* (after *electron*, *proton*)

neutron bomb
noun a nuclear weapon which releases a shower of neutrons but little blast, thus killing people but causing little damage to property

Word use: Another name is **clean bomb**.

never
adverb **1** not ever
2 not at all
3 to no extent or degree

Word history: Old English *nǣfre*

never-never
noun *Australian* desert country where hardly anyone lives

nevertheless (nev-uh-dhuh-les)
adverb a strong form of **however**

new
adjective **1** recently arrived, obtained or come into being (***avant-garde***, ***fresh***, ***innovative***, ***novel***, ***original***)
2 fresh or unused: *Turn to a **new** page.*

Word building: **newness** *noun*
Word history: Middle English and Old English *newe*

new / knew
Don't confuse **new** with **knew**, which is the past tense of the verb **know**, to feel certain that something is true, or to have learned and understood it:
I knew you'd be late!

newbie
noun Colloquial **1** a newcomer to the internet
2 a newcomer to any activity

news
noun **1** a report of something that has just happened (***information***, ***intelligence***, ***the dope***, ***the drum***)
phrase **2 bad news**, *Colloquial* someone or something from whom nothing good is to be expected: *Ideas like that are really **bad news**.*

Word history: Middle English *news*, plural of Middle English, Old English *newe* that which is new, noun use of *newe*, adjective

newsagency
noun a shop which sells newspapers, magazines, stationery, etc.

Word building: **newsagent** *noun*

newsgroup
noun Internet an online discussion forum about a particular topic, in which users can post messages, and read messages posted by others

newspaper
noun a printed publication issued at regular times, usually daily or weekly, and commonly containing news, comment, features and advertisements

newsprint
noun the paper used or made to print newspapers on

newsreader
noun **1** one who reads the news on radio, television, etc.
2 *Internet* a program which allows a user to access, read and post messages in a newsgroup

newsreel
noun a short film showing current news events

newt
noun a small amphibian with a long tail related to the salamander

Word history: Middle English

newton
noun the derived SI unit of force; the force needed to give an acceleration of one metre per second per second to a mass of one kilogram

Word use: The symbol is **N**, without a full stop.
Word history: named after Sir Isaac *Newton*, 1642–1727, English scientist, mathematician and philosopher

Newton's law of gravitation
noun a law stating that any two bodies attract each other with a force proportional to the product of their masses and inversely proportional to the square of the distance between them

Word history: look up *newton*

Newton's laws
plural noun three classical laws of motion: **1** all bodies continue in a state of rest or uniform motion unless they are acted upon by an external force
2 the rate of change of momentum of a body is proportional to force applied to it
3 to every action there is an equal and opposite reaction

Word history: look up *newton*

next
adjective **1** immediately following: *the **next** day* (***imminent***, ***impending***, ***prospective***)
2 nearest: *the **next** room* (***adjacent***, ***close***, ***neighbouring***)
adverb **3** in the nearest place: *Can I sit **next** to you?*

Word history: Old English *nēxt*

next of kin
noun your nearest relation or relations

nexus (nek-suhs)
noun **1** a tie or link
2 a connected series

Noun forms: The plural is **nexus**.
Word history: Latin

nib
noun the writing point of a pen

Word history: Old English *nybba* point (in a placename)

nibble
verb **1** to bite off small bits from: *I **nibbled** the chocolate.*
2 to bite gently: *The fish **nibbled** the bait.*

Word building: **nibble** *noun*
Word history: late Middle English

nice
adjective **1** pleasing or delightful: *a **nice** day* (***agreeable***, ***enjoyable***, ***lovely***, ***pleasant***, ***welcome***)
2 kind or pleasant: ***nice** people* (***considerate***, ***thoughtful***, ***unselfish***, ***well-intentioned***)
3 showing great accuracy, skill or exactness: *a **nice** analysis of the problem*

Word history: Middle English, from Old French word meaning 'simple', from Latin word meaning 'not knowing'

nicety (nuys-uh-tee)
noun a fine or small point: *the **nicety** of his argument*

Noun forms: The plural is **niceties**.

niche (nich, neesh)
noun **1** a small hollow set into a wall: *A lovely statue stood in the **niche**.*
2 a place or position suitable for a person or thing: *Everyone has their **niche** in society.*

Word history: French word meaning 'to make a nest', from Gallo-Romance, from Latin word meaning 'nest'

nick
noun **1** a small cut or notch
verb **2** to cut slightly
3 *Colloquial* to steal (***knock off***, ***pilfer***, ***pinch***, ***take***, ***thieve***)
phrase **4 in good nick**, in good condition
5 in the nick of time, at the last possible moment: *We arrived at the airport **in the nick of time**.*
6 nick off, *Australian Colloquial* to leave or disappear (***absent yourself***, ***flee***, ***run away***, ***take to your heels***)
Word history: late Middle English

nickel
noun a hard, silvery-white metal
Word history: Swedish

nickname
noun a name used instead of your real name: *Dad's **nickname** is Bluey because he has red hair!* (***alias***, ***pseudonym***)
Word building: **nickname** *verb*
Word history: Middle English

nicotine (nik-uh-teen, nik-uh-teen)
noun a poisonous substance in tobacco
Word history: French, from Jacques *Nicot*, 1530–1600, who introduced tobacco into France in 1560

niece (nees)
noun the daughter of your brother or sister, or of your husband's or wife's brother or sister
Word history: Middle English, from Old French

nifty
adjective Colloquial **1** smart or clever: *a **nifty** trick*
2 stylish: *a **nifty** outfit* (***chic***, ***dapper***, ***elegant***, ***fashionable***, ***smart***)
Adjective forms: **niftier**, **niftiest**
Word history: originally theatrical slang

niggard (nig-uhd)
noun someone who is very unwilling to spend money or give things
Word building: **niggardly** *adjective* **niggardly** *adverb*
Word history: Middle English

niggle (nig-uhl)
verb **1** to make constant small criticisms or demands: *to **niggle** at someone*
2 to irritate or annoy
Word building: **niggler** *noun*
Word history: Scandinavian

nigh (nuy)
adverb Old-fashioned **1** near in space, time or relation: *The time of judgement is **nigh**.*
2 nearly or almost: *It is **nigh** on 12 o'clock.*
preposition Old-fashioned **3** near
Word history: Middle English *nigh(e)*, *neye*, Old English *nēah*, *nēh*

night
noun the time of darkness between sunset and sunrise
Word history: Middle English; Old English *niht*, *neaht*

night / knight / nite
Nite is another spelling for **night** that is used in informal writing and advertising:
Buy Nite-Lites! Nite-Lites make night light!
You will also see it used in a word like **overnite**, as in *an overnite van.*
Don't confuse **night** with **knight**. A **knight** in medieval times was an armed soldier on horseback. Nowadays, a **knight** is someone who has an honour given to him by the king or queen of his country.

nightcap
noun **1** a drink, especially a hot one, you have before going to bed
2 a cap people used to wear to bed

nightclub
noun **1** a venue for watching singing, music or dancing acts, open until late, and usually serving food and drink
2 a venue for dancing, which opens from evening until early morning

nightingale (nuyt-ing-gayl)
noun a small bird known for the beautiful singing of the male, especially at night
Word history: Old English *nihtegale* literally, night singer (compare Old English *galan* sing)

nightly
adjective **1** coming, happening or active at night: *a **nightly** visit*
adverb **2** every night: *The play is performed **nightly** during May.*

nightmare
noun **1** a very frightening dream
2 any very upsetting or frightening experience: *Being in the city during the earthquake was a **nightmare**.*
Word building: **nightmarish** *adjective*
Word history: Middle English (*mare* evil spirit)

nihilism (nuy-uhl-iz-uhm, nee-uhl-iz-uhm)
noun **1** the total lack of belief in religion or moral principles and duties, or in established laws and institutions
2 *Philosophy*
a the belief that there is no objective basis of truth
b an extreme form of scepticism, saying that nothing really exists
3 the principles of a Russian revolutionary group in the latter half of the 19th century
Word use: You can also use **Nihilism** for definition 3.
Word building: **nihilist** *noun* **nihilistic** *adjective*
Word history: Latin

nil
noun nothing: *The result of my efforts was **nil**.*
Word history: Latin

nimble
adjective **1** able to move quickly and easily: *a **nimble** acrobat* | ***nimble** fingers* (***agile***, ***athletic***, ***light on one's feet***, ***sprightly***, ***spry***)
2 quick in understanding: *You need a **nimble** mind to do cryptic crosswords.*
Word building: **nimbleness** *noun* **nimbly** *adverb*
Word history: Middle English

nimbus
noun **1** a rain cloud
2 → **halo** (definition 1)

Noun forms: The plural is **nimbi** (nim-buy) or **nimbuses**.
Word history: from Latin word meaning 'rainstorm', 'thunder-cloud'

nine
noun **1** a cardinal number, eight plus one (8 + 1)
2 a symbol for this number, as 9 or IX
3 a set of nine persons or things
adjective **4** amounting to nine in number
phrase **5 dressed (up) to the nines**, *Colloquial* smartly dressed or overdressed

Word building: **ninth** *adjective* **ninth** *noun*
Word history: Middle English; Old English *nigen*

nineteen
noun **1** a cardinal number, ten plus nine (10 + 9)
2 a symbol for this number, as 19 or XIX
3 a set of nineteen people or things
adjective **4** amounting to nineteen in number
phrase **5 talk nineteen to the dozen**, to talk very quickly or excitedly

Word building: **nineteenth** *adjective* **nineteenth** *noun*
Word history: Middle English

ninety
noun **1** a cardinal number, ten times nine (10 × 9)
2 a symbol for this number, as 90 or XC
3 a set of ninety persons or things
4 nineties, the numbers from 90 to 99 of a series, especially with reference to the years of a person's age, or the years of a century
adjective **5** amounting to ninety in number

Noun forms: The plural is **nineties**.
Word building: **ninetieth** *adjective* **ninetieth** *noun*
Word history: Old English *nigontig*

ninny
noun Colloquial a foolish or stupid person

Noun forms: The plural is **ninnies**.

nip
verb **1** to press sharply between two surfaces or points
2 to take off by pinching, biting, or snipping
3 to affect sharply or painfully, as cold does
noun **4** a pinch
5 a biting quality: *There is a **nip** in the air on frosty winter mornings.*
6 a biting taste or tang, as in cheese
7 a small bit or quantity of anything
phrase **8 nip something in the bud**, to stop the development of something: *We need to **nip that plan in the bud**.*

Verb forms: I **nipped**, I have **nipped**, I am **nipping**
Word history: Middle English

nipple
noun **1** part of your breast and in women the part from which a baby sucks milk
2 something resembling this, such as the mouthpiece of a baby's bottle

nippy
adjective **1** very chilly or cold: *a **nippy** breeze* (***freezing***, ***frosty***, ***icy***, ***sharp***, ***wintry***)
2 active or nimble: *He's **nippy** on his feet.*

Adjective forms: **nippier**, **nippiest**

nirvana (ner-vah-nuh)
noun in Buddhism, the final state of happiness reached when, after much practice, freedom from human emotions and concerns is achieved

Word history: from a Sanskrit word meaning 'a blowing out' (as of a light)

nit
noun **1** the egg of an insect such as a louse
2 the young of such an insect, especially when it is living in human hair

Word history: Old English *hnitu*

nit / knit
Don't confuse **nit** with **knit**, which means 'to make something out of long strands of wool, using a pair of long needles'.

nite / knight / night
Look up **knight / night / nite**.

nitrogen (nuy-truh-juhn)
noun a colourless, odourless, gas which forms 78 per cent of the earth's atmosphere

Word building: **nitrogenous** *adjective*
Word history: French

nitroglycerine (nuy-troh-glis-uh-reen)
noun a colourless, highly explosive oil, the main chemical of dynamite and certain rocket powders

Word use: You can also use **nitroglycerin** (nuy-troh-glis-uh-ruhn).

nitty-gritty
noun Colloquial the centre of a matter: *Let's get down to the **nitty-gritty**.*

nitwit
noun Colloquial a slow-thinking or foolish person

nix
noun Colloquial nothing

Word history: from German word meaning 'nothing'

no[1]
adverb **1** a word used to express denial, disagreement, or refusal such as in a reply, or to add force to an earlier negative: ***No**, you may not go.* | *We will not give in, **no**, never!*
noun **2** a reply of 'no'

Noun forms: The plural is **noes**.
Word use: The opposite of this is **yes**.
Word history: Middle English; from Old English *nā*

Note that you shouldn't use **no** instead of *any*. It's wrong to say:

I don't want no more pavlova.

It should be:

I don't want any more pavlova.

For more information, look up **negatives**.

no[2]
adjective **1** not any: ***no** money*
2 very far from being a: *He is **no** genius.*

Word history: variant of *none*

no / know

Don't confuse **no** with **know**.

To **know** something is to feel certain that it is correct or true.

If you **know** someone, then you have met them before.

no ball
noun a ball bowled in cricket in a way not allowed by the rules and automatically giving the batsman a score of one run

nobble
verb Colloquial **1** to disable (a racehorse or greyhound), especially by drugging: *The horse was **nobbled** and ran last.*
2 to win over by underhand means
3 to swindle or cheat people out of money
4 to catch or seize

nobility
noun **1** the aristocracy or noble class of a country
2 noble birth or rank
3 high moral excellence
4 greatness or grandeur

noble
adjective **1** belonging to the aristocratic or ruling class of a country: *a **noble** family*
2 having high principles: *He has a **noble** character.*
3 stately in appearance: *a **noble** monument*
4 of a high quality; admirable (***commendable***, ***laudable***, ***praiseworthy***)
noun **5** a person of noble birth or rank

Word history: Middle English, from Old French, from Latin word meaning 'well-known', 'highborn'

nobleman
noun a man of noble birth or rank

noblewoman
noun a woman of noble birth or rank

nobody
pronoun **1** no person: *There was **nobody** in the room.*
noun **2** a person of no importance: *He made her feel like a complete **nobody**.*

Nobody is sometimes called an *indefinite pronoun*. For more information, look up **pronouns: indefinite pronouns**.

nobody / no-one

These words are singular, and so should be followed by singular verbs such as *is* or *has*:

Nobody has left yet.

For advice on the best pronoun to use with **nobody** and **no-one** (should it be *his? her? their?*), look up **somebody / someone**.

nocturnal (nok-ter-nuhl)
adjective **1** active by night: *Possums are **nocturnal** animals.*
2 done, happening or coming by night: *a **nocturnal** adventure*

Word use: The opposite of definition 1 is **diurnal**.
Word history: late Middle English, from Latin word meaning 'of or in the night'

nod
verb **1** to bow in a short, quick movement especially in agreement, greeting, command, etc.: *He **nodded** in agreement.* | *She **nodded** her head.*
2 to let the head fall forwards with a sudden movement when sleepy
3 to bend down with a swinging movement: *The trees **nodded** in the breeze.*
noun **4** a short, quick bending down of the head, especially in agreement, greeting, command or sleepiness
5 a bending or swinging movement of anything
phrase **6 get the nod**, *Colloquial* to gain approval or permission
7 give the nod to, *Colloquial* to allow or permit
8 nod off, *Colloquial* to go to sleep

Verb forms: I **nodded**, I have **nodded**, I am **nodding**
Word history: Middle English

node
noun **1** a knot, lump or knob: *a lymph **node** in your body*
2 a joint in the stem of a plant, especially where a leaf grows
3 *Computers* a host or gateway on the internet
4 *Computers* an end point of a branch or junction of two or more branches in a network

Word building: **nodal** *adjective* **nodose** *adjective*
Word history: from Latin word meaning 'knot'

nodule
noun a small, rounded mass or lump

Word building: **nodular** *adjective*
Word history: from Latin word meaning 'node'

no-fly zone
noun an area over which all or specified aircraft are forbidden to fly

no-frills
adjective Colloquial plain and simple; without any extra features: ***no-frills** service* | *She gave a **no-frills** account of the facts.*

noggin
noun **1** a small cup or mug
2 *Colloquial* the head

noise
noun any kind of sound, especially a sound which is too loud or which you don't like (***commotion***, ***din***, ***hubbub***, ***racket***, ***uproar***)

Word building: **noisily** *adverb* **noisiness** *noun*
Word history: Middle English, from Old French, from Latin word meaning 'seasickness'

noisome (noy-suhm)
adjective **1** offensive or sickening
2 injurious or harmful to health

Word use: Definition 1 is usually used about smell.
Word history: Middle English

noisy
adjective **1** making a lot of noise: *a **noisy** crowd*
2 full of noise: *a **noisy** street*

Adjective forms: **noisier**, **noisiest**
Word use: The opposite of this is **quiet**.
Word building: **noisily** *adverb* **noisiness** *noun*

nomad
noun **1** a member of a race or tribe that moves from one area to another hunting, food-gathering or grazing their animals
2 any wanderer

Word building: **nomadic** *adjective*
Word history: Latin, from Greek word meaning 'roaming' (like cattle)

nomenclature (nuh-men-kluh-chuh, noh-muhn-klay-chuh)
noun **1** a set or system of names or terms, especially those used in a particular science or art
2 the names or terms forming a set or system

Word history: Latin

nominal (nom-uhn-uhl)
adjective **1** being so in name only: ***nominal*** *peace*
2 named only as a matter of form, being small in comparison with the actual value: *The price he quoted was purely* ***nominal****.*
3 having to do with a name or names
4 *Grammar* having to do with a noun or nouns

Word history: Middle English, from Latin word meaning 'pertaining to names'

nominate
verb to name as a candidate in an election: *I* ***nominated*** *her as chairperson.*

Word building: **nomination** *noun* **nominator** *noun*
Word history: from Latin word meaning 'named'

nominee (nom-uh-nee)
noun **1** someone put forward usually to fill an office or stand for election
2 a person appointed by another to act in their place

non-action verb
noun → **stative verb**

nonagon
noun a flat shape with nine straight sides

Word history: from Latin word meaning 'ninth'

nonchalant (non-shuh-luhnt)
adjective calm and not worried: *He faced the angry crowd with a* ***nonchalant*** *air.*

Word building: **nonchalance** *noun*
Word history: French

noncommittal
adjective not showing your opinion or decision so that you won't be held to it: *a* ***noncommittal*** *answer*

nonconformist (non-kuhn-fawm-uhst)
noun a person who refuses to accept the usual or expected ideas, customs or ways of living

Word use: The opposite of this is **conformist**.
Word building: **nonconformity** *noun*

nondescript (non-duh-skript)
adjective very ordinary-looking, without any easily recognised qualities (***average***, ***fair***, ***mediocre***, ***standard***)

Word history: *non-* + Latin word meaning 'described'

none
pronoun **1** not one: *There is* ***none*** *to help.*
2 not any: *That is* ***none*** *of your business.*
3 no people or things: ***None*** *were suitable.*
adverb **4** in no way: *The supply is* ***none*** *too great.*

Word history: Old English *nān*

nonentity (non-en-tuh-tee)
noun someone of no importance: *He was a* ***nonentity*** *in the organisation.*

Word history: *non-* + entity

nonetheless (nun-dhuh-les)
adverb however or nevertheless

Word use: You can also use **none the less**.

nonfiction
noun something written about real people and facts, rather than made-up stories

Word use: The opposite is **fiction**.

nonflammable
adjective not easily set alight or burnt

nong
noun *Australian, NZ Colloquial* a fool or idiot

Word history: shortened form of the term *ning-nong*, a variation of *ning-nang*, a word in a dialect of British English meaning 'foolish person'

non-narrative genre
noun a variety or style of literature which does not involve the telling of a story

nonplus (non-plus)
verb **1** to puzzle completely
noun **2** a state of complete puzzlement

Verb forms: it **nonplussed**, it has **nonplussed**, it is **nonplussing**
Word history: from Latin word meaning 'not more', 'no further'

nonplussed (non-plust)
adjective puzzled (***confused***, ***undecided***)

non-renewable resource
noun a natural resource which, once it is depleted, cannot be replaced or restored

Word use: Compare this with **renewable resource.**

nonsense
noun words that are silly or without meaning (***bunkum***, ***gobbledygook***, ***hocus-pocus***, ***mumbo jumbo***, ***rubbish***)

Word building: **nonsensical** *adjective*

non sequitur (non-sek-wuh-ter)
noun a conclusion which does not come or follow sensibly from earlier statements

Word history: from Latin word meaning 'it does not follow'

non-sexist language
noun language which does not reflect discrimination against a person on the basis of their sex

> The aim of non-sexist language, or **inclusive language** as it is sometimes called, is to avoid unnecessary or irrelevant reference to a person's gender. The problem comes up in three ways:
> 1 words which describe a person's job, occupation or role
> 2 words or phrases which mention a person's gender when that information is unnecessary
> 3 pronouns like *his/her*

1 Many names of occupations have the suffix -man. (Look up **-man**.) Some people argue that this seems to mean that only men can hold these positions. So people have tried to avoid these words. One method is to replace -man with -person. (Look up **-person**.) So instead of *chairman* you could use *chairperson*. Another method is to find different words which are neutral as to gender.

So for *businessman*, we have *executive*, for *chairman*, *convener* or *moderator*, and for *policeman*, *police officer*.

There are other sets of words where there used to be paired forms, masculine and feminine, with the feminine form indicated by a feminine word ending attached to the masculine form. For example, we had *poet* and *poetess* and *author* and *authoress*. In these pairs the masculine form is neutral. It is the feminine form which has the gender marker. So the easiest solution is to drop the feminine form and use the neutral form for both male and female. Thus a poet is a man or a woman.

2 Even though you use words which are neutral with regard to gender, like *poet* or *doctor* or *plumber*, some people add words which indicate gender. Often this is not necessary. For example:

We interviewed a lawyer, a journalist and a lady doctor.

In this instance it is the professions of the people interviewed that is important, not their gender. If that had been important it would have been given for all of them, not just for the doctor.

In most cases sexist language is the unnecessary indication of female gender. But it is sometimes the reverse, as in *male nurse*.

3 Sometimes you can get into trouble with words like *his* and *her* that refer to someone already mentioned in your writing. For example:

A doctor keeps medicine in his/her bag.

Using *his/her* avoids assuming one gender or the other, but it's a rather clumsy expression. One simple way to avoid such problems is to turn this sentence into the plural.

Doctors keep medicine in their bags.

Another way out of the 'his or her' difficulty is to use the neutral *their* for the singular. For example:

Each child keeps their books in their desk.

There are still a number of people who disapprove of this solution on grammatical grounds, since *their* is normally a plural pronoun.

Nevertheless it is widely accepted in spoken language. It provides a simple solution to a real problem. Other solutions are on the whole more complicated and cumbersome, or they require a major re-working of the sentence.

There are no hard-and-fast rules to follow to avoid sexist language. The hardest part is to become aware of it as a problem and to form the habit of removing it from your writing.

noodle
noun a type of pasta cut in long thin strips

Word history: German

nook
noun **1** a corner, especially in a room
2 any small, private or hidden place

Word history: Middle English

noon
noun midday or 12 o'clock in the daytime

Word history: Old English *nōn*, from Latin word meaning 'ninth hour'

no-one
pronoun no person

Word use: You can also use **no one**.

No-one is sometimes called an *indefinite pronoun.*

For more information, look up **pronouns: indefinite pronouns.**

no-one / nobody

Look up **nobody / no-one.**

noose
noun a loop with a sliding knot which tightens as the rope is pulled

Word history: probably from Old French, from Latin word meaning 'knot'

nor
conjunction a negative conjunction used:
1 together with **neither**: *He could neither read **nor** write.*
2 to continue the force of a negative, such as *not, no, never*, etc., from a preceding clause: *I never saw him again, **nor** did I regret it.*
3 after a positive clause, in the sense of *and…not*: *Our daughter passed brilliantly, **nor** could we have wished for more.*

Word history: Old English *nōther*

norm
noun **1** a standard, model or pattern
2 an average or mean
3 a marked standard of average performance of people of a given age, background, etc.

Word history: from Latin word meaning 'carpenter's square', 'rule', 'pattern'

normal
adjective **1** ordinary or usual: *the **normal** way of doing it* | ***normal** behaviour* (***conventional, customary, orthodox, traditional***)
noun **2** anything normal: *Everything is back to **normal**.*
3 the average or mean

Word use: The opposite of this is **abnormal**.
Word building: **normalcy** *noun* **normality** *noun* **normally** *adverb*
Word history: from Latin word meaning 'made according to a carpenter's square or rule'

norovirus (nor-oh-vuy-ruhs)
noun a virus which causes severe, highly infectious gastroenteritis

north
noun the direction which is to your right when you face the setting sun or the west

Word use: The opposite direction is **south**.
Word building: **north** *adjective* **north** *adverb* **northern** *adjective*
Word history: Middle English and Old English

northerly
adjective **1** towards the north: *We travelled in a* ***northerly*** *direction.*
2 of the wind, from the north: *a* ***northerly*** *wind*
noun **3** a wind blowing from the north: *A light* ***northerly*** *is blowing along the coast.*

nose
noun **1** the part of your face you use for breathing and smelling
2 a sense of smell: *This cat has a good* ***nose*** *for mice.*
verb **3** to move or push forward: *The car* ***nosed*** *through the flock of sheep.*
4 to interfere or pry: *He likes to* ***nose*** *into other people's business.*
phrase **5 by a nose**, *Colloquial* by a very small amount
6 lead by the nose, to exercise complete control over
7 on the nose, *Australian, NZ Colloquial*
a smelly, especially because something has decayed
b unpleasant or distasteful
8 pay through the nose, to pay too high a price
9 turn your nose up, to reject something you don't like, especially when you really ought to be grateful
10 under your nose, in an obvious place

Word building: **nasal** *adjective*
Word history: Middle English; Old English *nosu*

nosedive
noun **1** a drop of an aeroplane with the front part of the craft straight downwards
2 any sudden drop
verb **3** to go into a nosedive

nosegay (nohz-gay)
noun a bunch of flowers or herbs (***bouquet***, ***posy***)

Word history: Middle English; literally, a *gay* (obsolete, something pretty) for the *nose* (that is, to smell)

nostalgia (nos-tal-juh)
noun a longing for the past and all the things that belonged to it

Word building: **nostalgic** *adjective* **nostalgically** *adverb*
Word history: Neo-Latin, from Greek word *nostos* meaning 'a return to home' combined with *algos* meaning 'pain'

nostril
noun one of the two openings of your nose

Word history: Old English *nosterl*

nostrum (nos-truhm)
noun **1** a medicine falsely claiming power to cure
2 a medicine made by the person who suggests its use or sells it
3 a pet plan or invention for doing something

Word history: from Latin word meaning 'our', 'ours'

nosy
adjective Colloquial interested in things that aren't your business (***curious***, ***enquiring***, ***questioning***, ***snoopy***)

Adjective forms: **nosier**, **nosiest**
Word use: You can also use **nosey**.

not
adverb a word expressing negation, denial or refusal: ***not*** *far* | *You must* ***not*** *do that.*

Word history: Middle English

not / knot

Don't confuse **not** with **knot**.

You can tie a **knot** in a piece of thread or rope.

If your hair is tangled it has **knots** in it.

A **knot** is also a measure of speed for ships.

not only ... but also

We use these words in a sentence to connect two related things:

I not only saw the movie but also read the book.

The sentence flows more easily when **not only** and **but also** both have the same kind of word after them. In the sentence above, each of them is followed by a verb (*saw* and *read*).

I not only saw the movie but also my friend gave me the book.

The second sentence sounds awkward because **not only** is followed by a verb and **but also** is followed by something different, a noun phrase.

notable
adjective **1** worthy of notice: *a* ***notable*** *success* (***celebrated***, ***important***, ***noted***, ***renowned***)
noun **2** an important person

Word use: The opposite of definition 1 is **insignificant**.
Word history: Middle English, from Latin

notable / noticeable

These words look similar but have different meanings.

A **notable** achievement is worth taking **note** of.

Something is **noticeable** if it grabs your attention, as in *a very noticeable hat*. This word relates to the verb **notice**.

notation
noun a way of writing down things like music or dance by using signs or symbols, such as notes or lines to stand for sounds or marks to stand for movement

Word history: from Latin word meaning 'a marking'

notch
noun a small, sharp cut on an edge or surface (***gash***, ***incision***, ***score***, ***slit***)

Word building: **notch** *verb*
Word history: Anglo-French

note
noun **1** something written down as a reminder to yourself
2 a short letter (***communiqué***, ***dispatch***, ***epistle***, ***message***)
3 a piece of paper money: *a $10* ***note***
4 importance or fame: *The mayor is a woman of* ***note*** *in our town.*
5 notice: *Take* ***note*** *of what I tell you.*
6 a musical sound, or the sign or symbol you use to write it down on paper
verb **7** to write down (***enter***, ***list***, ***log***, ***register***)
8 to notice or pay attention to

Word use: You can also use **banknote** for definition 3.
Word history: Middle English, from Latin word meaning 'a mark'

noted
adjective famous or honoured: *a* ***noted*** *author* (***celebrated***, ***important***, ***notable***, ***renowned***)

nothing (nuth-ing)
pronoun **1** no thing: *Say* ***nothing***.
2 no part, share or mark: *The place shows* ***nothing*** *of its former beauty.*
3 something that is non-existent
4 something or somebody of no importance
phrase **5 for nothing,** free of charge
6 make nothing of,
a to be unable to understand
b to cope easily with or treat lightly
7 next to nothing, very little
8 nothing doing, *Colloquial* definitely not

Nothing is a word that is often singular and so is followed by a singular verb:

Nothing is known about him.

Even when some plural words separate **nothing** from its verb, strictly speaking the verb should be singular too:

Nothing except a few isolated facts is known about him.

Notice that this sentence is equivalent to:

Nothing is known about him except a few isolated facts.

But you will often find a plural verb used in sentences like this:

Nothing except a few isolated facts are known.

Few people would object to this nowadays.

Nothing is sometimes called an *indefinite pronoun*. For more information, look up **pronouns: indefinite pronouns.**

notice
noun **1** a sign or note giving a warning or some information
2 a statement that an agreement of some sort is to end: *The landlady gave* ***notice*** *to her tenant to leave.* | *The boss gave a fortnight's* ***notice*** *to his workers because he was closing down.*
3 interested attention: *The new film is worthy of* ***notice***.
verb **4** to pay attention to or take notice of (***attend to***, ***note***, ***register***)

Word building: **noticeable** *adjective*
Word history: late Middle English, from Old French, from Latin word meaning 'a being known', 'fame', 'knowledge'

noticeable / notable
Look up **notable / noticeable.**

noticeboard
noun a board where people put notes and general information for others to see, such as at a school, in an office, or in another public place

notify
verb to inform, especially in an official way: *The School Committee* ***notified*** *the parents that the meeting time had changed.* (***advise***, ***instruct***, ***tell***)

Verb forms: I **notified,** I have **notified,** I am **notifying**
Word building: **notifiable** *adjective* **notification** *noun*
Word history: Middle English, from Old French, from Latin word meaning 'make known'

notion
noun **1** an idea, often not very clear in your mind: *I have a* ***notion*** *of what life in the year 2020 may be like.* (***brainstorm***, ***concept***, ***theory***, ***thought***)
2 a foolish or fanciful idea: *He's full of* ***notions*** *about ways to make a fortune.*

Word building: **notional** *adjective*
Word history: from Latin word meaning 'a becoming acquainted', 'conception', 'notion'

not negotiable
adjective having to do with a cheque which is crossed and has the words 'not negotiable' written on it, commonly held to mean that the cheque can be paid only into the account, the name of which appears on the cheque

notorious (nuh-taw-ree-uhs)
adjective famous or well-known for something bad: *He's a* ***notorious*** *liar.*

Word building: **notoriety** *noun*
Word history: Medieval Latin, from Latin word meaning 'known'

notwithstanding (not-with-stan-ding)
preposition **1** in spite of: ***Notwithstanding*** *her laziness, she passed the exam.*
adverb **2** nevertheless: *The match will continue* ***notwithstanding***.

Word history: Middle English

nougat (nooh-gar)
noun a hard paste-like sweet containing almonds or other nuts

Word history: French, from Provençal, from Late Latin word meaning 'nut'

nought (nawt)
noun the symbol '0', or zero

Word history: Old English *nōht*

nought / naught
Don't confuse **nought** with **naught,** which is an old-fashioned word for 'nothing':

It was naught but the wind.

It can also mean 'ruin', or 'complete failure', as in *to bring to naught* or *come to naught.*

noun
noun a type of word which names something

Word history: Middle English, from Anglo-French, from Latin word meaning 'name'

nouns

Nouns are words that are commonly said to name people, places or things. They often act as the subject or object in a sentence.

proper nouns

These nouns name individual people or places: *Tony, Ned Kelly, the Murray River, Uluru.* They start with capital letters. Occasionally the definite article *the* (without a capital) is part of the name: *the Murray River, the Adelaide Hills, the Opera House.* **Proper nouns** contrast with **common nouns.**

common nouns

These nouns start with lower-case letters and name things that are not unique: *butter, dog, beauty, flying.* Some common nouns are called **abstract nouns**, and refer to such things as ideas and feelings: *beauty, flying, rudeness.* Other common nouns are called **concrete nouns,** and refer to things your senses can directly experience: *butter, dog, skateboard, vice-captain.*

Most concrete nouns refer to things that you can count, and so are called **count nouns.** *Dog, skateboard* and *vice-captain* are all count nouns. *Butter*, on the other hand, is a **mass noun**, like *rice, mud* and *water.* You can talk about *two dogs*, but you can't talk about *two rices.*

collective nouns

A **collective noun** groups a number of items under the one heading. The word *team*, for instance, brings together a number of individuals into the one group, as do the words *government, company* and *crowd.* Does this mean that *team* is a singular word or a plural? Which of the following should we say?

The team are…

or

The team is…

Both ways are possible in Australian English. The thing to do is to decide whether you want to stress the group nature of the noun or the fact that it's a collection of individuals. For example:

The team is at the top of the competition this season.

The team are agreed on their tactics for this match.

There is another group of nouns that act rather like collectives. They are the names of fish and animals. For example:

The fish are ready to eat.

The deer are grazing in the park.

These are like collective nouns because the singular verb can be used when you are writing about more than one item. However, you always use a plural verb with these nouns if you are writing about more than one item. If you say *the deer is*, you can only be referring to one deer.

For a list of collective nouns, see appendixes, page 991.

nourish (nu-rish)

verb to give enough food to encourage or ensure growth

Word building: **nourishing** *adjective* **nourishment** *noun*
Word history: Middle English, from Old French, from Latin word meaning 'suckle', 'feed', 'maintain'

nous (nows)

noun Colloquial common sense

Word history: from Greek word meaning 'mind', 'intellect'

novel[1]

noun a long imaginative, story which fills a whole book

Word building: **novelist** *noun*
Word history: Italian, from Latin word meaning 'new kind of story'

novel[2]

adjective new or different: *a* ***novel*** *idea* (***fresh, innovative, original***)

Word history: Middle English, from Latin word meaning 'new'

novelty

noun **1** newness or strangeness: *the* ***novelty*** *of going to the beach instead of to the mountains*
2 a new or different experience
3 a new or unusual article in a shop

Noun forms: The plural is **novelties.**
Word history: Middle English, from Old French, from Late Latin word meaning 'newness'

November

noun the eleventh month of the year, containing thirty days

Word history: Middle English and Old English, from Latin: the ninth month of the early Roman year

novice (nov-uhs)

noun **1** someone who is new to the type of work or job they are doing
2 someone who is living in a religious order for a time of testing before taking final vows

Word use: The opposite of definition 1 is **veteran.**
Word history: Middle English, from Old French, from Latin word meaning 'new'

novitiate (nuh-vish-ee-uht, nuh-vish-ee-ayt)

noun **1** the state or period of being a newcomer to a religious order or church
2 the quarters taken up by religious newcomers during the period of testing
3 the state or period of being a beginner in anything
4 a novice

Word use: You can also use **noviciate.**
Word history: Medieval Latin, from Latin word meaning 'new'

now

adverb **1** at the present time or moment: *He is here* ***now.***
2 immediately or at once: ***now*** *or never*
3 at a certain time or point in some period under consideration: *The case* ***now*** *passes to the jury.*
4 at the time or moment only just past: *I saw him just* ***now*** *in the street.*
phrase **5 now and again** or **now and then,** occasionally

nowadays
adverb **1** in these times
noun **2** the present

Word history: Middle English

nowhere (noh-wair)
adverb **1** in, at, or to no place
noun **2** a state of seeming non-existence: *He disappeared into **nowhere**.*
phrase **3 get nowhere**, to achieve nothing

Word history: Middle English; Old English *nāhwær*

noxious (nok-shuhs)
adjective **1** harmful or hurtful: ***noxious** gases* (***poisonous**, **toxic***)
2 declared harmful by law and meant to be destroyed: ***noxious** plants*

Word history: from Latin word meaning 'hurtful'

nozzle
noun the end of a pipe or hose through which you can spray water

Word history: *nose* + *-le*, (suffix, small)

nuance (nyooh-ons)
noun a slight variation of colour, meaning, expression or feeling: *The **nuances** of his voice showed his growing anger.*

Word history: French

nub
noun **1** a knob or lump
2 the point or gist of anything: *the **nub** of the matter*

Word history: variant of *knob*

nubile (nyooh-buyl)
adjective physically mature or old enough to marry

Word use: This is used to describe a girl or young woman.
Word building: **nubility** *noun*
Word history: Latin

nuclear (nyooh-klee-uh)
adjective **1** having to do with or forming a nucleus
2 having to do with or powered by nuclear energy

nuclear disarmament
noun the dismantling of nuclear weapons, especially those of major military powers

nuclear energy
noun the energy or power which is obtained by causing changes within the atomic nucleus

Word use: Other names are **nuclear power**, **atomic energy** and **atomic power**.

nuclear fission
noun the breakdown of an atomic nucleus of an element, with conversion of part of its mass into energy

nuclear power
noun **1** → **nuclear energy**
2 a country which uses nuclear energy or nuclear weapons

nuclear reactor
noun an apparatus in which a chain reaction is maintained and controlled for the production of nuclear energy

Word use: You can also use **reactor**.

nuclear waste
noun the radioactive by-products of nuclear fission

nuclear weapon
noun any weapon in which the explosive power is derived from nuclear fission, fusion, or a combination of both

nucleus (nyooh-klee-uhs)
noun **1** the central part or thing about which other parts or things are grouped: *Helen and Jiro were the **nucleus** of a new rock band.* (***centre**, **core**, **focus**, **heart**, **hub***)
2 *Biology* a mass of protoplasm, encased in a delicate membrane, present inside nearly all living cells and containing the genetic material
3 *Physics* the central core of an atom, made of protons and neutrons, with a net positive charge equal to the number of protons

Noun forms: The plural is **nuclei** (nyooh-klee-uy) or **nucleuses**.
Word history: from Latin word meaning 'nut', 'kernel', 'fruit stone'

nude
adjective **1** unclothed or naked (***bald**, **bare**, **exposed***)
noun **2** an unclothed human figure, especially one that an artist has painted

Word building: **nudity** *noun*
Word history: from Latin word meaning 'bare'

nudge
verb to give a small push to, especially with your elbow

Word building: **nudge** *noun*

nudism (nyooh-diz-uhm)
noun the practice of going without clothes as a means of healthy living

Word building: **nudist** *noun*

nugget
noun a lump of something, especially of gold, found in the ground

Word history: apparently from British dialect *nug* lump, block

nuisance (nyooh-suhns)
noun someone or something that's very annoying (***annoyance**, **bother**, **pest**, **trial***)

Word history: Middle English, from Old French word meaning 'harm', from Latin

null
adjective **1** of no importance or use
phrase **2 null and void**, having no legal force or effect: *The contract was declared **null and void**.*

Word history: from Latin word meaning 'none'

nulla-nulla (nul-uh-nul-uh)
noun an Aboriginal wooden club

Word history: from Dharug, an Australian Aboriginal language spoken by the people living near Sydney Cove in the early days of European settlement

nullify (nul-uh-fuy)
verb **1** to make ineffective, not successful, or of no importance
2 to make or declare legally empty or inoperative: *to **nullify** a contract*

Verb forms: I **nullified**, I have **nullified**, I am **nullifying**
Word building: **nullification** *noun*
Word history: from Late Latin word meaning 'make null', 'dispose'

numb (num)
adjective unable to feel anything: *His fingers were* ***numb*** *with cold.*

Word building: **numb** *verb*
Word history: Old English *numen*, past participle of *niman* take

numbat (num-bat)
noun a small Australian marsupial, with a long bushy tail and a pointed snout, which feeds on insects, found in south-western Australia

Word history: from Nyungar, an Australian Aboriginal language of the Perth-Albany region

number
noun **1** a sign or symbol used to represent a place in a counting system: *7 is the* ***number*** *which comes after 6 and before 8.* | $\frac{1}{2}$, $\frac{1}{4}$ *and* $\frac{1}{3}$ *are all* ***numbers*** *smaller than 1.*
2 the sum or total of a collection of things: *This year's audience was only half the* ***number*** *of last year's.*
3 a collection or quantity, usually large: *A* ***number*** *of people came.*
4 the particular numeral or figure given to something to fix its place in a list or series or to identify it: *Our house* ***number*** *is 67.* | *What is your phone* ***number****?*
5 a telephone number
6 a song, especially on a concert program: *Hans will sing the next* ***number****.*
7 *Grammar* the number of persons or objects a noun, pronoun or verb refers to
verb **8** to mark with a number: *We* ***numbered*** *all the files.*
9 to amount to a certain number: *The crowd at the cricket match* ***numbered*** *80 000.*

Word history: Middle English, from Old French, from Latin

1 Numbers in figures. When you are writing large numbers there are two different ways to break them up, so that they are easy to read. One is to use spaces, the other is to use commas.

To use the first method, separate the figures with a space into groups of three to the left or right of the decimal point:

70 000
700 000
7 000 000
0.000 07
0.000 007
0.000 000 7

If the number only has four figures on either side of the decimal point there is no space:

700.007
7000.0007
70 000.0007
70 000.000 07

If you use commas, there are two main differences from what happens when you use spaces. Firstly, commas are never used *after* the decimal point. Secondly, you *do* use a comma with four-figure numbers.

700
7,000
70,000
7,000,000
7000.007
7,000.0007
70,000.00007

The use of a comma rather than a space has a number of disadvantages. As you can see from the examples, this style makes long numbers after the decimal point difficult to read. Another problem is that in some countries the comma is also used to indicate the decimal place.

Groups of numbers — pages. To write a group of page numbers you can use as few figures as possible for the last page, so long as your meaning is clear:

pp 184–9 i.e. pages 184 to 189
pp 184–99 i.e. pages 184 to 199
pp 184–209 i.e. pages 184 to 209

Note however that it is not usual to shorten the numbers between 10 and 19 in each hundred:

pp 10–14, *not* 10–4
pp 217–19, *not* 217–9

Groups of numbers — years. Writing groups of years follows the same rules, except that it is not usual to shorten the final year to three figures:

1884–6 1884–96 1884–1906, *not 1884–906*

2 Numbers in words. Numbers are usually written out as words in writing that is descriptive, or where numbers are unusual — writing such as English essays, history essays or stories. But writing in maths and science involves lots of numbers and therefore it is simpler and easier for the reader if you write them as figures.

Even in descriptive writing there are some kinds of numbers that you don't write out. For example, years and numbers used with abbreviations or symbols are usually written as figures:

Captain Cook landed in Australia in 1770.
He landed at Botany Bay, 34°S, 151°E.

numberplate
noun a flat, metal strip which shows the registration number of your car

numeral
noun a figure or letter, or a group of figures or letters, which represent a number: *The number of days in the week is expressed by the* ***numeral*** *7.* | *The Roman* ***numeral*** *for this is VII.*

Word history: Late Latin, from Latin word meaning 'number'

numerate (nyooh-muh-rayt)
adjective having basic skills in mathematics

Word building: **numeracy** *noun*
Word history: Latin

numerator
noun the number which is written above the line in a fraction to show how many parts of the whole are taken: *In the fraction* $\frac{3}{4}$, *3 is the* ***numerator****.*

Word use: Compare this with **denominator**.
Word history: from Late Latin word meaning 'a counter'

numerical (nyooh-me-rik-uhl)
adjective having to do with numbers

numerology (nyooh-muh-rol-uh-jee)
noun the study of numbers, to determine their supposed influence on your life and future

Word building: **numerological** *adjective*
Word history: from Latin word meaning 'number'

numerous
adjective very many: ***Numerous** people went to the concert*. (***countless**, **innumerable**, **legion**, **multiple**, **multitudinous***)

Word history: Latin

numismatics (nyooh-muhz-mat-iks)
noun the science of coins and medals

Word building: **numismatist** *noun*

nun
noun a woman who has devoted herself to a religious life, usually in a convent

Word history: Middle English and Old English *nunne*, from Late Latin

Nunga (nung-guh)
noun an Aboriginal person from southern SA

Word use: Compare this with **Anangu**, **Koori**, **Murri**, **Nyungar**, **Yamatji** and **Yolngu**.

nunnery (nun-uh-ree)
noun a religious house for nuns (***convent***)

Noun forms: The plural is **nunneries**.

nuptial (nup-shuhl)
adjective **1** having to do with marriage or the marriage ceremony: ***nuptial** vows*
noun **2 nuptials**, a marriage or wedding ceremony

Word history: from Latin word meaning 'relating to marriage'

nurse
noun **1** someone who looks after sick people, usually in a hospital
verb **2** to look after in time of sickness: *to **nurse** a patient*
3 to hold in your arms: *to **nurse** a baby* (***cradle**, **cuddle**, **embrace**, **hug***)
4 to look after carefully so as to help growth: *to **nurse** seedlings | to **nurse** an ambition*
5 to breastfeed

Word history: Middle English, from Old French, from Late Latin word meaning 'nurse'

nurse practitioner
noun a nurse who is legally qualified to take on some of the responsibilities of a doctor

nursery
noun **1** a room or place for babies
2 a school for very young children
3 a place where young plants can be bought

Noun forms: The plural is **nurseries**.

nursery rhyme
noun a short, simple poem or song for young children

nurture (ner-chuh)
verb to feed and look after when young: *to **nurture** children*

Word building: **nurture** *noun*
Word history: Middle English, from Old French, from Latin

nut
noun **1** a dry fruit consisting of a kernel that you can eat inside a hard shell
2 the kernel itself
3 a small metal block with a hole which has a thread in it, enabling it to be screwed on the end of a bolt
4 *Colloquial* your head
5 *Colloquial* someone who is odd or foolish

Word history: Old English *hnutu*

nutmeg
noun a spice made from the seed of a tree that grows in tropical countries

Word history: Middle English

nutrient (nyooh-tree-uhnt)
noun a substance that provides food and energy: *Vitamins and minerals are important **nutrients**.*

Word building: **nutrient** *adjective*
Word history: from Latin word meaning 'nourishing'

nutriment (nyooh-truh-muhnt)
noun **1** any matter that, taken into a living organism, serves to support it in its existence, helping growth, replacing loss, and providing energy
2 something that provides food

Word history: Latin

nutrition (nyooh-trish-uhn)
noun **1** eating or eating habits: *healthy **nutrition***
2 the process by which food is changed to nourish our bodies

Word building: **nutritionist** *noun* **nutritious** *adjective*

nuzzle
verb to touch or rub with the nose

Word history: Middle English

nylon
noun a strong material made from coal, which gives elastic threads that are useful in making fabrics or bristles, etc.

Word history: Trademark

nymph (nimf)
noun **1** a goddess, pictured as a beautiful young woman living in the sea, woods or mountains
2 a young, wingless insect

Word history: Middle English, from Old French, from Latin, from Greek word meaning 'nymph', 'pupa'

nymphomania (nim-fo-may-nee-a)
noun uncontrollable sexual desire in women

Word building: **nymphomaniac** *adjective* **nymphomaniac** *noun*
Word history: Neo-Latin, from Greek

Nyungar (nyoon-gah)
noun **1** an Aboriginal person from south-western WA
2 an Australian Aboriginal language from south-western WA

Word use: You can also use **Nyunga**, **Nyoongah** or **Noongar**. | Compare this with **Anangu**, **Koori**, **Murri**, **Nunga**, **Yamatji** and **Yolngu**.

oaf
noun someone who is clumsy, stupid or rude
Word history: Old English *ælf* elf

oak
noun a tree that bears acorns and is famous for its hard wood
Word history: Old English *āc*

oar (aw)
noun **1** a long pole with a wide, flattened end, used for rowing a boat
phrase **2 put your oar in,** to interfere or meddle
Word history: Old English *ār*

> **oar / or / ore / awe**
> Don't confuse **oar** with the other three words that sound the same.
> You use **or** to connect alternative words, phrases or clauses:
> *I don't know which colour to choose – red, yellow or green.*
> **Ore** is a rock or mineral which is mined for the metal it contains.
> **Awe** is a feeling of great respect mixed with fear:
> *The men were in awe of his bad temper.*

oasis (oh-ay-suhs)
noun a place in the desert where there is water and trees can grow
Noun forms: The plural is **oases** (oh-ay-seez).
Word history: Latin, from Greek, perhaps from Egyptian

oath
noun **1** a saying which uses God's name or anything holy to give importance to your words
2 a promise you make, such as in a court of law, that what you say will be true: *She said it under* ***oath.*** (***pledge, vow, word of honour***)
Word history: Old English *āth*

oats
plural noun a cereal which is used to make porridge and to feed horses
Word history: Old English *āte* (singular)

obdurate (ob-juh-ruht)
adjective **1** hardened against persuasion (***adamant, hard-hearted, immovable, inflexible, stubborn***)
2 refusing to change your ways: *an* ***obdurate*** *sinner*
Word history: Middle English, from Latin word meaning 'hardened'

obedient
adjective following someone else's wishes or commands: *an* ***obedient*** *dog* (***compliant, docile, submissive, tractable***)
Word building: **obedience** *noun* **obediently** *adverb*
Word history: Middle English, from Latin *obediens* obeying

obeisance (oh-bay-suhns)
noun **1** a movement of the body expressing deep respect, such as a bow or curtsy
2 obedience or respect, as that due to someone in a higher position
Word history: Middle English, from Old French word meaning 'obedience'

obelisk
noun a tall pillar of stone, put up as a monument
Word history: Latin, from Greek word meaning 'pointed pillar'

obese (oh-bees)
adjective very fat
Word building: **obesity** *noun*
Word history: Latin

obey (oh-bay)
verb to do as you are told (***comply, follow, heed, observe***)
Word history: Middle English, from Old French, from Latin

obituary (uh-bich-uh-ree)
noun a notice, usually in a newspaper, which says that someone has died and which often includes a short account of his or her life and achievements
Word history: Neo-Latin, from Latin word meaning 'death'

object (ob-jekt)
noun **1** something which can be seen or felt: *The shelf was crowded with* ***objects.***
2 the reason or purpose: *What is the real* ***object*** *of his visit?*
3 *Grammar* the person or thing which receives the action of a verb
verb (uhb-jekt) **4** to feel or say you don't agree with something
phrase **5 object to,**
a to say you don't like, or that you disapprove of, something: *I* ***object to*** *that idea.*
b to argue against: *He* ***objected to*** *a picnic being held on a rainy day.*
Word use: The opposite of definition 5 is **agree with.**
Word history: Middle English, from Latin word meaning 'thrown before', 'presented', 'exposed', 'opposed', 'reproached with'

objects in grammar

The **object** of a verb is the person or thing that is affected by the action of that verb.

There are two different types of object:

1 **direct object**. To find the direct object, we simply ask 'who?' or 'what?' after the verb:

She stroked the cat.

She stroked 'who?' or 'what?' The answer is the cat. So the cat is the direct object of the verb stroked. It is what is acted on by the verb.

2 **indirect object**. Some sentences have another kind of object as well. It is the person or thing that receives something through the action of the verb:

They sent him a book.

In this example, him is the indirect object (the person who gets the book). Look up **indirect object**.

Note that *book*, the thing being sent, is the **direct object**.

object code
noun a compiled computer code in machine-readable form, created from a source code

objection
noun an argument against something

objectionable
adjective unpleasant or offensive: ***objectionable*** *behaviour*

Word building: **objectionably** *adverb*

objective
noun **1** something to work towards: *Their* ***objective*** *is to grow all the food they need.*
2 the lens or combination of lenses through which the image is viewed in a telescope or microscope, or through which the picture is taken in a camera
adjective **3** having to do with actual objects or something real rather than thoughts or feelings
4 fair and free of prejudice: *He finds it hard to be* ***objective****.* (***impartial***, ***just***, ***neutral***, ***unbiased***)

Word use: The opposite of definition 3 is **subjective**.
Word building: **objectively** *adverb*
objectivity *noun*
Word history: Medieval Latin

objective case
noun Grammar the form of a noun or pronoun which shows it is the object of a verb, such as 'him' in *I can hear him.*

object-oriented
adjective Computers having to do with programming which groups together certain data and procedures into units (objects) which can then be manipulated in a modular manner: ***object-oriented*** *programming*

obligation
noun something which should be done out of duty or gratitude: *You have an* ***obligation*** *to be obedient to your parents.*

obligatory (o-blig-uh-tuh-ree, o-blig-uh-tree)
adjective required as a matter of obligation: *It is* ***obligatory*** *to attend.* (***compulsory***, ***essential***, ***mandatory***, ***necessary***)

Word use: The opposite of this is **optional** or **voluntary**.

oblige (uh-bluyj)
verb **1** to do a favour: *I needed a lift and he* ***obliged****.*
phrase **2 be obliged**,
a to be grateful for someone's kindness: *I* ***am*** *deeply* ***obliged*** *to you for treating me so well.*
b to be required to, out of duty or need, or by law: *He* ***was obliged*** *to pay for repairs.*

Word history: Middle English, from Old French, from Latin word meaning 'bind or tie around'

obliging
adjective willing to do favours or services: *The clerk was most* ***obliging****.* (***accommodating***, ***cooperative***, ***helpful***)

oblique (uh-bleek)
adjective **1** indirect: *There was only an* ***oblique*** *reference to what had happened.*
2 slanting or sloping: *an* ***oblique*** *line*

Word history: Middle English, from Latin

obliterate (uh-blit-uh-rayt)
verb to wipe out or destroy: *The waves* ***obliterated*** *their footprints.*

Word building: **obliteration** *noun*
Word history: from Latin word meaning 'erased'

oblivion
noun **1** the condition of being forgotten: *She was a popular writer but she has passed into* ***oblivion****.*
2 a state of forgetting something: *a few minutes of peaceful* ***oblivion***

oblivious
adjective **1** forgetful or not remembering: ***oblivious*** *of her promise*
phrase **2 oblivious of** (or **to**), not noticing: ***oblivious of*** *the cold* | ***oblivious to*** *the noise*

Word building: **obliviously** *adverb*
Word history: Middle English, from Latin

oblong
noun **1** a four-sided shape with all its angles right angles, longer than it is wide
2 a rectangular or oval shape that is longer than it is wide
adjective **3** elongated in shape

Word history: Middle English, from Latin word meaning 'rather long', 'oblong'

obnoxious (uhb-nok-shuhs)
adjective disagreeable or nasty: *an* ***obnoxious*** *person*

Word building: **obnoxiously** *adverb*
Word history: from Latin word meaning 'exposed to harm'

oboe
noun a tube-shaped, woodwind instrument with a double reed that you blow through

Word building: **oboist** *noun*
Word history: Italian, from French

obscene (uhb-seen)
adjective indecent or disgusting: ***obscene*** *violence*

Word building: **obscenity** *noun* (*plural* **obscenities**)
obscenely *adverb*
Word history: from Latin word meaning 'of evil omen', 'offensive', 'disgusting'

obscure
adjective **1** dark or shadowy: *an* ***obscure*** *corner* (***dim***, ***gloomy***, ***murky***)
2 uncertain or unclear: ***obscure*** *meaning*
verb **3** to darken or hide: *Clouds* ***obscured*** *the stars.* (***cover***, ***eclipse***, ***screen***, ***shade***)

Word building: **obscurity** *noun*
Word history: Middle English, from Latin word meaning 'dark', 'dim', 'unknown', 'ignoble'

obsequious (uhb-see-kwee-uhs)
adjective being over-eager to serve or please

Word history: Middle English, from Latin

observance
noun **1** the action of obeying or following: ***observance*** *of laws*
2 a keeping or celebration by proper procedure, ceremonies, etc.
3 observation

observant
adjective watchful or alert: *The* ***observant*** *child noticed where the lollies were kept.* (***attentive***, ***sharp-eyed***, ***vigilant***)

Word use: The opposite of this is **oblivious** or **unobservant**.
Word history: Middle English, from Latin

observation
noun **1** the act of noticing or watching
2 the state of being noticed: *You cannot escape* ***observation***.
3 the act of noting something carefully for a scientific, artistic or other special purpose
4 a remark or comment

observatory
noun a building equipped with powerful telescopes for observing the stars, planets and weather patterns

Noun forms: The plural is **observatories**.

observe
verb **1** to see, notice or watch: ***Observe*** *the detail.* | *He just goes along to* ***observe***. (***view***, ***witness***)
2 to study: *He's* ***observing*** *the bird life.*
3 to keep or follow: ***Observe*** *the rules.* (***comply with***, ***heed***, ***obey***)
4 to comment or remark: *'You're quite late', she* ***observed***.

Word building: **observer** *noun*
Word history: Middle English, from Latin word meaning 'watch', 'comply with', 'observe'

obsession
noun a strong idea or feeling which controls someone's behaviour (***complex***, ***fetish***, ***hang-up***, ***phobia***)

Word building: **obsess** *verb* **obsessed** *adjective* **obsessive** *adjective*

obsessive-compulsive disorder
noun a disorder of the mind in which the sufferer engages in repetitive rituals

obsolescent (ob-suh-les-uhnt)
adjective becoming out of date

Word building: **obsolescence** *noun*
Word history: Latin

obsolete
adjective out-of-date: *an* ***obsolete*** *weapon* (***antiquated***, ***archaic***, ***old-fashioned***)

Word use: The opposite of this is **current** or **up-to-date**.
Word history: Latin

obstacle
noun something which is in your way or which delays you (***barrier***, ***drawback***, ***handicap***, ***hindrance***, ***hitch***)

Word history: Middle English, from Old French, from Latin

obstetrics (uhb-stet-riks)
noun the type of medical practice that is concerned with caring for pregnant women before, during and after the birth of their babies

Word building: **obstetric** *adjective* **obstetrician** *noun*

obstinate
adjective stubborn or not willing to change your mind, even though you may be wrong (***adamant***, ***inflexible***, ***persistent***, ***stubborn***, ***uncompromising***)

Word building: **obstinacy** *noun* **obstinately** *adverb*
Word history: Middle English, from Latin word meaning 'determined'

obstreperous (uhb-strep-uh-ruhs)
adjective resisting control in a noisy way: ***obstreperous*** *behaviour* | ***obstreperous*** *children*

Word building: **obstreperously** *adverb*
Word history: from Latin word meaning 'clamorous'

obstruct
verb **1** to block or close off: *A landslide* ***obstructed*** *the road.* (***bar***, ***barricade***, ***cut off***)
2 to prevent or make difficult: *She* ***obstructed*** *our efforts to open the gate.* (***hamper***, ***hinder***, ***oppose***, ***resist***)

Word history: Latin

obstruction
noun **1** something that obstructs by forming a blockage
2 the act of obstructing

obtain
verb to get or acquire: *She managed to* ***obtain*** *fresh bread.*

Word history: Middle English, from Old French, from Latin word meaning 'take hold of', 'get', 'prevail', 'continue'

obtuse (uhb-tyoohs)
adjective stupid or slow to understand

Word building: **obtusely** *adverb* **obtuseness** *noun*
Word history: from Latin word meaning 'dulled'

obtuse angle
noun Geometry an angle greater than 90° and less than 180°

obviate
verb to get rid of or prevent by effective measures: *This plan will* ***obviate*** *the necessity of beginning again.*

Word history: from Late Latin word meaning 'met', 'opposed', 'prevented'

obvious
adjective clearly understood or seen (***apparent***, ***distinct***, ***evident***, ***plain***, ***visible***)

Word building: **obviously** *adverb*
Word history: from Latin word meaning 'in the way', 'meeting'

occasion
noun **1** a particular time or event: *He remembers the **occasion** when he met you.*
2 an opportunity: *I took the **occasion** to thank him.*
verb **3** to give cause for or bring about: *Her exam results **occasion** a celebration.*
phrase **4 rise to the occasion,** to show yourself able to meet the needs of a particular task

Word history: Middle English, from Latin word meaning 'opportunity', 'fit time'

occasional
adjective happening sometimes: ***occasional** showers* (***infrequent**, **sporadic***)

Word use: The opposite of this is **constant**.
Word building: **occasionally** *adverb*

occlude
verb **1** to close, shut or stop up: *to **occlude** a passageway*
2 to shut in, out or off
3 *Chemistry* in relation to some solids, to absorb and hold gases or liquids in tiny pores on their surfaces

Word history: from Latin word meaning 'shut up', 'close up'

occult (ok-ult, uh-kult)
adjective having to do with so-called sciences, such as magic or astrology, which say they use secret ways to gain knowledge

Word history: from Latin word meaning 'covered', 'concealed'

occupant
noun someone who lives in or occupies a house or a room

Word building: **occupancy** *noun*
Word history: Latin

occupation
noun **1** your usual job or employment: *What is her **occupation**?* (***business**, **career**, **profession**, **vocation**, **work***)
2 the possession of a place, either legally or illegally: *The tenant is in **occupation**.*
3 the taking over of a country or territory by force

Word history: Middle English, from Latin word meaning 'seizing', 'employment'

occupy
verb **1** of space or time, to fill or pass: *How does he **occupy** his time? | That building **occupies** a lot of space.*
2 to be in or live in: *Who **occupies** the house?* (***dwell in**, **inhabit**, **reside in***)
3 to take or hold by force: *to **occupy** a country* (***capture**, **invade**, **seize**, **take over***)

Verb forms: I **occupied**, I have **occupied**, I am **occupying**
Word history: Middle English, from Old French, from Latin word meaning 'take possession of', 'take up', 'employ'

occur
verb **1** to happen: *The incident **occurred** yesterday.* (***arise**, **come about**, **transpire***)
phrase **2 occur to,** to come into the mind of: *It **occurs to** me that you might not want to come.*

Verb forms: it **occurred**, it has **occurred**, it is **occurring**
Word building: **occurrence** *noun*
Word history: from Latin word meaning 'run against', 'go up to', 'meet', 'befall'

ocean (oh-shuhn)
noun one of the large areas of salt water between continents, such as the Atlantic Ocean or the Pacific Ocean

Word building: **oceanic** (oh-shee-an-ik, oh-see-an-ik) *adjective*
Word history: Latin, from Greek word meaning 'the ocean', originally 'the great stream supposed to encompass the earth'

oceanic crust
noun Geology that portion of the earth's lithosphere which forms the floor of much of the oceans

Word use: Look up **continental crust**.

oceanography (oh-shuhn-og-ruh-fee)
noun a branch of physical geography dealing with the ocean

ochre (oh-kuh)
noun **1** a yellowish clay used in paints and dyes
2 the yellowish or reddish colour of ochre

Word building: **ochre** *adjective*
Word history: Middle English, from Old French, from Latin, from Greek word meaning 'yellow ochre'

ocker
noun Colloquial **1** the uncultivated Australian working man considered as a type
2 an insensitive, narrow-minded Australian man who considers his ideas and values the only possible ones
3 an Australian male displaying qualities considered to be typically Australian, as good humour, helpfulness and ability to overcome difficulties
adjective **4** distinctively Australian: *an **ocker** sense of humour*

Word history: variant of *Oscar*, especially the character in the television comedy series *The Mavis Brampton Show* (1965–68)

o'clock
adverb of or by the clock: *It will be twelve **o'clock** in five minutes.*

octagon (ok-tuh-gon, ok-tuh-guhn)
noun a flat shape with eight straight sides

Word history: from Greek word meaning 'having eight angles'

octave (ok-tiv)
noun **1** the eight note distance between two musical notes of the same name but different pitch
2 these two notes played together

Word history: Middle English, from Latin word meaning 'eighth'

octet
noun **1** a group of eight
2 a piece of music for eight voices or eight performers

October
noun the tenth month of the year, containing 31 days

Word history: Middle English and Old English, from Latin: eighth month of the early Roman year

octopus
noun a soft-bodied sea animal which has eight arms with suckers on them

Noun forms: The plural is **octopuses**.
Word use: Some people use **octopi** for the plural of **octopus**. It is regarded by many people as incorrect, with the most accepted plural being **octopuses**.
Word history: Neo-Latin, from Greek word meaning 'eight-footed'

octopus strap
noun a stretchable rope with hooks on either end used for fastening luggage to roof-racks, etc.

ocular (ok-yuh-luh)
adjective **1** having to do with or like the eye: ***ocular** movements*
noun **2** the eyepiece of a viewing instrument, such as a microscope

Word history: from Late Latin word meaning 'of the eyes'

OD
noun, verb → **overdose**

Word history: abbreviation

odd
adjective **1** strange or unusual: ***odd** behaviour* (***abnormal**, **bizarre**, **peculiar**, **weird***)
2 unable to be exactly divided by two: *Seven is an **odd** number, and eight is an even number.*
3 part-time or casual: ***odd** jobs*
4 not matching, or left over: ***odd** socks | an **odd** glove*

Word history: Middle English, from Scandinavian

oddball
noun Colloquial someone who is unusual or peculiar

Word use: You can also use **odd bod**.
Word building: **oddball** *adjective*

oddity
noun **1** an odd characteristic or peculiarity
2 an odd person or thing

Noun forms: The plural is **oddities**.

oddment
noun **1** an odd article, bit, left-over, etc.
2 an article belonging to a broken or incomplete set

odds
plural noun **1** the chances of something happening, such as a horse winning a race: *The **odds** are five to one on Black Prince. | The **odds** are against you.*
phrase **2 at odds**, in disagreement: *They are always **at odds**.*
3 odds and ends, odd bits or scraps
4 over the odds, too much

odds-on
adjective of something that is a chance, likely to win, succeed, etc.

ode
noun a song or poem praising something: *an **ode** to love*

Word history: French, from Late Latin, from Greek word meaning 'song'

odious
adjective hateful or disgusting: *He's an **odious** character.*

Word history: Middle English, from Latin word meaning 'hateful'

odium
noun **1** hatred
2 the shame attached to something that is hated

Word history: from Latin word meaning 'hatred'

odour
noun a smell: *an unpleasant **odour***

Word use: You can also use **odor**.
Word building: **odorous** *adjective*
Word history: Middle English, from Old French, from Latin

odyssey (od-uh-see)
noun any long series of wanderings

Word building: **Odyssean** *adjective*
Word history: Greek *Odýsseia* from *Odysseús* Odysseus, whose ten years of wandering after the Trojan War were described in Homer's epic poem, the *Odyssey*

oedema (uh-dee-muh)
noun the leaking of fluid into tissue spaces and body cavities

Noun forms: The plural is **oedemata** (uh-dee-muh-tuh).
Word use: You can also use **edema**.
Word history: Neo-Latin, from Greek word meaning 'a swelling'

oesophagus (uh-sof-uh-guhs)
noun the tube connecting the back of the mouth with the stomach (***gullet***)

Noun forms: The plural is **oesophagi** (uh-sof-uh-guy).
Word use: You can also use **esophagus**.
Word history: Neo-Latin, from Greek

oestrogen (ees-truh-juhn, es-truh-juhn)
noun any one of a group of female sex hormones secreted by the ovaries and responsible for the female characteristics that develop after puberty

Word use: You can also use **estrogen**.

oestrous cycle (ees-truhs suy-kuhl)
noun a cycle of physiological changes in sexual and other organs in female mammals

Word use: You can also use **estrous cycle**.

of
preposition a word indicating: **1** distance or separation from: *within a metre **of** her house*
2 origin or source: ***of** good family*
3 cause or reason: *to die **of** hunger*
4 substance or contents: *a packet **of** sugar | a lump **of** wood*
5 identity: *the city **of** Canberra*
6 belonging, possession or association: *the queen **of** England | the property **of** us all*
7 inclusion in a number or group: *one **of** us*
8 what something is about or regarding: *talk **of** peace*
9 qualities or characteristics: *a man **of** tact*

Word history: Middle English and Old English

of / have

When you abbreviate **have** in contracted forms like *could have* (could've), *would have* (would've) and *should have* (should've), the 've sounds like **of**. It is a fairly common mistake to write *could of*, *would of* and *should of*, but this is not correct.

off

adverb **1** away from a position occupied, or from an attachment: *He took **off** his hat.* | *The handle has come **off**.*
2 to or at a distance away: *He ran **off**.* | *Summer is only a week **off**.*
3 less: *ten per cent **off***
4 away from normal employment: *We have four days **off** at Easter.*
5 completely: *to kill **off** rats*
preposition **6** away from: *to fall **off** a horse* | *to be **off** work*
7 not up to the usual standard of: ***off** his game*
8 *Colloquial* avoiding: ***off** her food*
9 distant from: ***off** the track*
adjective **10** cancelled or no longer in effect: *The agreement is **off**.*
11 not so good as usual: *an **off** year for apples*
12 unwell: *I am a bit **off** today.* (***ailing***, ***ill***, ***indisposed***, ***off-colour***, ***sick***)
13 unfit for eating or bad: *The milk is **off**.* (***inedible***, ***rancid***, ***rank***, ***stale***, ***unpalatable***)
noun **14** → **off side**
phrase **15 be off**, to depart or leave
16 off and on, occasionally: *It works **off and on**.*

Word use: You can also use **on and off** for definition 16.
Word history: Middle English and Old English *of* of, off

off / from

These words are both often used as prepositions in the following way:

I'll buy that book off you.

I'll buy that book from you.

Note that some people consider this use of **off** to be incorrect so it's better to avoid it in formal essays.

offal

noun animal intestines and other parts which are thrown away, or other organs such as the brain, liver and tripe which are used as food

Word history: Middle English

offbeat

adjective **1** unusual or unconventional: *That idea is a little **offbeat**, but we could give it a try.*
2 in jazz, etc., having a strong accent on the second and fourth beat of a four-beat bar

off-colour

adjective **1** unwell or sick (***ailing***, ***ill***, ***indisposed***)
2 in bad taste: *an **off-colour** joke*

Word use: You can also use **off-color**.

offcut

noun a small length of timber or other material, left over after special orders have been prepared

offence

noun **1** a wrongdoing or crime: *a traffic **offence***
2 an insult, or other wrong: *an **offence** against decency*

Word use: The US spelling is **offense**.
Word history: Middle English, from Latin

offend

verb **1** to annoy or displease (***insult***, ***irritate***, ***rile***, ***upset***, ***vex***)
2 to do wrong or commit a crime

Word building: **offender** *noun*
Word history: Middle English, from Old French, from Latin word meaning 'strike against', 'displease'

offensive

adjective **1** displeasing or disgusting: *an **offensive** book* | *an **offensive** smell*
2 insulting: *an **offensive** gesture*
3 attacking: ***offensive** movements*
noun **4** an attack: *The allied **offensive** was devastating.*

Word building: **offensively** *adverb*

offer

verb **1** to put forward hoping that it will be accepted: *She **offered** the plate of cakes.*
2 to show willingness: *She **offered** to help.*
3 to bid or suggest: *He is **offering** $100.*
noun **4** an act of offering, or something which is offered
5 a suggestion or proposal: *an **offer** of marriage* | *an **offer** of $10* (***bid***, ***proposition***, ***tender***)

Word history: Old English *offrian*, from Latin

offering

noun something offered, such as money offered in worship to God or the church

offhand

adjective vague or casual, sometimes in a rude way: *He nodded in an **offhand** manner.*

office

noun **1** a place where you work or do business
2 a place where you go to buy tickets or get information
3 rank or duty: *She holds the **office** of deputy manager.* (***position***, ***post***, ***station***)

Word history: Middle English, from Old French, from Latin word meaning 'service', 'duty', 'ceremony'

officer

noun **1** someone who holds a rank in the army, navy, air force, police force or similar organisation
2 someone chosen to do an important job in a particular organisation: *The society has to elect its **officers**.*

Word history: Middle English, from Old French, from Medieval Latin, from Latin word meaning 'office'

official (uh-fish-uhl)

noun **1** someone with a rank or who has authority to do a particular job
adjective **2** properly approved or arranged: *an **official** statement* (***authoritative***, ***formal***, ***legal***, ***legitimate***)

Word building: **officially** *adverb*
Word history: Late Latin, from Latin word meaning 'office'

officiate (uh-fish-ee-ayt)
verb to perform the duties of an office or position

Word history: Medieval Latin, from Latin word meaning 'office'

officious (uh-fish-uhs)
adjective **1** over-eager to force your services upon others: *an **officious** employee*
2 marked by or coming from such an attitude: ***officious** behaviour*

Word history: from Latin word meaning 'obliging', 'dutiful'

offing
phrase **in the offing 1** not very far away
2 ready to happen, appear, etc.

Word history: from the nautical word *offing* a position at a distance from the shore

off limits
adjective out of bounds

offline
adjective not connected to a computer network: *to work **offline***

Word use: You can also use **off-line**.

off-load
verb **1** to unload: *to **off-load** goods*
2 to get rid of
3 *Rugby, Australian Rules* to pass (the ball)

off-peak
adjective having to do with a time when there is less activity or lower demand: *an **off-peak** hot water service*

off-putting
adjective discouraging or unfriendly: *She has an **off-putting** manner.* (***daunting**, **disconcerting**, **unnerving**, **unsettling***)

off-season
noun a time of reduced activity for business or the manufacturing industry: *Some workers may lose their jobs in the **off-season**.*

offset (of-set, of-set)
verb to balance by something else: *The gains **offset** the losses.* (***cancel out**, **compensate for**, **counterbalance**, **neutralise***)

Verb forms: I **offset**, I have **offset**, I am **offsetting**

offshoot
noun **1** a shoot from a main stem, as of a plant
2 a branch, or a descendant, of a family or race
3 something produced in addition to the main product or main result of an activity

offshore
adverb **1** off or away from the shore
2 in or to another country: *to study **offshore** | to move operations **offshore***
adjective **3** moving or being away from the shore: *an **offshore** wind*

off side
noun Cricket that half of the field towards which the feet of the person who is batting point

Word use: You can also use **off**. | Compare this with **leg side**.

offside
adjective **1** in some team sports, placed illegally in relation to the ball, your own team, and the opposing team
2 *Australian, NZ* opposed or uncooperative: *I don't want him **offside**.*

offsider
noun Australian, NZ a partner or friend (***aide**, **assistant**, **associate**, **deputy**, **helper***)

offspring
noun the young of a particular parent (***issue**, **progeny***)

Word history: Middle English and Old English *ofspring*

off-the-record
adjective unofficial and not intended for public quotation: *an **off-the-record** discussion with the Prime Minister*

often (of-uhn, of-tuhn)
adverb **1** many times or frequently
2 in many cases

Word history: Middle English

ogle (oh-guhl)
verb to look at, especially with sexual interest

Word history: apparently from Dutch word meaning 'to eye'

ogre (oh-guh)
noun an imaginary monster of fairy tales and legends, which likes to eat people

Word history: French

ohm
noun a measure of electrical resistance

Word use: The symbol is Ω.
Word history: named after GS *Ohm*, 1787–1854, German physicist

oil
noun **1** a fatty liquid made from animal or vegetable fats, which is used in cooking
2 a thick, black liquid made from petroleum which is used to run and care for machinery
verb **3** to cover or fill with oil
phrase **4 burn the midnight oil**, to stay up late at night to study, work, etc.
5 pour oil on troubled waters, to calm

Word history: Middle English, from Old French, from Latin word *oleum* meaning '(olive) oil'

oilskin
noun a cloth treated with oil to make it waterproof so that it can be used for rain wear

ointment
noun a soft, greasy mixture used for healing your skin

Word history: Middle English, from Old French

okay
Colloquial
adjective **1** all right or satisfactory: *Are you **okay** now?*
adverb **2** well or correctly: *The car performed **okay**.*
verb **3** to pass or accept: *Will you **okay** this?*
noun **4** approval: *He gave the plan the **okay**.*
interjection **5** yes: ***Okay**, you can come if you like.*

Word use: You can also use **OK**, **ok** or **o.k.**
Word history: 19th century US slang; originally two letters *O.K.* standing for *orl korrect*, a jocular misspelling of 'all correct'

okra (<u>ok</u>-ruh, <u>ohk</u>-ruh)
noun a tall plant which produces pods that are used in soups and chutneys

Word history: a West African language

old
adjective **1** having lived for a long time: *an **old** man* (***aged***, ***elderly***, ***senior***)
2 having existed for a long time: ***old** buildings* (***ancient***, ***antique***)
3 aged in appearance: *She suddenly looks **old**.*
4 having reached a certain age: *five years **old***
5 worn out or out of date: ***old** clothes* | *an **old** car*
6 of an earlier time: *in the **old** days* | ***old** boys of the school* (***former***, ***past***, ***previous***)

Word history: Middle English; Old English *ald*, *eald*

olden
adjective having to do with the past: ***olden** days*

old-fashioned
adjective belonging to an earlier time or style: ***old-fashioned** clothes* (***antiquated***, ***archaic***, ***obsolete***, ***out-of-date***)

Word use: The opposite of this is **contemporary** or **modern**.

oleander (oh-lee-<u>an</u>-duh, ol-ee-<u>an</u>-duh)
noun a poisonous pink or white flowering shrub with dark green leaves

Word history: Medieval Latin

oligarchy (<u>ol</u>-uh-gah-kee)
noun a type of government in which a few people have all the power

Word history: Greek

olive
noun **1** a tree which grows in warm countries, or its fruit which can be eaten or crushed for its oil
2 a yellowish-green or brownish-green colour

Word building: **olive** *adjective*
Word history: Middle English, from Old French, from Latin

olive branch
noun **1** a branch of the olive tree, used as a symbol of peace
2 anything offered as a sign of peace

Olympic (uh-<u>lim</u>-pik)
adjective **1** having to do with the Olympic Games
2 of a standard suitable for the Olympic Games: *an **Olympic** athlete*

Word history: named after *Olympia*, a plain in Greece where a festival of games and sports was held every four years in ancient times

ombudsman (<u>om</u>-buhdz-muhn)
noun an official whose job is to look into people's complaints against the government and government agencies

Word history: from Swedish word meaning 'commissioner'

omelette (<u>om</u>-luht)
noun a food made of eggs beaten up and fried in a pan

Word use: You can also use **omelet**.
Word history: from French word meaning 'thin plate'

omen (<u>oh</u>-muhn)
noun a sign of good or bad luck to come (***augury***, ***portent***)

Word history: Latin

ominous (<u>om</u>-uh-nuhs)
adjective threatening: *an **ominous** silence* | ***ominous** clouds*

Word history: from Latin word meaning 'bearing omens', 'portentous'

omit
verb **1** to leave out: *You have **omitted** a word.*
2 to fail to do: *He **omits** to knock.* (***forget***, ***neglect***, ***overlook***)

Verb forms: I **omitted**, I have **omitted**, I am **omitting**
Word building: **omission** *noun*
Word history: Middle English, from Latin word meaning 'let go', 'neglect', 'omit'

omnibus
noun **1** an old-fashioned word for **bus**
2 a book of collected stories or writings by one writer or about one particular subject

Noun forms: The plural is **omnibuses.**
Word history: Latin word literally meaning 'for all'

omnipotent (om-<u>nip</u>-uh-tuhnt)
adjective having the power to do all things: *an **omnipotent** god*

Word building: **omnipotence** *noun*
Word history: Middle English, from Latin word meaning 'almighty'

omnipresent (om-nuh-<u>prez</u>-uhnt)
adjective present everywhere at the same time: *the **omnipresent** God*

Word building: **omnipresence** *noun*
Word history: Medieval Latin

omniscient (om-<u>nis</u>-ee-uhnt, om-<u>nish</u>-uhnt)
adjective knowing everything: *the **omniscient** author*

Word building: **omniscience** *noun*
Word history: *omni-* (a word part meaning 'all') + Latin *sciens* knowing

omnivore (<u>om</u>-nuh-vaw)
noun an animal that eats both animal and plant foods

Word use: Compare this with **carnivore, herbivore** and **insectivore**.

omnivorous (om-<u>niv</u>-uh-ruhs)
adjective **1** eating both animal and plant foods: *Humans are **omnivorous**.*
2 taking in everything, such as with your mind: *She is an **omnivorous** reader.*

Word history: Latin

on
preposition a word indicating: **1** position above and in contact with a supporting surface: ***on** the table*
2 contact with any surface: *the picture **on** the wall*
3 situation or place: *a house **on** the coast* | *a scar **on** the face* | *the person **on** the left*
4 state, condition, etc.: ***on** fire*
5 way or means: *to come **on** foot* | *to talk **on** the telephone*
6 time or occasion: ***on** Saturday*
7 object of action, thought, etc.: *to gaze **on** a scene*
8 what something is about: *an essay **on** animals*
9 ground or basis: ***on** good authority*

adverb **10** on yourself or itself: *to put your coat* ***on***
11 fast or tight: *to hold* ***on***
12 forwards or onwards: *further* ***on***
13 into active operation: *to turn the gas* ***on***
adjective **14** operating or in use: *The heating is* ***on.***
15 occurring: *What's* ***on*** *tomorrow?*
phrase **16 get on to,**
a to work on: *You need to* ***get on to*** *that project.*
b to make contact with
17 have yourself on, *Australian Colloquial* to think yourself better than you really are
18 on and off, occasionally

Word use: You can also use **off and on** for definition 18.
Word history: Old English *on, an* 'on', 'in', 'to'

once (wuns)
adverb **1** at a time in the past: *There was* ***once*** *a handsome prince.* (***formerly, once upon a time, previously***)
2 a single time: *The mail is delivered* ***once*** *a day.*
conjunction **3** if ever or whenever: *There'll be trouble* ***once*** *she finds out the truth.*
noun **4** a single occasion: ***Once*** *is enough.*
phrase **5 all at once,**
a suddenly: ***All at once*** *there was a loud crash and we all ran into the room.*
b at the same time: *Three things happened* ***all at once.***
6 at once,
a immediately: *Come* ***at once****! I need help!*
b at the same time: *Everything was happening* ***at once.***
7 once and for all, finally and decisively: *I've made up my mind* ***once and for all.***
8 once in a while, occasionally

Word history: Old English *ānes*

oncology (ong-kol-uh-jee)
noun the branch of medical science that deals with tumours

Word building: **oncologist** *noun* **oncological** *adjective*

one
adjective **1** being a single unit or individual, rather than two or more: ***one*** *apple*
2 being at some time in the future: *We'll meet again* ***one*** *day.*
3 single through union or agreement: *of* ***one*** *mind / with* ***one*** *voice*
4 particular: ***one*** *evening last week*
5 only: *the* ***one*** *person we can trust*
noun **6** the first and lowest whole number
7 a single person or thing
pronoun **8** a person or thing of a particular number or kind: ***one*** *of the poets*
9 anyone: *as good as* ***one*** *would hope*
10 a person like yourself: *What could* ***one*** *do in the situation?*
11 a person or thing of the kind just mentioned: *The paintings are fine* ***ones.***
phrase **12 at one,** in a state of unity and agreement: *We are* ***at one*** *on this question.*
13 one by one, singly and following each other

Word history: Old English

Some people like to avoid speaking too personally and directly, and instead of using *I* and *you*, they use **one**. You might say or write:

What can one possibly do about it?

It could mean *you* and it could mean *I* (or both of us).

One is rather a detached form of address, with no fixed or regular place in our pronoun system. This is why it often causes problems when you try to continue the sentence with it. Which possessive pronoun should you use?

1 One can only do his best.

2 One can only do her best.

3 One can only do their best.

4 One can only do one's best.

The first two sentences draw attention to gender, which many people prefer to avoid. (Look up **non-sexist language.**) The third sentence is neutral in gender, but moves from singular to plural in a way that some people feel is ungrammatical. The fourth sentence has an unusual and rather self-conscious tone because of the pronoun **one's**. Whichever pronoun you choose, you will need to stay with it, to be consistent. So after *his*, you would have to use *himself*, after *one's* it would have to be *oneself*, etc.

With all these complications, it is probably easier not to use **one** at all. For most Australians, it has a slightly old-fashioned and pompous ring to it these days.

one-eyed
adjective **1** having only one eye
2 having a strong preference in favour of someone or something

one-off
adjective individual, unique, or only occurring once

Word building: **one-off** *noun*

onerous (oh-nuh-ruhs)
adjective hard to bear: ***onerous*** *duties* (***burdensome, heavy, oppressive, taxing***)

Word history: Middle English, from Latin

oneself
pronoun **1** the reflexive form of the pronoun **one**: *It's hard to make* ***oneself*** *comfortable without a chair to sit on.*
2 your proper or normal self

For more information, look up **pronouns: reflexive pronouns.**

one-upmanship
noun the art or practice of gaining an advantage over others, by using money, position, etc.

onion
noun a strong-smelling bulb vegetable used in cooking and salads

Word history: Middle English, from Old French, from Latin word meaning 'large pearl', 'onion'

online
adjective **1** having direct access to a computer database: *an* ***online*** *branch of the bank*
2 (of information, etc.) able to be accessed directly by connection to a computer database, the internet, etc.: *The newspapers are* ***online.***
adverb **3** on the internet: *Let's chat* ***online.***
4 while interactively connected to a computer database: *to browse the data* ***online***

onlooker
noun someone who watches something happen: *A crowd of* ***onlookers*** *gathered around the scene of the accident.* (***observer***, ***spectator***, ***viewer***)

only (ohn-lee)
adverb **1** without others or alone: ***Only*** *he remained.*
2 merely or just: *If you would* ***only*** *go away.*
3 as recently as: *He was here* ***only*** *a moment ago.*
adjective **4** single or sole: *an* ***only*** *child*
conjunction **5** but: *I would have gone,* ***only*** *you objected.*
phrase **6 only too**, very: *She was* ***only too*** *pleased to come.*

Word history: Old English *ānlīc*

We often use **only** to spotlight something in a sentence:

John only got his work back today.

In speech it doesn't matter too much where we put the **only**, because we can show by the rising pitch of the voice just which word it is meant to spotlight. In our example, the speaker's voice could rise all the way from *only* to *today*, to show that *today* was the point of surprise.

But in writing there is no voice to guide the reader to the word we mean to spotlight. Instead it must be shown through the careful placement of words. **Only** draws most attention to the word straight after it. So to emphasise *today* we would have to write:

John got his work back only today.

Note the difference of meaning if we write:

John got only his work back today …

(Something else was kept back)

or

Only John got his work back today …

(Others didn't)

Other words which help to spotlight those next to them are:

even, exactly, just, merely, nearly, simply

Like **only**, they must be carefully placed to create the meaning you intend.

onomatopoeia (on-uh-mat-uh-pee-uh)
noun the use of a word or words which sound like the thing or sound they are describing, such as *crunch, splash* or *buzz*

Word building: **onomatopoeic** *adjective*
Word history: Late Latin, from Greek word meaning 'the making of words'

onsell
verb to sell (assets, securities, etc.) shortly after purchase: *to* ***onsell*** *shares*

Verb forms: I **onsold**, I have **onsold**, I am **onselling**
Word building: **onselling** *noun*

onset
noun a beginning: *the* ***onset*** *of a disease* (***commencement***, ***origin***, ***outbreak***, ***start***)

Word use: The opposite of this is **conclusion** or **end**.

onside
adjective **1** not offside
2 *Australian, NZ* in agreement

onslaught (on-slawt)
noun a fierce rush or attack (***assault***, ***blitz***, ***charge***)

onto
preposition to a place or position on (***upon***)

ontology
noun **1** the branch of metaphysics that investigates the nature of being
2 the structural framework for a computer database

onus (oh-nuhs)
noun a responsibility (***obligation***)

Word history: from Latin word meaning 'load', 'burden'

onward
adjective **1** directed or moving forwards
adverb **2** → **onwards**

Word history: Middle English, from *on* + *-ward* (a word part showing direction)

onwards
adverb **1** towards a point ahead or in front: *From that day* ***onwards*** *she kept a diary.*
2 at a position or point in front: *The train took us* ***onwards*** *to our destination.* (***ahead***, ***beyond***, ***forwards***)

Word use: You can also use **onward**.

oomph (oomf)
noun Colloquial **1** energy and vitality
2 sex appeal

ooze[1]
verb **1** to seep or leak slowly: *Gas* ***oozed*** *from the crack in the pipe.* (***dribble***, ***drip***, ***flow***, ***trickle***)
2 to give out slowly: *The wound is* ***oozing*** *blood. | She* ***oozes*** *charm.*

Word history: Old English *wōs* juice, moisture

ooze[2]
noun soft mud, such as on the bottom of the ocean

Word history: Old English *wāse* mud

opal
noun a valuable gem of various colours, streaked with red and blue

Word history: Latin, from Greek

opaque (oh-payk)
adjective not able to be seen through: *The water was muddy and* ***opaque***.

Word use: Compare this with **transparent** and **translucent**.
Word building: **opacity** *noun*
Word history: Middle English, from Latin word meaning 'shady', 'darkened'

open
adjective **1** not shut or locked (***agape***, ***ajar***, ***gaping***, ***unbarred***, ***unlocked***)
2 not limited or enclosed: ***open*** *fields* (***extensive***, ***spacious***, ***unfenced***, ***wide***)
3 not blocked or obstructed: *an* ***open*** *view*
4 friendly: *She has an* ***open*** *nature.* (***candid***, ***frank***, ***sincere***, ***spontaneous***, ***unreserved***)
5 able to be entered in, such as a competition, or applied for, such as a job
verb **6** to make or become open: *She* ***opened*** *the window. | The door* ***opened***.
7 to begin or start: *She* ***opened*** *the book at page ten. | Has school* ***opened***?
noun **8** an open or clear space, usually outside: *Let's have dinner in the* ***open***.

9 a competition in which both amateur and professional athletes can take part
phrase **10 open up**,
a to make ready for use: *to* ***open up*** *new land*
b to begin firing: *The artillery* ***opened up.***

Word use: The opposite of definition 1 is **closed.** | The opposite of definition 6 is **close.**
Word building: **openly** *adverb* **openness** *noun*
Word history: Middle English and Old English

open-and-shut
adjective easily decided or obvious

open-cut mine
noun a shallow, open pit allowing mining of rock layers near the surface

opener (ohp-nuh, ohp-uh-nuh)
noun **1** someone or something that opens: *You will need an* ***opener*** *to take the top off.*
2 *Cricket* a player who opens their side's innings by batting first
phrase **3 for openers,** to begin with: *I'll play a sonata* ***for openers.***

opening
noun **1** a making or becoming open
2 a space or place, not in use
3 a gap or hole
4 a beginning: *the* ***opening*** *of the opera*
5 an official beginning: *the* ***opening*** *of the new library by the minister*
6 a vacancy or opportunity: *There's an* ***opening*** *here for a hard worker.*

open-minded
adjective able to accept new and different ideas

open source software
noun Computers free software for which the source code is provided

opera
noun a play which is sung to music

Word building: **operatic** *adjective*
Word history: Italian, from Latin word meaning 'service', 'work', 'a work'

operable (op-uh-ruh-buhl, op-ruh-buhl)
adjective **1** able to be put into practice
2 able to be treated by a surgical operation

operate
verb **1** to work: *He can't* ***operate*** *the levers. | The escalator isn't* ***operating.***
2 to perform surgery: *The doctor will have to* ***operate*** *on her leg.*

Word history: from Latin word meaning 'having done work', 'having had effect'

operating profit
noun the profit, after income tax expense, resulting from the normal activities of a business over a particular period, occurring when the operating revenues and gains exceed the expenses and losses incurred in operating the business

operating system
noun Computers the essential program which enables all other programs to be run on a computer, and which establishes an interface between a user and the hardware of the computer

operation
noun **1** the way that something works
2 working order: *The lift isn't in* ***operation.***
3 a medical treatment on someone's body, using surgery
4 a military mission

Word building: **operational** *adjective*

operative
adjective **1** working or functional: *an* ***operative*** *life of two years*
2 having force or effect: *That law is only* ***operative*** *in Victoria.*

operator
noun **1** someone who works a machine: *a lift* ***operator***
2 someone who runs a big business: *the* ***operators*** *of a tourist resort*
3 *Mathematics, Computers, etc.* a symbol, character, word, etc., used to represent a particular action or logical relation, as the word 'and', or the plus symbol (+)

ophthalmic (of-thal-mik)
adjective having to do with the eye

ophthalmology (of-thal-mol-uh-jee)
noun the science dealing with the structure, functions and diseases of the eye

Word building: **ophthalmologist** *noun*

opiate
noun a medicinal drug containing opium that is able to put you to sleep

opinion
noun what you think or decide: *My* ***opinion*** *is that we should all help. | public* ***opinion*** (***attitude, conviction, outlook, stand, viewpoint***)

Word history: Middle English, from Old French, from Latin supposition

opinionated (uh-pin-yuhn-ay-tuhd)
adjective conceitedly full of your own ideas or opinions

opinion poll
noun the questioning of a selected number of the population, chosen so as to include a wide range of types of people, in order to find out public opinion on a particular issue, such as an election

Word use: You can also use **gallup poll.**

opium
noun a drug made from the juice of the poppy, which is used to relieve pain and put you to sleep

Word history: Middle English, from Latin, from Greek word meaning 'juice'

opponent
noun someone who is on the opposite side to you in a fight or contest (***adversary, antagonist, enemy, foe, rival***)

Word history: from Latin word meaning 'opposing'

opportune (op-uh-tyoohn)
adjective **1** favourable or appropriate: *an* ***opportune*** *moment to interrupt*
2 happening or coming at a good time: *an* ***opportune*** *arrival* (***auspicious, convenient, seasonable, timely, well-timed***)

Word history: Middle English, from Latin

opportunism (op-uh-tyoohn-iz-uhm, op-uh-choohn-iz-uhm)
noun the practice, as in politics, of changing actions, etc., to suit the occasion, often without thought of principles

Word building: **opportunist** *noun*

opportunistic (op-uh-chooh-nis-tik)
adjective **1** displaying opportunism: ***opportunistic*** *behaviour*
2 of an illness, developing as a result of a weakness in the immune system: *An* ***opportunistic*** *disease rendered her unwell.*

Word building: **opportunistically** *adverb*

opportunity
noun a suitable time or occasion: *She never had the* ***opportunity*** *to sing at a concert.*

Noun forms: The plural is **opportunities**.

opportunity shop
noun Australian, NZ a shop run by a church, charity, etc., for the sale of second-hand goods, especially clothes

oppose
verb to resist or fight: *They* ***opposed*** *her marriage.* (***counter***, ***defy***, ***obstruct***, ***withstand***)

Word use: The opposite of this is **support** or **agree with**.
Word history: Middle English, from Old French

opposite
adjective **1** completely different: *We hold* ***opposite*** *views on everything.* (***antithetical***, ***conflicting***, ***contradictory***, ***contrary***, ***converse***)
2 facing: *She lives in the* ***opposite*** *house.*
noun **3** the contrary: *I believe the* ***opposite***.

Word history: Middle English, from Latin word meaning 'put before or against', 'opposed'

opposition
noun **1** resistance or a fight: *They put up strong* ***opposition***.
2 the opposing side: *the* ***opposition*** *in a debate*
3 the major political party in parliament opposed to the party in power: *the leader of the* ***opposition***

Word use: The opposite of definition 1 is **agreement** or **support**. | You can also use **Opposition** for definition 3.
Word history: Latin

oppress
verb **1** to cause hardship to or weigh heavily upon: *Their poverty* ***oppressed*** *them.* (***afflict***, ***burden***)
2 to be cruel to: *The soldiers* ***oppressed*** *their prisoners.* (***maltreat***, ***persecute***, ***suppress***, ***tyrannise***)

Word building: **oppression** *noun*
oppressor *noun*
Word history: Middle English, from Latin word meaning 'press against', 'subdue'

oppressive
adjective **1** unjustly cruel or harsh: *an* ***oppressive*** *tyrant* | ***oppressive*** *taxes* (***brutal***, ***repressive***, ***tyrannical***)
2 so great or heavy as to make you uncomfortable: ***oppressive*** *heat* (***burdensome***, ***onerous***)

opt
verb **1** to choose: *He* ***opted*** *to join.* (***elect***)
phrase **2 opt out**, to decide not to join in or continue with

Word history: French, from Latin word meaning 'choose', 'wish'

optic
adjective **1** having to do with the eye as the organ of sight, or sight as a function of the brain
2 optical

Word history: Medieval Latin, from Greek word meaning 'of sight'

optical
adjective having to do with seeing: ***optical*** *glasses* | ***optical*** *illusion*

optician (op-tish-uhn)
noun someone who makes or sells glasses, according to prescription, to improve eyesight

Word history: French, from Medieval Latin

optimise
verb to make the best of, or make the most effective use of: *The big windows* ***optimised*** *the light.*

Verb forms: I **optimised**, I have **optimised**, I am **optimising**
Word use: You can also use **optimize**.
Word building: **optimisation** *noun*

optimism
noun hopefulness or the habit of expecting that things will turn out well: *She's not well but she's full of* ***optimism***.

Word use: The opposite is **pessimism**.
Word building: **optimistic** *adjective*
optimistically *adverb*
Word history: Neo-Latin, from Latin word meaning 'best'

optimist
noun someone who looks on the bright side and always hopes for the best

optimum
noun **1** the best point, degree, amount, etc., for the purpose
adjective **2** best or most favourable

Noun forms: The plural is **optima** or **optimums**.
Word building: **optimal** *adjective*
Word history: from Latin word meaning 'best'

option
noun a choice or the right to choose (***alternative***, ***elective***, ***preference***, ***selection***)

Word building: **optional** *adjective*
Word history: from Latin word meaning 'choice'

optional preferential voting
noun a form of preferential voting in which voters may vote for one candidate only, or choose to indicate preferences for others

Word use: Compare this with **full preferential voting** and **partial preferential voting**.

optometrist (op-tom-uh-truhst)
noun someone who tests your eyesight in order to supply glasses to improve it

Word building: **optometry** *noun*
Word history: based on *opt*(*ic*)

opulent (op-yuh-luhnt)
adjective rich or wealthy (***affluent***, ***luxurious***, ***prosperous***, ***sumptuous***)

Word building: **opulence** *noun* **opulently** *adverb*
Word history: from Latin word meaning 'rich', 'wealthy'

opus (oh-puhs)
noun a work, especially a musical composition

Word use: The plural is **opera** but it is not often used.
Word history: from Latin word meaning 'work', 'labour', 'a work'

or
conjunction indicates a connection between words, phrases, and clauses expressing choices: *blue* ***or*** *red* | *in love* ***or*** *in hate* | *to be* ***or*** *not to be*

> **or / oar / ore / awe**
> Look up **oar / or / ore / awe.**

oracle (o-ruh-kuhl)
noun **1** someone, especially a priest or priestess in ancient Greece, who answers difficult questions or reveals the future
2 a difficult saying given by such an oracle

Word building: **oracular** *adjective*
Word history: Middle English, from Old French, from Latin

oral
adjective **1** spoken: *an* ***oral*** *test in French*
2 having to do with your mouth or taken by mouth

Word history: from Latin word meaning 'mouth'

> **oral / aural**
> Don't confuse **oral** with **aural**, which means 'having to do with hearing or listening'.

orange
noun **1** a round, reddish-gold citrus fruit
2 a reddish-gold colour
adjective **3** made with or prepared from oranges: ***orange*** *juice*
4 of an orange colour: *the* ***orange*** *sun at sunset* (***amber***, ***ginger***, ***terracotta***)

Word history: Middle English, from Middle French, from Old Provençal, from Arabic, from Persian, from Sanskrit

orangutan (uh-rang-uh-tan)
noun a large ape found in Borneo and Sumatra, which climbs trees

Word use: You can also use **orang-utan** or **orang-outang**.
Word history: from Malay word meaning 'man of the woods'

oration
noun a formal speech, especially one given on a special occasion

Word history: Middle English, from Latin word meaning 'speech', 'discourse', 'prayer'

orator (o-ruh-tuh)
noun a public speaker, especially a skilful one

Word building: **oratorical** *adjective*
Word history: from Latin word meaning 'speaker', 'supplicant'

oratorio (o-ruh-taw-ree-oh)
noun a long, musical composition, usually based on a religious theme, for solo voices, chorus and orchestra

Noun forms: The plural is **oratorios.**

oratory (o-ruh-tree)
noun **1** skilful and powerful public speaking
2 the art of public speaking

orb
noun **1** chiefly in poetry, any of the heavenly bodies: *the* ***orb*** *of day (the sun)*
2 a sphere, globe or ball
3 a globe bearing a cross, as a sign of royalty

Word history: from Latin word meaning 'circle', 'disc', 'orb'

orbit
noun **1** the curved path or line of flight followed by a planet or satellite around the earth or sun
2 one complete circuit around such a curved path
verb **3** to travel around in an orbit-like course

Word building: **orbital** *adjective*
Word history: from Latin word meaning 'wheel track', 'course', 'circuit'

orchard
noun a paddock or farm where fruit trees are grown

Word building: **orchardist** *noun*
Word history: Old English *orceard*

orchestra (aw-kuhs-truh)
noun a large group of players of musical instruments, usually performing classical or semi-classical music

Word history: Latin, from Greek word meaning 'the space on which the chorus in Ancient Greek theatre danced'

orchestrate (aw-kuhs-trayt)
verb **1** to compose or arrange music to enable it to be performed by an orchestra
2 to put together in a well planned way: *to* ***orchestrate*** *a conference*

Word building: **orchestration** *noun*

orchid (aw-kuhd)
noun a plant that grows in warm climates and the beautiful waxy flower it produces

Word history: Neo-Latin

ordain
verb **1** to appoint to the church as a priest or minister
2 to order or declare: *The king* ***ordained*** *that the prisoner be banished for life.*

Word history: Middle English, from Old French, from Latin word meaning 'order', 'arrange', 'appoint'

ordeal
noun a severe test or hardship: *The funeral was an* ***ordeal*** *for her.*

Word history: Old English *ordēl*

order
noun **1** a command (***decree***, ***dictate***, ***direction***, ***edict***, ***instruction***)

2 the proper arrangement of things: *Restore* ***order*** *to your room.*
3 a a request to make or supply something, usually for money: *to place an* ***order*** *for shoes*
b the goods purchased: *Your* ***order*** *has arrived.*
c a written request to pay money or deliver goods
4 the way things are placed in relation to each other: *Did they come in that* ***order****?*
5 working condition: *It's out of* ***order****.*
6 a division into a particular group or kind: *the* ***order*** *of mammals*
7 a religious group living under the same rules: *the Dominican* ***order***
8 a lawful state or behaviour: *The police tried to restore* ***order****.*
verb **9** to command or give an instruction (***decree***, ***demand***, ***insist***, ***require***, ***stipulate***)
10 to request for something to be made or supplied: *Let us* ***order*** *tea.*
phrase **11 a tall order**, *Colloquial* a difficult task
12 call to order, to establish quiet and order among a group of people at a meeting or so on
13 in order,
a properly arranged
b suitable or appropriate
14 in order that, so that: *I gave him a list* ***in order that*** *he would remember everything.*
15 in order to, as a means to: *I ran* ***in order to*** *catch the bus.*
16 out of order,
a not working properly
b socially unacceptable, inappropriate: *That comment was completely out of order.*

Word history: Middle English, from Old French, from Latin word meaning 'row', 'rank', 'regular arrangement'

orderly
adjective **1** arranged in an approved order or tidy manner (***neat***, ***shipshape***, ***tidy***, ***trim***)
2 systematic or disciplined: *an* ***orderly*** *mind* (***methodical***)
3 willing to obey rules or laws: *an* ***orderly*** *citizen*
noun **4** someone, especially a soldier or hospital employee, who performs general duties

Noun forms: The plural is **orderlies**.
Word building: **orderliness** *noun*

ordinal number
noun a number which tells you the place of a thing in a series, such as 'first' in *the first child* or 'fourteenth' in *the fourteenth week*

Word use: Compare this with **cardinal number**. | For information on how to write and punctuate numbers, look up **number**.

ordinance (aw-duh-nuhns)
noun a rule or regulation: *an* ***ordinance*** *of the governor*

Word history: Middle English, from Old French word meaning 'to order', from Latin

ordinarily (aw-duhn-uh-ruh-li, aw-duh-nair-ruh-lee)
adverb usually: *He* ***ordinarily*** *arrives on time.*

ordinary
adjective **1** usual or normal: *an* ***ordinary*** *working day* (***average***, ***common***, ***customary***, ***routine***, ***standard***, ***unremarkable***)
2 of poor quality or inferior: *It looks rather* ***ordinary****.* (***indifferent***, ***mediocre***, ***nondescript***, ***pedestrian***, ***second-rate***)

Word building: **ordinariness** *noun*
Word history: Middle English, from Latin word meaning 'of the usual order'

ordure (aw-joouh)
noun filth or dung (***excrement***, ***manure***)

Word history: Middle English, from Old French word meaning 'filthy', from Latin word meaning 'horrid'

ore
noun a rock or mineral which contains a metal that is valuable enough to be mined

Word history: Old English *ār* brass

ore / or / oar / awe

Don't confuse **ore** with the other three words that sound the same.

You use **or** to connect alternative words, phrases or clauses:

I don't know which colour to choose — red, yellow or green.

You use an **oar** for rowing a boat.

Awe is a feeling of great respect mixed with fear:

The men were in awe of her bad temper.

oregano (o-ruh-gah-noh)
noun a herb of the mint family, used in cooking

organ
noun **1** a musical instrument with pipes and one or more keyboards
2 a part of your body which has a particular job, such as your heart which pumps blood or your liver which makes bile
3 something which can be used to express a particular viewpoint: *This newsletter is the official* ***organ*** *of our club.*

Word history: Middle English, from Latin, from Greek word meaning 'instrument', 'tool', 'bodily organ', 'musical instrument'

organdie
noun a fine but stiff cotton material

Word history: French

organic (aw-gan-ik)
adjective **1** having to do with living things or their organs
2 *Chemistry* having to do with a class of compounds consisting of all compounds of carbon except for its oxides, sulfides and metal carbonates
3 having to do with the way parts are organised in a complete structure
4 having to do with farming without chemicals: *They only use* ***organic*** *fertilisers.*

Word use: Compare definition 2 with **inorganic** (definition 2).
Word building: **organically** *adverb*
Word history: Latin, from Greek

organisation
noun **1** the skilful arrangement or running of something
2 something which is run or managed
3 a group of people organised for some purpose, such as a business firm or a club (***company***, ***corporation***, ***outfit***, ***syndicate***)
4 the people or structure involved in running a business, club, political party, etc.

Word use: You can also use **organization**.
Word building: **organisational** *adjective*

organise
verb **1** to form, especially into a group which works or does things together: *to* ***organise*** *a chess club*
2 to order or arrange neatly: *to* ***organise*** *my books*
3 to arrange or plan: *He* ***organised*** *the holiday.* (***engineer***, ***mastermind***, ***set up***)

Word use: You can also use **organize**.
Word building: **organiser** *noun*
Word history: Middle English, from Medieval Latin, from Latin word meaning 'organ'

organism
noun **1** *Biology* an individual composed of mutually dependent parts which work together to develop and support life
2 any form of animal or plant life: *She saw the tiny* ***organism*** *under the microscope.*

orgasm
noun the moment of greatest pleasure in sexual intercourse

Word history: Neo-Latin, from Greek word meaning 'swell', 'be excited'

orgy (aw-jee)
noun wild or drunken feasting, or other uncontrolled behaviour

Noun forms: The plural is **orgies**.
Word history: Latin, from Greek

orient (o-ree-uhnt, aw-ree-uhnt)
verb **1** to aim or direct
2 to adjust or adapt

Word building: **oriented** *adjective*
Word history: Middle English, from Latin word meaning 'the east', 'sunrise'

orient / orientate

These verbs can both be used to mean either 'to aim or direct' or 'to adjust or adapt':

The lesson was oriented (or *orientated*) *towards the younger students.*

The house was oriented (or *orientated*) *towards the north to catch the sun.*

They oriented (or *orientated*) *themselves quickly to their new school.*

The -ate ending adds nothing to the meaning of **orient**, which is the simpler and older verb, and does the same job perfectly as well.

oriental (o-ree-en-tuhl, aw-ree-en-tuhl)
adjective (*sometimes upper case*) of or from an Asian country

orientate (o-ree-uhn-tayt, aw-ree-uhn-tayt)
verb **1** to aim or direct
2 to adjust or adapt

Word building: **orientated** *adjective* **orientation** *noun*

orienteering
noun a sport in which you have to find your way as quickly as possible over a difficult course, using maps and a compass

orifice (o-ruh-fuhs)
noun the mouth or opening of a hole

Word history: French, from Latin

origami (or-uh-gah-mee)
noun the art of folding paper into interesting shapes, first developed in Japan

Word history: Japanese

origin
noun where something or someone comes from: *the* ***origin*** *of an idea* | *of Irish* ***origin*** (***beginning***, ***commencement***, ***derivation***, ***root***, ***source***)

Word history: from Latin word meaning 'beginning', 'source', 'rise'

original
adjective **1** first or earliest: *The* ***original*** *models are in the museum.*
2 newly thought up or invented, especially without a model: *an* ***original*** *design* (***avant-garde***, ***fresh***, ***innovative***, ***modern***, ***novel***)
noun **3** the earliest or first form from which copies are made: *He has kept the* ***original***.
4 a work which has not been copied from anything else

Word building: **originality** *noun* **originally** *adverb*

originate
verb **1** to invent or cause to start: *Who* ***originated*** *the idea?* (***conceive***, ***create***, ***devise***, ***generate***, ***initiate***, ***introduce***)
2 to start: *The idea* ***originated*** *with Mia.* (***arise***, ***begin***)

ornament
noun **1** an object or a decoration which is meant to be beautiful rather than useful
verb **2** to decorate

Word building: **ornamental** *adjective*
Word history: from Latin word meaning 'equipment', 'ornament'

ornate
adjective covered with ornaments, showy or fine: ***ornate*** *chairs*

Word use: The opposite of this is **plain** or **undecorated**.
Word history: Middle English, from Latin word meaning 'adorned'

ornithology
noun the study of birds and bird life

Word building: **ornithologist** *noun*

orphan
noun **1** someone, especially a child, whose parents have died
verb **2** to make an orphan of: *He was* ***orphaned*** *by a car accident.*

Word history: late Middle English, from Late Latin, from Greek word meaning 'without parents', 'bereaved'

orphanage
noun a place where children without parents live

orthodontics
noun that branch of dentistry concerned with straightening teeth or correcting irregularities of the jaw

Word building: **orthodontic** *adjective* **orthodontist** *noun*
Word history: Neo-Latin, from Greek

orthodox
adjective **1** usual or accepted: ***orthodox*** *dress* (***conventional***, ***customary***, ***normal***, ***traditional***)
2 according to usual religious teaching

Word use: The opposite of this is **unconventional** or **unorthodox**.
Word building: **orthodoxy** *noun*
Word history: Late Latin, from Greek word meaning 'right in opinion'

orthography (aw-thog-ruh-fee)
noun **1** the art or manner of spelling correctly
2 the study of spelling

Word history: Middle English, from Latin, from Greek word meaning 'correct writing'

orthopaedics (awth-uh-pee-diks)
noun the type of medicine that corrects or cures any problems or diseases of the spine and bones

Word use: You can also use **orthopedics**.
Word building: **orthopaedic** *adjective* **orthopaedist** *noun*
Word history: Greek

orthosis (aw-thoh-suhs)
noun a device applied to the body to modify position or motion: *Plaster casts are the most common type of* ***orthosis*** *for broken bones.*

Noun forms: The plural is **orthoses** (aw-thoh-seez).

orthotic (aw-thot-ik)
adjective **1** having to do with an orthosis: ***orthotic*** *footwear*
noun **2** an orthotic device, especially one for the foot

oscillate (os-uh-layt)
verb to move or swing to and fro

Word building: **oscillation** *noun* **oscillator** *noun*
Word history: Latin *oscillātus* swung

osmosis
noun the tendency of a liquid to pass through a semi-permeable membrane into a solution where its concentration is lower, so that in the end the solutions will be of equal strength on both sides of the wall

Word history: Neo-Latin, from Greek word meaning 'a thrusting'

ostensible
adjective outward, supposed or pretended: *The* ***ostensible*** *reason for her lateness was that she missed the train.* (***alleged***, ***professed***, ***purported***, ***seeming***)

Word building: **ostensibly** *adverb*
Word history: French, from Latin, displayed

ostentation
noun showiness or display: *He dresses with* ***ostentation.***

Word building: **ostentatious** *adjective* **ostentatiously** *adverb* **ostentatiousness** *noun*
Word history: Middle English, from Latin

osteoarthritis (os-tee-oh-ah-thruy-tuhs)
noun a degenerative type of chronic arthritis

osteopathy (os-tee-op-uh-thee)
noun the method of treating disease by pressing bones and muscles in your body

Word building: **osteopath** *noun* **osteopathic** *adjective*

ostracise (os-truh-suyz)
verb to keep away from, or send away, especially as a punishment (***cold-shoulder***, ***exclude***, ***exile***, ***expel***, ***isolate***)

Word use: You can also use **ostracize**.
Word building: **ostracism** *noun*
Word history: from Greek word meaning 'potsherd' (a pottery fragment), originally 'a piece of earthenware used as a token in a ballot'

ostrich
noun a large bird of Africa which runs fast but can't fly

Word history: Middle English, from Old French, from Late Latin, from Greek

other
adjective **1** additional or further: *He and one* ***other*** *person were there.*
2 different from the thing or things spoken of: *in some* ***other*** *city*
3 different in nature or kind: *I would not have her* ***other*** *than as she is.*
pronoun **4** the other one: *Each praises the* ***other.***
5 some other person or thing: *some day or* ***other***
phrase **6 every other**, every alternate: *a meeting* ***every other*** *week*

Word history: Middle English, from Old English *ōther*

otherwise
adverb **1** under other circumstances: *I might* ***otherwise*** *have come.*
2 in another manner or differently: *Try to see it* ***otherwise.***
3 in other respects: *an* ***otherwise*** *happy life*

otter
noun a furry water mammal with webbed feet and a flattened tail like a ship's rudder

Word history: Old English *oter, ot(o)r*

ottoman (ot-uh-muhn)
noun a low padded seat without a back or arms

ought (awt)
verb indicating obligation, duty, etc.: *You* ***ought*** *to help.*

Word use: This is an auxiliary verb, always used with another verb.

ought to

Both **ought to** and **should** mean that something has to be done:

You ought to turn the light on.

You should turn the light on.

So *ought to* and *should* both combine with other verbs to make statements expressing obligation.

(continued)

ought to *(continued)*

But when it comes to making questions or negative sentences, **ought to** seems awkward, and perhaps a little old-fashioned:

Ought you to turn the light on?

You oughtn't to turn the light on.

It's easier to say:

Should you turn the light on?

You shouldn't turn the light on.

ouija (wee-juh, wee-jee)
noun a board used in seances, which is supposed to tap out messages from dead people

Word history: French *oui* yes + German *ja* yes

ounce
noun a measure of weight in the imperial system, equal to about 29 grams

Word use: Look up **imperial system**.
Word history: Middle English, from Old French, from Latin word meaning 'twelfth part', 'inch', 'ounce'

our
pronoun the possessive form of **we**, used before a noun: *We took* ***our*** *dog for a walk.*

Our is a first person plural pronoun. It is sometimes called a *determiner* or a *possessive adjective.*

For more information, look up **pronouns: personal pronouns** and **pronouns: possessive pronouns.**

ours
pronoun **1** the possessive form of **we** used without a noun following: *The dog is* ***ours.***
2 the person(s) or thing(s) belonging to us: ***Ours*** *are those seats over there.*

Ours is a first person plural pronoun in the possessive case.

For more information, look up **pronouns: personal pronouns** and **pronouns: possessive pronouns.**

ourselves
pronoun **1** the reflexive form of **we**: *We hurt* ***ourselves.***
2 a form of **us** or **we** used for emphasis: *We did it* ***ourselves.***

For more information, look up **pronouns: reflexive pronouns.**

oust (owst)
verb to push out or expel: *The rebels* ***ousted*** *the king from the palace.*

Word history: Anglo-French, from Latin word meaning 'be in the way', 'protect against'

out
adverb **1** forth or away from a place, position, state, etc.: ***out*** *of the room* | ***out*** *of order* | *to hire* ***out*** | *to vote* ***out*** *of power*
2 away from your home: *to set* ***out*** *on a journey*
3 into the open: *to go* ***out*** *for a walk*
4 completely or to the end: *to dry* ***out*** | *to empty* ***out*** | *tired* ***out*** | *to fight it* ***out***
5 no longer burning or giving light: *The lamp went* ***out.***
6 not in fashion: *That style has gone* ***out.***
7 into sight or notice: *The stars came* ***out.*** | *The book came* ***out*** *in May.* | *He has been found* ***out.***
8 beyond a point or surface: *to stick* ***out***
9 into existence or activity: *War broke* ***out.***
10 away from existence or activity: *to fade* ***out*** | *to block* ***out***
11 from among many: *to pick* ***out***
12 from a centre: *to spread* ***out***
13 aloud: *to call* ***out***
adjective **14** incorrect: *He was* ***out*** *in his sums.*
15 not burning or giving light: *The fire is* ***out.***
16 unconscious: *The boxer was* ***out*** *for five minutes.*
17 torn or worn: *trousers* ***out*** *at the knee*
18 finished: *before the week is* ***out***
19 in tennis and other games, beyond the boundary lines
20 in cricket, removed from play
preposition **21** forth from: ***out*** *the door*
22 outside: ***out*** *the back*
phrase **23 go all out**, to try as hard as possible to do something
24 out-and-out, complete or absolute: *an* ***out-and-out*** *liar*
25 out of,
a from a source: *made* ***out of*** *scraps*
b to a state of lacking: *to run* ***out of*** *milk*

Word history: Middle English, from Old English *ūt*

outback
noun Australian, NZ the remote parts of the country or bush, far from the cities and the coast (***hinterland, the bush, the sticks***)

Word building: **outback** *adjective* **outback** *adverb*

outboard
adjective on the outside of a boat or plane: *an* ***outboard*** *motor*

outbreak
noun a sudden beginning or happening: *the* ***outbreak*** *of war* | *an* ***outbreak*** *of measles*

outbuilding
noun a building set apart from a main building

outburst
noun a sudden bursting or pouring out: *an* ***outburst*** *of violence* | *an* ***outburst*** *of laughter*

outcast
noun someone who is not accepted by people in a society

outcome
noun a result or consequence: *the* ***outcome*** *of the elections*

outcrop
noun **1** a part that shows above or beyond: *an* ***outcrop*** *of rock*
2 a sudden or unexpected occurrence: *an* ***outcrop*** *of labour unrest* (***eruption, flare-up, outbreak, upsurge***)

outcry
noun a loud noise or an uproar: *a public* ***outcry*** *against nuclear bombs*

Noun forms: The plural is **outcries.**

outdated
adjective out-of-date or old-fashioned

outdo
verb to surpass in doing or performance

Verb forms: I **outdid,** I have **outdone,** I am **outdoing**

outdoor
adjective occurring or used out of doors: *Playing soccer is an **outdoor** activity.*

outdoors
adverb **1** outside a house or in the open air: *We'll have breakfast **outdoors** today.*
noun **2** the open-air world outside houses
phrase **3 the great outdoors**, the natural environment, especially wild areas

outer
adjective **1** farther out or having to do with the outside: *the **outer** walls of a house*
noun **2** *Australian* that part of a sportsground which is without shelter
phrase **3 on the outer**, *Australian, NZ Colloquial* shut out from the group or mildly ostracised

Word history: comparative formation of *out*

outer space
noun the region of the universe outside the earth's atmosphere

outfit
noun **1** a set of clothes or equipment needed for an activity: *A skiing **outfit** consists of skis, poles, boots and appropriate clothes.*
2 a business or group of people working together: *a military **outfit*** (***company***, ***corporation***, ***firm***, ***organisation***)
verb **3** to equip or fit out

Verb forms: I **outfitted**, I have **outfitted**, I am **outfitting**

outfox
verb to get an advantage over (***outmanoeuvre***, ***outsmart***, ***outwit***)

outgoing
adjective **1** friendly and sociable: *He is **outgoing** and has lots of friends.* (***cordial***, ***extroverted***, ***genial***, ***gregarious***, ***warm***)
2 departing or going out: ***outgoing** trains*

Word use: The opposite of definition 1 is **shy**. The opposite of definition 2 is **incoming**.

outgrowth
noun **1** a natural development, product or result
2 an extra result
3 a growing out or forth

outing
noun a trip taken for fun: *an **outing** to the beach*

outlandish
adjective **1** very strange in appearance, behaviour, etc. (***bizarre***, ***eccentric***, ***fantastic***, ***freakish***)
2 out-of-the-way or remote

outlaw
noun **1** a criminal, especially in earlier times one who had been cut off from the protection of the law (***bandit***, ***bushranger***, ***highwayman***)
verb **2** to make someone an outlaw
3 to forbid by law: *The government **outlawed** smoking on public transport.* (***ban***, ***bar***, ***disallow***, ***proscribe***)

Word history: Old English *ūtlage*

outlay
noun **1** money, time or energy spent in getting something (***expenditure***)
verb **2** to spend (***expend***, ***pay***)

Verb forms: I **outlaid**, I have **outlaid**, I am **outlaying**

outlet
noun **1** an opening or way for letting something out: *A power point is an **outlet** for electricity.* | *Stamping your feet is an **outlet** for anger.*
2 a shop or market: *an **outlet** for handcrafts* (***stall***, ***store***, ***supermarket***)

outline
noun **1** a line showing the shape of something: *the **outline** of a circle*
2 a short description giving only the most important points: *an **outline** of a story* (***precis***, ***report***, ***résumé***, ***summary***, ***synopsis***)

Word building: **outline** *verb*

outlook
noun **1** a view: *an **outlook** over the park from the verandah* (***prospect***, ***scene***, ***vista***)
2 an attitude or point of view: *a gloomy **outlook** on life* (***opinion***, ***stand***, ***viewpoint***)
3 what is likely to happen in the future: *The weather **outlook** for tomorrow is good.*

outlying
adjective far from the centre or main body (***distant***, ***faraway***, ***isolated***, ***remote***)

out-of-pocket
adjective having to do with what has been spent in cash: ***out-of-pocket** expenses*

outpatient
noun a patient who comes to a hospital for medical treatment but does not have to stay overnight

outpost
noun **1** a group of soldiers stationed away from the main army
2 a settlement far away from the main town: *a desert **outpost***

output
noun **1** something that is produced: *to increase the **output** of a factory*
2 the information that a computer can put out, based on the information that has been put in

Word use: The opposite of this is **input**.

outrage
noun **1** something that shocks or offends people
2 a feeling of very strong anger

Word building: **outrageous** *adjective*
Word history: Middle English, from Old French word meaning 'push beyond bounds'

outright
adverb **1** completely or totally: *to refuse **outright***
2 immediately: *to be killed **outright***
adjective **3** complete or total: *an **outright** failure*

outset
noun the beginning or start: *Our team looked set to win from the **outset**.* (***commencement***, ***opening***)

outside
noun **1** the outer part or side: *to paint the **outside** of the house* | *She seems calm on the **outside** but inside she's angry.* (***exterior***, ***facade***, ***surface***)
adjective **2** on the outer side or part: *the **outside** walls*
3 coming from somewhere else: *a business funded by **outside** money*
adverb **4** on or to the outside: *It's cold **outside**.* | *Go **outside**.*
phrase **5 an outside chance**, scarcely any chance at all
6 at the outside, *Colloquial* at the limit: *You can spend not more than $10 **at the outside**.*

Word use: The opposite is **inside**.

outsider
noun someone who doesn't fit in to a group

outskirts
plural noun the outer areas: *small farms on the **outskirts** of the city* (***boundary***, ***edge***, ***periphery***)

outspoken
adjective saying openly what you think even if it offends people

Word use: The opposite of this is **tactful**.

outstanding
adjective **1** standing out from all others: *an **outstanding** swimmer* (***excellent***, ***exceptional***, ***great***, ***sensational***, ***superior***)
2 not settled or finished: ***outstanding** debts*

Word building: **outstandingly** *adverb*

outstrip
verb **1** to outdo, surpass or excel
2 to pass in running or travelling swiftly (***beat***, ***lap***, ***overtake***, ***pass***)

Verb forms: I **outstripped**, I have **outstripped**, I am **outstripping**

outward
adjective **1** able to be seen: ***outward** signs of fear*
2 outside or outer: *the **outward** surface*
3 away from a place: *a bus making an **outward** journey*
adverb **4** → **outwards**

Word use: The opposite of defninition 1 is **inward**.
Word history: Middle English; Old English *ūtweard*

outwardly
adverb on the outside: ***outwardly** shy*

Word use: The opposite of this is **inwardly**.

outwards
adverb towards the outside: *I last saw her heading **outwards** to the garden.*

Word use: You can also use **outward**.

outweigh (owt-<u>way</u>)
verb **1** to be more valuable, important, etc., than: *The advantages of the plan **outweighed** its faults.*
2 to weigh more than

outwit
verb to beat by being more cunning or clever: *If you can't be stronger than your opponents you must **outwit** them.*

Verb forms: I **outwitted**, I have **outwitted**, I am **outwitting**

ova
noun plural of **ovum**

oval
adjective **1** shaped like an egg
noun **2** an oval shape
3 *Australian* a field for playing sport on

Word history: Neo-Latin, from Latin word meaning 'egg'

ovary
noun the part of a female's body that produces eggs for reproduction

Noun forms: The plural is **ovaries**.
Word building: **ovarian** *adjective*
Word history: Neo-Latin, from Latin word meaning 'egg'

ovation
noun cheers and enthusiastic applause: *The audience gave the orchestra an **ovation**.*

Word history: from Latin word meaning 'rejoicing'

oven (<u>uv</u>-uhn)
noun a closed-in space, usually part of a stove, used for cooking, heating and drying

Word history: Middle English, from Old English *ofen*

ovenproof
adjective not damaged by being heated in a oven

ovenware
noun ovenproof dishes

over
preposition **1** above in place or position: *a roof **over** our heads*
2 above and to the other side of: *to jump **over** a wall*
3 above in power: *The manager is **over** the supervisor.*
4 on or upon: *Put a cloth **over** the food.*
5 on top of: *She hit him **over** the head.*
6 across: *to go **over** a bridge | lands **over** the sea*
7 throughout: ***over** a great distance*
8 more than: ***over** a kilometre*
9 rather than: *to choose this **over** that*
10 during: ***over** the holidays*
11 about: *to quarrel **over** it*
12 by means of: ***over** the radio*
adverb **13** through: *Read it **over**.*
14 at some distance in a direction pointed out: ***over** by the house*
15 across: *Come **over** and see us.*
16 down or upside down: *to knock **over***
17 in repetition: *two times **over***
adjective **18** finished: *when the war is **over***
noun **19** in cricket, a division of the game made up of a certain number of balls bowled successively by one bowler
phrase **20 all over**,
a everywhere
b thoroughly
c finished and done with
d typical of: *That's him **all over**.*
21 over and above, in addition to: *What he did was **over and above** his duty.*
22 over the fence, unreasonable: *His request was **over the fence**.*

Word history: Middle English, from Old English *ofer*

overall (<u>oh</u>-vuh-rawl)
adjective **1** from one extreme limit of a thing to another: *the **overall** length of a bridge*
2 with everything included: *an **overall** estimate*
noun **3 overalls**, a pair of trousers of strong material, usually with a bib and shoulder straps
adverb (oh-vuhr-<u>awl</u>) **4** covering or including everything: *the position viewed **overall***

overarm
adjective **1** performed with the arm raised above the shoulder, as bowling
2 having to do with a style of swimming similar to freestyle
adverb **3** in an overarm manner: *to swim **overarm***

overawe
verb to fill with fear and respect: *The presence of the famous actor **overawed** them.*

overbalance
verb to lose your balance and fall or trip over: *to **overbalance** while skating* (***capsize**, **keel over**, **tip over**, **tumble***)

overbearing
adjective bossy and arrogant (***authoritarian**, **autocratic**, **dictatorial**, **imperious**, **tyrannical***)

overboard
adverb **1** over the side of a boat or ship into the water: *to fall **overboard** and have to be rescued*
phrase **2 go overboard**, *Colloquial* to be over enthusiastic: *He's really **going overboard** about computers.*

overcast
adjective cloudy and grey: ***overcast** skies* (***dreary**, **dull**, **foggy**, **hazy**, **misty***)

overcharge
verb to charge too high a price

overcome
verb **1** to win the battle against: *to **overcome** an enemy | to **overcome** the fear of heights*
2 to make weak or helpless: *Weariness finally **overcame** the travellers*

Verb forms: I **overcame**, I have **overcome**, I am **overcoming**
Word history: Middle English, from Old English *ofercuman*

overdo
verb to do more than is sensible: *to **overdo** exercise*

Verb forms: I **overdid**, I have **overdone**, I am **overdoing**

overdone
adjective cooked too much: ***overdone** steak*

overdose
noun **1** a dose of a drug large enough to either kill you or make you seriously ill: *an **overdose** of heroin*
verb **2** to take an overdose of a drug: *She **overdosed** last night and is in hospital today fighting for her life.*

Word use: You can also use the colloquial **OD**.

overdraft
noun a banking arrangement that allows a customer to borrow money by taking more out of a cheque account than is in it, up to an agreed limit and with the payment of interest

overdraw
verb **1** to take more money out of a bank account than there is in it
2 to exaggerate: *His story was wildly **overdrawn**.*

Verb forms: I **overdrew**, I have **overdrawn**, I am **overdrawing**

overdue
adjective late or past the proper time: ***overdue** library books*

overflow
verb **1** to spill or flow over
noun **2** a flood: *the **overflow** of a river*
3 the area of land covered by water in times of flood

overgrown
adjective covered with weeds and long grass

Word building: **overgrow** *verb* **overgrowth** *noun*

overhang
verb **1** to hang over: *A tree **overhangs** the pool. | We can shelter where the cliff **overhangs**.*
2 to loom over or threaten: *Danger **overhung** their journey.*
noun **3** an overhanging projection

Verb forms: it **overhung**, it has **overhung**, it is **overhanging**

overhaul
verb to check, take apart, and repair: *to **overhaul** an engine*

Word building: **overhaul** *noun*

overhead
adverb **1** straight above: *birds flying **overhead***
adjective **2** above your head: ***overhead** telephone wires*
noun **3 overheads**, the fixed costs involved in running a business

overhear
verb to hear other people's conversation, especially by accident: *They were talking so loudly I **overheard** what was said.*

Verb forms: I **overheard**, I have **overheard**, I am **overhearing**

overkill
noun the use of more material or energy than is necessary to achieve an aim

overlap
verb **1** to partly cover: *Place the tiles on the roof so that one **overlaps** the other.*
noun **2** the amount of overlapping: *an **overlap** of two centimetres*
3 an overlapping part or place

Verb forms: it **overlapped**, it has **overlapped**, it is **overlapping**

overleaf
adverb on the other side of the page

overlook
verb **1** to miss or ignore: *to **overlook** a spelling mistake | I shall **overlook** your lateness this time.* (***discount**, **disregard**, **pass over**, **turn a blind eye to***)
2 to look down over: *The house **overlooks** the park.*

overly
adverb excessively or too: *a voyage not **overly** dangerous*

overnight (oh-vuh-nuyt)
adverb **1** during the night: *to stay **overnight***
2 *Australian* on the evening before: *Preparations were made **overnight**.*
3 suddenly or very quickly: *New towns sprang up **overnight**.*
adjective (oh-vuh-nuyt) **4** done, happening or continuing during the night: *an **overnight** stop*
5 staying for one night: ***overnight** guests*
6 designed to be used one night or very few nights: ***overnight** bag*
7 happening suddenly or rapidly: *an **overnight** success*
verb **8** to stay overnight at a place while in transit: *We overnighted in Singapore.*

overpass
noun a bridge for cars or pedestrians, which crosses over a busy road

overpower
verb to overcome by greater strength: *The wrestler **overpowered** his opponent.* (***conquer**, **crush**, **defeat**, **overwhelm**, **vanquish***)

overpowering
adjective very strong: *an **overpowering** personality | an **overpowering** perfume*

overreach
verb to defeat yourself by doing too much or being too clever: *He **overreached** himself in applying for the boss's job.*

overriding
adjective more important than any other: *an **overriding** consideration*

overrule
verb to rule or decide against: *to **overrule** a person | to **overrule** an objection*

overrun
verb to spread or swarm over: *The Pied Piper got rid of the rats which were **overrunning** the city.*

Verb forms: it **overran**, it has **overrun**, it is **overrunning**
Word history: Old English *oferyrnan*

overseas
adverb over or beyond the sea: *to travel **overseas***

Word building: **overseas** *adjective*

oversee
verb to supervise or manage: *to **oversee** workers*

Verb forms: I **oversaw**, I have **overseen**, I am **overseeing**
Word building: **overseer** *noun*
Word history: Old English *ofersēon*

overshadow
verb **1** to be more important, active or noticeable than: *She always **overshadowed** him at parties.*
2 to cast a shadow over
3 to make dark or gloomy
4 to shelter or protect

Word history: Old English *ofersceadwian*

overshoot
verb **1** to shoot or go beyond: *to **overshoot** the mark | to **overshoot** the landing*
2 to go further in anything than is intended or proper

Verb forms: I **overshot**, I have **overshot**, I am **overshooting**
Word history: Middle English

oversight
noun **1** a failure to notice or take something into account
2 something left out, or not done, by mistake

Word history: Middle English

overt
adjective open, and not hidden or secret: ***overt** hostility | **overt** behaviour* (***apparent**, **manifest**, **obvious**, **unconcealed**, **undisguised***)

Word use: The opposite of this is **covert** or **concealed.**
Word history: Middle English, from Old French word meaning 'open', from Latin

overtake
verb **1** to catch up and pass: *The police **overtook** the speeding car. | It is dangerous to **overtake** on a bridge.*
2 to come upon suddenly: *A storm **overtook** the yacht.*

Verb forms: I **overtook**, I have **overtaken**, I am **overtaking**
Word history: Middle English

overthrow
verb **1** to defeat or put an end to by force: *The army **overthrew** the government.*
2 to throw too far: *The fielder **overthrew** the ball and it missed the wicket.*

Verb forms: I **overthrew**, I have **overthrown**, I am **overthrowing**
Word building: **overthrow** *noun*

overtime
noun extra time worked before or after the usual working hours: *to get extra pay for **overtime***

Word building: **overtime** *adjective*

overtone
noun an extra meaning or implication: *There was an **overtone** of resentment in his voice.* (***connotation**, **flavour**, **hint**, **nuance**, **undercurrent***)

Word use: This is often used in the plural.

overture
noun **1** music played before the start of an opera, ballet or musical show
2 a first attempt to make an offer or establish a friendship with someone

Word history: Middle English, from Old French, from Latin word meaning 'opening'

overturn
verb **1** to turn over on its side, back or face: *to **overturn** the wheelbarrow | The car **overturned.*** (***bowl over**, **invert**, **skittle**, **tip over**, **upset***)
2 to reverse or turn the other way: *The High Court **overturned** the lower court's decision.*

Word history: Middle English

overview
noun a general view that takes everything into account

overweight
adjective weighing more than is normal or proper: *He came back from the holiday very **overweight**.*

overwhelm
verb **1** to be so strong as to crush or bury: *His feelings **overwhelmed** him.* (***engulf**, **flood**, **inundate**, **smother**, **swamp***)
2 to defeat: *The army **overwhelmed** the enemy.*

Word building: **overwhelming** *adjective*
Word history: Middle English

overwrought (oh-vuh-rawt)
adjective worked up with excitement or worry

ovoid (oh-voyd)
adjective **1** having the solid form of an egg
noun **2** an ovoid body

Word history: from Latin word meaning 'egg'

ovulate
verb to release eggs from your ovary: *Women **ovulate** every month.*

Word building: **ovulation** *noun*

ovum (oh-vuhm)
noun one of the cells produced by a female which can join with a sperm to develop into a new individual

Noun forms: The plural is **ova**.
Word history: from Latin word meaning 'egg'

owe
verb **1** to have to pay back: *I **owe** you $2.*
2 to have a duty to give: *I **owe** her an apology.*

Word history: Old English *āgan*

owing
adjective **1** due to be paid or given back: *the amount **owing***
phrase **2 owing to**, because of: *I was late **owing to** the heavy traffic.*

owl
noun **1** a bird with large eyes and a hooting call, which feeds mostly at night on small animals like birds and frogs
2 a solemn-looking or wise person

Word history: Old English *ūle*

own
verb **1** to possess or have for yourself (***hold***, ***keep***, ***retain***)
adjective **2** belonging to yourself: *her **own** bike*
noun **3** something belonging to yourself: *She has a bike of her **own**.*
phrase **4 come into your own,**
a to receive what rightfully belongs to you
b to reach a situation where you are respected and successful
5 get your own back, to have revenge
6 on your own, alone and without help
7 own up, to admit or confess

Word building: **owner** *noun* **ownership** *noun*
Word history: Old English *agnian*

ox
noun **1** → **bullock**
2 any member of the cattle family, especially one used for pulling loads in some countries

Noun forms: The plural is **oxen**.
Word history: Old English *oxa*

oxidant (ok-suh-duhnt)
noun the oxidising agent which supplies oxygen, or accepts electrons, in an oxidation reaction

oxidate (ok-suh-dayt)
verb to oxidise: *The metal **oxidated** when oxygen was added.*

Verb forms: I **oxidated**, I have **oxidated**, I am **oxidating**
Word building: **oxidative** *adjective*

oxidation
noun **1** the act or process of oxidising
adjective **2** having to do with oxidation: *an **oxidation** potential*

oxide
noun a compound, usually containing two elements only, one of which is oxygen, as *mercuric oxide*

Word history: French, from *ox(ygène)* oxygen + *(ac)ide* acid

oxidise
verb **1** to change an element into its oxide by combining with oxygen
2 to cover with a coating of oxide, or rust
3 to take away hydrogen from a substance
4 to increase the valency of an element by removing electrons

Word use: You can also use **oxidize**.

oxyacetylene torch (ok-see-uh-set-uh-leen tawch)
noun a device used for welding or cutting steel by burning a mixture of acetylene and oxygen in a special jet

Word use: You can also use **oxyacetylene burner**.

oxygen (ok-suh-juhn)
noun a gas with no colour or smell which is an essential part of the air we breathe

Word history: from French word meaning 'acid-producer'

oyster
noun a shellfish you can eat, having a double shell with a jagged edge, often found attached to rocks

Word history: Middle English, from Old French, from Latin, from Greek

Oz
noun Colloquial Australia

Word use: You can also use **oz**.

ozone
noun a poisonous form of oxygen which is found in the air in tiny quantities, formed when lightning passes through the atmosphere

ozone depletion
noun a decline in the amount of ozone in the earth's stratosphere

ozone layer
noun a layer of ozone in one of the outer parts of the atmosphere, at a height of about 30 kilometres, which partly blocks the harmful rays of the sun

Word use: You can also use **ozonosphere**.

Pp

PA
noun **1** a public-address system
2 power of attorney
Word history: abbreviation

pace
noun **1** a single step or the distance covered by it
2 speed or rate of movement
verb **3** to set the pace for: *A car will go beside the runners to* ***pace*** *them.*
4 to walk with regular steps: *He* ***paced*** *backwards and forwards.*
5 to measure by paces: *We* ***paced*** *the oval and found it to be about 50 metres long.*
phrase **6 put someone through their paces,** to make someone perform or show their abilities
Word history: Middle English, from Old French, from Latin word meaning 'a pace', 'a step', literally 'a stretch (of the leg)'

pacemaker
noun **1** someone or something that sets the pace, usually in a race
2 an instrument to control the rate of the heartbeat, which is implanted beneath the skin of someone with a diseased heart

pachyderm (<u>pak</u>-ee-derm)
noun a large mammal with thick skin and hooves, such as the elephant, hippopotamus and rhinoceros
Word history: French, from Greek word meaning 'thick-skinned'

pacific (puh-<u>sif</u>-ik)
adjective peaceful or peace-loving
Word history: from Latin word meaning 'peacemaking'

pacifism (<u>pas</u>-uh-fiz-uhm)
noun opposition to war or violence of any kind
Word building: **pacifist** *noun*
Word history: *pacif(ic)* + *-ism*

pacify (<u>pas</u>-uh-fuy)
verb to make peaceful or calm: *She quickly* ***pacified*** *the frightened horse.* (***appease, comfort, mollify, placate, quieten***)
Verb forms: I **pacified,** I have **pacified,** I am **pacifying**
Word use: The opposite of this is **excite** or **upset.**
Word history: late Middle English, from Latin word meaning 'make peace'

pack
noun **1** a parcel or bundle of things wrapped or tied up
2 a load carried on the back of people or animals: *The hikers put their* ***packs*** *on.*
3 a group of animals living and hunting together: *a* ***pack*** *of wolves*
4 a group of people or things: *a* ***pack*** *of thieves | a* ***pack*** *of lies* (***crowd, flock, herd, mob***)
5 a complete set: *a* ***pack*** *of playing cards*
verb **6** to put into a suitcase, parcel or box
7 to press together or crowd: *The people* ***packed*** *into the hall.*
phrase **8 go to the pack,** *Australian* to become worse in condition or performance: *My car won't start — it's finally* ***gone to the pack.***
9 pack off, to send away in a hurry: *She* ***packed*** *him* ***off*** *to school.*
Word history: Middle English, from Flemish, Dutch or Low German

package
noun a parcel or a bundle (***pack, packet***)
Word building: **package** *verb*

packet
noun **1** a small pack or package of anything
2 *Computers* a block of data which forms part of a message sent over a network link
Word history: diminutive of *pack*

packet switching
noun a method of sending data packets through a network link

pact
noun an agreement: *The two friends made a* ***pact*** *to help each other.* (***bargain, compact, treaty***)
Word history: Middle English, from Latin word meaning 'agreed'

pad[1]
noun **1** a wad or mass of soft material used to give comfort, protection or shape to something
2 a number of sheets of paper held together at one edge
3 a soft block of material soaked in ink used for inking a rubber stamp
4 the soft, cushion-like part on the underside of the feet of animals like dogs, foxes, etc.
5 a flat area that helicopters, and sometimes spaceships, take off from
6 *Old-fashioned, Colloquial* a place where someone lives, especially a single room
verb **7** to protect or fill out with a pad or padding: *to* ***pad*** *the shoulders of a suit*
8 to use too many words or too much unnecessary material: *to* ***pad*** *a speech* (***augment, fill out, flesh out, spin out, stretch***)
Verb forms: I **padded,** I have **padded,** I am **padding**
Word use: You can also use **writing pad** for definition 2. | You can also use **pad out** for definition 8.
Word history: special uses of old-fashioned *pad* bundle to lie on, perhaps blend of *pack* and *bed*

pad[2]
verb to walk with soft footsteps: *I'm* ***padding*** *around trying not to wake anyone.*

Verb forms: I **padded**, I have **padded**, I am **padding**
Word history: Dutch or Low German; originally beggars' and thieves' slang

paddle[1]
noun a short oar which you use in guiding a canoe through the water

Word building: **paddle** *verb*

paddle[2]
verb to walk or play with bare feet in shallow water

paddock
noun Australian, NZ a large area of land which has been fenced and is usually used for grazing sheep or other animals

Word history: variant of *parrock*, Old English *pearroc* enclosure (originally fence)

paddy[1]
noun **1** rice growing as a crop, before it is cut or gathered
2 the often flooded land on which rice is grown

Word use: You can also use **paddy field** for definition 2.
Word history: Malay

paddy[2]
noun Colloquial a fit of anger or rage

Word history: from *Paddy* an Irishman (the Irish being seen as quick-tempered)

paddy-wagon
noun a police van for carrying prisoners

paddywhack
noun Colloquial a spanking

pademelon (pad-ee-mel-uhn)
noun a type of small wallaby

padlock
noun a removable lock with a curved metal bar which passes through something and is then snapped shut

Word history: late Middle English

padre (pahd-ray)
noun **1** father, used especially to refer to a priest
2 a military or naval chaplain

Word history: Spanish, Portuguese, Italian, from Latin word meaning 'father'

paediatrics (pee-dee-at-riks)
noun the study and treatment of the diseases and illnesses of young children

Word use: You can also use **pediatrics**.
Word building: **paediatrician** *noun*
Word history: Greek

paedophile (ped-uh-fuyl, peed-uh-fuyl)
noun an adult who engages in or desires sexual activities with children

Word use: You can also use **pedophile**.
Word building: **paedophilia** *noun*
Word history: Greek *paed-* child + *-o-* + Greek *-phile* lover, friend

paedophilia (pe-duh-fil-ee-uh, peed-uh-fil-ee-uh)
noun sexual attraction in an adult towards children

Word use: You can also use **pedophilia**.

pagan (pay-guhn)
noun **1** a follower of an ancient religion or set of beliefs that includes more than one god
2 someone who does not follow an accepted religion (***heathen***, ***infidel***)
3 in Western history, someone who believes in a religion other than Christianity; used to describe the ancient Greeks and Romans, and sometimes the Jews
4 a person who has no respect for religion
5 a person who follows a modern set of beliefs modelled on ancient pagan religion

Word building: **pagan** *adjective*
Word history: Middle English, from Latin word meaning 'civilian', so called (by the Christians) because not a soldier of Christ

page[1]
noun **1** one of the sheets of paper making up a book, magazine, letter, etc.
2 one side of one of these sheets
3 *Computers* the amount of data which will print out as a single page
4 → web page

Word history: French, from Latin

page[2]
noun **1** a uniformed boy employee of a hotel or something similar
verb **2** to try to find someone in a hotel, hospital, shop, etc., by calling out their name on a microphone or public address system

Word history: Middle English, from Old French, from Italian, from Greek word meaning 'boy', 'servant'

pageant (paj-uhnt)
noun **1** a colourful public show, often including a procession of people in costume (***parade***, ***tableau***)
2 any showy display (***extravaganza***, ***spectacle***)

Word history: Middle English

pagoda (puh-goh-duh)
noun a sacred building or temple shaped like a tower and usually found in eastern countries such as India and China

Word history: Portuguese

paid
verb past tense and past participle of **pay**

pail
noun Old-fashioned a bucket

Word history: Old English *pægel* wine vessel

> **pail / pale**
> Don't confuse **pail** with **pale**, which means 'whitish, colourless or not very bright'.

pain
noun **1** suffering or hurt felt when you are injured or sick, or when you are unhappy (***ache***, ***pang***, ***spasm***, ***throb***, ***twinge***)
2 pains, very careful efforts: *Great **pains** were taken to make the wedding a happy occasion.*
verb **3** to cause pain or suffering to
phrase **4 pain in the neck**, *Colloquial* someone or something annoying or unpleasant
Word building: **painful** *adjective*
Word history: Middle English, from Old French, from Latin word meaning 'penalty', 'pain', from Greek word meaning 'fine'

pain / pane
Don't confuse **pain** with **pane**, which is a single plate or sheet of glass, usually in a window.

painkiller
noun a drug or medicine that takes away or lessens pain
Word building: **painkilling** *adjective*

painstaking
adjective extremely careful: ***painstaking** work*

paint
noun **1** a liquid colouring substance that you can put on a surface to give it colour
verb **2** to make a picture of someone or something using paint
3 to cover with paint: *She **painted** the ceiling red.* (***colour***, ***daub***, ***stain***, ***tint***)
Word history: Middle English, from Old French, from Latin word meaning 'paint', 'adorn'

painter[1]
noun **1** an artist who paints pictures
2 someone who coats the surfaces of buildings, etc., with paint
Word history: Middle English, from Old French, from Latin

painter[2]
noun a rope for tying a boat to a ship, wharf, etc.
Word history: Middle English, from Anglo-French, from Latin

painterly
adjective **1** having to do with painting that is of the highest standard in every way, showing both skill and an understanding of aesthetics
2 having to do with painting, sculpture and architecture in which form is expressed in masses of light and shade, whose edges merge and mingle, rather than in well-defined lines and outlines

painting
noun **1** a picture or pattern done in paints
2 the act, art or work of someone who paints

pair
noun **1** two things of the same kind that go together: *a **pair** of shoes*
2 a combination of two parts joined together to make a single thing: *a **pair** of scissors*
3 two people, things or animals thought of as connected to each other in some way: *a happily married **pair***
Noun forms: The plural is **pairs** or **pair**.
Word history: Middle English, from Old French, from Latin word meaning 'equal'

pair / pare / pear
Don't confuse **pair** with **pare** or **pear**.
You **pare** an apple when you peel off the skin.
A **pear** is a kind of fruit.

paisley (<u>payz</u>-lee)
noun **1** a soft, woollen cloth woven with a colourful and very detailed pattern
2 any pattern similar to that woven on paisley
Noun forms: The plural is **paisleys**.
Word history: named after *Paisley*, town in Scotland

pal
noun Colloquial a friend (***companion***, ***comrade***, ***mate***, ***playmate***)
Word use: The opposite of this is **enemy**.
Word history: from Romani word meaning 'brother'

palace
noun the official home of a king, queen, bishop or other very important person
Word history: Middle English, from Old French, from Latin word meaning 'palace'

palaeontology (pal-ee-on-<u>tol</u>-uh-jee, pay-lee-on-<u>tol</u>-uh-jee)
noun the science of the forms of life that existed in the geological periods before this one, as represented by fossil animals and plants
Word building: **palaeontologist** *noun*
Word history: French

palatable (<u>pal</u>-uh-tuh-buhl)
adjective pleasant to taste
Word use: The opposite of this is **unpalatable**.

palate (<u>pal</u>-uht)
noun **1** the roof of your mouth
2 the sense of taste
Word history: Middle English, from Latin

palate / palette / pallet
Don't confuse **palate** with **palette**, a thin board on which painters mix their colours, or with **pallet**, a large wooden packing tray which can be moved from place to place by a forklift truck.

palatial (puh-<u>lay</u>-shuhl)
adjective like a palace
Word history: from Latin

palaver (puh-<u>lah</u>-vuh)
noun **1** idle, useless or foolish talk
2 any unnecessarily long business or bother: *the **palaver** of writing out new instructions*
Word building: **palaver** *verb*
Word history: Portuguese, from Latin word meaning 'parable'

pale[1]
adjective **1** having a whitish or colourless appearance: *a **pale** face* (***ashen***, ***bleached***, ***faded***, ***pallid***)
2 not very bright in colour (***neutral***, ***pastel***, ***washed out***)
verb **3** to become pale

4 to become less in importance or strength: *Her unhappiness **paled** beside that of her friend.*

Word history: Middle English, from Old French, from Latin word meaning 'pallid'

pale[2]
noun **1** a long, pointed piece of wood, such as part of a fence (***paling***, ***picket***, ***stake***)
2 limits or bounds: *outside the **pale** of good manners*
phrase **3 beyond the pale**, outside the limits of what is socially or morally acceptable: *Our religion finds behaviour like that **beyond the pale**.*

Word history: Middle English, from French, from Latin word meaning 'stake'

pale / pail
Don't confuse **pale** with **pail**, which is another word for 'bucket'.

palette (pal-uht)
noun a thin board, usually with a thumb hole at one end, used by painters to mix colours on

Word history: French word meaning 'palette', 'flat-bladed implement', from Latin word meaning 'spade', 'shovel'

palindrome (pal-uhn-drohm)
noun a word or sentence which reads the same either backwards or forwards, such as the sentence 'Madam, I'm Adam.'

Word history: Greek *palíndromos* running back

paling (pay-ling)
noun a long pointed piece of wood, such as part of a fence

palisade (pal-uh-sayd)
noun a fence of tall pointed sticks set firmly in the ground as a defence around a fort or camp

Word history: French word meaning 'furnish with a paling', from Latin word meaning 'pale'

pall[1] (pawl)
noun **1** a cloth for spreading over a coffin
2 something that covers with darkness or gloominess: *A **pall** of smoke hung over the city.*

Word history: Middle English; Old English *pæll*, from Latin word meaning 'cloak', 'covering'

pall[2] (pawl)
verb to become tiring or boring: *Her talk began to **pall**.*

Word history: Middle English

pallbearer
noun someone who carries the coffin at a funeral

pallet
noun **1** a tool with a flat blade and a handle used for shaping and smoothing in pottery
2 a large, wooden packing tray on which things are stored, which can be moved from place to place by a forklift truck

Word history: Middle English, from Old French, from Latin word meaning 'chaff'

pallet / palette / palate
Don't confuse **pallet** with **palette**, a thin board on which painters mix their colours, or with **palate**, the roof of your mouth, and your sense of taste.

palliate (pal-ee-ayt)
verb **1** to excuse, or cause to appear less serious: *to **palliate** an offence*
2 to lessen the severity of: *to **palliate** a disease*

Word building: **palliative** *adjective*
Word history: from Latin word meaning 'covered with a cloak'

pallid
adjective pale or lacking in colour

Word history: Latin

palm[1] (pahm)
noun **1** the part of the inside of your hand that reaches from your wrist to the beginning of your fingers
phrase **2 cross** (or **grease**) (or **oil**) **someone's palm**, to bribe someone
3 palm off on (or **upon**), to get rid of by trickery: *He tried to **palm off** the broken watch **on** me.*

Word history: from Latin word meaning 'palm', 'hand', 'blade of an oar'

palm[2] (pahm)
noun a tall plant with no branches, usually with a crown of large, fan-shaped leaves at the top

Word use: You can also use **palm tree**.
Word history: Middle English and Old English, from Latin word meaning 'palm tree'; has the same word history as *palm*[1]

palmistry (pah-muh-stree)
noun the art of telling someone's fortune or character by the length and pattern of the lines on the palm of their hand

Word history: Middle English

palmtop
noun **1** a small handheld personal computer
adjective **2** having to do with a palmtop: ***palmtop** features*

palomino (pal-uh-mee-noh)
noun a tan or cream-coloured horse with a white mane and tail

Noun forms: The plural is **palominos**.
Word use: You can also use **palamino**.
Word history: Spanish

palpable (pal-puh-buhl)
adjective **1** so obvious that you can easily see, hear and understand it: *a **palpable** lie*
2 able to be touched or felt: *a **palpable** lump in the stomach*

Word building: **palpability** *noun*
Word history: Middle English, from Latin word meaning 'touch'

palpate (pal-payt)
verb to examine using your sense of touch, especially in medicine: *The doctor **palpated** the patient's stomach gently.*

Word building: **palpation** *noun*
Word history: from Latin word meaning 'touched', 'stroked'

palpitate
verb **1** to beat much faster than normal: *Her heart was **palpitating** with the effort of the long run.* (***drum***, ***flutter***, ***pulsate***, ***throb***, ***vibrate***)
2 to shake slightly or to tremble: *He **palpitated** with fear.*

Word building: **palpitation** *noun*
Word history: from Latin word meaning 'moved quickly'

paltry (pawl-tree)
adjective small or worthless: *a* ***paltry*** *sum of money | a* ***paltry*** *coward* (***meagre***, ***mean***, ***puny***, ***scant***, ***skimpy***, ***wretched***)

Word history: apparently from dialect *palt* rubbish

pamper
verb to treat too kindly: *He* ***pampers*** *the dogs by giving them chocolates.*

Word history: Middle English

pamphlet (pam-fluht)
noun **1** a very small, paper-covered book
2 a single sheet of paper with advertisements printed on it, which is handed out to you or put in your letterbox (***booklet***, ***brochure***, ***circular***, ***leaflet***)

Word history: Middle English

pan[1]
noun **1** a broad, shallow, open dish, which is usually used for cooking
2 any container shaped liked this: *Gold can be separated from gravel and sand by washing it in a* ***pan***.
verb **3** to wash gravel or sand in a pan to separate gold or other heavy metals
4 *Colloquial* to criticise severely: *The critics* ***panned*** *the new film.*

Verb forms: I **panned,** I have **panned,** I am **panning**
Word history: Middle English and Old English *panne*

pan[2]
verb of a camera in films, TV, etc., to operate so that it moves continuously in order to film a wide area, or to keep a moving person or object in view

Verb forms: I **panned,** I have **panned,** I am **panning**
Word history: abbreviation of *panorama*

panacea (pan-uh-see-uh)
noun a cure for all diseases, problems, etc.

Word building: **panacean** *adjective*
Word history: Latin, from Greek

panache (puh-nash, puh-nahsh)
noun flair, or a grand and stylish way of doing things (***dash***, ***flamboyance***)

Word history: French, from Italian, from Latin word meaning 'feather'

Panama hat (pan-uh-mah hat)
noun a fine plaited hat made of the young leaves of a South American palmlike plant

Word use: You can also use **panama hat**.
Word history: named after *Panama*, a republic in Central America

pancake
noun a thin, flat cake made of batter cooked in a frying pan

pancreas (pan-kree-uhs)
noun a gland near your stomach which produces the hormone insulin and important enzymes which help your digestion

Word history: Neo-Latin, from Greek word meaning 'sweetbread'

panda
noun a large, black-and-white, bear-like animal which is found mainly in China

Word history: French, perhaps from Nepalese

pandemonium (pan-duh-moh-nee-uhm)
noun wild and noisy confusion (***commotion***, ***din***, ***hubbub***, ***racket***, ***uproar***)

Word history: from *Pandaemonium*, name for the capital of hell in the epic poem *Paradise Lost* (1667; 1674) by John Milton

pander
phrase **pander to,** to go too far in satisfying: *to* ***pander to*** *a child's demands*

Pandora's box
noun anything that produces many troubles, especially something expected at first to give blessings

Word history: in classical mythology, a box or jar which contained all human ills, given by the god Zeus to *Pandora*, the first mortal woman. She was sent by Zeus to bring misery to humanity as punishment because Prometheus had stolen fire from heaven.

pane
noun a single plate or sheet of glass, usually part of a window

Word history: Middle English, from Old French, from Latin word meaning 'a cloth', 'rag'

pane / pain
Don't confuse **pane** with **pain**, which is the hurt or suffering you feel when you are injured, sick or unhappy.

panegyric (pan-uh-jir-ik)
noun a speech or writing in praise of a person or thing (***eulogy***, ***tribute***)

Word building: **panegyrical** *adjective* **panegyrist** *noun*
Word history: Latin, from Greek word meaning 'festival oration'

panel
noun **1** a separate section set into a ceiling, door or wall, that is sometimes raised above or sunk below the main surface
2 a thin, flat piece of wood
3 a separate section of material set into a dress
4 a board or section of a machine on which controls are fixed: *the instrument* ***panel*** *of a car*
5 a group of people selected to form a jury or brought together to discuss matters, judge competitions, etc.

Word building: **panel** *verb* (**panelled, panelling**)
Word history: Middle English, from Old French word meaning 'piece (of anything)', from Latin word meaning 'rag'

panel beater
noun someone who beats sheet metal into shapes for the bodywork of motor vehicles, etc.

pang
noun a sudden, short, sharp feeling of mental or bodily pain: *a* ***pang*** *of remorse | a* ***pang*** *of hunger*

panic
noun **1** a sudden terror, sometimes without an obvious reason
verb **2** to feel panic: *She **panicked** when she saw the gun.* (***freak out***, ***go to pieces***, ***lose your nerve***)
3 to cause to panic: *The falling branch **panicked** the horse.* (***alarm***, ***scare***, ***startle***, ***terrify***, ***unnerve***)

Verb forms: I **panicked**, I have **panicked**, I am **panicking**
Word history: French, from Latin, from Greek word meaning 'relating to or caused by Pan'

pannier (pan-ee-uh)
noun a basket, for carrying provisions, etc., usually carried on a person's back or on each side of the back of a bicycle or animal

Word history: Middle English, from Old French, from Latin word meaning 'basket for bread'

pannikin (pan-uh-kuhn)
noun **1** a small pan or metal cup
adjective **2** having to do with someone who acts importantly when in reality they are not: *a **pannikin** boss* | *a **pannikin** snob*

panoply (pan-uh-plee)
noun **1** a complete suit of armour
2 a complete covering or show of something

Noun forms: The plural is **panoplies**.
Word building: **panoplied** *adjective*
Word history: from Greek word meaning 'complete suit of armour'

panorama (pan-uh-rah-muh)
noun **1** a view over a wide area
2 a continually changing scene: *the **panorama** of city life*

Word building: **panoramic** *adjective*
Word history: Greek

panpipe
noun a musical instrument made up of pipes of different lengths which are played by blowing across their open ends

pansy
noun a garden plant with white, yellow or purple velvety flowers

Noun forms: The plural is **pansies**.
Word history: from French word meaning 'pansy', literally 'thought'

pant
verb **1** to breathe hard and quickly because of effort or emotion (***blow***, ***gasp***, ***heave***, ***puff***, ***wheeze***)
noun **2** a sudden short breath

Word history: Middle English, probably (with reference to the feeling of oppression in nightmare) from Latin word meaning 'phantasm', 'idea', 'fantasy'

pantechnicon (pan-tek-nik-uhn)
noun a large van for moving furniture

Word history: Greek; originally the name of a bazaar in 19th century London, which became a furniture warehouse

pantheism (pan-thee-iz-uhm)
noun the belief in which God is identified with the material universe or the forces of nature and therefore is thought to be impersonal

Word building: **pantheist** *noun* **pantheistic** *adjective*
Word history: Greek

pantheon (pan-thee-uhn)
noun **1** a public building containing tombs or memorials of the famous dead of a nation
2 all the gods believed in by a particular people thought of altogether

Word history: Middle English, from Latin, from Greek word meaning 'of all gods'

panther
noun a leopard, especially a black one

pantihose
noun women's tights, usually made out of stocking material

Word use: You can also use **pantyhose**. | This word is always used as a plural, with a plural verb: *My pantihose have a ladder in them.*

pantomime
noun a play in which the actors have to use actions and not words to tell the story (***mime***)

Word history: Latin, from Greek word meaning 'all-imitating'

pantry
noun a room or cupboard in which food is kept

Noun forms: The plural is **pantries**.
Word history: Middle English, Anglo-French, from Old French word meaning 'servant in charge of bread', from Latin word meaning 'bread'

pants
plural noun **1** trousers
2 underpants, especially women's

Word history: abbreviation of *pantaloons*

pap
noun **1** soft food for babies or people who are sick, such as bread soaked in water or milk
2 books, ideas, talk, etc., considered as demanding only a low standard of intelligence or attention

papacy (pay-puh-see)
noun **1** the office or position of the pope in the Roman Catholic Church
2 the period during which a particular pope rules

Noun forms: The plural is **papacies**.
Word history: Middle English, from Medieval Latin word meaning 'pope', 'father'

papal
adjective having to do with the pope or the papacy: *a **papal** decree*

Word history: Middle English, from Medieval Latin word meaning 'pope'

paparazzo (pap-uh-raht-soh, pah-puh-raht-soh)
noun a press photographer who pursues celebrities in order to photograph them

Noun forms: The plural is **paparazzi**.
Word history: Italian, from the surname of such a photographer in the 1960 film *La Dolce Vita.*

papaya (puh-puy-uh)
noun a pawpaw, especially of the smaller kind with reddish-pink flesh

paper
noun **1** a material made from straw, wood, etc., usually in thin sheets for writing or printing on, or wrapping things in
2 a newspaper
3 a written examination
4 papers, documents identifying who you are, what country you come from, etc.
phrase **5 on paper**,
a in writing
b in the planning stage
c in theory rather than in practice: *It looks fine **on paper**, but will it work?*

Word history: Middle English and Old English, from Latin word meaning 'paper', 'papyrus'

paperback
noun a book with a soft paper cover, usually cheaper than one with a hard cover

paperbark
noun a tree that bears a form of bark consisting of many thin layers of papery material, some parts of which peel off

papier-mâché (pay-puh-mash-ay)
noun a substance made of paper pulp sometimes mixed with glue and other materials and used when wet to make models, boxes, etc., which become hard and strong when dry

Word history: from French word meaning 'chewed paper'

papilla (puh-pil-uh)
noun any small, pointed, nipple-like structure on the body, such as a hair root

Noun forms: The plural is **papillae** (puh-pil-ee).
Word building: **papillary** *adjective* **papillose** *adjective*
Word history: from Latin word meaning 'nipple'

papillomavirus (pap-uh-loh-muh-vuy-ruhs)
noun any of various small species-specific viruses causing warts

pappadum
noun a thin, crisp, Indian wafer bread, made from spiced potato or rice flour

Word use: You can also use **pappadam** or **poppadum**.

paprika (pap-rik-uh, puh-pree-kuh)
noun powder made from a red pepper, used as a spice

Word history: Hungarian

Pap smear
noun a medical test in which a smear of cells from the cervix or vagina is put on a glass slide and looked at under the microscope; used to detect cancer

Word use: You can also use **cervical smear**.
Word history: abbreviation of *Pap(anicolaou) smear*, from George *Papanicolaou*, 1883–1962, US scientist, who devised this test

papyrus (puh-puy-ruhs)
noun **1** a tall water plant
2 material for writing on made out of this plant
3 an ancient document written on this material

Noun forms: The plural is **papyri**.
Word use: **Papyrus** usually stays singular for definitions 1 and 2, even when you are writing about more than one plant, or when you are talking about lots of papyrus as a writing material.
Word history: Middle English, from Latin, from Greek word meaning 'the plant papyrus', 'something made from papyrus'

par
noun **1** an equal level: *Her tennis playing is on a **par** with her sister's.*
2 an average or normal amount: *below **par** | above **par***
3 *Commerce*
a the legally established value of the unit of money of one country in terms of that of another using the same metal as a standard of value
b the state of the shares of any business, etc., when they may be bought at the original price or at the apparent value

Word history: from Latin word meaning 'equal'

parable (pa-ruh-buhl)
noun a short story used to teach a truth or moral lesson

Word history: Middle English, from Late Latin word meaning 'comparison', 'parable', 'proverb', 'word', from Greek word meaning 'a placing beside', 'comparison'

parabola (puh-rab-uh-luh)
noun a special kind of even curve, like the path of an object when it is thrown forwards into the air and falls back to the earth

Word use: This word is used in geometry.
Word history: Neo-Latin, from Greek

parachute (pa-ruh-shooht)
noun a large piece of cloth shaped like an umbrella and used to slow down the fall of someone jumping from an aircraft

Word building: **parachute** *verb* **parachutist** *noun*
Word history: French, from *para-* + *chute* a fall

parade
noun **1** a gathering of troops, scouts, etc., for inspection or display (***review***)
2 a group of people marching in the street to celebrate something (***cavalcade, procession***)

Word history: French, from Spanish, from Latin word meaning 'prepare'

paradigm (pa-ruh-duym)
noun a pattern or example

Word history: late Middle English, from Late Latin, from Greek word meaning 'pattern'

paradise
noun **1** heaven
2 a place of great beauty or delight

Word history: Middle English, from Late Latin, from Greek word meaning 'park', from Old Persian word meaning 'enclosure'

paradox
noun **1** a statement which is true although it contains two seemingly opposite ideas, such as the statement 'You have to be cruel to be kind.'
2 someone or something which seems to show contradictions

Word building: **paradoxical** *adjective*
Word history: Latin, from Greek word meaning 'contrary to received opinion', 'incredible'

paraffin (pa-ruh-fuhn)
noun **1** *Chemistry* any one of a series of saturated hydrocarbons
2 a mixture of hydrocarbons obtained from petroleum and used as a laxative
3 a British word for **kerosene**

Word use: You can also use **paraffin oil** or **liquid paraffin** for definition 2.
Word history: German, from Latin

paragon (pa-ruh-guhn)
noun someone or something good enough to copy: *She is a* ***paragon*** *of virtue.*

Word history: Middle French, from Italian word meaning 'touchstone', 'comparison', 'paragon'

paragraph
noun **1** a section of writing dealing with a particular subject or point, beginning on a new line
verb **2** to divide into paragraphs

Word history: Late Latin, from Greek word meaning 'line or mark in the margin'

parakeet
noun a kind of small parrot, such as the budgerigar, usually with a long pointed tail

Word history: from Italian word meaning 'parson'

parallax (pa-ruh-laks)
noun the change in position of objects that seems to happen when the person looking changes position

Word building: **parallactic** *adjective*
Word history: from Greek word meaning 'change'

parallel (pa-ruh-lel)
adjective **1** being the same distance from each other at every point: *A railway track is made up of two* ***parallel*** *lines.*
2 *Computers* having to do with a system in which several activities are carried on at the same time
noun **3** a line parallel with another
4 a comparison showing likeness: *You can draw a* ***parallel*** *between her and many great musicians before her.*

Word history: Latin, from Greek word meaning 'beside one another'

parallelogram (pa-ruh-lel-uh-gram)
noun a four-sided figure whose opposite sides are parallel to each other

Word history: from Greek word meaning 'bounded by parallel lines'

parallel port
noun *Computers* a port that enables several bits of data to be sent or received at a time

Word use: Compare this with **serial port**.

parallel universe
noun a postulated universe in another space and time continuum parallel to our own: *The story was set in a* ***parallel universe.***

parallel verb
noun a verb which expands the range of actions, processes, states, etc., but which is grammatically identical to the preceding verb

paralysis (puh-ral-uh-suhs)
noun an inability to move

Noun forms: The plural is **paralyses** (puh-ral-uh-seez).
Word building: **paralyse** *verb*
Word history: Latin, from Greek word meaning 'palsy'

paramedic
noun a person who provides emergency specialist first aid to someone who is injured or ill

paramedical
adjective having to do with health care workers other than doctors, dentists, nurses, etc., who have special training in the performance of supportive health treatments: *ambulances and other* ***paramedical*** *services*

parameter (puh-ram-uh-tuh)
noun **1** a factor or limit which affects the way something is done: *Write the assignment within the* ***parameters*** *of the topic.*
2 *Mathematics* one of the independent variables in a set of parametric equations
3 *Mathematics* a variable which may be kept constant while the effect of other variables is investigated

Word building: **parametric** *adjective*

parameter / perimeter
Don't confuse **parameter** with **perimeter**, which is the outside edge of a shape or an area, as in *the perimeter of a playing field.*

paramount
adjective above others in rank, authority or importance

Word history: Anglo-French word meaning 'above', from Latin

paramour (pa-ruh-maw)
noun an unlawful lover, especially of a married person

Word history: Middle English, from Old French, originally phrase *par amour* by love, by way of (sexual) love, from Latin

paranoia (pa-ruh-noy-uh)
noun a mental condition in which the patient suffers from delusions such as that of persecution or of being a very great person

Word building: **paranoiac** *noun* **paranoiac** *adjective*
Word history: Neo-Latin, from Greek word meaning 'derangement'

paranoid
adjective full of fears about things which are made up or imagined

parapet
noun a wall or barrier at the edge of a balcony, roof or bridge

Word history: Italian, from Latin

paraphernalia (pa-ruh-fuh-nay-lee-uh)
plural noun goods, equipment, baggage or other articles, especially unnecessary ones (***gear***, ***stuff***, ***things***)

Word history: Medieval Latin, from Late Latin, from Greek word meaning 'bride's belongings other than dowry'

paraphrase
verb to put in different words so that it's easier to understand

Word building: **paraphrase** *noun*
Word history: French, from Latin, from Greek

paraplegia (pa-ruh-plee-juh)
noun paralysis of the lower part of the body

Word history: Neo-Latin, from Greek word meaning 'paralysis on one side'

paraplegic (pa-ruh-plee-jik)
noun someone who has lost the use of the lower part of their body

Word building: **paraplegic** *adjective*

parasite
noun **1** an animal or plant which lives on or in another from which it obtains its food: *Fleas are **parasites**.*
2 someone who lives on the money earned by other people without doing anything in return

Word building: **parasitic** *adjective* **parasitism** *noun*
Word history: Latin, from Greek word meaning 'one who eats at the table of another'

parasol
noun a small sun umbrella

Word history: French, from Italian, from Latin

paratrooper
noun a soldier who reaches a battle by landing from an aeroplane by parachute

Word history: *para(chute)* + *trooper*

parboil (pah-boyl)
verb to boil until only half cooked

Word history: Middle English, from Old French, from Late Latin

parcel
noun **1** a package or wrapped bundle of goods
verb **2** to make up into a parcel

Verb forms: I **parcelled**, I have **parcelled**, I am **parcelling**
Word history: Middle English, from Old French, Latin word meaning 'particle'

parch
verb to make or become very dry

Word building: **parched** *adjective*
Word history: Middle English

parchment
noun **1** the skin of sheep, goats or similar animals prepared as a material to write on
2 paper which looks like this

Word history: Middle English, from Old French, blend of Late Latin word meaning 'parchment' and Latin word meaning 'Parthian (leather)'

pardon
noun **1** forgiveness, especially for a crime (***acquittal***, ***amnesty***, ***reprieve***)
verb **2** to forgive and not punish (***clear***, ***excuse***, ***let off***, ***spare***)
3 to excuse: *'**Pardon** me', I said when I walked in front of her.*

Word building: **pardonable** *adjective*
Word history: Middle English, from Old French, from Late Latin word meaning 'grant'

pare (pair)
verb **1** to peel or cut off the outer layer of: *to **pare** apples*
2 to cut down or make less: *to **pare** expenses*

Word history: Middle English, from Old French word meaning 'prepare', 'trim', from Latin

pare / pair / pear
Don't confuse **pare** with **pair** or **pear**.
Two things that go together, like shoes, are a **pair**.
A **pear** is a kind of fruit.

parent (pair-ruhnt)
noun a father or a mother

Word building: **parentage** *noun* **parental** *adjective* **parenthood** *noun*
Word history: Middle English, from Latin

parenthesis (puh-ren-thuh-suhs)
noun **1** one of the upright brackets () often used to mark off such a phrase or clause
2 a a descriptive or explanatory phrase or clause put into a sentence and marked off by commas, brackets or dashes, such as 'the blue one' in *He took your bag — the blue one — when he left.*
b a phrase, sentence or comment inserted into a conversation or written passage, which is not directly related to the main subject: *'He's married now, you know,' she said as a **parenthesis**.*

Noun forms: The plural is **parentheses** (puh-ren-thuh-seez).
Word building: **parenthetic** *adjective*
Word history: Medieval Latin, from Greek word meaning 'a putting in beside'

pariah (puh-ruy-uh)
noun any person or animal generally despised (***exile***, ***outcast***)

Word history: Tamil word literally meaning 'drummer' (from a hereditary duty of the caste)

parietal (puh-ruy-uh-tuhl)
adjective having to do with the side of the skull, or to any wall or wall-like structure: ***parietal** bones*

Word history: Late Latin, from Latin word meaning 'wall'

parish
noun **1** a district which has its own church and clergy member
2 the people of a parish

Word building: **parishioner** *noun*
Word history: Middle English, from Old French, from Late Latin, from Greek

parity (pa-ruh-tee)
noun **1** equality in amount, status, or character
2 similarity

Word history: Late Latin, from Latin word meaning 'equal'

park
noun **1** an area of land set aside for public use and kept in good order by the council or government: *Hyde **Park** | a national **park***
verb **2** to put or leave a car, bicycle or other vehicle in a particular spot, such as at the side of the road
3 in a computer, to move the read/write head of a hard disk drive to a safe landing zone before turning off the computer, so that the data is not corrupted

Word history: Middle English, from Old French; of Germanic origin

parka
noun a warm, waterproof jacket with a hood

Word history: Aleut, a language spoken by the Aleutian Indians of the Alaskan Peninsula

Parkinson's disease
noun a form of paralysis marked by uncontrollable shaking, stiff muscles and weak movement

Word history: named after James *Parkinson*, 1755–1824, English physician who first described it

parlance (pah-luhns)
noun a way of speaking, or language: *legal **parlance** (**idiom**, **vocabulary**)*

Word history: Anglo-French, from Latin

parley
noun a talk or discussion, especially between people who are fighting each other

Noun forms: The plural is **parleys**.
Word building: **parley** *verb*
Word history: from French word meaning 'speech'

parliament (pah-luh-muhnt)
noun the assembly of people elected to make the laws for a country or state

Word building: **parliamentary** *adjective*
Word history: Middle English, from Old French

parliamentarian
noun a Member of Parliament

parliamentary privilege (pah-luh-men-tree priv-uh-lij)
noun the special rights enjoyed by parliament and its members which allow members to say things freely in parliament that they could be prosecuted for outside, and which generally protect them from criticism

parlour
noun **1** *Old-fashioned* a formal room where you entertain visitors
2 a room where customers of certain businesses are attended to: *a beauty **parlour***

Word use: You can also use **parlor**.
Word history: Middle English, from Anglo-French

parmesan
noun a hard, dry, pale yellow cheese, often used for grating

Word history: named after *Parma*, city in northern Italy

parochial (puh-roh-kee-uhl)
adjective **1** having to do with a parish or parishes: ***parochial** duties*
2 confined to or interested only in your own parish, or some particular narrow place or field of activity: *She's very **parochial** in her outlook.*

Word building: **parochialism** *noun*
Word history: Middle English, from Late Latin, from Late Latin

parody (pa-ruh-dee)
noun a humorous imitation of a serious piece of writing or music

Noun forms: The plural is **parodies**.
Word building: **parody** *verb* (**parodied**, **parodying**)
Word history: Latin, from Greek word meaning 'burlesque poem'

parole
noun the early freeing of a prisoner on the condition of good behaviour: *He is out on **parole**.*

Word building: **parole** *verb*
Word history: French word meaning 'word', from Latin

paroxysm (pa-ruhk-siz-uhm)
noun a sudden violent fit: *a **paroxysm** of coughing | a **paroxysm** of anger*

Word history: Medieval Latin, from Greek word meaning 'irritation'

parquet (pah-kay, pah-kee)
adjective made of short pieces of wood fitted together to form a pattern: *a **parquet** coffee table*

Word building: **parquet** *noun* **parquetry** *noun*
Word history: from French word meaning 'part of a park', 'flooring'

parrot
noun **1** a hook-billed, often brightly coloured bird which can be taught to talk
verb **2** to repeat or imitate like a parrot

Word history: French, diminutive of *Pierre* Peter. We have a habit of giving birds human names, like Polly for the parrot, and Maggie for the magpie.

parry (pa-ree)
verb to turn aside or avoid: *She was able to **parry** my question.*

Verb forms: I **parried**, I have **parried**, I am **parrying**
Word history: probably from French, from Italian word meaning 'ward off', 'protect', from Latin word meaning 'make ready', 'prepare'

parse (pahz)
verb to describe by telling the part of speech, etc.: *to **parse** all the words in the sentence*

Word history: from Latin word meaning 'part', as in 'part of speech'

parsimony (pah-suh-muh-nee)
noun very great meanness in spending money

Word building: **parsimonious** *adjective*
Word history: Middle English, from Latin word literally meaning 'sparingness'

parsley
noun a herb used in cooking

Word history: Middle English, blend of Old French and Old English

parsnip
noun a whitish root vegetable that is shaped like a carrot

Word history: Middle English, from Old French, from Latin

parson
noun a member of the clergy (***chaplain*, *minister*, *priest*, *vicar***)

Word history: Middle English, from Medieval Latin word meaning 'parson', from Latin word meaning 'person'

part
noun **1** a piece or portion (***bit*, *fraction*, *proportion*, *section*, *segment***)
2 a replacement piece for something worn out or broken: *We always carry spare **parts** for our bicycles.*
3 a share in something, such as work, a duty, etc.: *to do your **part***
4 an actor's role: *a **part** in a play*
verb **5** to separate, or become separated into parts
phrase **6 part and parcel**, an essential part: *The character he plays is **part and parcel** of the play.*
7 part with, to give up: *He made me **part with** my favourite book.*
8 play a part,
a to pretend
b to make yourself active or useful in something: *Can you **play a part** in the school open day?*
9 take someone's part, to defend or support: *He **took my part** in an argument I was having about planting trees.*

Word history: Middle English, Old English, from Latin word meaning 'piece', 'portion'

partake
phrase **1 partake in**, to participate or act in something with other people: *to **partake in** the illegal activities*
2 partake of, to receive, take, or have a share: *to **partake of** her kindness*

Verb forms: I **partook**, I have **partaken**, I am **partaking**
Word building: **partaker** *noun*

partial (pah-shuhl)
adjective **1** not total or general: *He suffers from **partial** deafness.*
2 showing unfair support or favouritism: *Everyone could see the umpire was being **partial** in his decisions.* (***biased*, *discriminatory*, *inequitable*, *prejudiced*, *unjust***)
phrase **3 partial to**, having a strong liking for: *I am **partial to** cake.*

Word building: **partiality** *noun* **partially** *adverb*
Word history: Middle English, from Latin word meaning 'part'

partial preferential voting
noun a form of preferential voting in which voters must indicate their order of preference for a minimum number of candidates

Word use: Compare this with **full preferential voting** and **optional preferential voting.**

participant
noun someone who participates: *All the **participants** in the school play should meet in the hall at seven.*

participate (pah-tis-uh-payt)
verb to take part

Word building: **participation** *noun*
Word history: Latin

participle (pah-tuh-sip-uhl)
noun **1** a word formed from a verb and used as an adjective, such as 'burning' in *a burning candle* or 'added' in *added work*
2 a word formed from a verb and used in compound verbs, such as 'burning' in *the candle has been burning* or 'added' in *I have added*

Word building: **participial** *adjective*
Word history: Middle English, from Old French, from Latin word meaning 'a sharing'

We say that verbs have two **participles**, the past and the present. The verb *to walk* for example, has:

1 the present participle *walking* (the action is going on)
2 the past participle *walked* (the action is in the past)

You can usually recognise them by their -ing and -ed endings. But the past participles of some verbs have unpredictable forms, such as -en and -n:

Ride becomes *ridden* in *I have ridden.*

Tear becomes *torn* in *I have torn.*

Some even keep their basic form (infinitive):

Cut remains as *cut* in *I have cut.*

Participles combine with the verbs *be* and *have* (auxiliaries) to make new verb forms that express a completed or uncompleted action (aspect), or an action that may be in a past, present or future time (tense). Some examples of this are:

was walking

have walked

has been walking.

particle
noun a very small bit: *a **particle** of dust* (***crumb*, *fragment*, *grain*, *mite*, *morsel*, *scrap***)

Word history: Middle English, from Latin word meaning 'part'

particular
adjective **1** single, or one, rather than all: *I am interested in that **particular** book on dogs.*
2 more than usual, or special: *Take **particular** care of that book.*
noun **3** a point or detail: *The report was right in every **particular**.*
phrase **4 in particular**, especially: *There is one book **in particular** that I want to read.*

Word building: **particularly** *adverb*
Word history: from Latin word meaning 'of a part', 'partial'

particulate pollution
noun pollution in the form of fine particles of solids or liquids mixed in a gas, often from the burning of fossil fuels in vehicles, power plants, etc.

partisan (pah-tuh-zuhn, pah-tuh-zan)
noun **1** a supporter of a person, party or cause (***adherent*, *devotee*, *disciple*, *stalwart***)
2 a member of a party of light or irregular troops, especially when resisting an invader or conqueror (***guerilla***)

Word history: French, from Italian, from Latin

partition
noun **1** a separating wall
2 a division into shares or parts: *The* ***partition*** *of the city into East Berlin and West Berlin occurred in 1945.*
verb **3** to divide into parts

Word building: **partition** *verb*
Word history: Middle English, from Latin

partly
adverb in part or not wholly: *The house is* ***partly*** *brick but the rest is fibro.*

partner
noun someone who shares or takes part in something with someone else: *a business* ***partner*** | *a dancing* ***partner*** (***associate***, ***collaborator***, ***colleague***, ***comrade***, ***friend***)

Word building: **partner** *verb*
Word history: Middle English

partnership
noun a business that is not incorporated, formed by the association of people (from two to twenty) who share all the risks and profits. This form of business association is common in the professions for people such as solicitors, dentists, etc., as well as in small businesses where only small amounts of capital are required.

part of speech
noun any of the main grammatical classes of words in a language

> In English, we generally say that there are eight parts of speech:
>
> | | |
> |---|---|
> | nouns | *water, tree, wisdom* |
> | pronouns | *you, mine, them* |
> | adjectives | *yellow, wise, dog-eared* |
> | verbs | *walks, is, wondered* |
> | adverbs | *soon, never, quickly* |
> | prepositions | *in, through, under* |
> | conjunctions | *and, because, when* |
> | interjections | *hey! oh!* |
>
> Each of these is described in its alphabetical place in this dictionary, and extra information about the various types is given there.

partridge
noun a European bird that is hunted and eaten

Noun forms: The plural is **partridge** or **partridges**.
Word history: Middle English, from Old French, from Latin, from Greek

part-time
adjective **1** taking or working fewer than all the usual working hours: *a* ***part-time*** *job* | *a* ***part-time*** *gardener*
adverb **2** for less than normal working hours: *He works* ***part-time****.*

parturition (pah-chuh-<u>rish</u>-uhn)
noun childbirth

Word history: Latin

party
noun **1** a social gathering, often to celebrate something: *a birthday* ***party***
2 a group of people who work for the same political ideals: *the Australian Labor* ***Party***

Noun forms: The plural is **parties**.
Word history: Middle English, from Old French word meaning 'part'

party line
noun **1** a telephone line shared by two or more subscribers
2 the boundary line between adjoining houses or properties
3 the policies and practices of a group, stated with the authority of the group leaders: *the Communist* ***party line***

party machine
noun the organisation behind a political party which influences the choice of candidates, manages fundraising, etc.

pashmina (pash-<u>meen</u>-uh)
noun **1** a fine woollen fabric made from the fur of Himalayan goats
2 a shawl made from this fabric

paspalum (pas-<u>pay</u>-luhm)
noun a type of grass native to the southern US but now one of the most widespread grasses in the higher-rainfall areas of Australia

pass
verb **1** to go by or beyond
2 to do successfully: *to* ***pass*** *a test*
3 to send or hand to: *to* ***pass*** *a message* | ***Pass*** *me that book.* (***give***, ***transfer***)
4 to approve or make: *to* ***pass*** *laws*
noun **5** a narrow path or road through a low part in a mountain
6 a piece of paper that shows you are allowed to do something or go somewhere: *a theatre* ***pass*** | *a train* ***pass***
7 the handing or tossing of a ball to another player in some ball games
8 the passing of an examination
phrase **9 bring to pass**, to cause to happen
10 come to pass, to happen
11 let (**something**) **pass**, to ignore or overlook (something)
12 make a pass, to make a sign or gesture that shows you find someone attractive or desire them sexually
13 pass away, (*euphemistic*) to die
14 pass off, to cause to be accepted or received in disguise: *I* ***passed*** *my older brother* ***off*** *as my boyfriend.*
15 pass out, to faint
16 pass over, to take no notice of
17 pass the buck, to avoid responsibility by making another take it
18 pass up, *Colloquial* to refuse or reject: *to* ***pass up*** *an opportunity to study overseas*

Word history: Middle English

> **passed / past**
> These related words sound the same but they are different parts of speech.
> **Passed** is the past form of the verb **pass**:
> *We passed the shop.*
> *He passed me the ruler.*
> *That time has passed.*
>
> *(continued)*

passed / past *(continued)*
Past can be used as follows:

as an adjective:	*the past fifteen years*
as a noun:	*in the past*
as an adverb:	*the soldiers marched past*
as a preposition:	*the house past the shop*

passable
adjective **1** able to be passed
2 able to be gone through or over: *a **passable** stream | a **passable** road*
3 fair or moderate: *a **passable** knowledge of history* (***reasonable***, ***tolerable***)

Word history: Middle English, from French word meaning 'pass'

passage
noun **1** a corridor, channel or a way for going: *a **passage** between rooms | a **passage** between islands*
2 a part of a story or piece of music

Word history: Middle English, from Old French word meaning 'pass'

passbook
noun → **bankbook**

passé (pah-say)
adjective out-of-date

Word history: French

passenger
noun someone who travels on a ship, plane, bus or other vehicle

Word history: Middle English, from Old French

passion (pash-uhn)
noun **1** any strong feeling or emotion, especially love, anger or grief
2 a strong interest or enthusiasm: *He has a **passion** for football.*

Word history: Middle English, from Old French, from Latin word meaning 'suffering'

passionate
adjective showing passion: *a **passionate** advocate of conservation | a **passionate** speech | **passionate** grief* (***ardent***, ***fervent***, ***heartfelt***, ***impassioned***, ***intense***)

passionfruit
noun a small, purplish fruit, the seeds and pulp of which you can eat

Noun forms: The plural is **passionfruit**.

passive
adjective letting things happen without taking any action yourself (***apathetic***, ***inactive***, ***indifferent***, ***uninvolved***)

Word use: The opposite of this is **active** or **proactive**.
Word history: Middle English, from Latin word meaning 'capable of feeling'

passive aggressive
adjective **1** deliberately uncooperative: ***passive aggressive** behaviour*
noun **2** a person who behaves in such a manner

passive verb
noun a verb whose subject is having an action done to it, rather than doing the action itself

Look up **verbs: passive verbs.**

passport
noun a government document which identifies you and which you need to travel to foreign countries

Word history: French *passeport*, from *passe(r)* pass + *port* port

password
noun a secret word that lets you get into a place where others are not allowed

past
adjective **1** gone by in time: *The old lady's **past** activities included bushwalking.* (***bygone***, ***former***, ***previous***, ***sometime***)
noun **2** time gone by: *in the **past***
adverb **3** by: *The troops marched **past**.*
preposition **4** beyond, in time or position: ***past** noon | **past** the shop*

Word history: Middle English

past / passed
Look up **passed / past.**

pasta (pas-tuh, pahs-tuh)
noun a food made from flour, water and sometimes egg, cut into various shapes which have their own names, such as spaghetti and ravioli, and cooked by boiling, then usually served with a sauce

Word history: Italian, from Late Latin word meaning 'dough', 'paste'

paste
noun **1** a mixture of flour and water used for sticking paper onto other surfaces (***adhesive***, ***glue***, ***gum***)
2 something made into a soft smooth mass: *tooth**paste** | almond **paste***
verb **3** to stick with paste: *to **paste** pictures into a book*
4 *Computers* to insert (data) from one application or document into another, or from one location in a document to another

Word history: Middle English, from Old French, from Late Latin, from Greek word meaning 'barley porridge'

pastel (pas-tuhl)
noun **1** a soft, pale colour
2 a crayon, or a drawing made with crayons

Word building: **pastel** *adjective*
Word history: French, from Provençal, from Late Latin word meaning 'paste'

pasteurise (pahs-chuh-ruyz)
verb to destroy germs in, by heating to a very high temperature: *to **pasteurise** milk*

Word use: You can also use **pasteurize**.
Word building: **pasteurisation** *noun*
Word history: named after Louis *Pasteur*, 1822–95, French chemist and bacteriologist

pastie (pas-tee, pahs-tee)
noun a type of pie filled with meat and vegetables

Word use: You can also use **pasty**.
Word history: Middle English, from Old French

pastime
noun something you do to make time pass pleasantly: *Reading is a good **pastime**.*

Word history: late Middle English

pastor
noun a member of the clergy (***chaplain***, ***clergyman***, ***minister***, ***priest***, ***vicar***)
Word building: **pastorate** *noun*
Word history: from Latin word meaning 'shepherd'

pastoral
adjective **1** having to do with shepherds or country life: *a **pastoral** painting | **pastoral** music | **pastoral** scenery* (***agrarian***, ***bucolic***, ***rural***, ***rustic***)
2 used for pasture: ***pastoral** land*
3 having to do with a church minister or member of the clergy, or with their duties
Word building: **pastoralism** *noun*
Word history: Middle English, from Latin word meaning 'relating to a shepherd'

pastoral care
noun **1** the responsibility of a member of the clergy to attend to the needs of the congregation
2 the provisions made to advise students about personal wellbeing and their moral and ethical concerns

pastoralist
noun Australian, NZ one who owns land used for raising stock, especially sheep or cattle

pastry
noun a mixture of flour, water and fat cooked as a crust for pies and tarts
Noun forms: The plural is **pastries**.
Word history: *past(e)* + *-ry*

past tense
noun the form of a verb which shows that something has already happened such as 'ran' in *I ran away* and 'have run' in *I have run away*

Look up **verbs: past tense**.

pasture (pahs-chuh)
noun **1** land suitable for grazing cattle or sheep: *There is good **pasture** on the property.*
verb **2** to graze: *to put cattle out to **pasture***
Word history: Middle English, from Old French, from Late Latin word literally meaning 'feeding', 'grazing'

pasty[1] (pay-stee)
adjective whitish or sick-looking: *a **pasty** complexion*
Adjective forms: **pastier**, **pastiest**
Word history: *paste*, noun + *-y*

pasty[2] (pas-tee, pahs-tee)
noun → **pastie**
Noun forms: The plural is **pasties**.

PA system (pee ay sis-tuhm)
noun → **public-address system**

pat[1]
verb **1** to strike lightly with your hand (***dab***, ***tap***)
2 to stroke gently (***caress***, ***fondle***, ***pet***)
noun **3** a light strike or blow: *He gave me a **pat** on the shoulder.*
phrase **4 pat someone on the back**, *Colloquial* to congratulate or encourage with praise
Verb forms: I **patted**, I have **patted**, I am **patting**
Word history: Middle English; related to *putt*

pat[2]
adjective **1** exactly to the point: *He gave a **pat** reply.* (***accurate***, ***definite***, ***precise***, ***spot-on***)
adverb **2** exactly or perfectly: *Learn it off **pat**.*
Word history: apparently related to *pat[1]*

patch
noun **1** a piece of material used to mend a hole or a weak place
2 a piece of material used to cover a wound
3 a small piece: *a **patch** of land | a **patch** of sunlight*
verb **4** to mend or make strong with a patch or patches: *to **patch** a hole in your jeans*
phrase **5 hit a bad patch**, to suffer a lot of bad luck, especially in your finances
6 not a patch on, *Colloquial* not nearly as good as
7 patch up,
a to repair or restore, often in a hasty way: *to **patch up** a break in a pipe*
b to settle or smooth over: *to **patch up** a quarrel*
Word history: Middle English

patchwork
noun a type of work in which pieces of differently coloured or shaped cloth are sewn together

patchy
adjective **1** having patches or something like patches: ***patchy** jeans | **patchy** shade*
2 not equal in quality, some bad and some good: ***patchy** homework*
Adjective forms: **patchier**, **patchiest**

pate (payt)
noun **1** the head
2 the crown or top of your head: *a man with a bald **pate***
Word history: Middle English

pâté (pat-ay, pah-tay)
noun a paste or spread made out of finely minced liver, meat, fish, etc.
Word history: French

patella (puh-tel-uh)
noun your kneecap
Noun forms: The plural is **patellas** or **patellae** (puh-tel-ee).
Word building: **patellar** *adjective* **patellate** *adjective*
Word history: Latin word literally meaning 'small pan'

patent (pay-tuhnt)
noun **1** a government grant given to an inventor, which gives the right to make, use and sell an invention without competition from others
2 an invention, process, etc., which has a patent like this
Word building: **patent** *adjective* **patent** *verb*

patent leather
noun leather with a very shiny surface
Word building: **patent-leather** *adjective*

paternal (puh-ter-nuhl)
adjective having to do with, or being like, a father: ***paternal** love*
Word history: from Latin word meaning 'fatherly'

paternalism
noun the principle or practice where a government or any group or person in authority manages the affairs of the country or community by looking after them as a father looks after his children

Word use: This word is often used in a disapproving way, because it implies that the people treated in this way are children.
Word building: **paternalistic** *adjective* **paternalistically** *adverb*

paternity
noun fatherhood: *The man denied* ***paternity*** *of the child.*

Word history: Middle English, from Latin word meaning 'fatherly'

Paterson's curse
noun a biennial plant from the Mediterranean area, but widely growing in settled parts of Australia, having blue-purple flowers

Word use: Another name is **salvation Jane**.

path
noun **1** a narrow way for walking: *a garden* ***path*** (***footpath***, ***pathway***, ***track***, ***trail***)
2 any way or route: *the ship's* ***path*** *| He followed in his father's* ***path***. (***avenue***, ***course***, ***direction***, ***passage***, ***road***)

Word history: Middle English; Old English *pæth*

pathetic (puh-thet-ik)
adjective **1** causing feelings of pity or sadness: *a* ***pathetic*** *sight* (***miserable***, ***pitiable***, ***pitiful***, ***woeful***, ***wretched***)
2 *Colloquial* showing a great lack of ability: *It was a* ***pathetic*** *attempt.* (***feeble***, ***hopeless***, ***useless***, ***worthless***)

Word history: Late Latin, from Greek word meaning 'sensitive'

pathologist (puh-thol-uh-juhst)
noun a doctor who is an expert in the effects of diseases on the body

pathology (puh-thol-uh-jee)
noun **1** the science of the origin, nature and course of diseases
2 the conditions and processes of a disease

Noun forms: The plural is **pathologies**.
Word building: **pathological** *adjective*

pathos (pay-thos)
noun the quality or power, in speech, literature, music, etc., of arousing a feeling of pity or sympathetic sadness

Word history: from Greek word meaning 'suffering', 'disease', 'feeling'

patience
noun **1** endurance without complaining: ***patience*** *in all her suffering*
2 calmness while waiting: *Have* ***patience*** *a little longer.*
3 a card game, usually played by one person alone

patient (pay-shuhnt)
noun **1** someone who is being treated by a doctor or is in a hospital
adjective **2** waiting calmly: *She was a* ***patient*** *customer.* (***long-suffering***, ***resigned***, ***uncomplaining***)

Word history: from Latin word meaning 'suffering', 'enduring'

patio (pat-ee-oh, pay-shee-oh)
noun an outdoor living area next to a house

Noun forms: The plural is **patios**.
Word history: Spanish

patriarch (pay-tree-ahk, pat-ree-ahk)
noun a male leader in a family, tribe, or any field of activity

Word building: **patriarchal** *adjective*
Word history: Middle English, from Late Latin, from Greek word meaning 'head of a family'

patriarchy (pay-tree-ah-kee, pat-ree-ah-kee)
noun a form of social organisation in which the father is head of the family and in which descent is through the male line, the children belonging to the father's clan

Noun forms: The plural is **patriarchies**.

patrician (puh-trish-uhn)
noun **1** a member of the original senatorial aristocracy in ancient Rome
2 any noble or aristocrat
adjective **3** having to do with an ancient Roman senator or his family
4 having to do with, or like an aristocrat or noble

Word history: Middle English, from Latin word meaning 'of the rank of the senators', 'patricians'

patricide (pat-ruh-suyd)
noun the act of someone who kills his or her father

Word building: **patricidal** *adjective*
Word history: *patri-* + *-cide*

patriot (pay-tree-uht, pat-ree-uht)
noun someone who loves their country and is loyal to it

Word building: **patriotic** *adjective* **patriotism** *noun*
Word history: Late Latin, from Greek

patrol (puh-trohl)
verb to go around regularly to make sure there is no trouble: *The police car* ***patrolled*** *the streets.*

Verb forms: I **patrolled**, I have **patrolled**, I am **patrolling**
Word building: **patrol** *noun*
Word history: from French word meaning 'patrol'

patron (pay-truhn)
noun **1** a regular customer of a hotel, shop, cinema or similar place (***buyer***, ***consumer***, ***purchaser***, ***shopper***)
2 a supporter or helper: *a* ***patron*** *of art | The governor is the* ***patron*** *of the children's hospital.* (***benefactor***, ***champion***, ***defender***, ***protector***, ***sponsor***)

Word history: Middle English, from Old French, from Latin word meaning 'patron'

patronage
noun **1** the financial support that customers bring to a shop, hotel, etc.
2 the position, support or encouragement of a patron: *The theatre needs the* ***patronage*** *of big companies to keep it afloat.*
3 a favour done in a condescending way: *She has such an air of* ***patronage***.

patronise (pat-ruh-nuyz)
verb **1** to be a customer of: *I've been **patronising** that shop for years.*
2 to treat kindly, but as if inferior: *Older children often **patronise** the younger ones.*

Word use: You can also use **patronize**.

patter[1]
verb to strike or move with quick, light, tapping sounds: *She **pattered** down the hallway in bare feet.*

Word building: **patter** *noun*
Word history: verb expressing repetition of the action of *pat[1]*

patter[2]
noun rapid speech or chatter, especially of a salesperson or entertainer

Word history: variant of *pater* in *Pater noster* Our Father

pattern
noun **1** an ornamental design
2 a particular arrangement of forms and colours
3 a model or guide: *a paper **pattern** for a dress* (***design***, ***example***, ***plan***, ***sample***, ***specimen***)
4 a design or figure that's repeated indefinitely: *a number **pattern** in mathematics*
verb **5** to model: *to **pattern** yourself on your father*
6 to cover or mark with a pattern

Word history: Middle English, from Medieval Latin word meaning 'model', 'example', from Latin word meaning 'patron'

patty
noun a savoury mixture formed into a flattened ball and fried

Noun forms: The plural is **patties**.
Word history: French

paucity (paw-suh-tee)
noun scantiness or lack of something needed: ***paucity** of material*

Word history: Middle English, from Latin

paunch (pawnch)
noun **1** the belly or abdomen
2 a large, prominent belly

Word building: **paunchy** *adjective* (**paunchier**, **paunchiest**)
Word history: Middle English, from Old Northern French, from Latin

pauper (paw-puh)
noun a very poor person, sometimes supported by a community

Word history: from Latin word meaning 'poor (man)'

pause (pawz)
noun **1** a short rest or stop when you're speaking or doing something (***break***, ***interlude***, ***lull***, ***recess***)
verb **2** to make a pause, to stop or wait: *Halfway through her speech, she **paused**, and looked down at her notes.*
3 to temporarily halt (a computer game, DVD, etc.): *He **paused** the film while he answered the phone.*

Word history: late Middle English, from Latin, from Greek word meaning 'cessation'

pave
verb to make a firm, level surface by laying concrete, stones or bricks on: *to **pave** a path*

Word history: Middle English, from Old French, for Latin word meaning 'beat down'

pavement
noun a paved footpath at the side of a road

Word history: Middle English, from Old French word meaning 'a floor beaten down'

pavilion (puh-vil-yuhn)
noun an open shelter in a park or amusement area

Word history: Middle English, from Old French, from Latin word meaning 'tent', originally 'butterfly'

pavlova
noun a dessert made of a large, round meringue filled with cream and topped with fruit

Word history: named after Anna *Pavlova*, 1885–1931, Russian ballerina who toured Australia and New Zealand in 1926

paw
noun **1** the foot of an animal with nails or claws
verb **2** to strike or scrape with the paws

Word history: Middle English, from Old French, of Germanic origin

paw / poor / pore / pour
Don't confuse **paw** with **poor**, **pore** or **pour**.
Someone is **poor** if they have very little money or property.
A **pore** is a small hole. Sweat comes out through the **pores** in your skin.
To **pore** over something is to read or study it carefully:

He watched the pirates pore over the secret treasure map.

You can **pour** a liquid from one container to another.

pawl
noun a pivoted bar made so as to fit into the teeth of a ratchet wheel, especially to prevent it moving backwards

Word history: perhaps from Dutch *pal*

pawn[1]
verb to leave something with a pawnbroker when you borrow money, to make sure that you repay your debt: *I **pawned** my watch for $30.*

Word history: late Middle English, from Old French

pawn[2]
noun **1** one of the pieces of lowest value in chess
2 an unimportant person used as a tool of another: *He was only a **pawn** in the game.*

Word history: Middle English, from Anglo-French, variant of Old French, from Late Latin word meaning 'foot soldier'

pawn / porn
Don't confuse **pawn** with **porn**, which is art, photography or writing thought or designed to be obscene or indecent. **Porn** is short for **pornography**.

pawnbroker
noun someone who lends you money, but only if you leave something that can be sold if you don't return the money

pawpaw
noun a large, yellow, fleshy fruit which grows in tropical Australia

Word use: A smaller kind of pawpaw, with reddish-pink flesh, is the **papaya**.
Word history: Spanish, of Carib origin

pay
verb **1** to give money in return for something: *I **paid** for the milk yesterday.* (***expend***, ***outlay***)
2 to give or offer: *to **pay** a compliment*
3 to be worthwhile: *It **pays** to be honest.*
4 to suffer or be punished: *to **pay** for your mistakes*
noun **5** wages or salary (***commission***, ***fee***, ***income***)
phrase **6 pay off,**
a to pay the full amount of a debt
b to dismiss from employment and pay any wages, etc., due: *to **pay off** an employee*
c to give a profit or prove to be worthwhile: *The gamble **paid off**.*
7 pay out,
a to punish in revenge
b *Colloquial* to scold or criticise: *He really paid me out for being late.*
8 pay up,
a to pay when someone demands you to: ***Pay up** or else!*
b to pay in full and on time: *My loan is **paid up** now.*
9 put paid to, to prevent or put an end to: *Her new job **put paid to** her dream of travelling.*

Verb forms: I **paid**, I have **paid**, I am **paying**
Word building: **payable** *adjective* **payment** *noun*
Word history: Middle English, from French, from Latin word meaning 'pacify'

pay-and-display
adjective **1** having to do with a ticket vending machine in a parking area, where the driver must purchase a ticket and display it on the dashboard of the vehicle: *a **pay-and-display** zone*
2 having to do with using this system of payment for parking

pay-as-you-go tax
noun a form of withholding tax in which tax is deducted from income before it is paid to the recipient

Word use: You can also use **PAYG tax**.

payola (pay-oh-luh)
noun a bribe, especially for the promotion of a commercial product, particularly through the abuse of your position or influence

Word history: *pay* + *-ola* suffix used in commercial names

pay-per-view
noun **1** a system by which you can view films, programs, etc., on television as you pay for them
adjective **2** having to do with this system: ***pay-per-view** movies*

payroll
noun **1** a roll or list of people to be paid wages, with the amounts due
2 the money or salaries paid out

payroll tax
noun a tax levied by a government on employers, based on the salaries and wages paid out

pay TV
noun a television service to viewers who pay a subscription

Word use: You can also use **pay television**.

PDF
noun Computers a type of computer file containing words and images which can be sent on the internet and read on any computer

Word use: You use **.pdf** in filenames.
Word history: *P(ortable) D(ocument) F(ormat)*

pea
noun a small, round, green seed which grows in a pod; used as a vegetable

peace
noun **1** freedom from war
2 calm, quiet or stillness: ***peace** of mind* | *the **peace** of the countryside* (***serenity***, ***tranquillity***)
phrase **3 hold your peace,** to keep silent
4 keep the peace, to refrain from creating a disturbance
5 make your peace, to settle a quarrel and become friends again

Word history: Middle English, from Old French, from Latin word meaning 'peace'

peace / piece
Don't confuse **peace** with **piece**, which is a bit or part of something, as in a *piece of cake*.
It can also be a single or individual thing, as in *a piece of fruit*.

peaceable
adjective loving peace: *a **peaceable** nation*

peaceful
adjective free from commotion or strife: *a **peaceful** scene* (***calm***, ***harmonious***, ***quiet***, ***serene***, ***tranquil***)

peach
noun a round, sweet, pinkish-yellow fruit with a single seed and furry skin

Word history: Middle English, from Old French

peacock
noun a male peafowl, a type of pheasant noted for the colourful eye-like pattern on its tail feathers

Noun forms: The plural is **peacock** or **peacocks**.
Word history: Middle English, from Latin

peahen (pee-hen)
noun a female peafowl, a type of pheasant with brownish feathers

peak
noun **1** the pointed top of a mountain
2 the highest or greatest point: *the **peak** of her achievements* (***apex***, ***crest***, ***pinnacle***, ***summit***, ***top***)
verb **3** to reach its highest point: *The interest rate on home mortgages **peaked** at 19%.*

Word building: **peaked** *adjective*
Word history: blend of *pike* a shaft (or *pick* a pointed hand tool) and *beak* the pointed mouth of a bird

peak / peek / pique

Don't confuse **peak** with **peek** or **pique**.

To **peek** is to snatch a quick look, often when you are not supposed to.

Pique is a feeling of mild annoyance. To be **piqued** is to be a bit annoyed.

peak body
noun an organisation which represents a group of enterprises engaged in similar activities: *the recreational bushwalking **peak body***

peak hour
noun the time when there is most traffic on the road because people are going to or leaving work: *Let's try to leave before **peak hour**.*

Word use: You can also use **rush hour**.

peaky
adjective pale and sick-looking

Adjective forms: **peakier**, **peakiest**

peal
noun **1** a loud, long, drawn-out sound of bells (***chime***, ***knell***, ***toll***)
2 any other loud, long sound: *a **peal** of laughter*

Word building: **peal** *verb*
Word history: Middle English

peal / peel

Don't confuse **peal** with **peel**. To **peel** an apple is to remove the skin from it.

peanut
noun a small nut which ripens in a pod underground and which you can eat

peanut butter
noun a paste or spread made from ground peanuts

Word use: You can also use **peanut paste** or **peanut spread**.

pear
noun a thin-skinned, pale green or brownish fruit, round at its base and growing smaller towards the stem

Word history: Old English *pere*, from Late Latin

pear / pair / pare

Don't confuse **pear** with **pair** or **pare**.

Two things that go together, like shoes, are a **pair**.

You **pare** an apple when you peel the skin off.

pearl (perl)
noun a shiny, round, usually white growth, found in some oysters and used in jewellery

Word building: **pearly** *adjective* (**pearlier**, **pearliest**)
Word history: Middle English, from Old French, from Medieval Latin *perla*

pearl / purl

Don't confuse **pearl** with **purl**, which is a stitch in knitting. It can also be spelt **pearl**.

peasant (pez-uhnt)
noun someone who lives and works as a farm labourer

Word use: These days we mainly use this word when we are talking about the past or about people in countries where agriculture is the mainstay of the economy.
Word history: late Middle English, from Anglo-French, from Late Latin, from Latin word meaning 'district'

peat
noun **1** soil which consists of partially rotted leaves, roots, grasses and similar matter in marshy areas
2 blocks of this, dried and used as fuel

Word history: Middle English

pebble
noun a small, smooth, rounded stone

Word building: **pebbly** *adjective* (**pebblier**, **pebbliest**)

pecan (pee-kan, pee-kan)
noun a sweet, oily nut which grows on trees, and which you can eat

peccadillo (pek-uh-dil-oh)
noun a small sin, offence or fault

Noun forms: The plural is **peccadilloes** or **peccadillos**.
Word history: Spanish, from Latin word meaning 'a sin'

peck
verb **1** to strike or eat with the beak: *The bird **pecked** the branch. | The chickens **pecked** the corn.*
2 to pick or nibble at food
3 to kiss quickly on the cheek

Word building: **peck** *noun*
Word history: Middle English

pecking order
noun **1** the natural order of importance seen in a flock of poultry or in any birds that live in flocks
2 any order of importance or precedence

pectin (pek-tuhn)
noun a jelly-like substance found in ripe fruits, which dissolves in sugared boiling water and which forms a gel upon cooling; used in jam-making

Word building: **pectic** *adjective*
Word history: *pect(ic)* + *-in*

pectoral (pek-tuh-ruhl)
adjective **1** having to do with your breast or chest: *the **pectoral** muscle* (***thoracic***)
2 worn on your breast or chest: *the **pectoral** cross of a bishop*

Word history: late Middle English, from Latin word meaning 'relating to the breast'

peculiar (puh-kyooh-lee-uh, puh-kyooh-lyuh)
adjective **1** strange, odd, or queer (***abnormal***, ***bizarre***, ***unconventional***, ***unusual***, ***weird***)
phrase **2 peculiar to**, having to do with one particular person or thing: *Gathering shiny objects is a habit **peculiar to** magpies and bowerbirds.*

Word history: late Middle English, from Latin word meaning 'relating to one's own'

peculiarity (puh-kyooh-lee-ar-uh-tee)
noun an odd characteristic or quality, especially one that sets you apart from others

Noun forms: The plural is **peculiarities**.

pecuniary (puh-kyooh-nee-uh-ree, puh-kyooh-nuh-ree)
adjective **1** consisting of, or given or taken in money: ***pecuniary** penalties*
2 having to do with money: ***pecuniary** affairs*

Word history: from Latin word meaning 'relating to money'

pedagogue (ped-uh-gog)
noun **1** a teacher of children
2 someone who is formal, places too much importance on small things and who holds strong opinions that people are expected to accept without question

Word building: **pedagogic** *adjective* **pedagogy** *noun* (*plural* **pedagogies**)
Word history: Middle English, from Old French, from Latin, from Greek word meaning 'a teacher of boys'

pedal
noun a lever worked by the foot: *an organ **pedal** | a sewing machine **pedal** | a bicycle **pedal***

Word building: **pedal** *verb* (**pedalled**, **pedalling**)
Word history: French, from Italian, from Latin word meaning '(something) relating to the foot'

pedal / peddle
Don't confuse **pedal** with **peddle**. To **peddle** something is to sell it, usually in small quantities, to individual buyers. The person who peddles is a **pedlar** or **peddler**.

pedant (ped-uhnt)
noun **1** someone who puts too much importance on small details of learning, or who possesses mere book-learning without practical wisdom
2 someone who shows overly strict attention to rules, details, etc.

Word building: **pedantic** *adjective* **pedantry** *noun*
Word history: from Italian word meaning 'teacher', 'pedant'

peddle
verb to take around from place to place in order to sell (***hawk***)

pedestal
noun **1** a support for a statue or ornament
2 the supporting base of a column

Word history: French, from Italian

pedestrian (puh-des-tree-uhn)
noun someone who walks: *A **pedestrian** must be careful when crossing a busy street.*

Word history: from Latin word meaning 'on foot'

pedicure (ped-uh-kyooh-uh)
noun professional care or treatment of the feet

Word history: French, from Latin

pedigree
noun a line of direct relationship, showing, for example, the father, and his father before him, etc.: *My dog has a long **pedigree**.*

Word building: **pedigreed** *adjective*
Word history: Middle English, apparently from Old French word literally meaning 'foot of a crane', said to refer to a mark having three branching lines, used in old genealogical tables

pediment (ped-uh-muhnt)
noun Architecture a low triangular gable crowned with a projecting cornice, in the Greek, Roman or Renaissance style, especially over a portico or porch or at the ends of a gable-roofed building

Word building: **pedimental** *adjective*
Word history: perhaps from Latin, a prop of a vine

pedlar
noun someone who travels round selling things

Word history: Middle English

pedometer (puh-dom-uh-tuh)
noun an instrument for recording the number of steps taken in walking: *Her **pedometer** read a distance of 4.3 km at the end of the day.*

peek
verb **1** to peep or peer
noun **2** a peep

Word history: Middle English

peek / peak / pique
Don't confuse **peek** with **peak** or **pique**.
A **peak** is the top of a mountain.
Pique is a feeling of mild annoyance. To be **piqued** is to be slightly annoyed.

peel
verb **1** to take off the skin, rind or outer layer of
2 to come off: *My skin is **peeling** where I was sunburnt.*
noun **3** the skin or rind of a fruit: *an orange **peel***
phrase **4 keep your eyes peeled,** *Colloquial* to keep a close watch

Word history: Middle English

peel / peal
Don't confuse **peel** with **peal.** Bells **peal** when they ring out.

peep[1]
verb **1** to look through a small opening or from a hiding place
2 to come briefly or partly into view: *The sun **peeped** over the horizon.*

Word building: **peep** *noun*
Word history: perhaps assimilated variant of *peek*

peep[2]
verb **1** to utter the shrill little cry of a young bird, mouse, etc. (***cheep***, ***squeak***)
2 to speak in a thin, weak voice
noun **3** a peeping cry or sound

Word history: Middle English

peer[1]
noun **1** someone of your own age or rank
2 a nobleman

Word building: **peeress** *feminine noun*
Word history: Middle English, from Old French, from Latin word meaning 'equal'

peer[2]
verb **1** to look closely in order to see clearly
2 to peep: *to* ***peer*** *through a window*

Word history: late Middle English

peer / pier
Don't confuse **peer** with **pier**. A **pier** is a jetty.

peerage
noun the nobility

peer group
noun a group of people of about the same age, social background or class

peerless
adjective having no equal

peevish
adjective cross or easily annoyed

Word history: Middle English *pevysh*

peewee
noun → **magpie lark**

peg
noun **1** a small wooden, metal or plastic pin used to fasten things, to hang things on, or to mark a place: *a clothes* ***peg*** | *a tent* ***peg*** | *a hat* ***peg*** | *a surveyor's* ***peg***
verb **2** to fasten with a peg
3 *Colloquial* to identify as a particular type, having certain abilities, etc.: *I* ***pegged*** *her as a keen athlete.*
phrase **4 peg away**, to work steadily
5 take down a peg, to humble: *That girl needs* ***taking down a peg.***

Verb forms: I **pegged**, I have **pegged**, I am **pegging**
Word history: Middle English

pejorative (puh-jo-ruh-tiv)
adjective expressing disapproval: *a* ***pejorative*** *statement*

Word history: from Latin word meaning 'having been made worse'

Peking duck (pee-king duk)
noun a Chinese dish consisting of small pancakes wrapped around pieces of roast duck, spring onions, cucumber, and hoisin sauce

Pekingese (pee-kuh-neez)
noun a small, long-haired dog originally from China

Word use: You can also use **Pekinese**.

pelican
noun a large, web-footed seabird with a pouch hanging beneath its bill for holding the fish it catches

Word history: Middle English and Old English, from Late Latin, from Greek

pellet
noun **1** a small, rounded piece of anything: *a paper* ***pellet*** | *a* ***pellet*** *of food*
2 a small bullet fired from a shotgun

Word history: Middle English, from Old French, from Latin word meaning 'ball'

pellucid (puh-looh-suhd)
adjective **1** allowing light to come through (***translucent***, ***transparent***)
2 clear, like water

Word history: from Latin word meaning 'transparent'

pelmet
noun an ornamental covering which hides a curtain rail

pelt[1]
verb **1** to throw: *to* ***pelt*** *stones at a post* (***cast***, ***hurl***, ***sling***)
2 to come down heavily: *Rain* ***pelted*** *down.*
3 to hurry: *He* ***pelted*** *down the hill.* (***dash***, ***hurtle***, ***race***, ***shoot***, ***speed***)

Word history: origin uncertain; perhaps related to *pellet*

pelt[2]
noun the skin taken from a dead animal to be made into leather

Word history: Middle English, origin uncertain, ultimately from Latin *pellis*

pelvis
noun the ring of bone made up of the lower part of your backbone and your two hip bones and the cavity it forms

Word building: **pelvic** *adjective*
Word history: from Latin word meaning 'basin'

pen[1]
noun **1** an instrument for writing with ink: *a ballpoint* ***pen***
verb **2** to write: *to* ***pen*** *a message*

Verb forms: I **penned**, I have **penned**, I am **penning**
Word history: Middle English, from Old French, from Late Latin word meaning 'pen', from Latin word meaning 'feather'

pen[2]
noun **1** an enclosure for animals on a farm
verb **2** to put in a pen: *to* ***pen*** *the animals for the night*

Verb forms: I **penned** or I **pent**, I have **penned** or I have **pent**, I am **penning**
Word history: Old English *penn*

penal (pee-nuhl)
adjective having to do with the punishment of crimes: *the* ***penal*** *laws*

Word history: Middle English, from Latin word meaning 'relating to punishment'

penalise
verb to punish or put at a disadvantage: *to* ***penalise*** *a driver for speeding*

Word use: You can also use **penalize**.

penalty (pen-uhl-tee)
noun **1** the price you pay for breaking a law or rule
2 a free kick or shot allowed in some sports to one team or player because an opponent has broken a rule

Noun forms: The plural is **penalties**.
Word history: *penal* + *-ty*

penalty corner
noun *Hockey* a corner given as a penalty for an infringement by a player on the defending team

penalty goal
noun Soccer, Hockey, etc. a goal scored from a penalty kick or hit: *The game was won by a* ***penalty goal****.*

penalty shootout
noun Soccer, Hockey, etc. a method of deciding a match after a tied game, in which each team is given equal opportunity to score penalty goals

penalty shot
noun Soccer, Hockey, etc. a shot at goal awarded to one side as a penalty for an infringement by a player on the other side

penance (pen-uhns)
noun a punishment you agree to, or offer to accept to show you are sorry for doing wrong

Word history: Middle English, from Old French, from Latin

pence (pens)
noun plural of **penny**, usually used in compounds: *four****pence***

penchant (pen-shuhnt, pon-shon)
noun a taste or liking for something: *a* ***penchant*** *for opera*

Word history: French, from Latin word meaning 'hang'

pencil
noun a thin, pointed piece of wood enclosing a stick of graphite or crayon, and used for writing or drawing

Word building: **pencil** *verb* (**pencilled, pencilling**)
Word history: Middle English, from Old French, from Vulgar Latin variant of Latin word meaning 'brush'

pendant
noun **1** a hanging piece of jewellery such as a necklace
adjective **2** hanging: ***pendant*** *vines*

Word history: Middle English, from Old French word meaning 'hang', from Latin

pending (pen-ding)
preposition **1** until or while waiting for: ***pending*** *his return*
2 during: ***pending*** *the official talks*
adjective **3** waiting for a decision: *The jury's verdict is* ***pending****.*

Word history: *pend(ent)* + *-ing*

pendulous (pen-juh-luhs)
adjective hanging loosely: *a* ***pendulous*** *stomach*

Word history: from Latin word meaning 'hanging', 'swinging'

pendulum (pen-juh-luhm)
noun a weight swinging backwards and forwards, which makes some clocks work

Word history: from Neo-Latin, properly neuter of Latin word meaning 'hanging', 'swinging'

penetrate (pen-uh-trayt)
verb **1** to go into or through, especially with a sharp instrument: *The arrow* ***penetrated*** *his arm.* | *The army* ***penetrated*** *the enemy's defences.*
2 to enter, reach or pass through, as if by piercing: *The knife* ***penetrated*** *to the bone.*

Word building: **penetration** *noun* **penetrable** *adjective*
Word history: Latin

penetrating
adjective sharp or piercing: *a* ***penetrating*** *sound* | *a* ***penetrating*** *look*

penfriend
noun someone, usually in another country, you have become friends with through writing letters

penguin (peng-gwuhn, pen-gwuhn)
noun a bird which cannot fly, has webbed feet and lives in or near the cold southern parts of the world

penicillin (pen-uh-sil-uhn)
noun a strong, germ-fighting substance used in medicines and ointments

Word history: Latin *pēnicillus* small brush + *-in*

peninsula (puh-nin-shuh-luh)
noun a long piece of land jutting out into the sea

Word building: **peninsular** *adjective*
Word history: Latin

penis (pee-nuhs)
noun the part of a male's body with which he urinates and has sexual intercourse

Word history: Latin word originally meaning 'tail'

penitent (pen-uh-tuhnt)
adjective sorry for wrongdoing and willing to put things right (***ashamed, contrite, remorseful, repentant***)

Word building: **penitence** *noun*
Word history: from Latin word meaning 'repenting'

penitentiary (pen-uh-ten-shuh-ree)
noun a jail or prison

Word history: Middle English, from Medieval Latin, from Latin word meaning 'penitence'

penknife
noun a small knife with one or more blades that fold into the handle so that it can be carried safely in a pocket

Noun forms: The plural is **penknives.**
Word use: You can also use **pocket-knife.** | This was once used to clean and mend quill pens.

pennant
noun a triangular flag, used as a signal on ships or as an award in a sporting event

Word history: variant of *pendant*

penniless
adjective having no money

penny
noun **1** a bronze or copper coin worth only a small amount, that was once used in Australia and still is in Britain and some other countries
phrase **2 a bad penny**, a bad or undesirable person or thing
3 the penny drops, the remark or explanation is understood

Noun forms: The plural is **pennies** or **pence.**
Word history: Old English *penig, pening, pending*

pension[1]
noun a regular payment made by the government to someone who is old, sick or poor, or by a private company to someone who has retired from working for it

Word history: from Latin word meaning 'payment'

pension² (pon-syon, pen-see-on)
noun **1** in France and some other countries, a boarding house or small hotel
2 in France and some other countries, room and board

Word use: Compare this with **pensione**.

pensione (pen-see-oh-nay)
noun **1** in Italy, a boarding house or small hotel
2 in Italy, room and board

Word use: Compare this with **pension²**.

pensioner
noun someone who receives a pension, especially an old age pensioner

pensive
adjective seriously or sadly thoughtful: *a **pensive** stare*

Word history: from French word meaning 'think'

pent
phrase **pent up**, shut in tightly: ***pent up** feelings*

pentagon
noun a flat shape with five straight sides

Word building: **pentagonal** *adjective*
Word history: Latin, from Greek

pentathlon (pen-tath-luhn)
noun a competition of five different track and field events, won by the competitor having the highest total score

Word history: Greek

penthouse
noun a separate flat on the roof or top storey of a building

Word history: Middle English, apparently from Old French, from Latin word meaning 'hang to or on', 'append'

penultimate (puh-nul-tuh-muht)
adjective next to the last

penumbra (puh-num-bruh)
noun a partial or imperfect shadow outside the complete shadow (umbra) of a body, usually a planet, where the light from the source of illumination is only partly cut off

Noun forms: The plural is **penumbrae** (puh-num-bree) or **penumbras.**
Word building: **penumbral** *adjective*
Word history: Neo-Latin, from Latin

penury (pen-yuh-ree)
noun **1** great poverty (***deprivation***, ***destitution***, ***need***, ***want***)
2 lack of food, etc.

Word building: **penurious** *adjective*
Word history: Middle English, from Latin word meaning 'want', 'scarcity'

peony (pee-uh-nee)
noun a type of garden plant or shrub with large, showy pink, red or yellow flowers

Noun forms: The plural is **peonies**.
Word history: Latin, from Greek, from *Paián* the physician of the gods (because the plant was used in medicine)

people
noun **1** human beings in general
2 all the members of a tribe, race or nation: *a peace-loving **people** | a nomadic **people***
3 the members of a particular group or community: *the **people** of a neighbourhood | working **people***
4 your family or relatives: *Some of my **people** are coming to visit.*

Noun forms: The plural is **people**; the plural for definition 2 is **peoples**.
Word history: Middle English, from Anglo-French, from Latin word meaning 'people'

people smuggling
noun the illegal business of transporting people from one country to another country which they are not authorised to enter as immigrants

Word building: **people smuggler** *noun*

pep
noun Colloquial **1** spirit or life: *I need a cold shower to give me **pep** in the morning.* (***animation***, ***energy***, ***vigour***, ***vim***)
phrase **2 pep up**, to give spirit or energy to: ***Pep up** my drink with some more lemonade.*

Verb forms: I **pepped**, I have **pepped**, I am **pepping**
Word building: **peppy** *adjective* (**peppier**, **peppiest**)
Word history: abbreviation of *pepper*

pepper
noun **1** a spice with a hot taste, made from the dried berries of a tropical plant
2 a capsicum: *a green **pepper** | a red **pepper***

Word building: **peppery** *adjective*
Word history: Old English *piper*, from Latin, from Greek word meaning 'pepper'; of Eastern origin

peppercorn
noun a berry of the black pepper plant often dried and used as a condiment

Word history: Old English *piporcorn*

peppermint
noun a lolly made with a strong-tasting, strong-smelling oil from a plant

pepperoni (pep-uh-roh-nee)
noun a type of salami: *He ordered extra **pepperoni** on his pizza.*

Word use: You can also use **peperoni**.

pepper spray
noun → **capsicum spray**

peppertree
noun an evergreen tree, mostly native to South America and grown in subtropical areas as ornamentals because of their evergreen leaves and bright red fruit

peptic (pep-tik)
adjective **1** having to do with or helping digestion: ***peptic** juices to break down food*
2 associated with the action of digestive substances: *a **peptic** ulcer*

Word history: from Latin word meaning 'able to digest'

per
preposition through, by or for each: ***per** annum (by the year) | **per** diem (by the day) | **per** metre (for each metre)*

Word history: Latin

per capita
adverb by each single person

Word history: Latin

perceive
verb **1** to come to know of through one of the senses, such as sight or hearing: *He **perceived** a glimmer of light at the end of the tunnel.* (***be aware of***, ***discern***, ***experience***)
2 to understand: *I **perceive** that you do not agree.* (***appreciate***, ***comprehend***, ***gather***, ***realise***)

Word building: **perceivable** *adjective*
Word history: Middle English, from Old French, from Latin word meaning 'seize', 'receive', 'understand'

per cent
adverb **1** in every hundred: *My bank pays ten **per cent** interest so if I have $100 in my account for a year, I get paid $10 interest.*
noun **2** another word for **percentage**: *What **per cent** are you offering?*

Word use: You can also use **percent**. | The symbol for definition 1 is '%'.
Word history: originally *per cent.*, abbreviation of Latin *per centum* by the hundred

percentage
noun **1** a number which shows the rate in every hundred: *The **percentage** of dark-haired children in this class is 65.*
2 a part or proportion: *A large **percentage** of children at our school lives nearby.*

percentile (puh-<u>sen</u>-tuyl)
noun Statistics one of the values of a variable which divides the distribution of the variable into one hundred groups having equal frequencies. Thus, there are one hundred percentiles, each having the same number of people, things, etc., but a varying range of scores.

Word history: *per cent* + *-ile*

perceptible
adjective able to be perceived: *a **perceptible** difference*

perception
noun **1** the act of perceiving or the ability to perceive: *My **perception** of colour is not good.* (***awareness***, ***feeling***, ***impression***, ***sensation***, ***sense***)
2 the ability to understand the inner nature of something quickly and clearly: *She has a lot of **perception**.*
3 understanding or knowledge

Word history: late Middle English, from Latin word meaning 'a receiving', hence 'apprehension'

perceptive
adjective quick in perceiving: *a **perceptive** answer*

Word building: **perceptiveness** *noun*

perch[1]
noun **1** a rod for birds to roost on
verb **2** to settle or rest on a perch or something similar: *The birds **perched** on the roof. | I **perched** the vase on the top shelf.*

Word history: Middle English, from Old French, from Latin word meaning 'pole', 'measuring rod'

perch[2]
noun any of a number of types of Australian fish that you can eat, mainly freshwater but some living in the sea

Noun forms: The plural is **perches** or **perch**.
Word history: Middle English, from Old French, from Latin, from Greek word meaning 'perch'

percolate (<u>per</u>-kuh-layt)
verb **1** to make a liquid pass through a substance (***filter***, ***filtrate***, ***permeate***, ***seep***)
2 to spread or become known gradually: *The news **percolated** through the classroom.*

Word building: **percolation** *noun*
Word history: from Latin word meaning 'strained through'

percolator
noun a coffee-maker in which boiling water is percolated through ground coffee

percussion (puh-<u>kush</u>-uhn)
noun the hitting of one thing against another

percussion instrument
noun a musical instrument, such as a drum, cymbal, or piano, which produces notes when it is struck

Word building: **percussionist** *noun*

perdition (per-<u>dish</u>-uhn)
noun **1** the condition of final spiritual ruin or damnation
2 hell

Word history: Middle English, from Latin word meaning 'act of destroying'

peremptory (puh-<u>remp</u>-tree, puh-<u>remp</u>-tuh-ree)
adjective leaving no chance for denial or refusal: *a **peremptory** command* (***arbitrary***, ***authoritative***, ***compelling***, ***imperative***, ***imperious***)

Word building: **peremptoriness** *noun*
Word history: from Latin word meaning 'destructive', 'decisive'

perennial (puh-<u>ren</u>-ee-uhl)
adjective **1** lasting for a long time or continually coming back: *a **perennial** joke | a **perennial** trouble-maker* (***eternal***, ***everlasting***, ***immortal***, ***permanent***, ***perpetual***)
2 having a life cycle of more than two years: *a **perennial** plant*
noun **3** a perennial plant

Word building: **perennially** *adverb*
Word history: from Latin word meaning 'lasting through the year'

perfect (<u>per</u>-fuhkt)
adjective **1** with nothing missing and no faults (***complete***, ***faultless***, ***ideal***, ***immaculate***, ***impeccable***)
2 completely suited for a particular purpose: *He is the **perfect** choice for the job.*
3 complete or absolute: *a **perfect** stranger*
4 having to do with the form of a verb which shows that the action of the verb is complete
5 having to do with the harmonic or consonant intervals of a musical scale, an octave, a fourth and a fifth: *When you play a **perfect** fifth on the piano, you play the tonic note of a scale and the fifth note of that scale in unison.*
verb (per-<u>fekt</u>) **6** to make complete or perfect

Word building: **perfectly** *adverb*
Word history: from Latin word meaning 'performed', 'completed'

perfect aspect
noun the grammatical aspect which expresses a completed action

We use the term **perfect** in grammar to mean 'completed'. We say that a verb like *have run* is perfect because it expresses a completed action. This differs from *was running* which is **continuous.** For more information about these two grammatical categories, look up **verbs: aspect.**

You can express a completed action in the present or past tense:

have run (present perfect)
had run (past perfect)

Look up **verbs: past tense** also.

perfection
noun **1** a perfect quality or state
2 excellence, or utmost skill, especially in some art, such as painting

perfectionist
noun **1** someone who believes in some doctrine concerning perfection
2 someone who demands nothing less than perfection in any area of activity, behaviour, etc.
Word building: **perfectionism** *noun*

perfidy (per-fuh-dee)
noun the carefully considered breaking of the faith or trust that someone has in you (***betrayal***, ***faithlessness***, ***treachery***)
Word building: **perfidious** *adjective*
Word history: from Latin word meaning 'faithlessness'

perforate (per-fuh-rayt)
verb to make a hole or holes in: *He used the point of a pencil to **perforate** the paper.*
Word building: **perforated** *adjective* **perforation** *noun*
Word history: from Latin word meaning 'having been pierced through'

perform
verb **1** to do or carry out: *She **performed** a graceful arm movement. | He **performed** his duty.* (***effect***, ***execute***, ***fulfil***)
2 to play a piece of music, or do an act in front of an audience: *to **perform** a concerto with an orchestra*
Word history: Middle English, from Anglo-French

performance
noun **1** a musical, dramatic or other amusement: *What **performances** are happening in town?*
2 the performing of a piece of music, a play, a part, etc.: *My **performance** tonight wasn't up to my usual standard.*
3 the carrying out or doing of work, acts or deeds

performance-enhancing drug
noun a drug taken by an athlete or other competitive sportsperson to improve performance

performer
noun someone who performs in front of an audience (***entertainer***)

perfume
noun **1** a liquid prepared so that it gives out a pleasant smell
2 a pleasant smell: *the **perfume** of roses*
verb **3** to give a pleasant smell to: *The flowers **perfumed** the room.*
4 to put perfume on: *to **perfume** notepaper*
Word history: from French word meaning 'to scent'

perfunctory (puh-fungk-tuh-ree)
adjective **1** done only as an uninteresting or mechanical duty: ***perfunctory** courtesy*
2 acting only out of duty
Word history: Late Latin, from Latin word meaning 'performed'

pergola (per-guh-luh, puh-goh-luh)
noun a shelter made of bars supported on posts, over which climbing plants are grown
Word history: Italian, from Latin word meaning 'shed', 'vine arbour'

perhaps
adverb maybe or possibly
Word history: Middle English

peril
noun danger or risk: *Our lives are in **peril**.*
Word building: **perilous** *adjective*
Word history: Middle English, from French, from Latin

perimeter (puh-rim-uh-tuh)
noun **1** the outside edge of a shape or area: *the **perimeter** of a football field* (***boundary***, ***limit***, ***outskirts***, ***periphery***, ***rim***)
2 the length of this edge
Word history: Latin, from Greek

perimeter / parameter
Don't confuse **perimeter** with **parameter**. The **parameters** of something are the limits that restrict it:

I have to consider the parameters of your voice, like how high you can sing, before I write a song for you.

In maths and science, a **parameter** is a variable factor.

period
noun **1** any division or portion of time: *We will have a **period** of work and then a **period** of play.*
2 a particular division of time or history: *the colonial **period** in Australia*
3 the monthly flow of blood from the uterus of a girl or woman, or the time when this happens
4 → **full stop**
5 *Geology* the main division of a geological era, shown in the earth's crust by systems of rocks laid down during it
adjective **6** having to do with a particular period of history: ***period** costumes*
Word history: Middle English, from Latin, from Greek word meaning 'a going around', 'cycle', 'period'

periodic (pear-ree-od-ik)
adjective **1** marked by periods or rounds that come back again and again: ***periodic*** *droughts*
2 happening or appearing at regular intervals: ***periodic*** *check-ups at the dentist* (***intermittent***, ***recurrent***, ***repeated***)
3 ceasing and then beginning again, etc.: ***periodic*** *pains*

Word use: You can also use **periodical**.
Word history: Latin, from Greek

periodical
adjective **1** happening or appearing at regular intervals: ***periodical*** *shifts of mood*
noun **2** a magazine that comes out at regular intervals

Word use: You can also use **periodic** for definition 1.
Word building: **periodically** *adverb*

periodic table
noun Chemistry a table in which the chemical elements are arranged in order of their atomic numbers and in rows and columns so that elements with similar chemical properties are in the same column

peripheral (puh-rif-uh-ruhl)
adjective **1** not central in importance (***incidental***, ***marginal***, ***minor***, ***secondary***, ***unimportant***)
noun **2** a device attached to a computer, which transfers information into and out of it, such as a monitor, a printer or a modem

Word use: You can also use **peripheral device** for definition 2.

periphery (puh-rif-uh-ree)
noun the outside edge of an area or thing: *The chairs were arranged around the* ***periphery*** *of the room.* (***boundary***, ***limit***, ***outskirts***, ***perimeter***, ***rim***)

Word history: Late Latin, from Greek

periphrasis (puh-rif-ruh-suhs)
noun **1** a roundabout way of speaking
2 a roundabout expression

Noun forms: The plural is **periphrases** (puh-rif-ruh-seez).
Word use: You can also use **periphrase** (pe-ree-frayz).
Word building: **periphrastic** *adjective*
Word history: Latin, from Greek

periscope
noun an instrument made of a tube with an arrangement of mirrors, used to see something from a position below or behind it: *the* ***periscope*** *of a submarine*

Word history: from Greek word meaning 'look around'

perish
verb **1** to die: *The explorers* ***perished*** *in the desert.* (***expire***, ***pass away***)
2 to rot or decay: *Rubber* ***perishes***. (***decompose***, ***deteriorate***, ***fester***, ***putrefy***)

Word use: The opposite of definition 1 is **survive**.
Word history: Middle English, from Old French, from Latin word meaning 'pass away', 'perish'

perishable (pe-rish-uh-buhl)
adjective **1** likely to decay or perish
noun **2** **perishables**, perishable things, especially food: *Put the* ***perishables*** *straight into the fridge.*

peritoneum (pe-ruh-tuh-nee-uhm)
noun the membrane lining the abdominal cavity

Noun forms: The plural is **peritonea** (pe-ruh-tuh-nee-uh).
Word use: You can also use **peritonaeum**.
Word building: **peritoneal** *adjective*
Word history: Late Latin, from Greek word meaning 'stretched over'

periwinkle[1]
noun **1** any of various saltwater sea-snails, especially used for food
2 the shell of any of various other small creatures with shells made up of a single piece

Word history: Old English *pīnewincle*

periwinkle[2]
noun a plant with pink or blue flowers

Word history: Old English *perwince*, from Latin

perjure (per-juh)
verb to make guilty of swearing falsely or of intentionally making a false statement under oath: *to* ***perjure*** *yourself*

Word building: **perjurer** *noun*
Word history: late Middle English, from Latin

perjury
noun the crime of telling a lie while under an oath: *The witness in the court case committed* ***perjury***.

Word history: Middle English, from Anglo-French, from Latin

perk[1]
phrase **perk up**, to make or become lively, strong or active, especially after sadness or sickness

Word history: Middle English

perk[2]
noun Colloquial any special thing that you get because of your job or because you belong to a particular group: *One of the* ***perks*** *of working in town is that you can go shopping at lunch time. | This car is one of the* ***perks*** *of my new job.*

Word use: This word is often used in the phrase **lurks and perks**. Look up **lurk**.
Word history: abbreviation and respelling of *perquisite* an extra fee over and above normal salary, etc.

perl
noun Computers a high-level programming language, originally designed for text processing but now used for web programming

Word history: *p(ractical) e(xtraction and) r(eport) l(anguage)*

permaculture
noun a system, usually applied to farming, housing, transport, etc., made up of elements which are economically viable and environmentally sound, thus making the whole system sustainable in the long term

Word history: *perma(nent)* + *culture*

permanent
adjective lasting for a very long time or forever: *a* ***permanent*** *job |* ***permanent*** *snow on a mountain top* (***eternal***, ***everlasting***, ***immortal***, ***perennial***, ***perpetual***)

Word use: The opposite is **temporary**.
Word building: **permanence** *noun* **permanency** *noun* **permanently** *adverb*
Word history: Middle English, from Latin word meaning 'remaining throughout'

permeable
adjective able to be passed through, especially by liquids: *a **permeable** membrane*

Word use: The opposite of this is **impermeable**.

permeate (per-mee-ayt)
verb to pass or spread through: *A strange smell **permeated** the room.*

Word building: **permeation** *noun*
Word history: from Latin word meaning 'passed through'

permissible
adjective allowed or permitted: *Going into the city was **permissible** as long as they were back before dark.*

permissible / permissive
Don't confuse **permissible** with **permissive**. Someone is **permissive** if they permit lots of things that others wouldn't.

permission
noun **1** the act of permitting or allowing someone to do something (***approval***, ***clearance***, ***consent***, ***dispensation***, ***leave***)
2 *Computers* a particular level of access to computing resources

Word history: Middle English, from Latin

permissive
adjective allowing freedom, especially in sexual or moral matters: *a **permissive** society* (***broad-minded***, ***indulgent***, ***liberal***, ***tolerant***)

Word building: **permissiveness** *noun*

permit (puh-mit)
verb **1** to allow (***authorise***, ***license***, ***suffer***, ***tolerate***)
2 to give the chance for: *This oven door **permits** heat to escape.*
noun (per-mit) **3** an official certificate that gives permission (***licence***, ***warrant***)

Verb forms: I **permitted**, I have **permitted**, I am **permitting**
Word history: late Middle English, from Latin word meaning 'to let go through'

permutation
noun the changing of the order of the elements in a group or set: *ACB and BAC are some of the **permutations** of ABC.*

pernicious (puh-nish-uhs)
adjective **1** very hurtful or destructive: ***pernicious** teachings*
2 deadly or fatal: *a **pernicious** disease*
3 evil or wicked: ***pernicious** behaviour*

Word history: Latin

peroxide (puh-rok-suyd)
noun **1** *Chemistry*
a an oxide derived from hydrogen peroxide
b hydrogen peroxide, used as a bleach
adjective **2** of the hair, bleached by peroxide: *She's a **peroxide** blonde.*
verb **3** to use peroxide as a bleach: *to **peroxide** your hair*

perpendicular (per-puhn-dik-yuh-luh)
adjective **1** upright or vertical: *a **perpendicular** post*
2 meeting a line or surface at right angles

Word use: The opposite of definition 1 is **horizontal**. The opposite of definition 2 is **parallel**.
Word history: Latin

perpetrate (per-puh-trayt)
verb to do or carry out: *to **perpetrate** a crime*

Word building: **perpetration** *noun* **perpetrator** *noun*
Word history: Latin

perpetual (puh-pe-chooh-uhl)
adjective **1** lasting for ever (***eternal***, ***everlasting***, ***immortal***, ***perennial***, ***permanent***)
2 continuing without a break: *There has been a **perpetual** stream of visitors.*

Word history: Middle English, from Latin

perpetuate (puh-pe-chooh-ayt)
verb to make last for a very long time: *to **perpetuate** a rumour*

perpetuity (per-puh-tyooh-uh-tee)
noun **1** endless or long life or existence without fixed limit
2 something that is lasting
3 an annuity paid for life
phrase **4 in perpetuity**, forever

Noun forms: The plural is **perpetuities**.
Word history: Middle English, from French, from Latin

perplex (per-pleks)
verb to make puzzled: *This question **perplexes** me.* (***baffle***, ***bewilder***, ***confuse***, ***mystify***, ***puzzle***)

Word building: **perplexed** *adjective* **perplexing** *adjective* **perplexity** *noun*
Word history: Middle English, from Latin word meaning 'involved'

per se (per say)
adverb by or in itself: *It's not her lateness **per se** that annoys us. She is rude as well.*

Word history: Latin

persecute (per-suh-kyooht)
verb **1** to constantly treat unfairly or cruelly
2 to harm or punish for having certain ideas or religious beliefs (***oppress***, ***repress***, ***suppress***)

Word building: **persecution** *noun* **persecutor** *noun*

persecute / prosecute
Don't confuse **persecute** with **prosecute**. You **prosecute** someone if you take legal action against them.

persevere
verb to continue in spite of difficulty: *I am tired but I will **persevere** with my work.* (***carry on***, ***persist***)

Word building: **perseverance** *noun*
Word history: Middle English, from French, from Latin word meaning 'continue steadfastly'

Persian cat (per-zhuhn kat)
noun a variety of domestic cat with long, silky hair and a bushy tail, probably coming originally from Persia

persimmon (per-suh-muhn)
noun a red or orange fleshy fruit

persist
verb **1** to continue doing something, often in spite of difficulty: *He* ***persisted*** *with his questions until he got an answer.* (***carry on***, ***persevere***)
2 to go on and on: *Her toothache* ***persisted*** *for hours.* (***hang in***, ***last the distance***, ***persevere***, ***persist***, ***stick to your guns***)
Word building: **persistence** *noun* **persistent** *adjective*
Word history: from Latin word meaning 'to continue steadfastly'

person
noun **1** a human being
2 a type of verb or pronoun form that shows the difference between the speaker, the person spoken to, and anyone or anything spoken about
phrase **3 in person**, with the person actually present: *He brought the letter* ***in person***.
Word history: Middle English, from Old French, from Latin word meaning 'actor's mask', 'character acted', 'personage', 'being'

person in grammar

Person is a term we use in grammar to distinguish three kinds of pronouns. The **first person** is the person speaking (usually *I* or *we*). The **second person** is the person spoken to (*you*). The **third person** is the person or thing spoken about (*he*, *she*, *it*, *they*, or *him*, *her*, *it*, *them*):

I'll tell	*you about*	*her.*
(first person)	(second person)	(third person)

Some verbs also have a special ending for the third person. The third person singular of verbs in the present tense usually ends with -s or -es. For example:

I walk but *she walks*.
I finish but *it finishes*.

-person

This ending doesn't show the sex of whoever it refers to, so it can be useful as a way of avoiding sexist language. *Chairperson* can be used instead of *chairman* or *chairwoman*, either of which may draw attention to the sex of the person referred to. Other cases like this in which a word with -person may be used are *draftsperson*, *spokesperson* and *tradesperson*.

But as things are, -person words mostly get used when a woman is being mentioned (only rarely do they refer to a man). So the -person ending comes to mean 'female' for many people, and doesn't really beat the sexist problem.

It is perhaps better to find some other kind of non-sexist word. For some alternatives, look up **-man** and **non-sexist language**.

personable (per-suhn-uh-buhl)
adjective having a pleasing personal appearance and manner (***agreeable***, ***attractive***, ***likable***, ***presentable***)

personage (per-suhn-ij)
noun a person, especially someone important
Word history: late Middle English, from Old French

personal
adjective **1** private or having to do with a particular person: *a* ***personal*** *matter* | ***personal*** *attention*
2 a having to do with the physical presence or involvement of a person: *a* ***personal*** *appearance at the concert* | ***personal*** *service*
b having to do with what serves the advantage of a particular person: ***personal*** *gain*
3 directed to a particular person in a rude way: *You shouldn't make* ***personal*** *remarks about someone's appearance.*
Word building: **personally** *adverb*
Word history: Middle English, from Latin

personal / personnel

Don't confuse **personal** with **personnel**. The **personnel** of a business or an institution are the people employed there.

personal computer
noun a small computer that can be placed on a desk or table and is meant for use in the home or by small businesses

personal digital assistant
noun a handheld computer which stores a diary, organiser, address book, calendar, etc.
Word use: The abbreviation is **PDA**.

personalise (per-suhn-uh-luyz)
verb **1** to make personal
2 to mark to show the name or initials of the owner: *to* ***personalise*** *a towel*
Word use: You can also use **personalize**.

personality
noun **1** the qualities of character that make someone an individual: *My baby already has a* ***personality***.
2 strong or lively character: *She has plenty of* ***personality***.
3 someone who is well-known: *a television* ***personality*** (***celebrity***)
Noun forms: The plural is **personalities**.

personal organiser
noun **1** a folder or wallet containing a diary, address book, etc.
2 a small electronic device used to record appointments, store telephone numbers, etc.
3 a computer program comprising features such as a diary, address book, etc.
Word use: You can also use **personal organizer**.

personal pronoun
noun a pronoun used to substitute for any noun that refers to a person or thing already mentioned

Look up **pronouns: personal pronouns**.

personification (puh-son-uh-fuh-kay-shuhn)
noun **1** the treating of objects or ideas as if they were people, especially as a special effect in your writing, as in *The book was begging to be opened.*
2 in art, etc., the representation of a thing or an idea in the form of a person
3 a person or thing representing a quality or something like this: *Hamlet is the* ***personification*** *of unhappiness.*
4 an imaginary person or creature thought to represent a thing or an idea: *A man with horns and a tail is the popular* ***personification*** *of the Devil.*

personify
verb **1** to give a human nature or form to: *Some stories* ***personify*** *animals by making them talk.*
2 to be a perfect example of: *She* ***personifies*** *beauty.*

Verb forms: it **personified**, it has **personified**, it is **personifying**

personnel (per-suh-nel)
noun the group of people working for a particular organisation

Word history: French, noun use of adjective

perspective
noun **1** the appearance of distance as well as height and width, produced on a flat surface, such as in a painting: *The artist has achieved* ***perspective*** *in painting that row of trees.*
2 a mental point of view: *She has a new* ***perspective*** *on this problem.*
phrase **3 in perspective,** with a proper balance

Word history: Middle English, from Medieval Latin word meaning 'science of optics', from Latin word meaning 'see through'

perspective / prospective

Don't confuse **perspective** with **prospective.** Something that is **prospective** is likely to happen. You can look towards it as a **prospect:**

Your prospective increase in income will mean that you can buy a car.

A **prospective** student is someone who intends to become a student.

perspex
noun a clear plastic resin, which is soft and easily moved when heated, used instead of glass in certain cases, as in framing pictures, etc.

Word history: Trademark

perspicacious (per-spuh-kay-shuhs)
adjective having keen mental powers of understanding and recognition: *What a* ***perspicacious*** *comment.* (***acute, discerning, perceptive, shrewd***)

Word building: **perspicacity** *noun*
Word history: *perspicaci(ty)* + *-ous*

perspire
verb to get rid of a salty liquid through the pores of your skin (***sweat***)

Word building: **perspiration** *noun*
Word history: from Latin word meaning 'breathe through'

persuade (puh-swayd)
verb to cause to do or believe something by advice, argument or influence: *He* ***persuaded*** *her to come.* | *She* ***persuaded*** *him that he was wrong.* (***coax, convince, induce, inveigle, prevail upon, talk into***)

Word building: **persuasive** *adjective*
Word history: Latin

persuasion (puh-sway-zhuhn)
noun **1** the act or power of persuading
2 a belief, especially religious: *people of the Christian* ***persuasion***

Word history: Middle English, from Latin

pert
adjective **1** bold or impudent (***bold, brazen, forward, fresh, saucy***)
2 attractive in a lively way: *a* ***pert*** *hat*

Word history: Middle English, from Old French

pertain (puh-tayn)
verb **1** to have reference or to relate: *documents* ***pertaining*** *to the case*
2 to be appropriate: *comments* ***pertaining*** *to the argument*

Word history: Middle English, from Old French, from Latin word meaning 'extend', 'reach', 'relate'

pertinacious (per-tuh-nay-shuhs)
adjective **1** clinging faithfully to a purpose, course of action, or opinion
2 continued and often repeated: ***pertinacious*** *efforts*

Word building: **pertinacity** *noun*
Word history: Latin

pertinent (per-tuh-nuhnt)
adjective having to do with the matter being discussed or thought about: *a* ***pertinent*** *comment* (***apposite, apt, relevant, to the point***)

Word use: The opposite of this is **irrelevant.**
Word building: **pertinence** *noun*
Word history: Middle English, from Latin

perturb
verb to disturb or worry greatly

Word building: **perturbation** *noun*
Word history: Middle English, from Latin *perturbāre*

perusal (puh-rooh-zuhl)
noun **1** a reading: *She gave the document a quick* ***perusal.***
2 the act of perusing

peruse (puh-roohz)
verb **1** to read through, especially with thoroughness or care: *to* ***peruse*** *a report*
2 to read in a leisurely way, without much attention to detail: *to* ***peruse*** *the Sunday papers*

Word building: **perusal** *noun*
Word history: late Middle English

pervade (puh-vayd)
verb **1** to spread its presence, activities, influence, etc., throughout: *Spring* ***pervaded*** *the air.*
2 to go, pass or spread through

Word building: **pervasion** *noun*
pervasive *adjective*
Word history: Latin

perverse
adjective deliberately going against what is expected or wanted: *a **perverse** answer* | *a **perverse** mood* (***contrary, pig-headed, unobliging***)

Word building: **perversely** *adverb* **perverseness** *noun* **perversity** *noun*
Word history: Middle English, from Latin word meaning 'turned the wrong way', 'awry'

perversion (puh-ver-zhuhn)
noun **1** the act of perverting or the state of being perverted
2 a perverted or abnormal form of something: *a **perversion** of justice*
3 a type of behaviour, usually sexual, which is not generally considered normal or acceptable

pervert (puh-vert)
verb **1** to turn away from what is right, either in behaviour or in beliefs
noun (per-vert) **2** someone who has unusual or unpleasant sexual habits

Word building: **perverted** *adjective*
Word history: Middle English, from Latin

pessary (pes-uh-ree)
noun **1** *Medicine* a device worn in the vagina to treat displacement of the uterus or stop conception from taking place
2 a vaginal tablet placed so as to kill infection or prevent conception

Word history: Middle English, from Latin, from Greek word originally meaning 'oval stone used in a game'

pessimism
noun the habit of expecting that things will turn out badly

Word use: The opposite is **optimism**.
Word building: **pessimistic** *adjective*
Word history: Latin

pessimist
noun someone who looks on the gloomy side of things

pest
noun someone or something that is annoying or harmful

Word history: from Latin word meaning 'plague', 'disease'

pester
verb to annoy continually

Word history: perhaps from Old French word meaning 'hobble (a horse)'

pesticide
noun a chemical for killing pests, such as insects

pestilence (pes-tuh-luhns)
noun **1** a deadly disease spread from person to person
2 something that produces or tends to produce such a disease

pestilent (pes-tuh-luhnt)
adjective **1** infectious: *a **pestilent** disease*
2 deadly, or poisonous
3 troublesome or annoying

Word history: Middle English, from Latin

pestle (pes-uhl)
noun a club-shaped tool for grinding substances in a mortar

Word history: Middle English, from Old French, from Latin word meaning 'pounded'

pesto
noun a thick green sauce made of basil, pine nuts, garlic, parmesan cheese and oil, used in Italian cooking

Word history: Italian word meaning 'paste'

pet[1]
noun **1** an animal that is kept because it is loved rather than because it is useful
2 a person who is given special attention: *teacher's **pet***
verb **3** to treat in a special way, giving kisses and loving pats to, as if to a pet

Verb forms: I **petted**, I have **petted**, I am **petting**
Word history: perhaps from *pet lamb* hand reared lamb, itself perhaps a shortened variant of *petty lamb* little lamb, where *petty* marks affection

pet[2]
noun a fit of crossness: *to be in a **pet***

petal
noun any of the leaf-like parts of a flower which are usually of a colour different to green

Word history: Neo-Latin word meaning 'petal', from Greek word meaning 'leaf'

peter (pee-tuh)
phrase **peter out**, to gradually become smaller or weaker and then disappear or cease (***abate, decrease, diminish, moderate, wane***)

petite (puh-teet)
adjective small and slim: *a **petite** woman* (***dainty, delicate, elfin, slight***)

Word history: French

petition
noun a formal request, especially to someone or a group in power: *to sign a **petition** to the local council asking for more parks*

Word building: **petition** *verb* **petitioner** *noun*
Word history: Middle English, from Latin

petrel (pet-ruhl)
noun **1** a type of sea-bird, for example, the mutton-bird
2 → **storm-petrel**

Word history: French

> **petrel / petrol**
> Don't confuse **petrel** with **petrol**, which is a liquid made from petroleum.

Petri dish (pee-tree dish)
noun a shallow, round, glass dish, used especially for growing bacteria, etc.

Word history: named after JR *Petri*, died 1921, German biologist

petrify
verb **1** to turn into stone or something like stone: *Millions of years have **petrified** the tree trunk.* (***fossilise, freeze, set, solidify, stiffen***)
2 to make stiff or unable to move with fear (***alarm, frighten, scare, shock, terrify***)

Verb forms: it **petrified**, it has **petrified**, it is **petrifying**
Word history: French, from Latin word meaning 'rock', 'stone', from Greek

petrol
noun a liquid made from petroleum, used widely as a fuel in engines

Word history: French, from Medieval Latin word meaning 'petroleum'

petroleum
noun an oily liquid, usually obtained by drilling under the ground and used to make petrol or other fuels

Word history: from Medieval Latin word meaning 'rock oil'

petticoat
noun a light, skirt-like undergarment worn by women and girls (***slip***)

Word history: Middle English

petty
adjective **1** of little importance: ***petty** details* (***insignificant***, ***minor***, ***secondary***, ***slight***, ***trifling***, ***trivial***)
2 concerned with unimportant things or showing narrow ideas and interests: *a **petty** mind*

Adjective forms: **pettier**, **pettiest**
Word building: **pettily** *adverb* **pettiness** *noun*
Word history: Middle English, from Old French

petty cash
noun a small store of money kept to meet the day-to-day expenses of an office, etc.

petulant (<u>pech</u>-uh-luhnt)
adjective showing or feeling impatient annoyance, especially over something unimportant: *a **petulant** toss of the head* (***fretful***, ***peevish***, ***querulous***, ***sulky***, ***sullen***)

Word building: **petulance** *noun* **petulantly** *adverb*
Word history: from Latin word meaning 'forward', 'pert', 'wanton'

petunia (puh-<u>tyooh</u>-nee-uh)
noun a kind of plant with funnel-shaped flowers of different colours

Word history: Neo-Latin, from Guarani word meaning 'tobacco'

pew
noun a long, bench-like seat in a church

Word history: Middle English, from Old French word meaning 'balcony', from Latin word meaning 'elevated place', 'balcony'

pewter
noun a mixture of metals, including tin, used for making dishes, mugs, etc.

Word history: Middle English, from Old French

pH
noun a measure of the acidity or alkalinity of soil, water, etc., running from 1 (extreme acidity) to 14 (extreme alkalinity)

phaeton (<u>fay</u>-tuhn)
noun a light, four-wheeled carriage, usually having two seats facing forward

Word history: named after *Phaeton*, who, in classical mythology, was the son of Helios, the sun-god. For one day he was allowed to drive his father's chariot, but drove too near the earth, and had Zeus not killed him with a thunderbolt, would have set the world on fire.

phalanger (fuh-<u>lan</u>-juh)
noun a group of tree-living marsupials of Australia, most having tails which can wrap around branches, and including brush-tailed possums and cuscuses

Word history: Neo-Latin, from Greek word meaning 'bone of finger or toe'; with reference to the webbed digits of the hind feet

phallus (<u>fal</u>-uhs)
noun an image of the erect male penis, standing for the reproductive power of nature in some religious systems

Noun forms: The plural is **phalluses**.
Word building: **phallic** *adjective*
Word history: Latin, from Greek

phantom
noun **1** an image appearing in a dream or in the mind only
2 a ghost or ghostly appearance (***apparition***, ***spectre***, ***spook***, ***wraith***)

Word building: **phantasmal** *adjective*
Word history: Middle English, from Old French, from Late Latin *phantasm*

Pharaoh (<u>fair</u>-roh)
noun the title of the ancient Egyptian kings

Word building: **Pharaonic** *adjective*
Word history: Old English *Pharaon*, from Latin, from Greek, from Hebrew, from Egyptian word meaning 'great house'

pharisee (<u>fa</u>-ruh-see)
noun a person who strictly observes the outer forms and ceremonies of religion without following its spirit

Word building: **pharisaism** *noun* **pharisaic** *adjective*
Word history: from the *Pharisees*, members of an ancient Jewish sect which observed strictly religious traditions and the written law

pharmaceutical (fah-muh-<u>syooh</u>-tik-uhl)
adjective having to do with the preparing and dispensing of drugs use in medicine

Word use: You can also use **pharmaceutic**.
Word history: Latin, from Greek

pharmacology (fah-muh-<u>kol</u>-uh-jee)
noun the science of drugs, their properties, uses and effects

Word building: **pharmacological** *adjective* **pharmacologist** *noun*
Word history: Neo-Latin, from Greek

pharmacy
noun **1** the preparing and giving out of drugs used in medicine: *She is studying **pharmacy**.*
2 a chemist's shop

Noun forms: The plural is **pharmacies**.
Word building: **pharmacist** *noun*
Word history: Late Latin, from Greek word meaning 'the practice of a druggist'

pharynx (<u>fa</u>-ringks)
noun the tube which connects your mouth and nose passages with your throat

Noun forms: The plural is **pharynges** (fuh-<u>rin</u>-jees) or **pharynxes**.
Word history: Neo-Latin, from Greek word meaning 'throat'

phase
noun **1** a stage of change or development: *the **phase** of childhood*
phrase **2 phase in**, to introduce gradually so as to fit into a system, etc.: *to **phase in** wearing hats to school*
3 phase out, to take out gradually from a system or way of doing things: *to **phase out** school uniforms*

pheasant (fez-uhnt)
noun a kind of large, long-tailed bird, often eaten as food

Word history: Middle English, from Anglo-French, variant of Old French, from Provençal, from Latin, from Greek word meaning 'Phasian (bird)'

phenomenal (fuh-nom-uh-nuhl)
adjective extraordinary: *a **phenomenal** time for swimming the 100 metres freestyle* (***astonishing***, ***extraordinary***, ***fabulous***, ***marvellous***, ***wonderful***)

phenomenon (fuh-nom-uh-nuhn)
noun **1** anything which is seen or able to be seen: *The growth of new leaves in spring is a **phenomenon** of nature.*
2 something or someone that is beyond the ordinary

Noun forms: The plural is **phenomena**.
Word history: Late Latin, from Greek word meaning '(that which is) appearing'

phial (fuy-uhl)
noun a small glass container for liquids: *a **phial** of medicine*

Word use: You can also use **vial**.
Word history: Middle English, from Old French, from Late Latin, from Greek word meaning 'saucer-like drinking vessel'

philander (fuh-lan-duh)
verb to carry on flirtations, usually used about a man

Word building: **philanderer** *noun*
Word history: from Greek word meaning 'man-loving (person)', later used in fiction as proper name, given to a lover

philanthropy (fuh-lan-thruh-pee)
noun **1** love of humankind, especially shown in deeds of giving to charity, etc.
2 an action or work based on philanthropy

Noun forms: The plural is **philanthropies**.
Word building: **philanthropist** *noun* **philanthropic** *adjective*
Word history: Late Latin, from Greek

philately (fuh-lat-uh-lee)
noun the collecting and studying of postage stamps

Word building: **philatelic** *adjective* **philatelist** *noun*
Word history: French

philharmonic
adjective fond of music

Word use: This is used especially in the names of musical societies, choirs or orchestras.
Word history: French

philistine (fil-uh-stuyn)
noun someone who doesn't like beautiful things such as paintings, sculpture or music, and is proud to be that way

Word building: **philistine** *adjective* **philistinism** *noun*
Word history: named after a native or inhabitant of *Philistia*, an ancient country on the east coast of the Mediterranean; Middle English, from Late Latin, from Late Greek, from Hebrew

philology (fuh-lol-uh-jee)
noun **1** the study of written records
2 linguistics

Word building: **philologist** *noun* **philologic** *adjective*
Word history: Middle English, from Latin, from Greek word meaning 'love of learning and literature'

philosophical (fil-uh-sof-i-kuhl)
adjective **1** having to do with philosophy
2 rationally or sensibly calm in trying circumstances: *a **philosophical** acceptance of his fate*

philosophy (fuh-los-uh-fee)
noun **1** the search for knowledge and wisdom and the answers to questions such as 'Why do I exist?' and 'What is the purpose of life?'
2 a system of rules or principles by which you live: *a **philosophy** of life*

Noun forms: The plural is **philosophies**.
Word building: **philosopher** *noun* **philosophise** *verb*
Word history: Middle English, from Latin, from Greek word literally meaning 'love of wisdom'

phishing (fish-ing)
noun a form of internet fraud in which an email purporting to be from a legitimate sender, such as a bank, etc., encourages the recipient to provide personal information, passwords, etc.

Word building: **phisher** *noun*
Word history: This word was coined to sound like the word *fishing* but is spelt with an initial *ph* to stand for *p(assword) h(arvesting)*, because the aim of this form of fraud is to collect people's passwords and other personal information in order to gain access to their accounts.

phlegm (flem)
noun Physiology the thick mucus produced in the breathing passages and discharged by coughing, etc., especially during a cold

Word history: Middle English, from Old French, from Late Latin, from Greek

phlegmatic (fleg-mat-ik)
adjective calm and even-tempered

Word history: Late Latin, from Greek

phobia (foh-bee-uh)
noun an overpowering fear: *a **phobia** about spiders* (***complex***, ***fetish***, ***hang-up***, ***obsession***)

Word use: This word is often joined with another word part to mean 'fear of a particular thing', as in *claustrophobia* which means 'fear of being shut in a small space'.
Word building: **phobic** *adjective*
Word history: independent use of *-phobia*, normally a noun ending

phoenix (fee-niks)
noun a mythical bird of great beauty, said to have burnt itself on a funeral pyre, and to have risen afresh from its ashes to live again

Word use: You can also use **Phoenix**.
Word history: Middle English and Old English *fēnix*, from Medieval Latin, from Greek

phone
noun → **telephone**

Word building: **phone** *verb*
Word history: abbreviation

phonetic (fuh-net-ik)
adjective having to do with speech sounds and the way they are produced

phonetics
noun the study of the sounds used in speaking

phoney
adjective Colloquial false or not genuine: *a **phoney** $20 note* (***bogus**, **counterfeit**, **fake**, **sham***)

Word use: The opposite of this is **authentic** or **genuine**. | You can also use **phony**.
Word building: **phoney** *noun*
Word history: originally US slang; origin unknown

phonics (fon-iks)
noun a method of teaching reading, pronunciation and spelling based upon the phonetic interpretation of ordinary spelling

phosphate (fos-fayt)
noun Chemistry a compound containing phosphorus, and found in most fertilisers

phosphorescence (fos-fuh-res-uhns)
noun the property and appearance of being luminous at temperatures below white heat, as from slow oxidation, in the case of phosphorus, or after exposure to light or other radiation

phosphorescent (fos-fuh-res-uhnt)
adjective shining or giving out light without getting hot

Word building: **phosphoresce** *verb*

phosphorus (fos-fuh-ruhs)
noun a chemical element which is used in making match heads, detergents and garden fertilisers

Word history: Neo-Latin, special use of Latin word meaning 'the morning star', from Greek word meaning 'light-bringer'

photo
noun → **photograph**

Noun forms: The plural is **photos**.

photochemical
adjective having to do with the action of light triggering a chemical process: ***photochemical** pollutant*

photocopier
noun a machine which makes copies of written or printed material by use of a special camera and light-sensitive paper

photocopy
noun an exact copy of a page of writing or pictures, made by a machine using a special camera and paper which reacts to light (***photostat***)

Noun forms: The plural is **photocopies**.
Word building: **photocopy** *verb* (**photocopied**, **photocopying**)

photoelectric cell
noun a device used for the detection and measuring of light

photogenic
adjective looking attractive in photographs

photograph
noun an image produced by the chemical effect of light on a light-sensitive surface such as film

Word use: The short form is **photo**.
Word building: **photograph** *verb* **photographic** *adjective*

photographic
adjective **1** having to do with photography
2 extremely realistic and detailed: ***photographic** memory*

Word use: You can also use **photographical**.
Word building: **photographically** *adverb*

photography (fuh-tog-ruh-fee)
noun the process or art of producing images of objects on sensitised surfaces by the chemical action of light or of other forms of radiant energy

Word building: **photographer** *noun*

photoshop
verb to alter a digital image on a computer: *We planned to **photoshop** the image by deleting the clouds from the sky.*

Verb forms: I **photoshopped**, I have **photoshopped**, I am **photoshopping**
Word building: **photoshopping** *noun*

photostat (foh-tuh-stat)
noun **1** a special camera for making exact copies of maps, drawings, pages of books, etc., which photographs directly as a positive on sensitised paper
2 a copy or photograph made with such a camera
verb **3** to make a photostat copy or copies
adjective **4** having to do with such a camera or copy

Word history: Trademark

photosynthesis (foh-toh-sin-thuh-suhs)
noun the synthesis of carbohydrates by plants from carbon dioxide and water in the presence of light and chlorophyll

Word history: Neo-Latin

phrase
noun **1** a small group of words that go together, usually without a complete verb
2 a group of musical notes which go together to form part of a tune
verb **3** to say or write in a particular way: *Could you **phrase** your question differently?*

Word history: from *phrases*, plural of Late Latin *phrasis*, from Greek word meaning 'speech', 'phraseology', 'expression'

A **phrase** is a group of words that acts together as a unit within a sentence:

standing on the corner
the old man
was singing
at the top of his voice

are all phrases.

As you can see from the examples above, phrases can't stand on their own and make a sensible message, except in answer to a question: *What are you doing? Standing on the corner!*

(continued)

phrase *(continued)*

Note that **phrases** like those above are all different from clauses in that they don't have both a *subject* and a *predicate*. Thus the following words make a clause:

He (subject) *was standing on the corner* (predicate).

phraseology (fray-zee-ol-uh-jee)
noun **1** the manner or style of verbal expression: *the **phraseology** of lawyers*
2 phrases or expressions: *medical **phraseology***

Word history: Neo-Latin, from Greek

phrenetic (fruh-net-ik)
adjective → **frenetic**

Word history: Middle English, from Old French, from Latin, from Late Greek

phrenology (fruh-nol-uh-jee)
noun the study of the shape of the skull to determine someone's mental powers

Word building: **phrenologist** *noun*
Word history: Greek

phylum (fuy-luhm)
noun one of the main groups into which biologists classify animals and plants, for instance the arthropods, molluscs, etc.: *All animals with backbones are in the same **phylum**.*

Noun forms: The plural is **phyla**.
Word history: Neo-Latin, from Greek word meaning 'race', 'tribe'

physical
adjective **1** having to do with the human body: ***physical** exercise*
2 having to do with the material things in the world rather than spiritual things (***actual***, ***concrete***, ***real***, ***tangible***)

Word building: **physically** *adverb*
Word history: Middle English, from Medieval Latin word meaning 'physic (medicine)'

physical change
noun any change in a body or substance which does not involve an alteration in its chemical composition

physician (fuh-zish-uhn)
noun a medical doctor, especially one who does not do surgery but works in diagnosis and treatment with drugs

Word history: Middle English, from Old French, from Medieval Latin word meaning 'physic (medicine)'

physics
noun the science of heat, light, electricity, magnetism, motion and other forms of matter and energy

Word building: **physicist** *noun*

physiognomy (fiz-ee-on-uh-mee)
noun **1** the facial features, especially as considered as a guide to character
2 the art of determining personal characteristics from the facial features or body form
3 the general or characteristic appearance of anything

Noun forms: The plural is **physiognomies**.
Word history: from Greek word meaning 'the judging of one's nature'

physiology (fiz-ee-ol-uh-jee)
noun the science dealing with the working of living organisms or their parts

Word building: **physiologist** *noun* **physiological** *adjective*
Word history: Latin, from Greek

physiotherapy (fiz-ee-oh-the-ruh-pee)
noun the treatment of disease and injuries by physical means such as massage, exercise, etc.

Word building: **physiotherapist** *noun*

physique (fuh-zeek)
noun the shape of someone's body: *a muscular **physique***

Word history: French, from Latin, from Greek

pi (puy)
noun the number you always get, 3.141 592+, when you divide the circumference of a circle by its diameter; expressed by the symbol π

Word history: Greek

pianissimo (pee-uh-nis-uh-moh)
adverb very softly

Word use: This is an instruction in music written as 'pp'. | The opposite is **fortissimo**.
Word history: Italian, superlative of *piano* softly

pianist (pee-uh-nuhst)
noun someone who plays the piano

piano[1]
noun a large musical instrument played by striking keys which are connected to hammers which then strike metal strings

Noun forms: The plural is **pianos**.
Word use: You can also use **pianoforte**.
Word history: Italian, abbreviation of *pianoforte* or *fortepiano*, from *piano* soft, and *forte* loud, because of the instrument's ability, unlike the harpsichord, to produce both loud and soft sounds

piano[2]
adverb softly: *This music should be played **piano**.*

Word use: This is an instruction in music written as 'p'. | The opposite is **forte**.
Word history: Italian, from a Latin word meaning 'plain'

piano accordion
noun a kind of accordion which has keys like a piano

pianoforte (pee-a-noh-for-tay, pee-ah-noh-for-tay)
noun → **piano**[1]

Word history: Italian

pianola (pee-uh-noh-luh)
noun → **player piano**

Word history: Trademark

picador (pik-uh-daw)
noun a bullfighter on horseback who opens the bullfight by enraging the bull by pricking it with sharp lances

Word use: Compare this with **matador**.
Word history: from Spanish word meaning 'prick', 'pierce'

piccolo (pik-uh-loh)
noun a small flute with a very high sound

Noun forms: The plural is **piccolos**.
Word history: Italian word meaning 'small'

pick[1]
verb **1** to choose or select
2 to take or gather
3 to use a sharp object to break open or dig into
noun **4** a choice or selection: *Take your **pick**.*
5 a plectrum, used to play a guitar or banjo
phrase **6 pick at**, to eat hardly any of: *to **pick at** your food*
7 pick holes in, to find fault with (***criticise***, ***pick to pieces***)
8 pick on, to annoy or criticise
9 pick out,
a to choose or select
b to see separately from surrounding things
c to make out: *Can you **pick out** the meaning of the code?*
d to take out by picking
10 pick to pieces, to criticise, especially in unimportant detail
11 pick up,
a to call for: *I'll **pick** you **up** at 8.30.*
b to learn easily, without special teaching: *Children **pick up** foreign languages quickly.* (***absorb***, ***assimilate***, ***digest***, ***take in***)
c to get well again (***brighten***, ***rally***, ***recover***, ***recuperate***)
12 the pick, the best one

Word building: **picker**
Word history: Middle English

pick[2]
noun a tool made up of a metal bar with sharp ends, fitted to a wooden handle and used for breaking up hard ground

Word use: You can also use **pickaxe**.
Word history: Old English *pīc*

picket
noun **1** a pointed, wooden fence post
2 a group of members of a trade union who stand guard outside their workplace during a strike, to stop people from going in to work
verb **3** to stand outside a workplace to protest about something, to prevent people from going in, or to persuade other workers to join a strike: *The trade unionists **picketed** the factory.*

Verb forms: I **picketed**, I have **picketed**, I am **picketing**
Word history: from French word meaning 'pointed stake', 'military picket'

pickle
noun **1** an onion, cucumber or other vegetable preserved in vinegar or salt water
2 an awkward situation: *to get yourself into a **pickle***
verb **3** to preserve in salt or vinegar

Word history: Middle English, from Middle Dutch or Middle Low German

pickpocket
noun **1** someone who steals things out of people's pockets or handbags
verb **2** to act as a pickpocket; steal from a pocket, handbag, etc., in a public place

picnic
noun **1** an outing to the beach, park, etc., during which you eat a meal in the open air
2 *Colloquial* an easy thing to do: *It's no **picnic** doing all your Christmas shopping in one day.*

Word building: **picnic** *verb* (**picnicked**, **picnicking**)

pictorial
adjective **1** having to do with a picture or pictures: ***pictorial** writing*
2 illustrated: *a **pictorial** history*
adjective **3** a newspaper or magazine made up mainly of pictures or photographs

picture
noun **1** a drawing, painting, photo or something similar
2 someone or something that looks very beautiful: *She looks a **picture** in her new dress.*
verb **3** to imagine: *I can't **picture** myself being old.*
phrase **4 get the picture** or **be in the picture**, to understand the situation
5 go to the pictures, to go to a showing of a film at a cinema: *Let's **go to the pictures** tonight.*
6 put in the picture, to inform

Word history: Middle French, from Latin

picture / pitcher
Don't confuse **picture** with **pitcher**, which is a large jug. It can also be the baseball player who throws the ball to the batter.

picturesque (pik-chuh-resk)
adjective pretty or charming: *a **picturesque** village*

Word history: *picture* + *-esque*

pidgin (pij-uhn)
noun a language based on a mixture of other languages and used by people who have no other language in common

Word history: perhaps the Chinese pronunciation of *business*

pidgin / pigeon
Don't confuse **pidgin** with **pigeon**, which is a plump, small-headed bird which is easily tamed.

pie
noun a pastry case filled with fruit, vegetables or meat, and baked in an oven

Word history: Middle English

piebald
adjective covered with patches of black and white or other colours: *a **piebald** horse*

Word use: Compare this with **skewbald**.
Word history: *pie* (look up **pied**) + *bald* white spot

piece
noun **1** a bit or part of something (***fragment***, ***particle***, ***section***, ***segment***)
2 a single or individual thing: *a **piece** of fruit*
verb **3** to fit or join: *to **piece** together a jigsaw*
phrase **4 a piece of cake**, *Colloquial* something that is very easy to achieve
5 a piece of your mind, outspoken criticism: *He deserves **a piece of your mind** after that disgraceful behaviour.*

6 go to pieces, to lose emotional or physical control of yourself
7 say your piece, to express an opinion
8 take a piece out of, to scold severely

Word history: Middle English *pece*, from Old French, from Late Latin *pecia*, a fragment, a piece of land, thought to be of Celtic origin

piece / peace
Don't confuse **piece** with **peace**, which is freedom from war, as in *a march for peace.*
It can also be calm or quiet, as in *peace of mind.*

pièce de résistance (pee-es duh ruh-zis-tuhns)
noun the most important or exciting thing in a series, especially a dish in a meal
Word history: French

piecemeal
adverb bit by bit or piece by piece
Word building: **piecemeal** *adjective*
Word history: Middle English

pie chart
noun → **pie graph**

pied (puyd)
adjective covered with different coloured patches
Word history: *pie* magpie (with reference to its black-and-white feathers)

pie graph
noun a graph in the shape of a circle which you divide into sectors according to the size of the categories you are comparing
Word use: You can also use **pie chart, circle graph** or **sector graph.**

pier (pear)
noun **1** a jetty built out into the water, that you can tie a boat to or fish from
2 one of the wooden or concrete supports which are driven into the ground to hold up a bridge (***pile***, ***pillar***, ***post***)
Word history: Middle English, from Medieval Latin

pier / peer
Don't confuse **pier** with **peer.**
To **peer** at something is to look at it closely in an effort to see.
Your **peers** are your equals, in age or rank.

pierce
verb to go into or through sharply: *The needle* ***pierced*** *her finger. | Her screams* ***pierced*** *the night.*
Word history: Middle English, from Old French, from Latin word meaning 'pierced'

piercing
adjective loud and sharp: ***piercing*** *screams*

piety (puy-uh-tee)
noun deep honour and respect for religion
Word use: The opposite of this is **impiety.**
Word building: **pious** *adjective*
Word history: Middle English, from Latin word meaning 'duty'

pig
noun **1** a farm animal with a flat snout and curly tail, which is kept for its meat
2 *Colloquial* someone who is dirty, selfish or greedy (***hog***, ***swine***)
Word history: Old English *picg*

pigeon (pij-uhn)
noun a plump, small-headed bird which is easily tamed
Word history: Middle English, from Old French, from Late Latin word meaning 'pigeon'

pigeon / pidgin
Look up **pidgin / pigeon.**

pigeonhole
noun **1** a small compartment for papers in an old-fashioned desk
verb **2** to put away for future use or notice
3 to give a definite place to in some orderly system

pigeon-toed (pij-uhn-tohd)
adjective with the toes or feet turned inwards

piggery (pig-uh-ree)
noun a farm where pigs are kept
Noun forms: The plural is **piggeries.**

piggyback
noun a ride on the back or shoulders
Word building: **piggyback** *verb*

pig-headed
adjective stupidly stubborn or obstinate (***contrary***, ***inflexible***, ***perverse***)

piglet
noun a baby pig

pigment
noun **1** a coloured powder which can be mixed with water to make paint
2 the substance which gives animals and plants colour
Word building: **pigmentation** *noun*
Word history: Middle English, from Latin

pigmy (pig-mee)
noun → **pygmy**

pigsty (pig-stuy)
noun a pen with a shelter for pigs
Noun forms: The plural is **pigsties.**

pigtail
noun a plait or bunch of tied-up hair hanging from the side or back of your head

pike[1]
noun a large, fierce fish with a long, pointed snout, found in northern countries
Word history: Middle English, abbreviation of *pikefish*, so called from its pointed snout

pike[2]
noun **1** historically, a weapon with a long shaft and small metal head, used by foot soldiers
verb **2** to wound, or kill with a pike
Word history: French

pike[3]
phrase Australian Colloquial **1 pike on**, to let down or abandon: *Don't* ***pike on*** *me.*
2 pike out on, to opt out or go back on an arrangement: *He* ***piked out on*** *the deal.*

Word building: **piker** *noun*
Word history: Middle English *pyke*, meaning 'to depart' or 'to be off', referring to the fact that if you **pike on** or **pike out on** someone, you figuratively leave or abandon them at a time when they are relying on you

pikelet
noun a small, sweet pancake, often eaten with butter and jam

Pilates (puh-lah-teez)
noun a fitness regimen that introduces comprehensive stretching and strengthening movements into an exercise routine

Word use: You can also use **Pilates method.**
Word history: named after Joseph *Pilates*, who developed it during World War I, when he was a German national held in a British camp, to help rehabilitate injured soldiers. He believed that physical and mental health were linked, and recommended certain exercises to strengthen key muscle groups and improve overall wellbeing.

pilchard (pil-chuhd)
noun a small fish found in great numbers in shoals around the southern half of the Australian coast (***sardine***)

pile[1]
noun **1** a number of things heaped up in one place
2 a large amount or number: *I have a* ***pile*** *of homework.* (***collection***, ***heap***, ***mass***, ***stack***)
verb **3** to load or stack
phrase **4 pile up**, to heap up or accumulate (***amass***, ***collect***, ***gather***, ***stack up***, ***store***)

Word history: Middle English, from Old French, from Latin word meaning 'pillar', 'pier', 'mole'

pile[2]
noun a long, heavy beam driven into the ground to support a bridge or building (***pier***, ***pillar***, ***post***, ***upright***)

Word history: Middle English and Old English *pīl* shaft, stake, from Latin word meaning 'javelin'

pile[3]
noun the raised surface of carpet, towels, velvet and similar material

Word history: Middle English, from Latin word meaning 'hair'

piles
noun → **haemorrhoids**

Word history: Middle English

pilfer
verb to steal in small amounts: *to* ***pilfer*** *biscuits from the tin* (***filch***, ***nick***, ***pinch***, ***snitch***)

Word building: **pilferer** *noun*
Word history: apparently from Anglo-French or Old French word meaning 'pillage', 'rob'

pilgrim
noun someone who makes a long journey to visit a holy place

Word history: Middle English, from Anglo-French (unrecorded), from Medieval Latin word meaning 'pilgrim', Latin word meaning 'foreigner'

pilgrimage (pil-gruh-mij)
noun **1** journey made by a pilgrim
2 any long journey

pill
noun **1** a small, round solid containing medicine, to be swallowed whole (***capsule***, ***tablet***)
2 something unpleasant that has to be accepted or put up with: *a bitter* ***pill*** *to swallow*
3 *Colloquial* an unpleasant or uninteresting person: *I'm not talking to that little* ***pill!***
phrase **4 sugar the pill**, to make bearable some unpleasant experience
5 the pill, *Colloquial* oral contraceptive

Word history: late Middle English, probably from Middle Dutch or Middle Low German, from Latin word meaning 'ball'

pillage
verb to rob brutally and violently: *The enemy soldiers* ***pillaged*** *the city.* (***maraud***, ***plunder***, ***raid***, ***ransack***, ***ravage***)

Word building: **pillage** *noun*
Word history: Middle English, from Old French word meaning 'rob', 'plunder'

pillar
noun a column which supports part of a building

Word history: Middle English, from Old French, from Latin word meaning 'pillar', 'pile[1]'

pillion
noun the passenger seat behind the driver's seat on a motorcycle

Word building: **pillion** *adjective*
Word history: apparently from Gaelic word meaning 'cushion', from Latin word meaning 'skin', 'pelt'

pillory (pil-uh-ree)
noun **1** a wooden framework with holes for the head and hands, in which an offender was locked, and made to suffer public scorn
verb **2** to set in the pillory
3 to heap public scorn or abuse on

Noun forms: The plural is **pillories.**
Verb forms: they **pilloried**, they have **pilloried**, they are **pillorying**
Word history: Middle English, from Old French, from Provençal, perhaps from Medieval Latin word meaning 'court', literally 'mirror to the glory of God'

pillow
noun a soft cushion to rest your head on when you are in bed

Word history: Old English *pyle, pylu* from Latin

pilot
noun **1** someone who flies a plane
2 someone who steers a ship into or out of port
adjective **3** done as an experiment: *a* ***pilot*** *film for a new television series*
verb **4** to guide or steer

Word history: French, from Italian, from Medieval Greek word meaning 'rudder'

pimento (puh-men-toh)
noun the dried fruits of a West Indian tree, used as a spice

Noun forms: The plural is **pimentos.**
Word history: Spanish word meaning 'pepper', 'allspice', from Late Latin word meaning 'plant juice', 'pigment'

pimp (pimp)
noun **1** someone who finds customers for a prostitute or brothel (***pander***, ***procurer***)
2 someone who gives information about criminals to the police
verb **3** to procure or solicit
4 to inform: *He **pimped** on the gang.*

pimple
noun a pus-filled swelling, usually on the face

Word building: **pimply** *adjective*
Word history: Middle English

pin
noun **1** a thin piece of metal with a sharply pointed end, used to fasten things together
2 any type of fastener that looks or works like a pin: *Grandma broke her hip and had to have a **pin** put in it.*
verb **3** to fasten or hold securely in position: *to **pin** papers together | The fallen branch **pinned** him to the ground.*

Verb forms: I **pinned**, I have **pinned**, I am **pinning**
Word history: Middle English; Old English *pinn* peg

PIN
noun a sequence of numbers and/or letters used as part of an identification procedure in electronic banking, as with an automatic teller machine

Word use: You can also use **personal identification number** or **PIN number**.
Word history: an acronym for P(ersonal) I(dentification) N(umber)

pinafore
noun a dress with no sleeves and a low neck, worn over a blouse or jumper, often as a school uniform or apron

pinball
noun a game in which you pull levers and push buttons to shoot a ball up a sloping board and score points when the ball hits various objects on the board

pince-nez (pans-nay, pins-nay)
noun a pair of glasses which are kept in place by a spring which pinches your nose, instead of having the usual sort of frame which fits over your ears

Word history: from French word meaning 'pinch nose'

pincers
plural noun **1** a tool with a pair of hinged, pinching jaws, used for pulling nails out of wood
2 the pinching claws of crabs, lobsters, and some insects

Word history: Middle English, from Old French word meaning 'pinch'

pinch
verb **1** to press or squeeze tightly and painfully between two surfaces, such as your thumb and finger: *He **pinched** her arm.*
2 *Colloquial* to steal (***filch***, ***nick***, ***pilfer***, ***snitch***)
noun **3** a painful nip or squeeze
4 the very small amount that you can hold between your finger and thumb: *a **pinch** of salt* (***dash***, ***drop***, ***skerrick***, ***trace***)
phrase **5 at a pinch**, if absolutely necessary: *Eight people can fit into the car **at a pinch**.*

Word building: **pincher** *noun*
Word history: Middle English, from Old French, from Late Latin

pincushion
noun a small cushion in which pins can be stuck to keep them handy when sewing

pine[1]
noun an evergreen tree with needle-like leaves and cones instead of flowers

Word history: Middle English; Old English *pīn*, from Latin

pine[2]
verb **1** to have an intense longing, or to yearn: *to **pine** for home*
phrase **2 pine away**, to become sick from grief and longing (***droop***, ***languish***, ***waste away***)

Word history: Middle English; Old English *pīnian* to torture, from Latin word meaning 'punishment'

pineapple
noun a large, yellow, tropical fruit which is sweet and juicy inside and has a rough outer skin

pine nut
noun a small edible nut, found in the cone of some kinds of pine tree

ping[1] (ping)
verb **1** to produce a sharp, ringing, high-pitched sound like that of a bullet striking an object, or of a small bell
noun **2** a pinging sound

Word building: **pinger** *noun*
Word history: imitative

ping[2]
noun Computers a program used for testing if a particular IP address is accessible

Word building: **ping** *verb*
Word history: *p(acket) In(ternet) g(roper)*

ping-pong
noun a game rather like tennis but played indoors on a table, using small bats and a very light, hollow, plastic ball (***table tennis***)

Word history: Trademark; from *ping*[1], noun, on model of *ding-dong*, etc.

pinion[1]
noun a small, toothed wheel which locks together with a toothed bar or larger wheel, used in machinery

Word history: French word meaning 'pinion', from Old French word meaning 'battlement', from Latin word meaning 'pinnacle'

pinion[2]
noun **1** a bird's wing or feather
verb **2** to cut off part of a bird's wing to stop it flying away
3 to prevent escape by tying back the arms or hands

Word history: Middle English, from Old French word meaning 'feather', from Latin

pink[1]
adjective **1** of a pale, whitish-red colour
noun **2** a pink colour
phrase **3 in the pink**, feeling bright and healthy

pink[2]
verb to cut in a zigzag pattern

Word history: Middle English *pynke(n)* make points (marks) or holes (with a sharp instrument)

pinking shears
plural noun scissors with notched blades, used for giving a scalloped or notched edge to material to stop it fraying

pinnacle
noun **1** a high, pointed mountain peak, or a tall, pointed spire on the roof of a building
2 the highest point of anything (***apex***, ***crest***, ***peak***, ***summit***, ***top***)

Word history: Middle English, from Old French, from Late Latin word meaning 'pinnacle'

pinnate (pin-ayt, pin-uht)
adjective **1** looking like a feather
2 having parts arranged on each side of a common axis

Word building: **pinnately** *adverb* **pinnation** *noun*
Word history: from Latin word meaning 'feathered', 'pinnate'

pint (puynt)
noun a measure of liquid in the imperial system, equal to almost 600 millilitres

Word use: Look up **imperial system**.

pin-up
noun a picture of a favourite person, pinned or stuck up on a wall

pioneer
noun someone who first explores an area, going ahead of others and opening the way for them: ***pioneers*** *opening up the Australian bush* | *a* ***pioneer*** *of modern music*

Word building: **pioneer** *verb*
Word history: French word meaning 'pioneer', from Old French word meaning 'foot soldier'

pious (puy-uhs)
adjective deeply religious (***devout***, ***god-fearing***, ***holy***, ***reverent***)

Word building: **piety** *noun*
Word history: Latin

pip[1]
noun the small seed of an apple, orange or similar fruit

Word history: abbreviation of *pippin* seed

pip[2]
noun a short, high sound such as the ones used as time signals on the phone or on radio

Word history: Middle English, apparently from Middle Dutch, from Vulgar Latin, for Latin word meaning 'phlegm', 'pip'

pip[3]
verb Colloquial to beat narrowly in a race: *The favourite was* ***pipped*** *at the post.*

Verb forms: I **pipped**, I have **pipped**, I am **pipping**

pipe
noun **1** a hollow tube for carrying water, gas, etc.
2 a small bowl with a hollow tube or stem for smoking tobacco
3 a tube through which you can pump air to make musical notes, such as in an organ
4 *Computers* a keyboard symbol (|)
verb **5** to transport or carry using a pipe: *to* ***pipe*** *water from the dam to the house*
phrase **6 pipe down**, to keep quiet
7 pipe up, to start talking suddenly

Word history: Middle English and Old English *pīpe*, from Latin word meaning 'chirp'

pipedream
noun an impossible hope or fancy

pipeline
noun **1** a pipe for carrying gas, oil or water over a long distance
phrase **2 in the pipeline**, on the way, or in the process of being prepared

pipette (pi-pet)
noun a thin, glass tube for measuring and carrying liquids in small quantities

Word use: You can also use **pipet**.
Word history: from French word meaning 'pipe'

pipi (pi-pee)
noun a burrowing shellfish that can be eaten

Word history: Maori

piping
noun **1** a system of pipes such as for the plumbing of a house
2 the shrill sound made by birds
3 a thin strip of material for trimming the edges of cushions or clothes
phrase **4 piping hot**, very hot

pipsqueak
noun Colloquial someone thought to be small and unimportant

piquant (pee-kuhnt)
adjective **1** pleasantly sharp in taste (***pungent***, ***savoury***, ***spicy***, ***tasty***)
2 pleasantly sharp, interesting, attractive or stimulating

pique (peek)
verb **1** to annoy and upset: *Maria's refusal to see Evan* ***piqued*** *him.* (***goad***, ***irritate***, ***provoke***, ***vex***)
2 to excite or stimulate: *The large parcel* ***piqued*** *her curiosity.*
noun **3** anger, resentment or ill feeling over some slight offence or from hurt pride

Word history: from French word meaning 'prick', 'sting'

pique / peak / peek
Don't confuse **pique** with **peak** or **peek**.
A **peak** is the top of a mountain.
To **peek** is to snatch a quick look, often when you are not supposed to.

piranha (puh-rah-nuh)
noun a small South American fish which swims in schools that viciously attack animals, including people, and eat their flesh at great speed

Word history: Portuguese

pirate
noun **1** someone who attacks and robs ships at sea (***buccaneer***)
adjective **2** reproduced and published without permission from the copyright owner: *a **pirate** DVD | a **pirate** copy*
verb **3** to take and use without permission: *to **pirate** someone's ideas and pretend they are your own*

Word building: **piracy** *noun*
Word history: Middle English, from Latin, from Greek

pirouette (pi-rooh-et)
noun a quick turn in a dance, often on tiptoe

Word building: **pirouette** *verb*
Word history: from French word meaning 'top', 'whirl'

piscatorial (pis-kuh-taw-ree-uhl)
adjective having to do with fishing

Word history: Latin

pistachio (puh-stah-shee-oh)
noun the nut of the fruit of a small tree of southern Europe and western Asia, used for flavouring

Noun forms: The plural is **pistachios.**
Word history: Italian, from Latin, from Greek

pistil
noun the seed-bearing part of a flower

Word history: Neo-Latin word meaning 'pistil', from Latin word meaning 'pestle'

pistol
noun a gun with a short barrel that fits into a holster or pocket

Word history: French word meaning 'pistol', from German, from Czech

piston
noun a rod or disc inside a tube which is pumped up and down and is used in engines

Word history: French, from Italian word meaning 'pound', from Latin word meaning 'pounded'

pit[1]
noun **1** a large hole in the ground, such as a mine
2 a small hollow, such as a scar left on someone's face by acne
3 the space in front of and beneath the stage in a theatre, where the orchestra sits
4 an area beside a car racing track where the cars are repaired and filled with petrol
verb **5** to make pits or hollows in: *Acne can **pit** your face.*
6 to set against: *She **pitted** her wits against his strength.*

Verb forms: I **pitted,** I have **pitted,** I am **pitting**
Word building: **pitted** *adjective*
Word history: Middle English and Old English *pytt*, from Latin word meaning 'well', 'pit', 'shaft'

pit[2]
noun the stone of a fruit such as a peach or a date

Word building: **pit** *verb* (**pitted, pitting**)
Word history: from Dutch word meaning 'kernel'

pita (pit-uh)
noun a flat, round, usually leavened bread forming a pocket: *She filled her **pita** with lamb and salad.*

Word use: You can also use **pita bread** or **pitta.**

pitch[1]
verb **1** to set up: *to **pitch** a tent*
2 to throw (***chuck, fling, hurl, sling, toss***)
3 to make a sudden falling movement: *He tripped and **pitched** forward.*
4 to rise and fall, as a ship does
5 to set at a certain level of musical pitch: *She **pitched** her instrument too high.*
noun **6** a throw or toss
7 the quality of a musical note thought of in terms of its highness or lowness
8 the area for playing sport, particularly the area between the wickets in cricket
9 the degree of slope: *the steep **pitch** of the roof* (***gradient, incline, slant, tilt***)
phrase **10 pitch in,** *Colloquial*
a to join in
b to begin strongly
11 pitch into,
a to attack, using words or action
b to begin to do: *They **pitched into** the washing up straight after the meal.*

Word history: Middle English

pitch[2]
noun **1** a dark, sticky substance used for making paths, etc., derived from coal tar
2 any of certain bitumens
3 any of various resins

Word history: Old English *pic*, from Latin

pitchblende (pich-blend)
noun the main ore of uranium and radium

Word history: German

pitcher[1]
noun the baseball player who throws the ball to the batter

Word history: *pitch*[1], verb + *-er*

pitcher[2]
noun a large jug

Word history: Middle English, from Old French

pitcher / picture
Don't confuse **pitcher** with **picture,** which is a drawing, painting or photo.

pitchfork
noun a large fork used for lifting and tossing hay, etc.

piteous (pit-ee-uhs)
adjective arousing or deserving pity

Word building: **piteously** *adverb*

pitfall
noun an unexpected trap

pith
noun **1** any soft, spongy substance such as that between the skin and the flesh of an orange
2 the most important part

Word history: Middle English; Old English *pitha* pith

pithy (pith-ee)
adjective **1** full of strength, substance or meaning: *a **pithy** saying* (***succinct, terse, trenchant***)
2 of, like or filled with pith

Adjective forms: **pithier, pithiest**

pitiable
adjective **1** deserving pity
2 worthless

Word building: **pitiably** *adverb*

pitiful
adjective **1** causing or deserving pity (***miserable***, ***pathetic***, ***pitiable***, ***woeful***, ***wretched***)
2 unsuccessful or worthless: ***pitiful*** *efforts*

Word building: **pitifully** *adverb*

pittance
noun a very small amount of money

Word history: Middle English, from Old French

pituitary (puh-tyooh-uh-tree, puh-tyooh-uh-tuh-ree)
noun a small, oval endocrine gland at the base of the brain, which produces several hormones

Noun forms: The plural is **pituitaries**.
Word use: You can also use **pituitary gland**.
Word history: from Latin word meaning 'pertaining to', or 'secreting phlegm'

pity
noun **1** deep sympathy for the suffering or sorrow of other people (***compassion***)
2 a cause for sorrow: *It's a* ***pity*** *she can't come too.*

Word building: **pity** *verb* (**pitied**, **pitying**)
Word history: Middle English, from Old French, from Latin word meaning 'piety'

pivot
noun **1** someone or something on which something turns or depends
verb **2** to turn, as on a pivot

Verb forms: I **pivoted**, I have **pivoted**, I am **pivoting**
Word building: **pivotal** *adjective*
Word history: French

pixel (pik-suhl)
noun any of the extremely small discrete elements, known as dots, which together make a graphic image as on a television or computer screen or as produced by a digital camera

pixie
noun an elf or fairy

pixilation (pik-suh-lay-shuhn)
noun an animation technique in which the animator photographs real objects and people frame by frame: *The movie we saw was made using* ***pixilation****.*

pizza (peet-suh, pit-suh)
noun a thin dough base covered with tomato, salami, cheese or similar savoury foods, and baked in an oven

placard
noun a large notice or poster

Word history: French, from Dutch word meaning 'flat board'

placate
verb to make calm or happy: *They* ***placated*** *him with presents.* (***appease***, ***mollify***, ***pacify***, ***quieten***, ***soothe***)

Word building: **placatory** *adjective*
Word history: Latin

place
noun **1** a particular area or part of space: *He's gone to a* ***place*** *I don't know.* (***location***, ***position***, ***site***, ***spot***, ***venue***)
2 situation: *I wouldn't do it if I were in your* ***place****.*
3 the page or passage you are up to when reading: *Mark your* ***place*** *with a bookmark.*
4 a short street, court or square
5 position in a race: *second* ***place***
verb **6** to put or set: *She* ***placed*** *it on the table.* (***deposit***, ***lodge***, ***plant***, ***position***, ***rest***)
7 to remember: *I can't* ***place*** *her.* (***recall***, ***recognise***, ***recollect***)
phrase **8 go places**, *Colloquial* to be successful in your work
9 in place of, instead of
10 out of place,
a not in the proper position
b unsuitable
11 put someone in their place, to reduce a person's over-high opinion of themself
12 take place, to happen

Word history: Old English, from Latin word meaning 'street', from Greek

placebo (pluh-see-boh)
noun a medicine which apparently performs no physical function but may help the patient mentally

Noun forms: The plural is **placebos**.
Word history: Middle English, from Latin word meaning 'I shall be pleasing', 'acceptable'

placement
noun **1** the act of placing: *the careful* ***placement*** *of furniture*
2 the act of finding positions or jobs for people

placenta (pluh-sen-tuh)
noun the organ which gives food and oxygen to a baby in its mother's womb

Noun forms: The plural is **placentas** or **placentae** (pluh-sen-tee).
Word history: Neo-Latin word meaning 'something having a flat circular form', from Latin word meaning 'a cake', from Greek word meaning 'flat cake'

placid (plas-uhd)
adjective calm or peaceful (***composed***, ***even-tempered***, ***imperturbable***, ***relaxed***, ***serene***)

Word building: **placidity** *noun* **placidly** *adverb*
Word history: Latin *placidus*

plagiarise (play-juh-ruyz)
verb (in art, literature, etc.) to take ideas, passages, etc., or their manner of expression and pass them off as your own

Word use: You can also use **plagiarize**.
Word building: **plagiarism** *noun* **plagiarist** *noun*

plague (playg)
noun **1** any serious disease which spreads very quickly
2 a huge number of any pest: *a* ***plague*** *of mice*
verb **3** to trouble in any manner (***annoy***, ***bedevil***, ***harass***, ***pester***, ***torment***)

Word history: Middle English, from Late Latin, from Latin word meaning 'blow', 'wound'

plaid (plad)
noun tartan cloth

Word history: from Gaelic word meaning 'blanket', 'plaid'

plain
adjective **1** clearly seen, heard or understood (***apparent***, ***distinct***, ***evident***, ***obvious***, ***visible***)
2 simple and uncomplicated (***natural***, ***unpretentious***)
3 not beautiful
noun **4** a large, flat area of land

Word building: **plainly** *adverb*
Word history: Middle English, from Old French, from Latin word meaning 'flat', 'level', 'plane'

plain / plane
Don't confuse **plain** with **plane**, which is a tool for smoothing wood. It is also a short form of **aeroplane**.

plainsong
noun one-part liturgical music used in the Christian church from the earliest times (***Gregorian chant***, ***plainchant***)

plaintiff
noun a person who brings a court case against someone else known as the defendant

Word history: Middle English, from Old French

plaintive
adjective complaining or sorrowful: *a* ***plaintive*** *cry*

Word history: Middle English, from Old French

plait (plat)
verb to weave or braid together three or more strands or bunches, as of hair

Word building: **plait** *noun*
Word history: Middle English, from Old French, from Latin word meaning 'folded'

plan
noun a program or design for how something should be done or made: *He has a* ***plan*** *for our next outing.* | *Have you finished the* ***plans*** *for the house?* (***idea***, ***plot***, ***project***, ***proposal***, ***scheme***)

Word building: **plan** *verb* (**planned**, **planning**)
Word history: French, from Latin

plane[1]
noun **1** a flat or level surface
2 a level: *Her writing is on a higher* ***plane*** *than mine.*
3 a winged machine which is driven through the air by its propellers or jet engines

Word use: The full form of definition 3 is **aeroplane**.
Word building: **plane** *adjective*
Word history: from Latin word meaning 'level ground'

plane[2]
noun a tool for smoothing wood

Word building: **plane** *verb*
Word history: Middle English, from French, from Late Latin

planet
noun any of the large bodies in space revolving around the sun or around any star

Word building: **planetary** *adjective*
Word history: Middle English, from Late Latin, from Greek word literally meaning 'wanderer'

plank
noun a flat length of wood, such as one used in building

Word history: Middle English, from Old Northern French, from Latin

plankton
noun the mass of very tiny plants and animals which float in water

Word history: German, from Greek word meaning 'wandering'

plant
noun **1** a living thing which grows in the ground and which cannot move around
2 the machinery and equipment connected with an industry
verb **3** to put in the ground to grow
4 to put or fix: *to* ***plant*** *an idea*

Word history: Middle English and Old English *plante*, from Latin word meaning 'sprout', 'slip', 'graft'

plantation
noun a farm, especially in tropical areas where crops such as coffee, sugar or cotton are grown

Word history: late Middle English, from Latin word meaning 'a planting'

plaque (plahk, plak)
noun **1** a metal plate, such as one fastened to a wall, with a name, profession or memorial date on it
2 a coating on teeth which causes decay

Word history: French, from Dutch *plak* flat board

plasma
noun **1** the liquid part of blood which contains the blood cells
2 a gas which is highly conductive, and suitable for use in computerised screens

Word history: Late Latin, from Greek word meaning 'something formed or moulded'

plasma screen
noun a type of screen for a television set, computer, etc.: *My* ***plasma screen*** *has amazing resolution.*

plaster
noun **1** a thick mixture of lime, sand and water, used to cover walls and ceilings
2 a fine, white powder which swells and sets rapidly when mixed with water and is used in making moulds
3 a bandage soaked in such a mixture, which is put around a broken limb to hold it in place
4 a covering for a minor wound

Word use: You can also use **plaster of Paris** for definition 2.
Word building: **plaster** *verb*
Word history: Middle English and Old English, from Vulgar Latin and Medieval Latin word meaning 'plaster' (both medical and builder's senses), from Latin, from Greek word meaning 'salve'

plastic
noun **1** a substance which can be shaped when soft and then hardened
adjective **2** made of plastic: *a* ***plastic*** *cup*

Word building: **plasticity** *noun*
Word history: Latin word meaning 'that may be moulded', from Greek

plastic explosive
noun an explosive substance in the form of a malleable, dough-like material

plasticine (plas-tuh-seen)
noun plastic modelling clay, in various colours
Word history: Trademark

plastic surgery
noun surgery done to improve the look of a part of the body which was badly formed or has been damaged in some way, or which is affected by age
Word building: **plastic surgeon**

plate
noun **1** a flat, round dish for food
2 cutlery or dishes made of, or coated with, gold or silver
3 a thin, flat sheet of metal
4 a colour illustration in a book
5 a support for false teeth
verb **6** to cover with a thin film of gold, silver, etc.
Word history: Middle English, from Old French word meaning 'flat piece', 'plate', probably from Old French, from Late Latin, from Greek word meaning 'broad', 'flat'

plateau (plat-oh)
noun a large, flat stretch of high ground
Noun forms: The plural is **plateaus** or **plateaux**.
Word history: French, from Old French word meaning 'flat object'

platelet
noun one of many small, cell-like fragments formed from special white blood cells, which help blood to clot in wounds

plate tectonics
noun a theory concerning the movements of the crust of the earth that explains how tectonic plates move; supporting the theory of continental drift.
Word use: Look up **continental drift**.

platform
noun **1** a raised floor, as in a hall or theatre, for public speakers or performers
2 the raised area beside the tracks at a railway station
3 a *Computers* an operating system
b a telecommunications system: *an SMS* ***platform***
Word history: from French word meaning 'flat form', 'plan', 'flat area', 'terrace'

platinum (plat-uh-nuhm)
noun a greyish-white, metallic element used in making scientific equipment and jewellery
Word history: Neo-Latin, from Spanish word meaning 'silver'

platitude (plat-uh-tyoohd)
noun an expression which has been used too many times, especially one spoken as if it were fresh and wise
Word building: **platitudinous** *adjective*
Word history: from French word meaning 'flat'

platonic (pluh-ton-ik)
adjective having to do with a love that is deep but does not involve sexual desires: ***platonic*** *love*

platoon
noun a group or unit of soldiers
Word history: from French word meaning 'little ball', 'group', 'platoon'

platter
noun a large plate used for serving food
Word history: Middle English, from Anglo-French, from Old French word meaning 'plate', 'dish'

platypus
noun an Australian web-footed animal with a bill like a duck's, which lays eggs and feeds its young with its own milk
Noun forms: The plural is **platypuses**.
Word use: Some people use **platypi** for the plural of **platypus**, but the most accepted and commonly used plural is **platypuses**.
Word history: Neo-Latin, from Greek word meaning 'flat-footed', in reference to the expanded webs of the front feet. The naturalist George Shaw made up this name. In the early days of the colony in Australia the settlers made up various names which are no longer used, such as 'duck mole', 'water mole' and 'the paradox', this last name referring to its mix of bird and animal features.

plaudits (plaw-duhts)
plural noun applause, approval, etc., as for an admired performance
Word history: Latin

plausible (plawz-uh-buhl)
adjective believable or reasonable: *a* ***plausible*** *story* (***conceivable***, ***credible***, ***likely***, ***possible***, ***probable***)
Word use: The opposite of this is **implausible**.
Word building: **plausibility** *noun* **plausibly** *adverb*
Word history: Latin

play
noun **1** activity for fun or relaxation
2 a story which can be acted out by actors in a theatre
3 light, rapid movement: *the* ***play*** *of reflections on water*
verb **4** to act the part of: *He is* ***playing*** *Hamlet.*
5 to do or take part in for sport or amusement: *Do you* ***play*** *cards?*
6 to take part in a game
7 to pretend to be or imitate, as in children's games: *They are* ***playing*** *pirates.*
8 to perform on: *He* ***plays*** *the flute.*
9 to cause to produce music or other sound: *to play a CD.*
phrase **10 play ball**, to work in agreement with
11 play down, to lessen the importance of (***laugh off***, ***make light of***, ***minimise***, ***trivialise***)
12 play for time, to gain needed time by unnecessarily prolonging something
13 play into the hands of, to act in such a way as to give an advantage to
14 play off,
a to set up friction between two people or groups of people for your own advantage
b to play an extra game in order to settle a tie
15 play the game, *Colloquial* play in accordance with the rules
Word history: Old English *plegan*

player
noun **1** someone or something that plays: *a tennis* ***player*** *| a CD* ***player***
2 someone who plays a musical instrument: *a trumpet* ***player***

player piano
noun a piano in which a mechanism turns a perforated paper roll, causing the piano keys to move in a particular order (***pianola***)

playground
noun **1** an outside area with equipment like swings, slides, etc., for children to play on
2 an outside area at a school, where students can play at recess and lunch

playwright
noun someone who writes plays (***dramatist***)

plaza
noun an open space or square in a town

Word history: Spanish, from Latin

plea
noun an earnest request

Word history: Middle English, from Old French, from Medieval Latin word meaning 'court', 'plea', from Latin word meaning '(thing which) seemed good', 'prescription', 'maxim'

plea bargaining
noun negotiation between the prosecution and defence in a lawsuit for an agreement that the accused will face lesser charges if they plead guilty

plead
verb **1** to beg or earnestly ask
2 to say whether you are innocent or guilty in a court case
3 to use as an excuse: *He* ***pleaded*** *tiredness.*

Word history: Middle English, from Old French word meaning 'go to law', 'plead', from Vulgar Latin, from Latin word meaning 'thing which pleases'

pleasant (ple-zuhnt)
adjective agreeable or pleasing: *a* ***pleasant*** *outing | a* ***pleasant*** *manner* (***enjoyable, lovely, nice, satisfying, welcome***)

Word building: **pleasantly** *adverb*
Word history: Middle English, from Old French *please*

pleasantry (plez-uhn-tree)
noun **1** pleasant humour in conversation
2 a polite remark or action

Noun forms: The plural is **pleasantries**.

please
verb **1** to make happy or satisfied: *The gift* ***pleased*** *them greatly.* (***charm, delight, gladden, gratify***)
interjection **2** if you are willing: *Come here* ***please.***

Word use: The opposite of definition 1 is **displease**.
Word building: **pleasing** *adjective*
Word history: Middle English, from Old French *plaisir*, from the Latin word *placere* meaning 'to please', 'to seem good'

pleasurable (plezh-uh-ruh-buhl)
adjective giving pleasure (***agreeable, enjoyable, pleasant***)

pleasure (plezh-uh)
noun enjoyment or happiness (***delight, gladness, joy***)

Word history: Middle English, from Old French *please*

pleat (pleet)
noun a pressed or stitched fold in trousers or a skirt

Word building: **pleat** *verb*
Word history: variant of *plait*

plebeian (pluh-bee-uhn)
adjective **1** having to do with the common people, especially in ancient Rome
2 common or vulgar
noun **3** a plebeian person

Word history: from Latin word meaning 'of the people'

plectrum (plek-truhm)
noun a small piece of wood, plastic or metal, used to pluck the strings of instruments such as the guitar or banjo

Word history: Latin, from Greek

pledge
noun **1** a promise made very seriously (***oath, vow, word of honour***)
2 something given as a guarantee that you will return a loan: *He left $10 as a* ***pledge.***

Word building: **pledge** *verb*
Word history: Middle English, from Old French, from Medieval Latin, of Germanic origin

plenary (pleen-uh-ree)
adjective **1** complete
2 attended by all qualified members, as a council

Word history: late Middle English, from Late Latin

plenipotentiary (plen-uh-puh-ten-shuh-ree)
noun **1** a person with full powers to negotiate on behalf of a state
adjective **2** having full power or authority, as a diplomatic agent
3 giving full power, as a commission

Word history: Medieval Latin, from Late Latin

plenitude (plen-uh-tyoohd)
noun **1** fullness in quantity, measure or degree (***abundance, bounty, plenty, profusion***)
2 the condition of being full

Word history: Latin

plentiful
adjective great in amount or number: *a* ***plentiful*** *supply* (***abundant, bountiful, copious, numerous, prolific***)

Word use: The opposite of this is **scarce**.
Word building: **plentifully** *adverb*

plenty
noun an amount or supply which is large or sufficient: *Take some, we have* ***plenty.***

Word building: **plenteous** *adjective*
Word history: Middle English, from Old French, from Latin word meaning 'fullness', 'abundance'

plethora (pleth-uh-ruh)
noun overabundance

Word history: Neo-Latin, from Greek word meaning 'fullness'

pliable (pluy-uh-buhl)
adjective flexible or easily bent: *a **pliable** stem* | *a **pliable** nature* (***floppy***, ***malleable***, ***supple***)

Word use: The opposite of this is **stiff**.
Word building: **pliability** *noun* **pliably** *adverb*
Word history: from French word meaning 'fold', 'bend'

pliant (pluy-uhnt)
adjective **1** bending readily (***flexible***, ***supple***)
2 easily inclined or influenced (***compliant***, ***tractable***, ***yielding***)

Word history: Middle English, from Old French word meaning 'fold', 'bend'

pliers (pluy-uhz)
plural noun a tool used for gripping, and for twisting or cutting wire

plight
noun a state or situation, usually bad: *She left them in an awful **plight**.*

Word history: Middle English, from Anglo-French, variant of Old French word meaning 'fold', 'manner of folding', 'condition'

Plimsoll line
noun a line or mark required to be placed on the side of all British merchant vessels, showing the depth to which they may be legally loaded

Word use: You can also use **Plimsoll mark**.
Word history: named after Samuel *Plimsoll*, 1824–98, British politician and social reformer

plinth (plinth)
noun **1** *Architecture* the lower square part of the base of a column or pedestal
2 a course of stones, as at the base of a wall

Word history: Latin, from Greek word meaning 'plinth', 'squared stone'

plod
verb to go or continue in a slow, steady and unexciting way: *He **plods** off to work every day.* (***lumber***, ***march***, ***slog***, ***tramp***, ***trudge***)

Verb forms: I **plodded**, I have **plodded**, I am **plodding**
Word building: **plodder** *noun*
Word history: perhaps imitative

plonk[1]
verb **1** to place or drop heavily or suddenly: *He **plonked** down the bag.*
noun **2** the act or sound of plonking

Word use: You can also use **plunk**.
Word history: imitative

plonk[2]
noun *Colloquial* any alcoholic liquor, especially cheap wine

Word history: perhaps a variant of French (*vin*) *blanc* white (wine)

plop
verb **1** to make a sound like that of a flat object striking water without a splash
2 to fall heavily with such a sound
noun **3** a plopping sound or fall
adverb **4** with a plop

Verb forms: I **plopped**, I have **plopped**, I am **plopping**
Word history: imitative

plot[1]
noun **1** a secret plan or scheme (***conspiracy***, ***intrigue***)
2 the story of a novel or play
verb **3** to plan secretly (***collude***, ***connive***, ***conspire***, ***intrigue***, ***scheme***)
4 to mark out or map: *to **plot** a route*

Verb forms: I **plotted**, I have **plotted**, I am **plotting**
Word history: abbreviation of Old French *complot*, meaning 'crowd struggle', later meaning 'concerted plan'

plot[2]
noun a small piece of ground: *a vegetable **plot***

Word history: Middle English and Old English

plough (plow)
noun **1** a tool with a curved blade for digging the soil
verb **2** to dig with a plough
phrase **3** **plough into**, to attack energetically
4 **plough through**, to work steadily at: *He **ploughs through** the housework.*

Word history: Middle English; Old English *plōh* ploughland

ploy (ploy)
noun a scheme, as in conversation, to gain the advantage

Word history: French *ployer*, from Latin *plicāre* fold

pluck
verb **1** to pull at and remove: *to **pluck** an apple from the tree*
2 to play notes on the strings of an instrument by pulling at them with your fingers or by using a plectrum
noun **3** courage

Word building: **plucky** *adjective* (**pluckier**, **pluckiest**)
Word history: Old English *pluccian*

plug
noun **1** a stopper to prevent liquid escaping, as from a basin
2 something used to block a hole
3 the connection at the end of an electrical wire which you put into a power point
verb **4** to stop up: *He **plugged** the leak.*
5 *Colloquial* to mention often, as a kind of advertisement: *He is **plugging** their show.*

Verb forms: I **plugged**, I have **plugged**, I am **plugging**
Word history: from Middle Dutch word meaning 'plug', 'peg'

plug-and-play
adjective *Computers* having to do with a computer system which automatically adjusts the settings of certain devices connected to it, so that they may be used immediately upon being plugged in: *The **plug-and-play** feature made using new hardware much simpler.*

plug-in
noun a piece of software which adds a specific feature to a larger system

plum
noun **1** a soft, smooth-skinned fruit related to, but larger than the cherry
adjective **2** good or choice: *a **plum** job*

Word history: Middle English; Old English *plūme*, from Greek

plumage (ploohm-ij)
noun the feathers covering a bird's body

Word history: late Middle English, from Old French word meaning 'feather'

plumb (plum)
noun **1** a lead weight on a string, used in measuring depth or as a test of uprightness
2 an exactly upright or perpendicular line or position: *The post is out of* ***plumb****, so we'll have to straighten it.*
adverb **3** in an upright position
4 exactly: ***plumb*** *in the middle*
verb **5** to find the depth of something with the use of a plumbline
6 to make vertical

Word use: You can also use **plumbline** for definition 1.
Word history: Middle English, from Old French, from Latin word meaning 'lead'

plumber (plum-uh)
noun someone who puts into a building the pipes which are used to carry water and waste and fixes them when something goes wrong

Word history: Middle English, from Old French, from Late Latin, from Latin word meaning 'lead'

plumbing (plum-ing)
noun **1** the system of pipes, etc., for carrying water, liquid wastes, etc., as in a building
2 the work of a plumber

plumbline (plum-luyn)
noun a string with a metal weight tied to one end, used to mark vertical lines, find the depth of water, etc.

Word use: You can also use **plumb**.

plume
noun **1** a feather, especially a long or showy one
2 a flow of waste material or other pollutant, spreading from a source: ***Plumes*** *of smoke billowed up from the chimneys of the factory.*

Word history: Old French, from Latin word meaning 'feather'

plummet
verb to fall straight and fast, as something heavy does

Word history: Middle English, from Old French word meaning 'lead'

plump[1]
adjective rather fat and well-rounded (***chubby***, ***portly***, ***stocky***, ***stout***, ***tubby***)

Word history: Middle English

plump[2]
verb **1** to fall heavily or suddenly (***drop***, ***flop***, ***sink***, ***slump***)
2 to vote for or choose only one out of a number: *Which team are you* ***plumping*** *for?*
3 to drop or throw heavily or suddenly

Word history: Middle English; probably imitative

plunder
verb to rob violently, as in war (***maraud***, ***pillage***, ***raid***, ***ravage***)

Word building: **plunder** *noun*
Word history: German

plunge
verb **1** to dip or thrust: *She* ***plunged*** *her bucket into the river. | The storm* ***plunged*** *the town into darkness.*
2 to dive or fall, as into water (***drop***, ***plummet***)
3 to move quickly or suddenly: *to* ***plunge*** *into action*
noun **4** a sudden rush or move
5 a dive or fall
phrase **6 take the plunge**, to start to do something

Word history: Middle English, from Old French, from Latin word meaning 'lead'

plural
adjective **1** indicating more than one person or thing
noun **2** a word in the plural form: *'Cats' is the* ***plural*** *of 'cat'.*

Word history: Middle English, from Latin

> When a noun, verb or pronoun refers to more than one person or thing, we say it is **plural** in number. We call it **singular** if it refers to just one.
>
> For nouns in English, adding -s or -es is the most common way of forming the plural:
>
> *one cat* *five cats*
> *one box* *fifteen boxes*
>
> Some nouns form their plurals in a different way:
>
> | | | | |
> |---|---|---|---|
> | *child* | *children* | *criterion* | *criteria* |
> | *ox* | *oxen* | *thesis* | *theses* |
> | *man* | *men* | *mouse* | *mice* |
>
> Some don't change at all:
>
> *one sheep* *two sheep*
>
> All of these are known as *count nouns* because they refer to things you can count, and they usually have a distinct plural form. Other nouns (*mass nouns*) don't normally occur in the plural at all:
>
> *butter* *rice* *mud*
>
> Most pronouns have a special plural form. *I* is singular, for example, but *we* is plural.
>
> Verbs have different singular and plural forms, at least in the present tense. In these cases it's important to make sure that you follow a plural noun or pronoun with a plural verb:
>
> *She wants* … but *They want* …
>
> For more information on difficult cases, look up **agreement in grammar.**
>
> For a list of **singular and plural forms**, see appendixes, page 985.

plurality (plooh-ral-uh-tee)
noun **1** the condition or fact of being plural
2 more than half of the whole (***majority***)

Noun forms: The plural is **pluralities.**

plus
preposition **1** *Mathematics* more by the addition of: *5* ***plus*** *2 is 7.*
2 as well as: *This car comes with full air conditioning* ***plus*** *power steering.*
noun **3** an added advantage: *The fact that it was so cheap was another* ***plus****.*

Word history: from Latin word meaning 'more'

plush
adjective rich, fine or costly

Word history: French, from Latin word meaning 'hair'

plutocracy (plooh-tok-ruh-see)
noun **1** the rule or power of wealth
2 a government or state in which the wealthy class rules

Noun forms: The plural is **plutocracies**.
Word building: **plutocrat** *noun* **plutocratic** *adjective*
Word history: Greek

plutonium
noun a radioactive element which is obtained from uranium, and is a powerful source of energy

Word history: Greek

pluvial (plooh-vee-uhl)
adjective **1** rainy
2 due to rain

Word history: Latin

ply[1]
verb **1** to use or do, especially busily: *to **ply** the oars* | *to **ply** a trade*
2 to supply continuously: *She **plied** us with sandwiches.*
3 to travel or cross often: *to **ply** the harbour* | *to **ply** between Sydney and Auckland*

Verb forms: I **plied**, I have **plied**, I am **plying**
Word history: short form of Middle English *aplyen* apply

ply[2]
noun a strand or a thickness

Noun forms: The plural is **plies**.
Word history: Middle English, from Old French word meaning 'fold', 'bend', from Latin word meaning 'fold'

plywood
noun board made of layers of wood stuck together

p.m.
abbreviation short for *post meridiem*, Latin words meaning 'after noon'

Word use: You can also use **pm**.

pneumatic (nyooh-mat-ik)
noun worked by air or air pressure: *a **pneumatic** pump*

Word building: **pneumatically** *adverb*
Word history: Latin, from Greek

pneumonia (nyooh-mohn-yuh)
noun an illness caused by an infection or inflammation of the lungs, which gives you a fever and makes breathing difficult

Word history: Neo-Latin, from Greek

poach[1]
verb to take game or fish illegally from someone else's land

Word history: Middle French word meaning 'thrust or put out (eyes)', 'dig out with the fingers', probably from Germanic

poach[2]
verb to cook in liquid just below boiling point in a shallow pan (***braise***, ***coddle***, ***simmer***, ***stew***)

Word building: **poacher** *noun*
Word history: French

pock
noun **1** a small swelling on the body containing pus, caused by a disease such as smallpox
2 a mark or spot left by or looking like such a swelling

Word history: Old English *poc*

pocket
noun **1** a cloth fold or pouch sewn into a garment, for holding things
2 a small area of something: *a **pocket** of coal* | *a **pocket** of resistance*
adjective **3** small enough to fit in a pocket: *a **pocket** dictionary*
verb **4** to put into your own pocket, especially dishonestly
phrase **5 in your pocket**, under your control
6 line your pockets, to make money by dishonest means
7 out of pocket, without money or having made a loss

Word history: Middle English, from Anglo-French, variant of French word meaning 'bag'

pocket money
noun **1** money that children are regularly given by their parents or carers, often in return for doing chores
2 small amounts of money used to pay for personal items

pod
noun the long container in which seeds grow: *a pea **pod***

podcast
verb **1** to deliver a radio program over the internet: *The radio station **podcast** the interview, so people could listen to it later on their MP3 players.*
noun **2** such a program
adjective **3** having to do with such a program

Verb forms: I **podcast**, I have **podcasted**, I am **podcasting**
Word building: **podcasting** *noun, adjective*

poddy
noun a young animal, especially a calf, which needs to be fed by hand

Noun forms: The plural is **poddies**.
Word building: **poddy** *adjective*
Word history: perhaps British dialect *poddy* fat

podium (poh-dee-uhm)
noun a small platform for a speaker or the conductor of an orchestra

Noun forms: The plural is **podiums** or **podia** (poh-dee-uh).
Word history: Latin word meaning 'elevated place', 'balcony', from Greek word meaning 'foot'

poem
noun a piece of writing set out in a certain way, often with lines that match in length, rhythm or rhyme

Word history: Latin, from Greek word meaning 'poem', 'something made'

poet
noun someone who writes poems

Word history: Greek *poetes* meaning 'a maker' and then 'a poet', from *poiein* 'to make', 'create'

poet / poetess

The suffix -ess is a common feminine ending in English. So **poetess** is the feminine form of **poet**.

Nowadays it is desirable to avoid words that refer to gender unnecessarily, and there is no need to turn **poet** into **poetess**. **Poet** describes someone who writes poetry, either a man or a woman.

For more information, look up **non-sexist language**.

poetic licence
noun freedom taken by a poet in not following the rules of language, logic, or fact, in order to produce a literary effect

poetry
noun **1** a poem or poems: *She writes* ***poetry****.*
2 beauty or harmony

Word building: **poetic** *adjective*
Word history: Middle English, from Late Latin

pogrom (pog-ruhm)
noun an organised mass killing, especially of Jews

Word history: from Russian word meaning 'devastation', 'destruction'

poignant (poyn-yuhnt)
adjective deeply or keenly felt: ***poignant*** *sorrow*

Word building: **poignancy** *noun*
Word history: Middle English, from Old French, from Latin word meaning 'prick', 'pierce'

poinsettia (poyn-set-ee-uh)
noun a plant, native to Mexico and Central America, with bright, usually scarlet, petal-like bracts

Word history: Neo-Latin, named after JR *Poinsett*, 1779–1851, US minister to Mexico, who discovered the plant there in 1828

point
noun **1** a sharp end: *the needle's* ***point***
2 a written dot, as in punctuation or decimals
3 the level or place in a process at which something happens: *boiling* ***point***
4 any of the 32 compass positions
5 a fact, idea or opinion put forward in a discussion, speech, piece of writing, etc.: *I'll make one last* ***point*** *before finishing my talk.*
6 the main fact, idea, etc.: *I didn't understand the* ***point*** *of the story.* (***meaning***, ***message***)
7 reason or intention: *The* ***point*** *of this exercise is to strengthen your leg muscles. | I don't see the* ***point*** *of doing this any longer.* (***purpose***)
8 a unit for scoring in a game
verb **9** to show by a finger or sign: *The sign* ***points*** *north.*
10 to aim: *to* ***point*** *a gun*
phrase **11 make a point of**, insist upon
12 off the point, not relevant
13 on (or **upon**) **the point of**, close to: ***on the point of*** *cracking up*
14 to the point, pertinent

Word history: Middle English, from Old French

point-blank
adjective **1** aimed or fired at very close range: *a* ***point-blank*** *shot*
2 plain or straight-forward: *a* ***point-blank*** *answer*

Word building: **point-blank** *adverb*

pointer
noun Computers an identifier giving the location in storage of something of interest, as a data item, table, or so on

pointy
adjective **1** being pointed at the end: ***pointy*** *shoes*
phrase **2 at the pointy end**, at the moment of engagement or crisis: ***at the pointy end*** *of the competition*

Adjective forms: **pointier**, **pointiest**

poise
noun **1** confidence or ease when dealing with people and situations
verb **2** to hold steady or balanced

Word building: **poised** *adjective*
Word history: late Middle English, from Old French, from Latin word meaning 'weigh'

poison
noun **1** a substance which causes death or illness if you swallow it or absorb it
verb **2** to kill or harm with poison

Word building: **poisonous** *adjective*
Word history: Middle English, from Old French word meaning 'potion', 'draught', 'poison', from Latin

poisonous / venomous

These words have meanings that are similar but not the same.

If food or drink is **poisonous**, it contains a substance which can kill you or make you very sick if you swallow it:

Snow White didn't know that the apple was poisonous.

We say that an animal is **venomous** if its fangs contain a dangerous venom:

Tiger snakes are venomous but not normally aggressive to bushwalkers.

So, strictly speaking, a red-back spider is **venomous**, not **poisonous**.

poke
verb **1** to push or prod: *to* ***poke*** *someone with your finger*
2 to show or appear, especially from behind something: *He* ***poked*** *his head around the door.*

Word building: **poke** *noun*
Word history: Middle English

poker[1]
noun a metal rod for stirring the fire in a fireplace or oven

poker[2]
noun a card game in which the players bet money on the value of the cards they are holding

poker machine
noun a coin-operated gambling machine (***fruit machine***, ***slot machine***)

pokie
noun Colloquial a poker machine

Noun forms: The plural is **pokies**.
Word use: You can also use **pokey**.

poky
adjective cramped: *a* ***poky*** *little room*

Adjective forms: **pokier**, **pokiest**
Word use: The opposite of this is **spacious**.

polar
adjective **1** having to do with a pole, as of the earth, a magnet, an electric cell, etc.
2 opposite in character and action

polarisation (poh-luh-ruy-zay-shuhn)
noun **1** the process by which rays of light show different properties in different directions
2 *Chemistry* the separation of a molecule into positive and negative ions

Word use: You can also use **polarization**.

polarity (poh-la-ruh-tee)
noun **1** *Physics* the possession of positive or negative, or both poles, by magnets, batteries, etc.
2 the possession of two directly opposite ideas, principles or qualities

pole[1]
noun a long, thin piece of wood or other material: *a flag* ***pole***

Word history: Middle English; Old English *pāl*, from Latin word meaning 'stake'

pole[2]
noun **1** each of the extremities of the axis of the earth, or of any spherical body
phrase **2 poles apart**, having completely opposite or widely different opinions, interests, etc.

Word use: Definition 1 takes a capital letter in the terms **North Pole** and **South Pole**.
Word history: Middle English, from Latin, from Greek word meaning 'pivot', 'axis', 'pole'

pole / poll
Don't confuse **pole** with **poll**. When someone takes a **poll** they count and record the number of people, votes or opinions in favour of or opposed to an important issue.

poleaxe (pohl-aks)
noun **1** a medieval weapon combining axe, hammer and spike, used for fighting on foot
2 a similar axe, used in striking down animals
verb **3** to strike down with a poleaxe

Word history: Middle English

polecat (pohl-kat)
noun **1** a European mammal of the weasel family, with blackish brown fur, and which gives off an offensive smell
2 any of various North American skunks

Word history: Middle English *polcat*

polemic (puh-lem-ik)
noun **1** an argument about some opinion, teaching, etc.
adjective **2** having to do with argument or disputation

Word use: You can also use **polemical** for definition 2.
Word history: from Greek word meaning 'of or for war'

police
noun members of a force employed by the state or nation to keep order and to protect life and property: *The* ***police*** *are investigating the murder.*

Word building: **police** *verb* **policeman** *noun* **policewoman** *noun*
Word history: French word meaning 'government', 'civil administration', 'police', from Medieval Latin

police officer
noun a member of the police force

police state
noun a country in which the police force is employed to discover and stop any opposition to the government in power

policy[1] (pol-uh-see)
noun a plan of action: *What is their foreign* ***policy?*** *| It's good* ***policy*** *to save.*

Noun forms: The plural is **policies**.
Word history: Middle English, from Old French word meaning 'government', 'civil administration', from Latin

policy[2] (pol-uh-see)
noun a signed agreement with an insurance company

Noun forms: The plural is **policies**.
Word history: French, from Italian, from Medieval Latin, from Greek word meaning 'a showing or setting forth'

polio (poh-lee-oh)
noun an infectious viral disease, now rare, marked by inflammation of the nerve cells, mainly of the spinal cord, and causing paralysis

Word use: The full form is **poliomyelitis** (poh-lee-oh-muy-uh-luy-tuhs) .
Word history: Neo-Latin, from Greek word meaning 'grey marrow'

polish
verb **1** to make shiny by rubbing (***buff***, ***burnish***)
2 to put the final touches to: *She just needs to* ***polish*** *her performance.*
noun **3** a paste or liquid which gives a shine when it is rubbed on: *shoe* ***polish***
4 fineness or elegance: *He sings with* ***polish.***
phrase **5 polish off**, to finish: *Let's* ***polish off*** *those cakes.*

Word building: **polished** *adjective* **polisher** *noun*
Word history: Middle English, from French, from Latin

polite
adjective **1** having good manners (***civil***, ***courteous***, ***gracious***, ***well-mannered***)
2 refined: ***polite*** *society*

Word building: **politely** *adverb* **politeness** *noun*
Word history: late Middle English, from Latin word meaning 'polished'

politic (pol-uh-tik)
adjective wise in a practical way (***judicious***, ***prudent***)

Word history: Middle English, from Latin, from Greek word meaning 'relating to citizens or to the state'

political (puh-lit-ik-uhl)
adjective **1** having to do with politics: *a* ***political*** *writer*
2 having or trying to gain power in government or public affairs: *a* ***political*** *party*
3 having to do with political parties or government: ***political*** *measures*
4 *Colloquial* interested in politics: *He is not* ***political.***

Word building: **politically** *adverb*

political asylum
noun asylum (definition 1) provided by a foreign country for someone fleeing political persecution in their own country

politician (pol-uh-tish-uhn)
noun a person who is active in party politics, especially someone who is a member of parliament

politics
noun **1** the management of the affairs of a country or state
2 methods used to gain power or success: *He hates the **politics** of his job.*
Word use: You can treat this noun as singular or plural.

polka
noun a quick and lively dance
Word building: **polka** *verb* (**polkaed, polkaing**)
Word history: French and German, from Czech word meaning 'half-step'

poll
noun **1** a counting of people, votes or opinions
verb **2** to ask and record the opinions of: *to **poll** the nation on an important matter*
3 to receive a number of votes: *to **poll** badly in an election*
4 to cut off the hair or horns of
phrase **5 the polls,** the place where votes are taken
Word history: from Middle English word meaning 'head'

poll / pole
Don't confuse **poll** with **pole**.
One kind of **pole** is a long thin piece of wood.
The other kind of **pole** is one of the extremities of the axis of the earth.

pollen
noun the yellowish seed dust of flowers
Word history: from Latin word meaning 'fine flour', 'dust'

pollinate
verb to cause to produce seeds by adding pollen: *Bees **pollinate** flowers as they collect nectar.*
Word building: **pollination** *noun*

pollutant (puh-looh-tuhnt)
noun a substance causing pollution

pollute
verb to spoil or make dirty: *The heavy traffic **pollutes** the air.* (***contaminate, corrupt, damage, foul, taint***)
Word building: **polluted** *adjective* **pollution** *noun*
Word history: Latin

pollution (puh-loo-shuhn)
noun **1** the act of polluting
2 environmental pollutants, such as motor vehicle emissions, industrial waste, etc.
3 the results of these pollutants, as city smog, etc.

polo
noun a ball game on horseback, between two teams using long wooden mallets and a wooden ball
Word history: Baltī (language of Kashmir)

poltergeist (pol-tuh-guyst)
noun a troublesome ghost or spirit who is supposed to move things and make noises
Word history: German word literally meaning 'noise-ghost'

polyandry (pol-ee-and-ree)
noun the practice or condition of having more than one husband at one time
Word building: **polyandrous** *adjective*
Word history: Greek

polyester (pol-ee-es-tuh)
noun a synthetic polymer in which the structural units are linked by ester groups

polygamy (puh-lig-uh-mee)
noun marriage to more than one person at a time
Word use: Compare this with **monogamy** and **bigamy**.
Word building: **polygamist** *noun* **polygamous** *adjective*

polygon
noun a flat shape with many straight sides
Word history: Latin, from Greek word meaning 'many-angled'

polygyny (puh-lij-uh-nee)
noun the practice or condition of having more than one wife at one time
Word building: **polygynous** *adjective*
Word history: from Greek word meaning 'having many wives'

polyhedron (pol-ee-hee-druhn)
noun a solid figure having many faces
Noun forms: The plural is **polyhedrons** or **polyhedra** (pol-ee-hee-druh).
Word building: **polyhedral** *adjective*
Word history: from Greek word meaning 'having many bases'

polymer (pol-uh-muh)
noun a compound of high molecular weight made by chemical combination of many molecules, often of the same compound
Word history: from Greek word meaning 'of many parts'

polyp (pol-uhp)
noun **1 a** a type of coelenterate which has a base attached to a rock, etc., a tubelike body, and a free end with mouth and tentacles
b an independent animal body forming part of a compound or colonial organism
2 a growth from a mucous surface, as of the nostril
Word building: **polypoid** *adjective*
Word history: French, from Latin, from Greek word meaning 'octopus'

polyphonic (pol-uh-fon-ik)
adjective **1** consisting of many voices or sounds
2 *Music* having two or more voices or parts, each with an independent melody, but all harmonising (***contrapuntal***)
Word building: **polyphony** *noun*

polyphonic ringtone (pol-ee-fon-ik ring-tohn)
noun a ringtone for a mobile phone which can play multiple tones and emulate different musical instruments

polystyrene (pol-ee-stuy-reen)
noun a clear, plastic polymer of styrene easily coloured and moulded, used in the form of rigid, white foam as an insulating material

polythene
noun a firm, light plastic which is used for containers, packing and insulation

polytonality (pol-ee-toh-nal-uh-tee)
noun Music the simultaneous use of more than one key

polyunsaturated (pol-ee-un-sach-uh-ray-tuhd)
adjective **1** having to do with a fat or oil based on fatty acids which have two or more double bonds per molecule, such as linoleic acid
2 having to do with food based on polyunsaturated oil or fat, as safflower oil, etc., or margarine

pomegranate (pom-uh-gran-uht)
noun a thick-skinned, pinkish fruit which splits open when it is ripe to reveal many seeds and flesh that you can eat
Word history: Middle English, from Old French *pome* meaning 'apple' and *grenate* 'the fruit', from Latin *granatum* meaning 'having many seeds'

Pomeranian (pom-uh-ray-nee-uhn)
noun a small dog with long, thick, silky hair
Word history: originating in *Pomerania*, a region of northern central Europe, now largely in Poland

pommel
noun **1** the front peak of a saddle
2 a knob at the end of a sword or knife handle
Word history: Middle English, from Old French, from Latin word meaning 'fruit'

Pommy
noun Australian, NZ Colloquial an English person
Word use: This is also written **pommy**. | You can also use **Pom**. | The use of this word may offend people.
Noun forms: The plural is **Pommies**.
Word history: perhaps an abbreviation of *pomegranate*, rhyming slang for immigrant

pomp
noun **1** splendid display, as in a ceremony or parade
2 exaggerated outward show, especially of dignity or importance
Word history: Middle English, from Old French, from Latin, from Greek word originally meaning 'a sending'

pompom
noun a ball made of wool or other thread, often put on hats or caps as an ornament
Word history: imitative

pompous
adjective showing too much sense of your own importance: *a **pompous** speech* (***affected, grandiose, pretentious, self-important***)
Word use: The opposite of this is **modest**.
Word building: **pomposity** *noun* **pompously** *adjective*
Word history: Middle English, from Late Latin

poncho
noun a cloak with a hole in the centre to put your head through
Noun forms: The plural is **ponchos**.
Word history: South American Spanish, from Araucanian word meaning 'woollen fabric'

pond
noun an area of water smaller than a lake
Word history: Middle English, irregular variant of *pound*

ponder
verb to think about deeply or carefully: *to **ponder** the question* (***concentrate on, contemplate, meditate on, reflect on, weigh***)
Word history: Middle English, from Old French, from Latin word meaning 'ponder', 'weigh'

ponderous
adjective **1** large and heavy (***bulky, cumbersome, unwieldy, weighty***)
2 serious and dull: *a **ponderous** discussion* (***dreary, laboured, pedantic, stodgy***)
Word history: Middle English

pontiff
noun a pope
Word building: **pontifical** *adjective*
Word history: Latin

pontificate (pon-tif-uh-kuht)
noun **1** the time during which a pontiff holds office
verb (pon-tif-uh-kayt) **2** to speak in an important-sounding manner
Word history: Medieval Latin

pontoon[1]
noun a floating structure used to support a temporary bridge or dock
Word history: French, from Latin word meaning 'bridge', 'pontoon', 'punt'

pontoon[2]
noun a gambling card game in which you try to score 21 points (***blackjack, twenty-one***)
Word history: perhaps a humorous mispronunciation of French *vingt-et-un* twenty-one

pony
noun a small horse
Noun forms: The plural is **ponies**.
Word history: French, from Latin word meaning 'young animal'

ponytail
noun a hairstyle in which the hair is tied in a loose bunch at the back of the head

poodle
noun a dog with thick, curly hair often trimmed in special shapes
Word history: short for *poodle dog*, from German word meaning 'splash-dog' (because the poodle is a water-dog)

poofter (poof-tuh)
noun Colloquial a male homosexual
Word use: The use of this word may offend people.

pool[1]
noun **1** a small area of still water, especially one made for swimming in
2 a small collection of any liquid: *a **pool** of blood*
Word history: Middle English and Old English *pōl*

pool[2]
noun **1** a combination of possessions, money or services for the use of everyone in a group: *a car **pool***
2 the sum of money that can be won in some gambling games
3 a kind of billiards game
verb **4** to put together for the use of everyone in a group: *Let's **pool** our money and buy her a present from us all.*

Word history: from French word meaning 'hen'; probably at first slang for 'booty'

poop (poohp)
noun a deck at the back part of a ship, above the main deck

Word history: Middle English, from Old French, from Italian, from Latin

poor
adjective **1** having little money, property or means of producing wealth: *a **poor** person | a **poor** country* (***broke***, ***hard up***, ***impoverished***, ***needy***, ***underprivileged***)
2 low in quality or skill: *a **poor** piece of work* (***bad***, ***defective***, ***inferior***, ***shoddy***, ***worthless***)
3 small in amount or number: *a **poor** wage*
4 unfortunate or unlucky: *You **poor** thing!*
noun **5** poor people as a group: *I am collecting money for the **poor**.*

Word use: The opposite of this is **rich** or **affluent**.
Word building: **poorness** *noun* **poverty** *noun*
Word history: Middle English, from Old French, from Latin

poor / pour / paw / pore

Don't confuse **poor** with **pour**, **paw**, or **pore**.

You can **pour** a liquid from one container to another.

A **paw** is the foot of an animal with nails or claws.

A **pore** is a small hole. Sweat comes out through the **pores** in your skin.

To **pore** over something is to read or study it carefully:

He watched the pirates pore over the secret treasure map.

pop[1]
verb **1** to make a short, explosive sound
2 to come, go or put quickly or suddenly: *I'll **pop** in and visit him. | **Pop** the books on my desk.*
noun **3** a short, explosive sound

Verb forms: I **popped**, I have **popped**, I am **popping**
Word history: Middle English; imitative

pop[2]
noun **1** music that is very popular at a certain time, especially among young people, usually having a strong rhythm
adjective **2** having the sound of pop music

Word use: You can also use **pop music** for definition 1.
Word history: short for *popular*

pop[3]
noun **Dad**, a word used when you address your father

popcorn
noun corn grain which bursts open and puffs up when heated and which is then eaten

pope
noun the bishop of Rome as head of the Roman Catholic Church

Word use: This is often spelt with a capital letter.
Word history: Middle English; Old English *pāpa*, from Medieval Latin word meaning 'bishop', 'pope', originally 'father', from Greek word meaning 'father'

poplar (pop-luh)
noun a fast-growing, tall tree yielding a useful, light softwood

Word history: Middle English, from Old French

poplin (pop-luhn)
noun a strong, finely ribbed, cotton material, used for clothing

Word history: French, from Italian word meaning 'papal'; so called from being made at the papal city of Avignon

poppadum
noun → **pappadum**

poppet (pop-uht)
noun **1** a valve which in opening is lifted bodily from its seat instead of being hinged at one side
2 a term of affection for a girl or child

Word use: You can also use **poppet valve** for definition 1.
Word history: earlier form of *puppet*

poppy
noun a kind of brightly coloured flower

Noun forms: The plural is **poppies**.
Word history: Middle English; Old English, from Vulgar Latin

populace (pop-yuh-luhs)
noun the common people of a population, as opposed to the higher classes

Word history: French, from Italian word meaning 'people'

popular
adjective **1** widely liked by a particular group or people in general: *a **popular** song | a girl who is **popular** with her class*
2 having to do with the people in general: ***popular** beliefs* (***collective***, ***common***, ***communal***, ***public***)

Word building: **popularity** *noun* **popularly** *adverb*
Word history: Latin

populate (pop-yuh-layt)
verb **1** to live in: *Australia was **populated** entirely by Aboriginal people before the Europeans came.* (***inhabit***)
2 to fill up with people

Word history: from Medieval Latin word meaning 'inhabited'

population (pop-yuh-lay-shuhn)
noun the people living in a country, town or other area

population density
noun a measure of the number of people living in a set area of land

populous (<u>pop</u>-yuh-luhs)
adjective having a large number of people: *a **populous** city*

Word history: Latin

porcelain (<u>paw</u>-suh-luhn)
noun a kind of fine china, used for dishes and ornaments

Word history: French, from Italian

porch
noun a covered area at the entrance of a building

Word history: Middle English, from Old French, from Latin word meaning 'porch', 'portico'

porcupine (<u>pawk</u>-yuh-puyn)
noun a small animal covered with stiff, sharp spines

Word history: Middle English, from Old French word meaning 'spine-pig', from Latin *porcus spinosus* meaning 'prickly pig'

pore[1]
phrase **pore over**, to read or study carefully: *The students **pored over** their books.*

Word history: Middle English

pore[2]
noun a very small opening, especially in the skin, for liquid to be taken in or come out through: *Sweat comes out through your **pores**.*

Word history: Middle English, from French, from Latin, from Greek word meaning 'passage'

> **pore / pour / paw / poor**
> Don't confuse **pore** with **pour**, **paw** or **poor**.
> You can **pour** a liquid from one container to another.
> A **paw** is the foot of an animal with nails or claws.
> Someone is **poor** if they don't have much money or property.

pork
noun the meat of a pig

Word history: Middle English, from Old French, from Latin word meaning 'hog', 'pig'

porn
noun Colloquial pornography

> **porn / pawn**
> Look up **pawn / porn**.

pornography
noun art, photography or writing that is thought to be indecent or obscene

Word building: **pornographer** *noun* **pornographic** *adjective*
Word history: from Greek word meaning 'writing of prostitutes'

porous
adjective having lots of small holes or spaces that allow air or water to pass through: ***porous** soil* | *Sandstone is a **porous** type of rock.*

Word building: **porousness** *noun*

porpoise (<u>paw</u>-puhs)
noun a sea mammal with a rounded snout, usually blackish on top and paler beneath, which often leaps from the water

Noun forms: The plural is **porpoises** or **porpoise**.
Word history: Middle English, from Old French, from Late Latin word meaning 'hog fish'

porridge
noun oats cooked with water or milk, often eaten for breakfast

Word history: variant of *pottage*

port[1]
noun **1** a harbour where ships load and unload
2 a town with a harbour

Word history: Middle English and Old English, from Latin word meaning 'harbour', 'haven'

port[2]
noun the left-hand side of a ship or plane when you are facing the front

Word use: The opposite is **starboard**.
Word history: origin uncertain; perhaps because the larboard side was customarily next to the shore in port

port[3]
noun a sweet, dark red wine

Word history: from *Oporto* (from Portuguese word meaning 'the port'), city in Portugal

port[4]
noun **1** an opening, such as a porthole in a ship
2 a connection point in a computer for the entry or exit of data

Word history: Middle English and Old English, from Latin word meaning 'gate'

port[5]
noun Australian a suitcase or school bag

portable
adjective able to be easily carried or moved: *a **portable** television*

Word building: **portability** *noun*
Word history: Middle English, from Late Latin

portal (<u>paw</u>-tuhl)
noun **1** a door, gate or entrance, especially one of grand appearance, as in a palace
2 → **web portal**

Word history: Middle English, from Medieval Latin, from Latin word meaning 'gate'

portal site
noun → **web portal**

portend (paw-<u>tend</u>)
verb **1** to indicate beforehand (often something undesirable), as an omen, etc.
2 *Old-fashioned* to signify

Word history: Middle English, from Latin word meaning 'point out', 'indicate', 'portend'

portent (<u>paw</u>-tent)
noun **1** an indication of something about to happen, especially something of great effect
2 meaning: *a happening of evil **portent***

Word building: **portentous** *adjective*
Word history: from Latin word meaning 'presaged'

porter[1]
noun someone whose job is carrying bags or other loads: *a railway* ***porter***
Word history: Middle English, from Old French, from Latin word meaning 'carry'

porter[2]
noun someone who has charge of a door or gate (***doorkeeper***, ***gatekeeper***, ***janitor***)
Word history: Middle English, from Anglo-French, from Latin word meaning 'gate'

portfolio
noun **1** *Old-fashioned* a case for carrying loose papers or letters
2 the duties of a minister in a government: *The Premier gave her the Education* ***portfolio.***
3 a collection of an artist's drawings, photographs, etc., which may be shown to prospective employers etc., as examples of their work
4 a collection of company shares or other investments owned by someone
Word history: Italian, from Latin

porthole
noun a round opening like a window in the side of a ship that gives light and air

portico (paw-tuh-koh)
noun a structure consisting of a roof supported by pillars, forming the entrance to a temple, church, house, etc.
Noun forms: The plural is **porticoes** or **porticos**.
Word history: Italian, from Latin word meaning 'porch', 'portico'

portion
noun a part or share of something (***fraction***, ***piece***, ***proportion***, ***section***, ***segment***)
Word building: **portion** *verb*
Word history: Middle English, from Old French, from Latin word meaning 'share', 'part'

portion / potion
Don't confuse **portion** with **potion**, which is an old-fashioned word for something you drink, often something poisonous or magical.

portly
adjective large and fat (***heavily-built***, ***plump***, ***stocky***, ***stout***, ***tubby***)
Word building: **portliness** *noun*

portmanteau (pawt-man-toh)
noun Old-fashioned a suitcase for travelling which opens into two halves
Noun forms: The plural is **portmanteaus** or **portmanteaux**.
Word history: from French word meaning 'cloak-carrier'

portrait (paw-truht)
noun **1** a painting, drawing or photograph of someone, especially of their face
2 a written or spoken description: *a* ***portrait*** *of life in the Middle Ages*
Word building: **portraiture** *noun*
Word history: French, from Late Latin word meaning 'portray', from Latin word meaning 'bring forward'

portray
verb **1** to make a painting or drawing of
2 to act the part of: *He* ***portrayed*** *a king in his class play.*
3 to describe in words (***depict***, ***express***, ***illustrate***, ***represent***)
Word building: **portrayal** *noun*
Word history: Middle English, from Old French, from Late Latin word meaning 'depict', from Latin word meaning 'draw forth'

Portuguese man-of-war (paw-chuh-geez man-uhv-waw)
noun **1** → **bluebottle** (definition 1)
2 a jellyfish

pose
verb **1** to take up a particular position: *The model* ***posed*** *for the camera.*
2 to pretend to be something or someone
3 to present or put forward: *The teacher* ***posed*** *a hard question.*
Word building: **pose** *noun* **poser** *noun*
Word history: Middle English, from Old French, from Late Latin word meaning 'lay down'

posh
adjective Colloquial smart, expensive-looking or high-class: *a* ***posh*** *car*
Word history: origin unknown; ? obsolete *posh* a dandy. The supposed acronym from *p(ort) o(ut,) s(tarboard) h(ome)*, a reference to the better (i.e. cooler) accommodation on vessels sailing from Britain to India, Australia, etc. is not supported by available evidence

position
noun **1** a place or location: *Take any* ***position*** *in the back row.*
2 proper place: *I am putting these chairs into* ***position.***
3 the manner in which something is placed or arranged
4 a situation or state: *My lack of money puts me in a difficult* ***position.***
5 rank or standing: *a high* ***position*** *in society*
6 a job (***duty***, ***employment***, ***office***, ***post***, ***station***)
7 a point of view: *What is your* ***position*** *in this argument?*
Word building: **position** *verb*
Word history: Middle English, from Latin

positive
adjective **1** absolutely sure or certain (***clear***, ***confident***, ***convinced***, ***definite***)
2 expressing agreement: *a* ***positive*** *answer*
3 actual or real: *This has been of* ***positive*** *good to us.* (***concrete***, ***material***, ***tangible***)
4 tending to see what is good or gives hope: ***positive*** *criticism of a pupil's work | a* ***positive*** *attitude towards a problem* (***constructive***, ***forward-looking***, ***productive***)
5 greater than zero in quantity
6 having a deficiency or lack of electrons: *the* ***positive*** *pole of an electric cell*
Word building: **positiveness** *noun*
Word history: Latin

posse (pos-ee)
noun a group of people that helps a sheriff keep peace

Word use: This word is mainly used in the US.
Word history: from Medieval Latin word meaning 'power', 'force', noun use of Latin infinitive, 'to be able', 'have power'

possess
verb **1** to own or have: *to* ***possess*** *a lot of books | to* ***possess*** *courage*
2 to take over and control: *Rage* ***possessed*** *her.* (***seize***)

Word building: **possessor** *noun*

possessed
adjective taken over by a strong feeling, madness or an apparently supernatural force: *She screamed as though* ***possessed.***

possession
noun **1** ownership or the act of possessing: *I took* ***possession*** *of my new car yesterday.*
2 something possessed: *This game is my favourite* ***possession.***
3 possessions, the group of things possessed by someone (***assets***, ***belongings***, ***effects***, ***property***)
4 in certain ball sports, control of the ball by a player or team during play

Word history: Middle English, from Latin

possessive
adjective wanting to possess or control all by yourself (***acquisitive***, ***grasping***, ***selfish***)

Word building: **possessively** *adverb* **possessiveness** *noun*

possessive adjective
noun the adjectival form of a possessive pronoun, as *my*, *his*, *her*, *our*, etc.

possessive case
noun the form of a noun or pronoun which shows ownership, such as 'hers', in *the book is hers*, which is the possessive case of 'she'

possessive pronoun
noun a personal pronoun indicating possession

Look up **pronouns: possessive pronouns**.

possible
adjective able to be, happen, be done, or be used: *a* ***possible*** *cure for a disease | Is it* ***possible*** *to drive there in one day?* (***conceivable***, ***imaginable***, ***potential***)

Word building: **possibility** *noun* (*plural* **possibilities**)
Word history: Middle English, from Latin

possum
noun an Australian marsupial that lives in trees and has well-developed limbs for climbing and grasping, a long tail for climbing and is active at night

post[1]
noun **1** an upright piece of wood or metal used as a support: *a fence* ***post***
2 a post marking the start or finish of a race
verb **3** to put up on a post or wall for public attention: *They* ***posted*** *a list of the new prices.*
4 *Computers* to place a message or other information on a network, especially the internet

Word history: Middle English and Old English, from Latin

post[2]
noun **1** a job or duty: *She has a teaching* ***post.*** (***appointment***, ***place***, ***position***, ***situation***, ***station***)
2 the place where a job or duty is done, especially guard duty
verb **3** to post a guard at the gate

Word history: French, from Italian, from Latin word meaning 'placed', 'put'

post[3]
noun **1** delivery of letters or other mail
2 the letters themselves
3 the system of carrying letters and other mail
verb **4** to send by post: *I am* ***posting*** *a letter to you tomorrow.*

Word building: **postal** *adjective*
Word history: French, from Italian word meaning 'placed', 'put'

postage
noun the cost of sending something by post

postcard
noun a card for sending by post with a picture on one side and a space for a message on the other side

postcode
noun a group of numbers added to your address to help speed the delivery of mail

postdate (pohst-dayt)
verb **1** to date (a document, cheque, invoice, etc.) with a date later than the current date
2 to follow in time

poster
noun a large notice, often illustrated

Word history: *post*[1], verb + *-er*

poster child
noun **1** a child used to advertise or bring attention to some community sentiment or aspiration
2 any person, organisation, or entity, regarded as representative of a cause, development, etc.

Noun forms: The plural is **poster children**.

posterior (pos-tear-ree-uh)
adjective **1** from or at the back: *a* ***posterior*** *view of the spine*
noun **2** *Colloquial* your bottom

Word use: The opposite of definition 1 is **anterior**.
Word history: from Latin word meaning 'coming after'

posterity (po-ste-ruh-tee)
noun the people who will live in the future: *His work will be remembered by* ***posterity.***

Word history: Middle English, from Latin

posterity / prosperity
Don't confuse **posterity** with **prosperity**, which is success or good fortune, often in relation to wealth:

The farmers have enjoyed two years of prosperity after the drought broke.

postgraduate (pohst-<u>graj</u>-ooh-uht)
noun **1** someone studying at a university for a higher degree, that is, one taken after a first degree
adjective **2** having to do with courses of study offered for a higher degree

Word use: You can also use **post-graduate**.

posthaste (pohst-<u>hayst</u>)
adverb with all possible speed

Word history: *post*[3] + *haste*

posthumous (<u>pos</u>-chuh-muhs)
adjective published, given, or happening after someone's death: *his **posthumous** writings* | *a **posthumous** award*

Word building: **posthumously** *adverb*
Word history: Latin

posting
noun Accounting the entering of an item into an accounts ledger

postmark
noun an official mark stamped on letters or other mail, to cancel the postage stamp, indicate the place and date of sending or of receipt, etc.

post-mortem
noun the medical examination of a dead body (***autopsy***)

Word building: **post-mortem** *adjective*
Word history: from Latin word meaning 'after death'

postpone
verb to put off to a later time: *They **postponed** the game because of rain.* (***adjourn***, ***defer***, ***delay***, ***put back***)

Word building: **postponement** *noun*
Word history: Latin

postscript
noun an extra message written on the end of a finished and signed letter

Word use: The abbreviation is **PS**.
Word history: from Latin word meaning 'written after'

postulate (<u>pos</u>-chuh-layt)
verb **1** to ask, demand or claim
2 to claim or take for granted the existence or truth of, especially as a basis for reasoning
noun (<u>pos</u>-chuh-luht) **3** something taken to be the case, without proof as a basis for reasoning, or as self-evident

Word building: **postulation** *noun*
Word history: from Latin word meaning 'thing requested'

posture
noun position of your body: *a kneeling **posture*** (***attitude***, ***bearing***, ***carriage***, ***pose***, ***stance***)

Word history: French, from Latin

posy
noun a small, neatly arranged bunch of flowers

Noun forms: The plural is **posies.**
Word history: variant of *poesy*

pot
noun **1** a container, usually round and deep: *a cooking **pot*** | *a flower **pot***
verb **2** to put or plant in a pot

Verb forms: I **potted**, I have **potted**, I am **potting**
Word history: Middle English and Old English *pott*

potash (<u>pot</u>-ash)
noun **1** potassium carbonate, especially the crude impure form obtained from wood ashes
2 oxide of potassium
3 potassium: *carbonate of **potash***

Word history: earlier *pot-ashes*, plural, translation of early Dutch

potassium (puh-<u>tas</u>-ee-uhm)
noun a silvery-white, metallic element, which oxidises rapidly in air, and whose compounds are used especially as fertiliser

Word history: Neo-Latin

potato
noun a white plant root which you can eat as a vegetable

Noun forms: The plural is **potatoes.**
Word history: Spanish word meaning 'white potato', from Haitian

potch (poch)
noun opal lacking the fine play of colour which is seen in gem-quality opal; it is commonly the stone in which precious opal is found

potent (<u>poh</u>-tuhnt)
adjective powerful or strong: *a **potent** king* | *a **potent** medicine* (***forceful***, ***mighty***)

Word building: **potency** *noun*
Word history: from Latin word meaning 'powerful'

potentate (<u>poh</u>-tuhn-tayt)
noun someone who possesses great power, such as a sovereign, monarch or ruler

Word history: Late Latin word meaning 'potentate', from Latin word meaning 'power', 'dominion'

potential
adjective **1** capable of becoming in the future: *I think this song is a **potential** hit.*
noun **2** possible or likely ability: *She is a pianist with a lot of **potential**.*

Word building: **potentiality** *noun* **potentially** *adverb*
Word history: Middle English, from Medieval Latin

potential difference
noun the difference in potential between two points, defined as the work performed when unit positive charge is moved from one point to the other

potential energy
noun energy which is due to position rather than motion, as a coiled spring, or a raised weight

Word use: Compare this with **kinetic energy**.

pothole
noun a hole in the ground, especially one in a road

potion
noun Old-fashioned a drink, especially medicine, or one that's poisonous or magical in some way

Word history: Latin

potion / portion
Don't confuse **potion** with **portion**, which is a part or share of something, as in my *portion of dessert.*

potoroo
noun a small, long-nosed, Australian animal with a pointed head like a bandicoot, found in low thick scrub and grassland

Word history: from Dharug, an Australian Aboriginal language spoken by the people living near Sydney Cove in the early days of European settlement

potpourri (pot-poouh-ree, poh-puh-ree)
noun **1** a mixture of dried flower petals used to give a perfume
2 any collection or mixture of different things: *This book is a **potpourri** of stories, poems and plays.*

Word history: from French word meaning 'rotten pot', translation of Spanish

potter[1]
noun someone who shapes pots, dishes, etc., out of clay, and then hardens them by baking

Word history: Middle English; Old English *pottere*

potter[2]
verb to busy or occupy yourself without getting much done: *I spent the day **pottering** about the house.*

Word history: Old English *potian* push, thrust

pottery
noun **1** the things a potter makes
2 a place where earthen pots or vessels are made

potty[1]
adjective Colloquial foolish or crazy

Adjective forms: **pottier, pottiest**

potty[2]
noun a pot used as a toilet, especially for small children

Word use: You can also use **pottie**.

pouch
noun **1** a small bag or sack, used for carrying things like money
2 a part of the body shaped like a bag or pocket: *the **pouch** of a kangaroo | **pouches** of skin beneath the eyes*

Word history: Middle English, from Old Northern French

poultice (pohl-tuhs)
noun **1** a soft, moist mass of bread, meal, linseed, etc., applied to the body as a means of curing an ailment
verb **2** to apply a poultice to

Word history: from originally *pultes*, Latin word meaning 'thick pap'

poultry (pohl-tree)
noun birds such as chickens, turkey, ducks, and geese, which are used as food or for egg production

Word history: Middle English, from Old French word meaning 'pullet'

pounce
verb to move or leap suddenly and seize: *The lion **pounced** on the zebra.*

Word building: **pounce** *noun*

pound[1]
verb **1** to hit hard and many times
2 to crush into a powder or small pieces (***crumble, grind, mill, pulverise***)
3 to beat or throb violently: *My heart was **pounding** with excitement.*
4 to go with quick, heavy steps: *They **pounded** along the corridor.*

Word history: Old English *pūnian*

pound[2]
noun **1** a measure of weight in the imperial system, equal to just under half a kilogram
2 a unit of money used in Australia until 1966 and still used in Britain and some other countries

Word use: The symbol for definition 1 is **lb** (*plural* **lbs**). | The symbol for definition 2 is **£**. | For definition 1 look up **imperial system**.
Word history: Middle English and Old English *pund*, from Latin

pound[3]
noun a place where animals are sheltered or kept, especially if they are homeless

Word history: Middle English and Old English *pund-*

pour
verb **1** to send flowing or falling: *She **poured** milk into a glass.*
2 to move or flow in great numbers: *The children **poured** out of the bus.*
3 to rain heavily (***come down in torrents, rain cats and dogs, teem***)

Word history: Middle English

pour / paw / poor / pore
Don't confuse **pour** with **paw, poor** or **pore.**

A **paw** is the foot of an animal with nails or claws.

Someone is **poor** if they don't have much money or property.

A **pore** is a small hole. Sweat comes out through the **pores** in your skin.

To **pore** over something is to read or study it carefully:

He watched the pirates pore over the secret treasure map.

pout
verb to push out the lips showing disappointment or sulkiness

Word building: **pout** *noun*
Word history: Middle English

poverty
noun **1** the condition of being poor: *They lived in **poverty** for years.* (***deprivation, destitution, need, penury, want***)
2 a shortage of something needed or wanted: *a **poverty** of ideas*

Word use: The opposite of definition 1 is **affluence**. The opposite of definition 2 is **wealth**.
Word history: Middle English, from Old French, from Latin

poverty line
noun the lowest income level at which it is possible to maintain an adequate standard of living

powder
noun **1** the very small, loose bits of something dry that has been crushed or ground: *talcum **powder** | a **powder** of dust | tablets crushed to a **powder***
verb **2** to crush into a powder (***grind***, ***mill***, ***pulverise***)
3 to cover with a powder: *to **powder** your face*

Word building: **powdery** *adjective*
Word history: Middle English, from Old French, from Latin word meaning 'dust'

power
noun **1** the ability to do something
2 control over others, especially the control that rulers or governments have: *The election put a new government into **power**. | Britain had **power** over its colonies in the days of the British Empire.* (***dominion***, ***rule***, ***sovereignty***, ***supremacy***, ***sway***)
3 strength or force: *a punch with a lot of **power*** (***might***, ***muscle***, ***vigour***)
4 someone who is very powerful: *This man is the **power** behind the throne.*
5 a country that has a lot of power: *There was a meeting of world **powers** in London.* (***superpower***)
6 the number that is the result of multiplying a number by itself one or more times: *Four is the second **power** of two, and eight is the third **power** of two.*
7 energy or force that can be used for doing work: *electrical **power***
verb **8** to supply with electricity or another kind of power: *to **power** a machine*

Word history: Middle English, from Anglo-French, from Vulgar Latin, for Latin

power board
noun a single moulded plastic unit comprising a number of power points

Word use: You can also use **powerboard**.

powerful
adjective **1** having, using or producing great power, force or effect
2 physically strong
3 potent, as a drug
4 having great influence, as a speech, speaker, description, reason, etc.
5 having great power, authority, or influence, as a nation
6 *Colloquial* great in number or amount: *a **powerful** lot of money*

Word use: The opposite of definition 1 is **powerless**. The opposite of definition 2 is **weak** or **feeble**.

power nap
noun a short sleep taken during the day in order to restore one's energy: *a refreshing **power nap***

power play
noun a strategy designed to gain the upper hand over an opponent in politics, business, etc.: *an underhand **power play***

Word building: **power player** *noun*

power point
noun a device, usually on a wall, to plug electrical power leads into

P-plate
noun one of a pair of identification plates which by law must be displayed, at the front and rear, on any motor vehicle driven by a driver with a provisional licence

PR
noun → **public relations**

Word history: abbreviation of *p(ublic) r(elations)*

practicable (prak-tik-uh-buhl)
adjective **1** able to be put into practice or done, especially sensibly or with the means you have: *a **practicable** idea | a **practicable** plan* (***achievable***, ***feasible***, ***possible***, ***viable***, ***workable***)
2 able or possible to be used or travelled over: *a **practicable** road*

Word history: Medieval Latin

practical
adjective **1** having to do with actual practice or action, rather than ideas: *an invention with a **practical** use | You need **practical** experience for this job.*
2 interested in and good at useful work: *a **practical** person*
3 sensible and realistic: *He always has a **practical** answer.* (***down-to-earth***, ***matter-of-fact***, ***pragmatic***)

Word use: The opposite of definition 1 is **academic** or **theoretical**.
Word building: **practicality** *noun*

practical joke
noun a trick played upon a person, often involving some physical action

practically
adverb **1** in a practical way
2 nearly or almost: *We're **practically** there.*

practice
noun **1** actual action or performance: *His idea sounded good but didn't work in **practice**.*
2 an action or performance that is repeated regularly to improve skill: *Aimée does her piano **practice** every morning.* (***drill***, ***rehearsal***, ***run-through***, ***training***)
3 the usual way of doing something: *It is the **practice** at our school to have assembly every Wednesday.*
4 the business of someone such as a doctor or lawyer

Word history: noun use of *practise*, verb

practise
verb **1** to do or carry out as a usual habit: *You should always **practise** truthfulness.*
2 to work in as a profession: *to **practise** law*
3 to do or perform repeatedly in order to improve skill: *He is **practising** his cricket strokes.*

Word building: **practised** *adjective*
Word history: Middle English, from Old French, *pra(c)tiser*, from Late Latin word meaning 'practical'

practitioner
noun someone working in a practice, particularly a doctor: *a medical **practitioner***

Word history: modified form of *practician*

pragmatic
adjective thinking about the results or usefulness of actions: *She is too **pragmatic** to waste time wanting what she can't have.* (***down-to-earth***, ***matter-of-fact***, ***practical***, ***realistic***, ***sensible***)

Word building: **pragmatically** *adverb*
Word history: Latin, from Greek word meaning 'active', 'versed in state affairs'; as noun, 'a man of business or action'

pragmatics
noun Linguistics the study of those aspects of language which relate to the conventions which regulate its use in a language community

prairie
noun a flat, grassy, treeless plain, especially in the US and Canada

Word history: French word meaning 'field', from Latin word meaning 'meadow'

praise
verb to say that you admire and approve of (***acclaim***, ***commend***, ***compliment***, ***laud***, ***speak well of***)

Word building: **praise** *noun*
Word history: Middle English, from Old French word meaning 'value', 'prize', from Latin word meaning 'price'

praline (prah-leen, pray-leen)
noun a confection of nuts and caramelised sugar

pram
noun a small, four-wheeled baby carriage which you push along

Word history: short form of *perambulator*

prance
verb to leap about (***caper***, ***dance***, ***frisk***, ***gambol***, ***skip***)

Word history: Middle English, perhaps an alliterative alteration of *dance*

prang (prang)
verb Colloquial **1** to crash: *He* ***pranged*** *the car.* | *If you drive like that, you will* ***prang***.
noun Colloquial **2** a crash, as in a car

prank
noun **1** a playful trick (***antic***, ***caper***, ***practical joke***)
2 a call to a mobile phone that cuts out before it can be answered, leaving a phone number listed for a return call

prate (prayt)
verb **1** to talk too much
noun **2** empty or foolish talk

Word building: **prater** *noun*

prattle
verb to chatter in a stupid way

Word building: **prattle** *noun*
Word history: variant of *prate*

prawn
noun a small shellfish used for food

Word history: Middle English

pray
verb **1** to talk to God to thank, praise or ask for something
2 to ask earnestly: *She* ***prayed*** *him to forgive her.* (***appeal***, ***beg***, ***beseech***, ***plead***)

Word history: Middle English, from Old French, from Latin word meaning 'beg', 'pray'

> **pray / prey**
> Don't confuse **pray** with **prey**. To **prey on** something is to hunt and eat it. It can also mean 'to affect something harmfully':
> *Cats prey on mice.*
> *The cause of his death still preys on my mind.*

prayer (prair)
noun **1** a sincere and earnest petition that someone makes to the god they believe in, often for help or forgiveness: *He said a* ***prayer*** *for his sister's safety.*
2 the act or practice of praying: *They joined together in* ***prayer*** *for the victims of the earthquake.*

praying mantis
noun → **mantis**

preach
verb **1** to give a sermon: *She* ***preaches*** *every Sunday.*
2 to give advice in a boring way: *He is always* ***preaching*** *about keeping the place tidy.*

Word history: Middle English, from Old French, from Late Latin

preamble (pree-am-buhl)
noun an introduction explaining the purpose of the book or document which follows

Word history: Middle English, from French, from Medieval Latin word meaning 'walking before'

precarious (pruh-kair-ree-uhs)
adjective **1** uncertain or depending on conditions you can't control: *His position in the company is* ***precarious***.
2 unsafe or risky: *a* ***precarious*** *position on top of a ladder* (***dangerous***, ***hazardous***, ***perilous***)

Word history: from Latin word meaning 'obtained by entreaty or by mere favour', hence 'uncertain', 'precarious'

precaution
noun something done in advance to prevent problems: ***precautions*** *against burglary*

Word building: **precautionary** *adjective*
Word history: Late Latin, from Latin word meaning 'guard against'

precede
verb to go before: *He* ***preceded*** *her into the room.*

Word history: Middle English, from Latin

> **precede / proceed**
> Don't confuse **precede** with **proceed**. To **proceed** is to go on or forwards:
> *The winners will proceed to the victory stand.*

precedence (pres-uh-duhns, prees-uh-duhns)
noun the right to go before something or someone else

precedent (prees-uh-duhnt, pres-uh-duhnt)
noun an event or case which may be used as an example for future action: *She set a* ***precedent*** *when she joined the soccer team, and soon lots of girls were signing up.*

precept (<u>pree</u>-sept)
noun a rule of action: *'Look before you leap' is a wise* ***precept***. (***commandment, direction, law, principle, regulation***)
Word history: Middle English, from Latin word meaning 'instructed'

precinct (<u>pree</u>-singkt)
noun **1** a place or area with definite limits: *shopping* ***precinct***
2 the surrounding area: *the* ***precincts*** *of the city*
Word history: Middle English, from Medieval Latin word meaning 'girded about', 'surrounded'

precious
adjective **1** having a high cost or value: ***precious*** *stones* (***valuable***)
2 deeply loved: *a* ***precious*** *friend* (***dear, cherished, treasured***)
Word history: Middle English, from Old French, from Latin word meaning 'costly'

precipice (<u>pres</u>-uh-puhs)
noun a steep cliff
Word history: French, from Latin

precipitate (pruh-<u>sip</u>-uh-tayt)
verb **1** to bring about quickly: *His arrival* ***precipitated*** *the quarrel.*
2 to change from vapour into dew, rain or snow
3 *Chemistry* to separate out a dissolved substance in solid form from a solution
Word building: **precipitate** *noun*
Word history: from Latin word meaning 'cast headlong'

precipitation (pruh-sip-uh-<u>tay</u>-shuhn)
noun **1** the water which forms as vapour changes into liquid and falls to earth as dew, rain or snow
2 the amount of dew, rain or snow in any one time and place

precipitous (pruh-<u>sip</u>-uh-tuhs)
adjective **1** of the nature of a precipice
2 very steep
3 over-hasty or rash
Word history: *precipit(ate)*, adjective, + *-ous*

precis (<u>pray</u>-see)
noun a brief piece of writing containing the main points of a larger work (***outline, report, résumé, summary, synopsis***)
Word history: French, noun use of adjective, cut short, *precise*

precise (pruh-<u>suys</u>)
adjective exact: ***precise*** *measurement* | ***precise*** *instructions* (***accurate, correct, explicit, specific***)
Word use: The opposite this is **approximate** or **general**.
Word building: **precision** *noun*
Word history: from Latin word meaning 'cut short', 'brief'

preclude
verb to rule out or exclude: *The new rules will not* ***preclude*** *women members from joining.* (***ban, bar, prevent, prohibit***)
Word history: from Latin word meaning 'shut off', 'close'

precocious (pruh-<u>koh</u>-shuhs)
adjective **1** more advanced than others of the same age: *a* ***precocious*** *child*
2 cheeky, impertinent
Word building: **precociousness** *noun* **precocity** *noun*
Word history: *precoci(ty)* (from French word meaning 'early maturity') + *-ous*

preconceive (pree-kuhn-<u>seev</u>)
verb to form an idea of in advance
Word building: **preconception** *noun*

precursor (pree-<u>ker</u>-suh)
noun someone or something that comes before (***antecedent, forerunner, predecessor***)
Word building: **precursory** *adjective* **precursive** *adjective*
Word history: Latin

predate (pree-<u>dayt</u>)
verb **1** to date before the actual time: *He* ***predated*** *the cheque by three days.*
2 to come before in date

predatory (<u>pred</u>-uh-tuh-ree, <u>pred</u>-uh-tree)
adjective hunting other animals for food: *An eagle is a* ***predatory*** *bird.*
Word building: **predator** *noun*
Word history: Latin

predecessor (<u>pree</u>-duh-ses-uh)
noun someone who had the job before you: *He was my* ***predecessor*** *as captain of the team.* (***antecedent, forerunner, precursor***)
Word history: Middle English, from Late Latin

predestine (pree-<u>des</u>-tuhn)
verb to determine beforehand: *Her fate was* ***predestined.***

predetermine (pree-duh-<u>ter</u>-muhn)
verb to determine or decide beforehand
Word building: **predetermination** *noun*

predicament (pruh-<u>dik</u>-uh-muhnt)
noun a difficult or dangerous situation
Word history: Middle English, from Late Latin, from Latin word meaning 'proclaim'

predicate (<u>pred</u>-i-kuht)
noun **1** the word or words which say something about the subject of a sentence
verb (<u>pred</u>-i-kayt) **2** to declare or proclaim
Word history: from Latin word meaning 'declared publicly', 'asserted', in Late Latin 'preached'

We commonly divide sentences into two parts:
1 What is being talked about (the **subject**)
2 What is being said about it (the **predicate**)

She (**subject**) *laughs a lot* (**predicate**).

Really ordinary people that you meet in the street (**subject**) *are nice* (**predicate**).

The snowy peaks (**subject**) *were beginning to turn pink in the sunset* (**predicate**).

Usually the **predicate** is the latter part of the sentence (that is everything that follows the **subject**). But occasionally, especially in literary styles of writing, the **predicate** can come first:

With great ceremony, and without a flicker of emotion, in walked (**predicate**) *Lu* (**subject**).

predict
verb to tell what is going to happen in the future (***forecast***, ***foresee***, ***prophesy***)
Word building: **predictable** *adjective* **prediction** *noun*
Word history: Latin

predilection (pree-duh-lek-shuhn)
noun a tendency of the mind in favour of something (***inclination***, ***leaning***, ***partiality***, ***predisposition***, ***preference***)
Word history: *pre-* + Latin word meaning 'love', 'choice'

predispose (pree-duhs-pohz)
verb **1** to give a previous inclination or tendency to **2** to make subject or liable: *He is **predisposed** to catching a cold.*
Word building: **predisposition** *noun*

predominate
verb **1** to be stronger or more important **2** to control or lead: *She **predominates** in class discussions.*
Word building: **predominance** *noun* **predominant** *adjective*
Word history: *pre-* + Latin word meaning 'ruled', 'dominated'

pre-eminent
adjective superior to or better than others: *He is the **pre-eminent** scientist in his field.* (***chief***, ***foremost***, ***outstanding***, ***paramount***, ***supreme***)
Word building: **pre-eminence** *noun*
Word history: Middle English, from Latin word meaning 'standing out', 'rising above'

pre-empt (pree-empt)
verb **1** to occupy (land) in order to prove an established right to buy **2** to get or gain beforehand **3** to act before someone else or someone else's action (***anticipate***)
Word building: **pre-emptive** *adjective* **pre-emptory** *adjective* **pre-emption** *noun*
Word history: *pre-emption* from *pre-* + Latin *emptio* a buying

preen
verb **1** to trim or arrange feathers with the beak **2** to prepare or dress yourself carefully **3** to pride yourself on something well done
Word history: Middle English

prefabricate
verb to make in a factory in parts, ready for putting together somewhere else at a later time: *The house was **prefabricated** to save money.*
Word building: **prefabrication** *noun*

preface (pref-uhs)
noun an introduction or statement at the front of a book, explaining its purpose
Word building: **preface** *verb* **prefatory** *adjective*
Word history: Middle English, from Old French, from Medieval Latin

prefect
noun a senior pupil with certain responsibilities in a school
Word history: Middle English, from Latin word meaning 'overseer', 'director', 'appointed as a superior'

prefer
verb to like better (***favour***)
Verb forms: I **preferred**, I have **preferred**, I am **preferring**
Word building: **preferable** *adjective*
Word history: Middle English, from Latin word meaning 'bear before', 'set before', 'prefer'

preference (pref-uh-ruhns, pref-ruhns)
noun **1** the act or fact of preferring: *My **preference** is for the home team.* **2** something that is preferred: *Is your **preference** tea or coffee?* (***choice***, ***option***, ***selection***)

preference share
noun in the share market, shares which receive preferred treatment, in that dividends are paid to holders of preferred shares before being paid to holders of ordinary shares

prefix
noun a word part which is put in front of a word to change the meaning, such as 'un-' in *unkind*
Word history: Middle English, from Latin word meaning 'fixed before'

For a list of **prefixes and suffixes**, see appendixes, page 975.

pregnant
adjective having a baby growing in the womb
Word building: **pregnancy** *noun*
Word history: Middle English, from Latin

prehensile (pree-hen-suyl)
adjective **1** suited for seizing or grasping anything **2** fitted for grasping by folding round an object
Word history: French, from Latin word meaning 'seized'

prehistoric
adjective belonging to the time before history was written or records were kept

prejudice (prej-uh-duhs)
noun **1** an opinion unfairly formed beforehand, without reason or evidence **2** harm or unfair treatment which is caused by an opinion like this
verb **3** to influence without sensible reason: *His curly hair **prejudiced** her in his favour.* (***bias***, ***jaundice***, ***slant***, ***sway***)
Word history: Middle English, from French, from Latin

prelate (prel-uht)
noun a senior member of the clergy, as an archbishop, bishop, etc.
Word history: Middle English, from Medieval Latin word meaning 'a civil or ecclesiastical dignitary'

preliminary
adjective coming before and leading up to the main matter: *a **preliminary** test*
Word history: Neo-Latin, from Latin word meaning 'of a threshold'

prelude (prel-yoohd)
noun **1** something that comes before: *Thought should be a **prelude** to action.* **2** a short piece of music written for an instrument
Word history: French, from Medieval Latin, from Latin word meaning 'play beforehand'

premarital (pree-ma-ruh-tuhl)
adjective before marriage

premature (prem-uh-chuh, prem-uh-tyooh-uh)
adjective coming or happening too soon: *a **premature** baby | a **premature** decision*

Word history: Latin

premeditate
verb to plan beforehand

Word building: **premeditation** *noun*
Word history: from Latin word meaning 'meditated beforehand'

premier (prem-ee-uh)
noun **1** the leader of a State government
adjective **2** first or leading: *the **premier** team in the championship*

Word building: **premiership** *noun*
Word history: French word meaning 'first', from Latin word meaning 'of the first rank'

premiere (prem-ee-air)
noun the first public performance of a play, film, or something similar

Word building: **premiere** *verb*
Word history: French word literally meaning 'first' (feminine)

premise (prem-uhs)
noun **1** a proposition (or one of several) from which a conclusion is drawn
2 a basis for reasoned argument

Word use: You can also use **premiss** for definition 1.
Word history: Middle English, from Medieval Latin word meaning 'sent before'

premises (prem-uh-suhz)
plural noun a building or house with the land belonging to it

premium (pree-mee-uhm)
noun **1** a bonus, gift or additional sum
2 a payment made for insurance
phrase **3 at a premium,**
a in high regard
b at a high price

Word history: from Latin word meaning 'profit'

premonition (prem-uh-nish-uhn, pree-muh-nish-uhn)
noun a feeling that something bad is about to happen: *I had a **premonition** about the accident.*

Word history: French (obsolete), from Late Latin

prenuptial agreement (pree-nup-chuhl uh-gree-muhnt)
noun a legal contract made by two people before their wedding: *The **prenuptial agreement** outlined the division of property in event of divorce.*

Word use: You can also use the colloquial word **prenup**.

preoccupied
adjective completely taken up in thought: *She seemed **preoccupied** and did not listen to a word I said.* (***absorbed**, **engrossed**, **faraway**, **in a brown study**, **lost in thought***)

Word building: **preoccupation** *noun*

prepare
verb to make or get ready: *to **prepare** a garden for planting | to **prepare** for a trip*

Word building: **preparation** *noun* **preparatory** *adjective*
Word history: from Latin word meaning 'make ready beforehand'

prepayment
noun payment in advance of receipt of goods or services

preponderant (pruh-pon-duh-ruhnt, pruh-pon-druhnt)
adjective greater in weight, force, influence, number, etc. (***paramount**, **predominant**, **prevailing***)

Word building: **preponderate** *verb* **preponderance** *noun*

preposition (prep-uh-zish-uhn)
noun a word placed before a noun to show its relation to other words in the sentence, such as 'to' and 'from' in *He gave an apple to Len and took a sandwich from him.*

Word history: Middle English, from Latin

common prepositions

above	after	among	at	before
beside	by	for	from	in
near	of	off	on	over
through	to	under	up	upon

preposition / proposition

Don't confuse **preposition** with **proposition**, which is a suggestion or proposal:

Your proposition that we should have a picnic lunch is a good one.

prepossessing (pree-puh-zes-ing)
adjective able to impress, especially favourably

preposterous
adjective absurd or far from what is normal or sensible: *a **preposterous** scheme for recycling oyster shells* (***farcical**, **ludicrous**, **nonsensical**, **ridiculous**, **silly***)

Word history: from Latin word meaning 'with the hinder part foremost'

prepuce (pree-pyoohs)
noun the fold of skin which covers the head of the penis or clitoris (***foreskin***)

Word history: Middle English, from French, from Latin

prerequisite (pree-rek-wuh-zuht)
adjective **1** needed beforehand
noun **2** something prerequisite: *A knowledge of French was the only **prerequisite** for obtaining the job.*

prerogative (pruh-rog-uh-tiv)
noun a right or privilege: *It is the captain's **prerogative** to choose the team.*

Word history: Middle English, from Latin word meaning 'voting first'

presage (pres-ij)
noun **1** a feeling of something about to happen (***boding**, **foreboding**, **premonition**, **presentiment***)

2 something that foreshadows a future event (***harbinger***, ***omen***, ***portent***)
3 a forecast or prediction (***prognostication***, ***prophecy***)
verb (<u>pres</u>-ij, pruh-<u>sayj</u>) **4** to have a feeling that something is about to happen
5 to forecast or make a forecast

Word building: **presager** *noun*
Word history: Middle English, from Latin

preschool
noun a school where some young children go for a year or so before they start primary school

prescribe
verb to order for use as a treatment: *The doctor **prescribed** some cough medicine.*

Word history: from Latin word meaning 'write before', 'direct'

prescribe / proscribe
Don't confuse **prescribe** with **proscribe**. To **proscribe** something is to condemn it and forbid people to do it.

prescription
noun a written order by a doctor to a chemist for medicine

Word use: The short form is **script**.
Word history: Middle English, from Latin

presence
noun attendance or being in a place: *Your **presence** is requested at the party.*

Word use: The opposite of this is **absence**.
Word history: Middle English, from Old French, from Latin

present[1] (<u>prez</u>-uhnt)
adjective **1** happening or existing now: *the **present** Prime Minister*
2 being in a place: *Is everyone **present**?*
noun **3** the present time

Word history: Middle English, from Latin word meaning 'being before (one)'

present[2] (pruh-<u>zent</u>)
verb **1** to give, especially in a formal way: *The mayor **presented** the prizes.* (***award***, ***confer***, ***donate***)
noun (<u>prez</u>-uhnt) **2** something given: *birthday **presents*** (***gift***)

Word building: **presentation** *noun*
Word history: Middle English, from Old French, from Latin

presentable
adjective fit to be seen: *Have a shower and make yourself **presentable**.*

presentiment (pruh-<u>zent</u>-uh-muhnt)
noun a feeling of something about to happen, especially something evil (***boding***, ***foreboding***, ***premonition***)

Word history: French (obsolete), from Latin word meaning 'perceive beforehand'

presently
adverb **1** in a short time: *The manager will see you **presently**.*
2 at this time: *He is **presently** living in Bendigo.*

present tense
noun the form of a verb which shows that something is happening in the present

Look up **verbs: present tense.**

preservative
noun a substance that prevents something, such as food, from going bad

preserve (pruh-<u>zerv</u>)
verb **1** to keep in existence or alive: *to **preserve** old customs* (***maintain***, ***perpetuate***, ***prolong***, ***retain***, ***sustain***)
2 to keep from going bad: *to **preserve** fruit* (***conserve***)
3 to keep safe: *Heaven **preserve** us!* (***protect***, ***rescue***, ***safeguard***, ***save***, ***shelter***)
noun **4** fruit cooked with sugar so that it can be stored

Word use: You can also use **preserves** for definition 4.
Word building: **preservation** *noun*
Word history: Middle English, from Latin

preside (pruh-<u>zuyd</u>)
verb **1** to occupy the place of authority or control, especially at a meeting (***chair***, ***direct***, ***head***, ***manage***, ***officiate***)
2 to exercise control

Word history: from Latin word meaning 'sit before', 'guard', 'preside over'

president
noun **1** the elected head of a republic
2 someone chosen to have control over the meetings of a society or something similar

Word building: **presidential** *adjective*
Word history: Middle English, from Latin word meaning 'presiding', 'ruling'

press
verb **1** to act upon with weight or force: ***Press** down the lid.* (***compress***, ***jam***, ***push***, ***squash***, ***squeeze***)
2 to squeeze: *She **pressed** his hand.*
3 to urge: *She **pressed** them to come.*
4 to use an iron to remove creases from clothes
noun **5** a machine used for printing
6 newspapers, magazines, etc., or the people who write for them

Word history: Old English *press*, from Medieval Latin

press conference
noun an interview of a famous person, public official, etc., by a group of journalists

press gallery
noun **1** a gallery kept apart for journalists, especially in a house of parliament
2 the group of reporters allowed to enter such a gallery

press release
noun a piece of news prepared for and given to the press

pressure (<u>presh</u>-uh)
noun **1** the weight or force with which something presses on something else: *to put **pressure** on a lever*
2 a force applied to something, measured as so much weight on a unit of area: *air **pressure***
3 continual worry: *He is under **pressure** at work.*

Word history: Middle English, from French, from Latin

pressure group
noun a group, in politics, business, etc., which attempts to protect or advance its own interests

pressure point
noun **1** any of the points in the body at which pressure applied with the fingers, a tourniquet, etc., will control bleeding from an artery at a point further away from the heart
2 a healing point in the body, stimulated by a special type of massage

pressurise
verb to keep normal air pressure in: *to **pressurise** the cabin of a plane*

Word use: You can also use **pressurize**.

prestige (pres-<u>teezh</u>)
noun high reputation or standing: *Don Bradman has enormous **prestige** in the world of cricket.*

Word building: **prestigious** *adjective*
Word history: French word meaning 'illusion', 'glamour', from Latin word meaning 'illusion'

presume
verb **1** to take for granted: *I **presume** you're tired after your walk.* (***assume***, ***infer***, ***suppose***, ***take it***)
2 to dare: *I would not **presume** to tell you how to do it.*
3 to act with inexcusable boldness or rudeness

Word building: **presumption** *noun*
Word history: Middle English, from Latin word meaning 'take beforehand', 'venture'

presumptuous
adjective **1** taking something for granted without reasonable cause
2 inexcusably bold or rude

pretence
noun **1** a false show: *a **pretence** of friendship*
2 a pretended reason

Word history: Middle English, from Anglo-French, from Medieval Latin word meaning 'pretend'

pretend
verb **1** to make a false claim: *She **pretended** to be interested in his speech. | The burglar **pretended** he was reading the meter.*
2 to make believe (***dream***, ***feign***, ***imagine***)

Word history: Middle English, from Latin word meaning 'stretch forth', 'pretend'

pretension
noun **1** a laying claim to something
2 a claim to something
3 the act of pretending
4 **pretensions**, a claim made, especially indirectly, to some quality, merit, etc.: *He has **pretensions** to good judgement.*

pretentious (pruh-<u>ten</u>-shuhs)
adjective having an exaggerated outward show of importance, wealth, etc. (***affected***, ***grandiose***, ***ostentatious***, ***pompous***, ***showy***)

Word history: from Latin word meaning 'pretension'

preterm
adjective **1** born or occurring before a pregnancy has reached its full term: *a **preterm** baby*
2 held before the elected body has reached its full term: *a **preterm** election*

Word use: You can also use **pre-term**.

pretext (<u>pree</u>-tekst)
noun something that is put forward to hide a true purpose or object: *He stayed out late on the **pretext** that his car had broken down.* (***excuse***, ***guise***, ***pretence***)

Word history: Latin

pretty
adjective **1** pleasant or attractive (***beautiful***, ***comely***, ***fair***, ***good-looking***, ***lovely***)
adverb **2** rather or quite: ***pretty** good*
phrase **3** **pretty much** (or **well**),
a to a large extent: *His version of what happened **pretty much** agrees with hers.*
b very nearly: *The exams are **pretty much** over, now.*

Adjective forms: **prettier, prettiest**
Word building: **prettiness** *noun*
Word history: Old English *prættig* cunning, wily

pretzel
noun a small, crisp, salted biscuit, often in the shape of a knot

Word history: German

prevail
verb **1** to win or triumph: *In spite of the objections, good sense **prevailed**.*
2 to be most numerous or strong: *Stunted gum trees **prevail** on these dry hillsides.*
phrase **3** **prevail upon**, to persuade successfully: *I **prevailed upon** him to change his mind.*

Word history: Middle English, from Latin word meaning 'be more able'

prevalent (<u>prev</u>-uh-luhnt)
adjective widespread: *an opinion **prevalent** in the community | a **prevalent** weed*

Word building: **prevalence** *noun*
Word history: from Latin word meaning 'prevailing'

prevaricate (pruh-<u>va</u>-ruh-kayt)
verb to speak in a way which tries to avoid the point by using various ploys

Word building: **prevarication** *noun*
Word history: from Latin word meaning 'walked crookedly', 'deviated'

prevent
verb **1** to keep someone from doing something: *He had to act quickly to **prevent** the baby from swallowing the beads.* (***bar***, ***hinder***, ***impede***, ***obstruct***, ***restrain***)
2 to keep from happening: *She was just in time to **prevent** an accident.* (***avert***, ***block***, ***forestall***, ***stave off***)

Word building: **prevention** *noun*
Word history: Middle English, from Latin word meaning 'come before'

preventive
adjective **1** serving to prevent or stop something, especially a disease
noun **2** a substance or measure designed to prevent something

Word use: You can also use **preventative**.

preventive medicine
noun medical strategies and practices designed to prevent the onset of disease

preview
noun a showing of a film or exhibition before the public is allowed to see it

previous
adjective happening before: *the **previous** day*
Word history: Latin

prey (pray)
noun **1** an animal hunted for food by another: *Mice are the **prey** of cats.*
2 a victim
phrase **3 bird of prey,** a bird which hunts smaller birds and animals as its prey
4 prey on,
a to hunt and eat: *Cats **prey on** mice.*
b to affect harmfully: *The problem is **preying on** my mind.*
Word history: Middle English, from Old French, from Latin word meaning 'booty', 'prey'

prey / pray
Don't confuse **prey** with **pray**. **Pray** means 'to talk to God'.

price
noun **1** the amount of money for which something is bought or sold (***charge***, ***cost***, ***rate***)
verb **2** to give or guess the price of: *to **price** a jewel*
Word history: Middle English, from Old French, from Latin word meaning 'price', 'value', 'worth'

price-fixing
noun the setting of a price for a commodity or service by agreement between business competitors: *The high prices were a result of **price-fixing**.*
Word building: **price-fixer** *noun*

priceless
adjective having a value beyond all price: *a **priceless** talent*

prick
noun **1** a small hole made by a needle, thorn or something sharp
2 the feeling of being pricked
verb **3** to pierce with a sharp point
phrase **4 prick up your ears,** to start listening, especially to something of particular interest
Word history: from Old English word meaning 'puncture'

prickle
noun a sharp point or thorn
Word building: **prickly** *adjective* (**pricklier**, **prickliest**)
Word history: Old English

pride
noun **1** well-earned pleasure or satisfaction: *She takes **pride** in her work.*
2 a high, or too high, opinion of your own dignity or importance
phrase **3 pride yourself on,** to take well-earned pleasure or satisfaction in: *He **prided himself on** a job well done.*
Word history: Middle English; Old English *prȳde*

priest
noun someone whose job is to perform religious ceremonies (***chaplain***, ***clergyman***, ***minister***, ***parson***, ***vicar***)
Word building: **priesthood** *noun* **priestly** *adjective*
Word history: Old English *prēost*, from Latin

priestess
noun a woman whose job it is to perform religious ceremonies

Look up **non-sexist language.**

prig
noun someone who is too concerned about duty and who always thinks they are right
Word building: **priggish** *adjective*
Word history: perhaps related to *prink* to dress fussily and for show

prim
adjective stiff and very proper in manner
Adjective forms: **primmer**, **primmest**
Word use: The opposite of this is **casual** and **relaxed**.

primacy (pruy-muh-see)
noun the condition of being first in order, rank, importance, etc.
Word history: Middle English, from Medieval Latin, from Latin word meaning 'primate'

primal
adjective **1** first or original (***initial***, ***primeval***, ***primordial***)
2 of first or highest importance (***central***, ***chief***, ***fundamental***, ***prime***, ***principal***)
Word history: Medieval Latin, from Latin word meaning 'first'

primary
adjective first in order or importance: ***primary** education | the **primary** reason for her success* (***chief***, ***fundamental***, ***key***, ***leading***, ***main***, ***major***)
Word history: late Middle English, from Latin word meaning 'of the first rank'

primary forest
noun Ecology forest that has not been logged or cleared in the past
Word use: Compare this with **secondary forest**.

primary industry
noun any industry such as dairy farming, forestry, mining, etc., which involves the growing, producing, extracting, etc., of natural resources

primary source
noun in the study of history, a document or other piece of evidence coming directly from the time being studied
Word use: Compare this with **secondary source**.

primate
noun **1** any mammal of the group that includes humans, apes and monkeys
2 the head bishop of a country
Word history: Middle English, from Medieval Latin word meaning 'chief bishop', Late Latin word meaning 'chief', 'head'

prime
adjective **1** of the first importance or quality: ***prime** time* | ***prime** beef*
2 typical: *a **prime** example*
noun **3** the period or condition of greatest vigour: *the **prime** of life*
verb **4** to cover with a coat of paint in preparation for a further coat
5 to prepare by supplying information, etc.: *The official **primed** the minister before the cabinet meeting.*
Word history: Old English, from Latin word meaning 'first'

prime minister
noun the leader of the government in some countries, including Australia
Word use: You can also use **Prime Minister**.

prime number
noun a number which cannot be divided except by itself and 1

primer[1] (prim-uh, pruy-muh)
noun a simple book for teaching the beginnings of any subject, especially reading
Word history: Middle English, from Medieval Latin

primer[2] (pruy-muh)
noun a coat of paint used to prepare a surface for the next coat
Word history: *prime* + *-er*

primeval (pruy-meev-uhl)
adjective belonging to the earliest period of the earth
Word history: from Latin word meaning 'young' + *-al*

primitive
adjective **1** being the earliest in existence: ***primitive** forms of life*
2 belonging to an early stage of civilisation: ***primitive** art*
Word history: Latin word meaning 'first of its kind'; replacing Middle English *primitif*, from Old French

primrose
noun **1** a common, perennial European plant, usually with pale yellow flowers
2 a pale yellow colour
Word building: **primrose** *adjective*
Word history: Middle English, from Medieval Latin word meaning 'first rose'

prince
noun a son or near male relation of a king or queen
Word building: **princely** *adjective*
Word history: Middle English, from Old French, from Latin word meaning 'principal person'

princess
noun **1** a daughter or near female relation of a king or queen
2 someone married to a prince
Word history: Middle English, from French, feminine of *prince*

principal (prin-suh-puhl)
adjective **1** main or leading: *the **principal** thing to remember* (***chief, fundamental, key, major, primary***)
noun **2** the head of a school
Word history: Middle English, from Latin word meaning 'first', 'chief'

principal / principle
Don't confuse **principal** with **principle,** which means a guiding rule of right behaviour.

principality
noun a small state ruled by a prince
Noun forms: The plural is **principalities**.

principle (prin-suh-puhl)
noun **1** a general truth or rule: *the **principles** of government*
2 a basic belief, teaching or opinion: *the **principles** of Christianity*
3 an inner guiding sense of right behaviour: *a person of **principle***
4 principles, guiding rules of right behaviour
phrase **5 in principle**, having to do with the basic ideas or principles: *I accept your plan **in principle**.*
6 on principle, according to a personal rule for right behaviour: *He doesn't eat meat **on principle**.*
Word history: Middle English, from French, from Latin

print
verb **1** to make copies of by pressing an inked surface on to paper or other material: *to **print** newspapers*
2 to write in separate letters rather than in running writing: *Please **print** your name and address.*
noun **3** the condition of being printed: *The book appeared in **print** last week.*
phrase **4 in print**,
a published
b of a book, still able to be bought from the publisher
5 out of print, of a book, sold out by the publisher
Word history: Middle English, from Old French word meaning 'impression', 'print', from Latin word meaning 'press'

printer
noun **1** a person or business engaged in the printing industry
2 *Computers* a device which outputs information in printed form

printout
noun information printed by a computer so that it can be read

prior[1] (pruy-uh)
adjective **1** earlier: *a **prior** engagement*
phrase **2 prior to**, before: ***prior to** my going away*
Word history: Latin word earlier meaning 'former'

prior[2]
noun a head monk or friar
Word building: **priory** *noun* (*plural* **priories**) **prioress** *feminine noun*
Word history: Middle English and Old English, from Medieval Latin word meaning 'superior', 'head'

priority (pruy-o-ruh-tee)
noun the right to go before someone or something else, because of urgency or importance: *The sickest people will be given **priority**.*

prise (pruyz)
verb to raise, move or force with a lever: ***Prise** open the lid with a screw driver.*

Word use: The US spelling is **prize**.
Word history: Middle English, from French word meaning 'a taking hold', from Latin word meaning 'seized'

prise / prize
Don't confuse **prise** with **prize**, which is a reward for success.

prism
noun a transparent object, usually of glass and with triangular ends, used for breaking light down into the colours of the rainbow

Word building: **prismatic** *adjective*
Word history: Late Latin, from Greek word meaning 'something sawed'

prison
noun a place where criminals are kept locked up (***compound***, ***jail***, ***lockup***, ***penitentiary***)

Word building: **imprison** *verb*
Word history: Middle English, from Old French, from Latin word meaning 'seizure', 'arrest'

prisoner
noun **1** someone who is kept in prison (***captive***, ***convict***, ***criminal***, ***inmate***, ***internee***)
2 someone who is caught or seized: *The gang took him **prisoner**.*

prissy
adjective Colloquial fussy and prim

Adjective forms: **prissier**, **prissiest**
Word history: blend of *prim* and *sissy*

pristine (pris-teen)
adjective **1** so clean as to appear new: ***pristine** white sheets* | *The house was in **pristine** condition.*
2 having to do with the earliest period or condition: *the earth's **pristine** landscape*
3 having its original purity: ***pristine** loveliness*

Word history: from Latin word meaning 'early'

privacy (pruy-vuh-see, priv-uh-see)
noun **1** the condition of being private (***seclusion***)
2 secrecy

Noun forms: The plural is **privacies**.
Word history: *priv(ate)* + *-acy*

private
adjective **1** belonging to someone in particular: ***private** property* (***personal***)
2 concerned with personal affairs: *My diary is **private**.* (***confidential***, ***secret***)

Word history: Middle English, from Latin word meaning 'separate'

private enterprise
noun **1** business activities not under state ownership or control
2 the principle of free business enterprise as in a capitalist system

privation
noun lack or loss of the usual comforts or necessary things of life: *to lead a life of **privation*** (***deprivation***, ***destitution***, ***hardship***, ***neediness***, ***poverty***)

Word history: Middle English, from Latin

privatise
verb to change the ownership of (land, industries, etc.) from government to private enterprise: *The electricity industry has been **privatised**.*

Word use: You can also use **privatize**.
Word building: **privatisation** *noun*

privet (priv-uht)
noun a European evergreen shrub or small tree, of unusual hardiness, with small, strong-smelling white flowers, now considered a pest in Australia, because it overgrows areas of bush

privilege (priv-uh-lij)
noun **1** a special right or advantage enjoyed by only a limited number of people: *We had the **privilege** of meeting the great poet.*
2 a special right or protection given to people in authority or office: *parliamentary **privilege***

Word building: **privileged** *adjective*
Word history: Middle English, from Latin word meaning 'a law in favour of or against an individual'

privy (priv-ee)
noun **1** an outhouse serving as a toilet
phrase **2 privy to**, sharing in the knowledge of something private or secret: *Many people were **privy to** the plan.*

Noun forms: The plural is **privies**.
Word history: Middle English, from Old French, from Latin word meaning 'separated', 'private'

prize[1]
noun **1** a reward for winning a race or competition (***award***, ***trophy***)
2 something won in a lottery or raffle

Word history: Middle English, from Old French word meaning 'price', 'value', 'glory', from Latin

prize[2]
verb to value highly

Word history: Middle English, from Old French word meaning 'praise', from Latin

prize / prise
Don't confuse **prize** with **prise**. To **prise** something open is to force it open, usually with a lever.

pro[1]
preposition **1** in favour of: *I am **pro** peace.*
phrase **2 pros and cons**, the arguments for and against something; the good points and the bad points: *Let's run through all the **pros and cons** of the proposal.*

Word history: from Latin word meaning 'in favour of', 'for'

pro[2]
noun Colloquial someone who is professional at something

Noun forms: The plural is **pros**.
Word history: short form of *professional*

proactive (proh-ak-tiv)
adjective taking direct action, rather than waiting until things happen and then reacting: *The government has taken a **proactive** attitude towards crime.*

Word use: The opposite of this is **passive**.

probability
noun **1** chance or likelihood: *There is the **probability** of rain.*
2 something that is probable or likely
Noun forms: The plural is **probabilities**.

probable
adjective likely or expected to happen or be true
Word building: **probably** *adverb*
Word history: Middle English, from Latin

probate (proh-bayt)
Law
noun **1** the official proving of a will as validly made according to the law
2 an officially certified copy of a will so proved
adjective **3** having to do with probate or a court of probate
Word history: Middle English, from Latin word meaning '(a thing) proved'

probation
noun **1** a period of trial: *She is new in the job and still on **probation**.*
2 a system of punishment in which certain people who have broken the law can stay free on condition of good behaviour: *He has been put on **probation** for shop-lifting.*
Word building: **probationary** *adjective*
Word history: Middle English, from Latin

probe
verb **1** to examine or search thoroughly: *to **probe** a wound | to **probe** evidence* (***delve into, explore, investigate, scrutinise, test***)
noun **2** the act of probing
3 an official inquiry: *The opposition is calling for a **probe** into government spending.*
4 a thin surgical instrument for exploring the depth or direction of a wound, sinus, etc.
Word building: **probe** *noun*
Word history: from Medieval Latin word meaning 'test', in Late Latin word meaning 'proof'

probiotic (proh-buy-ot-ik)
adjective **1** having to do with a food containing live bacteria: ***Probiotic** yoghurts contain bacteria which are good for you.*
noun **2** such a food

probity (proh-buh-tee)
noun honesty (***honour, integrity, rectitude, uprightness***)
Word history: Latin

problem
noun **1** something which is difficult or uncertain: *His health is a **problem**.* (***complication, difficulty, trouble***)
2 a question to be answered: *a maths **problem*** (***conundrum, puzzle***)
Word building: **problematic** *adjective*
Word history: Middle English, from Latin, from Greek

pro bono (proh boh-noh)
adjective **1** especially in legal work, performed without charge: *A proportion of her time is spent on **pro bono** work.*
adverb **2** without charging a fee: *He is working **pro bono** for this client.*

proboscis (pruh-bos-kuhs, pruh-boh-suhs)
noun **1** an elephant's trunk
2 any long, flexible nose, as of the tapir
3 in insects, a long, tubelike mouthpart used for feeding
Noun forms: The plural is **proboscises** (pruh-bos-kuh-suhz, pruh-bos-uh-suhz).
Word history: Latin, from Greek

procedural (pruh-see-juh-ruhl)
adjective **1** having to do with procedure
2 having to do with a type of text which shows how something can be done: *Recipes are **procedural** texts.*
Word building: **procedurally** *adverb*

procedure (pruh-see-juh)
noun a way of doing something: *the usual **procedure** for applying for a job | parliamentary **procedure*** (***approach, means, method, technique***)
Word history: French

proceed
verb **1** to move forward, especially after stopping (***advance, forge ahead, make headway, progress, push on***)
2 to go on or continue
noun **3 proceeds**, money brought in by selling, etc. (***dividend, pay, profit, return***)
Word history: Middle English, from Latin

> **proceed / precede**
> Don't confuse **proceed** with **precede**. To **precede** someone is to go in front of them.

proceeding
noun **1** behaviour or way of acting: *This is a strange **proceeding**.*
2 proceedings, records of the activities and meetings of a club or society

process
noun **1** a series of actions carried out for a particular purpose: *the **process** of making butter*
verb **2** to treat, prepare or deal with in a certain way: *to **process** iron ore | to **process** film | to **process** data*
Word building: **processor** *noun*
Word history: Middle English, from French, from Latin word meaning 'a going forward'

procession
noun an orderly line of people, cars or floats moving along in a ceremony or as a show (***cavalcade, parade***)
Word history: early Middle English, from Medieval Latin word meaning 'a religious procession', in Latin, 'a marching on'

proclaim
verb to announce publicly: *The Governor-General **proclaimed** three new laws this morning. | She **proclaimed** her innocence to the crowded courtroom.* (***declare, profess, promulgate, publish***)
Word building: **proclamation** *noun*
Word history: Middle English, from Latin

proclivity (pruh-kliv-uh-tee)
noun a natural or habitual inclination or tendency: *a **proclivity** to fault-finding* (***leaning, predilection, predisposition, propensity***)
Noun forms: The plural is **proclivities**.
Word history: from Latin word meaning 'tendency', 'propensity'

procrastinate
verb to put off doing something until another time

Word building: **procrastination** *noun*
Word history: from Latin word meaning 'put off till the next day'

procreate
verb to produce offspring

Word building: **procreation** *noun*
Word history: Latin

procure
verb to obtain: *to* ***procure*** *food* | *to* ***procure*** *a result* (***acquire***, ***gain***, ***get***, ***secure***, ***win***)

Word building: **procurable** *adjective*
Word history: Middle English, from Latin word meaning 'take care of', 'manage'

prod
verb to poke or jab

Verb forms: I **prodded**, I have **prodded**, I am **prodding**
Word building: **prod** *noun*

prodigal
adjective wasteful or extravagant: *a* ***prodigal*** *use of materials* | *the* ***prodigal*** *son*

Word building: **prodigal** *noun*
Word history: Middle English, from Latin

prodigious (pruh-dij-uhs)
adjective extraordinary in size, amount or force: *a* ***prodigious*** *noise*

Word history: Latin

prodigy (prod-uh-jee)
noun **1** someone, especially a child, who has extraordinary talent: *Mozart was a musical* ***prodigy***. (***genius***, ***wonder child***)
2 an extraordinary or wonderful thing

Noun forms: The plural is **prodigies**.
Word history: from Latin word meaning 'prophetic sign', 'omen'

produce (pruh-dyoohs)
verb **1** to bring into being: *This soil* ***produces*** *good crops.* (***bear***, ***breed***, ***grow***, ***supply***, ***yield***)
2 to pull out and present: *He* ***produced*** *a letter from his pocket.*
3 to assemble the cast for and generally organise and control: *to* ***produce*** *a play*
noun (proj-oohs) **4** farm or natural products: *Farmers take their* ***produce*** *to market.*

Word history: from Latin word meaning 'lead or bring forward'

producer
noun **1** someone who produces articles, agricultural products, etc.
2 someone who arranges the financing of a film production
3 someone who is responsible for a film, television or radio production, or a music recording, who controls the performers, and who has the final decision on artistic matters
4 *Science* an apparatus used for making producer gas

producer gas
noun a fuel gas produced by combining cheap solid fuel with steam; used in the place of petrol, natural gas, etc.

product
noun **1** something made or brought into existence: *the* ***product*** *of labour* | *household* ***products***
2 the result you get by multiplying two or more numbers together
3 *Chemistry* a substance obtained from another substance through chemical change
4 a substance sold commercially for a particular use: *How are we going to advertise this* ***product***?

Word history: Middle English, from Latin *prōductum* (thing) produced

production
noun **1** the act of producing or creating
2 something that is produced
3 *Economics* the producing of articles able to be bought and sold
4 the total amount produced
5 the staging of a play

productive
adjective **1** producing or tending to produce
2 producing easily or abundantly

Word use: The opposite of definition 1 is **infertile** or **unproductive**. The opposite of definition 2 is **unfruitful** or **unproductive**.
Word building: **productivity** *noun*

profane
adjective showing deep lack of respect for religion: ***profane*** *language* (***blasphemous***, ***impious***, ***irreverent***, ***sacrilegious***, ***unholy***)

Word use: The opposite of this is **sacred**.
Word building: **profanity** *noun*
Word history: Middle English, from French, from Latin word meaning 'before (outside) the temple'

profess
verb to declare or show, often insincerely: *He* ***professed*** *great sorrow.*

profession
noun **1** an occupation in which advanced and special knowledge of a subject is needed: *She is a lawyer by* ***profession***.
2 the people in a profession taken as a whole: *the legal* ***profession***
3 a declaration, whether true or false: *a* ***profession*** *of love*

Word history: Middle English, from Latin word meaning 'public declaration'

professional
adjective **1** following an occupation to earn a living from it: *a* ***professional*** *golfer*
2 belonging to a profession: ***professional*** *studies*
3 expert or competent: *Her painting is very* ***professional***. (***adept***, ***masterly***, ***polished***, ***proficient***)

Word use: Compare this with **amateur**.
Word building: **professional** *noun*
professionalism *noun*

professor
noun a university teacher of the highest rank

Word building: **professorial** (prof-uh-saw-ree-uhl) *adjective*
Word history: Middle English, from Latin

proffer
verb to place before someone, for acceptance: *He* ***proffered*** *his resignation to the board.*

Word history: Middle English, from Old French

proficient (pruh-fish-uhnt)
adjective skilled or expert: *a **proficient** carpenter* (***able, accomplished, capable, competent, gifted***)

Word building: **proficiency** *noun*
Word history: from Latin word meaning 'making progress'

profile
noun **1** an outline of a face, especially a side view
2 a drawing, painting or photograph of the side view of a face
3 a short account of someone's life and character: *There is a **profile** of the Treasurer in today's paper.*
4 on a website, personal details of a user made available to particular people or to all other users: *I've set up my profile so that only people I know can view it – that's the safest option.*
phrase **5 keep a low profile**, to act so as not to be noticed

Word history: Italian word meaning 'draw in outline', from Latin word meaning 'pro-' + Late Latin word meaning 'thread'

profit
noun **1** money made from selling something at a higher price than you paid for it (***bonus, dividend, return***)
2 advantage or benefit: *There is no **profit** in regretting the past.*

Word use: Look up **operating profit** also.
Word building: **profit** *verb* **profitable** *adjective*
Word history: Middle English, from Old French, from Latin word meaning 'progress', 'profit'

> **profit / prophet**
> Don't confuse **profit** with **prophet**. A **prophet** in biblical times was someone who spoke on behalf of God. It can also mean 'a great teacher or leader'.

profiteer
noun **1** someone who makes money in a greedy way, often by taking unfair advantage of people
verb **2** to act as a profiteer

profiterole (pruh-fit-uh-rohl)
noun a small pastry ball filled with cream and custard, and coated with chocolate

profligate (prof-luh-guht)
adjective **1** extremely and shamelessly immoral
2 carelessly wasteful (***extravagant, spendthrift***)
noun **3** a profligate person

Word history: from Latin word meaning 'overthrown', 'ruined'

profound
adjective **1** going deeply into ideas or thought: *a **profound** thinker* (***discerning, penetrating, wise***)
2 deep, intense or absolute: ***profound** sleep* | ***profound** regret* (***acute, extreme***)

Word use: The opposite of this is **shallow** or **superficial**.
Word building: **profundity** *noun*
Word history: Middle English, from Old French, from Latin

profuse (pruh-fyoohs)
adjective plentiful: *a **profuse** flow of blood* | ***profuse** apologies*

Word building: **profusion** *noun*
Word history: Middle English, from Latin word meaning 'poured forth'

progenitor (pruh-jen-uh-tuh)
noun an ancestor (***antecedent, forebear, forefather***)

progeny (proj-uh-nee)
noun offspring or descendants: *the **progeny** of my pet rabbits* | *the **progeny** of kings* (***issue, young***)

Word history: Middle English, from Old French, from Latin

prognosis
noun a doctor's opinion on how a disease will develop (***forecast, prediction***)

Noun forms: The plural is **prognoses** (prog-noh-seez).
Word history: Late Latin, from Greek word meaning 'foreknowledge'

> **prognosis / diagnosis**
> These are both medical terms, although they also have more general meanings.
> A **diagnosis** is a doctor's analysis of what is wrong with a patient.
> A **prognosis** is the next step that the doctor takes after making a **diagnosis.** It is an informed opinion as to what course the illness will take:
> *The doctor's prognosis is that you will have a fever for two weeks.*

prognosticate
verb to make a forecast (***predict, presage, prophesy***)

program
noun **1** a plan to be followed: *a **program** of study*
2 a list of items and performers in a concert or play
3 a particular entertainment or production: *There's a good **program** on TV tonight.*
4 a set of instructions that makes a computer deal with certain data and solve problems
verb **5** to enter instructions into (a device) to make it perform a certain task: *to **program** the DVD player*
6 to write a computer program

Verb forms: I **programmed**, I have **programmed**, I am **programming**
Word use: You can also use **programme** for definitions 1, 2 and 3.
Word building: **programmer** *noun*
Word history: Late Latin, from Greek word meaning 'public notice in writing'

programming language
noun → **computer language**

progress (proh-gres)
noun **1** advance or improvement: ***progress** along a road* | ***progress** in studies* (***advancement, headway, progression***)
phrase **2 in progress**, going on or under way: *work **in progress***

Word building: **progress** (pruh-gres) *verb*
Word history: Middle English, from Latin word meaning 'a going forward'

progression
noun **1** forward or onward movement
2 *Mathematics* a sequence of numbers in which there is a constant relation between each number and its successor

Word use: The opposite of definition 1 is **regression**.

progressive
adjective favouring or making change, improvement or reform: *a **progressive** policy | a **progressive** school*

Word use: The opposite of this is **conservative**.

prohibit
verb to forbid by law: *The government has **prohibited** smoking on trains.* (***ban***, ***bar***, ***block***, ***proscribe***, ***veto***)

Word history: Middle English, from Latin word meaning 'held back'

prohibition (proh-uh-bish-uhn)
noun **1** the act of forbidding
2 a law or order that forbids something

prohibitive (pruh-hib-uh-tiv)
adjective serving to prevent the use, purchase, etc., of something: *the **prohibitive** price of meat*

Word use: You can also use **prohibitory**.

project (proh-jekt, pro-jekt)
noun **1** a plan or scheme: *a **project** for making money* (***enterprise***, ***undertaking***, ***venture***)
2 a special piece of work that you do for school, usually by researching something: *The students did a **project** on wheat.*
verb (pruh-jekt) **3** to throw: *to **project** your voice*
4 to show on a screen: *to **project** a film*
5 to jut out: *The table **projects** too far into the hall.* (***protrude***)

Word history: Middle English, from Latin word meaning '(thing) thrown out'

projectile (pruh-jek-tuyl)
noun **1** something thrown: *Stones and other **projectiles** were hurled at the speaker.*
2 something fired from a gun (***bullet***, ***missile***, ***rocket***, ***shell***)

Word history: from Neo-Latin word meaning 'projecting'

projection
noun **1** a part that sticks out
2 the condition of sticking out
3 in mapping, a representation of the earth's surface drawn over lines of latitude and longitude on a flat surface

projector
noun a piece of equipment for showing a film or a slide on a screen

prolapse (proh-laps)
noun Medicine a falling down of an organ or part, such as the uterus, from its normal position

Word history: from Late Latin word meaning 'a falling down'

proletariat (proh-luh-tair-ree-uht)
noun the class in society that owns no large property but has to work to live

Word history: French, from Latin word meaning 'a Roman citizen of the lowest class'

proliferate (pruh-lif-uh-rayt)
verb to grow by multiplying: *The weeds have **proliferated** since the rain.*

Word building: **proliferation** *noun*

prolific (pruh-lif-ik)
adjective producing plentifully: *a **prolific** tree | a **prolific** writer* (***copious***, ***fertile***, ***fruitful***, ***profuse***)

Word history: Medieval Latin, from Latin *prōli-* offspring + *-ficus* making

prolix (proh-liks)
adjective **1** long and with too many words: *a **prolix** speech*
2 speaking or writing at great or boring length (***verbose***, ***wordy***)

Word history: Middle English, from Latin word meaning 'extended', 'long'

prologue (proh-log)
noun **1** a speech at the beginning of a play
2 anything that introduces something else

Word history: Middle English, from Latin, from Greek

prolong
verb to make last longer: *to **prolong** a speech | to **prolong** a pleasure* (***draw out***, ***extend***, ***protract***, ***stretch out***)

Word use: The opposite of this is **shorten**.
Word building: **prolongation** *noun*
Word history: Middle English, from Late Latin

promenade (prom-uh-nahd)
noun **1** an unhurried walk, especially in a public place
2 a place where people walk to and fro, especially next to a beach (***esplanade***)

Word building: **promenade** *verb*
Word history: from French word meaning 'lead out', 'take for a walk or airing'

prominent (prom-uh-nuhnt)
adjective **1** sticking out: ***prominent** teeth* (***jutting***, ***projecting***, ***protruding***, ***protuberant***)
2 outstanding or important: *a **prominent** citizen* (***distinguished***, ***eminent***, ***famous***, ***leading***, ***renowned***)

Word building: **prominence** *noun*
Word history: from Latin word meaning 'jutting out'

promiscuous (pruh-mis-kyooh-uhs)
adjective having several casual sexual partners

Word building: **promiscuity** (pro-muh-skyooh-uh-tee) *noun*
Word history: Latin

promise
noun **1** a declaration or statement that you will do, or keep from doing something (***oath***, ***pledge***, ***vow***, ***word of honour***)
2 signs of future excellence: *to show **promise***

Word building: **promise** *verb*
Word history: Middle English, from Latin

promissory note (prom-uh-suh-ree noht)
noun a written promise to pay a stated sum of money to a particular person

promontory (prom-uhn-tree)
noun a high point of land or rock jutting out into the sea

Noun forms: The plural is **promontories**.
Word history: Medieval Latin

promote
verb **1** to raise or advance in rank or position: *You have been* ***promoted*** *to general manager.* (***elevate***, ***forward***, ***upgrade***)
2 to try to increase the sales of by advertising: *They are* ***promoting*** *the new product on television.*

Word use: The opposite of definition 1 is **demote**.
Word building: **promotion** *noun*
Word history: Middle English, from Latin word meaning 'moved forward', 'advanced'

prompt
adjective **1** immediate: *a* ***prompt*** *reply to a letter*
verb **2** to encourage or urge to action: *A desire to help* ***prompted*** *him to speak.*
3 to remind of the next words in a play

Word building: **prompter** *noun* **promptitude** *noun*
Word history: Middle English, from Latin word meaning 'taken out', 'at hand'

promulgate (prom-uhl-gayt)
verb **1** to make known by public declaration: *to* ***promulgate*** *a law*
2 to spread widely among people: *to* ***promulgate*** *a belief*

Word history: from Latin word meaning 'made publicly known', 'published'

prone
adjective **1** liable or likely to have or do: ***prone*** *to headaches*
2 lying flat with your face downwards

Word history: Middle English, from Latin word meaning 'turned or leaning forwards', 'inclined downwards'

prong
noun a thin, sharp point on a fork

Word history: Middle English

pronoun
noun a word which stands for a noun

Word history: French, from Latin

pronouns

Pronouns are words like *it*, *them* or *who*. They often stand in place of *nouns* we have mentioned before:

The surfers finished waxing their surfboards. Then they ran into the water with them.

The pronouns *they* and *them* (in the second sentence) stand for *surfers* and *surfboards* (in the first sentence).

The six types of pronouns are:

personal pronouns
me, our, them, etc.
possessive pronouns
mine, ours, theirs, etc.
reflexive pronouns
myself, ourselves, themselves, etc.
interrogative pronouns
who, which, etc.
relative pronouns
who, that, etc.
demonstrative pronouns
that, these, etc.

Note that some words appear in more than one list.

personal pronouns

We use personal pronouns to substitute for any noun that refers to a person or thing already mentioned:

Where's Helen? I need her.

The personal pronoun *her* stands for *Helen* in the example above. The full set of personal pronouns in English is listed below:

I	*me*	*my*	*mine*
we	*us*	*our*	*ours*
you	*your*	*yours*	
he	*him*	*his*	
she	*her*	*hers*	
it	*its*		
they	*them*	*their*	*theirs*

possessive pronouns

Some pronouns that indicate ownership (possession) can be used instead of a noun which has already been mentioned, and they take a special form. These pronouns are called possessive pronouns:

That book is mine.

Is that one yours?

Yours is the red one.

They contrast with personal pronouns in the possessive case which are sometimes called **possessive adjectives**. These always come with a noun:

That's my book.

Is your umbrella the one with stripes?

reflexive pronouns

These pronouns end in -self or -selves. We use them to show that both the subject and the object of a verb refer to the same person or thing. That is, the reflexive pronoun refers back to the subject:

She cut herself.

In this sentence, *she* (personal pronoun) is the subject, while *herself* (reflexive pronoun) is the object, but they both refer to the same person.

They surprised themselves.

In this sentence, *they* (personal pronoun) and *themselves* (reflexive pronoun) both refer to the same people. Similarly, in the following sentence, *Mario* (noun) and *himself* (reflexive pronoun) refer to the same person.

Mario hurt himself.

The full set of reflexive pronouns in English is listed below.

myself	*ourselves*
yourself	*yourselves*
himself	*themselves*
herself	
itself	

interrogative pronouns

Many questions are introduced by the words *who*, *whom*, *which*, *whose* and *what*. In such questions, these words are interrogative pronouns:

Who can come?

Whom do you want?

Which is the one?
Whose is that?
What do you want?

They all stand in for nouns, so they're **pronouns**. And they all identify what follows as a question, so they're **interrogative** words.

relative pronouns
These pronouns are *who, whom, whose, which* and *that*. They begin adjectival clauses in the following examples:

the lady who/that lost her umbrella
the man whose dog was run over
the amplifier which/that overloaded
the teacher whom/that you like the least

Note that in the last example you don't actually need a relative pronoun at all:

the teacher you like the least

Except for the use of *whose* in the second example, you have a choice of relative pronouns. Some writers feel that you should choose *that* only when you are writing informally, but in fact your writing will be quite acceptable no matter which you use.

demonstrative pronouns / adjectives
We use demonstratives in English to point out specific persons or things. There are only four, and all begin with th-:

this that these those

They can act as either adjectives or pronouns.

This is what I mean. (pronoun)
Those are the ones. (pronoun)
That guitar… (adjective)
Are those books yours? (adjective)

They are important because they create links with other words in the text.

pronounce
verb **1** to make the sound of: *Australians **pronounce** 'dance' in two ways.*
2 to declare formally: *to **pronounce** a judgement* (***proclaim, utter***)

Word building: **pronouncement** *noun* **pronunciation** *noun*
Word history: Middle English, from Old French, from Latin word meaning 'proclaim', 'announce', 'recite'

pronounced
adjective strongly marked: *a **pronounced** tendency*

proof
noun **1** something that shows a thing is true
adjective **2** strong enough to resist: *It is **proof** against fire.*
verb **3** to treat or coat to make resistant: *This carpet has been **proofed** against stains.*

Word history: Middle English, from Old French, from Latin word meaning 'prove'

proofread
verb to read in order to find and mark mistakes to be corrected

Verb forms: I **proofread**, I have **proofread**, I am **proofreading**

prop[1]
verb **1** to rest against a support: *to **prop** a ladder against a wall*
noun **2** a stick, pole or beam, or other support
3 a person or thing serving as a support
phrase **4 prop up**, to support or prevent from falling: *to **prop up** a wall* | *to **prop up** someone on cushions* (***brace, fortify, reinforce, shore up, steady, strengthen***)

Verb forms: I **propped**, I have **propped**, I am **propping**
Word history: Middle English

prop[2]
noun any object used as part of a stage or film setting, except scenery or costumes

Word history: short for *property*

propaganda
noun information which is used to try and convince you of a certain point of view: *political **propaganda***

Word building: **propagandise** *verb*
Word history: Italian, from use of Latin *propāgandā* in the Neo-Latin title, *Sacra Congregatio de Propaganda Fide*, a committee of cardinals established in 1622 by Pope Gregory XV for the propagation of the faith

propagate (prop-uh-gayt)
verb **1** to increase or multiply: *Some plants can be **propagated** by cuttings.*
2 to spread: *to **propagate** ideas*

Word building: **propagation** *noun*
Word history: Latin word meaning 'propagated' (originally referring to the growing of plants from cuttings or slips)

propane (proh-payn)
noun a gas which is used for fuel for cooking or heating; found in petroleum

Word history: *prop(ionic acid)* + *-ane*

propel
verb to drive forwards: *The boat was **propelled** by oars.* (***force, push, ram, shove, thrust***)

Verb forms: I **propelled**, I have **propelled**, I am **propelling**
Word history: Latin

propellant
noun the fuel used to propel a rocket

propeller
noun a device with revolving blades used for driving a plane or ship

propensity (pruh-pen-suh-tee)
noun a natural or habitual tendency or inclination: *a **propensity** to find fault*

Noun forms: The plural is **propensities**.

proper
adjective **1** accepted or right: *the **proper** way to write* | *the **proper** time to sleep*
2 correct in behaviour: *She is always very **proper** when she comes to tea.* (***decent, polite, refined, respectable***)
3 real or genuine: *I need some **proper** tools, not these toys.* (***actual, authentic, legitimate, proven, true***)

Word history: Middle English, from Old French, from Latin word meaning 'your own'

proper noun
noun a noun that is the name of a particular place, person or thing

Word use: Compare this with **common noun**.

Look up **nouns: proper nouns.**

property
noun **1** something that is owned: *This book is my* ***property****.* | *National parks are public* ***property****.* (***assets***, ***belongings***, ***possessions***)
2 a piece of land or building that may be owned
3 *Australian*, *NZ* a station or farm: *a cattle* ***property***

Noun forms: The plural is **properties.**
Word use: You can also use **country property** for definition 3.
Word history: Middle English

prophecy (<u>prof</u>-uh-see)
noun **1** a statement telling what is going to happen in the future
2 a message from God, or the act of proclaiming such a message

Noun forms: The plural is **prophecies.**
Word history: Middle English, from Old French, from Late Latin, from Greek

prophesy (<u>prof</u>-uh-suy)
verb to deliver a prophecy, or to predict: *He* ***prophesied*** *a terrible storm.* (***divine***, ***forecast***, ***foresee***)

Verb forms: I **prophesied,** I have **prophesied,** I am **prophesying**
Word history: verb use of and variant of *prophecy*

prophet
noun **1** someone who speaks on behalf of God
2 someone who predicts the future
3 a great teacher or leader

Word building: **prophetic** *adjective*
Word history: Middle English, from Latin, from Greek word meaning 'spokesman', 'interpreter', 'prophet'

prophet / profit
Don't confuse **prophet** with **profit,** which is the money you make from selling something at a higher price than you paid for it. It can also be an advantage or benefit:

There is no profit in regretting the mistakes you made in your youth.

prophylactic (prof-uh-<u>lak</u>-tik)
adjective **1** of a drug, defending or protecting from disease
2 preventive or protective
noun **3** a prophylactic medicine or action
4 a contraceptive agent or device, such as a pill, foam, condom, etc.

Word history: Greek

propitiate (pruh-<u>pish</u>-ee-ayt)
verb to appease or conciliate

Word history: Latin

propitious (pruh-<u>pish</u>-uhs)
adjective **1** favourable: ***propitious*** *weather* | ***propitious*** *omens*
2 favourably inclined or disposed

Word history: Middle English, from Latin

proponent (pruh-<u>poh</u>-nuhnt)
noun **1** someone who puts forward a proposal
2 someone who supports a cause

proportion
noun **1** the relation or comparison of one thing to another according to its size, number, etc.: *the* ***proportion*** *of girls to boys in the class*
2 a proper or correct relationship between things: *The dog's small head was not in* ***proportion*** *to his large body.*
3 a part, compared to the whole: *a large* ***proportion*** *of the total* (***fraction***, ***piece***, ***section***, ***segment***, ***share***)

Word building: **proportion** *verb* **proportionate** *adjective*
Word history: Middle English, from Latin

proposal
noun **1** the act of proposing for acceptance, adoption or performance
2 a plan or scheme offered (***bid***, ***offer***, ***proposition***, ***suggestion***, ***tender***)
3 an offer, especially of marriage

propose
verb **1** to put forward or suggest
2 to plan or intend
3 to suggest marriage: *He* ***proposed*** *to her.*

Word history: Middle English, from French

proposition
noun **1** the act of proposing something
2 a plan put forward (***proposal***, ***recommendation***, ***suggestion***)
3 a suggestion for sexual intercourse

Word history: Middle English, from Latin word meaning 'a setting forth'

proposition / preposition
Don't confuse **proposition** with **preposition,** which is a part of speech.

propound
verb to put forward to be considered, accepted, or acted on: *He* ***propounded*** *a theory.*

Word history: Middle English, from Latin word meaning 'set forth'

proprietary (pruh-<u>pruy</u>-uh-tree)
adjective **1** belonging to a proprietor or proprietors
2 being a proprietor or proprietors: *the* ***proprietary*** *class*
3 having to do with property or ownership: ***proprietary*** *rights*
4 belonging or controlled as property: ***proprietary*** *company*
5 manufactured and sold only by the owner of the patent, formula, brand name or trademark: ***proprietary*** *medicine*

Word history: Middle English, from Late Latin, from Latin word meaning 'ownership'

proprietary limited company
noun a company with a limit of fifty shareholders, which cannot issue shares for public subscription and which is not listed on the stock exchange

Word use: You can also use **proprietary company.**

proprietor (pruh-pruy-uh-tuh)
noun the person who owns a business or a property

Word building: **proprietorship** *noun*
Word history: *propriet(y)* + *-or*

propriety (pruh-pruy-uh-tee)
noun good manners or proper behaviour

Word history: Middle English, from Latin word meaning 'peculiarity', 'ownership'

propulsion (pruh-pul-shuhn)
noun a driving or propelling force: *Many planes are driven by jet* ***propulsion.***

Word history: from Latin word meaning 'driven forward' + *-ion*

pro rata (proh rah-tuh)
adverb **1** according to a certain rate: *I will count up how many newspapers each person sold and then share out the money* ***pro rata.***
adjective **2** proportionate

Word history: from Medieval Latin word meaning 'according to rate'

prorogue (pruh-rohg)
verb to temporarily discontinue meetings of: *to* ***prorogue*** *parliament*

Word history: Middle English, from French, from Latin word meaning 'prolong', 'protract', 'defer'

prosaic (proh-zay-ik, pruh-zay-ik)
adjective dull and unimaginative

Word history: Medieval Latin, from Latin word meaning 'prose'

proscenium (pruh-see-nee-uhm)
noun **1** in the modern theatre, the decorative arch or opening between the stage and the auditorium
2 in the ancient theatre, the stage

Noun forms: The plural is **proscenia** (pruh-see-nee-uh).
Word use: You can also use **proscenium arch**.
Word history: Latin, from Greek *proskénion*

proscribe
verb to forbid

Word use: The opposite of this is **permit**.
Word history: from Latin word meaning 'write before', 'publish', 'proscribe'

proscribe / prescribe
Don't confuse **proscribe** with **prescribe**. A doctor **prescribes** medicine to take when you are ill.

prose
noun ordinary written or spoken language rather than poetry

Word history: Middle English, from French, from Latin word meaning 'straightforward (speech)'

prosecute (pros-uh-kyooht)
verb to take legal action against: *The police* ***prosecuted*** *her for shoplifting*

Word building: **prosecution** *noun* **prosecutor** *noun*
Word history: Middle English, from Latin word meaning 'pursued', 'continued'

prosecute / persecute
Don't confuse **prosecute** with **persecute**. You **persecute** people if you treat them cruelly or unjustly, often because of their political or religious beliefs.

proselyte (pros-uh-luyt)
noun a convert or someone who has changed from one opinion to another

Word history: Middle English, from Late Latin, from Greek word meaning 'newcomer'

prosody (pros-uh-dee, proz-uh-dee)
noun **1** the science or study of writing poetry
2 a particular system of poetic writing: *Milton's* ***prosody***

Word history: late Middle English, from Latin, from Greek word meaning 'tone or accent', 'modulation of voice', 'song sung to music'

prospect
noun **1** something looked forward to or expected, especially something successful: *A holiday is a pleasant* ***prospect.*** | *He has good* ***prospects*** *in his job.*
2 someone who may be a customer, contestant, etc.: *Try him, he looks a likely* ***prospect.***
3 a view or a scene (***landscape, outlook, vista***)
verb **4** to search for gold or other minerals

Word building: **prospector** *noun*
Word history: Middle English, from Latin word meaning 'outlook', 'view'

prospective
adjective likely to happen or be: ***prospective*** *benefits* | *her* ***prospective*** *husband* (***anticipated, expected, future, impending, potential***)

prospective / perspective
Don't confuse **prospective** with **perspective**, which is a particular view you have of something. This can be what you see with your eyes, or a way of thinking about something. To have things in the right perspective is to be looking at things the right way.

prospectus
noun **1** a statement or pamphlet which advertises something new or gives more details about an institution like a school or university
2 *Commerce* an official brochure through which a company offers its securities for sale to the public

Word history: from Latin word meaning 'outlook', 'view'

prosper
verb to be successful or thrive: *Her career* ***prospered.*** (***bloom, blossom, boom, flower, succeed***)

Word history: late Middle English, from Latin word meaning 'make prosperous'

prosperity
noun success or good fortune, often in relation to money

prosperity / posterity
Don't confuse **prosperity** with **posterity**, which refers to all the people who will live in the future.

prosperous
adjective successful or wealthy: *a **prosperous** business* (***affluent***, ***opulent***, ***rich***, ***thriving***, ***well-off***)
Word history: Middle English, from Latin

prostate gland
noun a gland which surrounds the urethra of males at the base of the bladder

prosthesis (pros-thee-suhs, pruhs-thee-suhs)
noun **1** the use of an artificial part to replace a damaged or missing part of the body
2 an artificial body part
Noun forms: The plural is **prostheses** (pros-thee-seez).
Word history: Late Latin, from Greek word meaning 'a putting to', 'addition'

prostitute
noun someone who has sexual intercourse with someone else for money
Word building: **prostitution** *noun*
Word history: from Latin word meaning 'placed before', 'exposed publicly', 'prostituted'

prostrate
phrase **prostrate yourself**, to throw or lay yourself face down: *The prisoners **prostrated themselves** at the feet of the general.*
Word building: **prostrate** *adjective*
Word history: Middle English, from Latin word meaning 'spread out'

protagonist (pruh-tag-uh-nuhst)
noun the main character in a story or play
Word history: Greek

protea (proh-tee-uh)
noun any of various southern African shrubs or trees with large, showy flowers
Word history: Neo-Latin, from Greek; named after *Proteus*, a sea-god of classical mythology, who was able to assume different shapes at will

protean (pruh-tee-uhn, proh-tee-uhn)
adjective readily taking on different forms or characters
Word history: from *Proteus*. Look up **protea**.

protect
verb to guard or defend from injury, danger or annoyance (***safeguard***, ***screen***, ***shelter***, ***shield***)
Word building: **protective** *adjective* **protector** *noun*
Word history: from Latin word meaning 'covered over'

protection
noun **1** the act of protecting (***defence***, ***safeguard***, ***security***, ***shield***)
2 *Colloquial* money paid to criminals to stop their threatened violence
3 *Economics* the system or theory of protecting home industries from foreign competition through duties placed on imports

protection money
noun money extorted by criminals from victims, supposedly as payment for protecting them from other criminals: *The gang went around the neighbourhood collecting **protection money**.*

protection racket
noun a criminal scheme based on the extortion of protection money

protectorate (pruh-tek-tuh-ruht, pruh-tek-truht)
noun a country protected and controlled by another stronger state

protégé (proh-tuh-zhay)
noun someone who is protected or supported by someone else (***charge***, ***dependant***, ***ward***)
Word history: French word meaning 'protect', from Latin

protein (proh-teen)
noun any of a group of substances which are present in such foods as milk, meat and cheese and which are important to our diet
Word history: German, from Greek word meaning 'primary'

protest (proh-test)
noun **1** an expression of disapproval or disagreement (***complaint***, ***dissent***, ***objection***, ***opposition***)
verb (pruh-test, proh-test) **2** to express disapproval or disagreement (***complain***, ***object***)
3 to state strongly and positively: *She **protested** her innocence to the end.*
Word building: **protestation** *noun*
Word history: Middle English, from French, from Latin word meaning 'declare publicly'

protocol (proh-tuh-kol)
noun **1** the rules of behaviour used on official occasions involving kings, queens, or other important people
2 in computer networking, a set of rules governing the format in which messages are sent from one computer to another
Word history: Medieval Latin, from Late Greek word originally meaning 'a first leaf glued to the front of a manuscript containing notes as to contents'

proton (proh-ton)
noun an elementary particle present in every atomic nucleus, the number of protons being different for each element. It has a positive electric charge equal in magnitude to that of the electron's negative charge.
Word use: Compare this with **electron** and **neutron**.
Word history: from Greek word meaning 'first'

protoplasm (proh-tuh-plaz-uhm)
noun a complex, colourless, semiliquid substance regarded as the physical basis of all vegetable and animal life, having the power of movement, reproduction, etc.

prototype (proh-tuh-tuyp)
noun the original or the model of something which is later copied
Word history: Neo-Latin, from Greek word meaning 'original', 'primitive'

protract
verb to draw out or lengthen in time

Word use: The opposite of this is **shorten**.
Word history: from Latin word meaning 'drawn forth', 'drawn out'

protractor
noun an instrument used to measure or mark off angles

protrude
verb to jut out (***bulge***, ***stand out***, ***stick out***)

Word history: Latin

protuberant (pruh-tyooh-buh-ruhnt, pruh-tyooh-bruhnt)
adjective swelling or bulging out beyond the surrounding surface

Word building: **protuberance** *noun*
Word history: from Late Latin word meaning 'swelling'

proud
adjective **1** feeling pleased or satisfied: *She was* ***proud*** *that her mother was so clever.*
2 having too high an opinion of your own importance (***arrogant***, ***conceited***, ***haughty***, ***pompous***, ***smug***, ***supercilious***)

Word history: Middle English; late Old English *prūd*, apparently from Vulgar Latin

prove (proohv)
verb **1** to show to be true or genuine (***bear out***, ***confirm***, ***corroborate***, ***substantiate***, ***verify***)
2 to show to be capable of something: *He* ***proved*** *himself an expert driver.*
3 to turn out: *The report* ***proved*** *to be false.*

Verb forms: I **proved**, I have **proved** or I have **proven**, I am **proving**
Word history: Middle English, from Latin word meaning 'try', 'test', 'prove', 'approve'

provenance (prov-uh-nuhns)
noun the place of origin, as of a work of art, etc.

Word history: French, from Latin word meaning 'come forth'

provender (prov-uhn-duh)
noun **1** dry food, such as hay, for livestock (***feed***, ***fodder***, ***forage***)
2 food in general

Word history: Middle English, from Old French word meaning 'provender', from Late Latin

proverb
noun a short, popular, usually wise saying that has been used by people for a long time, such as *A stitch in time saves nine.* (***adage***, ***epigram***, ***maxim***, ***motto***)

Word building: **proverbial** *adjective*
Word history: Middle English, from Old French, from Latin

provide
verb **1** to make available or to supply: *I will* ***provide*** *the food. | He will* ***provide*** *us with the drink.*
2 to supply what is needed to live: *Parents usually* ***provide*** *for their children.*

Word history: Middle English, from Latin word meaning 'foresee', 'look after', 'provide for'

provided (pruh-vuy-duhd)
conjunction on the condition or understanding: *I will consent,* ***provided*** *(that) all the others agree.*

Word use: You can also use **providing**.

providence (prov-uh-duhns)
noun **1** the care and protection of God, nature or fate (***chance***, ***destiny***, ***fortune***, ***luck***)
2 the careful management of things like money, in preparation for the future

provident (prov-uh-duhnt)
adjective **1** careful in providing for the future
2 careful in the management of money (***economical***, ***frugal***, ***thrifty***)

provider
noun **1** someone who supplies something
2 → internet service provider

province
noun **1** a section or division of a country, territory or region
2 a range or field of knowledge: *The history of South Australia is outside my* ***province****.*

Word history: Middle English, from French, from Latin word meaning 'province', 'official charge'

provincial (pruh-vin-shuhl)
adjective **1** belonging to or characteristic of some particular province or provinces: ***provincial*** *customs*
2 having the manners characteristic of people living in a province or the provinces (***narrow***, ***parochial***, ***unsophisticated***)
noun **3** someone who lives in or comes from the provinces

Word building: **provincialism** *noun*

provision
noun **1** a section of a document which sets out a condition (***proviso***, ***qualification***, ***reservation***, ***rider***, ***stipulation***)
2 the providing or supplying of something such as food
3 an arrangement made beforehand
4 provisions, supplies of food and other necessities

Word history: Middle English, from Latin

provisional
adjective temporary, or for the time being only: *a* ***provisional*** *government* (***casual***, ***fill-in***, ***interim***, ***makeshift***)

proviso (pruh-vuy-zoh)
noun **1** a clause stating a condition in a legal or similar document
2 a condition or stipulation

Noun forms: The plural is **provisos** or **provisoes**.
Word building: **provisory** *adjective*
Word history: late Middle English, from Medieval Latin word meaning 'it being provided that'

provoke
verb **1** to make angry or annoyed: *He* ***provoked*** *the dog by teasing it.* (***goad***, ***irritate***, ***pique***, ***vex***)
2 to stir up or cause: *His behaviour* ***provoked*** *his parents' anger.* (***evoke***, ***induce***, ***inspire***, ***produce***, ***stimulate***)

Word building: **provocation** *noun* **provocative** *adjective*
Word history: Middle English, from Latin word meaning 'call forth', 'challenge', 'provoke'

provost (prov-uhst)
noun **1** the head officer of a governing body of certain religious foundations
2 the head of certain colleges, schools, etc.

Word history: Middle English; Old English *profost*, from Medieval Latin word meaning 'one placed before', 'president'

prow (prow)
noun the front part of a ship or boat above the waterline (***bow***)

Word history: French, from dialect Italian (Genoese), from Latin, from Greek

prowess (prow-es, prow-es)
noun **1** bravery
2 outstanding ability or skill

Word history: Middle English, from Old French word meaning 'good', 'valiant', from Latin word meaning 'be useful'

prowl
verb to go about quietly, as if in search of prey or something to steal

Word building: **prowl** *noun*
Word history: Middle English

proximity (prok-sim-uh-tee)
noun nearness in place, time, etc.

Word history: late Middle English, from Latin

proxy
noun someone who is officially allowed to act for someone else: *He acted as* ***proxy*** *for his mother at the ceremony.*

Noun forms: The plural is **proxies.**
Word history: Middle English

prude
noun someone who is too modest or proper

Word history: French word meaning 'a prude', as adjective, 'prudish', from Old French word meaning 'worthy or respectable woman'

prudence
noun careful practical wisdom or good sound judgement

Word building: **prudent** *adjective*

prune[1]
noun a dried plum

Word history: late Middle English, from French, from Latin word meaning 'plum', from Greek word meaning 'plum'

prune[2]
verb to cut off twigs or branches from

Word history: Middle English, from Old French word meaning 'prune (vines)', from Latin

prurient (prooh-ree-uhnt)
adjective **1** obsessed by or causing sexual thoughts to an unusual degree
2 itching

Word building: **prurience** *noun* **pruriency** *noun*
Word history: from Latin word meaning 'itching'

pry
verb to look or search with too much curiosity: *He is always* ***prying*** *into our affairs.*

Verb forms: I **pried**, I have **pried**, I am **prying**
Word building: **prying** *adjective*
Word history: Middle English

psalm (sahm)
noun a sacred song, hymn or poem

Word history: Old English *ps(e)alm, sealm*, from Late Latin, from Greek word meaning 'song sung to the harp', originally 'a plucking' (as of strings)

pseudonym (syooh-duh-nim)
noun an invented name used by a writer (***alias, nickname, pen-name, title***)

Word history: from Greek word meaning 'false name'

psych (suyk)
Colloquial
verb **1** to persuade by psychological means rather than overtly by argument: *He tried to* ***psych*** *them into playing better.*
phrase **2 psych up**, to bring to a state of intense focus and keen motivation: *The coach tried to* ***psych up*** *the team*
3 psych you out, to disturb your composure: *The booing was an effort to* ***psych him out.***

psyche (suy-kee)
noun the human soul, spirit or mind

Word history: Latin, from Greek word literally meaning 'breath'

psychedelic (suy-kuh-del-ik)
adjective **1** causing or having to do with a mental state of enlarged consciousness, involving a sense of joy and increased awareness
2 having to do with a group of drugs inducing such a state, especially LSD
3 *Colloquial* having bright colours and an imaginative pattern
4 having to do with music which is played very loudly and accompanied by a lightshow

Word history: Greek

psychiatry (suh-kuy-uh-tree, suy-kuy-uh-tree)
noun the study and treatment of mental illness

Word building: **psychiatric** *adjective* **psychiatrist** *noun*
Word history: Greek

psychic (suy-kik)
adjective **1** having to do with the human soul or mind
2 having the power to tell the future or what others are thinking

Word building: **psychic** *noun*
Word history: from Greek word meaning 'of the soul'

psychoanalysis (suy-koh-uh-nal-uh-suhs)
noun a method of examining unconscious mental processes, and of treating neuroses, etc., based on a system of theories concerning the relation of conscious and unconscious psychological processes

Word building: **psychoanalytic** *adjective* **psychoanalytical** *adjective* **psychoanalyse** *verb* **psychoanalyst** *noun*

psychology (suy-kol-uh-jee)
noun the study of the mind, how it works, and why people behave as they do

Word building: **psychological** *adjective* **psychologist** *noun*
Word history: Neo-Latin, from Greek

psychopathic (suy-kuh-path-ik)
adjective having to do with a mental disease or disorder in which an apparently normal person behaves with no sense of social responsibility

Word building: **psychopath** *noun*

psychosis (suy-koh-suhs)
noun any severe form of mental disorder or disease

Noun forms: The plural is **psychoses** (suy-koh-seez).
Word building: **psychotic** *adjective* **psychotic** *noun*
Word history: Neo-Latin, from Late Greek

psychosomatic (suy-koh-suh-mat-ik)
adjective having to do with an illness of your body which is caused by or made worse by your emotional state

pterodactyl (te-ruh-dak-tuhl)
noun an extinct flying reptile

ptomaine (tuh-mayn)
noun any of a class of basic nitrogenous substances, some very poisonous, produced during the decay of animal or plant matter

Word use: You can also use **ptomain**.
Word history: Italian, from Greek word meaning 'dead body'

pub
noun Colloquial a hotel

Word history: short for *public house*

puberty (pyooh-buh-tee)
noun the stage of life or physical development when someone is first capable of producing children

Word history: Middle English, from Latin

pubic (pyooh-bik)
adjective having to do with the lower part of your abdomen where the genitals are: ***pubic** hair*

Word history: from Latin word meaning 'pubic hair', 'groin'

public
adjective **1** having to do with or used by the people of a community or the people as a whole: ***public** affairs* | ***public** transport* (***collective***, ***common***, ***communal***, ***general***, ***popular***)
noun **2** the people of a community
phrase **3 go public**,
a to make known things which were previously secret or private
b to sell part or all of a company's capital to the public
c to seek listing for a company on the stock exchange

Word history: Latin

public-address system
noun an electronic system consisting of microphone, amplifier, and a loudspeaker, which serves to amplify sound

Word use: You can also use **PA system** or **PA**.

publican
noun the owner or manager of a hotel

Word history: Latin

publication
noun **1** the publishing of a book, magazine, newspaper or other printed work
2 something which is published (***book***, ***gazette***, ***journal***, ***magazine***, ***pamphlet***)

Word history: Middle English, from Latin

publicise (pub-luh-suyz)
verb to bring to public notice (***advertise***, ***broadcast***, ***promote***)

Word use: You can also use **publicize**.

publicity (pub-lis-uh-tee)
noun any advertisement, information, etc., which is meant to attract the attention of the public

Word building: **publicist** *noun*

public relations
plural noun the methods used to give the public a good impression of a particular business or company

Word use: The abbreviation is **PR**.

public service
noun the departments of government responsible for the administration of laws and government policy, and the people who work in these departments: *My parents both work for the **public service** — Mum is in the Department of Foreign Affairs and Dad is in the Department of Defence.*

Word building: **public servant** *noun*

publish
verb **1** to prepare and issue a book, magazine, etc., in printed copies for sale to the public
2 to announce to the public (***advertise***, ***broadcast***, ***proclaim***, ***promulgate***)

Word building: **publisher** *noun*
Word history: Middle English, from French

puce (pyoohs)
adjective of a dark purplish-brown colour

Word building: **puce** *noun*
Word history: French word literally meaning 'flea', from Latin

pucker
verb to gather into small folds or wrinkles

Word building: **pucker** *noun*
Word history: apparently connected with *poke* (bag)

pudding
noun a soft, sweet dish usually served as a dessert

Word history: Middle English

puddle
noun a small pool of liquid, such as dirty water left after rain

Word history: Middle English, apparently from Old English *pudd* ditch

puerile (pyoouh-ruyl)
adjective childish or foolish: *a piece of **puerile** writing*

Word building: **puerility** *noun*
Word history: Latin

puff
noun **1** a short, quick, sending out of air, wind or breath
2 a light pastry with a filling of jam, cream, etc.: *a cream **puff***
verb **3** to blow with puffs: *The smoke **puffed** into the air. | The train **puffed** steam out of its funnel.*
4 to breathe quickly after violent exercise (***blow***, ***gasp***, ***heave***, ***pant***, ***wheeze***)
5 to smoke a cigarette, cigar or pipe
phrase **6 puff up**, to become swollen

Word history: Middle English, Old English *pyff*; of imitative origin

puffer
noun a device for puffing medicine into the mouth to help make breathing easier (***inhaler***)

puffin
noun a seabird found in the northern Atlantic, with a duck-like body and a narrow brightly coloured bill

Word history: Middle English

pug
noun a small dog with a smooth coat, a very wrinkled face, a snub nose and a tightly curled tail

pugilist (pyooh-juh-luhst)
noun someone who fights with the fists (***boxer***, ***prizefighter***)

Word building: **pugilism** *noun* **pugilistic** *adjective*

pugnacious (pug-nay-shuhs)
adjective tending to quarrel or fight (***aggressive***, ***argumentative***, ***belligerent***, ***combative***, ***warlike***)

Word history: from Latin word meaning 'combativeness'

pull
verb **1** to move something by tugging or drawing it towards you (***drag***, ***haul***, ***lug***, ***tow***)
2 to tear apart: *to **pull** something to pieces*
3 to strain: *to **pull** a muscle*
4 *Colloquial* to withdraw: *After receiving complaints from their viewers, the TV network **pulled** the program.*
phrase **5 pull apart** or **pull to pieces**, to examine in critical detail: *The teacher **pulled** his essay **apart**.*
6 pull in, to move your vehicle to the side of the road to stop
7 pull off, *Colloquial* to succeed in gaining or performing something
8 pull out,
a to leave or depart
b *Colloquial* to withdraw from an agreement or undertaking
9 pull up, to stop
10 pull yourself together, to regain your self-control
11 pull your weight, to take a full and fair share of work, responsibility, etc.

Word building: **pull** *noun*
Word history: Old English *pullian* pull, pluck

pull-down menu
noun a computer menu which is instantly accessible and which leaves the screen exactly as it was once an option has been chosen

Word use: You can also use **drop-down menu**.
Word history: from the notion that accessing the menu is comparable to pulling down a physical screen which then rolls back leaving the previous screen in view

pullet (pool-uht)
noun a hen less than one year old

Word history: Middle English from Old French word meaning 'young hen', from Late Latin word meaning 'young animal', 'chicken'

pulley (pool-ee)
noun a wheel or system of wheels with ropes or chains, used to lift heavy things

Word history: Middle English, from Old French, from a derivative of Greek word meaning 'axle'

pullover
noun → **jumper**[1]

pulmonary (pul-muhn-ree, pool-)
adjective having to do with the lungs

Word use: You can also use **pulmonic**.
Word history: from Latin word meaning 'lung'

pulp
noun **1** the soft, juicy part of a fruit
2 any soft, wet mass: *Paper is made out of the **pulp** from wood, linen and similar materials.*

Word building: **pulp** *verb*
Word history: Latin

pulpit (pool-puht)
noun a raised platform in a church where the priest or minister stands to give a sermon

Word history: Middle English, from Medieval Latin, from Latin word meaning 'stage', 'platform'

pulsate (pul-sayt)
verb to beat or throb like your heart (***drum***, ***palpitate***, ***pound***, ***quiver***, ***vibrate***)

Word history: from Latin word meaning 'pushed', 'struck', 'beaten'

pulse
noun **1** the regular beating in your arteries caused by the pumping of blood by your heart
2 any regular stroke, beat or vibration, as the underlying beat in music

Word building: **pulse** *verb*
Word history: from Latin word meaning 'a pushing', 'beating', 'pulse'

pulverise
verb **1** to pound or grind into dust or powder: *He **pulverised** the rock into sand.* (***crumble***, ***crush***, ***mill***)
2 to destroy completely (***annihilate***, ***demolish***, ***eradicate***, ***exterminate***, ***wipe out***)

Word use: You can also use **pulverize**.
Word history: Middle English, from Latin word meaning 'dust'

puma (pyooh-muh)
noun a large animal of the cat family found in America (***cougar***, ***mountain lion***)

Word history: Spanish, from Quechua

pumice (pum-uhs)
noun a light-weight form of volcanic stone used for rubbing and cleaning things

Word history: Middle English, from Old French, from Latin

pummel
verb to beat with rapid blows of the fists

Verb forms: I **pummelled**, I have **pummelled**, I am **pummelling**

pump[1]
noun **1** a device that forces a liquid or gas in or out of something
verb **2** to move by using a pump: *to* ***pump*** *water out of the dam*
3 to move or operate by an up-and-down hand action
phrase **4 pump up**, to fill with air: *to* ***pump up*** *your tyres*

Word history: Middle English

pump[2]
noun a low, light shoe worn for dancing, etc.

pumpkin
noun a large, roundish, yellow-orange vegetable

Word history: French word meaning 'a melon', from Latin, from Greek

pun
noun a play on words which sound alike but are different in meaning, as in *Our photography shop is a developing business.*

Word building: **pun** *verb* (**punned, punning**)
Word history: perhaps short for obsolete *pundigrion*, from Italian word meaning 'fine point', 'quibble'

punch[1]
noun **1** a hit or blow, especially with your fist
2 a strong or forceful effect

Word building: **punch** *verb*
Word history: perhaps a variant of *pounce*

punch[2]
noun a device for making holes in tickets, leather or similar materials

Word history: short for *puncheon* pointed tool

punch[3]
noun a drink made of water, fruit juice, pieces of fruit and sometimes wine, rum, or other spirit

Word history: perhaps short for *puncheon* a cask

punchline
noun the culminating sentence, line, etc., of a joke: *He forgot the* ***punchline*** *so no-one got the joke.*

punctilious (pungk-til-ee-uhs)
adjective being very exact about doing things correctly: *He was* ***punctilious*** *in carrying out his duties.*

punctual (pungk-chooh-uhl)
adjective careful about being on time

Word building: **punctuality** *noun* **punctually** *adverb*
Word history: Middle English, from Medieval Latin, from Latin word meaning 'a pricking', 'a point'

punctuate (pungk-chooh-ayt)
verb **1** to mark with punctuation marks in order to make the meaning clear: *to* ***punctuate*** *a sentence*
2 to interrupt every so often: *They* ***punctuated*** *his speech with cheers.*

punctuation (pungk-chooh-ay-shuhn)
noun commas, semi-colons, colons, full stops, etc., used in writing to make the meaning clear

These are the punctuation marks used in writing:

Punctuation for sentences

brackets ( ) (parentheses)	exclamation mark !
	full stop .
colon :	question mark ?
comma ,	quotation marks ' ' (inverted commas)
dash —	
ellipsis ...	semicolon ;

Punctuation for words

apostrophe ' hyphen - slash /

accents:

acute ´	grave `
cedilla ¸	háček ˇ
circumflex ˆ	tilde ~
dieresis ¨	umlaut ¨

puncture (pungk-chuh)
verb to prick or make a hole in: *to* ***puncture*** *the skin with a pin | to* ***puncture*** *a tyre*

Word building: **puncture** *noun*
Word history: Latin

pundit (pun-duht)
noun someone who knows a lot about a subject

Word history: from Hindustani *pandit*, from Sanskrit word meaning 'learned'

pungent (pun-juhnt)
adjective having a sharp taste or smell: *the* ***pungent*** *odour of vinegar* (***piquant, savoury, spicy, tasty***)

Word building: **pungency** *noun*
Word history: from Latin word meaning 'pricking'

punish
verb **1** to make suffer in some way because of wrongdoing: *to* ***punish*** *criminals by putting them in jail* (***chastise, correct, discipline, penalise***)
2 to handle severely or roughly: *The boxer really* ***punished*** *his opponent.*

Word building: **punishment** *noun*
punitive *adjective*
Word history: Middle English, from Old French, from Latin

punk
noun **1** a type of hard and fast rock music with aggressive lyrics
2 a person who is a fan of this music and who wears typical punk clothing such as leather jackets, torn black jeans, silver chains, body piercings, with a short spiked hairdo
verb **3** to embarrass (someone) by playing an elaborate practical joke on them

Word use: You can also use **punk rock** or **punk music** for definition 1.

punnet
noun a small, shallow box or basket for small fruits, especially strawberries

Word history: diminutive of British dialect *pun* pound

punt[1]
noun **1** a shallow, flat-bottomed boat with square ends, which is usually driven by pushing with a pole against the bottom of the river
verb **2** to carry in a punt: *He* ***punted*** *them down the river.*

Word history: Old English *punt*, from Latin word meaning 'punt', 'pontoon[1]'

punt[2]
noun a kick which you give to a dropped football before it has hit the ground

Word building: **punt** *verb*
Word history: British dialect *bunt, punt* push with force

punt[3]
noun **1** a bet: *She had a* ***punt*** *on the last race and won $20.*
verb **2** to bet or wager
phrase **3 take a punt**, *Colloquial* to take a chance: *He* ***took a punt*** *on the weather and left his umbrella at home.*

Word building: **punt** *verb*
Word history: French, from Spanish word meaning 'point', from Latin

puny (pyooh-nee)
adjective **1** small and weak (***frail***, ***sickly***, ***slight***, ***thin***)
2 of little importance: ***puny*** *efforts*

pup
noun **1** a young dog less than one year old
2 a young seal

Word use: You can also use **puppy** for definition 1.

pupa (pyooh-puh)
noun an insect in the cocoon between the larva and mature adult stages

Noun forms: The plural is **pupae** (pyooh-pee).
Word building: **pupal** *adjective* **pupate** *verb*
Word history: Neo-Latin, from Latin word meaning 'girl', 'doll', 'puppet'

pupil[1]
noun someone who is being taught

Word history: Middle English, from Old French, from Latin word meaning 'orphan', 'ward'

pupil[2]
noun the small, dark spot on the iris of your eye, which expands to allow more light into the retina

Word history: Latin word literally meaning 'little doll'

puppet
noun **1** a doll or figure of some kind which is moved by wires or your hand, usually on a small stage
2 someone who is controlled by others (***serf***, ***servant***, ***slave***, ***subject***, ***vassal***)

Word building: **puppeteer** *noun* **puppetry** *noun*
Word history: Middle English, apparently from Middle Low German word meaning 'doll', of Roman origin

purchase (per-chuhs)
verb **1** to pay for or buy
noun **2** something which is bought
3 an effective hold or position for applying leverage: *I can't get any* ***purchase*** *on this screw — I need a different screwdriver.*

Word use: The opposite of definition 1 is **sell**.
Word history: Middle English, from Anglo-French word meaning 'seek to obtain', 'procure'

purdah
noun an outfit of black clothing, shoes and gloves, and a covering for the face, worn by some Muslim women

Word history: from an Urdu word meaning 'curtain'

pure
adjective **1** having nothing mixed with it, especially anything which might spoil it: ***pure*** *gold* | ***pure*** *silk*
2 clear and true: *the* ***pure*** *notes of a flute*
3 clean and spotless: *a* ***pure*** *reputation* (***hygienic***, ***immaculate***, ***spick-and-span***, ***stainless***)

Word building: **purification** *noun* **purity** *noun*
Word history: Middle English, from Old French, from Latin word meaning 'clean', 'unmixed', 'plain', 'pure'

puree (pyooh-ray)
noun vegetables or fruit cooked and then sieved or blended

Word use: You can also use **purée**.
Word building: **puree** *verb*
Word history: from French word meaning 'strain'

purgative (per-guh-tiv)
noun **1** a medicine causing emptying or cleansing of the bowels
adjective **2** cleansing or purging, particularly in causing emptying of the bowels

Word history: Middle English, from Late Latin word meaning 'cleansed'

purgatory (per-guh-tree)
noun **1 Purgatory**, a place of temporary punishment where some Christians believe you go after death but before you go to heaven
2 any place or situation in your life which causes a lot of suffering

Word use: Definition 1 is part of the belief of the Roman Catholic Church.
Word history: Middle English, from Late Latin word meaning 'cleanse'

purge (perj)
verb to purify or get rid of what is unwanted or not good

Word building: **purge** *noun*
Word history: Middle English, from Old French, from Latin word meaning 'cleanse'

purify (pyooh-ruh-fuy)
verb to make pure (***cleanse***, ***decontaminate***, ***refine***)

Verb forms: I **purified**, I have **purified**, I am **purifying**
Word history: Middle English, from Old French, from Latin

purism (pyooh-riz-uhm)
noun **1** very careful keeping of or insistence on purity in language, style, etc.
2 a theory and practice in art, originated in 1918, which reduces all natural appearances to a geometric simplicity typical of machines

Word building: **purist** *noun* **puristic** *adjective*
Word history: *pure* + *-ism*

puritan (pyooh-ruh-tuhn)
noun **1** someone who tries to be very pure and strict in moral and religious matters
adjective **2** having to do with puritans

Word building: **puritanism** *noun*
Word history: from Late Latin word meaning 'purity'

puritanical (pyooh-ruh-tan-uh-kuhl)
adjective behaving like a puritan

purl
noun a stitch used in knitting

Word building: **purl** *verb*

purl / pearl
Don't confuse **purl** with **pearl**, which is a precious bead that you find in an oyster.

purloin (per-loyn)
verb to take dishonestly or steal: *They* ***purloined*** *the car.*

Word building: **purloiner** *noun*
Word history: Middle English, from Anglo-French word meaning 'put off', 'remove'

purple
adjective of a dark reddish-blue colour

Word building: **purple** *noun*
Word history: Old English (Northumbrian) *purpl(e)*, from Latin, from Greek word meaning 'kind of shellfish yielding purple dye'

purport (per-pawt, per-pawt)
verb **1** to say or claim: *a document* ***purporting*** *to be official*
2 to bring to the mind as the meaning or thing meant (***denote***, ***express***, ***imply***, ***signify***)
noun (per-pawt, per-puht) **3** tenor, import or meaning: *the* ***purport*** *of my words*
4 purpose or object

Word history: late Middle English, from Anglo-French word meaning 'convey'

purpose
noun **1** the reason something is done or made: *The* ***purpose*** *of this device is to make potato peeling easier.* (***aim***, ***function***, ***intention***, ***object***, ***point***)
phrase **2 on purpose**, intentionally (***deliberately***)

Word building: **purposely** *adverb* **purposeful** *adjective* **purposefully** *adverb*
Word history: Middle English, from Old French word meaning 'propose'

purposely / purposefully
These related adverbs are both linked to **purpose** but they have different meanings.
If you do something **purposely**, you do it intentionally and not by chance:
They purposely went early to avoid the crowds.
If you do something **purposefully**, you do it with determination and resolution:
She began walking towards him slowly but purposefully.

purr
verb to make a low, continuous, murmuring sound as a cat does

Word building: **purr** *noun*
Word history: imitative

purse
noun **1** a small bag for carrying money
verb **2** to draw into folds or wrinkles: *She* ***pursed*** *her lips in annoyance.*

Word history: Middle English and Old English *purs*, from Late Latin word meaning 'bag', from Greek word meaning 'hide', 'leather'

purser
noun a ship's officer who looks after the accounts

pursuant (puh-syooh-uhnt)
adjective **1** going along with or agreeing
2 pursuing
phrase **3 pursuant to**, according: *to do something* ***pursuant to*** *an agreement*

Word building: **pursuance** *noun*

pursue (puh-syooh)
verb **1** to follow so as to catch (***chase***, ***seek***, ***shadow***, ***tag***, ***track***)
2 to try hard for or seek: *to* ***pursue*** *happiness | to* ***pursue*** *a career* (***hunt for***, ***quest after***, ***search for***, ***strive for***)

Word building: **pursuit** *noun*
Word history: Middle English, from Anglo-French, from Latin word meaning 'follow', 'continue'

purvey (puh-vay)
verb to provide or supply, especially food

Word building: **purveyance** *noun* **purveyor** *noun*
Word history: Middle English, from Anglo-French, from Latin word meaning 'foresee', 'provide for'

pus (pus)
noun the yellowish-white substance in a boil or sore

Word building: **pussy** (pus-ee) *adjective*
Word history: Latin

push
verb **1** to move by pressing or leaning against (***drive***, ***propel***, ***push***, ***ram***, ***shove***, ***thrust***)
2 to force from behind: *We* ***pushed*** *our way through the crowd.*
3 to recommend or to insist on earnestly: *She* ***pushed*** *me to agree with her. | He* ***pushed*** *his plan.*
noun **4** the act of pushing
phrase **5 push off**,
a to move away from the shore, etc., as the result of a push
b *Colloquial* to leave
6 push on, to continue or go forward (***advance***, ***forge ahead***, ***make headway***, ***proceed***, ***progress***)
7 the push, *Colloquial* the sack: *He was given* ***the push***.

Word history: Middle English, from Old French, from Latin

pushover
noun **1** something easily done
2 an easily defeated person or team

push-up
noun an exercise in which you raise your body from a lying down position by pushing against the floor, leaving your feet on the ground and keeping your body and legs in a straight line

pusillanimous (pyooh-suh-lan-uh-muhs)
adjective lacking strength of mind or courage (***cowardly***, ***craven***, ***fainthearted***, ***feeble***, ***spineless***)

Word building: **pusillanimity** *noun*
Word history: Late Latin, from Latin

puss
noun a cat

Word use: You can also use **pussy**.

pussyfoot
verb to act timidly as if afraid to make a decision

pustule (pus-tyoohl)
noun a pimple

Word building: **pustulant** *adjective* **pustular** *adjective*
Word history: Middle English, from Latin

put
verb **1** to place or set down
2 to cause to suffer: *The king **put** her to death.*
3 to cause to begin: *I **put** her to work.*
4 to express in words: *to **put** a question*
phrase **5 put about,**
a to spread, especially a rumour or a story
b to change direction or course: *The yacht **put about** to avoid the storm.*
6 put across, to communicate or explain effectively
7 put down,
a to stamp out: *to **put down** a rebellion*
b to kill as an act of mercy: *We had to **put down** our old sick dog.*
8 put forward, to suggest or propose
9 put off, to postpone
10 put on, to pretend to have or to be: *He **puts on** his aches and pains.*
11 put out, to annoy or make difficulties for
12 put paid to, *Colloquial* to destroy finally: *Rain **put paid to** the picnic.*
13 put through,
a to connect by telephone
b to organise or carry into effect
14 put upon, to impose on or take advantage of
15 put up with, to bear or endure (***suffer***, ***tolerate***)

Verb forms: I **put**, I have **put**, I am **putting**
Word history: Middle English

putative (pyooh-tuh-tiv)
adjective commonly thought of as such (***assumed***, ***presumed***, ***reputed***, ***supposed***)

Word history: late Middle English, from Latin word meaning 'think'

putrefy (pyooh-truh-fuy)
verb to rot or decay (***decompose***, ***deteriorate***, ***fester***, ***perish***)

Verb forms: it **putrefied**, it has **putrefied**, it is **putrefying**

putrid (pyooh-truhd)
adjective decaying or rotten, especially when foul-smelling (***fetid***, ***high***, ***rank***, ***smelly***, ***stinking***)

Word history: Latin

putt (put)
verb to strike a golf ball gently along the green towards the hole

Word history: variant of *put*

putter
noun a golf club, usually with a relatively short, stiff shaft and a wooden or iron head, which is used in putting

putty
noun a kind of cement used for fixing glass into frames or filling holes in wood

Word building: **putty** *verb* (**puttied**, **puttying**)
Word history: from French word meaning 'a potful'

puzzle
noun **1** a toy or game which entertains by giving you an interesting problem to solve
2 something that is difficult to understand: *Her rudeness is a **puzzle** to me.* (***conundrum***, ***enigma***, ***mystery***, ***riddle***)

Word building: **puzzle** *verb* **puzzlement** *noun*

PVA
noun polyvinyl acetate, a transparent resin produced by the polymerisation of vinyl acetate, which is used as an adhesive, in paints and lacquers, etc.

Word history: abbreviation of *p(oly)v(inyl) a(cetate)*

PVC
noun polyvinyl chloride, a colourless water-resistant resin, produced by polymerisation of vinyl chloride, used in many products, including rain wear, garden hoses and floor tiles

Word history: abbreviation of *p(oly)v(inyl) c(hloride)*

pygmy (pig-mee)
noun **1** a member of a tribe of African people who are mostly under 1.5 metres tall
2 any small, dwarf-like person or thing

Word use: You can also use **pigmy**.
Word history: Middle English, from Latin, from Greek word meaning 'dwarfish'

pyjama party
noun a party you go to in your pyjamas and stay the whole night (***sleepover***, ***slumber party***)

pyjamas
plural noun loose trousers and jacket worn in bed

Word history: Hindustani, from Persian word meaning 'leg garment'

pylon (puy-lon)
noun **1** a tall, steel tower carrying electric or telephone wires
2 one of the two tall structures on either side of a bridge or of a gateway

Word history: from Greek word meaning 'gateway'

pyramid (pi-ruh-mid)
noun a structure with a square base and with sides sloping to a point, such as the huge stone ones built by the ancient Egyptians

Word history: Latin *pyramis*, from Greek, of Egyptian origin; replacing Middle English *pyramis*, from Latin

pyre (puy-uh)
noun a pile of wood used for burning dead bodies in some countries

Word history: Latin, from Greek

pyromania (puy-ruh-may-nee-uh)
noun a very great desire for setting things on fire

Word building: **pyromaniac** *noun*

pyrotechnics (puy-roh-tek-niks)
noun **1** the art of making and using fireworks
2 a brilliant or sensational display, of speaking, etc.

Pyrrhic victory (pi-rik vik-tuh-ree)
noun a victory gained at too great a cost

Word history: from *Pyrrhus*, 319–272 BC, king of Epirus, who won such a victory over the Romans at Asculum in 279 BC

Pythagoras's theorem
noun the geometrical theorem which states that, in a right-angled triangle, the square on the hypotenuse is equal to the sum of the squares on the other two sides

Word history: named after *Pythagoras*, about 582 to about 500 BC, Greek philosopher, mathematician and religious reformer

python (puy-thuhn)
noun a large snake which crushes its prey but is not venomous

Word history: Latin, from Greek

QC
noun → **Queen's Counsel**
Word history: abbreviation

QED
abbreviation which was to be shown or proved
Word history: abbreviation of Latin *q(uod) e(rat) d(ēmonstrandum)*

quack[1]
noun the sound a duck makes
Word building: **quack** *verb*
Word history: imitative

quack[2]
noun someone with no proper training who pretends to have medical skills and to be able to cure people (***charlatan***)
Word building: **quackery** *noun*
Word history: Dutch *quacksalver* related to *quack[1]* and *salve*

quad[1]
noun Colloquial a quadrangle, originally of a college
Word history: short for *quadrangle*; originally university slang

quad[2]
noun → **quadruplet**

quad bike
noun a four-wheeled motorcycle designed to travel over rough terrain

quadrangle
noun a square or rectangular courtyard surrounded by buildings
Word history: Middle English, from Late Latin word meaning 'four-cornered (thing)'

quadrant
noun **1** a quarter of a circle
2 an instrument for measuring altitudes, especially in astronomy and navigation
Word history: Middle English, from Latin word meaning 'fourth part'

quadratic
adjective **1** square
2 *Algebra* involving a number or numbers that are squared, but not raised to any higher power: *a **quadratic** equation*
noun **3** *Algebra* a quadratic equation

quadriceps (kwod-ruh-seps)
noun the great muscle of the front of the thigh, which extends the leg and is considered as having four points of connection
Word history: from Latin *quadri-* four + *-ceps* head, point of origin

quadrilateral
noun a closed, plane figure with four sides
Word building: **quadrilateral** *adjective*
Word history: from Latin word meaning 'four-sided'

quadrille (kwuh-dril)
noun a dance where four couples dance in a square pattern
Word history: French, from Spanish word meaning 'company', 'troop', from Latin

quadriplegia (kwo-druh-plee-juh)
noun a condition in which the arms and legs are paralysed
Word building: **quadriplegic** *adjective*
quadriplegic *noun*
Word history: *quadri-* (a word part meaning 'four') + *(para)plegia*

quadruped (kwo-druh-ped)
noun an animal with four feet
Word building: **quadruped** *adjective*
Word history: Latin

quadruple (kwo-drooh-puhl, kwo-druh-puhl)
verb **1** to multiply by four
adjective **2** made up of four parts
3 four times bigger
Word building: **quadruple** *noun*
Word history: Middle English, from Latin

quadruplet
noun one of four children born at the same time to the same mother
Word use: The abbreviation is **quad.**
Word history: *quadruple* + *-et*

quaff (kwof)
verb to drink thirstily (***guzzle***)
Word history: blend of *quench* and *draught*

quagmire (kwog-muyuh)
noun a muddy patch of ground: *The rain has turned the yard into a **quagmire**.* (***bog***, ***marsh***, ***swamp***)
Word history: *quag* (of obscure origin) boggy ground + *mire*

quail[1]
noun a small bird that builds its nest on the ground and is hunted for sport and food
Noun forms: The plural is **quails** or **quail.**
Word history: Middle English, from Old French; of Germanic origin

quail[2]
verb to show fear when danger threatens (***chicken out***, ***cower***, ***cringe***, ***flinch***, ***waver***)
Word history: Middle English

quaint
adjective charmingly strange or old-fashioned: *a **quaint** little country town*

Word history: Middle English, from Old French word meaning 'clever', 'beautiful', from Latin word meaning 'known'

quake
verb **1** to tremble or shake: *to **quake** with fear | The city **quaked** with the force of the explosion.* (***quiver***, ***shiver***, ***shudder***, ***vibrate***)
noun **2** an earthquake

Word history: Middle English, from Old English *cwacian* shake, tremble

qualification (kwol-uh-fuh-kay-shuhn)
noun **1** an ability or achievement which makes a person fit for a particular job or position, etc.
2 the act of qualifying
3 a modification or limitation: *I give you my promise without any **qualification**.*

qualify (kwol-uh-fuy)
verb **1** to make or become suitable for: *Her teaching experience **qualifies** her for the job. | To **qualify** for the final you must do well in the heats.*
2 to change or limit the meaning of: *to **qualify** a remark | An adjective **qualifies** a noun.*

Verb forms: I **qualified**, I have **qualified**, I am **qualifying**
Word building: **qualified** *adjective*
Word history: Medieval Latin

qualitative (kwol-uh-tay-tiv, kwol-uh-tuh-tiv)
adjective having to do with quality or qualities

Word history: Late Latin

quality (kwol-uh-tee)
noun **1** a feature or characteristic: *The sound of an echo has a hollow **quality**.*
2 value or worth: *food of poor **quality***
3 high grade or value: *clothes of **quality***
adjective **4** of fine or good quality: ***quality** clothes* (***excellent***, ***high class***, ***superior***)

Noun forms: The plural is **qualities**.
Word history: Middle English, from Latin

qualm (kwahm)
noun a slightly guilty feeling: *They had some **qualms** about being late.*

Word history: Old English *cwealm* torment, pain, plague

quandary (kwon-dree)
noun confusion about what is the best thing to do: *I'm in a **quandary** about this invitation.*

Noun forms: The plural is **quandaries**.

quandong (kwon-dong)
noun an Australian tree with fruit which can be eaten raw or made into jams and jellies

Word history: from Wiradjuri, an Australian Aboriginal language of the Murrumbidgee-Lachlan region

quantify (kwon-tuh-fuy)
verb to measure or find the quantity of

Word history: Medieval Latin

quantitative (kwon-tuh-tay-tiv, kwon-tuh-tuh-tiv)
adjective **1** measured or able to be measured
2 having to do with the describing or measuring of quantity

quantity (kwon-tuh-tee)
noun an amount or measure: *What **quantity** does this bottle hold?*

Noun forms: The plural is **quantities**.
Word history: Middle English *quantite*, from Latin *quantitas*

quantum (kwon-tuhm)
noun **1** a quantity or amount
2 *Physics*
a one of the discrete quantities of energy or momentum of an atomic system which is characteristic of the quantum theory
b this amount of energy regarded as a unit

Noun forms: The plural is **quanta**.
Word history: from Latin word meaning 'how great', 'how much'

quantum number
noun one of a set of integers or half-integers which defines the energy state of a system, or its components, in quantum theory

quantum physics
noun the branch of physics that uses quantum theory

quantum theory
noun *Physics* a theory that describes electromagnetic radiation in terms of quanta

quarantine (kwo-ruhn-teen)
noun the isolating of people, animals or plants for a certain period of time to make sure they don't spread a disease to others

Word building: **quarantine** *verb*
Word history: Italian, from Latin word meaning 'forty'

quarrel (kwo-ruhl)
noun an angry argument (***altercation***, ***conflict***, ***controversy***, ***difference***, ***dispute***)

Word building: **quarrel** *verb* (**quarrelled**, **quarrelling**) **quarrelsome** *adjective*
Word history: Middle English, from Old French, from Latin word meaning 'a complaint'

quarry[1] (kwo-ree)
noun a large open pit where stone used for building is cut or blasted out of the ground: *a sandstone **quarry***

Noun forms: The plural is **quarries**.
Word building: **quarry** *verb* (**quarried**, **quarrying**)
Word history: Middle English, from Medieval Latin word meaning 'place where stone is squared', from Latin word meaning 'to square'

quarry[2] (kwo-ree)
noun an animal or bird that is being hunted or chased: *The hounds tracked down their **quarry**.*

Noun forms: The plural is **quarries**.
Word history: Middle English, from Old French word meaning 'skin', 'hide', from Latin

quarter (kwaw-tuh)
noun **1** one of the parts you get when you divide something equally into four: *a **quarter** of an apple*
2 a district in a town: *the business **quarter***
3 quarters, a place to live: *the nurses' **quarters***
verb **4** to divide into four equal parts
5 to provide with a place to live or sleep: *The soldiers were **quartered** in the barracks.*

Word history: Middle English, from Old French, from Latin word meaning 'fourth part'

quarterdeck
noun the part of the top deck of a ship between the mast and the stern, used by the officers

quarterly
adjective **1** happening or done every three months
noun **2** a magazine or the like appearing every three months

Noun forms: The plural is **quarterlies**.
Word building: **quarterly** *adverb*
Word history: late Middle English

quartermaster
noun an army officer in charge of food, clothing, housing and equipment

Word history: late Middle English

quartet
noun **1** a group of four people, especially musicians or singers
2 a musical piece for four voices or four performers: *a* ***quartet*** *for string instruments*

Word history: French, from Italian word meaning 'fourth', from Latin

quarto (kwaw-toh)
noun a medium paper size

Noun forms: The plural is **quartos**.
Word history: Neo-Latin

quartz (kwawts)
noun a common mineral which has many different forms and colours, and which can be used to make very accurate clocks and watches

Word history: German

> **quartz / quarts**
> Don't confuse **quartz** with **quarts**, which is the plural of **quart**, a measure of liquid in the imperial system. One **quart** is equal to 1.136 litres.

quartzite
noun a coarse-grained rock consisting basically of quartz in interlocking grains

quasar (kway-zah, kway-sah)
noun Physics one of many extremely distant, very massive sources of high-energy radio-frequency electromagnetic radiation, of unknown structure

Word history: short for *quas(i-stell)ar (source)*

quash[1] (kwosh)
verb to put down completely (***crush***, ***quell***, ***subdue***, ***suppress***)

Word history: Middle English, from Old French, from Latin word meaning 'shake'

quash[2] (kwosh)
verb to make void or set aside: *to* ***quash*** *a law* | *to* ***quash*** *a decision*

Word history: Middle English, from Old French, from Latin word meaning 'shake'

quasi (kwah-zee)
adjective resembling but not actual: *a* ***quasi-****smile*

Word use: This is usually joined to the word it describes by a hyphen.
Word building: **quasi** *adverb*
Word history: Middle English, from Latin

quaternary (kwo-ter-nuh-ree)
adjective **1** consisting of four
2 arranged in fours

Word building: **quaternary** *noun*
Word history: Middle English, from Latin *quaternārius*

quaver (kway-vuh)
noun **1** a shaking or trembling voice: *The old man spoke in a* ***quaver***.
2 a musical note which is half as long as a crotchet
verb **3** to say or sing in a trembling voice

Word building: **quavery** *adjective*
Word history: Middle English; blend of *quake* and *waver*

quay (kee)
noun a wharf where ships and ferries load or unload passengers and cargo

Word history: Old French

> **quay / key**
> Don't confuse **quay** with **key**, which is most often a small, specially shaped piece of metal that can open a lock.

queasy
adjective feeling as if you are going to vomit

Adjective forms: **queasier**, **queasiest**
Word history: late Middle English

queen
noun **1** a woman who is the sovereign of a country
2 the wife of a king
3 the large egg-laying female of such creatures as bees, ants, and termites
4 a playing card with a picture of a queen on it
5 the most powerful chess piece

Word history: Middle English; wife, queen

Queensberry rules
plural noun the set of rules followed in modern boxing

Word history: named after the 8th Marquis of *Queensberry*, 1844–1900, British sportsman

Queen's Counsel
noun (in some legal systems) a member of the senior of the two ranks of barrister

Word use: When the reigning monarch is a man, this is called **King's Counsel**. | This title has been replaced by **Senior Counsel** in some legal systems. | Look up **silk** also. | The abbreviation is **QC**.

queer
adjective **1** strange or odd: *a* ***queer*** *idea* (***abnormal***, ***atypical***, ***peculiar***, ***unusual***, ***weird***)
2 unwell: *I feel* ***queer***. (***nauseous***, ***queasy***, ***sick***)
3 *Colloquial* homosexual

Word building: **queerly** *adverb*
Word history: from German word meaning 'oblique', 'cross', 'adverse'

> This word used to be used disapprovingly about homosexuals, but nowadays is quite a positive term used by gay people themselves.

quell
verb to stop or calm: *to **quell** riots* | *to **quell** your fears*

Word history: from Old English word meaning 'kill'

quench
verb **1** to put out: *to **quench** a fire*
2 to satisfy or make less: *A cool drink will **quench** your thirst.*

Word history: Old English

querulous (kwe-ruh-luhs)
adjective irritable and complaining (***cantankerous***, ***discontented***, ***dissatisfied***, ***fretful***, ***plaintive***)

Word history: Latin

query (kwear-ree)
noun **1** a question or enquiry
2 a doubt or problem: *a **query** about the electricity bill*
verb **3** to ask questions about or doubt (***challenge***, ***question***, ***suspect***)

Noun forms: The plural is **queries**.
Word history: from Latin word meaning 'ask'

quest
noun a search: *a talent **quest*** | *a **quest** for gold*

Word history: Middle English, from Old French, from Latin word meaning 'sought', 'asked'

question
noun **1** a request for information: *The police asked the witnesses many **questions** about the accident.*
2 a doubt or problem: *There is no **question** about her honesty.*
phrase **3 call in** (or **into**) **question**, to raise doubts about or demand an explanation about
4 out of the question, impossible

Word building: **question** *verb*
Word history: Middle English, from Anglo-French, from Latin

Questions may differ from statements in several ways. Often, instead of the subject of the verb beginning the sentence, part of the verb itself is placed first:

He is leaving home. (statement)
becomes
Is he leaving home? (question)

Alternatively, a question word such as *who*, *what* or *where* may begin the sentence:

Where is he going?

Sometimes, a question tag such as *won't you* or *doesn't she* ends the sentence:

He's leaving home, isn't he?

Note that all these forms have one thing in common: they end with a question mark.

Sometimes in speech the only difference between a statement and a question is the pitch of your voice. And when you write them down, the only difference would be the punctuation you use:

He's leaving now. (statement)
He's leaving now? (question)

For more information, look up **indirect question** and **question mark**.

questionable
adjective **1** of doubtful honesty or respectability: *a **questionable** person*
2 doubtful or uncertain: *Whether this is true is **questionable**.* (***debatable***, ***dubious***, ***open to question***, ***unproven***)

question mark
noun a punctuation mark (?) put at the end of a written question

A **question mark** can be used in a number of ways to indicate a question:

1 *How are you going?*
2 *Well? What?*
3 *That's all you've got to say?*
4 *I said, 'How are you going?'*
5 *'Are you going to answer me?' I asked.*

Example 1 shows the most common use of the question mark, at the end of a sentence which is a question.

Example 2 shows that you can use a question mark for a question that isn't a complete sentence — it may only be one word.

Questions sometimes use the same word order as statements. But when they are spoken, you know they are questions by the special pitch of the voice of the speaker. When such questions are written, the only indication that they are questions is the question mark at the end, as in example 3.

Examples 4 and 5 show how to use question marks with quotation marks. The question mark comes just before the final quotation mark, and there is no need for a comma if the sentence continues after the quotation.

Note that there is no need for a question mark when you write an indirect question:

I asked how she was going.

Note also that it is not necessary to use a question mark when the sentence is a request:

Would you pass the butter, please.

questionnaire (kwes-chuhn-air, kes-chuhn-air)
noun a list of questions set out on a printed form with spaces for the answers to be written in

Word history: French

queue (kyooh)
noun a single line of people, cars or animals waiting in turn for something: *a **queue** for tickets*

Word building: **queue** *verb*
Word history: French, from Latin word meaning 'tail'

queue / cue
Don't confuse **queue** and **cue**, which can be anything said or done as a signal for what follows or a long stick used in billiards and similar games.

quibble
verb to argue, especially over things that don't matter: *to **quibble** over a few cents change*

Word history: perhaps from *quib* gibe, apparently variant of *quip*

quiche (keesh)
noun a tart filled with a mixture of cooked eggs, cream and other savoury ingredients, such as cheese, ham, or so on, often eaten cold

Word history: French, from German word meaning 'cake'

quick
adjective **1** fast, rapid or impatient: *a* ***quick*** *movement | a* ***quick*** *temper* (***brisk***, ***prompt***, ***speedy***, ***swift***)
2 done, completed or happening in a short time: *a* ***quick*** *job*
noun **3** the sensitive skin under your nails: *nails bitten down to the* ***quick***
phrase **4 cut to the quick**, to hurt the feelings of someone deeply

Word building: **quick** *adverb* **quickly** *adverb*
Word history: from Old English word meaning 'living'

quicken
verb to make or become faster

Word history: Middle English

quicksand
noun an area of loose, wet sand of considerable depth, which traps anyone who falls into it and sucks them down

Word history: Middle English, from archaic *quick* shifting + *sand*

quicksilver
adjective **1** changing quickly
noun **2** → **mercury**

Word history: from Old English word meaning 'living silver'

quid
noun Colloquial **1** one pound in money, used before decimal currency
phrase **2 a quick quid**, money earned with little effort, often by dishonest means
3 not the full quid, dull or mentally slow

Word history: from Old English word meaning 'cud'

quiescent (kwee-es-uhnt)
adjective being at rest, quiet, or still

Word history: from Latin word meaning 'keeping quiet'

quiet
adjective **1** still or silent: *a* ***quiet*** *stream | a* ***quiet*** *voice* (***hushed***, ***low***, ***muffled***, ***noiseless***, ***soft***)
2 calm and peaceful: *a* ***quiet*** *weekend | a* ***quiet*** *street* (***restful***, ***serene***, ***tranquil***, ***untroubled***)
3 shy: *The new girl is rather* ***quiet***. (***reserved***, ***reticent***)
noun **4** calmness or peace
phrase **5 on the quiet**, *Colloquial* secretly

Word building: **quietly** *adverb*
Word history: Middle English, from Latin word meaning 'rest', 'repose'

> **quiet / quite**
> Don't confuse **quiet** with **quite**, which means 'completely' or 'fairly or considerably'.

quieten
verb to make or become quiet

quill
noun **1** a large feather
2 an old-fashioned pen, made from a goose's feather
3 a sharp spine of an echidna or porcupine

Word history: Middle English

quilt
noun a light, warm bed-cover usually filled with feathers

Word history: Middle English, from Old French, from Latin word meaning 'mattress', 'cushion'

quince
noun a sour yellow fruit, rather like a large pear, which is so hard it has to be cooked before you can eat it

Word history: Middle English, from Old French, from Latin, from Greek word meaning 'quince', literally '(apple) of *Cydonia*' (ancient city of Crete)

quinine (kwin-een, kwuh-neen)
noun a bitter medicine used to treat malaria

Word history: Spanish (from Quechua word meaning 'bark') + *-ine*

quintessential (kwin-tuh-sen-shuhl)
adjective being the most perfect example of something: *the* ***quintessential*** *outback setting*

Word history: Middle English, from Medieval Latin word meaning 'fifth essence'

quintet
noun **1** a group of five people, especially musicians or singers
2 a musical piece for five voices or five performers

Word history: French, from Italian, from Latin word meaning 'fifth'

quintuple (kwin-tup-uhl, kwin-tyoohp-uhl)
verb **1** to multiply by five
adjective **2** made up of five parts
3 five times bigger

Word building: **quintuple** *noun*
Word history: French

quintuplet (kwin-tup-luht)
noun one of five children born at the same time to the same mother

quip
noun a clever or sarcastic remark (***gibe***, ***joke***, ***pun***, ***wisecrack***, ***witticism***)

Word building: **quip** *verb* (**quipped**, **quipping**)
Word history: from Latin word meaning 'indeed'

quirk
noun **1** a particular habit or way of acting: *a* ***quirk*** *of his nature*
2 a sudden twist or turn: ***quirk*** *of fate*

quirky
adjective odd or eccentric

Adjective forms: **quirkier**, **quirkiest**

quisling
noun a person who is disloyal to his or her own country by helping an occupying enemy force

Word history: from Vidkun *Quisling*, 1887–1945, pro-Nazi Norwegian leader

quit
verb **1** to give up or leave: *to **quit** a job | The wages were very low so she **quit**.* (***abdicate, pull out, resign, retire***)
phrase **2 call it quits,**
a to decide to stop doing something
b to end an argument by agreeing that both sides are even

Verb forms: I **quit** or I **quitted**, I have **quit** or I have **quitted**, I am **quitting**
Word history: Middle English, from Old French, from Medieval Latin word meaning 'release', 'discharge', from Late Latin word meaning 'quiet'

quite
adverb **1** completely or entirely: *to be **quite** right*
2 fairly or reasonably: ***quite** pretty*

Word history: adverb use of Middle English adjective *quite* quit

quiver[1]
verb to tremble or shake slightly: *to **quiver** with fear | The leaves **quiver** in the breeze.*

Word building: **quiver** *noun*
Word history: Middle English

quiver[2]
noun a case for holding arrows

Word history: Middle English, from Old French *quivre*

quixotic (kwik-<u>so</u>-tik)
adjective having romantic ideas about doing brave and wonderful deeds

Word history: from Don *Quixote*, the hero of a romance by Miguel de Cervantes, 1547–1616, Spanish novelist

quiz
noun **1** a test to see who knows the most about a particular subject: *a general knowledge **quiz** on TV | a spelling **quiz***
verb **2** to ask a series of questions of (***grill, interrogate, interview***)

Noun forms: The plural is **quizzes**.
Verb forms: I **quizzed**, I have **quizzed**, I am **quizzing**

quizzical
adjective teasing, or suggesting you know something the other person doesn't: *a **quizzical** smile*

quoin (koyn)
noun **1** the outer solid angle of a wall or the like
2 one of the stones forming it
3 a wedge-shaped piece of wood, stone, etc.

Word history: variant of *coin*

quoit (koyt)
noun **1** a flattish ring of iron or some other material thrown in play to encircle an upright peg
2 quoits, the game played this way

Word use: You can also use **deck quoit** for definition 1 or **deck quoits** for definition 2. | Definition 2 is plural in form but treated as singular.
Word history: Middle English *coyte*

quokka (<u>kwok</u>-uh)
noun a small wallaby, *Setonix brachyurus*, found in considerable numbers on Rottnest and Bald Islands, off Western Australia, and as small colonies in south-western mainland Western Australia

Word history: from Nyungar, an Australian Aboriginal language of the Perth-Albany region

quoll (kwol)
noun an Australian marsupial with a long tail and spots, about the size of a cat

Word history: from Guugu Yimidhirr, an Australian Aboriginal language from the Cooktown region in Queensland

quorum (<u>kwaw</u>-ruhm)
noun the number of people that have to be at a meeting before decisions can be made

Word history: Latin word meaning 'of whom'; from a use of the word in commissions written in Latin

quota
noun the share that you are entitled to: *Because of the drought, the farmers needed more than their **quota** of water.* (***allocation, allowance, ration***)

Word history: Medieval Latin, short for Latin *quota pars* how great a part?

quotable
adjective worth repeating

quotation
noun **1** a passage copied exactly from a book or speech
2 a price quoted

quotation mark
noun one of the punctuation marks (" ") or (' ') used before and after a quotation

Quotation marks are also known as **quote marks, quotes** and **inverted commas**. Their main use is to show that you are quoting someone exactly, and especially to show that you are quoting someone's spoken words:

George told them to 'rack off'.

This shows that 'rack' and 'off' are exactly the words that George spoke. Compare:

George told them to rack off.

Here George still tells the people to go away, but because there are no quotation marks it may be that he used some expression other than 'rack off'.

Quotation marks can sometimes be used to indicate the titles of short pieces of writing — for example, essays, poems, or the chapters of a book. The names of planes, trains and other vehicles can similarly be written with quotation marks.

Another use for quotes is to highlight a word or to show that you've made it up:

I think the word 'ocker' is a bit old-fashioned.

Why don't we call them 'yappies' — for <u>y</u>okelish <u>A</u>ustralian <u>p</u>eople?

When using quotation marks, there are two things to consider: (**1**) whether to use double quotes (" ") or single quotes (' '), and (**2**) how to punctuate with quotation marks.

(continued)

quotation marks *(continued)*

1 Double quotes or single quotes?

In your writing you must choose one or other as your basic system. There are good arguments in favour of each.

Double quotes are useful because you can tell them apart easily from apostrophes:

'I've visited all my friends' houses,' Maria said.

"I've visited all my friends' houses," Maria said.

The main argument for single quotes is that they are less fussy, both to look at and to write.

Once you have chosen one style as your basic quotation marks, you should use it throughout your written work. The second style can then be used for quotations within quotations:

She told me, "George saw them and said 'rack off' to them."

She told me, 'George saw them and said "rack off" to them.'

2 Punctuation with quotations

When you are writing speech you often introduce a quotation with a phrase like *he said*, *she replied*, etc. There are three common ways to punctuate between the phrase and the quote. You can simply leave a space, add a comma, or add a colon:

George said "Rack off."

George said, "Rack off."

George said: "Rack off."

Once you are inside the quotation marks you should use exactly the same punctuation as you would in your normal writing. If the quotation is a sentence, it should start with a capital letter, and should usually end with a full stop:

George said "You've all got to rack off."

If the sentence continues after the quotation is ended, the full stop changes to a comma:

George said "You've all got to rack off," and went home.

quote
verb **1** to repeat exactly: *to* ***quote*** *a phrase from Shakespeare*
2 to name a price: *The mechanic* ***quoted*** *$100 to fix the car.*
noun **3** a quotation

Word history: Middle English, from Medieval Latin word meaning 'divide into chapters and verses', from Latin word meaning 'how many'

quotient (kwoh-shuhnt)
noun the number or result you get when one number is divided by another: *In the sum 12 ÷ 4, the* ***quotient*** *is 3.*

Word use: Compare this with **divisor** and **dividend**.
Word history: Middle English, from Latin word meaning 'how many times'

q.v.
abbreviation short for *quod vide*, Latin words meaning 'which see', used as an instruction to look up a cross-reference in a book, article, etc.

rabbi (<u>rab</u>-uy)
noun a Jewish priest or leader
Word history: Middle English and Old English, from Latin, from Hebrew word meaning 'my master'

rabbit
noun **1** a small, long-eared, burrowing animal
verb **2** to hunt rabbits
phrase **3 rabbit on,** *Colloquial* to talk a lot of nonsense
Word history: Middle English

rabble
noun a noisy crowd or mob
Word history: Middle English

rabid (<u>rab</u>-uhd)
adjective **1** extraordinarily unreasoning in your opinions or in what you do: *a* ***rabid*** *isolationist*
2 furious or raging: ***rabid*** *hunger*
3 affected with or having to do with rabies
Word history: from Latin word meaning 'raving', 'mad'

rabies
noun a fatal disease that is spread to people by the bite of a dog or of some other animal which has the disease
Word history: from Latin word meaning 'madness', 'rage'

raccoon (ruh-<u>koohn</u>)
noun a small flesh-eating animal found mainly in North America, living in or among trees and having greyish fur, a sharp snout, and a bushy ringed tail
Word use: You can also use **racoon**.
Word history: from Native American word meaning 'he scratches with the hands'

race[1]
noun **1** a contest of speed
2 any kind of competition: *the arms* ***race***
3 a narrow passageway for animals, such as one leading to a sheep dip
verb **4** to run or move very quickly (***hurry, hurtle, pelt, speed, tear***)
5 to compete with in running: *I* ***raced*** *him to the shop.*
Word history: Middle English, from Scandinavian

race[2]
noun a group of tribes or nations with the same ancestors, the same language and culture or the same skin colour
Word history: French, from Italian word meaning 'race', 'breed', 'lineage'

racecourse (<u>rays</u>-caws)
noun a piece of ground on which horseraces are held for public entertainment

racial (<u>ray</u>-shuhl)
adjective **1** having to do with or typical of a race: *White skin is a* ***racial*** *characteristic of Scandinavian people.*
2 having to do with relations between people of different races: ***racial*** *harmony*

racism (<u>ray</u>-siz-uhm)
noun **1** the belief that your own race is better than any other
2 unpleasant or violent behaviour towards members of another race
Word building: **racist** *noun* **racist** *adjective*

racist language
noun words that express racial prejudice

The use of racist terms such as *boong*, *slope* and *nigger* reflects the speaker's unjustified attitude of their own race's superiority over another race. These words are offensive and damaging and the use of such derogatory terms puts people of other races and nationalities at an immediate disadvantage. Whether you mean it or not, the words suggest a bias against those people — or at least a readiness to stereotype them. You should avoid them whether you are writing or speaking.

rack[1]
noun **1** a framework of bars, wires or pegs for holding things
2 a frame on which people used to be tortured by having their bodies stretched
verb **3** to cause great pain to: *Fever* ***racked*** *her body.*
Word history: Middle English, from Middle Dutch or Middle Low German

rack[2]
noun **1** wreck or destruction
phrase **2 rack and ruin,** disrepair or collapse, especially owing to neglect

rack[3]
phrase **rack off,** *Australian Colloquial* to leave or go: *He* ***racked off*** *ages ago.* | ***Rack off,*** *hairy legs!*

racket[1]
noun **1** a loud confused noise (***commotion, din, hubbub, pandemonium, uproar***)
2 an illegal business or way of making money: *an organised car-stealing* ***racket***

racket[2]
noun → **racquet**

raconteur (rak-on-ter)
noun someone who is very good at telling interesting and amusing stories, especially true ones

Word history: French

racquet (rak-uht)
noun a bat with a network of nylon or cord stretched across an oval frame, which is used in tennis and similar games

Word use: You can also use **racket**.
Word history: French

racy (ray-see)
adjective **1** lively or vigorous
2 suggestive or risqué: *a **racy** story*

Adjective forms: **racier**, **raciest**
Word building: **racily** *adverb* **raciness** *noun*

radar
noun a device which tells you the position and speed of objects like cars, ships or planes, by sending out radio waves and measuring the time the echo takes to come back and the direction it comes from

Word history: an acronym for *ra(dio) d(etecting) a(nd) r(anging)*

radar trap
noun a place beside a road where police have set up radar equipment to detect speeding motorists

radial (ray-dee-uhl)
adjective arranged like rays or radii

Word history: from Latin word meaning 'radius'

radian (ray-dee-uhn)
noun a supplementary SI unit of measurement of a plane angle, being the angle between two radii of a circle which cut off on the circumference an arc equal to the length of the radius

Word use: The symbol is **rad**, without a full stop.

radiant (ray-dee-uhnt)
adjective **1** shining or sending out rays: *the **radiant** sun*
2 bright with joy: *a **radiant** smile*

Word building: **radiance** *noun*
Word history: Middle English, from Latin word meaning 'emitting rays'

radiate
verb **1** to spread out like rays from a centre
2 to send out in rays: *The stove **radiated** heat.*

Word history: Latin

radiation
noun the sending and spreading out of rays, particles or waves, especially by a radioactive substance

radiator
noun **1** an electric room heater with a rod or rods which become red-hot
2 a device which cools the engine of a motor vehicle

radical (rad-ik-uhl)
adjective **1** being in favour of extreme social or political reforms: *a **radical** political party*
2 going to the root or bottom of things: *a **radical** change in education | **radical** ideas about religion* (***basic***, ***fundamental***)
noun **3** someone who holds or follows principles which are far from the ordinary, especially left-wing political principles

Word use: The opposite of definitions 1 and 3 is **conservative**. The opposite of definition 2 is **minor** or **superficial**.
Word history: Middle English, from Late Latin, from Latin word meaning 'root'

radicle (rad-ik-uhl)
noun the largest and most important root of a young plant

Word history: from Latin word meaning 'little root'

radio
noun **1** the sending of electrical signals through the air to a set which receives them: *The message came by **radio**.*
2 a device for picking up radio broadcasts: *We turned on the **radio** for the news.*
verb **3** to send a message by radio: *We **radioed** for help.*

Noun forms: The plural is **radios**.
Verb forms: I **radioed**, I have **radioed**, I am **radioing**
Word use: An old-fashioned word for definition 2 is **wireless**.
Word history: combining form of *radius*

radioactivity
noun the ability of some atomic elements, like uranium, to release harmful radiation

Word building: **radioactive** *adjective*

radiocarbon dating
noun finding the age of objects of plant or animal origin from their content of radioactive carbon

Word use: You can also use **carbon dating**.

radiography (ray-dee-og-ruh-fee)
noun the production of pictures caused by the action of X-rays on a photographic plate, especially as used in medicine (***X-ray photography***)

Word building: **radiographer** *noun* **radiographic** *adjective*

radiology (ray-dee-ol-uh-jee)
noun **1** the science dealing with X-rays or rays from radioactive substances, especially for medical uses
2 the examining or photographing of organs, etc., with such rays

Word building: **radiologist** *noun* **radiological** *adjective*

radiotherapy (ray-dee-oh-ther-uh-pee)
noun the treatment of disease by X-rays or radioactive substances

radish
noun a hot-tasting, red-skinned vegetable eaten raw in salads

Word history: Old English, from Latin word meaning 'root', 'radish'

radium
noun a naturally occurring radioactive element sometimes used to treat cancer

Word history: Neo-Latin, from Latin *radius* ray

radius (ray-dee-uhs)
noun **1** a straight line going from the centre of a circle to its circumference or edge
2 a circular area around some point: *every house within a **radius** of ten kilometres of the school*

Noun forms: The plural is **radii** (<u>ray</u>-dee-uy) or **radiuses.**
Word history: from Latin word meaning 'staff', 'rod', 'spoke of a wheel', 'radius', 'ray or beam of light'

Rafferty's rules
plural noun Australian, NZ no rules at all, such as something organised in a slipshod way
Word use: You can also use **Rafferty rules.**

raffia
noun a fibre obtained from the leaves of a palm tree, used in weaving baskets and in other crafts
Word history: Malagasy

raffle
noun a lottery in which the prizes are usually goods, not money
Word building: **raffle** *verb*
Word history: Middle English, from Old French word meaning 'kind of game at dice', 'net', 'plundering', from Dutch word meaning 'ravel'

raft[1]
noun a floating platform, often made of logs, for carrying goods or people on the water
Word history: Middle English *rafte* beam, rafter, from Scandinavian

raft[2]
noun a collection or set of items: *a whole* ***raft*** *of issues to consider*

rafter
noun a piece of wood forming part of the framework of a roof
Word history: Old English *ræfterer*

rag[1]
noun **1** an old torn piece of cloth that you use for cleaning
2 a newspaper or magazine, especially one thought to be of low quality
3 rags, worn and shabby clothing
Word history: Middle English *ragg(e)*, from Scandinavian

rag[2]
verb Colloquial **1** to tease or torment
noun Colloquial **2** any disorderly or high-spirited behaviour, especially by a group of young people
Verb forms: I **ragged**, I have **ragged**, I am **ragging**

ragamuffin
noun Old-fashioned someone who is ragged and dirty, especially a child

rage
noun **1** violent anger: *to get into a* ***rage*** (***fury***, ***ire***, ***temper***, ***wrath***)
verb **2** to act or speak angrily
3 to move or happen violently: *The storm* ***raged*** *for days.*
4 *Colloquial* to set about enjoying yourself (***celebrate***, ***party on***, ***revel***, ***whoop it up***)
phrase **5 all the rage**, fashionable or popular (***cool***, ***hip***, ***trendy***, ***vogueish***)
Word history: Middle English, from Old French, from Vulgar Latin, from Latin *rabies* madness, rage

ragged (<u>rag</u>-uhd)
adjective **1** wearing old and torn clothes
2 torn or worn to rags: ***ragged*** *clothing*

raglan (<u>rag</u>-luhn)
noun **1** a loose overcoat whose sleeves are cut so as to continue up to the collar
adjective **2** made in such a way
Word history: named after Lord *Raglan*, 1788–1855, British field marshal

raid
noun a sudden invasion or attack: *a police* ***raid*** *on a gambling house* | *a* ***raid*** *on an enemy airfield*
Word history: Old English *rād* expedition, literally, riding

rail[1]
noun **1** a rod or bar used as a support or barrier
2 the railway: *We will travel by* ***rail.***
3 rails, the railway lines that a train runs on
phrase **4 off the rails**, out of control
Word history: Middle English, from Old French, from Latin word meaning 'rule', 'straight stick', 'bar'

rail[2]
phrase **rail at**, to complain bitterly about: *to* ***rail at*** *fate*
Word history: Middle English, from French word meaning 'deride', from Provençal word meaning 'chatter', from Latin word meaning 'shriek'

raillery (<u>ray</u>-luh-ree)
noun Old-fashioned good-humoured teasing (***banter***, ***leg-pulling***)
Noun forms: The plural is **railleries.**
Word history: French

railway
noun **1** the track or way laid with parallel metal rails for trains to run on
2 all these tracks together with their trains, buildings and land

raiment (<u>ray</u>-muhnt)
noun Old-fashioned clothing or apparel (***attire***, ***dress***)
Word history: Middle English

rain
noun **1** water falling from the sky in drops (***drizzle***, ***pour***, ***spit***, ***sprinkle***, ***teem***)
2 a large quantity of anything which keeps on falling for some time: *a* ***rain*** *of confetti*
verb **3** to come down from the sky in drops of water
4 to fall constantly like rain: *Tears* ***rained*** *down her cheeks.*
phrase **5 rain cats and dogs**, to rain heavily
6 right as rain, perfectly all right
Word history: Old English *regn*

rain / reign / rein
Don't confuse **rain** with **reign** or **rein.**
The **reign** of a king or queen is the period during which they rule.
A rider uses a **rein** to guide a horse.

rainbow
noun **1** an arc of colours that appears in the sky when the sun is shining after rain
adjective **2** having many colours
Word history: Old English *regnboga*

rainbow lorikeet
noun a brightly coloured, noisy, sociable parrot, orange and green with a bright blue head and a red beak

rainbow serpent
noun (in Aboriginal mythology) a spirit of creation which appeared as a great snake in the Dreaming, made the earth, and then returned to a spot at a place where the rainbow meets the earth
Word use: You can also use **rainbow snake** or **rainbow spirit**.

rainfall
noun the amount of water falling as rain, snow, etc., within a given time and area: *a **rainfall** of 1210 mm a year*

rainforest
noun thick forest in moderately warm to very hot areas which has heavy rainfall and high humidity

raise
verb **1** to lift up (***elevate, hoist, jack up***)
2 to bring up or produce: *to **raise** a family | to **raise** cattle*
3 to gather together or collect: *to **raise** an army | to **raise** money*
4 to cause to stick out: *The sun **raised** blisters on my arms.*
5 to increase in amount: *to **raise** prices*
noun **6** an increase in wages
Word history: Middle English, from Scandinavian

raise / rise
Don't confuse **raise** with **rise**. To **rise** is to get up, or go upwards:
I rise at dawn each morning.
Their voices rise when they get angry.
A **rise** is an upward movement, or an upward slope, as in *a price rise* or *a rise in the ground.*

raise / raze
Don't confuse **raise** with **raze**. To **raze** something is to knock it down flat:
The wreckers have been told to raze the damaged building.

raisin
noun a dried sweet grape
Word history: Middle English, from Old French, from Latin word meaning 'cluster of grapes'

rake[1]
noun **1** a long-handled gardening tool used for gathering cut grass and leaves or for levelling and smoothing the ground
verb **2** to clear or level with a rake: *to **rake** the lawn*
3 to use a rake: *He's out in the garden **raking**.*
4 to search thoroughly through
phrase **5 rake in**, to gather or collect: *to **rake in** donations* (***accumulate, amass, pile up***)
Word history: Old English *raca*

rake[2]
noun a dissolute, immoral man, especially one in fashionable society
Word history: short for *rakehell*, from *rake[1]* + *hell*

rally[1]
verb **1** to bring together: *to **rally** an army* (***assemble, raise***)
2 to come together: *The people **rallied** behind their leader.*
3 to revive or recover: *She **rallied** briefly before becoming unconscious.*
noun **4** a public meeting to discuss an important or worrying topic
5 a recovery from illness
6 a long exchange of strokes in tennis and similar games
7 a motor vehicle competition testing skill rather than speed
Verb forms: I **rallied**, I have **rallied**, I am **rallying**
Noun forms: The plural is **rallies**.
Word history: French

rally[2]
verb to tease good-humouredly
Verb forms: I **rallied**, I have **rallied**, I am **rallying**
Word history: from French word meaning 'rail[2]'

ram
noun **1** a male sheep
2 a device for battering or forcefully pushing something
verb **3** to strike with great force: *The car **rammed** the wall.* (***collide with, hit***)
4 to drive or force by heavy blows: *to **ram** down the earth*
Verb forms: I **rammed**, I have **rammed**, I am **ramming**
Word history: Middle English and Old English

RAM (ram)
noun computer memory from which each item can be accessed or found equally quickly
Word history: an acronym for *r(andom) a(ccess) m(emory)*

ramble
verb **1** to wander about in an unhurried way (***digress, diverge, stray***)
2 to talk or write without keeping to the subject
noun **3** a pleasant slow walk, especially in the country
Word building: **rambling** *adjective*
Word history: perhaps derived from and expressing repetition of *roam*

ramification (ram-uh-fuh-kay-shuhn)
noun **1** the act or manner of ramifying
2 a branch: *the **ramifications** of a nerve*
3 one of a number of results or consequences, especially one which complicates an issue

ramify (ram-uh-fuy)
verb to divide or spread out into branches or branch-like parts
Verb forms: it **ramified**, it has **ramified**, it is **ramifying**

ramp
noun a sloping surface connecting two levels: *a pedestrian **ramp** | a loading **ramp***
Word history: Middle English, from French word meaning 'creep', 'crawl', 'climb'

rampage (ram-payj)
noun **1** violent or angry behaviour
verb (ram-payj) **2** to move or act violently and angrily
Word building: **rampageous** *adjective*
Word history: originally Scottish; apparently variant of *ramp-rage*

rampant (ram-puhnt)
adjective **1** violent or raging
2 unchecked: *Looting was **rampant** in the bombed city.*
Word history: Middle English, from Old French word meaning 'climb'

rampart (ram-paht)
noun a mound of earth used as a fortification or defence
Word history: from French word meaning 'fortify'

ram raid
noun a robbery involving gaining access to a property, such as a shop, service station, etc., by driving a vehicle into the front window

ramrod (ram-rod)
noun **1** a rod for pushing down the charge of a muzzle-loading gun
2 a cleaning rod for the barrel of a rifle, etc.
phrase **3 stiff as a ramrod,** unbending or rigid: *He stood as **stiff as a ramrod**.*

ramshackle
adjective shaky or likely to collapse: *a **ramshackle** old building*
Word use: The opposite of this is **sound** or **robust**.

ran
verb past tense of **run**

ranch
noun a large farm or station for grazing cattle, horses or sheep
Word use: This word is mostly used in the US.
Word building: **rancher** *noun*
Word history: Spanish *rancho*, group of people who eat together

rancid (ran-suhd)
adjective having a stale, sour smell or taste: ***rancid** fat (**inedible**, **off**, **rank**)*
Word building: **rancidity** *noun*
Word history: Latin

rancour (rang-kuh)
noun continuing resentment or ill will
Word use: You can also use **rancor**.
Word building: **rancorous** *adjective*
Word history: Middle English, from Old French, from Late Latin word meaning 'rank smell or taste', from Latin word meaning 'to be rank'

random
adjective **1** happening or being done without a plan or purpose: *a **random** choice (**accidental**, **chance**, **coincidental**, **fluky**, **haphazard**)*
2 *Colloquial* ordinary, uninteresting: *That party was pretty random.*
3 *Colloquial* having to do with someone or something not known to the speaker: *This total random at the party accused me of taking her bag!*
phrase **4 at random,** without a plan or purpose
Word history: Middle English, from Old French word meaning 'rushing movement', 'disorder'

random drug test
noun a test to detect the presence of drugs in someone's system, usually by saliva, blood or urine sampling, applied to randomly selected motorists, athletes, workers, etc.
Word use: The abbreviation is **RDT**.

randy (ran-dee)
adjective Colloquial **1** lecherous or continually looking for sexual experiences
2 sexually excited

rang
verb past tense of **ring**[2]

ranga
noun Colloquial a red-headed person
Word use: The use of this word may offend people.
Word history: shortened form of the word *orangutan*, with reference to the reddish hair of an orangutan

range
noun **1** a line or row of mountains
2 a large area of land, especially one used for shooting practice: *a rifle **range***
3 the distance that a bullet or rocket can travel
4 the limits within which there can be differences: *You are within the normal **range** for height.*
5 a collection or variety: *a **range** of goods | a **range** of opinions*
6 a cooking stove
verb **7** to vary or change within stated limits: *Prices **ranged** from $5 to $10.*
8 to go, move or wander: *We **ranged** over a wide area on our holidays.*
Word history: Middle English, from Old French word meaning 'arrange in line'

ranger
noun someone who looks after a national park or any other public area like this

rank[1]
noun **1** social class: *people of every **rank***
2 official position or grade: *the **rank** of colonel (**class**, **level**, **stage**, **step**)*
3 a row or line: *The soldiers stood in **ranks**.*
phrase **4 pull rank** or **pull rank on,** to resort to the use of a position of authority to force action or behaviour
Word building: **rank** *verb*
Word history: Old French *renc, reng*, of Germanic origin

rank[2]
adjective **1** growing too tall or coarse: ***rank** weeds*
2 having a strong unpleasant taste or smell: *the **rank** smell of cigar smoke (**fetid**, **high**, **putrid**, **smelly**, **stinking**)*
Word history: Old English *ranc* proud, bold

rankle (rang-kuhl)
verb to produce or continue to produce irritation or resentment in your mind: *Her harsh words of the previous visit still* ***rankled.*** (***fester***, ***smart***)

Word history: Middle English, from Old French, from Medieval Latin word meaning 'ulcer', from Latin word meaning 'little serpent'

ransack
verb to search and rob: *to* ***ransack*** *a house*

Word history: Middle English, from Scandinavian

ransom
noun money which must be paid for the return of someone who has been kidnapped or captured in a battle

Word building: **ransom** *verb* (**ransomed**, **ransoming**)
Word history: Middle English, from Old French, from Latin word meaning 'redemption'

rant
verb to speak loudly or angrily (***rave***, ***roar***, ***scream blue murder***, ***thunder***, ***yammer***)

Word building: **ranter** *noun*
Word history: Middle Dutch *ranten* rave

rap[1]
verb to strike with a quick, light blow: *She* ***rapped*** *my knuckles.* | *to* ***rap*** *on the door*

Verb forms: I **rapped**, I have **rapped**, I am **rapping**
Word building: **rap** *noun*
Word history: Middle English

rap / wrap

Don't confuse **rap** with **wrap**. To **wrap** something is to fold paper or material around it:

I'll wrap the present for you.

rapped / rapt / wrapped

Don't confuse **rapped** with **rapt** or **wrapped**.

Rapped is the past form of the verb **rap**, to hit or knock sharply or lightly:

She rapped my knuckles.

Wrapped is the past form of the verb **wrap**, to fold something around someone or something:

I wrapped the blanket around him.

When someone says that they're really **wrapped** in someone or something, it means that they're very enthusiastic about them. You can also spell this **rapt**.

Note that **wrapped** implies being wrapped up in someone and **rapt** describes being enraptured by someone. When used in this way, both these words are part of everyday language, and you should try to avoid them in your essay writing.

rap[2]
noun **1** a type of music that has strong rhythms in which the words rhyme and are spoken, not sung
verb **2** to perform this kind of music

Word use: You can also use **rap music** for definition 1.
Verb forms: I **rapped**, I have **rapped**, I am **rapping**

rapacious (ruh-pay-shuhs)
adjective greedy in a violent and unpleasant way (***avaricious***, ***grasping***, ***insatiable***, ***voracious***)

Word building: **rapacity** *noun*
Word history: from Latin word meaning 'greediness'

rape
noun the crime of having sexual intercourse with someone against their will

Word building: **rape** *verb* **rapist** *noun*
Word history: Middle English, from Latin word meaning 'seize', 'carry off'

rapid
adjective fast or quick: ***rapid*** *growth* | *a* ***rapid*** *worker* (***express***, ***speedy***, ***swift***)

Word building: **rapidity** *noun*
Word history: Latin

rapier (ray-pee-uh)
noun a sword with a long, thin, pointed blade

Word history: French

rapport (ruh-paw)
noun close connection and sympathy between people or between people and things

Word history: from French word meaning 'bring back', 'refer'

rapt
adjective **1** deeply occupied with your own thoughts and unaware of what is going on around you
2 overpowered by strong feelings: *She was* ***rapt*** *with joy.*

Word history: Middle English, from Latin word meaning 'seized', 'transported'

rapture
noun great joy or happiness

Word building: **rapturous** *adjective*

rare[1]
adjective **1** unusual or uncommon: *a* ***rare*** *disease* (***extraordinary***, ***remarkable***, ***singular***, ***strange***)
2 thin: ***rare*** *mountain air*

Word use: The opposite of definition 1 is **common**.
Word history: Middle English, from Latin word meaning 'thin', 'not dense'

rare[2]
adjective underdone or cooked so that it is still very red inside: *a* ***rare*** *grilled steak*

Word building: **rareness** *noun*
Word history: Old English *hrēr* lightly boiled (said of eggs)

rarefied (rair-ruh-fuyd)
adjective **1** belonging to or reserved for a small group; esoteric: *The invitations only went out to a* ***rarefied*** *group of scientists.*
2 (of air) having only a small amount of oxygen present: *The air at the mountain's peak was* ***rarefied.***
3 (of language) high-sounding; lofty: *a* ***rarefied*** *speech*

rarefy (rair-ruh-fuy)
verb **1** to make or become thin, or less dense
2 to refine

Verb forms: it **rarefied**, it has **rarefied**, it is **rarefying**
Word building: **rarefaction** *noun* **rarefactive** *adjective*

rarity (rair-ruh-tee)
noun **1** something interesting and uncommon: *A whale in the harbour is a great **rarity** these days.*
2 rare state or quality
3 thinness, as of air or a gas

Noun forms: The plural is **rarities.**

rascal (rahs-kuhl)
noun **1** *Old-fashioned* a dishonest person
2 a mischievous child or scamp

Word history: Middle English, from Old French word meaning 'rabble', from Latin word meaning 'scratch'

rash[1]
adjective **1** acting too quickly and without thinking: *a **rash** person* (***foolhardy, harebrained, hasty, impetuous, reckless***)
2 done without thinking about what might happen: *a **rash** move*

Word building: **rashness** *noun*
Word history: Middle English

rash[2]
noun red itchy spots or patches on the skin

Word history: French, from Latin word meaning 'scratch'

rasher
noun a thin slice of bacon

rash shirt
noun → **surf shirt** (definition 1)

Word use: You can also use the colloquial word **rashie.**

rasp (rahsp, rasp)
noun **1** a coarse metal file
verb **2** to use a rasp: *to **rasp** wood*
3 to scrape or rub roughly: *The cat's tongue **rasped** my hand.* (***chafe, coarsen, roughen, ruffle***)
4 to make a grating sound: *The door **rasped** on its hinges.*

Word history: Middle English, from Old French word meaning 'scrape', 'grate', from Germanic

raspberry[1] (rahz-buh-ree, rahz-bree)
noun a soft, juicy, reddish-purple berry

Noun forms: The plural is **raspberries.**
Word building: **raspberry** *adjective*
Word history: *rasp(is)* raspberry (origin uncertain) + *berry*

raspberry[2] (rahz-buh-ree, rahz-bree)
noun Colloquial a rude sound expressing contempt, made with the tongue and lips

Noun forms: The plural is **raspberries.**

rat
noun **1** a long-tailed animal similar to, but larger than, a mouse
2 *Colloquial* someone who leaves a friend who is in trouble
phrase **3 smell a rat,** *Colloquial* to be suspicious

Word history: Old English *rat*

ratchet (rach-uht)
noun a mechanism having a toothed bar and wheel which engages with a pivoted bar

Word history: French word meaning 'ratchet', 'bobbin', from Italian, from Germanic

rate
noun **1** speed: *to work at a steady **rate** | to travel at a **rate** of 100 kilometres an hour*
2 a charge or payment: *The interest **rate** on the loan is 10% per year.* (***cost, expense, outlay***)
3 rates, the tax paid by people who own land to their local council
verb **4** to set a value on, or consider as: *The council **rated** the land at $20 000. | I **rate** him a very good friend.* (***calculate at, estimate at, gauge, judge***)
phrase **5 at any rate,** in any case
6 at this rate, if things go on like this

Word history: Middle English, from Medieval Latin word meaning 'fixed amount or portion', 'rate', from Latin word meaning 'fixed by calculation', 'determined'

rather
adverb **1** to a certain extent: ***rather** good*
2 with better reason: *The opposite position is **rather** to be supported.*
3 sooner or more willingly: *I would **rather** go today.*
4 instead of: *He is a hindrance **rather** than a help.*

Word history: Old English *hrathor*, comparative of *hrathe* quickly

ratify
verb to confirm or approve

Verb forms: I **ratified,** I have **ratified,** I am **ratifying**
Word building: **ratification** *noun* **ratifier** *noun*
Word history: Middle English, from Old French, from Latin

rating
noun the value or standing that someone or something has

ratio (ray-shee-oh)
noun the relationship between two amounts or quantities expressed in the lowest possible whole numbers: *The pupil-teacher **ratio** at our school is 30 to 1. | the **ratio** of good apples to bad*

Word history: from Latin word meaning 'reckoning', 'relation', 'reason'

ration (rash-uhn)
noun **1** a fixed amount allowed to one person or group: *a **ration** of sultanas*
verb **2** to share out as a ration: *to **ration** tea when it is in short supply* (***allocate, allot, dispense, distribute, issue***)

Word history: French, from Medieval Latin word meaning 'allowance of provisions', Latin word meaning 'account'

rational (rash-nuhl, rash-uh-nuhl)
adjective **1** sensible or reasonable: *a **rational** decision*
2 sane or in possession of your reason: *He was quite **rational** when he regained consciousness.*

Word use: The opposite of this is **irrational.**
Word history: Latin

rationale (rash-uh-nahl)
noun **1** a statement of reasons or principles
2 fundamental reasons for the existence of something

Word history: Latin

rationalise (<u>rash</u>-nuh-luyz)
verb **1** to invent a rational, acceptable explanation for behaviour which appears unusual
2 to make economical or efficient
Word use: You can also use **rationalize.**

rational number
noun one of a set of numbers which includes integers and fractions

rat-race
noun **1** a fiercely competitive struggle for success, especially in careers
2 the fast pace of city life

rat run
noun Colloquial a circuitous route through suburban streets, usually taken by a driver wishing to avoid major thoroughfares
Word building: **rat-runner** *noun* **rat-running** *noun*

rattan (ruh-<u>tan</u>)
noun **1** a kind of climbing palm
2 the tough stems of such palms, used for wickerwork, canes, etc.
3 a stick or switch of this material
Word history: Malay

rattle
verb **1** to make, or cause to make, a series of short, sharp, clattering sounds: *The window **rattled**. | He **rattled** the doorknob.*
2 to confuse or upset: *The examiner **rattled** him with her questions.*
noun **3** a number of short, sharp, clattering sounds
4 a baby's toy which makes a noise like this
Word building: **rattly** *adjective* (**rattlier, rattliest**)
Word history: Middle English

rattlesnake
noun a venomous American snake that has a tail with horny rings which make a rattling sound

raucous (<u>raw</u>-kuhs)
adjective harsh-sounding: *a **raucous** laugh* (***blaring, deafening, loud, resonant, shrill***)
Word history: Latin

ravage
verb to damage badly: *Sorrow **ravaged** her face.*
Word history: French

ravages
plural noun great damage or devastation: *the **ravages** of war*

rave
verb **1** to talk wildly making little sense, especially when you are very ill (***babble, jabber, talk rubbish, waffle, yak***)
2 *Colloquial* to talk or write excitedly
Word building: **rave** *noun*
Word history: Middle English, probably from Old French word meaning 'wander', 'be delirious'

ravel (<u>rav</u>-uhl)
verb **1** to tangle or become entangled
noun **2** a tangle or complication
Verb forms: it **ravelled**, it has **ravelled**, it is **ravelling**
Word history: from Middle Dutch word meaning 'entangle'

raven
noun **1** a large, shiny, black bird with a harsh call
adjective **2** shiny black: ***raven** hair*
Word history: Old English

ravenous (<u>rav</u>-uh-nuhs)
adjective very hungry
Word history: Middle English, from Old French

rave party
noun an entertainment event, generally lasting throughout the night, at which people dance to loud dance music in a large empty space (such as a warehouse or an outdoor clearing) and often take drugs
Word use: The short form is **rave.**

ravine (ruh-<u>veen</u>)
noun a long, deep, narrow valley, especially one made by a river
Word history: French

ravioli (rav-ee-<u>ohl</u>-ee)
plural noun small squares of pasta wrapped around minced meat or vegetables, cooked, and served in a sauce
Word history: Italian, from Latin word meaning 'turnip', 'beet'

ravishing
adjective very beautiful

raw
adjective **1** not cooked
2 not treated or processed: ***raw** leather*
3 inexperienced or untrained: *a **raw** recruit* (***amateur, callow, green, incompetent, naive***)
4 painfully open: *a **raw** wound*
5 very cold: *a **raw** wind* (***bleak, chilly, wintry***)

> **raw / roar**
> Don't confuse **raw** with **roar.** Lions **roar** when they make a loud deep sound.

ray[1]
noun **1** a beam of light
2 a small amount: *a **ray** of hope*
Word history: Middle English, from Old French, from Latin

ray[2]
noun a fish related to the sharks, with a flat body suited for life on the sea bottom, and with its gill openings on its lower surface
Word history: Middle English, from French, from Latin

rayon
noun an artificial fabric, similar to silk
Word history: French word meaning 'ray', from Old French

raze
verb to knock down level to the ground: *The wreckers had to **raze** the building after the fire.*
Word history: Middle English, from French, from Vulgar Latin, from Latin word meaning 'scraped'

raze / raise

Don't confuse **raze** with **raise**. To **raise** something is to lift it up, or to increase it:

Raise your hands above your head.

We will have to raise prices from next week.

razor
noun a sharp-edged instrument or a small electrical instrument for shaving hair from your skin

Word history: Middle English, from Old French word meaning 'scrape', 'shave'

razor wire
noun coiled stainless-steel wire having pieces of protruding metal with razor-sharp points attached at intervals along the wire

re (ree, ray)
preposition with reference to

Word history: Latin

reach
verb **1** to get to or arrive at (***come to***, ***surface at***, ***turn up at***)
2 to succeed in touching: *I can **reach** the high shelf.*
noun **3** the distance you can reach: *She left the water within the patient's **reach**.*
4 a straight part of a river between bends

Word history: Old English *rǣcan*

react (ree-akt)
verb **1** to act in answer or reply: *We all **react** to danger in different ways.* (***behave***, ***respond***)
2 to act upon each other, as chemicals do when combined

reaction (ree-ak-shuhn)
noun **1** something done as a result of an action by someone else: *Her **reaction** to my rudeness was to walk away.* (***reply***, ***response***)
2 *Chemistry* the action of chemical agents upon each other

Word use: Another name for definition 2 is **chemical change**.

reactionary (ree-ak-shun-uh-ree, ree-ak-shun-ree)
noun **1** a person opposed to progress or reform
adjective **2** opposing progressive policies

Noun forms: The plural is **reactionaries**.

reactive (ree-ak-tiv)
adjective readily entering into chemical reactions

Word building: **reactivity** *noun*

reactor (ree-ak-tuh)
noun **1** a substance or person undergoing a reaction
2 → **nuclear reactor**

read[1] (reed)
verb **1** to look at and understand: *to **read** a sign* | *to **read** French*
2 to look at and say aloud: *She is going to **read** him a story.*
3 to understand: *to **read** her character from her face*
4 to take in information from: *My computer can't **read** that disk.*
phrase **5 read between the lines**, to see the hidden truth or meaning

Verb forms: I **read**, I have **read** (*pronounced* red), I am **reading**

Word history: Old English *rǣdan* counsel, consider, read

read / reed

Don't confuse **read** with **reed**, which is a tall kind of grass growing in marshes and swamps.

read[2] (red)
adjective having knowledge gained by reading: *a widely **read** person*

Word history: past participle of *read*[1]

read / red

Don't confuse **read** with **red**, which is the colour of a ripe tomato.

ready
adjective **1** completely prepared: ***ready** to leave* (***equipped***, ***fitted***)
2 quick: *a **ready** answer*
3 likely at any moment: *a tree **ready** to fall*
verb **4** to prepare: *She **readied** herself for the children's return.*

Adjective forms: **readier**, **readiest**
Verb forms: I **readied**, I have **readied**, I am **readying**
Word building: **readily** *adverb* **readiness** *noun*
Word history: Old English *rǣde* ready

reagent (ree-ay-juhnt)
noun a substance which, because of the reactions it causes, is used in chemical analysis

real
adjective **1** true or actual: *the **real** reason* | *a story from **real** life*
2 having existence as a material object (***concrete***, ***physical***, ***tangible***)
3 genuine or not artificial: ***real** diamonds*

Word history: Middle English, from Late Latin, from Latin word meaning 'thing', 'matter'

real / reel

Don't confuse **real** with **reel**, which is a cylinder or wheel-like device onto which something is wound.

To **reel** is to sway or stagger, often from a blow.

A **reel** can also be a lively Scottish dance or the music for it.

real estate
noun land and the buildings on it

realisation (ree-uh-luy-zay-shuhn)
noun **1** the making real of something imagined or planned: *the **realisation** of a dream*
2 knowledge and awareness: *the **realisation** of his guilt*

Word use: You can also use **realization**.

realise
verb **1** to come to understand: *I now **realise** that it was the wrong thing to do.* (***perceive***, ***see***)
2 to make real or bring to pass: *His worst fears were **realised**.*

Word use: You can also use **realize**.

realism
noun **1** the facing of life as it really is
2 painting nature or writing about life as it really is

Word use: Compare this with **idealism**.

realist
noun someone who accepts situations as they really are and behaves in a practical way

Word use: Compare this with **idealist**.
Word building: **realistic** *adjective*

realistic (ree-uh-list-ik)
adjective **1** tending to face facts and deal with things as they really are
2 tending to take a practical view of human problems rather than one based on principles of right and wrong

reality (ree-al-uh-tee)
noun **1** the state or fact of being real: *the **reality** of death*
2 a real thing or fact: *Her win was **reality**, not a dream.*

Noun forms: The plural is **realities**.

reality check
noun Colloquial **1** an assessment of the facts of a situation, often providing someone with a set of expectations different to their earlier ones which were based on wishful thinking
2 any event which causes someone's expectations, beliefs, etc., to be more realistic: *Looking at how much money was left in my bank account was a huge **reality check**.*

reality TV
noun a television program format which uses actual footage of events as they occur, often in a contrived situation and with some competitive element providing the motivation for people to interact

Word use: You can also use **reality television**.

really
adverb **1** in reality: *to see things as they **really** are*
2 truly: *a **really** honest man | I **really** want to go.*
3 indeed: ***Really**, this is too much.*
4 extremely: ***really** hot*

realm (relm)
noun **1** a kingdom
2 a particular area of interest or knowledge: *the **realm** of literature*

Word history: Middle English, from Old French word meaning 'regal', from Latin

real number
noun one of the set of numbers which include all rational and irrational numbers

real-time
adjective Computers **1** happening immediately, with no delay: ***real-time** processing*
2 happening at the same speed that the event would happen in real life

ream (reem)
noun **1** a standard quantity of paper equal to 500 sheets
2 reams, *Colloquial* a large quantity

Word history: Middle English, from Old French, through Spanish, from Arabic word meaning 'bundle or bale'

reap
verb **1** to cut with a sickle or machine: *to **reap** the wheat*
2 to get as a return for work: *to **reap** the benefit*

Word building: **reaper** *noun*
Word history: Old English

rear[1] (rear)
noun **1** the back of anything
2 the buttocks
adjective **3** situated at or having to do with the rear: *a **rear** window*

Word history: variant of *arrear*, noun

rear[2] (rear, rair)
verb **1** to look after and support: *to **rear** a family*
2 to rise up on the hind legs: *The horse **reared** when it saw the snake.*

Word history: Old English *rǣran* raise

reason
noun **1** the cause of an action or happening
2 a statement or explanation of these causes
3 the ability to use your mind to form opinions
4 sound judgement or good sense
verb **5** to come to a logical conclusion about: *She **reasoned** that the earth was round.* (***conclude**, **infer**, **work out***)
6 to argue in a logical way: *I will **reason** with him.*
phrase **7 in** (or **within**) **reason**, within the limits of what may be expected
8 it stands to reason, it is obvious

Word history: Middle English, from Old French, from Latin word meaning 'reckoning', 'account'

reasonable
adjective **1** sensible or showing sound judgement: *a **reasonable** man | a **reasonable** choice* (***sage**, **sane**, **shrewd**, **wise***)
2 fair or moderate: *a **reasonable** price*

reasoning
noun **1** the act of process of someone who reasons
2 the reasons or arguments used in arriving at a conclusion: *What is the **reasoning** behind the decision to abandon school uniforms?*

reassure (ree-uh-shaw)
verb to give confidence to

Word building: **reassurance** *noun*

rebate (ree-bayt)
noun **1** the return of part of an original amount paid for some service or commodity
verb **2** to allow as a discount
3 to take away, as from a total

Word history: Middle English, from Old French word meaning 'beat or put down'

rebel (reb-uhl)
noun **1** someone who fights the government or resists those in authority: *She was a bit of a **rebel** in her youth.*
verb (ruh-bel) **2** to fight against the government or resist those who rule or have power (***mutiny**, **rebel**, **revolt**, **rise up***)

Verb forms: I **rebelled**, I have **rebelled**, I am **rebelling**
Word building: **rebel** *adjective* **rebellious** *adjective*
Word history: Middle English, from Old French, from Latin word meaning 'wage war again (as conquered people)'

rebellion (ruh-bel-yuhn)
noun **1** open, organised, and armed resistance to the government or ruler (***mutiny***, ***revolt***, ***revolution***, ***uprising***)
2 resistance against any authority or control
3 refusal to obey established customs, culture, etc.

Word history: Middle English, from Latin

rebound (ruh-bownd)
verb **1** to bounce or spring back: *The ball **rebounded** off the wall.*
noun (ree-bownd, ruh-bownd) **2** the action of rebounding: *to catch a ball on the **rebound***

Word history: Middle English, from Old French

rebuff
noun a refusal to accept offers or suggestions: *His **rebuff** hurt my feelings.* (***rejection***, ***snub***)

Word building: **rebuff** *verb*
Word history: French, from Italian

rebuke (ruh-byoohk)
verb to scold or show you disapprove of (***admonish***, ***find fault with***, ***reprimand***, ***rouse on***, ***tick off***)

Word building: **rebuke** *noun*
Word history: Middle English, from Old French word meaning 'beat back'

rebut (ruh-but)
verb to oppose or prove false by proof or argument (***contradict***, ***demolish***, ***disprove***, ***invalidate***, ***refute***)

Verb forms: I **rebutted**, I have **rebutted**, I am **rebutting**
Word building: **rebuttal** *noun*
Word history: Middle English, from Anglo-French

recalcitrant (ruh-kal-suh-truhnt)
adjective **1** resisting authority or control (***defiant***, ***disobedient***, ***dissident***, ***militant***, ***rebellious***)
2 describing a pollutant which is not easily biodegradable
noun **3** a recalcitrant person

Word building: **recalcitrance** *noun*
Word history: from Latin word meaning 'kicking back'

recall (ruh-kawl)
verb **1** to remember (***place***, ***recognise***, ***recollect***)
2 to bring or order back: *to **recall** an ambassador*
noun (ree-kawl) **3** ability to remember

Word use: The opposite of definition 1 is **forget**.

recant (ruh-kant)
verb to formally withdraw or disown a statement or opinion (***retract***, ***take back***)

Word building: **recantation** *noun*
Word history: Latin

recap
verb Colloquial to repeat the main points of a discussion, lesson, etc.: *To **recap**, the most important thing is to practise every day.*

Verb forms: I **recapped**, I have **recapped**, I am **recapping**
Word history: short form of *recapitulate*

recapitulate (ree-kuh-pich-uh-layt)
verb **1** to summarise, as at the end of a speech
2 *Zoology* to repeat ancestral evolutionary stages during development
3 to sum up statements or matters

Word history: Late Latin

recede (ruh-seed)
verb to move back and become more distant (***ebb***, ***disappear***)

Word history: Middle English, from Latin word meaning 'go back'

receipt (ruh-seet)
noun **1** a signed piece of paper proving that you have received goods sent or have paid money
2 the receiving of something: *On **receipt** of your letter I sent the parcel.*
3 receipts, money received, especially in a shop: *The firm's **receipts** fell last year.*

Word history: Middle English, from Anglo-French, from Latin word meaning 'received'

receipt / recipe
Don't confuse **receipt** with **recipe**, which is a list of ingredients and the instructions for cooking something.

receive
verb **1** to get or be given: *to **receive** a gift | to **receive** news* (***acquire***, ***gain***)
2 to admit or allow to enter: *to **receive** into a club*

Word history: Middle English, from Old Northern French, from Latin word meaning 'take back', 'take to one's self', 'receive'

receiver
noun **1** someone or something that receives
2 someone who receives things which they know have been stolen
3 someone who is appointed to take over a bankrupt company
4 the player receiving the balls served in tennis and similar games

Word use: The opposite of definition 1 is **giver** or **sender**.

recent
adjective happening or done not long ago (***contemporary***, ***current***, ***modern***, ***new***, ***up-to-date***)

Word history: Latin

receptacle (ruh-sep-tuh-kuhl)
noun a container or something that holds things: *a **receptacle** for rubbish*

Word history: Middle English, from Latin

reception
noun **1** a formal party in honour of someone
2 an office or desk in a business or hotel where guests or callers are met and looked after
3 the result or act of receiving or being received: ***Reception** on our TV is not very clear. | Her friends gave her a warm **reception** when she returned.*

Word history: Middle English, from Latin

receptionist
noun someone employed in an office or hotel to look after callers or guests

receptive
adjective quick to take in new ideas or knowledge: *a **receptive** mind*

recess (ruh-<u>ses</u>, <u>ree</u>-ses)
noun **1** a part of a room where the wall is set back for shelves or cupboards
2 a short time or break when work stops: *a* ***recess*** *for morning tea*

Word building: **recess** (ruh-<u>ses</u>) *verb*
Word history: from Latin word meaning 'a going back'

recession (ruh-<u>se</u>-shuhn)
noun a time when business affairs in a nation are bad and many people do not have a job

recession / depression
When used in economics, these terms refer to similar circumstances, but there is a difference.
A **recession** is a downturn in the economy for a small period of time.
A **depression** is a downturn in the economy lasting for a long period of time. It is a major economic and social crisis.

recessive (ruh-<u>ses</u>-iv)
adjective **1** tending to move back
2 *Biology* having to do with a hereditary character resulting from a gene which has less biochemical activity than another dominant gene, and therefore is kept inactive when paired with it: *Blue eye colour is* ***recessive,*** *whereas brown is dominant.*

recidivism (ruh-<u>sid</u>-uh-viz-uhm)
noun repeated or habitual relapse into crime

Word building: **recidivist** *noun* **recidivistic** *adjective*
Word history: from Latin word meaning 'relapsing'

recipe (<u>res</u>-uh-pee)
noun a list of ingredients and the instructions telling you how to cook something

Word history: Middle English, from Latin word meaning 'take', as used at the head of prescriptions

recipe / receipt
Don't confuse **recipe** with **receipt.** You get a **receipt** to prove that you have paid for goods in a shop.

recipient (ruh-<u>sip</u>-ee-uhnt)
noun someone or something that receives

Word history: from Latin word meaning 'receiving'

reciprocal (ruh-<u>sip</u>-ruh-kuhl)
adjective **1** given, felt or done by one person to another: ***reciprocal*** *aid* | ***reciprocal*** *love*
noun **2** *Mathematics* the number by which a given quantity is multiplied to produce one: *The* ***reciprocal*** *of 4 is* $\frac{1}{4}$.

Word history: from Latin word meaning 'returning', 'reciprocal'

reciprocate (ruh-<u>sip</u>-ruh-kayt)
verb **1** to give, feel, etc., in return: *The audience* ***reciprocated*** *with applause.* (***reply, respond***)
2 to give and receive mutually: *to* ***reciprocate*** *favours* (***exchange, interchange, swap***)

Word building: **reciprocative** *adjective* **reciprocation** *noun*
Word history: Latin

recital (ruh-<u>suyt</u>-uhl)
noun **1** a concert or entertainment given by one performer or by the pupils of one teacher
2 a long explanation or statement: *We listened to a* ***recital*** *of his problems.*

recite
verb **1** to repeat from memory the words of: *She* ***recited*** *a poem in class on Open Day.*
2 to repeat poetry or something similar from memory: *He is going to* ***recite*** *now.*

Word building: **recitation** *noun*
Word history: Middle English, from Latin word meaning 'read aloud', 'repeat'

reckless
adjective not caring about danger, especially in a foolish way: *He's a* ***reckless*** *climber.* (***foolhardy, harebrained, hasty, impetuous, rash***)

Word use: The opposite of this is **cautious.**
Word history: Old English *rēcelēas* careless

reckon
verb **1** to think or believe: *I* ***reckon*** *she is clever.* (***guess, imagine, suppose, suspect***)
2 to calculate or count up: *I* ***reckon*** *the total to be $210.* (***compute, figure***)
3 *Colloquial* to think or suppose: *I* ***reckon*** *we ought to go now.*
4 to depend or rely: *We can* ***reckon*** *on his help I am sure.*

Verb forms: I **reckoned,** I have **reckoned,** I am **reckoning**
Word history: Old English *(ge)recenian*

reckoning
noun **1** a count or calculation
2 the settlement of accounts, such as between two people or groups
3 a statement of an amount due

reclaim
verb **1** to make suitable for farming or some other use: *We* ***reclaimed*** *the swamp land for a park.*
2 to get back: *I* ***reclaimed*** *my cases at the airport.*

Word history: Middle English, from Old French, from Latin word meaning 'cry out against'

recline
verb to lean or lie back

Word history: Middle English, from Latin

recluse (ruh-<u>kloohs</u>)
noun someone who lives alone and does not mix with other people (***hermit, introvert, loner***)

Word history: Middle English, from Old French, from Late Latin word meaning 'shut up'

recognise (<u>rek</u>-uhg-nuyz)
verb **1** to know again: *I hardly* ***recognised*** *her when she came back.*
2 to understand or realise: *I* ***recognise*** *the truth of what you say.* (***acknowledge, perceive, sense***)

Word use: You can also use **recognize.**
Word building: **recognisable** *adjective* **recognition** *noun*
Word history: *recogn(ition)* + *-ise*

recoil
verb **1** to draw back: *She* ***recoiled*** *in fear when she saw the snake.*
2 to spring back: *The rifle* ***recoiled*** *against his shoulder when he fired it.*
Word building: **recoil** *noun*
Word history: Middle English, from Old French, from Latin *re-*, prefix indicating backward movement + *cūlus* the buttocks

recollect (rek-uh-lekt)
verb to remember or bring back to your mind
Word building: **recollection** *noun*
Word history: from Latin word meaning 'collected again'

recommend
verb **1** to suggest as being good or worthwhile
2 to urge strongly: *I* ***recommend*** *that you be very careful.* (***advise, advocate, propose, suggest***)
Word building: **recommendation** *noun*
Word history: Middle English, from Medieval Latin, from Latin word meaning 'commend again'

recompense (rek-uhm-pens)
verb to make a repayment to: *I will* ***recompense*** *you for the trouble you have had.* (***compensate, pay, reimburse, repay, reward***)
Word building: **recompense** *noun*
Word history: Middle English, from Late Latin, from Latin

reconcile (rek-uhn-suyl)
verb **1** to cause to agree or make friendly: *to* ***reconcile*** *the two opinions | to* ***reconcile*** *the quarrelling brothers.* (***conciliate***)
2 to be no longer opposed: *I am* ***reconciled*** *to moving to another town.*
Word history: Middle English, from Latin

reconciliation
noun **1** the settling of a lingering dispute, grievance, etc., held by one group of society against another
2 *Accounting* the making of one account consistent with another by balancing apparent discrepancies

recondition
verb to repair or bring back to a good condition: *to* ***recondition*** *a motor*

reconnaissance (ruh-kon-uh-suhns)
noun **1** the act of reconnoitring
2 an air or ground search made to assess military information, such as troop movements and position
3 an examination or survey of the general geological characteristics of an area
Word history: French

reconnoitre (rek-uh-noy-tuh)
verb **1** to look carefully at in order to gain useful information: *Scouts* ***reconnoitred*** *the area before the army attacked.*
2 to study or examine an area or situation before taking action: *Scouts were sent out to* ***reconnoitre*** *the track.* (***inspect, look over, scan, survey***)
Word building: **reconnoitre** *noun*
Word history: from French word meaning 'recognise'

reconsider
verb to consider again with a view to a change of decision or action: *She thought she should* ***reconsider*** *going to Africa until the epidemic was over.*

record (ruh-kawd)
verb **1** to write down so that the information can be kept: *to* ***record*** *a sale* (***enter, list, log, make a note of, register***)
2 to put music or other sounds on a CD, tape, etc.
noun (rek-awd) **3** something that has been recorded in writing or print
4 a black plastic disc on which music has been recorded
5 the best performance so far in a sport or any other activity: *She broke the* ***record*** *for the long jump.*
6 a self-contained group of data on a computer, such as an employee's name, address and salary
phrase **7 off the record**, unofficially
8 on record, recorded publicly: *My disapproval is* ***on record****.*
Word building: **record** *adjective* **recording** *noun*
Word history: Middle English, from Old French, from Latin word meaning 'remember'

recorder
noun **1** an official who keeps records
2 a machine for recording sound
3 a type of wooden or plastic flute with a soft sound

recount (ruh-kownt)
verb **1** to narrate or tell about: *to* ***recount*** *the events of the day* (***describe, outline, relate***)
noun **2** a written or spoken text type or form which typically records events in the order in which they happened
Word history: Middle English, from Anglo-French word meaning 'repeat', 'relate'

recoup (ruh-koohp)
verb **1** to regain or recover: *to* ***recoup*** *your losses*
2 to pay back: *The company* ***recouped*** *them for the damage.* (***indemnify, reimburse***)
noun (ree-koohp) **3** the act of recouping
Word history: Middle English, from French word meaning 'cut again'

recourse (ruh-kaws)
noun a turning to a person or thing for help or protection: ***recourse*** *to the law*
Word history: Middle English, from Old French, from Latin word meaning 'a running back'

recover
verb **1** to regain or get again: *to* ***recover*** *lost property*
2 to get well again after being sick (***brighten up, convalesce, pick up, rally, recuperate***)
Word building: **recovery** *noun*
Word history: Middle English, from Anglo-French, from Latin word meaning 'recuperate'

recreation (rek-ree-ay-shuhn)
noun a game, hobby or sport which is an enjoyable change from your daily work
Word history: Middle English, from Latin

recriminate (ruh-krim-uh-nayt)
verb to bring a countercharge against someone who blames you of wrongdoing
Word building: **recrimination** *noun* **recriminator** *noun*
Word history: Medieval Latin

recruit (ruh-<u>krooht</u>)
noun **1** someone who has just joined the army, navy or air force
2 someone who has just joined an organisation or group: *a new **recruit** to the choir*
verb **3** to enlist or enrol: *We are **recruiting** new members for our club.*
4 to enlist people for service: *The army is **recruiting** now.*

Word history: from French word meaning 'a new growth'

rectangle
noun a four-sided shape with all its angles right angles

Word building: **rectangular** *adjective*
Word history: from Late Latin word meaning 'right-angled'

rectangular prism
noun a three-dimensional figure which has two ends which are rectangles in parallel planes, joined by sides which are parallelograms

rectify (<u>rek</u>-tuh-fuy)
verb to make or put right: *to **rectify** a mistake* (***amend**, **correct**, **remedy**, **repair**, **revise***)

Verb forms: I **rectified**, I have **rectified**, I am **rectifying**
Word building: **rectification** *noun*
Word history: Middle English, from Late Latin

rectitude (<u>rek</u>-tuh-tyoohd)
noun rightness or correctness of principle or practice: *the **rectitude** of your actions* | ***rectitude** of judgement*

Word history: Middle English, from Late Latin, from Latin

rector
noun a member of the clergy who is in charge of a parish, congregation or college

Word history: Middle English, from Latin word meaning 'ruler'

rectory (<u>rek</u>-tuh-ree)
noun a rector's house

Noun forms: The plural is **rectories**.

rectum
noun the short final section of your large intestine leading to your anus

Noun forms: The plural is **recta**.
Word building: **rectal** *adjective*
Word history: Neo-Latin

recumbent (ruh-<u>kum</u>-buhnt)
adjective **1** lying down (***leaning**, **reclining***)
2 inactive or idle

Word building: **recumbency** *noun*
Word history: Latin

recuperate (ruh-<u>kooh</u>-puh-rayt)
verb to recover from sickness or tiredness (***brighten up**, **convalesce**, **pick up**, **rally**, **recover***)

Word building: **recuperation** *noun* **recuperative** *adjective*
Word history: from Latin word meaning 'regained', 'recovered'

recur (ree-<u>ker</u>, ruh-<u>ker</u>)
verb to happen again

Verb forms: it **recurred**, it has **recurred**, it is **recurring**
Word building: **recurrence** *noun* **recurrent** *adjective*
Word history: Middle English, from Latin word meaning 'run back'

recycle
verb to use again, usually in another form: *to **recycle** waste paper into cardboard*

Word building: **recyclable** *adjective*

red
adjective **1** of the colour of a ripe tomato
2 having communist or radical left-wing political views
noun **3** a red colour
phrase **4 see red**, *Colloquial* to become very angry
5 the red,
a red ink as used in accounting for recording losses and deficits
b loss or debt: *to be in **the red***

Word history: Middle English *red(e)*, Old English *rēad*

red / read
Don't confuse **red** with **read** (rhymes with *bed*), which is the past form of the verb **read** (rhymes with *feed*):
I read her a fairy story last night.

red-back spider
noun a small, very venomous, Australian spider with a red or orange streak on it

red-bellied black snake
noun a poisonous snake of eastern Australian forests and scrubs, shiny black above and pale pink to red below

red blood cell
noun one of the red cells in the blood, which are rich in iron and have the function of carrying oxygen around the body

red-blooded (<u>red</u>-blud-uhd)
adjective strong or virile

red card
noun **1** *Sport* a red card shown by a referee to a player who has committed a serious infringement of the rules as an indication that the player is to leave the field for the remainder of the game
phrase **2 give someone the red card**, to dismiss or reject someone, as from a job, a relationship, etc.

Word use: Compare this with **yellow card**.

red dwarf
noun *Astronomy* a type of small, relatively cool, very faint star

redeem
verb **1** to pay off: *to **redeem** a debt*
2 to get back by paying money owed on: *to **redeem** a pawned watch*
3 a to claim (an item) by presenting a coupon, voucher, etc.
b to claim (a prize) by presenting a winning ticket
4 to make up for past misbehaviour: *She **redeemed** herself in my opinion by apologising.*

Word building: **redeemable** *adjective* **redeemer** *noun*
Word history: Middle English, from Latin word meaning 'buy back'

redemption
noun **1** the act or result of redeeming
2 deliverance or rescue

redeploy (ree-duh-ploy)
verb to rearrange or reorganise a person, military unit, etc., in order to create more effective results

Word building: **redeployment** *noun*

red-handed
adjective in the very act of doing something wrong: *They investigated the noise and caught him **red-handed**.*

Word use: This adjective follows the noun it describes.

red herring
noun a false clue or something that takes your attention away from what is really important: *The blood-stained knife was a **red herring**.*

red-letter day
noun a memorable or especially happy occasion

Word history: from the day in the Christian church calendar marked by red letters, on which judges wear red robes

redolent (red-uh-luhnt)
adjective **1** having a pleasant smell (***fragrant***, ***perfumed***)
phrase **2 redolent of,**
a smelling of: ***redolent of*** *roses*
b suggestive or reminiscent of: *stories* ***redolent of*** *mystery*

Word building: **redolence** *noun*
Word history: Middle English, from Latin word meaning 'giving back a smell'

redoubtable (ruh-dow-tuh-buhl)
adjective **1** that is to be feared
2 commanding respect (***awe-inspiring***, ***formidable***)

Word history: Middle English, from Old French word meaning 'fear'

redound (ruh-downd)
verb **1** to have an effect, as to the advantage or disadvantage of a person or thing
2 to come back, as upon a person

Word history: Middle English, from Old French, from Latin word meaning 'overflow'

redress (ruh-dres)
noun **1** the setting right of what is wrong
2 relief from wrong or injury
verb **3** to set right or correct
4 to adjust evenly again, as a balance

Word history: Middle English, from French

red tape
noun **1** tape of a reddish colour, much used for tying up official papers
2 unnecessary attention to formality and rules

reduce
verb **1** to make lower, less or fewer: *to **reduce** the price of milk | to **reduce** speed | to **reduce** the number of pupils in a class* (***cut back***, ***decrease***, ***lessen***, ***lower***)
2 to bring to another condition: *to **reduce** someone to tears*

Word history: Middle English, from Latin word meaning 'bring back', 'restore', 'replace'

reduction
noun **1** the act or result of reducing
2 the amount by which something is reduced
3 a copy on a smaller scale

Word building: **reductive** *adjective*

redundant
adjective no longer needed (***excessive***, ***extra***, ***superfluous***, ***surplus***, ***unnecessary***)

Word building: **redundancy** *noun*
Word history: from Latin word meaning 'overflowing'

reed
noun **1** a tall, straight-stemmed grass growing in marshes or swamps
2 a musical pipe made from a reed or something like it
3 a vibrating piece of cane or metal set in the mouthpiece of some wind instruments such as an oboe

Word history: Old English *hrēod*

reed / read
Don't confuse **reed** with **read**. Children learn to **read** books at school.

reef
noun a narrow ridge of rock, sand or coral at or near the ocean surface

Word history: Dutch or Low German *rif*, from Scandinavian

reefer (reef-uh)
noun Colloquial a marijuana cigarette

reef knot
noun a kind of double knot which does not slip

reek
verb to have a strong unpleasant smell: *He **reeks** of stale tobacco.*

Word building: **reek** *noun*
Word history: Old English *rēc*

reek / wreak
Don't confuse **reek** with **wreak**.
To **wreak your revenge** on someone is to carry out a vengeful act against them.
To **wreak havoc** is to bring about ruinous damage.
Wreak is an old-fashioned word so both phrases sound rather formal.

reel[1]
noun **1** a cylinder or wheel-like device onto which something is wound: *a **reel** of thread*
2 a roll or spool of film
verb **3** to wind on a reel
phrase **4 reel off**, to say or write in a smooth rapid way: *to **reel off** instructions*

Word history: Old English *hrēol*

reel[2]
verb to sway or stagger, especially from a blow or an attack of giddiness (***lurch***, ***wobble***)

reel[3]
noun a lively Scottish dance or the music for it
Word history: Middle English

reel / real
Don't confuse **reel** with **real**. Something is **real** if it is true or genuine.

refectory (ruh-fek-tuh-ree)
noun the dining hall in a religious house, university, etc.
Noun forms: The plural is **refectories**.
Word history: Medieval Latin, from Latin word meaning 'restore'

refer (ruh-fer)
verb **1** to go or send for information or help: *to **refer** to a map for directions | to **refer** a patient to a specialist*
2 (of a doctor) to direct (a patient) to another doctor, usually a specialist, for further consultation or treatment
phrase **3 refer to,** to mention: *to **refer** to past events*
Verb forms: I **referred**, I have **referred,** I am **referring**
Word building: **referral** *noun*
Word history: Middle English, from Latin word meaning 'carry back'

referee
noun **1** someone who decides or settles matters which could be argued about, especially in sport (***umpire***)
verb **2** to act as referee
Verb forms: I **refereed**, I have **refereed**, I am **refereeing**

reference
noun **1** a mention
2 a book or a place in a book or other writing where information may be found
3 the act of looking for information: *to make **reference** to an encyclopedia | a library for public **reference***
4 a letter giving a description of someone's character and abilities: *You will need two **references** to apply for this job.*
adjective **5** used to give information: ***reference** books*
phrase **6 terms of reference,** the range allowed for the study of something
7 with reference to, having to do with: *I will ask you some questions **with reference to** your family.*

referendum
noun a public vote taken on a question of government or law
Noun forms: The plural is **referendums** or **referenda.**
Word history: Latin

refine
verb **1** to make more fine or pure: *to **refine** sugar*
2 to make more elegant or polite: *to **refine** your manners*
Word building: **refined** *adjective*
Word history: *re-* + *fine*[1], verb

refinement
noun **1** fineness of feeling, taste, etc.
2 elegance of manners or language
3 the act of refining
4 improvement on something

refinery
noun an establishment for refining something, such as metal, sugar, petroleum, etc.
Noun forms: The plural is **refineries**.

reflect
verb **1** to throw back: *Metal **reflects** light.*
2 to show an image of: *The mirror **reflected** her dirty face.*
3 to show: *The children's good results **reflected** their teacher's hard work.*
phrase **4 reflect on,** to think carefully about: *I will **reflect on** what she said.* (***concentrate on***, ***contemplate***, ***meditate on***, ***ponder***, ***weigh***)
Word building: **reflective** *adjective* **reflector** *noun*
Word history: Middle English, from Latin word meaning 'bend back'

reflection
noun **1** the state of being reflected
2 an image or representation
3 the casting back, or the change of direction, of light, heat, sound, etc., after striking a surface

reflex (ree-fleks)
noun an action done without thinking as a response to something: *Sneezing and blinking are **reflexes**.*
Word building: **reflex** *adjective*
Word history: from Latin word meaning 'reflected', 'bent back'

reflex angle
noun an angle greater than 180° but less than 360°

reflexive (ruh-flek-siv)
adjective **1** of a verb, whose subject and object are identical, such as *shave* in *He shaved himself.*
2 of a pronoun, which is the object of a reflexive verb, such as *himself* in the example above
noun **3** a reflexive verb or pronoun, such as *tricked* or *himself* in *He tricked himself.*

Look up **pronouns: reflexive pronouns.**

reform
verb **1** to improve by changing what is wrong or bad: *You need to **reform** your behaviour.* (***amend***, ***correct***, ***rectify***, ***remedy***, ***revise***)
noun **2** improvement or correction of what is wrong, evil, etc.
Word building: **reformer** *noun*
Word history: Middle English, from Latin

reformation (ref-uh-may-shuhn)
noun the act or result of reforming

reformatory (ruh-fawm-uh-tree)
adjective **1** having to do with reform
noun **2** an institution for the reformation of young offenders
Noun forms: The plural is **reformatories.**

refraction (ruh-frak-shuhn)
noun the change of direction of a ray of light, heat, or something like this, in passing obliquely from one medium into another in which its speed is different

refractory (ruh-frak-tuh-ree)
adjective **1** unmanageable or stubborn: *a **refractory** child*
2 difficult to fuse, reduce, or work, such as an ore or metal

refrain[1]
verb to keep yourself back: *to **refrain** from eating more cake*

Word history: Middle English, from Old French, from Latin word meaning 'to bridle'

refrain[2]
noun a line or verse that is repeated regularly in a song or poem (***chorus***)

Word history: Middle English, from Old French, from Latin word meaning 'refract'

refresh
verb **1** to make fresh and strong again: *That cold drink has **refreshed** me.*
2 to update the image on a computer screen

Word building: **refreshing** *adjective*
Word history: Middle English, from Old French

refreshment
noun something that refreshes, especially food and drink or a light meal: *The **refreshments** are in the next room.*

refrigerant
adjective **1** refrigerating; cooling: *An effective **refrigerant** system kept the food fresh.*
noun **2** a liquid capable of vaporising at a low temperature like ammonia, used in mechanical refrigeration
3 a cooling substance, as ice, solid carbon dioxide, ammonia, hydrofluorocarbon, hydrochlorofluorocarbon, etc., used in a refrigerator

refrigerate
verb to make or keep cold or frozen: *to **refrigerate** food* (***chill***, ***cool***, ***freeze***)

Word building: **refrigeration** *noun*
Word history: from Latin word meaning 'made cool again'

refrigerator
noun a cabinet or room where food and drink are kept cool

Word use: The short form is **fridge**.

refuge (<u>ref</u>-yoohj)
noun **1** shelter or protection from danger or trouble: *They found a **refuge** from the storm in a cave.* (***asylum***, ***haven***, ***retreat***, ***sanctuary***)
2 a place that gives shelter or protection: *a **refuge** for homeless people*

Word history: Middle English, from Old French, from Latin

refugee (ref-yooh-<u>jee</u>)
noun someone who escapes to another country for safety, especially during a war

Word history: from French word meaning 'take refuge'

refund (ruh-<u>fund</u>)
verb **1** to give back or repay: *I asked the shop to **refund** my money because the toy I bought was broken.* (***pay back***, ***reimburse***)
noun (<u>ree</u>-fund) **2** a repayment of money

Word history: Middle English, from Latin word meaning 'pour back'

refurbish
verb to make clean or new-looking: *to **refurbish** an old armchair*

refusal (ruh-<u>fyooh</u>-zuhl)
noun **1** the act of refusing
2 the first right in refusing or taking something (***option***)

Word use: You can also use **first refusal** for definition 2.

refuse[1] (ruh-<u>fyoohz</u>)
verb to say you will not accept or do: *He **refused** her invitation to the party. | He **refused** to speak.* (***decline***, ***knock back***, ***rebuff***, ***reject***)

Word use: The opposite of this is **accept**.
Word history: Middle English, from Old French, from Vulgar Latin, from Latin word meaning 'poured back'

refuse[2] (<u>ref</u>-yoohs)
noun rubbish: *The gutters were filled with **refuse**.* (***debris***, ***garbage***, ***junk***, ***rubbish***, ***trash***)

Word history: Middle English, from Old French word meaning 'refused'

refute (ruh-<u>fyooht</u>)
verb to prove to be false: *I **refuted** all her arguments.* (***contradict***, ***demolish***, ***disprove***, ***invalidate***, ***rebut***)

Word use: The opposite of this is **affirm**.
Word building: **refutation** *noun*
Word history: from Latin word meaning 'repel', 'refute'

regain
verb to get back again: *I stopped at the top of the hill to **regain** my breath.*

regal
adjective having to do with or like a king or queen: *a **regal** visit | **regal** appearance*

Word history: Middle English, from Latin

regale (ruh-<u>gayl</u>)
verb to entertain agreeably, especially with good food or drink

Word history: French, from Old French word meaning 'feast', from *gale* pleasure, from Middle Dutch word meaning 'wealth'

regard
verb **1** to think of or consider: *I **regard** her as a hard worker.*
2 to look at or observe: *She **regarded** him with a frown.*
noun **3** thought or attention: *He gives no **regard** to what I say.*
4 a feeling of kindness or liking: *I hold them in high **regard**.* (***esteem***, ***honour***, ***respect***, ***veneration***)
5 regards, expressions of respect or friendship: *Please give your sister my **regards**.*
phrase **6 as regards**, in relation to
7 with (or **in**) **regard to**, having to do with or concerning: *I am writing **with regard to** your party.*

Word history: Middle English, from French

regatta
noun a meeting for boat races

Word history: Italian

regenerate (ruh-<u>jen</u>-uh-rayt)
verb **1** to bring about a change for the better
2 to bring into existence again
3 to come into existence or be formed again
adjective (ruh-<u>jen</u>-uh-ruht) **4** remade in a better form
5 changed for a better character

Word building: **regeneration** *noun* **regenerative** *adjective*
Word history: Middle English, from Latin word meaning 'made over', 'produced anew'

regent
noun someone who rules a kingdom while the king or queen is sick or too young

Word building: **regency** *noun*
Word history: Middle English, from Latin word meaning 'ruling'

reggae (<u>reg</u>-ay)
noun a kind of pop music which started in the West Indies

Word history: West Indian

regime (ray-<u>zheem</u>)
noun **1** a system of rule or government: *The new principal brought in a different* ***regime.***
2 a particular government: *This* ***regime*** *has not done much for unemployed people.*

Word use: You can also use **régime**.
Word history: French, from Latin word meaning 'direction', 'government'

regimen (<u>rej</u>-uh-muhn)
noun **1** a controlled course of diet, exercise, or manner of living, intended to preserve or restore health or to gain some result
2 a particular form or system of government
3 the prevailing system

Word history: Middle English, from Latin

regiment (<u>rej</u>-uh-muhnt)
noun **1** a division of an army consisting of two or more battalions
verb (<u>rej</u>-uh-ment) **2** to group together and treat with strict discipline: *The camp leaders* ***regimented*** *us too much.*

Word building: **regimental** *adjective* **regimentation** *noun*
Word history: Middle English, from Late Latin word meaning 'rule'

region
noun **1** any part or area: *a* ***region*** *of your body | a country* ***region***
2 an area of the earth with particular features: *the tropical* ***regions***

Word history: Middle English, from Latin word meaning 'line', 'district'

register
noun **1** a list of names, belongings, or events, kept as a record: *a* ***register*** *of births and marriages*
2 a book for keeping such lists: *a hotel* ***register***
3 a machine which records information: *a cash* ***register***
4 the musical range of a voice or instrument
verb **5** to write down or have written down in a register: *He* ***registered*** *his name on the waiting list. | You have to* ***register*** *your car every year.* (***enter, list, record***)
6 to show or indicate: *The thermometer* ***registered*** *a very low temperature. | Her face* ***registered*** *surprise.*

Word building: **registration** *noun*
Word history: Middle English, from Medieval Latin, from Latin word meaning 'recorded'

registered nurse
noun a nurse who holds a degree in nursing from a university

Word use: The abbreviation is **RN**. | Compare this with **enrolled nurse**.

registrar
noun **1** someone who keeps records
2 a doctor in a hospital who is training to be a specialist

registry
noun **1** the place where a register is kept
2 the act of registering

Noun forms: The plural for definition 1 is **registries**.

registry office
noun the office where births, marriages and deaths are recorded, and non-religious marriages are performed

regress
verb to move or go back: *He has* ***regressed*** *to his bad old ways.*

Word use: The opposite of this is **progress** or **advance**.
Word building: **regress** *noun* **regression** *noun* **regressive** *adjective*
Word history: Middle English, from Latin word meaning 'a going back'

regret
verb **1** to feel sorry or sad about: *I* ***regret*** *that I got angry with you. | She* ***regretted*** *the end of the holiday.*
noun **2** a feeling of loss or disappointment or of being sorry about something you have done
3 regrets, polite expressions of being sorry: *Please give her my* ***regrets*** *that I cannot come.*

Verb forms: I **regretted,** I have **regretted,** I am **regretting**
Word building: **regretful** *adjective* **regretfulness** *noun* **regrettable** *adjective*
Word history: Middle English, from Old French, from Germanic

regretful / regrettable

These words are both linked to **regret** but they mean different things.

Someone is **regretful** if they are sad about something that has happened. They are full of **regret**.

Something is **regrettable** if it has happened but you wish it hadn't. It is to be **regretted**.

regrowth
noun **1** a growing again: *This forest is undergoing* ***regrowth.***
2 new hair growth, especially that which contrasts in colour with previously dyed hair: *Her* ***regrowth*** *revealed that she didn't really have blond hair.*

regular
adjective **1** usual or normal: *Let's go to school the* ***regular*** *way.*
2 arranged evenly: ***regular*** *teeth*

3 following a rule or pattern, especially having to do with fixed times: *He is **regular** in his habits.* | ***regular** meals* | *a **regular** sight*
noun **4** *Colloquial* a regular visitor or customer

Word use: The opposite of definitions 1–3 is **irregular**.
Word building: **regularity** *noun* **regularly** *adverb*
Word history: Latin

regulate
verb to control or change so that a rule or standard is kept to: *to **regulate** behaviour* | *to **regulate** the temperature of a room*

Word building: **regulative** *adjective* **regulator** *noun* **regulatory** *adjective*
Word history: Late Latin, from Latin word meaning 'rule'

regulation
noun **1** a rule or law: *school **regulations*** (***convention**, **precept***)
2 control, or correction and adjustment: *the **regulation** of traffic*

regurgitate (ruh-gerj-uh-tayt)
verb **1** to bring back from the stomach, especially before digestion has taken place: *Mother birds **regurgitate** food for their young.* (***disgorge***)
2 to repeat, usually without understanding: *To **regurgitate** information from a book.*

Word building: **regurgitation** *noun*
Word history: Medieval Latin

rehabilitate
verb to help return to normal activities, especially after an illness, accident or addiction

Word building: **rehabilitation** *noun*
Word history: from Medieval Latin word meaning 'restored'

rehash (ree-hash)
verb **1** to work up in a new form: *The composer **rehashed** the score for the next production.*
noun (ree-hash) **2** the act of rehashing
3 something rehashed

rehearse (ruh-hers)
verb to practise in private before giving a public performance

Word building: **rehearsal** *noun*
Word history: Middle English, from Old French word meaning 'harrow again'

reign (rayn)
noun **1** the time during which a king or queen rules: *the **reign** of Queen Elizabeth*
verb **2** to rule as a king or queen
3 to be in control: *Peace **reigned** throughout the world.*

Word history: Middle English, from Old French, from Latin

reign / rain / rein
Don't confuse **reign** with **rain** or **rein**.
Rain is water falling from the sky in drops.
A rider uses a **rein** to guide a horse.

reimburse (ree-im-bers)
verb to pay back: *I will **reimburse** your expenses.* (***refund**, **repay***)

Word building: **reimbursement** *noun*
Word history: *re-* + *imburse* (from Medieval Latin word meaning 'purse', 'bag')

rein (rayn)
noun **1** a long thin strap which a rider uses to guide a horse or other animal
2 any kind of control or check: *She keeps a tight **rein** on her feelings.*

Word building: **rein** *verb*
Word history: Middle English, from Old French, from Latin word meaning 'hold back'

reincarnation (ree-in-kah-nay-shuhn)
noun the belief that when the body dies the soul moves to a new body or form

reindeer (rayn-dear)
noun a kind of deer with large antlers, which lives in the cold northern areas of the world

Noun forms: The plural is **reindeer** or **reindeers**.
Word history: Middle English, from Scandinavian

reinforce (ree-in-faws)
verb to strengthen, by adding someone or something: *Extra soldiers were sent to **reinforce** the garrison.* | *These facts will **reinforce** my argument.* (***fortify**, **prop up**, **shore up**, **strengthen***)

Word building: **reinforcement** *noun*

reinforcements (ree-in-faws-muhnts)
plural noun an additional supply of troops, ships, etc., for a military or naval force

reinstate (ree-in-stayt)
verb to put back or establish again, usually to a former position

Word building: **reinstatement** *noun*

reiterate (ree-it-uh-rayt)
verb to say or do again or repeatedly (***go over again**, **reduplicate**, **repeat***)

Word building: **reiteration** *noun* **reiterative** *adjective*
Word history: Latin

reject (ruh-jekt)
verb **1** to refuse to accept or use: *He **rejected** her invitation.* | *They **rejected** his work.* (***decline**, **knock back**, **rebuff**, **renounce***)
noun (ree-jekt) **2** someone or something that has been rejected: *We will use these pictures and throw out the **rejects**.*

Word building: **rejection** *noun*
Word history: from Latin word meaning 'thrown back'

rejoice
verb to be glad or delighted: *They **rejoiced** over her success.* (***celebrate**, **cheer***)

Word building: **rejoicing** *noun*
Word history: Middle English, from Old French

rejoin[1] (ruh-joyn)
verb to come again into the company of: *to **rejoin** a party after a brief absence*

rejoin[2] (ruh-joyn)
verb to answer

Word history: Middle English, from Anglo-French

rejoinder
noun a spoken answer or response: *a quick **rejoinder***

Word history: Middle English, from Anglo-French

rejuvenate (ruh-jooh-vuh-nayt)
verb to make young again: *I need a holiday to* ***rejuvenate*** *me.*

Word building: **rejuvenation** *noun*
Word history: from Late Latin word meaning 'become young again' + *-ate*

relapse
verb to return or fall back: *to* ***relapse*** *into sickness | to* ***relapse*** *into bad behaviour*

Word building: **relapse** *noun*
Word history: from Latin word meaning 'slipped back'

relate
verb **1** to tell: *to* ***relate*** *a story* (***narrate, outline, recount***)
2 to connect, in your mind: *The police* ***related*** *his absence to the time of the murder.*
3 to be friends or understand each other: *Some parents and teenagers find it hard to* ***relate.***
phrase **4 relate to,** to understand and often identify with: *to* ***relate to*** *a character in a film*

Word history: from Latin word meaning 'reported', 'carried back'

related
adjective **1** associated or connected: *The two questions are* ***related.*** (***allied, interconnected***)
2 part of the same family

relation
noun **1** the way things or people are connected: *the* ***relation*** *between two numbers*
2 a family relative (***family, flesh and blood, kin***)
3 *Mathematics* a property which connects two quantities or functions

Word building: **relationship** *noun*
Word history: Middle English, from Latin word meaning 'a bringing back', 'report'

relative
noun **1** someone who is part of your family: *Cousins, aunts and uncles are some of our* ***relatives.*** (***family, flesh and blood, kin, relations***)
adjective **2** thought about in comparison with something else: *They live in* ***relative*** *poverty.* (***comparative***)
phrase **3 relative to,** having a connection with: *The loudness of his voice is* ***relative to*** *his anger.*

Word building: **relativity** *noun*
Word history: Middle English, from Late Latin, from Latin word meaning 'carried back'

relatively
adverb comparatively: *a* ***relatively*** *small difference*

relative pronoun
noun a pronoun which introduces a dependent clause and refers to a person or thing in the main clause

Look up **pronouns: relative pronouns.**

relax
verb **1** to loosen or make less firm: *to* ***relax*** *your arm*
2 to make or become less strict: *to* ***relax*** *discipline*
3 to rest and feel at ease: *to sit down and* ***relax*** (***laze, put your feet up, take it easy, wind down***)

Word history: Middle English, from Latin

relaxation
noun **1** a stopping of bodily or mental effort
2 something done for enjoyment or entertainment
3 a loosening or slackening
4 a reduction of strictness or severity

relay (ree-lay)
noun **1** a group which takes its turn with others to keep some activity going: *to work in* ***relays***
2 a team race in which each member runs or swims a part of the distance
verb (ruh-lay, ree-lay) **3** to pass or carry forward: *to* ***relay*** *a message* (***dispatch, forward, pass on, send, transmit***)

Word history: Middle English, from Old French word meaning 'leave behind' (originally 'hounds in reserve along the line of the hunt')

release
verb **1** to set free: *to* ***release*** *the prisoner | to* ***release*** *from pain* (***deliver, emancipate, free, liberate, rescue***)
2 to make public: *to* ***release*** *a news story*
noun **3** the act of releasing
4 a statement, news story, etc., released to the public

Word history: Middle English, from Old French, from Latin word meaning 'relax'

relegate (rel-uh-gayt)
verb **1** to send to some lower position, place, or condition
2 to hand over to someone

Word building: **relegation** *noun*
Word history: from Latin word meaning 'sent back'

relent
verb to soften or become more forgiving than you meant to be: *I* ***relented*** *when I saw how sorry he was.*

Word history: Middle English word meaning 'melt', from Latin word meaning 'grow slack or soft'

relentless
adjective never stopping or becoming softer: *a* ***relentless*** *enemy |* ***relentless*** *heat |* ***relentless*** *questioning* (***pitiless, unrelenting***)

Word building: **relentlessly** *adverb*
relentlessness *noun*

relevant
adjective connected with what is being discussed: *a* ***relevant*** *remark* (***allied, associated, pertinent, related***)

Word use: The opposite of this is **irrelevant**.
Word building: **relevance** *noun* **relevancy** *noun*
Word history: Medieval Latin, from Latin word meaning 'raise up'

reliable
adjective trusted or able to be relied on: *a* ***reliable*** *friend | a* ***reliable*** *encyclopedia* (***dependable, faithful***)

Word building: **reliability** *noun*

reliant
adjective having trust, or depending: *We are* ***reliant*** *on him for money.*

Word building: **reliance** *noun*

relic
noun something left over from the past: *These statues are* ***relics*** *of a great civilisation.*

Word history: Old English, from Latin

relief
noun **1** freedom or release from pain, unhappiness or worry (***comfort***, ***consolation***, ***solace***)
2 something that gives relief or help (***aid***, ***assistance***, ***help***)
3 someone who replaces someone else in a job or on a duty
4 a figure or shape in a sculpture carved so that it stands out above its background
5 *Physical Geography* the departure of the land surface in any area from that of a level surface

Word history: Middle English, from Old French

relieve
verb **1** to remove or lessen: *to* ***relieve*** *pain* (***alleviate***, ***ease***, ***soothe***)
2 to free from pain, unhappiness or worry: *Her safe arrival* ***relieved*** *them.*
3 to free from duty by coming as a replacement: *He* ***relieved*** *the soldier on guard.*
4 to bring help to: *Food was sent to* ***relieve*** *the drought victims.*

Word use: The opposite of definition 1 is **aggravate**.
Word history: Middle English, from Old French, from Latin word meaning 'raise again', 'assist'

religion
noun **1** belief in a supernatural power that made and controls the world and that you should worship and obey
2 the way this belief is expressed in your way of life, worship, or service
3 any formal system on which this belief has been based: *the Jewish* ***religion***

Word history: Middle English, from Latin word meaning 'fear of the gods', 'sacredness', 'scrupulousness'

religious (ruh-<u>lij</u>-uhs)
adjective **1** having to do with religion
2 believing in religion (***devout***, ***god-fearing***, ***pious***)
3 very conscientious: *to do something with* ***religious*** *care*

Word use: The opposite of definition 1 is **secular**. The opposite of definition 2 is **irreligious**.
Word history: Middle English, from Latin

relinquish (ruh-<u>ling</u>-kwish)
verb to give up, put aside, or surrender: *He was forced to* ***relinquish*** *his position.*

Word history: Middle English, from Old French

relish
noun **1** a liking or enjoyment of something: *He looked forward to his holidays with* ***relish***.
2 something that adds taste to food, such as a sauce
verb **3** to enjoy, or take pleasure in: *She* ***relished*** *the attention her success brought her.* (***appreciate***, ***like***, ***welcome***)

Word history: Middle English, from Old French word meaning 'what is left', 'remainder'

reluctant
adjective unwilling or not prepared: *She was* ***reluctant*** *to help.* (***averse***, ***disinclined***, ***hesitant***, ***loath***)

Word use: The opposite of this is **enthusiastic**.
Word building: **reluctance** *noun* **reluctantly** *adverb*
Word history: from Latin word meaning 'struggling against'

rely (ruh-<u>luy</u>)
verb to depend upon or put trust in: *I am* ***relying*** *on you to help me.*

Verb forms: I **relied**, I have **relied**, I am **relying**
Word history: Middle English, from Old French word meaning 'bind together', from Latin word meaning 'bind back'

remain
verb **1** to stay: *to* ***remain*** *at home | to* ***remain*** *happy* (***continue***)
2 to be left: *Some food* ***remained*** *after the party.*

Word history: Middle English, from Anglo-French, from Latin

remainder
noun what remains or is left: *How will we spend the* ***remainder*** *of the day? | If you subtract 4 from 6 the* ***remainder*** *is 2.*

Word history: Middle English, from Anglo-French, from Latin

remains
plural noun **1** what is left: *the* ***remains*** *of a meal*
2 someone's dead body: *They buried his* ***remains***. *| human* ***remains***

Word history: Middle English, from Anglo-French, from Latin

remand (ruh-<u>mand</u>, ruh-<u>mahnd</u>)
verb **1** to send back into custody to await further proceedings: *The court* ***remanded*** *the prisoner until the next session of the court.*
noun **2** the act of remanding
3 the condition of being remanded

Word history: Middle English, from Late Latin word meaning 'to send back word', 'repeat a command'

remark
verb **1** to comment or say casually: *He* ***remarked*** *that it was a fine day.* (***exclaim***, ***let drop***, ***observe***)
noun **2** the act of taking notice: *an event worthy of* ***remark***
3 a comment

Word history: from French word meaning 'note', 'heed'

remarkable
adjective worthy of remark or notice because unusual or extraordinary: *a* ***remarkable*** *achievement* (***amazing***, ***astonishing***, ***astounding***)

remedial (ruh-<u>mee</u>-dee-uhl)
adjective **1** providing a remedy
2 designed to meet the needs of children who are disadvantaged or have particular learning problems

remediation
noun **1** the act or process of remedying
2 *Ecology* the restoration of an environment to its pristine state, as by the removal of pollutants, contaminants, etc.

remedy (<u>rem</u>-uh-dee)
noun **1** a cure for a disease
2 something that corrects anything that is wrong or bad: *a **remedy** for unemployment*
verb **3** to put right: *to **remedy** a fault* (***amend, correct, rectify***)

Noun forms: The plural is **remedies**.
Verb forms: I **remedied**, I have **remedied**, I am **remedying**
Word history: Middle English, from Latin

remember
verb to bring back to or keep in your mind: *I can't **remember** the answer. | Please **remember** to bring your books.* (***place, recall, recognise, recollect***)

Word history: Middle English, from Old French, from Late Latin, from Latin word meaning 'call to mind'

remembrance
noun **1** an impression kept in your memory: *fond **remembrance** of the past*
2 an object, such as a gift, that serves to keep someone or something in your mind

remind
verb to make remember: *I always have to **remind** you to take your key.*

Word building: **reminder** *noun*

reminiscence (rem-uh-<u>nis</u>-uhns)
noun **1** a remembering of the past
2 something remembered: *He recounted **reminiscences** of his childhood.*

Word building: **reminisce** *verb* **reminiscent** *adjective*
Word history: Latin

remiss (ruh-<u>mis</u>)
adjective careless in duty, business, etc. (***irresponsible, negligent***)

Word building: **remissness** *noun*
Word history: Middle English, from Latin word meaning 'sent back'

remission
noun **1** a period during which a disease is less severe: *His cancer has gone into **remission**.*
2 a shortening of a prison sentence
3 an exemption from paying a fee

Word history: Middle English, from Old French, from Latin

remit (ruh-<u>mit</u>)
verb **1** to send to a person or place: *All funds should be **remitted** to the treasurer.*
2 to decide not to enforce or demand
3 to pardon or forgive: *to **remit** a prisoner's sentence*
4 to lessen or abate: *to **remit** watchfulness | Her fever has **remitted**.*
5 to send money, etc., as payment

Verb forms: I **remitted**, I have **remitted**, I am **remitting**
Word history: Middle English, from Latin word meaning 'send back'

remittance (ruh-<u>mit</u>-uhns)
noun **1** the sending of money, etc., as payment
2 money, etc., sent from one place to another

remnant
noun a part or amount that is left: *a **remnant** of material* (***leavings, leftovers, odds and ends, remains, residue***)

Word history: Middle English, from Old French word meaning 'remain'

remonstrate (<u>rem</u>-uhns-trayt)
verb to make an objection or protest: *He **remonstrated** with the teacher about the examination mark.*

Word building: **remonstration** *noun* **remonstrative** *adjective*
Word history: from Medieval Latin word meaning 'exhibited'

remorse (ruh-<u>maws</u>)
noun deep and painful sorrow or regret for having done wrong (***compunction, guilt***)

Word building: **remorseful** *adjective* **remorseless** *adjective*
Word history: Middle English, from Latin word meaning 'a biting back'

remote
adjective **1** far away or distant: *a **remote** planet | the **remote** past* (***faraway, isolated, outlying***)
2 slight: *a **remote** chance | I haven't the **remotest** idea.*

Word history: Middle English, from Latin word meaning 'removed'

remote sensing
noun the identification of data, usually concerning features of the earth or other bodies in space, from a satellite, aeroplane, etc.

removalist
noun Australian a person or firm whose work is moving furniture, etc., to a new home or office

remove
verb **1** to take off or away: *Please **remove** your shoes. | Someone has **removed** my book.*
2 to dismiss from a job or official position: *to **remove** a manager*

Word building: **removal** *noun*
Word history: Middle English, from Old French, from Latin

removed (ruh-<u>moohvd</u>)
adjective **1** unconnected, remote, or separate: *His way of life is far **removed** from mine.*
2 distant, used in expressing degrees of relationship: *A first cousin twice **removed** is a cousin's grandchild.*

remunerate (ruh-<u>myoohn</u>-uh-rayt)
verb to pay or reward for work, trouble, etc.

Word building: **remuneration** *noun* **remunerative** *adjective*
Word history: from Latin word meaning 'given back'

renaissance (ruh-<u>nay</u>-suhns, ruh-<u>nas</u>-uhns)
noun a revival

Word history: from French word meaning 'rebirth'

renal
adjective having to do with your kidneys: ***renal** disease*

Word history: Late Latin, from Latin word meaning 'kidney'

rend
verb to pull or tear violently
Verb forms: I **rent**, I have **rent**, I am **rending**
Word history: Old English

render
verb **1** to cause to be or become: *His jokes* ***rendered*** *them helpless with laughter.*
2 to give: *to* ***render*** *help* | *to* ***render*** *payment*
3 to perform: *to* ***render*** *a song*
4 to cover with a coat of plaster: *to* ***render*** *a wall*
Word building: **rendering** *noun*
Word history: Middle English, from Old French, from Romance word meaning 'give back'

rendezvous (ron-day-vooh)
noun **1** a meeting arranged beforehand, sometimes secretly: *They had a* ***rendezvous*** *behind the hall to discuss the surprise party.* (***appointment***, ***assignation***, ***date***)
2 a place for meeting or assembling, especially of troops, ships, or spacecraft
Word use: This word comes from French which is why the 's' is not sounded.
Word building: **rendezvous** *verb* (**rendezvoused** (ron-day-voohd), **rendezvousing** (ron-day-vooh-ing))
Word history: from French word meaning 'present or betake yourself (yourselves)'

rendition (ren-dish-uhn)
noun **1** a performance
2 a translation
3 an interpretation, as of a role or a piece of music
Word history: French, from Latin

renegade (ren-uh-gayd)
noun **1** someone who deserts one party or cause for another (***deserter***, ***traitor***)
2 someone who does not conform to social expectations
verb **3** to become a renegade
Word history: Spanish word meaning 'renounce', from Medieval Latin, from Latin word meaning 'deny'

renege (ruh-neg, ruh-nig)
verb **1** *Cards* to fail to follow suit when you can and should do so
2 *Colloquial* to go back on your word
Word building: **reneger** *noun*
Word history: Medieval Latin, from Latin

renew
verb **1** to begin again: *They* ***renewed*** *their friendship.*
2 to build up again: *to* ***renew*** *supplies*
Word building: **renewal** *noun*

renewable resource
noun a natural resource which is not finite but can be renewed, such as the sun, wind, or biomass
Word use: Compare this with **non-renewable resource**.

renounce
verb to give up or put aside: *to* ***renounce*** *their evil ways* | *to* ***renounce*** *a legal claim* (***reject***, ***turn one's back on***)
Word history: Middle English, from French, from Latin word meaning 'make known', 'report'

renovate
verb to repair or restore to good condition: *to* ***renovate*** *an old house* (***fix***, ***improve***, ***mend***, ***patch up***)
Word building: **renovation** *noun* **renovator** *noun*
Word history: Latin

renown
noun fame: *a singer of great* ***renown***
Word use: The opposite of this is **anonymity**.
Word building: **renowned** *adjective*
Word history: Middle English, from Anglo-French, from Old French word meaning 'name over again', from Latin

rent[1]
noun **1** payment that you make regularly for a house, flat or other property that you use
verb **2** to allow the use of in return for regular payment: *I have decided to* ***rent*** *my house to them.*
3 to have the use of in return for regular payment: *I have* ***rented*** *a flat in the city.*
Word building: **rental** *noun*
Word history: Middle English, from Old French, from Romance, from Latin

rent / lease / let / hire

These words have similar meanings but there are some differences.

To **rent** or **lease** property is to have the use of it in return for payments made to the owner:

I am renting a flat in town from a millionaire.

I am leasing a television rather than buying it.

To **rent** or **lease** property is also to give temporary possession of it to someone else. Sometimes this is **rent out**:

I will rent (out) my flat in town to you.

The verb **rent** has developed from the noun **rent**, the payment made to the owner. The document you sign when **renting** a property is a **lease**.

To **let** property is to put it up for rent:

I have made the decision to let my flat in town. If you want it I will rent it to you.

Property which is available for rental in this way is said to be **to let**:

My flat in town is to let.

To **hire** something is to have temporary use of it in return for payment:

We are hiring a hall for the wedding.

To **hire** something is also to give others the temporary use of it in return for payment. Often this is **hire out**:

I will hire out this hall to you for the wedding.

To **hire** someone is to employ them:

We are hiring a band for the occasion.

rent[2]
noun Old-fashioned **1** an opening or tear made by rending
2 a break or split in relations or union
verb **3** past tense and past participle of **rend**

rental
noun an amount received or paid as rent
Word history: Middle English

renunciation (ruh-nun-see-ay-shuhn)
noun **1** the act of renouncing
2 a formal declaration renouncing something

Word building: **renunciative** *adjective* **renunciatory** *adjective*

rep
noun Colloquial a representative, especially a travelling salesperson, trade union delegate or sporting representative

Word history: abbreviation

repair[1]
verb **1** to bring back to good condition: *to **repair** an old bike* (***fix***, ***mend***, ***patch up***, ***renovate***, ***restore***)
2 to put right: *I will **repair** the damage.*
noun **3** the work of repairing
4 condition: *a house in good **repair** | a car in bad **repair***

Word building: **repairable** *adjective*
Word history: Middle English, from Latin word meaning 'put in order'

repair[2]
Old-fashioned
verb **1** to go: *He soon **repaired** to Adelaide.*
noun **2** the act of repairing or going: *to make **repair** to Adelaide*

Word history: Middle English, from Old French word meaning 'return', from Late Latin word meaning 'return to one's country'

reparation
noun **1** the making up for doing something wrong or harmful: *injury for which there can be no **reparation*** (***compensation***, ***pay-back***)
2 something done or money paid as compensation

Word history: Middle English, from Latin

repartee (rep-ah-tee)
noun **1** a quick and clever or witty reply
2 talk marked by quickness and wittiness of reply

Word history: from French word meaning 'an answering thrust'

repast (ruh-pahst)
noun Old-fashioned a meal

Word history: Middle English, from Old French, from Late Latin word meaning 'feed regularly'

repatriate (ree-pat-ree-ayt)
verb **1** to bring or send back to their own country: *to **repatriate** prisoners of war*
noun (ree-pat-ree-uht) **2** someone who has been repatriated

Word history: Late Latin

repatriation (ree-pat-ree-ay-shuhn)
noun **1** the act of repatriating
2 *Australian* assistance given to people who have served in the armed forces on their return to civilian life, in the form of pensions, medical care, allowances for dependants, etc.

repay
verb to pay back or return: *to **repay** a loan | to **repay** a visit*

Verb forms: I **repaid**, I have **repaid**, I am **repaying**
Word building: **repayment** *noun*

repeal
verb to officially put an end to: *to **repeal** a law* (***abolish***, ***annul***, ***break off***, ***cancel***, ***dissolve***)

Word building: **repeal** *noun* **repealable** *adjective*
Word history: Middle English, from Anglo-French

repeat
verb **1** to say or do again: *to **repeat** a sentence | to **repeat** a piece of music*
2 to tell something you have heard to someone else: *Please don't **repeat** what I've just told you — it could get me into terrible trouble.*
noun **3** something that is repeated, such as a television program that has been shown before

Word building: **repeated** *adjective* **repeatedly** *adverb* **repetitive** *adjective*
Word history: Middle English, from Latin word meaning 'do or say again'

repel
verb **1** to drive back: *They **repelled** the enemy.* (***dispel***, ***rebuff***, ***repulse***, ***scare off***)
2 to disgust: *Her cruelty **repels**. | The bad smell **repelled** them.* (***horrify***, ***offend***, ***revolt***, ***sicken***)
3 to keep away: *This spray **repels** mosquitoes.*

Verb forms: I **repelled**, I have **repelled**, I am **repelling**
Word building: **repelling** *adjective*
Word history: Middle English, from Latin word meaning 'drive back'

repellent (ruh-pel-uhnt)
adjective **1** causing distaste or disgust (***abhorrent***, ***repulsive***)
2 driving back
noun **3** something that repels

Word use: You can also use **repellant** for definition 3.

repent
verb to regret or feel sorry: *He **repents** his harsh words. | She **repents** that she was so cruel.*

Word building: **repentance** *noun* **repentant** *adjective*
Word history: Middle English, from Old French

repercussion (ree-puh-kush-uhn)
noun **1** the indirect effect or result of some event or action: *The **repercussions** of the plan were very widely felt.*
2 the condition of being driven or thrown back
3 a springing back or rebounding of something, such as an echo

Word history: Middle English, from Latin

repertoire (rep-uh-twah)
noun the plays, musical pieces or other items which an entertainer, such as an actor or musician, is prepared to perform in public: *She has a huge **repertoire** of songs.*

Word history: French, from Latin word meaning 'inventory', 'catalogue'

repertory (rep-uh-tree)
noun **1** a type of theatrical company, which prepares several plays, operas, etc., and produces them in turn, for a limited run only
2 a store of things available

Noun forms: The plural is **repertories**.
Word history: Latin

repetition
noun **1** the act of repeating: ***Repetition** becomes tedious.*
2 the thing which is repeated: *His speech was a **repetition** of mine.*
Word building: **repetitious** *adjective* **repetitive** *adjective*
Word history: Latin

replace
verb **1** to take the place of: *Ky-Long will **replace** him today.*
2 to renew or exchange, especially something damaged: *He has to **replace** the old tyres.* (***substitute for***, ***transpose***)
3 to put back: *She **replaced** the toys in the cupboard.*
Word building: **replacement** *noun*

replace / substitute
These words describe the same event from different angles.
You **replace** an existing person or thing with something else:
We'll replace Andrew with Ashan as fullback.
You **substitute** a new person or thing for something else:
We'll substitute Ashan for Andrew as fullback.
In these two sentences exactly the same thing is happening. Andrew is going and Ashan is coming. Note that the names appear in a different order.

replay
noun **1** a previously tied match or game that is played again to decide the winner
2 a repeat, especially on television, of the important parts of a game, often straight after they have happened

replenish
verb to refill or restore: *to **replenish** a jug | to **replenish** your strength*
Word building: **replenishment** *noun*
Word history: Middle English, from Old French, from Latin

replete (ruh-pleet)
adjective **1** fully supplied or provided: ***replete** with all they needed for the trip*
2 having had enough food and drink
Word building: **repletion** *noun*
Word history: Middle English, from Latin word meaning 'filled'

replica
noun an exact copy: *The museum had a **replica** of the painting.* (***duplicate***, ***effigy***, ***likeness***, ***model***)
Word history: Italian

reply
verb to give an answer or response: *Did you **reply** to the letter? | She **replied** with a nod.* (***answer***, ***react***, ***respond***)
Verb forms: I **replied**, I have **replied**, I am **replying**
Word building: **reply** *noun* (*plural* **replies**)
Word history: Middle English, from Old French word meaning 'fold again', 'turn back', 'reply', from Latin word meaning 'unfold', 'reply'

report
noun **1** an account of the important facts, especially of a meeting, an event, or someone's progress at work or school (***assessment***, ***briefing***, ***summary***)
2 a loud sudden noise, like a gun firing
verb **3** to describe or give an account of: *He **reported** his discovery.* (***declare***, ***proclaim***, ***publish***, ***reveal***)
4 to complain about or tell on: *She is going to **report** them.* (***dob on***, ***inform on***)
5 to appear for duty: *Sergio **reported** to his commanding officer.*
6 to act as a reporter: *Pina **reports** for the local newspaper.*
Word history: Middle English, from Old French, from Latin

reporter
noun **1** someone who works for radio, television or a newspaper, gathering and describing the news
2 someone who makes a report of what is said, such as in a law court

repose
noun **1** peaceful rest: *to lie in **repose***
verb **2** to lay to rest: *to **repose** on a grassy bank*
Word building: **repose** *verb*
Word history: Middle English, from French, from Latin

repository (ruh-poz-uh-tree)
noun **1** a container or place where things are put, stored, or offered for sale, such as a warehouse
2 someone to whom something is entrusted or confided
Noun forms: The plural is **repositories**.
Word history: Latin

repossess
verb to take back again, usually because payments have not been made when they should: *The store **repossessed** the television set.*
Word building: **repossession** *noun*

reprehensible (rep-ruh-hen-suh-buhl)
adjective deserving to be rebuked: ***reprehensible** conduct* (***blameworthy***, ***guilty***)
Word building: **reprehensibility** *noun*

represent
verb **1** to stand for or mean: *A yellow flag **represents** sickness on board a ship.*
2 to act on behalf of: *She **represents** her country at the United Nations.*
3 to show or portray: *The painting **represents** a country scene.* (***depict***, ***illustrate***)
Word history: Middle English, from Latin

representation
noun **1** the act of representing: *a fair **representation** of the facts*
2 the state of being represented: ***representation** of the electorate by elected members of parliament*
3 something representing another thing, such as a statue, picture or figure
4 a speech or action on behalf of a person, body, business house, district, or the like by an agent or deputy: *She made **representation** on behalf of the parents' group.*

representative
adjective **1** serving to represent
2 typical of a class or group: *a **representative** selection of Australian verse*
3 representing a constituency or community or the people generally, in the making and passing of laws or in government: *a **representative** assembly*
noun **4** someone or something that represents another or others, especially an agent, travelling salesperson, elected member of parliament or a member of a sporting team

repress
verb to keep under control by effort or force: *She **repressed** her anger.*
Word building: **repressed** *adjective* **repression** *noun* **repressive** *adjective*
Word history: Middle English, from Latin

reprieve
noun a delay, especially in carrying out a punishment: *The judge granted him a **reprieve** from execution.* (***amnesty***)
Word building: **reprieve** *verb*
Word history: from Middle English word meaning 'reprove', apparently taken in literal sense of 'test again' (involving postponement)

reprimand
noun a scolding or rebuke, especially from someone in charge (***admonishment***, ***ticking off***)
Word building: **reprimand** *verb*
Word history: from French word meaning 'repress', 'reprove'

reprisal
noun an act which causes hurt or damage to someone as punishment for what they have done
Word history: Middle English, from Anglo-French word meaning 'taken back'

reproach
noun **1** blame or disapproval: *She was full of **reproach** for our misbehavior.*
verb **2** to blame
Word building: **reproachful** *adjective* **reproachfully** *adverb*
Word history: late Middle English, from French, from Latin word meaning 'reprove'

reprobate (rep-ruh-bayt)
noun an unprincipled, immoral or wicked person
Word building: **reprobation** *noun*
Word history: Middle English, from Late Latin word meaning 'reproved'

reproduce
verb **1** to copy: *to **reproduce** a picture* (***duplicate***, ***match***, ***replicate***)
2 to produce offspring or young, by some process of generation or propagation, sexual or asexual
Word building: **reproducer** *noun* **reproducible** *adjective* **reproduction** *noun* **reproductive** *adjective*

reproof (ruh-proohf)
noun an act or example of blaming, finding fault with, or scolding in a sharp way

reprove (ruh-proohv)
verb to scold or blame: *She **reproved** them for being impatient.*
Word use: The opposite of this is **praise**.
Word building: **reprover** *noun* **reprovingly** *adverb*
Word history: Middle English, from Old French, from Latin

reptile
noun a cold-blooded animal such as a lizard, snake, turtle or crocodile that lays eggs and crawls close to or on the ground
Word building: **reptilian** *adjective*
Word history: Middle English, from Late Latin

republic
noun a nation which has a president, not a hereditary monarch, as head of state
Word history: from Latin word meaning 'public matter'

republican
adjective **1** having to do with a republic: *a **republican** government*
2 favouring a republican form of government
noun **3** someone who favours or supports a republican form of government
Word building: **republicanism** *noun*

repudiate (ruh-pyooh-dee-ayt)
verb **1** to refuse to recognise as having power or binding force
2 to throw off or disown: *to **repudiate** a son*
3 to reject with disapproval, especially a belief, etc.
4 to refuse to accept as true, especially a charge or accusation (***deny***, ***rebut***)
5 to refuse to accept knowledge of and pay, especially a debt, etc.
Word building: **repudiation** *noun*
Word history: from Late Latin word meaning 'rejected', 'divorced'

repugnant
adjective unpleasant or distasteful: *a **repugnant** job | She finds the idea **repugnant**.*
Word building: **repugnance** *noun* **repugnantly** *adverb*
Word history: from Latin word meaning 'fighting against'

repulse
verb **1** to drive back: *They **repulsed** the attack.* (***dispel***, ***repel***, ***scare off***)
2 to reject or refuse: *He **repulsed** her offer of help.* (***decline***, ***knock back***, ***rebuff***, ***spurn***)
3 to produce a feeling of strong dislike or disgust
Word building: **repulse** *noun*
Word history: from Latin word meaning 'repelled'

repulsion
noun **1** the act of driving back
2 a feeling of being driven away by your own distaste for someone or something (***aversion***, ***repugnance***)
3 in physics, a force which repels two or more objects from each other
Word use: The opposite of this is **attraction**.

repulsive
adjective dreadful, horrible and disgusting (***revolting***, ***vile***, ***yucky***)

reputable (rep-yuh-tuh-buhl)
adjective able to be trusted: *a **reputable** firm of lawyers*
Word use: The opposite of this is **disreputable**.

reputation
noun **1** the way in which people regard someone or something: *a good* ***reputation*** *as an actor*
2 honesty or good name: *She spoiled her* ***reputation.***

repute (ruh-pyooht)
noun **1** regard in the view of others
verb **2** to consider to be as stated: *He was* ***reputed*** *to be a millionaire.*

reputed
adjective supposed or thought to be: *He's a* ***reputed*** *champion.*
Word building: **reputedly** *adverb*

request
noun **1** the act of asking
2 the thing asked for
verb **3** to ask for or seek, especially politely or formally
Word history: Middle English, from Old French, from Gallo-Roman word meaning '(things) asked for', from Late Latin word meaning 'seek'

requiem (rek-wee-uhm)
noun a church service, especially in the Roman Catholic Church, where prayers are said for someone who has died
Word history: Middle English, from Latin word meaning 'rest', the first word of the Latin mass for the dead

require
verb **1** to need: *Skiing* ***requires*** *practice.*
2 to demand or insist on: *He will do as you* ***require.*** | *She* ***requires*** *silence.* (***demand, order, stipulate***)
Word building: **requirement** *noun*
Word history: Middle English, from Latin word meaning 'search for', 'require'

requisition (rek-wuh-zish-uhn)
noun **1** the demanding formally that something be done, given, etc. (***call, claim, demand, order, ultimatum***)
2 the form on which such a demand is written
verb **3** to demand or take for official use

rescind (ruh-sind)
verb **1** to withdraw formally (***abrogate, annul, revoke***)
2 to cause to have no legal force, by a later action or a higher power
Word building: **rescindable** *adjective* **rescission** *noun*
Word history: from Latin word meaning 'cut off', 'annul'

rescue
verb to save from danger or set free from confinement (***deliver, emancipate, free, liberate, release***)
Word building: **rescue** *noun* **rescuer** *noun*
Word history: Middle English, from Old French, from Latin *re-* + *excutere* shake out or off

research
noun close study or scientific experiment in order to understand or learn more about a subject
Word building: **research** *verb* **researcher** *noun*
Word history: French

resemblance
noun **1** the state or fact of resembling: *There is a distinct* ***resemblance*** *between her and her cousin.* (***likeness, similarity***)
2 the degree, kind, or point of likeness: *The* ***resemblance*** *is most obvious in their hair colour.*

resemble
verb to be like: *She* ***resembles*** *her mother.*
Word history: Middle English, from Old French, from Latin word meaning 'simulate', 'imitate', 'copy'

resent
verb to feel jealous, hurt, or angry about: *They* ***resent*** *his success.* | *She* ***resents*** *his rudeness.*
Word building: **resentful** *adjective* **resentment** *noun*
Word history: French, from Latin word meaning 'feel'

reservation
noun **1** something which has been held or set aside for you, such as seats in a theatre or a room in a motel
2 a doubt: *She has* ***reservations*** *about her ability to do the job.*

reserve
verb **1** to save or keep for later
2 to book in advance: *You have to* ***reserve*** *your seat.*
noun **3** someone or something kept as a replacement, especially an extra member of a sports team
4 public land set aside for a special use, especially as a park or wildlife sanctuary
5 an amount of capital retained by a company to meet needs that may arise, or for any other purpose to which the profits of the company may usefully be applied
6 shyness or reticence
Word building: **reserve** *adjective*
Word history: Middle English, from Latin word meaning 'keep back'

reserve / reverse
Don't confuse **reserve** with **reverse**. To **reverse** is to make something go backwards:
She reversed the car up the drive.

reserve bank
noun the national banking organisation of a country, which carries out the monetary policy of a government, receives tax and other revenue, pays government costs, and issues money, both paper and coin, as legal tender

reserved
adjective **1** kept or set aside: ***reserved*** *seats*
2 shy and not wanting to talk about yourself: *He has a very* ***reserved*** *nature.* (***laconic, quiet, reticent, taciturn***)
Word use: The opposite of definition 2 is **outgoing** or **gregarious**.

reserve price
noun the lowest price at which a person is willing to sell his or her property at auction
Word use: You can also use **reserve**.

reservoir (<u>rez</u>-uh-vwah)
noun **1** a place where water is stored: *the town **reservoir** (**dam**, **weir**)*
2 a container, especially for oil or gas

Word history: from French word meaning 'keep', 'reserve'

reshuffle
verb to change around: *The Prime Minister will **reshuffle** cabinet.*

Word building: **reshuffle** *noun*

reside
verb to live or dwell, especially over a long period: *He **resides** in Australia now.*

Word history: Middle English, from Latin

residence
noun **1** the place where someone lives, especially a large house
2 the time you live in a place: *They threatened to cut short his **residence** in Australia.*

Word building: **resident** *noun* **residential** *adjective*

residual (ruh-<u>zij</u>-ooh-uhl)
adjective **1** left over
2 formed by the subtraction of one quantity from another: *a **residual** quantity*
noun **3** *Commerce* the remainder left after the main part is subtracted or accounted for: *a **residual** in the balance of payments*

residue
noun what is left (***leavings***, ***leftovers***, ***odds and ends***, ***remainder***, ***remnants***)

Word history: Middle English, from French, from Latin

resign
verb **1** to give up or step down: *He **resigned** his job.* | *She wants to **resign** from the committee.*
2 to surrender or give in to: *We **resigned** ourselves to whatever might happen.*

Word building: **resignation** *noun* **resigned** *adjective*
Word history: Middle English, from Old French, from Latin word meaning 'unseal', 'annul'

resilient
adjective able to bounce back: *Rubber is a **resilient** material.* | *She has a **resilient** nature.* (***bouncy***, ***elastic***, ***rubbery***, ***springy***)

Word building: **resilience** *noun*
Word history: from Latin word meaning 'rebounding'

resin (<u>rez</u>-uhn)
noun a sap produced by some plants, which can be used in medicines and varnishes

Word building: **resinous** *adjective*
Word history: Middle English, from Latin

resist
verb to withstand or fight against: *to **resist** temptation* (***counter***, ***defy***, ***obstruct***, ***oppose***)

Word building: **resistant** *adjective*
Word history: Middle English, from Latin word meaning 'withstand'

resistance (ruh-<u>zis</u>-tuhns)
noun **1** the act or power of resisting, opposing, or withstanding
2 *Electricity*
a that property of a device which opposes the flow of an electric current
b a measure of the ability of a device to oppose the flow of an electric current

Word history: Middle English, from French

resolute
adjective firm or determined: *a **resolute** character* | *a **resolute** approach*

Word use: The opposite of this is **doubtful** or **irresolute**.
Word history: Middle English, from Latin word meaning 'resolved'

resolution
noun **1** a decision, especially one made by a group or committee: *They passed a **resolution** to meet every month.*
2 determination or firmness: *She wore an expression of stubborn **resolution**.*
3 the degree of fineness in the reproduction of an image: *The photo was of such high **resolution** that you could see the bee's stinger.*

Word history: Middle English, from Latin

resolve
verb **1** to decide
2 to solve or settle: *They couldn't **resolve** the problem.* | *to **resolve** doubts* (***crack***, ***figure out***, ***puzzle out***, ***work out***)
noun **3** firmness of purpose, especially to follow some course of action

Word history: Middle English, from Latin word meaning 'loosen', 'dissolve'

resonance (<u>rez</u>-uh-nuhns)
noun **1** the condition or quality of being resonant
2 the amplification of the voice by the bones of the head and upper chest, together with the air cavities of the pharynx, mouth, and nasal passages
3 a similarity between two or more objects, ideas, words, etc.
4 *Physics* the amplification of a vibration in a machine or electrical system at a particular frequency as an external stimulus approaches the same frequency

resonant
adjective **1** resounding or ringing: *She played a **resonant** chord on the piano.*
2 deep and rich in tone: *He has a **resonant** baritone voice.*

Word building: **resonantly** *adverb*
Word history: from Latin word meaning 'resounding'

resonate
verb to ring or resound: *The strings on her cello **resonated** when she plucked them.*

Word history: from Latin word meaning 'resounded'

resort (ruh-<u>zawt</u>)
verb **1** to fall back on, in time of need: *He **resorted** to begging for money.*
noun **2** a holiday place: *a seaside **resort***
3 a large hotel with special facilities offered, as sporting activities, health and fitness equipment, and a large pool or pools
4 someone or something turned to for help: *a last **resort***

Word history: Middle English, from Old French word meaning 'go out again'

resound
verb to boom, ring or echo: *The hills **resounded** with their voices.*
Word building: **resounding** *adjective*
Word history: Middle English *re-* + *soun(en)* sound[1]

resource
noun **1** a source of supply, support, or aid
2 the ability to manage in a difficult situation
3 a source of information: *Use books, the internet and other **resources** to research your assignment.*
4 resources, *Commerce* assets such as money, or property which can be converted into money
Word history: French, from Old French, from Latin word meaning 'rise again'

resourceful (ruh-zaws-fuhl, ruh-saws-fuhl)
adjective skilful in overcoming difficulties (***adaptable***, ***flexible***, ***ingenious***)

respect
noun **1** admiration or high regard (***esteem***, ***honour***, ***veneration***)
2 politeness or consideration: *You should show more **respect**.*
3 respects, friendly greetings: *Give my **respects** to your wife.*
4 a matter or detail: *In some **respects** it would have been better.*
Word history: Middle English, from Latin word meaning 'having been regarded'

respectable
adjective **1** good or worthy of respect, especially in the sense of being socially acceptable: *a **respectable** person | a **respectable** job* (***decent***, ***moral***, ***proper***, ***right***)
2 fairly good: *a **respectable** mark*
Word building: **respectability** *noun*

respectable / respectful
Don't confuse **respectable** with **respectful**. You are **respectful** if you are full of respect or admiration for someone else and behave in a way that shows this.

respectful
adjective full of respect or admiration: *They walked at a **respectful** distance behind the president.*
Word building: **respectfully** *adverb*

respective
adjective having to do with each one: *They went their **respective** ways.*
Word building: **respectively** *adverb*

respectively / respectfully
These words look similar but they mean different things.
Respectively is the adverb from **respective**. It is used in situations where you have a number of things which have to be matched up with other things in corresponding order:
Mice, horses, and rabbits eat cheese, hay, and carrots respectively.
Respectfully is the adverb from **respectful**, meaning 'full of respect or admiration':
She bowed her head respectfully.

respiration
noun breathing: *His **respiration** is very rapid.*
Word building: **respiratory** *adjective*

respirator (res-puh-ray-tuh)
noun **1** a device worn over the mouth, or nose and mouth, to prevent the breathing in of poisonous or harmful substances, etc., for example, a gasmask
2 an apparatus to induce artificial respiration

respite (res-puht, res-puyt)
noun **1** an interval of relief, especially from anything upsetting or trying: *to work without **respite***
2 a temporary putting off of the execution of a person condemned to death (***reprieve***, ***stay of execution***)
verb **3** to set free temporarily, especially from anything upsetting or trying
Word history: Middle English, from Old French, from Late Latin word meaning 'delay', from Latin word meaning 'look for', 'wait for'

resplendent (ruh-splen-duhnt)
adjective shining brightly: ***resplendent** in white uniforms* (***bright***, ***gleaming***, ***shiny***, ***splendid***)
Word building: **resplendence** *noun*
Word history: from Latin word meaning 'shining'

respond
verb **1** to answer, using words or actions: *She **responded** 'yes'. | He **responded** with a nod.* (***react***, ***reply***, ***retort***)
2 to react: *He did not **respond** to my pleas.*
Word history: Middle English, from Latin

respondent (ruh-spon-duhnt)
noun **1** *Law* a defendant
adjective **2** answering or responsive
Word history: from Latin word meaning 'answering'

response
noun **1** a reply in words or actions: *They had a big **response** to their appeal for clothes.*
2 a reaction: *The sunflower turns in **response** to light.* (***acknowledgement***, ***answer***, ***feedback***, ***reply***)
3 a line or verse sung by a church choir or congregation in reply to the priest
Word building: **responsive** *adjective*
Word history: Latin

responsibility
noun a duty or care: *It is her **responsibility** to lock up. | He shares in the **responsibility** of looking after the children.*
Noun forms: The plural is **responsibilities**.

responsible
adjective **1** reliable or capable: *a **responsible** person* (***conscientious***, ***dependable***, ***dutiful***)
2 answerable for something or to someone: *Who is **responsible** for the mistake? | I am **responsible** to my boss if anything goes wrong.*
Word building: **responsibly** *adverb*

rest[1]
noun **1** a time of sleep or recovery (***break, loaf, spell***)
2 time off, especially from something tiring or troubling
3 a stopping of movement: *The wheels came to* ***rest****.*
4 the time of silence between notes in music
5 a support: *a foot* ***rest***
verb **6** to sleep or relax (***laze, put your feet up, take it easy, wind down***)
7 to stop or have a break
8 to lie or position: *to* ***rest*** *your arm on the table* (***deposit, lodge, park, place, set***)
9 to depend or let depend: *The outcome* ***rests*** *on you. | They* ***rest*** *their case on new evidence.*
10 to stay or let stay: *The torch light* ***rested*** *on one spot. | He* ***rested*** *his gaze on the clock.*
phrase **11 at rest,**
a dead: *He is* ***at rest*** *in his grave.*
b peaceful or unworried: *His mind is* ***at rest****.*
12 let rest, to leave alone: *He* ***let*** *the matter* ***rest****.*

Word history: Old English

rest[2]
noun everyone or everything remaining: *The* ***rest*** *had to go.*

Word history: Middle English, from French, from Latin word meaning 'remain'

rest / wrest
Don't confuse **rest** with **wrest**. To **wrest** something is to remove it with difficulty, especially by giving it a violent twist or pull.

restaurant (res-tuh-ront)
noun a place where you can buy and eat a meal

Word history: from French word meaning 'restore'

restitution (res-tuh-tyooh-shuhn)
noun **1** repayment made by giving back a similar or equal amount in money or goods to that lost, damaged, or harmed (***indemnification***)
2 the giving back of property or rights previously taken, carried away, or given up
3 the bringing back to the former or original condition or position

Word history: Middle English, from Latin word meaning 'a restoring'

restive (res-tiv)
adjective **1** restless or uneasy
2 unmanageable, or hard to control

Word history: *rest*[2] + *-ive*

restoration
noun **1** the act of restoring, reviving, or re-establishing
2 something which is renewed

restore
verb **1** to give or bring back: *to* ***restore*** *lost property to its owner | to* ***restore*** *order*
2 to bring back to good condition: *to* ***restore*** *a building* (***fix, improve, mend, patch up, renovate, repair***)

Word building: **restorer** *noun*
Word history: Middle English, from Old French, from Latin word meaning 'restore', 'repair'

restrain
verb to control or prevent: *It was hard to* ***restrain*** *the horse. | She* ***restrained*** *him from running onto the road.* (***check, hold back***)

Word history: Middle English, from Old French, from Latin word meaning 'restrain'

restraint (ruh-straynt)
noun **1** restraining action or influence: *freedom from* ***restraint***
2 a means of restraining
3 the condition or fact of being restrained (***confinement, inhibition***)
4 a holding back of feelings: *She showed considerable* ***restraint*** *in a potentially explosive situation.*

Word use: The opposite of definition 3 is **abandon**.
Word history: Middle English, from Old French word meaning 'restrain'

restrict
verb to limit or confine: *He* ***restricts*** *his food intake. | The doctor* ***restricted*** *her to light exercise.* (***control, curb, inhibit, limit***)

Word building: **restricted** *adjective* **restriction** *noun*
Word history: from Latin word meaning 'restrained', 'restricted'

restructure
verb **1** to change the organisation or structure of: *to* ***restructure*** *the hospital's committee system.*
2 (in business, manufacturing, etc.) to change an existing pattern of employment, distribution, etc., often resulting in job losses
3 to reformulate, as when redrafting a document, policy, wage award, etc.
noun **4** the act or process of restructuring: *an award* ***restructure*** *among the factory workers.*

Word building: **restructuring** *noun*

result
noun **1** the effect of an action or event (***conclusion, consequence, outcome, sequel***)
2 the answer to a sum
verb **3** to end in a particular way: *The match* ***resulted*** *in a draw.*

Word history: late Middle English, from Latin word meaning 'spring back'

resume
verb **1** to continue: *They* ***resumed*** *their journey after a break. | Now that you are quiet, let us* ***resume****.*
2 to take back, or go back to: *The council* ***resumed*** *our land. | He* ***resumed*** *his seat.*

Word building: **resumption** *noun*
Word history: late Middle English, from Latin word meaning 'take up again'

résumé (rez-yuh-may)
noun a summing up or summary (***outline, precis, report, synopsis***)

Word history: French

resurrect
verb **1** to bring back from the dead: *Some religions believe it is possible to* ***resurrect*** *the dead.*
2 to bring back into use: *We* ***resurrected*** *our old clothes.*

Word building: **resurrection** *noun*

resuscitate (ruh-sus-uh-tayt)
verb to bring back to life, especially from unconsciousness: *He* ***resuscitated*** *the drowning man.*

Word building: **resuscitation** *noun*
Word history: from Latin word meaning 'revived'

retail
noun **1** the sale of goods to the public, not to shops
verb **2** to sell to the user
3 to be sold: *It* ***retails*** *at $5.*

Word use: Compare this with **wholesale.**
Word building: **retail** *adjective* **retailer** *noun*
Word history: Middle English, from Anglo-French word meaning 'cut', 'clip', 'pare'

retail bank
noun a bank which deals with transactions made by individual customers rather than businesses or other banks

Word use: Compare this with **merchant bank.**
Word building: **retail banker** *noun* **retail banking** *noun*

retain
verb **1** to keep or keep on: *She is managing to* ***retain*** *her old home. | to* ***retain*** *an old servant* (***maintain, preserve, sustain***)
2 to remember: *She doesn't* ***retain*** *names.*
3 to hold in place: *Her hair is* ***retained*** *by a net.*

Word history: Middle English, from Old French, from Roman

retainer[1] (ruh-tay-nuh)
noun **1** someone or something that retains
2 in former times, someone attached to a noble household or owing it service
3 any servant, especially a personal or family servant of long standing
4 a special, removable device worn in the mouth to help keep teeth in their new, straightened position after braces have been removed

Word history: *retain* + *-er*

retainer[2] (ruh-tay-nuh)
noun a fee paid to ensure services, for instance to a lawyer

Word history: French

retaliate
verb to strike back: *If you tease him he will* ***retaliate.*** (***get even, reciprocate, take revenge***)

Word building: **retaliation** *noun*
Word history: from Late Latin word meaning 'requited'

retard
verb **1** to hinder or make slower: *The muddy road* ***retarded*** *our progress.* (***frustrate, hamper, hinder, impede, inhibit***)
2 to slow down or limit (a person's development)

Word use: The opposite of definition 1 is **hasten.**
Word building: **retarded** *adjective*
Word history: Latin

retardation
noun **1** the act of slowing down
2 the condition of being retarded

retch
verb to try to vomit

Word building: **retching** *noun*
Word history: from Old English word meaning 'clear the throat'

retch / wretch
Don't confuse **retch** with **wretch**, a poor miserable person.

retention (ruh-ten-shuhn)
noun **1** the act of retaining
2 the condition of being retained
3 the power to retain
4 the act or power of remembering things (***memory, recall***)

Word history: Middle English, from Latin

retentive (ruh-ten-tiv)
adjective **1** tending or working to retain something
2 having the power or ability to retain
3 having the power or ability to remember

reticent (ret-uh-suhnt)
adjective inclined to be silent (***laconic, quiet, reserved, shy, taciturn***)

Word building: **reticence** *noun*
Word history: from Latin word meaning 'keeping silent'

reticulate (ruh-tik-yuh-luht)
adjective **1** like a network or net
verb (ruh-tik-yuh-layt) **2** to form into a network

Word building: **reticulation** *noun*
Word history: from Latin word meaning 'made like a net'

retina (ret-uh-nuh)
noun the coating on the back part of your eyeball which receives the image of what you see

Noun forms: The plural is **retinas** or **retinae** (ret-uh-nee).
Word history: Middle English, from Latin word meaning 'net'

retinue (ret-uh-nyooh)
noun a body of servants in attendance upon an important person

Word history: Middle English, from Old French word meaning 'retain'

retire
verb **1** to leave work, especially because you are getting old
2 to go away from other people, especially to go to bed: *We* ***retired*** *early, after a long hard day.*
3 to leave the sports field or ring early, usually because you are injured: *The cricketer had to* ***retire*** *hurt.*

Word building: **retired** *adjective* **retirement** *noun*
Word history: from French word meaning 'withdraw'

retiring
adjective withdrawing from relations with others (***reserved, shy***)

retort
noun a quick or sharp reply

Word building: **retort** *verb*
Word history: from Latin word meaning 'twisted back'

retrace
verb to go over again: *She **retraced** her steps. | He tried to **retrace** the events of that day long ago.*
Word building: **retraceable** *adjective*
Word history: French

retract[1] (ruh-<u>trakt</u>)
verb to draw back or in: *The snail **retracted** its feelers.*
Word building: **retractor** *noun*
Word history: Middle English, from Latin word meaning 'drawn back'

retract[2] (ruh-<u>trakt</u>)
verb to withdraw: *She must **retract** her statement immediately.*
Word building: **retractable** *adjective* **retraction** *noun*
Word history: from Latin word meaning 'recall'

retread
verb **1** to repair or bring back to good condition, by moulding on a new tread: *to **retread** a worn car tyre*
noun **2** a retreaded tyre

retreat
noun **1** withdrawal from a difficult or dangerous situation, usually in war: *The troops had to make a **retreat** from the enemy.*
2 withdrawal from people or activity
3 a place which is sheltered or remote: *They have a **retreat** in the bush.* (***asylum***, ***haven***, ***refuge***, ***sanctuary***, ***shelter***)
Word building: **retreat** *verb*
Word history: Middle English

retrench
verb to dismiss from employment, in order to save money: *The factory has to **retrench** half its workers.*
Word building: **retrenchment** *noun*
Word history: French

retribution (ret-ruh-<u>byooh</u>-shuhn)
noun repayment for your actions, especially in the form of punishment
Word history: Middle English, from Latin

retrieve
verb **1** to get, or bring back: *I **retrieved** my watch from the office. | The dog **retrieved** the ball.*
2 to save: *to **retrieve** a difficult situation*
Word building: **retrievable** *adjective* **retrieval** *noun*
Word history: Middle English, from Old French word meaning 'find again'

retriever
noun a type of dog that can be trained to bring birds and small animals back to the hunter

retro
adjective having to do with a style of fashion or music which combines aspects of previous styles: *She loved **retro** music because it brought back memories of when she was younger.*

retroactive (ret-roh-<u>ak</u>-tiv)
adjective operating as from a past date: *a **retroactive** tax law* (***retrospective***)
Word building: **retroactivity** *noun*

retrofit
verb **1** to fit out anew as part of repairs or maintenance, especially by replacing old or worn parts with new and up-to-date ones
2 to fit out at a later time as part of a secondary stage of development: *to **retrofit** the inner suburbs with green spaces*
Verb forms: I **retrofitted**, I have **retrofitted**, I am **retrofitting**

retrograde (<u>ret</u>-ruh-grayd)
adjective **1** having a backward motion or direction
2 returning to an earlier and lesser state: *a **retrograde** step*
verb **3** to move or go backwards
Word history: Middle English, from Latin word meaning 'going backwards'

retrogress (ret-roh-<u>gres</u>)
verb to go backwards, especially into a worse or earlier condition
Word building: **retrogression** *noun*

retrospect (<u>ret</u>-ruh-spekt)
noun a survey of past times, events, etc.
Word building: **retrospection** *noun*

retrospective (ret-ruh-<u>spek</u>-tiv)
adjective **1** having to do with or coming from the past: *a **retrospective** exhibition of paintings*
2 taking effect from a date before the present: *a **retrospective** wage rise*
Word building: **retrospective** *noun* **retrospectively** *adverb*

return
verb **1** to go or come back: *They have to **return** home now. | She continually **returns** to the same idea.*
2 to give or send back: *He **returned** the insult. | She will **return** the books.*
noun **3** an act of returning: *An effective **return** of service is an asset in tennis.*
4 a repetition or recurrence: *Many happy **returns** of the day!*
5 a report or paper which has to be sent: *a tax **return***
6 a yield or profit, as from labour, land, business, investment, etc. (***dividend***, ***pay-out***)
phrase **7 by return**, by the next post
Word building: **return** *adjective*
Word history: Middle English, from Old French

reunion
noun a special meeting, usually of a family, or of people who have not seen each other for a long time

rev
noun **1** a turning round or revolution, usually of an engine
verb **2** to make turn over faster: *to **rev** your engine*
Verb forms: I **revved**, I have **revved**, I am **revving**
Word history: abbreviation of *rev(olution)*

revalue (ree-<u>val</u>-yooh)
verb **1** to value again, especially to raise the legal value of: *The new government **revalued** the currency.*
2 to reconsider or review
Word use: The opposite is **devalue**.
Word building: **revaluation** *noun*

reveal
verb to show or make known: *to **reveal** the dirt* | *to **reveal** a secret* (***admit***, ***disclose***, ***expose***, ***make public***)

Word use: The opposite of this is **conceal**.
Word building: **revealing** *adjective*
Word history: Middle English, from Latin word meaning 'unveil', 'reveal'

reveille (ruh-val-ee)
noun the signal sounded on a bugle or drum to wake up soldiers in the morning

Word history: French word meaning 'awaken', from *re-* again + Latin word meaning 'keep watch'

revel (rev-uhl)
verb **1** to take great pleasure or delight in something: *to **revel** in good food*
2 to have a wild party (***celebrate***, ***party on***, ***rage***, ***rejoice***, ***whoop it up***)
noun **3** a wild party or festivity
4 revels, an occasion of merrymaking or noisy festivity with dancing, etc.

Verb forms: I **revelled**, I have **revelled**, I am **revelling**
Word building: **reveller** *noun* **revelry** *noun*
Word history: Middle English, from Old French word meaning 'to make noise', 'rebel', from Latin

revelation (rev-uh-lay-shuhn)
noun **1** the act of revealing
2 something revealed, especially causing astonishment (***disclosure***, ***eye-opener***)

Word history: Middle English, from Latin

revenge
noun the hurt or damage done to pay someone back for the bad things they have done to you (***retaliation***, ***vengeance***)

Word building: **revenge** *verb*
Word history: Middle English, from Old French

revenge / avenge

These words have the same basic meanings but are usually different parts of speech.

Revenge is most often used as a noun. You can use **revenge** as a verb if you want to, although it isn't very common.

Avenge is always used as a verb. It means 'to pay someone back for a wrong they have done':

'I will avenge my father's murder!' cried the princess.

revenue
noun the money a government makes from taxes and other sources

Word history: Middle English, from French word meaning 'return'

reverberate
verb **1** to echo over and over again
2 to linger in the memory: *words that **reverberate** through our history*

Word building: **reverberation** *noun*
Word history: from Latin word meaning 'beaten back'

revere (ruh-vear)
verb to feel deep respect for (***honour***, ***venerate***, ***worship***)

Word building: **reverence** *noun* **reverence** *verb* **reverent** *adjective* **reverential** *adjective*
Word history: from Latin word meaning 'feel awe of', 'fear', 'revere'

Reverend
noun a title of respect for a member of the clergy

reverie (rev-uh-ree)
noun **1** a daydream
2 *Music* an instrumental composition of a vague and dreamy character

Word use: You can also use **revery**.
Word history: from French word meaning 'to dream'

reverse
noun **1** the opposite: *No, the **reverse** is true.*
2 the back or rear of anything
3 a gear which drives a car backwards
4 the side of a coin, medal, etc., which does not bear the the head or main design (opposed to *obverse*)
verb **5** to turn back, or drive backwards, or put in the opposite direction: *He took two steps forward then **reversed**.* | *She **reversed** the car into the drive.*
6 to cancel or wipe out: *The judge **reversed** the decision.* (***annul***, ***dissolve***, ***repeal***)

Word building: **reversal** *noun* **reverse** *adjective*
Word history: Middle English, from Latin word meaning 'turned about'

reverse / reserve

Don't confuse **reverse** with **reserve**. To **reserve** something is to keep it for a particular person or use:

I'll reserve you a seat next to mine.

She wants to reserve this book for her project.

reverse-cycle
adjective having to do with an air conditioner able to cool an area in summer and heat it in winter: *a **reverse-cycle** air-conditioning system*

revert
verb to go back to: *to **revert** to an old habit*

Word building: **reversion** *noun*
Word history: Middle English, from Old French, from Late Latin

review
noun **1** a newspaper or magazine article which describes and gives you an opinion of a book, a film, a performance, or an art exhibition
2 a magazine which contains articles about recent happenings or discoveries, often in a particular area of interest: *a scientific **review***
3 an inspection or examination: *The matter is under **review**.*
verb **4** to look over: *The general **reviewed** the troops.* (***assess***, ***examine***, ***inspect***, ***vet***)
5 to write about: *to **review** a book*
6 to reconsider or think about again: *She **reviewed** her decision.*

Word building: **reviewer** *noun*

review / revue

Don't confuse **review** with **revue**, which is a musical show with songs, dances and skits making fun of recent events or popular fashions.

revile (ruh-vuyl)
verb to speak strongly to, with contempt and abuse: *The man **reviled** the stranger.*

Word history: Middle English, from Old French word meaning 'treat or regard as vile'

revise
verb **1** to check or correct: *She **revised** her manuscript.* (***amend, correct, improve, rectify***)
2 to go back over in order to learn: *He is **revising** his maths.*

Word building: **revision** *noun*
Word history: French, from Latin word meaning 'go to see again', 'look back on'

revive
verb **1** to return to life or energy: *She **revived** when she had finished her rest.*
2 to set going again or bring back into use: *to **revive** an argument | to **revive** a play*

Word building: **revival** *noun*
Word history: Middle English, from Latin word meaning 'live again'

revoke (ruh-vohk)
verb to take back or withdraw: *to **revoke** a decree*

Word building: **revocation** *noun*
Word history: Middle English, from Latin word meaning 'call back'

revolt
verb **1** to rebel or rise up against those with power over you: *The prisoners **revolted** against their captors.* (***mutiny, rise up, run riot***)
2 to disgust: *The food **revolted** her.* (***nauseate, offend, sicken***)

Word building: **revolt** *noun* **revolting** *adjective*
Word history: French, from Italian word meaning 'revolt', 'turning', from Latin word meaning 'overturn', 'revolve'

revolution
noun **1** a complete change: *There's been a **revolution** in the business.*
2 the complete overthrow of a government or a form of government (***coup, mutiny, rebellion, revolt, uprising***)
3 in mechanics
a a turning round or rotating on an axis, especially in a car engine
b a single cycle in such a course

Word history: Middle English, from Latin

revolutionary
adjective **1** having to do with a complete change or revolution: *a **revolutionary** invention | a **revolutionary** government*
noun **2** someone who supports a revolution
Noun forms: The plural is **revolutionaries.**

revolutionise
verb to bring about a revolutionary change in: *to **revolutionise** car production*

Word use: You can also use **revolutionize.**

revolve
verb **1** to turn in a circle or move in an orbit: *He **revolved** the wheel. | The moon **revolves** around the earth.*
2 to move in a cycle: *The seasons **revolve**.*

Word history: Middle English, from Latin word meaning 'roll', 'turn'

revolver
noun a pistol with a revolving section for bullets, which can be fired without having to reload between shots

revue
noun a musical show with songs, dances and items which make fun of recent events or popular fashions

Word history: French

revue / review
Don't confuse **revue** with **review.** A **review** is a newspaper or magazine article which describes a book or film and gives you the reviewer's opinion of it.

revulsion
noun a sudden and violent change of feeling against someone or something: *She felt a **revulsion** for her old habits.*

Word history: from Latin word meaning 'a plucking away'

reward
noun **1** something given or received in return for work or help
2 money offered to encourage people to give information about a crime or lost property

Word building: **reward** *verb*
Word history: Middle English, from Old French

rewarding
adjective giving such satisfaction that the effort made was worthwhile: *Growing your own vegetables can be very **rewarding**.*

rhapsody
noun **1** *Music* an instrumental composition irregular in form and suggesting improvisation: *Liszt's Hungarian **Rhapsodies***
2 an epic poem or part of an epic poem, suitable for recitation at one time
3 an exaggerated expression of enthusiasm: *to go into **rhapsodies** about something*

Noun forms: The plural is **rhapsodies.**
Word history: Latin, from Greek word meaning 'epic recital'

rhesus monkey
noun a monkey common in India, used greatly in medical research

rhetoric (ret-uh-rik)
noun **1** the art of using specially literary language in prose or verse, including figures of speech
2 the study of such language
3 exaggeration or display in writing or speech

Word history: Middle English, from Latin, from Greek word meaning 'the rhetorical art of speaking so as to influence the thoughts of the hearers'

rhetorical question
noun a question which does not seek an answer but is designed to produce an effect

rheumatic fever (rooh-mat-ik fee-vuh)
noun a disease, usually affecting children, involving fever, inflammation of the joints and muscle pains

rheumatism (<u>rooh</u>-muh-tiz-uhm)
noun a painful disease affecting the joints or muscles

Word building: **rheumatic** *adjective*
Word history: Late Latin, from Greek word meaning 'a suffering from a bodily discharge'

rhinestone
noun an artificial gem made of a mixture of clay, water, etc.

Word history: translation of French *caillou du Rhin* pebble of the Rhine

rhinoceros
noun a large thick-skinned mammal of Africa and Asia, with one or two horns on its nose

Noun forms: The plural is **rhinoceroses** or **rhinoceros.**
Word use: The short form is **rhino.**
Word history: Middle English, from Late Latin, from Greek *rhīno-* (a word part meaning 'nose') + *-kerōs* horned

rhodium (<u>roh</u>-dee-uhm)
noun a silvery-white metallic element similar to platinum, used in alloys and catalysts

Word history: Neo-Latin

rhododendron (roh-duh-<u>den</u>-druhn)
noun a large shrub with pink, purple or white flowers

Word history: Neo-Latin, from Greek word meaning 'rose tree'

rhombus
noun a parallelogram with four equal sides and angles that are not right angles

Noun forms: The plural is **rhombuses** or **rhombi.**
Word history: Latin, from Greek

rhubarb (<u>rooh</u>-bahb)
noun a plant whose stalks are cooked with sugar and water to make a dessert

Word history: Middle English, from Old French, from Medieval Latin, from Greek word meaning 'foreign rhubarb'

rhyme (ruym)
noun **1** an agreement or a likeness in the sounds at the end of words, as in 'cat' and 'bat'
2 a word which rhymes with another
3 a poem or verse that has rhymes
phrase **4 rhyme or reason**, logic or meaning: *There was no* ***rhyme or reason*** *in her behaviour.*

Word building: **rhyme** *verb*
Word history: Middle English, from Old French word meaning 'to rhyme', from Old High German word meaning 'series', 'row'

rhythm (<u>ridh</u>-uhm)
noun **1** the pattern of beats in music or speech (***beat***, ***swing***, ***tempo***, ***time***)
2 an even or regular movement: *He has no sense of* ***rhythm.***

Word building: **rhythmic** *adjective* **rhythmical** *adjective* **rhythmically** *adverb*
Word history: Latin, from Greek

rhythm and blues
noun a style of music using both vocal and instrumental elements based on the guitar, and from the African-American blues style, but faster and with more complex rhythms

Word use: The abbreviation is **R & B**.

rib[1]
noun **1** one of the set of curved bones partly enclosing the chest
2 the main vein of a leaf
3 a raised or ridged pattern in knitting

Word building: **rib** *verb* (**ribbed**, **ribbing**) **ribbed** *adjective*
Word history: Old English

rib[2]
verb Colloquial to tease or make fun of (***heckle***, ***insult***, ***mock***, ***ridicule***, ***taunt***)

Verb forms: I **ribbed**, I have **ribbed**, I am **ribbing**
Word history: short for *rib-tickle*

ribald (<u>rib</u>-uhld, <u>ruy</u>-buhld)
adjective crude, coarse, or indecent: ***ribald*** *language* | *a* ***ribald*** *person*

Word building: **ribaldry** *noun*
Word history: Middle English, from Old French word meaning 'dissipate', from Middle High German word meaning 'be on heat', or from Middle Dutch word meaning 'whore'

ribbon
noun **1** a band of thin material used for tying or decorating: *Her hair was tied with* ***ribbons.***
2 anything like a ribbon: *a* ***ribbon*** *of moonlight*
3 the ink-soaked tape used in a typewriter

Word history: Middle English, from Old French

rice
noun white or brown grain grown in warm wet climates and widely used for food

Word history: Middle English, from Old French, from Italian, from Greek, of Eastern origin

rice paper
noun **1** thin paper made from the straw of rice, which can be eaten
2 Chinese paper consisting of the pith of certain plants cut and pressed into thin sheets

rich
adjective **1** having a great deal of anything, especially money: *a* ***rich*** *woman* | *a* ***rich*** *country* (***affluent***, ***loaded***, ***prosperous***, ***wealthy***, ***well-off***)
2 of fine full quality, such as materials, sounds, smells and colours: *a* ***rich*** *tone* | *a* ***rich*** *velvet* (***bright***, ***intense***, ***vivid***)
3 fatty or hard to digest: ***rich*** *foods*
noun **4 riches**, wealth (***capital***, ***money***, ***treasure***)

Word history: Old English

Richter scale (rik-tuh <u>skayl</u>)
noun a scale used to measure the energy of disturbances in the earth, such as earthquakes

Word history: named after Charles French *Richter*, 1900–85, US seismologist

rich text format
noun Computers a format which is essentially ASCII with special commands, which makes it possible to exchange documents between different document preparation systems

Word use: You use **.rtf** in filenames.

rick[1]
noun a stack of hay, straw, etc.

Word history: Old English

rick[2]
verb to sprain or strain: *to* ***rick*** *your neck*

rickety
adjective weak or shaky: *a* ***rickety*** *old chair*

rickshaw
noun a light cart drawn by one or two people, which is used in some Asian countries as a form of transport

ricochet (rik-uh-shay)
noun the movement of an object, such as a bullet, when it hits something, bounces off, and keeps travelling in another direction
Word building: **ricochet** *verb* (**ricocheted, ricocheting**)
Word history: French

ricotta
noun a soft, white cottage cheese with a mild taste, made from whey and used in cooking
Word history: Italian word meaning 'cooked again'

rid
verb **1** to clear of something unwanted: *to* ***rid*** *the house of white ants*
phrase **2 get rid of,** to get free of
Verb forms: I **rid,** I have **rid,** I am **ridding**
Word history: from Old English word meaning 'clear (land)'

riddance
noun a freeing or clearing: *She's gone and good* ***riddance!***

ridden
verb past participle of **ride**

riddle[1]
noun **1** a cleverly worded question usually asked as a joke
2 any puzzling thing or person
Word history: from Old English word meaning 'enigma'

riddle[2]
verb to pierce with many holes, like those of a sieve: *The body was* ***riddled*** *with bullets.*
Word history: Old English

ride
verb **1** to sit on and control while in motion: *to* ***ride*** *a horse | to* ***ride*** *a bike*
2 to travel or be carried along: *to* ***ride*** *in a train*
noun **3** a short journey: *a* ***ride*** *on a horse | a bus* ***ride***
phrase **4 ride out,** to survive a difficulty by not giving up: *They* ***rode out*** *the storm in a shed. | to* ***ride out*** *the recession*
5 ride up, of clothes such as skirts, to move up the body when worn
6 take for a ride, to deceive or trick
Verb forms: I **rode,** I have **ridden,** I am **riding**
Word history: Old English

rider
noun **1** someone who rides a horse, bicycle, etc.
2 an addition or amendment to a document, etc.

ridge
noun **1** a long narrow range of mountains
2 any long narrow strip: ***ridges*** *of earth left by a plough*
Word building: **ridge** *verb*
Word history: from Old English word meaning 'spine', 'crest'

ridicule
verb to make fun of: *to* ***ridicule*** *their strange way of speaking* (***deride, mock***)
Word building: **ridicule** *noun*
Word history: French, from Latin word meaning 'laughable (thing)'

ridiculous
adjective funny or causing people to laugh: *a* ***ridiculous*** *hat* (***absurd, farcical, ludicrous, preposterous, silly***)

riesling (reez-ling, rees-ling)
noun a dry, white wine
Word history: German

rife
adjective common or widespread: *Dishonesty is* ***rife*** *in our society.*
Word history: late Old English

riffraff
noun the worthless or disreputable part of society: *the* ***riffraff*** *of the city* (***rabble, scum***)
Word history: Middle English *rif and raf* every particle, things of small value, from Old French *rifler* spoil, *raffler* ravage, snatch away

rifle[1]
noun a gun that is held against the shoulder, with a long barrel which is specially designed to give spin to the bullet so its flight will be more accurate
Word history: from Low German word meaning 'to groove'

rifle[2]
verb to search quickly through, leaving a mess: *to* ***rifle*** *through drawers | to* ***rifle*** *the house*
Word history: Middle English, from Old French word meaning 'scrape', 'graze', 'plunder', from Dutch word meaning 'scrape'

rift
noun **1** a narrow opening made by splitting: *a* ***rift*** *in the earth* (***crack, crevice, fissure, split***)
2 a breaking down in the friendly relations between people or countries
Word history: Middle English, from Scandinavian

rig
verb **1** to equip with the necessary ropes and lines: *to* ***rig*** *a yacht*
2 to control dishonestly: *to* ***rig*** *an election*
phrase **3 rig up,** to put together or in proper working order: *to* ***rig up*** *a dance floor | to* ***rig up*** *a tent*
Verb forms: I **rigged,** I have **rigged,** I am **rigging**
Word building: **rig** *noun* **rigger** *noun*
Word history: probably from Scandinavian

rigger / rigour

These words look similar but have different meanings.

A **rigger** is someone who fits sails and rigging to the mast of a ship. It can also be a construction worker on a building site who works with cranes.

Rigour is strictness, or hardship:

You'll have to train for the Olympics with the utmost rigour.

I hope he'll survive the rigours of prison life.

Another way of spelling this is **rigor.**

rigging
noun the ropes, wires, chains, etc., used to support and work the masts, yards, sails, etc., on a ship

right
adjective **1** fair and good (***impartial, just, neutral, objective***)
2 correct (***accurate, certain, true, valid***)
3 not left: *your **right** hand*
4 straight or upright: *to put things **right** | a **right** angle*
5 having to do with the Right (definition 16) (***conservative, reactionary***)
noun **6** what is fair and good: *We must hope that **right** will win.*
7 a fair claim: *He has a **right** to some time off.*
8 the right side: *the third house on the **right***
adverb **9** to the right side: *Turn **right** at the post office.*
10 directly or straight: ***right** to the bottom*
11 exactly or immediately: ***right** here | **right** now*
verb **12** to put in an upright or proper position
13 to correct or make up for: *to **right** a wrong*
phrase **14 by rights**, in all fairness
15 right as rain, *Colloquial* safe, or in good health (***protected, secure, well***)
16 the Right, the party, or the section of a party, or the body of people in general, with the more conservative viewpoint in a political system
17 to rights, in proper order: *to set a room **to rights***

Word use: The opposite of definitions 3, 5, 8, 9 and 16 is **left.** | You can also use **the right** or **right wing** for definition 16.
Word history: Old English

right / write / rite / wright

Don't confuse **right** with **write, rite** or **wright**.

To **write** is to form letters or words with a pen or something similar. You **write** a poem when you create it using words.

A **rite** is a ceremony, often a religious one, as in *the holy rite of baptism.*

A **wright** is an old-fashioned word for a worker who constructs things. You will find it nowadays only as a suffix in words like *wheelwright* and *playwright.*

right angle
noun an angle of 90°

right-angled
adjective having one or more right angles: *a **right-angled** triangle*

right-click
verb to activate a computer function by pressing on the right-hand button on the mouse: *If you **right-click** on delete, the file will go.*

righteous (ruy-chuhs)
adjective **1** good and upright: *a **righteous** man*
2 having a good cause or reason: ***righteous** indignation*

Word building: **righteousness** *noun*
Word history: Old English from *riht* right + *wīs* manner, fashion

rightful
adjective having a valid or just claim: *the **rightful** owner*

right-handed
adjective naturally inclined to use the right hand to do things: *He plays tennis **right-handed**.*

right wing
noun → **right** (definition 16)

Word building: **right-wing** *adjective* **right-winger** *noun*

rigid
adjective **1** stiff and inflexible: *The handrail should be **rigid**.* (***firm, hard, tough, unyielding***)
2 strict or unbending: ***rigid** discipline* (***austere, firm, harsh, straitlaced***)

Word building: **rigidity** *noun*
Word history: Latin

rigmarole
noun **1** a confused and rambling story
2 a long and complicated process

Word history: from obsolete *ragman roll* a roll, list, or catalogue

rigor mortis
noun the stiffening of the body after death

Word history: from Latin word meaning 'stiffness of death'

rigour
noun **1** strictness: *He trained with the utmost **rigour**.*
2 hardship or severity: *Some animals can survive the **rigours** of desert life.*

Word use: You can also use **rigor.**
Word building: **rigorous** *adjective*
Word history: Middle English, from Old English, from Latin

rile
verb Colloquial to irritate or vex

rim
noun the outer edge, especially of a circular or round object: *the **rim** of a glass | the **rim** of a wheel | the Pacific **rim*** (***border, brim, brink, edge, margin***)

Word history: Old English

rind
noun a fairly thick and firm skin: *lemon **rind** | the **rind** of cheese*

ring[1]
noun **1** a circular band for wearing on the finger: *a wedding **ring***
2 anything shaped like a ring: *a key **ring***
3 a circular line or shape: *to draw a **ring***
4 an enclosed area, not necessarily circular: *a circus **ring** | a boxing **ring***
phrase **5 run rings around**, *Colloquial* to be much better than

Word building: **ring** *verb*
Word history: Old English

ring[2]
verb **1** to give out a clear musical sound: *The bells are **ringing**. | His voice **rang** out.* (***chime***, ***peal***)
2 to make a bell sound, especially as a signal: *to **ring** a doorbell*
3 to telephone: ***Ring** me on Wednesday.*
phrase **4 ring a bell**, to bring back a memory or sound familiar
5 ring up,
a to telephone
b to record the cost of on a cash register
Verb forms: I **rang**, I have **rung**, I am **ringing**
Word building: **ring** *noun*
Word history: Old English

ring / wring
Don't confuse **ring** with **wring**. To **wring** is to twist and squeeze something:
I'll wring the water out of my wet socks.
I saw her wring her hands in grief.

ringbark
verb to cut away a ring of bark from a tree trunk or branch in order to kill it by cutting off the flow of sap

ringer[1]
noun Australian a station hand, especially a stockworker or drover

ringer[2]
noun Australian, NZ **1** the fastest shearer of a group
2 anyone who is the fastest or best at anything
Word history: from British dialect word meaning 'anything superlatively good'

ring-in
noun Australian, NZ Colloquial someone or something taking the place of another at the last moment

ringleader
noun someone who leads others in opposition to authority, law, etc.
Word history: from the phrase *to lead the ring* to be first

ringlet
noun a long curl of hair shaped like a corkscrew

ringmaster
noun someone in charge of a circus performance

ringtone
noun Telecommunications **1** a tone that a person hears when they ring up that tells them that the called telephone is ringing
2 the sound produced by a mobile phone to indicate that a call is being received: *Her mobile has a really cool **ringtone**.*

ringworm
noun a skin disease with ring-shaped patches, caused by fungi

rink
noun **1** a sheet of ice prepared for skating
2 a smooth floor for rollerskating
Word history: Scottish

rinse
verb **1** to wash lightly in clean water to remove scra ps of food or soap
noun **2** a liquid for colouring hair
Word history: Middle English, from Old French, from Latin word meaning 'fresh', 'recent'

riot
noun **1** a disturbance of the peace by a group of people
2 wild disorder or confusion (***commotion***, ***hullaballoo***, ***tumult***, ***turmoil***)
Word building: **riot** *verb* **rioter** *noun* **riotous** *adjective*
Word history: Middle English, from Old French word meaning 'to quarrel', from Latin word meaning 'roar'

rip[1]
verb **1** to tear in a rough way (***cut***, ***gash***, ***lacerate***, ***slash***, ***slit***)
2 *Computers* to copy (digital data) from a CD or DVD to the hard drive of a computer
phrase **3 let it rip**, *Colloquial* to allow something, such as a car engine, to go as fast as possible
4 let rip, *Colloquial* to give way to anger or other strong emotion
5 rip into, *Colloquial* to begin rapidly and eagerly: *Let's **rip into** the housework.*
6 rip off, *Colloquial* to defraud or take money from by cheating (***fleece***, ***swindle***, ***take for a ride***)
Verb forms: I **ripped**, I have **ripped**, I am **ripping**
Word building: **rip** *noun*
Word history: Middle English

rip[2]
noun a disturbance in the sea resulting in a fast current, especially at a beach

RIP
abbreviation may he or she (or they) rest in peace
Word history: abbreviation of Latin *requiescat* (or *requiescant*) *in pace*

ripcord
noun a cord or ring which opens a parachute during a descent

ripe
adjective ready for harvesting, picking or eating: ***ripe** wheat | **ripe** fruit*
Word building: **ripen** *verb* **ripeness** *noun*
Word history: Old English

rip-off
noun Colloquial a price or charge that is too much

riposte (ruh-post)
noun a quick, sharp return in speech or action
Word building: **riposte** *verb*
Word history: French, from Italian word meaning 'response', from Latin

ripper
noun **1** a tool used for breaking up rock, usually on the back of a bulldozer
2 *Computers* a software program that copies data from a CD or DVD to the hard drive
3 *Colloquial* someone or something that you admire a lot

ripple
verb **1** to make small waves on: *The wind is **rippling** the water.*

noun **2** a small wave
3 a sound coming as though in a wave: *a **ripple** of laughter*

rise
verb **1** to get up or get out of bed (***arise***)
2 to extend or go upwards, or swell up: *The tower **rises** to a great height. | Her voice **rose**. | The cake has **risen**.*
3 to rebel or revolt: *The people **rose** against the tyrant.*
noun **4** an upward movement: *a **rise** in temperature | a **rise** in prices* (***escalation***, ***increase***, ***jump***)
5 an upward slope: *a **rise** in the ground*
phrase **6 get** (or **take**) **a rise out of**, to provoke a reaction, such as anger or annoyance, by teasing, etc.
7 give rise to, to cause or produce

Verb forms: I **rose**, I have **risen**, I am **rising**
Word building: **rising** *noun*
Word history: Old English

rise / raise

Don't confuse **rise** with **raise**.

To **raise** is to lift up, or bring up:

He tried to raise the bucket from the well.

I'm trying to raise this family by myself.

A **raise** is an increase in wages, as in *a raise in salary*. For this meaning, you may also use the word **rise**.

risk
noun the possibility of being injured, hurt or losing something (***chance***, ***danger***)

Word building: **risky** *adjective* (**riskier**, **riskiest**) **risk** *verb*
Word history: French, from Italian word meaning 'to risk', 'dare', perhaps from Greek word meaning 'cliff' (through meaning of to sail around a cliff)

risotto
noun a dish consisting of rice cooked slowly with meat, seafood or vegetables and flavoured with cheese and herbs, originating in Italy

risqué (ris-kay, ris-kay)
adjective daringly close to being improper or indelicate: *a **risqué** joke*

Word history: from French word meaning 'risk'

rissole
noun a fried ball or small cake of minced food: *a meat **rissole***

Word history: French, perhaps from Vulgar Latin word meaning 'reddish'

rite
noun a ceremony, especially a religious one

Word history: Middle English, from Latin word meaning 'ceremony'

rite / write / right / wright

Look up **right / write / rite / wright.**

ritual
noun **1** a set procedure for a religious or other ceremony
2 an often repeated series of actions: *the **ritual** of getting up in the morning*

Word history: Latin

rival
noun **1** someone who is aiming at the same thing as another person: *He was her **rival** for the championship.* (***adversary***, ***antagonist***, ***opponent***)
verb **2** to compete with: *No-one **rivals** her in mathematics.*

Verb forms: I **rivalled**, I have **rivalled**, I am **rivalling**
Word building: **rivalry** *noun* (*plural* **rivalries**)
Word history: from Latin word meaning 'one living by or using the same stream as another'

river
noun a large natural stream of water flowing in a definite course or channel

Word history: Middle English, from Old French, from Latin word meaning 'bank'

rivet
noun **1** a bolt for holding pieces of metal together
verb **2** to fasten with a rivet
3 to fix firmly: *He was **riveted** to the spot. | The scene **riveted** her attention.*

Verb forms: I **riveted**, I have **riveted**, I am **riveting**
Word history: Middle English, from Old French word meaning 'fix', 'clinch', from Romance word meaning 'to make firm', 'come to shore', from Latin word meaning 'shore'

rivulet
noun a small stream or brook

Word history: Italian, from Latin word meaning 'small stream'

RMO
noun a medical officer who has graduated recently and who is appointed to and resident in a hospital

Word history: abbreviation of *r(esident) m(edical) o(fficer)*

RNA
noun ribonucleic acid, one of a class of large molecules (ribonucleotides) found in all living cells and some viruses, which translates the genetic code (DNA) during protein synthesis

Word history: abbreviation of *r(ibo)n(ucleic) a(cid)*

road
noun **1** a way or track suitable for cars, people and animals to travel along
phrase **2 on the road**,
a travelling
b of a theatrical company or musical band, on tour
3 take to the road,
a to begin a journey
b to move about with no regular place of sleeping or living

Word history: from Old English word meaning 'a riding', 'journey on horseback'

road / rode / rowed

Don't confuse **road** with **rode** or **rowed**.

Rode is the past tense of the verb **ride**, to sit on and control something:

I fell off that horse the first time I rode it.

Rowed is the past form of the verb **row**, to move using oars:

I rowed the boat right around the island.

roadie
noun someone who looks after the sound equipment for a pop group on tour

road kill
noun the remains of any animal or animals struck and killed by a motor vehicle and lying on or beside a road

Word use: You can also use **roadkill**.
Word building: **road-killed** *adjective*

road train
noun Australian a truck towing a number of large trailers, used for carrying cattle or other freight

roam
verb to walk or travel with no particular purpose (***rove***, ***wander***)

Word history: Middle English

roan
adjective of a reddish-brown colour with splashes of grey or white: *a **roan** horse*

Word building: **roan** *noun*
Word history: Middle English, from French, from Spanish, from Latin word meaning 'yellow-grey'

roar
verb **1** to make a loud deep sound: *A lion **roared**. | The wind **roared**.* (***bawl***, ***bellow***)
2 to laugh loudly (***break up***, ***guffaw***)

Word building: **roar** *noun*
Word history: Old English

roar / raw
Don't confuse **roar** with **raw**. Food is **raw** if it hasn't been cooked.

roast
verb **1** to cook over a fire or bake in an oven (***barbecue***, ***grill***)
noun **2** a piece of meat that has been or is going to be roasted

Word history: Middle English, from Old French, from Germanic

rob
verb to steal from, often using force

Verb forms: I **robbed**, I have **robbed**, I am **robbing**
Word building: **robbery** *noun* (*plural* **robberies**)
Word history: Middle English, from Old French, Old High German

robe
noun a long loose gown worn by men or women

Word use: This is often used in the plural, as in **coronation robes**.
Word history: Middle English, from Old French

robin
noun **1** any of a group of Australian birds with brightly coloured breasts
2 a European bird with a red breast, often painted on Christmas cards

Word history: Middle English *Robyn*, from Old French *Robin*, little Robert

robot (roh-bot)
noun a machine programmed to do a job usually done by a person

Word history: first used in the play *R.U.R.* by Karel Capek, 1890–1938, Czech dramatist and novelist; apparently from Czech *robotnik* serf

robust (roh-bust, ruh-bust)
adjective strong: *a **robust** frame | in **robust** health* (***brawny***, ***hardy***, ***husky***, ***muscly***)

Word use: The opposite of this is **frail** or **weak**.
Word history: Latin

rock[1]
noun **1** a large mass of stone (***boulder***, ***monolith***)
2 a stone of any size

Word history: Old English, from Medieval Latin

rock[2]
verb **1** to move from side to side: *The boat is **rocking** on the waves.* (***quake***, ***shake***, ***shudder***, ***sway***, ***tremble***)
2 to cause to move from side to side: *to **rock** a cradle*
3 to dance to rock'n'roll music
noun **4** a kind of loud popular music with a strong rhythm and electronically amplified sound, usually more complicated than rock'n'roll
5 → **rock'n'roll**

Word use: You can also use **rock music** for definition 4.
Word history: Old English

rock art
noun **1** the art of creating pictures on rock surfaces by painting, drawing, or carving out sections of rock, traditionally practised by Australian Aboriginal peoples
2 a picture created on a rock surface

rocker
noun **1** one of the curved pieces on which a cradle or a rocking chair rocks
2 a rocking chair

rockery
noun part of a garden where plants are grown in between rocks

Noun forms: The plural is **rockeries**.

rocket
noun **1** a cylinder full of gunpowder or something similar, fired into the air as a signal or as a firework
2 a space vehicle driven by hot gas that shoots out from the rear
verb **3** to move rapidly like a rocket

Word history: French

rockmelon
noun Australian, *NZ* a small round melon with orange-coloured flesh

Word use: Another name is **cantaloupe**.

rock'n'roll
noun **1** a simple kind of popular music with a strong beat
2 a dance performed to this music

Word use: You can also use **rock-and-roll** or **rock**.

rococo (ruh-koh-koh)
noun **1** a style of art, architecture and decoration of the 18th century, with use of ornate scrolls and curves
adjective **2** in the rococo style
3 over-elaborately decorated

Word history: from French word meaning 'rockwork', 'pebblework or shellwork'

rod
noun a long stick of wood, metal or other material

Word history: Old English

rode
verb past tense of **ride**

rode / road / rowed
Don't confuse **rode** with **road** or **rowed**.
Cars, people and animals travel along a **road**.
Rowed is the past form of the verb **row**, to move using oars:
I rowed the boat right around the island.

rodent
noun one of a group of animals, including rats, mice, and guinea pigs, with sharp teeth for gnawing

Word history: from Latin word meaning 'gnawing'

rodeo (roh-day-oh, roh-dee-oh)
noun a display of cowboy skills, like riding horses and lassoing cattle, for public entertainment

Word history: Spanish word meaning 'cattle ring', from Latin

roe
noun **1** the mass of eggs inside a female fish
2 the sperm of the male fish

Word history: Middle English

roe / row
Don't confuse **roe** with **row**, which is a line of people or things, as in *a row of houses*. Also, you **row** a boat with oars.
When **row** means 'a noisy quarrel or fight' we pronounce it to rhyme with *cow*.

roger
interjection message received and understood, used in signalling and telecommunications

Word history: the personal name *Roger* used in telecommunications as a name for *r*, used as an abbreviation for *received*

rogue (rohg)
noun **1** *Old-fashioned* a dishonest person (***cheat***, ***crook***, ***fraud***, ***knave***, ***shark***)
2 someone who plays tricks for fun

Word building: **roguery** *noun*
Word history: apparently short for obsolete *roger* begging vagabond

roguish (roh-gish)
adjective mischievous

role
noun **1** the part or character that an actor plays
2 the expected or usual part played in life: *a mother's **role** | a husband's **role***

Word history: from French word meaning 'the roll of paper containing an actor's part'

role / roll
Don't confuse **role** with **roll**, which is something made into the shape of a cylinder.

role-play
noun the imagining and acting out of the behaviour and feelings of a particular role (definition 2), used as a method of counselling, teaching, etc.

role reversal
noun the playing of a role by somebody which is in some way the opposite of a role they usually play, such as when a leader acts as a follower, etc.: *It was a case of **role reversal** when the so-called 'brain' had to ask the others how to do the question.*

roll
verb **1** to move or cause to move by turning over and over like a ball or a wheel
2 to be carried along on wheels: *The truck **rolled** down the hill.*
3 to press or flatten with a particular tool made for the purpose: *to **roll** pastry | to **roll** a cricket pitch*
4 to sway or cause to sway from side to side
noun **5** a piece of paper, material or food made into the shape of a cylinder: *a **roll** of carpet | a sponge **roll***
6 a list or register: *a class **roll***
7 a low continuous sound: *a **roll** of thunder*
phrase **8 roll in**, to arrive or appear in large numbers
9 roll up,
a to make into the shape of a cylinder: *to **roll up** a map*
b to come along: *A big crowd **rolled up** to the meeting.*

Word history: Middle English, from Old French, from Latin word meaning 'little wheel'

roll / role
Don't confuse **roll** with **role**, which is the part or character that an actor plays.

roller
noun **1** a cylinder or wheel on which something is rolled
2 a cylinder used for flattening: *a road **roller** | the **rollers** in a mangle*
3 a cylinder around which something is rolled: *a hair **roller***
4 a long swelling wave advancing steadily

rollerblade
noun **1** one of a pair of rollerskates designed in imitation of an ice-skating shoe with a single row of rollers instead of a skate
verb **2** to move on rollerblades: *He **rollerblades** to school.*

Word use: Another name is **inline skate**.
Word history: Trademark
Word building: **rollerblading** *noun* **rollerblader** *noun*

roller-coaster
noun an amusement park ride, on a steep twisting track

rollerskate
noun a kind of skate running on small wheels or rollers
Word building: **rollerskate** *verb*

rollicking
adjective jolly and carefree: *a **rollicking** song*
Word history: from *romp* and *frolic* + *-ing*

rolling strike
noun industrial action against an employer in which groups of employees go on strike one after the other without interruption

rollout
noun the launch of a new product, service, etc.: *The **rollout** of the new software was well publicised.*

roly-poly
adjective fat and fleshy

ROM (rom)
noun computer memory which can be read but not changed
Word history: an acronym for *r(ead) o(nly) m(emory)*

roman
adjective having to do with the upright style of printing types most commonly used in modern books, etc.
Word history: from *Roman* belonging to or having to do with Rome, ancient or modern

romance
noun **1** feelings of great love and affection or behaviour suited to these feelings: *There was no **romance** in their relationship.*
2 a novel or movie about people falling in love
3 a love affair: *It was only a brief **romance**, but it affected him deeply.*
Word history: Middle English, from Old French, from Vulgar Latin word meaning 'in one of the Romance languages', from Latin word meaning 'Romanic'

Romanesque (roh-muh-nesk)
adjective indicating the style of European architecture of the late 10th until the 13th century, characterised by towers, heavy walls, small windows, and the use of open timber roofs

Romani (rom-uh-nee)
noun **1** someone who belongs to a group of people once from India but now found mainly in Europe, many of whom do not live in any one place but wander about
adjective **2** having to do with the Romanies, their language or customs
Noun forms: The plural is **Romanies**.
Word use: You can also use **Romany**. | Romani people are sometimes called **gypsies**, but this term may offend some people.

Roman numerals
plural noun the numbers used by the ancient Romans, and still used for some purposes, like royal titles and chapter headings in books

romantic
adjective **1** having to do with or like romance: *a **romantic** adventure*
2 fanciful or suited to romance rather than to real or practical life: ***romantic** ideas*
3 showing or expressing love, strong affection, etc.
4 having to do with a style of literature, art, and music of the late 18th and 19th centuries, characterised by freedom of treatment, a viewing of form as less important than matter, imagination, experimentation with form, etc.
5 imaginary or made-up
noun **6** a romantic person
Word use: You can also use **Romantic** for definition 4. | Compare definition 4 with **classical**.
Word history: from French word meaning 'romance', 'novel'

romanticise
verb **1** to give a romantic character to: *The true story has been greatly **romanticised**.*
2 to have romantic ideas
Word use: You can also use **romanticize**.

romp
verb **1** to play in an active noisy way
phrase **2 romp in**, to win easily
Word history: from obsolete *ramp* rough woman

roo (rooh)
noun Australian Colloquial a kangaroo
Word history: abbreviation

roof (roohf)
noun **1** the top covering of a building or car
2 the overhead or upper surface of a hollow space: *the **roof** of a cave | the **roof** of your mouth*
phrase **3 hit the roof**, *Colloquial* to become very angry
4 raise the roof, to make a loud noise, especially in complaint
Noun forms: The plural is **roofs**.
Word history: Old English

rook[1] (rook)
noun a large black European bird like a crow that nests in groups in tall trees
Word history: Old English

rook[2] (rook)
noun a chess piece which can travel only in straight lines (***castle***)
Word history: Middle English, from Old French, from Persian

rookery (rook-uh-ree)
noun **1** a place where rooks nest
2 a breeding place for other birds or animals: *a penguin **rookery***
Noun forms: The plural is **rookeries**.

rookie (rook-ee)
noun Colloquial someone who is new at something, originally in the army, and now in any service, sporting team, etc.
Word use: You can also use **rooky**.

room (roohm)
noun **1** a part of a building separated by walls from other parts (***cell***, ***chamber***, ***compartment***, ***cubicle***)
2 space: *Move up and give me some **room**.*
Word history: Old English

roomy (roohm-ee)
adjective spacious (***commodious***, ***expansive***)
Adjective forms: **roomier**, **roomiest**
Word use: The opposite of this is **cramped** or **small**.

roost (roohst)
noun a resting place for birds at night
Word building: **roost** *verb*
Word history: Old English

rooster (roohst-uh)
noun → **cock**[1]

root[1] (rooht)
noun **1** the part of a plant which usually grows downwards into the soil and supplies the plant with food and water
2 the origin or beginning: *Money is the* ***root*** *of all evil.*
3 a number which, when multiplied by itself a certain number of times, produces a given quantity: *2 is the square* ***root*** *of 4 and the cube* ***root*** *of 8.*
4 roots, a feeling of belonging: *He has lived here for ten years but his* ***roots*** *are in New Zealand.*
verb **5** to send down roots and begin to grow: *A strange plant has* ***rooted*** *in our garden.*
6 to fix as if by roots: *She was* ***rooted*** *to the spot.*
phrase **7 root out,**
a to pull up by the roots: *to* ***root out*** *weeds*
b to remove completely: *to* ***root out*** *wickedness*
8 take (or **strike**) **root,**
a to send out roots and begin to grow
b to become fixed or established
Word use: For definition 3 also look up **square root** and **cube root.**
Word building: **rootless** *adjective*
Word history: Old English, from Scandinavian

root[2] (rooht)
verb **1** to turn up the soil with the snout, as pigs do
phrase **2 root around**, to search as if to find something
Word history: Old English

root / route
Don't confuse **root** with **route**, which is a way or road from one place to another:
The bus takes the longest possible route to the station.

rope
noun **1** a strong thick cord made of twisted fibre or wire
verb **2** to tie up with a rope
Word history: Old English

ropeable
adjective Colloquial angry
Word use: You can also use **ropable.**

rort
noun Australian Colloquial **1** an incident or series of incidents involving reprehensible or suspect behaviour, especially by officials or politicians
2 a wild party

rosary
noun **1** a string of beads used for counting a series of prayers, usually in the Roman Catholic Church
2 the series of prayers that are said
Noun forms: The plural is **rosaries.**
Word history: Middle English, from Latin word meaning 'rose garden'

rose[1]
noun **1** a wild or garden shrub with attractive, usually sweet-smelling, flowers and thorny stems
2 a deep pink colour
Word building: **rose** *adjective*
Word history: Middle English and Old English, from Latin

rose[2]
verb past tense of **rise**

rosé (roh-zay)
noun a light wine of an almost transparent pale red colour
Word history: French

rosella
noun a parrot with bright red, green and blue feathers
Word use: Another name is **lowry.**
Word history: from *Rosehill*, an early settlement in New South Wales, now Parramatta, where the birds were first seen by the colonial settlers

rosemary
noun a bushy plant with strongly-scented leaves used as a herb
Word history: Middle English *rose mary*, from Latin word meaning 'dew of the sea'

rosette
noun a decoration made of ribbons tied so as to look like the petals of a rose
Word history: from French word meaning 'rose[1]'

rosin (roz-uhn)
noun resin made from the dried sap of pine trees, used for rubbing on violin bows
Word history: Middle English, from Old French word meaning 'resin'

roster
noun a list of people's names and the times they are on duty: *a* ***roster*** *for the school tuckshop*
Word history: from Dutch word meaning 'list'

rostrum
noun a raised platform for a speaker or the conductor of an orchestra
Noun forms: The plural is **rostrums** or **rostra.**
Word history: from Latin word meaning 'beak', in plural, 'speakers' platform'

rosy
adjective **1** pink and healthy-looking: ***rosy*** *cheeks*
2 likely to turn out well: *a* ***rosy*** *future*
Adjective forms: **rosier, rosiest**

rot
verb **1** to make or go bad: *Sweets* ***rot*** *your teeth. | The garbage is* ***rotting.*** (***decay, decompose, perish***)
noun **2** a type of disease that makes things decay or go bad: *This timber has dry* ***rot.*** *| The cow has foot* ***rot.***
3 *Colloquial* nonsense or rubbish: *He talks a lot of* ***rot.*** (***bunkum, mumbo jumbo, piffle***)
Verb forms: it **rotted**, it has **rotted**, it is **rotting**
Word history: Middle English, from Scandinavian

rotary
adjective **1** turning around as on an axis: *a* ***rotary*** *clothes hoist*
2 of a machine, having a part or parts that turn like a wheel: *a* ***rotary*** *hoe*

rotate
verb **1** to turn round like a wheel (***spin***, ***twist***, ***wind***)
2 to go, or cause to go, through a series of changes: *to* ***rotate*** *the crops each year*

Word history: from Latin word meaning 'swung round', 'revolved'

rotation
noun **1** the act of turning around as on an axis
2 a the turning of the earth or other body in space about its own axis
b one complete turning or revolution of such a body

rote
noun **1** *Old-fashioned* a routine or fixed course of procedure
phrase **2 by rote**, in a mechanical way without thinking about the meaning: *to learn* ***by rote***

> **rote / wrote**
> Don't confuse **rote** with **wrote**, which is the past tense of the verb **write**, to form words with a pen, or to compose something with words:
> *She wrote a long letter to her friend in New Zealand.*

rotisserie (roh-tis-uh-ree)
noun a skewer which turns round and round in an oven, for cooking chickens and other food

Word history: from French word meaning 'roasting place'

rotor
noun **1** the rotating part of a machine
2 *Aeronautics* a system of rotating flaps, usually horizontal, as those of a helicopter

Word history: short for *rotator*

rotten
adjective **1** gone bad or decaying: *a* ***rotten*** *apple* (***decayed***, ***off***, ***putrid***)
2 *Colloquial* sick or unhappy: *to feel* ***rotten*** (***crook***, ***ill***, ***indisposed***, ***off-colour***)
3 *Colloquial* wicked: ***rotten*** *to the core*
4 *Colloquial* so incapable as to cause dismay: *a* ***rotten*** *shot* (***abominable***, ***abysmal***, ***atrocious***)

Word history: Middle English, from Scandinavian

rotund (roh-tund)
adjective plump and rounded: *a* ***rotund*** *belly*

Word building: **rotundity** *noun* **rotundness** *noun*
Word history: Latin

rotunda
noun a round building or room, especially one with a dome

Word history: from Latin word meaning 'rotund'

rouge (roohzh)
noun pinkish-red make-up used on the cheeks

Word building: **rouge** *verb*
Word history: French word meaning (properly adjective) 'red', from Latin

rough (ruf)
adjective **1** bumpy or uneven (***bristly***, ***coarse***, ***gnarled***, ***shaggy***)
2 wild or violent: ***rough*** *weather* | *a* ***rough*** *football match*
3 not properly finished: *a* ***rough*** *sketch*
4 difficult: *It was* ***rough on*** *the family when their dog died.*
phrase **5 rough it**, to make do without the usual home comforts: *to* ***rough it*** *camping in the bush*

Word building: **roughen** *verb*
Word history: Middle English, from Old English *ruh*

roughage
noun the fibre in food that has little nutritional value but helps in digestion

roughly
adverb **1** in a rough or violent manner
2 approximately: *The storm lasted* ***roughly*** *two hours.*

roulette (rooh-let)
noun a gambling game in which players bet on a small ball which runs around a revolving wheel

Word history: from French word meaning 'round slice'

round
adjective **1** shaped like a circle or ball (***circular***, ***spherical***)
2 completed by returning to the starting point: *a* ***round*** *trip* (***return***)
3 whole or complete: *a* ***round*** *dozen*
noun **4** an outburst: *a* ***round*** *of applause*
5 a period of boxing or wrestling: *He was knocked out in the third* ***round***.
6 a song for several singers, each joining in at a different time
adverb **7** in a circular direction: *to spin* ***round*** | *a tree 40 centimetres* ***round***
8 here and there: *to travel* ***round***
9 in some other direction: *to turn* ***round***
phrase **10 round down**, to reduce an amount to the nearest larger unit below it: *to* ***round down*** *92 cents to 90 cents*
11 round on (or **upon**), to attack suddenly, especially with words
12 round out, to add more detail to
13 round up,
a to gather in one place: *to* ***round up*** *sheep*
b to increase an amount to the nearest larger unit above: *to* ***round up*** *87 cents to 90 cents*

Word history: Middle English, from Old French, from Latin word meaning 'wheel-shaped'

roundabout
noun **1** a circular intersection for controlling traffic
2 → **merry-go-round**
adjective **3** going the long way round: *a* ***roundabout*** *way home*

rounders
plural noun a game like baseball, played with a soft ball

Word use: This word takes a singular verb: *Rounders is a good game.*

roundly
adverb strongly or energetically: *She scolded him* ***roundly***.

rouse[1] (rowz)
verb **1** to wake up: *The phone* ***roused*** *her.*
2 to stir up or arouse: *to* ***rouse*** *her anger*

rouse / rows

Don't confuse **rouse** with **rows.** If people have lots of **rows** (rhyming with *cows*), they have many noisy fights or quarrels.

Rows (rhyming with *hose*) means 'lines of people or things', as in *rows of potatoes.*

Rows with this pronunciation can also be a form of the verb **row**:

She often rows the boat.

rouse[2] (rows)
phrase **rouse on**, *Australian*, *NZ* to be angry with: *to* ***rouse on*** *the children for getting home late* (***admonish***, ***rebuke***, ***reprimand***, ***scold***, ***tick off***)
Word history: from Scottish word meaning 'to shout'

rouseabout (rows-uh-bowt)
noun Australian, *NZ* someone hired to do odd jobs on a farm, in a hotel, etc.
Word history: *rouse*[1] + *about*

rousing (row-zing)
adjective energetic and stirring: *a* ***rousing*** *song* (***breathtaking***, ***exciting***, ***exhilarating***, ***stimulating***, ***thrilling***)
Word history: from *rouse*[1]

rout (rowt)
verb **1** to defeat and force to run away: *to* ***rout*** *an army*
noun **2** a total defeat
Word history: Middle English, from Anglo-French, from Latin word meaning 'broken'

route (rooht)
noun **1** a way or road from one place to another: *The bus takes the long* ***route*** *home.* (***beeline***, ***course***, ***path***, ***track***)
2 (rowt) *Computers* a path, such as that between hosts in a computer network
verb **3** to send by a particular route
Verb forms: I **routed**, I have **routed**, I am **routeing** or I am **routing**
Word history: Middle English, from French, from Latin word meaning 'broken (road)'

route / root

Look up **root / route.**

router (row-tuh)
noun Computers a piece of hardware for connecting networks
Word use: Another name is **gateway**.
Word history: French, from Latin

routine (rooh-teen)
noun **1** something which is always done in the same way or at the same time or place: *a dance* ***routine***
adjective **2** done by routine: *I've put the car in for a* ***routine*** *safety inspection.*
3 (of an activity) dull or boring due to its unchanging nature
Word use: The opposite of definition 3 is **interesting** or **varied.**
Word history: from French word meaning 'route'

routing (row-ting, rooh-ting)
noun Computers the process of sending data packets to the required destination over a network

rove
verb to wander or roam (***journey***, ***travel***, ***voyage***)
Word building: **rover** *noun*
Word history: Middle English, from Scandinavian

row[1] (roh)
noun a line of people or things (***file***, ***queue***, ***rank***, ***string***)
Word history: Old English *rāw*

row[2] (roh)
verb to move using oars: *to* ***row*** *a boat* | *to learn how to* ***row***
Word history: Middle English; Old English *rōwan*

row / roe

Don't confuse **row** with **roe**, which is the mass of eggs inside a female fish. This word rhymes with *slow.*

rowed / road / rode

Don't confuse **rowed** with **road** or **rode.**

Cars, people and animals travel along a **road.**

Rode is the past tense of the verb **ride,** to sit on and control something.

row[3] (row)
noun **1** a noisy quarrel or fight (***argument***, ***bust-up***, ***disagreement***)
2 shouting and loud noise: *I can't sleep with that* ***row*** *going on.* (***commotion***, ***din***, ***hubbub***, ***racket***, ***uproar***)
verb **3** to quarrel loudly (***argue***, ***clash***, ***conflict***, ***disagree***, ***squabble***)

rows / rouse

Look up **rouse / rows.**

rowdy (row-dee)
adjective wild and noisy: *a bunch of* ***rowdy*** *kids*
Adjective forms: **rowdier**, **rowdiest**
Word building: **rowdily** *adverb* **rowdiness** *noun*

rowlock (rol-uhk)
noun a metal ring that supports an oar in a rowing boat
Word history: variant of *oarlock*, by association with *row*[2]

royal
adjective having to do with a king or queen: *a* ***royal*** *visit*
Word history: Middle English, from Old French, from Latin

royalist
noun a supporter of a monarchy, especially in times of rebellion or civil war
Word building: **royalist** *adjective*

royalty
noun **1** kings, queens and members of their families
2 a share of the profits made from their work, paid to an inventor, author or composer
Word history: Middle English, from Old French

rtf
noun → **rich text format**

rub
verb **1** to move back and forth while pressing down: *to **rub** polish on your shoes | I have blisters where my shoes **rubbed**.*
phrase **2 rub down,**
a to rub so as to smooth or clean: *to **rub down** a bench* (***plane***, ***polish***, ***sand***, ***smooth***)
b to rub or massage: *to **rub down** a footballer*
3 rub it in, to keep on reminding someone about their mistakes
4 rub off, to be passed on, especially as a result of close contact: *His love of music **rubbed off** on her.*
5 rub out, to clean off by rubbing: *to **rub out** a pencil mark*
6 rub (**up**) **the wrong way,** to annoy (***get on someone's nerves***, ***irritate***)
7 rub up, to polish (***buff***, ***burnish***, ***shine***)
8 rub up on, to refresh your memory about
Verb forms: I **rubbed**, I have **rubbed**, I am **rubbing**
Word history: Middle English

rubber
noun **1** elastic material made from the thick sap of some tropical trees, used to make things like car tyres, bouncing balls and elastic bands
2 a small piece of soft rubber used to rub out pencil marks (***eraser***)
Word building: **rubbery** *adjective*
Word history: *rub* + *-er*

rubber plant
noun a plant with oblong, shining, leathery leaves, often grown as a house plant

rubbish
noun **1** useless left-over material or matter (***debris***, ***garbage***, ***junk***, ***refuse***, ***trash***)
2 nonsense: *Don't talk **rubbish**.* (***bunkum***, ***mumbo jumbo***, ***piffle***, ***rot***)
verb **3** *Colloquial* to scoff at or make fun of
Word history: Middle English

rubbishy
adjective worthless

rubble
noun rough pieces of broken stone or brick
Word history: Middle English

rubella (rooh-bel-uh)
noun → **German measles**
Word history: from Neo-Latin word meaning 'reddish'

rubric
noun a title, heading, or direction in a book, etc., written or printed in red or otherwise made different from the rest of the text
Word history: from Latin word meaning 'red earth'

ruby
noun **1** a precious stone of a rich red colour
2 a rich red colour
Noun forms: The plural is **rubies**.
Word building: **ruby** *adjective*
Word history: Middle English, from Old French, from Latin word meaning 'red'

rucksack
noun Old-fashioned a backpack
Word history: German word literally meaning 'back sack'

ruction
noun Colloquial a noisy interruption, quarrel or row

rudder
noun a flat movable plate at the back of a boat or plane, used for steering
Word history: Old English *rōthor*

ruddy
adjective having a healthy red colour: *a **ruddy** face* (***bloodshot***, ***florid***, ***flushed***, ***inflamed***, ***rosy***)
Adjective forms: **ruddier**, **ruddiest**
Word history: Old English *rudig*, from *rudu* redness

rude
adjective **1** bad-mannered or impolite (***impudent***, ***insolent***, ***insulting***, ***vulgar***)
2 *Old-fashioned* rough: *a **rude** bush hut*
Word use: The opposite of definition 1 is **courteous**.
Word building: **rudeness** *noun*
Word history: Middle English, from Latin

rudiments
plural noun **1** the basic elements or first principles of a subject: *the **rudiments** of grammar*
2 the first slight appearance, or undeveloped form of something: *an embryo with the **rudiments** of limbs*
Word building: **rudimentary** *adjective*
Word history: from Latin word meaning 'beginning'

rue
verb to feel sorrow over or regret bitterly: *In later years he **rued** his decision not to complete his education.*
Word history: Old English *hrēowan*

ruffian
noun Old-fashioned someone who is rough or rowdy
Word history: earlier *rufian*, from French

ruffle
verb **1** to spoil the calmness or smoothness of: *Don't **ruffle** his temper. | Birds **ruffle** their feathers.* (***chafe***, ***coarsen***, ***rasp***, ***roughen***)
noun **2** a frill on a skirt, blouse or curtains
Word building: **ruffled** *adjective*
Word history: Middle English

rug
noun **1** a thick warm blanket
2 a small carpet
Word history: Scandinavian

Rugby football
noun (*also lower case*) **1** → **Rugby Union**
2 → **Rugby League**

Word history: invented at *Rugby* school, Warwickshire, England

Rugby League
noun (*also lower case*) one of the two forms of Rugby football, played by teams of thirteen players each, differing from Rugby Union in certain details of the rules and, formerly, in allowing professionalism

Word use: The short form is **League**.

Rugby Union
noun (*also lower case*) one of the two forms of Rugby football, played by teams of fifteen players each, differing from Rugby League in certain details of the rules and formerly being restricted to amateurs

Word use: The short form is **Union**.

rugged (rug-uhd)
adjective **1** rough or uneven: *a **rugged** mountain range*
2 tough and strong: *a **rugged** mountain climber* (***hardy***, ***sturdy***)

Word history: Middle English, from Scandinavian

ruin
verb **1** to wreck or destroy: *The rain **ruined** the harvest.* (***demolish***, ***wipe out***)
noun **2** complete destruction: *the **ruin** of my hopes*
3 ruins, the remains of fallen buildings: *the **ruins** of an ancient castle*

Word building: **ruination** *noun* **ruined** *adjective*
Word history: Middle English, from Old French, from Latin word meaning 'overthrow', 'ruin'

rule
noun **1** an instruction about behaviour, actions, etc.: *to play according to the **rules*** (***convention***, ***formula***, ***law***, ***precept***, ***regulation***)
verb **2** to govern, control or reign: *The king **ruled** his country wisely.*
3 to decide or direct: *The referee **ruled** that she was offside.*
4 to draw, using a ruler: *to **rule** a straight line*
phrase **5 as a rule**, usually: *We walk to school **as a rule**.*
6 rule off, to mark the end of by ruling a line beneath
7 rule out, to declare out of the question

Word history: Middle English, from Old French, from Latin word meaning 'straight stick', 'pattern'

ruler
noun **1** someone who rules or governs
2 a strip of wood or plastic with a straight edge, used for measuring and drawing straight lines

ruling
noun **1** a decision made by someone with authority
adjective **2** governing or in charge: *the **ruling** party*

rum
noun a strong alcoholic drink made from sugar cane

Word history: perhaps short for obsolete *rumbullion* from French *rebouillir* boil again

rumble
noun **1** a deep rolling sound: *the **rumble** of thunder*
2 *Colloquial* a gang fight
verb **3** to make a deep rolling sound: *Thunder **rumbled**.*
4 to move with such a sound: *The train **rumbled** along the track.*

Word history: Middle English; probably imitative

rumbustious (rum-bus-chuhs)
adjective rowdy or boisterous

Word history: probably from *robustious* from *robust*

ruminant (rooh-muh-nuhnt)
noun an animal that chews its cud, such as a cow, deer, sheep, etc.

Word history: Latin

ruminate
verb **1** to chew the cud, like a cow
2 to consider very carefully or meditate: *to **ruminate** on a problem*

Word history: Latin

rummage
verb to search by moving everything around: *to **rummage** through a bag to find a pen*

Word history: from French word meaning 'stow goods in hold of ship'

rummy
noun a card game in which you put cards into matching sets and ordered groups

rumour (rooh-muh)
noun **1** a story that spreads which may or may not be true (***gossip***, ***hearsay***, ***talk***, ***the whisper***)
verb **2** to spread or report by rumour: *It is **rumoured** that you are going overseas.*

Word use: You can also use **rumor**.
Word history: Middle English, from Old French, from Latin

rump
noun **1** the back part of a cow, horse, or similar animal
2 meat taken from this part: *grilled **rump***

Word history: Middle English, from Scandinavian

rumple
verb **1** to crush or mess up: *Please don't **rumple** the bed cover.*
noun **2** a crease or wrinkle

Word history: perhaps from Middle Dutch

rumpus
noun a loud noise and commotion

run
verb **1** to move quickly by foot
2 to go or make go: *The bus **runs** every half hour. | to **run** a car*
3 to pass quickly: *to **run** your fingers through your hair | to have ideas **running** through your mind*
4 to flow or fill with water: *to leave a tap **running** | to **run** a bath*
5 to extend or continue: *to **run** a net across the river | A crack **runs** down the wall.*
6 to conduct or manage: *to **run** a business* (***control***, ***direct***, ***govern***, ***supervise***)
noun **7** the action of running: *to go for a **run***
8 a trip or journey: *a **run** in the car*
9 a pen for animals: *a chicken **run***
10 a course for a particular service or activity, etc.: *a milk **run** | paper **run***
11 *Australian*, *NZ* a large area of grazing land; a rural property
12 a score in cricket: *Our team made 120 **runs**.*
13 a series of happenings: *a **run** of good luck*

phrase **14 in the long run**, in the end: *It turned out well* ***in the long run.***
15 on the run, escaped: *A dangerous prisoner is* ***on the run.***
16 run across, to meet or find unexpectedly (***come across***, ***encounter***)
17 run down,
a to slow down before stopping, as a clock or a watch
b of a car, driver, etc., to knock down and injure
c to criticise
18 run in,
a to run at a reduced load and speed for a period so that the machine gradually becomes ready for full operation: *to* ***run in*** *a car*
b *Colloquial* to arrest
19 run into,
a to meet unexpectedly (***bump into***, ***come across***, ***encounter***)
b to collide with
c to amount to: *an income* ***running into*** *hundreds of thousands*
20 run off,
a to go away quickly
b to produce copies of by a printing process
21 run off with, to steal (***knock off***, ***nick***, ***pilfer***, ***pinch***, ***take***)
22 run out,
a to use up completely: *We've* ***run out*** *of food.*
b to be all used up: *The food has* ***run out.***
23 run over,
a of a car, driver, etc., to knock down and injure
b to go beyond: *to* ***run over*** *a time limit*
24 run short,
a to become scarce or nearly used up
b to be used up almost completely: *We're* ***running short*** *of bread.*
25 run through,
a to practise: *to* ***run through*** *a speech*
b to stab with a sword
26 run up,
a to climb quickly (***clamber up***, ***scale***, ***shin***)
b to put up: *to* ***run up*** *a flag* | *to* ***run up*** *a sail*
c to collect or incur: *to* ***run up*** *a large bill*
d to make, especially quickly: *to* ***run up*** *a dress*

Verb forms: I **ran**, I have **run**, I am **running**
Word history: Old English *rinnan*

runaway
adjective **1** running out of control: *a* ***runaway*** *horse*
2 very easy: *a* ***runaway*** *win over the other team*
noun **3** someone who has escaped or run away

run-down
adjective **1** tired or weak because of not being healthy: *She has been looking very* ***run-down*** *since her operation.*
2 in poor condition; needing repair: *a* ***run-down*** *old house*
noun **3** a summary of information or the main points of a discussion, etc.: *I'll give you a* ***run-down*** *of what was said before you arrived.*

Word use: You can also use **rundown**.

rung[1]
verb past participle of **ring**[2]

rung[2]
noun one of the steps of a ladder

> **rung / wrung**
> Don't confuse **rung** with **wrung**. **Wrung** is the past form of the verb **wring**, to twist and squeeze something:
> *They wrung their hands in grief.*
> *I have wrung the water out of the washer.*

run-in
noun Colloquial a disagreement or argument

runner
noun **1** someone who runs well and competes in races
2 a messenger
3 something in or on which something else moves, as one of the smooth strips of wood on which a drawer slides
4 a type of sports shoe worn for jogging and some other types of exercise

Word use: You can also use **jogger** or **jogging shoe** for definition 4.

runner-up
noun someone who comes second in a contest

running
adjective **1** able to run or suitable for running: *a machine in* ***running*** *order* | ***running*** *shoes*
2 flowing: ***running*** *water*
3 in a row: *to be late three days* ***running***
noun **4** management or organisation: *the* ***running*** *of a shop*
phrase **5 out of the running**, with no chance of winning

running writing
noun writing where all the letters of a word are joined together

runny
adjective flowing or pouring out liquid: ***runny*** *custard* | *a* ***runny*** *nose* (***fluid***, ***liquid***, ***molten***, ***sloppy***)

Adjective forms: **runnier**, **runniest**

run-of-the-mill
adjective mediocre: *It's a very* ***run-of-the-mill*** *film.* (***average***, ***commonplace***, ***nondescript***, ***ordinary***, ***standard***)

runt
noun a person or animal that is the smallest in their group: *This piglet is the* ***runt*** *of the litter.*

Word history: Old English *hrunta* (in *Hrunting* name of sword in epic poem *Beowulf*)

runway
noun **1** a paved or cleared strip on which aeroplanes land and take off (***airstrip***)
2 → **catwalk**

rupture
verb to break or burst: *to* ***rupture*** *a friendship* | *Her appendix* ***ruptured.***

Word history: Latin

rural
adjective having to do with the countryside or farming: ***rural*** *land* (***agrarian***, ***country***, ***outback***, ***pastoral***, ***rustic***)

Word use: The opposite of this is **urban**.
Word history: Middle English, from Latin

ruse (roohz)
noun a dishonest trick or scheme (***con***, ***hoax***, ***swindle***)

Word history: Middle English, noun use of obsolete *ruse* to detour, from French

rush[1]
verb **1** to move in a great hurry: *The river* ***rushed*** *over the rocks.* (***dart***, ***dash***, ***hasten***, ***hurry***, ***speed***)
2 to do in a great hurry: *Don't* ***rush*** *your dinner.*
3 to hurry into doing something or making a decision: *Don't* ***rush*** *me.*
noun **4** a time of great hurry and movement: *the gold* ***rush*** | *a* ***rush*** *of wind*

Word history: Middle English, from Anglo-French, from Late Latin word meaning 'push back', Latin word meaning 'refuse'

rush[2]
noun a type of long grass that grows in wet ground along river banks

Word history: Old English *rysc(e)*

rush hour
noun → **peak hour**

rusk
noun **1** a piece of bread or cake crisped in the oven
2 a similar factory-made product, given especially to babies when teething

Word history: from Spanish or Portuguese word meaning 'twist of bread', literally 'screw'

russet
adjective having a reddish-brown colour

Word building: **russet** *noun*
Word history: Middle English, from Old French word meaning 'red', from Latin

rust
noun **1** the red or orange coating which forms on the surface of iron when exposed to air and water, consisting chiefly of ferric hydroxide and ferric oxide
2 any film or coating on metal due to oxidation
3 *Botany* any of the various plant diseases caused by fungi, in which the leaves and stems become spotted and turn a red to brown colour
4 a reddish-brown or orange colour
verb **5** to grow or become rusty

Word building: **rust** *adjective*
Word history: Middle English and Old English

rustic
adjective **1** having to do with the country as distinguished from the city (***agrarian***, ***country***, ***outback***, ***pastoral***, ***rural***)
2 simple and unsophisticated
noun **3** a country person, especially of simple tastes

Word history: late Middle English, from Latin

rustle
verb **1** to make a series of slight, soft sounds, such as leaves, papers, etc., rubbing gently together
2 to cause such sounds by moving something
3 to move so as to cause a rustling sound
4 to steal cattle, horses, etc.
noun **5** the sound made by anything that rustles (***murmur***, ***sigh***, ***undertone***, ***whisper***)
phrase **6 rustle up**, *Colloquial* to move, bring, get, etc., by energetic action: *to* ***rustle up*** *breakfast*

Word history: Middle English; Old English *hrūxlian* 'make a noise'

rut
noun **1** a groove made in the ground by the wheels of a car (***channel***, ***ditch***, ***furrow***, ***trench***)
phrase **2 in a rut**, doing the same thing all the time

Word history: origin uncertain; perhaps a variant of *route*

ruthless (roohth-luhs)
adjective showing no pity or mercy: *a* ***ruthless*** *tyrant* (***brutal***, ***callous***, ***cruel***)

Word use: The opposite of this is **compassionate** or **kind**.
Word building: **ruthlessness** *noun* **ruthlessly** *adverb*

rye (ruy)
noun **1** a grain which grows like wheat and is ground into flour
adjective **2** made from rye: ***rye*** *bread*

Word history: Middle English; Old English *ryge*

rye / wry
Don't confuse **rye** with **wry**. You make a **wry** face to show displeasure or disgust.

Ss

Sabbath
noun **1** the seventh day of the week, Saturday, which is the day of worship for Jews and for some Christians
2 the first day of the week, Sunday, which is the day of worship for most Christians

sabbatical (suh-bat-ik-uhl)
adjective **1** bringing a period of rest
noun **2** a year, term, or other period of freedom from teaching, given to a teacher in certain universities, etc., for study or travel

Word use: You can also use **sabbatical leave** for definition 2.

sable (say-buhl)
noun a weasel-like mammal of cold areas, valued for its dark brown fur

Word history: Middle English, from Old French, from Slavic

sabotage (sab-uh-tahzh)
noun damage done on purpose to stop somebody else being successful: *the* ***sabotage*** *of the enemy's arms factory*

Word building: **sabotage** *verb* **saboteur** *noun*
Word history: French *saboter*, to make a deliberate noise with sabots (wooden shoes) to drown out a speaker or performer. From there it extended to any work done badly, but in particular to the action of French workmen in destroying machines during a strike.

sabre (say-buh)
noun a heavy, slightly curved, one-edged sword

Word use: The US spelling is **saber**.
Word history: French, from German, from Hungarian

sac / sack
Don't confuse **sac** with **sack**, which can be a large bag made of strongly woven material or dismissal from your job.

sac (sak)
noun a bag-like structure in an animal or plant, often one containing fluid

Word history: Latin

saccharin (sak-uh-ruhn, sak-ruhn)
noun a sweet chemical used instead of sugar

Word building: **saccharine** *adjective*

sachet (sash-ay)
noun a small sealed packet or bag used to contain small servings of food, or shampoo for your hair, or perfumed herbs to keep cupboards smelling fresh

Word use: This comes from French which is why the 't' is not sounded.
Word history: French, from Latin

sack[1]
noun **1** a large bag made of strongly woven material
2 dismissal from your job: *I've been given the* ***sack****.*
phrase **3 hit the sack**, *Colloquial* to go to bed

Word building: **sack** *verb*
Word history: Old English *sacc*, from Latin word meaning 'bag', 'sackcloth', from Greek, from Hebrew

sack[2]
verb **1** to rob, or plunder, using violence after capture: *to* ***sack*** *a city*
noun **2** the violent robbing of a captured place: *the* ***sack*** *of Troy* (***looting***, ***pillage***)

Word history: French, from Italian

sacrament (sak-ruh-muhnt)
noun a Christian religious ceremony which is the outward show of a spiritual event or change: *the* ***sacrament*** *of baptism*

Word building: **sacramental** *adjective*
Word history: Middle English, from Latin word meaning 'oath', 'solemn engagement'

sacred (say-kruhd)
adjective **1** holy or worthy of religious respect: *a* ***sacred*** *city* (***blessed***, ***hallowed***)
2 having to do with religion: ***sacred*** *music*

Word history: Middle English, from Latin

sacrifice
verb **1** to give up at a loss to yourself: *He* ***sacrificed*** *his chance of winning to help his friend.*
2 to offer to a god, especially your life or your goods

Word building: **sacrifice** *noun* **sacrificial** *adjective*
Word history: Middle English, from French, from Latin

sacrilege (sak-ruh-lij)
noun disrespect shown to something sacred

Word building: **sacrilegious** *adjective*
Word history: Middle English, from Old French, from Latin

sacrosanct (sak-ruh-sangkt)
adjective especially sacred (***blessed***, ***hallowed***, ***holy***)

Word history: Latin

sad
adjective **1** sorrowful, or mournful: *to feel* ***sad*** (***glum***, ***low***, ***miserable***, ***unhappy***, ***upset***)
2 expressing or showing sorrow: ***sad*** *looks*
3 causing sorrow: *a* ***sad*** *disappointment*
4 shocking or deplorable: *a* ***sad*** *state of affairs*

Adjective forms: **sadder**, **saddest**
Word building: **sadden** *verb* **sadness** *noun*
Word history: Middle English; Old English *sæd*

saddle
noun **1** a seat for the rider of a horse
2 the seat on a bicycle
3 a piece of meat including part of the backbone and the ribs: *a **saddle** of mutton*
verb **4** to put a saddle on
5 to load or burden: *He **saddled** me with a nasty job.*
phrase **6 in the saddle**, in control of a situation

Word building: **saddler** *noun*
Word history: Old English *sadol*

saddlery
noun **1** saddles and all the other equipment used for riding horses
2 the work or shop of a saddler

Noun forms: The plural is **saddleries**.

sadism (sad-iz-uhm, sayd-iz-uhm)
noun **1** sexual satisfaction gained through inflicting physical pain and shame
2 any unhealthy enjoyment in causing mental or physical pain

Word building: **sadist** *noun* **sadist** *adjective* **sadistic** *adjective*
Word history: French *sadisme*, from the Marquis de Sade, 1740–1814, French soldier and novelist, notorious for the mixture of sex and cruelty in his books

safari (suh-fah-ree)
noun a long journey, usually for hunting wild animals

Noun forms: The plural is **safaris**.
Word history: Swahili, from Arabic

safe
adjective **1** free from danger or risk: *You are **safe** now.* (***immune***, ***protected***, ***right as rain***, ***secure***, ***sheltered***)
2 careful in avoiding danger: *a **safe** driver*
3 beyond or away from danger: *in a **safe** place*
noun **4** a steel or iron box that you keep money, jewels or valuable papers in

Word use: The opposite of definitions 1 to 3 is **dangerous** or **unsafe**.
Word building: **safety** *noun*
Word history: Middle English, from Old French, from Latin word meaning 'uninjured'

safeguard
noun **1** something that helps to protect or defend you (***defence***, ***protection***, ***security***, ***shield***)
2 a permit for safe travel through politically dangerous areas
verb **3** to protect, or guard: *to **safeguard** your economic interests* (***preserve***, ***save***)

Word history: Middle English, from Old French

safe sex
noun sexual practices in which precautions are taken to prevent the spread of disease, especially AIDS, through sexual intercourse

safety pin
noun **1** a pin bent back on itself to form a spring, with a guard to cover the point
2 a locking device on grenades, mines, etc., to keep them safe until they need to be used

safflower
noun a plant with large orange-red flowers which is grown for the oil obtained from its seeds

Word history: Dutch, from Old French, from Italian

saffron
noun an orange-coloured powder made from flowers; used to colour food

Word history: Middle English, from French, from Arabic

sag
verb **1** to bend down, especially in the middle: *The mattress **sagged** from the weight of his body.* (***collapse***, ***droop***, ***loll***, ***slump***)
2 to droop or hang loosely: *Her shoulders **sagged**.*

Verb forms: I **sagged**, I have **sagged**, I am **sagging**
Word building: **sag** *noun*
Word history: Middle English

saga (sah-guh)
noun **1** a long novel about the lives of a family or group of people
2 any long story

Word history: from Icelandic word meaning 'story', 'history'

sagacious (suh-gay-shuhs)
adjective having good judgement and understanding (***astute***, ***shrewd***)

Word building: **sagacity** *noun*
Word history: Latin

sage[1]
noun Old-fashioned **1** a very wise person (***philosopher***, ***scholar***)
adjective **2** wise, or prudent: ***sage** comments* (***level-headed***, ***reasonable***, ***sane***, ***sensible***, ***shrewd***)

Word history: Middle English, from Old French, from Latin word meaning 'wise'

sage[2]
noun a herb used in cooking

Word history: Middle English, from Old French, from Latin

sago (say-goh)
noun a starchy food made from the soft inside of the trunk of some palm trees

Word history: Malay

said
verb **1** past tense and past participle of **say**
adjective **2** named or mentioned before: *the **said** witness* | *the **said** amount*

sail
noun **1** a sheet of canvas or nylon which catches the wind and makes a boat move through the water
2 a voyage in a ship or boat
verb **3** to travel in a ship or boat
4 to move or be carried along on water: *Ships **sail** to Hobart from Melbourne.*
5 to move along quickly: *Clouds **sailed** overhead.* (***cruise***, ***float***, ***glide***, ***skim***)
6 to cause to sail: *He **sails** his boat on the harbour.*
phrase **7 set sail**, to start a voyage
8 under sail, with the sails set

Word history: Middle English

sail / sale
Don't confuse **sail** with **sale.** A **sale** is when something such as a house is sold. If you go to a **sale**, you can buy things at a specially low price.

sailboard
noun a light-weight surfboard with a mast and sail, on which the rider stands to control the sail (***windsurfer***)

sailor
noun a member of a ship's crew (***marine***, ***mariner***, ***seafarer***, ***seaman***, ***tar***)

saint
noun **1** someone who has been declared to be holy by the Christian church
2 a very good person
Word use: Definition 1 is shortened to 'St' and used as a title as in *St John.*
Word building: **sainthood** *noun*
saintly *adjective*
Word history: Middle English, from Old French, from Latin word meaning 'consecrated'

Saint Bernard (suhnt <u>bern</u>-uhd)
noun one of a breed of large dogs with a huge head, noted for their intelligence
Word history: named after the hospice of *St Bernard*, on the pass of the Great St Bernard in the Alps, between Switzerland and Italy, where the dogs are kept by the monks for rescuing travellers from the snow

sake[1] (sayk)
noun **1** purpose: *For the **sake** of peace, let's not argue.*
2 benefit or good: *For your own **sake**, do your best.*
Word history: Middle English; Old English *sacu* lawsuit, cause

sake[2] (<u>sah</u>-kee)
noun a Japanese alcoholic drink made from rice
Word history: Japanese

salacious (suh-<u>lay</u>-shuhs)
adjective **1** lustful or lecherous
2 obscene, or erotic: ***salacious** writing*
Word history: from Latin word meaning 'lust'

salad
noun **1** a dish of raw vegetables such as lettuce, tomatoes and celery
2 a dish of raw or cooked food served cold, usually with a dressing: *rice **salad** | fruit **salad***
Word history: Middle English, from Old French, from Old Provençal word meaning 'to salt', from Latin word meaning 'salt'

salamander (<u>sal</u>-uh-man-duh)
noun a type of amphibian with a tail, which lives in the water when very young, but later lives on land
Word history: Middle English, from Old French, from Latin, from Greek

salami (suh-<u>lah</u>-mee)
noun a kind of sausage with a strong, salty taste
Word history: Italian (plural), from Latin word meaning 'to salt'

salary
noun the regular pay you get for your job, especially for office work
Noun forms: The plural is **salaries**.
Word use: Compare this with **wage**.
Word history: Middle English, from Anglo-French, from Latin word originally meaning 'money allowed to soldiers for the purchase of salt'

sale
noun **1** the act of selling: *the **sale** of a house*
2 a special selling at a low price: *a **sale** of summer clothes | The end of year **sales** always attract crowds of eager buyers.*
phrase **3 for sale** or **on sale**, able to be bought: *Our house is **for sale**. | Her latest book is **on sale** now.*
Word history: Middle English; late Old English *sala*

sale / sail
Don't confuse **sale** with **sail**, which is the part of a boat which catches the wind and makes it move through the water.

salesperson
noun someone who sells things
Word building: **salesman** *masculine noun*
saleswoman *feminine noun*

The non-sexist word **salesperson** is often used to refer to a person who sells goods in a shop. The ending <u>-person</u> applies equally to both men and women. It is replacing the traditional names **salesman** and **saleswoman**. The endings <u>-man</u> and <u>-woman</u> are being avoided nowadays because they draw unnecessary attention to whether the person is a man or woman.
Another option is to use a different expression altogether, such as *shop assistant.*
For more information, look up **non-sexist language**.

sales tax
noun a tax added to the retail price of goods

salient (<u>say</u>-lee-uhnt)
adjective **1** standing out or easily seen: ***salient** features*
2 jutting or pointing outwards, as an angle does
Word building: **salience** *noun* **saliency** *noun*
Word history: from Latin word meaning 'leaping forth'

saline (<u>say</u>-luyn, <u>say</u>-leen)
adjective containing or tasting like salt: *a **saline** solution*
Word building: **salinity** *noun*
Word history: from Latin word meaning 'salt'

salinity (suh-<u>lin</u>-uh-tee)
noun **1** the degree of salt present in a substance
2 a level of salt rising to the surface of the earth which turns surface fresh water into brackish water and reduces the value of the soil for agriculture

saliva (suh-luy-vuh)
noun the watery liquid in your mouth, which helps you swallow and begin to digest food

Word building: **salivate** *verb*
Word history: Middle English, from Latin

salivary
adjective having to do with saliva: *the **salivary** glands*

sallow
adjective having a sickly yellowish colour: ***sallow** skin*

Word history: Old English *salo*

sally[1] (sal-ee)
noun **1** a sudden rushing forth, especially of soldiers upon an enemy (***attack**, **sortie***)
2 an excursion, or expedition
3 a lively or clever remark
verb **4** to rush or set out: *The soldiers **sallied** forth from the ruined tower. | to **sally** forth on a shopping spree*

Noun forms: The plural is **sallies**.
Verb forms: I **sallied**, I have **sallied**, I am **sallying**
Word history: French word meaning 'issuing forth', 'outrush', from Latin

sally[2] (sal-ee)
noun an Australian tree thought to look like the willow, especially one of the wattles and gum trees

Noun forms: The plural is **sallies**.

salmon (sam-uhn)
noun a sea and freshwater food fish with pink flesh, common in the northern Atlantic Ocean near the mouths of large rivers, or in lakes; introduced into Australia

Noun forms: The plural is **salmons** or **salmon**.
Word history: Middle English, from Anglo-French, from Latin

salmonella (sal-muh-nel-uh)
noun a type of bacterium causing sickness in humans and animals, by food poisoning

Word history: named after Daniel E *Salmon*, 1850–1914, US pathologist

salon (sal-on)
noun a fashionable shop: *a frock **salon** | a beauty **salon***

Word history: French, from Italian word meaning 'hall', from Germanic

saloon
noun a well-furnished bar room in a hotel

Word history: from French word meaning 'salon'

salsa
noun **1** a spicy sauce made from tomatoes and chilli, used in Mexican cooking
2 a type of dance music from Central America which blends lively rhythms with jazz and rock music

Word history: from American Spanish word meaning 'sauce'

salt
noun **1** white crystals obtained from sea water and used to flavour or preserve food
2 a chemical compound formed from an acid and an alkali
phrase **3 rub salt into the wound**, to make things worse than they already are
4 take with a grain of salt, to have little belief in
5 the salt of the earth, the best kind of people
6 worth your salt, so capable and efficient that you are thought to deserve your pay

Word use: You can also use the scientific name **sodium chloride** for definition 1.
Word building: **salty** *adjective* (**saltier**, **saltiest**)
Word history: Middle English; Old English *sealt*

saltbush
noun a plant which can grow in very dry parts of Australia and which horses and cattle eat

saltcellar
noun a container for salt, used at a meal table

Word history: Middle English, from Old French word meaning 'salt', from Latin

salt-lick
noun **1** a place to which wild animals go to lick salt found naturally there
2 *Agriculture* a block of salt, and sometimes minerals, etc., given to grazing animals to lick

salt pan
noun a small basin flooded by salt deposits, the remains of an evaporated salt lake which may have entirely disappeared

Word use: You can also use **salt flat**.

saltpetre (solt-pee-tuh)
noun white potassium nitrate, used in making things such as gunpowder

Word use: You can also use **nitre**.
Word history: Middle English, from Medieval Latin word meaning 'salt of the rock'

saltwater
adjective of or living in sea water: *a **saltwater** crocodile.*

salubrious (suh-looh-bree-uhs)
adjective healthy, or health-giving: ***salubrious** air | a **salubrious** climate*

Word building: **salubrity** *noun*
Word history: Latin

salutary (sal-yuh-tree)
adjective **1** health-giving or wholesome
2 beneficial or doing good: ***salutary** advice*

Word history: Latin, from *Salus*, Roman goddess of health and prosperity

salutation
noun **1** the act of greeting
2 something said, written, or done as a greeting

Word building: **salutatory** *adjective*

salute
verb **1** to greet
2 to raise your right hand to the side of your head as a mark of respect for: *The soldier **saluted** the Prime Minister.*

Word building: **salute** *noun*
Word history: Middle English, from Latin word meaning 'greet'

salvage (sal-vij)
noun the saving of a ship or its cargo from fire, shipwreck, or other damage

Word building: **salvage** *verb*
Word history: Medieval Latin, from Latin word meaning 'save'

> **salvage / selvage**
> Don't confuse **salvage** with **selvage**, which is the edge of fabric or wallpaper sewn or finished to stop it from fraying. Another way of spelling this is **selvedge**.

salvation
noun **1** the act of saving
2 the cause or means of saving: *The ladder against the wall of the burning house was his* ***salvation.***

Word history: Middle English, from Late Latin

salve (salv, sahv)
noun **1** a healing ointment
2 anything that soothes
verb **3** to soothe as if with salve: *to* ***salve*** *your conscience*

Word history: Middle English; Old English *sealf*

salver (sal-vuh)
noun a tray

Word history: Spanish, from Latin

salvo
noun the firing of guns a number of times, often as a salute

Noun forms: The plural is **salvo** or **salvoes**.
Word history: Italian, from Old French, from Latin word meaning 'be in good health'

same
adjective **1** being the very one just spoken of: *the very* ***same*** *day*
2 agreeing, or corresponding: *two boxes of the* ***same*** *size*
3 unchanged: *She has the* ***same*** *lovely smile she always had.*
pronoun **4** the same person or thing: *She's the* ***same*** *as ever.*
phrase **5 all the same,**
a even so: ***All the same,*** *I do think you should come.*
b unimportant: *Whether you come or not is* ***all the same*** *to me.*
6 just the same,
a in the same way: *She parts her hair* ***just the same*** *as she's always done.*
b even so

Word history: Middle English and Old French

Samoyed (sam-oyd)
noun a breed of Russian dogs, medium in size, with a coat of long, thick, white hair

Word history: from Russian word meaning 'self-eater'

sampan
noun a small Chinese boat, with one oar at the stern

Word history: from Chinese word meaning 'three boards'

sample
noun **1** a part or piece which shows what the whole is like: *a* ***sample*** *of her writing* (***example, specimen***)
verb **2** to test or judge by a sample: *to* ***sample*** *a cake*
adjective **3** acting as a specimen: *a* ***sample*** *packet*

Word history: Middle English

sampler
noun **1** someone who samples
2 a piece of embroidery showing a beginner's skill in needlework

Word history: Middle English, from Old French, from Latin word meaning 'example'

samurai (sam-yuh-ruy)
noun a Japanese warrior who lived in medieval times

Noun forms: The plural is **samurai**.
Word history: Japanese

sanatorium
noun a hospital for sick people who need to rest and live for a time in a healthy climate

Noun forms: The plural is **sanatoriums** or **sanatoria**.
Word use: You can also use **sanitarium**.
Word history: Neo-Latin, from Latin word meaning 'healed'

sanctify
verb to make holy or set apart as holy

Verb forms: I **sanctified**, I have **sanctified**, I am **sanctifying**
Word history: from Latin word meaning 'make holy'

sanctimonious (sangk-tuh-moh-nee-uhs)
adjective making a show of holiness

Word building: **sanctimony** *noun*

sanction
verb **1** to give approval or support to: *We are prepared to* ***sanction*** *its use.* (***advocate, approve, endorse, praise***)
noun **2** approval, or authorisation: *The plans now have the* ***sanction*** *of the council.*
3 strong feelings among people about what is right and what is wrong: *social* ***sanctions*** *against smoking and taking drugs*
4 action by a country, or countries towards another, designed to make it keep to certain laws: *trade* ***sanctions***

Word history: Latin

sanctity (sangk-tuh-tee)
noun holiness

Noun forms: The plural is **sanctities**.
Word history: Latin

sanctuary (sangk-chuh-ree, sangk-chooh-uh-ree)
noun **1** a holy place
2 a place of safety: *a bird* ***sanctuary*** (***asylum, haven, refuge, retreat, shelter***)
3 protection given to someone running away from ill-treatment

Noun forms: The plural is **sanctuaries**.
Word history: Middle English, from Latin

sanctum (sangk-tuhm)
noun **1** a sacred or holy place
2 an especially private place, or retreat: *the inner* ***sanctum***

Noun forms: The plural is **sanctums** or **sancta**.
Word history: from Latin (neuter) word meaning 'holy'

sand
noun **1** fine grains of rocks that have been broken up or worn away
verb **2** to smooth or polish with sand or sandpaper
Word building: **sandy** *adjective* (**sandier**, **sandiest**)
Word history: Middle English and Old English

sandal
noun a kind of shoe made of a flat sole fastened to the foot with straps
Word history: French

sandalwood
noun a sweet-smelling wood used for carving ornaments, or burnt as incense
Word history: *sandal* (from Medieval Latin, from Sanskrit) + *wood*

sandbank
noun a bank of sand in the sea or a river, formed by currents and often uncovered at low tide
Word use: You can also use **sandbar**.

sandblast
noun **1** a blast of air or steam loaded with sand, used to clean, grind, cut, or decorate hard surfaces
verb **2** to clean, etc., with a sandblast: *to **sandblast** an old stone building*

sandhill
noun a low hill of piled up sand

sandpaper
noun a strong paper coated with a layer of sand and used for smoothing rough surfaces
Word building: **sandpaper** *verb*

sandshoe
noun Australian, NZ a canvas shoe with a rubber sole, usually worn for sport

sandsoap
noun an abrasive soap for removing stains

sandstone
noun a type of rock formed by the consolidation of sand, the grains being held together by a cement of silica, lime, gypsum, or iron salts

sandwich
noun **1** two slices of bread with a filling between them
verb **2** to crowd or place between two other things: *We **sandwiched** the child between the two adults on the small seat.*
Word history: named after the 4th Earl of *Sandwich*, 1718–92

sane
adjective **1** having a healthy mind (***sound***, ***well-balanced***)
2 sensible or based on common sense: *a **sane** decision*
Word building: **sanity** *noun*
Word history: from Latin word meaning 'sound', 'healthy'

sang
verb past tense of **sing**

sangfroid (sõng-<u>frwah</u>)
noun coolness of mind (***calmness***, ***composure***)
Word history: from French word meaning 'cold blood'

sanguine (<u>sang</u>-gwuhn)
adjective **1** naturally cheerful and hopeful: *a **sanguine** temperament*
2 hopeful or confident: ***sanguine** expectations*
3 ruddy: *a **sanguine** complexion*
Word history: Middle English, from Latin word meaning 'blood'

sanitary
adjective having to do with cleanliness or care in preventing disease
Word use: The opposite of this is **unsanitary**.
Word history: from Latin word meaning 'health'

sanitation
noun the protection of public health using sanitary methods

sanitise
verb to make hygienic: *He **sanitised** the bench with disinfectant.*
Word use: You can also use **sanitize**.

sank
verb past tense of **sink**

sap[1]
noun the juice circulating in a plant
Word history: Middle English; Old English *sæp*

sap[2]
verb to weaken or destroy gradually: *Worry **sapped** her health.* (***drain***, ***tire***, ***wear down***)
Verb forms: I **sapped**, I have **sapped**, I am **sapping**
Word history: earlier *zappe*, from Italian word meaning 'spade', 'hoe'

sapling
noun a young tree

sapphire (<u>saf</u>-uy-uh)
noun **1** a clear blue gemstone
2 a deep blue colour
Word building: **sapphire** *adjective*
Word history: Latin, from Greek

saprophyte (<u>sap</u>-ruh-fuyt)
noun any vegetable organism that lives on dead organic matter, as certain fungi and bacteria
Word building: **saprophytic** (sap-ruh-<u>fit</u>-ik) *adjective*

sarcasm
noun the saying of harsh and bitter things, especially by using the trick of saying the opposite of what you really mean, so as to hurt someone's feelings
Word building: **sarcastic** *adjective*
Word history: Late Latin, from Late Greek word meaning 'sneer'

sarcophagus (sah-<u>kof</u>-uh-guhs)
noun a stone coffin
Noun forms: The plural is **sarcophagi** or **sarcophaguses**.
Word history: Latin, from Greek word originally meaning adjective 'flesh-eating'

sardine
noun a young sea-fish usually cooked in oil and tinned
Word history: Middle English, from Italian, from Latin word meaning 'type of fish'

sardonic
adjective sarcastic or mockingly scornful: *a **sardonic** remark*

Word history: French, from Latin, from Greek word meaning 'Sardinian', from a Sardinian plant (said to bring on convulsions resembling laughter)

sari (sah-ree)
noun a long piece of cotton or silk material worn by a Hindu woman, which she drapes around her body with one end over her head or shoulders

Word history: Hindustani

sarong (suh-rong)
noun a length of cloth wrapped around the body like a skirt and worn by both men and women in Malaysia and some Pacific islands

Word history: Malay

sarsaparilla (sahs-puh-ril-uh)
noun **1** a climbing or trailing plant with a root that is used in making medicine
2 an extract or other preparation made of it

Word history: Spanish

sartorial (sah-taw-ree-uhl)
adjective having to do with clothes or dress, usually a man's: ***sartorial** splendour*

Word history: from Latin word meaning 'of a tailor'

sash[1]
noun a long band of cloth worn round your waist or over your shoulder

Word history: from Arabic word meaning 'turban'

sash[2]
noun a window frame which slides up and down

Word history: Middle English; alteration of *chassis*

sashimi (sa-shee-mee)
noun a Japanese dish of fresh seafood fillets cut into bite-sized, oblong strips, and eaten raw with soy sauce and Japanese horseradish

sassafras (sas-uh-fras)
noun **1** an American tree known for the aromatic bark of its root, often used in making medicine and for flavouring
2 an Australian tree with sweet-smelling bark

Word history: Spanish

satanic (suh-tan-ik)
adjective **1** of Satan, the chief evil spirit, the great enemy of humankind
2 extremely wicked, as Satan is (***devilish**, **diabolical**, **evil***)

Word use: You can also use **satanical**.

satay (sah-tay)
noun cubes of spiced meat grilled on a skewer and covered with a hot peanut or soybean-based sauce

Word history: Malay

satchel
noun a school bag with straps, carried on your back

Word history: Middle English, from Old French word meaning 'sack', from Latin

sate (sayt)
verb **1** to satisfy to the full: *to **sate** any appetite or desire*
2 to fill uncomfortably full (***glut**, **surfeit***)

Word building: **sated** *adjective*
Word history: blend of obsolete *sade* satiate (Old English *sadian*) and Latin *sat* enough

satellite
noun **1** an object in space, such as a moon, which moves around a larger one, such as a planet
2 a machine sent into orbit around the earth or another planet to transmit information back to earth
adjective **3** produced by the use of a satellite in the transmission of signals: ***satellite** imaging* | ***satellite** broadcasting*

Word history: from Latin word meaning 'attendant', 'guard'

satellite TV
noun a television service in which a signal is transmitted via an artificial satellite to a satellite dish and then to the television set of a householder

satiate (say-shee-ayt)
verb **1** to supply with too much of something, so as to cause disgust or weariness (***cloy**, **pall**, **surfeit***)
2 to satisfy to the full (***glut**, **quench**, **sate***)

Word history: from Latin word meaning 'filled full'

satin
noun **1** a very smooth shiny cloth
adjective **2** made of satin
3 smooth and shiny: *a **satin** finish* (***glossy**, **lustrous**, **silky**, **sleek***)

Word history: Middle English, from Old French, from Italian, from Latin word meaning 'silk'

satire
noun **1** the use of sarcasm or humour to draw people's attention to something which is silly or bad
2 any poem, book or play which does this

Word building: **satiric** *adjective* **satirical** *adjective*
Word history: from Latin word meaning 'medley'

satirise (sat-uh-ruyz)
verb to make the object of satire: *to **satirise** an old story*

Word use: You can also use **satirize**.
Word building: **satirist** *noun*

satisfaction
noun **1** the act of satisfying, or the condition of being satisfied
2 the making good of a wrong

Word use: The opposite of definition 1 is **dissatisfaction**.
Word history: Middle English, from Latin

satisfactory
adjective fulfilling all demands or requirements: *to give a **satisfactory** answer* (***adequate**, **decent**, **sufficient***)

satisfy
verb **1** to please or make happy: *to **satisfy** an employer* (***appeal to**, **meet the demands of***)
2 to bring to an end by supplying what is needed: *to **satisfy** someone's hunger*
3 to convince: *to **satisfy** yourself that a job has been done*

Verb forms: I **satisfied**, I have **satisfied**, I am **satisfying**
Word history: Middle English, from Old French, from Latin word meaning 'do enough'

saturate
verb **1** to soak thoroughly: *The rain **saturated** the ground.*
2 to fill or load completely: *The market is **saturated** with goods.*
3 *Chemistry* to cause to unite with the greatest possible amount of another substance, through solution, chemical combination, or something like this: *to **saturate** a fat*

Word building: **saturated** *adjective* **saturable** *adjective* **saturation** *noun*
Word history: from Latin word meaning 'satisfied', 'saturated'

Saturday
noun the seventh day of the week, following Friday

Word history: Middle English; Old English *Sæterdæg*, *Sætern(es)dæg* meaning 'day of Saturn'

saturnine (sat-uh-nuyn)
adjective having an inactive, gloomy, or sullen nature

Word history: *Saturn* + *-ine*, the planet which is supposed to give a gloomy nature to those born under its sign

satyr (sat-uh, say-tuh)
noun a god, pictured in old stories as part goat and part human

Word history: Middle English, from Latin, from Greek

sauce
noun **1** a liquid put on food as a flavouring
2 *Colloquial* rudeness or impertinence

Word history: Middle English, from Old French, from Vulgar Latin word meaning 'salted'

sauce / source

Don't confuse **sauce** with **source**. The **source** of something is the place, thing or person from which it comes:

The Murray River has its source in the Snowy Mountains.

Which book was the source of your information?

My mother is the source of that rumour.

saucepan
noun a cooking pot with a lid and a long handle

saucer
noun a small, round plate used under a cup

Word history: Middle English, from Old French word meaning 'vessel for holding sauce'

saucy (saw-see)
adjective *Old-fashioned* cheeky and suggestive of sexuality: *a **saucy** remark | a **saucy** grin | a **saucy** novel* (***bold***, ***brazen***, ***forward***)

Adjective forms: **saucier**, **sauciest**

sauerkraut (sow-uh-krowt)
noun cabbage cut fine, salted, and allowed to ferment until sour

Word history: German

sauna (saw-nuh)
noun a room with a kind of steam bath in which you become clean by perspiring

Word history: Finnish

saunter (sawn-tuh)
verb to walk in an unhurried way (***amble***, ***stroll***)

Word building: **saunter** *noun*
Word history: late Middle English

sausage
noun finely minced meat packed into a thin skin

Word history: Middle English, from Old Northern French, from Late Latin, from Latin word meaning 'salted'

sausage roll
noun a roll of baked pastry filled with sausage meat

sauté (soh-tay)
verb to brown or cook gently in a pan with a little fat

Verb forms: I **sautéed**, I have **sautéed**, I am **sautéing**
Word use: There is a accent over the 'e' because this was originally a French word.
Word history: French word meaning 'tossed', from Latin

sauterne (soh-tern, suh-tern)
noun a rich, sweet, white table wine

Word history: named after the district *Sauternes*, near Bordeaux, where it is made

savage
adjective **1** untamed or wild
2 fierce or cruel: ***savage** punishment* (***barbaric***, ***brutal***, ***callous***, ***ruthless***)
noun **3** an uncivilised person who has no experience of the modern world
4 a rude or cruel person

Word building: **savagery** *noun*
Word history: Middle English, from Old French, from Late Latin word meaning 'of the woods', 'wild'

savanna (suh-van-uh)
noun a grassland region with scattered trees, usually in subtropical or tropical regions

Word use: You can also use **savannah**.
Word history: Spanish, from Carib

save[1]
verb **1** to rescue from danger or harm (***preserve***, ***protect***, ***safeguard***, ***salvage***)
2 to avoid spending or using up: *to **save** $100 | to **save** electricity* (***bank***, ***hoard***, ***stockpile***, ***store***, ***stow away***)
phrase **3 save up**, to put aside money: *to **save up** for a bicycle*

Word history: Middle English, from Old French, from Late Latin

save[2]
preposition except, or but: *Nothing **save** a miracle could help her now.*

Word history: Middle English; variant of *safe* adjective, an obsolete sense of reserving, making exception of

saveloy (<u>sav</u>-uh-loy)
noun a frankfurt

Word history: French, from Italian word meaning 'brain', from Latin

saving
adjective **1** rescuing, or preserving
2 making acceptable in spite of other bad qualities; redeeming: *He's a coward, but he has a **saving** sense of humour.*
3 making an exception: *a **saving** clause*
noun **4** a lessening of expense: *a **saving** of 10 per cent*
5 something that is saved
6 savings, sums of money saved and put aside
preposition **7** except: *Everyone came, **saving** Rui.*
8 with all due respect to or for: ***saving** your presence*
conjunction **9** except, or but

saviour (<u>sayv</u>-yuh)
noun someone who saves or rescues

Word use: You can also use **savior**.
Word history: Middle English, from Old French, from Late Latin

savoir-faire (sav-wah-<u>fair</u>, suv-wah-<u>fair</u>)
noun knowledge of what to do in any situation

Word history: French word literally meaning 'to know how to act'

savour (<u>say</u>-vuh)
verb to taste or smell, especially with pleasure

Word use: You can also use **savor**.
Word building: **savour** *noun*
Word history: Middle English, from Old French, from Latin word meaning 'taste', 'savour'

savoury (<u>say</u>-vuh-ree)
adjective **1** having a delicious taste or smell (***piquant***, ***pungent***, ***sharp***, ***spicy***, ***tasty***)
2 salty or sharp-tasting rather than sweet: *a **savoury** filling*
noun **3** a salty or unsweet bite-sized piece of food on a small biscuit or piece of toast

Word use: You can also use **savory**.
Noun forms: The plural is **savouries**.
Word history: Middle English, from Old French

savvy (<u>sav</u>-ee)
verb Colloquial to know, or understand

Verb forms: I **savvied**, I have **savvied**, I am **savvying**
Word history: Spanish

saw[1]
noun **1** a cutting tool with sharp teeth on a thin blade
verb **2** to cut with a saw
3 to cut as a saw does: *He **sawed** at the meat with his blunt old knife.*

Verb forms: I **sawed**, I have **sawn** or I have **sawed**, I am **sawing**
Word history: Old English *saga, sagu*

saw[2]
verb past tense of **see**[1]

saw / sore / soar
Don't confuse **saw** with **sore** or **soar**.
If your leg is **sore**, it hurts or feels painful. If you feel **sore** about something, you are annoyed or offended.
To **soar** is to fly upwards, or to rise to a great height:
Jets soar into the air.
House prices are about to soar.

saxophone
noun a wind instrument with a curved brass body

Word building: **saxophonist** *noun*

say
verb **1** to speak or utter
2 to express in words: *to **say** that you are happy*
3 to assert or declare: *They **said** he would go.*
noun **4** a turn to speak: *You can have your **say** now.*

Verb forms: I **said**, I have **said**, I am **saying**
Word history: Middle English; Old English *secgan*

saying
noun **1** something wise that's often said (***adage***, ***epigram***, ***maxim***, ***motto***, ***proverb***)
phrase **2 go without saying**, to be very obvious

S-bend
noun an S-shaped bend, as in a pipe or road

scab
noun **1** the crust which forms over a sore when it is healing
2 someone who goes on working during a strike

Word use: You can also use **blackleg** for definition 2.
Word building: **scab** *verb* (**scabbed**, **scabbing**)
Word history: Middle English, from Scandinavian

scabbard (<u>skab</u>-uhd)
noun a holder for the blade of a sword or dagger

Word history: Middle English, from Anglo-French; probably of Germanic origin

scabies (<u>skay</u>-beez)
noun an infectious skin disease in sheep and cattle, and in humans, caused by parasitic mites

Word history: from Latin word meaning 'roughness', 'the itch'

scaffold
noun **1** a framework to stand on when you are doing work on a building
2 a raised platform on which criminals are executed

Word use: You can also use **scaffolding**.
Word history: Middle English, from Old French, from Late Latin

scald (skawld)
verb **1** to burn with hot liquid or steam
2 to heat to almost boiling point: *to **scald** milk*
noun **3** a burn caused by hot liquid or steam

Word history: Middle English, from Old Northern French word meaning 'burn', 'scald', from Late Latin word meaning 'wash in hot water'

scale[1]
noun **1** one of the thin, flat, fingernail-like plates which form the covering of fish and some other animals

2 any thin flaky coating or flake that peels off from a surface
verb **3** to remove scale or scales from

Word building: **scaly** *adjective* (**scalier**, **scaliest**)
Word history: Middle English, from Old French; of Germanic origin

scale²
noun **1** a set of marks along a line for measuring: *the* ***scale*** *of a thermometer*
2 a marked line on a map showing how to measure distances
3 size, compared to something else: *Our new house is on a larger* ***scale*** *than our old one.*
4 a series of musical notes going up or down at fixed intervals, usually one that begins on a particular note: *the* ***scale*** *of C major*
verb **5** to climb: *to* ***scale*** *a mountain | to* ***scale*** *a wall* (***ascend***, ***mount***, ***shin up***)
6 to arrange according to a scale: *to* ***scale*** *exam marks*

Word history: Middle English, from Latin word meaning 'staircase', 'ladder'

scalene (skay-leen)
adjective with three unequal sides: *a* ***scalene*** *triangle*

Word history: Late Latin, from Greek word meaning 'unequal'

scales
plural noun a weighing machine

Word history: Middle English, from Scandinavian

scallop (skol-uhp)
noun **1** a type of shellfish which has two wavy shells and is good to eat
2 one of the regular curves along the edge of pastry, a garment, or cloth

Word building: **scallop** *verb* (**scalloped**, **scalloping**)
Word history: Middle English, from Old French word meaning 'shell'; of Germanic origin

scallywag (skal-ee-wag)
noun a scamp, or rascal, often used playfully of children

Word use: You can also use **scalawag** or **scallawag**.

scalp
noun **1** the skin of your head where the hair grows
verb **2** to cut the scalp from

Word history: Middle English, from Scandinavian

scalpel
noun a small, very sharp knife used by surgeons in operations

Word history: Latin

scam
noun Colloquial a trick, especially one involving money

scamp
noun Old-fashioned a rascal or mischievous person

Word history: special use of obsolete *scamp*, verb, 'go (on highways)', apparently from Dutch, from Old French word meaning 'decamp'

scamper
verb to run or hurry away quickly (***dart***, ***scoot***, ***scurry***, ***speed***)

Word building: **scamper** *noun*
Word history: obsolete *scamp*, verb, go + *-er*

scan
verb **1** to look at closely (***examine***, ***inspect***, ***look over***, ***survey***)
2 to look over quickly: *to* ***scan*** *a page*
3 to go over with a radar beam: *They* ***scanned*** *the area for the lost boat.*
4 *Computers* to use a scanner to input text or graphics
5 *Medicine* to examine (a part of the body) using a moving detector to produce an image of that body part, sometimes after an injection of a radioactive substance which can enhance the image

Verb forms: I **scanned**, I have **scanned**, I am **scanning**
Word building: **scan** *noun*
Word history: Middle English, from Late Latin word meaning 'scan verse', from Latin word meaning 'climb'

scandal
noun **1** talk or gossip that harms someone's reputation
2 a disgraceful or dreadful happening

Word building: **scandalous** *adjective*
Word history: Late Latin word meaning 'cause of offence', from Greek word meaning 'trap'

scandalise
verb to shock or horrify by something considered disgraceful

Word use: You can also use **scandalize**.

scanner
noun **1** *Medicine* a machine used to scan (definition 5) a part of the body
2 *Computers* a device used to scan an image or text and convert it into digital form for storage, etc., on a computer

Word use: You can also use **optical scanner**.

scant
adjective **1** hardly enough: *There is* ***scant*** *time in which to finish.*
2 barely as much as there's supposed to be: *He lingered over his* ***scant*** *meal.* (***meagre***, ***measly***, ***paltry***, ***skimpy***)

Word history: Middle English, from Scandinavian

scanty
adjective **1** barely enough: *a* ***scanty*** *supply*
2 brief: ***scanty*** *clothing |* ***scanty*** *information*

Adjective forms: **scantier**, **scantiest**

scapegoat
noun someone who is made to take the blame for others

Word history: *(e)scape*, verb + *goat*; originally with reference to the goat, in ancient Jewish ritual, sent into the wilderness after the chief priest on the Day of Atonement had symbolically laid the sins of the people upon it (in the Bible, look up Leviticus 16)

scapula (skap-yuh-luh)
noun either of two flat, triangular bones, each forming the back part of a shoulder

Noun forms: The plural is **scapulas** or **scapulae** (skap-yuh-lee).
Word use: A more common name for this is **shoulderblade**.
Word history: from Neo-Latin word meaning 'shoulderblade' (in Latin only in plural)

scar
noun **1** a mark left on your skin by a healed sore or burn
verb **2** to leave a scar: *to **scar** for life*

Verb forms: it **scarred**, it has **scarred**, it is **scarring**
Word history: Middle English, from Old French, from Late Latin word meaning 'scab', from Greek word literally meaning 'hearth'

scarab (<u>ska</u>-ruhb)
noun **1** a type of beetle, regarded as sacred by the ancient Egyptians
2 the image of this beetle, much used in jewellery, etc.

Word history: Latin

scarce
adjective **1** not enough to fill the need
2 rarely seen or found: *Leather-covered books are **scarce** now.* (***infrequent***, ***occasional***, ***rare***, ***unusual***)

Word building: **scarcity** *noun* (*plural* **scarcities**)
Word history: Middle English, from Old Northern French word meaning 'scanty', 'stingy', from Late Latin

scarcely
adverb barely or not quite

Like *hardly*, **scarcely** is an adverb that has negative meaning, so it should not be used after the word *without* (which already has a negative meaning).
For example:
We can fix it <u>with</u> <u>scarcely</u> any effort. QHFGS
We can fix it <u>without</u> <u>scarcely</u> any effort. VQNMF
Note that *scarcely* is one of the few adverbs that require you to change around the word order when a verb follows it:
Scarcely <u>had I</u> gone when … QHFGS
Scarcely <u>I had</u> gone when … VQNMF

scare
verb **1** to frighten (***alarm***, ***petrify***, ***shock***, ***terrify***)
2 to become frightened: *I don't **scare** easily.*
noun **3** a sudden fright or alarm, sometimes for no reason
4 widespread fear or worry: *a **scare** about pollution in the sea*

Word building: **scary** *adjective* (**scarier**, **scariest**)
Word history: Middle English, from Scandinavian

scarecrow
noun a figure dressed in old clothes, put up to frighten birds away from crops

scarf
noun a piece of material worn around your neck or head for warmth or ornament

Noun forms: The plural is **scarfs** or **scarves**.
Word history: perhaps from Old Northern French word meaning 'sash', 'sling for arm', probably variant of Old French word meaning 'a pilgrim's bag hung round the neck'

scarify (<u>ska</u>-ruh-fuy, <u>skair</u>-ruh-fuy)
verb **1** to make scratches or small cuts on the surface of
2 to hurt by severe criticism
3 to loosen with a type of cultivator: *to **scarify** soil*

Verb forms: it **scarified**, it has **scarified**, it is **scarifying**
Word building: **scarification** *noun*
Word history: late Middle English, from Late Latin, from Greek word meaning 'scratch an outline'

scarlet
adjective of a bright red colour (***crimson***, ***rosy***, ***ruby***)

Word building: **scarlet** *noun*
Word history: Middle English, from Old French, perhaps from Persian word meaning 'a rich cloth'

scarlet fever
noun a disease that spreads easily, causing a high fever and a scarlet rash

scat
verb Colloquial to go off hastily

Verb forms: it **scatted**, it has **scatted**, it is **scatting**
Word use: This is usually used as a command.

scathing (<u>skay</u>-dhing)
adjective meant to hurt your feelings by criticising you: *a **scathing** remark*

Word history: Middle English, from Scandinavian word meaning 'harm'

scatter
verb **1** to throw loosely about (***dissipate***, ***distribute***, ***spread***, ***strew***)
2 to drive off or go in different directions: *The runaway car **scattered** the crowd. | The crowd **scattered**.*

Word building: **scatter** *noun*
Word history: Middle English

scattergun
noun **1** a gun, such as a shotgun, which does not shoot a single missile but many smaller missiles in a scatter
phrase **2 scattergun approach**, an approach to a problem, argument, etc., which relies on a broad range of counter measures that are not necessarily well thought out

scattering
noun a small spread-out number or quantity: *a **scattering** of people living so far from the city*

scavenge (<u>skav</u>-uhnj)
verb to search for, or amongst rubbish or other disused material to find something you can take and use: *to **scavenge** driftwood from the beach | to **scavenge** for clothing at the tip*

scavenger
noun **1** someone who searches in rubbish for useful things
2 an animal which eats flesh from dead animals

scenario (suh-<u>nah</u>-ree-oh, suh-<u>nair</u>-ree-oh)
noun **1** an outline of a dramatic work, giving details about scenes, characters, situations, etc.
2 an outline or script of a film, giving the action in the order in which it takes place, description of scenes and characters, etc.
3 an outline of a general situation or plan

Noun forms: The plural is **scenarios**.
Word history: Italian, from Late Latin word meaning 'having to do with stage scenes'

scene (seen)
noun **1** a place where something happens: *the **scene** of the crime* (***location***, ***setting***)
2 a view or a picture of a view (***landscape***, ***outlook***, ***prospect***, ***vista***)
3 one of the divisions of a play
4 a real or imaginary event, especially one described in writing
5 a noisy outburst of excitement or anger in front of other people
Word history: Latin, from Greek word meaning 'tent', 'stage'

scene / seen
Don't confuse **scene** with **seen**. **Seen** is a past form of the verb **see**, to take things in with your eyes or mind. It is the past participle:
Have you seen the circus?
He hasn't seen the joke yet.

scenery (seen-uh-ree)
noun **1** the natural features of a place: *beautiful coastal **scenery***
2 paintings, hangings and structures put on a stage to show the place where a play is meant to take place
Noun forms: The plural is **sceneries**.

scenic (seen-ik)
adjective having beautiful scenery: *a **scenic** journey through the woods*

scent (sent)
noun **1** a pleasant smell: *the **scent** of flowers* (***aroma***, ***bouquet***, ***fragrance***, ***odour***)
2 the particular smell of an animal or person which enables other animals to follow them
3 perfume: *a bottle of **scent***
verb **4** to become aware of by smelling, or any other way: *The hounds **scented** a fox. | to **scent** trouble*
5 to put perfume on or into
Word building: **scented** *adjective*
Word history: Middle English, from French word meaning 'perceive', from Latin

scent / sent / cent
Don't confuse **scent** with **sent** or **cent**.
Sent is the past form of the verb **send**:
He sent me this postcard.
A **cent** is one-hundredth of a dollar.

sceptic (skep-tik)
noun someone who doesn't believe things that most other people accept without question
Word building: **scepticism** *noun*
Word history: Latin word meaning 'inquiring', 'reflective', from Greek

sceptic / septic
Don't confuse **sceptic** with **septic**. When something is **septic** it is infected with germs, as in *a septic wound.*

sceptical
adjective having or showing doubt: *a **sceptical** attitude to falling in love | a **sceptical** smile*

sceptre (sep-tuh)
noun a rod carried by a king, queen or emperor as a symbol of royal or imperial power
Word history: Middle English, from Old French, from Latin, from Greek

schedule (shed-zhoohl, sked-joohl)
noun **1** a plan which shows you how a project is to be done and sets out a timetable for it
2 a list of things to be done
Word building: **schedule** *verb*
Word history: Late Latin, from Latin word meaning 'leaf of paper', 'probably from Latin' word meaning 'split'

scheme (skeem)
noun **1** a plan of action: *a **scheme** for raising money*
2 a secret plot: *a **scheme** to kidnap the president* (***conspiracy***, ***intrigue***, ***ruse***, ***stratagem***, ***trick***)
Word building: **scheme** *verb*
Word history: Medieval Latin, from Greek

scheming
adjective crafty or cunning

schism (skiz-uhm, siz-uhm)
noun a division into opposed parties, especially within a church
Word building: **schismatic** *adjective*
Word history: Latin, from Greek

schizophrenia (skit-suh-free-nee-uh)
noun a disorder of a person's mind in which they experience disconnected thought, behaviour and functioning of their personality, withdrawal from reality, emotional dullness and distortion of reality
Word use: You will sometimes find **split personality** used but its use is not generally approved.
Word building: **schizophrenic** *noun* **schizophrenic** *adjective*
Word history: Greek *schizo-*, meaning 'split', and *phrēn*, meaning 'mind', with the suffix *-ia*, used in the names of certain diseases

schizophrenic (skit-suh-fren-ik, skit-suh-free-nik)
noun **1** a person who is suffering from schizophrenia
adjective **2** having to do with schizophrenia
3 suffering from schizophrenia
4 (in popular but erroneous use) suffering from multiple personality disorder
5 *Colloquial* having an unpredictable or extremely changeable personality
6 *Colloquial* unable to choose between two courses of action
Word use: You can also use **schizophrene** for definition 1.

schnapper (snap-uh)
noun → **snapper**

schnapps (shnaps)
noun a type of gin
Word history: from German word meaning 'dram', 'nip'

scholar (<u>skol</u>-uh)
noun **1** a student or pupil
2 a learned person: *a Latin* ***scholar*** (***intellectual***, ***philosopher***, ***sage***)

Word building: **scholarly** *adjective*
Word history: Late Latin

scholarship (<u>skol</u>-uh-ship)
noun **1** a sum of money won by a student which helps to pay school or university fees
2 knowledge gained by study: *He is a man of great* ***scholarship***.

scholastic (skuh-<u>las</u>-tik)
adjective having to do with schools, students, or education: ***scholastic*** *achievements*

Word history: Latin, from Greek word meaning 'studious', 'learned'

school[1]
noun **1** a place where children are taught
2 the children who go to a school: *The* ***school*** *went to the zoo today.*
3 any place or time of teaching: *a dancing* ***school*** | *a tennis* ***school***
verb **4** to train or teach: *to* ***school*** *a horse in showjumping*

Word history: Old English *scōl*, from Latin, from Greek word originally meaning 'leisure', hence employment of 'leisure', 'study'

school[2]
noun a large number of fish, whales, or dolphins swimming together

Word history: Middle English, from Dutch word meaning 'troop', 'multitude'

schooling
noun education or training

schooner (<u>skooh</u>-nuh)
noun **1** a sailing ship with two or more masts
2 *Australian*, *NZ* a large beer glass

Word history: origin uncertain; said to be from New England (US) dialect verb *scoon* skim along

sciatica (suy-<u>at</u>-ik-uh)
noun pain and tenderness at some points of the sciatic nerve, which extends from the hip down the back of the thigh

Word history: late Middle English, from Medieval Latin, properly feminine of adjective word meaning 'sciatic'

science
noun **1** the study of the physical world in an organised way, by measuring, testing and experimenting
2 knowledge gained in this way
3 a particular branch of this study: *the* ***science*** *of botany*

Word history: Middle English, from Old French, from Latin word meaning 'knowledge'

science fiction
noun a form of fiction which uses scientific knowledge and theory in its plot, setting, etc., in an imaginative way

scientific (suy-uhn-<u>tif</u>-ik)
adjective **1** having to do with science or the sciences: ***scientific*** *studies*
2 in accordance with the principles of exact science: *a* ***scientific*** *method*
3 systematic or accurate

Word history: Late Latin

scientific method
noun a method of research in which you identify a problem, collect the relevant data, formulate a hypothesis on the basis of this data, and, finally, test the hypothesis to prove if it is valid

scientist (<u>suy</u>-uhnt-uhst)
noun someone skilled in or working in the field of science, especially physical or natural science

scimitar (<u>sim</u>-uh-tuh)
noun a curved, single-edged sword of Middle Eastern origin

Word use: You can also use **scimiter**.
Word history: Italian

scintillate (<u>sin</u>-tuh-layt)
verb **1** to flash, or give out sparks
2 to twinkle, as the stars do
3 to be bright and amusing in conversation

Word history: Latin

scion (<u>suy</u>-uhn)
noun **1** a descendant or young member of a family, especially a noble or ancient one
2 a shoot, especially one cut for grafting or planting

Word history: Middle English, from Old French, from Latin

scissors (<u>siz</u>-uhz)
plural noun a cutting instrument made of two blades joined together: *My* ***scissors*** *are blunt.*

Word use: The expression *a pair of scissors* is often used.
Word history: Middle English, from Old French, from Late Latin, from Latin word meaning 'cut', 'slain'

sclerophyll (<u>skler</u>-uh-fil, <u>sklear</u>-uh-fil)
noun a type of plant, usually found in low rainfall areas, having tough leaves which help to reduce water loss

sclerophyll forest
noun a forest comprising sclerophyll plants

sclerosis (skluh-<u>roh</u>-suhs)
noun *Medicine* a hardening of a tissue or part

Noun forms: The plural is **scleroses** (skluh-<u>roh</u>-seez).
Word history: Medieval Latin, from Greek word meaning 'hardening'

scoff[1]
verb to mock or jeer

Word history: Middle English, from Scandinavian

scoff[2]
verb *Colloquial* to eat greedily and quickly

Word history: Afrikaans word meaning 'meal', from Dutch word meaning 'quarter (of the day)'

scold
verb to find fault with: *She* ***scolded*** *me for being careless.* (***admonish***, ***rebuke***, ***reprimand***, ***rouse on***, ***tick off***)

Word history: Middle English, from Scandinavian

scoliosis (skol-ee-oh-suhs)
noun abnormal lateral curvature of the spine, more common in females than males, and developing at any age but often accelerating in puberty in periods of growth spurts

scone (skon)
noun a small plain cake made from dough, often split open and spread with butter or jam and cream

Word history: from Middle Dutch word meaning 'fine bread'

scoop
noun **1** a small spoon-like ladle: *a flour* ***scoop***
2 the bucket of a dredge
3 a hollow made or an amount taken by a scoop
4 a news story published or broadcast before any other newspaper or radio or television station

Word building: **scoop** *verb*
Word history: Middle English, from Middle Low German or Middle Dutch word meaning 'container for drawing or bailing water'

scoot
verb Colloquial to go or move quickly (***dart***, ***hurry***, ***scamper***, ***scurry***, ***speed***)

Word history: of Scandinavian origin

scooter
noun a child's toy with two wheels, one in front of the other, and a board between them on which you stand

scope
noun **1** range or reach: *This comes within the* ***scope*** *of my work.*
2 space or room: ***scope*** *for improvement*

Word history: Italian, from Greek word meaning 'mark', 'aim'

scorch
verb **1** to burn slightly, often with an iron
2 to cause to dry up with heat: *The sun* ***scorched*** *the desert.*
noun **3** a burn on the surface

Word history: Scandinavian

score
noun **1** the total of points made by a competitor or team in a game
2 a scratch, especially a deep one in wood or metal (***cut***, ***gash***, ***incision***, ***notch***, ***slit***)
3 *Old-fashioned* a set of twenty: *to live three* ***score*** *years*
4 a written or printed piece of music with all parts included and written one under the other
verb **5** to make (a point, goal, etc.) in a game: *He* ***scored*** *all his team's points.*
6 to compose the music for, or write for orchestra: *to* ***score*** *a film* | *to* ***score*** *music suited to that period of time*
7 to make scratches, cuts, or lines in or on (***cut***, ***nick***)
8 *Colloquial* to gain or win: *to* ***score*** *millions of birthday presents* | *to* ***score*** *a big success*
phrase **9 score off**, to gain an advantage over: *to* ***score off*** *someone's misfortune*

Word history: Middle English; late Old English *scoru*, from Scandinavian

scorn
noun an open show of disgust or contempt (***derision***, ***disdain***, ***disrespect***)

Word building: **scorn** *verb* **scornful** *adjective*
Word history: Middle English, from Old French word meaning 'mockery', 'derision'; of Germanic origin

scorpion
noun a spider-like invertebrate with a long narrow tail that ends in a venomous stinger

Word history: Middle English, from Latin, from Greek

scotch
verb **1** to injure so as to make harmless
2 to put an end to: *Her mother soon* ***scotched*** *her plans for going out.*

Word history: blend of *score* and *notch*

Scotch
noun whisky made in Scotland

Word use: You can also use **Scotch whisky**.

scot-free (skot-free)
adjective free from punishment, payment, or harm: *to get off* ***scot-free***

Scottish terrier
noun a breed of terrier with short legs and wiry hair, originally from Scotland

Word use: You can also use **Scottie**.

scoundrel (skown-druhl)
noun Old-fashioned a wicked or dishonourable person

scour[1] (skow-uh)
verb to clean by rubbing hard, usually in soap and water

Word history: Middle English, probably from Middle Dutch or Middle Low German, probably from Old French, from Latin word meaning 'care for', 'clean'

scour[2] (skow-uh)
verb to range about, as in search of something: *He* ***scoured*** *the countryside for her.*

Word history: Middle English

scourge (skerj)
noun **1** a cause of severe suffering: *the* ***scourge*** *of disease*
2 *Old-fashioned* a whip or lash, especially for punishment or torture
verb Old-fashioned **3** to whip with a scourge (***flog***, ***lash***)

Word history: Middle English, from Anglo-French, from Late Latin word meaning 'strip off the hide'

scout
noun **1** someone sent to find out information, especially about an enemy
2 a member of the Scout Association, a worldwide organisation which aims at developing character, self-reliance and usefulness to others

Word use: You can also use **Scout** for definition 2.
Word building: **scout** *verb*
Word history: Middle English, from Old French word meaning 'action of listening', from Latin

scowl
verb to have an angry look on your face (***frown***, ***glare***, ***glower***)

Word building: **scowl** *noun*
Word history: Middle English, from Scandinavian

scrabble
verb to scratch or scrape with claws or your hands: *to **scrabble** in the dirt*
Word history: from Dutch word meaning 'scratch'

scraggly (<u>skrag</u>-lee)
adjective ragged, or straggling
Adjective forms: **scragglier**, **scraggliest**

scraggy (<u>scrag</u>-ee)
adjective **1** thin or bony
2 lacking in quantity: *a **scraggy** meal* (***meagre***, ***scrappy***)
Adjective forms: **scraggier**, **scraggiest**

scram
verb Colloquial to go away, or leave quickly
Verb forms: I **scrammed**, I have **scrammed**, I am **scramming**
Word history: alteration of *scramble*

scramble
verb **1** to climb or walk quickly and awkwardly
2 of eggs, to cook by mixing yolks and whites with milk, and heating
3 to mix together in a confused way
noun **4** a hurried climb or movement over rough ground
5 a disorderly struggle to get something: *a **scramble** for seats in the back row*
Word history: variant of *scrabble*

scrap[1]
noun **1** a small piece (***fragment***, ***morsel***, ***part***, ***particle***, ***trace***)
2 anything useless or worn out, especially old metal
3 scraps, bits of food left over from a meal
adjective **4** consisting of scraps: *a **scrap** heap*
verb **5** to make into scrap: *to **scrap** a ship for its metal*
6 to put aside as useless (***discard***, ***ditch***, ***dump***, ***jettison***, ***shed***)
Verb forms: I **scrapped**, I have **scrapped**, I am **scrapping**
Word history: Middle English, from Scandinavian

scrap[2]
noun Old-fashioned a fight or quarrel (***altercation***, ***argument***, ***dispute***)
Word building: **scrap** *verb* (**scrapped**, **scrapping**)
Word history: variant of *scrape*

scrape
verb **1** to drag or rub something sharp or rough over something, usually to remove a layer: *We **scraped** the wall to remove the old paint.*
2 to scratch: *The knife **scraped** the table.*
3 to rub harshly or noisily: *The chalk **scraped** on the blackboard.*
noun **4** the act or sound of scraping
5 a scraped place
6 an awkward situation
phrase **7 scrape through**, to manage with difficulty
8 scrape up, to gather together
Word history: Middle English, from Scandinavian

scratch
verb **1** to mark or cut roughly: *to **scratch** polished wood* | *The kitten **scratched** my skin.* (***graze***, ***nick***, ***score***, ***tear***)
2 to draw a line through an item on a list in order to cancel it: *to **scratch** a name from a list*
3 to withdraw: *to **scratch** a horse from a race*
4 to lessen itching by rubbing with the nails or claws: *That dog is always **scratching**.*
5 to make a slight grating noise
noun **6** a mark made by scratching
phrase **7 from scratch**, from the beginning or from nothing
8 up to scratch, of a satisfactory standard
Word building: **scratchy** *adjective* (**scratchier**, **scratchiest**)
Word history: blend of obsolete *scrat* and *cratch*, both meaning scratch

scrawl
verb to write untidily (***scratch***, ***scribble***)
Word building: **scrawl** *noun*
Word history: special use of obsolete *scrawl* sprawl, influenced by *scribble*, etc.

scrawny (<u>skraw</u>-nee)
adjective thin, bony or, scraggy: *a long **scrawny** neck*
Adjective forms: **scrawnier**, **scrawniest**
Word history: variant of *scranny*

scream
verb **1** to make a loud piercing cry or sound: *The hyena **screamed** with pain.* (***screech***, ***shriek***, ***squawk***, ***squeal***, ***yelp***)
noun **2** such a cry or sound
3 *Colloquial* someone or something that is very funny: *He's a real **scream**.*
Word history: Middle English

scree
noun a steep mass of broken rocks on the side of a mountain
Word history: Scandinavian

screech
verb to make a harsh high-pitched cry or noise: *The owl **screeched** overhead.* | *The tyres **screeched** on the wet road.* (***scream***, ***shriek***, ***squawk***, ***squeal***)
Word building: **screech** *noun*
Word history: variant of archaic *scritch*; probably imitative

screed
noun a long speech or piece of writing (***essay***, ***harangue***, ***tirade***)
Word history: Old English *scrēade* shred

screen
noun **1** a large, flat surface on which a film can be shown
2 the part of a TV set or the video terminal of a computer on which the picture appears
3 a frame covered with wire mesh, placed over a window to keep out insects
4 a covered frame or a curtain used to hide something or to protect something
5 anything that shelters or hides: *They stood behind a **screen** of shrubs.*
verb **6** to show on a screen: *to **screen** a film*
7 to examine the loyalty, character, or ability of: *to **screen** people for a job* (***check***, ***investigate***)
Word history: Middle English, from Old French, from Old High German

screen capture
noun the process of copying what is displayed on a computer screen to a computer file or printer

screen grab
noun an image taken from a computer screen and saved as a pdf file

screenplay
noun the story of a film in written form, including the details of camera positions and movement, action, speech, lighting, etc.

screenshot
noun an image of a web page

screw
noun **1** a kind of nail with a slot in its flat end and a spiral thread above its point
verb **2** to turn along a thread: *to **screw** a lid on*
3 to turn sharply: *She **screwed** her head around to see.* (***rotate***, ***twist***)
4 to twist or wrinkle: *He **screwed** up his eyes in the sun.*
phrase **5 have a screw loose**, *Colloquial* to be slightly odd, or have crazy ideas
6 put the screws on, *Colloquial* to put pressure on

Word history: Middle English

screwdriver
noun a tool which fits into the end of a screw and is turned to drive the screw in or take it out

scribble
verb **1** to write hastily or carelessly (***scratch***, ***scrawl***)
2 to make meaningless marks with a pen or pencil

Word building: **scribble** *noun* **scribbler** *noun*
Word history: Middle English, from Medieval Latin

scribe
noun **1** a writer or author
2 someone who used to make copies of books before the invention of printing
3 a teacher who used to explain the Jewish law
4 someone who writes or types something which another dictates: *He injured his arm and so needed a **scribe** for the exam.*

Word history: Middle English, from Latin word meaning 'writer'

scrimmage (<u>skrim</u>-ij)
noun **1** a rough or lively struggle
2 in some football codes, the action of a number of players struggling for the ball in no set pattern of play
verb **3** to take part in a scrimmage

Word use: You can also use **scrummage**.
Word history: variant of *scrimish*, variant of *skirmish*

scrimp
verb to use less of something in order to save money: *They **scrimped** on butter to save a few cents.*

scrip
noun **1** a written certificate or receipt
2 *Finance* a certificate representing a provisional purchase of shares or stock where the purchase price is paid in parts according to an agreed schedule of payments

script
noun **1** the words written down for the actors to say in a play or film
2 handwriting
3 a set of computer instructions that is interpreted line by line each time it is run
4 → **prescription**

Word history: from Latin word meaning '(something) written'

scripture
noun a holy writing or book

Word building: **scriptural** *adjective*
Word history: Middle English, from Latin word meaning 'writing'

scroll
noun **1** a roll of parchment or paper with writing on it
verb **2** *Computers* to move (text, images, etc.) up, down, left or right on a computer screen in order to view material which is outside the limits of the screen

Word history: Middle English, from Anglo-French, of Germanic origin

scrooge (skroohj)
noun a mean ill-tempered person (***cheapskate***, ***miser***, ***skinflint***, ***tightwad***)

Word history: after Ebenezer *Scrooge*, a character in Dickens's story *A Christmas Carol* (1843)

scrotum
noun the pouch of skin in males which contains their testicles

Word history: Latin

scrounge
verb Colloquial to obtain by borrowing, begging or stealing

Word building: **scrounger** *noun*
Word history: perhaps variant of dialect *scringe* to glean

scrub[1]
verb **1** to rub hard with a brush, soap and water in order to clean
2 *Colloquial* to decide not to do: *We have to **scrub** the school concert.* (***call off***, ***cancel***)

Verb forms: I **scrubbed**, I have **scrubbed**, I am **scrubbing**
Word building: **scrub** *noun*
Word history: Middle English, apparently from Middle Dutch word meaning 'scratch', 'rub', 'scrub'

scrub[2]
noun a bush area of low trees or shrubs

Word history: variant of *shrub*, a low, stunted bush. From the type of plants growing there, the word extends in meaning to refer to the land covered by these plants. Just as we have 'bush' and 'the Bush', so too we have 'scrub' and 'the Scrub', to mean the remote parts of Australia and the people who live there

scruff
noun the back of your neck

Word history: from Dutch word meaning 'horse's withers'

scruffy
adjective dirty, shabby, and uncared for (***bedraggled***, ***dishevelled***, ***unkempt***, ***untidy***)

Adjective forms: **scruffier**, **scruffiest**

scrum
noun **1** a way of restarting the play in a game of Rugby Union and Rugby League football, in which some of the players pack together and push, one side against the other, until the ball is thrown in and the hookers try to kick it back to their team-mates
2 the formation of players in a scrum

Word history: short for *scrummage*

scrummage (<u>skrum</u>-ij)
noun **1** → **scrum**
2 → **scrimmage**

scrumptious (<u>skrump</u>-shuhs)
adjective very tasty or delicious: *a **scrumptious** dinner* (***appetising***, ***luscious***, ***more-ish***, ***mouth-watering***)

Word history: originally dialect, meaning 'stingy', from *scrimp*

scruple
noun a doubt that you have about a matter of deciding between right and wrong

scrupulous (<u>skroohp</u>-yuh-luhs)
adjective **1** careful or exact in every detail: *He is **scrupulous** in his work.* (***honest***, ***truthful***, ***upright***)
2 being strict about doing what is right: *She is **scrupulous** in her dealings with her customers.*

scrutineer (skrooh-tuh-<u>near</u>)
noun **1** someone who inspects the counting of votes by electoral officers
2 an official in a race, contest, etc., who checks that the rules are obeyed

scrutinise (<u>skrooh</u>-tuh-nuyz)
verb to examine closely and carefully (***delve into***, ***explore***, ***investigate***, ***probe***, ***research***)

Word use: You can also use **scrutinize**.
Word building: **scrutiny** *noun* (*plural* **scrutinies**)

SCSI (<u>skuz</u>-ee)
noun Computers a standard system for attaching peripheral devices to computers

Word history: *S(mall) C(omputer) S(ystem) I(nterface)*

scuba (<u>skooh</u>-buh)
noun a system that lets a diver breathe air through a mouthpiece connected by tubes to an air tank

Word history: an acronym for *s(elf-)c(ontained) u(nderwater) b(reathing) a(pparatus)*

scud
verb **1** to run or move quickly or hurriedly
2 to run before a gale with little or no sail set
noun **3** clouds, spray, etc., driven by the wind

Word history: Scandinavian

scuff
verb **1** to scrape with your feet
2 to make a mark on by scraping: *to **scuff** your shoes | to **scuff** furniture*

Word history: perhaps short for *scuffle*

scuffle
verb to struggle or fight in a confused way (***come to blows***, ***grapple***, ***tussle***)

Word building: **scuffle** *noun*
Word history: perhaps of Scandinavian origin

scull[1] (skul)
noun **1 a** an oar worked from side to side over the stern of a boat as a means of moving forwards
b one of a pair of oars operated, one on each side, by one person
2 a boat propelled by a scull or sculls
verb **3** to move by means of a scull or sculls

Word history: Middle English

scull[2]
verb Colloquial to consume (a drink) without stopping for a breath

Word use: You can also use **skol**.
Word history: Scandinavian languages in which the word *skol*, which means 'cup' or 'bowl'. It is said as drinkers raise their glasses in a toast, in a similar way to the English expression *cheers*.

scull / skull
Don't confuse **scull** with **skull**. Your **skull** is the bony part of your head.

scullery
noun a small room where the rough, dirty, kitchen work is done

Noun forms: The plural is **sculleries.**
Word history: Middle English, from Old French word meaning 'dish', from Latin word meaning 'salver'

sculpt
verb to carve: *to **sculpt** a bird out of wood*

sculpture
noun **1** the art or work of making figures or designs in marble, clay, bronze or similar materials
2 something made this way
verb **3** to form sculptures

Word building: **sculptor** *noun* **sculptural** *adjective*
Word history: Middle English, from Latin

scum
noun **1** a thin layer of froth or dirt on the top of a liquid
2 someone who is low or worthless: *the **scum** of the earth*

Word history: Middle English, from Middle Dutch

scungies (<u>skun</u>-jeez)
plural noun short pants worn by men or women under board shorts, sports uniforms or similar garments

Word history: Trademark

scurrilous (<u>sku</u>-ruh-luhs)
adjective **1** coarsely rude and nasty: *a **scurrilous** attack*
2 coarsely jocular or derisive: *a **scurrilous** jest*

scurry
verb to move quickly: *The children **scurried** back to bed.* (***dart***, ***dive***, ***scamper***, ***scoot***, ***speed***)

Verb forms: I **scurried**, I have **scurried**, I am **scurrying**
Word building: **scurry** *noun* (*plural* **scurries**)

scurvy
noun a disease marked by swollen and bleeding gums, dull blue spots on the skin, inability to stand, etc., caused by lack of vitamin C in your diet

scuttle
verb to run with quick steps: *The mice* ***scuttled*** *away.*
Word building: **scuttle** *noun*

scythe (suydh)
noun a tool with a long curved blade joined at an angle to a long handle: *He used a* ***scythe*** *to cut the long grass.*
Word history: Old English *sīthe*

sea
noun **1** the salt waters that cover most of the earth's surface
2 a particular part of these waters, usually near or almost surrounded by land: *the Tasman* ***Sea***
3 a large quantity: *a* ***sea*** *of troubles*
phrase **4 at sea,**
a sailing or on the ocean
b uncertain or confused
Word use: You can also use **all at sea** for definition 4b.
Word history: English *sǣ*

sea / see
Don't confuse **sea** with **see.**
You **see** things with your eyes.
See can also mean 'to understand'.

seas / sees / seize
Look up **sees / seize / seas.**

sea anemone (see uh-nem-uh-nee)
noun a sea animal which stays in one place and catches food with one or more tentacles growing on top of its tube-shaped body

seabird
noun a bird frequenting the sea or coast

seafarer
noun a traveller on the sea (***mariner***, ***sailor***, ***seaman***)
Word building: **seafaring** *adjective*

seafood
noun food which comes from the sea, such as fish, squid and shellfish

seagoing
adjective **1** designed or fit for sailing in the open sea: *a* ***seagoing*** *vessel* (***maritime***, ***nautical***, ***naval***, ***seafaring***, ***seaworthy***)
2 going to sea

seagrass matting
noun matting made using certain grass fibres

seagull
noun a bird which lives near or on the sea and is usually white with a grey back and wings and has a harsh cry
Word use: The short form is **gull.**

seahorse
noun a small fish with a curved tail and a head shaped like a horse's

seal[1]
noun **1** a design pressed into a piece of wax, or a stamp engraved with such a design, used for making a document official
2 a piece of wax for closing an envelope or document, which has to be broken before the contents can be read
3 anything used to close something
verb **4** to close so that entry is impossible except by force: *He* ***sealed*** *the envelope.* | *The police* ***sealed*** *off the road.*
5 to cover with tar: *to* ***seal*** *a road*
6 to decide finally: *to* ***seal*** *someone's fate*
Word history: Middle English, from Old French, from Late Latin

seal[2]
noun a sea mammal with smooth fur, a long rounded body and large flippers
Word history: Old English *seolh*

sea level
noun the average level of the sea, used as a base to measure height: *The town is 1000 metres above* ***sea level.***

sea lion
noun a type of large Australian seal which has white hair on the back of its neck

seam
noun **1** the line where two pieces of material have been joined together: *The* ***seam*** *isn't sewn straight.*
2 a thin layer of a different kind of rock or mineral in the ground: *a coal* ***seam*** (***band***, ***deposit***, ***stratum***, ***vein***)
Word history: Middle English *seme*, Old English *sēam*

seam / seem
Don't confuse **seam** with **seem.** To **seem** is to appear to be a certain way:
They seem happy together.

seaman
noun a sailor (***mariner***, ***seafarer***)
Noun forms: The plural is **seamen.**
Word building: **seamanship** *noun*

seamstress
noun a woman whose job is sewing

seamy (see-mee)
adjective bad, or sordid: *the* ***seamy*** *side of life*
Adjective forms: **seamier, seamiest**

seance (say-ons)
noun a meeting of people who are trying to contact the spirits of dead people
Word history: French word meaning 'a sitting', from Old French, from Latin word meaning 'sit'

seaplane
noun a plane with floats, which can take off and land on water

sear
verb **1** to burn or blacken the outside of: *to* ***sear*** *a piece of meat*
2 to cause to dry up or wither: *The sun* ***seared*** *the wheat.*

Word building: **searing** *adjective*
Word history: Old English *sēar*

search
verb **1** to go through or look through thoroughly in order to find something or someone: *He* ***searched*** *the house for his watch.* (***examine, go over, turn upside down***)
2 to examine, usually for hidden or illegal objects: *Guards* ***searched*** *everyone's bags.* (***inspect, look over, vet***)

Word building: **search** *noun*
Word history: Middle English, from Old French, from Late Latin, from Latin word meaning 'circle'

search warrant
noun an order by a court which allows the police to search your house, usually for stolen goods

seasickness
noun a feeling of sickness in your stomach, or vomiting caused by the movement of a ship at sea

Word building: **seasick** *adjective*

season
noun **1** one of the four divisions of the year into spring, summer, autumn, and winter
2 a period of time, especially when it is connected with some event or activity: *the Christmas* ***season*** | *the football* ***season*** | *It's been a good* ***season*** *for strawberries.*
verb **3** to add flavour or interest to: *She* ***seasons*** *her cooking with pepper and herbs.*
4 to treat or let stand until ready for use: *to* ***season*** *timber*

Word building: **seasonal** *adjective*
Word history: Middle English, from Old French, from Latin word meaning '(time of) sowing'

seasoning
noun something like salt, herbs or spices, which adds flavour

seat
noun **1** something for sitting on: *a garden* ***seat***
2 a part for sitting on: *the* ***seat*** *of a chair* | *the* ***seat*** *of your pants*
3 a centre of some educational activity: *a* ***seat*** *of learning*
4 a large country house
5 the right to sit in parliament: *She won a* ***seat*** *in the last election.*

Word building: **seat** *verb* **seated** *adjective*
Word history: Middle English, from Scandinavian

seatbelt
noun a belt attached to the frame of a motor vehicle, or to a seat in an aeroplane, etc., for holding a person safely in place against sudden turns, stops, collision, etc.

Word use: You can also use **safety belt.**

sea urchin
noun a sea animal with a round, spiky shell

sea wasp
noun → **box jellyfish**

seaweed
noun any plant that grows in the ocean

seaworthy
adjective of a ship, adequately and safely built and fitted out to sail at sea

Word building: **seaworthiness** *noun*

secant (<u>seek</u>-uhnt)
noun Mathematics a straight line which cuts a circle or other curve

Word history: from Latin word meaning 'cutting'

secateurs (<u>sek</u>-uh-tuhz, sek-uh-<u>terz</u>)
plural noun gardening shears for clipping and pruning

Word history: French, from Latin word meaning 'cut'

secede (suh-<u>seed</u>)
verb to withdraw formally from a friendship, alliance or association, such as from a political or religious organisation

Word building: **secession** *noun*
Word history: from Latin word meaning 'go back', 'withdraw'

seclude
verb to shut away: *She* ***secludes*** *herself in her room.*

Word building: **seclusion** *noun*
Word history: Latin

secluded
adjective quiet and private: *a* ***secluded*** *garden*

second[1]
adjective **1** next after the first
2 another: *a* ***second*** *chance*
3 alternate: *every* ***second*** *weekend*
verb **4** to express support of: *Who will* ***second*** *this proposal so we can vote on it?*

Word building: **second** *noun* **seconder** *noun*
Word history: Middle English, from French, from Latin

second[2]
noun one sixtieth part of a minute of time

Word history: Middle English, from French, from Medieval Latin *secunda (minūta)*, that is, the result of the second division of the hour into sixty

second[3] (suh-<u>kond</u>)
verb to move for a limited time to another post, organisation, or responsibility: *to* ***second*** *a military officer to another post*

secondary
adjective **1** next after the first in order or importance: *a* ***secondary*** *matter* (***minor, petty, subordinate, trivial***)
2 taken from something other than the original: *a* ***secondary*** *source*
3 having to do with the processing of primary products, such as meat, wheat, coal, and wool: *a* ***secondary*** *industry*

Word history: Middle English, from Latin

secondary forest
noun Ecology forest that has regrown after logging or clearing activities

Word use: Compare this with **primary forest.**

secondary industry
noun an industry which involves the processing of primary products, such as wheat, iron ore, and wool into manufactured goods, such as flour, steel, and cloth

secondary school
noun a school providing education after the finish of primary school

Word use: You can also use **high school**.

secondary source
noun in the study of history, a book, person, statement, etc., supplying information which is not firsthand but relies on reported accounts or hearsay

Word use: Compare this with **primary source**.

second-hand
adjective bought or got from someone else: *a **second-hand** car | a **second-hand** jumper* (***used***)

Word use: The opposite of this is **new** or **unused**.
Word building: **second-hand** *adverb*

second nature
noun a habit, tendency, etc., that you have been practising so long that it is firmly fixed in your character: *Correcting other people's grammar is **second nature** to him.*

second person
noun a grammatical category for pronouns, indicating the person or thing being spoken to

Pronouns such as *you*, *yourself* and *yourselves* are said to be in the **second person**, which is the person being spoken to. (**First person** is the one speaking; **third person** is the one spoken about.) For more information, look up **person in grammar**.

seconds
plural noun (at a meal)
1 a second helping
2 a second course

second wind
noun **1** the return of more comfortable breathing and the lessening of strain on your muscles in an ongoing energetic activity, after you have got over the initial stresses
2 a return of interest, enthusiasm, etc.

secret
adjective **1** done or made without others knowing: *a **secret** plan* (***confidential***, ***hush-hush***)
2 having to do with a place or object that is culturally very important: *I'll take you to the **secret** spring.*
3 designed to escape notice: *a **secret** door*
noun **4** something hidden or concealed
5 a mystery: *the **secrets** of nature*
phrase **6 in secret**, with no-one else knowing

Word building: **secrecy** *noun* **secretly** *adverb*
Word history: Middle English, from French, from Latin word meaning 'divided off'

secretariat (sek-ruh-<u>tair</u>-ree-uht)
noun the officials or office entrusted with keeping records and carrying out secretarial duties, especially for an international organisation, government, etc.

Word history: French, from Medieval Latin word meaning 'the office of a secretary'

secretary
noun someone whose job is to write letters, keep records or make phone calls for an employer

Noun forms: The plural is **secretaries**.
Word building: **secretarial** *adjective*
Word history: Medieval Latin word meaning 'confidential officer', from Latin word meaning '(something) secret'

secrete (suh-<u>kreet</u>)
verb **1** to produce, such as by a gland: *to **secrete** saliva*
2 to hide away: *He has **secreted** the treasure under the floor.*

Word building: **secretion** *noun*
Word history: from Latin word meaning 'put apart'

secretive
adjective liking to keep things to yourself: *a **secretive** nature* (***cagey***, ***furtive***, ***stealthy***)

secret service
noun the department of government concerned with national security, especially with espionage

sect
noun a religious group, especially one which has broken away from a larger group

Word building: **sectarian** *adjective*
Word history: Middle English, from Latin word meaning 'following'

section
noun **1** a part or division of something (***fraction***, ***piece***, ***portion***, ***proportion***, ***segment***)
2 a picture of how something would look if you cut it from top to bottom or across and showed the inside

Word history: from Latin word meaning 'a cutting'

sector
noun **1** a division of a circle, shaped like a wedge of cake
2 a large division or an area of activity: *the public **sector***
3 *Computers*
a the smallest part of a track on a magnetic disk or tape that can be addressed, usually 128 or 256 bytes
b the block of data stored on a sector

Word history: Late Latin, special use of Latin *sector* cutter

sector graph
noun → **pie graph**

secular (<u>sek</u>-yuh-luh)
adjective worldly, as opposed to religious or spiritual: *She doesn't like to hear **secular** music in church.*

Word history: Late Latin word meaning 'worldly', from Latin word meaning 'belonging to an age'

secularism (<u>sek</u>-yuh-luh-riz-uhm)
noun **1** secular spirit or tendencies, especially a system of political or social philosophy which refuses to accept all forms of religious faith and worship
2 the view that public education and other matters of state or government policy should be carried out without the introduction of religion

Word building: **secularist** *noun* **secularistic** *adjective*

secure
adjective **1** free from care or danger (***protected***, ***right as rain***, ***safe***, ***sheltered***)
2 firmly fastened or in place (***firm***, ***fixed***, ***stable***, ***steady***)
3 in safe keeping: *Your money will be* ***secure*** *in the bank.*
verb **4** to get: *He was unable to* ***secure*** *tickets.* (***acquire***, ***gain***, ***procure***)
5 to tie up tightly: *to* ***secure*** *the knots*
6 to make safe: *to* ***secure*** *your future* (***defend***, ***guard***, ***protect***)
Word building: **securely** *adverb*
Word history: Latin word meaning 'free from care'

secure server
noun Computers a website which can prevent information such as a purchaser's credit card number or a respondent's personal information being obtained by someone other than the person who is supposed to receive it

security
noun **1** safety, or confidence: *He escaped to a place of* ***security***. | *She has the* ***security*** *she needs to start a new life.*
2 protection, or defence: *Window locks are my* ***security*** *against burglars.* (***safeguard***, ***shield***)
3 *Law* something given or left to ensure that a promise or a debt is kept or repaid
4 securities, stocks and shares, or something similar

sedan (suh-dan)
noun a car with four doors, which seats from four to six people
Word history: perhaps from Italian, from Latin word meaning 'seat'

sedate
adjective **1** calm and steady: *They walked at a* ***sedate*** *pace.*
verb **2** to calm or put to sleep by means of sedatives that relax the body: *The doctor* ***sedated*** *the hysterical child.*
Word building: **sedation** *noun*
Word history: from Latin word meaning 'calmed'

sedative
noun **1** a drug which lessens pain or excitement
adjective **2** calming or soothing

sedentary (sed-uhn-tree)
adjective **1** having to do with or needing a sitting position: *a* ***sedentary*** *occupation*
2 used to sitting a great deal and taking little exercise
3 *Zoology*
a staying in one place, or not migratory
b of animals, not often moving about, or joined to an object that does not move
Word history: Latin

sediment
noun **1** solid material that falls to the bottom of a liquid (***dregs***, ***lees***)
2 *Geology* mineral or organic material laid down or deposited by water, ice or air
Word building: **sedimentary** *adjective*
Word history: French, from Latin word meaning 'a setting'

sedimentary rock
noun Geology a rock formed by the depositing of layers of sediment
Word use: Compare this with **igneous rock** and **metamorphic rock**.

sedimentation
noun the depositing or accumulating of sediment

sedition (suh-dish-uhn)
noun **1** the urging to discontent or rebellion against the government
2 actions or language promoting such discontent or rebellion
Word building: **seditious** *adjective*
Word history: Middle English, from Latin word meaning 'a going apart'

seduce
verb to persuade or entice to do something considered wrong
Word building: **seducer** *noun* **seduction** *noun* **seductive** *adjective* **seductively** *adverb*
Word history: Middle English, from Latin word meaning 'lead aside'

see[1]
verb **1** to take things in with your eyes or your mind: *to* ***see*** *clearly* | *I* ***see*** *what you mean.* (***notice***, ***observe***, ***perceive***)
2 to consider or think of: *We shall* ***see***. | *I* ***see*** *it like this.*
3 to find out: ***See*** *who it is.*
4 to meet or visit: *to* ***see*** *a friend* | *to* ***see*** *the doctor*
5 to go with: *She'll* ***see*** *you to the door.*
6 to imagine or remember: *I can just* ***see*** *her laughing the way she used to.*
7 to know or experience: *He must have* ***seen*** *a lot.*
phrase **8 see through**,
a to detect: *She* ***saw through*** *the disguise.*
b to stay until the end of: *He always* ***sees*** *a job* ***through***.
Verb forms: I **saw**, I have **seen**, I am **seeing**
Word history: Middle English; Old English *sēon*

The verb **to see** is an irregular verb in English. That is, it does not follow the normal and regular pattern of forming its past tense and past participle by simply adding -ed.

The past tense is *saw*: *I saw a star.*

The past participle is *seen*: *I have seen a star.*

Note that the use of *seen* as a past tense is not acceptable in writing:

I seen him this morning. WRONG
I have seen him this morning. RIGHT

see / sea

Don't confuse **see** with **sea**, which is a large stretch of water.

sees / seize / seas

Don't confuse **sees** with **seize** or **seas**.

Sees is a part of the present tense of **see**:

He sees the pen on the table.

To **seize** something is to grab hold of it:

He seized the pen and wouldn't let it go.

Seas is the plural of **sea**:

We went sailing on the high seas.

see[2]
noun the office or jurisdiction of a bishop
Word use: Compare this with **bishopric**.
Word history: Middle English, from Old French, from Latin

seed
noun **1** the part produced by a plant from which a new plant grows
2 seeds, the beginnings or start: *the **seeds** of their quarrel*
verb **3** to sow with seed: *to **seed** land*
4 to remove the seeds from: *to **seed** fruit*
phrase **5 go** (or **run**) **to seed**,
a of a plant, to come to the stage of producing seed
b to come near the end of your vigour, usefulness, etc.
Word history: Middle English; Old English

seedling
noun a young plant

seedy
adjective **1** shabby and untidy: *a **seedy** appearance*
2 unwell: *I'm feeling quite **seedy** this morning.*
Adjective forms: **seedier**, **seediest**

seek
verb **1** to try to find or get: *to **seek** an answer | to **seek** fame* (***hunt for***, ***pursue***, ***quest after***, ***search for***, ***strive for***)
2 to try: *She **seeks** to help.* (***attempt***, ***undertake***)
Verb forms: I **sought**, I have **sought**, I am **seeking**
Word history: Old English *sēcan*

seem
verb **1** to have the look of being: *She **seems** happy.*
2 to appear to yourself: *I **seem** to be dizzy.*
Word history: Middle English, from Scandinavian

seem / seam
Don't confuse **seem** with **seam**. A **seam** is the line where two pieces of material like fabric or metal have been joined together. It can also be a layer of rock or mineral in the ground, as in *a coal seam.*

seemly (seem-lee)
adjective **1** becoming, or decent: ***seemly** behaviour*
2 handsome
Adjective forms: **seemlier**, **seemliest**
Word history: Middle English, from Scandinavian

seen
verb past participle and past tense of **see**[1]

seen / scene
Don't confuse **seen** with **scene**, which is a place where something happens, as in *the scene of a crime.*
In a stage play, a number of **scenes** make an act.

seep
verb to leak or drip slowly: *Water **seeps** from the pipe.* (***dribble***, ***ooze***, ***trickle***)
Word building: **seepage** *noun*
Word history: perhaps variant of dialect *sipe*, Old English *sīpian*

seer
noun Old-fashioned someone who can see into the future

seesaw
noun **1** a plank balanced in the middle, so that the child sitting at one end rises when the child at the other end goes down
verb **2** to move like a seesaw
Word history: varied reduplication suggested by *saw*[1]

seethe
verb **1** to bubble and foam: *The sea was **seething** far below.*
2 to be excited or disturbed: *She is **seething** with rage.*
Word history: Middle English; Old English *sēothan*

segment
noun **1** a piece or section: *a **segment** of orange* (***fraction***, ***part***, ***portion***, ***proportion***)
verb **2** to separate into pieces
Word building: **segmentation** *noun*
Word history: Latin

segregate
verb to set or keep apart, especially one race or group of people from another
Word use: The opposite of this is **unite**.
Word building: **segregation** *noun*
Word history: Middle English, from Latin word meaning 'separated from the flock'

seismic (suyz-mik)
adjective having to do with or caused by an earthquake
Word history: Greek

seismograph (suyz-muh-graf, suyz-muh-grahf)
noun an instrument for measuring and recording vibrations within the earth, such as earthquakes

seismology (suyz-mol-uh-jee)
noun the science or study of earthquakes and their phenomena
Word building: **seismologic** *adjective* **seismologist** *noun*

seize (seez)
verb **1** to take hold of suddenly, or by force: *to **seize** an idea or an opportunity | to **seize** a knife* (***grab***, ***nab***, ***nail***, ***snap up***, ***snatch***)
2 to become stuck or jammed: *The engine **seized**.*
Word history: Middle English, from Old French, from Vulgar Latin word meaning 'set', 'put (in possession)', from Germanic

seize / seas / sees
Look up **sees / seize / seas**.

seizure (see-zhuh)
noun **1** the act of seizing
2 a sudden attack of disease

seldom
adverb rarely or not often: *He **seldom** takes part.*
Word history: Middle English; Old English *seldum*

select
verb **1** to choose: ***Select** your favourite recipe.* (***choose**, **decide on**, **pick**, **take***)
adjective **2** carefully chosen: *a **select** few*
3 of special value or excellence

Word building: **selective** *adjective* **selectively** *adverb*
Word history: from Latin word meaning 'chosen'

selection
noun **1** choice: *This course is my **selection**.*
2 a range of goods, etc., to choose from: *a wide **selection** of ice-creams*
3 *Australian* in the past, a block of land acquired under the system of free selection
4 *Biology* the singling out of certain animals and plants for reproduction and continuing the species, either naturally or artificially

selective
adjective **1** having the function or power of selection: *The panel was able to be quite **selective** about who were given interviews.*
2 fastidious; discriminating
3 characterised by selection: ***selective** deafness*
4 biased: ***selective** reporting*
5 *Education* describing a school to which entry is restricted to those applicants who perform best on a set of tests

Word building: **selectively** *adverb*

self
noun **1** your own person
2 your nature, character, etc.: *his better **self***
adjective **3** uniform, or being the same throughout
pronoun **4** myself, himself, etc.: *to make a cheque payable to **self***

Noun forms: The plural is **selves**.

self-centred
adjective always thinking of yourself first and other people second: *a **self-centred** person*

self-confidence
noun belief in your own ability: *to be full of **self-confidence***

Word building: **self-confident** *adjective*

self-conscious (self-<u>kon</u>-shuhs)
adjective **1** too aware of other people noticing you
2 conscious of yourself or your own thoughts, etc.

self-contained
adjective **1** not needing a lot of help or support from other people: *She doesn't mind living by herself as she is very **self-contained**.*
2 of a flat, house, etc., having all the necessary facilities, such as its own bathroom, toilet and kitchen

self-control
noun the ability to stop yourself from doing something: *She hasn't much **self-control** when it comes to sweets.*

Word building: **self-controlled** *adjective*

self-defence
noun the ability to protect yourself against attack

self-effacing
adjective not liking to have people praise you or pay attention to you: *People thought she was **self-effacing** because she shied away from attention.* (***modest***)

self-esteem
noun confident belief in your own abilities and your value as a person: *It is important for a child to develop **self-esteem**.*

self-evident
adjective evident in itself without proof

Word building: **self-evidence** *noun*

self-funded
adjective **1** paid for out of someone's own money rather than in some other way, for instance by government, etc.: *a **self-funded** trip*
2 being supported financially by your own money, rather than by something like a pension: *a **self-funded** retiree*

Word building: **self-funding** *adjective*

self-government
noun **1** government of a state or community by its own members
2 political independence of a country, people, region, etc.

Word building: **self-governed** *adjective*

self-indulgent
adjective not attempting to restrict your own desires or pleasure in any way at all: *Watching three DVDs when there was work to be done was very **self-indulgent**.*

self-interest
noun regard for your own advantage, especially with disregard of others

Word building: **self-interested** *adjective*

selfish
adjective thinking only of your own interests: *a **selfish** act* (***inconsiderate**, **self-centred***)

Word building: **selfishly** *adverb* **selfishness** *noun*

self-made
adjective having succeeded in life, without help from inheritance, class background, or other people: *a **self-made** woman*

self-opinionated
adjective **1** vain, or conceited
2 giving your own opinion often

self-pity
noun too much pity or sympathy for yourself; feeling sorry for yourself: *He shouldn't waste so much time on **self-pity** — he should do something about his problems.*

self-possessed
adjective showing control of your feelings, behaviour, etc.

Word building: **self-possession** *noun*

self-raising flour
noun flour with baking powder already added to it, so that it makes bread or cakes rise

self-respect
noun pride and confidence in yourself and the way you behave: *She wished she hadn't been so rude as she felt she had lost her **self-respect**.*

self-righteous
adjective convinced that you know and do what is morally right in a way that annoys others: *Telling everyone what they should do was quite **self-righteous** of her.*

self-sacrifice
noun a giving up of your interests, desires, etc., for the good of another
Word building: **self-sacrificing** *adjective*

self-satisfied
adjective very impressed with yourself or your own actions: *a **self-satisfied** grin*

self-service
adjective having to do with a shop or restaurant where the customers serve themselves and then pay a cashier

self-sufficient
adjective **1** able to supply your own needs (***autonomous***, ***independent***, ***separate***)
2 having too much confidence in your own abilities, powers, etc.
Word building: **self-sufficiency** *noun*

sell
verb **1** to give up for money: *He **sold** his car.* (***auction***, ***flog***, ***hawk***, ***peddle***)
2 to have for sale: *Do you **sell** goldfish here?*
Verb forms: I **sold**, I have **sold**, I am **selling**
Word building: **seller** *noun*
Word history: Old English *sellan*

sell / cell
Don't confuse **sell** with **cell**, which is a small bare room, like a *prison cell*. A **cell** is also a small unit of living matter, as in a *plant cell*.

seller / cellar
Don't confuse **seller** with **cellar**, which is an underground room for storing goods like wine.

sellout
noun Colloquial **1** a betrayal: *That was a total **betrayal** — telling my secrets when she swore she wouldn't tell a soul!*
2 a play, show, etc., for which all seats are sold

selvage (sel-vij)
noun the edge of woven fabric finished to prevent fraying
Word use: You can also use **selvedge**.
Word history: late Middle English

selvage / salvage
Don't confuse **selvage** or **selvedge** with **salvage**. To **salvage** something is to rescue it from fire, shipwreck or other damage.

semantic (suh-man-tik)
adjective having to do with signs or meaning
Word history: from Greek word meaning 'significant'

semantics (suh-man-tiks)
noun Linguistics the systematic study of the meanings of words and changes in them

semaphore (sem-uh-faw)
noun a system for signalling messages using flags
Word building: **semaphore** *verb*
Word history: Greek

semblance (sem-bluhns)
noun **1** an outward appearance or likeness: *a **semblance** of the girl I knew*
2 an unreal appearance: *a **semblance** of sorrow*
Word history: Middle English, from Old French word meaning 'be like', 'seem', from Latin

semen (see-muhn)
noun liquid containing sperm, which is produced by the testicles
Word history: from Latin word meaning 'seed'

semester (suh-mes-tuh)
noun in educational institutions, one of the two divisions of the academic year
Word history: German, from Latin word meaning 'six monthly'

semibreve
noun a musical note which is four crotchets long

semicircle
noun a half circle
Word building: **semicircular** *adjective*

semicolon
noun a punctuation mark (;) which is used to show more of a break between parts of a sentence than a comma does

You generally use a **semicolon** to divide parts of a sentence which could each stand on their own as separate sentences. The semicolon shows that the separate parts are related in some way:

The telephone rang; his sister ran inside.

The telephone rang. His sister ran inside.

The first example suggests much more strongly than the second that the two events are related (perhaps the sister ran inside because the telephone rang).

Note that it is quite acceptable to use connecting words like *and*, *but* and *however* after a **semicolon**:

The telephone rang; and his sister ran inside.

Semicolons can also be used to separate lists of different sets of things — that is, to form a large list made up of smaller lists:

At the jumble sale there were books, magazines and newspapers; records, cassettes and CDs; and tables, chairs and sofas.

The small lists in this sentence are the lists of printed works, musical recordings and furniture. The individual items in these small lists are separated by a comma. The small lists together make up the larger list of 'kinds of things sold', and the three kinds of things are separated by a **semicolon**.

semidetached
adjective partly separate, used especially about two houses sharing one wall while remaining separate from other buildings

seminal (sem-uhn-uhl)
adjective **1** having to do with the nature of semen
2 *Botany* having to do with seed
3 highly original and influential
4 undeveloped, or rudimentary
Word history: Middle English, from Latin word meaning 'seed'

seminar (<u>sem</u>-uh-nah)
noun **1** a meeting of students, such as in a university, engaged in advanced study and original research under a professor, lecturer, etc.
2 a course or subject of study for advanced students
3 a meeting organised to discuss a specific topic: *a public* ***seminar*** *on uranium mining*
Word history: German, from Latin word meaning 'of or for seed'

seminary (<u>sem</u>-uhn-ree)
noun a college for training Roman Catholic priests
Word building: **seminarian** (sem-uh-<u>nair</u>-ree-uhn) *noun*
Word history: late Middle English, from Latin word meaning 'nursery'

semiquaver
noun a musical note which is equal to half a quaver

semitone
noun half a tone, or the difference between the notes which are next to each other on the piano

semitrailer
noun a large truck which consists of a long trailer connected to the cabin and a powerful engine

semolina (sem-uh-<u>lee</u>-nuh)
noun the large hard bits of wheat grains left over after the fine flour has been separated
Word history: Italian word meaning 'bran', from Latin word meaning 'fine flour'

senate (<u>sen</u>-uht)
noun one of the decision-making bodies in the government of a country (***congress***, ***council***)
Word building: **senator** *noun*
Word history: Middle English, from Latin

send
verb **1** to cause to go: *She* ***sent*** *him away.* | *He* ***sends*** *a letter every week.*
2 to cause to become: *He* ***sends*** *her mad with rage.*
3 to send a message: *He will* ***send*** *for you.*
phrase **4 send up,** to mock, usually by imitating in an exaggerated way: *They* ***send up*** *her accent.* (***ape***, ***caricature***, ***mimic***)
Verb forms: I **sent**, I have **sent**, I am **sending**
Word building: **sender** *noun*
Word history: Old English *sendan*

senile
adjective weak in the body or mind because of old age (***aged***, ***elderly***, ***geriatric***)
Word building: **senility** *noun*
Word history: Latin

senior
adjective of greater age, or importance: *She is* ***senior*** *to me by twenty years.* | *a* ***senior*** *lecturer*
Word building: **senior** *noun* **seniority** *noun*
Word history: Middle English, from Latin word meaning 'old'

Senior Counsel
noun (in some legal systems) a member of the senior of the two ranks of barrister
Word use: In the systems where this title is used, it has replaced **Queen's Counsel**. | The abbreviation is **SC**.

sensation
noun **1** feeling: *The accident has left her with no* ***sensation*** *in her hand.* | *He had the* ***sensation*** *that he was being followed.* (***awareness***, ***impression***, ***perception***, ***sense***)
2 a cause or feeling of excitement: *The pop star was a* ***sensation.*** | *The news flash caused a* ***sensation.***
Word building: **sensational** *adjective* **sensationally** *adverb*
Word history: Medieval Latin, from Late Latin word meaning 'having sense'

sensationalism (sen-<u>say</u>-shuhn-uhl-iz-uhm)
noun the producing of cheap emotional excitement by popular newspapers, novels, etc.
Word building: **sensationalist** *noun*

sense
noun **1** one of the powers or abilities by which we taste, touch, hear, see and smell: *His* ***sense*** *of smell is impaired.* (***awareness***, ***feeling***, ***perception***, ***sensation***)
2 any physical or mental feeling or ability: *a* ***sense*** *of tiredness* | *a* ***sense*** *of humour*
3 the ability to think and act sensibly and intelligently: *She has no* ***sense.***
4 meaning: *Could you explain the* ***sense*** *of this remark?* (***essence***, ***gist***, ***meaning***, ***significance***)
verb **5** to notice or feel with your senses: *You could* ***sense*** *the tension between the players.* (***perceive***, ***realise***, ***recognise***, ***understand***)
Word history: Middle English, from Latin

sensibility
noun the ability to feel
Noun forms: The plural is **sensibilities.**

sensible
adjective **1** full of good sense: *a* ***sensible*** *move* (***level-headed***, ***practical***, ***prudent***, ***reasonable***, ***sage***)
2 *Old-fashioned* knowing or aware: *She is* ***sensible*** *of her responsibility.*
Word building: **sensibly** *adverb*
Word history: Middle English, from Late Latin

sensitise (<u>sen</u>-suh-tuyz)
verb to make sensitive
Word use: You can also use **sensitize.**
Word building: **sensitisation** *noun* **sensitiser** *noun*

sensitive
adjective **1** having feeling: ***sensitive*** *to the cold*
2 easily affected by something: *The film is* ***sensitive*** *to light.*
3 overly reacting, especially to what others say: *Don't be so* ***sensitive!*** (***prickly***, ***thin-skinned***, ***touchy***)
4 causing strong feelings: *a* ***sensitive*** *matter*
Word use: The opposite of definition 1 is **insensitive.**
Word building: **sensitivity** *noun* (*plural* **sensitivities**) **sensitively** *adverb*
Word history: Middle English, from Medieval Latin, from Latin word meaning 'sense'

sensor (<u>sen</u>-suh)
noun a device which detects a variable quantity and converts it into a signal for measuring, recording, etc.

sensor / censor

Don't confuse **sensor** with **censor**. A **censor** is a person who is appointed to examine films, plays, news reports and the like, to see whether they are suitable for the general public.

sensory
adjective having to do with feeling: *Tentacles are the **sensory** organs of some animals.*

sensual
adjective having to do with feeling or with your senses: *Listening to the music was a **sensual** pleasure.*

Word building: **sensualist** *noun* **sensuality** *noun* **sensually** *adverb*
Word history: late Middle English, from Late Latin

sensuous (sen-shooh-uhs)
adjective **1** having to do with your senses
2 perceived by or affecting your senses: *the **sensuous** qualities of music*
3 aware of the physical senses: *a **sensuous** temperament*

sent
verb past tense and past participle of **send**

sent / scent / cent

Don't confuse **sent** with **scent** or **cent**.

Scent is the smell that flowers and perfume have.

A **cent** is one-hundredth of a dollar.

sentence
noun **1** a group of words which form a complete statement, question, comment, or exclamation
2 the punishment of a criminal: *The judge passed a **sentence** of five years' jail.*
verb **3** to condemn to punishment

Word history: Middle English, from French, from Latin word meaning 'opinion'

sentences

In writing, **sentences** always begin with a capital letter and end with a full stop, a question mark or an exclamation mark.

What we call 'fully formed' sentences are those which have a main clause (with a subject and a predicate).

There are three main types of sentences:

1 **Simple sentence** This consists of a single main clause (that is, a clause that can stand on its own):

They	*are going home now.*
subject	predicate

2 **Compound sentence** This consists of at least two main clauses, joined by a conjunction:

They are going home now	*and*	*I'm going with them.*
main clause 1	conjunction	main clause 2

The conjunction has to be what is called a coordinating conjunction — for more information, look up **conjunctions.**

3 **Complex sentence** This consists of at least two clauses, one of which is a dependent clause (that is, a clause that can't stand on its own):

They are going home now	*because it's so late.*
main clause	dependent clause

From time to time you may discover groups of words which are punctuated as if they were sentences but which do not have both subject and predicate and so do not fall into any of the three categories above. These pieces of sentences are often called **sentence fragments** or **fragmentary sentences.** They usually occur as answers to questions, and some parts of their structure are left out, so the readers have to complete the rest of the sentence for themselves.

When are you getting home?

Question: simple sentence

Sometime after nine.

Answer: fragmentary sentence

The fragmentary answer is really saying:

I'm getting home sometime after nine.

This is what actually happens in real conversation, so you'll find it particularly in written dialogue.

sententious (sen-ten-shuhs)
adjective **1** having many pithy sayings or maxims: *a **sententious** style of writing*
2 arrogant and judgemental in speech (***moralising***, ***self-righteous***)

Word history: late Middle English, from Latin

sentient (sen-tee-uhnt, sen-shuhnt)
adjective **1** having the power of perception by the senses
2 marked by sensation
noun **3** someone or something that is sentient
4 the mind

Word building: **sentience** *noun*
Word history: from Latin word meaning 'feeling'

sentiment
noun **1** an attitude or opinion: *What is the public **sentiment** about this new law?*
2 a mental feeling or emotion

Word history: Late Latin, from Latin word meaning 'feel'

sentimental
adjective showing or having to do with tender feelings: ***sentimental** tears | a **sentimental** song*

Word building: **sentimentality** *noun* **sentimentally** *adverb*

sentinel
noun a soldier who acts as a lookout

Word history: French, from Italian, from Late Latin word meaning 'avoid danger', from Latin word meaning 'perceive'

sentry
noun a soldier who stands guard to keep people out

Noun forms: The plural is **sentries.**
Word history: perhaps short for obsolete *centrinel*, variant of *sentinel*

separate (sep-uh-rayt)
verb **1** to put or keep apart (***break off***, ***detach***, ***disconnect***, ***divide***)
2 to stop living with a marriage partner, without actually divorcing
adjective (sep-ruht) **3** not connected (***autonomous***, ***self-sufficient***, ***unattached***)

Word use: The opposite of definition 1 is **join**, **combine** or **amalgamate.**
Word history: Middle English, from Latin

separatist (sep-ruh-tuhst, sep-uh-ruh-tuhst)
noun **1** someone who separates or withdraws, especially from an established church
2 in former times, someone who wanted the separation from England of the administrative and judicial functions of the colonies in Australia, and their independence of each other

Word building: **separatism** *noun*

sepia (see-pee-uh)
noun **1** a brown colouring matter obtained from the ink-like substance produced by various cuttlefish, and used in drawing
2 a dark brown colour
adjective **3** of a dark brown colour: *a sketch in **sepia** tones* (***beige, brown, fawn, tan***)

Word history: Latin, from Greek

sepsis (sep-suhs)
noun a poisoning of some part of the body by bacterial organisms: *dental **sepsis***

Word history: Neo-Latin, from Greek

September
noun the ninth month of the year, containing thirty days

Word history: Middle English, Old English, from Latin, the seventh month in the early Roman calendar

septet
noun **1** any group or set of seven
2 a musical piece for seven voices or seven performers

Word history: German

septic
adjective infected with germs: *a **septic** wound*

Word history: Latin, from Greek

septic / sceptic
Don't confuse **septic** with **sceptic**. A **sceptic** is someone who doesn't believe things that most other people accept without question.

septicaemia (sep-tuh-see-mee-uh)
noun the entry of disease-producing bacteria into the bloodstream

Word use: You can also use **septicemia**.
Word building: **septicaemic** *adjective*
Word history: Neo-Latin, from Greek

septic tank
noun a tank in which solid waste matter is broken down by bacteria which do not need oxygen to be present

septum (sep-tuhm)
noun **1** a dividing wall, membrane, etc., especially between your nostrils
2 a membrane which allows osmosis

Noun forms: The plural is **septa**.
Word history: from Latin word meaning 'enclosure'

sepulchre (sep-uhl-kuh)
noun *Old-fashioned* a tomb or a grave

Word history: Middle English, from Old French, from Latin

sequel (see-kwuhl)
noun **1** a book or film which continues on from an earlier work
2 anything which follows or results from something (***consequence, outcome***)

Word history: Middle English, from Latin

sequence (see-kwuhns)
noun a series of things following each other (***chain, cycle, succession***)

Word building: **sequential** *adjective*
Word history: Middle English, from Latin word meaning 'following'

sequester (suh-kwes-tuh, see-kwes-tuh)
verb **1** to withdraw away or into retirement (***hide away, seclude***)
2 to remove or separate
3 to remove (a gas) from the atmosphere and store it to minimise the effects of greenhouse gases
4 *Law* to remove for a time from the owner until legal claims are satisfied: *to **sequester** property*

Word building: **sequestered** *adjective*
Word history: Middle English, from Late Latin word meaning 'separate', from Latin word meaning 'trustee'

sequestration (se-kwes-tray-shun)
noun **1** a removal or separation from a group
2 withdrawal; retirement or seclusion
3 removal of a substance for storage elsewhere
4 *Law* the sequestering of property

sequin (see-kwuhn)
noun a small shiny disc sewn as a decoration onto bags, evening clothes, or fancy dress

Word building: **sequined** *adjective*
Word history: French, from Italian *zecchino*, a Venetian coin

sere (sear)
adjective dry, or withered

Word history: variant of *sear*

serenade (se-ruh-nayd)
noun music traditionally played or sung in the open air at night, as by a man under the window of his lover

Word building: **serenade** *verb*
Word history: French, from Italian

serene
adjective calm and peaceful (***gentle, harmonious, quiet, tranquil***)

Word building: **serenely** *adverb* **serenity** *noun*
Word history: Latin

serf
noun someone who in feudal times was not free but was thought of as belonging to the land that a lord owned, and was sold with it

Noun forms: The plural is **serfs**.
Word history: Middle English, from French, from Latin word meaning 'slave'

serf / surf
Don't confuse **serf** with **surf**, which means the waves which break along the shoreline.

serge (serj)
noun **1** a strong woollen cloth used especially for clothing
2 cotton, rayon or silk with parallel woven lines

Word history: French

serge / surge
Don't confuse **serge** with **surge**, which is a sudden rush or upward sweep, as of water.

sergeant (sah-juhnt)
noun **1** an officer in the army who ranks next above a corporal
2 a police officer ranking between a constable and an inspector

Word history: Middle English, from Old French, from Latin word meaning 'serving'

serial (sear-ree-uhl)
noun **1** a story that is published or broadcast one part at a time at regular intervals
adjective **2** published in instalments or parts appearing one after the other: *a **serial** story*
3 *Computers* having to do with data transfer in which information is carried along a path one bit at a time

Word history: Neo-Latin, from Latin word meaning 'series'

serial / cereal
Don't confuse **serial** with **cereal**, which is grain, such as wheat or rice. A **cereal** is the breakfast food made from this.

serial killer
noun someone who kills a number of people over time all in a similar way

serial number
noun an individual number given to a particular person, article, etc., for identification

serial port
noun Computers a port that enables data to be sent or received one bit at a time

Word use: Compare this with **parallel port**.

series (sear-reez)
noun **1** a number of things or events arranged or happening in a certain order or sequence (***chain***, ***course***, ***cycle***)
2 a set of something: *This coin will now complete the **series** in my collection.*
3 a number of programs on radio or television which are linked in some way, either by subject matter or by being about the same group of people
4 *Geology* a division of a system of rocks, marked by sedimentary deposits formed during a geological epoch

Noun forms: The plural is **series**.
Word history: Latin

serious (sear-ree-uhs)
adjective **1** solemn or thoughtful: *The judge had a **serious** expression on her face.* (***dour***, ***grave***, ***sober***, ***stern***)
2 sincere and not joking: *Are you **serious**?*
3 important or needing a lot of thought: *Buying a new house is a **serious** matter.* (***momentous***, ***significant***)
4 giving cause for concern or worry: *His condition after the operation was **serious**.*

Word history: Middle English, from Late Latin, from Latin

sermon
noun **1** a serious talk, usually one preached in church: *Sunday's **sermon** was about loving your neighbour.* (***lecture***, ***lesson***)
2 a long boring speech: *Her father gave her a **sermon** about riding her bike on the busy road.*

Word history: Middle English, from Old French, from Latin word meaning 'discourse'

serpent
noun **1** *Old-fashioned* a snake
2 someone who is cunning, untrustworthy, or evil: *Satan, or the Devil, is often described as a **serpent**.*

Word history: Middle English, from Latin word meaning 'creeping thing'

serrated (suh-ray-tuhd)
adjective having notches or teeth along the edge: *A saw has a **serrated** blade.*

Word building: **serrate** *verb* **serration** *noun*
Word history: from Latin word meaning 'saw-shaped'

serum (sear-ruhm)
noun **1** a clear, pale yellow liquid that separates from your blood when it clots
2 this liquid used as a base for vaccines

Noun forms: The plural is **sera** or **serums**.
Word history: from Latin word meaning 'whey'

servant
noun **1** someone who works for or is in the service of someone else (***subject***, ***vassal***)
2 someone who is employed to live in your house and help look after it

Word history: Middle English, from Old French word meaning 'serving'

serve
verb **1** to work for
2 to put on a table: *to **serve** the dinner*
3 to supply or answer the needs of: *The shop assistant **served** me.*
4 to give help or assistance: *to **serve** in a shop*
5 to go through a term of service such as in the army or in a jail
6 to be of use: *That tree will **serve** as a shelter from the rain.* (***fill the bill***, ***qualify***, ***suffice***, ***suit***)
7 to start playing for a point in tennis by hitting the ball over the net
noun **8** the act of serving a ball in tennis

Word history: Middle English, from Old French, from Latin

server
noun **1** a computer which provides services to another computer via a network
2 a program which provides services to another computer via a network

servery (serv-uh-ree)
noun a room or area near the kitchen in which food is set out on plates

service
noun **1** a helpful act: *to perform a* ***service*** *for someone*
2 the supplying of something either useful to, or needed by, a large group of people: *a telephone* ***service*** | *a bus* ***service***
3 a department of public employment or the group of people in it: *the diplomatic* ***service***
4 the way you serve food: *The* ***service*** *in this restaurant is bad.*
5 the act of getting a car or other machinery into good order: *I put my car in the garage for a* ***service***.
noun **6** a religious ceremony: *a marriage* ***service***
7 a set of dishes for a particular use: *a dinner* ***service***
8 the act of serving a ball in tennis
verb **9** to make fit for use: *The garage* ***serviced*** *my car.*
Word history: Old English *serfise*, from Old French, from Latin

servicing / serving
Don't confuse **servicing** with **serving**.
Servicing is the present participle of **service** meaning 'to repair, or make fit for use':
The garage is servicing my car.
Serving is the present participle of **serve** meaning 'to attend or wait on someone':
The waiter is serving me now.

serviceable
adjective useful: *My old sandshoes are still* ***serviceable***.

service provider
noun → **internet service provider**

services
plural noun **1** things such as public transport, schools, hospitals, etc.: *essential* ***services***
phrase **2 the services,** the armed forces: *in* ***the services***

service station
noun a place where you can buy petrol, oil, etc., for motor vehicles, and where mechanical repairs are carried out
Word use: You can also use **petrol station**.

serviette
noun a piece of cloth or paper, used during a meal to wipe your lips and hands and to protect your clothes (***napkin***, ***table napkin***)
Word history: from French word meaning 'serve'

servile (ser-vuyl)
adjective **1** weakly allowing another to have control: ***servile*** *manners* (***downtrodden***, ***submissive***, ***subservient***, ***weak-willed***)
2 abject, in the way slaves are: ***servile*** *obedience*
Word building: **servility** *noun*
Word history: Middle English, from Latin

serving
noun **1** the act of someone or something that serves
2 a portion or helping of food or drink
adjective **3** having to do with dishing out food: *a* ***serving*** *spoon*

serving / servicing
Look up **servicing / serving**.

servitude (ser-vuh-tyoohd)
noun **1** slavery, or bondage: *political* ***servitude***
2 forced service or labour as a punishment for criminals: *penal* ***servitude***
Word history: Middle English, from Latin

servlet
noun Computers a small Java program which runs as part of a web server

sesame (ses-uh-mee)
noun a tropical herb, whose small oval seeds are used for food and oil
Word history: Greek

session (sesh-uhn)
noun **1** the sitting or meeting together of a court, council or parliament
2 a period of time for any particular activity: *a dancing* ***session***
Word history: Middle English, from Latin

set
verb **1** to put in a particular place or position: *She* ***set*** *the vase on the table.* (***deposit***, ***lodge***, ***park***, ***place***, ***rest***)
2 to cause to begin: *The accident really* ***set*** *him thinking.* (***get going***, ***start***)
3 to fix or appoint: *The officials* ***set*** *a time for the race.*
4 to provide for others to follow: *She* ***set*** *an excellent example.*
5 to give, assign, or make up: *The teacher* ***set*** *the homework.* | *He* ***set*** *the maths exam.*
6 to arrange in proper order: *She* ***set*** *the table for dinner.*
7 to adjust or regulate: *I* ***set*** *the clock.*
8 to put something into a fixed place or position: *The doctor* ***set*** *her broken arm.*
9 to become hard or solid: *The jelly* ***set*** *in the bowl.* (***harden***, ***solidify***, ***stiffen***)
10 to pass or sink below the horizon: *The sun* ***sets*** *every evening.*
noun **11** a number of things that are used together, or form a collection: *a* ***set*** *of dishes*
12 a radio or television receiver
13 a group of games that make up one of the sections of a tennis match
14 a number of pieces of scenery arranged together, used for a play or film
15 any collection of numbers or objects in maths which have something in common
adjective **16** fixed beforehand: *a* ***set*** *time* | ***set*** *rules*
17 fixed or rigid: *a* ***set*** *smile* | ***set*** *in your ways*
18 ready or prepared: *all* ***set*** *to go*
phrase **19 set off,**
a to explode: *to* ***set off*** *a bomb*
b to begin a journey
20 set out,
a to arrange
b to explain carefully
c to start a journey (***begin***, ***get going***, ***get off***, ***start***)
21 set up,
a to build or erect (***construct***, ***put up***)
b to provide with: *His parents* ***set*** *him* ***up*** *with a house.*
c to claim to be: *He* ***sets*** *himself* ***up*** *as an expert.*

Verb forms: I **set**, I have **set**, I am **setting**
Word history: Middle English *sette(n)* to set, place, from Old English *settan*

setback
noun something that hinders or slows down your progress (***blow***, ***difficulty***, ***obstruction***)

set square
noun a flat piece of wood or plastic in the shape of a right-angled triangle, used in drawing technical things like plans for buildings

settee (set-ee, suh-tee)
noun a seat or sofa for two or more people

Word history: perhaps from *seat*

setter (set-uh)
noun a long-haired hunting dog trained to stand stiffly and point its nose towards the animal being hunted

setting
noun **1** the surroundings of anything: *The house was situated in a pretty country* ***setting****.* (***environment***, ***environs***, ***scene***)
2 the time and place in which a play or film takes place
3 a group of things such as a knife, fork, and plate used to set someone's place at the table
4 a position to which a device is adjusted for a particular function: *Is the modem on the correct* ***setting****? | Adjust the* ***settings*** *on the television to improve reception.*

settle
verb **1** to decide or agree: *They* ***settled*** *on a suitable time.* (***assent***, ***concur***, ***see eye to eye***, ***shake hands***)
2 to put in order or arrange: *She* ***settled*** *all her affairs before she went away.* (***organise***, ***sort out***)
3 to pay: *He* ***settled*** *the bill.*
4 to set up a home: *The family* ***settled*** *in Tasmania.*
5 to sink down gradually: *The dust slowly* ***settled****.*
phrase **6 settle down,**
a to put to bed
b to begin to do serious work
c to begin to live an ordered life, especially after marrying

Word history: Old English *setlan* from *setl* a seat

settlement
noun **1** the act or result of settling
2 an arrangement or adjustment
3 a colony
4 a small village, usually in an area with not many people

settler
noun someone who settles in a new country

set-top box
noun a device, connected to a conventional television set, which receives and decodes digital television broadcasts

Word use: The abbreviation is **STB**.

set-up
noun **1** organisation or arrangement: *The* ***set-up*** *of the library is clear.*
2 *Colloquial* something which has been arranged dishonestly
3 *Colloquial* a trap

Word building: **set-up** *adjective*

seven
noun **1** a cardinal number, six plus one (6 + 1)
2 the symbol for this number, as 7 or VII
3 a set of seven persons or things
adjective **4** amounting to seven in number

Word building: **seventh** *adjective* **seventh** *noun*
Word history: Old English *seofon*

seventeen (sev-uhn-teen)
noun **1** a cardinal number, ten plus seven (10 + 7)
2 the symbol for this number, as 17 or XVII
3 a set of seventeen people or things
adjective **4** amounting to seventeen in number

Word building: **seventeenth** *adjective* **seventeenth** *noun*
Word history: Old English *seofontene*

seventy
noun **1** cardinal number, ten times seven (10 × 7)
2 symbol for this number, as 70 or LXX
3 a set of seventy persons or things
4 seventies, the numbers from 70 to 79 of a series, especially with reference to the years of a person's age, or the years of a century
adjective **5** amounting to seventy in number

Noun forms: The plural is **seventies.**
Word building: **seventieth** *adjective* **seventieth** *noun*
Word history: Old English *seofontig*

sever (sev-uh)
verb **1** to cut or separate
2 to break off: *The countries have* ***severed*** *all relations.*

Word history: Middle English, from Anglo-French, from Late Latin

several
adjective **1** more than two, but not many
2 individual, different or respective: *They went their* ***several*** *ways.*

Word history: Middle English, from Anglo-French, from Latin word meaning 'distinct'

severance pay (sev-uh-ruhns pay)
noun money paid by a firm to workers or directors to make up for the loss of their jobs

severe (suh-vear)
adjective **1** harsh or extreme: ***severe*** *punishment*
2 unsmiling or stern: *a* ***severe*** *face*
3 serious or grave: *a* ***severe*** *illness*
4 simple, plain, and without decoration: *She wears* ***severe*** *clothes.* (***plain***, ***quiet***, ***unadorned***, ***unobtrusive***)

Word building: **severity** *noun*
Word history: Latin

sew (soh)
verb **1** to join with stitches, using a needle and thread (***darn***, ***embroider***, ***stitch***, ***tack***, ***work***)
2 to make or repair clothes with a needle and thread

Word history: Old English *siw(i)an*

sew / so / sow

Don't confuse **sew** with **so** or **sow**.

So means 'therefore'.

To **sow**, rhyming with *go*, is to scatter seed on the ground. But a **sow**, rhyming with *cow*, is a female pig.

sewage
noun the waste matter which passes through drains and sewers

> **sewage / sewerage**
> Don't confuse **sewage** with **sewerage**, which is the process of taking the **sewage** away.

sewer (<u>sooh</u>-uh)
noun a pipeline, usually underground, made to carry away waste water and waste matter

Word history: Middle English, from Old French word meaning 'channel from a fishpond', from Romance, from Latin

sewerage (<u>sooh</u>-rij, <u>soo</u>-uh-rij)
noun the removal of waste water and waste matter using sewers

> **sewerage / sewage**
> Don't confuse **sewerage** with **sewage**, which is the waste matter which passes through the **sewerage** system.

sex
noun **1** one of the two divisions of either male or female in humans and animals
2 the characteristic or condition of being either male or female
3 the instinct which causes sexual attraction between two people
4 the arousal of sexual interest by the way people are portrayed in films, books, etc.: ***sex** on TV*
5 → **sexual intercourse**

Word history: Middle English, from Latin *sexus* sex, perhaps originally, division

sexist
adjective having to do with an attitude which judges someone by their sex rather than by their own individual qualities

Word building: **sexism** *noun* **sexist** *noun*

sexist language
noun language which presents a view of the world which either excludes or demeans one or other sex

> Given our social history, **sexist language** usually refers to language which presents a world dominated by men, in which men are the real people and women are shadowy figures in the background. For example, terms like *businessman* or *newsman* inevitably give the impression that only men can have jobs in business or can report the news. Look up **-man**.
>
> The attitude of mind that is behind sexist language is revealed in other less obvious ways. Look at the following examples and note the underlying assumptions about men and women which they reveal:
>
> **1** *A boy and his sister were sitting in their father's fine watermelon patch. The gingerbread man ran past. 'Stop!' commanded the boy. 'Oh please stop!' pleaded the little girl.*
>
> In this example the assumption is that boys command and that girls plead. That is, that men have the authority to give orders but women should just ask very nicely.
>
> **2** *The Abkhazian people of Georgia are famous for their longevity. Many of them live vigorous lives well past their hundredth birthday. Most have their own teeth, under flamboyant silver moustaches.*
>
> In this example the writer has drifted from talking about people, which ought to mean men and women, to talking about men with their 'flamboyant silver moustaches'. This implies that the only people who count are the men.
>
> For ways to avoid sexist language, look up **non-sexist language**.

sextant
noun an instrument which measures the angles between the sun, moon, stars, and earth to help sailors work out their position

Word history: from Latin word meaning 'sixth part'

sextet
noun **1** any group or set of six
2 a musical piece for six voices or six performers

Word history: alteration of *sestet*, from Latin *sex* six

sexual
adjective having to do with sex

Word history: Late Latin

sexual harassment
noun unwanted sexual advances, usually made to a woman by a man, especially one who holds a superior position in an organisation for which they both work

sexual intercourse
noun a sexual act between two people, usually one in which a man's penis enters a woman's vagina

Word use: You can also use **intercourse** or **sex**.

sexualise
verb to fill with sexual character: *The community objected to the way the company was **sexualising** the images of young girls.*

Verb forms: it **sexualised**, it had **sexualised**, it is **sexualising**
Word use: You can also use **sexualize**.
Word building: **sexualisation** *noun* **sexualised** *adjective*

sexy
adjective **1** having a great concern with sex: *a **sexy** book*
2 having an attractiveness or charm that attracts the members of the opposite sex

Adjective forms: **sexier**, **sexiest**

SGML
noun a computer mark-up language, designed to be a general standard, in which various elements of a document, database, etc., are given tags, providing flexible structure and data retrieval

shabby
adjective **1** very worn: ***shabby** clothes*
2 wearing old or very worn clothes
3 mean or unfair: *It was a **shabby** trick to play on a friend.* (***contemptible***, ***despicable***, ***nasty***, ***unkind***)

Adjective forms: **shabbier**, **shabbiest**
Word history: *shab* (Middle English; Old English *sceabb* scab) + *-y*

shack
noun a rough cabin or hut
Word history: short for *shackle* in same sense, itself short for *ramshackle*

shackle
noun **1** a ring of iron, usually one of a pair, for holding the wrist or ankle of a prisoner or slave
2 anything that stops someone's free thought or action
Word history: Middle English *shackle*, Old English *sceacel* fetter

shade
noun **1** a slight darkness or an area of slight darkness caused by the blocking off of rays of light
2 something that shuts out, or protects from, light or heat: *Pull down the **shades** on those windows.*
3 a darker or lighter kind of one colour: *Her dress was in three **shades** of green.*
verb **4** to dim or darken (***fog***, ***obscure***)
5 to protect from heat or light
Word history: Old English *sceadu*

shadow
noun **1** the dark figure or area of shade made by something blocking out light
2 shade or slight darkness
verb **3** to shade, or protect from heat or light
4 to follow secretly (***tag***, ***track***)
Word building: **shadowy** *adjective*
Word history: Old English *scead(u)we*, form of *sceadu* shade

shady
adjective **1** in the shade: *a **shady** spot*
2 giving shade: *a **shady** tree*
3 *Colloquial* of doubtful honesty or character: *a **shady** deal*
Adjective forms: **shadier**, **shadiest**

shaft
noun **1** a long pole or rod: *the **shaft** of a spear | the **shaft** of an arrow*
2 a ray or beam: *a **shaft** of sunlight*
3 a passage that is like a well, or an enclosed vertical or sloping space: *a lift **shaft** | a mine **shaft***
Word history: Old English *sceaft*

shag[1]
noun **1** rough, matted hair, wool, etc.
2 a heavy or rough woollen cloth, with short, fuzzy fibres
3 coarse tobacco cut into fine shreds
Word history: Old English *sceacga* wool, etc.

shag[2]
noun **1** → **cormorant**
phrase **2 like a shag on a rock**, *Australian*, *NZ Colloquial* alone, or deserted
Word history: perhaps from the shaggy crest of the bird

shaggy
adjective **1** covered with or having long rough hair: *a **shaggy** dog*
2 rough, coarse, or untidy: *The lion had a **shaggy** appearance.*
Adjective forms: **shaggier**, **shaggiest**

shake
verb **1** to move backwards and forwards with quick short movements (***quake***, ***rock***, ***shudder***, ***sway***, ***tremble***)
2 to fall or scatter by using such movements: *Sand **shakes** off easily.*
3 to tremble with fear or cold
4 to make unsteady or unsettled: *Her faith in his honesty was **shaken** by his behaviour.*
noun **5** the act of shaking or an unsteady movement
6 a milkshake
phrase **7 no great shakes**, *Colloquial* of no particular importance
8 shake hands, to grip hands as a greeting, or to show agreement
Verb forms: I **shook**, I have **shaken**, I am **shaking**
Word history: Old English *sceacan*

shaky
adjective **1** shaking, or trembling: ***shaky** legs*
2 likely to break down or give way: *a **shaky** ladder | a **shaky** friendship*
Adjective forms: **shakier**, **shakiest**
Word building: **shakiness** *noun*

shale
noun a rock of layered or easily split structure formed by the consolidation of clay or very tiny particles
Word building: **shaly** *adjective* (**shalier**, **shaliest**)
Word history: special use of obsolete *shale* scale (of a fish, etc.)

shall
auxiliary verb **1** used, generally, in the first person to show simple future time: *I **shall** go today.*
2 used, generally in the second and third persons, to show promise or determination: *You **shall** do it.*
3 used in questions that allow for *shall* in the answer: ***Shall** he be told? He **shall**.*
4 used conditionally in all persons to show future time: *if he **shall** come*
Verb forms: I **shall**, I **should**
Word use: The old forms of the verb are **thou shalt**, **thou shouldst** or **shouldest**.
Word history: Old English *sceal*

shallot (shuh-lot)
noun an onion-like plant used for flavouring in cooking and as a vegetable
Word history: variant of *eschalot*, from Old French

shallow
adjective **1** not deep: ***shallow** water*
2 without any serious thought: *a **shallow** mind | a **shallow** argument*
Word history: Middle English *schalowe*

sham
noun **1** something that is not what it appears to be (***fake***, ***fraud***)
verb **2** to pretend: *to **sham** illness*
adjective **3** not real or true (***bogus***, ***counterfeit***, ***fake***, ***false***, ***phoney***)
Verb forms: I **shammed**, I have **shammed**, I am **shamming**
Word history: special use of British dialect *sham*, northern variant of *shame*

shamble
verb **1** to shuffle
noun **2** a shambling walk

Word history: verb use of *shamble*, adjective, awkward

shambles
noun any place or thing in confusion or disorder: *The office is in a* ***shambles***. (***mess***, ***muddle***)

Word use: This word is usually treated as a singular.
Word history: Old English *sc(e)amel* stool, table, later counter for selling meat, later slaughtering place

shame
noun **1** a mentally painful feeling that comes after you know you have said or done something wrong or silly
2 a disgrace or dishonour: *Her crime brought* ***shame*** *to her family.*
3 a pity or something to be sorry about: *It's a* ***shame*** *he can't come today.*
4 *Aboriginal English* a mixture of embarrassment and shyness, felt by some people in different situations, such as when they are singled out from a group to be either praised or scolded
verb **5** to cause to feel shame: *Their behaviour* ***shamed*** *their parents.*
phrase **6 put to shame,**
a to disgrace or make ashamed
b to do better than: *Robert* ***puts*** *Raoul* ***to shame*** *in swimming.*

Word building: **shameful** *adjective* **shameless** *adjective*
Word history: Old English *sc(e)amu*

shampoo
noun **1** a liquid soap, for washing hair, carpet, etc.
verb **2** to wash with shampoo: *to* ***shampoo*** *your hair* | *to* ***shampoo*** *a carpet*

Verb forms: I **shampooed**, I have **shampooed**, I am **shampooing**
Word history: from Hindustani word meaning 'to shampoo', literally 'to press', 'squeeze'

shamrock
noun a bright green plant with three small leaves grouped on one stem: *The* ***shamrock*** *is the national emblem of Ireland.*

Word history: Irish *seamróg*, little clover

shandy
noun a drink which is a mixture of beer with either ginger beer or lemonade

Noun forms: The plural is **shandies**.

shanghai[1] (shang-huy, shang-huy)
verb **1** to take someone forcibly to join a ship as a member of the crew
2 *Colloquial* to steal

Verb forms: I **shanghaied**, I have **shanghaied**, I am **shanghaiing**
Word history: apparently short for 'to ship to *Shanghai*', a port city in eastern China

shanghai[2] (shang-huy)
noun Australian, NZ a child's catapult or slingshot

Word history: British dialect *shangan* a cleft stick for putting on a dog's tail

shank
noun **1** the whole leg
2 a cut of meat from the top part of the leg, from the front or back
3 that part of an instrument, tool, etc., connecting the acting part with the handle

Word history: Old English *sc(e)anca*

shan't
contraction of **shall not**

Look up **contractions in grammar.**

shantung (shan-tung)
noun **1** a heavy silk cloth made of rough, spun wild silk
2 a fabric like this made of rayon or cotton

Word history: from *Shantung*, maritime province in north-eastern China

shanty[1]
noun a roughly built hut, cabin or house

Noun forms: The plural is **shanties.**
Word history: probably from Canadian French *chantier* log hut, from French word meaning 'shed', from Latin word meaning 'framework'

shanty[2]
noun a sailors' song, usually sung in rhythm to the work they are doing

Noun forms: The plural is **shanties.**
Word history: French *chanter* sing

shape
noun **1** the outline or form of something or someone (***design***, ***figure***, ***structure***)
2 proper order: *The house is now in* ***shape*** *for our visitors.*
3 condition: *His business affairs were in bad* ***shape.***
verb **4** to give definite form, shape or character to: *The potter carefully* ***shaped*** *his pots.* (***construct***, ***fashion***, ***form***)
phrase **5 shape up,** to develop: *The new worker is* ***shaping up*** *well.*

Word building: **shapeless** *adjective*
Word history: Middle English

shapely
adjective having a pleasing shape

Adjective forms: **shapelier**, **shapeliest**

shard
noun a small piece, especially of broken earthenware

Word use: You can also use **sherd.**
Word history: Old English *sceard*

share (shair)
noun **1** the part given to or owned by someone (***allocation***, ***allotment***, ***cut***, ***distribution***, ***quota***)
2 each of the equal parts into which the ownership of a company is divided: *to buy 500* ***shares*** *in BHP*
verb **3** to divide into parts with each person receiving a part (***allocate***, ***distribute***, ***divvy up***, ***dole out***, ***split***)
4 to use or enjoy together: *The whole family* ***shares*** *the car.*

Word history: Old English *scearu* cutting, division

shareholder
noun someone who owns a share or shares in a company

sharia (shah-ree-uh, shu-ree-uh)
noun **1** the law based on the Koran, the Sunna, and Arabic tradition, followed by Muslims
adjective **2** having to do with this system: *a **sharia** court*

Word use: You can also use **shariah**.

shark[1]
noun any of a number of large fish which are very fierce and sometimes dangerous to humans, and which have soft skeletons and five to seven pairs of gill openings

shark[2]
noun a person who dishonestly profits from others, as through false or unfair money dealings (***cheat***, ***crook***, ***fraud***)

Word building: **shark** *verb*
Word history: from German word meaning 'rascal'

sharp
adjective **1** having a thin cutting edge or a fine point: *a **sharp** knife | a **sharp** needle*
2 sudden or abrupt: *a **sharp** rise in temperature | a **sharp** bend in the road*
3 clearly outlined or distinct: *a **sharp** picture on TV*
4 strong or biting in taste (***piquant***, ***pungent***, ***savoury***, ***spicy***, ***tasty***)
5 very cold or piercing: *a **sharp** wind* (***frosty***, ***icy***, ***nippy***, ***wintry***)
6 mentally quick and alert: *a **sharp** mind* (***astute***, ***canny***, ***clever***, ***knowing***, ***shrewd***)
7 keen or sensitive: *a **sharp** ear*
8 higher in pitch by a semitone, or too high in pitch: *B **sharp** | Your recorder is a bit **sharp** in the low notes.*
adverb **9** precisely: *at one o'clock **sharp***
noun **10 a** a note that is one semitone above a given note
b the music sign (♯) which raises a note by a semitone when it is placed before it

Word use: The opposite of definitions 8 and 10 is **flat**.
Word building: **sharpness** *noun*
Word history: Old English *scearp*

sharpen
verb to make or become sharp or sharper

Word building: **sharpener** *noun*

shashlik (shash-lik)
noun → **shish kebab**

Word use: You can also use **shashlick** or **shaslick**.
Word history: Russian *shashlyk*, of Turkic origin

shatter
verb **1** to break into pieces
2 to weaken or destroy: *His health was **shattered** by the accident.*

Word history: Middle English

shave
verb **1** to remove hair with a razor
2 to take thin slices from, especially so as to smooth: *The carpenter **shaved** the wood.*
3 to graze or come very near: *The car just **shaved** the corner.*
noun **4** the act or process of shaving
phrase **5 a close shave**, a narrow miss or escape

Verb forms: I **shaved**, I have **shaved** or I have **shaven**, I am **shaving**
Word history: Old English *sceafan*

shaving
noun a very thin piece, especially of wood: *The **shavings** from the door covered the floor.*

shawl
noun a piece of material worn as a covering for your shoulders or head

Word history: Persian

she
pronoun the personal pronoun used to refer to a particular female: ***She** walked towards me.*

She is a third person singular pronoun in the subjective case.
For more information, look up **pronouns: personal pronouns**.

sheaf
noun **1** one of the bundles into which cereal plants, like wheat and rye, are bound after they are cut in the field
2 any bundle, group, or collection: *a **sheaf** of papers*

Noun forms: The plural is **sheaves**.
Word history: Old English *scēaf*

shear
verb **1** to remove by cutting with a sharp instrument: *He **sheared** all the wool from the sheep.* (***clip***, ***cut***, ***mow***, ***snip***, ***trim***)
2 to cut hair or fleece from something: *to **shear** sheep*
noun **3 shears**, large scissors or another similar cutting tool

Verb forms: I **sheared**, I have **sheared** or I have **shorn**, I am **shearing**
Word building: **shearer** *noun*
Word history: Old English *sceran*

shear / sheer
Don't confuse **shear** with **sheer.**
Cloth is **sheer** if it is so thin that you can see through it.
A **sheer** cliff is very steep.
To **sheer** away is to change course suddenly.

sheath
noun **1** a covering for the blade of a sword, dagger or bayonet
2 any similar covering
3 a close-fitting dress which follows the shape of your body

Noun forms: The plural is **sheaths**.
Word history: Old English *scēath*

sheathe
verb **1** to put into a sheath: *to **sheathe** a sword*
2 to enclose in or as though in a covering
3 to cover with a layer that protects

Word history: Middle English *shethe*

shed[1]
noun a simple or roughly-built building used for storage or sheltering animals

Word history: Old English *scead, sced* shelter, shade

shed[2]
verb **1** to pour forth or let fall: *to **shed** blood | to **shed** tears*
2 to give forth or send out light, sound, or smell: *This lamp **sheds** a soft glow of light.*
3 to cast or throw off: *A snake regularly **sheds** its skin and grows another one.* (***discard, ditch, dump, jettison, scrap***)

Verb forms: it **shed**, it has **shed**, it is **shedding**
Word history: Old English

she'd
contraction of **she had** or **she would**

Look up **contractions in grammar.**

sheen
noun brightness: *He polished the furniture to a glowing **sheen.*** (***lustre, polish***)

Word history: Old English *scēne* beautiful, bright

sheep
noun **1** an animal, closely related to the goat, which is kept for its meat and thick wool
2 someone who is shy, timid or stupid

Noun forms: The plural is **sheep.**
Word history: Old English *scēp* (Anglian), *scēap*

sheep dip
noun a deep trough containing a liquid which kills harmful insects on sheep as they are driven through it

sheepdog
noun a dog trained to guard and round up sheep

sheepish
adjective awkwardly shy or embarrassed

sheer[1]
adjective **1** very thin so that you can see through: *The curtains on the window were almost **sheer.*** (***gauzy, transparent***)
2 absolute, or unmixed with anything else: *You won by **sheer** luck.*
3 very steep: *a **sheer** cliff*

sheer[2]
verb **1** to swerve or change course: *The ship **sheered** away from the rocks.*
noun **2** a swerve

Word history: special use of *shear*, verb

sheer / shear
Look up **shear / sheer.**

sheet
noun **1** one of two large pieces of cloth used on a bed, one under you and the other over you
2 any layer or covering: *a **sheet** of water*
3 a broad thin piece of something: *a **sheet** of glass | a **sheet** of paper*

Word history: Old English *scēat* lap

sheikh (sheek, shayk)
noun in Arab and other Muslim use, a chief or head, such as of a religious group, village, or tribe

Word history: from Arabic word meaning 'old man'

shelf
noun **1** a thin flat piece of wood, glass, or something similar, fixed horizontally to a wall or in a frame and used for holding things like books or ornaments
2 a ledge: *a **shelf** of rock*

Noun forms: The plural is **shelves.**
Word history: Middle English

shell
noun **1** the hard outer covering of things like nuts, eggs and certain animals
2 something like a shell: *Just the **shell** of the building remained after the fire.*
3 a hollow bullet-like case filled with explosives, to be fired from a large gun
4 *Computers* an interface program which executes commands
verb **5** to take out of the shell: *to **shell** peas*
6 to fire shells on: *The soldiers **shelled** the enemy.*
phrase **7 shell out,** *Colloquial* to hand over or pay up

Word history: Old English *scell* (Anglian), *sciell*

she'll
contraction of **she will** or **she shall**

Look up **contractions in grammar.**

shellfish
noun an animal like an oyster or lobster that is not a fish but lives in water and has a shell

Noun forms: The plural is **shellfishes** or **shellfish.**
Word history: Old English *scilfisc*

shelter
noun **1** protection from bad weather, danger, etc.: *We took **shelter** from the rain.*
2 a place of safety and protection: *a bomb **shelter*** (***asylum, haven, refuge, retreat, sanctuary***)

Word building: **shelter** *verb*

shelve
verb **1** to place on a shelf or shelves
2 to stop considering or thinking about: *He **shelved** the problem for a few days.* (***defer, set aside***)

Word history: from *shelves*, plural of *shelf*

shepherd (<u>shep</u>-uhd)
noun **1** someone who looks after sheep
verb **2** to take care of or to guard, especially when moving along: *The police **shepherded** the pop star through the crowd.*

Word history: Old English *scēphyrde*

sherbet
noun a sweet, fizzy powder that you can eat dry or use to make a fizzy drink

Word history: Turkish and Persian, from Arabic word meaning 'a drink'

sheriff
noun **1** in Australia, an officer in some courts of law who has duties such as organising juries
2 in the US, the chief law enforcement officer in a county

Word history: Old English *scīrgerēfa*

sherry
noun a strong sweet or dry wine

Noun forms: The plural is **sherries.**
Word history: earlier *sherris*, taken as plural, from Spanish (*vino de*) *Xeres* (wine of) Xeres, now Jerez in southern Spain

she's
contraction of **she is** or **she has**

Look up **contractions in grammar.**

Shetland pony
noun a pony of a small, sturdy, rough-coated breed

Word use: You can also use **sheltie.**
Word history: from the *Shetland* Islands, a Scottish island group north-east of the mainland, where the ponies were originally bred

shield
noun **1** a flat piece of metal, leather, or wood, carried to protect your body in a battle
2 anything used for protection: *She held her hands to her eyes as a **shield** against the sun.* (***defence***, ***protection***, ***safeguard***)

Word building: **shield** *verb*
Word history: Old English *sceld*

shift
verb **1** to move from one place or position to another (***budge***, ***give way***, ***stir***)
2 to manage to get along or succeed: *She'll **shift** for herself.*
noun **3** a change or a move: *a **shift** in the wind*
4 the period of time worked by someone in a place of work which operates 24 hours a day: *I have to do the night **shift** at the hospital tomorrow.*
5 the people who work during this time: *The day **shift** takes over now.*
6 a loose-fitting dress

Word history: Middle English; Old English *sciftan*, related to German *schichten* arrange

shifting agriculture
noun a form of agriculture in which people clear and cultivate an area of land and then move on to another area, for various reasons, such as nomadic habits

Word use: You can also use **shifting cultivation**.

shiftless
adjective lazy, or lacking in resource or ambition

shifty
adjective deceitful and looking as if you've got something to hide: *The burglar had **shifty** eyes.* (***crooked***, ***cunning***, ***dishonest***)

Adjective forms: **shiftier**, **shiftiest**

shiitake mushroom (shit-ah-kee mush-roohm)
noun an edible mushroom native to Japan and thought to have health-giving properties

shilling
noun a silver coin used in Australia before decimal currency

Word history: Old English *scilling*

shimmer
verb to shine or gleam with a dim unsteady light (***flicker***, ***glimmer***)

Word history: Old English *scimerian*, from *scīmian* shine

shin
noun **1** the front part of your leg between your knee and your ankle
phrase **2 shin up**, to climb up by gripping with your hands and your feet: *He **shinned** quickly **up** the rope.* (***ascend***, ***mount***, ***scale***)

Verb forms: I **shinned**, I have **shinned**, I am **shinning**
Word history: Old English *scinu*

shine
verb **1** to glow or give out light (***beam***, ***blaze***, ***burn***, ***flare***)
2 to polish: *He **shined** his shoes.* (***buff***, ***burnish***, ***smooth***, ***wax***)
3 to be very good at something: *She **shines** at tennis.* (***make the grade***, ***steal the show***, ***succeed***, ***triumph***, ***win***)
4 to direct the light of: ***Shine** the torch over here.*
noun **5** polished brightness

Verb forms: it **shone** or it **shined**, it has **shone** or it has **shined**, it is **shining**
Word building: **shiny** *adjective* (**shinier**, **shiniest**)
Word history: Old English *scīnan*

shiner
noun **1** someone or something that shines
2 *Colloquial* a black eye

shingle[1]
noun **1** a thin piece of wood, slate, etc., used in rows to cover the roofs and sides of houses
verb **2** to cover with shingles

Word history: Middle English; variant of *shindle*, from Latin

shingle[2]
noun small, water-worn stones or pebbles lying in masses on the seashore

Word history: earlier *chingle*; perhaps of imitative origin

shingles
noun a skin disease which affects the nerves and causes a painful rash, often around the middle of the body

Word history: Middle English, from Medieval Latin, from Latin *cingulum* girdle

Shinto
noun a native religion of Japan in which nature and ancestors are worshipped and held sacred

Word building: **Shintoist** *noun*, *adjective*
Word history: Japanese, from Chinese word meaning 'way of the gods'

ship
noun **1** a large boat for carrying people or goods over deep water
verb **2** to send by ship, train, truck, etc.

Verb forms: I **shipped**, I have **shipped**, I am **shipping**
Word history: Old English *scip*

shipment
noun a load of goods shipped at one time

shipshape
adjective neat and tidy (***orderly***, ***trim***)

shipwreck
noun **1** the destruction of a ship by running into land or sinking
2 the remains of a wrecked ship
verb **3** to suffer or cause to suffer a shipwreck: *We were* ***shipwrecked*** *on the rocks.*

shiralee (shi-ruh-lee, shi-ruh-lee)
noun Australian a swag

shiraz (shuh-raz)
noun **1** a red grape variety grown in Australia
2 a wine made from this grape
Word history: from *Shiraz*, city in Iran

shire
noun a local government area
Word history: Old English *scīr*

shire council
noun the local administrative body which serves a shire
Word use: Compare this with **city council** and **municipal council.**

shirk
verb to get out of doing: *to* ***shirk*** *your job* (***avoid***, ***evade***)
Word use: The opposite of this is **fulfil.**
Word building: **shirker** *noun*
Word history: perhaps from German word meaning 'parasite', 'sharper'

shirt (shert)
noun **1** a garment for the upper part of your body, usually with buttons down the front, a collar, and long or short sleeves
phrase **2 keep your shirt on**, to keep your temper or be patient
Word history: Old English *scyrte*

shish kebab
noun → **kebab** (definition 1)
Word use: You can also use **shashlik.**
Word history: Turkish

shiver
verb to shake with fear, cold or excitement (***quiver***, ***shudder***, ***tremble***)
Word building: **shiver** *noun* **shivery** *adjective*
Word history: Middle English *chivere*

shoal[1]
noun a sandbank under shallow water
Word history: Old English *sceald* shallow

shoal[2]
noun a group of fish swimming together
Word history: Old English *scolu* shoal (of fishes), multitude, troop

shock[1]
noun **1** a sudden and violent fright or upset
2 pain and injury caused by an electric current passing through the body
Word building: **shock** *verb*
Word history: French word meaning 'strike against', 'shock', from Middle Dutch

shock[2]
noun a thick bushy mass: *a* ***shock*** *of hair*
Word history: perhaps variant of *shag*[1]

shocking
adjective **1** causing very great surprise, disgust, horror, etc.: ***shocking*** *news*
2 *Colloquial* very bad: ***shocking*** *weather*

shoddy
adjective **1** bad or made badly: ***shoddy*** *work | a* ***shoddy*** *house* (***crummy***, ***defective***, ***dud***, ***inferior***)
2 mean: *a* ***shoddy*** *thing to do*
Adjective forms: **shoddier, shoddiest**
Word building: **shoddily** *adverb* **shoddiness** *noun*

shoe (shooh)
noun **1** an external covering, usually made of leather, for your foot
2 a thing or part looking like a shoe in form, position, or use
verb **3** to provide or fit with shoes: *to* ***shoe*** *a horse*
phrase **4 in someone's shoes**, in the position or situation of another: *I shouldn't like to be* ***in his shoes.***
Noun forms: The plural is **shoes.**
Verb forms: I **shoed,** I have **shoed,** I am **shoeing**
Word history: Old English *scōh*

shoehorn
noun a long piece of metal or plastic that you put into the heel of your shoe to make it go on more easily

shone
verb past tense and past participle of **shine**

shook
verb past tense of **shake**

shoot
verb **1** to hit or kill with a bullet, arrow, or something else fired from a weapon: *The policeman* ***shot*** *the bank robber.*
2 to fire from a weapon: *to* ***shoot*** *an arrow*
3 to send out quickly and accurately like an arrow or bullet: *to* ***shoot*** *questions | to* ***shoot*** *a ball into the goal*
4 to move quickly: *He* ***shot*** *along the path.*
5 to photograph or film: *to* ***shoot*** *a scene*
6 to put out new growths: *Plants* ***shoot*** *in spring.*
noun **7** a new growth on a plant
phrase **8 shoot down,**
a to bring down by gunfire: *to* ***shoot down*** *an aircraft*
b to defeat completely: *The panel will easily* ***shoot down*** *your argument.*
9 shoot through, *Australian, NZ Colloquial* to go away, usually when you are supposed to stay: *Instead of going to the exam, he* ***shot through.***
Verb forms: I **shot,** I have **shot,** I am **shooting**
Word building: **shooter** *noun*
Word history: Old English *scēotan*

shoot / chute
Don't confuse **shoot** with **chute,** which is a sloping channel for sending things like water, grain, rubbish or coal to a lower level.

shop
noun **1** a building where goods are sold (***stall***, ***store***, ***supermarket***)
2 a place where work is done, usually mechanical work
3 an act of shopping for goods: *We do a big weekly* ***shop.***
verb **4** to go looking for and buying goods

phrase **5 shop around**, to visit a number of shops comparing quality and price before buying
6 talk shop, to discuss your trade, profession, or business

Verb forms: I **shopped**, I have **shopped**, I am **shopping**
Word use: You can also use **workshop** for definition 2.
Word building: **shopper** *noun*
Word history: Old English *sceoppa* booth

shoplift
verb to steal from a shop while pretending to be shopping

Word building: **shoplifter** *noun* **shoplifting** *noun*

shoplifting
noun the crime of stealing goods from a shop while appearing to be a legitimate customer

Word use: You can also use **shop stealing**.

shop stealing
noun → **shoplifting**

Word building: **shop stealer** *noun*

shop steward
noun a trade-union official representing workers in a factory, workshop, etc.

shore[1]
noun the land along the edge of the sea or a lake

Word history: Middle English *schore*, probably from Middle Low German

shore[2]
noun **1** a supporting post or beam used as a prop (***strut***)
phrase **2 shore up**, to prop up or support by a shore or shores (***brace up***, ***steady***)

shore / sure
Don't confuse **shore** with **sure**. If you are **sure** of something, you are certain or confident of it, as in *sure of success*.

shorn
verb past participle of **shear**

short
adjective **1** not long (***abridged***, ***brief***, ***concise***, ***condensed***)
2 not tall (***little***, ***small***, ***tiny***)
3 rude and abrupt: *He was **short** with me.* (***blunt***, ***brusque***, ***curt***, ***terse***)
4 not having enough: *We are **short** of water.* (***deficient in***, ***lacking in***, ***wanting in***)
adverb **5** suddenly: *to **stop** short*
6 without going the full length: *The ball fell **short** of the goal.*
noun **7** a short film, especially one advertising a program or film to be shown later (***preview***, ***trailer***)
phrase **8 cut short**, to interrupt, or end suddenly
9 for short, as an abbreviation: *A telephone is called a 'phone' **for short**.*
10 in short, in a few words: *In short, it was a fabulous holiday.*
11 make short work of, to finish or get rid of quickly: *to **make short work of** your homework*
12 short for, being a shortened form of: *'Phone' is **short for** 'telephone'.*
13 sell yourself short, *Colloquial* to think too poorly of yourself or of your achievements

Word building: **shortness** *noun*
Word history: Old English *sc(e)ort*

shortage
noun a lack in amount: *a **shortage** of food* (***dearth***, ***deficiency***, ***deficit***, ***insufficiency***)

Word use: The opposite of this is **glut**.

shortbread
noun a thick biscuit made with a lot of butter

short-change
verb Colloquial **1** to give less than proper change to
2 to cheat

short circuit
noun a fault in an electrical circuit causing the current to flow between two points only instead of through the whole circuit

Word building: **short-circuit** *adjective*

shortcoming
noun a failure or fault: *Laziness is his worst **shortcoming**.*

short cut
noun a shorter or quicker way

shorten
verb to make short or shorter (***abbreviate***, ***abridge***, ***condense***)

shortening
noun fat, such as butter or margarine, used in making pastry

shorthand
noun a system of fast handwriting using lines, curves and dots instead of letters

Word building: **shorthand** *adjective*

shorthanded
adjective not having enough helpers or workers

short list
noun a list of specially favoured candidates for a position, who have been chosen from a larger group

shortly
adverb soon: *I am coming **shortly**.*

shorts
plural noun short trousers, not going beyond the knee

short-sighted
adjective **1** not able to clearly see things that are far away (***myopic***)
2 not thinking about the future: *a **short-sighted** answer to a problem*

Word building: **short-sightedness** *noun*

short story
noun a type of fiction written in prose, which is much shorter than a novel and which usually has a small number of characters and explores one idea or topic

Noun forms: The plural is **short stories**.

short-tempered
adjective becoming angry easily

Word use: The opposite of this is **patient** or **calm**.

shot[1]
noun **1** the shooting of a gun, bow, or other weapon: *He took three **shots** at the target. | I think I heard a **shot**.*
2 bullets or other lead ammunition
3 the heavy metal ball thrown in shot-put contests
4 a stroke or throw in sports: *a **shot** at goal*
5 a try, attempt or guess
6 *Colloquial* an injection: *The doctor gave her a tetanus **shot**.*
7 *Colloquial* a photograph: *We took some **shots** of our house.*
phrase **8 big shot**, *Colloquial* an important person
9 call the shots,
a to direct the camera angles, etc., in a television production
b *Colloquial* to be in command
10 like a shot, *Colloquial* instantly, or very quickly

Word history: Old English *sc(e)ot, gesceot*

shot[2]
verb **1** past tense and past participle of **shoot**
adjective **2** woven so as to present a play of colours: ***shot** silk*

shotgun
noun a gun that fires small shot and is used for shooting animals for sport

shot-put (shot-poot)
noun **1** the sport of throwing a heavy metal ball as far as possible
2 the ball itself

Word building: **shot-putter** *noun* **shot-putting** *noun*

should (shood)
verb **1** past tense of **shall**
2 specially used:
a to indicate obligation, duty, etc.: *You **should** not do that.*
b to make a more polite statement: *I **should** hardly say that.*
c to express uncertainty: *if it **should** be true | He **should** come soon.*

Word history: Old English *sc(e)olde*

shoulder (shohl-duh)
noun **1** the part of your body that joins your neck to your arm
verb **2** to push with your shoulders: *He **shouldered** his way through the crowd.*
3 to support or carry on your shoulders: *to **shoulder** the load of wood*
4 to take upon yourself: *to **shoulder** a responsibility*
phrase **5 give the cold shoulder to**, to snub, ignore, or treat coldly

Word history: Old English *sculdor*

shoulderblade
noun → **scapula**

shouldn't
contraction of **should not**

Look up **contractions in grammar**.

should've
contraction of **should have**

When you say **should've** it may sound like the words 'should of', but in fact it is short for 'should have'.

While it is correct to use **should've**, it is wrong to use *should of* because *should* is never followed by *of*.

Look up **contractions in grammar**.

shout
verb **1** to call or cry out loudly (***bawl***, ***bellow***, ***belt out***, ***roar***, ***yell***)
2 *Australian, NZ Colloquial* to buy or pay for: *I'll **shout** the ice-creams.*

Word building: **shout** *noun*
Word history: Middle English

shove (shuv)
verb to push roughly (***drive***, ***propel***, ***ram***, ***thrust***)

Word building: **shove** *noun*
Word history: Old English *scūfan*

shovel (shuv-uhl)
noun **1** a tool or machine with a wide blade for moving things like soil or rubbish
verb **2** to move with a shovel: *to **shovel** sand into a truck*

Verb forms: I **shovelled,** I have **shovelled,** I am **shovelling**
Word history: Old English *scofl*

show
verb **1** to cause or allow to be seen: *He **showed** his drawing to his mother.* (***demonstrate***, ***display***, ***exhibit***, ***flaunt***, ***parade***)
2 to point out or explain: *Please **show** me how to do it.*
3 to guide: ***Show** him to the kitchen.*
4 to prove by demonstrating: *I'll **show** that it is true.*
noun **5** a public showing or exhibition: *an art **show***
6 an entertainment, such as a play or television program
7 a false showing or pretence: *He was bored but he made a **show** of interest.*
phrase **8 show off,**
a to show proudly: *He **showed off** his new bike.*
b to behave so as to get attention or praise for yourself: *Stop **showing off**!*
9 show up,
a to make stand out clearly: *White clothes **show up** dirt.*
b to appear or arrive: *He didn't **show up** till after dinner.* (***come***, ***emerge***, ***materialise***, ***turn up***)
c to reveal or expose: *The shoddy work **showed up** his carelessness.* (***disclose***, ***display***, ***make plain***, ***make public***)

Verb forms: I **showed,** I have **showed** or I have **shown,** I am **showing**
Word history: Old English *scēawian* look at

showdown
noun an open showing of disagreements, in order to clear up a situation: *I've decided to have a **showdown** with the boss this week.*

shower
noun **1** a brief fall of rain
2 a fall of anything in large numbers: *a **shower** of sparks | a **shower** of questions*

3 a spout that sends out fine streams of water for washing your body
4 the use of such a shower to wash yourself
verb **5** to wet with a shower: *He **showered** us with the hose.*
6 to wash yourself under a shower
7 to fall in a shower: *Bullets **showered** down on us.*
phrase **8 shower on**, to give generously to: *He **showered** presents **on** her.*

Word building: **showery** *adjective*
Word history: Old English *scūr*

shower tea
noun Australian a party for a bride-to-be to which the guests, usually other women, bring a present for her future home

show-off
noun someone who behaves so as to get attention or praise (***boaster***, ***exhibitionist***, ***know-all***, ***skite***, ***smart alec***)

showroom
noun a room where goods for sale are shown

showy
adjective attracting attention by looking striking or colourful: ***showy** dressing* | ***showy** flowers* (***flashy***, ***spectacular***)

Adjective forms: **showier**, **showiest**
Word building: **showiness** *noun*

shrank
verb past tense of **shrink**

shrapnel
noun the small parts of an exploded cannon shell: *He was wounded by **shrapnel**.*

Word history: named after the inventor, H *Shrapnel*, 1761–1842, an officer in the British army

shred
noun **1** a narrow strip cut or torn off: *a dress torn to **shreds***
2 a very small bit: *There was not a **shred** of food left.* | *He did not feel a **shred** of pity for her.*
verb **3** to tear into small pieces: *We can **shred** this material and use it to stuff cushions.*

Verb forms: I **shredded** or I **shred**, I have **shredded** or I have **shred**, I am **shredding**
Word history: Old English *scrēade*

shrew
noun **1** a small mouse-like animal that eats insects
2 *Old-fashioned* a very bad-tempered woman

Word building: **shrewish** *adjective*
Word history: Old English *scrēawa*

shrewd
adjective clever, and with good practical judgement: *a **shrewd** investor* (***astute***, ***canny***, ***clever***, ***knowing***, ***sharp***)

Word building: **shrewdly** *adverb* **shrewdness** *noun*
Word history: Middle English *shrewed*, past participle of *shrew* curse (now obsolete), verb use of *shrew*, noun

shriek (shreek)
noun a loud, sharp, high-pitched cry or noise: *a **shriek** of fright* | *the **shriek** of a whistle* (***scream***, ***screech***, ***squawk***, ***squeal***)

Word building: **shriek** *verb*
Word history: Middle English *schriche*

shrift
noun **1** *Old-fashioned* a confession of sins to a priest
phrase **2 short shrift**, little time or attention in dealing with someone: *The teacher gave the pupil **short shrift**.*

Word history: Old English *scrift* from *shrive*

shrill
adjective loud and high-pitched: *a **shrill** voice* (***falsetto***, ***high***, ***high-pitched***, ***soprano***, ***treble***)

Word building: **shrilly** *adverb* **shrillness** *noun*
Word history: Middle English *shrille*

shrimp
noun a kind of prawn

Word history: Middle English *shrimpe*

shrine
noun a sacred or holy place: *a **shrine** of remembrance for those killed in the war*

Word history: Old English *scrīn* from Latin word meaning 'case for books and papers'

shrink
verb **1** to become smaller: *The number of children at our school is **shrinking**.* (***atrophy***, ***contract***, ***dwindle***, ***shrivel***, ***wither***)
2 to draw back: *The frightened child **shrank** into a corner.*

Verb forms: I **shrank**, I have **shrunk** or I have **shrunken**, I am **shrinking**
Word building: **shrinkage** *noun*
Word history: Old English *scrincan*

shrink-wrap
verb to enclose (an object) in a flexible plastic wrapping which shrinks to the shape of the object, sealing it in: *The meat trays in the supermarket are all **shrink-wrapped**.*

Verb forms: I **shrink-wrapped**, I have **shrink-wrapped**, I am **shrink-wrapping**

shrivel
verb to shrink and wrinkle: *Heat **shrivels** grass.* | *He is **shrivelling** with age.* (***atrophy***, ***contract***, ***dwindle***, ***shrink***, ***wither***)

Verb forms: I **shrivelled**, I have **shrivelled**, I am **shrivelling**

shroud
noun **1** a cloth for wrapping a dead body in
2 something which covers and hides like a cloth: *a **shroud** of rain*
verb **3** to cover or hide: *Darkness **shrouded** the town.* | *Mystery **shrouded** her past life.* (***blanket***, ***envelop***, ***wrap***, ***wreathe***)

Word history: Old English *scrūd*

shrub
noun a small, low, tree-like plant

Word building: **shrubby** *adjective* (**shrubbier**, **shrubbiest**)
Word history: Old English *scrybb* brushwood

shrubbery
noun a group of shrubs or a garden area where they are grown

Noun forms: The plural is **shrubberies**.

shrug
verb to raise and lower your shoulders to show doubt, scorn or lack of interest

Verb forms: I **shrugged**, I have **shrugged**, I am **shrugging**
Word building: **shrug** *noun*
Word history: Middle English

shudder
noun to shake suddenly from fear, cold or horror (***quake***, ***rock***, ***sway***, ***tremble***)

Word building: **shudder** *noun*
Word history: Middle English *shodder, shuder* from Old English *scūdan* move, shake

shuffle
verb **1** to walk slowly without lifting the feet
2 to move about: *He **shuffled** the papers on his desk. | They **shuffled** him from one class to another.*
3 to mix up the order of cards in a pack

Word building: **shuffle** *noun* **shuffler** *noun*
Word history: from Low German word meaning 'walk clumsily or with dragging feet'

shun
verb to keep away from deliberately: *He **shunned** me for a week after our fight.*

Verb forms: I **shunned**, I have **shunned**, I am **shunning**
Word history: Old English *scunian*

shunt
verb **1** to move aside or turn aside or out of the way
2 to move from one line of rails to another: *The train was **shunted** onto the northern line.*
noun **3** the act of shunting
4 a railway siding

Word history: Middle English; origin obscure, perhaps from *shun*

shush
interjection **1** a command to be quiet or silent
verb **2** to make or become silent

shut
verb **1** to close or put something in or across an opening: *to **shut** a book | to **shut** a door*
adjective **2** closed
phrase **3 shut down**, to close down or stop for a while: *Schools **shut down** during the holidays.*
4 shut in, to keep in or confine: *to **shut** a bird **in** a cage* (***imprison***, ***intern***, ***jail***, ***lock up***, ***restrain***)
5 shut off, to stop the flow of: *to **shut off** electricity*
6 shut out, to keep out or bar: *She **shut** him **out** of her room.*
7 shut up, *Colloquial* to stop talking

Verb forms: I **shut**, I have **shut**, I am **shutting**
Word history: Old English *scyttan* 'bolt (a door)'

shutter
noun **1** a movable wooden cover for the outside of a window
2 a part of a camera which opens and shuts over the lens to allow light through to the film

Word building: **shutter** *verb*

shuttle
noun the part of a loom that carries the thread backwards and forwards in weaving

Word history: Old English *scytel* dart, arrow

shuttlecock
noun **1** a piece of cork or light plastic with feathers stuck in it that is hit backwards and forwards in games such as badminton
2 a game played with a shuttlecock

shy[1]
adjective **1** bashful or not feeling relaxed with other people (***coy***, ***demure***, ***diffident***, ***modest***, ***reticent***)
2 timid or easily frightened
verb **3** to move suddenly back or aside: *The horse **shied** when the car went past.*

Verb forms: it **shied**, it has **shied**, it is **shying**
Word history: Old English *scēoh*

shy[2]
verb **1** to throw with a sudden swift movement: *to **shy** a stone*
noun **2** a sudden swift throw

Verb forms: I **shied**, I have **shied**, I am **shying**
Noun forms: The plural is **shies**.

SI
noun → **International System of Units**

Word history: abbreviation of French *S(ystème) I(nternational) (d' Unités)*

Siamese cat (suy-uh-meez <u>kat</u>)
noun a short-haired cat, coming originally from Siam (the former name of Thailand), with blue eyes, a small head, and coloured fawn or grey with dark ears, legs and tail

Siamese twins (suy-uh-meez <u>twinz</u>)
plural noun → **conjoined twins**

Word use: This term is not used much nowadays.
Word history: from two Chinese men, Chang and Eng (1811–74), who were born in *Siam* (the former name of Thailand) joined together at the waist

sibilant (<u>sib</u>-uh-luhnt)
adjective **1** hissing
noun **2** in phonetics, a hissing sound, as in the four sounds indicated by 's' or 'ss' which occur in *this, rose, pressure, pleasure*

Word building: **sibilance** *noun*
Word history: Latin

sibling
noun a brother or sister

Word history: Old English

sic (sik)
adverb so; thus (often used in brackets to show that something has been copied exactly from the original)

Word history: Latin

sick
adjective **1** ill or having a disease (***ailing***, ***crook***, ***indisposed***, ***off-colour***)
2 vomiting, or feeling like vomiting (***bilious***, ***nauseous***)
3 for sick people: ***sick** leave*
4 having to do with something horrible or disgusting: *a **sick** joke*
phrase **5 be sick**, to vomit
6 be sick of, to be annoyed or fed up with: *I am **sick of** your untidiness.*

Word building: **sickness** *noun*
Word history: Old English *sēoc*

sick bay
noun a place in a school where students go if they are ill or injured

sicken
verb to make sick: *Such violence on television **sickens** me.* (***disgust***, ***horrify***, ***nauseate***, ***offend***, ***revolt***)

Word building: **sickening** *noun*

sickie
noun Australian, NZ Colloquial a day taken off work with pay because of real or pretended sickness

sickle
noun a curved short-handled tool for cutting grass or grain

Word history: Old English *sicol*, from Latin

sickly
adjective **1** unhealthy or getting sick easily: *a **sickly** child*
2 having to do with sickness: *a **sickly** colour of the face*
3 making you feel sick: *a **sickly** smell* (***nauseating***, ***sick-making***)

Adjective forms: **sicklier**, **sickliest**
Word building: **sickliness** *noun*

side
noun **1** one of the outer edges or lines of something usually not the top, bottom, front, or back: *the **side** of a house | the **side** of a rectangle*
2 one of the two surfaces of a material like paper or cloth: *Write on one **side** only.*
3 either half of your body: *I've got a stitch in my **side**.*
4 the space next to someone or something: *She stood at his **side**.*
5 one of two or more groups that are against each other: *Which **side** are you on?*
6 a position or way of thinking about something: *to look at a question from all **sides***
7 a part or area: *the east **side** of a city*
adjective **8** at the side: *a **side** door*
9 from the side: *a **side** view*
phrase **10 on the side**,
a separate from the main subject
b *Colloquial* as an addition, especially a secret one
11 side with, to place yourself with a side or a party to support an issue (***befriend***, ***champion***, ***defend***, ***stand by***, ***stick up for***)
12 take sides, to show support for one person in an argument, contest, etc.

Word history: Middle English and Old English

sideboard
noun a piece of furniture with shelves and drawers for holding things like plates and cups

sideburns
plural noun whiskers extending from the hairline down below the ears

Word use: You can also use **sidelevers** or **sideboards**.

sidecar
noun **1** a small car attached on one side to a motorcycle and supported on the other by a wheel of its own, used for a passenger, etc.
adverb **2** in a sidecar: *He rode **sidecar**.*

side effect
noun any effect produced other than those originally intended

sideline
noun **1** an additional or auxiliary line of goods or of business: *The farmer tried growing macadamias as a **sideline** to his usual crop.*
2 *Sport*
a a line or mark defining the limit of play on the side of the field in football, etc.
b (*plural*) the area immediately beyond any of the sidelines
verb **3** *Sport* to cause (a player) to stop participating or to become an observer from the sidelines: *The accident **sidelined** him for eight months.*
4 to put outside the group involved in the main activity of an enterprise, organisation, etc.
phrase **5 on the sidelines**,
a not playing in a contest or game
b not involved in the main action

Verb forms: I **sidelined**, I have **sidelined**, I am **sidelining**

sidelong
adjective **1** directed to one side (***aslant***, ***oblique***)
adverb **2** towards the side

sideshow
noun a small show that is part of a larger fair or circus

sidestep
verb **1** to step to one side to avoid: *to **sidestep** a puddle*
2 to avoid: *He **sidestepped** making a decision.*

Verb forms: I **sidestepped**, I have **sidestepped**, I am **sidestepping**

sidetrack
verb **1** to pull or move away from the main subject or course
noun **2** a diversion or distraction
3 a temporary road or detour

sideways
adverb **1** with the side going first or forwards: *A crab moves **sideways**.*
2 facing or leaning to the side
3 towards or from one side
adjective **4** towards or from one side: *a **sideways** tilt*

Word use: You can also use **sidewise**.

sidle (<u>suy</u>-duhl)
verb to move sideways, usually hoping not to be noticed: *He **sidled** into the room late.*

SIDS (sidz)
noun → **sudden infant death syndrome**

Word history: an acronym for *s(udden) i(nfant) d(eath) s(yndrome)*

siege (seej)
noun the surrounding of a place in order to capture it: *The city was under **siege** for three days during the war.*

Word history: Middle English, from Old French, from Latin word meaning 'sit'

siemens (<u>see</u>-muhnz)
noun the SI unit of electrical conductance

Noun forms: The plural is **siemens**.
Word use: The symbol is **S**, without a full stop. | This unit used to be known as the **mho**.
Word history: named after EW von *Siemens*, 1816–92, German electrical engineer and inventor

sierra (see-<u>air</u>-ruh)
noun a chain of hills or mountains, the tops of which look like the teeth of a saw

Word history: Spanish word literally meaning 'saw', from Latin

siesta (see-<u>es</u>-tuh)
noun a midday or afternoon rest

Word history: Spanish, from Latin word meaning 'sixth (hour)', 'midday'

sieve (siv)
noun **1** a container with mesh or holes at the bottom, used for straining liquids or separating thick from thin, or large from small
verb **2** to separate or strain with a sieve (***sift***)

Word history: Old English *sife*

sift
verb **1** to separate the thick or coarse parts of with a sieve: *to **sift** flour* (***sieve***)
2 to scatter with a sieve: *to **sift** icing sugar onto a cake*
3 to sort through carefully: *I **sifted** all the information to find the piece of evidence I wanted.*

Word history: Old English *siftan*

sigh (suy)
verb to let out your breath slowly and with a soft sound, from tiredness, sadness, or relief

Word building: **sigh** *noun*
Word history: Old English *sīcan*

sight (suyt)
noun **1** the ability to see (***eyesight***, ***vision***)
2 something which is seen or should be seen: *She was a beautiful **sight**. | the **sights** of the city*
3 something that looks odd or unattractive: *He looked a **sight** in his ragged jeans.*
verb **4** to get sight of: *They **sighted** a ship on the horizon.*
phrase **5 in sight of**, in a position where it is possible to see: *We are now **in sight of** land.*
6 lower your sights, to be less ambitious
7 on sight, as soon as you see a thing
8 raise your sights, to be more ambitious
9 sight unseen, without any previous inspection: *to buy a car **sight unseen***

Word history: Middle English; Old English *gesiht*

> **sight / site / cite**
> Don't confuse **sight** with **site** or **cite**.
> A **site** is the land where something is built or will soon be built.
> To **cite** something is to quote it as an authority, or to refer to it as an example.

sightseeing
noun the act of visiting or seeing places and things of interest

Word building: **sightseer** *noun*

sign (suyn)
noun **1** anything that shows that something exists or is likely to happen: *Clouds are a **sign** of rain.* (***indication***, ***pointer***, ***token***)
2 a mark, figure, or symbol used to stand for a word, idea, or mathematical value: *a dollar **sign** | a plus **sign***
3 a movement that expresses an idea or feeling: *He made a **sign** for me to leave the room.*
4 a notice that gives information, warns or advertises: *a house with a 'for sale' **sign***
verb **5** to write your signature on: *to **sign** a letter*
6 to write as a signature: *She **signed** her name.*
phrase **7 sign off**, to stop broadcasting a radio or television program
8 sign on,
a to employ or hire: *to **sign on** some new workers*
b to bind yourself to employment: *to **sign on** as ship's cook*
9 sign up,
a to enter the military services
b to take on by a signed agreement: *The club **signed up** two new players.*

Word history: Middle English, from Old French, from Latin word meaning 'mark', 'signal'

> **sign / sine**
> Don't confuse **sign** with **sine. Sine** is a mathematical term used in trigonometry. It is the ratio of the side opposite a given angle in a right-angled triangle to the hypotenuse.

signal (<u>sig</u>-nuhl)
noun **1** any action or object that warns, points a direction, or gives an order: *He gave the **signal** for them to start. | We stopped at the traffic **signals**.*
2 the waves by which sound or pictures are sent in radio and television
verb **3** to make a signal to: *She **signalled** him to stop talking.*
4 to make known by signal: *We **signalled** the good news.*

Verb forms: I **signalled**, I have **signalled**, I am **signalling**
Word history: Middle English, from Medieval Latin, from Latin word meaning 'sign'

signatory (<u>sig</u>-nuh-tree)
adjective **1** signing, or joining in signing, a document: *the **signatory** powers to a treaty*
noun **2** someone who signs, or has the power to sign, a document, cheque, etc.

Noun forms: The plural is **signatories**.

signature (<u>sig</u>-nuh-chuh)
noun **1** the way you write your own name
2 *Music* the sign or signs written at the beginning of a piece of music to tell its key and time
adjective **3** typical of a style: *Would you like to taste my **signature** dish?*

Word history: Medieval Latin

signet
noun a raised engraved design used as an official stamp or set into a finger ring

Word history: Middle English, from Medieval Latin, from Latin word meaning 'sign'

significance
noun **1** importance: *Do you understand the **significance** of these vows?*
2 meaning: *What is the **significance** of the question?* (***drift***, ***essence***, ***gist***, ***sense***)
3 the quality of being important or having a special meaning: *She's a woman of **significance**.*

significant
adjective **1** important: *a* ***significant*** *event in Australia's history* (***critical***, ***fateful***, ***memorable***, ***momentous***, ***serious***)
2 full of meaning: *a* ***significant*** *look*
Word building: **significantly** *adverb*

signify
verb **1** to be a sign of: *Black clouds* ***signify*** *a storm.*
2 to make known by signs: *He* ***signified*** *his anger with a frown.*
Verb forms: I **signified**, I have **signified**, I am **signifying**
Word building: **signification** *noun*
Word history: Middle English, from Latin word meaning 'show by signs'

silence
noun **1** absence of any sound or noise
verb **2** to bring to silence: *She* ***silenced*** *the class.*
Word history: Middle English, from Old French, from Latin

silencer
noun **1** a person or thing that silences
2 a device for softening the noise of a firearm

silent
adjective **1** making no sound or not talking: *He remained* ***silent***. (***hushed***, ***quiet***, ***still***)
2 having no sound: *a* ***silent*** *room | a* ***silent*** *movie*
3 not pronounced: *In the word 'know' the letter 'k' is* ***silent***.
Word history: from Latin word meaning 'being silent'

silent partner
noun a partner taking no active or public part in the conduct of a business

silhouette (sil-ooh-<u>et</u>, sil-uh-<u>wet</u>)
noun **1** an outline drawing filled in with black, like a shadow
verb **2** to show up like a silhouette or shadow: *The tree was* ***silhouetted*** *against the sky.*
Word history: named after Etienne de *Silhouette*, 1709–67, French author and politician

silicon
noun an element found in minerals and rocks, used in making such things as glass and steel
Word history: *silic-* + *-on*, modelled on *boron*, *carbon*

> **silicon / silicone**
> Don't confuse **silicon** with **silicone**, which is the name for any of a group of chemical <u>compounds</u> that include the element **silicon** as part of their structure. Some oils and synthetic rubbers are **silicones**.

silk
noun **1** a soft, shiny cloth made from the threads of the cocoon of the silkworm
2 the gown of such material, worn by a Queen's or King's Counsel in a law court
phrase **3 take silk**, to become a Queen's or King's Counsel
Word building: **silk** *adjective* **silken** *adjective* **silkiness** *noun* **silky** *adjective*
Word history: Middle English; Old English *sioloc*, *seoloc*, from Baltic or Slavic

silk-screen
noun a way of printing in which ink is passed over a stencil attached to a screen of silk or other fine cloth
Word building: **silk-screen** *verb*

silkworm
noun a kind of caterpillar which spins a fine soft thread to make a cocoon
Word history: Old English *seolcwyrm*

sill
noun a flat piece of wood or other material beneath a window or door
Word history: Old English *syl*, *syll(e)*

silly
adjective foolish or stupid (***fatuous***, ***idiotic***, ***inane***, ***ridiculous***, ***senseless***)
Adjective forms: **sillier**, **silliest**
Word building: **silliness** *noun*
Word history: Old English *sēlig* (Anglian), *sælig*

silo
noun a tower-like building for storing grain
Noun forms: The plural is **silos**.
Word history: Spanish from Latin, from Greek word meaning 'pit in which grain is stored'

silt
noun earthy matter like very fine sand which is carried by running water and then left behind on the river bottom
Word history: Middle English

silver
noun **1** a white metal used for making things like jewellery, coins, mirrors and cutlery
2 things made from silver or similar metal, such as coins or cutlery: *I have a $5 note but no* ***silver***. *| We put the* ***silver*** *on the dining table on special occasions.*
3 a shiny whitish-grey colour
adjective **4** made of silver or of a metallic mixture similar to it
5 producing silver: *a* ***silver*** *mine*
6 of a silver colour
Word building: **silver** *verb* **silvery** *adjective*
Word history: Middle English; Old English *siolfor*

silverbeet
noun a vegetable with large, firm, dark-green leaves and a long fleshy, white stalk
Word use: Another name is **spinach**.

silver bullet
noun a certain and effective remedy, like a drug, defence system, etc., usually not believed to be achievable: *If only there was a* ***silver bullet*** *for cancer.*
Word history: from the idea in popular mythology that witches, vampires, werewolves, etc. can only be killed with a silver bullet

silverfish
noun a small, wingless insect which feeds on paper and some fabrics, and so damages books and household goods
Noun forms: The plural is **silverfishes** or **silverfish**.

silver plate
noun **1** a thin silver coating put on the surface of another metal, usually by electrolysis
2 tableware plated with such a coating

silverside
noun a cut of beef from the outside top part of a hind leg

SIM card (sim kahd)
noun a circuit-bearing card that you insert into a mobile phone which contains your authorisation to use a certain mobile phone network

Word use: You can also use **sim card**.
Word history: an acronym for *S(ubscriber) I(dentity) M(odule)*

simian (sim-ee-uhn)
adjective **1** having to do with or like an ape or monkey
noun **2** an ape or monkey

Word history: from Latin word meaning 'ape'

similar
adjective **1** having a general likeness: *Their faces are **similar**. | His bike is **similar** to hers.* (***akin***, ***alike***, ***comparable***)
2 *Geometry* of figures, having corresponding sides proportional and corresponding angles equal

Word building: **similarity** *noun* (*plural* **similarities**)
Word history: from Latin word meaning 'like'

simile (sim-uh-lee)
noun a figure of speech which points out a likeness between two generally unlike things, as in *to sing like a bird* and *He's as strong as an ox.*

Word use: Compare this with **metaphor**.
Word history: Middle English, from Latin word meaning 'like'

simmer
verb **1** to cook in a liquid just below boiling point
2 to be full of strong but controlled feelings: *She was **simmering** with rage.*
phrase **3 simmer down,** to become calm or calmer

Word history: earlier *simber*, Middle English *simper*

simper
verb to smile in a silly or unnatural way

Word building: **simper** *noun*

simple
adjective **1** easy to understand, do, or use: *a **simple** explanation | a **simple** test | a **simple** tool* (***cinchy***, ***easy***, ***effortless***, ***foolproof***, ***uncomplicated***)
2 plain and uncomplicated: *a **simple** writing style | **simple** clothes* (***natural***, ***quiet***, ***unadorned***, ***unaffected***, ***unobtrusive***)
3 mentally weak (***dull***, ***slow***, ***stupid***, ***thick***)
4 having to do with the most basic one-word form of a verb such as 'ran' in *I ran*: *the **simple** past tense*

Word use: The opposite of definitions 1 and 2 is **complex** or **complicated**. | Compare definition 4 with **continuous** and **perfect** which talk about verbs of more than one word such as 'am running' and 'have run'.
Word building: **simpleness** *noun*
simplicity *noun*
Word history: Middle English, from Old French, from Latin

simple interest
noun interest that is only payable on the principal amount of the debt

Word use: Compare this with **compound interest**.

simple past tense
noun Grammar the form of the past tense which signifies an action which has occurred and has been completed in the past, as in *He cooked dinner* contrasted with *He has been cooking dinner.*

simple present tense
noun Grammar the form of the present tense which signifies an action happening now with no indication as to whether it is continuing, as in *She goes to school* contrasted with the continuous form *She is going to school.*

simple sentence
noun a sentence that consists of just one main clause: *'They are going home now' is a **simple sentence**.*

Simple sentences contrast with **compound sentences** and **complex sentences**.
For more information, look up **sentences**.

simpleton
noun Old-fashioned a foolish person

simplify
verb to make easier or more simple (***disentangle***, ***sort out***, ***streamline***, ***unravel***)

Verb forms: I **simplified**, I have **simplified**, I am **simplifying**
Word history: French, from Medieval Latin

simplistic
adjective being so simple as to lose accuracy: *He gave a **simplistic** account of the causes of unemployment.*

simply
adverb **1** in a plain and straightforward way: *She answered **simply**. | He dressed **simply**.*
2 merely: *He is **simply** going for a walk.*
3 absolutely: *She was **simply** wonderful in the emergency.*

Word history: Middle English

simulate (sim-yuh-layt)
verb **1** to make a pretence of: *He **simulated** admiration to flatter her.*
2 to imitate or make a copy of: *They **simulated** diamonds to make the cheap jewellery.*

Word building: **simulation** *noun*
Word history: from Latin word meaning 'made like'

simulator
noun a device used in training or experiments that simulates movement or flight

simulcast (sim-uhl-kahst)
noun a program broadcast at the same time on both television and radio

simultaneous (sim-uhl-tay-nee-uhs)
adjective happening at the same time

Word building: **simultaneously** *adverb*
Word history: from Medieval Latin word meaning 'simulated'

sin
noun **1** an act of breaking one of God's laws
2 any serious crime or offence
Word building: **sin** *verb* (**sinned**, **sinning**)
sinful *adjective*
Word history: Old English *syn(n)*

since
adverb **1** from then until now: *Ever* ***since*** *I discovered his identity, I have regarded him with suspicion.*
2 between a particular past time and the present time: *He at first refused, but has* ***since*** *agreed.*
3 ago: *long* ***since***
preposition **4** counting from: ***since*** *noon*
conjunction **5** in the period following the time when: *Has he written* ***since*** *he left?*
Word history: Middle English *syns*, *synnes*, from Old English *siththan* then

sincere
adjective having and expressing true feelings: *She was* ***sincere*** *in her wishes for his success.* (***frank***, ***honest***, ***truthful***)
Word building: **sincerity** *noun*
Word history: Latin

sine (suyn)
noun Mathematics a function in trigonometry defined for an acute angle in a right-angled triangle as the ratio of the side opposite the angle to the hypotenuse
Word use: The short form is **sin**.
Word history: from Latin word meaning 'curve'

> **sine / sign**
> Don't confuse **sine** with **sign**.
> Anything that shows that something exists or is likely to happen is a **sign**. A **sign** can also be something such as a mark or symbol that stands for a word, idea or mathematical value:
> *Don't forget to add a dollar sign in front of the amount of money on this form.*
> A notice giving information is a **sign**.

sinecure (<u>sin</u>-uh-kyoohuh, <u>suyn</u>-uh-kyoohuh)
noun a position requiring little or no work, especially one yielding profitable returns
Word history: short for Latin phrase (*beneficium*) *sine cūrā*

sinew (<u>sin</u>-yooh)
noun a piece of tough tissue joining a muscle to a bone
Word history: Old English *sinu* (nominative), *sinuwe* (genitive)

sing
verb **1** to give out musical sounds with your voice
2 to perform in this way: *She* ***sang*** *in the choir.*
Verb forms: I **sang**, I have **sung**, I am **singing**
Word history: Old English *singan*

singe (sinj)
verb to burn slightly
Word history: Old English *sencgan*

single
adjective **1** one and only: *my* ***single*** *reason for going* (***exclusive***, ***only***, ***sole***, ***unique***)
2 for one person: *a* ***single*** *bed*
3 unmarried (***celibate***, ***lone***, ***unattached***, ***unwed***)
4 one song from an album released for sale on its own, or with one or two other songs
phrase **5 single out**, to choose alone: *They* ***singled*** *her* ***out*** *for promotion.* (***elect***, ***favour***, ***opt for***, ***prefer***, ***select***)
Word building: **single** *noun* **singleness** *noun*
Word history: Middle English, from Old French, from Latin

single file
noun a line of people or things arranged one behind the other (***Indian file***)

single-handed
adverb by working alone: *He built the house* ***single-handed.***

single-minded
adjective **1** having or showing undivided purpose (***determined***, ***dogged***, ***persistent***, ***stubborn***, ***tenacious***)
2 steadfast, or sincere in what you do

singlet
noun a garment with narrow shoulder straps, worn on the upper part of your body, usually under your other clothes (***vest***)

singsong
adjective with a regular up and down pattern in the tone: *a* ***singsong*** *voice*

singular
adjective **1** indicating one person or thing
2 unusual or odd: *He had a very* ***singular*** *appearance.* (***extraordinary***, ***rare***, ***remarkable***, ***uncommon***)
Word use: The opposite of definition 2 is **commonplace**.
Word history: Middle English, from Latin

> If a noun, verb or pronoun refers to one single person or thing, we say it is **singular** in number. The words 'teacher', 'hears' and 'she' in the sentence *She hears the teacher* are singular. If a word refers to more than one, we say it is *plural* in number.
> Look up **plural**. For a list of **singular and plural forms**, see appendixes, page 985.

sinister
adjective suggesting a threat of evil: *a* ***sinister*** *remark*
Word history: Middle English, from Latin; originally referring to omens observed on the left (the unlucky) side

sink
verb **1** to go down gradually, as in water: *The ship* ***sank.*** | *The sun is* ***sinking.***
2 to cause to go down: *They* ***sank*** *an enemy ship.*
noun **3** a kitchen basin with a drain
phrase **4 sink in**, to become understood: *The importance of the letter at last* ***sank in.***
Verb forms: I **sank**, I have **sunk**, I am **sinking**
Word building: **sunken** *adjective*
Word history: Old English *sincan*

sinker
noun a weight, usually of lead, for making a fishing line sink below the surface

sinuous (sin-yooh-uhs)
adjective **1** moving with smooth twists and turns, like a snake: *the **sinuous** body of the dancer*
2 winding: *a **sinuous** trail of slime* (***coiled, squiggly, twisted, wavy, winding***)
Word history: Latin

sinus (suy-nuhs)
noun one of the air-filled holes in the skull, connecting with the nose
Word history: Latin

sinusitis (suy-nuh-suy-tuhs)
noun an inflammation of a sinus or sinuses

sip
verb to drink in small mouthfuls
Verb forms: I **sipped**, I have **sipped**, I am **sipping**
Word building: **sip** *noun*
Word history: Old English *sypian* drink in

siphon (suy-fuhn)
noun a tube through which liquid flows up over the edge of a higher container to a lower one, using the force of gravity to draw the water out at the lower end
Word use: You can also use **syphon**.
Word building: **siphon** *verb*
Word history: Latin, from Greek word meaning 'pipe', 'tube'

sir
noun **1** a respectful or formal word used when speaking to a man
2 Sir, the title belonging to a knight or baronet
Word history: variant of *sire*

sire
noun the male parent of an animal
Word history: Middle English, from Old French, from Latin word meaning 'senior'

siren
noun a device that makes a loud warning sound, used on ambulances, police cars, etc.
Word history: Middle English, from Latin, from Greek word meaning 'sea nymph'

sirloin (ser-loyn)
noun the part of the loin of beef in front of the rump
Word history: earlier *surloyn*, from Old French *surlonge*, from *sur* over, above + *longe* loin

sissy
noun Colloquial **1** a man or boy with mannerisms of the opposite sex
2 a cowardly person (***chicken, coward, cry-baby, scaredy-cat, sook***)
Word history: from *sister*

sister
noun **1** a female relative who has the same parents as you
2 a senior nurse
3 a nun
4 a term used, especially in Aboriginal English, to express solidarity with a woman, even if she is not a relative
Word building: **sisterhood** *noun*
Word history: Middle English, from Scandinavian

sister-in-law
noun **1** the sister of your husband or wife
2 the wife of your brother
3 the wife of the brother of your husband or wife
Noun forms: The plural is **sisters-in-law**.

sit
verb **1** to rest on the lower part of your body
2 to rest or be placed: *The teapot is **sitting** on the table.*
3 to try to answer the questions in: *to **sit** an exam*
4 to pose: *to **sit** for a portrait*
5 to be in the process of meeting: *Parliament is **sitting**.*
phrase **6 be sitting pretty**, *Colloquial* to be at an advantage: *I **am sitting pretty** now that I've won the lottery.*
7 sit in for, to take the place of for a short time: *I'm **sitting in for** my boss for a day.*
8 sit on,
a to have a place: *to **sit on** a committee*
b *Colloquial* to check or repress: *to **sit on** information*
c *Colloquial* to prevent from becoming public knowledge: *to **sit on** a document*
9 sit out,
a to stay to the end of: *Though the film was boring, we had to **sit it out**.*
b to take no part in: *to **sit out** a dance*
10 sit tight, to take no action: *to **sit tight** until a decision is reached*
11 sit up,
a to raise yourself from a lying to a sitting position
b to stay up later than usual
c to become alert: *to **sit up** when the newsflash came*
Verb forms: I **sat**, I have **sat**, I am **sitting**
Word history: Old English *sittan*

sitar (si-tah, see-tah)
noun an Indian musical instrument which you play by plucking its three strings
Word history: Hindustani

sitcom
noun → **situation comedy**
Word history: formed from *sit(uation) com(edy)*

site
noun **1** the piece of land on which something is or will be built: *a house on a **site** overlooking the ocean*
2 a place where something happens or has happened: *the **site** of the annual picnic* (***location, position, spot, venue***)
3 → **website**
Word history: from Latin word meaning 'position'

site / sight / cite
Don't confuse **site** with **sight** or **cite.**
Your **sight** is your ability to see things. It can also be something worth seeing.
To **cite** something is to quote it as an authority, or to refer to it as an example.

site map
noun **1** a map of a building site showing the location of different buildings, areas of interest, etc.
2 a map of a website showing the various pages and links between them

situate
verb to place in a position
Word history: from Late Latin word meaning 'located'

situation
noun **1** a position in relation to the surroundings: *The shop has a good **situation**.*
2 a state of affairs: *The **situation** has been difficult since he left.*

situation comedy
noun **1** comedy derived from the situations of ordinary life
2 a movie, show, series, etc., involving situation comedy
Word use: The short form is **sitcom**.

SI unit
noun a unit of the International System of Units
Word history: from the French, *Système International d'Unités*

six
noun **1** a cardinal number, five plus one (5 + 1)
2 a symbol for this number, as 6 or VI
3 a set of six persons or things
4 *Cricket* a hit scoring six runs, the ball clearing the boundary without touching the ground
adjective **5** amounting to six in number
phrase **6 at sixes and sevens**, in confusion
7 go for six, to suffer a major setback
8 hit for six, to dispose of completely
Word building: **sixth** *adjective* **sixth** *noun*
Word history: Middle English and Old English

sixteen
noun **1** a cardinal number, ten plus six (10 + 6)
2 a symbol for this number, as 16 or XVI
3 a set of sixteen people or things
adjective **4** amounting to sixteen in number
Word building: **sixteenth** *adjective* **sixteenth** *noun*
Word history: Middle English *sixtene*, Old English *sixtēne*

sixty
noun **1** a cardinal number, ten times six (10 × 6)
2 a symbol for this number as 60 or LX
3 a set of sixty persons or things
4 sixties, the numbers from 60 to 69 of a series, especially with reference to the years of a person's age, or the years of a century
adjective **5** amounting to sixty in number
Noun forms: The plural is **sixties**.
Word building: **sixtieth** *adjective* **sixtieth** *noun*
Word history: Old English *sixtig*

size[1]
noun the dimensions or extent of something
Word history: Middle English, from Old French

size[2]
noun **1** a sticky or jelly-like preparation made from glue, starch, etc., used for coating paper and cloth
verb **2** to coat or treat with size
Word use: You can also use **sizing** for definition 1.
Word history: Middle English *syse*; perhaps special use of *size*[1]

sizeable
adjective quite big

sizzle
verb to make a hissing sound while cooking: *The sausages are **sizzling** in the pan.*
Word history: imitative

skate
noun **1** a boot with a blade attached to the bottom, which you wear to move on ice
2 a rollerskate
3 a rollerblade
Word building: **skate** *verb* **skater** *noun*
Word history: Dutch, from Old Northern French word meaning 'stilt'

skateboard
noun a narrow wooden board on rollerskate wheels, which you usually ride standing up

skein (skayn)
noun a length of thread or wool wound in a coil
Word history: Middle English, from Old French

skeleton
noun **1** all the bones of a human or animal body, connected together
2 a bare framework of something (***base***, ***foundation***, ***support***)
adjective **3** cut back to the smallest number that can cope: *a **skeleton** staff*
Word building: **skeletal** *adjective*
Word history: Neo-Latin, from Greek word meaning 'dried up'

skeleton key
noun a key with nearly the whole substance of the bit filed away, so that it may open various locks

skerrick (ske-rik)
noun Australian, *NZ* a very small quantity: *not a **skerrick** left* (***dash***, ***drop***, ***hint***, ***pinch***, ***trace***)
Word history: British dialect

sketch
noun **1** a drawing or painting done roughly or quickly
2 any rough plan or outline
Word building: **sketchy** *adjective* (**sketchier**, **sketchiest**) **sketch** *verb*
Word history: Dutch, from Italian, from Latin word meaning 'impromptu poem', from Greek word meaning 'without preparation'

skew (skyooh)
verb **1** to turn aside or twist
2 to give a sloping direction to
3 to distort, or describe unfairly
adjective **4** slanting
5 *Geometry* not lying in the same plane
noun **6** a twisting or sloping movement, direction, or position
Word history: Middle English, from Old Northern French word meaning 'escape'

skewbald
adjective having patches of different colours, especially of white and brown: *a **skewbald** horse*
Word use: Compare this with **piebald**.
Word history: obsolete English *skewed* skewbald

skewer
noun a long pin of wood or metal, especially one for holding meat while it is being cooked
Word building: **skewer** *verb*
Word history: earlier *skiver*

ski
noun one of a pair of long narrow pieces of wood, metal or plastic, which you fasten to your shoes and use for moving on snow

Word building: **ski** *verb* (**ski'd** or **skied**, **skiing**) **skier** *noun*
Word history: Norwegian

skid
verb **1** to slide forward when the wheels of your car or bike are no longer gripping the road surface: *The car **skidded** on the icy road.*
noun **2** a plank or bar for supporting, rolling, or sliding something heavy along
3 an act of skidding: *The car went into a **skid**.*
phrase **4 on the skids**, getting worse fast: *The company is **on the skids**.*
5 put the skids under, to place in a dangerous position: *to **put the skids under** someone*

Verb forms: I **skidded**, I have **skidded**, I am **skidding**
Word history: origin uncertain; perhaps from Scandinavian

skiff
noun any of various types of small boat, usually propelled by oars or sails

Word history: French, from Italian, from Old High German word meaning 'ship'

skill
noun the ability to do something well (***capability***, ***competency***, ***efficiency***, ***proficiency***, ***talent***)

Word building: **skilful** *adjective* **skilled** *adjective*
Word history: Middle English, from Scandinavian

skillet
noun a small frying pan

skim
verb **1** to remove floating matter from: *to **skim** soup stock*
2 to remove from the surface of something: *to **skim** fat from gravy*
3 to move lightly over the surface or top of: *The birds **skimmed** across the lake.* (***float***, ***glide***, ***sail***)
4 to read quickly without taking everything in: *I have just **skimmed** the newspaper.* (***browse through***, ***leaf through***)
5 *Colloquial* to take the details of (a plastic card, such as a credit card) so as to steal money from the account of the owner

Verb forms: I **skimmed**, I have **skimmed**, I am **skimming**
Word history: dialect variant of obsolete *scum*, verb, skim

skim milk
noun milk from which the cream has been removed

skimp
verb **1** to do hastily, or without attention
2 to allow only a little
phrase **3 skimp on**, to use less of: *to **skimp on** milk | don't **skimp on** sleep*

skimpy
adjective **1** hardly enough in quantity, size, etc.: *a **skimpy** meal | a **skimpy** jumper*
2 stingy or mean with money

Word building: **skimpily** *adverb* **skimpiness** *noun*
Adjective forms: **skimpier**, **skimpiest**

skin
noun **1** the outer covering of an animal or human
2 any surface layer: *the **skin** on hot milk* (***coating***, ***crust***, ***film***, ***glaze***, ***veneer***)
verb **3** to remove the skin of

Verb forms: I **skinned**, I have **skinned**, I am **skinning**
Word history: Middle English, from Scandinavian

skindiving
noun underwater swimming for which you use a snorkel, mask, and flippers

Word building: **skindiver** *noun*

skinflint
noun a mean stingy person

skinhead
noun a person with their hair cut very short or totally shaved off

skink
noun any of many different, usually smooth-scaled lizards

Word history: Latin, from Greek

skinny
adjective thin (***lean***, ***slender***, ***slight***, ***slim***, ***spindly***)

Adjective forms: **skinnier**, **skinniest**
Word building: **skinniness** *noun*

skip
verb **1** to jump lightly from one foot to the other (***caper***, ***dance***, ***frisk***, ***gambol***, ***prance***)
2 to jump over a twirling rope
3 to leave out: *He often **skips** bits when he's reading.* (***drop***, ***exclude***)

Verb forms: I **skipped**, I have **skipped**, I am **skipping**
Word building: **skip** *noun*
Word history: Middle English

skipper
noun the captain of a ship or a team

Word history: Middle English, from Middle Dutch word meaning 'ship'

skirmish
noun a small battle (***brawl***, ***combat***, ***conflict***, ***fight***, ***fray***)

Word building: **skirmish** *verb*
Word history: Middle English, from Old French, from Old High German word meaning 'shield'

skirt
noun **1** a piece of outer clothing, worn by women and girls, that hangs from the waist
verb **2** to go round the edge of: *He **skirted** the dam.*

Word history: Middle English, from Scandinavian

skirting board
noun a board running round a room at the base of the walls

skit
noun a short play or other piece of writing which makes fun of something

Word history: from Middle English word meaning 'harlot'

skite
noun Australian, *NZ* someone who boasts a lot (***boaster***, ***exhibitionist***, ***know-all***, ***show-off***, ***smart alec***)

Word building: **skite** *verb*
Word history: Scottish and northern dialect *skite* (derogatory) from *bletherskate* a person who talks too much. The word *blether* comes from Old Norse and means talk nonsense. The word *skate* is from Old Scottish and means a sudden movement or slip, and from there, a trick that you play on someone, and so, in the end, a trickster.

skittish
adjective **1** tending to take fright or be shy
2 restlessly lively
3 uncertain

Word building: **skittishness** *noun*
Word history: Middle English

skittle
verb **1** to knock over, or send flying (***bowl over***, ***overturn***, ***tip over***, ***upset***)
noun **2 skittles**, a game played with bottle-shaped pieces of wood and a ball to knock them down

Word history: Scandinavian

skivvy
noun Australian, *NZ* a close-fitting piece of clothing of knitted material, with long sleeves and a high collar

Noun forms: The plural is **skivvies**.

skulduggery (skul-<u>dug</u>-uh-ree)
noun mean dishonesty or trickery

Word use: You can also use **skullduggery**.

skulk
verb to stay nearby, trying not to let anyone know you are there: *Someone was **skulking** about the place before the burglary.*

Word history: Middle English, from Scandinavian

skull
noun the bony framework of the head, enclosing the brain and supporting the face

Word history: Middle English, from Scandinavian

skull / scull
Don't confuse **skull** with **scull**, which is a type of oar used for rowing a boat.

skullcap
noun a close-fitting, brimless cap, especially one worn by a Jewish man or boy

Word use: Another word for this, when worn by a Jewish person, is **yarmulke**.

skunk
noun a small, furry, North American animal that lets out a foul-smelling fluid when attacked

Word history: Native American

sky
noun the area of the clouds or the upper air

Noun forms: The plural is **skies**.
Word history: Middle English, from Scandinavian

skyboard
noun **1** a lightweight board similar to a snowboard, used for skysurfing
verb **2** to skydive on such a skyboard

skydive
verb **1** to engage in the sport of skydiving: *They **skydived** early in the morning when there was no wind.*
noun **2** an instance of skydiving

Word building: **skydiver** *noun*

skydiving
noun the sport of falling from a plane for some distance before opening your parachute

skylark[1]
noun **1** → **lark**[1]
2 a native Australian bird known for singing in flight

skylark[2]
verb to play about or play tricks, especially in high spirits

skylight
noun a flat window in a roof

skyscraper
noun a very tall building, especially an office block

skysurf
verb to skydive on a skyboard: *She wanted to **skysurf** from a higher altitude next time.*

Word use: You can also use **skyboard**.
Word building: **skysurfer** *noun*

skysurfing
noun **1** a sport in which a person skydives with a skyboard attached to the feet making surfing-like actions during freefall and then releasing a parachute
adjective **2** having to do with skysurfing

slab
noun **1** a large flat piece: *a stone **slab** | a **slab** of cake*
2 *Colloquial* a carton of 24 drink cans

Word history: Middle English

slack
adjective **1** loose: *a **slack** rope*
2 lazy (***idle***, ***indolent***, ***slothful***)

Word building: **slack** *verb* **slackness** *noun*
Word history: Old English *sleac, slæc*

slacken
verb **1** to make or become less active, intense, etc.
2 to make or become looser

slacks
plural noun long trousers

slag
noun the waste material from a mine, or from metal-bearing rock when it is melted down

Word history: Middle Low German *slagge*

slain (slayn)
verb past participle of **slay**

slake
verb **1** to lessen by satisfying: *to **slake** your thirst | to **slake** your desire for revenge*
2 to treat with water or moist air: *to **slake** lime*

Word history: Old English *slacian*, from *slæc* slack

slalom (<u>slay</u>-luhm, <u>slah</u>-luhm)
noun a downhill skiing race with a winding course

slam
verb **1** to shut hard with a loud noise: *to **slam** a door*
2 to hit or throw hard or noisily: *to **slam** a ball into a net*

Verb forms: I **slammed**, I have **slammed**, I am **slamming**

slander
noun a false spoken statement which damages someone's reputation or good name (***defamation***, ***slur***, ***smear***)

Word building: **slander** *verb* **slanderous** *adjective*
Word history: Middle English, from Anglo-French, from Latin word meaning 'cause of offence'

slander / libel
Don't confuse **slander** with **libel**, which is a written or printed statement which damages someone's reputation.

slang
noun everyday or colloquial language that is not fitting for formal use

Word building: **slangy** *adjective* (**slangier**, **slangiest**)

slant
noun **1** a slope or angle (***gradient***, ***incline***, ***pitch***)
2 an aspect or point of view: *This news gives a new **slant** to the problem.*

Word building: **slant** *verb* **slantwise** *adverb*
Word history: Scandinavian

slap
noun **1** a quick hit, especially with the open hand
verb **2** to hit smartly, especially with the open hand
3 to put carelessly: *to **slap** on paint | to **slap** a book on the table*
phrase **4 slap down**, to crush the enthusiasm of

Verb forms: I **slapped**, I have **slapped**, I am **slapping**
Word history: Low German; imitative

slapdash
adverb **1** in a hasty careless manner
adjective **2** carelessly hasty

slapstick
noun rough and noisy comedy

slash
verb **1** to cut violently and unevenly: *Vandals have **slashed** the train seats.* (***gash***, ***lacerate***, ***rip***, ***slit***, ***tear***)
2 to reduce greatly: *to **slash** prices*
noun **3** a a cut or wound
4 a punctuation mark (/) sometimes used to separate items that are equally good alternatives
5 to clear (a piece of land) by cutting down weeds and old growth: *to slash the paddock*

Word history: Middle English, perhaps from Old French word meaning 'break'

If you use slashes when you write *he/she/it comes*, this means that *he*, *she* and *it* are all possible as pronouns with the verb *comes*.
Slashes are a convenient way of conveying this information, though some writers prefer to avoid them if possible in formal essay writing.
Note that the technical name of the **slash** is the *solidus*.

slash-and-burn
adjective having to do with a method of cultivating land in which natural vegetation is cut down before sowing crops or pasture: *a **slash-and-burn** approach to farming*

slat
noun a long strip of wood or metal: *the **slats** of a blind*

Word history: Middle English, from Old French word meaning 'piece broken or split off'

slate[1]
noun a dark bluish-grey rock which splits easily into layers and is used on roofs and floors

Word history: Middle English, from Old French word meaning 'piece broken off'

slate[2]
verb Colloquial to criticise severely, especially in a newspaper review, etc.

Word history: special use of *slate[1]*

slather
verb **1** to use thickly or in large quantities: *to **slather** on sunscreen*
noun **2** a large quantity
phrase **3 open slather**, *Australian*, *NZ Colloquial*
a complete freedom
b an argument or fight in which anyone may join

Word building: **slathering** *noun*
Word history: British dialect *slather* to slip, slide, related to *slidder* slippery, *sludder* mud

slaughter (slaw-tuh)
verb **1** to kill for food: *to **slaughter** cattle*
2 to kill violently in great numbers

Word building: **slaughter** *noun*
Word history: Middle English, from Scandinavian

slave
noun **1** someone who works without being paid and is the prisoner of someone else (***puppet***, ***serf***, ***servant***, ***subject***, ***vassal***)
verb **2** to work very hard, like a slave (***labour***, ***slog***, ***toil***)

Word building: **slavery** *noun* **slavish** *adjective*
Word history: Middle English, from Old French, from Medieval Latin word meaning 'slave', 'Slav'; from the fact that many Slavs (people from eastern and central Europe) were reduced to slavery

slaver (slav-uh)
verb **1** to slobber, or let saliva run from the mouth
2 to show great desire for something by slavering, the way a dog does
noun **3** saliva coming from the mouth

Word history: Middle English, from Scandinavian

slay
verb Old-fashioned to kill (***assassinate***, ***execute***, ***murder***)

Verb forms: I **slew**, I have **slain**, I am **slaying**
Word history: Old English *slēan*

> **slay / sleigh**
> Don't confuse **slay** with **sleigh**, which is a large sled, usually one pulled by animals.

sleaze
noun Colloquial **1** sleazy or sordid activity, especially having to do with sexual behaviour: *That film was full of* ***sleaze.***
2 a sleazy person, especially a man, who constantly relates to people on a sexual level: *Keep away from him — he's a real* ***sleaze.***

Word use: You can also use **sleazebag** for definition 2.

sleazy
adjective **1** untidy and dirty (***bedraggled, dishevelled, scruffy, sloppy, unkempt***)
2 having to do with morally dubious behaviour, especially open sexual behaviour or conversation: *a* ***sleazy*** *bar* | *a* ***sleazy*** *character*

Adjective forms: **sleazier, sleaziest**
Word building: **sleaziness** *noun*

sled
noun a vehicle on runners for travelling or carrying loads over snow, ice, rough ground, etc.

Word use: You can also use **sledge**.
Word history: Middle English, from Middle Flemish or Middle Low German

sledge
noun → **sled**

Word history: Middle Dutch

sledgehammer
noun a large heavy hammer

sleek
adjective smooth and shiny: ***sleek*** *hair* (***glossy, lustrous, satiny, silky***)

Word building: **sleekness** *noun*
Word history: variant of *slick*

sleep
verb **1** to rest with your eyes closed and your mind unconscious: *Did you* ***sleep*** *well last night?* (***nap, slumber, snooze***)
2 to have beds for: *The caravan* ***sleeps*** *four.*
phrase **3 sleep in,** to sleep later than usual
4 sleep on it, to put off making a decision, etc., overnight

Verb forms: I **slept**, I have **slept**, I am **sleeping**
Word building: **sleepy** *adjective* (**sleepier, sleepiest**) **sleep** *noun* **sleepiness** *noun* **sleepless** *adjective*
Word history: Old English *slēpan, slāpan*

sleep apnoea (sleep ap-nee-uh)
noun a temporary stopping of breathing during sleep, often caused by obstruction of the airway

Word use: You can also use **sleep apnea**.

sleeper
noun **1** a wooden, concrete, or steel beam on which railway lines rest
2 a small ring worn in a pierced ear to prevent the hole from closing

sleeper cell
noun a small group of people, committed to a cause, who infiltrate a community waiting for an instruction to carry out sabotage, undertake a specific terrorist activity, etc.

sleeping-bag
noun a large bag, usually waterproof and warmly lined, for sleeping in, especially for use out of doors

sleepover
noun an occasion when you spend the night sleeping at a friend's home

sleet
noun rain mixed with snow or hail

Word building: **sleet** *verb*
Word history: Middle English

sleeve
noun the part of a garment that covers the arm

Word history: Old English

sleigh (slay)
noun a large sled, especially one pulled by animals

Word history: Dutch

sleight (sluyt)
noun **1** skill (***adroitness, dexterity***)
phrase **2 sleight of hand,** skill in using your hands quickly in tricks, etc., often in a performance

Word history: Middle English, from Scandinavian

slender
adjective slim or thin: *a* ***slender*** *girl* | *a* ***slender*** *branch* (***lean, skinny, slight, spindly***)

Word building: **slenderness** *noun*
Word history: Middle English; origin uncertain

sleuth (sloohth)
noun Old-fashioned a detective

Word history: Middle English, from Scandinavian

slew[1] (slooh)
verb past tense of **slay**

slew[2] (slooh)
verb **1** to swing or twist round
noun **2** a slewing movement
3 a position reached by slewing

slew[3] (slooh)
noun Colloquial a large number: *a whole* ***slew*** *of DVDs*

slice
verb **1** to cut into thin pieces: *to* ***slice*** *bread*
2 to hit a ball so that it curves to the right if you are right-handed

Word use: The opposite of definition 2 is **hook**.
Word building: **slice** *noun* **sliced** *adjective*
Word history: Middle English, from Old French word meaning 'splinter', 'sliver of wood', from Germanic

slick
adjective **1** clever and smooth, but not sincere: *a* ***slick*** *salesman*
2 smart or skilful: *a* ***slick*** *answer* (***silver-tongued, smooth***)
noun **3** a shiny patch of oil on water
phrase **4 slick down,** to smooth down: *to* ***slick down*** *hair with oil*

Word history: Middle English

slide
verb **1** to move along smoothly: *to **slide** a drawer in and out | to **slide** down a slippery dip*
noun **2** a sliding movement: *She slipped on a banana peel and went for a **slide**.*
3 a see-through photograph which can be shown on a screen using a projector
4 a thin sheet of glass used for holding things that you look at under a microscope

Verb forms: I **slid**, I have **slid**, I am **sliding**
Word history: Old English *slīdan*

slide rule
noun an instrument to help you calculate numbers rapidly, consisting of a rule with a sliding piece moving along it, both marked with graduated logarithmic scales

slight
adjective **1** small: *a **slight** cough* (***insignificant**, **minor**, **trifling**, **trivial***)
2 thin: *a man of **slight** build* (***lean**, **skinny**, **slender**, **slim**, **spindly***)
verb **3** to treat rudely: *They **slighted** her by not inviting her to the party.* (***affront**, **humiliate**, **insult**, **snub***)
noun **4** an insult

Word history: Old English *sliht* smooth (in *eorthslihtes* close to earth)

slightly
adverb not very much: *You are only **slightly** taller than me.*

slim
adjective **1** slender: ***slim** legs* (***lean**, **slight**, **thin***)
2 slight: *a **slim** chance* (***negligible**, **one-in-a-million***)

Adjective forms: **slimmer**, **slimmest**
Word building: **slim** *verb* (**slimmed**, **slimming**)
Word history: Dutch or Low German

slime
noun slippery wet matter, usually unpleasant: *Snails leave a trail of **slime**.*

Word building: **slimy** *adjective* (**slimier**, **slimiest**) **sliminess** *noun*
Word history: Old English *slīm*

sling
noun **1** a piece of cloth looped around your neck to support your arm if it is injured
2 an old-fashioned weapon for throwing stones, made of a leather strap which is swung quickly round and round before releasing the stone
verb **3** to throw or fling: *to **sling** a stone*
4 to hang loosely: *to **sling** a coat across your shoulders*

Verb forms: I **slung**, I have **slung**, I am **slinging**
Word history: Middle English, from Scandinavian

slingshot
noun → **catapult**

slink
verb to creep quietly so as not to be noticed: *The dog **slunk** away with its tail between its legs.*

Verb forms: I **slunk**, I have **slunk**, I am **slinking**
Word history: Old English *slincan* creep, crawl

slip[1]
verb **1** to slide easily: *to **slip** a note under the door | The wet glass **slipped** from her hand.*
2 to fall over: *to **slip** on a polished floor* (***overbalance**, **pitch forward**, **stumble**, **topple**, **trip***)
3 to escape from: *The dog **slipped** its leash. | Your birthday **slipped** my mind.*
noun **4** a mistake: *to make a **slip** in adding up the bill* (***blue**, **blunder**, **boo-boo**, **error***)
5 a petticoat
6 a small sheet or piece: *a **slip** of paper*
phrase **7 let slip**, to say or reveal without meaning to (***admit**, **disclose***)

Verb forms: I **slipped**, I have **slipped**, I am **slipping**
Word history: Middle English, from Midlle Low German

slip[2]
noun **1** a piece cut from a plant for planting or grafting; a cutting
2 any long narrow piece, as of wood, paper, land, etc.
3 a young person, especially one of slender form: *a **slip** of a girl*

Word history: Middle English, from Middle Dutch or Middle Low German word meaning 'cut', 'slit', 'strip', etc.

slipper
noun a soft comfortable shoe for wearing indoors

slippery
adjective too smooth or wet to get a hold on: ***slippery** ice* (***glassy**, **polished***)

Word history: Old English *slipor*

slippery dip
noun Australian a structure with a smooth slope for children to slide down for amusement

slipshod
adjective untidy, careless, or negligent

slip-stitch
noun **1** a type of stitch used for dress hems, etc., in which only a few threads of material are caught up from the outer material
2 a stitch slipped, or not worked, in knitting, crocheting, etc.

slipstream
noun an air current forced back by a moving object, especially an aircraft propeller or jet

slit
noun **1** a long straight cut or opening (***gash**, **incision**, **notch**, **score***)
verb **2** to cut apart or open along a line: *to **slit** open an envelope* (***lacerate**, **rip**, **slash**, **tear***)

Verb forms: I **slit**, I have **slit**, I am **slitting**
Word history: Old English *-slittan* (northern dialect)

slither
verb to slide along like a snake

Word history: Middle English; variant of dialect *slidder*, from Old English *slīdan* slide

sliver (<u>sli</u>-vuh)
noun a small thin piece: *a **sliver** of wood* (***fragment**, **particle**, **scrap***)

Word building: **sliver** *verb*
Word history: Old English *slīfan* split

slob
noun someone who is lazy and untidy

Word use: This word is used as an insult.
Word history: Irish *slab* mud, from obsolete English *slab* thick in consistency

slobber
verb to dribble or drool

Word building: **slobbery** *adjective*

slog
verb **1** to hit hard: *She* ***slogged*** *the ball.* (***knock for six***, ***strike at***)
2 to plod along heavily: *The weary hikers* ***slogged*** *up the hill.* (***lumber***, ***toil***, ***tramp***, ***trudge***)

Verb forms: I **slogged**, I have **slogged**, I am **slogging**
Word history: variant of *slug*^{2}, verb

slogan (sloh-guhn)
noun a clever catchy saying used to advertise something

Word history: Scottish Gaelic *sluagh-ghairm* warcry

sloop (sloohp)
noun a single-masted sailing vessel carrying fore-and-aft sails

Word history: Dutch

slop
verb to spill or splash: *Don't* ***slop*** *water over the side of the bath.* | *The milk* ***slopped*** *out of the cup.*

Verb forms: I **slopped**, I have **slopped**, I am **slopping**
Word history: Middle English *sloppe* mudhole, Old English -*sloppe* (in *cusloppe* cowslip, literally, cow slime)

slope
verb **1** to be higher at one end than the other: *The hill* ***slopes*** *steeply.* (***lean***, ***list***, ***slant***, ***tilt***, ***tip***)
noun **2** a slant or tilt: *the* ***slope*** *of a roof* (***gradient***, ***incline***, ***pitch***)
3 slopes, a hilly area: *There will be snow on the southern* ***slopes***.

Word building: **sloping** *adjective*
Word history: from *aslope*, adverb, on a slant

sloppy
adjective **1** wet and runny (***fluid***, ***liquid***)
2 too sentimental: *a* ***sloppy*** *love story*
3 loose or untidy: *a* ***sloppy*** *jumper* | ***sloppy*** *school work* (***bedraggled***, ***dishevelled***, ***scruffy***, ***sleazy***, ***unkempt***)

Adjective forms: **sloppier**, **sloppiest**
Word building: **sloppily** *adverb* **sloppiness** *noun*

slosh
verb to pour or splash sloppily: *to* ***slosh*** *water over the floor* | *to* ***slosh*** *around in the mud*

Word history: blend of *slop* and *slush*

slot
noun a small narrow slit or opening: *Put a coin in the* ***slot***.

Word history: Middle English, from Old French word meaning 'hollow between breasts'

sloth (slohth)
noun **1** great laziness
2 a slow clumsy mammal which lives in the jungles of South America

Word building: **slothful** *adjective*
Word history: Middle English *slowth*

slouch
verb to walk or sit without holding yourself up straight (***droop***, ***loll***, ***sag***, ***slump***)

Word building: **slouch** *noun*

slouch hat
noun an army hat with the brim designed to be turned up on one side

slough[1] (slow)
noun **1** a piece of soft muddy ground
2 a condition of despair, helplessness, etc.

Word history: Old English *slōh*

slough[2] (sluf)
noun **1** the skin of a snake, especially the outer skin which is shed periodically
verb **2** to be shed or thrown off, as the slough of a snake is
phrase **3 slough off**, to shed or throw: *He decided to* ***slough off*** *his bad habits.* | *The snake* ***sloughed off*** *its skin.*

Word history: Middle English

sloven (sluv-uhn)
noun someone who is dirty, careless or untidy

Word history: Middle English

slovenly (sluv-uhn-lee)
adjective dirty, careless and untidy in your habits

Word building: **slovenliness** *noun*

slow
adjective **1** taking a long time: *a* ***slow*** *train* | *a* ***slow*** *learner* (***leisurely***, ***plodding***, ***unhurried***)
2 behind the right time: *The clock is five minutes* ***slow***.
phrase **3 slow down**, to make or become slower

Word building: **slowly** *adverb* **slowness** *noun*
Word history: Old English *slāw* sluggish, dull

slow-mo
noun Colloquial (in film or television) slow motion

Word use: You can also use **slomo**.

slow motion
noun the process or technique used in films or television in which the images move more slowly than in real life, due to having been photographed at a greater number of frames per second than normal, or being projected more slowly than normal

sludge
noun soft muddy substance: *The drain is clogged with* ***sludge***.

Word building: **sludgy** *adjective* (**sludgier**, **sludgiest**)
Word history: Middle English *slich* slime; perhaps imitative

slug[1]
noun **1** a slimy creature like a snail without its shell
2 a small bullet

Word history: Middle English, from Scandinavian

slug[2]
verb Colloquial **1** to punch hard: *to **slug** him in the eye*
2 to charge far too much: *They **slugged** me for fixing my bike.*

Verb forms: I **slugged**, I have **slugged**, I am **slugging**
Word building: **slug** *noun*
Word history: perhaps originally, hit with a slug (piece of lead)

sluggard (slug-uhd)
noun **1** someone who is habitually inactive or lazy
adjective **2** lazy

Word building: **sluggardly** *adjective*
Word history: Middle English *slogard(e)*, from obsolete *sluggy* sluggish + *-ard*

sluggish
adjective moving slowly with no energy (***apathetic***, ***inert***, ***lethargic***, ***listless***, ***tired***)

Word use: The opposite of this is **energetic** or **active**.

sluice (sloohs)
noun **1** a channel for water, fitted with a gate to control the water flow
verb **2** to drain: *to **sluice** water from a pond*
3 to wash with running water

Word history: Middle English, from Old French, from Late Latin word meaning 'shut out'

slum
noun a dirty overcrowded place in which poor people live

Word building: **slummy** *adjective* (**slummier**, **slummiest**)
Word history: first occurs as slang word for room

slumber
noun deep sleep

Word building: **slumber** *verb*
Word history: Old English *slūma*

slump
verb to drop heavily: *to **slump** into a chair* (***collapse***, ***droop***, ***loll***, ***sag***, ***slouch***)

Word building: **slump** *noun*
Word history: verb use of British dialect *slump* bog

slur
verb **1** to pronounce unclearly: *Don't **slur** your words.*
2 to harm the good name of: *The newspaper article **slurred** the politician.*
noun **3** unclear sound or speech
4 *Music*
a a combination of two or more different notes, played or sung without a break
b a curved mark showing this
5 harm done to your good name, often caused by a remark: *a **slur** on his reputation*

Verb forms: I **slurred**, I have **slurred**, I am **slurring**
Word history: British dialect *slur* fluid mud

slurp (slerp)
verb **1** to eat or drink with a lot of noise
noun **2** the noise thus produced

Word history: Middle Dutch *slorpen* to sip

slush
noun snow which is partly melted

Word building: **slushy** *adjective* (**slushier**, **slushiest**)
Word history: Scandinavian

slut
noun a woman who has many sexual partners

Word use: The use of this word will offend people.
Word building: **sluttish** *adjective*
Word history: Middle English

sly
adjective **1** cunning or deceitful (***artful***, ***crafty***, ***devious***, ***dishonest***, ***wily***)
phrase **2 on the sly**, secretly: *to take money **on the sly***

Adjective forms: **slyer** or **slier**, **slyest** or **sliest**
Word history: Middle English, from Scandinavian

smack[1]
phrase **smack of**, to have a touch of: *His behaviour **smacks of** selfishness.*

Word building: **smack** *noun*
Word history: Old English *smæc*

smack[2]
verb **1** to hit with the hand open
phrase **2 smack your lips**, to make a noise with your lips as if you are looking forward to eating something good

Word building: **smack** *noun*
Word history: of imitative origin

small
adjective **1** not big or great (***little***, ***short***, ***tiny***)
2 ashamed or embarrassed: *to feel **small***
adverb **3** into small pieces: *to cut the fruit up **small***
phrase **4 small talk**, conversation about things which are not important

Word history: Old English *smæl*

smallgoods
plural noun Australian, NZ goods sold in a delicatessen, especially meats such as salami and frankfurts

smallpox
noun a serious infectious disease with a rash which leaves deep scars

smarmy
adjective falsely charming or flattering

smart
adjective **1** clever or intelligent (***brainy***, ***bright***, ***brilliant***)
2 quick
3 neat and fashionable: *a **smart** new suit* (***chic***, ***dapper***, ***elegant***, ***nifty***)
4 (of a computerised device) performing some functions without the human input usually required: *a **smart** air conditioner*
verb **5** to sting or hurt: *A cut **smarts** if you bathe it with salt water. | to **smart** from an insult*

Word building: **smartly** *adverb*
Word history: Old English *smeortan*

smarten
phrase **smarten up 1** to make more neat and tidy: *I'll have to **smarten up** before I go to the dinner. | I'd like to **smarten up** the house before the guests arrive.*
2 to begin to behave better: *If you don't **smarten up** young man, you'll end up getting the sack.*

smash
verb **1** to break loudly into pieces: *to **smash** a plate*
2 to hit with great force: *to **smash** the ball over the net | The car **smashed** into the fence.*
noun **3** a loud crash
4 a film, play, recording, etc., that is a great success

Word use: You can also use **smash-hit** for definition 4.
Word history: perhaps a blend of *smack*[2] and *mash*

smashing
adjective Old-fashioned, Colloquial excellent, or extremely good

smattering
noun a slight knowledge: *I have only a **smattering** of French.*

Word history: Middle English, from Scandinavian

smear
verb **1** to rub or spread: *to **smear** grease over the walls* (***coat***, ***daub***, ***plaster***)
noun **2** a dirty mark or stain: *a **smear** of paint*
3 a slur on your good name

Word history: Old English *smeoru*

smell
verb **1** to sense through the nose
2 to give off an odour: *The dinner **smells** delicious.*
noun **3** the ability to sense odours through the nose
4 an odour or scent: *flowers with a strong **smell*** (***aroma***, ***bouquet***, ***fragrance***)

Verb forms: I **smelt** or I **smelled**, I have **smelt** or I have **smelled**, I am **smelling**
Word building: **smelly** *adjective* (**smellier**, **smelliest**)
Word history: Middle English

smelt
verb to melt or refine ore in order to obtain metal: *to **smelt** iron*

Word history: Middle Dutch or Middle Low German

smelter
noun the place where ore is refined into metal

smidgen (<u>smij</u>-uhn)
noun a very small quantity or bit. *She only likes a **smidgen** of vegemite on her toast.*

Word use: You can also use **smidgin** or **smidgeon**.
Word history: British dialect

smile
verb **1** to show you are happy or amused by widening your mouth and turning it up at the corners (***grin***)
noun **2** the act of smiling: *a **smile** from ear to ear* (***grin***)

Word history: Middle English

smirk
verb to smile in a smug way that annoys people (***snigger***, ***titter***)

Word building: **smirk** *noun*
Word history: Old English *sme(a)rcian*

smithereens
plural noun tiny pieces: *The cup smashed into **smithereens**.*

smithy
noun a blacksmith's workshop

Noun forms: The plural is **smithies**.

smitten
adjective **1** affected suddenly and strongly by a particular feeling: *She was **smitten** with guilt.*
2 suddenly liking something very much or suddenly falling in love with someone: *He is completely **smitten** by her.*

Word history: past participle of *smite* to strike or hit

smock
noun a long, loose shirt worn on top of your clothes to stop them getting dirty

Word building: **smock** *verb*
Word history: Old English *smocc*; originally name of garment with a hole for the head

smocking
noun a sort of embroidery used on baby's clothes

smog
noun a dirty cloud of smoke and fog: *Their vision was restricted by the **smog**.*

Word building: **smoggy** *adjective* (**smoggier**, **smoggiest**)

smoke
noun **1** the cloud of gas and tiny particles given off when something burns: *Bushfires filled the air with **smoke**.*
2 a cigarette: *a packet of **smokes***
verb **3** to give off smoke: *The chimney is **smoking**.*
4 to breathe in the smoke of a cigarette while holding it between your lips
5 to treat with wood smoke as a preservative: *to **smoke** meat*
phrase **6 go** (or **end**) **up in smoke,**
a to be burnt up completely
b to end or disappear without coming to anything: *My career has **ended up in smoke**.*

Word building: **smoky** *adjective* (**smokier**, **smokiest**)
Word history: Old English *smoca*

smokescreen
noun anything used to hide the truth or what you are really doing: *His excuse was simply a **smokescreen**.*

smoking ceremony
noun an Aboriginal cleansing ritual in which green leaves from local plants are burnt creating smoke which is said to cleanse and heal the area

smoking gun
noun a piece of evidence which clearly points to the perpetrator of a crime, the cause of a disaster, etc.: *The email was a **smoking gun** proving that the politician was taking bribes.*

smoodge (smoohj)
verb Colloquial **1** to kiss or caress
2 to praise in an insincere way

Word use: You can also use **smooge**.
Word history: probably from British dialect

smooth
adjective **1** even and without bumps or lumps
2 very pleasant in manner, especially when insincere: *a* ***smooth*** *talker* (***silver-tongued***, ***slick***)
verb **3** to make even or level (***grind down***, ***iron out***, ***plane***, ***rub down***, ***sand***)

Word building: **smoothly** *adverb* **smoothness** *noun*
Word history: Old English *smōth*

smorgasbord
noun a meal where you help yourself to a great variety of meats and salads

Word history: Swedish *smörgås* sandwich + *bord* table

smother (smu-dhuh)
verb **1** to choke by keeping out air: *to* ***smother*** *a fire with sand | Don't cover your head with a plastic bag because you might* ***smother***. (***asphyxiate***, ***stifle***, ***suffocate***)
2 to cover all over: *She* ***smothered*** *her face with make-up.*
3 to protect too closely: *Her parents* ***smother*** *her and never allow her to play outside.*

Word history: Old English *smorian* suffocate

smoulder (smohl-duh)
verb to burn slowly giving off smoke but no flame

Word history: from Middle English word meaning 'smoky vapour'

SMS (es-em-es)
noun **1** a service which allows you to key in a message on a mobile phone and send it to another mobile phone where someone else can read it on the screen
2 → **text message**
3 → **SMS code**
verb **4** to send a message using this system: *I'll* ***SMS*** *the address to you. | I'll* ***SMS*** *you the address.*

Verb forms: I **SMS'ed** or I **SMSed**, I have **SMS'ed** or I have **SMSed**, I am **SMS'ing** or I am **SMSing**

SMS code
noun a code designed to reduce the length of words when sending SMS messages, such as *u* for *you*, *b4* for *before*, etc.

SMS message
→ **text message**

Word building: **SMS messaging** *noun*

smudge
noun a dirty mark or smear

Word building: **smudge** *verb*
Word history: Middle English

smug
adjective very pleased with yourself: *a* ***smug*** *grin* (***arrogant***, ***conceited***)

Word use: The opposite of this is **humble**.
Word building: **smugly** *adverb*
Word history: perhaps from Dutch word meaning 'neat'

smuggle
verb to carry secretly and illegally: *to* ***smuggle*** *rare birds out of the country*

Word building: **smuggler** *noun* **smuggling** *noun*
Word history: Low German

smut
noun **1** a smudge of soot or dirt
2 offensive or obscene talk

Word building: **smutty** *adjective* (**smuttier**, **smuttiest**)
Word history: Old English *smitte*

snack
noun **1** a small quick meal: *a* ***snack*** *after school*
2 *Colloquial* something that is very easy to do: *That test was a* ***snack***.
verb **3** to eat small portions of food at times other than meal times: *I* ***snacked*** *throughout the day.*

Word history: noun use of *snack*, verb, snap

snag[1]
noun **1** something sharp sticking out or lying on the bottom of a river
2 a problem or difficulty: *a* ***snag*** *in our plans*
verb **3** to catch on, or damage by, a snag: *to* ***snag*** *your stockings*
4 to obstruct or hinder, the way a snag does

Verb forms: it **snagged**, it has **snagged**, it is **snagging**
Word history: Scandinavian

snag[2]
noun Australian, *NZ Colloquial* a sausage

Word history: perhaps from British dialect word meaning 'a small meal'

snail
noun a small slow-moving animal with a soft body and a coiled shell, often found in gardens

Word history: Old English *snegel*

snake
noun **1** a long scaly creature without legs which slithers silently along the ground
verb **2** to twist and wind like the body of a snake
phrase **3 snake in the grass**, someone who secretly does you harm

Word history: Old English *snaca*

snaky
adjective Australian, *NZ Colloquial* spiteful or angry: *a* ***snaky*** *remark*

Adjective forms: **snakier**, **snakiest**

snap
verb **1** to break with a sudden sharp sound: *to* ***snap*** *a biscuit in two | The rubber band* ***snapped***.
2 to make a sudden biting movement: *The dog will* ***snap*** *if you tease it.*
3 to speak angrily and sharply
noun **4** a sudden sharp sound or movement
5 an easy card game in which you try to be the first to call out when you see two matching cards
adjective **6** sudden: *a* ***snap*** *decision* (***abrupt***, ***impromptu***, ***impulsive***)
phrase **7 snap up**, to grab quickly: *to* ***snap up*** *a bargain* (***nab***, ***nail***, ***seize***, ***snatch***)

Verb forms: I **snapped**, I have **snapped**, I am **snapping**
Word history: Dutch or Low German

snapper
noun an Australian and New Zealand saltwater fish belonging to the bream family, which is good to eat

Word use: You can also use **schnapper**.

snappy
adjective **1** quick or brisk: *a **snappy** decision*
2 *Colloquial* stylish: *a **snappy** dresser*

Adjective forms: **snappier**, **snappiest**

snapshot
noun an informal photograph taken quickly

snare (snair)
noun a trap for catching birds and small animals (***booby trap***, ***lure***, ***net***)

Word building: **snare** *verb*
Word history: Middle English, from Scandinavian

snarl[1]
verb to growl angrily or fiercely

Word building: **snarl** *noun*
Word history: obsolete *snar* snarl

snarl[2]
noun a tangle or knot

Word building: **snarl** *verb*
Word history: Middle English *snarle* snare, from Scandinavian

snatch
verb **1** to take hold of suddenly: *to **snatch** a purse* (***grab***, ***nab***, ***nail***, ***seize***, ***snap up***)
noun **2** a sudden grab
3 a scrap or small part: *to overhear **snatches** of conversation* (***hint***, ***piece***)

Word history: Middle English

sneak
verb **1** to move or act in a sly and furtive way: *to **sneak** into the room | to **sneak** a chocolate*
noun **2** someone mean who tells tales and can't be trusted

Verb forms: I **sneaked**, I have **sneaked**, I am **sneaking**
Word building: **sneaky** *adjective* (**sneakier**, **sneakiest**) **sneakily** *adverb*
Word history: related to Old English *snīcan* sneak along

sneaker
noun a rubber-soled shoe made of canvas

sneer
verb to say or look in a nasty mocking way (***leer***, ***smirk***)

Word building: **sneer** *noun*
Word history: Middle English *snere*

sneeze
verb **1** to have a sudden noisy explosion of air, mostly through your mouth, because of irritation in your nose
phrase **2 not to be sneezed at,** *Colloquial* worth thinking about: *This offer is **not to be sneezed at**.*

Word building: **sneeze** *noun*
Word history: Old English *fnēosan*

snib
noun **1** a mechanism which is usually part of a lock and which can be operated from only one side of a door. It holds the lock in position without using a key.
2 a latch (definition 1)
verb **3** to hold by means of a snib: *to **snib** a lock*

Verb forms: it **snibbed**, it has **snibbed**, it is **snibbing**

snick
verb **1** to cut, snip, or nick
2 to strike sharply
3 *Cricket* to hit, especially accidentally, with the edge of the bat: *to **snick** the ball*
noun **4** a small cut
5 *Cricket* a glancing blow given to the ball

Word history: origin uncertain

snicker
verb **1** of a horse, to make a low, snorting neigh
2 → **snigger**

Word building: **snicker** *noun*

snide
adjective insulting in a nasty indirect way: ***snide** remarks about the Mayor*

Word history: British dialect *snidy* treacherous

sniff
verb to breathe in through the nose in a short sharp burst: *to **sniff** the air | to **sniff** with a cold*

Word building: **sniff** *noun*
Word history: Middle English; from *snivel*

sniffle
verb **1** to sniff continually because you have a cold or are trying not to cry
phrase **2 the sniffles,** a cold with a runny nose

Word history: from *sniff*

snigger
verb to give a rather rude laugh or giggle which you try to hide: *to **snigger** at a dirty joke* (***smirk***, ***snicker***, ***titter***)

Word building: **snigger** *noun*
Word history: imitative

snip
verb to cut using small quick strokes of the scissors

Verb forms: I **snipped**, I have **snipped**, I am **snipping**
Word building: **snip** *noun*
Word history: from Dutch and Low German word meaning 'snatch', 'clip'

snipe
noun **1** a small shorebird with a plump body, striped head and long straight bill, found in swamps and wet grasslands
phrase **2 snipe at,** to make critical or damaging comments about without entering into open conflict

Word history: Middle English, from Scandinavian

sniper
noun someone who shoots from a place which is hidden or some distance from the target

snippet (snip-uht)
noun a small bit, scrap, or fragment: *a **snippet** of information*

snitch[1]
verb Colloquial to snatch or steal

Word history: perhaps variant of *snatch*

snitch[2]
Colloquial
verb **1** to tell tales
noun **2** an informer

snivel
verb to sniffle noisily while you are crying

Verb forms: I **snivelled**, I have **snivelled**, I am **snivelling**
Word history: Old English *snofl* mucus

snob
noun someone who looks down on people who are not wealthy, important, or clever

Word building: **snobbery** *noun* **snobbish** *adjective*

snooker
noun a game like billiards, played with balls of many colours

snoop
verb to creep around, prying into things

Word building: **snoopy** *adjective* (**snoopier**, **snoopiest**)
Word history: from Dutch word meaning 'take and eat (food or drink) on the sly'

snooze
noun Colloquial a rest or short sleep (***doze***, ***drowse***, ***nap***)

Word building: **snooze** *verb*

snore
verb to breathe with a loud rumbling noise while you're asleep

Word building: **snore** *noun*
Word history: Middle English; perhaps blend of *sniff* and *roar*

snorkel
noun a tube through which you can breathe air as you swim face downwards in the water

Word building: **snorkel** *verb* (**snorkelled**, **snorkelling**)
Word history: German

snort
verb to force your breath out of your nose so that it makes a rough rumbling sound: *to **snort** with anger*

Word history: Middle English

snot
noun Colloquial mucus from the nose

Word history: Old English

snout
noun the front part of an animal's face where the nose and jaws are

Word history: Middle English

snow
noun **1** frozen rain drops which fall to the ground as tiny white flakes
verb **2** of snow, to fall: *It **snowed** for two whole weeks.*
phrase **3 be snowed under**, to be overcome by something: ***I am snowed under** with work at the moment.*

Word building: **snowy** *adjective*
Word history: Old English *snaw*

snowball
noun **1** a pile of snow pressed into a ball
verb **2** to pile up at a great rate: *The work is **snowballing**.*

snowboard
noun **1** a board for gliding over the snow, which resembles a surfboard in that the rider stands on it, the feet being strapped to it as with skis
verb **2** to glide over the snow on a snowboard: *She **snowboarded** down the run in record time.*

Word building: **snowboarder** *noun* **snowboarding** *noun*

snowman
noun a human-like figure made of hard packed snow

Noun forms: The plural is **snowmen**.

snub
verb **1** to show dislike or contempt for, especially by ignoring
noun **2** an instance of this: *a deliberate **snub*** (***put-down***, ***rebuff***)
adjective **3** short and turned up at the tip: *a **snub** nose*

Verb forms: I **snubbed**, I have **snubbed**, I am **snubbing**
Word history: Middle English, from Scandinavian

snuff
noun powdered tobacco used for sniffing

Word history: Middle Dutch

snuffle
verb **1** of pigs, etc., to breathe in, in a noisy way
2 to speak through your nose or with a nasal twang
3 to sniff, or snivel
noun **4** an act or sound of snuffling
phrase **5 the snuffles**, *Colloquial* a nasal condition, such as from a cold

Word history: Dutch or Flemish

snug
adjective comfortable and warm: *Our strong tent was **snug** despite the rain.*

Adjective forms: **snugger**, **snuggest**
Word history: from Middle Dutch word meaning 'smart', 'ship-shape'

snuggle
phrase **snuggle up**, to lie closely together for warmth or comfort: *The kittens **snuggled up** in their basket.*

Word history: from *snug*, verb

so
adverb **1** in the way shown or described: *Do it **so**.*
2 as told or described: *Is that **so**?*
3 to that extent: *Do not walk **so** fast.*
4 very: *You are **so** kind.*
5 for this reason: *Bananas are nutritious and **so** you should eat them often.*
6 about that number or amount: *a day or **so** ago*
7 so-so, only fair: *I'm feeling **so-so** today.*
phrase **8 and so forth**, and the rest
9 just so, in perfect order
10 so not, *Colloquial* definitely not: *That is **so not** cool.*
11 so over, *Colloquial* completely sick of or bored with: *I'm **so over** your continual complaining.*
12 so that,
a with the result that
b in order that
13 so to speak, in a manner of speaking

Word history: Old English *swā*

so /sew / sow

Don't confuse **so** with **sew** or **sow**.

To **sew** is to stitch something with a needle and thread.

To **sow**, rhyming with *go*, is to scatter seed on the ground.

But a **sow**, rhyming with *cow*, is a female pig.

soak
verb **1** to lie or leave in liquid for a long time: *I like to* ***soak*** *in a bath after sport. | She* ***soaked*** *the clothes to loosen the dirt.*
2 to wet thoroughly (***dampen***, ***irrigate***, ***moisten***, ***water***)
phrase **3 soak up**, to take in or absorb

Word building: **soak** *noun*
Word history: Old English *socian*

soap
noun a substance made out of fat, used for washing yourself or cleaning things

Word building: **soap** *verb* **soapy** *adjective* (**soapier**, **soapiest**)
Word history: Old English *sāpe*

soapbox
noun **1** a box used as a platform by street speakers
2 any place, means, etc., used by a person to make a speech, say what they think, or make any kind of public statement

soap opera
noun Colloquial a television series which tells a story about people's lives and problems, often in an over-emotional way

Word history: so called because originally sponsored on US radio networks by soap manufacturers

soar
verb **1** to fly upwards, quickly and effortlessly (***ascend***, ***climb***, ***mount***, ***rise***)
2 to fly at a great height hardly moving the wings: *The eagle* ***soared*** *over the valley.*
3 to rise to a great height: *Our hopes* ***soared***. *| Prices are* ***soaring***. (***climb***, ***mount***)

Word history: Middle English, from Old French word meaning 'fly up', 'soar', from Late Latin

soar / saw / sore

Don't confuse **soar** with **saw** or **sore**.

A **saw** is a cutting tool with sharp teeth on a thin blade.

Saw is also the past tense of the verb **see**, to take things in with your eyes or your mind.

If your leg is **sore**, it hurts or feels painful.

sob
verb **1** to cry making a gulping noise as you breathe (***bawl***, ***blubber***, ***wail***)
2 to speak while doing this: *She* ***sobbed*** *her words of pity.*

Verb forms: I **sobbed**, I have **sobbed**, I am **sobbing**
Word building: **sob** *noun*
Word history: Middle English; imitative

sober
adjective **1** not drunk
2 quiet and serious: *The sad news put us in a* ***sober*** *mood.* (***grave***, ***solemn***)

Word building: **sober** *verb*
Word history: Middle English, from Old French, from Latin

sobriety
noun **1** the state or quality of being sober
2 moderation, especially in the use of alcohol
3 seriousness

soccer
noun a form of football played with a round ball in which the players, except for the goalkeeper, are not allowed to use their hands or arms to play the ball

Word history: *(as)soc(iation)* + *-er* (from *association football*, a British term for the sport)

sociable (<u>soh</u>-shuh-buhl)
adjective friendly, or wanting to be with other people (***agreeable***, ***genial***, ***neighbourly***, ***outgoing***, ***warm***)

Word use: The opposite of this is **reserved** or **unsociable**.
Word building: **sociability** *noun* **sociableness** *noun* **sociably** *adverb*
Word history: Latin

social
adjective **1** having to do with friendliness: *Our tennis club is as much a* ***social*** *club as a sporting one.*
2 having to do with fashionable people: *a* ***social*** *page in a newspaper*
3 having to do with human society, or the way it is organised: ***social*** *problems |* ***social*** *status*
noun **4** a party or gathering: *a church* ***social***

Word history: Latin

socialise (<u>soh</u>-shul-uyz)
verb **1** to train or educate so as to live according to the customs of society
2 to be friendly and mix with others as at a party

Word use: You can also use **socialize**.
Word building: **socialisation** *noun*

socialism (<u>soh</u>-shuh-liz-uhm)
noun the political belief that all industry and wealth should be owned and controlled by the people as a whole

Word use: Compare this with **capitalism** and **communism**.
Word building: **socialist** *noun*

socialite (<u>soh</u>-shuh-luyt)
noun someone who regularly goes to fashionable society functions

social security
noun money and services provided by the government to disadvantaged members of the public by means of old-age pensions, sickness and unemployment benefits, etc.

social welfare
noun a system of community services set up by a state to help disadvantaged people

social work
noun **1** organised work directed towards improving social conditions
2 the study of methods by which this can be done

Word building: **social worker** *noun*

society (suh-<u>suy</u>-uh-tee)
noun **1** people as a whole: *human* ***society***
2 people as a group in which there are divisions according to birth, education, and occupation: *the middle class of* ***society***
3 a group of people with a common interest: *a* ***society*** *for coin collectors*
4 companionship or company: *She enjoyed his* ***society.***
5 rich people and their activities: *Some people enjoy reading about* ***society*** *in the social column of newspapers.*

Noun forms: The plural is **societies**.
Word history: Latin

sociology (soh-see-<u>ol</u>-uh-jee)
noun the study of the development and organisation of human society

Word building: **sociologist** *noun*

sock[1]
noun **1** a garment that you wear under a shoe, covering the foot and the ankle and sometimes reaching up to the knee
phrase **2 pull your socks up**, to make an effort to improve

Word history: Old English *socc*

sock[2]
verb Colloquial to hit hard

Word building: **sock** *noun*

socket
noun **1** a hollow area which holds some part or thing: *an eye* ***socket***
2 a place on the wall or a machine into which you plug an electric cord or cable

Word history: Middle English, from Anglo-French word meaning 'little ploughshare'; of Celtic origin

sod
noun a square or oblong piece of grass which has been cut or torn out of a lawn or other turf

Word history: Middle English, from Middle Dutch or Middle Low German word meaning 'turf'

soda
noun **1** a chemical compound containing sodium used for various purposes, such as baking soda, caustic soda, etc.
2 → soda water
3 a drink made with soda water, fruit juices, and ice-cream

Word history: Medieval Latin, from Italian, from Arabic

soda water
noun a fizzy drink made by filling water with bubbles of carbon dioxide

Word use: The short form is **soda**.

sodden
adjective soaked with a liquid: ***sodden*** *washing hanging in the rain* (***dank***, ***moist***, ***soggy***, ***wet***)

Word history: Middle English *sothen*, past participle of *seethe*

sodium (<u>soh</u>-dee-uhm)
noun a soft, silver-white, metallic element found in salt

Word history: *sod(a)* + *-ium*

sodium bicarbonate (soh-dee-uhm buy-<u>kah</u>-buh-nuht)
noun a white, crystalline compound, used in cooking, medicine, etc.

Word use: Another name is **baking soda**.

sodium chloride
noun common salt

sofa
noun a long couch with a back and two sides

Word history: from Arabic word meaning 'raised floor for use as seat'

soft
adjective **1** easily cut or pressed out of shape
2 smooth and pleasant to touch: *the* ***soft*** *fur of a kitten* (***downy***, ***silky***, ***velvet***)
3 low in sound: *We could hardly hear her* ***soft*** *voice.* (***faint***, ***indistinct***, ***muffled***, ***quiet***)
4 not harsh or glaring: ***soft*** *light*
5 gentle or pitying: *She has a* ***soft*** *heart.*
6 not able to bear hardship: *He's too* ***soft*** *for a farmer's life.*
7 (of water) having a low level of salts from minerals, so that soap lathers easily in it
phrase **8 a soft touch**, *Colloquial* someone who gives money too easily
9 be soft on someone, *Colloquial*
a to fancy someone in a romantic way
b to act towards someone less harshly than expected

Word building: **soften** *verb*
Word history: Old English *softe*

softball
noun a form of baseball played with a larger softer ball which is bowled underarm

soft drink
noun a drink which has no alcohol in it

soft pedal
noun a pedal, such as the one on a piano, for lessening the volume

soft-pedal
verb **1** to soften the sound by means of the soft pedal: *to* ***soft-pedal*** *a piano*
2 *Colloquial* to make less strong or harsh: *The government is* ***soft-pedalling*** *on the new tax until after the election.*

Verb forms: I **soft-pedalled**, I have **soft-pedalled**, I am **soft-pedalling**

soft sell
noun a method of advertising or selling which is quietly persuasive and indirect

Word use: Compare this with **hard sell**.

soft target
noun an enemy target without military protection

software
noun a collection of programs used to control a computer

Word use: Compare this with **hardware**.

softwood
noun a cone-bearing tree or its wood

soggy
adjective **1** soaked or thoroughly wet: ***soggy*** *ground* (***moist***, ***sodden***)
2 damp and heavy like bread when it is not cooked enough

Adjective forms: **soggier**, **soggiest**
Word history: British dialect *sog* bog

soil[1]
noun ground or earth, especially of the kind plants can grow in (***dirt***, ***loam***)

Word history: Middle English, from Anglo-French, from Latin

soil[2]
verb to make dirty or stained (***dirty***, ***smear***, ***smudge***, ***spoil***, ***spot***)

Word history: Middle English, from Old French word meaning 'pigsty', from Latin word meaning 'pig'

soil profile
noun Geography a section through the soil, extending downwards from the surface to the underlying material, that shows the different layers, or horizons, often marked by the letters A, B, or C

solace (sol-uhs)
noun **1** comfort in sorrow or trouble (***consolation***, ***relief***)
2 something that provides this
verb **3** to comfort, console, or cheer (***relieve***, ***soothe***)

Word history: Middle English, from Old French, from Latin

solar
adjective **1** having to do with the sun: *a **solar** eclipse*
2 operated or produced by the heat of the sun: ***solar** energy*

Word history: Latin

solar heating
noun the use of solar energy to provide heating for air or water in a building

Word building: **solar-heated** *adjective*

solar panel
noun a glass sheet behind which are an interconnected set of solar cells which convert energy from the sun into electricity as part of a solar heating system

solar plexus
noun **1** a network of nerves in the upper part of your abdomen, behind your stomach and in front of your aorta
2 *Colloquial* a point on your body, just below the sternum, where a blow will affect this nerve centre

solar system
noun the sun together with all the planets, moons, etc., which revolve around it

sold
verb past tense and past participle of **sell**

solder
noun an alloy which can be melted easily and used to join metals together

Word building: **solder** *verb*
Word history: Middle English, from Old French word meaning 'to solder', from Latin word meaning 'make firm'

soldier
noun **1** someone who serves in an army
2 someone who serves any cause: *a **soldier** against poverty*
verb **3** to serve as a soldier
phrase **4 soldier on**, to continue doing something you have started

Word building: **soldierly** *adjective*
Word history: Middle English, from Old French word meaning 'pay', from Latin

sole[1]
adjective **1** being the only one: *the **sole** remaining member of his family* (***exclusive***, ***single***, ***unique***)
2 not shared: *the **sole** right to sell a property*

Word history: from Latin word meaning 'alone'

sole[2]
noun the underneath or bottom of your foot or shoe

Word history: Middle English and Old English, from Latin word meaning 'sandal', 'shoe'

sole[3]
noun any of a number of types of flat-bodied fishes with both eyes on the upper side

Noun forms: The plural is **sole** or **soles.**
Word history: Middle English, from French, from Latin

> **sole / soul**
> Don't confuse **sole** with **soul**. Your **soul** is the spiritual part of you, contrasted with your body.

solecism (sol-uh-siz-uhm)
noun **1** a lapsing into incorrect grammar as in *they was*
2 a breach of good manners or etiquette

Word building: **solecistic** *adjective*
Word history: Latin, from Greek

solemn (sol-uhm)
adjective **1** serious or sincere: *a **solemn** promise* (***grave***, ***sober***, ***stern***)
2 causing a grave mood or serious thoughts: ***solemn** music*
3 marked by formality or ritual: *a **solemn** ceremony*

Word building: **solemnity** *noun* (*plural* **solemnities**) **solemnly** *adverb*
Word history: Middle English, from Latin

solemnise (sol-uhm-nuyz)
verb to perform a ceremony or rite, especially that of marriage

Word use: You can also use **solemnize**.

solenoid (soh-luh-noyd, sol-uh-noyd)
noun a coil or wire in which a magnetic field is set up when electricity flows through it

Word history: from Greek word meaning 'channel', 'pipe', 'shellfish'

sole trader
noun a person who owns their own business

solicit (suh-lis-uht)
verb **1** to seek seriously and respectfully: *to **solicit** funds*
2 of a prostitute, etc., to seek the custom of
3 to try to get for business: *to **solicit** orders or trade*

Word building: **solicitation** *noun*
Word history: Middle English, from Latin word meaning 'disturb', 'incite'

solicitor (suh-lis-uh-tuh)
noun a lawyer who advises clients and prepares cases for a barrister to present in court

solicitous (suh-lis-uh-tuhs)
adjective **1** anxious or concerned over something: ***solicitous*** *about a person's health*
2 anxiously wanting: ***solicitous*** *of the esteem of others*

Word building: **solicitude** *noun*
Word history: Latin

solid
adjective **1** having length, breadth, and thickness: *a* ***solid*** *shape*
2 having the inside filled: *a* ***solid*** *rubber ball*
3 consisting only of: ***solid*** *gold*
noun **4** something solid
5 solids, food that is not in liquid form

Word building: **solidity** *noun* **solidly** *adverb*
Word history: Middle English, from Latin

solidarity (sol-uh-da-ruh-tee)
noun a united front presented by members of a group with strongly-held common ideas and interests

Word history: French, from Latin word meaning 'solid'

solidify
verb to become solid (***harden***, ***petrify***, ***set***, ***stiffen***)

Verb forms: it **solidified**, it has **solidified**, it is **solidifying**

solid-state
adjective **1** *Physics* having to do with the structure and properties of solids
2 in electronics, having to do with electronic devices which are composed of components in the solid state such as transistors, semiconductor diodes, integrated circuits, etc.

soliloquy (suh-lil-uh-kwee)
noun the act of talking when you are alone, or when you are pretending to be alone as happens in a play

Noun forms: The plural is **soliloquies**.
Word building: **soliloquise** *verb*
Word history: Late Latin

solitaire (sol-uh-tair)
noun **1** a game played by one person, with marbles or pegs on a board with holes
2 a card game played by one person
3 a single precious stone, especially a diamond, set in a ring, brooch, etc.

Word history: French, from Latin word meaning 'alone'

solitary (sol-uh-tree)
adjective **1** quite alone (***lonely***, ***reclusive***)
2 being the only one: *a* ***solitary*** *exception*

Word history: Middle English, from Latin

solitude (sol-uh-tyoohd)
noun a state of being alone: *to enjoy a brief time of* ***solitude***

Word history: Middle English, from Latin

solo
noun **1** a musical performance by one person
adjective **2** performed or done alone: *a* ***solo*** *item* | *a* ***solo*** *flight*
adverb **3** alone: *He flew* ***solo***.

Word history: Italian, from Latin word meaning 'alone'

soloist (soh-loh-uhst)
noun someone who performs a solo, often on a musical instrument (***instrumentalist***, ***virtuoso***)

solstice (sol-stuhs)
noun Astronomy either of the two times in the year when the sun is at its greatest distance from the celestial equator, about June 21 when it enters the sign of Cancer, and about December 22, when it enters the sign of Capricorn

Word building: **solstitial** *adjective*
Word history: Middle English, from Old French, from Latin

solubility (sol-yuh-bil-uh-tee)
noun the property of being able to be dissolved

Noun forms: The plural is **solubilities**.

soluble (sol-yuh-buhl)
adjective **1** able to be dissolved: *Sugar is* ***soluble*** *in water.*
2 able to be solved: *a* ***soluble*** *problem*

Word use: The opposite of this is **insoluble**.
Word history: Middle English, from Latin

solute
noun a substance dissolved in a given solution

Word history: Latin

solution
noun **1** the solving of, or answer to a problem
2 a substance which is made up of one chemical, usually a solid, spread perfectly throughout another chemical, usually a liquid: *Sugar can be dissolved in tea to make a* ***solution***.

Word history: Middle English, from Latin

solve
verb to explain or find the answer to: *He* ***solved*** *the mystery.* (***crack***, ***figure out***, ***puzzle out***, ***resolve***, ***work out***)

Word building: **solvable** *adjective*
Word history: Middle English, from Latin word meaning 'loosen', 'dissolve'

solvent
adjective **1** able to pay off all your debts
noun **2** a substance, usually a liquid, that can dissolve other substances in it: *Water is a* ***solvent*** *for sugar.*

sombre (som-buh)
adjective gloomily dark or dull: *the* ***sombre*** *interior of the deserted castle* | ***sombre*** *clothes* (***dingy***, ***drab***, ***dull***, ***gloomy***, ***mousy***)

Word use: The US spelling is **somber**.
Word history: French, from Vulgar Latin word meaning 'to shade', from Latin

sombrero (som-brair-roh)
noun a broad-brimmed hat worn in Spain, Mexico, and some other countries

Noun forms: The plural is **sombreros**.
Word history: from Spanish word meaning 'shade'

some
adjective **1** being one thing or person that is not named: ***some*** *poor woman*
2 of a certain number, amount, extent, etc., that is not specified but is often large: ***some*** *variation in temperature* | *He was here for* ***some*** *weeks.*

3 *Colloquial* great or important: *That was* ***some*** *storm!*
pronoun **4** certain people, or instances, etc., that are not named: ***Some*** *think he is dead.*
5 an unstated number, amount, etc., that is marked out from the rest: ***Some*** *of this work is good.*

Word history: Old English *sum*

some / sum
Don't confuse **some** with **sum**. A **sum** is a calculation in arithmetic:
I am doing my sums now.
It is also an amount of money:
That is a big sum to pay out.

somebody
pronoun **1** some person
noun **2** a person of some importance: *He thinks he is* ***somebody****.*

Noun forms: The plural is **somebodies**.

Somebody is sometimes called an *indefinite pronoun*.
For more information, look up **pronouns: indefinite pronouns**.

somebody / someone
These words are singular and so should be followed by singular verbs such as *is* and *has*:
Somebody has left.
The real problem arises when you have to choose the right pronoun to follow. You could write
Somebody has left his headlights on.
which assumes the person is male, or
Somebody has left her headlights on.
which assumes the person is female, or
Somebody has left his or her headlights on.
which doesn't assume the sex of the person, but is awkward to write all the time.
One solution is to break the singular agreement and use the plural pronoun *their*:
Somebody has left their headlights on.
This is the usual way of solving the problem in our speech, and is increasingly common even in formal writing. Some people, however, object to this and would prefer you to rewrite the sentence:
Somebody's headlights have been left on.
For more information on this, look up **agreement in grammar**.

somehow
adverb in some way not specified, apparent, or known: ***Somehow*** *the prisoner escaped.*

someone
pronoun some person

Someone is sometimes called an *indefinite pronoun*.
For more information, look up **pronouns: indefinite pronouns**.

somersault (sum-uh-sawlt, sum-uh-solt)
noun a gymnastic movement in which your body rolls end over end

Word building: **somersault** *verb*
Word history: Old French, from Provençal word meaning 'leap above', from Latin

something
pronoun some thing; a certain thing which is not named

This is sometimes called an *indefinite pronoun*.
For more information, look up **pronouns: indefinite pronoun.**

sometimes
adverb on some occasions; now and then: ***Sometimes*** *she arrives on time –* ***sometimes*** *she's late.* (***occasionally***, ***every so often***, ***at times***, ***intermittently***)

somewhat
adverb in some measure or degree; to some extent: *The news* ***somewhat*** *lessened his anxiety.*

somewhere
adverb in, at or to some place not specified, determined, or known: *I've put my glasses down* ***somewhere****.*

somnambulism (som-nam-yuh-liz-uhm)
noun the fact or habit of walking about, and often of doing other things, while asleep

Word building: **somnambulist** *noun*
somnambulistic *adjective*

son
noun **1** the male child of someone
2 a man looked upon as being the product or result of a particular thing: *a* ***son*** *of the land*

Word history: Old English *sunu*

sonar (soh-nah)
noun a device for finding depth under water by measuring the time it takes to receive an echo from a sound

Word history: an acronym for *so(und) n(avigation) a(nd) r(anging)*

sonata (suh-nah-tuh)
noun a musical composition in several movements usually for the piano

Word history: Italian

song
noun **1** a short musical composition with words (***anthem***, ***ballad***, ***carol***, ***hymn***, ***lullaby***)
2 musical sounds produced by birds
phrase **3 for a song**, at a very low price

Word history: Old English

sonic
adjective **1** having to do with sound waves
2 having to do with the speed of sound

son-in-law
noun the husband of your daughter

Noun forms: The plural is **sons-in-law**.

sonnet
noun a poem of fourteen lines in which the lines have to rhyme in a certain way

Word history: French, from Italian, from Old Persian word meaning 'sound', from Latin

sonorous (son-uh-ruhs)
adjective sounding deep, loud, and rich: *a **sonorous** voice*

Word building: **sonority** *noun*
Word history: Latin

sook (sook)
noun Australian, NZ someone who is shy, timid, or cowardly (***chicken, coward, cry-baby, scaredy-cat, sissy***)

Word use: This is mostly used about children.
Word building: **sooky** *adjective* (**sookier, sookiest**)

soon (soohn)
adverb **1** within a short time
2 quickly or promptly: *She will be back **soon**.*

Word history: Old English *sōna* at once

soot (soot)
noun the black substance which sticks to the inside of a chimney when coal, wood, oil, or other fuels are burnt

Word building: **sooty** *adjective* (**sootier, sootiest**)
Word history: Old English *sōt*

soothe (soohdh)
verb **1** to calm or comfort: *He **soothed** the frightened child.* (***pacify, quiet, quieten***)
2 to relieve or lessen: *to **soothe** pain* (***allay, alleviate, ease***)

Word use: The opposite of this is **aggravate**.
Word building: **soothing** *adjective*
Word history: Old English *sōth* sooth

sop
noun **1** piece of bread, etc., dipped in milk, soup, or any other liquid like this
2 anything thoroughly soaked
3 something given to pacify or quieten, or as a bribe: *They gave me this job as a **sop** to my pride.*
4 *Colloquial* a weak or cowardly person
verb **5** to dip or soak
phrase **6 sop up**, to take or soak: *The cloth will **sop up** the water.*

Verb forms: it **sopped**, it has **sopped**, it is **sopping**
Word history: Middle English; Old English *sopp*

sophisticated (suh-fis-tuh-kay-tuhd)
adjective **1** wise and experienced in the interests and pleasures of the world
2 intricate or complex: ***sophisticated** machinery*

Word use: The opposite of definition 1 is **unsophisticated**. The opposite of definition 2 is **simple** or **crude**.
Word building: **sophistication** *noun*

soporific (sop-uh-rif-ik)
adjective causing sleep or sleepiness

Word history: Latin *sopor* sleep + *-i-* + *-fic*

sopping
adjective very wet

soppy
adjective Colloquial too sentimental: *a **soppy** love story*

Adjective forms: **soppier, soppiest**

soprano (suh-prah-noh)
noun **1** the range of notes which can be sung by a woman or boy with a high voice
2 a woman or boy who sings in this range
adjective **3** having a soprano voice or range of notes: *a **soprano** cornet* (***high, high-pitched, shrill, treble***)

Noun forms: The plural is **sopranos**.
Word use: **Soprano** is the highest range of singing voices, with **alto** next below.
Word history: Italian word meaning 'above', from Latin

sorbet (saw-bay, saw-buht)
noun a frozen dessert made with fruit and eggwhites, sometimes eaten to refresh your mouth between courses of a meal

Word history: French word meaning 'water-ice', from Turkish and Persian

sorcery (saw-suh-ree)
noun Old-fashioned magic, especially black magic using evil spirits

Word building: **sorcerer** *noun* **sorceress** *noun*
Word history: Middle English, from Medieval Latin, from Latin word meaning 'lot'

sordid
adjective **1** morally mean or nasty: *a **sordid** way of life*
2 dirty or filthy: ***sordid** surroundings*

Word building: **sordidness** *noun*
Word history: from Latin word meaning 'dirty', 'base'

sore
adjective **1** painful or hurting (***aching, sensitive, tender***)
2 *Colloquial* annoyed or offended: *What are you **sore** about?*
noun **3** a sore spot or place on your body

Word history: Old English *sār*

sore / saw / soar

Don't confuse **sore** with **saw** or **soar**.

A **saw** is a cutting tool with sharp teeth on a thin blade. **Saw** is also the past tense of the verb **see**, to take things in with your eyes or your mind:

I saw your photo in the paper.

To **soar** is to fly upwards, or to rise to a great height:

Jets soar into the air.

House prices are about to soar.

sorrow
noun grief, sadness, or the feeling of being sorry (***anguish, depression, gloom, melancholy, misery***)

Word use: The opposite of this is **joy** or **happiness**.
Word building: **sorrowful** *adjective*
Word history: Old English *sorg*

sorry
adjective **1** feeling sad because you have done something wrong (***ashamed, contrite, penitent, remorseful, repentant***)
2 feeling pity

Adjective forms: **sorrier, sorriest**
Word history: Old English *sār* sore

sort
noun **1** a particular kind or type: *Cod are a* ***sort*** *of fish.*
verb **2** to arrange or group according to type or kind: *to* ***sort*** *the sheep from the goats* (***arrange***, ***classify***, ***grade***)
phrase **3 of sorts**, of a kind that is neither good nor bad: *He is a friend* ***of sorts****.*
4 out of sorts, not in good health or in a good mood
5 sort of, in some way: *I* ***sort of*** *hoped he would come.*
Word history: Middle English, from Old French, from Latin word meaning 'lot', 'condition', Late Latin word meaning 'class', 'order'

sortie (saw-tee)
noun **1** an attack by troops from a besieged place
2 the flying of a military aircraft on a mission
Word history: from French word meaning 'go out'

SOS (es-oh-es)
noun an urgent call for help: *The ship sent an* ***SOS*** *by radio.*
Word history: probably chosen because the Morse code for these letters is clear and easy, but some people say the letters stand for 'Save Our Souls'

sotto voce (sot-oh voh-chay)
adverb in a low voice meant not to be overheard
Word history: Italian word meaning 'under (normal) voice (level)'

soufflé (sooh-flay)
noun a light baked dish, either savoury or sweet, made fluffy with beaten eggwhites
Word use: The accent over the 'e' is a clue that this word was originally French.
Word history: French, from Latin word meaning 'blow up'

sought (sawt)
verb past tense and past participle of **seek**

soul
noun **1** the unseen or spiritual part of a person believed to survive after they die
2 human being: *She's a kind* ***soul****.*
3 a type of modern African American blues music with songs about emotions and personal experiences
Word use: Another name for definition 1 is **spirit**. | You can also use **soul music** for definition 3.
Word history: Old English *sāwl*

soul / sole
Don't confuse **soul** with **sole**, which is the underneath part of your foot.

sound[1]
noun **1** something heard as a result of vibrations in the air reaching your ear
2 the effect on your ears of a particular sound: *the* ***sound*** *of music*
verb **3** to make a sound: *The trumpet* ***sounded****.*
4 to cause to make a sound: ***Sound*** *the trumpets.*
5 to give a certain feeling when heard or read: *That* ***sounds*** *strange.*
Word history: Middle English, from Old French, from Latin

sound[2]
adjective **1** healthy or in good condition: *a* ***sound*** *heart* (***fine***, ***fit***, ***robust***)
2 unbroken or deep: ***sound*** *sleep*
3 reliable or good: ***sound*** *advice*
phrase **4 sound as a bell**, in perfect condition
Word building: **soundly** *adverb*
Word history: Old English *gesund*

sound[3]
verb **1** to measure or try the depth of by letting down a lead weight on the end of a line
phrase **2 sound out**, to try by indirect ways to find the feelings of: ***Sound*** *her* ***out*** *about going for a swim.*
Word history: Old English *sundgyrd* sounding pole, from Scandinavian

sound[4]
noun a narrow stretch of water joining two larger bodies of water or between an island and the mainland
Word history: Old English *sund* channel, sea

sound system
noun a set of items used for playing recorded music, usually having a radio, tape deck, turntable, CD player, and a set of speakers

soundtrack
noun **1** the strip beside a moving picture film which carries the sound recording
2 all the songs and music of a film, released on a CD, tape, etc.

soup
noun **1** a liquid food made from meat, fish, or vegetables
phrase **2 in the soup**, *Colloquial* in trouble
Word history: from French word meaning 'sop', 'broth', of Germanic origin

sour
adjective **1** having an acid taste, such as that of lemons (***bitter***, ***dry***, ***green***, ***tart***)
2 cross or irritable: *He's in a* ***sour*** *mood today.*
Word building: **sour** *verb* **sourish** *adjective*
Word history: Old English *sūr*

source
noun **1** the place or thing from which something comes: *Those countries are the main* ***source*** *of the world's oil.* (***origin***)
2 the beginning or place of origin of a river: *The Murray River has its* ***source*** *in the Snowy Mountains.* (***start***)
3 a book, person or statement which supplies information: *That book was one of the primary* ***sources*** *of my history essay. | We heard it from a reliable* ***source****.*
Word history: Middle English, from Old French word meaning 'spring up', from Latin word meaning 'rise'

source / sauce
Don't confuse **source** with **sauce**, which is a liquid used to flavour food, such as *tomato sauce.*

source code
noun Computers the high-level programming language version of a program, which has to be translated into machine language to be executed

Word use: Compare this with **executable code**.

souse (sows)
verb **1** to plunge into water or other liquid
2 to soak or become soaked with water, etc.
noun **3** the act of sousing

Word history: Middle English, from Old French, from Old High German word meaning 'brine'

south
noun the direction which is to your left when you face the setting sun in the west

Word use: The opposite direction is **north**.
Word building: **south** *adverb* **south** *adjective* **southern** *adjective*
Word history: Old English *sūth*

southerly
adjective **1** towards the south: *We travelled in a **southerly** direction.*
2 of the wind, from the south: *a **southerly** wind*
noun **3** a wind blowing from the south: *A strong **southerly** is forecast for this afternoon.*

souvenir (sooh-vuh-near)
noun something you keep as a memory of a place or event (***keepsake, memento, token, trophy***)

Word history: French word meaning 'remember', from Latin word meaning 'come to mind'

souvlaki (soohv-lah-kee)
plural noun a Greek dish of diced lamb and vegetables cooked on skewers

sovereign (sov-ruhn)
noun **1** a king or queen (***lord, monarch, ruler***)
adjective **2** having highest rank, power, or authority

Word building: **sovereignty** *noun*
Word history: Middle English, from Old French, from Latin word meaning 'above'

soviet
noun **1** in the former Soviet Union, a local governing council
2 any similar socialist assembly

Word history: from Russian word meaning 'council'

sow[1] (soh)
verb **1** to scatter in the earth for growth: *to **sow** wheat seeds*
2 to scatter seeds over: *to **sow** a field*

Verb forms: I **sowed**, I have **sown** or I have **sowed**, I am **sowing**
Word history: Old English *sāwan*

> **sow / so / sew**
> Don't confuse **sow** with **so** or **sew**.
> **So** means 'therefore'.
> To **sew** is to stitch something with a needle and thread.

sow[2] (sow)
noun an adult female pig

Word history: Middle English, from Old English *sugu*

soybean
noun a kind of plant seed which can be eaten as a bean or grown for its oil

Word use: You can also use **soy** or **soya bean**.

soy sauce
noun a salty dark brown sauce, made by fermenting soybeans in brine

Word use: You can also use **soya sauce**.
Word history: Japanese, from Chinese word meaning 'bean oil'

spa
noun **1** a place where there is a flow of mineral water from the earth
2 a bath or swimming pool which has heated bubbly water pumped into it
3 a place where you can get mind and body treatments such as massages and beauty therapies

Word history: from *Spa*, town in eastern Belgium, famous for its mineral springs

space
noun **1** the continuous openness in which everything exists: *There is **space** all around us.*
2 the space outside the earth's atmosphere: *to send a rocket into **space***
3 a part or area of space: *This table takes up a lot of **space**.* (***room***)
4 the distance between things: *The trees were planted at equal **spaces** apart.*
5 a blank area on a surface: *We put a **space** between each word when we write.*
6 a period of time: *He arrived after a **space** of two hours.*
verb **7** to arrange with spaces in between: ***Space** yourselves so that you have room to swing your arms.*

Word use: You can also use **outer space** for definition 2.
Word history: Middle English, from Old French, from Latin

spacecraft
noun a vehicle which can travel outside the earth's atmosphere

spaceship
noun a vehicle that can travel to outer space

space shuttle
noun a spaceship that carries people and equipment between earth and a satellite and which can land and be used again

spacious
adjective having a lot of space: *a **spacious** house* (***commodious, expansive, open, roomy***)

Word use: The opposite of this is **cramped** or **small**.
Word building: **spaciousness** *noun*
Word history: Middle English, from Latin

spade[1]
noun a tool for digging, with a long handle and a metal blade that you push into the ground with your foot

Word history: Old English *spadu*

spade[2]
noun a black shape like an upside-down heart with a stem, used on playing cards

Word history: Italian word originally meaning 'sword', later used as a mark on cards, from Latin, from Greek word meaning 'wooden blade'

spadework
noun work, especially laborious or boring, done to prepare for further work

spaghetti (spuh-get-ee)
noun a kind of pasta formed into long, thin, rounded strips

Word history: Italian word meaning 'little cords'

spam
noun **1** a type of cooked tinned meat
2 *Colloquial* unsolicited email, especially advertising material
verb **3** *Colloquial* to send spam (definition 2): *Our company put a block on the source that kept* ***spamming*** *the employees.*

Word building: **spammer** *noun* **spamming** *noun*

span
noun **1** the distance between the two furthest edges or ends of something: *the* ***span*** *of a bridge | the* ***span*** *of your hand*
2 the full stretch of anything: *Humans have a longer life* ***span*** *than animals.*
verb **3** to stretch over or across: *The bridge* ***spans*** *the river.* (***cross***, ***traverse***)

Verb forms: it **spanned**, it has **spanned**, it is **spanning**
Word history: Old English

spangle
noun a small piece of something that glitters: *an evening dress covered with* ***spangles***

Word building: **spangled** *adjective*
Word history: Middle English, from Middle Dutch

spaniel
noun a kind of dog with a long, silky coat and drooping ears

Word history: Middle English, from Old French word meaning 'Spanish (dog)', from Latin

spank
verb to hit as a punishment, usually with the open hand

Word building: **spank** *noun* **spanking** *noun*
Word history: imitative

spanner
noun a tool for gripping and turning something, such as a nut on a bolt

Word history: German

spar[1]
noun a strong pole, such as a mast on a ship

Word history: Middle English

spar[2]
verb to punch lightly or make punching movements: *The boxers* ***sparred*** *at each other for practice.*

Verb forms: I **sparred**, I have **sparred**, I am **sparring**
Word building: **spar** *noun*
Word history: Middle English; originally meaning thrust (noun and verb)

spare
verb **1** to stop yourself from destroying or hurting: *The king* ***spared*** *his enemy.* (***excuse***, ***forgive***, ***let off***, ***pardon***)
2 to show consideration for: *I* ***spared*** *his feelings.*
3 to part with or let go: *Can you* ***spare*** *a few dollars?*
adjective **4** extra: *a* ***spare*** *tyre*
5 free for extra use: ***spare*** *time*
6 lean or thin: *a* ***spare*** *physique* (***skinny***, ***slender***, ***slight***)
noun **7** something that is extra: *This light bulb is blown and we haven't a* ***spare***.

Word history: Old English *sparian*

sparing
adjective **1** using in small amounts: *Be* ***sparing*** *with the sugar.* (***economical***, ***frugal***)
2 showing mercy

Word building: **sparingly** *adverb*

spark
noun **1** a tiny piece of burning material thrown up by a fire
2 a sudden letting out of electricity, usually with a flash of light (***flare***, ***flash***, ***flicker***, ***sparkle***)
3 a small showing of something: *a* ***spark*** *of intelligence*
verb **4** to send out sparks (***flare***, ***flash***, ***flicker***, ***sparkle***)
5 to set going: *His speech* ***sparked*** *some interest.* (***initiate***)

Word history: Old English *spearca*

sparkle
verb **1** to burn or shine with little flashes of light (***flicker***, ***glimmer***, ***glitter***, ***shimmer***, ***twinkle***)
2 to be lively or brilliant: *The conversation* ***sparkled***.

Word building: **sparkle** *noun*
Word history: from *spark*

spark plug
noun a part in an engine that gives out an electric spark which sets fire to the fuel in each cylinder

sparrow
noun a small brown bird, common in many parts of the world

Word history: Old English *spearwa*

sparse
adjective thinly spread out or scattered: *a* ***sparse*** *population*

Word building: **sparsely** *adverb* **sparseness** *noun* **sparsity** *noun*
Word history: from Latin word meaning 'scattered'

spartan (spah-tuhn)
adjective **1** unbendingly simple in lifestyle, or sternly disciplined
noun **2** a person of spartan characteristics

Word history: from *Sparta*, an ancient city in southern Greece, famous for strict discipline and training of soldiers

spasm
noun **1** a sudden uncontrolled movement of your muscles (***cramp***, ***twitch***)
2 a sudden short burst of activity or feeling: *to work in* ***spasms*** *| a* ***spasm*** *of rage*

Word building: **spasmodic** *adjective*
Word history: Middle English, from Latin, from Greek

spastic
noun someone suffering from cerebral palsy

Word use: Because some people use **spastic** to refer informally to someone they think is foolish, the term has taken on negative and offensive overtones. For that reason, it is avoided by many people when referring to sufferers of cerebral palsy.
Word history: Latin, from Greek

spat[1]
noun **1** a light blow, slap, or smack
2 a small quarrel (***altercation***, ***argument***, ***difference***, ***dispute***)

spat[2]
verb past tense and past participle of **spit**[1]

spate
noun a sudden pouring out: *a **spate** of words*

Word history: Middle English

spatial (spay-shuhl)
adjective having to do with space: *That famous painter has a good **spatial** sense.*

spatter
verb **1** to scatter or splash in small particles or drops: *to **spatter** mud*
2 to send out small particles or drops
noun **3** the act or sound of spattering: *the **spatter** of rain on a roof*
4 a splash or spot of something spattered

Word history: from Dutch and Low German word meaning 'burst', 'spout'

spatula (spat-chuh-luh)
noun a tool with a flat, bendable blade, used for mixing or spreading such things as paint or food

Word history: Latin

spawn
noun a mass of eggs given out by fish and other water creatures

Word history: Middle English, from Anglo-French word meaning 'spill', from Latin word meaning 'expand'

spay
verb to remove the ovaries of: *to **spay** a female animal*

Word history: Middle English, from Anglo-French word meaning 'cut with a sword'

speak
verb **1** to give out the sounds of words in an ordinary voice
2 to have a conversation or tell by speaking
3 to give a speech or lecture
verb **4** to be able to use a particular language: *Can you **speak** Italian?*
phrase **5 so to speak**, as one might say
6 speak for,
a to recommend or put your case forward
b to reserve or put aside: *This dress is already **spoken for**.*

Verb forms: I **spoke**, I have **spoken**, I am **speaking**
Word history: Old English *sprecan*

speaker
noun **1** someone who speaks, especially before an audience
2 the part of a sound system that produces the sound
phrase **3 the Speaker**, the person who controls the meeting of a house of parliament

spear
noun a weapon which consists of a long pole with a sharp, pointed end

Word building: **spear** *verb*
Word history: Old English *spere*

spear gun
noun a gun that throws out a spear, used in underwater fishing

spearmint
noun a garden herb much used for flavouring

special
adjective **1** of a particular or distinct kind: *a **special** bus for schoolchildren | a new car with **special** fittings*
2 more important than or different from what is ordinary or usual: ***special** circumstances* (***exceptional***)
noun **3** something which is special, particularly something sold at a special cheap price

Word history: Middle English, from Latin

specialise
verb to concentrate on a special kind of work or study: *She **specialises** in Australian history.*

Word use: You can also use **specialize**.
Word building: **specialisation** *noun*

specialist
noun someone who studies or is good at a particular subject or area of work, particularly a doctor: *to go and see a skin **specialist*** (***authority***, ***consultant***, ***expert***)

speciality (spesh-ee-al-uh-tee)
noun something you are very good at making or doing: *My **speciality** is pavlova.*

Word use: Compare **specialty**.
Word history: Middle English, from Old French, from Late Latin

specially
adverb particularly

specialty (spesh-uhl-tee)
noun a particular kind of study, work, or product that someone specialises in: *The surgeon's **specialty** is heart operations. | This restaurant's **specialty** is spaghetti.*

Word use: Compare this with **speciality**. The distinction between these two words seems to be disappearing.
Word history: Middle English, from Old French word meaning 'speciality'

species (spee-seez, spee-sheez)
noun one of the groups into which animals and plants are divided according to their characteristics

Noun forms: The plural is **species**.
Word history: from Latin word meaning 'appearance', 'sort'

specific (spuh-sif-ik)
adjective **1** particular: *I want the **specific** kind of paper I mentioned, not something similar.*
2 giving definite details: *a **specific** description*

Word use: The opposite of definition 2 is **vague**.
Word building: **specifically** *adverb*

specification (spes-uh-fuh-kay-shuhn)
noun **1** the act of specifying: *the* ***specification*** *of your requirements*
2 an item in a detailed description of the measurements and materials to be used for something you plan to make: *the builder's* ***specifications*** *for the extensions to our house*

specific gravity
noun the ratio of the density of any substance to that of a standard substance (usually water for solids and liquids and hydrogen or air for gases)

Word use: You can also use **specific density**.

specify (spes-uh-fuy)
verb to state with definite details: *You must* ***specify*** *how many chairs you will need.*

Verb forms: I **specified**, I have **specified**, I am **specifying**
Word history: Middle English, from Medieval Latin word meaning 'specific', from Latin word meaning 'sort', 'kind'

specimen (spes-uh-muhn)
noun a single thing or part taken as being typical of a whole group or mass: *This poem is a* ***specimen*** *of my work. | The doctor took a* ***specimen*** *of my blood for tests.* (***example***, ***model***, ***pattern***, ***sample***)

Word history: Latin

specious (spee-shuhs)
adjective **1** seemingly good or right but without real worth: ***specious*** *arguments*
2 pleasing to the eye, but deceptive or not really so

Word building: **speciosity** *noun*
Word history: Middle English, from Latin word meaning 'fair', 'fair-seeming'

speck
noun a very small spot or bit: *a brown dress with* ***specks*** *of green | a* ***speck*** *of dust*

Word building: **specked** *adjective*
Word history: Old English *specca*

speckle
noun **1** a small spot or mark
verb **2** to mark with speckles: *Dust* ***speckled*** *his coat.*

Word building: **speckled** *adjective*
Word history: from *speck*

spectacle
noun **1** anything seen, especially something that draws your attention: *The storm made a great* ***spectacle***.
2 a large public show or display

Word history: Middle English, from Latin

spectacles
plural noun Old-fashioned a pair of reading glasses

spectacular
adjective **1** striking, dramatic, or thrilling: *a* ***spectacular*** *display of skill* (***eye-catching***, ***flamboyant***, ***ostentatious***, ***resplendent***)
noun **2** a film, television show, etc., that is expensive to produce

spectator
noun someone who watches something: ***spectators*** *at a football game* (***observer***, ***onlooker***, ***viewer***)

Word history: Latin

spectre (spek-tuh)
noun → **ghost** (***apparition***, ***ghost***, ***phantom***, ***spook***, ***wraith***)

Word building: **spectral** *adjective*
Word history: from Latin word meaning 'apparition'

spectroscope (spek-truh-skohp)
noun an optical instrument for producing and examining the spectrum of light or other forms of electromagnetic radiation

Word building: **spectroscopic** *adjective* **spectroscopy** *noun*

spectrum
noun **1** the band of colours which is produced when white light is split up
2 a range of ideas, beliefs, or types: *the* ***spectrum*** *of public opinion*

Noun forms: The plural is **spectrums** or **spectra**.
Word history: from Latin word meaning 'appearance', 'form'

speculate
verb to think or have an opinion without certain knowledge: *She* ***speculated*** *on her chances of winning.*

Word building: **speculation** *noun* **speculative** *adjective* **speculator** *noun*
Word history: from Latin word meaning 'observed', 'examined'

sped
verb past tense and past participle of **speed**

speech
noun **1** the ability to speak
2 a talk given in front of an audience: *The principal made a long* ***speech*** *at assembly.*
3 the way someone speaks: *Your* ***speech*** *is not clear enough.*

Word history: Old English *spǣc*

speed
noun **1** quickness in moving, going, or doing something
verb **2** to move or make move quickly: *He* ***sped*** *on his way.* (***hurry***, ***hurtle***, ***pelt***, ***race***, ***streak***, ***tear***)
3 to drive a vehicle faster than is allowed by law
phrase **4 speed up**, to go or do more quickly

Verb forms: I **sped** or I **speeded**, I have **sped** or I have **speeded**, I am **speeding**
Word building: **speedy** *adjective* (**speedier**, **speediest**) **speedily** *adverb* **speedster** *noun*
Word history: Old English *spēd*

speedometer
noun an instrument on a vehicle that shows how fast it is travelling

speedway
noun **1** a racing track for motor vehicles, especially motorcycles
2 a road on which more than the ordinary speed is allowed

speleology (spee-lee-ol-uh-jee)
noun the exploration and study of caves

Word building: **speleologist** *noun*
Word history: Greek

spell[1]
verb **1** to say or write the letters of a word in order: *She can* ***spell*** *well.*
2 to be the letters that make up a word: *The letters 'm-a-t'* ***spell*** *'mat'.*
3 to mean: *That noise in the engine* ***spells*** *trouble.*
phrase **4 spell out,**
a to read with difficulty
b to explain clearly (***clarify***, ***elucidate***)

Verb forms: I **spelt** or I **spelled,** I have **spelt** or I have **spelled,** I am **spelling**
Word history: Middle English, from Old French, of Germanic origin

spell[2]
noun **1** *Old-fashioned* a group of words that is supposed to have magic power: *The witch chanted a* ***spell.***
2 a fascinating power: *She has him in her* ***spell.***

Word history: Old English *spell* discourse

spell[3]
noun **1** a period of work: *I will take a* ***spell*** *at digging now.*
2 a short period of anything: *a* ***spell*** *of cold weather*
3 a period of rest: *You should take a* ***spell*** *or you will get tired.* (***break***, ***rest***)

Word history: Old English *spelian* represent

spellbound
adjective enchanted or fascinated: *a* ***spellbound*** *audience*

spelling
noun **1** the way in which words are spelt
2 a group of letters representing a word
3 the act of a speller
4 your ability to spell

For **a guide to spelling** and a list of **spelling demons**, see appendixes, pages 978 and 984.

spencer
noun Australian, NZ a woman's singlet, worn for extra warmth

Word history: named after George John *Spencer*, 1758–1834, 2nd Earl Spencer

spend
verb **1** to pay out: *I* ***spent*** *a lot of money today.* (***expend***, ***fork out***, ***outlay***)
2 to pass: *They* ***spent*** *the holidays at the beach.*
3 to use up: *He has* ***spent*** *all his anger.*

Verb forms: I **spent,** I have **spent,** I am **spending**
Word building: **spender** *noun*
Word history: Old English *spendan*, from Latin word meaning 'expend'

spendthrift
noun someone who spends their money wastefully

Word use: The opposite of this is **miser**.

sperm
noun one of the cells produced by a male, that can join with an egg or ovum to develop into a new individual

Word history: Middle English, from Latin, from Greek

spermatozoon (sper-muh-toh-zoh-on)
noun one of the tiny, usually actively moving, gametes (male reproductive cells) in semen, whose job is to fertilise the ovum

Noun forms: The plural is **spermatozoa**.
Word building: **spermatozoan** *adjective*

spew
verb Colloquial to vomit

Word history: Old English *spīwan*

sphere (sfear)
noun **1** something completely round in shape, such as a ball or a planet (***globe***, ***globule***, ***orb***)
2 an area of activity: *He works in the* ***sphere*** *of education.*

Word building: **spherical** *adjective*
Word history: Middle English, from Latin, from Greek

sphincter (sfingk-tuh)
noun a circular band of muscle around an opening of the body or one of its hollow organs

Word history: Latin, from Greek word meaning 'band'

spice
noun **1** a substance made from a plant, which is used to flavour or preserve food: *Pepper and cinnamon are* ***spices.***
2 something that adds interest: *You need to give your story some* ***spice.***

Word building: **spicy** *adjective* (**spicier**, **spiciest**) **spiciness** *noun* **spice** *verb*
Word history: Middle English, from Old French, from Latin word meaning 'species'

spick-and-span
adjective **1** neat and clean (***immaculate***, ***spotless***)
2 perfectly new and fresh

Word use: You can also use **spick and span.**
Word history: variant of *span-new*, from Scandinavian

spider
noun an eight-legged creature, like an insect but without wings, which usually spins a web and is sometimes venomous

Word building: **spidery** *adjective*
Word history: Old English *spīthra*

spiel (speel, shpeel)
noun Colloquial **1** smooth or reasonable-sounding talk, especially for the purpose of selling, persuasion, cheating, seduction, etc.
2 any talk or speech

Word building: **spieler** *noun*
Word history: from German word meaning 'play'

spigot (spig-uht)
noun **1** a small peg or plug for closing the outlet of a cask, etc.
2 the end of a pipe which enters the enlarged end of another pipe to form a joint

Word history: Middle English, from *spike*[1]

spike[1]
noun **1** a sharp pointed piece or part: *a fence with* ***spikes*** *on it*
2 spikes, a pair of shoes with sharp metal pieces on the bottom, worn by runners or other athletes to stop them slipping

Word building: **spiky** *adjective* (**spikier**, **spikiest**) **spike** *verb*
Word history: Middle English, from Scandinavian

spike[2]
noun the part of a cereal plant, such as wheat, that contains the grains
Word history: Middle English, from Latin word meaning 'ear of grain'

spill
verb **1** to run or fall from a container: *The milk is **spilling** over.*
2 to make run or fall from a container: *I have **spilt** the cereal.*
Verb forms: I **spilt** or I **spilled**, I have **spilt** or I have **spilled**, I am **spilling**
Word building: **spill** *noun* **spillage** *noun*
Word history: Old English *spillan*

spin
verb **1** to make thread by twisting and winding fibres, such as cotton or wool
2 to form by producing a long moist thread from the body: *Spiders **spin** webs.*
3 to turn around and around very fast: *The top is **spinning**.* (***gyrate***, ***swirl***, ***twirl***, ***whirl***, ***whirr***)
4 to cause to turn around and around very fast: *She **spun** a coin.*
5 to produce or make up in a manner suggestive of spinning thread, such as a story: *She **spins** a good yarn.*
6 *Colloquial* to give a desired slant to (a story) in the media so as to win public approval
noun **7** a spinning or whirling movement
8 a short quick journey: *Let's take the car for a **spin**.*
phrase **9 spin out**, to make last a long time: *to **spin out** a story.*
Verb forms: I **spun**, I have **spun**, I am **spinning**
Word building: **spinner** *noun* **spinning** *noun*
Word history: Old English *spinnan*

spina bifida (spuy-nuh bif-uh-duh)
noun a defect existing from birth in the development of the spinal column in which it fails to join up properly

spinach (spin-ich)
noun **1** a plant with large, green leaves which are eaten as a vegetable
2 → **silverbeet**
Word use: You can also use **English spinach** for definition 1.
Word history: Old French, from Medieval Latin, from Spanish, from Arabic

spinal
adjective having to do with your spine

spinal cord
noun in the body, the cord of nervous tissue extending through the spinal column

spin control
noun a method of controlling the point of view presented in the media, especially in relation to politics: *The politician's media staff attempted **spin control** after he made a public blunder in his speech.*

spindle
noun **1** a rod used to twist or wind the thread in spinning
2 a part of a machine which turns round or on which something turns
Word history: Old English *spinnan* spin

spindly
adjective long and thin: *a **spindly** plant* (***lean***, ***skinny***, ***slight***)
Adjective forms: **spindlier**, **spindliest**

spin-dry
verb to dry by spinning in a machine so that the moisture is taken out: *to **spin-dry** clothes*
Verb forms: I **spin-dried**, I have **spin-dried**, I am **spin-drying**
Word building: **spin-drier** *noun* **spin-dryer** *noun*

spine
noun **1** the column of bones in your back
2 a thorn on a plant
3 a stiff pointed part on an animal, such as on an echidna
4 the part of a book's cover that holds the front and back together
Word history: Middle English, from Latin

spinet (spin-uht)
noun a small keyboard instrument rather like the harpsichord, the main difference being that the strings run across the instrument more or less in the direction of the keyboard, not at right angles to it
Word history: French, perhaps named after Giovanni *Spinetti*, lived about 1500, Venetian inventor

spinifex (spin-uh-feks)
noun a kind of spiny grass
Word history: from Neo-Latin word meaning 'spine maker'

spinnaker (spin-uh-kuh)
noun a large triangular sail
Word history: supposedly from *Sphinx* (mispronounced *spinks*), a yacht on which this sail was first regularly used

spinning wheel
noun a machine for spinning wool, flax, etc., into yarn or thread, consisting of a spindle turned around by a large wheel driven by your hand or foot

spin-off
noun **1** an object, product, or undertaking developed from or because of a larger development: *The non-stick frying pan is a commercially valuable **spin-off** of space research.*
2 *Economics* the formation of a new company by an existing company, with shareholders in the existing company entitled to subscribe for shares in the new company

spinster
noun a woman who has not been married
Word history: Middle English, from *spin* + *-ster*

spiny
adjective having spines or leaves shaped like spines
Adjective forms: **spinier**, **spiniest**

spiny anteater
noun → **echidna**

spiral
noun **1** a curve that winds around and around away from a centre: *a spring in the shape of a **spiral*** (***coil***, ***curl***, ***loop***, ***twist***)
verb **2** to move in the shape of a spiral: *Smoke **spiralled** from the chimney.*
adjective **3** like or having a spiral or spirals: *a **spiral** staircase*

Verb forms: it **spiralled**, it has **spiralled**, it is **spiralling**
Word history: Medieval Latin

spire
noun a tall, pointed part of a building, usually on a roof or tower: *the **spire** of a church*

Word history: Old English *spīr*

spirit
noun **1** → **soul** (definition 1)
2 a supernatural being
3 temper or character: *a woman with a generous **spirit***
4 feeling or mood: *team **spirit** | the **spirit** of Christmas*
noun **5** general meaning or intention: *the **spirit** of an agreement*
6 lively courage: *I like him for his **spirit**.*
7 spirits,
a the state of your mind: *She is in high **spirits** today.*
b strong alcoholic drink
phrase **8 spirit away**, to carry mysteriously or secretly: *He was **spirited away** by his friends before the police arrived.*

Word history: Middle English, from Latin word meaning 'breathing'

spirited
adjective showing lively courage (***dynamic***, ***energetic***, ***full of beans***, ***vigorous***)

spiritual
adjective **1** having to do with or interested in the spirit rather than the body: *a **spiritual** attitude | a **spiritual** person*
2 having to do with holy, religious, or supernatural things: *a **spiritual** leader*

Word use: The opposite of definition 2 is **physical**.
Word building: **spirituality** *noun*
Word history: Latin

spiritualism
noun **1** a belief or doctrine that the spirits of the dead keep living after the mortal life, and communicate with the living, especially through a person (a medium) particularly open to their influence
2 the practices or phenomena associated with this belief

Word building: **spiritualist** *noun* **spiritualist** *adjective*

spit[1]
verb **1** to force out saliva from your mouth: *Don't **spit** on the footpath.*
2 to send out from your mouth: *She **spat** her lolly out.*
3 to fall in light scattered drops: *It is **spitting** with rain.* (***drizzle***, ***sprinkle***)
4 to make a noise like spitting: *Fat was **spitting** in the pan.*
noun **5** saliva, especially when spat out

Verb forms: I **spat**, I have **spat**, I am **spitting**
Word history: Old English *spittan*

spit[2]
noun **1** a sharp pointed rod which is pushed through meat for roasting it over a fire or grilling it in an oven
2 a narrow area of land jutting out into the water

Word history: Old English *spitu*

spite
noun **1** a bad-tempered wish to annoy or hurt someone else: *He had no reason for hitting her except **spite**.* (***ill-will***, ***malice***)
phrase **2 in spite of**, without taking notice of: *We will play **in spite of** the bad weather.*

Word building: **spite** *verb* **spiteful** *adjective*
Word history: Middle English

spittle (<u>spit</u>-uhl)
noun saliva or spit

Word history: Old English *spātl*

spittoon (spi-<u>toohn</u>)
noun a bowl, or something similar, for spitting into

splash
verb **1** to wet by scattering with drops of liquid or mud
2 to fall in drops: *Rain **splashed** on the window.*
3 to make fly about in drops: *The baby **splashed** the bath water.*
noun **4** the act or sound of splashing
5 a mark made by splashing
6 a patch of colour or light: *a **splash** of red on a white background*
phrase **7 make a splash**, to be widely noticed: *She **made a splash** in her new clothes.*

Word building: **splashy** *adjective*
Word history: from Old English, perhaps imitative

splatter
verb to splash

splay
verb **1** to spread out, expand, or extend
2 to make slanting
3 to have a sloping or slanting direction

Word building: **splay** *noun* **splay** *adjective*
Word history: variant of *display*

spleen
noun **1** a vascular, glandlike organ in which blood is modified. It is found at the end of the stomach nearest the heart.
2 bad temper or spite: *venting his **spleen** on his unfortunate wife*

Word history: Middle English, from Latin, from Greek

splendid
adjective **1** magnificent or grand: *a **splendid** sight | a **splendid** victory* (***bonzer***, ***excellent***, ***great***, ***super***, ***superb***)
2 extremely good: *a **splendid** performance*

Word building: **splendidly** *adverb*
Word history: Latin *splendidus* shining brightly

splendour
noun **1** a brilliant or gorgeous appearance, colouring, etc.: *the **splendour** of his coronation* (***grandeur***, ***magnificence***, ***pomp***)
2 glory: *the **splendour** of ancient Roman architecture*
3 great brightness: *the **splendour** of the sun*

Word use: You can also use **splendor**.
Word history: Middle English, from Latin

splice
verb to join by twisting threads together, or overlapping timber: *to* ***splice*** *ropes* | *to* ***splice*** *pieces of wood*

Word history: Middle Dutch

splint
noun a thin piece of something stiff, such as wood, used to hold a broken or injured bone in position

Word history: Middle English, from Middle Low German word meaning 'metal pin'

splinter
noun a long, thin, sharp piece broken off from something hard, such as wood, metal or glass

Word building: **splinter** *verb*
Word history: Middle English, from Middle Dutch or Middle Low German

split
verb **1** to separate or break apart, especially from end to end: *The ends of my hair are* ***splitting****.* | *He* ***split*** *the apple in two.*
2 to divide up in any way (***distribute***, ***divvy up***, ***dole out***, ***share***)
3 to divide in opinion or feeling: *The argument* ***split*** *the family.*
noun **4** the act of splitting
5 a break or division caused by splitting: *a* ***split*** *in a dress* | *a* ***split*** *in public opinion* (***break***, ***crack***, ***crevice***, ***fissure***, ***rift***)
phrase **6 split up**, to stop living together or stop being friends
7 the splits, an exercise in which you spread your legs apart while sinking to the floor until they stretch out at right angles to your body

Verb forms: I **split**, I have **split**, I am **splitting**
Word history: Middle Dutch

split infinitive
noun an infinitive in which a word or phrase is inserted between *to* and the verb

When a verb starts with the word *to*, it's called an **infinitive**: *to walk*, *to respond*, *to develop*. Yet the infinitive is also found without *to* beside it at all — whenever it is used with an auxiliary verb, as in: *can walk*, *do respond* or *will develop*. Those who think of the infinitive as *to walk* have been inclined to say that it is a single unit which should never be split up. So they object to **split infinitives**.

To split an infinitive is to insert a word between *to* and the verb, as in *to slowly walk*, *to quickly respond*. It happens quite often when we speak and often seems the most natural thing to write.

Your efforts not to split infinitives can sometimes alter the meaning of a sentence. Compare:

I like to really understand things.

with

I like really to understand things.

The second sentence keeps the infinitive unsplit, but does it mean quite the same as the first sentence?

Getting the meaning right is the most important thing, and you will find that splitting the infinitive is accepted without comment these days.

split personality
noun Colloquial an unpredictable or extremely changeable personality

Word use: Look up **schizophrenia** and **multiple personality disorder**.

splurge
verb to spend extravagantly or wastefully: *She* ***splurged*** *all her money on a taxi.* (***blow***, ***fritter away***, ***squander***, ***waste***)

Word building: **splurge** *noun*
Word history: perhaps blend of *splash* and *surge*

splutter
verb **1** to talk quickly or in a confused way: *He* ***spluttered*** *with rage.* (***mutter***, ***stammer***, ***stutter***)
2 to make a popping noise, as boiling fat does

Word building: **splutter** *noun* **splutterer** *noun*
Word history: blend of *splash* and *sputter*

spoil
verb **1** to damage or ruin (***contaminate***, ***corrupt***, ***foul***, ***pollute***, ***taint***)
2 to damage the nature or character of by giving way to demands or temper: *to* ***spoil*** *a child*
3 to go bad: *The food will* ***spoil*** *if you don't put it away.*

Verb forms: I **spoiled** or I **spoilt**, I have **spoiled** or I have **spoilt**, I am **spoiling**
Word history: Middle English, from Old French, from Latin

spoilsport
noun someone who interferes with the pleasure of others

spoke
noun one of the rods, bars, or wires that connects the rim of a wheel to the hub or centre, as on a bicycle or steering wheel

spoken
verb **1** past participle of **speak**
adjective **2** oral, or expressed by speaking
3 in compound words, speaking, or using speech, as indicated: *fair-****spoken*** | *plain-****spoken***

Word use: The opposite of definition 2 is **written**.

spokesperson
noun someone who speaks on behalf of someone else

This word has been made up to avoid referring to the gender of the person speaking. After all, the important thing usually is that the person is speaking on behalf of others. It generally doesn't matter in the least whether the person is a man or a woman.

Sometimes **spokesman** or **spokeswoman** is used when it is clear what gender the speaker is.

Look up **non-sexist language**.

sponge (spunj)
noun **1** a material with lots of holes for soaking up liquid, used especially for wiping and cleaning
2 a kind of sea creature whose rubbery absorbent skeleton can be used for washing and cleaning
3 a light cake made from well-beaten eggs, flour and sugar
verb **4** to wash, wipe, and clean with a sponge (***blot***, ***mop***, ***swab***)

5 *Colloquial* to live at someone else's expense: *He* ***sponged*** *on his uncle.*

Word building: **spongy** *adjective* (**spongier**, **spongiest**)
Word history: Middle English and Old English, from Latin, from Greek

sponsor
noun a person or group who supports someone or something, often with money

Word building: **sponsor** *verb* **sponsorship** *noun*
Word history: Latin

spontaneous
adjective happening naturally and, often, unexpectedly: ***spontaneous*** *growth* | ***spontaneous*** *applause* (***free***, ***open***, ***unconventional***, ***uninhibited***)

Word use: The opposite of this is **considered** or **planned.**
Word building: **spontaneity** *noun* **spontaneously** *adverb*
Word history: Latin

spoof (spoohf)
noun Colloquial a humorous imitation: *He did a* ***spoof*** *of the Prime Minister.*

Noun forms: The plural is **spoofs.**
Word building: **spoof** *verb*
Word history: coined by Arthur Roberts, 1852–1933, British comedian

spook
noun Colloquial a ghost: *The attic is full of* ***spooks.*** (***apparition***, ***phantom***, ***spectre***, ***wraith***)

Word building: **spook** *verb* **spooked** *adjective* **spooky** *adjective* (**spookier**, **spookiest**)
Word history: Dutch

spooky
adjective Colloquial like or suggesting a spook or ghost; eerie: *a* ***spooky*** *noise*

Adjective forms: **spookier**, **spookiest**
Word building: **spookily** *adverb* **spookiness** *noun*

spool
noun the cylinder or bobbin on which something, such as wire, thread or film, is wound

Word history: Middle English, from Middle Dutch or Middle Low German

spoon
noun a utensil with a rounded end attached to a handle, which is used for stirring or lifting food and other things

Word history: Middle English and Old English *spōn*

spoonerism (spooh-nuh-riz-uhm)
noun a deliberate slip of the tongue where sounds of words are transposed, as in 'our queer old dean' for 'our dear old queen'

Word history: named after Rev WA *Spooner*, 1844–1930, of New College, Oxford, noted for such slips

spoor
noun the track left by a wild animal

Word history: Afrikaans, from Dutch

sporadic (spuh-rad-ik)
adjective irregular and not very frequent: *Apart from the* ***sporadic*** *rain the weather was marvellous.* (***erratic***, ***fitful***, ***intermittent***, ***occasional***)

Word building: **sporadically** *adverb*
Word history: Medieval Latin, from Greek

spore
noun a seed or germ cell

Word history: Neo-Latin, from Greek word meaning 'seed'

sporran
noun the pouch of fur worn by Scottish Highlanders at the front of the kilt

Word history: Gaelic

sport
noun **1** any game or contest that requires physical activity: *Netball is one of the largest* ***sports*** *in the country.*
phrase **2 a bad sport**, a person who does not play fair and complains when they lose
3 a good sport,
a a person who always plays fair
b a person who is pleasant and agreeable: *You'll like her — she's* ***a good sport***
4 be a sport, a expression asking someone to act fairly or to give in to a request: ***Be a sport*** *and admit you were out!*

Word building: **sportive** *adjective*
Word history: Middle English

sporting
adjective **1** taking part in, given to, or interested in sport
2 concerned with or suitable for such sport: *a* ***sporting*** *glove*
3 showing qualities such as fairness, good humour when losing, etc.
4 even or fair: *a* ***sporting*** *chance*

sports
noun **1** athletics or other similar sporting activities
adjective **2** having to do with sport or sports: ***sports*** *day*
3 of clothes, etc., casual: *a* ***sports*** *coat*

sports car
noun a fast car, usually a two-seater

sportsman
noun **1** a man who takes part in sport
2 any person who shows the qualities that are admired in sport, such as courage and fairness

Noun forms: The plural is **sportsmen.**
Word building: **sportsmanlike** *adjective* **sportsmanship** *noun*

Note that definition 2 can be used about women, along with **sportsmanlike** and **sportsmanship.** However, because these terms include the word *man*, they can be seen to not include women.

Another expression you could use for **sportsman** is **a good sport**, and for **sportsmanlike** you could use **sporting** or **fair. Sportsmanship** has two senses: you can use **skill** for one (ability in playing a sport) and **fairness** for the other (qualities such as are admired in sport).

sportsperson
noun a person who regularly plays sport

Noun forms: The plural is **sportspeople.**

sportswoman
noun a woman who takes part in sport
Noun forms: The plural is **sportswomen**.

If you don't know the sex of the person you are referring to, or if you are talking about a group which includes both men and women, it is inappropriate to use the terms **sportsman** and **sportswoman**. It is better to choose a term such as **competitor**, **player**, **athlete**, etc. The word **sportsperson** (with the plural **sportspeople**) is also used from time to time.

The adjective **sportsmanlike** is similarly problematic, so it is better to use the word **sporting** when you are talking about qualities such as fairness, courage, etc. If you are referring to someone who has these qualities you could use the expression **a (good) sport**.

Look up **non-sexist language**.

sporty
adjective Colloquial **1** flashy, or showy: *a **sporty** car*
2 having a lot of style: *a **sporty** look*
3 like or suited to a sportsman or a sportswoman: ***sporty** shoes*
Adjective forms: **sportier**, **sportiest**

spot
noun **1** a small, usually round, mark: *There's a **spot** on your tie.*
2 a place: *We found a nice **spot** to have a picnic.* (***location***, ***position***, ***site***, ***venue***)
verb **3** to mark or stain: *This material **spots** easily.* | *You have **spotted** your jacket.* (***dirty***, ***smear***, ***smudge***, ***soil***, ***spoil***)
4 to see or notice: *I couldn't **spot** him in the crowd.*
phrase **5 change your spots**, to alter your basic character
6 on the spot,
a instantly: *She bought it **on the spot**.*
b in an awkward situation: *Her question put him **on the spot**.*
7 soft spot, special sympathy or affection: *a **soft spot** for small animals*
8 tight spot, a serious problem or difficulty
Verb forms: I **spotted**, I have **spotted**, I am **spotting**
Word building: **spotted** *adjective* **spotty** *adjective* (**spottier**, **spottiest**)
Word history: Middle English

spotlight
noun a lamp with a strong narrow beam, such as used in the theatre or attached to cars
Word building: **spotlight** *verb* (**spotlighted** or **spotlit**, **spotlighting**)

spouse (spows, spowz)
noun your husband or wife
Word history: Middle English, from Old French, from Latin word meaning 'betrothed'

spout
noun **1** the tube or lip-like part of a container from which water or other contents are poured
verb **2** to pour out
Word history: Middle English

sprain
verb to twist and bruise, without actually putting out of place or breaking: *She **sprained** her ankle.*
Word building: **sprain** *noun*

sprang
verb past tense of **spring**

sprat
noun a small herring-like fish that lives in the waters off the coast of Europe
Word history: Middle English and Old English *sprott*

sprawl
verb **1** to lie or sit with your limbs stretched out: *He **sprawled** all over the couch.* (***loll***, ***lounge***, ***recline***, ***repose***, ***stretch out***)
2 to spread out in an untidy or careless way: *Her writing **sprawled** all over the page.*
noun **3** a scattered or irregular grouping of something: *urban **sprawl***
Word history: Old English *sprēawlian*

spray[1]
noun a fine stream of droplets, such as one thrown by a wave or jet of water
Word building: **spray** *verb*

spray[2]
noun a single stem, or a small bunch of flowers: *She had a **spray** of jasmine pinned to her dress.*
Word history: Middle English

spray can
noun → **aerosol** (definition 2)

spread (spred)
verb **1** to extend, or stretch out: *The rain is **spreading** south.* | *She **spread** the cloth on the table.*
2 to scatter, or send around: *to **spread** germs* | *to **spread** the news* (***disperse***, ***dissipate***, ***distribute***, ***strew***)
3 to put on in a thin layer: *to **spread** butter* (***coat***, ***daub***, ***plaster***, ***smear***)
4 to cover with a thin layer: *She **spread** the bread with jam.*
noun **5** anything which is spread on bread, such as jam or soft cheese
6 *Colloquial* a large meal or feast (***banquet***, ***feed***, ***repast***)
Verb forms: I **spread**, I have **spread**, I am **spreading**
Word history: Old English *sprǣdan*

spread-eagled
adjective having your arms and legs stretched out widely: *I found her **spread-eagled** on the floor.*

spreadsheet
noun Computers **1** a program for organising large amounts of data in tables, allowing quick calculations
2 a table produced by such a program

spree
noun **1** a lively time of fun
2 an extravagant outing: *a shopping **spree***

sprig
noun **1** a shoot, twig, or small branch: *a **sprig** of holly*
2 a person, usually young, such as a descendant or offshoot of a family
verb **3** to decorate with a design of sprigs: *to **sprig** cloth, pottery, etc.*
Verb forms: I **sprigged**, I have **sprigged**, I am **sprigging**
Word history: Middle English

sprightly
adjective lively and quick: *a **sprightly** tune* (***agile***, ***nimble***, ***spry***)
Adjective forms: **sprightlier**, **sprightliest**
Word use: The opposite of this is **frail** or **slow**.
Word history: from *spright*, variant of *sprite*

spring
verb **1** to move or leap upwards with sudden energy: *to **spring** into the air* | *The dog **springs** into her arms.* (***bound***, ***frisk***, ***jump***, ***vault***)
2 to arise or happen: *Farms are **springing** up on the city's outskirts.*
3 to come: *Where do you **spring** from?*
noun **4** a leap or pounce
5 a coil of wire which bounces back when it is stretched
6 the season of the year after winter and before summer
7 the ability to bounce back: *The mattress hasn't much **spring** left.*
8 a flow of water from the ground: *a hot **spring***
Verb forms: I **sprang**, I have **sprung**, I am **springing**
Word building: **spring** *adjective*
Word history: Middle English; Old English *springan*

springboard
noun a board with a lot of bounce in it, used for diving or vaulting

spring-clean
verb to clean thoroughly, as people used to do each spring: *to **spring-clean** a house*
Word building: **spring-clean** *noun* **spring-cleaning** *noun*

spring roll
noun **1** in Chinese cooking, a deep-fried roll of thin dough with a savoury filling
2 in Vietnamese cooking, a roll of raw vegetables and seafood or tofu, wrapped in rice paper and eaten cold
Word history: In Chinese tradition, this is eaten at the spring festival.

springy
adjective bouncy, or elastic: *a **springy** step* (***resilient***, ***rubbery***, ***stretchy***)
Adjective forms: **springier**, **springiest**
Word building: **springiness** *adjective*

sprinkle
verb **1** to scatter here and there, or in small quantities
2 to rain slightly (***drizzle***, ***spit***)
Word building: **sprinkle** *noun* **sprinkler** *noun*
Word history: Middle English

sprint
verb to race at top speed, especially over a short distance
Word building: **sprint** *noun* **sprinter** *noun*
Word history: Scandinavian

sprite
noun an elf, fairy, or goblin
Word history: Middle English, from Old French

sprocket
noun a toothed wheel that meshes with the links of a chain such as the one on a bicycle
Word history: from *sprock* (of obscure origin)

sprout
verb **1** to grow, or send up shoots: *He is trying to **sprout** plants from seed.* | *The bulb has **sprouted**.*
noun **2** a shoot
3 → **brussels sprout**
Word history: Old English *sprūtan*

spruce[1]
noun an evergreen tree with fine needle-like leaves and cones
Word history: Middle English, variant of *Pruce* Prussia

spruce[2]
adjective **1** stylish or smart: *He looks very **spruce** in his new suit.*
phrase **2 spruce up**, to smarten up: ***Spruce** yourself **up** before you go to the interview.*
Word history: perhaps special use of *spruce[1]* through (obsolete) *Spruce leather*, a leather from Prussia used in jerkins, etc.

sprung
verb past tense and past participle of **spring**

spry
adjective nimble or active: *The old man is still very **spry**.* (***agile***, ***sprightly***)
Adjective forms: **spryer**, **spryest**
Word building: **spryly** *adverb*

spud
noun **1** *Colloquial* a potato
2 a spade-like tool for digging up weeds
Word history: Middle English *spudde* kind of knife

spume (spyoohm)
noun **1** foam, froth, or scum
verb **2** to foam or froth
Word history: Middle English, from Latin

spun
verb **1** past tense and past participle of **spin**
adjective **2** formed by or as if by spinning: ***spun** rayon*

spunk
noun *Colloquial* **1** courage
2 *Australian* someone who is good-looking
Word history: blend of *spark* and obsolete *funk* spark, touchwood

spunky
Colloquial
adjective **1** plucky; spirited: *a **spunky** attitude*
2 *Australian* good-looking; attractive: *They all agreed that the new student was pretty **spunky**.*
Adjective forms: **spunkier**, **spunkiest**
Word building: **spunkily** *adverb* **spunkiness** *noun*

spur
noun **1** a sharp instrument worn on the heel of a riding boot to urge a horse to go faster
2 anything which makes work go faster or urges you on
3 something looking like a spur, such as the horny piece on some birds' feet or a ridge rising up to a mountain range
verb **4** to prick with, or as if with, a spur: *to **spur** a horse*

phrase **5 on the spur of the moment**, suddenly or without preparation

Verb forms: I **spurred**, I have **spurred**, I am **spurring**
Word history: Middle English; Old English *spura*

spurious (<u>spyooh</u>-ree-uhs)
adjective not real or true (***counterfeit***, ***fake***)

Word history: from Latin word meaning 'false'

spurn (spern)
verb to reject or scorn: *She **spurned** his offer of help.* (***deride***, ***disdain***, ***ridicule***)

Word use: The opposite of this is **accept** or **welcome.**
Word history: Middle English; Old English *spurnan*

spurt
verb **1** to flow suddenly: *Blood **spurted** from the wound.* (***gush***, ***stream***)
noun **2** a sudden rush

Word history: Old English *spryttan* come forth

sputnik (<u>sput</u>-nik, <u>spoot</u>-nik)
noun a satellite placed in orbit around the earth, especially an early Soviet model

Word history: from Russian word meaning 'companion'

sputter
verb **1** to give off particles of anything in an explosive manner, as a candle does in burning
2 to spit particles of saliva, food, etc., from the mouth in a similar manner
3 to utter words or sounds in an explosive, meaningless manner
noun **4** the act, process, or sound of sputtering
5 explosive, meaningless sound

Word history: from *spout*

sputum (<u>spyooh</u>-tuhm)
noun saliva, especially mixed with mucus

Word history: Latin

spy
noun **1** someone who secretly watches and reports on the activities of others
verb **2** to watch secretly, and report
3 to see: *I can't **spy** her yet.*

Noun forms: The plural is **spies.**
Verb forms: I **spied**, I have **spied**, I am **spying**
Word building: **spying** *noun*
Word history: Middle English, from Old French word meaning 'espy' (to see)

spyware
noun a piece of software that performs tasks like taking note of the computer user's internet access, redirecting the user to unwanted sites, etc., without the user's knowledge or consent

squabble (<u>skwo</u>-buhl)
noun a small unimportant quarrel: *They are good friends in spite of their **squabbles**.* (***altercation***, ***argument***, ***difference***, ***dispute***)

Word building: **squabble** *verb*
Word history: perhaps imitative

squad (skwod)
noun a small group taking part in a shared activity: *a **squad** of cleaners | the football **squad***

Word history: French, from Italian word meaning 'square'

squadron (<u>skwod</u>-ruhn)
noun a fighting unit in the navy or the airforce

Word history: from Italian word meaning 'square'

squalid (<u>skwol</u>-uhd)
adjective dirty or filthy: *a **squalid** hovel*

Word history: Latin

squall[1]
noun a sudden strong wind

Word building: **squall** *verb*
Word history: perhaps related to *squall*[2]

squall[2]
verb **1** to cry out or scream loudly
noun **2** the act or sound of squalling

Word history: imitative

squalor (<u>skwol</u>-uh)
noun dirt and poverty

Word history: Latin

squander (<u>skwon</u>-duh)
verb to spend or use wastefully (***blow***, ***fritter away***, ***splurge***, ***waste***)

square
noun **1** a shape with four equal sides and four right angles
2 an open public place in a town
3 an instrument which is used to draw and check right angles
4 a number multiplied by itself: *The **square** of 2 is 2 × 2, or 4.*
5 *Old-fashioned*, *Colloquial* someone who is old-fashioned in what they like and the way they look
verb **6** to make straight or square
7 to multiply by itself: *If you add 2 and 3 then **square** the result, you get 25.*
8 to agree: *It doesn't **square** with the facts.*
adjective **9** in the form of a right angle: *a **square** corner*
10 cube-shaped or nearly so: *a **square** box*
11 equal to a square with sides of the stated length: *a **square** metre*
12 even or level: *The two sides aren't quite **square**.*
13 paid up: *We are **square** now.*
14 fair: *a **square** deal*
15 full or complete: *a **square** meal*
16 *Old-fashioned*, *Colloquial* old-fashioned in looks or behaviour (***antiquated***, ***archaic***, ***out-of-date***)
phrase **17 square off with,**
a *Australian*, *NZ* to apologise
b *Australian* to get revenge
18 square up, to pay a bill, debt, etc.

Word building: **square** *adverb* **squarely** *adverb*
Word history: Middle English, from Old French, from Latin word meaning 'to square'

square dance
noun a country dance for couples, in which someone calls or sings the steps to be followed

square root
noun the number which, when multiplied by itself, gives the stated number: *The **square root** of 16 is 4.*

squash[1] (skwosh)
verb **1** to flatten or crush: *The wheel **squashed** his hat.* (***compress, jam, press, squeeze, trample***)
2 to put down: *to **squash** the rebellion*
noun **3** a game for two players with racquets and a small rubber ball, played in a small court with walls
4 a fizzy fruit drink
Word history: Old French, perhaps partly imitative

squash[2] (skwosh)
noun a round vegetable like a marrow

squat (skwot)
verb **1** to sit in a crouching position
2 to live without permission on land or property which you don't own
adjective **3** short and thickset: *a **squat** figure* (***stocky, stumpy***)
Verb forms: I **squatted,** I have **squatted,** I am **squatting**
Word building: **squat** *noun* **squatness** *noun*
Word history: Middle English, from Old French

squatter (skwot-uh)
noun **1** *Australian, NZ* in the past, someone who settled on crown land to run sheep, etc., first without government permission, but later with a lease or licence
2 *Australian, NZ* a rich rural landowner
3 someone who lives without permission in a place they don't own

squatter settlement
noun an area of human habitation in which the inhabitants have no legal right to occupy the site and which is usually characterised by slum housing and lack of government services, such as power and water

squaw
noun a Native American woman
Word use: The use of this word will offend people.

squawk
verb to make a loud unpleasant cry: *The chickens **squawked** when the fox chased them.* (***screech, shriek, squeal***)
Word building: **squawk** *noun*
Word history: blend of *squall*[2] and *croak*

squeak
verb to make a high-pitched cry or a creaking noise: *A mouse **squeaked**. | The gate **squeaks**.*
Word building: **squeaky** *adjective* (**squeakier, squeakiest**) **squeak** *noun* **squeakily** *adverb*
Word history: Middle English, apparently from Scandinavian

squeal
verb to make a sudden high-pitched cry, as if in pain or fright (***scream, shriek, yelp***)
Word building: **squeal** *noun*
Word history: imitative

squeamish (skwee-mish)
adjective **1** easily sickened
2 overly sensitive and soft-hearted
Word history: late Middle English

squeeze
verb **1** to press hard, so as to remove something: *to **squeeze** an orange* (***compress, jam, squash***)
2 to cram: *to **squeeze** clothes into a bag*
3 to hug or hold close (***cuddle, embrace***)
4 to force a way: *They **squeezed** through the crowd.*
noun **5** a tight fit: *She's wearing the jacket but it's a bit of a **squeeze**.*
6 a small amount of something got by squeezing: *a **squeeze** of lemon*
7 *Colloquial* a boyfriend or girlfriend: *He's taking his new **squeeze** to the movies.*
phrase **8 a tight squeeze**, a difficult situation
Word history: Old English *cwȳsan*

squelch
verb **1** to crush down, or squash: *to **squelch** a strawberry between your teeth*
2 *Colloquial* to silence, with a crushing reply, or something like this
3 to make a splashing sound: *Water **squelched** in her shoes.*
4 to tread heavily in water, mud, etc., with a sound like this
noun **5** a squelched mass of anything
6 a squelching sound
Word history: variant of *quelch*

squid
noun a sea animal with a soft body and no backbone, which has tentacles attached to its head
Word use: Another name is **calamari**, especially as a food.

squint
verb **1** to have both your eyes turned towards your nose
2 to look indirectly, such as by a quick glance or with half-closed eyes
Word building: **squint** *noun* **squinting** *adjective*

squire
Old-fashioned
noun **1** an English country gentleman
2 a young nobleman attending a medieval knight
verb **3** to attend as a squire
Word history: Middle English, from Old French

squirm
verb to wriggle uncomfortably: *to **squirm** with embarrassment* (***fidget, toss and turn, writhe***)
Word history: blend of *skew* and *worm* verb

squirrel
noun a bushy-tailed animal found in Europe, Asia, and North America which lives in trees and hoards nuts and acorns
Word history: Middle English, from Anglo-French, from Late Latin, from Greek

squirt
verb **1** to wet with a jet of liquid: *They **squirted** each other with hoses.*
noun **2** an act of squirting: *I gave him a **squirt** with the hose.*
3 *Colloquial* a small person

stab
verb **1** to wound, pierce, or push, with, or as if with, a pointed weapon: *She **stabbed** herself with the needle. | He **stabbed** at his food.*
noun **2** a sudden painful blow or feeling: *a **stab** of regret*
3 an attempt: *Now you have a **stab** at it.* (***crack, go, try***)

Verb forms: I **stabbed**, I have **stabbed**, I am **stabbing**
Word building: **stabbing** *adjective*
Word history: Middle English

stable[1]
noun **1** a place where horses are kept and fed
verb **2** to put or keep in a stable

Word history: Middle English, from Old French, from Latin

stable[2]
adjective firm and steady: *a **stable** relationship* (***fixed***, ***secure***)

Word building: **stabilise** *noun* **stability** *noun*
Word history: Middle English, from French, from Latin

staccato (stuh-kah-toh)
adjective an instruction in music to make notes sharply separate

Word history: Italian word meaning 'detach'

stack
noun **1** a large pile of things on top of each other
2 a tall chimney
3 a large number or quantity: *There was a **stack** of people there.*
verb **4** to pile up: ***Stack** the plates.*
5 to arrange unfairly: *to **stack** the cards*
phrase **6 stack a meeting**, to influence the decisions of a meeting unfairly by organising people to attend who will vote the way you want

Word building: **stacked** *adjective*
Word history: Middle English, from Scandinavian

stadium
noun a large, often indoor, sports arena, with seats for spectators and parking available

Noun forms: The plural is **stadiums** or **stadia**.
Word history: Latin, from Greek

staff (stahf)
noun **1** the people who work in a business or an institution, such as a school or hospital
2 a large stick or rod

Noun forms: The plural for definition 2 is **staves** (stayvz).
Word building: **staff** *verb* **staff** *adjective*
Word history: Middle English; Old English *stæf*

Staff can be used to refer to a group of people helping or working for the same leader or employer. In this case it is a **collective noun.**

It can be used with either a singular or plural verb:

The staff were keen to finish the job.

The staff at our school is most conscientious.

The plural of this kind of **staff** is spelt **staffs.**

The staffs of the two schools held a joint end-of-term party.

In music, **stave** is an equally good spelling for **staff** when the word refers to the lines and spaces on which music is written. The plural of this kind of **staff** is also spelt **staves.**

stag
noun a male deer

Word history: Middle English *stagge*, related to Icelandic *steggr* male fox, tomcat

stage
noun **1** a raised floor, usually in a theatre, on which public performances take place
2 a step in a process: *Now we can go on to the next **stage**.* (***class***, ***grade***, ***level***, ***rank***)
3 a period of development: *an early **stage***
4 a section of a rocket which drops off after firing
verb **5** to do or perform, especially on a stage: *to **stage** a play*
6 to plan or carry out: *to **stage** a riot*
phrase **7 hold the stage**, to be the centre of attention

Word history: Middle English, from Old French, from Latin word meaning 'stand'

stagecoach
noun a passenger and goods coach which used to cover a particular route, changing horses regularly on long trips

stagger
verb **1** to stand or go unsteadily (***totter***)
2 to arrange so that things don't occur at the same time: *They **stagger** their holidays.*
3 to shock: *The news **staggered** me.*

Word building: **stagger** *noun*
Word history: Middle English, from Scandinavian

staggered
adjective amazed: *I'm **staggered** to hear that.*

stagnant
adjective still and dirty: ***stagnant** water*

Word building: **stagnancy** *noun*
Word history: Latin

stagnate
verb **1** to stop running or flowing: *The water has **stagnated**.*
2 to become dull and inactive: *She feels she is **stagnating** at home.*

Word building: **stagnation** *noun*
Word history: Latin

staid (stayd)
adjective of settled or calm character

Word building: **staidness** *noun*
Word history: variant of *stayed*, past participle of *stay[1]*

stain
noun **1** a mark or blemish (***blot***, ***blotch***, ***spot***)
2 a clear colouring, such as that used on wood

Word building: **stain** *verb*
Word history: Middle English, from Scandinavian

stainless steel
noun a steel mixed with a certain amount of chromium and which resists rust and many corrosive agents

stair
noun one of a series of steps

Word history: Old English *stǣger*

stair / stare

Don't confuse **stair** with **stare.** To **stare** at someone is to look directly at them for a long time with your eyes wide open.

staircase
noun a series of steps with its handrail or banister

stairwell
noun a vertical shaft or opening containing a flight of stairs

stake[1]
noun **1** a stick which is often pointed at one end: *She put in* ***stakes*** *to support the vine.*
verb **2** to put stakes in the ground as a marker, or for support
3 to make a claim for: *He has* ***staked*** *his share.*
phrase **4 stake out**, to surround, in order to keep watch or make a raid: *to* ***stake out*** *a building*
5 the stake, death by burning while tied to a stake

Word history: Middle English; Old English *staca*

stake[2]
noun **1** the amount bet in a race or game: *The* ***stakes*** *were high.*
2 a personal interest or involvement: *He has a* ***stake*** *in the shop.*
verb **3** to bet
phrase **4 at stake**, at risk: *A lot is* ***at stake***.

> **stake / steak**
> Don't confuse **stake** with **steak**, which is a thick slice of meat or fish which is usually grilled or fried.

stalactite (stal-uhk-tuyt)
noun a deposit formed by dripping water, which hangs from the roof of a limestone cave

Word history: Neo-Latin

stalagmite (stal-uhg-muyt)
noun a deposit formed by dripping water, which builds up on the floor of a limestone cave

Word history: Neo-Latin

stale
adjective not fresh or new (***inedible***, ***off***, ***old***)

Word history: Middle English, perhaps from Anglo-French word meaning 'stop'

stalemate
noun a situation where no progress can be made (***deadlock***, ***halt***, ***standstill***)

Word use: This comes from chess, when the pieces are in a position where no move can be made by a player without putting the king in check, the result being a draw.
Word history: Old French *estal* standstill + *mat* checkmated (from Arabic)

stalk[1] (stawk)
noun the stem of a plant

Word history: Middle English, from Old English *stæla* stalk

stalk[2] (stawk)
verb **1** to follow quietly and carefully: *The cat was* ***stalking*** *a mouse.*
2 to walk slowly and proudly: *He* ***stalked*** *out of the room in a rage.*
3 to follow secretly and constantly: *She was* ***stalked*** *by her ex-boyfriend.*

Word history: Old English *-stealcian* move stealthily

> **stalk / stork**
> Don't confuse **stalk** with **stork**, which is a large bird with long legs and a long beak.

stall[1]
noun **1** a stand, tent, or table where goods are sold, such as at a fete
2 a section of a stable or shed where one horse or cow is kept
verb **3** to lose power, especially when unintended: *The car* ***stalled*** *at the lights.* (***come to a halt***, ***stop***)
phrase **4 the stalls**, the front seats on the ground floor of a theatre

Word history: Middle English; Old English *steall*

stall[2]
noun Colloquial **1** anything used to gain time, or to deceive
verb Colloquial **2** to act in a way that intends to deceive
3 to put off, avoid, or deceive: ***Stall*** *the visitors until next week.*

Word history: Middle English, from Anglo-French, from Old English *stæl*

stallion (stal-yuhn)
noun a male horse kept for breeding

Word history: Middle English, from Old French; of Germanic origin

stalwart (stawl-wuht)
adjective **1** strong and brave (***trusty***, ***valiant***)
2 firm, dependable, or unyielding
noun **3** a stalwart person

Word history: Middle English

stamen
noun the part of a flower that produces the pollen

Noun forms: The plural is **stamens** or **stamina**.
Word history: from Latin word meaning 'thread', 'warp in the upright loom'

stamina[1] (stam-uh-nuh)
noun physical strength or power, especially to fight off sickness or tiredness (***endurance***, ***grit***, ***perseverance***, ***persistence***, ***tenacity***)

Word history: from Latin word meaning 'threads' (specifically, those spun by the Fates determining length of life)

stamina[2] (stam-uh-nuh)
noun a plural of **stamen**

stammer
noun → **stutter**

Word building: **stammer** *verb*
Word history: Middle English; Old English *stamerian*

stamp
verb **1** to strike, beat, or crush by a downward push of your foot
2 to put a mark on something to show that it has been approved or is genuine: *The customs officer* ***stamped*** *my passport.*
3 to mark something with a pattern or design: *They* ***stamped*** *the emblem on the shirt.*
noun **4** a small sticky piece of paper printed by the government for attaching to letters or documents

5 an official mark showing something is genuine or has been approved
6 an engraved block or instrument, usually of rubber, used for making a mark on something

Word history: early Middle English

stamp duty
noun a tax placed on certain legal documents, such as cheques, receipts, etc., payment of which is shown by a stamp

stampede
noun a sudden scattering or headlong flight of a group of animals or people, often in fright

Word building: **stampede** *verb*
Word history: from Mexican Spanish word meaning 'press', of Germanic origin

stance
noun **1** a way of standing: *a boxer's* ***stance*** (***attitude***, ***bearing***, ***carriage***, ***manner***, ***posture***)
2 your way of thinking: *My* ***stance*** *on saving rainforests is well-known.*

Word history: French, from Italian *stanza* station, stopping place, room, from Latin word meaning 'standing'

stanchion (stan-shuhn, stan-chuhn, stahn-shuhn, stahn-chuhn)
noun an upright bar, beam, post or support

Word building: **stanchion** *verb*
Word history: Middle English, from Old French word meaning 'stance'

stand
verb **1** to take or keep an upright position on your feet
2 to stop moving or halt: ***Stand*** *and deliver!*
3 to be placed or situated: *The house* ***stands*** *at the end of the street.*
4 to be unchanged or to continue the same: *The law still* ***stands.***
5 to become a candidate: *He* ***stood*** *for the position of mayor.*
6 to undergo: *She* ***stood*** *trial.*
7 to bear or tolerate: *I can't* ***stand*** *him.*
noun **8** opposition to, or support for a cause: *My father takes a strong* ***stand*** *against smoking.*
9 a platform or raised place, such as for spectators or a display of goods
10 a framework to support something
phrase **11 stand by,**
a to wait or be ready
b to help: *I'll* ***stand by*** *him.*
c to keep to: *She always* ***stands by*** *her promises.*
12 stand down,
a to go off duty
b to withdraw, especially from a contest
c to put off because of a strike: *Ten more workers were* ***stood down*** *this morning.*
13 stand for, to represent: *A police officer* ***stands for*** *the law.*
14 stand in for, to act in place of
15 stand up for, to defend the cause of
16 stand up to,
a to remain in good condition in spite of: *to* ***stand up to*** *hard wear*
b to oppose, especially bravely: *to* ***stand up to*** *the enemy*

Verb forms: I **stood,** I have **stood,** I am **standing**
Word history: Middle English; Old English *standan*

standard
noun **1** anything taken as a rule or basis for comparing other things (***criterion***, ***model***)
2 a grade or level of excellence or achievement: *a high* ***standard*** *of living*
3 a flag, emblem, or symbol
adjective **4** used as a standard or rule: ***standard*** *spelling*
5 normal, acceptable, or average: *The shirt was the* ***standard*** *size for a ten year old.*

Word history: Middle English, from Old French, modification of *estandard*, from Germanic

standardise
verb **1** to make standard in size, weight, or quality, etc.
2 to compare with or test by a standard: *This car has been* ***standardised*** *with the original model.*

Word use: You can also use **standarize.**
Word building: **standardisation** *noun*

stand-by
noun someone or something kept ready to be used when needed or in an emergency

Noun forms: The plural is **stand-bys.**

stand-in
noun any substitute, but especially one used to replace someone for a short time in a play or film

standing
noun **1** position, status, or reputation: *a woman of good* ***standing***
2 duration or length of existence or membership: *a member of long* ***standing***
adjective **3** in an upright position
4 continuing without stopping or changing: *a* ***standing*** *rule*

standout
Colloquial
noun **1** a person in a team, competition, etc., who impresses as having abilities greater than all the others
adjective **2** outstanding; obvious: *a* ***standout*** *choice*
3 brilliant, excellent: *a* ***standout*** *season*

standstill
noun a stop or halt: *Work came to a* ***standstill.***

stank
verb past tense of **stink**

stanza
noun a group of lines of poetry arranged in a pattern or verse

Word history: Italian, from Latin word meaning 'standing'

staphylococcus (staf-uh-luh-kok-uhs)
noun any of a certain common group of bacteria in which the individual organisms form irregular clusters, causing boils, septic infections of wounds, etc.

Noun forms: The plural is **staphylococci** (staf-uh-luh-kok-uy, staf-uh-luh-kok-ee).
Word building: **staphylococcal** *adjective*
Word history: Greek *staphylē* bunch of grapes + *coccus* a sphere-shaped bacterial organism

staple[1]
noun **1** a bent piece of wire used to bind papers and similar things together
2 a U-shaped piece of metal with pointed ends for driving into a surface

Word building: **staple** *verb*
Word history: Middle English; Old English *stapol* support

staple[2]
noun **1** a most important or main item, especially food which is used or needed continually
2 a fibre of wool or cotton
adjective **3** regarded as a basic necessity: *Rice is the* ***staple*** *food in India.*

Word history: late Middle English, from Middle Dutch word meaning 'support'

stapler
noun a small machine used to join papers with staples

Word history: *staple[1]* + *-er*

star
noun **1** any of the large bodies in space like our sun, which we see as bright points of light in the night sky
2 a shape resembling a star in the sky, with five or six points which look like rays of light
3 someone who is excellent in something or who is famous in an art or profession: *She is a swimming* ***star***. | *He is a film* ***star***. (***celebrity***, ***hero***, ***household name***, ***leading light***, ***VIP***)
adjective **4** brilliant or best: *She is the* ***star*** *swimmer in the team.* (***leading***, ***main***, ***principal***, ***top***)
verb **5** to appear as, or to present someone as, a leading performer: *She* ***starred*** *in the film.* | *The play* ***starred*** *the son of the director.*

Verb forms: I **starred**, I have **starred**, I am **starring**
Word building: **starred** *adjective* **starry** *adjective* (**starrier, starriest**)
Word history: Old English *steorra*

starboard (stah-buhd)
noun the right-hand side of a ship when you are facing the front or bow of the ship

Word use: The opposite is **port**.
Word history: Old English *stēorbord*, from *stēor* steering + *bord* side (of a ship)

starch
noun **1** a white tasteless substance found in foods like potatoes, wheat and rice
2 a preparation of this used to stiffen clothes and materials
verb **3** to stiffen with starch

Word history: Old English *stercean* make stiff or resolute

stare
verb **1** to look directly for a long time, especially with your eyes wide open (***gape***, ***gawk***, ***gaze***, ***goggle***)
noun **2** a long, fixed look with your eyes wide open

Word history: Middle English; Old English *starian*

> **stare / stair**
> Don't confuse **stare** with **stair**, which is one of a series of steps.

starfish
noun a sea animal with a body in the shape of a star

Noun forms: The plural is **starfish** or **starfishes**.

stark
adjective **1** complete or total: ***stark*** *madness*
2 harsh or barren: *A desert is a* ***stark*** *landscape.*
adverb **3** absolutely or utterly: ***stark*** *naked*

Word history: Middle English; Old English *stearc* stiff

starling
noun a noisy bird with dark shiny feathers

Word history: Middle English; Old English *stærling*

start
verb **1** to begin to move or to set moving: *I* ***started*** *on my journey.* | *He* ***started*** *the engine.* (***get going***, ***get off***, ***set out***)
2 to begin: *When did you* ***start*** *on your career?* | *Will you* ***start*** *the letter?* (***commence***, ***embark on***, ***initiate***, ***open***, ***set about***)
3 to move suddenly or with a sudden jerk from a position or place: *The rabbit* ***started*** *up from the undergrowth.*
4 to be among the competitors in a race or contest: *How many are* ***starting*** *in the long jump?*
noun **5** a beginning (***commencement***, ***onset***, ***origin***, ***outset***)
6 the first part of anything: *the* ***start*** *of a book*
7 a sudden jerk of your body: *I woke with a* ***start***.

Word history: Middle English

starter
noun **1** someone entering a race
2 someone who gives a signal to begin a race
3 the first course of a large meal: *We'll have soup as the* ***starter***.
4 an electrical device that makes an engine start working, especially one that starts the engine of a vehicle
phrase **5 for starters**, *Colloquial* in the first place: *I can't come out tonight for many reasons —* ***for starters***, *I broke my leg this morning.*

startle
verb **1** to disturb, surprise or frighten suddenly (***bowl over***, ***shock***, ***take aback***)
2 to move with a sudden jerk such as from a fright or surprise

Word history: Old English *steartlian* kick, struggle

starve
verb **1** to die or cause to die from hunger: *Many babies* ***starve*** *in poor countries.* | *Some people* ***starve*** *their pets.*
2 to be suffering severely from hunger
3 to cause to suffer from the lack of something needed: *The strike* ***starved*** *the city of petrol.*

Word building: **starvation** *noun*
Word history: Old English *steorfan* die

state
noun **1** the condition of someone or something: *a* ***state*** *of unhappiness*
2 a tense, excited, or nervous condition: *She has got herself into quite a* ***state*** *about this.*
3 a number of people living in a definite territory and organised under one government
4 the territory itself: *Tasmania is a* ***state*** *of Australia.*

adjective **5** having to do with ceremonies, special occasions, or the government
verb **6** to say or express in speech or writing

Word history: Middle English

stately
adjective formal, grand or majestic: *a* ***stately*** *palace* (***dignified***, ***distinguished***, ***lofty***, ***lordly***)

Adjective forms: **statelier**, **stateliest**

statement
noun **1** the stating or declaring of facts or ideas
2 the thing or things stated: *I don't think that* ***statement*** *is true.*

Statements are sentences in which you state or declare something:

I'm going home.

It's getting pretty late.

Statements contrast with *questions*, *commands* and *exclamations* as one of the four functions of sentences. A statement is perhaps the most basic type of sentence and in writing usually begins with a capital letter and ends with a full stop.

statesman
noun someone who is skilled in, or whose work is, directing the affairs of the government

Noun forms: The plural is **statesmen**.
Word building: **statesmanship** *noun*
Word history: from *state's*, possessive of *state* + *man*

Because the word **statesman** seems to exclude women, you could use another term such as **leader** or **political leader**.

Look up **non-sexist language**.

static
adjective **1** at rest or still
2 having to do with electricity which is not flowing, especially that caused by friction
noun **3** noise or interference with sound waves such as crackling caused by electrical activity in the air

Word history: Neo-Latin, from Greek

static electricity
noun electricity at rest, as distinct from dynamic or current electricity, for example electricity produced by friction

station
noun **1** a place at which a train or bus regularly stops
2 *Australian*, *NZ* a farm for raising sheep or cattle
3 a place set up for some particular kind of work or service: *a police* ***station***
4 the place or the equipment used for broadcasting or transmitting for radio or television
verb **5** to place or post in a position for a particular reason: *The guard was* ***stationed*** *at the gate.* (***establish***, ***install***, ***locate***, ***position***, ***site***)

Word history: Middle English, from Latin. The special Australian use of this word for a rural property comes from its military use for an outpost of the colonial government, a place where troops were stationed for a particular purpose. In the early days of settlement that purpose was to superintend the work of convicts which gave rise to the term *convict station*. A very remote location was called an *outstation*. This military use was adopted in church use as *mission station* and in agricultural use as *cattle station* and *sheep station*.

stationary (stay-shuhn-ree)
adjective not moving: *The car was* ***stationary*** *at the red light.* (***immobile***, ***motionless***, ***still***)

Word use: This should not be confused with **stationery**.
Word history: Middle English, from Latin

stationary / stationery
Don't confuse **stationary** with **stationery**, which is writing materials.

stationery (stay-shuhn-ree, stay-shuhn-uh-ree)
noun writing paper and writing materials such as pens and pencils

Word use: This should not be confused with **stationary**.
Word building: **stationer** *noun*

station wagon
noun a car which has extra space behind the back seat and a door at the back

statistics
plural noun the science which deals with the collection, classification and use of numerical facts

Word building: **statistical** *adjective* **statistician** *noun*
Word history: plural of *statistic*, from German, from Neo-Latin

stative verb
noun *Grammar* a verb which indicates a state or condition which is not changing, as in *I own a house*, or *I hate vegetables.*

Word use: You can also use **non-action verb**. | Compare this with **dynamic verb**.

statue (sta-chooh)
noun an image of a person or animal made out of stone, wood or bronze

Word history: Middle English, from French, from Latin

statuesque (stach-ooh-esk)
adjective like or suggesting a statue, such as in dignity, grace, beauty, etc.

stature (sta-chuh)
noun **1** someone's height
2 achievement or distinction reached by someone: *She was a woman of high* ***stature*** *in the computing business.*

Word history: Middle English, from Old French, from Latin

status (stay-tuhs)
noun **1** someone's social or professional position, rank or importance
2 the state or condition of something

Word history: Latin

status quo (stay-tuhs kwoh)
noun an existing state or condition

Word history: from Latin word meaning 'state in which'

statute (sta-chooht)
noun **1 a** a law made by a law-making body and expressed in a formal document
b the document in which the law is expressed
2 a rule established by an organisation, etc., for the conduct of its own affairs

Word building: **statutory** *adjective*
Word history: Middle English, from French, from Latin word meaning 'decreed', 'set up'

statutory declaration (sta-chuh-tree dek-luh-ray-shuhn, sta-chuh-tuh-ree dek-luh-ray-shuhn)
noun a written statement taken, declared and witnessed by an authorised official, such as a justice of the peace, etc., but not sworn on oath and therefore not recognised as evidence in a court of law

staunch[1] (stawnch)
verb Old-fashioned to stop the flow of blood from: *to* ***staunch*** *a wound*

staunch[2] (stawnch)
adjective **1** loyal or steadfast: *a* ***staunch*** *friend* (***enduring***, ***faithful***, ***firm***, ***reliable***, ***stout-hearted***)
2 strong or substantial

Word history: late Middle English, from Old French

stave
noun **1** a thin, narrow, curved piece of wood that is part of the side of a barrel or tub
2 the set of five horizontal lines used in music, on which the notes are written
phrase **3 stave in,** to break a hole in
4 stave off, to put off or prevent: *We* ***staved off*** *our hunger during the hike with boiled lollies.*

Verb forms: I **staved** or I **stove**, I have **staved** or I have **stove**, I am **staving**
Word use: You can also use **staff** for definition 2.
Word history: Middle English

stay[1]
verb **1** to remain in a place (***wait***)
2 to continue to be: *Children cannot* ***stay*** *clean.* (***remain***)
noun **3** a time of living somewhere: *We had a short* ***stay*** *in Queensland.*
phrase **4 stay put,** to remain where placed

Word history: late Middle English, probably Old French word meaning 'stand', from Latin

stay[2]
noun a support, especially used to keep something steady (***brace***, ***prop***)

Word history: apparently Old English *stæg*

STD
noun a system for making long distance calls in which the person ringing is automatically connected

Word history: abbreviation of *s(ubscriber) t(runk) d(ialling)*

stead (sted)
noun **1** place or position: *Since he couldn't come, he sent his brother in his* ***stead.***
phrase **2 stand in good stead,** to be useful: *His extra study* ***stood*** *him* ***in good stead*** *in the exam.*

Word history: Middle English and Old English *stede*

steadfast (sted-fahst)
adjective firmly fixed, constant, or unchanging: *a* ***steadfast*** *gaze* | *a* ***steadfast*** *friend* (***enduring***, ***faithful***, ***firm***, ***reliable***, ***staunch***)

Word history: Old English

steady (sted-ee)
adjective **1** firmly placed or fixed: *a* ***steady*** *ladder* (***firm***, ***fixed***, ***secure***, ***stable***, ***still***)
2 constant or regular: ***steady*** *progress at school* (***permanent***, ***persistent***)
3 free from excitement or upset: ***steady*** *nerves*
4 reliable, or having good habits: *Her friend seems a* ***steady*** *little girl.* (***dependable***, ***responsible***)
noun Old-fashioned, Colloquial **5** a regular girlfriend or boyfriend
adverb **6** in a firm or regular manner
phrase **7 go steady,** *Colloquial* to go out regularly with the same boyfriend or girlfriend

Adjective forms: **steadier, steadiest**
Noun forms: The plural is **steadies.**
Word building: **steady** *verb* (**steadied, steadying**)
Word history: *stead + -y*

steak (stayk)
noun a thick slice of meat or fish usually used for grilling or frying

Word history: Middle English, from Old Norse

steak / stake

Don't confuse **steak** with **stake.**

A **stake** is a stick with a pointed end.

A **stake** can also be the amount bet in a race or game.

steal
verb **1** to take something that does not belong to you, especially secretly (***knock off***, ***nick***, ***pilfer***, ***pinch***, ***thieve***)
2 to get, take, or do secretly: *She* ***stole*** *a nap during the show.*
3 *Old-fashioned* to move or go secretly: *He* ***stole*** *away quietly in the night.*
noun **4** *Colloquial* something obtained cheaply or below its true cost: *This dress is a real* ***steal.***

Verb forms: **I stole,** I have **stolen,** I am **stealing**
Word history: Old English *stelan*

steal / steel

Don't confuse **steal** with **steel,** which is iron mixed with other metals and carbon to make it very hard and strong.

stealth (stelth)
noun secret, hidden or sly action or behaviour

Word building: **stealthy** *adjective*
Word history: Middle English

steam
noun **1** a colourless gas or vapour produced by boiling water and used for driving machinery and for heating
verb **2** to give off steam: *The hot food was* ***steaming.***
3 to treat with steam in order to cook, soften or heat
phrase **4 let off steam,** to release or let go of stored-up feelings

5 run out of steam, to lose power or energy
6 steam up, to become covered with steam: *The kitchen windows had all* ***steamed up.***

Word building: **steamy** *adjective* (**steamier**, **steamiest**)
Word history: Old English *stēam*

steam-engine
noun an engine which is powered by steam, especially a locomotive

steamroller
noun **1** a heavy vehicle with a large roller, used for crushing and levelling rocks and earth in road-making
2 an overpowering force which crushes anything in its path

Word building: **steamroller** *verb*

steed
noun Old-fashioned a horse, especially one for fast riding

Word history: Old English *stēda* stallion

steel
noun **1** iron mixed with carbon and other metals so that it is very hard and strong
verb **2** to make hard, unfeeling or determined: *She* ***steeled*** *herself against their rudeness.*

Word building: **steely** *adjective* (**steelier**, **steeliest**) **steel** *adjective*
Word history: Middle English and dialect Old English *stēle*

steel / steal
Look up **steal / steel.**

steep[1]
adjective **1** having a sharp slope (***precipitous***, ***sheer***)
2 too high: *a* ***steep*** *price*
3 *Colloquial* extreme or extravagant: *It's a bit* ***steep*** *to do something like that.* (***excessive***, ***unreasonable***)

Word history: Old English *stēap*

steep[2]
verb **1** to soak or lie soaking in water or other liquid (***brew***, ***infuse***, ***stand***)
2 to be filled with: *a mind* ***steeped*** *in romance* (***infuse***)

Word history: Middle English

steeple
noun a tall tower attached to a church, often with a spire on top

Word history: Old English *stēpel*

steeplechase
noun a race over a course which has obstacles such as jumps and ditches

Word building: **steeplechase** *verb*

steer[1]
verb **1** to guide the course of by using a rudder or wheel: *He* ***steered*** *the boat.* (***direct***, ***pilot***)
2 to be guided in a particular direction: *This plane* ***steers*** *easily.*

Word history: Old English *stēoran*

steer[2]
noun a sterilised male of the cattle family, especially one raised for beef

Word history: Middle English; Old English *steor*

steerage (<u>stear</u>-rij)
noun **1** a part or division of a ship, originally that containing the steering apparatus, later varying in use
2 the part in a passenger ship given to the passengers who travel at the cheapest rate

stegosaurus (steg-uh-<u>saw</u>-ruhs)
noun a large plant-eating dinosaur with a heavy bony armour

stellar (<u>stel</u>-uh)
adjective **1** having to do with a star or stars
2 *Colloquial* special, outstanding: *a* ***stellar*** *person | a* ***stellar*** *performance*

Word building: **stellate** *adjective* **stelliform** *adjective*
Word history: Late Latin, from Latin word meaning 'star'

stem[1]
noun **1** the central stalk of a plant, that grows upwards from the root
2 the stalk which supports or joins a flower, leaf, or fruit to a plant
3 a long thin part like the stem of a plant: *the* ***stem*** *of a pipe | the* ***stem*** *of a wineglass*
verb **4** to originate or come from: *This model* ***stems*** *from an earlier invention of mine.*

Verb forms: it **stemmed**, it has **stemmed**, it is **stemming**
Word history: Middle English; Old English *stemn*

In English the **stem** of a word is the base part to which prefixes and suffixes are added. So <u>educat-</u> is the stem in all the following:

educated education educator
re-educating uneducated

As the examples show, the stem remains unchanged, whatever is added to it.

For a list of **prefixes and suffixes.** see appendixes, page 975.

stem[2]
verb to stop, check, or dam up: *She* ***stemmed*** *the flow of blood with a towel.*

Verb forms: I **stemmed**, I have **stemmed**, I am **stemming**
Word history: Middle English, from Scandinavian

stem cell
noun a form of cell (definition 2) taken from a person or animal early in its development which, though not having a particular function at that point, is capable of dividing and developing into cells of various types such as nerve cells or blood cells

stench
noun an offensive smell (***stink***)

Word history: Middle English; Old English *stenc*

stencil (<u>sten</u>-suhl)
noun **1** a thin sheet of paper, cardboard or metal with designs or letters cut out of it: *The children painted over the **stencils** leaving colourful patterns on the paper underneath.*
2 the actual letters or designs produced
verb **3** to mark, paint or produce letters or designs by using a stencil

Verb forms: I **stencilled**, I have **stencilled**, I am **stencilling**
Word history: apparently from Middle English, from Old French, from Latin word meaning 'spark'

stenographer (stuh-<u>nog</u>-ruh-fuh)
noun someone who can write in shorthand what someone else is saying and then type it out

step
noun **1** a movement made by lifting your foot and putting it down again in a new position
2 the distance measured by one such movement: *Move a **step** nearer.*
3 a move or action: *the first **step** towards peace*
4 a support for your foot in going up or coming down: *a **step** of a ladder or stair*
verb **5** to walk or tread: *Please **step** this way. | Don't **step** on my toe!*
phrase **6 step down,**
a to decrease
b to resign
7 step in, to become involved
8 step on it, *Colloquial* to hurry
9 step up, to increase
10 watch your step, to go or behave carefully

Verb forms: I **stepped**, I have **stepped**, I am **stepping**
Word history: Middle English; dialect Old English *steppe*

step-
a word part that indicates that you are related to someone because of the remarriage of a parent, rather than by birth, as in *stepmother*

stepfamily
noun **1** the family of your step-parent
2 a family in which at least one of the parents has had children with a previous partner

stepladder
noun a ladder which has flat steps instead of rungs and has a pair of hinged legs to keep it upright

steppe (step)
noun a large plain, especially one without trees

Word history: from Russian word meaning 'step'

stereo (<u>ste</u>-ree-oh, <u>stear</u>-ree-oh)
adjective **1** having to do with a system of recording and reproducing sound that uses two channels and two speakers
noun **2** a sound system equipped to reproduce sound in this way: *We've just bought a new **stereo**.*

Noun forms: The plural is **stereos**.

stereophonic (ste-ree-uh-<u>fon</u>-ik, stear-ree-uh-<u>fon</u>-ik)
adjective having to do with using two channels and two speakers to transmit and broadcast sound

Word history: *stereo-* + *phonic*

stereotype
noun an oversimplified and conventional idea or image, used to label or define people

sterile (<u>ste</u>-ruyl)
adjective **1** free from living germs: *a **sterile** bandage*
2 of a person, not able to have children
3 of land, not able to produce crops

Word use: The opposite for definitions 2 and 3 is **fertile**.
Word building: **sterility** *noun*
Word history: from Latin word meaning 'barren'

sterilise
verb **1** to destroy germs in something, often by boiling it
2 to make unable to reproduce young, especially by surgery: *The vet **sterilised** my dog.*

Word use: You can also use **sterilize**.
Word building: **sterilisation** *noun*

sterling
adjective **1** having to do with British money
2 being of a certain standard quality of silver
3 made of this sterling silver: *a **sterling** cutlery set*
4 thoroughly excellent: ***sterling** character*

Word history: Middle English

stern[1]
adjective **1** firm or strict: ***stern** discipline* (***harsh**, **rigid**, **stringent***)
2 hard, harsh, or severe: *a **stern** warning*

Word history: Middle English; Old English *styrne*

stern[2]
noun the back part of anything, but especially of a ship or boat (***back**, **rear***)

Word history: Middle English, perhaps from Scandinavian

sternum (<u>ster</u>-nuhm)
noun a bone or series or bones extending along the mid-line of the front of the chest and attached to the ribs

Noun forms: The plural is **sterna** (<u>ster</u>-nuh) or **sternums.**
Word use: A more common word is **breastbone.**
Word building: **sternal** *adjective*
Word history: Neo-Latin, from Greek word meaning 'chest', 'breast'

steroid (<u>ste</u>-roid)
noun **1** any of a large group of chemical substances found in the body, including many hormones
2 a hormone used by athletes, etc., to develop their muscles

stethoscope (<u>steth</u>-uh-skohp)
noun an instrument used by doctors to listen to the sounds made by your heart and lungs

stetson (<u>stet</u>-suhn)
noun a hat with a broad brim and a wide crown, as worn by cowboys

Word history: named after the designer, John *Stetson*, 1830–1906, US hatmaker

stevedore (<u>stee</u>-vuh-daw)
noun a firm or individual engaged in the loading or unloading of ships

Word history: Spanish word meaning 'pack', 'stow', from Latin word meaning 'press'

stew
verb **1** to cook by slow boiling (***braise***, ***poach***, ***simmer***)
2 *Colloquial* to worry or fuss
noun **3** food cooked by stewing, especially a dish of meat and vegetables cooked together
4 *Colloquial* a condition or state of worrying or uneasiness

Word history: Middle English, from Old French, from Vulgar Latin word meaning 'perspire'

steward
noun **1** someone who looks after others in a club or on a ship or plane
2 someone who manages someone else's affairs or property

Word history: Middle English; Old English *stīweard, stigweard*

stick[1]
noun **1** a branch or long thin piece of wood, sometimes used for a special purpose: *a walking* ***stick***
2 something shaped like a stick: *a* ***stick*** *of celery*
phrase **3 the sticks**, *Colloquial* the country, especially when thought of as backward and dull

Word history: Old English *sticca*

stick[2]
verb **1** to pierce with a pointed instrument
2 to thrust something pointed in or through something: *If you* ***stick*** *a pin into a balloon it will burst.*
3 to put into a place or position: *Just* ***stick*** *your head out of the window.*
4 to fasten into position by piercing or gluing: *He* ***stuck*** *a picture to the wall.*
5 to be prevented from moving: *The car will* ***stick*** *in the mud if it keeps raining.*
6 to stay attached as if by glue: *The mud* ***sticks*** *to his shoes.*
7 to remain firm in opinion, attachment, etc.: *She* ***sticks*** *to her word. | I will* ***stick*** *by my friends.*
phrase **8 stick around**, *Colloquial* to stay nearby
9 stick by (or **to**) (or **with**), to remain loyal to
10 stick out,
a to stand out, or be in the way (***jut out***, ***protrude***)
b to be obvious or conspicuous: *The facts* ***stick out*** *clearly.*
11 stick (**something**) **out**, to put up with until the very end: *They were bored by the film but* ***stuck it out*** *for two hours.* (***endure***, ***suffer***, ***tolerate***)
12 stick together, to remain friendly, loyal, etc., to one another
13 stick up for, to speak or act in favour of (***champion***, ***defend***, ***stand by***)

Verb forms: I **stuck**, I have **stuck**, I am **sticking**
Word building: **stick** *noun*
Word history: Middle English *stike(n)*, Old English *stician*

sticker
noun an adhesive or gummed label, usually with an advertisement or other message printed on it (***tab***, ***tag***, ***ticket***)

stick insect
noun an insect, often without wings, with a long, thin, twig-like body

stickleback (stik-uhl-bak)
noun a type of small, aggressive, spiny-backed fish found in fresh waters and sea inlets of the northern hemisphere

Word history: Middle English, from Old English *sticol* scaly + *bæc* back

stickler
noun someone who unbendingly insists on something: *My teacher is a* ***stickler*** *for correct spelling.*

sticky
adjective **1** adhesive or gluey
2 hot and humid: *a* ***sticky*** *day*
3 *Colloquial* awkward or difficult to deal with: *a* ***sticky*** *situation*

Adjective forms: **stickier**, **stickiest**
Word building: **stickily** *adverb* **stickiness** *noun*

stickybeak
noun Australian, NZ someone who is curious about things that aren't their business

Word building: **stickybeak** *verb*

stiff
adjective **1** hard or firm and not easily bent (***rigid***, ***tough***)
2 not moving or working easily: *a* ***stiff*** *hinge*
3 not able to move easily: *Her legs were* ***stiff*** *with the cold.*
4 strong and with steady force: *a* ***stiff*** *wind*
5 severe or hard to deal with: *He gave us a* ***stiff*** *punishment.*
6 unusually high in price or demand: *That's a* ***stiff*** *price for that vase.*
7 *Australian, NZ Colloquial* unfortunate or unlucky: *That's* ***stiff****!*
noun **8** *Colloquial* a dead body

Word building: **stiff** *adverb* **stiffen** *verb* **stiffness** *noun*
Word history: Middle English; Old English *stīf*

stifle
verb **1** to smother or prevent the breathing of (***asphyxiate***, ***choke***, ***suffocate***)
2 to keep back, or to stop, especially with difficulty: *He* ***stifled*** *a yawn.*
3 to become stifled or be unable to breathe

Word building: **stifling** *adjective*
Word history: Scandinavian

stigma
noun a mark of shame or a stain on your reputation

Word history: Latin, from Greek

stile
noun a step or steps for climbing over a fence where there is no gate

Word history: Middle English; Old English *stigel*

stile / style
Don't confuse **stile** with **style**, which means 'a kind of design' or 'a way of making something'.

stiletto (stuh-let-oh)
noun **1** a dagger with a narrow, pointed blade
2 a high, very narrow heel on a woman's shoe

Noun forms: The plural is **stilettos**.
Word history: Italian word meaning 'dagger', from Latin word meaning 'pointed instrument'

still[1]
adjective **1** free from movement: ***still*** *water* (***immobile***, ***motionless***, ***stationary***, ***steady***)
2 free from sound or noise: *a* ***still*** *night*
noun **3** stillness or silence: *in the* ***still*** *of the night*
4 a single photographic picture
adverb **5** up to or even at this time: *Is she* ***still*** *here?*
6 without sound or movement: *She stood* ***still.***
verb **7** to make or become quiet or silent

Word building: **stillness** *noun*
Word history: Middle English and Old English *stille*

still[2]
noun equipment for distilling a liquid, especially a liquor

stillbirth
noun the birth of a dead baby

Word building: **stillborn** *adjective*

still life
noun a picture representing inanimate objects, such as fruit, flowers, etc.

Noun forms: The plural is **still lifes** (stil luyfs).
Word building: **still-life** *adjective*

stilt
noun **1** one of a pair of poles used for walking on, each with a support for your foot at some distance above the ground
2 a high supporting post under a building

Word history: Middle English

stilted
adjective too formal because you are not at ease: *The new captain spoke in a very* ***stilted*** *manner.*

stimulant (stim-yuh-luhnt)
noun something that makes you more likely to stay awake or that makes some parts of your body act faster, such as a medicine or food

Word history: from Latin word meaning 'stimulating', 'inciting'

stimulate (stim-yuh-layt)
verb **1** to spur on, or excite: *The dancers were* ***stimulated*** *by the music and bright lights.*
2 to act as a stimulus or stimulant

Word use: The opposite of this is **dampen**.
Word building: **stimulation** *noun* **stimulator** *noun*
Word history: from Latin word meaning 'goaded on'

stimulus (stim-yuh-luhs)
noun something that starts action, effort or thought: *Seeing the exhibition was the* ***stimulus*** *she needed to start painting again.*

Noun forms: The plural is **stimuli** or **stimuluses**.
Word history: from Neo-Latin, special use of Latin word meaning 'goad', 'sting'

sting
verb **1** to prick or wound with a sharp-pointed, often venomous organ which some animals have: *A bee* ***stung*** *me.*
2 to hurt the feelings of: *Her unkind words* ***stung*** *me.*
noun **3** an act of stinging
4 the wound or pain caused by stinging
5 a sharp-pointed, often venomous organ of insects and other animals, able to cause painful wounds
6 *Colloquial* an undercover operation set up by police to trap a criminal

Verb forms: I **stung**, I have **stung**, I am **stinging**
Word use: You can also use **stinger** for definition 5.
Word history: Old English *stingan*

stingray
noun any of the rays, a type of fish which have a long, flexible tail with a strong, saw-like bony spine near the base, with which they can inflict severe and very painful wounds

stingy (stin-jee)
adjective mean about spending money (***mingy***, ***miserly***, ***penny-pinching***, ***thrifty***, ***tight***)

Adjective forms: **stingier**, **stingiest**
Word history: originally meaning 'having a sting', 'bad-tempered'

stink
verb **1** to give off a bad smell
noun **2** a bad smell
3 *Colloquial* a fuss: *She kicked up a* ***stink*** *when she heard the news.*

Verb forms: it **stank**, it has **stunk**, it is **stinking**
Word history: Middle English; Old English *stincan*

stint[1]
verb **1** to cut to a certain amount, number, share, or allowance, often unreasonably (***limit***, ***restrict***)
2 to be limited in spending or frugal
noun **3** limitation or restriction, especially as to amount: *to give without* ***stint***
4 a limited or stated quantity, share, rate, etc.: *to exceed your* ***stint***
5 a set amount or piece of work: *to do your daily* ***stint***

Word history: Middle English; Old English *styntan* make blunt, dull

stint[2]
noun a small bird that lives on the shores of seas, rivers and lakes

stipend (stuy-pend)
noun fixed or regular pay (***salary***, ***wage***)

Word history: Middle English, from Latin

stipple (stip-uhl)
verb **1** to paint, engrave or draw by means of dots or small touches
noun **2** the method of painting, engraving, etc., done in this way
3 a painting, engraving, etc., made by means of dots or small spots

Word use: You can also use **stippling** for definition 2.
Word history: from Dutch word meaning 'dot', 'speckle'

stipulate (stip-yuh-layt)
verb **1** to make a stated demand or arrangement as a condition of agreement (***demand***, ***insist on***, ***order***, ***require***)
2 to arrange specially, or state clearly, in terms of agreement: *to* ***stipulate*** *a price*
3 to require as a necessary condition in making an agreement

Word building: **stipulation** *noun*
Word history: Latin

stir
verb **1** to mix something by moving a spoon, stick, or something similar around in it (***beat***, ***fold***, ***mash***, ***whip***)
2 to move: *The rock won't **stir**.* (***budge***, ***give way***, ***shift***)
3 to cause to move: *The breeze **stirred** the leaves.*
4 to excite: *He **stirred** up the party by singing.*
5 *Colloquial* to deliberately mention things likely to cause an argument
noun **6** the act or sound of stirring or moving
7 excitement or commotion: *Her arrival caused quite a **stir**.*

Verb forms: I **stirred**, I have **stirred**, I am **stirring**
Word history: Middle English; Old English *styrian*

stir-fry
verb **1** to fry (food) by stirring in a pan with a small amount of hot oil or fat
noun **2** a dish that has been cooked in this way: *We're having a **stir-fry** for dinner tonight.*

Word building: **stir-fried** *adjective*

stirrup
noun a loop or ring of metal hung from the saddle of a horse to support the rider's foot

Word history: Middle English; Old English *stigrāp*

stitch
noun **1** a complete movement of a threaded needle through a piece of material
2 the loop of thread left in the material
3 one complete movement with needles in knitting, crochet, etc.
4 a sudden, sharp pain, especially between your ribs (***ache***, ***cramp***, ***spasm***, ***twinge***)
phrase **5 in stitches**, laughing uncontrollably

Word building: **stitch** *verb*
Word history: Old English *stice*

stoat
noun a type of weasel which has a brown coat of fur in summer

Word use: The white winter coat of the stoat is called **ermine**.
Word history: Middle English

stock
noun **1** the total quantity of goods kept by a business shop for selling to customers
2 a quantity of something kept for future use: *We kept a good **stock** of food in the house.*
3 → **livestock**
4 a tribe, family, or race: *He is of Italian **stock**.*
5 liquid in which meat, fish, vegetables, etc., have been cooked, often used as a base for sauces or soups
6 the shares of a business company
verb **7** to provide with or collect a stock or supply
8 to provide with horses, cattle, etc.: *to **stock** the property with fine merinos*
adjective **9** kept regularly in store: ***stock** articles*
10 in common use or ordinary: *a **stock** argument*
phrase **11 take stock**, to make a judgement or survey of resources, prospects, etc.: *to **take stock** of a situation*

Word history: Middle English; Old English *stoc(c)*

stockade
noun a strong wooden fence built for defence

Word history: French, from Old Provençal word meaning 'stake', of Germanic origin

stockbroker
noun an agent or broker who buys and sells stocks and shares for customers for a commission

stock exchange
noun **1** a building or place where stocks and shares are bought and sold
2 an association of brokers and dealers in stocks and bonds, who meet to transact their business

stocking
noun a tight-fitting item of women's clothing that covers the foot and leg

stockman
noun a man whose job is to look after the animals, especially the cattle, on a property

Noun forms: The plural is **stockmen**.

stockpile
verb to save up in large amounts for future use: *to **stockpile** wood for the winter* (***bank***, ***gather***, ***hoard***, ***store***, ***stow away***)

Word building: **stockpile** *noun*

stock-still
adverb without moving at all: *to stand **stock-still*** (***immobile***, ***motionless***, ***stationary***, ***steady***)

stocktake
noun the examination and listing of goods, assets, and other things like this, in a shop, business, etc.

Word use: You can also use **stocktaking**.

stockworker
noun someone whose job is to look after the animals, especially the cattle, on a property

stocky
adjective short, solid and strong: *a **stocky** young footballer* (***beefy***, ***burly***, ***squat***, ***stumpy***, ***thickset***)

Adjective forms: **stockier**, **stockiest**

stoic (<u>stoh</u>-ik)
adjective **1** noted for calm or silent strength and courage
noun **2** someone who is always mentally strong, patient and uncomplaining

Word use: You can also use **stoical** for definition 1.
Word building: **stoicism** *noun*
Word history: from the *Stoic* school of philosophy founded by Zeno, who lived about 475 BC, and who taught that people should be free from strong feelings and bear without complaint anything that happens to them. The name *Stoic* was Greek for 'porch', specifically the porch in Athens from which Zeno lectured.

stoke
verb to stir up and add fuel to: *to **stoke** a fire*

stoked
adjective *Colloquial* extremely pleased: *I was **stoked** when I found out I had come first in the class.*

stoker
noun someone employed to tend a furnace used in generating steam, such as on a steamship

stole
noun a long, wide scarf worn around your shoulders for warmth

Word history: Middle English and Old English, from Latin, from Greek word meaning 'clothing', 'robe'

stolen
verb past participle of **steal**

stolid (stol-uhd)
adjective not easily moved or stirred (***dull***, ***unimaginative***)

Word history: Latin

stomach (stum-uhk)
noun the bag-like organ in the body that receives food after it is swallowed and starts to digest it

Word history: Middle English, from Old French, from Latin, from Greek word meaning 'throat', 'gullet', 'stomach'

stone
noun **1** the hard substance which rocks are made of: *a house built of* ***stone***
2 a piece of rock (***boulder***, ***cobble***, ***pebble***)
3 a gem
4 the hard seed inside a cherry, peach, plum or similar fruit
5 a unit of weight in the imperial system, equal to a little more than six kilograms
verb **6** to throw stones at
7 to take the stones out of: *to* ***stone*** *peaches*

Word use: For definition 5, look up **imperial system.**
Word history: Middle English; Old English *stān*

stoned
adjective Colloquial completely drunk or drugged

stony
adjective **1** full of or having many stones or rocks
2 like or suggesting stone, especially when it is hard like stone
3 unfeeling or merciless: *a* ***stony*** *heart* (***callous***, ***cold-blooded***, ***cruel***, ***hard-hearted***)

Adjective forms: **stonier**, **stoniest**

stood
verb past tense and past participle of **stand**

stooge (stoohj)
noun Colloquial **1** an entertainer who feeds lines to a comedian and is often the object of his or her jokes
2 someone who acts on behalf of another, especially in a flattering, dishonest, corrupt or secretive fashion

stool
noun a seat with no arms or back

Word history: Middle English; Old English *stōl*

stoop
verb **1** to bend forwards
2 to lower yourself: *to* ***stoop*** *to lying*

Word history: Old English *stūpian*

stop
verb **1** to end or finish (***cease***, ***terminate***)
2 to come to a halt: *The car* ***stopped*** *in the driveway.*
3 to bring to a halt: *to* ***stop*** *the car*
4 to prevent: *to* ***stop*** *them from leaving* (***block***, ***forbid***, ***prevent***, ***prohibit***)
5 to close or block up: *to* ***stop*** *a leak*
6 to stay: *to* ***stop*** *overnight with friends*
noun **7** a finish or end: *to put a* ***stop*** *to the noise* (***close***, ***conclusion***, ***termination***)
8 the place where a bus, tram or other vehicle stops to pick up and set down passengers
phrase **9 stop by**, to call somewhere for a short time on the way to another place (***blow in***, ***drop in***, ***look in***, ***visit***)
10 stop off at, to halt for a short stay in before leaving for another place: ***Stop off at*** *Katoomba on your way west.*
11 stop over, to make a brief stop during a long plane flight

Verb forms: I **stopped**, I have **stopped**, I am **stopping**
Word history: Old English *stoppian*, from Vulgar Latin

stopgap
noun **1** something that fills the place of something lacking
adjective **2** makeshift

stoppage
noun cessation of activity

stopper
noun something that fits into the top of a bottle to close it

stop press
noun news put into a newspaper at the last minute, after printing has already begun

stopwatch
noun a watch which can be stopped and started by pressing a button, used for timing races, etc.

storage
noun room to keep things: *The cupboard has plenty of* ***storage***.

store
noun **1** things put away for use in the future: *a* ***store*** *of groceries* (***bank***, ***hoard***, ***stockpile***)
2 a place for keeping a supply of things: *Get some pencils from the* ***store***.
3 a shop: *the corner* ***store*** (***market***, ***outlet***, ***stall***)
verb **4** to put in a warehouse, etc., for keeping
phrase **5 in store**, coming soon: *There is a surprise* ***in store*** *for you.*

Word history: Middle English, from Old French word meaning 'build', 'furnish', 'stock', from Latin word meaning 'renew', 'restore'

storehouse
noun a building in which things are stored or kept

storey
noun one whole level of a building (***floor***)

Noun forms: The plural is **storeys**.
Word use: The US spelling is **story**.
Word history: Middle English, from Old French word meaning 'build'

storey / story
Don't confuse **storey** with **story**, which is the telling of something that has happened, either made up or in real life.

stork
noun a large bird with long legs and a long beak, which feeds in shallow water

Word history: Old English *storc*

stork / stalk
Don't confuse **stork** with **stalk**, which is the stem of a plant. To **stalk** something is to follow it quietly and carefully.

storm
noun **1** a violent change in the weather bringing wind, rain, thunder and lightning
2 a strong outburst: *a **storm** of applause*
verb **3** to rush angrily: *He **stormed** out of the room.*
4 to attack suddenly and violently: *The warriors **stormed** the castle.*
phrase **5 take by storm**,
a to take by military attack
b to be a great success in: *The pop singer **took** Sydney **by storm**.*

Word building: **stormy** *adjective* (**stormier**, **stormiest**)
Word history: Middle English and Old English

storm-petrel
noun a type of small dark seabird

Word use: You can also use **petrel**.

story
noun **1** the telling of something that has happened, either made up or in real life: *the **story** of Robinson Crusoe*
2 a lie or fib

Noun forms: The plural is **stories**.
Word history: Middle English, from Anglo-French, from Latin

stout (stowt)
adjective **1** rather overweight (***fat***, ***heavy***, ***plump***, ***portly***, ***tubby***)
2 strong and heavy: *a **stout** stick*
3 brave and fearless: *a **stout** heart* (***bold***, ***courageous***, ***fearless***, ***heroic***, ***valiant***)
noun **4** a strong, dark-brown beer

Word history: Middle English, from Old French word meaning 'brave', 'proud', from Germanic

stove
noun a device which uses wood, gas or electricity to produce heat for cooking or warming a room

Word history: Old English *stofa* hot air bathroom

stow (stoh)
verb to pack or store away: ***Stow** your luggage in the boot of the car.* (***gather***, ***hoard***, ***save***, ***stockpile***)

Word history: Middle English, from *stowe* place, Old English *stow*

stowaway (stoh-uh-way)
noun someone who hides on a ship or plane to get a free trip

Word building: **stowaway** *verb*

STP
noun standard temperature and pressure; temperature of 0°C and a pressure of 101 325 pascals

Word history: abbreviation of *s(tandard) t(emperature and) p(ressure)*

straddle
verb to sit or stand with one leg on each side of: *to **straddle** a horse*

Word history: British dialect, from *stride*

strafe (strahf, strayf)
verb **1** to attack a target on the ground by aircraft with machine-gun fire
2 to bombard heavily

Word history: German; from the phrase *Gott strafe England* God punish England

straggle
verb **1** to lag behind or walk out of line
2 to grow or spread untidily: *Overgrown vines **straggled** over the fence.*

Word building: **straggler** *noun* **straggly** *adjective* (**stragglier**, **straggliest**)
Word history: Middle English; blend of *stray* and *draggle*

straight
adjective **1** not bent or curved
2 honest and reliable: *a **straight** answer*
3 serious: *to keep a **straight** face | to have a **straight** talk*
adverb **4** without bending, curving, or twisting: *The road runs **straight** for five kilometres.*
5 in the proper order: *to set your room **straight***
6 directly or immediately: *I'll come **straight** over.*
phrase **7 go straight**, to lead an honest life, especially after being in prison

Word history: Middle English, originally past participle of *stretch*

straight / strait
Don't confuse **straight** with **strait**, which is a narrow channel connecting two large bodies of water.

straight angle
noun an angle of 180°

straightaway
adverb at once: *I'll come **straightaway**.*

Word use: The opposite of this is **at leisure**.

straighten
verb to make or become straight

straightforward
adjective **1** honest and open (***candid***, ***direct***, ***forthright***, ***frank***, ***genuine***)
2 not difficult or complicated: *a **straightforward** problem* (***clear***, ***evident***, ***explicit***, ***obvious***, ***plain***)

Word use: The opposite of definition 1 is **vague** and **evasive**.

strain[1]
verb **1** to pull, push or stretch hard or too far: *to **strain** a muscle | The dog **strained** at its leash.*
2 to pour through a sieve: *to **strain** orange juice*
noun **3** great effort, pressure or stress: *He looked tired from the **strain** of work. | The **strain** on the rope made it snap.*
4 strains, musical sounds: *the sweet **strains** of a violin*

Word history: Middle English, from Old French word meaning 'bind tightly', 'clasp', 'squeeze', from Latin word meaning 'draw tight'

strain[2]
noun breed or family line: *This **strain** of cat has no tail.*

Word history: Old English *gestrēon* acquisition

strainer
noun a filter or sieve: *a tea* ***strainer***

strait
noun a narrow channel connecting two large bodies of water: *Bass* ***Strait***

Word history: Middle English, from Old French word meaning 'tight', 'narrow', from Latin word meaning 'bound'

straitened (stray-tuhnd)
adjective pinched or restricting: *in* ***straitened*** *circumstances*

straitjacket
noun a coat which is wrapped around mentally ill people to restrain them, if they are acting violently enough to hurt themselves or others

Word use: You can also use **straightjacket**.

straitlaced
adjective rather strict and proper in your attitude to life (***austere***, ***prim***)

strand[1]
verb **1** to drive or run aground on a beach
2 to bring into a helpless position: *He is* ***stranded*** *in Darwin without money.*
noun **3** the shore of the sea or a river, often used in poetry

Word history: Middle English and Old English

strand[2]
noun **1** one of the threads which are twisted together to form a rope, cord, wire, etc.
2 a single thread in cloth
3 a lock of hair
4 a string of pearls, beads, etc.

Word history: Middle English

stranded
adjective **1** washed up on the beach: *a* ***stranded*** *whale*
2 alone and helpless: ***stranded*** *in the middle of the desert*

strange
adjective **1** queer or odd: *a* ***strange*** *way of walking* (***abnormal***, ***bizarre***, ***peculiar***, ***unusual***, ***weird***)
2 not seen or heard of before: *a* ***strange*** *part of town* (***new***, ***unfamiliar***)

Word history: Middle English, from Old French, from Latin word meaning 'external', 'foreign'

stranger
noun **1** someone you haven't met before
2 someone who has not been in a place before: *I'm a* ***stranger*** *in town.*

strangle
verb to kill by squeezing the throat and cutting off the air supply (***asphyxiate***, ***choke***, ***strangulate***)

Word building: **strangler** *noun* **strangulation** *noun*
Word history: Middle English, from Old French, from Latin, from Greek

stranglehold
noun **1** a tight hold around the neck, especially in wrestling
2 anything which prevents movement or development

strap
noun **1** a strip of leather or cloth used for tying or holding things in place: *a watch* ***strap***
verb **2** to fasten with a strap

Verb forms: I **strapped**, I have **strapped**, I am **strapping**

strapping
adjective tall and strong: *a* ***strapping*** *young athlete*

stratagem (strat-uh-jem)
noun **1** a plan, scheme or trick for deceiving an enemy (***artifice***, ***plot***, ***ruse***)
2 any trick (***hoax***, ***prank***, ***ruse***)

Word history: French, from Latin, from Greek

strategic
adjective important in a strategy

strategy (strat-uh-jee)
noun **1** a clever scheme
2 the planning and tactics used in war

Noun forms: The plural is **strategies**.
Word building: **strategist** *noun*
Word history: from Greek word meaning 'generalship'

stratify (strat-uh-fuy)
verb **1** to form in strata or layers
2 to develop horizontal status groups in society: *a rigidly* ***stratified*** *society*

Verb forms: it **stratified**, it has **stratified**, it is **stratifying**
Word history: Neo-Latin

stratosphere
noun the region of the earth's atmosphere ouside the troposphere but within the ionosphere, beginning at about 20 km above the earth's surface

stratum (strah-tuhm)
noun a layer or level: *The cliff face shows several different rock* ***strata***. (***band***, ***deposit***, ***seam***, ***vein***)

Noun forms: The plural is **strata** or **stratums**.
Word history: from Neo-Latin; Latin word meaning 'something spread out'

straw
noun **1** a thin, hollow tube through which you can suck a drink
2 cut, dried stalks of wheat, oats, corn, or other grain
phrase **3 the last straw**, a final act or circumstance, etc., which makes a situation unbearable

Word history: Old English *strēaw*

strawberry
noun a small, juicy, red fruit which has many tiny seeds on its surface

Noun forms: The plural is **strawberries**.

stray
verb **1** to wander off and get lost (***digress***, ***diverge***, ***ramble***)
adjective **2** straying, or having strayed: *We found a* ***stray*** *cat behind the house.*
noun **3** a domestic animal found wandering without an owner

Word history: Middle English, from Old French, from Latin word meaning 'wander outside'

streak
noun **1** a long, thin mark or line: *a **streak** of lightning | a **streak** of paint*
verb **2** to mark with streaks
3 to move very quickly: *The dog **streaked** across the road.* (***dart***, ***hurtle***, ***pelt***, ***race***, ***tear***)

Word building: **streaky** *adjective* (**streakier**, **streakiest**)
Word history: Old English *strica*

stream
noun **1** a small river or creek
2 a continuous flow: *a **stream** of air | a **stream** of words*
verb **3** to flow or run: *Tears **streamed** from his eyes.* (***gush***, ***spurt***, ***surge***, ***wash***)
4 to group according to ability: *The school **streamed** the children into different classes.*

Word history: Old English *strēam*

streamer
noun a long strip of brightly coloured paper

streaming
noun **1** the process of dividing schoolchildren into groups, usually on the basis of ability
2 the process of transmitting digital data in a continuous, steady flow, so that it may be processed and displayed as it is received, rather than being stored and only displayed when the entire file has been received and processed

streamline
verb to simplify, especially to improve efficiency: *to **streamline** the hospital's admission system*

streamlined
adjective **1** shaped to move quickly and smoothly through air or water
2 simplified, especially to improve efficiency: *the new **streamlined** regulations*

street
noun **1** a road lined with buildings
2 the people who live in a street: *The whole **street** gathered around the bonfire.*

Word history: Old English *strǣt*

streetwise
adjective skilled in living in an urban environment; knowing how to survive on the streets: *She is pretty **streetwise** so she shouldn't have any trouble going to New York by herself.*

strength
noun **1** the quality of being strong: *Do you have enough **strength** to move the piano?* (***force***, ***might***, ***muscle***, ***power***, ***vigour***)
phrase **2 on the strength of**, on the basis of

Word history: Old English *strength(u)*

strengthen
verb to make stronger (***brace***, ***fortify***, ***prop up***, ***reinforce***, ***shore up***)

strenuous (stren-yooh-uhs)
adjective needing a great effort: ***strenuous** exercise*

Word building: **strenuously** *adverb*
Word history: Latin

streptococcus (strep-tuh-kok-uhs)
noun any of a group of bacteria typically forming chains which may cause scarlet fever and other infectious diseases

Noun forms: The plural is **streptococci** (strep-tuh-kok-uy, strep-tuh-kok-ee).
Word building: **streptococcal** *adjective*

stress
verb **1** to emphasise: *to **stress** the need for caution*
2 to pronounce strongly: *You should **stress** the second syllable in 'pronounce'.*
3 to put pressure or strain on
4 to work yourself into a state of nervousness or anxiety: *Don't **stress** about it.*
noun **5** great importance: *to lay **stress** on the need for safety*
6 accent or emphasis: *to pronounce a word with the **stress** on the first syllable*
7 strain or pressure: *the **stress** of work*

Word building: **stress** *verb*
Word history: variant of *distress*

stressful
adjective causing anxiety and tension: *An exam can be a very **stressful** thing.*

stretch
verb **1** to pull out or extend (***run***, ***spread***)
2 to spread: *The desert seems to **stretch** forever.*
3 to widen or enlarge: *to **stretch** a jumper*
noun **4** the action of stretching: *to have a yawn and a **stretch***
5 a continuous spread or period of time: *a **stretch** of land | a **stretch** of ten years*
phrase **6 stretch out**, to lie down at full length
7 stretch your legs, to go for a walk

Word building: **stretchy** *adjective* (**stretchier**, **stretchiest**)
Word history: Old English *streccan*

stretcher
noun a light frame covered with canvas for carrying sick people

strew
verb to scatter or throw everywhere: *to **strew** the floor with clothes* (***disperse***, ***dissipate***, ***distribute***, ***spread***)

Verb forms: I **strewed**, I have **strewn**, I am **strewing**
Word history: Old English *strēowian*

stricken
adjective struck down or overcome: ***stricken** with fear*

Word history: old past participle of *strike*

strict
adjective **1** demanding that you behave well and obey the rules: *a **strict** teacher* (***austere***, ***firm***, ***harsh***, ***rigid***, ***straitlaced***)
2 complete or total: *in **strict** secrecy*

Word building: **strictly** *adverb*
Word history: from Latin word meaning 'drawn together', 'tight', 'severe'

stricture (strik-chuh)
noun **1** a strongly negative comment (***censure***, ***criticism***)
2 the narrowing of any passage of the body as a result of disease

Word history: Middle English, from Latin

stride
verb **1** to walk confidently with long steps (***march***, ***strut***, ***swagger***)
noun **2** a big step forward: *to take ten* ***strides*** *to reach the end of the room | to make great* ***strides*** *in learning to read*
3 strides, *Colloquial* trousers

Verb forms: I **strode**, I have **stridden**, I am **striding**
Word history: Old English *strīdan*

strident (<u>struy</u>-duhnt)
adjective making or having a hard and unpleasant sound (***grating***, ***harsh***)

Word building: **stridence** *noun* **stridency** *noun*
Word history: from Latin word meaning 'creaking'

strife
noun **1** fighting and quarrelling: *a country torn with* ***strife***
phrase **2 in strife**, *Australian, NZ Colloquial* in trouble: *You'll be* ***in strife*** *for being so late.*

Word history: Middle English, from Old French

strike
verb **1** to hit (***bat***, ***beat***, ***clip***, ***knock***, ***tap***)
2 to attack: *A snake sometimes* ***strikes*** *without warning.*
3 to come across or find: *to* ***strike*** *gold*
4 to affect strongly: *The ghost story* ***struck*** *them with terror.*
5 to sound by hitting a gong: *The clock* ***struck*** *three.*
6 to light: *to* ***strike*** *a match*
noun **7** a hit or blow
8 a work stoppage, usually in protest against low pay and poor working conditions

Verb forms: I **struck**, I have **struck**, I am **striking**
Word history: Old English *strīcan*

striking
adjective impressive or noticeable

strine (struyn)
noun Colloquial **1** Australian English, especially its colloquial words
2 the form of it which appeared in the books of Alastair Morrison, pen-name 'Afferbeck Lauder', where it was written in scrambled form to suggest extreme omission of sounds, running of words into each other, etc., as in *Gloria Soame* for *glorious home, muncer go* for *months ago*

string
noun **1** a thread or cord
2 a row or line of things: *a* ***string*** *of cars*
3 one of the pieces of wire stretched across a violin, guitar or similar instrument, which produces musical sounds when it is made to vibrate
4 strings, musical instruments with strings, especially those played with a bow
verb **5** to hang or thread on a string
phrase **6 pull strings**, *Colloquial* to seek your own advancement by using undue influence
7 string along (or **on**), *Colloquial* to deceive in a series of falsehoods
8 string out, to spread out or lengthen: *The people* ***strung out*** *along the beach to watch the surfers. | to* ***string out*** *a conversation*

Verb forms: I **strung**, I have **strung**, I am **stringing**
Word history: Old English *streng*

stringent (<u>strin</u>-juhnt)
adjective **1** rigorously exacting: ***stringent*** *laws*
2 urgent or compelling: ***stringent*** *necessity*
3 tight: *a* ***stringent*** *money market*

Word building: **stringency** *noun*
Word history: from Latin word meaning 'drawing tight'

stringy
adjective tough, wiry, or fibrous

strip[1]
verb **1** to remove or take away: *to* ***strip*** *the paint from a table*
2 to take off all your clothes

Verb forms: I **stripped**, I have **stripped**, I am **stripping**
Word building: **stripper** *noun*
Word history: Old English *-strzpan*

strip[2]
noun **1** a long, narrow piece or area: *a* ***strip*** *of paper | the coastal* ***strip***
2 a series of cartoons telling a story

Word use: You can also use **comic strip** for definition 2.
Word history: Middle English

stripe
noun **1** a long, narrow band of a different colour from the rest of a thing: *red* ***stripes*** *on a blue background*
2 stripes, strips of braid worn on a military uniform to show rank

Word building: **striped** *adjective*
Word history: Middle Dutch

striptease (<u>strip</u>-teez)
noun an act in which a person, usually a woman, takes off their clothes slowly before an audience

strive
phrase **strive for**, to try hard for: *to* ***strive for*** *success* (***pursue***, ***quest after***, ***search for***, ***seek***)

Verb forms: I **strove**, I have **striven**, I am **striving**
Word history: Middle English, from Old French word meaning 'quarrel', 'contend'

strobe
noun a device which gives out a series of brilliant flashes of light

strobe lighting
noun a flashing light of great intensity, as at a theatre, dance, etc., obtained by using a strobe

strode
verb past tense of **stride**

stroganoff (<u>strog</u>-uh-nof)
noun a Russian dish of meat cooked in a sauce of sour cream and mushrooms

Word history: named after Count Paul *Stroganoff*, a Russian diplomat in the 19th century

stroke[1]
noun **1** a hit or blow
2 a style of swimming
3 an action or event: *a* ***stroke*** *of good luck*
4 a sudden break in the circulation of blood in the brain which can cause paralysis or other disabilities

Word history: Middle English

stroke²
verb to pass your hand over gently (***feel***, ***finger***, ***handle***, ***pat***, ***touch***)

Word building: **stroke** *noun*
Word history: Old English *strācian*

stroll
verb to walk slowly (***amble***, ***saunter***)

Word building: **stroll** *noun*

stroller
noun a chair on wheels used for carrying small children

strong
adjective **1** having great power or effect: *a **strong** wind* | *a **strong** will* (***dominant***, ***forceful***, ***mighty***, ***potent***, ***powerful***)
2 not easily broken: *a **strong** fence* (***hardy***, ***robust***)
3 having a lot of flavour or smell: ***strong** coffee*
adverb **4** in number: *The army was 10 000 **strong**.*

Word building: **strongly** *adverb*
Word history: Old English

stronghold
noun a fortress

stroppy
adjective Colloquial **1** difficult to control (***aggressive***, ***contrary***, ***defiant***, ***quarrelsome***, ***wilful***)
2 annoyed or angry

Adjective forms: **stroppier**, **stroppiest**
Word history: from *obstreperous*

strove (strohv)
verb past tense of **strive**

struck
verb past tense and a past participle of **strike**

structure
noun **1** something that has been built or constructed: *Bridges and buildings are both **structures**.*
2 the way something is put together: *the **structure** of a sentence* (***build***, ***design***, ***form***, ***shape***)

Word building: **structural** *adjective* **structure** *verb*
Word history: Latin

struggle
verb **1** to fight very hard: *She **struggled** against her attacker.* (***battle***, ***grapple***, ***scuffle***, ***tussle***, ***wrestle***)
2 to try very hard to do something difficult: *She **struggled** to get to the top of the mountain.* (***battle***, ***labour***, ***strain***, ***strive***, ***toil***)

Word building: **struggle** *noun* **struggler** *noun*
Word history: Middle English

strum
verb to play by running your fingers across the strings of: *to **strum** a guitar*

Verb forms: I **strummed**, I have **strummed**, I am **strumming**
Word history: blend of *string* and *thumb*

strung
verb past tense and past participle of **string**

strut¹
verb to walk proudly or pompously, with your back straight and your chin pushed forward (***parade***, ***stride***, ***swagger***)

Verb forms: I **strutted**, I have **strutted**, I am **strutting**
Word building: **strut** *noun*
Word history: Old English *strūtian* stand stiffly

strut²
noun a wooden or metal bar that supports part of a building

Word history: related to *strut¹*

strychnine (strik-neen, strik-nuhn)
noun a colourless, crystalline poison which is a powerful stimulant to the central nervous system

Word history: French, from Latin, from Greek word meaning 'kind of nightshade'

stub
noun **1** a short end piece: *the **stub** of a pencil*
verb **2** to bump against something hard: *to **stub** your toe*

Verb forms: I **stubbed**, I have **stubbed**, I am **stubbing**
Word history: Old English

stubble
noun **1** the short stalks left in the ground after wheat or corn has been harvested
2 the short, prickly hairs growing on the face of a man who hasn't shaved for a few days

Word building: **stubbly** *adjective*
Word history: Middle English, from Old French, from Late Latin

stubborn (stub-uhn)
adjective determined not to give way or change your mind (***adamant***, ***inflexible***, ***obstinate***, ***persistent***, ***pig-headed***)

Word building: **stubbornness** *noun*
Word history: Middle English, from Old English *stybb* stub

stubby
adjective **1** short and thick
2 bristly, as the hair or beard
noun **3** *Australian*, *NZ* a small, squat beer bottle

Adjective forms: **stubbier**, **stubbiest**
Noun forms: The plural is **stubbies**.

stuck
verb **1** past tense and past participle of **stick²**
phrase **2 get stuck into**, *Colloquial*
a to set about with great energy
b to attack energetically

stuck-up
adjective Colloquial snobbish or conceited (***big-headed***, ***conceited***, ***pompous***, ***proud***, ***vain***)

stud¹
noun a small knob or button: *Football boots have **studs** underneath.* | *This shirt fastens with **studs**.*

Word history: Old English *studu*

stud²
noun a farm where horses or cattle are kept for breeding

Word history: Old English *stōd*

student
noun someone who is studying, especially at a school, college or university

Word history: Middle English, from Latin word meaning 'being eager', 'studying'

studio (styooh-dee-oh)
noun **1** the workroom of an artist or musician
2 a place where films or radio and television programs are made

Word history: Italian, from Latin word meaning 'zeal', 'study', Late Latin 'a place for study'

studious
adjective **1** eager or given to study: *a* ***studious*** *boy*
2 having to do with study: ***studious*** *tastes*
3 painstaking: ***studious*** *care* (***assiduous***, ***zealous***)

study (stu-dee)
verb **1** to spend time learning
2 to look at closely: *to* ***study*** *a document* (***analyse***, ***assess***, ***examine***, ***inspect***)
noun **3** the careful learning of a subject
4 a room with a desk and books for studying
5 a short piece of music often used for practising technique

Verb forms: I **studied**, I have **studied**, I am **studying**
Noun forms: The plural is **studies**.
Word history: Middle English, from Latin word meaning 'zeal', 'application', 'study', Late Latin word meaning 'a place for study'

stuff
noun **1** the material from which things are made: *cushions filled with soft* ***stuff*** (***cloth***, ***fabric***, ***textile***)
2 *Colloquial* belongings: *Put your* ***stuff*** *in your locker.* (***belongings***, ***gear***, ***paraphernalia***, ***possessions***, ***property***)
verb **3** to fill tightly or cram: *to* ***stuff*** *clothes into a drawer*

Word history: Middle English, from Old French word meaning 'provide', from Germanic, from Late Latin word meaning 'tow'

stuffing
noun **1** material used for filling: *the* ***stuffing*** *of a pillow*
2 a tasty mixture put inside a chicken or other poultry before it is cooked

stuffy
adjective **1** not having enough air: *a* ***stuffy*** *room*
2 prim or easily shocked

Adjective forms: **stuffier**, **stuffiest**
Word building: **stuffiness** *noun*

stumble
verb **1** to trip and nearly fall (***overbalance***, ***pitch forward***, ***slip***)
2 to walk unsteadily (***hobble***, ***limp***, ***shuffle***, ***stagger***, ***totter***)
3 to act or speak in an unsteady and hesitating way

Word history: Middle English

stump
noun **1** a short part left after the main part has been cut off: *a tree* ***stump*** | *the* ***stump*** *of a pencil*
2 one of the three upright sticks forming the wicket in cricket
verb **3** to baffle completely: *The question* ***stumped*** *him.*

Word history: Middle English *stomp*

stumpy
adjective short and thick (***squat***, ***stocky***, ***stubby***, ***thickset***)

Adjective forms: **stumpier**, **stumpiest**

stun
verb **1** to make unconscious: *The blow* ***stunned*** *him.*
2 to shock or astonish

Verb forms: I **stunned**, I have **stunned**, I am **stunning**
Word history: Old English *stunian* resound, crash

stung
verb **1** past tense and past participle of **sting**
adjective Colloquial **2** *Australian* drunk
3 tricked or cheated

stunt[1]
verb to stop or slow down the growth of: *Lack of food* ***stunts*** *children in some countries.*

Word history: verb use of *stunt*, adjective (now dialect), dwarfed, stubborn (in Middle English and Old English foolish)

stunt[2]
noun **1** a spectacular and often dangerous performance
2 something done to attract publicity or attention

Word history: origin uncertain

stunt double
noun someone who is paid to perform hazardous or acrobatic feats, especially one who replaces a film actor in scenes requiring such feats

stuntman
noun a male stunt double

stuntwoman
noun a female stunt double

stupefy (styooh-puh-fuy)
verb **1** to make senseless or unconscious: *The blow on her head* ***stupefied*** *her.*
2 to astound or overcome with amazement

Verb forms: it **stupefied**, it has **stupefied**, it is **stupefying**
Word building: **stupefaction** *noun*
Word history: Latin

stupendous
adjective amazingly good: *The singer's performance was* ***stupendous***. (***astonishing***, ***astounding***, ***remarkable***, ***staggering***, ***wonderful***)

Word history: from Latin word meaning 'to be wondered at'

stupid
adjective **1** not clever or quick to understand: *a* ***stupid*** *dog* (***dense***, ***dull***, ***dumb***, ***slow***, ***thick***)
2 showing a lack of good sense: *a* ***stupid*** *thing to do*

Word building: **stupidity** *noun*
Word history: Latin

stupor (styooh-puh)
noun a state in which the mind or senses are deadened or not working, as a result of illness or drugs

Word history: Middle English, from Latin

sturdy
adjective strong or able to stand up to rough use or handling: *a* ***sturdy*** *little boy* | *a* ***sturdy*** *garden tool* (***durable***, ***hardy***, ***heavy-duty***, ***rugged***, ***tough***)

Adjective forms: **sturdier, sturdiest**
Word history: Middle English, from Old French word meaning 'dazed', 'reckless', from Late Latin word meaning 'deafen (with chatter)', from *turdus* 'turtledove'

sturgeon (ster-juhn)
noun a large fish found in the northern areas of the world, the eggs of which can be salted and eaten as caviar

Word history: Middle English, from Anglo-French, variant of Old French, from Vulgar Latin, from Germanic

Sturt's desert pea
noun an Australian plant with brilliant scarlet and black flowers, found in inland desert country; floral emblem of South Australia

Word history: named after Charles *Sturt*, 1795–1869, Australian explorer, born in India

Sturt's desert rose
noun a shrub of inland Australia with attractive mauve flowers; the floral emblem of the Northern Territory

Word history: named after Charles *Sturt*, 1795–1869, Australian explorer, born in India

stutter
noun a speech problem in which the rhythm of speech is blocked and sounds, especially the first consonants in words, are repeated

Word use: You can also use **stammer**.
Word building: **stutter** *verb*
Word history: British dialect *stut*, Middle English *stutte(n)*

sty[1]
noun a place to keep pigs in

Noun forms: The plural is **sties**.
Word history: Old English *stig*

sty[2]
noun a small, red and painful swelling on the eyelid

Noun forms: The plural is **sties**.
Word use: You can also use **stye**.
Word history: Middle English *styan* (Old English *stīgend* sty, literally, rising)

style
noun **1** a particular kind, sort, or type, especially of music, art, architecture, etc.: *The church is built in the Gothic **style**. | music in the baroque **style***
2 a way of doing something: *Shakespeare's **style** of writing | a **style** of living*
3 an elegant or fashionable way of doing things

Word building: **style** *verb*
Word history: Middle English, from Old French, from Latin

style / stile
Look up **stile / style**.

stylise (stuy-uh-luyz)
verb to make something match or conform with a particular and usually simplified style or form, often to achieve an effect rather than being true to life

Word use: You can also use **stylize.**
Verb forms: it **stylised**, it has **stylised**, it is **stylising**
Word building: **stylised** *adjective* **stylisation** *noun*

stylish
adjective fashionable or elegant

stylus
noun **1** a pointed tool for drawing or writing
2 a needle used to play a record (definition 4)

Noun forms: The plural is **styluses** or **styli**.
Word history: Latin

suave (swahv)
adjective smooth and sophisticated in manner: *The famous actor was very **suave**.*

Word use: The opposite of this is **awkward** and **unsophisticated**.
Word history: from Latin word meaning 'gentle'

sub
noun Colloquial **1** subeditor
2 submarine
3 subscription
4 substitute

Word history: abbreviation

subconscious (sub-kon-shuhs)
noun the part of your mind below consciousness or awareness: *Your dreams can come from your **subconscious**.*

Word building: **subconscious** *adjective*

subcontract (sub-kon-tract)
noun **1** a contract to do, or provide materials for, one section of a larger job or contract
verb (sub-kuhn-trakt) **2** to make a subcontract for

Word building: **subcontractor** *noun*

subculture
noun a network of behaviour, beliefs and attitudes existing within and different from a larger culture

subcutaneous (sub-kyooh-tay-nee-uhs)
adjective **1** situated or lying under the skin
2 given under the skin: *A **subcutaneous** injection was administered to him.*

subdivide
verb to divide again into smaller divisions, especially land

Word building: **subdivision** *noun*

subdominant
noun Music the fourth note of a scale, next below the dominant

subdue
verb to overcome, usually by force (***dominate***, ***oppress***, ***overpower***, ***repress***)

subdued
adjective unusually quiet and low-key (***depressed***, ***down***, ***low***)

Word history: Middle English, from Old French word meaning 'seduce', from Latin word meaning 'remove by stealth'

subeditor (sub-ed-uh-tuh)
noun **1** in journalism, someone who prepares material written by others and makes it ready for printing
2 an assistant editor

subheading
noun the title or heading of a section in a chapter, essay, newspaper article, etc.

subject (sub-jekt)
noun **1** a matter under discussion: *the **subject** of a book*
2 a branch of study: *My favourite **subject** is maths.*
3 something chosen by an artist for painting
4 someone who is under the rule of a monarch or state: *a British **subject***
5 the part of a sentence about which something is said, such as 'the roof of the house' in *The roof of the house was red.*
phrase **6 subject to,**
a open to or likely to receive: ***subject to** teasing*
b depending on: *The excursion to the beach is **subject to** the teacher's approval.*
7 subject to (sub-jekt), to cause to undergo: *He was **subjected to** harsh treatment.*
Word history: from Latin word meaning 'placed under'

subjects in grammar

We commonly divide sentences into two parts: what is being talked about, and what is being said about it:

She / laughs a lot.

The elephant in the corner that keeps waving its trunk / eats strawberries.

The first part (what's being talked about) is called the **subject** of the sentence. The rest is called the **predicate**.

The easiest way to find the subject is to ask the question *who?* or *what?* before the main verb of the sentence (*laughs* and *eats* in the examples above).

1 Who or what laughs?

She …

2 Who or what eats?

The elephant in the corner that keeps waving its trunk …

subjective
adjective having to do with the thinker rather than the thing thought about: *a **subjective** opinion*
Word use: The opposite is **objective**.

subjective case
noun the form of a noun or pronoun which shows it is the subject of a verb such as 'I' in *I can hear him.*

subjugate (sub-juh-gayt)
verb to bring under complete control or into subjection (***conquer**, **subdue***)
Word building: **subjugation** *noun* **subjugator** *noun*
Word history: from Latin word meaning 'brought under the yoke'

subjunctive
adjective Grammar having to do with the mood expressing hypothetical action

For more information about the **subjunctive** mood, look up **verbs: mood.**

sublimate (sub-luh-mayt)
verb **1** to redirect socially inappropriate impulses into socially constructive or creative activities
2 → **sublime** (definition 5)
Word building: **sublimation** *noun*
Word history: from Latin word meaning 'elevated'

sublime
adjective **1** elevated or lofty in thought, language, bearing, etc.: ***sublime** poetry*
2 impressing the mind with a sense of greatness or power: ***sublime** scenery*
3 perfect or supreme: *a **sublime** moment*
noun **4** that which is sublime: *from the **sublime** to the ridiculous*
verb **5** *Chemistry* to change a solid by heat directly into a vapour, which on cooling condenses back to solid form, without becoming liquid first
Word use: You can also use **sublimate** for definition 5.
Word building: **sublimeness** *noun* **sublimity** *noun*
Word history: Middle English, from Latin word meaning 'elevate'

subliminal (suh-blim-uh-nuhl)
adjective being at a level below the threshold of consciousness or perception: ***Subliminal** advertising tempts us without our awareness.*

submarine
adjective **1** being under water: ***submarine** cables*
noun **2** a type of ship that can travel under water

submediant
noun Music the sixth note of a musical scale, being midway between the subdominant and the upper tonic

submerge
verb to sink, or make sink: *The submarine **submerged.** / **Submerge** the clothes in the water.*
Word building: **submersion** *noun*
Word history: Latin

submissive
adjective tending to yield (***downtrodden**, **obedient**, **servile**, **subservient**, **unresisting***)
Word use: The opposite of this is **assertive**.
Word building: **submissiveness** *noun*

submit
verb **1** to yield or give in: *to **submit** to orders / to **submit** to punishment* (***capitulate**, **succumb**, **surrender***)
2 to hand in or offer for acceptance or judgement: *to **submit** an entry in a competition*
Verb forms: I **submitted**, I have **submitted**, I am **submitting**
Word building: **submission** *noun*
Word history: Middle English, from Latin word meaning 'lower', 'put under'

subordinate
adjective placed in or belonging to a lower order or rank: *a **subordinate** employee* (***junior**, **lowly**, **minor**, **subsidiary***)
Word building: **subordinate** *noun* **subordination** *noun*
Word history: late Middle English, from Medieval Latin word meaning 'subordinated'

subpoena (suh-pee-nuh)
noun **1** a legal document ordering a person to appear in court, usually as a witness
verb **2** to send a subpoena: *The court **subpoenaed** the neighbour of the dead man.*

Word history: Middle English, from Latin word meaning 'under penalty', the first words of the writ

subprime
adjective *US* having to do with a loan, usually for a house, which is risky for the organisation which lends the money because the person who has been given the loan has not been properly assessed and may not be able to repay it: *They were granted a **subprime** loan over the phone.*

subscribe (suhb-skruyb)
verb **1** to promise to give or pay a sum of money as a contribution, payment, share, etc.: *They **subscribed** a percentage of their salary to the fund.*
2 to express agreement to by signing your name
3 to sign your name to a document
4 to obtain a subscription to a magazine, newspaper, etc.: *I **subscribe** to several magazines.*

Word building: **subscriber** *noun*
Word history: Middle English, from Latin

subscription
noun **1** a payment you make for club membership, a series of concert tickets, a regular magazine, etc.
2 an amount of money given: ***subscription** to the bushfire appeal*

Word history: late Middle English, from Latin

subsequent (sub-suh-kwuhnt)
adjective happening later: ***subsequent** events*

Word building: **subsequently** *adverb*
Word history: late Middle English, from Latin

subservient (suhb-serv-ee-uhnt)
adjective very submissive (***downtrodden***, ***obsequious***, ***servile***)

Word building: **subservience** *noun*
subserviency *noun*
Word history: Latin

subside
verb to sink to a lower level: *The rain has made the road **subside**. | The laughter **subsided**.*

Word building: **subsidence** *noun*
Word history: from Latin word meaning 'settle down'

subsidiary (suhb-sij-uh-ree)
adjective **1** less important: *a **subsidiary** role* (***junior***, ***lowly***, ***minor***, ***subordinate***)
noun **2** a company legally controlled by another company or companies

Noun forms: The plural is **subsidiaries**.
Word history: from Latin word meaning 'belonging to a reserve'

subsidy (sub-suh-dee)
noun a supporting payment made by a government or other organisation: *a **subsidy** to farmers*

Noun forms: The plural is **subsidies**.
Word building: **subsidise** *verb*

subsist
verb to continue to live or stay alive, especially when food and other needs are in short supply

Word building: **subsistence** *noun*
Word history: from Latin word meaning 'stand firm', 'be adequate to'

subsistence farming
noun farming in which the produce is consumed by the farmer and his or her family leaving little or no surplus for marketing

Word use: You can also use **subsistence agriculture**.

subsoil
noun the bed or layer of earth just below the surface soil

substance
noun **1** anything of which a thing is made
2 a particular kind of matter: *This **substance** will remove paint.*
3 the main or basic part: *the **substance** of an argument*
phrase **4 in substance**,
a mainly or substantially: *The reports, **in substance**, supported what I had claimed.*
b actually or really

Word history: Middle English, from Old French, from Latin

substantial
adjective large or solid: *a **substantial** sum of money | a **substantial** building* (***ample***, ***big***, ***bulky***, ***generous***, ***huge***)

Word use: The opposite of this is **insubstantial**.
Word building: **substantially** *adverb*
Word history: Middle English, from Late Latin

substantiate (suhb-stan-shee-ayt)
verb to establish by proof or evidence: *to **substantiate** a charge* (***bear out***, ***confirm***, ***corroborate***, ***prove***, ***verify***)

Word building: **substantiation** *noun*

substantive (sub-stan-tiv, sub-stuhn-tiv)
noun **1** a noun, pronoun, or other word or phrase which acts like a noun
adjective **2** having independent existence
3 real or actual
4 of considerable amount: *a **substantive** quantity of goods*

Word history: Middle English, from Late Latin word meaning 'standing by itself', from Latin word meaning 'substance'

substitute
noun **1** someone or something acting in place of another
verb **2** to put in the place of: *She **substituted** margarine for butter.* (***exchange***, ***replace***, ***swap***, ***transpose***)

Word building: **substitution** *noun*
Word history: Middle English, from Latin

substitute / replace
Look up **replace / substitute**.

subsume (suhb-syoohm)
verb to consider or include as part of a larger group: *The skills imparted at the summer science course are not easily **subsumed** within the normal school curriculum.*

Word history: Neo-Latin

subterfuge (sub-tuh-fyoohj)
noun a plan or trick used to hide or avoid something (***deceit***, ***ruse***)

Word history: Late Latin, from Latin word meaning 'flee secretly'

subterranean (sub-tuh-ray-nee-uhn)
adjective underground: *a **subterranean** passage*

Word history: from Latin word meaning 'below the earth'

subtitle
noun **1** a secondary title of a book or a play: *The **subtitle** of 'The Mikado' is 'The Town of Titipu'.*
2 subtitles, a translation in words on the screen of what is being said in a foreign-language film or opera

subtle (sut-uhl)
adjective **1** so fine or slight as to not be obvious or clear: *a **subtle** difference*
2 skilful or clever: ***subtle** humour*

Word building: **subtlety** *noun* (*plural* **subtleties**) **subtly** *adverb*
Word history: Middle English, from Old French, from Latin word meaning 'fine', 'delicate'

subtract
verb to take away: ***Subtract** 2 from 7, and you get 5.*

Word history: from Latin word meaning 'carried away'

subtraction
noun Mathematics the operation of finding the difference between two numbers or quantities (denoted by the symbol –)

Word use: The opposite of this is **addition**.

subtropical (sub-trop-ik-uhl)
adjective having to do with a region between tropical and temperate

suburb
noun a district of a city with its own shopping centre, school and other facilities: *a bayside **suburb** | an industrial **suburb***

Word building: **suburban** *adjective*
Word history: Middle English, from Latin

suburbia (suh-berb-ee-uh)
noun **1** the suburbs as a group, especially as they seem to represent the middle range of community standards and values
2 the characteristic life of people in suburbs

subvert (suhb-vert)
verb **1** to overthrow: *Rampant unrest is **subverting** the influence of the governing party.*
2 to undermine the principles of

Word building: **subversion** *noun* **subversive** *noun* **subversive** *adjective*
Word history: Middle English, from Latin

subway
noun a tunnel under a street or railway for people to walk through

succeed (suhk-seed)
verb **1** to do or accomplish what you have attempted: *After an effort he **succeeded** in opening the box.* (***make the grade***, ***shine***, ***steal the show***, ***triumph***, ***win through***)
2 to come after and take the place of: *She **succeeded** her father in the family business.*

Word history: Middle English, from Latin word meaning 'go up', 'be successful'

success (suhk-ses)
noun **1** a good or desired result (***accomplishment***, ***achievement***, ***feat***)
2 someone who has achieved a great deal in their field

Word building: **successful** *adjective*
Word history: Latin

succession (suhk-sesh-uhn)
noun **1** the coming of one after another in order or in the course of events
2 a number of people or things following one another in order (***chain***, ***course***, ***cycle***, ***sequence***, ***series***)
3 the right, act or process, by which one person succeeds to the office, rank, estate, etc., of another
4 the order or line of those entitled to succeed
5 *Ecology* the gradual replacement of one community by another in development towards a stable community of vegetation

Word building: **successional** *adjective*
Word history: Middle English, from Latin

successive (suhk-ses-iv)
adjective following uninterrupted or in a regular order: *three **successive** days*

successor (suhk-ses-uh)
noun someone or something that comes after and takes the place of: *He is my **successor** as president of the debating society.*

Word history: Latin; replacing Middle English *successour*, from Anglo-French

succinct (suhk-singkt)
adjective expressed or expressing in few words (***brief***, ***concise***)

Word history: Middle English, from Latin word meaning 'girded up'

succour (suk-uh)
noun **1** someone or something that gives help, relief or aid
verb **2** to help or relieve in difficulty, need, or distress

Word use: You can also use **succor**.
Word history: Middle English, from Anglo-French, Old French word meaning 'to help', from Latin

succulent (suk-yuh-luhnt)
adjective juicy: *a **succulent** steak*

Word building: **succulence** *noun*
Word history: Latin

succumb (suh-kum)
verb to yield or give way: *She **succumbed** to the disease. | He **succumbed** to temptation.* (***capitulate***, ***give in***, ***submit***, ***surrender***)

Word history: late Middle English, from Latin

such
adjective **1** of the kind, type, degree, extent, etc., shown or suggested: ***Such** a man is dangerous.*
2 of that particular kind or type: *The food, **such** as it was, was plentiful.*
3 similar: *tea, coffee and **such** goods*
phrase **4 such as**,
a of the kind named: *People **such as** these are not to be trusted.*
b for example: *He likes outdoor sports **such as** tennis and football.*

suck
verb **1** to draw in with the mouth: *to **suck** lemonade through a straw*
2 to hold and move about in the mouth until melted or dissolved: *to **suck** a lolly*
3 to draw in: *Cold air is **sucked** in through the window.*

Word building: **suck** *noun*
Word history: Old English *sūcan*

sucker
noun **1** someone or something that sucks
2 a baby or a young animal that is suckled
3 a part or organ of an animal adapted for sucking nourishment or for sticking to an object as by suction
4 *Colloquial* a person easily deceived or taken advantage of
5 a shoot rising from an underground stem or a root

suckle
verb to nurse or feed milk to from the breast: *The cow **suckled** her calf.*

Word history: from *suck*

sucrose (soohk-rohz, soohk-rohs)
noun a crystalline carbohydrate, obtained from sugar cane, sugar beet, etc.

Word history: French *sucr(e)* sugar + *-ose*

suction
noun the power of sucking produced when the pressure of the air inside something is less than the outside pressure

Word history: Latin

sudden
adjective happening quickly and without warning (***abrupt***, ***impromptu***, ***impulsive***, ***snap***)

Word use: The opposite of this is **gradual**.
Word building: **suddenly** *adverb* **suddenness** *noun*
Word history: Middle English, from Anglo-French, from Latin

sudden infant death syndrome
noun the sudden, unexplained death of an apparently healthy baby, usually while asleep

Word use: The abbreviation is **SIDS**. | A **cot death** is an instance of this syndrome.

sudoku (suh-doh-kooh)
noun a logic puzzle in which the solution depends on correctly inserting digits from 1 to 9 in a grid so that in each row and each column and in each marked subset within the grid each digit occurs only once

Word history: Japanese: single digit

suds
plural noun soapy water with bubbles

Word history: from Middle Dutch word meaning 'marsh'

sue
verb to bring a legal action against: *He is **suing** the makers of the faulty machine.*

Word history: Middle English, from Anglo-French, from Vulgar Latin

suede (swayd)
noun a soft leather with a slightly furry surface

Word history: French word literally meaning 'Sweden'

suet (sooh-uht)
noun a hard, dry fat surrounding the kidneys of animals and used in cooking

Word history: Middle English, from Anglo-French

suffer
verb **1** to feel pain or unhappiness: *She **suffers** from asthma.* | *He has **suffered** for a long time.*
2 to put up with: *She **suffered** their insults quietly.* (***endure***, ***stick out***, ***tolerate***)

Word history: Latin

sufferance (suf-uh-ruhns, suf-ruhns)
noun **1** tolerance
phrase **2 on sufferance**, reluctantly tolerated: *I had the distinct feeling that I was there **on sufferance** and that they would have preferred me to stay away.*

suffice
verb to be enough: *Three lamingtons will **suffice**, thank you.* (***fill the bill***, ***qualify***, ***serve***, ***suit***)

Word history: Latin

sufficient
adjective enough (***adequate***, ***decent***, ***satisfactory***)

Word use: The opposite of this is **insufficient** or **deficient**.
Word building: **sufficiency** *noun*
Word history: Middle English, from Latin word meaning 'sufficing'

suffix
noun a word part added to the end of a word, such as '-ness' in *kindness*

Word history: from Neo-Latin word meaning 'fastened on'

For a list of **prefixes and suffixes**, see appendixes, page 975.

suffocate
verb **1** to kill by stopping from breathing: *The murderer **suffocated** the victim with a pillow.* (***asphyxiate***, ***choke***, ***smother***, ***stifle***, ***strangle***)
2 to die from lack of air

Word building: **suffocation** *noun*
Word history: from Latin word meaning 'choked'

suffrage (suf-rij)
noun the right of voting, especially in political elections

Word history: Middle English, from Latin

suffuse (suh-fyoohz)
verb to lightly spread with or as if with a liquid, colour, etc.: *Her face was **suffused** with pink.*

Word building: **suffusion** *noun* **suffusive** *adjective*
Word history: from Latin word meaning 'overspread'

sugar
noun a sweet substance made mainly from cane and beet and used widely in food

Word building: **sugary** *adjective*
Word history: Middle English, from Medieval Latin, from Arabic

sugar beet
noun a variety of beet with a white root, grown for its sugar

sugar cane
noun a tall grass, of tropical and warm areas, having a stout, jointed stalk, being the chief source of sugar

Word use: You can also use **sugarcane**.

suggest (suh-<u>jest</u>)
verb to put forward the idea of: *She **suggested** a game of chess.* (***advise***, ***advocate***, ***propose***, ***recommend***)

Word history: from Latin word meaning 'placed under', 'added'

suggestible
adjective easily influenced

suggestion
noun **1** the act or result of suggesting
2 something suggested (***piece of advice***, ***pointer***, ***recommendation***, ***tip***)
3 a slight trace: *just a **suggestion** of a foreign accent*

suggestive
adjective suggesting something, especially something improper

suicide (<u>sooh</u>-uh-suyd)
noun **1** the act of killing yourself deliberately: *to commit **suicide***
2 someone who does this

Word building: **suicidal** *adjective* **suicide** *verb*
Word history: Neo-Latin

suit (sooht)
noun **1** a set of clothes meant to be worn together
2 one of the four sets in a pack of cards
verb **3** to fit or be convenient: *Tomorrow will **suit** quite well.* (***fill the bill***, ***qualify***, ***serve***, ***suffice***)
4 to be convenient to: *It **suits** me to go on Thursday.*
5 to look attractive on: *That colour **suits** you.*

Word history: Middle English, from Anglo-French word meaning 'follow'

> **suit / suite**
> Don't confuse **suit** with **suite**, which is a group of rooms.

suitable
adjective **1** fitting or convenient: *a **suitable** time*
2 appropriate or right for the occasion: ***suitable** clothes*

Word building: **suitability** *noun*

suitcase
noun an oblong bag for carrying clothes and other things when you travel

suite (sweet)
noun a series or set, especially of furniture or rooms

Word history: French

> **suite / suit**
> Don't confuse **suite** with **suit**, which is a set of clothes.

> **suite / sweet**
> Don't confuse **suite** with **sweet**, which is a lolly or a dessert.

sukiyaki (soo-kee-<u>ah</u>-kee)
noun a Japanese dish of fried meat, vegetables etc., usually cooked with soy sauce

sulfur (<u>sul</u>-fuh)
noun a non-metallic element which exists in several forms, usually a yellow crystalline solid, and which burns with a blue flame and a suffocating smell; used in making gunpowder, matches, rubber, medicine, etc.

Word use: This scientific meaning used to be written **sulphur**.

sulk
verb to be bad-tempered and silent because you feel that you have been unfairly treated

Word building: **sulky** *adjective* (**sulkier**, **sulkiest**)

sullen
adjective angry, silent, and ill-mannered (***gloomy***, ***moody***, ***morose***, ***surly***)

Word building: **sullenness** *noun*
Word history: Middle English, from Anglo-French word meaning 'sole[1]'

sully (<u>sul</u>-ee)
verb **1** to soil, stain or tarnish: ***sullied** goods*
2 to spoil the purity of: *He **sullied** the good name of the family.* (***defile***, ***disgrace***, ***dishonour***)

Word history: Old English *(ā)solian* become dirty

sulphur (<u>sul</u>-fuh)
noun → **sulfur**

sulphur-crested cockatoo
noun a large common parrot, mainly white, with yellow under the wings and tail, and a forward curving yellow crest, found in Australia, New Guinea and nearby islands

Word use: Another name is **white cockatoo**.

sultan
noun a Muslim ruler

Word building: **sultanate** *noun*
Word history: Medieval Latin, from Arabic word meaning 'king', 'ruler', 'power'

sultana
noun **1** a small, green, seedless grape
2 dried fruit made from such a grape
3 a wife or any close female relative of a sultan

Word history: Italian word for a female sultan

sultry
adjective hot and humid: *It was a **sultry** day, before the thunderstorm.* (***close***, ***muggy***, ***oppressive***)

Word building: **sultriness** *noun*
Word history: *sulter* (variant of *swelter*) + *-y*

sum
noun **1** a total: *The **sum** of 183 and 17 is 200.*
2 an exercise or problem in arithmetic
3 an amount: *a **sum** of money*
phrase **4 sum up**,
a to add up
b to express in a shortened form: *It is difficult to **sum up** what he said.* (***condense***, ***summarise***)
c to form an opinion about: *She **summed** him **up** at once.*

Verb forms: I **summed**, I have **summed**, I am **summing**
Word history: from Latin word meaning 'highest'

sum / some
Don't confuse **sum** with **some**, which means 'a few or a little'.

summarise
verb **1** to state or express in a clear, short form: *The secretary* ***summarised*** *the points raised in the meeting.* (***condense***, ***sum up***)
2 to be a summary of: *The concluding remarks* ***summarised*** *the gist of the speech.*
Word use: You can also use **summarize**.

summary
noun a short statement in speech or writing giving the main points of something (***precis***, ***synopsis***)
Noun forms: The plural is **summaries**.
Word history: Middle English, from Medieval Latin, from Latin word meaning 'sum'

summer
noun the warmest season of the year
Word building: **summery** *adjective*
Word history: Old English *sumor*

summit
noun the top or highest point: *the* ***summit*** *of a hill* | *the* ***summit*** *of her career* (***apex***, ***crest***, ***peak***, ***pinnacle***)
Word history: late Middle English, from French, from Latin word meaning 'highest'

summon
verb to send for officially: *They* ***summoned*** *him to appear before the committee.*
Word history: from Latin word meaning 'suggest'

summons
noun an order to appear at a particular place, especially a court of law (***command***, ***decree***)
Noun forms: The plural is **summonses**.
Word history: Middle English, from Anglo-French, Old French word meaning 'summon'

sump
noun **1** a pit, well, etc., in which water or other liquid is collected
2 a container situated at the lowest point in a circulating system, such as an internal-combustion engine, which collects oil
Word history: Middle English, from Middle Low German or Middle Dutch

sumptuous (sump-chooh-uhs)
adjective rich and luxurious: *a* ***sumptuous*** *home*
Word history: late Middle English, from Latin word meaning 'expensive'

sun
noun **1** the star which is the centre of our solar system and which gives light and warmth to the earth
2 sunshine: *a seat in the* ***sun***
phrase **3 under the sun**, anywhere on earth
Word building: **sunny** *adjective* (**sunnier**, **sunniest**) **sunless** *adjective* **sunlight** *noun*
Word use: **Solar** is the adjective meaning 'having to do with the sun'.
Word history: Middle English and Old English *sunne*

sunbake
verb Australian to lie or sit in the sun in order to become tanned

sunblock
noun → **sunscreen** (definition 1)

sunburn
noun painful reddening of the skin caused by being burnt by the heat of the sun
Word building: **sunburnt** *adjective*

suncream
noun → **sunscreen** (definition 1)

sundae
noun an ice-cream served with flavoured syrup and chopped nuts

Sunday
noun the first day of the week, following Saturday
Word history: Middle English; Old English *sunnandæg*

sunder
verb to separate or become separated
Word history: Middle English; late Old English *sundrian*

sundial
noun an instrument which tells the time by a shadow cast on its face, which is marked in hours like a clock

sundry (sun-dree)
adjective **1** various or miscellaneous: ***sundry*** *persons* | ***sundry*** *expenses*
noun **2 sundries**,
a sundry things or items
b *Cricket* a score made other than by hitting the ball with the bat, such as a bye or wide
phrase **3 all and sundry**, everyone
Word history: Middle English; Old English *syndrig* private, separate

sunflower
noun a tall plant with big yellow flowers and seeds which you can eat

sung
verb past tense and past participle of **sing**

sunglasses
plural noun spectacles with darkened lenses to protect your eyes from the glare of the sun

sunk
verb a past tense and past participle of **sink**

sunken
verb **1** a past participle of **sink**
adjective **2** sunk or having been sunk beneath the surface: *a* ***sunken*** *ship* (***submerged***, ***underwater***)
3 having settled down to a lower level: ***sunken*** *walls*
4 lying below the general level: *a* ***sunken*** *garden*
5 hollow: ***sunken*** *cheeks*

Sunna (sun-uh)
noun the traditional part of Muslim law, claimed to be based on the words and acts of Mohammed

sunrise
noun the appearance of the sun above the horizon in the morning or the time when this happens

sunscreen
noun **1** a cream which protects the skin against damage from the rays of the sun
2 a screen which gives shelter from the sun

Word use: Other names for definition 1 are **sunblock**, **suncream** and **blockout**.

sunset
noun the disappearance of the sun below the horizon at night or the time when this happens

sunshine
noun **1** the light of the sun
2 cheerfulness or brightness

sunspot
noun one of the dark patches on the surface of the sun which is believed to affect some things on earth, such as the weather

sunstroke
noun a sickness with weakness and a high temperature caused by being in the sun for too long

suntan
noun brownness of the skin caused by being out in the sun

Word building: **suntanned** *adjective*

super
adjective Colloquial extremely good or pleasing: *a **super** effort | a **super** holiday* (***excellent***, ***great***, ***splendid***, ***superb***)

superannuation (sooh-puh-ran-yooh-ay-shuhn)
noun Australian, NZ **1** a pension or allowance paid to a person, especially someone who has retired from work on account of age and infirmity
2 a sum of money paid regularly by an employee to a superannuation fund

superb
adjective excellent or splendid: *a **superb** performance | **superb** beauty* (***great***, ***wonderful***)

Word history: from Latin word meaning 'proud', 'distinguished'

superbug
noun a bacterium which has adapted so that it has become resistant to all existing antibiotics

supercilious (sooh-puh-sil-ee-uhs)
adjective proud and scornful: *a **supercilious** person | a **supercilious** look* (***arrogant***, ***contemptuous***, ***disdainful***, ***haughty***, ***snobbish***)

Word building: **superciliously** *adverb* **superciliousness** *noun*
Word history: Latin

supercontinent
noun any great landmass that existed in the geological past and split into smaller landmasses

superficial
adjective **1** having to do with the outside or surface: *a **superficial** cut*
2 being on the outside only, rather than real or deep: *a **superficial** similarity between two people | **superficial** sorrow*
3 caring only about how things appear on the surface: *a **superficial** writer*

Word building: **superficiality** *noun*
Word history: Middle English, from Late Latin, from Latin

superfluous (sooh-per-flooh-uhs)
adjective more than is needed: *There were so many helpers that he was **superfluous**.* (***excessive***, ***extra***, ***redundant***, ***surplus***, ***unnecessary***)

Word building: **superfluity** *noun* **superfluously** *adverb* **superfluousness** *noun*
Word history: Middle English, from Latin word meaning 'overflowing'

superimpose (sooh-puh-rim-pohz)
verb **1** to place, or set on or over something else
2 to put or join as an addition

superintend
verb to supervise

superintendent
noun someone who is in charge of work, a business, or a building (***administrator***, ***boss***, ***director***, ***manager***)

superior (suh-pear-ree-uh)
adjective **1** higher in position or rank: *a **superior** officer*
2 better or of higher quality: ***superior** intelligence*
3 greater in amount: *They beat us because of **superior** numbers.*
noun **4** someone who is higher in rank than you: *You have to be careful how you speak to your **superiors**.*

Word building: **superiority** *noun*
Word history: Middle English, from Latin word meaning 'above'

superlative (sooh-per-luh-tiv)
adjective **1** of the highest or best kind: *a **superlative** voice | **superlative** skill*
2 having to do with the form of an adjective or adverb which expresses the greatest degree of comparison: *'Smoothest' is the **superlative** form of 'smooth' and 'most easily' is the **superlative** form of 'easily'.*

Word use: Compare definition 2 with **comparative.**
Word history: Middle English, from Late Latin, from Latin word meaning 'carried beyond'

supermarket
noun a large, self-service shop selling food and other household goods

supernatural
adjective not able to be explained in terms of the laws of nature: *A ghost is a **supernatural** being.*

Word building: **supernatural** *noun*

supernova
noun Astronomy the sudden collapse of a giant star resulting in an explosion of stellar matter and energy into space

Noun forms: The plural is **supernovas** or **supernovae** (sooh-puh-noh-vee).

superpower
noun an extremely powerful and influential nation

supersede (sooh-puh-seed)
verb **1** to replace in power, office, effectiveness, acceptance, use, etc.: *Electricity has **superseded***

gas as a means of lighting. (***replace***, ***supplant***)
2 to set aside as useless or out of date

Word history: from Latin word meaning 'sit above'

supersize
adjective unusually large: ***supersize*** *ice-creams*

supersonic
adjective moving faster than the speed of sound: *a* ***supersonic*** *jet*

superstar
noun an entertainer or actor who is very famous

superstition
noun a belief about the meaning of a thing or event that does not stem from reason or sensible thought: *There is a* ***superstition*** *that if you break a mirror you get seven years' bad luck.*

Word building: **superstitious** *adjective* **superstitiously** *adverb*
Word history: Middle English, from Latin word meaning 'a standing over', as in wonder or awe

superstitious / suspicious

Don't confuse **superstitious** with **suspicious**.

People who are **superstitious** believe that certain things or events bring them good or bad luck.

When a person is **suspicious** of someone or something, they feel wary and distrustful of them.

superstructure (<u>sooh</u>-puh-struk-chuh)
noun **1** all of a structure above the basement or foundation
2 any structure built on something else
3 the parts of a ship built above the main deck

supertonic
noun the second note of a musical scale, being the next above the tonic

supervise
verb to direct, or manage: *to* ***supervise*** *a class | to* ***supervise*** *a job* (***control***, ***govern***, ***rule***, ***run***)

Word building: **supervision** *noun* **supervisor** *noun* **supervisory** *adjective*
Word history: Medieval Latin

supine (<u>sooh</u>-puyn)
adjective **1** lying on the back, with the face or front upwards
2 inactive or passive, especially from laziness or lack of interest

Word history: Latin

supper
noun a light meal eaten in the evening

Word history: Middle English, from Old French word meaning 'sup' (to eat the evening meal)

supplant
verb to take the place of: *He has* ***supplanted*** *her as captain of the team.*

Word history: Middle English, from Latin word meaning 'trip up', 'overthrow'

supple
adjective flexible or bending easily: *an athlete with a* ***supple*** *body | a* ***supple*** *cane* (***floppy***, ***malleable***, ***pliable***)

Word history: Middle English, from Old French, from Latin word meaning 'bending under'

supplement (<u>sup</u>-luh-muhnt)
noun **1** something added to complete or correct: *Two hundred new words are listed in the* ***supplement*** *of the dictionary.*
2 an extra part of a newspaper on a particular subject: *an educational* ***supplement***
verb (<u>sup</u>-luh-ment) **3** to add to: *She* ***supplements*** *her pocket money by babysitting.*

Word building: **supplementation** *noun*
Word history: Middle English, from Latin

supplementary
adjective additional: ***supplementary*** *information*

supplicate (<u>sup</u>-luh-kayt)
verb to pray or ask humbly

Word building: **supplication** *noun* **supplicatory** *adjective*
Word history: late Middle English, from Latin word meaning 'begged'

supply
verb **1** to provide: *to* ***supply*** *a school with books | to* ***supply*** *books to a school* (***equip***, ***furnish***)
noun **2** an amount of something provided or available for use: *We have a good* ***supply*** *of paper.* (***quantity***, ***stock***, ***store***)
3 supplies, a store of materials, food, etc.: *He was in charge of the army's* ***supplies***.

Verb forms: I **supplied**, I have **supplied**, I am **supplying**
Noun forms: The plural is **supplies**.
Word building: **supplier** *noun*
Word history: Middle English, from Old French, from Latin word meaning 'fill up'

supply bill
noun in parliament, a bill to organise the money which the government needs to carry out its business

support
verb **1** to hold up: *to* ***support*** *a weight | a wall that* ***supports*** *a building* (***secure***, ***stabilise***, ***steady***)
2 to give help or strength to: *He* ***supported*** *her with kindness and advice. | I have information to* ***support*** *my argument.* (***aid***, ***assist***)
3 to believe in and help: *They* ***support*** *the Labor Party. | He* ***supports*** *the local football team.*
4 to supply with money or other things needed for living: *He works to* ***support*** *his family.*
noun **5** the providing of support: *I need your* ***support***.
6 something that gives support: *This pole is one of the* ***supports*** *of the tent.* (***base***, ***foundation***, ***framework***, ***skeleton***)

Word building: **supporter** *noun* **supportive** *adjective*
Word history: Middle English, from Old French word meaning 'bear', from Latin word meaning 'convey'

suppose
verb **1** to assume or take as being a fact: *Let us* ***suppose*** *that everything will go well.*
2 to think or believe without having actual knowledge: *I* ***suppose*** *that you are right. | Do you* ***suppose*** *it was an accident?* (***conclude***, ***guess***, ***reckon***, ***suspect***)

Word building: **supposition** *noun*
Word history: Middle English, from Old French

supposed
adjective **1** thought to be probable: *his **supposed** victory*
phrase **2 supposed to**, expected or meant to: *You are **supposed to** be here at 9 o'clock every morning.*

Word building: **supposedly** *adverb*

suppository (suh-poz-uh-tree)
noun a solid, medicinal substance put into the rectum or vagina where it dissolves

Noun forms: The plural is **suppositories**.
Word history: Late Latin, from Latin word meaning 'placed under'

suppress
verb **1** to abolish or put an end to: *The government **suppressed** street demonstrations.*
2 to keep inside or hidden: *He **suppressed** a yawn. | They **suppressed** the news of his death.*

Word building: **suppression** *noun* **suppressive** *adjective* **suppressor** *noun*
Word history: Middle English, from Latin word meaning 'put down'

suppurate (sup-yuh-rayt)
verb to produce or discharge pus: *a **suppurating** wound*

Word building: **suppuration** *noun* **suppurative** *adjective*
Word history: from Latin word meaning 'caused to secrete pus'

supreme
adjective **1** highest in position or power: *the **supreme** commander*
2 greatest: ***supreme** courage | **supreme** hatred*

Word building: **supremacy** *noun*
Word history: from Latin word meaning 'that is above'

surcharge (ser-chahj)
noun **1** an additional charge for payment, tax, etc.
2 an excessive sum or price charged
3 a mark printed over a postage stamp which alters or restates its face value
verb (ser-chahj, ser-chahj) **4** to charge an additional sum for payment
5 to over-charge
6 to overload

Word history: Middle English, from Old French

sure
adjective **1** certain, or confident: *I am **sure** of what I am saying. | He is **sure** of success.* (***clear***, ***definite***, ***positive***)
2 able to be trusted: *a **sure** messenger*
3 firm: *to stand on **sure** ground*
4 never missing or slipping: *a **sure** aim with a gun*
adverb **5** *Colloquial* surely or certainly: *You **sure** were lucky.*
phrase **6 for sure**, as a certainty
7 make sure, to be certain: ***Make sure** that you lock the door when you leave.*

Word building: **sureness** *noun*
Word history: Middle English, from Old French, from Latin word meaning 'secure'

sure / shore
Don't confuse **sure** with **shore**, which is the land along the edge of the sea or a lake.

surely
adverb **1** firmly or steadily: *He ran slowly but **surely**.*
2 almost certainly: *It will **surely** be fine tomorrow.*

surely / surly
Don't confuse **surely** with **surly**, which rhymes with *curly*, and means 'gruff and bad-tempered'.

surety (shaw-ruh-tee, shooh-ruh-tee)
noun **1** security against loss, damage, non-fulfilment of an obligation, non-payment of a debt, etc. (***bond***, ***guarantee***)
2 a certainty
3 something which gives confidence or safety
4 someone who is legally answerable for the debt, etc., of another

Noun forms: The plural is **sureties**.
Word history: Middle English, from Old French, from Latin

surf
noun **1** the swell of the sea which breaks upon a shore: *We could see the line of the **surf** up ahead.*
2 the mass or line of foamy water caused by the breaking of the sea upon a shore, etc.: *The **surf** is very rough today.*
3 a time spent in the surf, swimming, etc., or especially riding a surfboard: *Let's go for a **surf**.*
verb **4** to take part in surfing: *They **surfed** all day Sunday.*
5 *Colloquial* to explore an information network: *I've learned to **surf** the internet.*

surf / serf
Don't confuse **surf** with **serf**, which was a peasant in medieval times.

surface
noun **1** the outer part or side of anything: *a polished **surface** | the six **surfaces** of a cube* (***exterior***, ***facade***, ***outside***)
2 the top, especially of water or other liquid: *I swam up to the **surface**.*
3 outside appearance: *He was calm on the **surface** but felt frightened inside.*
verb **4** to rise to the surface: *The diver **surfaced**.*
5 to give a surface to: *He **surfaced** the path with gravel.*

Word history: French

surface tension
noun a property of liquids due to unbalanced molecular forces near the surface, leading to the apparent presence of a surface film

surfboard
noun a long narrow board used to ride waves towards the shore

surfeit (ser-fuht)
noun **1** too great an amount (***excess***, ***glut***, ***superabundance***)
2 disgust caused by too much of anything

Word history: Middle English, from Old French word meaning 'excess'

surfing
noun the sport of riding waves towards the shore, either by standing on a surfboard or by allowing your body to be carried along by the wave

Word use: You can also use **bodysurfing** when you do not use a surfboard.
Word building: **surfer** *noun*

surf lifesaving
noun lifesaving which is appropriate for emergency situations occurring on surf beaches

surf shirt
noun **1** a garment worn with a swimming costume to protect the upper body from sunburn, usually made from a light synthetic fabric and having short or long sleeves
2 a loose, short-sleeved, men's casual shirt, usually brightly patterned

Word use: You can also use **rash shirt** for definition 1.

surge
noun **1** a wave-like rush or forward movement: *a **surge** of anger | the **surge** of a crowd*
verb **2** to rush forwards or upwards in waves or like waves: *The crowd **surged** around the Prime Minister's car. | Blood **surged** to his face.* (***flow***, ***gush***, ***spurt***, ***stream***, ***wash***)

> **surge / serge**
> Don't confuse **surge** with **serge**, which is a kind of rough material.

surgeon (<u>ser</u>-juhn)
noun a doctor who does surgery

Word history: Middle English, from Anglo-French

surgery
noun **1** the treatment of diseases or injuries by using instruments to cut into the body
2 the room of a doctor or dentist, where patients go for treatment

Word building: **surgical** *adjective*
Word history: Middle English, from Old French

surly
adjective unfriendly and bad-tempered: *a **surly** person | a **surly** voice* (***gloomy***, ***miserable***, ***morose***, ***sullen***)

Adjective forms: **surlier**, **surliest**
Word history: variant of obsolete *sirly* lordly

surmise (ser-<u>muyz</u>)
verb to think something without certain or strong evidence (***conjecture***, ***guess***)

Word history: Middle English from Old French word meaning 'accuse'

surmount (ser-<u>mownt</u>)
verb **1** to get on the top of: *The walkers **surmounted** the hill.*
2 to get over or across: *If you can **surmount** these problems, you will be in a far better position.* (***overcome***, ***triumph over***)
3 to be on top of or above: *a statue **surmounting** a pillar*

Word history: Middle English, from Old French

surname
noun someone's family name: *Her first name is Jane and her **surname** is Brown.*

Word history: Middle English, from French

surpass
verb to be better than: *This painting **surpasses** all your other ones.*

Word history: French

surplice (<u>ser</u>-pluhs)
noun a loose, white piece of clothing, worn in church by choir singers and by some priests and ministers on top of their other clothes

Word history: Middle English, from Anglo-French, from Old French word meaning 'over-fur (garment)'

surplus (<u>ser</u>-pluhs)
noun an amount that is more than what is needed or used: *Australia has a wheat **surplus** after several seasons of good rainfall.* (***excess***, ***glut***, ***oversupply***)

Word use: The opposite of this is **deficit**.
Word building: **surplus** *adjective*
Word history: Middle English, from Old French

surprise
verb **1** to fill with a feeling of shock and wonder because of being unexpected or very unusual: *Her sudden outburst of anger **surprised** me.* (***amaze***, ***astonish***, ***astound***, ***stun***)
2 to come upon suddenly and unexpectedly: *He **surprised** me as I was creeping out the back door.* (***catch***)
noun **3** something that surprises: *Your present was a lovely **surprise**.*
4 the feeling of being surprised: *She shouted with **surprise**.*
adjective **5** sudden and unexpected: *a **surprise** attack*

Word history: late Middle English, from French word meaning 'surprise'

surprising
adjective astonishing or extraordinary: *What a **surprising** thing to happen!*

surrender
verb to give up to the ownership or power of someone or something else: *He **surrendered** his gun to the policeman. | I have **surrendered** to despair.* (***capitulate***, ***give in***, ***submit***, ***succumb***, ***yield***)

Word building: **surrender** *noun*
Word history: late Middle English, from Anglo-French

surreptitious (sur-uhp-<u>tish</u>-uhs)
adjective **1** obtained, done, or made in a secret or stealthy way: *a **surreptitious** glance* (***cagey***, ***furtive***, ***secret***, ***secretive***, ***underhand***)
2 acting in a secret or stealthy way

Word history: late Middle English, from Latin word meaning 'snatched away secretly'

surrogate (<u>su</u>-ruh-guht)
noun **1** someone appointed to act for another (***deputy***, ***stand-in***)
2 something that takes the place of another thing (***replacement***, ***substitute***)

Word history: from Latin word meaning 'put in another's place'

surround
verb to encompass or go around completely: *A wooden fence **surrounds** our house.* | *A feeling of sadness **surrounded** them.* (***box in***, ***confine***, ***encircle***, ***enclose***)

Word history: late Middle English, from Anglo-French, from Late Latin word meaning 'overflow'

surroundings
plural noun everything that is around or near someone or something: *Everyone is affected by their **surroundings**.* (***environs***, ***scene***, ***setting***)

surveillance (ser-vay-luhns)
noun a watch kept over a person, especially a suspect, prisoner, or someone like this

Word building: **surveillant** *adjective*
Word history: French

survey (ser-vay, ser-vay)
verb **1** to take a general view of: *We **surveyed** the surrounding countryside from the hill.* (***examine***, ***inspect***, ***look over***, ***scan***)
2 to ask the views of, in order to write a report about what people think or do: *You need to **survey** the public on this matter.*
3 to find out the form and boundaries of land by measuring: *The council **surveyed** the area.*
noun (ser-vay) **4** an act of surveying: *They did a **survey** to see what people thought about daylight saving.* (***analysis***, ***examination***, ***inquiry***, ***investigation***, ***poll***)
5 a report or map made after surveying

Noun forms: The plural is **surveys**.
Word history: Middle English, from Old French, from Latin

surveyor
noun someone whose job is taking surveys, particularly of land

survive
verb to remain alive or in existence, especially after someone else's death, or after something has ended or died out: *Of the four who set out on the expedition, only one **survived**.* | *The singer's popularity has **survived** through many music fads.* (***continue***, ***endure***, ***hold out***, ***last***, ***persist***)

Word building: **survival** *noun* **survivor** *noun*
Word history: late Middle English, from Anglo-French

surviving
adjective remaining: *He is the only **surviving** member of the family.*

susceptible (suh-sep-tuh-buhl)
phrase **susceptible to**, easily affected by: *He is **susceptible to** colds.* | *She is **susceptible to** praise.* (***open to***, ***vulnerable to***)

Word building: **susceptibility** *noun*
Word history: Medieval Latin, from Latin word meaning 'taken up'

sushi (soosh-ee, soohsh-ee)
noun (in Japanese cookery) any of various preparations of boiled Japanese rice flavoured with a sweetened rice vinegar and combined with toppings or fillings of raw seafood, vegetables, seaweed, etc.

Word history: Japanese, meaning literally 'it is sour', with reference to the fact that food is flavoured or eaten with condiments such as rice vinegar and pickled vegetables

suspect (suh-spekt)
verb **1** to think to be guilty or bad without certain knowledge: *I **suspected** him of being a thief.* (***believe***, ***reckon***)
2 to think to be likely: *I **suspect** that he is not very happy.*
noun (sus-pekt) **3** someone who is suspected, especially of a crime: *The police have three **suspects**.*
adjective (sus-pekt) **4** open to suspicion: *Your story is very **suspect**.*

Word history: Middle English, from Latin

suspend
verb **1** to hang by being joined to something above: *I will **suspend** the curtains from this rail.*
2 to put off until a later time: *The judge **suspended** the criminal's sentence for six months.* (***adjourn***, ***defer***, ***delay***, ***postpone***, ***shelve***)
3 to remove for a time from a position or membership: *The principal **suspended** him for bad behaviour.*

Word history: Middle English, from Latin

suspended
adjective hanging: *light bulbs **suspended** from the ceiling*

suspender
noun an elastic strap with fasteners to hold up a woman's stockings

suspense
noun an anxious state of mind caused by having to wait to find something out: *He was in **suspense** until he heard the results of the exams.*

Word building: **suspenseful** *adjective*
Word history: Middle English, from Anglo-French word meaning 'in suspense', from Latin word meaning 'suspended'

suspension
noun **1** a suspending or being suspended
2 a liquid in which very small parts of a solid substance are mixed but not dissolved
3 the system of springs, etc., used in a vehicle to limit the effect of the jolting of the wheels, etc.

Word history: Late Latin

suspicion (suh-spish-uhn)
noun **1** the feeling of suspecting: *He looked at her with **suspicion**.*
2 the condition of being suspected: *He is under **suspicion**.*
3 a slight trace showing: *She gave the **suspicion** of a smile.*

Word history: late Middle English, from Latin

suspicious (suh-spish-uhs)
adjective **1** distrustful: *a **suspicious** mind*
2 causing you to believe that something bad is happening: *the **suspicious** activities of the local gang*

Word use: The opposite of definition 1 is **trusting**.
Word building: **suspiciously** *adverb*

suspicious / superstitious
Look up **superstitious / suspicious**.

suss
adjective Colloquial **1** suspect or suspicious: *Her story was pretty* ***suss.***
phrase **2 suss out,** to find out about something: *See if you can* ***suss out*** *how much she earns.*

Word history: independent use of first element of *suspect* or *suspicious*

sustain
verb **1** to hold up or support: *I can't* ***sustain*** *your weight for long.* (***keep, maintain, preserve, prolong, retain***)
2 to suffer or have happen to you: *She* ***sustained*** *a terrible injury in the car accident.*
3 to keep up, or keep going: *It's hard to* ***sustain*** *a conversation with him. | This drink should* ***sustain*** *you until we get there.*

Word history: Middle English, from Old French, from Latin

sustainable
adjective **1** able to be sustained
2 designed or having the capacity to continue operating perpetually, by avoiding adverse effects on the natural environment and depletion of natural resources: *a* ***sustainable*** *transport system |* ***sustainable*** *forestry*

Word building: **sustainability** *noun* **sustainably** *adverb*

sustainable development
noun economic development that takes into account the future cost of impacts on the environment and the decline of natural resources

sustenance
noun things that make living possible, such as food and money

suture (sooh-chuh)
noun **1** *Surgery*
a the joining of the edges of a wound, etc., by stitching or some similar process
b one of the stitches used
2 *Anatomy* the line where two bones meet, especially in the skull
verb **3** to join by or as if by a suture

Word history: Latin

svelte (svelt, sfelt)
adjective slender: *a* ***svelte*** *figure*

swab (swob)
noun a piece of sponge, cloth or cottonwool, often on a stick, used for cleaning parts of your body, such as your mouth, or applying a medicine, etc.

swaddle (swod-uhl)
verb to wrap up tightly with clothes or strips of cloth: *to* ***swaddle*** *a newborn baby*

Word history: Old English *swæthel* swaddling band

swag
noun Australian, NZ a bundle or roll of belongings carried on the shoulders by someone travelling in the bush (***shiralee***)

Word building: **swagman** *noun*
Word history: British dialect *swag* to sway from side to side. The idea behind it is that the swaying is caused by a heavy burden so an overladen cart might swag, and so too might an overladen person. The word transferred to the burden or bundle that was causing the person to sway.

swagger
verb to walk pompously and proudly (***march, parade, stride, strut***)

Word building: **swagger** *noun*

swallow[1] (swol-oh)
verb **1** to take into the stomach through the throat
2 to take in and make disappear: *Darkness* ***swallowed*** *the hills. | My new car* ***swallowed*** *up most of my money.*
3 to believe without questioning: *Don't* ***swallow*** *everything he tells you.* (***accept, credit, take for granted, take on trust***)

Word building: **swallow** *noun*
Word history: Old English *swelgan*

swallow[2]
noun a small bird with long wings and a forked tail

Word history: Old English *swealwe*

swam
verb past tense of **swim**

swami (swah-mee)
noun a title for a Hindu religious teacher

Noun forms: The plural is **swamis.**
Word history: Hindustani word meaning 'master', from Sanskrit

swamp (swomp)
noun **1** an area of wet, soft ground (***bog, marsh, mire, quagmire***)
verb **2** to flood: *Water* ***swamped*** *our tent.* (***engulf, inundate, overwhelm***)

Word history: Middle English

swan (swon)
noun a large waterbird with a long, thin neck, either black or white in colour

Word history: Middle English and Old English

swank
noun Colloquial showy smartness in appearance or behaviour: *a person with a lot of* ***swank***

Word building: **swanky** *adjective* (**swankier, swankiest**)

swan song
noun the last appearance, work, achievement, etc., of someone, especially a composer, writer or actor, before their retirement or death

Word history: fabled last song of the dying swan

swap (swop)
verb to exchange: *We* ***swapped*** *beds for the night.* (***substitute, transpose***)

Verb forms: I **swapped,** I have **swapped,** I am **swapping**
Word building: **swap** *noun*
Word history: Middle English

swarm (swawm)
noun **1** a large group of bees
2 a large number of people or things, especially when moving together
verb **3** to move in great numbers: *People* ***swarmed*** *into the cinema.*
phrase **4 swarm with,** to be covered or filled with: *This grass is* ***swarming with*** *ants.*

Word history: Middle English; Old English *swearm*

swarthy (swaw-dhee)
adjective dark in skin-colour

Adjective forms: **swarthier**, **swarthiest**
Word building: **swarthiness** *noun*
Word history: variant of *swarty*

swastika (swos-tik-uh)
noun **1** an ancient symbol or ornament in the form of a cross with arms of equal length, each continuing at right angles, and all pointing in the same direction, clockwise or anticlockwise
2 this figure adapted with clockwise arms as the official emblem of the Nazi Party and the Third Reich

Word history: from Sanskrit word meaning 'wellbeing'

swat (swot)
verb to hit with a hard, quick blow

Verb forms: I **swatted**, I have **swatted**, I am **swatting**
Word history: originally variant of *squat*

swathe (swaydh)
verb to wrap up with strips of material or other wrappings: *She **swathed** her neck with a scarf.*

Word history: Middle English; late Old English *swathian*

sway
verb **1** to move or swing from side to side: *She **swayed** in time to the music.* | *The wind **swayed** the trees.*
2 to cause to think or act in a particular way: *His speech **swayed** most people to vote for him.*
noun **3** a swaying movement
4 control or rule: *The Prime Minister has held **sway** for many years.* (***clout***, ***hold***, ***influence***, ***power***)

Word history: Middle English, from Scandinavian

swear
verb **1** to make a very serious promise or oath: *I **swear** that I am speaking the truth.* | *He **swore** to keep the secret.*
2 to make swear: *I **swore** him to secrecy.*
3 to use language that is generally thought unpleasant or rude
4 to admit to office or service by administering an oath
phrase **5 swear by**,
a to name some sacred being or thing, as your witness for an action or statement
b to have confidence in

Verb forms: I **swore**, I have **sworn**, I am **swearing**
Word building: **swearer** *noun*
Word history: Old English *swerian*

sweat (swet)
verb **1** to give out a salty liquid through the skin: *This work has made me **sweat**.* (***perspire***)
noun **2** the liquid produced in sweating
phrase **3 sweat on**, to feel worried about losing: *I was **sweating on** getting that job.*

Word building: **sweaty** *adjective*
Word history: Old English *swǣtan*

sweater (swet-uh)
noun a knitted jumper

sweatshirt
noun a loose light jumper

sweep
verb **1** to clean or move away with a broom or brush: *to **sweep** a floor* | *to **sweep** dust away*
2 to push or touch with a light stroke: *She **swept** the hair from her face.* | *Her long dress **swept** the floor.*
3 to pass over or make pass over with a continuous movement: *Fire **swept** the countryside.* | *He **swept** a brush over the table.*
4 to move quickly and smoothly: *She **swept** out of the room.* | *His glance **swept** over the page.*
5 to stretch continuously: *The mountains **sweep** down to the sea.*
noun **6** the act of sweeping: *This floor needs a **sweep**.*
7 a swinging movement: *He gave a **sweep** of his arm.*
8 steady, forceful movement: *the **sweep** of the waves*
9 a continuous stretch: *a long **sweep** of sand*
10 someone whose job is sweeping, especially cleaning out chimneys

Word history: Middle English

sweeping
adjective wide-ranging: *a **sweeping** report*

sweepstake (sweep-stayk)
noun a type of lottery in which participants buy tickets giving them the chance of drawing the name of a competitor in a race or other contest, the outcome of the lottery depending on the result of the race

Word history: *sweep* + *stake*[2]

sweet
adjective **1** having a pleasant taste like that of sugar or honey (***candied***, ***glacé***, ***sugary***)
2 pleasant in any way: ***sweet** sounds* | *a **sweet** girl* | *a **sweet** face*
noun **3** something that is sweet, such as a lolly
4 a beloved person or sweetheart: *my sweet*
5 sweets, a dessert
interjection **6** *Colloquial* an exclamation of delight, reassurance or approval

Word building: **sweetly** *adverb* **sweetness** *noun*
Word history: Middle English and Old English *swēte*

> **sweet / suite**
> Don't confuse **sweet** with **suite**, which is a set of connecting rooms that makes one living area. It is also a set of furniture. In music it is a set of pieces written to go together.

sweetbread (sweet-bred)
noun the pancreas or thymus gland of an animal, especially a calf or a lamb, used for food

sweet corn
noun the yellow kernels or seeds of corn, which you can eat as a vegetable

sweeten
verb to make sweet

sweetheart
noun someone loved by a person

Word use: This is often used as a way of addressing someone.

sweet potato
noun a tropical plant with a root that you can eat as a vegetable

Noun forms: The plural is **sweet potatoes**.

swell
verb **1** to grow or make grow in size, amount or force: *The music **swelled** and then died away. | Rain **swelled** the river till it overflowed.*
2 to bulge out: *The sails **swelled** in the breeze.* (***billow***, ***fill out***, ***round out***)
noun **3** an increase in size, amount or force
4 the movement of the waves of the sea: *There is a big **swell** today.*
5 *Colloquial* someone who is rich and fashionably dressed
adjective **6** *Colloquial* excellent: *What a **swell** day for a picnic!*

Verb forms: it **swelled**, it has **swollen** or it has **swelled**, it is **swelling**
Word history: Middle English; Old English *swellan*

swelling
noun a swollen part

swelter
verb to feel very hot: *We **sweltered** all summer.* (***boil***, ***burn***, ***roast***)

Word building: **sweltering** *adjective*
Word history: Old English *sweltan*

swept
verb past tense and past participle of **sweep**

swerve
verb to turn aside suddenly: *The car **swerved** to miss the dog.* (***swing***, ***twist***, ***veer***)

Word building: **swerve** *noun*
Word history: Middle English; Old English *sweorfan* rub, file

swift
adjective fast or quick: *a **swift** ship | He is always **swift** to help.* (***express***, ***rapid***, ***speedy***)

Word building: **swiftly** *adjective* **swiftness** *noun*
Word history: Middle English and Old English

swill
noun **1** any liquid or partly liquid food for animals, especially pigs
verb **2** to drink greedily

Word history: Old English *swilian*

swim
verb **1** to move through water by movements of the arms, legs, fins or tail
2 to move across or along by swimming: *to **swim** a river*
3 to be dizzy or giddy: *My head was **swimming**.*
4 to be covered or flooded with a liquid: *My meat was **swimming** in gravy.*

Verb forms: I **swam**, I have **swum**, I am **swimming**
Word building: **swim** *noun* **swimmer** *noun*
Word history: Old English *swimman*

swimming costume
noun a piece of clothing to wear when you're swimming

swimsuit
noun a swimming costume

swindle
verb to cheat out of money (***defraud***, ***fleece***, ***rip off***)

Word building: **swindle** *noun* **swindler** *noun*

swine
noun **1** *Old-fashioned* a pig
2 *Colloquial* someone who is unpleasant or nasty

Noun forms: The plural is **swine**.
Word history: Middle English; Old English *swīn*

swing[1]
verb **1** to move or make move to and fro
2 to move or make move in a curve: *The car **swung** around the corner. | He **swung** open the door.*
noun **3** a swinging movement
4 a change, especially in the number of votes for a political party in an election: *a **swing** to Labor*
5 a seat hung from above on which you sit and swing to and fro for fun

Verb forms: I **swung**, I have **swung**, I am **swinging**
Word history: Middle English; Old English *swingan*

swing[2]
noun a kind of jazz music, often played by big bands

Word history: special use of *swing*[1]

swipe
verb *Colloquial* **1** to hit after taking a full swing with the arm: *He **swiped** me across the face.*
2 to steal: *She **swiped** my rubber.*

Word building: **swipe** *noun*
Word history: like *sweep*

swirl
verb **1** to move in a whirling way: *Water **swirled** around the rock.* (***gyrate***, ***spin***, ***twirl***, ***whirl***)
noun **2** a swirling movement or whirl
3 a pattern created by a whirling movement, as in a painting or the icing on a cake

Word building: **swirl** *noun* **swirly** *adjective*
Word history: perhaps imitative

swish
verb to move or make move with a hissing sound: *The whip **swished** through the air. | The horse **swished** its tail.*

Word building: **swish** *noun*
Word history: imitative

switch
verb **1** to change or turn: *to **switch** classes | to **switch** directions | to **switch** a conversation to another subject*
noun **2** a changing or turning: *a **switch** of plans*
3 a button for turning an electric current on or off, directing an electric current, or making or breaking a circuit
4 a thin cane used for whipping
5 *Australian Colloquial* → **switchboard**
phrase **6 switch off**, to make an electrical appliance stop: *to **switch off** a toaster*
7 switch on, to make an electrical appliance start: *to **switch on** a light*

switchboard
noun an arrangement of switches on a board, especially one that is used to connect telephone calls

Word use: You can also use the colloquial word **switch**.

swivel (swiv-uhl)
verb to turn around: *He **swivelled** around to have a better look.*

Word history: Middle English, from Scandinavian

swollen
verb past participle of **swell**

swoon
verb **1** *Old-fashioned* to faint or become unconscious: *The pain made her **swoon**.*
2 to have such a strong feeling as to almost faint: *She **swooned** over her favourite rock star.*

Word history: Old English *geswōgen* in a swoon

swoop
verb **1** to sweep down through the air: *The eagle **swooped** on the mouse.*
2 to come down in a sudden attack: *The army **swooped** down on the town.*

Word building: **swoop** *noun*
Word history: Old English *swāpan* sweep

sword (sawd)
noun **1** a weapon with a long, pointed blade fixed in a handle
phrase **2 cross swords,**
a to join in combat
b to disagree violently

Word history: Middle English; Old English *sweord*

swordfish (sawd-fish)
noun a large sea fish with a long, sharp upper jaw, like a sword

Noun forms: The plural is **swordfish** or **swordfishes.**

swore
verb past tense of **swear**

sworn
verb **1** past participle of **swear**
adjective **2** bound by or as if by an oath
3 determined or confirmed: *a **sworn** enemy*

swot
verb **1** to study hard: *You should not **swot** all the time. | **Swotting** books on fish psychology is not my idea of fun.*
noun **2** someone who studies hard

Word history: dialect variant of *sweat*

swum
verb past participle of **swim**

swung
verb past tense and past participle of **swing**[1]

sycophant (sik-uh-fant)
noun a self-seeking flatterer

Word building: **sycophancy** *noun* **sycophantic** *adjective*
Word history: Latin, from Greek word meaning 'slanderer', 'false accuser'

syllable (sil-uh-buhl)
noun a part of a word which consists of a vowel sound and possibly consonant sounds around the vowel: *'Along' has two **syllables** and 'wonderful' has three.*

Word building: **syllabic** (suh-lab-ik) *adjective*
Word history: Middle English, from Anglo-French, from Latin, from Greek

syllabus (sil-uh-buhs)
noun an outline of what is to be taught in a course of lessons

Noun forms: The plural is **syllabuses** or **syllabi.**
Word history: Neo-Latin

symbol
noun **1** something that stands for or means something else: *The dove is a **symbol** of peace.* (***emblem, sign, token, totem***)
2 a letter, number or other mark used to stand for something: *The **symbol** for degrees is '°'.*

Word building: **symbolic** *adjective*
Word history: Late Latin, from Greek word meaning 'mark', 'token', 'ticket'

symbol / cymbal
Look up **cymbal / symbol.**

symbolise
verb **1** to stand for or represent
2 to represent by a symbol, or symbols

Word use: You can also use **symbolize.**

symbolism (sim-buhl-iz-uhm)
noun **1** the practice of representing things by symbols or of giving things a symbolic meaning
2 a set or system of symbols
3 symbolic meaning or character

symmetry (sim-uh-tree)
noun the arrangement of the parts of something so that they are all balanced in size and shape: *a design with perfect **symmetry***

Word building: **symmetrical** *adjective*
Word history: Late Latin, from Greek

sympathetic
adjective **1** marked by or showing sympathy (***compassionate, kindly***)
2 having a natural feeling for: *I am **sympathetic** to your idea.*
3 agreeing with or liking something: *He is **sympathetic** to the project.*

Word building: **sympathetically** *adverb*

sympathise
verb **1** to share in a feeling of sorrow or trouble with someone: *He **sympathised** with her when he heard of her mother's death.* (***commiserate, empathise, feel for***)
2 to understand and agree with: *I **sympathise** with your ideas.*

Word use: You can also use **sympathize.**
Word building: **sympathiser** *noun*
Word history: from French word meaning 'sympathy'

sympathy (sim-puh-thee)
noun **1** a feeling shared with someone else, especially in sorrow or trouble: *I felt great **sympathy** for her.* (***compassion, tenderness***)
2 an agreement in ideas, likes or dislikes: *They were in **sympathy** on that matter.*

Word history: Latin, from Greek word meaning 'feeling with another'

symphony (sim-fuh-nee)
noun a musical composition for a full orchestra, usually with several movements or major sections

Noun forms: The plural is **symphonies.**
Word building: **symphonic** *adjective*
Word history: Middle English, from Latin, from Greek word literally meaning 'a sounding together'

symposium (sim-<u>poh</u>-zee-uhm)
noun a meeting for discussion

Noun forms: The plural is **symposiums** or **symposia**.
Word history: Latin, from Greek

symptom
noun **1** something that shows that you have a disease or illness of some kind: *A sore throat is a* ***symptom*** *of a cold.*
2 any sign that shows that something is happening: *Unemployment is a* ***symptom*** *of a weak economy.*

Word history: Late Latin, from Greek

symptomatic
adjective **1** having to do with a symptom or symptoms
2 indicative: *It is* ***symptomatic*** *of flu that you get a runny nose.*

synagogue (<u>sin</u>-uh-gog)
noun a Jewish place of worship

Word history: Middle English, from Late Latin, from Greek word meaning 'meeting', 'assembly'

synchronise (<u>sink</u>-ruh-nuyz)
verb **1** to happen or make happen at the same time: *Let's* ***synchronise*** *our arrival.*
2 to make show the same time: *We'd better* ***synchronise*** *our watches.*

Word use: You can also use **synchronize**.
Word building: **synchronisation** *noun*
Word history: from Greek word meaning 'be contemporary with'

syncopate (<u>sink</u>-uh-payt)
verb to change the rhythm of, by putting the beat in unexpected places: *to* ***syncopate*** *a piece of music*

Word building: **syncopation** *noun*
Word history: from Late Latin word meaning 'cut short'

syndicate (<u>sin</u>-di-kuht)
noun **1** a combination of people, such as business associates, commercial firms, etc., formed to carry out some project, especially one needing a lot of capital (***company***, ***firm***, ***organisation***, ***outfit***)
2 any agency which buys and supplies articles, stories, etc., for publication in a number of newspapers, or other news media, at the same time
verb (<u>sin</u>-di-kayt) **3** to combine into a syndicate
4 to publish in different newspapers at the same time

Word building: **syndication** *noun*
Word history: French *syndicat*

syndrome (<u>sin</u>-drohm)
noun a pattern of symptoms in a disease, condition, etc.

Word building: **syndromic** *adjective*
Word history: Neo-Latin, from Greek word meaning 'a running together'

synod (<u>sin</u>-uhd)
noun **1** an assembly of church officials brought together to discuss and decide church affairs
2 any council

Word history: Middle English, from Late Latin, from Greek word meaning 'assembly'

synonym (<u>sin</u>-uh-nim)
noun a word having the same or very similar meaning as another: *'Joyful' and 'glad' are* ***synonyms****.*

Word building: **synonymous** *adjective*
Word history: Middle English, from Late Latin, from Greek word meaning 'synonymous'

synopsis (suh-<u>nop</u>-suhs)
noun **1** a short statement giving a general view of some subject (***outline***, ***plan***, ***precis***, ***résumé***, ***summary***)
2 a summary of headings or short paragraphs giving a view of the whole
3 the outline of the plot of a novel, play, film, etc.

Noun forms: The plural is **synopses** (suh-<u>nop</u>-seez).
Word history: Late Latin, from Greek word meaning 'general view'

synoptic chart
noun a chart showing the distribution of weather conditions over a region at a given moment

syntax (<u>sin</u>-taks)
noun **1 a** the patterns of formation of sentences and phrases from words in a particular language
b the study and description of these
2 the rules governing the order or structure, as opposed to the meaning, of symbols or expressions used in a computer language

Word building: **syntactic** *adjective* **syntactical** *adjective*
Word history: Late Latin, from Greek word meaning 'arrangement'

synthesis (<u>sin</u>-thuh-suhs)
noun the blending together of parts into a whole: *The plan was the result of a* ***synthesis*** *of our ideas.* | *This cloth is made by a* ***synthesis*** *of different materials.*

Word use: Compare this with **analysis**.
Word history: Latin, from Greek word literally meaning 'a taking together'

synthesise
verb to make up by grouping parts together

Word use: You can also use **synthesize**.

synthesiser
noun a machine which makes speech or music

synthetic (sin-<u>thet</u>-ik)
adjective **1** made by people; artificial: ***synthetic*** *rubber*
2 having to do with synthesis

Word history: Neo-Latin, from Greek

syphilis
noun a chronic, infectious venereal disease, caused by a microorganism and communicated by contact or heredity

Word building: **syphilitic** *adjective*
syphilitic *noun*
Word history: Neo-Latin, from *Syphilus*, name of the shepherd suffering from the disease in a Latin poem of 16th century by German Fracastoro

syphon
noun → **siphon**

syringe (suh-rinj, si-rinj)
noun a small tube with either a piston or a rubber bulb for drawing in and squirting out liquid, used to clean wounds or, when fitted to a needle, to inject liquid into or take it out of the body

Word building: **syringe** *verb*
Word history: from Greek word meaning 'pipe'

syrup
noun a thick, sweet, sticky liquid: *strawberry* ***syrup***

Word building: **syrupy** *adjective*
Word history: Middle English, from Old French, from Arabic word meaning 'beverage'

sysadmin (sis-ad-min)
noun → **system administrator**

Word history: *sys(tem) admin(istrator)*

sysop (sis-op)
noun → **system operator**

Word history: *sys(tem) op(erator)*

system
noun **1** the way something is organised or arranged: *the decimal* ***system*** *of currency | the parliamentary* ***system*** *of government | a new* ***system*** *of marking exam papers*
2 an organised way of doing something: *You must have more* ***system*** *in your work.*
3 a set of connected parts: *a railway* ***system***
4 an assemblage of parts of organs of the same or similar tissues or concerned with the same function: *the nervous* ***system****, the digestive* ***system***

Word history: Late Latin, from Greek word meaning 'organised whole'

system administrator
noun Computers the person responsible for maintaining a multi-user system

Word use: You can also use **systems administrator** or **sysadmin**.

systematic
adjective **1** having, showing or involving a system, method, or plan: *a* ***systematic*** *course of reading |* ***systematic*** *efforts*
2 arranged in or marking an ordered system: ***systematic*** *theology*
3 concerned with classification: ***systematic*** *botany*

Word use: You can also use **systematical**.

systematise
verb to arrange in or according to a system

Word use: You can also use **systematize**.
Word building: **systematisation** *noun*

systemic (sis-tem-ik, sis-tee-mik)
adjective **1** having to do with a system
2 a having to do with the whole bodily system
b having to do with a particular system of parts or organs of the body

system operator
noun Computers a person who assists in the operation of a computer system

Word use: You can also use **systems operator** or **sysop**.

systems analysis
noun the analysis of an activity or project, usually with the help of a computer, to find out its aims, methods and effectiveness

Word building: **systems analyst** *noun*

systole (sis-tuh-lee, sis-tohl)
noun the normal rhythmical contraction of the heart

Word use: Compare this with **diastole**.
Word building: **systolic** *adjective*
Word history: Neo-Latin, from Greek word meaning 'contraction'

Tt

tab[1]
noun **1** a small flap or loop attached to a piece of clothing or something similar (***label***, ***sticker***, ***tag***, ***ticket***)
2 a tag for a name or label
phrase **3 keep tabs on**, to keep a watch or a check on: *The coach **keeps tabs on** promising players.*

tab[2]
noun → **tab key**

tabby
noun a grey or brownish-yellow cat with a striped coat
Noun forms: The plural is **tabbies**.
Word building: **tabby** *adjective*
Word history: Middle English, from Old French, from Arabic word meaning 'rich watered silk', from 'Attābīya (district of Baghdad where this was first made)

tab key
noun a key on a computer keyboard which is depressed to set the point at which the next section of the line of type begins or to move to a new field on a record: *Set the **tab key** to make four columns.* | *Press the **tab key** and it will take you to the next box on the form.*
Word use: You can also use **tab**.

table
noun **1** a piece of furniture which has a flat top resting on one or more legs
2 a plan or chart setting out items or numbers: *a **table** of contents* | *a multiplication **table***
verb **3** to set out a subject for discussion in parliament
phrase **4 turn the tables**, to cause a complete about-turn in circumstances
Word history: Middle English; Old English *tablu*, from Latin word meaning 'board'

tableau (<u>tab</u>-loh)
noun a scene, or a group of people or objects arranged to form a picture or scene: *They made a charming **tableau**.*
Noun forms: The plural is **tableaus** or **tableaux**.
Word history: from French word meaning 'a table', 'picture'

tableland
noun a high and generally level region of a wide area (***plateau***)

tablespoon
noun a large spoon used for measuring or serving

tablet
noun **1** a small, flat, solid piece of medicine or soap
2 a flat slab or surface that you can carve or write on: *People used to write on **tablets** made of stone.*
Word history: Middle English, from French

tabloid (<u>tab</u>-loyd)
noun a newspaper, about one half the ordinary page size, emphasising pictures and short, rather than detailed, articles
Word history: *tabl(et)* + *-oid*

taboo (tuh-<u>booh</u>)
adjective strictly forbidden: *Kicking and biting are **taboo**.*
Word building: **taboo** *verb* (**tabooed**, **tabooing**) **taboo** *noun*
Word history: Tongan *tabu*

tabouli (tuh-<u>booh</u>-lee)
noun a salad of cracked wheat, chopped parsley, mint, tomato, oil and lemon juice, originating in Middle Eastern cooking
Word use: You can also use **tabouleh** or **tabbouli**.
Word history: Arabic

tabulate (<u>tab</u>-yuh-layt)
verb to put or form into a table, plan, etc. (***categorise***, ***chart***, ***codify***, ***index***, ***itemise***)
Word building: **tabulation** *noun* **tabular** *adjective*
Word history: from Latin word meaning 'boarded', 'planked'

tachometer (ta-<u>kom</u>-uh-tuh)
noun an instrument for measuring the number of revolutions per minute made by a revolving shaft, such as in a car
Word use: You can also use **tacheometer** or **tachymeter**.
Word building: **tachometric** (tak-uh-<u>met</u>-rik), **tachometrical** (tak-uh-<u>met</u>-rik-uhl) *adjective* **tachometrically** (tak-uh-<u>met</u>-rik-lee) *adverb* **tachometry** *noun*
Word history: *tacho-* (a word part meaning 'swift') + *-meter*

tacit (<u>tas</u>-uht)
adjective not openly expressed, but understood (***implicit***, ***implied***, ***inferred***)
Word history: Latin

taciturn (<u>tas</u>-uh-tern)
adjective not inclined to talk much or enter into conversations (***laconic***, ***quiet***, ***reserved***, ***reticent***, ***withdrawn***)
Word building: **taciturnity** *noun*
Word history: Latin

tack
noun **1** a small nail with a flat head, such as is used in laying carpet or for putting up pictures
2 a zigzag movement or sharp turn, as in sailing against the wind
verb **3** to fasten with tacks
4 to zigzag or change direction: *The yacht* ***tacked*** *across the harbour.*
5 to sew loosely with large stitches
6 to join loosely or roughly: *They've* ***tacked*** *a bathroom onto the laundry. | The last paragraph seems to have been* ***tacked*** *on as an afterthought.*

Word history: Middle English, from Anglo-French word meaning 'a fastening', 'clasp', 'nail', from Germanic

tackle
noun **1** equipment, especially for fishing or sailing
2 the ropes and blocks used for lifting, lowering or moving heavy weights
verb **3** to take on and struggle with: *to* ***tackle*** *a problem* (***attack, come to grips with, confront, take on***)
4 to seize and bring to a stop, especially in football: *He was heavily* ***tackled*** *by three opposing forwards.*
5 to try to get the ball from, especially in soccer and hockey

Word building: **tackler** *noun*
Word history: Middle English word meaning 'gear', from Middle Low German

tacky
adjective sticky: *Their fingers were* ***tacky*** *from eating toffee.*

Adjective forms: **tackier, tackiest**
Word building: **tackiness** *noun*

taco (tah-koh, tak-oh)
noun a dish of Mexican origin consisting of a flat piece of crisp corn bread folded around a spicy savoury filling

tact
noun a sense of the right time to do or say something: *She showed great* ***tact*** *in handling a delicate situation.*

Word building: **tactful** *noun* **tactfully** *adverb* **tactfulness** *noun* **tactless** *adjective* **tactlessly** *adverb*
Word history: from Latin word meaning 'sense of touch'

tactic
noun a plan for gaining something you desire

Word building: **tactical** *adjective*
Word history: Neo-Latin, from Greek word meaning 'ordered'

tactics
plural noun a plan of action, especially for placing and moving troops and ships during a battle: *They outwitted the enemy with their superior* ***tactics****.*

Word building: **tactical** *adjective* **tactician** *noun*

tactile
adjective **1** having a sense of touch: *The fingertips are especially* ***tactile****.*
2 inviting to the touch: *a* ***tactile*** *surface*

Word building: **tactility** *noun*
Word history: from Latin word meaning 'tangible'

tad
noun Colloquial a small amount: *I'll have just a* ***tad*** *more please.*

Word history: originally US, meaning 'a small boy'; perhaps from *tadpole* or from British dialect *taddick* a small amount

tadpole
noun a young frog or toad in the earliest stage of its life during which it develops legs and becomes able to leave the water

Word history: Middle English, from *tadde* toad + *pol* poll (head)

taffeta (taf-uh-tuh)
noun a shiny silk or rayon fabric of plain weave

Word history: Middle English, from Medieval Latin, from Persian word meaning 'silken or linen cloth'

tag
noun **1** a small loop or label (***sticker, tab, ticket***)
2 something, such as a binding of plastic, metal, etc., at the end of a cord such as on a shoelace
verb **3** to put a label on (***brand, identify, mark***)
4 to label or describe someone with a word or phrase: *They* ***tagged*** *her a coward.* (***call, christen, dub, name***)
5 to follow closely, especially without being invited: *The dog* ***tagged*** *along wherever she went.* (***tail, trail***)

Verb forms: I **tagged**, I have **tagged**, I am **tagging**
Word history: Middle English

tagine (tah-zheen)
noun (in Moroccan cookery) a slow-cooked stew, featuring meat or poultry, with vegetables, olives, preserved lemon and spices, served with couscous

Word use: You can also use **tajine**.

tai chi (tuy chee)
noun a form of stylised exercises based on Chinese martial arts which emphasises moving smoothly from one movement to another while not losing balance

tail
noun **1** the end of the backbone in some animals, especially when it forms a separate, flexible part of the body, as with cats, dogs, horses, etc.
2 the end or bottom of anything: *a shirt* ***tail***
3 tails,
a a black formal suit for men with a long-tailed coat
b the side of a coin opposite that with the picture of a head on it: *Heads or* ***tails****?*
verb **4** to follow closely: *The police* ***tailed*** *his car to the airport.*

Word history: Old English

tail / tale
Don't confuse **tail** with **tale**, which is a story, as in *a romantic tale.*

tailgate
noun the board at the back of a truck, wagon, etc., which can be removed or let down for ease in loading and unloading

tailor
noun **1** someone who mends or makes clothes, especially for men
2 an Australian fish, named because of its scissor-like teeth
verb **3** to provide or design for a particular need or situation, as a tailor makes clothes to fit each customer: *We'll **tailor** our prices to suit the market.*
Word history: Middle English, from Old French word meaning 'cutter'

tailor-made
adjective **1** made especially to order by a tailor for an individual customer
2 designed for a particular need or taste

taint
verb **1** to spoil slightly: *His bad mood **tainted** their enjoyment.*
2 to make or become bad or corrupt (***contaminate***, ***corrupt***, ***damage***, ***pollute***, ***ruin***)
Word building: **taint** *noun*
Word history: Middle English

taipan (tuy-pan)
noun a venomous brown snake with long fangs, found in Australia and New Guinea
Word history: from Wik-Mungkan, an Australian Aboriginal language of northern Queensland

take
verb **1** to get or receive: *He **took** it from me.* | *They **took** $10 for the chair.*
2 to have or use: *to **take** a rest*
3 to subtract: ***Take** 2 from 4.* (***deduct***, ***remove***)
4 to bring or carry: ***Take** your coat with you.*
5 to travel on or lead: *She **takes** a train.* | *Where will it **take** us?*
6 to feel or experience: *to **take** pride* | *to **take** it personally*
7 to make use of: *to **take** an opportunity*
8 to use up: *This **takes** time.*
9 to write down: ***Take** a note.*
10 to make: *to **take** a photo* | *to **take** a copy*
11 to regard or consider: *They **take** me to be a fool.*
12 to require or need: *It **takes** nerve to do that.*
13 to have the desired effect: *The dye didn't **take**, and now the colour's all wrong.*
14 to become: *She **took** ill.*
phrase **15 take after**, to be or look like: *She **takes after** her aunt.*
16 take for, to believe to be, usually mistakenly: *I **took** him **for** the postman.*
17 take in,
a to deceive or trick
b to make smaller: *She had to **take in** the waist.*
18 take it, *Colloquial*
a to put up with pain, misfortune, etc., with strength: *I just can't **take it** any more.*
b to react in a way shown or described: *When I told him the news, he **took it** badly.*
c to assume or suppose: *I **take it** from your silence that all this is true.*
19 take off,
a to leave
b to imitate: *They **take off** his accent.*
20 take on,
a to hire: *to **take on** a worker*
b to handle or agree to do
c to get or acquire: *to **take on** a new aspect*
d *Colloquial* to stand up to, oppose, or quarrel with: *We **took on** the council and won.*
21 take out,
a to remove or extract: *to **take out** a tooth*
b to treat to dinner, a film, etc.: *to **take** a friend **out***
c to apply for and get: *to **take out** an insurance policy*
d to release: *Don't **take** you anger **out** on him!*
22 take to,
a to devote or addict yourself to: *to **take to** drink*
b to respond well to: *I did not **take to** the new boss.*
c to go to: *to **take to** your bed*
23 take up,
a to lift or pick up
b to begin to study, practise, etc.: *to **take up** ancient Greek*
c to occupy: *to **take up** time*
d to continue: *to **take up** where you left off*
Verb forms: I **took**, I have **taken**, I am **taking**
Word history: Old English, from Scandinavian

takeaway
noun food that you can buy in a shop or restaurant and take home or somewhere else to eat

take-off
noun the action of an aircraft or spaceship in leaving the ground and flying into the air at the beginning of its journey: *It's five minutes to **take-off**.*

takeover
noun the gaining or taking of control, especially of another business or country

talc
noun a soft, greenish-grey mineral that is oily to the touch and that is used in making talcum powder, electrical insulation, etc.
Word use: You can also use **talcum**.
Word history: Medieval Latin, from Arabic

talcum powder
noun a scented powder, used after a bath or shower

tale
noun a story, which may be true or false
Word history: from Old English word meaning 'reckoning', 'speech'

talent
noun skill or ability: *Her drawings show **talent**.*
Word building: **talented** *adjective*
Word history: Old English, from Latin, from Greek

talisman (tal-uhz-muhn)
noun something considered to be lucky or magical
Word history: Arabic, from Late Greek word meaning 'talisman', earlier 'religious rite', 'performance', 'completion'

talk
verb **1** to speak, or express in words
2 to give or reveal information: *They tried to make him **talk**.*
3 to discuss: *They are **talking** politics.*
noun **4** an occasion for talking, such as a speech, lecture or conference
5 a conversation or discussion: *They had a good **talk**.*
6 gossip, or the topic of gossip: *the **talk** of the town* (***hearsay***, ***rumour***)
phrase **7 talk down to**, to speak to in a way that suggests that you are superior: *to **talk down to** a friend*

8 talk into, to persuade someone to do something they were not originally intending to do: *We **talked** her **into** coming to the party.* (***coax***, ***convince***, ***induce***, ***prevail upon***)
9 talk round,
a to discuss in general terms without coming to the main point
b to bring around to your way of thinking

Word building: **talkative** *adjective* **talker** *noun*
Word history: Middle English

tall
adjective **1** of more than average height: ***tall*** *grass* (***high***, ***lofty***, ***towering***)
2 having a particular height: *a man 1.9 metres* ***tall***
3 *Colloquial* difficult to believe: *a* ***tall*** *story*
4 *Colloquial* difficult to carry out: *a* ***tall*** *order*

Word history: from Old English word meaning 'prompt'

tallow (tal-oh)
noun the fatty tissue of animals, especially sheep, cattle, etc., used to make candles, soap, etc.

Word building: **tallowy** *adjective*
Word history: Middle English

tall poppy
noun Australian, *NZ* a person who is outstanding in any way, especially someone with great wealth or status

tally
noun **1** a record or account of an amount counted or owed: *The shearers keep a* ***tally*** *of the sheep they shear.*
verb **2** to count or record (***add up***, ***calculate***, ***total***)
3 to agree: *His story doesn't* ***tally*** *with the facts.*

Noun forms: The plural is **tallies.**
Verb forms: I **tallied**, I have **tallied**, I am **tallying**
Word history: Middle English, from Anglo-French, from Latin word meaning 'rod'

talon
noun the claw, especially of birds of prey such as the eagle

Word history: Middle English, from Old French word meaning 'heel', from Late Latin word meaning 'talon'

tambourine (tam-buh-reen)
noun a small drum with a skin-covered frame which has metal discs set into it, played by hitting and shaking it

Word history: from French word meaning 'little drum'

tame
adjective **1** used to being handled by humans: *a* ***tame*** *bird*
2 dull: *The film was very* ***tame.***
verb **3** to bring under human control: *to* ***tame*** *a lion cub*

Word building: **tameness** *noun* **tamer** *noun*
Word history: Old English

tamper
verb to interfere so as to change or damage

tampon
noun a cotton plug used to absorb the flow of blood from the vagina during menstruation

Word history: French

tan
verb **1** to turn or become brown in the sun: *She* ***tans*** *her legs. | His back* ***tans*** *easily.*
2 to change into leather by soaking and treating: *to* ***tan*** *a hide*
noun **3** a suntan
4 a yellowish-brown colour

Verb forms: I **tanned**, I have **tanned**, I am **tanning**
Word building: **tan** *adjective* **tanner** *noun*
Word history: Old English, from Medieval Latin

tanbark
noun **1** bark used in tanning hide
2 such bark broken up in chips and used as a ground-cover, usually in playgrounds, landscape gardening, etc.

tandem
adverb **1** one behind another
noun **2** a bicycle for two riders

Word building: **tandem** *adjective*
Word history: from Latin word meaning 'at length (in time)', probably humorously used at first

tandoori (tan-doo-uh-ree)
adjective having to do with Indian-style food cooked in a very hot clay oven: ***tandoori*** *chicken*

Word history: from Urdu *tandoor* an oven

tang
noun a strong, salty or sharp flavour or smell: *the* ***tang*** *of the sea*

Word building: **tangy** *adjective* (**tangier, tangiest**)
Word history: Middle English, from Scandinavian

tangent (tan-juhnt)
noun **1** a straight line which touches a curve
2 a sudden new direction: *He keeps flying off at a* ***tangent.***
adjective **3** touching

Word history: from Latin word meaning 'touching'

tangent ratio
noun Mathematics a trigonometric function, defined for an acute angle in a right-angled triangle as the ratio of the opposite side to the adjacent side

Word use: The short form is **tan.**

tangerine (tan-juh-reen)
noun **1** a type of mandarin
2 of a reddish-orange colour

Word building: **tangerine** *adjective*
Word history: *Tangier* (a seaport in northern Morocco) + *-ine*

tangible (tan-juh-buhl)
adjective real, or able to be touched or felt (***actual***, ***concrete***, ***material***, ***physical***)

Word use: The opposite of this is **intangible.**
Word history: Latin

tangle
verb to put or get in a confused muddle: *The kitten has* ***tangled*** *the threads.*

Word building: **tangle** *noun*
Word history: Middle English word meaning 'entangle', from Scandinavian

tango
noun a South American ballroom dance

Noun forms: The plural is **tangos**.
Word building: **tango** *verb* (**tangoed**, **tangoing**)
Word history: American Spanish

tank
noun **1** a container for liquid, such as petrol or water
2 a heavy fighting vehicle armed with cannons and machine-guns
Word history: perhaps from Gujarati (an Indian language) word meaning 'pool'

tankard
noun a beer mug, or other large cup, sometimes with a lid
Word history: Middle English

tanker
noun a large vehicle or vessel for carrying oil or other liquids in large quantities

tannin (tan-uhn)
noun a harsh and bitter vegetable substance, such as the one which gives the tanning properties to wattle bark, or the one in grape skins, stalks and seeds which gives a characteristic tannin taste to some wines
Word history: Medieval Latin

tantalise
verb to tease or torment with the sight of something wished for but out of reach
Word use: You can also use **tantalize**.
Word building: **tantalising** *adjective*
tantalisingly *adverb*
Word history: from *Tantalus*, who, in Greek mythology, was condemned to stand, hungry and thirsty, in water up to his chin, under a tree laden with fruit, because he had revealed secrets of the gods

tantamount
adjective equivalent, usually in value, force, effect or meaning: *Taking her purse without asking was **tantamount** to robbery.*
Word history: French

tantrum
noun a violent outburst of temper

Taoism (tow-iz-uhm)
noun a Chinese philosophy which encourages people not to interfere with nature and to be sincere and honest
Word building: **Taoist** *noun*, *adjective*

tap[1]
verb to hit lightly (***bat***, ***beat***, ***clip***, ***pat***, ***rap***)
Verb forms: I **tapped**, I have **tapped**, I am **tapping**
Word building: **tap** *noun*
Word history: Middle English, from French word meaning 'strike', 'slap'; of Germanic origin

tap[2]
noun **1** something used to control the flow of liquid: *a bath **tap***
2 a connection to a telephone line, usually made secretly, so that a person can listen to a conversation on the line without the speakers knowing
verb **3** to draw on, as from a supply of water, or other resources: *He was able to **tap** his reserves of energy.*
4 to connect with secretly, in order to overhear conversation: *They have **tapped** her phone.*
phrase **5 on tap**,
a of a drink, such as beer in a cask, ready to be drawn off and served
b ready to be used immediately
Verb forms: I **tapped**, I have **tapped**, I am **tapping**
Word history: Old English

tape
noun **1** a long strip of paper, cloth or a similar material such as you use in sewing or in typewriters
2 a plastic strip coated with magnetic powder, used to record sound and video signals and to store information from computers
3 → tape measure
verb **4** to record on tape: *He **taped** my copy of the opera.*
Word history: Middle English

tape deck
noun a tape recorder without built-in amplifiers or speakers

tape measure
noun a long strip or ribbon made of linen or steel, marked with millimetres and centimetres for measuring
Word use: The short form is **tape**.

taper
verb **1** to gradually narrow or thin at one end: *The road **tapers** into a track. | She **tapered** her nails to a point.*
noun **2** a very thin candle
Word building: **tapering** *adjective*
Word history: from Middle English word meaning 'candle'

tape recorder
noun a machine which records sound on magnetic tape

tapestry
noun a piece of cloth with a design which has been woven or embroidered
Noun forms: The plural is **tapestries**.
Word history: Middle English, from French word meaning 'maker of tapestry'

tapeworm
noun a flat or tapelike worm which lives in the intestines of people and animals

tapioca (tap-ee-oh-kuh)
noun floury grains of cassava starch used for puddings and thickening sauce
Word history: Portuguese, from Brazilian (Tupi-Guarani) *tipioca*, from *tipi* residue + *og, ók* squeeze out

taproot
noun the big main root of a plant from which the other roots branch

tar
noun **1** a thick, black, sticky substance obtained from wood or coal, especially used for making roads
verb **2** to cover or smear with tar
Verb forms: it **tarred**, it has **tarred**, it is **tarring**
Word history: Old English

tarantula (tuh-ran-chuh-luh)
noun **1** a large, furry Australian spider which often shelters indoors when it's raining (***huntsman***)
2 a venomous spider of Europe

Word history: Medieval Latin, from Italian, from *Taranto* sea-port in south-eastern Italy, where the European spider is common

tardy
adjective **1** moving or acting slowly (***dilatory***, ***lethargic***, ***sluggish***)
2 late or behindhand
3 delaying through reluctance

Adjective forms: **tardier**, **tardiest**
Word building: **tardily** *adverb* **tardiness** *noun*
Word history: Middle English, from French, from Latin word meaning 'slow'

tare (tair)
noun **1** the weight of the wrapping or the container holding goods
2 the unloaded weight of a vehicle, especially a truck

Word history: Middle English, from Medieval Latin, from Arabic word meaning 'deduction'

target
noun **1** something which you aim at in order to hit or reach: *Her arrow hit the centre of the* ***target***. | *They set a* ***target*** *of ten days to finish work.* (***goal***)
2 a victim: *He is the* ***target*** *of their jokes.* (***butt***)

Word history: Middle English, from French

tariff
noun **1** a charge for importing something into a country
2 the price charged for a room in a hotel

Word history: Italian, from Arabic word meaning 'notification', 'information'

tarmac
noun **1** a mixture of tar and gravel used to seal roads
2 an airport runway

tarnish
verb to dull, discolour or spoil: *Silver* ***tarnishes*** *in the salt air.* | *to* ***tarnish*** *a reputation*

Word building: **tarnish** *noun* **tarnished** *adjective*
Word history: from French word meaning 'dull', 'dark', probably of Germanic origin

tarot (ta-roh)
noun **1** one of a pack of 78 playing cards
2 a trump card in such a pack, bearing a symbolic or mythological character, now chiefly used in fortune telling, etc.

Word history: French, from Italian

tarpaulin (tah-paw-luhn)
noun a large canvas or other waterproof cover

Word history: earlier *tarpauling*, from *tar* + *pall* + *-ing*

tarragon
noun a strong-smelling herb used in cooking and salads

Word history: Spanish, from Arabic, probably from Greek

tarry
verb Old-fashioned to linger or loiter (***dally***, ***dawdle***, ***delay***)

Verb forms: I **tarried**, I have **tarried**, I am **tarrying**
Word history: Middle English

tart[1]
adjective sour or sharp: *a* ***tart*** *taste* | *a* ***tart*** *retort* (***acid***, ***bitter***)

Word building: **tartly** *adverb* **tartness** *noun*
Word history: from Old English word meaning 'sharp', 'rough'

tart[2]
noun a shallow fruit or jam pie without a top

Word history: Middle English, from Old French, from Latin

tartan
noun the checked woollen cloth in the colours of the different Scottish Highland clans, or any similar checked cloth

Word building: **tartan** *adjective*
Word history: apparently from French word meaning 'linsey-woolsey' (a coarse fabric of cotton or linen woven under wool)

tartar[1] (tah-tuh)
noun **1** a hard substance deposited on the teeth by the saliva
2 a potassium salt forming a deposit in wines

Word building: **tartaric** *adjective*
Word history: Medieval Latin, from Greek

tartar[2] (tah-tuh)
noun a savage person who cannot be reasoned with

Word history: from *Tartar*, a member of a Mongolian people, who, under the leadership of Genghis Khan, overran Asia and eastern Europe during the Middle Ages

taser (tay-zuh)
noun a form of stun gun which fires projectiles with a wire attached through which an electric current passes

Word use: You can also use **taser gun**.
Word building: **tasered** *adjective*

task
noun **1** a piece of work, or a duty (***assignment***, ***chore***, ***errand***, ***job***, ***mission***)
phrase **2 take to task**, to blame or scold

Word history: Middle English, from Medieval Latin

Tasmanian blue gum
noun a tall smooth-barked gum tree, native to Tasmania and Victoria; floral emblem of Tasmania

Tasmanian devil
noun a fierce, black-and-white, meat-eating marsupial, found in Tasmania

Tasmanian scallop
noun → **scallop** (definition 1)

Tasmanian tiger
noun → **thylacine**

Word use: You can also use **Tasmanian wolf**.

Tasmanian wolf
noun → **thylacine**

Word use: You can also use **Tasmanian tiger**.

tassel
noun a bunch of silk, or other threads, hanging as an ornament

Word history: Middle English, from Old French word meaning 'fastening for a cloak'

taste
noun **1** the sense which experiences flavour
2 flavour: *It has a sweet* ***taste****.*
3 a liking or enjoyment: *I've acquired a* ***taste*** *for olives.*
4 a sense of what belongs or is attractive: *I like her* ***taste*** *in clothes.*
5 a first experience or sample: *She had a* ***taste*** *of city life.*
verb **6** to try by eating: *He* ***tasted*** *the soup to see if it was ready.* (***savour***)
7 to experience or feel, especially through your sense of taste
8 to have a certain flavour: *This* ***tastes*** *like chicken.*

Word history: Middle English, from Old French word meaning 'try by touching'

tastebud
noun any of a number of small bodies on the surface of the tongue, which perceive taste

tasty
adjective full of flavour: *a* ***tasty*** *sauce* (***piquant****,* ***pungent****,* ***savoury****,* ***sharp****,* ***spicy***)

Adjective forms: **tastier, tastiest**
Word use: The opposite of this is **bland** or **tasteless.**

tatters
plural noun torn or ragged pieces, especially of clothing: *His shirt was in* ***tatters****.*

tatting
noun **1** the process or work of making a type of knotted lace, with a shuttle
2 such lace

tattle
verb **1** to let out secrets
2 to chatter or gossip
noun **3** chatter or gossip

Word history: Middle English, apparently from Middle Flemish

tattoo[1]
noun **1** a signal on a trumpet or drum: *to beat a* ***tattoo***
2 an outdoor military display

Word history: Dutch word literally meaning 'the tap is to' meaning 'the bar is shut'

tattoo[2]
noun an ink picture permanently printed into someone's skin with needles

Word building: **tattoo** *verb* (**tattooed, tattooing**)
Word history: earlier *tattow*, from Polynesian

taught (tawt)
verb past tense and past participle of **teach**

taunt
verb to insult or tease cruelly (***heckle****,* ***mock****,* ***rib****,* ***ridicule****,* ***tease***)

Word building: **taunt** *noun* **taunting** *adjective* **tauntingly** *adverb*

taut
adjective stretched tight: *They held the rope* ***taut****.*

Word building: **tautly** *adverb* **tautness** *noun*
Word history: Middle English

tautology (taw-tol-uh-jee)
noun the needless repetition of an idea, usually in the same sentence, without giving extra clearness, as in *to descend down*

Noun forms: The plural is **tautologies.**
Word building: **tautological** *adjective*
Word history: Late Latin, from Greek

tavern
noun a place where food and alcoholic drink can be bought

taw
noun **1** a favoured or fancy marble with which to shoot
2 taws, the game of marbles

Word history: perhaps Scandinavian

taw / tor / tore
Don't confuse **taw** with **tor** or **tore.**
A **taw** is a kind of marble or a token used in games like hopscotch.
A **tor** is a rocky outcrop or hill.
Tore is the past form of **tear**, to pull apart.

tawdry
adjective cheap and showy: ***tawdry*** *jewellery* (***flashy****,* ***gaudy****,* ***tinselly***)

Word history: short for *(Sain)t Audrey lace*, that is, lace bought at her fair in the Isle of Ely, England

tawny
adjective of a yellowish-brown colour, like a lion's coat

Adjective forms: **tawnier, tawniest**
Word history: Middle English, from Old French word meaning 'tanned'

tawny frogmouth
noun a medium-sized Australian night bird, with differently coloured mottled plumage, and a low but penetrating call

tax
noun **1** money people have to pay each year to the government to pay for public services, and which is usually a percentage of the value of income, property, goods purchased, etc.
verb **2** to put a tax on
3 to burden or exhaust: *The work* ***taxes*** *her strength.* (***drain****,* ***sap****,* ***strain****,* ***weaken****,* ***weary***)

Word building: **taxable** *adjective*
Word history: Middle English, from Latin word meaning 'reprove', 'appraise'

taxation
noun **1** the act or fact of taxing, or of being taxed
2 a tax imposed
3 the money raised by taxes

taxi
noun **1** a car for hire, with a driver and a meter which calculates the fare
verb **2** of aircraft, to move along the runway before taking off, or after landing: *The plane* ***taxied*** *to the terminal.*

Noun forms: The plural is **taxis.**
Verb forms: it **taxied,** it has **taxied,** it is **taxiing**
Word history: short for *taxicab*

taxidermy (tak-suh-derm-ee)
noun the art of preparing and preserving the skins of animals, and stuffing and mounting them in lifelike form

Word building: **taxidermist** *noun*
Word history: from Greek word meaning 'arrangement of skin'

taxonomy (tak-son-uh-mee)
noun the classification of types of plants, animals, etc.

Word building: **taxonomic** *adjective* **taxonomist** *noun* **taxonomer** *noun*
Word history: French, from Greek

tax return
noun a statement of personal income required every year by government tax authorities, used in calculating the amount of tax to be paid

TB
noun tuberculosis

Word history: abbreviation

TCP/IP (tee-see-pee uy-pee)
noun Computers the suite of protocols used to connect hosts on the internet

Word history: an acronym for *t(ransmission) c(ontrol) p(rotocol)/i(nternet) p(rotocol)*

tea
noun **1** a drink made by pouring boiling water onto the dried leaves of a shrub grown mainly in China, India and Sri Lanka
2 the dried leaves of this shrub
3 a late afternoon or evening meal: *They had **tea** at six.*

Word history: Chinese *ch'a*

> **tea / tee**
> Don't confuse **tea** with **tee**, which is a small support for the ball that you use in golf.

tea bag
noun a small bag made of paper filled with tea leaves which is placed in boiling water to make tea

teach
verb **1** to instruct or give knowledge to: *He **teaches** kindergarten children.* (***coach***, ***drill***, ***educate***, ***train***)
2 to give knowledge of or skill in: *She **teaches** maths.*

Verb forms: I **taught**, I have **taught**, I am **teaching**
Word building: **teacher** *noun*
Word history: Old English

> **teach / learn**
> Look up **learn / teach**.

teak
noun a hard, long-lasting wood used for shipbuilding and furniture

teal
noun a type of small, freshwater duck which ranges widely over Australia, Indonesia, New Zealand and the Pacific islands

Noun forms: The plural is **teals** or **teal**.

tea light
noun a small candle, often in a metal or plastic casing

team
noun **1** a group of people who share an activity, such as sport or work: *A new doctor joined the **team**.*
2 a number of animals harnessed together to do work: *a **team** of oxen*

Word history: Old English

> **team / teem**
> Don't confuse **team** with **teem**. To **teem** is to rain very hard. It can also mean 'to swarm with small animals':
> *This river teems with fish.*

tear[1] (tear)
noun **1** a drop of water that falls from the eyes, caused by sadness or pain
phrase **2 in tears**, crying: *We were **in tears** by the end of the sad film.*

Word building: **tearful** *adjective* **tearfully** *adverb*
Word history: Old English *tēar*

> **tear / tier**
> Don't confuse **tear** with **tier**, which is one level in a series of levels:
> *The wedding cake had three tiers in it.*

tear[2] (tair)
verb **1** to rip: *She **tore** her skirt. | The paper **tears** easily.* (***cut***, ***gash***, ***lacerate***, ***slash***, ***slit***)
2 to remove or pull away: *He will **tear** the food from your hands. | He couldn't **tear** himself from the game.*
noun **3** a rip
phrase **4 tear into**, to attack violently, either with the body or with words
5 tear off, to hurry away

Verb forms: I **tore**, I have **torn**, I am **tearing**
Word history: Old English *teran*

tear gas (tear gas)
noun a gas used in warfare or in riots, which makes the eyes sting and water, producing short-term blindness

tease (teez)
verb **1** to mock or pester in a light-hearted but embarrassing way (***heckle***, ***rib***, ***taunt***)
2 to separate the strands of: *to **tease** wool*

Word building: **tease** *noun* **teasing** *adjective* **teasingly** *adverb*
Word history: Old English *tǣsan* tear up

teaspoon
noun a small spoon which holds about five millilitres

teat
noun the rubber top on a baby's bottle which is shaped like a nipple

Word history: Middle English *tete*, Old French

tea-tree
noun a shrub with small leaves and red, white or pink flowers, found in Australia and New Zealand

Word history: so called from its use as a tea substitute in the early days of European settlement in Australia

tech (tek)
noun **1** *Colloquial* a technical college or school
2 → **techie**

techie (tek-ee)
noun *Colloquial* someone with a professional or passionate interest in technology, especially computing: *When the computer breaks down I get a **techie** to fix it.*

Word use: You can also use **tech head** or **tech**.

technical (tek-nik-uhl)
adjective **1** having to do with practical science and machinery: *a **technical** education*
2 using words or covering topics that only an expert would understand

Word building: **technically** *adverb*

technicality
noun **1** a technical point or detail
2 an exact, often narrow-minded, following of a rule, law, etc.: *He could not apply due to a **technicality**.*

technician (tek-nish-uhn)
noun **1** someone skilled in the technical side of a subject
2 someone skilled in the technique of an art, as music or painting

technicolour (tek-ni-kul-uh, tek-nuh-kul-uh)
noun **1** the process of making cinema films in colour
adjective **2** bright or striking, especially colours

Word use: You can also use **technicolor**.
Word history: Trademark *Technicolor*

technique (tek-neek)
noun **1** the way of doing or performing: *His **technique** is influenced by his teacher.* (***approach***, ***means***, ***method***, ***procedure***)
2 practical skill or knowledge: *She has good ideas but not much **technique**.*

Word history: French

technology (tek-nol-uh-jee)
noun **1** the use of practical or mechanical science in industry, etc.
2 the methods, practices or equipment by which this is done: *a country with a developed **technology***

Word building: **technological** *adjective* **technologically** *adverb* **technologist** *noun*
Word history: from Greek word meaning 'systematic treatment'

tectonic (tek-ton-ik)
adjective **1** having to do with building
2 *Geology*
a having to do with the structure of the earth's crust
b having to do with the forces or conditions within the earth that cause movements of the crust, such as earthquakes, folds, faults, etc.
c indicating the results of such movements: ***tectonic** valleys*

Word history: Late Latin, from Greek

tectonic plate
noun one of the sections of the earth's surface, beneath the land and the oceans, which moves in relation to other sections

Word use: You can also use **crustal plate**.

tedious
adjective long and boring: *a **tedious** wait | a **tedious** lecture* (***dull***, ***monotonous***, ***uninteresting***)

Word building: **tediously** *adverb* **tedium** *noun*
Word history: Middle English, from Late Latin

tee
noun **1** the starting place for each hole in golf
2 a plastic or wooden holder from which a player drives a golf ball
phrase **3 tee off**, to strike the ball from a tee
4 tee up, to organise or arrange: *We've **teed up** a partner for you.*

tee / tea
Look up **tea / tee**.

teem[1]
phrase **teem with**, to be full of: *The park **teems with** wildlife.*

Word building: **teeming** *adjective*
Word history: Old English *tēman, tīeman* produce (offspring)

teem[2]
verb to rain very hard (***come down in torrents***, ***pour***, ***rain cats and dogs***)

Word history: Middle English, from Scandinavian

teem / team
Look up **team / teem**.

teen
Colloquial
adjective **1** teenage: *a **teen** movie*
noun **2** a teenager

teenager
noun someone who is aged between 12 and 20

Word building: **teenage** *adjective*

teens
plural noun the period of a person's life between the ages of 12 and 20

teepee
noun a tent or wigwam of the indigenous people of North America: *The children rigged up a pretend **teepee** with some sheets and broomsticks.*

Word use: You can also use **tepee**.

teeter
verb to move or hang unsteadily

Word history: variant of *titter*, from Scandinavian

teeth
noun **1** plural of **tooth**
2 power or effectiveness: *to give a law **teeth***
phrase **3 get your teeth into**, to start to manage effectively
4 in the teeth of, in defiance of
5 to the teeth, fully: *armed **to the teeth***

teethe (teedh)
verb to grow teeth

Verb forms: it **teethed**, it has **teethed**, it is **teething**

teething
noun **1** the first growth of teeth
phrase **2 teething troubles**, difficulties, usually temporary, which often occur at the beginning of a project or enterprise

teetotal
adjective opposed to the drinking of alcohol or practising the total non-drinking of alcohol: *a **teetotal** organisation*

Word building: **teetotalism** *noun* **teetotaller** *noun*
Word history: from *total*, with reduplication of initial *t-* for emphasis

teflon
noun a lining for saucepans, frying pans, etc., to which food does not stick

Word history: Trademark

telco (tel-koh)
noun a telecommunications company

telecast
noun a television broadcast

telecommunications
plural noun the sending of messages by telephone, radio, cable or satellite

teleconference
noun a conference in which people who are far apart from each other can talk via an audiovisual telecommunications system

telegram
noun a message sent by telegraph

telegraph
noun a system or device for sending messages by electric signals along wire

Word building: **telegraph** *verb* **telegraphic** *adjective* **telegraphy** *noun*

telepathy (tuh-lep-uh-thee)
noun the sharing or passing on of information or thoughts between one person's mind and another's without speaking, writing or using actions: *We didn't tell him so he must have known by **telepathy**.*

Word building: **telepathic** *adjective* **telepathically** *adverb* **telepathist** *noun*

telephone
noun **1** a system for speaking to someone else over a long distance, usually powered by electricity
2 an electrical device consisting of a microphone and a receiver with a handset, used to connect to this system

Word use: The short form is **phone**.
Word building: **telephone** *verb* **telephonic** *adjective* **telephonically** *adverb*

telephoto lens
noun a lens for a camera which gives a larger picture of distant objects

teleprinter
noun an instrument with a typewriter keyboard which sends and receives messages by changing typed information into electrical signals

telescope
noun **1** a tube-shaped instrument with powerful lenses which make distant objects seem closer
verb **2** to force together, one into another, the way the sliding tubes of a jointed telescope fit together
3 to shorten or condense

Word building: **telescopic** *adjective*
Word history: Neo-Latin, from Greek word meaning 'far-seeing'

televise
verb to broadcast by television

television
noun **1** the sending of pictures by radio waves which are picked up by the receiving sets of viewers
2 a television set or receiver
3 the programs transmitted to a television set: *to watch too much **television***

Word use: The abbreviation is **TV**.

telex
noun **1** a postal service in which teleprinters are rented to businesses which can send and receive their own messages
2 the message sent or received

Word building: **telex** *verb*

tell
verb **1** to give an account or description of (***describe***, ***inform***, ***narrate***, ***recount***, ***relate***)
2 to express or say: *to **tell** a lie*
3 to know or recognise: *Can you **tell** which is yours?*
4 to order: ***Tell** him to go.*
5 to have or show an effect: *The strain is **telling** on her.*
phrase **6 tell off**, to scold
7 tell on, to tell tales about

Verb forms: I **told**, I have **told**, I am **telling**
Word history: Old English *tellan*

teller
noun someone who works in a bank receiving and paying out the customers' money

telltale
adjective revealing, especially of what is not meant to be known: *There were **telltale** footprints under the window.*

Word building: **telltale** *noun*

telnet
noun Computers a program which opens a shell (definition 4) on a remote computer

temerity (tuh-me-ruh-tee)
noun foolish boldness, or rashness

Word history: late Middle English, from Latin

temper
noun **1** the particular state of mind or mood someone is in: *She's in a good **temper**.*
2 an angry or resentful mood: *a fit of **temper*** (***anger***, ***fury***, ***ire***, ***rage***, ***wrath***)
verb **3** to strengthen by changes of temperature: *to **temper** steel*
4 to make less severe: *She **tempered** her criticism.*

Word history: Middle English; Old English *temprian*, from Latin word meaning 'divide or proportion duly', 'temper'

tempera (<u>tem</u>-puh-ruh)
noun paint made from colouring matter ground in water and mixed with egg yolk or some similar substance

Word history: Italian word meaning 'paint in distemper', from Latin

temperament (<u>tem</u>-pruh-muhnt)
noun a type of personality or character: *She has a cheerful **temperament**.* (***constitution***, ***disposition***, ***make-up***)

Word history: late Middle English, from Latin word meaning 'due mixture'

temperamental (tem-pruh-<u>ment</u>-uhl)
adjective moody (***capricious***, ***changeable***, ***flighty***, ***mercurial***, ***volatile***)

Word building: **temperamentally** *adverb*

temperance (<u>tem</u>-puh-ruhns, <u>tem</u>-pruhns)
noun **1** moderation and self-control, especially in drinking alcohol
2 the complete avoidance of alcohol

Word history: Middle English, from Anglo-French, from Latin word meaning 'moderation'

temperate (<u>tem</u>-puh-ruht, <u>tem</u>-pruht)
adjective moderate and steady: *a **temperate** use of alcohol | a **temperate** winter* (***mild***, ***reasonable***, ***restrained***)

Word building: **temperately** *adverb* **temperateness** *noun*
Word history: Middle English, from Latin

temperate rainforest
noun a coniferous or broadleaf forest occurring in coastal mountains with high rainfall: *There are **temperate rainforests** in the south-east of the Australian mainland and Tasmania.*

Word use: Look up **cool temperate rainforest** and **warm temperate rainforest**. | Compare **tropical rainforest**.

temperature (<u>temp</u>-ruh-chuh)
noun **1** a measure of the degree of heat or cold of something or someone
2 an abnormally high amount of heat in the body: *to have a **temperature***

Word history: Latin

tempest
noun a violent storm or a violent disturbance: *The ship sank in the **tempest**. | a **tempest** of tears*

Word building: **tempestuous** *adjective* **tempestuously** *adverb*
Word history: Middle English, from Old French, from Romance word meaning 'time', 'storm', from Latin word meaning 'season'

template (<u>tem</u>-pluht, <u>tem</u>-playt)
noun **1** a pattern or mould(s) usually consisting of a thin plate of wood, metal or plastic, used as a guide in mechanical work or for putting a design onto a work surface, etc.
2 a horizontal piece of timber, stone, or the like, in a wall, to receive and distribute the pressure of a beam, etc.

Word history: perhaps from French word meaning 'stretcher', from Latin word meaning 'small timber'

temple[1]
noun a large building where people worship

Word history: Old English *templ*, from Latin

temple[2]
noun the flat part on either side of the forehead

Word history: Middle English, from Old French, from Romance

tempo
noun speed, rhythm or pattern: *music with a fast **tempo** | the **tempo** of modern life* (***beat***, ***swing***)

Noun forms: The plural is **tempos** or **tempi**.
Word history: Italian, from Latin word meaning 'time'

temporal[1] (<u>tem</u>-puh-ruhl, <u>tem</u>-pruhl)
adjective **1** having to do with time
2 having to do with the present life or with this world

Word history: Middle English, from Latin word meaning 'relating to or enduring for a time'

temporal[2] (<u>tem</u>-puh-ruhl, <u>tem</u>-pruhl)
adjective Anatomy having to do with or situated near the temple: ***temporal** bone*

Word history: Latin

temporary (<u>tem</u>-pree, <u>tem</u>-pruh-ree)
adjective lasting for a short time: *a **temporary** job* (***interim***, ***passing***, ***provisional***, ***transient***)

Word use: The opposite is **permanent**.
Word building: **temporarily** *adverb*

temporise (<u>temp</u>-uh-ruyz)
verb **1** to avoid making a decision in order to gain time or delay matters
2 to give in for the moment to the demands of a situation

Word use: You can also use **temporize**.
Word building: **temporisation** *noun*
Word history: from Medieval Latin word meaning 'delay'

tempt
verb **1** to attract or persuade, especially to something unwise or forbidden
2 to dare or provoke: *Don't **tempt** fate.*

Word building: **tempter** *noun* **temptress** *feminine noun* **tempting** *adjective* **temptingly** *adverb*
Word history: Middle English, from Latin word meaning 'touch', 'test'

temptation
noun **1** the act of tempting (***allurement***, ***enticement***, ***inducement***, ***seduction***)
2 something that tempts, entices or allures

Word history: Middle English *temptacion*, from Latin *templātio*

tempura (tem-<u>pooh</u>-ruh)
noun a Japanese food made from seafood or vegetables coated in a light batter and deep-fried in oil

Word history: Japanese, probably from Portuguese word meaning 'seasoning'

ten
noun **1** a cardinal number, nine plus one (9 + 1)
2 the symbol for this number, as 10 or X
3 a set of ten persons or things
adjective **4** amounting to ten in number

Word building: **tenth** *adjective* **tenth** *noun*
Word history: Middle English; Old English *tēn*

tenable
adjective able to be held, supported or defended, as against attack or objection: *a* ***tenable*** *theory*

Word building: **tenability** *noun*
Word history: French, from Latin word meaning 'hold', 'keep'

tenacious (tuh-nay-shuhs)
adjective **1** holding on firmly: *a* ***tenacious*** *grip*
2 stubbornly persistent: *a* ***tenacious*** *person* (***determined***, ***dogged***, ***resolute***, ***single-minded***, ***unflagging***)

Word building: **tenaciously** *adverb* **tenacity** *noun*
Word history: *tenaci(ty)* + *-ous*

tenant
noun someone who pays rent for the use of a house, land or a flat

Word building: **tenancy** *noun*
Word history: Middle English, from French word meaning 'hold', from Latin

tend[1]
verb **1** to be likely or inclined: *I* ***tend*** *to be cross when I'm tired.*
2 to move in a certain direction: *The sunflower* ***tends*** *towards the light.*

Word history: Middle English, from French, from Latin word meaning 'stretch', 'go', 'strive'

tend[2]
verb to watch or look after: *to* ***tend*** *a fire | The nurse is* ***tending*** *him.*

Word history: Middle English, variant of *attend*

tendency
noun a natural movement in some direction or towards some point, end or result

Noun forms: The plural is **tendencies**.
Word history: Medieval Latin, from Latin word meaning 'tend[1]'

tendentious (ten-den-shuhs)
adjective presented so as to influence in a desired direction or present a particular point of view: *a* ***tendentious*** *novel*

tender[1]
adjective **1** not tough or hard: ***tender*** *steak*
2 warm and affectionate: ***tender*** *parents* (***caring***, ***loving***, ***soft-hearted***, ***tender-hearted***)
3 gentle or delicate: *a* ***tender*** *touch*
4 painful to feel or discuss: ***tender*** *to the touch | It's a* ***tender*** *subject.*

Word building: **tenderly** *adverb* **tenderness** *noun*
Word history: Middle English, from French, from Latin word meaning 'soft', 'delicate', 'tender'

tender[2]
verb **1** to offer: *He* ***tendered*** *his resignation.* (***extend***, ***give***, ***hand in***, ***present***, ***submit***)
noun **2** an offer of payment or of doing a job for a certain price: *They will accept the lowest* ***tender***.

Word history: Anglo-French, from Latin

tendon
noun a cord of tough body tissue joining a muscle to a bone (***sinew***)

Word history: Medieval Latin, from Greek word meaning 'sinew'

tendril
noun a coiling, threadlike part of a climbing plant

Word history: French word meaning 'tender shoot', from Late Latin word meaning 'tender'

tenement (ten-uh-muhnt)
noun a building divided into flats, especially one in the poorer, crowded parts of a large city

Word history: Middle English, from Old French, from Latin

tenet (ten-uht)
noun any opinion, principle, teaching, etc., held as true

Word history: from Latin word meaning 'he holds'

tennis
noun a game in which two players, or two pairs of players, use racquets to hit a ball over a central net

Word history: Middle English, from Anglo-French word meaning 'hold', 'take'

tenon (ten-uhn)
noun a piece shaped to stick out on the end of a piece of wood, etc., to fit into a mortise (corresponding cavity) in another piece

Word history: Middle English, from Old French word meaning 'hold', from Latin

tenor (ten-uh)
noun **1** the range of musical notes which can be sung by a male singer with a high voice: *He sings* ***tenor*** *in the choir.*
2 a man with a high singing voice
3 the course of thought or meaning running through something spoken or written: *I didn't hear all the speech but I caught the* ***tenor*** *of it.* (***drift***, ***gist***, ***intent***, ***theme***)
adjective **4** having to do with, or having the range of a tenor: *a* ***tenor*** *saxophone*

Word use: **Tenor** range is higher than **baritone** and **bass** and lower than **soprano** and **alto**.
Word history: Middle English, from Medieval Latin word meaning 'course'

tenpin bowling
noun an indoor sport in which the player bowls a heavy ball down a wooden alley at ten upright objects (pins), trying to knock down as many as possible

tense[1]
adjective **1** rigid or stretched tight
2 suffering from nervous strain: *He has been very* ***tense*** *since his illness.*

Word use: The opposite of this is **relaxed**.
Word building: **tense** *verb*
Word history: from Latin word meaning 'stretched', 'taut'

tense[2]
noun the form of a verb which shows the time of an action

Word history: Middle English, from Old French, from Latin word meaning 'time'

For more information on **tense**, look up **verbs**.

tensile (ten-suyl)
adjective **1** having to do with tension: ***tensile*** *stress*
2 able to be stretched or drawn out (***ductile***)

Word history: Neo-Latin, from Latin word meaning 'stretch'

tension (<u>ten</u>-shuhn)
noun **1** the act of stretching or straining
2 the condition of being stretched or strained
3 a strained feeling of anxiety or excitement
4 a strained relationship between individuals, groups, countries, etc.
5 voltage

Word history: from Late Latin word meaning 'act of stretching'

tent
noun a movable shelter made of cloth, held up by poles

Word history: Middle English, from Old French, from Latin word meaning 'stretched'

tentacle
noun a thin, easily-bent, arm-like part on an animal such as an octopus, used for feeling and grasping

Word history: Neo-Latin, from Latin

tentative
adjective unsure or cautious: *He made a **tentative** attempt to join in the conversation.*

Word history: Medieval Latin, from Latin word meaning 'try'

tenterhooks
phrase **on tenterhooks**, in a condition of anxious waiting

tenuous
adjective weak or vague: *a **tenuous** connection*

Word history: from Latin word meaning 'slender'

tenure (<u>ten</u>-yuh)
noun **1** the holding or possession of anything: *the **tenure** of an office*
2 the holding of property, especially real property, in return for services
3 the time for which something is held

Word history: Middle English, from Old French, from Latin word meaning 'hold'

tepee
noun → **teepee**

tepid (<u>tep</u>-uhd)
adjective lukewarm or slightly warm

Word history: Middle English, from Latin

teppanyaki (te-pan-<u>yah</u>-kee)
noun a Japanese dish in which pieces of meat or fish are roasted on a hot iron plate

Word history: from Japanese words meaning 'iron' and 'roast' or 'bake'

teriyaki (te-ree-<u>yah</u>-kee)
noun a Japanese dish consisting of meat, chicken or seafood, marinated in a mixture containing soy sauce, and grilled

term
noun **1** a division of the year in schools and colleges
2 a period of time: *in the long **term***
3 a descriptive or naming word or group of words: *This book is full of technical **terms**.*
4 terms, conditions of agreement

Word history: Middle English, from Old French, from Latin word meaning 'boundary', 'limit', 'end'

terminal
adjective **1** marking the end: *the **terminal** chapter of a book* | *a **terminal** illness* (***final***, ***last***, ***ultimate***)
noun **2** the end of a railway line or other travel route where passengers and goods arrive and leave: *an air **terminal***
3 a point where current enters or leaves in an electrical circuit
4 → **computer terminal**

Word history: from Latin word meaning 'pertaining to an end or boundary'

terminally
adverb **1** incurably: ***terminally** ill*
2 *Colloquial* incessantly: ***terminally** bewildered*

terminate
verb **1** to bring to an end: *They have **terminated** his job at the factory.* (***close***, ***conclude***, ***cut off***, ***discontinue***, ***finish***)
2 to come to the end of a journey at a certain place: *This train **terminates** here.* (***cease***, ***finish***, ***stop***)
3 to end (a pregnancy) by causing the foetus to be expelled before it is developed enough to live

Word history: from Latin word meaning 'ended', 'limited'

terminology (ter-muh-<u>nol</u>-uh-jee)
noun the system of special words or phrases belonging to a science, art or subject: *the **terminology** of physics*

Noun forms: The plural is **terminologies**.
Word building: **terminological** *adjective*
Word history: German

terminus
noun a station at the end of a railway line or bus route

Noun forms: The plural is **terminuses** or **termini**.
Word history: from Latin word meaning 'boundary', 'limit'

termite
noun a pale-coloured insect which can destroy wooden buildings and furniture

Word use: A termite is often called a **white ant**, although it is not really an ant.
Word history: Neo-Latin, from Latin word meaning 'woodworm'

tern
noun a gull-like water bird with a slender body and beak, small feet, a long and deeply forked tail, and graceful flight

Word history: Scandinavian

ternary
adjective **1** consisting of or having to do with three (***treble***, ***triple***)
2 third in order or rank
3 based on the number three

Word history: Middle English, from Late Latin word meaning 'made up of three'

terrace
noun **1** a narrow, flattened area on the side of a hill: *a rice **terrace***
2 a row of houses joined together
3 one of these houses: *the end **terrace***

Word history: Old French word meaning 'terrace', 'pile of earth', from French word meaning 'earth', from Latin

terracotta
noun **1** a clay used for pipes, roof tiles and other similar things
2 a brownish-red colour

Word building: **terracotta** *adjective*
Word history: Italian word meaning 'baked earth', from Latin

terrain
noun a part of the land surface, with its natural features in mind: *rough **terrain***

Word history: French word meaning 'earth', from Latin

terrarium (tuh-rair-ree-uhm)
noun **1** a closed glass container in which moisture-loving plants are grown
2 a container in which small animals, such as lizards, turtles, etc., are kept

Noun forms: The plural is **terrariums** or **terraria** (tuh-rair-ree-uh).
Word history: from Neo-Latin word meaning 'earth'

terrazzo (tuh-raht-soh, tuh-rahz-oh)
noun a type of floor material of chippings of broken stone and cement, polished when in place

Word history: Italian word meaning 'terrace', 'balcony'

terrestrial
adjective living or growing on land

Word history: Middle English, from Latin word meaning 'having to do with earth'

terrible
adjective **1** causing great fear: *a **terrible** monster* (***dreadful***, ***frightening***, ***frightful***, ***horrendous***, ***horrible***)
2 very bad: *a **terrible** noise*

Word history: Middle English, from Latin

terrier
noun a kind of small dog, originally used for hunting

Word history: Middle English, from French

terrific
adjective **1** very great: ***terrific** speed*
2 very good: *a **terrific** game* (***excellent***, ***exceptional***, ***fantastic***, ***great***, ***outstanding***)

Word history: from Latin word meaning 'frightening'

terrify
verb to frighten very much (***alarm***, ***petrify***, ***scare***)

Verb forms: I **terrified**, I have **terrified**, I am **terrifying**
Word history: Latin

terrine (tuh-reen)
noun **1** an earthenware cooking dish
2 pâté served in such a dish

Word history: French

territory
noun **1** any area of land, especially a region thought of as belonging to someone: *enemy **territory***
2 the land and waters under the control of a particular government, ruler, etc.: *Australian **territory***
3 an area controlled by a country in whose government it is not fully represented: *the **territories** of Australia*

Noun forms: The plural is **territories**.
Word building: **territorial** *adjective*
Word history: Middle English, from Latin word meaning 'land round a town', 'district'

terror
noun an overpowering fear

Word history: Latin

terrorise
verb to control or force by the use of fear: *The bully **terrorised** the younger children.* (***frighten***, ***intimidate***, ***menace***, ***terrify***, ***threaten***)

Word use: You can also use **terrorize**.

terrorist
noun someone who uses violence for political purposes: *After the bombing, the government stated it would not give in to the demands of **terrorists**.*

Word building: **terrorism** *noun*

terry towelling
noun a cotton cloth with loops on both sides

terse
adjective short and to the point: *a **terse** comment* (***abrupt***, ***blunt***, ***brusque***, ***curt***, ***succinct***)

Word use: The opposite of this is **wordy**.
Word history: from Latin word meaning 'polished'

tertiary (ter-shuh-ree)
adjective belonging to the third order, rank, formation, etc.

Word history: from Latin word meaning 'of third part or rank'

tertiary education (ter-shuh-ree ej-uh-kay-shuhn)
noun education at college or university, which follows secondary education

terylene (te-ruh-leen)
noun a synthetic polyester fibre, used in clothing manufacture

Word history: Trademark

test
noun **1** a trial to decide something: *a **test** of strength* (***assessment***, ***check-up***, ***investigation***)
2 a set of questions to answer, designed to show how much you know about something: *a maths **test*** (***exam***, ***examination***)
3 → **test match**
verb **4** to try in order to find out: *to **test** if the water is hot enough | to **test** the class's knowledge* (***assay***, ***check***, ***examine***, ***investigate***, ***screen***)

Word history: Middle English, from Old French, from Latin word meaning 'tile', 'earthen vessel', 'pot'

testament
noun a will

Word use: This is used mostly in the phrase 'last will and testament'.
Word building: **testamentary** *adjective*
Word history: Middle English, from Latin word meaning 'will'

testes (tes-teez)
plural noun the testicles

Noun forms: The singular is **testis**.

testicle (tes-tik-uhl)
noun one of the two, round, male sex glands in the scrotum

Word use: Another name is **testis**.
Word history: from Latin *testis*

testify
verb **1** to swear as true: *The witness **testified** that he had seen a blue sedan near the bank.*
2 to give evidence: *The barren land **testifies** to a hard winter.*

Verb forms: I **testified**, I have **testified**, I am **testifying**
Word history: Middle English, from Latin word meaning 'bear witness'

testimonial
noun **1** a reference for a job
2 something given as an expression of appreciation: *He was given a watch as a **testimonial** from his workmates.*

testimony (test-uh-muh-nee)
noun the statement of a witness who is under oath to tell the truth

Noun forms: The plural is **testimonies**.
Word history: late Middle English, from Latin word meaning 'evidence', 'attestation'

testis (tes-tuhs)
noun → **testicle**

Noun forms: The plural is **testes** (tes-teez).
Word history: Latin

test match
noun one of a series of international sporting events, usually cricket or Rugby football

Word use: You can also use **test**.

test tube
noun a hollow glass cylinder with one end closed, used in chemical tests

testy
adjective touchy or irritably impatient

Adjective forms: **testier**, **testiest**
Word history: Middle English, from Anglo-French word meaning 'headstrong', from Old French word meaning 'head'

tetanus (tet-uh-nuhs)
noun an infectious, often deadly, disease which causes extreme stiffness of the muscles of the jaw and other parts of the body

Word use: An old-fashioned word for this is **lockjaw**.
Word history: Latin, from Greek word meaning 'spasm (of muscles)'

tether
noun a rope or chain for tying up an animal

Word building: **tether** *verb*
Word history: Middle English, apparently from Scandinavian

text
noun **1** the main body of words in a book, not including notes, the index and other extra material
2 a written, spoken or visual work, especially one with special features shared with other works of the same type
3 → **textbook**
verb **4** to send a text message: *He sat there **texting** all through dinner.* | ***Text** me when you arrive.* | *I'll **text** the information to you.*

Word building: **textual** *adjective*
Word history: Middle English, from Medieval Latin word meaning 'wording (of the Gospel)', Latin word meaning 'structure (of a discourse)', originally 'texture'

texta
noun → **felt pen**

Word history: Trademark

textaholic
noun Colloquial someone who sends an excessive number of text messages

Word building: **textaholism** *noun*

textbook
noun a book setting out the information for a course of study in a subject

Word use: You can also use **text**.

textile
noun any woven material used for clothing, curtains, etc. (***cloth***, ***fabric***, ***stuff***)

Word history: from Latin word meaning 'woven'

text message
noun a message sent by mobile phone using SMS

Word use: You can also use **SMS message** or **SMS**.
Word building: **text messaging** *noun*

texture
noun the roughness or smoothness of a material: *The pebbles next to the concrete give a contrast in **texture**.*

Word history: late Middle English, from Latin word meaning 'weaving'

thalidomide (thuh-lid-uh-muyd)
noun a drug, formerly used as a sedative until it was found to affect normal growth of the foetus if taken during pregnancy

Word history: formed from *thal(lic)* + *(im)ido-* + *(glutari)mide* (from *glut(en)* + *(tart)ar(ic)* + *imide*)

thallus
noun a simple plant body that does not have true leaves, stem and root

Noun forms: The plural is **thalli** (thal-uy) or **thalluses**.
Word history: Neo-Latin, from Greek word meaning 'young shoot', 'twig'

than
conjunction **1** used after adjectives, adverbs and certain other comparative words, such as *other, otherwise, else*, etc., to introduce the second part of the comparison: *He is taller **than** I am.*
preposition **2** in comparison with: *He is taller **than** me.*

Word history: Middle English and Old English

Sometimes people use *than what* when a simple **than** is all that's needed.

They always stay longer than what I do.

The sentence above is not acceptable usage. Write instead:

They always stay longer than I do.

thank
verb **1** to give thanks to: *to **thank** them for their kindness*
noun **2 thanks**, words saying how grateful you are

Word building: **thankful** *adjective* **thankless** *adjective*
Word history: Middle English; Old English *thanc* gratitude

thanks
plural noun **1** acknowledgement of gratitude for a benefit or favour, by words or otherwise: *to return a borrowed book with **thanks***
interjection **2** an expression used in acknowledging a favour, service or courtesy that someone receives
phrase **3 thanks a million** (or **a bunch**), (*often ironic*) an emphatic expression of thanks
4 thanks but no thanks, (*sometimes ironic*) an expression of polite rejection: *We said **thanks but no thanks** when he offered to help with the painting — last time he helped was a disaster.*
5 thanks to,
a thanks are due to: ***Thanks to** Graeme, we finished the painting on time.*
b as a result or consequence of
6 vote of thanks, a formal expression of appreciation, usually on behalf of a group of people

thanksgiving
noun **1** the act of giving thanks
2 an expression of thanks, especially to God

thank you
interjection an expression used to tell someone that you are grateful to them: ***Thank you**, I would really like to come.*

that
pronoun **1** a demonstrative pronoun used to show:
a a person, thing or idea, etc., pointed out, mentioned or suggested to you: ***That** is my husband.*
b one of two or more people, things, etc., already mentioned, referring to the one that is further away: ***That** is riper than this.*
2 a relative pronoun used:
a as the subjective or object of a relative clause: *How old is the car **that** was stolen?*
b in various special forms: *fool **that** he is*
adjective **3** a demonstrative adjective used to show:
a a person, thing or idea: ***That** man is my husband.*
b the one of two or more people, things, etc., that is further away: *It was **that** book I wanted, not this one.*
adverb **4** used with other adverbs and adjectives to show the precise degree, extent, etc.: ***that** much* | ***that** far*
conjunction **5** used to introduce a noun clause: ***That** he will come is certain.*
phrase **6 at that**, besides, or additionally: *It's an idea, and a good one **at that**.*
7 that is, more exactly and precisely: *I see him often: well, **that is**, once a week.*
8 that's that, that is the end of the matter: *I've lost it, so **that's that**.*

Pronoun forms: (*plural* **those**)
Word history: Middle English; Old English *thæt* that, the

For more information about **that** as a pronoun, look up **pronouns: demonstrative pronouns** and **pronouns: relative pronouns.**

Demonstrative adjectives (see definition 3) are sometimes called *determiners.*

thatch
verb to cover a roof with straw, reeds or palm leaves

Word building: **thatch** *noun*
Word history: Old English *thæc* roof, thatch

thaw
verb to melt: *The ice has **thawed**.* (***defrost**, **dissolve**, **liquefy**, **unfreeze***)

Word building: **thaw** *noun*
Word history: Old English *thawian*

the
definite article a particular person or thing, already referred to or about to be identified

Look up **articles in grammar: definite articles.**

theatre (<u>thear</u>-tuh)
noun **1** a building or hall for presenting plays, opera, ballet, etc.
2 a cinema
3 a room in a hospital where operations are performed

Word use: The US spelling is **theater**.
Word history: Middle English, from Latin, from Greek word meaning 'seeing place', 'theatre'

theatrical (thee-<u>at</u>-rik-uhl)
adjective **1** in or belonging to a theatre: *a **theatrical** presentation*
2 aiming to create an effect: *She made a **theatrical** entrance into the restaurant.*

theft
noun the act or crime of stealing

Word history: Middle English; Old English *thēoft*

their
pronoun the possessive form of **they** used before a noun: ***their** dog*

Their is a third person plural pronoun. It is sometimes called a *determiner* or a *possessive adjective.*

See the note at **they** regarding the use of **their** as a singular pronoun, as in *If anyone has lost their form, please come to the information desk.*

For more information, look up **pronouns: personal pronouns** and **pronouns: possessive pronouns.**

their / there / they're

Don't confuse **their** with **there** or **they're.**

There is used to indicate or call attention to a place or point:

Please move over there.

They're is a form of *they are*:

They're going to visit us today.

Look up **contractions in grammar.**

For more information about **their,** look up **pronouns: personal pronouns** and **pronouns: possessive pronouns.**

theirs
pronoun **1** the possessive form of **they**, used without a noun following: *Those books are* ***theirs****.*
2 the person(s) or thing(s) belonging to them: ***Theirs*** *is the red car parked around the back.*

Theirs is a third person plural pronoun in the possessive case.
See the note at **they** regarding the use of **theirs** as a singular pronoun, as in *If anyone thinks this watch is theirs, please see me after school.*
For more information, look up **pronouns: personal pronouns** and **pronouns: possessive pronouns.**

theism (<u>thee</u>-iz-uhm)
noun belief in the existence of a God or gods
Word use: The opposite is **atheism**.
Word building: **theist** *noun* **theist** *adjective* **theistic** *adjective*
Word history: from Greek word meaning 'god'

them
pronoun **1** the personal pronoun used, usually after a verb or preposition, to refer to a number of people or things: *I'll put* ***them*** *in my bag. | Get it from* ***them*** *tomorrow.*
2 a personal pronoun used, usually after a verb or preposition, to refer to a single person when the sex of the person is unknown: *If anyone needs a new form, I am happy to supply* ***them*** *with one.*

Them is a third person plural pronoun in the objective case.
See the note at **they** regarding the use of **them** as a singular pronoun, as in definition 2.
For more information, look up **pronouns: personal pronouns**.

theme
noun the subject of a speech, a book or a piece of music
Word history: Middle English, from Latin, from Greek

themself
pronoun a reflexive form of **they** used as a singular pronoun when the sex of the person being referred to is unknown

This is regarded as incorrect by many people. See the note at **themselves**.

themselves
pronoun **1** the reflexive form of **they**: *They hurt* ***themselves****.*
2 a form of **them** or **they** used for emphasis: *They did it* ***themselves****.*

For more information, look up **pronouns: reflexive pronouns**.
Like **they** and **them**, **themselves** can be used as a singular pronoun when the sex of the person being referred to is unknown (*If someone comes to the door they can let themselves in*). Sometimes, the form **themself** is used in this situation (*A child might hurt themself on this equipment*). Note, however, that some people would still regard **themself** as an incorrect use.

then
adverb **1** at the time: *Prices were lower* ***then****.*
2 immediately or soon afterwards: *He stopped, and* ***then*** *began again.*
3 next in order of time, or of place: *He unlocked the door,* ***then*** *walked inside. | Down the road there's a shop,* ***then*** *a garage.*
4 at another time
5 in addition: *She gave me ten dollars,* ***then*** *another three dollars.*
6 in that case: *If it gets hot,* ***then*** *I'll wear a hat.*
adjective **7** being at that time: *the* ***then*** *prime minister*
noun **8** that time: *till* ***then***
Word history: Old English *thæn*

thence
adverb Old-fashioned **1** from that place: *Julius Caesar marched to Gaul and* ***thence*** *to Spain.*
2 from that time: *The bill was passed in parliament and* ***thence*** *became law.*
3 for that reason: *He had the stolen jewels in his possession, and* ***thence*** *the police believed him to be the robber.*
Word history: Old English *thanone* thence

theodolite (thee-<u>od</u>-uh-luyt)
noun an instrument used in surveying land

theology
noun **1** the study of God and religion
2 a collection of beliefs held by a particular religion: *Christian* ***theology*** (***creed***, ***doctrine***, ***dogma***, ***teachings***)
Noun forms: The plural is **theologies**.
Word building: **theologian** *noun* **theological** *adjective*
Word history: Middle English, from Latin, from Greek

theorem (<u>thear</u>-ruhm)
noun a statement containing something to be proved in mathematics
Word history: Late Latin, from Greek word meaning 'spectacle', 'theory', 'thesis (to be proved)'

theoretical (thee-uh-<u>ret</u>-ik-uhl)
adjective **1** having to do with theory as opposed to practice: *a* ***theoretical*** *approach to a topic*
2 existing only in theory: *a* ***theoretical*** *star in space* (***conjectural***, ***hypothetical***, ***problematical***)
3 given to, forming or dealing with theories: *a* ***theoretical*** *explanation* (***speculative***)
Word use: The opposite of definition 1 is **practical**. | You can also use **theoretic**.

theorise (<u>thear</u>-ruyz)
verb **1** to form a theory
2 to think, or speculate
Word use: You can also use **theorize**.
Word building: **theorisation** *noun* **theorist** *noun*

theory (<u>thear</u>-ree)
noun **1** an explanation based on observation and reason: *atomic* ***theory*** (***hypothesis***, ***thesis***)
2 a suggested explanation with little or no basis in fact: *a* ***theory*** *about ghosts* (***conjecture***, ***speculation***, ***supposition***)
3 the part of a subject which deals with underlying principles rather than practice: *You can put a new element in an electric jug without knowing the* ***theory*** *of electricity.*
Noun forms: The plural is **theories**.
Word history: Late Latin, from Greek word meaning 'contemplation', 'theory'

therapeutic (ther-uh-pyooh-tik)
adjective having to do with the treating or curing of disease (***curative, remedial***)

Word use: You can also use **therapeutical**.
Word history: Neo-Latin, from Greek word meaning 'one who treats medically'

therapy
noun healing treatment: *water **therapy** | speech **therapy***

Noun forms: The plural is **therapies**.
Word building: **therapist** *noun*
Word history: Neo-Latin, from Greek word meaning 'healing'

there
adverb **1** in or at that place: *The book is **there**, on the top shelf.*
2 at that particular point: *He finished **there**, ready to start again.*
3 in that matter, etc.: *I must agree with you **there**.*
4 into or to that place: *Go in **there**.*
5 used to call attention to something: ***There** they go.*
adjective **6** used for emphasis: *that man **there***
pronoun **7** that place: *He comes from **there** too.*
8 used to begin a sentence or clause in which the verb comes before its subject: ***There** is no hope.*
interjection **9** an exclamation used to show satisfaction, etc.: ***There**! It's done!*
phrase **10 all there**, *Colloquial* of sound mind: *Are you sure he's **all there**?*

Word history: Middle English; Old English *thær*

there / their / they're
Look up **their / there / they're**.

thereabouts
adverb **1** about or near that place or time
2 about that number, amount, etc.

Word use: You can also use **thereabout**.

thereby
adverb Old-fashioned **1** by means of that: *She studied hard, and **thereby** passed her exams.*
2 in that connection or relation: ***Thereby** hangs a tale.*
3 by or near that place

therefore
adverb as a result

Word history: Middle English

thereupon
adverb Old-fashioned as a following action or immediate result: *The winner was announced. **Thereupon** the audience started clapping and cheering.*

thermal (ther-muhl)
adjective **1** having to do with heat or temperature: ***thermal** energy*
noun **2** a rising current of air caused by local heating, used by glider pilots, birds, etc., to go higher

Word use: You can also use **thermic** for definition 1.
Word history: from Greek word meaning 'heat'

thermodynamics (ther-moh-duy-nam-iks)
noun the science concerned with processes involving heat changes and conversion of energy

Word building: **thermodynamic** *adjective* **thermodynamical** *adjective* **thermodynamically** *adverb*

thermometer
noun an instrument for measuring temperature

thermos
noun a double-walled container, usually made of silvered glass and having a vacuum between the two walls, used to keep substances at a constant temperature

Word history: Trademark; Greek word meaning 'hot'

thermostat
noun a device for keeping a temperature steady: *an oven **thermostat***

thesaurus (thuh-saw-ruhs)
noun a book of words arranged in groups which have a similar meaning

Noun forms: The plural is **thesauruses**.
Word history: Latin, from Greek word meaning 'treasure', 'treasury'

these
pronoun, adjective plural of **this**: ***These** are my favourite paintings. | **These** plates are dirty.*

For more information, look up **pronouns: demonstrative pronouns / adjectives**.

thesis (thee-suhs)
noun **1** an idea, argument or explanation, especially one to be discussed and proved
2 a book-length essay presented by a student for a higher university degree

Noun forms: The plural is **theses** (thee-seez).
Word history: Middle English, from Greek word meaning 'setting down', 'something set down'

thespian (thes-pee-uhn)
adjective **1** having to do with tragedy or with dramatic art in general (***dramatic, tragic***)
noun **2** an actor or actress

Word use: You will also see this written **Thespian**.
Word history: from *Thespis*, a poet living in the sixth century BC

they
pronoun **1** the personal pronoun used to refer to a number of people or things, not including the speaker or the person spoken to. It is the plural of **he**, **she** and **it**.
2 a personal pronoun used to refer to a single person when the sex of the person is unknown: *If anyone wants to go, **they** should let me know.*

They (definition 1) is a third person plural pronoun in the subjective case. Definition 2 is used as a singular pronoun.

The use of **they** as a singular pronoun (definition 2) is becoming more widespread when the sex of the person being referred to is unknown. Nowadays, speakers try to avoid using *he* because it can be considered sexist, and *he or she* because it is clumsy. Instead of saying *If anyone knows the answer, he should speak up* or *If anyone knows the answer, he or she should speak up*, it is neater to say *If anyone knows the answer, they should speak up*. The other forms of the pronoun (**them, their** and **theirs**) are used in the same way. Also look up **themselves**.

For more information, look up **pronouns: personal pronouns**.

they'd
contraction of **they had** or **they would**

Look up **contractions in grammar.**

they'll
contraction of **they will** or **they shall**

Look up **contractions in grammar.**

they're
contraction of **they are**

Look up **contractions in grammar.**

they're / their / there
Look up **their / there / they're.**

they've
contraction of **they have**

Look up **contractions in grammar.**

thiamine (thuy-uh-meen)
noun vitamin B_1, part of vitamin B complex, needed by the nervous system, the absence of which causes beri-beri, etc.

Word use: You can also use **thiamin.**
Word history: *thi(o)- + (vit)amin*

thick
adjective **1** measuring rather a lot from one surface to the other: *a **thick** slice of bread | a **thick** blanket* (***chunky, dense, heavy, solid***)
2 measuring as stated between opposite surfaces: *a board two centimetres **thick***
3 dense or packed close together: ***thick** bush | a **thick** crowd*
4 not runny or pouring easily: *a **thick** sauce* (***gelatinous, gluey, viscous***)
5 with the particles close together: ***thick** smoke*

Word building: **thicken** *verb* **thickness** *noun*
Word history: Middle English; Old English *thicce*

thicket
noun a thick growth of shrubs or small trees

Word history: Old English *thiccet*

thickset
adjective **1** dense: *a **thickset** hedge*
2 with thick form or build: *a **thickset** person* (***beefy, burly, heavy, stocky, stumpy***)

thief
noun someone who steals (***bandit, burglar, kleptomaniac, pickpocket, robber, shoplifter***)

Noun forms: The plural is **thieves.**
Word history: Middle English; Old English *thēof*

thieve
verb to steal (***knock off, nick, pilfer, pinch, take***)

Word history: Old English *thēofian*

thigh
noun in humans, the part of the leg between the groin and the knee

Word history: Middle English; Old English *thēoh*

thimble
noun a protective cover for the finger, worn when sewing

Word history: Old English *thymel*

thin
adjective **1** measuring not much from one surface or side to the other: *a **thin** slice of bread | a **thin** line* (***fine, narrow***)
2 slim or lean: *He keeps **thin** by exercising.* (***skinny, slender, slight, spindly***)
3 barely covering or scattered: ***thin** hair | a **thin** crowd*
4 runny or watery: ***thin** gravy*
5 easily seen through: ***thin** curtains | a **thin** excuse* (***delicate, filmy, sheer, transparent, unsubstantial***)

Word building: **thin** *verb* (**thinned, thinning**) **thinness** *noun*
Word history: Middle English and Old English *thynne*

thing
noun **1** a real object that is not alive
2 some object which is not or cannot be easily described: *The stick had a brass **thing** on it.*
3 a matter or affair: ***Things** are going well.*
4 things, utensils or personal belongings: *the tea **things** | Your **things** are on the table.*

Word history: Middle English and Old Dutch

think
verb **1** to form or turn over in your mind: *to **think** pleasant thoughts | He was **thinking** what to do.*
2 to imagine or have an idea of: ***Think** what it would be like to be rich.*
3 to have a purpose in mind: *She **thought** she would go home.*
4 to consider or have an opinion: *He **thought** the film was good.*
5 to take account: ***Think** of other people's feelings.*
phrase **6 think aloud,** to say what your thoughts are as they come into your mind
7 think better of, to decide against something that you had originally intended
8 think little of, to have a low opinion of
9 think nothing of,
a to have a low opinion of: *I **think nothing of** him because he is so rude.*
b to not be worried or hesitant about: ***Think nothing of** asking for my help.*

Verb forms: I **thought,** I have **thought,** I am **thinking**
Word history: Middle English; Old English *thencan*

third
adjective **1** next after the second
2 being one of three equal parts
noun **3** a third part
4 the third member of a series

third party
noun any person other than those directly involved in some agreement, business affair, etc.

third person
noun a grammatical category for pronouns, indicating the person or thing being spoken about

Pronouns such as *she, him* and *themselves* are said to be in the *third person,* which is the person being spoken about. (**First person** is the one speaking, **second person** is the one spoken to.) For more information, look up **person in grammar.**

third world
noun developing countries thought of as one group, especially those of Africa, South America, and South-East Asia

Word use: You can also use **Third World**.

thirst
noun **1** an uncomfortable feeling of dryness in the mouth and throat caused by the need for a drink
2 an eager desire: *a* ***thirst*** *for knowledge*

Word building: **thirsty** *adjective* (**thirstier**, **thirstiest**) **thirst** *verb*
Word history: Old English *thyrstan*

thirteen
noun **1** a cardinal number, ten plus three (10 + 3)
2 a symbol for this number, as 13 or XIII
3 a set of thirteen people or things
adjective **4** amounting to thirteen in number

Word building: **thirteenth** *adjective* **thirteenth** *noun*
Word history: Old English *thrēotēne*

thirty
noun **1** a cardinal number, ten times three (10 × 3)
2 a symbol for this number, as 30 or XXX
3 a set of thirty persons or things
4 thirties, the numbers from 30 to 39 of a series, especially with reference to the years of a person's age, or the years of a century
adjective **5** amounting to thirty in number

Noun forms: The plural is **thirties**.
Word building: **thirtieth** *adjective* **thirtieth** *noun*
Word history: Old English *thrītig*

this
pronoun **1** a demonstrative pronoun used to show:
a a person, thing or idea pointed out, mentioned, etc.: ***This*** *is your seat.*
b the nearest of one or two people, things, etc.: ***This*** *is a prettier hat than that.*
adjective **2** a demonstrative adjective used to show:
a a person, thing or idea pointed out, mentioned, etc.: ***This*** *book is very boring.*
b the nearest of one or two people, things, etc.: ***This*** *way is quicker than that.*
adverb **3** an adverb used with adjectives and adverbs of quantity or extent: *Do you like* ***this*** *much milk in your tea?*
phrase **4 with this**, immediately after this: *He said goodbye, and* ***with this*** *went into the garden to read.*

Pronoun forms: (*plural* **these**)
Word history: Middle English and Old English

For more information, look up **pronouns: demonstrative pronouns**.
Demonstrative adjectives (see definition 2) are sometimes called *determiners*.

thistle
noun a plant with prickly leaves and purple or white flowers

Word history: Middle English and Old English *thistel*

thither (<u>dhidh</u>-uh)
adverb to or towards that place or point: *The path runs* ***thither***.

Word history: Middle English; Old English *thider*

thong
noun **1** *Australian* a simple kind of sandal, usually made of rubber or leather
2 a narrow strip of leather
3 *US* → **G-string**

thorax (<u>thaw</u>-raks)
noun **1** the chest in human beings or a similar part in other animals
2 the part of an insect's body between its head and abdomen

Noun forms: The plural is **thoraces** (<u>thaw</u>-ruh-seez, thaw-<u>ray</u>-seez) or **thoraxes**.
Word building: **thoracic** (thuh-<u>ras</u>-ik) *adjective*
Word history: Middle English, from Latin, from Greek word meaning 'breastplate', 'chest'

thorn
noun a sharp-pointed prickle on the stem of a plant

Word building: **thorny** *adjective* (**thornier**, **thorniest**)
Word history: Middle English and Old English

thorough (<u>thu</u>-ruh)
adjective complete, careful or without missing anything: *a* ***thorough*** *search | a* ***thorough*** *wash* (***comprehensive***, ***detailed***, ***exhaustive***, ***in-depth***, ***intensive***)

Word building: **thoroughness** *noun*
Word history: Middle English; Old English *thuruh*

thoroughfare
noun a public road or way open at both ends

those
pronoun, *adjective* plural of **that**: ***Those*** *are my shoes. | Do you like* ***those*** *colours?*

For more information, look up **pronouns: demonstrative pronouns / adjectives**.

though
conjunction **1** in spite of the fact that: ***Though*** *we had no money, we had a good time.*
2 yet, still or nevertheless: *I will go* ***though*** *I fear it will be useless.*
adverb **3** for all that or however
phrase **4 as though**, as if: *It rained* ***as though*** *it would never stop.*

Word history: Middle English, from Scandinavian

thought[1]
noun **1** the forming of ideas in your mind
2 an idea (***concept***, ***notion***, ***theory***)
3 consideration or reflection: *Give it* ***thought*** *before you agree.*

Word history: Old English *thoht*

thought[2]
verb past tense and past participle of **think**

thoughtful
adjective **1** thinking hard about something in particular, or tending to do a lot of thinking in general: *The bad news made him* ***thoughtful***. *| She's a* ***thoughtful*** *sort of person, always taking the time to think things through.*
2 showing that someone had done a lot of thinking: *a* ***thoughtful*** *piece of writing*
3 kind and considerate, always thinking about other people's needs and feelings: *It was very* ***thoughtful*** *of you to send me a Christmas card.*

Word building: **thoughtfully** *adverb*
thoughtfulness *noun*

thoughtless
adjective not thinking about or caring about other people's needs and feelings: *Her **thoughtless** remark hurt many people's feelings.*

Word building: **thoughtlessly** *adverb*
thoughtlessness *noun*

thousand
noun **1** a cardinal number, ten times one hundred (10×100)
2 a symbol for this number, as 1000 or M
3 a great number or amount
adjective **4** amounting to one thousand in number

Word building: **thousandth** *adjective*
thousandth *noun*
Word history: Middle English; Old English *thūsend*

thrash
verb **1** to beat soundly as a punishment (***cane***, ***flog***, ***lash***, ***scourge***, ***whip***)
2 to defeat utterly (***beat***, ***conquer***, ***lick***, ***vanquish***, ***wipe out***)

Word history: variant of *thresh*

thread (thred)
noun **1** a very thin cord of cotton, wool or other fibre spun out to a great length and used for weaving cloth
2 a very thin cord of any fibre used for sewing
3 a thin strand
4 the spiral part on a screw
5 *Internet* a newsgroup posting and its set of replies, forming a group of related messages
verb **6** to pass a thread through

Word history: Old English *thrǣd*

threadbare
adjective worn and thin: ***threadbare** trousers* | *a **threadbare** argument* (***ragged***, ***shabby***, ***tattered***, ***worn out***)

threat (thret)
noun **1** a warning that you intend to hurt or rob someone: *Terrified by his **threats**, she handed over the money.*
2 a possible danger: *a **threat** of war*

Word building: **threaten** *verb*
Word history: Old English *thrēat* throng, threat, distress

threatened species
noun a species that is considered to be at risk of extinction in its natural habitat. Depending on the level of this risk, an endangered species may be classified as critically endangered, endangered or vulnerable.

Word use: Compare this with **endangered species**, **critically endangered species**, and **vulnerable species**.

three
noun **1** a cardinal number, two plus one ($2 + 1$)
2 a symbol for this number, as 3 or III
3 a set of three people or things
adjective **4** amounting to three in number

Word building: **third** *adjective* **third** *noun*
Word history: Middle English; Old English *thrēo*

three-dimensional
adjective having, or seeming to have, length, breadth and height and therefore a solid look

thresh
verb to separate grain or seeds from a plant, by beating: *to **thresh** corn*

Word history: Old English *threscan*

threshold (<u>thresh</u>-hohld)
noun **1** the bottom part of an entrance or doorway: *He paused on the **threshold**.*
2 a beginning point: *the **threshold** of a career*

Word history: Old English *threscold, -wold*

threw (throoh)
verb past tense of **throw**

threw / through
Don't confuse **threw** with **through**. The most common meaning of the preposition **through** is 'in at one place and out at the other':
The train went through the tunnel.

thrice
adverb three times, or on three occasions

Word history: Old English *thrīga*

thrift
noun careful management of money and supplies

Word use: The opposite of this is **extravagance**.
Word building: **thrifty** *adjective* (**thriftier**, **thriftiest**) **thriftless** *adjective*
Word history: Middle English, from *thrive*

thrill
verb **1** to feel a sudden wave of strong emotion: *to **thrill** with terror*
2 to excite very much: *She was **thrilled** at winning the prize.*

Word building: **thrill** *noun* **thrilling** *adjective*
Word history: Middle English, from Old English *thyrlian*

thriller
noun an exciting story, especially one about a crime

thrive
verb **1** to grow strongly
2 to do well or prosper: *The business is **thriving**.* (***bloom***, ***blossom***, ***boom***, ***flower***, ***succeed***)

Word history: Middle English, from Scandinavian

throat
noun **1** the front of the neck below the chin
2 the passage from the mouth to the stomach or lungs

Word history: Middle English and Old English *throte*

throb
verb to beat regularly and strongly: *His heart **throbbed**.* | *The engine **throbbed**.* (***drum***, ***palpitate***, ***pulsate***, ***vibrate***, ***whirr***)

Verb forms: it **throbbed**, it has **throbbed**, it is **throbbing**
Word history: Middle English

throes (throhz)
plural noun **1** any violent disturbance or struggle
phrase **2 in the throes of**, fully involved and struggling with: *She was **in the throes of** writing her latest novel.*
Word history: Middle English

thrombosis
noun a clotting of the blood within the blood vessels

Word history: Neo-Latin, from Greek word meaning 'curdling', 'clotting'

throne
noun **1** the special chair used by a king, queen or bishop on important occasions
2 the office or power of a king or queen: *to be loyal to the* ***throne***

Word history: Middle English, from Latin, from Greek word meaning 'high seat'

> **throne / thrown**
> Don't confuse **throne** with **thrown**, which is a past form of the verb **throw**. It is the past participle:
> *My ball was thrown over the fence by my brother.*

throng
noun **1** a crowd: ***Throngs*** *of people watched the parade.* (***flock***, ***herd***, ***mob***, ***multitude***, ***pack***)
verb **2** to crowd, or crowd upon: *People* ***thronged*** *to the show.*

Word history: Middle English; Old English *gethrang*

throttle
verb **1** to choke or strangle
noun **2** a device such as a lever which controls the flow of petrol into a engine

Word history: late Middle English

through (throoh)
preposition **1** in at one end, side, etc., and out the other, of: *The bullet passed* ***through*** *his body.*
2 past: *The car went* ***through*** *the red light without stopping.*
3 between or among the parts of: *to swing* ***through*** *the trees*
4 over the surface of: *to travel* ***through*** *a country*
5 during the whole period of: *to work* ***through*** *the night*
6 having reached the end of, often successfully: *to be* ***through*** *your work | to get* ***through*** *your exams*
adverb **7** all the way: *The train goes right* ***through*** *to Perth.*
8 throughout: *wet* ***through***
9 from the beginning to the end: *to read a letter right* ***through*** *| to carry the matter* ***through***
adjective **10** going through the whole of a distance without stopping: *a* ***through*** *train*
phrase **11 go through**, to wear out: *to* ***go through*** *three pairs of shoes*
12 through with, finished or done with: *Are you* ***through with*** *the bathroom?*

Word use: You can also use **thro, thro'** or **thru**, but generally not in formal writing.
Word history: Middle English; variant of *thourgh*, Old English *thurh*

throughout
preposition **1** everywhere in
2 from the beginning to the end of
adverb **3** in every part: *In this building there are lifts* ***throughout.***
4 at every moment or point

throw
verb **1** to fling or send through the air (***chuck***, ***hurl***, ***pitch***, ***sling***, ***toss***)
2 to arrange: *to* ***throw*** *a party*
phrase **3 throw in**, to add as an extra: *If you buy these jeans, we'll* ***throw in*** *a sweater as well.*
4 throw out,
a to say indirectly or casually: *to* ***throw out*** *a remark or hint*
b to refuse to accept
c to cause to make a mistake
d to expel (***cast out***, ***evict***, ***exile***, ***jettison***, ***reject***)
5 throw over, to abandon or leave behind
6 throw together, to put together in a quick or casual way: *to* ***throw together*** *a delicious meal*
7 throw up, to vomit

Verb forms: I **threw**, I have **thrown**, I am **throwing**
Word building: **throw** *noun*
Word history: Middle English; Old English *thrāwan* turn, twist

thrush[1]
noun a type of migratory bird, of medium size, not brightly coloured, but noted for its song

Word history: Old English *thrȳsce*

thrush[2]
noun a disease caused by a parasitic fungus, with whitish spots and ulcers found on the membranes of the mouth, throat, vagina, etc.

thrust
verb to force or push hard: *to* ***thrust*** *a dagger into his back | to* ***thrust*** *through the crowds* (***drive***, ***propel***, ***ram***, ***shove***)

Verb forms: I **thrust**, I have **thrust**, I am **thrusting**
Word building: **thrust** *noun*
Word history: Middle English, from Scandinavian

thud
noun a heavy bumping sound: *to fall to the ground with a* ***thud***

Word building: **thud** *verb* (**thudded, thudding**)
Word history: Middle English; Old English *thyddan*, verb

thug
noun someone who is brutal and violent

Word history: from *Thugs*, a former body of professional robbers and murderers in India who strangled their victims; Hindustani *thag*

thumb (thum)
noun **1** the inner finger that is much shorter and thicker than the rest
verb **2** to turn over using your thumb: *to* ***thumb*** *through the pages of a book*
phrase **3 all thumbs**, clumsy and awkward

Word history: Middle English; Old English *thūma*

thumbnail
noun **1** the nail of the thumb
2 *Computers* a small preview image of a page, usually prior to printing

Word history: definition 2 from *thumbnail sketch* a rough drawing of something

thump
verb to hit heavily or beat: *to* ***thump*** *on the back | My heart is* ***thumping.*** (***bang***, ***hammer***, ***pound***, ***thud***)

Word building: **thump** *noun*
Word history: imitative

thunder
noun **1** the loud booming noise that follows a flash of lightning in a storm, caused by the violent disturbance of the air by electricity
2 any loud noise like this: *the **thunder** of applause*
verb **3** to give out thunder or a noise as loud as thunder: *It **thundered** last night. | The horses **thundered** down the track.*

Word building: **thunderous** *adjective* **thundery** *adjective*
Word history: Middle English; Old English *thunor*

thunderbolt
noun **1** a flash of lightning and thunder
2 something that suddenly frightens or surprises you

Thursday
noun the fifth day of the week, following Wednesday

Word history: Middle English, from Scandinavian

thus
adverb **1** in this way
2 in the following manner
3 as a result

thwart (thwawt)
verb to oppose or stop from succeeding: *to **thwart** their plans*

Word history: Middle English *thwert*, adverb, from Scandinavian

thylacine (thuy-luh-seen)
noun a meat-eating, wolf-like marsupial of Tasmania, tan-coloured, with black stripes across the back, now thought to be extinct

Word use: Other names are **Tasmanian tiger** or **Tasmanian wolf**.

thyme (tuym)
noun a common garden herb of the mint family

Word history: Middle English, from Latin, from Greek

thyme / time
Don't confuse **thyme** with **time**, which is a particular period or moment.

thyroid (thuy-royd)
adjective **1** indicating or having to do with the thyroid gland
2 indicating or having to do with the most important cartilage of the larynx, known in men as the Adam's apple

Word history: variant of *thyreoid*, from Greek word meaning 'shield-shaped'

thyroid gland
noun a two-lobed, ductless gland lying on either side of the windpipe, or trachea, and connected below the larynx by a thin link of tissue. It gives out thyroxine which regulates metabolism and growth.

tiara (tee-ah-ruh)
noun a piece of women's jewellery that looks like a tiny crown

Word history: Latin, from Greek

tibia (tib-ee-uh)
noun the inner of the two bones of the lower leg, from knee to ankle (***shinbone***)

Noun forms: The plural is **tibias** or **tibiae** (tib-ee-ee).
Word building: **tibial** *adjective*
Word history: from Latin word meaning 'shinbone', 'flute'

tic (tik)
noun Medicine a sudden painless twitching in the muscles of the face or hand

Word history: French, from Italian; of Germanic origin

tick[1]
noun **1** the clicking sound made by a clock
2 a small mark (✓) used to show that something has been done correctly
3 *Colloquial* a moment or instant: *I'll be there in a **tick**.*
verb **4** to make ticking sounds
5 to mark correct with a tick
phrase **6 tick off**, to scold or speak crossly to (***admonish***, ***rebuke***, ***reprimand***, ***rouse on***)

Word history: late Middle English

tick[2]
noun a tiny, blood-sucking creature whose poison can paralyse animals such as dogs and cats

Word history: Old English *ticia*

ticker
noun Colloquial the heart: *He's got something wrong with his **ticker**.*

ticket
noun **1** a small printed card which shows that you have paid for something: *a bus **ticket***
2 a label or tag showing how much something costs (***sticker***, ***tab***)

Word history: from French word meaning 'ticket', 'label'

tickle
verb to stroke or poke lightly, causing itching or irritation

Word building: **tickle** *noun*
Word history: Middle English

ticklish
adjective **1** sensitive to being tickled: *I'm **ticklish** under the arms.*
2 difficult and needing to be handled carefully: *a **ticklish** situation*

tidal wave
noun a huge ocean wave which rises up after an earthquake in the sea bed or near the shore (***tsunami***)

tiddler
noun **1** a very small fish, especially a stickleback or minnow
2 *Colloquial* an unusually small child

tiddlywinks
noun a game in which you flick coloured discs into a cup

tide
noun **1** the rise and fall of the ocean, twice each day
2 a trend which comes and goes like a tide: *the **tide** of good fortune*
phrase **3 tide over,** to help through a difficult time: *This money will **tide** you **over** until pay day.*

Word building: **tidal** *adjective*
Word history: Middle English; Old English *tīd*, related to German *Zeit* time

tidings
plural noun Old-fashioned news or information: *to bring glad **tidings***

Word history: Middle English; Old English *tīdung*

tidy
adjective **1** neat, with everything kept in its right place: *a **tidy** desk | a **tidy** student* (***methodical***, ***neat***, ***orderly***, ***shipshape***, ***trim***)
noun **2** a rubbish container: *a kitchen **tidy***

Adjective forms: **tidier, tidiest**
Noun forms: The plural is **tidies.**
Word building: **tidy** *verb* (**tidied, tidying**)
Word history: Middle English

tie
verb **1** to fasten with cord or string: *to **tie** a parcel* (***bind***, ***lash***, ***rope***, ***secure***, ***strap***)
2 to loop into a knot or bow: *to **tie** a ribbon around your hair*
3 to get the same score in a contest: *They **tied** for first place.*
noun **4** a ribbon or string
5 a strip of cloth worn around your neck and knotted under your collar
phrase **6 tie in,** to relate to or fit in: *That doesn't **tie in** with the rest of his story.*
7 tie up,
a to fasten securely by tying: *to **tie up** a ship to a wharf*
b to bind or wrap up: *to **tie up** a parcel*
c to block or hinder
d to be busy: *I can't do it because I'm **tied up**.*

Verb forms: I **tied,** I have **tied,** I am **tying**
Word history: Middle English; Old English *tīgan* bind

tier (tear)
noun a row or layer: ***tiers** of seats in a theatre*

Word history: from French word meaning 'sequence'

tier / tear
Don't confuse **tier** with **tear**. **Tears** are the drops that fall from your eyes when you are crying.

tiff
noun **1** a slight quarrel
2 a slight fit of bad temper

TIFF (tif)
noun Computers **1** a standard format used to store images as data
2 a file in this format

Word history: *T(agged) I(mage) F(ile) F(ormat)*

tiger
noun a large wild animal of the cat family, which has yellow-brown fur with black stripes

Word history: Old English *tīgras* (plural), from Latin, from Greek

tiger snake
noun a very venomous Australian snake with striped markings

tight
adjective **1** fitting very closely: ***tight** shoes* (***close***, ***confined***, ***cramped***, ***narrow***)
2 pulled or stretched as far as it can go: *a **tight** knot*
3 *Colloquial* drunk
4 *Colloquial* mean with money (***mingy***, ***miserly***, ***penny-pinching***, ***stingy***)

Word building: **tight** *adverb* **tighten** *verb* **tightness** *noun* **tightly** *adverb*
Word history: Middle English, variant of *thight* dense, solid

tightrope
noun a wire stretched tightly above the ground for acrobats to balance on

tights
plural noun a close-fitting, skin-tight garment covering the body from the waist to the feet (***pantihose***)

tigress
noun a female tiger

tilde (til-duh)
noun a mark (~) placed over a letter, as over the letter *n* in Spanish to indicate a palatal nasal sound, as in *señor*

Word history: Spanish

tile
noun **1** a thin slab of baked clay for covering roofs, floors, walls and other surfaces
verb **2** to put tiles on: *to **tile** a roof*

Word history: Middle English; Old English *tīgele*

till[1]
preposition → **until**

Word building: **till** *conjunction*
Word history: Middle English; Old English *til*, from Scandinavian

till / until
These words are both correct. In more formal writing you usually use **until**:

Until he was deposed in the Rum Rebellion of 1808, William Bligh was the Governor of New South Wales.

If you were to use **till** in this sentence, it would sound more informal.

Note that **till** shouldn't be written **'til** or **'till** because it is not an abbreviation of **until** but is a word in its own right.

till[2]
verb to dig and prepare for planting crops: *to **till** the soil* (***cultivate***, ***turn over***, ***work***)

Word history: Old English *tilian* strive, get

till[3]
noun a drawer for keeping money in, in a shop, usually with compartments for notes and coins of different denominations

Word history: Old English *tyllan*

tiller
noun a handle joined to a boat's rudder, used for steering

Word history: Middle English, from Old French word meaning 'weaver's beam', from Latin word meaning 'web'

tilt
verb **1** to lean or slant: *to* ***tilt*** *the ladder against the wall | to* ***tilt*** *to the left* (***incline***, ***list***, ***slope***, ***tip***)
2 to fight in a jousting tournament

Word building: **tilt** *noun*
Word history: Middle English, from Old English *tealt* unsteady

timber
noun **1** wood that has been sawn ready for building (***boards***, ***lumber***, ***planks***)
adjective **2** made of timber: *a* ***timber*** *house* (***wood***)

Word history: Middle English and Old English; originally building, material for building

timbered
adjective covered with trees: *a* ***timbered*** *hillside*

timbre (tim-buh, tam-buh)
noun the particular sound an instrument makes: *The flute and clarinet have different* ***timbres***.

Word use: The US spelling is **timber**.
Word history: French word meaning 'quality of sound', originally 'kind of tambourine', from Latin, from Greek word meaning 'kettledrum'

time
noun **1** the passing of the hours, days, weeks, months and years
2 a particular moment shown by a clock: *What is the* ***time****?*
3 a particular period or moment: *It is* ***time*** *to go home.*
4 the rhythm or tempo of a piece of music (***beat***, ***swing***)
5 times, lots of, or multiplied by: *I know that 5* ***times*** *4 is 20.*
verb **6** to measure or record the time or speed of: *to* ***time*** *a race*
7 to choose the moment for: *She* ***timed*** *her arrival perfectly.*
phrase **8 behind the times**, old-fashioned
9 for the time being, temporarily, or just for the moment
10 from time to time, occasionally
11 in good time, early, with plenty of time to spare
12 in time,
a soon or early enough
b after some time
c following the correct rhythm or tempo
13 kill time, to occupy yourself so as to make the time pass quickly
14 on time, punctually or at the right time
15 take time out, to spare the time: *to* ***take time out*** *to weed the garden*
16 take your time, to be slow or leisurely
17 time after time, again and again

Word building: **timer** *noun*
Word history: Middle English; Old English *tīma*

time / thyme
Don't confuse **time** with **thyme**, which is a common garden herb.

time clause
noun **1** a clause in a contract which limits it or some aspect of it to a certain time period
2 *Grammar* a subordinate clause which specifies the time at which the action of the main clause takes place, as in *When you arrive, go straight to bed.*

timeless
adjective **1** everlasting
2 referring to no particular time: *The film has a* ***timeless*** *quality.*

time line
noun a line marked with dates to show the order in which events have happened

timely
adjective happening at just the right time: *a* ***timely*** *arrival*

Adjective forms: **timelier, timeliest**
Word building: **timeliness** *noun*

timepiece
noun a clock or watch, especially an old-fashioned one

time signature
noun a sign of two numbers written one above the other at the beginning of a piece of music, showing the rhythm

Word use: Compare **key signature**.

timetable
noun **1** a list of the times when buses, trains, ferries, etc., arrive and depart
2 a list of the times when school lessons, university lectures, etc., begin

timid
adjective easily frightened (***apprehensive***, ***fearful***, ***nervous***, ***shrinking***, ***timorous***)

Word building: **timidity** *noun* **timidly** *adverb*
Word history: from Latin word meaning 'frightened'

timing
noun control of the best time for something to happen: *The* ***timing*** *of the announcement was perfect.*

timorous (tim-uh-ruhs)
adjective timid or fearful

Word building: **timorously** *adverb*
Word history: late Middle English, from Medieval Latin word meaning 'fearful', 'frightened'

timpani (tim-puh-nee)
plural noun a set of kettledrums

Word history: Italian, from Latin, from Greek

tin
noun **1** a light, silver-coloured metal used in making alloys and in plating
2 a metal container, such as a can or a pan: *a* ***tin*** *of apricots | a cake* ***tin***
verb **3** to seal up and preserve in a tin: *to* ***tin*** *peaches*

Verb forms: I **tinned**, I have **tinned**, I am **tinning**
Word history: Middle English and Old English

tincture (<u>ting</u>-chuh)
noun **1** a solution made up of a medicine in alcohol
2 a trace or smattering
verb **3** to give a dye or colour to (***stain***, ***tinge***)
Word history: Middle English, from Latin word meaning 'dyeing', 'tingeing'

tinder
noun dry paper or twigs that catch fire easily
Word history: Middle English; Old English *tynder*

tine (tuyn)
noun a sharp projecting point or prong, such as of a fork, etc.
Word history: Middle English *tyne*, variant of Middle English and Old English *tind*, appearing at the same time as Middle High German *zint*

tinea (<u>tin</u>-ee-uh)
noun a skin disease, caused by a fungus, which makes the skin between the toes red and sore
Word history: from Neo-Latin, in Latin word meaning 'gnawing worm'

tinge (tinj)
verb **1** to tint or give a small amount of colour to
2 to give a small amount of anything to: *His acceptance was* ***tinged*** *with distrust.*
noun **3** a small amount of colour
4 a small amount of anything: *The soup had just a* ***tinge*** *of garlic.*
Verb forms: it **tinged**, it has **tinged**, it is **tingeing** or it is **tinging**
Word history: late Middle English, from Latin word meaning 'dye', 'colour'

tingle
verb to have a prickly feeling: *to* ***tingle*** *with cold | to* ***tingle*** *with excitement*
Word building: **tingle** *noun* **tingling** *adjective*
Word history: Middle English; apparently variant of *tinkle*

tinker
noun **1** a person who used to go from door to door mending old pots and pans
verb **2** to fiddle around trying to mend something without much success: *to* ***tinker*** *with the car engine*
Word history: Middle English variant of *tinekere* worker in tin

tinkle
verb to jingle or ring lightly: *to* ***tinkle*** *a bell*
Word building: **tinkle** *noun*
Word history: Middle English; imitative

tinnie
noun Australian Colloquial a can of beer
Word use: You can also use **tinny**.

tinny
adjective **1** not made strongly and likely to fall apart: *a* ***tinny*** *bicycle*
2 having a hollow metallic sound
Adjective forms: **tinnier**, **tinniest**

tinsel
noun glittering metal strips used for decoration: *to hang* ***tinsel*** *on the Christmas tree*
Word building: **tinselly** *adjective*
Word history: French word meaning 'spark flash', from Latin

tint
noun **1** a colour, especially a delicate or pale colour (***hue***, ***shade***, ***tone***)
2 a dye for the hair
verb **3** to dye or colour slightly: *to* ***tint*** *your hair*
Word history: Latin *tinctus* coloured, tinged

tiny
adjective very small or minute (***diminutive***, ***little***, ***microscopic***, ***miniature***)
Adjective forms: **tinier**, **tiniest**
Word history: obsolete *tine* very small

tip[1]
noun the pointed part at the end: *the* ***tip*** *of my nose*
Word history: Middle English

tip[2]
verb **1** to make slope, tilt or fall over: *If you* ***tip*** *the cup the milk will spill.* (***incline***, ***lean***, ***slant***)
2 to fall or make fall: *My lunch* ***tipped*** *out of my bag. | I* ***tipped*** *the water out of the glass.*
noun **3** a rubbish dump
phrase **4 tip over**, to fall over or overturn: *The vase of flowers* ***tipped over***. (***capsize***, ***overbalance***, ***topple***)
Verb forms: I **tipped**, I have **tipped**, I am **tipping**
Word history: Middle English

tip[3]
noun **1** money given in thanks to someone who has done something for you: *to leave a* ***tip*** *for the waiter*
2 a piece of useful information: *a* ***tip*** *on how to solve a problem* (***hint***, ***pointer***, ***recommendation***, ***suggestion***)
phrase **3 tip off**, to warn of trouble or danger (***alert***, ***caution***, ***forewarn***, ***warn***)
Verb forms: I **tipped**, I have **tipped**, I am **tipping**

tip[4]
verb to touch lightly or tap
Verb forms: I **tipped**, I have **tipped**, I am **tipping**

tipple
verb to drink, especially repeatedly and in small quantities: *to* ***tipple*** *wine and spirits*

tipsy
adjective a bit drunk: *She gets* ***tipsy*** *after only one glass of wine.*
Adjective forms: **tipsier**, **tipsiest**

tiptoe
verb to walk softly and carefully on the tips of the toes

tirade (tuy-<u>rayd</u>, tuh-<u>rayd</u>)
noun a long angry speech
Word history: French word meaning 'draught', 'shot', from Italian word meaning 'volley'

tire
verb to make or become sleepy or weak: *The long walk* ***tired*** *the children. | She has been ill and* ***tires*** *easily.* (***exhaust***, ***fatigue***, ***strain***, ***tax***, ***weary***)
Word building: **tired** *adjective*
Word history: Middle English *tyre*, Old English *tȳrian*

tiring
adjective making you feel sleepy or weak: *Gardening in the heat is very **tiring**.*

tissue (tish-ooh)
noun **1** the substance of which living things are made: *muscle **tissue***
2 soft thin paper, especially a piece used as a paper handkerchief: *Give me a **tissue** to blow my nose.*

Word history: Middle English, from Old French word meaning 'rich kind of cloth', from Latin

tit
noun a small Australian bird, especially a thornbill, blue tit, etc.

Word history: Middle English

titan (tuy-tuhn)
noun a person or thing of enormous size and strength

Word use: You can also use **Titan**.
Word building: **titanic** *adjective*
Word history: from the *Titans*, who, in Greek mythology, were a family of gods, thought of as lawless beings of gigantic size and enormous strength

titanium (tuy-tay-nee-uhm)
noun a dark grey metal used to remove oxygen and nitrogen from steel and to toughen it

Word history: *titan* + *-ium*

titbit
noun **1** a delicious morsel of food
2 an especially interesting piece of gossip or other information

Word history: from *tidbit*, from British dialect *tyd* nice + *bit*[2]

tithe (tuydh)
noun **1** a tenth part of income, profits, agricultural produce, etc., due or paid as a tax to the church
2 a tenth part of anything
verb **3** to give or pay a tithe

Word history: Old English *te(o)g(o)thian*

titian (tish-uhn, tee-uhn)
adjective having a deep reddish or reddish-brown colour, especially hair

Word building: **titian** *noun*
Word history: made famous by the Italian painter *Titian*

titillate
verb **1** to tickle, or cause a tingling sensation in
2 to excite pleasantly: *to **titillate** the fancy*

Word building: **titillation** *noun*
Word history: from Latin word meaning 'tickled'

titivate
verb Colloquial to spruce up: *to **titivate** yourself in front of the mirror*

Word building: **titivation** *noun* **titivator** *noun*
Word history: earlier *tiddivate*, perhaps from *tidy*

title
noun **1** the name of a book, film or piece of music
2 a name showing someone's occupation or rank in society, such as Mr, Ms, Doctor, Sir or Lord
3 the legal right to own property or a certificate stating this: *the **title** to a house*
verb **4** to call or name: *to **title** a book*

Word building: **titled** *adjective*
Word history: Middle English, from Old French, from Latin

titter
verb to giggle in a silly or nervous way (***snigger***)

Word building: **titter** *noun*

tittle-tattle
noun **1** gossip
verb **2** to gossip or talk about other people's private affairs

titular (tich-uh-luh)
adjective **1** having to do with a title
2 having a title, especially of rank
3 being such in title only: *a **titular** head of government*

Word history: Latin

TNT
noun in chemistry, trinitrotoluene, a high explosive set off by detonators, but not affected by ordinary friction or shock

Word history: abbreviation of *t(ri)n(itro)t(oluene)*

to
preposition **1** expressing movement or direction towards something: *from east **to** west*
2 showing a limit of extent, time or amount: *rotten **to** the core* | ***to** this day* | *goods **to** the value of $100*
3 expressing contact or attachment: *Apply varnish **to** a surface.* | *The paper stuck **to** the wall.* | *He held **to** his opinions.*
4 expressing time up to and including: *Monday **to** Friday*
5 expressing an aim, purpose or intention: *going **to** the rescue*
6 showing result: ***to** his dismay* | ***to** my surprise*
7 indicating addition or amount: *adding insult **to** injury*
8 expressing comparison or opposition: *The score was nine **to** five.*
9 expressing reference or relation: *What will he say **to** this?*
adverb **10** to a contact point or closed position: *Pull the door **to**.*
phrase **11 to and fro,**
a to and from some place or thing
b in opposite or different directions alternately

Word history: Middle English and Old English tō

to / too / two
Don't confuse **to** with **too** or **two**.
The most common meanings of the adverb **too** are 'also' or 'in addition' and 'more than is required':

I want to come too.

Your voice is too soft to hear.

Two is a number, and is a noun or an adjective.

toad
noun an amphibian, living on land, similar to a frog, but bigger

Word history: Old English *tādige*

toadfish
noun Australia the toado

toado (<u>toh</u>-doh)
noun a type of poisonous fish that can puff itself out, found in the warm seas around Australia and elsewhere

Word history: *toad* + *-o*

toadstool
noun a type of fungus like a mushroom, but usually poisonous

toast[1]
noun sliced bread cooked till it is brown on both sides

Word building: **toast** *verb* **toaster** *noun*
Word history: Middle English, from Old French, from Latin word meaning 'dry', 'parch'

toast[2]
noun **1** someone or something you honour with a special drink: *The Queen will be our next* ***toast****.*
2 the act of drinking in this way: *a* ***toast*** *to the Queen*
3 someone who suddenly becomes very popular and famous: *She was the* ***toast*** *of the town.*

Word building: **toast** *verb*
Word history: figurative use of *toast*[1], with reference to a piece of toast being put into a beverage to flavour it

tobacco
noun **1** a plant whose leaves are dried and used for smoking in cigarettes, cigars and pipes
2 the dried leaves themselves

Word history: Spanish, from Arawak (from Guarani) word meaning 'pipe for smoking', or 'roll of leaves smoked', or 'plant'

toboggan
noun **1** a small, light sled
verb **2** to ride on a toboggan

Verb forms: I **tobogganed**, I have **tobogganed**, I am **tobogganing**
Word building: **tobogganing** *noun*
Word history: Canadian French, from Abnaki (Algonquian) word meaning '(what is) used for dragging'

today
noun **1** this present day
2 this present time or age
adverb **3** on this present day
4 at the present time

Word history: Middle English; Old English *to dæg*

toddle
verb to walk slowly and unsteadily, like a child or old person

Word history: blend of *totter* and *waddle*

toddler
noun a very young child

toddy
noun **1** a drink made of spirits and hot water, sweetened and sometimes spiced
2 the sap, especially when fermented, of various species of palm, used as a drink

Noun forms: The plural is **toddies**.
Word history: from Hindustani word meaning 'palm tree'

to-die-for
adjective Colloquial extremely desirable: *the biggest* ***to-die-for*** *hunk at school* | *a* ***to-die-for*** *outfit.*

to-do
noun Colloquial bustle or fuss

Noun forms: The plural is **to-dos**.

toe
noun **1** in humans and other animals, one of the end members or digits of the foot
2 a part of a stocking or shoe, to cover the toes
3 a part like a toe
verb **4** to kick or strike with your toe: *to* ***toe*** *the ground*
phrase **5 on your toes**, wide-awake or prepared to act
6 toe the line, *Colloquial* to conform or behave according to the rules
7 tread on someone's toes, to offend, especially by acting in another person's area of responsibility

Word history: Middle English; Old English *tā*

toe / tow
Don't confuse **toe** with **tow**. To **tow** a vehicle is to drag or pull it along using a rope or chain.

toey (<u>toh</u>-ee)
adjective Australian, NZ Colloquial keen or anxious to go: *The horse was very* ***toey*** *as we waited by the gate.*

toff
noun Colloquial a rich, upper-class, usually well-dressed person

Word use: This word is used especially in British English.
Word building: **toffy** *adjective* (**toffier, toffiest**)

toffee
noun a sticky sweet made from sugar, water and sometimes butter

Word history: earlier *taffy, tuffy*

tofu (<u>toh</u>-fooh)
noun a food made from white soybeans

Word history: Japanese *tōfu*, from Chinese word meaning fermented bean

toga (<u>toh</u>-guh)
noun a loose robe worn by people in ancient Rome
Word history: Latin

together
adverb **1** into or to one place, gathering, mass, etc.: *to call the people* ***together***
2 into or in contact, union, etc.: *to sew two things* ***together*** | *multiply these numbers* ***together***
3 into or in a relationship: *to bring strangers* ***together***
4 taken or thought of together: *This one cost more than all the others* ***together****.*
5 at the same time: *You cannot have both* ***together****.*
adjective **6** *Colloquial* capable and calm: *He is quite* ***together*** *these days.*

Word building: **togetherness** *noun*
Word history: Old English *tōgædere*

toggle
noun **1** a type of fastener, made of a small bar or pin which fits through a loop of rope or chain
adjective **2** *Computers* having to do with a key or a command that has the opposite effect each time you use it, such as switching between upper and lower case letters
Word history: perhaps related to *tackle*

togs
plural noun Colloquial a swimming costume

toil
verb **1** to work hard for a long time (***labour***, ***slave***, ***sweat***)
2 to walk with great difficulty: *to* ***toil*** *up the hill* (***lumber***, ***plod***, ***slog***, ***trudge***)

Word building: **toil** *noun*
Word history: Middle English, from Anglo-French word meaning 'strive', 'dispute', 'wrangle', from Latin word meaning 'stir'

toilet
noun **1** a receptacle for the disposal of urine and waste matter from the bowel, especially one connected to a drain in which the waste is flushed away with water (***latrine***, ***lavatory***, ***loo***, ***urinal***, ***water closet***, ***WC***)
2 a room where people go to use a toilet (***bathroom***, ***lavatory***, ***washroom***)
3 the process of washing, shaving and getting dressed

Word history: from French word meaning 'cloth'

toiletries
plural noun soap, toothpaste, deodorant and other similar things used for washing, dressing, etc.

token
noun **1** a ticket or disc used instead of money to pay for something
2 a sign or symbol of something: *A wedding ring is a* ***token*** *of love.* (***emblem***, ***mark***, ***representation***)

Word history: Middle English; Old English *tācen*

told
verb **1** past tense and past participle of **tell**
phrase **2 all told**, in all

tolerance
noun **1** the ability to accept opinions, practices, etc., that are different from your own
2 the ability to put up with unpleasant circumstances
3 *Medicine* the increasing resistance of the human body to the effects of a drug such as morphine, etc., so that bigger and bigger doses are needed to have the same effect

tolerate
verb to put up with or allow: *She can't* ***tolerate*** *loud noise. | He won't* ***tolerate*** *bad behaviour.* (***abide***, ***permit***, ***stand***, ***suffer***)

Word building: **tolerable** *adjective* **tolerant** *adjective* **tolerance** *noun*
Word history: from Latin word meaning 'endured'

toll[1]
verb to ring slowly: *to* ***toll*** *a bell*

Word history: Middle English

toll[2]
noun **1** a fee paid for crossing a bridge or driving on an expressway
2 the price paid in terms of numbers of people dead: *the death* ***toll*** *in war | the road* ***toll***

Word history: Middle English and Old English, from Latin, from Greek word meaning 'toll house'

tom
noun a male cat

Word history: short for *Thomas*

tomahawk
noun a small axe, used by Native Americans

Word history: from Algonquian (Native American) word meaning 'war club', 'ceremonial object'

tomato
noun a juicy red fruit which can be cooked or eaten raw in salads

Noun forms: The plural is **tomatoes**.
Word history: Spanish, from Nahuatl

tomb (toohm)
noun a grave, especially a grand one where an important person is buried

Word history: Middle English, from Old French, from Late Latin, from Greek

tomboy
noun an adventurous, high-spirited girl

tombstone
noun a stone over someone's grave, usually with their name and dates of birth and death carved on it

tome (tohm)
noun **1** a single book forming a part of a larger work (***volume***)
2 a large book, especially a learned one

Word history: French, from Latin, from Greek word meaning 'volume', 'section of book'

tomfoolery
noun foolish or silly behaviour

Noun forms: The plural is **tomfooleries**.

tomorrow
noun the day after today

Word history: Old English *tō morgen(ne)* on the *morrow*, in the morning

tom-tom
noun an African or Indian drum

Word history: Hindustani or other East Indian vernacular; imitative

ton[1] (tun)
noun **1** a unit of mass in the imperial system, equal to approximately 1016 kg
2 → **tonne**
3 *Colloquial* any heavy weight: *That book weighs a* ***ton***.
4 tons, *Colloquial* very many or a good deal: ***tons*** *of things to see*

Word use: For definition 1 look up **imperial system**.
Word history: Middle English

ton[2] (tun)
noun Colloquial **1** a score of a hundred
2 a speed of 100 mph or 100 km/h, especially on a motorcycle

tonality
noun **1** *Music* all the relations, to do with both melody and harmony, that exist between the notes of a scale or a musical system
2 in painting, the system of tones and colours of a picture, etc.

tone
noun **1** a musical sound: *a violin with a mellow* ***tone***
2 a musical interval equal to two semitones
3 the lightness or darkness of a colour: *a blue* ***tone***
4 the style or quality of something: *Bad behaviour lowers the* ***tone*** *of the school.*
phrase **5 tone down**,
a in painting, to make less bright
b to soften or make less: *to* ***tone down*** *your efforts*
6 tone in, to match: *Those shoes will* ***tone in*** *with your new shorts.*
7 tone up, to make strong and fit: *Exercise* ***tones up*** *your body.*

Word history: Middle English, from Medieval Latin, from Greek word meaning 'tension', 'pitch', 'key'

tongs
plural noun a tool with two arms hinged together, used for picking up things

Word history: Middle English; Old English *tang*

tongue (tung)
noun **1** the mass of muscle in the mouth that helps in eating food and shaping the sounds of human speech
2 a language or dialect: *a foreign* ***tongue***
3 the loose flap of leather under the laces of some shoes
4 the clapper, or piece of metal, that hangs inside a bell and makes a sound when it hits the side
phrase **5 hold your tongue**, to be quiet
6 mind your tongue, to be careful what you say

Word history: Middle English and Old English *tunge*

tonic
noun **1** something that makes you stronger, healthier and more cheerful
2 *Music* the first note or degree of a scale

Word building: **tonic** *adjective*
Word history: from Greek word meaning 'pertaining to tone'

tonight
noun **1** the night of this present day
adverb **2** on the night of this present day

Word history: Middle English; Old English *tō niht*

tonne (ton)
noun a measure of mass in the metric system, equal to 1000 kilograms

Word use: The symbol is **t**, without a full stop. | Look up **metric system**.

tonsil
noun either of the two oval-shaped masses of tissue at the back of the throat

Word history: Latin

tonsillitis
noun an infection which makes the tonsils sore and inflamed

Word history: Neo-Latin, from Latin

tonsure (ton-shuh)
noun **1** the act of shaving the hair on top of the head, especially formerly as a sign of becoming a priest or monk
2 the shaved top of the head

Word building: **tonsured** *adjective*
Word history: Middle English, from Latin word meaning 'shearing'

too
adverb **1** also or in addition: *young, clever and rich* ***too***
2 more than is wanted or than should be: ***too*** *long |* ***too*** *many pupils*
phrase **3 only too**, very: *I'm* ***only too*** *glad to help you.*

Word history: variant of *to*, adverb

too / to / two
Don't confuse **too** with **to** or **two**.
The most common way **to** is used is to indicate movement in the direction of a place or person:
Tomorrow I'm flying from Adelaide to Perth.
Two is a number and is a noun or an adjective.

took
verb past tense of **take**

tool
noun **1** any instrument used for doing some mechanical work, such as a hammer, saw or knife
2 anything used like a tool to do work or to cause some result: *Books are a* ***tool*** *for gaining knowledge.*

Word history: Middle English word from Old English

toolbar
noun Computers a row of icons on a computer screen used for accessing frequently used features of an application

toolkit
noun **1** a collection of tools kept together, usually containing all the tools likely to be needed for some particular work such as plumbing, electrical repair, etc.
2 the actual storage device for holding those tools

toot
verb to sound or cause to sound in short blasts, like a horn or whistle

Word building: **toot** *noun*
Word history: late Middle English

tooth
noun **1** one of the hard, bonelike parts or growths inside the mouths of humans and animals, used for eating
2 any toothlike part of a comb, rake or saw

Noun forms: The plural is **teeth**.
Word history: Middle English; Old English *tōth*

top[1]
noun **1** the highest point or surface of anything (***apex***, ***crest***, ***peak***, ***pinnacle***, ***summit***)
2 the part of a plant above the ground: *carrot* ***tops***
3 a part thought of as higher: *the* ***top*** *of the street*
4 a covering or lid such as on a box or a jar
5 an outer piece of clothing for the upper part of the body
adjective **6** highest or upper: *the* ***top*** *shelf*
7 *Colloquial* best or excellent: *He's a* ***top*** *student.* (***fine***, ***great***, ***leading***, ***outstanding***, ***star***)
verb **8** to give a top to or put a top on
9 to be at or reach the top of: *to* ***top*** *the class in maths*
phrase **10 blow your top**, *Colloquial* to lose your temper
11 from the top, from the beginning
12 on top, successful

13 on top of,
a upon
b following very closely upon
14 top off with, to complete by adding a finishing touch: *He **topped off** his dinner **with** a large ice-cream.*
15 top up, to fill up a partly filled container

Verb forms: I **topped**, I have **topped**, I am **topping**
Word history: Middle English and Old English

top[2]
noun a cone-shaped toy which is made to spin on its pointed end

Word history: Middle English and Old English

topaz (toh-paz)
noun a mineral occurring in crystals of various colours, and used as a gem

Word history: Latin, from Greek

topiary (toh-pee-uh-ree)
adjective **1** of hedges, trees, etc., clipped or trimmed into ornamental shapes
noun **2** a garden containing topiary work

Word building: **topiarian** *adjective*
Word history: Latin

topic
noun the subject of a speech, discussion, conversation or piece of writing (***theme***)

Word history: singular of *topics*, from Latin, from Greek

topical
adjective dealing with things that are happening now

topography (tuh-pog-ruf-ee)
noun a detailed description and analysis of the geographical features of a fairly small area

Noun forms: The plural is **topographies.**
Word building: **topographer** *noun* **topographic** *adjective* **topographical** *adjective*
Word history: Middle English, from Late Latin, from Greek

topple
verb **1** to fall forward or to tumble down (***overbalance***, ***overturn***, ***pitch forward***, ***slip over***, ***tip over***)
2 to make fall

Word history: from *top*

tops
adjective Colloquial very good or excellent: *That film was **tops**. | We had a **tops** time at the zoo.*

topsoil
noun **1** the valuable upper part of the soil where most plants grow
verb **2** to cover with topsoil: *to **topsoil** land*

topsy-turvy
adverb upside down, backwards or back to front

Word building: **topsy-turvy** *adjective*

tor
noun a rocky outcrop or hill

tor / tore / taw
Look up **taw / tor / tore.**

torch
noun **1** a portable light which is run by batteries
2 something with a burning flame or flare which can be carried around or set into a holder
3 an instrument like a lamp which produces a very hot flame used for burning off paint or melting metal

Word history: Middle English, from Old French

tore (taw)
verb past tense of **tear**[2]

toreador (to-ree-uh-daw)
noun a Spanish bullfighter

Word history: from Spanish word meaning 'fight bulls'

torment (taw-ment)
verb **1** to torture or give great pain to: *Headaches **tormented** her day after day.* (***afflict***, ***harrow***, ***rack***)
2 to worry or annoy greatly: *The dog **tormented** the cat all morning.* (***harass***, ***hound***, ***persecute***, ***plague***)
noun (taw-ment) **3** great pain or agony
4 something that causes pain or is a source of worry or trouble: *His bad knee was a **torment** to him.*

Word history: Middle English, from Old French word meaning 'torment', from Latin word meaning 'something operated by twisting'

torn (tawn)
verb **1** past participle of **tear**[2]
phrase **2 that's torn it,** everything is ruined
3 torn between, unable to choose between: ***torn between** conflicting duties*

tornado
noun a violent whirlwind

Noun forms: The plural is **tornadoes** or **tornados.**
Word history: Spanish

torpedo
noun **1** a cigar-shaped missile containing explosives, which can travel by itself under water when fired by a submarine or torpedo-boat
verb **2** to attack or destroy by torpedo or torpedoes

Noun forms: The plural is **torpedoes.**
Word history: from Latin word meaning 'electric ray', which disables its prey by electric discharge

torpor (taw-puh)
noun **1** a state in which your physical and mental powers are not active
2 sluggish inactivity or inability to move or act (***apathy***, ***languor***, ***lethargy***, ***stupor***)

Word building: **torpid** *adjective*
Word history: from Latin word meaning 'numbness'

torque (tawk)
noun **1** something which produces rotation
2 the turning power of a shaft

Word history: from Latin word meaning 'twisted metal necklace'

torrent
noun **1** a stream of water flowing with great speed or violence, or a violent downpour of rain
2 a violent stream or flow of anything: *a* ***torrent*** *of words*

Word history: from Latin word meaning 'torrent', literally 'boiling'

torrid (tor-uhd)
adjective **1** of regions, etc., subject to burning heat
2 of climate, weather, etc., unpleasantly hot
3 passionate or ardent

Word history: Latin

torsion (taw-shuhn)
noun an act of twisting or the state of being twisted

Word building: **torsional** *adjective*
Word history: Middle English, from Late Latin word meaning 'twist'

torso (taw-soh)
noun the trunk of the human body

Noun forms: The plural is **torsos.**
Word history: Italian word meaning 'trunk', 'stump', 'stalk', 'trunk of statue', from Latin

tort (tawt)
noun Law **1** a civil injury, where legal action is undertaken by a private individual, as opposed to a criminal wrong, where legal action is undertaken by the state
2 torts, the branch of law concerned with civil injuries

Word history: from French word meaning 'a wrong'

tortilla (taw-tee-yuh)
noun a Mexican flat bread made from ground corn

Word history: from Spanish word meaning 'little cake'

tortoise (taw-tuhs)
noun any of various reptiles which have feet with toes, a hard shell covering their bodies and most of which live on land

Word use: Compare this with **turtle.**
Word history: Middle English, from Medieval Latin, from Latin word meaning 'twisted'

tortoiseshell
noun **1** a hard, yellow-brown covering of a turtle, used in the past to make combs, etc.
2 an artificial substance resembling this

tortuous (taw-chooh-uhs)
adjective **1** twisting, winding or crooked: *a* ***tortuous*** *mountain road*
2 not direct or straightforward: *a* ***tortuous*** *procedure* | ***tortuous*** *writing*

Word history: Middle English, from Latin word meaning 'full of turns or twists'

torture
noun **1** an act or method of causing severe pain, especially so as to gain information
verb **2** to cause severe pain to: *The soldiers* ***tortured*** *the spies to find out what they knew.* | *Earache* ***tortured*** *her all night.* (***agonise***, ***harrow***, ***torment***)

Word history: from Latin word meaning 'twisting', 'torment', 'torture'

toss
verb **1** to throw or fling, especially lightly: *She* ***tossed*** *the paper into the bin.* (***chuck***, ***hurl***, ***pitch***, ***sling***)
2 to fling or jerk about: *The wind* ***tossed*** *the branches of the tree.* | *The ship was* ***tossing*** *in the waves.* (***agitate***, ***jolt***, ***rock***, ***shake***, ***thrash***)
3 to move around or mix: *He* ***tossed*** *the salad.*
4 to throw a coin to decide something according to which side falls face up: ***Toss*** *for it, and heads I win!*

Word building: **toss** *noun*
Word history: apparently from Scandinavian

tosser
noun Colloquial a stupid person

tot[1]
noun **1** a small child
2 a small amount of drink
3 a small quantity of anything

Word history: perhaps short for *totterer* child learning to walk

tot[2]
phrase **tot up**, *Colloquial* to add: *to* ***tot up*** *a bill*

Verb forms: I **totted**, I have **totted**, I am **totting**
Word history: from Latin word meaning 'so much', 'so many'

total
adjective **1** whole or entire: *This is the* ***total*** *bill.* (***comprehensive***, ***full***)
2 complete or absolute: *a* ***total*** *failure* (***all-out***, ***downright***, ***unmitigated***, ***utter***)
noun **3** the sum or whole amount
verb **4** to add up or find the total of (***calculate***, ***count***, ***tally***)
5 to reach an amount of: *The bills for the outfit* ***total*** *$200.*

Verb forms: I **totalled**, I have **totalled**, I am **totalling**
Word history: Middle English, from Medieval Latin, from Latin word meaning 'entire'

totalisator (toh-tuh-luy-zay-tuh)
noun **1** a machine for registering and indicating the total of operations, measurements, etc.
2 a form of betting, such as on horseraces, in which those who bet on the winners divide the bets or stakes, less a percentage for the management, taxes, etc.

Word use: You can also use **totalizator.** | You can also use **tote** for definition 2.

totalitarian (toh-tal-uh-tair-ree-uhn)
adjective having to do with a government which has complete control and doesn't allow any opposition (***autocratic***, ***despotic***, ***repressive***, ***tyrannical***)

Word building: **totalitarianism** *noun*

totality (toh-tal-uh-tee)
noun **1** the state of being total
2 a whole or total amount

Noun forms: The plural is **totalities.**

totally
adverb **1** wholly; entirely; completely
2 *Colloquial* absolutely: *He just* ***totally*** *doesn't get it!*

tote[1] (toht)
verb Colloquial **1** to carry: *to **tote** books around*
2 to wear or be armed with: *to **tote** a gun*

tote[2] (toht)
noun → **totalisator** (definition 2)

totem
noun **1** something, often an animal, used as the token or emblem of a family or group (***sign***, ***symbol***)
2 a statue or drawing of such an emblem
adjective **3** having to do with a totem: *a **totem** pole*
Word history: from Algonquian (Native American) word meaning 'his brother-sister kin'

totter
verb to sway or walk unsteadily (***hobble***, ***limp***, ***lurch***, ***stagger***, ***toddle***)
Word history: Middle English, from Scandinavian

toucan (<u>tooh</u>-kan)
noun a fruit-eating bird of tropical America, brightly coloured and with a very large beak

touch
verb **1** to feel with your hand or finger (***brush***, ***contact***, ***finger***, ***handle***, ***pat***, ***stroke***)
2 to come into contact: *The two wires are **touching**.*
3 to strike or hit gently or lightly: *She **touched** him on the shoulder.*
4 to affect with a feeling or emotion: *Their sad story **touched** his heart.*
noun **5** the act of touching or being touched
6 one of the five bodily senses which is used to feel or handle things
7 close communication: *Have you been in **touch** with your mother lately?*
phrase **8 touch on,**
a to talk about for a short time: *I can only **touch on** that subject today.*
b to refer to: *Don't be so cruel as to **touch on** his failure.*
9 touch up,
a to put finishing details to
b to repair, renew or add points of detail to: *to **touch up** a photograph*
Word history: Middle English, from Old French

touching
adjective **1** pathetic or moving
preposition **2** about or concerning

touchy
adjective **1** irritable or easily offended: *Be careful because he's very **touchy** today.* (***moody***, ***prickly***, ***sensitive***, ***thin-skinned***)
2 likely to irritate or offend: *Don't talk about that because it's a **touchy** subject.*
Adjective forms: **touchier**, **touchiest**

tough (tuf)
adjective **1** not easily broken or cut (***durable***, ***firm***, ***hard***, ***resistant***, ***strong***)
2 difficult to chew
3 able to put up with bad conditions (***hardy***, ***resilient***, ***rugged***, ***sturdy***)
4 hard or difficult to deal with: *a **tough** exam* (***arduous***, ***complex***, ***demanding***, ***exacting***)
5 rough or aggressive: ***tough** behaviour*
Word building: **toughness** *noun*
Word history: Middle English; Old English *tōh*

toupee (<u>tooh</u>-pay)
noun a wig or patch of false hair worn to cover a bald spot
Word use: You can also use **toupée**.
Word history: French, from Old French word meaning 'tuft of hair'

tour (<u>toouh</u>, <u>tooh</u>-uh, taw)
verb to travel through a place or to travel from one place to another: *The band **toured** America. | They are **touring** all this summer.*
Word building: **tour** *noun*
Word history: Middle English, from French, from Latin word meaning 'tool for making a circle'

tourism
noun **1** the practice of touring, especially for pleasure
2 the work and industry of providing food, accommodation, entertainment, etc., for tourists

tourist
noun someone who travels or tours for pleasure (***sightseer***, ***traveller***, ***tripper***)

tournament (<u>taw</u>-nuh-muhnt)
noun **1** a meeting for contests in sports, cards, and other similar things: *a tennis **tournament** | a bridge **tournament***
2 a contest in medieval times where two knights on horseback fought for a prize
Word history: Middle English, from Old French

tourniquet (<u>taw</u>-nuh-kay, <u>toouh</u>-nuh-kay)
noun a tight bandage or band, twisted or wrapped around your arm or leg to stop bleeding
Word history: French, from *tourner* turn

tousle (<u>towz</u>-uhl)
verb to make untidy or dishevelled: *His hair was **tousled**.*
Word history: Middle English

tout (towt)
verb **1** to try urgently or persistently to get business, employment, votes, etc.
2 to spy on a racehorse, etc., to get (and sell) information for betting purposes
3 to describe or declare, especially favourably: *to **tout** a politician as a friend of the people*
noun **4** someone who touts
Word history: Middle English

tow (toh)
verb **1** to drag or pull using a rope or chain: *to **tow** a car* (***draw***, ***haul***, ***lug***, ***trail***)
phrase **2 in tow,**
a in the condition of being towed
b in someone's charge
c following someone around
Word building: **tow** *noun*
Word history: Old English *togian* pull by force, drag

tow / toe
Don't confuse **tow** with **toe**. People have **toes** at the end of their feet.

toward
preposition towards
Word history: Old English *tō-* to + *-weard* -ward

towards
preposition **1** in the direction of: *to walk **towards** the north*
2 with respect to or as regards: *My attitude **towards** you is unchanged.*
3 shortly before: ***towards** 2 o'clock*
4 close to: *situated **towards** the front*
5 as a help or contribution to: *to give money **towards** a gift*
Word use: You can also use **toward**.

towel
noun **1** a piece of cloth used for wiping and drying something wet
phrase **2 throw in the towel**, to give up or admit defeat (***capitulate***, ***submit***, ***succumb***, ***surrender***, ***yield***)
Word history: Middle English, from Old French word meaning 'cloth for washing or wiping', from Germanic

towelling
noun **1** a type of cloth used for making towels, clothes for the beach, etc.
2 a rubbing with a towel
3 *Australian Colloquial* a thrashing

tower (tow-uh)
noun **1** a tall, narrow structure that is usually part of a building such as a church, but which sometimes stands alone
verb **2** to rise and stretch far upwards: *The mountain **towers** into the sky.*
Word history: Old English *tūr*, from Old French

town
noun **1** a large area of houses, shops and offices where many people live and work, larger than a village and smaller than a city
2 the main shopping and business centre or area of a city: *I'm going to **town** to do my shopping.*
3 the people of a town: *The whole **town** is worried about the traffic problem.*
Word history: Middle English; Old English *tūn*

town hall
noun a large public building belonging to a town, for meetings and gatherings

town house
noun **1** *Australian* a house built as part of a small block of similar houses with its own entrance at ground floor
2 an extra house in a city, owned by someone who lives in the country

township
noun a small town or settlement
Word history: Old English *tūnscipe*

toxaemia (tok-see-mee-uh)
noun the presence in the bloodstream of bacterial poisons which are carried around to all parts of the body
Word use: You can also use **toxemia**.
Word building: **toxaemic** *adjective*
Word history: Neo-Latin

toxic
adjective **1** having to do with, affected with, or caused by a poison
2 poisonous (***noxious***)
Word building: **toxically** *adverb* **toxicity** *noun*
Word history: Middle Latin, poison, from Greek

toxin
noun a poison produced by some animal or vegetable organisms which can cause diseases such as tetanus or diphtheria
Word history: *tox(ic)* + *-in(e)*

toy
noun **1** an object, often a small imitation of some familiar thing, for children or others to play with
2 something of little value or importance
3 anything very small, especially a dog of a small breed
adjective **4** of or like a toy, especially in size
5 made as a toy: *a **toy** train*
phrase **6 toy with**,
a to handle idly or carelessly: *He sat there **toying with** his bread.*
b to think or act without plan or seriousness: *to **toy with** an idea*
Word history: Middle English

TPI
noun Australian a person who has injuries from war service which are judged to have totally and permanently incapacitated the person
Word building: **TPI** *adjective*
Word history: abbreviation of *t(otally and) p(ermanently) i(ncapacitated)*

trace[1]
noun **1** a mark that shows that something has been present, often a footprint or a track: *There was a **trace** of blood on his shirt. | The robbers left **traces** in the snow.*
2 a very small amount: *The earth contained only a **trace** of iron.* (***dash***, ***drop***, ***hint***, ***pinch***, ***skerrick***, ***tinge***)
verb **3** to follow the footprints, or make out the course of: *They **traced** the robbers to their hideout. | She **traced** the history of the wool industry in Australia.* (***pursue***, ***shadow***, ***tag***, ***track***, ***trail***)
4 to copy by following the lines of the original on transparent paper placed over it: *If you can't draw the map of Australia, you'd better **trace** one.*
Word building: **tracing** *noun*
Word history: Middle English, from Old French word meaning 'delineate', 'trace', 'pursue', from Latin

trace[2]
noun **1** each of the two straps, ropes or chains by which a carriage, wagon, etc., is drawn by a horse, etc.
phrase **2 kick over the traces**, to free yourself from discipline, authority, etc.
Word history: Middle English, from Old French word meaning 'strap for harness', 'act of drawing', from Latin

tracery
noun **1** ornamental work consisting of branching ribs, bars, etc., as in the upper part of a Gothic window or in panels, screens, etc.
2 any delicate interlacing pattern: *a **tracery** of leaves*
Noun forms: The plural is **traceries**.

trachea (truh-kee-uh)
noun in vertebrates that breathe air, the tube stretching from the larynx to the bronchi, serving as the main passage for sending air to and from the lungs

Noun forms: The plural is **tracheas** or **tracheae** (truh-kee-ee).
Word use: A more common term is **windpipe**.
Word building: **tracheal** *adjective*
Word history: Medieval Latin, from Greek

track
noun **1** a rough path or trail
2 a structure of metal rails and sleepers on which a train runs
3 a mark or series of marks like footprints, left by anything that has passed along
4 a path or course laid out for racing
5 any pathway or course (***line***, ***road***, ***route***, ***trajectory***, ***way***)
6 one of the separate sections on a recording, such as a CD, containing one song or piece of music
7 *Computers* the band or path on a tape or disk along which data is stored: *On a tape the* ***tracks*** *are parallel, but on a disk they are like the* ***tracks*** *on a vinyl record.*
verb **8** to follow, or hunt by following, the tracks or footprints of (***chase***, ***pursue***, ***seek***, ***shadow***, ***tag***, ***trail***)
9 to follow the course of by radar or sonar
adjective **10** having to do with athletic sports performed on a running track: ***track*** *events*
phrase **11 in your tracks**, just where you are standing: *He was stopped* ***in his tracks***.
12 keep track of, to keep sight or knowledge of
13 lose track of, to fail to stay in touch with
14 off the track, away from what is being talked or written about

Word history: late Middle English, from French *trac*, perhaps from Germanic

tracksuit
noun a loose, two-piece set of clothing worn by athletes in training or between events

tract[1]
noun **1** a stretch of land or water
2 a system or series of connected parts in the body: *digestive* ***tract***

Word history: late Middle English, from Latin word meaning 'drawing', 'stretch', 'extent', 'tract'

tract[2]
noun a short piece of writing, often on a religious subject

Word history: Middle English *tracte*

tractable (trak-tuh-buhl)
adjective **1** easily managed: ***tractable*** *people* (***amenable***, ***compliant***, ***docile***, ***obedient***, ***submissive***)
2 easily handled or dealt with: ***tractable*** *metals* (***ductile***, ***malleable***, ***pliable***, ***workable***)

Word building: **tractability** *noun* **tractably** *adverb*
Word history: Latin

traction
noun **1** the act of drawing or pulling something, especially along a surface
2 the force that prevents a wheel slipping: *These* ***tyres*** *have good traction.*

Word history: Medieval Latin word meaning 'act of drawing', from Latin word meaning 'draw'

tractor
noun a powerful motor vehicle used to pull farm machinery, etc.

Word history: obsolete *tract*, verb, draw + *-or*

trade
noun **1** the buying, selling or exchanging of goods (***commerce***)
2 a particular kind of work or, sometimes, the people who are involved in this work: *the* ***trade*** *of a carpenter | This magazine is for the electrical* ***trade***. (***business***, ***craft***, ***profession***)
verb **3** to buy, sell or exchange goods or other desirable things: *They* ***traded*** *in wheat. | They* ***traded*** *seats with each other.*
adjective **4** having to do with commerce or a particular job
phrase **5 trade in**, to give as a part payment in exchange for something new: *She* ***traded in*** *her old car for a new one.*
6 trade on, to take advantage of, especially in an unfair way: *He* ***traded on*** *the fact that he was the boss's son.* (***exploit***, ***play on***)

Word history: Middle English, from Middle Low German word meaning 'a track'

trade-in
noun **1** goods given in part payment: *I had my old car as a* ***trade-in***.
adjective **2** having to do with goods like these or with such a method of payment

trademark
noun a name, sign or mark used to show that goods have been made by a particular manufacturer

trade name
noun **1** the name under which a firm does business
2 a word or phrase used in trade indicating a business or a particular class of goods, but which is not a trademark

trade price
noun the price at which goods are sold to members of the same trade or to retail dealers by wholesalers

trader
noun **1** a merchant or business executive
2 a ship used in trade, especially to carry goods among a chain of islands

tradesperson
noun a person working in a trade

Noun forms: The plural is **tradespeople**.
Word building: **tradesman** *masculine noun*

trade union
noun an organisation or association of workers set up to help its members with any work problems, such as wages, working conditions, etc., and for dealing with employers

Word use: You can also use **union**.
Word building: **trade unionism** *noun* **trade unionist** *noun*

tradition
noun **1** the handing down of beliefs, customs and stories from one generation to another
2 the beliefs or customs that are handed down

Word history: Middle English, from Latin word meaning 'delivery', 'handing down'

traditional
adjective having to do with or handed down by tradition (***conventional***, ***customary***, ***normal***, ***orthodox***, ***usual***)

traditional custodian
noun an Indigenous Australian who has the responsibility of looking after their land

traditional owner
noun an Indigenous Australian who has, in accordance with Aboriginal tradition, social, economic, and spiritual ties with, and responsibility for their lands

traffic
noun **1** the coming and going of people or vehicles along a road, waterway, railway line or airway
2 the people or vehicles that travel along such a route
3 the business, trade or dealings carried out between countries or people, sometimes illegally: ***traffic*** *in drugs*
verb **4** to carry on trade or commercial dealings, often illegally

Verb forms: I **trafficked**, I have **trafficked**, I am **trafficking**
Word building: **trafficker** *noun*
Word history: French, from Italian

tragedy (traj-uh-dee)
noun **1** a sad or serious play with an unhappy ending: *Shakespeare's* ***tragedy*** *of 'Hamlet'*
2 any very sad or dreadful happening (***affliction***, ***calamity***, ***catastrophe***, ***disaster***, ***misfortune***)

Word building: **tragic** *adjective*
Word history: Middle English, from Latin, from Greek word meaning 'goat song' (reason for name variously explained)

trail
verb **1** to drag or be dragged along the ground
2 to have floating or coming out behind: *The car was* ***trailing*** *clouds of smoke.*
3 to follow the track of
4 to hang down loosely from something
5 to follow: *The little girl* ***trailed*** *after her sister.*
noun **6** a path or a track made across rough country
7 footprints or smell left by a hunted animal or person
8 a stream of dust or smoke left behind something moving

Word history: Middle English, from Anglo-French word meaning 'trail', Old French word meaning 'tow (a boat)', from Latin word meaning 'dragnet'

> **trail / trial**
> Don't confuse **trail** with **trial**. A **trial** is the testing of something, especially a case to test a person's guilt or innocence in a law court.

trail bike
noun → **dirt bike**

trailer
noun **1** a vehicle, made to be towed by a car or a truck, used to carry loads
2 an advertisement for a film soon to be shown, usually made up of scenes from it (***short***, ***shorts***)

train
noun **1** a number of railway carriages joined together and pulled by an engine
2 a line of people, cars or animals travelling together: *a camel* ***train***
3 something that is drawn or trails along: *the* ***train*** *on a wedding dress*
4 a group of followers: *The king and his* ***train*** *entered.*
5 a series of connected ideas: *a* ***train*** *of thought*
verb **6** to teach a person or animal to know or do something (***coach***, ***drill***, ***educate***, ***instruct***)
7 to become or make fit by exercise or diet for some sport or a contest

Word history: Middle English from Old French, from Latin word meaning 'draw'

trainee
noun **1** someone receiving training
adjective **2** receiving training: *a* ***trainee*** *pilot*

trainer
noun **1** someone who trains horses for racing
2 someone who trains athletes
3 a shoe designed for use during exercise or sport

training
noun **1** the development in yourself or in another of certain skills, habits and attitudes (***drill***, ***practice***, ***rehearsal***, ***run-through***)
2 the condition that results from this, especially in regard to your physical condition

train wreck
noun **1** the wreck of a train
2 *Colloquial* a complete disaster: *Her life is a* ***train wreck***.

traipse (trayps)
verb *Colloquial* to trudge or walk tiredly

trait (tray, trayt)
noun **1** an inherited physical mark or feature
2 that feature or quality that sets something apart from others: *a bad character* ***trait*** (***attribute***, ***characteristic***)

Word history: late Middle English, from French word meaning 'draught', from Latin

> **trait / tray**
> Don't confuse **trait** (sometimes pronounced *tray*) with **tray**. A **tray** is a flat piece of wood, plastic or metal used for holding or carrying things.

traitor
noun someone who betrays a person or a country

Word history: Middle English, from Old French, from Latin word meaning 'betrayer'

trajectory (truh-jek-tuh-ree)
noun the curved flight path of a bullet or other body

Noun forms: The plural is **trajectories**.
Word history: from Medieval Latin word meaning 'casting over'

tram
noun a passenger car running on rails, usually powered by electricity from an overhead wire

Word history: from Middle Low German or Middle Dutch word meaning 'beam', 'rung', etc.

trammel (tram-uhl)
verb **1** to restrain or hamper
noun **2** **trammels**, anything that stops or gets in the way of free action: *the* ***trammels*** *of custom*
3 a three-layered fishing net

Verb forms: I **trammelled**, I have **trammelled**, I am **trammelling**
Word history: Middle English, from Old French word meaning 'net with three layers of meshes', from Latin

tramp
verb **1** to tread or walk heavily or steadily: *The soldiers **tramped** down the road.* (***march***, ***plod***, ***slog***, ***trudge***)
2 to tread heavily: *The horse **tramped** on his toes.*
noun **3** the act of tramping: *a **tramp** through the bush*
4 the sound of a firm heavy tread
5 someone who travels about from place to place on foot, with no fixed home (***drifter***, ***vagabond***, ***vagrant***)

Word history: Middle English

trample
verb **1** to crush or tread heavily on (***compress***, ***jam***, ***press***, ***squash***, ***squeeze***)
2 to treat cruelly: *She **trampled** on his feelings.*

Word history: Middle English, from *tramp*

trampoline
noun a frame with tightly stretched material attached to it by springs, on which you can jump and tumble for pleasure or sport

Word building: **trampoline** *verb*
Word history: from Italian word meaning 'springboard'

trance
noun **1** a state of being dazed or not fully conscious
2 the condition of being completely lost in thought

Word history: Middle English, from Old French word meaning 'passage', especially from life to death, 'deadly suspense or fear', from Latin

tranquil (trang-kwuhl)
adjective peaceful, quiet or calm (***harmonious***, ***placid***, ***restful***, ***serene***)

Word use: The opposite of this is **agitated** or **disturbed**.
Word building: **tranquillity** *noun*
Word history: earlier *tranquill*, from Latin

tranquilliser (trang-kwuh-luy-zuh)
noun a drug that has a calming effect without inducing sleep

Word use: You can also use **tranquillizer**.

transact
verb to carry through to a successful conclusion: *It won't take long to **transact** our business.*

Word history: from Latin word meaning 'carried out', 'driven through', 'accomplished'

transaction
noun **1** a piece of business
2 the managing or carrying on of business

transcend (tran-send)
verb to go or be above or beyond: *to **transcend** a limit* (***exceed***, ***rise above***, ***surpass***)

Word history: Middle English, from Latin word meaning 'climb over or beyond'

transcendental (tran-sen-den-tuhl)
adjective **1** going above, surpassing or superior
2 going beyond ordinary experience, thought or belief

transcribe
verb **1** to make a copy of in writing: *to **transcribe** a letter*
2 to reproduce in writing or print from speech
3 to write out in other characters: *to **transcribe** shorthand notes*
4 *Music* to arrange for a different instrument or voice: *to **transcribe** a violin piece for piano*

Word building: **transcription** *noun* **transcript** *noun*
Word history: from Latin word meaning 'copy across'

trans fat (tranz fat)
noun fat composed of trans fatty acid

trans fatty acid
noun a type of unsaturated fat occurring naturally in meat and dairy products which is thought to increase the risk of coronary heart disease

transfer
verb **1** to carry or send from one place or person to another (***convey***, ***deliver***, ***transport***)
2 to take or move from one surface to another
noun **3** the act of transferring or the fact of being transferred: *The **transfer** of soldiers is complete.*
4 a drawing or pattern which can be put onto another surface: *These **transfers** can be put onto your T-shirt.*

Verb forms: I **transferred**, I have **transferred**, I am **transferring**
Word building: **transference** *noun* **transferral** *noun*
Word history: Middle English, from Latin word meaning 'carry across'

transfigure
verb **1** to change or alter in outward form or appearance
2 to change so as to glorify, exalt or idealise

Word history: Middle English, from Latin

transfix
verb **1** to pierce through or fix fast with something sharp or pointed
2 to make unable to move, such as with amazement or terror: *I was absolutely **transfixed** at the sight of the shark.*

Word history: from Latin word meaning 'pierced', 'transfixed'

transform
verb **1** to change in form or appearance: *The new suit **transformed** him into an important looking person.* (***alter***, ***convert***, ***transfigure***)
2 to change in condition or character: *Her new job **transformed** her life.* (***alter***, ***reconstruct***, ***revolutionise***)

Word building: **transformation** *noun*
Word history: Middle English, from Latin word meaning 'change form'

transformer
noun an electrical device used for changing one voltage to another

transfuse
verb **1** to pour in or spread through
2 to take from one person or animal and inject into another: *to **transfuse** blood*

Word building: **transfusion** *noun*
Word history: Middle English, from Latin word meaning 'poured across'

transgress
verb **1** to pass over or go beyond: *to* ***transgress*** *the bounds of what is sensible*
2 to break: *to* ***transgress*** *a law, command, etc.*
phrase **3 transgress against**, to break a law, command, etc. (***defy***, ***disobey***, ***flout***, ***infringe***, ***violate***)

Word building: **transgression** *noun* **transgressor** *noun*
Word history: from Latin word meaning 'having stepped across'

transient (<u>tran</u>-zee-uhnt)
adjective **1** passing with time or not lasting: *a* ***transient*** *feeling of loneliness*
2 temporary: *a* ***transient*** *guest at a hotel*
noun **3** someone or something that is transient

Word building: **transiency** *noun*

transistor
noun **1** a small electronic device used in computers, radios, etc., for controlling the flow of current
2 a small radio equipped with these devices

Word history: *trans(fer)* + *(res)istor*

transit
noun **1** passing across or through: *the* ***transit*** *of passengers from Sydney to Perth*
2 the state of being carried from one place to another: *The parcel was lost in* ***transit***.

Word history: Middle English, from Latin word meaning 'act of crossing'

transition (tran-<u>zish</u>-uhn)
noun **1** a passing from one position, state, stage, etc., to another
2 *Music*
a a passing from one key to another (***modulation***)
b a passage serving as a connecting link between two more important passages

Word building: **transitionary** *adjective*
Word history: from Latin word meaning 'act of going across'

transitive verb
noun a verb like 'bring' that needs an object for it to make sense

Word use: The opposite is an **intransitive verb**.

transit lane
noun a traffic lane which is restricted during peak hours to vehicles carrying more than a certain number of people

transitory (<u>tranz</u>-uh-tree)
adjective **1** passing away or not lasting
2 brief or lasting for a short time

translate
verb to change from one language into another: *He* ***translated*** *the book from Italian into English.*

Word building: **translation** *noun* **translator** *noun*
Word history: Middle English, from Latin word meaning 'carried over'

translucent (tranz-<u>looh</u>-suhnt)
adjective allowing some light to come through

Word use: Compare this with **opaque** and **transparent**.
Word history: from Latin word meaning 'shining through'

> **translucent / transparent**
> Don't confuse **translucent** with **transparent**. A **transparent** substance allows light to pass through so that you can see through it.

transmission
noun **1** the act of transmitting
2 something that is transmitted
3 the broadcasting of a radio or television program
4 the part of a motor which transmits the power from the engine to the wheels

Word history: Latin

transmit
verb **1** to send over or along: *The money was* ***transmitted*** *electronically.* (***carry***, ***dispatch***, ***forward***, ***pass on***, ***relay***, ***transfer***)
2 to pass on to someone else: *to* ***transmit*** *a disease*
3 to broadcast

Verb forms: I **transmitted**, I have **transmitted**, I am **transmitting**
Word history: Middle English, from Latin word meaning 'send across'

transmitter
noun Radio that part of the broadcasting apparatus which produces and changes the radio waves and sends them out to the aerial

Word use: You can also use **transmitting set**.

transmute
verb to change from one nature or form to another

Word building: **transmutation** *noun*
Word history: Middle English, from Latin

transom (<u>tran</u>-suhm)
noun **1** a crosspiece separating a door, window, etc., from a window above it
2 a window above a door

Word building: **transomed** *adjective*
Word history: Middle English, from Latin

transparency
noun **1** the quality of being transparent or able to be seen through
2 something which is transparent, especially a transparent photograph projected onto a screen or looked at by light shining through from behind
3 the policy of making all operations in an organisation open and visible, and being accountable to the public for them

Noun forms: The plural is **transparencies**.

transparent
adjective **1** allowing light to pass through so that you can see through: ***transparent*** *material* (***clear***, ***limpid***, ***sheer***)
2 easily understood or seen through: *She gave a* ***transparent*** *excuse.*

Word use: Compare definition 1 with **opaque** and **translucent**.
Word history: Middle English, from Medieval Latin, from Latin

> **transparent / translucent**
> Look up **translucent / transparent**.

transpire (trans-puy-uh)
verb **1** to happen or take place (***arise***, ***come about***, ***come to pass***, ***fall***, ***occur***)
2 of the body, a leaf, etc., to give off waste matter, etc., through the surface

Word building: **transpiration** *noun* **transpiratory** *adjective*
Word history: Medieval Latin, from Latin

transplant (trans-plant, trans-plahnt)
verb **1** to remove from one place to another: *to* ***transplant*** *carrots | to* ***transplant*** *a heart*
noun (trans-plant, trans-plahnt) **2** the act of transplanting
3 something transplanted, such as a part of someone's body: *He died before a suitable kidney* ***transplant*** *could be found.*

Word history: late Middle English, from Late Latin

transport (trans-pawt, trans-pawt)
verb **1** to carry from one place to another (***convey***, ***deliver***, ***move***, ***send***, ***transfer***)
2 to carry away by strong emotion: *She was* ***transported*** *with happiness.*
3 to send to another country to live: *to* ***transport*** *criminals*
noun (trans-pawt) **4** a system or method of transporting: *public* ***transport***
5 a ship, plane or truck used to transport people or goods

Word history: Middle English, from Latin word meaning 'carry across'

transportation
noun **1** the act of transporting or the state of being transported
2 a means of transport
3 in the past, the sending or carrying of a criminal to a penal colony: ***transportation*** *for life*

transpose
verb **1** to change the order of something in a series: *to* ***transpose*** *a paragraph so that a story is easier to follow*
2 to make change places: *If you* ***transpose*** *the letters in the word 'on', you get 'no'.* (***exchange***, ***reverse***, ***swap***)

Word building: **transposition** *noun*
Word history: Middle English, from French

transsexual (tran-sek-shooh-uhl)
noun someone who feels himself or herself, though physically of one sex, to be of the other sex psychologically

transverse (tranz-vers, tranz-vers)
adjective **1** lying or being across or in a crosswise direction
noun **2** something which is transverse
3 *Geometry* an axis that passes through the foci of a hyperbola

Word history: from Latin word meaning 'turned or directed across'

transvestite
noun someone who gets sexual pleasure from wearing the clothing of the opposite sex

trap
noun **1** a device for catching animals (***ambush***, ***booby trap***, ***lure***, ***net***, ***snare***)
2 a trick or any other way of catching someone by surprise
3 a two-wheeled carriage drawn by a horse
4 *Colloquial* the mouth
verb **5** to catch in a trap (***ambush***, ***corner***, ***snare***, ***take by surprise***, ***waylay***)
6 to trick or lead by tricking: *She* ***trapped*** *him into telling the truth.*

Verb forms: I **trapped**, I have **trapped**, I am **trapping**
Word history: Old English *træppe*

trapdoor
noun a door cut into a floor, ceiling or roof

trapdoor spider
noun a type of spider that digs tunnels in the ground that are sometimes fitted with a lid which it can open or keep tightly closed. It has a painful bite.

trapeze (truh-peez)
noun a short bar joined to the ends of two hanging ropes, on which gymnasts and acrobats perform

Word history: French, from Latin word meaning 'small table', from Greek

trapezium
noun a four-sided figure, two of whose sides are parallel

Noun forms: The plural is **trapeziums** or **trapezia**.
Word history: Neo-Latin

trappings
plural noun **1** articles of equipment or dress, especially ornamental
2 the things, especially ornamental, which necessarily go with a position, office, etc.: *the* ***trappings*** *of power*
3 the coverings, harness, etc., for a horse, especially ornamental

Word history: Middle English

trash
noun **1** rubbish or anything worthless or useless (***debris***, ***garbage***, ***junk***, ***refuse***)
2 nonsense or silly ideas or talk (***bunkum***, ***mumbo jumbo***, ***piffle***, ***rot***, ***rubbish***)
3 people thought of as worthless
verb Colloquial **4** to destroy completely, especially as an act of vandalism

Word history: Middle English

trauma (traw-muh)
noun **1** a wound or injury to the body
2 an emotional shock which has a lasting effect on the mind

Noun forms: The plural is **traumas** or **traumata**.
Word building: **traumatic** *adjective*
Word history: from Greek word meaning 'wound'

travail (trav-ayl)
noun **1** physical or mental hard work
2 the labour and pain of childbirth

travel
verb **1** to go from one place to another or to journey throughout: *She* ***travelled*** *across India. | He* ***travelled*** *the world.* (***roam***, ***rove***, ***tour***, ***voyage***, ***wander***)
2 to go from place to place for a business firm
3 *Colloquial* to move with speed: *That car was really* ***travelling****!*

noun **4** the act of travelling: ***Travel** is his main interest in life.*
5 travels, journeys

Verb forms: I **travelled**, I have **travelled**, I am **travelling**
Word history: Middle English; from *travail*

travel advisory
noun a notice, such as one issued by a government authority, giving advice on the degree of risk involved in travelling to certain parts of the world affected by war, diseases, etc.

travelogue (trav-uh-log)
noun a film or illustrated talk describing a country, travels, etc.

traverse
verb to pass across, over or through (***bridge**, **cross**, **ford**, **span**, **travel across***)

Word history: Middle English

travesty (trav-uhs-tee)
noun **1** any inferior or distorted likeness or imitation: *a **travesty** of justice*
verb **2** to make or be a travesty of

Noun forms: The plural is **travesties**.
Verb forms: it **travestied**, it has **travestied**, it is **travestying**
Word history: French word meaning 'disguised', from Italian word meaning 'disguise'

trawl
noun a strong net which is dragged along the sea bottom to catch fish

Word building: **trawl** *verb*

trawler
noun a type of boat used in fishing with a trawl

tray
noun a flat piece of wood, plastic or metal used for holding or carrying things: *He brought the tea on a **tray**.*

Word history: Middle English; Old English *trēg*

tray / trait
Don't confuse **tray** with **trait** (sometimes pronounced *tray*).
A **trait** is a particular quality or characteristic that someone has:
Being boastful is one of the bad traits of his personality.
Note that you will sometimes hear **trait** pronounced to rhyme with *plate*.

treacherous (trech-uh-ruhs)
adjective **1** disloyal or not to be trusted: *a **treacherous** enemy | **treacherous** weather* (***false**, **fickle**, **traitorous**, **unfaithful***)
2 dangerous and unpredictable: ***treacherous** weather | **treacherous** reefs*

Word building: **treacherously** *adverb*

treachery (trech-uh-ree)
noun the act of breaking faith or trust (***betrayal**, **disloyalty**, **infidelity**, **treason***)

Noun forms: The plural is **treacheries**.
Word history: Middle English, from Old French word meaning 'cheat'

treacle
noun a dark, sticky liquid made from sugar

Word building: **treacly** *adjective*
Word history: Middle English, from Old French word meaning 'antidote', from Latin, from Greek

tread (tred)
verb **1** to walk or step on: *He **treads** heavily. | She **treads** the same path every day.*
noun **2** a step or the sound it makes: *You could hear his **tread** on the stairs.*
3 the part, especially of a tyre, which touches the road or any other surface
phrase **4 tread water**, to keep your head above water by moving your arms and legs

Verb forms: I **trod**, I have **trod** or I have **trodden**, I am **treading**
Word history: Middle English

treadle
noun a lever, etc., worked by the foot to give movement to a machine

Word history: Middle English and Old English *tredel*

treadmill
noun **1** an apparatus for producing rotating movement by the weight of people or animals treading on a series of moving steps that form a kind of continuous path, as around the outside of a wheel
2 your life, work, etc., seen as a boring round of repetitive activities

treason
noun the crime of betraying your country, such as by spying for another country

Word building: **treasonable** *adjective*
Word history: Middle English, from Anglo-French, from Latin word meaning 'act of betraying'

treasure (trezh-uh)
noun **1** something worth a lot of money, such as gold and jewels, or anything which is highly valued: *His bike is his greatest **treasure**.* (***riches**, **valuables**, **wealth***)
verb **2** to value highly: *He **treasures** your praise.*
3 to store up for later use

Word building: **treasured** *adjective*
Word history: Middle English, from Old French, from Latin

treasurer (trezh-uh-ruh)
noun **1** someone in charge of the money belonging to a company, club or city: *The **treasurer** reported that funds were low.*
2 Treasurer, the head of the Treasury: *The **Treasurer** announced the budget.*

treasury (trezh-uh-ree)
noun **1** a place where money or valuables are kept
2 Treasury, the government department which manages a country's finances

treat
verb **1** to behave towards, in a particular way: *They **treated** the boy kindly.*
2 to try to cure: *to **treat** a patient*
3 to deal with or discuss: *They are **treating** the matter seriously.*
4 to change by chemical or other process: *to **treat** sewage*

5 to pay for some special pleasure for: *Juan's father **treated** him to an ice-cream.*
noun **6** the gift of a drink, dinner or entertainment: *It's my **treat** this time.*

Word building: **treatment** *noun*
Word history: Middle English, from Old French, from Latin word meaning 'drag', 'handle', 'treat'

treatise (treet-uhs)
noun a book or writing dealing with some particular subject, especially in a formal or detailed way

Word history: Middle English, from Anglo-French word meaning 'treat'

treaty
noun an agreement: *After the war both countries signed the peace **treaty**.*

Noun forms: The plural is **treaties**.
Word history: Middle English, from Anglo-French word meaning 'handled', 'treated'

treble
adjective **1** high-pitched: *a **treble** voice | a **treble** recorder (**falsetto**, **soprano**)*
2 three times as much as: *He paid **treble** the amount.*
noun **3** a piano part for the right hand
4 a high-pitched voice or sound
verb **5** to triple: *to **treble** the amount you study*

Word history: Middle English, from Old French, from Latin word meaning 'triple'

tree
noun a plant with leaves and woody branches, trunk and roots

Word history: Middle English; Old English *trēo(w)*

tree change
noun a move from a city environment to a rural location away from the coast, as part of a lifestyle change, usually to escape stressful aspects of city life: *Life was getting too hectic and they decided to opt for a **tree change**.*

Word building: **tree changer** *noun*

trek
verb to walk or travel especially over a long distance or with much difficulty: *We are going to **trek** across the mountains.*

Verb forms: I **trekked**, I have **trekked**, I am **trekking**
Word building: **trek** *noun* **trekker** *noun*
Word history: from Dutch word meaning 'draw', 'travel'

trellis
noun a support made of crossing wooden or other strips, such as for a vine or creeper (***lattice***)

Word history: Middle English, from Old French, from Late Latin

tremble
verb to shake, especially from fear, weakness or cold: *Her voice **trembled**.* (***quake***, ***quiver***, ***shudder***, ***vibrate***)

Word building: **tremble** *noun* **trembly** *adjective* (**tremblier**, **trembliest**)
Word history: Middle English, from French, from Latin

tremendous
adjective **1** large or great: *a **tremendous** size* (***colossal***, ***enormous***, ***gigantic***, ***huge***, ***massive***)
2 wonderful or remarkable: *She's a **tremendous** character.*

Word building: **tremendously** *adverb*
Word history: from Latin word meaning 'dreadful'

tremolo (trem-uh-loh)
noun a trembling effect in someone's voice or in a musical instrument

Noun forms: The plural is **tremolos**.
Word history: Italian word meaning 'trembling', from Latin

tremor
noun a shaking movement or vibration: *She has a **tremor** in her hand. | The earth **tremor** damaged our wall.*

Word history: Middle English, from Latin word meaning 'trembling', 'terror'

tremulous (trem-yuh-luhs)
adjective shaky or uncertain: *His voice was **tremulous** with excitement.*

Word building: **tremulously** *adverb*
Word history: Latin

trench
noun a deep ditch, especially one dug to protect soldiers from enemy fire

Word history: Middle English, from Old French word meaning 'act of cutting', 'slice', from Latin word meaning 'cut off'

trenchant (tren-chuhnt)
adjective keenly effective: *a **trenchant** argument | a **trenchant** policy* (***forceful***, ***incisive***, ***vigorous***)

Word building: **trenchancy** *noun*
Word history: Middle English, from Old French word meaning 'cut'

trend
noun a tendency or movement in a certain direction, which leads to a fashion: *There's a **trend** towards buying smaller cars.* (***current***, ***drift***, ***inclination***, ***leaning***)

Word history: Old English *trendan*

trendy
adjective fashionable: ***trendy** clothes*

Adjective forms: **trendier**, **trendiest**
Word use: The opposite of this is **unfashionable**.
Word building: **trendiness** *noun*

trepidation (trep-uh-day-shuhn)
noun fearful alarm or agitation

Word history: from Latin word meaning 'act of hurrying', or 'of being alarmed'

trespass
verb to enter a place illegally and without permission

Word building: **trespass** *noun* **trespasser** *noun*
Word history: Middle English, from Old French, from Latin

tress
noun a long lock or curl of hair, especially of a woman

Word use: The plural **tresses** is usually used, as in *her long golden tresses.*
Word history: Middle English, from French word meaning 'plait or braid of hair'

trestle (tres-uhl)
noun a plank supported by legs at each end
Word history: Middle English, from Old French word meaning 'transom', 'beam', from Latin

trevally (truh-val-ee)
noun a type of Australian sport and food fish, usually fast-swimming and having a forked or crescent-shaped tail

triad (truy-ad)
noun a group of three closely connected things, such as musical notes in a chord
Word building: **triadic** *adjective*
Word history: Latin, from Greek word meaning 'group of three'

trial
noun **1** a hearing of the facts or a trying of someone's guilt or innocence in a law court: *a **trial** by jury*
2 a test or contest: *a **trial** of strength*
3 an experiment: *The **trial** was unsuccessful.*
4 a cause of suffering: *His asthma was a **trial** to him.*
phrase **5 on trial**, undergoing a test or trial, especially in court
Word history: from Anglo-French word meaning 'try'

trial / trail
Look up **trail / trial.**

trial balance
noun a two-column list of all the balances kept in a ledger, with the debit balance and the credit balance being listed separately so that it is easy to check that the totals of each column agree

triangle
noun **1** a flat, three-sided shape, formed by three straight lines which meet so as to form three angles
2 a percussion instrument made of a steel rod bent into a triangle, which is struck with a small steel rod
Word building: **triangular** *adjective*
Word history: Middle English, from Latin word literally meaning 'three-cornered object'

triathlon
noun an athletic contest consisting of three events, usually swimming, cycling, and running, one immediately after the other
Word building: **triathlete** *noun*

tribe
noun **1** a group of people who believe they have a common ancestor, have many of the same customs, and who usually live in the same area
2 any large group with something in common: *He brought a **tribe** of friends home.*
Word building: **tribal** *adjective* **tribally** *adverb*
Word history: Latin

tribulation (trib-yuh-lay-shuhn)
noun great trouble, trial or sadness
Word history: Middle English, from Latin word meaning 'afflict'

tribunal (truy-byooh-nuhl)
noun a court of justice or a place where judgements are made
Word history: from Latin word meaning 'judgement seat'

tributary (trib-yuh-tree)
noun a stream flowing into a larger river
Noun forms: The plural is **tributaries.**
Word building: **tributary** *adjective*

tribute
noun a gift or speech made to show respect or regard for someone
Word history: Middle English, from Latin

trice (truys)
noun Old-fashioned a very short time: *I'll be back in a **trice**.* (***flash***, ***instant***, ***second***, ***split second***)
Word history: Middle English

triceps (truy-seps)
noun a muscle having three points of origin, especially the one at the back of the upper arm
Word history: from Latin word meaning 'three-headed'

triceratops (truy-se-ruh-tops)
noun a large plant-eating dinosaur with a heavily armoured neck and three horns on the skull

trick
noun **1** something done to deceive or amuse (***con***, ***hoax***, ***plot***, ***prank***, ***ruse***, ***swindle***)
2 a skilful or clever act, such as juggling
3 something which deceives your senses: *A mirage is just a **trick** of your eyes.*
4 a habit or mannerism: *She has a **trick** of nodding while you speak.*
verb **5** to deceive or cheat by a trick (***bluff***, ***dupe***, ***fool***, ***hoax***, ***kid***)
phrase **6 do the trick**, to bring about the desired result
Word building: **trickery** *noun* **trickster** *noun*
Word history: Middle English, from Old French word meaning 'deceit'

trickle
verb to flow in a very small or slow stream: *Tears **trickled** down her cheeks.* (***dribble***, ***drip***)
Word building: **trickle** *noun*
Word history: variant of obsolete *strickle*, from *strike*

tricky
adjective **1** difficult to handle or deal with: *a **tricky** question*
2 given to playing tricks, especially in order to cheat or deceive
Adjective forms: **trickier, trickiest**

tricolour (trik-uh-luh, truy-kul-uh)
noun a flag, etc., with three colours
Word use: You can also use **tricolor.**
Word history: French, from Late Latin

tricycle (truy-sik-uhl)
noun a cycle with three wheels, usually two at the back
Word history: French

trident (truy-duhnt)
noun **1** a three-pronged instrument or weapon
2 a spear having three prongs

Word history: from Latin word meaning 'having three teeth'

tried
verb past tense and past participle of **try**

triennial (truy-en-ee-uhl)
adjective **1** lasting three years
2 happening every three years
noun **3** a period of three years
4 a third anniversary

Word use: You can also use **triennium** for definition 3.
Word history: from Latin word meaning 'period of three years'

trifle
noun **1** a small or worthless amount or thing
2 a dessert usually made of sponge cake with sherry or wine, jelly, jam, fruit and custard
verb **3** to waste time: *She spends all day **trifling**.*
phrase **4 trifle with**, to treat too lightly: *Can't you see she's **trifling with** you?*

Word building: **trifler** *noun*
Word history: Middle English *treoflen*, from Old French *trufler* make sport of, deceive

trigger
noun **1** the lever on a gun which you press to fire the bullet
verb **2** to start off: *to **trigger** a reaction*

Word history: earlier *tricker*, from Dutch word meaning 'pull'

trigonometry (trig-uh-nom-uh-tree)
noun that branch of mathematics that deals with the relations between the sides and angles of triangles, and with calculations, etc., based on these

Word building: **trigonometric** *adjective* **trigonometrical** *adjective*
Word history: Neo-Latin, from Greek

trill
noun a vibrating sound, especially when made up of two notes being rapidly repeated one after the other

Word building: **trill** *verb*
Word history: from Italian word meaning 'quaver or warble in singing'; of Germanic origin

trillion (tril-yuhn)
noun **1** a million times a million, or 10^{12}
2 less commonly in Australia, a million times a billion, or 10^{18}

Word building: **trillionth** *noun* **trillionth** *adjective*
Word history: French

trilogy (tril-uh-jee)
noun a series of three related works, such as novels or plays

Word history: Greek

trim
verb **1** to shorten, such as by cutting or tightening: *He needs to **trim** his beard. | to **trim** a sail* (***clip**, **cut**, **mow**, **shear**, **snip***)
2 to decorate: *to **trim** a Christmas tree*
adjective **3** neat and smart (***dapper**, **orderly**, **shipshape**, **spick-and-span**, **tidy***)
4 healthily slim

Verb forms: I **trimmed**, I have **trimmed**, I am **trimming**
Word history: Old English *trymman, trymian* strengthen, prepare

trimaran (truy-muh-ran)
noun a sailing boat with three hulls

Word history: *tri-* + *(cata)maran*

trinity
noun a group of three

Word history: Middle English, from Old French, from Latin word meaning 'triad', 'trio', 'trinity'

trinket
noun a cheap ornament

trinomial
adjective *Algebra* consisting of or having to do with three terms connected by the sign +, the sign −, or both of these

Word building: **trinomial** *noun*

trio (tree-oh)
noun **1** a group of three
2 a group of three musicians
3 a musical piece for three voices or performers

Word history: from Italian word meaning 'three'

trip
noun **1** a journey or outing: *He is going on a world **trip**. | We took a **trip** on a ferry.* (***excursion**, **expedition**, **jaunt**, **tour**, **voyage***)
verb **2** to stumble: *She **tripped** and fell.* (***lose your footing**, **overbalance**, **pitch forward**, **slip***)
3 to cause to stumble or fall: *The wire **tripped** him.*
4 to set off: *He trod on the wire which **trips** the alarm.*
phrase **5 trip up**, to cause to make a mistake: *The barrister's questions **tripped** me **up**.* (***catch out**, **confuse**, **disconcert**, **trap***)

Verb forms: I **tripped**, I have **tripped**, I am **tripping**
Word history: Middle English, from Old French word meaning 'strike with the feet', from Germanic

tripartite (truy-pah-tuyt)
adjective **1** divided into or consisting of three parts
2 involving three parties: *a **tripartite** treaty*

Word history: Middle English, from Latin word meaning 'divided into three parts'

tripe
noun **1** the stomach of cattle when cleaned and sold as meat
2 *Colloquial* worthless rubbish

Word history: Middle English, from Old French, ultimately from Arabic

triple
verb **1** to multiply by three
adjective **2** having three parts: *a **triple** program*
3 three times as great: *a **triple** quantity*

Word use: You can also use **treble** for definition 3.
Word history: Middle English, from Latin, from Greek word meaning 'threefold'

triplet
noun **1** one of three children born at the same time to the same mother
2 a three-line verse of poetry

Word history: from *triple*

triplicate (trip-luh-kayt)
verb **1** to triple or make threefold
2 to make or produce a third time
adjective (trip-luh-kuht) **3** threefold or triple
noun (trip-luh-kuht) **4** one of three identical things

Word building: **triplication** *noun*
Word history: from Latin word meaning 'tripled'

tripod (truy-pod)
noun a three-legged stool or support

Word history: Latin, from Greek word meaning 'three-footed'

triptych (trip-tik)
noun in art, a set of three-hinged panels featuring pictures, carvings, etc.

Word history: from Greek word meaning 'of three plates'

trite (truyt)
adjective repeated too often: *a **trite** saying* (***banal***, ***clichéd***, ***hackneyed***, ***unoriginal***)

Word history: from Latin word meaning 'rubbed', 'worn'

triton (truy-tuhn)
noun **1** a sea mollusc with a large, spiral, often beautifully coloured shell
2 the shell of a triton

Word history: from *Triton*, a sea-god in classical mythology, represented as having the head and trunk of a man and the tail of a fish, and bearing a conch-shell trumpet; Latin, from Greek

triumph (truy-umf, truy-uhmf)
noun a victory or success (***conquest***, ***win***)

Word building: **triumph** *verb* **triumphant** *adjective* **triumphantly** *adverb*
Word history: Old English *triumpha*, from Latin

trivia (triv-ee-uh)
noun inessential, unimportant or inconsequential things

Word building: **triviality** *noun*

Trivia can be either singular or plural:
Such trivia is of interest to me.
These trivia are not worth collecting.
There is no plural *trivias.*

trivial
adjective unimportant: ***trivial** details* (***insignificant***, ***minor***, ***petty***, ***slight***, ***trifling***)

Word building: **triviality** *noun*
Word history: Middle English, from Latin word meaning 'belonging to the crossroads', hence 'common'

trochee (troh-kee)
noun Poetry a metrical foot of two syllables, a long followed by a short, or an accented followed by an unaccented

Word history: Latin, from Greek word meaning 'running'

trod
verb past tense and past participle of **tread**

trodden
verb past participle of **tread**

troglodyte (trog-luh-duyt)
noun **1** a prehistoric cave-dweller
2 *Colloquial* anyone thought to be primitive, unintelligent or insensitive

Word history: Latin, from Greek word meaning 'one who creeps into holes'

troll
noun an imaginary being in fairy stories, either a dwarf or a giant, who lives underground

Word history: Scandinavian

trolley
noun **1** a cart on wheels, used for carrying goods in a supermarket
2 a small table on wheels for carrying food or crockery
3 a truck with low sides which runs on rails: *The miners loaded the **trolley** with coal.*

trollop (trol-uhp)
noun **1** an untidy or slovenly woman (***slattern***)
2 a sexually immoral woman, especially a prostitute

trombone
noun a brass wind instrument like a trumpet, on which the note is changed by sliding a section of tube in or out

Word building: **trombonist** *noun*
Word history: Italian word meaning 'trumpet', from Old High German

troop
noun **1** a group or band of people, animals or things: *a circus **troop** | a **troop** of scouts* (***company***, ***gang***, ***team***)
2 troops, a large number of soldiers
verb **3** to come or go in large numbers

Word building: **trooper** *noun*
Word history: French, from Late Latin word meaning 'flock', from Germanic

troop / troupe
Don't confuse **troop** with **troupe**, which is a group of entertainers, as in *a troupe of actors.*

trophy (troh-fee)
noun **1** a prize won in a contest, usually a small metal statue or a cup with an inscription
2 a souvenir kept from a war or a hunting expedition (***booty***, ***keepsake***, ***memento***, ***spoils***, ***token***)

Noun forms: The plural is **trophies**.
Word history: French, from Latin, from Greek word meaning 'putting to flight'

tropic
noun **1** either of two lines of latitude about 23½° north and south of the equator, known as the *Tropic of Cancer* and the *Tropic of Capricorn*
phrase **2 the tropics**, the area of land lying between these bands

Word building: **tropical** *adjective*
Word history: Middle English, from Latin, from Greek word meaning 'having to do with a turn'

tropical rainforest
noun rainforest occurring in tropical areas, as in northern Australia

Word use: Compare **temperate rainforest.**

troposphere
noun the inner layer of the atmosphere, between the heights of about 10 km and 19 km, within which nearly all clouds are formed

trot
verb **1** to go at a fast but steady pace, as horses do when they move, so that a front leg moves at the same time as the opposite back leg
noun **2** a fast but steady pace: *She set off at a* ***trot***.
3 trots, trotting races for horses
phrase **4 trot out**, *Colloquial*
a to bring forward for or as if for inspection
b to say in a meaningless or boring way: *to* ***trot out*** *the same old arguments*

Verb forms: it **trotted**, it has **trotted**, it is **trotting**
Word history: Middle English, from Old French, from Middle High German word meaning 'run', originally 'tread'

troth (trohth)
noun Old-fashioned **1** faithfulness, fidelity or loyalty: *by my* ***troth***
2 truth: *in* ***troth***
3 your word or promise, especially in engaging yourself to marry: *to pledge your* ***troth***

Word history: Old English *trēowth*

trotter
noun **1** a horse bred for trotting races
2 an animal's foot, especially that of a pig or sheep when it is used for food

troubadour (trooh-buh-daw)
noun a singer or song-writer, especially in medieval France (***minstrel***)

Word history: French, from Provençal, perhaps from Late Latin word meaning 'figure of speech'

trouble (trub-uhl)
verb **1** to disturb, bother or worry: *It's a shame to* ***trouble*** *him when he's tired.*
2 to put to inconvenience: *May I* ***trouble*** *you to tell me the time?*
noun **3** a difficulty or an unhappy situation: *to make* ***trouble*** | *to be in* ***trouble***
4 inconvenience: *She went to a lot of* ***trouble*** *to find it.*
5 any problem or disorder: *industrial* ***trouble*** | *heart* ***trouble***

Word building: **troublesome** *adjective*
Word history: Middle English, from Old French, from Late Latin

trough (trof)
noun **1** a long, low container for animal feed or water or any similar trench or hollow
2 an area of low pressure on a weather map

Word history: Middle English; Old English *trōh*

trounce (trowns)
verb **1** to beat or thrash
2 *Colloquial* to defeat convincingly

troupe (troohp)
noun a band or group of entertainers: *a* ***troupe*** *of actors*

Word building: **trouper** *noun*
Word history: French

trousers
plural noun clothing for the lower half of the body from waist to ankle, divided into two parts for the legs

trousseau (trooh-soh)
noun linen and clothes collected by a bride for her marriage

Noun forms: The plural is **trousseaus** or **trousseaux**.
Word history: French word literally meaning 'bundle'

trout
noun a freshwater fish related to the salmon

Noun forms: The plural is **trout**.
Word history: Old English *truht*, from Latin, from Greek word meaning 'gnawer', 'a sea fish'

trowel
noun **1** a flat tool with a handle used for spreading cement or plaster
2 a small garden spade

Word history: Middle English, from Old French, from Late Latin

truant
noun someone who stays away from school without permission

Word building: **truancy** *noun* **truant** *adjective*
Word history: Middle English, from Old French, probably of Celtic origin

truce
noun an agreement to end fighting for a time: *Both sides agreed to call a* ***truce*** *over Christmas.* (***armistice***, ***ceasefire***)

Word history: Old English *trēow* treaty, good faith

truck
noun **1** a motor vehicle with a back section for carrying goods (***lorry***, ***van***)
2 a railway goods carriage

Word building: **truck** *verb*

truckie
noun Colloquial a truck driver

truculent (truk-yuh-luhnt)
adjective fierce (***aggressive***, ***belligerent***, ***combative***, ***hostile***, ***pugnacious***)

Word building: **truculence** *noun* **truculency** *noun*
Word history: Latin

trudge
verb to tread heavily or slowly: *He* ***trudged*** *upstairs in his boots.* (***lumber***, ***plod***, ***slog***, ***tramp***)

true
adjective **1** full of truth or not false: *a* ***true*** *story* (***accurate***, ***correct***, ***factual***, ***right***, ***valid***)
2 real or being what it seems: ***true*** *gold*
3 loyal or faithful: *a* ***true*** *friend*
4 exact: *She measured the sides to see if they were* ***true***.
adverb **5** truly, or in a true manner: *Tell me* ***true***.

Word building: **truly** *adverb*
Word history: Middle English; Old English *trēowe*

truffle
noun **1** a fungus that grows underground and which can be eaten
2 a chocolate sweet usually filled with rum

Word history: French, from Provençal or from Italian perhaps, from Late Latin

truism (trooh-iz-uhm)
noun a self-evident, obvious truth

Word building: **truistic** *adjective*

trump
noun **1 trumps**, in card games such as bridge, a specially chosen suit, all the cards of which rank higher than any card of the other suits for a particular round of the game
2 any card of such a suit
verb **3** to take or win with a trump: *I played an ace but he **trumped** it.*
phrase **4 trump up**, to invent dishonestly: *She **trumped up** some story to get out of trouble.*

Word history: unexplained variant of *triumph*

trumpet
noun **1** a brass wind instrument with a curved tube and three valves
verb **2** to sound a trumpet or make a similar loud noise: *The elephants **trumpeted** in the forest.*
3 to tell far and wide: *He **trumpeted** the news all through the neighbourhood.*

Word building: **trumpeter** *noun*
Word history: Middle English, from Old French

truncate (trung-kayt)
verb **1** to shorten by cutting off a part
2 to cut off the corners or angles of: *a **truncated** pyramid*

Word building: **truncation** *noun*
Word history: from Latin word meaning 'cut'

truncheon (trun-shuhn)
noun a short stick or club, such as one used by police to keep order or defend themselves

Word history: Middle English, from Old French word meaning 'piece cut off', from Latin word meaning 'stump'

trundle
verb to roll along, or move on wheels: *to **trundle** a hoop | The trolley **trundled** along the aisle.*

Word history: Old English *tryndel* wheel

trunk
noun **1** the main or central part: *the **trunk** of a tree*
2 the main part of the body without the head, legs or arms
3 a box or chest for storing or transporting possessions
4 the long, flexible nose of an elephant
5 trunks, shorts worn by men and boys while swimming
adjective **6** main or central

Word history: late Middle English, from Latin

trunk line
noun **1** a telephone line between two exchanges in different parts of a country or the world, used for making long-distance calls
2 a main railway line

Word use: You can also use **trunkline**.

truss
verb **1** to bind or secure: *They **trussed** her hands tightly. | He **trussed** the turkey.*
2 to support, such as with bars and beams: *to **truss** a bridge*

Word building: **truss** *noun*
Word history: Middle English, from Old French, from Latin word meaning 'bundle'

trust
noun **1** belief or confidence: *to lose someone's **trust***
2 the expectation that someone can or will pay: *He will let you buy on **trust**.*
3 reliability or responsibility: *a position of **trust***
4 money or property held and managed by one person for another or others
verb **5** to believe or have confidence in (***count on**, **have faith in**, **rely on***)
6 to hope or expect: *They **trust** you will come.*

Word history: Middle English, from Scandinavian

trustee
noun someone who manages business or property for another

trustworthy
adjective deserving trust: *a **trustworthy** ally* (***constant**, **faithful**, **loyal**, **reliable**, **steadfast**, **trusty***)

Word use: The opposite of this is **untrustworthy**.
Word building: **trustworthiness** *noun*

truth
noun **1** what has really happened: *He doesn't always tell the **truth**.* (***facts**, **reality***)
2 a fact or principle: *a scientific **truth*** (***axiom**, **certainty**, **law***)
3 honesty or reliability: *There's not much **truth** in what she says.*

Word building: **truthful** *adjective* **truthfully** *adverb*
Word history: Old English *trēowth*

try
verb **1** to make an effort or attempt to do: *You must **try** harder before you give it up. | **Try** it.*
2 to test or find out: *Did you **try** it for size?* (***check**, **examine**, **investigate**, **sample**, **screen***)
3 to examine in a court of law: *Don't judge her until she is **tried**.*
4 to strain or exhaust: *He **tries** my patience.*
noun **5** an attempt or effort
6 a score in rugby, made by a player touching the ball down on the ground behind the opponent's goal line

Verb forms: I **tried**, I have **tried**, I am **trying**
Noun forms: The plural is **tries**.
Word history: Middle English, from Old French word meaning 'pick', 'cull'

try to / try and

There is some argument about whether you should use *and* or *to* after **try**. Some people don't like **try and** because, they argue, *try* in this situation is followed by a verb in its infinitive form which should be indicated by *to*. For example, *try and climb the mountain* should be *try to climb the mountain*. But there is no doubt that **try and** is a common expression, and widely accepted and understood.

try-hard
noun Colloquial a person who tries strongly to fit in or be good at something but fails

trying
adjective annoying: *His nagging is very **trying**.* (***exasperating**, **infuriating**, **irritating**, **maddening**, **vexing***)

tryst (trist)
noun a planned meeting, especially between lovers (***appointment**, **assignation**, **date**, **rendezvous***)

Word history: Middle English, from Old French

tsar (zah)
noun **1** an emperor or king
2 an autocratic ruler or dictator

Word use: You can also use **czar** or **tzar**.
Word building: **tsarina** *feminine noun*
Word history: Russian, from Latin *Caesar*

tsetse fly (tset-see fluy, set-see fluy)
noun any of the African blood-sucking flies, some of which carry parasites which cause sleeping sickness

Word use: You can also use **tzetze fly**.

T-shirt
noun a light, short-sleeved shirt without a collar

T square
noun a T-shaped ruler used in mechanical drawing to make parallel lines, etc.

tsunami (tsooh-nah-mee)
noun a tidal wave

Word history: Japanese, from *tsu* harbour + *nami* wave

tuan
noun a small mouse-like marsupial, mostly tree-dwelling, with a hairy-tipped tail

Word history: from Wathawuring, an Australian Aboriginal language of an area around Geelong and inland to the Ballarat region

tub
noun a round, flat-bottomed container: *a wash **tub** | a **tub** of butter*

Word history: Middle English

tuba (tyooh-buh)
noun a very low-pitched, brass wind instrument

Word history: from Latin word meaning 'trumpet'

tubby
adjective short and fat (***chubby***, ***plump***, ***portly***, ***stocky***, ***stout***)

Adjective forms: **tubbier**, **tubbiest**
Word building: **tubbiness** *noun*

tube
noun **1** a narrow, hollow pipe which liquid or gas can flow through
2 a soft narrow, container, sealed at one end, with a screw top at the other: *a toothpaste **tube** | a **tube** of paint*

Word building: **tubular** *adjective*
Word history: from Latin word meaning 'pipe'

tuber (tyooh-buh)
noun an underground stem, such as a potato, from which new plants may grow

Word history: from Latin word meaning 'bump', 'swelling'

tuberculosis (tuh-ber-kyuh-loh-suhs)
noun a disease of the lungs in which small lumps or swellings are produced

Word building: **tubercular** *adjective* **tuberculous** *adjective*
Word history: Neo-Latin, from Latin word meaning 'tubercle' (a nodule)

tuck
verb **1** to put into or fold away: *to **tuck** something in your pocket*
2 to sew in a narrow fold to improve the fit of a garment
noun **3** a narrow fold: *You'll need to make a **tuck** in the hem.*
phrase **4** **tuck in**,
a to fold tightly into the bed clothes: *She **tucked** them **in**.*
b *Colloquial* to eat heartily

Word history: Old English *tūcian* torment

tucker
noun Australian, NZ Colloquial food: *The **tucker**'s good.* (***grub***, ***provisions***, ***victuals***)

Word history: *tuck* + *-er*

tuckshop
noun a shop, usually in a school, which sells lunches and snacks

Tuesday
noun the third day of the week, following Monday

Word history: Middle English, Old English *Tiwesdæg* Tiw's day (translation of Latin: day of Mars)

tuft
noun an upright bunch, such as of hair, grass or feathers

Word building: **tuft** *verb* **tufted** *adjective*
Word history: Middle English

tug
verb **1** to pull hard: *to **tug** on the reins | to **tug** the rope twice*
2 to tow, such as with a tugboat
noun **3** a hard pull
4 a tugboat

Verb forms: I **tugged**, I have **tugged**, I am **tugging**
Word history: Middle English

tugboat
noun a small, powerful boat which is used to tow other ships

tuition (tyooh-ish-uhn)
noun teaching: *She needs more **tuition** before the exam.*

Word history: late Middle English, from Latin word meaning 'guardianship'

tulip
noun a cup-shaped flower, which grows from a bulb

Word history: earlier *tulipa(n)*, from Turkish word meaning 'turban'

tulle (tyoohl)
noun a thin silk or netlike material, used in making hats, veils, dresses, etc.

Word history: French; from *Tulle*, a town in central France

tumble
verb **1** to fall or roll: *Prices are **tumbling**. | to **tumble** downstairs* (***fall head over heels***, ***plummet***, ***somersault***, ***topple***)
2 to toss: *to **tumble** clothes in a drier*

Word building: **tumble** *noun*
Word history: Old English *tumbian* dance

tumbler
noun a drinking glass

tumbrel
noun a cart used during the French Revolution to carry victims to the guillotine

Word history: Middle English, from Medieval Latin, from Old Low German word meaning 'fall'

tummy
noun *Colloquial* your stomach, where food is partly digested

Noun forms: The plural is **tummies**.

tumour
noun a swelling in someone's body, especially one made up of an unusual growth of cells

Word use: You can also use **tumor**.
Word history: from Latin word meaning 'swollen state'

tumult (tyooh-mult)
noun **1** a noisy disturbance or uproar (***commotion***, ***fuss***, ***hullaballoo***, ***riot***, ***turmoil***)
2 a mental or emotional disturbance: *These words caused a **tumult** in her mind.*

Word building: **tumultuous** *adjective*
Word history: Middle English, from Latin

tuna
noun a large sea fish with pink flesh, used for food

Word history: American Spanish

tundra
noun a treeless Arctic plain with mosses, lichens and dwarfed plants

Word history: from Russian word meaning 'marshy plain'

tune
noun **1** a number of musical sounds of different pitch, one after the other, that form a pattern
2 correct adjustment of pitch: *Is your violin in **tune**?*
verb **3** to set to a correct or usual musical pitch: *to **tune** an instrument*
4 to put into smooth running order: *to **tune** an engine*
5 to adjust so as to get an incoming signal at its strongest: *to **tune** a radio*
phrase **6 call the tune**, to be in a position to command or control
7 change your tune, to change your opinions, etc.
8 to the tune of, to the amount of

Word building: **tuneful** *adjective*
Word history: Middle English; unexplained variant of *tone*

tuner (tyooh-nuh)
noun **1** part of a radio receiver which picks up any chosen radio frequency and feeds it into an amplifier
2 a computer component that can receive digital television transmission

tungsten (tung-stuhn)
noun rare, bright-grey metal with a high melting point (3410°C), used to make high-speed, steel cutting tools, electric-lamp filaments, etc.

Word history: from Swedish word meaning 'heavy stone'

tunic
noun **1** a soldier's or police officer's jacket
2 a sleeveless dress worn by girls as part of a school uniform

Word history: Old English *tunice*, from Latin

tuning
noun the set of pitches for the individual strings of instruments such as lutes and zithers

tunnel
noun an underground passage, especially a large one for trains or cars

Word building: **tunnel** *verb* (**tunnelled**, **tunnelling**)
Word history: late Middle English

turban
noun a form of headdress made of a long piece of cloth wound around the head in folds

Word history: earlier *turband*, from Turkish *tülbend*, from Arabic *dulband*, from Persian, Hindi

turbid (ter-buhd)
adjective **1** muddy, with stirred-up particles: ***turbid** liquid*
2 not clear, but thick and dense, as smoke or clouds (***muddy***, ***murky***, ***opaque***)
3 disturbed, confused or muddled

Word history: Latin *turbidus* disturbed

turbine
noun a revolving motor in which a wheel with blades is driven by a liquid or gas passing through it

Word history: French, from Latin word meaning 'anything that spins'

turbojet
noun **1** an aircraft engine where air is compressed then forced into a combustion chamber and burnt with fuel, the expanding hot gases providing the force for driving the turbine and compressor
2 any vehicle, usually aircraft, driven by such an engine

turbulence
noun a violent commotion or storminess

Word building: **turbulent** *adjective*

tureen (tuh-reen, tyooh-reen)
noun a large deep dish with a cover, for holding soup, etc., at the table

Word history: earlier *terrine*, from French word meaning earthenware dish, from Latin word meaning 'earth'

turf
noun **1** a grass surface with its matted roots
2 a piece of this

Noun forms: The plural for definition 2 is **turfs** or **turves**.
Word history: Old English

turgid (ter-juhd)
adjective **1** high-sounding or pompous: ***turgid** language*
2 swollen or distended

Word building: **turgidity** *noun* **turgidness** *noun*
Word history: Latin

turkey
noun a large bird, originally from America, bred for eating

Turkish delight
noun a cubed, gelatine-stiffened sweet covered with icing sugar

turmeric (term-uh-rik)
noun **1** the strongly-smelling, root-like underground stem of an East Indian plant

2 powder prepared from it, used as a seasoning, a dye, in medicine, etc.

Word history: from Medieval Latin word meaning 'deserving earth'

turmoil
noun wild disorder: *Everything is in **turmoil** because he is leaving at a moment's notice.* (***commotion***, ***fuss***, ***hullaballoo***, ***riot***, ***tumult***)

Word history: apparently from *turn* + British dialect *moil* confusion

turn
verb **1** to revolve or spin: *The wheels are **turning** slowly.* (***rotate***, ***twist***, ***wind***)
2 to go round: *The truck **turned** the corner.*
3 to point or aim in a certain direction: *They **turned** the ship into the wind.* | *She **turned** her face to the wall.*
4 to move to the other side or the opposite position: ***Turn** the page quietly.* | *She tossed and **turned** all night.*
5 to become: *He **turned** red.*
6 to change or be changed: *The witch **turned** his car into a pumpkin.* | *He **turned** into a mouse.*
noun **7** a movement of rotation, whether complete or not: *a slight **turn** of the handle*
8 a chance to do something or get something and which comes in due order to each of a number of people: *It's my **turn** to choose.*
9 a change of direction: *He made a **turn** to the right.*
phrase **10 out of turn,**
a out of proper order
b at the wrong time
11 take turns, to do in order one after another
12 turn down,
a to refuse or reject: *to **turn down** an offer*
b to lessen the strength of: *to **turn down** a radio*
13 turn off,
a to stop the flow of: *to **turn off** the tap*
b to switch off: *to **turn off** the light*
c to start a strong dislike in: *His bad manners **turned** me **off**.*
d to lose interest in: *to **turn off** gardening*
14 turn on,
a to start the supply of: *to **turn on** the electricity*
b to excite or interest: *That jazz really **turns** me **on**.*
15 turn out,
a to switch off: ***Turn out** the lights.*
b to produce or make: *The factory **turns out** 300 packets an hour.*
c to force to leave: *The landlord **turned** them **out** into the street.*
d to empty: *He **turned out** his pockets.*
e to become or develop: *She has **turned out** well.*
f to come along: *A large crowd **turned out** to hear her.*
16 turn over,
a to move or be moved from one side to another
b to start: *The engine **turned over**.*
c to transfer or hand over
d to buy and then sell: *to **turn over** goods*
17 turn up,
a to fold, especially so as to shorten: *She **turned up** the hem of her dress.*
b to be found: *That pen I lost has **turned up** at last.*
c to increase the strength of: ***Turn up** the gas.*
d to arrive: *He **turned up** unexpectedly.* (***come***, ***put in an appearance***, ***show up***)

Word history: Middle English; Old English *turnian*, from Latin word meaning 'turn (in a lathe)'

turnip
noun a plant with a thick, white or yellow root which is eaten as a vegetable

Word history: earlier *turnepe*, perhaps from *turn* (with reference to its neatly rounded shape) + Middle English *nepe* turnip

turnout
noun **1** all the people who come to a meeting, show, concert, etc.
2 a quantity or output produced
3 the act of turning out
4 the manner or style in which a person or thing is dressed, equipped, etc.
5 an outfit
6 *Australian Colloquial* a party, show, entertainment, etc.

turnover
noun **1** an upset
2 the total number of worker replacements in a given period of time in a given business or industry
3 the number of times that capital is invested and reinvested in a line of goods during a particular period of time
4 the total amount of business done in a given time
5 the rate at which items are sold or stock is used up and replaced
6 a small, semicircular pastry case filled with fruit

turnstile
noun a revolving gate that allows one person to pass at a time

turntable
noun **1** the surface on which a record (definition 4) turns when it is played
2 the rotating plate on which food is placed in a microwave oven

turpentine
noun **1** an oil used for dissolving paint, originally from a tree, now usually made from petroleum
2 a very tall Australian tree with stringy bark and leaves which are whitish underneath

Word use: The short form of definition 1 is **turps**.
Word history: Middle English, from Latin, from Greek

turpitude
noun the condition of being wicked (***criminality***, ***depravity***, ***iniquity***, ***villainy***)

Word history: Latin *turpitūdo* baseness

turps
noun Colloquial → **turpentine** (definition 1)

turquoise (ter-kwoyz)
noun **1** a greenish-blue stone used in jewellery
2 a greenish-blue colour (***aqua***, ***aquamarine***)

Word building: **turquoise** *adjective*
Word history: from French word meaning 'Turkish (stone)'

turret
noun a small tower at a corner of a building

Word history: Middle English, from Old French word meaning 'tower'

turtle
noun any of various reptiles which have flippers, a hard shell covering their bodies, and most of which live in the sea

Word use: Compare this with **tortoise**.
Word history: Spanish, from Late Latin word meaning 'twisted'

turtleneck
adjective of a sweater, etc., having a high, close-fitting neck

tusk
noun the very long tooth, usually one of a pair, that certain animals such as the elephant or walrus have

Word history: variant of Middle English and Old English *tux*

tussle
verb to fight roughly (***brawl***, ***come to blows***, ***grapple***, ***scuffle***, ***struggle***)

Word building: **tussle** *noun*
Word history: variant of *tousle*

tussock
noun a tuft or clump of grass

tutelage (tyooh-tuh-lij)
noun **1** the office or function of a guardian
2 instruction
3 the condition of being under a guardian or tutor

Word building: **tutelary** *adjective*
Word history: from Latin word meaning 'watching'

tutor
noun a teacher, especially a private one or one in a university (***adviser***, ***coach***, ***guide***, ***mentor***, ***trainer***)

Word history: Middle English, from Latin word meaning 'protector'

tutorial (tyooh-taw-ree-uhl)
adjective **1** having to do with or exercised by a tutor: ***tutorial*** *functions or authority*
noun **2** a period of instruction given by a university tutor to a single student or a small group of students

tutu
noun a short ballet skirt, usually made out of layers of net-like material

Word history: French

tuxedo (tuk-see-doh)
noun a man's dinner jacket

Word history: short for *Tuxedo coat*, named after the country club at *Tuxedo* Park, in New York State, US

TV
noun → **television**

Word history: abbreviation

twaddle (twod-uhl)
noun **1** unimportant, silly or tiring talk or writing
verb **2** to talk in a trivial, silly or tiring manner

Word history: variant of *twattle*, blend of *twiddle* and *tattle*

twain (twayn)
noun *Old-fashioned* two

Word history: Old English *twēgen*

twang
verb **1** to make a sharp, ringing sound, such as that made by the string of a musical instrument when plucked
noun **2** a sharp, ringing sound produced by plucking or suddenly releasing a tightly stretched string
3 a sound like this
4 a sharp, nasal tone, as of the human voice

Word building: **twangy** *adjective*
Word history: imitative

tweak (tweek)
verb **1** to seize and pull with a sharp jerk and twist: *to* ***tweak*** *someone's ear*
2 to make minor adjustments to

Word building: **tweak** *noun*
Word history: Old English *twician*

twee
adjective *Colloquial* too delicate, affected, or excessively dainty

tweed
noun a rough woollen cloth

tweezers
plural noun small pincers or nippers for plucking out hairs or picking up small objects

twelve
noun **1** a cardinal number, ten plus two (10 + 2)
2 a symbol for this number, as 12 or XII
3 a set of twelve people or things
adjective **4** amounting to twelve in number

Word building: **twelfth** *adjective* **twelfth** *noun*
Word history: Middle English; Old English *twelf*

twenty
noun **1** a cardinal number, ten times two (10 × 2)
2 a symbol for this number, as 20 or XX
3 a set of twenty people or things
4 **twenties**, the numbers from 20 to 29 of a series, especially with reference to the years of a person's age, or the years of a century
adjective **5** amounting to twenty in number

Noun forms: The plural is **twenties.**
Word building: **twentieth** *adjective* **twentieth** *noun*
Word history: Middle English; Old English *twēntig*

24/7 (twen-tee-faw sev-uhn)
adverb *Colloquial* continuously: *This channel broadcasts news* ***24/7****.*

Word use: You can also use **24-7** or **twenty-four seven.**
Word history: abbreviation of *24 hours a day, 7 days a week*

twice
adverb **1** two times, one after the other: *Write* ***twice*** *a week.*
2 on two occasions, or in two instances
3 doubly, or in twofold quantity or degree: ***twice*** *as much*

twiddle
verb to turn round and round, especially in a pointless or irritating way: *to* ***twiddle*** *your thumbs*

Word history: blend of *twitch* and *fiddle*

twig[1]
noun a small, thin branch of a tree
Word history: Middle English and Old English *twigge*

twig[2]
verb Colloquial to understand
Verb forms: I **twigged**, I have **twigged**, I am **twigging**

twilight (twuy-luyt)
noun the dim light from the sky after sunset
Word history: Middle English

twill
noun **1** fabric woven so as to produce an effect of parallel diagonal lines
2 the characteristic weave or pattern of such fabrics
Word building: **twilled** *adjective*
Word history: Old English *twili(c)*, from Latin word meaning 'having double thread'

twin
noun **1** one of two children or animals born at the same birth
2 one of two things that match or look alike
Word building: **twin** *adjective*
Word history: Middle English; Old English *(ge)twinn*

twine
verb **1** to twist or wind
noun **2** string made of two or more strands twisted together
Word history: Middle English; Old English *twin*

twinge
noun a pain that lasts only a moment: *a **twinge** of rheumatism* (***pang***, ***prick***, ***spasm***, ***stab***)
Word history: Old English *twengan* pinch

twinkle
verb to shine with flickering gleams of light (***glimmer***, ***glitter***, ***shimmer***, ***sparkle***)
Word building: **twinkle** *noun*
Word history: Middle English; Old English *twinclian*

twirl
verb to spin rapidly (***gyrate***, ***rotate***, ***swirl***, ***whirl***)
Word history: blend of *twist* and *whirl*

twist
verb **1** to combine by winding together: *fibres **twisted** to make a rope*
2 to turn about to face another direction: *She **twisted** to see who was walking behind her.* (***do an about-face***, ***spin around***)
3 to wring or squeeze out of place or shape
4 to sprain or put out of place: *He **twisted** his ankle.*
5 to change the meaning of: *You have **twisted** my argument.* (***distort***, ***falsify***, ***misrepresent***, ***slant***)
Word building: **twist** *noun*
Word history: Old English *-twist*

twitch
verb **1** to jerk or give a short sudden pull at: *He **twitched** the rope out of her hands.*
2 to give a slight but sudden movement: *His mouth **twitched**.*
Word building: **twitch** *noun*
Word history: Middle English *twicchen*

twitchy
adjective nervous
Adjective forms: **twitchier**, **twitchiest**

twitter
verb **1** to give out a series of small, trembling sounds, the way a bird does
2 to giggle
3 to tremble with excitement, etc.
noun **4** the act or sound of twittering
5 a state of trembling or shaky excitement
Word building: **twittery** *adjective*
Word history: Middle English, German

two
noun **1** a cardinal number, one plus one (1 + 1)
2 a symbol for this number, as 2 or II
3 a set of two people or things
adjective **4** amounting to two in number
phrase **5 put two and two together**, to draw an answer or judgement from certain facts, events, etc.
Word history: Middle English; Old English *twā*

two / to / too
Don't confuse **two** with **to** or **too**.
To indicates movement in the direction of a place or person:
Can you walk over here to me?
Too means 'also' or 'in addition', and 'more than is required'.
I want to come too.
Your voice is too soft to hear.

two-dimensional
adjective having two different planes of measurement, such as height and width

two-up
noun a game in which two coins are spun in the air and bets are laid on both falling either heads up or tails up

tycoon
noun a rich and powerful owner of a business
Word history: Japanese, from Chinese

type
noun **1** a kind: *a **type** of literature* (***branch***, ***category***, ***class***, ***fashion***, ***genre***, ***sort***, ***style***, ***variety***)
2 metal letters for printing
3 printed letters: *a headline in large **type***
verb **4** to write with a typewriter
Word history: late Middle English, from Latin, from Greek word meaning 'blow', 'impression'

typecast
verb to cast continually in the same kind of part: *to **typecast** an actor*

typeface
noun the style or appearance of printing type

typescript
noun a typewritten copy of a piece of formal or legal writing

typeset
verb in printing, to set type
Verb forms: I **typeset**, I have **typeset**, I am **typesetting**
Word building: **typesetter** *noun*

typewriter
noun a machine with a keyboard, which produces numbers and letters like those used in printing

typhoid fever (tuy-foyd fee-vuh)
noun a severe infectious disease, often resulting in death, caused by a type of bacteria which infects food or drink

Word use: You can also use **typhoid**.

typhoon (tuy-foohn)
noun a violent storm like a cyclone or hurricane

Word history: from Chinese word meaning 'great wind'

typhus (tuy-fuhs)
noun an acute infectious disease marked by extreme exhaustion, severe nervous symptoms and an outbreak of reddish spots on the body, thought to be carried by lice and fleas

Word use: You can also use **typhus fever**.
Word building: **typhous** *adjective*
Word history: Neo-Latin, from Greek word meaning 'vapour'

typical
adjective **1** belonging to a particular kind and having the main characteristics of that kind: ***typical*** *desert plants*
2 expected, normal or characteristic: ***typical*** *behaviour*

Word use: The opposite of this is **atypical**.

typify
verb **1** to be a typical sign of: *His sloppy clothes* ***typify*** *his careless attitude.*
2 to represent or show all the main characteristics of: *She* ***typifies*** *university students in general.*
3 to represent by a type, etc.

Verb forms: it **typified**, it has **typified**, it is **typifying**
Word history: Latin

typist
noun someone who uses a typewriter

tyrannosaurus (tuh-ran-uh-saw-ruhs)
noun a large, aggressive, meat-eating dinosaur, which walked erect on its hind legs

Word history: New Latin, from Greek *turannos* tyrant + *sauros* lizard

tyranny (ti-ruh-nee)
noun **1** complete or unchecked power
2 unjustly harsh government

Word building: **tyrannise** *verb*
Word history: Middle English, from Medieval Latin word meaning 'tyrant'

tyrant (tuy-ruhnt)
noun **1** a king or ruler with unlimited power
2 anyone in a position of power who uses it cruelly and unjustly

Word history: Middle English, from Old French, from Latin, from Greek

tyre
noun a band of rubber, fitted round the rim of a wheel

Word use: The US spelling is **tire**.
Word history: late Middle English

tzar (zah)
noun → **tsar**

tzetze fly (tset-see, set-see)
noun → **tsetse fly**

ubiquity (yooh-<u>bik</u>-wuh-tee)
noun **1** the state of being everywhere at the same time (***omnipresence***)
2 the ability to be everywhere at the same time
3 the state of being very widespread

Word building: **ubiquitous** *adjective*
Word history: Neo-Latin, from Latin word meaning 'everywhere'

U-boat
noun a German submarine

Word history: from German word meaning 'undersea boat'

udder
noun the part of the body which produces milk in such animals as cows and goats, usually hanging and bag-like and with more than one teat

Word history: Old English *ūder*

UFO
noun something unknown seen in the sky, especially if thought to be a spaceship

Noun forms: The plural is **UFOs** or **UFO's**.
Word history: abbreviation of *u(nidentified) f(lying) o(bject)*

ugg boot
noun a comfortable shoe made from sheepskin with the soft fleece being on the inside of the boot and the leather on the outside

Word use: You can also use **ug boot** or **ugh boot**.

ugly
adjective **1** unpleasant in appearance (***grotesque***, ***hideous***, ***monstrous***, ***repulsive***)
2 nasty or threatening: *an **ugly** situation*

Word use: The opposite of definition 1 is **beautiful**.
Adjective forms: **uglier, ugliest**
Word building: **ugliness** *noun*
Word history: Middle English, from Scandinavian

ukulele (yooh-kuh-<u>lay</u>-lee)
noun a musical instrument like a small guitar but with only four strings

Word use: You can also use **ukelele**.
Word history: Hawaiian word literally meaning 'flea'

ulcer
noun a sore which is hard to heal, on the skin or on an internal part of the body, such as the lining of the stomach

Word building: **ulcerate** *verb* **ulcerous** *adjective*
Word history: Middle English, from Latin

ulterior (ul-<u>tear</u>-ree-uh)
adjective concealed behind what is seen or openly declared: ***ulterior** motives*

Word history: from Latin word meaning 'farther'

ultimate
adjective final or most important: *his **ultimate** aim in life*

Word history: Late Latin word meaning 'ended', from Latin word meaning 'last'

ultimatum (ul-tuh-<u>may</u>-tuhm)
noun a final statement of terms or conditions: *After the third broken window his father gave him an **ultimatum**.*

Noun forms: The plural is **ultimatums** or **ultimata**.
Word history: from Neo-Latin word meaning 'ultimate'

ultralight
adjective **1** extremely lightweight: *an **ultralight** tent*
2 having to do with an ultralight aircraft
noun **3** an ultralight aircraft

ultralight aircraft
noun a powered aircraft of limited weight, designed to carry not more than two people

Word use: You can also use **ultralight** or **ultralight plane**.

ultramarine
adjective of a deep blue colour

Word building: **ultramarine** *noun*
Word history: Medieval Latin

ultrasound
noun sound vibrations sometimes used in medical therapy or used instead of X-rays to make images of internal parts of the body

ultraviolet
adjective beyond the violet end of the visible spectrum of light: *The **ultraviolet** light rays from the sun can burn you.*

Word use: The abbreviation is **UV**.

ululate (<u>yoohl</u>-yuh-layt)
verb **1** to howl, as a dog, wolf, etc., does
2 to loudly express deep sorrow

Word history: Latin

umber
adjective having a dark reddish brown colour

Word building: **umber** *noun*
Word history: from Italian word meaning 'shade'

umbilical cord (um-<u>bil</u>-uh-kuhl kawd, um-buh-<u>luy</u>-kuhl kawd)
noun the tube which connects an unborn baby or animal to the lining of its mother's womb, and through which nourishment passes

umbra
noun **1** a shade or shadow
2 *Astronomy* the complete or perfect shadow of a body, such as a planet, which does not let any light through

Word history: Latin

umbrage
noun offence or resentful displeasure: *He took* ***umbrage*** *at her remarks.*

Word history: late Middle English, from French, from Latin word meaning 'of or in the shade'

umbrella
noun a circular screen on a metal framework which is used for a shelter against rain or sun

Word history: Italian word meaning 'shade', from Latin

umlaut
noun an accent sometimes placed above the vowels 'a', 'o' or 'u' in German and some languages related to German

An **umlaut** shows that the vowel should be pronounced differently from the unaccented vowel. The German word *Mann* rhymes with *sun*, while *Männer* is pronounced *menner*.

This accent is only rarely used in English, mainly when a proper noun from German is written. An example is the word **Führer**, meaning 'a leader' or referring particularly to Adolf Hitler.

Sometimes an extra e is added in English instead of using the umlaut. For example, the Swiss German word *müsli* has become *muesli*.

Note that while the umlaut looks the same as the dieresis, they work in different ways. Look up **dieresis**.

umpire
noun **1** someone who makes sure that a game is played according to the rules
2 someone asked to make a decision in an argument between two or more other people or parties (***referee***)

Word building: **umpire** *verb*
Word history: Middle English, from Old French word meaning 'uneven', 'odd'

unanimous (yooh-nan-uh-muhs)
adjective **1** all having the same opinion: *The committee members were* ***unanimous*** *in their support.*
2 showing complete agreement: *a* ***unanimous*** *vote*

Word building: **unanimity** *noun*
Word history: Latin

unassuming
adjective modest or not making any special claims about yourself: *an* ***unassuming*** *manner*

unaware
adjective not aware of something: *I was* ***unaware*** *that my shoelace was undone.*

unawares
adverb **1** while not aware of a thing yourself: *to pass through danger* ***unawares***
2 while another is not aware: *to come upon someone* ***unawares***

unbecoming
adjective **1** not appropriate or suitable: *behaviour* ***unbecoming*** *to the situation*
2 unattractive: *That dress is* ***unbecoming*** *on her.*

unbelief
noun lack of belief in religion

unbending
adjective firm or determined: *He was quite* ***unbending*** *about the rules.*

unburden
verb to free from a load: *She* ***unburdened*** *herself of her worries by ringing me last night.*

uncalled-for
adjective unnecessary and improper: *an* ***uncalled-for*** *insult*

uncanny
adjective weird or unnatural: *It was quite* ***uncanny*** *that we both had the same dream.*

Word building: **uncanniness** *noun*

uncertain
adjective **1** not sure: *I am* ***uncertain*** *about the date today.* (***doubtful, dubious, vague***)
2 not to be depended on: *The weather is so* ***uncertain.***

Word use: The opposite of definition 1 is **certain**. The opposite of definition 2 is **reliable**.

uncle
noun **1** the brother of your father or mother
2 your aunt's husband

Word history: Middle English, from Anglo-French, from Latin word meaning 'mother's brother'

uncomfortable
adjective **1** lacking in comfort: *an* ***uncomfortable*** *chair*
2 uneasy: *Your staring makes me feel* ***uncomfortable.***

uncommon
adjective **1** not common; unusual or rare
2 unusual in amount or degree; above the ordinary: *intelligence* ***uncommon*** *in a young child*

unconscionable (un-kon-shuh-nuh-buhl)
adjective **1** unreasonably overdone or excessive: ***unconscionable*** *expense*
2 not guided by conscience: ***unconscionable*** *behaviour* (***unprincipled, unscrupulous***)

unconscious (un-kon-shuhs)
adjective **1** unaware: *He is* ***unconscious*** *of his surroundings when reading.*
2 having fainted or lost consciousness: *She lay* ***unconscious*** *at the foot of the cliff.* (***comatose, out cold, stunned***)
3 below the level of awareness: *The* ***unconscious*** *mind holds a lot of information we cannot recall.*

uncouth (un-koohth)
adjective rough and ill-mannered (***coarse, common, crude, tasteless, vulgar***)

Word use: The opposite of this is **polite** and **well-mannered**.
Word history: Middle English, from Old English *uncūth* known

uncover
verb **1** to take the cover or covering off
2 to find out or discover something secret or unknown: *They* ***uncovered*** *the truth about their grandfather.*

unction (<u>ungk</u>-shuhn)
noun **1** the act of anointing, especially for medical purposes or as a religious rite
2 something soothing or comforting

Word history: Middle English, from Latin

unctuous (<u>ungk</u>-shooh-uhs)
adjective **1** oily or greasy like an ointment
2 having an excessively smooth, earnest manner, especially of an insincere kind

Word history: Middle English, from Medieval Latin, from Latin word meaning 'ointment'

undecipherable (un-duh-<u>suy</u>-fuh-ruh-buhl, un-duh-<u>suy</u>-fruh-buhl)
adjective unable to be read: *If he writes too fast his writing becomes* ***undecipherable****.*

under
preposition **1** beneath and covered by: ***under*** *a table |* ***under*** *a tree*
2 below the surface of: ***under*** *the sea*
3 in a position lower than: *to stand* ***under*** *a window*
4 in a condition of supporting, bearing, undergoing, etc.: *to sink* ***under*** *a load | a matter* ***under*** *consideration*
5 as designated or indicated: ***under*** *a new name*
6 less than: ***under*** *one dollar*
7 subject to the power, direction, etc., of: ***under*** *someone's influence |* ***under*** *supervision | born* ***under*** *Leo*
8 during the rule or reign of
9 in accordance with: ***under*** *the provisions of the law*
10 in the process of: ***under*** *repair*
adverb **11** under something
12 beneath the surface
13 in a lower degree, amount, etc.
14 in a lower position or condition
phrase **15 down under**, *Colloquial* in or to Australia or New Zealand

Word building: **under** *adjective*
Word history: Middle English and Old English

under-age
adjective below the customary or required age, especially legal age, as for entering licensed premises, marrying, etc.

underarm
adverb with your arm remaining below the shoulder: *to bowl* ***underarm***

undercarriage
noun the parts of an aeroplane under the body, supporting it on the ground, or when taking off and landing

undercurrent
noun **1** a current under the surface
2 a hidden tendency or movement: *There was an* ***undercurrent*** *of feeling against him.*

undercut
verb **1** to cut under or beneath
2 to sell or work at a lower price than: *Supermarkets often* ***undercut*** *corner shops.*
3 *Sport* to hit so as to give backspin to the ball

Verb forms: I **undercut**, I have **undercut**, I am **undercutting**

underdeveloped
adjective **1** of a country, in the early stages of building an industrial economy
2 less fully developed than average

Word use: You can also use **developing** for definition 1.

underdog
noun **1** someone who is ill-treated
2 the loser or expected loser in a competitive situation, fight, etc.

underdone
adjective cooked lightly or less than completely: ***underdone*** *meat*

underestimate
verb to work out or calculate at too low a rate, value or amount: *I* ***underestimated*** *the time needed for the job.*

undergo
verb **1** to experience or go through: *to* ***undergo*** *a medical examination*
2 to suffer: *He has* ***undergone*** *many hardships.*

Verb forms: I **underwent**, I have **undergone**, I am **undergoing**

undergraduate
noun a university student who has not yet received a degree

underground
adjective **1** lying underground: *an* ***underground*** *river* (***subterranean***)
2 secret: ***underground*** *work for the cause* (***clandestine, hidden***)

Word building: **underground** *adverb*

undergrowth
noun shrubs and low plants growing beneath or among trees

underhand
adjective secret and sly: ***underhand*** *dealings* (***cagey, furtive, secretive, stealthy, surreptitious***)

underline
verb **1** to draw a line underneath
2 to stress the importance of (***emphasise, highlight***)

undermine
verb **1** to make unstable by digging into or wearing away supports or foundations
2 to harm or weaken by secret or underhand means
3 to destroy gradually: *to* ***undermine*** *her confidence*

underneath
preposition **1** under or beneath
noun **2** the under or lowest part or view

Word building: **underneath** *adverb* **underneath** *adjective*
Word history: Old English *underneothan*

underpants
plural noun an undergarment covering the lower part of the body from the waist to the top of the thighs

underpass
noun a road or pathway which goes under a railway or another road

underprivileged (un-duh-<u>priv</u>-uh-lijd)
adjective not having the normal privileges or rights of a society because of lack of money and low social status

understand
verb **1** to grasp the idea of: *I am trying to **understand** what you are saying.* (***comprehend***, ***fathom***, ***make out***)
2 to know the nature of thoroughly: *We **understand** her very well.*
3 to get the idea of by knowing the meaning of the words used: *Do you **understand** Greek?*
4 to be sympathetic: *He knew that whatever he did she would **understand**.*

Verb forms: I **understood**, I have **understood**, I am **understanding**
Word use: The opposite of definition 1 is **misunderstand**.
Word history: Middle English; Old English

understanding
noun **1** ability to understand or grasp ideas
2 knowledge: *He has a good **understanding** of the subject.*
3 a private agreement: *They came to an **understanding** about the profits.*
adjective **4** sympathetic: *He gave her an **understanding** look.*
phrase **5 on the understanding that**, on condition that

understate
verb to describe as less than is true: *He **understated** his income to the Taxation Office. | To say she is angry is to **understate** the case.*

Word use: The opposite of this is **exaggerate**.
Word building: **understatement** *noun*

understudy
noun an actor or singer who stands by to replace someone who is unable to perform, usually because of illness

Noun forms: The plural is **understudies**.
Word building: **understudy** *verb* (**understudied**, **understudying**)

undertake
verb to promise: *He **undertook** to have the job finished within a year.*

Verb forms: I **undertook**, I have **undertaken**, I am **undertaking**

undertaker
noun someone who prepares bodies for burial or cremation and arranges funerals

undertaking
noun **1** a solemn promise to do something
2 a task: *a difficult **undertaking*** (***enterprise***, ***job***, ***project***, ***venture***)

under-the-counter
adjective having to do with goods kept hidden for sale in some improper way, such as on the black market

undertone
noun **1** a low or quietened tone of speaking (***murmur***, ***sigh***, ***whisper***)
2 an underlying quality, element or tendency
3 background colour

undertow
noun **1** backward flow of water below the surface of waves breaking on a beach
2 any strong current below the surface of water, moving in a direction different from that of the surface current

underwear
noun clothing such as singlets, underpants and petticoats, worn under other clothes

underworld
noun **1** the world of criminals and criminal activities
2 in mythology, a world beneath the earth which is inhabited by the spirits of all the people who have died

underwrite
verb **1** to agree to meet the cost of
2 *Insurance*
a to sign, thus becoming responsible for payment in case of certain losses: *to **underwrite** an insurance policy*
b to take on responsibility for insuring an amount up to: *to **underwrite** the sum of $3000*

Verb forms: I **underwrote**, I have **underwritten**, I am **underwriting**
Word history: Middle English, from Old English, from Latin

undo
verb **1** to open or untie: *to **undo** a parcel*
2 to ruin or spoil: *The storm **undid** all our work in the garden.*

Verb forms: I **undid**, I have **undone**, I am **undoing**
Word history: Middle English, from Old English

undoing
noun **1** downfall: *Greed led to her **undoing**.*
2 the cause of downfall: *Greed was her **undoing**.*

undress
verb to take clothes off: *to **undress** the baby | Please **undress** for bed.*

undue
adjective **1** too great or excessive: ***undue** haste* (***unnecessary***, ***unwarranted***)
2 not proper, fitting or right: *to exercise **undue** influence* (***improper***, ***unjustified***)

Word building: **unduly** *adverb*

undulate (<u>un</u>-juh-layt)
verb **1** to rise and fall in waves
2 to have a wavy form or surface: *The hills **undulated** into the distance.*

Word history: from Latin word meaning 'wavy'

unearth
verb to dig up or find after searching: *Anka **unearthed** her old school photos.* (***discover***, ***locate***, ***trace***, ***track down***)

Word use: The opposite of this is **bury**.

unearthly
adjective **1** not of this earth or world
2 unnaturally strange or weird: *an **unearthly** scream*
3 *Colloquial* unreasonable or absurd: *to get up at an **unearthly** hour*

uneasy
adjective worried or uncomfortable

Adjective forms: **uneasier**, **uneasiest**
Word building: **uneasily** *adverb* **uneasiness** *noun*

unemployed
adjective **1** out of work, especially of someone who wants to find work
2 not in use

unemployment
noun **1** the condition of being unemployed
2 the number of people out of work: ***Unemployment*** *rose last year.*

unequivocal (un-ee-kwiv-uh-kuhl, un-uh-kwiv-uh-kuhl)
adjective having a single, definite, clear meaning: *an **unequivocal** reply*

unerring (un-er-ring)
adjective without error or mistake: *an **unerring** instinct for the truth*

uneven
adjective **1** not flat, level or straight: ***uneven*** *ground* (***irregular***, ***lopsided***, ***unbalanced***, ***unequal***)
2 not equally balanced: *an **uneven** contest*

Word building: **unevenly** *adverb* **unevenness** *noun*
Word history: Middle English; Old English

unfair
adjective not fair or just (***discriminatory***, ***inequitable***, ***partial***, ***prejudiced***)

Word building: **unfairly** *adverb* **unfairness** *noun*
Word history: Middle English; Old English *unfæger*

unfamiliar
adjective **1** not having knowledge of: *I am **unfamiliar** with his poetry.*
2 not known or seen before: *Her face is **unfamiliar** to me.*

Word building: **unfamiliarity** *noun*

unfeeling
adjective cold and hard-hearted (***callous***, ***cold-blooded***, ***cruel***, ***insensitive***, ***stony***)

Word use: The opposite of this is **caring**.

unfold
verb **1** to spread or open out
2 to become known little by little: *Listen as the story **unfolds**.* (***develop***, ***evolve***)

Word history: Middle English; Old English *unfealdan*

unforeseen
adjective not expected: *an **unforeseen** delay*

unfortunate
adjective **1** unlucky (***cursed***, ***hapless***, ***star-crossed***)
2 likely to turn out badly: *an **unfortunate** decision*

Word building: **unfortunately** *adverb*

ungainly
adjective clumsy or awkward

Word building: **ungainliness** *noun*
Word history: Middle English

unguent (ung-gwuhnt)
noun an ointment

Word history: Middle English, from Latin

uni
noun → **university**

Word history: abbreviation

unicameral (yooh-nee-kam-uh-ruhl)
adjective having a single parliamentary chamber: *Many countries with **unicameral** legislatures are only small.*

Word use: Compare this with **bicameral**.
Word building: **unicameralism** *noun* **unicameralist** *noun*

unicorn (yooh-nuh-kawn)
noun an imaginary animal like a horse with a single horn growing in the middle of its forehead

Word history: Middle English, from Latin word meaning 'having one horn'

uniform
adjective **1** the same in appearance: *bottles of **uniform** size and colour* (***equal***, ***equivalent***, ***level***, ***similar***, ***symmetrical***)
noun **2** special clothes worn by people to show they have a particular job or go to a particular school or other institution

Word building: **uniformity** *noun* **uniformly** *adverb*
Word history: Latin

unify (yooh-nuh-fuy)
verb to form into one whole

Verb forms: I **unified**, I have **unified**, I am **unifying**
Word use: The opposite of this is **separate** or **split**.
Word building: **unification** *noun*
Word history: Medieval Latin, from Latin

unilateral
adjective **1** having to do with or affecting one side only: ***unilateral*** *paralysis*
2 done by one side only: ***unilateral*** *disarmament*
3 in legal contracts, etc., binding one party only

uninhibited
adjective behaving just as you like without worrying about what other people think, or being held back by feelings of guilt, etc. (***free***, ***open***, ***spontaneous***, ***unconventional***, ***wild***)

uninstall
verb Computers to remove (a software application): *Something was wrong with the program — so we tried **uninstalling** it and installing it again.*

uninterested
adjective not wanting to know about something (***apathetic***, ***bored***, ***indifferent***)

uninterested / disinterested

Don't confuse **uninterested** with **disinterested**.

A **disinterested** person is one who is free from bias and self-interest:

A judge has to act as the disinterested controller of a court.

Uninterested means 'not interested':

She was so uninterested in the proceedings that she left the courtroom.

union (yoohn-yuhn)
noun **1** a number of things joined together as one
2 → **trade union**
3 in universities, a student organisation

Word history: Middle English, from Latin

unionise
verb to organise into a trade union

Word use: You can also use **unionize**.

unionist
noun **1** someone who supports the idea of union, for example, the union of states or regions to form one country
2 a member of a trade union

unique (yooh-neek)
adjective different from all the others: *Your fingerprints are **unique**.* (***exclusive***, ***only***, ***single***, ***sole***)

Word history: French, from Latin

unisex
adjective suitable for both females and males: *a **unisex** hairstyle*

unison (yooh-nuh-suhn)
phrase **in unison**, singing or saying the same thing all together: *The choir sang **in unison**.*

Word history: Late Latin word meaning 'having one sound', from Latin

unit
noun **1** a single person or thing or the whole of a group of people or things
2 an amount used in measurement: *A metre is a **unit** of length.*
3 one complete part of a school subject: *two **units** of maths*
4 *Australian*, *NZ* one out of a number of separately owned homes in the same multi-storey building (***apartment***, ***condominium***, ***flat***, ***home unit***)

Word history: apparently short form of *unity*

unite
verb to join together as one: *The two clubs **united**. | The fight to save the koalas **united** the community.* (***combine***, ***connect***, ***knit***, ***link***)

Word building: **united** *adjective*
Word history: Middle English, from Latin word meaning 'joined together', 'made one'

unity
noun **1** the state of being one or a united whole
2 a feeling of belonging or harmony in a group

Word use: The opposite of this is **disunity**.
Word history: Middle English, from Latin

universal
adjective including and affecting everyone, everything and every place

Word history: Middle English, from Latin *ūniversālis*

universe
noun the whole of space and everything that exists in it (***cosmos***)

Word history: Latin

university
noun a place where you can study to earn a degree and do research after secondary education

Noun forms: The plural is **universities**.
Word use: The short form is **uni**.
Word history: Middle English, from Medieval Latin word meaning 'guild (of teachers and students)'

UNIX (yooh-niks)
noun Computers a multi-user, multi-tasking operating system

Word use: You can also use **Unix**.
Word history: Trademark

unkempt
adjective **1** not combed: ***unkempt** hair*
2 in an uncared-for or untidy condition (***bedraggled***, ***dishevelled***, ***scruffy***, ***sleazy***, ***sloppy***)

Word history: from obsolete *kemb* (Middle English *kembe*, Old English *cemban*) comb

unknown
adjective unfamiliar or not known: *an **unknown** face*

unleaded petrol
noun petrol that does not contain the metal lead and is therefore not as environmentally damaging as petrol with lead

unless
conjunction except on condition that: *I won't come **unless** you promise to be there.*

unlike
adjective **1** different or dissimilar: *My daughters are very **unlike**. | **unlike** quantities*
preposition **2** different from: *You are **unlike** your mother.*
3 uncharacteristic: *It is **unlike** you to be cheerful.*

unlikely
adjective **1** probably not true: *an **unlikely** story* (***far-fetched***, ***implausible***, ***improbable***, ***incredible***, ***unbelievable***)
2 probably not going to happen: *Rain is **unlikely**.*

Word building: **unlikelihood** *noun*

unload
verb to take things off or out of: *to **unload** a truck | to **unload** a gun*

unmitigated
adjective **1** not softened or lessened: ***unmitigated** anger*
2 total or absolute: *an **unmitigated** fool*

unnatural
adjective not normal, natural or usual: *an **unnatural** light in the sky*

unnerve
verb to upset or make nervous: *The scornful crowd **unnerved** the speaker.*

Word building: **unnerving** *adjective*

unprepossessing
adjective not impressive; ordinary: *Her **unprepossessing** appearance and manner hid a brilliant and creative mind.*

unpresented
adjective not handed or sent into a bank, etc., for payment: *an **unpresented** cheque*

unravel
verb to untangle or work out: *to **unravel** the knitting | to **unravel** a mystery* (***disentangle***, ***solve***, ***sort out***)

Verb forms: I **unravelled**, I have **unravelled**, I am **unravelling**

unreal
adjective **1** imaginary or non-existent
2 *Colloquial* amazing or unbelievable: *That song is **unreal**.* (***excellent***, ***great***, ***wonderful***)

unreasonable
adjective **1** not guided by reason or good sense (***arbitrary***, ***groundless***, ***illogical***, ***irrational***)
2 not agreeable to or willing to listen to reason
3 excessive or immoderate: ***unreasonable*** *expense*

unrelenting
adjective **1** not yielding to feelings of kindness or compassion: *The judge was* ***unrelenting*** *in his decision.*
2 not slackening in speed or rate of advance: *the* ***unrelenting*** *approach of the storm*

unrequited
adjective not returned or reciprocated: ***unrequited*** *love*

unrest
noun an angry, restless feeling: ***unrest*** *among the prisoners*

Word use: The opposite of this is **contentment**.

unruly
adjective disobedient or uncontrollable: *an* ***unruly*** *class* (***defiant***, ***delinquent***, ***headstrong***, ***wilful***)

Word use: The opposite of this is **obedient**.

unsavoury
adjective **1** unpleasant in taste or smell
2 socially or morally unpleasant or offensive

Word use: You can also use **unsavory**.

unscathed
adjective not hurt or injured: *They survived the battle* ***unscathed.***

unscrew
verb **1** to unfasten by taking the screws out of: *to* ***unscrew*** *the brass plate from his door*
2 to take off by turning round and round: *to* ***unscrew*** *the lid from a bottle*

unsecured
adjective **1** not made secure or fastened
2 not insured against loss, such as by a mortgage, bond, pledge, etc.

unseemly
adjective not proper or decent: ***unseemly*** *behaviour*

Word building: **unseemliness** *noun*

unseen
adjective **1** not seen or observed (***concealed***, ***hidden***, ***imperceptible***, ***inconspicuous***, ***invisible***)
noun **2** an unprepared passage for translation, or a piece of music for playing, such as in an examination

unsettle
verb to disturb or upset: *The thunder* ***unsettled*** *the dogs.*

Word building: **unsettling** *adjective*

unsettled
adjective **1** not settled or fixed in a place
2 not populated, as a region
3 liable to change: ***unsettled*** *opinions* | ***unsettled*** *times* | ***unsettled*** *weather*
4 undetermined: *an* ***unsettled*** *question*
5 not paid, adjusted or closed: *an* ***unsettled*** *account*

unsightly
adjective not pleasant to look at: *an* ***unsightly*** *scar*

unsound
adjective **1** diseased: ***unsound*** *in body or mind*
2 decayed: ***unsound*** *timber or fruit*
3 faulty or impaired: ***unsound*** *goods* (***defective***, ***inferior***, ***shoddy***, ***substandard***)
4 not solid or firm: ***unsound*** *foundations*
5 not well-founded or valid: *an* ***unsound*** *argument*
6 not financially strong: *an* ***unsound*** *business*

unstable
adjective **1** not stable or steady
2 lacking emotional stability
3 *Chemistry* indicating compounds which easily decompose

untapped
adjective not used, as resources, possibilities, etc.: *an* ***untapped*** *fund of money* | ***untapped*** *enthusiasm*

untenable
adjective **1** not able to be held against attack
2 not able to be defended against argument, as an opinion, scheme, etc.

unthinkable
adjective not deserving to be considered or thought about: *It is* ***unthinkable*** *that we would leave the children alone.*

unthinking
adjective **1** thoughtless or heedless
2 indicating lack of thought or reflection
3 not given to critical or reflective thought

untidy
adjective **1** not tidy or neat (***chaotic***, ***disorganised***, ***haywire***, ***higgledy-piggledy***, ***messy***)
verb **2** to make untidy

Adjective forms: **untidier**, **untidiest**
Verb forms: I **untidied**, I have **untidied**, I am **untidying**
Word building: **untidily** *adverb* **untidiness** *noun*

untie
verb to loosen or set loose by undoing a knot: *She* ***untied*** *her scarf.* | *He* ***untied*** *the dog.*

Verb forms: I **untied**, I have **untied**, I am **untying**

until
conjunction **1** up to the time that or when: *I will wait* ***until*** *you come.*
2 before: *He did not arrive* ***until*** *the meeting was over.*
preposition **3** up to the time of: *He stayed* ***until*** *midnight.*
4 before: *He did not go* ***until*** *midnight.*

Word use: You can also use **till**. | Definitions 2 and 4 are always used in negative ('not') sentences.

until / till
Look up **till / until**.

untimely
adjective **1** not happening at a suitable time or season (***inappropriate***, ***inopportune***)
2 not fully mature or ripe (***premature***, ***unripe***)
adverb **3** at the wrong time or season

untold
adjective **1** not told: *an* ***untold*** *story*
2 more than can be counted or measured: *a man of* ***untold*** *wealth* (***countless***, ***endless***, ***infinite***)

untoward (un-tuh-wawd)
adjective **1** unexpected or unpleasant: *We should arrive by midday unless anything **untoward** happens.*
2 *Old-fashioned* not proper or suitable: ***untoward** behaviour*

Word history: *un-* + *toward*

untruth
noun a lie or falsehood

unusual
adjective not usual, common or ordinary: *It is **unusual** for her to be late. | That shirt is an **unusual** colour.* (***uncommon***, ***out of the ordinary***, ***extraordinary***, ***exceptional***, ***rare***, ***strange***)

unwarranted
adjective **1** not supported, justified or confirmed: *an **unwarranted** supposition*
2 not authorised: ***unwarranted** actions*

unwieldy
adjective **1** difficult to handle or manage: *an **unwieldy** load*
2 awkward: *an **unwieldy** movement of the arm*

unwind (un-wuynd)
verb **1** to undo (something wound)
2 to disentangle
3 to become unwound
4 to calm down

Verb forms: I **unwound**, I have **unwound**, I am **unwinding**

unwitting
adjective **1** not meant or intended: *an **unwitting** insult*
2 not knowing, or unaware: *an **unwitting** victim*

Word building: **unwittingly** *adverb*

unworldly
adjective **1** not seeking material advantage or gain
2 simple or naive in nature (***gullible***, ***innocent***, ***unsophisticated***)
3 unearthly or not of this world

unwritten
adjective **1** not written
2 customary rather than actually expressed or given form: *It is an **unwritten** rule that you take your shoes off at the door.*

Word history: Old English

unzip
verb **1** to unfasten with a zip: *to **unzip** a dress*
2 → **decompress** (definition 3)

Verb forms: I **unzipped**, I have **unzipped**, I am **unzipping**

up
adverb **1** to or in a higher place: *to climb **up** to the top of a ladder | the vase is **up** out of the way*
2 into the air: *to throw **up** a ball*
3 to or in an upright position: *put the ladder **up***
4 to, near or at a higher rank or condition: *to move **up** in the world*
preposition **5** to or at a higher place on or in: ***up** the stairs*
6 to or at a higher or farther point of: ***up** the street*
adjective **7** going upwards: *an **up** escalator*
8 standing and speaking: *The Prime Minister was **up** for three hours.*
9 out of bed
10 well informed: *She is **up** in scientific matters.*
11 on offer: *a house **up** for sale*
12 appearing before a court on a charge: *He is **up** for speeding again.*
13 in the process of happening: *They wondered what was **up**.*
14 ahead: *She was three points **up** in the game.*
verb **15** to raise: *to **up** the bet*
16 *Colloquial* to get or start up: *to **up** and away*
phrase **17 up against**, *Colloquial* faced with: *They are **up against** enormous problems.*
18 up and about, active
19 up to,
a doing: *What are you **up to**?*
b resting on as a duty: *It is **up to** you to make the next move.*
c as many as: *It will carry **up to** eight people.*
d as far as: ***up to** their knees in water*
e *Colloquial* capable of: *not **up to** the job*

Verb forms: I **upped**, I have **upped**, I am **upping**
Word use: This word is often combined with a verb to form a compound as in *set up*, *add up*, *catch up*, etc. Look up the main verb to find the meanings of these and other compounds.
Word history: Old English

upbraid
verb to speak angrily to about doing something wrong: *She **upbraided** him for his lateness.* (***reprove***, ***scold***)

Word history: Old English

upbringing
noun the care and education that is given by parents or similar people to someone during their childhood

update
verb **1** to give the latest news to: *I will **update** you on what has happened recently.*
2 to make more modern: *They are **updating** the shop.*
noun **3** the act of updating: *I need an **update** on the situation.*
4 a more recent version: *I am installing some software **updates** on my computer.*

Word building: **update** *noun*

up-end
verb **1** to set on end: *to **up-end** the barrel*
2 to upset or change greatly: *to **up-end** the plans*

upgrade
verb **1** to promote or make more important: *His boss **upgraded** him to a new job. | The company **upgraded** his position.*
2 to improve: *You must **upgrade** your work.* (***better***, ***correct***, ***enhance***)
3 to allocate to (someone) a better seat on a plane, a better room in a hotel, or something similar: *When we checked in, we were **upgraded** to first class!*
noun **4** *Computers* a new version of a product: *You can download an **upgrade** of your anti-virus software.*

Word use: The opposite of definition 1 is **downgrade**.

upheaval
noun a complete change or great disturbance: *We were in a state of **upheaval** after we moved house.*

uphill
adjective **1** going upwards: *an **uphill** path*
2 very difficult: *an **uphill** task*

Word building: **uphill** *adverb*

uphold
verb to support or keep unchanged: *The principal* ***upheld*** *the rule that the teacher had made.*

Verb forms: I **upheld**, I have **upheld**, I am **upholding**

upholster
verb to provide with coverings, stuffing and springs: *to* ***upholster*** *a chair*

Word building: **upholsterer** *noun*

upholstery
noun **1** the cushions, furniture coverings and other material used to stuff and cover furniture and cushions
2 the interior padding and lining for the seats, etc., of a car

Noun forms: The plural is **upholsteries.**

upkeep
noun the work or cost of looking after something or someone

uplift
verb **1** to lift up
2 to cause to feel better, especially spiritually or mentally: *The beautiful singing* ***uplifted*** *him.*

Word building: **uplift** *noun*

uplifting
adjective making you feel happy or think about doing good things: *We were all inspired by his* ***uplifting*** *speech about what we can do to stop environmental damage.*

upload
Computers
verb **1** to transfer or copy (data) from a computer to a larger system, as from a personal computer to a network or mainframe computer: *to* ***upload*** *new software*
noun **2** the act of uploading data
3 data that has been uploaded

up-market
adjective **1** having to do with commercial services and goods of high status, quality and price
2 superior or pretentious in style or production

Word use: The opposite of this is **down-market**.

upon
preposition **1** up and on: *to climb* ***upon*** *a table*
2 in a raised position on: *The hat is* ***upon*** *his head.*
3 on

Word history: Middle English

upper
adjective **1** higher or highest in place, position or rank: *the* ***upper*** *slopes of a mountain | the* ***upper*** *class*
2 facing upwards: *the* ***upper*** *side of a coin*

upper case
noun the printing type that makes capital letters

Word use: Compare this with **lower case**.

upper class
noun the wealthiest group of people in a society

Word use: Compare this with **lower class** and **middle class**.
Word building: **upper-class** *adjective*

upper hand
noun the controlling position or advantage: *She has the* ***upper hand*** *in their relationship.*

upper house
noun one of the bodies in a parliament of two houses (upper and lower), generally smaller and less representative than the lower branch, usually acting as a house of review, rarely introducing legislation and lacking the constitutional power to initiate any financial legislation

Word use: You can also use **upper chamber**.

uppermost
adjective highest in place, order, rank, power, etc.

Word building: **uppermost** *adverb*

upright
adjective **1** straight upward or vertical: *an* ***upright*** *position*
2 *Old-fashioned* honest and just: *an* ***upright*** *person* (***decent***, ***honourable***)

Word building: **upright** *adverb*
Word history: Old English

uprising
noun a violent rebellion against a government or other authority by a large number of people (***revolt***, ***revolution***)

uproar
noun a noisy disturbance: *There was an* ***uproar*** *in the classroom before the teacher came.* (***commotion***, ***din***, ***hubbub***, ***pandemonium***, ***racket***)

Word history: from Dutch word meaning 'tumult'

uproot
verb **1** to tear up by or as if by the roots
2 to remove completely
3 to displace: *We were* ***uprooted*** *every few years when our father was sent to a new posting.*

upset
verb **1** to turn or knock over: *to* ***upset*** *a boat | to* ***upset*** *a cup of tea* (***bowl over***, ***overturn***, ***skittle***, ***tip over***)
2 to put out of order: *to* ***upset*** *someone's plans* (***disorganise***, ***disrupt***, ***disturb***, ***mess up***, ***mix up***)
3 to make feel sad or hurt: *His insults* ***upset*** *me.* (***annoy***, ***distress***, ***hurt***, ***sadden***, ***trouble***)
4 to make feel sick in the stomach: *That food* ***upset*** *me.*
noun **5** the act of overturning or the state of being overturned
6 the act of disordering or the state of being disordered
7 a slight illness, especially of the stomach
8 an emotional disturbance
9 an unexpected defeat

Verb forms: I **upset**, I have **upset**, I am **upsetting**
Word building: **upset** *adjective*

upshot
noun the final conclusion or result: *the* ***upshot*** *of the argument*

upstage
adverb **1** on or to the back of the stage
verb **2** to steal attention from, by placing yourself in a more favourable position in word or action

upstairs
adverb **1** up the stairs
2 to or in a higher rank or office
adjective **3** on an upper floor: *an* ***upstairs*** *toilet*
noun **4** an upper storey or storeys: ***Upstairs*** *was damaged during the storm.*
phrase **5 kick upstairs**, to promote in order to get out of the way

upstanding
adjective **1** upright or erect
2 straightforward, open or honourable
3 *Colloquial* standing up: *Be **upstanding** and charge your glasses.*

upstart
noun someone who has risen suddenly from a low position to wealth or power, especially one who is self-important and unpleasant

uptake
noun the act of understanding or grasping facts: *He is quick on the **uptake** so you won't have to tell him twice.*

uptight
adjective Colloquial nervous or worried: *He felt **uptight** before his music exam.* (***agitated***, ***disturbed***, ***flustered***, ***het-up***, ***upset***)

up-to-date
adjective **1** including the most recent facts: *an **up-to-date** news report*
2 modern: ***up-to-date** clothes* | ***up-to-date** ideas* (***contemporary***, ***current***, ***new***, ***recent***)

Word use: The opposite of this is **outdated**.

upturn
verb **1** to turn up or over: *The boat was **upturned**.*
2 to direct or turn upwards
noun **3** an upward turn, or a changing and rising movement, as in prices, business, etc.

upward
adjective **1** directed or moving towards a higher point or level
adverb **2** → **upwards**

Word history: Old English

upwards
adverb **1** towards a higher place, position, level or degree
phrase **2 upwards of**, more than or above: *He is **upwards of** 60 years of age.*

Word use: You can also use **upward** for definition 1.

uranium (yooh-ray-nee-uhm)
noun a white, radioactive metal which comes from a yellow ore and which can be used to produce nuclear weapons and energy

Word history: Neo-Latin

urban (er-buhn)
adjective having to do with a city or town: *the **urban** population* (***citified***, ***civic***, ***metropolitan***, ***suburban***)

Word use: The opposite of this is **rural**.
Word history: Latin

urban area
noun an area of human habitation in which most of the working inhabitants are engaged in non-agricultural activities

urbane (er-bayn)
adjective having or showing the good taste and manners considered to be characteristic of city-dwellers (***sophisticated***, ***suave***)

Word history: Latin

urban fringe
noun the area on the periphery of a city or town where the built-up area extends into the rural countryside

urban sprawl
noun the outer areas of a city, especially where development is considered to have been unplanned and undesirable

urchin
noun a small boy, especially one who is mischievous or poorly dressed

Word history: Middle English, from a dialect of Old French, from Latin word meaning 'hedgehog'

urethra (yooh-reeth-ruh)
noun Anatomy the tube-like part by which urine is carried from the bladder and passed from the body

Noun forms: The plural is **urethras** or **urethrae** (yooh-reeth-ree).
Word history: Late Latin, from Greek

urge
verb **1** to try hard to persuade: *I **urged** him to be very careful.* (***encourage***, ***inspire***, ***motivate***, ***persuade***)
2 to push, drive or force: *She **urged** the horse along the path.* | *Hunger **urged** us to keep going.*
noun **3** a strong natural desire: *I felt an **urge** to eat some fruit.*

Word history: from Latin word meaning 'press', 'drive'

urgent
adjective needing immediate action or attention: *an **urgent** message*

Word building: **urgency** *noun* **urgently** *adverb*
Word history: Latin

urinal (yooh-ruhn-uhl, yuh-ruyn-uhl)
noun a fixture, room or building to urinate in, especially a men's toilet

Word history: Middle English, from Latin

urinate
verb to pass urine from the body

Word building: **urination** *noun*

urine (yooh-ruhn, yooh-ruyn)
noun liquid produced by the kidneys and passed from the body as a waste product

Word building: **urinary** *adjective*
Word history: Middle English, from Latin

URL
noun Computers the address of a document on the internet

Word history: an acronym meaning *u(niform) r(esource) l(ocator)*

urn (ern)
noun **1** a kind of vase, especially one for holding the ashes of someone who has been cremated
2 a container with a tap, used for heating water

Word history: Middle English, from Latin

urn / earn

Don't confuse **urn** with **earn**. To **earn** is to receive something in return for working, or to deserve to get something.

ursine (er-suyn)
adjective **1** having to do with a bear or bears
2 bear-like

Word history: Latin

us
pronoun the personal pronoun used, usually after a verb or preposition, by a speaker to refer to himself or herself along with at least one other person: *Could you please take **us** home? | He ran to **us**.*

Us is a first person plural pronoun in the objective case.
For more information, look up **pronouns: personal pronouns**.

usage
noun **1** the way of using or treating: *rough **usage***
2 a custom or practice
3 the way in which a language is used: *English **usage***
Word history: Middle English, from Old French word meaning 'use', from Latin

USB (yooh es bee)
noun Computers a standard for connection sockets
Word history: an acronym for *u(niversal) s(erial) b(us)*

USB stick
noun → **memory stick**

use (yoohz)
verb **1** to employ or put into action for some purpose: *I will **use** a knife to cut this rope. | Do you know how to **use** this machine?* (**utilise**)
2 to take advantage of someone's feeling for you in order to get them to do something you want: *She doesn't love Kanye, she is simply **using** him.* (**exploit**)
noun (yoohs) **3** the act of using: *This shows the **use** of common sense. | You should clean those brushes after each **use**.*
4 the state of being used: *Is this seat in **use**?*
5 a way of being used: *You will find that this bag has a lot of **uses**.*
6 the ability to use something: *She lost the **use** of her legs after the accident.*
7 a need for using something: *Do you have any **use** for these clothes?* (**call**, **want**)
8 the ability to be used in a helpful way: *This book is of **use** to me.*
phrase (yoohz) **9 use up**, to take or wear out the entire supply of: *I've **used up** the toothpaste. | He's **used up** his strength.* (**exhaust**, **expend**, **consume**)
Word building: **usable** *adjective* **useful** *adjective* **useless** *adjective* **user** *noun*
Word history: Middle English, from Old French, from Latin

use / utilise
The original distinction between these words is disappearing.
Strictly speaking, to **utilise** something is a formal way of saying to use it in a practical or effective way.
Nowadays, many people choose **utilise** in a context where **use** would be clearer. This has the effect of making what they say sound pretentious — why use a long word when a short word is better? It would be better to say:
If you use your brain, you'll find the answer to the riddle.
rather than:
If you utilise your brain, you'll find the answer to the riddle.

use / youse
Don't confuse **use** with **youse**.
Youse is a slang form of **you** and usually refers to more than one person. It should be avoided in essays and conversation because it is considered ungrammatical.

used[1] (yoohzd)
adjective **1** having been made use of, especially showing signs of wear: *We bought a new lounge as our old one looked very **used**.*
2 second-hand: *a **used** car | **used** clothing*
Word history: past form of *use*

used[2] (yoohst)
phrase **used to 1** was or were accustomed: *We **used to** go there every summer.*
2 in the habit of, or accustomed to: *I am **used to** getting up early.*
Word history: special use of *use*

user group
noun a group of people linked by their use of a particular product, sometimes forming an association for the sharing of information about that product

userid (yooh-zuhr-uy-dee)
noun a personal identification code entered into a computer when signing on
Word use: You can also use **username**.

username
noun → **userid**

usher
noun someone who shows people to their seats at a meeting, in church, or at another public gathering
Word history: Middle English, from Anglo-French, from Late Latin word meaning 'doorkeeper'

usual
adjective normal or customary: *We went to school the **usual** way.* (**conventional**, **orthodox**, **traditional**)
Word building: **usually** *adverb*
Word history: Middle English, from Latin

usurp
verb to seize and hold by force or without right: *to **usurp** power | to **usurp** the throne*
Word history: Middle English, from Latin

usury (yooh-zhuh-ree)
noun **1** a very high rate of interest, especially in excess of the legal rate
2 the lending, or practice of lending money at a very high rate of interest
Noun forms: The plural is **usuries**.
Word history: Middle English, from Medieval Latin word meaning 'interest'

utensil (yooh-ten-suhl)
noun an instrument, tool or container, especially one of those used for cooking or eating: *Pots and pans are kitchen **utensils**.*
Word history: Middle English, from Medieval Latin word meaning 'useful'

uterus (yooh-tuh-ruhs)
noun the part of the body of a female in which a baby grows (***womb***)

Noun forms: The plural is **uteri** (yooh-tuh-ruy).
Word history: Latin

utilise
verb to put into use: *We can **utilise** the sun's power to make electricity.* (***employ***, ***exploit***)

Word use: You can also use **utilize**.
Word building: **utilisation** *noun*

utilitarian (yooh-til-uh-tair-ree-uhn)
adjective **1** having to do with practical or material things: *a **utilitarian** idea*
2 designed for usefulness rather than beauty, etc.: ***utilitarian** clothes*

Word building: **utilitarian** *noun*

utility
noun **1** usefulness
2 a public service, such as a bus or railway service, gas or electricity supply
3 *Australian*, *NZ* a small truck

Word use: You can also use the colloquial word **ute** for definition 3.
Word history: Middle English, from Latin

utmost
adjective **1** greatest: *This is of the **utmost** importance.*
2 farthest: *He went to the **utmost** boundary of the property.*
noun **3** the greatest amount possible: *This is the **utmost** that can be said.*
4 the best that you can do: *Try your **utmost**.*

Word use: You can also use **uttermost**.
Word history: Old English

utopia (yooh-toh-pee-uh)
noun a completely perfect place or society

Word building: **utopian** *adjective*
Word history: from *Utopia*, the name of a book written in 1516 by Sir Thomas More (1478–1535) about an imaginary island on which there is the utmost perfection in law, politics, etc.; the word is Neo-Latin, from Greek *ou* not + *-topia*, from *tópas* place

utter[1]
verb to speak: *He was sorry he had **uttered** angry words.* (***articulate***, ***enunciate***, ***pronounce***, ***voice***)

Word building: **utterance** *noun*
Word history: Middle English

utter[2]
adjective complete or total: ***utter** happiness* | *The room was **utter** luxury.*

Word building: **utterly** *adverb*
Word history: from Old English word meaning 'outer'

U-turn
noun a turn made by a car or other vehicle so that it faces the way it has just come

UV
adjective → **ultraviolet**

Word history: abbreviation

uvula (yoohv-yuh-luh)
noun *Anatomy* the small, fleshy, cone-shaped body part projecting downwards above the back of the tongue

Noun forms: The plural is **uvulas** or **uvulae** (yoohv-yuh-lee).
Word history: Middle English, from Medieval Latin, from Latin word meaning 'little grape'

uxorious (uk-saw-ree-uhs)
adjective greatly or foolishly fond of your wife

Word history: Latin

Vv

vacant (<u>vay</u>-kuhnt)
adjective **1** empty: ***vacant** space* (***blank***, ***deserted***, ***void***)
2 not occupied by anyone: *a **vacant** chair | a **vacant** job*

Word building: **vacancy** *noun* (*plural* **vacancies**)
Word history: Middle English, from Latin

vacate (vuh-<u>kayt</u>, vay-<u>kayt</u>)
verb to leave or make empty: *You must **vacate** your room by 10 o'clock.* (***evacuate***, ***quit***)

Word history: from Latin word meaning 'freed', 'emptied'

vacation
noun **1** a holiday
2 the time of the year when a place such as a university is closed (***break***, ***recess***)

Word history: Middle English, from Latin

vaccinate (<u>vak</u>-suh-nayt)
verb to administer a vaccine to in order to prevent illness: *The nurse **vaccinated** the child.*

Word building: **vaccination** *noun*

vaccine (<u>vak</u>-seen)
noun a liquid made from the germs that give you a disease, which is given to you to stop you getting that disease

Word history: from Latin word meaning 'pertaining to cows'

vacillate (<u>vas</u>-uh-layt)
verb **1** to move back and forth
2 to change continually from one course, position, etc., to another (***change your tune***, ***chop and change***, ***fluctuate***, ***hesitate***, ***waver***)
3 to be indecisive or hesitant

Word building: **vacillation** *noun*
Word history: Latin

vacuole (<u>vak</u>-yooh-ohl)
noun **1** a tiny space within a cell containing fluid
2 a tiny space in organic tissue

vacuous (<u>vak</u>-yooh-uhs)
adjective empty, especially of ideas or intelligence

Word building: **vacuousness** *noun*
Word history: Latin

vacuum (<u>vak</u>-yoohm)
noun **1** a space completely free of matter
2 an enclosed space from which air or other gas has been removed, such as by an air pump

Word use: You can also use **perfect vacuum** or **complete vacuum** for definition 1. | You can also use **partial vacuum** for definition 2.
Word history: from Latin word meaning 'empty'

vacuum cleaner
noun a machine for cleaning floors, carpets, etc., which functions by sucking up dirt and dust

vagabond (<u>vag</u>-uh-bond)
adjective **1** wandering from place to place without being settled
2 good-for-nothing or worthless: ***vagabond** friends*
noun **3** someone who is without a fixed home and who wanders from place to place, especially one thought to be idle or worthless (***itinerant***, ***tramp***, ***vagrant***)

Word history: Middle English, from Latin word meaning 'strolling about'

vagary (<u>vay</u>-guh-ree)
noun **1** an unusual, quaint or extravagant idea
2 a wild, fanciful or fantastic action

Noun forms: The plural is **vagaries**.
Word history: apparently from Latin word meaning 'wander'

vagina (vuh-<u>juy</u>-nuh)
noun the passage in the body of a female that leads from the uterus to the outside of the body

Noun forms: The plural is **vaginas**.
Word building: **vaginal** *adjective*
Word history: from Latin word meaning 'sheath'

vagrant (<u>vay</u>-gruhnt)
noun a homeless person (***itinerant***, ***swagman***, ***tramp***)

Word history: late Middle English, from Latin

vague (vayg)
adjective not clear or certain: ***vague** shapes | **vague** feelings* (***approximate***, ***faint***, ***hazy***, ***indefinite***, ***uncertain***)

Word building: **vaguely** *adverb* **vagueness** *noun*
Word history: from Latin word meaning 'wandering'

vain
adjective **1** very proud of yourself, especially about the way you look (***big-headed***, ***conceited***, ***egotistic***, ***narcissistic***, ***stuck-up***)
2 useless or having no effect: *He made a **vain** attempt to stop the dogs fighting.* (***futile***, ***impossible***, ***ineffective***, ***ineffectual***)
phrase **3 in vain**, uselessly or without effect: *They tried **in vain** to save her.*

Word building: **vanity** *noun*
Word history: Middle English, from Old French, from Latin word meaning 'empty', 'idle'

vain / vane / vein

Don't confuse **vain** with **vane** or **vein**.

A **vane** is a flat piece of metal, or something similar, designed to move with the wind. A **weather vane** shows the direction the wind is blowing.

A **vein** is a blood vessel taking the blood back to the heart.

vale
noun an old-fashioned word for **valley**

vale / veil

Don't confuse **vale** with **veil**, which is a piece of material worn by women to cover their head or face, or a verb meaning to hide or disguise.

valediction (val-uh-dik-shuhn)
noun **1** a saying goodbye
2 a speech, etc., made at the time of or by way of leave-taking

Word building: **valedictory** *adjective* **valedictory** *noun*
Word history: from Latin word meaning 'bidden goodbye'

valedictory (val-uh-dik-tuh-ree)
adjective **1** bidding farewell: *a **valedictory** speech*
2 having to do with an occasion of leave-taking: *a **valedictory** gift*
noun **3** a valedictory speech: *She wrote a **valedictory** for him when he was about to retire.*

Noun forms: The plural is **valedictories**.

valency (vay-luhn-see)
noun the combining power of an atom or radical compared with the hydrogen atom: *a **valency** of one (the ability to combine with or replace one atom of hydrogen)*

Word use: You can also use **valence**.
Word history: from Latin word meaning 'strength'

valentine
noun **1** a present or message of love or friendship sent to someone on St Valentine's Day, 14 February
2 the person you choose to send this message to

Word history: named after St *Valentine*, died about AD 270, Christian martyr at Rome

valet (val-ay, val-uht)
noun a male servant who looks after his employer's clothes and other personal things

Word history: French, variant of Middle French

valet parking
noun a service provided, for instance in a hotel, in which patrons drive to the door and leave their cars for an attendant to park

valiant
adjective brave or courageous: *a **valiant** person | a **valiant** attempt to save his life* (***bold***, ***courageous***, ***fearless***, ***heroic***)

Word use: The opposite of this is **cowardly** or **fearful**.
Word building: **valiantly** *adverb*
Word history: Middle English, from Old French word meaning 'be strong', from Latin

valid
adjective **1** made with good reasons: *a **valid** excuse to leave the room* (***correct***, ***reasonable***, ***right***)
2 having legal or official force: *This ticket is **valid** for two rides.*

Word use: The opposite of this is **invalid**.
Word building: **validity** *noun*
Word history: from Latin word meaning 'strong'

validate
verb to confirm

valley
noun the low land between hills or mountains, usually with a river flowing through it (***canyon***, ***gorge***, ***gully***, ***ravine***)

Noun forms: The plural is **valleys**.
Word history: Middle English, from Old French, from Latin

valour
noun braveness or courage

Word use: You can also use **valor**.
Word building: **valorous** *adjective*
Word history: Middle English, from Old French, from Latin word meaning 'be strong', 'be worth'

valuable
adjective **1** worth a lot of money: ***valuable** jewels*
2 of great use or importance: ***valuable** help* (***handy***, ***helpful***, ***useful***)
noun **3 valuables**, things that are valuable, such as jewellery: *Don't leave any **valuables** in the changing rooms.*

valuable / invaluable / valueless

Don't confuse **valuable** with **invaluable** or **valueless**.

Something **invaluable** is so precious that no value or price can be attached to it. It is not, as you might think, the opposite of **valuable**.

Something **valueless** is worthless and has no value at all.

valuation (val-yooh-ay-shuhn)
noun **1** the fixing of the value of a thing
2 the value decided or fixed

value
noun **1** the amount of money something is worth: *the **value** of your house*
2 what makes something worthwhile or useful: *He talked about the **value** of education.*
3 values, the beliefs and ideas about what is important, held by a person or community of people: *We like each other because we have the same **values**.*
verb **4** to decide the value of: *His job is to **value** jewellery.* (***appraise***, ***evaluate***, ***judge***, ***measure***, ***size up***)
5 to think to be valuable: *I **value** your friendship.*

Word building: **valuer** *noun* **valueless** *adjective*
Word history: Middle English, from Old French word meaning 'be worth', from Latin

value-add
verb to add to the value of a product or service at any stage of production: *The grocer looked at ways to **value-add** his organic range.*

Word building: **value-added** *adjective* **value-adding** *noun*

valueless / valuable / invaluable
Look up **valuable / invaluable / valueless.**

valve
noun **1** the part of a pipe or other passage that opens and shuts to control the flow of liquid or gas
2 one of the two or more separable parts of the shell of a sea animal, such as a mussel

Word history: Middle English, from Latin word meaning 'leaf of a door', (plural) 'folding doors'

vamp
noun **1** the front part of the upper of a shoe or boot
2 anything patched up or pieced together
3 *Music* an accompaniment, usually improvised, consisting of a succession of simple chords
verb **4** to patch up or repair: *to **vamp** up the house*
5 *Music* to improvise an accompaniment or tune

Word history: Middle English, from Old French word meaning 'forepart of the foot', from Latin

vampire
noun an imaginary being, usually thought of as a dead person come back to life, believed to suck blood from people while they are sleeping

Word history: French, from German, perhaps from Turkish word meaning 'witch'

van
noun a covered vehicle for carrying goods: *a removal **van***

vandal
noun someone who deliberately destroys or damages things

Word building: **vandalise** *verb* **vandalism** *noun*
Word history: Late Latin *Vandalus*, Latinisation of native tribal name

vane
noun **1** a blade on a windmill
2 a flat piece of metal or other material on a roof, which turns with the wind to show which direction it is blowing from

Word use: You can also use **weathervane** for definition 2.
Word history: Middle English; Old English *fana* flag

vane / vein / vain
Look up **vain / vane / vein.**

vanguard
noun **1** the front part of an army
2 any leading position: *She is in the **vanguard** of fashion.*

Word history: late Middle English, from Old French

vanilla
noun a liquid made from a plant, used to flavour food

Word history: Neo-Latin, from Spanish word meaning 'little pod', from Latin

vanish
verb to disappear, especially quickly: *When I turned around she had **vanished**.* (***dematerialise, dissolve, fade, melt***)

Word history: Middle English, from Old French

vanity
noun **1** extreme pride in yourself: *She is too full of **vanity**.*
2 something that someone is vain about: *His hair was one of his **vanities**.*

Noun forms: The plural is **vanities**.
Word history: Middle English, from Old French, from Latin word meaning 'emptiness'

vanquish
verb to defeat: *The Roman army **vanquished** the enemy. | Our team **vanquished** all the others.* (***beat, conquer, lick, thrash***)

Word history: Middle English, from Old French from Latin

vantage (van-tij, vahn-tij)
noun **1** a position or condition giving a benefit: *With the **vantage** of height he was able to see above the crowd.*
2 an opportunity likely to give a benefit
adjective **3** giving or being a vantage: *a **vantage** point | **vantage** ground*

Word history: Middle English; short for *advantage*

vapid (vap-uhd)
adjective **1** having lost sharpness or flavour (***insipid, pale, tasteless***)
2 dull or uninteresting: ***vapid** talk*

Word building: **vapidity** *noun* **vapidness** *noun*
Word history: Latin

vaporise
verb to change into vapour: *Liquid **vaporises** when it is boiled.*

Word use: You can also use **vaporize**.
Word building: **vaporisation** *noun* **vaporiser** *noun*

vapour
noun a cloud of a gas-like substance, such as fog, mist or steam

Word use: You can also use **vapor**.
Word building: **vaporous** *adjective*
Word history: Middle English, from Anglo-French, from Latin word meaning 'steam'

variable
adjective **1** likely to vary or change: ***variable** weather | a person with **variable** moods*
2 able to be changed: *The length of this table is **variable**.*
noun **3** something which varies
4 *Mathematics* a symbol, or the quantity or function which it signifies, which may represent any one of a given set of numbers and other objects

Word history: Latin

variance (vair-ree-uhns)
noun **1** the condition or fact of varying (***divergence, separation***)
2 an instance of this
3 in statistics, the square of the standard deviation
4 a disagreement or quarrel
phrase **5 at variance**, not agreeing or differing

Word history: Middle English, from Old French

variant (vair-ree-uhnt)
adjective **1** tending to change or alter
2 being an altered form of something: *a **variant** spelling of a word*
noun **3** a variant form

Word history: Middle English, from Latin word meaning 'varying'

variation
noun **1** a change or alteration: *There is a lot of **variation** in the weather at this time of the year.*
2 a different form of something: *This novel is just a **variation** of all his other books.*

Word history: Middle English, from Latin

varicose (va-ruh-kohs, va-ruh-kuhs)
adjective abnormally or unusually enlarged or swollen, such as veins in the body

Word building: **varicosity** *noun*
Word history: Latin

varicose veins
plural noun veins close to the skin, especially in your legs, which become knotted and swollen; caused by a defect in the valves that control blood-flow to these veins, or the pumping system that normally moves the blood from the legs when you are standing for a long time

variegate (vair-ree-uh-gayt, vair-ruh-gayt)
verb to make varied in appearance, especially with different colours

Word building: **variegation** *noun*
Word history: Late Latin

variegated (vair-ree-uh-gayt-uhd)
adjective marked with different colours: ***variegated** leaves*

variety
noun **1** a variation or a change from what usually happens: *You enjoy work more if there is some **variety** in it.*
2 a number of things of different kinds: *a shop with a **variety** of cakes* (***assortment***, ***diversity***, ***mix***, ***mixture***)
3 kind or sort: *This **variety** of ice-cream is my favourite.*

Word history: Latin

various
adjective **1** different: *His talents are many and **various**.* (***assorted***, ***diverse***, ***miscellaneous***, ***mixed***, ***motley***)
2 several: *I visited **various** parts of the country.*

Word building: **variously** *adverb* **variousness** *noun*
Word history: Latin

varnish
noun a liquid coating which, when dry, gives a hard, glossy look to a surface

Word building: **varnish** *verb*
Word history: Middle English, from Old French word meaning 'varnish', from Medieval Latin word meaning 'sweet-smelling resin', from Medieval Greek

vary
verb **1** to change: *She never **varies** her habits.* (***adapt***, ***alter***)
2 to be different or cause to be different: *Opinions **vary** as to whether this is a good idea. | You should **vary** what you read.*

Verb forms: I **varied**, I have **varied**, I am **varying**
Word history: Middle English, from Latin word meaning 'various'

vascular (vas-kyuh-luh)
adjective having to do with vessels or ducts in animals or plants which carry fluids, like blood, lymph or sap

Word building: **vascularity** *noun*
Word history: Neo-Latin, from Latin word meaning 'little vessel'

vas deferens (vas def-uh-ruhns)
noun the duct in the male body, which carries the sperm from the testis to the urethra

Noun forms: The plural is **vasa deferentia** (vay-suh def-uh-ren-shee-uh).
Word history: from Latin word meaning 'vessel carrying down'

vase (vahz)
noun a container for flowers

Word history: French, from Latin word meaning 'vessel'

vasectomy (vuh-sek-tuh-mee)
noun the cutting of the vas deferens, or of a part of it, as a method of male sterilisation

Noun forms: The plural is **vasectomies**.

vaseline (vas-uh-leen, vas-uh-leen)
noun a jelly made from petroleum, used in medicine and as a lubricant

Word history: Trademark

vassal
noun someone in feudal times, who lived on and used a nobleman's land and had to fight and work for him in return (***serf***)

Word history: Middle English, from Old French, from Late Latin word meaning 'servant'; of Celtic origin

vast
adjective very great: *a **vast** country | a **vast** amount of money* (***colossal***, ***enormous***, ***gigantic***, ***massive***)

Word building: **vastly** *adverb* **vastness** *noun*
Word history: Latin

vat
noun a very large container for liquids

Word history: Old English

vaudeville (vawd-vil, vaw-duh-vil)
noun a light theatrical entertainment, mainly with musical and comedy acts

Word history: French, from *chanson du Vau de Vire*, type of satirical song popular in the 15th century in the Valley of Vire, a region in Normandy, France

vault[1] (vawlt, volt)
noun **1** an underground room, especially one for storing valuable things, or one where dead people are buried
2 an arched roof or something thought to be similar: *the **vault** of a church | the **vault** of the sky*

Word building: **vaulted** *adjective*
Word history: Middle English, from Old French, from Romance

vault[2] (vawlt, volt)
verb to leap or jump over: *He **vaulted** the fence.* (***bound***, ***spring***)

Word building: **vault** *noun*
Word history: Old French, from Italian, from Latin word meaning 'roll'

vaunt (vawnt)
verb to speak boastfully of: *to **vaunt** your abilities*

Word building: **vaunted** *adjective*
Word history: Middle English, from Late Latin, from Latin word meaning 'vain'

VCR
noun → **video** (definition 3)

Word history: short for *video cassette recorder*

VD
noun → **venereal disease**

Word history: abbreviation

VDU
noun a computer terminal which shows information on a screen

Word use: You can also use **visual display unit, visual display terminal** or **VDT**.
Word history: abbreviation of *v(isual) d(isplay) u(nit)*

veal
noun the flesh of a calf used for food

Word history: Middle English, from Old French, from Latin word meaning 'little calf'

vector (<u>vek</u>-tuh)
noun a quantity which possesses both magnitude and direction, for instance, velocity

Word building: **vectorial** *adjective*
Word history: from Latin word meaning 'carrier'

veejay
noun → **V-jay**

veer
verb to change direction: *The road suddenly **veered** to the left. | I **veered** to avoid the dog.*

Word history: French, from Latin

vegan (<u>vee</u>-guhn)
noun a strict vegetarian who not only does not eat meat or fish, but who does not eat or use anything at all that comes from an animal, such as eggs, cheese or leather

Word history: from *veg(etari)an*

vegetable
noun **1** any herbaceous plant, annual, biennial or perennial, whose fruits, seeds, roots, tubers, bulbs, stems, leaves or flower parts are used as food: *Carrots, beans and potatoes are **vegetables**.*
adjective **2** of or having to do with plants: *the **vegetable** kingdom*

Word history: Middle English, from Late Latin word meaning 'vivifying'

vegetarian
noun someone who refuses to eat meat or fish and lives mainly on vegetable food

vegetate (<u>vej</u>-uh-tayt)
verb to be inactive, dull or unthinking: *You would **vegetate** in a backwater like that!*

Word history: from Latin word meaning 'enlivened'

vegetation
noun the whole plant life of a particular area: *Tropical places usually have thick **vegetation**.*

vehement (<u>vee</u>-uh-muhnt)
adjective strong or passionate: *a **vehement** dislike*

Word building: **vehemence** *noun* **vehemently** *adverb*
Word history: Middle English, from Latin

vehicle (<u>vee</u>-ik-uhl, <u>vee</u>-uhk-uhl)
noun a form of transport, such as a car or bicycle

Word building: **vehicular** *adjective*
Word history: from Latin word meaning 'conveyance'

veil (vayl)
noun **1** a piece of material worn over the head and face
verb **2** to hide or disguise: *The mountains were **veiled** in mist.*

Word history: Middle English, from Anglo-French, from Latin word meaning 'sail', 'covering'

veil / vale
Don't confuse **veil** with **vale**, which is an old-fashioned word for 'valley'.

vein (vayn)
noun **1** one of the small tubes that carries blood through your body
2 a line on a leaf or insect's wing
3 a layer of coal or gold in the middle of rock (***band***, ***deposit***, ***seam***, ***stratum***)

Word history: Middle English, from Old French, from Latin

vein / vain / vane
Look up **vain / vane / vein.**

velcro
noun a type of fastening tape made of two fabric strips, one with many tiny nylon hooks and the other with a nylon pile, that stick firmly together when pressed

Word history: Trademark

veldt (velt)
noun open country, with grass, bushes or shrubs, or thinly forested, typical of parts of southern Africa

Word use: You can also use **veld**.
Word history: Afrikaans, from Dutch word meaning 'field'

velocity (vuh-<u>los</u>-uh-tee)
noun rate of motion in a given direction: *a wind **velocity** of 100 kilometres an hour*

Noun forms: The plural is **velocities**.
Word history: from Latin word meaning 'swiftness'

velodrome (<u>vel</u>-uh-drohm)
noun an arena with a banked track for cycle races

velour (vuh-<u>looh</u>-uh)
noun any of various cloths with a fine, raised finish

Word use: You can also use **velours**.
Word history: French word meaning 'velvet', from Provençal, from Latin word meaning 'hair'

velvet
noun a kind of soft, thick material that feels rather like fur
Word building: **velvet** *adjective* **velvety** *adjective*
Word history: Middle English, from Medieval Latin, from Latin word meaning 'shaggy hair'

venal (vee-nuhl)
adjective open to, or marked by, bribery and corruption
Word building: **venality** *noun*
Word history: from Latin word meaning 'for sale'

vendetta
noun **1** a feud in which the family of a murder victim tries to get revenge by killing the murderer or one of the murderer's family
2 any long or persistent quarrel, rivalry, etc.
3 *Colloquial* a firm stand taken on an issue and strictly enforced: *The police conducted a* ***vendetta*** *against vandalism.*
Word history: Italian, from Latin word meaning 'vengeance'

vendor
noun someone whose business is selling things: *We bought some fruit from the street* ***vendor****.*
Word building: **vend** *verb*
Word history: from Latin word meaning 'sell'

veneer (vuh-near)
noun **1** a thin layer of wood or plastic used to cover the surface underneath (***coating***, ***crust***, ***film***, ***glaze***, ***skin***)
2 outwardly pleasant behaviour, disguising what is really underneath: *a* ***veneer*** *of good manners*
Word history: German, from French

venerable
adjective worthy of respect because of age or importance
Word history: Middle English, from Latin *venerābilis*

venerate
verb to have a reverent respect for (***honour***, ***idolise***, ***revere***, ***worship***)

venereal disease (vuh-near-ree-uhl)
noun a disease, especially syphilis and gonorrhoea, picked up by having sexual intercourse with someone who is infected
Word use: You can also use **sexually transmitted disease** or the abbreviation **VD**.

vengeance (ven-juhns)
noun **1** the act of paying someone back for harm they have done to you (***retaliation***, ***revenge***)
phrase **2 with a vengeance**, very strongly or forcefully
Word history: Middle English, from Old French

venial (vee-nee-uhl)
adjective excusable or pardonable
Word building: **veniality** *noun* **venialness** *noun*
Word history: Middle English, from Latin word meaning 'pardon'

venison
noun the meat of a deer, eaten as food
Word history: Middle English, from Old French, from Latin word meaning 'hunting'

Venn diagram (ven duy-uh-gram)
noun Mathematics a diagram which represents sets of elements as circles whose overlap indicates the overlap of the sets
Word history: named after John *Venn*, 1834–1923, English logician

venom
noun the poison that spiders and snakes inject into their victims (***toxin***)
Word history: Middle English, from Old French, from Latin word meaning 'poison'

venomous
adjective **1** inflicting a poisoned bite, sting or wound
2 spiteful or malignant

venomous / poisonous
Look up **poisonous / venomous.**

vent
noun **1** an opening to let smoke or fumes out
verb **2** to express or show: *to* ***vent*** *anger*
Word history: Old French, from Latin

ventilate
verb to bring fresh air into and let stale air out of: *Open the windows to* ***ventilate*** *the room.*
Word building: **ventilation** *noun* **ventilator** *noun*
Word history: from Latin word meaning 'fanned'

ventral
adjective **1** having to do with the belly (***abdominal***)
2 of or on the lower side or surface, as of an organ or part: *a* ***ventral*** *fin*
Word history: Latin

ventricle (ven-trik-uhl)
noun **1** any of various hollow organs or parts in an animal body
2 one of the two main cavities of the heart, which receives the blood from the auricles and sends it into the arteries
Word building: **ventricular** *adjective*
Word history: Middle English, from Latin word meaning 'belly'

ventriloquism (ven-tril-uh-kwiz-uhm)
noun a way of speaking without moving your lips so that your voice seems to come from somewhere else
Word building: **ventriloquist** *noun*
Word history: Late Latin word meaning 'one who apparently speaks from the belly'

venture
noun **1** something you set out to do, especially something which has risks attached: *a business* ***venture*** (***enterprise***, ***project***, ***undertaking***)
verb **2** to risk or dare: *to* ***venture*** *an opinion*
Word history: Middle English, earlier form of *adventure*

venturesome
adjective tending to take risks, sometimes rashly (***adventurous***, ***daring***)

venue (ven-yooh)
noun the place where a particular event is held: *The new hall is the* ***venue*** *for the school concert.* (***location, site, spot***)

Word history: Middle English, from Old French word meaning 'coming'

veracity (vuh-ras-uh-tee)
noun **1** truthfulness or honesty
2 accuracy or precision

Noun forms: The plural is **veracities**.
Word building: **veracious** *adjective*
Word history: Medieval Latin, from Latin word meaning 'true'

verandah
noun a partly open section on the outside of a house, usually covered by the main roof

Word use: You can also use **veranda**.
Word history: apparently from Portuguese and Old Spanish word meaning 'railing', from Latin word meaning 'rod'

verb
noun a word in a sentence which tells you what someone or something does or feels, such as 'hear' and 'walks' in *If anyone walks past, I'll hear them.*

Word history: Middle English, from Latin word meaning 'word', 'verb'

verbs

It is often said that a **verb** is the most important word in a sentence. Some sentences (those that express commands) may consist of verbs alone:

Go!

Shoot!

Verbs usually come after the subject of a sentence. Many sentences are made up of just the subject and a verb:

She arrived.

The cat left.

Some verbs are made up of more than one word (and are referred to as compound verbs or verb phrases):

She has arrived.

The cat must have left.

The last word in each case (*arrived* and *left*) is the **main verb**. The other words that help make up the full verb (*has, must* and *have*) are called **auxiliaries.**

main verbs

A main verb tells what action or process is or was taking place in a sentence:

He sings softly.

We ate the cheese.

They were running.

In these sentences *sings, ate* and *running* are **main verbs**. *Were* is different — it is an **auxiliary verb**. Its job is simply to join with *running* to make up a complete verb. *Running* on its own would not be enough.

auxiliary verbs

We use auxiliary verbs all the time in speaking and writing, to help make a complete verb. Here are some examples:

I can make pavlovas.

I am making one now.

Who will eat my pavlova?

Auxiliaries are used with other verbs for extra shades of meaning. We can use them to show if something is possible or allowable:

I can eat the pavlova.

I could eat the pavlova.

I may eat the pavlova.

I might eat the pavlova.

We can use auxiliaries to show when something happens (in the future, present or past tense):

I will eat the pavlova.

I am eating the pavlova.

I have eaten the pavlova.

Here are some examples of other uses of auxiliaries, including the forming of questions and negatives:

Do you like pavlova? (question)

I do like pavlova. (emphasis)

I should finish my pavlova. (obligation)

Did I eat the pavlova? (question)

You like pavlova, don't you? (question negative)

I don't like pavlova anymore. (negative)

Auxiliaries are often contracted with pronouns and the word *not*. For example:

I am eating. — I'm eating.

I had eaten. — I'd eaten.

I will eat. — I'll eat.

I will not eat. — I won't eat.

active verbs

The most common way of writing a sentence is to have the subject doing the action of the verb. When this happens the verb is called an active verb:

Kate put her surfboard on the roofracks.

In this sentence, *put* is an active verb because Kate, the subject of the sentence, is carrying out the action.

Even though they're called 'active', these verbs don't necessarily involve movement. For example, both *paddled* and *waited* are active verbs in the following sentence:

She paddled her board past the breakers and waited for a good wave.

Active verbs contrast with passive verbs, in which the subject is acted on by the action of the verb.

Kate fell off the board and was dumped by a wave.

In this sentence, *fell* is an active verb and *was dumped* is a passive verb.

passive verbs

A passive verb is one whose subject is having an action done to it, rather than doing the action itself.

(continued)

passive verbs *(continued)*

In the sentence:

The dog was hit by a car.

the dog is not doing the hitting. It is being hit by the car. Because the subject of the sentence (*the dog*) is not the 'doer' of the action, we say that the verb is **passive**.

When the subject of a sentence carries out the action, we say that the verb is **active**. You can see an example of an active verb in the following sentence:

A car hit the dog.

When we change from passive to active or vice versa, the focus of our attention shifts. In the case of our two examples, it shifts from *the dog* (in the passive sentence) to *the car* (in the active sentence).

Note that using passive verbs is a way of making your writing more impersonal.

reflexive verbs

Reflexive verbs are made simply by adding a reflexive pronoun after the verb.

For example:

He taught himself to play the guitar.

Himself is a reflexive pronoun which refers to *he*. For more about this, look up **pronouns: reflexive pronouns**.

tense

We are able to show in English whether events have happened (past time), are happening (present time), or will happen (future time). We do this in one of two ways:

1 by changing the verb a little: *sing*, *sang*, *sung*; or adding an ending to it: *walk*, *walks*, *walked*.
2 by bringing in an auxiliary (or helping) verb: *I will sing*.

The examples above are the simple tenses — present, past and future.

present tense

You use the present tense of the verb to show or suggest that actions and events are happening at the time you are writing. The following sentence is in the present tense:

I walk to work every day.

The present tense suggests to the reader that things are going on at the very time they are reading. So you can use it to bring the past into the present.

For example:

He comes into the room and is blinded by the light. He puts on his dark glasses and sees ...
This is called the **narrative present**.

We can also distinguish whether the events are completed or are continuing by using the present tense in its *perfect* or *continuous* forms:

I walk (present — simple form)

I am walking (present continuous)

I have walked (present perfect)

I have been walking (present perfect continuous)

The perfect and the continuous forms of a verb are called *aspects* of tense, and they are indicated by the auxiliary verbs *be* and *have*. You can see them used with the verb *walk* in the examples above.

past tense

We use the past tense of a verb for actions and events that have happened in the past.

We show this either by adding endings to the basic (infinitive) form of the verb (*walk* becomes *walked* and *finish* becomes *finished*) or by changing the spellings within the word itself (*fight* becomes *fought* and *run* becomes *ran*).

We can also show whether the events are completed or continuing by using the past tense in its *perfect* or *continuous* forms:

I walked (past — simple form)

I was walking (past continuous)

I had walked (past perfect)

I had been walking (past perfect continuous)

As you can see in the examples above, we use the verbs *be* and *have* to indicate the perfect and continuous aspects of the past tense.

future tense

In English we show that the action of a verb takes place in the future by using words such as *will* and *shall* (modals) and *tomorrow* and *soon* (adverbs of time):

He will come.

He comes tomorrow.

compound tense

There are other more complicated forms of present, past and future tenses which we call compound tenses:

I am walking *I have walked*
I have been walking

I was walking *I had walked*
I had been walking

I will be walking *I will have walked*
I will have been walking

Compound tenses use the auxiliaries *have* and *be*, and the present or past participles. Look up **participle**.

These tenses express different ways of looking at the action of the verb. This is called **aspect**.

aspect

In English, verbs can show that the action is either *continuous* or *complete*.

Continuous aspect is shown by ending the verb with -ing, and by preceding it with a form of the verb *be*:

I was walking.

I am eating.

The **continuous** aspect is also known as the **imperfect** aspect.

If the action is complete, we can use the **perfect** aspect. This is shown by using the past participle of the verb (with an -ed or -en ending for most verbs) preceded by a form of the verb *have*:

I have walked.

I have eaten.

If the verb is neither continuous nor perfect, it is called a **simple** verb:

I walked.

I eat.

Some languages that you may study have what is called a **conditional** aspect of the verb. It expresses what may happen if certain conditions are true.

English doesn't have the conditional aspect, so we use certain conjunctions like *if* and *unless* to do the job. Clauses with these conjunctions can be called **conditional clauses.**

If it rains, the barbecue's off.

You can't do that unless you've got a licence.

mood

Mood is a term of grammar that is applied to verbs. In English, verbs can be **indicative** (making factual statements or asking questions), **imperative** (giving commands) or, more rarely, **subjunctive** (expressing wishes or possibilities).

indicative mood

She is going. (statement)

Are you going? (question)

imperative mood

Go on!

subjunctive mood

I wish I were going.

irregular verbs

Some of the most common verbs in English form their different tenses in an unpredictable way. The majority of verbs (**regular verbs**) add -ed to give both the past tense and the past participle. For instance, *to walk*:

I walked (past tense)

I have walked (past participle)

Any verb which does not use this method of creating its past participle and its past tense is known as an **irregular verb.**

An example of an irregular verb is *to draw*, where the past forms are:

I drew not *I drawed*

I have drawn not *I have drawed*

Another example is the verb *to hit*, which doesn't change at all for its past tense and past participle:

I hit the ball so hard it broke the window.

I have hit it so many times my arm's sore.

Some irregular verbs

begin, began, begun
bite, bit, bitten
blow, blew, blown
break, broke, broken
drink, drank, drunk
drive, drove, driven
eat, ate, eaten
fall, fell, fallen
fly, flew, flown
forget, forgot, forgotten
freeze, froze, frozen
give, gave, given
go, went, gone
hide, hid, hidden
know, knew, known
ride, rode, ridden
ring, rang, rung
rise, rose, risen
see, saw, seen
shake, shook, shaken
sing, sang, sung
sink, sank, sunk
speak, spoke, spoken
swim, swam, swum
take, took, taken
tear, tore, torn
throw, threw, thrown
tread, trod, trodden
wear, wore, worn
write, wrote, written

verb phrases

Verb phrases are groups of words which contain a main verb as the most important word:

The cat must have left.

In the sentence above *must have left* is a **verb phrase.** *Left* is the **main verb** while *must* and *have* are **auxiliary verbs.**

verbal
adjective **1** spoken rather than written: *a **verbal** message*
2 having to do with words: ***verbal** skills*

Word history: Middle English, from Latin word meaning 'word'

verbalise (ver-buhl-uyz)
verb to express in words

Word use: You can also use **verbalize.**
Word building: **verbalisation** *noun*

verbatim (ver-bay-tuhm)
adverb using exactly the same words: *to quote her words **verbatim***

Word history: Medieval Latin, from Latin word meaning 'word'

verbiage (ver-bee-ij)
noun a mass of useless words, in writing or speech

Word history: French word meaning 'gabble', from Latin word meaning 'word'

verbose (ver-bohs)
adjective using too many words, making the listener bored or annoyed: *a **verbose** person* | *a **verbose** account* (***garrulous, loquacious, wordy***)

Word building: **verbosity** *noun*
Word history: from Latin word meaning 'full of words'

verdant (ver-duhnt)
adjective green with vegetation: *a **verdant** valley*

Word building: **verdancy** *noun*
Word history: *verd(ure)* + *-ant*

verdict
noun the judge's or jury's decision or answer in a law court

Word history: blend of Medieval Latin and Middle English

verdure (ver-jooh-uh)
noun **1** greenness, especially of fresh, flourishing vegetation
2 green vegetation, especially grass or herbage

Word history: Middle English, from Old French word meaning 'green', from Latin

verge
noun **1** the very edge: *on the **verge** of tears*
2 the strip of dirt or grass at the edge of a road
phrase **3 verge on**, to come close to: *to **verge on** stupidity*

Word history: Middle English, from French, from Latin word meaning 'rod'

verify
verb to prove to be true or correct: *You can **verify** the spelling of a word by looking it up in the dictionary.* (***bear out, confirm, corroborate, substantiate***)

Verb forms: I **verified**, I have **verified**, I am **verifying**
Word use: The opposite of this is **disprove**.
Word building: **verification** *noun*
Word history: Middle English, from Old French, from Latin word meaning 'true'

veritable (ve-ruht-uh-buhl)
adjective genuine or real: *a **veritable** triumph*

Word history: Middle English, from Anglo-French, from Latin word meaning 'truth'

verity (ve-ruh-tee)
noun **1** the quality of being true or in accordance with fact or reality
2 a truth or true statement, principle, belief, idea, or the like

Word history: Middle English, from Latin

verjuice (ver-joohs)
noun an acid liquid made from the sour juice of unripe grapes, etc., used especially in cooking

vermicelli (ver-muh-sel-ee, ver-muh-chel-ee)
noun pasta in the shape of thin spaghetti

Word history: Italian, plural word meaning 'little worm', from Latin

vermiform (ver-muh-fawm)
adjective long and thin, like a worm

Word history: Medieval Latin

vermiform appendix
noun → **appendix** (definition 2)

vermilion (vuh-mil-yuhn)
noun **1** a brilliant scarlet red colour
2 bright red pigment consisting of mercuric sulfide

Word building: **vermilion** *adjective*
Word history: Middle English, from Old French word meaning 'bright red'

vermin
plural noun harmful or troublesome animals collectively, such as rats, cockroaches and fleas

Word history: Middle English, from Old French word meaning 'worm', from Latin

vermouth (ver-muhth, vuh-moohth)
noun a fortified white wine flavoured by herbs, roots, barks, bitters, etc.

Word history: French, from German word meaning 'wormwood' (a bitter herb)

vernacular (vuh-nak-yuh-luh)
noun **1** the native speech or language of a place
2 the language used by a class or profession: *Punters have their own **vernacular**.*
3 everyday or colloquial language, as opposed to formal or learned language

Word building: **vernacular** *adjective* **vernacularism** *noun*
Word history: from Latin word meaning 'native' + *-ar*

versatile
adjective able to do a variety of things: *a **versatile** performer | a **versatile** tool*

Word building: **versatility** *noun*
Word history: from Latin word meaning 'turning about'

verse[1]
noun **1** poetry: *a play written in **verse***
2 a group of lines that go together in a song or poem
3 a numbered part of a chapter in the Bible

Word history: Old English, from Latin word meaning 'line', 'row'

verse[2]
verb Colloquial Sport to play against (somebody) in a game or competition: *Who are we **versing** this week?*

Word history: from *versus*, misunderstood as a verb form *verses*, with the infinitive *verse*

versed (verst)
adjective experienced: *well **versed** in a subject* (***practised, skilled***)

Word history: from Latin word meaning 'busied', 'engaged'

version
noun **1** someone's description of what happened compared with someone else's: *What's your **version** of the accident?*
2 a particular form of something: *the film **version** of 'Alice in Wonderland'*

Word history: from Latin word meaning 'turning'

versus (ver-suhs)
preposition against

Word use: This word is used especially in law with reference to the opposing sides in a case and in sport with reference to the two opposing teams or players. | The abbreviation is **v.** or **vs.**
Word history: Latin

vertebra (ver-tuh-bruh)
noun one of the bones of the spine or backbone

Noun forms: The plural is **vertebrae** (ver-tuh-bree).
Word history: Latin

vertebrate (ver-tuh-brayt, ver-tuh-bruht)
adjective having a backbone: *Fish are **vertebrate** creatures but prawns are not.*

Word building: **vertebrate** *noun*
Word history: from Latin word meaning 'jointed'

vertex
noun the top or highest point of something: *the **vertex** of a pyramid*

Noun forms: The plural is **vertices** or **vertexes**.
Word history: from Latin word meaning 'whirl', 'crown of the head', 'summit'

vertical
adjective standing straight up or at right angles to the horizon: *a **vertical** line* (***perpendicular, upright***)

Word use: Compare this with **horizontal** and **diagonal**.
Word building: **vertically** *adverb*
Word history: from Late Latin word meaning 'vertex'

vertigo (<u>ver</u>-tuh-goh)
noun a feeling of sickness or dizziness, often caused by looking down from a height

Word building: **vertiginous** *adjective*
Word history: from Latin word meaning 'whirling round'

verve
noun lively enthusiasm: *to speak with* ***verve***

Word history: from French word meaning 'enthusiasm', 'fancy'

very
adverb **1** a word used to add emphasis to an adjective or adverb: ***very*** *fast* | ***very*** *slow* | ***very*** *quietly* | *Thank you* ***very*** *much.* (***decidedly***, ***exceedingly***, ***exceptionally***, ***extremely***, ***particularly***, ***really***, ***remarkably***)
adjective **2** a word used to add emphasis to a noun, meaning:
a actual, particular or exact: *the* ***very*** *thing you should've done* | *the* ***very*** *man himself*
b mere: *The* ***very*** *thought is distressing.* | *They grew to fear his* ***very*** *name.*

Word history: Middle English, from Old French, from Latin word meaning 'true'

vessel
noun **1** a ship or boat
2 *Old-fashioned* a hollow container, such as a cup or bottle
3 a tube which carries fluid inside your body, such as a blood vessel

Word history: Middle English, from Old French, from Latin word meaning 'small vase'

vest
noun **1** a waistcoat
2 a singlet

Word history: Middle English, from Old French, from Latin word meaning 'clothe'

vestal (<u>ves</u>-tuhl)
adjective **1** virginal or chaste
noun **2** a chaste, unmarried woman

Word history: from the four (later six) virgins, consecrated by the ancient Romans to *Vesta*, the goddess of the hearth

vestibule (<u>vest</u>-uh-byoohl)
noun an entrance hall

Word history: Latin

vestige (<u>vest</u>-ij)
noun the last trace of something that was once there

Word building: **vestigial** *adjective*
Word history: French, from Latin word meaning 'footprint'

vestment (<u>vest</u>-muhnt)
noun an outer garment, especially a ceremonial one

Word building: **vestmental** *adjective*
Word history: Middle English, from Old French, from Latin word meaning 'clothing'

vet
noun **1** → **veterinary surgeon**
verb **2** to check or examine carefully: *to* ***vet*** *the people applying for a job* (***assess***, ***examine***, ***inspect***, ***review***)

veteran
noun **1** someone who has worked for a long time in a particular job
2 a returned soldier
adjective **3** with long experience: *a* ***veteran*** *bushwalker* (***experienced***, ***practised***)
phrase **4 veteran car**, a car built before 1918

Word use: The opposite of definitions 1 and 3 is **beginner**.
Word history: from Latin word meaning 'old'

veterinary science (vet-uhn-ree <u>suy</u>-uhns, vet-uh-ruhn-ree <u>suy</u>-uhns)
noun that branch of medicine dealing with the study, prevention and treatment of animal diseases and injuries

Word use: You can also use **veterinary medicine**.

veterinary surgeon
noun someone whose job is to treat sick animals

Word use: You can also use **veterinarian** or **vet**.

veto (<u>vee</u>-toh)
verb **1** to refuse to agree to: *to* ***veto*** *a plan*
noun **2** the power or right to prevent something

Verb forms: I **vetoed**, I have **vetoed**, I am **vetoing**
Noun forms: The plural is **vetos** or **vetoes**.
Word history: from Latin word meaning 'I forbid'

vex
verb to annoy or worry: *to* ***vex*** *your parents* (***bug***, ***goad***, ***irritate***, ***pique***, ***provoke***)

Word building: **vexation** *noun* **vexatious** *adjective* **vexed** *adjective*
Word history: Middle English, from Latin word meaning 'agitate'

via (<u>vuy</u>-uh)
preposition **1** by way of: *Go to Italy* ***via*** *Singapore.*
2 by means of: *to reach a conclusion* ***via*** *three logical steps*

Word history: from Latin word meaning 'way'

viable (<u>vuy</u>-uh-buhl)
adjective **1** practicable or workable (***feasible***, ***likely***, ***possible***)
2 physically able to live

Word building: **viability** *noun*
Word history: French word meaning 'life', from Latin

viaduct (<u>vuy</u>-uh-dukt)
noun a bridge with many arches, which carries a road or railway over a valley

Word history: Latin *via* way + *-duct* as in *aqueduct*

vial (<u>vuy</u>-uhl)
noun → **phial**

Word history: Middle English, variant of *fiole* phial

vibes[1]
noun → **vibraphone**

Word history: abbreviation

vibes[2]
plural noun *Colloquial* the feeling you get, good or bad, just from being in a place: *I don't like the* ***vibes*** *in this meeting.*

vibrant
adjective **1** bright, lively and exciting: *a* ***vibrant*** *colour* | *a* ***vibrant*** *personality*
2 vibrating or quickly moving to and fro

Word history: Latin

vibraphone
noun an electronic musical instrument like a xylophone, often used in jazz

Word use: You can also use **vibes**.
Word history: from Latin word meaning 'shake', 'vibrate' + *-phone*

vibrate
verb **1** to keep on moving quickly up and down or to and fro (***quake***, ***rock***, ***shake***, ***shudder***, ***tremble***)
2 to make a buzzing or quivering sound

Word history: from Latin word meaning 'shaken'

vibration
noun **1** the act of vibrating
2 the moving from side to side of a string, etc., to produce musical sound

vibrato (vuh-brah-toh)
noun the pulsating effect produced in the singing voice or in an instrumental tone by rapid small oscillations in pitch about the given note

Noun forms: The plural is **vibratos.**
Word history: Italian word meaning 'vibrate', from Latin

vicar
noun a priest, especially one in charge of an Anglican parish

Word history: Middle English, from Anglo-French, from Latin word meaning 'substitute'

vicarage (vik-uh-rij)
noun the house of a vicar

vicarious (vuh-kair-ree-uhs)
adjective **1** done or experienced by one person in place of another
2 felt at second-hand, by identifying with the experiences of another: ***vicarious*** *pleasure*

Word history: from Latin word meaning 'substituted'

vice[1]
noun **1** wickedness or evil
2 a fault or bad habit

Word history: Middle English, from Old French, from Latin word meaning 'fault'

vice[2]
noun a tool which closes around something and holds it tightly in place while you work on it

Word history: Middle English, from Old French word meaning 'screw', from Latin word meaning 'vine'

vice-regal
adjective having to do with someone appointed as a deputy by a king or queen, such as a governor-general or governor of a state

vice versa (vuy-suh ver-suh, vuys ver-suh, vuy-see ver-suh)
adverb the other way round from what you've just said, as in *I like him and vice versa*, which means *I like him and he likes me.*

Word history: Latin

vicinity
noun neighbourhood or area nearby: *There is no swimming pool in our* ***vicinity.***

Noun forms: The plural is **vicinities.**
Word history: Latin

vicious (vish-uhs)
adjective very cruel or harmful: *a* ***vicious*** *dog | a* ***vicious*** *attack* (***barbaric***, ***brutal***, ***savage***, ***violent***)

Word building: **viciously** *adverb* **viciousness** *noun*
Word history: Middle English, from Latin word meaning 'faulty'

vicissitude (vuh-sis-uh-tyoohd)
noun **1** a change, or something different, occurring in the course of something
2 vicissitudes, ups and downs: ***vicissitudes*** *of life*

Word history: from Latin word meaning 'change'

victim
noun someone who suffers harm or injury: *a* ***victim*** *of a car accident* (***casualty***)

Word history: from Latin word meaning 'beast for sacrifice'

victimise
verb to punish or harm unfairly (***abuse***, ***hound***, ***maltreat***, ***torment***, ***torture***)

Word use: You can also use **victimize.**
Word building: **victimisation** *noun*

victor
noun **1** someone who has defeated an enemy (***conqueror***, ***subjugator***)
2 the winner in any fight or race, etc. (***champion***, ***master***)

victory
noun a win or success in a contest (***conquest***, ***triumph***)

Noun forms: The plural is **victories.**
Word building: **victorious** *adjective*
Word history: Middle English, from Latin

video
noun **1** a recording on a videotape of a film, television show, or the like
2 a videotape
3 a tape recorder which records both images and sounds
adjective **4** having to do with television

Word use: The full form of definition 3 is **video recorder** or **video cassette recorder**. You can also use the abbreviation **VCR.**
Word history: from Latin word meaning 'I see'

video clip
noun a short film made to accompany a popular song, usually featuring the performers of the song

Word use: The short form is **clip.**

video referee
noun a referee who adjudicates with the aid of video footage of the game

videostreaming
noun the streaming of video data

Word use: Look up **streaming.**

videotape
noun magnetic tape used for recording film or television pictures and sound

vie
phrase **vie with**, to compete against or try to beat: *to* ***vie with*** *one's opponent*

Verb forms: I **vied**, I have **vied**, I am **vying**
Word history: French word meaning 'challenge', from Latin word meaning 'invite'

view
noun **1** whatever you can see from a particular place: *a spectacular **view** from the top of the tower* (***outlook**, **prospect**, **vista***)
2 an idea or opinion: *What is your **view** on homework?* (***attitude**, **conviction**, **outlook**, **viewpoint***)
verb **3** to look at or see: *I will **view** the new building tomorrow.*
phrase **4 in view of**, because of
5 on view, displayed for all to see

Word building: **viewer** *noun*
Word history: Middle English, from Anglo-French word meaning 'see', from Latin

viewpoint
noun **1** a place giving a view of something
2 a point of view or attitude of mind: *An artist and a surgeon have different **viewpoints** of the human body.*

vigil (vij-uhl)
noun the act of keeping watch at night: *to keep **vigil** by a sick child's bed*

Word history: Middle English, from Anglo-French, from Latin word meaning 'watch'

vigilant (vij-uh-luhnt)
adjective alert and watchful

Word building: **vigilance** *noun* **vigilantly** *adverb*

vigilante (vij-uh-lant-ee)
noun a member of an unauthorised committee of citizens organised to keep order and punish crime in the absence of regular law enforcement

Word history: from Spanish word meaning 'vigilant'

vignette (vin-yet)
noun **1** a decorative design or small illustration used on the titlepage of a book or at the beginning or end of a chapter
2 an engraving, drawing, photograph, etc., shading off gradually at the edges
3 any small, pleasing picture or view
4 a small, graceful, literary sketch

Word history: from French word meaning 'vine'

vigorous
adjective strong, energetic and full of life (***dynamic**, **full of beans**, **lively**, **spirited***)

vigour
noun energy and strength (***force**, **might**, **muscle**, **power***)

Word use: You can also use **vigor**.

vile
adjective disgustingly bad: *a **vile** smell / **vile** language* (***awful**, **horrible**, **repulsive**, **revolting***)

Word building: **vileness** *noun*
Word history: Middle English, from Anglo-French, from Latin word meaning 'cheap', 'base'

vilify (vil-uh-fuy)
verb to speak evil of or defame

Verb forms: I **vilified**, I have **vilified**, I am **vilifying**
Word building: **vilification** *noun* **vilifier** *noun*
Word history: Middle English, from Late Latin

villa (vil-uh)
noun **1** a country house, usually a large or important one, especially in a Mediterranean country
2 *Australian* a small house, often one of a set of connected dwellings
3 an ancient Roman country house associated with agriculture, usually built round a courtyard

Word history: Latin or Italian

village
noun a small town in the country (***hamlet**, **township***)

Word building: **villager** *noun*
Word history: Middle English, from Old French, from Latin word meaning 'villa'

villain (vil-uhn)
noun **1** *Old-fashioned* a wicked person or scoundrel (***rascal**, **rogue***)
2 in a story, film, etc., the evil character

Word building: **villainous** *adjective*
Word history: Middle English, from Old French, from Latin word meaning 'farm servant'

villainy
noun **1** the action or conduct of a villain or scoundrel
2 a villainous action or deed

villein (vil-uhn)
noun someone in feudal times, with a little more freedom than a serf

Word history: variant of *villain*

vim
noun Colloquial energy or vigour

Word history: Latin

vindicate (vin-duh-kayt)
verb **1** to show to be right or innocent: *to **vindicate** an accused person*
2 to provide the reason for: *to **vindicate** her outburst* (***excuse**, **justify**, **warrant***)

Word use: The opposite of definition 1 is **convict**.
Word building: **vindication** *noun*
Word history: Latin

vindictive
adjective spiteful or full of revenge: *a **vindictive** remark* (***bitter**, **malicious**, **resentful**, **vengeful***)

Word history: Latin

vine
noun a climbing plant, such as a grape

Word history: Middle English, from Old French, from Latin

vinegar
noun a sour liquid made from wine or cider and used to flavour food

Word history: Middle English, from Old French, from *vin* wine + *egre* sour

vineyard (vin-yuhd)
noun a farm where grapevines are grown

Word history: Middle English; from *vine* + *yard*[2]

vintage
noun **1** the wine or grapes grown in one particular year: *the 1999* ***vintage***
adjective **2** of very high quality, though perhaps in an old-fashioned way: ***vintage*** *rock'n'roll*
phrase **3 vintage car**, a car built between 1918 and 1930
Word history: Middle English, from Anglo-French, from Latin word meaning 'grape gathering'

vinyl (vuy-nuhl)
noun a type of plastic
Word history: Latin *vinum* wine + *-yl*

viol (vuy-uhl)
noun a six-stringed musical instrument, played with a bow and having frets, common in the 16th and 17th centuries
Word history: from Old French word meaning 'instrument'

viola (vee-oh-luh)
noun a stringed instrument, like a violin but a little bigger
Word use: The **viola** is lower in pitch than the **violin** and higher than the **cello** and **double bass**.
Word history: Italian

violate
verb **1** to disobey: *to* ***violate*** *the law* (***flout***, ***infringe***, ***transgress***)
2 to treat brutally, showing no respect: *to* ***violate*** *a holy place*
Word building: **violation** *noun*
Word history: late Middle English, from Latin

violent
adjective powerful and causing damage: *a* ***violent*** *storm* | *a* ***violent*** *temper* (***ferocious***, ***fierce***, ***forceful***, ***furious***, ***wild***)
Word building: **violence** *noun* **violently** *adverb*
Word history: Middle English, from Old French, from Latin word meaning 'vehemence'

violet
noun **1** a small plant with purplish-blue flowers
2 a purplish-blue colour
Word building: **violet** *adjective*
Word history: Middle English, from Old French, from Latin

violin
noun a stringed instrument played with a bow and held between your shoulder and chin
Word use: The **violin** is higher in pitch than the **viola, cello** and **double bass**.
Word building: **violinist** *noun*
Word history: from Italian word meaning 'little viol' (a bowed intrument)

violoncello (vuy-uh-luhn-chel-oh)
noun → **cello**
Word history: from Italian word meaning 'little bass viol' (a bowed instrument)

VIP
noun Colloquial a very important person (***big shot***, ***big wheel***, ***bigwig***, ***star***)
Word history: abbreviation

viper
noun one of various highly venomous snakes found in Africa, Asia and Europe, including the common vipers, the adders, etc.
Word history: from Latin word meaning 'bringing forth living young' (vipers were formerly thought to be viviparous)

virago (vuh-rah-goh)
noun a violent or bad-tempered woman (***shrew***, ***vixen***)
Word history: Old English, from Latin word meaning 'manlike woman'

viral (vuy-ruhl)
adjective having to do with or caused by a virus

virgin
noun **1** someone who has never had sexual intercourse
adjective **2** completely natural or unspoiled: ***virgin*** *bush* | ***virgin*** *wool*
Word use: Definition 1 is mostly used of girls and women.
Word building: **virginity** *noun*
Word history: Middle English, from Old French, from Latin word meaning 'maiden'

virginal[1] (verj-uh-nuhl)
adjective **1** having to do with a virgin
2 pure or untouched
Word history: Latin *virginālis* maidenly

virginal[2]
noun a small, rectangular harpsichord with the strings parallel to the keyboard, the earlier types placed on a table, common in the 16th and 17th centuries

virile (vi-ruyl)
adjective strong, forceful and masculine
Word building: **virility** *noun*
Word history: Latin, from *vir* man

virology (vuy-rol-uh-jee)
noun the study of viruses and the diseases caused by them
Word building: **virological** *adjective* **virologist** *noun*
Word history: *viro-* (combining form of *virus*) + *-logy*, body of knowledge

virtual
adjective **1** as if it were really so: *His family made him a* ***virtual*** *slave.*
2 *Computers* existing only as a computer representation, and not as a physical thing: *a virtual bookshop*
Word history: Middle English, from Medieval Latin

virtually
adverb **1** in effect, although not in fact: *Although his family was rich, he was* ***virtually*** *a beggar.*
2 *Colloquial* almost

virtual reality
noun **1** an artificial environment represented by a computer which produces visual and auditory stimuli to make the environment seem real to the user, and which the user can interact with as if it were physically real
2 any artificial environment represented by a computer

virtue
noun **1** goodness or proper behaviour
2 a good quality: *Patience is a **virtue**.*

Word history: Middle English, from Latin word meaning 'manliness'

virtuoso (ver-chooh-oh-soh, ver-chooh-oh-zoh)
noun a highly skilled person, especially a musician

Noun forms: The plural is **virtuosos** or **virtuosi**.
Word building: **virtuoso** *adjective* **virtuosity** *noun*
Word history: Italian word meaning 'learned', 'skilful'

virtuous
adjective good, honourable and obedient

virulent (vi-ruh-luhnt)
adjective **1** very harmful: *a **virulent** disease*
2 bitter and spiteful: ***virulent** criticism*

Word building: **virulence** *noun*
Word history: Middle English, from Latin word meaning 'poisonous'

virus
noun **1** a very small organism that causes disease
2 any disease caused by a virus
3 *Computers* a small program which is let loose in the operating system with the intention of wreaking havoc, normally by destroying files

Word history: from Latin word meaning 'slimy liquid', 'poison'

virus / germ / bacterium

These words all refer to the cause of a disease.

A **virus** is a strand of genetic material (DNA or RNA). It reproduces by infecting living cells and undermining their cellular structure so as to make more virus. As viruses do not use up energy, it is debatable whether they are living things or merely complicated biochemical molecules.

A **germ** is an everyday term that non-scientists might use to describe a bacterium or virus which causes an infectious illness.

A **bacterium** is a single-celled microorganism. Some bacteria cause infectious diseases and others take part in the process of fermentation or rotting.

visa (vee-zuh)
noun a stamp or written notice put in your passport, giving you permission to enter a certain country

Word history: Latin, short for *carta vīsa* paper (has been) seen

visage (viz-ij)
noun **1** a face, especially of a human being (***countenance***)
2 appearance or aspect

Word history: Middle English, from Anglo-French and Old French word meaning 'face', from Latin word meaning 'to see'

viscera (vis-uh-ruh)
plural noun Anatomy the soft interior organs of the body, including the brain, lungs, heart, stomach, intestines, etc.

Word building: **visceral** *adjective*
Word history: Latin

viscose (vis-kohs, vis-kohz)
noun a viscous solution prepared by treating cellulose, which is used in making rayon or cellophane, etc.

Word building: **viscose** *adjective*
Word history: Latin

viscount (vuy-kownt)
noun a British nobleman ranking below an earl and above a baron

Word building: **viscountess** *feminine noun*
Word history: Middle English, from Anglo-French, from *vis* vice- + *counte* count[2]

viscous (vis-kuhs)
adjective thick and sticky, like glue: *a **viscous** liquid*

Word history: Middle English, from Latin

visibility
noun the distance you can see, given the weather conditions or time of day: *Drive slowly because **visibility** is bad.*

visible
adjective able to be seen: *The lighthouse is **visible** from a long distance.* (***conspicuous***, ***noticeable***)

Word history: Middle English, from Latin

vision
noun **1** the power of sight or the sense of seeing: *His **vision** is impaired.* (***eyesight***)
2 the power of imagining: *It was Colonel Light's **vision** that led to Adelaide being built.*
3 a mental image: ***visions** of power | a **vision** of God* (***dream***)

Word history: Middle English, from Latin word meaning 'sight'

visionary (vizh-uhn-ree)
adjective **1** given to or concerned with seeing visions: *a **visionary** mystic*
2 unreal or imaginary: ***visionary** evils*
3 given to, or based on, imagination or theory: *a **visionary** thinker | a **visionary** plan*
noun **4** someone who sees visions
5 someone who is given to ideas or plans which are not immediately practical

Noun forms: The plural is **visionaries**.

vision-impaired
adjective **1** deficient in sight, ranging from complete blindness to partial vision: *He wasn't allowed to drive as he was **vision-impaired**.*
2 having to do with a person with partial vision (opposed to *blind*)

Word building: **visually-impaired** *adjective*

visit
verb **1** to call on to see: *to **visit** friends*
2 to stay with as a guest: *My cousin is **visiting** me this week.*
3 to access a site on the internet: *I visited the school's site this morning — it's looking great!*

Word building: **visit** *noun* **visitor** *noun*
Word history: Middle English, from Latin word meaning 'go to see'

visitation (viz-uh-tay-shuhn)
noun a visit, especially for the purpose of making an official inspection, etc.

visor (vuy-zuh)
noun the movable part of a helmet, which can be pulled down over your eyes

Word history: Middle English, from Anglo-French, from *vis* face

vista (vis-tuh)
noun **1** a view, especially one seen through a long, narrow passage, such as between rows of trees, houses, etc. (***outlook***, ***prospect***, ***scene***, ***view***)
2 a mental view stretching over a long time or over a series of remembered or imagined experiences: ***vistas*** *of the past*

Word history: Italian word meaning 'view', from Latin

visual
adjective **1** of or having to do with sight: ***visual*** *ability*
2 able to be seen: *Teachers use pictures as* ***visual*** *aids.*

Word history: Middle English, from Late Latin word meaning 'belonging to sight'

visual display unit
noun a computer terminal which shows information on a screen

Word use: The abbreviation is **VDU**.

visualise
verb to form a mental picture of: *I recognise her name, but I can't* ***visualise*** *her face.*

Word use: You can also use **visualize**.

vital
adjective **1** having to do with or necessary to life: *the* ***vital*** *parts of the body*
2 full of life: *She is a very* ***vital*** *person.*
3 absolutely necessary: *It is* ***vital*** *that we stick together.* (***crucial***, ***essential***, ***imperative***, ***obligatory***)

Word history: Middle English, from Latin

vitality
noun energy or vigour

vitamin (vuy-tuh-muhn, vit-uh-muhn)
noun any of a number of substances present in food and necessary in small quantities for good health

Word history: from Latin word meaning 'life' + *amin(e)*

vitiate (vish-ee-ayt)
verb **1** to lower the quality of or spoil
2 to make legally ineffective or invalidate

Word building: **vitiation** *noun* **vitiator** *noun*
Word history: from Latin word meaning 'spoiled'

viticulture (vit-ee-kul-chuh)
noun **1** the cultivation of the grapevine
2 the study of grapevine cultivation

Word building: **viticultural** *adjective* **viticulturist** *noun*
Word history: from Latin word meaning 'vine' + *culture*

vitreous (vit-ree-uhs)
adjective **1** hard and transparent like glass: ***vitreous*** *china*
2 having to do with glass
3 obtained from glass

Word building: **vitreosity** *noun*
Word history: from Latin word meaning 'glass'

vitrify (vit-ruh-fuy)
verb **1** to change or be changed into glass, so that all the particles of clay, sand, etc., are fused together, becoming waterproof
2 to make or become like glass

Verb forms: it **vitrified**, it has **vitrified**, it is **vitrifying**
Word building: **vitrification** *noun*

vitriol (vit-ree-ol)
noun **1** any of certain glassy, metallic sulfates, such as of copper (blue vitriol) or of iron (green vitriol), etc.
2 sulfuric acid
3 something sharp, bitter or severe, such as criticism, speech, etc.

Word building: **vitriolic** *adjective*
Word history: Middle English, from Medieval Latin, from Latin word meaning 'glass'

vituperate (vuh-tyooh-puh-rayt, vuy-tyooh-puh-rayt)
verb to find fault with, using rough language (***abuse***, ***revile***)

Word building: **vituperation** *noun* **vituperative** *adjective*
Word history: Latin

vivacious (vuh-vay-shuhs)
adjective lively or energetic: *a* ***vivacious*** *talker* (***frisky***, ***frolicsome***, ***jaunty***, ***playful***)

Word building: **vivacity** *noun*

vivid
adjective **1** bright or dazzling: ***vivid*** *colours* (***colourful***, ***gaudy***, ***gay***, ***rich***)
2 strong and clear: *a* ***vivid*** *imagination* (***bright***, ***intense***)

Word building: **vividness** *noun*
Word history: Latin *vīvidus* animated

viviparous (vuh-vip-uh-ruhs)
adjective bringing forth living young, rather than laying eggs, as most mammals and some reptiles and fishes do

Word history: from Latin word meaning 'bringing forth living young'

vivisection (viv-uh-sek-shuhn)
noun the practice of cutting up living animals, especially in order to advance medical knowledge

Word building: **vivisect** *verb* **vivisectionist** *noun*

vixen
noun **1** a female fox
2 a bad-tempered woman

Word history: southern dialect variant of Middle English word meaning 'she-fox', from Old English

V-jay
noun a presenter of music video clips

Word use: You can also use **VJ** or **veejay**.

vlog (vlog)
noun a blog with video streaming

Word building: **vlogging** *noun* **vlogger** *noun*

vocabulary (vuh-kab-yuh-luh-ree)
noun the total number of words used by someone or by a particular group of people: *She has a large* ***vocabulary***.

Word history: Medieval Latin, from Latin word meaning 'vocable' (a name or term)

vocal
adjective **1** of or having to do with your voice: *the **vocal** cords*
2 talkative: *He was very **vocal** on the subject of holidays.*
3 sung or for singing: ***vocal** music*
Word history: Middle English, from Latin word meaning 'voice'

vocal cords
plural noun the folds of tissue lining your larynx which vibrate as air from your lungs passes them, making voiced sounds

vocalise
verb **1** to express with the voice: *to **vocalise** ideas*
2 to speak or sing
Word use: You can also use **vocalize**.
Word building: **vocalisation** *noun*

vocalist
noun a singer

vocation
noun an occupation, business or profession, especially one which you seriously believe in: *a **vocation** to be a nun* (***career***, ***life's work***)
Word history: Middle English, from Latin word meaning 'calling'

vociferous (vuh-sif-uh-ruhs)
adjective noisy or clamorous: *a **vociferous** crowd | a **vociferous** protest*
Word building: **vociferousness** *noun*

vodcasting
noun the online delivery of video on demand

vodka
noun a Russian alcoholic drink made from grain and potatoes
Word history: from Russian word meaning 'little water'

vogue (vohg)
noun fashion: *the **vogue** fifty years ago* (***craze***, ***fad***, ***rage***, ***trend***)
Word history: French word meaning 'row', 'go along smoothly', from Italian, perhaps from Latin word meaning 'call' (through use in sailors' shanties)

voice
noun **1** the sound or sounds you make with your mouth especially when you speak or sing
2 the right to express an opinion: *He had no **voice** in the matter.*
3 the quality or condition of the voice for singing: *in good **voice***
verb **4** to utter or give voice to: *to **voice** an opinion* (***articulate***, ***enunciate***, ***pronounce***, ***sound***)
Word history: Middle English, from Anglo-French, from Latin

voice box
noun → **larynx**

voicemail
noun **1** a system for recording messages over the telephone to be played back later
2 a message received on such a system

void
adjective **1** without legal force: *The contract is null and **void**.*
2 empty: *This statement is **void** of meaning.* (***blank***, ***deserted***)
noun **3** an empty space: *They peered over the edge of the cliff into the **void**.*
Word history: Middle English, from Old French, from Latin word meaning 'be empty'

volatile (vol-uh-tuyl)
adjective **1** evaporating quickly: *Methylated spirits is a **volatile** substance.*
2 of a person, changeable, flighty, or easily provoked to anger
Word history: Middle English, from Latin word meaning 'flying'

volcano
noun a mountain with an opening in the top, through which molten rock, steam and ashes burst out when it is active
Noun forms: The plural is **volcanoes** or **volcanos**.
Word building: **volcanic** *adjective*
Word history: Italian, from Latin word meaning 'Vulcan', 'god of fire'

volcanology (vol-kuh-nol-uh-jee)
noun the scientific study of volcanoes and phenomena associated with them
Word use: You can also use **vulcanology**.
Word building: **volcanological** (vol-kuh-nuh-loj-i-kuhl) *adjective* **volcanologist** *noun*

vole
noun a kind of rodent similar to and belonging to the same family as the common rats and mice and usually of heavy build with short limbs and tail
Word history: short for *volemouse* field mouse, from Scandinavian

volition (vuh-lish-uhn)
noun an act of will or purpose: *He did it quite of his own **volition**.*
Word history: Medieval Latin, from Latin word meaning 'I wish'

volley (vol-ee)
noun **1** the firing of a number of guns together
2 an outpouring at one time: *a **volley** of words*
3 in a game such as tennis, the return of a ball before it bounces
verb **4** to return a ball before it bounces
Word history: French word meaning 'flight', from Latin

volleyball
noun a team game in which a large ball is volleyed by hand or arm over a net

volt
noun a measurement of electric force
Word use: The symbol is **V**, without a full stop.
Word history: named after Count Alessandro *Volta*, 1745–1827, Italian physicist

voltage (vol-tij)
noun electromotive force or potential expressed in volts

voluble
adjective marked by a ready and continuous flow of words: *a **voluble** explanation* (***chatty***, ***communicative***, ***garrulous***, ***loquacious***, ***talkative***)
Word building: **volubility** *noun*
Word history: from Latin word meaning 'roll', 'turn'

volume
noun **1** a book, especially one of a series
2 the space occupied by a body or substance, measured in cubic units
3 amount, especially a large amount: *the **volume** of traffic | **volumes** of smoke*
4 loudness: *Turn down the **volume** on the TV.*

Word history: Middle English, from Old French, from Latin word meaning 'roll (of papyrus or parchment)'

volumetric (vol-yuh-met-rik)
adjective having to do with, or depending upon measurement by volume

Word use: You can also use **volumetrical**.

voluminous (vuh-looh-muh-nuhs)
adjective **1** forming enough to fill a book: ***voluminous** letters*
2 large or full: *a **voluminous** skirt*

Word history: from Late Latin word meaning 'full of folds'

voluntary
adjective **1** done or made by free will or choice: *a **voluntary** decision*
2 unpaid: ***voluntary** work*

Word use: The opposite of definition 1 is **compulsory**.
Word history: Middle English, from Latin

volunteer
noun **1** someone who offers to do something, such as to join the army, of their own free will
verb **2** to offer without being asked: *He **volunteered** to make the tea.*
3 to join the army as a volunteer

Word building: **volunteer** *adjective*
Word history: French, from Latin word meaning 'voluntary'

voluptuary (vuh-lup-chooh-uh-ree)
noun someone who delights in luxury and the pleasures of the senses

Word history: Latin word meaning *voluptuārius*, variant of *voluptārius*, from *voluptas* pleasure

voluptuous (vuh-lup-chooh-uhs)
adjective **1** full of, suggesting, or producing sensual, especially sexual, pleasure: *a **voluptuous** dance*
2 arising from enjoyment of the pleasures of the senses: *the **voluptuous** pleasure of a warm bath*
3 full and shapely: *a **voluptuous** figure*

Word use: Definition 3 is used in relation to the female body.
Word history: Middle English, from Latin word meaning 'pleasure'

vomit
verb to throw up the contents of the stomach through the mouth

Verb forms: I **vomited**, I have **vomited**, I am **vomiting**
Word building: **vomit** *noun*
Word history: late Middle English, from Latin

voodoo (vooh-dooh)
noun **1** mysterious practices, like sorcery, witchcraft and fetishism, probably of African origin
2 a fetish or other object of voodoo worship
adjective **3** having to do with, or practising voodoo

Word building: **voodooism** *noun* **voodoo** *verb*
Word history: Haitian Creole *vodu*, from an African language

voracious (vuh-ray-shuhs)
adjective **1** wanting food in large quantities: *a **voracious** appetite*
2 eager or greedy in some activity: *a **voracious** reader* (***insatiable**, **rapacious***)

Word building: **voracity** *noun* **voraciousness** *noun*
Word history: from Latin word meaning 'greediness' + *-ous*

vortex (vaw-teks)
noun **1** a whirling mass of water, air, fire, etc.
2 a state of affairs likened to this for violent activity, irresistible force, etc.

Noun forms: The plural is **vortexes** or **vortices** (vaw-tuh-seez).
Word building: **vortical** *adjective*
Word history: Latin

votary (voh-tuh-ree)
noun **1** someone who is bound by a vow to a religious life
2 someone devoted to some activity, study, etc.

Noun forms: The plural is **votaries**.
Word history: from Latin word meaning 'vow' + *-ary*

vote
noun **1** a formal expression, such as putting your hand up or ticking a piece of paper, indicating a wish or choice (***ballot**, **election***)
2 the total number of votes: *the Labor **vote***

Word building: **vote** *verb*
Word history: Middle English, from Latin word meaning 'vow', 'wish'

votive (voh-tiv)
adjective **1** done, given, etc., in accordance with a vow: *a **votive** offering*
2 expressive of a wish or desire

Word history: from Latin word meaning 'having to do with a vow'

vouch
phrase **vouch for**, to guarantee or make yourself responsible for: *I can **vouch for** her.*

Word history: Middle English, from Anglo-French

voucher
noun **1** a piece of paper that proves how money has been spent: *a shopping **voucher***
2 a ticket used instead of money: *a gift **voucher***

vouchsafe (vowch-sayf)
verb to have the graciousness to do something

Word history: from Middle English word meaning 'guarantee as safe'

vow
noun a solemn promise (***oath**, **pact**, **pledge**, **word of honour***)

Word building: **vow** *verb*
Word history: Middle English, from Anglo-French, from Latin

vowel (vow-uhl)
noun **1** a speech sound made by allowing air to pass through the middle of your mouth without being blocked by your tongue or lips

2 a letter, *a*, *e*, *i*, *o* or *u*, used to represent the sound of a vowel

Word use: Compare this with **consonant**.
Word history: Middle English, from Old French, from Latin word meaning 'vocal'

voyage
noun a journey by sea or air to somewhere quite far away (***cruise***, ***trip***)

Word building: **voyage** *verb*
Word history: Middle English, from Old French, from Latin word meaning 'provision for a journey'

voyeur (voy-er, vwah-yer)
noun someone who satisfies sexual desires by looking on at sexual acts

Word building: **voyeurism** *noun*
Word history: from French word meaning 'see'

VRML
noun a computer language used for programming virtual reality applications

Word history: *v(irtual) r(eality) m(odelling) l(anguage)*

vulcanise (vul-kuh-nuyz)
verb to treat substances such as rubber with sulfur and heat to make them solid, hard, long-wearing and able to stretch

Word use: You can also use **vulcanize**.

vulcanology (vul-kuh-nol-uh-jee)
noun the scientific study of volcanoes

Word use: You can also use **volcanology**.
Word building: **vulcanological** *adjective* **vulcanologist** *noun*

vulgar
adjective coarse, crude or ill-mannered: ***vulgar*** *manners* (***common***, ***tasteless***, ***uncouth***)

Word use: The opposite of this is **polite** or **refined**.
Word building: **vulgarity** *noun*
Word history: Middle English, from Latin word meaning 'having to do with the common people'

vulnerable
adjective able or liable to be hurt (***exposed***, ***insecure***, ***open***, ***susceptible***)

Word building: **vulnerability** *noun*
Word history: from Late Latin word meaning 'wounding'

vulnerable species
noun a threatened species that is facing a high risk of extinction in the wild in the medium-term future

Word use: Compare this with **endangered species** and **critically endangered species**.

vulture
noun a large, carrion-eating bird usually with a bald head

Word history: Middle English, from Latin

vulva (vul-vuh)
noun the external female sexual organs

Noun forms: The plural is **vulvas** or **vulvae** (vul-vee).
Word history: from Latin word meaning 'wrapper'

vying (vuy-ing)
verb present participle of **vie**

Ww

wad (wod)
noun **1** a small lump or pad of anything soft: *a **wad** of cottonwool*
2 a roll or bundle: *a **wad** of banknotes*

wadding (wod-ing)
noun any soft material for stuffing, padding, packing, etc.

waddle (wod-uhl)
verb to walk with short steps, swaying from side to side like a duck (***lurch, reel, sway, wobble***)

Word building: **waddle** *noun*
Word history: from *wade*

waddy (wod-ee)
noun a heavy, wooden, Aboriginal war club

Noun forms: The plural is **waddies.**
Word history: from Dharug, an Australian Aboriginal language spoken by the people living near Sydney Cove in the early days of European settlement

wade
verb to walk through water

Word history: from Old English word meaning 'go'

wadi (wod-ee)
noun in Arabia, Syria, northern Africa, etc., a watercourse which is dry except during periods of rainfall

Word history: Arabic

wafer
noun a thin, crisp biscuit

Word history: Middle English, from Old French, from Middle Low German word meaning 'honeycomb'

waffle[1] (wof-uhl)
noun a crisp batter cake with a pattern of squares left by the hinged appliance in which it is cooked

Word history: Dutch

waffle[2] (wof-uhl)
verb Colloquial **1** to speak or write vaguely, to no purpose, and at length (***babble, jabber, rave, talk rubbish***)
noun Colloquial **2** lengthy and vague speech or writing
3 nonsense, or twaddle

Word history: from British dialect *waff* to yelp

waft (woft)
verb to blow lightly: *The breeze **wafted** the leaves. | The sounds of music **wafted** across the lake.*

Word building: **waft** *noun*
Word history: from obsolete *wafter*, Middle English word meaning 'armed escort vessel', from Dutch or Low German word meaning 'guard'

wag[1]
verb **1** to move from side to side
2 to play truant from: *to **wag** school*

Verb forms: I **wagged**, I have **wagged**, I am **wagging**
Word history: Middle English, from Scandinavian

wag[2]
noun a funny person (***card, comedian, joker***)

Word building: **waggish** *adjective*

wage
noun **1** the money an employee is paid regularly for working, especially in a factory or as a labourer
verb **2** to carry on: *to **wage** war*

Word use: Compare definition 1 with **salary.**
Word history: Middle English, from Old French word meaning 'pledge'

wage indexation
noun the adjustment of wages in accordance with changes in prices as shown in the consumer price index

wager
noun a bet

Word building: **wager** *verb*
Word history: Middle English, from Anglo-French

waggle
verb to wag with short, quick movements

Word history: from *wag*[1]

wagon
noun **1** a four-wheeled heavy cart
2 a railway truck

Word history: Dutch

wagtail
noun a small bird with a slender body and a long, narrow tail which is frequently wagged

waif
noun a person without a home or friends, especially a child

Word history: Middle English, from Anglo-French, probably from Scandinavian

wail
verb to give a long, sad cry or to cry continuously

Word building: **wail** *noun*
Word history: Middle English, from Scandinavian

wail / whale

Don't confuse **wail** with **whale,** which is a very large mammal that lives in the sea.

wainscot (<u>wayns</u>-kuht, <u>wayns</u>-koht)
noun panels of wood used to line the walls of a room, etc.

Word use: You can also use **wainscotting** or **wainscoting**.
Word history: Middle English, from Middle Low German

waist
noun the part of your body between your ribs and hips

Word history: Middle English

waist / waste
Don't confuse **waist** with **waste**. To **waste** something is to use it up or spend it without much result:

Try not to waste too much money on cheap gimmicks.

waistcoat
noun a close-fitting, sleeveless piece of clothing which reaches to the waist and buttons down the front, often worn under a jacket (***vest***)

wait
verb **1** to stay or rest until something happens
2 to be ready: *Your dinner is **waiting**.*
phrase **3 wait on**, to act as a waiter to: *to **wait on** someone*

Word building: **wait** *noun*
Word history: Middle English, from Old French, from Old High German word meaning 'watch'

wait / weight
Don't confuse **wait** with **weight**, which is how heavy something is. Your **weight** is how heavy you are.

wait on / wait for
There is a difference in meaning between **wait on** and **wait for**.

To **wait on** someone is to serve them, particularly by serving meals to them.

To **wait for** someone is to stop so that someone else can catch up.

People sometimes use **wait on** to mean **wait for**. For example:

We are waiting on Frank. He's always late.

But this has a colloquial or informal flavour.

waiter
noun a person who serves food and drink to you at your table in a restaurant or hotel

Look up **non-sexist language**.

waive (wayv)
verb **1** to decide not to insist on: *to **waive** a fine* (***forgo***, ***relinquish***)
2 to defer or put aside for the time
3 to put aside or dismiss from discussion: *He **waived** my attempts to explain.*

Word history: Middle English, from Anglo-French word meaning 'abandon'

waive / wave
Don't confuse **waive** with **wave**. To **wave** is to move something up and down or from side to side, as in *to wave a flag* or *to wave your hand.*

wake[1]
verb **1** to stop being asleep: *I like to **wake** to the sound of music.* (***awake***, ***awaken***)
2 to rouse from sleep: *His mother always **wakes** him at seven.*

Verb forms: I **woke**, I have **woken**, I am **waking**
Word building: **wakeful** *adjective* **waken** *verb*
Word history: Old English

wake[2]
noun the track left by a ship moving through the water (***wash***)

Word history: Scandinavian

walk
verb **1** to go along by putting one foot after the other (***amble***, ***march***, ***pace***, ***pad***, ***saunter***)
phrase **2 walk out**,
a to go on strike
b to leave angrily
3 walk out on, to abandon or desert

Word building: **walk** *noun*
Word history: from Old English word meaning 'roll', 'toss', 'go'

walkabout
noun **1** a period of nomadic wandering, undertaken by Aboriginal people who feel the need to leave white society and return for spiritual replenishment to their traditional way of life
phrase **2 go walkabout**, to wander around the country in a nomadic manner

walkie-talkie
noun a light radio that you can carry, used by police, soldiers, etc., to send and receive messages

walkman
noun a small portable radio, cassette player, etc., with earphones

Word history: Trademark

walkover
noun an easy victory

wall
noun **1** one of the sides of a building or room
2 a brick or stone structure acting as a boundary fence or barrier (***barricade***, ***partition***, ***screen***)
3 anything that closes off or divides
phrase **4 go to the wall**,
a to give way or be defeated
b to fail in business or become bankrupt
5 with your back to the wall, in a very difficult or desperate situation

Word history: Old English, from Latin

wallaby
noun any of several types of plant-eating marsupial, related and similar to the kangaroo

Noun forms: The plural is **wallabies**.
Word use: The wallaby belongs to a class of animals called **marsupials**.
Word history: from Dharug, an Australian Aboriginal language spoken by the people living near Sydney Cove in the early days of European settlement

wallaroo
noun a type of stocky kangaroo with coarse hair, that lives in rocky areas

Word use: The wallaroo belongs to a class of animals called **marsupials**.
Word history: from Dharug, an Australian Aboriginal language spoken by the people living near Sydney Cove in the early days of European settlement

wallet
noun a small folding case for papers, banknotes, etc., carried in your pocket or handbag

Word history: Middle English

wall-eyed (wol-uyd)
adjective **1** having eyes in which a squint causes an unusual amount of white to show
2 having eyes with little or no colour

Word history: Middle English, from Scandinavian

wallflower
noun **1** a European perennial plant, growing wild on old walls, cliffs, etc., and also cultivated in gardens, with sweet-scented red or yellow flowers
2 *Colloquial* a person at a dance, especially a woman, who is not chosen as a partner

wallop
verb Colloquial to beat soundly

Word building: **wallop** *noun*
Word history: Middle English, from Old French

wallow
verb to lie or roll about: *The hippopotamuses were **wallowing** in the mud. | I **wallowed** in a hot bath.*

Word history: from Old English word meaning 'roll'

wallpaper
noun **1** paper, usually with printed decorative patterns in colour, for pasting on and covering walls or ceilings of rooms, etc.
verb **2** to put wallpaper on

walnut
noun **1** a type of nut which you can eat, grown on a European tree
2 the wood of this tree, used for making furniture

Word history: from Old English word meaning 'foreign nuts'

walrus
noun a large, warm-blooded sea animal with flippers and large tusks

Word history: from Dutch word meaning 'whale horse'

waltz (wawls)
noun **1** a type of dance in which you and your partner move in circles to music with a 1-2-3 beat
2 a piece of music for this dance

Word building: **waltz** *verb*
Word history: from German word meaning 'roll', 'dance a waltz'

wan (won)
adjective **1** pale or lacking in colour: *a **wan** complexion | a **wan** light*
2 sickly: *a **wan** smile*

Word history: from Old English word meaning 'dark', 'gloomy'

wand (wond)
noun a thin stick or rod, especially one supposedly used by a magician or fairy to work magic

Word history: Middle English, from Scandinavian

wander (won-duh)
verb **1** to go about with no definite aim or fixed course (***digress***, ***diverge***, ***ramble***, ***stray***)
2 to move or turn idly: *His eyes **wandered** from the page.*

Word history: Old English

wander / wonder
Don't confuse **wander** with **wonder**. To **wonder** (rhymes with *under*) is to think about something with curiosity or surprise:

I wonder why she decided to change schools.

wane (wayn)
verb to grow, or seem to grow, smaller or less: *Her enthusiasm has **waned**. | The moon is **waning**.* (***abate***, ***decrease***, ***diminish***, ***moderate***, ***peter out***)

Word use: The opposite of this is **wax**.
Word history: from Old English word meaning 'lessen'

wangle
verb Colloquial to do or get something by cunning or trickery: *He **wangled** an extra day's holiday.*

Word building: **wangle** *noun*
Word history: blend of *wag*[1] and *dangle*

want
verb **1** to feel a need or a desire for (something): *to **want** your dinner | always **wanting** something new* (***covet***, ***crave***, ***desire***, ***fancy***, ***long for***)
2 to feel a need or desire (to do something): *I **want** to see you.*
3 to have none or little of: *He **wants** common sense.*
4 to require or need: *The car **wants** cleaning.*
5 to wish or feel inclined to: *They can go out if they **want**.*
6 to be in a condition of need or poverty
noun **7** something wanted or needed: *to see to someone's **wants***
8 an absence or lack of something necessary: *plants dying for **want** of rain*
9 poverty: *to live in **want*** (***deprivation***, ***destitution***, ***distress***, ***need***)

Word history: Middle English, from Scandinavian

wanting
adjective **1** lacking or absent: *an apparatus with some of the parts **wanting*** (***deficient***, ***incomplete***, ***short***)
2 lacking some part, thing or respect: *to be **wanting** in courtesy*

wanton (won-tuhn)
adjective **1** done or behaving in an uncontrolled, selfish way, with bad results: *a **wanton** attacker | **wanton** cruelty*
2 *Old-fashioned* uncontrolled in your sexual behaviour (***lascivious***, ***loose***)

Word history: from Middle English word meaning 'undisciplined'

war
noun **1** fighting with weapons between countries, or between groups within a nation (***battle***, ***clash***, ***combat***, ***conflict***, ***contest***, ***fight***, ***struggle***)
2 any other fighting: *a **war** of words*

Word building: **war** *verb* (**warred, warring**) **warlike** *adjective*
Word history: Middle English, from Old French, from Old High German word meaning 'strife'

war / wore

Don't confuse **war** with **wore**, which is the past tense of the verb **wear**, to carry or have on your body:

I wore a red dress to the disco.

waratah (wo-ruh-tah, wo-ruh-tah)
noun an Australian shrub with large, red flowers; the floral emblem of New South Wales

Word history: from Dharug, an Australian Aboriginal language spoken by the people living near Sydney Cove in the early days of European settlement

warble
verb to sing with trills, like a bird

Word history: Middle English, from Old French word meaning 'quaver', from Germanic

warbler (wawb-luh)
noun a small songbird, chiefly found in the Northern Hemisphere, with a few species found in Australia and New Zealand

ward
noun **1** a division of a municipality, city or town, used in elections: *She is standing for the East **ward**.*
2 a room or division in a hospital
3 a young person who has been legally placed under the care or control of a guardian: *a state **ward***
phrase **4 ward off**, to turn aside: *to **ward off** a blow*

Word history: Old English

warden
noun someone who is given the care or responsibility of something

Word history: Middle English, from Old French

warder
noun a prison officer

Word history: Middle English, from *ward*

wardrobe
noun **1** a cupboard for keeping clothes in
2 someone's set of clothes, or the costumes used by actors

Word history: Middle English, from Old French

ware (wair)
noun **1 wares**, *Old-fashioned* articles for sale: *a shopkeeper displaying his **wares***
2 a particular kind of manufactured article for sale: *tin**ware** | silver**ware***

Word use: Definition 2 is now chiefly used in combination with some other word.
Word history: Old English

warehouse
noun a large building for storing goods

warfare
noun **1** the act of waging war
2 armed conflict

warhead
noun the section of a rocket, bomb or torpedo containing the explosive

warlock
noun a wizard or sorcerer

Word history: from Old English word meaning 'oath-breaker', 'devil'

warm
adjective **1** having some heat that can be felt: ***warm** water*
2 keeping heat in: ***warm** clothes | a **warm** house*
3 kind and affectionate: *a **warm** welcome* (***friendly, genial, sociable***)

Word building: **warm** *verb* **warmth** *noun*
Word history: Old English

warm-blooded
adjective having a body temperature which stays more or less the same regardless of the surrounding temperature: ***warm-blooded** animals*

Word use: The opposite is **cold-blooded**.

warmonger (waw-mung-guh)
noun someone who advises war as the best action to take

Word building: **warmongering** *noun*

warm temperate rainforest
noun an evergreen broad-leaved forest favoured by a mild climate and steady rainfall, and exhibiting great biodiversity; in Australia dominated by evergreen eucalypts, with green ferns and moisture-loving conifers also present

Word use: You can also use **warm temperate forest**. | Compare **cool temperate rainforest**.

warn
verb to tell or signal of a possible danger: *They **warned** us that the road was icy. | Flashing lights **warn** of fog.* (***advise, caution, forewarn, tip off***)

Word building: **warning** *noun*
Word history: Old English

warn / worn

Don't confuse **warn** with **worn**.

Something is **worn** if it is shabby or damaged from frequent use, as in *a worn bedspread.*

Worn is also a past form of the verb **wear**:

I have worn the same coat for four winters.

warning
noun **1** the act of warning, giving notice, or cautioning: *Next time she does that, it won't be just a **warning** she gets!*
2 something serving to warn, give notice, or caution: *When we saw the **warning** on the fence we weren't game to go any closer.*
adjective **3** that warns: *a **warning** sign*

Word building: **warningly** *adverb*

warp
verb **1** to bend or become bent out of shape: *Rain has **warped** the timber. | The boards **warped** in the sun.*
noun **2** a bend or twist
3 the lengthwise threads in weaving

Word history: Old English

warrant (<u>wo</u>-ruhnt)
noun **1** a paper issued by a magistrate allowing a police officer to make an arrest or a search of a building
verb **2** to give a formal promise or guarantee: *The company has **warranted** to repair or replace the car if it breaks down in the first three months.*
3 to require: *The circumstances **warrant** immediate action.* (***call for***, ***demand***, ***justify***)
Word history: Middle English from Old French word meaning 'defender', from Germanic

warranty
noun a formal promise or assurance of reliability: *Do not buy an electric heater without a **warranty**.*
Noun forms: The plural is **warranties.**
Word history: Middle English, from Old French

warranty / guarantee
Look up **guarantee / warranty.**

warren
noun a series of connecting burrows where many rabbits live
Word history: Middle English, from Anglo-French word meaning 'game park'

warrigal (<u>wo</u>-ruh-guhl)
Australian
noun **1** → **dingo**
adjective **2** wild or untamed
Word history: from Dharug, an Australian Aboriginal language spoken by the people living near Sydney Cove in the early days of European settlement

warrior
noun a soldier or fighter (***combatant***)
Word history: Middle English, from Old Northern French

wart
noun a small, hard lump on the skin, caused by a virus
Word history: Old English

wary (<u>wair</u>-ree)
adjective watchful or careful (***alert***, ***cautious***)

was (woz)
verb first and third person singular past tense indicative of **be**
Word history: Old English

wasabi (wuh-<u>sah</u>-bee)
noun a green paste with a hot, spicy taste, eaten with Japanese food

wash
verb **1** to wet and rub, usually with soap or detergent, in order to clean (***cleanse***, ***launder***, ***mop up***, ***scrub***)
2 to carry along by water: *The bottle was **washed** ashore in New Zealand.*
noun **3** an act of washing
4 clothes which are ready to be washed, or have just been washed: *I have lost a sock in the **wash**.*
5 waves made by a ship: *The dinghy rocked in the liner's **wash**.*
phrase **6 wash down,**
a to clean completely by washing
b to swallow with the help of liquid: *to **wash down** food*
7 wash out,
a to remove by washing
b to cause to be cancelled: *The rain **washed out** the football match.*
8 wash up, to wash after a meal: *to **wash up** the dishes*
Word building: **washable** *adjective*
Word history: Middle English

washer
noun a flat ring of rubber or metal to make a joint or a nut fit tightly
Word use: Look up **face washer**.

wasn't
contraction of **was not**

Look up **contractions in grammar.**

wasp
noun a four-winged insect that stings
Word history: Old English

waspish
adjective sharp and spiteful: *a **waspish** remark*

wastage
noun loss by use, wear, decay, wastefulness, etc.

waste
verb **1** to use up or spend without much result: *to **waste** food | to **waste** money on gambling* (***fritter away***, ***splurge***, ***squander***)
2 to wear away: *Illness has **wasted** his muscles.*
noun **3** useless spending or use without enough result: *a **waste** of material | a **waste** of money*
phrase **4 go to waste,** to fail to be used
5 lay waste, to destroy, devastate or ruin
Word building: **wasteful** *adjective*
Word history: Middle English, from Old Northern French, from Latin word meaning 'make empty', 'lay waste'

waste / waist
Look up **waist / waste.**

wastewater
noun water that has been used in residences, businesses, factories, etc., containing waste such as faeces, chemicals, etc.
Word use: You can also use **waste water.** | Compare this with **greywater**.

watch
verb **1** to look at attentively: *The students **watched** a film.* (***observe***, ***see***, ***view***)
2 to be careful of: ***Watch** your step.*
3 to guard: *They **watch** the place at night.*
noun **4** a lookout or guard: *to keep **watch***
5 a small timepiece which you wear on your wrist
phrase **6 watch out,** to be alert or be on your guard
7 watch out for,
a to avoid, or beware of: ***Watch out for** broken glass.*
b to look for: *I like to **watch out for** my father when he comes home.*
8 watch over, to guard or protect
Word building: **watchful** *adjective*
Word history: Old English *wacian* wake

watchman
noun someone who keeps guard over a building, usually at night, to protect it from fire and burglary
Noun forms: The plural is **watchmen**.

Look up **non-sexist language**.

water
noun **1** the colourless, transparent liquid which forms rain, rivers, lakes and oceans
verb **2** to pour water on: *to* ***water*** *the garden* (***dampen***, ***irrigate***, ***moisten***, ***soak***, ***wet***)
3 to supply with water: *to* ***water*** *a horse*
phrase **4 in deep** (or **hot**) **water**, in trouble
5 like water, freely: *to spend money* ***like water***
6 throw cold water on, to discourage
7 water down,
a to make weaker by adding water
b to weaken: *to* ***water down*** *an argument*
Word history: Middle English

waterbed
noun a hard-wearing, plastic bag filled with water, used as a mattress in a supporting wooden frame

waterbomb
verb to fight (a bushfire) by means of dropping large volumes of water from the air onto strategic points: *The helicopter passed over the fire* ***waterbombing*** *it.*

water buffalo
noun a large buffalo domesticated in India, introduced into Australia and living in great numbers in the Northern Territory
Word use: You can also use **water ox**.

water closet
noun → **toilet** (definition 1)
Word use: The abbreviation is **WC**.

watercolour
noun **1** paint made from colour diluted with water and gum instead of oil
2 a painting done in watercolour
Word use: You can also use **watercolor**.
Word building: **watercolourist** *noun*

watercourse
noun **1** a stream of water, such as a river or brook
2 the bed of such a stream
3 a natural or artificial channel carrying water

watercress
noun a leafy salad vegetable with a peppery taste

water cycle
noun the continuous circulation of water on earth, through the process of evaporation from the sea, condensation into clouds, and precipitation falling on the land and returning to the sea
Word use: You can also use **hydrological cycle**.

waterfall
noun a steep fall or flow of water, usually from a great height (***cascade***)

waterfront
noun **1** land next to a body of water
2 the wharves in a port

waterhole
noun a natural hole or hollow in which water collects, such as a spring in a desert, or a cavity in the dried-up course of a river

waterlily
noun a water plant with large flowers and flat leaves that float on the surface
Noun forms: The plural is **waterlilies**.

waterlogged
adjective **1** completely soaked with water
2 flooded

waterloo (waw-tuh-looh)
noun a final and complete defeat: *The team met their* ***waterloo*** *in Saturday's game.*
Word history: from *Waterloo*, a village in Belgium where Napoleon Bonaparte was decisively defeated by the British and the Prussians in 1815

watermark
noun **1** a line showing the greatest height that water has risen to
2 a mark, usually the maker's name or trademark, made in paper and able to be seen when held up to the light

watermelon
noun a large melon with green skin and dark pink flesh

water police
noun a civil force whose function is to police waterways, coordinating incidents involving vessels on the water, dealing with criminal activity and assisting in rescue operations, security operations, etc.

water polo
noun a game played by two teams of seven swimmers each, in which the object is to pass a ball into the opposing team's goal

waterproof
adjective made of, or coated with, material which prevents water getting through
Word building: **waterproof** *verb*

watershed
noun **1** the ridge line at the top of a range of hills, dividing two drainage areas or river basins
2 a crucial event or time in a career, venture, etc.

waterski
verb to travel on special skis over water, towed by a speedboat
Verb forms: I **waterskied**, I have **waterskied**, I am **waterskiing**

watertight
adjective **1** completely sealed against water
2 having no fault or weakness: *a* ***watertight*** *argument*

watery
adjective **1** having to do with or like water: *a* ***watery*** *fluid*
2 full of or containing too much water: ***watery*** *soup*

watt (wot)
noun a unit of electrical power
Word use: The symbol is **W**, without a full stop.
Word history: named after James *Watt*, 1736–1819, Scottish engineer and inventor

watt / what
Don't confuse **watt** with **what**. **What** is a word that introduces a question:
What bird is that?

wattle
noun **1** → **acacia**
2 rods or twigs interwoven and used for fences, walls or roofs
3 a coloured fleshy part hanging from the throat of certain birds such as the turkey

Word history: from Old English word meaning 'covering'. Later on in English it came to refer to the twigs that were woven together to make fences or walls for buildings.

wattle and daub
noun interwoven sticks or twigs covered with mud, used as a building material

wave
noun **1** a movement in the form of a ridge on the surface of a liquid, especially the sea
2 a vibration that travels through air or water and which we experience as light, sound, etc.: *a sound* ***wave***
3 a surge of feeling: *A* ***wave*** *of anger went through him.*
4 an up-and-down or side-to-side movement of the hand used as a sign of greeting or farewell
verb **5** to move up and down or from side to side: *to* ***wave*** *a flag* (***brandish***, ***shake***)
6 to move the hand in greeting

Word building: **wavy** *adjective* (**wavier**, **waviest**)
Word history: Old English

> **wave / waive**
> Look up **waive / wave**.

wavelength
noun **1** one full wave movement, such as from the top of one wave to the top of the next
2 a way of thinking: *We're on the same* ***wavelength***.

waver
verb **1** to flutter, or sway to and fro: *Leaves* ***wavered*** *in the breeze.*
2 to become unsteady or begin to fail or give way: *His mind is* ***wavering***. | *His voice is* ***wavering***. (***fluctuate***, ***vacillate***)
3 to feel or show doubt or indecision: *He* ***wavered*** *in his determination.* (***hesitate***, ***quail***)

Word history: from Old English word meaning 'wave'

wax[1]
noun **1** a fairly hard, greasy substance that is easy to melt
verb **2** to rub or polish with wax (***buff***, ***burnish***, ***shine***)

Word history: Old English

wax[2]
verb to grow, or seem to grow, bigger: *The moon is* ***waxing***.

Word use: The opposite of this is **wane**.

waxwork
noun **1 a** figures, ornaments, etc., made of wax: *He deals in* ***waxwork***.
b one such figure: *a* ***waxwork*** *of the Queen*
2 waxworks, a public showing of wax figures, ornaments, etc.

Word use: Definition 2 is treated as singular: *The* ***waxworks*** *is open now.*

way
noun **1** manner or means: *the right* ***way*** *to do it*
2 direction: *Come this* ***way***.
3 passage or progress: *They made their* ***way*** *through the bush.*
4 road, path, route or passage: *a* ***way*** *through the forest*
adverb Colloquial **5** extremely: *way cool*
phrase **6 by the way**, incidentally: ***By the way***, *have you got that letter yet?*
7 by way of,
a through or via
b as a method or means of
8 give way,
a to withdraw or retreat
b to collapse or yield
9 go out of your way, to make a special effort
10 on the way out,
a ready for rest or retirement
b losing popularity
11 out of the way,
a so as not to block or keep back: *Get your smelly feet* ***out of the way***.
b dealt with: *I'm glad to have that essay* ***out of the way***.
c off the beaten track
d unusual
12 under way,
a moving along: *Once the track is checked, the train will be* ***under way***.
b in progress: *The conference is* ***under way***.

Word history: Old English

> **way / weigh / whey**
> Don't confuse **way** with **weigh** or **whey**.
> To **weigh** something is to measure how heavy it is:
> *The greengrocer weighed the apples on the scales.*
> **Whey** is the watery part of milk separated from the curd, formed in cheese-making.

wayfarer
noun a traveller, especially on foot

waylay
verb to lie in wait for, especially in order to attack: *They* ***waylaid*** *him outside his house.* (***ambush***, ***catch***, ***snare***, ***take by surprise***, ***trap***)

Verb forms: I **waylaid**, I have **waylaid**, I am **waylaying**

way-out
adjective quite different from the usual: ***way-out*** *clothes*

wayward
adjective acting in a way that people don't think right or proper: *a* ***wayward*** *child*

Word history: Middle English

WC
noun Colloquial a toilet

Word history: *w(ater-)c(loset)*

we
pronoun the personal pronoun used by a speaker to refer to himself or herself along with at least one other person: *I'm ready and you're ready so* ***we*** *can go.* | ***We*** *need to elect a new mayor.*

We is a first person plural pronoun in the subjective case.

For more information, look up **pronouns: personal pronouns**.

weak
adjective **1** liable to break or fall down: *a **weak** framework*
2 not healthy or strong (***feeble***, ***frail***)
3 lacking in force or strength: *a **weak** leader | a **weak** argument*

Word building: **weaken** *verb* **weakness** *noun*
Word history: Middle English, from Scandinavian

weak / week

Don't confuse **weak** with **week**. A **week** is seven days.

weakling
noun a weak person or animal

weal
noun a mark or swelling on the skin made by a blow (***welt***)

Word history: Old English *walu* weal, ridge

wealth
noun **1** a large store of money and property (***capital***, ***riches***, ***treasure***)
2 a rich supply: *a **wealth** of ideas*

Word building: **wealthy** *adjective*
Word history: Middle English, from *wel* well + *-th*

wean
verb to make (a child or animal) used to food other than its mother's milk: *to **wean** a baby*

Word history: Old English

weapon (wep-uhn)
noun an instrument used in fighting

Word history: Old English

wear
verb **1** to carry or have on your body: *to **wear** a dress | to **wear** a brooch*
noun **2** a gradual using up: *The carpet shows signs of **wear**.*
3 clothing: *beach **wear***
phrase **4 wear away**, to get rid of bit by bit: *The rain has **worn away** the paint.*
5 wear off, to gradually reduce or get less: *The effect of the aspirin is **wearing off** and my headache is returning.* (***decrease***, ***diminish***, ***ease***, ***ebb***, ***lessen***, ***reduce***)
6 wear out,
a to wear or use until no longer fit for use: *to **wear out** clothes*
b to tire out because of continuous strain: *You have finally **worn out** my patience.* (***deplete***, ***exhaust***)

Verb forms: I **wore**, I have **worn**, I am **wearing**
Word building: **wearable** *adjective*
Word history: Old English

wear / where

Don't confuse **wear** with **where**.

Where asks the question 'at what place?':

Where has my bicycle gone to?

wearing
adjective **1** gradually damaging or wasting
2 tiring or exhausting

weary
adjective tired (***bushed***, ***exhausted***, ***fatigued***, ***lethargic***, ***worn***)

Adjective forms: **wearier**, **weariest**
Word building: **weary** *verb* (**wearied**, **wearying**)
Word history: Old English

weasel
noun a small, fierce, European animal that eats mice, rabbits and other small animals

Word history: Old English

weather
noun **1** the state of the atmosphere as far as heat and cold, wetness and dryness are concerned (***climate***)
verb **2** to be affected by the weather: *The fence has **weathered** to a grey colour.*
3 to come safely through: *to **weather** a storm* (***endure***, ***survive***, ***withstand***)
phrase **4 under the weather**, *Colloquial* ill, drunk, etc.

Word history: Old English

weather / whether / wether

Don't confuse **weather** with **whether** or **wether**.

Whether is a word which introduces the first of two alternatives. For example:

I do not know whether to come or to go.

A **wether** is a sheep. In particular, it is a ram castrated when young.

weatherboard
adjective having a covering of overlapping boards: *a **weatherboard** cottage*

weathering
noun the breakdown of rocks within the earth's mantle by the chemical and physical effects of climate

weathervane
noun a flat piece of metal fixed on a roof, which moves with the wind and shows its direction

weave
verb **1** to thread fibres together in order to make cloth, baskets or anything like this (***interlace***, ***intertwine***, ***knit***)
2 to go by moving from side to side: *She **weaves** through the crowd.*

Verb forms: I **wove** or, for definition 2, I **weaved**, I have **woven** or, for definition 2, I have **wove**, I am **weaving**
Word history: Old English

web
noun **1** the fine, silk-like net made by spiders to catch insects
2 → **World Wide Web**

Word history: Old English

webbed
adjective having skin between the toes, usually to help in swimming, as the feet of some animals and birds

Word use: An animal with webbed feet is **web-footed**.

webbing
noun **1** a woven material of hemp, cotton or jute, in bands of various widths, for use where strength is needed
2 such woven bands nailed on furniture under springs or upholstery, for support
3 the membrane forming a web or webs

web browser
noun → **browser**

webcam
noun → **web camera**

Word use: You can also use **web cam**.

web camera
noun a digital video camera, the images from which are transmitted via the internet

Word use: The short form is **webcam**.

webcast
verb **1** to broadcast on the internet to multiple recipients simultaneously: *The online business will start **webcasting** as soon as possible.*
2 to broadcast (information) on the internet in such a way: *He intends to **webcast** his surf travel films.*
noun **3** such a broadcast on the internet

Verb forms: I **webcast**, I have **webcasted**, I am **webcasting**
Word building: **webcaster** *noun* **webcasting** *noun*

web crawler
noun an internet search engine, originally designed to search keywords specified at URLs to locate required websites, but now capable of searching for other kinds of information, such as email addresses

web log
noun → **blog**

Word use: You can also use **weblog**.

webmaster
noun a person responsible for the development and maintenance of a web server or website

web page
noun Computers a document on the World Wide Web

Word use: You can also use **webpage**.

web portal
noun a website which offers information and sometimes direct links to other websites along with a range of services such as email, online shopping, etc.

Word use: You can also use **portal**, **portal site** or **internet portal**.

web server
noun Computers a program which connects a user to a web page when requested

Word use: You can also use **webserver**.

website
noun a place on the World Wide Web that can be looked up for information, etc.

Word use: You can also use **web site** or **site**.

webzine (<u>web</u>-zeen)
noun a magazine published on the internet

wed
verb to marry: *They will **wed** tomorrow morning. | The minister **wed** them.*

Verb forms: I **wed**, I have **wed**, I am **wedding**
Word history: from Old English word meaning 'pledge'

we'd
contraction of **we had** or **we would**

Look up **contractions in grammar.**

wedding
noun a marriage ceremony

Word history: Old English

wedge
noun a piece of wood or metal, thinner at one end than the other and used when you want to split wood or make something secure

Word building: **wedge** *verb*
Word history: Old English

wedge politics
noun a political strategy in which one group seeks to weaken opposing groups by forcing them to divide over a particular issue

wedlock
noun the state of being married

Word history: Old English

Wednesday (<u>wenz</u>-day)
noun the fourth day of the week, following Tuesday

Word history: Middle English, Old English meaning 'Woden's day', (translation of Latin: day of mercury)

wee
adjective very small

Word history: from Middle English word meaning '(small) quantity', Old English word meaning 'weight', 'amount'

weed
noun **1** a useless plant growing where it is not wanted
verb **2** to pull weeds out of: *to **weed** the garden*

Word history: Old English

weedy
adjective thin and weak (***feeble***, ***frail***, ***helpless***, ***invalid***)

Adjective forms: **weedier**, **weediest**

week
noun a period of seven days, especially from Sunday to Saturday

Word history: Old English

week / weak
Look up **weak / week.**

weekday
noun any day of the week except Saturday or Sunday

weekend
noun the time from Friday evening to Sunday evening, when most people do not have to work or go to school

weekender
noun a holiday cottage used at weekends or during holidays

weekly
adjective **1** happening once a week: *the **weekly** wash*
adverb **2** once a week: *The garbage is collected **weekly**.*
noun **3** a paper or magazine that comes out once a week

Noun forms: The plural is **weeklies**.

weep
verb to show sorrow or any emotion by crying (***bawl***, ***blubber***, ***cry***, ***howl***, ***sob***, ***wail***, ***whimper***)

Verb forms: I **wept**, I have **wept**, I am **weeping**
Word history: from Old English word meaning 'wail'

weeping
adjective **1** passing out liquid: *a **weeping** wound*
2 showing sorrow by shedding tears
3 having narrow, graceful branches that hang down: *a **weeping** elm*

weevil
noun a kind of beetle which destroys grain, nuts, fruit and trees

Word history: Old English

weft
noun the threads woven across the warp in cloth

Word history: Old English

weigh (way)
verb **1** to measure the heaviness of by means of a scale or balance
2 to press heavily: *The affair **weighed** on her conscience.* (***burden***, ***oppress***, ***torment***, ***worry***)
phrase **3 weigh into**, to attack, with words or with your hands or feet
4 weigh your words, to consider and choose your words carefully when you speak or write

Word history: from Old English word meaning 'carry', 'weigh'

> **weigh / way / whey**
> Don't confuse **weigh** with **way** or **whey**.
> A **way** of doing something is the manner or fashion in which you do it:
> *Are you sure that's the right way to ride a skateboard?*
> **Way** can also mean 'direction':
> *You should go that way.*
> **Whey** is the watery part of milk separated from the curd, formed in cheese-making.

weight (wayt)
noun **1** an amount of heaviness
2 the force of gravity on something, which varies with its position on the earth
3 a heavy object (***burden***, ***encumbrance***, ***load***)
4 something serious and worrying: *That lifts a **weight** from my mind.*
phrase **5 carry weight**, to have influence or importance
6 pull your weight, to do your fair share of work
7 throw your weight around (or **about**),
a to behave in a quarrelsome or selfish way
b to use your authority, influence, etc., when it is not necessary

Word building: **weighty** *adjective* (**weightier**, **weightiest**)
Word history: Old English

> **weight / wait**
> Don't confuse **weight** with **wait**. To **wait** is to stay or rest until something happens.

weightlessness
noun a state of being without apparent weight, as experienced by astronauts at great distances from earth, due to the absence of any apparent pull of gravity (***zero gravity***)

weir (wear)
noun a small lake made by damming a river

Word history: Old English

weird
adjective very odd or strange (***abnormal***, ***bizarre***, ***peculiar***, ***unusual***)

Word history: from Old English word meaning 'fate'

weirdo (wear-doh)
noun Colloquial an odd, strange or eccentric person: *What do you think of her new boyfriend? He seems a **weirdo** to me.*

welch (welsh)
verb → **welsh**

welcome
adjective **1** giving rise to pleasure or happiness: *Your kind remarks are **welcome**.* (***agreeable***, ***pleasing***)
noun **2** a kindly greeting: *a warm **welcome***

Word building: **welcome** *verb* **welcome** *adjective*
Word history: Old English, from *wil-* pleasure + *cuma* guest

welcome to country
noun a welcoming speech, performance, etc., given by a representative or representatives of the traditional Indigenous custodians of the land on which a public event, meeting, etc., is taking place

weld
verb to join together by heat and pressure: *to **weld** metal*

Word history: variant of *well*[2]

welfare
noun the state of being healthy and having a good way of life: *He is interested in the **welfare** of old people.*

Word history: Middle English

welfare state
noun a state in which the wellbeing of the people in social security, health, education, housing and working conditions is the responsibility of the government

well[1]
adverb **1** in a good way: *She sings **well**.*
2 thoroughly: *Shake the bottle **well**.*
3 clearly: *I can see it **well**.*
adjective **4** in good health (***fine***, ***fit***, ***healthy***, ***robust***, ***sound***)
5 satisfactory: *All is **well**.*
phrase **6 as well**, in addition: *She is bringing a friend **as well**.*
7 as well as, in addition to: *He was handsome **as well as** rich.*

Adverb forms: **better**, **best**
Adjective forms: **better**, **best**
Word history: Old English

well / good
Look up **good / well**.

well[2]
noun **1** a hole drilled or dug in the ground to obtain water, oil, natural gas or other substances
verb **2** to spring or gush: *Tears **welled** up in his eyes.*

Word history: Old English

we'll
contraction of **we will** or **we shall**

Look up **contractions in grammar**.

well-appointed
adjective of a hotel, house, etc., comfortably and well equipped, decorated or furnished

wellbeing
noun the state of being healthy and contented

well-done
adjective of meat, cooked thoroughly: *I like steak **well-done**.*

well-heeled
adjective Colloquial wealthy or prosperous

well-meaning
adjective having good intentions (***considerate***, ***kindly***, ***thoughtful***, ***well-disposed***)

Word building: **well-meant** *adjective*

well-off
adjective wealthy or prosperous (***affluent***, ***loaded***, ***rich***)

Word use: You can also use **well-to-do**.

well-spoken
adjective **1** having a carefully developed, refined way of speaking
2 speaking well, fittingly or pleasingly
3 polite in speech

well-to-do
adjective well-off, or having enough money to be able to live comfortably (***in the money***, ***prosperous***, ***rich***)

welsh
verb Colloquial **1** to cheat by escaping payment, especially of a gambling debt
2 to inform or tell on someone: *to **welsh** on a friend.*

Word use: You can also use **welch**.

welt
noun a raised mark on the skin made by a blow with a stick or whip (***weal***)

Word history: Middle English

welter
verb Old-fashioned **1** to lie bathed or soaked in something, especially blood
noun **2** a rolling or tumbling about: *in the **welter** of the sea*
3 a race in which the horses carry weights which are not less than 51 kilograms

Word history: Middle English, from obsolete *welt* roll

wend
verb to direct or make: *He **wended** his way to the riverside.*

Word history: Old English

went
verb past tense of **go**

wept
verb past tense and past participle of **weep**

were
verb past tense indicative plural and subjunctive singular and plural of **be**

Word history: Old English

we're
contraction of **we are**

Look up **contractions in grammar**.

weren't
contraction of **were not**

Look up **contractions in grammar**.

werewolf (wair-woolf)
noun a man who, according to old superstition, changed into a wolf when there was a full moon

Noun forms: The plural is **werewolves**.
Word history: Old English, from *wer* man + *wolf*

west
noun the direction in which the sun sets

Word use: The opposite direction is **east**.
Word building: **west** *adjective* **west** *adverb*
Word history: Old English

westerly
adjective **1** towards the west: *We travelled in a **westerly** direction.*
2 of the wind, from the west: *a **westerly** wind*
noun **3** a wind blowing from the west: *A strong **westerly** is forecast for this afternoon.*

western
adjective **1** lying in or towards the west: ***western** suburbs*
noun **2** a film or story about cowboys and Indians in the American west

Word history: Old English

Westminster system
noun a system of parliamentary government originating in Britain, with two houses in which ministers are members of parliament and are responsible to it, and in which the head of state is not also head of government, and the judiciary is independent of the executive and legislature

Word history: so named because the British Houses of Parliament are situated in *Westminster* in central London

wet
adjective **1** covered or soaked with water or some other liquid (***damp***, ***dank***, ***moist***, ***sodden***, ***soggy***)
2 not yet dry: ***wet** paint*
3 rainy: *a **wet** summer*
verb **4** to make wet (***dampen***, ***irrigate***, ***moisten***, ***soak***, ***water***)
5 to make wet by urinating: *Baby has **wet** his nappy.*
phrase **6 the wet**, the rainy season in central and northern Australia, from December to March

Adjective forms: **wetter**, **wettest**
Verb forms: I **wet**, I have **wet**, I am **wetting**
Word history: from Old English word meaning 'to wet'

> **wet / whet**
> Don't confuse **wet** with **whet.** To **whet** a knife is to sharpen it. If something **whets** your appetite then it sharpens your hunger.

wet blanket
noun someone who stops you enjoying yourself

wether
noun a castrated ram

Word history: Old English

> **wether / weather / whether**
> Don't confuse **wether** with **weather** or **whether.**
> The **weather** is sunshine or rain.
> **Whether** is the word that introduces the first of two alternatives. For example:
> *I do not know whether to come or go.*

wetland
noun **1** an area in which the soil is frequently or permanently saturated with or under water, as a swamp, marsh, etc.
2 (*plural*) an ecological system made up of such areas

wet nurse
noun a woman paid to breastfeed another woman's baby

wet season
noun the period of an annual cycle in the tropics when rainfall and humidity increase markedly, usually as a result of the change in the prevailing winds

Word use: Compare this with **dry season**.

wetsuit
noun a tight rubber garment worn by divers and surfers to keep in body heat

we've
contraction of **we have**

> Look up **contractions in grammar.**

whack
noun a sharp blow

Word building: **whack** *verb*
Word history: perhaps imitative; perhaps variant of *thwack*

whale
noun a very large sea mammal that used to be hunted for its valuable oil

Word building: **whaler** *noun* **whaling** *noun*
Word history: Old English

> **whale / wail**
> Don't confuse **whale** with **wail.** To **wail** is to give a long, sad cry or to cry continuously.

whalebone
noun an elastic horny substance growing in place of teeth in the upper jaw of certain whales (***baleen***)

wham (wam)
noun **1** a forceful stroke or blow
verb **2** to hit forcefully, especially with a single loud noise

Verb forms: I **whammed**, I have **whammed**, I am **whamming**

wharf (wawf)
noun a structure built along or out from the shore of a harbour, where ships can load and unload (***dock***, ***jetty***, ***pier***, ***quay***)

Noun forms: The plural is **wharves** or **wharfs.**
Word history: from Old English word meaning 'dam'

wharfie
noun Australian, *NZ Colloquial* someone who works on the wharves, loading and unloading ships in port

what
pronoun **1** asking for something to be named or stated: ***What** is your name?* | ***What** did he do?*
2 asking about the nature, character, class, origin, etc., of a thing or person: ***What** is that animal?*
3 asking about the importance of something: ***What** is wealth without health?*
4 the thing that: *This is **what** he says.*
5 anything that: *Say **what** you please.*
adverb **6** how much?: ***What** does it matter?*
phrase **7 what's what,**
a the true position
b the correct procedure: *He knows **what's what**.*

Word history: Old English

> **what / watt**
> Don't confuse **what** with **watt.** A **watt** is a unit of electrical power.

whatever
pronoun **1 a** anything that: *Do **whatever** you like.*
b no matter what: *Do it, **whatever** happens.*
2 *Colloquial* what ever? what?: ***Whatever** do you mean?*
adjective **3** any…that: ***Whatever** worth the work has is to John's credit.*
4 no matter what: ***Whatever** blame he might receive, he'll still carry on.*
5 what or who…it may be: *For **whatever** reason, he is unwilling.* | *any person **whatever***

Word use: You will also find **whate'er** used in some poetry. | Definition 2 is used to give force to a question.

what's
contraction of **what is** or **what has**

> Look up **contractions in grammar.**

wheat
noun the grain of a widely grown cereal plant, used for making flour

Word history: Old English

wheatgerm
noun a part of the wheat grain, rich in vitamins, which is removed when the wheat is ground

wheedle
verb to get by coaxing or persuasion: *They **wheedled** some money from their mother for the movies.*

wheel
noun **1** a circular frame or solid disc turning on an axle, used in machinery and on vehicles
verb **2** to roll or push on wheels: *to **wheel** a bicycle*
3 to turn around: *He **wheeled** on his followers.*

Word history: Old English

wheelbarrow
noun a small cart, usually with one wheel at the front and two legs, which you lift when you wheel it along

wheelchair
noun a chair on wheels, used by people unable to walk

wheeze
verb to breathe with difficulty, making a whistling sound (***blow***, ***gasp***, ***heave***, ***pant***, ***puff***)

Word building: **wheeze** *noun* **wheezy** *adjective*
Word history: Middle English *whese*, probably from Scandinavian; compare Icelandic *hvæsa* hiss

whelk
noun a shellfish with a spiral shell

Word history: Old English

whelp
noun **1** the young of the dog, wolf, bear, lion, tiger, seal, etc.
verb **2** of a bitch, lioness, etc., to bear young

Word history: Old English

when
adverb **1** at what time?: ***When** are you coming?*
conjunction **2** at what time: *to know **when** he is coming*
3 at the time that: ***when** we are ready to go*
4 at any time: *He gets impatient **when** he is kept waiting.*
5 whereas: *You made him sit up **when** you should have left him lying still.*
pronoun **6** what time: *Since **when** have you known this?*

Word history: Old English

whenever
conjunction **1** at any time when: *Come **whenever** you like.*
adverb **2** when?: ***Whenever** did he say that?*

Word use: You will also see **whene'er** used, especially in poetry. | Definition 2 is used to give force to a question.

where
adverb **1** in or at what place?: ***Where** is he?*
2 in what position?: ***Where** do you want to stand?*
3 to what place?: ***Where** are you going?*
4 from what source?: ***Where** did you get this information?*
conjunction **5** in, at, or to what place or point: *Find **where** the trouble is.* | *Find out **where** he's gone.*
6 in a position, or place in which: *There are streets **where** it is better not to go.* | *The book is **where** you left it.*
7 *Colloquial* that: *I read **where** they were going to increase train fares.*
pronoun **8** what place: ***Where** have you come from?*
9 the place in which: *This is **where** we live.*

Word history: Old English

> **where / wear**
> Don't confuse **where** with **wear**, which is to carry or have something on your body, as in *to wear a hat.*

whereabouts
noun the place where someone or something is: *His **whereabouts** are unknown.*

whereas
conjunction **1** while on the other hand: *Frederico came, **whereas** the others didn't.*
2 it being the case that

Word use: Definition 2 is used especially in legal documents.

wherefore
adverb **1** for what?; why?
conjunction **2** for what or which cause or reason?
noun **3** the cause or reason: *the whys and **wherefores***

Word history: Middle English; from *where* + *fore* because of, *for*

whereupon
conjunction at or after which: *He failed his driving test, **whereupon** he did it again later.*

wherever
conjunction **1** in, at or to whatever place
adverb **2** where?: ***Wherever** did you find that?*

Word use: You will also see **where'er** used in some poetry. | Definition 2 is used to give force to a question.

wherewithal
noun the means or supplies for the purpose or need, especially money: *the **wherewithal** to pay my rent*

whet
verb to sharpen: *to **whet** a knife* | *to **whet** your appetite*

Verb forms: I **whetted**, I have **whetted**, I am **whetting**
Word history: Old English

> **whet / wet**
> Look up **wet / whet**.

whether
conjunction **1** a word introducing the first of two or more possible happenings, and sometimes repeated before the second one: *It matters little **whether** we go or **whether** we stay.*
2 used to introduce a single happening, the other being understood: *See **whether** he has come (or not).*

phrase **3 whether or no,** in any case: *He threatens to go,* ***whether or no.***

Word history: Old English

whether / weather / wether

Don't confuse **whether** with **weather** or **wether**.

The **weather** is sunshine or rain.

A **wether** is a sheep. In particular, it is a ram castrated when young.

whey

noun the watery part of milk separated from the curd, formed in cheese-making

Word history: Old English

whey / way / weigh

Don't confuse **whey** with **way** or **weigh**.

A **way** of doing something is the manner or fashion in which you do it:

Are you sure that's the right way to ride a skateboard?

Way can also mean 'direction':

You should go that way.

To **weigh** something is to measure how heavy it is.

which

pronoun **1** of a certain number, what one?: ***Which*** *of these do you want?*
2 what particular one or any one that: *She knows* ***which*** *she wants. | Choose* ***which*** *you like.*
3 a thing that: *And,* ***which*** *is worse, your work is wrong.*
adjective **4** of a certain number, what one of: ***Which*** *book do you want?*

Word history: Old English

which / witch

Don't confuse **which** with **witch**. A **witch** is the female equivalent of a wizard.

whichever

pronoun **1** of those in question, any one that: *Take* ***whichever*** *you like.*
2 no matter which: ***Whichever*** *you choose, the others will be hurt.*
adjective **3** no matter which: ***whichever*** *day |* ***whichever*** *person*

whiff

noun a slight puff: *a* ***whiff*** *of smoke | a* ***whiff*** *of perfume*

Word history: perhaps blend of *whip* and *puff*

while

noun **1** a space of time: *a long* ***while***
conjunction **2** during or in the time that: *Stay here* ***while*** *I'm out.*
phrase **3 once in a while,** occasionally
4 while away, to cause to pass, usually in a pleasant way: *to* ***while away*** *the day in the sun*
5 worth your while, worth your time, effort or expense

Word use: You can also use **whilst** for definition 2.
Word history: Old English

while / wile

Don't confuse **while** with **wile.** A **wile** is a cunning trick. It is a rather old-fashioned word, although the adjective from it, **wily,** is still well-known.

whilst

conjunction while

whim

noun a sudden change of mind without an obvious reason

Word history: probably from Scandinavian

whimper

verb to cry weakly

Word building: **whimper** *noun*
Word history: from *whimp* (now British dialect) whine

whimsical

adjective amusingly odd

whimsy (<u>wim</u>-zee)

noun **1** an odd or fanciful notion
2 a product of playful fancy, such as a small written piece

Noun forms: The plural is **whimsies.**
Word use: You can also use **whimsey.**

whine

verb to make a constant complaint, especially in a high-pitched and nasal voice (***complain, gripe, nag, whinge***)

Word building: **whine** *noun*
Word history: Old English

whine / wine

Don't confuse **whine** with **wine,** which is an alcoholic drink that is made from grapes and sometimes from other fruit.

whinge

verb to complain in a tiresome way (***gripe, grumble, moan, nag, whine***)

Word history: northern British dialect variant of *whine*

whinny

noun the sound a horse makes

Noun forms: The plural is **whinnies.**
Word building: **whinny** *verb* (**whinnied, whinnying**)
Word history: from Old English *whine* in (now obsolete) sense 'whinny'

whip

noun **1** a long piece of rope or leather attached to a handle, used to hit animals or people
verb **2** to beat with a whip (***flog, lash, scourge, thrash***)
3 to beat with light, quick strokes: *to* ***whip*** *cream*
phrase **4 whip out,** to bring out with a sudden movement: *He* ***whipped out*** *a gun.*
5 whip up, to rouse: *to* ***whip up*** *enthusiasm*

Verb forms: I **whipped,** I have **whipped,** I am **whipping**
Word history: Middle English

whiplash
noun **1** the lash of a whip
2 an injury to the spine, usually in the neck area, caused by sudden movement forwards or backwards, especially in a car accident

whippet
noun a dog like a greyhound, used especially in rabbit hunting and racing
Word history: noun use of obsolete verb, to frisk, originally in the phrase *whip it* move briskly

whirl
verb to turn round or spin rapidly (***gyrate***, ***spin***, ***swirl***, ***twirl***, ***whirr***)
Word building: **whirl** *noun*
Word history: Middle English, from Scandinavian

whirlpool
noun a circular current in a river or sea

whirlwind
noun a strong wind that blows in a spiral
Word history: Middle English, from Scandinavian

whirr
verb to make a low buzzing sound while moving or working: *The machinery **whirred** constantly.*
Word use: You can also use **whir**.
Word building: **whirr** *noun*
Word history: Middle English, from Scandinavian

whisk
noun **1** a light, sweeping stroke: *a **whisk** with a duster*
2 a kitchen tool used for beating eggs, cream, etc.
verb **3** to move lightly and rapidly: *to **whisk** something out of the way | to **whisk** out of the room*
Word history: Middle English, from Scandinavian word meaning 'wipe'

whisker
noun **1** one of the long bristles on the face of a cat or similar animal
2 whiskers, a man's beard and moustache
Word history: Middle English

whisky
noun an alcoholic drink distilled from grain, especially barley
Noun forms: The plural is **whiskies.**
Word history: short for *whiskybae*, from Gaelic word meaning 'water of life'

whisper
verb to speak very softly with your breath rather than your voice (***murmur***, ***mutter***)
Word building: **whisper** *noun*
Word history: Old English

whist
noun a card game played by two pairs of people
Word history: earlier *whisk*, perhaps special use of *whisk*, altered by confusion with *whist* silence!

whistle
verb **1** to make a shrill sound by forcing your breath through a small opening that you form between your lips and your teeth
2 to make a similar sound by blowing through a whistle
3 to make a shrill sound: *The wind **whistles** in the trees.*
noun **4** a small pipe which produces one or more notes when you blow through it
5 the sound produced by a whistle or by whistling
Word history: Old English

white
adjective **1** of the colour of milk (***ivory***, ***lily-white***, ***pale***, ***snowy***)
2 light or fairly light in colour: ***white** wine | **white** coffee | **white** meat*
3 having light skin like a European: *a **white** man*
Word building: **white** *noun* **whiten** *verb* **whiteness** *noun*
Word history: Old English

white ant
noun an insect which eats through wood
Word use: Scientists classify it as a **termite**, not as an ant.

white-ant
verb Colloquial to subvert or undermine from within (an organisation or enterprise): *They **white-anted** his leadership by refusing to back him on issues he thought were important.*
Word building: **white-anter** *noun* **white-anting** *noun*

white blood cell
noun one of the white or colourless cells in the blood, which have the function of fighting disease in the body by destroying disease-producing microorganisms

whiteboard
noun a board with a white plastic surface which you write on with an erasable felt pen, used for teaching or presentations

white cockatoo
noun → **sulphur-crested cockatoo**

white-collar
adjective having to do with workers in professional or business positions: *a **white-collar** job | **white-collar** crime*
Word use: Compare this with **blue-collar.**
Word history: from the clothing traditionally worn by men in these positions; word meaning 'suit', 'white shirt and tie.'

white elephant
noun something useless which can cost a lot of money to maintain: *The big new theatre is a **white elephant** because nobody uses it.*

white flag
noun an all-white flag, used to indicate surrender or truce

white gold
noun any of several gold alloys with a white colour due to the presence of nickel or platinum

whitegoods
plural noun electrical goods such as fridges, washing machines, etc., which have a white enamel surface
Word building: **whitegoods** *adjective*

white heat
noun great heat which causes a substance, usually metal, to glow with white light

white lie
noun a lie told for reasons of kindness or politeness

white-out
noun a thin white paint that is used to cover written mistakes on paper

whitewash
noun **1** a white liquid that people used to paint walls and ceilings with
2 anything used to cover up faults and give a good appearance on the surface

Word building: **whitewash** *verb*

white water
noun water with a broken, foaming surface, as shallow water rushing over rocks

whither
adverb Old-fashioned to what place or to what?

Word use: This word has now been replaced by **where**.
Word building: **whither** *conjunction*
Word history: Old English

whiting
noun **1** in Australia, a species of edible fish that lives in the estuaries of rivers and in the sea, highly prized for sport
2 elsewhere, a European species of the cod family

Word history: from Middle English, perhaps alteration of Old English word meaning 'kind of fish'

whittle
verb **1** to cut, trim or shape by taking off bits with a knife
2 to make less, a little at a time: *We've managed to **whittle** down our costs.*

Word history: alteration of Middle English word meaning 'knife', from Old English word meaning 'whittle'

whiz[1]
verb to move with a humming or hissing sound: *A bullet **whizzed** past his ear.* (***zoom***)

Verb forms: it **whizzed**, it has **whizzed**, it is **whizzing**
Word history: imitative

whiz[2]
noun Colloquial someone who is very good at something: *a **whiz** at maths*

Word history: perhaps abbreviation of *wizard*

who
pronoun **1** an interrogative pronoun used when
a asking the question 'what person?': ***Who** told you so?*
b asking 'what?', as to the character, origin, position, importance, etc., of a person: ***Who** is the man in uniform?*
2 a relative pronoun introducing an adjectival clause describing a person: *I know **who** did it.* | *The woman **who** sold it to me has gone to lunch.*

Word history: Old English

Who is used as the subject of a verb (*Who gave it to you?*), while, strictly speaking, **whom** is used as the object (*Whom did you see?*). However, many people use **who** instead of **whom** (*Who did you see?*), and it is generally regarded as acceptable. In fact, many people would regard the use of **whom** as slightly pompous.

For more information, look up **pronouns: interrogative pronouns** and **pronouns: relative pronouns.**

who'd
contraction of **who had** or **who would**

Look up **contractions in grammar.**

whoever
pronoun **1** whatever person, or anyone that: ***Whoever** wants it may have it.*
2 who ever?, or who?; used to give force to a question: ***Whoever** is that?*

Word use: You will also see **whoe'er** used in some poetry.

whole (hohl)
adjective **1** making up the full quantity, number or thing (***complete***, ***entire***, ***total***)
2 in one piece: *He swallowed the cherry **whole**.*
noun **3** the entire quantity, amount or number
4 a thing complete in itself
phrase **5 on the whole**, in general

Word history: Old English

whole / hole
Don't confuse **whole** with **hole**. You can have a **hole** in your pocket or dig a **hole** in the ground.

wholehearted
adjective sincere or earnest: *You have my **wholehearted** support.*

wholemeal
noun flour made from the whole grain of wheat

whole number
noun a number without fractions, such as 0, 1, 2, 3, etc. (***integer***)

wholesale
noun the sale of goods, usually in large quantities, to shop owners rather than directly to the public

Word use: Compare this with **retail.**
Word building: **wholesale** *adjective* **wholesale** *verb* **wholesaler** *noun*

wholesome
adjective good for you

Word history: Middle English, from *hol* whole + *-sum* -some

who'll
contraction of **who will** or **who shall**

Look up **contractions in grammar.**

wholly
adverb entirely or totally

wholly / holey / holy
Don't confuse **wholly** with **holey** or **holy.**
Something is **holey** if it is full of holes.
A **holy** person is saintly and good.

whom (hoohm)
pronoun objective case of the pronoun **who**: ***Whom** did you see last night?*

Strictly speaking, **whom** is used as the object of a verb instead of **who** (*Whom did you see?*). However, many people use **who** instead of **whom** (*Who did you see?*), and it is generally regarded as acceptable. In fact, many people would regard the use of **whom** in everyday speech as slightly pompous.

For more information, look up **pronouns: interrogative pronouns** and **pronouns: relative pronouns.**

whoop (woohp)
noun a loud cry or shout: *She gave a **whoop** of glee.*

Word building: **whoop** *verb*
Word history: from Old English word meaning 'threaten'

whooping cough (hooh-ping kof)
noun an infectious disease of the air passages, caught mostly by children, marked by a series of short, sharp coughs followed by the taking-in of a deep breath accompanied by a whooping sound

whoops (woops)
interjection an exclamation of mild surprise, upset, etc.

Word use: You can also use **whoops-a-daisy**.

whoosh (woosh)
noun a loud rushing noise, usually of water or air

whopper
noun Colloquial **1** something unusually large of its kind
2 a big lie

whore (haw)
noun Old-fashioned a female prostitute

Word history: Old English

whorl (werl)
noun **1** a circular arrangement of parts that are alike, such as those in leaves, flowers, etc., round a point
2 one of the turns of a spiral shell
3 one of the principal ridge-shapes of a fingerprint, forming at least one complete circle

Word building: **whorled** *adjective*
Word history: Middle English

who's
contraction of **who is** or **who has**

Look up **contractions in grammar**.

who's / whose

These words sound the same but mean different things.

Who's is a short form of **who is** or **who has**:

Who's ready for sweets?

For more information, look up **contractions in grammar**.

Whose is a word which introduces a question:

Whose car is that?

whose (hoohz)
pronoun **1** possessive case of the pronoun **who**: *the girl **whose** book I borrowed*
2 possessive case of the pronoun **which**: *the pen **whose** point is broken*

For more information, look up **pronouns: interrogative pronouns** and **pronouns: relative pronouns.**

who've
contraction of **who have**

Look up **contractions in grammar.**

wh-question (dub-uhl-yooh-aytch-kwes-chuhn)
noun Grammar a question that begins with an interrogative pronoun, such as *who, what, when, where, which,* or *how*

why
adverb **1** for what cause, reason or purpose?: ***Why** did you go?*
conjunction **2** for what cause or reason
3 for which: *the reason **why** she refused*
4 the reason for which: *That is **why** I raised this question again.*
interjection **5** an expression of surprise, hesitation, etc.: ***Why**, it's all gone!*

Word history: Old English

wick
noun the twisted threads in a candle or lamp which absorb the melted wax or oil to be burnt

Word history: Old English

wicked (wik-uhd)
adjective **1** evil and harmful (***black, evil, heinous, sinful, villainous***)
2 bad or wrong: *Stealing is **wicked**.*

Word history: Middle English

wicker
noun **1** a slender, but strong, flexible twig of willow easily bent or woven
adjective **2** consisting or made of wicker, especially when woven: *a **wicker** table*

Word use: You can also use **wickerwork** for definition 2.
Word history: Middle English, from Scandinavian

wicket
noun **1** one of the two sets of three stumps with two bails on top, at which the bowler aims the ball in cricket
2 the area between the two wickets, especially when referring to the state of the ground: *a wet **wicket***
3 the dismissal of a batsman: *3 **wickets** for 90 runs*

Word history: Middle English, from Anglo-French, from Scandinavian

wide
adjective **1** having a large size from side to side (***broad, extensive, outspread***)
2 having a certain size from side to side: *30 centimetres **wide***
adverb **3** fully: *Open **wide**!* | *He is **wide** awake.*
4 far to the side: *The shot went **wide**.*

Word building: **widen** *verb* **width** *noun*
Word history: Old English

widespread
adjective **1** spread over a wide space
2 happening in many places or among many people
Word use: The opposite of this is **limited**.

widget (wij-uht)
noun **1** *Colloquial (humorous)* a mechanical device or gadget, the name of which you do not know or cannot think of: *Where's that **widget** to clean the barbecue?*
2 *Computers* a component of a graphical user interface that displays information that a user can interact with to change the information, such as a window or a text box

widow
noun a woman whose husband is dead and who has not married again
Word history: Old English

widower
noun a man whose wife is dead and who has not married again

widow's peak
noun a point formed by the hair growing down in the middle of the forehead

wield
verb to control and use: *to **wield** a weapon | to **wield** influence* (***employ**, **ply**, **utilise***)
Word history: Middle English *welde(n)*, Old English *wieldan* control, from *wealdan* rule, govern, related to German *walten*

wife
noun the woman to whom a man is married (***partner**, **spouse***)
Noun forms: The plural is **wives**.
Word history: from Old English word meaning 'woman', 'wife'

wi-fi (wuy-fuy)
noun **1** a communications networking standard which is used to create high-speed wireless local area networks
adjective **2** having to do with a wi-fi: ***Wi-fi** products can be tested to ensure that they communicate effectively between themselves.*

wig
noun a specially made covering of hair for the head
Word history: short for *periwig*, from French

wiggle
verb to move with short motions from side to side
Word history: Middle English, from *wig* (now British dialect) wag

wigwam (wig-wom)
noun a Native American hut made of poles with bark, mats or skins laid over them
Word history: from Native American word meaning 'dwelling'

wiki (wik-ee)
noun a website in which the contents are contributed and edited by visitors to the site

wild
adjective **1** living or growing in a natural state without human interference or care: ***wild** animals | **wild** strawberries* (***feral**, **free**, **native***)
2 unruly or disorderly: ***wild** hair | a **wild** party*
adverb **3** in a wild way
noun **4 wilds**, a waste or wilderness: *in the **wilds** of Africa*
phrase **5 in the wild**, in natural surroundings, usually a long way from civilisation or other people: *She is fond of camping **in the wild**.*
6 run wild,
a to grow without care or control
b to behave in an uncontrolled way
Word history: Old English

wildcard
noun **1** in some card games, a playing card which can be given the value of any other card
2 in computer searches, a special character that is not a letter or number, used to stand for any character or set of characters
3 in sport, a player or team allowed into a competition without having to compete in qualifying matches
Word building: **wildcard** *adjective*

wildcat
noun **1** a large, undomesticated cat
2 a quick-tempered or fierce person
3 an exploratory well drilled in an effort to discover deposits of oil or gas

wildcat strike
noun a strike which has not been called or approved by officials of a trade union

wilderness
noun **1** a natural area of country, such as forest, desert, etc., without roads or houses, which may be very beautiful but difficult to reach
2 an occupied and dismal stretch of country
Word history: from Old English word meaning 'of wild beasts'

wildflower
noun the flower of a plant that grows in a natural or uncultivated state
Word use: You can also use **wild flower**.

wildlife
noun animals, birds and insects living in their natural surroundings

wile
noun a trick or something done to persuade someone
Word history: Middle English, probably from Scandinavian

wile / while
Don't confuse **wile** with **while. While** is a conjunction meaning 'during the time that':
While I cook dinner you can tell me the news.
While is also a noun meaning 'a space of time':
He was here for a long while.

wilful
adjective **1** done on purpose: *a **wilful** murder*
2 headstrong or obstinate: *a **wilful** child* (***defiant**, **insubordinate**, **unruly***)
Word history: from Old English word meaning 'willing'

will[1]
verb **1** to be going to: *I **will** cut your hair.*
2 to be willing to: *I **will** help you.*
3 to be accustomed or likely to: *He **would** sit for hours and hours.*

Word use: This is an auxiliary, or helping verb, always used with another one in the form **will** or **would**.
Word history: Old English *wyllan*

will[2]
noun **1** the power of choosing your own actions
2 wish or desire: *against his **will*** (***choice**, **inclination***)
3 purpose or determination: *the **will** to win*
4 a legal document stating what a person wants done with their property after their death
phrase **5 at will**, at someone's own choice: *to wander **at will***

Word building: **will** *verb*
Word history: Old English *willa*

willie wagtail
noun a common black-and-white Australian bird with a fan-like tail

Word use: You can also use **willy-wagtail**.

willing
adjective agreeing quite happily: *He was **willing** to help.* (***anxious**, **avid**, **eager**, **enthusiastic**, **keen***)

willow
noun **1** a tree which has tough but easily bent branches which are used for basketwork, etc.
2 *Colloquial* a cricket bat

Word history: Old English

willpower
noun **1** control over your own desires and actions: *It takes a lot of **willpower** to stay on a diet.*
2 strength of will: *He has great **willpower**.*

will've
contraction of **will have**

Look up **contractions in grammar**.

willy-willy
noun Australian a strong wind that moves around in circles, often collecting dust, waste matter, etc.

Word history: from Yindjibarndi, an Australian Aboriginal language of the Fortescue River district of Western Australia

wilt
verb to become limp: *These flowers will **wilt** without water.*

Word history: dialect variant of *wilk* wither

wily (wuy-lee)
adjective crafty or cunning (***artful**, **devious**, **dishonest**, **sly***)

Adjective forms: **wilier**, **wiliest**
Word building: **wiliness** *noun*
Word history: Middle English, from *wil(e)* + *-y*

wimp
noun Colloquial a weak, cowardly person

Word history: perhaps from *Wimpy* the timid character in the comic strip *Popeye*

wimple (wim-puhl)
noun a woman's headcloth drawn in folds about the chin, formerly worn out of doors, and still in use by some nuns

Word history: Old English

win
verb **1** to gain a victory (***succeed**, **triumph***)
2 to achieve by effort: *to **win** fame* (***earn**, **gain**, **obtain**, **procure***)
3 to be successful in: *to **win** a game* | *to **win** a lottery*
phrase **4 win over**, to persuade, or gain the favour or support of: *She **won** him **over** with her sound arguments.* (***coax**, **convince**, **influence**, **persuade***)

Verb forms: I **won**, I have **won**, I am **winning**
Word building: **win** *noun* **winner** *noun*
Word history: from Old English word meaning 'work', 'fight', 'bear'

wince
verb to start or flinch because of pain or a blow

Word building: **wince** *noun*
Word history: Middle English

winch
noun a device for hauling or hoisting, consisting of a cable wound round a drum turned by a crank or motor

Word building: **winch** *verb*
Word history: Old English

wind[1] (wind)
noun **1** moving air
2 a gale or storm
3 breath: *He can't run because he's short of **wind**.*
4 gas coming from your stomach or bowel
verb **5** to take away the breath of: *The blow **winded** him.*
phrase **6 in the wind**,
a likely to happen: *A marriage is **in the wind**.*
b spreading as a rumour: *His promotion is **in the wind**.*

Word building: **windy** *adjective* (**windier**, **windiest**)
Word history: Old English

wind[2] (wuynd)
verb **1** to turn first one way and then another: *The path **winds** up the hill.* (***bend**, **twist***)
2 to roll into a ball: *to **wind** wool*
3 to tighten the spring of: *to **wind** a clock*
phrase **4 wind down**,
a to rest after a very active time (***laze**, **put your feet up**, **relax**, **take it easy***)
b of a clock, to run down
c to reduce the size or force of: *to **wind down** an operation*
d to lower by winding
e to end action, speech, etc.

Verb forms: I **wound**, I have **wound**, I am **winding**
Word history: Old English

windbreak
noun a protection from the wind such as a fence or row of trees

windcheater
noun a close-fitting jacket or jumper worn for protection against the wind

wind energy
noun energy derived from the wind, as by wind turbines in a wind farm

windfall
noun **1** something, such as fruit, blown down by the wind
2 an unexpected piece of good luck

wind farm
noun an array of wind turbines set up in a windy location to produce electricity
Word use: You can also use **windfarm**.

wind instrument
noun a musical instrument that you play by blowing

windjammer (<u>wind</u>-jam-uh)
noun a large sailing ship

windlass (<u>wind</u>-luhs)
noun **1** a device for raising weights, etc., usually consisting of a horizontal cylinder or barrel turned by a crank, lever, etc., upon which something like a cable winds
verb **2** to raise or move by means of a windlass
Word history: Middle English from *windel* to wind + *-as* pole (from Scandinavian)

windmill
noun a mill for grinding or pumping, worked by the wind turning a set of arms or sails

window
noun **1** an opening in a wall for letting in light and air and usually having panes of glass
2 *Computers*
a part of the screen, such as the area taken up with the pull-down menu
b the part of a large document currently visible on a screen
Word history: Middle English, from Scandinavian

window-shop
verb to look at articles in shop windows instead of actually buying them
Verb forms: I **window-shopped**, I have **window-shopped**, I am **window-shopping**
Word building: **window-shopper** *noun* **window-shopping** *adjective* **window-shopping** *noun*

windpipe
noun → **trachea**

windscreen
noun the sheet of glass which forms the front window of a motor vehicle

windsock
noun a wind-direction indicator, used at airports and elsewhere, consisting of a long cone of textile material, flown from a mast
Word use: You can also use **airsock, wind cone** or **wind sleeve**.

windsurfer
noun **1** → **sailboard**
2 a person who windsurfs
Word building: **windsurf** *verb*
Word history: Trademark

wind turbine
noun a modern windmill, usually with blades designed like aeroplane wings, which drives a generator to produce electricity when wind turns the blades

windward (<u>wind</u>-wuhd)
adverb **1** towards the wind: *to sail **windward***
adjective **2** facing the wind: *the **windward** side*
Word use: The opposite of this is **leeward**.
Word building: **windward** *noun*

wine
noun an alcoholic drink made from grapes and sometimes from other fruit
Word history: Old English

wine / whine
Don't confuse **wine** with **whine**. When animals like dogs **whine**, they make a noise that means they are unhappy.

wing
noun **1** the part of the body of a bird or insect that is used for flying
2 one of the long, flat parts that project from either side of an aeroplane
3 a part of a building which is joined to the main part: *A new **wing** was added to the school.*
4 a political group within a larger group: *the left **wing** of the Labor Party*
5 one of the two side areas of play in games of football, hockey, soccer and similar sports
6 someone who plays in this place on the field
verb **7** to fly: *The bird **winged** its way home.*
phrase **8 in the wings**, quietly ready to do something when needed
9 on the wing, flying: *birds **on the wing***
Word history: Middle English, from Scandinavian

wink
verb to close and open one eye quickly: *He **winked** at me to show we were friends again.*
Word building: **wink** *noun*
Word history: Old English

winning
adjective **1** being the winner: *the **winning** team*
2 charming: *a **winning** smile*
noun **3 winnings**, something won, especially money: *He counted his **winnings**.*

winnow (<u>win</u>-oh)
verb **1** to free from chaff, dirt, etc., by means of wind or driven air: *to **winnow** grain*
2 to blow upon, as the wind does upon grain in this process
3 to analyse in a critical way: *to **winnow** a mass of statements*
noun **4** a device for winnowing grain, etc.
5 the act of winnowing
Word building: **winnower** *noun*
Word history: Old English, from *wind*[1]

winsome (<u>win</u>-suhm)
adjective pleasing or charming: *a **winsome** smile*
Word building: **winsomeness** *noun*
Word history: Old English, from *wyn* joy + *-sum* -some

winter
noun the coldest season of the year
Word building: **wintry** *adjective*
Word history: Old English

win-win
adjective having to do with a situation in which both parties to a dispute can achieve a satisfactory outcome: *The* ***win-win*** *situation left both parties happy.*

wipe
verb **1** to rub lightly in order to clean or dry (***blot***, ***mop***, ***sponge***, ***swab***, ***towel***)
2 to remove by wiping: *He* ***wiped*** *the crumbs off the chair.*
phrase **3 wipe out**, to destroy or defeat completely (***annihilate***, ***demolish***, ***eradicate***, ***exterminate***)

Word building: **wipe** *noun* **wiper** *noun*
Word history: Old English

wire
noun **1** a long piece of thin metal that can be bent: *a fence made of* ***wire*** *| an electric* ***wire***
2 a hidden microphone that allows others to listen in to a conversation secretly: *The agent got the information by wearing a* ***wire***.
verb **3** to fasten with wire: *He* ***wired*** *the gate to the fence.*
4 to provide with an electric system of wiring such as for lighting

Word history: Old English

wireless
noun an old-fashioned word for **radio**

wireless technology
noun telecommunications technology which does not need telephone lines, cables, etc.

wire tap
noun a telephone tap

Word use: Look up **tap** (definition 2). | You can also use **wiretap**.

wiry
adjective **1** like wire in shape or stiffness: ***wiry*** *grass |* ***wiry*** *hair*
2 thin and strong: *a* ***wiry*** *person*

Adjective forms: **wirier, wiriest**

wisdom
noun **1** the quality of being wise: *There is* ***wisdom*** *in what she says.*
2 knowledge or learning: *Books pass on the* ***wisdom*** *of the past.*

Word use: The opposite of this is **foolishness**.
Word history: Old English

wise
adjective **1** able to judge what is true or right: *a* ***wise*** *person*
2 showing good judgement: *a* ***wise*** *decision* (***level-headed***, ***prudent***, ***sage***, ***sensible***, ***shrewd***)
3 having knowledge or information: *He is* ***wise*** *in the law. | His explanation did not make us any* ***wiser***.

Word history: Old English

wisecrack
noun a smart or amusing remark (***gibe***, ***joke***, ***quip***, ***witticism***)

Word building: **wisecrack** *verb*

wish
verb **1** to want or desire: *I* ***wish*** *to be a concert pianist.*
2 to express a desire for something, sometimes silently: *I* ***wish*** *we could go swimming. | to* ***wish*** *upon a star*
3 to say to as a greeting: *He* ***wished*** *her good morning.*
noun **4** something you wish for: *Did you get your* ***wish****?*
5 the act of wishing: *Shut your eyes and make a* ***wish***

Word history: Old English

wishbone
noun a bone shaped like a Y in the chest of birds such as chickens

Word history: this bone got its name from the belief that when two people pull it apart, the one getting the longer piece will have their wish come true

wishful
adjective **1** having or showing a wish (***desirous***, ***hopeful***)
phrase **2 wishful thinking**, a belief that a thing will happen or be so, based on your hopes rather than on reality

wishy-washy
adjective without strength or force: *a* ***wishy-washy*** *speech*

wisp
noun someone or something that is small or thin: *a* ***wisp*** *of a girl | a* ***wisp*** *of hair | a* ***wisp*** *of smoke*

Word building: **wispy** *adjective* (**wispier, wispiest**)
Word history: Middle English

wisteria (wis-tear-ree-uh)
noun a climbing shrub, with handsome bunches of purple or white flowers, often used to cover verandahs and walls

Word history: after Caspar *Wistar*, 1761–1818, US anatomist

wistful
adjective thoughtful in a sad way: *a* ***wistful*** *stare*

Word building: **wistfully** *adjective* **wistfulness** *noun*
Word history: obsolete *wist* attentive

wit
noun **1** the ability to be amusing in a clever way
2 someone with this ability
3 wits, mental abilities or common sense: *She always has her* ***wits*** *about her.*

Word history: Old English

witch
noun **1** a woman who practises magic, especially to do evil
2 an ugly or bad old woman

Word history: from Old English word meaning 'practise sorcery'

witch / which
Don't confuse **witch** with **which**. **Which** is a pronoun that introduces a question:
Which witch did you like best?

witchcraft
noun the sorcery or magic that a witch uses

witchdoctor
noun (in some societies) a person supposed to have magical powers for healing or harming others (***medicine man***)

witchetty grub
noun a large, white, wood-boring grub that can be eaten

Word use: You can also use **witchety grub.**
Word history: from Adnyamathanha, an Australian Aboriginal language of the Flinders Ranges area in South Australia

witch-hunt
noun **1** in the past, the searching out of people to be accused of, and killed for, witchcraft
2 a strong effort to discover and accuse people of disloyalty, dishonesty, etc., usually based on slight, doubtful or unimportant evidence

with
preposition **1** in the company of: *I will go **with** you.*
2 in some particular relation to: *to mix water **with** milk | to talk **with** a friend*
3 showing agreement or similarity: *in harmony **with** him*
4 *Colloquial* understanding the thinking of: *Are you **with** me?*
5 in the same direction as: ***with** the stream*
6 by the use or means of: *Cut it **with** a knife.*
7 at the same time as: *to rise **with** the dawn*
8 against: *to wage a war **with** evil*
9 in the care or keeping of: *Leave it **with** me.*
phrase **10 be** (or **get**) **with it,**
a to be or become aware of a situation: ***Get with it.** He's already got a girlfriend.*
b to concentrate: *I can't **get with it** today.*
c to be or become fashionable: *She **is with it** doing that new dancing.*

Word history: Old English

withdraw
verb **1** to move back or away: *She **withdrew** to the kitchen.* (***retire***, ***retreat***)
2 to take back: *I **withdraw** what I said about you.*
3 to take out: *to **withdraw** some money from the bank* (***extract***, ***remove***)

Verb forms: I **withdrew**, I have **withdrawn**, I am **withdrawing**
Word building: **withdrawal** *noun*

withdrawn
verb **1** past participle of **withdraw**
adjective **2** shy, or modest

wither
verb to become dried up and shrunken: *The grass **withered** in the hot sun. | Our friendship has **withered** away.* (***atrophy***, ***contract***, ***dwindle***, ***shrink***, ***shrivel***)

Word history: Middle English; perhaps variant of *weather*

withers
plural noun the highest part of a horse's or other animal's back, behind the neck

withhold
verb to hold back: *They will **withhold** payment until they are satisfied with the goods.*

Verb forms: I **withheld**, I have **withheld**, I am **withholding**
Word history: Middle English

within
preposition **1** inside: *The bookmark goes **within** the book.*
2 inside yourself: *He rejoiced **within**.*
3 in or into the interior of: ***within** a city*
4 not beyond: ***within** view*

Word history: Old English

without
preposition **1** lacking or not with: ***without** help*
2 free from: ***without** pain*
adverb **3** lacking: *We must take this or go **without**.*

Word building: **without** *adjective*
Word history: Old English

withstand
verb to stand or hold firm against: *She **withstood** his requests for more money. | This material will **withstand** heavy use.* (***counter***, ***defy***, ***oppose***, ***resist***)

Verb forms: I **withstood**, I have **withstood**, I am **withstanding**
Word history: Old English

witness
noun **1** someone who sees or hears something by being present: *I was a **witness** to the accident.*
2 a person who gives evidence, especially in a law court
verb **3** to be present at and see: *We all **witnessed** the fight.* (***notice***, ***observe***, ***see***, ***view***, ***watch***)

Word history: Old English *witnes*

witticism
noun a joke or a witty remark (***gibe***, ***pun***, ***quip***, ***wisecrack***)

Word history: from *witty*; modelled on *criticism*

witty
adjective amusingly clever in what you write or say

Adjective forms: **wittier**, **wittiest**
Word building: **wittily** *adverb* **wittiness** *noun*
Word history: Old English, from

wives
noun plural of **wife**

wizard
noun **1** someone who practises magic (***enchanter***, ***magician***, ***sorcerer***, ***warlock***)
2 someone who is very good at something: *a **wizard** at maths* (***expert***, ***genius***)

Word building: **wizardry** *noun*
Word history: Middle English, from *wys* wise + *-ard*

wizened (wiz-uhnd)
adjective dried up and shrunken: *the **wizened** face of an old man*

wobbegong (wob-ee-gong)
noun a shark, of the eastern Australian coast, having a flattened body and mottled skin and living on the bottom of the sea

Word history: from an Australian Aboriginal language, perhaps of eastern NSW

wobble
verb to move or make move unsteadily from side to side: *The cup **wobbled** and then fell off the table. | She **wobbled** her loose tooth.* (***lurch***, ***reel***, ***shake***, ***sway***)

Word building: **wobble** *noun* **wobbly** *adjective* (**wobblier**, **wobbliest**)
Word history: Low German

woe
noun great sadness
Word building: **woeful** *adjective*
Word history: Old English

woebegone (woh-buh-gon)
adjective sad or miserable: *a **woebegone** look*

wog[1]
noun someone from another country, especially someone with olive-brown skin
Word use: The use of this word will offend people.
Word history: perhaps short for *golliwog*, a black-faced doll

wog[2]
noun Australian Colloquial a germ that causes a sickness: *Almost everyone in our class has caught the **wog**.*

wok
noun a large, round-bottomed frying pan used in Asian cookery
Word history: from Cantonese word meaning 'cooking pot'

woke
verb past tense of **wake**[1]

woken
verb past participle of **wake**[1]

wolf
noun **1** a large, wild, flesh-eating dog-like animal of Europe, Asia and North America
verb **2** *Colloquial* to eat hungrily
phrase **3 cry wolf,** to give false alarms continually
Noun forms: The plural is **wolves**.
Word history: Old English

wolves (woolvz)
noun plural of **wolf**

woman (woom-uhn)
noun an adult, female human being
Noun forms: The plural is **women** (wim-uhn).
Word building: **womanhood** *noun* **womanish** *adjective* **womanly** *adjective*
Word history: Old English from *wīf* female + *man* human being

womb (woohm)
noun → **uterus**
Word history: Old English

wombat
noun a short-legged, heavy marsupial that burrows holes
Word history: from Dharug, an Australian Aboriginal language spoken by the people living near Sydney Cove in the early days of European settlement

women (wim-uhn)
noun plural of **woman**

women's business
noun **1** in Aboriginal societies, matters, especially cultural traditions, which are the exclusive domain of women
2 *Colloquial (humorous)* activities seen to be especially favoured or understood by women
Word use: You can also use **secret women's business**.

women's liberation
noun a movement seeking to end inequality between the sexes
Word use: You can also use the colloquial term **women's lib**.

won (wun)
verb past tense and past participle of **win**

wonder (wun-duh)
verb **1** to think about with curiosity or surprise: *I **wonder** why he decided to go.*
2 to think about with admiration: *I **wonder** at his courage.*
noun **3** something strange and surprising: *It is a **wonder** that you arrived on time.*
4 the feeling caused by something strange and surprising: *He looked at her work with **wonder**.*
Word history: Old English

wonder / wander
Don't confuse **wonder** with **wander**. To **wander** (rhymes with *yonder*) is to go about with no definite aim or fixed course.

wonderful
adjective extremely good or excellent (***astonishing***, ***fabulous***, ***incredible***, ***marvellous***, ***phenomenal***)
Word history: Old English

wondrous (wun-druhs)
adjective **1** wonderful or marvellous
adverb **2** in a wonderful or surprising degree
Word history: variant of Middle English word meaning 'wonderful'

wonky (wong-kee)
adjective Colloquial **1** shaky or unsound
2 to one side
3 unwell or upset
Word history: variant of British dialect *wanky*, from Old English word meaning 'shaky', 'unsteady'

wont (wohnt)
Old-fashioned
adjective **1** accustomed or used: *She is **wont** to speak her mind.*
noun **2** custom or habit: *She spoke her mind, as is her **wont**.*
Word history: from Old English word meaning 'be accustomed'

won't
contraction of **will not**

Look up **contractions in grammar**.

won ton (won ton)
noun a small ball of spicy pork wrapped in thin dough, usually boiled and served in soup in Chinese cooking
Word history: from a Cantonese word meaning 'pastry'

woo
verb Old-fashioned to try to win the love of, especially so as to marry: *He is **wooing** the girl next door.*
Word building: **wooer** *noun*
Word history: Old English

wood
noun **1** the hard substance that makes up most of the trunk and branches of a tree
2 this substance cut up and used in various ways, such as building houses and making furniture
3 an area covered thickly with trees: *I went for a walk in the **wood**.*
4 a golf club with a wooden head

Word use: When wood is sawn or shaped into pieces for building it is called **timber**.
Word history: Old English

wood / would

Don't confuse **wood** with **would. Would** is an auxiliary verb, so you will always find it used with another verb:

I would like to help you.

I would have helped you if you'd asked me.

woodblock
noun **1** a block of wood with a raised design on it for printing from
2 a print made in this way

Word use: You can also use **woodcut**.

woodchip
noun **1** (*plural*) small pieces of wood, made by mechanically reducing trees to fragments for later industrial use
adjective **2** having to do with an industry, company, etc., which deals in woodchips

Word building: **woodchipping** *noun*

wooden
adjective **1** made of wood: *a **wooden** table*
2 stiff and clumsy: *a **wooden** way of walking*
3 without interest or liveliness: *a **wooden** stare | a **wooden** performance*

woodpecker
noun a bird with a hard, strong beak for digging into wood after insects

woodwind
noun the group of musical wind instruments that includes the flutes, clarinets, oboes and bassoons

woodwork
noun **1** things made of wood
2 the making of wooden things: *He is good at **woodwork**.*

Word use: Another name for definition 2 is **carpentry**.

wool
noun **1** the soft, curly hair of sheep and some other animals
2 thread or cloth made from sheep's wool: *a dress of **wool***

Word history: Old English

wool clip
noun the amount of wool yielded from the yearly shearing season, by a farm, district, etc.

Word use: You can also use **clip**.

woollen
adjective **1** made or consisting of wool
2 having to do with wool, products made of wool, or their manufacture
noun **3 woollens**, knitted woollen clothing, especially jumpers

woolly
adjective **1** made of wool or something similar: *a **woolly** jumper*
2 not clear or firm: ***woolly** thinking* (***indefinite, uncertain, vague***)

woolshed
noun a large shed for shearing and baling wool

woomera (woom-uh-ruh)
noun a stick with a notch at one end, traditionally used by Aboriginal people to throw spears

Word history: from Dharug, an Australian Aboriginal language spoken by the people living near Sydney Cove in the early days of European settlement

Woop Woop
noun an imaginary remote or backward town or district

woozy (wooh-zee)
adjective Colloquial **1** muddled, or stupidly confused
2 dizzy, nauseous, etc.
3 slightly drunk

Word building: **woozily** *adverb* **wooziness** *noun*

word
noun **1** a sound or group of sounds which stands for an idea, action or object, and which is one of the building blocks of a language
2 the group of letters you use to write down these sounds
3 speech or talk: *He said a quick **word** about his favourite topic.*
4 an utterance or remark: *I will give you a **word** of warning.*
5 a promise: *He gave his **word**.* (***oath, pact, pledge, vow, word of honour***)
6 order or command: *Start moving when I give the **word**.*
7 news: *I have just got **word** of the accident.*
verb **8** to choose words to express: *She **worded** her speech very carefully.*
phrase **9 eat your words,** *Colloquial* to take back something you have said or written
10 have words with, to argue with
11 in a word,
a briefly, or in short
b as a summary
12 in so many words, so openly and plainly that there should be no mistake
13 the last word,
a the final remark in an argument
b the very latest or best: *This computer is **the last word** in modern technology.*
14 word for word,
a of a repeated message, report, etc., using exactly the same words as the original
b translated exactly, word by word, instead of thinking of the general sense of the whole

Word history: Old English

wordbreak
noun the dividing of a word between the end of one line and the beginning of the next, when it is too long to fit completely on the first line

When the word you want to write is too long for the rest of the line, you can often divide it into two, and put the second part on the next line. You simply put a hyphen after the first part to show that there's more to come on the next line.

(continued)

wordbreak *(continued)*

Where to break words

It's important to divide words without misleading your reader. Don't, for example, divide *mother* into *moth-er*! Some of the guiding rules are:

1 Don't divide words of less than six letters.
2 Don't divide words of one syllable.
3 Try to have a least three letters of the word on each line.
4 Don't separate vowels which are part of the same syllable. For example, *crea-ture* is fine, but *cre-ature* is not.
5 Try to have a consonant at the beginning of the second part — except when it's misleading, as with a word like *dra-wing*.
6 Only break hyphenated words at the hyphen.

wording
noun the way you use words: *He used polite* ***wording*** *in his letter.*

word order
noun the order of words in a sentence

In English, getting the words of a sentence in the right order is important. For example, the normal position for the subject of a sentence is before the verb:

subject verb
You will go.

Changing the order of the words turns the statement into a question:

Will you go?

There are some adverbs too, like *hardly* and *scarcely*, that change the usual order of words in a sentence:

Scarcely had you gone when…

And words like *only*, which are used to emphasise other words in a sentence, must be carefully placed or they will have the wrong effect. For more information, look up **hardly, scarcely** and **only**.

word processor
noun a computer program used for writing and formatting documents, letters, etc.
Word building: **word processing** *noun*

word wrap
noun Computers the automatic formatting of lines of text to fit onto a screen

wordy
adjective using too many words: *a* ***wordy*** *explanation* (***lengthy***, ***long-drawn-out***, ***longwinded***, ***rambling***, ***tedious***)
Adjective forms: **wordier, wordiest**
Word use: The opposite of this is **succinct** or **brief**.
Word building: **wordiness** *noun*

wore
verb past tense of **wear**

wore / war

Don't confuse **wore** with **war**, which is any fighting or conflict between countries.

work
noun **1** effort made by the body or mind to do something: *It will take hours of* ***work*** *to finish this job.* (***exertion***, ***industry***, ***labour***)
2 something that needs to be done by effort: *I've brought some* ***work*** *home from school.*
3 something made by effort: *a* ***work*** *of art | a musical* ***work***
4 a job by which you earn money: *Her* ***work*** *is teaching.* (***occupation***, ***position***, ***profession***)
verb **5** to do work: *You should* ***work*** *when you're in class.* (***labour***, ***slave***, ***slog***, ***toil***)
6 to have a job by which you earn money: *She* ***works*** *in a bookshop.*
7 to act or operate properly: *This toaster isn't* ***working***.
8 to use or manage: *Do you know how to* ***work*** *this machine?*
phrase **9 at work,**
a at the place of your employment
b in the middle of working: *Danger, men* ***at work***.
c operating: *Strange forces have been* ***at work*** *in the neighbourhood.*
10 make short work of, to finish quickly
11 the works, the whole lot
12 work at, to keep on making an effort to achieve or master
13 work back, *Australian* to work longer than usual at your place of employment
14 work in,
a to put in or introduce gradually: *to* ***work in*** *the butter and sugar*
b to find room for or fit in: *Take the existing program and see if you can* ***work*** *this new material* ***in***.
15 work out,
a to solve, find out or calculate by thinking: *to* ***work out*** *an answer | to* ***work out*** *a sum* (***crack***, ***figure out***, ***puzzle out***, ***resolve***)
b to turn out: *I hope our plan* ***works out*** *all right.*
c to train or practise a sport or exercise: *He* ***works out*** *every morning.*
16 work up,
a to excite the feelings of: *She* ***worked*** *herself* ***up*** *into a rage.*
b to make increase: *I've* ***worked up*** *an appetite with all this running.*
c to move gradually towards: *I'm* ***working up*** *to telling you the surprise.*
Word history: from Old English word meaning 'act', 'deed'

workable
adjective able to be put into operation: *a* ***workable*** *machine | a* ***workable*** *plan* (***feasible***, ***possible***, ***practicable***, ***viable***)

workaday
adjective **1** working, practical or everyday: ***workaday*** *shoes*
2 dull and ordinary: *a* ***workaday*** *mind* (***commonplace***, ***humdrum***)

worker
noun **1** someone or something that works
2 someone who has a particular job: *an office* ***worker***
3 someone who is employed in a factory or does work with their hands: *The* ***workers*** *here get on well with the bosses.*

workers compensation
noun **1** an insurance scheme for employers to cover compensation to employees suffering injury or disease either at work or in travel to and from work: *The boss had set up* ***workers compensation*** *years before.*
2 a payment made under such a scheme: *She is hoping the* ***workers compensation*** *comes through quickly.*

Word use: You can also use the colloquial term **workers comp**.

workflow
noun the chain of events in a work process

workforce
noun all the people in a country, city, etc., who are employed

Word use: You can also use **work force**.

working capital
noun **1** the amount of money you need to carry on a business
2 *Accounting* your current assets minus your current liabilities

working class
noun the class of people made up mainly of manual workers and labourers (***proletariat***, ***the masses***)

work-in-progress
noun work that is being done at the present time

work-out
noun **1** a trial match, race, etc.
2 energetic physical exercise: *He has a* ***work-out*** *in the gym once a week.*

workplace
noun a place of employment

workplace agreement
noun a written formal agreement made between an employer and employees at a particular workplace about pay and other employment conditions

workshop
noun **1** a room or building in which work, especially mechanical work, is carried on, thought of as smaller than a factory
2 a group meeting to exchange ideas and study techniques, skills, etc.: *a theatre* ***workshop***

world
noun **1** the earth and everything that lives on it (***globe***)
2 a particular area of life or interest: *the animal* ***world*** | *the* ***world*** *of sport* (***domain***, ***field***, ***realm***, ***sphere***, ***territory***)
phrase **3 for all the world,**
a for any reason, no matter how great: *He wouldn't come* ***for all the world.***
b exactly or in every way: *He looks* ***for all the world*** *like a rock star.*
4 on top of the world, as delighted as you could possibly be
5 out of this world, excellent or as good as you could imagine
6 think the world of, to think very highly of

Word history: Old English

world-class
adjective among the best in the world: *a* ***world-class*** *athlete*

worldly
adjective **1** interested only in the things that concern us in our life on earth, rather than in any other life after death
2 used to the ways of the world

Adjective forms: **worldlier**, **worldliest**
Word building: **worldliness** *noun*

world music
noun the popular or folk music of different cultures and nationalities from around the world, outside the tradition of Western rock or pop music

World Wide Web
noun a large-scale hypertext information system, available on the internet

Word use: You can also use **the web** or the abbreviation **www**.

worm (werm)
noun **1** a long, thin animal with a soft body and no legs, that moves by slithering along
2 someone whom you do not respect
3 *Computers* a program which, once it is loaded on a computer, does damage by copying itself until it takes up all the available memory, bringing the whole system to a standstill
verb **4** to creep or crawl like a worm: *to* ***worm*** *your way under a hedge*
5 to free from worms: *to* ***worm*** *a cat*
phrase **6 a can of worms**, *Colloquial* a difficult or complicated situation
7 worm into, to get by roundabout means: *to* ***worm into*** *a teacher's good books*
8 worm out of,
a to get, by persistent roundabout methods: *to* ***worm*** *a secret* ***out of*** *a person*
b to avoid: *to* ***worm out of*** *your responsibilities*

Word history: from Old English word meaning 'worm', 'serpent'

worn
verb **1** past participle of **wear**
adjective **2** shabby or damaged by wear or use
3 very tired (***bushed***, ***exhausted***, ***fatigued***, ***weary***)

> **worn / warn**
> Don't confuse **worn** with **warn**. To **warn** is to tell someone of possible danger.

worrisome (<u>wu</u>-ree-suhm)
adjective worrying or annoying

worry (<u>wu</u>-ree)
verb **1** to feel anxious or upset: *Our parents* ***worry*** *if we stay out late.* (***fret***, ***fuss***)
2 to bother or annoy: *Don't* ***worry*** *me now, I'm busy.* (***hassle***, ***irritate***, ***upset***)
3 to grab with the teeth and shake: *The cat is* ***worrying*** *a mouse.*

Verb forms: I **worried**, I have **worried**, I am **worrying**
Word history: from Old English word meaning 'strangle'

worse
adjective **1** bad to a greater degree: *My cold is* ***worse*** *than it was yesterday.*
noun **2** someone or something which is worse
adverb **3** in a more unpleasant, evil or severe way

phrase **4 for the worse**, in a worse condition: *a change **for the worse***
5 none the worse for, not harmed by: *He's **none the worse for** a night out on the mountain.*
6 the worse for wear,
a shabby: *That sofa is **the worse for wear**.*
b *Colloquial* drunk
7 worse off, less fortunate or well placed

Word use: This is a form of the adjective **bad**.
Word history: Old English *wyrsa*

worsen
verb to become worse (***decline***, ***degenerate***, ***deteriorate***, ***go to the pack***)

Word use: The opposite of this is **improve**.

worship
noun **1** great love, honour, and respect
2 the showing of deep honour and respect for God in a ceremony or prayer: *to go to church for evening **worship***

Word building: **worship** *verb* (**worshipped, worshipping**)
Word history: Old English *weorth* worth + *-scipe* -ship

worst
adjective bad to the greatest degree: *the **worst** winter for years*

Word use: This is a form of the adjective **bad**.
Word building: **worst** *adverb*
Word history: Old English *wurresta*

worsted (woos-tuhd)
noun **1** a firmly twisted yarn or thread spun from combed wool, used for weaving, etc.
2 wool cloth woven from such yarns, having a hard, smooth surface, and no nap
adjective **3** consisting or made of worsted

Word history: named after Middle English *Worsted*, parish in Norfolk, England (now Worstead)

worth
adjective **1** equal in value to: *It isn't **worth** $10.*
2 good enough for: *a place **worth** visiting*
noun **3** value or importance: *a painting of great **worth***
4 quantity or amount: *$10 **worth** of petrol*

Word building: **worthless** *adjective*
Word history: Old English

worthwhile
adjective useful or good enough to spend time on: *a **worthwhile** hobby*

worthy (wer-dhee)
adjective **1** deserving respect or admiration: *a **worthy** effort*
phrase **2 worthy of**, good enough for: *a meal **worthy of** a king*

Adjective forms: **worthier, worthiest**
Word building: **worthiness** *noun*

would (wood)
verb **1** the past tense of **will**[1]
2 specially used:
a in expressing a wish: *I **would** it were true.*
b used to express condition: *I **would** have come had you asked me.*
c often used to make a statement or question less direct or blunt: *That **would** scarcely be fair. | **Would** you be so kind?*

Word history: Old English *wolde*

would / wood
Look up **wood / would**.

would-be
adjective wishing or planning to be: *a **would-be** actor*

wouldn't
contraction of **would not**

Look up **contractions in grammar**.

would've
contraction of **would have**

When you say **would've** it may sound like the words 'would of', but in fact it is short for 'would have'. While it is correct to use **would've**, it is wrong to use **would of** because **would** is never followed by **of**.
Look up **contractions in grammar**.

wound[1] (woohnd)
noun **1** an injury, especially a cut
verb **2** to cause such an injury in someone
3 to hurt someone's feelings (***offend***, ***upset***)

Word history: Old English *wund*

wound[2] (wownd)
verb past tense and past participle of **wind**[2]

wove (wohv)
verb past tense and occasional past participle of **weave**

woven (woh-vuhn)
verb usual past participle of **weave**

wow factor
noun Colloquial a quality of a product, person, entertainment, etc., which excites instant admiration: *A large part of the teen idol's **wow factor** was his style of dress and dance routines.*

wowser (wow-zuh)
noun Australian, NZ Colloquial a person who does not drink alcohol or indulge in any other worldly pleasures and doesn't want others to enjoy these things either

Word history: perhaps British dialect *wow* to make a complaint; whine; popularly supposed to be an acronym of *w(e) o(nly) w(ant) s(ocial) e(vils) r(emedied)*, a slogan invented by John Norton, Australian journalist and politician, 1862–1916

wraith (rayth)
noun **1** a ghostlike appearance of a living person, supposed to be seen just before, or as a sign of, that person's death
2 a ghost (***apparition***, ***phantom***, ***spectre***, ***spook***)
3 someone or something pale, thin and not solid

wrangle (rang-guhl)
verb to argue or quarrel noisily (***bicker***, ***differ***, ***disagree***, ***dispute***)

Word building: **wrangle** *noun*
Word history: from Low German word meaning 'struggle', 'make uproar'

wrap
verb **1** to fold paper or material around: *I'll **wrap** the parcel.* (***enclose***, ***envelop***, ***shroud***, ***wreathe***)
2 to fold so as to cover: ***Wrap** the blanket round you to keep warm.*

noun **3** a scarf, shawl, etc.
4 a food item in which various fillings are wrapped in a base such as lavash, pita bread, etc.

Verb forms: I **wrapped**, I have **wrapped**, I am **wrapping**
Word history: blend of obsolete *wry* to cover, and *lap*[2]

wrap / rap

Don't confuse **wrap** with **rap.** To **rap** something is to strike it with a quick light blow. **Rap** is also a type of music.

wrapped / rapped / rapt

Don't confuse **wrapped** with **rapped** or **rapt.**

Rapped is the past form of the verb **rap**, to hit or knock sharply or lightly:

She rapped my knuckles.

If you are **rapt** in your own thoughts, you are thinking so deeply that you're unaware of what is happening around you.

Note that **wrapped** implies being wrapped up in someone or something and **rapt** describes being enraptured by someone or something. When used in this way, both these words are part of everyday language and you should try to avoid them in your essay writing.

wrapper
noun covering: *a bread **wrapper***

wrath (roth)
noun anger or revenge

Word building: **wrathful** *adjective*
Word history: from Old English word meaning 'wroth'

wreak (reek)
verb to carry out or inflict: *The storm **wreaked** havoc on the garden.*

Word history: Old English *wrecan*

wreak / reek

Don't confuse **wreak** with **reek,** which is to give off a terrible smell.

wreath (reeth)
noun flowers and leaves tied together to make a ring

Word history: Old English *wrǣth*

wreathe (reedh)
verb to surround: *Mist **wreathed** the valley.*

wreck
verb **1** to ruin or destroy (***mar***, ***sabotage***, ***spoil***, ***vandalise***)
noun **2** something, especially a ship, that has been wrecked

Word building: **wrecker** *noun*
Word history: Middle English, from Scandinavian

wreckage
noun the broken parts of a wreck

wren
noun a very small bird with a long, upright tail

Word history: Old English *wrenna*

wrench
verb **1** to twist roughly: *to **wrench** the door open | to **wrench** your ankle*
noun **2** a sudden, sharp twist
3 a type of spanner

Word history: from Old English word meaning 'twist', 'turn'

wrest (rest)
verb to pull or grab roughly: *to **wrest** the gun from his grasp*

Word history: Old English *wrǣstan*

wrest / rest

Don't confuse **wrest** with **rest,** which is to relax and take life easy.

wrestle
verb **1** to struggle with someone and try to throw them to the ground (***fight***, ***grapple***, ***scuffle***, ***tussle***)
2 to struggle or make a great effort: *to **wrestle** with a difficult problem* (***battle***, ***fight***)

Word building: **wrestler** *noun*
Word history: Middle English, from *wrest*

wrestling (res-ling)
noun **1** an exercise or sport in which two people struggle hand to hand, each trying to throw or force the other to the ground
2 the act of someone who wrestles

wretch
noun someone who is very miserable and unfortunate

Word history: from Old English word meaning 'exile', 'adventurer'

wretch / retch

Don't confuse **wretch** with **retch,** which is to try to vomit.

wretched (rech-uhd)
adjective **1** poor, miserable and pitiful: *a **wretched** slum* (***dismal***, ***pathetic***, ***woeful***)
2 worthless or irritating: *The **wretched** door won't open.*

wriggle
verb **1** to twist and turn like a snake or worm (***fidget***, ***squirm***, ***toss and turn***, ***writhe***)
phrase **2 get a wriggle on,** to hurry up

Word building: **wriggly** *adjective* (**wrigglier**, **wriggliest**)
Word history: Middle Low German

wright (ruyt)
noun Old-fashioned a worker who makes things

Word use: Nowadays you will only find this as an ending on words like **wheelwright** and **playwright**.

wright / right / write / rite

Don't confuse **wright** with **right, write** or **rite.**

If you get an answer **right** then it is correct. If an action is **right**, it is thought to be good or acceptable. Your **right** hand is the opposite of your left hand.

(continued)

wright / right / write / rite *(continued)*

To **write** is to form letters or words with a pen or something similar. You **write** a poem when you create it using words.

A **rite** is a ceremony, often a religious one, as in *the holy rite of baptism.*

wring
verb to twist and squeeze: *to **wring** water out of the floor mop | to **wring** your hands in grief*
Verb forms: I **wrung**, I have **wrung**, I am **wringing**
Word building: **wringer** *noun*
Word history: Old English *wringan*

wring / ring

Don't confuse **wring** with **ring**.

You wear a **ring** on your finger.

Bells **ring** when they give out a clear musical sound.

When you **ring** someone, you telephone them.

wrinkle
noun a crease on something that is usually smooth (***crinkle***, ***fold***, ***furrow***, ***ridge***)
Word building: **wrinkle** *verb*
Word history: Old English *gewrinclod* serrate

wrist
noun the joint where your hand meets your arm
Word history: Old English

writ (rit)
noun Law a written order issued in connection with a judgement in a law court (***decree***, ***order***, ***summons***, ***warrant***)
Word history: Old English

write
verb **1** to form letters or words with a pen, pencil, or something similar: *to **write** on the blackboard*
2 to compose or create using words: *to **write** a poem* (***dash off***, ***draft***, ***pen***, ***set down***)
3 to write a letter and send it: *I **wrote** to my sister last week.*
4 (of a computer) to copy (information) from its primary storage area to a secondary device such as a magnetic tape or disk
phrase **5 write down,**
a to put down in writing
b to harm by writing something nasty about
6 write down to, to write in a simple way so it can be easily understood
7 write off,
a to cancel: *to **write off** an entry in an account*
b to treat as a loss that cannot be recovered
c to consider as dead
8 write out,
a to put in writing
b to write in full or in its complete form
c to write so much that there is nothing left to write
9 write up,
a to write out in full or in detail: *to **write up** an essay from notes*
b to bring up to date: *to **write up** a diary*
c to bring to the notice of the public by writing
d to praise in writing
Verb forms: I **wrote**, I have **written**, I am **writing**
Word building: **writer** *noun* **writing** *noun*
Word history: Old English *wrītan*

write-off
noun Colloquial a car that has been so badly smashed that it can't be repaired

writhe (ruyth)
verb to twist, as if in pain or embarrassment (***squirm***, ***wriggle***)
Word history: from Old English word meaning 'twist', 'wind'

writing process
noun the process of putting your ideas on paper. The main stages you go through when you do this are brainstorming, drafting, revising and proofreading, and publishing your finished work.

written
verb past participle of **write**

wrong
adjective **1** bad or evil: *It is **wrong** to tell lies.*
2 not correct: *the **wrong** answer*
verb **3** to hurt or treat unfairly
phrase **4 get on the wrong side of,** to bring the anger or disfavour of upon yourself: *to **get on the wrong side of** my father*
5 get someone wrong, to misunderstand: *I was so flustered, I **got him** all **wrong**.*
6 in the wrong,
a guilty: *You should say sorry because you are **in the wrong**.*
b mistaken or in error
Word building: **wrongly** *adverb*
Word history: Old English *wrang*, from Scandinavian

wrong-foot
verb **1** (in various sports, as football, tennis, etc.) to trick (an opponent) into moving the wrong way
2 to catch unprepared: *They **wrong-footed** the celebrity when they asked why she felt the need for 2000 outfits.*

wrote (roht)
verb past tense of **write**

wrote / rote

Don't confuse **wrote** with **rote**. When you learn something **by rote**, you repeat it over and over again until you memorise it, but you don't try to understand what it means.

wrought (rawt)
verb **1** *Old-fashioned past tense and past participle of* **work**
adjective **2** made or formed by manufacture
3 produced or shaped by beating with a hammer, etc.
4 ornamented or elaborated: *a highly **wrought** design*

wrought iron
noun a fairly pure form of iron which contains almost no carbon, which is easily forged, welded, etc., and which does not harden when suddenly cooled

wrung (rung)
verb past tense and past participle of **wring**

wrung / rung

Don't confuse **wrung** with **rung**, which is a past form of the verb **ring**, to make clear musical sounds. It is the past participle:

They have rung the bell but no-one's answering.

wry (ruy)
adjective **1** showing displeasure or disgust: *She made a **wry** face as she tasted the soup.*
2 crooked or twisted: *a **wry** neck*

Adjective forms: **wrier, wriest**
Word history: Old English *wrīgian* swerve

wry / rye

Don't confuse **wry** with **rye**. **Rye** is a grain like wheat, that is ground into flour.

wurley (wer-lee)
noun an Aboriginal hut or shelter made of boughs, leaves and plaited grass

Word use: You can also use **wurlie**.
Word history: from Kaurna, an Australian Aboriginal language of the Adelaide region

wuss (woos)
noun Colloquial a weak, cowardly person

Word building: **wussy** *adjective*
Word history: perhaps blend of *woman* and *puss*

X-axis
noun the horizontal axis in a two-dimensional Cartesian coordinate system

X chromosome
noun one of two sex chromosomes controlling sex determination, often paired with a Y chromosome. In humans and most mammals, the XX pairing controls femaleness and the XY pairing controls maleness; in poultry and some insects the opposite is true.

Word use: Look up **chromosome**.

xenophobia (zen-uh-foh-bee-uh)
noun the fear or hatred of foreigners or strangers

Word building: **xenophobe** *noun* **xenophobic** *adjective*

xerox (zear-roks)
noun a copy of a document, etc., made by a machine using a special photographic process

Word history: Trademark

X-ray
noun **1** a ray that can pass through something solid **2** a photograph of the inside of someone's body, used by doctors to help diagnose disease
verb **3** to make a photograph with an X-ray

Word history: so called because their nature was not known, *X* being a symbol generally used to indicate this

X-ray crystallography
noun the study of a crystalline substance by observing diffraction patterns which occur when a beam of X-rays is passed through it

X-ray tube
noun a tube with a vacuum inside in which a heavy metal target is bombarded with a high-velocity stream of electrons to produce X-rays

xylophone (zuy-luh-fohn)
noun a musical instrument made of a row of wooden bars of different lengths which you hit with small, wooden hammers

Yy

yabber
Colloquial
verb **1** to talk or converse
noun **2** talk or conversation
Word history: perhaps from Wuywurrung, an Australian Aboriginal language of the Melbourne region

yabby
noun a small Australian crayfish
Noun forms: The plural is **yabbies.**
Word history: from Wembawemba, an Australian Aboriginal language of western Victoria

yacht (yot)
noun a sailing boat used for sport or pleasure
Word building: **yachting** *noun*
Word history: early modern Dutch, short for *jaghtschip* ship for chasing

yahoo (yah-hooh, yah-hooh)
noun **1** a rough, coarse or uncouth person
verb **2** to behave in a rough, uncouth manner: *Will you stop **yahooing** around.*
interjection **3** an exclamation expressing enthusiasm or delight
Word history: from *Yahoo*, one of a race of brutes having the form of humans and all their degrading passions (but none of their better qualities), in *Gulliver's Travels* (1726) by Jonathan Swift

yak[1]
noun a long-haired wild ox found in the highlands of the Xizang Autonomous Region (Tibet)
Word history: Tibetan

yak[2]
verb Colloquial to talk on and on without saying anything very important (***chatter***, ***gasbag***, ***gush***, ***rant***, ***rave***)
Verb forms: I **yakked,** I have **yakked,** I am **yakking**
Word building: **yak** *noun*
Word history: imitative

yakka
noun Australian, NZ Colloquial work
Word history: from Yagara, an Australian Aboriginal language of the Brisbane region

yam
noun a potato-like vegetable which grows in warmer parts of the world
Word history: Spanish, ultimately of African origin

Yamatji (yam-uh-jee)
noun an Aboriginal person from mid-western WA
Word use: Compare this with **Anangu**, **Koori**, **Murri**, **Nunga**, **Nyungar** and **Yolngu**.

yank
verb to pull or tug suddenly
Word building: **yank** *noun*

yap
verb to bark with short, high sounds
Verb forms: it **yapped**, it has **yapped**, it is **yapping**
Word building: **yap** *noun* **yapping** *noun*
Word history: imitative

yard[1]
noun **1** a unit of length in the imperial system, equal to about 91 centimetres
2 on a boat or ship, a long, round pole tapering towards each end, slung crosswise to a mast and suspending a sail
Word use: For definition 1 look up **imperial system.**
Word history: Old English *gerd*

yard[2]
noun **1** the fenced ground around a house or other building
2 a fenced or walled area in which any work or business is carried on
Word history: Old English *geard* enclosure

yardarm
noun either end of the yard of a square sail

yardstick
noun **1** a measuring stick one yard long
2 any standard of measurement

yarmulke (yah-mool-kuh)
noun a skullcap worn by some Jewish men and boys, especially on religious occasions
Word use: You can also use **yarmulka**.

yarn
noun **1** nylon, cotton or wool thread used for knitting and weaving
2 a long story, especially one about unlikely happenings
verb **3** to tell such stories
Word history: Old English *gearn*

yaw
verb **1** to move temporarily back and forth from a straight course: *The ship **yawed** to starboard.*
2 to swing around its vertical axis: *The aircraft, because of its design, tends to roll and **yaw**.*

yawn
verb **1** to take a long, deep breath through your mouth, especially when you are bored or tired
2 to be wide open like a mouth: *The cave* ***yawned*** *before them.*

Word building: **yawn** *noun*
Word history: Old English *geonian*

Y-axis
noun the vertical axis in a two-dimensional Cartesian coordinate system

Y chromosome
noun one of a pair with the X chromosome in the male of many animals including humans. In humans and most mammals, the XX pairing controls femaleness and the XY pairing controls maleness; in poultry and some insects the opposite is true.

Word use: Look up **chromosome.**

yeah (yair)
adverb Colloquial yes

yeah-no
interjection Colloquial an expression used to indicate emphatic agreement or polite disagreement, or to downplay the force of what has been put forward by the other speaker: *He had no idea why the teacher looked bamboozled when he said '****Yeah-no****, you're right about that'.*

year
noun **1** the period of twelve months from 1 January to 31 December
2 any period of twelve months: *I saw him a* ***year*** *ago.*

Word history: Old English *gēar*

If you're writing about **years of age**, the punctuation depends on how you've phrased it. There are no hyphens if it is a simple phrase:

He is sixteen years old.

But when the expression becomes a compound noun or adjective, it needs hyphens:

He is a sixteen-year-old. (compound noun)

a group of sixteen-year-olds (compound noun)

a sixteen-year-old student (compound adjective)

It's the same whether you write the number in words or letters:

a 16-year-old student (compound adjective)

Note that in **years of time**, there's no need for an apostrophe if it's more than one year:

two years time

Only when it's a single year do you need an apostrophe:

a year's time

yearling
noun an animal one year old or in the second year of its age

yearly
adjective **1** done, made, happening, appearing, etc., once a year, or every year
2 continuing for a year
adverb **3** once a year or annually
noun **4** a publication appearing once a year

yearn (yern)
verb to want very much: *She* ***yearns*** *to go back to her home town.*

Word building: **yearning** *noun*
Word history: Old English *giernan*

yeast (yeest)
noun a substance which causes the dough to rise when you make bread

Word history: Old English *gist*

yell
verb to call out loudly or shout: *He* ***yelled*** *with pain.* | *She* ***yelled*** *her answer.* (***bawl***, ***bellow***, ***roar***, ***shriek***)

Word building: **yell** *noun*
Word history: Old English *gellan*

yellow
adjective **1** of a bright colour like that of butter, lemons, etc.; between green and orange in the spectrum (***lemon***, ***saffron***)
2 having the almost yellow skin of the Mongoloid peoples
3 *Colloquial* cowardly (***fearful***, ***frightened***, ***gutless***, ***spineless***)
noun **4** a yellow colour
5 a yellow pigment or dye
verb **6** to make or become yellow

Word building: **yellowish** *adjective*
Word history: Old English *geolu*

yellow box
noun a large, spreading type of gum tree, common on the western slopes in eastern Australia, and valued as a source of honey

yellowcake
noun uranium in the form in which it is dug out of the ground

yellow card
noun Sport a yellow card shown by the referee to a player who has committed a foul as an indication that the player has been cautioned

Word use: Compare this with **red card.**

yellow fever
noun an infectious disease found in warm countries, caused by a virus carried by a mosquito and marked by fever, jaundice, etc., and sometimes resulting in death

yelp
verb to give a quick, sharp cry: *The dog* ***yelped*** *when the boy hit him.* (***squawk***, ***squeal***)

Word building: **yelp** *noun*
Word history: Old English *gelpan* boast

yen[1]
noun the unit of currency in Japan

Noun forms: The plural is **yen.**
Word history: Japanese, from Chinese word meaning 'a round thing', 'a dollar'

yen[2]
noun a strong desire or longing (***craving***, ***inclination***, ***wish***)

Word history: Chinese (Cantonese) *yan* craving

yes
adverb **1** a word used to express agreement or assent, or to mark the addition of something emphasising a previous statement: ***Yes****, you may go.* | *I know,* ***yes****, I know.*
noun **2** a reply of 'yes'

Noun forms: The plural is **yeses**.
Word use: The opposite of this is **no**.
Word history: Old English *gēse*; perhaps from *gēa* yes + *sī* be it

yes/no question
noun Grammar a question which can only be answered by 'yes' or 'no', as *Is today Sunday?*

yesterday
noun the day before today

Word building: **yesterday** *adverb*
Word history: Old English *geostrandæg*

yet
adverb **1** at the present time: *Don't leave* ***yet****.*
2 up to a particular time: *He had not* ***yet*** *arrived.*

yeti (yet-ee)
noun a human-like creature supposed to live in the mountains of Tibet (Xizang AR)

Noun forms: The plural is **yetis**.
Word use: Another name is **abominable snowman**.
Word history: Tibetan

yew (yooh)
noun an evergreen, cone-bearing tree found through most of the Northern Hemisphere, of medium height and having dense, dark leaves and a fine-grained wood

Word history: Old English *īw, ēow*

yew / ewe / you
Don't confuse **yew** with **ewe** or **you**.
A **ewe** is a female sheep.
You is the person being spoken to.

yield
verb **1** to produce: *This type of wheat* ***yields*** *a good crop.* (***bear, grow***)
2 to give in or surrender: *I* ***yielded*** *to his argument.* | *The country* ***yielded*** *to the invader.* (***capitulate, submit, succumb***)
noun **3** the quantity of something yielded

Word history: Old English *g(i)eldan* pay

yob
noun Colloquial a rude, uncultivated or aggressive young man

Word use: You can also use **yobbo**.
Word history: perhaps *boy* spelt backwards

yobbo
noun Colloquial **1** an unrefined, uncultured, slovenly young man
2 a hooligan or lout

Word use: The short form is **yob**.

yodel
verb to sing with rapid changes between your normal voice and falsetto (a very high voice), in a manner popular with Swiss mountaineers

Verb forms: I **yodelled**, I have **yodelled**, I am **yodelling**
Word building: **yodel** *noun* **yodeller** *noun*
Word history: German

yoga (yoh-guh)
noun a set of exercises which involve deep breathing and holding unusual body positions, in order to reach a calm, peaceful state of mind

Word history: Hindustani, from Sanskrit word meaning 'union'

yoghurt (yoh-guht, yog-uht)
noun a food made by the controlled curdling of milk

Word use: You can also use **yogurt**.
Word history: Turkish

yogi (yoh-gee)
noun someone who is a master of yoga

Noun forms: The plural is **yogis**.

yoke (yohk)
noun **1** a device consisting of a wooden crosspiece with curved ends fitting over the necks of two oxen pulling a load
2 a shaped piece in a garment, fitted about the neck, shoulders or hips, from which the rest of the garment hangs

Word building: **yoke** *verb*
Word history: Old English *geoc*

yoke / yolk
Don't confuse **yoke** with **yolk**, which is the yellow part of an egg.

yokel (yoh-kuhl)
noun a country person or rustic

yolk (yohk)
noun the yellow part of an egg

Word history: Old English *geolca*, from *geolu* yellow

yolk / yoke
Look up **yoke / yolk**.

Yolngu (yolng-ooh)
noun **1** an Aboriginal person from the north-eastern part of NT
2 a group of closely related Australian Aboriginal languages from the north-eastern part of the NT

Word use: Compare this with **Anangu**, **Koori**, **Murri**, **Nunga**, **Nyungar** and **Yamatji**.

yonder
adjective Old-fashioned being in that place or over there: ***yonder*** *farm on the hill*

Word building: **yonder** *adverb*
Word history: Middle English

yonks
plural noun Colloquial a long, long time: *I haven't seen him for* ***yonks****.*

Word history: possibly a spoonerism of *donkey's years*

yore (yaw)
phrase **of yore**, time long past: *in days of* ***yore***

Word history: Old English *geāra*, perhaps from *gēar* year

Yorkshire pudding

noun a batter baked and served with roast beef

Word history: from *Yorkshire*, a former county in northern England

you

pronoun **1** the personal pronoun used to refer to the person or people spoken to: ***You** are coming.* | *I'll take **you** tomorrow.*
2 anyone; people in general: ***You** can tell he's genuine.* | *It really makes **you** mad when **you** hear that kind of thing.*

You is a second person pronoun. It is used for one person (singular) or more than one (plural). It is also used in both the subjective and objective case. The following are some examples:

You need to be alone for a while (singular subject).

You can come in one at a time, children (plural subject).

I'll call you later, Mum (singular object).

I'll see you tomorrow, everyone (plural object).

For more information, look up **pronouns: personal pronouns.**

you / youse

Youse is a slang form of you and usually refers to more than person. It should be avoided in essays and conversation because it is considered ungrammatical.

For more information about **you**, look up **pronouns: personal pronouns.**

you'd

contraction of **you had** or **you would**

Look up **contractions in grammar.**

you'll

contraction of **you will** or **you shall**

Look up **contractions in grammar.**

young

adjective **1** being in the early stage of life, growth or existence: *a **young** animal* | *a **young** nation* (***childish***, ***junior***, ***juvenile***, ***youthful***)
noun **2** offspring: *Calves are the **young** of cows.* (***descendant***, ***issue***, ***progeny***)
3 young children: *the high spirits of the **young***

Word history: Old English *geong*

youngster

noun a child or young person

your

pronoun the possessive form of **you**, used before a noun: ***your** dog*

Your is a second person singular or plural pronoun. It sometimes called a *determiner* or a *possessive adjective.*

For more information, look up **pronouns: personal pronouns** and **pronouns: possessive pronouns.**

your / you're

Don't confuse **your** with **you're.**

You're is short for **you are.** Look up **contractions in grammar.**

For more information, look up **pronouns: personal pronouns** and **pronouns: possessive pronouns.**

you're

contraction of **you are**

Look up **contractions in grammar.**

yours

pronoun **1** the possessive form of **you** used without a noun following: *The dog is **yours**.*
2 the person(s) or thing(s) belonging to you: ***Yours** is the plate on the left.*

Yours is a second person pronoun in the possessive case. It can be singular or plural.

For more information, look up **pronouns: personal pronouns** and **pronouns: possessive pronouns.**

yourself

pronoun **1** the reflexive form of **you** (singular): *You've cut **yourself**.*
2 a form of **you** (singular) used for emphasis: *You did it **yourself**.*
3 your proper or normal self

For more information, look up **pronouns: reflexive pronouns.**

yourselves

pronoun **1** the reflexive form of **you** (plural): *Have you washed **yourselves**?*
2 a form of **you** (plural) used for emphasis: *You've done it all **yourselves**.*

For more information, look up **pronouns: reflexive pronouns.**

youse (yoohz)

pronoun Colloquial slang form of **you**

youse / use

Look up **use / youse.**

youth

noun **1** a young man
2 young people
3 the time when you are young: *She spent her **youth** on a farm.*

Word building: **youth** *adjective* **youthful** *adjective*
Word history: Old English *geoguth*

youth hostel

noun a cheap place for travellers to stay, intended for young people with not much money

you've

contraction of **you have**

Look up **contractions in grammar.**

yoyo (yoh-yoh)
noun a toy made of two, round, flat-sided pieces of wood or plastic with a length of string wound between them by which you can make it spin up and down

Noun forms: The plural is **yoyos**.
Word history: Trademark

yucky
adjective Colloquial disgusting or unpleasant (***horrible***, ***nasty***, ***repulsive***, ***revolting***, ***vile***)

yum cha
noun a Chinese meal in which you choose small individual serves of many different dishes displayed on trolleys

Word history: from a Cantonese word meaning literally 'drink tea'

yummy
adjective Colloquial delicious or very good to the taste

yuppie
noun Colloquial a young urban professional person, having a good income and luxurious lifestyle: *We don't go to that restaurant anymore — it's always full of* ***yuppies****.*

Word history: *y*(*oung*) *u*(*rban*) *p*(*rofessional*) + *-ie*

Zz

zany
adjective funny in a silly or crazy way: *She has a **zany** sense of humour.*

Adjective forms: **zanier**, **zaniest**
Word history: French, from dialect Italian (Venetian) word meaning 'clown', literally 'Johnny' (Italian *Giovanni* John)

zap
verb Colloquial **1** to destroy with a sudden burst of violence (***annihilate***, ***obliterate***)
2 to move quickly
3 to cook or heat in a microwave oven: *I'll just **zap** this corn.*

zeal (zeel)
noun eagerness or enthusiasm: ***zeal** for the conservation movement*

Word building: **zealous** (zel-uhs) *adjective*
Word history: Middle English, from Latin, from Greek word meaning 'boil'

zealot (zel-uht)
noun **1** someone who shows zeal
2 someone carried away by too much zeal, especially for a religious cause (***fanatic***)

Word building: **zealotry** *noun*
Word history: Late Latin, from Greek word meaning 'zeal'

zebra
noun a wild, horse-like, African animal with a black-and-white striped body

Word history: Italian or Portuguese

zebra crossing
noun a street crossing marked with broad black and white or black and yellow stripes

Zen
noun a Buddhist sect, popular in Japan, which believes in self-contemplation by meditation as the key to the understanding of the universe

Word history: from a Sanskrit word meaning 'religious meditation'

zenith (zen-uhth)
noun **1** the point of the celestial sphere vertically above any place or observer
2 the highest point or state of anything: *She's at the **zenith** of her career.* (***apex***, ***culmination***, ***height***)

Word use: Compare this with **nadir**.
Word history: Middle English, from Medieval Latin, from Arabic

zephyr (zef-uh)
noun a soft, mild breeze

Word history: Latin, from Greek

zeppelin (zep-uh-luhn)
noun a large airship consisting of a long, covered framework containing compartments filled with gas, and various structures for holding the engines, passengers, etc.

Word history: named after French von *Zeppelin*, 1838–1917, German general and airship builder

zero
noun **1** the figure or symbol '0'
2 nothing (***nil***, ***nought***)

Noun forms: The plural is **zeros** or **zeroes**.
Word history: Italian, from Arabic word meaning 'cipher'

zero population growth
noun the minimum population increase needed to maintain the existing level of population

Word use: The abbreviation is **ZPG**.

zest
noun keen enjoyment: *She does her work with **zest**.*

Word building: **zestful** *adjective*
Word history: from French word meaning 'orange or lemon peel' (used for flavouring)

ziggurat (zig-uh-rat)
noun among the ancient Babylonians and Assyrians, a temple in the form of a pyramidal tower, having a broad ascent winding round the outside of the structure and presenting the appearance of a series of terraces or steps

Word use: You can also use **zikkurat** or **zikurat**.
Word history: from Assyrian word meaning 'pinnacle'

zigzag
noun a line with sharp turns first to one side and then to the other

Word building: **zigzag** *verb* (**zigzagged**, **zigzagging**)
Word history: French, from German, reduplication of *Zacke* point, tooth

zinc
noun a bluish-white metal, used in making galvanised iron and some alloys

Word history: German

zine (zeen)
noun Colloquial a magazine, especially one about an alternative subculture, or one in electronic form published on the internet

Word use: You can also use **'zine** or **ezine**.
Word history: short form of *magazine*

zip
noun **1** a fastener consisting of two rows of interlocking metal or plastic teeth and a sliding piece which joins or separates them
verb **2** to fasten with a zip
3 → **compress** (definition 2)

Word use: You can also use **zipper** or **zip-fastener**.
Verb forms: I **zipped**, I have **zipped**, I am **zipping**
Word history: imitative

zip file
noun a compressed version of a computer file

Word use: In filenames you use **.zip**.

zircon (<u>zer</u>-kon)
noun a common mineral, zirconium silicate, occurring in various colours, used industrially as a refractory when opaque and as a gem when transparent

Word history: perhaps from Persian word meaning 'gold-coloured'

zit
noun Colloquial a pimple

zither (<u>zidh</u>-uh)
noun a musical stringed instrument played with a plectrum and your finger tips

Word history: German, from Latin

zodiac (<u>zoh</u>-dee-ak)
noun a part of the sky forming an imaginary belt through which the sun, moon and planets appear to travel, and which contains twelve constellations which are named and used in astrology

Word history: Middle English, from Latin, from Greek word meaning '(circle) of the signs', 'little animals'

zombie
noun **1** a dead body brought back to life by supernatural means
2 someone who looks like a zombie and seems to have no mind

Word history: from West African word meaning 'good-luck fetish'

zone
noun an area marked off and used for a special purpose: *a military **zone***

Word building: **zone** *verb* **zoning** *noun*
Word history: Latin, from Greek word meaning 'girdle'

zonked
adjective Colloquial extremely tired or exhausted: *They were completely **zonked** after gardening all day.*

Word use: You can also use **zonked out**.
Word history: *zonk*, imitative of a heavy fall + *-ed*

zoo
noun a large area of land with enclosed areas or cages where live animals are kept for public viewing

Word history: from *zoological garden*

zoology (zoh-<u>ol</u>-uh-jee)
noun the science or study of animal life

Word history: Neo-Latin or New Greek

zoom
verb **1** to move quickly with a humming sound: *He **zoomed** by on his motorcycle.*
2 to go up suddenly: *The aeroplane **zoomed** into the clouds.*

Word building: **zoom** *noun*
Word history: imitative

zot
verb Colloquial **1** to depart quickly: *She **zotted** off to find her friends.*
2 to knock, or kill: *Quickly, **zot** that fly.*

Verb forms: I **zotted**, I have **zotted**, I am **zotting**

ZPG
noun → **zero population growth**

Word history: abbreviation

zucchini (zuh-<u>kee</u>-nee)
noun a small vegetable marrow, usually picked when very young

Noun forms: The plural is **zucchini** or **zucchinis**.
Word use: Another name is **courgette**.
Word history: Italian

zygote (<u>zuy</u>-goht, <u>zig</u>-oht)
noun a cell produced by the union of two gametes

Word building: **zygotic** *adjective*
Word history: from Greek word meaning 'yoked'

Appendixes

Quick usage troubleshooting guide

between or **among**

Use *between* for two and *among* for more than two. For example:

Geoff and Maria divided the proceeds of the garage sale ***between*** *them.*

The last of the water was divided ***among*** *the four hikers.*

best or **better**

If you are comparing two things, you say one is *better* than the other. If you are comparing more than two things, you say that one is *best*. For example:

Our team proved itself the ***better*** *side on the day.*

Michael Jackson was considered by his fans the ***best*** *singer in the world.*

between you and I/between you and me

Between is a preposition and must be followed in the sentence by *me*. Similarly, *between him and her* is correct, and *between he and she* is incorrect.

can or **may**

Can means *to be able to*. For example:

Once you ***can*** *swim, the beach becomes a safer place.*

May means *to be allowed* or *to be permitted*. For example:

You ***may*** *watch TV after you have finished your homework.*

different from/different to/different than

Both *different from* and *different to* are considered acceptable, although *different from* is traditionally favoured in writing. *Different than* is common in American English, and in spoken Australian English but is regarded as incorrect by some.

fewer or **less**

Use *fewer* for number (things that can be counted individually) and *less* for quantity (things that can't be counted). For example:

There were ***fewer*** *than thirty people at the party.*

We have had ***less*** *rain this year than last year.*

good or **well**

Good is an adjective and *well* is an adverb. In the following example *good* (an adjective) is used as an adverb. This sentence is therefore incorrect.

She did ***good*** *at the athletics meet.*

Correct usage is:

She did ***well*** *at the athletics meet.*

loan or **lend**

Both *lend* and *loan* can be used as verbs, but only *loan* should be used as a noun, and not *lend*. The correct usage is as follows:

Pieta gave me a ***loan*** *of ten dollars.*

It is considered incorrect to say:

Pieta gave me a ***lend*** *of ten dollars.*

that/which/who

Use *who* for people. For example:

Juanita is the girl ***who*** *was elected as class captain.*

On some occasions it is appropriate to use *that* for people. For example:

Juanita was the best friend ***that*** *I ever had.*

Use *which* or *that* for things, for example:

Katrina's car, ***which*** *she loved, was a write-off.*

The strawberries ***that*** *we picked were sweet and tasty.*

should have/could have/would have

In speech or writing we may contract these to *should've, could've, would've*. In each contraction the *'ve* takes the place of *have*. Never write them as *should* ***of***, *could* ***of***, *would* ***of***. For example:

I ***should have*** *brought my umbrella* is correct.

Never write *I* ***should of*** *brought my umbrella.*

try and/try to

Try and is used in casual speech. In writing it would be edited as:

Try to come to my party on Saturday.

who or **whom**

Nowadays the rule about the usage of *whom* is less strictly applied than in the past. Some examples of usage of *who* and *whom* are:

This is the boy who threw the ball.

(*Who* must be used in this sentence because it is the subject of the verb *threw*.)

This is the boy whom the teacher asked to collect the books.

This is the boy who the teacher asked to collect the books.

(Because *whom* is the object of the verb *is*, *whom* was traditionally considered correct. However, both are considered acceptable today when used as the object of a clause.)

Whom should always be used after a preposition. For example:

Mandy was the person ***to whom*** *I gave the extra ticket.*

Greek and Latin roots

Root	Meaning	Examples
Greek roots		
aster	a star	astronomy, astronaut
bios	life	biography, biology
chronos	time	chronology, synchronise
demos	the people	democracy, epidemic
gē	the earth	geography, geology
grapho	I write	autograph, paragraph
logos	a word, a speech, or a study	dialogue, catalogue
mikros	small	microscope, microbe
phonē	sound	telephone, microphone
skopeo	I view	telescope, periscope
tēle	far	telephone, telegraph
Latin roots		
aequus	equal, fair, just	equivalent, equilateral
annus	a year	anniversary, annuity
audio	I hear	audience, auditorium
cado	I fall	accident, deciduous
cedo	I go	succeed, antecedent
centum	a hundred	century, centipede
corpus	the body	corpse, incorporate
credo	I believe	credible, credential
decem	ten	decimal, decimate
dico	I say	diction, verdict

Root	Meaning	Examples
finis	the end	define, finalist
frango	I break	fraction, fragile
gradus	step	gradual, degree
jungo	I join	conjunction, joint
lego	I read, I choose	elect, legible
loquor	I speak	loquacious, soliloquy
magnus	great	magnify, magnificent
manus	the hand	manufacture, manual
mater	mother	maternal, matron
mitto	I send	transmit, remit
modus	a manner, a measure	mode, modern
novus	new	novelty, innovate
pars	part	particle, participate
pater	father	paternal, patriarch
pax	peace	pact, pacify
pello	I drive	propel, compulsion
pono	place	preposition, deposit
porto	I carry	portable, transport
scribo	I write	prescribe, describe
solus	alone	solitary, desolate
specio	I see	spectator, suspect
spiro	I breathe	respiration, perspire
tango	I touch	contagious, contact
unus	one	unanimous, union
vivo	I live	survive, vital
volvo	I roll	involve, revolt

Prefixes and suffixes

Prefixes

Prefix	What it means or indicates	Base word	New word formed
ab-	away, from	normal	abnormal
an-	not, lacking	(mon)archy	anarchy
ante-	before	(pre)cedent	antecedent
anti-	against	clockwise	anticlockwise
auto-	self	biography	autobiography
be-	to make become	friend	befriend
co-, com-, con-	together	(in)habit	cohabit
contra-	against	(con)ception	contraception
counter-	opposite; contrary	terrorism	counterterrorism
cyber-	internet, computers	threat	cyberthreat
de-	(i) a separating	horn	dehorn
	(ii) down, back, not	(a)scend	descend
dis	(i) a taking apart	member	dismember
	(ii) not, back	ability	disability
e-	internet	mail	email
	electronic	tag	e-tag
eco-	ecology, ecological	system	ecosystem
en-, em-	in, into	gulf	engulf
ex-	(i) out of, from	(im)port	export
	(ii) former	wife	ex-wife
extra-	outside, besides	ordinary	extraordinary
hyper-	over	active	hyperactive
hypo-	under, less than	thermal	hypothermia
in-	in, into	land	inland
in-, il-, ir-	not	expensive	inexpensive
		legal	illegal
		regular	irregular
infra-	below, beneath	structure	infrastructure
inter-	between, among	national	international
intra-	within	state	intrastate
macro-	long, large	climate	macroclimate
mal-	bad, wrong	treat	maltreat
micro-	very small	film	microfilm
mis-	fault, failure, not	trust	mistrust
mono-	alone, single	tone	monotone
multi-	many	national	multinational
non-	not	fiction	non-fiction
omni-	all	potent	omnipotent
poly-	much, many	(octa)gon	polygon
post-	behind, after	war	postwar
pre-	before	historic	prehistoric
pro-	in favour of	Labor	pro-Labor
quasi-	resembling	official	quasi-official
re-	again, back	pay	repay
retro-	backwards	(a)spect	retrospect
semi-	half	circle	semicircle
sub-	under, not quite	way	subway
super-	over	natural	supernatural
supra-	above	national	supranational
trans-	across, beyond	(ex)port	transport
ultra-	(i) beyond	violet	ultraviolet
	(ii) excessively	fashionable	ultrafashionable
un-	(i) not	certain	uncertain
	(ii) reversal of an action	bend	unbend

Suffixes

Suffixes that give you nouns

Suffix	What it means or indicates	Base word	New word formed
-age	(i) condition or state (ii) result	bond wreck	bondage wreckage
-al	an action	deny	denial
-an	someone concerned with	republic	republican
-ance	an action, state or quality	assist	assistance
-ant	someone or something that	serve	servant
-ary	a place, person or relationship	grain	granary
-ate	condition or office	consul	consulate
-cy	condition or character	accurate	accuracy
-dom	(i) an area ruled over (ii) condition	king free	kingdom freedom
-ee	the object or receiver of some action	evacuate	evacuee
-eer	someone concerned with	engine	engineer
-en	a plural	ox	oxen
-ence	an action, state or quality	prudent	prudence
-ent	someone or something that	reside	resident
-er[1]	(i) someone or something that (ii) something or someone with a particular quality	drive island	driver islander
-er[2]	someone connected with	office	officer
-er[3]	an action or process	remind	reminder
-ery	type or place of work	bake	bakery
-ess	feminine form	count	countess
-ful	as much as will fill	spoon	spoonful
-hood	state, condition or character	child	childhood
-ian	someone connected with a place, person or thing	Christ	Christian
-ics	a body of facts or principles	electron	electronics
-ing	an action, result or product	build	building
-ion (-sion, -tion, -ation, -ution, -ition)	a process, state or result	commune compel deduce tempt revolve render	communion compulsion deduction temptation revolution rendition
-ism	action, condition, principles	baptise	baptism
-ist	someone concerned with	piano	pianist
-ite	someone associated with	Israel	Israelite
-logy	science or knowledge	zoo	zoology
-ology	science or knowledge	music	musicology
-ment	an action, state or result	refresh	refreshment
-ness	a quality or state	happy	happiness
-or	someone or something that	act	actor
-ory	a place or thing for	direct	directory
-ship	(i) condition (ii) skill or position	friend leader	friendship leadership

Suffixes that give you adjectives

Suffix	What it means or indicates	Base word	New word formed
-able	ability or likelihood	perish	perishable
-al	connected with or like	nature	natural
-an	belonging to or having to do with	Australia	Australian
-ant	having the quality of	please	pleasant
-ar, -ary	of or like	supplement	supplementary
-en	with the appearance of or made of	wood	wooden
-ent	having the quality or character of	depend	dependent
-er	comparative degree	small	smaller
-est	superlative degree	small	smallest
-ful	full of or marked by	beauty	beautiful
-ible	ability or likelihood	reduce	reducible
-ic, -ical	having to do with	poet	poetic
-ish	(i) belonging to or having to do with	Britain	British
	(ii) somewhat or rather	red	reddish
-ive	serving to or able to	correct	corrective
-less	without	care	careless
-like	similar to or like	life	lifelike
-ly	(i) for, by or through each	hour	hourly
	(ii) like	saint	saintly
-ory	serving to or having the effect of	advise	advisory
-ous,	full of or marked by	joy	joyous
-eous		plenty	plenteous
-some	a tendency or leaning towards	quarrel	quarrelsome

Suffixes that give you adverbs

Suffix	What it means or indicates	Base word	New word formed
-er	comparative degree	fast	faster
-est	superlative degree	fast	fastest
-ly	manner	glad	gladly
-ward(s)	direction	up	upward(s)
-ways	manner	length	lengthways
-wise	direction of	length	lengthwise

Suffixes that give you verbs

Suffix	What it means or indicates	Base word	New word formed
-ate	cause or do	active	activate
-en	make or do	length	lengthen
-er	(forms repeating verbs)	flick	flicker
-ise	make or do	legal	legalise

A guide to spelling

If you can't easily find the word you're looking up, it might be that the word begins with a letter or letters that you say in a different way to normal or which may be completely silent.

Here is a table to help you track down those tricky words.

Sound that the word begins with	The word could begin with this	Example
ch	c	cello
f	ph	photo
g	gh	ghost
g	gu	guide
h	wh	whole
j	g	gem
k	ch	character
k	qu	quiche
k	kh	khaki
kw	qu	quite
n	gn	gnash
n	kn	knee
n	pn	pneumonia
r	rh	rhyme
r	wr	write
s	c	cereal
s	ps	psychology
s	sc	science
s	sw	sword
sh	s	sugar
sh	sch	schedule
sh	ch	champagne
sk	sch	school
t	th	thyme
t	tw	two
w	wh	white
z	x	xylophone

The 26 letters of the English alphabet can be combined in many different sequences to form many thousands of words. Five of those 26 letters are called **vowels** (*a*, *e*, *i*, *o*, *u*), and the other 21 are called **consonants**. The letter *y* can act as a consonant or a vowel, depending on where it is located in the word.

Many sounds in English words can be spelt in different ways. Some simple rules will help with spelling if you do not want to refer to a dictionary all the time.

Consonant sounds

f
The sound *f* (as in *fame*) can also be spelt:
ph as in *photo*
ff as in *giraffe*
gh as in *laugh.*

g
The sound *g* (as in *grin*) can also be spelt:
gh as in *ghost*
gg as in *egg*
gu as in *guide.*

j
The sound *j* (as in *job*) can also be spelt:
g as in *gem*
dg as in *fudge.*

k
The sound *k* (as in *keep*) can also be spelt:
c as in *cat*
ch as in *character*
qu as in *quiche*
ck as in *duck*
que as in *cheque*
kh as in *khaki.*

s
The sound *s* (as in *sister*) can also be spelt:
ce as in *ice*
sc as in *scene*
ss as in *hiss.*

sh
The sound *sh* (as in *ship*) can also be spelt:
ch as in *champagne*
ci as in *special*
s as in *sugar*
si as in *dimension*
ssi as in *mission*
ss as in *tissue*
ti as in *lotion.*

z
The sound *z* (as in *zoo*) can also be spelt:
s as in *daisy*
x as in *xylophone.*

Hard and soft *c* and *g*

The letter *c* can be either soft (*cereal*, *citizen*, *cycle*) or hard (*cap*, *count*).

The letter *g* can also be soft (*gentle*, *ginger*, *gym*) or hard (*gate*, *goggles*). Notice that both letters are usually soft when followed by an *e*, *i*, or *y*.

Silent letters

b

The letter *b* is sometimes silent:
after *m* — *limb, bomb, comb*
before *t* — *subtle, debt.*

g

The letter *g* is often silent:
before *n* — *gnaw, gnome, sign.*

gh

The letters *gh* are silent:
at the end of a word — *through, neigh*
before *t* — *light, sought.*

h

The letter *h* is sometimes silent:
at the beginning of a word — *hour, honour, honest*
after *w* — *whisk, whittle, whip.*

k

The letter *k* is silent:
always before *n* — *knife, knit, knee.*

l

The letter *l* is silent:
in the words *calf, palm, chalk.*

n

The letter *n* is sometimes silent:
after *m* — *autumn, solemn.*

p

The letter *p* is sometimes silent:
before *s*, *n* or *t* — *psychiatrist, pneumonia, pterodactyl, receipt.*

s

The letter *s* is silent:
in the words *aisle, island.*

t

The letter *t* is silent:
after *s* in many words — *listen, bustle, castle.*

w

The letter *w* is silent:
before *r* — *wrap, wrist*
before *h* — *what, whole.*

Vowel sounds

The vowel sounds in English can be spelt in a number of different ways, as the following list shows.

a sounds

The sound *a* as in *hat* is nearly always spelt with an *a*.

The sound *a* as in *vase* can be spelt:
a as in *pass*
al as in *calf*
ar as in *jar*
au as in *laugh*.

The sound *a* as in *plate* can be spelt:
a as in *late*
ai as in *rain*
ay as in *crayon*
ea as in *break*
ei as in *eight*
ey as in *grey*.

e sounds

The sound *e* as in *spell* can be spelt:
e as in *red*
ea as in *bread*.

The sound *ee* as in *see* can be spelt:
e as in *demon*
ea as in *flea*
ee as in *teen*
ei as in *ceiling*
ey as in *key*
i as in *sardine*
ie as in *infield*.

The sound *air* as in *hair* can be spelt:
air as in *chair*
are as in *share*
ear as in *pear*
ere as in *there*
eir as in *their*.

i sounds

The sound *i* as in *hit* can be spelt:
i as in *bin*
ui as in *build*
y as in *pyramid*.

The sound *i* as in *drive* can be spelt:
i as in *lime*
igh as in *high*
ie as in *pie*
ye as in *goodbye*
y as in *fly*.

The sound *ear* as in *appear* can be spelt:
ear as in *fear*
eer as in *beer*
ere as in *here*
ier as in *pier*.

o sounds

The sound *o* as in *drop* can be spelt:
a as in *wasp*
au as in *sausage*
o as in *plot*
ou as in *cough*.

The sound *o* as in *joke* can be spelt:
o as in *phone*
oa as in *soap*
oe as in *toe*
ow as in *flow*.

The sound *aw* as in *yawn* can be spelt:
al as in *talk*
augh as in *caught*
aw as in *jaw*
oar as in *roar*
or as in *sword*
ough as in *ought*
ure as in *sure*
oor as in *door*.

The sound *ow* as in *clown* can be spelt:
ou as in *loud*
ow as in *frown*.

The sound *oy* as in *toy* can be spelt:
oi as in *coin*
oy as in *boy*.

u sounds

The sound *u* as in *luck* can be spelt:
o as in *come*
ou as in *touch*
u as in *much*.

The sound *u* as in *push* can be spelt:
oo as in *look*
ou as in *could*
u as in *full*.

The sound *u* as in *rude* can be spelt:
ew as in *flew*
o as in *do*
oo as in *boot*
ou as in *soup*
u as in *flute*
ui as in *fruit*.

The sound *u* ('you') as in *use* can be spelt:
ew as in *new*
u as in *duty*.

er sound

The sound *er* as in *perk* can be spelt:
ear as in *learn*
er as in *service*
ir as in *bird*
or as in *work*
our as in *journey*
ur as in *purse*.

Spelling tips

Here are some tips to help you deal with spelling challenges.

- Use *i* before *e* except after *c* — *believe*, *field*, *piece*, *achieve*, and *receive*, *deceive*, *ceiling*. Exceptions are *foreign*, *seize* and *weird*. The rule holds in most cases where the sound is *ee* as in *see*.
- When *y* is at the start of a word, it acts like a consonant — *yard*, *yell*. If it is at the end of a word, or has an *i* sound, it acts as a vowel — *valley*, *gym*.
- Many words ending in *our*, such as *colour*, *honour* and *vigour*, can also be spelt with *or*. In Australia, the most common spelling is with *our* but some magazines and newspapers use the variant *or*. Whichever spelling variant you choose, be consistent throughout your writing.
- Some words ending in *ise* can also be spelt with *ize*. In Australia, the more common usage is *ise* — for example, *organise* rather than *organize*.
- Double the last letter of a word which ends in a single consonant before adding endings beginning with a vowel, for example *sad*, *sadder*, *saddest*; *thin*, *thinner*, *thinnest*; *clap*, *clapped*, *clapping*.
- If the vowel of the word is spelt with two letters, the final consonant is not doubled, for example *sweet*, *sweeter*, *sweetest* and *soak*, *soaked*, *soaking*.
- With two-syllable words, for example *begin*, double the last consonant (*beginning*) if the second syllable is stressed. If the word has a strong stress on the first syllable, the final consonant is not doubled before an ending, for example *offer*, *offering*, *offered*.
- Whether to double the final *l* in a word like *equal* (*equalled* or *equaled*) or *medal* (*medallist* and *medalist*) is a point of discussion. In Australian spelling, the double *ll* is commonly used.
  Note: The *l* is never doubled before *ise*, for example *formalise* and *legalise*.
- Some words ending in *c*, for example *picnic*, *panic*, have a *k* added before an ending: *picnicker*, *panicked*. This avoids the confusion of thinking the *c* has an *s* sound as it does in many other words.

Singular and plural words

A **singular** word is a word which refers to one person or thing. A **plural** word refers to more than one person or thing.

- The plural form of most words is formed by adding *s* to the singular form.
- Singular words ending in *s*, *sh*, *tch*, *x* and *z* have *es* added to them to form the plural.

dress	*dresses*	*watch*	*watches*	*waltz*	*waltzes*
wish	*wishes*	*box*	*boxes*		

- Singular words ending in *ch* usually have *es* added to them to form the plural. However, if the *ch* is pronounced *k*, the plural is formed with just *s*.

church	*churches*	*monarch*	*monarchs*

- Singular words that end in *y* normally have *s* added to them to form the plural — for example, *toy* becomes *toys*. If there is a consonant before the *y*, the *y* changes to an *i* before adding *es* — for example, *hobby* becomes *hobbies*.
- Some singular words ending in *f* and *fe* drop the ending and add *ves* to form the plural — *leaf* becomes *leaves*, *knife* becomes *knives*.
- Some singular words do not change in their plural form, for example *sheep*, *deer*, *series*, *species*.

Some plural forms of words just don't follow the rules at all! On page 985 is a table of plural forms, including some irregular forms.

Spelling demons

accommodate
antarctic
awkward
believe
burglar
business
catastrophe
ceremony
colloquial
column
committee
convalesce
deceive
definitely
devastate
eucalypt
exaggerate
explanation
foreign
genre
government
harass
heirloom
hierarchy
indigenous
initiate
jeopardy
knowledge
language
leisure
liaison
livelihood
loneliness
longitude
martyr
mediocre
miscellaneous
necessary
nuisance
occasion
pamphlet
parliament
psychiatrist
physician
possess
receive
rhyme
rhythm
secretary
separate
success
terrain
tyranny
umbrella
unique
vacuum
whinge
woollen
wield
zephyr

Singular and plural forms

Singular	Plural
analysis	analyses
antithesis	antitheses
apex	apexes apices
appendix	appendixes appendices
axis	axes
bacterium	bacteria
basis	bases
bonus	bonuses
cactus	cacti
cargo	cargoes
crisis	crises
criterion	criteria
curriculum	curricula curriculums
datum	data
dwarf	dwarfs dwarves
echo	echoes
elf	elves
erratum	errata
fish	fish fishes
formula	formulae
fungus	fungi
gas	gases
genre	genres
hero	heroes
hippopotamus	hippopotamuses hippopotami
hoof	hoofs hooves
index	indexes indices
larva	larvae
matrix	matrices matrixes
maximum	maximums maxima
medium	media
menu	menus
minimum	minimums minima

Singular	Plural
mosquito	mosquitoes
mother-in-law	mothers-in-law
motto	mottos mottoes
nucleus	nuclei
oasis	oases
octopus	octopuses
phenomenon	phenomena
photo	photos
piano	pianos
platypus	platypuses
plus	pluses
potato	potatoes
quiz	quizzes
quota	quotas
radius	radii
referendum	referendums referenda
rhinoceros	rhinoceroses rhinoceros
roof	roofs
salmon	salmon
scenario	scenarios
series	series
shampoo	shampoos
ski	skis
species	species
stimulus	stimuli
syllabus	syllabuses syllabi
taxi	taxis
tomato	tomatoes
tornado	tornadoes
virus	viruses
volcano	volcanoes
wharf	wharves wharfs
zero	zeros zeroes

Prepositions

A preposition is a word placed before a noun to show its relation to other words in the sentence. Here are some common prepositions with illustrations to show their meaning.

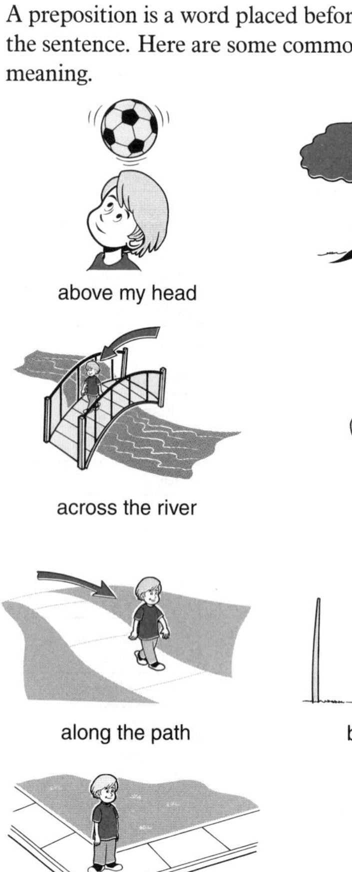

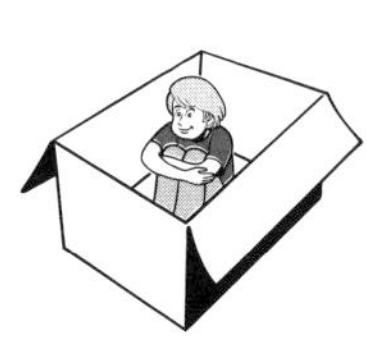

above my head

beneath the trees

inside the box

across the river

beside the chair

on the table

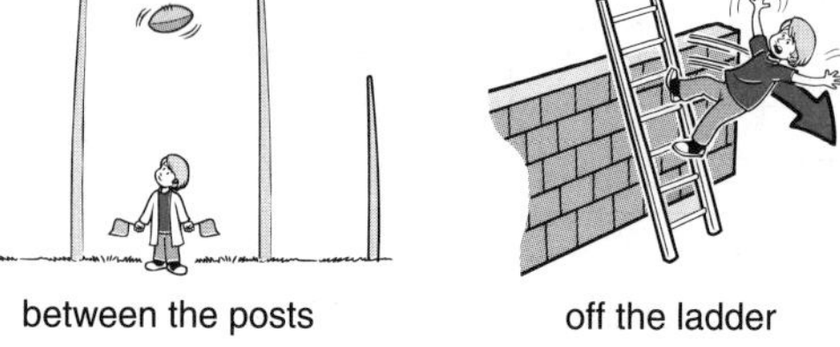

along the path

between the posts

off the ladder

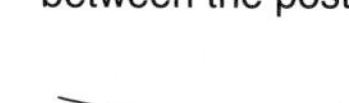

at the corner

by the window

over the wall

behind the door

down the hole

through the window

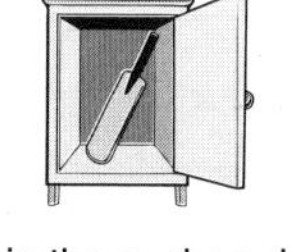

below the bridge

in the cupboard

up the hill

Abbreviations

A'asia	Australasia
ABC	Australian Broadcasting Corporation
ABN	Australian Business Number
ABS	Australian Bureau of Statistics
a.c., AC	alternating current
a/c	account
AC	Companion of the Order of Australia
ACCC	Australian Competition and Consumer Commission
ACN	Australian Company Number
ACT	Australian Capital Territory
ACTU	Australian Council of Trade Unions
AD	in the year of our Lord (Latin *Anno Domini*)
AEDST	Australian Eastern Daylight Saving Time
AEST	Australian Eastern Standard Time
AFL	Australian Football League
AFP	Australian Federal Police
AGM	annual general meeting
a.h., AH	after hours
AIS	Australian Institute of Sport
ALP	Australian Labor Party
a.m.	before noon (Latin *ante meridiem*)
AM	Member of the Order of Australia; (*Radio*) amplitude modulation
AMA	Australian Medical Association
amt	amount
anon.	anonymous
ANZAAS	Australian and New Zealand Association for the Advancement of Science
ANZAC	Australian and New Zealand Army Corps
ANZUS	Australia, New Zealand and the United States (Security Treaty)
AO	Officer of the Order of Australia
APEC	Asia-Pacific Economic Cooperation (group)
approx.	approximate; approximately
ARL	Australian Rugby League
ARU	Australian Rugby Union
ASAP	as soon as possible
ASEAN	Association of South-East Asian Nations
ASIC	Australian Securities and Investments Commission
ASIO	Australian Security Intelligence Organisation
ASIS	Australian Secret Intelligence Service
Assn, assn	association
assoc.	associate; associated; association
ASX	Australian Securities Exchange
ATAR	Australian Tertiary Admission Rank
Aus., Aust.	Australia; Australian
Av., Ave	Avenue (in street names)
AV	audio-visual
AWA	Australian Workplace Agreement
AWDST	Australian Western Daylight Saving Time
AWST	Australian Western Standard Time
b.	born; (*Cricket*) bowled; breadth
BA	Bachelor of Arts
B & B	bed and breakfast
B & W	black and white
BAS	Business Activity Statement
BBQ	barbecue
BC	Before Christ
bcc	blind carbon copy; (in emails) blind courtesy copy
BCE	Before the Common Era
BH	business hours
bps	bits per second; bytes per second
BP	Before Present (before 1950, in dating system used in geology, archaeology, etc.)
Bro.	brother
Bros	brothers
BSc	Bachelor of Science
B/W	black and white
BYO	bring your own
c.	cent; century; (before dates) about (Latin *circa*)
C	Cape; Celsius; Centigrade; century
C/–	care of
Cap., Capt.	Captain
CB	(*Radio*) citizen band
CBD	Central Business District
cc	carbon copy; (in emails) courtesy copy
CCS	carbon capture and storage
CCTV	closed-circuit television
Cdr	Commander
CE	Common Era
CEO	Chief Executive Officer
cf.	compare (Latin *confer*)
c/f	(*Accounting*) carried forward; carry forward
CFC	chlorofluorocarbon
ch., chap.	chapter
CIA	(in the US) Central Intelligence Agency
CIB	Criminal Investigation Branch
circ.	about (Latin *circa*)
Cllr	Councillor
CMF	Citizen Military Forces
cnr	corner
c/o	care of
Co., Coy	company
CO	Commanding Officer
COAG	Council of Australian Governments
COB	close of business
COD	cash on delivery

C of E	Church of England
Col.	Colonel
Comm.	Commonwealth
cont., contd	continued
co-op	cooperative
Corp.	corporation; Corporal
CPA	certified practising accountant
CPI	Consumer Price Index
Cpl	Corporal
CPU	central processing unit
Cr	Councillor
Cres.	Crescent (in street names)
CRT	cathode-ray tube
CSIRO	Commonwealth Scientific and Industrial Research Organisation
CST	Central Standard Time
Cwlth, Cwth	Commonwealth
CWA	Country Women's Association
d.c., DC	direct current
DC	(in the US) District of Columbia
Dept, dept	department
dip.	diploma
Dip. Ed.	Diploma of Education
DIY	do-it-yourself
DMZ	demilitarised zone
DOB	date of birth
Dr	Doctor
Dr.	Drive (in street names)
E	east; eastern
ea.	each
ECG	electrocardiogram; electrocardiograph
EEG	electroencephalogram; electroencephalograph
EFL	English as a foreign language
EFT	electronic funds transfer
e.g.	for example (Latin *exempli gratia*)
enc., encl.	enclosed; enclosure
ENSO	El Niño-Southern Oscillation
ENT	(*Medicine*) ear, nose and throat
ESL	English as a second language
Esq.	Esquire
est.	established; estimated
EST	Eastern Standard Time
estab.	established
ETA	estimated time of arrival
etc.	and so on (Latin *et cetera*)
ETD	estimated time of departure
EU	European Union
F	Fahrenheit
FAHA	Fellow of the Australian Academy of the Humanities
FAQ	frequently asked question
FBI	(in the US) Federal Bureau of Investigation
fig.	figure
figs	figures
fl.	flourished
FM	(*Radio*) frequency modulation
FOI	freedom of information
fol.	following
Fr	Father
fwd	forward
FYI	for your information
G	gigabyte; (*Film classification*) general viewing
GB	gigabyte; Great Britain
GDP	Gross Domestic Product
Gen.	(*Military*) General
GFC	global financial crisis
G-G, GG	Governor-General
GI	glycaemic index
GM	genetically-modified; General Manager
GMT	Greenwich Mean Time
GNP	Gross National Product
Gov.	Governor
Govt, govt	government
GP	general practitioner
GPS	global positioning system
GST	goods and services tax
h.c.f.	highest common factor
hcp	handicap
HMAS	Her (or His) Majesty's Australian Ship
Hon.	honourable; honorary
HQ	headquarters
hr	hour
HR	human resources; House of Representatives
HRH	Her (or His) Royal Highness
Hts	Heights
hwy	highway
ID	identification
i.e.	that is (Latin *id est*)
illus.	illustrated; illustration
IMF	International Monetary Fund
Inc.	Incorporated
I/O	input/output
IOU	I owe you
IP	intellectual property; internet protocol
IR	industrial relations
IRC	internet relay chat
Is., is., isl.	Island; Isle
ISBN	International Standard Book Number
ISP	internet service provider
IT	information technology
jnr, jr	junior
JP	Justice of the Peace
K	thousand; kilometre; kilobyte
Kb, kb	kilobit
KB, Kb, kb	kilobyte
kbps	kilobits per second
kBps	kilobytes per second
kbyte	kilobyte
KO	knockout
KPI	key performance indicator

L	learner (driver)
LAN	local area network
lat.	latitude
l.b.w.	(*Cricket*) leg before wicket
l.c.d.	lowest common denominator
LCD	liquid crystal display
l.c.m.	lowest common multiple
LED	light-emitting diode
lic'd	licensed
Lieut.	Lieutenant
LNG	liquefied natural gas
long.	longitude
LPG	liquefied petroleum gas
Ltd	Limited
l.y.	light-year
m.	male; masculine; married
M	(*Film classification*) mature
MA	Master of Arts; (*Film classification*) mature accompanied
Maj.	Major
masc.	masculine
max.	maximum
Mb	megabit
MB	megabyte
Mbps	megabits per second
MBps	megabytes per second
mbyte	megabyte
MC	Master of Ceremonies
Messrs	Gentlemen (French *Messieurs*)
mfd	manufactured
MHR	Member of the House of Representatives
min.	minute; minimum
misc.	miscellaneous
MP	Member of Parliament; Military Police
MS	manuscript; multiple sclerosis
MSG	monosodium glutamate
Msgr	Monsignor
MSS	manuscripts
Mt	Mount; Mountain
MV	Merchant Vessel; Motor Vessel
n.	born (Latin *natus*)
N	north; northern
n/a, n.a.	not applicable; not available
NATO	North Atlantic Treaty Organisation
NB	note well (Latin *nota bene*)
NCP	National Country Party
NE	north-east; north-eastern
neg.	negative
NGO	non-government organisation
no., No.	number
nos, Nos	numbers
NPA	National Party of Australia
NSW	New South Wales
NT	Northern Territory
NW	north-west; north-western
NZ	New Zealand
OA	Order of Australia
OAM	Medal of the Order of Australia
O/D	overdraft; overdrawn
OECD	Organisation for Economic Cooperation and Development
OHMS	On Her (or His) Majesty's Service
o.n.o.	or near(est) offer
op.	opus
OPEC	Organisation of the Petroleum Exporting Countries
opp.	opposite
p.	page
P	provisional (driver's licence)
p.a.	yearly (Latin *per annum*)
para.	paragraph
Parl., Parlt	Parliament
PAYE	pay-as-you-earn
PAYG	pay-as-you-go
PB	personal best
p.c.	per cent
PC	personal computer; politically correct; personnel carrier
PE	physical education
PG	(*Film classification*) parental guidance recommended
PhD	Doctor of Philosophy
Pl.	Place (in street names)
P/L	Proprietary Limited
p.m.	afternoon (Latin *post meridiem*)
PM	Prime Minister
PNG	Papua New Guinea
PO	postal order; Post Office
pop.	population
pos.	position
POW	prisoner of war
pp.	pages
PPS	additional postscript (Latin *post post scriptum*)
PPP	public-private partnership
pr	pair
Prof.	Professor
PS	postscript (Latin *post scriptum*)
PTO, p.t.o.	please turn over
Pty	Proprietary
PVA	polyvinyl acetate
PVC	polyvinyl chloride
QC	Queen's Counsel
Qld	Queensland
qtr	quarter; quarterly
q.v.	which see (Latin *quod vide*)
r.	(*Cricket*) runs
R	(*Film classification*) restricted (to those aged 18 and over)
RAAF	Royal Australian Air Force
RAN	Royal Australian Navy
RBA	Reserve Bank of Australia
RBT	random breath test
RC	Red Cross; Roman Catholic; (*Film classification*) refused classification
Rd	Road (in street names)
RD	rural delivery (used in addresses)

RDI	recommended dietary intake
RDO	rostered day off
ref.	reference; referee
reg.	registration; registered; regulation
retd	retired
Rev., Revd	Reverend
RFDS	Royal Flying Doctor Service
RIP	may he or she (or they) rest in peace (Latin *requiescat in pace*)
RMB	Roadside Mail Box
RSL	Returned and Services League of Australia
RSPCA	Royal Society for the Prevention of Cruelty to Animals
RSVP	please reply (French *répondez s'il vous plaît*)
Rt Hon.	Right Honourable
s.	singular; second(s)
S	south; southern
SA	South Australia
s.a.e., SAE	stamped addressed envelope; self-addressed envelope
SBS	Special Broadcasting Service
SC	Senior Counsel
sci-fi, SF	science fiction
SE	south-east; south-eastern
sec.	second; secondary; secretary
sect.	section
sen., snr, sr	senior
Sergt, Sgt	Sergeant
SI	International System of Units (French *Système International d'Unités*)
SIEV	suspected illegal entry vessel
SM	stipendiary magistrate
SMS	short messaging service
snr, sr	senior
Soc.	Society
SOI	Southern Oscillation Index
SPF	sun protection factor
Sqn Ldr	Squadron Leader
Sr	Senior
SRC	Students' Representative Council
St	Street; Saint; Strait
STD	sexually transmitted disease; Subscriber Trunk Dialling
Sth	south
Sthn	southern
SW	south-west; south-western
TAB	Totalisator Agency Board
TAFE	Technical and Further Education
Tas.	Tasmania
TBA	to be announced
TBC	to be confirmed
tbs., tbsp.	tablespoon
tel.	telephone
temp.	temporary; temperature
TFN	tax file number
tsp., t.	teaspoon
U	Union; United; University
UAC	Universities Admissions Centre
UAE	United Arab Emirates
u/c	under cover
UHF, u.h.f.	ultra high frequency
UHT	ultra heat treated
UK	United Kingdom
ULP	unleaded petrol
UN	United Nations
UNESCO	United Nations Educational, Scientific and Cultural Organisation
UNHCR	United Nations High Commissioner for Refugees
UNICEF	United Nations International Children's Emergency Fund
US(A)	United States (of America)
UV	ultraviolet
v.	verb; verse; versus
VC	Victoria Cross
VCR	video cassette recorder
VFL	Victorian Football League (former name of the Australian Football League)
VHF, v.h.f.	very high frequency
Vic.	Victoria
vol.	volume
vs.	versus
w.	week; weight; wide; width; with
W	west; western
WA	Western Australia
WAN	wide area network
WC	toilet (water closet)
WEA	Workers' Educational Association
WEL	Women's Electoral Lobby
Wg Cdr	Wing Commander
WHO	World Health Organisation
wk	week; work
wkt	wicket
WO	Warrant Officer
w.p.m.	words per minute
WST	Western Standard Time
wt	weight
WTO	World Trade Organisation
www	World Wide Web
X	Cross; (*Film classification*) restricted (to age 18 and over; contains sexually explicit material)
Xmas	Christmas
y.	year
YHA	Youth Hostels Association
YMCA	Young Men's Christian Association
yr	year
YWCA	Young Women's Christian Association

Collective nouns

a shrewdness of apes

a cete of badgers

a sloth of bears

a swarm of bees

a flock of birds

a herd of buffalo

a clowder of cats

a mob of cattle

a murder of crows

a brood of chickens

a rake of colts

a litter of cubs

a pack of dogs

a clutch of eggs

a herd of elephants

a business of ferrets

a shoal of fish

a cloud of flies

a skulk of foxes

an army of frogs

a gaggle of geese

a siege of herons

a team of horses

a smack of jellyfish

a troop of kangaroos

a kindle of kittens

an exaltation of larks

a leap of leopards

a pride of lions

a tiding of magpies

a troop of monkeys

a watch of nightingales

a parliament of owls

a covey of partridges

a school of porpoises

a bevy of quail

a warren of rabbits

a string of racehorses

a flock of sheep

a wedge of swans

a convoy of trucks

a rafter of turkeys

a pod of whales

a pack of wolves

Literary terms

Allegory
A story in which the characters and events stand for something or someone else.

Alliteration
The repetition of the first letter of a word in the word or words following it — for example, *the whistling wind.*

Assonance
The repetition of the same vowel sound in a sequence of words to create a special effect — for example, *the slow blowing of the bellows.*

Hyperbole
A figure of speech using exaggeration for emphasis — for example, *I've told you a million times not to do that.*

Irony
A form of humour in speech or writing in which what is said is the opposite of what is actually meant.

Metaphor
A word picture in which the thing you want to describe is replaced with another image — for example, *He was a lion on the football field.*

Onomatopoeia
The name given to the way the sound of a word can echo its meaning or sense — for example, *the buzzing of bees.*

Oxymoron
A figure of speech in which two words or phrases of opposite or contrasting meaning are placed together for special effect — for example, *bitter sweet, agonising joy.*

Parody
The humorous imitation of a serious piece of writing.

Personification
A device used in writing by which objects are treated as if they have human qualities — for example, *The sun smiled on the parade.*

Satire
A literary style which uses irony and sarcasm to ridicule corrupt or foolish behaviour.

Simile
A word picture in which something is likened to something else — for example, *as thin as a stick-insect.*

Symbolism
This is when people or things stand for something other than themselves — for example, a rose can be seen as a symbol of beauty.

Tautology
This is saying the same thing over again in another way — for example, *She was the captain and the leader of the team.*

Prime Ministers of Australia

1901–03	Edmund Barton	Protectionist
1903–04	Alfred Deakin	Liberal
1904	John Christian Watson	Labor Party
1904–05	George Houston Reid	Free Trader
1905–08	Alfred Deakin	Liberal
1908–09	Andrew Fisher	Labor Party
1909–10	Alfred Deakin	Liberal
1910–13	Andrew Fisher	Labor Party
1913–14	Joseph Cook	Free Trader/Liberal
1914–15	Andrew Fisher	Labor Party
1915–23	William Morris Hughes	Labor/Nationalist Party
1923–29	Stanley Melbourne Bruce	Nationalist Party
1929–32	James Henry Scullin	Labor Party
1932–39	Joseph Aloysius Lyons	United Australia Party
1939	Earle Christmas Grafton Page (caretaker)	Country Party
1939–41	Robert Gordon Menzies	United Australia Party
1941	Arthur William Fadden	Country Party
1941–45	John Joseph Curtin	Labor Party
1945	Francis Michael Forde (caretaker)	Labor Party
1945–49	Joseph Benedict Chifley	Labor Party
1949–66	Robert Gordon Menzies	Liberal Party
1966–67	Harold Edward Holt	Liberal Party
1967–68	John McEwen (caretaker)	Country Party
1968–71	John Grey Gorton	Liberal Party
1971–72	William McMahon	Liberal Party
1972–75	Edward Gough Whitlam	Labor Party
1975–83	John Malcolm Fraser	Liberal Party
1983–91	Robert James Lee Hawke	Labor Party
1991–96	Paul John Keating	Labor Party
1996–2007	John Winston Howard	Liberal Party
2007–2010	Kevin Michael Rudd	Labor Party
2010–	Julia Eileen Gillard	Labor Party

Map showing the Aboriginal languages referred to in this dictionary

taipan
6.
kangaroo
quoll
13.
Uluru
15.
willy-willy
16.
churinga
kadaitja
1.
bung
currawong
dillybag
humpy
yakka
11.
bindi-eye
brigalow
brolga
budgerigar
coolamon
mulga
Murri
3.
kowari
8.
euro
witchetty grub
12.
10.
mulgara
dibbler
dunnart
jarrah
karri
kylie
numbat
Nyungar
quokka
4.
billabong
kookabura
quandong
9.
7.
bilby
bindi-eye
coolibah
galah
18.
Koori
2.
19.
wurley
5.
bunyip
mallee
yabby
14.
tuan
17.
bogong
bettong
cooee
kurrajong
nulla-nulla
potoroo
waddy
wallaroo
woomera
bogey
boomerang
corroboree
dingo
gibber
gunyah
koala
wallaby
waratah
warrigal
wombat

Languages:

1. Arrernte
2. Dharug
3. Kamilaroi
4. Nyungar
5. Wembawemba
6. Wik-Mungkan
7. Yuwaalaraay
8. Diyari
9. Wiradjuri
10. Wangganguru
11. Yagara
12. Adnyamathanha
13. Guugu Yimidhirr
14. Wathawurung
15. Luritja
16. Yindjibarndi
17. Ngarigo
18. Awabakal
19. Kaurna

(The arrows show which words come from that language.)

A guide to the Macquarie School Dictionary

Guideword

bacteria

Headword

bacteria

plural noun microscopic living bodies with one cell, which multiply by dividing themselves in two and which can cause disease and decay

Noun forms: The singular is **bacterium**.
Word building: **bacterial** *adjective*
Word history: Neo-Latin, from Greek word meaning 'little stick'

Word building — other members of the headword's family

Usage notes in shaded entries

You will sometimes see **bacteria** used with a singular verb. Some people feel that this is not acceptable as **bacteria** is the plural form of **bacterium**.

Look up **germ / bacterium / virus**.

ballistic

adjective **1** having to do with ballistics
phrase **2 go ballistic**, *Colloquial* to become extremely angry: *Dad will* ***go ballistic*** *when he sees this mess.*

Idiomatic phrase

Label telling you how the phrase is used

Balmain bug

noun an edible flattened crustacean first discovered in Port Jackson (Sydney Harbour); similar to the Moreton Bay bug

Word history: named after *Balmain*, a suburb of Sydney, New South Wales

Part of speech

balmy (bah-mee)

adjective fine or pleasant: *In the* ***balmy*** *spring weather they often ate outdoors.* (***fair***, ***mild***, ***sunny***, ***temperate***)

Adjective forms: **balmier**, **balmiest**

Adjective forms — those not formed by simply adding ***-er*** *or* ***-est***, *or by using the words* ***more*** *or* ***most***

ban

verb to bar or forbid: *Our teacher* ***banned*** *chewing gum from the classroom.* (***censor***, ***disqualify***, ***exclude***, ***outlaw***, ***prevent***)

Word use: The opposite of this is **allow**.
Verb forms: I **banned**, I have **banned**, I am **banning**
Word history: Middle English, from Scandinavian

Verb forms giving you other tenses of the verb

Word use telling you something interesting about the word

banal (buh-nahl, bay-nuhl)

adjective ordinary and unoriginal: *The TV film was so* ***banal*** *that we turned it off.* (***clichéd***, ***commonplace***, ***hackneyed***, ***trite***, ***unimaginative***)

Word building: **banality** *noun*
Word history: French, from Germanic word meaning 'proclamation'

How to say the word — see the pronunciation key on page v

band[1]

noun **1** a group of people acting together: *a* ***band*** *of outlaws* (***bunch***, ***crowd***, ***gang***, ***huddle***, ***troop***)
2 a group of musicians: *a rock* ***band*** | *a* ***brass*** *band*
verb **3** to join in a group: *to* ***band*** *together to protect the environment*

Word history: French, from Germanic

Change of part of speech

Words that are spelt the same but have different histories

band[2]

noun **1** a strip of material for tying, binding or decorating: *a hat* ***band*** | *a rubber* ***band***
2 a narrow strip that contrasts with its surroundings: *a* ***band*** *of red paint* (***line***, ***stripe***)
3 *Mining* a layer of stone containing ore or a similar valuable material, such as opal (***deposit***, ***seam***, ***stratum***, ***vein***)
4 *Radio* a defined or specified range of frequencies: *The radio station I listen to is part of the FM* ***band***.

Word history: Middle English, from French

Label telling you the subject area of the word (as used in a particular definition)